WRITING THROUGH LITERATURE

Linda Anstendig
PACE UNIVERSITY

David Hicks
PACE UNIVERSITY

PRENTICE HALL
Upper Saddle River, New Jersey 07458

Library of Congress Cataloging-in-Publication Data

Anstendig, Linda (date)
Writing through literature / Linda Anstendig, David Hicks.
p. cm.
Includes indexes.
ISBN 0-02-303564-1
1. College readers. 2. Literature—History and criticism—Theory, etc. 3. English language—Rhetoric. 4. Criticism—Authorship.
I. Hicks, David (date) . II. Title.
PE1417.A57 1996
808′.0427—dc20 95-34512
CIP

Acquisitions Editor: D. Anthony English
Editorial/Production Supervision: Karen Trost
Interior Design: Joan Greenfield
Copy Editor: Katherine Hieatt
Buyer: Mary Ann Gloriande
Editorial Assistant: Joan Polk
Cover Photo: Georgia O'Keeffe, "Red Hills, Lake George" 1927
Oil on Canvas 27 x 32 (68.5 x 81.2 cm)
Signed and dated.
Acquired 1945, The Phillips Collection,
Washington, D.C.

Simon & Schuster/A Viacom Company
Upper Saddle River, New Jersey 07458

Printed in the United States of America
10 9 8 7 6 5 4 3 2 1

ISBN 0-02-303564-1

Prentice-Hall International (UK) Limited, *London*
Prentice-Hall of Australia Pty. Limited, *Sydney*
Prentice-Hall Canada Inc., *Toronto*
Prentice-Hall Hispanoamericana, S.A., *Mexico*
Prentice-Hall of India Private Limited, *New Delhi*
Prentice-Hall of Japan, Inc., *Tokyo*
Simon & Schuster Asia Pte. Ltd., *Singapore*
Editora Prentice-Hall do Brasil, Ltda., *Rio de Janeiro*

For Howard and Maggie

CONTENTS

PREFACE

[The literary work] must be thought of as an event in time. It is not an object or an ideal entity. It happens during a coming-together, a compenetration, of a reader and a text. The reader brings to the text his past experience and present personality. Under the magnetism of the ordered symbols of the text, he marshals his resources and crystallizes out from the stuff of memory, thought, and feeling a new order, a new experience, which he sees as the [literary work]. This becomes part of the ongoing stream of his experience, to be reflected on from any angle important to him as a human being.

—Louise Rosenblatt, *The Reader, the Text, the Poem*

Writing Through Literature is not simply an anthology of readings, nor is it solely a writing text, but a true combination of the two. It has been designed with one goal in mind: to help students become better writers—and better readers—through literature.

Increasingly, the teaching of writing and the teaching of literature are seen as interrelated. As more and more people recognize this, and as schools provide increasing support and encouragement for interdisciplinary studies and writing-across-the-curriculum programs, composition and literature are becoming mutually supportive and increasingly interwoven fields. Hence the time is right for a book that integrates the two disciplines.

Designed for any composition course that includes literary readings, *Writing Through Literature* contains process writing assignment sequences wrapped around "clusters" of five to nine readings each. Preceding and following the clusters, which are contained in sections organized under five broad themes, each of these informal to formal writing assignment sequences begins by asking students to express their opinions about the topic (growing up, modern love, religion, etc.) and ends with a broad writing project that combines their opinions with what they have learned from the readings.

In addition, following each individual reading are questions designed to help students react to it—in reading journals, notebooks, or class discussions—and focus on particular elements. Questions under the heading "Probing the Work" encourage students to look closely at particular passages or literary devices in the work; questions under the heading "Identifying Issues" ask them to see the larger issues that the work raises, which can be considered outside the text.

Students who are assigned a cluster will be asked to do the following:

1. Write from their own experience with the topic.
2. Creatively express and share their views.
3. Read an essay, poems, stories, and perhaps a play on the topic.
4. React to each reading in a journal, or through some other method.
5. Discuss the readings in class.
6. Write a draft of an essay that combines their opinions with what they learned from the readings.
7. Incorporate critical sources and document correctly (optional).
8. Get peer reaction to their draft.
9. Revise their draft to its final form.

Aside from the unique format of the book's assignment sequences, *Writing Through Literature* has other innovative and noteworthy features.

AN EXTENDED SECTION ON THE READING/WRITING PROCESS

Part 1 is devoted to explaining the interrelated reading and writing processes, and provides student samples as illustration. It also explains in detail just how the assignment sequences should work in conjunction with literature.

A SECTION DEVOTED TO LITERARY TERMS

The last chapter of Part 1, "Talking Literature," categorizes and defines literary terms in easy-to-understand language and provides examples of those terms from the readings in the book.

WRITING INTEGRATED THROUGHOUT THE TEXT

Instead of being appended to the end of each reading, or relegated to the back pages, writing questions and suggestions are integrated throughout this text:

- It begins with several chapters on the writing process.
- No works are provided just for "additional reading"—the only readings included here are meant to be used in the students' writing assignments.

- After each reading students are encouraged to *write* their reactions to it, preferably in a reading journal.
- The objective of every reading cluster is to arrive at a comprehensive essay.
- *Writing Tips* are included in each "Putting It All Together" step.

THEMATIC ARRANGEMENT OF READINGS

Four genres (essays, poems, fiction, and drama) are integrated and grouped according to five main themes: "Identities," "Families," "Love," "Frames of Mind," and "The Individual and the Cosmos."

The small reading clusters within each section are designed for two-week lesson plans focused on interrelated texts. They are arranged chronologically, with the exception of the essays, which are placed at the beginning of the clusters, and the plays, which are placed at the end.

CRITICAL COMMENTARY

In almost every cluster there will be at least one poem, short story, or play for which we will provide some critical perspective—the writer's own comments, a contemporary review, or a critical opinion about the work—usually in the "Probing the Work" or "Identifying Issues" steps. After many of the plays we have reprinted reviews or commentaries.

STUDENT MODELS

Samples of student reactions, drafts of essays, and responses to readings appear throughout the book. These were written not by the "star" students necessarily but by students who consider themselves "average" readers and writers. Some samples are revised over several drafts, so that students can identify with the struggle, and the complete nature of the investment they are challenged to make in their writing.

"USER-FRIENDLY" FORMAT

We have incorporated much of what would normally appear in a teacher's guide, so that instructors need only assign the clusters to the students, then do what they do best: help students work on their writing. The readings are for the most part short and accessible. The assignments are clearly written, with step-by-step directions. Also, there is constant cross-referencing so that students can find more information on what they are being asked to do in Part 2 by looking at the appropriate chapter of Part 1. If, for example, a student is asked to identify an *image* in a poem, the page number for the definition of *image* is included.

NONTRADITIONAL ASSIGNMENTS

Under "Enacting the Topic," the second step in the assignment sequence, students are asked to take an unusual approach to the topic before they read the literary selections: interview a family member, watch television, write a scene from a play, role-play, and so on. This not only makes learning more enjoyable, but forces students to find other points of view on the topic, or other ways of looking at the topic, before reading the works.

ACCESSIBLE READINGS

Many of our favorite literary works were cut from this book because they weren't "accessible" enough. We did not want to publish a literature anthology with complex works that would baffle first-year students until the professor could explicate them. Works were chosen for their quality, if they fit the theme of the cluster, but primarily we chose works that could be said to be "good for writing." The readings included here have all been successfully class-tested in a variety of composition courses, from remedial to advanced levels.

MULTICULTURAL SELECTIONS

Although many of the readings in *Writing Through Literature* are by twentieth-century American writers, other cultures are well represented. When writing and reading about the issue of individualism versus conformity (in the "Self-Reliance" cluster, p. 126), for example, students will read not only Robert Frost's perspective, but also those of Chinua Achebe and Kitty Tsui. Almost every one of the clusters provides nonwhite, non-European/American perspectives, and there are as many works by women as there are by men.

INSTRUCTOR'S MANUAL

Available with this text is an instructor's guide that provides tips on using this book in the class, sample syllabi, alternative tables of contents, and more writing samples.

ACKNOWLEDGMENTS

Finding the time to work on this book in the midst of our busy university and child-rearing schedules often meant meeting in the evenings and on weekends, and our families showed great patience as it took longer than we had expected. Our love and thanks, then, to Howard, Mark, and Karin Anstendig, and to Maggie, Stephen, and Caitlin Hicks. We would also like to thank our chairperson at Pace University, Robert Klaeger, for his cooperation and patience.

The seeds for this book were planted by scholars and professors we read and worked with during our development: Mina Shaugnessy, Louise Rosenblatt, Harvey Weiner, Peter Elbow, Donald Bartholomae, and Lil Brannon. They, as well as such scholar/friends as Isabel Kimmel and James Seitz, have unknowingly contributed to this book.

We were fortunate to receive valuable feedback along the way from our reviewers: Katherine Ackley, University of Wisconsin, Stevens Point; Harriette C. Buchanan, Appalachian State University; James Bynum, Georgia Institute of Technology; Margaret Hallissy, Long Island University; Stanley J. Kozikowski, Bryant College; Sue Pine, Florida Community College; Merritt W. Starke, Jr., Henderson State University; Susan D. Tilka, Southwest Texas State University.

The person who knew better than we which questions to ask these reviewers, Morgan Lance, proved a dependable source of quick advice and professional courtesy at Macmillan, now Prentice Hall. We are grateful for Morgan's help, for Barbara Heinssen's enthusiasm for our idea, and for Tony English's supervision. We are indebted to Fred Courtright, our permissions editor, for invaluable and friendly assistance above and beyond the call of duty. We are fortunate, too, in that our production editor, Karen Trost, was just the patient and experienced person we needed to supervise the completion of the project. And we are thankful for the help of Joan Polk, and the excellent work of our copy editor, Katherine Hieatt.

Our gratitude goes out to our colleagues at Pace who provided support and feedback, especially our friend and "coach," Robert DiYanni. Bob Beuka provided us with enthusiastic and invaluable feedback on the practical uses of this book in the classroom, and with student samples when we needed them. We are indebted as well to our wonderful students at Pace, who provided us with many literary insights, opinions regarding the merits and demerits of our selections, and more exceptional writing samples than we could possibly include.

Finally, we reserve our special thanks to a student, Stacy DiLoreto, who was our consultant, copyist, blurb-finder, manuscript-organizer, and friend, and to Eunice Cunha, whose photographs enhance each section of Part 2.

PART 1

WRITING THROUGH LITERATURE

Books . . . are for nothing but to inspire.

—Ralph Waldo Emerson

1

INTRODUCTION: WRITING *THROUGH* LITERATURE

WHY *WRITING THROUGH LITERATURE?*

We decided on this title—instead of *Writing About Literature,* or *Writing and Literature*—because it most accurately communicates the goal of this book. *Through* reading and discussing the following essays, poems, stories, and plays, you will improve your *writing.* Along the way, of course, we hope you will learn a thing or two about life and art. But primarily the object of this book is to enable you in many ways to write *through,* and not just *about,* literature.

Now, you are probably used to writing "through" your experiences, or writing "through" argument: you may have done so in other writing courses. You may have also written "through" the lenses of your teachers—explaining what a poem means, for example, after having it explained to you. But writing "through" *literature?*

Let us explain. Too often, we have found, students perceive literature—especially poetry—as an interesting but somewhat obscure batch of frightfully "deep" words containing hidden meanings that require assistance (from a teacher or a critic) to be fully understood. Too often the challenge for students is to "assess," "analyze," "evaluate," or "interpret" the story or poem as the teacher or critic would, as objectively as possible, in dry, authoritative terms: *"Araby," by James Joyce, is about . . . ; In Frost's "Stopping By Woods," the road represents . . ."*

As we see it, there are two fundamental problems with this perception and practice:

1. Students are asked to write authoritatively about something they may not have much authority to write about. They are being asked to play a game: to pretend they are critics and to write as if they know everything about the work.
2. In first-semester writing courses, students are typically asked to write personally, to argue from their experience and research, to write about what they are interested in, and to make an investment in their subjects. In the second semester they are suddenly expected to drop all that and write in detached prose, treating their subject with awe and avoiding the mention of personal experiences. This can be confusing.

In contrast, this book asks you to consider literature and writing from many perspectives, including your own. When you write an essay on a literary topic, you will not be sitting at your desk with an open book and a blank pad of paper (or a blank computer screen) in front of you; rather, you will have available to you several perspectives on that topic: your own, from your reading journals and in-class writing; your classmates', from class discussions and peer reviews of your rough drafts; your instructor's; and those of a variety of writers whose works you have just read. So you will be writing about a topic *through* the literature you have read about that topic. You may learn from the poems and stories, and learn how to write critically *about* them from your instructor, but you may also draw from these works to support or illustrate the point *you* want to make, based on your own ideas and experiences.

So let's do away with the old-fashioned notion that you need to be literary critics writing in academic prose. You probably don't enjoy reading such writing yourself. When you read a well-written article or book for your own intellectual enjoyment, chances are that the writer has combined personal opinion and experience with some research and references to other works on that topic. Such writing and such an objective are what we are asking of you.

In order to accomplish this, of course, you will need to arm yourself with the tools of the trade: the terminology of literary criticism and an understanding of writers' methods. If you are not exactly sure how to explain the *theme* of a story, if you do not recognize how *rhyme* and *meter* contribute to a complete understanding of a poem, if you are not aware of how *symbolism* and *imagery* enrich a work, then you are not getting all you could out of your reading experience, nor are you writing as knowledgeably as you could be. It would then be advantageous for you to learn, recognize, and use these and other literary terms and devices, spelled out for you in Chapter 8 (beginning on page 63).

Still, many students find these terms bothersome. If you are wondering why you need to learn them, consider the following analogies. When many people have "car trouble," they bring the car in for repair, and rely upon the mechanic to find the trouble and fix it. Some very intelligent people in this situation find themselves embarrassed and helpless due to their ignorance. But people who understand the details of how a car engine works are more confident drivers and customers as a result of their technical knowledge. Similarly, anyone who has played a particular sport and knows it well can watch it being played by professionals with real appreciation. In contrast to the casual fan, this person knows the fine points of the game, and appreciates every element of the action, or even of the seeming *inaction.*

In the same way, an understanding of the technique of a poem, story, or play leads to a greater understanding of literature, and will go far to eliminate the helplessness many feel when they confront a "difficult" poem or story. The reader who has learned the technical strategies of writing will be more confident and more intellectually active than will the casual reader with no such knowledge. In the case of the poem, as with the car repair and the sporting event, the person's level of understanding and confidence depends on the level of his or her comprehension of the technique behind the product.

Moreover, by examining the method behind a literary work, you learn how to evaluate, more generally, a "text"—which can be not only a story, but a marketing survey, a household discussion, a television show, or someone's facial expression. Thus the questions in our book that ask you to assess the technique of a work will be stimulating a type of thinking that will not only help you succeed in other disciplines while at college, but will also help you better perceive the world—and yourself—beyond a college composition or literature course. And on the more aesthetic level, to truly understand a literary work is to better appreciate the beauty of poetry and tale-telling—a worthwhile endeavor in its own right.

We hope the assignments in this book will encourage you to value your initial reactions to the readings you are assigned, contribute (through discussion questions, writing suggestions, and excerpts from criticism) to your knowledge of them, and ultimately connect your own feelings about the topics and works with what you discovered about them through dialogues with your classmates, instructor, and critics.

Thus, you will be exploring and using literature to write more knowledgeably about topics—*self-identity, family, love, the mind, religion, nature, death*—about which you care a great deal. Through literature, then, you will see your own views on these topics expressed or illustrated; through literature, you will discover new writing techniques and strategies; through literature, you will find a variety of viewpoints on a single particular issue; *through literature you will improve your writing.*

2

READING/WRITING: THE READING PROCESS

One must be an inventor to read well. . . . There is then creative reading as well as creative writing.

—Ralph Waldo Emerson

Reading is very much a "before, during, and after" process. When you read a magazine or newspaper you may be merely gathering information or entertaining yourself, depending on the nature of the article. But when you are reading an *assigned* poem, story, or play for a college class, your approach to your subject is probably very different.

In contrast to a newspaper, magazine, or book you pick out yourself, an assigned reading may trigger agitation or apprehension. Now, instead of casually thinking, "What's the news today?" or "This is something I'm interested in," you are thinking, "What do I *have to read* for class?" You are being forced to read, even if you enjoy reading anyway, so your reading experience and mental preparedness are different.

Given these circumstances, there are several possible approaches students may take to an assigned text:

1. They read it through quickly, shrug their shoulders, and wait until their instructor goes over it in class to "understand" it. If they are called on in class to give their opinion of it, they shrug their shoulders again and mumble something about it being too complicated, deep, or depressing.

2. They read it so that they understand much of what happens in it, then put it aside and wait to hear what it is "about" from their teacher.

3. They read with intelligence and curiosity, write down questions and comments, are ready to speak about what they've read, and then share their perspectives and questions with their classmates and instructor.

Students who follow option 3 will be developing the kinds of thinking skills that may be applied to many aspects of school and life.

THE "BEFORE, DURING, AND AFTER" METHOD

Have you ever seen a film without knowing much about it beforehand? The way you act and react *before, during,* and *after* you see this film is similar to the way we are going to ask you to consider a literary text you are seeing and reading for the first time.

BEFORE the film begins, you know the title, the film's stars, and what, generally, it is about. In your mind you are predicting what will happen in it and whether you will like it.

DURING the film, your first predictions about what it is about are altered or confirmed. You notice the familiar story line or directorial touches you've noticed in other films; you compare it to other romantic, comedic, or dramatic movies you've seen; and you take note of particularly unusual camera shots, lines of dialogue, or images.

AFTER the film, you discuss the merits and/or demerits of it, and use examples to illustrate your praise or criticism. You might wonder about a particular sequence or scene that confused you, and assess it relative to your original expectations: "That was better than I expected!"; "The ending didn't make sense."

It may seem far-fetched to you, but we'd like you to see how the same process may be appropriate when reading literature.

BEFORE you read a work, *be curious* about it. Ask yourself questions:

What does the title suggest?

What are your expectations about the reading?

What can you predict about the reading in front of you?

What are you going to be reading about?

Who is the author? Is she or he familiar to you?

In other words, flex your brain muscles. Don't be a passive reader: make assumptions and predictions, just as you do before viewing a movie. Be open-minded and flexible.

DURING your reading, *engage* with the work. Do not merely ingest words; taste them. Be alert to what the author is getting across and how you are being led or influenced by him or her—how you are being guided to respond in certain ways.

Ask questions, and investigate the answers.
Wonder out loud, or in writing, about what is being written, and confess your confusion about things you don't understand. If there's a word, image, or reference you don't know, look it up! You have a dictionary, and your library has reference books, for this very purpose.

Extend, or change, your first impressions of the work.
Reconsider your initial reactions or expectations, adjusting them to what you are encountering as you read. Note how the writer is influencing your reactions.

Make connections with the work as you read.
What does it remind you of? Have you ever experienced a similar event or feeling? Do you know anyone else who has? Does a character remind you of someone you know?

Formulate generalizations about the reading.
What "type" of story, play, or poem is it? What category or genre does it fit into? What other works does it remind you of?

Notice literary features and conventions.
Writers draw upon them and expect you to be consciously or unconsciously influenced by them. In a good poem, story, or play, as in a good film, nothing is wasted. What devices is the writer using? What is the point of view? What kinds of images or symbols do you notice?

Meet the author halfway.
From what perspective, from what background and with what purpose is the author approaching this work? Rather than agreeing with everything you read, question some of it; see what the author is trying to get across, and how you are being influenced. Is there another side to the story that's not being told? Why not?

Be "within and without."
F. Scott Fitzgerald's *The Great Gatsby* is narrated by Nick Carroway, a young man who describes himself as being "both within and without" the society he is describing. Nick feels that even while he is immersed in the world he can distance himself from it enough to evaluate it. In this manner you should be reading these works: get caught up in a story but always be appreciating and/or evaluating it as a critic.

AFTER reading, step back and put the work in a broad perspective. Shift from being "within" to being "without." Do not just put the book down and wait to hear what the work is "about." You know you can talk specifically about the attributes and/or demerits of a particular movie, television show, or person. You can do so as well with words on a page that remain available to you for one or more rereadings. So treat literature as if it were a new movie, or a new CD from a musical artist or group: evaluate it, react to it, explain why you have the opinion you do about it, and why you reacted as you did when you first experienced it.

Reread, review.
Most of the works in this book are short enough to read at least twice. And just as you notice more interesting aspects of a film the second time you see it, so do the techniques and strategies behind a literary work become clearer upon each reviewing. So read it again, then step back and evaluate it.

Reassess, expand, or reject your initial impressions.
Think about your original expectations. Have they come true? What have you learned that would change or expand what you thought in the beginning?

Translate basic themes.
What is it about? What are some of the interesting issues the writer is illustrating? What seem to be his or her judgments of them? What do you think of the writer's depictions of them?

Put the reading in cultural/historical perspective.
Is the writer working with or describing the same cultural values as your own? Have social mores or opinions changed since the work was written? Can you share or understand the universal themes despite the cultural/historical differences?

Find the larger meanings.
What is the main point of the work? What seems to be the author's purpose? What do you think of it? Be careful here not to jump to an "interpretation" that cannot be justified by the details of the reading. Try instead to evaluate it sensibly, making sure that evidence in the text supports your ideas.

Compare to other works.
How does this literary work compare with others of its type? Are you reminded of other similar works? Evaluate it in relation to them.

A POEM AND A STORY: ILLUSTRATING THE BEFORE, DURING, AND AFTER METHOD

To illustrate these steps, let's consider two fairly unfamiliar works by established contemporary writers. For the first, Sharon Olds's "Photograph of the Girl," we've transcribed the oral and written reading notes of some students who were seeing the poem for the first time. (The oral comments are in quotation marks, the written comments in italics.) If you think, and write, as you read, then the reading and writing processes blend. As a result, you become a better reader and a more reflective writer.

SHARON OLDS

Photograph of the Girl

The girl sits on the hard ground,
the dry pan of Russia, in the drought
of 1921, stunned,
eyes closed, mouth open,
raw hot wind blowing
sand in her face. Hunger and puberty are
taking her together. She leans on a sack,
layers of clothes fluttering in the heat,
the new radius of her arm curved.
She cannot be beautiful, but she is
starving. Each day she grows thinner, and her bones
grow longer, porous. The caption says
she is going to starve to death that winter
with millions of others. Deep in her body
the ovaries let out her first eggs,
golden as drops of rain.

—1983

BEFORE

Here are some sample comments from students as they looked at just the author and title of the above poem (spoken comments in quotation marks, written comments in italic):

Author/Title/Prediction

- "It's a photograph, so, we'll get a picture, a snapshot. We'll have to figure out what it means."
- *Olds is always writing about adolescent females and thoughts on coming through puberty. Often sexual. Often ambiguous. Safe to say this is going to be about an adolescent female, probably something about her outward image vs. inward image.*
- *What girl? What time? What look? What society?*
- *This poem will be about a girl's innocence and possibly the ending of her innocence.*

DURING

As students read the poem, they commented on it, and asked questions about it:

Make Connections

- "This reminds me of a photograph of a Bosnian woman, or a homeless woman I saw once. She can be anyone, I guess."
- "Like a picture on a UNICEF poster."
- *This is like those TV ads about starving children in Africa.*
- *Although this is about the 1920s it could be written about many present-day issues of suffering—for example children suffering in a cancer ward.*
- *I feel a direct connection between myself and this young girl—except with the difficult time. I remember my premenstrual stage. I also notice that this picture of the girl and today's headlines are not very different. These children are timeless. How heartbreaking!*

Ask Questions, Investigate

- *What's up in Russia circa 1921?*
- "Why is the 'radius of her arm curved'"?
- "What does the poet mean by ovaries and eggs falling?"
- *Why the word "stunned"? It's a drought which must have been going on for quite a while. "Stunned" is an immediate reaction.*

Notice Literary Features

Irony

- "In a way you feel her crying out for help. But she can't because she is weak. A good example of tragedy. Tragic irony."
- "There's potential for new life and hope is dying. Kind of ironic."

Paradox

- *The many contrasts between the creation of new life and the approach of death is startling. The poem gives you hope and at the same instant snatches it away with cold reality.*
- *This girl is in a drought, dying while inside her is growing the potential for life that is like rain. The internal versus external contrast illustrates ironic tragedy.*

Tone

- *Tone is mournful, regretful: regret for the girl's sake.*
- "The speaker seems very distant."
- "Just as the speaker is empathizing for this poor girl, the reader is also led to empathize."

Imagery

- "Startling imagery. Hard ground, open mouth."

Extend Impressions

- *Other ironies: layers of clothes on a starving girl? Her arm's curved as if she's holding a baby and she's ovulating.*
- *It was very moving, filled with irony and contrast and made me feel for this girl and those people who starved that winter. . . . It caused me to think of the inner beauty all of us have, starving in poverty or not.*

Meet the Author Halfway

- "The poet is looking at the picture and describing it. She is somewhat distant from the subject."
- "She takes a personal interest in the girl; seems to feel deeply about the subject. She makes us empathize with her."
- "It's important that the speaker is a woman. The girl is changing. The speaker can relate to this woman's changing."
- *Seems like there is a photograph, and when we look closer and closer we see things that aren't visible: her bones and then even her ovaries. So she's not just an observer, she's creating this.*
- *I feel the girl's pain and the sympathy of the author. It seems the author wishes she could have done something but knows she cannot.*

AFTER

Now here are the comments students made after having read the poem, and some written comments made after a class discussion of the poem.

Reread, Review; Focus on Particular Lines

"eyes closed, mouth open, / raw hot wind blowing / in her face"

- *In this image the author creates a feeling of desperation.*

"She cannot be beautiful but she is / starving."

- "For every image there is irony and contrast. Just when it's hopeful, you're shot down and it's painful."

"layers of clothes fluttering in the heat"

- *The image I have is layers of tatters: one shirt has unconcealable holes where it's worn out, so another is added for coverage.*

"the ovaries let out her first eggs, / golden as drops of rain."

- "The chance of raining might be as slim as the girl's surviving."
- "The last lines take hope away."
- "I think of new life coming. There's death in the air but potential for life."
- *I was not sure how to interpret the last two lines of the poem. During the discussion I came to a conclusion—I believe the lines are to show the reader the sadness and hardship the girl has to deal with. The ovaries are letting out the girl's first eggs under such terrible conditions. This should be a beautiful, blossoming time in a young girl's life, where in this poem it isn't.*
- *I believe there is no hope for this young girl just as there is no hope for rain at this time either. On the other hand her "coming of age" also signifies happiness just like rain would at this time as well. Her "eggs" are letting her know that her body is still alive even if her will isn't.*

Put into Cultural Context

- *The poet compares the difficulties of the girl to that of Russia. The drought of 1921 in Russia and miserable conditions prevailing: these are similar to those of the girl. But people are still fighting to overcome it; there is still hope.*

Translate Themes

- "It's tragic in that point in time. The girl is starting out puberty but she's dying. Her arm has a new curve to it, her bones are growing, there's a contrast in the lines."
- *The hopelessness of the girl's situation with yet a new beginning which should take place but may not. . . .*

Reassess Original Impressions

- *It's not what I thought it would be, a picture with no judgments. The poet is trying to do more than just show a picture.*
- *As I read it again I get a different understanding of it. Now I see that the author is explaining that this girl, just at the age of puberty and adolescence, will starve to death. As if taken without really having been able to live. There seems to be a female-to-female bond between the author and the girl in the picture. This girl will die before reaching womanhood.*

Compare to Other Works

- "*Grapes of Wrath*. How the drought forces the family to move. 'She leans on a sack' reminds me of how families have to carry belongings."

As you can see, without a teacher's help, these students arrived at their own assessments of the poem, simply by asking questions, reassessing their views, and discussing it among themselves.

BE AN INQUIRING READER

By contrast with poems, the reading/writing process is different with stories, as you typically have more time to reflect. But there may be more ways for the author to lead and manipulate you in a story, so you should not unthinkingly allow yourself to be swept along. Be an inquiring reader.

We reprint the following story with some student questions and observations alongside the text, to show how the steps outlined on page 5 may be applied to the reading of a short story. The comments and questions you see in the right column were made by one student, Stacy DiLoreto, as she read the story for the first time. As you will see from her comments, Stacy began to see the story from a particular angle, and developed a particular interpretation of it—one that you do not necessarily have to share. The "Before" and "After" sections also include comments made by a variety of students in a freshman composition class.

The story, written by Gabriel García Márquez, is titled "The Handsomest Drowned Man in the World." García Márquez, Nobel Prize winner (1982) and Colombia's most famous writer, was born in a small coastal town in 1928, which he depicted in his most famous novel, *One Hundred Years of Solitude* (1967)—one of the many examples of his "magic realism."

BEFORE

Title: "The Handsomest Drowned Man in the World"

- *At this point, it doesn't matter what he looks like—he's in over his head!* (irony)
- *"Handsomest"—according to whom?*
- "Sounds like something a kid would say: you're my best friend in the world, you're the prettiest mommy in the world."

Expectations/Predictions

- "I'm expecting a bizarre story, sort of morbid."

DURING

Now here is the text of the story, with Stacy's comments alongside. (She circled or underlined critical or confusing words.)

GABRIEL GARCÍA MÁRQUEZ

The Handsomest Drowned Man in the World

(translated by Gregory Rabassa)

The first children who saw the dark and slinky bulge approaching through the sea let themselves think it was an empty ship. Then they saw it had no flags or masts and they thought it was a whale. But when it washed up on the beach, they removed the clumps of seaweed, the jellyfish tentacles, and the remains of fish and flotsam, and only then did they see that it was a drowned man.

"dark" = mysterious?

"slinky" = sneaky? quiet?

deluding themselves? (Fantasy better than reality)

progression from inanimate object to creature to human being.

Yuck!

They had been playing with him all afternoon, burying him in the sand and digging him up again, when someone chanced to see them and spread the alarm in the village. The men who carried him to the nearest house noticed that he weighed more than any dead man they had ever known, almost as much as a horse, and they said to each other that maybe he'd been floating too long and the water had got into his bones. When they laid him on the floor they said he'd been taller than all other men because there was barely enough room for him in the house, but they thought that maybe the ability to keep on growing after death was part of the nature of certain drowned men. He had the smell of the sea about him and only his shape gave one to suppose that it was the corpse of a human being, because the skin was covered with a crust of mud and scales.

the children don't understand the gravity of this?

"The Heaviest Drowned Man in the World?"

not very scientific; primitive speculations; not based on any solid evidence (like the title)

They did not even have to clean off his face to know that the dead man was a stranger. The village was made up of only twenty-odd wooden houses that had stone courtyards with no flowers and which were spread about on the end of a desertlike cape. There was so little land that mothers always went about with the fear that the wind would carry off their children and the few dead that the years had caused among them had to be thrown off the cliffs. But the sea was calm and bountiful and all the men fit into seven boats. So when they found the drowned man they simply had to look at one another to see that they were all there. That night they did

could not be given proper burial

not go out to work at sea. While the men went to find out if anyone was missing in neighboring villages, the women stayed behind to care for the drowned man. They took the mud off with grass swabs, they removed the underwater stones entangled in his hair, and they scraped the crust off with tools used for scaling fish. As they were doing that they noticed that the vegetation on him came from faraway oceans and deep water and that his clothes were in tatters, as if he had sailed through labyrinths of coral. They noticed too that he bore his death with pride, for he did not have the lonely look of other drowned men who came out of the sea or that haggard, needy look of men who drowned in rivers. But only when they finished cleaning him off did they become aware of the kind of man he was and it left them breathless. Not only was he the tallest, strongest, most virile, and best built man they had ever seen, but even though they were looking at him there was no room for him in their imagination.

religious image

he seems noble

their ideals on beauty

They could not find a bed in the village large enough to lay him on nor was there a table solid enough to use for his wake. The tallest men's holiday pants would not fit him, not the fattest ones' Sunday shirts, nor the shoes of the one with the biggest feet. Fascinated by his huge size and beauty, the women then decided to make him some pants from a large piece of sail and a shirt from some bridal brabant linen so that he could continue through his death with dignity. As they sewed, sitting in a circle and gazing at the corpse between stitches, it seemed to them that the wind had never been so steady nor the sea so restless as on that night and they supposed that the change had something to do with the dead man. They thought that if that magnificent man had lived in the village, his house would have had the widest doors, the highest ceiling, and the strongest floor, his bedstead would have been made from a midship frame held together by iron bolts, and his wife would have been the happiest woman. They thought that he would have had so much authority that he could have drawn fish out of the sea simply by calling their names and that he would have put so much work into his land that springs would have burst forth from among the rocks so that he would have been able to

they show respect for the dead, even though they don't know him

belief in afterlife? death as journey?

community event? seems like a ritual

attempt to explain nature by things they can understand and relate to ("this is what causes that")

superhuman quality! Jesus caught fish although his apostles could not at first (fisher of men). They think of him as a god

Jesus supposedly drew water from a stone

plant flowers on the cliffs. They secretly compared him to their own men, thinking that for all their lives theirs were incapable of doing what he could do in one night, and they ended up dismissing them deep in their hearts as the weakest, meanest, and most useless creatures on earth. They were wandering through that maze of fantasy when the oldest woman, who as the oldest had looked upon the drowned man with more compassion than passion, sighed:

What did he do?

disillusionment/pessimism—men are basically evil

"He has the face of someone called Esteban."

It was true. Most of them had only to take another look at him to see that he could not have any other name. The more stubborn among them, who were the youngest, still lived for a few hours with the illusion that when they put his clothes on and he lay among the flowers in patent leather shoes his name might be Lautaro. But it was a vain illusion. There had not been enough canvas, the poorly cut and worse sewn pants were too tight, and the hidden strength of his heart popped the buttons on his shirt. After midnight the whistling of the wind died down and the sea fell into its Wednesday drowsiness. The silence put an end to any last doubts: he was Esteban. The women who had dressed him, who had combed his hair, had cut his nails and shaved him were unable to hold back a shudder of pity when they had to resign themselves to his being dragged along the ground. It was then that they understood how unhappy he must have been with that huge body since it bothered him even after death. They could see him in life, condemned to going through doors sideways, cracking his head on crossbeams, remaining on his feet during visits, not knowing what to do with his soft, pink, sea lion hands while the lady of the house looked for her most resistant chair and begged him, frightened to death, sit here, Esteban, please, and he, leaning against the wall, smiling, don't bother ma'am, I'm fine where I am, his heels raw and his back roasted from having done the same thing so many times whenever he paid a visit, don't bother, ma'am, I'm fine where I am, just to avoid the embarrassment of breaking the chair, and never knowing perhaps that the one who said don't go, Es-

He's dead! Do they believe he can still feel?

their village is the whole world to them—they assume that every place is like their village and people are like themselves

Change from last description: "his wife the happiest woman, he the biggest, most virile . . ." Is this no longer a good quality in their eyes? Being great, or chosen, has its burdens.

teban, at least wait till the coffee's ready, were the ones who later on would whisper the big boob finally left, how nice, the handsome fool has gone. That was what the women were thinking beside the body a little before dawn. Later, when they covered his face with a handkerchief so that the light would not bother him, he looked so forever dead, so defenseless, so much like their men that the first furrows of tears opened in their hearts. It was one of the younger ones who began the weeping. The others, coming to, went from sighs to wails, and the more they sobbed the more they felt like weeping, because the drowned man was becoming all the more Esteban for them, and so they wept so much, for he was the most destitute, most peaceful, and most obliging man on earth, poor Esteban. So when the men returned with the news that the drowned man was not from the neighboring villages either, the women felt an opening of jubilation in the midst of their tears.

They always compare this man to the men in the village—this seems to bring out their men's shortcomings

humble, meek, lamb of God

note religious reference

"Praise the Lord," they sighed, "he's ours!"

The men thought the fuss was only womanish frivolity. Fatigued because of the difficult nighttime inquiries, all they wanted was to get rid of the bother of the newcomer once and for all before the sun grew strong on that arid, windless day. They improvised a litter with the remains of foremasts and gaffs, tying it together with rigging so that it would bear the weight of the body until they reached the cliffs. They wanted to tie the anchor from a cargo ship to him so that he would sink easily into the deepest waves, where fish are blind and divers die of nostalgia, and bad currents would not bring him back to shore, as had happened with other bodies. But the more they hurried, the more the women thought of ways to waste time. They walked about like startled hens, pecking with the sea charms on their breasts, some interfering on one side to put a scapular of the good wind on the drowned man, some on the other side to put a wrist compass on him, and after a great deal of *get away from there, woman, stay out of the way, look, you almost made me fall on top of the dead man,* the men began to feel mistrust in their livers and started grumbling about why so many main altar decorations for a stranger, because no matter how many nails and holy-water jars

went from water references and steady wind, to this

this seems significant, but I can't figure out exactly what it means/implies

is this common?

superstitious

great image!

"nails"—Christ

he had on him, the sharks would chew him all the same, but the women kept piling on their junk relics, running back and forth, stumbling, while they released in sighs what they did not in tears, so that the men finally exploded with *since when has there ever been such a fuss over a drifting corpse, a drowned nobody, a piece of cold Wednesday meat.* One of the women, mortified by so much lack of care, then removed the handkerchief from the dead man's face and the men were left breathless too.

Death the only certainty in life. Does this imply that no matter how religious we are, we all go to the same place anyway? Or just that we all die?

but is he a nobody?

Another religious ref.? Can't eat meat on Ash Wed. Veronica wiped Jesus' face with a handkerchief.

He was Esteban. It was not necessary to repeat it for them to recognize him. If they had been told Sir Walter Raleigh, even they might have been impressed with his gringo accent, the macaw on his shoulder, his cannibal-killing blunderbuss, but there could be only one Esteban in the world and there he was, stretched out like a sperm whale, shoeless, wearing the pants of an undersized child, and with those stony nails that had to be cut with a knife. They only had to take the handkerchief off his face to see that he was ashamed, that it was not his fault that he was so big or so heavy or so handsome, and if he had known that this was going to happen, he would have looked for a more discreet place to drown in, seriously, I even would have tied the anchor off a galleon around my neck and staggered off a cliff like someone who doesn't like things in order not to be upsetting people now with this Wednesday dead body, as you people say, in order not to be bothering anyone with this filthy piece of cold meat that doesn't have anything to do with me. There was so much truth in his manner that even the most mistrustful men, the ones who felt the bitterness of endless nights at sea fearing that their women would tire of dreaming about them and begin to dream of drowned men, even they and others who were harder still shuddered in the marrow of their bones at Esteban's sincerity.

a great man who has been reduced to this

Jesus nailed to the cross?

Or does it?

even "Doubting Thomases"

That was how they came to hold the most splendid funeral they could conceive of for an abandoned drowned man. Some women who had gone to get flowers in the neighboring villages returned with other women who could not believe what they had been told, and those women went back for more flowers

Now lots of flowers; before there were no flowers at all

when they saw the dead man, and they brought more and more until there were so many flowers and so many people that it was hard to walk about. At the final moment it pained them to return him to the waters as an orphan and they chose a father and mother from among the best people, and aunts and uncles and cousins, so that through him all the inhabitants of the village became kinsmen. Some sailors who heard weeping from a distance went off course and people heard of one who had himself tied to the mainmast, remembering ancient fables about sirens. While they fought for the privilege of carrying him on their shoulders along the steep escarpment by the cliffs, men and women became aware for the first time of the desolation of their streets, the dryness of their courtyards, the narrowness of their dreams as they faced the splendor and beauty of their drowned man. They let him go without an anchor so that he could come back if he wished and whenever he wished, and they all held their breath for the fraction of centuries the body took to fall into the abyss. They did not need to look at one another to realize that they were no longer all present, that they would never be. But they also knew that everything would be different from then on, that their houses would have wider doors, higher ceilings, and stronger floors so that Esteban's memory could go everywhere without bumping into beams and so that no one in the future would dare whisper the big boob finally died, too bad, the handsome fool has finally died, because they were going to paint their house fronts gay colors to make Esteban's memory eternal and they were going to break their backs digging for springs among the stones and planting flowers on the cliffs so that in future years at dawn the passengers on great liners would awaken, suffocated by the smell of gardens on the high seas, and the captain would have to come down from the bridge in his dress uniform, with his astrolabe, his pole star, and his row of war medals and, pointing to the promontory of roses on the horizon, he would say in fourteen languages, look there, where the wind is so peaceful now that it's gone to sleep beneath the beds, over there, where the sun's so bright that the sunflowers don't know which way to turn, yes, that's Esteban's village.

"waters"—cleansing, baptismal
Joseph and Mary were "chosen"

We're all brothers and sisters? Children of God

allusion to Odysseus in The Odyssey

Perhaps a metaphor for their souls; they realize, now, they are lacking in spirituality and see the beauty of the way of God, who had to die as a human to redeem them.

They've opened their hearts, minds and souls, so that "Esteban" may enter

People from other places could not help but hear the "Good News"

ref. to how 3 wise men found Jesus?

Which war did he fight? Battle with evil?

14 languages—for the whole world to hear

enlightenment can come from every direction if you're open to it.

AFTER

This story may be appreciated for what it illustrates and suggests about fiction, myth, legends, and storytelling. Stacy, because of her knowledge of Christianity, focused on the rich religious implications of the tale and raised several intriguing questions (it's quite useful to ask questions or to admit to confusion while reading). It's important to note that while Stacy has found a fascinating angle on the story, other readings are possible. Here is her reaction after reading and responding to the story:

> Esteban was there from the beginning of the story, but nobody immediately realized it. He was even considered a toy by the children in the village. It seemed strange to me that people who made up wives' tales and half-believed them, did not immediately have faith that this was Esteban.
>
> On the whole, I thought the story was difficult to understand. It wasn't until I read about 1/4 of it that I had any ideas on what it is about. However, it is laden with images that support my theory. It is about salvation and enlightenment. Why the women were the first to see the light, I don't know. I also don't know why the author chose to make him a drowned man. Because he was supposed to drift into their lives? Because of the significance of water as being spiritual?
>
> I am also not clear on the captain at the end. He must symbolize someone, or thing, but I'm not sure who or what. This story leaves me with unanswered questions like the one mentioned, but also gave me clues, like the ones I wrote in the margins.

Now here are some of the spoken and written comments from other students after they read the story for the first time:

Reassess initial impressions

- "At first, I was surprised that the women were taking so much care with him. Then I realized that they were actually creating a personality for this stranger."
- "As I continued to read, I realized that not only the beginning was based on a child's game of imagination, but the rest of the story was too."

Translate basic themes

- "It seems that these people aren't very satisfied with their own lives and are jealous. The women compare their husbands to him and the men probably feel a bit threatened."

Find the larger meanings

- "The story almost makes Esteban out to be a savior of some sort because of the production the women made and the result his death had on them and their land. They were treating him as if he were still alive which was weird."

- *The drowned man who acquired the name Esteban made these villagers soften and feel pity for someone they didn't even know. In doing so they saw how "bleak and dry their own village was." They saw how easily such a great life could be lost and caused them to value their own existence and improve their lives.*

As you can see, not all the steps listed in the "AFTER" section on page 10 have been followed in the student reactions to "Photograph of the Girl" and "The Handsomest Drowned Man in the World." If some are inappropriate to the work, or beyond your understanding during your first reading, that's fine. It should be evident from these student samples that even if you follow a few of the steps, your understanding of the work you are reading will be greatly increased.

3

READING/WRITING: READING JOURNALS

How do I know what I think until I see what I say?
—W. H. Auden

We suggest you keep a separate section of your class notebook or a separate notebook in which you can respond in writing to what you read. You might want to add to your journal after class discussion, but you should get in the habit of spending some private time right after reading so that you can:

- Think on paper about what you read
- Ask yourself questions about what you don't understand or what you find confusing
- Speculate about the meaning of a work and note patterns
- Collect observations, quotes, and literary images
- Try out and generate ideas for more formal essays
- Prepare for class discussion
- Examine your own attitudes about a work, an author, or a style
- Make connections with other readings, and your own knowledge
- Practice your writing
- Remember what you read

A journal serves primarily as a place to use writing as a tool for learning, discovering what you think, and becoming a more critical reader. You need not be too concerned about "getting it right."

There are different ways of keeping a reading journal, depending on your instructor's directions and your inclinations and limitations. Here are some models for you to try out. You need not limit yourself to one kind.

THE DOUBLE-ENTRY JOURNAL

In a *double-entry journal* you have a chance to talk back to the work you are reading. *You should try to write at least one page for every reading*. Fold the page in half, or draw a line vertically down the center. On one side list what you observe in the poem, story, or play you are reading or have just read: facts, names, quotations, and so on. On the other side, reflect, ask questions, make connections, evaluate, and convey your feelings about what you observed.

What I Say (Reflections on Notes)	*What the Work Says (Notes—use page number and/or line number for poems)*
Questions I want to ask	Main points
Arguments I want to make	Details
Ideas I want to know more about	Quotable quotes
What I already know about this	Images, symbols
My experiences that relate to this	Names, places
Connections to other readings I know	About the author
How I feel about this	
What I see as the effects of the author's ideas	

Here is an excerpt from a student's double-entry journal on Alice Munro's story "Boys and Girls" (p. 109 in this text):

This story is touching and is one that I feel many young girls can relate to. The girl looked down upon her mother's job of homemaking as boring and insignificant. She wanted to be appreciated and trusted by her father. After she sees the negative aspects of her father's job, she begins to mature and lean more toward her "feminine" side. I went through this myself when I was younger.	This is the story of a young girl who lives on a fox ranch w/her parents and younger brother. In the beginning she's very tomboyish and interested in her father's work. As the story progresses she realizes it may not be so bad being a girl.
The young girl does not realize that her mother was envious of her daughter's interest in the father. She thinks her mother is out to get her, as many kids do. Her mother may also be trying to protect her from the unpleasant aspects of the job.	"She was plotting now to get me to stay in the house more, although she knew I hated it. . . . It did not occur to me that she could be lonely, or jealous" (113–114)
The girl feels it is a job to be a girl or it is something she unfortunately has to work for.	"A girl was not, as I had supposed, simply what I was; it was what I had to become" (114).
The girl realizes that she is maturing and and becoming a lady, and maybe it's not so bad after all.	"I didn't protest that, even in my heart. Maybe it was true" (120).

The student has focused well on the main movement of the story, but has not become comfortable enough using her journal to react more specifically or more freely. Still, she has used her journal to identify important passages and to sum up the story's theme, *as she sees it*. When it comes time to discuss or write about "Boys and Girls," she will be one step ahead of students who did not use a reading journal.

THE SUMMARY/REFLECTION JOURNAL

The *summary/reflection journal* is a variation of the double-entry journal, but instead of dividing the page, you write your own summary in paragraph form, focusing on many of the same issues and questions you would in a double-entry journal. Then below that summary, write your reflections in paragraph form.

Here is an excerpt from a student's summary/reflection on Charlotte Perkins Gilman's "The Yellow Wallpaper" (p. 842).

> The woman in "The Yellow Wallpaper" is writing about her life. She feels as though she is ill, though there is nothing wrong with her. Her husband thinks that it is just a nervous condition and all she needs is rest. It seems as though her husband doesn't believe there is anything wrong because he doesn't want to admit that there might be something mentally wrong with her. Mental illnesses are very hard to understand and often can't really be cured.
>
> > John is practical in the extreme. He has no patience with faith, an intense horror of superstition, and he scoffs openly at any talk of things not to be felt and seen and put down in figures. (843)
>
> Throughout the story, the woman describes, in great detail, yellow wallpaper that graces the walls of her bedroom. The wallpaper is confusing, and seems to have no direction. I think the yellow wallpaper symbolizes what goes on in the woman's mind. "By daylight she is subdued, quiet. I fancy it is the pattern that keeps her so still. It is so puzzling. It keeps me quiet by the hour" (850). During the day the wallpaper is quiet as is the woman. However at night the paper is very different:
>
> > At night in any kind of light, in twilight, candlelight, lamplight, and worst of all by moonlight, it becomes bars. The outside pattern, I mean, and the woman behind it is as plain as can be. (850)
>
> Like wallpaper, at night when her husband returns home, the woman feels trapped as though she were behind bars. Her own husband is trapping her in a world where she cannot survive; she has to get out. "[S]he is all the time trying to climb through. But nobody could climb through that pattern—it strangles so; I think that is why it has so many heads" (852).

This student, Rosy, has patiently reflected on the story, and picked out some passages that impressed her as significant. As a result, were she to use "The Yellow Wallpaper" in her paper on the subject of *Madness* (see the cluster beginning on page 830), she has already done much of the work and fleshed out some of her ideas.

THE FREEWRITING JOURNAL

A *freewriting journal* is more like a diary of a reading, where you can write informally about your initial reactions to the work. If you are intrigued by certain statements, characters, issues or problems, write about them. Spend at least 10 to 15 minutes writing whenever you have finished reading, or when you have put your book down for a break.

By the end of the following freewriting-journal reaction to Sharon Olds's "Photograph of the Girl" (p. 8), Annette has not only guessed what must have been the source of the poem, but also arrives at a greater understanding of the poem than when she began her journal entry. And that's what reading journals are all about!

> I envision a poor little girl sitting on a stump. The kind of people you see in *Time Magazine* and they are explaining what is happening in their country and what it is doing to the children and people. You feel sorry for this girl because she cannot live her full life unless some miracle happens. She has to be about 13–15 and she is already dying because of lack of nourishment. You envision the picture to look very deathly looking, and to think she is younger than us and has nothing to look forward to. She has no body, and she will starve to death, at least she won't die alone.
>
> The last two lines are very confusing. Forget it, I got it! Her body is trying to adjust to being a woman. But it is sad to think she may never reach the day to see herself as a woman.
>
> This is a very sad poem, and it makes you grateful that you are not suffering like her. This is not a poem I would preferably want to read.

Whatever journal you use—double-entry, summary/reflection, or freewriting—keep it close by you when you read. You may want to write something as it strikes you, rather than waiting until you are finished. But do try to write immediately after you finish as well. As you can see from the preceding samples, reading journals increase comprehension of a work, and *begin the writing process*. When it came time for these students to write the first draft of their essay, they found it much easier than they would have without a reading journal. In effect, they had already begun writing their paper, by articulating their thoughts on each work that they had read.

4

THE WRITING PROCESS

Writing is a deliberate act;
one has to make up one's mind to do it.

—James Britton

Writing is not just one process, but several. You are constantly handling many different demands: composing ideas, organizing thoughts, writing complete sentences. Like a busy switchboard operator, you are trying to keep the wires uncrossed and the communication clear.

Although we talk about the stages of the process—prewriting, drafting, revising, and editing—we know that when you write, you do not really proceed in such a lockstep fashion. Rather, you go back and forth, gathering ideas and thinking about the essay, clarifying your thoughts as you write, refining and correcting as you revise and edit.

It is important, however, to actually experience each stage as you write an essay about literature—or about any subject. The process is individual and complex, but there are certain rituals that many writers follow, and certain techniques that can help you write effectively.

PREWRITING

Perhaps *percolating* is a better term since ideas bubble up throughout the process as you try to discover what you want to say. A writer percolates ideas, stirs words together, and mixes the right amount of spicy ingredients into sentences and paragraphs so they work together to create a palatable essay.

Even as you do other things—get something to eat, listen to music, stare out the window—you can half-consciously generate ideas. It is best to deliberately collect information, begin to focus, relate new to old information, and begin to ask and answer questions. You can set goals for yourself and make a commitment to your subject. Spend some time playing with ideas, allowing yourself to be creative and experimental.

Some examples follow of techniques to use. Try each of them. One or two will work better for you than others, depending on your purpose, needs, and thinking style.

Freewriting

Put yourself on automatic pilot and write out your thoughts nonstop: write everything you already know or would like to know about your topic. Give yourself 10 to 20 minutes and don't stop writing, not even for a moment, until you're done. You can include your frustrations—"I just don't have any good ideas"—as well as information and, of course, gems of wisdom.

Here is Joanne's response to the *freewriting* assignment at the beginning of the assignment sequence for the "Becoming a Person" cluster (Chapter 9, p.86). The assignment asks students to write about an *epiphany* in their lives:

> A time in my life when I was disillusioned by the world was when I got my first job. I was fourteen years old and really never knew what the world was really about. I began to realize that nothing comes easy in this world and a person has to work very hard for every penny they earn. I realized this because of the people I worked with. They were mostly all married or had children on the way, or both. For them it's harder to survive than normal. They have bills to pay and children to feed. A supermarket salary is not the greatest one around, but these people all had problems when they were younger and never got the proper education or the chance to work for a better job. This world can be cruel to people who deserve better. Living in this world today a person really has to work their butt off just to live comfortably. I realized that the world is cruel and heartless and has no sympathy for people in need.

Beginning with her own experience of disillusionment, Joanne arrived at what could later become the focus of a longer paper on the cluster: the theme of an individual learning about the heartlessness of the world.

In a freewriting exercise, try to write out both facts and feelings as you seek to explore the topic. Don't stop to correct spelling or grammar.

Brainstorming

Make lists creatively by emptying your head about the topic onto the page—a kind of "data dumping." You can work alone or with others, jotting down words, not sentences, related to the topic. Phrasing and ordering can be flexible. You can use code words. As with freewriting, you need not commit to any of these ideas. You might end up throwing this list away, but some of the items might become key phrases.

In the following sample, Joanne *brainstorms* about "Photograph of the Girl":

Puberty/menstrual cycle

Photo, Ethiopia—TV commercial Dead already

autobiographical suffering from inevitable

sexist? uncontrollable

no parents lonesome

While this may seem like a random list of words, in fact there is real insight revealed here: Joanne has made a connection between the poem and the late-night television commercials for charity organizations, in that both play on our emotions by presenting an upsetting image that arouses our sympathies; she has also questioned whether the portrayal of the girl is sexist (would the poem be as moving if it were about a boy?), and has emphasized the "inevitable" doom of the girl in addition to her consequent isolation.

Clustering

Clustering, or *mapping,* is the process by which you create a visual map springing from one word or phrase that serves as a nucleus. This is a nonlinear brainstorming process through which you can free-associate ideas and details. You might even be able to see categories of ideas. Concrete words can trigger more details that make for lively writing.

The following is Joanne's clustering reaction to Gabriel García Márquez's "The Handsomest Drowned Man in the World" (p. 13):

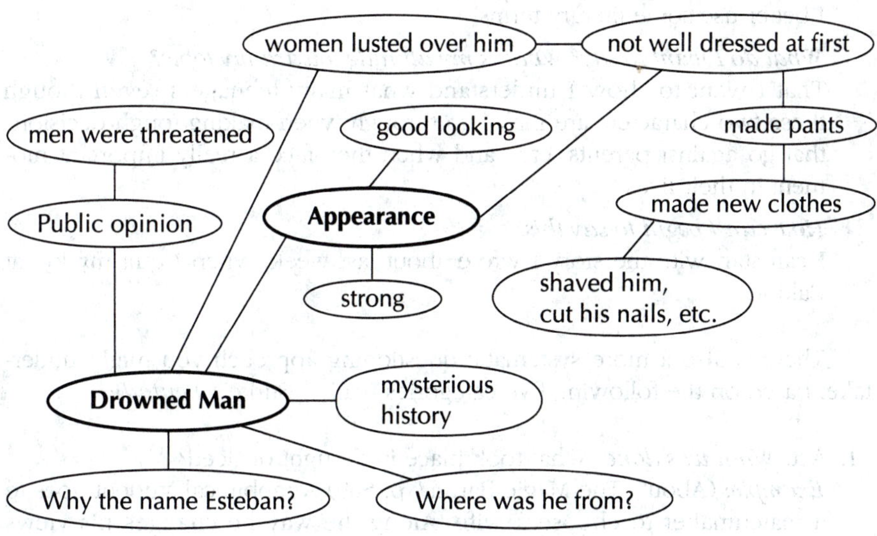

Asking a Series of Questions

Another alternative is to sit down with the following questions in front of you and write down some informal answers to them:

- What do I know already?
- What is my purpose? Why am I writing this?
- Who will read this?
- What might I want to say? What is my attitude toward my topic?
- How can I begin to say this?

The following is the thinking process Kim went through before writing her paper for the "Becoming a Person" cluster (p. 86). In her first draft she focused on Updike's "A & P," but in subsequent drafts she expanded the scope of her paper to include more of her own experiences and other works in the cluster:

> *What do I know already?*
> I know that Sammy experiences an *epiphany* when he says, "My stomach kind of fell." (p. 108). This quote is important.
>
> *What is my purpose?*
> To talk about what "becoming a person" means to Sammy and to me—and maybe connect Sammy's experience with the boy's in "Araby."
>
> *Who will read this?*
> My classmates, so I better make it interesting for them, and [my teacher], so I better use some literary terms!
>
> *What do I want to say? What is my attitude toward my topic?*
> That I want to show I understand what many teenagers (even though these two characters are male) go through when making tough decisions that go against parents, etc., and when they face a really important moment in their lives.
>
> *How can I begin to say this?*
> I can start with the story I wrote about last week, when I quit my job at Caldor.

There is also a more systematic questioning approach you might undertake, based on the following five categories (called Burke's *Pentad*):

1. Act. *What was done?* What took place in thought or deed?
   Example: (About "The Magic Barrel," p. 569) A rabbinical student goes to a matchmaker to choose a wife. Along the way he changes his views about love and marriage, and about himself.

2. Scene. *When or where was it done?*
   Example: In New York, in Finkle's dingy apartment and the neighborhood streets.
3. Agent. *Who did it?* What person or kind of person performed the act?
   Example: Leo Finkle is the protagonist, but the agent may be the matchmaker, Saltzman, since he manipulates Finkle through the prospects he introduces to him, until Finkle falls in love with a photograph of Saltzman's daughter.
4. Agency. *How did he or she do it?* What means or instruments were used?
   Example: Saltzman plants a photograph of his daughter in a folder he gives Finkle.
5. Purpose. *Why did it happen?* What was the main motivation?
   Example: The purpose of Saltzman's act is to provide an excellent match for his wayward daughter. He may have been motivated as well to help Finkle, whose faith was wavering: Finkle could focus on the redemption of Stella rather than on his own troubled state.

Notice that you can use the answer to any one of the five questions as the focus of your paper. As you answer these questions your thesis may become clear, even while others may crop up as possibilities. Other examples regarding the same story might have focused on Finkle as the agent, Saltzman (or one of the women) as the instrument, and his need to find a spouse as his purpose.

Note-Taking

Once you've come up with a topic, go back to your journal and to the texts and begin to reread, jotting down all the information related to your topic and what interests you. Be sure to copy notes exactly, with page numbers. Go back with direction, with a "nutshell sentence" (see p. 31) in your head.

DRAFTING

Just as most artists make sketches before they paint, most writers need to map out their ideas in an organized way. You can discover whether you are saying what you want to when you actually organize your ideas in writing or on the computer screen. This act of writing should be seen not as a final step, but as an interim stage between gathering ideas and revising and editing, all of which are probably going on at the same time. You should try to separate this act of composing from trying to get your writing into perfectly correct English; that will come later. Here the emphasis is on composing—being spontaneous.

This is the time when you need to ask yourself, "How do I know what I think until I say what I mean?"

There are no simple rules, but there are certain guidelines and strategies you can use as you compose a draft of your paper.

Avoiding Generalizations and Unsupported Opinions

Generalizations are only as worthwhile as the evidence behind them. The writer who wants to be believed should have facts, concrete details, evidence, and often the authority of genuine experience. Remember, the more specific and particular your writing, the more universal it will be. If you give details, no matter how personal, it is easier for the reader to relate to what you've written.

It can be quite useless simply to state generally known facts (since the reader already knows them) or to state a strong opinion without any evidence. In fact, such statements work *against* your chances of successfully engaging the reader. Consider the following opening sentence to one student's essay on the "Married Love" cluster (pp. 630–722):

> A marriage relies on many different things to make it last. The most important of these is effective communication. If a couple cannot communicate effectively then it becomes difficult for one member to express any problems that exist. The problem of lack of communication exists in the play *A Doll's House* and the short story "The Yellow Wallpaper."

Since everyone knows that "a marriage relies on many different things to make it last," and since most people would agree that communication is important, this student might as well have begun with the last sentence of the paragraph, either leaving out the first three or improving upon her introduction (see pp. 33–38 for introduction ideas). Indeed, even the last sentence is a bit too general: a lack of communication "exists" in the two works she will be writing about, but perhaps a clearer statement would be that those works *emphasize* that particular marital problem.

Here is another problematic introduction:

> In John Updike's "A & P" many images are used. Authors use images to create pictures in the reader's mind. Most of these images deal with food or sex. However, I will focus on other images not dealing with food or sex which are just as important. These images focus on a town. This town is old, boring and unwilling to change.

While this paper might have an interesting focus—the *setting* of Updike's story rather than the main character's actions or opinions—there is no need for the general sentences on images that begin the paper. In attempting to introduce his paper using a general-to-specific format, this student has fallen prey to an all-too-common tendency to present broad, general statements.

Using a Nutshell Sentence

Using a *nutshell sentence* is a good way to get started. Summarize what you want to say—make the most important assertion you can make about the topic—in one sentence or a few sentences, and use that as a working thesis or focus statement. Actually, it is a good idea to try out a few of these sentences, and then to choose the best one to work with.

The following is a nutshell sentence from the outline of a student paper on the "Seeing" cluster, focusing on Elizabeth Bishop's poem "The Fish":

> Any creature that is hanging on a line, totally defenseless, can make someone think about ending a living thing's life. The fish was taken from its territory intentionally for death, and is in pain. Obviously the creature gave a great struggle, leaving the "green line frayed at the end," showing the extent to which living things heroically hang on to life to the end.

Although this nutshell sentence is more than a sentence long, it's more important to get your thoughts down in an organized way than to adhere to a one-sentence format. The sentences may not be as focused or well articulated as a single sentence, but that's all right too. Nutshell sentences are meant to be flexible (see p. 43).

Using Organizing Strategies

Some strategies help you move from the beginning into the middle and to the end of your essay. At some point in your education you might have learned the formula of the five-paragraph essay: one idea (thesis), three supporting paragraphs (three major reasons, causes, factors, or points), introduction, and conclusion. Although that approach can serve as a starting point—serving the same purpose as training wheels on a bike—it too often limits the real thinking and exploring necessary for essay writing. How often do you find articles in the "real world" written in this way? Instead, try to think of writing as a journey of exploration; you need logical starting and ending points, and a map of the route you will take, with *signposts* (see below). Here are some patterns of organization that might help you as you structure your paragraphs and/or your entire essay.

Description: show how something looks, feels, smells, and so forth. Use detail until you complete the picture.

Chronology: tell what comes first, second, or next, in chronological order.

Illustration: make a point and give specific examples.

Use of Analogies: compare your point to something more familiar to your reader. (See p. 63 for our own use of *analogy* to explain the importance of understanding literary technique.)

Definition: explain what something means.

Classification: divide your subject into groups or categories.

Comparison/Contrast: put two things together to show significant similarities and differences.

Cause and Effect: explain how one thing leads to another.

Argumentation: persuade the reader to adopt an opinion.

Problem/Solution: frame or present a problem and offer solutions.

These strategies can help you as you generate ideas and also as you organize your writing. Usually, you would combine a few of these methods as you write; they are not always distinguishable, but you should be able to call upon them as organizing strategies.

You also need to think about organizing strategies within paragraphs. Do you start with your least important idea and build up to the most important, or vice versa? Do you start with a simple idea and work up to one that is more complex? You need to think about how you will present your ideas to make them as clear, persuasive, and interesting as they can be. Refer to one of the sample essays in Appendix A or B (pp. 1016–1019). What organizing strategies does the writer use?

Using Signposts

Signposts, also known as *transitional* or *bridge* words, help guide the reader between and within sentences and paragraphs, showing how sentences and/or paragraphs relate to each other. However (there's a signpost word!), these words need to be chosen carefully and used judiciously. As a writer you need to make the connections logically; the signpost words can help clarify these connections but should not clutter up your prose.

Many different kinds of words, phrases, and clauses can serve as signposts: synonyms, pronouns (which always need clear referents), repetition of key words, and word patterns. Here is a brief list of those connecting words that can illustrate different kinds of relationships:

Adding a Point: furthermore, besides, finally, in addition to, moreover, also

Emphasis: above all, indeed, in fact, in other words, most important

Time: then, afterwards, eventually, next, immediately, meanwhile, previously, often, later, usually

Cause and Effect: as a result, consequently, therefore, thus, hence

Examples: for example, for instance

Progression: first, second, third, furthermore

Contrast: but, however, in contrast, instead, nevertheless, on the contrary, on the other hand, still, unfortunately, rather, at least

Conclusions: therefore, to sum up, in brief, in general, for these reasons, finally, in conclusion

Signposts can be used poorly, especially when the sentences that are being connected merely repeat themselves, as in this example from a student essay: "The girl in this poem ['Photograph of the Girl,' p. 8)] is starving. Moreover, she has probably not had anything to eat in a long time."

But for the most part, students don't use signposts frequently enough. Properly used, they can give your writing unity and coherence—what many students call "flow." Here is an example from Elizabeth's paper on the "Phenomenal Woman" cluster (pp. 192–233):

> Through Angelou's poem ["Phenomenal Woman"], we can see that she is aware of the male feelings toward women, but that she rises above their low expectations. Rushin, *on the other hand,* writes [in "The Tired Poem"] about her frustration regarding male attitudes toward women, placing all her focus on the wrongs that men do *rather than* the good that women are capable of.

Writing Introductions and Conclusions

The *introduction* helps to engage readers and orient them for the journey. It serves as both advertisement and map for the trip, in that the writer is both enticing (or "hooking") the travellers/readers, and giving them specific directions. (See page 37 for more on introductions and conclusions.)

Here is an introduction from Heather's paper that succeeds in both attracting and directing the reader:

> "Make sure you call me when you get there and be home by 11:30." For years these, and many other words, have drifted off my mother's lips and formed chains around my wrists and ankles. Each time I receive a warning, the chains get heavier and heavier, and I struggle even harder for my independence and freedom. These chains of love (as my mother calls them) create conflict between the two of us. The poem "Today," by Margaret Atwood, describes some of these conflicts and struggles through the eyes of a mother—a mother trying to protect her daughter from her own innocence.

The *conclusion* marks the final destination. It can reflect on the journey or serve to make a climactic point. It should never just repeat what was said in the opening. Try not to use your conclusion merely as a wrap-up: instead, use it to urge your point home, punctuate your essay, or appeal to the reader's emotions.

At the end of his long paper on the "Death & Co." readings (pp. 989–1015), Patrick uses his last paragraph to urge a new confrontational attitude toward death, as the works in that cluster encourage:

> Death is a harsh reality that we all have to come to terms with. We must come to accept the fact that death is inevitable, unchallengeable, and uncontrollable. We must begin to see death as an everyday reality instead of a taboo subject, for only through acceptance will we truly be able to come to terms with it. And while it may seem dreary, we must take the time to analyze and learn from the human process of mourning. For only then will we be able to conquer our greatest fear of all: Death.

Asking the Right Questions

As you begin to revise, think about questions that a reader might ask to see whether you have answered them in your writing. (The following are adapted from Mina Shaughnessy, *Errors and Expectations,* New York: Oxford University Press, 1977.)

Reader's Questions	*Writer's Response*
What are you going to say?	Introduction, lead
What's your point?	Thesis, main idea statement
What do you mean?	Qualifying statements, examples
Can you prove it? Show me.	Examples, quotations, information, details
So what?	Conclusion

REVISING

Revising means reseeing. This is the stage when you reshape and bring into focus what you really want to say, and see whether you have said it effectively. You need to shift your perspective from writer to critical reader, from your "writing self" to your "reading self." How do you gain this kind of distance?

One way is to *leave enough time*. Many professional writers put their writing away for weeks. Ray Bradbury, the science fiction writer, tries to leave his stories for one year before he revises them. Your instructor may not give you that luxury, but you should give yourself at least a day or night before you attempt to rework your draft.

This is when you think hard about those questions your readers might ask (see the list above). Think also about how each page, paragraph, sentence, line, and word fits in with what you really want to say. Often, a chain reaction is set off; you change one sentence or word and that affects a whole paragraph.

Another way to become more critically detached is to *seek help from others*. Although as the writer you have the ultimate responsibility for making decisions about what works best in your essay, you would benefit from having someone else read it, or reading it to another person. Often a friend can see flaws you can't in your own work. Even the very best writers get feedback on their work from other writers, friends, and editors. There are many ways you can share your essays with your peers, both giving and getting feedback.

Here are some more detailed guidelines and techniques you may find helpful when you are revising your papers. (See also the Revision Checklist on page 40.) Some are designed for working alone and some for working with at least one other person.

Making a Descriptive Outline

By yourself or with someone else, you might make a *descriptive outline* of your essay. For many people, outlining before beginning to write is difficult. But at the drafting stage outlining is critical. Start by writing your main idea, or nutshell sentence (p. 31), which usually appears in your introduction. Then write a one-sentence summary of each paragraph. You might also write a second sentence that sums up what each paragraph does.

Below is an example of a descriptive outline of a draft of Deirdre's short paper focusing on Roethke's "My Papa's Waltz" (see p. 470):

1. I want to compare my father to Roethke's—difference in time spent with me.
2. Roethke shows that he cares deeply about his father and looks back fondly in spite of his father's alcoholism.
3. I can remember "romping" with my father when I was three just as Roethke's father danced and played with him.
4. Poem is about an abused son who looks back at father with contentment; but from my perspective I see myself waltzing through life with my father.

Now here is the draft of Deirdre's paper from which she made her outline. Can you point out the weaknesses that she will need to address when she prepares to revise it?

> My father was not an alcoholic, nor was he an abusive man. But when reading Theodore Roethke's poem "My Papa's Waltz" I saw characteristics of him. Yet he differs from the interpretation of Roethke's father we discussed in class. Roethke's father abused him; mine was simply spending quality time with me.
>
> Roethke describes his father as a drinker: "the whiskey on your breath / Could make a small boy dizzy." A common association with alcoholics is that they are vicious and beat their children. One would understandingly assume that their children would inherit the same characteristics. But in Roethke's poem the tone is not of an angry, abused child, yet one of contentment; the speaker looks back on his childhood fondly. As much as society looks down upon alcoholics and child abusers, Roethke shows that though it may not have been a wonderful experience, he did come to care for his father deeply.
>
> Roethke's work is interpreted from a male point of view—understandably so, considering it was a man who wrote. But when I read it, I took it from a female perspective as well as a personal one. The work returned me to a time when I was three to five years old. At that age we are still so young and naive and still see our parents as the "be all and end all" of our tiny universes. Taking into consideration that I am the youngest and only girl, one can assume that I was Daddy's little girl. "My Papa's Waltz" was not about a drunk father beating his son but of a happy one sharing a dance with his little boy. My father and I did "romp until the pans slid from the kitchen shelf."
>
> My father taught me that hard work was the only kind of work worth doing. He proved it to me because "the hand that held my wrist was battered on one knuckle; with a palm caked hard by dirt." The hand was not battered by alcoholic rages but by hard work. Furthermore, after a night of waltzing, a young girl is sure to be tired as her father tucks her in for a night's rest; he "then waltzed me off to bed, still clinging to [his] shirt."
>
> "My Papa's Waltz" by Theodore Roethke is a poem about an abused son looking back on his life with an abusive father and seeing it contentedly. From where I stand, it is about a father waltzing with his little girl and teaching her how to dance through life.

Deirdre has appropriated some of the Roethke poem to her own experiences and feelings, which is one way of writing "through" literature. Following the assignment sequence in the cluster "My Father's Life" (pp. 446–474), her outline will be expanded to bring in other works and other ideas. What strengths and weaknesses do you recognize in this draft? What suggestions for revision might you make as Deirdre moves from personal experience to literary analysis?

Changing the Introduction and/or Conclusion

Have you begun your essay so that you have engaged, oriented, and directed the reader in the most interesting way possible? You might consider using one of the following:

- A lively quotation
- An analogy
- A problem or dilemma to be solved
- An anecdote
- A striking image
- An intriguing question (that you will attempt to answer in your essay)
- A strong assertion

You might also use one of these devices to improve your *conclusion*. The conclusion need not be too long or drawn out, but it might have a twist, or a provocative statement that leaves the reader thinking about the implications of your essay.

Checking for Signposts and Transitions

You might circle them: the words that help you to show logical connections, and the words that help you link one sentence or paragraph to the next (see page 32 for more details). Do you have enough? Too many? What patterns of organization have you used?

Gathering Peer Review Ideas

You can solve many problems with your writing by exchanging drafts-in-progress with one or more of your classmates. No matter how accomplished a writer you are, you can benefit from peer review, since what is clear to you, the writer, is not always clear to the reader. And often what you *think* is clear to the reader actually isn't.

There are various ways you can work on your papers in stages and get feedback from your peers, depending on your instructor's directions. It is always important to make suggestions to your classmates that will be helpful and positive. Remember, the writer has the final authority and responsibility for making any changes.

Here are some strategies to use, followed by a list of questions that can be asked about drafts. Not all questions need to be answered each time.

- Comments should always be descriptive and specific rather than general: "In this sentence you effectively show why . . ." or, "I had trouble following this paragraph because . . ." and *not* "This is a good paper," or "I liked it."
- *The writer* may first ask for help on specific parts of a draft, or ask if a point seems to be clear.
- *The reader* might write a descriptive outline of his or her partner's essay, summarizing in one sentence what each paragraph says and, perhaps, summarizing in another sentence what each paragraph does (illustrates, explains, etc.).
- When working with peers, it is usually helpful to combine *reading* essays aloud (and conferring about them) with *writing* your specific suggestions.

Here is a list of questions to guide peer review groups. As you critique a fellow student's draft, you might ask these questions:

1. What does the writer want to say in this essay? Retell and/or underline the main point of the paper.
2. What is the most effective part of this essay, and why?
3. What is the least effective part of this essay, and why?
4. How does the writer develop and support his or her main ideas? Point to specific evidence used.
5. Are there places where more evidence is needed?
6. Does the introduction "hook" you into the essay? Is the conclusion effective, or does it merely repeat the introduction?
7. What, specifically, can be done to improve this essay?
8. What is your overall evaluation of this essay? What grade would you give it and why?

EDITING

Now we come to the final stage, at which you closely examine your writing to detect and correct violations in writing conventions, inaccuracies in word meanings, and problems in grammar and spelling. Although you have probably begun to monitor these things from the beginning, it is better to give yourself permission to be more spontaneous when you begin to write, and set aside special proofreading time at the very end of the writing process.

Proofreading How-Tos

1. Force yourself to read your essay slowly and, preferably, out loud. You might even use something (a ruler, or index card) to prevent you from reading more than one line at a time.
2. Be systematic and use a brightly colored pen or pencil. Make both marginal (in the margins alongside your draft) and internal (within the text of the paper) notes, and write questions. Although you will focus more on proofreading for spelling and grammar a bit later, you could begin to circle problematic words and phrases.

Using the Computer

Most of you have probably done some word-processing and know how useful a tool the computer is for a writer. It allows you to write freely, without worrying about errors at first or retyping whole drafts. You can move whole blocks of text, fill in new information, check spelling and grammar, and then store your writing on disks for future reference.

Some people are more comfortable writing first by hand, while others choose to type directly onto the computer. Whatever method you use, revising becomes much more feasible with a computer. It is still important, however, to print out a copy to edit, perhaps with someone else, and not to rely on the computer to find all the problems. After all it is just a machine. It can't tell the difference between *their* and *there,* or between other homophones. It can't recognize a word left out nor can it solve stylistic flaws.

But most important, a computer doesn't beep when you don't support your ideas or when you write very simplistically or lazily. Some students hand in papers with elaborately designed title pages and enormous lettering, forgetting that what counts most is *what* they are writing, not how it looks. The best computer and fanciest laser printer can't make up for flat writing.

Some very exciting ideas and strategies combining computers and writing have been tried out in colleges and universities; the possibilities keep expanding. Now, many people at one time can read a draft of your essay on their computer monitors and offer suggestions to improve it, and many college libraries offer the capacity for computer research that brings a staggering amount of information to the screen, and to hard copy, in seconds. Be sure to find out just what your college library has to offer.

The more practice you get using your computer, the more efficient you will become and the more shortcuts you will find. Just don't wait until five minutes before the essay is due to print it!

A REVISION CHECKLIST

Here are some questions you might ask yourself after you have written a draft of your paper:

1. Do I have a title that is fitting?
2. Do I include the title and author of the work(s) I am discussing the first time I mention them?
3. What is my main idea, or my thesis? Do I make it clear soon enough and keep my focus throughout the essay?
4. Do I develop my thesis and main points enough? Are my general statements and ideas supported by appropriate concrete details, especially by brief quotations from the text?
5. Is each paragraph unified by a topic sentence or topic idea? Are there adequate transitions from one paragraph to the next? How many paragraphs do I have?
6. Is my organization reasonable? Does each point lead to the next? Do I follow a plan, according to categories I have set up, according to degree of importance, and so on? Are there any irrelevant parts?
7. Is my introduction interesting and focused? Is my conclusion appropriate and provocative without being repetitive?
8. Is my tone formal enough? Not too formal? Am I too tentative, sarcastic, or apologetic? Is my style effective, my vocabulary adequate?
9. Are my quotations accurate? Do they serve a real purpose rather than just adding words? Do I document the quotations with page numbers in parentheses?
10. Have I proofread carefully? Are there any editing problems—spelling, mechanics, and so forth?

AN EDITING CHECKLIST

Sentences: 1. Is every sentence "healthy"? No run-ons, fragments?

Agreement: 2. Do nouns (subjects) and verbs agree in every sentence?

3. Do nouns and pronouns agree?

Tense: 4. Are verb tenses consistent, rather than shifting from sentence to sentence?

5. Do verb tenses match correctly within sentences?

Conventions:

6. Are all new paragraphs indented?
7. Is the spelling accurate?
8. Are all apostrophes included (to show ownership and for contractions)?

Pronouns:

9. Do we know to whom each pronoun refers?
10. Are pronouns consistent in person throughout the essay?

Sentences:

11. Is the sentence style varied rather than monotonous?
12. Are there some short, some long, some compound, and some complex sentences?
13. Should some short sentences be combined?

Prose Style:

14. Are the verbs carefully chosen? Do they reflect what I really want to say, or are they commonly used words that don't convey my meaning exactly?
15. Am I writing in the active, rather than the passive, voice?
16. Have I eliminated prepositional phrases and nouns that I don't really need?

It may seem like painstaking work to actually ask yourself all these questions after you have expended a great deal of time and energy writing your essay. But taking the time to go over this list not only will improve your grade, it will also give you practice with the kind of work habits that will make you a better, more polished writer.

5

FROM PERSONAL RESPONSE TO CRITICAL INQUIRY

You have seen how the reading and writing processes are intersecting and complementary; you have to cross paths and travel in many directions on the way. If you experience each stage, you can ultimately complete a journey through a literary work that rewards you as readers and writers.

Let's look at how you can make this journey from a personal response to a poem toward a more coherent interpretation, and finally toward the completion of a critical analysis that might include integrating outside sources.

GWENDOLYN BROOKS

We Real Cool

The Pool Players.
Seven at the Golden Shovel.

We real cool. We
Left school. We

Lurk late. We
Strike straight. We

Sing sin. We
Thin gin. We

Jazz June. We
Die soon.

—1960

Your first reading of this interesting poem will probably be tentative: you might want to write a journal entry where you record your initial observations, reflections, and questions.

JOURNAL RESPONSES

Here is an excerpt from Kate's journal:

> ["We Real Cool"] is a poem that describes the attitude of juvenile delinquents or any adolescents that are having trouble and falling into patterns where they feel it is better to "live fast and die young."
>
> This poem has great significance for me since I just graduated from high school one year ago (less than that!). I have seen many of my friends go through the pattern of saying "Why bother?" and then going out to get drunk and play pool. My one experience with this came when I was 16 and had culture shock when I got back from Australia after being an exchange student. I had great difficulty adjusting to my parents' strict rules and regulations . . . I did a lot of pool playing that year . . .
>
> The only line I did not understand was: "We/ Jazz June." Does it mean they graduate?

Here is an excerpt from Don's journal:

> I liked Gwendolyn Brooks's poem "We Real Cool." I think the poem is referring to young black men who left school early and are now not doing much with their lives.
>
> This poem was written by one of the community and it shows the author's disgust and disdain for these men, not making anything of their lives. She seems to be saying that they are fooling only themselves that they are "cool" but finally losing by dying soon.

You might try to read the poem again at this point, now with your classmates. Does it sound like a funeral dirge? A jazz tune? Rap? How much do the *meter* (p. 68) and *rhyme* (p. 68) affect its meaning? Have you noticed the play of *alliteration* (p. 68)? What *images* (p. 77) and/or patterns of images strike you?

NUTSHELL SENTENCES

After you have a chance to discuss your journals and the poem with your classmates, you might try to put together a *nutshell sentence* (see page 31)—a one-sentence statement that sums up and captures for you the significant meaning of the poem. This sentence can help you summarize and focus your thoughts as you strive for a comprehensive interpretation, taking into account all that you might say about what the poem means and *how* the poem means (how the poet conveys her meaning, what techniques she uses, etc.).

Kate got together with a small group of students and they came up with this nutshell sentence:

> "We Real Cool" by Gwendolyn Brooks is a poem that describes the attitude of people who live life on the edge, drop-outs or musicians trying to make it—people who feel it is better to "live fast and die young."

Lisa's group came up with two nutshell sentences:

1. The kids in "We Real Cool" by Gwendolyn Brooks are living for the moment; unfortunately, when the moment you live for is over, so are you.
2. "We Real Cool" can be read on two different levels—the first meaning of cool is "with it" and knows what's going on; the other meaning can be interpreted as cold, indifferent, mean and impenetrable—this may be their attitude towards society.

Which nutshell sentence do you prefer? Could you use one of them to help you focus an extended analysis of the poem?

CRITICAL COMMENTARY

At this point you might want to extend your critical inquiry of the poem to include outside sources. Did the discussion provoke any questions about the author? Do you want to further investigate ideas about how the rhythm of the poem affects its meaning? This seemingly simple poem can be quite intriguing and complex. You can read what other scholars have written about the poem to add another dimension to your understanding.

It is usually a good idea to read critical sources *after* you have done your own thinking about a literary work. Then, you can decide what information is most useful, which ideas make sense, and whether scholars substantiate your own conclusions or offer different ways of looking at the work. Interaction between the ideas you develop yourself and the material you find in any sources you use is important.

The following are a few excerpts from scholars writing about Gwendolyn Brooks as a poet, all taken from Maria K. Mootry and Gary Smith, eds., *A Life Distilled: Gwendolyn Brooks, Her Poetry and Fiction* (Chicago: University of Chicago Press, 1989). Take a few minutes to read them:

1. [Hortense J. Spillers, from "Gwendolyn the Terrible"]
   [Gwendolyn Brooks has said,] "My aim, in my next future, is to write poems that will somehow successfully 'call' . . . all black people: black people in taverns, black people in alleys, black people in gutters, schools, offices, fac-

tories, prisons, the consulate . . . ; *not* always to 'teach'—I shall wish often to entertain, to illumine. My newish voice will not be an imitation of the contemporary young black voice, which I so admire, but an extending adaptation of today's G. B. voice."

"Today's G. B. voice" is one of the most complex on the American scene precisely because Brooks refuses to make easy judgments. In fact, her disposition to preserve judgment is directly mirrored in a poetry of cunning, laconic surprise. Any descriptive catalog can be . . . strained in her case: I have tried "uncluttered," "clean," "robust," ingenious," "unorthodox," and in each case a handful of poems will fit. This method of grading and cataloging, however, is essentially busywork, and we are still left with the main business. What in this poetry is stunning and evasive?

To begin with . . . "We Real Cool" illustrates the wealth of implication that the poet can achieve in a very spare poem. . . . The simplicity of the poem is stark to the point of elaborateness. Less than lean, it is virtually coded. Made up entirely of monosyllables and end-stops, the poem is no non-sense at all. Gathered in eight units of three-beat lines, it does not necessarily invite inflection, but its persistent bump on "we" suggests waltz time to my ear. If the reader chooses to render the poem that way, she runs out of breath, or trips her tongue, but it seems that such "breathlessness" is exactly required of dudes hastening toward their death. Deliberately subverting the romance of sociological pathos, Brooks presents the pool players—"seven in the golden shovel"—in their own words and time. They make no excuse for themselves and apparently invite no one else to do so. The poem is their situation as *they* see it. In eight (could be nonstop) lines, here is their total destiny. Perhaps comic geniuses, they could well drink to this poem, making it a drinking/revelry song.

Brooks's poetry, then, is not weighed down by egoistic debris, nor is her world one of private symbolisms alone, or even foremost; rather, she presents a range of temperaments and situations.

2. [Kenny J. Williams, from *The World of Satin Legs, Mrs Sallie and the Blackstone Rangers: The Restricted Chicago of Gwendolyn Brooks*]
Thus in many ways several literary movements seemed to converge in Brooks. Like the early novelists of Chicago, she tacitly accepted the notion of the city's power. She has also acknowledged that she saw in the work of Langston Hughes "that writing about the ordinary aspects of black life was important."[1] The economy of language that marked, for example, Sandburg's "Fog" and the celebration of jazz rhythms that one finds in Langston Hughes seem to meet in Brooks's study of the seven urban pool players in "We Real

[1]Brooks, Gwendolyn, *Report from Part One* (Detroit: Broadside Press, 1972), p. 170.

Cool." Blyden Jackson has spoken perceptively of her increased usage of language compression.

> Her craftsmanship is careful. [She] belongs to the school of writers who do not believe in wasting a single word. Selection and significance—one can divine in her diction how she has brooded over them, how every word has been chosen with due regard for the several functions it may be called upon to perform in the dispensation of a poem. But the brooding goes deep and it affects not only words. The words must be put together. And the principle of dire economy which governs her choice of diction disciplines severely all of her poetic maneuvers. Terseness, a judicious understatement combined with pregnant ellipses, often guides the reader into an adventure which permits a revelation of Miss Brooks' capacity for sensitive interpretations of the human comedy.[2]

In addition to a superb sense of language, Gwendolyn Brooks has a clear vision that permits her to observe her people in a particular setting that articulates a consciousness of the relationship between *place* and *life*. No reader of urban literature can ever again be satisfied with such simplistic assumptions that begin with *"the city is."* Arthur P. Davis has called Brooks "the poet of the unheroic." He has noted that "for her the modern world [is] *unheroic."* Her people "lack bigness; we are little creatures contented with little things and little moments," but Davis says "she understands and sympathizes with our littleness." Yet, despite her acute sense of observation that readily sees the many ironies of her characters and their lives, Brooks never pokes fun at them. In fact, many of her people even seem suspended in time, place, and history. Thus she has the ability to endow simple facts with complex meanings, and the importance of her work ultimately rests in the wealth of interpretations that result from her view of urban life.

3. [Houston A. Baker, Jr., from *The Achievement of Gwendolyn Brooks*] [Brooks's chiding] is not always in the derisive mode. She often turns an irony of loving kindness on black Americans. "We Real Cool" would fit easily into the canon of [Langston] Hughes or Sterling Brown. . . . The irony is patent, but the poet's sympathy and admiration for the folk are no less obvious (the bold relief of "We," for example). A sympathetic irony in dealing with the folk has characterized some of the most outstanding works in the black American literary tradition. . . . All manifest a concern with the black man living in the "promised land" of the American city, and Brooks's [poems] likewise reveal the employment of kindly laughter to veil the tears of a desperate situation. In her autobiography, *Report from Part One,* she

[2]"From One 'New Negro' to Another, 1923–1972," in *Black Poetry in America: Two Essays in Historical Interpretation,* ed. Blyden Jackson and Louis Rubin, Jr. (Baton Rouge: Louisiana State University Press, 1974), p. 84.

> attests to having been in the situation and to having felt its deeper pulsations: "I lived on 63rd Street [in Chicago] . . . and there was a good deal of life in the raw all about me. You might feel that this would be disturbing, but it was not. It contributed to my writing progress. I wrote about what I saw and heard in the street."

We will be referring to these critical excerpts in Chapter 6, "The Research Process."

6

THE RESEARCH PROCESS

Authentic research begins with your curiosity to find something out.
—Toby Fulweiler

Once you have written a draft of your paper and expanded your ideas, you might see what others have said about the works you are discussing. Remember, your paper should be *your* paper; don't give over your authority to a critic for lack of self-confidence. Often critics publish articles or books on topics because they have intriguing new angles on them, but that doesn't mean that their way of seeing things should be yours, or that what they are focusing on is what you should focus on.

But a critic does have experience you might lack in examining literature and might have much to offer your paper, in the form of an opinion that supports your argument, or one that you can argue against. So if you choose to incorporate critical (secondary) sources in your paper, it would help to take a systematic approach to the research process.

PRIMARY/SECONDARY SOURCES

A *primary source* is the text itself, the source of your information; a *secondary source* is a work that comments on, analyzes, or interprets the primary text. Ideally, you will focus on the primary sources, while using secondary sources selectively and advantageously.

In a news story, a reporter, whether on television or in a newspaper, will typically (1) state what happened, (2) quote someone directly involved in the incident *(primary source),* (3) explain the implications, (4) quote an expert who provides some analysis *(secondary source),* then (5) finish the report himself or herself. Thus, the reporter controls the report while at the same time providing the audience with valuable firsthand and secondhand information. And the reader or viewer ends up crediting the reporter for a good report, not the experts quoted. The same process, the same maintenance of authority, should apply to your papers involving secondary sources.

When you analyze a poem such as "We Real Cool," you are writing about a *primary source* (the work itself) and you should use examples and quotations to support your ideas.

When you extend your ideas about a work to include outside reading, you are consulting *secondary sources.* You might learn about an author's background: for example, Gwendolyn Brooks's African-American heritage and

Chicago home are central to her poetry. You can learn more about the author's literary influences and techniques too. For example, Brooks's strong narrative voice, her connection to Langston Hughes, and her fascination with irony all play roles in her poetry.

As you research secondary sources, we recommend you take notes, take care to integrate critical quotations, and document meticulously. Here are some suggestions to help as you research for your paper.

TAKING NOTES WHILE RESEARCHING

Do not simply scan an article or book to pluck out a quote you can use: be sure you first understand the critic's thesis before you excerpt his or her work. While you read through the work, you should take notes. We can use the excerpts above of critical sources about "We Real Cool" to illustrate the kind of note-taking method you might use.

Using Index Cards

Always write down the author and title of the secondary source. Keep a separate page or index card and copy information exactly. Unless your instructor tells you otherwise, use the documentation format of the Modern Language Association (MLA). The Spillers passage quoted on pages 44–45, for example, would look like this on your index card (See *The MLA Handbook for Writers of Research Papers,* Fourth Edition. Joseph Gibaldi. New York: Modern Language Association, 1995.):

> Spillers, Hortense. "Gwendolyn the Terrible: Propositions on Eleven Poems." *A Life Distilled: Gwendolyn Brooks, Her Poetry and Fiction.* Ed. Maria K. Mootry and Gary Smith. Chicago: University of Chicago Press, 1989.

Summarizing Main Ideas

If you come to a particularly important paragraph, you might want to *paraphrase* or *summarize* it. You should record the page numbers of the passage. Here are two examples: the first summarizes, the second paraphrases.

Summary	Williams talks about the different literary movements that have affected Gwendolyn Brooks's writing. He also says that she is able to make a connection between "place and life." (46)
Paraphrase	Williams refers to Jackson's view of the way Gwendolyn Brooks compresses her language. Jackson states that Brooks

> chooses her words with much care. She only uses words that are important in her writing, making sure not to add any superfluous words. Each word performs a function in her poetry. (46)

Copying Direct Quotations

Choose a few quotations that you might use as textual evidence to support the points you want to make. Choose passages carefully and copy them exactly. Look for sentences that are particularly effective or that make a controversial or provocative point.

INTEGRATING QUOTATIONS

Too many students simply insert quotations without properly setting them up beforehand and spelling out their implications afterwards. The following suggestions will help you to better integrate quotations with your own prose. First, here are some general rules.

Avoid Successive Quotations

Try not to have two or more quotations in a row, since it takes away from your authority and bogs down your paper. Include your own words of explanation in lieu of successive quotes. Build bridges among quotations with your own writing.

Make Grammatical Sense

Quoted passages should be grammatically integrated with your own prose; the passage you are quoting should be treated as part of your sentence. Consider the following passage from a student essay on the "Growing Up" cluster. (This sentence is taken from the student's discussion of Anne Sexton's "The Fury of Overshoes," p. 359):

> Every time my mother went out, I would lie in bed awaiting her safe return. "Under your bed sat the wolf and he made a shadow when cars passed by in the night" flashes fear before my eyes (360).

Here in the second sentence there is no obvious subject, verb, or predicate, so the syntax is confusing. The writer has mistakenly considered the quotation as an entity separate, grammatically, from her sentence. *This image,* she wants to say, flashes fear before my eyes. So to correct her flawed quotation, she might write,

Anne Sexton's image of a wolf under the bed, "[making] a shadow / when cars passed by in the night," flashes fear before my eyes (360).

Use the Present Tense

Use the present, not past tense, when writing about literature, as if it is always made to "come alive" when you read it. For example, write, "In 'We Real Cool' Brooks *describes* some kids who *don't* care about going to school," *not* "In 'We Real Cool' Brooks *described* some kids who *didn't* care about going to school." Consider the following sentence from the same essay:

> When Sexton wrote, "They made you give up your nightlight and your teddy and your thumb," I remembered when as a child I was forced to enter an adult world I was not ready for.

According to the wording of this sentence, the student was present when Sexton wrote her poem and remembered what happened when she was a child. Since this is obviously not the case, she needs to correct the wording and the tense. She might write the following corrected version:

> Sexton writes, "They made you give up your nightlight / and your teddy and your thumb." As I read this, I remembered when as a child I, like the subject of Sexton's poem, was forced to enter an adult world I was not ready for.

Here are some more techniques you can use to improve your quoting. Once again we have used examples from the criticism of Brooks's "We Real Cool."

Introducing Quotations: Credit the Author

When you integrate into your text a *summary* of a passage, you might want to introduce it by giving credit to the author. (For examples, see the list below.)

Introducing Quotations: Use the Correct Punctuation

1. Use a comma for a brief introduction:
   According to Hortense Spillers, "Brooks refuses to make easy judgments" of her characters (46).

2. Use a colon to separate your own grammatically complete introduction or statement from the quotation.

One critic, Kenny Williams, speaks of Brooks's understanding of the people she writes about: "Gwendolyn Brooks has a clear vision that permits her to observe her people in a particular setting that articulates a consciousness of the relationship between *place* and *life*" (46).

3. Use the word *that* with no punctuation between it and the quotation. Houston Baker, Jr. suggests that Brooks "often turns an irony of loving kindness on black Americans" (46).

Putting the Quotation into Context

Avoid simply typing in quotations merely to enhance your paper, or sprinkling quotations indiscriminately throughout your paper. Take the time to put the quotation in context and to explain and comment on the quotation, as the student does in the example below:

> Gwendolyn Brooks's "We Real Cool" uses words in an exact and deliberate manner. The staccato beat befits the ideas in the poem perfectly. As Spillers notes, "The simplicity of the poem is stark to the point of elaborateness" (45). The monosyllabic rhythm denotes the young pool players living life in the fast lane.

Overquoting

Many students don't quote *primary sources* (the poems, stories, or plays you are writing about) often enough, and *overquote* their *secondary sources*. If you quote too frequently without directing the quotations with your own prose, you run the risk of overwhelming your reader and losing control of your paper. The reader will be reading secondhand, unoriginal information, and might as well read the articles or books you are quoting, rather than your paper.

When you use secondary sources, try to provide a good balance of paraphrase, quotation, and summary. Try to incorporate brief quoted phrases into your own sentence structure, as in the following example:

> They live life for the moment, grasping at whatever pleasure they can according to "their total destiny" (Spillers, 45).

Indenting Long Quotations

When a quotation is over four typed lines long, it should be indented according to the format recommended by your instructor. Quotation marks are not needed, and the parenthetical citation comes two spaces after, not just before, the final punctuation. The following example uses the MLA format:

According to Williams, Brooks's ability to portray African-Americans in a truthful, not stereotypical, fashion gives her poetry the power to change the way we see urban African-Americans:

> In addition to a superb sense of language, Gwendolyn Brooks has a clear vision that permits her to observe her people in a particular setting that articulates a consciousness of the relationship between place and life. No reader of urban literature can ever again be satisfied with such simplistic assumptions that begin with "The city is." (Williams 46)

Quoting Poetry

Separate quoted lines of poetry with a slash (/) mark.

> The opening of Brooks's poem establishes the speakers' attitude and situation: "We real cool. We / Left school" (42).

More than three lines of poetry should be indented, and arranged according to the line arrangement of the poem itself.

> The opening of Brooks's poem establishes the speakers' attitude and situation:
>
> We real cool. We
> Left school. We
> Lurk late. We
> Strike straight.

Using Ellipses or Brackets

You may occasionally need to change a quotation, using ellipses or brackets. Sometimes you may need to make a quotation shorter, clearer, or more effective by changing it. There are two ways:

1. Indicate omissions with an ellipsis (. . .). (See the example after 2, below.) If omitted material ends a sentence then you need a period also.
2. Indicate any additions or changes in wording within a quotation with brackets ([ ]), not by parentheses. Remember, the quote must fit in with the syntax of your own sentence. The following example illustrates how to use both *ellipses* and *brackets*.

> I see her poem as sarcastic. The pool players think they are cool, but they die young, "[making] no excuse for themselves. . . . The poem is *their* situation as *they* see it" (Spillers 45).

You need to follow a number of steps when consulting an outside source so that you will accurately incorporate the evidence you find, strengthen your own analysis, and be able to make a clear distinction between your own thesis, interpretation, conclusions, and those of the literary critic.

Documentation: Avoid Plagiarism

Documentation, or "giving credit" means identifying the sources you consult when you prepare your essays. Failure to document properly might result in plagiarism, which is the presentation of someone else's ideas, work, or facts as your own. Most of the cases of student plagiarism arise because of uncertainties about, or insufficient attention to, correct research procedures.

Here are examples of incorrect documentation, some of which might be considered examples of plagiarism.

1. Citing a quotation without listing the source on the *Works Cited* page.
2. Copying an author's words (more than three in succession) without using quotation marks.
3. Quoting inaccurately: skipping words, inverting order.
4. Summarizing inaccurately or failing to document summarized material.
5. Citing inaccurately—for example, if there is no connection between the page cited and the information where the citation occurs in the research paper.
6. Collaborating with another person in an unauthorized manner.

Read the following paragraph written after students had read the excerpt from Hortense Spillers (see p. 45). Do you think this student needs to give credit in this paragraph? If so, where and how?

> Gwendolyn Brooks makes no judgments in her poetry but just describes what she sees. This poem is virtually coded and straightforward—to the point. It is up to each reader individually to interpret what she thinks is meant.

Did you notice that this paragraph effectively summarizes some of the points that Spillers makes? Even though the student hasn't quoted more than three words in succession, her use of the terms "makes no judgments" and "virtually coded" indicates that she has presented Spillers's words and ideas as her own. She needs to add "(Spillers 44–45)" at the end of her paragraph.

7

THE ASSIGNMENT SEQUENCE

Each section in this book is organized according to a general theme: "Identities," "Families," "Love," "Frames of Mind," "The Individual and the Cosmos." Within each section there are clusters of readings focused on a more particular topic within each theme: in the "Family" section, for example, there is a cluster of poems and stories about the mother-child relationship; in the "Frames of Mind" section there is a cluster of readings on ways of learning.

Preceding and following each cluster is an "Assignment Sequence"—a progression of assignments with the objective of helping you to write a good essay on the topic and readings of that cluster. The broad plan of each of these assignment sequences is to start with informal writing, to work out your ideas on the topic and on the readings, and end up with a comprehensive, formal essay that *combines the clear expression of your ideas and a specific understanding of the literary works.*

Each assignment sequence has been arranged so that it sandwiches the readings of the cluster. You are first asked to write about the specific *topic* of the cluster, then to read—and react to—the specific readings in it, and finally to "put it all together" in a draft of an essay. Simply put, the assignment sequence asks you to take the following general steps toward writing a good essay:

- Think about the general topic of the readings before you read; write from your own experiences and knowledge of the topic.
- After each reading, jot down notes and questions about it, and consider the questions posed afterwards.
- After completing all of the readings, follow directions for the remainder of the assignment sequence until you complete your essay on the topic.

Typically, the assignment sequence will ask you to share your informal writing with your classmates, to try some creative exercise that should help you clarify your feelings on the cluster theme, and perhaps to consider what a literary critic has written about one of the works. Generally, the methods spelled out in Chapter 4, "The Writing Process," have been applied to assignments geared toward helping you write through literature. The philosophy is simple. Rather than write about a story or poem in five paragraphs, due on a certain day, without any "practice," you will take your time and arrive at the final draft through trial and error—lots of practice—and through a development of your ideas.

STEP 1: THINKING ABOUT THE TOPIC

You will begin by *thinking about* the topic (growing up, feminism, education, love, etc.). What's your opinion? What have you been through? What do you think about . . . ? In this step, you will be *freewriting, brainstorming, clustering,* or *asking a series of questions* (see "Prewriting," beginning on page 25) to get your thoughts in motion. Often in this informal step the seeds of your essay are planted.

STEP 2: "ENACTING" THE TOPIC

Next, you will be asked to *enact* the topic—through some non-traditional exercise, like creating a television sitcom, interviewing a professor, writing a letter to someone—to illustrate the real-life implications and applications of the subject, and to test and amend your ideas.

STEP 3: RESPONDING TO THE READINGS

Then you will *respond to the readings* informally—in your journals or notebooks—to see what your reactions and opinions are regarding the authors' version of the topic you've been writing about and enacting. There are questions (under the headings "Probing the Work" and "Identifying Issues") following each reading to prompt you, but most often your questions and answers will arise from your own responses to the literature.

STEP 4: MAKING CONNECTIONS

Next, you will be asked to *make connections* among the works in the cluster, and between what *you* think about the cluster theme and what you have just *read* in the cluster readings. You might be asked to write impromptu essays making such connections.

STEP 5: PUTTING IT ALL TOGETHER

Finally, you will *put it all together* in a rough draft of your essay; you will share your writing with your classmates, get their opinions and criticisms, and revise your essay until you are satisfied with it *and* your peers understand what you intend to get across.

Included in the "Putting It All Together" section is a "Writing Tip," suggesting a particular way you could improve your paper. For example, one suggests you try a new kind of introduction; another suggests ways of improving transitions.

There is then a section called "CrossClusters"—a list of works found elsewhere in the book that deals with the cluster topic you are writing about. We include such a list at the end of every assignment sequence so that you might, if your instructor approves, look at other works in our book that address the particular theme of this cluster.

At this point you are ready to write the final draft of the essay on this topic that you will hand in.

This may seem like a lot of work, and it *is,* but your chances of successfully communicating your ideas and showing an intelligent understanding of the literature—and earning a good evaluation from your instructor—are much greater if you take your time and work on your essay in phases, and are receiving reactions and criticisms *before* the essay is handed in—not afterwards, when criticism of that paper is not as useful.

SAMPLE ASSIGNMENT SEQUENCE

The following samples are taken from an assignment sequence on the "Growing Up" cluster of readings (pp. 343–369), which features poems and stories about growing up. Maddy's responses were chosen not for their particular flaws or attributes, but for the way they illustrate how an essay might *evolve* from informal thoughts to formal writing. If you have been used to thinking of a topic and writing in a frenzy the night before your paper is due, you should be ready for a change in your essay-writing method.

Maddy's directions are printed in italics.

Step 1: Thinking About "Growing Up"

Freewrite about a childhood memory you have that captures what you feel is the most prominent characteristic of your younger years. Focus on your relationship with a particular friend or family member.

> At the young age of 39 my mother became widowed with three children under thirteen years of age. I can remember how strong she looked at my father's funeral, but now I realize that she was merely in shock.
>
> After she took over my father's business, my routine went like clockwork. I was dropped off at elementary school, and off my mother drove to pick up my grandfather for their long commute. Quickly she learned the ropes, fighting to gain respect in a man's field. . . .

My relationship with my mother is a stormy yet close one. As the youngest, I have always been treated with more attention and protection. My mother has worked since I was six, and I believe watching over me is considered another job to her.

I identify mostly with my nephew. As a five-year-old, he seems rebellious and very anxious. His defiant behavior reminds me of how I was, full of anger and yearning for attention. His outbursts began when his sister was born when he was three.

Maddy's focus shifts a bit in this freewriting exercise, but through further thought and class discussion she will narrow her focus.

Step 2: Enacting the Topic

Write a diary entry from the perspective of yourself as a young boy or girl, focusing on a particularly meaningful day in your early life.

Why didn't I listen to Mommy yesterday? She begged me not to go into Butler woods on my way home from Cynthia's house, but I did anyway.

I wanted to show Rebecca the secret path Linda and I found last week when we walked Lacy, and now we are both stiff and puffy. We watched the sun disappear as we walked deeper into the woods, and we felt like explorers searching new lands. I don't know when Rebecca kicked the beehive, but she started yelling real loud. She was covered with bees and trying to knock them off, but they wouldn't budge. All of a sudden they began stinging me . . .

At the hospital, they pulled out over 100 stingers. The doctor told Mom I could have been blinded if the stingers were just a bit closer to my eyes. I guess Mom won't let me into the woods again. Not even when I'm grown up.

As you can see, when writing about a traumatic incident that has nothing, on the surface, to do with her mother, Maddy focuses on their relationship nonetheless. In the draft of her paper, she will end up writing mostly about the works that address the mother-child relationship, and about her own relationship with her mother.

Step 3: Responding to the Readings

Here are some excerpts from Maddy's reading-journal reactions to the "Growing Up" readings. As you can see, Maddy included in her consideration of this topic one of the works mentioned in the "CrossClusters" section (see p. 369), Naguib Mahfouz's "Half a Day" (p. 763).

Frank O'Connor, "My Oedipus Complex"

Did the author fight for his own mother's affections while growing up as the main character does?

Although the child "Larry" mentions he wants to marry and bear children with his mother, few sexual desires are detailed. His urges to keep his mother to himself and not share his affections towards her sound normal. As a child he had little paternal contact, and his parents should have noticed to understand that his father posed a threat. My father passed away when I was six, and when my mom remarried it was difficult to accept that I too had to "share" her.

Anne Sexton, "The Fury of Overshoes"

The author uses typical childhood obstacles as not being able to buckle your shoes or properly feed yourself and quickly reminds us how dependent youngsters are on their parents. As a child, learning to ride my bicycle seemed like the biggest and hardest thing to do, yet it's only a building block for what the world has in store for us.

As a child, I remember hiding under my blanket as a car passed, since it created such horrible shadows on my ceiling. This poem hits home with me: so entertaining yet so realistic.

Audre Lorde, "Hanging Fire"

This poem is so charming because at the age of fourteen, skin problems and braces seem to ruin our lives. As a child, some obstacles seem so magnified, and it is easy to believe they are the worst things that will ever happen.

The repeated line, "And Momma's in the bedroom with the door closed" has many meanings. Is the door closed, signifying that these are the child's battles and only she can overcome them? Or can the child be from a dysfunctional family and have nobody to turn to for help and advice? Is the child fatherless? Since not any information is detailed about "Daddy," does he exist?

Naguib Mahfouz, "Half a Day" (p. 763)

The quick transition from child to adult seems a bit confusing, yet interesting. I view it as this: it seems we grow up so fast, and yet it seems like only yesterday that we were youngsters. Sometimes it's easier to remember childhood feelings and episodes than things we did only yesterday.

It sounds as if "Grandpa" suddenly forgot his age and was suddenly thrown back into his hometown. This can explain being "lost" and not recognizing the area. I wonder if I will see myself as a child in 40 years when positioned in a setting from my youth.

In the above reactions, Maddy has made sense of the readings and reacted specifically to some of the images or important lines. Her personal connection to the fear conveyed in Lorde's "Hanging Fire" will serve her well in the paper she writes on this cluster, parts of which are excerpted in Step 5.

Step 4: Making Connections

Select one of the following questions and write an informal response in which you connect your own ideas with those conveyed in the works of this cluster, and/or make connections among the works themselves.

A. What are the different aspects of childhood experiences illustrated in this cluster? Which ones seem most believable? Which do you most easily identify with, and why?

B. Many people talk about childhood as being the most carefree time of their lives. But what problematic aspects of growing up do these writers depict?

C. How does the experience you described in your freewriting exercise compare with the moments of growth described by these writers?

Of the three choices, Maddy chose to respond to B:

In response to this, Maddy wrote about the difficulties she had adjusting to her father's death and the feelings of loneliness that resulted from her mother's immersion in the business world. She saw similarities between her own difficulties and those depicted in Sexton's "The Fury of Overshoes" and Lorde's "Hanging Fire." The informal written response to this step of the writing process evolved rather easily into the final version of her essay, excerpted in "Step 5: Putting it All Together."

Step 5: Putting it All Together

The following is excerpted from the second draft of Maddy's paper on the "Hanging Fire" cluster.

> Why do some children never experience death, while others have loved ones drop like flies? I'll bet my childhood closet was filled with black dresses, since it seems as if I attended more funerals than anyone I knew. Although most people would associate death with sadness, I often experienced anger. Why did people I love leave me? Was I a bad person? Of course not. Unfortunately, life is seen very differently through a six-year-old's eyes, and they are not always capable of reasoning. The result can be anger and bitterness. . . .

Anne Sexton's poem, "The Fury of Overshoes," brought me back in time to when the pain and suffering devoured me. Reading the line, "They made you give up your nightlight and your teddy and your thumb," I remembered when as a child I was forced to enter an adult world I was not ready for. My father's death orphaned me, removing both parents from my life. My mother transformed from a happy homemaker to a provider overnight. Every day, she had to drive to pick up my grandfather and make a long commute, taking over my father's business. . . .

Why did my mother leave me alone when I needed her the most? When I came home from school every day, it was the housekeeper, the television and myself. I felt so lonely, yearning for my mother to be home, waiting to greet me with hugs and cookies. She no longer made me lunch and picked me up from school. Sexton asks, "Remember when you couldn't buckle your own overshoe or tie your own shoe or cut your own meat?" Sexton evokes the mixed feelings of frustration and powerlessness of not being in control of your life: "The world wasn't yours" back then, but there was something wonderful about being so dependent. Sexton's words do not apply to my childhood, since at age six I had to care for myself. At that age, however, I didn't want to be an adult. Maybe I didn't want to bathe myself, tie my own shoes, cut my own meat or give up my teddy. Where is my nightlight? Did my father take it with him? "Oh thumb, I want a drink." These are Sexton's words, but they were also mine, reflecting a feeling that carried me through the second grade. Did I suck my thumb because I was thirsty for love?

Eventually, my mother started dating, and I would wait forever for her to return from these dates. Sexton describes the shadow "the wolf" under the child's bed makes as cars drive by at night, capturing perfectly what happens when fear and imagination are heightened by a lonely child. How I used to count the hours for my mother's return, braving the creatures of my closet as I found shelter under my safe blankets, my "overshoe." It's funny, but I always knew which shadow on my bedroom ceiling was my mother's car entering the driveway.

As I grew up, I realized that death was a normal part of life, uncontrollable and inevitable. As an adult, reading "Half a Day" by Naguib Mahfouz, has made me five years old again. Life is simple again, my father alive, and again we walk hand in hand. Mahfouz's description of kindergarten life matches my memory of it: "We played all sorts of different games: swings, the vaulting horse, ball games" (764). We acted like children, not adults. "We ate delicious food, took a little nap, and woke up to go on with friendship and love, play and learning."

As I walk through my school playground now, walking my friend's dog, I suddenly see that frightened six-year-old girl again, waiting for her housekeeper to pick her up. As the dog jerks the leash, she disappears. Suddenly I ask myself, "Where was the street lined with gardens? Where had it disappeared to?" (765). As Mahfouz knows, time is both culprit and savior. Although it was only time before my father was to leave me, it was only time before all healing could occur. As Mahfouz shows, memories are a great gift, bringing back both happiness and sadness. I wonder if I'll see that little girl again as she waits for her ride home.

8

TALKING LITERATURE

LITERARY TERMS

To write confidently about literary works, you need to become familiar with *literary terms*. Like any other field of study, literature has a specialized vocabulary, and if you become familiar with it, you will be able to write with more authority and confidence.

In the assignment sequences in this book, you are asked to "prewrite" about the themes of the clusters (in the first step, "Thinking About . . ."). Next, you might *enact the topic,* by creatively exploring your own views and the views of others. Then you are asked to read the cluster of works, and *respond to the readings.*

In this third step of the assignment sequence, you will be jotting down your immediate reactions to the literature, asking questions, and noting passages of interest. But you should also be taking note of the literary devices the authors are employing. Once you understand even a few of these, you will be reading with far less confusion than you may be now, especially when it comes to poetry. Comprehending the method behind the meaning of literary works grants you a specific appreciation of them—just as a familiarity with the technique of a musical instrument allows you to listen to a recording or concert with greater insight and appreciation. Moreover, understanding literary techniques and terminology enables you to view other kinds of texts, and indeed the world, with more intelligence, perception, and understanding. Watching a political event, listening to music, or experiencing an everyday human encounter acquires much more meaning when you appreciate its *symbolism,* understand *imagery,* and can discuss its *metaphorical* significance. These are not just terms for understanding literature; they are empowering ways of seeing life.

To illustrate how an understanding of literary terms can benefit your writing as you go through the assignment sequence, read the excerpt below taken from Patrick's writing on Emily Dickinson's "There's a certain Slant of light." Patrick combines his feelings on the topic of religion, a close look at Dickinson's poem, and an understanding of how writers employ *image, symbol,* and *allusion.*

EMILY DICKINSON

There's a certain Slant of light

There's a certain Slant of light,
Winter Afternoons —
That oppresses, like the Heft
Of Cathedral Tunes —

Heavenly Hurt, it gives us —
We can find no scar,
But internal difference,
Where the Meanings, are —

None may touch it, Any —
'Tis the Seal Despair —
An imperial affliction
Sent us of the Air —

When it comes, the Landscape listens —
Shadows — hold their breath —
When it goes, 'tis like the Distance
On the look of Death —

Some religious standards instill massive feelings of guilt within every follower, for not even the most pious individuals can live their lives without sinning (violating a standard) at least a few times. Thus, to be accepted by God, we must limit our everyday desires and concede to anything and everything that he (supposedly) wants, and must constantly monitor actions to God's liking. Ask yourself this: could that ever be the basis for a loving relationship? I think not.

Various writers who have confronted this topic would agree with my statements; one is Emily Dickinson. In "There's a certain Slant of light," Dickinson (a fairly religious person herself) paints an **image** of a slant of light, perhaps entering a church through a stained-glass window. (The mention of "cathedral tunes" indicates that the light is slanting in a church.) Note that the window has taken the light and forced it to conform to its design and structure. The coming and going of the light might [**symbolically**] represent the birth and death of Christ. Dickinson **alludes** to a comparison between the altering force (again, perhaps, a stained-glass window) and the forces of religion (what Christ stands for). For like the (church) window, religion forces us to conform to its standards and expectations. Continuing this **metaphor,** Dickinson goes on to call religion an "imperial affliction" that oppresses its many followers.

Below are some literary terms you should know to be able to intelligently consider literature in your writing. We provide an example of each one from the works in this book, and whenever appropriate from the three works that appear in Part 1—"Photograph of the Girl," by Sharon Olds (p. 8), "The Handsomest Drowned Man in the World," by Gabriel García Márquez (p.13), and "We Real Cool," by Gwendolyn Brooks (p. 42). As, or after, you read each poem, story, or play in this book, you should be able to locate and understand how the author is using some of these devices.

PERSPECTIVE

Narrator: the person telling the story

Point of View: the perspective from which a story is told

Speaker: the person who is narrating the poem

Persona: the assumed identity of the writer, or of the fictional "I"

Writers manipulate us by presenting their works from a particular *perspective*. Just as we need to remind ourselves that there are two sides to every story our friends tell us, as readers we need to understand that what we are reading could very well be told from another angle. And the perspective from which the work is being presented usually figures greatly in the overall purpose and meaning of the work.

Narrator

The "voice" that is telling you the story is typically *not* the author; don't make the mistake of equating authors with their *narrators*. After all, you have no problem distinguishing between the two if the narrator is a psychopathic murderer (see Poe's "The Tell-Tale Heart," p. 834); do the same even when the narrator seems fairly believable. Furthermore, try to distinguish between *reliable narrators* and *unreliable narrators*. Reliable narrators are so called because they are telling the story with objectivity and seem fair-minded; unreliable narrators cannot be trusted to tell the "truth," because they have a stake in how you perceive the story, or because they are, for whatever reason, incapable of presenting a balanced view of what happens.

The *narrator* of "The Handsomest Drowned Man in the World" (p. 13) seems mature and reliable, because he or she puts the story in perspective, detached from the action. But if that story were narrated by one of the children who plays with the dead body as it washes up on shore or by one of the women who become emotionally attached to the drowned man, it would not be nearly so "reliable."

Points of View

The most common types of narrations, or *points of view,* are as follows:

First-person narration:
The narrator is a character, referring to himself or herself as "I." (See "The Tell-Tale Heart," p. 834.)

Third-person omniscient narration:
The story is told as if it were seen through the eyes of a "god." This narrator knows what every character thinks, what is happening beyond what the characters are aware of, and what will happen in the future. This is the narration of "The Handsomest Drowned Man in the World" (p. 13): the narrator tells us what the women imagine, how the children play with the body out of sight of the adult characters, and what the men think.

Third-person limited omniscient narration:
The narrator's knowledge is limited: the narrator may tell you what one of the characters thinks, and some of what is happening beyond the scope of the characters' knowledge, but not everything. In James Joyce's "Araby," for example (p. 89), we are told what the boy thinks of himself, but we don't hear anything about what the other characters are thinking—only what they do or say in the boy's presence.

Third-person objective narration:
The narrator reports the events of the story with no insight into the character's thoughts or motivations, as if the narrator were a fly on the wall. (See, for example, Shirley Jackson's "The Lottery," p. 131.)

Speaker/Persona

Use the term *speaker* when you are discussing the "narrator" of a poem, and use *point of view* or *narrator* for fiction. (Generally, you won't need a corresponding term for plays, which don't have narrators: the plot unfolds through the use of dialogue and stage direction.) Again, you need to understand that the *speaker* of a poem—the voice that is narrating it—is not the poet. Some poets like to "body-snatch" and speak through someone else's mouth: they've created a *persona*. In "We Real Cool" (p. 42) the *speaker* is actually plural: a group of seven dropouts speaking as one.

In Joanne's paper on the "Growing Up" cluster she includes a consideration of a work listed in the "CrossClusters" section, Olds's "Photograph of the Girl":

> The speaker is looking at a picture of the Russian drought in 1921, of a girl who is dying of starvation. She notices the pain that this girl has experienced, a greater pain, certainly, than that of most other girls.

VOICE

Tone: the expression of the author's (or speaker's or narrator's) attitude

Diction: the writer's choice of words

Denotation: a word's literal meaning, exclusive of images or feelings it evokes

Connotation: the implications or suggestions evoked by a word

Hyperbole: deliberate exaggeration

Understatement: presenting something as less significant than it is

Tone

The implied *attitude* of the speaker or narrator toward his or her subject and toward the reader is what we call the *tone* of the work. While the tone of Brooks's "We Real Cool" seems defiant, the tone of "The Handsomest Drowned Man in the World" (p. 13), especially at the end of that story, seems rather romantic and even majestic.

Diction

The words the writer chooses, called *diction,* have much to do with the *tone* of the work. When the group of school dropouts say, "We / Jazz June," it doesn't, for the moment, matter if you know what they mean by "jazz," because the tone is established from the use of that slang. We know this isn't a group of sophisticated debutantes speaking.

Denotation/Connotation

A word can have a *connotative* as well as *denotative* meaning, depending on its context and emphasis. Consider the following words, in "Photograph of the Girl": "The girl sits on the hard ground, / the dry pan of Russia." Here, the *denotative* meaning of "pan" (a cooking utensil) doesn't suffice; the word *connotes* flatness, or even a gruesome feeling that the girl is, in a sense, "frying" in this dreary, arid landscape. Similarly, the word "hard" *denotes* solidity, but its *connotation* gives the word more resonance: the ground is especially hard for a starving girl, cruel as well.

Hyperbole/Understatement

The work's *tone* may also be affected if the writer is exaggerating *(hyperbole)* or *understating,* to achieve a desired effect. The title of García Márquez's "The Handsomest Drowned Man in the World" (p. 13) is an example of *hy-*

perbole; its effect is to heighten the aura of a story that is really about a bloated dead body that washes up on shore near a village where people are living pathetically boring lives. In contrast, much of the poem "Photograph of the Girl" (p. 8), including its title, is *understated.* The effect is to allow the visual image to speak for itself, and to let us feel for ourselves the tragedy of the girl's situation.

LANGUAGE/TECHNIQUE

Metaphor: a figure of speech in which one thing is said to be another

Simile: a figure of speech in which one thing is said to be like another

Alliteration: the close repetition of consonant sounds

Assonance: the close repetition of vowel sounds

Meter: regular rhythmic patterns in poetry, measured in units called **feet**

Stress: the emphasis placed on a syllable

Feet: a group of syllables containing one stressed syllable

Rhyme: the repetition of identical sounds

Metaphor/Simile

When writers write metaphorically (using either *metaphors* or *similes*), they are attempting to define some experience by comparing it to another. It is almost impossible to accurately convey most intense human emotions or experiences. What words can be used to define what it feels like to be in love? To have been in a dreadful accident? To have given birth to a child? So writers use metaphors and similes for reasons both practical (to get their point across in a way the reader will understand) and artistic (to bring to life those feelings).

All verbal human expression, it can be argued, is necessarily metaphorical, since all words are "signifiers" of what we experience, think, or feel. What most people consider good writing is usually a matter of creative and/or accurate use of *metaphorical language.*

Metaphorical language doesn't merely make comparisons but implies something about the subject of the comparison. For example, when the drowned man in García Márquez's story is described as "stretched out like a sperm whale" (a *simile*) and as having "stony nails" (a *metaphor*), those expressions not only help you understand how large he is but also suggest the rare, wondrous and treasured aspect of his appearance, and perhaps too the sexual virility the women were seeing in him.

Given a particularly meaningful moment, or a situation rich with implications, writers will grope for or experiment with the right metaphor to convey their meaning. In her poem "Metaphors," Sylvia Plath lists a series of metaphors to make a point about both society's view and her own view of her condition:

Metaphors

I'm a riddle in nine syllables,
An elephant, a ponderous house,
A melon strolling on two tendrils.
A red fruit, ivory, fine timbers!
This loaf's big with its yeasty rising.
Money's new-minted in this fat purse.
I'm a means, a stage, a cow in calf.
I've eaten a bag of green apples,
Boarded the train there's no getting off.

Alliteration/Assonance

Writers will often play with sounds in their writing, whether in fiction, drama, or poetry. Combining consonant sounds *(alliteration)* or vowel sounds *(assonance)* creates unity among lines of poetry and adds poetic character to a narrative description. When Gwendolyn Brooks writes, "We / Jazz June," she is employing *alliteration* (the letter *j*); when she combines "Sing Sin" and "Thin Gin," she is using *assonance* (the short *i* sound).

You will not be able to write about a poem with complete understanding if you are unable to discuss its *form* and *technique* as well as its content. In poetry, form contributes to meaning. A poet chooses every word with an eye—and an ear—toward the overall *theme* or purpose of the poem as well as its *meter,* often revising many times.

Meter/Stress/Feet

The *meter* of a poem is the pattern, sometimes recurrent, of *stressed* and unstressed syllables. Each unit of this pattern is called a *foot,* and the number of *feet* per line determines the poem's meter. A *caesura* is a pause or break in the metrical or rhythmic progress of a line of poetry. Here is a list of patterns:

- *iambic:* unstressed syllable followed by a stressed syllable

    Example: "He *kind*ly *Stopped* for *Me*" (p. 993).

- *trochaic:* stressed syllable followed by an unstressed syllable

  Example: *Rus*-sia (p. 8)
- *anapestic:* two unstressed syllables followed by a stressed syllable

  Example: "in the *drought*" (p. 8)
- *dactylic:* stressed syllable followed by two unstressed syllables

  Example: *Pho*-to-graph (p. 8)
- *spondaic:* two stressed syllables

  Example: "*Jazz June*" (p. 42)

A poem by Samuel Taylor Coleridge sums it all up for us:

> Trochee trips from long to short.
> From long to long in solemn sort.
> Slow Spondee stalks; strong foot! yet ill able
> Ever to come up with Dactyl trisyllable
> Iambics march from short to long
> With a leap and a bound the swift Anapests throng

The following terms refer to the number of *feet* in a single line of a poem:

monometer: one foot

dimeter: two feet

trimeter: three feet

tetrameter: four feet

pentameter: five feet

hexameter: six feet

heptameter: seven feet

Take a look now at the first *stanza* of Dickinson's "Because I could not stop for Death."

> Because I could not stop for Death—
> He kindly Stopped for Me—
> The Carriage held but just Ourselves—
> And Immortality.

Each foot is *iambic* (an unstressed, followed by stressed, syllable), but the first and third lines are written in *tetrameter* (four feet), while the second and fourth lines in *trimeter* (three feet). The effect of the poem's meter is to reflect a comfortable carriage ride—that is, until the meter falters later in the poem.

Rhyme

Most of us can recognize *end rhymes,* since the rhyming words are easily found right smack at the end of the lines. But many poems in this book, when they do rhyme, do so less obviously.

Exact rhyme: the words match exactly, as in "We Real Cool" (p. 42)

Near rhyme: the end consonants are the same, but the vowel sounds differ, or the end vowel sounds are the same, but the consonants differ—as in "Photograph of the Girl":

> The girl sits on the hard *ground,*
> the dry pan of Russia, in the *drought*
> of 1921, *stunned* . . .

As you can see, *ground* and *drought* share a vowel sound *(ow),* while the *nd* sound of *stunned* matches the same sound in *ground.*

Internal rhyme: rhymes or near-rhymes that occur in the middle of lines, as in this line from the same poem, which repeats the long *o* sound three times: "eyes *closed,* mouth *op*en, raw hot wind / *blow*ing sand . . .

The *rhyme scheme* of a poem is the fixed pattern of rhyme for the whole poem. For example, the rhyme scheme of "Stopping By Woods on a Snowy Evening" (p. 949) is aaba, bbcb, ccdc, dddd. Each letter stands for a word at the end of a line (e.g., *know* = a).

POETIC FORM

Stanza: a group of lines that form a division of a poem

Dramatic Monologue: a character's speech to an unseen listener that reveals the dramatic situation and the speaker's true nature

Sonnet: a verse containing 14 lines and a complicated rhyme scheme

Free Verse (or, *Blank Verse*): poetry with no set rhyme or meter

Poetic form (or *structure*) and meaning go hand in hand. Note the line arrangement of Brooks's "We Real Cool" (p. 42), which is critical to the poem. The effect is a cadence of "street kids."

Stanza

Poetic lines are grouped in *stanzas;* each stanza of "We Real Cool" is just two lines long. The poet arranges stanzas either according to a set form (as in a *sonnet,* for example) and/or according to the sequence of ideas or images of the poem.

Dramatic Monologue

"We Real Cool" is also a *dramatic monologue* in that a group of kids, speaking in a single voice to an unseen listener, reveal through their speech their real character and dramatic circumstance. Sometimes a story can be referred to as a dramatic monologue—for example, "Girl" (p. 377), "The Tell-Tale Heart," (p. 834), or "The Yellow Wallpaper," (p. 842)—but the term is most often used in discussions of poetry.

Sonnet

The *Shakespearean* or *English* sonnet has three *quatrains* (four lines of verse) followed by a *couplet* (two lines, which usually rhyme). In these sonnets the *rhyme scheme* is *abab, cdcd, efef,* and *gg.* (See Shakespeare's "Let Me Not To the Marriage of True Minds", p. 567.) The *Petrarchan* or *Italian* sonnet is divided into one *octave* (eight lines) with a rhyme scheme of *abbaabba,* and one *sestet* (six lines) with a rhyme scheme of *cdecde, cdccdc,* or *cdedce.* See Frost's "Once by the Pacific" for a variation of the Shakespearean sonnet form (p. 950).

Free Verse

Many of the poems in this book are written in *free verse* or *blank verse*—meaning they have no set structure or rhyme scheme; however, that does not mean they are without cadence. Often poets will use the rhythm of speech, or match the meter to the subject, to unify it rhythmically.

STORY FORM

Structure: the organization of a literary work

Plot: the events of a narrative or play, and the organization of those events

Setting: the time and place at which a literary work occurs

Conflict: the opposition of two forces or characters in fiction or drama

Climax: a moment of great intensity; the turning point in the plot, when the conflict is resolved

Structure

The organization, or *structure,* of a story or poem may have much to do with the success of the work. The structure of "The Handsomest Drowned Man in the World" (p. 13) is pretty straightforward, moving chronologically from the time the drowned man washes up on shore to the villagers' elaborate "funeral" for him at the end, with a quick projection into the future in the last sentence. But some stories begin in the present tense, flash back to a past event, and end back in the present. Ernest Hemingway's "Fathers and Sons" (p. 454), for example, begins and ends with the narrator driving, his son in the seat next to him: the "story" takes the form of several flashbacks, as the narrator daydreams about his youth. In a story that is organized this way, it is important to recognize how the story's *structure* affects your feelings about and understanding of it.

Plot

Related to the structure is the story's *plot,* or sequence of events. A typical plot will follow this general pattern:

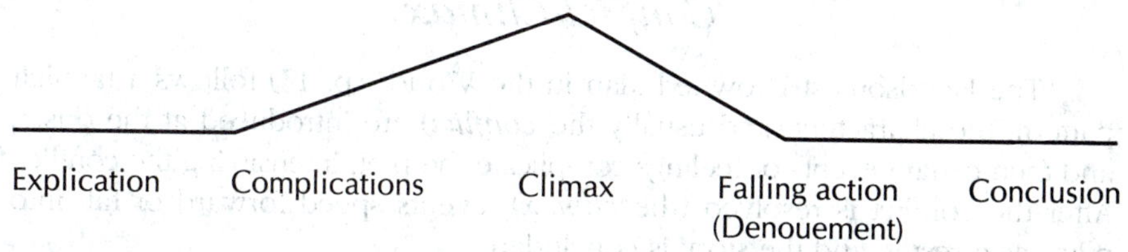

Of course, many stories don't follow such a neat, formulaic structure. A story that does will begin with an *explication* of what the story will be about, introducing the characters, *setting,* and "problem" of the story. The *explication* of García Márquez's "The Handsomest Drowned Man in the World" (p. 13) begins with the children "playing" with the drowned man: we soon realized that the story will revolve around the villagers' reaction to this corpse. It appears the village women will be cleaning the body off, and finding out whether the dead man was a resident of a neighboring village.

There is some *foreshadowing*—a warning of things to come—when the children note that the body had "the ability to keep on growing after death"

(p. 13). *Complications* begin when the men discover that nobody claims the body and that their women have become emotionally attached to it, claiming it for themselves and giving it a name. They become resentful of the women's adoration of the corpse, and the women see their men as inadequate in comparison to it.

A *conflict* develops as the villagers begin to question their own lives (the conflict between their real lives and the romantic life of "Esteban") and between the men and the women. The *climax* might be said to occur when the men see the corpse's face and are, like the women, "left breathless." From that point on, any conflicts are resolved, since both the men and women recognize the value of Esteban and they work together at his funeral *(falling action,* often called *denouement)* heightening their visions of themselves and their village in the process, to the point that it becomes a magical place that future ships will gaze at with wonder *(conclusion).*

Now let's spell out some of the terms we just used.

Setting

A writer usually establishes the *setting* early on. The setting might be incidental, but might also be a major "character," and take on symbolic significance, as in Gilman's "The Yellow Wallpaper" (p. 842). In "The Handsomest Drowned Man in the World" (p. 13), the *setting,* an unnamed secluded village, is an important factor in the story, for it is transformed by the story's end.

Conflict/Climax

"The Handsomest Drowned Man in the World" (p. 13) follows a familiar pattern: the characters (and usually the *conflict*) are introduced at the onset, and then certain events or feelings complicate the plot, intensifying the conflict. After the conflict is resolved (the *climax*), events speed forward or fall into place as a result, and the story is concluded.

When you write about or summarize the *plot* of one of your readings, be careful not to spend too much time merely recounting the story's action. Instead, focus on the *conflict* that the author develops to move the plot along. The conflict may occur (1) within one character; (2) between a character and society; (3) between a character and the forces of nature and the universe; or (4) between two characters, one the *protagonist* (the main character, or the *hero*) and the *antagonist* (the main character in opposition to the hero). But many interesting stories have more than one conflict, or a character who has both an internal and external conflict. In "The Handsomest Drowned Man in the World," the villagers are collectively in conflict between their real, dull lives and the romantic dreams of their lives that Esteban awakens in them. But you can also see a conflict between the men and the women in the village.

When the *conflict* is resolved, the *climax* has occurred. The climax is not always the most exciting point of the work—indeed, quite often it occurs subtly. But after the climax, everything rushes to a close.

DRAMATIC FORM

Tragedy: a drama of high importance involving an elevated character (the tragic hero) who, due to a character flaw (the tragic flaw), dies, evoking sorrow and pity from the audience

Comedy: a literary work that is less exalted and less serious than a tragedy, ending happily, usually with a marriage

Tragicomedy: a play that combines elements of tragedy and comedy, either by providing a happy ending to a potentially tragic story or by some more complex blending of serious and light moods

Absurdist Drama (or **Theatre of the Absurd**): a play illustrating the modern sense of human purposelessness in a universe without meaning or value

Tragedy

Tragedies depict individuals whose death or ruin evokes great admiration and pity in audiences. *Tragic heroes* are traditionally characters of high rank, like princes or kings, since then they have a long way to fall, so to speak (see *Antigone,* p. 144). In the twentieth century some playwrights have attempted to portray common men and women as tragic heroes (a well-known example being Willy Loman—a "low man"—in Arthur Miller's *Death of a Salesman*), suggesting that there is something noble in a tragic hero's character, not social rank. Whatever the case, a *tragic hero* (the main character who dies or is ruined at the end of the play) typically causes his or her own demise by way of a *tragic flaw:* in most cases, the hero is guilty of excessive pride—called *hubris*—and is unable to "settle" for being "average." This unwillingness to settle for a mundane existence arouses admiration in the audience, and pity for the hero at the play's conclusion.

Comedy

The end of a *comedy,* in contrast, is happy. Most comedies depict the intriguing game-playing and wit involved in the development of at least one, but sometimes several couples, and usually end with the couples getting married. (see *A Midsummer Night's Dream*, p. 766.)

Other Dramatic Forms

A *tragicomedy* is a play that combines elements of tragedy and comedy. *Theatre of the absurd,* or *absurdist drama,* is a term used to describe plays that act out existentialist philosophy by depicting characters absurdly faced with living in a world without meaning. Eugène Ionesco's *The Lesson* (p. 904) is an example of absurdist drama.

CHARACTER

Protagonist: the main character

Antagonist: the character in opposition to the main character

Dynamic Character: a character who changes over the course of the work

Static Character: a character who does not change over the course of the work

Epiphany: a sudden, perhaps seemingly trivial event or moment that acquires great significance when, because of it, a character achieves a higher level of self-awareness

Characterization: a telling detail that reveals the nature of a character

Protagonist/Antagonist, Dynamic/Static Character

In most stories, plays, and narrative poems, one of the characters, usually the main character or *protagonist,* changes (a *character* is anyone who appears in a literary work). That character is called *dynamic* (or sometimes *round*). The characters who do not change are called *static* (or sometimes *flat*). Among the static characters is usually the *antagonist,* the character in opposition to the protagonist. The character who changes is usually the one whom the story is "about," and the moment of change, if it involves a seemingly trivial event that is heightened in importance by the character's recognition of its spiritual implications, may be termed his or her *epiphany*. At the end of James Joyce's "Araby" (p. 89), for example, the young boy experiences just such an epiphany when he recognizes the emotional and spiritual implications of a seemingly commonplace moment in his life.

Characterization

Writers give their characters particular traits that indicate what they want you to think of the characters. If a character is described as having "ice-blue eyes," then you can be pretty sure that character is meant to be seen as cold-hearted; if another has "a slithery voice," then you may infer that character to be smooth-talking and untrustworthy. Of course, the best characters are multi-dimensional and may have many *characterizations*. Esteban, in "The Handsomest Drowned Man in the World" (p. 13), is an obviously *static* character who is *characterized* by his enormous body, the observation of which evokes pity in the women, and compels them to think of him as one of those people who are embarrassed by their size and exceedingly polite and deferential to others. But it also gives him a godlike nobility and grandeur.

MEANING

Theme: the central meaning of a literary work

Symbol: an object or event that suggests meanings beyond its literal meaning

Allegory: a form of symbolism in which objects, setting, and characters stand for (represent) abstract ideas

Ambiguity: a word, image, theme, or object that has more than one meaning

Image: the verbal representation of a sensory impression or experience

Irony: 1. the use of words to convey the opposite of their literal meaning 2. an incongruity between what is expected and what actually occurs

Dramatic Irony: When the reader or audience of a play knows more about a character's situation than the character does

Paradox: a statement that, though it appears self-contradictory, contains a basis of truth that reconciles the seeming opposites

Oxymoron: a figure of speech containing two apparently contradictory terms

Theme

There may be many *themes*, or important issues, in any one work. But the main theme of a work, stated as a generalization, combines what it is about and what seems to be the overall purpose of the work. A friend who asks, "What is this reading *about?*" may be asking for the *plot;* but when your teacher asks, "What is this reading *about?*" she or he may be asking for an overall *theme*—its central idea or statement. You should try to understand a work's theme before you write about it, because to do so is to understand the work's essential meaning. For example, the students who assessed Sharon Olds's "Photograph of the Girl" were attempting to articulate what they saw as the theme of the poem. (See page 8.) As you can see from those student samples, themes don't have to be articulated in perfect sentences, nor is there one "correct" theme to every work.

Symbol

A *symbol* is a figure of speech that has concrete meaning but that also resonates with abstract meaning. Symbols may be direct and particular, or vague, suggestive, and universal: a valentine is a symbol of love; a river might represent the subconscious.

A sign—an object that signifies something else, such as a traffic light—has only one meaning. A *symbol* serves a similar purpose, but is more complex and at times more abstract. Most students seized upon the last image in Olds's "Photograph of the Girl" as symbolic of the ironic tragedy of her death just as she is entering a new phase of life (p. 8). Some symbols are fairly conventional (the rose that represents love, for example), but many are open-ended and complicated. The drowned man in García Márquez's story, for example, at first represents a plaything to the children, the ideal masculinity for the women, and an annoying burden for the men; but by the story's end he seems to represent both what is missing in the village and what they all yearn for.

Students sometimes become too preoccupied with finding symbols in a story, at the expense of a good understanding of how the story is depicting real human experience. To unequivocally say, for example, that Esteban represents male virility would not only be presumptuous but would also take the symbol out of the context of the story as a whole, since it is clear that Esteban represents more than mere virility to the villagers, and to the captain at the end of the story.

Allegory

If a poem, story, or play is *entirely* symbolic—that is, if the primary function of the characters, events, and setting are symbolic, not literal—then it is an *allegory*. Emily Dickinson's "Because I could not stop for Death" (p. 993), Sylvia Plath's "Death & Co." (p. 995) and Woody Allen's *Death Knocks* (p. 1005) are among the works in this book that may be seen as *allegories,* since most of the characters and events of those works could not plausibly exist or happen and are obviously symbolic.

Ambiguity

Multiple meanings of a word, phrase or situation in a literary work often create *ambiguity,* or uncertainty. As readers, we are invited to consider two or more contrary ideas at the same time. In John Updike's story "A&P," Sammy's decision may be considered ambiguous. Does he quit for the girls, "hoping they'll stop and watch . . . their unsuspected hero"? Or does he suspect they haven't noticed him, as he realizes, in that split second, he needs to quit for other reasons? The language the author uses reflects the uncertainty and complexity of Sammy's motivation.

Image

Writers sometimes use *images*—of sight most commonly, but also of sound, taste, smell, or touch—to appeal to our senses. Note how Sharon Olds, in "Photograph of the Girl" creates a *visual image* that also appeals to our senses of touch, taste, and sound, when she describes the girl sitting on the ground, "eyes closed, mouth open, raw hot / wind blowing sand in her face." Through her imagery, we can *feel* the sand on her face, *taste* it in her open mouth, and *hear* it blowing on her, as we *see* the scene as a whole.

Irony

It is difficult to define irony, because there are many types and because much depends on the reader inferring it. When a writer is being ironic there is usually a discrepancy between what is said and what the reader knows to be true. You probably recognize irony when an expression strikes you as being oddly but appropriately "coincidental": "How ironic," you might say, when a race-car driver is killed in a highway accident.

In "Photograph of the Girl" (p. 8) there is verbal irony in the line "Hunger and puberty are / taking her together," as several students noted since there is (as in definition 2 on p. 77) an incongruity between what is expected and what actually occurs; one doesn't expect those two events—hunger and puberty—to occur simultaneously. The same is true for the line "She cannot be beautiful, but she is / starving," and for the final image of the poem.

Dramatic Irony

Playwrights most often use *dramatic irony,* but it occurs in fiction and narrative poetry as well. You've all seen a movie in which the audience cringes as one of the stars tremblingly opens a door on the other side of which lurks the villain. The audience knows what's behind the door, but the character doesn't: this is known as *dramatic irony.* In *A Doll's House* (p. 659), for example, the audience knows that Krogstad has blackmailed Nora, but Torvald doesn't.

Paradox/Oxymoron

Writers use seemingly contradictory expressions to convey certain truths about characters or events. If such an expression is put in sentence or paragraph form, it is called a *paradox;* if in an expression, or neat turn of phrase, it is called an *oxymoron*. It is a *paradox* that the girl in Sharon Olds's poem is ovulating as she is starving. And Gwendolyn Brooks uses an *oxymoron* when she has her speakers say, "We / Sing sin," since we are not used to thinking of sinning as something worth celebrating.

As you read the works you are assigned in this book, use this section as a reference guide to assist you in the understanding, and use, of literary terms—or to get some ideas, if you feel that you like a work, but would like to be able to write more specifically about the techniques behind it. The better you understand the way writers employ these strategies and the way these terms are used, the more confidently and intelligently you will be writing through literature.

PART 2

READINGS FOR WRITING

SECTION 1 (CHAPTERS 9–12)

IDENTITIES

In this section are a wide variety of perspectives on the subject of *identity*. They offer an array of responses to some basic questions we ask of ourselves: What makes us who we are? What roles are we forced to play, and what roles do we willingly take on? What are our *real* selves, as opposed to the selves we seem to be to our family, friends, or the larger society? At what point in our lives did we come of age? In what ways are our selves defined by, or set in contrast to, the community in which we live? What are the distinctive qualities of being a woman? Of being an African-American?

You are asked to write about your own sense of self and your own identity, then to read the various ways in which some authors have depicted such self-discovery. Afterwards, you will be able to bring these many perspectives together in an essay on the subject.

GETTING STARTED: WRITING EXERCISES ON IDENTITIES

Informally write in response to one of the following questions:

1. If someone asked, "Who are you?" what would you say? Write a list of roles you play and/or qualities you have that identify you and make you who you are.
2. Describe how you see yourself in relation to your friends and family, and then in relation to society in general. What are the differences among these relationships?
3. Write a quick reaction to one or more of the following quotations:
   - "Resolve to be thyself; and know that he who finds himself, loses his misery."—Matthew Arnold
   - "The unexamined life is not worth living."—Socrates
   - "I want by understanding myself to understand others. I want to be all that I am capable of becoming."—Katherine Mansfield
   - "Human beings are more alike than unalike, and what is true anywhere is true everywhere."—Maya Angelou
4. READ the following *section essay* by Rollo May, from "The Experience of Becoming a Person." Some key terms used in this essay follow: *conformity, potential, empathy, joy, self, relationship*. After reading the essay, select one of the terms, and summarize (a) what Rollo May says about it, and (b) what you think about what May says.

SECTION ESSAY

ROLLO MAY

The Experience of Becoming a Person (excerpt)

Rollo May (b. 1909), psychologist, is best known for his role in the self-actualization movement of the 1950s. His works include The Meaning of Anxiety *(1950),* Psy-

chology and the Human Dilemma (1967), and Freedom and Destiny (1981). The following excerpt is taken from Man's Search for Himself (1953), an influential book for its time.

This consciousness of self, this capacity to see one's self as though from the outside, is the distinctive characteristic of man. A friend of mine has a dog who waits at his studio door all morning and, when anybody comes to the door, he jumps up and barks, wanting to play. My friend holds that the dog is saying in his barking: "Here is a dog who has been waiting all morning for someone to come to play with him. Are you the one?" This is a nice sentiment, and all of us who like dogs enjoy projecting such cozy thoughts into their heads. But actually this is exactly what the dog cannot say. He can show that he wants to play and entice you into throwing his ball for him, but he cannot stand outside himself and see himself as a dog doing these things. He is not blessed with the consciousness of self.

Inasmuch as this means the dog is also free from neurotic anxiety and guilt feelings, which are the doubtful blessings of the human being, some people would prefer to say the dog is not cursed with the consciousness of self. Walt Whitman, echoing this thought, envies the animals:

> I think I could turn and live with animals. . . .
> They do not sweat and whine about their condition,
> They do not lie awake in the dark and weep for their sins . . .

But actually man's consciousness of himself is the source of his highest qualities. It underlies his ability to distinguish between "I" and the world. It gives him the capacity to keep time, which is simply the ability to stand outside the present and to imagine oneself back in yesterday or ahead in the day after tomorrow. Thus human beings can learn from the past and plan for the future. And thus man is the historical mammal in that he can stand outside and look at his history; and thereby he can influence his own development as a person, and to a minor extent he can influence the march of history in his nation and society as a whole. The capacity for consciousness of self also underlies man's ability to use symbols, which is a way of disengaging something from what it is, such as the two sounds which make up the word "table" and agreeing that these sounds will stand for a whole class of things. Thus man can think in abstractions like "beauty," "reason," and "goodness."

This capacity for consciousness of ourselves gives us the ability to see ourselves as others see us and to have empathy with others. It underlies our remarkable capacity to transport ourselves into someone else's parlor where we will be in reality next week, and then in imagination to think and plan how we will act. And it enables us to imagine ourselves in someone else's place, and to ask how we would feel and what we would do if we were this other person.

No matter how poorly we use or fail to use or even abuse these capacities, they are the rudiments of our ability to begin to love our neighbor, to have ethical sensitivity, to see truth, to create beauty, to devote ourselves to ideals, and to die for them if need be.

To fulfill these potentialities is to be a person. This is what is meant when it is stated in the Hebrew-Christian religious tradition that man is created in the image of God.

But these gifts come only at a high price, the price of anxiety and inward crises. The birth of the self is no simple and easy matter. For the child now faces the frightful prospect of being out on his own, alone, and without the full protection of the decisions of his parents. It is no wonder that when he begins to feel himself an identity in his own right, he may feel terribly powerless in comparison with the great and strong adults around him. In the midst of a struggle over her dependency on her mother, one person had this eloquent dream: "I was in a little boat tied to a big boat. We were going through the ocean and big waves came up, piling over the sides of my boat. I wondered whether it was still tied to the big boat."

The healthy child, who is loved and supported but not coddled by his parents, will proceed in his development despite this anxiety and the crises that face him. And there may be no particular external signs of trauma or special rebelliousness. But when his parents consciously or unconsciously exploit him for their own ends or pleasure, or hate or reject him, so that he cannot be sure of minimal support when he tries out his new independence, the child will cling to the parents and will use his capacity for independence only in the forms of negativity and stubbornness. If, when he first begins tentatively to say "No," his parents beat him down rather than love and encourage him, he thereafter will say "No" not as a form of true independent strength but as a mere rebellion.

Or if, as in the majority of cases in the present day, the parents themselves are anxious and bewildered in the tumultuous seas of the changing times, unsure of themselves and beset by self-doubts, their anxiety will carry over and lead the child to feel that he lives in a world in which it is dangerous to venture into becoming one's self.

This brief sketch is schematic, to be sure, and it is meant to give us as adults a kind of retrospective picture in the light of which we can better understand how one fails to achieve selfhood. Most of the data for these conflicts of childhood come from adults who are struggling, in dreams, memories or in present-day relations, to overcome what in their past lives originally blocked them in becoming fully born as persons. Almost every adult is, in greater or lesser degree, still struggling on the long journey to achieve selfhood on the basis of the patterns which were set in his early experiences in the family.

Nor do we for a moment overlook the fact that selfhood is always born in a social context. Genetically, Auden[1] is quite right:

> . . . for the ego is a dream
> Till a neighbor's need by
> name create it.

Or, as we put it above, the self is always born and grows in interpersonal relationships. But no "ego" moves on into responsible selfhood if it remains chiefly the reflection of the social context around it. In our particular world in which conformity is the great destroyer of selfhood—in our society in which fitting the "pattern" tends to be accepted as the norm, and being "well liked" is the alleged ticket to salvation—what needs to be emphasized is not only the admitted fact that we are to some extent created by each other but also our capacity to experience, and create, ourselves.

—1953

[1]W. H. Auden (1907–1973), an English poet [Ed.]

9

BECOMING A PERSON

WRITING ASSIGNMENT SEQUENCE

1. Thinking About . . . Becoming a Person

Focused Freewriting: Write about a particular *moment of recognition,* or *epiphany* (see page 76) that has occurred in your life: a time or event when your perception of yourself changed, when you grew from child to adult, or when you became disillusioned by the realities of the world. How much of that self-awareness had to do with your gender? (For more on *freewriting,* see page 26.)

2. Enacting the Topic

Write a diary entry from the perspective of your younger self about that same *epiphany.* The date of the entry should correspond to the actual event.

3. Responding to the Readings

As you read the works in this cluster, jot down in your response journals questions you have about the works, and comment on passages you find provocative or puzzling. Consider the questions following each reading for journal writing and prepare to discuss your reactions in class.

CLUSTER ESSAY

LANGSTON HUGHES

Salvation

Langston Hughes (1902–1967) was born in Joplin, Missouri, but grew up mainly in Lawrence, Kansas (probably the setting for the essay below), then in Cleveland. After a year in Mexico, where his father lived, he spent a year at Columbia University from 1921 to 1922. After working at odd jobs he entered Lincoln University (in Pennsylvania) in 1926. By the time he graduated three years later, he had published two books of poetry (including The Weary Blues) *and established himself as the best poet of the Harlem Re-*

naissance (then called the "New Negro" Renaissance). Reflecting on his long career as a poet, political activist, dramatist, short-story writer, journalist (for more than 20 years for the Chicago Defender*), songwriter, and translator, Hughes wrote two autobiographies. The essay below, "Salvation," is excerpted from the first of these,* The Big Sea *(1940).*

I was saved from sin when I was going on thirteen. But not really saved. It happened like this. There was a big revival at my Auntie Reed's church. Every night for weeks there had been much preaching, singing, praying, and shouting, and some very hardened sinners had been brought to Christ, and the membership of the church had grown by leaps and bounds. Then just before the revival ended, they held a special meeting for children, "to bring the young lambs to the fold." My aunt spoke of it for days ahead. That night I was escorted to the front row and placed on the mourners' bench with all the other young sinners, who had not yet been brought to Jesus.

My aunt told me that when you were saved you saw a light, and something happened to you inside! And Jesus came into your life! And God was with you from then on! She said you could see and hear and feel Jesus in your soul. I believed her. I have heard a great many old people say the same thing and it seemed to me they ought to know. So I sat there calmly in the hot, crowded church, waiting for Jesus to come to me.

The preacher preached a wonderful rhythmical sermon, all moans and shouts and lonely cries and dire pictures of hell, and then he sang a song about the ninety and nine safe in the fold, but one little lamb was left out in the cold. Then he said: "Won't you come? Won't you come to Jesus? Young lambs, won't you come?" And he held out his arms to all us young sinners there on the mourners' bench. And the little girls cried. And some of them jumped up and went to Jesus right away. But most of us just sat there.

A great many old people came and knelt around us and prayed, old women with jet-black faces and braided hair, old men with work-gnarled hands. And the church sang a song about the lower lights are burning, some poor sinners to be saved. And the whole building rocked with prayer and song.

Still I kept waiting to *see* Jesus.

Finally all the young people had gone to the altar and were saved, but one boy and me. He was a rounder's son named Westley. Westley and I were surrounded by sisters and deacons praying. It was very hot in the church, and getting late now. Finally Westley said to me in a whisper: "God damn! I'm tired o' sitting here. Let's get up and be saved." So he got up and was saved.

Then I was left all alone on the mourners' bench. My aunt came and knelt at my knees and cried, while prayers and songs swirled all around me in the little church. The whole congregation prayed for me alone, in a mighty wail of moans and voices. And I kept waiting serenely for Jesus, waiting, waiting—but he didn't come. I wanted to see him, but nothing happened to me. Nothing! I wanted something to happen to me, but nothing happened.

I heard the songs and the minister saying: "Why don't you come? My dear child, why don't you come to Jesus? Jesus is waiting for you. He wants you. Why don't you come? Sister Reed, what is this child's name?"

"Langston," my aunt sobbed.

"Langston, why don't you come? Why don't you come and be saved? Oh, Lamb of God! Why don't you come?"

Now it was really getting late. I began to be ashamed of myself, holding everything up so long. I began to wonder what God thought about Westley, who certainly hadn't seen Jesus either, but who was now sitting proudly on the platform, swinging his knickerbockered legs and grinning down at me, surrounded by deacons and old women on their knees praying. God had not struck Westley dead for taking his name in vain or for lying in the temple. So I decided that maybe to save further trouble, I'd better lie, too, and say that Jesus had come, and get up and be saved.

So I got up.

Suddenly the whole room broke into a sea of shouting, as they saw me rise. Waves of rejoicing swept the place. Women leaped in the air. My aunt threw her arms around me. The minister took me by the hand and led me to the platform.

When things quited down, in a hushed silence, punctuated by a few ecstatic "Amens," all the new young lambs were blessed in the name of God. Then joyous singing filled the room.

That night, for the last time in my life but one—for I was a big boy twelve years old—I cried. I cried, in bed alone, and couldn't stop. I buried my head under the quilts, but my aunt heard me. She woke up and told my uncle I was crying because the Holy Ghost had come into my life, and because I had seen Jesus. But I was really crying because I couldn't bear to tell her that I had lied, that I had deceived everybody in the church, that I hadn't seen Jesus, and that now I didn't believe there was a Jesus any more, since he didn't come to help me.

—1940

What are your reactions to and questions about this work? The following questions may help provoke some ideas.

Probing the Work

1. How is Hughes's expectation of being saved different from his actual experience? What does he learn from his experience?

Identifying Issues

2. To what degree do institutions (churches, schools, families, etc.) that are supposed to help young people find their way instead help them sometimes to *lose* their way?

JAMES JOYCE

Araby

James Joyce (1882–1941) was born in Dublin, Ireland. His father's drinking contributed to the family's financial deterioration, but Joyce was well educated at Jesuit schools and University College, Dublin. In 1902 he left Ireland and lived in Europe, teaching English and writing stories (including "Araby"), later publishing them in a collection called Dubliners *(1916). He dedicated much of the rest of his life to writing novels, including* Portrait of the Artist as a Young Man *(1916),* Ulysses *(1922), and* Finnegan's Wake *(1939).*

North Richmond Street, being blind, was a quiet street except at the hour when the Christian Brothers' School set the boys free. An uninhabited house of two storeys stood at the blind end, detached from its neighbours in a square ground. The other houses of the street, conscious of decent lives within them, gazed at one another with brown imperturbable faces.

The former tenant of our house, a priest, had died in the back drawing-room. Air, musty from having been long enclosed, hung in all the rooms, and the waste room behind the kitchen was littered with old useless papers. Among these I found a few paper-covered books, the pages of which were curled and damp: *The Abbot,* by Walter Scott, *The Devout Communicant* and *The Memoirs of Vidocq.* I liked the last best because its leaves were yellow. The wild garden behind the house contained a central apple-tree and a few straggling bushes under one of which I found the late tenant's rusty bicycle-pump. He had been a very charitable priest; in his will he had left all his money to institutions and the furniture of his house to his sister.

When the short days of winter came dusk fell before we had well eaten our dinners. When we met in the street the houses had grown sombre. The space of sky above us was the colour of ever-changing violet and towards it the lamps of the street lifted their feeble lanterns. The cold air stung us and we played till our bodies glowed. Our shouts echoed in the silent street. The career of our play brought us through the dark muddy lanes behind the houses where we ran the gauntlet of the rough tribes from the cottages, to the back doors of the dark dripping gardens where odours arose from the ashpits, to the dark odorous stables where a coachman smoothed and combed the horse or shook music from the buckled harness. When we returned to the street light from the kitchen windows had filled the areas. If my uncle was seen turning the corner we hid in the shadow until we had seen him safely housed. Or if Mangan's sister came out on the doorstep to call her brother in to his tea we watched her from our shadow peer up and down the street. We waited to see whether she would remain or go in and, if she remained, we left our shadow and walked up to Mangan's steps resignedly. She was waiting for us, her figure defined by the light from the half-opened door. Her brother always teased her before he obeyed and I stood by the railings looking at her.

Her dress swung as she moved her body and the soft rope of her hair tossed from side to side.

Every morning I lay on the floor in the front parlour watching her door. The blind was pulled down to within an inch of the sash so that I could not be seen. When she came out on the doorstep my heart leaped. I ran to the hall, seized my books and followed her. I kept her brown figure always in my eye and, when we came near the point at which our ways diverged, I quickened my pace and passed her. This happened morning after morning. I had never spoken to her, except for a few casual words, and yet her name was like a summons to all my foolish blood.

Her image accompanied me even in places the most hostile to romance. On Saturday evenings when my aunt went marketing I had to go to carry some of the parcels. We walked through the flaring streets, jostled by drunken men and bargaining women, amid the curses of labourers, the shrill litanies of shop-boys who stood on guard by the barrels of pigs' cheeks, the nasal chanting of street-singers, who sang a *come-all-you* about O'Donovan Rossa, or a ballad about the troubles in our native land. These noises converged in a single sensation of life for me: I imagined that I bore my chalice safely through a throng of foes. Her name sprang to my lips at moments in strange prayers and praises which I myself did not understand. My eyes were often full of tears (I could not tell why) and at times a flood from my heart seemed to pour itself out into my bosom. I thought little of the future. I did not know whether I would ever speak to her or not or, if I spoke to her, how I could tell her of my confused adoration. But my body was like a harp and her words and gestures were like fingers running upon the wires.

One evening I went into the back drawing-room in which the priest had died. It was a dark rainy evening and there was no sound in the house. Through one of the broken panes I heard the rain impinge upon the earth, the fine incessant needles of water playing in the sodden beds. Some distant lamp or lighted window gleamed below me. I was thankful that I could see so little. All my senses seemed to desire to veil themselves and, feeling that I was about to slip from them, I pressed the palms of my hands together until they trembled, murmuring: *"O love! O love!"* many times.

At last she spoke to me. When she addressed the first words to me I was so confused that I did not know what to answer. She asked me was I going to *Araby*. I forgot whether I answered yes or no. It would be a splendid bazaar, she said she would love to go.

"And why can't you?" I asked.

While she spoke she turned a silver bracelet round and round her wrist. She could not go, she said, because there would be a retreat that week in her convent. Her brother and two other boys were fighting for their caps and I was alone at the railings. She held one of the spikes, bowing her head towards me. The light from the lamp opposite our door caught the white curve of her neck, lit up her hair that rested there and, falling, lit up the hand upon the railing. It fell over one side of her dress and caught the white border of a petticoat, just visible as she stood at ease.

"It's well for you," she said.

"If I go," I said, "I will bring you something."

What innumerable follies laid waste my waking and sleeping thoughts after that evening! I wished to annihilate the tedious intervening days. I chafed against the work of school. At night in my bedroom and by day in the classroom her image came between me and the page I strove to read. The syllables of the word *Araby* were called to me through the silence in which my soul luxuriated and cast an Eastern enchantment over me. I asked for leave to go to the bazaar on Saturday night. My aunt was surprised and hoped it was not some Freemason affair. I answered few questions in class. I watched my master's face pass from amiability to sternness; he hoped I was not beginning to idle. I could not call my wandering thoughts together. I had hardly any patience with the serious work of life which, now that it stood between me and my desire, seemed to me child's play, ugly monotonous child's play.

On Saturday morning I reminded my uncle that I wished to go to the bazaar in the evening. He was fussing at the hallstand, looking for the hatbrush, and answered me curtly:

"Yes, boy, I know."

As he was in the hall I could not go into the front parlour and lie at the window. I left the house in bad humour and walked slowly towards the school. The air was pitilessly raw and already my heart misgave me.

When I came home to dinner my uncle had not yet been home. Still it was early. I sat staring at the clock for some time and, when its ticking began to irritate me, I left the room. I mounted the staircase and gained the upper part of the house. The high cold empty gloomy rooms liberated me and I went from room to room singing. From the front window I saw my companions playing below in the street. Their cries reached me weakened and indistinct and, leaning my forehead against the cool glass, I looked over at the dark house where she lived. I may have stood there for an hour, seeing nothing but the brown-clad figure cast by my imagination, touched discreetly by the lamplight at the curved neck, at the hand upon the railings and at the border below the dress.

When I came downstairs again I found Mrs. Mercer sitting at the fire. She was an old garrulous woman, a pawnbroker's widow, who collected used stamps for some pious purpose. I had to endure the gossip of the tea-table. The meal was prolonged beyond an hour and still my uncle did not come. Mrs. Mercer stood up to go: she was sorry she couldn't wait any longer, but it was after eight o'clock and she did not like to be out late, as the night air was bad for her. When she had gone I began to walk up and down the room, clenching my fists. My aunt said:

"I'm afraid you may put off your bazaar for this night of Our Lord."

At nine o'clock I heard my uncle's latchkey in the halldoor. I heard him talking to himself and heard the hallstand rocking when it had received the weight of his overcoat. I could interpret these signs. When he was midway through his dinner I asked him to give me the money to go to the bazaar. He had forgotten.

"The people are in bed and after their first sleep now," he said.

I did not smile. My aunt said to him energetically:

"Can't you give him the money and let him go? You've kept him late enough as it is."

My uncle said he was very sorry he had forgotten. He said he believed in the old saying: "All work and no play makes Jack a dull boy." He asked me where I was going and, when I had told him a second time he asked me did I know *The Arab's Farewell to his Steed*. When I left the kitchen he was about to recite the opening lines of the piece to my aunt.

I held a florin tightly in my hand as I strode down Buckingham Street towards the station. The sight of the streets thronged with buyers and glaring with gas recalled to me the purpose of my journey. I took my seat in a third-class carriage of a deserted train. After an intolerable delay the train moved out of the station slowly. It crept onward among ruinous houses and over the twinkling river. At Westland Row Station a crowd of people pressed to the carriage doors; but the porters moved them back, saying that it was a special train for the bazaar. I remained alone in the bare carriage. In a few minutes the train drew up beside an improvised wooden platform. I passed out on to the road and saw by the lighted dial of a clock that it was ten minutes to ten. In front of me was a large building which displayed the magical name.

I could not find any sixpenny entrance and, fearing that the bazaar would be closed, I passed in quickly through a turnstile, handing a shilling to a weary-looking man. I found myself in a big hall girdled at half its height by a gallery. Nearly all the stalls were closed and the greater part of the hall was in darkness. I recognised a silence like that which pervades a church after a service. I walked into the centre of the bazaar timidly. A few people were gathered about the stalls which were still open. Before a curtain, over which the words *Café Chantant* were written in coloured lamps, two men were counting money on a salver. I listened to the fall of the coins.

Remembering with difficulty why I had come I went over to one of the stalls and examined porcelain vases and flowered tea-sets. At the door of the stall a young lady was talking and laughing with two young gentlemen. I remarked their English accents and listened vaguely to their conversation.

"O, I never said such a thing!"

"O, but you did!"

"O, but I didn't!"

"Didn't she say that?"

"Yes. I heard her."

"O, there's a . . . fib!"

Observing me the young lady came over and asked me did I wish to buy anything. The tone of her voice was not encouraging; she seemed to have spoken to me out of a sense of duty. I looked humbly at the great jars that stood like eastern guards at either side of the dark entrance to the stall and murmured:

"No, thank you."

The young lady changed the position of one of the vases and went back to the two young men. They began to talk of the same subject. Once or twice the young lady glanced at me over her shoulder.

I lingered before her stall, though I knew my stay was useless, to make my interest in her wares seem the more real. Then I turned away slowly and walked down the middle of the bazaar. I allowed the two pennies to fall against the sixpence in my pocket. I heard a voice call from one end of the gallery that the light was out. The upper part of the hall was now completely dark.

Gazing up into the darkness I saw myself as a creature driven and derided by vanity; and my eyes burned with anguish and anger.

—1916

What are your reactions to and questions about this work? The following questions may help provoke some ideas.

Probing the Work

1. Assess the *plot* and *conflict* (p. 73) of "Araby": what is the boy like in the beginning, and at the end? What forces is he struggling against? At what point is this struggle resolved (the *climax*)?
2. At the end of the story the boy says, "I saw myself as a creature driven and derided by vanity; and my eyes burned with anguish and anger." What does he realize at this point? How might this realization, or *epiphany* (see page 76), affect his life?

Identifying Issues

3. Langston Hughes (in "Salvation") and the boy in "Araby" are both disillusioned and influenced by their religious background and surroundings. How might you compare and contrast their religious influences?

RICHARD WRIGHT

The Man Who Was Almost a Man

Richard Wright (1908–1960) grew up among African-American sharecroppers in Mississippi, Arkansas, and Tennessee, then among the urban poor in Chicago and New York. He wrote mostly about issues of race and poverty, in newspapers (for the communist cause, which he later renounced), novels (e.g., Native Son, *1940), and autobiographical works (e.g.,* Black Boy, *1945). In 1946 with his wife and daughter Wright deliberately exiled himself to Paris, where he continued to write.*

Dave struck out across the fields, looking homeward through paling light. Whut's the use talkin wid em niggers in the field? Anyhow, his mother was putting supper on the table. Them niggers can't understan nothing. One of these days he was going to get a gun and practice shooting, then they couldn't talk to him as though he were a little boy. He slowed, looking at the ground. Shucks, Ah ain scareda them even ef they are biggern me! Aw, Ah know whut Ahma do. Ahm going by ol Joe's sto n git that Sears Roebuck catlog n look at them guns. Mebbe Ma will lemme buy one when she gits mah pay from ol man Hawkins. Ahma beg her t gimme some money. Ahm ol ernough to hava gun. Ahm seventeen. Almost a man. He strode, feeling his long loose-jointed limbs. Shucks, a man oughta hava little gun aftah he done worked hard all day.

He came in sight of Joe's store. A yellow lantern glowed on the front porch. He mounted steps and went through the screen door, hearing it bang behind him. There was a strong smell of coal oil and mackerel fish. He felt very confident until he saw fat Joe walk in through the rear door, then his courage began to ooze.

"Howdy, Dave! Whutcha want?"

"How yuh. Mistah Joe? Aw, Ah don wanna buy nothing. Ah jus wanted t see ef yuhd lemme look at tha catlog erwhile."

"Sure! You wanna see it here?"

"Nawsuh. Ah wants t take it home wid me. Ah'll bring it back termorrow when Ah come in from the fiels."

"You plannin on buying something?"

"Yessuh."

"Your ma lettin you have your own money now?"

"Shucks. Mistah Joe, Ahm gittin t be a man like anybody else!"

Joe laughed and wiped his greasy white face with a red bandanna.

"Whut you plannin on buyin?"

Dave looked at the floor, scratched his head, scratched his thigh, and smiled. Then he looked up shyly.

"Ah'll tell yuh, Mistah Joe, ef yuh promise yuh won't tell."

"I promise."

"Waal, Ahma buy a gun."

"A gun? What you want with a gun?"

"Ah wanna keep it."

"You ain't nothing but a boy. You don't need a gun."

"Aw, lemme have the catalog, Mistah Joe. Ah'll bring it back."

Joe walked through the rear door. Dave was elated. He looked around at barrels of sugar and flour. He heard Joe coming back. He craned his neck to see if he were bringing the book. Yeah, he's got it. Gawddog, he's got it!

"Here, but be sure you bring it back. It's the only one I got."

"Sho, Mistah Joe."

"Say, if you wanna buy a gun, why don't you buy one from me? I gotta gun to sell."

"Will it shoot?"

"Sure it'll shoot."

"Whut kind is it?"

"Oh, it's kinda old . . . a left-hand Wheeler. A pistol. A big one."

"Is it got bullets in it?"

"It's loaded."

"Kin Ah see it?"

"Where's your money?"

"What yuh wan fer it?"

"I'll let you have it for two dollars."

"Just two dollahs? Shucks, Ah, could buy tha when Ah git mah pay."

"I'll have it here when you want it."

"Awright, suh. Ah be in fer it."

He went through the door, hearing it slam again behind him. Ahma git some money from Ma n buy me a gun! Only two dollahs! He tucked the thick catalogue under his arm and hurried.

"Where yuh been, boy?" His mother held a steaming dish of black-eyed peas.

"Aw, Ma, Ah just stopped down the road t talk wid the boys."

"Yuh know bettah t keep suppah waitin."

He sat down, resting the catalogue on the edge of the table.

"Yuh git up from there and git to the well n wash yosef! Ah ain feedin no hogs in mah house!"

She grabbed his shoulder and pushed him. He stumbled out of the room, then came back to get the catalogue.

"Whut this?"

"Aw, Ma, it's jusa catlog."

"Who yuh git it from?"

"From Joe, down at the sto."

"Waal, thas good. We kin use it in the outhouse."

"Naw, Ma." He grabbed for it. "Gimme ma catlog, Ma."

She held onto it and glared at him.

"Quit hollerin at me! Whu's wrong wid yuh? Yuh crazy?"

"But Ma, please. It ain mine! It's Joe's! He tol me t bring it back t im termorrow."

She gave up the book. He stumbled down the back steps, hugging the thick book under his arm. When he had splashed water on his face and hands, he groped back to the kitchen and fumbled in a corner for the towel. He bumped into a chair; it clattered to the floor. The catalogue sprawled at his feet. When he had dried his eyes he snatched up the book and held it again under his arm. His mother stood watching him.

"Now, ef yuh gonna act a fool over that ol book, Ah'll take it n burn it up."

"Naw, Ma, please."

"Waal, set down n be still!"

He sat down and drew the oil lamp close. He thumbled page after page, unaware of the food his mother set on the table. His father came in. Then his small brother.

"Whutcha got there, Dave?" his father asked.

"Jusa catlog," he answered, not looking up.

"Yeah, here they is!" His eyes glowed at blue-and-black revolvers. He glanced up, feeling sudden guilt. His father was watching him. He eased the book under the table and rested it on his knees. After the blessing was asked, he ate. He scooped up peas and swallowed fat meat without chewing. Buttermilk helped to wash it down. He did not want to mention money before his father. He would do much better by cornering his mother when she was alone. He looked at his father uneasily out of the edge of his eye.

"Boy, how come yuh don quit foolin wid tha book n eat yo suppah?"

"Yessuh."

"How you n ol man Hawkins gitten erlong?"

"Suh?"

"Can't yuh hear? Why don yuh lissen? Ah ast yu how wuz yuh n ol man hawkins gittin erlong?"

"Oh, swell, Pa. Ah plows mo lan than anybody over there."

"Waal, yuh oughta keep you mind on whut yuh doin."

"Yessuh."

He poured his plate full of molasses and sopped it up slowly with a chunk of cornbread. When his father and brother had left the kitchen, he still sat and looked again at the guns in the catalogue, longing to muster courage enough to present his case to his mother. Lawd, ef Ah only had tha pretty one! He could almost feel the slickness of the weapon with his fingers. If he had a gun like that he would polish it and keep it shining so it would never rust. N Ah'd keep it loaded, by Gawd!

"Ma?" His voice was hesitant.

"Hunh?"

"Ol man Hawkins give yuh mah money yit?"

"Yeah, but ain no usa yuh thinking bout throwin nona it erway. Ahm keepin tha money sos yuh kin have cloes go t school this winter."

He rose and went to her side with the open catalogue in his palms. She was washing dishes, her head bent low over a pan. Shyly he raised the book. When he spoke, his voice was husky, faint.

"Ma, Gawd knows Ah wans one of these."

"One of whut?" she asked, not raising her eyes.

"One of these," he said again, not daring even to point. She glanced up at the page, then at him with wide eyes.

"Nigger, is yuh gone plumb crazy?"

"Aw, Ma—"

"Git outta here! Don yuh talk t me bout no gun! Yuh a fool!"

"Ma, Ah kin buy one fer two dollahs."

"Not ef Ah knows it, yuh ain!"

"But yuh promised me one—"

"Ah don care what Ah promised! Yuh ain nothing but a boy yit!"

"Ma, ef yuh lemme buy one Ah'll *never* ast yuh fer nothing no mo."

"Ah tol yuh t git outta here! Yuh ain gonna toucha penny of tha money fer no gun! Thas how come Ah has Mistah Hawkins t pay yo wages t me, cause Ah knows yuh ain't got no sense."

"But, Ma, we needa gun. Pa ain got no gun. We needa gun in the house. Yuh kin never tell whut might happen."

"Now don yuh try to maka fool outta me, boy! Ef we did hava gun, yuh wouldn't have it!"

He laid the catalogue down and slipped his arm around her waist.

"Aw, Ma, Ah done worked hard alla summer n ain ast yuh fer nothing, is Ah, now?"

"Thas whut yuh spose t do!"

"But Ma, Ah wans a gun. Yuh kin lemme have two dollahs outta mah money. Please, Ma. I kin give it to Pa . . . Please, Ma! Ah loves yuh, Ma."

When she spoke her voice came soft and low.

"What yuh wan wida gun, Dave? Yuh don need no gun. Yuh'll git in trouble. N ef yo pa jus thought Ah let yuh have money t buy a gun he'd hava fit."

"Ah'll hide it, Ma. It ain't but two dollahs."

"Lawd, chil, whut's wrong wid yuh?"

"Ain nothing wrong, Ma. Ahm almos a man now. Ah wans a gun."

"Who gonna sell yuh a gun?"

"Ol Joe at the sto."

"N it don cos but two dollahs?"

"Thas all, Ma. Just two dollahs. Please, Ma."

She was stacking the plates away; her hands moved slowly, reflectively. Dave kept an anxious silence. Finally, she turned to him.

"Ah'll let yuh git tha gun ef yuh promise me one thing."

"What's tha, Ma?"

"Yuh bring it straight back t me, yuh hear? It be fer Pa."

"Yessum! Lemme go now, Ma."

She stooped, turned slightly to one side, raised the hem of her dress, rolled down the top of her stocking, and came up with a slender wad of bills.

"Here," she said. "Lawd knows yuh don need no gun. But yer pa does.

Yuh bring it right back t me, yuh hear? Ahma put it up. Now ef yuh don, Ahma have yuh pa pick yuh so hard yuh won fergit it."

"Yessum."

He took the money, ran down the steps, and across the yard.

"Dave! Yuuuuuh Daaaaave!"

He heard, but he was not going to stop now. "Naw, Lawd!"

The first movement he made the following morning was to reach under his pillow for the gun. In the gray light of dawn he held it loosely, feeling a sense of power. Could kill a man with a gun like this. Kill anybody, black or white. And if he were holding his gun in his hand, nobody could run over him; they would have to respect him. It was a big gun, with a long barrel and a heavy handle. He raised and lowered it in his hand, marveling at its weight.

He had not come straight home with it as his mother had asked; instead he had stayed out in the fields, holding the weapon in his hand, aiming it now and then at some imaginary foe. But he had not fired it; he had been afraid that his father might hear. Also he was not sure he knew how to fire it.

To avoid surrendering the pistol he had not come into the house until he knew that they were all asleep. When his mother had tiptoed to his bedside late that night and demanded the gun, he had first played possum; then he had told her that the gun was hidden outdoors, that he would bring it to her in the morning. Now he lay turning it slowly in his hands. He broke it, took out the cartridges, felt them, and then put them back.

He slid out of bed, got a long strip of old flannel from a trunk, wrapped the gun in it, and tied it to his naked thigh while it was still loaded. He did not go in to breakfast. Even though it was not yet daylight, he started for Jim Hawkins' plantation. Just as the sun was rising he reached the barns where the mules and plows were kept.

"Hey! That you, Dave?"

He turned. Jim Hawkins stood eyeing him suspiciously.

"What're yuh doing here so early?"

"Ah didn't know Ah was gittin up so early, Mistah Hawkins. Ah was fixin t hitch up ol Jenny n take her t the fiels."

"Good. Since you're so early, how about plowing that stretch down by the woods?"

"Suits me, Mistah Hawkins."

"O.K. Go to it!"

He hitched Jenny to a plow and started across the fields. Hot dog! This was just what he wanted. If he could get down by the woods, he could shoot his gun and nobody would hear. He walked behind the plow, hearing the traces creaking, feeling the gun tied tight to his thigh.

When he reached the woods, he plowed two whole rows before he decided to take out the gun. Finally, he stopped, looked in all directions, then untied the gun and held it in his hand. He turned to the mule and smiled.

"Know whut this is, Jenny? Naw, yuh wouldn know! Yuhs jusa ol mule! Anyhow, this is a gun, n it kin shoot, by Gawd!"

He held the gun at arm's length. Whut t hell, Ahma shoot this thing! He looked at Jenny again.

"Lissen here, Jenny! When Ah pull this ol trigger, Ah don wan yuh to run n acka fool now!"

Jenny stood with head down, her short ears pricked straight. Dave walked off about twenty feet, held the gun far out from him at arm's length, and turned his head. Hell, he told himself, Ah ain afraid. The gun felt loose in his fingers; he waved it wildly for a moment. Then he shut his eyes and tightened his forefinger. Bloom! A report half deafened him and he thought his right hand was torn from his arm. He heard Jenny whinnying and galloping over the field, and he found himself on his knees, squeezing his fingers hard between his legs. His hand was numb; he jammed it into his mouth, trying to warm it, trying to stop the pain. The gun lay at his feet. He did not quite know what had happened. He stood up and stared at the gun as though it were a living thing. He gritted his teeth and kicked the gun. Yuh almos broke mah arm! He turned to look for Jenny; she was far over the fields, tossing her head and kicking wildly.

"Hol on there, ol mule!"

When he caught up with her she stood trembling, walling her big white eyes at him. The plow was far away; the traces had broken. Then Dave stopped short, looking, not believing. Jenny was bleeding. Her left side was red and wet with blood. He went closer. Lawd, have mercy! Wondah did Ah shoot this mule? He grabbed for Jenny's mane. She flinched, snorted, whirled, tossing her head.

"Hol on now! Hol on."

Then he saw the hole in Jenny's side, right between the ribs. It was round, wet, red. A crimson stream streaked down the front leg, flowing fast. Good Gawd! Ah wuzn't shootin at tha mule. He felt panic. He knew he had to stop that blood, or Jenny would bleed to death. He had never seen so much blood in all his life. He chased the mule for a half a mile, trying to catch her. Finally she stopped, breathing hard, stumpy tail half arched. He caught her mane and led her back to where the plow and gun lay. Then he stooped and grabbed handfuls of damp black earth and tried to plug the bullet hole. Jenny shuddered, whinnied, and broke from him.

"Hol on! Hol on now!"

He tried to plug it again, but blood came anyhow. His fingers were hot and sticky. He rubbed dirt into his palms, trying to dry them. Then again he attempted to plug the bullet hole, but Jenny shied away, kicking her heels high. He stood helpless. He had to do something. He ran at Jenny; she dodged him. He watched a red stream of blood flow down Jenny's leg and form a bright pool at her feet.

"Jenny . . . Jenny," he called weakly.

His lips trembled. She's bleeding t death! He looked in the direction of home, wanting to go back, wanting to get help. But he saw the pistol lying in the damp black clay. He had a queer feeling that if he only did something, this would not be; Jenny would not be there bleeding to death.

When he went to her this time, she did not move. She stood with sleepy, dreamy eyes; and when he touched her she gave a low-pitched whinny and knelt to the ground, her front knees slopping in blood.

"Jenny . . . Jenny . . ." he whispered.

For a long time she held her neck erect; then her head sank, slowly. Her ribs swelled with a mighty heave and she went over.

Dave's stomach felt empty, very empty. He picked up the gun and held it gingerly between his thumb and forefinger. He buried it at the foot of a tree. He took a stick and tried to cover the pool of blood with dirt—but what was the use? There was Jenny lying with her mouth open and her eyes walled and glassy. He could not tell Jim Hawkins he had shot his mule. But he had to tell something. Yeah, Ah'll tell em Jenny started gittin wil n fell on the joint of the plow. . . . But that would hardly happen to a mule. He walked across the field slowly, head down.

It was sunset. Two of Jim Hawkins' men were over near the edge of the woods digging a hole in which to bury Jenny. Dave was surrounded by a knot of people, all of whom were looking down at the dead mule.

"I don't see how in the world it happened," said Jim Hawkins for the tenth time.

The crowd parted and Dave's mother, father, and small brother pushed into the center.

"Where Dave?" his mother called.

"There he is," said Jim Hawkins.

His mother grabbed him.

"Whut happened, Dave? Whut yuh done?"

"Nothin."

"C mon, boy, talk," his father said.

Dave took a deep breath and told the story he knew nobody believed.

"Waal," he drawled. "Ah brung ol Jenny down here sos Ah could do mah plowin. Ah plowed bout two rows, just like yuh see." He stopped and pointed at the long rows of upturned earth. "Then somethin musta been wrong wid ol Jenny. She wouldn ack right a-tall. She started snortin n kicking her heels. Ah tried t hol her, but she pulled erway, rearin n goin in. Then when the point of the plow was sticking up in the air, she swung erroun n twisted herself back on it . . . She stuck herself n started t bleed. N fo Ah could do anything, she wuz dead."

"Did you ever hear of anything like that in all your life?" asked Jim Hawkins.

There were white and black standing in the crowd. They murmured. Dave's mother came close to him and looked hard into his face. "Tell the truth, Dave," she said.

"Looks like a bullet hole to me," said one man.
"Dave, whut yuh do wit the gun?" his mother asked.

The crowd surged in, looking at him. He jammed his hands into his pockets, shook his head slowly from left to right, and backed away. His eyes were wide and painful.

"Did he hava gun?" asked Jim Hawkins.

"By Gawd, Ah tol yuh tha wud a gun wound," said a man, slapping his thigh.

His father caught his shoulders and shook him till his teeth rattled.

"Tell whut happened, yuh rascal! Tell whut . . ."

Dave looked at Jenny's stiff legs and began to cry.

"Whut yuh do wid tha gun?" his mother asked.

"Whut wul he doin wida gun?" his father asked.

"Come on and tell the truth," said Hawkins. "Ain't nobody going to hurt you . . ."

His mother crowded close to him.

"Did yuh shoot tha mule, Dave?"

Dave cried, seeing blurred white and black faces.

"Ahh ddinn gggo tt sshooot hher . . . Ah ssswear ffo Gawd Ahh ddin. . . . Ah wul a-tryin t sssee ef the old gggun would sshoot—"

"Where yuh git the gun from?" his father asked.

"Ah got it from Joe, at the sto."

"Where yuh git the money?"

"Ma give it t me."

"He kept worryin me, Bob. Ah had t. Ah tol im t bring the gun right back to me . . . It was fer yuh, the gun."

"But howyuh happen to shoot that mule?" asked Jim Hawkins.

"Ah wuznt shootin at the mule, Mistah Hawkins. The gun jumped when Ah pulled the trigger . . . N fo Ah knowed anythin Jenny was there a-bleedin."

Somebody in the crowd laughed. Jim Hawkins walked close to Dave and looked into his face.

"Well, looks like you have bought you a mule, Dave."

"Ah swear fo Gawd, Ah didn go t kill the mule, Mistah Hawkins!"

"But you killed her!"

All the crowd was laughing now. They stood on tiptoe and poked heads over one another's shoulders.

"Well, boy, looks like yuh done bought a dead mule! Hahaha!"

"Ain tha ershame."

"Hohohohoho."

Dave stood, head down, twisting his feet in the dirt.

"Well, you needn't worry about it, Bob," said Jim Hawkins to Dave's father. "Just let the boy keep on working and pay me two dollars a month."

"Whut yuh wan fer yo mule, Mistah Hawkins?"

Jim Hawkins screwed up his eyes.

"Fifty dollars."

"Whut yuh do wid tha gun?" Dave's father demanded.

Dave said nothing.

"Yuh wan me t take a tree n beat yuh till yuh talk!"

"Nawsuh!"

"Whut yuh do wid it?"

"Ah throwed it erway."

"Where?"

"Ah . . . Ah throwed it in the creek."

"Waal, c mon home. N firs thing in the mawning git to tha creek n fin tha gun."

"Yessuh."

"Whut yuh pay fer it?"

"Two dollahs."

"Take tha gun n git yo money back n carry it t Mistah Hawkins, yuh near? N don fergit Ahma lam you black bottom good fer this! Now march yosef on home, suh!"

Dave turned and walked slowly. He heard people laughing. Dave glared, his eyes welling with tears. Hot anger bubbled in him. Then he swallowed and stumbled on.

That night Dave did not sleep. He was glad that he had gotten out of killing the mule so easily, but he was hurt. Something hot seemed to turn over inside him each time he remembered how they had laughed. He tossed on his bed, feeling his hard pillow. N Pa says he's gonna beat me . . . He remembered other beatings, and his back quivered. Naw, naw, Ah sho don wan im t beat me tha way no mo. Dam em all! Nobody ever gave him anything. All he did was work. They treat me like a mule, n then they beat me. He gritted his teeth. N Ma had t tell on me.

Well, if he had to, he would take old man Hawkins that two dollars. But that meant selling the gun. And he wanted to keep that gun. Fifty dollars for a dead mule.

He turned over, thinking how he had fired the gun. He had an itch to fire it again. Ef other men kin shoota gun, by Gawd, Ah kin! He was still, listening. Mebbe they all sleepin now. The house was still. He heard the soft breathing of his brother. Yes, now! He would go down and get that gun and see if he could fire it! He eased out of bed and slipped into overalls.

The moon was bright. He ran almost all the way to the edge of the woods.He stumbled over the ground, looking for the spot where he had buried the gun. Yeah, here it is. Like a hungry dog scratching for a bone, he pawed it up. He puffed his black cheeks and blew dirt from the trigger and barrel. He broke it and found four cartridges unshot. He looked around; the fields were filled with silence and moonlight. He clutched the gun stiff and hard in his fingers. But, as soon as he wanted to pull the trigger, he shut his eyes and turned his head. Naw, An can't shoot wid mah eyes closed n mah head turned. With effort he held his eyes open; then he squeezed. *Bloooom!* He was stiff, not breathing. The gun was still in his hands. Dammit, he'd done it! He fired again. *Blooooom!* He smiled. *Blooooom! Blooooom! Click, click.* There! It was empty. If anybody could shoot a gun, he could. He put the gun into his hip pocket and started across the fields.

When he reached the top of a ridge he stood straight and proud in the moonlight, looking at Jim Hawkins' big white house, feeling the gun sagging in his pocket. Lawd, ef Ah had just one mo bullet Ah'd taka shot at tha house. Ah'd like t scare ol man Hawkins jusa little . . . Jusa enough t let im know Dave Saunders is a man.

To his left the road curved, running to the tracks of the Illinois Central. He jerked his head, listening. From far off came a faint *hooof-hoooof; hoooof-hoooof.* . . . He stood rigid. Two dollahs a mont. Les see now . . . That means it'll take bout two years. Shucks! Ah'll be dam!

He started down the road, toward the tracks. Yeah, here she comes! He stood beside the track and held himself stiffly. Here she comes, erroun the ben . . . C mon, yuh slow poke! C mon! He had his hand on his gun; something quivered in his stomach. Then the train thundered past, the gray and brown box cars rumbling and clinking. He gripped the gun tightly; then he jerked his hand out of his pocket. Ah betcha Bill wouldn't do it! Ah betcha. . . . The cars slid past, steel grinding upon steel. Ahm riding yuh ternight, so hep me Gawd! He was hot all over. He hesitated just a moment; then he grabbed, pulled atop of a car, and lay flat. He felt his pocket; the gun was still there. Ahead the long rails were glinting in the moonlight, stretching away, away to somewhere, somewhere where he could be a man . . .

—*1939*

What are your reactions to and questions about this work? The following questions may help provoke some ideas.

Probing the Work

1. Dave has such an overwhelming desire to own a gun; when he obtains one he gains "a sense of power." He says, "Could kill a man with a gun like this. Kill anybody, black or white." Why does he feel this way? What are the consequences of such an attitude?

Identifying Issues

2. To what extent do issues of race enter into Dave's feelings and actions? Compare Dave's dreams to those of boys you know.

JOHN UPDIKE

A & P

*John Updike (b. 1932) grew up in a working-class household in Shillington, Pennsylvania; his father was a math teacher at his school. Updike excelled at Harvard, then began his writing career with—and continues to contribute to—*The New Yorker. *He has written 16 novels, including* Rabbit, Run *(1960),* Rabbit Is Rich *(1981),* Couples *(1968),* The Witches of Eastwick *(1984), and* Brazil *(1994); 6 books of poetry; 5 books of criticism; and 11 collections of short stories, including* Pigeon Feathers *(1962), where the following story is found, and* The Afterlife and Other Stories *(1994).*

In walks these three girls in nothing but bathing suits. I'm in the third check-out slot, with my back to the door, so I don't see them until they're over by the bread. The one that caught my eye first was the one in the plaid green two-piece. She was a chunky kid, with a good tan and a sweet broad soft-looking can with those two crescents of white just under it, where the sun never seems to hit, at the top of the backs of her legs. I stood there with my hand on a box of HiHo crackers trying to remember if I rang it up or not. I ring it up again and the customer starts giving me hell. She's one of these cash-register-watchers, a witch about fifty with rouge on her cheekbones and no eyebrows, and I know it made her day to trip me up. She'd been watching cash registers for fifty years and probably never seen a mistake before.

By the time I got her feathers smoothed and her goodies into a bag—she gives me a little snort in passing, if she'd been born at the right time they would have burned her over in Salem—by the time I get her on her way the girls had circled around the bread and were coming back, without a pushcart, back my way along the counters, in the aisle between the check-outs and the Special bins. They didn't even have shoes on. There was this chunky one, with the two-piece—it was bright green and the seams on the bra were still sharp and her belly was still pretty pale so I guessed she just got it (the suit)—there was this one, with one of those chubby berry-faces, the lips all bunched together under her nose, this one, and a tall one, with black hair that hadn't quite frizzed right, and one of these sunburns right across under the eyes, and a chin that was too long—you know, the kind of girl other girls think is very "striking" and "attractive" but never quite makes it, as they very well know, which is why they like her so much—and then the third one, that wasn't quite so tall. She was the queen. She kind of led them, the other two peeking around and making their shoulders round. She didn't look around, not this queen, she just walked straight on slowly, on these long white prima donna legs. She came down a little hard on her heels, as if she didn't walk in her bare feet that much, putting down her heels and then letting the weight move along to her toes as if she was testing the floor with every step, putting a little deliberate extra action into it. You never know for sure how girls' minds work (do you really think it's a mind in there or just a little buzz like a bee in a glass jar?) but you got the idea she had talked the other two into coming in here with her, and now she was showing them how to do it, walk slow and hold yourself straight.

She had on a kind of dirty-pink—beige maybe, I don't know—bathing suit with a little nubble all over it and, what got me, the straps were down. They were off her shoulders looped loose around the cool tops of her arms, and I guess as a result the suit had slipped a little on her, so all around the top of the cloth there was this shining rim. If it hadn't been there you wouldn't have known there could have been anything whiter than those shoulders. With the straps pushed off, there was nothing between the top of the suit and the top of her head except just *her,* this clean bare plane of the top of her chest down from the shoulder bones like a dented sheet of metal tilted in the light. I mean, it was more than pretty.

She had sort of oaky hair that the sun and salt had bleached, done up in a bun that was unraveling, and a kind of prim face. Walking into the A & P with your straps down, I suppose it's the only kind of face you *can* have. She held her head so high her neck, coming up out of those white shoulders, looked kind of stretched, but I didn't mind. The longer her neck was, the more of her there was.

She must have felt in the corner of her eye me and over my shoulder Stokesie in the second slot watching, but she didn't tip. Not this queen. She kept her eyes moving across the racks, and stopped, and turned so slow it made my stomach rub the inside of my apron, and buzzed to the other two, who kind of huddled against her for relief, and they all three of them went up the cat-and-dog-food-breakfast-cereal-macaroni-rice-raisins-seasonings-spreads-spaghetti-soft-drinks-crackers-and-cookies aisle. From the third slot I look straight up this aisle to the meat counter, and I watched them all the way. The fat one with the tan sort of fumbled with the cookies, but on second thought she put the packages back. The sheep pushing their carts down the aisle—the girls were walking against the usual traffic (not that we have one-way signs or anything)—were pretty hilarious. You could see them, when Queenie's white shoulders dawned on them, kind of jerk, or hop, or hiccup, but their eyes snapped back to their own baskets and on they pushed. I bet you could set off dynamite in an A & P and the people would by and large keep reaching and checking oatmeal off their lists and muttering "Let me see, there was a third thing, began with A, asparagus, no, ah, yes, applesauce!" or whatever it is they do mutter. But there was no doubt, this jiggled them. A few houseslaves in pin curlers even looked around after pushing their carts past to make sure what they had seen was correct.

You know, it's one thing to have a girl in a bathing suit down on the beach, where what with the glare nobody can look at each other much anyway, and another thing in the cool of the A & P, under the fluorescent lights, against all those stacked packages, with her feet paddling along naked over our checkerboard green-and-cream rubber-tile floor.

"Oh Daddy," Stokesie said beside me. "I feel so faint."

"Darling," I said. "Hold me tight." Stokesie's married, with two babies chalked up on his fuselage already, but as far as I can tell that's the only difference. He's twenty-two, and I was nineteen this April.

"Is it done?" he asks, the responsible married man finding his voice. I forgot to say he thinks he's going to be manager some sunny day, maybe in 1990 when it's called the Great Alexandrov and Petrooshki Tea Company or something.

What he meant was, our town is five miles from a beach, with a big summer colony out on the Point, but we're right in the middle of town, and the women generally put on a shirt or shorts or something before they get out of the car into the street. And anyway these are usually women with six children and varicose veins mapping their legs and nobody, including them, could care less. As I say, we're right in the middle of town, and if you stand at our front doors you can see two banks and the Congregational church and the newspaper store and three real-estate offices and about twenty-seven old freeloaders tearing up Central Street because the sewer broke again. It's not as if we're on the Cape; we're north of Boston and there's people in this town haven't seen the ocean for twenty years.

The girls had reached the meat counter and were asking McMahon something. He pointed, they pointed, and they shuffled out of sight behind a pyramid of Diet Delight peaches. All that was left for us to see was old McMahon patting his mouth and looking after them sizing up their joints. Poor kids, I began to feel sorry for them, they couldn't help it.

Now here comes the sad part of the story, at least my family says it's sad but I don't think it's sad myself. The store's pretty empty, it being Thursday afternoon, so there was nothing much to do except lean on the register and wait for the girls to show up again. The whole store was like a pinball machine and I didn't know which tunnel they'd come out of. After a while they come around out of the far aisle, around the light bulbs, records at discount of the Caribbean Six or Tony Martin Sings or some such gunk you wonder they waste the wax on, sixpacks of candy bars, and plastic toys done up in cellophane that fall apart when a kid looks at them anyway. Around they come, Queenie still leading the way, and holding a little gray jar in her hand. Slots Three through Seven are unmanned and I could see her wondering between Stokes and me, but Stokesie with his usual luck draws an old party in baggy gray pants who stumbles up with four giant cans of pineapple juice (what do these bums *do* with all that pineapple juice? I've often asked myself) so the girls come to me. Queenie puts down the jar and I take it into my fingers icy cold. Kingfish Fancy Herring Snacks in Pure Sour Cream: 49¢. Now her hands are empty, not a ring or a bracelet, bare as God made them, and I wonder where the money's coming from. Still with that prim look she lifts a folded dollar bill out of the hollow at the center of her nubbled pink top. The jar went heavy in my hand. Really, I thought that was so cute.

Then everybody's luck begins to run out. Lengel comes in from haggling with a truck full of cabbages on the lot and is about to scuttle into that door marked MANAGER behind which he hides all day when the girls touch his eye. Lengel's pretty dreary, teaches Sunday school and the rest, but he doesn't miss that much. He comes over and says, "Girls, this isn't the beach."

Queenie blushes, though maybe it's just a brush of sunburn I was noticing for the first time, now that she was so close. "My mother asked me to pick up a jar of herring snacks." Her voice kind of startled me, the way voices do when you see the people first, coming out so flat and dumb yet kind of tony, too, the way it ticked over "pick up" and "snacks." All of a sudden I slid right down her voice into her living room. Her father and the other men were standing around in ice-cream coats and bow ties and the women were in sandals picking up herring snacks on toothpicks off a big plate and they were all holding drinks the color of water with olives and sprigs of mint in them. When my parents have somebody over they get lemonade and if it's a real racy affair Schlitz in tall glasses with "They'll Do It Every Time" cartoons stencilled on.

"That's all right," Lengel said. "But this isn't the beach." His repeating this struck me as funny, as if it had just occurred to him, and he had been thinking all these years the A & P was a great big dune and he was the head lifeguard. He didn't like my smiling—as I say he doesn't miss much—but he concentrates on giving the girls that sad Sunday-school-superintendent stare.

Queenie's blush is no sunburn now, and the plump one in plaid, that I liked better from the back—a really sweet can—pipes up, "We weren't doing any shopping. We just came in for the one thing."

"That makes no difference," Lengel tells her, and I could see from the way his eyes went that he hadn't noticed she was wearing a two-piece before. "We want you decently dressed when you come in here."

"We *are* decent," Queenie says suddenly, her lower lip pushing, getting sore now that she remembers her place, a place from which the crowd that runs the A & P must look pretty crummy. Fancy Herring Snacks flashed in her very blue eyes.

"Girls, I don't want to argue with you. After this come in here with your shoulders covered. It's our policy." He turns his back. That's policy for you. Policy is what the kingpins want. What the others want is juvenile delinquency.

All this while, the customers had been showing up with their carts but, you know, sheep, seeing a scene, they had all bunched up on Stokesie, who shook open a paper bag as gently as peeling a peach, not wanting to miss a word. I could feel in the silence everybody getting nervous, most of all Lengel, who asks me, "Sammy, have you rung up this purchase?"

I thought and said "No" but it wasn't about that I was thinking. I go through the punches, 4, 9, GROC, TOT—it's more complicated than you think, and after you do it often enough, it begins to make a little song, that you hear words to, in my case "Hello *(bing)* there, you *(gung)* hap-py *pee*-pul *(splat)!*"—the *splat* being the drawer flying out. I uncrease the bill, tenderly as you may imagine, it just having come from between the two smoothest scoops of vanilla I had ever known were there, and pass a half and a penny into her narrow pink palm, and nestle the herrings in a bag and twist its neck and hand it over, all the time thinking.

The girls, and who'd blame them, are in a hurry to get out, so I say "I quit" to Lengel quick enough for them to hear, hoping they'll stop and watch me, their unsuspected hero. They keep right on going, into the electric eye; the door flies open and they flicker across the lot to their car, Queenie and Plaid and Big Tall Goony-Goony (not that as raw material she was so bad), leaving me with Lengel and a kink in his eyebrow.

"Did you say something, Sammy?"

"I said I quit."

"I thought you did."

"You didn't have to embarrass them."

"It was they who were embarrassing us."

I started to say something that came out "Fiddle-de-doo." It's a saying of my grandmother's, and I know she would have been pleased.

"I don't think you know what you're saying," Lengel said.

"I know you don't," I said. "But I do." I pull the bow at the back of my apron and start shrugging it off my shoulders. A couple customers that had been heading for my slot begin to knock against each other, like scared pigs in a chute.

Lengel sighs and begins to look very patient and old and gray. He's been a friend of my parents for years. "Sammy, you don't want to do this to your Mom and Dad," he tells me. It's true, I don't. But it seems to me that once you begin a gesture it's fatal not to go through with it. I fold the apron, "Sammy" stitched in red on the pocket, and put it on the counter, and drop the bow tie on top of it. The bow tie is theirs, if you've ever wondered. "You'll feel this for the rest of your life," Lengel says, and I know that's true, too, but remembering how he made that pretty girl blush makes me so scrunchy inside I punch the No Sale tab and the machine whirs "pee-pul" and the drawer splats out. One advantage to this scene taking place in summer, I can follow this up with a clean exit, there's no fumbling around getting your coat and galoshes, I just saunter into the electric eye in my white shirt that my mother ironed the night before, and the door heaves itself open, and outside the sunshine is skating around on the asphalt.

I look around for my girls, but they're gone, of course. There wasn't anybody but some young married screaming with her children about some candy they didn't get by the door of a powder-blue Falcon station wagon. Looking back in the big windows, over the bags of peat moss and aluminum lawn furniture stacked on the pavement, I could see Lengel in my place in the slot, checking the sheep through. His face was dark gray and his back stiff, as if he'd just had an injection of iron, and my stomach kind of fell as I felt how hard the world was going to be to me hereafter.

—1962

What are your reactions to and questions about this work? The following questions may help provoke some ideas.

Probing the Work

1. You can see Sammy's decision to quit his job from many different perspectives, depending on your interpretation of his motives, your attitude toward him, and your own values and background. How do you explain his actions and their consequences? How wise a decision does he make? What is his motivation?

Identifying Issues

2. What are the ties of family and class that Sammy seems surrounded and confined by? How successful is Sammy in going against them?

ALICE MUNRO

Boys and Girls

Alice Munro (b. 1931) grew up on an impoverished farm in Ontario, Canada, where her father raised silver foxes and her mother battled Parkinson's disease. She and her first husband moved to British Columbia, where she founded a bookstore and raised three daughters. Her first book of stories, Dance of the Happy Shades *(1968), was a critical but not popular success. Her work has since found a large audience, often in* The New Yorker *and* Redbook. *Other collections include* The Progress of Love *(1986),* Friend of My Youth *(1990), and* Open Secrets *(1994).*

My father was a fox farmer. That is, he raised silver foxes, in pens; and in the fall and early winter, when their fur was prime, he killed them and skinned them and sold their pelts to the Hudson's Bay Company or the Montreal Fur Traders. These companies supplied us with heroic calendars to hang, one on each side of the kitchen door. Against a background of cold blue sky and black pine forests and treacherous northern rivers, plumed adventurers planted the flags of England or of France; magnificent savages bent their backs to the portage.

For several weeks before Christmas, my father worked after supper in the cellar of our house. The cellar was whitewashed, and lit by a hundred-watt bulb over the worktable. My brother Laird and I sat on the top step and watched. My father removed the pelt inside-out from the body of the fox, which looked surprisingly small, mean and rat-like, deprived of its arrogant weight of fur. The naked, slippery bodies were collected in a sack and buried at the dump. One time the hired man, Henry Bailey, had taken a swipe at me with his sack saying, "Christmas present!" My mother thought that was not funny. In fact she disliked the whole pelting operation—that was what the killing, skinning, and preparation of the furs was called—and wished it did not have to take place in the house. There was the smell. After the pelt had been stretched inside-out on a long board my father scraped away delicately, removing the little clotted webs of blood vessels, the bubbles of fat; the smell of blood and animal fat, with the strong primitive odour of the fox itself, penetrated all parts of the house. I found it reassuringly seasonal, like the smell of oranges and pine needles.

Henry Bailey suffered from bronchial troubles. He would cough and cough until his narrow face turned scarlet, and his light blue, derisive eyes filled up with tears; then he took the lid off the stove, and, standing well back, shot out a great clot of phlegm—hsss—straight into the heart of the flames. We admired him for this performance and for his ability to make his stomach growl at will, and for his laughter, which was full of high whistlings and gurglings and involved the whole faulty machinery of his chest. It was sometimes hard to tell what he was laughing at, and always possible that it might be us.

After we had been sent to bed we could still smell fox and still hear Henry's laugh, but these things, reminders of the warm, safe, brightly lit downstairs world, seemed lost and diminished, floating on the stale cold air upstairs. We were afraid at night in the winter. We were not afraid of *outside* though this was the time of year when snowdrifts curled around our house like sleeping whales and the wind harassed us all night, coming up from the buried fields, the frozen swamp, with its old bugbear chorus of threats and misery. We were afraid of *inside,* the room where we slept. At this time the upstairs of our house was not finished. A brick chimney went up one wall. In the middle of the floor was a square hole, with a wooden railing around it; that was where the stairs came up. On the other side of the stairwell were the things that nobody had any use for any more—a soldiery roll of linoleum, standing on end, a wicker baby carriage, a fern basket, china jugs and basins with cracks in them, a picture of the Battle of Balaclava, very sad to look at. I had told Laird, as soon as he was old enough to understand such things, that bats and skeletons lived over there; whenever a man escaped from the county jail, twenty miles away, I imagined that he had somehow let himself in the window and was hiding behind the linoleum. But we had rules to keep us safe. When the light was on, we were safe as long as we did not step off the square of worn carpet which defined our bedroom-space; when the light was off no place was safe but the beds themselves. I had to turn out the light kneeling on the end of my bed, and stretching as far as I could to reach the cord.

In the dark we lay on our beds, our narrow life rafts, and fixed our eyes on the faint light coming up the stairwell, and sang songs. Laird sang "Jingle Bells," which he would sing any time, whether it was Christmas or not, and I sang "Danny Boy." I loved the sound of my own voice, frail and supplicating, rising in the dark. We could make out the tall frosted shapes of the windows now, gloomy and white. When I came to the part, *When I am dead, as dead I well may be*—a fit of shivering caused not by the cold sheets but by pleasurable emotion almost silenced me. *You'll kneel and say, an Ave there above me*—What was an Ave? Every day I forgot to find out.

Laird went straight from singing to sleep. I could hear his long, satisfied, bubbly breaths. Now for the time that remained to me, the most perfectly private and perhaps the best time of the whole day, I arranged myself tightly under the covers and went on with one of the stories I was telling myself from night to night. These stories were about myself, when I had grown a little older; they took place in a world that was recognizably mine, yet one that presented opportunities for courage, boldness and self-sacrifice, as mine never did. I rescued people from a bombed building (it discouraged me that the real war had gone on so far away from Jubilee). I shot two rabid wolves who were menacing the schoolyard (the teachers cowered terrified at my back). I rode a fine horse spiritedly down the main street of Jubilee, acknowledging the townspeople's gratitude for some yet-to-be-worked-out piece of heroism (nobody ever rode a horse there, except King Billy in the Orangemen's Day parade).[1] There was always riding and shooting in these stories, though I had only been on a horse twice—bareback because we did not own a saddle—and the second time I had slid right around and dropped under the horse's feet; it had stepped placidly over me. I really was learning to shoot, but I could not hit anything yet, not even tin cans on fence posts.

Alive, the foxes inhabited a world my father made for them. It was surrounded by a high guard fence, like a medieval town, with a gate that was padlocked at night. Along the streets of this town were ranged large, sturdy pens. Each of them had a real door that a man could go through, a wooden ramp along the wire, for the foxes to run up and down on, and a kennel—something like a clothes chest with airholes—where they slept and stayed in winter and had their young. There were feeding and watering dishes attached to the wire in such a way that they could be emptied and cleaned from the outside. The dishes were made of old tin cans, and the ramps and kennels of odds and ends of old lumber. Everything was tidy and ingenious; my father was tirelessly inventive and his favourite book in the world was Robinson Crusoe. He had fitted a tin drum on a wheelbarrow, for bringing water down to the pens. This was my job in summer, when the foxes had to have water twice a day. Between nine and ten o'clock in the morning, and again after supper, I filled the drum at the pump and trundled it down through the barnyard to the pens, where I parked it, and filled my watering can and went along the streets. Laird came too, with his little cream and green gardening can, filled too full and knocking against his legs and slopping water on his canvas shoes. I had the real watering can, my father's, though I could only carry it three-quarters full.

[1]King Billy: William III of Great Britain, also known as the Prince of Orange, whose coronation in 1689 ensured that Britain would become a Protestant nation and a parliamentary democracy.

The foxes all had names, which were printed on a tin plate and hung beside their doors. They were not named when they were born, but when they survived the first year's pelting and were added to the breeding stock. Those my father had named were called names like Prince, Bob, Wally and Betty. Those I had named were called Star or Turk, or Maureen or Diana. Laird named one Maud after a hired girl we had when he was little, one Harold after a boy at school, and one Mexico, he did not say why.

Naming them did not make pets out of them, or anything like it. Nobody but my father ever went into the pens, and he had twice had blood-poisoning from bites. When I was bringing them their water they prowled up and down on the paths they had made inside their pens, barking seldom—they saved that for nighttime, when they might get up a chorus of community frenzy—but always watching me, their eyes burning, clear gold, in their pointed, malevolent faces. They were beautiful for their delicate legs and heavy, aristocratic tails and the bright fur sprinkled on dark down their backs—which gave them their name—but especially for their faces, drawn exquisitely sharp in pure hostility, and their golden eyes.

Besides carrying water I helped my father when he cut the long grass, and the lamb's quarter and flowering money-musk, that grew between the pens. He cut with the scythe and I raked into piles. Then he took a pitchfork and threw fresh-cut grass all over the top of the pens, to keep the foxes cooler and shade their coats, which were browned by too much sun. My father did not talk to me unless it was about the job we were doing. In this he was quite different from my mother, who, if she was feeling cheerful, would tell me all sorts of things—the name of a dog she had had when she was a little girl, the names of boys she had gone out with later on when she was grown up, and what certain dresses of hers had looked like—she could not imagine now what had become of them. Whatever thoughts and stories my father had were private, and I was shy of him and would never ask him questions. Nevertheless I worked willingly under his eyes, and with a feeling of pride. One time a feed salesman came down into the pens to talk to him and my father said, "Like to have you meet my new hired man." I turned away and raked furiously, red in the face with pleasure.

"Could of fooled me," said the salesman. "I thought it was only a girl."

After the grass was cut, it seemed suddenly much later in the year. I walked on stubble in the earlier evening, aware of the reddening skies, the entering silences, of fall. When I wheeled the tank out of the gate and put the padlock on, it was almost dark. One night at this time I saw my mother and father standing talking on the little rise of ground we called the gangway, in front of the barn. My father had just come from the meathouse; he had his stiff bloody apron on, and a pail of cut-up meat in his hand.

It was an odd thing to see my mother down at the barn. She did not often come out of the house unless it was to do something—hang out the wash or dig potatoes in the garden. She looked out of place, with her bare lumpy legs, not touched by the sun, her apron still on and damp across the stomach from the supper dishes. Her hair was tied up in a kerchief, wisps of it falling out. She would tie her hair up like this in the morning, saying she did not have time to do it properly, and it would stay tied up all day. It was true, too; she really did not have time. These days our back porch was piled with baskets of peaches and grapes and pears, bought in town, and onions and tomatoes and cucumbers grown at home, all waiting to be made into jelly and jam and preserves, pickles and chili sauce. In the kitchen there was a fire in the stove all day, jars clinked in boiling water, sometimes a cheesecloth bag was strung on a pole between two chairs, straining blue-black grape pulp for jelly. I was given jobs to do and I would sit at the table peeling peaches that had been soaked in the hot water, or cutting up onions, my eyes smarting and streaming. As soon as I was done I ran out of the house, trying to get out of earshot before my mother thought of what she wanted me to do next. I hated the hot dark kitchen in summer, the green blinds and the flypapers, the same old oilcloth table and wavy mirror and bumpy linoleum. My mother was too tired and preoccupied to talk to me, she had no heart to tell about the Normal School Graduation Dance; sweat trickled over her face and she was always counting under her breath, pointing at jars, dumping cups of sugar. It seemed to me that work in the house was endless, dreary and peculiarly depressing; work done out of doors, and in my father's service, was ritualistically important.

I wheeled the tank up to the barn, where it was kept, and I heard my mother saying, "Wait till Laird gets a little bigger, then you'll have a real help."

What my father said I did not hear. I was pleased by the way he stood listening, politely as he would to a salesman or a stranger, but with an air of wanting to get on with his real work. I felt my mother had no business down here and I wanted him to feel the same way. What did she mean about Laird? He was no help to anybody. Where was he now? Swinging himself sick on the swing, going around in circles, or trying to catch caterpillars. He never once stayed with me till I was finished.

"And then I can use her more in the house," I heard my mother say. She had a dead-quiet, regretful way of talking about me that always made me uneasy. "I just get my back turned and she runs off. It's not like I had a girl in the family at all."

I went and sat on a feedbag in the corner of the barn, not wanting to appear when this conversation was going on. My mother, I felt, was not to be trusted. She was kinder than my father and more easily fooled, but you could not depend on her, and the real reasons for the things she said and did were not to be known. She loved me, and she sat up late at night making a dress of the difficult style I wanted, for me to wear when school started, but she was also my enemy. She was always plotting. She was plotting now to get me to stay in the house more, although she knew I hated it (*because* she knew I hated it) and keep me from working for my father. It seemed to me she would do this simply out of perversity, and to try her power. It did not occur to me that she could be lonely, or jealous. No grown-up could be; they were too fortunate. I sat and kicked my heels monotonously against a feedbag, raising dust, and did not come out till she was gone.

At any rate, I did not expect my father to pay any attention to what she said. Who could imagine Laird doing my work—Laird remembering the padlock and cleaning out the watering-dishes with a leaf on the end of a stick, or even wheeling the tank without it tumbling over? It showed how little my mother knew about the way things really were.

I have forgotten to say what the foxes were fed. My father's bloody apron reminded me. They were fed horsemeat. At this time most farmers still kept horses, and when a horse got too old to work, or broke a leg or got down and would not get up, as they sometimes did, the owner would call my father, and he and Henry went out to the farm in the truck. Usually they shot and butchered the horse there, paying the farmer from five to twelve dollars. If they had already too much meat on hand, they would bring the horse back alive, and keep it for a few days or weeks in our stable, until the meat was needed. After the war the farmers were buying tractors and gradually getting rid of horses altogether, so it sometimes happened that we got a good healthy horse, that there was just no use for any more. If this happened in the winter we might keep the horse in our stable till spring, for we had plenty of hay and if there was a lot of snow—and the plow did not always get our road cleared—it was convenient to be able to go to town with a horse and cutter.

The winter I was eleven years old we had two horses in the stable. We did not know what names they had before, so we called them Mack and Flora. Mack was an old black workhorse, sooty and indifferent. Flora was a sorrel mare, a driver. We took them both out in the cutter. Mack was slow and easy to handle. Flora was given to fits of violent alarm, veering at cars and even at other horses, but we loved her speed and high-stepping, her general air of gallantry and abandon. On Saturdays we went down to the stable and as soon as we opened the door on its cosy, animal-smelling darkness Flora threw up her head, rolled her eyes, whinnied despairingly and pulled herself through a crisis of nerves on the spot. It was not safe to go into her stall; she would kick.

This winter also I began to hear a great deal more on the theme my mother had sounded when she had been talking in front of the barn. I no longer felt safe. It seemed that in the minds of the people around me there was a steady undercurrent of thought, not to be deflected, on this one subject. The word *girl* had formerly seemed to me innocent and unburdened, like the word *child;* now it appeared that it was no such thing. A girl was not, as I had supposed, simply what I was; it was what I had to become. It was a definition, always touched with emphasis, with reproach and disappointment. Also it was a joke on me. Once Laird and I were fighting, and for the first time ever I had to use all my strength against him; even so, he caught and pinned my arm for a moment, really hurting me. Henry saw this, and laughed, saying, "Oh, that there Laird's gonna show you, one of these days!" Laird was getting a lot bigger. But I was getting bigger too.

My grandmother came to stay with us for a few weeks and I heard other things. "Girls don't slam doors like that." "Girls keep their knees together when they sit down." And worse still, when I asked some questions, "That's none of girls' business." I continued to slam the doors and sit as awkwardly as possible, thinking that by such measures I kept myself free.

When spring came, the horses were let out in the barnyard. Mack stood against the barn wall trying to scratch his neck and haunches, but Flora trotted up and down and reared at the fences, clattering her hooves against the rails. Snow drifts dwindled quickly, revealing the hard grey and brown earth, the familiar rise and fall of the ground, plain and bare after the fantastic landscape of winter. There was a great feeling of opening-out, of release. We just wore rubbers now, over our shoes; our feet felt ridiculously light. One Saturday we went out to the stable and found all the doors open, letting in the unaccustomed sunlight and fresh air. Henry was there, just idling around looking at his collection of calendars which were tacked up behind the stalls in a part of the stable my mother had probably never seen.

"Come to say goodbye to your old friend Mack?" Henry said. "Here, you give him a taste of oats." He poured some oats into Laird's cupped hands and Laird went to feed Mack. Mack's teeth were in bad shape. He ate very slowly, patiently shifting the oats around in his mouth, trying to find a stump of a molar to grind it on. "Poor old Mack," said Henry mournfully. "When a horse's teeth's gone, he's gone. That's about the way."

"Are you going to shoot him today?" I said. Mack and Flora had been in the stable so long I had almost forgotten they were going to be shot.

Henry didn't answer me. Instead he started to sing in a high, trembly, mocking-sorrowful voice, *Oh, there's no more work, for poor Uncle Ned, he's gone where the good darkies go.* Mack's thick, blackish tongue worked diligently at Laird's hand. I went out before the song was ended and sat down on the gangway.

I had never seen them shoot a horse, but I knew where it was done. Last summer Laird and I had come upon a horse's entrails before they were buried. We had thought it was a big black snake, coiled up in the sun. That was around in the field that ran up beside the barn. I thought that if we went inside the barn, and found a wide crack or knothole to look through, we would be able to see them do it. It was not something I wanted to see; just the same, if a thing really happened, it was better to see it, and know.

My father came down from the house, carrying the gun.

"What are you doing here?" he said.

"Nothing."

"Go on up and play around the house."

He sent Laird out of the stable. I said to Laird, "Do you want to see them shoot Mack?" and without waiting for an answer led him around to the front door of the barn, opened it carefully, and went in. "Be quiet or they'll hear us," I said. We could hear Henry and my father talking in the stable, then the heavy, shuffling steps of Mack being backed out of his stall.

In the loft it was cold and dark. Thin, crisscrossed beams of sunlight fell through the cracks. The hay was low. It was a rolling country, hills and hollows, slipping under our feet. About four feet up was a beam going around the walls. We piled hay up in one corner and I boosted Laird up and hoisted myself. The beam was not very wide; we crept along it with our hands flat on the barn walls. There were plenty of knotholes, and I found one that gave me the view I wanted—a corner of the barnyard, the gate, part of the field. Laird did not have a knothole and began to complain.

I showed him a widened crack between two boards. "Be quiet and wait. If they hear you you'll get us in trouble."

My father came in sight carrying the gun. Henry was leading Mack by the halter. He dropped it and took out his cigarette papers and tobacco; he rolled cigarettes for my father and himself. While this was going on Mack nosed around in the old, dead grass along the fence. Then my father opened the gate and they took Mack through. Henry led Mack away from the path to a patch of ground and they talked together, not loud enough for us to hear. Mack again began searching for a mouthful of fresh grass, which was not to be found. My father walked away in a straight line, and stopped short at a distance which seemed to suit him. Henry was walking away from Mack too, but sideways, still negligently holding on to the halter. My father raised the gun and Mack looked up as if he had noticed something and my father shot him.

Mack did not collapse at once but swayed, lurched sideways and fell, first on his side; then he rolled over on his back and, amazingly, kicked his legs for a few seconds in the air. At this Henry laughed, as if Mack had done a trick for him. Laird, who had drawn a long, groaning breath of surprise when the shot was fired, said out loud, "He's not dead." And it seemed to me it might be true. But his legs stopped, he rolled on his side again, his muscles quivered and sank. The two men walked over and looked at him in a businesslike way; they bent down and examined his forehead where the bullet had gone in, and now I saw his blood on the brown grass.

"Now they just skin him and cut him up," I said. "Let's go." My legs were a little shaky and I jumped gratefully down into the hay. "Now you've seen how they shoot a horse," I said in a congratulatory way, as if I had seen it many times before. "Let's see if any barn cat's had kittens in the hay." Laird jumped. He seemed young and obedient again. Suddenly I remembered how, when he was little, I had brought him into the barn and told him to climb the ladder to the top beam. That was in the spring, too, when the hay was low. I had done it out of a need for excitement, a desire for something to happen so that I could tell about it. He was wearing a little bulky brown and white checked coat, made down from one of mine. He went all the way up, just as I told him, and sat down on the top beam with the hay far below him on one side, and the barn floor and some old machinery on the other. Then I ran screaming to my father, "Laird's up on the top beam!" My father came, my mother came, my father went up the ladder talking very quietly and brought Laird down under his arm, at which my mother leaned against the ladder and began to cry. They said to me, "Why weren't you watching him?" but nobody ever knew the truth. Laird did not know enough to tell. But whenever I saw the brown and white checked coat hanging in the closet, or at the bottom of the rag bag, which was where it ended up, I felt a weight in my stomach, the sadness of unexorcized guilt.

I looked at Laird who did not even remember this, and I did not like the look on this thin, winter-pale face. His expression was not frightened or upset, but remote, concentrating. "Listen," I said, in an unusually bright and friendly voice, "you aren't going to tell, are you?"

"No," he said absently.

"Promise."

"Promise," he said. I grabbed the hand behind his back to make sure he was not crossing his fingers. Even so, he might have a nightmare; it might come out that way. I decided I had better work hard to get all thoughts of what he had seen out of his mind—which, it seemed to me, could not hold very many things at a time. I got some money I had saved and that afternoon we went into Jubilee and saw a show, with Judy Canova, at which we both laughed a great deal. After that I thought it would be all right.

Two weeks later I knew they were going to shoot Flora. I knew from the night before, when I heard my mother ask if the hay was holding out all right, and my father said, "Well, after to-morrow there'll just be the cow, and we should be able to put her out to grass in another week." So I knew it was Flora's turn in the morning.

This time I didn't think of watching it. That was something to see just one time. I had not thought about it very often since, but sometimes when I was busy, working at school, or standing in front of the mirror combing my hair and wondering if I would be pretty when I grew up, the whole scene would flash into my mind: I would see the easy, practised way my father raised the gun, and hear Henry laughing when Mack kicked his legs in the air. I did not have any great feeling of horror and opposition, such as a city child might have had; I was too used to seeing the death of animals as a necessity by which we lived. Yet I felt a little ashamed, and there was a new wariness, a sense of holding-off, in my attitude to my father and his work.

It was a fine day, and we were going around the yard picking up tree branches that had been torn off in winter storms. This was something we had been told to do, and also we wanted to use them to make a teepee. We heard Flora whinny, and then my father's voice and Henry's shouting, and we ran down to the barnyard to see what was going on.

The stable door was open. Henry had just brought Flora out, and she had broken away from him. She was running free in the barnyard, from one end to the other. We climbed up on the fence. It was exciting to see her running, whinnying, going up on her hind legs, prancing and threatening like a horse in a Western movie, an unbroken ranch horse, though she was just an old driver, an old sorrel mare. My father and Henry ran after her and tried to grab the dangling halter. They tried to work her into a corner, and they had almost succeeded when she made a run between them, wild-eyed, and disappeared around the corner of the barn. We heard the rails clatter down as she got over the fence, and Henry yelled, "She's into the field now!"

That meant she was in the long L-shaped field that ran up by the house. If she got around the center, heading towards the lane, the gate was open; the truck had been driven into the field this morning. My father shouted to me, because I was on the other side of the fence, nearest the lane, "Go shut the gate!"

I could run very fast. I ran across the garden, past the tree where our swing was hung, and jumped across a ditch into the lane. There was the open gate. She had not got out, I could not see her up on the road; she must have run to the other end of the field. The gate was heavy. I lifted it out of the gravel and carried it across the roadway. I had it half-way across when she came in sight, galloping straight towards me. There was just time to get the chain on. Laird came scrambling through the ditch to help me.

Instead of shutting the gate, I opened it as wide as I could. I did not make any decision to do this, it was just what I did. Flora never slowed down; she galloped straight past me, and Laird jumped up and down, yelling, "Shut it, shut it!" even after it was too late. My father and Henry appeared in the field a moment too late to see what I had done. They only saw Flora heading for the township road. They would think I had not got there in time.

They did not waste any time asking about it. They went back to the barn and got the gun and knives they used, and put these in the truck; then they turned the truck around and came bouncing up the field toward us. Laird called to them, "Let me go too, let me go too!" and Henry stopped the truck and they took him in. I shut the gate after they were all gone.

I supposed Laird would tell. I wondered what would happen to me. I had never disobeyed my father before, and I could not understand why I had done it. Flora would not really get away. They would catch up with her in the truck. Or if they did not catch her this morning somebody would see her and telephone us this afternoon or tomorrow. There was no wild country here for her to run to, only farms. What was more, my father had paid for her, we needed the meat to feed the foxes, we needed the foxes to make our living. All I had done was make more work for my father who worked hard enough already. And when my father found out about it he was not going to trust me any more; he would know that I was not entirely on his side. I was on Flora's side, and that made me no use to anybody, not even to her. Just the same, I did not regret it; when she came running at me and I held the gate open, that was the only thing I could do.

I went back to the house, and my mother said, "What's all the commotion?" I told her that Flora had kicked down the fence and got away. "Your poor father," she said, "now he'll have to go chasing over the countryside. Well, there isn't any use planning dinner before one." She put up the ironing board. I wanted to tell her, but thought better of it and went upstairs and sat on my bed.

Lately I had been trying to make my part of the room fancy, spreading the bed with old lace curtains, and fixing myself a dressing-table with some leftovers of cretonne for a skirt. I planned to put up some kind of barricade between my bed and Laird's, to keep my section separate from his. In the sunlight, the lace curtains were just dusty rags. We did not sing at night any more. One night when I was singing Laird said, "You sound silly," and I went right on but the next night I did not start. There was not so much need to anyway, we were no longer afraid. We knew it was just old furniture over there, old jumble and confusion. We did not keep to the rules. I still stayed awake after Laird was asleep and told myself stories, but even in these stories something different was happening, mysterious alterations took place. A story might start off in the old way, with a spectacular danger, a fire or wild animals, and for a while I might rescue people; then things would change around, and instead, somebody would be rescuing me. It might be a boy from our class at school, or even Mr. Campbell, our teacher, who tickled girls under the arms. And at this point the story concerned itself at great length what what I looked like—how long my hair was, and what kind of dress I had on; by the time I had these details worked out the real excitement of the story was lost.

It was later than one o'clock when the truck came back. The tarpaulin was over the back, which meant there was meat in it. My mother had to heat dinner up all over again. Henry and my father had changed from their bloody overalls into ordinary working overalls in the barn, and they washed their arms and necks and faces at the sink, and splashed water on their hair and combed it. Laird lifted his arm to show off a streak of blood. "We shot old Flora," he said, "and cut her up in fifty pieces."

"Well I don't want to hear about it," my mother said. "And don't come to my table like that."

My father made him go and wash the blood off.

We sat down and my father said grace and Henry pasted his chewing-gum on the end of his fork, the way he always did; when he took it off he would have us admire the pattern. We began to pass the bowls of steaming, overcooked vegetables. Laird looked across the table at me and said proudly, distinctly, "Anyway it was her fault Flora got away."

"What?" my father said.

"She could of shut the gate and she didn't. She just open' it up and Flora run out."

"Is that right?" my father said.

Everybody at the table was looking at me. I nodded, swallowing food with great difficulty. To my shame, tears flooded my eyes.

My father made a curt sound of disgust. "What did you do that for?"

I did not answer. I put down my fork and waited to be sent from the table, still not looking up.

But this did not happen. For some time nobody said anything, then Laird said matter-of-factly, "She's crying."

"Never mind," my father said. He spoke with resignation, even good humour, the words which absolved and dismissed me for good. "She's only a girl," he said.

I didn't protest that, even in my heart. Maybe it was true.

—1968

What are your reactions to and questions about this work? The following questions may help provoke some ideas.

Probing the Work

1. What is your reaction to the father's words at the end of the story—"She's only a girl"—and the narrator's response, "I didn't protest that, even in my heart. Maybe it was true"?

Identifying Issues

2. What has the narrator learned from her painful experience? What does the story seem to be saying about the nature of men and women, and what do you think of the distinctions made about gender roles?

RITA DOVE

Adolescence III

Rita Dove (b. 1952) was born in Akron and educated at Miami University, the University of Tübingen, and the University of Iowa. Her books of poetry include Museum *(1983), the Pulitzer Prize-winning* Thomas and Beulah *(1986), and* Mother Love *(1995). Dove was Poet Laureate of the United States from 1993 to 1995.*

With Dad gone, Mom and I worked
The dusky rows of tomatoes.
As they glowed orange in sunlight
And rotted in shadow, I too
Grew orange and softer, swelling out
Starched cotton slips.

The texture of twilight made me think of
Lengths of Dotted Swiss. In my room
I wrapped scarred knees in dresses

That once went to big-band dances;
I baptized my earlobes with rosewater.
Along the window-sill, the lipstick stubs
Glittered in their steel shells.

Looking out at the rows of clay
And chicken manure, I dreamed how it would happen:
He would meet me by the blue spruce,
A carnation over his heart, saying,
"I have come for you, Madam;
I have loved you in my dreams."
At his touch, the scabs would fall away.
Over his shoulder, I see my father coming toward us:
He carries his tears in a bowl,
And blood hangs in the pine-soaked air.

—1980

What are your reactions to and questions about this work? The following questions may help provoke some ideas.

Probing the Work

1. Can you identify a few different kinds of sensory *images* in the poem (of smell, taste, touch, sight, or sound)? (See page 79 for more on imagery.) Pick one of the images and discuss how it reflects what the speaker feels.

Identifying Issues

2. What are the various pulls of adolescence that the speaker is expressing? To what extent can you relate to the conflicts among family members and lovers (imagined or real) that are depicted here?

STEPHEN DUNN

Tenderness

Stephen Dunn (b. 1939) was born in Forest Hills, New York, and attended Hofstra University and Syracuse University. His books of poetry include Looking for Holes in the Ceiling *(1974),* Not Dancing *(1984),* Between Angels *(1989) and* New and Selected Poems *(1995). Dunn currently teaches creative writing at Stockton State College in New Jersey.*

Back then when so much was clear
  and I hadn't learned
young men learn from women

what it feels like to feel just right,
  I was twenty-three,
she thirty-four, two children, a husband

in prison for breaking someone's head.
  Yelled at, slapped
around, all she knew of tenderness

was how much she wanted it, and all
  I knew
were back seats and a night or two

in a sleeping bag in the furtive dark.
  We worked
in the same office, banter and loneliness

leading to the shared secret
  that to help
National Biscuit sell biscuits

was wildly comic, which led to my body
  existing with hers
like rain water that's found its way

underground to water it naturally joins.
  I can't remember
ever saying the exact word, tenderness,

though she did. It's a word I see now
  you must be older to use,
you must have experienced the absence of it

often enough to know what silk and deep balm
  it is
when at last it comes. I think it was terror

at first that drove me to touch her
  so softly,
then selfishness, the clear benefit

of doing something that would come back
  to me twofold,
and finally, sometime later, it became

reflexive and motiveless in the high
  ignorance of love.
Oh abstractions are just abstract

until they have an ache in them. I met
  a woman never touched
gently, and when it ended between us,

I had new hands and new sorrow,
  everything it meant
to be a man changed, unheroic, floating.

—1988

What are your reactions to and questions about this work? The following questions may help provoke some ideas.

Probing the Work

1. The speaker of this poem says that he is forever changed by his love affair; he has "new hands and new sorrow." Explain what you think he learned, how he learned it, and what was different about him afterwards.

Identifying Issues

2. To what degree can love and/or sexual experience commonly bring about a broad change in attitude toward men or women?

WRITING ASSIGNMENT SEQUENCE (CONTINUED FROM PAGE 86)

4. Making Connections

Select one of the following questions and write an informal response in which you connect your own ideas with those conveyed in the works of this cluster, and/or make connections among the works themselves.

A. A few of the works in this cluster deal with painful rites of initiation that boys and girls inevitably go through on their way toward adulthood. To what degree do you believe these rites are necessary to one's identity? With which of these characters have you shared similar kinds of initiation?

B. What are the most critical conflicts and issues that the characters deal with as they come of age? How successfully do they resolve these issues?

C. With which character(s) in this cluster do you identify most, and why?

D. What advice might you give to one or more of these characters to help see them through their difficulties?

5. Putting It All Together

Write an essay that combines what you think about the topic *Becoming a Person* with what you now understand about the readings.

- Collect your informal writing, notes, and reading-journal entries on this topic and decide what will be the focus of your essay.
- Outline your essay. Select the literary passages and personal details you might use to illustrate and support your main focus.
- Write a draft of your essay in which you bring together what you think about the subject with what you understand about the readings. Try to include in your draft one or more *literary terms*.
- Share what you've written with your classmates and instructor, then revise it according to their recommendations.

Writing Tip: Using a Nutshell Sentence

A *nutshell sentence* (see page 31) draws upon the notes, passages, and comments entered in your response journal and notebook. It expresses the focus and direction of your paper. The nutshell sentence helps you guide your thoughts as you develop your essay, but may be modified or expanded as you proceed. As you write your essay, use your nutshell sentence to test your ideas and arguments. For example, Heather came up with a nutshell sentence to help her focus and to test her ideas about epiphanies:

> My purpose will be to show that some individuals need to be blinded in the present in order to see more clearly in the future.

CrossClusters

In your paper you might want to consider how the following works located elsewhere in this book depict a character becoming a person:

- Sharon Olds, "Photograph of the Girl" (p. 8)
- Langston Hughes, "As I Grew Older" (p. 239)
- Russell Baker, from *Growing Up* (p. 343)
- Liliana Heker, "The Stolen Party" (p. 362)
- Michael Dorris, "The Contest" (p. 374)
- Raymond Carver, "My Father's Life" (p. 446)
- Ernest Hemingway, "Fathers and Sons" (p. 454)
- Kazuo Ishiguro, "The Family Supper" (p. 493)

- Henrik Ibsen, *A Doll's House* (p. 659)
- Toni Cade Bambara, "The Lesson" (p. 887)
- Doris Lessing, "A Sunrise on the Veld" (p. 953)
- Isabel Allende, "And of Clay Are We Created" (p. 996)

Sample Essay

The following is an excerpt from a student essay that combines the student's own feelings and experiences on "Becoming a Person" with a close look at Hughes's "Salvation":

> Langston Hughes explains that he had to lose his faith in God to find his identity. He is taken to his Aunt's church to be saved; that is, to bring Jesus into his life. He is told that once he is saved, his life will be better: "My aunt told me that when you were saved you saw a light . . . you could *see* and hear and feel Jesus" (6). For a thirteen-year old, these claims seem pretty dramatic, especially coming from his aunt and other knowledgeable adults. He is going on the word of others on what their interpretation of being saved is. "I wanted something to happen to me, but nothing happened" (7). Hughes truly believes that he is going to see Jesus; in fact he waits to see him. . . . But nothing happens. . . .
>
> Finding one's identity is a continuous process that parallels education and learning of life experiences. My father, who served in Vietnam, once told me before I left for Korea that he was discriminated against there, and that Asians do not like blacks. . . . According to what my father said, I was expecting to be harassed and persecuted once I stepped off the plane. I had no reason to doubt him. My father is someone I trust who would not misinform me. Like Hughes, I was relying on a reliable source. While I did indeed experience forms of prejudice when I got there (they didn't like women to be seen with a black man, for example), mostly it was from ignorance: many Koreans from the small villages had never seen a black person before. Mostly I met Koreans who became good friends with me and tried to make my stay as comfortable as possible. Just because my father has a bad memory about serving in an Asian country, that does not mean that I would have the same experience.
>
> Sometimes the process of growing up does not happen at a particular time. Not everyone matures the same. I believe that Langston does get saved, not in church but in his room. He feels so guilty for lying that he cries. He cries not because of the fact that he did not see Jesus, but for the fact that he knows he did something wrong. And when you realize what is wrong and right, in a sense you become "Saved."

10

SELF-RELIANCE

WRITING ASSIGNMENT SEQUENCE

1. Thinking About . . . Self-Reliance

Clustering: Make a diagram that illustrates your status in your world. Draw a circle with your name in it, and then branches with smaller circles showing all the people who have a role in shaping your world and your*self*. If you'd like, add descriptive words about their influences on you, and later explain why you wrote what you did. (For more on *clustering*, see page 27.) Here is a sample:

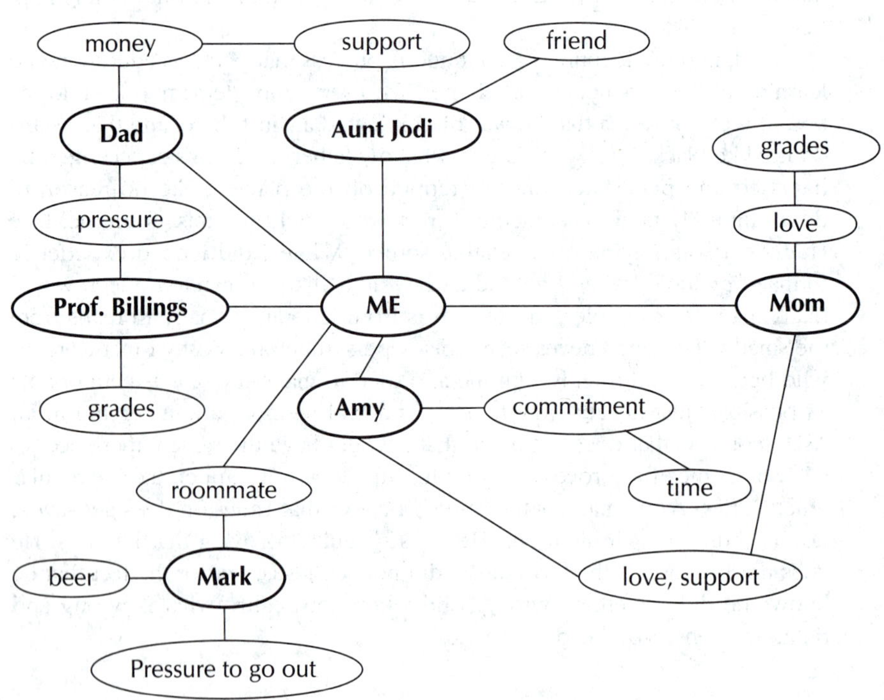

2. *Enacting the Topic*

Along with two or three of your classmates, *write a scene from a play,* in which a character has to choose whether to be self-reliant (following his or her conscience) or to do what family, friends and/or institutions say to do. Give your classmates their acting parts and play it out in front of the class.

3. *Responding to the Readings*

As you read the works in this cluster, jot down in your response journals questions you have about the works, and comment on passages you find provocative or puzzling. Consider the questions following each reading for journal writing and prepare to discuss your reactions in class.

CLUSTER ESSAY

RALPH WALDO EMERSON

Self-Reliance (excerpt)

Ralph Waldo Emerson (1803–1882), born in Boston and ordained as a minister, left the ministry after three years and made a career as a lecturer. After moving to Concord and publishing Nature *in 1836, Emerson became the chief spokesperson for the transcendentalist movement, which emphasized the primacy of following one's intuition, or conscience (the divine voice within) in order to be virtuous. His thinking profoundly influenced many of his younger contemporaries, such as Henry Thoreau and Walt Whitman, and scores of writers since.*

To believe your own thought, to believe that what is true for you in your private heart, is true for all men,—that is genius. Speak your latent conviction and it shall be the universal sense; for the inmost in due time becomes the outmost,—and our first thought is rendered back to us by the trumpets of the Last Judgment. Familiar as the voice of the mind is to each, the highest merit we ascribe to Moses, Plato, and Milton, is that they set at naught books and traditions, and spoke not what men but what they thought. A man should learn to detect and watch that gleam of light which flashes across his mind from within, more than the lustre of the firmament of bards and sages. Yet he dismisses without notice his thought, because it is his. In every work of genius we recognize our own rejected thoughts: they come back to us with a certain alienated majesty. Great works of art have no more affecting lesson for us than this. They teach us to abide by our spontaneous impression with good-humored inflexibility then most when the whole cry of voices is on the other side. Else, tomorrow a stranger will say with masterly good sense precisely what we have thought and felt all the time, and we shall be forced to take with shame our own opinion from another.

There is a time in every man's education when he arrives at the conviction that envy is ignorance; that imitation is suicide; that he must take himself for better, for worse, as his portion; that though the wide universe is full of good, no kernel of nourishing corn can come to him but through his toil bestowed on that plot of ground which is given to him to till. . . .

Society everywhere is in conspiracy against the manhood of every one of its members. Society is a joint-stock company in which the members agree for the better securing of his bread to each shareholder, to surrender the liberty and culture of the eater. The virtue in most request is conformity. Self-reliance is its aversion. It loves not realities and creators, but names and customs.

Whoso would be a man must be a nonconformist. He who would gather immortal palms must not be hindered by the name of goodness, but must explore if it be goodness. Nothing is at last sacred but the integrity of your own mind. Absolve you to yourself, and you shall have the suffrage of the world. I remember an answer which when quite young I was prompted to make to a valued adviser who was wont to importune me with the dear old doctrines of the church. On my saying, What have I to do with the sacredness of traditions, if I live wholly from within? my friend suggested—"But these impulses may be from below, not from above." I replied, "They do not seem to me to be such; but if I am the Devil's child, I will live then from the Devil." No law can be sacred to me but that of my nature. Good and bad are but names very readily transferable to that or this; the only right is what is after my constitution, the only wrong what is against it. A man is to carry himself in the presence of all opposition as if every thing were titular and ephemeral but he. I am ashamed to think how easily we capitulate to badges and names, to large societies and dead institutions. Every decent and well-spoken individual affects and sways me more than is right. I ought to go upright and vital, and speak the rude truth in all ways. . . .

For nonconformity the world whips you with its displeasure. And therefore a man must know how to estimate a sour face. The bystanders look askance on him in the public street or in the friend's parlor. If this aversation had its origin in contempt and resistance like his own, he might well go home with a sad countenance; but the sour faces of the multitude, like their sweet faces, have no deep cause, but are put on and off as the wind blows, and a newspaper directs. . . .

A foolish consistency is the hobgoblin of little minds, adored by little statesmen and philosophers and divines. With consistency a great soul has simply nothing to do. He may as well concern himself with his shadow on the wall. Speak what you think now in hard words, and to-morrow speak what to-morrow thinks in hard words again, though it contradict every thing you said to-day.—'Ah, so you shall be sure to be misunderstood.'—Is it so bad then to be misunderstood? Pythagoras was misunderstood, and Socrates, and Jesus, and Luther, and Copernicus, and Galileo, and Newton, and every pure and wise spirit that ever took flesh. To be great is to be misunderstood.

—1841

What are your reactions to and questions about this work? The following questions may help provoke some ideas.

Probing the Work

1. Pick a sentence or passage from Emerson's essay and consider the implications of it should someone follow through on his advice. Consider both positive and negative implications, and how it might apply to your life.
2. How does Emerson define self-reliance? How does he view conformity?

Identifying Issues

3. What are the potential conflicts resulting from pursuing self-reliant aims? Can you describe any situations in which pursuit of self-reliance might need to be balanced by familial or social responsibilities?

ROBERT FROST

Mending Wall

Robert Frost (1874–1963) was born in San Francisco but moved with his mother to New England after his father died. Frost married his high school co-valedictorian, and in 1900 he moved to a farm in New Hampshire, where he farmed without success for about 12 years. After selling the property, Frost and his family moved to England, where he published two books of poems: A Boy's Will *(1913) and* North of Boston *(1914). Frost returned to America in 1915 and fast became the nation's most popular poet.*

Something there is that doesn't love a wall,
That sends the frozen ground-swell under it,
And spills the upper boulders in the sun;
And makes gaps even two can pass abreast.
The work of hunters is another thing:
I have come after them and made repair
Where they have left not one stone on a stone,

But they would have the rabbit out of hiding,
To please the yelping dogs. The gaps I mean,
No one has seen them made or heard them made,
But at spring mending-time we find them there.
I let my neighbor know beyond the hill;
And on a day we meet to walk the line
And set the wall between us once again.
We keep the wall between us as we go.
To each the boulders that have fallen to each.
And some are loaves and some so nearly balls
We have to use a spell to make them balance:
'Stay where you are until our backs are turned!'
We wear our fingers rough with handling them.
Oh, just another kind of outdoor game.
One on a side. It comes to little more:
There where it is we do not need the wall:
He is all pine and I am apple orchard.
My apple trees will never get across
And eat the cones under his pines, I tell him.
He only says, 'Good fences make good neighbors.'
Spring is the mischief in me, and I wonder
If I could put a notion in his head:
'*Why* do they make good neighbors? Isn't it
Where there are cows? But here there are no cows.
Before I built a wall I'd ask to know
What I was walling in or walling out,
And to whom I was like to give offense.
Something there is that doesn't love a wall,
That wants it down.' I could say 'Elves' to him,
But it's not elves exactly, and I'd rather
He said it for himself. I see him there
Bringing a stone grasped firmly by the top
In each hand, like an old-stone savage armed.
He moves in darkness as it seems to me,
Not of woods only and the shade of trees.
He will not go behind his father's saying,
And he likes having thought of it so well
He says again, 'Good fences make good neighbors.'

—1914

What are your reactions to and questions about this work? The following questions may help provoke some ideas.

Probing the Work

1. What is the difference between the speaker's attitude toward the wall and his neighbor's? Is there any ambivalence on the speaker's part? Explain.

Identifying Issues

2. What do you think the mending wall represents? What kinds of walls exist in the relationships you mapped out in the "Enacting the Topic" exercise (p. 126)?

SHIRLEY JACKSON

The Lottery

Shirley Jackson (1919–1965) was born in San Francisco and attended college at the University of Rochester and Syracuse University. Living in Vermont with her husband, she wrote two autobiographical books on middle-class New England life, and several novels in addition to short fiction. When "The Lottery" was first published in The New Yorker *in 1948, it elicited an unprecedented response from readers.*

The morning of June 27th was clear and sunny, with the fresh warmth of a full-summer day; the flowers were blossoming profusely and the grass was richly green. The people of the village began to gather in the square, between the post office and the bank, around ten o'clock; in some towns there were so many people that the lottery took two days and had to be started on June 26th, but in this village, where there were only about three hundred people, the whole lottery took less than two hours, so it could begin at ten o'clock in the morning and still be through in time to allow the villagers to get home for noon dinner.

The children assembled first, of course. School was recently over for the summer, and the feeling of liberty sat uneasily on most of them; they tended to gather together quietly for a while before they broke into boisterous play, and their talk was still of the classroom and the teacher, of books and reprimands. Bobby Martin had already stuffed his pockets full of stones, and the other boys soon followed his example, selecting the smoothest and roundest stones; Bobby and Harry Jones and Dickie Delacroix—the villagers pronounced this name "Dellacroy"—eventually made a great pile of stones in one corner of the square and guarded it against the raids of the other boys. The girls stood aside, talking among themselves, looking over their shoulders at the boys, and the very small children rolled in the dust or clung to the hands of their older brothers or sisters.

Soon the men began to gather, surveying their own children, speaking of planting and rain, tractors and taxes. They stood together, away from the pile of stones in the corner, and their jokes were quiet and they smiled rather than laughed. The women, wearing faded house dresses and sweaters, came shortly after their menfolk. They greeted one another and exchanged bits of gossip as they went to join their husbands. Soon the women, standing by their husbands, began to call to their children, and the children came reluctantly, having to be called four or five times. Bobby Martin ducked under his mother's grasping hand and ran, laughing, back to the pile of stones. His father spoke up sharply, and Bobby came quickly and took his place between his father and his oldest brother.

The lottery was conducted—as were the square dances, the teenage club, the Halloween program—by Mr. Summers, who had time and energy to devote to civic activities. He was a round-faced, jovial man and he ran the coal business, and people were sorry for him, because he had no children and his wife was a scold. When he arrived in the square, carrying the black wooden box, there was a murmur of conversation among the villagers, and he waved and called, "Little late today, folks." The postmaster, Mr. Graves, followed him, carrying a three-legged stool, and the stool was put in the center of the square and Mr. Summers set the black box down on it. The villagers kept their distance, leaving a space between themselves and the stool, and when Mr. Summers said, "Some of you fellows want to give me a hand?" there was a hesitation before two men, Mr. Martin and his oldest son, Baxter, came forward to hold the box steady on the stool while Mr. Summers stirred up the papers inside it.

The original paraphernalia for the lottery had been lost long ago, and the black box now resting on the stool had been put into use even before Old Man Warner, the oldest man in town, was born. Mr. Summers spoke frequently to the villagers about making a new box, but no one liked to upset even as much tradition as was represented by the black box. There was a story that the present box had been made with some pieces of the box that had preceded it, the one that had been constructed when the first people settled down to make a village here. Every year, after the lottery, Mr. Summers began talking again about a new box, but every year the subject was allowed to fade off without anything's being done. The black box grew shabbier each year; by now it was no longer completely black but splintered badly along one side to show the original wood color, and in some places faded or stained.

Mr. Martin and his oldest son, Baxter, held the black box securely on the stool until Mr. Summers had stirred the papers thoroughly with his hand. Because so much of the ritual had been forgotten or discarded, Mr. Summers had been successful in having slips of paper substituted for the chips of wood that had been used for generations. Chips of wood, Mr. Summers had argued, had been all very well when the village was tiny, but now that the population was more than three hundred and likely to keep on growing, it was necessary to use something that would fit more easily into the black box. The night before the lottery, Mr. Summers and Mr. Graves made up the slips of paper and put them in the box, and it was then taken to the safe of Mr. Summers' coal company and locked up until Mr. Summers was ready to take it to the square next morning. The rest of the year, the box was put away, sometimes one place, sometimes another; it had spent one year in Mr. Graves's barn and another year underfoot in the post office, and sometimes it was set on a shelf in the Martin grocery and left there.

There was a great deal of fussing to be done before Mr. Summers declared the lottery open. There were the lists to make up—of heads of families, heads of households in each family, members of each household in each family. There was the proper swearing-in of Mr. Summers by the postmaster, as the official of the lottery; at one time, some people remembered, there had been a recital of some sort, performed by the official of the lottery, a perfunctory, tuneless chant that had been rattled off duly each year; some people believed that the official of the lottery used to stand just so when he said or sang it, others believed that he was supposed to walk among the people, but years and years ago this part of the ritual had been allowed to lapse. There had been, also, a ritual salute, which the official of the lottery had had to use in addressing each person who came up to draw from the box, but this also had changed with time, until now it was felt necessary only for the official to speak to each person approaching. Mr. Summers was very good at all this; in his clean white shirt and blue jeans, with one hand resting carelessly on the black box, he seemed very proper and important as he talked interminably to Mr. Graves and the Martins.

Just as Mr. Summers finally left off talking and turned to the assembled villagers, Mrs. Hutchinson came hurriedly along the path to the square, her sweater thrown over her shoulders, and slid into place in the back of the crowd. "Clean forgot what day it was," she said to Mrs. Delacroix, who stood next to her, and they both laughed softly. "Thought my old man was out back stacking wood," Mrs. Hutchinson went on, "and then I looked out the window and the kids were gone, and then I remembered it was the twenty-seventh and came a-running." She dried her hands on her apron, and Mrs. Delacroix said, "You're in time, though. They're still talking away up there."

Mrs. Hutchinson craned her neck to see through the crowd and found her husband and children standing near the front. She tapped Mrs. Delacroix on the arm as a farewell and began to make her way through the crowd. The people separated good-humoredly to let her through; two or three people said, in voices just loud enough to be heard across the crowd, "Here comes your Missus, Hutchinson," and "Bill, she made it after all." Mrs. Hutchinson reached her husband, and Mr. Summers, who had been waiting, said cheerfully, "Thought we were going to have to get on without you, Tessie." Mrs. Hutchinson said, grinning, "Wouldn't have me leave m'dishes in the sink, now, would you, Joe?" and soft laughter ran through the crowd as the people stirred back into position after Mrs. Hutchinson's arrival.

"Well, now," Mr. Summers said soberly, "guess we better get started, get this over with, so's we can go back to work. Anybody ain't here?"

"Dunbar," several people said. "Dunbar, Dunbar."

Mr. Summers consulted his list. "Clyde Dunbar," he said. "That's right. He's broke his leg, hasn't he? Who's drawing for him?"

"Me, I guess," a woman said, and Mr. Summers turned to look at her. "Wife draws for her husband," Mr. Summers said. "Don't you have a grown boy to do it for you, Janey?" Although Mr. Summers and everyone else in the village knew the answer perfectly well, it was the business of the official of the lottery to ask such questions formally. Mr. Summers waited with an expression of polite interest while Mrs. Dunbar answered.

"Horace's not but sixteen yet," Mrs. Dunbar said regretfully. "Guess I gotta fill in for the old man this year."

"Right," Mr. Summers said. He made a note on the list he was holding. Then he asked, "Watson boy drawing this year?"

A tall boy in the crowd raised his hand. "Here," he said. "I'm drawing for m'mother and me." He blinked his eyes nervously and ducked his head as several voices in the crowd said things like "Good fellow, Jack," and "Glad to see your mother's got a man to do it."

"Well," Mr. Summers said, "guess that's everyone. Old Man Warner make it?"

"Here," a voice said, and Mr. Summers nodded.

A sudden hush fell on the crowd as Mr. Summers cleared his throat and looked at the list. "All ready?" he called. "Now, I'll read the names—heads of families first—and the men come up and take a paper out of the box. Keep the paper folded in your hand without looking at it until everyone has had a turn. Everything clear?"

The people had done it so many times that they only half listened to the directions; most of them were quiet, wetting their lips, not looking around. Then Mr. Summers raised one hand high and said, "Adams." A man disengaged himself from the crowd and came forward. "Hi, Steve," Mr. Summers said, and Mr. Adams said, "Hi, Joe." They grinned at one another humorlessly and nervously. Then Mr. Adams reached into the black box and took out a folded paper. He held it firmly by one corner as he turned and went hastily back to his place in the crowd, where he stood a little apart from his family, not looking down at his hand.

"Allen," Mr. Summers said. "Anderson . . . Bentham."

"Seems like there's no time at all between lotteries any more," Mrs. Delacroix said to Mrs. Graves in the back row. "Seems like we got through with the last one only last week."

"Time sure goes fast," Mrs. Graves said.

"Clark . . . Delacroix."

"There goes my old man," Mrs. Delacroix said. She held her breath while her husband went forward.

"Dunbar," Mr. Summers said, and Mrs. Dunbar went steadily to the box while one of the women said, "Go on, Janey," and another said, "There she goes."

"We're next," Mrs. Graves said. She watched while Mr. Graves came around from the side of the box, greeted Mr. Summers gravely, and selected a slip of paper from the box. By now, all through the crowd there were men holding the small folded papers in their large hands, turning them over and over nervously. Mrs. Dunbar and her two sons stood together, Mrs. Dunbar holding the slip of paper.

"Harburt . . . Hutchinson."

"Get up there, Bill," Mrs. Hutchinson said, and the people near her laughed.

"Jones."

"They do say," Mr. Adams said to Old Man Warner, who stood next to him, "that over in the north village they're talking of giving up the lottery."

Old Man Warner snorted. "Pack of crazy fools," he said. "Listening to the young folks, nothing's good enough for *them*. Next thing you know, they'll be wanting to go back to living in caves, nobody work any more, live *that* way for a while. Used to be a saying about 'Lottery in June, corn be heavy soon.' First thing you know, we'd all be eating stewed chickweed and acorns. There's *always* been a lottery," he added petulantly. "Bad enough to see young Joe Summers up there joking with everybody."

"Some places have already quit lotteries," Mrs. Adams said.

"Nothing but trouble in *that,*" Old Man Warner said stoutly. "Pack of young fools."

"Martin." And Bobby Martin watched his father go forward. "Overdyke . . . Percy."

"I wish they'd hurry," Mrs. Dunbar said to her older son. "I wish they'd hurry."

"They're almost through," her son said.

"You get ready to run tell Dad," Mrs. Dunbar said.

Mr. Summers called his own name and then stepped forward precisely and selected a slip from the box. Then he called, "Warner."

"Seventy-seventh year I been in the lottery," Old Man Warner said as he went through the crowd. "Seventy-seventh time."

"Watson." The tall boy came awkwardly through the crowd. Someone said, "Don't be nervous, Jack," and Mr. Summers said, "Take your time, son."

"Zanini."

After that, there was a long pause, a breathless pause, until Mr. Summers, holding his slip of paper in the air, said, "All right, fellows." For a minute, no one moved, and then all the slips of paper were opened. Suddenly, all the women began to speak at once, saying, "Who is it?" "Who's got it?" "Is it the Dunbars?" "Is it the Watsons?" Then the voices began to say, "It's Hutchinson. It's Bill," "Bill Hutchinson's got it."

"Go tell your father," Mrs. Dunbar said to her older son.

People began to look around to see the Hutchinsons. Bill Hutchinson was standing quiet, staring down at the paper in his hand. Suddenly, Tessie Hutchinson shouted to Mr. Summers, "You didn't give him time enough to take any paper he wanted. I saw you. It wasn't fair."

"Be a good sport, Tessie," Mrs. Delacroix called, and Mrs. Graves said, "All of us took the same chance."

"Shut up, Tessie," Bill Hutchinson said.

"Well, everyone," Mr. Summers said, "that was done pretty fast, and now we've got to be hurrying a little more to get done in time." He consulted his next list. "Bill," he said, "you draw for the Hutchinson family. You got any other households in the Hutchinsons?"

"There's Don and Eva," Mrs. Hutchinson yelled. "Make *them* take their chance!"

"Daughters draw with their husbands' families, Tessie," Mr. Summers said gently. "You know that as well as anyone else."

"It wasn't *fair,"* Tessie said.

"I guess not, Joe," Bill Hutchinson said regretfully. "My daughter draws with her husband's family, that's only fair. And I've got no other family except the kids."

"Then, as far as drawing for families is concerned, it's you," Mr. Summers said in explanation, "and as far as drawing for households is concerned, that's you, too. Right?"

"Right," Bill Hutchinson said.

"How many kids, Bill?" Mr. Summers asked formally.

"Three," Bill Hutchinson said. "There's Bill, Jr., and Nancy, and little Dave. And Tessie and me."

"All right, then," Mr. Summers said. "Harry, you got their tickets back?"

Mr. Graves nodded and held up the slips of paper. "Put them in the box, then," Mr. Summers directed. "Take Bill's and put it in."

"I think we ought to start over," Mrs. Hutchinson said, as quietly as she could. "I tell you it wasn't *fair*. You didn't give him time enough to choose. *Every*body saw that."

Mr. Graves had selected the five slips and put them in the box, and he dropped all the papers but those onto the ground, where the breeze caught them and lifted them off.

"Listen, everybody," Mrs. Hutchinson was saying to the people around her.

"Ready, Bill?" Mr. Summers asked, and Bill Hutchinson, with one quick glance around at his wife and children, nodded.

"Remember," Mr. Summers said, "take the slips and keep them folded until each person has taken one. Harry, you help little Dave." Mr. Graves took the hand of the little boy, who came willingly with him up to the box. "Take a paper out of the box, Davy," Mr. Summers said. Davy put his hand into the box and laughed. "Take just *one* paper," Mr. Summers said. "Harry, you hold it for him." Mr. Graves took the child's hand and removed the folded paper from the tight fist and held it while little Dave stood next to him and looked up at him wonderingly.

"Nancy next," Mr. Summers said. Nancy was twelve, and her school friends breathed heavily as she went forward, switching her skirt, and took a slip daintily from the box. "Bill, Jr.," Mr. Summers said, and Billy, his face red and his feet over-large, nearly knocked the box over as he got a paper out. "Tessie," Mr. Summers said. She hesitated for a minute, looking around defiantly, and then set her lips and went up to the box. She snatched a paper out and held it behind her.

"Bill," Mr. Summers said, and Bill Hutchinson reached into the box and felt around, bringing his hand out at last with the slip of paper in it.

The crowd was quiet. A girl whispered, "I hope it's not Nancy," and the sound of the whisper reached the edges of the crowd.

"It's not the way it used to be," Old Man Warner said clearly. "People ain't the way they used to be."

"All right," Mr. Summers said. "Open the papers. Harry, you open little Dave's."

Mr. Graves opened the slip of paper and there was a general sigh through the crowd as he held it up and everyone could see that it was blank. Nancy and Bill, Jr., opened theirs at the same time, and both beamed and laughed, turning around to the crowd and holding their slips of paper above their heads.

"Tessie," Mr. Summers said. There was a pause, and then Mr. Summers looked at Bill Hutchinson, and Bill unfolded his paper and showed it. It was blank.

"It's Tessie," Mr. Summers said, and his voice was hushed. "Show us her paper, Bill."

Bill Hutchinson went over to his wife and forced the slip of paper out of her hand. It had a black spot on it, the black spot Mr. Summers had made the night before with the heavy pencil in the coal-company office. Bill Hutchinson held it up, and there was a stir in the crowd.

"All right, folks," Mr. Summers said. "Let's finish quickly."

Although the villagers had forgotten the ritual and lost the original black box, they still remembered to use stones. The pile of stones the boys had made earlier was ready; there were stones on the ground with the blowing scraps of paper that had come out of the box. Mrs. Delacroix selected a stone so large she had to pick it up with both hands and turned to Mrs. Dunbar. "Come on," she said. "Hurry up."

Mrs. Dunbar had small stones in both hands, and she said, gasping for breath, "I can't run at all. You'll have to go ahead and I'll catch up with you."

The children had stones already, and someone gave little Davy Hutchinson a few pebbles.

Tessie Hutchinson was in the center of a cleared space by now, and she held her hands out desperately as the villagers moved in on her. "It isn't fair," she said. A stone hit her on the side of the head.

Old Man Warner was saying, "Come on, come on, everyone." Steve Adams was in the front of the crowd of villagers, with Mrs. Graves beside him.

"It isn't fair, it isn't right," Mrs. Hutchinson screamed, and then they were upon her.

—1948

What are your reactions to and questions about this work? The following questions may help provoke some ideas.

Probing the Work

1. What is the *point of view* of this work (p. 66)? The *setting* (p. 74)? *Tone* (p. 67)? *Plot* (p. 73)? How do these elements work together to shape your reaction to what happens to Tessie?

Identifying Issues

2. What is Jackson illustrating about the power of societal laws, traditions, and pressures? How do her ideas fit in with your own beliefs about community?

CHINUA ACHEBE

Dead Men's Path

Chinua Achebe (b. 1930) was born in Ogidi, Nigeria, a member of the Ibo tribe. He learned English, and attended University College of Ibadan and London University. After beginning a radio career, Achebe left Nigeria when it came under military rule. He has taught at the Universities of Massachusetts/Amherst, Connecticut, and Guelph in Ontario, Canada. Achebe has written novels, including Things Fall Apart *(1958) and* Anthills of the Savannah *(1988), as well as essays, short stories—one collection is* Girls at War and Other Stories *(1991)—and poetry.*

Michael Obi's hopes were fulfilled much earlier than he expected. He was appointed headmaster of Ndume Central School in January 1949. It had always been an unprogressive school, so the Mission authorities decided to send a young and energetic man to run it. Obi accepted this responsibility with enthusiasm. He had many wonderful ideas and this was an opportunity to put them into practice. He had had sound secondary school education which designated him a "pivotal teacher" in the official records and set him apart from the other headmasters in the mission field. He was outspoken in his condemnation of the narrow views of these older and often less-educated ones.

"We shall make a good job of it, shan't we?" he asked his young wife when they first heard the joyful news of his promotion.

"We shall do our best," she replied. "We shall have such beautiful gardens and everything will be just *modern* and delightful . . ." In their two years of married life she had become completely infected by his passion for "modern methods" and his denigration of "these old and superannuated people in the teaching field who would be better employed as traders in the Onitsha market." She began to see herself already as the admired wife of the young headmaster, the queen of the school.

The wives of the other teachers would envy her position. She would set the fashion in everything . . . Then, suddenly, it occurred to her that there might not be other wives. Wavering between hope and fear, she asked her husband, looking anxiously at him.

"All our colleagues are young and unmarried," he said with enthusiasm which for once she did not share. "Which is a good thing," he continued.

"Why?"

"Why? They will give all their time and energy to the school."

Nancy was downcast. For a few minutes she became sceptical about the new school; but it was only for a few minutes. Her little personal misfortune could not blind her to her husband's happy prospects. She looked at him as he sat folded up in a chair. He was stoop-shouldered and looked frail. But he sometimes surprised people with sudden bursts of physical energy. In his present posture, however, all his bodily strength seemed to have retired behind his deep-set eyes, giving them an extraordinary power of penetration. He was only twenty-six, but looked thirty or more. On the whole, he was not unhandsome.

"A penny for your thoughts, Mike," said Nancy after a while, imitating the woman's magazine she read.

"I was thinking what a grand opportunity we've got at last to show these people how a school should be run."

Ndume School was backward in every sense of the word. Mr. Obi put his whole life into the work, and his wife hers too. He had two aims. A high standard of teaching was insisted upon, and the school compound was to be turned into a place of beauty. Nancy's dream-gardens came to life with the coming of the rains, and blossomed. Beautiful hibiscus and allamanda hedges in brilliant red and yellow marked out the carefully tended school compound from the rank neighbourhood bushes.

One evening as Obi was admiring his work he was scandalized to see an old woman from the village hobble right across the compound, through a marigold flower-bed and the hedges. On going up there he found faint signs of an almost disused path from the village across the school compound to the bush on the other side.

"It amazes me," said Obi to one of his teachers who had been three years in the school, "that you people allowed the villagers to make use of this footpath. It is simply incredible." He shook his head.

"The path," said the teacher apologetically, "appears to be very important to them. Although it is hardly used, it connects the village shrine with their place of burial."

"And what has that got to do with the school?" asked the headmaster.

"Well, I don't know," replied the other with a shrug of the shoulders. "But I remember there was a big row some time ago when we attempted to close it."

"That was some time ago. But it will not be used now," said Obi as he walked away. "What will the Government Education Officer think of this when he comes to inspect the school next week? The villagers might, for all I know, decide to use the schoolroom for a pagan ritual during the inspection."

Heavy sticks were planted closely across the path at the two places where it entered and left the school premises. These were further strengthened with barbed wire.

Three days later the village priest of *Ani* called on the headmaster. He was an old man and walked with a slight stoop. He carried a stout walking-stick which he usually tapped on the floor, by way of emphasis, each time he made a new point in his argument.

"I have heard," he said after the usual exchange of cordialities, "that our ancestral footpath has recently been closed . . ."

"Yes," replied Mr. Obi. "We cannot allow people to make a highway of our school compound."

"Look here, my son," said the priest bringing down his walking-stick, "this path was here before you were born and before your father was born. The whole life of this village depends on it. Our dead relatives depart by it and our ancestors visit us by it. But most important, it is the path of children coming in to be born . . ."

Mr. Obi listened with a satisfied smile on his face.

"The whole purpose of our school," he said finally, "is to eradicate just such beliefs as that. Dead men do not require footpaths. The whole idea is just fantastic. Our duty is to teach your children to laugh at such ideas."

"What you say may be true," replied the priest, "but we follow the practices of our fathers. If you re-open the path we shall have nothing to quarrel about. What I always say is: let the hawk perch and let the eagle perch." He rose to go.

"I am sorry," said the young headmaster. "But the school compound cannot be a thoroughfare. It is against our regulations. I would suggest your constructing another path, skirting our premises. We can even get our boys to help in building it. I don't suppose the ancestors will find the little detour too burdensome."

"I have no more words to say," said the old priest, already outside.

Two days later a young woman in the village died in childbed. A diviner was immediately consulted and he prescribed heavy sacrifices to propitiate ancestors insulted by the fence.

Obi woke up next morning among the ruins of his work. The beautiful hedges were torn up not just near the path but right round the school, the flowers trampled to death and one of the school buildings pulled down . . . That day, the white Supervisor came to inspect the school and wrote a nasty report on the state of the premises but more seriously about the "tribal-war situation developing between the school and the village, arising in part from the misguided zeal of the new headmaster."

—1972

What are your reactions to and questions about this work? The following questions may help provoke some ideas.

Probing the Work

1. What are the different kinds of *conflicts* (p. 74) in this work?

Identifying Issues

2. Compare and contrast the treatment of tradition in this story with that in "The Lottery."

KITTY TSUI

It's in the Name

*Kitty Tsui (b. 1952) was born in Kowloon, Hong Kong, grew up in England, and in 1969 moved to the United States with her family. Tsui is not only a gifted poet (*The Words of a Woman Who Breathes Fire, *1983), she is also an actress and competitive bodybuilder.*

I've been called sway
  sue
  suey
  suzy
  tissue
  ha-chiew.

my father pronounced it choy
so i grew up saying choy,
always careful to add: t-s-u-i.

the first name is kit fan,
fragrant purity.
but can also mean
marriage.

in chinese, choy
can also mean hurry, fast, *faidee.*

i am constantly
chased by the chant
hurry to get married . . .

if it's not bad enough
it's in the name
it's also in the face.

one day a woman instructor
insisted i had been
one of her guest speakers
in a class.

she was so sure of herself
she had me convinced
it was during my alcohol days
when memory was gone.

genny lim was the speaker.

it happens all the time.
orientals so hard to tell apart.

the same day
a woman stopped
to wish me a good opening.

i was not in a play or an art show.

zand gee, nancy hom and stephanie lowe
had a three-woman show.

that's not all.
i've been called
willyce kim,
canyon sam,
louise low.

it happens all the time.

a newspaper woman thought
i was willyce kim for months.

willyce kim gets called susan kwong.
nellie wong is made nellie kim
or not mentioned by name at all.
merle woo is called merle wong
or smeared as yellow woman
in a gay male publication.

it happens all the time.
it's in the name.
it's in the face.

orientals so hard to tell apart.

our faces,
strong, brown,
different as
the bumps
on the skin of
bittermelon.
our tongues,
sharp and fragrant
as ginger,

telling our history,
our experiences
as asian american women,
workers and poets,
cutting the ropes
that bind us,
breaking from
the silence of centuries

to write
our dreams into action,
give voice to our visions
and tongues
to our foreparents,
those who entered
at chinese hospital
or the paper sons
who came by way of
angel island,
forced to take
false names.

the sewing shop worker,
the secretary,

the doctor,
the *deem sum* girl,
the lesbian,
the bike messenger,
the typesetter,
the boxer,
the student.

each with a name.
each with a face,

blood, bone, breath.

—1983

What are your reactions to and questions about this work? The following questions may help provoke some ideas.

Probing the Work

1. What phrases are repeated in this poem? What is the effect of such repetition?

Identifying Issues

2. How important *are* names, especially with regard to one's cultural or ethnic identity? Consider the difference between one's name (Kitty Tsui) and the *label* one acquires ("oriental"): what are the positive and negative aspects of such labeling?

SOPHOCLES

Antigone

(translated by Robert Fagles)

Sophocles (496?–406 B.C.) was born into a respectable family in Colonus (near Athens, where he was to live most of his life) of ancient Greece. When he was 27 he won a competition for writing a tragic play, defeating another great Greek tragedian, Aeschylus. Out of some 120 plays that he is said to have written, only seven survive, among them Oedipus Rex. *He died an honored citizen in his ninetieth year.*

Summary:

Antigone, Ismene, Polynices and Etiocles were the children of Oedipus, King of Thebes. (Oedipus, the protagonist of Sophocles' play, Oedipus Rex, *was the son of Laius, king of Thebes, and Jocasta. However, he was brought up in Corinth as son and heir to Polybus, due, indirectly, to an oracle's prophesy. Unwittingly, Oedipus killed his father,*

Laius, and married his mother, Jocasta, and upon learning the horrible truth, blinded himself and was led into exile by Antigone.)

The two brothers, Eteocles (a defender of the city of Thebes) and Polynices (one of its attackers), are killed in battle against each other. Creon, their uncle, on becoming king, immediately denies Polynices burial rites and orders that anyone who tries to bury him be punished with death. Defiantly, Antigone asks her sister Ismene to help her bury their brother, but Ismene, too afraid, refuses. Creon becomes enraged when he hears that his decree has been disobeyed, and when Antigone is captured and brought before him, he refuses to listen to any of her arguments or to those of her sister, even when Ismene reminds him that Antigone is engaged to his son Haemon. Antigone also stands firm in her belief that she was obeying divine law in burying her brother. Creon decides that Antigone must die, and his son Haemon is not able to persuade him to show leniency. Haemon vows revenge, but Creon goes ahead and orders Antigone be imprisoned in a cave and left to die for her crime against the state. The prophet Tiresias warns Creon that the gods are angry with him and that he should allow Polynices to be buried. Finally, Creon begins to understand Tiresias' prophesy and tries to free Antigone. But when he gets to the tomb he finds it is too late. Antigone has hung herself, and he must watch Haemon kill himself. Eurydice, Creon's wife, also commits suicide after hearing of her son's death. At the end of the play Creon is led away into exile.

The role of the chorus in Greek Tragedies and in Antigone *is to give background information, comment on events, give thematic observations, and sometimes mark the division of scenes.*

Characters

ANTIGONE, *daughter of Oedipus and Jocasta*
ISMENE, *sister of Antigone*
A CHORUS *of old Theban citizens and their Leader*
CREON, *king of Thebes, uncle of Antigone and Ismene*
A SENTRY
HAEMON, *son of Creon and Eurydice*
TIRESIAS, *a blind prophet*
A MESSENGER
EURYDICE, *wife of Creon*
GUARDS, ATTENDANTS, *and* A BOY

TIME AND SCENE. *The royal house of Thebes. It is still night, and the invading armies of Argos have just been driven from the city. Fighting on opposite sides, the sons of Oedipus, Eteocles and Polynices, have killed each other in combat. Their uncle, Creon, is now king of Thebes.*

Enter ANTIGONE, *slipping through the central doors of the palace. She motions to her sister,* ISMENE, *who follows her cautiously toward an altar at the center of the stage.*

ANTIGONE: My own flesh and blood — dear sister, dear Ismene,
how many griefs our father Oedipus handed down!
Do you know one, I ask you, one grief
that Zeus will not perfect for the two of us
while we still live and breathe? There's nothing,

no pain—our lives are pain—no private shame,
no public disgrace, nothing I haven't seen
in your griefs and mine. And now this:
an emergency decree, they say, the Commander
has just declared for all of Thebes.
What, haven't you heard? Don't you see?
The doom reserved for enemies
marches on the ones we love the most.

ISMENE: Not I, I haven't heard a word, Antigone.
Nothing of loved ones,
no joy or pain has come my way, not since
the two of us were robbed of our two brothers,
both gone in a day, a double blow—
not since the armies of Argos vanished,
just this very night. I know nothing more,
whether our luck's improved or ruin's still to come.

ANTIGONE: I thought so. That's why I brought you out here,
past the gates, so you could hear in private.

ISMENE: What's the matter? Trouble, clearly . . .
you sound so dark, so grim.

ANTIGONE: Why not? Our own brothers' burial!
Hasn't Creon graced one with all the rites,
disgraced the other? Eteocles, they say,
has been given full military honors,
rightly so—Creon's laid him in the earth,
and he goes with glory down among the dead.
But the body of Polynices, who died miserably—
why, a city-wide proclamation, rumor has it,
forbids anyone to bury him, even mourn him.
He's to be left unwept, unburied, a lovely treasure
for birds that scan the field and feast to their heart's
content.
Such, I hear, is the martial law our good Creon
lays down for you and me—yes, me, I tell you—
and he's coming here to alert the uninformed
in no uncertain terms,
and he won't treat the matter lightly. Whoever
disobeys in the least will die, his doom is sealed:
stoning to death inside the city walls!

There you have it. You'll soon show what you are,
worth your breeding, Ismene, or a coward—
for all your royal blood.

ISMENE: My poor sister, if things have come to this,

who am I to make or mend them, tell me,
what good am I to you?
ANTIGONE: Decide.
Will you share the labor, share the work?
ISMENE: What work, what's the risk? What do you mean?
ANTIGONE *(raising her hands)*: Will you lift up his body with these
bare hands and lower it with me?
ISMENE: What? You'd bury him—
when a law forbids the city?
ANTIGONE: Yes!
He is my brother and—deny it as you will—
your brother too.
No one will ever convict me for a traitor.
ISMENE: So desperate, and Creon has expressly—
ANTIGONE: No,
he has no right to keep me from my own.
ISMENE: Oh my sister, think—
think how our own father died, hated,
his reputation in ruins, driven on
by the crimes he brought to light himself
to gouge out his eyes with his own hands—
then mother . . . his mother and wife, both in one,
mutilating her life in the twisted noose—°
and last, our two brothers dead in a single day,
both shedding their own blood, poor suffering boys,
battling out their common destiny hand-to-hand.
Now look at the two of us, left so alone . . .
think what a death we'll die, the worst of all
if we violate the laws and override
the fixed decree of the throne, its power—
we must be sensible. Remember we are women,
we're not born to contend with men. Then too,
we're underlings, ruled by much stronger hands,
so we must submit in this, and things still worse.

I, for one, I'll beg the dead to forgive me—
I'm forced, I have no choice—I must obey
the ones who stand in power. Why rush to extremes?
It's madness, madness.
ANTIGONE: I won't insist,

60–66 think . . . noose: Although he tried to avoid his fate, Oedipus unknowingly killed his father and married his mother, Jocasta. When they learned of his crime, Oedipus blinded himself and Jocasta committed suicide. (This story is told in Sophocles' *Oedipus Rex.*)

no, even if you should have a change of heart,
I'd never welcome you in the labor, not with me.
So, do as you like, whatever suits you best—
I'll bury him myself.
And even if I die in the act, that death will be a glory.
I'll lie with the one I love and loved by him—
an outrage sacred to the gods! I have longer
to please the dead than please the living here:
in the kingdom down below I'll lie forever.
Do as you like, dishonor the laws
the gods hold in honor.

ISMENE: I'd do them no dishonor . . .
but defy the city? I have no strength for that.

ANTIGONE: You have your excuses. I am on my way,
I'll raise a mound for him, for my dear brother.

ISMENE: Oh Antigone, you're so rash—I'm so afraid for you!

ANTIGONE: Don't fear for me. Set your own life in order.

ISMENE: Then don't, at least, blurt this out to anyone.
Keep it a secret. I'll join you in that, I promise.

ANTIGONE: Dear god, shout it from the rooftops. I'll hate you
all the more for silence—tell the world!

ISMENE: So fiery—and it ought to chill your heart.

ANTIGONE: I know I please where I must please the most.

ISMENE: Yes, if you can, but you're in love with impossibility.

ANTIGONE: Very well then, once my strength gives out
I will be done at last.

ISMENE: You're wrong from the start,
you're off on a hopeless quest.

ANTIGONE: If you say so, you will make me hate you,
and the hatred of the dead, by all rights,
will haunt you night and day.
But leave me to my own absurdity, leave me
to suffer this—dreadful thing. I'll suffer
nothing as great as death without glory.

Exit to the side.

ISMENE: Then go if you must, but rest assured,
wild, irrational as you are, my sister,
you are truly dear to the ones who love you.

Withdrawing to the palace. Enter a CHORUS, *the old citizens of Thebes, chanting as the sun begins to rise.*

CHORUS: Glory!—great beam of sun, brightest of all
that ever rose on the seven gates of Thebes,

you burn through night at last!
Great eye of the golden day,
mounting the Dirce's banks you throw him back—
the enemy out of Argos, the white shield, the man of bronze—
he's flying headlong now
the bridle of fate stampeding him with pain!

And he had driven against our borders,
launched by the warring claims of Polynices—
like an eagle screaming, winging havoc
over the land, wings of armor
shielded white as snow,
a huge army massing,
crested helmets bristling for assault.

He hovered above our roofs, his vast maw gaping
closing down around our seven gates,
his spears thirsting for the kill
but now he's gone, look,
before he could glut his jaws with Theban blood
or the god of fire put our crown of towers to the torch.
He grappled the Dragon none can master—Thebes—
the clang of our arms like thunder at his back!

Zeus hates with a vengeance all bravado,
the mighty boasts of men. He watched them
coming on in a rising flood, the pride
of their golden armor ringing shrill—
and brandishing his lightning
blasted the fighter just at the goal,
rushing to shout his triumph from our walls.
Down from the heights he crashed, pounding down on the earth!
And a moment ago, blazing torch in hand—
mad for attack, ecstatic
he breathed his rage, the storm
of his fury hurling at our heads!
But now his high hopes have laid him low
and down the enemy ranks the iron god of war
deals his rewards, his stunning blows—Ares
rapture of battle, our right arm in the crisis.
Seven captains marshaled at seven gates
seven against their equals, gave
their brazen trophies up to Zeus,
god of the breaking rout of battle,
all but two: those blood brothers,

one father, one mother—matched in rage,
spears matched for the twin conquest—
clashed and won the common prize of death.

But now for Victory! Glorious in the morning,
joy in her eyes to meet our joy
she is winging down to Thebes,
our fleets of chariots wheeling in her wake—
Now let us win oblivion from the wars,
thronging the temples of the gods
in singing, dancing choirs through the night!
Lord Dionysus, god of the dance
that shakes the land of Thebes, now lead the way!

Enter CREON *from the palace, attended by his* GUARD.

But look, the king of the realm is coming,
Creon, the new man for the new day,
whatever the gods are sending now . . .
what new plan will he launch?
Why this, this special session?
Why this sudden call to the old men
summoned at one command?

CREON: My countrymen,
the ship of state is safe. The gods who rocked her,
after a long, merciless pounding in the storm,
have righted her once more.
Out of the whole city
I have called you here alone. Well I know,
first, your undeviating respect
for the throne and royal power of King Laius.°
Next, while Oedipus steered the land of Thebes,
and even after he died, your loyalty was unshakable,
you still stood by their children. Now then,
since the two sons are dead—two blows of fate
in the same day, cut down by each other's hands,
both killers, both brothers stained with blood—
as I am next in kin to the dead,
I now possess the throne and all its powers.

Of course you cannot know a man completely,
his character, his principles, sense of judgment,
not till he's shown his colors, ruling the people,

185 Laius: The father of Oedipus.

making laws. Experience, there's the test.
As I see it, whoever assumes the task,
the awesome task of setting the city's course,
and refuses to adopt the soundest policies
but fearing someone, keeps his lips locked tight,
he's utterly worthless. So I rate him now,
I always have. And whoever places a friend
above the good of his own country, he is nothing:
I have no use for him. Zeus my witness,
Zeus who sees all things, always—
I could never stand by silent, watching destruction
march against our city, putting safety to rout,
nor could I ever make that man a friend of mine
who menaces our country. Remember this:
our country *is* our safety.
Only while she voyages true on course
can we establish friendships, truer than blood itself.
Such are my standards. They make our city great.

Closely akin to them I have proclaimed,
just now, the following decree to our people
concerning the two sons of Oedipus.
Eteocles, who died fighting for Thebes,
excelling all in arms: he shall be buried,
crowned with a hero's honors, the cups we pour
to soak the earth and reach the famous dead.

But as for his blood brother, Polynices,
who returned from exile, home to his father-city
and the gods of his race, consumed with one desire—
to burn them roof to roots—who thirsted to drink
his kinsmen's blood and sell the rest to slavery:
that man—a proclamation has forbidden the city
to dignify him with burial, mourn him at all.
No, he must be left unburied, his corpse
carrion for the birds and dogs to tear,
an obscenity for the citizens to behold!

These are my principles. Never at my hands
will the traitor be honored above the patriot.
But whoever proves his loyalty to the state:
I'll prize that man in death as well as life.

LEADER: If this is your pleasure, Creon, treating
our city's enemy and our friend this way . . .

The power is yours, I suppose, to enforce it
with the laws, both for the dead and all of us,
the living.

CREON: Follow my orders closely then,
be on your guard.

LEADER: We're too old.
Lay that burden on younger shoulders.

CREON: No, no,
I don't mean the body—I've posted guards already.

LEADER: What commands for us then? What other service?

CREON: See that you never side with those who break my orders.

LEADER: Never. Only a fool could be in love with death.

CREON: Death is the price—you're right. But all too often
the mere hope of money has ruined many men.

A SENTRY *enters from the side.*

SENTRY: My lord,
I can't say I'm winded from running, or set out
with any spring in my legs either—no sir,
I was lost in thought, and it made me stop, often,
dead in my tracks, wheeling, turning back,
and all the time a voice inside me muttering,
"Idiot, why? You're going straight to your death."
Then muttering, "Stopped again, poor fool?
If somebody gets the news to Creon first,
what's to save your neck?"
And so,
mulling it over, on I trudged, dragging my feet,
you can make a short road take forever . . .
but at last, look, common sense won out,
I'm here, and I'm all yours,
and even though I come empty-handed
I'll tell my story just the same, because
I've come with a good grip on one hope,
what will come will come, whatever fate—

CREON: Come to the point!
What's wrong—why so afraid?

SENTRY: First, myself, I've got to tell you,
I didn't do it, didn't see who did—
Be fair, don't take it out on me.

CREON: You're playing it safe, soldier,
barricading yourself from any trouble.
It's obvious, you've something strange to tell.

SENTRY: Dangerous too, and danger makes you delay
    for all you're worth
CREON: Out with it—then dismiss!
SENTRY: All right, here it comes. The body—
    someone's just buried it, then run off . . .
    sprinkled some dry dust on the flesh,
    given it proper rites.
CREON: What?
    What man alive would dare—
SENTRY: I've no idea, I swear it.
    There was no mark of a spade, no pickaxe there,
    no earth turned up, the ground packed hard and dry,
    unbroken, no tracks, no wheelruts, nothing,
    the workman left no trace. Just at sunup
    the first watch of the day points it out—
    it was a wonder! We were stunned . . .
    a terrific burden too, for all of us, listen:
    you can't see the corpse, not that it's buried,
    really, just a light cover of road-dust on it,
    as if someone meant to lay the dead to rest
    and keep from getting cursed.
    Not a sign in sight that dogs or wild beasts
    had worried the body, even torn the skin.

    But what came next! Rough talk flew thick and fast,
    guard grilling guard—we'd have come to blows
    at last, nothing to stop it; each man for himself
    and each the culprit, no one caught red-handed,
    all of us pleading ignorance, dodging the charges,
    ready to take up red-hot iron in our fists,
    go through fire, swear oaths to the gods—
    "I didn't do it, I had no hand in it either,
    not in the plotting, not in the work itself!"

    Finally, after all this wrangling came to nothing,
    one man spoke out and made us stare at the
      ground,
    hanging our heads in fear. No way to counter him,
    no way to take his advice and come through
    safe and sound. Here's what he said:
    "Look, we've got to report the facts to Creon,
    we can't keep this hidden." Well, that won out,
    and the lot fell on me, condemned me,
    unlucky as ever, I got the prize. So here I am,

against my will and yours too, well I know—
no one wants the man who brings bad news.

LEADER: My king,
ever since he began I've been debating in my mind,
could this possibly be the work of the gods?

CREON: Stop—
before you make me choke with anger—the gods!
You, you're senile, must you be insane?
You say—why it's intolerable—say the gods
could have the slightest concern for that corpse?
Tell me, was it for meritorious service
they proceeded to bury him, prized him so? The hero
who came to burn their temples ringed with pillars,
their golden treasures—scorch their hallowed earth
and fling their laws to the winds.
Exactly when did you last see the gods
celebrating traitors? Inconceivable!

No, from the first there were certain citizens
who could hardly stand the spirit of my regime,
grumbling against me in the dark, heads together,
tossing wildly, never keeping their necks beneath
the yoke, loyally submitting to their king.
These are the instigators, I'm convinced—
they've perverted my own guard, bribed them
to do their work.
Money! Nothing worse
in our lives, so current, rampant, so corrupting.
Money—you demolish cities, root men from their homes,
you train and twist good minds and set them on
to the most atrocious schemes. No limit,
you make them adept at every kind of outrage,
every godless crime—money!
Everyone—
the whole crew bribed to commit this crime,
they've made one thing sure at least:
sooner or later they will pay the price.

Wheeling on the SENTRY.

You—
I swear to Zeus as I still believe in Zeus,
if you don't find the man who buried that corpse,
the very man, and produce him before my eyes,
simple death won't be enough for you,

not till we string you up alive
and wring the immorality out of you.
Then you can steal the rest of your days,
better informed about where to make a killing.
You'll have learned, at last, it doesn't pay
to itch for rewards from every hand that beckons.
Filthy profits wreck most men, you'll see—
they'll never save your life.

SENTRY: Please,
may I say a word or two, or just turn and go?

CREON: Can't you tell? Everything you say offends me.

SENTRY: Where does it hurt you, in the ears or in the heart?

CREON: And who are you to pinpoint my displeasure?

SENTRY: The culprit grates on your feelings,
I just annoy your ears.

CREON: Still talking?
You talk too much! A born nuisance—

SENTRY: Maybe so,
but I never did this thing, so help me!

CREON: Yes you did—
what's more, you squandered your life for silver!

SENTRY: Oh it's terrible when the one who does the judging
judges things all wrong.

CREON: Well now,
you just be clever about your judgments—
if you fail to produce the criminals for me,
you'll swear your dirty money brought you pain.

Turning sharply, reentering the palace.

SENTRY: I hope he's found. Best thing by far.
But caught or not, that's in the lap of fortune;
I'll never come back, you've seen the last of me.
I'm saved, even now, and I never thought,
I never hoped—
dear gods, I owe you all my thanks!

Rushing out.

CHORUS: Numberless wonders
terrible wonders walk the world but none the match for man—
that great wonder crossing the heaving gray sea,
driven on by the blasts of winter
on through breakers crashing left and right,
holds his steady course
and the oldest of the gods he wears away—

the Earth, the immortal, the inexhaustible—
as his plows go back and forth, year in, year out
with the breed of stallions turning up the furrows.

And the blithe, lightheaded race of birds he snares,
the tribes of savage beasts, the life that swarms the depths—
with one fling of his nets
woven and coiled tight, he takes them all,
man the skilled, the brilliant!
He conquers all, taming with his techniques
the prey that roams the cliffs and wild lairs,
training the stallion, clamping the yoke across
his shaggy neck, and the tireless mountain bull.

And speech and thought, quick as the wind
and the mood and mind for law that rules the city—
all these he has taught himself
and shelter from the arrows of the frost
when there's rough lodging under the cold clear sky
and the shafts of lashing rain—
ready, resourceful man!
Never without resources
never an impasse as he marches on the future—
only Death, from Death alone he will find no rescue
but from desperate plagues he has plotted his escapes.

Man the master, ingenious past all measure
past all dreams, the skills within his grasp—
he forges on, now to destruction
now again to greatness. When he weaves in
the laws of the land, and the justice of the gods
that binds his oaths together
he and his city rise high—
but the city casts out
that man who weds himself to inhumanity
thanks to reckless daring. Never share my hearth
never think my thoughts, whoever does such things.

Enter ANTIGONE *from the side, accompanied by the* SENTRY.

Here is a dark sign from the gods—
what to make of this? I know her,
how can I deny it? That young girl's Antigone!
Wretched, child of a wretched father,
Oedipus. Look, is it possible?

They bring you in like a prisoner—
why? did you break the king's laws?
Did they take you in some act of mad defiance?
SENTRY: She's the one, she did it single-handed—
we caught her burying the body. Where's Creon?

Enter CREON *from the palace.*

LEADER: Back again, just in time when you need him.
CREON: In time for what? What is it?
SENTRY: My king,
there's nothing you can swear you'll never do—
second thoughts make liars of us all.
I could have sworn I wouldn't hurry back
(what with your threats, the buffeting I just took),
but a stroke of luck beyond our wildest hopes,
what a joy, there's nothing like it. So,
back I've come, breaking my oath, who cares?
I'm bringing in our prisoner—this young girl—
we took her giving the dead the last rites.
But no casting lots this time; this is *my* luck,
my prize, no one else's.
Now, my lord,
here she is. Take her, question her,
cross-examine her to your heart's content.
But set me free, it's only right—
I'm rid of this dreadful business once for all.
CREON: Prisoner! Her? You took her—where, doing what?
SENTRY: Burying the man. That's the whole story.
CREON: What?
You mean what you say, you're telling me the truth?
SENTRY: She's the one. With my own eyes I saw her
bury the body, just what you've forbidden.
There. Is that plain and clear?
CREON: What did you see? Did you catch her in the act?
SENTRY: Here's what happened. We went back to our post,
those threats of yours breathing down our necks—
we brushed the corpse clean of the dust that covered it,
stripped it bare . . . it was slimy, going soft,
and we took to high ground, backs to the wind
so the stink of him couldn't hit us;
jostling, baiting each other to keep awake,
shouting back and forth—no napping on the job,
not this time. And so the hours dragged by
until the sun stood dead above our heads,

a huge white ball in the noon sky, beating,
blazing down, and then it happened—
suddenly, a whirlwind!
Twisting a great dust-storm up from the earth,
a black plague of the heavens, filling the plain,
ripping the leaves off every tree in sight,
choking the air and sky. We squinted hard
and took our whipping from the gods.

And after the storm passed—it seemed endless—
there, we saw the girl!
And she cried out a sharp, piercing cry,
like a bird come back to an empty nest,
peering into its bed, and all the babies gone . . .
Just so, when she sees the corpse bare
she bursts into a long, shattering wail
and calls down withering curses on the heads
of all who did the work. And she scoops up dry dust,
handfuls, quickly, and lifting a fine bronze urn,
lifting it high and pouring, she crowns the dead
with three full libations.

Soon as we saw
we rushed her, closed on the kill like hunters,
and she, she didn't flinch. We interrogated her,
charging her with offenses past and present—
she stood up to it all, denied nothing. I tell you,
it made me ache and laugh in the same breath.
It's pure joy to escape the worst yourself,
it hurts a man to bring down his friends.
But all that, I'm afraid, means less to me
than my own skin. That's the way I'm made.

CREON *(wheeling on* ANTIGONE): You,
with your eyes fixed on the ground—speak up.
Do you deny you did this, yes or no?

ANTIGONE: I did it. I don't deny a thing.

CREON *(to the* SENTRY): You, get out, wherever you please—
you're clear of a very heavy charge.

He leaves; CREON *turns back to* ANTIGONE.

You, tell me briefly, no long speeches—
were you aware a decree had forbidden this?

ANTIGONE: Well aware. How could I avoid it? It was public.

CREON: And still you had the gall to break this law?
ANTIGONE: Of course I did. It wasn't Zeus, not in the least,
who made this proclamation—not to me.
Nor did that Justice, dwelling with the gods
beneath the earth, ordain such laws for men.
Nor did I think your edict had such force
that you, a mere mortal, could override the gods,
the great unwritten, unshakable traditions.
They are alive, not just today or yesterday:
they live forever, from the first of time,
and no one knows when they first saw the light.

These laws—I was not about to break them,
not out of fear of some man's wounded pride,
and face the retribution of the gods.
Die I must, I've known it all my life —
how could I keep from knowing?—even without
your death-sentence ringing in my ears.
And if I am to die before my time
I consider that a gain. Who on earth,
alive in the midst of so much grief as I,
could fail to find his death a rich reward?
So for me, at least, to meet this doom of yours
is precious little pain. But if I had allowed
my own mother's son to rot, an unburied corpse—
that would have been an agony! This is nothing.
And if my present actions strike you as foolish,
let's just say I've been accused of folly
by a fool.
LEADER: Like father like daughter,
passionate, wild . . .
she hasn't learned to bend before adversity.
CREON: No? Believe me, the stiffest stubborn wills
fall the hardest; the toughest iron,
tempered strong in the white-hot fire,
you'll see it crack and shatter first of all.
And I've known spirited horses you can break
with a light bit—proud, rebellious horses.
There's no room for pride, not in a slave,
not with the lord and master standing by.

This girl was an old hand at insolence
when she overrode the edicts we made public.

But once she'd done it—the insolence,
twice over—to glory in it, laughing,
mocking us to our face with what she'd done.
I'm not the man, not now: she is the man
if this victory goes to her and she goes free.

Never! Sister's child or closer in blood
than all my family clustered at my altar
worshiping Guardian Zeus—she'll never escape,
she and her blood sister, the most barbaric death.
Yes, I accuse her sister of an equal part
in scheming this, this burial.

To his ATTENDANTS.

Bring her here!
I just saw her inside, hysterical, gone to pieces.
It never fails; the mind convicts itself
in advance, when scoundrels are up to no good,
plotting in the dark. Oh but I hate it more
when a traitor, caught red-handed,
tries to glorify his crimes.

ANTIGONE: Creon, what more do you want
than my arrest and execution?

CREON: Nothing. Then I have it all.

ANTIGONE: Then why delay? Your moralizing repels me,
every word you say—pray god it always will.
So naturally all I say repels you too.
Enough.
Give me glory! What greater glory could I win
than to give my own brother decent burial?
These citizens here would all agree,

To the CHORUS.

they'd praise me too
if their lips weren't locked in fear.

Pointing to CREON.

Lucky tyrants—the perquisites of power!
Ruthless power to do and say whatever pleases *them*.

CREON: You alone, of all the people in Thebes,
see things that way.

ANTIGONE: They see it just that way
but defer to you and keep their tongues in leash.

CREON: And you, aren't you ashamed to differ so from them?
So disloyal!
ANTIGONE: Not ashamed for a moment,
not to honor my brother, my own flesh and blood.
CREON: Wasn't Eteocles a brother too—cut down, facing him?
ANTIGONE: Brother, yes, by the same mother, the same father.
CREON: Then how can you render his enemy such honors,
such impieties in his eyes?
ANTIGONE: He'll never testify to that,
Eteocles dead and buried.
CREON: He will—
if you honor the traitor just as much as him.
ANTIGONE: But it was his brother, not some slave that died—
CREON: Ravaging our country!—
but Eteocles died fighting in our behalf.
ANTIGONE: No matter—Death longs for the same rites for all.
CREON: Never the same for the patriot and the traitor.
ANTIGONE: Who, Creon, who on earth can say the ones below
don't find this pure and uncorrupt?
CREON: Never. Once an enemy, never a friend,
not even after death.
ANTIGONE: I was born to join in love, not hate—
that is my nature.
CREON: Go down below and love,
if love you must—love the dead! While I'm alive,
no woman is going to lord it over me.

Enter ISMENE *from the palace, under guard.*

CHORUS: Look,
Ismene's coming, weeping a sister's tears,
loving sister, under a cloud . . .
her face is flushed, her cheeks streaming.
Sorrow puts her lovely radiance in the dark.
CREON: You—
in my house, you viper, slinking undetected,
sucking my life-blood! I never knew
I was breeding twin disasters, the two of you
rising up against my throne. Come, tell me,
will you confess your part in the crime or not?
Answer me. Swear to me.
ISMENE: I did it, yes—

if only she consents—I share the guilt,
the consequences too.

ANTIGONE: No,
Justice will never suffer that—not you,
you were unwilling. I never brought you in.

ISMENE: But now you face such dangers . . . I'm not ashamed
to sail through trouble with you,
make your troubles mine.

ANTIGONE: Who did the work?
Let the dead and the god of death bear witness!
I've no love for a friend who loves in words alone.

ISMENE: Oh no, my sister, don't reject me, please,
let me die beside you, consecrating
the dead together.

ANTIGONE: Never share my dying,
don't lay claim to what you never touched.
My death will be enough.

ISMENE: What do I care for life, cut off from you?

ANTIGONE: Ask Creon. Your concern is all for him.

ISMENE: Why abuse me so? It doesn't help you now.

ANTIGONE: You're right—
if I mock you, I get no pleasure from it,
only pain.

ISMENE: Tell me, dear one,
what can I do to help you, even now?

ANTIGONE: Save yourself. I don't grudge you your survival.

ISMENE: Oh no, no, denied my portion in your death?

ANTIGONE: You chose to live, I chose to die.

ISMENE: Not, at least,
without every kind of caution I could voice.

ANTIGONE: Your wisdom appealed to one world—mine, another.

ISMENE: But look, we're both guilty, both condemned to death.

ANTIGONE: Courage! Live your life. I gave myself to death,
long ago, so I might serve the dead.

CREON: They're both mad, I tell you, the two of them.
One's just shown it, the other's been that way
since she was born.

ISMENE: True, my king,
the sense we were born with cannot last forever . . .
commit cruelty on a person long enough
and the mind begins to go.

CREON: Yours did,
when you chose to commit your crimes with her.

ISMENE: How can I live alone, without her?

CREON: Her?
Don't even mention her—she no longer exists.
ISMENE: What? You'd kill your own son's bride?
CREON: Absolutely:
there are other fields for him to plow.
ISMENE: Perhaps,
but never as true, as close a bond as theirs.
CREON: A worthless woman for my son? It repels me.
ISMENE: Dearest Haemon, your father wrongs you so!
CREON: Enough, enough—you and your talk of marriage!
ISMENE: Creon—you're really going to rob your son of Antigone?
CREON: Death will do it for me—break their marriage off.
LEADER: So, it's settled then? Antigone must die?
CREON: Settled, yes—we both know that.

To the GUARDS.

Stop wasting time. Take them in.
From now on they'll act like women.
Tie them up, no more running loose;
even the bravest will cut and run,
once they see Death coming for their lives.

The GUARDS *escort* ANTIGONE *and* ISMENE *into the palace.* CREON *remains while the old citizens form their chorus.*

CHORUS: Blest, they are the truly blest who all their lives
have never tasted devastation. For others, once
the gods have rocked a house to its foundations
the ruin will never cease, cresting on and on
from one generation on throughout the race—
like a great mounting tide
driven on by savage northern gales,
surging over the dead black depths
roiling up from the bottom dark heaves of sand
and the headlands, taking the storm's onslaught full-force,
roar, and the low moaning
echoes on and on
and now
as in ancient times I see the sorrows of the house,
the living heirs of the old ancestral kings,
piling on the sorrows of the dead
and one generation cannot free the next—
some god will bring them crashing down,
the race finds no release.
And now the light, the hope

springing up from the late last root
in the house of Oedipus, that hope's cut down in turn
by the long, bloody knife swung by the gods of death
by a senseless word
by fury at the heart.
Zeus,
yours is the power, Zeus, what man on earth
can override it, who can hold it back?
Power that neither Sleep, the all-ensnaring
no, nor the tireless months of heaven
can ever overmaster—young through all time,
mighty lord of power, you hold fast
the dazzling crystal mansions of Olympus.
And throughout the future, late and soon
as through the past, your law prevails:
no towering form of greatness
enters into the lives of mortals
free and clear of ruin.
True,
our dreams, our high hopes voyaging far and wide
bring sheer delight to many, to many others
delusion, blithe, mindless lusts
and the fraud steals on one slowly . . . unaware
till he trips and puts his foot into the fire.
He was a wise old man who coined
the famous saying: "Sooner or later
foul is fair, fair is foul
to the man the gods will ruin"—
He goes his way for a moment only
free of blinding ruin.

Enter HAEMON *from the palace.*

Here's Haemon now, the last of all your sons.
Does he come in tears for his bride,
his doomed bride, Antigone—
bitter at being cheated of their marriage?

CREON: We'll soon know, better than seers could tell us.

Turning to HAEMON.

Son, you've heard the final verdict on your bride?
Are you coming now, raving against your father?
Or do you love me, no matter what I do?

HAEMON: Father, I'm your *son* . . . you in your wisdom
set my bearings for me—I obey you.

the gift of eloquence, he and no one else,
and character too . . . such men, I tell you,
spread them open—you will find them empty.
No,
it's no disgrace for a man, even a wise man,
to learn many things and not to be too rigid.
You've seen trees by a raging winter torrent,
how many sway with the flood and salvage every twig,
but not the stubborn—they're ripped out, roots and all.
Bend or break. The same when a man is sailing:
haul your sheets too taut, never give an inch,
you'll capsize, go the rest of the voyage
keel up and the rowing-benches under.
Oh give way. Relax your anger—change!
I'm young, I know, but let me offer this:
it would be best by far, I admit,
if a man were born infallible, right by nature.
If not—and things don't often go that way,
it's best to learn from those with good advice.

LEADER: You'd do well, my lord, if he's speaking to the point,
to learn from him,

Turning to HAEMON.

and you, my boy, from him.
You both are talking sense.

CREON: So,
men our age, we're to be lectured, are we?—
schooled by a boy his age?

HAEMON: Only in what is right. But if I seem young,
look less to my years and more to what I do.

CREON: Do? Is admiring rebels an achievement?

HAEMON: I'd never suggest that you admire treason.

CREON: Oh?—
isn't that just the sickness that's attacked her?

HAEMON: The whole city of Thebes denies it, to a man.

CREON: And is Thebes about to tell me how to rule?

HAEMON: Now, you see? Who's talking like a child?

CREON: Am I to rule this land for others—or myself?

HAEMON: It's no city at all, owned by one man alone.

CREON: What? The city *is* the king's—that's the law!

HAEMON: What a splendid king you'd make of a desert island—
you and you alone.

CREON *(to the* CHORUS*)*: This boy, I do believe,
is fighting on her side, the woman's side.

HAEMON: If you are a woman, yes;
  my concern is all for you.
CREON: Why, you degenerate—bandying accusations,
  threatening me with justice, your own father!
HAEMON: I see my father offending justice—wrong.
CREON: Wrong?
  To protect my royal rights?
HAEMON: Protect your rights?
  When you trample down the honors of the gods?
CREON: You, you soul of corruption, rotten through—
  woman's accomplice!
HAEMON: That may be,
  but you'll never find me accomplice to a criminal.
CREON: That's what *she* is,
  and every word you say is a blatant appeal for her—
HAEMON: And you, and me, and the gods beneath the earth.
CREON: You'll never marry her, not while she's alive.
HAEMON: Then she'll die . . . but her death will kill another.
CREON: What, brazen threats? You go too far!
HAEMON: What threat?
  Combating your empty, mindless judgments with a word?
CREON: You'll suffer for your sermons, you and your empty
  wisdom!
HAEMON: If you weren't my father, I'd say you were insane.
CREON: Don't flatter me with Father—you woman's slave!
HAEMON: You really expect to fling abuse at me
  and not receive the same?
CREON: Is that so!
  Now, by heaven, I promise you, you'll pay—
  taunting, insulting me! Bring her out,
  that hateful—she'll die now, here,
  in front of his eyes, beside her groom!
HAEMON: No, no, she will never die beside me—
  don't delude yourself. And you will never
  see me, never set eyes on my face again.
  Rage your heart out, rage with friends
  who can stand the sight of you.

Rushing out.

LEADER: Gone, my king, in a burst of anger.
  A temper young as his . . . hurt him once,
  he may do something violent.
CREON: Let him do—
  dream up something desperate, past all human limit!

Good riddance. Rest assured,
he'll never save those two young girls from death.
LEADER: Both of them, you really intend to kill them both?
CREON: No, not her, the one whose hands are clean;
you're quite right.
LEADER: But Antigone—
what sort of death do you have in mind for her?
CREON: I'll take her down some wild, desolate path
never trod by men, and wall her up alive
in a rocky vault, and set out short rations,
just a gesture of piety
to keep the entire city free of defilement.
There let her pray to the one god she worships:
Death—who knows?—may just reprieve her from death.
Or she may learn at last, better late than never,
what a waste of breath it is to worship Death.

Exit to the palace.

CHORUS: Love, never conquered in battle
Love the plunderer laying waste the rich!
Love standing the night-watch
guarding a girl's soft cheek,
you range the seas, the shepherds' steadings off in the wilds—
not even the deathless gods can flee your onset,
nothing human born for a day—
whoever feels your grip is driven mad.
Love
you wrench the minds of the righteous into outrage,
swerve them to their ruin—you have ignited this,
this kindred strife, father and son at war
and Love alone the victor—
warm glance of the bride triumphant, burning with desire!
Throned in power, side-by-side with the mighty laws!
Irresistible Aphrodite, never conquered—
Love, you mock us for your sport.

ANTIGONE *is brought from the palace under guard.*

But now, even I'd rebel against the king,
I'd break all bounds when I see this—
I fill with tears, can't hold them back,
not any more . . . I see Antigone make her way
to the bridal vault where all are laid to rest.
ANTIGONE: Look at me, men of my fatherland,
setting out on the last road

looking into the last light of day
the last I'll ever see . . .
the god of death who puts us all to bed
takes me down to the banks of Acheron alive—
denied my part in the wedding-songs,
no wedding-song in the dusk has crowned my marriage—
I go to wed the lord of the dark waters.
CHORUS: Not crowned with glory, crowned with a dirge,
you leave for the deep pit of the dead.
No withering illness laid you low,
no strokes of the sword—a law to yourself,
alone, no mortal like you, ever, you go down
to the halls of Death alive and breathing.
ANTIGONE: But think of Niobe—well I know her story—
think what a living death she died,
Tantalus' daughter, stranger queen from the east:
there on the mountain heights, growing stone
binding as ivy, slowly walled her round
and the rains will never cease, the legends say
the snows will never leave her . . .
wasting away, under her brows the tears
showering down her breasting ridge and slopes—
a rocky death like hers puts me to sleep.°
CHORUS: But she was a god, born of gods,
and we are only mortals born to die.
And yet, of course, it's a great thing
for a dying girl to hear, just hear
she shares a destiny equal to the gods,
during life and later, once she's dead.
ANTIGONE: O you mock me!
Why, in the name of all my fathers' gods
why can't you wait till I am gone—
must you abuse me to my face?
O my city, all your fine rich sons!
And you, you springs of the Dirce,
holy grove of Thebes where the chariots gather,
you at least, you'll bear me witness, look,
unmourned by friends and forced by such crude laws
I go to my rockbound prison, strange new tomb—
always a stranger, O dear god,

915–924 Niobe . . . sleep: Because of her pride, the gods killed Niobe's children and turned Niobe into a rock on Mount Sipylus, where she wept continuously.

I have no home on earth and none below,
not with the living, not with the breathless dead.
CHORUS: You went too far, the last limits of daring—
smashing against the high throne of Justice!
Your life's in ruins, child—I wonder . . .
do you pay for your father's terrible ordeal?
ANTIGONE: There—at last you've touched it, the worst pain
the worst anguish! Raking up the grief for father
three times over, for all the doom
that's truck us down, the brilliant house of Laius.
O mother, your marriage-bed
the coiling horrors, the coupling there—
you with your own son, my father—doomstruck mother!
Such, such were my parents, and I their wretched child.
I go to them now, cursed, unwed, to share their home—
I am a stranger! O dear brother, doomed
in your marriage—your marriage murders mine,
your dying drags me down to death alive!

Enter CREON.

CHORUS: Reverence asks some reverence in return—
but attacks on power never go unchecked,
not by the man who holds the reins of power.
Your own blind will, your passion has destroyed you.
ANTIGONE: No one to weep for me, my friends,
no wedding-song—they take me away
in all my pain . . . the road lies open, waiting.
Never again, the law forbids me to see
the sacred eye of day. I am agony!
No tears for the destiny that's mine,
no loved one mourns my death.
CHORUS: Can't you see?
If a man could wail his own dirge *before* he dies,
he'd never finish.

To the GUARDS.

Take her away, quickly!
Wall her up in the tomb, you have your orders.
Abandon her there, alone, and let her choose—
death or a buried life with a good roof for shelter.
As for myself, my hands are clean. This young girl—
dead or alive, she will be stripped of her rights,
her stranger's rights, here in the world above.

ANTIGONE: O tomb, my bridal-bed—my house, my prison
cut in the hollow rock, my everlasting watch!
I'll soon be there, soon embrace my own,
the great growing family of our dead
Persephone has received among her ghosts.

I,

the last of them all, the most reviled by far,
go down before my destined time's run out.
But still I go, cherishing one good hope:
my arrival may be dear to father,
dear to you, my mother,
dear to you, my loving brother, Eteocles—
When you died I washed you with my hands,
I dressed you all, I poured the cups
across your tombs. But now, Polynices,
because I laid your body out as well,
this, this is my reward. Nevertheless
I honored you—the decent will admit it—
well and wisely too.

Never, I tell you,

if I had been the mother of children
or if my husband died, exposed and rotting—
I'd never have taken this ordeal upon myself,
never defied our people's will. What law,
you ask, do I satisfy with what I say?
A husband dead, there might have been another.
A child by another too, if I had lost the first.
But mother and father both lost in the halls of
Death,
no brother could ever spring to light again.

For this law alone I held you first in honor.
For this, Creon, the king, judges me a criminal
guilty of dreadful outrage, my dear brother!
And now he leads me off, a captive in his hands,
with no part in the bridal-song, the bridal-bed,
denied all joy of marriage, raising children—
deserted so by loved ones, struck by fate,
I descend alive to the caverns of the dead.

What law of the mighty gods have I transgressed?
Why look to the heavens any more, tormented as I am?
Whom to call, what comrades now? Just think,
my reverence only brands me for irreverence!

Very well: if this is the pleasure of the gods,
once I suffer I will know that I was wrong.
But if these men are wrong, let them suffer
nothing worse than they mete out to me—
these masters of injustice!

LEADER: Still the same rough winds, the wild passion
raging through the girl.

CREON *(to the* GUARDS*)*: Take her away.
You're wasting time—you'll pay for it too.

ANTIGONE: Oh god, the voice of death. It's come, it's here.

CREON: True. Not a word of hope—your doom is sealed.

ANTIGONE: Land of Thebes, city of all my fathers—
O you gods, the first gods of the race!
They drag me away, now, no more delay.
Look on me, you noble sons of Thebes—
the last of a great line of kings,
I alone, see what I suffer now
at the hands of what breed of men—
all for reverence, my reverence for the gods!

She leaves under guard; the CHORUS *gathers.*

CHORUS: Danaë, Danaë—
even she endured a fate like yours,
in all her lovely strength she traded
the light of day for the bolted brazen vault—
buried within her tomb, her bridal-chamber,
wed to the yoke and broken.
But she was of glorious birth
my child, my child
and treasured the seed of Zeus within her womb,
the cloudburst streaming gold!°
The power of fate is a wonder,
dark, terrible wonder—
neither wealth nor armies
towered walls nor ships
black hulls lashed by the salt
can save us from that force.
The yoke tamed him too
young Lycurgus flaming in anger
king of Edonia, all for his mad taunts

1035–44 Danaë . . . gold: Her father imprisoned Danaë in an underground house of bronze when he learned that she would have a son who would kill him. But Zeus came to her in a shower of gold and she gave birth to Perseus.

Dionysus clamped him down, encased
in the chain-mail of rock
and there his rage
his terrible flowering rage burst—
sobbing, dying away . . . at last that madman
came to know his god—
the power he mocked, the power
he taunted in all his frenzy
trying to stamp out
the women strong with the god—
the torch, the raving sacred cries—
enraging the Muses who adore the flute.°

And far north where the Black Rocks
cut the sea in half
and murderous straits
split the coast of Thrace
a forbidding city stands
where once, hard by the walls
the savage Ares thrilled to watch
a king's new queen, a Fury rearing in rage
against his two royal sons—
her bloody hands, her dagger-shuttle
stabbing out their eyes—cursed, blinding wounds—
their eyes blind sockets screaming for revenge!°

They wailed in agony, cries echoing cries
the princes doomed at birth . . .
and their mother doomed to chains,
walled off in a tomb of stone—
but she traced her own birth back
to a proud Athenian line and the high gods
and off in caverns half the world away,
born of the wild North Wind
she sprang on her father's gales,
racing stallions up the leaping cliffs—
child of the heavens. But even on her the Fates
the gray everlasting Fates rode hard
my child, my child.

1051–65 The yoke . . . the flute: According to various legends Lycurgus was imprisoned in the stone cell or driven mad by the gods for insulting Dionysus and the Muses.

1066–77 And far north . . . screaming for revenge: Eidothea, second wife of King Phineas, blinded her stepsons after the king had imprisoned their mother in a cave. Ares is the god of war.

Enter TIRESIAS, *the blind prophet, led by a* BOY.

TIRESIAS: Lords of Thebes,
I and the boy have come together,
hand in hand. Two see with the eyes of one . . .
so the blind must go, with a guide to lead the way.
CREON: What is it, old Tiresias? What news now?
TIRESIAS: I will teach you. And you obey the seer.
CREON: I will,
I've never wavered from your advice before.
TIRESIAS: And so you kept the city straight on course.
CREON: I owe you a great deal, I swear to that.
TIRESIAS: Then reflect, my son: you are poised,
once more on the razor-edge of fate.
CREON: What is it? I shudder to hear you.
TIRESIAS: You will learn
when you listen to the warnings of my craft.
As I sat on the ancient seat of augury,
in the sanctuary where every bird I know
will hover at my hands—suddenly I heard it,
a strange voice in the wingbeats, unintelligible,
barbaric, a mad scream! Talons flashing, ripping,
they were killing each other—that much I knew—
the murderous fury whirring in those wings
made that much clear!
I was afraid,
I turned quickly, tested the burnt-sacrifice,
ignited the altar at all points—but no fire,
the god in the fire never blazed.
Not from those offerings . . . over the embers
slid a heavy ooze from the long thighbones,
smoking, sputtering out, and the bladder
puffed and burst—spraying gall into the air—
and the fat wrapping the bones slithered off
and left them glistening white. No fire!
The rites failed that might have blazed the future
with a sign. So I learned from the boy here;
he is my guide, as I am guide to others.
And it's you—
your high resolve that sets this plague on Thebes.
The public altars and sacred hearths are fouled,
one and all, by the birds and dogs with carrion
torn from the corpse, the doomstruck son of Oedipus!
And so the gods are deaf to our prayers, they spurn

the offerings in our hands, the flame of holy flesh.
No birds cry out an omen clear and true—
they're gorged with the murdered victim's blood
and fat.
Take these things to heart, my son, I warn you.
All men make mistakes, it is only human.
But once the wrong is done, a man
can turn his back on folly, misfortune too,
if he tries to make amends, however low he's fallen,
and stops his bullnecked ways. Stubbornness
brands you for stupidity—pride is a crime.
No, yield to the dead!
Never stab the fighter when he's down.
Where's the glory, killing the dead twice over?

I mean you well. I give you sound advice.
It's best to learn from a good adviser
when he speaks for your own good:
it's pure gain.

CREON: Old man—all of you! So,
you shoot your arrows at my head like archers at the target—
I even have *him* loosed on me, this fortune-teller.
Oh his ilk has tried to sell me short
and ship me off for years. Well,
drive your bargains, traffic—much as you like—
in the gold of India, silver-gold of Sardis.
You'll never bury that body in the grave,
not even if Zeus's eagles rip the corpse
and wing their rotten pickings off to the throne of god!
Never, not even in fear of such defilement
will I tolerate his burial, that traitor.
Well I know, we can't defile the gods—
no mortal has the power.
No,
reverend old Tiresias, all men fall,
it's only human, but the wisest fall obscenely
when they glorify obscene advice with rhetoric—
all for their own gain.

TIRESIAS: Oh god, is there a man alive
who knows, who actually believes . . .

CREON: What now?
What earth-shattering truth are you about to utter?

TIRESIAS: . . . just how much a sense of judgment, wisdom
is the greatest gift we have?

CREON: Just as much, I'd say,
as a twisted mind is the worst affliction going.
TIRESIAS: You are the one who's sick, Creon, sick to death.
CREON: I am in no mood to trade insults with a seer.
TIRESIAS: You have already, calling my prophecies a lie.
CREON: Why not?
You and the whole breed of seers are mad for money!
TIRESIAS: And the whole race of tyrants lusts to rake it in.
CREON: This slander of yours—
are you aware you're speaking to the king?
TIRESIAS: Well aware. Who helped you save the city?
CREON: You—
you have your skills, old seer, but you lust for injustice!
TIRESIAS: You will drive me to utter the dreadful secret in my heart.
CREON: Spit it out! Just don't speak it out for profit.
TIRESIAS: Profit? No, not a bit of profit, not for you.
CREON: Know full well, you'll never buy off my resolve.
TIRESIAS: Then know this too, learn this by heart!
The chariot of the sun will not race through
so many circuits more, before you have surrendered
one born of your own loins, your own flesh and blood,
a corpse for corpses given in return, since you have thrust
to the world below a child sprung for the world above,
ruthlessly lodged a living soul within the grave—
then you've robbed the gods below the earth,
keeping a dead body here in the bright air,
unburied, unsung, unhallowed by the rites.

You, you have no business with the dead,
nor do the gods above—this is violence
you have forced upon the heavens.
And so the avengers, the dark destroyers late
but true to the mark, now lie in wait for you,
the Furies sent by the gods and the god of death
to strike you down with the pains that you perfected!

There. Reflect on that, tell me I've been bribed.
The day comes soon, no long test of time, not now,
that wakes the wails for men and women in your halls.
Great hatred rises against you—
cities in tumult, all whose mutilated sons
the dogs have graced with burial, or the wild beasts,
some wheeling crow that wings the ungodly stench of carrion
back to each city, each warrior's hearth and home.

These arrows for your heart! Since you've raked me
I loose them like an archer in my anger,
arrows deadly true. You'll never escape
their burning, searing force.

Motioning to his escort.

Come, boy, take me home.
So he can vent his rage on younger men,
and learn to keep a gentler tongue in his head
and better sense than what he carries now.

Exit to the side.

LEADER: The old man's gone, my king—
terrible prophecies. Well I know,
since the hair on this old head went gray,
he's never lied to Thebes.
CREON: I know it myself—I'm shaken, torn.
It's a dreadful thing to yield . . . but resist now?
Lay my pride bare to the blows of ruin?
That's dreadful too.
LEADER: But good advice,
Creon, take it now, you must.
CREON: What should I do? Tell me . . . I'll obey.
LEADER: Go! Free the girl from the rocky vault
and raise a mound for the body you exposed.
CREON: That's your advice? You think I should give in?
LEADER: Yes, my king, quickly. Disasters sent by the gods
cut short our follies in a flash.
CREON: Oh it's hard,
giving up the heart's desire . . . but I will do it—
no more fighting a losing battle with necessity.
LEADER: Do it now, go, don't leave it to others.
CREON: Now—I'm on my way! Come, each of you,
take up axes, make for the high ground,
over there, quickly! I and my better judgment
have come round to this—I shackled her,
I'll set her free myself. I am afraid . . .
it's best to keep the established laws
to the very day we die.

Rushing out, followed by his entourage. The CHORUS *clusters around the altar.*

CHORUS: God of a hundred names!
Great Dionysus—
Son and glory of Semele! Pride of Thebes—
Child of Zeus whose thunder rocks the clouds—
Lord of the famous lands of evening—
King of the Mysteries!
King of Eleusis, Demeter's plain
her breasting hills that welcome in the world—
Great Dionysus!
Bacchus, living in Thebes
the mother-city of all your frenzied women—
Bacchus
living along the Ismenus' rippling waters
standing over the field sown with the Dragon's teeth!°

You—we have seen you through the flaring smoky fires,
your torches blazing over the twin peaks
where nymphs of the hallowed cave climb onward
fired with you, your sacred rage—
we have seen you at Castalia's running spring
and down from the heights of Nysa crowned with ivy
the greening shore rioting vines and grapes
down you come in your storm of wild women
ecstatic, mystic cries—
Dionysus—
down to watch and ward the roads of Thebes!

First of all cities, Thebes you honor first
you and your mother, bride of the lightning—
come, Dionysus! now your people lie
in the iron grip of plague,
come in your racing, healing stride
down Parnassus' slopes
or across the moaning straits.
Lord of the dancing—
dance, dance the constellations breathing fire!
Great master of the voices of the night!
Child of Zeus, God's offspring, come, come forth!
Lord, king, dance with your nymphs, swirling, raving
arm-in-arm in frenzy through the night

1247–48 Ismenus . . . Dragon's teeth: Cadmus killed a dragon here and sowed the field with its teeth, from which the builders of Thebes arose.

they dance you, Iacchus°—
Dance, Dionysus
giver of all good things!

Enter a MESSENGER *from the side.*

MESSENGER: Neighbors,
friends of the house of Cadmus° and the kings,
there's not a thing in this life of ours
I'd praise or blame as settled once for all.
Fortune lifts and Fortune fells the lucky
and unlucky every day. No prophet on earth
can tell a man his fate. Take Creon:
there was a man to rouse your envy once,
as I see it. He saved the realm from enemies;
taking power, he alone, the lord of the fatherland,
he set us true on course—flourished like a tree
with the noble line of sons he bred and reared . . .
and now it's lost, all gone.
Believe me,
when a man has squandered his true joys,
he's good as dead, I tell you, a living corpse.
Pile up riches in your house, as much as you like
—live like a king with a huge show of pomp,
but if real delight is missing from the lot,
I wouldn't give you a wisp of smoke for it,
not compared with joy.

LEADER: What now?
What new grief do you bring the house of kings?

MESSENGER: Dead, dead—and the living are guilty of their death!

LEADER: Who's the murderer? Who is dead? Tell us.

MESSENGER: Haemon's gone, his blood spilled by the very hand—

LEADER: His father's or his own?

MESSENGER: His own . . .
raging mad with his father for the death—

LEADER: Oh great seer,
you saw it all, you brought your word to birth!

MESSENGER: Those are the facts. Deal with them as you will.

As he turns to go, EURYDICE *enters from the palace.*

1271 Iacchus: Another name for Dionysus. (see also 1247–48n.).
1273 Cadmus: The legendary founder of Thebes (see also 1247–48n.).

LEADER: Look, Eurydice. Poor woman, Creon's wife,
so close at hand. By chance perhaps,
unless she's heard the news about her son.
EURYDICE: My countrymen,
all of you—I caught the sound of your words
as I was leaving to do my part,
to appeal to queen Athena with my prayers.
I was just loosing the bolts, opening the doors,
when a voice filled with sorrow, family sorrow,
struck my ears, and I fell back, terrified,
into the women's arms—everything went black.
Tell me the news, again, whatever it is . . .
sorrow and I are hardly strangers;
I can bear the worst.
MESSENGER: I—dear lady,
I'll speak as an eye-witness. I was there.
And I won't pass over one word of the truth.
Why should I try to soothe you with a story,
only to prove a liar in a moment?
Truth is always best.
So,
I escorted your lord, I guided him
to the edge of the plain where the body lay,
Polynices, torn by the dogs and still unmourned.
And saying a prayer to Hecate of the Crossroads,
Pluto too, to hold their anger and be kind,
we washed the dead in a bath of holy water
and plucking some fresh branches, gathering . . .
what was left of him, we burned them all together
and raised a high mound of native earth, and then
we turned and made for that rocky vault of hers,
the hollow, empty bed of the bride of Death.
And far off, one of us heard a voice,
a long wail rising, echoing
out of that unhallowed wedding-chamber;
he ran to alert the master and Creon pressed on,
closer—the strange, inscrutable cry came sharper,
throbbing around him now, and he let loose
a cry of his own, enough to wrench the heart,
"Oh god, am I the prophet now? going down
the darkest road I've ever gone? My son—
it's *his* dear voice, he greets me! Go, men,
closer, quickly! Go through the gap,
the rocks are dragged back—

right to the tomb's very mouth—and look,
see if it's Haemon's voice I think I hear,
or the gods have robbed me of my senses."

The king was shattered. We took his orders,
went and searched, and there in the deepest,
dark recesses of the tomb we found her . . .
hanged by the neck in a fine linen noose,
strangled in her veils—and the boy,
his arms flung around her waist,
clinging to her, wailing for his bride,
dead and down below, for his father's crimes
and the bed of his marriage blighted by misfortune.
When Creon saw him, he gave a deep sob,
he ran in, shouting, crying out to him,
"Oh my child—what have you done? what seized
    you,
what insanity? what disaster drove you mad?
Come out, my son! I beg you on my knees!"
But the boy gave him a wild burning glance,
spat in his face, not a word in reply,
he drew his sword—his father rushed out,
running as Haemon lunged and missed!—
and then, doomed, desperate with himself,
suddenly leaning his full weight on the blade,
he buried it in his body, halfway to the hilt.
And still in his senses, pouring his arms around her,
he embraced the girl and breathing hard,
released a quick rush of blood,
bright red on her cheek glistening white.
And there he lies, body enfolding body . . .
he has won his bride at last, poor boy,
not here but in the houses of the dead.

Creon shows the world that of all the ills
afflicting men the worst is lack of judgment.

EURYDICE *turns and reenters the palace.*

LEADER: What do you make of that? The lady's gone,
    without a word, good or bad.

MESSENGER: I'm alarmed too
    but here's my hope—faced with her son's death,
    she finds it unbecoming to mourn in public.
    Inside, under her roof, she'll set her women

to the task and wail the sorrow of the house.
She's too discreet. She won't do something rash.
LEADER: I'm not so sure. To me, at least,
a long heavy silence promises danger,
just as much as a lot of empty outcries.
MESSENGER: We'll see if she's holding something back,
hiding some passion in her heart.
I'm going in. You may be right—who knows?
Even too much silence has its dangers.

Exit to the palace. Enter CREON *from the side, escorted by* ATTENDANTS *carrying* HAEMON*'s body on a bier.*

LEADER: The king himself! Coming toward us,
look, holding the boy's head in his hands.
Clear, damning proof, if it's right to say so—
proof of his own madness, no one else's,
no, his own blind wrongs.
CREON: Ohhh,
so senseless, so insane . . . my crimes,
my stubborn, deadly—
Look at us, the killer, the killed,
father and son, the same blood—the misery!
My plans, my mad fanatic heart,
my son, cut off so young!
Ai, dead, lost to the world,
not through your stupidity, no, my own.
LEADER: Too late,
too late, you see what justice means.
CREON: Oh I've learned
through blood and tears! Then, it was then,
when the god came down and struck me—a great weight
shattering, driving me down that wild savage path,
ruining, trampling down my joy. Oh the agony,
the heartbreaking agonies of our lives.

Enter the MESSENGER *from the palace.*

MESSENGER: Master,
what a hoard of grief you have, and you'll have more.
The grief that lies to hand you've brought yourself—

Pointing to HAEMON*'s body.*

the rest, in the house, you'll see it all too soon.
CREON: What now? What's worse than this?
MESSENGER: The queen is dead.

The mother of this dead body . . . mother to the end—
poor thing, her wounds are fresh.

CREON: No, no,
harbor of Death, so choked, so hard to cleanse!—
why me? why are you killing me?
Herald of pain, more words, more grief?
I died once, you kill me again and again!
What's the report, boy . . . some news for me?
My wife dead? O dear god!
Slaughter heaped on slaughter?

The doors open; the body of EURYDICE *is brought out on her bier.*

MESSENGER: See for yourself:
now they bring her body from the palace.

CREON: Oh, no,
another, a second loss to break the heart.
What next, what fate still waits for me?
I just held my son in my arms and now,
look, a new corpse rising before my eyes—
wretched, helpless mother—O my son!

MESSENGER: She stabbed herself at the altar,
then her eyes went dark, after she'd raised
a cry for the noble fate of Megareus,° the hero
killed in the first assault, then for Haemon,
then with her dying breath she called down
torments on your head—you killed her sons.

CREON: Oh the dread,
I shudder with dread! Why not kill me too?—
run me through with a good sharp sword?
Oh god, the misery, anguish—
I, I'm churning with it, going under.

MESSENGER: Yes, and the dead, the woman lying there,
piles the guilt of all their deaths on you.

CREON: How did she end her life, what bloody stroke?

MESSENGER: She drove home to the heart with her own hand,
once she learned her son was dead . . . that agony.

CREON: And the guilt is all mine—
can never be fixed on another man,
no escape for me. I killed you,
I, god help me, I admit it all!

1428 Megareus: One of Creon and Eurydice's sons, slain when Thebes was attacked.

To his ATTENDANTS.

Take me away, quickly, out of sight.
I don't even exist—I'm no one. Nothing.
LEADER: Good advice, if there's any good in suffering.
Quickest is best when troubles block the way.
CREON *(kneeling in prayer)*:
Come, let it come—that best of fates for me
that brings the final day, best fate of all.
Oh quickly, now—
so I never have to see another sunrise.
LEADER: That will come when it comes;
we must deal with all that lies before us.
The future rests with the ones who tend the future.
CREON: That prayer—I poured my heart into that prayer!
LEADER: No more prayers now. For mortal men
there is no escape from the doom we must endure.
CREON: Take me away, I beg you, out of sight.
A rash, indiscriminate fool!
I murdered you, my son, against my will—
you too, my wife . . .
Wailing wreck of a man,
whom to look to? where to lean for support?

Desperately turning from HAEMON *to* EURYDICE *on their biers.*

Whatever I touch goes wrong—once more
a crushing fate's come down upon my head.

The MESSENGER *and* ATTENDANTS *lead* CREON *into the palace.*

CHORUS: Wisdom is by far the greatest part of joy,
and reverence toward the gods must be safeguarded.
The mighty words of the proud are paid in full
with mighty blows of fate, and at long last
those blows will teach us wisdom.

The old citizens exit to the side.

—441 B.C.

What are your reactions to and questions about this work? The following questions may help provoke some ideas.

Probing the Work

1. Look closely at a scene that depicts one of the following confrontations: Creon and Antigone, Antigone and Ismene, Creon and Haemon. Pick out

one or two of the most significant lines and interpret the issues being debated according to your beliefs and the characters' motivations.

Identifying Issues

2. Consider how the play deals with either of the following issues: (a) individual conscience versus the law; (b) loyalty to state and ruler versus loyalty to family.
3. Read the following critical excerpt by Charles Paul Segal and see how it adds to or contradicts your feelings about the play. Select a passage from Segal's article that you either agree or disagree with, and find evidence in the play to support your stance. Alternatively, pick out one of the issues Segal explores and find more examples in the play to support (or refute) his point.

Commentary

CHARLES PAUL SEGAL

Sophocles' Praise of Man and the Conflicts of the Antigone *(excerpt)*[1]

It is no coincidence that the most influential interpretation of the *Antigone*—and one of the most influential interpretations of a Greek tragedy—comes from a philosopher of idealism and dialectics. The *Antigone* is certainly a play of antitheses and conflicts, and this state of conflict is embodied in the presence on stage of two protagonists, each diametrically opposed to the other. Yet as a result of Hegel's famous analysis much discussion of the play has focused on the question of which of the two protagonists has more of "the right" on his side. This approach runs the risk of conceptualizing the protagonists too simply into antithetical "principles" which somehow are, and dialectically must be, ultimately reconciled.

This is not to say that there are not conceptual issues involved in the characters of Creon and Antigone. But the issues are too complex to be satisfactorily reduced to a single antithetical formulation. We must avoid seeing the protagonists as one-dimensional representatives of simple oppositions: right and wrong, reason and emotion, state and individual, or the like. Such oppositions have some validity, but a validity purchased at the price of oversimplification and ultimately a misunderstanding of Sophocles' sense of the tragic. The characters, like the play itself, have many levels which fuse organically, sometimes indistinguishably, into a complex unity; and here the confrontations of the two protagonists create an ever-ramifying interplay between interlocking and expanding issues.

It is the essence and the marvel of works of the Classical period that con-

[1]Line numbers and quotations refer to the version of *Antigone* that appears on pp. 144–185 of this text [Ed.].

crete and generic so perfectly meet and unite. In this quality Sophocles is preeminent. In the *Antigone* the characters *are* the issues, and the issues the characters. But the characters are not only "issues." They are individuals moving as all men do in a complex entanglement of will and circumstance, passion and altruism, guilt and innocence. Their searching, suffering, growth to understanding, and death give to the "philosophical" issues substance and the breath of life. Hence they can move us with a statement that does not falsify the intertwining of idea with particular, concept with action, loss with attainment, that forms the structure of our reality.

Recent critics, abandoning the simple thesis-antithesis opposition and looking at the play in terms of the action itself, have made it clear that it is hard to find much pure "right" on Creon's side, though this is not to say that his fate entirely lacks a tragic dimension or that the conflict is settled merely by a kind of moral default. Antigone, on the other hand, is vindicated by the end of the play, but only at the cost of tremendous suffering, her own and that of those closest to her. Indeed, since she disappears a little after the half-way point of the drama, one may wonder whether it is not the gods, Tiresias, and the rights of the corpse, which are vindicated rather than Antigone herself.

But Antigone and Creon are clearly the central focus of the play. Yet together they give the play a double focus. The "double center of gravity" in the work, as one critic has called it, creates a tension and richness which makes it possible for the action to reflect back upon itself in complex ways. And, as another critic has aptly pointed out, the decisive quality of the moral judgment expressed at the end of the tragedy requires a movement in which there can be sufficient complexity to make the play an adequate artistic expression of the complexity which exists in life.

The complexity lies in part in the fact that the two protagonists, though totally opposed in their views, are nevertheless each bound to the other, "demonically bound,". . . . Each is necessary to define the other. On the one hand, as Whitman has well remarked, "Antigone is the balance in which Creon is weighed, and found wanting"; on the other, Antigone's harshness would make no sense without Creon's authoritarian willfulness. It is the essence of the tragedy that the one figure seems to generate the other, that the two coexist as complementary parts of a whole. This whole is not necessarily a Hegelian "synthesis" of two opposing "spiritual substances," but something both infinitely simpler and infinitely more complex, something which is antecedent to and more basic than the conceptual formulations about spirit and absolutes. It is nothing less than the nature of man, his place in the world, and the possibilities and limitations of his actions. Around these issues and derivative from them revolve the antinomies which have been conceptualized in so many different ways: divine versus human law, individual versus state, religious versus secular, private versus public morality.

The conflict between Creon and Antigone has its starting point in the problems of law and justice. At any rate, the difference is most explicitly formulated in these terms in Antigone's great speech on the divine laws [lines 500 ff], a speech which is both confession and defence, both plea of guilt and self-vindication, almost encomium. Against the limited and relative "decrees" of men she sets the eternal laws of Zeus, the "unwritten laws of the gods." She couples her assertion of these absolute "laws" with her own resolute acceptance of death . . . . Thus she begins to extend the conflict outward into issues of wider scope. She chooses the divine command over the human compulsion, and rejects life with its compromises for the absolutes of death. Indeed, in her terms these absolutes are, paradoxically, just the things which "live always" . . . .

This speech is also the focal point for themes that reverberate throughout the play. Antigone opposes the "decrees" . . . of Creon to the "laws" . . . of the gods, and thus sharpens the issue of what constitutes "law". . . . By implication she introduces the distinction between the man-made and the "natural," the artificial and the eternally existent. The two words, "decree" and "law," have been used confusedly and indiscriminately by Creon . . . ; and they now are seen to diverge.

The same divergence occurs with "justice". . . . Antigone here appeals to the [". . .Justice, dwelling with the gods beneath the earth. . ." (501–502)] whereas Creon is later to define the justice of a man solely in relation to the *polis*, the state, and to identify justice in private life with that in public life: ["Show me the man who rules his household well: I'll show you someone fit to rule the state" (739–740)]. The certainty of this identification is severely shaken in the following scene, where the question of justice comes up in the most intimate of Creon's domestic relations and drives a wedge between "public" and "private" justice. Creon taunts his son with ["threatening me with justice" (832)] and is told in reply that he is mistaken in the matter of what is just. . . . The chorus is to accuse Antigone of ["smashing against the high throne of justice" (944)], but will exclaim, at the end, to Creon, ["reverence toward the gods must be safeguarded" (1467)].

Antigone's unqualified declaration for absolute values thus precipitates a redefinition of some basic moral and ethical categories. They do not fit her and have consequently to be remade. She is "a law to herself" . . . ; and, as she is well aware (499 ff.), she must pay the price for standing outside the conventional definitions of "law" and "justice." She challenges human law with an absolute which she backs up with the resolve of her own death, for this is the fullest assertion she can make of the intensity of her moral convictions. She can assert what she is only by staking her entire being, her life. It is by this extreme defense of her beliefs that she rises to heroic and deeply tragic stature; and, simultaneously, by the same gesture she makes herself incomprehensible to the other actors, Creon, Ismene, the chorus. Only Haemon, who, at a lower level, makes and fulfils a similar resolve to die, comes close to understanding her; and in his final act, affirming himself truly her betrothed, he is indeed "married" to her in death. Death is the only possible union of such natures:

And there he lies, body enfolding body. . .
he has won his bride at last, poor boy,
not here but in the houses of the dead (1369–1371).

In Antigone's speech on the "unwritten laws," emphasis naturally falls upon law and justice, for the setting is a juridical one and Antigone is, as it were, on trial. But in the close-knit fifth-century city-state, "law" and "legality" have a far wider range of application than they would in the more compartmentalized ethics of modern civilization. For Sophocles and his contemporaries they involve the entire public and private life of the citizen, his relations with the gods and with his fellow-men, and all the responsibilities, moral, political, social, implied in those relations.

It is again among the tragic paradoxes of Antigone's position that she who accepts the absolutes of death has a far fuller sense of the complexities of life. Creon, who lacks a true "reverence" for the gods, the powers beyond human life, also lacks a deep awareness of the complexities within the human realm. Hence he tends to see the world in terms of harshly opposed categories, right and wrong, reason and folly, youth and age, male and female. He scornfully joins old age with foolishness in speaking to the chorus . . . and refuses to listen to his son's advice because he is younger . . . . Yet his opposition of old and young is later to be turned against him by Tiresias . . . , and he is, in the end, to be "taught" by the young son . . . who dies, Creon laments, ["cut off so young" (1397)].

All these categories imply the relation of superior and inferior, stronger and weaker. This highly structured and aggressive view of the world Creon expresses perhaps most strikingly in repeatedly formulating the conflict between Antigone and himself in terms of the woman trying to conquer the man . . . . He sees in Antigone a challenge to his whole way of living and his basic attitudes toward the world. And of course he is right, for Antigone's full acceptance of her womanly nature, her absolute valuation of the bonds of blood and affection, is a total denial of Creon's obsessively masculine rationality.

—1964

WRITING ASSIGNMENT SEQUENCE (CONTINUED FROM PAGE 126)

4. Making Connections

Select one of the following questions and write an informal response in which you connect your own ideas with those conveyed in the works of this cluster, and/or make connections among the works themselves.

A. What are the varying degrees of individualism shown in the works of this cluster, and what are the consequences of such nonconformity?

B. What are the difficult kinds of peer/community pressures exerted in these works, and to what extent are they justified or not?

C. How would you amend or add to either the diagram you made of yourself and the people in your life (in the "Clustering" exercise, p. 126), or the scene you wrote depicting the conflict between individualistic and community needs ("Enacting the Topic," p. 127)?

5. *Putting It All Together*

Write an essay that combines what you think about the topic *Self-Reliance* with what you now understand about the readings.

- Collect your informal writing, notes, and reading-journal entries on this topic and decide what will be the focus of your essay.
- Outline your essay. Select the literary passages and personal details you might use to illustrate and support your main focus.
- Write a draft of your essay in which you bring together what you think about the subject with what you understand about the readings. Try to include in your draft one or more *literary terms.*
- Share what you've written with your classmates and instructor, then revise it according to their recommendations.

Writing Tip: Changing Your Introduction

After you write the first draft of your essay, take a look at your first paragraph. Have you begun your essay so that you have engaged, oriented, and directed the reader in the most interesting way possible? You might consider using one of the following:

- a lively quotation
- a problem or dilemma to be solved
- an anecdote
- a striking image
- an intriguing question (that you will answer in your essay)

Samples

Joanne begins her essay with *an intriguing question*:

Is it possible to be *truly* self-reliant?

Phaedra begins with a *quotation* from pop culture:

> "Reality . . . what a concept." This phrase, popularized by Robin Williams, is an ironically simplified view of a complex idea.

Laurel begins her essay with a dramatic *anecdote*:

> "Mom?"
>
> "What is it now? I've read you three books. I've brought you water and have kissed you goodnight."
>
> "Close my closet door. I'm scared of that monster."

CrossClusters

In your paper you might want to consider how the following works located elsewhere in this book deal with the tension between self-reliance and conformity:

- John Updike, "A & P" (p. 104)
- Richard Wright, "The Man Who Was Almost a Man" (p. 93)
- Susan Glaspell, *Trifles* (p. 220)
- Audre Lorde, "Power" (p. 251)
- Raymond Carver, "My Father's Life" (p. 446)
- James Baldwin, "The Rockpile" (p. 462)
- Sam Shepard, *True West* (p. 502)
- Tony Kushner, from *Angels in America* (p. 621)
- Nathaniel Hawthorne, "The Birth-mark" (p. 633)
- Henrik Ibsen, *A Doll's House* (p. 659)
- Mme. de Beaumont, "Beauty and the Beast" (p. 732)
- Ursula LeGuin, "The Ones Who Walk Away From Omelas" (p. 757)
- William Shakespeare, *A Midsummer-Night's Dream* (p. 766)
- Robert Browning, "Porphyria's Lover" (p. 840)
- Charlotte Perkins Gilman, "The Yellow Wallpaper" (p. 842)
- Sylvia Plath, "Lady Lazarus" (p. 856)
- Eugène Ionesco, *The Lesson* (p. 904)
- William Blake, "Proverbs of Hell" (p. 968)
- Woody Allen, *Death Knocks* (p. 1005)

11

PHENOMENAL WOMAN

WRITING ASSIGNMENT SEQUENCE

1. Thinking About . . . Women

Brainstorming: Write *feminist* on the top left side of a piece of paper, and *female* on the right. Then write whatever words you think of in reaction to or in association with those two words. (Some may apply to both words.) Afterwards, jot down your observations regarding why you thought of the words you did. (For more on *brainstorming,* see page 26.)

2. Enacting the Topic

Make a collage, or clip articles and advertisements, illustrating different images of women in today's newspapers and magazines. Prepare to present to the class a summary of what you found, and draw some conclusions about these images.

3. Responding to the Readings

As you read the works in this cluster, jot down in your response journals questions you have about the works, and comment on passages you find provocative or puzzling. Consider the questions following each reading for journal writing and prepare to discuss your reactions in class.

CLUSTER ESSAY

VIRGINIA WOOLF

Professions for Women[1]

Virginia Woolf (1882–1941) cofounded the Hogarth Press and wrote several novels (among them Mrs. Dalloway, *1925 and* To the Lighthouse, *1927). She also wrote es-*

1. "A paper read to the Women's Service League" [Woolf's note].

says, such as "A Room of One's Own" (1929) that have become staples of contemporary feminist theory.

When your secretary invited me to come here, she told me that your Society is concerned with the employment of women and she suggested that I might tell you something about my own professional experiences. It is true I am a woman; it is true I am employed; but what professional experiences have I had? It is difficult to say. My profession is literature; and in that profession there are fewer experiences for women than in any other, with the exception of the stage—fewer, I mean, that are peculiar to women. For the road was cut many years ago—by Fanny Burney, by Aphra Behn, by Harriet Martineau, by Jane Austen, by George Eliot—many famous women, and many more unknown and forgotten, have been before me, making the path smooth, and regulating my steps. Thus, when I came to write, there were very few material obstacles in my way. Writing was a reputable and harmless occupation. The family peace was not broken by the scratching of a pen. No demand was made upon the family purse. For ten and sixpence one can buy paper enough to write all the plays of Shakespeare—if one has a mind that way. Pianos and models, Paris, Vienna, and Berlin, masters and mistresses, are not needed by a writer. The cheapness of writing paper is, of course, the reason why women have succeeded as writers before they have succeeded in the other professions.

But to tell you my story—it is a simple one. You have only got to figure to yourselves a girl in a bedroom with a pen in her hand. She had only to move that pen from left to right—from ten o'clock to one. Then it occurred to her to do what is simple and cheap enough after all—to slip a few of those pages into an envelope, fix a penny stamp in the corner, and drop the envelope into the red box at the corner. It was thus that I became a journalist; and my effort was rewarded on the first day of the following month—a very glorious day it was for me—by a letter from an editor containing a cheque for one pound ten shillings and sixpence. But to show you how little I deserve to be called a professional woman, how little I know of the struggles and difficulties of such lives, I have to admit that instead of spending that sum upon bread and butter, rent, shoes and stockings, or butcher's bills, I went out and bought a cat—a beautiful cat, a Persian cat, which very soon involved me in bitter disputes with my neighbours.

What could be easier than to write articles and to buy Persian cats with the profits? But wait a moment. Articles have to be about something. Mine, I seem to remember, was about a novel by a famous man. And while I was writing this review, I discovered that if I were going to review books I should need to do battle with a certain phantom. And the phantom was a woman, and when I came to know her better I called her after the heroine of a famous poem, The Angel in the House.[2] It was she who used to come between me and my paper

[2]By Coventry Patmore (1823–1896), published 1854–62.

when I was writing reviews. It was she who bothered me and wasted my time and so tormented me that at last I killed her. You who come of a younger and happier generation may not have heard of her—you may not know what I mean by The Angel in the House. I will describe her as shortly as I can. She was intensely sympathetic. She was immensely charming. She was utterly unselfish. She excelled in the difficult arts of family life. She sacrificed herself daily. If there was chicken, she took the leg; if there was a draught she sat in it—in short she was so constituted that she never had a mind or a wish of her own, but preferred to sympathize always with the minds and wishes of others. Above all—I need not say it—she was pure. Her purity was supposed to be her chief beauty—her blushes, her great grace. In those days—the last of Queen Victoria—every house had its Angel. And when I came to write I encountered her with the very first words. The shadow of her wings fell on my page; I heard the rustling of her skirts in the room. Directly, that is to say, I took my pen in my hand to review that novel by a famous man, she slipped behind me and whispered: 'My dear, you are a young woman. You are writing about a book that has been written by a man. Be sympathetic; be tender; flatter; deceive; use all the arts and wiles of our sex. Never let anybody guess that you have a mind of your own. Above all, be pure.' And she made as if to guide my pen. I now record the one act for which I take some credit to myself, though the credit rightly belongs to some excellent ancestors of mine who left me a certain sum of money—shall we say five hundred pounds a year?—so that it was not necessary for me to depend solely on charm for my living. I turned upon her and caught her by the throat. I did my best to kill her. My excuse, if I were to be had up in a court of law, would be that I acted in self-defence. Had I not killed her she would have killed me. She would have plucked the heart out of my writing. For, as I found, directly I put pen to paper, you cannot review even a novel without having a mind of your own, without expressing what you think to be the truth about human relations, morality, sex. And all these questions, according to the Angel of the House, cannot be dealt with freely and openly by women; they must charm, they must conciliate, they must—to put it bluntly—tell lies if they are to succeed. Thus, whenever I felt the shadow of her wing or the radiance of her halo upon my page, I took up the inkpot and flung it at her. She died hard. Her fictitious nature was of great assistance to her. It is far harder to kill a phantom than a reality. She was always creeping back when I thought I had despatched her. Though I flatter myself that I killed her in the end, the struggle was severe; it took much time that had better have been spent upon learning Greek grammar; or in roaming the world in search of adventures. But it was a real experience; it was an experience that was bound to befall all women writers at that time. Killing the Angel in the House was part of the occupation of a woman writer.

But to continue my story. The Angel was dead; what then remained? You may say that what remained was a simple and common object—a young woman in a bedroom with an inkpot. In other words, now that she had rid herself of falsehood, that young woman had only to be herself. Ah, but what is 'herself'? I mean, what is a woman? I assure you, I do not know. I do not believe that you know. I do not believe that anybody can know until she has expressed herself in all the arts and professions open to human skill. That indeed is one of the reasons why I have come here—out of respect for you, who are in process of showing us by your experiments what a woman is, who are in process of providing us, by your failures and successes, with that extremely important piece of information.

But to continue the story of my professional experiences. I made one pound ten and six by my first review; and I bought a Persian cat with the proceeds. Then I grew ambitious. A Persian cat is all very well, I said; but a Persian cat is not enough. I must have a motor-car. And it was thus that I became a novelist—for it is a very strange thing that people will give you a motor-car if you will tell them a story. It is a still stranger thing that there is nothing so delightful in the world as telling stories. It is far pleasanter than writing reviews of famous novels. And yet, if I am to obey your secretary and tell you my professional experiences as a novelist, I must tell you about a very strange experience that befell me as a novelist. And to understand it you must try first to imagine a novelist's state of mind. I hope I am not giving away professional secrets if I say that a novelist's chief desire is to be as unconscious as possible. He has to induce in himself a state of perpetual lethargy. He wants life to proceed with the utmost quiet and regularity. He wants to see the same faces, to read the same books, to do the same things day after day, month after month, while he is writing, so that nothing may break the illusion in which he is living—so that nothing may disturb or disquiet the mysterious nosings about, feelings round, darts, dashes, and sudden discoveries of that very shy and illusive spirit, the imagination. I suspect that this state is the same both for men and women. Be that as it may, I want you to imagine me writing a novel in a state of trance. I want you to figure to yourselves a girl sitting with a pen in her hand, which for minutes, and indeed for hours, she never dips into the inkpot. The image that comes to my mind when I think of this girl is the image of a fisherman lying sunk in dreams on the verge of a deep lake with a rod held out over the water. She was letting her imagination sweep unchecked round every rock and cranny of the world that lies submerged in the depths of our unconscious being. Now came the experience that I believe to be far commoner with women writers than with men. The line raced through the girl's fingers. Her imagination had rushed away. It had sought the pools, the depths, the dark places where the largest fish slumber. And then there was a smash. There was an explosion. There was foam and confusion. The imagination had dashed itself against something hard. The girl was roused from her dream. She was indeed in a state of the most acute and difficult distress. To speak without figure, she had thought of something, something about the body, about the passions which it was unfitting for her as a woman to say. Men, her reason told her, would be shocked. The consciousness of what men will say of a woman who speaks the truth about her passions had roused her from her artist's state of unconsciousness. She could write no more. The trance was over. Her imagination could work no longer. This I believe to be a very common experience with women writers—they are impeded by the extreme conventionality of the other sex. For though men sensibly allow themselves great freedom in these respects, I doubt that they realize or can control the extreme severity with which they condemn such freedom in women.

These then were two very genuine experiences of my own. These were two of the adventures of my professional life. The first—killing the Angel in the House—I think I solved. She died. But the second, telling the truth about my own experiences as a body, I do not think I solved. I doubt that any woman has solved it yet. The obstacles against her are still immensely powerful—and yet they are very difficult to define. Outwardly, what is simpler than to write books? Outwardly, what obstacles are there for a woman rather than for a man? Inwardly, I think, the case is very different; she has still many ghosts to fight, many prejudices to overcome. Indeed it will be a long time still, I think, before a woman can sit down to write a book without finding a phantom to be slain, a rock to be dashed against. And if this is so in literature, the freest of all professions for women, how is it in the new professions which you are now for the first time entering?

Those are the questions that I should like, had I time, to ask you. And indeed, if I have laid stress upon these professional experiences of mine, it is because I believe that they are, though in different forms, yours also. Even when the path is nominally open—when there is nothing to prevent a woman from being a doctor, a lawyer, a civil servant—there are many phantoms and obstacles, as I believe, looming in her way. To discuss and define them is I think of great value and importance; for thus only can the labour be shared, the difficulties be solved. But besides this, it is necessary also to discuss the ends and the aims for which we are fighting, for which we are doing battle with these formidable obstacles. Those aims cannot be taken for granted; they must be perpetually questioned and examined. The whole position, as I see it—here in this hall surrounded by women practising for the first time in history I know not how many different professions—is one of extraordinary interest and importance. You have won rooms of your own in the house hitherto exclusively owned by men. You are able, though not without great labour and effort, to pay the rent. You are earning your five hundred pounds a year. But this freedom is only a beginning; the room is your own, but it is still bare. It has to be furnished; it has to be decorated; it has to be shared. How are you going to furnish it, how are you going to decorate it? With whom are you going to share it, and upon what terms? These, I think are questions of the utmost importance and interest. For the first time in history you are able to ask them; for the first time you are able to decide for yourselves what the answers should be. Willingly would I stay and discuss those questions and answers—but not tonight. My time is up; and I must cease.

—1942

What are your reactions to and questions about this work? The following questions may help provoke some ideas.

Probing the Work

1. Reread the last paragraph and think about the *metaphor* (see page 68) Woolf uses: how *has* the "room" been furnished since the essay was written over 50 years ago?

Identifying Issues

2. How does Woolf depict the struggle between socially imposed expectations and women's own individualistic inclinations? Apply the conflict Woolf describes to one of the other works in the cluster and to real world examples.

ADRIENNE RICH

Aunt Jennifer's Tigers

Adrienne Rich (b. 1929) was born in Baltimore and educated at Radcliffe College; while a senior there she had her first book of poems, A Change of World *(1951), published. She married and had three sons. Her many collections include* Snapshots of a Daughter-in-Law *(1963) and* Diving Into the Wreck *(1973). After her husband's suicide in 1970, Rich became increasingly involved in the woman's movement. She continues to write politically charged essays and poetry, living in California and teaching at Stanford University.*

Aunt Jennifer's tigers prance across a screen,
Bright topaz denizens of a world of green.
They do not fear the men beneath the tree;
They pace in sleek chivalric certainty.

Aunt Jennifer's fingers fluttering through her wool
Find even the ivory needle hard to pull.
The massive weight of Uncle's wedding band
Sits heavily upon Aunt Jennifer's hand.

When Aunt is dead, her terrified hands will lie
Still ringed with ordeals she was mastered by.
The tigers in the panel that she made
Will go on prancing, proud and unafraid.

—1951

What are your reactions to and questions about this work? The following questions may help provoke some ideas.

Probing the Work

1. What does the tiger, ring, or quilt represent for Aunt Jennifer? What does it reveal about the type of woman she is?

Identifying Issues

2. What kinds of choices do women like Aunt Jennifer have, given their circumstances? To what extent can they find real fulfillment in these kinds of choices?

JOYCE CAROL OATES

Where Are You Going, Where Have You Been?

Joyce Carol Oates (b. 1938) is an astoundingly prolific writer who has written over 20 novels and dozens of short stories and poems, many of them set in upstate New York, where she grew up. Since her first book of stories in 1963 she has produced a least one volume every year (except 1965), about topics ranging from farming to boxing. Among her novels are Son of the Morning *(1978),* Bellefleur *(1980),* Solstice *(1985),* Raven's Wing *(1987), and* Foxfire *(1993).*

For Bob Dylan

Her name was Connie. She was fifteen and she had a quick nervous giggling habit of craning her neck to glance into mirrors, or checking other people's faces to make sure her own was all right. Her mother, who noticed everything and knew everything and who hadn't much reason any longer to look at her own face, always scolded Connie about it. "Stop gawking at yourself, who are you? You think you're so pretty?" she would say. Connie would raise her eyebrows at these familiar complaints and look right through her mother, into a shadowy vision of herself as she was right at that moment: she knew she was pretty and that was everything. Her mother had been pretty once too, if you could believe those old snapshots in the album, but now her looks were gone and that was why she was always after Connie.

"Why don't you keep your room clean like your sister? How've you got your hair fixed—what the hell stinks? Hair spray? You don't see your sister using that junk."

Her sister June was twenty-four and still lived at home. She was a secretary in the high school Connie attended, and if that wasn't bad enough—with her in the same building—she was so plain and chunky and steady that Connie had to hear her praised all the time by her mother and her mother's sisters. June did this, June did that, she saved money and helped clean the house and cooked and Connie couldn't do a thing, her mind was all filled with trashy daydreams. Their father was away at work most of the time and when he came home he wanted supper and he read the newspaper at supper and after supper he went to bed. He didn't bother talking much to them, but around his bent head Connie's mother kept picking at her until Connie wished her mother was dead and she herself was dead and it was all over. "She makes me want to throw up sometimes," she complained to her friends. She had a high, breathless, amused voice which made everything she said sound a little forced, whether it was sincere or not.

There was one good thing: June went places with girl friends of hers, girls who were just as plain and steady as she, and so when Connie wanted to do that her mother had no objections. The father of Connie's best girl friend drove the girls the three miles to town and left them off at a shopping plaze, so that they could walk through the stores or go to a movie, and when he came to pick them up again at eleven he never bothered to ask what they had done.

They must have been familiar sights, walking around that shopping plaza in their shorts and flat ballerina slippers that always scuffed the sidewalk, with charm bracelets jingling on their thin wrists; they would lean together to whisper and laugh secretly if someone passed by who amused or interested them. Connie had long dark blond hair that drew anyone's eye to it, and she wore part of it pulled up on her head and puffed out and the rest of it she let fall down her back. She wore a pull-over jersey blouse that looked one way when she was at home and another way when she was away from home. Everything about her had two sides to it, one for home and one for anywhere that was not home: her walk that could be childlike and bobbing, or languid enough to make anyone think she was hearing music in her head, her mouth which was pale and smirking most of the time, but bright and pink on these evenings out, her laugh which was cynical and drawling at home—"Ha, ha, very funny"—but high-pitched and nervous anywhere else, like the jingling of the charms on her bracelet.

Sometimes they did go shopping or to a movie, but sometimes they went across the highway, ducking fast across the busy road, to a drive-in restaurant where older kids hung out. The restaurant was shaped like a big bottle, though squatter than a real bottle, and on its cap was a revolving figure of a grinning boy who held a hamburger aloft. One night in mid-summer they ran across, breathless with daring, and right away someone leaned out a car window and invited them over, but it was just a boy from high school they didn't like. It made them feel good to be able to ignore him. They went up through the maze of parked and cruising cars to the bright-lit, fly-infested restaurant, their faces pleased and expectant as if they were entering a sacred building that loomed out of the night to give them what haven and what blessing they yearned for. They sat at the counter and crossed their legs at the ankles, their thin shoulders rigid with excitement, and listened to the music that made everything so good: the music was always in the background like music at a church service, it was something to depend upon.

A boy named Eddie came in to talk with them. He sat backwards on his stool, turning himself jerkily around in semi-circles and then stopping and turning again, and after a while he asked Connie if she would like something to eat. She said she did and so she tapped her friend's arm on her way out—her friend pulled her face up into a brave droll look—and Connie said she would meet her at eleven, across the way. "I just hate to leave her like that," Connie said earnestly, but the boy said that she wouldn't be alone for long. So they went out to his car and on the way Connie couldn't help but let her eyes wander over the windshields and faces all around her, her face gleaming with a joy that had nothing to do with Eddie or even this place; it might have been the music. She drew her shoulders up and sucked in her breath with the pure pleasure of being alive, and just at that moment she happened to glance at a face just a few feet from hers. It was a boy with shaggy black hair, in a convertible jalopy painted gold. He stared at her and then his lips widened into a grin. Connie slit her eyes at him and turned away, but she couldn't help glancing back and there he was still watching her. He wagged a finger and laughed and said, "Gonna get you, baby," and Connie turned away again without Eddie noticing anything.

She spent three hours with him, at the restaurant where they ate hamburgers and drank Cokes in wax cups that were always sweating, and then down an alley a mile or so away, and when he left her off at five to eleven only the movie house was still open at the plaza. Her girl friend was there, talking with a boy. When Connie came up the two girls smiled at each other and Connie said, "How was the movie?" and the girl said, "*You* should know." They rode off with the girl's father, sleepy and pleased, and Connie couldn't help but look at the darkened shopping plaza with its big empty parking lot and its signs that were faded and ghostly now, and over at the drive-in restaurant where cars were still circling tirelessly. She couldn't hear the music at this distance.

Next morning June asked her how the movie was and Connie said, "So-so."

She and that girl and occasionally another girl went out several times a week that way, and the rest of the time Connie spent around the house—it was summer vacation—getting in her mother's way and thinking, dreaming, about the boys she met. But all the boys fell back and dissolved into a single face that was not even a face, but an idea, a feeling, mixed up with the urgent insistent pounding of the music and the humid night air of July. Connie's mother kept dragging her back to the daylight by finding things for her to do or saying, suddenly, "What's this about the Pettinger girl?"

And Connie would say nervously, "Oh, her. That dope." She always drew thick clear lines between herself and such girls, and her mother was simple and kindly enough to believe her. Her mother was so simple, Connie thought, that it was maybe cruel to fool her so much. Her mother went scuffling around the house in old bedroom slippers and complained over the telephone to one sister about the other, then the other called up and the two of them complained about the third one. If June's name was mentioned her mother's tone was approving, and if Connie's name was mentioned it was disapproving. This did not really mean she disliked Connie and actually Connie thought that her mother preferred her to June because she was prettier, but the two of them kept up a pretense of exasperation, a sense that they were tugging and struggling over something of little value to either of them. Sometimes, over coffee, they were almost friends, but something would come up—some vexation that was like a fly buzzing suddenly around their heads—and their faces went hard with contempt.

One Sunday Connie got up at eleven—none of them bothered with church—and washed her hair so that it could dry all day long, in the sun. Her parents and sister were going to a barbecue at an aunt's house and Connie said no, she wasn't interested, rolling her eyes to let her mother know just what she thought of it. "Stay home alone then," her mother said sharply. Connie sat out back in a lawn chair and watched them drive away, her father quiet and bald, hunched around so that he could back the car out, her mother with a look that was still angry and not at all softened through the windshield, and in the back seat poor old June all dressed up as if she didn't know what a barbecue was, with all the running yelling kids and the flies. Connie sat with her eyes closed in the sun, dreaming and dazed with the warmth about her as if this were a kind of love, the caresses of love, and her mind slipped over onto thoughts of the boy she had been with the night before and how nice he had been, how sweet it always was, not the way someone like June would suppose but sweet, gentle, the way it was in movies and promised in songs; and when she opened her eyes she hardly knew where she was, the back yard ran off into weeds and a fence-line of trees and behind it the sky was perfectly blue and still. The asbestos "ranch house" that was now three years old startled her—it looked small. She shook her head as if to get awake.

It was too hot. She went inside the house and turned on the radio to drown out the quiet. She sat on the edge of her bed, barefoot, and listened for an hour and a half to a program called XYZ Sunday Jamboree, record after record of hard, fast, shrieking songs she sang along with, interspersed by exclamations from "Bobby King": "An' look here you girls at Napoleon's—Son and Charley want you to pay real close attention to this song coming up!"

And Connie paid close attention herself, bathed in a glow of slow-pulsed joy that seemed to rise mysteriously out of the music itself and lay languidly about the airless little room, breathed in and breathed out with each gentle rise and fall of her chest.

After a while she heard a car coming up the drive. She sat up at once, startled, because it couldn't be her father so soon. The gravel kept crunching all the way in from the road—the driveway was long—and Connie ran to the window. It was a car she didn't know. It was an open jalopy, painted a bright gold that caught the sunlight opaquely. Her heart began to pound and her fingers snatched at her hair, checking it, and she whispered "Christ. Christ," wondering how bad she looked. The car came to a stop at the side door and the horn sounded four short taps as if this were a signal Connie knew.

She went into the kitchen and approached the door slowly, then hung out the screen door, her bare toes curling down off the step. There were two boys in the car and now she recognized the driver: he had shaggy, shabby black hair that looked crazy as a wig and he was grinning at her.

"I ain't late, am I?" he said.

"Who the hell do you think you are?" Connie said.

"Toldja I'd be out, didn't I?"

"I don't even know who you are."

She spoke sullenly, careful to show no interest or pleasure, and he spoke in a fast bright monotone. Connie looked past him to the other boy, taking her time. He had fair brown hair, with a lock that fell onto his forehead. His sideburns gave him a fierce, embarrassed look, but so far he hadn't even bothered to glance at her. Both boys wore sunglasses. The driver's glasses were metallic and mirrored everything in miniature.

"You wanta come for a ride?" he said.

Connie smirked and let her hair fall loose over one shoulder.

"Don'tcha like my car? New paint job," he said. "Hey."

"What?"

"You're cute."

She pretended to fidget, chasing flies away from the door.

"Don'tcha believe me, or what?" he said.

"Look, I don't even know who you are," Connie said in disgust.

"Hey, Ellie's got a radio, see. Mine's broke down." He lifted his friend's arm and showed her the little transistor the boy was holding, and now Connie began to hear the music. It was the same program that was playing inside the house.

"Bobby King?" she said.

"I listen to him all the time. I think he's great."

"He's kind of great," Connie said reluctantly.

"Listen, that guy's *great*. He knows where the action is."

Connie blushed a little, because the glasses made it impossible for her to see just what this boy was looking at. She couldn't decide if she liked him or if he was just a jerk, and so she dawdled in the doorway and wouldn't come down or go back inside. She said, "What's all that stuff painted on your car?"

"Can'tcha read it?" He opened the door very carefully, as if he was afraid it might fall off. He slid out just as carefully, planting his feet firmly on the ground, the tiny metallic world in his glasses slowing down like gelatine hardening and in the midst of it Connie's bright green blouse. "This here is my name, to begin with," he said. ARNOLD FRIEND was written in tarlike black letters on the side, with a drawing of a round grinning face that reminded Connie of a pumpkin, except it wore sunglasses. "I wanta introduce myself, I'm Arnold Friend and that's my real name and I'm gonna be your friend, honey, and inside the car's Ellie Oscar, he's kinda shy." Ellie brought his transistor radio up to his shoulder and balanced it there. "Now these numbers are a secret code, honey," Arnold Friend explained. He read off the numbers 33, 19, 17 and raised his eyebrows at her to see what she thought of that, but she didn't think much of it. The left rear fender had been smashed and around it was written, on the gleaming gold background: DONE BY CRAZY WOMAN DRIVER. Connie had to laugh at that. Arnold Friend was pleased at her laughter and looked up at her. "Around the other side's a lot more—you wanta come and see them?"

"No."

"Why not?"

"Why should I?"

"Don'tcha wanta see what's on the car? Don'tcha wanta go for a ride?"

"I don't know."

"Why not?"

"I got things to do."

"Like what?"

"Things."

He laughed as if she had said something funny. He slapped his thighs. He was standing in a strange way, leaning back against the car as if he were balancing himself. He wasn't tall, only an inch or so taller than she would be if she came down to him. Connie liked the way he was dressed, which was the way all of them dressed: tight faded jeans stuffed into black, scuffed boots, a belt that pulled his waist in and showed how lean he was, and a white pull-over shirt that was a little soiled and showed the hard small muscles of his arms and shoulders. He looked as if he probably did hard work, lifting and carrying things. Even his neck looked muscular. And his face was a familiar face, somehow: the jaw and chin and cheeks slightly darkened, because he hadn't shaved for a day or two, and the nose long and hawklike, sniffing as if she were a treat he was going to gobble up and it was all a joke.

"Connie, you ain't telling the truth. This is your day set aside for a ride with me and you know it," he said, still laughing. The way he straightened and recovered from his fit of laughing showed that it had been all fake.

"How do you know what my name is?" she said suspiciously.

"It's Connie."

"Maybe and maybe not."

"I know my Connie," he said, wagging his finger. Now she remembered him even better, back at the restaurant, and her cheeks warmed at the thought of how she sucked in her breath just at the moment she passed him—how she must have looked to him. And he had remembered her. "Ellie and I come out here especially for you," he said. "Ellie can sit in back. How about it?"

"Where?"

"Where what?"

"Where're we going?"

He looked at her. He took off the sunglasses and she saw how pale the skin around his eyes was, like holes that were not in shadow but instead in light. His eyes were chips of broken glass that catch the light in an amiable way. He smiled. It was as if the idea of going for a ride somewhere, to some place, was a new idea to him.

"Just for a ride, Connie sweetheart."

"I never said my name was Connie," she said.

"But I know what it is. I know your name and all about you, lots of things," Arnold Friend said. He had not moved yet but stood still leaning back against the side of his jalopy. "I took a special interest in you, such a pretty girl, and found out all about you like I know your parents and sister are gone somewheres and I know where and how long they're going to be gone, and I know who you were with last night, and your best girl friend's name is Betty. Right?"

He spoke in a simple lilting voice, exactly as if he were reciting the words to a song. His smile assured her that everything was fine. In the car Ellie turned up the volume on his radio and did not bother to look around at them.

"Ellie can sit in the back seat," Arnold Friend said. He indicated his friend with a casual jerk of his chin, as if Ellie did not count and she should not bother with him.

"How'd you find out all that stuff?" Connie said.

"Listen: Betty Schultz and Tony Fitch and Jimmy Pettinger and Nancy Pettinger," he said, in a chant. "Raymond Stanley and Bob Hutter—"

"Do you know all those kids?"

"I know everybody."

"Look, you're kidding. You're not from around here."

"Sure."

"But—how come we never saw you before?"

"Sure you saw me before," he said. He looked down at his boots, as if he were a little offended. "You just don't remember."

"I guess I'd remember you," Connie said.

"Yeah?" He looked up at this, beaming. He was pleased. He began to mark time with the music from Ellie's radio, tapping his fists lightly together. Connie looked away from his smile to the car, which was painted so bright it almost hurt her eyes to look at it. She looked at that name, ARNOLD FRIEND. And up at the front fender was an expression that was familiar—MAN THE FLYING SAUCERS. It was an expression kids had used the year before, but didn't use this year. She looked at it for a while as if the words meant something to her that she did not yet know.

"What're you thinking about? Huh?" Arnold Friend demanded. "Not worried about your hair blowing around in the car, are you?"

"No."

"Think I maybe can't drive good?"

"How do I know?"

"You're a hard girl to handle. How come?" he said. "Don't you know I'm your friend? Didn't you see me put my sign in the air when you walked by?"

"What sign?"

"My sign." And he drew an X in the air, leaning out toward her. They were maybe ten feet apart. After his hand fell back to his side the X was still in the air, almost visible. Connie let the screen door close and stood perfectly still inside it, listening to the music from her radio and the boy's blend together. She stared at Arnold Friend. He stood there so stiffly relaxed, pretending to be relaxed, with one hand idly on the door handle as if he were keeping himself up that way and had no intention of ever moving again. She recognized most things about him, the tight jeans that showed his thighs and buttocks and the greasy leather boots and the tight shirt, and even that slippery friendly smile of his, that sleepy dreamy smile that all the boys used to get across ideas they didn't want to put into words. She recognized all this and also the singsong way he talked, slightly mocking, kidding, but serious and a little melancholy, and she recognized the way he tapped one fist against the other in homage to the perpetual music behind him. But all these things did not come together.

She said suddenly, "Hey, how old are you?"

His smile faded. She could see then that he wasn't a kid, he was much older—thirty, maybe more. At this knowledge her heart began to pound faster.

"That's a crazy thing to ask. Can'tcha see I'm your own age?"

"Like hell you are."

"Or maybe a couple years older, I'm eighteen."

"Eighteen?" she said doubtfully.

He grinned to reassure her and lines appeared at the corners of his mouth. His teeth were big and white. He grinned so broadly his eyes became slits and she saw how thick the lashes were, thick and black as if painted with a black tarlike material. Then he seemed to become embarrassed, abruptly, and looked over his shoulder at Ellie. *"Him,* he's crazy," he said. "Ain't he a riot, he's a nut, a real character." Ellie was still listening to the music. His sunglasses told nothing about what he was thinking. He wore a bright orange shirt unbuttoned halfway to show his chest, which was a pale, bluish chest and not muscular like Arnold Friend's. His shirt collar was turned up all around and the very tips of the collar pointed out past his chin as if they were protecting him. He was pressing the transistor radio up against his ear and sat there in a kind of daze, right in the sun.

"He's kinda strange," Connie said.

"Hey, she says you're kinda strange! Kinda strange!" Arnold Friend cried. He pounded on the car to get Ellie's attention. Ellie turned for the first time and Connie saw with shock that he wasn't a kid either—he had a fair hairless face, cheeks reddened slightly as if the veins grew too close to the surface of his skin, the face of a forty-year-old baby. Connie felt a wave of dizziness rise in her at this sight and she stared at him as if waiting for something to change the shock of the moment, make it all right again. Ellie's lips kept shaping words, mumbling along with the words blasting in his ear.

"Maybe you two better go away," Connie said faintly.

"What? How come?" Arnold Friend cried. "We come out here to take you for a ride. It's Sunday." He had the voice of the man on the radio now. It was the same voice, Connie thought. "Don'tcha know it's Sunday all day and honey, no matter who you were with last night today you're with Arnold Friend and don't you forget it!—Maybe you better step out here," he said, and this last was in a different voice. It was a little flatter, as if the heat was finally getting to him.

"No. I got things to do."

"Hey."

"You two better leave."

"We ain't leaving until you come with us."

"Like hell I am—"

"Connie, don't fool around with me. I mean, I mean, don't fool *around,"* he said, shaking his head. He laughed incredulously. He placed his sunglasses on top of his head, carefully, as if he were indeed wearing a wig, and brought the stems down behind his ears. Connie stared at him, another wave of dizziness and fear rising in her so that for a moment he wasn't even in focus but was just a blur, standing there against his gold car, and she had the idea that he had driven up the driveway all right but had come from nowhere before that and belonged nowhere and that everything about him and even about the music that was so familiar to her was only half real.

"If my father comes and sees you—"

"He ain't coming. He's at a barbecue."

"How do you know that?"

"Aunt Tillie's. Right now they're—uh—they're drinking. Sitting around," he said vaguely, squinting as if he were staring all the way to town and over to Aunt Tillie's backyard. Then the vision seemed to get clear and he nodded energetically. "Yeah. Sitting around. There's your sister in a blue dress, huh? And high heels, the poor sad bitch—nothing like you, sweetheart! And your mother's helping some fat woman with the corn, they're cleaning the corn—husking the corn—"

"What fat woman?" Connie cried.

"How do I know what fat woman. I don't know every goddam fat woman in the world!" Arnold Friend laughed.

"Oh, that's Mrs. Hornby. . . . Who invited her?" Connie said. She felt a little lightheaded. Her breath was coming quickly.

"She's too fat. I don't like them fat. I like them the way you are, honey," he said, smiling sleepily at her. They stared at each other for a while, through the screen door. He said softly, "Now what you're going to do is this: you're going to come out that door. You're going to sit up front with me and Ellie's going to sit in the back, the hell with Ellie, right? This isn't Ellie's date. You're my date. I'm your lover, honey."

"What? You're crazy—"

"Yes, I'm your lover. You don't know what that is but you will," he said. "I know that too. I know all about you. But look: it's real nice and you couldn't ask for nobody better than me, or more polite. I always keep my word. I'll tell you how it is, I'm always nice at first, the first time. I'll hold you so tight you won't think you have to try to get away or pretend anything because you'll know you can't. And I'll come inside you where it's all secret and you'll give in to me and you'll love me—"

"Shut up! You're crazy!" Connie said. She backed away from the door. She put her hands against her ears as if she'd heard something terrible, something not meant for her. "People don't talk like that, you're crazy," she muttered. Her heart was almost too big now for her chest and its pumping made sweat break out all over her. She looked out to see Arnold Friend pause and then take a step toward the porch lurching. He almost fell. But, like a clever drunken man, he managed to catch his balance. He wobbled in his high boots and grabbed hold of one of the porch posts.

"Honey?" he said. "You still listening?"

"Get the hell out of here!"

"Be nice, honey. Listen."

"I'm going to call the police—"

He wobbled again and out of the side of his mouth came a fast spat curse, an aside not meant for her to hear. But even this "Christ!" sounded forced. Then he began to smile again. She watched this smile come, awkward as if he were smiling from inside a mask. His whole face was a mask, she thought wildly, tanned down onto his throat but then running out as if he had plastered make-up on his face but had forgotten about his throat.

"Honey—? Listen, here's how it is. I always tell the truth and I promise you this: I ain't coming in that house after you."

"You better not! I'm going to call the police if you—if you don't—"

"Honey," he said, talking right through her voice, "honey, I'm not coming in there but you are coming out here. You know why?"

She was panting. The kitchen looked like a place she had never seen before, some room she had run inside but which wasn't good enough, wasn't going to help her. The kitchen window had never had a curtain, after three years, and there were dishes in the sink for her to do—probably—and if you ran your hand across the table you'd probably feel something sticky there.

"You listening, honey? Hey?"

"—going to call the police—"

"Soon as you touch the phone I don't need to keep my promise and can come inside. You won't want that."

She rushed forward and tried to lock the door. Her fingers were shaking. "But why lock it," Arnold Friend said gently, talking right into her face. "It's just a screen door. It's just nothing." One of his boots was at a strange angle, as if his foot wasn't in it. It pointed out to the left, bent at the ankle. "I mean, anybody can break through a screen door and glass and wood and iron or anything else if he needs to, anybody at all and specially Arnold Friend. If the place got lit up with a fire honey you'd come running out into my arms, right into my arms and safe at home—like you knew I was your lover and'd stopped fooling around. I don't mind a nice shy girl but I don't like no fooling around." Part of those words were spoken with a slight rhythmic lilt, and Connie somehow recognized them—the echo of a song from last year, about a girl rushing into her boy friend's arms and coming home again—

Connie stood barefoot on the linoleum floor, staring at him. "What do you want?" she whispered.

"I want you," he said.

"What?"

"Seen you that night and thought, that's the one, yes sir. I never needed to look any more."

"But my father's coming back. He's coming to get me. I had to wash my hair first—" She spoke in a dry, rapid voice, hardly raising it for him to hear.

"No, your daddy is not coming and yes, you had to wash your hair and you washed it for me. It's nice and shining and all for me, I thank you, sweetheart," he said, with a mock bow, but again he almost lost his balance. He had to bend and adjust his boots. Evidently his feet did not go all the way down; the boots must have been stuffed with something so that he would seem taller. Connie stared out at him and behind him Ellie in the car, who seemed to be looking off toward Connie's right, into nothing. This Ellie said, pulling the words out of the air one after another as if he were just discovering them, "You want me to pull out the phone?"

"Shut your mouth and keep it shut," Arnold Friend said, his face red from bending over or maybe from embarrassment because Connie had seen his boots. "This ain't none of your business."

"What—what are you doing? What do you want?" Connie said. "If I call the police they'll get you, they'll arrest you—"

"Promise was not to come in unless you touch that phone, and I'll keep that promise," he said. He resumed his erect position and tried to force his shoulders back. He sounded like a hero in a movie, declaring something important. He spoke too loudly and it was as if he were speaking to someone behind Connie. "I ain't made plans for coming in that house where I don't belong but just for you to come out to me, the way you should. Don't you know who I am?"

"You're crazy," she whispered. She backed away from the door but did not want to go into another part of the house, as if this would give him permission to come through the door. "What do you. . . . You're crazy, you . . ."

"Huh? What're you saying, honey?"

Her eyes darted everywhere in the kitchen. She could not remember what it was, this room.

"This is how it is, honey: you come out and we'll drive away, have a nice ride. But if you don't come out we're gonna wait till your people come home and then they're all going to get it."

"You want that telephone pulled out?" Ellie said. He held the radio away from his ear and grimaced, as if without the radio the air was too much for him.

"I toldja shut up, Ellie," Arnold Friend said, "you're deaf, get a hearing aid, right? Fix yourself up. This little girl's no trouble and's gonna be nice to me, so Ellie keep to yourself, this ain't your date—right? Don't hem in on me. Don't hog. Don't crush. Don't bird dog. Don't trail me," he said in a rapid meaningless voice, as if he were running through all the expressions he'd learned but was no longer sure which one of them was in style, then rushing on to new ones, making them up with his eyes closed, "Don't crawl under my fence, don't squeeze in my chipmunk hole, don't sniff my glue, suck my popsicle, keep your own greasy fingers on yourself!" He shaded his eyes and peered in at Connie, who was backed against the kitchen table. "Don't mind him honey he's just a creep. He's a dope. Right? I'm the boy for you and like I said you come out here nice like a lady and give me your hand, and nobody else gets hurt, I mean, your nice old bald-headed daddy and your mummy and your sister in her high heels. Because listen: why bring them in this?"

"Leave me alone," Connie whispered.

"Hey, you know that old woman down the road, the one with the chickens and stuff—you know her?"

"She's dead!"

"Dead? What? You know her?" Arnold Friend said.

"She's dead—"

"Don't you like her?"

"She's dead—she's—she isn't here any more—"

"But don't you like her, I mean, you got something against her? Some grudge or something?" Then his voice dipped as if he were conscious of a rudeness. He touched the sunglasses perched on top of his head as if to make sure they were still there. "Now you be a good girl."

"What are you going to do?"

"Just two things, or maybe three," Arnold Friend said. "But I promise it won't last long and you'll like me that way you get to like people you're close to. You will. It's all over for you here, so come on out. You don't want your people in any trouble, do you?"

She turned and bumped against a chair or something, hurting her leg, but she ran into the back room and picked up the telephone. Something roared in her ear, a tiny roaring, and she was so sick with fear that she could do nothing but listen to it—the telephone was clammy and very heavy and her fingers groped down to the dial but were too weak to touch it. She began to scream into the phone, into the roaring. She cried out, she cried for her mother, she felt her breath start jerking back and forth in her lungs as if it were something Arnold Friend were stabbing her with again and again with no tenderness. A noisy sorrowful wailing rose all about her and she was locked inside it the way she was locked inside the house.

After a while she could hear again. She was sitting on the floor with her wet back against the wall.

Arnold Friend was saying from the door, "That's a good girl. Put the phone back."

She kicked the phone away from her.

"No, honey. Pick it up. Put it back right."

She picked it up and put it back. The dial tone stopped.

"That's a good girl. Now you come outside."

She was hollow with what had been fear, but what was now just an emptiness. All that screaming had blasted it out of her. She sat, one leg cramped under her, and deep inside her brain was something like a pinpoint of light that kept going and would not let her relax. She thought, I'm not going to see my mother again. She thought, I'm not going to sleep in my bed again. Her bright green blouse was all wet.

Arnold Friend said, in a gentle-loud voice that was like a stage voice, "The place where you came from ain't there any more, and where you had in mind to go is cancelled out. This place you are now—inside your daddy's house—is nothing but a cardboard box I can knock down any time. You know that and always did know it. You hear me?"

She thought, I have got to think. I have to know what to do.

"We'll go out to a nice field, out in the country here where it smells so nice and it's sunny," Arnold Friend said. "I'll have my arms around you so you won't need to try to get away and I'll show you what love is like, what it does. The hell with this house! It looks solid all right," he said. He ran a fingernail down the screen and the noise did not make Connie shiver, as it would have the day before. "Now put your hand on your heart, honey. Feel that? That feels solid too but we know better, be nice to me, be sweet like you can because what else is there for a girl like you but to be sweet and pretty and give in?—and get away before her people come back?"

She felt her pounding heart. Her hand seemed to enclose it. She thought for the first time in her life that it was nothing that was hers, that belonged to her, but just a pounding, living thing inside this body that wasn't really hers either.

"You don't want them to get hurt," Arnold Friend went on. "Now get up, honey. Get up all by yourself."

She stood.

"Now turn this way. That's right. Come over here to me—Ellie, put that away, didn't I tell you? You dope. You miserable creepy dope," Arnold Friend said. His words were not angry but only part of an incantation. The incantation was kindly. "Now come out through the kitchen to me honey and let's see a smile, try it, you're a brave sweet little girl and now they're eating corn and hotdogs cooked to bursting over an outdoor fire, and they don't know one thing about you and never did and honey you're better than them because not a one of them would have done this for you."

Connie felt the linoleum under her feet; it was cool. She brushed her hair back out of her eyes. Arnold Friend let go of the post tentatively and opened his arms for her, his elbows pointing in toward each other and his wrists limp, to show that this was an embarrassed embrace and a little mocking, he didn't want to make her self-conscious.

She put out her hand against the screen. She watched herself push the door slowly open as if she were safe back somewhere in the other doorway, watching this body and this head of long hair moving out into the sunlight where Arnold Friend waited.

"My sweet little blue-eyed girl," he said, in a half-sung sigh that had nothing to do with her brown eyes but was taken up just the same by the vast sunlit reaches of the land behind him and on all sides of him, so much land that Connie had never seen before and did not recognize except to know that she was going to it.

—1965

What are your reactions to and questions about this work? The following questions may help provoke some ideas.

Probing the Work

1. How does Connie define the difference between her world at home and the world outside her home, before and after the visit by Arnold?
2. How old is Arnold? How much of his speech reflects a typical adolescent male attitude? How much reflects the experience of adulthood? What does his *tone* reveal about his character?

Identifying Issues

3. What causes a girl like Connie to be caught up in rebellious, flirty behavior? To what extent is it "safe" to be that way, and under what circumstances?

MARGE PIERCY

Barbie Doll

Marge Piercy (b. 1936) was born in a poor neighborhood in Detroit and attended the University of Michigan—the first member of her family to attend college. After getting her master's degree from Northwestern University she moved to Chicago and was active in the antiwar, civil rights, and feminist movements. In 1970 she moved to Massachusetts, where she devoted her energies to her writing; her poetry collections include To Be Of Use *(1973) and* Stone, Paper, Knife *(1983).*

This girlchild was born as usual
and presented dolls that did pee-pee
and miniature GE stoves and irons
and wee lipsticks the color of cherry candy.
Then in the magic of puberty, a classmate said:
You have a great big nose and fat legs.

She was healthy, tested intelligent,
possessed strong arms and back,
abundant sexual drive and manual dexterity.
She went to and fro apologizing.
Everyone saw a fat nose on thick legs.

She was advised to play coy,
exhorted to come on hearty,
exercise, diet, smile and wheedle.
Her good nature wore out
like a fan belt.
So she cut off her nose and her legs
and offered them up.

In the casket displayed on satin she lay
with the undertaker's cosmetics painted on,
a turned-up putty nose,
dressed in a pink and white nightie.
Doesn't she look pretty? everyone said.
Consummation at last.
To every woman a happy ending.

—1973

What are your reactions to and questions about this work? The following questions may help provoke some ideas.

Probing the Work

1. What feeling is Piercy expressing about social demands on girls, and what kinds of *images* (p. 79) does she use to convey that feeling?

Identifying Issues

2. What does this poem illustrate about society's standards of beauty for women, and how do these standards influence your life?

MAYA ANGELOU

Phenomenal Woman

In addition to being a poet, Maya Angelou (b. 1928) has been a singer, dancer, actress, playwright, screenwriter, newspaper editor (in Egypt), university administrator (in Ghana), lecturer, and professor (at Wake Forest University). She has written several autobiographical texts, including I Know Why the Caged Bird Sings *(1969), the inspirational* Wouldn't Take Nothing for My Journey Now *(1994), and five collections of poetry, including* Oh Pray My Wings Are Gonna Fit Me Well *and* I Shall Not Be Moved. *She has become a national figure, appearing on talk shows, and reading her poem "On the Pulse of Morning" at President Bill Clinton's inauguration in 1993. Her recent book on women's writing is* Phenomenal Woman *(1995).*

Pretty women wonder where my secret lies.
I'm not cute or built to suit a fashion model's size
But when I start to tell them,
They think I'm telling lies.
I say,
It's in the reach of my arms,
The span of my hips,
The stride of my step,
The curl of my lips.
I'm a woman
Phenomenally.
Phenomenal woman,
That's me.

I walk into a room
Just as cool as you please,
And to a man,
The fellows stand or
Fall down on their knees.
Then they swarm around me,

A hive of honey bees.
I say,
It's the fire in my eyes,
And the flash of my teeth,
The swing in my waist,
And the joy in my feet.
I'm a woman
Phenomenally.
Phenomenal woman,
That's me.

Men themselves have wondered
What they see in me.
They try so much
But they can't touch
My inner mystery.
When I try to show them
They say they still can't see.
I say,
It's in the arch of my back,
The sun of my smile,
The ride of my breasts,
The grace of my style.
I'm a woman
Phenomenally.
Phenomenal woman,
That's me.

Now you understand
Just why my head's not bowed.
I don't shout or jump about
Or have to talk real loud.
When you see me passing
It ought to make you proud.
I say,
It's in the click of my heels,
The bend of my hair,
the palm of my hand,
The need for my care.
'Cause I'm a woman
Phenomenally.
Phenomenal woman,
That's me.

—*1978*

What are your reactions to and questions about this work? The following questions may help provoke some ideas.

Probing the Work

1. What particular aspects of women does Angelou pinpoint as worth celebrating, and what do they represent?

Identifying Issues

2. Contrast Angelou's depiction of feminine beauty with Piercy's. What would Angelou say to the girl described in Piercy's poem?

LINDA PASTAN

Marks

Linda Pastan (b. 1932) was born in New York City and studied at Brandeis and Radcliffe. Her poetry collections include Five Stages of Grief *(1978),* AM/PM *(1982), and* Heroes in Disguise *(1991). She resides in the suburbs of Washington, and is Maryland's poet laureate.*

My husband gives me an A
for last night's supper,
an incomplete for my ironing,
a B plus in bed.
My son says I am average,
an average mother, but if
I put my mind to it
I could improve.
My daughter believes
in Pass/Fail and tells me
I pass. Wait 'til they learn
I'm dropping out.

—1978

What are your reactions to and questions about this work? The following questions may help provoke some ideas.

Probing the Work

1. What does the *speaker* mean when she says, "I'm dropping out"? Why might she be dropping out?

Identifying Issues

2. How does this poem illustrate the variety of pressures and judgments faced by women in traditional roles (even in our own time)?

KATE RUSHIN

The Tired Poem: Last Letter from a Typical Unemployed Black Professional Woman

Kate Rushin (b. 1951) was born in Syracuse, New York, and grew up in Lawnside and Camden, New Jersey. She attended Oberlin College and has taught poetry workshops for both adults and children. A collection of her poems is called The Black Back-Up *(1993).*

So it's a gorgeous afternoon in the park
It's so nice you forget your Attitude
The one your mama taught you
The one that says Don't-Mess-With-Me
You forget until you hear all this
Whistling and lip smacking
You whip around and say
I ain't no damn dog
It's a young guy
His mouth drops open
Excuse me Sister
How you doing
You lie and smile and say
I'm doing good
Everything's cool Brother

Then five minutes later
Hey you Sweet Devil
Hey Girl come here
You tense   sigh   calculate
You know the lean boys and bearded men
Are only cousins and lovers and friends
Sometimes when you say Hey
You get a beautiful surprised smile
Or a good talk

And you've listened to your uncle when he was drunk
Talking about how he has to scuffle to get by and
How he'd wanted to be an engineer
And you talk to Joko who wants to be a singer and
Buy some clothes and get a house for his mother

The Soc. and Psych. books say you're domineering
And you've been to enough
Sisters-Are-Not-Taking-Care-Of-Business discussions
To know where you went wrong
It's decided it had to be the day you decided to go to school
Still you remember the last time you said hey
So you keep on walking
What   you too good to speak
Don't nobody want you no way

You go home   sit on the front steps   listen to
The neighbor boy brag about
How many girls he has pregnant
You ask him if he's going to take care of the babies
And what if he gets taken to court
And what are the girls going to do
He has pictures of them all
This real cute one was supposed to go to college
Dumb broad knew she could get pregnant
I'll just say it's not mine
On the back of this picture of a girl in a cap and gown
It says something like
I love you in my own strange way
Thank you

Then you go in the house
Flip through a magazine and there is
An-Ode-To-My-Black-Queen poem
The kind where the Brother
Thanks all of the Sisters Who Endured
Way back when he didn't have his Shit Together
And you have to wonder where they are now
And you know what happens when you try to resist
All of this Enduring
And you think how this
Thank-you poem is really
No consolation at all
Unless you believe
What the man you met on the train told you
The Black man who worked for the State Department
And had lived in five countries
He said Dear
You were born to suffer
Why don't you give me your address
And I'll come visit

So you try to talk to your friend
About the train and the park and everything
And how it all seems somehow connected
And he says
You're just a Typical Black Professional Woman
Some sisters know how to deal
Right about here
Your end of the conversation phases out
He goes on to say how
Black Professional Women have always had the advantage
You have to stop and think about that one
Maybe you are supposed to be grateful for those sweaty
Beefy-faced white businessmen who try to
Pick you up at lunchtime
And you wonder how many times your friend had
Pennies thrown at him
How many times he's been felt up in the subway
How many times he's been cussed out on the street
You wonder how many times he's been offered
$10 for a piece of himself
$10 for a piece
So you're waiting for the bus
And you look at this young Black man
Asking if you want to make some money
You look at him for a long time
You imagine the little dingy room
It would take twenty minutes or less
You only get $15 for spending all day with thirty kids
Nobody is offering you
Any cash for your poems
You remember again how you have the advantage
How you're not taking care of business
How this man is somebody's kid brother or cousin
And could be your own
So you try to explain how $10 wouldn't pay for
What you'd have to give up
He pushes a handful of sticky crumpled dollars
Into your face and says

Why not
You think I can't pay
Look at that roll
Don't tell me you don't need the money

Cause I know you do
I'll give you fifteen

You maintain your sense of humor
You remember a joke you heard
Well no matter what
A Black Woman never has to starve
Just as long as there are
Dirty toilets and . . .
It isn't funny
Then you wonder if he would at least
Give you the money
And not beat you up
But you're very cool and say
No thanks
You tell him he should spend his time
Looking for someone he cares about
Who cares about him
He waves you off
Get outta my face
I don't have time for that bullshit
You blew it Bitch

Then
(Is it suddenly)
Your voice gets loud
And fills the night street
Your voice gets louder and louder
Your bus comes
The second-shift people file on
The security guards and nurse's aides
Look at you like you're crazy
Get on the damn bus
And remember
You blew it
He turns away
Your bus pulls off
There is no one on the street but you

And then
It is
Very
Quiet

—1979

What are your reactions to and questions about this work? The following questions may help provoke some ideas.

Probing the Work

1. What does each man in the poem represent in terms of male attitudes toward women?

Identifying Issues

2. How does this poem illustrate the extra pressures on poor black women? How do class and ethnicity worsen the situation for women?

SUSAN GLASPELL

Trifles

Susan Glaspell (1882–1948) was born and raised in Davenport, Iowa, and educated at Drake University. She was a columnist for the Des Moines Daily News, *and a prolific writer of short fiction—mostly romances that appeared in popular magazines. Glaspell was married and moved to Greenwich Village in New York, where she began to write—and act in, and produce—her own plays. In the first performance of* Trifles, *she played the role of Mrs. Hale.*

SCENE: *The kitchen in the now abandoned farmhouse of* JOHN WRIGHT, *a gloomy kitchen, and left without having been put in order—unwashed pans under the sink, a loaf of bread outside the breadbox, a dish towel on the table—other signs of incompleted work. At the rear the outer door opens, and the* SHERIFF *comes in, followed by the* COUNTY ATTORNEY *and* HALE. *The* SHERIFF *and* HALE *are men in middle life, the* COUNTY ATTORNEY *is a young man; all are much bundled up and go at once to the stove. They are followed by the two women—the* SHERIFF'S WIFE *first; she is a slight wiry woman, a thin nervous face.* MRS. HALE *is larger and would ordinarily be called more comfortable looking, but she is disturbed now and looks fearfully about as she enters. The women have come in slowly and stand close together near the door.*

COUNTY ATTORNEY: [*rubbing his hands*] This feels good. Come up to the fire, ladies.

MRS. PETERS: [*after taking a step forward*] I'm not—cold.

SHERIFF: [*unbuttoning his overcoat and stepping away from the stove as if to the beginning of official business*] Now, Mr. Hale, before we move things about, you explain to Mr. Henderson just what you saw when you came here yesterday morning.

COUNTY ATTORNEY: By the way, has anything been moved? Are things just as you left them yesterday?

SHERIFF: [*looking about*] It's just the same. When it dropped below zero last night, I thought I'd better send Frank out this morning to make a fire for us—no use getting pneumonia with a big case on; but I told him not to touch anything except the stove—and you know Frank.

COUNTY ATTORNEY: Somebody should have been left here yesterday.

SHERIFF: Oh—yesterday.When I had to send Frank to Morris Center for that man who went crazy—I want you to know I had my hands full yesterday. I knew you could get back from Omaha by today, and as long as I went over everything here myself—

COUNTY ATTORNEY: Well, Mr. Hale, tell just what happened when you came here yesterday morning.

HALE: Harry and I had started to town with a load of potatoes. We came along the road from my place; and as I got here, I said, "I'm going to see if I can't get John Wright to go in with me on a party telephone." I spoke to Wright about it once before, and he put me off, saying folks talked too much anyway, and all he asked was peace and quiet—I guess you know about how much he talked himself; but I thought maybe if I went to the house and talked about it before his wife, though I said to Harry that I didn't know as what his wife wanted made much difference to John—

COUNTY ATTORNEY: Let's talk about that later, Mr. Hale. I do want to talk about that, but tell now just what happened when you got to the house.

HALE: I didn't hear or see anything; I knocked at the door, and still it was all quiet inside. I knew they must be up, it was past eight o'clock. So I knocked again, and I thought I heard somebody say, "Come in." I wasn't sure, I'm not sure yet, but I opened the door—this door [*indicating the door by which the two women are still standing*], and there in that rocker—[*pointing to it*] sat Mrs. Wright. [*They all look at the rocker.*]

COUNTY ATTORNEY: What—was she doing?

HALE: She was rockin' back and forth. She had her apron in her hand and was kind of—pleating it.

COUNTY ATTORNEY: And how did she—look?

HALE: Well, she looked queer.

COUNTY ATTORNEY: How do you mean—queer?

HALE: Well, as if she didn't know what she was going to do next. And kind of done up.

COUNTY ATTORNEY: How did she seem to feel about your coming?

HALE: Why, I don't think she minded—one way or other. She didn't pay much attention. I said, "How do, Mrs. Wright, it's cold, ain't it?" And she said, "Is it?"—and went on kind of pleating at her apron. Well, I was surprised; she didn't ask me to come up to the stove, or to set down, but just sat there, not even looking at me, so I said, "I want to see John." And then she—laughed. I guess you would call it a laugh. I thought of Harry and the team outside, so I said a little sharp: "Can't I see John?" "No," she says, kind o' dull like. "Ain't he home?" says I. "Yes," says she, "he's home." "Then why can't I see him?" I asked her, out of patience. " 'Cause he's dead," says she. *"Dead?"* says I. She just nodded her head, not getting a bit excited, but rockin' back and forth. "Why—where is he?" says I, not knowing what to say. She just pointed upstairs—like that [*himself pointing to the room above*]. I got up, with the idea of going up there. I walked from there to here—then I says, "Why, what did he die of?" "He died of a rope around his neck," says she, and just went on pleatin' at her apron. Well, I went out and called Harry. I thought I might—need help. We went upstairs, and there he was lyin'—

COUNTY ATTORNEY: I think I'd rather have you go into that upstairs, where you can point it all out. Just go on now with the rest of the story.

HALE: Well, my first thought was to get that rope off. I looked . . . [*Stops, his face twitches.*] . . . but Harry, he went up to him, and he said, "No, he's dead all right, and we'd better not touch anything." So we went back downstairs. She was still sitting that same way. "Has anybody been notified?" I asked. "No," says she, unconcerned. "Who did this, Mrs. Wright?" said Harry. He said it businesslike—and she stopped pleatin' of her apron. "I don't know," she says. "You don't *know?"* says Harry. "No," says she, "Weren't you sleepin' in the bed with him?" says Harry. "Yes," says she, "but I was on the inside." "Somebody slipped a rope round his neck and strangled him, and you didn't wake up?" says Harry. "I didn't wake up," she said after him. We must 'a looked as if we didn't see how that could be, for after a minute she said, "I sleep sound." Harry was going to ask her more questions, but I said maybe we ought to let her tell her story first to the coroner, or the sheriff, so Harry went fast as he could to Rivers' place, where there's a telephone.

COUNTY ATTORNEY: And what did Mrs. Wright do when she knew that you had gone for the coroner?

HALE: She moved from that chair to this over here . . . [*Pointing to a small chair in the corner.*] . . . and just sat there with her hands held together and looking down. I got a feeling that I ought to make some conversation, so I said I had come in to see if John wanted to put in a telephone, and at that she started to laugh, and then she stopped and looked at me—scared. [*The* COUNTY ATTORNEY, *who has had his notebook out, makes a note.*] I dunno, maybe it wasn't scared. I wouldn't like to say it was. Soon Harry got back, and then Dr. Lloyd came, and you, Mr. Peters, and so I guess that's all I know that you don't.

COUNTY ATTORNEY: [*looking around*] I guess we'll go upstairs first—and then out to the barn and around there. [*To the* SHERIFF.] You're convinced that there was nothing important here—nothing that would point to any motive?

SHERIFF: Nothing here but kitchen things.

[*The* COUNTY ATTORNEY, *after again looking around the kitchen, opens the door of a cupboard closet. He gets up on a chair and looks on a shelf. Pulls his hand away, sticky.*]

COUNTY ATTORNEY: Here's a nice mess.

[*The women draw nearer.*]

MRS. PETERS: [*to the other woman*] Oh, her fruit; it did freeze. [*To the* LAWYER.] She worried about that when it turned so cold. She said the fir'd go out and her jars would break.

SHERIFF: Well, can you beat the women! Held for murder and worryin' about her preserves.

COUNTY ATTORNEY: I guess before we're through she may have something more serious than preserves to worry about.

HALE: Well, women are used to worrying over trifles. [*The two women move a little closer together.*]

COUNTY ATTORNEY: [*with the gallantry of a young politician*] And yet, for all their worries, what would we do without the ladies? [*The women do not unbend. He goes to the sink, takes a dipperful of water from the pail and, pouring it into a basin, washes his hands. Starts to wipe them on the roller towel, turns it for a cleaner place.*] Dirty towels! [*Kicks his foot against the pans under the sink.*] Not much of a housekeeper, would you say, ladies?

MRS. HALE: [*stiffly*] There's a great deal of work to be done on a farm.

COUNTY ATTORNEY: To be sure. And yet . . . [*With a little bow to her.*] . . . I know there are some Dickson county farmhouses which do not have such roller towels. [*He gives it a pull to expose its full length again.*]

MRS. HALE: Those towels get dirty awful quick. Men's hands aren't always as clean as they might be.

COUNTY ATTORNEY: Ah, loyal to your sex, I see. But you and Mrs. Wright were neighbors. I suppose you were friends, too.

MRS. HALE: [*shaking her head*] I've not seen much of her of late years. I've not been in this house—it's more than a year.

COUNTY ATTORNEY: And why was that? You didn't like her?

MRS. HALE: I liked her all well enough. Farmers' wives have their hands full, Mr. Henderson. And then—

COUNTY ATTORNEY: Yes—?

MRS. HALE: [*looking about*] It never seemed a very cheerful place.

COUNTY ATTORNEY: No—it's not cheerful. I shouldn't say she had the home-making instinct.

MRS. HALE: Well, I don't know as Wright had, either.

COUNTY ATTORNEY: You mean that they didn't get on very well?

MRS. HALE: No, I don't mean anything. But I don't think a place'd be any cheerfuler for John Wright's being in it.

COUNTY ATTORNEY: I'd like to talk more of that a little later. I want to get the lay of things upstairs now. [*He goes to the left, where three steps lead to a stair door.*]

SHERIFF: I suppose anything Mrs. Peters does'll be all right. She was to take in some clothes for her, you know, and a few little things. We left in such a hurry yesterday.

COUNTY ATTORNEY: Yes, but I would like to see what you take, Mrs. Peters, and keep an eye out for anything that might be of use to us.

MRS. PETERS: Yes, Mr. Henderson.

[*The women listen to the men's steps on the stairs, then look about the kitchen.*]

MRS. HALE: I'd hate to have men coming into my kitchen, snooping around and criticizing. [*She arranges the pans under sink which the* LAWYER *had shoved out of place.*]

MRS. PETERS: Of course it's no more than their duty.

MRS. HALE: Duty's all right, but I guess that deputy sheriff that came out to make the fire might have got a little of this on. [*Gives the roller towel a pull.*] Wish I'd thought of that sooner. Seems mean to talk about her for not having things slicked up when she had to come away in such a hurry.

MRS. PETERS: [*who has gone to a small table in the left rear corner of the room, and lifted one end of a towel that covers a pan*] She had bread set. [*Stands still.*]

MRS. HALE: [*eyes fixed on a loaf of bread beside the breadbox, which is on a low shelf at the other side of the room. Moves slowly toward it*] She was going to put this in there. [*Picks up loaf, then abruptly drops it. In a manner of returning to familiar things.*] It's a shame about her fruit. I wonder if it's all gone. [*Gets up on the chair and looks.*] I think there's some here that's all right, Mrs. Peters. Yes—here; [*Holding it toward the window.*] this is cherries, too. [*Looking again.*] I declare I believe that's the only one. [*Gets down, bottle in her hand. Goes to the sink and wipes it off on the outside.*] She'll feel awful bad after all her hard work in the hot weather. I remember the afternoon I put up my cherries last summer. [*She puts the bottle on the big kitchen table, center of the room, front table. With a sigh, is about to sit down in the rocking chair. Before she is seated realizes what chair it is; with a slow look at it, steps back. The chair, which she has touched, rocks back and forth.*]

MRS. PETERS: Well, I must get those things from the front room closet. [*She goes to the door at the right, but after looking into the other room steps back.*] You coming with me, Mrs. Hale? You could help me carry them. [*They go into the other room; reappear,* MRS. PETERS *carrying a dress and skirt,* MRS. HALE *following with a pair of shoes.*]

MRS. PETERS: My, it's cold in there. [*She puts the cloth on the big table, and hurries to the stove.*]

MRS. HALE: [*examining the skirt*] Wright was close. I think maybe that's why she kept so much to herself. She didn't even belong to the Ladies' Aid. I suppose she felt she couldn't do her part, and then you don't enjoy things when you feel shabby. She used to wear pretty clothes and be lively, when she was Minnie Foster, one of the town girls singing in the choir. But that—oh, that was thirty years ago. This all you was to take in?

MRS. PETERS: She said she wanted an apron. Funny thing to want, for there isn't much to get you dirty in jail, goodness knows. But I suppose just to make her feel more natural. She said they was in the top drawer in this cupboard. Yes, here. And then her little shawl that always hung behind the door. [*Opens stair door and looks.*] Yes, here it is. [*Quickly shuts door leading upstairs.*]

MRS. HALE: [*abruptly moving toward her*] Mrs. Peters?

MRS. PETERS: Yes, Mrs. Hale?

MRS. HALE: Do you think she did it?

MRS. PETERS: [*in a frightened voice*] Oh, I don't know.

MRS. HALE: Well, I don't think she did. Asking for an apron and her little shawl. Worrying about her fruit.

MRS. PETERS: [*starts to speak, glances up, where footsteps are heard in the room above. In a low voice*] Mr. Peters says it looks bad for her. Mr. Henderson is awful sarcastic in speech, and he'll make fun of her sayin' she didn't wake up.

MRS. HALE: Well, I guess John Wright didn't wake when they was slipping that rope under his neck.

MRS. PETERS: No, it's strange. It must have been done awful crafty and still. They say it was such a—funny way to kill a man, rigging it all up like that.

MRS. HALE: That's just what Mr. Hale said. There was a gun in the house. He says that's what he can't understand.

MRS. PETERS: Mr. Henderson said coming out that what was needed for the case was a motive; something to show anger, or—sudden feeling.

MRS. HALE: [*who is standing by the table*] Well, I don't see any signs of anger around here. [*She puts her hand on the dish towel which lies on the table, stands looking down at the table, one half of which is clean, the other half messy.*] It's wiped here. [*Makes a move as if to finish work, then turns and looks at loaf of bread outside the breadbox. Drops towel. In that voice of coming back to familiar things.*] Wonder how they are finding things upstairs? I hope she had it a little more red-up there. You know, it seems kind of *sneaking*. Locking her up in town and then coming out here and trying to get her own house to turn against her!

MRS. PETERS: But, Mrs. Hale, the law is the law.

MRS. HALE: I s'pose 'tis. [*Unbuttoning her coat.*] Better loosen up your things, Mrs. Peters. You won't feel them when you go out. [MRS. PETERS *takes off her fur tippet, goes to hang it on hook at the back of room, stands looking at the under part of the small corner table.*]

MRS. PETERS: She was piecing a quilt. [*She brings the large sewing basket, and they look at the bright pieces.*]

MRS. HALE: It's log cabin pattern. Pretty, isn't it? I wonder if she was goin' to quilt or just knot it? [*Footsteps have been heard coming down the stairs. The* SHERIFF *enters, followed by* HALE *and the* COUNTY ATTORNEY.]

SHERIFF: They wonder if she was going to quilt it or just knot it. [*The men laugh, the women look abashed.*]

COUNTY ATTORNEY: [*rubbing his hands over the stove*] Frank's fire didn't do much up there, did it? Well, let's go out to the barn and get that cleared up. [*The men go outside.*]

MRS. HALE: [*resentfully*] I don't know as there's anything so strange, our takin' up our time with little things while we're waiting for them to get the evidence. [*She sits down at the big table, smoothing out a block with decision.*] I don't see as it's anything to laugh about.

MRS. PETERS: [*apologetically*] Of course they've got awful important things on their minds. [*Pulls up a chair and joins* MRS. HALE *at the table.*]

MRS. HALE: [*examining another block*] Mrs. Peters, look at this one. Here, this is the one she was working on, and look at the sewing! All the rest of it has been so nice and even. And look at this! It's all over the place! Why, it looks as if she didn't know what she was about! [*After she has said this, they look at each other, then started to glance back at the door. After an instant* MRS. HALE *has pulled at a knot and ripped the sewing.*]

MRS. PETERS: Oh, what are you doing, Mrs. Hale?

MRS. HALE: [*mildly*] Just pulling out a stitch or two that's not sewed very good. [*Threading a needle.*] Bad sewing always made me fidgety.

MRS. PETERS: [*nervously*] I don't think we ought to touch things.

MRS. HALE: I'll just finish up this end. [*Suddenly stopping and leaning forward.*] Mrs. Peters?

MRS. PETERS: Yes, Mrs. Hale?

MRS. HALE: What do you suppose she was so nervous about?

MRS. PETERS: Oh—I don't know. I don't know as she was nervous. I sometimes sew awful queer when I'm just tired. [MRS. HALE *starts to say something, looks at* MRS. PETERS, *then goes on sewing.*] Well, I must get these things wrapped up. They may be through sooner than we think. [*Putting apron and other things together.*] I wonder where I can find a piece of paper, and string.

MRS. HALE: In that cupboard, maybe.

MRS. PETERS: [*looking in cupboard*] Why, here's a birdcage. [*Holds it up.*] Did she have a bird, Mrs. Hale?

MRS. HALE: Why, I don't know whether she did or not—I've not been here for so long. There was a man around last year selling canaries cheap, but I don't know as she took one; maybe she did. She used to sing real pretty herself.

MRS. PETERS: [*glancing around*] Seems funny to think of a bird here. But she must have had one, or why should she have a cage? I wonder what happened to it?

MRS. HALE: I s'pose maybe the cat got it.

MRS. PETERS: No, she didn't have a cat. She's got that feeling some people have about cats—being afraid of them. My cat got in her room, and she was real upset and asked me to take it out.

MRS. HALE: My sister Bessie was like that. Queer, ain't it?

MRS. PETERS: [*examining the cage*] Why, look at this door. It's broke. One hinge is pulled apart.

MRS. HALE: [*looking, too*] Looks as if someone must have been rough with it.

MRS. PETERS: Why, yes. [*She brings the cage forward and puts it on the table.*]

MRS. HALE: I wish if they're going to find any evidence they'd be about it. I don't like this place.

MRS. PETERS: But I'm awful glad you came with me, Mrs. Hale. It would be lonesome for me sitting here alone.

MRS. HALE: It would, wouldn't it? [*Dropping her sewing.*] But I tell you what I do wish, Mrs. Peters. I wish I had come over sometimes when *she* was here. I—[*Looking around the room.*]—wish I had.

MRS. PETERS: But of course you were awful busy, Mrs. Hale—your house and your children.

MRS. HALE: I could've come. I stayed away because it weren't cheerful—and that's why I ought to have come. I—I've never liked this place. Maybe because it's down in a hollow, and you don't see the road. I dunno what it is, but it's a lonesome place and always was. I wish I had come over to see Minnie Foster sometimes. I can see now—[*Shakes her head.*]

MRS. PETERS: Well, you mustn't reproach yourself, Mrs. Hale. Somehow we just don't see how it is with other folks until—something comes up.

MRS. HALE: Not having children makes less work—but it makes a quiet house, and Wright out to work all day, and no company when he did come in. Did you know John Wright, Mrs. Peters?

MRS. PETERS: Not to know him; I've seen him in town. They say he was a good man.

MRS. HALE: Yes—good; he didn't drink, and kept his word as well as most, I guess, and paid his debts. But he was a hard man, Mrs. Peters. Just to pass the time of day with him. [*Shivers.*] Like a raw wind that gets to the bone. [*Pauses, her eye falling on the cage.*] I should think she would 'a wanted a bird. But what do you suppose went with it?

MRS. PETERS: I don't know, unless it got sick and died. [*She reaches over and swings the broken door, swings it again; both women watch it.*]

MRS. HALE: You weren't raised round here, were you? [MRS. PETERS *shakes her head.*] You didn't know—her?

MRS. PETERS: Not till they brought her yesterday.

MRS. HALE: She—come to think of it, she was kind of like a bird herself—real sweet and pretty, but kind of timid and—fluttery. How—she—did—

change. [*Silence; then as if struck by a happy thought and relieved to get back to everyday things.*] Tell you what, Mrs. Peters, why don't you take the quilt in with you? It might take up her mind.

MRS. PETERS: Why, I think that's a real nice idea, Mrs. Hale. There couldn't possible be any objection to it, could there? Now, just what would I take? I wonder if her patches are in here—and her things. [*They look in the sewing basket.*]

MRS. HALE: Here's some red. I expect this has got sewing things in it [*Brings out a fancy box.*] What a pretty box. Looks like something somebody would give you. Maybe her scissors are in here. [*Opens box. Suddenly puts her hand to her nose.*] Why—[MRS. PETERS *bends nearer, then turns her face away.*] There's something wrapped up in this piece of silk.

MRS. PETERS: Why, this isn't her scissors.

MRS. HALE: [*lifting the silk*]. Oh, Mrs. Peters—it's—[MRS. PETERS *bends closer.*]

MRS. PETERS: It's the bird.

MRS. HALE: [*jumping up*]. But, Mrs. Peters—look at it. Its neck! Look at its neck! It's all—other side *to.*

MRS. PETERS: Somebody—wrung—its neck. [*Their eyes meet. A look of growing comprehension of horror. Steps are heard outside.* MRS. HALE *slips box under quilt pieces, and sinks into her chair. Enter* SHERIFF *and* COUNTY ATTORNEY. MRS. PETERS *rises.*]

COUNTY ATTORNEY: [*as one turning from serious things to little pleasantries*] Well, ladies, have you decided whether she was going to quilt it or knot it?

MRS. PETERS: We think she was going to—knot it.

COUNTY ATTORNEY: Well, that's interesting, I'm sure. [*Seeing the birdcage.*] Has the bird flown?

MRS. HALE: [*putting more quilt pieces over the box*] We think the—cat got it.

COUNTY ATTORNEY: [*preoccupied*]. Is there a cat?

[MRS. HALE *glances in a quick covert way at* MRS. PETERS.]

MRS. PETERS: Well, not now. They're superstitious, you know. They leave.

COUNTY ATTORNEY: [*to* SHERIFF PETERS, *continuing an interrupted conversation*] No sign at all of anyone having come from the outside. Their own rope. Now let's go up again and go over it piece by piece. [*They start upstairs.*] It would have to have been someone who knew just the—

[MRS. PETERS *sits down. The two women sit there not looking at one another, but as if peering into something and at the same time holding back. When they talk now, it is the manner of feeling their way over strange ground, as if afraid of what they are saying, but as if they cannot help saying it.*]

MRS. HALE: She liked the bird. She was going to bury it in that pretty box.

MRS. PETERS: [*in a whisper*] When I was a girl—my kitten—there was a boy took a hatchet, and before my eyes—and before I could get there—[*Covers her face an instant.*] If they hadn't held me back, I would have—[*Catches herself, looks upstairs where steps are heard, falters weakly.*]—hurt him.

MRS. HALE: [*with a slow look around her*]. I wonder how it would seem never to have had any children around. [*Pause.*] No, Wright wouldn't like the bird—a thing that sang. She used to sing. He killed that, too.

MRS. PETERS: [*moving uneasily*] We don't know who killed the bird.

MRS. HALE: I knew John Wright.

MRS. PETERS: It was an awful thing was done in this house that night, Mrs. Hale. Killing a man while he slept, slipping a rope around his neck that choked the life out of him.

MRS. HALE: His neck. Choked the life out of him.

[*Her hand goes out and rests on the birdcage.*]

MRS. PETERS: [*with a rising voice*] We don't know who killed him. We don't *know.*

MRS. HALE: [*her own feeling not interrupted*] If there'd been years and years of nothing, then a bird to sing to you, it would be awful—still, after the bird was still.

MRS. PETERS: [*something within her speaking*] I know what stillness is. When we homesteaded in Dakota, and my first baby died—after he was two years old, and me with no other then—

MRS. HALE: [*moving*] How soon do you suppose they'll be through, looking for evidence?

MRS. PETERS: I know what stillness is. [*Pulling herself back.*] The law has got to punish crime, Mrs. Hale.

MRS. HALE: [*not as if answering that*] I wish you'd seen Minnie Foster when she wore a white dress with blue ribbons and stood up there in the choir and sang. [*A look around the room.*] Oh, I *wish* I'd come over here once in a while! That was a crime! That was a crime! Who's going to punish that?

MRS. PETERS: [*looking upstairs*] We mustn't—take on.

MRS. HALE: I might have known she needed help! I know how things can be—for women. I tell you, it's queer, Mrs. Peters. We live close together and we live far apart. We all go through the same things—it's all just a different kind of the same thing. [*Brushes her eyes, noticing the bottle of fruit, reaches out for it.*] If I was you, I wouldn't tell her her fruit was gone. Tell her it *ain't.* Tell her it's all right. Take this in to prove it to her. She—she may never know whether it was broke or not.

MRS. PETERS: [*takes the bottle, looks about for something to wrap it in; takes petticoat from the clothes brought from the other room, very nervously begins winding this around the bottle. In a false voice*] My, it's a good thing the men couldn't hear us. Wouldn't they just laugh! Getting all stirred up over a little thing like a—dead canary. As if that could have anything to do with—with—wouldn't they *laugh!*

[*The men are heard coming downstairs.*]

MRS. HALE: [*under her breath*] Maybe they would—maybe they wouldn't.

COUNTY ATTORNEY: No, Peters, it's all perfectly clear except a reason for doing it. But you know juries when it comes to women. If there was some definite thing. Something to show—something to make a story about—a thing that would connect up with this strange way of doing it.

[*The women's eyes meet for an instant. Enter* HALE *from outer door.*]

MRS. HALE: Well, I've got the team around. Pretty cold out there.

COUNTY ATTORNEY: I'm going to stay here awhile by myself. [*To the* SHERIFF.] You can send Frank out for me, can't you? I want to go over everything. I'm not satisfied that we can't do better.

SHERIFF: Do you want to see what Mrs. Peters is going to take in?

[*The* LAWYER *goes to the table, picks up the apron, laughs.*]

COUNTY ATTORNEY: Oh I guess they're not very dangerous things the ladies have picked up. [*Moves a few things about, disturbing the quilt pieces which cover the box. Steps back.*] No, Mrs. Peters doesn't need supervising. For that matter, a sheriff's wife is married to the law. Ever think of it that way, Mrs. Peters?

MRS. PETERS: Not—just that way.

SHERIFF: [*chuckling*] Married to the law. [*Moves toward the other room.*] I just want you to come in here a minute, George. We ought to take a look at these windows.

COUNTY ATTORNEY: [*scoffingly*] Oh, windows!

SHERIFF: We'll be right out, Mr. Hale.

[HALE *goes outside. The* SHERIFF *follows the* COUNTY ATTORNEY *into the other room. Then* MRS. HALE *rises, hands tight together, looking intensely at* MRS. PETERS, *whose eyes take a slow turn, finally meeting* MRS. HALE'S. *A moment* MRS. HALE *holds her, then her own eyes point the way to where the box is concealed. Suddenly* MRS. PETERS *throws back quilt pieces and tries to put the box in the bag she is wearing. It is too big. She opens box, starts to take the bird out, cannot touch it, goes to pieces, stands there helpless. Sound of a knob turning in the other room.* MRS. HALE *snatches the box and puts it in the pocket of her big coat. Enter* COUNTY ATTORNEY *and* SHERIFF.]

COUNTY ATTORNEY: [*facetiously*] Well, Henry, at least we found out that she was not going to quilt it. She was going to—what is it you call it, ladies?

MRS. HALE: [*her hand against her pocket*] We call it—knot it, Mr. Henderson.

Curtain

—1916

What are your reactions to and questions about this work? The following questions may help provoke some ideas.

Probing the Work

1. Mr. Hale says, "Women are used to worrying about trifles." What does he mean by this? What do the women in this play worry about? What "clues" can they see that the men can't?
2. Is the crime justified, according to the author? According to you?
3. In *Sister's Choice* critic Elaine Showalter points out that the quilt in women's fiction often represents the common threads of women's culture; piecing and patchwork have become *metaphors* "for a Female Aesthetic, for sisterhood, and for a politics of feminist survival." [See "Aunt Jennifer's Tigers" (p. 197) and "Everyday Use" (p. 483) for other illustrations of this.] If so, what does it signify when the women say, in response to Mr. Hale's question about how Minnie was going to finish the unsewn parts of the quilt, "We think she was going to—knot it"?

Identifying Issues

4. The play points out the differences between men's and women's perception, behavior, and judgments. Do you agree with the author's implied conclusion?
5. This play was written in 1916; to what extent could it be written today? What changes would have to be made to update it? How do the gender differences described here still obstruct understanding between the sexes?

WRITING ASSIGNMENT SEQUENCE (CONTINUED FROM PAGE 192)

4. Making Connections

Select one of the following questions and write an informal response in which you connect your own ideas with those conveyed in the works of this cluster, and/or make connections among the works themselves.

A. What are the various states of mind among the women depicted in the works of this cluster as they act out traditional feminine roles? How are they coping with their oppressed status? What are the conflicts they are experiencing between the demands of traditional gender roles and their individualistic yearnings?

B. How have women "furnished the rooms" that they have claimed for themselves, as Virginia Woolf describes it? What are the various accommodations women have found for themselves, as described in the works in this cluster?

C. Have the depictions of women in this cluster changed the perception of women, or of feminism, that you expressed in your *brainstorming* exercise?

5. Putting It All Together

Write an essay that combines what you think about the topic *Phenomenal Woman* with what you now understand about the readings.

- Collect your informal writing, notes, and reading-journal entries on this topic and decide what will be the focus of your essay.
- Outline your essay. Select the literary passages and personal details you might use to illustrate and support your main focus.
- Write a draft of your essay in which you bring together what you think about the subject with what you understand about the readings. Try to include in your draft one or more *literary terms*.
- Share what you've written with your classmates and instructor, then revise it according to their recommendations.

Writing Tip: Rules to Question

Sometimes you need to rethink those rules you may have learned in the past:

- Never use "*I*".
  Why not? It's okay to write about yourself, so long as you don't call more attention to yourself than to the focus of your essay.
- Never start a sentence with *and* or *because*.
  Because your teachers didn't want you to write sentence fragments, they taught you this rule. *And* if you tend to write fragments, it might be a good idea to obey it still. But it isn't illegal to do so. Just remember that when you begin a sentence with either word, punctuate properly.
- Don't use contractions.
  Oops, we just did. Your decision to use contractions depends on your audience, and your subject. If the writing is fairly informal, as it is here, you could use an occasional contraction. Just don't make it a habit.
- Never write one- or two-sentence paragraphs.
  You need to support your points, so this is a good rule in general, but

sometimes you can use a one-sentence paragraph for emphasis or for shock value. (See "The Yellow Wallpaper," p. 842.)

When good writers break rules, they understand the original purpose of those rules!

CrossClusters

In your paper you might want to consider how the following works located elsewhere in this book deal with women's issues:

- Alice Munro, "Boys and Girls" (p. 109)
- Rita Dove, "Adolescence III" (p. 120)
- Michael Dorris, "The Contest" (p. 374)
- Jamaica Kincaid, "Girl" (p. 377)
- Fawziyya Abu-Khalid, "Mother's Inheritance" (p. 379)
- Marsha Norman, *'Night, Mother* (p. 400)
- Ernest Hemingway, "Hills Like White Elephants" (p. 611)
- Muriel Rukeyser, "Looking at Each Other" (p. 619)
- Nathaniel Hawthorne, "The Birth-mark" (p. 633)
- Kate Chopin, "The Story of an Hour" (p. 646)
- John Updike, "Wife Wooing" (p. 653)
- Henrik Ibsen, *A Doll's House* (p. 659)
- Mme. de Beaumont, "Beauty and the Beast" (p. 732)
- William Shakespeare, *A Midsummer Night's Dream* (p. 766)
- Robert Browning, "Porphyria's Lover" (p. 840)
- Charlotte Perkins Gilman, "The Yellow Wallpaper" (p. 842)
- Eugène Ionesco, *The Lesson* (p. 904)

12

A DREAM DEFERRED

WRITING ASSIGNMENT SEQUENCE

1. Thinking About . . . a Dream Deferred

Brainstorming: Write down the term *a Dream Deferred,* and ask yourself how it applies to the African-American experience. Write down the possible results that come to mind when you speculate what happens when a person has to continually defer his or her dream of freedom and equality because of societal barriers and prejudices. (Keep in mind the many variations possible, since there is no single condition that applies to all people of a particular race. For more on *brainstorming,* see page 26.)

2. Enacting the Topic

Role-Playing: Two people answer an ad for an apartment to rent: one is white, one is black. Write a dialogue that illustrates one possible way the real estate agent might treat each of the two applicants.

3. Responding to the Readings

As you read the works in this cluster, jot down in your response journals questions you have about the works, and comment on passages you find provocative or puzzling. Consider the questions following each reading for journal writing and prepare to discuss your reactions in class.

CLUSTER ESSAY

MARTIN LUTHER KING, JR.

I Have a Dream

Martin Luther King, Jr. (1929–1968) was born in Atlanta, and was pastor of a Baptist church in Montgomery, Alabama. In 1956, as president of the Montgomery Improvement Association, he helped organize a transportation boycott in response to the arrest of Rosa Parks, and as president of the Southern Christian Leadership Conference he led nonviolent marches and protests throughout the South, to Chicago, and to Washington, D.C. In 1963 he delivered the following speech to over 200,000 people in front of the Lincoln Memorial in Washington. The next year he was awarded the Nobel Peace Prize. King wrote several books including The Measure of a Man *(1968) and* Trumpet of Conscience *(1968). He was assassinated on April 3, 1968.*

Five score years ago, a great American, in whose symbolic shadow we stand, signed the Emancipation Proclamation. This momentous decree came as a great beacon light of hope to millions of Negro slaves who had been seared in the flames of withering injustice. It came as a joyous daybreak to end the long night of captivity.

But one hundred years later, we must face the tragic fact that the Negro is still not free. One hundred years later, the life of the Negro is still sadly crippled by the manacles of segregation and the chains of discrimination. One hundred years later, the Negro lives on a lonely island of poverty in the midst of a vast ocean of material prosperity. One hundred years later, the Negro is still languished in the corners of American society and finds himself an exile in his own land. So we have come here today to dramatize an appalling condition.

In a sense we have come to our nation's Capital to cash a check. When the architects of our republic wrote the magnificent words of the Constitution and the Declaration of Independence, they were signing a promissory note to which every American was to fall heir. This note was a promise that all men would be guaranteed the unalienable rights of life, liberty, and the pursuit of happiness.

It is obvious today that America has defaulted on this promissory note insofar as her citizens of color are concerned. Instead of honoring this sacred obligation, America has given the Negro people a bad check; a check which has come back marked "insufficient funds." But we refuse to believe that the bank of justice is bankrupt. We refuse to believe that there are insufficient funds in the great vaults of opportunity of this nation. So we have come to cash this check—a check that will give us upon demand the riches of freedom and the security of justice. We have also come to this hallowed spot to remind America of the fierce urgency of *now*. This is no time to engage in the luxury of cooling off or to take the tranquilizing drugs of gradualism. *Now* is the time to make real the promises of Democracy. *Now* is the time to rise from the dark and desolate valley of segregation to the sunlit path of racial justice. *Now* is the time to open the doors of opportunity to all of God's children. *Now* is the time to lift our nation from the quicksands of racial injustice to the solid rock of brotherhood.

It would be fatal for the nation to overlook the urgency of the moment and to underestimate the determination of the Negro. This sweltering summer of the Negro's legitimate discontent will not pass until there is an invigorating autumn of freedom and equality. 1963 is not an end, but a beginning. Those who hope that the Negro needed to blow off steam and will now be content will have a rude awakening if the nation returns to business as usual. There will be neither rest nor tranquility in America until the Negro is granted his citizenship rights. The whirlwinds of revolt will continue to shake the foundation of our nation until the bright day of justice emerges.

But there is something that I must say to my people who stand on the warm threshold which leads into the palace of justice. In the process of gaining our rightful place we must not be guilty of wrongful deeds. Let us not seek to satisfy our thirst for freedom by drinking from the cup of bitterness and hatred. We must forever conduct our struggle on the high plane of dignity and discipline. We must not allow our creative protest to degenerate into physical violence. Again and again we must rise to the majestic heights of meeting physical force with soul force. The marvelous new militancy which has engulfed the Negro community must not lead us to a distrust of all white people, for many of our white brothers, as evidenced by their presence here today, have come to realize that their destiny is tied up with our destiny and their freedom in inextricably bound to our freedom. We cannot walk alone.

And as we walk, we must make the pledge that we shall march ahead. We cannot turn back. There are those who are asking the devotees of civil rights, "When will you be satisfied?" We can never be satisfied as long as the Negro is the victim of the unspeakable horrors of police brutality. We can never be satisfied as long as our bodies, heavy with the fatigue of travel, cannot gain lodging in the motels of the highways and the hotels of the cities. We cannot be satisfied as long as the Negro's basic mobility is from a smaller ghetto to a larger one. We can never be satisfied as long as a Negro in Mississippi cannot vote and a Negro in New York believes he has nothing for which to vote. No, no, we are not satisfied, and we will not be satisfied until justice rolls down like waters and righteousness like a mighty stream.

I am not unmindful that some of you have come here out of great trials and tribulations. Some of you have come fresh from narrow jail cells. Some of you have come from areas where your quest for freedom left you battered by the storms of persecution and staggered by the winds of police brutality. You have been the veterans of creative suffering. Continue to work with the faith that unearned suffering is redemptive.

Go back to Mississippi, go back to Alabama, go back to South Carolina, go back to Georgia, go back to Louisiana, go back to the slums and ghettos of our northern cities, knowing that somehow this situation can and will be changed. Let us not wallow in the valley of despair.

I say to you today, my friends, that in spite of the difficulties and frustrations of the moment I still have a dream. It is a dream deeply rooted in the American dream.

I have a dream that one day this nation will rise up and live out the true meaning of its creed: "We hold these truths to be self-evident; that all men are created equal."

I have a dream that one day in the red hills of Georgia the sons of former slaves and the sons of former slaveowners will be able to sit down together at the table of brotherhood.

I have a dream that one day even the state of Mississippi, a desert state sweltering with the heat of injustice and oppression, will be transformed into an oasis of freedom and justice.

I have a dream that my four little children will one day live in a nation where they will not be judged by the color of their skin but by the content of their character.

I have a dream today.

I have a dream that one day the state of Alabama, whose governor's lips are presently dripping with the words of interposition and nullification, will be transformed into a situation where little black boys and black girls will be able to join hands with little white boys and white girls and walk together as sisters and brothers.

I have a dream today.

I have a dream that one day every valley shall be exalted, every hill and mountain shall be made low, the rough places will be made plain, and the crooked places will be made straight, and the glory of the Lord shall be revealed, and all flesh shall see it together.

This is our hope. This is the faith with which I return to the South. With this faith we will be able to hew out of the mountain of despair a stone of hope. With this faith we will be able to transform the jangling discords of our nation into a beautiful symphony of brotherhood. With this faith we will be able to work together, to pray together, to struggle together, to go to jail together, to stand up for freedom together, knowing that we will be free one day.

This will be the day when all of God's children will be able to sing with new meaning

My country, 'tis of thee,
Sweet land of liberty,
    Of thee I sing:
Land where my fathers died,
Land of the pilgrims' pride,
From every mountain-side
    Let freedom ring.

And if America is to be a great nation this must become true. So let freedom ring from the prodigious hilltops of New Hampshire. Let freedom ring from the mighty mountains of New York. Let freedom ring from the heightening Alleghenies of Pennsylvania!

Let freedom ring from the snowcapped Rockies of Colorado!

Let freedom ring from the curvaceous peaks of California!

But not only that; let freedom ring from Stone Mountain of Georgia!

Let freedom ring from Lookout Mountain of Tennessee!

Let freedom ring from every hill and molehill of Mississippi. From every mountainside, let freedom ring.

When we let freedom ring, when we let it ring from every village and every hamlet, from every state and every city, we will be able to speed up that day when all of God's children, black men and white men, Jews and Gentiles, Protestants and Catholics, will be able to join hands and sing in the words of the old Negro spiritual, "Free at last! free at last! thank God almighty, we are free at last!"

—1963

What are your reactions to and questions about this work? The following questions may help provoke some ideas.

Probing the Work

1. What is the dream King speaks of and to what extent has it been fulfilled?

Identifying Issues

2. What would Martin Luther King, Jr. say about the condition of blacks in America today?

LANGSTON HUGHES

Harlem

Langston Hughes (1902–1967) was born in Joplin, Missouri, but grew up mainly in Lawrence, Kansas then in Cleveland. After a year in Mexico, where his father lived, he spent a year at Columbia University from 1921 to 1922. After working at odd jobs he entered Lincoln University (Pennsylvania) in 1926. By the time he graduated three years later, he had published two books of poetry (including The Weary Blues*) and established himself as the best poet of the Harlem Renaissance (then called the "New Negro" Renaissance). Hughes was not only a poet but also a political activist, dramatist, short-story writer, journalist, songwriter, translator, and autobiographer.*

What happens to a dream deferred?

Does it dry up
like a raisin in the sun?
Or fester like a sore—
And then run?
Does it stink like rotten meat?
Or crust and sugar over—

like a syrupy sweet?

Maybe it just sags
like a heavy load.

Or does it explode?

—1951

What are your reactions to and questions about this work? The following questions may help provoke some ideas.

Probing the Work

1. What are the different *metaphors* and *similes* (p. 68) Hughes uses to describe the possible consequences of deferring dreams, and what does each one imply about that option?

Identifying Issues

2. In what ways has the dream "exploded" in our time?
3. According to Jean Wagner in *Black Poets of the United States,* the dream that Hughes writes of represents the democratic ideal of liberty and equality; the history of the dream is actually the history of the founding and building of America. The dream of black people has always been closely blended with the American dream, which is not yet a reality for all. The dream, according to Wagner, is no longer exalted; it is a vision degraded through trampling and abuse. Wagner also suggests that jazz has influenced the tone and structure of Hughes's poetry: it softens the acrid disillusionment that the poems voice.

   What evidence have you seen in our world today to confirm or contradict what Wagner says about the significance and expression of the "dream"?

LANGSTON HUGHES

As I Grew Older

(See biographical information on page 238.)

It was a long time ago.
I have almost forgotten my dream.
But it was there then,
In front of me,
Bright like a sun—
My dream.

And then the wall rose,
Rose slowly,
Slowly,
Between me and my dream.
Rose slowly, slowly,
Dimming,
Hiding,
The light of my dream.
Rose until it touched the sky—
The wall

Shadow.
I am black.

I lie down in the shadow.
No longer the light of my dream before me,
Above me.
Only the thick wall.
Only the shadow.

My hands!
My dark hands!
Break through the wall!
Find my dream!
Help me to shatter this darkness,
To smash this night,
To break this shadow
Into a thousand lights of sun,
Into a thousand whirling dreams
Of sun!

—1925

What are your reactions to and questions about this work? The following questions may help provoke some ideas.

Probing the Work

1. What are the positive and negative elements of this speaker's experiences? How does Hughes employ *images* (see page 79) of shadow and sun?

Identifying Issues

2. Which *metaphor* (see page 68), if any, from "Harlem," applies best to the speaker's experience in this poem, and to the experience of some African-Americans today?

GWENDOLYN BROOKS

Sadie and Maud

Gwendolyn Brooks (b. 1917) was born in Topeka but grew up in Chicago. She had her first poem published at age 10, and in high school published several more. Focusing on the lives of the urban poor, especially women, her first collection of poetry (A Street in Bronzeville) *was published in 1947; in 1950 she became the first African-American woman to win a Pulitzer Prize for poetry, for her second book,* Annie Allen. *In the late 1960s Brooks turned to more politically radical themes. From 1985 to 1986 she served as Poetry Consultant to the Library of Congress, the first black woman to do so.*

Maud went to college.
Sadie stayed at home.
Sadie scraped life
With a fine-tooth comb.

She didn't leave a tangle in.
Her comb found every strand.
Sadie was one of the livingest chits°
In all the land.

Sadie bore two babies
Under her maiden name.
Maud and Ma and Papa
Nearly died of shame.
Every one but Sadie
Nearly died of shame.

When Sadie said her last so-long
Her girls struck out from home.
(Sadie had left as heritage
Her fine-tooth comb.)

Maud, who went to college,
Is a thin brown mouse.
She is living all alone
In this old house.

—1945

What are your reactions to and questions about this work? The following questions may help provoke some ideas.

7 chits: Pert young women.

Probing the Work

1. How does Brooks depict *irony*—the difference between what you would expect of each girl and what actually happens?
2. Is Maud less "successful," than Sadie? Why or why not? What is Brooks trying to show by her last stanza?

Identifying Issues

3. What are the ingredients of the "dream" that Martin Luther King, Jr. and Langston Hughes refer to? Is college one of them?
4. What kind of education is more worthwhile, the kind experienced by Sadie or the kind experienced by Maud? Can you point to examples of individuals who have been successful regardless of, or because of, their educational credentials?

WOLE SOYINKA

Telephone Conversation

Wole Soyinka (b. 1934) was born in Nigeria, and studied first at University College at Ibadan, then at Leeds University, where his plays were first performed. He became a successful playwright in the late 1950s (e.g., for The Swamp Dwellers, The Lion and the Jewel*), and in the 1960s became a social activist and was imprisoned for two years (including 15 months in solitary confinement).*

The price seemed reasonable, location
Indifferent. The landlady swore she lived
Off premises. Nothing remained
But self-confession. 'Madam,' I warned,
'I hate a wasted journey—I am African.'
Silence. Silenced transmission of
Pressurized good-breeding. Voice, when it came,
Lipstick coated, long gold-rolled
Cigarette-holder pipped. Caught I was, foully.
"HOW DARK?" . . . I had not misheard. . . . "ARE YOU LIGHT
OR VERY DARK?" Button B. Button A. Stench
Of rancid breath of public hide-and-speak.
Red booth. Red pillar-box. Red double-tiered
Omnibus squelching tar. It *was* real! Shamed
By ill-mannered silence, surrender
Pushed dumbfoundment to beg simplification.
Considerate she was, varying the emphasis—
"ARE YOU DARK? OR VERY LIGHT?" Revelation came.
"You mean—like plain or milk chocolate?"

Her assent was clinical, crushing in its light
Impersonality. Rapidly, wave-length adjusted,
I chose. "West African sepia"—and as afterthought,
"Down in my passport." Silence for spectroscopic
Flight of fancy, till truthfulness clanged her accent
Hard on the mouthpiece. "WHAT'S THAT?" conceding
"DON'T KNOW WHAT THAT IS." "Like brunette."
"THAT'S DARK, ISN'T IT?" "Not altogether.
Facially, I am brunette, but madam, you should see
The rest of me. Palm of my hand, soles of my feet
Are a peroxide blonde. Friction, caused—
Foolishly madam—by sitting down, has turned
My bottom raven black—One moment madam!"—sensing
Her receiver rearing on the thunderclap
About my ears—"Madam," I pleaded, "wouldn't you rather
See for yourself?"

—1960

What are your reactions to and questions about this work? The following questions may help provoke some ideas.

Probing the Work

1. Look at the sensory *imagery* (see page 79) of the poem. How do the various images illustrate the feelings of the speaker?

Identifying Issues

2. This poem illustrates an issue not commonly discussed (there's even a term for it: *pigmentocracy*), that leads to a specific kind of discrimination among African-Americans. Have you noticed such discrimination among blacks based on the lightness or darkness of skin? How might this affect an individual's goals and dreams?

CHARLES JOHNSON

Exchange Value

Charles Johnson grew up in Chicago, but now resides in Seattle. Among his works are three novels, a number of short stories, and cartoons. His novel Middle Passage *won the 1990 National Book Award. He also teaches and writes for television.*

Me and my brother Loftis came in by the old lady's window. There was some kinda boobytrap—boxes of broken glass—that shoulda warned us Miss Bailey wasn't the easy mark we made her to be. She had been living alone for twenty years in 4-B down the hall from Loftis and me, long before our folks died—a hincty, half-bald West Indian woman with a craglike face, who kept her door barricaded, shutters closed, and wore the same sorrylooking outfit—black wingtip shoes, cropfingered gloves in winter, and a man's floppy hat—like maybe she dressed half-asleep or in a dark attic. Loftis, he figured Miss Bailey had some grandtheft dough stashed inside, jim, or leastways a shoebox full of money, cause she never spent a nickel on herself, not even for food, and only left her place at night.

Anyway, we figured Miss Bailey was gone. Her mailbox be full, and Pookie White, who run the Thirty-ninth Street Creole restaurant, he say she ain't dropped by in days to collect the handouts he give her so she can get by. So here's me and Loftis, tipping around Miss Bailey's blackdark kitchen. The floor be littered with fruitrinds, roaches, old food furred with blue mold. Her dirty dishes be stacked in a sink spidered with cracks, and it looks like the old lady been living, lately, on Ritz crackers and Department of Agriculture (Welfare Office) peanut butter. Her toilet be stopped up, too, and, on the bathroom floor, there's five Maxwell House coffee cans full of shit. Me, I was closing her bathroom door when I whiffed this evil smell so bad, so thick, I could hardly breathe, and what breath I drew was horrible, like a solid thing in my throatpipes, like soup. "Cooter," Loftis whisper, low, across the room, "you smell that?" He went right on sniffing it, like people do for some reason when something be smelling stanky, then took out his headrag and held it over his mouth. "That's the awfulest stink I *ever* smelled!" Then, head low, he slipped his long self into the livingroom. Me, I stayed by the window, gulping air, and do you know why?

You oughta know, up front, that I ain't too good at this gangster stuff, and I had a real bad feeling about Miss Bailey from the get-go. Mama used to say it was Loftis, not me, who'd go places—I see her standing at the sideboard by the sink now, big as a Frigidaire, white with flour to her elbows, a washtowel over her shoulder, while we ate a breakfast of cornbread and syrup. He graduated fifth at DuSable High School, had two gigs, and, like Papa, he be always wanting the things white people had out in Hyde Park, where Mama did daywork. Loftis, he the kinda brother who buys *Esquire,* sews Hart, Schaffner and Marx labels in Robert Hall suits, talks properlike, packs his hair with Murrays, and took classes in politics and stuff at the Black People's Topographical Library in the late 1960s; who, at thirty, makes his bed military style, reads *Black Scholar* on the bus he takes to the plant, and, come hell or high water, plans to make a Big Score. Loftis, he say I'm bout as useful on a hustle—or when it comes to getting ahead—as a headcold, and he say he has to count my legs sometimes to be sure I ain't a mule, seeing how, for all my eighteen years, I can't keep no job and sorta stay close to home, watching TV or reading *World's Finest* comic books, or maybe just laying dead, listening to music, imagining I see faces or foreign places in water stains on the wallpaper, cause somedays when I remember Papa, then Mama killing theyselves for chump change—a pitiful li'l bowl of porridge— I get to thinking that even if I ain't had all I wanted, maybe I've had, you know, all I'm ever gonna get.

"Cooter," Loftis say from the livingroom. "You best get in here quick."

Loftis, he'd switched on Miss Bailey's sulfurcolored livingroom lights, so for a second I couldn't see and started coughing—the smell be so powerful it hit my nostrils like coke—and when my eyes cleared, shapes evolved from the light, and I thought for an instant like I'd slipped in space. I seen why Loftis called me, and went back two steps. See, 4-B is so small, if you ring Miss Bailey's doorbell the toilet'd flush. But her livingroom, webbed in dust, be filled to the max with dollars of all denominations, stacks of stock in General Motors, Gulf Oil, and 3M Corporation in old White Owl cigar boxes, battered purses, or bound in pink rubber bands. It be like the kind of cubbyhole kids play in, but filled with . . . *things*—everything—like a world within the world, you take it from me, so like picturebook scenes of plentifulness you could seal yourself off in here and settle forever. Loftis and me both drew breath suddenly. There be unopened cases of Jack Daniel's, three safes cemented to the floor, hundreds of matchbooks, unworn clothes, a zinc laundry tub, dozens of wedding rings, rubbish, World War II magazines, a carton of one hundred canned sardines, mink stoles, old rags, a birdcage, a bucket of silver dollars, thousands of books, paintings, quarters in tobacco cans, two pianos, glass jars of pennies, a set of bagpipes, an almost complete Model A Ford dappled with rust, and, I swear, three sections of a dead tree.

"Godamighty damn!" My head be light; I sat on an upended peachcrate and picked me up a bottle of Jack Daniel's.

"Don't you touch *anything*!" Loftis, he panting a little; he slap both hands on a table. "Not until we inventory this stuff."

"Inventory? Aw Lord, Loftis," I say, "something ain't *right* about this stash. There could be a curse on it . . ."

"Boy, sometimes you act weakminded."

"For real, Loftis, I got a feeling . . ."

Loftis, he shucked off his shoes and sat down heavily on the lumpy arm of a stuffed chair. "Don't say *anything*." He chewed his knuckles, and for the first time Loftis looked like he didn't know his next move. "Let me think, okay?" He squeezed his nose in a way he has when thinking hard, sighed, then stood up, and say, "There's something you better see in that bedroom yonder. Cover up your mouth."

"Loftis, I ain't going in there."

He look at me right funny then. "She's a miser, that's all. She saves things."

"But a tree?" I say. "Loftis, a *tree* ain't normal!"

"Cooter, I ain't gonna tell you twice."

Like always, I followed Loftis, who swung his flashlight from the plant—he a nightwatchman—into Miss Bailey's bedroom, but me, I'm thinking how trippy this thing is getting, remembering how, last year, when I had a paper route, the old lady, with her queer crablike walk, pulled my coat for some change in the hallway, and when I give her a handful of dimes, she say in her old Inner Sanctum voice, "Thank you, Co-o-oter," then gulped the coins down like aspirin, no lie, and scurried off like a hunchback. Me, I wanted no parts of this squirrelly old broad, but Loftis, he holding my wrist now, beaming his light onto a low bed. The room had a funny, museumlike smell. Real sour. It was full of dirty laundry. And I be sure the old lady's stuff had a terrible string attached when Loftis, looking away, lifted her bedsheets and a knot of black flies rose. I stepped back and held my breath. Miss Bailey be in her long-sleeved flannel nightgown, bloated, like she'd been inflated by a tire pump, her crazy putty face bald with rot, flyblown, her fingers big as bananas. Her wristwatch be ticking softly beside a stump of half-eaten bread. Above the bed, her wall had roaches squashed in little circles of bloodstain. Maggots clustered in her eyes, her ears, and one fistsized rat rattled in her flesh. My eyes snapped shut. My knees failed, then I did a Hollywood faint. When I surfaced, Loftis, he be sitting beside me in the livingroom, where he'd drug me, reading a wrinkled, yellow article from the Chicago *Daily Defender.*

"Listen to this," Loftis say. " 'Elnora Bailey, forty-five, a Negro housemaid in the Highland Park home of Henry Conners, is the beneficiary of her employer's will. An old American family, the Connerses arrived in this country on the *Providence,* shortly after the voyage of the *Mayflower.* The family flourished in the early days of the 1900s'! . . ." He went on, getting breath. " 'A distinguished and wealthy industrialist, without heirs or a wife, Conners willed his entire estate to Miss Bailey of 3347 N. Clark Street for her twenty years of service to his family' . . ." Loftis, he give that Geoffrey Holder laugh of his, low and deep, then it eased up his throat until it hit a high note and tipped his head back onto his shoulders. "Cooter, that was before we was born! Miss Bailey kept this in the Bible next to her bed."

Standing, I braced myself with one hand against the wall. "She didn't earn it?"

"Naw." Loftis, he folded the paper—"Not one penny"—and stuffed it in his shirt pocket. His jaw looked tight as a horseshoe. "Way *I* see it," he say, "this was her one shot in a lifetime to be rich, but, being country, she had backward ways and blew it." Rubbing his hands, he stood up to survey the livingroom. "Somebody's gonna find Miss Bailey soon, but if we stay on the case—Cooter, don't you square up on me now—we can tote everything to our place before daybreak. Best we start with the big stuff."

"But why didn't she *use* it, huh? Tell me that?"

Loftis, he don't pay me no mind. When he gets an idea in his head, you can't dig it out with a chisel. How long it took me and Loftis to inventory, then haul Miss Bailey's queer old stuff to our crib, I can't say, but that decrepit old ninnyhammer's hoard come to $879,543 in cash money, thirty-two bank books (some deposits be only $5), and me, I wasn't sure I was dreaming or what, but I suddenly flashed on this feeling, once we left her flat, that all the fears Loftis and me had about the future be gone, cause Miss Bailey's property was the past—the power of that fellah Henry Conners trapped like a bottle spirit, which we could live off, so it was the future, too, pure potential: can *do*. Loftis got to talking on about how that piano we pushed home be equal to a thousand bills, jim, which equals, say, a bad TEAC A-3340 tape deck, or a down payment on a deuce-and-a-quarter. Its value be (Loftis say) that of a universal standard of measure, relational, unreal as number, so that tape deck could turn, magically, into two gold lamé suits, a trip to Tijuana, or twenty-five rimjobs from a ho—we had $879,543 worth of wishes, if you can deal with that. Be like Miss Bailey's stuff is raw energy, and Loftis and me, like wizards, can transform her stuff into anything else at will. All we had to do, it seemed to me, was decide exactly what to exchange it for.

While Loftis studied this over (he looked funny, like a potato trying to say something, after the inventory, and sat, real quiet, in the kitchen), I filled my pockets with fifties, grabbed me a cab downtown to grease, yum, at one of them high-hat restaurants in the Loop . . . But then I thought better of it, you know, like I'd be out of place—just another jig putting on airs—and scarfed instead at a ribjoint till both my eyes bubbled. This fat lady making fishburgers in the back favored an old hardleg babysitter I once had, a Mrs. Paine who made me eat ochre, and I wanted so bad to say, "Loftis and me Got Ovuh," but I couldn't put that in the wind, could I, so I hatted up. Then I copped a boss silk necktie, cashmere socks, and a whistle-slick maxie leather jacket on State Street, took cabs *everywhere*, but when I got home that evening a funny, Pandoralike feeling hit me. I took off the jacket, boxed it—it looked so trifling in the hallway's weak light—and, tired, turned my key in the door. I couldn't get in. Loftis, he'd changed the lock and, when he finally let me in, looking vaguer, crabby, like something out of the Book of Revelations, I seen this elaborate boobytrapped tunnel of cardboard and razor blades behind him, with a two-foot space just big enough for him or me to crawl through. That wasn't all. Two bags of trash from the furnace room be sitting inside the door. Loftis, he give my leather jacket this evil look, hauled me inside, and hit me upside the head.

"How much this thing set us back?"

"Two fifty." My jaws be tight; I toss him my receipt. "You want me to take it back? Maybe I can get something else . . ."

Loftis, he say, not to me, but to the receipt, "Remember the time Mama give me that ring we had in the family for fifty years? And I took it to Merchandise Mart and sold it for a few pieces of candy?" He hitched his chair forward, and sat with his elbows on his knees. "That's what you did, Cooter. You crawled into a Clark bar." He commence to rip up my receipt, then picked up his flashlight and keys. "The instant you buy something you *lose* the power to buy something." He button up his coat with holes in the elbows, showing his blue shirt, then turned round at the tunnel to say: "Don't touch Miss Bailey's money, or drink her splo, or do *anything* until I get back."

"Where you going?"

"To work. It's Wednesday, ain't it?"

"You going to work?"

"Yeah."

"You got to go *really?* Loftis," I say, "what you brang them bags of trash in here for?"

"It ain't trash!" He cut his eyes at me. "There's good clothes in there. Mr. Peterson tossed them out, he don't care, but I saw some use in them, that's all."

"Loftis . . ."

"Yeah?"

"What we gonna do with all this money?"

Loftis pressed his fingers to his eyelids, and for a second he look caged, or like somebody's kicked him in his stomach. Then he cut me some slack: "Let me think on it tonight—it don't pay to rush—then we can TCB, okay?"

Five hours after Loftis leave for work, that old blister Mr. Peterson, our landlord, he come collecting rent, find Miss Bailey's body in apartment 4-B, and phoned the Fire Department. Me, I be folding my new jacket in tissue paper to keep it fresh, adding the box to Miss Bailey's unsunned treasures, when two paramedics squeezed her on a long stretcher through a crowd in the hallway. See, I had to pin her from the stairhead, looking down one last time at this dizzy old lady, and I seen something in her face, like maybe she'd been poor as Job's turkey for thirty years, suffering that special Negro fear of using up what little we get in this life—Loftis, he call that entropy—believing in her belly, and for all her faith, jim, there just ain't no more coming tomorrow from grace, or the Lord, or from her own labor, like she can't kill nothing, and won't nothing die . . . so when Conners will her his wealth, it put her through changes, she be spellbound, possessed by the promise of life, panicky about depletion, and locked now in the past cause *every* purchase, you know, has to be a poor buy: a loss of life. Me, I wasn't worried none. Loftis, he got a brain trained by years of talking trash with people in Frog Hudson's Barber Shop on Thirty-fifth Street. By morning, I knew, he'd have some kinda wheeze worked out.

But Loftis, he don't come home. Me, I got plenty worried. I listen to the hi-fi all day Thursday, only pawing outside to peep down the stairs, like that'd make Loftis come sooner. So Thursday go by; and come Friday the head's out of kilter—first there's an ogrelike belch from the toiletbowl, then water bursts from the bathroom into the kitchen—and me, I can't call the super (How do I explain the tunnel?), so I gave up and quit bailing. But on Sat'day, I could smell greens cooking next door. Twice I almost opened Miss Bailey's sardines, even though starving be less an evil than eating up our stash, but I waited till it was dark and, lightheaded with hunger, I stepped outside to Pookie White's, lay a hardluck story on him, and Pookie, he give me some jambalaya and gumbo. Back home in the livingroom, fingerfeeding myself, barricaded in by all that hope made material, the Kid felt like a king in his countingroom, or God in February, the month before He made the world (Mama's saying), and I copped some z's in an armchair till I heard the door move on its hinges, then bumping in the tunnel, and a heavy-footed walk thumped into the bedroom.

"Loftis?" I rubbed my eyes. "You back?" It be Sunday morning. Six-thirty sharp. Darkness dissolved slowly into the strangeness of twilight, with the rays of sunlight flaring at exactly the same angle they fall each night, as if the hour be an island, a moment, outside time. Me, I'm afraid Loftis gonna fuss bout my not straightening up, letting things go. I went into the bathroom, poured water in the one-spigot washstand—brown rust come bursting out in flakes—and rinsed my face. "Loftis, you supposed to be home four days ago. Hey," I say, toweling my face, "you okay, brah?" How come he don't answer me? Wiping my hands on the seat of my trousers, I tipped into Loftis's room. He sleeping with his mouth open. His legs be drawn up, both fists clenched between his knees. He'd kicked his blanket on the floor. In his sleep, Loftis laughed, or moaned, it be hard to tell. His eyelids, not quite shut, show slits of white. I decided to wait till Loftis wake up for his decision, but turning, I seen his watch, keys, and what looked in the first stain of sunlight to be a carefully wrapped piece of newspaper on his nightstand. The sun surged up in a bright shimmer, focusing the bedroom slowly like solution do a photographic image in the developer. And then something so freakish went down I ain't sure it took place. Fumblefingered, I unfolded the paper and inside be a blemished penny. It be like somebody hit me hard between the shoulderblades. Taped on the penny be a slip of paper, and on the paper be the note, "Found while walking down Devon Avenue." I hear Loftis mumble like he trapped in a nightmare. "Hold tight," I whisper, "it's all right." Me, I wanted to tell Loftis how Miss Bailey looked four days ago, that maybe it didn't have to be like that for us—did it?—because we could change. Couldn't we? Me, I pull his packed sheets over him, wrap up the penny, and, when I locate Miss Bailey's glass jar in the livingroom, put it away carefully, for now, with the rest of our things.

—1986

What are your reactions to and questions about this work? The following questions may help provoke some ideas.

Probing the Work

1. What does Miss Bailey represent?
2. Look at the passage on page 247 that begins, "I wasn't sure I was dreaming." What does this passage reveal about the difference between the way the two brothers deal with the money, and their goals?

Identifying Issues

3. How does the title reflect the *theme* (see page 77) of the story? What has "exchange value"? What are the values, monetary or other, that are depicted here?

LUCILLE CLIFTON

for de Lawd

Lucille Clifton (b. 1936) was born in Depew, New York, and was educated at Fredonia State Teachers College (New York) and at Howard University (Washington, D.C.). While married and with six children under ten years old, she published her first collection of poetry, Good Times, *in 1969. She has since published several more books of poetry as well as more than 16 books for young readers, and has taught at a number of colleges and universities.*

people say they have a hard time
understanding how I
go on about my business
playing my Ray Charles
hollering at the kids—
seem like my Afro
cut off in some old image
would show I got a long memory
and I come from a line
of black and going on women
who got used to making it through murdered sons
and who grief kept on pushing
who fried chicken
ironed
swept off the back steps
who grief kept
for their still alive sons
for their sons coming
for their sons gone
just pushing
in the inner city
or
like we call it
home
we think a lot about uptown
and the silent nights
and the houses straight as

dead men
and the pastel lights
and we hang on to our no place
happy to be alive
and in the inner city
or
like we call it
home

—*1969*

What are your reactions to and questions about this work? The following questions may help provoke some ideas.

Probing the Work

1. What significance does the repeated phrase *inner city* have for the speaker? What do you think the speaker's attitude is toward the inner city in contrast to "uptown"?

Identifying Issues

2. What are some stereotypes about inner-city life that the poet is addressing here? How is the speaker dealing with her life? How might you deal with it if you were in her position?

AUDRE LORDE

Power

Audre Lorde (1934–1992) was born in New York City of West Indian parents, and attended Hunter College and Columbia University. She worked as a librarian and then taught at several colleges before becoming a professor of English at Hunter College in New York City. She was a poet as well as a spokesperson for human rights. Her books include The First Cities *(1968) and* The Marvellous Arithmetics of Distance: Poems 1987–1992 *(1993).*

The difference between poetry and rhetoric
is being
ready to kill
yourself
instead of your children.

I am trapped on a desert of raw gunshot wounds
and a dead child dragging his shattered black

face off the edge of my sleep
blood from his punctured cheeks and shoulders
is the only liquid for miles and my stomach
churns at the imagined taste while
my mouth splits into dry lips
without loyalty or reason
thirsting for the wetness of his blood
as it sinks into the whiteness
of the desert where I am lost
without imagery or magic
trying to make power out of hatred and destruction
trying to heal my dying son with kisses
only the sun will bleach his bones quicker.

The policeman who shot down a 10-year-old in Queens
stood over the boy with his cop shoes in childish blood
and a voice said "Die you little motherfucker" and
there are tapes to prove that. At his trial
this policeman said in his own defense
"I didn't notice the size or nothing else
only the color." and
there are tapes to prove that, too.

Today that 37-year-old white man with 13 years of police forcing
has been set free
by 11 white men who said they were satisfied
justice had been done
and one black woman who said
"They convinced me" meaning
they had dragged her 4′10″ black woman's frame
over the hot coals of four centuries of white male approval
until she let go the first real power she ever had
and lined her own womb with cement
to make a graveyard for our children.

I have not been able to touch the destruction within me.
But unless I learn to use
the difference between poetry and rhetoric
my power too will run corrupt as poisonous mold
or lie limp and useless as an unconnected wire
and one day I will take my teenaged plug
and connect it to the nearest socket
raping an 85-year-old white woman
who is somebody's mother

and as I beat her senseless and set a torch to her bed
a greek chorus will be singing in 3/4 time
"Poor thing. She never hurt a soul. What beasts they are."

—1978

What are your reactions to and questions about this work? The following questions may help provoke some ideas.

Probing the Work

1. How would you characterize the relationship between the speaker and the situation or experiences of this poem? What is the speaker's *tone* (see page 67)? What is her attitude toward the conditions she describes?
2. What does the poet mean by "the difference between poetry and rhetoric"?

Identifying Issues

3. What kinds of power is the poet describing here? Who wields it, and what are its consequences? What are the implications for and connections to real-life situations that you might know of or have read or heard about?

LORRAINE HANSBERRY

A Raisin in the Sun

Lorraine Hansberry (1930–1965) was born in Chicago to a well-to-do family that entertained such famous African-Americans as W. E. B. DuBois and Langston Hughes. But in 1938, when they moved into a white neighborhood, violence erupted and their lives changed. Even though the Supreme Court had declared restrictive housing laws illegal in 1940, Hansberry's father was psychologically and financially destroyed by the injustices he suffered, and died in 1946. Hansberry attended the University of Wisconsin, then the New School in New York City, where she became a civil rights activist. In 1953 she married, and a few years later began writing this play. She died of cancer at age 34.

What happens to a dream deferred?
Does it dry up
Like a raisin in the sun?
Or fester like a sore—
And then run?
Does it stink like rotten meat?

Or crust and sugar over—
Like a syrupy sweet?

Maybe it just sags
Like a heavy load.

Or does it explode?

—Langston Hughes

Characters
(In order of appearance)

RUTH YOUNGER
TRAVIS YOUNGER
WALTER LEE YOUNGER (BROTHER)
BENEATHA YOUNGER
LENA YOUNGER (MAMA)
JOSEPH ASAGAI
GEORGE MURCHISON
KARL LINDNER
BOBO
MOVING MEN

The action of the play is set in Chicago's Southside, sometime between World War II and the present.

Act I

Scene One: Friday morning.

Scene Two: The following morning.

Act II

Scene One: Later, the same day.

Scene Two: Friday night, a few weeks later.

Scene Three: Moving day, one week later.

Act III

An hour later.

ACT I

Scene I

The YOUNGER *living room would be a comfortable and well-ordered room if it were not for a number of indestructible contradictions to this state of being. Its furnishings are typical and undistinguished and their primary feature now is that they have clearly had to accommodate the living of too many people for too many years—and they are tired. Still, we can see that at some time, a time probably no longer remembered by the family (except perhaps for* MAMA*), the furnishings of this room were actually selected with care and love* *and even hope—and brought to this apartment and arranged with taste and pride.*

That was a long time ago. Now the once loved pattern of the couch upholstery has to fight to show itself from under acres of crocheted doilies and couch covers which have themselves finally come to be more important than the upholstery. And here a table or a chair has been moved to disguise the worn places in the carpet; but the carpet has fought back by showing its weariness, with depressing uniformity, elsewhere on its surface.

Weariness has, in fact, won in this room. Everything has been polished, washed, sat on, used, scrubbed too often. All pretenses but living itself have long since vanished from the very atmosphere of this room.

Moreover, a section of this room, for it is not really a room unto itself, though the landlord's lease would make it seem so, slopes backward to provide a small kitchen area, where the family prepares the meals that are eaten in the living room proper, which must also serve as dining room. The single window that has been provided for these "two" rooms is located in this kitchen area. The sole natural light the family may enjoy in the course of a day is only that which fights its way through this little window.

At left, a door leads to a bedroom which is shared by Mama *and her daughter,* Beneatha. *At right, opposite, is a second room (which in the beginning of the life of this apartment was probably a breakfast room) which serves as a bedroom for* Walter *and his wife,* Ruth.

Time: Sometime between World War II and the present.

Place: Chicago's Southside.

At Rise: It is morning dark in the living room. Travis *is asleep on the make-down bed at center. An alarm clock sounds from within the bedroom at right, and presently* Ruth *enters from that room and closes the door behind her. She crosses sleepily toward the window. As she passes her sleeping son she reaches down and shakes him a little. At the window she raises the shade and a dusky Southside morning light comes in feebly. She fills a pot with water and puts it on to boil. She calls to the boy, between yawns, in a slightly muffled voice.*

Ruth *is about thirty. We can see that she was a pretty girl, even exceptionally so, but now it is apparent that life has been little that she expected, and disappointment has already begun to hang in her face. In a few years, before thirty-five even, she will be known among her people as a "settled woman."*

She crosses to her son and gives him a good, final, rousing shake.

Ruth: Come on now, boy, it's seven thirty! *(Her son sits up at last, in a stupor of sleepiness)* I say hurry up, Travis! You ain't the only person in the world got to use a bathroom! *(The child, a sturdy, handsome little boy of ten or eleven, drags himself out of the bed and almost blindly takes his towels and "today's clothes" from drawers and a closet and goes out to the bathroom, which is in an outside hall and which is shared by another family or families on the same floor.* RUTH *crosses to the bedroom door at right and opens it and calls in to her husband)* Walter Lee! . . . It's after seven thirty! Lemme see you do some waking up in there now! *(She waits)* You better get up from there, man! It's after seven thirty I tell you. *(She waits again)* All right, you just go ahead and lay there and next thing you know Travis be finished and Mr. Johnson'll be in there and you'll be fussing and cussing round here like a madman! And be late too! *(She waits, at the end of patience)* Walter Lee—it's time for you to GET UP!

(She waits another second and then starts to go into the bedroom, but is apparently satisfied that her husband has begun to get up. She stops, pulls the door to, and returns to the kitchen area. She wipes her face with a moist cloth and runs her fingers through her sleep-disheveled hair in a vain effort and ties an apron around her housecoat. The bedroom door at right opens and her husband stands in the doorway in his pajamas, which are rumpled and mismated. He is a lean, intense young man in his middle thirties, inclined to quick nervous movements and erratic speech habits—and always in his voice there is a quality of indictment)

WALTER: Is he out yet?

RUTH: What you mean *out?* He ain't hardly got in there good yet.

WALTER *(wandering in, still more oriented to sleep than to a new day):* Well, what was you doing all that yelling for if I can't even get in there yet? *(Stopping and thinking)* Check coming today?

RUTH: They *said* Saturday and this is just Friday and I hopes to God you ain't going to get up here first thing this morning and start talking to me 'bout no money—'cause I 'bout don't want to hear it.

WALTER: Something the matter with you this morning?

RUTH: No—I'm just sleepy as the devil. What kind of eggs you want?

WALTER: Not scrambled. *(*RUTH *starts to scramble eggs)* Paper come? *(*RUTH *points impatiently to the rolled up* Tribune *on the table, and he gets it and spreads it out and vaguely reads the front page)* Set off another bomb yesterday.

RUTH *(maximum indifference):* Did they?

WALTER *(looking up):* What's the matter with you?

RUTH: Ain't nothing the matter with me. And don't keep asking me that this morning.

WALTER: Ain't nobody bothering you. *(Reading the news of the day absently again)* Say Colonel McCormick is sick.

RUTH *(affecting tea-party interest):* Is he now? Poor thing.

WALTER *(sighing and looking at his watch):* Oh, me. *(He waits)* Now what is that boy doing in that bathroom all this time? He just going to have to start getting up earlier. I can't be being late to work on account of him fooling around in there.

RUTH *(turning on him):* Oh, no he ain't going to be getting up no earlier no such thing! It ain't his fault that he can't get to bed no earlier nights 'cause he got a bunch of crazy good-for-nothing clowns sitting up running their mouths in what is supposed to be his bedroom after ten o'clock at night . . .

WALTER: That's what you mad about, ain't it? The things I want to talk about with my friends just couldn't be important in your mind, could they?

(He rises and finds a cigarette in her handbag on the table and crosses to the little window and looks out, smoking and deeply enjoying this first one)

RUTH *(almost matter of factly, a complaint too automatic to deserve emphasis):* Why you always got to smoke before you eat in the morning?

WALTER *(at the window):* Just look at 'em down there . . . Running and racing to work . . . *(He turns and faces his wife and watches her a moment at the stove, and then, suddenly)* You look young this morning, baby.

RUTH *(indifferently):* Yeah?

WALTER: Just for a second—stirring them eggs. Just for a second it was—you looked real young again. *(He reaches for her; she crosses away. Then, drily)* It's gone now—you look like yourself again!

RUTH: Man, if you don't shut up and leave me alone.

WALTER *(looking out to the street again):* First thing a man ought to learn in life is not to make love to no colored woman first thing in the morning. You all some eeeevil people at eight o'clock in the morning.

*(*TRAVIS *appears in the hall doorway, almost fully dressed and quite wide awake now, his towels and pajamas across his shoulders. He opens the door and signals for his father to make the bathroom in a hurry)*

TRAVIS *(watching the bathroom):* Daddy, come on!

*(*WALTER *gets his bathroom utensils and flies out to the bathroom)*

RUTH: Sit down and have your breakfast, Travis.

TRAVIS: Mama, this is Friday. *(Gleefully)* Check coming tomorrow, huh?

RUTH: You get your mind off money and eat your breakfast.

TRAVIS *(eating):* This is the morning we supposed to bring the fifty cents to school.

RUTH: Well, I ain't got no fifty cents this morning.

TRAVIS: Teacher say we have to.

RUTH: I don't care what teacher say. I ain't got it. Eat your breakfast, Travis.

TRAVIS: I *am* eating.

RUTH: Hush up now and just eat!

(The boy gives her an exasperated look for her lack of understanding, and eats grudgingly)

TRAVIS: You think Grandmama would have it?

RUTH: No! And I want you to stop asking your grandmother for money, you hear me?

TRAVIS *(outraged):* Gaaaleee! I don't ask her, she just gimme it sometimes!

RUTH: Travis Willard Younger—I got too much on me this morning to be—

TRAVIS: Maybe Daddy—

RUTH: *Travis!*

(The boy hushes abruptly. They are both quiet and tense for several seconds)

TRAVIS *(presently):* Could I maybe go carry some groceries in front of the supermarket for a little while after school then?

RUTH: Just hush, I said. *(*TRAVIS *jabs his spoon into his cereal bowl viciously, and rests his head in anger upon his fists)* If you through eating, you can get over there and make up your bed.

(The boy obeys stiffly and crosses the room, almost mechanically, to the bed and more or less folds the bedding into a heap, then angrily gets his books and cap)

TRAVIS *(sulking and standing apart from her unnaturally):* I'm gone.

RUTH *(looking up from the stove to inspect him automatically):* Come here. *(He crosses to her and she studies his head)* If you don't take this comb and fix this here head, you better! *(*TRAVIS *puts down his books with a great sigh of oppression, and crosses to the mirror. His mother mutters under her breath about his "slubbornness")* 'Bout to march out of here with that head looking just like chickens slept in it! I just don't know where you get your slubborn ways . . . And get your jacket, too. Looks chilly out this morning.

TRAVIS *(with conspicuously brushed hair and jacket):* I'm gone.

RUTH: Get carfare and milk money—*(Waving one finger)*—and not a single penny for no caps, you hear me?

TRAVIS *(with sullen politeness):* Yes'm.

(He turns in outrage to leave. His mother watches after him as in his frustration he approaches the door almost comically. When she speaks to him, her voice has become a very gentle tease)

RUTH *(mocking; as she thinks he would say it):* Oh, Mama makes me so mad sometimes, I don't know what to do! *(She waits and continues to his back as he stands stock-still in front of the door)* I wouldn't kiss that woman good-bye for nothing in this world this morning! *(The boy finally turns around and rolls his eyes at her, knowing the mood has changed and he is vindicated; he does not, however, move toward her yet)* Not for nothing in this world! *(She finally laughs aloud at him and holds out her arms to him and we see that it is a way between them, very old and practiced. He crosses to her and allows her to embrace him warmly but keeps his face fixed with masculine rigidity. She holds him back from her presently and looks at him and runs her fingers over the features of his face. With utter gentleness—)* Now—whose little old angry man are you?

TRAVIS *(the masculinity and gruffness start to fade at last):* Aw gaalee—Mama . . .

RUTH *(Mimicking):* Aw—gaaaaalleeeee, Mama! *(She pushes him, with rough playfulness and finality, toward the door)* Get on out of here or you going to be late.

TRAVIS *(in the face of love, new aggressiveness):* Mama, could I *please* go carry groceries?

RUTH: Honey, it's starting to get so cold evenings.

WALTER *(coming in from the bathroom and drawing a make-believe gun from a make-believe holster and shooting at his son):* What is it he wants to do?

RUTH: Go carry groceries after school at the supermarket.

WALTER: Well, let him go . . .

TRAVIS *(quickly, to the ally):* I *have* to—she won't gimme the fifty cents . . .

WALTER *(to his wife only):* Why not?

RUTH *(simply, and with flavor):* 'Cause we don't have it.

WALTER *(to* RUTH *only):* What you tell the boy things like that for? *(Reaching down into his pants with a rather important gesture)* Here, son—

(He hands the boy the coin, but his eyes are directed to his wife's. TRAVIS *takes the money happily)*

TRAVIS: Thanks, Daddy.

(He starts out. RUTH *watches both of them with murder in her eyes.* WALTER *stands and stares back at her with defiance, and suddenly reaches into his pocket again on an afterthought)*

WALTER *(without even looking at his son, still staring hard at his wife):* In fact, here's another fifty cents . . . Buy yourself some fruit today—or take a taxicab to school or something!

TRAVIS: Whoopee—

(He leaps up and clasps his father around the middle with his legs, and they face each other in mutual appreciation; slowly WALTER LEE *peeks around the boy to catch the violent rays from his wife's eyes and draws his head back as if shot)*

WALTER: You better get down now—and get to school, man.

TRAVIS *(at the door):* O.K. Good-bye.

(He exits)

WALTER *(after him, pointing with pride):* That's *my* boy. *(She looks at him in disgust and turns back to her work)* You know what I was thinking 'bout in the bathroom this morning?

RUTH: No.

WALTER: How come you always try to be so pleasant!

RUTH: What is there to be pleasant 'bout!

WALTER: You want to know what I was thinking 'bout in the bathroom or not!

RUTH: I know what you thinking 'bout.

WALTER *(ignoring her):* 'Bout what me and Willy Harris was talking about last night.

RUTH *(immediately—a refrain):* Willy Harris is a good-for-nothing loudmouth.

WALTER: Anybody who talks to me has got to be a good-for-nothing loudmouth, ain't he? And what you know about who is just a good-for-nothing loudmouth? Charlie Atkins was just a "good-for-nothing loudmouth" too, wasn't he! When he wanted me to go in the dry-cleaning business with him. And now—he's grossing a hundred thousand a year. A hundred thousand dollars a year! You still call *him* a loudmouth!

RUTH *(bitterly):* Oh, Walter Lee . . .

(She folds her head on her arms over the table)

WALTER *(rising and coming to her and standing over her):* You tired, ain't you? Tired of everything. Me, the boy, the way we live—this beat-up hole—everything. Ain't you? *(She doesn't look up, doesn't answer)* So tired—moaning and groaning all the time, but you wouldn't do nothing to help, would you? You couldn't be on my side that long for nothing, could you?

RUTH: Walter, please leave me alone.

WALTER: A man needs for a woman to back him up . . .

RUTH: Walter—

WALTER: Mama would listen to you. You know she listen to you more than she do me and Bennie. She think more of you. All you have to do is just sit down with her when you drinking your coffee one morning and talking 'bout things like you do and—*(He sits down beside her and demonstrates graphically what he thinks her methods and tone should be)*—you just sip your coffee, see, and say easy like that you been thinking 'bout that deal Walter Lee is so interested in, 'bout the store and all, and sip some more coffee, like what you saying ain't really that important to you—And the next thing you know, she be listening good and asking you questions and when I come home—I can tell her the details. This ain't no fly-by-night proposition, baby. I mean we figured it out, me and Willy and Bobo.

RUTH *(with a frown):* Bobo?

WALTER: Yeah. You see, this little liquor store we got in mind cost seventy-five thousand and we figured the initial investment on the place be 'bout thirty thousand, see. That be ten thousand each. Course, there's a couple of hundred you got to pay so's you don't spend your life just waiting for them clowns to let your license get approved—

RUTH: You mean graft?

WALTER *(frowning impatiently):* Don't call it that. See there, that just goes to show you what women understand about the world. Baby, don't *nothing* happen for you in this world 'less you pay *somebody* off!

RUTH: Walter, leave me alone! *(She raises her head and stares at him vigorously—then says, more quietly) Eat* your eggs, they gonna be cold.

WALTER *(straightening up from her and looking off):* That's it. There you are. Man say to his woman: I got me a dream. His woman say: Eat your eggs. *(Sadly, but gaining in power)* Man say: I got to take hold of this here world, baby! And a woman will say: Eat your eggs and go to work. *(Passionately now)* Man say: I got to change my life, I'm choking to death, baby! And his woman say—*(In utter anguish as he brings his fists down on his thighs)*—Your eggs is getting cold!

RUTH *(softly):* Walter, that ain't none of our money.

WALTER *(not listening at all or even looking at her):* This morning, I was lookin' in the mirror and thinking about it . . . I'm thirty-five years old; I been married eleven years and I got a boy who sleeps in the living room—*(Very, very quietly)*—and all I got to give him is stories about how rich white people live . . .

RUTH: Eat your eggs, Walter.

WALTER *(slams the table and jumps up):* —DAMN MY EGGS—DAMN ALL THE EGGS THAT EVER WAS!

RUTH: Then go to work.

WALTER *(looking up at her):* See—I'm trying to talk to you 'bout myself—*(Shaking his head with the repetition)*—and all you can say is eat them eggs and go to work.

RUTH *(wearily):* Honey, you never say nothing new. I listen to you every day, every night and every morning, and you never say nothing new. *(Shrugging)* So you would rather *be* Mr. Arnold than be his chauffeur. So—I would *rather* be living in Buckingham Palace.

WALTER: That is just what is wrong with the colored woman in this world . . . Don't understand about building their men up and making 'em feel like they somebody. Like they can do something.

RUTH *(drily, but to hurt):* There *are* colored men who do things.

WALTER: No thanks to the colored woman.

RUTH: Well, being a colored woman, I guess I can't help myself none.

(She rises and gets the ironing board and sets it up and attacks a huge pile of rough-dried clothes, sprinkling them in preparation for the ironing and then rolling them into tight fat balls)

WALTER *(mumbling):* We one group of men tied to a race of women with small minds!

(His sister BENEATHA *enters. She is about twenty, as slim and intense as her brother. She is not as pretty as her sister-in-law, but her lean, almost intellectual face has a handsomeness of its own. She wears a bright-red flannel nightie, and her thick hair stands wildly about her head. Her speech is a mixture of many things; it is different from the rest of the family's insofar as education has permeated her sense of English—and perhaps the Midwest rather than the South has finally—at last—won out in her inflection; but not altogether, because over all of it is a soft slurring and transformed use of vowels which is the decided influence of the Southside. She passes through the room without looking at either* RUTH *or* WALTER *and goes to the outside door and looks, a little blindly, out to the bathroom. She sees that it has been lost to the Johnsons. She closes the door with a sleepy vengeance and crosses to the table and sits down a little defeated)*

BENEATHA: I am going to start timing those people.

WALTER: You should get up earlier.

BENEATHA *(her face in her hands. She is still fighting the urge to go back to bed):* Really—would you suggest dawn? Where's the paper?

WALTER *(pushing the paper across the table to her as he studies her almost clinically, as though he has never seen her before):* You a horrible-looking chick at this hour.

BENEATHA *(drily):* Good morning, everybody.

WALTER *(senselessly):* How is school coming?

BENEATHA *(in the same spirit):* Lovely. Lovely. And you know, biology is the greatest. *(Looking up at him)* I dissected something that looked just like you yesterday.

WALTER: I just wondered if you've made up your mind and everything.

BENEATHA *(gaining in sharpness and impatience):* And what did I answer yesterday morning—and the day before that?

RUTH *(from the ironing board, like someone disinterested and old):* Don't be so nasty, Bennie.

BENEATHA *(still to her brother):* And the day before that and the day before that!

WALTER *(defensively):* I'm interested in you. Something wrong with that? Ain't many girls who decide—

WALTER *and* BENEATHA *(in unison):* —"to be a doctor."

(Silence)

WALTER: Have we figured out yet just exactly how much medical school is going to cost?

RUTH: Walter Lee, why don't you leave that girl alone and get out of here to work?

BENEATHA *(exits to the bathroom and bangs on the door):* Come on out of there, please!

(She comes back into the room)

WALTER *(looking at his sister intently):* You know the check is coming tomorrow.

BENEATHA *(turning on him with a sharpness all her own):* That money belongs to Mama, Walter, and it's for her to decide how she wants to use it. I don't care if she wants to buy a house or a rocket ship or just nail it up somewhere and look at it. It's hers. Not ours—*hers.*

WALTER *(bitterly):* Now ain't that fine! You just got your mother's interest at heart, ain't you, girl? You such a nice girl—but if Mama got that money she can always take a few thousand and help you through school too—can't she?

BENEATHA: I have never asked anyone around here to do anything for me!

WALTER: No! And the line between asking and just accepting when the time comes is big and wide—ain't it!

BENEATHA *(with fury):* What do you want from me, Brother—that I quit school or just drop dead, which!

WALTER: I don't want nothing but for you to stop acting holy 'round here. Me and Ruth done made some sacrifices for you—why can't you do something for the family?

RUTH: Walter, don't be dragging me in it.

WALTER: You are in it—Don't you get up and go work in somebody's kitchen for the last three years to help put clothes on her back?

RUTH: Oh, Walter—that's not fair . . .

WALTER: It ain't that nobody expects you to get on your knees and say thank you, Brother; thank you, Ruth; thank you, Mama—and thank you, Travis, for wearing the same pair of shoes for two semesters—

BENEATHA *(dropping to her knees):* Well—I *do*—all right?—thank everybody! And forgive me for ever wanting to be anything at all! *(Pursuing him on her knees across the floor)* FORGIVE ME, FORGIVE ME, FORGIVE ME!

RUTH: Please stop it! Your mama'll hear you.

WALTER: Who the hell told you you had to be a doctor? If you so crazy 'bout messing 'round with sick people—then go be a nurse like other women—or just get married and be quiet . . .

BENEATHA: Well—you finally got it said . . . It took you three years but you finally got it said. Walter, give up; leave me alone—it's Mama's money.

WALTER: *He was my father, too!*

BENEATHA: So what? He was mine, too—and Travis' grandfather—but the insurance money belongs to Mama. Picking on me is not going to make her give it to you to invest in any liquor stores—*(Underbreath, dropping into a chair)*—and I for one say, God bless Mama for that!

WALTER *(to* RUTH*):* See—did you hear? Did you hear!

RUTH: Honey, please go to work.

WALTER: Nobody in this house is ever going to understand me.

BENEATHA: Because you're a nut.

WALTER: Who's a nut?

BENEATHA: You—you are a nut. Thee is mad, boy.

WALTER *(looking at his wife and his sister from the door, very sadly):* The world's most backward race of people, and that's a fact.

BENEATHA *(turning slowly in her chair):* And then there are all those prophets who would lead us out of the wilderness—*(*WALTER *slams out of the house)*—into the swamps!

RUTH: Bennie, why you always gotta be pickin' on your brother? Can't you be a little sweeter sometimes? *(Door opens.* WALTER *walks in. He fumbles with his cap, starts to speak, clears throat, looks everywhere but at* RUTH. *Finally:)*

WALTER *(to* RUTH*):* I need some money for carfare.

RUTH *(looks at him, then warms; teasing, but tenderly):* Fifty cents? *(She goes to her bag and gets money)* Here—take a taxi!

*(*WALTER *exits.* MAMA *enters. She is a woman in her early sixties, full-bodied and strong. She is one of those women of a certain grace and beauty who wear it so unobtrusively that it takes a while to notice. Her dark-brown face is surrounded by the total whiteness of her hair, and, being a woman who has adjusted to many things in life and overcome many more, her face is full of strength. She has, we can see, wit and faith of a kind that keep her eyes lit and full of interest and expectancy. She is, in a word, a beautiful woman. Her bearing is perhaps most like the noble bearing of the women of the Hereros of Southwest Africa—rather as if she imagines that as she walks she still bears a basket or a vessel upon her head. Her speech, on the other hand, is as careless as her carriage is precise—she is inclined to slur everything—but her voice is perhaps not so much quiet as simply soft)*

MAMA: Who that 'round here slamming doors at this hour?

(She crosses through the room, goes to the window, opens it, and brings in a feeble little plant growing doggedly in a small pot on the window sill. She feels the dirt and puts it back out)

RUTH: That was Walter Lee. He and Bennie was at it again.

MAMA: My children and they tempers. Lord, if this little old plant don't get more sun than it's been getting it ain't never going to see spring again. *(She turns from the window)* What's the matter with you this morning, Ruth? You looks right peaked. You aiming to iron all them things? Leave some for me. I'll get to 'em this afternoon. Bennie honey, it's too drafty for you to be sitting 'round half dressed. Where's your robe?

BENEATHA: In the cleaners.

MAMA: Well, go get mine and put it on.

BENEATHA: I'm not cold, Mama, honest.

MAMA: I know—but you so thin . . .

BENEATHA *(irritably):* Mama, I'm not cold.

MAMA *(seeing the make-down bed as* TRAVIS *has left it):* Lord have mercy, look at that poor bed. Bless his heart—he tries, don't he?

(She moves to the bed TRAVIS *has sloppily made up)*

RUTH: No—he don't half try at all 'cause he knows you going to come along behind him and fix everything. That's just how come he don't know how to do nothing right now—you done spoiled that boy so.

MAMA *(folding bedding):* Well—he's a little boy. Ain't supposed to know 'bout housekeeping. My baby, that's what he is. What you fix for his breakfast this morning?

RUTH *(angrily):* I feed my son, Lena!

MAMA: I ain't meddling—*(Underbreath; busy-bodyish)* I just noticed all last week he had cold cereal, and when it starts getting this chilly in the fall a child ought to have some hot grits or something when he goes out in the cold—

RUTH *(furious):* I gave him hot oats—is that all right!

MAMA: I ain't meddling. *(Pause)* Put a lot of nice butter on it? *(*RUTH *shoots her an angry look and does not reply)* He likes lots of butter.

RUTH *(exasperated):* Lena—

MAMA *(to* BENEATHA. MAMA *is inclined to wander conversationally sometimes):* What was you and your brother fussing 'bout this morning?

BENEATHA: It's not important, Mama.

(She gets up and goes to look out at the bathroom, which is apparently free, and she picks up her towels and rushes out)

MAMA: What was they fighting about?

RUTH: Now you know as well as I do.

MAMA *(shaking her head):* Brother still worrying hisself sick about that money?

RUTH: You know he is.

MAMA: You had breakfast?

RUTH: Some coffee.

MAMA: Girl, you better start eating and looking after yourself better. You almost thin as Travis.

RUTH: Lena—

MAMA: Uh-hunh?

RUTH: What are you going to do with it?

MAMA: Now don't you start, child. It's too early in the morning to be talking about money. It ain't Christian.

RUTH: It's just that he got his heart set on that store—

MAMA: You mean that liquor store that Willy Harris want him to invest in?

RUTH: Yes—

MAMA: We ain't no business people, Ruth. We just plain working folks.

RUTH: Ain't nobody business people till they go into business. Walter Lee say colored people ain't never going to start getting ahead till they start gambling on some different kinds of things in the world—investments and things.

MAMA: What done got into you, girl? Walter Lee done finally sold you on investing.

RUTH: No. Mama, something is happening between Walter and me. I don't know what it is—but he needs something—something I can't give him any more. He needs this chance, Lena.

MAMA *(frowning deeply):* But liquor, honey—

RUTH: Well—like Walter say—I spec people going to always be drinking themselves some liquor.

MAMA: Well—whether they drinks it or not ain't none of my business. But whether I go into business selling it to 'em *is,* and I don't want that on my ledger this late in life. *(Stopping suddenly and studying her daughter-in-law)* Ruth Younger, what's the matter with you today? You look like you could fall over right there.

RUTH: I'm tired.

MAMA: Then you better stay home from work today.

RUTH: I can't stay home. She'd be calling up the agency and screaming at them, "My girl didn't come in today—send me somebody! My girl didn't come in!" Oh, she just have a fit . . .

MAMA: Well, let her have it. I'll just call her up and say you got the flu—

RUTH *(laughing):* Why the flu?

MAMA: 'Cause it sounds respectable to 'em. Something white people get, too. They know 'bout the flu. Otherwise they think you been cut up or something when you tell 'em you sick.

RUTH: I got to go in. We need the money.

MAMA: Somebody would of thought my children done all but starved to death the way they talk about money here late. Child, we got a great big old check coming tomorrow.

RUTH *(sincerely, but also self-righteously):* Now that's your money. It ain't got nothing to do with me. We all feel like that—Walter and Bennie and me—even Travis.

MAMA *(thoughtfully, and suddenly very far away):* Ten thousand dollars—

RUTH: Sure is wonderful.

MAMA: Ten thousand dollars.

RUTH: You know what you should do, Miss Lena? You should take yourself a trip somewhere. To Europe or South America or someplace—

MAMA *(throwing up her hands at the thought):* Oh, child!

RUTH: I'm serious. Just pack up and leave! Go on away and enjoy yourself some. Forget about the family and have yourself a ball for once in your life—

MAMA *(drily):* You shound like I'm just about ready to die. Who'd go with me? What I look like wandering 'round Europe by myself?

RUTH: Shoot—these here rich white women do it all the time. They don't think nothing of packing up they suitcases and piling on one of them big steamships and—swoosh!—they gone, child.

MAMA: Something always told me I wasn't no rich white woman.

RUTH: Well—what are you going to do with it then?

MAMA: I ain't rightly decided. *(Thinking. She speaks now with emphasis)* Some of it got to be put away for Beneatha and her schoolin'—and ain't nothing going to touch that part of it. Nothing. *(She waits several seconds, trying to make up her mind about something, and looks at* RUTH *a little tentatively before going on)* Been thinking that we maybe could meet the notes on a little old two-story somewhere, with a yard where Travis could play in the summertime, if we use part of the insurance for a down payment and everybody kind of pitch in. I could maybe take on a little day work again, few days a week—

RUTH *(studying her mother-in-law furtively and concentrating on her ironing, anxious to encourage without seeming to):* Well, Lord knows, we've put enough rent into this here rat trap to pay for four houses by now . . .

MAMA *(looking up at the words "rat trap" and then looking around and leaning back and sighing—in a suddenly reflective mood—):* "Rat trap"—yes, that's all it is. *(Smiling)* I remember just as well the day me and Big Walter moved in here. Hadn't been married but two weeks and wasn't planning on living here no more than a year. *(She shakes her head at the dissolved dream)* We was going to set away, little by little, don't you know, and buy a little place out in Morgan Park. We had even picked out the house. *(Chuckling a little)* Looks right dumpy today. But Lord, child, you should know all the dreams I had 'bout buying that house and fixing it up and making me a little garden in the back—*(She waits and stops smiling)* And didn't none of it happen.

(Dropping her hands in a futile gesture)

RUTH *(keeps her head down, ironing):* Yes, life can be a barrel of disappointments, sometimes.

MAMA: Honey, Big Walter would come in here some nights back then and slump down on that couch there and just look at the rug, and look at me and look at the rug and then back at me—and I'd know he was down then . . . really down. *(After a second very long and thoughtful pause; she is seeing back to times that only she can see)* And then, Lord, when I lost that baby—little Claude—I almost thought I was going to lose Big Walter too. Oh, that man grieved hisself! He was one man to love his children.

RUTH: Ain't nothin' can tear at you like losin' your baby.

MAMA: I guess that's how come that man finally worked hisself to death like he done. Like he was fighting his own war with this here world that took his baby from him.

RUTH: He sure was a fine man, all right. I always liked Mr. Younger.

MAMA: Crazy 'bout his children! God knows there was plenty wrong with Walter Younger—hard-headed, mean, kind of wild with women—plenty wrong with him. But he sure loved his children. Always wanted them to have something—be something. That's where Brother gets all these notions, I reckon. Big Walter used to say, he'd get right wet in the eyes sometimes, lean his head back with the water standing in his eyes and say, "Seem like God didn't see fit to give the black man nothing but dreams—but He did give us children to make them dreams seem worth while." *(She smiles)* He could talk like that, don't you know.

RUTH: Yes, he sure could. He was a good man, Mr. Younger.

MAMA: Yes, a fine man—just couldn't never catch up with his dreams, that's all.

*(*BENEATHA *comes in, brushing her hair and looking up to the ceiling, where the sound of a vacuum cleaner has started up)*

BENEATHA: What could be so dirty on that woman's rugs that she has to vacuum them every single day?

RUTH: I wish certain young women 'round here who I could name would take inspiration about certain rugs in a certain apartment I could also mention.

BENEATHA *(shrugging):* How much cleaning can a house need, for Christ's sakes.

MAMA *(not liking the Lord's name used thus):* Bennie!

RUTH: Just listen to her—just listen!

BENEATHA: Oh, God!

MAMA: If you use the Lord's name just one more time—

BENEATHA *(a bit of a whine):* Oh, Mama—

RUTH: Fresh—just fresh as salt, this girl!

BENEATHA *(drily):* Well—if the salt loses its savor—

MAMA: Now that will do. I just ain't going to have you 'round here reciting the scriptures in vain—you hear me?

BENEATHA: How did I manage to get on everybody's wrong side by just walking into a room?

RUTH: If you weren't so fresh—

BENEATHA: Ruth, I'm twenty years old.

MAMA: What time you be home from school today?

BENEATHA: Kind of late. *(With enthusiasm)* Madeline is going to start my guitar lessons today.

*(*MAMA *and* RUTH *look up with the same expression)*

MAMA: Your *what* kind of lessons?

BENEATHA: Guitar.

RUTH: Oh, Father!

MAMA: How come you done taken it in your mind to learn to play the guitar?

BENEATHA: I just want to, that's all.

MAMA *(smiling):* Lord, child, don't you know what to do with yourself? How long it going to be before you get tired of this now—like you got tired of that little play-acting group you joined last year? *(Looking at* RUTH*)* And what was it the year before that?

RUTH: The horseback-riding club for which she bought that fifty-five-dollar riding habit that's been hanging in the closet ever since!

MAMA *(to* BENEATHA*):* Why you got to flit so from one thing to another, baby?

BENEATHA *(sharply):* I just want to learn to play the guitar. Is there anything wrong with that?

MAMA: Ain't nobody trying to stop you. I just wonders sometimes why you has to flit so from one thing to another all the time. You ain't never done nothing with all that camera equipment you brought home—

BENEATHA: I don't flit! I—I experiment with different forms of expression—

RUTH: Like riding a horse?

BENEATHA: —People have to express themselves one way or another.

MAMA: What is it you want to express?

BENEATHA *(angrily):* Me! *(*MAMA *and* RUTH *look at each other and burst into raucous laughter)* Don't worry—I don't expect you to understand.

MAMA *(to change the subject):* Who you going out with tomorrow night?

BENEATHA *(with displeasure):* George Murchison again.

MAMA *(pleased):* Oh—you getting a little sweet on him?

RUTH: You ask me, this child ain't sweet on nobody but herself—*(Underbreath)* Express herself!

(They laugh)

BENEATHA: Oh—I like George all right, Mama. I mean I like him enough to go out with him and stuff, but—

RUTH *(for devilment):* What does *and stuff* mean?

BENEATHA: Mind your own business.

MAMA: Stop picking at her now, Ruth. *(She chuckles—then a suspicious sudden look at her daughter as she turns in her chair for emphasis)* What DOES it mean?

BENEATHA *(wearily):* Oh, I just mean I couldn't ever really be serious about George. He's—he's so shallow.

RUTH: Shallow—what do you mean he's shallow? He's *Rich!*

MAMA: Hush, Ruth.

BENEATHA: I know he's rich. He knows he's rich, too.

RUTH: Well—what other qualities a man got to have to satisfy you, little girl?

BENEATHA: You wouldn't even begin to understand. Anybody who married Walter could not possibly understand.

MAMA *(outraged):* What kind of way is that to talk about your brother?

BENEATHA: Brother is a flip—let's face it.

MAMA *(to* RUTH*, helplessly):* What's a flip?

RUTH *(glad to add kindling):* She's saying he's crazy.

BENEATHA: Not crazy. Brother isn't really crazy yet—he—he's an elaborate neurotic.

MAMA: Hush your mouth!

BENEATHA: As for George. Well. George looks good—he's got a beautiful car and he takes me to nice places and, as my sister-in-law says, he is probably the richest boy I will ever get to know and I even like him sometimes—but if the Youngers are sitting around waiting to see if their little Bennie is going to tie up the family with the Murchisons, they are wasting their time.

RUTH: You mean you wouldn't marry George Murchison if he asked you someday? That pretty, rich thing? Honey, I knew you was odd—

BENEATHA: No I would not marry him if all I felt for him was what I feel now. Besides, George's family wouldn't really like it.

MAMA: Why not?

BENEATHA: Oh, Mama—The Murchisons are honest-to-God-real-*live*-rich colored people, and the only people in the world who are more snobbish than rich white people are rich colored people. I thought everybody knew that. I've met Mrs. Murchison. She's a scene!

MAMA: You must not dislike people 'cause they well off, honey.

BENEATHA: Why not? It makes just as much sense as disliking people 'cause they are poor, and lots of people do that.

RUTH *(a wisdom-of-the-ages manner. To* MAMA*)*: Well, she'll get over some of this—

BENEATHA: Get over it? What are you talking about, Ruth? Listen, I'm going to be a doctor. I'm not worried about who I'm going to marry yet—if I ever get married.

MAMA *and* RUTH: *If!*

MAMA: Now, Bennie—

BENEATHA: Oh, I probably will . . . but first I'm going to be a doctor, and George, for one, still thinks that's pretty funny. I couldn't be bothered with that. I am going to be a doctor and everybody around here better understand that!

MAMA *(kindly)*: 'Course you going to be a doctor, honey, God willing.

BENEATHA *(drily)*: God hasn't got a thing to do with it.

MAMA: Beneatha—that just wasn't necessary.

BENEATHA: Well—neither is God. I get sick of hearing about God.

MAMA: Beneatha!

BENEATHA: I mean it! I'm just tired of hearing about God all the time. What has He got to do with anything? Does he pay tuition?

MAMA: You 'bout to get your fresh little jaw slapped!

RUTH: That's just what she needs, all right!

BENEATHA: Why? Why can't I say what I want to around here, like everybody else?

MAMA: It don't sound nice for a young girl to say things like that—you wasn't brought up that way. Me and your father went to trouble to get you and Brother to church every Sunday.

BENEATHA: Mama, you don't understand. It's all a matter of ideas, and God is just one idea I don't accept. It's not important. I am not going out and be immoral or commit crimes because I don't believe in God. I don't even think about it. It's just that I get tired of Him getting credit for all the things the human race achieves through its own stubborn effort. There simply is no blasted God—there is only man and it is *he* who makes miracles!

*(*Mama *absorbs this speech, studies her daughter and rises slowly and crosses to* Beneatha *and slaps her powerfully across the face. After, there is only silence and the daughter drops her eyes from her mother's face, and* Mama *is very tall before her)*

Mama: Now—you say after me, in my mother's house there is still God. *(There is a long pause and* Beneatha *stares at the floor wordlessly.* Mama *repeats the phrase with precision and cool emotion)* In my mother's house there is still God.

Beneatha: In my mother's house there is still God.

(A long pause)

Mama *(walking away from* Beneatha, *too disturbed for triumphant posture. Stopping and turning back to her daughter):* There are some ideas we ain't going to have in this house. Not long as I am at the head of this family.

Beneatha: Yes, ma'am.

*(*Mama *walks out of the room)*

Ruth *(almost gently, with profound understanding):* You think you a woman, Bennie—but you still a little girl. What you did was childish—so you got treated like a child.

Beneatha: I see. *(Quietly)* I also see that everybody thinks it's all right for Mama to be a tyrant. But all the tyranny in the world will never put a God in the heavens!

(She picks up her books and goes out. Pause)

Ruth *(goes to* Mama*'s door):* She said she was sorry.

Mama *(coming out, going to her plant):* They frightens me, Ruth. My children.

Ruth: You got good children, Lena. They just a little off sometimes—but they're good.

Mama: No—there's something come down between me and them that don't let us understand each other and I don't know what it is. One done almost lost his mind thinking 'bout money all the time and the other done commence to talk about things I can't seem to understand in no form or fashion. What is it that's changing, Ruth.

Ruth *(soothingly, older than her years):* Now . . . you taking it all too seriously. You just got strong-willed children and it takes a strong woman like you to keep 'em in hand.

Mama *(looking at her plant and sprinkling a little water on it):* They spirited all right, my children. Got to admit they got spirit—Bennie and Walter. Like this little old plant that ain't never had enough sunshine or nothing—and look at it . . .

(She has her back to Ruth, *who has had to stop ironing and lean against something and put the back of her hand to her forehead)*

Ruth *(trying to keep* Mama *from noticing):* You . . . sure . . . loves that little old thing, don't you? . . .

Mama: Well, I always wanted me a garden like I used to see sometimes at the back of the houses down home. This plant is close as I ever got to having one. *(She looks out of the window as she replaces the plant)* Lord, ain't nothing as dreary as the view from this window on a dreary day, is there? Why ain't you singing this morning, Ruth? Sing that "No Ways Tired." That song always lifts me up so—*(She turns at last to see that* Ruth *has slipped quietly to the floor, in a state of semiconsciousness)* Ruth! Ruth honey—what's the matter with you . . . Ruth!

Curtain

Scene II

It is the following morning; a Saturday morning, and house cleaning is in progress at the Youngers. *Furniture has been shoved hither and yon and* Mama *is giving the kitchen-area walls a washing down.* Beneatha, *in dungarees, with a handkerchief tied around her face, is spraying insecticide into the cracks in the walls. As they work, the radio is on and a Southside disk-jockey program is inappropriately filling the house with a rather exotic saxophone blues.* Travis, *the sole idle one, is leaning on his arms, looking out of the window.*

Travis: Grandmama, that stuff Bennie is using smells awful. Can I go downstairs, please?

Mama: Did you get all them chores done already? I ain't seen you doing much.

Travis: Yes'm—finished early. Where did Mama go this morning?

Mama *(looking at* Beneatha*):* She had to go on a little errand.

(The phone rings. Beneatha *runs to answer it and reaches it before* Walter, *who has entered from bedroom)*

Travis: Where?

Mama: To tend to her business.

Beneatha: Haylo . . . *(Disappointed)* Yes, he is. *(She tosses the phone to* Walter, *who barely catches it)* It's Willie Harris again.

Walter *(as privately as possible under* Mama*'s gaze):* Hello, Willie. Did you get the papers from the lawyer? . . . No, not yet. I told you the mailman doesn't get here till ten-thirty . . . No, I'll come there . . . Yeah! Right away. *(He hangs up and goes for his coat)*

Beneatha: Brother, where did Ruth go?

WALTER *(as he exits):* How should I know!

TRAVIS: Aw come on, Grandma. Can I go outside?

MAMA: Oh, I guess so. You stay right in front of the house, though, and keep a good lookout for the postman.

TRAVIS: Yes'm. *(He darts into bedroom for stickball and bat, reenters, and sees* BENEATHA *on her knees spraying under sofa with behind upraised. He edges closer to the target, takes aim, and lets her have it. She screams)* Leave them poor little cockroaches alone, they ain't bothering you none! *(He runs as she swings the spray-gun at him viciously and playfully)* Grandma! Grandma!

MAMA: Look out there, girl, before you be spilling some of that stuff on that child!

TRAVIS *(safely behind the bastion of* MAMA*):* That's right—look out, now! *(He exits)*

BENEATHA *(drily):* I can't imagine that it would hurt him—it has never hurt the roaches.

MAMA: Well, little boys' hides ain't as tough as Southside roaches. You better get over there behind the bureau. I seen one marching out of there like Napoleon yesterday.

BENEATHA: There's really only one way to get rid of them, Mama—

MAMA: How?

BENEATHA: Set fire to this building! Mama, where did Ruth go?

MAMA *(looking at her with meaning):* To the doctor, I think.

BENEATHA: The doctor? What's the matter? *(They exchange glances)* You don't think—

MAMA *(with her sense of drama):* Now I ain't saying what I think. But I ain't never been wrong 'bout a woman neither.

(The phone rings)

BENEATHA *(at the phone):* Hay-lo . . . *(Pause, and a moment of recognition)* Well—when did you get back! . . . And how was it? . . . Of course I've missed you—in my way . . . This morning? No . . . house cleaning and all that and Mama hates it if I let people come over when the house is like this . . . You *have?* Well, that's different . . . What is it—Oh, what the hell, come on over . . . Right, see you then. *Arrividerci.*

(She hangs up)

MAMA *(who has listened vigorously, as is her habit):* Who is that you inviting over here with this house looking like this? You ain't got the pride you was born with!

BENEATHA: Asagai doesn't care how houses look, Mama—he's an intellectual.

MAMA: *Who?*

BENEATHA: Asagai—Joseph Asagai. He's an African boy I met on campus. He's been studying in Canada all summer.

MAMA: What's his name?

BENEATHA: Asagai, Joseph. Ah-sah-guy . . . He's from Nigeria.
MAMA: Oh, that's the little country that was founded by slaves way back . . .
BENEATHA: No, Mama—that's Liberia.
MAMA: I don't think I never met no African before.
BENEATHA: Well, do me a favor and don't ask him a whole lot of ignorant questions about Africans. I mean, do they wear clothes and all that—
MAMA: Well, now, I guess if you think we so ignorant 'round here maybe you shouldn't bring your friends here—
BENEATHA: It's just that people ask such crazy things. All anyone seems to know about when it comes to Africa is Tarzan—
MAMA *(indignantly):* Why should I know anything about Africa?
BENEATHA: Why do you give money at church for the missionary work?
MAMA: Well, that's to help save people.
BENEATHA: You mean save them from *heathenism*—
MAMA *(innocently):* Yes.
BENEATHA: I'm afraid they need more salvation from the British and the French.

(RUTH *comes in forlornly and pulls off her coat with dejection. They both turn to look at her)*

RUTH *(dispiritedly):* Well, I guess from all the happy faces—everybody knows.
BENEATHA: You pregnant?
MAMA: Lord have mercy, I sure hope it's a little old girl. Travis ought to have a sister.

(BENEATHA *and* RUTH *give her a hopeless look for this grandmotherly enthusiasm)*

BENEATHA: How far along are you?
RUTH: Two months.
BENEATHA: Did you mean to? I mean did you plan it or was it an accident?
MAMA: What do you know about planning or not planning?
BENEATHA: Oh, Mama.
RUTH *(wearily):* She's twenty years old, Lena.
BENEATHA: Did you plan it, Ruth?
RUTH: Mind your own business.
BENEATHA: It is my business—where is he going to live, on the *roof? (There is silence following the remark as the three women react to the sense of it)* Gee—I didn't mean that, Ruth, honest. Gee, I don't feel like that at all. I—I think it is wonderful.
RUTH *(dully):* Wonderful.
BENEATHA: Yes—really.
MAMA *(looking at* RUTH, *worried):* Doctor say everything going to be all right?
RUTH *(Far away):* Yes—she says everything is going to be fine . . .
MAMA *(immediately suspicious):* "She"—What doctor you went to?

*(*Ruth *folds over, near hysteria)*

Mama *(worriedly hovering over* Ruth*):* Ruth honey—what's the matter with you—you sick?

*(*Ruth *has her fists clenched on her thighs and is fighting hard to suppress a scream that seems to be rising in her)*

Beneatha: What's the matter with her, Mama?

Mama *(working her fingers in* Ruth*'s shoulders to relax her):* She be all right. Women gets right depressed sometimes when they get her way. *(Speaking softly, expertly, rapidly)* Now you just relax. That's right . . . just lean back, don't think 'bout nothing at all . . . nothing at all—

Ruth: I'm all right . . .

(The glassy-eyed look melts and then she collapses into a fit of heavy sobbing. The bell rings)

Beneatha: Oh, my God—that must be Asagai.

Mama *(to* Ruth*):* Come on now, honey. You need to lie down and rest awhile . . . then have some nice hot food.

(They exit, Ruth*'s weight on her mother-in-law.* Beneatha, *herself profoundly disturbed, opens the door to admit a rather dramatic-looking young man with a large package)*

Asagai: Hello, Alaiyo—

Beneatha *(holding the door open and regarding him with pleasure):* Hello . . . *(Long pause)* Well—come in. And please excuse everything. My mother was very upset about my letting anyone come here with the place like this.

Asagai *(coming into the room):* You look disturbed too . . . Is something wrong?

Beneatha *(still at the door, absently):* Yes . . . we've all got acute ghetto-itus. *(She smiles and comes toward him, finding a cigarette and sitting)* So—sit down! No! Wait! *(She whips the spraygun off sofa where she had left it and puts the cushions back. At last perches on arm of sofa. He sits)* So, how was Canada?

Asagai *(a sophisticate):* Canadian.

Beneatha *(looking at him):* Asagai, I'm very glad you are back.

Asagai *(looking back at her in turn):* Are you really?

Beneatha: Yes—very.

Asagai: Why?—you were quite glad when I went away. What happened?

Beneatha: You went away.

Asagai: Ahhhhhhhh.

Beneatha: Before—you wanted to be so serious before there was time.

Asagai: How much time must there be before one knows what one feels?

BENEATHA *(stalling this particular conversation. Her hands pressed together, in a deliberately childish gesture):* What did you bring me?

ASAGAI *(handing her the package):* Open it and see.

BENEATHA *(eagerly opening the package and drawing out some records and the colorful robes of a Nigerian woman):* Oh, Asagai! . . . You got them for me! . . . How beautiful . . . and the records too! *(She lifts out the robes and runs to the mirror with them and holds the drapery up in front of herself)*

ASAGAI *(coming to her at the mirror):* I shall have to teach you how to drape it properly. *(He flings the material about her for the moment and stands back to look at her)* Ah—*Oh-pay-gay-day, oh-gbah-mu-shay. (A Yoruba exclamation for admiration)* You wear it well . . . very well . . . mutilated hair and all.

BENEATHA *(turning suddenly):* My hair—what's wrong with my hair?

ASAGAI *(shrugging):* Were you born with it like that?

BENEATHA *(reaching up to touch it):* No . . . of course not.

(She looks back to the mirror, disturbed)

ASAGAI *(smiling):* How then?

BENEATHA: You know perfectly well how . . . as crinkly as yours . . . that's how.

ASAGAI: And it is ugly to you that way?

BENEATHA *(quickly):* Oh, no—not ugly . . . *(More slowly, apologetically)* But it's so hard to manage when it's, well—raw.

ASAGAI: And so to accommodate that—you mutilate it every week?

BENEATHA: It's not mutilation!

ASAGAI *(laughing aloud at her seriousness):* Oh . . . please! I am only teasing you because you are so very serious about these things. *(He stands back from her and folds his arms across his chest as he watches her pulling at her hair and frowning in the mirror)* Do you remember the first time you met me at school? . . . *(He laughs)* You came up to me and you said—and I thought you were the most serious little thing I had ever seen—you said: *(He imitates her)* "Mr. Asagai—I want very much to talk with you. About Africa. You see, Mr. Asagai, I am looking for my *identity!"*

(He laughs)

BENEATHA *(turning to him, not laughing):* Yes—

(Her face is quizzical, profoundly disturbed)

ASAGAI *(still teasing and reaching out and taking her face in his hands and turning her profile to him):* Well . . . it is true that this is not so much a profile of a Hollywood queen as perhaps a queen of the Nile—*(A mock dismissal of the importance of the question)* But what does it matter? Assimilationism is so popular in your country.

BENEATHA *(wheeling, passionately, sharply):* I am not an assimilationist!

ASAGAI *(the protest hangs in the room for a moment and* ASAGAI *studies her, his laughter fading):* Such a serious one. *(There is a pause)* So—you like the robes? You must take excellent care of them—they are from my sister's personal wardrobe.

BENEATHA *(with incredulity):* You—you sent all the way home—for me?

ASAGAI *(with charm):* For you—I would do much more . . . Well, that is what I came for. I must go.

BENEATHA: Will you call me Monday?

ASAGAI: Yes . . . We have a great deal to talk about. I mean about identity and time and all that.

BENEATHA: Time?

ASAGAI: Yes. About how much time one needs to know what one feels.

BENEATHA: You see! You never understood that there is more than one kind of feeling which can exist between a man and a woman—or, at least, there should be.

ASAGAI *(shaking his head negatively but gently):* No. Between a man and a woman there need be only one kind of feeling. I have that for you . . . Now even . . . right this moment . . .

BENEATHA: I know—and by itself—it won't do. I can find that anywhere.

ASAGAI: For a woman it should be enough.

BENEATHA: I know—because that's what it says in all the novels that men write. But it isn't. Go ahead and laugh—but I'm not interested in being someone's little episode in America or—*(With feminine vengeance)*—one of them! *(*ASAGAI *has burst into laughter again)* That's funny as hell, huh!

ASAGAI: It's just that every American girl I have known has said that to me. White—black—in this you are all the same. And the same speech, too!

BENEATHA *(angrily):* Yuk, yuk, yuk!

ASAGAI: It's how you can be sure that the world's most liberated women are not liberated at all. You all talk about it too much!

*(*MAMA *enters and is immediately all social charm because of the presence of a guest)*

BENEATHA: Oh—Mama—this is Mr. Asagai.

MAMA: How do you do?

ASAGAI *(total politeness to an elder):* How do you do, Mrs. Younger. Please forgive me for coming at such an outrageous hour on a Saturday.

MAMA: Well, you are quite welcome. I just hope you understand that our house don't always look like this. *(Chatterish)* You must come again. I would love to hear all about—*(Not sure of the name)*—your country. I think it's so sad the way our American Negroes don't know nothing about Africa 'cept Tarzan and all that. And all that money they pour into these churches when they ought to be helping you people over there drive out them French and Englishmen done taken away your land.

(The mother flashes a slightly superior look at her daughter upon completion of the recitation)

ASAGAI *(taken aback by this sudden and acutely unrelated expression of sympathy):* Yes . . . yes . . .

MAMA *(smiling at him suddenly and relaxing and looking him over):* How many miles is it from here to where you come from?

ASAGAI: Many thousands.

MAMA *(looking at him as she would* WALTER*):* I bet you don't half look after yourself, being away from your Mama either. I spec you better come 'round here from time to time to get yourself some decent home-cooked meals . . .

ASAGAI *(moved):* Thank you. Thank you very much. *(They are all quiet, then—)* Well . . . I must go. I will call you Monday, Alaiyo.

MAMA: What's that he call you?

ASAGAI: Oh—"Alaiyo." I hope you don't mind. It is what you would call a nickname, I think. It is a Yoruba word. I am a Yoruba.

MAMA *(looking at* BENEATHA*):* I—I thought he was from—*(Uncertain)*

ASAGAI *(understanding):* Nigeria is my country. Yoruba is my tribal origin—

BENEATHA: You didn't tell us what Alaiyo means . . . for all I know, you might be calling me Little Idiot or something . . .

ASAGAI: Well . . . let me see . . . I do not know how just to explain it . . . The sense of a thing can be so different when it changes languages.

BENEATHA: You're evading.

ASAGAI: No—really it is difficult . . . *(Thinking)* It means . . . it means One for Whom Bread—Food—Is Not Enough. *(He looks at her)* Is that all right?

BENEATHA *(understanding, softly):* Thank you.

MAMA *(looking from one to the other and not understanding any of it):* Well . . . that's nice . . . You must come see us again—Mr.——

ASAGAI: Ah-sah-guy . . .

MAMA: Yes . . . Do come again.

ASAGAI: Good-bye.

(He exits)

MAMA *(after him):* Lord, that's a pretty thing just went out here! *(Insinuatingly, to her daughter)* Yes, I guess I see why we done commence to get so interested in Africa 'round here. Missionaries my aunt Jenny!

(She exits)

BENEATHA: Oh, Mama! . . .

(She picks up the Nigerian dress and holds it up to her in front of the mirror again. She sets the headdress on haphazardly and then notices her hair again and clutches at it and then replaces the headdress and frowns at herself. Then she starts to wriggle in front of the mirror as she thinks a Nigerian woman might. TRAVIS *enters and stands regarding her)*

TRAVIS: What's the matter, girl, you cracking up?
BENEATHA: Shut up.

(She pulls the headdress off and looks at herself in the mirror and clutches at her hair again and squinches her eyes as if trying to imagine something. Then, suddenly, she gets her raincoat and kerchief and hurriedly prepares for going out)

MAMA *(coming back into the room):* She's resting now. Travis, baby, run next door and ask Miss Johnson to please let me have a little kitchen cleanser. This here can is empty as Jacob's kettle.
TRAVIS: I just came in.
MAMA: Do as you told. *(He exits and she looks at her daughter)* Where you going?
BENEATHA *(halting at the door):* To become a queen of the Nile!

(She exits in a breathless blaze of glory. RUTH *appears in the bedroom doorway)*

MAMA: Who told you to get up?
RUTH: Ain't nothing wrong with me to be lying in no bed for. Where did Bennie go?
MAMA *(drumming her fingers):* Far as I could make out—to Egypt. *(*RUTH *just looks at her)* What time is it getting to?
RUTH: Ten twenty. And the mailman going to ring that bell this morning just like he done every morning for the last umpteen years.

*(*TRAVIS *comes in with the cleanser can)*

TRAVIS: She say to tell you that she don't have much.
MAMA *(angrily):* Lord, some people I could name sure is tight-fisted! *(Directing her grandson)* Mark two cans of cleanser down on the list there. If she that hard up for kitchen cleanser, I sure don't want to forget to get her none!
RUTH: Lena—maybe the woman is just short on cleanser—
MAMA *(not listening):* —Much baking powder as she done borrowed from me all these years, she could of done gone into the baking business!

(The bell sounds suddenly and sharply and all three are stunned—serious and silent—mid-speech. In spite of all the other conversations and distractions of the morning, this is what they have been waiting for, even TRAVIS, *who looks helplessly from his mother to his grandmother.* RUTH *is the first to come to life again)*

RUTH *(to* TRAVIS*): Get down them steps, boy!*

*(*TRAVIS *snaps to life and flies out to get the mail)*

MAMA *(her eyes wide, her hand to her breast):* You mean it done really come?
RUTH *(excited):* Oh, Miss Lena!

Mama *(collecting herself):* Well . . . I don't know what we all so excited about 'round here for. We known it was coming for months.

Ruth: That's a whole lot different from having it come and being able to hold it in your hands . . . a piece of paper worth ten thousand dollars . . . *(*Travis *bursts back into the room. He holds the envelope high above his head, like a little dancer, his face is radiant and he is breathless. He moves to his grandmother with sudden slow ceremony and puts the envelope into her hands. She accepts it, and then merely holds it and looks at it)* Come on! Open it . . . Lord have mercy, I wish Walter Lee was here!

Travis: Open it, Grandmama!

Mama *(staring at it):* Now you all be quiet. It's just a check.

Ruth: Open it . . .

Mama *(still staring at it):* Now don't act silly . . . We ain't never been no people to act silly 'bout no money—

Ruth *(swiftly):* We ain't never had none before—OPEN IT!

*(*Mama *finally makes a good strong tear and pulls out the thin blue slice of paper and inspects it closely. The boy and his mother study it raptly over* Mama*'s shoulders)*

Mama: *Travis! (She is counting off with doubt)* Is that the right number of zeros.

Travis: Yes'm . . . ten thousand dollars. Gaalee, Grandmama, you rich.

Mama *(she holds the check away from her, still looking at it. Slowly her face sobers into a mask of unhappiness):* Ten thousand dollars. *(She hands it to* Ruth*):* Put it away somewhere, Ruth. *(She does not look at* Ruth; *her eyes seem to be seeing something somewhere very far off)* Ten thousand dollars they give you. Ten thousand dollars.

Travis *(to his mother, sincerely):* What's the matter with Grandmama—don't she want to be rich?

Ruth *(distractedly):* You go on out and play now, baby. *(*Travis *exits.* Mama *starts wiping dishes absently, humming intently to herself.* Ruth *turns to her, with kind exasperation)* You've gone and got yourself upset.

Mama *(not looking at her):* I spec if it wasn't for you all . . . I would just put that money away or give it to the church or something.

Ruth: Now what kind of talk is that. Mr. Younger would just be plain mad if he could hear you talking foolish like that.

Mama *(stopping and staring off):* Yes . . . he sure would. *(Sighing)* We got enough to do with that money, all right. *(She halts then, and turns and looks at her daughter-in-law hard;* Ruth *avoids her eyes and* Mama *wipes her hands with finality and starts to speak firmly to* Ruth*)* Where did you go today, girl?

Ruth: To the doctor.

Mama *(impatiently):* Now, Ruth . . . you know better than that. Old Doctor Jones is strange enough in his way but there ain't nothing 'bout him make somebody slip and call him "she"—like you done this morning.

RUTH: Well, that's what happened—my tongue slipped.
MAMA: You went to see that woman, didn't you?
RUTH *(defensively, giving herself away):* What woman you talking about?
MAMA *(angrily):* That woman who—

(WALTER enters in great excitement)

WALTER: Did it come?
MAMA *(quietly):* Can't you give people a Christian greeting before you start asking about money?
WALTER *(to RUTH):* Did it come? *(RUTH unfolds the check and lays it quietly before him, watching him intently with thoughts of her own. WALTER sits down and grasps it close and counts off the zeros)* Ten thousand dollars—*(He turns suddenly, frantically to his mother and draws some papers out of his breast pocket)* Mama—look. Old Willy Harris put everything on paper—
MAMA: Son—I think you ought to talk to your wife . . . I'll go on out and leave you alone if you want—
WALTER: I can talk to her later—Mama, look—
MAMA: Son—
WALTER: WILL SOMEBODY PLEASE LISTEN TO ME TODAY!
MAMA *(quietly):* I don't 'low no yellin' in this house, Walter Lee, and you know it—*(WALTER stares at them in frustration and starts to speak several times)* And there ain't going to be no investing in no liquor stores.
WALTER: But, Mama, you ain't even looked at it.
MAMA: I don't aim to have to speak on that again.

(A long pause)

WALTER: You ain't looked at it and you don't aim to have to speak on that again? You ain't even looked at it and *you* have decided—*(Crumpling his papers)* Well, *you* tell that to my boy tonight when you put him to sleep on the living-room couch . . . *(Turning to MAMA and speaking directly to her)* Yeah—and tell it to my wife, Mama, tomorrow when she has to go out of here to look after somebody else's kids. And tell it to *me,* Mama, every time we need a new pair of curtains and I have to watch *you* go out and work in somebody's kitchen. Yeah, you tell me then!

(WALTER starts out)

RUTH: Where you going?
WALTER: I'm going out!
RUTH: Where?
WALTER: Just out of this house somewhere—
RUTH *(getting her coat):* I'll come too.
WALTER: I don't want you to come!
RUTH: I got something to talk to you about, Walter.
WALTER: That's too bad.

MAMA *(still quietly):* Walter Lee—*(She waits and he finally turns and looks at her)* Sit down.

WALTER: I'm a grown man, Mama.

MAMA: Ain't nobody said you wasn't grown. But you still in my house and my presence. And as long as you are—you'll talk to your wife civil. Now sit down.

RUTH *(suddenly):* Oh, let him go on out and drink himself to death! He makes me sick to my stomach! *(She flings her coat against him and exits to bedroom)*

WALTER *(violently flinging the coat after her):* And you turn mine too, baby! *(The door slams behind her)* That was my biggest mistake—

MAMA *(still quietly):* Walter, what is the matter with you?

WALTER: Matter with me? Ain't nothing the matter with *me!*

MAMA: Yes there is. Something eating you up like a crazy man. Something more than me not giving you this money. The past few years I been watching it happen to you. You get all nervous acting and kind of wild in the eyes—*(WALTER jumps up impatiently at her words)* I said sit there now, I'm talking to you!

WALTER: Mama—I don't need no nagging at me today.

MAMA: Seem like you getting to a place where you always tied up in some kind of knot about something. But if anybody ask you 'bout it you just yell at 'em and bust out the house and go out and drink somewheres. Walter Lee, people can't live with that. Ruth's a good, patient girl in her way—but you getting to be too much. Boy, don't make the mistake of driving that girl away from you.

WALTER: Why—what she do for me?

MAMA: She loves you.

WALTER: Mama—I'm going out. I want to go off somewhere and be by myself for a while.

MAMA: I'm sorry 'bout your liquor store, son. It just wasn't the thing for us to do. That's what I want to tell you about—

WALTER: I got to go out, Mama—

(He rises)

MAMA: It's dangerous, son.

WALTER: What's dangerous?

MAMA: When a man goes outside his home to look for peace.

WALTER *(beseechingly):* Then why can't there never be no peace in this house then?

MAMA: You done found it in some other house?

WALTER: No—there ain't no woman! Why do women always think there's a woman somewhere when a man gets restless. *(Picks up the check)* Do you know what this money means to me? Do you know what this money can do for us? *(Puts it back)* Mama—Mama—I want so many things . . .

MAMA: Yes, son—

WALTER: I want so many things that they are driving me kind of crazy . . . Mama—look at me.

MAMA: I'm looking at you. You a good-looking boy. You got a job, a nice wife, a fine boy and—

WALTER: A job. *(Looks at her)* Mama, a job? I open and close car doors all day long. I drive a man around in his limousine and I say, "Yes, sir; no, sir; very good, sir; shall I take the Drive, sir?" Mama, that ain't no kind of job . . . that ain't nothing at all. *(Very quietly)* Mama, I don't know if I can make you understand.

MAMA: Understand what, baby?

WALTER *(quietly):* Sometimes it's like I can see the future stretched out in front of me—just plain as day. The future, Mama. Hanging over there at the edge of my days. Just waiting for me—a big, looming blank space—full of *nothing*. Just waiting for *me*. But it don't have to be. *(Pause. Kneeling beside her chair)* Mama—sometimes when I'm downtown and I pass them cool, quiet-looking restaurants where them white boys are sitting back and talking 'bout things . . . sitting there turning deals worth millions of dollars . . . sometimes I see guys don't look much older than me—

MAMA: Son—how come you talk so much 'bout money?

WALTER *(with immense passion):* Because it is life, Mama!

MAMA *(quietly):* Oh—*(Very quietly)* So now it's life. Money is life. Once upon a time freedom used to be life—now it's money. I guess the world really do change . . .

WALTER: No—it was always money, Mama. We just didn't know about it.

MAMA: No . . . something has changed. *(She looks at him)* You something new, boy. In my time we was worried about not being lynched and getting to the North if we could and how to stay alive and still have a pinch of dignity too . . . Now here come you and Beneatha—talking 'bout things we ain't never even thought about hardly, me and your daddy. You ain't satisfied or proud of nothing we done. I mean that you had a home; that we kept you out of trouble till you was grown; that you don't have to ride to work on the back of nobody's streetcar—You my children—but how different we done become.

WALTER *(a long beat. He pats her hand and gets up):* You just don't understand, Mama, you just don't understand.

MAMA: Son—do you know your wife is expecting another baby? *(WALTER stands, stunned, and absorbs what his mother has said)* That's what she wanted to talk to you about. *(WALTER sinks down into a chair)* This ain't for me to be telling—but you ought to know. *(She waits)* I think Ruth is thinking 'bout getting rid of that child.

WALTER *(slowly understanding):* —No—no—Ruth wouldn't do that.

MAMA: When the world gets ugly enough—a woman will do anything for her family. *The part that's already living.*

WALTER: You don't know Ruth, Mama, if you think she would do that.

*(*RUTH *opens the bedroom door and stands there a little limp)*

RUTH *(beaten):* Yes I would too, Walter. *(Pause)* I gave her a five-dollar down payment.

(There is total silence as the man stares at his wife and the mother stares at her son)

MAMA *(presently):* Well—*(Tightly)* Well—son, I'm waiting to hear you say something . . . *(She waits)* I'm waiting to hear how you be your father's son. Be the man he was . . . *(Pause. The silence shouts)* Your wife say she going to destroy your child. And I'm waiting to hear you talk like him and say we a people who give children life, not who destroys them—*(She rises)* I'm waiting to see you stand up and look like your daddy and say we done give up one baby to poverty and that we ain't going to give up nary another one . . . I'm waiting.

WALTER: Ruth—*(He can say nothing)*

MAMA: If you a son of mine, tell her! *(*WALTER *picks up his keys and his coat and walks out. She continues, bitterly)* You . . . you are a disgrace to your father's memory. Somebody get me my hat!

Curtain

ACT II

Scene I

Time: Later the same day.

At rise: RUTH *is ironing again. She has the radio going. Presently* BENEATHA*'s bedroom door opens and* RUTH*'s mouth falls and she puts down the iron in fascination.*

RUTH: What have we got on tonight!

BENEATHA *(emerging grandly from the doorway so that we can see her thoroughly robed in the costume Asagai brought):* You are looking at what a well-dressed Nigerian woman wears—*(She parades for* RUTH*, her hair completely hidden by the headdress; she is coquettishly fanning herself with an ornate oriental fan, mistakenly more like Butterfly than any Nigerian that ever was)* Isn't it beautiful? *(She promenades to the radio and, with an arrogant flourish, turns off the good loud blues that is playing)* Enough of this assimilationist junk! *(*RUTH *follows her with her eyes as* *she goes to the phonograph and puts on a record and turns and waits ceremoniously for the music to come up. Then, with a shout—)* OCOMOGOSIAY!

*(*RUTH *jumps. The music comes up, a lovely Nigerian melody.* BENEATHA *listens, enraptured, her eyes far away—"back to the past." She begins to dance.* RUTH *is dumbfounded)*

RUTH: What kind of dance is that?
BENEATHA: A folk dance.
RUTH *(Pearl Bailey):* What kind of folks do that, honey?
BENEATHA: It's from Nigeria. It's a dance of welcome.
RUTH: Who you welcoming?
BENEATHA: The men back to the village.
RUTH: Where they been?
BENEATHA: How should I know—out hunting or something. Anyway, they are coming back now . . .
RUTH: Well, that's good.
BENEATHA *(with the record):* Alundi, alundi
Alundi alunya
Jop pu à jeepua
Ang gu soooooooooo

Ai yai yae . . .
Ayehaye—alundi . . .

*(*WALTER *comes in during this performance; he has obviously been drinking. He leans against the door heavily and watches his sister, at first with distaste. Then his eyes look off—"back to the past"—as he lifts both his fists to the roof, screaming)*

WALTER: YEAH . . . AND ETHIOPIA STRETCH FORTH HER HANDS AGAIN! . . .
RUTH *(drily, looking at him):* Yes—and Africa sure is claiming her own tonight. *(She gives them both up and starts ironing again)*
WALTER *(all in a drunken, dramatic shout):* Shut up! . . . I'm digging them drums . . . them drums move me! . . . *(He makes his weaving way to his wife's face and leans in close to her)* In my *heart of hearts—(He thumps his chest)*—I am much warrior!
RUTH *(without even looking up):* In your heart of hearts you are much drunkard.
WALTER *(coming away from her and starting to wander around the room, shouting):* Me and Jomo . . . *(Intently, in his sister's face. She has stopped dancing to watch him in this unknown mood)* That's my man, Kenyatta. *(Shouting and thumping his chest)* FLAMING SPEAR! HOT DAMN! *(He is suddenly in possession of an imaginary spear and actively spearing enemies all over the room) OCOMOGOSIAY . . .*

BENEATHA *(to encourage* WALTER, *thoroughly caught up with this side of him): OCOMOGOSIAY,* FLAMING SPEAR!

WALTER: THE LION IS WAKING . . . OWIMOWEH!

(He pulls his shirt open and leaps up on the table and gestures with his spear)

BENEATHA: OWIMOWEH!

WALTER *(on the table, very far gone, his eyes pure glass sheets. He sees what we cannot, that he is a leader of his people, a great chief, a descendant of Chaka, and that the hour to march has come):* Listen, my black brothers—

BENEATHA: OCOMOGOSIAY!

WALTER: —Do you hear the waters rushing against the shores of the coastlands—

BENEATHA: OCOMOGOSIAY!

WALTER: —Do you hear the screeching of the cocks in yonder hills beyond where the chiefs meet in council for the coming of the mighty war—

BENEATHA: OCOMOGOSIAY!

(And now the lighting shifts subtly to suggest the world of WALTER*'s imagination, and the mood shifts from pure comedy. It is the inner* WALTER *speaking: the Southside chauffeur has assumed an unexpected majesty)*

WALTER: —Do you hear the beating of the wings of the birds flying low over the mountains and the low places of our land—

BENEATHA: OCOMOGOSIAY!

WALTER: —Do you hear the singing of the women, singing the war songs of our fathers to the babies in the great houses? Singing the sweet war songs! *(The doorbell rings)* OH, DO YOU HEAR, MY *BLACK* BROTHERS!

BENEATHA *(completely gone):* We hear you, Flaming Spear—

*(*RUTH *shuts off the phonograph and opens the door.* GEORGE MURCHISON *enters)*

WALTER: Telling us to prepare for the GREATNESS OF THE TIME! *(Lights back to normal. He turns and sees* GEORGE*)* Black Brother!

(He extends his hand for the fraternal clasp)

GEORGE: Black Brother, hell!

RUTH *(having had enough, and embarrassed for the family):* Beneatha, you got company—what's the matter with you? Walter Lee Younger, get down off that table and stop acting like a fool . . .

*(*WALTER *comes down off the table suddenly and makes a quick exit to the bathroom)*

RUTH: He's had a little to drink . . . I don't know what her excuse is.

GEORGE *(to* BENEATHA*):* Look honey, we're going *to* the theatre—we're not going to be *in* it . . . so go change, huh?

*(*Beneatha *looks at him and slowly, ceremoniously, lifts her hands and pulls off the headdress. Her hair is close-cropped and unstraightened.* George *freezes mid-sentence and* Ruth*'s eyes all but fall out of her head)*

George: What in the name of—

Ruth *(touching* Beneatha*'s hair):* Girl, you done lost your natural mind!? Look at your head!

George: What have you done to your head—I mean your hair!

Beneatha: Nothing—except cut it off.

Ruth: Now that's the truth—it's what ain't been done to it! You expect this boy to go out with you with your head all nappy like that?

Beneatha *(looking at* George*):* That's up to George. If he's ashamed of his heritage—

George: Oh, don't be so proud of yourself, Bennie—just because you look eccentric.

Beneatha: How can something that's natural be eccentric?

George: That's what being eccentric means—being natural. Get dressed.

Beneatha: I don't like that, George.

Ruth: Why must you and your brother make an argument out of everything people say?

Beneatha: Because I hate assimilationist Negroes!

Ruth: Will somebody please tell me what assimila-who-ever means!

George: Oh, it's just a college girl's way of calling people Uncle Toms—but that isn't what it means at all.

Ruth: Well, what does it mean?

Beneatha *(cutting* George *off and staring at him as she replies to* Ruth*):* It means someone who is willing to give up his own culture and submerge himself completely in the dominant, and in this case *oppressive* culture!

George: Oh, dear, dear, dear! Here we go! A lecture on the African past! On our Great West African Heritage! In one second we will hear all about the great Ashanti empires; the great Songhay civilizations; and the great sculpture of Bénin—and then some poetry in the Bantu—and the whole monologue will end with the word *heritage! (Nastily)* Let's face it, baby, your heritage is nothing but a bunch of raggedy-assed spirituals and some grass huts!

Beneatha: GRASS HUTS! *(*Ruth *crosses to her and forcibly pushes her toward the bedroom)* See there . . . you are standing there in your splendid ignorance talking about people who were the first to smelt iron on the face of the earth! *(*Ruth *is pushing her through the door)* The Ashanti were performing surgical operations when the English—*(*Ruth *pulls the door to, with* Beneatha *on the other side, and smiles graciously at* George. Beneatha *opens the door and shouts the end of the sentence defiantly at* George*)*—were still tatooing themselves with blue dragons! *(She goes back inside)*

Ruth: Have a seat, George. *(They both sit.* Ruth *folds her hands rather primly on her lap, determined to demonstrate the civilization of the family)* Warm, ain't it? I mean for September. *(Pause)* Just like they always say about Chicago weather: If it's too hot or cold for you, just wait a minute and it'll change. *(She smiles happily at this cliché of clichés)* Everybody say it's got to do with them bombs and things they keep setting off. *(Pause)* Would you like a nice cold beer?

GEORGE: No, thank you. I don't care for beer. *(He looks at his watch)* I hope she hurries up.

RUTH: What time is the show?

GEORGE: It's an eight-thirty curtain. That's just Chicago, though. In New York standard curtain time is eight forty.

(He is rather proud of this knowledge)

RUTH *(properly appreciating it):* You get to New York a lot?

GEORGE *(offhand):* Few times a year.

RUTH: Oh—that's nice. I've never been to New York.

*(*WALTER *enters. We feel he has relieved himself, but the edge of unreality is still with him)*

WALTER: New York ain't got nothing Chicago ain't. Just a bunch of hustling people all squeezed up together—being "Eastern."

(He turns his face into a screw of displeasure)

GEORGE: Oh—you've been?

WALTER: *Plenty* of times.

RUTH *(shocked at the lie):* Walter Lee Younger!

WALTER *(staring her down):* Plenty! *(Pause)* What we got to drink in this house? Why don't you offer this man some refreshment. *(To* GEORGE*)* They don't know how to entertain people in this house, man.

GEORGE: Thank you—I don't really care for anything.

WALTER *(feeling his head; sobriety coming):* Where's Mama?

RUTH: She ain't come back yet.

WALTER *(looking* MURCHISON *over from head to toe, scrutinizing his carefully casual tweed sports jacket over cashmere V-neck sweater over soft eyelet shirt and tie, and soft slacks, finished off with white buckskin shoes):* Why all you college boys wear them faggoty-looking white shoes?

RUTH: Walter Lee!

*(*GEORGE MURCHISON *ignores the remark)*

WALTER *(to* RUTH*):* Well, they look crazy as hell—white shoes, cold as it is.

RUTH *(crushed):* You have to excuse him—

WALTER: No he don't! Excuse me for what? What you always excusing me for! I'll excuse myself when I needs to be excused! *(A pause)* They look as funny as them black knee socks Beneatha wears out of here all the time.

RUTH: It's the college *style,* Walter.

WALTER: Style, hell. She looks like she got burnt legs or something!

RUTH: Oh, Walter—

WALTER *(an irritable mimic):* Oh, Walter! Oh, Walter! *(To* MURCHISON*)* How's your old man making out? I understand you all going to buy that big hotel on the Drive? *(He finds a beer in the refrigerator, wanders over to* MURCHISON, *sipping and wiping his lips with the back of his hand, and straddling a choir backwards to talk to the other man)* Shrewd move. Your old man is all right, man. *(Tapping his head and half winking for emphasis)* I mean he knows how to operate. I mean he thinks *big,* you know what I mean, I mean for a *home,* you know? But I think he's kind of running out of ideas now. I'd like to talk to him. Listen, man, I got some plans that could turn this city upside down. I mean think like he does. *Big.* Invest big, gamble big, hell, lose *big* if you have to, you know what I mean. It's hard to find a man on this whole Southside who understands my kind of thinking—you dig? *(He scrutinizes* MURCHISON *again, drinks his beer, squints his eyes and leans in close, confidential, man to man)* Me and you ought to sit down and talk sometimes, man. Man, I got me some ideas . . .

MURCHISON *(with boredom):* Yeah—sometimes we'll have to do that, Walter.

WALTER *(understanding the indifference, and offended):* Yeah—well, when you get the time, man. I know you a busy little boy.

RUTH: Walter, please—

WALTER *(bitterly, hurt):* I know ain't nothing in this world as busy as you colored college boys with your fraternity pins and white shoes . . .

RUTH *(covering her face with humiliation):* Oh, Walter Lee—

WALTER: I see you all all the time—with the books tucked under your arms—going to your *(British A—a mimic)* "clahsses." And for what! What the hell you learning over there? Filling up your heads—*(Counting off on his fingers)*—with the sociology and the psychology—but they teaching you how to be a man? How to take over and run the world? They teaching you how to run a rubber plantation or a steel mill? Naw—just to talk proper and read books and wear them faggoty-looking white shoes . . .

GEORGE *(looking at him with distaste, a little above it all):* You're all wacked up with bitterness, man.

WALTER *(intently, almost quietly, between the teeth, glaring at the boy):* And you—ain't you bitter, man? Ain't you just about had it yet? Don't you see no stars gleaming that you can't reach out and grab? You happy?—You contented son-of-a-bitch—you happy? You got it made? Bitter? Man, I'm a volcano. Bitter? Here I am a giant—surrounded by ants! Ants who can't even understand what it is the giant is talking about.

RUTH *(passionately and suddenly):* Oh, Walter—ain't you with nobody!

WALTER *(violently):* No! 'Cause ain't nobody with me! Not even my own mother!

RUTH: Walter, that's a terrible thing to say!

*(*BENEATHA *enters, dressed for the evening in a cocktail dress and earrings, hair natural)*

GEORGE: Well—hey—*(Crosses to* BENEATHA; *thoughtful, with emphasis, since this is a reversal)* You look great!

WALTER *(seeing his sister's hair for the first time):* What's the matter with your head?

BENEATHA *(tired of the jokes now):* I cut it off, Brother.

WALTER *(coming close to inspect it and walking around her):* Well, I'll be damned. So that's what they mean by the African bush . . .

BENEATHA: Ha ha. Let's go, George.

GEORGE *(looking at her):* You know something? I like it. It's sharp. I mean it really is. *(Helps her into her wrap)*

RUTH: Yes—I think so, too. *(She goes to the mirror and starts to clutch at her hair)*

WALTER: Oh no! You leave yours alone, baby. You might turn out to have a pin-shaped head or something!

BENEATHA: See you all later.

RUTH: Have a nice time.

GEORGE: Thanks. Good night. *(Half out the door, he reopens it. To* WALTER*)* Good night, Prometheus!

*(*BENEATHA *and* GEORGE *exit)*

WALTER *(to* RUTH*):* Who is Prometheus?

RUTH: I don't know. Don't worry about it.

WALTER *(in fury, pointing after* GEORGE*):* See there—they get to a point where they can't insult you man to man—they got to go talk about something ain't nobody never heard of!

RUTH: How do you know it was an insult? *(To humor him)* Maybe Prometheus is a nice fellow.

WALTER: Prometheus! I bet there ain't even no such thing! I bet that simple-minded clown—

RUTH: Walter—

(She stops what she is doing and looks at him)

WALTER *(yelling):* Don't start!

RUTH: Start what?

WALTER: Your nagging! Where was I? Who was I with? How much money did I spend?

RUTH *(plaintively):* Walter Lee—why don't we just try to talk about it . . .

WALTER *(not listening):* I been out talking with people who understand me. People who care about the things I got on my mind.

RUTH *(wearily):* I guess that means people like Willy Harris.

WALTER: Yes, people like Willy Harris.

RUTH *(with a sudden flash of impatience):* Why don't you all just hurry up and go into the banking business and stop talking about it!

WALTER: Why? You want to know why? 'Cause we all tied up in a race of people that don't know how to do nothing but moan, pray and have babies!

(The line is too bitter even for him and he looks at her and sits down)

RUTH: Oh, Walter . . . *(Softly)* Honey, why can't you stop fighting me?

WALTER *(without thinking):* Who's fighting you? Who even cares about you?

(This line begins the retardation of his mood)

RUTH: Well—*(She waits a long time, and then with resignation starts to put away her things)* I guess I might as well go on to bed . . . *(More or less to herself)* I don't know where we lost it . . . but we have . . . *(Then, to him)* I—I'm sorry about this new baby, Walter. I guess maybe I better go on and do what I started . . . I guess I just didn't realize how bad things was with us . . . I guess I just didn't really realize—*(She starts out to the bedroom and stops)* You want some hot milk?

WALTER: Hot milk?

RUTH: Yes—hot milk.

WALTER: Why hot milk?

RUTH: 'Cause after all that liquor you come home with you ought to have something hot in your stomach.

WALTER: I don't want no milk.

RUTH: You want some coffee then?

WALTER: No, I don't want no coffee. I don't want nothing hot to drink. *(Almost plaintively)* Why you always trying to give me something to eat?

RUTH *(standing and looking at him helplessly):* What *else* can I give you, Walter Lee Younger?

(She stands and looks at him and presently turns to go out again. He lifts his head and watches her going away from him in a new mood which began to emerge when he asked her "Who cares about you?")

WALTER: It's been rough, ain't it, baby? *(She hears and stops but does not turn around and he continues to her back)* I guess between two people there ain't never as much understood as folks generally thinks there is. I mean like between me and you—*(She turns to face him)* How we gets to the place where we scared to talk softness to each other. *(He waits, thinking hard himself)* Why you think it got to be like that? *(He is thoughtful, almost as a child would be)* Ruth, what is it gets into people ought to be close?

RUTH: I don't know, honey. I think about it a lot.

WALTER: On account of you and me, you mean? The way things are with us. The way something done come down between us.

RUTH: There ain't so much between us, Walter . . . Not when you come to me and try to talk to me. Try to be with me . . . a little even.

WALTER *(total honesty):* Sometimes . . . sometimes . . . I don't even know how to try.

RUTH: Walter—

WALTER: Yes?

RUTH *(coming to him, gently and with misgiving, but coming to him):* Honey . . . life don't have to be like this. I mean sometimes people can do things so that things are better . . . You remember how we used to talk when Travis was born . . . about the way we were going to live . . . the kind of house . . . *(She is stroking his head)* Well, it's all starting to slip away from us . . .

(He turns her to him and they look at each other and kiss, tenderly and hungrily. The door opens and MAMA *enters—*WALTER *breaks away and jumps up. A beat)*

WALTER: Mama, where have you been?

MAMA: My—them steps is longer than they used to be. Whew! *(She sits down and ignores him)* How you feeling this evening, Ruth?

*(*RUTH *shrugs, disturbed at having been interrupted and watching her husband knowingly)*

WALTER: Mama, where have you been all day?

MAMA *(still ignoring him and leaning on the table and changing to more comfortable shoes):* Where's Travis?

RUTH: I let him go out earlier and he ain't come back yet. Boy, is he going to get it!

WALTER: Mama!

MAMA *(as if she has heard him for the first time):* Yes, son?

WALTER: Where did you go this afternoon?

MAMA: I went downtown to tend to some business that I had to tend to.

WALTER: What kind of business?

MAMA: You know better than to question me like a child, Brother.

WALTER *(rising and bending over the table):* Where were you, Mama? *(Bringing his fists down and shouting)* Mama, you didn't go do something with that insurance money, something crazy?

(The front door opens slowly, interrupting him, and TRAVIS *peeks his head in, less than hopefully)*

TRAVIS *(to his mother):* Mama, I—

RUTH: "Mama I" nothing! You're going to get it, boy! Get on in that bedroom and get yourself ready!

TRAVIS: But I—

MAMA: Why don't you all never let the child explain hisself.

RUTH: Keep out of it now, Lena.

*(*MAMA *clamps her lips together, and* RUTH *advances toward her son menacingly)*

RUTH: A thousand times I have told you not to go off like that—

MAMA *(holding out her arms to her grandson):* Well—at least let me tell him something. I want him to be the first one to hear . . . Come here, Travis. *(The boy obeys, gladly)* Travis—*(She takes him by the shoulder and looks into his face)*—you know that money we got in the mail this morning?

TRAVIS: Yes'm—

MAMA: Well—what you think your grandmama gone and done with that money?

TRAVIS: I don't know, Grandmama.

MAMA *(putting her finger on his nose for emphasis):* She went out and she bought you a house! *(The explosion comes from* WALTER *at the end of the revelation and he jumps up and turns away from all of them in a fury.* MAMA *continues, to* TRAVIS*)* You glad about the house? It's going to be yours when you get to be a man.

TRAVIS: Yeah—I always wanted to live in a house.

MAMA: All right, gimme some sugar then—*(*TRAVIS *puts his arms around her neck as she watches her son over the boy's shoulder. Then, to* TRAVIS, *after the embrace)* Now when you say your prayers tonight, you thank God and your grandfather—'cause it was him who give you the house—in his way.

RUTH *(taking the boy from* MAMA *and pushing him toward the bedroom):* Now you get out of here and get ready for your beating.

TRAVIS: Aw, Mama—

RUTH: Get on in there—*(Closing the door behind him and turning radiantly to her mother-in-law)* So you went and did it!

MAMA *(quietly, looking at her son with pain):* Yes, I did.

RUTH *(raising both arms classically):* PRAISE GOD! *(Looks at* WALTER *a moment, who says nothing. She crosses rapidly to her husband)* Please, honey—let me be glad . . . you be glad too. *(She has laid her hands on his shoulders, but he shakes himself free of her roughly, without turning to face her)* Oh, Walter . . . a home . . . *a home. (She comes back to* MAMA*)* Well—where is it? How big is it? How much it going to cost?

MAMA: Well—

RUTH: When we moving?

MAMA *(smiling at her):* First of the month.

RUTH *(throwing back her head with jubilance): Praise God!*

MAMA *(tentatively, still looking at her son's back turned against her and* RUTH*):* It's—it's a nice house too . . . *(She cannot help speaking directly to him. An imploring quality in her voice, her manner, makes her almost like a girl now)* Three bedrooms—nice big one for you and Ruth. . . . Me and

Beneatha still have to share our room, but Travis have one of his own—and *(With difficulty)* I figure if the—new baby—is a boy, we could get one of them double-decker outfits . . . And there's a yard with a little patch of dirt where I could maybe get to grow me a few flowers . . . And a nice big basement . . .

Ruth: Walter honey, be glad—

Mama *(still to his back, fingering things on the table):* 'Course I don't want to make it sound fancier than it is . . . It's just a plain little old house—but it's made good and solid—and it will be *ours.* Walter Lee—it makes a difference in a man when he can walk on floors that belong to *him* . . .

Ruth: Where is it?

Mama *(frightened at this telling):* Well—well—it's out there in Clybourne Park—

*(*Ruth*'s radiance fades abruptly, and* Walter *finally turns slowly to face his mother with incredulity and hostility)*

Ruth: Where?

Mama *(matter-of-factly):* Four o six Clybourne Street, Clybourne Park.

Ruth: Clybourne Park? Mama, there ain't no colored people living in Clybourne Park.

Mama *(almost idiotically):* Well, I guess there's going to be some now.

Walter *(bitterly):* So that's the peace and comfort you went out and bought for us today!

Mama *(raising her eyes to meet his finally):* Son—I just tried to find the nicest place for the least amount of money for my family.

Ruth *(trying to recover from the shock):* Well—well—'course I ain't one never been 'fraid of no crackers, mind you—but—well, wasn't there no other houses nowhere?

Mama: Them houses they put up for colored in them areas way out all seem to cost twice as much as other houses. I did the best I could.

Ruth *(struck senseless with the news, in its various degrees of goodness and trouble, she sits a moment, her fists propping her chin in thought, and then she starts to rise, bringing her fists down with vigor, the radiance spreading from cheek to cheek again):* Well—well!—All I can say is—if this is my time in life—*MY TIME*—to say good-bye—*(And she builds with momentum as she starts to circle the room with an exuberant, almost tearfully happy release)*—to these Goddamned cracking walls!—*(She pounds the walls)*—and these marching roaches!—*(She wipes at an imaginary army of marching roaches)*—and this cramped little closet which ain't now or never was no kitchen! . . . then I say it loud and good, HALLELUJAH! AND GOOD-BYE MISERY . . . I DON'T NEVER WANT TO SEE YOUR UGLY FACE AGAIN! *(She laughs joyously, having practically destroyed the apartment, and flings her arms up and lets them come down happily, slowly, reflectively, over her abdomen, aware for the first time perhaps that the life therein pulses with happiness and not despair)* Lena?

MAMA *(moved, watching her happiness):* Yes, honey?
RUTH *(looking off):* Is there—is there a whole lot of sunlight?
MAMA *(understanding):* Yes, child, there's a whole lot of sunlight.

(Long pause)

RUTH *(collecting herself and going to the door of the room* TRAVIS *is in):* Well—I guess I better see 'bout Travis. *(To* MAMA*)* Lord, I sure don't feel like whipping nobody today!

(She exits)

MAMA *(the mother and son are left alone now and the mother waits a long time, considering deeply, before she speaks):* Son—you—you understand what I done, don't you? *(*WALTER *is silent and sullen)* I—I just seen my family falling apart today . . . just falling to pieces in front of my eyes . . . We couldn't of gone on like we was today. We was going backwards 'stead of forwards—talking 'bout killing babies and wishing each other was dead . . . When it gets like that in life—you just got to do something different, push on out and do something bigger . . . *(She waits)* I wish you say something, son . . . I wish you'd say how deep inside you you think I done the right thing—
WALTER *(crossing slowly to his bedroom door and finally turning there and speaking measuredly):* What you need me to say you done right for? *You* the head of this family. You run our lives like you want to. It was your money and you did what you wanted with it. So what you need for me to say it was all right for? *(Bitterly, to hurt her as deeply as he knows is possible)* So you butchered up a dream of mine—you—who always talking 'bout your children's dreams . . .
MAMA: Walter Lee—

(He just closes the door behind him. MAMA *sits alone, thinking heavily)*

Curtain

Scene II

Time: Friday night. A few weeks later.

At rise: Packing crates mark the intention of the family to move. BENEATHA *and* GEORGE *come in, presumably from an evening out again.*

GEORGE: O.K. . . . O.K., whatever you say . . . *(They both sit on the couch. He tries to kiss her. She moves away)* Look, we've had a nice evening; let's not spoil it, huh? . . .

(He again turns her head and tries to nuzzle in and she turns away from him, not with distaste but with momentary lack of interest; in a mood to pursue what they were talking about)

BENEATHA: I'm *trying* to talk to you.

GEORGE: We always talk.

BENEATHA: Yes—and I love to talk.

GEORGE *(exasperated; rising):* I know it and I don't mind it sometimes . . . I want you to cut it out, see—The moody stuff, I mean. I don't like it. You're a nice-looking girl . . . all over. That's all you need, honey, forget the atmosphere. Guys aren't going to go for the atmosphere—they're going to go for what they see. Be glad for that. Drop the Garbo routine. It doesn't go with you. As for myself, I want a nice—*(Groping)*—simple *(Thoughtfully)*—sophisticated girl . . . not a poet—O.K.?

(He starts to kiss her, she rebuffs him again and he jumps up)

BENEATHA: Why are you angry, George?

GEORGE: Because this is stupid! I don't go out with you to discuss the nature of "quiet desperation" or to hear all about your thoughts—because the world will go on thinking what it thinks regardless—

BENEATHA: Then why read books? Why go to school?

GEORGE *(with artificial patience, counting on his fingers):* It's simple. You read books—to learn facts—to get grades—to pass the course—to get a degree. That's all—it has nothing to do with thoughts.

(A long pause)

BENEATHA: I see. *(He starts to sit)* Good night, George.

*(*GEORGE *looks at her a little oddly, and starts to exit. He meets* MAMA *coming in)*

GEORGE: Oh—hello, Mrs. Younger.

MAMA: Hello, George, how you feeling?

GEORGE: Fine—fine, how are you?

MAMA: Oh, a little tired. You know them steps can get you after a day's work. You all have a nice time tonight?

GEORGE: Yes—a fine time. A fine time.

MAMA: Well, good night.

GEORGE: Good night. *(He exits.* MAMA *closes the door behind her)* Hello, honey. What you sitting like that for?

BENEATHA: I'm just sitting.

MAMA: Didn't you have a nice time?

BENEATHA: No.

MAMA: No? What's the matter?

BENEATHA: Mama, George is a fool—honest. *(She rises)*

MAMA *(bustling around unloading the packages she has entered with. She stops):* Is he, baby?

BENEATHA: Yes.

*(*Beneatha *makes up* Travis' *bed as she talks)*

Mama: You sure?
Beneatha: Yes.
Mama: Well—I guess you better not waste your time with no fools.

*(*Beneatha *looks up at her mother, watching her put groceries in the refrigerator. Finally she gathers up her things and starts into the bedroom. At the door she stops and looks back at her mother)*

Beneatha: Mama—
Mama: Yes, baby—
Beneatha: Thank you.
Mama: For what?
Beneatha: For understanding me this time.

(She exits quickly and the mother stands, smiling a little, looking at the place where Beneatha *just stood.* Ruth *enters)*

Ruth: Now don't you fool with any of this stuff, Lena—
Mama: Oh, I just thought I'd sort a few things out. Is Brother here?
Ruth: Yes.
Mama *(with concern):* Is he—
Ruth *(reading her eyes):* Yes.

*(*Mama *is silent and someone knocks on the door.* Mama *and* Ruth *exchange weary and knowing glances and* Ruth *opens it to admit the neighbor,* Mrs. Johnson,* *who is a rather squeaky wide-eyed lady of no particular age, with a newspaper under her arm)*

Mama *(changing her expression to acute delight and a ringing cheerful greeting):* Oh—hello there, Johnson.
Johnson *(This is a woman who decided long ago to be enthusiastic about EVERYTHING in life and she is inclined to wave her wrist vigorously at the height of her exclamatory comments):* Hello there, yourself! H'you this evening, Ruth?
Ruth *(not much of a deceptive type):* Fine, Mis' Johnson, h'you?
Johnson: Fine. *(Reaching out quickly, playfully, and patting* Ruth*'s stomach)* Ain't you starting to poke out none yet! *(She mugs with delight at the over-familiar remark and her eyes dart around looking at the crates and packing preparation;* Mama*'s face is a cold sheet of endurance)* Oh, ain't we getting ready round here, though! Yessir! Lookathere! I'm telling you the Youngers is really getting ready to "move on up a little higher!"—Bless God!
Mama *(a little drily, doubting the total sincerity of the Blesser):* Bless God.

*This character and the scene of her visit were cut from the original production and early editions of the play.

JOHNSON: He's good, ain't He?

MAMA: Oh yes, He's good.

JOHNSON: I mean sometimes He works in mysterious ways . . . but He works, don't He!

MAMA *(the same):* Yes, he does.

JOHNSON: I'm just soooooo happy for y'all. And this here child—*(About* RUTH*)* looks like she could just pop open with happiness, don't she. Where's all the rest of the family?

MAMA: Bennie's gone to bed—

JOHNSON: Ain't no . . . *(The implication is pregnancy)* sickness done hit you—I hope . . . ?

MAMA: No—she just tired. She was out this evening.

JOHNSON *(all is a coo, an emphatic coo):* Aw—ain't that lovely. She still going out with the little Murchison boy?

MAMA *(drily):* Ummmm huh.

JOHNSON: That's lovely. You sure got lovely children, Younger. Me and Isaiah talks all the time 'bout what fine children you was blessed with. We sure do.

MAMA: Ruth, give Mis' Johnson a piece of sweet potato pie and some milk.

JOHNSON: Oh honey, I can't stay hardly a minute—I just dropped in to see if there was anything I could do. *(Accepting the food easily)* I guess y'all seen the news what's all over the colored paper this week . . .

MAMA: No—didn't get mine yet this week.

JOHNSON *(lifting her head and blinking with the spirit of catastrophe):* You mean you ain't read 'bout them colored people that was bombed out their place out there?

*(*RUTH *straightens with concern and takes the paper and reads it.* JOHNSON *notices her and feeds commentary)*

JOHNSON: Ain't it something how bad these here white folks is getting here in Chicago! Lord, getting so you think you right down in Mississippi! *(With a tremendous and rather insincere sense of melodrama)* 'Course I thinks it's wonderful how our folks keeps on pushing out. You hear some of these Negroes round here talking 'bout how they don't go where they ain't wanted and all that—but not me, honey! *(This is a lie)* Wilhemenia Othella Johnson goes anywhere, any time she feels like it! *(With head movement for emphasis)* Yes I do! Why if we left it up to these here crackers, the poor niggers wouldn't have nothing—*(She clasps her hand over her mouth)* Oh, I always forgets you don't 'low that word in your house.

MAMA *(quietly, looking at her):* No—I don't 'low it.

JOHNSON *(vigorously again):* Me neither! I was just telling Isaiah yesterday when he come using it in front of me—I said, "Isaiah, it's just like Mis' Younger says all the time—"

MAMA: Don't you want some more pie?

JOHNSON: No—no thank you; this was lovely. I got to get on over home and have my midnight coffee. I hear some people say it don't let them sleep but I finds I can't close my eyes right lessen I done had that laaaast cup of coffee . . . *(She waits. A beat. Undaunted)* My Goodnight coffee, I calls it!

MAMA *(with much eye-rolling and communication between herself and* RUTH*)*: Ruth, why don't you give Mis' Johnson some coffee.

*(*RUTH *gives* MAMA *an unpleasant look for her kindness)*

JOHNSON *(accepting the coffee)*: Where's Brother tonight?

MAMA: He's lying down.

JOHNSON: MMmmmmm, he sure gets his beauty rest, don't he? Good-looking man. Sure is a good-looking man! *(Reaching out to pat* RUTH*'s stomach again)* I guess that's how come we keep on having babies around here. *(She winks at* MAMA*)* One thing 'bout Brother, he always know how to have a *good* time. And soooooo ambitious! I bet it was his idea y'all moving out to Clybourne Park. Lord—I bet this time next month y'all's names will have been in the papers plenty—*(Holding up her hands to mark off each word of the headline she can see in front of her)* "NEGROES INVADE CLYBOURNE PARK—BOMBED!"

MAMA *(she and* RUTH *look at the woman in amazement)*: We ain't exactly moving out there to get bombed.

JOHNSON: Oh, honey—you know I'm praying to God every day that don't nothing like that happen! But you have to think of life like it is—and these here Chicago peckerwoods is some baaaad peckerwoods.

MAMA *(wearily)*: We done thought about all that Mis' Johnson.

*(*BENEATHA *comes out of the bedroom in her robe and passes through to the bathroom.* MRS. JOHNSON *turns)*

JOHNSON: Hello there, Bennie!

BENEATHA *(crisply)*: Hello, Mrs. Johnson.

JOHNSON: How is school?

BENEATHA *(crisply)*: Fine, thank you. *(She goes out.)*

JOHNSON *(insulted)*: Getting so she don't have much to say to nobody.

MAMA: The child was on her way to the bathroom.

JOHNSON: I know—but sometimes she act like ain't got time to pass the time of day with nobody ain't been to college. Oh—I ain't criticizing her none. It's just—you know how some of our young people gets when they get a little education. *(*MAMA *and* RUTH *say nothing, just look at her)* Yes—well. Well, I guess I better get on home. *(Unmoving)* 'Course I can understand how she must be proud and everything—being the only one in the family to make something of herself. I know just being a chauffeur ain't never satisfied Brother none. He shouldn't feel like that, though. Ain't nothing wrong with being a chauffeur.

Mama: There's plenty wrong with it.

Johnson: What?

Mama: Plenty. My husband always said being any kind of a servant wasn't a fit thing for a man to have to be. He always said a man's hands was made to make things, or to turn the earth with—not to drive nobody's car for 'em—or—*(She looks at her own hands)* carry they slop jars. And my boy is just like him—he wasn't meant to wait on nobody.

Johnson *(rising, somewhat offended):* Mmmmmmmmm. The Youngers is too much for me! *(She looks around)* You sure one proud-acting bunch of colored folks. Well—I always thinks like Booker T. Washington said that time—"Education has spoiled many a good plow hand"—

Mama: Is that what old Booker T. said?

Johnson: He sure did.

Mama: Well, it sounds just like him. The fool.

Johnson *(indignantly):* Well—he was one of our great men.

Mama: Who said so?

Johnson *(nonplussed):* You know, me and you ain't never agreed about some things, Lena Younger. I guess I better be going—

Ruth *(quickly):* Good night.

Johnson: Good night. Oh—*(Thrusting it at her)* You can keep the paper! *(With a trill)* 'Night.

Mama: Good night, Mis' Johnson.

*(*Mrs. Johnson *exits)*

Ruth: If ignorance was gold . . .

Mama: Shush. Don't talk about folks behind their backs.

Ruth: You do.

Mama: I'm old and corrupted. *(*Beneatha *enters)* You was rude to Mis' Johnson, Beneatha, and I don't like it at all.

Beneatha *(at her door):* Mama, if there are two things we, as a people, have got to overcome, one is the Ku Klux Klan—and the other is Mrs. Johnson. *(She exits)*

Mama: Smart aleck.

(The phone rings)

Ruth: I'll get it.

Mama: Lord, ain't this a popular place tonight.

Ruth *(at the phone):* Hello—Just a minute. *(Goes to door)* Walter, it's Mrs. Arnold. *(Waits. Goes back to the phone. Tense)* Hello. Yes, this is his wife speaking . . . He's lying down now. Yes . . . well, he'll be in tomorrow. He's been very sick. Yes—I know we should have called, but we were so sure he'd be able to come in today. Yes—yes, I'm very sorry. Yes . . . Thank you very much. *(She hangs up.* Walter *is standing in the doorway of the bedroom behind her)* That was Mrs. Arnold.

WALTER *(indifferently):* Was it?

RUTH: She said if you don't come in tomorrow that they are getting a new man . . .

WALTER: Ain't that sad—ain't that crying sad.

RUTH: She said Mr. Arnold has had to take a cab for three days . . . Walter, you ain't been to work for three days! *(This is a revelation to her)* Where you been, Walter Lee Younger? *(WALTER looks at her and starts to laugh)* You're going to lose your job.

WALTER: That's right . . . *(He turns on the radio)*

RUTH: Oh, Walter, and with your mother working like a dog every day—

(A steamy, deep blues pours into the room)

WALTER: That's sad too—Everything is sad.

MAMA: What you been doing for these three days, son?

WALTER: Mama—you don't know all the things a man what got leisure can find to do in this city . . . What's this—Friday night? Well—Wednesday I borrowed Willy Harris' car and I went for a drive . . . just me and myself and I drove and drove . . . Way out . . . way past South Chicago, and I parked the car and I sat and looked at the steel mills all day long. I just sat in the car and looked at them big black chimneys for hours. Then I drove back and I went to the Green Hat. *(Pause)* And Thursday—Thursday I borrowed the car again and I got in it and I pointed it the other way and I drove the other way—for hours—way, way up to Wisconsin, and I looked at the farms. I just drove and looked at the farms. Then I drove back and I went to the Green Hat. *(Pause)* And today—today I didn't get the car. Today I just walked. All over the Southside. And I looked at the Negroes and they looked at me and finally I just sat down on the curb at Thirty-ninth and South Parkway and I just sat there and watched the Negroes go by. And then I went to the Green Hat. You all sad? You all depressed? And you know where I am going right now—

(RUTH goes out quietly)

MAMA: Oh, Big Walter, is this the harvest of our days?

WALTER: You know what I like about the Green Hat? I like this little cat they got there who blows a sax . . . He blows. He talks to me. He ain't but 'bout five feet tall and he's got a conked head and his eyes is always closed and he's all music—

MAMA *(rising and getting some papers out of her handbag):* Walter—

WALTER: And there's this other guy who plays the piano . . . and they got a sound. I mean they can work on some music . . . They got the best little combo in the world in the Green Hat . . . You can just sit there and drink and listen to them three men play and you realize that don't nothing matter worth a damn, but just being there—

MAMA: I've helped do it to you, haven't I, son? Walter I been wrong.

WALTER: Naw—you ain't never been wrong about nothing, Mama.

MAMA: Listen to me, now. I say I been wrong, son. That I been doing to you what the rest of the world been doing to you. *(She turns off the radio)* Walter—*(She stops and he looks up slowly at her and she meets his eyes pleadingly)* What you ain't never understood is that I ain't got nothing, don't own nothing, ain't never really wanted nothing that wasn't for you. There ain't nothing as precious to me . . . There ain't nothing worth holding on to, money, dreams, nothing else—if it means—if it means it's going to destroy my boy. *(She takes an envelope out of her handbag and puts it in front of him and he watches her without speaking or moving)* I paid the man thirty-five hundred dollars down on the house. That leaves sixty-five hundred dollars. Monday morning I want you to take this money and take three thousand dollars and put it in a savings account for Beneath's medical schooling. The rest you put in a checking account—with your name on it. And from now on any penny that come out of it or that go in it is for you to look after. For you to decide. *(She drops her hands a little helplessly)* It ain't much, but it's all I got in the world and I'm putting it in your hands. I'm telling you to be the head of this family from now on like you supposed to be.

WALTER *(stares at the money):* You trust me like that, Mama?

MAMA: I ain't never stop trusting you. Like I ain't never stop loving you.

(She goes out, and WALTER *sits looking at the money on the table. Finally, in a decisive gesture, he gets up, and, in mingled joy and desperation, picks up the money. At the same moment,* TRAVIS *enters for bed)*

TRAVIS: What's the matter, Daddy? You drunk?

WALTER *(sweetly, more sweetly than we have ever known him):* No, Daddy ain't drunk. Daddy ain't going to never be drunk again. . . .

TRAVIS: Well, good night, Daddy.

(The father has come from behind the couch and leans over, embracing his son)

WALTER: Son, I feel like talking to you tonight.

TRAVIS: About what?

WALTER: Oh, about a lot of things. About you and what kind of man you going to be when you grow up. . . . Son—son, what do you want to be when you grow up?

TRAVIS: A bus driver.

WALTER *(laughing a little):* A what? Man, that ain't nothing to want to be!

TRAVIS: Why not?

WALTER: 'Cause, man—it ain't big enough—you know what I mean.

TRAVIS: I don't know then. I can't make up my mind. Sometimes Mama asks me that too. And sometimes when I tell her I just want to be like you—she says she don't want me to be like that and sometimes she says she does. . . .

Walter *(gathering him up in his arms):* You know what, Travis? In seven years you going to be seventeen years old. And things is going to be very different with us in seven years, Travis. . . . One day when you are seventeen I'll come home—home from my office downtown somewhere—

Travis: You don't work in no office, Daddy.

Walter: No—but after tonight. After what your daddy gonna do tonight, there's going to be offices—a whole lot of offices. . . .

Travis: What you gonna do tonight, Daddy?

Walter: You wouldn't understand yet, son, but your daddy's gonna make a transaction . . . a business transaction that's going to change our lives. . . . That's how come one day when you 'bout seventeen years old I'll come home and I'll be pretty tired, you know what I mean, after a day of conferences and secretaries getting things wrong the way they do . . . 'cause an executive's life is hell, man—*(The more he talks the farther away he gets)* And I'll pull the car up on the driveway . . . just a plain black Chrysler, I think, with white walls—no—black tires. More elegant. Rich people don't have to be flashy . . . though I'll have to get something a little sportier for Ruth—maybe a Cadillac convertible to do her shopping in. . . . And I'll come up the steps to the house and the gardener will be clipping away at the hedges and he'll say, "Good evening, Mr. Younger." And I'll say, "Hello, Jefferson, how are you this evening?" And I'll go inside and Ruth will come downstairs and meet me at the door and we'll kiss each other and she'll take my arm and we'll go up to your room to see you sitting on the floor with the catalogues of all the great schools in America around you. . . . All the great schools in the world! And—and I'll say, all right son—it's your seventeenth birthday, what is it you've decided? . . . Just tell me where you want to go to school and you'll *go*. Just tell me, what it is you want to be—and you'll *be* it. . . . Whatever you want to be—Yessir! *(He holds his arms open for* Travis*)* You just name it, son . . . *(*Travis *leaps into them)* and I hand you the world!

*(*Walter*'s voice has risen in pitch and hysterical promise and on the last line he lifts* Travis *high)*

(Blackout)

Scene III

Time: Saturday, moving day, one week later.

Before the curtain rises, Ruth*'s voice, a strident, dramatic church alto, cuts through the silence.*

It is, in the darkness, a triumphant surge, a penetrating statement of expectation: "Oh, Lord, I don't feel no ways tired! Children, oh, glory hallelujah!"

As the curtain rises we see that RUTH *is alone in the living room, finishing up the family's packing. It is moving day. She is nailing crates and tying cartons.* BENEATHA *enters, carrying a guitar case, and watches her exuberant sister-in-law.*

RUTH: Hey!

BENEATHA *(putting away the case):* Hi.

RUTH *(pointing at a package):* Honey—look in that package there and see what I found on sale this morning at the South Center. *(*RUTH *gets up and moves to the package and draws out some curtains)* Lookahere—hand-turned hems!

BENEATHA: How do you know the window size out there?

RUTH *(who hadn't thought of that):* Oh—Well, they bound to fit something in the whole house. Anyhow, they was too good a bargain to pass up. *(*RUTH *slaps her head, suddenly remembering something)* Oh, Bennie—I meant to put a special note on that carton over there. That's your mama's good china and she wants 'em to be very careful with it.

BENEATHA: I'll do it.

*(*BENEATHA *finds a piece of paper and starts to draw large letters on it)*

RUTH: You know what I'm going to do soon as I get in that new house?

BENEATHA: What?

RUTH: Honey—I'm going to run me a tub of water up to here . . . *(With her fingers practically up to her nostrils)* And I'm going to get in it—and I am going to sit . . . and sit . . . and sit in that hot water and the first person who knocks to tell *me* to hurry up and come out—

BENEATHA: Gets shot at sunrise.

RUTH *(laughing happily):* You said it, sister! *(Noticing how large* BENEATHA *is absent-mindedly making the note)* Honey, they ain't going to read that from no airplane.

BENEATHA *(laughing herself):* I guess I always think things have more emphasis if they are big, somehow.

RUTH *(looking up at her and smiling):* You and your brother seem to have that as a philosophy of life. Lord, that man—done changed so 'round here. You know—you know what we did last night? Me and Walter Lee?

BENEATHA: What?

RUTH *(smiling to herself):* We went to the movies. *(Looking at* BENEATHA *to see if she understands)* We went to the movies. You know the last time me and Walter went to the movies together?

BENEATHA: No.

RUTH: Me neither. That's how long it been. *(Smiling again)* But we went last night. The picture wasn't much good, but that didn't seem to matter. We went—and we held hands.

BENEATHA: Oh, Lord!

RUTH: We held hands—and you know what?

BENEATHA: What?

RUTH: When we come out of the show it was late and dark and all the stores and things was closed up . . . and it was kind of chilly and there wasn't many people on the streets . . . and we was still holding hands, me and Walter.

BENEATHA: You're killing me.

*(*WALTER *enters with a large package. His happiness is deep in him; he cannot keep still with his new-found exuberance. He is singing and wiggling and snapping his fingers. He puts his package in a corner and puts a phonograph record, which he has brought in with him, on the record player. As the music, soulful and sensuous, comes up he dances over to* RUTH *and tries to get her to dance with him. She gives in at last to his raunchiness and in a fit of giggling allows herself to be drawn into his mood. They dip and she melts into his arms in a classic, body-melding "slow drag")*

BENEATHA *(regarding them a long time as they dance, then drawing in her breath for a deeply exaggerated comment which she does not particularly mean):* Talk about—olddddddddd-fashionedddddd—Negroes!

WALTER *(stopping momentarily):* What kind of Negroes? *(He says this in fun. He is not angry with her today, nor with anyone. He starts to dance with his wife again)*

BENEATHA: Old-fashioned.

WALTER *(as he dances with* RUTH*):* You know, when these *New Negroes* have their convention—*(Pointing at his sister)*—that is going to be the chairman of the Committee on Unending Agitation. *(He goes on dancing, then stops)* Race, race, race! . . . Girl, I do believe you are the first person in the history of the entire human race to successfully brainwash yourself. *(*BENEATHA *breaks up and he goes on dancing. He stops again, enjoying his tease)* Damn, even the N double A C P takes a holiday sometimes! *(*BENEATHA *and* RUTH *laugh. He dances with* RUTH *some more and starts to laugh and stops and pantomimes someone over an operating table)* I can just see that chick someday looking down at some poor cat on an operating table and before she starts to slice him, she says . . . *(Pulling his sleeves back maliciously)* "By the way, what are your views on civil rights down there? . . ."

(He laughs at her again and starts to dance happily. The bell sounds)

BENEATHA: Sticks and stones may break my bones but . . . words will never hurt me!

*(*BENEATHA *goes to the door and opens it as* WALTER *and* RUTH *go on with the clowning.* BENEATHA *is somewhat surprised to see a quiet-looking middle-aged white man in a business suit holding his hat and a briefcase in his hand and consulting a small piece of paper)*

MAN: Uh—how do you do, miss. I am looking for a Mrs.—*(He looks at the slip of paper)* Mrs. Lena Younger? *(He stops short, struck dumb at the sight of the oblivious* WALTER *and* RUTH*)*

BENEATHA *(smoothing her hair with slight embarrassment):* Oh—yes, that's my mother. Excuse me *(She closes the door and turns to quiet the other two)* Ruth! Brother! *(Enunciating precisely but soundlessly: "There's a white man at the door!" They stop dancing,* RUTH *cuts off the phonograph,* BENEATHA *opens the door. The man casts a curious quick glance at all of them)* Uh—come in please.

MAN *(coming in):* Thank you.

BENEATHA: My mother isn't here just now. Is it business?

MAN: Yes . . . well, of a sort.

WALTER *(freely, the Man of the House):* Have a seat. I'm Mrs. Younger's son. I look after most of her business matters.

*(*RUTH *and* BENEATHA *exchange amused glances)*

MAN *(regarding* WALTER, *and sitting):* Well—My name is Karl Lindner . . .

WALTER *(stretching out his hand):* Walter Younger. This is my wife—*(*RUTH *nods politely)*—and my sister.

LINDNER: How do you do.

WALTER *(amiably, as he sits himself easily on a chair, leaning forward on his knees with interest and looking expectantly into the newcomer's face):* What can we do for you, Mr. Lindner!

LINDNER *(some minor shuffling of the hat and briefcase on his knees):* Well—I am a representative of the Clybourne Park Improvement Association—

WALTER *(pointing):* Why don't you sit your things on the floor?

LINDNER: Oh—yes. Thank you. *(He slides the briefcase and hat under the chair)* And as I was saying—I am from the Clybourne Park Improvement Association and we have had it brought to our attention at the last meeting that you people—or at least your mother—has bought a piece of residential property at—*(He digs for the slip of paper again)*—four o six Clybourne Street . . .

WALTER: That's right. Care for something to drink? Ruth, get Mr. Lindner a beer.

LINDNER *(upset for some reason):* Oh—no, really. I mean thank you very much, but no thank you.

RUTH *(innocently):* Some coffee?

LINDNER: Thank you, nothing at all.

*(*BENEATHA *is watching the man carefully)*

LINDNER: Well, I don't know how much you folks know about our organization. *(He is a gentle man; thoughtful and somewhat labored in his manner)* It is one of these community organizations set up to look after—oh, you know, things like block upkeep and special projects and we also have what we call our New Neighbors Orientation Committee . . .

BENEATHA *(drily):* Yes—and what do they do?

LINDNER *(turning a little to her and then returning the main force to* WALTER*):* Well—it's what you might call a sort of welcoming committee, I guess. I mean they, we—I'm the chairman of the committee—go around and see the new people who move into the neighborhood and sort of give them the lowdown on the way we do things in Clybourne Park.

BENEATHA *(with appreciation of the two meanings, which escape* RUTH *and* WALTER*):* Un-huh.

LINDNER: And we also have the category of what the association calls—*(He looks elsewhere)*—uh—special community problems . . .

BENEATHA: Yes—and what are some of those?

WALTER: Girl, let the man talk.

LINDNER *(with understated relief):* Thank you. I would sort of like to explain this thing in my own way. I mean I want to explain to you in a certain way.

WALTER: Go ahead.

LINDNER: Yes. Well. I'm going to try to get right to the point. I'm sure we'll all appreciate that in the long run.

BENEATHA: Yes.

WALTER: Be still now!

LINDNER: Well—

RUTH *(still innocently):* Would you like another chair—you don't look comfortable.

LINDNER *(more frustrated than annoyed):* No, thank you very much. Please. Well—to get right to the point I—*(A great breath, and he is off at last)* I am sure you people must be aware of some of the incidents which have happened in various parts of the city when colored people have moved into certain areas—*(*BENEATHA *exhales heavily and starts tossing a piece of fruit up and down in the air)* Well—because we have what I think is going to be a unique type of organization in American community life—not only do we deplore that kind of thing—but we are trying to do something about it. *(*BENEATHA *stops tossing and turns with a new and quizzical interest to the man)* We feel—*(gaining confidence in his mission because of the interest in the faces of the people he is talking to)*—we feel that most of the trouble in this world, when you come right down to it—*(He hits his knee for emphasis)*—most of the trouble exists because people just don't sit down and talk to each other.

RUTH *(nodding as she might in church, pleased with the remark):* You can say that again, mister.

LINDNER *(more encouraged by such affirmation):* That we don't try hard enough in this world to understand the other fellow's problem. The other guy's point of view.

RUTH: Now that's right.

*(*BENEATHA *and* WALTER *merely watch and listen with genuine interest)*

LINDNER: Yes—that's the way we feel out in Clybourne Park. And that's why I was elected to come here this afternoon and talk to you people. Friendly like, you know, the way people should talk to each other and see if we couldn't find some way to work this thing out. As I say, the whole business is a matter of *caring* about the other fellow. Anybody can see that you are a nice family of folks, hard working and honest I'm sure. *(*BENEATHA *frowns slightly, quizzically, her head tilted regarding him)* Today everybody knows what it means to be on the outside of *something*. And of course, there is always somebody who is out to take advantage of people who don't always understand.

WALTER: What do you mean?

LINDNER: Well—you see our community is made up of people who've worked hard as the dickens for years to build up that little community. They're not rich and fancy people; just hard-working, honest people who don't really have much but those little homes and a dream of the kind of community they want to raise their children in. Now, I don't say we are perfect and there is a lot wrong in some of the things they want. But you've got to admit that a man, right or wrong, has the right to want to have the neighborhood he lives in a certain kind of way. And at the moment the overwhelming majority of our people out there feel that people get along better, take more of a common interest in the life of the community, when they share a common background. I want you to believe me when I tell you that race prejudice simply doesn't enter into it. It is a matter of the people of Clybourne Park believing, rightly or wrongly, as I say, that for the happiness of all concerned that our Negro families are happier when they live in their *own* communities.

BENEATHA *(with a grand and bitter gesture):* This, friends, is the Welcoming Committee!

WALTER *(dumbfounded, looking at* LINDNER*):* Is this what you came marching all the way over here to tell us?

LINDNER: Well, now we've been having a fine conversation. I hope you'll hear me all the way through.

WALTER *(tightly):* Go ahead, man.

LINDNER: You see—in the face of all the things I have said, we are prepared to make your family a very generous offer . . .

BENEATHA: Thirty pieces and not a coin less!

WALTER: Yeah?

LINDNER *(putting on his glasses and drawing a form out of the briefcase):* Our association is prepared, through the collective effort of our people, to buy the house from you at a financial gain to your family.

RUTH: Lord have mercy, ain't this the living gall!

WALTER: All right, you through?

LINDNER: Well, I want to give you the exact terms of the financial arrangement—

WALTER: We don't want to hear no exact terms of no arrangements. I want to know if you got any more to tell us 'bout getting together?

LINDNER *(taking off his glasses):* Well—I don't suppose that you feel . . .

WALTER: Never mind how I feel—you got any more to say 'bout how people ought to sit down and talk to each other? . . . Get out of my house, man.

(He turns his back and walks to the door)

LINDNER *(Looking around at the hostile faces and reaching and assembling his hat and briefcase):* Well—I don't understand why you people are reacting this way. What do you think you are going to gain by moving into a neighborhood where you just aren't wanted and where some elements—well—people can get awful worked up when they feel that their whole way of life and everything they've ever worked for is threatened.

WALTER: Get out.

LINDNER *(at the door, holding a small card):* Well—I'm sorry it went like this.

WALTER: Get out.

LINDNER *(almost sadly regarding* WALTER*):* You just can't force people to change their hearts, son.

(He turns and put his card on a table and exits. WALTER *pushes the door to with stinging hatred, and stands looking at it.* RUTH *just sits and* BENEATHA *just stands. They say nothing.* MAMA *and* TRAVIS *enter)*

MAMA: Well—this all the packing got done since I left out of here this morning. I testify before God that my children got all the energy of the *dead!* What time the moving men due?

BENEATHA: Four o'clock. You had a caller, Mama.

(She is smiling, teasingly)

MAMA: Sure enough—who?

BENEATHA *(her arms folded saucily):* The Welcoming Committee.

*(*WALTER *and* RUTH *giggle)*

MAMA *(innocently):* Who?

BENEATHA: The Welcoming Committee. They said they're sure going to be glad to see you when you get there.

WALTER *(devilishly):* Yeah, they said they can't hardly wait to see your face.

(Laughter)

MAMA *(sensing their facetiousness):* What's the matter with you all?

WALTER: Ain't nothing the matter with us. We just telling you 'bout the gentleman who came to see you this afternoon. From the Clybourne Park Improvement Association.

MAMA: What he want?

RUTH *(in the same mood as* BENEATHA *and* WALTER*):* To welcome you, honey.

WALTER: He said they can't hardly wait. He said the one thing they don't have, that they just *dying* to have out there is a fine family of fine colored people! *(To* RUTH *and* BENEATHA*)* Ain't that right!

RUTH *(mockingly):* Yeah! He left his card—

BENEATHA *(handing card to* MAMA*):* In case.

*(*MAMA *reads and throws it on the floor—understanding and looking off as she draws her chair up to the table on which she has put her plant and some sticks and some cord)*

MAMA: Father, give us strength. *(knowingly—and without fun)* Did he threaten us?

BENEATHA: Oh—Mama—they don't do it like that any more. He talked Brotherhood. He said everybody ought to learn how to sit down and hate each other with good Christian fellowship.

(She and WALTER *shake hands to ridicule the remark)*

MAMA *(sadly):* Lord, protect us . . .

RUTH: You should hear the money those folks raised to buy the house from us. All we paid and then some.

BENEATHA: What they think we going to do—eat 'em?

RUTH: No, honey, marry 'em.

MAMA *(shaking her head):* Lord, Lord, Lord . . .

RUTH: Well—that's the way the crackers crumble. *(A beat)* Joke.

BENEATHA *(laughingly noticing what her mother is doing):* Mama, what are you doing?

MAMA: Fixing my plant so it won't get hurt none on the way . . .

BENEATHA: Mama, you going to take *that* to the new house?

MAMA: Un-huh—

BENEATHA: That raggedy-looking old thing?

MAMA *(stopping and looking at her):* It expresses ME!

RUTH *(with delight, to* BENEATHA*):* So there, Miss Thing!

*(*WALTER *comes to* MAMA *suddenly and bends down behind her and squeezes her in his arms with all his strength. She is overwhelmed by the suddenness of it and, though delighted, her manner is like that of* RUTH *and* TRAVIS*)*

MAMA: Look out now, boy! You make me mess up my thing here!

WALTER *(his face lit, he slips down on his knees beside her, his arms still about her):* Mama . . . you know what it means to climb up in the chariot?

MAMA *(gruffly, very happy):* Get on away from me now . . .

RUTH *(near the gift-wrapped package, trying to catch* WALTER*'s eye):* Psst—

WALTER: What the old song say, Mama . . .

RUTH: Walter—Now?

(She is pointing at the package)

WALTER *(speaking the lines, sweetly, playfully, in his mother's face)*
I got wings . . . you got wings . . .
All God's Children got wings . . .

MAMA: Boy—get out of my face and do some work . . .

WALTER: When I get to heaven gonna put on my wings,
Gonna fly all over God's heaven . . .

BENEATHA *(teasingly, from across the room):* Everybody talking 'bout heaven ain't going there!

WALTER *(to* RUTH, *who is carrying the box across to them):* I don't know, you think we ought to give her that . . . Seems to me she ain't been very appreciative around here.

MAMA *(eying the box, which is obviously a gift):* What is that?

WALTER *(taking it from* RUTH *and putting it on the table in front of* MAMA*):* Well—what you all think? Should we give it to her?

RUTH: Oh—she was pretty good today.

MAMA: I'll good you—

(She turns her eyes to the box again)

BENEATHA: Open it, Mama.

(She stands up, looks at it, turns and looks at all of them, and then presses her hands together and does not open the package)

WALTER *(sweetly):* Open it, Mama. It's for you. *(*MAMA *looks in his eyes. It is the first present in her life without its being Christmas. Slowly she opens her package and lifts out, one by one, a brand-new sparkling set of gardening tools.* WALTER *continues, prodding)* Ruth made up the note—read it . . .

MAMA *(picking up the card and adjusting her glasses):* "To our own Mrs. Miniver—Love from Brother, Ruth and Beneatha." Ain't that lovely . . .

TRAVIS *(tugging at his father's sleeve):* Daddy, can I give her mine now?

WALTER: All right, son. *(*TRAVIS *flies to get his gift)*

MAMA: Now I don't have to use my knives and forks no more . . .

WALTER: Travis didn't want to go in with the rest of us, Mama. He got his own. *(Somewhat amused)* We don't know what it is . . .

TRAVIS *(racing back in the room with a large hatbox and putting it in front of his grandmother):* Here!

MAMA: Lord have mercy, baby. You done gone and bought your grandmother a hat?

TRAVIS *(very proud):* Open it!

(She does and lifts out an elaborate, but very elaborate, wide gardening hat, and all the adults break up at the sight of it)

RUTH: Travis, honey, what is that?

TRAVIS *(who thinks it is beautiful and appropriate):* It's a gardening hat! Like the ladies always have on in the magazines when they work in their gardens.

BENEATHA *(giggling fiercely):* Travis—we were trying to make Mama Mrs. Miniver—not Scarlet O'Hara!

MAMA *(indignantly):* What's the matter with you all! This here is a beautiful hat! *(Absurdly)* I always wanted me one just like it!

(She pops it on her head to prove it to her grandson, and the hat is ludicrous and considerably oversized)

RUTH: Hot dog! Go, Mama!

WALTER *(doubled over with laughter):* I'm sorry, Mama—but you look like you ready to go out and chop you some cotton sure enough!

(They all laugh except MAMA, *out of deference to* TRAVIS' *feelings)*

MAMA *(gathering the boy up to her):* Bless your heart—this is the prettiest hat I ever owned—*(*WALTER, RUTH *and* BENEATHA *chime in—noisily, festively and insincerely congratulating* TRAVIS *on his gift)* What are we all standing around here for? We ain't finished packin' yet. Bennie, you ain't packed one book.

(The bell rings)

BENEATHA: That couldn't be the movers . . . it's not hardly two good yet—

*(*BENEATHA *goes into her room.* MAMA *starts for door)*

WALTER *(turning, stiffening):* Wait—wait—I'll get it.

(He stands and looks at the door)

MAMA: You expecting company, son?

WALTER *(just looking at the door):* Yeah—yeah . . .

*(*MAMA *looks at* RUTH, *and they exchange innocent and unfrightened glances)*

MAMA *(not understanding):* Well, let them in, son.

BENEATHA *(from her room):* We need some more string.

MAMA: Travis—you run to the hardware and get me some string cord.

*(*MAMA *goes out and* WALTER *turns and looks at* RUTH. TRAVIS *goes to a dish for money)*

RUTH: Why don't you answer the door, man?

WALTER *(suddenly bounding across the floor to embrace her):* 'Cause sometimes it hard to let the future begin!

(Stooping down in her face)

I got wings! You got wings!
All God's children got wings!

(He crosses to the door and throws it open. Standing there is a very slight little man in a not too prosperous business suit and with haunted frightened eyes and a hat pulled down tightly, brim up, around his forehead. TRAVIS *passes between the men and exits.* WALTER *leans deep in the man's face, still in his jubilance)*

When I get to heaven gonna put on my wings,
Gonna fly all over God's heaven . . .

(The little man just stares at him)

Heaven—

(Suddenly he stops and looks past the little man into the empty hallway) Where's Willy, man?

BOBO: He ain't with me.
WALTER *(not disturbed):* Oh—come on in. You know my wife.
BOBO *(dumbly, taking off his hat):* Yes—h'you, Miss Ruth.
RUTH *(quietly, a mood apart from her husband already, seeing* BOBO*):* Hello, Bobo.
WALTER: You right on time today . . . Right on time. That's the way! *(He slaps* BOBO *on his back)* Sit down . . . lemme hear.

*(*RUTH *stands stiffly and quietly in back of them, as though somehow she senses death, her eyes fixed on her husband)*

BOBO *(his frightened eyes on the floor, his hat in his hands):* Could I please get a drink of water, before I tell you about it, Walter Lee?

*(*WALTER *does not take his eyes off the man.* RUTH *goes blindly to the tap and gets a glass of water and brings it to* BOBO*)*

WALTER: There ain't nothing wrong, is there?
BOBO: Lemme tell you—
WALTER: Man—didn't nothing go wrong?
BOBO: Lemme tell you—Walter Lee. *(Looking at* RUTH *and talking to her more than to* WALTER*)* You know how it was. I got to tell you how it was. I mean first I got to tell you how it was all the way . . . I mean about the money I put in, Walter Lee . . .
WALTER *(with taut agitation now):* What about the money you put in?
BOBO: Well—it wasn't much as we told you—me and Willy—*(He stops)* I'm sorry, Walter. I got a bad feeling about it. I got a real bad feeling about it . . .
WALTER: Man, what you telling me about all this for? . . . Tell me what happened in Springfield . . .

BOBO: Springfield.

RUTH *(like a dead woman):* What was supposed to happen in Springfield?

BOBO *(to her):* This deal that me and Walter went into with Willy—Me and Willy was going to go down to Springfield and spread some money 'round so's we wouldn't have to wait so long for the liquor license . . . That's what we were going to do. Everybody said that was the way you had to do, you understand, Miss Ruth?

WALTER: Man—what happened down there?

BOBO *(a pitiful man, near tears):* I'm trying to tell you, Walter.

WALTER *(screaming at him suddenly):* THEN TELL ME, GODDAMMIT . . . WHAT'S THE MATTER WITH YOU?

BOBO: Man . . . I didn't go to no Springfield, yesterday.

WALTER *(halted, life hanging in the moment):* Why not?

BOBO *(the long way, the hard way to tell):* 'Cause I didn't have no reasons to . . .

WALTER: Man, what are you talking about!

BOBO: I'm talking about the fact that when I got to the train station yesterday morning—eight o'clock like we planned . . . Man—*Willy didn't never show up.*

WALTER: Why . . . where was he . . . where is he?

BOBO: That's what I'm trying to tell you . . . I don't know . . . I waited six hours . . . I called his house . . . and I waited . . . six hours . . . I waited in that train station six hours . . . *(Breaking into tears)* That was all the extra money I had in the world . . . *(Looking up at* WALTER *with the tears running down his face)* Man, *Willy is gone.*

WALTER: Gone, what you mean Willy is gone? Gone where? You mean he went by himself. You mean he went off to Springfield by himself—to take care of getting the license—*(Turns and looks anxiously at* RUTH*)* You mean maybe he didn't want too many people in on the business down there? *(Looks to* RUTH *again, as before)* You know Willy got his own ways. *(Looks back to* BOBO*)* Maybe you was late yesterday and he just went on down there without you. Maybe—maybe—he's been callin' you at home tryin' to tell you what happened or something. Maybe—maybe—he just got sick. He's somewhere—he's got to be somewhere. We just got to find him—me and you got to find him. *(Grabs* BOBO *senselessly by the collar and starts to shake him)* We got to!

BOBO *(in sudden angry, frightened agony):* What's the matter with you, Walter! *When a cat take off with your money he don't leave you no road maps!*

WALTER *(turning madly, as though he is leading for* WILLY *in the very room):* Willy! . . . Willy . . . don't do it . . . Please don't do it . . . Man, not with that money . . . Man, please, not with that money . . . Oh, God . . . Don't let it be true . . . *(He is wandering around, crying out for* WILLY *and looking for him or perhaps for help from God)* Man . . . I trusted you . . . Man, I put my life in your hands . . . *(He starts to crumple down on the floor as* Ruth *just covers her face in horror.* Mama *opens the door and comes into the room, with* Beneatha *behind her)* Man . . . *(He starts to pound the floor with his fists, sobbing wildly)* THAT MONEY IS MADE OUT OF MY FATHER'S FLESH——

Bobo *(standing over him helplessly):* I'm sorry, Walter . . . *(Only* Walter's *sobs reply.* Bobo *puts on his hat)* I had my life staked on this deal, too . . .

(He exits)

Mama *(to* Walter*):* Son—*(She goes to him, bends down to him, talks to his bent head)* Son . . . Is it gone? Son, I gave you sixty-five hundred dollars. Is it gone? All of it? Beneatha's money too?

Walter *(lifting his head slowly):* Mama . . . I never . . . went to the bank at all . . .

Mama *(not wanting to believe him):* You mean . . . your sister's school money . . . you used that too . . . Walter? . . .

Walter: Yessss! All of it . . . It's all gone . . .

(There is total silence. Ruth *stands with her face covered with her hands;* Beneatha *leans forlornly against a wall, fingering a piece of red ribbon from the mother's gift.* Mama *stops and looks at her son without recognition and then, quite without thinking about it, starts to beat him senselessly in the face.* Beneatha *goes to them and stops it)*

Beneatha: Mama!

*(*Mama *stops and looks at both of her children and rises slowly and wanders vaguely, aimlessly away from them)*

Mama: I seen . . . him . . . night after night . . . come in . . . and look at that rug . . . and then look at me . . . the red showing in his eyes . . . the veins moving in his head . . . I seen him grow thin and old before he was forty . . . working and working and working like somebody's old horse . . . killing himself . . . and you—you give it all away in a day—*(She raises her arms to strike him again)*

Beneatha: Mama—

Mama: Oh, God . . . *(She looks up to Him)* Look down here—and show me the strength.

Beneatha: Mama—

Mama *(folding over):* Strength . . .

Beneatha *(plaintively):* Mama . . .

Mama: Strength!

Curtain

ACT III

An hour later.

At curtain, there is a sullen light of gloom in the living room, gray light not unlike that which began the first scene of Act One. At left we can see WALTER *within his room, alone with himself. He is stretched out on the bed, his shirt out and open, his arms under his head. He does not smoke, he does not cry out, he merely lies there, looking up at the ceiling, much as if he were alone in the world.*

In the living room BENEATHA *sits at the table, still surrounded by the now almost ominous packing crates. She sits looking off. We feel that this is a mood struck perhaps an hour before, and it lingers now, full of the empty sound of profound disappointment. We see on a line from her brother's bedroom the sameness of their attitudes. Presently the bell rings and* BENEATHA *rises without ambition or interest in answering. It is* ASAGAI, *smiling broadly, striding into the room with energy and happy expectation and conversation.*

ASAGAI: I came over . . . I had some free time. I thought I might help with the packing. Ah, I like the look of packing crates! A household in preparation for a journey! It depresses some people . . . but for me . . . it is another feeling. Something full of the flow of life, do you understand? Movement, progress . . . It makes me think of Africa.

BENEATHA: Africa!

ASAGAI: What kind of a mood is this? Have I told you how deeply you move me?

BENEATHA: He gave away the money, Asagai . . .

ASAGAI: Who gave away what money?

BENEATHA: The insurance money. My brother gave it away.

ASAGAI: Gave it away?

BENEATHA: He made an investment! With a man even Travis wouldn't have trusted with his most worn-out marbles.

ASAGAI: And it's gone?

BENEATHA: Gone!

ASAGAI: I'm very sorry . . . And you, now?

BENEATHA: Me? . . . Me? . . . Me, I'm nothing . . . Me. When I was very small . . . we used to take our sleds out in the wintertime and the only hills we had were the ice-covered stone steps of some houses down the street. And we used to fill them in with snow and make them smooth and slide down them all day . . . and it was very dangerous, you know . . . far too steep . . . and sure enough one day a kid named Rufus came down too fast and hit the sidewalk and we saw his face just split open right there in front of us . . . And I remember standing there looking at his bloody open face thinking that was the end of Rufus. But the ambulance came and they took him to the hospital and they fixed the broken bones and they sewed it all up . . . and the next time I saw Rufus he just had a little line down the middle of his face . . . I never got over that . . .

ASAGAI: What?

BENEATHA: That that was what one person could do for another, fix him up—sew up the problem, make him all right again. That was the most marvelous thing in the world . . . I wanted to do that. I always thought it was the one concrete thing in the world that a human being could do. Fix up the sick, you know—and make them whole again. This was truly being God . . .

ASAGAI: You wanted to be God?

BENEATHA: No—I wanted to cure. It used to be so important to me. I wanted to cure. It used to matter. I used to care. I mean about people and how their bodies hurt . . .

ASAGAI: And you've stopped caring?

BENEATHA: Yes—I think so.

ASAGAI: Why?

BENEATHA *(bitterly):* Because it doesn't seem deep enough, close enough to what ails mankind! It was a child's way of seeing things—or an idealist's.

ASAGAI: Children see things very well sometimes—and idealists even better.

BENEATHA: I know that's what you think. Because you are still where I left off. You with all your talk and dreams about Africa! You still think you can patch up the world. Cure the Great Sore of Colonialism—*(Loftily, mocking it)* with the Penicillin of Independence—!

ASAGAI: Yes!

BENEATHA: Independence *and then what?* What about all the crooks and thieves and just plain idiots who will come into power and steal and plunder the same as before—only now they will be black and do it in the name of the new Independence—WHAT ABOUT THEM?!

ASAGAI: That will be the problem for another time. First we must get there.

BENEATHA: And where does it end?

ASAGAI: End? Who even spoke of an end? To life? To living?

BENEATHA: An end to misery! To stupidity! Don't you see there isn't any real progress, Asagai, there is only one large circle that we march in, around and around, each of us with our own little picture in front of us—our own little mirage that we think is the future.

ASAGAI: That is the mistake.

BENEATHA: What?

ASAGAI: What you just said—about the circle. It isn't a circle—it is simply a long line—as in geometry, you know, one that reaches into infinity. And because we cannot see the end—we also cannot see how it changes. And it is very odd but those who see the changes—who dream, who will not give up—are called idealists . . . and those who see only the circle—we call *them* the "realists"!

BENEATHA: Asagai, while I was sleeping in that bed in there, people went out and took the future right out of my hands! And nobody asked me, nobody consulted me—they just went out and changed my life!

ASAGAI: Was it your money?

BENEATHA: What?

ASAGAI: Was it your money he gave away?

BENEATHA: It belonged to all of us.

ASAGAI: But did you earn it? Would you have had it at all if your father had not died?

BENEATHA: No.

ASAGAI: Then isn't there something wrong in a house—in a world—where all dreams, good or bad, must depend on the death of a man? I never thought to see *you* like this, Alaiyo. You! Your brother made a mistake and you are grateful to him so that now you can give up the ailing human race on account of it! You talk about what good is struggle, what good is anything! Where are we all going and why are we bothering!

BENEATHA: AND YOU CANNOT ANSWER IT!

ASAGAI *(shouting over her): I LIVE THE ANSWER! (Pause)* In my village at home it is the exceptional man who can even read a newspaper . . . or who ever sees a book at all. I will go home and much of what I will have to say will seem strange to the people of my village. But I will teach and work and things will happen, slowly and swiftly. At times it will seem that nothing changes at all . . . and then again the sudden dramatic events which make history leap into the future. And then quiet again. Retrogression even. Guns, murder, revolution. And I even will have moments when I wonder if the quiet was not better than all that death and hatred. But I will look about my village at the illiteracy and disease and ignorance and I will not wonder long. And perhaps . . . perhaps I will be a great man . . . I mean perhaps I will hold on to the substance of truth and find my way always with the right course . . . and perhaps for it I will be butchered in my bed some night by the servants of empire . . .

BENEATHA: *The martyr!*

ASAGAI *(he smiles):* . . . or perhaps I shall live to be a very old man, respected and esteemed in my new nation . . . And perhaps I shall hold office and this is what I'm trying to tell you, Alaiyo: Perhaps the things I believe now for my country will be wrong and outmoded, and I will not understand and do terrible things to have things my way or merely to keep my power. Don't you see that there will be young men and women—not British soldiers then, but my own black countrymen—to step out of the shadows some evening and slit my then useless throat? Don't you see they have always been there . . . that they always will be. And that such a thing as my own death will be an advance? They who might kill me even . . . actually replenish all that I was.

BENEATHA: Oh, Asagai, I know all that.

ASAGAI: Good! Then stop moaning and groaning and tell me what you plan to do.

BENEATHA: Do?

ASAGAI: I have a bit of a suggestion.

BENEATHA: What?

ASAGAI *(rather quietly for him):* That when it is all over—that you come home with me—

BENEATHA *(staring at him and crossing away with exasperation):* Oh—Asagai—at this moment you decide to be romantic!

ASAGAI *(quickly understanding the misunderstanding):* My dear, young creature of the New World—I do not mean across the city—I mean across the ocean: home—to Africa.

BENEATHA *(slowly understanding and turning to him with murmured amazement):* To Africa?

ASAGAI: Yes! . . . *(Smiling and lifting his arms playfully)* Three hundred years later the African Prince rose up out of the seas and swept the maiden back across the middle passage over which her ancestors had come—

BENEATHA *(unable to play):* To—to Nigeria?

ASAGAI: Nigeria. Home. *(Coming to her with genuine romantic flippancy)* I will show you our mountains and our stars; and give you cool drinks from gourds and teach you the old songs and the ways of our people—and, in time, we will pretend that—*(Very Softly)*—you have only been away for a day. Say that you'll come—*(He swings her around and takes her full in his arms in a kiss which proceeds to passion)*

BENEATHA *(pulling away suddenly):* You're getting me all mixed up—

ASAGAI: Why?

BENEATHA: Too many things—too many things have happened today. I must sit down and think. I don't know what I feel about anything right this minute.

(She promptly sits down and props her chin on her fist)

ASAGAI *(charmed):* All right, I shall leave you. No—don't get up. *(Touching her, gently, sweetly)* Just sit awhile and think . . . Never be afraid to sit awhile and think. *(He goes to door and looks at her)* How often I have looked at you and said, "Ah—so this is what the New World hath finally wrought . . ."

(He exits. BENEATHA *sits on alone. Presently* WALTER *enters from his room and starts to rummage through things, feverishly looking for something. She looks up and turns in her seat)*

BENEATHA *(hissingly):* Yes—just look at what the New World hath wrought! . . . Just look! *(She gestures with bitter disgust)* There he is! *Monsieur le petit bourgeois noir*—himself! There he is—Symbol of a Rising Class! Entrepreneur! Titan of the system! *(*WALTER *ignores her completely and continues frantically and destructively looking for something and hurling* *things to floor and tearing things out of their place in his search.* Beneatha *ignores the eccentricity of his actions and goes on with the monologue of insult)* Did you dream of yachts on Lake Michigan, Brother? Did you see yourself on that Great Day sitting down at the Conference Table, surrounded by all the mighty bald-headed men in America? All halted, waiting, breathless, waiting for your pronouncements on industry? Waiting for you—Chairman of the Board! *(*Walter *finds what he is looking for—a small piece of white paper—and pushes it in his pocket and puts on his coat and rushes out without ever having looked at her. She shouts after him)* I look at you and I see the final triumph of stupidity in the world!

(The door slams and she returns to just sitting again. Ruth *comes quickly out of* Mama*'s room)*

Ruth: Who was that?
Beneatha: Your husband.
Ruth: Where did he go?
Beneatha: Who knows—maybe he has an appointment at U.S. Steel.
Ruth *(anxiously, with frightened eyes):* You didn't say nothing bad to him, did you?
Beneatha: Bad? Say anything bad to him? No—I told him he was a sweet boy and full of dreams and everything is strictly peachy keen, as the ofay kids say!

*(*Mama *enters from her bedroom. She is lost, vague, trying to catch hold, to make some sense of her former command of the world, but it still eludes her. A sense of waste overwhelms her gait; a measure of apology rides on her shoulders. She goes to her plant, which has remained on the table, looks at it, picks it up and takes it to the window sill and sits it outside, and she stands and looks at it a long moment. Then she closes the window, straightens her body with effort and turns around to her children)*

Mama: Well—ain't it a mess in here, though? *(A false cheerfulness, a beginning of something)* I guess we all better stop moping around and get some work done. All this unpacking and everything we got to do. *(*Ruth *raises her head slowly in response to the sense of the line; and* Beneatha *in similar manner turns very slowly to look at her mother)* One of you all better call the moving people and tell 'em not to come.
Ruth: Tell 'em not to come?
Mama: Of course, baby. Ain't no need in 'em coming all the way here and having to go back. They charges for that too. *(She sits down, fingers to her brow, thinking)* Lord, ever since I was a little girl, I always remembers people saying, "Lena—Lena Eggleston, you aims too high all the time. You needs to slow down and see life a little more like it is. Just slow down some." That's what they always used to say down home—"Lord, that Lena Eggleston is a high-minded thing. She'll get her due one day!"

RUTH: No, Lena . . .

MAMA: Me and Big Walter just didn't never learn right.

RUTH: Lena, no! We gotta go. Bennie—tell her . . . *(She rises and crosses to* BENEATHA *with her arms outstretched.* BENEATHA *doesn't respond)* Tell her we can still move . . . the notes ain't but a hundred and twenty-five a month. We got four grown people in this house—we can work . . .

MAMA *(to herself):* Just aimed too high all the time—

RUTH *(turning and going to* MAMA *fast—the words pouring out with urgency and desperation):* Lena—I'll work . . . I'll work twenty hours a day in all the kitchens in Chicago . . . I'll strap my baby on my back if I have to and scrub all the floors in America and wash all the sheets in America if I have to—but we got to MOVE! We got to get OUT OF HERE!!

*(*MAMA *reaches out absently and pats* RUTH*'s hand)*

MAMA: No—I sees things differently now. Been thinking 'bout some of the things we could do to fix this place up some. I seen a second-hand bureau over on Maxwell Street just the other day that could fit right there. *(She points to where the new furniture might go.* RUTH *wanders away from her)* Would need some new handles on it and then a little varnish and it look like something brand-new. And—we can put up them new curtains in the kitchen . . . Why this place be looking fine. Cheer us all up so that we forget trouble ever come . . . *(To* RUTH*)* And you could get some nice screens to put up in your room round the baby's bassinet . . . *(She looks at both of them, pleadingly)* Sometimes you just got to know when to give up some things . . . and hold on to what you got. . . .

*(*WALTER *enters from the outside, looking spent and leaning against the door, his coat hanging from him)*

MAMA: Where you been, son?

WALTER *(breathing hard):* Made a call.

MAMA: To who, son?

WALTER: To The Man. *(He heads for his room)*

MAMA: What man, baby?

WALTER *(stops in the door):* The Man, Mama. Don't you know who The Man is?

RUTH: Walter Lee?

WALTER: *The Man*. Like the guys in the streets say—The Man. Captain Boss—Mistuh Charley . . . Old Cap'n Please Mr. Bossman . . .

BENEATHA *(suddenly):* Lindner!

WALTER: That's right! That's good. I told him to come right over.

BENEATHA *(fiercely, understanding):* For what? What do you want to see him for!

WALTER *(looking at his sister):* We going to do business with him.

MAMA: What you talking 'bout, son?

WALTER: Talking 'bout life, Mama. You all always telling me to see life like it is.

Well—I laid in there on my back today . . . and I figured it out. Life just like it is. Who gets and who don't get. *(He sits down with his coat on and laughs)* Mama, you know it's all divided up. Life is. Sure enough. Between the takers and the "tooken." *(He laughs)* I've figured it out finally. *(He looks around at them)* Yeah. Some of us always getting "tooken." *(He laughs)* People like Willy Harris, they don't never get "tooken." And you know why the rest of us do? 'Cause we all mixed up. Mixed up bad. We get to looking 'round for the right and the wrong; and we worry about it and cry about it and stay up nights trying to figure out 'bout the wrong and the right of things all the time . . . And all the time, man, them takers is out there operating, just taking and taking. Willy Harris? Shoot—Willy Harris don't even count. He don't even count in the big scheme of things. But I'll say one thing for old Willy Harris . . . he's taught me something. He's taught me to keep my eye on what counts in this world. Yeah—*(Shouting out a little)* Thanks, Willy!

RUTH: What did you call that man for, Walter Lee?

WALTER: Called him to tell him to come on over to the show. Gonna put on a show for the man. Just what he wants to see. You see, Mama, the man came here today and he told us that them people out there where you want us to move—well they so upset they willing to pay us *not* to move! *(He laughs again)* And—and oh, Mama—you would of been proud of the way me and Ruth and Bennie acted. We told him to get out . . . Lord have mercy! We told the man to get out! Oh, we was some proud folks this afternoon, yeah. *(He lights a cigarette)* We were still full of that old-time stuff . . .

RUTH *(coming toward him slowly)*: You talking 'bout taking them people's money to keep us from moving in that house?

WALTER: I ain't just talking 'bout it, baby—I'm telling you that's what's going to happen!

BENEATHA: Oh, God! Where is the bottom! Where is the real honest-to-God bottom so he can't go any farther!

WALTER: See—that's the old stuff. You and that boy that was here today. You all want everybody to carry a flag and a spear and sing some marching songs, huh? You wanna spend your life looking into things and trying to find the right and the wrong part, huh? Yeah. You know what's going to happen to that boy someday—he'll find himself sitting in a dungeon, locked in forever—and the takers will have the key! Forget it, baby! There ain't no causes—there ain't nothing but taking in this world, and he who takes most is smartest—and it don't make a damn bit of difference *how.*

MAMA: You making something inside me cry, son. Some awful pain inside me.

WALTER: Don't cry, Mama. Understand. That white man is going to walk in that door able to write checks for more money than we ever had. It's important to him and I'm going to help him . . . I'm going to put on the show, Mama.

MAMA: Son—I come from five generations of people who was slaves and sharecroppers—but ain't nobody in my family never let nobody pay 'em no money that was a way of telling us we wasn't fit to walk the earth. We ain't never been that poor. *(Raising her eyes and looking at him)* We ain't never been that—dead inside.

Beneatha: Well—we are dead now. All the talk about dreams and sunlight that goes on in this house. It's all dead now.

Walter: What's the matter with you all! I didn't make this world! It was give to me this way! Hell, yes, I want me some yachts someday! Yes, I want to hang some real pearls 'round my wife's neck. Ain't she supposed to wear no pearls? Somebody tell me—tell me, who decides which women is suppose to wear pearls in this world. I tell you I am a *man*—and I think my wife should wear some pearls in this world!

(This last line hangs a good while and Walter *begins to move about the room. The word "Man" has penetrated his consciousness; he mumbles it to himself repeatedly between strange agitated pauses as he moves about)*

Mama: Baby, how you going to feel on the inside?

Walter: Fine! . . . Going to feel fine . . . a man . . .

Mama: You won't have nothing left then, Walter Lee.

Walter *(coming to her):* I'm going to feel fine, Mama. I'm going to look that son-of-a-bitch in the eyes and say—*(He falters)*—and say, "All right, Mr. Lindner—*(He falters even more)*—that's *your* neighborhood out there! You got the right to keep it like you want! You got the right to have it like you want! Just write the check and—the house is yours." And—and I am going to say—*(His voice almost breaks)* "And you—you people just put the money in my hand and you won't have to live next to this bunch of stinking niggers! . . ." *(He straightens up and moves away from his mother, walking around the room)* And maybe—maybe I'll just get down on my black knees . . . *(He does so;* Ruth *and* Bennie *and* Mama *watch him in frozen horror)* "Captain, Mistuh, Bossman—*(Groveling and grinning and wringing his hands in profoundly anguished imitation of the slow-witted movie stereotype)* A-hee-hee-hee! Oh, yassuh boss! Yasssssuh! Great white—*(Voice breaking, he forces himself to go on)*—Father, just gi' ussen de money, fo' God's sake, and we's—we's ain't gwine come out deh and dirty up yo' white folks neighborhood . . ." *(He breaks down completely)* And I'll feel fine! Fine! FINE! *(He gets up and goes into the bedroom)*

Beneatha: That is not a man. That is nothing but a toothless rat.

Mama: Yes—death done come in this here house. *(She is nodding, slowly, reflectively)* Done come walking in my house on the lips of my children. You what supposed to be my beginning again. You—what supposed to be my harvest. *(To* Beneatha*)* You—you mourning your brother?

Beneatha: He's no brother of mine.

Mama: What you say?

Beneatha: I said that that individual in that room is no brother of mine.

MAMA: That's what I thought you said. You feeling like you better than he is today? *(*BENEATHA *does not answer)* Yes? What you tell him a minute ago? That he wasn't a man? Yes? You give him up for me? You done wrote his epitaph too—like the rest of the world? Well, who give you the privilege?

BENEATHA: Be on my side for once! You saw what he just did, Mama! You saw him—down on his knees. Wasn't it you who taught me to despise any man who would do that? Do what he's going to do?

MAMA: Yes—I taught you that. Me and your daddy. But I thought I taught you something else too . . . I thought I taught you to love him.

BENEATHA: Love him? There is nothing left to love.

MAMA: There is *always* something left to love. And if you ain't learned that, you ain't learned nothing. *(Looking at her)* Have you cried for that boy today? I don't mean for yourself and for the family 'cause we lost the money. I mean for him: what he been through and what it done to him. Child, when do you think is the time to love somebody the most? When they done good and made things easy for everybody? Well then, you ain't through learning—because that ain't the time at all. It's when he's at his lowest and can't believe in hisself 'cause the world done whipped him so! When you starts measuring somebody, measure him right, child, measure him right. Make sure you done taken into account what hills and valleys he come through before he got to wherever he is.

*(*TRAVIS *bursts into the room at the end of the speech, leaving the door open)*

TRAVIS: Grandmama—the moving men are downstairs! The truck just pulled up.

MAMA *(turning and looking at him):* Are they, baby? They downstairs?

(She sighs and sits. LINDNER *appears in the doorway. He peers in and knocks lightly, to gain attention, and comes in. All turn to look at him)*

LINDNER *(hat and briefcase in hand):* Uh—hello . . .

*(*RUTH *crosses mechanically to the bedroom door and opens it and lets it swing open freely and slowly as the lights come up on* WALTER *within, still in his coat, sitting at the far corner of the room. He looks up and out through the room to* LINDNER*)*

RUTH: He's here.

(A long minute passes and WALTER *slowly gets up)*

LINDNER *(coming to the table with efficiency, putting his briefcase on the table and starting to unfold papers and unscrew fountain pens):* Well, I certainly was glad to hear from you people. *(*WALTER *has begun the trek out of the room, slowly and awkwardly, rather like a small boy, passing the back of his sleeve across his mouth from time to time)* Life can really be so much simpler than people let it be most of the time. Well—with whom do I negotiate? You, Mrs. Younger, or your son here? *(*MAMA *sits with her* *hands folded on her lap and her eyes closed as* Walter *advances.* Travis *goes closer to* Lindner *and looks at the papers curiously)* Just some official papers, sonny.

Ruth: Travis, you go downstairs—

Mama *(opening her eyes and looking into* Walter's*):* No. Travis, you stay right here. And you make him understand what you doing, Walter Lee. You teach him good. Like Willy Harris taught you. You show where our five generations done come to. *(*Walter *looks from her to the boy, who grins at him innocently)* Go ahead, son—*(She folds her hands and closes her eyes)* Go ahead.

Walter *(at last crosses to* Lindner, *who is reviewing the contract):* Well, Mr. Lindner. *(*Beneatha *turns away)* We called you—*(There is a profound, simple groping quality in his speech)*—because, well, me and my family *(He looks around and shifts from one foot to the other)* Well—we are very plain people . . .

Lindner: Yes—

Walter: I mean—I have worked as a chauffeur most of my life—and my wife here, she does domestic work in people's kitchens. So does my mother. I mean—we are plain people . . .

Lindner: Yes, Mr. Younger—

Walter *(really like a small boy, looking down at his shoes and then up at the man):* And—uh—well, my father, well, he was a laborer most of his life. . . .

Lindner *(absolutely confused):* Uh, yes—yes, I understand. *(He turns back to the contract)*

Walter *(a beat; staring at him):* And my father—*(With sudden intensity)* My father almost *beat a man to death* once because this man called him a bad name or something, you know what I mean?

Lindner *(looking up, frozen):* No, no, I'm afraid I don't—

Walter *(a beat. The tension hangs; then* Walter *steps back from it):* Yeah. Well—what I mean is that we come from people who had a lot of *pride.* I mean—we are very proud people. And that's my sister over there and she's going to be a doctor—and we are very proud—

Lindner: Well—I am sure that is very nice, but—

Walter: What I am telling you is that we called you over here to tell you that we are very proud and that this—*(Signaling to* Travis*)* Travis, come here. *(*Travis *crosses and* Walter *draws him before him facing the man)* This is my son, and he makes the sixth generation our family in this country. And we have all thought about your offer—

Lindner: Well, good . . . good—

Walter: And we have decided to move into our house because my father—my father—he earned it for us brick by brick. *(*Mama *has her eyes closed and is rocking back and forth as though she were in church, with her head nodding the Amen yes)* We don't want to make no trouble for nobody or fight no causes, and we will try to be good neighbors. And that's *all* we got to say about that. *(He looks the man absolutely in the eyes)* We don't want your money. *(He turns and walks away)*

LINDNER *(looking around at all of them):* I take it then—that you have decided to occupy . . .

BENEATHA: That's what the man said.

LINDNER *(to* MAMA *in her reverie):* Then I would like to appeal to you, Mrs. Younger. You are older and wiser and understand things better, I am sure . . .

MAMA: I am afraid you don't understand. My son said we was going to move and there ain't nothing left for me to say. *(Briskly)* You know how these young folks is nowadays, mister. Can't do a thing with 'em! *(As he opens his mouth, she rises)* Good-bye.

LINDNER *(folding up his materials):* Well—if you are that final about it . . . there is nothing left for me to say. *(He finishes, almost ignored by the family, who are concentrating on* WALTER LEE. *At the door* LINDNER *halts and looks around)* I sure hope you people know what you're getting into.

(He shakes his head and exits)

RUTH *(looking around and coming to life):* Well, for God's sake—if the moving men are here—LET'S GET THE HELL OUT OF HERE!

MAMA *(into action):* Ain't it the truth! Look at all this here mess. Ruth, put Travis' good jacket on him . . . Walter Lee, fix your tie and tuck your shirt in, you look like somebody's hoodlum! Lord have mercy, where is my plant? *(She flies to get it amid the general bustling of the family, who are deliberately trying to ignore the nobility of the past moment)* You all start on down . . . Travis child, don't go empty-handed . . . Ruth, where did I put that box with my skillets in it? I want to be in charge of it myself . . . I'm going to make us the biggest dinner we ever ate tonight . . . Beneatha, what's the matter with them stockings? Pull them things up, girl . . .

(The family starts to file out as two moving men appear and begin to carry out the heavier pieces of furniture, bumping into the family as they move about)

BENEATHA: Mama, Asagai asked me to marry him today and go to Africa—

MAMA *(in the middle of her getting-ready activity):* He did? You ain't old enough to marry nobody—*(Seeing the moving men lifting one of her chairs precariously)* Darling, that ain't no bale of cotton, please handle it so we can sit in it again! I had that chair twenty-five years . . .

(The movers sigh with exasperation and go on with their work)

BENEATHA *(girlishly and unreasonably trying to pursue the conversation):* To go to Africa, Mama—be a doctor in Africa . . .

MAMA *(distracted):* Yes, baby—

WALTER: *Africa!* What he want you to go to Africa for?

Beneatha: To practice there . . .

Walter: Girl, if you don't get all them silly ideas out your head! You better marry yourself a man with some loot . . .

Beneatha *(angrily, precisely as in the first scene of the play):* What have you got to do with who I marry!

Walter: Plenty. Now I think George Murchison—

Beneatha: *George Murchison!* I wouldn't marry him if he was Adam and I was Eve!

*(*Walter *and* Beneatha *go out yelling at each other vigorously and the anger is loud and real till their voices diminish.* Ruth *stands at the door and turns to* Mama *and smiles knowingly)*

Mama *(fixing her hat at last):* Yeah—they something all right, my children . . .

Ruth: Yeah—they're something. Let's go, Lena.

Mama *(stalling, starting to look around at the house):* Yes—I'm coming. Ruth—

Ruth: Yes?

Mama *(quietly, woman to woman):* He finally come into his manhood today, didn't he? Kind of like a rainbow after the rain . . .

Ruth *(biting her lip lest her own pride explode in front of* Mama*):* Yes, Lena.

*(*Walter*'s voice calls for them raucously)*

Walter *(off stage):* Y'all come on! These people charges by the hour, you know!

Mama *(waving* Ruth *out vaguely):* All right, honey—go on down. I be down directly.

*(*Ruth *hesitates, then exits.* Mama *stands, at last alone in the living room, her plant on the table before her as the lights start to come down. She looks around at all the walls and ceilings and suddenly, despite herself, while the children call below, a great heaving thing rises in her and she puts her fist to her mouth to stifle it, takes a final desperate look, pulls her coat about her, pats her hat and goes out. The lights dim down. The door opens and she comes back in, grabs her plant, and goes out for the last time)*

Curtain

—1958

What are your reactions to and questions about this work? The following questions may help provoke some ideas.

Probing the Work

1. What is the role of the family in this play? How does each member of the family interpret the American dream?

2. What are some of the *symbols* (p.78) in this play? What, for example, might the plant represent?
3. What is the primary *conflict* (p. 79) of the play? When is it resolved?
4. At the end of the play, Walter, according to Hansberry, "has finally reached out in his tiny moment and caught that sweet essence which is human dignity, and it shines like the old star-touched dream that is in his eyes." Explain what Hansberry means here: do you agree with her?
5. What is the difference between how Walter identifies himself at the beginning of the play and how he does so at the end?

Identifying Issues

6. Why does Asagai say of Beneatha, "So this is what the new world has wrought"? Why does Beneatha say to Asagai, "I am looking for my identity." What does Beneatha represent with regard to American women in general, or African-American women in particular?
7. React to one of the following comments Lorraine Hansberry has made:
   - "There is simply no reason why dreams should dry up like raisins or prunes or anything else in America. . . . I believe that we can *impose* beauty on our future."
   - "We must come out of the ghettos of America, because the ghettos are killing us: not only our 'dreams' . . . but our very bodies."
8. Read the following *critical commentary* by Amiri Baraka and summarize its main points. What do you find most enlightening? Are there any favorable comments he makes about the play that you would disagree with? What do you think of his assessment of the George/Walter conflict (p. 333), or of his conclusion that Hansberry "created a family on the cutting edge of the same class and ideological struggles as existed in the [civil rights] movement itself and among the people" (p. 333)?

Commentary

AMIRI BARAKA

"A Raisin in the Sun's" Enduring Passion (excerpt)

Raisin typifies American society in a way that reflects more accurately the real lives of the black U.S. majority than any work that ever received commercial exposure before it, and few if any since. It has the life that only classics can maintain. Any useful re-appreciation of it cannot be limited, therefore, to the passages restored or the new values discovered, important though these are: it is the play itself, as a dramatic (and sociopolitical) whole, that demands our confirmation of its grandeur.

When *Raisin* first appeared in 1959, the Civil Rights Movement was in its earlier stages. And as a document reflecting the *essence* of those struggles, the play is unexcelled. For many of us it was—and remains—the quintessential civil rights drama. But any attempt to confine the play to an era, mind-set, an issue ("Housing") or set of topical concerns was, as we now see, a mistake. The truth is that Hansberry's dramatic skills have yet to be properly appreciated—and not just by those guardians of the status quo who pass themselves off as dramatic critics. For black theater artists and would-be theorists especially, this is ironic because the play is probably the most widely appreciated—particularly by African Americans—black drama that we have.

Raisin lives in large measure because black people have kept it alive. And because Hansberry has done *more* than document, which is the most limited form of realism. She is a *critical realist,* in a way that Langston Hughes, Richard Wright, and Margaret Walker are. That is, she *analyzes* and *assesses* reality and shapes her statement as an aesthetically powerful and politically advanced work of art. Her statement cannot be separated from the characters she creates to embody, in their totality, the life she observes: it becomes, in short, the living material of the work, part of its breathing body, integral and alive. . . .

Hansberry's play . . . dealt with the very same issues of democratic rights and quality that were being aired in the streets. It dealt with them with an unabating dramatic force, vision, political concreteness and clarity that, in retrospect, are awesome. But it dealt with them not as abstractions, fit only for infantile-left pamphlets, but as they are *lived.* In reality.

All of *Raisin*'s characters speak *to* the text and are critical to its dramatic tensions and understanding. They are necessarily larger than life—in impact—but crafted meticulously from living social material.

When the play opened on Broadway, Lena Younger, the emotional adhesive of the family, was given a broad, aggressive reading by Claudia McNeil. Indeed, her reading has been taken as the model and somewhat institutionalized in various productions I've seen.

The role itself—of family head, folksy counsel, upholder of tradition—has caused many people to see her as the stereotyped "black matriarch" of establishment and commercial sociological fame. Carrying with them (or rebelling against) the preconceived baggage of that stereotype, and recalling the play through the haze of memory (or from the compromised movie version), they have not bothered to look more closely at the actual woman Hansberry created—and at *what* tradition she in fact upholds.

[In the recent New York revival of the play, Olivia Cole's reading of Lena] was revelation and renewal.

Ms. Cole came at the role from the inside out. Her Lena is a woman, black, poor, struggle-worn but proud and loving. She was in the world *before* the rest of the family, before many of us viewing the play. She has seen and felt what we have not, or what we cannot yet identify. She is no quaint, folksy artifact; she is truth, history, love—and struggle—as they can be manifest only in real life.

Similarly, the new interpreters of Walter Lee . . . are something "fresh," like our kids say. They bring a contemporary flavoring to the work that consists of knowing—with more certainty than, say, Sidney Poitier could have in the original—the frustration and rage animating the healthy black male, *post*-civil rights era. They play Walter Lee more aggressively, more self-consciously, so that when he does fall we can actually hate him—hate the frivolous, selfish male-chauvinist part of ourselves. And when he stands up at the finale and will not be beaten, we can cry with joy. . . .

A Raisin in the Sun is about *dreams,* ironically enough. And how those psychological projections of human life can come into conflict like any other product of that life. For Lena, a new house, the stability and happiness of her children, are her principal dream. And as such this is the completion of a dream she and her late husband—who has literally, like the slaves, been *worked* to death—conceived together.

Ruth's dream, as mother and wife, is somewhat similar. A room for her son, an inside toilet. She dreams as one of those triply oppressed by society—as worker, as African American, and as woman. But her dream, and her mother-in-law's, conflicts with Walter Lee's. He is the chauffeur to a rich white man and dreams of owning all and doing all the things he sees "Mr. Arnold" do and own. On one level Walter Lee is merely aspiring to full and acknowledged humanity; on another level he yearns to strut his "manhood," a predictable mix of *machismo* and fantasy. But Hansberry takes it even further to show us that on still another level Walter Lee, worker though he be, has the "realizable" dream of the black petty bourgeoisie. "There he is! *Monsieur le petit bourgeois noir*—himself!," cries Beneatha, the other of Lena Younger's children. "There he is—Symbol of a Rising Class! Entrepreneur! Titan of the system!" The deepness of this is that Hansberry can see that the conflict of dreams is not just that of individuals but, more importantly, of classes. Not since Theodore Ward's *Big White Fog* (1938) has there been a play so thoroughly and expertly reflective of class struggle within a black family.

Beneatha dreams of medical school. She is already socially mobile, finding a place, as her family cannot, among other petty bourgeois aspirants on the rungs of "education," where their hard work has put her. Her aspiration is less caustic, more attainable than Walter's. But she yearns for something more. Her name Beneatha (as who ain't?) should instruct us. She is, on the one hand, secure in the collegiate world of "ideas" and elitism, above the mass; on the other, undeceived by the myths and symbols of class and status. Part militant, part dilletante, "liberated" woman, little girl, she questions everything and dreams of service to humanity, an identity beyond self and family in the liberation struggles of her people. Ah, but will she have the strength to stay the course?

Hansberry has Beneatha grappling with key controversies of the period, but also some that had yet to clearly surface. And she grapples with some that will remain with us until society itself is changed: The relationship of the intellectual to the masses. The relationship of African Americans to Africans. The liberation movement itself and the gnawing necessity of black self-respect in its many guises (e.g., "straightened" hair vs. "the natural"). Written in 1956 and first seen by audiences in the new revivals, the part of the text in which Beneatha unveils her hair—the "perm" cut off and she glowing with her original woolly crown—precedes the "Afro" by a decade. Dialogue between Beneatha and her mother, brother, Asagai and George Murchison digs into all these still-burning concerns.

Similarly, Walter Lee and Ruth's dialogues lay out his male chauvinism and even self- and group-hate born of the frustration of too many dreams too long deferred: the powerlessness of black people to control their own fate or that of their families in capitalist America where race is place, white is right, and money makes and defines the man. Walter dreams of using his father's insurance money to buy a liquor store. This dream is in conflict not only with the dreams of the Younger women, but with reality. But Walter appreciates only his differences with—and blames—the women. Throughout the work, Hansberry addresses herself to issues that the very young might feel only *The Color Purple* has raised. Walter's relationship to his wife and sister, and Beneatha's with George and Asagai, gives us a variety of male chauvinism—working class, petty bourgeois, African.

Asagai, the Nigerian student who courts Beneatha, dreams of the liberation of Africa and even of taking Beneatha there: "We will pretend that . . . you have only been away for a day." But that's not reality either, though his discussion of the dynamics and dialectics of revolution—and of the continuity of human struggle, the only means of progress—still rings with truth!

Hansberry's warnings about neo-colonialism and the growth (and corruption) of a post-colonial African bourgeoisie—"the servants of empire," as Asagai calls them—are dazzling because of their subsequent replication by reality. As is, above all, her sense of the pressures mounting inexorably in this one typical household, and in Walter Lee especially, and of where they must surely lead. It was the "explosion" Langston Hughes talked about in his great poem "Harlem"—centerpiece of his incomparable *Montage of a Dream Deferred,* from which the play's title was taken—and it informs the play as its twinned projection: dream or coming reality.

These are the categories Langston proposes for the dream:

> Does it dry up
> Like a raisin in the sun?

Dried up is what Walter Lee and Ruth's marriage had become, because their respective dreams have been deferred. When Mama Lena and Beneatha are felled by news of Walter Lee's weakness and dishonesty, their life's will—the desired greening of their humanity—is defoliated.

> Or fester like a sore—
> And then run?

Walter Lee's dream has festered, and in his dealings with the slack-jawed con man Willie (merchant of the stuff of dreams), his dream is "running."

We speak of the American Dream. Malcolm X said that for the Afro-American it was the American Nightmare. The little ferret man . . . is the dream's messenger, and the only white person in the play. His name is Lindner (as in "neither a borrower nor a Lindner be"), and the thirty or so "pieces of silver" he proffers are meant to help the niggers understand the dichotomous dream.

"But you've got to admit that a man, right or wrong, has the right to want to have the neighborhood he lives in a certain kind of way," says Lindner. Except black folks. Yes, these "not rich and fancy" representatives of white lower-middle America have a dream, too. A class dream, though it does not even serve them. But they are kept ignorant enough not to understand that the real dimensions of that dream—white supremacy, black "inferiority," and with them ultimately, though they know it not, fascism and war—are revealed every day throughout the world as deadly to human life and development—even their own.

In the post-civil rights era, in "polite" society, theirs is a dream too gross even to speak of *directly* anymore. And this is another legacy of the play: It was one of the shots fired (and still being fired) at the aberrant white-supremacy dream that is American reality. And the play is also a summation of those shots, that battle, its heightened statement. Yet the man, Lindner, explains him/them self, and there is even a hint of compassion for Lindner the man as he bumbles on in outrageous innocence of all he is actually saying—that "innocence" for which Americans are famous, which begs you to love and understand me for hating you, the innocence that kills. Through him we see this other dream:

> Does it stink like rotten meat?
> Or crust and sugar over—
> Like a syrupy sweet?

Almost everyone else in the play would sound like Martin Luther King at the march on Washington were we to read their speeches closely and project them broadly. An exception is George Murchison (merchant's son), the "assimilated" good bourgeois whose boldest dream, if one can call it that, is to "get the grades . . . to pass the course . . . to get a degree" en route to making it the American way. George wants only to "pop" Beneatha after she, looking good, can be seen with him in the "proper" places. He is opposed to a woman's "thinking" at all, and black heritage to him "is nothing but a bunch of raggedy-ass spirituals and some grass huts." The truth of this portrait is one reason the black bourgeoisie has not created the black national theaters, publishing houses, journals, galleries, film corporations, and newspapers the African American people desperately need. So lacking in self-respect are members of this class of George's, they even let the Kentucky Colonel sell us fried chicken and giblets.

The clash between Walter Lee and George, one of the high points of class struggle in the play and a dramatic tour de force, gives us the dialogue between the *sons* of the house and of the field slaves.

When *Raisin* appeared the movement itself was in transition, which is why Hansberry could sum up its throbbing profile with such clarity. The baton was ready to pass from "George's father" as leader of the "Freedom Movement" (when its real muscle was always the Lena Youngers and their husbands) to the Walter Lees and Beneathas and Asagais and even the Georges.

In February 1960, black students at North Carolina A & T began to "sit in" at Woolworth's in a more forceful attack on segregated public facilities. By the end of 1960, some 96,000 students across the country had gotten involved in these sit-ins. In 1961, Patrice Lumumba was assassinated, and black intellectuals and activists in New York stormed the United Nations gallery. While Ralph Bunche (George's spiritual father) shrank back "embarrassed"—probably more so than by slavery and colonialism! But the Pan African thrust had definitely returned.

And by this time, too, Malcolm X, "the fire prophet," had emerged as the truest reflector of black mass feelings. It was of someone like Malcolm that Walter Lee spoke as in a trance in prophecy while he mounts the table to deliver his liquor-fired call to arms. (Nation of Islam headquarters was Chicago where the play is set!) Walter Lee embodies the explosion to be—what happens when the dream is deferred past even the patience of the Lena Youngers.

Young militants like myself were taken with Malcolm's coming, with the immanence of explosion.

We thought Hansberry's play was part of the "passive resistance" phase of the movement, which was over the minute Malcolm's penetrating eyes and words began to charge through the media with deadly force. We thought her play "middle class" in that its focus seemed to be on "moving into white folks' neighborhoods," when most blacks were just trying to pay their rent in ghetto shacks.

We missed the essence of the work—that Hansberry had created a family on the cutting edge of the same class and ideological struggles as existed in the movement itself and among the people. What is most telling about our ignorance is that Hansberry's play still remains overwhelmingly popular and evocative of black and white reality, and the masses of black people dug it true. . . .

It is Lorraine Hansberry's play which, though it seems "conservative" in form and content to the radical petty bourgeoisie (as opposed to revolutionaries), is the accurate telling and stunning vision of the real struggle. . . . The Younger family is part of the black majority, and the concerns I once dismissed as "middle class"—buying a house and moving into "white folks' neighborhoods"—are actually reflective of the essence of black people's striving and the will to defeat segregation, discrimination, and national oppression. There is no such thing as a "white folks' neighborhood" except to racists *and to those submitting to racism.*

The Younger family is the incarnation—*before* they burst from the bloody Southern backroads and the burning streets of Watts and Newark onto TV screens and the *world* stage—of our common ghetto-variety Fanny Lou Hamers, Malcolm X's, and Angela Davises. And their burden surely will be lifted, or one day it certainly will "explode."

—1987

WRITING ASSIGNMENT SEQUENCE (CONTINUED FROM PAGE 234)

4. Making Connections

Select one of the following questions and write an informal response in which you connect your own ideas with those conveyed in the works of this cluster, and/or make connections among the works themselves.

A. What are the elements of the "dream," according to the works in this cluster?

B. To what degree is *money* the main obstacle to the achievement of the dream, as illustrated by the works in this cluster?

C. What are the various ways in which the "dream" is "deferred" in the works of this cluster?

D. Which of the words you wrote in your *brainstorming* exercise was illustrated most frequently or most vividly in this cluster?

5. Putting It All Together

Write an essay that combines what you think about the topic *A Dream Deferred* with what you now understand about the readings.

- Collect your informal writing, notes, and reading-journal entries on this topic and decide what will be the focus of your essay.
- Outline your essay. Select the literary passages and personal details you might use to illustrate and support your main focus.

- Write a draft of your essay in which you bring together what you think about the subject with what you understand about the readings. Try to include in your draft one or more *literary terms.*
- Share what you've written with your classmates and instructor, then revise it according to their recommendations.

Writing Tip: Changing Your Conclusion

The *conclusion* is sometimes the most aggravating part of the essay for students to write, and too often it flatly repeats the introduction. An effective conclusion should make a climactic point, or, in a long paper, remind the reader of your most important point(s). Use it to appeal to the reader's emotions. You might use alternatives similar to those suggested for your introductions to improve your conclusion:

- a lively quotation
- the solution to the problem you've been describing
- an anecdote
- a striking image
- an intriguing question (that you want to leave your reader with)
- a strong assertion

Compare your conclusion with your introduction. Do they work together? Does the conclusion unnecessarily echo the introduction? Might your conclusion instead make a great introduction? For example, Baraka's essay on *A Raisin in the Sun* (p. 328) ends with both a *strong assertion* and a *quotation*—of the Langston Hughes poem (p. 238) that the play takes its title from:

> The Younger family is the incarnation . . . of our common ghetto-variety Fanny Lou Hamers, Malcolm X's, and Angela Davises. And their burden shall be lifted, or one day it certainly will "explode."

CrossClusters

In your paper you might want to consider how the following works located elsewhere in this book deal with the topic of a dream deferred:

- Richard Wright, "The Man Who Was Almost a Man" (p. 93)
- Kate Rushin, "The Tired Poem: Last Letter from a Typical Unemployed Black Professional Woman" (p. 216)
- Alice Walker, "Everyday Use" (p. 483)
- Langston Hughes, "Theme from English B" (p. 886)

- Toni Cade Bambara, "The Lesson" (p. 887)
- Shirley Lauro, *Open Admission* (p. 894)

SYNTHESIS PAPER FOR SECTION 1: IDENTITIES

How do your preliminary ideas about identities hold up now that you have read a variety of works on the topic? Adding to, expanding on, and revising the writing that you have already done on the subject of identities, write a long paper in which you examine some of the literature in this section, bringing together your early writing with the knowledge you have gained from your class discussions. The paper might combine research and critical analysis with your personal opinions and experiences. You might even bring in references to films, music, books, and/or magazine articles. There are many possibilities for topics relating to the complexities of *becoming a person, self-reliance versus conformity, being a woman,* and *being African-American.*

Here are some questions to consider:

- What are the most significant factors influencing the development of a strong identity?
- How important a role do outside forces play in enabling an individual to make his or her own way? Which forces are most significant?
- What does it mean to be self-reliant? What are the costs?
- Under what circumstances do being African-American and/or being female hinder or help an individual's capacity to grow as a person or to be self-reliant?

SECTION 2 (CHAPTERS 13–16)

FAMILIES

The readings in this section focus on the dynamics of several different familial relationships. The perspectives range from a child's view of her unseen mother to a mother's view of a departing child, from a boy's idolatry of his father to a young woman's poetic remembrances of a drunk, perverted uncle. You will be asked to think and write about your own experiences with family and friends, your view of your parents, and your definition of *family*. Finally, your task will be to combine your thoughts with the issues and ideas illustrated in the works of this section.

GETTING STARTED: WRITING EXERCISES ON FAMILIES

1. Write about the most problematic and/or the most rewarding relationship you have with a particular member of your family.

2. What are your "family values"?
3. Explain and agree/disagree with one of the following quotations:
   - "All happy families resemble one another; every unhappy family is unhappy in its own fashion."—Leo Tolstoy
   - "There are secrets in all families."—George Farquhar
   - "Instead of trying to make women—and men—adapt to an outworn institution, we should adapt our institutions to the lives people actually live."—Katha Pollit
4. Read the following section essay, "Families," by Jane Howard. Go through Howard's categories and identify those qualities that your family has and hasn't. Amend, or disagree with, some of them.

SECTION ESSAY

JANE HOWARD

Families (excerpt)

Jane Howard (b. 1935) was born in Springfield, Illinois. She is a reporter, editor, writer, and professor. Her books include Please Touch: A Guided Tour of the Human Potential Movement *(1970),* Families *(1978), which is excerpted below, and* Margaret Mead: A Life *(1984).*

Each of us is born into one family not of our choosing. If we're going to go around devising new ones, we might as well have the luxury of picking their members ourselves. Clever picking might result in new families whose benefits would surpass or at least equal those of the old. The new ones by definition cannot spawn us—as soon as they do that, they stop being new—but there is plenty they can do. I have seen them work wonders. As a member in reasonable standing of six or seven tribes in addition to the one I was born to, I have been trying to figure which earmarks are common to both kinds of families.

(1) Good families have a chief, or a heroine, or a founder—someone around whom others cluster, whose achievements as the Yiddish word has it, let them *kvell,* and whose example spurs them on to like feats. Some blood dynasties produce such figures regularly; others languish for as many as five generations between demigods, wondering with each new pregnancy whether this, at last, might be the messianic baby who will redeem us. Look, is there not something gubernatorial about her footstep, or musical about the way he bangs with his spoon on his cup? All clans, of all kinds, need such a figure now and then. Sometimes clans based on water rather than blood harbor several such personages at one time. The Bloomsbury Group in Lon-

don six decades ago was not much hampered by its lack of a temporal history.

(2) Good families have a switchboard operator—someone like my mother who cannot help but keep track of what all the others are up to, who plays Houston Mission Control to everyone else's Apollo. This role, like the foregoing one, is assumed rather than assigned. Someone always volunteers for it. That person often also has the instincts of an archivist, and feels driven to keep scrapbooks and photograph albums up to date, so that the clan can see proof of its own continuity.

(3) Good families are much to all their members, but everything to none. Good families are fortresses with many windows and doors to the outer world. The blood clans I feel most drawn to were founded by parents who are nearly as devoted to whatever it is they do outside as they are to each other and their children. Their curiosity and passion are contagious. Everybody, where they live, is busy. Paint is spattered on eyeglasses. Mud lurks under fingernails. Person-to-person calls come in the middle of the night from Tokyo and Brussels. Catchers' mitts, ballet slippers, overdue library books and other signs of extrafamilial concerns are everywhere.

(4) Good families are hospitable. Knowing that hosts need guests as much as guests need hosts, they are generous with honorary memberships for friends, whom they urge to come early and often and to stay late. Such clans exude a vivid sense of surrounding rings of relatives, neighbors, teachers, students and godparents, any of whom at any time might break or slide into the inner circle. Inside that circle a wholesome, tacit emotional feudalism develops: you give me protection, I'll give you fealty. Such treaties begin with, but soon go far beyond, the jolly exchange of pie at Thanksgiving for cake on birthdays. It means you can ask me to supervise your children for the fortnight you will be in the hospital, and that however inconvenient this might be for me, I shall manage to. It means I can phone you on what for me is a dreary, wretched Sunday afternoon and for you is the eve of a deadline, knowing you will tell me to come right over, if only to watch you type. It means we need not dissemble. ("To yield to seeming," as Buber wrote, "is man's essential cowardice, to resist it is his essential courage . . . one must at times pay dearly for life lived from the being, but it is never too dear.")

(5) Good families deal squarely with direness. Pity the tribe that doesn't have, and cherish, at least one flamboyant eccentric. Pity too the one that supposes it can avoid for long the woes to which all flesh is heir. Lunacy, bankruptcy, suicide and other unthinkable fates sooner or later afflict the noblest of clans with an undertow of gloom. Family life is a set of givens, someone once told me, and it takes courage to see certain givens as blessings rather than as curses. Contradictions and inconsistencies are givens, too. So is the war against what the Oregon patriarch Kenneth Babbs calls malarkey. "There's always malarkey lurking, bubbles in the cesspool, fetid bubbles that pop and smell.

But I don't put up with malarkey, between my stepkids and my natural ones or anywhere else in the family."

(6) Good families prize their rituals. Nothing welds a family more than these. Rituals are vital especially for clans without histories, because they evoke a past, imply a future, and hint at continuity. No line in the Seder service at Passover reassures more than the last: "Next year in Jerusalem!" A clan becomes more of a clan each time it gathers to observe a fixed ritual (Christmas, birthdays, Thanksgiving, and so on), grieve at a funeral (anyone may come to most funerals; those who do declare their tribalness), and devises a new rite of its own. Equinox breakfasts and all-white dinners can be at least as welding as Memorial Day parades. Several of us in the old *Life* magazine years used to meet for lunch every Pearl Harbor Day, preferably to eat some politically neutral fare like smorgasbord, to "forgive" our only ancestrally Japanese colleague Irene Kubota Neves. For that and other reasons we became, and remain, a sort of family.

"Rituals," a California friend of mine said, "aren't just externals and holidays. They are the performances of our lives. They are a kind of shorthand. They can't be decreed. My mother used to try to decree them. She'd make such a goddamn fuss over what we talked about at dinner, aiming at Topics of Common Interest, topics that celebrated our cohesion as a family. These performances were always hollow, because the phenomenology of the moment got sacrificed for the *idea* of the moment. Real rituals are discovered in retrospect. They emerge around constitutive moments, moments that only happen once, around whose memory meanings cluster. You don't choose those moments. They choose themselves." A lucky clan includes a born mythologizer, like my blood sister, who has the gift of apprehending such a moment when she sees it, and who cannot help but invent new rituals every where she goes.

(7) Good families are affectionate. This is of course a matter of style. I know clans whose members greet each other with gingerly handshakes or, in what pass for kisses, with hurried brushes of side jawbones, as if the object were to touch not the lips but the ears. I don't see how such people manage. "The tribe that does not hug," as someone who has been part of many *ad hoc* families recently wrote to me, "is no tribe at all. More and more I realize that everybody, regardless of age, needs to be hugged and comforted in a brotherly or sisterly way now and then. Preferably now."

(8) Good families have a sense of place, which these days is not achieved easily. As Susanne Langer wrote in 1957, "Most people have no home that is a symbol of their childhood, not even a definite memory of one place to serve that purpose . . . all the old symbols are gone." Once I asked a roomful of supper guests who, if anyone, felt any strong pull to any certain spot on the face of the earth. Everyone was silent, except for a visitor from Bavaria. The rest of us seemed to know all too well what Walker Percy means in *The Moviegoer* when he tells of the "genie-soul of the place which every place has or else is

not a place [and which] wherever you go, you must meet and master or else be met and mastered." All that meeting and mastering saps plenty of strength. It also underscores our need for tribal bases of the sort which soaring real estate taxes and splintering families have made all but obsolete.

So what are we to do, those of us whose habit and pleasure and doom is our tendency, as a Georgia lady put it, to "fly off at every other whipstitch?" Think in terms of movable feasts, for a start. Live here, wherever here may be, as if we were going to belong here for the rest of our lives. Learn to hallow whatever ground we happen to stand on or land on. Like medieval knights who took their tapestries along on Crusades, like modern Afghanis with their yurts, we must pack such totems and icons as we can to make short-term quarters feel like home. Pillows, small rugs, watercolors can dispel much of the chilling anonymity of a sublet apartment or motel room. When we can, we should live in rooms with stoves or fireplaces or anyway candlelight. The ancient saying still is true: Extinguished hearth, extinguished family. Round tables help, too, and as a friend of mine once put it, so do "too many comfortable chairs, with surfaces to put feet on, arranged so as to encourage a maximum of eye contact." Such rooms inspire good talk, of which good clans can never have enough.

(9) Good families, not just the blood kind, find some way to connect with posterity. "To forge a link in the humble chain of being, encircling heirs to ancestors," as Michael Novak has written, "is to walk within a circle of magic as primitive as humans knew in caves." He is talking of course about babies, feeling them leap in wombs, giving them suck. Parenthood, however, is a state which some miss by chance and others by design, and a vocation to which not all are called. Some of us, like the novelist Richard P. Brickner, "look on as others name their children who in turn name their own lives, devising their own flags from their parents' cloth." What are we who lack children to do? Build houses? Plant trees? Write books or symphonies or laws? Perhaps, but even if we do these things, there still should be children on the sidelines, if not at the center, of our lives. It is a sadly impoverished tribe that does not allow access to, and make much of, some children. Not too much, of course: it has truly been said that never in history have so many educated people devoted so much attention to so few children. Attention, in excess, can turn to fawning, which isn't much better than neglect. Still, if we don't regularly see and talk to and laugh with people who can expect to outlive us by twenty years or so, we had better get busy and find some.

(10) Good families also honor their elders. The wider the age range, the stronger the tribe. Jean-Paul Sartre and Margaret Mead, to name two spectacularly confident former children, have both remarked on the central importance of grandparents in their own early lives. Grandparents now are in much more abundant supply than they were a generation or two ago when old age was more rare. If actual grandparents are not at hand, no family should have too

hard a time finding substitute ones to whom to give unfeigned homage. The Soviet Union's enchantment with day care centers, I have heard, stems at least in part from the state's eagerness to keep children away from their presumably subversive grandparents. Let that be a lesson to clans based on interest as well as to those based on genes.

—*1978*

13

GROWING UP

WRITING ASSIGNMENT SEQUENCE

1. Thinking About . . . Growing Up

Freewriting: Write about a moment in your childhood that represents what life was like for you when you were growing up. (For more on freewriting, see p. 26.)

2. Enacting the Topic

Write a diary entry dated sometime during your childhood. Adopt the point of view of yourself as a child, and write an entry about the incident you described in the freewriting exercise above.

3. Responding to the Readings

As you read the works in this cluster, jot down in your response journals questions you have about the works, and comment on passages you find provocative or puzzling. Consider the questions following each reading for journal writing and prepare to discuss your reactions in class.

CLUSTER ESSAY

RUSSELL BAKER

Growing Up (excerpt)

Russell Baker (b. 1925) has written the "Observer" column in the New York Times *for over 30 years, a column that is syndicated to over 450 newspapers. Known for his satiric humor, Baker has published several collections of his essays and a Pulitzer Prize-winning autobiography,* Growing Up *(1982) from which the following reading is excerpted. His second volume of memoirs,* Good Times, *was published in 1989.*

I began working in journalism when I was eight years old. It was my mother's idea. She wanted me to "make something" of myself and, after a levelheaded appraisal of my strengths, decided I had better start young if I was to have any chance of keeping up with the competition.

The flaw in my character which she had already spotted was lack of "gumption." My idea of a perfect afternoon was lying in front of the radio rereading my favorite Big Little Book, *Dick Tracy Meets Stooge Viller.* My mother despised inactivity. Seeing me having a good time in repose, she was powerless to hide her disgust. "You've got no more gumption than a bump on a log," she said. "Get out in the kitchen and help Doris do those dirty dishes."

My sister Doris, though two years younger than I, had enough gumption for a dozen people. She positively enjoyed washing dishes, making beds, and cleaning the house. When she was only seven she could carry a piece of short-weighted cheese back to the A&P, threaten the manager with legal action, and come back triumphantly with the full quarter-pound we'd paid for and a few ounces extra thrown in for forgiveness. Doris could have made something of herself if she hadn't been a girl. Because of this defect, however, the best she could hope for was a career as a nurse or schoolteacher, the only work that capable females were considered up to in those days.

This must have saddened my mother, this twist of fate that had allocated all the gumption to the daughter and left her with a son who was content with Dick Tracy and Stooge Viller. If disappointed, though, she wasted no energy on self-pity. She would make me make something of myself whether I wanted to or not. "The Lord helps those who help themselves," she said. That was the way her mind worked.

She was realistic about the difficulty. Having sized up the material the Lord had given her to mold, she didn't overestimate what she could do with it. She didn't insist that I grow up to be President of the United States.

Fifty years ago parents still asked boys if they wanted to grow up to be President, and asked it not jokingly but seriously. Many parents who were hardly more than paupers still believed their sons could do it. Abraham Lincoln had done it. We were only sixty-five years from Lincoln. Many a grandfather who walked among us could remember Lincoln's time. Men of grandfatherly age were the worst for asking if you wanted to grow up to be President. A surprising number of little boys said yes and meant it.

I was asked many times myself. No, I would say, I didn't want to grow up to be President. My mother was present during one of these interrogations. An elderly uncle, having posed the usual question and exposed my lack of interest in the Presidency, asked, "Well, what *do* you want to be when you grow up?"

I loved to pick through trash piles and collect empty bottles, tin cans with pretty labels, and discarded magazines. The most desirable job on earth sprang instantly to mind. "I want to be a garbage man," I said.

My uncle smiled, but my mother had seen the first distressing evidence of a bump budding on a log. "Have a little gumption, Russell," she said. Her calling me Russell was a signal of unhappiness. When she approved of me I was always "Buddy."

When I turned eight years old she decided that the job of starting me on the road toward making something of myself could no longer be safely delayed. "Buddy," she said one day, "I want you to come home right after school this afternoon. Somebody's coming and I want you to meet him."

When I burst in that afternoon she was in conference in the parlor with an executive of the Curtis Publishing Company. She introduced me. He bent low from the waist and shook my hand. Was it true as my mother had told him, he asked, that I longed for the opportunity to conquer the world of business?

My mother replied that I was blessed with a rare determination to make something of myself.

"That's right," I whispered.

"But have you got the grit, the character, the never-say-quit spirit it takes to succeed in business?"

My mother said I certainly did.

"That's right," I said.

He eyed me silently for a long pause, as though weighing whether I could be trusted to keep his confidence, then spoke man-to-man. Before taking a crucial step, he said, he wanted to advise me that working for the Curtis Publishing Company placed enormous responsibility on a young man. It was one of the great companies of America. Perhaps the greatest publishing house in the world. I had heard, no doubt, of the *Saturday Evening Post?*

Heard of it? My mother said that everyone in our house had heard of the *Saturday Post* and that I, in fact, read it with religious devotion.

Then doubtless, he said, we were also familiar with those two monthly pillars of the magazine world, the *Ladies Home Journal* and the *Country Gentleman.*

Indeed we were familiar with them, said my mother.

Representing the *Saturday Evening Post* was one of the weightiest honors that could be bestowed in the world of business, he said. He was personally proud of being a part of that great corporation.

My mother said he had every right to be.

Again he studied me as though debating whether I was worthy of a knighthood. Finally: "Are you trustworthy?"

My mother said I was the soul of honesty.

"That's right," I said.

The caller smiled for the first time. He told me I was a lucky young man. He admired my spunk. Too many young men thought life was all play. Those young men would not go far in this world. Only a young man willing to work and save and keep his face washed and his hair neatly combed could hope to come out on top in a world such as ours. Did I truly and sincerely believe that I was such a young man?

"He certainly does," said my mother.

"That's right," I said.

He said he had been so impressed by what he had seen of me that he was going to make me a representative of the Curtis Publishing Company. On the following Tuesday, he said, thirty freshly printed copies of the *Saturday Evening Post* would be delivered at our door. I would place these magazines, still damp with the ink of the presses, in a handsome canvas bag, sling it over my shoulder, and set forth through the streets to bring the best in journalism, fiction, and cartoons to the American public.

He had brought the canvas bag with him. He presented it with reverence fit for a chasuble. He showed me how to drape the sling over my left shoulder and across the chest so that the pouch lay easily accessible to my right hand, allowing the best in journalism, fiction, and cartoons to be swiftly extracted and sold to a citizenry whose happiness and security depended upon us soldiers of the free press.

The following Tuesday I raced home from school, put the canvas bag over my shoulder, dumped the magazines in, and, tilting to the left to balance their weight on my right hip, embarked on the highway of journalism.

We lived in Belleville, New Jersey, a commuter town at the northern fringe of Newark. It was 1932, the bleakest year of the Depression. My father had died two years before, leaving us with a few pieces of Sears, Roebuck furniture and not much else, and my mother had taken Doris and me to live with one of her younger brothers. This was my Uncle Allen. Uncle Allen had made something of himself by 1932. As salesman for a soft-drink bottler in Newark, he had an income of $30 a week; wore pearl-gray spats, detachable collars, and a three-piece suit; was happily married; and took in threadbare relatives.

With my load of magazines I headed toward Belleville Avenue. That's where the people were. There were two filling stations at the intersection with Union Avenue, as well as an A&P, a fruit stand, a bakery, a barber shop, Zuccarelli's drugstore, and a diner shaped like a railroad car. For several hours I made myself highly visible, shifting position now and then from corner to corner, from shop window to shop window, to make sure everyone could see the heavy black lettering on the canvas bag that said THE SATURDAY EVENING POST. When the angle of the light indicated it was suppertime, I walked back to the house.

"How many did you sell, Buddy?" my mother asked.

"None."

"Where did you go?"

"The corner of Belleville and Union Avenues."

"What did you do?"

"Stood on the corner waiting for somebody to buy a *Saturday Evening Post.*"

"You just stood there?"

"Didn't sell a single one."

"For God's sake, Russell!"

Uncle Allen intervened. "I've been thinking about it for some time," he said, "and I've about decided to take the *Post* regularly. Put me down as a regular customer." I handed him a magazine and he paid me a nickel. It was the first nickel I earned.

Afterwards my mother instructed me in salesmanship. I would have to ring doorbells, address adults with charming self-confidence, and break down resistance with a sales talk pointing out that no one, no matter how poor, could afford to be without the *Saturday Evening Post* in the home.

I told my mother I'd changed my mind about wanting to succeed in the magazine business.

"If you think I'm going to raise a good-for-nothing," she replied, "you've got another think coming." She told me to hit the streets with the canvas bag and start ringing doorbells the instant school was out next day. When I objected that I didn't feel any aptitude for salesmanship, she asked how I'd like to lend her my leather belt so she could whack some sense into me. I bowed to superior will and entered journalism with a heavy heart.

My mother and I had fought this battle almost as long as I could remember. It probably started even before memory began, when I was a country child in northern Virginia and my mother, dissatisfied with my father's plain workman's life, determined that I would not grow up like him and his people, with calluses on their hands, overalls on their backs, and fourth-grade educations in their heads. She had fancier ideas of life's possibilities. Introducing me to the *Saturday Evening Post,* she was trying to wean me as early as possible from my father's world where men left with their lunch pails at sunup, worked with their hands until the grime ate into the pores, and died with a few sticks of mail-order furniture as their legacy. In my mother's vision of the better life there were desks and white collars, well-pressed suits, evenings of reading and lively talk, and perhaps—if a man were very, very lucky and hit the jackpot, really made something important of himself—perhaps there might be a fantastic salary of $5,000 a year to support a big house and a Buick with a rumble seat and a vacation in Atlantic City.

And so I set forth with my sack of magazines. I was afraid of the dogs that snarled behind the doors of potential buyers. I was timid about ringing the doorbells of strangers, relieved when no one came to the door, and scared when someone did. Despite my mother's instructions, I could not deliver an engaging sales pitch. When a door opened I simply asked, "Want to buy a *Saturday Evening Post?*" In Belleville few persons did. It was a town of 30,000 people, and most weeks I rang a fair majority of its doorbells. But I rarely sold my thirty copies. Some weeks I canvassed the entire town for six days and still had four or five unsold magazines on Monday evening; then I dreaded the coming of Tuesday morning, when a batch of thirty fresh *Saturday Evening Posts* was due at the front door.

"Better get out there and sell the rest of those magazines tonight," my mother would say.

I usually posted myself then at a busy intersection where a traffic light controlled commuter flow from Newark. When the light turned red I stood on the curb and shouted my sales pitch at the motorists.

"Want to buy a *Saturday Evening Post?*"

One rainy night when car windows were sealed against me I came back soaked and with not a single sale to report. My mother beckoned to Doris.

"Go back down there with Buddy and show him how to sell these magazines," she said.

Brimming with zest, Doris, who was then seven years old, returned with me to the corner. She took a magazine from the bag, and when the light turned red she strode to the nearest car and banged her small fist against the closed window. The driver, probably startled at what he took to be a midget assaulting his car, lowered the window to stare, and Doris thrust a *Saturday Evening Post* at him.

"You need this magazine," she piped, "and it only costs a nickel."

Her salesmanship was irresistible. Before the light changed half a dozen times she disposed of the entire batch. I didn't feel humiliated. To the contrary. I was so happy I decided to give her a treat. Leading her to the vegetable store on Belleville Avenue, I bought three apples, which cost a nickel, and gave her one.

"You shouldn't waste money," she said.

"Eat your apple," I bit into mine.

"You shouldn't eat before supper," she said. "It'll spoil your appetite."

Back at the house that evening, she dutifully reported me for wasting a nickel. Instead of a scolding, I was rewarded with a pat on the back for having the good sense to buy fruit instead of candy. My mother reached into her bottomless supply of maxims and told Doris, "An apple a day keeps the doctor away."

By the time I was ten I had learned all my mother's maxims by heart. Asking to stay up past normal bedtime, I knew that a refusal would be explained with, "Early to bed and early to rise, makes a man healthy, wealthy, and wise." If I whimpered about having to get up early in the morning, I could depend on her to say, "The early bird gets the worm."

The one I most despised was, "If at first you don't succeed, try, try again." This was the battle cry with which she constantly sent me back into the hopeless struggle whenever I moaned that I had rung every doorbell in town and knew there wasn't a single potential buyer left in Belleville that week. After listening to my explanation, she handed me the canvas bag and said, "If at first you don't succeed . . ."

Three years in that job, which I would gladly have quit after the first day except for her insistence, produced at least one valuable result. My mother finally concluded that I would never make something of myself by pursuing a life in business and started considering careers that demanded less competitive zeal.

One evening when I was eleven I brought home a short "composition" on my summer vacation which the teacher had graded with an A. Reading it with her own schoolteacher's eye, my mother agreed that it was top-drawer seventh grade prose and complimented me. Nothing more was said about it immediately, but a new idea had taken life in her mind. Halfway through supper she suddenly interrupted the conversation.

"Buddy," she said, "maybe you could be a writer."

I clasped the idea to my heart. I had never met a writer, had shown no previous urge to write, and hadn't a notion how to become a writer, but I loved stories and thought that making up stories must surely be almost as much fun as reading them. Best of all, though, and what really gladdened my heart, was the ease of the writer's life. Writers did not have to trudge through the town peddling from canvas bags, defending themselves against angry dogs, being rejected by surly strangers. Writers did not have to ring doorbells. So far as I could make out, what writers did couldn't even be classified as work.

I was enchanted. Writers didn't have to have any gumption at all. I did not dare tell anybody for fear of being laughed at in the schoolyard, but secretly I decided that what I'd like to be when I grew up was a writer.

—1982

What are your reactions to and questions about this work? The following questions may help provoke some ideas.

Probing the Work

1. Russell's mother accuses him of not having "gumption." Do you agree with her? What else might be "wrong" with him?
2. Describe the family dynamics as Baker presents them. What do you think is his purpose in presenting his family as he does?

Identifying Issues

3. To what extent do you think that Baker's experience was shaped by the times in which he lived (during the Depression)? What contemporary childhood experience might be said to parallel Russell's? How different would the mother, sister, or Russell be today?

FRANK O'CONNOR

My Oedipus Complex

Frank O'Connor, pen name of Michael O'Donovan (1903–1966), was born in Cork, Ireland, and had to leave school after the fourth grade to make money for his family. He served in the Irish Republican Army during the armed conflict of 1918–1921, and was captured by the British. After his release from prison he worked as a librarian and as director of the Abbey Theatre in Dublin. In the 1950s he taught at Northwestern and Harvard Universities in the United States.

Father was in the army all through the war—the first war, I mean—so, up to the age of five, I never saw much of him, and what I saw did not worry me. Sometimes I woke and there was a big figure in khaki peering down at me in the candlelight. Sometimes in the early morning I heard the slamming of the front door and the clatter of nailed boots down the cobbles of the lane. These were Father's entrances and exits. Like Santa Claus he came and went mysteriously.

In fact, I rather liked his visits, though it was an uncomfortable squeeze between Mother and him when I got into the big bed in the early morning. He smoked, which gave him a pleasant musty smell, and shaved, an operation of astounding interest. Each time he left a trail of souvenirs—model tanks and Gurkha knives with handles made of bullet cases, and German helmets and cap badges and button-sticks, and all sorts of military equipment—carefully stowed away in a long box on top of the wardrobe, in case they ever came in handy. There was a bit of the magpie about Father; he expected everything to come in handy. When his back was turned, Mother let me get a chair and rummage through his treasures. She didn't seem to think so highly of them as he did.

The war was the most peaceful period of my life. The window of my attic faced southeast. My mother had curtained it, but that had small effect. I always woke with the first light and, with all the responsibilities of the previous day melted, feeling myself rather like the sun, ready to illumine and rejoice. Life never seemed so simple and clear and full of possibilities as then. I put my feet out from under the clothes—I called them Mrs. Left and Mrs. Right—and invented dramatic situations for them in which they discussed the problems of the day. At least Mrs. Right did; she was very demonstrative, but I hadn't the same control of Mrs. Left, so she mostly contented herself with nodding agreement.

They discussed what Mother and I should do during the day, what Santa Claus should give a fellow for Christmas, and what steps should be taken to brighten the home. There was that little matter of the baby, for instance. Mother and I could never agree about that. Ours was the only house in the terrace without a new baby, and Mother said we couldn't afford one till Father came back from the war because they cost seventeen and six. That showed how simple she was. The Geneys up the road had a baby, and everyone knew they couldn't afford seventeen and six. It was probably a cheap baby, and Mother wanted something really good, but I felt she was too exclusive. The Geneys' baby would have done us fine.

Having settled my plans for the day, I got up, put a chair under the attic window, and lifted the frame high enough to stick out my head. The window overlooked the front gardens of the terrace behind ours, and beyond these it looked over a deep valley to the tall, red-brick houses terraced up the opposite hillside, which were all still in shadow, while those at our side of the valley were all lit up, though with long strange shadows that made them seem unfamiliar; rigid and painted.

After that I went into Mother's room and climbed into the big bed. She woke and I began to tell her of my schemes. By this time, though I never seem to have noticed it, I was petrified in my nightshirt, and I thawed as I talked until, the last frost melted, I fell asleep beside her and woke again only when I heard her below in the kitchen, making the breakfast.

After breakfast we went into town; heard Mass at St. Augustine's and said a prayer for Father, and did the shopping. If the afternoon was fine we either went for a walk in the country or a visit to Mother's great friend in the convent, Mother St. Dominic. Mother had them all praying for Father, and every night, going to bed, I asked God to send him back safe from the war to us. Little, indeed, did I know what I was praying for!

One morning, I got into the big bed, and there, sure enough, was Father in his usual Santa Claus manner, but later, instead of uniform, he put on his best blue suit, and Mother was as pleased as anything. I saw nothing to be pleased about, because, out of uniform, Father was altogether less interesting, but she only beamed, and explained that our prayers had been answered, and off we went to Mass to thank God for having brought Father safely home.

The irony of it! That very day when he came in to dinner he took off his boots and put on his slippers, donned the dirty old cap he wore about the house to save him from colds, crossed his legs, and began to talk gravely to Mother, who looked anxious. Naturally, I disliked her looking anxious, because it destroyed her good looks, so I interrupted him.

"Just a moment, Larry!" she said gently.

This was only what she said when we had boring visitors, so I attached no importance to it and went on talking.

"Do be quiet, Larry!" she said impatiently. "Don't you hear me talking to Daddy?"

This was the first time I had heard those ominous words, "talking to Daddy," and I couldn't help feeling that if this was how God answered prayers, he couldn't listen to them very attentively.

"Why are you talking to Daddy?" I asked with as great a show of indifference as I could muster.

"Because Daddy and I have business to discuss. Now, don't interrupt again!"

In the afternoon, at Mother's request, Father took me for a walk. This time we went into town instead of out the country, and I thought at first, in my usual optimistic way, that it might be an improvement. It was nothing of the sort. Father and I had quite different notions of a walk in town. He had no proper interest in trams, ships, and horses, and the only thing that seemed to divert him was talking to fellows as old as himself. When I wanted to stop he simply went on, dragging me behind him by the hand; when he wanted to stop I had no alternative but to do the same. I noticed that it seemed to be a sign that he wanted to stop for a long time whenever he leaned against a wall. The second time I saw him do it I got wild. He seemed to be settling himself forever. I pulled him by the coat and trousers, but, unlike Mother who, if you were too persistent, got into a wax and said: "Larry, if you don't behave yourself, I'll give you a good slap," Father had an extraordinary capacity for amiable inattention. I sized him up and wondered would I cry, but he seemed to be too remote to be annoyed even by that. Really, it was like going for a walk with a mountain! He either ignored the wrenching and pummelling entirely, or else glanced down with a grin of amusement from his peak. I had never met anyone so absorbed in himself as he seemed.

At teatime, "talking to Daddy" began again, complicated this time by the fact that he had an evening paper, and every few minutes he put it down and told Mother something new out of it. I felt this was foul play. Man for man, I was prepared to compete with him any time for Mother's attention, but when he had it all made up for him by other people it left me no chance. Several times I tried to change the subject without success.

"You must be quiet while Daddy is reading, Larry," Mother said impatiently.

It was clear that she either genuinely liked talking to Father better than talking to me, or else that he had some terrible hold on her which made her afraid to admit the truth.

"Mummy," I said that night when she was tucking me up, "do you think if I prayed hard God would send Daddy back to the war?"

She seemed to think about that for a moment.

"No, dear," she said with a smile. "I don't think he would."

"Why wouldn't he, Mummy?"

"Because there isn't a war any longer, dear."

"But, Mummy, couldn't God make another war, if He liked?"

"He wouldn't like to, dear. It's not God who makes wars, but bad people."

"Oh!" I said.

I was disappointed about that. I began to think that God wasn't quite what he was cracked up to be.

Next morning I woke at my usual hour, feeling like a bottle of champagne. I put out my feet and invented a long conversation in which Mrs. Right talked of the trouble she had with her own father till she put him in the Home. I didn't quite know what the Home was but it sounded the right place for Father. Then I got my chair and stuck my head out of the attic window. Dawn was just breaking, with a guilty air that made me feel I had caught it in the act. My head bursting with stories and schemes, I stumbled in next door, and in the half-darkness scrambled into the big bed. There was no room at Mother's side so I had to get between her and Father. For the time being I had forgotten about him, and for several minutes I sat bolt upright, racking my brains to know what I could do with him. He was taking up more than his fair share of the bed, and I couldn't get comfortable, so I gave him several kicks that made him grunt and stretch. He made room all right, though. Mother waked and felt for me. I settled back comfortably in the warmth of the bed with my thumb in my mouth.

"Mummy!" I hummed, loudly and contentedly.

"Sssh! dear," she whispered. "Don't wake Daddy!"

This was a new development, which threatened to be even more serious than "talking to Daddy." Life without my early-morning conferences was unthinkable.

"Why?" I asked severely.

"Because poor Daddy is tired."

This seemed to me a quite inadequate reason, and I was sickened by the sentimentality of her "poor Daddy." I never liked that sort of gush; it always struck me as insincere.

"Oh!" I said lightly. Then in my most winning tone: "Do you know where I want to go with you today, Mummy?"

"No dear," she sighed.

"I want to go down the Glen and fish for thornybacks with my new net, and then I want to go out to the Fox and Hounds, and—"

"Don't-wake-Daddy!" she hissed angrily, clapping her hand across my mouth.

But it was too late. He was awake, or nearly so. He grunted and reached for the matches. Then he stared incredulously at his watch.

"Like a cup of tea, dear?" asked Mother in a meek, hushed voice I had never heard her use before. It sounded almost as though she were afraid.

"Tea?" he exclaimed indignantly. "Do you know what the time is?"

"And after that I want to go up the Rathcooney Road," I said loudly, afraid I'd forget something in all those interruptions.

"Go to sleep at once, Larry!" she said sharply.

I began to snivel. I couldn't concentrate, the way that pair went on, and smothering my early-morning schemes was like burying a family from the cradle.

Father said nothing, but lit his pipe and sucked it, looking out into the shadows without minding Mother or me. I knew he was mad. Every time I made a remark Mother hushed me irritably. I was mortified. I felt it wasn't fair; there was even something sinister in it. Every time I had pointed out to her the waste of making two beds when we could both sleep in one, she had told me it was healthier like that, and now here was this man, this stranger, sleeping with her without the least regard for her health!

He got up early and made tea, but though he brought Mother a cup he brought none for me.

"Mummy," I shouted, "I want a cup of tea, too."

"Yes, dear," she said patiently. "You can drink from Mummy's saucer."

That settled it. Either Father or I would have to leave the house. I didn't want to drink from Mother's saucer; I wanted to be treated as an equal in my own home, so, just to spite her, I drank it all and left none for her. She took that quietly, too.

But that night when she was putting me to bed she said gently:

"Larry, I want you to promise me something."

"What is it?" I asked.

"Not to come in and disturb poor Daddy in the morning. Promise?"

"Poor Daddy" again! I was becoming suspicious of everything involving that quite impossible man.

"Why?" I asked.

"Because poor Daddy is worried and tired and he doesn't sleep well."

"Why doesn't he, Mummy?"

"Well, you know, don't you, that while he was at the war Mummy got the pennies from the Post Office?"

"From Miss MacCarthy?"

"That's right. But now, you see, Miss MacCarthy hasn't any more pennies, so Daddy must go out and find us some. You know what would happen if he couldn't?"

"No," I said, "tell us."

"Well, I think we might have to go out and beg for them like the poor old woman on Fridays. We wouldn't like that, would we?"

"No," I agreed. "We wouldn't."

"So you'll promise not to come in and wake him?"

"Promise."

Mind you, I meant that. I knew pennies were a serious matter, and I was all against having to go out and beg like the old woman on Fridays. Mother laid out all my toys in a complete ring round the bed so that, whatever way I got out, I was bound to fall over one of them.

When I woke I remembered my promise all right. I got up and sat on the floor and played—for hours, it seemed to me. Then I got my chair and looked out the attic window for more hours. I wished it was time for Father to wake; I wished someone would make me a cup of tea. I didn't feel in the least like the sun; instead, I was bored and so very, very cold! I simply longed for the warmth and depth of the big featherbed.

At last I could stand it no longer. I went into the next room. As there was still no room at Mother's side I climbed over her and she woke with a start.

"Larry," she whispered, gripping my arm very tightly, "what did you promise?"

"But I did, Mummy," I wailed, caught in the very act. "I was quiet for ever so long."

"Oh, dear, and you're perished!" she said sadly, feeling me all over. "Now, if I let you stay will you promise not to talk?"

"But I want to talk, Mummy," I wailed.

"That has nothing to do with it," she said with a firmness that was new to me. "Daddy wants to sleep. Now, do you understand that?"

I understood it only too well. I wanted to talk, he wanted to sleep—whose house was it, anyway?

"Mummy," I said with equal firmness, "I think it would be healthier for Daddy to sleep in his own bed."

That seemed to stagger her, because she said nothing for a while.

"Now, once for all," she went on, "you're to be perfectly quiet or go back to your own bed. Which is it to be?"

The injustice of it got me down. I had convicted her out of her own mouth of inconsistency and unreasonableness, and she hadn't even attempted to reply. Full of spite, I gave Father a kick, which she didn't notice but which made him grunt and open his eyes in alarm.

"What time is it?" he asked in a panic-stricken voice, not looking at Mother but at the door, as if he saw someone there.

"It's early yet," she replied soothingly. "It's only the child. Go to sleep again. . . . Now, Larry," she added, getting out of bed, "you've wakened Daddy and you must go back."

This time, for all her quiet air, I knew she meant it, and knew that my principal rights and privileges were as good as lost unless I asserted them at once. As she lifted me, I gave a screech, enough to wake the dead, not to mind Father. He groaned.

"That damn child! Doesn't he ever sleep?"

"It's only a habit, dear," she said quietly, though I could see she was vexed.

"Well, it's time he got out of it," shouted Father, beginning to heave in the bed. He suddenly gathered all the bedclothes about him, turned to the wall, and then looked back over his shoulder with nothing showing only two small, spiteful, dark eyes. The man looked very wicked.

To open the bedroom door, Mother had to let me down, and I broke free and dashed for the farthest corner, screeching. Father sat bolt upright in bed.

"Shut up, you little puppy!" he said in a choking voice.

I was so astonished that I stopped screeching. Never, never had anyone spoken to me in that tone before. I looked at him incredulously and saw his face convulsed with rage. It was only then that I fully realized how God had codded me, listening to my prayers for the safe return of this monster.

"Shut up, you!" I bawled, beside myself.

"What's that you said?" shouted Father, making a wild leap out of the bed.

"Mick, Mick!" cried Mother. "Don't you see the child isn't used to you?"

"I see he's better fed than taught," snarled Father, waving his arms wildly. "He wants his bottom smacked."

All his previous shouting was as nothing to these obscene words referring to my person. They really made my blood boil.

"Smack your own!" I screamed hysterically. "Smack your own! Shut up! Shut up!"

At this he lost his patience and let fly at me. He did it with the lack of conviction you'd expect of a man under Mother's horrified eyes, and it ended up as a mere tap, but the sheer indignity of being struck at all by a stranger, a total stranger who had cajoled his way back from the war into our big bed as a result of my innocent intercession, made me completely dotty. I shrieked and shrieked, and danced in my bare feet, and Father, looking awkward and hairy in nothing but a short gray army shirt, glared down at me like a mountain out for murder. I think it must have been then that I realized he was jealous too. And there stood Mother in her nightdress, looking as if her heart was broken between us. I hoped she felt as she looked. It seemed to me that she deserved it all.

From that morning out my life was a hell. Father and I were enemies, open and avowed. We conducted a series of skirmishes against one another, he trying to steal my time with Mother and I his. When she was sitting on my bed, telling me a story, he took to looking for some pair of old boots which he alleged he had left behind him at the beginning of the war. While he talked to Mother I played loudly with my toys to show my total lack of concern. He created a terrible scene one evening when he came in from work and found me at his box, playing with his regimental badges, Gurkha knives, and button-sticks. Mother got up and took the box from me.

"You mustn't play with Daddy's toys unless he lets you, Larry," she said severely. "Daddy doesn't play with yours."

For some reason Father looked at her as if she had struck him and then turned away with a scowl.

"Those are not toys," he growled, taking down the box again to see had I lifted anything. "Some of those curios are very rare and valuable."

But as time went on I saw more and more how he managed to alienate Mother and me. What made it worse was that I couldn't grasp his method or see what attraction he had for Mother. In every possible way he was less winning than I. He had a common accent and made noises at his tea. I thought for a while that it might be the newspapers she was interested in, so I made up bits of news of my own to read to her. Then I thought it might be the smoking, which I personally thought attractive, and took his pipes and went round the house dribbling into them till he caught me. I even made noises at my tea, but Mother only told me I was disgusting. It all seemed to hinge round that unhealthy habit of sleeping together, so I made a point of dropping into their

bedroom and nosing round, talking to myself, so that they wouldn't know I was watching them, but they were never up to anything that I could see. In the end it beat me. It seemed to depend on being grown-up and giving people rings, and I realized I'd have to wait.

But at the same time I wanted him to see that I was only waiting, not giving up the fight. One evening when he was being particularly obnoxious, chattering away well above my head, I let him have it.

"Mummy," I said, "do you know what I'm going to do when I grow up?"

"No, dear," she replied. "What?"

"I'm going to marry you," I said quietly.

Father gave a great guffaw out of him, but he didn't take me in. I knew it must only be pretense. And Mother, in spite of everything, was pleased. I felt she was probably relieved to know that one day Father's hold on her would be broken.

"Won't that be nice?" she said with a smile.

"It'll be very nice," I said confidently. "Because we're going to have lots and lots of babies."

"That's right, dear," she said placidly. "I think we'll have one soon, and then you'll have plenty of company."

I was no end pleased about that because it showed that in spite of the way she gave in to Father she still considered my wishes. Besides, it would put the Geneys in their place.

It didn't turn out like that, though. To begin with, she was very preoccupied—I supposed about where she would get the seventeen and six—and though Father took to staying out late in the evenings it did me no particular good. She stopped taking me for walks, became as touchy as blazes, and smacked me for nothing at all. Sometimes I wished I'd never mentioned the confounded baby—I seemed to have a genius for bringing calamity on myself.

And calamity it was! Sonny arrived in the most appalling hullabaloo—even that much he couldn't do without a fuss—and from the first moment I disliked him. He was a difficult child—so far as I was concerned he was always difficult—and demanded far too much attention. Mother was simply silly about him, and couldn't see when he was only showing off. As company he was worse than useless. He slept all day, and I had to go round the house on tiptoe to avoid waking him. It wasn't any longer a question of not waking Father. The slogan now was "Don't-wake-Sonny!" I couldn't understand why the child wouldn't sleep at the proper time, so whenever Mother's back was turned I woke him. Sometimes to keep him awake I pinched him as well. Mother caught me at it one day and gave me a most unmerciful flaking.

One evening, when Father was coming in from work, I was playing trains in the front garden. I let on not to notice him; instead, I pretended to be talking to myself, and said in a loud voice: "If another bloody baby comes into this house, I'm going out."

Father stopped dead and looked at me over his shoulder.

"What's that you said?" he asked sternly.

"I was only talking to myself," I replied, trying to conceal my panic. "It's private."

He turned and went in without a word. Mind you, I intended it as a solemn warning, but its effect was quite different. Father started being quite nice to me. I could understand that, of course. Mother was quite sickening about Sonny. Even at mealtimes she'd get up and gawk at him in the cradle with an idiotic smile, and tell Father to do the same. He was always polite about it, but he looked so puzzled you could see he didn't know what she was talking about. He complained of the way Sonny cried at night, but she only got cross and said that Sonny never cried except when there was something up with him—which was a flaming lie, because Sonny never had anything up with him, and only cried for attention. It was really painful to see how simple-minded she was. Father wasn't attractive, but he had a fine intelligence. He saw through Sonny, and now he knew that I saw through him as well.

One night I woke with a start. There was someone beside me in the bed. For one wild moment I felt sure it must be Mother, having come to her senses and left Father for good, but then I heard Sonny in convulsions in the next room, and Mother saying: "There! There! There!" and I knew it wasn't she. It was Father. He was lying beside me, wide awake, breathing hard and apparently as mad as hell.

After a while it came to me what he was mad about. It was his turn now. After turning me out of the big bed, he had been turned out himself. Mother had no consideration now for anyone but that poisonous pup, Sonny. I couldn't help feeling sorry for Father. I had been through it all myself, and even at that age I was magnanimous. I began to stroke him down and say: "There! There!" He wasn't exactly responsive.

"Aren't you asleep either?" he snarled.

"Ah, come on and put your arm around us, can't you?" I said, and he did, in a sort of way. Gingerly, I suppose, is how you'd describe it. He was very bony but better than nothing.

At Christmas he went out of his way to buy me a really nice model railway.

—1950

What are your reactions to and questions about this work? The following questions may help provoke some ideas.

Probing the Work

1. How reliable is Larry as the narrator of events? What are his strengths and shortcomings? According to biographer William Tomory (in *Frank*

O'Connor), O'Connor presents a "balanced" view of the child/parent relationship in this story. Do you agree? Why or why not?

Identifying Issues

2. According to Sigmund Freud, early in childhood a boy loves his mother and identifies with his father. As he gets older and his sexual urge begins to develop, the boy begins to crave exclusive sexual possession of his mother and starts to hate his rival, his father. Named after the Greek tragic hero who kills his father and marries his mother, the Oedipus complex begins to go away when the boy (1) becomes afraid of being physically harmed by his father (a fear called *castration anxiety*), (2) realizes he can never have sex with his mother, and (3) senses his mother's disappointment in him. According to Freud, when the boy renounces the mother, he may intensify his identification with his father.

   Are Freud's theory and O'Connor's representation of it true to life? What other kinds of conflicts and complexes arise in the various relationships between young children and their parents?

ANNE SEXTON

The Fury of Overshoes

Anne Sexton (1928–1974) was born in Newton, Massachusetts, and attended Garland Junior College. After marrying, she worked as a fashion model, teacher, and professor. She was an accomplished poet: her books include To Bedlam and Part Way Back *(1960),* Live or Die *(1967),* Transformations *(1972), and* The Death Notebooks *(1974). Sexton committed suicide in 1974.*

They sit in a row
outside the kindergarten,
black, red, brown, all
with those brass buckles.
Remember when you couldn't
buckle your own
overshoe
or tie your own
shoe
or cut your own meat
and the tears
running down like mud
because you fell off your
tricycle?
Remember, big fish,

when you couldn't swim
and simply slipped under
like a stone frog?
The world wasn't
yours.
It belonged to
the big people.
Under your bed
sat the wolf
and he made a shadow
when cars passed by
at night.
They made you give up
your nightlight
and your teddy
and your thumb.
Oh overshoes,
don't you
remember me,
pushing you up and down
in the winter snow?
Oh thumb,
I want a drink,
it is dark,
where are the big people,
when will I get there,
taking giant steps
all day,
each day
and thinking
nothing of it?

—1974

What are your reactions to and questions about this work? The following questions may help provoke some ideas.

Probing the Work

1. Take a close look at one of the several *images* (see page 79) Sexton has included to evoke the complex feelings of childhood: what kinds of emotions does the image arouse in you?
2. Why do you think Sexton titled her poem "The Fury of Overshoes"?

Identifying Issues

3. To what extent does this poem's complex depiction of childhood ring true? To what degree could your childhood, or that of someone you know, be characterized by the sort of emotions depicted here?

AUDRE LORDE

Hanging Fire

Audre Lorde (1934–1992), born in New York City of West Indian parents, attended Hunter College and Columbia University. She worked as a librarian and then taught at several colleges before becoming a professor of English at Hunter College in New York City. She was simultaneously a poet and spokesperson for human rights. Her books include The First Cities *(1968),* Between Our Selves, Zami—A New Spelling of My Name, *and* The Marvelous Arithmetics of Distance: Poems 1987–1992.

I am fourteen
and my skin has betrayed me
the boy I cannot live without
still sucks his thumb
in secret
how come my knees are
always so ashy
what if I die
before morning
and momma's in the bedroom
with the door closed.

I have to learn how to dance
in time for the next party
my room is too small for me
suppose I die before graduation
they will sing sad melodies
but finally
tell the truth about me
There is nothing I want to do
and too much
that has to be done
and momma's in the bedroom
with the door closed.

Nobody even stops to think
about my side of it
I should have been on Math Team

my marks were better than his
why do I have to be
the one
wearing braces
I have nothing to wear tomorrow
will I live long enough
to grow up
and momma's in the bedroom
with the door closed.

—1978

What are your reactions to and questions about this work? The following questions may help provoke some ideas.

Probing the Work

1. According to the Oxford English Dictionary, *to hang fire* is a term used for firearms that are "slow in communicating the fire through the vent to the charge." Figuratively, the term means "to hesitate or be slow in acting." How does this information about the term used in the title help or change your understanding of the poem?
2. What are the different sources of this adolescent's frustrations?

Identifying Issues

3. How believably does Lorde identify the feelings and particular dilemmas of adolescents? To what extent do the gender distinctions pointed out by this poem apply to your own experiences?

LILIANA HEKER

The Stolen Party

(translated by Alberto Manguel)

Liliana Heker (b. 1943) was born in Argentina, and achieved fame in 1966 with the publication of her first book. She writes fiction and edits a literary magazine. The story below, first published in Spanish in 1982, was translated and printed in Other Fires: Short Fiction by Latin American Women *(1985), edited by Alberto Manguel.*

As soon as she arrived she went straight to the kitchen to see if the monkey was there. It was: what a relief! She wouldn't have liked to admit that her mother had been right. *Monkeys at a birthday?* her mother had sneered. *Get away with you, believing any nonsense you're told!* She was cross, but not because of the monkey, the girl thought; it's just because of the party.

"I don't like you going," she told her. "It's a rich people's party."

"Rich people go to Heaven too," said the girl, who studied religion at school.

"Get away with Heaven," said the mother. "The problem with you, young lady, is that you like to fart higher than your ass."

The girl didn't approve of the way her mother spoke. She was barely nine, and one of the best in her class.

"I'm going because I've been invited," she said. "And I've been invited because Luciana is my friend. So there."

"Ah yes, your friend," her mother grumbled. She paused. "Listen, Rosaura," she said at last. "That one's not your friend. You know what you are to them? The maid's daughter, that's what."

Rosaura blinked hard: she wasn't going to cry. Then she yelled: "Shut up! You know nothing about being friends!"

Every afternoon she used to go to Luciana's house and they would both finish their homework while Rosaura's mother did the cleaning. They had their tea in the kitchen and they told each other secrets. Rosaura loved everything in the big house, and she also loved the people who lived there.

"I'm going because it will be the most lovely party in the whole world, Luciana told me it would. There will be a magician, and he will bring a monkey and everything."

The mother swung around to take a good look at her child, and pompously put her hands on her hips.

"Monkeys at a birthday?" she said. "Get away with you, believing any nonsense you're told!"

Rosaura was deeply offended. She thought it unfair of her mother to accuse other people of being liars simply because they were rich. Rosaura too wanted to be rich, of course. If one day she managed to live in a beautiful palace, would her mother stop loving her? She felt very sad. She wanted to go to that party more than anything else in the world.

"I'll die if I don't go," she whispered, almost without moving her lips.

And she wasn't sure whether she had been heard, but on the morning of the party she discovered that her mother had starched her Christmas dress. And in the afternoon, after washing her hair, her mother rinsed it in apple vinegar so that it would be all nice and shiny. Before going out, Rosaura admired herself in the mirror, with her white dress and glossy hair, and thought she looked terribly pretty.

Señora Ines also seemed to notice. As soon as she saw her, she said:

"How lovely you look today, Rosaura."

Rosaura gave her starched skirt a slight toss with her hands and walked into the party with a firm step. She said hello to Luciana and asked about the monkey. Luciana put on a secretive look and whispered into Rosaura's ear: "He's in the kitchen. But don't tell anyone, because it's a surprise."

Rosaura wanted to make sure. Carefully she entered the kitchen and there she saw it: deep in thought, inside its cage. It looked so funny that the girl

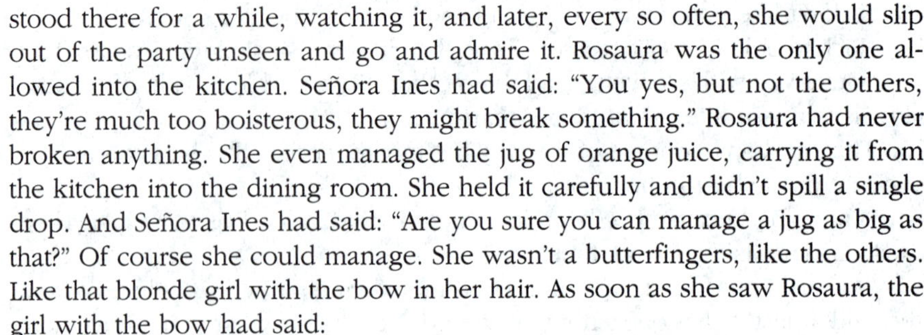

stood there for a while, watching it, and later, every so often, she would slip out of the party unseen and go and admire it. Rosaura was the only one allowed into the kitchen. Señora Ines had said: "You yes, but not the others, they're much too boisterous, they might break something." Rosaura had never broken anything. She even managed the jug of orange juice, carrying it from the kitchen into the dining room. She held it carefully and didn't spill a single drop. And Señora Ines had said: "Are you sure you can manage a jug as big as that?" Of course she could manage. She wasn't a butterfingers, like the others. Like that blonde girl with the bow in her hair. As soon as she saw Rosaura, the girl with the bow had said:

"And you? Who are you?"

"I'm a friend of Luciana," said Rosaura.

"No," said the girl with the bow, "you are not a friend of Luciana because I'm her cousin and I know all her friends. And I don't know you."

"So what," said Rosaura. "I come here every afternoon with my mother and we do our homework together."

"You and your mother do your homework together?" asked the girl, laughing.

"I and Luciana do our homework together," said Rosaura, very seriously.

The girl with the bow shrugged her shoulders.

"That's not being friends," she said. "Do you go to school together?"

"No."

"So where do you know her from?" said the girl, getting impatient.

Rosaura remembered her mother's words perfectly. She took a deep breath.

"I'm the daughter of the employee," she said.

Her mother had said very clearly: "If someone asks, you say you're the daughter of the employee; that's all." She also told her to add: "And proud of it." But Rosaura thought that never in her life would she dare say something of the sort.

"What employee?" said the girl with the bow. "Employee in a shop?"

"No," said Rosaura angrily. "My mother doesn't sell anything in any shop, so there."

"So how come she's an employee?" said the girl with the bow.

Just then Señora Ines arrived saying *shh shh,* and asked Rosaura if she wouldn't mind helping serve out the hotdogs, as she knew the house so much better than the others.

"See?" said Rosaura to the girl with the bow, and when no one was looking she kicked her in the shin.

Apart from the girl with the bow, all the others were delightful. The one she liked best was Luciana, with her golden birthday crown; and then the boys. Rosaura won the sack race, and nobody managed to catch her when they played tag. When they split into two teams to play charades, all the boys wanted her for their side. Rosaura felt she had never been so happy in all her life.

But the best was still to come. The best came after Luciana blew out the candles. First the cake. Señora Ines had asked her to help pass the cake around, and Rosaura had enjoyed the task immensely, because everyone called out to her, shouting "Me, me!" Rosaura remembered a story in which there was a queen who had the power of life or death over her subjects. She had always loved that, having the power of life or death. To Luciana and the boys she gave the largest pieces, and to the girl with the bow she gave a slice so thin one could see through it.

After the cake came the magician, tall and bony, with a fine red cape. A true magician: he could untie handkerchiefs by blowing on them and make a chain with links that had no openings. He could guess what cards were pulled out from a pack, and the monkey was his assistant. He called the monkey "partner." "Let's see here, partner," he would say, "turn over a card." And, "Don't run away, partner: time to work now."

The final trick was wonderful. One of the children had to hold the monkey in his arms and the magician said he would make him disappear.

"What, the boy?" they all shouted.

"No, the monkey!" shouted back the magician.

Rosaura thought that this was truly the most amusing party in the whole world.

The magician asked a small fat boy to come and help, but the small fat boy got frightened almost at once and dropped the monkey on the floor. The magician picked him up carefully, whispered something in his ear, and the monkey nodded almost as if he understood.

"You mustn't be so unmanly, my friend," the magician said to the fat boy.

"What's unmanly?" said the fat boy.

The magician turned around as if to look for spies.

"A sissy," said the magician. "Go sit down."

Then he stared at all the faces, one by one. Rosaura felt her heart tremble.

"You, with the Spanish eyes," said the magician. And everyone saw that he was pointing at her.

She wasn't afraid. Neither holding the monkey, nor when the magician made him vanish; not even when, at the end, the magician flung his red cape over Rosaura's head and uttered a few magic words . . . and the monkey reappeared, chattering happily, in her arms. The children clapped furiously. And before Rosaura returned to her seat, the magician said:

"Thank you very much, my little countess."

She was so pleased with the compliment that a while later, when her mother came to fetch her, that was the first thing she told her.

"I helped the magician and he said to me, 'Thank you very much, my little countess.' "

It was strange because up to then Rosaura had thought that she was angry with her mother. All along Rosaura had imagined that she would say to her: "See that the monkey wasn't a lie?" But instead she was so thrilled that she told her mother all about the wonderful magician.

Her mother tapped her on the head and said: "So now we're a countess!"

But one could see that she was beaming.

And now they both stood in the entrance, because a moment ago Señora Ines, smiling, had said: "Please wait here a second."

Her mother suddenly seemed worried.

"What is it?" she asked Rosaura.

"What is what?" said Rosaura. "It's nothing; she just wants to get the presents for those who are leaving, see?"

She pointed at the fat boy and at a girl with pigtails who were also waiting there, next to their mothers. And she explained about the presents. She knew, because she had been watching those who left before her. When one of the girls was about to leave, Señora Ines would give her a bracelet. When a boy left, Señora Ines gave him a yo-yo. Rosaura preferred the yo-yo because it sparkled, but she didn't mention that to her mother. Her mother might have said: "So why don't you ask for one, you blockhead?" That's what her mother was like. Rosaura didn't feel like explaining that she'd be horribly ashamed to be the odd one out. Instead she said:

"I was the best-behaved at the party."

And she said no more because Señora Ines came out into the hall with two bags, one pink and one blue.

First she went up to the fat boy, gave him a yo-yo out of the blue bag, and the fat boy left with his mother. Then she went up to the girl and gave her a bracelet out of the pink bag, and the girl with the pigtails left as well.

Finally she came up to Rosaura and her mother. She had a big smile on her face and Rosaura liked that. Señora Ines looked down at her, then looked up at her mother, and then said something that made Rosaura proud:

"What a marvelous daughter you have, Herminia."

For an instant, Rosaura thought that she'd give her two presents: the bracelet and the yo-yo. Señora Ines bent down as if about to look for something. Rosaura also leaned forward, stretching out her arm. But she never completed the movement.

Señora Ines didn't look in the pink bag. Nor did she look in the blue bag. Instead she rummaged in her purse. In her hand appeared two bills.

"You really and truly earned this," she said handing them over. "Thank you for all your help, my pet."

Rosaura felt her arms stiffen, stick close to her body, and then she noticed her mother's hand on her shoulder. Instinctively she pressed herself against her mother's body. That was all. Except her eyes. Rosaura's eyes had a cold, clear look that fixed itself on Señora Ines's face.

Señora Ines, motionless, stood there with her hand outstretched. As if she didn't dare draw it back. As if the slightest change might shatter an infinitely delicate balance.

—1982

What are your reactions to and questions about this work? The following questions may help provoke some ideas.

Probing the Work

1. Why does Señora Ines stand with her hand outstretched, "As if the slightest change might shatter an infinitely delicate balance"?
2. Why is this story called "The Stolen Party"?

Identifying Issues

3. To what extent is the recognition of class distinctions an integral part of one's sense of self and one's development as a child growing up?

WRITING ASSIGNMENT SEQUENCE (CONTINUED FROM PAGE 343)

4. Making Connections

Select one of the following questions and write an informal response in which you connect your own ideas with those conveyed in the works of this cluster, and/or make connections among the works themselves.

A. What are the different aspects of childhood experiences illustrated in this cluster? Which ones seem most believable? Which do you most easily identify with, and why?

B. Many people talk about childhood as being the most carefree time of their lives. But what problematic aspects of growing up do these writers depict?

C. How does the experience you described in your *freewriting* exercise compare with the moments of growth described by these writers?

5. Putting It All Together

Write an essay that combines what you think about the topic *Growing Up* with what you now understand about the readings.

- Collect your informal writing, notes, and reading-journal entries on this topic and decide what will be the focus of your essay.

- Outline your essay. Select the literary passages and personal details you might use to illustrate and support your main focus.
- Write a draft of your essay in which you bring together what you think about the subject with what you understand about the readings. Try to include in your draft one or more *literary terms.*
- Share what you've written with your classmates and instructor, then revise it according to their recommendations.

Writing Tip: Building Paragraphs

Like an architect, you should build each paragraph with a firm foundation (a focus sentence or a strong point) and all sentences should be arranged according to a logical plan so the whole structure stays and works together. Check your paragraphs. Use your eyes to check their length—they shouldn't all be the same size. Break up a very long paragraph if it contains more than one idea. Expand very short paragraphs; they can make your thoughts seem incomplete. Add examples or quotations.

How many sentences do you have? Are they all linked together? Have you made decisions about where you are shifting your point? Most healthy paragraphs should have

- a central point stated in a clear sentence
- adequate supporting and illustrative details, and perhaps the reason your examples are appropriate
- no irrelevant material

Notice the way in which Trevor builds his paragraphs in this excerpt from his essay, "Sharing the Family," related to the works in the "Growing Up" cluster. The second sentence of the first paragraph, and the first sentence of the second paragraph establish his central point: in each paragraph he provides relevant examples and details to support his point.

> When I married my first wife, she had an eight-year-old son who had spent most of his early years in daycare centers, schools or with baby-sitters. Consequently, when we settled into a routine, he was always jealous of the relationship between his mother and me, and no matter how hard I tried I was unable to establish a kinship with him. This seems to be very similar to Larry's situation in "My Oedipus Complex" when his father enters his life for the first time at the age of five. Up to this point Larry was treated as the man of the house by his mother, and they had settled into a routine. Instead of his mother's undivided attention, whereby they did everything exclusively together, he now has to contend with being told "do be quiet,

Larry! Don't you hear me talking to Daddy" (351). At this point his mother seems to ignore their previous relationship and concentrates on making Larry conform to the new situation. In trying to stop him from coming into the master bed in the morning she tells him "not to come in and disturb poor Daddy" (354). She is again breaking from the earlier tradition and promoting her husband above the child.

The relationship deteriorates, especially after a fight between father and child, whereby the father tries to establish some authority by smacking Larry. It seems that Larry's mother is unable to reconcile the two men in her life. Larry's life gets worse as he and his father "conducted a series of skirmishes against one another" (356). Larry's mother is inconsistent, allowing him to play with his father's war memorabilia, but when he is caught by his father his mother takes them away, saying "you mustn't play with Daddy's toys unless he lets you" (356). Her scornful belittlement of the father's war relics hurts him equally.

CrossClusters

In your paper you might want to consider how the following works located elsewhere in this book depict growing up:

- Sharon Olds, "Photograph of the Girl" (p. 8)
- Langston Hughes, "Salvation" (p. 86)
- James Joyce, "Araby" (p. 89)
- Richard Wright, "The Man Who Was Almost a Man" (p. 93)
- John Updike, "A & P" (p. 104)
- Alice Munro, "Boys and Girls" (p. 109)
- Rita Dove, "Adolescence III" (p. 120)
- Marge Piercy, "Barbie Doll" (p. 212)
- Charles Johnston, "Exchange Value" (p. 243)
- Michael Dorris, "The Contest" (p. 374)
- Jamaica Kincaid, "Girl" (p. 377)
- Amy Tan, "Two Kinds" (p. 385)
- Raymond Carver, "My Father's Life" (p. 446)
- Ernest Hemingway, "Fathers and Sons" (p. 454)
- Theodore Roethke, "My Papa's Waltz" (p. 470)
- Bruno Bettleheim, "The Child's Need for Magic" (p. 729)
- Naguito Mahfouz, "Half a Day" (p. 763)
- Grace Paley, "The Loudest Voice" (p. 971)

Sample Essay

Here is Trevor's completed essay.

"Sharing the Family," by Trevor Hughes

Reading the stories, essays and poems in this cluster and comparing some of the salient points with my own life, I was surprised at some of the parallels. The ten points that Jane Howard raises in "Families" are of particular interest, but I find one to be very pertinent: "Good families are much to all their members but everything to none" (339). "My Oedipus complex" by Frank O'Connor and the poem "Hanging Fire" by Audre Lorde show dysfunctional families where the parents' self interest manifests itself in problematic relationships.

When I married my first wife she had an eight-year-old son who had spent most of his early years in daycare centers, schools or with babysitters. Consequently, when we settled into a routine he was always jealous of the relationship between his mother and me, and no matter how hard I tried I was unable to establish a kinship with him. This seems to be very similar to Larry's situation in "My Oedipus Complex" when his father enters his life for the first time at the age of five. Up to this point Larry was treated as the man of the house by his mother, and they had settled into a routine. Instead of his mother's undivided attention, whereby they did everything exclusively together, he now has to contend with being told "do be quiet, Larry! Don't you hear me talking to Daddy" (351). His mother at this point seems to ignore their previous relationship and concentrates on making Larry conform to the new situation. In trying to stop him from coming into the master bed in the morning she tells him "not to come in and disturb poor Daddy" (354). She is again breaking from the earlier tradition and promoting her husband above the child.

The relationship deteriorates, especially after a fight between father and child, whereby the father tries to establish some authority by smacking Larry. It seems Larry's mother is unable to reconcile the two men in her life. Larry's life gets worse as he and his father "conducted a series of skirmishes against one another" (356). Larry's mother is inconsistent, allowing him to play with his father's war memorabilia, but when caught by his father his mother takes them away, saying "you mustn't play with Daddy's toys unless he lets you" (356). Her scornful belittlement of the father's war relics hurts him equally.

At this point my story and Larry's diverge. His mother has another child to whom she now devotes all her attention, much to the chagrin of both father and son. Larry feels very antagonistic towards his new sibling lamenting, "Mother had no consideration now for anyone but that poisonous pup" (358). His mother's egocentrism has an ironic bright side, as she has only room in her life for one person. It is now Sonny who monopolizes her.

The father, in order to escape his son's nightly tantrum, joins Larry in his bed, and in order to comfort each other puts his arm around him. Larry wistfully muses "after turning me out of the big bed, he had been turned out himself." This reversal causes a relationship to develop which keeps the men in the family together. In my case, however, I was unable to overcome the problems, and after five years we were divorced.

In "Hanging Fire" by Audre Lorde we again see a child, in this case a fourteen year old girl, who has multiple problems. We read that her "skin has betrayed her" (line 2). Though this could have been caused by acne, it might be a reference to racial or gender problems. Two recurring themes, however, manifest themselves in the poem. The first is her repeated fear of dying—at the beginning before morning, then before graduation and finally before growing up. Secondly, and probably most seriously, she repeatedly laments "and momma's in the bedroom with the door closed" (lines 10–11, 22–23 & 34–35). I can recall the inaccessibility of my parents and the lack of their concern or attention in my school or private life, when I was growing up.

What if we apply Jane Howard's advice "Good families are much to all their members but everything to none" (339). It appears Larry's mother puts all her energies into one person at the time, basically to the exclusion of everyone else. If she had tried to share her time between father and son, the outcome could have been one of shared love and joy. This is true in my third (and hopefully last) marriage. My son was six years old when [my present wife and I] got married; she and I had lived together since he was two. This was a very similar scenario to Larry's, except that I did not keep myself chained to the house, but had to work and consequently put my son in a daycare center where he was able to interact with other children. My new wife realized that for the relationship to work she had to forge a union with my son. She has striven to do this, and has succeeded to such an extent that my son calls her Mummy, and treats her as if she were his natural mother. I do not have any problems that revolve around jealousy.

In "Hanging Fire" it would be easy to see a lot of the teenager's frustrations being dissipated if the speaker's mother was not constantly in the bedroom. Whether this is a metaphor for the inaccessibility of the mother or the actual situation, the poem leaves ambiguous. Maybe the cause is an illness, but no mention is made of the father. A question arises if the father is nonexistent or as unapproachable as the mother. Anyway, the poem gives the definite impression of abandonment that could easily have been reversed if the mother showed more interest in the daughter. The problems would still be there but the anger to a large degree is eliminated. As adults we have more control over how the family operates; it is therefore up to us to establish the rules of good family life.

In conclusion I would like to expand my feelings on Howard's homily,

"Nobody in the family is more important than anybody else." I do not suggest that the hierarchy of the family be forsaken, as discipline and respect for elders are essential for children. What I am saying is that each family member contributes in their own way, and nobody should be put above anybody else. It is essential that each member contribute and support all other members to the best of their ability. Homer said "light is the task where many share the toil" and dividing the work among all family members makes life more satisfying for all. Ogden Nash is quoted as saying "a family is a unit composed not only of children but of men, women, an occasional animal, and the common cold." If the parents are selfish in their energies or commitments, then everyone is a loser.

14

MOTHER'S INHERITANCE

WRITING ASSIGNMENT SEQUENCE

1. Thinking About . . . Mothers

Asking a Series of Questions: Respond in a quick, informal manner to the following questions:

- What happens to a woman when she becomes a mother? Does her identity change?
- What, besides the fact of giving birth, identifies a woman as a mother?
- Do you think of your mother as if she were a different person before you were born? As if she is a different person at her job? As if she is different in a friendship or relationship?

2. Enacting the Topic

Think of television shows, past or present, that depict mothers (e.g. "The Cosby Show" or "Roseanne"). Act out or describe one that features a stereotypical depiction and one that seems to go against the stereotype. For the show that depicts a stereotype, what qualities of motherhood are exaggerated? Create a show that reflects your own experiences. What qualities of the mother would you stress?

3. Responding to the Readings

As you read the works in this cluster, jot down in your response journals questions you have about the works, and comment on passages you find provocative or puzzling. Consider the questions following each reading for journal writing and prepare to discuss your reactions in class.

CLUSTER ESSAY

MICHAEL DORRIS

The Contest

Michael Dorris (b. 1945) is of Irish, French, and Modoc Indian descent. He published his first, highly acclaimed novel in 1987. Two years later his nonfiction book The Broken Cord, *about his adopted son's fetal alcohol syndrome, won the National Book Critics' Circle Prize. He and his wife, Louise Erdrich (see page 491), wrote* The Crown of Columbus *together. The following essay is from his book of essays,* Paper Trail *(1994).*

My mother and two of her older sisters were all quite ill during their late teens and early twenties, and as a result my mother married relatively late. She and my father, a young army lieutenant, met on a blind date while he was stationed at Fort Knox. In almost every respect—ethnicity, religion, background—he was romantically, complicatedly different from other men she knew, and characteristically my mother had high hopes, as she traveled alone to California for her wedding and then lived on army bases in Texas and Washington State during their first year together.

In 1947, my father was killed in a jeep accident near Passau, Germany, and my mother returned to live with my grandmother and Aunt Marion in Louisville. I was two, and my mother was in her thirties, more than ten years younger than my current age. A widow after less than five years—one long war—as a wife, she must have been lonely and terribly disappointed, but I never heard her complain or question the sharp turn in her future. My father's insurance money was divided between donations for masses said in his name and my mother's share of a down payment on the house in which she and my aunt still live. Then, with the small monthly stipend from my father's military pension and social security to supplement my aunt's salary, my mother stayed home, devoting herself to the perfection of my childhood.

Before her marriage, according to uncensored snips of stories and to the evidence of the family photo album, my mother was infamous in her circle as a free spirit. She swam at midnight in the Ohio River, spent her vacations from Colgate Palmolive as a below-decks passenger on United Fruit Company boats in the Caribbean, even once sang on a local radio station as part of a trio that included Dale Evans. In the snapshots from her early twenties, she often has flowers tucked in her long, curly black hair or sports an off-the-shoulder blouse. With her strong brow and deeply lidded eyes she has the look of a youthful Loretta Young, with a smile as wide as Lena Horne's.

There wasn't much money during the depression for store-bought clothes, and early on my mother taught herself to sew—she needed a wardrobe for the fun she intended to have. In my favorite picture of her from the period, she has glamorized a cloth coat with epaulets fashioned from pieces of an old carpet, meant to resemble pressed fur. Her expression is bold, interested to see what comes next.

I personally first encountered this adventurous side of my mother when I was nine years old. A friend of my Aunt Ginny's, Henry Lea, had a job as assistant stage manager at the Memorial Coliseum downtown, the theater where nationally touring Broadway plays were presented. One January day Henry called to offer my mother and me passes to see a matinee of *The Dark Is Light Enough,* a drama starring Katherine Cornell and my mother's all-time favorite actor, Tyrone Power.

My mother took a long time to get ready that morning, and when she finally appeared, perfumed and made up, she was transformed in my eyes into a movie star herself. She seemed almost distant, enveloped in a cloud of graciousness, as if her enthusiasm had reached some plateau of calm from which she could review all that followed with serene detachment. The day, for her, was an occasion, an opportunity to step out of the role she normally played and into a brighter, less constricting version of her possibilities.

The last thing my mother did before we departed was to write a few words on a piece of note paper, stare at it for a moment, make a correction or two, then slip it into her purse. When I asked for an explanation, she would only say, mysteriously, "Just in case, Honey."

I don't recall a single detail about the play—its dialogue was far over my head—but I do remember that my mother sat at attention for the whole performance, her back straight, her full concentration on the rhythm of the lines and the flow of the action on the stage. During intermission we remained in our seats, didn't talk much. I looked at the program, and once or twice my mother checked the paper she had stuck in her purse—but she still refused to let me see the words. There were curtain calls, many of them, yet we didn't leave when the house lights went up.

"A surprise," my mother whispered. "Henry's going to sneak us in backstage." Her voice was tense, and she seemed less thrilled than terrified by the prospect. I followed her to a small door near the orchestra pit, and our friend met the knock.

"It'll have to be quick," Henry warned us. "He's beat. I'll put you in wardrobe and he'll try to drop in to say hello."

We waited in a room filled with wonderful costumes in brilliant colors, drawers overflowing with masks and capes, the props from many productions stacked upon every surface. But instead of exclaiming at each new thing I pointed out, my mother dug once again into her purse and found the now familiar paper. She was still looking at it when we heard someone at the door, and quickly she crumpled it in her fist.

Tyrone Power was the first famous person I ever met, and what I remember about him were his eyelashes: unnaturally long. I shook hands when we were introduced, but I hung my head, tongue-tied with shyness, incapable of uttering a sound.

"Ty," Henry said. "This is my friend Mary Besy and her little boy, Michael."

I glanced up to see my mother step forward without hesitation.

"Oh, Mr. Power." She spoke smoothly, confidently, each syllable enunciated, distinct and clear. "We missed you every moment you were offstage."

It was just the right compliment. Tyrone Power smiled—that was the other thing he had besides eyelashes: teeth—and lingered for a few minutes longer than I think he'd planned.

It was a cold, raw winter dusk. My mother drove with one hand on the wheel and with the other she absently combed her hair. As we made our way down Frankfort Avenue, she sang along with the music on the radio. Somehow I knew that if she ever smoked, which she never did, she would have had a cigarette.

At home, I ran ahead into the house, showed my grandmother and aunt the program, raved about our excursion backstage, our hobnob with celebrity. My mother stood by the door, listened, nodded, even reluctantly consented to repeat her opening remark to Tyrone Power, but when she went into the kitchen to fix supper she seemed returned to the routine of her life, almost as though nothing out of the ordinary had happened.

But next morning, there was evidence to the contrary. In search of a glove, I went out to our car, parked in the alley beside our house. The door on the driver's side was open and the overhead light was still dimly lit, illuminating a layer of gray frost that covered the inside of the windshield. The turn signal blinked, my mother's winter coat lay abandoned across the seat, the keys were still in the ignition, and the tank had run out of gas.

It must have been a year or two later when my mother heard about a competition run by the local Singer Sewing Machine outlet. Each registered contestant paid a $20 fee to enroll in an advanced class during which she would design and construct an outfit called an "afternoon ensemble." Eventually a fashion show would take place, with official judges. The grand prize was an airplane dream trip to Florida for two, all expenses paid.

The tuition put a strain on our finances, but my mother regarded this as an investment. Every Tuesday night for three months she went to her seminar, discussed the intricacies of basting and pleating and tucks with other women, and returned with ideas that she translated into sketches. She took me along when she shopped for her material, examining each flat bolt with an eye toward the cloth's drape and texture, as well as price.

On the big night, however, my mother wouldn't let anyone accompany her to the finals. She had made a blue linen sundress—ideal for Florida, she had decided—with an ivory bolero jacket. She even dyed a pair of shoes the same shade of blue and covered a pillbox hat frame to match. My aunt contributed her good white gloves, and my grandmother came up with a pair of pearl-drop earrings to complete the effect. My mother had gotten a beauty parlor permanent wave that afternoon, dressed early, and stood during supper so as not to wrinkle. We all applauded when she did a last twirl before walking out the door alone.

My mother has suffered many disappointments, big and small, in her life, and borne them all bravely, but that night was a triumph. She arrived home at ten o'clock with a red velveteen crown, a silver plastic scepter, and a certificate worth two airplane tickets, four days at the Belmar Hotel in Miami Beach, a cabana by the pool, and a welcome dinner that included shrimp cocktails and dessert.

I vividly recall that trip of thirty-five years ago—for I was my mother's chosen companion, the chief beneficiary as always of her labor. She found a pattern, made an orange plaid sports coat for me, along with a new pair of long pants, and she bought me a clip-on bow tie. After dinner, that first night in the tropics, we sat together on our private balcony, listening until well past my usual bedtime as the hotel band played tune after tune of the music from my mother's youth: "Harbor Lights," "Stormy Weather," "The Heart of a Fool." She was wearing the linen dress, of course, and her hair was blowing free in the ocean wind. Her head was back, her eyes were closed, and she was smiling, harmonizing the familiar words to herself.

—1993

What are your reactions to and questions about this work? The following questions may help provoke some ideas.

Probing the Work

1. How is Dorris's mother *characterized* (p. 77)? Select a detail that Dorris uses to describe or define his mother, and discuss what it reveals about her.

Identifying Issues

2. What are the distinguishing features of a mother/son relationship implied by this essay? To what extent can you relate to or disagree with Dorris's depiction of this relationship?

JAMAICA KINCAID

Girl

Jamaica Kincaid (b. 1949) was born in Antigua (West Indies) and immigrated to the United States. She has been a contributor and staff writer for The New Yorker *since 1976. The story below comes from her collection,* At the Bottom of the River *(1984). She has also published* Annie John *(1985),* A Small Place *(1988), and* Lucy *(1990).*

Wash the white clothes on Monday and put them on the stone heap; wash the color clothes on Tuesday and put them on the clothesline to dry; don't walk barehead in the hot sun; cook pumpkin fritters in very hot sweet oil; soak your little clothes right after you take them off; when buying cotton to make yourself a nice blouse, be sure that it doesn't have gum on it, because that way it won't hold up well after a wash; soak salt fish overnight before you cook it; is it true that you sing benna[1] in Sunday School?; always eat your food in such a way that it won't turn someone else's stomach; on Sundays try to walk like a lady and not like the slut you are so bent on becoming; don't sing benna in Sunday School; you mustn't speak to wharf-rat boys, not even to give directions; don't eat fruits on the street—flies will follow you; *but I don't sing benna on Sundays at all and never in Sunday school;* this is how to sew on a button; this is how to make a buttonhole for the button you have just sewed on; this is how to hem a dress when you see the hem coming down and so to prevent yourself from looking like the slut I know you are so bent on becoming; this is how you iron your father's khaki shirt so that it doesn't have a crease; this is how you iron your father's khaki pants so that they don't have a crease; this is how you grow okra—far from the house, because okra tree harbors red ants; when you are growing dasheen, make sure it gets plenty of water or else it makes your throat itch when you are eating it; this is how you sweep a corner; this is how you sweep a whole house; this is how you sweep a yard; this is how you smile to someone you don't like too much; this is how you set a table for dinner with an important guest; this is how you smile to someone you don't like at all; this is how you smile to someone you like completely; this is how you set a table for tea; this is how you set a table for dinner; this is how you set a table for lunch; this is how you set a table for breakfast; this is how to behave in the presence of men who don't know you very well, and this way they won't recognize immediately the slut I have warned you against becoming; be sure to wash every day, even if it is with your own spit; don't squat down to play marbles—you are not a boy, you know; don't pick people's flowers—you might catch something; don't throw stones at blackbirds, because it might not be a blackbird at all; this is how to make a bread pudding; this is how to make doukona[2]; this is how to make pepper pot; this is how to make a good medicine for a cold; this is how to make a good medicine to throw away a child before it even becomes a child; this is how to catch a fish; this is how to throw back a fish you don't like, and that way something bad won't fall on you; this is how to bully a man; this is how a man bullies you; this is how to love a man, and if this doesn't work there are other ways, and if they don't work don't feel too bad about giving up; this is how to spit up in the air if you feel like it, and this is how to move quick so that it doesn't fall on you; this is how to make ends meet; always squeeze bread to make sure it's fresh; *but what if the baker won't let me feel the bread?;* you mean to say that after all you are really going to be the kind of woman who the baker won't let near the bread?

—1978

[1]Calypso music.

[2]Spicy pudding made of plantains.

What are your reactions to and questions about this work? The following questions may help provoke some ideas.

Probing the Work

1. How do the *diction* (see page 67) and *point of view* (see page 66) of "Girl" contribute to our understanding of this mother/daughter relationship?

Identifying Issues

2. Explain the kinds of values the mother wishes to pass on to her daughter. To what degree do you think her advice is helpful? To what degree is it harmful?

FAWZIYYA ABU-KHALID

Mother's Inheritance

(translated by Kamal Boullata)

Fawziyya Abu-Khalid (b. 1955) was born in Riyadh, Saudi Arabia, to a Westernized upper-middle-class family. She studied sociology at American University in Beirut, then attended Lewis and Clark College in the United States. She published some of her poems in local newspapers when she was a girl, then collected them (including the one below) in her first book, Until When Will They Go on Raping You on Your Wedding Night? *This collection was published in Lebanon but banned in her native country. She has also published* Reading the Secret of the History of Arab Silence.

Mother,
You did not leave me an inheritance of necklaces for a wedding
but a neck
        that towers above the guillotine
Not an embroidered veil for my face
but the eyes of a falcon
        that glitter like the daggers
        in the belts of our men.
Not a piece of land large enough
        to plant a single date palm
but the primal fruit of The Fertile Crescent:°
My Womb.
You let me sleep with all the children
        of our neighborhood

11. The Fertile Crescent, The Middle East, flanked by the Nile and the Tigris and Euphrates Rivers; historically and symbolically the cradle of civilization.

that my agony may give birth
        to new rebels

In the bundle of your will
I thought I could find
        a seed from The Garden of Eden
        that I may plant in my heart
        forsaken by the seasons
Instead
You left me with a sheathless sword
        the name of an obscure child carved on its blade
Every pore in me
        every crack
        opened up:

A sheath.

I plunged the sword into my heart
        but the wall could not contain it
I thrust it into my lungs
        but the window could not box it
I dipped it into my waist
        but the house was too small for it
It lengthened into the streets
        defoliating the decorations
        of official holidays
Tilling asphalt
Announcing the season of
The Coming Feast.

Mother,
Today, they came to confiscate the inheritance
        you left me.
They could not decipher the children's fingerprints
They could not walk the road that stretches
        between the arteries of my heart
        and the cord that feeds the babe
        in every mother's womb.
They seized the children of the neighborhood
        for interrogation
They could not convict the innocence in their eyes.
They searched my pockets
        took off my clothes
        peeled my skin
But they failed to reach
        the glistening silk that nestles

the twin doves
in my breast.

—1978

What are your reactions to and questions about this work? The following questions may help provoke some ideas.

Probing the Work

1. Explain at least three of the powerful images of this poem and what connections you can make among them. What do they seem to reveal about the speaker's attitude toward her mother's inheritance?

Identifying Issues

2. To what degree can or should a mother protect her children from the larger society? To what degree is this speaker's anger justified? To what degree can or should mothers control their children's destiny?

CYNTHIA OZICK

The Shawl

Cynthia Ozick (b. 1928) was born in the Bronx, New York, and began her writing career relatively late, but armed with an impressive knowledge of Jewish history and learning. Her books include the short-story collection The Pagan Rabbi and Other Stories *(1971), the essay collections* Art and Ardor *(1983) and* Metaphor and Memory *(1989), and the novels* Levitation *(1982) and* The Messiah of Stockholm *(1987). "The Shawl" first appeared as a short story, then was expanded to a novel by the same name in 1989.*

Stella, cold, cold, the coldness of hell. How they walked on the roads together, Rosa with Magda curled up between sore breasts, Magda wound up in the shawl. Sometimes Stella carried Magda. But she was jealous of Magda. A thin girl of fourteen, too small, with thin breasts of her own, Stella wanted to be wrapped in a shawl, hidden away, asleep, rocked by the march, a baby, a round infant in arms. Magda took Rosa's nipple, and Rosa never stopped walking, a walking cradle. There was not enough milk; sometimes Magda sucked air; then she screamed. Stella was ravenous. Her knees were tumors on sticks, her elbows chicken bones.

Rosa did not feel hunger; she felt light, not like someone walking but like someone in a faint, in trance, arrested in a fit, someone who is already a floating angel, alert and seeing everything, but in the air, not there, not touching the road. As if teetering on the tips of her fingernails. She looked into Magda's face through a gap in the shawl: a squirrel in a nest, safe, no one could reach her inside the little house of the shawl's windings. The face, very round, a pocket mirror of a face: but it was not Rosa's bleak complexion, dark like cholera, it was another kind of face altogether, eyes blue as air, smooth feathers of hair nearly as yellow as the Star sewn into Rosa's coat. You could think she was one of *their* babies.

Rosa, floating, dreamed of giving Magda away in one of the villages. She could leave the line for a minute and push Magda into the hands of any woman on the side of the road. But if she moved out of line they might shoot. And even if she fled the line for half a second and pushed the shawl-bundle at a stranger, would the woman take it? She might be surprised, or afraid; she might drop the shawl, and Magda would fall out and strike her head and die. The little round head. Such a good child, she gave up screaming, and sucked now only for the taste of the drying nipple itself. The neat grip of the tiny gums. One mite of a tooth tip sticking up in the bottom gum, how shining, an elfin tombstone of white marble gleaming there. Without complaining, Magda relinquished Rosa's teats, first the left, then the right; both were cracked, not a sniff of milk. The duct-crevice extinct, a dead volcano, blind eye, chill hole, so Magda took the corner of the shawl and milked it instead. She sucked and sucked, flooding the threads with wetness. The shawl's good flavor, milk of linen.

It was a magic shawl, it could nourish an infant for three days and three nights. Magda did not die, she stayed alive, although very quiet. A peculiar smell, of cinnamon and almonds, lifted out of her mouth. She held her eyes open every moment, forgetting how to blink or nap, and Rosa and sometimes Stella studied their blueness. On the road they raised one burden of a leg after another and studied Magda's face. "Aryan," Stella said, in a voice grown as thin as a string; and Rosa thought how Stella gazed at Magda like a young cannibal. And the time that Stella said "Aryan," it sounded to Rosa as if Stella had really said "Let us devour her."

But Magda lived to walk. She lived that long, but she did not walk very well, partly because she was only fifteen months old, and partly because the spindles of her legs could not hold up her fat belly. It was fat with air, full and round. Rosa gave almost all her food to Magda, Stella gave nothing; Stella was ravenous, a growing child herself, but not growing much. Stella did not menstruate. Rosa did not menstruate. Rosa was ravenous, but also not; she learned from Magda how to drink the taste of a finger in one's mouth. They were in a place without pity, all pity was annihilated in Rosa, she looked at Stella's bones without pity. She was sure that Stella was waiting for Magda to die so she could put her teeth into the little thighs.

Rosa knew Magda was going to die very soon; she should have been dead already, but she had been buried away deep inside the magic shawl, mistaken there for the shivering mound of Rosa's breasts; Rosa clung to the shawl as if it covered only herself. No one took it away from her. Magda was mute. She never cried. Rosa hid her in the barracks, under the shawl, but she knew that one day someone would inform; or one day someone, not even Stella, would steal Magda to eat her. When Magda began to walk Rosa knew that Magda was going to die very soon, something would happen. She was afraid to fall asleep; she slept with the weight of her thigh on Magda's body; she was afraid she would smother Magda under her thigh. The weight of Rosa was becoming less and less; Rosa and Stella were slowly turning into air.

Magda was quiet, but her eyes were horribly alive, like blue tigers. She watched. Sometimes she laughed—it seemed a laugh, but how could it be? Magda had never seen anyone laugh. Still, Magda laughed at her shawl when the wind blew its corners, the bad wind with pieces of black in it, that made Stella's and Rosa's eyes tear. Magda's eyes were always clear and tearless. She watched like a tiger. She guarded her shawl. No one could touch it; only Rosa could touch it. Stella was not allowed. The shawl was Magda's own baby, her pet, her little sister. She tangled herself up in it and sucked on one of the corners when she wanted to be very still.

Then Stella took the shawl away and made Magda die.

Afterward Stella said: "I was cold."

And afterward she was always cold, always. The cold went into her heart: Rosa saw that Stella's heart was cold. Magda flopped onward with her little pencil legs scribbling this way and that, in search of the shawl; the pencils faltered at the barracks opening, where the light began. Rosa saw and pursued. But already Magda was in the square outside the barracks, in the jolly light. It was the roll-call arena. Every morning Rosa had to conceal Magda under the shawl against a wall of the barracks and go out and stand in the arena with Stella and hundreds of others, sometimes for hours, and Magda, deserted, was quiet under the shawl, sucking on her corner. Every day Magda was silent, and so she did not die. Rosa saw that today Magda was going to die, and at the same time a fearful joy ran in Rosa's two palms, her fingers were on fire, she was astonished, febrile: Magda, in the sunlight, swaying on her pencil legs, was howling. Ever since the drying up of Rosa's nipples, ever since Magda's last scream on the road, Magda had been devoid of any syllable; Magda was a mute. Rosa believed that something had gone wrong with her vocal cords, with her windpipe, with the cave of her larynx; Magda was defective, without a voice; perhaps she was deaf; there might be something amiss with her intelligence; Magda was dumb. Even the laugh that came when the ash-stippled wind made a clown out of Magda's shawl was only the air-blown showing of her teeth. Even when the lice, head lice and body lice, crazed her so that she became as wild as one of the big rats that plundered the barracks at daybreak looking for carrion, she rubbed and scratched and kicked and bit and rolled without a whimper. But now Magda's mouth was spilling a long viscous rope of clamor.

"Maaaa—"

It was the first noise Magda had ever sent out from her throat since the drying up of Rosa's nipples.

"Maaaa . . . aaa!"

Again! Magda was wavering in the perilous sunlight of the arena, scribbling on such pitiful little bent shins. Rosa saw. She saw that Magda was grieving for the loss of her shawl, she saw that Magda was going to die. A tide of commands hammered in Rosa's nipples: Fetch, get, bring! But she did not know which to go after first, Magda or the shawl. If she jumped out into the arena to snatch Magda up, the howling would not stop, because Magda would still not have the shawl; but if she ran back into the barracks to find the shawl, and if she found it, and if she came after Magda holding it and shaking it, then she would get Magda back, Magda would put the shawl in her mouth and turn dumb again.

Rosa entered the dark. It was easy to discover the shawl. Stella was heaped under it, asleep in her thin bones. Rosa tore the shawl free and flew—she could fly, she was only air—into the arena. The sunheat murmured of another life, of butterflies in summer. The light was placid, mellow. On the other side of the steel fence, far away, there were green meadows speckled with dandelions and deep-colored violets; beyond them, even farther, innocent tiger lilies, tall, lifting their orange bonnets. In the barracks they spoke of "flowers," of "rain": excrement, thick turd-braids, and the slow stinking maroon waterfall that slunk down from the upper bunks, the stink mixed with a bitter fatty floating smoke that greased Rosa's skin. She stood for an instant at the margin of the arena. Sometimes the electricity inside the fence would seem to hum; even Stella said it was only an imagining, but Rosa heard real sounds in the wire: grainy sad voices. The farther she was from the fence, the more clearly the voices crowded at her. The lamenting voices strummed so convincingly, so passionately, it was impossible to suspect them of being phantoms. The voices told her to hold up the shawl, high; the voices told her to shake it, to whip with it, to unfurl it like a flag. Rosa lifted, shook, whipped, unfurled. Far off, very far, Magda leaned across her air-fed belly, reaching out with the rods of her arms. She was high up, elevated, riding someone's shoulder. But the shoulder that carried Magda was not coming toward Rosa and the shawl, it was drifting away, the speck of Magda was moving more and more into the smoky distance. Above the shoulder a helmet glinted. The light tapped the helmet and sparkled it into a goblet. Below the helmet a black body like a domino and a pair of black boots hurled themselves in the direction of the electrified fence. The electric voices began to chatter wildly. "Maamaa, maaamaaa," they all hummed together. How far Magda was from Rosa now, across the whole square, past a dozen barracks, all the way on the other side! She was no bigger than a moth.

All at once Magda was swimming through the air. The whole of Magda traveled through loftiness. She looked like a butterfly touching a silver vine. And the moment Magda's feathered round head and her pencil legs and balloonish belly and zigzag arms splashed against the fence, the steel voices went mad in their growling, urging Rosa to run and run to the spot where Magda had fallen from her flight against the electrified fence; but of course Rosa did not obey them. She only stood, because if she ran they would shoot, and if she tried to pick up the sticks of Magda's body they would shoot, and if she let the wolf's screech ascending now through the ladder of her skeleton break out, they would shoot; so she took Magda's shawl and filled her own mouth with it, stuffed it in and stuffed it in, until she was swallowing up the wolf's screech and tasting the cinnamon and almond depth of Magda's saliva; and Rosa drank Magda's shawl until it dried.

—1989

What are your reactions to and questions about this work? The following questions may help provoke some ideas.

Probing the Work

1. Why is the shawl described as magical? What is its significance for Rosa? For Magda? For Stella?
2. Look closely at the description of the last two paragraphs: What feelings are evoked? How does the author convey these feelings?

Identifying Issues

3. How do the circumstances of this story help determine the intensity of the mother/child relationship? Can you connect this tragedy to any other real-life or historical incidents?

AMY TAN

Two Kinds

Amy Tan (b. 1952) was born in California shortly after her parents immigrated to the United States from China. She started writing as a child and won a writing contest at age 8. As an adult, Tan made her living as a freelance business writer for many years, but turned to fiction in 1985. In 1987 Tan traveled to China for the first time, an experience that contributed to the writing of her best-selling novel, The Joy Luck Club *(1989), from which the following selection is excerpted.*

My mother believed you could be anything you wanted to be in America. You could open a restaurant. You could work for the government and get good retirement. You could buy a house with almost no money down. You could become rich. You could become instantly famous.

"Of course, you can be prodigy, too," my mother told me when I was nine. "You can be best anything. What does Auntie Lindo know? Her daughter, she is only best tricky."

America was where all my mother's hopes lay. She had come to San Francisco in 1949 after losing everything in China: her mother and father, her family home, her first husband, and two daughters, twin baby girls. But she never looked back with regret. Things could get better in so many ways.

We didn't immediately pick the right kind of prodigy. At first my mother thought I could be a Chinese Shirley Temple. We'd watch Shirley's old movies on TV as though they were training films. My mother would poke my arm and say, *"Ni kan.* You watch." And I would see Shirley tapping her feet, or singing a sailor song, or pursing her lips into a very round O while saying "Oh, my goodness."

"Ni kan," my mother said, as Shirley's eyes flooded with tears. "You already know how. Don't need talent for crying!"

Soon after my mother got this idea about Shirley Temple, she took me to the beauty training school in the Mission District and put me in the hands of a student who could barely hold the scissors without shaking. Instead of getting big fat curls, I emerged with an uneven mass of crinkly black fuzz. My mother dragged me off to the bathroom and tried to wet down my hair.

"You look like Negro Chinese," she lamented, as if I had done this on purpose.

The instructor of the beauty training school had to lop off these soggy clumps to make my hair even again. "Peter Pan is very popular these days," the instructor assured my mother. I now had hair the length of a boy's, with curly bangs that hung at a slant two inches above my eyebrows. I liked the haircut, and it made me actually look forward to my future fame.

In fact, in the beginning I was just as excited as my mother, maybe even more so. I pictured this prodigy part of me as many different images, and I tried each one on for size. I was a dainty ballerina girl standing by the curtain, waiting to hear the music that would send me floating on my tiptoes. I was like the Christ child lifted out of the straw manger, crying with holy indignity. I was Cinderella stepping from her pumpkin carriage with sparkly cartoon music filling the air.

In all of my imaginings I was filled with a sense that I would soon become perfect. My mother and father would adore me. I would be beyond reproach. I would never feel the need to sulk, or to clamor for anything.

But sometimes the prodigy in me became impatient. "If you don't hurry up and get me out of here, I'm disappearing for good," it warned. "And then you'll always be nothing."

Every night after dinner my mother and I would sit at the Formica-topped kitchen table. She would present new tests, taking her examples from stories of amazing children that she read in *Ripley's Believe It or Not* or *Good Housekeeping, Reader's Digest,* or any of a dozen other magazines she kept in a pile in our bathroom. My mother got these magazines from people whose houses she cleaned. And since she cleaned many houses each week, we had a great assortment. She would look through them all, searching for stories about remarkable children.

The first night she brought out a story about a three-year-old boy who knew the capitals of all the states and even of most of the European countries. A teacher was quoted as saying that the little boy could also pronounce the names of the foreign cities correctly. "What's the capital of Finland?" my mother asked me, looking at the story.

All I knew was the capital of California, because Sacramento was the name of the street we lived on in Chinatown. "Nairobi!" I guessed, saying the most foreign word I could think of. She checked to see if that might be one way to pronounce *Helsinki* before showing me the answer.

The tests got harder—multiplying numbers in my head, finding the queen of hearts in a deck of cards, trying to stand on my head without using my hands, predicting the daily temperatures in Los Angeles, New York, and London. One night I had to look at a page from the Bible for three minutes and then report everything I could remember. "Now Jehoshaphat had riches and honor in abundance and . . . that's all I remember, Ma," I said.

And after seeing, once again, my mother's disappointed face, something inside me began to die. I hated the tests, the raised hopes and failed expectations. Before going to bed that night I looked in the mirror above the bathroom sink, and when I saw only my face staring back—and understood that it would always be this ordinary face—I began to cry. Such a sad, ugly girl! I made high-pitched noises like a crazed animal, trying to scratch out the face in the mirror.

And then I saw what seemed to be the prodigy side of me—a face I had never seen before. I looked at my reflection, blinking so that I could see more clearly. The girl staring back at me was angry, powerful. She and I were the same. I had new thoughts, willful thoughts—or, rather, thoughts filled with lots of won'ts. I won't let her change me, I promised myself. I won't be what I'm not.

So now when my mother presented her tests, I performed listlessly, my head propped on one arm. I pretended to be bored. And I was. I got so bored that I started counting the bellows of the foghorns out on the bay while my mother drilled me in other areas. The sound was comforting and reminded me of the cow jumping over the moon. And the next day I played a game with myself, seeing if my mother would give up on me before eight bellows. After a while I usually counted only one bellow, maybe two at most. At last she was beginning to give up hope.

Two or three months went by without any mention of my being a prodigy. And then one day my mother was watching the *Ed Sullivan Show* on TV. The TV was old and the sound kept shorting out. Every time my mother got halfway up from the sofa to adjust the set, the sound would come back on and Sullivan would be talking. As soon as she sat down, Sullivan would go silent again. She got up—the TV broke into loud piano music. She sat down—silence. Up and down, back and forth, quiet and loud. It was like a stiff, embraceless dance between her and the TV set. Finally, she stood by the set with her hand on the sound dial.

She seemed entranced by the music, a frenzied little piano piece with a mesmerizing quality, which alternated between quick, playful passages and teasing, lilting ones.

"Ni kan," my mother said, calling me over with hurried hand gestures. "Look here."

I could see why my mother was fascinated by the music. It was being pounded out by a little Chinese girl, about nine years old, with a Peter Pan haircut. The girl had the sauciness of a Shirley Temple. She was proudly modest, like a proper Chinese child. And she also did a fancy sweep of a curtsy, so that the fluffy skirt of her white dress cascaded to the floor like the petals of a large carnation.

In spite of these warning signs, I wasn't worried. Our family had no piano and we couldn't afford to buy one, let alone reams of sheet music and piano lessons. So I could be generous in my comments when my mother badmouthed the little girl on TV.

"Play note right, but doesn't sound good!" my mother complained. "No singing sound."

"What are you picking on her for?" I said carelessly. "She's pretty good. Maybe she's not the best, but she's trying hard." I knew almost immediately that I would be sorry I had said that.

"Just like you," she said. "Not the best. Because you not trying." She gave a little huff as she let go of the sound dial and sat down on the sofa.

The little Chinese girl sat down also, to play an encore of "Anitra's Tanz," by Grieg.[1] I remember the song, because later on I had to learn how to play it.

Three days after watching the *Ed Sullivan Show* my mother told me what my schedule would be for piano lessons and piano practice. She had talked to Mr. Chong, who lived on the first floor of our apartment building. Mr. Chong was a retired piano teacher, and my mother had traded housecleaning services for weekly lessons and a piano for me to practice on every day, two hours a day, from four until six.

When my mother told me this, I felt as though I had been sent to hell. I whined, and then kicked my foot a little when I couldn't stand it anymore.

"Why don't you like me the way I am?" I cried. "I'm *not* a genius! I can't play the piano. And even if I could, I wouldn't go on TV if you paid me a million dollars!"

My mother slapped me. "Who ask you to be genius?" she shouted. "Only

[1]A section from the incidental music that Edvard Grieg (1843–1907) wrote for *Peer Gynt,* a play by Henrik Ibsen.

ask you be your best. For you sake. You think I want you to be genius? Hnnh! What for! Who ask you!"

"So ungrateful," I heard her mutter in Chinese. "If she had as much talent as she has temper, she'd be famous now."

Mr. Chong, whom I secretly nicknamed Old Chong, was very strange, always tapping his fingers to the silent music of an invisible orchestra. He looked ancient in my eyes. He had lost most of the hair on the top of his head, and he wore thick glasses and had eyes that always looked tired. But he must have been younger than I thought, since he lived with his mother and was not yet married.

I met Old Lady Chong once, and that was enough. She had a peculiar smell, like a baby that had done something in its pants, and her fingers felt like a dead person's, like an old peach I once found in the back of the refrigerator; its skin just slid off the flesh when I picked it up.

I soon found out why Old Chong had retired from teaching piano. He was deaf. "Like Beethoven!" he shouted to me. "We're both listening only in our head!" And he would start to conduct his frantic silent sonatas.

Our lessons went like this. He would open the book and point to different things, explaining their purpose: "Key! Treble! Bass! No sharps or flats! So this is C major! Listen now and play after me!"

And then he would play the C scale a few times, a simple cord, and then, as if inspired by an old unreachable itch, he would gradually add more notes and running trills and a pounding bass until the music was really something quite grand.

I would play after him, the simple scale, the simple chord, and then just play some nonsense that sounded like a cat running up and down on top of garbage cans. Old Chong would smile and applaud and say, "Very good! But now you must learn to keep time!"

So that's how I discovered that Old Chong's eyes were too slow to keep up with the wrong notes I was playing. He went through the motions in half time. To help me keep rhythm, he stood behind me and pushed down on my right shoulder for every beat. He balanced pennies on top of my wrists so that I would keep them still as I slowly played scales and arpeggios. He had me curve my hand around an apple and keep that shape when playing chords. He marched stiffly to show me how to make each finger dance up and down, staccato, like an obedient little soldier.

He taught me all these things, and that was how I also learned I could be lazy and get away with mistakes, lots of mistakes. If I hit the wrong notes because I hadn't practiced enough, I never corrected myself. I just kept playing in rhythm. And Old Chong kept conducting his own private reverie.

So maybe I never really gave myself a fair chance. I did pick up the basics pretty quickly, and I might have become a good pianist at that young age. But I was so determined not to try, not to be anybody different, and I learned to play only the most ear-splitting preludes, the most discordant hymns.

Over the next year I practiced like this, dutifully in my own way. And then one day I heard my mother and her friend Lindo Jong both talking in a loud, bragging tone of voice so that others could hear. It was after church, and I was leaning against a brick wall, wearing a dress with stiff white petticoats. Auntie Lindo's daughter, Waverly, who was my age, was standing farther down the wall, about five feet away. We had grown up together and shared all the closeness of two sisters, squabbling over crayons and dolls. In other words, for the most part, we hated each other. I thought she was snotty. Waverly Jong had gained a certain amount of fame as "Chinatown's Littlest Chinese Chess Champion."

"She bring home too many trophy," Auntie Lindo lamented that Sunday. "All day she play chess. All day I have no time do nothing but dust off her winnings." She threw a scolding look at Waverly, who pretended not to see her.

"You lucky you don't have this problem," Auntie Lindo said with a sigh to my mother.

And my mother squared her shoulders and bragged: "Our problem worser than yours. If we ask Jing-mei wash dish, she hear nothing but music. It's like you can't stop this natural talent."

And right then I was determined to put a stop to her foolish pride.

A few weeks later Old Chong and my mother conspired to have me play in a talent show that was to be held in the church hall. But then my parents had saved up enough to buy me a secondhand piano, a black Wurlitzer spinet with a scarred bench. It was the showpiece of our living room.

For the talent show I was to play a piece called "Pleading Child," from Schumann's *Scenes From Childhood*.[2] It was a simple, moody piece that sounded more difficult than it was. I was supposed to memorize the whole thing. But I dawdled over it, playing a few bars and then cheating, looking up to see what notes followed. I never really listened to what I was playing. I daydreamed about being somewhere else, about being someone else.

The part I liked to practice best was the fancy curtsy: right foot out, touch the rose on the carpet with a pointed foot, sweep to the side, bend left leg, look up, and smile.

My parents invited all the couples from their social club to witness my debut. Auntie Lindo and Uncle Tin were there. Waverly and her two older brothers had also come. The first two rows were filled with children either younger or older than I was. The littlest ones got to go first. They recited simple nursery rhymes, squawked out tunes on miniature violins, and twirled hula hoops in pink ballet tutus, and when they bowed or curtsied, the audience would sigh in unison, *"Awww,"* and then clap enthusiastically.

When my turn came, I was very confident. I remember my childish excitement. It was as if I knew, without a doubt, that the prodigy side of me re-

[2]Piano work by Robert Schumann (1810–1856) with twelve titled sections and an epilogue.

ally did exist. I had no fear whatsoever, no nervousness. I remember thinking, This is it! This is it! I looked out over the audience, at my mother's blank face, my father's yawn, Auntie Lindo's stiff-lipped smile, Waverly's sulky expression. I had on a white dress, layered with sheets of lace, and a pink bow in my Peter Pan haircut. As I sat down, I envisioned people jumping to their feet and Ed Sullivan rushing up to introduce me to everyone on TV.

And I started to play. Everything was so beautiful. I was so caught up in how lovely I looked that I wasn't worried about how I would sound. So I was surprised when I hit the first wrong note. And then I hit another, and another. A chill started at the top of my head and began to trickle down. Yet I couldn't stop playing, as though my hands were bewitched. I kept thinking my fingers would adjust themselves back, like a train switching to the right track. I played this strange jumble through to the end, the sour notes staying with me all the way.

When I stood up, I discovered my legs were shaking. Maybe I had just been nervous, and the audience, like Old Chong, had seen me go through the right motions and had not heard anything wrong at all. I swept my right foot out, went down on my knee, looked up, and smiled. The room was quiet, except for Old Chong, who was beaming and shouting, "Bravo! Bravo! Well done!" But then I saw my mother's face, her stricken face. The audience clapped weakly, and as I walked back to my chair, with my whole face quivering as I tried not to cry, I heard a little boy whisper loudly to his mother, "That was awful," and the mother whispered, "Well, she certainly tried."

And now I realized how many people were in the audience—the whole world, it seemed. I was aware of eyes burning into my back. I felt the shame of my mother and father as they sat stiffly through the rest of the show.

We could have escaped during intermission. Pride and some strange sense of honor must have anchored my parents to their chairs. And so we watched it all: The eighteen-year-old boy with a fake moustache who did a magic show and juggled flaming hoops while riding a unicycle. The breasted girl with white makeup who sang an aria from *Madame Butterfly* and got an honorable mention. And the eleven-year-old boy who won first prize playing a tricky violin song that sounded like a busy bee.

After the show the Hsus, the Jongs, and the St. Clairs, from the Joy Luck Club, came up to my mother and father.

"Lots of talented kids," Auntie Lindo said vaguely, smiling broadly.

"That was somethin' else," my father said, and I wondered if he was referring to me in a humorous way, or whether he even remembered what I had done.

Waverly looked at me and shrugged her shoulders. "You aren't a genius like me," she said matter-of-factly. And if I hadn't felt so bad, I would have pulled her braids and punched her stomach.

But my mother's expression was what devastated me: a quiet, blank look that said she had lost everything. I felt the same way, and everybody seemed now to be coming up, like gawkers at the scene of an accident, to see what parts were actually missing.

When we got on the bus to go home, my father was humming the busy-bee tune and my mother was silent. I kept thinking she wanted to wait until we got home before shouting at me. But when my father unlocked the door to our apartment, my mother walked in and went straight to the back, into the bedroom. No accusations. No blame. And in a way, I felt disappointed. I had been waiting for her to start shouting, so that I could shout back and cry and blame her for all my misery.

I had assumed that my talent-show fiasco meant that I would never have to play the piano again. But two days later, after school, my mother came out of the kitchen and saw me watching TV.

"Four clock," she reminded me, as if it were any other day. I was stunned, as though she were asking me to go through the talent-show torture again. I planted myself more squarely in front of the TV.

"Turn off TV," she called from the kitchen five minutes later.

I didn't budge. And then I decided. I didn't have to do what my mother said anymore. I wasn't her slave. This wasn't China. I had listened to her before, and look what happened. She was the stupid one.

She came out of the kitchen and stood in the arched entryway of the living room. "Four clock," she said once again, louder.

"I'm not going to play anymore," I said nonchalantly. "Why should I? I'm not a genius."

She stood in front of the TV. I saw that her chest was heaving up and down in an angry way.

"No!" I said, and I now felt stronger, as if my true self had finally emerged. So this was what had been inside me all along.

"No! I won't!" I screamed.

She snapped off the TV, yanked me by the arm and pulled me off the floor. She was frighteningly strong, half pulling, half carrying me toward the piano as I kicked the throw rugs under my feet. She lifted me up and onto the hard bench. I was sobbing by now, looking at her bitterly. Her chest was heaving even more and her mouth was open, smiling crazily as if she were pleased that I was crying.

"You want me to be someone that I'm not!" I sobbed. "I'll never be the kind of daughter you want me to be!"

"Only two kinds of daughters," she shouted in Chinese. "Those who are obedient and those who follow their own mind! Only one kind of daughter can live in this house. Obedient daughter!"

"Then I wish I weren't your daughter. I wish you weren't my mother," I shouted. As I said these things I got scared. It felt like worms and toads and slimy things crawling out of my chest, but it also felt good, that this awful side of me had surfaced, at last.

"Too late change this," my mother said shrilly.

And I could sense her anger rising to its breaking point. I wanted to see it spill over. And that's when I remembered the babies she had lost in China, the ones we never talked about. "Then I wish I'd never been born!" I shouted. "I wish I were dead! Like them."

It was as if I had said magic words. Alakazam!—her face went blank, her mouth closed, her arms went slack, and she backed out of the room, stunned, as if she were blowing away like a small brown leaf, thin, brittle, lifeless.

It was not the only disappointment my mother felt in me. In the years that followed, I failed her many times, each time asserting my will, my right to fall short of expectations. I didn't get straight *A*s. I didn't become class president. I didn't get into Stanford. I dropped out of college.

Unlike my mother, I did not believe I could be anything I wanted to be. I could only be me.

And for all those years we never talked about the disaster at the recital or my terrible declarations afterward at the piano bench. Neither of us talked about it again, as if it were a betrayal that was now unspeakable. So I never found a way to ask her why she had hoped for something so large that failure was inevitable.

And even worse, I never asked her about what frightened me the most: Why had she given up hope? For after our struggle at the piano, she never mentioned my playing again. The lessons stopped. The lid to the piano was closed, shutting out the dust, my misery, and her dreams.

So she surprised me. A few years ago she offered to give me the piano, for my thirtieth birthday. I had not played in all those years. I saw the offer as a sign of forgiveness, a tremendous burden removed.

"Are you sure?" I asked shyly. "I mean, won't you and Dad miss it?"

"No, this your piano," she said firmly. "Always your piano. You only one can play."

"Well, I probably can't play anymore," I said. "It's been years."

"You pick up fast," my mother said, as if she knew this was certain. "You have natural talent. You could be genius if you want to."

"No, I couldn't."

"You just not trying," my mother said. And she was neither angry nor sad. She said it as if announcing a fact that could never be disproved. "Take it," she said.

But I didn't at first. It was enough that she had offered it to me. And after that, every time I saw it in my parents' living room, standing in front of the bay window, it made me feel proud, as if it were a shiny trophy that I had won back.

Last week I sent a tuner over to my parents' apartment and had the piano reconditioned, for purely sentimental reasons. My mother had died a few months before, and I had been getting things in order for my father, a little bit at a time. I put the jewelry in special silk pouches. The sweaters she had knitted in yellow, pink, bright orange—all the colors I hated—I put in moth-proof boxes. I found some old Chinese silk dresses, the kind with little slits up the sides. I rubbed the old silk against my skin, and then wrapped them in tissue and decided to take them home with me.

After I had the piano tuned, I opened the lid and touched the keys. It sounded even richer than I remembered. Really, it was a very good piano. Inside the bench were the same exercise notes with handwritten scales, the same secondhand music books with their covers held together with yellow tape.

I opened up the Schumann book to the dark little piece I had played at the recital. It was on the left-hand page, "Pleading Child." It looked more difficult than I remembered. I played a few bars, surprised at how easily the notes came back to me.

And for the first time, or so it seemed, I noticed the piece on the right-hand side. It was called "Perfectly Contented." I tried to play this one as well. It had a lighter melody but with the same flowing rhythm and turned out to be quite easy. "Pleading Child" was shorter but slower; "Perfectly Contented" was longer but faster. And after I had played them both a few times, I realized they were two halves of the same song.

—1989

What are your reactions to and questions about this work? The following questions may help provoke some ideas.

Probing the Work

1. Describe the conflicts between mother and daughter: to what extent are they resolved? What discoveries are made by each?

Identifying Issues

2. To what extent do you think a mother should push a child to excel? What are the consequences of *not* "pushing"?

DAVID LEAVITT

Gravity

David Leavitt (b. 1961) was born in Palo Alto, California, and was educated at Yale. He began his writing career at a young age, publishing his first collection of short stories at age 23 and two novels by age 28. His work often focuses on homosexual men and the tensions created within the family structure. The following story is from the collection A Place I've Never Been *(1990).*

Theo had a choice between a drug that would save his sight and a drug that would keep him alive, so he chose not to go blind. He stopped the pills and started the injections—these required the implantation of an unpleasant and painful catheter just above his heart—and within a few days the clouds in his eyes started to clear up; he could see again. He remembered going into New York City to a show with his mother, when he was twelve and didn't want to admit he needed glasses. "Can you read that?" she'd shouted, pointing to a Broadway marquee, and when he'd squinted, making out only one or two letters, she'd taken off her own glasses—harlequins with tiny rhinestones in the corners—and shoved them onto his face. The world came into focus, and he gasped, astonished at the precision around the edges of things, the legibility, the hard, sharp, colorful landscape. Sylvia had to squint through *Fiddler on the Roof* that day, but for Theo, his face masked by his mother's huge glasses, everything was as bright and vivid as a comic book. Even though people stared at him, and muttered things, Sylvia didn't care; he could *see*.

Because he was dying again, Theo moved back to his mother's house in New Jersey. The DHPG injections she took in stride—she'd seen her own mother through *her* dying, after all. Four times a day, with the equanimity of a nurse, she cleaned out the plastic tube implanted in his chest, inserted a sterilized hypodermic and slowly dripped the bag of sight-giving liquid into his veins. They endured this procedure silently, Sylvia sitting on the side of the hospital bed she'd rented for the duration of Theo's stay—his life, he sometimes thought—watching reruns of *I Love Lucy* or the news, while he tried not to think about the hard piece of pipe stuck into him, even though it was a constant reminder of how wide and unswimmable the gulf was becoming between him and the ever-receding shoreline of the well. And Sylvia was intricately cheerful. Each day she urged him to go out with her somewhere—to the library, or the little museum with the dinosaur replicas he'd been fond of as a child—and when his thinness and the cane drew stares, she'd maneuver him around the people who were staring, determined to shield him from whatever they might say or do. It had been the same that afternoon so many years ago, when she'd pushed him through a lobbyful of curious and laughing faces, determined that nothing should interfere with the spectacle of his seeing. What a pair they must have made, a boy in ugly glasses and a mother daring the world to say a word about it!

This warm, breezy afternoon in May they were shopping for revenge. "Your cousin Howard's engagement party is next month," Sylvia explained in the car. "A very nice girl from Livingston. I met her a few weeks ago, and really, she's a superior person."

"I'm glad," Theo said. "Congratulate Howie for me."

"Do you think you'll be up to going to the party?"

"I'm not sure. Would it be okay for me just to give him a gift?"

"You already have. A lovely silver tray, if I say so myself. The thank-you note's in the living room."

"Mom," Theo said, "why do you always have to—"

Sylvia honked her horn at a truck making an illegal left turn. "Better they should get something than no present at all, is what I say," she said. "But now, the problem is, *I* have to give Howie something, to be from me, and it better be good. It better be very, very good."

"Why?"

"Don't you remember that cheap little nothing Bibi gave you for your graduation? It was disgusting."

"I can't remember what she gave me."

"Of course you can't. It was a tacky pen-and-pencil set. Not even a real leather box. So naturally, it stands to reason that I have to get something truly spectacular for Howard's engagement. Something that will make Bibi blanch. Anyway, I think I've found just the thing, but I need your advice."

"Advice? Well, when my old roommate Nick got married, I gave him a garlic press. It cost five dollars and reflected exactly how much I felt, at that moment, our friendship was worth."

Sylvia laughed. "Clever. But my idea is much more brilliant, because it makes it possible for me to get back at Bibi *and* give Howard the nice gift he and his girl deserve." She smiled, clearly pleased with herself. "Ah, you live and learn."

"You live," Theo said.

Sylvia blinked. "Well, look, here we are." She pulled the car into a handicapped-parking place on Morris Avenue and got out to help Theo, but he was already hoisting himself up out of his seat, using the door handle for leverage. "I can manage myself," he said with some irritation. Sylvia stepped back.

"Clearly one advantage to all this for you," Theo said, balancing on his cane, "is that it's suddenly so much easier to get a parking place."

"Oh Theo, please," Sylvia said. "Look, here's where we're going."

She leaned him into a gift shop filled with porcelain statuettes of Snow White and all seven of the dwarves, music boxes which, when you opened them, played "The Shadow of Your Smile," complicated-smelling potpourris in purple wallpapered boxes, and stuffed snakes you were supposed to push up against drafty windows and doors.

"Mrs. Greenman," said an expansive, gray-haired man in a cream-colored cardigan sweater. "Look who's here, Archie, it's Mrs. Greenman."

Another man, this one thinner and balding, but dressed in an identical cardigan, peered out from the back of the shop. "Hello there!" he said, smiling. He looked at Theo, and his expression changed.

"Mr. Sherman, Mr. Baker. This is my son, Theo."

"Hello," Mr. Sherman and Mr. Baker said. They didn't offer to shake hands.

"Are you here for that item we discussed last week?" Mr. Sherman asked.

"Yes," Sylvia said. "I want advice from my son here." She walked over to a large ridged crystal bowl, a very fifties sort of bowl, stalwart and square-jawed. "What do you think? Beautiful, isn't it?"

"Mom, to tell the truth, I think it's kind of ugly."

"Four hundred and twenty-five dollars," Sylvia said admiringly. "You have to feel it."

Then she picked up the big bowl and tossed it to Theo, like a football.

The gentlemen in the cardigan sweaters gasped and did not exhale. When Theo caught it, it sank his hands. His cane rattled as it hit the floor.

"That's heavy," Sylvia said, observing with satisfaction how the bowl had weighted Theo's arms down. "And where crystal is concerned, heavy is impressive."

She took the bowl back from him and carried it to the counter. Mr. Sherman was mopping his brow. Theo looked at the floor, still surprised not to see shards of glass around his feet.

Since no one else seemed to be volunteering, he bent over and picked up the cane.

"Four hundred and fifty-nine, with tax," Mr. Sherman said, his voice still a bit shaky, and a look of relish came over Sylvia's face as she pulled out her checkbook to pay. Behind the counter, Theo could see Mr. Baker put his hand on his forehead and cast his eyes to the ceiling.

It seemed Sylvia had been looking a long time for something like this, something heavy enough to leave an impression, yet so fragile it could make you sorry.

They headed back out to the car.

"Where can we go now?" Sylvia asked, as she got in. "There must be someplace else to go."

"Home," Theo said. "It's almost time for my medicine."

"Really? Oh. All right." She pulled on her seat belt, inserted the car key in the ignition and sat there.

For just a moment, but perceptibly, her face broke. She squeezed her eyes shut so tight the blue shadow on the lids cracked.

Almost as quickly she was back to normal again, and they were driving. "It's getting hotter," Sylvia said. "Shall I put on the air?"

"Sure," Theo said. He was thinking about the bowl, or more specifically, about how surprising its weight had been, pulling his hands down. For a while now he'd been worried about his mother, worried about what damage his illness might secretly be doing to her that of course she would never admit. On the surface things seemed all right. She still broiled herself a skinned chicken breast for dinner every night, still swam a mile and a half a day, still kept used teabags wrapped in foil in the refrigerator. Yet she had also, at about three o'clock one morning, woken him up to tell him she was going to the twenty-four-hour supermarket, and was there anything he wanted. Then there was the gift shop: She had literally pitched that bowl toward him, pitched it like a ball, and as that great gleam of flight and potential regret came sailing his direction, it had occurred to him that she was trusting his two feeble hands, out of the whole world, to keep it from shattering. What was she trying to test? Was it his newly regained vision? Was it the assurance that he was there, alive, that he hadn't yet slipped past all her caring, a little lost boy in rhinestone-studded glasses? There are certain things you've already done before you even think how to do them—a child pulled from in front of a car, for instance, or the bowl, which Theo was holding before he could even begin to calculate its brief trajectory. It had pulled his arms down, and from that apish posture he'd looked at his mother, who smiled broadly, as if, in the war between heaviness and shattering, he'd just helped her win some small but sustaining victory.

—1990

What are your reactions to and questions about this work? The following questions may help provoke some ideas.

Probing the Work

1. Complete the following statement by Theo: "Mom, why do you always have to—" (p. 396). Explain what Theo's incomplete complaint, along with your completion of it, illustrates about his relationship with his mother.
2. Why does Sylvia throw the crystal bowl to Theo? What does this act seem to represent, in the context of the whole story?

Identifying Issues

3. How is Sylvia dealing with her son's fatal illness? How does Leavitt's depiction compare to the reactions of people you have known in similar circumstances, or to your conception of how it should be handled?

MARGARET ATWOOD

Today

Margaret Atwood (b. 1939) was born in Ottawa, Ontario, and grew up in northern Ontario and the Quebec bush. She was educated at the University of Toronto and Radcliffe College. Among her many works are the poetry collections The Circle Game *(1966) and* True Stories *(1981); the novels* The Edible Woman *(1969),* The Handmaid's Tale *(1985),* Cat's Eye *(1988), and* The Robber Bride *(1994); and the short-story collections* Dancing Girls and Other Stories *(1978) and* Bluebeard's Egg *(1983).*

Today the lawn holds
my daughter like a hostage
where she walks, not as high
as the wrecked picnic table,
through the scant grass, burdock leaves

made ragged by the mower,
tripping, stopping
to pick up and put down.

(Watch the slope, hard clay with bladed
stones, posing
innocuous as daisies:
it leads down to the pond,
where the ducks beckon, eleven
of them, they are saying:
    feathers.   feathers.)

The lure of eleven birds
on water, the glitter
and true shine, how can I tell her
that white, that bluegreen gold
is treachery?

Each of these rescues
costs me something,
a loss, a dulling
of this bluegold eye.

Later she will learn
about edges. Or better, find
by luck or a longer journey
the shadow of that liquid
gold place, which can be
so single and clear for her
only now, when it means danger
only to me.

—1991

What are your reactions to and questions about this work? The following questions may help provoke some ideas.

Probing the Work

1. What are the contrasts expressed between the mother's thoughts (as she watches her daughter) and her actions? Explain in your own words the stanza that begins, "Each of these rescues / costs me something."

Identifying Issues

2. How does this mother feel about sheltering and protecting her daughter? What is your attitude toward a child's need to be "held back"? Do boys need less protecting than girls? Explain why or why not.

MARSHA NORMAN

'night, Mother

Marsha Norman (b. 1947) was born in Kentucky and educated at Agnes Scott College in Georgia. A "better than average amateur musician" (in her own words), she settled on playwriting as a career instead of one as a composer. Included among Norman's other plays are Getting Out *(1977),* Circus Valentine *(1979), and* Traveler in the Dark *(1984).*

Characters

JESSIE CATES, *in her late thirties or early forties, is pale and vaguely unsteady physically. It is only in the last year that Jessie has gained control of her mind and body, and tonight she is determined to hold on to that control. She wears pants and a long black sweater with deep pockets, which contain scraps of paper, and there may be a pencil behind her ear or a pen clipped to one of the pockets of the sweater.*

As a rule, Jessie doesn't feel much like talking. Other people have rarely found her quirky sense of humor amusing. She has a peaceful energy on this night, a sense of purpose, but is clearly aware of the time passing moment by moment. Oddly enough, Jessie has never been as communicative or as enjoyable as she is on this evening, but we must know she has not always been this way. There is a familiarity between these two women that comes from having lived together for a long time. There is a shorthand to the talk and a sense of routine comfort in the way they relate to each other physically. Naturally, there are also routine aggravations.

THELMA CATES, "MAMA," *is Jessie's mother, in her late fifties or early sixties. She has begun to feel her age and so takes it easy when she can, or when it serves her purpose to let someone help her. But she speaks quickly and enjoys talking. She believes that things* are *what she says they are. Her sturdiness is more a mental quality than a physical one, finally. She is chatty and nosy, and this is* her *house.*

The play takes place in a relatively new house built way out on a country road, with a living room and connecting kitchen, and a center hall that leads off to the bedrooms. A pull cord in the hall ceiling releases a ladder which leads to the attic. One of these bedrooms opens directly onto the hall, and its entry should be visible to everyone in the audience. It should be, in fact, the focal point of the entire set, and the lighting should make it disappear completely at times and draw the entire set into it at others. It is a point of both threat and promise. It is an ordinary door that opens onto absolute nothingness. That door is the point of all the action, and the utmost care should be given to its design and construction.

The living room is cluttered with magazines and needlework catalogues, ashtrays and candy dishes. Examples of Mama's *needlework are everywhere—pillows, afghans, and quilts, doilies and rugs, and they are quite nice examples. The house is more comfortable than messy, but there is quite a lot to keep in place here. It is more personal than charming. It is not quaint. Under no circumstances should the set and its dressing make a judgment about the intelligence or taste of* Jessie *and* Mama. *It should simply indicate that they are very specific real people who happen to live in a particular part of the country. Heavy accents, which would further distance the audience from* Jessie *and* Mama, *are also wrong.*

The time is the present, with the action beginning about 8:15. Clocks onstage in the kitchen and on a table in the living room should run throughout the performance and be visible to the audience.

There will be no intermission.

Mama *stretches to reach the cupcakes in a cabinet in the kitchen. She can't see them, but she can feel around for them, and she's eager to have one, so she's working pretty hard at it. This may be the most serious exercise* Mama *ever gets. She finds a cupcake, the coconut-covered, raspberry-and-marshmallow-filled kind known as a snowball, but sees that there's one missing from the package. She calls to* Jessie, *who is apparently somewhere else in the house.*

Mama *(Unwrapping the cupcake):* Jessie, it's the last snowball, sugar. Put it on the list, O.K.? And we're out of Hershey bars, and where's that peanut brittle? I think maybe Dawson's been in it again. I ought to put a big mirror on the refrigerator door. That'll keep him out of my treats, won't it? You hear me, honey? *(Then more to herself)* I hate it when the coconut falls off. Why does the coconut fall off?

*(*Jessie *enters from her bedroom, carrying a stack of newspapers)*

Jessie: We got any old towels?

Mama: There you are!

Jessie *(Holding a towel that was on the stack of newspapers):* Towels you don't want anymore. *(Picking up* Mama*'s snowball wrapper)* How about this swimming towel Loretta gave us? Beach towel, that's the name of it. You want it? *(*Mama *shakes her head no)*

Mama: What have you been doing in there?

Jessie: And a big piece of plastic like a rubber sheet or something. Garbage bags would do if there's enough.

Mama: Don't go making a big mess, Jessie. It's eight o'clock already.

Jessie: Maybe an old blanket or towels we got in a soap box sometime?

Mama: I said don't make a mess. Your hair is black enough, hon.

Jessie *(Continuing to search the kitchen cabinets, finding two or three more tow-*

els to add to her stack): It's not for my hair, Mama. What about some old pillows anywhere, or a foam cushion out of a yard chair would be real good.

MAMA: You haven't forgot what night it is, have you? *(Holding up her fingernails)* They're all chipped, see? I've been waiting all week, Jess. It's Saturday night, sugar.

JESSIE: I know. I got it on the schedule.

MAMA *(Crossing to the living room):* You want me to wash 'em now or are you making your mess first? *(Looking at the snowball)* We're out of these. Did I say that already?

JESSIE: There's more coming tomorrow. I ordered you a whole case.

MAMA *(Checking the TV Guide):* A whole case will go stale, Jessie.

JESSIE: They can go in the freezer till you're ready for them. Where's Daddy's gun?

MAMA: In the attic.

JESSIE: Where in the attic? I looked your whole nap and couldn't find it anywhere.

MAMA: One of his shoeboxes, I think.

JESSIE: Full of shoes. I looked already.

MAMA: Well, you didn't look good enough, then. There's that box from the ones he wore to the hospital. When he died, they told me I could have them back, but I never did like those shoes.

JESSIE *(Pulling them out of her pocket):* I found the bullets. They were in an old milk can.

MAMA *(As* JESSIE *starts for the hall):* Dawson took the shotgun, didn't he? Hand me that basket, hon.

JESSIE *(Getting the basket for her):* Dawson better not've taken that pistol.

MAMA *(Stopping her again):* Now my glasses, please. *(*JESSIE *returns to get the glasses)* I told him to take those rubber boots, too, but he said they were for fishing. I told him to take up fishing.

*(*JESSIE *reaches for the cleaning spray, and cleans* MAMA'S *glasses for her)*

JESSIE: He's just too lazy to climb up there, Mama. Or maybe he's just being smart. That floor's not very steady.

MAMA *(Getting out a piece of knitting):* It's not a floor at all, hon, it's a board now and then. Measure this for me. I need six inches.

JESSIE *(As she measures):* Dawson could probably use some of those clothes up there. Somebody should have them. You ought to call the Salvation Army before the whole thing falls in on you. Six inches exactly.

MAMA: It's plenty safe! As long as you don't go up there.

JESSIE *(Turning to go again):* I'm careful.

MAMA: What do you want the gun for, Jess?

JESSIE *(Not returning this time. Opening the ladder in the hall):* Protection. *(She steadies the ladder as* MAMA *talks)*

MAMA: You take the TV way too serious, hon. I've never seen a criminal in my life. This is way too far to come for what's out here to steal. Never seen a one.

JESSIE *(Taking her first step up):* Except for Ricky.

MAMA: Ricky is mixed up. That's not a crime.

JESSIE: Get your hands washed. I'll be right back. And get 'em real dry. You dry your hands till I get back or it's no go, all right?

MAMA: I thought Dawson told you not to go up those stairs.

JESSIE *(Going up):* He did.

MAMA: I don't like the idea of a gun, Jess.

JESSIE *(Calling down from the attic):* Which shoebox, do you remember?

MAMA: Black.

JESSIE: The box was black?

MAMA: The shoes were black.

JESSIE: That doesn't help much, Mother.

MAMA: I'm not trying to help, sugar. *(No answer)* We don't have anything anybody'd want, Jessie. I mean, I don't even want what we got, Jessie.

JESSIE: Neither do I. Wash your hands. *(*MAMA *gets up and crosses to stand under the ladder)*

MAMA: You come down from there before you have a fit. I can't come up and get you, you know.

JESSIE: I know.

MAMA: We'll just hand it over to them when they come, how's that? Whatever they want, the criminals.

JESSIE: That's a good idea, Mama.

MAMA: Ricky will grow out of this and be a real fine boy, Jess. But I have to tell you, I wouldn't want Ricky to know we had a gun in the house.

JESSIE: Here it is. I found it.

MAMA: It's just something Ricky's going through. Maybe he's in with some bad people. He just needs some time, sugar. He'll get back in school or get a job or one day you'll get a call and he'll say he's sorry for all the trouble he's caused and invite you out for supper someplace dress-up.

JESSIE *(Coming back down the steps):* Don't worry. It's not for him, it's for me.

MAMA: I didn't think you would shoot your own boy, Jessie. I know you've felt like it, well, we've all felt like shooting somebody, but we don't do it. I just don't think we need . . .

JESSIE *(Interrupting):* Your hands aren't washed. Do you want a manicure or not?

MAMA: Yes, I do, but . . .

JESSIE *(Crossing to the chair):* Then wash your hands and don't talk to me any more about Ricky. Those two rings he took were the last valuable things *I* had, so now he's started in on other people, door to door. I hope they put him away sometime. I'd turn him in myself if I knew where he was.

MAMA: You don't mean that.

JESSIE: Every word. Wash your hands and that's that last time I'm telling you.

*(*JESSIE *sits down with the gun and starts cleaning it, pushing the cylinder out, checking to see that the chambers and barrel are empty, then putting some oil on a small patch of cloth and pushing it through the barrel with the push rod that was in the box.* MAMA *goes to the kitchen and washes hands, as instructed, trying not to show her concern about the gun)*

MAMA: I shoulda got you to bring down that milk can. Agnes Fletcher sold hers to somebody with a flea market for forty dollars apiece.

JESSIE: I'll go back and get it in a minute. There's a wagon wheel up there, too. There's even a churn. I'll get it all if you want.

MAMA *(Coming over, taking over now):* What are you doing?

JESSIE: The barrel has to be clean, Mama. Old powder, dust gets in it . . .

MAMA: What for?

JESSIE: I told you.

MAMA *(Reaching for the gun):* And I told you, we don't get criminals out here.

JESSIE *(Quickly pulling it to her):* And I told you . . . *(Then trying to be calm)* The gun is for me.

MAMA: Well, you can have it if you want. When I die, you'll get it all, anyway.

JESSIE: I'm going to kill myself, Mama.

MAMA *(Returning to the sofa):* Very funny. Very funny.

JESSIE: I am.

MAMA: You are not! Don't even say such a thing, Jessie.

JESSIE: How would you know if I didn't say it? You want it to be a surprise? You're lying there in your bed or maybe you're just brushing your teeth and you hear this . . . noise down the hall?

MAMA: Kill yourself.

JESSIE: Shoot myself. In a couple of hours.

MAMA: It must be time for your medicine.

JESSIE: Took it already.

MAMA: What's the matter with you?

JESSIE: Not a thing. Feel fine.

MAMA: You feel fine. You're just going to kill yourself.

JESSIE: Waited until I felt good enough, in fact.

MAMA: Don't make jokes, Jessie. I'm too old for jokes.

JESSIE: It's not a joke, Mama.

*(*MAMA *watches for a moment in silence)*

MAMA: That gun's no good, you know. He broke it right before he died. He dropped it in the mud one day.

JESSIE: Seems O.K. *(She spins the chamber, cocks the pistol, and pulls the trigger. The gun is not yet loaded, so all we hear is the click, but it will definitely work. It's also obvious that* JESSIE *knows her way around a gun.* MAMA *cannot speak)* I had Cecil's all ready in there, just in case I couldn't find this one, but I'd rather use Daddy's.

MAMA: Those bullets are at least fifteen years old.

JESSIE *(Pulling out another box):* These are from last week.

MAMA: Where did you get those?

JESSIE: Feed store Dawson told me about.

MAMA: Dawson!

JESSIE: I told him I was worried about prowlers. He said he thought it was a good idea. He told me what kind to ask for.

MAMA: If he had any idea . . .

JESSIE: He took it as a compliment. He thought I might be taking an interest in things. He got through telling me all about the bullets and then he said we ought to talk like this more often.

MAMA: And where was I while this was going on?

JESSIE: On the phone with Agnes. About the milk can, I guess. Anyway, I asked Dawson if he thought they'd send me some bullets and he said he'd just call for me, because he knew they'd send them if he told them to. And he was absolutely right. Here they are.

MAMA: How could he do that?

JESSIE: Just trying to help, Mama.

MAMA: And then I told you where the gun was.

JESSIE *(Smiling, enjoying this joke):* See? Everybody's doing what they can.

MAMA: You told me it was for protection!

JESSIE: It *is!* I'm still doing your nails, though. Want to try that new Chinaberry color?

MAMA: Well, I'm calling Dawson right now. We'll just see what he has to say about this little stunt.

JESSIE: Dawson doesn't have any more to do with this.

MAMA: He's your brother.

JESSIE: And that's all.

MAMA *(Stands up, moves toward the phone):* Dawson will put a stop to this. Yes he will. He'll take the gun away.

JESSIE: If you call him, I'll just have to do it before he gets here. Soon as you hang up the phone, I'll just walk in the bedroom and lock the door. Dawson will get here just in time to help you clean up. Go ahead, call him. Then call the police. Then call the funeral home. Then call Loretta and see if *she'll* do your nails.

MAMA: You will not! This is crazy talk, Jessie!

*(*MAMA *goes directly to the telephone and starts to dial, but* JESSIE *is fast, coming up behind her and taking the receiver out of her hand, putting it back down)*

JESSIE *(Firm and quiet):* I said no. This is private. Dawson is not invited.

MAMA: Just me.

JESSIE: I don't want anybody else over here. Just you and me. If Dawson comes over, it'll make me feel stupid for not doing it ten years ago.

MAMA: I think we better call the doctor. Or how about the ambulance. You like that one driver, I know. What's his name, Timmy? Get you somebody to talk to.

JESSIE *(Going back to her chair):* I'm through talking, Mama. You're it. No more.

MAMA: We're just going to sit around like every other night in the world and then you're going to kill yourself? *(*JESSIE *doesn't answer)* You'll miss. *(Again there is no response)* You'll just wind up a vegetable. How would you like that? Shoot your ear off? You know what the doctor said about getting excited. You'll cock the pistol and have a fit.

JESSIE: I think I can kill myself, Mama.

MAMA: You're not going to kill yourself, Jessie. You're not even upset! *(*JESSIE *smiles, or laughs quietly, and* MAMA *tries a different approach)* People don't really kill themselves, Jessie. No, mam, doesn't make sense, unless you're retarded or deranged, and you're as normal as they come, Jessie, for the most part. We're all *afraid* to die.

JESSIE: I'm not, Mama. I'm cold all the time, anyway.

MAMA: That's ridiculous.

JESSIE: It's exactly what I want. It's dark and quiet.

MAMA: So is the back yard, Jessie! Close your eyes. Stuff cotton in your ears. Take a nap! It's quiet in your room. I'll leave the TV off all night.

JESSIE: So quiet I don't know it's quiet. So nobody can get me.

MAMA: You don't know what dead is like. It might not be quiet at all. What if it's like an alarm clock, and you can't wake up so you can't shut it off. Ever.

JESSIE: Dead is everybody and everything I ever knew, gone. Dead is dead quiet.

MAMA: It's a sin. You'll go to hell.

JESSIE: Uh-huh.

MAMA: You will!

JESSIE: Jesus was a suicide, if you ask me.

MAMA: You'll go to hell just for saying that, Jessie!

JESSIE *(With genuine surprise):* I didn't know I thought that.

MAMA: Jessie!

*(*JESSIE *doesn't answer. She puts the now-loaded gun back in the box and crosses to the kitchen. But* MAMA *is afraid she's headed for the bedroom)*

MAMA *(In a panic):* You can't use my towels! They're my towels. I've had them for a long time. I like my towels.

JESSIE: I asked you if you wanted that swimming towel and you said you didn't.

MAMA: And you can't use your father's gun, either. It's mine now, too. And you can't do it in my house.

JESSIE: Oh, come on.

MAMA: No. You can't do it. I won't let you. The house is in my name.

JESSIE: I have to go in the bedroom and lock the door behind me so they won't arrest you for killing me. They'll probably test your hands for gunpowder, anyway, but you'll pass.

MAMA: Not in my house!

JESSIE: If I'd known you were going to act like this, I wouldn't have told you.

MAMA: How am I supposed to act? Tell you to go ahead? O.K. by me, sugar? Might try it myself. What took you so long?

JESSIE: There's just no point in fighting me over it, that's all. Want some coffee?

MAMA: Your birthday's coming up, Jessie. Don't you want to know what we got you?

JESSIE: You got me dusting powder, Loretta got me a new housecoat, pink probably, and Dawson got me new slippers, too small, but they go with the robe, he'll say. *(*MAMA *cannot speak)* Right? *(Apparently* JESSIE *is right)* Be back in a minute.

*(*JESSIE *takes the gun box, puts it on top of the stack of towels and garbage bags, and takes them into her bedroom.* MAMA*, alone for a moment, goes to the phone, picks up the receiver, looks toward the bedroom, starts to dial, and then replaces the receiver in its cradle as* JESSIE *walks back into the room.* JESSIE *wonders, silently. They have lived together for so long there is very rarely any reason for one to ask what the other was about to do)*

MAMA: I started to, but I didn't. I didn't call him.

JESSIE: Good. Thank you.

MAMA *(Starting over, a new approach):* What's this all about, Jessie?

JESSIE: About?

*(*JESSIE *now begins the next task she had "on the schedule," which is refilling all the candy jars, taking the empty papers out of the boxes of chocolates, etc.* MAMA *generally snitches when* JESSIE *does this. Not tonight, though. Nevertheless,* JESSIE *offers)*

MAMA: What did I do?

JESSIE: Nothing. Want a caramel?

MAMA *(Ignoring the candy):* You're mad at me.

JESSIE: Not a bit. I am worried about you, but I'm going to do what I can before I go. We're not just going to sit around tonight. I made a list of things.

MAMA: What things?

JESSIE: How the washer works. Things like that.

MAMA: I know how the washer works. You put the clothes in. You put the soap in. You turn it on. You wait.

JESSIE: You do something else. You don't just wait.

MAMA: Whatever else you find to do, you're still mainly waiting. The waiting's the worst part of it. The waiting's what you pay somebody else to do, if you can.

JESSIE *(Nodding)*: O.K. Where do we keep the soap?

MAMA: I could find it.

JESSIE: See?

MAMA: If you're mad about doing the wash, we can get Loretta to do it.

JESSIE: Oh now, that might be worth staying to see.

MAMA: She'd never in her life, would she?

JESSIE: Nope.

MAMA: What's the matter with her?

JESSIE: She thinks she's better than we are. She's not.

MAMA: Maybe if she didn't wear that yellow all the time.

JESSIE: The washer repair number is on a little card taped to the side of the machine.

MAMA: Loretta doesn't ever have to come over here again. Dawson can just leave her at home when he comes. And we don't ever have to see Dawson either if he bothers you. Does he bother you?

JESSIE: Sure he does. Be sure you clean out the lint tray every time you use the dryer. But don't ever put your house shoes in, it'll melt the soles.

MAMA: What does Dawson do, that bothers you?

JESSIE: He just calls me Jess like he knows who he's talking to. He's always wondering what I do all day. I mean, I wonder that myself, but it's my day, so it's mine to wonder about, not his.

MAMA: Family is just accident, Jessie. It's nothing personal, hon. They don't mean to get on your nerves. They don't even mean to be your family, they just are.

JESSIE: They know too much.

MAMA: About what?

JESSIE: They know things about you, and they learned it before you had a chance to say whether you wanted them to know it or not. They were there when it happened and it don't belong to them, it belongs to you, only they got it. Like my mail-order bra got delivered to their house.

MAMA: By accident!

JESSIE: All the same . . . they opened it. They saw the little rosebuds on it. *(Offering her another candy)* Chewy mint?

MAMA *(Shaking her head no)*: What do they know about you? I'll tell them never to talk about it again. Is it Ricky or Cecil or your fits or your hair is falling out or you drink too much coffee or you never go out of the house or what?

JESSIE: I just don't like their talk. The account at the grocery is in Dawson's name when you call. The number's on a whole list of numbers on the back cover of the phone book.

MAMA: Well! Now we're getting somewhere. They're none of them ever setting foot in this house again.

JESSIE: It's not them, Mother. I wouldn't kill myself just to get away from them.

MAMA: You leave the room when they come over, anyway.

JESSIE: I stay as long as I can. Besides, it's you they come to see.

MAMA: That's because I stay in the room when they come.

JESSIE: It's not them.

MAMA: Then what is it?

JESSIE *(Checking the list on her note pad):* The grocery won't deliver on Saturday anymore. And if you want your order the same day, you have to call before ten. And they won't deliver less than fifteen dollars' worth. What I do is tell them what we need and tell them to add on cigarettes until it gets to fifteen dollars.

MAMA: It's Ricky. You're trying to get through to him.

JESSIE: If I thought I could do that, I would stay.

MAMA: Make him sorry he hurt you, then. That's it, isn't it?

JESSIE: He's hurt me, I've hurt him. We're about even.

MAMA: You'll be telling him killing is O.K. with you, you know. Want him to start killing next? Nothing wrong with it. Mom did it.

JESSIE: Only a matter of time, anyway, Mama. When the call comes, you let Dawson handle it.

MAMA: Honey, nothing says those calls are always going to be some new trouble he's into. You could get one that he's got a job, that he's getting married, or how about he's joined the army, wouldn't that be nice?

JESSIE: If you call the Sweet Tooth before you call the grocery, that Susie will take your fudge next door to the grocery and it'll all come out together. Be sure you talk to Susie, though. She won't let them put it in the bottom of a sack like that one time, remember?

MAMA: Ricky could come over, you know. What if he calls us?

JESSIE: It's not Ricky, Mama.

MAMA: Or anybody could call us, Jessie.

JESSIE: Not on Saturday night, Mama.

MAMA: Then what is it? Are you sick? If your gums are swelling again, we can get you to the dentist in the morning.

JESSIE: No. Can you order your medicine or do you want Dawson to? I've got a note to him. I'll add that to it if you want.

MAMA: Your eyes don't look right. I thought so yesterday.

JESSIE: That was just the ragweed. I'm not sick.

MAMA: Epilepsy is sick, Jessie.

JESSIE: It won't kill me. *(A pause)* If it would, I wouldn't have to.

MAMA: You don't *have* to.

JESSIE: No, I don't. That's what I like about it.

MAMA: Well, I won't let you!

JESSIE: It's not up to you.

MAMA: Jessie!

JESSIE: I want to hang a big sign around my neck, like Daddy's on the barn. GONE FISHING.

MAMA: You don't like it here.

JESSIE *(Smiling):* Exactly.

MAMA: I meant here in my house.

JESSIE: I know you did.

MAMA: You never should have moved back in here with me. If you'd kept your little house or found another place when Cecil left you, you'd have made some new friends at least. Had a life to lead. Had your own things around you. Give Ricky a place to come see you. You never should've come here.

JESSIE: Maybe.

MAMA: But I didn't force you, did I?

JESSIE: If it was a mistake, we made it together. You took me in. I appreciate that.

MAMA: You didn't have any business being by yourself right then, but I can see how you might want a place of your own. A grown woman should . . .

JESSIE: Mama . . . I'm just not having a very good time and I don't have any reason to think it'll get anything but worse. I'm tired. I'm hurt. I'm sad. I feel used.

MAMA: Tired of what?

JESSIE: It all.

MAMA: What does that mean?

JESSIE: I can't say it any better.

MAMA: Well, you'll have to say it better because I'm not letting you alone till you do. What were those other things? Hurt . . . *(Before* JESSIE *can answer)* You had this all ready to say to me, didn't you? Did you write this down? How long have you been thinking about this?

JESSIE: Off and on, ten years. On all the time, since Christmas.

MAMA: What happened at Christmas?

JESSIE: Nothing.

MAMA: So why Christmas?

JESSIE: That's it. On the nose.

(A pause. MAMA *knows exactly what* JESSIE *means. She was there, too, after all)*

JESSIE *(Putting the candy sacks away):* See where all this is? Red hots up front, sour balls and horehound mixed together in this one sack. New packages of toffee and licorice right in back there.

MAMA: Go back to your list. You're hurt by what?

JESSIE *(*MAMA *knows perfectly well):* Mama . . .

MAMA: O.K. Sad about what? There's nothing real sad going on right now. If it was after your divorce or something, that would make sense.

JESSIE *(Looking at her list, then opening the drawer):* Now, this drawer has everything in it that there's no better place for. Extension cords, batteries for the radio, extra lighters, sandpaper, masking tape, Elmer's glue, thumbtacks, that kind of stuff. The mousetraps are under the sink, but you call Dawson if you've got one and let him do it.

MAMA: Sad about what?

JESSIE: The way things are.

MAMA: Not good enough. What things?

JESSIE: Oh, everything from you and me to Red China.

MAMA: I think we can leave the Chinese out of this.

JESSIE *(Crosses back into the living room):* There's extra light bulbs in a box in the hall closet. And we've got a couple of packages of fuses in the fuse box. There's candles and matches in the top of the broom closet, but if the lights go out, just call Dawson and sit tight. But don't open the refrigerator door. Things will stay cool in there as long as you keep the door shut.

MAMA: I asked you a question.

JESSIE: I read the paper. I don't like how things are. And they're not any better out there than they are here.

MAMA: If you're doing this because of the newspapers, I can sure fix that!

JESSIE: There's just more of it on TV.

MAMA *(Kicking the television set):* Take it out, then!

JESSIE: You wouldn't do that.

MAMA: Watch me.

JESSIE: What would you do all day?

MAMA *(Desperately):* Sing. *(*JESSIE *laughs)* I would, too. You want to watch? I'll sing till morning to keep you alive, Jessie, please!

JESSIE: No. *(Then affectionately)* It's a funny idea, though. What do you sing?

MAMA *(Has no idea how to answer this):* We've got a good life here!

JESSIE *(Going back into the kitchen):* I called this morning and canceled the papers, except for Sunday, for your puzzles; you'll still get that one.

MAMA: Let's get another dog, Jessie! You liked a big dog, now, didn't you? That King dog, didn't you?

JESSIE *(Washing her hands):* I did like that King dog, yes.

MAMA: I'm so dumb. He's the one run under the tractor.

JESSIE: That makes him dumb, not you.

MAMA: For bringing it up.

JESSIE: It's O.K. Handi-Wipes and sponges under the sink.

MAMA: We could get a new dog and keep him in the house. Dogs are cheap!

JESSIE *(Getting big pill jars out of the cabinet):* No.

MAMA: Something for you to take care of.

JESSIE: I've had you, Mama.

MAMA *(Frantically starting to fill pill bottles):* You do too much for me. I can fill pill bottles all day, Jessie, and change the shelf paper and wash the floor when I get through. You just watch me. You don't have to do another thing in this house if you don't want to. You don't have to take care of me, Jessie.

JESSIE: I know that. You've just been letting me do it so I'll have something to do, haven't you?

MAMA *(Realizing this was a mistake):* I don't do it as well as you. I just meant if it tires you out or makes you feel used . . .

JESSIE: Mama, I know you used to ride the bus. Riding the bus and it's hot and bumpy and crowded and too noisy and more than anything in the world you want to get off and the only reason in the world you don't get off is it's still fifty blocks from where you're going? Well, I can get off right now if I want to, because even if I ride fifty more years and get off then, it's the same place when I step down to it. Whenever I feel like it, I can get off. As soon as I've had enough, it's my stop. I've had enough.

MAMA: You're feeling sorry for yourself!

JESSIE: The plumber's helper is under the sink, too.

MAMA: You're not having a good time! Whoever promised you a good time? Do you think I've had a good time?

JESSIE: I think you're pretty happy, yeah. You have things you like to do.

MAMA: Like what?

JESSIE: Like crochet.

MAMA: I'll teach you to crochet.

JESSIE: I can't do any of that nice work, Mama.

MAMA: Good time don't come looking for you, Jessie. You could work some puzzles or put in a garden or go to the store. Let's call a taxi and go to the A&P!

JESSIE: I shopped you up for about two weeks already. You're not going to need toilet paper till Thanksgiving.

MAMA *(Interrupting):* You're acting like some little brat, Jessie. You're mad and everybody's boring and you don't have anything to do and you don't like me and you don't like going out and you don't like staying in and you never talk on the phone and you don't watch TV and you're miserable and it's your own sweet fault.

JESSIE: And it's time I did something about it.

MAMA: Not something like killing yourself. Something like . . . buying us all new dishes! I'd like that. Or maybe the doctor would let you get a driver's license now, or I know what let's do right this minute, let's rearrange the furniture.

JESSIE: I'll do that. If you want. I always thought if the TV was somewhere else, you wouldn't get such a glare on it during the day. I'll do whatever you want before I go.

MAMA *(Badly frightened by those words):* You could get a job!

JESSIE: I took that telephone sales job and I didn't even make enough money to pay the phone bill, and I tried to work at the gift shop at the hospital and they said I made people real uncomfortable smiling at them the way I did.

MAMA: You could keep books. You kept your dad's books.

JESSIE: But nobody ever checked them.

MAMA: When he died, they checked them.

JESSIE: And that's when they took the books away from me.

MAMA: That's because without him there wasn't any business, Jessie!

JESSIE *(Putting the pill bottles away):* You know I couldn't work. I can't do anything. I've never been around people my whole life except when I went to the hospital. I could have a seizure any time. What good would a job do? The kind of job I could get would make me feel worse.

MAMA: Jessie!

JESSIE: It's true!

MAMA: It's what you think is true!

JESSIE *(Struck by the clarity of that):* That's right. It's what I think is true.

MAMA *(Hysterically):* But I can't do anything about that!

JESSIE *(Quietly):* No. You can't. *(*MAMA *slumps, if not physically, at least emotionally)* And I can't do anything either, about my life, to change it, make it better, make me feel better about it. Like it better, make it work. But I can stop it. Shut it down, turn it off like the radio when there's nothing on I want to listen to. It's all I really have that belongs to me and I'm going to say what happens to it. And it's going to stop. And I'm going to stop it. So. Let's just have a good time.

MAMA: Have a good time.

JESSIE: We can't go on fussing all night. I mean, I could ask you things I always wanted to know and you could make me some hot chocolate. The old way.

MAMA *(In despair):* It takes cocoa, Jessie.

JESSIE *(Gets it out of the cabinet):* I bought cocoa, Mama. And I'd like to have a caramel apple and do your nails.

MAMA: You didn't eat a bit of supper.

JESSIE: Does that mean I can't have a caramel apple?

MAMA: Of course not. I mean . . . *(Smiling a little)* Of course you can have a caramel apple.

JESSIE: I thought I could.

MAMA: I make the best caramel apples in the world.

JESSIE: I know you do.

MAMA: Or used to. And you don't get cocoa like mine anywhere anymore.

JESSIE: It takes time, I know, but . . .

MAMA: The salt is the trick.

JESSIE: Trouble and everything.

MAMA *(Backing away toward the stove):* It's no trouble. What trouble? You put it in the pan and stir it up. All right. Fine. Caramel apples. Cocoa. O.K.

*(*JESSIE *walks to the counter to retrieve her cigarettes as* MAMA *looks for the right pan. There are brief near-smiles, and maybe* MAMA *clears her throat. We have a truce, for the moment. A genuine but nevertheless uneasy one.* JESSIE*, who has been in constant motion since the beginning, now seems content to sit.*

MAMA *starts looking for a pan to make the cocoa, getting out all the pans in the cabinets in the process. It looks like she's making a mess on purpose so* JESSIE *will have to put them all away again.* MAMA *is buying time, or trying to, and entertaining)*

JESSIE: You talk to Agnes today?

MAMA: She's calling me from a pay phone this week. God only knows why. She has a perfectly good Trimline at home.

JESSIE *(Laughing):* Well, how is she?

MAMA: How is she every day, Jessie? Nuts.

JESSIE: Is she really crazy or just silly?

MAMA: No, she's really crazy. She was probably using the pay phone because she had another little fire problem at home.

JESSIE: Mother . . .

MAMA: I'm serious! Agnes Fletcher's burned down every house she ever lived in. Eight fires, and she's due for a new one any day now.

JESSIE *(Laughing):* No!

MAMA: Wouldn't surprise me a bit.

JESSIE *(Laughing):* Why didn't you tell me this before? Why isn't she locked up somewhere?

MAMA: 'Cause nobody ever got hurt, I guess. Agnes woke everybody up to watch the fires as soon as she set 'em. One time she set out porch chairs and served lemonade.

JESSIE *(Shaking her head):* Real lemonade?

MAMA: The houses they lived in, you knew they were going to fall down anyway, so why wait for it, is all I could ever make out about it. Agnes likes a feeling of accomplishment.

JESSIE: Good for her.

MAMA *(Finding the pan she wants):* Why are you asking about Agnes? One cup or two?

JESSIE: One. She's your friend. No marshmallows.

MAMA *(Getting the milk, etc.):* You have to have marshmallows. That's the old way, Jess. Two or three? Three is better.

JESSIE: Three, then. Her whole house burns up? Her clothes and pillows and everything? I'm not sure I believe this.

MAMA: When she was a girl, Jess, not now. Long time ago. But she's still got it in her, I'm sure of it.

JESSIE: She wouldn't burn her house down now. Where would she go? She can't get Buster to build her a new one, he's dead. How could she burn it up?

MAMA: Be exciting, though if she did. You never know.

JESSIE: You do too know, Mama. She wouldn't do it.

MAMA *(Forced to admit, but reluctant):* I guess not.

JESSIE: What else? Why does she wear all those whistles around her neck?

MAMA: Why does she have a house full of birds?

JESSIE: I didn't know she had a house full of birds!

MAMA: Well, she does. And she says they just follow her home. Well, I know for a fact that she's still paying on the last parrot she bought. You gotta keep your life filled up, she says. She says a lot of stupid things. *(JESSIE laughs, MAMA continues, convinced she's getting somewhere)* It's all that okra she eats. You can't just willy-nilly eat okra two meals a day and expect to get away with it. Made her crazy.

JESSIE: She really eats okra twice a day? Where does she get it in the winter?

MAMA: Well, she eats it a lot. Maybe not two meals but . . .

JESSIE: More than the average person.

MAMA *(Beginning to get irritated)*: I don't know how much okra the average person eats.

JESSIE: Do you know how much okra Agnes eats?

MAMA: No.

JESSIE: How many birds does she have?

MAMA: Two.

JESSIE: Then what are the whistles for?

MAMA: They're not real whistles. Just little plastic ones on a necklace she won playing Bingo, and I only told you about it because I thought I might get a laugh out of you for once even if it wasn't the truth, Jessie. Things don't have to be true to talk about 'em, you know.

JESSIE: Why won't she come over here?

(MAMA is suddenly quiet, but the cocoa and milk are in the pan now, so she lights the stove and starts stirring)

MAMA: Well now, what a good idea. We should've had more cocoa. Cocoa is perfect.

JESSIE: Except you don't like milk.

MAMA *(Another attempt, but not as energetic)*: I hate milk. Coats your throat as bad as okra. Something just downright disgusting about it.

JESSIE: It's because of me, isn't it?

MAMA: No, Jess.

JESSIE: Yes, Mama.

MAMA: O.K. Yes, then, but she's crazy. She's as crazy as they come. She's a lunatic.

JESSIE: What is it exactly? Did I say something, sometime? Or did she see me have a fit and's afraid I might have another one if she came over, or what?

MAMA: I guess.

JESSIE: You guess what? What's she ever said? She must've given you some reason.

MAMA: Your hands are cold.

JESSIE: What difference does that make?

MAMA: "Like a corpse," she says, "and I'm gonna be one soon enough as it is."

JESSIE: That's crazy.

MAMA: That's Agnes. "Jessie's shook the hand of death and I can't take the chance it's catching, Thelma, so I ain't comin' over, and you can understand or not, but I ain't comin'. I'll come up the driveway, but that's as far as I go."

JESSIE *(Laughing, relieved):* I thought she didn't like me! She's scared of me! How about that! Scared of me.

MAMA: I could make her come over here, Jessie. I could call her up right now and she could bring the birds and come visit. I didn't know you ever thought about her at all. I'll tell her she just has to come and she'll come, all right. She owes me one.

JESSIE: No, that's all right. I just wondered about it. When I'm in the hospital, does she come over here?

MAMA: Her kitchen is just a tiny thing. When she comes over here, she feels like . . . *(Toning it down a little)* Well, we all like a change of scene, don't we.

JESSIE *(Playing along):* Sure we do. Plus there's no birds diving around.

MAMA: I hate those birds. She says I don't understand them. What's there to understand about birds?

JESSIE: Why Agnes likes them, for one thing. Why they stay with her when they could be outside with the other birds. What their singing means. How they fly. What they think Agnes is.

MAMA: Why do you have to know so much about things, Jessie? There's just not that much *to* things that I could ever see.

JESSIE: That you could ever *tell,* you mean. You didn't have to lie to me about Agnes.

MAMA: I didn't lie. You never asked before!

JESSIE: You lied about setting fire to all those houses and about how many birds she has and how much okra she eats and why she won't come over here. If I have to keep dragging the truth out of you, this is going to take all night.

MAMA: That's fine with me. I'm not a bit sleepy.

JESSIE: Mama . . .

MAMA: All right. Ask me whatever you want. Here.

(They come to an awkward stop, as the cocoa is ready and MAMA *pours it into the cups* JESSIE *has set on the table)*

JESSIE *(As* MAMA *takes her first sip):* Did you love Daddy?

MAMA: No.

JESSIE *(Pleased that* MAMA *understands the rules better now):* I didn't think so. Were you really fifteen when you married him?

MAMA: The way he told it? I'm sitting in the mud, he comes along, drags me in the kitchen, "She's been there ever since"?

JESSIE: Yes.

MAMA: No. It was a big fat lie, the whole thing. He just thought it was funnier that way. God, this milk in here.

JESSIE: The cocoa helps.

MAMA *(Pleased that they agree on this, at least):* Not enough, though, does it? You can still taste it, can't you?

JESSIE: Yeah, it's pretty bad. I thought it was my memory that was bad, but it's not. It's the milk, all right.

MAMA: It's a real waste of chocolate. You don't have to finish it.

JESSIE *(Putting her cup down):* Thanks, though.

MAMA: I should've known not to make it. I knew you wouldn't like it. You never did like it.

JESSIE: You didn't ever love him, or he did something and you stopped loving him, or what?

MAMA: He felt sorry for me. He wanted a plain country woman and that's what he married, and then he held it against me the rest of my life like I was supposed to change and surprise him somehow. Like I remember this one day he was standing on the porch and I told him to get a shirt on and he went in and got one and then he said, real peaceful, but to the point, "You're right, Thelma. If God had meant for people to go around without any clothes on, they'd have been born that way."

JESSIE *(Sees MAMA's hurt):* He didn't mean anything by that, Mama.

MAMA: He never said a word he didn't have to, Jessie. That was probably all he'd said to me all day, Jessie. So if he said it, there was something to it, but I never did figure that one out. What did that mean?

JESSIE: I don't know. I liked him better than you did, but I didn't know him any better.

MAMA: How could I love him, Jessie. I didn't have a thing he wanted. *(JESSIE doesn't answer)* He got his share, though. You loved him enough for both of us. You followed him around like some . . . Jessie, all the man ever did was farm and sit . . . and try to think of somebody to sell the farm to.

JESSIE: Or make me a boyfriend out of pipe cleaners and sit back and smile like the stick man was about to dance and wasn't I going to get a kick out of that. Or sit up with a sick cow all night and leave me a chain of sleepy stick elephants on my bed in the morning.

MAMA: Or just sit.

JESSIE: I liked him sitting. Big old faded blue man in the chair. Quiet.

MAMA: Agnes gets more talk out of her birds than I got from the two of you. He could've had that GONE FISHING sign around his neck in that chair. I saw him stare off at the water. I saw him look at the weather rolling in. I got where I could practically see the boat myself. But you, you knew what he was thinking about and you're going to tell me.

JESSIE: I don't know, Mama! His life, I guess. His corn. His boots. Us. Things. You know.

MAMA: No, I don't know, Jessie! You had those quiet little conversations after supper every night. What were you whispering about?

JESSIE: We weren't whispering, you were just across the room.

MAMA: What did you talk about?

JESSIE: We talked about why black socks are warmer than blue socks. Is that something to go tell Mother? You were just jealous because I'd rather talk to him than wash the dishes with you.

MAMA: I was jealous because you'd rather talk to him than anything! (JESSIE *reaches across the table for the small clock and starts to wind it)* If I had died instead of him, he wouldn't have taken you in like I did.

JESSIE: I wouldn't have expected him to.

MAMA: Then what would you have done?

JESSIE: Come visit.

MAMA: Oh, I see. He died and left you stuck with me and you're mad about it.

JESSIE *(Getting up from the table):* Not anymore. He didn't mean to. I didn't have to come here. We've been through this.

MAMA: He felt sorry for you, too, Jessie, don't kid yourself about that. He said you were a runt and he said it from the day you were born and he said you didn't have a chance.

JESSIE *(Getting the canister of sugar and starting to refill the sugar bowl):* I know he loved me.

MAMA: What if he did? It didn't change anything.

JESSIE: It didn't have to. I miss him.

MAMA: He never really went fishing, you know. Never once. His tackle box was full of chewing tobacco and all he ever did was drive out to the lake and sit in his car. Dawson told me. And Bennie at the bait shop, he told Dawson. They all laughed about it. And he'd come back from fishing and all he'd have to show for it was . . . a whole pipe-cleaner *family*—chickens, pigs, a dog with a bad leg—it was creepy strange. It made me sick to look at them and I hid his pipe cleaners a couple of times but he always had more somewhere.

JESSIE: I thought it might be better for you after he died. You'd get interested in things. Breathe better. Change somehow.

MAMA: Into what? The Queen? A clerk in a shoe store? Why should I? Because he said to? Because you said to? (JESSIE *shakes her head)* Well I wasn't here for his entertainment and I'm not here for yours either, Jessie. I don't know what I'm here for, but then I don't think about it. *(Realizing what all this means)* But I bet you wouldn't be killing yourself if he were still alive. That's a fine thing to figure out, isn't it?

JESSIE *(Filling the honey jar now):* That's not true.

MAMA: Oh no? Then what were you asking about him for? Why did you want to know if I loved him?

JESSIE: I didn't think you did, that's all.

MAMA: Fine then. You were right. Do you feel better now?

JESSIE *(Cleaning the honey jar carefully):* It feels good to be right about it.

MAMA: It didn't matter whether I loved him. It didn't matter to me and it didn't matter to him. And it didn't mean we didn't get along. It wasn't important.

We didn't talk about it. *(Sweeping the pots off the cabinet)* Take all these pots out to the porch!

JESSIE: What for?

MAMA: Just leave me this one pan. *(She jerks the silverware drawer open)* Get me one knife, one fork, one big spoon, and the can opener, and put them out where I can get them. *(Starts throwing knives and forks in one of the pans)*

JESSIE: Don't do that! I just straightened that drawer!

MAMA *(Throwing the pan in the sink):* And throw out all the plates and cups. I'll use paper. Loretta can have what she wants and Dawson can sell the rest.

JESSIE *(Calmly):* What are you doing?

MAMA: I'm not going to cook. I never liked it, anyway. I like candy. Wrapped in plastic or coming in sacks. And tuna. I like tuna. I'll eat tuna, thank you.

JESSIE *(Taking the pan out of the sink):* What if you want to make apple butter? You can't make apple butter in that little pan. What if you leave carrots on cooking and burn up that pan?

MAMA: I don't like carrots.

JESSIE: What if the strawberries are good this year and you want to go picking with Agnes.

MAMA: I'll tell her to bring a pan. You said you would do whatever I wanted! I don't want a bunch of pans cluttering up my cabinets I can't get down to, anyway. Throw them out. Every last one.

JESSIE *(Gathering up the pots):* I'm putting them all back in. I'm not taking them to the porch. If you want them, they'll be here. You'll bend down and get them, like you got the one for the cocoa. And if somebody else comes over here to cook, they'll have something to cook in, and that's the end of it!

MAMA: Who's going to come cook here?

JESSIE: Agnes.

MAMA: In my pots. Not on your life.

JESSIE: There's no reason why the two of you couldn't just live here together. Be cheaper for both of you and somebody to talk to. And if the birds bothered you, well, one day when Agnes is out getting her hair done, you could take them all for a walk!

MAMA *(As JESSIE straightens the silverware):* So that's why you're pestering me about Agnes. You think you can rest easy if you get me a new babysitter? Well, I don't want to live with Agnes. I barely want to talk with Agnes. She's just around. We go back, that's all. I'm not letting Agnes near this place. You don't get off as easy as that, child.

JESSIE: O.K. then. It's just something to think about.

MAMA: I don't like things to think about. I like things to go on.

JESSIE *(Closing the silverware drawer):* I want to know what Daddy said to you the night he died. You came storming out of his room and said I could wait it out with him if I wanted to, but you were going to watch *Gunsmoke*. What did he say to you?

MAMA: He didn't have *anything* to say to me, Jessie. That's why I left. He didn't say a thing. It was his last chance not to talk to me and he took full advantage of it.

JESSIE *(After a moment):* I'm sorry you didn't love him. Sorry for you, I mean. He seemed like a nice man.

MAMA *(As* JESSIE *walks to the refrigerator):* Ready for your apple now?

JESSIE: Soon as I'm through here, Mama.

MAMA: You won't like the apple, either. It'll be just like the cocoa. You never liked eating at all, did you? Any of it! What have you been living on all these years, toothpaste?

JESSIE *(As she starts to clean out the refrigerator):* Now, you know the milkman comes on Wednesdays and Saturdays, and he leaves the order blank in an egg box, and you give the bills to Dawson once a month.

MAMA: Do they still make that orangeade?

JESSIE: It's not orangeade, it's just orange.

MAMA: I'm going to get some. I thought they stopped making it. You just stopped ordering it.

JESSIE: You should drink milk.

MAMA: Not anymore, I'm not. That hot chocolate was the last. Hooray.

JESSIE *(Getting the garbage can from under the sink):* I told them to keep delivering a quart a week no matter what you said. I told them you'd run out of Cokes and you'd have to drink it. I told them I knew you wouldn't pour it on the ground . . .

MAMA *(Finishing her sentence):* And you told them you weren't going to be ordering anymore?

JESSIE: I told them I was taking a little holiday and to look after you.

MAMA: And they didn't think something was funny about that? You who doesn't go to the front steps? You, who only sees the driveway looking down from a stretcher passed out cold?

JESSIE *(Enjoying this, but not laughing):* They said it was about time, but why didn't I take you with me? And I said I didn't think you'd want to go, and they said, "Yeah, everybody's got their own idea of vacation."

MAMA: I guess you think that's funny.

JESSIE *(Pulling jars out of the refrigerator):* You know there never was any reason to call the ambulance for me. All they ever did for me in the emergency room was let me wake up. I could've done that here. Now, I'll just call them out and you say yes or no. I know you like pickles. Ketchup?

MAMA: Keep it.

JESSIE: We've had this since last Fourth of July.

MAMA: Keep the ketchup. Keep it all.

JESSIE: Are you going to drink ketchup from the bottle or what? How can you want your food and not want your pots to cook it in? This stuff will all spoil in here, Mother.

Mama: Nothing I ever did was good enough for you and I want to know why.

Jessie: That's not true.

Mama: And I want to know why you've lived here this long feeling the way you do.

Jessie: You have no earthly idea how I feel.

Mama: Well, how could I? You're real far back there, Jessie.

Jessie: Back where?

Mama: What's it like over there, where you are? Do people always say the right thing or get whatever they want, or what?

Jessie: What are you talking about?

Mama: Why do you read the newspaper? Why don't you wear that sweater I made for you? Do you remember how I used to look, or am I just any old woman now? When you have a fit, do you see stars or what? How did you fall off the horse, really? Why did Cecil leave you? Where did you put my old glasses?

Jessie *(Stunned by* Mama*'s intensity):* They're in the bottom drawer of your dresser in an old Milk of Magnesia box. Cecil left me because he made me choose between him and smoking.

Mama: Jessie, I know he wasn't that dumb.

Jessie: I never understood why he hated it so much when it's so good. Smoking is the only thing I know that's always just what you think it's going to be. Just like it was the last time, right there when you want it and real quiet.

Mama: Your fits made him sick and you know it.

Jessie: Say seizures, not fits. Seizures.

Mama: It's the same thing. A seizure in the hospital is a fit at home.

Jessie: They didn't bother him at all. Except he did feel responsible for it. It *was* his idea to go horseback riding that day. It was his idea I could do *anything* if I just made up my mind to. I fell off the horse because I didn't know how to hold on. Cecil left for pretty much the same reason.

Mama: He had a girl, Jessie. I walked right in on them in the toolshed.

Jessie *(After a moment):* O.K. That's fair. *(Lighting another cigarette)* Was she very pretty?

Mama: She was Agnes's girl, Carlene. Judge for yourself.

Jessie *(As she walks to the living room):* I guess you and Agnes had a good talk about that, huh?

Mama: I never thought he was good enough for you. They moved here from Tennessee, you know.

Jessie: What are you talking about? You liked him better than I did. You flirted him out here to build your porch or I'd never even met him at all. You thought maybe he'd help you out around the place, come in and get some coffee and talk to you. God knows what you thought. All that curly hair.

Mama: He's the best carpenter I ever saw. That little house of yours will still be standing at the end of the world, Jessie.

JESSIE: You didn't need a porch, Mama.

MAMA: All right! I wanted you to have a husband.

JESSIE: And I couldn't get one on my own, of course.

MAMA: How were you going to get a husband never opening your mouth to a living soul?

JESSIE: So I was quiet about it, so what?

MAMA: So I should have let you just sit here? Sit like your daddy? Sit here?

JESSIE: Maybe.

MAMA: Well, I didn't think so.

JESSIE: Well, what did you know?

MAMA: I never said I knew much. How was I supposed to learn anything living out here? I didn't know enough to do half the things I did in my life. Things happen. You do what you can about them and you see what happens next. I married you off to the wrong man, I admit that. So I took you in when he left. I'm sorry.

JESSIE: He wasn't the wrong man.

MAMA: He didn't love you, Jessie, or he wouldn't have left.

JESSIE: He wasn't the wrong man, Mama. I loved Cecil so much. And I tried to get more exercise and I tried to stay awake. I tried to learn to ride a horse. And I tried to stay outside with him, but he always knew I was trying, so it didn't work.

MAMA: He was a selfish man. He told me once he hated to see people move into his houses after he built them. He knew they'd mess them up.

JESSIE: I loved that bridge he built over the creek in back of the house. It didn't have to be anything special, a couple of boards would have been just fine, but he used that yellow pine and rubbed it so smooth . . .

MAMA: He had responsibilities here. He had a wife and son here and he failed you.

JESSIE: Or that baby bed he built for Ricky. I told him he didn't have to spend so much time on it, but he said it had to last, and the thing ended up weighing two hundred pounds and I couldn't move it. I said, "How long does a baby bed have to last, anyway?" But maybe he thought if it was strong enough, it might keep Ricky a baby.

MAMA: Ricky is too much like Cecil.

JESSIE: He is not. Ricky is as much like me as it's possible for any human to be. We even wear the same size pants. These are his, I think.

MAMA: That's just the same size. That's not you're the same person.

JESSIE: I see it on his face. I hear it when he talks. We look out at the world and we see the same thing: Not Fair. And the only difference between us is Ricky's out there trying to get even. And he knows not to trust anybody and he got it straight from me. And he knows not to try to get work, and guess where he got that. He walks around like there's loose boards in the floor, and you know who laid that floor, I did.

MAMA: Ricky isn't through yet. You don't know how he'll turn out!

JESSIE *(Going back to the kitchen):* Yes I do and so did Cecil. Ricky is the two of us together for all time in too small a space. And we're tearing each other apart, like always, inside that boy, and if you don't see it, then you're just blind.

MAMA: Give him time, Jess.

JESSIE: Oh, he'll have plenty of that. Five years for forgery, ten years for armed assault . . .

MAMA *(Furious):* Stop that! *(Then pleading)* Jessie, Cecil might be ready to try it again, honey, that happens sometimes. Go downtown. Find him. Talk to him. He didn't know what he had in you. Maybe he sees things different now, but you're not going to know that till you go see him. Or call him up! Right now! He might be home.

JESSIE: And say what? Nothing's changed, Cecil, I'd just like to look at you, if you don't mind? No. He loved me, Mama. He just didn't know how things fall down around me like they do. I think he did the right thing. He gave himself another chance, that's all. But I did beg him to take me with him. I did tell him I would leave Ricky and you and everything I loved out here if only he would take me with him, but he couldn't and I understood that. *(Pause)* I wrote that note I showed you. I wrote it. Not Cecil. I said "I'm sorry, Jessie, I can't fix it all for you." I said I'd always love me, not Cecil. But that's how he felt.

MAMA: Then he should've taken you with him!

JESSIE *(Picking up the garbage bag she has filled):* Mama, you don't pack your garbage when you move.

MAMA: You will not call yourself garbage, Jessie.

JESSIE *(Taking the bag to the big garbage can near the back door):* Just a way of saying it, Mama. Thinking about my list, that's all. *(Opening the can, putting the garbage in, then securing the lid)* Well, a little more than that, I was trying to say it's all right that Cecil left. It was . . . a relief in a way. I never was what he wanted to see, so it was better when he wasn't looking at me all the time.

MAMA: I'll make your apple now.

JESSIE: No thanks. You get the manicure stuff and I'll be right there.

*(*JESSIE *ties up the big garbage bag in the can and replaces the small garbage bag under the sink, all the time trying desperately to regain her calm.* MAMA *watches, from a distance, her hand reaching unconsciously for the phone. Then she has a better idea. Or rather she thinks of the only other thing left and is willing to try it. Maybe she is even convinced it will work)*

MAMA: Jessie, I think your daddy had little . . .

JESSIE *(Interrupting her):* Garbage night is Tuesday. Put it out as late as you can. The Davis's dogs get in it if you don't. *(Replacing the garbage bag in the can under the sink)* And keep ordering the heavy black bags. It doesn't pay to buy the cheap ones. And I've got all the ties here with the hammers and all. Take them out of the box as soon as you open a new one and put them in this drawer. They'll get lost if you don't, and rubber bands or something else won't work.

MAMA: I think your daddy had fits, too. I think he sat in his chair and had little fits. I read this a long time ago in a magazine, how little fits go, just little blackouts where maybe their eyes don't even close and people just call them "thinking spells."

JESSIE *(Getting the slipcover out of the laundry basket):* I don't think you want this manicure we've been looking forward to. I washed this cover for the sofa, but it'll take both of us to get it back on.

MAMA: I watched his eyes. I know that's what it was. The magazine said some people don't even know they've had one.

JESSIE: Daddy would've known if he'd had fits, Mama.

MAMA: The lady in this story had kept track of hers and she'd had eighty thousand of them in the last eleven years.

JESSIE: Next time you wash this cover, it'll dry better if you put it on wet.

MAMA: Jessie, listen to what I'm telling you. This lady had anywhere between five and five hundred fits a day and they lasted maybe fifteen seconds apiece, so that out of her life, she'd only lost about two weeks altogether, and she had a full-time secretary job and an IQ of 120.

JESSIE *(Amused by* MAMA'S *approach):* You want to talk about fits, is that it?

MAMA: Yes. I do. I want to say . . .

JESSIE *(Interrupting):* Most of the time I wouldn't even know I'd had one, except I wake up with different clothes on, feeling like I've been run over. Sometimes I feel my head start to turn around or hear myself scream. And sometimes there *is* this dizzy stupid feeling a little before it, but if the TV's on, well, it's easy to miss.

(As JESSIE *and* MAMA *replace the slipcover on the sofa and the afghan on the chair, the physical struggle somehow mirrors the emotional one in the conversation)*

MAMA: I can tell when you're about to have one. Your eyes get this big! But, Jessie, you haven't . . .

JESSIE *(Taking charge of this):* What do they look like? The seizures.

MAMA *(Reluctant):* Different each time, Jess.

JESSIE: O.K. Pick one, then. A good one. I think I want to know now.

MAMA: There's not much to tell. You just . . . crumple, in a heap, like a puppet and somebody cut the strings all at once, or like the firing squad in some Mexican movie, you just slide down the wall, you know. You don't know what happens? How can you not know what happens?

JESSIE: I'm busy.

MAMA: That's not funny.

JESSIE: I'm not laughing. My head turns around and I fall down and then what?

MAMA: Well, your chest squeezes in and out, and you sound like you're gagging, sucking air in and out like you can't breathe.

JESSIE: Do it for me. Make the sound for me.

MAMA: I will not. It's awful-sounding.

JESSIE: Yeah. It felt like it might be. What's next?

MAMA: Your mouth bites down and I have to get your tongue out of the way fast, so you don't bite yourself.

JESSIE: Or you. I bite you, too, don't I?

MAMA: You got me once real good. I had to get a tetanus! But I know what to watch for now. And then you turn blue and the jerks start up. Like I'm standing there poking you with a cattle prod or you're sticking your finger in a light socket as fast as you can . . .

JESSIE: Foaming like a mad dog the whole time.

MAMA: It's bubbling, Jess, not foam like the washer overflowed, for God's sake; it's bubbling like a baby spitting up. I go get a wet washcloth, that's all. And then the jerks slow down and you wet yourself and it's over. Two minutes tops.

JESSIE: How do I get to the bed?

MAMA: How do you think?

JESSIE: I'm too heavy for you now. How do you do it?

MAMA: I call Dawson. But I get you cleaned up before he gets here and I make him leave before you wake up.

JESSIE: You could just leave me on the floor.

MAMA: I want you to wake up someplace nice, O.K.? *(Then making a real effort)* But, Jessie, and this is the reason I even brought this up! You haven't had a seizure for a solid year. A whole year, do you realize that?

JESSIE: Yeah, the phenobarb's about right now, I guess.

MAMA: You bet it is. You might never have another one, ever! You might be through with it for all time!

JESSIE: Could be.

MAMA: You are. I know you are!

JESSIE: I sure am feeling good. I really am. The double vision's gone and my gums aren't swelling. No rashes or anything. I'm feeling as good as I ever felt in my life. I'm even feeling like worrying or getting mad and I'm not afraid it will start a fit if I do, I just go ahead.

MAMA: Of course you do! You can even scream at me, if you want to. I can take it. You don't have to act like you're just visiting here, Jessie. This is your house, too.

JESSIE: The best part is, my memory's back.

MAMA: Your memory's always been good. When couldn't you remember things? You're always reminding me what . . .

JESSIE: Because I've made lists for everything. But now I remember what things mean on my lists. I see "dish towels," and I used to wonder whether I was supposed to wash them, buy them, or look for them because I wouldn't remember where I put them after I washed them, but now I know it means wrap them up, they're a present for Loretta's birthday.

MAMA *(Finished with the sofa now):* You used to go looking for your lists, too. I've noticed that. You always know where they are now! *(Then suddenly worried)* Loretta's birthday isn't coming up, is it?

JESSIE: I made a list of all the birthdays for you. I even put yours on it. *(A small smile)* So you can call Loretta and remind her.

MAMA: Let's take Loretta to Howard Johnson's and have those fried clams. I *know* you love that clam roll.

JESSIE *(Slight pause):* I won't be here, Mama.

MAMA: What have we just been talking about? You'll be here. You're well, Jessie. You're starting all over. You said it yourself. You're remembering things and . . .

JESSIE: I won't be here. If I'd ever had a year like this, to think straight and all, before now, I'd be gone already.

MAMA *(Not pleading, commanding):* No. Jessie.

JESSIE *(Folding the rest of the laundry):* Yes, Mama. Once I started remembering, I could see what it all added up to.

MAMA: The fits are over!

JESSIE: It's not the fits, Mama.

MAMA: Then it's me for giving them to you, but I didn't do it!

JESSIE: It's not the fits! You said it yourself, the medicine takes care of the fits.

MAMA *(Interrupting):* Your daddy gave you those fits, Jessie. He passed it down to you like your green eyes and your straight hair. It's not my fault!

JESSIE: So what if he had little fits? It's not inherited. I fell off the horse. It was an accident.

MAMA: The horse wasn't the first time, Jessie. You had a fit when you were five years old.

JESSIE: I did not.

MAMA: You did! You were eating a popsicle and down you went. He gave it to you. It's *his* fault, not mine.

JESSIE: Well, you took your time telling me.

MAMA: How do you tell that to a five-year-old?

JESSIE: What did the doctor say?

MAMA: He said kids have them all the time. He said there wasn't anything to do but wait for another one.

JESSIE: But I didn't have another one.

(Now there is a real silence)

JESSIE: You mean to tell me I had fits all the time as a kid and you just told me I fell down or something and it wasn't till I had the fit when Cecil was looking that anybody bothered to find out what was the matter with me?

MAMA: It wasn't *all the time,* Jessie. And they changed when you started to school. More like your daddy's. Oh, that was some swell time, sitting here with the two of you turning off and on like light bulbs some nights.

JESSIE: How many fits did I have?

MAMA: You never hurt yourself. I never let you out of my sight. I caught you every time.

JESSIE: But you didn't tell anybody.

MAMA: It was none of their business.

JESSIE: You were ashamed.

MAMA: I didn't want anybody to know. Least of all you.

JESSIE: Least of all me. Oh, right. That was mine to know, Mama, not yours. Did Daddy know?

MAMA: He thought you were . . . you fell down a lot. That's what he thought. You were careless. Or maybe he thought I beat you. I don't know what he thought. He didn't think about it.

JESSIE: Because you didn't tell him!

MAMA: If I told him about you, I'd have to tell him about him!

JESSIE: I don't like this. I don't like this one bit.

MAMA: I didn't think you'd like it. That's why I didn't tell you.

JESSIE: If I'd known I was an epileptic, Mama, I wouldn't have ridden any horses.

MAMA: Make you feel like a freak, is that what I should have done?

JESSIE: Just get the manicure tray and sit down!

MAMA *(Throwing it to the floor):* I don't want a manicure!

JESSIE: Doesn't look like you do, no.

MAMA: Maybe I did drop you, you don't knnow.

JESSIE: If you say you didn't you didn't.

MAMA *(Beginning to break down):* Maybe I fed you the wrong thing. Maybe you had a fever sometime and I didn't know it soon enough. Maybe it's a punishment.

JESSIE: For what?

MAMA: I don't know. Because of how I felt about your father. Because I didn't want any more children. Because I smoked too much or didn't eat right when I was carrying you. It has to be something I did.

JESSIE: It does not. It's just a sickness, not a curse. Epilepsy doesn't mean anything. It just is.

MAMA: I'm not talking about the fits here, Jessie! I'm talking about this killing yourself. It has to be me that's the matter here. You wouldn't be doing this if it wasn't. I didn't tell you things or I married you off to the wrong man or I took you in and let your life get away from you or all of it put together. I don't know what I did, but I did it, I know this is all my fault, Jessie, but I don't know what to do about it now!

JESSIE *(Exasperated at having to say this again):* It doesn't have anything to do with you!

MAMA: Everything you do has to do with me, Jessie. You can't do *anything,* wash your face or cut your finger, without doing it to me. That's right! You might as well kill me as you, Jessie, it's the same thing. This has to do with me, Jessie.

JESSIE: Then what if it does! What if it has everything to do with you! What if you are all I have and you're not enough? What if I could take all the rest of it if only I didn't have you here? What if the only way I can get away from you for good is to kill myself? What if it is? I can *still* do it!

MAMA *(In desperate tears):* Don't leave me, Jessie! *(*JESSIE *stands for a moment, then turns for the bedroom)* No! *(She grabs* JESSIE*'s arm)*

JESSIE *(Carefully taking her arm away):* I have a box of things I want people to have. I'm just going to go get it for you. You . . . just rest a minute.

*(*JESSIE *is gone.* MAMA *heads for the telephone, but she can't even pick up the receiver this time and, instead, stoops to clean up the bottles that have spilled out of the manicure tray*

JESSIE *returns, carrying a box that groceries were delivered in. It probably says Hershey Kisses or Starkist Tuna.* MAMA *is still down on the floor cleaning up, hoping that maybe if she just makes it look nice enough,* JESSIE *will stay)*

MAMA: Jessie, how can I live here without you? I need you! You're supposed to tell me to stand up straight and say how nice I look in my pink dress, and drink my milk. You're supposed to go around and lock up so I know we're safe for the night, and when I wake up, you're supposed to be out there making the coffee and watching me get older every day, and you're supposed to help me die when the time comes. I can't do that by myself, Jessie. I'm not like you, Jessie. I hate the quiet and I don't want to die and I don't want you to go, Jessie. How can I . . . *(Has to stop a moment)* How can I get up every day knowing you had to kill yourself to make it stop hurting and I was here all the time and I never even saw it. And then you gave me this chance to make it better, convince you to stay alive, and I couldn't do it. How can I live with myself after this, Jessie?

JESSIE: I only told you so I could explain it, so you wouldn't blame yourself, so you wouldn't feel bad. There wasn't anything you could say to change my mind. I didn't want you to save me. I just wanted you to know.

MAMA: Stay with me just a little longer. Just a few more years. I don't have that many more to go, Jessie. And as soon as I'm dead, you can do whatever you want. Maybe with me gone, you'll have all the quiet you want, right here in the house. And maybe one day you'll put in some begonias up the walk and get just the right rain for them all summer. And Ricky will be married by then and he'll bring your grandbabies over and you can sneak them a piece of candy when their daddy's not looking and then be real glad when they've gone home and left you to your quiet again.

JESSIE: Don't you see, Mama, everything I do winds up like this. How could I think you would understand? How could I think you would want a manicure? We could hold hands for an hour and then I could go shoot myself? I'm sorry about tonight, Mama, but it's exactly why I'm doing it.

MAMA: If you've got the guts to kill yourself, Jessie, you've got the guts to stay alive.

JESSIE: I know that. So it's really just a matter of where I'd rather be.

MAMA: Look, maybe I can't think of what you should do, but that doesn't mean there isn't something that would help. *You* find it. *You* think of it. You can keep trying. You can get brave and try some more. You don't have to give up!

JESSIE: I'm *not* giving up! This *is* the other thing I'm trying. And I'm sure there are some other things that might work, but *might* work isn't good enough anymore. I need something that *will* work. *This* will work. That's why I picked it.

MAMA: But something might happen. Something that could change everything. Who knows what it might be, but it might be worth waiting for! *(*JESSIE *doesn't respond)* Try it for two more weeks. We could have more talks like tonight.

JESSIE: No, Mama.

MAMA: I'll pay more attention to you. Tell the truth when you ask me. Let you have your say.

JESSIE: No, Mama! We wouldn't have more talks like tonight, because it's this next part that's made this last part so good, Mama. No, Mama. *This* is how I have my say. This is how I say what I thought about it *all* and I say no. To Dawson and Loretta and the Red Chinese and epilepsy and Ricky and Cecil and you. And me. And hope. I say no! *(Then going to* MAMA *on the sofa)* Just let me go easy, Mama.

MAMA: How can I let you go?

JESSIE: You can because you have to. It's what you've always done.

MAMA: You are my child!

JESSIE: I am what became of your child. *(*MAMA *cannot answer)* I found an old baby picture of me. And it was somebody else, not me. It was somebody pink and fat who never heard of sick or lonely, somebody who cried and got fed, and reached up and got held and kicked but didn't hurt anybody, and slept whenever she wanted to, just by closing her eyes. Somebody who mainly just laid there and laughed at the colors waving around over her head and chewed on a polka-dot whale and woke up knowing some new trick nearly every day, and rolled over and drooled on the sheet and felt your hand pulling my quilt back up over me. That's who I started out and this is who is left. *(There is no self-pity here)* That's what this is about. It's somebody I lost, all right, it's my own self. Who I never was. Or who I tried to be and never got there. Somebody I waited for who never came. And never will. So, see, it doesn't much matter what else happens in the world or in this house, even. I'm what was worth waiting for and I didn't make it. Me . . . who might have made a difference to me . . . I'm not going to show up, so there's no reason to stay, except to keep you company, and that's . . . not reason enough because I'm not . . . very good company. *(Pause)* Am I.

MAMA *(Knowing she must tell the truth):* No. And neither am I.

JESSIE: I had this strange little thought, well, maybe it's not so strange. Anyway, after Christmas, after I decided to do this, I would wonder, sometimes, what might keep me here, what might be worth staying for, and you know what it was? It was maybe if there was something I really liked, like maybe if I really liked rice pudding or cornflakes for breakfast or something, that might be enough.

MAMA: Rice pudding is good.

JESSIE: Not to me.

MAMA: And you're not afraid?

JESSIE: Afraid of what?

MAMA: I'm afraid of it, for me, I mean. When my time comes. I know it's coming, but . . .

JESSIE: You don't know when. Like in a scary movie.

MAMA: Yeah, sneaking up on me like some killer on the loose, hiding out in the back yard just waiting for me to have my hands full someday and how am I supposed to protect myself anyhow when I don't know what he looks like and I don't know how he sounds coming up behind me like that or if it will hurt or take very long or what I don't get done before it happens.

JESSIE: You've got plenty of time left.

MAMA: I forget what for, right now.

JESSIE: For whatever happens, I don't know. For the rest of your life. For Agnes burning down one more house or Dawson losing his hair or . . .

MAMA *(Quickly):* Jessie. I can't just sit here and say O.K., kill yourself if you want to.

JESSIE: Sure you can. You just did. Say it again.

MAMA *(Really startled):* Jessie! *(Quiet horror)* How dare you! *(Furious)* How dare you! You think you can just leave whenever you want, like you're watching television here? No, you can't, Jessie. You make me feel like a fool for being alive, child, and you are so wrong! I like it here, and I will stay here until they make me go, until they drag me screaming and I mean screeching into my grave, and you're real smart to get away before then because, I mean, honey, you've never heard noise like that in your life. (JESSIE *turns away)* Who am I talking to? You're gone already, aren't you? I'm looking right through you! I can't stop you because you're already gone! I guess you think they'll all have to talk about you now! I guess you think this will really confuse them. Oh yes, ever since Christmas you've been laughing to yourself and thinking, "Boy, are they all in for a surprise." Well, nobody's going to be a bit surprised, sweetheart. This is just like you. Do it the hard way, that's my girl, all right. (JESSIE *gets up and goes into the kitchen, but* MAMA *follows her)* You know who they're going to feel sorry for? Me! How about that! Not you, me! They're going to be *ashamed* of you. Yes. *Ashamed!* If somebody asks Dawson about it, he'll change the subject as fast as he can. He'll talk about how much he has to pay to park his car these days.

JESSIE: Leave me alone.

MAMA: It's the truth!

JESSIE: I should've just left you a note!

MAMA *(Screaming):* Yes! *(Then suddenly understanding what she has said, nearly paralyzed by the thought of it, she turns slowly to face* JESSIE, *nearly whispering)* No. No. I . . . might not have thought of all the things you've said.

JESSIE: It's O.K., Mama.

*(*MAMA *is nearly unconscious from the emotional devastation of these last few moments. She sits down at the kitchen table, hurt and angry and desperately afraid. But she looks almost numb. She is so far beyond what is known as pain that she is virtually unreachable and* JESSIE *knows this, and talks quietly, watching for signs of recovery)*

JESSIE *(Washes her hands in the sink):* I remember you liked that preacher who did Daddy's, so if you want to ask him to the service, that's O.K. with me.

MAMA *(Not an answer, just a word):* What.

JESSIE *(Putting on hand lotion as she talks):* And pick some songs you like or let Agnes pick, she'll know exactly which ones. Oh, and I had your dress cleaned that you wore to Daddy's. You looked real good in that.

MAMA: I don't remember, hon.

JESSIE: And it won't be so bad once your friends start coming to the funeral home. You'll probably see people you haven't seen for years, but I thought about what you should say to get you over that nervous part when they first come in.

MAMA *(Simply repeating):* Come in.

JESSIE: Take them up to see their flowers, they'd like that. And when they say, "I'm so sorry, Thelma," you just say, "I appreciate your coming, Connie." And then ask how their garden was this summer or what they're doing for Thanksgiving or how their children . . .

MAMA: I don't think I should ask about their children. I'll talk about what they have on, that's always good. And I'll have some crochet work with me.

JESSIE: And Agnes will be there, so you might not have to talk at all.

MAMA: Maybe if Connie Richards does come, I can get her to tell me where she gets that Irish yarn, she calls it. I know it doesn't come from Ireland. I think it just comes with a green wrapper.

JESSIE: And be sure to invite enough people home afterward so you get enough food to feed them all and have some left for you. But don't let anybody take anything home, especially Loretta.

MAMA: Loretta will get all the food set up, honey. It's only fair to let her have some macaroni or something.

JESSIE: No, Mama. You have to be more selfish from now on. *(Sitting at the table with* MAMA*)* Now, somebody's bound to ask you why I did it and you just say you don't know. That you loved me and you know I loved you and we just sat around tonight like every other night of our lives, and then I came over and kissed you and said, " 'Night, Mother," and you heard me close my bedroom door and the next thing you heard was the shot. And whatever reasons I had, well, you guess I just took them with me.

MAMA *(Quietly):* It was something personal.

JESSIE: Good. That's good, Mama.

MAMA: That's what I'll say, then.

JESSIE: Personal. Yeah.

MAMA: Is that what I tell Dawson and Loretta, too? We sat around, you kissed me, " 'Night, Mother"? They'll want to know more, Jessie. They won't believe it.

JESSIE: Well, then, tell them what we did. I filled up the candy jars. I cleaned out the refrigerator. We made some hot chocolate and put the cover back on the sofa. You had no idea. All right? I really think it's better that way. If they knew we talked about it, they really won't understand how you let me go.

MAMA: I guess not.

JESSIE: It's private. Tonight is private, yours and mine, and I don't want anybody else to have any of it.

MAMA: O.K., then.

JESSIE *(Standing behind* MAMA *now, holding her shoulders):* Now, when you hear the shot, I don't want you to come in. First of all, you won't be able to get in by yourself, but I don't want you trying. Call Dawson, then call the police, and then call Agnes. And then you'll need something to do till somebody gets here, so wash the hot-chocolate pan. You wash that pan till you hear the doorbell ring and I don't care if it's an hour, you keep washing that pan.

MAMA: I'll make my calls and then I'll just sit. I won't need something to do. What will the police say?

JESSIE: They'll do that gunpowder test, I guess, and ask you what happened, and by that time, the ambulance will be here and they'll come in and get me and you know how that goes. You stay out here with Dawson and Loretta. You keep Dawson out here. I want the police in the room first, not Dawson, O.K.?

MAMA: What if Dawson and Loretta want me to go home with them?

JESSIE *(Returning to the living room):* That's up to you.

MAMA: I think I'll stay here. All they've got is Sanka.

JESSIE: Maybe Agnes could come stay with you for a few days.

MAMA *(Standing up, looking into the living room):* I'd rather be by myself, I think. *(Walking toward the box* JESSIE *brought in earlier)* You want me to give people those things?

JESSIE *(They sit down on the sofa,* JESSIE *holding the box on her lap):* I want Loretta to have my little calculator. Dawson bought it for himself, you know, but then he saw one he liked better and he couldn't bring both of them home with Loretta counting every penny the way she does, so he gave the first one to me. Be funny for her to have it now, don't you think? And all my house slippers are in a sack for her in my closet. Tell her I know they'll fit and I've never worn any of them, and make sure Dawson hears you tell her that. I'm glad he loves Loretta so much, but I wish he knew not everybody has her size feet.

MAMA *(Taking the calculator):* O.K.

JESSIE *(Reaching into the box again):* This letter is for Dawson, but it's mostly about you, so read it if you want. There's a list of presents for you for at least twenty more Christmases and birthdays, so if you want anything special you better add it to this list before you give it to him. Or if you want to be surprised, just don't read that page. This Christmas, you're getting mostly stuff for the house, like a new rug in your bathroom and needlework, but next Christmas, you're really going to cost him next Christmas. I think you'll like it a lot and you'd never think of it.

MAMA: And you think he'll go for it?

JESSIE: I think he'll feel like a real jerk if he doesn't. Me telling him to, like this and all. Now, this number's where you call Cecil. I called it last week and he answered, so I know he still lives there.

MAMA: What do you want me to tell him?

JESSIE: Tell him we talked about him and I only had good things to say about him, but mainly tell him to find Ricky and tell him what I did, and tell Ricky you have something for him, out here, from me, and to come get it. *(Pulls a sack out of the box)*

MAMA *(The sack feels empty):* What is it?

JESSIE *(Taking it off):* My watch. *(Putting it in the sack and taking a ribbon out of the sack to tie around the top of it)*

MAMA: He'll sell it!

JESSIE: That's the idea. I appreciate him not stealing it already. I'd like to buy him a good meal.

MAMA: He'll buy dope with it!

JESSIE: Well, then, I hope he gets some good dope with it, Mama. And the rest of this is for you. *(Handing* MAMA *the box now.* MAMA *picks up the things and looks at them)*

MAMA *(Surprised and pleased):* When did you do all this? During my naps, I guess.

JESSIE: I guess. I tried to be quiet about it. *(As* MAMA *is puzzled by the presents)* Those are just little presents. For whenever you need one. They're not bought presents, just things I thought you might like to look at, pictures or things you think you've lost. Things you didn't know you had, even. You'll see.

MAMA: I'm not sure I want them. They'll make me think of you.

JESSIE: No they won't. They're just things, like a free tube of toothpaste I found hanging on the door one day.

MAMA: Oh. All right, then.

JESSIE: Well, maybe there's one nice present in there somewhere. It's Granny's ring she gave me and I thought you might like to have it, but I didn't think you'd wear it if I gave it to you right now.

MAMA *(Taking the box to a table nearby):* No. Probably not. *(Turning back to face her)* I'm ready for my manicure, I guess. Want me to wash my hands again?

JESSIE *(Standing up):* It's time for me to go, Mama.

MAMA *(Starting for her):* No, Jessie, you've got all night!

JESSIE *(As* MAMA *grabs her):* No, Mama.

MAMA: It's not even ten o'clock.

JESSIE *(Very calm):* Let me go, Mama.

MAMA: I can't. You can't go. You can't do this. You didn't say it would be so soon, Jessie. I'm scared. I love you.

JESSIE *(Takes her hands away):* Let go of me, Mama. I've said everything I had to say.

MAMA *(Standing still a minute):* You said you wanted to do my nails.

JESSIE *(Taking a small step backward):* I can't. It's too late.

MAMA: It's not too late!

JESSIE: I don't want you to wake Dawson and Loretta when you call. I want them to still be up and dressed so they can get right over.

MAMA *(As* JESSIE *backs up,* MAMA *moves in on her, but carefully):* They wake up fast, Jessie, if they have to. They don't matter here, Jessie. You do. I do. We're not through yet. We've got a lot of things to take care of here. I don't know where my prescriptions are and you didn't tell me what to tell Dr. Davis when he calls or how much you want me to tell Ricky or who I call to rake the leaves or . . .

JESSIE: Don't try and stop me, Mama, you can't do it.

MAMA *(Grabbing her again, this time hard):* I can too! I'll stand in front of this hall and you can't get past me. *(They struggle)* You'll have to knock me down to get away from me, Jessie. I'm not about to let you . . .

*(*MAMA *struggles with* JESSIE *at the door and in the struggle* JESSIE *gets away from her and—*

JESSIE *(Almost a whisper):* 'Night, Mother. *(She vanishes into her bedroom and we hear the door lock just as* MAMA *gets to it)*

MAMA *(Screams):* Jessie! *(Pounding on the door)* Jessie, you let me in there. Don't you do this, Jessie. I'm not going to stop screaming until you open this door, Jessie. Jessie! Jessie! What if I don't do any of the things you told me to do! I'll tell Cecil what a miserable man he was to make you feel the way he did and I'll give Ricky's watch to Dawson if I feel like it and the only way you can make sure I do what you want is you come out here and make me, Jessie! *(Pounding again)* Jessie! Stop this! I didn't know! I was here with you all the time. How could I know you were so alone?

(And MAMA *stops for a moment, breathless and frantic, putting her ear to the door, and when she doesn't hear anything, she stands up straight again and screams once more)*

Jessie! Please!

(And we hear the shot, and it sounds like an answer, it sounds like No. MAMA *collapses against the door, tears streaming down her face, but not screaming anymore. In shock now)*

Jessie, Jessie, child . . . Forgive me. *(Pause)* I thought you were mine.

(And she leaves the door and makes her way through the living room, around the furniture, as though she didn't know where it was, not knowing what to do. Finally, she goes to the stove in the kitchen and picks up the hot-chocolate pan and carries it with her to the telephone, and holds on to it while she dials the number. She looks down at the pan, holding it tight like her life depended on it. She hears Loretta answer)

MAMA: Loretta, let me talk to Dawson, honey.

—1983

What are your reactions to and questions about this work? The following questions may help provoke some ideas.

Probing the Work

1. Find an exchange between Jessie and Mama that reveals an important quality of their relationship. From this passage, what can you infer about the following:
   - their past relationship
   - their present relationship
   - their individual personalities
2. Look carefully at some of Norman's stage directions:
   - What kind of information do you gain from them?
   - How do the stage directions influence your understanding of the characters?
3. What is the function of Jessie's brother Dawson in this play? How is he *characterized* (see p. 77)? How does he affect the outcome of the play?

4. In an interview, Marsha Norman said that even though Jessie has her way and commits suicide, "Mama does gain other things in the course of the evening." What does she "gain"?
5. At the end of the play Thelma and Jessie struggle at the door, but, according to Norman, "Thelma's crucial letting go has occurred earlier in the [play]." At what point does Thelma "let go" of Jessie?
6. According to Norman, *'night, Mother* is "a play of nearly total triumph." Do you agree or disagree, and why?

Identifying Issues

7. To what extent is it a child's responsibility to care for a parent as each gets older? What are the ramifications and implications of such a role-reversal, both in the play and in life?
8. How sympathetic toward Jessie do you think Norman wants us to be? Do you think her suicide is justified? Under what circumstances, if any, do you think suicide is justifiable in "real life"?
9. "Americans have a life-at-all-costs attitude," Norman has said, as opposed to, say, the Japanese, who believe suicide is more of a civil right. What do you think about American attitudes toward life and suicide? How do such attitudes affect laws, or personal decisions, about one's right to die? (See Ishiguro's "Family Supper," p. 493.)
10. The question the play asks, according to Norman, is " 'What does it take to survive? What does it take to save your life?' Now Jessie's answer is 'It takes killing myself.' Mama's answer is 'It takes cocoa and marshmallows and doilies and the *TV Guide* and Agnes and the birds and trips to the grocery.' Jessie feels, 'No, I'm sorry. That's not enough.' " What is your answer to the play's question? What does it take to save your life?
11. Read the following two reviews of *'night, Mother*, the first by Frank Rich, the second by Stanley Kauffmann. Which of the reviews better reflects your opinions of the play? With what specific points of each review do you agree or disagree, and why?

Commentary

FRANK RICH

Suicide Talk in 'night, Mother

"We've got a good life here," says Thelma Cates to her daughter, Jessie, in Marsha Norman's new play, " 'Night, Mother." Many would agree. Thelma, who is a widow, and Jessie, who is divorced, live together in a spick-and-span house on a country road somewhere in the New South. There are no money problems. Nights are spent in such relaxed pursuits as crocheting and watching television.

But on the particular, ordinary Saturday night that we meet Thelma (Anne Pitoniak) and Jessie (Kathy Bates), we learn that the good life may not be so good after all. As the daughter prepares to perform her weekly ritual of giving her mother a manicure, she says calmly, almost as a throwaway line, "I'm going to kill myself, Mama." And, over the next 90 minutes, Mama—and the rest of us—must face the fact that Jessie is not kidding.

" 'Night, Mother," which has traveled to Broadway's John Golden Theater from Harvard's American Repertory Theater, is a shattering evening, but it looks like simplicity itself. A totally realistic play, set in real time counted by onstage clocks, it shows us what happens after Jessie makes her announcement. What happens, unsurprisingly, is that the first skeptical and then terrified mother tries to cajole and talk her child out of suicide. "People don't really kill themselves," argues Thelma, "unless they're retarded or deranged."

But Jessie isn't deranged—she's never felt better in her life—and that's why " 'Night, Mother" is more complex than it looks, more harrowing than even its plot suggests. Miss Norman's play is simple only in the way that an Edward Hopper painting is simple. As she perfectly captures the intimate details of two individual, ordinary women, this playwright locates the emptiness that fills too many ordinary homes on too many faceless streets in the vast country we live in now.

Why does Jessie want to kill herself? There are many conceivable motives. She's a fat, lumpy, anonymous-looking woman in her 30's who spends her days indoors, eating junk food. Her son is a hoodlum. Her last job, working at a gift shop in a hospital, didn't work out. She misses her dead father, as well as the husband who left her. She suffers from epilepsy, though it's now been brought under control by medication.

As the play progresses, her mother enumerates all these disappointments, desperately offering to solve any of them she can. But Jessie will have none of it. She instead wants to use her last hours to help her mother get the house in order and to sit around chatting "like every other night of our lives." The daughter insists that they make cocoa, re-cover the couch and clean out the refrigerator.

Jessie is at peace about her decision because she has decided that nothing can change it. "It doesn't really matter what else happens in the world or in this house," she says, for the real problem is "nobody out there, but my own self." In Jessie's opinion, that self—her interior life—is something that she "lost" and that will "never show up." It is also the only "real" possession she has; and she claims the right to "stop it, shut it down, turn it off."

Although it is likely to kindle many debates about the subject, " 'Night, Mother" is not a message play about the choice to commit suicide. It's about contemporary life and what gives it—or fails to give it—value. We first get a sense of the Cates's existence before " 'Night, Mother" begins. Heidi Landesman's disturbing set, in view as we enter the theater, is an all-American living room and kitchen, right out of a television sitcom: homey, appointed with the right appliances, conventionally tasteful. But, when James F. Ingalls's cruelly bright lighting comes up, we see the house is colorless and dead—a pair of antiseptic model rooms, framed like a department-store window.

Miss Norman's dialogue maps the rest of the vacuum. When Thelma at first mistakes Jessie's preoccupation with guns for a fear of burglars, she says, "We don't have anything people would want." And we come to see that neither mother nor daughter does. Their lives are built on neighborhood gossip, ritualized familial obligations and housekeeping. Before tonight—when a gun is literally to their heads—they've never expressed their real feelings to one another or to anybody else. The more loneliness that is exposed the more we realize that the most horrifying aspect of " 'Night, Mother" is not Jessie's decision to end her life but her mother's gradual awakening—and ours—to the inexorable logic of that decision.

The play would never work, never make that logic real, if Miss Norman for a second condescended to her characters by painting them as fools—or if she stuck in authorial speeches that commented on or judged their predicament. As she previously demonstrated in "Getting Out," Miss Norman is far too honest a writer to fall into those traps.

Jessie and Thelma are not caricatured as stupid yokels. They are not without wit; When the mother begs the daughter to stay around "for a few more years" until her own death, she uses every argument that the smartest member of the audience might muster . . . Jessie, meanwhile, knocks those arguments down with brutal, eloquent force.

The strongest argument, of course, is the blood tie. Miss Norman draws the mother-daughter relationship painfully, with all the guilt and anger and twisted passion it can contain. During the course of the play, Thelma and Jessie ask each other every question they've ever wanted to ask—from "Why did your husband leave you?" to "Why did you never wear the sweater I made you?" As they do, the women often switch roles, to the excruciating point at which Thelma becomes a tantrum-throwing infant, lashing out at Jessie any way she can.

At more tender times, we see the love between these women, but we also see that it's not enough to make a difference to Jessie, who has no self-love. "You are my child!" cries the mother, in a primal plea. "No," says the daughter. "I am what became of your child."

Under the brilliant, unerring choreographic hand of the director Tom Moore—who follows the playwright by refusing to gild or theatricalize any moment—the superb actresses, both veterans of Louisville's Actors Theater, circle each other in a grueling dance of death that ebbs and flows so naturally that every violent transition catches us by surprise. There are pockets of humor—the mother even gets a laugh describing her daughter's youthful epileptic fits—and there is warmth.

But there is also the sight of Miss Pitoniak's Thelma, a gabby "plain country woman," turning white and dumb with fear as she realizes that the daughter through whom she's lived by proxy is beyond her reach—"already gone," even though still alive. And there is the moment when the otherwise deliberate Miss Bates turns away from her whimpering mother to wail defiantly, "I say *no* to hope."

Does " 'Night, Mother" say no to hope? It's easy to feel that way after reeling from this play's crushing blow. But there can be hope if there is understanding, and it is Marsha Norman's profound achievement that she brings both understanding and dignity to forgotten and tragic American lives.

—1983

STANLEY KAUFFMANN

More Trick than Tragedy

If the hoopla about Marsha Norman's new play were credible, the current state of American drama would be better than it is. *'night, Mother* has lately been garlanded with a Pulitzer after lusty cheering by many critics. Because the play has only two characters, is in one long act, and ends with a death, some commentators have called it classical and have invoked Aristotle. I envy their rapture; the play itself keeps me from sharing it. *'night, Mother* is certainly better written and constructed than Norman's last New York production, *Getting Out,* but like that earlier play, the new one is fundamentally a stunt. Moreover, I think it has been misconstrued by most who have written about it, and apparently by the author herself.

Getting Out, which was done off-Broadway in 1979, dealt with an unruly Southern girl, her troubles with the law, and her struggle for rehabilitation after prison. The protagonist was shown at two ages, teens and twenties, and was played by two actresses. This tired ingenuity, which was embossed with tired candor, camouflaged the fact that the play was only a gussied-up rehash of a 1930s Girls-in-the-Big-House movie. Inarguably *'night, Mother* addresses deeper themes, is less flashy, and has a number of sharp lines; nonetheless it too is a device, a stunt, and not an authentic drama; and it fails at being even the drama that it claims to be.

The play *seems* to be about a woman in her thirties for whom life has lost savor and point and who decides to make a quick exit with one bullet: it seems to be a drama of the courage to face nullity, to recognize and reject it. Jessie is a plump, divorced country woman who lives with her widowed mother in the family home. (The dead father/husband was a hardworking farmer. Norman never explains how he left enough money, insurance or otherwise, for these two women to live on without worries.) At the moment that the play begins, Jessie comes into the parlor-and-kitchen set carrying a beach towel and asks her mother whether there's a sheet of plastic around. The question is matter-of-fact, as is her question about where Daddy's gun is. She climbs to the attic, gets the pistol, and announces as she cleans it that she is going to kill herself. At the end of an hour and a half, by the clock on the wall crammed with doodads, she goes into the bedroom, locks the door, and does it. (The play could have used the same title as the last Norman work.)

After Jessie's calm announcement of intent, her mother, Thelma, goes through recurring stages of disbelief, fright, panic, near-petulance, near-acceptance, and dismay. Jessie just plows ahead through the last ninety minutes of her life, occasionally pierced by stabs of feeling, but mostly making careful preparations or informing Thelma of preparations already made, including much trivia about deliveries of groceries, milk, and candy.

The trivia are used as light background for the dark matters that are revealed. Jessie has been divorced by the husband she still loves; her teenage son is a thief and drug addict living on the loose; she has epilepsy, as her father had. She has had a year's remission of the illness, which apparently is meant to underscore that she is not committing suicide to escape it. Nor is she killing herself because of any other circumstance of her life that we learn about. Why, then, is she doing it? She is empty. She has been waiting for herself all these years, and " 'I' never got here." Her life is so unvaryingly flavorless that, she says, death will only be like getting off a bus fifty blocks before the end of the line. She is quitting life fifty years before the end because she will be in the same "place" then as she is now.

Despite her mother's increasing terror, Jessie is obdurate. "You are my child!" cries Thelma. "No," Jessie replies, "I am what became of your child." At the last, a self-determined last, she tears herself from her mother's grasp, goes into the bedroom, locks the door so that Thelma can't be suspected of murdering her, and after a moment, shoots.

Ostensibly we have been watching the last moments of a present-day spiritual aristocrat, a woman who can look on life and death with a judicious eye and can choose courageously, a woman who recognizes desolation and declines to be humiliated by it even if her choice costs her life. But is that really what we have seen?

How can we accept Jessie's statements about herself: accept her condition of emancipated despair? If these things were true, what possible reason would she have to *announce* her decision, then put her mother through those ninety minutes? She says she is doing it to spare Thelma the pain of discovery after the event. Is this a rational way to spare another person pain: to subject her mother to these ninety minutes and leave her with a memory of them in *addition* to the suicide? Could a nobly philosophic, privately resolved Jessie really come in calmly with that blanket, calmly ask for a plastic sheet and a pistol, and calmly sit there cleaning the pistol in front of her mother?

In reality, we are watching an act of vengeance. Jessie is not, as implied, our vicar in a Slough of Despond that possibly threatens us all. Jessie is a case. She is a woman haunted by an illness that may recur, a woman parted from the husband she loves because, she says, he asked her to choose between him and smoking! As for her relationship with her mother, Thelma says she got tired of watching Jessie and her father, whom Jessie loved, "going on and off like electric lights" because of their illness. This is the same Thelma who walked away from her husband's deathbed to watch *Gunsmoke* because he wouldn't talk to her.

Add up all these elements, and Jessie stands clear as a vengeful neurotic, not a tragic heroine. It's a truism that suicides are committed *at* someone, and this play, intentionally or not, dramatizes it. Jessie's last utterance, which is the title of the work, is the last twist of the knife. Instead of a woman quietly exalted by her ultra-rational choice and by her will to carry it out, we see a woman deceptively serene (as serenity often is), whose life has been made impossible by ill luck and warped values, whose buried hatred for her mother has italicized her despair, who is bent on suicide, and who comes in to torture her mother for ninety minutes before doing it. That grim, twisted Jessie is latent in the script, of course, or she couldn't be perceived; but Norman, deliberately or unwittingly, has chosen to present Jessie as a rustic female samurai who speaks implicitly to the residual nobility in us all.

Thelma, too, is contradictorily drawn. From Moment One she is almost a caricature of a self-centered old baby, with no more brain than she needs to make hot chocolate and watch TV. And what does this silly old woman do when she hears her daughter's suicide plan? She plunges into deterrent chat, in domestic light-comedy style. Instead of the hysteria we might expect from this dodo, instead of the screaming or fainting or struggle or even a transparent ruse to get the gun, she casts herself as a partner in a "clever" cat-and-mouse duet, as if she were accustomed to such crises and were competent to handle them. When she sees deterrence failing, she thinks more of the threat to herself than to Jessie, of the disturbance of her cozy life, and in childish pique she makes a mess—she throws pots on the floor. Thelma's actions result not from the complexity of a character, but from the traffic-management of a character by its author to make the play possible.

That is the pervasive flaw of the whole play: manipulation. To put it another way, if the play were true—true to Norman's characters as she wants us to think of them—it wouldn't exist. Either Jessie would shoot herself before it begins, or, as soon as she discloses her plans, Thelma would collapse. Thus, though *'night, Mother* is more subtle than *Getting Out,* it is at bottom equally a stunt, a contrivance, and the author's tyrannical governance of characters in order to flesh out a gimmicky framework: the suicide announcement at the start and the pistol shot at the finish.

Thelma's one impeccable line comes right after the shot. Against the locked bedroom door she sobs: "Forgive me. I thought you were mine." The drama that really leads to that line—of a clawing Electra complex, of the mother's mirror-image hatreds, and of the pity overarching both—has not been written.

—1983

WRITING ASSIGNMENT SEQUENCE (CONTINUED FROM PAGE 373)

4. Making Connections

Select one of the following questions and write an informal response in which you connect your own ideas with those conveyed in the works of this cluster, and/or make connections among the works themselves.

A. After reading the works in this cluster, have the ideas you expressed in your earlier exercise regarding a mother's identity changed? If so, how? If not, why not?

B. What are the strengths and weaknesses of the different mothers portrayed here? Which mothers can you most readily connect with? With which do you sympathize? Explain your answers.

C. Compare and contrast the different ways that *culture* (the place where you live, its values and common ideals) and *context* (the situation you are in) influence these mothers' actions and attitudes.

D. What conflicts between mothers and children are expressed in the works of this cluster? Which ones seem most intriguing? Provocative? Believable? Damaging?

5. Putting It All Together

Write an essay that combines what you think about the topic *Mother's Inheritance* with what you now understand about the readings.

- Collect your informal writing, notes, and reading-journal entries on this topic and decide what will be the focus of your essay.
- Outline your essay. Select the literary passages and personal details you might use to illustrate and support your main focus.
- Write a draft of your essay in which you bring together what you think about the subject with what you understand about the readings. Try to include in your draft one or more *literary terms.*

- Share what you've written with your classmates and instructor, then revise it according to their recommendations.

Writing Tip: Signposts

Make a list or circle the transitional *(signpost)* words you have used (1) between paragraphs and (2) within paragraphs to link ideas, achieve coherence, and help the reader more easily follow your train of thought. (See the explanation and list of *signpost* words on page 32.) Try to use a combination of devices; try not to overuse the same words.

Here are two paragraphs from Michelle's essay related to mothers—with some of the *signposts* underlined. Has she used transitions effectively?

> In Saudian Arabian society, women are not treated equally and have very few rights. According to the Muslim religion, women are weak, emotional, and subject to temptation (Nyrop 94). Therefore, all decisions must be made by the men in the household, mainly the father. The primary decision to be made in a young woman's life is that of marriage. However, according to Hala (who was born and raised in Jordan), the women had no choice in the selection of their marriage partners: "Representatives of both the bride and groom negotiate the marriage" (Nyrop 93). In fact, many women did not even see the groom until the marriage agreement had been finalized (Hala).
>
> Also a tradition in this Arabic society is how the woman is brought into the man's family. The groom's family comes to the bride's house to get her and then the ceremony takes place at his house. Hence, "they confiscated the inheritance" according to Abu-Khalid (380). However, she is left with the strength found in her mother's "Garden of Eden" (1. 19) and her soul, which they can not reach. Traditionally, the woman does not inherit property or material goods. The speaker needs a connection with her mother after the wedding takes place. Her only "inheritance" and reminder of her mother is her body and the ability to reproduce.

CrossClusters

In your paper you might want to consider how the following works located elsewhere in this book depict mothers:

- Richard Wright, "The Man Who Was Almost a Man" (p. 93)
- Alice Munro, "Boys and Girls" (p. 109)
- Shirley Jackson, "The Lottery" (p. 131)
- Lorraine Hansberry, *A Raisin in the Sun* (p. 253)
- Frank O'Connor, "My Oedipus Complex" (p. 350)

- Russell Baker, from *Growing Up* (p. 343)
- Audre Lorde, "Hanging Fire" (p. 361)
- Raymond Carver, "My Father's Life" (p. 446)
- James Baldwin, "The Rockpile" (p. 462)
- Alice Walker, "Everyday Use" (p. 483)
- Sam Shepard, *True West* (p. 502)
- Henrik Ibsen, *A Doll's House* (p. 659)
- Grace Paley, "The Loudest Voice" (p. 971)

Sample Essay

Here is a draft of Eugene's essay. He decided to focus on "The Shawl" and incorporate some ideas he gained from reading other sources and seeing the film *Schindler's List.*

"The Magic of Life," by Eugene Antonov

When I read the story "The Shawl" by Cynthia Ozick I was impressed and slightly shocked. I was shocked not only by the events reflected in the story, but by the language, the expressions, the words being used to describe the physical and especially mental sufferings of the characters. I have never thought it possible to convey human emotions on paper so closely, so touchingly that you feel as if you have suffered through this yourself. I was sure that the author of the story was a real participant and that the work is a kind of memoir—otherwise it would be preposterous to assume that it was a result of someone's fantasy.

Reading the story reminded me of "Schindler's List"—the movie I saw just a few weeks ago. The written words of the story sounded for me like a soundtrack of the movie. I saw those "glinting helmets" and electrified fences and exhausted people; I smelled the gunpowder smoke and the scent of human fear. I remembered other movies and books based on the facts of World War II, when more than 20 million Russians were killed by Nazis; my grandfather was one of them.

I was impressed for the second time when I looked up the biography of Cynthia Ozick. She never was there! She tells a tale directly from the consciousness of a Holocaust survivor, using the facts gleaned from the history and events derived from memoirs. She manages to create a successful combination of biography and fiction, realism and imagery in order to deviate from the mere depiction of the documentary facts. That is why the place and the time of the events in the story are not mentioned, creating the terrifying feeling of timelessness, as if it may happen right now, in the real world. The wars in former Yugoslavia and the former Soviet Union can serve as real world examples.

As Robert Harris says, "[Ozick's] stories are elusive, mysterious, and disturbing. They shimmer with intelligence, they glory in language, and they puzzle" (25). That is true; there are a few vague moments in the story that can be clarified only by thorough research, which, of course, makes it more exciting and challenging. Only in the second paragraph, Cynthia Ozick mentions the yellow Star of David sewn into Rosa's coat and reveals that these three people are Jews on a march whose destination is a Nazi concentration camp. But what does the sentence "You could think [Magda] was one of their babies" (Ozick 382) mean, and why does Stella call Magda "Aryan"? Presumably, Magda was born of a German father, which sounds quite strange (Germans would never mix with Jews). In my research I learned that Rosa was raped by an S.S. officer in a conçentration camp. This fact intensifies Rosa's struggle to conceal Magda from Nazis. It also explains the hostile attitude of Stella, Rosa's niece—the sequel story "Rosa" expands on this relationship—who desires to "devour" her.

This is not a metaphor. In an interview Cynthia Ozick says, "Only once did I ever put a real dream in a piece of writing. It was a nightmare. A long and horrifying set of teeth appeared up and down a human thigh" ("Authors" 299). She doesn't mention where exactly she used it, but I think that it results in the depiction of Stella's cannibalism. Stella studies the blueness of the baby's eyes, gazes at the roundness of its face, "waiting for Magda to die"—an event that the shawl delays.

The talented use of metaphors starts from the very title—the shawl is an epitome of safety and peace. Wrapped in the shawl in the "place without pits," Magda is safe because it is quiet. It is guarded by Magda: "No one could touch it. . . . The shawl was Magda's own baby, her pet, her little sister" (Ozick, 383). When Rosa's teats dry out of milk, Ozick calls it the "duct-crevice extinct, a dead volcano, blind eye, chill hole" (382), stressing its inability to nourish the child any more. Mentioning the fence with "grainy sad voices", she, presumably, intimates the "voices" of numbers of people who died from the fence. They are warning Rosa not to approach the fence, to stay away from it. Magda doesn't avoid it: "She looked like a butterfly touching a silver vine" (Ozick, 384). The rhythm of these words can melt any heart, even the sturdiest one.

15

MY FATHER'S LIFE

WRITING ASSIGNMENT SEQUENCE

1. Thinking About . . . Fathers

Brainstorming: Write the word *father* on a piece of paper and jot down any words that come to mind. Which words fit the conventional image of a father? Which are unusual, or suggest other ways of seeing that word?

2. Enacting the Topic

Role Playing: From the perspective of your father (even if unknown, or deceased), *write a letter* to your child (you, the writer) in which you describe a meaningful incident in your lives from *his* perspective, and attempt to define your relationship (past or present) from *his* point of view.

3. Responding to the Readings

As you read the works in this cluster, jot down in your response journals questions you have about the works, and comment on passages you find provocative or puzzling. Consider the questions following each reading for journal writing and prepare to discuss your reactions in class.

CLUSTER ESSAY

RAYMOND CARVER

My Father's Life

Raymond Carver (1939–1988) was born in Oregon and grew up in Yakima, a working-class town in Washington. He was married at 19 and moved to California, where he worked nights and attended Chico State College and then Humboldt State College. He worked at many jobs, of both the unskilled and literary variety, and wrote about the lives of blue-collar people. In the late 1970s, after years of unhappiness and a great deal of smoking and drinking, Carver met, fell in love with, and later married the writer Tess Gallagher (see page 620). With her he spent a happy final decade of his life. Among his publications are What We Talk About When We Talk About Love *(1981),* Cathedral *(1983), and* Where I'm Calling From *(1988).*

My dad's name was Clevie Raymond Carver. His family called him Raymond and friends called him C.R. I was named Raymond Clevie Carver, Jr. I hated the "Junior" part. When I was little my dad called me Frog, which was okay. But later, like everybody else in the family, he began calling me Junior. He went on calling me this until I was thirteen or fourteen and announced that I wouldn't answer to that name any longer. So he began calling me Doc. From then until his death, on June 17, 1967, he called me Doc, or else Son.

When he died, my mother telephoned my wife with the news. I was away from my family at the time, between lives, trying to enroll in the School of Library Science at the University of Iowa. When my wife answered the phone, my mother blurted out, "Raymond's dead!" For a moment, my wife thought my mother was telling her that I was dead. Then my mother made it clear *which* Raymond she was talking about and my wife said, "Thank God. I thought you meant *my* Raymond."

My dad walked, hitched rides, and rode in empty boxcars when he went from Arkansas to Washington State in 1934, looking for work. I don't know whether he was pursuing a dream when he went out to Washington. I doubt it. I don't think he dreamed much. I believe he was simply looking for steady work at decent pay. Steady work was meaningful work. He picked apples for a time and then landed a construction laborer's job on the Grand Coulee Dam. After he'd put aside a little money, he bought a car and drove back to Arkansas to help his folks, my grandparents, pack up for the move west. He said later that they were about to starve down there, and this wasn't meant as a figure of speech. It was during that short while in Arkansas, in a town called Leola, that my mother met my dad on the sidewalk as he came out of a tavern.

"He was drunk," she said. "I don't know why I let him talk to me. His eyes were glittery. I wish I'd had a crystal ball." They'd met once, a year or so before, at a dance. He'd had girlfriends before her, my mother told me. "Your dad always had a girlfriend, even after we married. He was my first and last. I never had another man. But I didn't miss anything."

They were married by a justice of the peace on the day they left for Washington, this big, tall country girl and a farmhand-turned-construction worker. My mother spent her wedding night with my dad and his folks, all of them camped beside the road in Arkansas.

In Omak, Washington, my dad and mother lived in a little place not much bigger than a cabin. My grandparents lived next door. My dad was still working on the dam, and later, with the huge turbines producing electricity and the water backed up for a hundred miles into Canada, he stood in the crowd and heard Franklin D. Roosevelt when he spoke at the construction site. "He never mentioned those guys who died building that dam," my dad said. Some of his friends had died there, men from Arkansas, Oklahoma, and Missouri.

He then took a job in a sawmill in Clatskanie, Oregon, a little town alongside the Columbia River. I was born there, and my mother has a picture of my dad standing in front of the gate to the mill, proudly holding me up to face the camera. My bonnet is on crooked and about to come untied. His hat is pushed back on his forehead, and he's wearing a big grin. Was he going in to work or just finishing his shift? It doesn't matter. In either case, he had a job and a family. These were his salad days.

In 1941 we moved to Yakima, Washington, where my dad went to work as a saw filer, a skilled trade he'd learned in Clatskanie. When war broke out, he was given a deferment because his work was considered necessary to the war effort. Finished lumber was in demand by the armed services, and he kept his saws so sharp they could shave the hair off your arm.

After my dad had moved us to Yakima, he moved his folks into the same neighborhood. By the mid-1940s the rest of my dad's family—his brother, his sister, and her husband, as well as uncles, cousins, nephews, and most of their extended family and friends—had come out from Arkansas. All because my dad came out first. The men went to work at Boise Cascade, where my dad worked, and the women packed apples in the canneries. And in just a little while, it seemed—according to my mother—everybody was better off than my dad. "Your dad couldn't keep money," my mother said. "Money burned a hole in his pocket. He was always doing for others."

The first house I clearly remember living in, at 1515 South Fifteenth Street, in Yakima, had an outdoor toilet. On Halloween night, or just any night, for the hell of it, neighbor kids, kids in their early teens, would carry our toilet away and leave it next to the road. My dad would have to get somebody to help him bring it home. Or these kids would take the toilet and stand it in somebody else's backyard. Once they actually set it on fire. But ours wasn't the only house that had an outdoor toilet. When I was old enough to know what I was doing, I threw rocks at the other toilets when I'd see someone go inside. This was called bombing the toilets. After a while, though, everyone went to indoor plumbing until, suddenly, our toilet was the last outdoor one in the neighborhood. I remember the shame I felt when my third-grade teacher, Mr. Wise, drove me home from school one day. I asked him to stop at the house just before ours, claiming I lived there.

I can recall what happened one night when my dad came home late to find that my mother had locked all the doors on him from the inside. He was drunk, and we could feel the house shudder as he rattled the door. When he'd managed to force open a window, she hit him between the eyes with a colander and knocked him out. We could see him down there on the grass. For years afterward, I used to pick up this colander—it was as heavy as a rolling pin—and imagine what it would feel like to be hit in the head with something like that.

It was during this period that I remember my dad taking me into the bedroom, sitting me down on the bed, and telling me that I might have to go live with my Aunt LaVon for a while. I couldn't understand what I'd done that meant I'd have to go away from home to live. But this, too—whatever prompted it—must have blown over, more or less, anyway, because we stayed together, and I didn't have to go live with her or anyone else.

I remember my mother pouring his whiskey down the sink. Sometimes she'd pour it all out and sometimes, if she was afraid of getting caught, she'd only pour half of it out and then add water to the rest. I tasted some of his whiskey once myself. It was terrible stuff, and I don't see how anybody could drink it.

After a long time without one, we finally got a car, in 1949 or 1950, a 1938 Ford. But it threw a rod the first week we had it, and my dad had to have the motor rebuilt.

"We drove the oldest car in town," my mother said. "We could have had a Cadillac for all he spent on car repairs." One time she found someone else's tube of lipstick on the floorboard, along with a lacy handkerchief. "See this?" she said to me. "Some floozy left this in the car."

Once I saw her take a pan of warm water into the bedroom where my dad was sleeping. She took his hand from under the covers and held it in the water. I stood in the doorway and watched. I wanted to know what was going on. This would make him talk in his sleep, she told me. There were things she needed to know, things she was sure he was keeping from her.

Every year or so, when I was little, we would take the North Coast Limited across the Cascade Range from Yakima to Seattle and stay in the Vance Hotel and eat, I remember, at a place called the Dinner Bell Cafe. Once we went to Ivar's Acres of Clams and drank glasses of warm clam broth.

In 1956, the year I was to graduate from high school, my dad quit his job at the mill in Yakima and took a job in Chester, a little sawmill town in northern California. The reasons given at the time for his taking the job had to do with a higher hourly wage and the vague promise that he might, in a few years' time, succeed to the job of head filer in this new mill. But I think, in the main, that my dad had grown restless and simply wanted to try his luck elsewhere. Things had gotten a little too predictable for him in Yakima. Also, the year before, there had been the deaths, within six months of each other, of both his parents.

But just a few days after graduation, when my mother and I were packed to move to Chester, my dad penciled a letter to say he'd been sick for a while. He didn't want us to worry, he said, but he'd cut himself on a saw. Maybe he'd got a tiny sliver of steel in his blood. Anyway, something had happened and he'd had to miss work, he said. In the same mail was an unsigned post-card from somebody down there telling my mother that my dad was about to die and that he was drinking "raw whiskey."

When we arrived in Chester, my dad was living in a trailer that belonged to the company. I didn't recognize him immediately. I guess for a moment I didn't want to recognize him. He was skinny and pale and looked bewildered. His pants wouldn't stay up. He didn't look like my dad. My mother began to cry. My dad put his arm around her and patted her shoulder vaguely, like he didn't know what this was all about, either. The three of us took up life together in the trailer, and we looked after him as best we could. But my dad was sick, and he couldn't get any better. I worked with him in the mill that summer and part of the fall. We'd get up in the mornings and eat eggs and toast while we listened to the radio, and then go out the door with our lunch pails. We'd pass through the gate together at eight in the morning, and I wouldn't see him again until quitting time. In November I went back to Yakima to be closer to my girlfriend, the girl I'd made up my mind I was going to marry.

He worked at the mill in Chester until the following February, when he collapsed on the job and was taken to the hospital. My mother asked if I would come down there and help. I caught a bus from Yakima to Chester, intending to drive them back to Yakima. But now, in addition to being physically sick, my dad was in the midst of a nervous breakdown, though none of us knew to call it that at the time. During the entire trip back to Yakima, he didn't speak, not even when asked a direct question. ("How do you feel, Raymond?" "You okay, Dad?") He'd communicate, if he communicated at all, by moving his head or by turning his palms up as if to say he didn't know or care. The only time he said anything on the trip, and for nearly a month afterward, was when I was speeding down a gravel road in Oregon and the car muffler came loose. "You were going too fast," he said.

Back in Yakima a doctor saw to it that my dad went to a psychiatrist. My mother and dad had to go on relief, as it was called, and the county paid for the psychiatrist. The psychiatrist asked my dad, "Who is the President?" He'd had a question put to him that he could answer. "Ike," my dad said. Nevertheless, they put him on the fifth floor of Valley Memorial Hospital and began giving him electroshock treatments. I was married by then and about to start my own family. My dad was still locked up when my wife went into this same hospital, just one floor down, to have our first baby. After she had delivered, I went upstairs to give my dad the news. They let me in through a steel door and showed me where I could find him. He was sitting on a couch with a blanket over his lap. *Hey,* I thought. *What in hell is happening to my dad?* I sat down next to him and told him he was a grandfather. He waited a minute and then he said, "I feel like a grandfather." That's all he said. He didn't smile or move. He was in a big room with a lot of other people. Then I hugged him, and he began to cry.

Somehow he got out of there. But now came the years when he couldn't work and just sat around the house trying to figure what next and what he'd done wrong in his life that he'd wound up like this. My mother went from job to crummy job. Much later she referred to that time he was in the hospital, and those years just afterward, as "when Raymond was sick." The word *sick* was never the same for me again.

In 1964, through the help of a friend, he was lucky enough to be hired on at a mill in Klamath, California. He moved down there by himself to see if he could hack it. He lived not far from the mill, in a one-room cabin not much different from the place he and my mother had started out living in when they went west. He scrawled letters to my mother, and if I called she'd read them aloud to me over the phone. In the letters, he said it was touch and go. Every day that he went to work, he felt like it was the most important day of his life. But every day, he told her, made the next day that much easier. He said for her to tell me he said hello. If he couldn't sleep at night, he said, he thought about me and the good times we used to have. Finally, after a couple of months, he regained some of his confidence. He could do the work and didn't think he had to worry that he'd let anybody down ever again. When he was sure, he sent for my mother.

He'd been off from work for six years and had lost everything in that time—home, car, furniture, and appliances, including the big freezer that had been my mother's pride and joy. He'd lost his good name too—Raymond Carver was someone who couldn't pay his bills—and his self-respect was gone. He'd even lost his virility. My mother told my wife, "All during that time Raymond was sick we slept together in the same bed, but we didn't have relations. He wanted to a few times, but nothing happened. I didn't miss it, but I think he wanted to, you know."

During those years I was trying to raise my own family and earn a living. But, one thing and another, we found ourselves having to move a lot. I couldn't keep track of what was going down in my dad's life. But I did have a chance one Christmas to tell him I wanted to be a writer. I might as well have told him I wanted to become a plastic surgeon. "What are you going to write about?" he wanted to know. Then, as if to help me out, he said, "Write about stuff you know about. Write about some of those fishing trips we took." I said I would, but I knew I wouldn't. "Send me what you write," he said. I said I'd do that, but then I didn't. I wasn't writing anything about fishing, and I didn't think he'd particularly care about, or even necessarily understand, what I was writing in those days. Besides, he wasn't a reader. Not the sort, anyway, I imagined I was writing for.

Then he died. I was a long way off, in Iowa City, with things still to say to him. I didn't have the chance to tell him goodbye, or that I thought he was doing great at his new job. That I was proud of him for making a comeback.

My mother said he came in from work that night and ate a big supper. Then he sat at the table by himself and finished what was left of a bottle of whiskey, a bottle she found hidden in the bottom of the garbage under some coffee grounds a day or so later. Then he got up and went to bed, where my mother joined him a little later. But in the night she had to get up and make a bed for herself on the couch. "He was snoring so loud I couldn't sleep," she said. The next morning when she looked in on him, he was on his back with his mouth open, his cheeks caved in. *Graylooking,* she said. She knew he was dead—she didn't need a doctor to tell her that. But she called one anyway, and then she called my wife.

Among the pictures my mother kept of my dad and herself during those early days in Washington was a photograph of him standing in front of a car, holding a beer and a stringer of fish. In the photograph he is wearing his hat back on his forehead and has this awkward grin on his face. I asked her for it and she gave it to me, along with some others. I put it up on my wall, and each time we moved, I took the picture along and put it up on another wall. I looked at it carefully from time to time, trying to figure out some things about my dad, and maybe myself in the process. But I couldn't. My dad just kept moving further and further away from me and back into time. Finally, in the course of another move, I lost the photograph. It was then that I tried to recall it, and at the same time make an attempt to say something about my dad, and how I thought that in some important ways we might be alike. I wrote the poem when I was living in an apartment house in an urban area south of San Francisco, at a time when I found myself, like my dad, having trouble with alcohol. The poem was a way of trying to connect up with him.

Photograph of My Father in His Twenty-Second Year

October. Here in this dank, unfamiliar kitchen
I study my father's embarrassed young man's face.
Sheepish grin, he holds in one hand a string
of spiny yellow perch, in the other
a bottle of Carlsberg beer.

In jeans and flannel shirt, he leans
against the front fender of a 1934 Ford.
He would like to pose brave and hearty for his posterity,
wear his old hat cocked over his ear.
All his life my father wanted to be bold.

But the eyes give him away, and the hands
that limply offer the string of dead perch
and the bottle of beer. Father, I love you,
yet how can I say thank you, I who can't hold my liquor either
and don't even know the places to fish.

The poem is true in its particulars, except that my dad died in June and not October, as the first word of the poem says. I wanted a word with more than one syllable to it to make it linger a little. But more than that, I wanted a month appropriate to what I felt at the time I wrote the poem—a month of short days and failing light, smoke in the air, things perishing. June was summer nights and days, graduations, my wedding anniversary, the birthday of one of my children. June wasn't a month your father died in.

After the service at the funeral home, after we had moved outside, a woman I didn't know came over to me and said, "He's happier where he is now." I stared at this woman until she moved away. I still remember the little knob of a hat she was wearing. Then one of my dad's cousins—I didn't know the man's name—reached out and took my hand, "We all miss him," he said, and I knew he wasn't saying it just to be polite.

I began to weep for the first time since receiving the news. I hadn't been able to before. I hadn't had the time, for one thing. Now, suddenly, I couldn't stop. I held my wife and wept while she said and did what she could do to comfort me there in the middle of that summer afternoon.

I listened to people say consoling things to my mother, and I was glad that my dad's family had turned up, had come to where he was. I thought I'd remember everything that was said and done that day and maybe find a way to tell it sometime. But I didn't. I forgot it all, or nearly. What I do remember is that I heard our name used a lot that afternoon, my dad's name and mine. But I knew they were talking about my dad. *Raymond,* these people kept saying in their beautiful voices out of my childhood. *Raymond.*

—1984

What are your reactions to and questions about this work? The following questions may help provoke some ideas.

Probing the Work

1. What details from this essay contribute to the definition of Carver's actual relationship with his father? Which signify the level of the relationship he would *like* to have?
2. What details in this essay *characterize* (p. 77) Carver's father? What statements does Carver make that sum up his father's character?

Identifying Issues

3. What are the examples of the qualities shared between son and father? What details illustrate both the tensions and the attachment that exist between father and son? How does the kind of relationship illustrated in Carver's tribute match with other father/son relationships you are familiar with?

ERNEST HEMINGWAY

Fathers and Sons

Ernest Hemingway (1899–1961) was born in Oak Park, Illinois, where his father was a doctor whose patients included the Native American residents. He worked for two newspapers and was wounded in World War I. In the 1920s he lived overseas and published a collection of short stories, In Our Time *(1925) and* The Sun Also Rises *(1926). In 1954 he received the Nobel Prize for Literature, but in 1961 he took his own life, as his father had. His works include* A Farewell to Arms *(1929),* For Whom the Bell Tolls *(1940), and* The Old Man and the Sea *(1952).*

There had been a sign to detour in the center of the main street of this town, but cars had obviously gone through, so, believing it was some repair which had been completed, Nicholas Adams drove on through the town along the empty, brick-paved street, stopped by traffic lights that flashed on and off on this traffic-less Sunday, and would be gone next year when the payments on the system were not met; on under the heavy trees of the small town that are a part of your heart if it is your town and you have walked under them, but that are only too heavy, that shut out the sun and that dampen the houses for a stranger; out past the last house and onto the highway that rose and fell straight away ahead with banks of red dirt sliced cleanly away and the second-growth timber on both sides. It was not his country but it was the middle of fall and all of this country was good to drive through and to see. The cotton was picked and in the clearings there were patches of corn, some cut with streaks of red sorghum, and, driving easily, his son asleep on the seat by his side, the day's run made, knowing the town he would reach for the night, Nick noticed which corn fields had soy beans or peas in them, how the thickets and the cut-over land lay, where the cabins and houses were in relation to the fields and the thickets; hunting the country in his mind as he went by; sizing up each clearing as to feed and cover and figuring where you would find a covey and which way they would fly.

In shooting quail you must not get between them and their habitual cover, once the dogs have found them, or when they flush they will come pouring at you, some rising steep, some skimming by your ears, whirring into a size you have never seen them in the air as they pass, the only way being to turn and take them over your shoulder as they go, before they set their wings and angle down into the thicket. Hunting this country for quail as his father had taught him, Nicholas Adams started thinking about his father. When he first thought about him it was always the eyes. The big frame, the quick movements, the wide shoulders, the hooked, hawk nose, the beard that covered the weak chin, you never thought about—it was always the eyes. They were protected in his head by the formation of the brows; set deep as though a special protection had been devised for some very valuable instrument. They saw much farther and much quicker than the human eye sees and they were the great gift his father had. His father saw as a big-horn ram or as an eagle sees, literally.

He would be standing with his father on one shore of the lake, his own eyes were very good then, and his father would say, "They've run up the flag." Nick could not see the flag or the flag pole. "There," his father would say, "it's your sister Dorothy. She's got the flag up and she's walking out onto the dock."

Nick would look across the lake and he could see the long wooded shoreline, the higher timber behind, the point that guarded the bay, the clear hills of the farm and the white of their cottage in the trees but he could not see any flag pole, or any dock, only the white of the beach and the curve of the shore.

"Can you see the sheep on the hillside toward the point?"

"Yes."

They were a whitish patch on the gray-green of the hill.

"I can count them," his father said.

Like all men with a faculty that surpasses human requirements, his father was very nervous. Then, too, he was sentimental, and, like most sentimental people, he was both cruel and abused. Also, he had much bad luck, and it was not all of it his own. He had died in a trap that he had helped only a little to set, and they had all betrayed him in their various ways before he died. All sentimental people are betrayed so many times. Nick could not write about him yet, although he would, later, but the quail country made him remember him as he was when Nick was a boy and he was very grateful to him for two things: fishing and shooting. His father was as sound on those two things as he was unsound on sex, for instance, and Nick was glad that it had been that way; for some one has to give you your first gun or the opportunity to get it and use it, and you have to live where there is game or fish if you are to learn about them, and now, at thirty-eight, he loved to fish and to shoot exactly as much as when he first had gone with his father. It was a passion that had never slackened and he was very grateful to his father for bringing him to know it.

While for the other, that his father was not sound about, all the equipment you will ever have is provided and each man learns all there is for him to know about it without advice; and it makes no difference where you live. He remembered very clearly the only two pieces of information his father had given him about that. Once when they were out shooting together Nick shot a red squirrel out of a hemlock tree. The squirrel fell, wounded, and when Nick picked him up bit the boy clean through the ball of the thumb.

"The dirty little bugger," Nick said and smacked the squirrel's head against the tree. "Look how he bit me."

His father looked and said, "Suck it out clean and put some iodine on when you get home."

"The little bugger," Nick said.

"Do you know what a bugger is?" his father asked him.

"We call anything a bugger," Nick said.

"A bugger is a man who has intercourse with animals."

"Why?" Nick said.

"I don't know," his father said. "But it is a heinous crime."

Nick's imagination was both stirred and horrified by this and he thought of various animals but none seemed attractive or practical and that was the sum total of direct sexual knowledge bequeathed him by his father except on one other subject. One morning he read in the paper that Enrico Caruso had been arrested for mashing.

"What is mashing?"

"It is one of the most heinous of crimes," his father answered. Nick's imagination pictured the great tenor doing something strange, bizarre, and heinous with a potato masher to a beautiful lady who looked like the pictures of Anna Held on the inside of cigar boxes. He resolved, with considerable horror, that when he was old enough he would try mashing at least once.

His father had summed up the whole matter by stating that masturbation produced blindness, insanity, and death, while a man who went with prostitutes would contract hideous venereal diseases and that the thing to do was to keep your hands off of people. On the other hand his father had the finest pair of eyes he had ever seen and Nick had loved him very much and for a long time. Now, knowing how it had all been, even remembering the earliest times before things had gone badly was not good remembering. If he wrote it he could get rid of it. He had gotten rid of many things by writing them. But it was still too early for that. There were still too many people. So he decided to think of something else. There was nothing to do about his father and he had thought it all through many times. The handsome job the undertaker had done on his father's face had not blurred in his mind and all the rest of it was quite clear, including the responsibilities. He had complimented the undertaker. The undertaker had been both proud and smugly pleased. But it was not the undertaker that had given him that last face. The undertaker had only made certain dashingly executed repairs of doubtful artistic merit. The face had been making itself and being made for a long time. It had modelled fast in the last three years. It was a good story but there were still too many people alive for him to write it.

Nick's own education in those earlier matters had been acquired in the hemlock woods behind the Indian camp. This was reached by a trail which ran from the cottage through the woods to the farm and then by a road which wound through the slashings to the camp. Now if he could still feel all of that trail with bare feet. First there was the pine-needle loam through the hemlock woods behind the cottage where the fallen logs crumbled into wood dust and long splintered pieces of wood hung like javelins in the tree that had been struck by lightning. You crossed the creek on a log and if you stepped off there was the black muck of the swamp. You climbed a fence out of the woods and the trail was hard in the sun across the field with cropped grass and sheep sorrel and mullen growing and to the left the quaky bog of the creek bottom where the killdeer plover fed. The spring house was in that creek. Below the barn there was fresh warm manure and the other older manure that was caked dry on top. Then there was another fence and the hard, hot trail from the barn to the house and the hot sandy road that ran down to the woods, crossing the creek, on a bridge this time, where the cat-tails grew that you soaked in kerosene to make jack-lights with for spearing fish at night.

Then the main road went off to the left, skirting the woods and climbing the hill, while you went into the woods on the wide clay and shale road, cool under the trees, and broadened for them to skid out the hemlock bark the Indians cut. The hemlock bark was piled in long rows of stacks, roofed over with more bark, like houses, and the peeled logs lay huge and yellow where the trees had been felled. They left the logs in the woods to rot, they did not even clear away or burn the tops. It was only the bark they wanted for the tannery at Boyne City; hauling it across the lake on the ice in winter, and each year there was less forest and more open, hot, shadeless, weed-grown slashing.

But there was still much forest then, virgin forest where the trees grew high before there were any branches and you walked on the brown, clean, springy-needled ground with no undergrowth and it was cool on the hottest days and they three lay against the trunk of a hemlock wider than two beds are long, with the breeze high in the tops and the cool light that came in patches, and Billy said:

"You want Trudy again?"

"You want to?"

"Un Huh."

"Come on."

"No, here."

"But Billy—"

"I no mind Billy. He my brother."

Then afterwards they sat, the three of them, listening for a black squirrel that was in the top branches where they could not see him. They were waiting for him to bark again because when he barked he would jerk his tail and Nick would shoot where he saw any movement. His father gave him only three cartridges a day to hunt with and he had a single-barrel twenty-gauge shotgun with a very long barrel.

"Son of a bitch never move," Billy said.

"You shoot, Nickie. Scare him. We see him jump. Shoot him again," Trudy said. It was a long speech for her.

"I've only got two shells," Nick said.

"Son of a bitch," said Billy.

They sat against the tree and were quiet. Nick was feeling hollow and happy.

"Eddie says he going to come some night sleep in bed with you sister Dorothy."

"What?"

"He said."

Trudy nodded.

"That's all he want do," she said. Eddie was their older half-brother. He was seventeen.

"If Eddie Gilby ever comes at night and even speaks to Dorothy you know what I'd do to him? I'd kill him like this." Nick cocked the gun and hardly taking aim pulled the trigger, blowing a hole as big as your hand in the head or belly of that half-breed bastard Eddie Gilby. "Like that. I'd kill him like that."

"He better not come then," Trudy said. She put her hand in Nick's pocket.

"He better watch out plenty," said Billy.

"He's big bluff," Trudy was exploring with her hand in Nick's pocket. "But don't you kill him. You get plenty trouble."

"I'd kill him like that," Nick said. Eddie Gilby lay on the ground with all his chest shot away. Nick put his foot on him proudly.

"I'd scalp him," he said happily.

"No," said Trudy. "That's dirty."

"I'd scalp him and send it to his mother."

"His mother dead," Trudy said. "Don't you kill him, Nickie. Don't you kill him for me."

"After I scalped him I'd throw him to the dogs."

Billy was very depressed. "He better watch out," he said gloomily.

"They'd tear him to pieces," Nick said, pleased with the picture. Then, having scalped that half-breed renegade and standing, watching the dogs tear him, his face unchanging, he fell backward against the tree, held tight around the neck, Trudy holding, choking him, and crying, "No kill him! No kill him! No kill him! No. No. No. Nickie. Nickie. Nickie!"

"What's the matter with you?"

"No kill him."

"I got to kill him."

"He just a big bluff."

"All right," Nickie said. "I won't kill him unless he comes around the house. Let go of me."

"That's good," Trudy said. "You want to do anything now? I feel good now."

"If Billy goes away." Nick had killed Eddie Gilby, then pardoned him his life, and he was a man now.

"You go, Billy. You hang around all the time. Go on."

"Son a bitch," Billy said. "I get tired this. What we come? Hunt or what?"

"You can take the gun. There's one shell."

"All right. I get a big black one all right."

"I'll holler," Nick said.

Then, later, it was a long time after and Billy was still away.

"You think we make a baby?" Trudy folded her brown legs together happily and rubbed against him. Something inside Nick had gone a long way away.

"I don't think so," he said.

"Make plenty baby what the hell."

They heard Billy shoot.

"I wonder if he got one."

"Don't care," said Trudy.

Billy came through the trees. He had the gun over his shoulder and he held a black squirrel by the front paws.

"Look," he said. "Bigger than a cat. You all through?"

"Where'd you get him?"

"Over there. Saw him jump first."

"Got to go home," Nick said.

"No," said Trudy.

"I got to get there for supper."

"All right."

"Want to hunt tomorrow?"

"All right."

"You can have the squirrel."

"All right."

"Come out after supper?"

"No."

"How you feel?"

"Good."

"All right."

"Give me kiss on the face," said Trudy.

Now, as he rode along the highway in the car and it was getting dark, Nick was all through thinking about his father. The end of the day never made him think of him. The end of the day had always belonged to Nick alone and he never felt right unless he was alone at it. His father came back to him in the fall of the year, or in the early spring when there had been jacksnipe on the prairie, or when he saw shocks of corn, or when he saw a lake, or if he ever saw a horse and buggy, or when he saw, or heard, wild geese, or in a duck blind; remembering the time an eagle dropped through the whirling snow to strike a canvas-covered decoy, rising, his wings beating, the talons caught in the canvas. His father was with him, suddenly, in deserted orchards and in new-plowed fields, in thickets, on small hills, or when going through dead grass, whenever splitting wood or hauling water, by grist mills, cider mills and dams and always with open fires. The towns he lived in were not towns his father knew. After he was fifteen he had shared nothing with him.

His father had frost in his beard in cold weather and in hot weather he sweated very much. He liked to work in the sun on the farm because he did not have to and he loved manual work, which Nick did not. Nick loved his father but hated the smell of him and once when he had to wear a suit of his father's underwear that had gotten too small for his father it made him feel sick and he took it off and put it under two stones in the creek and said that he had lost it. He had told his father how it was when his father had made him put it on but his father had said it was freshly washed. It had been, too. When Nick had asked him to smell of it his father sniffed at it indignantly and said that it was clean and fresh. When Nick came home from fishing without it and said he lost it he was whipped for lying.

Afterwards he had sat inside the woodshed with the door open, his shotgun loaded and cocked, looking across at his father sitting on the screen porch reading the paper, and thought, "I can blow him to hell. I can kill him." Finally he felt his anger go out of him and he felt a little sick about it being the gun that his father had given him. Then he had gone to the Indian camp, walking there in the dark, to get rid of the smell. There was only one person in his family that he liked the smell of; one sister. All the others he avoided all contact with. That sense blunted when he started to smoke. It was a good thing. It was good for a bird dog but it did not help a man.

"What was it like, Papa, when you were a little boy and used to hunt with the Indians?"

"I don't know," Nick was startled. He had not even noticed the boy was awake. He looked at him sitting beside him on the seat. He had felt quite alone but this boy had been with him. He wondered for how long. "We used to go all day to hunt black squirrels," he said. "My father only gave me three shells a day because he said that would teach me to hunt and it wasn't good for a boy to go banging around. I went with a boy named Billy Gilby and his sister Trudy. We used to go out nearly every day all one summer."

"Those are funny names for Indians."

"Yes, aren't they," Nick said.

"But tell me what they were like."

"They were Ojibways," Nick said. "And they were very nice."

"But what were they like to be with?"

"It's hard to say," Nick Adams said. Could you say she did first what no one has ever done better and mention plump brown legs, flat belly, hard little breasts, well holding arms, quick searching tongue, the flat eyes, the good taste of mouth, then uncomfortably, tightly, sweetly, moistly, lovely, tightly, achingly, fully, finally, unendingly, never-endingly, never-to-endingly, suddenly ended, the great bird flown like an owl in the twilight, only it daylight in the woods and hemlock needles stuck against your belly. So that when you go in a place where Indians have lived you smell them gone and all the empty pain killer bottles and the flies that buzz do not kill the sweetgrass smell, the smoke smell and that other like a fresh cased marten skin. Nor any jokes about them nor old squaws take that away. Nor the sick sweet smell they get to have. Nor what they did finally. It wasn't how they ended. They all ended the same. Long time ago good. Now no good.

And about the other. When you have shot one bird flying you have shot all birds flying. They are all different and they fly in different ways but the sensation is the same and the last one is as good as the first. He could thank his father for that.

"You might not like them," Nick said to the boy. "But I think you would."

"And my grandfather lived with them too when he was a boy, didn't he?"

"Yes. When I asked him what they were like he said that he had many friends among them."

"Will I ever live with them?"

"I don't know," Nick said. "That's up to you."

"How old will I be when I get a shotgun and can hunt by myself?"

"Twelve years old if I see you are careful."

"I wish I was twelve now."

"You will be, soon enough."

"What was my grandfather like? I can't remember him except that he gave me an air rifle and an American flag when I came over from France that time. What was he like?"

"He's hard to describe. He was a great hunter and fisherman and he had wonderful eyes."

"Was he greater than you?"

"He was a much better shot and his father was a great wing shot too."

"I'll bet he wasn't better than you."

"Oh, yes he was. He shot very quickly and beautifully. I'd rather see him shoot than any man I ever knew. He was always very disappointed in the way I shot."

"Why do we never go to pray at the tomb of my grandfather?"

"We live in a different part of the country. It's a long way from here."

"In France that wouldn't make any difference. In France we'd go. I think I ought to go to pray at the tomb of my grandfather."

"Sometime we'll go."

"I hope we won't live somewhere so that I can never go to pray at your tomb when you are dead."

"We'll have to arrange it."

"Don't you think we might all be buried at a convenient place? We could all be buried in France. That would be fine."

"I don't want to be buried in France," Nick said.

"Well, then, we'll have to get some convenient place in America. Couldn't we all be buried out at the ranch?"

"That's an idea."

"Then I could stop and pray at the tomb of my grandfather on the way to the ranch."

"You're awfully practical."

"Well, I don't feel good never to have even visited the tomb of my grandfather."

"We'll have to go," Nick said. "I can see we'll have to go."

—1933

What are your reactions to and questions about this work? The following questions may help provoke some ideas.

Probing the Work

1. How is the father *characterized* in this story (see page 77)? What details are provided by the narrator that influence your judgment of his father?
2. What does Hemingway's depiction of adolescent sex reveal about Nick's character? Is it accurate, or distorted by the male perspective? Explain.

Identifying Issues

3. In what ways does the bond between father and son, such as the one Hemingway describes, differ from that between mother and daughter?
4. What are the various differences among generations depicted in this story? How important to you is the connection among generations that is stressed at the end? Explain.

JAMES BALDWIN

The Rockpile

*James Baldwin (1924–1987) was born in Harlem and lived as a young man in New Jersey and in the Greenwich Village section of New York City. In 1948 he moved to Paris. While in France and Switzerland, he published two novels—*Go Tell It on the Mountain *(1953) and* Giovanni's Room *(1956)—and a collection of essays,* Notes of a Native Son *(1955). He returned to America in 1957 and continued to publish (*The Fire Next Time *appeared in 1963), travel, and teach at universities until his death of cancer in France.*

Across the street from their house, in an empty lot between two houses, stood the rockpile. It was a strange place to find a mass of natural rock jutting out of the ground; and someone, probably Aunt Florence, had once told them that the rock was there and could not be taken away because without it the subway cars underground would fly apart, killing all the people. This, touching on some natural mystery concerning the surface and the center of the earth, was far too intriguing an explanation to be challenged, and it invested the rockpile, moreover, with such mysterious importance that Roy felt it to be his right, not to say his duty, to play there.

Other boys were to be seen there each afternoon after school and all day Saturday and Sunday. They fought on the rockpile. Sure footed, dangerous, and reckless, they rushed each other and grappled on the heights, sometimes disappearing down the other side in a confusion of dust and screams and upended, flying feet. "It's a wonder they don't kill themselves," their mother said, watching sometimes from the fire escape. "You children stay away from there, you hear me?" Though she said "children" she was looking at Roy, where he sat beside John on the fire escape. "The good Lord knows," she continued. "I don't want you to come home bleeding like a hog every day the Lord sends." Roy shifted impatiently, and continued to stare at the street, as though in this gazing he might somehow acquire wings. John said nothing. He had not really been spoken to: he was afraid of the rockpile and of the boys who played there.

Each Saturday morning John and Roy sat on the fire escape and watched the forbidden street below. Sometimes their mother sat in the room behind them, sewing, or dressing their younger sister, or nursing the baby, Paul. The sun fell across them and across the fire escape with a high, benevolent indifference; below them, men and women, and boys and girls, sinners all, loitered; sometimes one of the church-members passed and saw them and waved. Then, for the moment that they waved decorously back, they were intimidated. They watched the saint, man or woman, until he or she had disappeared from sight. The passage of one of the redeemed made them consider, however vacantly, the wickedness of the street, their own latent wickedness in sitting where they sat; and made them think of their father, who came home early on Saturdays and who would soon be turning this corner and entering the dark hall below them.

But until he came to end their freedom, they sat, watching and longing above the street. At the end of the street nearest their house was the bridge which spanned the Harlem River and led to a city called the Bronx; which was where Aunt Florence lived. Nevertheless, when they saw her coming, she did not come from the bridge, but from the opposite end of the street. This, weakly, to their minds, she explained by saying that she had taken the subway, not wishing to walk, and that, besides, she did not live in *that* section of the Bronx. Knowing that the Bronx was across the river, they did not believe this story ever, but, adopting toward her their father's attitude, assumed that she had just left some sinful place which she dared not name, as, for example, a movie palace.

In the summertime boys swam in the river, diving off the wooden dock, or wading in from the garbage-heavy bank. Once a boy, whose name was Richard, drowned in the river. His mother had not known where he was; she had even come to their house, to ask if he was there. Then, in the evening, at six o'clock, they had heard from the street a woman screaming and wailing; and they ran to the windows and looked out. Down the street came the woman, Richard's mother, screaming, her face raised to the sky and tears running down her face. A woman walked beside her, trying to make her quiet and trying to hold her up. Behind them walked a man, Richard's father, with Richard's body in his arms. There were two white policemen walking in the gutter, who did not seem to know what should be done. Richard's father and Richard were wet, and Richard's body lay across his father's arms like a cotton baby. The woman's screaming filled all the street; cars slowed down and the people in the cars stared; people opened their windows and looked out and came rushing out of doors to stand in the gutter, watching. Then the small procession disappeared within the house which stood beside the rockpile. Then, *"Lord, Lord, Lord!"* cried Elizabeth, their mother, and slammed the window down.

One Saturday, an hour before his father would be coming home, Roy was wounded on the rockpile and brought screaming upstairs. He and John had been sitting on the fire escape and their mother had gone into the kitchen to sip tea with Sister McCandless. By and by Roy became bored and sat beside John in restless silence; and John began drawing into his schoolbook a newspaper advertisement which featured a new electric locomotive. Some friends of Roy passed beneath the fire escape and called him. Roy began to fidget, yelling down to them through the bars. Then a silence fell. John looked up. Roy stood looking at him.

"I'm going downstairs," he said.

"You better stay where you is, boy. You know Mama don't want you going downstairs."

"I be right *back.* She won't even know I'm gone, less you run and tell her."

"I ain't *got* to tell her. What's going to stop her from coming in here and looking out the window?"

"She's talking," Roy said. He started into the house.

"But Daddy's going to be home soon!"

"I be back before *that.* What you all the time got to be so *scared* for?" He was already in the house and he now turned, leaning on the windowsill, to swear impatiently, "I be back in *five* minutes."

John watched him sourly as he carefully unlocked the door and disappeared. In a moment he saw him on the sidewalk with his friends. He did not dare to go and tell his mother that Roy had left the fire escape because he had practically promised not to. He started to shout, *Remember, you said five minutes!* but one of Roy's friends was looking up at the fire escape. John looked down at his schoolbook: he became engrossed again in the problem of the locomotive.

When he looked up again he did not know how much time had passed, but now there was a gang fight on the rockpile. Dozens of boys fought each other in the harsh sun: clambering up the rocks and battling hand to hand, scuffed shoes sliding on the slippery rock; filling the bright air with curses and jubilant cries. They filled the air, too, with flying weapons: stones, sticks, tin cans, garbage, whatever could be picked up and thrown. John watched in a kind of absent amazement—until he remembered that Roy was still downstairs, and that he was one of the boys on the rockpile. Then he was afraid; he could not see his brother among the figures in the sun; and he stood up, leaning over the fire-escape railing. Then Roy appeared from the other side of the rocks; John saw that his shirt was torn; he was laughing. He moved until he stood at the very top of the rockpile. Then, something, an empty tin can, flew out of the air and hit him on the forehead, just above the eye. Immediately, one side of Roy's face ran with blood, he fell and rolled on his face down the rocks. Then for a moment there was no movement at all, no sound, the sun, arrested, lay on the street and the sidewalk and the arrested boys. Then someone screamed or shouted; boys began to run away down the street, toward the bridge. The figure on the ground, having caught its breath and felt its own blood, began to shout. John cried, "Mama! Mama!" and ran inside.

"Don't fret, don't fret," panted Sister McCandless as they rushed down the dark, narrow, swaying stairs, "don't fret. Ain't a boy been born don't get his knocks every now and again. *Lord!"* they hurried into the sun. A man had picked Roy up and now walked slowly toward them. One or two boys sat silent on their stoops; at either end of the street there was a group of boys watching. "He ain't hurt bad," the man said, "wouldn't be making this kind of noise if he was hurt real bad."

Elizabeth, trembling, reached out to take Roy, but Sister McCandless, bigger, calmer, took him from the man and threw him over her shoulder as she once might have handled a sack of cotton. "God bless you," she said to the man, "God bless you, son." Roy was still screaming. Elizabeth stood behind Sister McCandless to stare at his bloody face.

"It's just a flesh wound," the man kept saying, "just broke the skin, that's all." They were moving across the sidewalk, toward the house. John, not now afraid of the staring boys, looked toward the corner to see if his father was yet in sight.

Upstairs, they hushed Roy's crying. They bathed the blood away, to find, just above the left eyebrow, the jagged, superficial scar. "Lord, have mercy," murmured Elizabeth, "another inch and it would've been his eye." And she looked with apprehension toward the clock. "Ain't it the truth," said Sister McCandless, busy with bandages and iodine.

"When did he go downstairs?" his mother asked at last.

Sister McCandless now sat fanning herself in the easy chair, at the head of the sofa where Roy lay, bound and silent. She paused for a moment to look sharply at John. John stood near the window, holding the newspaper advertisement and the drawing he had done.

"We was sitting on the fire escape," he said. "Some boys he knew called him."

"When?"

"He said he'd be back in five minutes."

"Why didn't you tell me he was downstairs?"

He looked at his hands, clasping his notebook, and did not answer.

"Boy," said Sister McCandless, "you hear your mother a-talking to you?"

He looked at his mother. He repeated:

"He said he'd be back in five minutes."

"He said he'd be back in five minutes," said Sister McCandless with scorn, "don't look to me like that's no right answer. You's the man of the house, you supposed to look after your baby brothers and sisters—you ain't supposed to let them run off and get half-killed. But I expect," she added, rising from the chair, dropping the cardboard fan, "your Daddy'll make you tell the truth. Your Ma's way too soft with you."

He did not look at her, but at the fan where it lay in the dark red, depressed seat where she had been. The fan advertised a pomade for the hair and showed a brown woman and her baby, both with glistening hair, smiling happily at each other.

"Honey," said Sister McCandless, "I got to be moving along. Maybe I drop in later tonight. I don't reckon you going to be at Tarry Service tonight?"

Tarry Service was the prayer meeting held every Saturday night at church to strengthen believers and prepare the church for the coming of the Holy Ghost on Sunday.

"I don't reckon," said Elizabeth. She stood up; she and Sister McCandless kissed each other on the cheek. "But you be sure to remember me in your prayers."

"I surely will do that." She paused, with her hand on the door knob, and looked down at Roy and laughed. "Poor little man," she said, "reckon he'll be content to stay on the fire escape *now.*"

Elizabeth laughed with her. "It sure ought to be a lesson to him. You don't reckon," she asked nervously, still smiling, "he going to keep that scar, do you?"

"Lord, no," said Sister McCandless, "ain't nothing but a scratch. I declare, Sister Grimes, you worse than a child. Another couple of weeks and you won't be able to see no scar. No, you go on about your housework, honey, and thank the Lord it weren't no worse." She opened the door; they heard the sound of feet on the stairs. "I expect that's the Reverend," said Sister McCandless, placidly, "I *bet* he going to raise cain."

"Maybe it's Florence," Elizabeth said. "Sometimes she get here about this time." They stood in the doorway, staring, while the steps reached the landing below and began again climbing to their floor. "No," said Elizabeth then, "that ain't her walk. That's Gabriel."

"Well, I'll just go on," said Sister McCandless, "and kind of prepare his mind." She pressed Elizabeth's hand as she spoke and started into the hall, leaving the door behind her slightly ajar. Elizabeth turned slowly back into the room. Roy did not open his eyes, or move; but she knew that he was not sleeping; he wished to delay until the last possible moment any contact with his father. John put his newspaper and his notebook on the table and stood, leaning on the table, staring at her.

"It wasn't my fault," he said. "I couldn't stop him from going downstairs."

"No," she said, "you ain't got nothing to worry about. You just tell your Daddy the truth."

He looked directly at her, and she turned to the window, staring into the street. What was Sister McCandless saying? Then from her bedroom she heard Delilah's thin wail and she turned, frowning, looking toward the bedroom and toward the still open door. She knew that John was watching her. Delilah continued to wail, she thought, angrily, *Now that girl's getting too big for that,* but she feared that Delilah would awaken Paul and she hurried into the bedroom. She tried to soothe Delilah back to sleep. Then she heard the front door open and close—too loud, Delilah raised her voice, with an exasperated sigh Elizabeth picked the child up. Her child and Gabriel's, her children and Gabriel's: Roy, Delilah, Paul. Only John was nameless and a stranger, living, unalterable testimony to his mother's days in sin.

"What happened?" Gabriel demanded. He stood, enormous, in the center of the room, his black lunchbox dangling from his hand, staring at the sofa where Roy lay. John stood just before him, it seemed to her astonished vision just below him, beneath his fist, his heavy shoe. The child stared at the man in fascination and terror—when a girl down home she had seen rabbits stand so paralyzed before the barking dog. She hurried past Gabriel to the sofa, feeling the weight of Delilah in her arms like the weight of a shield, and stood over Roy, saying:

"Now, ain't a thing to get upset about, Gabriel. This boy sneaked downstairs while I had my back turned and got hisself hurt a little. He's alright now."

Roy, as though in confirmation, now opened his eyes and looked gravely at his father. Gabriel dropped his lunchbox with a clatter and knelt by the sofa.

"How you feel, son? Tell your Daddy what happened?"

Roy opened his mouth to speak and then, relapsing into panic, began to cry. His father held him by the shoulder.

"You don't want to cry. You's Daddy's little man. Tell your Daddy what happened."

"He went downstairs," said Elizabeth, "where he didn't have no business to be, and got to fighting with them bad boys playing on that rockpile. That's what happened and it's a mercy it weren't nothing worse."

He looked up at her. "Can't you let this boy answer me for hisself?"

Ignoring this, she went on, more gently: "He got cut on the forehead, but it ain't nothing to worry about."

"You call a doctor? How you know it ain't nothing to worry about?"

"Is you got money to be throwing away on doctors? No, I ain't called no doctor. Ain't nothing wrong with my eyes that I can't tell whether he's hurt bad or not. He got a fright more'n anything else, and you ought to pray God it teaches him a lesson."

"You got a lot to say *now,"* he said, "but I'll have *me* something to say in a minute. I'll be wanting to know when all this happened, what you was doing with your eyes *then."* He turned back to Roy, who had lain quietly sobbing eyes wide open and body held rigid: and who now, at his father's touch, remembered the height, the sharp, sliding rock beneath his feet, the sun, the explosion of the sun, his plunge into darkness and his salty blood; and recoiled, beginning to scream, as his father touched his forehead. "Hold still, hold still," crooned his father, shaking, "hold still. Don't cry. Daddy ain't going to hurt you, he just wants to see this bandage, see what they've done to his little man." But Roy continued to scream and would not be still and Gabriel dared not lift the bandage for fear of hurting him more. And he looked at Elizabeth in fury: "Can't you put that child down and help me with this boy? John, take your baby sister from your mother—don't look like neither of you got good sense."

John took Delilah and sat down with her in the easy chair. His mother bent over Roy, and held him still, while his father, carefully—but still Roy screamed—lifted the bandage and stared at the wound. Roy's sobs began to lessen. Gabriel readjusted the bandage. "You see," said Elizabeth, finally, "he ain't nowhere near dead."

"It sure ain't your fault that he ain't dead." He and Elizabeth considered each other for a moment in silence. "He came mightly close to losing an eye. Course, his eyes ain't as big as your'n, so I reckon you don't think it matters so much." At this her face hardened; he smiled. "Lord, have mercy," he said, "you think you ever going to learn to do right? Where was you when all this happened? Who let him go downstairs?"

"Ain't nobody let him go downstairs, he just went. He got a head just like his father, it got to be broken before it'll bow. I was in the kitchen."

"Where was Johnnie?"

"He was in here?"

"Where?"

"He was on the fire escape."

"Didn't he know Roy was downstairs?"

"I reckon."

"What you mean, you reckon? He ain't got your big eyes for nothing, does he?" He looked over at John. "Boy, you see your brother go downstairs?"

"Gabriel, ain't no sense in trying to blame Johnnie. You know right well if you have trouble making Roy behave, he ain't going to listen to his brother. He don't hardly listen to me."

"How come you didn't tell your mother Roy was downstairs?"

John said nothing, staring at the blanket which covered Delilah.

"Boy, you hear me? You want me to take a strap to you?"

"No, you ain't," she said. "You ain't going to take no strap to this boy, not today you ain't. Ain't a soul to blame for Roy's lying up there now but you—you because you done spoiled him so that he thinks he can do just anything and get away with it. I'm here to tell you that ain't no way to raise no child. You don't pray to the Lord to help you do better than you been doing, you going to live to shed bitter tears that the Lord didn't take his soul today." And she was trembling. She moved, unseeing, toward John and took Delilah from his arms. She looked back at Gabriel, who had risen, who stood near the sofa, staring at her. And she found in his face not fury alone, which would not have surprised her; but hatred so deep as to become insupportable in its lack of personality. His eyes were struck alive, unmoving, blind with malevolence—she felt, like the pull of the earth at her feet, his longing to witness her perdition. Again, as though it might be propitiation, she moved the child in her arms. And at this his eyes changed, he looked at Elizabeth, the mother of his children, the helpmeet given by the Lord. Then her eyes clouded; she moved to leave the room; her foot struck the lunchbox lying on the floor.

"John," she said, "pick up your father's lunchbox like a good boy."

She heard, behind her, his scrambling movement as he left the easy chair, the scrape and jangle of the lunchbox as he picked it up, bending his dark head near the toe of his father's heavy shoe.

—1957

What are your reactions to and questions about this work? The following questions may help provoke some ideas.

Probing the Work

1. How is the father *characterized* here? What details are given about his dress and mannerisms that indicate the kind of person he is?
2. Why is the title of the story, and its focal point, the rockpile? What does it represent?
3. Where does the "hatred" in Gabriel's eyes come from? Why hate his wife over this? What has been building up within him? With her? How much of a role does her past play in the way they treat each other?

Identifying Issues

4. Who, if anyone, is most responsible for Roy's injury? John? Roy? The mother? The father? According to the father, the mother is at fault. But is the mother right, at the end? In general, which kind of attitude and be-

havior—the mother's or the father's—is more likely to be responsible for Roy's rebelliousness?

5. What are some of the religious references or names that you noticed? What is Baldwin attempting to show about the influence of religion on this family and on this society? In what sense is the Christian faith distinctly patriarchal, and how does that aspect of the religion influence the father's role in a Christian household?

THEODORE ROETHKE

My Papa's Waltz

Theodore Roethke (1908–1963) was born in Saginaw, Michigan, and grew up around his father's 25-acre greenhouse complex. He worked at Lafayette College as professor of English and tennis coach. Roethke suffered from periodic mental breakdowns and depression. His books include Open House *(1942) and* The Far Field *(1964).*

The whiskey on your breath
Could make a small boy dizzy;
But I hung on like death;
Such waltzing was not easy.

We romped until the pans
Slid from the kitchen shelf;
My mother's countenance
Could not unfrown itself.

The hand that held my wrist
Was battered on one knuckle;
At every step you missed
My right ear scraped a buckle.

You beat time on my head
With a palm caked hard by dirt,
Then waltzed me off to bed
Still clinging to your shirt.

—1942

What are your reactions to and questions about this work? The following questions may help provoke some ideas.

Probing the Work

1. Pick out the *diction* that suggests this is a playful event, and the *diction* that suggests this is a violent act. What can you conclude about the son's relationship with his father?

Identifying Issues

2. What are the ambivalent qualities of most father/son relationships? What factors tend to make this particular relationship so complex?

RONALD KOERTGE

Orientation Week

Ronald Koertge (pronounced Kur-chee*) was born in Olney, Illinois, in 1940, an only child. He started writing in the 1960s and joined the faculty of Pasadena City College in 1965, where he still teaches. He writes most of his full-length works for young adults:* Where the Kissing Never Stops *(1986),* The Arizona Kid *(1988), and* The Harmony Arms *(1992) are three examples. One exception is his 1980 novel for adults,* The Boogeyman. *Some of his best poems are found in* The Selected Poems of Ronald Koertge *(1982). He has also published a college textbook,* 100 Things to Write About *(1990).*

and a family of two is exploring the Student Union.
Dad is all decked out in the shirt she bought with
her own money. Joyce is wearing snug cutoffs and
her freshman breasts stir as she walks.

Dad knows that all the boys plan to slip some LSD
in her cocoa as soon as he is out of sight. He
takes in the monsters, their hair down to there,
a fuselage in every pair of pants.

Worse than he expected, certainly not the eunuchs
and mild wethers that he hoped for. And where is
The Jake Barnes Dormitory?

He sees them do it to her even as they stand by the
car. Worse, he sees her ask for it, coaxing with
her expensive teeth. Why can't he
lock those vivid hips in her room?
Follow her everywhere, revolvers drawn?
Punch a few of those furry bastards in the chops?

So he does what he can—lips to chaste brow, hand
to bare arm saying,

Good-by now. Be good.

—1982

What are your reactions to and questions about this work? The following questions may help provoke some ideas.

Probing the Work

1. Why doesn't "Dad" tell Joyce what he is thinking?

Identifying Issues

2. To what extent does the father/daughter relationship revolve around protective and fearful impulses regarding sex? How typical is this father's attitude toward his daughter's sexuality, and toward every young man at the college?

SHARON OLDS

The Victims

Sharon Olds (b. 1942) was born in San Francisco and educated at Stanford and Columbia. Her books of poetry include Satan Says *(1980),* The Dead and the Living *(1982),* The Gold Cell *(1987), and* The Father *(1992).*

When Mother divorced you, we were glad. She took it and
took it, in silence, all those years and then
kicked you out, suddenly, and her
kids loved it. Then you were fired, and we
grinned inside, the way people grinned when
Nixon's helicopter lifted off the South
Lawn for the last time.° We were tickled
to think of your office taken away,
your secretaries taken away,
your lunches with three double bourbons,
your pencils, your reams of paper. Would they take your
suits back, too, those dark
carcasses hung in your closet, and the black
noses of your shoes with their large pores?
She had taught us to take it, to hate you and take it
until we pricked with her for your
annihilation, Father. Now I
pass the bums in doorways, the white
slugs of their bodies gleaming through slits in their
suits of compressed silt, the stained
flippers of their hands, the underwater
fire of their eyes, ships gone down with the
lanterns lit, and I wonder who took it and

6–7. Nixon's helicopter . . .last time, when Richard Nixon resigned the U.S. presidency on August 8, 1974, his exit from the White House (by helicopter from the lawn) was televised live.

took it from them in silence until they had
given it all away and had nothing
left but this.

—1984

What are your reactions to and questions about this work? The following questions may help provoke some ideas.

Probing the Work

1. What do you think Olds means by the underwater *metaphors* (see page 68) and *images* (see page 79) she uses in lines 19–23?

Identifying Issues

2. Children of divorced parents at times are led to turn against one of them, most often against the father. Why does this occur? What could bring about a more evenhanded understanding of that parent's perspective?

WRITING ASSIGNMENT SEQUENCE (CONTINUED FROM PAGE 446)

4. Making Connections

Select one of the following questions and write an informal response in which you connect your own ideas with those conveyed in the works of this cluster, and/or make connections among the works themselves.

A. What traits distinguish fathers from mothers?

B. Which of the perspectives on fathers in the works of this cluster comes closest to your own? Why?

C. What are the various roles fathers play in their children's lives?

5. Putting It All Together

Write an essay that combines what you think about the topic *My Father's Life* with what you now understand about the readings.

- Collect your informal writing, notes, and reading-journal entries on this topic and decide what will be the focus of your essay.
- Outline your essay. Select the literary passages and personal details you might use to illustrate and support your main focus.

- Write a draft of your essay in which you bring together what you think about the subject with what you understand about the readings. Try to include in your draft one or more *literary terms.*
- Share what you've written with your classmates and instructor, then revise it according to their recommendations.

Writing Tip: Avoid General Statements

General statements convey messages more clearly as they become more precise. Sentences like "Everybody needs love" waste the reader's time because they don't make a real point. Keep asking yourself, "What do I really want to say about this? How can I *qualify* this statement?" (For example, you might begin to revise the statement above by writing, "Many writers express the pain associated with love," and then continue to narrow your focus.) *Rule of thumb:* effective writers supply specific supporting details and concrete language for every stated opinion or assertion. *Be suspicious of generalizations that are unsupported.* (See page 30 for more on avoiding generalizations.)

CrossClusters

In your paper you might want to consider how the following works located elsewhere in this book depict fathers:

- Alice Munro, "Boys and Girls" (p. 109)
- Rita Dove, "Adolescence III" (p. 120)
- Shirley Jackson, "The Lottery" (p. 131)
- Lorraine Hansberry, *A Raisin in the Sun* (p. 253)
- Frank O'Connor, "My Oedipus Complex" (p. 350)
- Barbara Dafoe Whitehead, "Dan Quayle Was Right" (p. 475)
- Kazuo Ishiguro, "A Family Supper" (p. 493)
- John Updike, "Wife Wooing" (p. 653)
- Henrik Ibsen, *A Doll's House* (p. 659)
- Mme. de Beaumont, "Beauty and the Beast" (p. 732)
- Edgar A. Poe, "The Tell-Tale Heart" (p. 834)
- Grace Paley, "The Loudest Voice" (p. 971)

16

FAMILY REUNION

WRITING ASSIGNMENT SEQUENCE

1. Thinking About . . . the Family

Focused Freewriting: Define *family*. Then describe a familial relationship you have or know of that illustrates the qualities you list in your definition.

2. Enacting the Topic

Interview a family member. With the help of a classmate or friend, write down a list of questions you can ask a family member that will lead him or her to share their concept of *family*. Try to pick the family member you know the least about. Interview him or her, record the responses, and write an assessment of what that person's concept of family is.

3. Responding to the Readings

As you read the works in this cluster, jot down in your response journals questions you have about the works, and comment on passages you find provocative or puzzling. Consider the questions following each reading for journal writing and prepare to discuss your reactions in class.

CLUSTER ESSAY

BARBARA DAFOE WHITEHEAD

Dan Quayle Was Right (excerpt)

Barbara Dafoe Whitehead (b. 1944) is the oldest of eight children; since both her parents worked, she had to look after her younger siblings. Today she has three children of her own. After receiving her B.A. at the University of Wisconsin at Madison, she earned an M.A. and Ph.D. in American Social History at the University of Chicago. Currently she is a social historian and vice president of the Institute for American Values, a nonpartisan research organization devoted to issues of family and civic well-

being. She directs the Institute's project on "The Family in American Culture." She is writing a book called The Divorce Culture *and is co-author of another,* Fatherless America *(1995). Her Mother's Day 1992 article in the Washington Post gave birth to the "Murphy Brown" controversy of that year's presidential campaign.*

Divorce and out-of-wedlock childbirth are transforming the lives of American children. In the postwar generation more than 80 percent of children grew up in a family with two biological parents who were married to each other. By 1980 only 50 percent could expect to spend their entire childhood in an intact family. If current trends continue, less than half of all children born today will live continuously with their own mother and father throughout childhood. Most American children will spend several years in a single-mother family. Some will eventually live in stepparent families, but because stepfamilies are more likely to break up than intact (by which I mean two-biological-parent) families, an increasing number of children will experience family breakup two or even three times during childhood.

According to a growing body of social-scientific evidence, children in families disrupted by divorce and out-of-wedlock birth do worse than children in intact families on several measures of well-being. Children in single-parent families are six times as likely to be poor. They are also likely to stay poor longer. Twenty-two percent of children in one-parent families will experience poverty during childhood for seven years or more, as compared with only two percent of children in two-parent families. A 1988 survey by the National Center for Health Statistics found that children in single-parent families are two to three times as likely as children in two-parent families to have emotional and behavioral problems. They are also more likely to drop out of high school, to get pregnant as teenagers, to abuse drugs, and to be in trouble with the law. Compared with children in intact families, children from disrupted families are at a much higher risk for physical or sexual abuse.

Contrary to popular belief, many children do not "bounce back" after divorce or remarriage. Difficulties that are associated with family breakup often persist into adulthood. Children who grow up in single-parent or stepparent families are less successful as adults, particularly in the two domains of life—love and work—that are most essential to happiness. Needless to say, not all children experience such negative effects. However, research shows that many children from disrupted families have a harder time achieving intimacy in a relationship, forming a stable marriage, or even holding a steady job.

Despite this growing body of evidence, it is nearly impossible to discuss changes in family structure without provoking angry protest. Many people see the discussion as no more than an attack on struggling single mothers and their children: Why blame single mothers when they are doing the very best they can? After all, the decision to end a marriage or a relationship is wrenching, and few parents are indifferent to the painful burden this decision imposes on their children. Many take the perilous step toward single parenthood as a last resort, after their best efforts to hold a marriage together have failed. Consequently, it can seem particularly cruel and unfeeling to remind parents of the hardships their children might suffer as a result of family breakup. Other people believe that the dramatic changes in family structure, though regrettable, are impossible to reverse. Family breakup is an inevitable feature of American life, and anyone who thinks otherwise is indulging in nostalgia or trying to turn back the clock. Since these new family forms are here to stay, the reasoning goes, we must accord respect to single parents, not criticize them. Typical is the view expressed by a Brooklyn woman in a recent letter to *The New York Times:* "Let's stop moralizing or blaming single parents and unwed mothers, and give them the respect they have earned and the support they deserve."

Such views are not to be dismissed. Indeed, they help to explain why family structure is such an explosive issue for Americans. The debate about it is not simply about the social-scientific evidence, although that is surely an important part of the discussion. It is also a debate over deeply held and often conflicting values. How do we begin to reconcile our long-standing belief in equality and diversity with an impressive body of evidence that suggests that not all family structures produce equal outcomes for children? How can we square traditional notions of public support for dependent women and children with a belief in women's right to pursue autonomy and independence in childbearing and child-rearing? How do we uphold the freedom of adults to pursue individual happiness in their private relationships and at the same time respond to the needs of children for stability, security, and permanence in their family lives? What do we do when the interests of adults and children conflict? These are the difficult issues at stake in the debate over family structure.

In the past these issues have turned out to be too difficult and too politically risky for debate. In the mid-1960s Daniel Patrick Moynihan, then an assistant secretary of labor, was denounced as a racist for calling attention to the relationship between the prevalence of black single-mother families and the lower socioeconomic standing of black children. For nearly twenty years the policy and research communities backed away from the entire issue. In 1980 the Carter Administration convened a historic White House Conference on Families, designed to address the growing problems of children and families in America. The result was a prolonged, publicly subsidized quarrel over the definition of "family." No President since has tried to hold a national family conference. Last year, at a time when the rate of out-of-wedlock births had reached a historic high, Vice President Dan Quayle was ridiculed for criticizing Murphy Brown. In short, every time the issue of family structure has been raised, the response has been first controversy, then retreat, and finally silence.

Yet it is also risky to ignore the issue of changing family structure. In recent years the problems associated with family disruption have grown. Overall child well-being has declined, despite a decrease in the number of children per family, an increase in the educational level of parents, and historically high levels of public spending. After dropping in the 1960s and 1970s, the proportion of children in poverty has increased dramatically, from 15 percent in 1970 to 20 percent in 1990, while the percentage of adult Americans in poverty has remained roughly constant. The teen suicide rate has more than tripled. Juvenile crime has increased and become more violent. School performance has continued to decline. There are no signs that these trends are about to reverse themselves.

If we fail to come to terms with the relationship between family structure and declining child well-being, then it will be increasingly difficult to improve children's life prospects, no matter how many new programs the federal government funds. Nor will we be able to make progress in bettering school performance or reducing crime or improving the quality of the nation's future work force—all domestic problems closely connected to family breakup. Worse, we may contribute to the problem by pursuing policies that actually increase family instability and breakup.

The Missing Father

Judith Wallerstein is one of the pioneers in research on the long-term psychological impact of family disruption on children. The California Children of Divorce Study, which she directs, remains the most enduring study of the long-term effects of divorce on children and their parents. Moreover, it represents the best-known effort to look at the impact of divorce on middle-class children. The California children entered the study without pathological family histories. Before divorce they lived in stable, protected homes. And although some of the children did experience economic insecurity as the result of divorce, they were generally free from the most severe forms of poverty associated with family breakup. Thus the study and the resulting book (which Wallerstein wrote with Sandra Blakeslee), *Second Chances: Men, Women, and Children a Decade After Divorce* (1989), provide new insight into the consequences of divorce which are not associated with extreme forms of economic or emotional deprivation.

When, in 1971, Wallerstein and her colleagues set out to conduct clinical interviews with 131 children from the San Francisco area, they thought they were embarking on a short-term study. Most experts believed that divorce was like a bad cold. There was a phase of acute discomfort, and then a short recovery phase. According to the conventional wisdom, kids would be back on their feet in no time at all. Yet when Wallerstein met these children for a second interview more than a year later, she was amazed to discover that there had been no miraculous recovery. In fact, the children seemed to be doing worse.

The news that children did not "get over" divorce was not particularly welcome at the time. Wallerstein recalls, "We got angry letters from therapists, parents, and lawyers saying we were undoubtedly wrong. They said children are really much better off being released from an unhappy marriage. Divorce, they said, is a liberating experience." One of the main results of the California study was to overturn this optimistic view. In Wallerstein's cautionary words, "Divorce is deceptive. Legally it is a single event, but psychologically it is a chain—sometimes a never-ending chain—of events, relocations, and radically shifting relationships strung through time, a process that forever changes the lives of the people involved."

Five years after divorce more than a third of the children experienced moderate or severe depression. At ten years a significant number of the now young men and women appeared to be troubled, drifting, and underachieving. At fifteen years many of the thirtyish adults were struggling to establish strong love relationships of their own. In short, far from recovering from their parents' divorce, a significant percentage of these grownups were still suffering from its effects. In fact, according to Wallerstein, the long-term effects of divorce emerge at a time when young adults are trying to make their own decisions about love, marriage, and family. Not all children in the study suffered negative consequences. But Wallerstein's research presents a sobering picture of divorce. "The child of divorce faces many additional psychological burdens in addition to the normative tasks of growing up," she says.

Divorce not only makes it more difficult for young adults to establish new relationships. It also weakens the oldest primary relationship: that between parent and child. According to Wallerstein, "Parent-child relationships are permanently altered by divorce in ways that our society has not anticipated." Not only do children experience a loss of parental attention at the onset of divorce, but they soon find that at every stage of their development their parents are not available in the same way they once were. "In a reasonably happy intact family," Wallerstein observes, "the child gravitates first to one parent and then to the other, using skills and attributes from each in climbing the developmental ladder." In a divorced family, children find it "harder to find the needed parent at needed times." This may help explain why very young children suffer the most as the result of family disruption. Their opportunities to engage in this kind of ongoing process are the most truncated and compromised.

The father-child bond is severely, often irreparably, damaged in disrupted families. In a situation without historical precedent, an astonishing and disheartening number of American fathers are failing to provide financial support to their children. Often, more than the father's support check is missing. Increasingly, children are bereft of any contact with their fathers. According to the National Survey of Children, in disrupted families only one child in six, on average, saw his or her father as often as once a week in the past year. Close to half did not see their father at all in the past year. As time goes on, contact becomes even more infrequent. Ten years after a marriage breaks up, more than two thirds of children report not having seen their father for a year. Not surprisingly, when asked to name the "adults you look up to and admire," only 20 percent of children in single-parent families named their father, as compared with 52 percent of children in two-parent families. A favorite complaint among Baby Boom Americans is that their fathers were emotionally remote guys who worked hard, came home at night to eat supper, and didn't have much to say to or do with the kids. But the current generation has a far worse father problem: many of their fathers are vanishing entirely.

Even for fathers who maintain regular contact, the pattern of father-child relationships changes. The sociologists Andrew Cherlin and Frank Furstenberg, who have studied broken families, write that the fathers behave more like other relatives than like parents. Rather than helping with homework or carrying out a project with their children, nonresidential fathers are likely to take the kids shopping, to the movies, or out to dinner. Instead of providing steady advice and guidance, divorced fathers become "treat" dads.

Apparently—and paradoxically—it is the visiting relationship itself, rather than the frequency of visits, that is the real source of the problem. According to Wallerstein, the few children in the California study who reported visiting with their fathers once or twice a week over a ten-year period still felt rejected. The need to schedule a special time to be with the child, the repeated leave-takings, and the lack of connection to the child's regular, daily schedule leaves many fathers adrift, frustrated, and confused. Wallerstein calls the visiting father a parent without portfolio.

The deterioration in father-child bonds is most severe among children who experience divorce at an early age, according to a recent study. Nearly three quarters of the respondents, now young men and women, report having poor relationships with their fathers. Close to half have received psychological help, nearly a third have dropped out of high school, and about a quarter report having experienced high levels of problem behavior or emotional distress by the time they became young adults.

Long-Term Effects

Since most children live with their mothers after divorce, one might expect that the mother-child bond would remain unaltered and might even be strengthened. Yet research shows that the mother-child bond is also weakened as the result of divorce. Only half of the children who were close to their mothers before a divorce remained equally close after the divorce. Boys, particularly, had difficulties with their mothers. Moreover, mother-child relationships deteriorated over time. Whereas teenagers in disrupted families were no more likely than teenagers in intact families to report poor relationships with their mothers, 30 percent of young adults from disrupted families have poor relationships with their mothers, as compared with 16 percent of young adults from intact families. Mother-daughter relationships often deteriorate as the daughter reaches young adulthood. The only group in society that derives any benefit from these weakened parent-child ties is the therapeutic community.

Young adults from disrupted families are nearly twice as likely as those from intact families to receive psychological help.

Some social scientists have criticized Judith Wallerstein's research because her study is based on a small clinical sample and does not include a control group of children from intact families. However, other studies generally support and strengthen her findings. Nicholas Zill has found similar long-term effects on children of divorce, reporting that "effects of marital discord and family disruption are visible twelve to twenty-two years later in poor relationships with parents, high levels of problem behavior, and an increased likelihood of dropping out of high school and receiving psychological help." Moreover, Zill's research also found signs of distress in young women who seemed relatively well adjusted in middle childhood and adolescence. Girls in single-parent families are also at much greater risk for precocious sexuality, teenage marriage, teenage pregnancy, nonmarital birth, and divorce than are girls in two-parent families.

Zill's research shows that family disruption strongly affects school achievement as well. Children in disrupted families are nearly twice as likely as those in intact families to drop out of high school; among children who do drop out, those from disrupted families are less likely eventually to earn a diploma or a GED. Boys are at greater risk for dropping out than girls, and are also more likely to exhibit aggressive, acting-out behaviors. Other research confirms these findings. According to a study by the National Association of Elementary School Principals, 33 percent of two-parent elementary school students are ranked as high achievers, as compared with 17 percent of single-parent students. The children in single-parent families are also more likely to be truant or late or to have disciplinary action taken against them. Even after controlling for race, income, and religion, scholars find significant differences in educational attainment between children who grow up in intact families and children who do not. In his 1992 study *America's Smallest School: The Family,* Paul Barton shows that the proportion of two-parent families varies widely from state to state and is related to variations in academic achievement. North Dakota, for example, scores highest on the math-proficiency test and second highest on the two-parent-family scale. The District of Columbia is second lowest on the math test and lowest in the nation on the two-parent-family scale.

Zill notes that "while coming from a disrupted family significantly increases a young adult's risks of experiencing social, emotional or academic difficulties, it does not foreordain such difficulties. The majority of young people from disrupted families have successfully completed high school, do *not* currently display high levels of emotional distress or problem behavior, and enjoy reasonable relationships with their mothers." Nevertheless, a majority of these young adults do show maladjustment in their relationships with their fathers.

These findings underscore the importance of both a mother and a father in fostering the emotional well-being of children. Obviously, not all children in two-parent families are free from emotional turmoil, but few are burdened with the troubles that accompany family breakup. Moreover, as the sociologist Amitai Etzioni explains in a new book, *The Spirit of Community,* two parents in an intact family make up what might be called a mutually supportive education coalition. When both parents are present, they can play different, even contradictory, roles. One parent may goad the child to achieve, while the other may encourage the child to take time out to daydream or toss a football around. One may emphasize taking intellectual risks, while the other may insist on following the teacher's guidelines. At the same time the parents regularly exchange information about the child's school problems and achievements, and have a sense of the overall educational mission. However, Etzioni writes,

> The sequence of divorce followed by a succession of boy or girlfriends, a second marriage, and frequently another divorce and another turnover of partners often means a repeatedly disrupted educational coalition. Each change in participants involves a change in the educational agenda for the child. Each new partner cannot be expected to pick up the previous one's educational post and program. . . . As a result, changes in parenting partners mean, at best, a deep disruption in a child's education, though of course several disruptions cut deeper into the effectiveness of the educational coalition than just one.

—1993

What are your reactions to and questions about this work? The following questions may help provoke some ideas.

Probing the Work

1. What statistic in this essay is most surprising to you? Least surprising?
2. Some people would argue that children are often better off being raised by a single parent, or by one custodial parent and another contributing to their upbringing, than by an unhappy couple. Select a conclusive statement Whitehead makes and speculate on how the information or statistics might be interpreted to arrive at the opposite conclusion, or how the terms she uses might be problematic.

Identifying Issues

3. Whitehead shows that divorce, while typically good for the adults, is destructive for the children. Have you found this to be true? Explain.
4. Should parents who are unhappy with their marriage stay together for their children's sake? Explain and support your opinion with evidence from real-life experience, readings, and so forth.

ALICE WALKER

Everyday Use

Alice Walker (b. 1944) was born in Eatonton, Georgia, and was educated at Spelman College and Sarah Lawrence. She is best known for her 1983 novel The Color Purple *and collection of essays,* In Search of Our Mothers' Gardens. *Among her other books are several volumes of poetry (including* Her Blue Body: Everything We Know, *1993), a children's biography of Langston Hughes, and the novels* The Temple of My Familiar *(1989) and* Possessing the Secret of Joy *(1993).*

For Your Grandmama

I will wait for her in the yard that Maggie and I made so clean and wavy yesterday afternoon. A yard like this is more comfortable than most people know. It is not just a yard. It is like an extended living room. When the hard clay is swept clean as a floor and the fine sand around the edges lined with tiny, irregular grooves anyone can come and sit and look up into the elm tree and wait for the breezes that never come inside the house.

Maggie will be nervous until after her sister goes: she will stand hopelessly in corners homely and ashamed of the burn scars down her arms and legs, eyeing her sister with a mixture of envy and awe. She thinks her sister has held life always in the palm of one hand, that "no" is a word the world never learned to say to her.

You've no doubt seen those TV shows where the child who has "made it" is confronted, as a surprise, by her own mother and father, tottering in weakly from backstage. (A pleasant surprise, of course: What would they do if parent and child came on the show only to curse out and insult each other?) On TV mother and child embrace and smile into each other's faces. Sometimes the mother and father weep, the child wraps them in her arms and leans across the table to tell how she would not have made it without their help. I have seen these programs.

Sometimes I dream a dream in which Dee and I are suddenly brought together on a TV program of this sort. Out of a dark and soft-seated limousine I am ushered into a bright room filled with many people. There I meet a smiling, gray, sporty man like Johnny Carson who shakes my hand and tells me what a fine girl I have. Then we are on the stage and Dee is embracing me with tears in her eyes. She pins on my dress a large orchid, even though she has told me once that she thinks orchids are tacky flowers.

In real life I am a large, big-boned woman with rough, man-working hands. In the winter I wear flannel nightgowns to bed and overalls during the day. I can kill and clean a hog as mercilessly as a man. My fat keeps me hot in zero weather. I can work outside all day, breaking ice to get water for washing; I can eat pork liver cooked over the open fire minutes after it comes steaming from the hog. One winter I knocked a bull calf straight in the brain between the eyes with a sledge hammer and had the meat hung up to chill before nightfall. But of course all this does not show on television. I am the way my daughter would want me to be: a hundred pounds lighter, my skin like an uncooked barley pancake. My hair glistens in the hot bright lights. Johnny Carson has much to do to keep up with my quick and witty tongue.

But that is a mistake. I know even before I wake up. Who ever knew a Johnson with a quick tongue? Who can even imagine me looking a strange white man in the eye? It seems to me I have talked to them always with one foot raised in flight, with my head turned in whichever way is farthest from them. Dee, though. She would always look anyone in the eye. Hesitation was no part of her nature.

"How do I look, Mama?" Maggie says, showing just enough of her thin body enveloped in pink skirt and red blouse for me to know she's there, almost hidden by the door.

"Come out into the yard," I say.

Have you ever seen a lame animal, perhaps a dog run over by some careless person rich enough to own a car, sidle up to someone who is ignorant enough to be kind to him? That is the way my Maggie walks. She has been like this, chin on chest, eyes on ground, feet in shuffle, ever since the fire that burned the other house to the ground.

Dee is lighter than Maggie, with nicer hair and a fuller figure. She's a woman now, though sometimes I forget. How long ago was it that the other house burned? Ten, twelve years? Sometimes I can still hear the flames and feel Maggie's arms sticking to me, her hair smoking and her dress falling off her in little black papery flakes. Her eyes seemed stretched open, blazed open by the flames reflected in them. And Dee. I see her standing off under the sweet gum tree she used to dig gum out of; a look of concentration on her face as she watched the last dingy gray board of the house fall in toward the red-hot brick chimney. Why don't you do a dance around the ashes? I'd wanted to ask her. She had hated the house that much.

I used to think she hated Maggie, too. But that was before we raised the money, the church and me, to send her to Augusta to school. She used to read to us without pity; forcing words, lies, other folks' habits, whole lives upon us two, sitting trapped and ignorant underneath her voice. She washed us in a river of make-believe, burned us with a lot of knowledge we didn't necessarily need to know. Pressed us to her with the serious way she read, to shove us away at just the moment, like dimwits, we seemed about to understand.

Dee wanted nice things. A yellow organdy dress to wear to her graduation from high school; black pumps to match a green suit she'd made from an old suit somebody gave me. She was determined to stare down any disaster in her efforts. Her eyelids would not flicker for minutes at a time. Often I fought off the temptation to shake her. At sixteen she had a style of her own: and knew what style was.

I never had an education myself. After second grade the school was closed down. Don't ask me why: in 1927 colored asked fewer questions than they do now. Sometimes Maggie reads to me. She stumbles along good-naturedly but can't see well. She knows she is not bright. Like good looks and money, quickness passed her by. She will marry John Thomas (who has mossy teeth in an earnest face) and then I'll be free to sit here and I guess just sing church songs to myself. Although I never was a good singer. Never could carry a tune. I was always better at a man's job. I used to love to milk till I was hooked in the side in '49. Cows are soothing and slow and don't bother you, unless you try to milk them the wrong way.

I have deliberately turned my back on the house. It is three rooms, just like the one that burned, except the roof is tin; they don't make shingle roofs any more. There are no real windows, just some holes cut in the sides, like the portholes in a ship, but not round and not square, with rawhide holding the shutters up on the outside. This house is in a pasture, too, like the other one. No doubt when Dee sees it she will want to tear it down. She wrote me once that no matter where we "choose" to live, she will manage to come see us. But she will never bring her friends. Maggie and I thought about this and Maggie asked me, "Mama, when did Dee ever *have* any friends?"

She had a few. Furtive boys in pink shirts hanging about on washday after school. Nervous girls who never laughed. Impressed with her they worshiped the well-turned phrase, the cute shape, the scalding humor that erupted like bubbles in lye. She read to them.

When she was courting Jimmy T she didn't have much time to pay to us, but turned all her faultfinding power on him. He *flew* to marry a cheap gal from a family of ignorant flashy people. She hardly had time to recompose herself.

When she comes I will meet—but there they are!

Maggie attempts to make a dash for the house, in her shuffling way, but I stay her with my hand. "Come back here," I say. And she stops and tries to dig a well in the sand with her toe.

It is hard to see them clearly through the strong sun. But even the first glimpse of leg out of the car tells me it is Dee. Her feet were always neat-looking, as if God himself had shaped them with a certain style. From the other side of the car comes a short, stocky man. Hair is all over his head a foot long and hanging from his chin like a kinky mule tail. I hear Maggie suck in her breath. "Uhnnnh," is what it sounds like. Like when you see the wriggling end of a snake just in front of your foot on the road. "Uhnnnh."

Dee next. A dress down to the ground, in this hot weather. A dress so loud it hurts my eyes. There are yellows and oranges enough to throw back the light of the sun. I feel my whole face warming from the heat waves it throws out. Earrings gold, too, and hanging down to her shoulders. Bracelets dangling and making noises when she moves her arm up to shake the folds of the dress out of her armpits. The dress is loose and flows, and as she walks closer, I like it. I hear Maggie go "Uhnnnh" again. It is her sister's hair. It stands straight up like the wool on a sheep. It is black as night and around the edges are two long pigtails that rope about like small lizards disappearing behind her ears.

"Wa-su-zo-Tean-o!" she says, coming on in that gliding way the dress makes her move. The short stocky fellow with the hair to his navel is all grinning and he follows up with "Asalamalakim, my mother and sister!" He moves to hug Maggie but she falls back, right up against the back of my chair. I feel her trembling there and when I look up I see the perspiration falling off her chin.

"Don't get up," says Dee. Since I am stout it takes something of a push. You can see me trying to move a second or two before I make it. She turns, showing white heels through her sandals, and goes back to the car. Out she peeks next with a Polaroid. She stoops down quickly and lines up picture after picture of me sitting there in front of the house with Maggie cowering behind me. She never takes a shot without making sure the house is included. When a cow comes nibbling around the edge of the yard she snaps it and me and Maggie *and* the house. Then she puts the Polaroid in the back seat of the car, and comes up and kisses me on the forehead.

Meanwhile Asalamalakim is going through the motions with Maggie's hand. Maggie's hand is as limp as a fish, and probably as cold, despite the sweat, and she keeps trying to pull it back. It looks like Asalamalakim wants to shake hands but wants to do it fancy. Or maybe he don't know how people shake hands. Anyhow, he soon gives up on Maggie.

"Well," I say. "Dee."

"No, Mama," she says. "Not 'Dee,' Wangero Leewanika Kemanjo!"

"What happened to 'Dee'?" I wanted to know.

"She's dead," Wangero said. "I couldn't bear it any longer being named after the people who oppress me."

"You know as well as me you was named after your aunt Dicie," I said. Dicie is my sister. She named Dee. We called her "Big Dee" after Dee was born.

"But who was *she* named after?" asked Wangero.

"I guess after Grandma Dee," I said.

"And who was she named after?" asked Wangero.

"Her mother," I said, and saw Wangero was getting tired. "That's about as far back as I can trace it," I said. Though, in fact, I probably could have carried it back beyond the Civil War through the branches.

"Well," said Asalamalakim, "there you are."

"Uhnnnh," I heard Maggie say.

"There I was not," I said, "before 'Dicie' cropped up in our family, so why should I try to trace it that far back?"

He just stood there grinning, looking down on me like somebody inspecting a Model A car. Every once in a while he and Wangero sent eye signals over my head.

"How do you pronounce this name?" I asked.

"You don't have to call me by it if you don't want to," said Wangero.

"Why shouldn't I?" I asked. "If that's what you want us to call you, we'll call you."

"I know it might sound awkward at first," said Wangero.

"I'll get used to it," I said. "Ream it out again."

Well, soon we got the name out of the way. Asalamalakim had a name twice as long and three times as hard. After I tripped over it two or three times he told me to just call him Hakim-a-barber. I wanted to ask him was he a barber, but I didn't really think he was, so I didn't ask.

"You must belong to those beef-cattle peoples down the road," I said. They said "Asalamalakim" when they met you, too, but they didn't shake hands. Always too busy: feeding the cattle, fixing the fences, putting up salt-lick shelters, throwing down hay. When the white folks poisoned some of the herd the men stayed up all night with rifles in their hands. I walked a mile and a half just to see the sight.

Hakim-a-barber said, "I accept some of their doctrines, but farming and raising cattle is not my style." (They didn't tell me, and I didn't ask, whether Wangero [Dee] had really gone and married him.)

We sat down to eat and right away he said he didn't eat collards and pork was unclean. Wangero, though, went on through the chitlins and corn bread, the greens and everything else. She talked a blue streak over the sweet potatoes. Everything delighted her. Even the fact that we still used the benches her daddy made for the table when we couldn't afford to buy chairs.

"Oh, Mama!" she cried. Then turned to Hakim-a-barber. "I never knew how lovely these benches are. You can feel the rump prints," she said, running her hands underneath her and along the bench. Then she gave a sigh and her hand closed over Grandma Dee's butter dish. "That's it!" she said. "I knew there was something I wanted to ask you if I could have." She jumped up from the table and went over in the corner where the churn stood, the milk in it clabber by now. She looked at the churn and looked at it.

"This churn top is what I need," she said. "Didn't Uncle Buddy whittle it out of a tree you all used to have?"

"Yes," I said.

"Uh huh," she said happily. "And I want the dasher, too."

"Uncle Buddy whittle that, too?" asked the barber.

Dee (Wangero) looked up at me.

"Aunt Dee's first husband whittled the dash," said Maggie so low you almost couldn't hear her. "His name was Henry, but they called him Stash."

"Maggie's brain is like an elephant's," Wangero said, laughing. "I can use the churn top as a centerpiece for the alcove table," she said, sliding a plate over the churn, "and I'll think of something artistic to do with the dasher."

When she finished wrapping the dasher the handle stuck out. I took it for a moment in my hands. You didn't even have to look close to see where hands pushing the dasher up and down to make butter had left a kind of sink in the wood. In fact, there were a lot of small sinks; you could see where thumbs and fingers had sunk into the wood. It was beautiful light yellow wood, from a tree that grew in the yard where Big Dee and Stash had lived.

After dinner Dee (Wangero) went to the trunk at the foot of my bed and started rifling through it. Maggie hung back in the kitchen over the dishpan. Out came Wangero with two quilts. They had been pieced by Grandma Dee and then Big Dee and me had hung them on the quilt frames on the front porch and quilted them. One was in the Lone Star pattern. The other was Walk Around the Mountain. In both of them were scraps of dresses Grandma Dee had worn fifty and more years ago. Bits and pieces of Grandpa Jarrell's Paisley shirts. And one teeny faded blue piece, about the size of a penny matchbox, that was from Great Grandpa Ezra's uniform that he wore in the Civil War.

"Mama," Wangero said sweet as a bird. "Can I have these old quilts?"

I heard something fall in the kitchen, and a minute later the kitchen door slammed.

"Why don't you take one or two of the others?" I asked. "These old things was just done by me and Big Dee from some tops your grandma pieced before she died."

"That'll make them last better," I said.

"That's not the point," said Wangero. "These are all pieces of dresses Grandma used to wear. She did all this stitching by hand. Imagine!" She held the quilts securely in her arms, stroking them.

"Some of the pieces, like those lavender ones, come from old clothes her mother handed down to her," I said, moving up to touch the quilts. Dee (Wangero) moved back just enough so that I couldn't reach the quilts. They already belonged to her.

"Imagine!" she breathed again, clutching them closely to her bosom.

"The truth is," I said, "I promised to give them quilts to Maggie, for when she marries John Thomas."

She gasped like a bee had stung her.

"Maggie can't appreciate these quilts!" she said. "She'd probably be backward enough to put them to everyday use."

"I reckon she would," I said. "God knows I been saving 'em for long enough with nobody using 'em. I hope she will!" I didn't want to bring up how I had offered Dee (Wangero) a quilt when she went away to college. Then she had told me they were old-fashioned, out of style.

"But they're *priceless!"* she was saying now, furiously; for she has a temper. "Maggie would put them on the bed and in five years they'd be in rags. Less than that!"

"She can always make some more," I said. "Maggie knows how to quilt."

Dee (Wangero) looked at me with hatred. "You just will not understand. The point is these quilts, *these* quilts!"

"Well," I said, stumped. "What would *you* do with them?"

"Hang them," she said. As if that was the only thing you *could* do with quilts.

Maggie by now was standing in the door. I could almost hear the sound her feet made as they scraped over each other.

"She can have them, Mama," she said, like somebody used to never winning anything, or having anything reserved for her. "I can 'member Grandma Dee without the quilts."

I looked at her hard. She had filled her bottom lip with checkerberry snuff and it gave her face a kind of dopey, hangdog look. It was Grandma Dee and Big Dee who taught her how to quilt herself. She stood there with her scarred hands hidden in the folds of her skirt. She looked at her sister with something like fear but she wasn't mad at her. This was Maggie's portion. This was the way she knew God to work.

When I looked at her like that something hit me in the top of my head and ran down to the soles of my feet. Just like when I'm in church and the spirit of God touches me and I get happy and shout. I did something I never had done before: hugged Maggie to me, then dragged her on into the room, snatched the quilts out of Miss Wangero's hands and dumped them into Maggie's lap. Maggie just sat there on my bed with her mouth open.

"Take one or two of the others," I said to Dee.

But she turned without a word and went out to Hakim-a-barber.

"You just don't understand," she said, as Maggie and I came out to the car.

"What don't I understand?" I wanted to know.

"Your heritage," she said. And then she turned to Maggie, kissed her, and said, "You ought to try to make something of yourself, too, Maggie. It's really a new day for us. But from the way you and Mama still live you'd never know it."

She put on some sunglasses that hid everything above the tip of her nose and her chin.

Maggie smiled; maybe at the sunglasses. But a real smile, not scared. After we watched the car dust settle I asked Maggie to bring me a dip of snuff. And then the two of us sat there just enjoying, until it was time to go in the house and go to bed.

—1973

What are your reactions to and questions about this work? The following questions may help provoke some ideas.

Probing the Work

1. Identify and explain the significance of one or two *symbols* (see page 78) in this story? How do they help you understand the *theme* (see page 77) of the story?

Identifying Issues

2. What is the difference between the two sisters' perceptions of their familial heritage? To what extent can and should families preserve their own ethnic traditions?

SEAMUS HEANEY

Mid-Term Break

Seamus Heaney (b. 1939) was born to a rural Catholic family in County Derry in Northern Ireland, received a B.A. from Queen's University in Belfast, then taught in secondary schools and universities. His first book, Death of a Naturalist *(1966), established his reputation as a rural poet, but later books, such as* Wintering Out *(1973) and* North *(1975), focus on other themes, such as Irish mythology. In 1995, Heaney received the Nobel Prize for Literature.*

I sat all morning in the college sick bay
Counting bells knelling classes to a close.
At two o'clock our neighbors drove me home.

In the porch I met my father crying—
He had always taken funerals in his stride—
And Big Jim Evans saying it was a hard blow.

The baby cooed and laughed and rocked the pram
When I came in, and I was embarrassed
By old men standing up to shake my hand

And tell me they were "sorry for my trouble,"
Whispers informed strangers I was the eldest,
Away at school, as my mother held my hand

In hers and coughed out angry tearless sighs.
At ten o'clock the ambulance arrived
With the corpse, stanched and bandaged by the nurses.

Next morning I went up into the room. Snowdrops
And candles soothed the bedside; I saw him
For the first time in six weeks. Paler now,

Wearing a poppy bruise on his left temple,
He lay in the four foot box as in his cot.
No gaudy scars, the bumper knocked him clear.

A four foot box, a foot for every year.

—1966

What are your reactions to and questions about this work? The following questions may help provoke some ideas.

Probing the Work

1. What is the speaker's reaction to the death, and how does it contrast with that of the other family members? What do we learn about their personalities from their reactions?
2. What effect does this poem have on you? How much of your response to it is influenced by the poem's *tone* (see page 67)? By its subject? What makes the death of a young sibling at such a young age especially tragic?

Identifying Issues

3. In what ways does a death in the family shift the dynamics of family relationships?

LOUISE ERDRICH

Family Reunion

Louise Erdrich (b. 1954), a Native American of Chippewa and German-American descent, was born in Little Falls, Minnesota, and grew up near the Turtle Mountain Chippewa Reservation in North Dakota, where her father taught school. She was educated at Dartmouth, where she now teaches, and at Johns Hopkins. Among her books are Love Medicine (1984), The Beet Queen (1986), Tracks (1988), The Bingo Palace (1993), a poetry collection entitled Jacklight (1984), and, with her husband Michael Dorris, The Crown of Columbus.

Ray's third new car in half as many years.
Full cooler in the trunk, Ray sogging the beer
as I solemnly chauffeur us through the bush
and up the backroads, hardly cowpaths and hub-deep in mud.
All day the sky lowers, clears, lowers again.
Somewhere in the bush near Saint John
there are uncles, a family, one mysterious brother
who stayed on the land when Ray left for the cities.
One week Ray is crocked. We've been through this before.
Even, as a little girl, hands in my dress,
Ah punka, you's my Debby, come and ki me.

Then the road ends in a yard full of dogs.
Them's Indian dogs, Ray says, lookit how they know me.
And they do seem to know him, like I do. His odor—
rank beef of fierce turtle pulled dripping from Metagoshe,
and the inflammable mansmell: hair tonic, ashes, alcohol.
Ray dances an old woman up in his arms.
Fiddles reel on the phonograph and I sink apart
in a corner, start knocking the Blue Ribbons down.
Four generations of people live here.
No one remembers Raymond Twobears.

So what. The walls shiver, the old house caulked with mud
sails back into the middle of Metagoshe.
A three-foot-long snapper is hooked on a troutline,
so mean that we do not dare wrestle him in
but tow him to shore, heavy as an old engine.
Then somehow Ray pries the beak open and shoves
down a cherry bomb. Lights the string tongue.

Headless and clenched in its armor, the snapper
is lugged home in the trunk for tomorrow's soup.
Ray rolls it beneath a bush in the backyard and goes in
to sleep his own head off. Tomorrow I find
that the animal has dragged itself off.
I follow torn tracks up a slight hill and over
into a small stream that deepens and widens into a marsh.

Ray finds his way back through the room into his arms.
When the phonograph stops, he slumps hard in his hands
and the boys and their old man fold him into the car
where he curls around his bad heart, hearing how it knocks
and rattles at the bars of his ribs to break out.

Somehow we find our way back. Uncle Ray
sings an old song to the body that pulls him
toward home. The gray fins that his hands have become
screw their bones in the dashboard. His face
has the odd, calm patience of a child who has always
let bad wounds alone, or a creature that has lived
for a long time underwater. And the angels come
lowering their slings and litters.

—*1980*

What are your reactions to and questions about this work? The following questions may help provoke some ideas.

Probing the Work

1. Why is the uncle in this poem compared to a turtle? In what other ways is he *characterized* (see page 77)? What feelings do you have about him by the end of the poem? What feelings does the *speaker* seem to have about him?

Identifying Issues

2. Explain how the family described here may be seen in some ways as dysfunctional, in some ways as typical.

KAZUO ISHIGURO

A Family Supper

Kazuo Ishiguro (b. 1954) was born in Nagasaki, and was brought to England by his parents when he was 6. Ishiguro's knowledge of his native country was acquired almost solely from reading a monthly quota of Japanese books. After studying at the University of Kent, Ishiguro hitchhiked throughout Canada and the United States, then studied fiction writing at the University of East Anglia. His books include the novels A Pale View of Hills *(1982),* The Remains of the Day *(1989), and* The Unconsoled *(1995).*

Fugu is a fish caught off the Pacific shores of Japan. The fish has held a special significance for me ever since my mother died after eating one. The poison resides in the sex glands of the fish, inside two fragile bags. These bags must be removed with caution when preparing the fish, for any clumsiness will result in the poison leaking into the veins. Regrettably, it is not easy to tell whether or not this operation has been carried out successfully. The proof is, as it were, in the eating.

Fugu poisoning is hideously painful and almost always fatal. If the fish has been eaten during the evening, the victim is usually overtaken by pain during his sleep. He rolls about in agony for a few hours and is dead by morning. The fish became extremely popular in Japan after the war. Until stricter regulations were imposed, it was all the rage to perform the hazardous gutting operation in one's own kitchen, then to invite neighbors and friends round for the feast.

At the time of my mother's death, I was living in California. My relationship with my parents had become somewhat strained around that period and consequently I did not learn of the circumstances of her death until I returned to Tokyo two years later. Apparently, my mother had always refused to eat fugu, but on this particular occasion she had made an exception, having been invited by an old school friend whom she was anxious not to offend. It was my father who supplied me with the details as we drove from the airport to his house in the Kamakura district. When we finally arrived, it was nearing the end of a sunny autumn day.

"Did you eat on the plane?" my father asked. We were sitting on the tatami floor of his tearoom.

"They gave me a light snack."

"You must be hungry. We'll eat as soon as Kikuko arrives."

My father was a formidable-looking man with a large stony jaw and furious black eyebrows. I think now, in retrospect, that he much resembled Chou En-lai, although he would not have cherished such a comparison, being particularly proud of the pure samurai blood that ran in the family. His general presence was not one that encouraged relaxed conversation; neither were things helped much by his odd way of stating each remark as if it were the concluding one. In fact, as I sat opposite him that afternoon, a boyhood memory came back to me of the time he had struck me several times around the head for "chattering like an old woman." Inevitably, our conversation since my arrival at the airport had been punctuated by long pauses.

"I'm sorry to hear about the firm," I said when neither of us had spoken for some time. He nodded gravely.

"In fact, the story didn't end there," he said. "After the firm's collapse, Watanabe killed himself. He didn't wish to live with the disgrace."

"I see."

"We were partners for seventeen years. A man of principle and honor. I respected him very much."

"Will you go into business again?" I asked.

"I am . . . in retirement. I'm too old to involve myself in new ventures now. Business these days has become so different. Dealing with foreigners. Doing things their way. I don't understand how we've come to this. Neither did Watanabe." He sighed. "A fine man. A man of principle."

The tearoom looked out over the garden. From where I sat I could make out the ancient well that as a child I had believed to be haunted. It was just visible now through the thick foliage. The sun had sunk low and much of the garden had fallen into shadow.

"I'm glad in any case that you've decided to come back," my father said. "More than a short visit, I hope."

"I'm not sure what my plans will be."

"I, for one, am prepared to forget the past. Your mother, too, was always ready to welcome you back—upset as she was by your behavior."

"I appreciate your sympathy. As I say, I'm not sure what my plans are."

"I've come to believe now that there were no evil intentions in your mind," my father continued. "You were swayed by certain . . . influences. Like so many others."

"Perhaps we should forget it, as you suggest."

"As you will. More tea?"

Just then a girl's voice came echoing through the house.

"At last." My father rose to his feet. "Kikuko has arrived."

Despite our difference in years, my sister and I had always been close.

Seeing me again seemed to make her excessively excited, and for a while she did nothing but giggle nervously. But she calmed down somewhat when my father started to question her about Osaka and her university. She answered him with short, formal replies. She in turn asked me a few questions, but she seemed inhibited by the fear that her question might lead to awkward topics. After a while, the conversation had become even sparser than prior to Kikuko's arrival. Then my father stood up, saying: "I must attend to the supper. Please excuse me for being burdened by such matters. Kikuko will look after you."

My sister relaxed quite visibly once he had left the room. Within a few minutes, she was chatting freely about her friends in Osaka and about her classes at university. Then quite suddenly she decided we should walk in the garden and went striding out onto the veranda. We put on some straw sandals that had been left along the veranda rail and stepped out into the garden. The light in the garden had grown very dim.

"I've been dying for a smoke for the last half hour," she said, lighting a cigarette.

"Then why didn't you smoke?"

She made a furtive gesture back toward the house, then grinned mischievously.

"Oh, I see," I said.

"Guess what? I've got a boyfriend now."

"Oh, yes?"

"Except I'm wondering what to do. I haven't made up my mind yet."

"Quite understandable."

"You see, he's making plans to go to America. He wants me to go with him as soon as I finish studying."

"I see. And you want to go to America?"

"If we go, we're going to hitchhike." Kikuko waved a thumb in front of my face. "People say it's dangerous, but I've done it in Osaka and it's fine."

"I see. So what is it you're unsure about?"

We were following a narrow path that wound through the shrubs and finished by the old well. As we walked, Kikuko persisted in taking unnecessarily theatrical puffs on her cigarette.

"Well, I've got lots of friends now in Osaka. I like it there. I'm not sure I want to leave them all behind just yet. And Suichi . . . I like him, but I'm not sure I want to spend so much time with him. Do you understand?"

"Oh, perfectly."

She grinned again, then skipped on ahead of me until she had reached the well. "Do you remember," she said as I came walking up to her, "how you used to say this well was haunted?"

"Yes, I remember."

We both peered over the side.

"Mother always told me it was the old woman from the vegetable store you'd seen that night," she said. "But I never believed her and never came out here alone."

"Mother used to tell me that too. She even told me once the old woman had confessed to being the ghost. Apparently, she'd been taking a shortcut through our garden. I imagine she had some trouble clambering over these walls."

Kikuko gave a giggle. She then turned her back to the well, casting her gaze about the garden.

"Mother never really blamed you, you know," she said, in a new voice. I remained silent. "She always used to say to me how it was their fault, hers and Father's, for not bringing you up correctly. She used to tell me how much more careful they'd been with me, and that's why I was so good." She looked up and the mischievous grin had returned to her face. "Poor Mother," she said.

"Yes. Poor Mother."

"Are you going back to California?"

"I don't know. I'll have to see."

"What happened to . . . to her? To Vicki?"

"That's all finished with," I said. "There's nothing much left for me now in California."

"Do you think I ought to go there?"

"Why not? I don't know. You'll probably like it." I glanced toward the house. "Perhaps we'd better go in soon. Father might need a hand with the supper."

But my sister was once more peering down into the well. "I can't see any ghosts," she said. Her voice echoed a little.

"Is Father very upset about his firm collapsing?"

"Don't know. You never can tell with Father." Then suddenly she straightened up and turned to me. "Did he tell you about old Watanabe? What he did?"

"I heard he committed suicide."

"Well, that wasn't all. He took his whole family with him. His wife and his two little girls."

"Oh, yes?"

"Those two beautiful little girls. He turned on the gas while they were all asleep. Then he cut his stomach with a meat knife."

"Yes, Father was just telling me how Watanabe was a man of principle."

"Sick." My sister turned back to the well.

"Careful. You'll fall right in."

"I can't see any ghost," she said. "You were lying to me all that time."

"But I never said it lived down the well."

"Where is it then?"

We both looked around at the trees and shrubs. The daylight had almost gone. Eventually I pointed to a small clearing some ten yards away.

"Just there I saw it. Just there."

We stared at the spot.

"What did it look like?"

"I couldn't see very well. It was dark."

"But you must have seen something."

"It was an old woman. She was just standing there, watching me."

We kept staring at the spot as if mesmerized.

"She was wearing a white kimono," I said. "Some of her hair came undone. It was blowing around a little."

Kikuko pushed her elbow against my arm. "Oh, be quiet. You're trying to frighten me all over again." She trod on the remains of her cigarette, then for a brief moment stood regarding it with a perplexed expression. She kicked some pine needles over it, then once more displayed her grin. "Let's see if supper's ready," she said.

We found my father in the kitchen. He gave us a quick glance, then carried on with what he was doing.

"Father's become quite a chef since he's had to manage on his own," Kikuko said with a laugh.

He turned and looked at my sister coldly. "Hardly a skill I'm proud of," he said. "Kikuko, come here and help."

For some moments my sister did not move. Then she stepped forward and took an apron hanging from a drawer.

"Just these vegetables need cooking now," he said to her. "The rest just needs watching." Then he looked up and regarded me strangely for some seconds. "I expect you want to look around the house," he said eventually. He put down the chopsticks he had been holding. "It's a long time since you've seen it."

As we left the kitchen I glanced toward Kikuko, but her back was turned.

"She's a good girl," my father said.

I followed my father from room to room. I had forgotten how large the house was. A panel would slide open and another room would appear. But the rooms were all startlingly empty. In one of the rooms the lights did not come on, and we stared at the stark walls and tatami in the pale light that came from the windows.

"This house is too large for a man to live in alone," my father said. "I don't have much use for most of these rooms now."

But eventually my father opened the door to a room packed full of books and papers. There were flowers in vases and pictures on the walls. Then I noticed something on a low table in the corner of the room. I came nearer and saw it was a plastic model of a battleship, the kind constructed by children. It had been placed on some newspaper; scattered around it were assorted pieces of gray plastic.

My father gave a laugh. He came up to the table and picked up the model.

"Since the firm folded," he said, "I have a little more time on my hands." He laughed again, rather strangely. For a moment his face looked almost gentle. "A little more time."

"That seems odd," I said. "You were always so busy."

"Too busy, perhaps." He looked at me with a small smile. "Perhaps I should have been a more attentive father."

I laughed. He went on contemplating his battleship. Then he looked up. "I hadn't meant to tell you this, but perhaps it's best that I do. It's my belief that your mother's death was no accident. She had many worries. And some disappointments."

We both gazed at the plastic battleship.

"Surely," I said eventually, "my mother didn't expect me to live here forever."

"Obviously you don't see. You don't see how it is for some parents. Not only must they lose their children, they must lose them to things they don't understand." He spun the battleship in his fingers. "These little gunboats here could have been better glued, don't you think?"

"Perhaps. I think it looks fine."

"During the war I spent some time on a ship rather like this. But my ambition was always the air force. I figured it like this: If your ship was struck by the enemy, all you could do was struggle in the water hoping for a lifeline. But in an airplane—well, there was always the final weapon." He put the model back onto the table. "I don't suppose you believe in war."

"Not particularly."

He cast an eye around the room. "Supper should be ready by now," he said. "You must be hungry."

Supper was waiting in a dimly lit room next to the kitchen. The only source of light was a big lantern that hung over the table, casting the rest of the room in shadow. We bowed to each other before starting the meal.

There was little conversation. When I made some polite comment about the food, Kikuko giggled a little. Her earlier nervousness seemed to have returned to her. My father did not speak for several minutes. Finally he said:

"It must feel strange for you, being back in Japan."

"Yes, it is a little strange."

"Already, perhaps, you regret leaving America."

"A little. Not so much. I didn't leave behind much. Just some empty rooms."

"I see."

I glanced across the table. My father's face looked stony and forbidding in the half-light. We ate on in silence.

Then my eye caught something at the back of the room. At first I continued eating, then my hands became still. The others noticed and looked at me. I went on gazing into the darkness past my father's shoulder.

"Who is that? In that photograph there?"

"Which photograph?" My father turned slightly, trying to follow my gaze.

"The lowest one. The old woman in the white kimono."

My father put down his chopsticks. He looked first at the photograph, then at me.

"Your mother." His voice had become very hard. "Can't you recognize your own mother?"

"My mother. You see, it's dark. I can't see it very well."

No one spoke for a few seconds, then Kikuko rose to her feet. She took the photograph down from the wall, came back to the table, and gave it to me.

"She looks a lot older," I said.

"It was taken shortly before her death," said my father.

"It was the dark. I couldn't see very well."

I looked up and noticed my father holding out a hand. I gave him the photograph. He looked at it intently, then held it toward Kikuko. Obediently, my sister rose to her feet once more and returned the picture to the wall.

There was a large pot left unopened at the center of the table. When Kikuko had seated herself again, my father reached forward and lifted the lid. A cloud of steam rose up and curled toward the lantern. He pushed the pot a little toward me.

"You must be hungry," he said. One side of his face had fallen into shadow.

"Thank you." I reached forward with my chopsticks. The steam was almost scalding. "What is it?"

"Fish."

"It smells very good."

In the soup were strips of fish that had curled almost into balls. I picked one out and brought it to my bowl.

"Help yourself. There's plenty."

"Thank you." I took a little more, then pushed the pot toward my father. I watched him take several pieces to his bowl. Then we both watched as Kikuko served herself.

My father bowed slightly. "You must be hungry," he said again. He took some fish to his mouth and started to eat. Then I, too, chose a piece and put it in my mouth. It felt soft, quite fleshy against my tongue.

The three of us ate in silence. Several minutes went by. My father lifted the lid and once more steam rose up. We all reached forward and helped ourselves.

"Here," I said to my father, "you have this last piece."

"Thank you."

When we had finished the meal, my father stretched out his arms and yawned with an air of satisfaction. "Kikuko," he said, "prepare a pot of tea, please."

My sister looked at him, then left the room without comment. My father stood up.

"Let's retire to the other room. It's rather warm in here."

I got to my feet and followed him into the tearoom. The large sliding windows had been left open, bringing in a breeze from the garden. For a while we sat in silence.

"Father," I said, finally.

"Yes?"

"Kikuko tells me Watanabe-san took his whole family with him."

My father lowered his eyes and nodded. For some moments he seemed deep in thought. "Watanabe was very devoted to his work," he said at last. "The collapse of the firm was a great blow to him. I fear it must have weakened his judgment."

"You think what he did . . . it was a mistake?"

"Why, of course. Do you see it otherwise?"

"No, no. Of course not."

"There are other things besides work," my father said.

"Yes."

We fell silent again. The sound of locusts came in from the garden. I looked out into the darkness. The well was no longer visible.

"What do you think you will do now?" my father asked. "Will you stay in Japan for a while?"

"To be honest, I hadn't thought that far ahead."

"If you wish to stay here, I mean here in this house, you would be very welcome. That is, if you don't mind living with an old man."

"Thank you. I'll have to think about it."

I gazed out once more into the darkness.

"But of course," said my father, "this house is so dreary now. You'll no doubt return to America before long."

"Perhaps. I don't know yet."

"No doubt you will."

For some time my father seemed to be studying the back of his hands. Then he looked up and sighed.

"Kikuko is due to complete her studies next spring," he said. "Perhaps she will want to come home then. She's a good girl."

"Perhaps she will."

"Things will improve then."

"Yes, I'm sure they will."

We fell silent once more, waiting for Kikuko to bring the tea.

—1990

What are your reactions to and questions about this work? The following questions may help provoke some ideas.

Probing the Work

1. Ishiguro says that he puts as little *plot* (see page 73) as possible in his stories. What is the *plot* of this story? What are the conflicts? How do these and other elements make the story interesting to follow?
2. Why does the narrator ask his father if he thinks what Watanabe did was a mistake (p. 500)? What do that question and his father's response to it say about both the narrator's and the father's attitudes toward each other and toward themselves?

Identifying Issues

3. How does this story illustrate the cultural differences, if any, between Eastern and Western family attitudes?

GARDNER MCFALL

Four Corners

Gardner McFall resides in New York City, where she teaches literature at Cooper Union. Her poems have appeared in such journals as The Nation *and* The New Yorker. *She received the Thomas McAfee Prize in poetry from* The Missouri Review *in 1987 and a "Discovery"/*The Nation *award in 1989. She has also written two children's books. The following poem first appeared in* The Missouri Review.

Two parents in front, two children in back
driving west in the hottest part of summer.
The dog's ears flapped in the wind.
Nothing could relieve that heat, not even

the soft drinks fished from our ice-chest.
In Kansas we counted the silos and fields;
then after the Rockies, all the trading posts
whose outdoor curios and blanket displays

gathered dust from the speeding trucks.
Late afternoon, our interest in scenery
fell on the possibility of a motel pool.
That's when we happened to spot the sign,

Four Corners. We found it described
in *Fodor's Guide:* marked by a low, square
monument, the state lines of Arizona, Utah,
Colorado, and New Mexico meeting in the middle.

It could have been anywhere if you believe
what you read. Hardly anything distinguished

that point where four states touch,
but we stopped the car. A man took our picture

to prove we were there, balanced together
on a concrete slab small as a kitchen table,
shoulder to shoulder, each in a different state,
our hair blowing in the same direction.

—1989

What are your reactions to and questions about this work? The following questions may help provoke some ideas.

Probing the Work

1. Examine the positions of the family members, both in the car and on the concrete slab. What is McFall trying to show about the direction and "state" of each person?

Identifying Issues

2. Do you think McFall is describing an ideal, or flawed, family structure?
3. Can you think of a *metaphor* or *simile* (p. 68) that would describe the status of your own family? You might start with, "My family is . . . "; or, "My family is like . . ."

SAM SHEPARD

True West[1]

Sam Shepard (b. 1943) has written more than 40 plays, 11 of which have won Obie Awards. In 1979 he won the Pulitzer Prize for Buried Child. *Other plays include* La Turista *(1967),* Curse of the Starving Class *(1978), and* Fool for Love. *He is also an accomplished actor.*

Characters

AUSTIN: *early thirties, light blue sports shirt, light tan cardigan sweater, clean blue jeans, white tennis shoes*

LEE: *his older brother, early forties, filthy white t-shirt, tattered brown overcoat covered with dust, dark blue baggy suit pants from the Salvation Army, pink suede belt, pointed black forties dress shoes scuffed up, holes in the soles, no socks, no hat, long pronounced sideburns, "Gene Vincent" hairdo, two days' growth of beard, bad teeth*

[1]The text is that of *Seven Plays* (1984).

SAUL KIMMER: *late forties, Hollywood producer, pink and white flower print sports shirt, white sports coat with matching polyester slacks, black and white loafers*

MOM: *early sixties, mother of the brothers, small woman, conservative white skirt and matching jacket, red shoulder bag, two pieces of matching red luggage*

SCENE: *All nine scenes take place on the same set; a kitchen and adjoining alcove of an older home in a Southern California suburb, about 40 miles east of Los Angeles. The kitchen takes up most of the playing area to stage left. The kitchen consists of a sink, upstage center,*[2] *surrounded by counter space, a wall telephone, cupboards, and a small window just above it bordered by neat yellow curtains. Stage left of sink is a stove. Stage right, a refrigerator. The alcove adjoins the kitchen to stage right.*[3] *There is no wall division or door to the alcove. It is open and easily accessible from the kitchen and defined only by the objects in it: a small round glass breakfast table mounted on white iron legs, two matching white iron chairs set across from each other. The two exterior walls of the alcove which prescribe a corner in the upstage right are composed of many small windows, beginning from a solid wall about three feet high and extending to the ceiling. The windows look out to bushes and citrus trees. The alcove is filled with all sorts of house plants in various pots, mostly Boston ferns hanging in planters at different levels. The floor of the alcove is composed of green synthetic grass.*

All entrances and exits are made stage left from the kitchen. There is no door. The actors simply go off and come onto the playing area.

NOTE ON SET AND COSTUME: *The set should be constructed realistically with no attempt to distort its dimensions, shapes, objects, or colors. No objects should be introduced which might draw special attention to themselves other than the props demanded by the script. If a stylistic "concept" is grafted onto the set design it will only serve to confuse the evolution of the characters' situation, which is the most important focus of the play.*

Likewise, the costumes should be exactly representative of who the characters are and not added onto for the sake of making a point to the audience.

NOTE ON SOUND: *The Coyote of Southern California has a distinct yapping, dog-like bark, similar to a Hyena. This yapping grows more intense and maniacal as the pack grows in numbers, which is usually the case when they lure and kill pets from suburban yards. The sense of growing frenzy in the pack should be felt in the background, particularly in Scenes 7 and 8. In any case, these Coyotes never make the long, mournful, solitary howl of the Hollywood stereotype.*

The sound of Crickets can speak for itself.

[2]I.e., toward the back of the setting ("downstage" is closer to the audience).
[3]"Stage left" and "stage right" are traditionally from the actors' point of view.

These sounds should also be treated realistically even though they sometimes grow in volume and numbers.

ACT ONE

Scene 1

Night. Sound of crickets in dark. Candlelight appears in alcove, illuminating AUSTIN, *seated at glass table hunched over a writing notebook, pen in hand, cigarette burning in ashtray, cup of coffee, typewriter on table, stacks of paper, candle burning on table.*

Soft moonlight fills kitchen illuminating LEE, *beer in hand, six-pack on counter behind him. He's leaning against the sink, mildly drunk; takes a slug of beer.*

LEE: So, Mom took off for Alaska, huh?
AUSTIN: Yeah.
LEE: Sorta' left you in charge.
AUSTIN: Well, she knew I was coming down here so she offered me the place.
LEE: You keepin' the plants watered?
AUSTIN: Yeah.
LEE: Keepin' the sink clean? She don't like even a single tea leaf in the sink ya' know.
AUSTIN: [*trying to concentrate on writing*] Yeah, I know.

[*pause*]

LEE: She gonna' be up there a long time?
AUSTIN: I don't know.
LEE: Kinda' nice for you, huh? Whole place to yourself.
AUSTIN: Yeah, it's great.
LEE: Ya' got crickets anyway. Tons a' crickets out there. [*looks around kitchen*] Ya' got groceries? Coffee?
AUSTIN: [*looking up from writing*] What?
LEE: You got coffee?
AUSTIN: Yeah.
LEE: At's good. [*short pause*] Real coffee? From the bean?
AUSTIN: Yeah. You want some?
LEE: Naw. I brought some uh—[*motions to beer*]
AUSTIN: Help yourself to whatever's—[*motions to refrigerator*]
LEE: I will. Don't worry about me. I'm not the one to worry about. I mean I can uh—[*pause*] You always work by candlelight?
AUSTIN: No—uh—Not always.
LEE: Just sometimes?
AUSTIN: [*puts pen down, rubs his eyes*] Yeah. Sometimes it's soothing.
LEE: Isn't that what the old guys did?
AUSTIN: What old guys?

Lee: The Forefathers. You know.

Austin: Forefathers?

Lee: Isn't that what they did? Candlelight burning into the night? Cabins in the wilderness.

Austin: [*rubs hand through his hair*] I suppose.

Lee: I'm not botherin' you am I? I mean I don't wanna break into yer uh—concentration or nothin'.

Austin: No, it's all right.

Lee: That's good. I mean I realize that yer line a' work demands a lota' concentration.

Austin: It's okay.

Lee: You probably think that I'm not fully able to comprehend somethin' like that, huh?

Austin: Like what?

Lee: That stuff yer doin'. That art. You know. Whatever you call it.

Austin: It's just a little research.

Lee: You may not know it but I did a little art myself once.

Austin: You did?

Lee: Yeah! I did some a' that. I fooled around with it. No future in it.

Austin: What'd you do?

Lee: Never mind what I did! Just never mind about that. [*pause*] It was ahead of its time.

[*pause*]

Austin: So, you went out to see the old man, huh?

Lee: Yeah, I seen him.

Austin: How's he doing?

Lee: Same. He's doin' just about the same.

Austin: I was down there too, you know.

Lee: What d'ya' want, an award? You want some kinda' medal? You were down there. He told me all about you.

Austin: What'd he say?

Lee: He told me. Don't worry.

[*pause*]

Austin: Well—

Lee: You don't have to say nothin'.

Austin: I wasn't.

Lee: Yeah, you were gonna' make somethin' up. Somethin' brilliant.

[*pause*]

Austin: You going to be down here very long, Lee?

Lee: Might be. Depends on a few things.

Austin: You got some friends down here?

LEE: [*laughs*] I know a few people. Yeah.
AUSTIN: Well, you can stay here as long as I'm here.
LEE: I don't need your permission do I?
AUSTIN: No.
LEE: I mean she's my mother too, right?
AUSTIN: Right.
LEE: She might've just as easily asked me to take care of her place as you.
AUSTIN: That's right.
LEE: I mean I know how to water plants.

[*long pause*]

AUSTIN: So you don't know how long you'll be staying then?
LEE: Depends mostly on houses, ya' know.
AUSTIN: Houses?
LEE: Yeah. Houses. Electric devices. Stuff like that. I gotta' make a little tour first.

[*short pause*]

AUSTIN: Lee, why don't you just try another neighborhood, all right?
LEE: [*laughs*] What'sa' matter with this neighborhood? This is a great neighborhood. Lush. Good class a' people. Not many dogs.
AUSTIN: Well, our uh—Our mother just happens to live here. That's all.
LEE: Nobody's gonna' know. All they know is somethin's missing. That's all. She'll never even hear about it. Nobody's gonna' know.
AUSTIN: You're going to get picked up if you start walking around here at night.
LEE: Me? I'm gonna' git picked up? What about you? You stick out like a sore thumb. Look at you. You think yer regular lookin'?
AUSTIN: I've got too much to deal with here to be worrying about—
LEE: Yer not gonna' have to worry about me! I've been doin' all right without you. I haven't been anywhere near you for five years! Now isn't that true?
AUSTIN: Yeah.
LEE: So you don't have to worry about me. I'm a free agent.
AUSTIN: All right.
LEE: Now all I wanna' do is borrow yer car.
AUSTIN: No!
LEE: Just fer a day. One day.
AUSTIN: No!
LEE: I won't take it outside a twenty mile radius. I promise ya'. You can check the speedometer.
AUSTIN: You're not borrowing my car! That's all there is to it.

[*pause*]

LEE: Then I'll just take the damn thing.
AUSTIN: Lee, look—I don't want any trouble, all right?

LEE: That's a dumb line. That is a dumb fuckin' line. You git paid fer dreamin' up a line like that?

AUSTIN: Look, I can give you some money if you need money.

[LEE *suddenly lunges at* AUSTIN, *grabs him violently by the shirt and shakes him with tremendous power*]

LEE: Don't you say that to me! Don't you ever say that to me! [*just as suddenly he turns him loose, pushes him away and backs off*] You may be able to git away with that with the Old Man. Git him tanked up for a week! Buy him off with yer Hollywood blood money, but not me! I can git my own money my own way. Big money!

AUSTIN: I was just making an offer.

LEE: Yeah, well keep it to yourself!

[*long pause*]

Those are the most monotonous fuckin' crickets I ever heard in my life.

AUSTIN: I kinda' like the sound.

LEE: Yeah. Supposed to be able to tell the temperature by the number a' pulses. You believe that?

AUSTIN: The temperature?

LEE: Yeah. The air. How hot it is.

AUSTIN: How do you do that?

LEE: I don't know. Some woman told me that. She was a Botanist. So I believed her.

AUSTIN: Where'd you meet her?

LEE: What?

AUSTIN: The woman Botanist?

LEE: I met her on the desert. I been spendin' a lota' time on the desert.

AUSTIN: What were you doing out there?

LEE: [*pause, stares in space*] I forgit. Had me a Pit Bull there for a while but I lost him.

AUSTIN: Pit Bull?

LEE: Fightin' dog. Damn I made some good money off that little dog. Real good money.

[*pause*]

AUSTIN: You could come up north with me, you know.

LEE: What's up there?

AUSTIN: My family.

LEE: Oh, that's right, you got the wife and kiddies now don't ya'. The house, the car, the whole slam. That's right.

AUSTIN: You could spend a couple days. See how you like it. I've got an extra room.

LEE: Too cold up there.

[*pause*]

AUSTIN: You want to sleep for a while?
LEE: [*pause, stares at* AUSTIN] I don't sleep.

[*lights to black*]

Scene 2

Morning. AUSTIN *is watering plants with a vaporizer,* LEE *sits at glass table in alcove drinking beer.*

LEE: I never realized the old lady was so security-minded.
AUSTIN: How do you mean?
LEE: Made a little tour this morning. She's got locks on everything. Locks and double-locks and chain locks and—What's she got that's so valuable?
AUSTIN: Antiques I guess. I don't know.
LEE: Antiques? Brought everything with her from the old place, huh. Just the same crap we always had around. Plates and spoons.
AUSTIN: I guess they have personal value to her.
LEE: Personal value. Yeah. Just a lota' junk. Most of it's phony anyway. Idaho decals. Now who in the hell wants to eat offa' plate with the State of Idaho starin' ya' in the face. Every time ya' take a bite ya' get to see a little bit more.
AUSTIN: Well it must mean something to her or she wouldn't save it.
LEE: Yeah, well personally I don't wann' be invaded by Idaho when I'm eatin'. When I'm eatin' I'm home. Ya' know what I'm sayin'? I'm not driftin', I'm home. I don't need my thoughts swept off to Idaho. I don't need that!

[*pause*]

AUSTIN: Did you go out last night?
LEE: Why?
AUSTIN: I thought I heard you go out.
LEE: Yeah, I went out. What about it?
AUSTIN: Just wondered.
LEE: Damn coyotes kept me awake.
AUSTIN: Oh yeah, I heard them. They must've killed somebody's dog or something.
LEE: Yappin' their fool heads off. They don't yap like that on the desert. They howl. These are city coyotes here.
AUSTIN: Well, you don't sleep anyway do you?

[*pause,* LEE *stares at him*]

LEE: You're pretty smart aren't ya?
AUSTIN: How do you mean?

LEE: I mean you never had any more on the ball than I did. But here you are gettin' invited into prominent people's houses. Sittin' around talkin' like you know somethin'.

AUSTIN: They're not so prominent.

LEE: They're a helluva' lot more prominent than the houses I get invited into.

AUSTIN: Well you invite yourself.

LEE: That's right. I do. In fact I probably got a wider range a' choices than you do, come to think of it.

AUSTIN: I wouldn't doubt it.

LEE: In fact I been inside some pretty classy places in my time. And I never even went to an Ivy League school either.

AUSTIN: You want some breakfast or something?

LEE: Breakfast?

AUSTIN: Yeah. Don't you eat breakfast?

LEE: Look, don't worry about me pal. I can take care a' myself. You just go ahead as though I wasn't even here, all right?

[AUSTIN *goes into kitchen, makes coffee*]

AUSTIN: Where'd you walk to last night?

[*pause*]

LEE: I went up in the foothills there. Up in the San Gabriels. Heat was drivin' me crazy.

AUSTIN: Well, wasn't it hot out on the desert?

LEE: Different kinda' heat. Out there it's clean. Cools off at night. There's a nice little breeze.

AUSTIN: Where were you, the Mojave?

LEE: Yeah. The Mojave. That's right.

AUSTIN: I haven't been out there in years.

LEE: Out past Needles there.

AUSTIN: Oh yeah.

LEE: Up here it's different. This country's real different.

AUSTIN: Well, it's been built up.

LEE: Built up? Wiped out is more like it. I don't even hardly recognize it.

AUSTIN: Yeah. Foothills are the same though, aren't they?

LEE: Pretty much. It's funny goin' up in there. The smells and everything. Used to catch snakes up there, remember?

AUSTIN: You caught snakes.

LEE: Yeah. And you'd pretend you were Geronimo° or some damn thing. You used to go right out to lunch.

AUSTIN: I enjoyed my imagination.

LEE: That what you call it? Looks like yer still enjoyin' it.

209. Geronimo, colorful Indian chieftain who led sensational raids against whites.

AUSTIN: So you just wandered around up there, huh?
LEE: Yeah. With a purpose.
AUSTIN: See any houses?

[*pause*]

LEE: Couple. Couple a' real nice ones. One of 'em didn't even have a dog. Walked right up and stuck my head in the window. Not a peep. Just a sweet kinda' suburban silence.
AUSTIN: What kind of a place was it?
LEE: Like a paradise. Kinda' place that sorta' kills ya' inside. Warm yellow lights. Mexican tile all around. Copper pots hangin' over the stove. Ya' know like they got in the magazines. Blonde people movin' in and outa' the rooms, talkin' to each other. [*pause*] Kinda' place you wish you sorta' grew up in, ya' know.
AUSTIN: That's the kind of place you wish you'd grown up in?
LEE: Yeah, why not?
AUSTIN: I thought you hated that kind of stuff.
LEE: Yeah, well you never knew too much about me did ya'?

[*pause*]

AUSTIN: Why'd you go out to the desert in the first place?
LEE: I was on my way to see the old man.
AUSTIN: You mean you just passed through there?
LEE: Yeah. That's right. Three months of passin' through.
AUSTIN: Three months?
LEE: Somethin' like that. Maybe more. Why?
AUSTIN: You lived on the Mojave for three months?
LEE: Yeah. What'sa' matter with that?
AUSTIN: By yourself?
LEE: Mostly. Had a couple a' visitors. Had that dog for a while.
AUSTIN: Didn't you miss people?
LEE: [*laughs*] People?
AUSTIN: Yeah. I mean I go crazy if I have to spend three nights in a motel by myself.
LEE: Yer not in a motel now.
AUSTIN: No, I know. But sometimes I have to stay in motels.
LEE: Well, they got people in motels don't they?
AUSTIN: Strangers.
LEE: Yer friendly aren't ya? Aren't you the friendly type?

[*pause*]

AUSTIN: I'm going to have somebody coming by here later, Lee.
LEE: Ah! Lady friend?
AUSTIN: No, a producer.

LEE: Aha! What's he produce?

AUSTIN: Film. Movies. You know.

LEE: Oh, movies. Motion Pictures! A Big Wig huh?

AUSTIN: Yeah.

LEE: What's he comin' by here for?

AUSTIN: We have to talk about a project.

LEE: Whadya' mean, "a project"? What's "a project"?

AUSTIN: A script.

LEE: Oh. That's what yer doin' with all these papers?

AUSTIN: Yeah.

LEE: Well, what's the project about?

AUSTIN: We're uh—it's a period piece.

LEE: What's "a period piece"?

AUSTIN: Look, it doesn't matter. The main thing is we need to discuss this alone. I mean—

LEE: Oh, I get it. You want me outa' the picture.

AUSTIN: Not exactly. I just need to be alone with him for a couple of hours. So we can talk.

LEE: Yer afraid I'll embarrass ya' huh?

AUSTIN: I'm not afraid you'll embarrass me!

LEE: Well, I tell ya' what— Why don't you just gimme the keys to yer car and I'll be back here around six o'clock or so. That give ya' enough time?

AUSTIN: I'm not loaning you my car, Lee.

LEE: You want me to just git lost huh? Take a hike? Is that it? Pound the pavement for a few hours while you bullshit yer way into a million bucks.

AUSTIN: Look, it's going to be hard enough for me to face this character on my own without—

LEE: You don't know this guy?

AUSTIN: No I don't know—He's a producer. I mean I've been meeting with him for months but you never get to know a producer.

LEE: Yer tryin' to hustle him? Is that it?

AUSTIN: I'm not trying to hustle him! I'm trying to work out a deal! It's not easy.

LEE: What kinda' deal?

AUSTIN: Convince him it's a worthwhile story.

LEE: He's not convinced? How come he's comin' over here if he's not convinced? I'll convince him for ya'.

AUSTIN: You don't understand the way things work down here.

LEE: How do things work down here?

[*pause*]

AUSTIN: Look, if I loan you my car will you have it back here by six?

LEE: On the button. With a full tank a' gas.

AUSTIN: [*digging in his pocket for keys*] Forget about the gas.

LEE: Hey, these days gas is gold, old buddy.

[AUSTIN *hands the keys to* LEE]

You remember that car I used to loan you?
AUSTIN: Yeah.
LEE: Forty Ford. Flathead.
AUSTIN: Yeah.
LEE: Sucker hauled ass didn't it?
AUSTIN: Lee, it's not that I don't want to loan you my car—
LEE: You are loanin' me yer car.

[LEE *gives* AUSTIN *a pat on the shoulder, pause*]

AUSTIN: I know. I just wish—
LEE: What? You wish what?
AUSTIN: I don't know. I wish I wasn't— I wish I didn't have to be doing business down here. I'd like to just spend some time with you.
LEE: I thought it was "Art" you were doin'.

[LEE *moves across kitchen toward exit, tosses keys in his hand*]

AUSTIN: Try to get it back here by six, okay?
LEE: No sweat. Hey, ya' know, if that uh—story of yours doesn't go over with the guy—tell him I got a couple a' "projects" he might be interested in. Real commercial. Full a' suspense. True-to-life stuff.

[LEE *exits,* AUSTIN *stares after* LEE *then turns, goes to papers at table, leafs through pages, lights fade to black*]

Scene 3

Afternoon. Alcove, SAUL KIMMER *and* AUSTIN *seated across from each other at table.*

SAUL: Well, to tell you the truth Austin, I have never felt so confident about a project in quite a long time.
AUSTIN: Well, that's good to hear, Saul.
SAUL: I am absolutely convinced we can get this thing off the ground. I mean we'll have to make a sale to television and that means getting a major star. Somebody bankable. But I think we can do it. I really do.
AUSTIN: Don't you think we need a first draft before we approach a star?
SAUL: No, no, not at all. I don't think it's necessary. Maybe a brief synopsis. I don't want you to touch the typewriter until we have some seed money.
AUSTIN: That's fine with me.
SAUL: I mean it's a great story. Just the story alone. You've really managed to capture something this time.
AUSTIN: I'm glad you like it, Saul.

[LEE *enters abruptly into the kitchen carrying a stolen television set, short pause*]

LEE: Aw shit, I'm sorry about that. I am really sorry Austin.
AUSTIN: [*standing*] That's all right.
LEE: [*moving toward them*] I mean I thought it was way past six already. You said to have it back here by six.
AUSTIN: We were just finishing up. [*to* SAUL] This is my, uh—brother, Lee.
SAUL: [*standing*] Oh, I'm very happy to meet you.

[LEE *sets T.V. on sink counter, shakes hands with* SAUL]

LEE: I can't tell ya' how happy I am to meet you sir.
SAUL: Saul Kimmer.
LEE: Mr. Kipper.
SAUL: Kimmer.
LEE: Lee's been living out on the desert and he just uh—
SAUL: Oh, that's terrific! [*to* LEE] Palm Springs?
LEE: Yeah. Yeah, right. Right around in that area. Near uh—Bob Hope. Drive there.
SAUL: Oh I love it out there. I just love it. The air is wonderful.
LEE: Yeah. Sure is. Healthy.
SAUL: And the golf. I don't know if you play golf, but the golf is just about the best.
LEE: I play a lota' golf.
SAUL: Is that right?
LEE: Yeah. In fact I was hoping I'd run into somebody out here who played a little golf. I've been lookin' for a partner.
SAUL: Well, I uh—
AUSTIN: Lee's just down for a visit while our mother's in Alaska.
SAUL: Oh, your mother's in Alaska?
AUSTIN: Yes. She went up there on a little vacation. This is her place.
SAUL: I see. Well isn't that something. Alaska.
LEE: What kinda' handicap do ya' have, Mr. Kimmer?
SAUL: Oh I'm just a Sunday duffer really. You know.
LEE: That's good 'cause I haven't swung a club in months.
SAUL: Well we ought to get together sometime and have a little game. Austin, do you play?

[SAUL *mimes a Johnny Carson golf swing for* AUSTIN]

AUSTIN: No. I don't uh—I've watched it on T.V.
LEE: [*to* SAUL] How 'bout tomorrow morning? Bright and early. We could get out there and put in eighteen holes before breakfast.
SAUL: Well, I've got uh—I have several appointments—

LEE: No, I mean real early. Crack a'dawn. While the dew's still thick on the fairway.

SAUL: Sounds really great.

LEE: Austin could be our caddie.

SAUL: Now that's an idea. [*laughs*]

AUSTIN: I don't know the first thing about golf.

LEE: There's nothin' to it. Isn't that right, Saul? He'd pick it up in fifteen minutes.

SAUL: Sure. Doesn't take long. 'Course you have to play for years to find your true form. [*chuckles*]

LEE: [*to* AUSTIN] We'll give ya' a quick run-down on the club faces. The irons, the woods. Show ya' a couple pointers on the basic swing. Might even let ya' hit the ball a couple times. Whatdya' think, Saul?

SAUL: Why not. I think it'd be great. I haven't had any exercise in weeks.

LEE: 'At's the spirit! We'll have a little orange juice right afterwards.

[*pause*]

SAUL: Orange juice?

LEE: Yeah! Vitamin C! Nothin' like a shot a' orange juice after a round a' golf. Hot shower. Snappin' towels at each others' privates. Real sense a' fraternity.

SAUL: [*smiles at* AUSTIN] Well, you make it sound very inviting, I must say. It really does sound great.

LEE: Then it's a date.

SAUL: Well, I'll call the country club and see if I can arrange something.

LEE: Great! Boy, I sure am sorry that I busted in on ya' all in the middle of yer meeting.

SAUL: Oh that's quite all right. We were just about finished anyway.

LEE: I can wait out in the other room if you want.

SAUL: No really—

LEE: Just got Austin's color T.V. back from the shop. I can watch a little amateur boxing now.

[LEE *and* AUSTIN *exchange looks*]

SAUL: Oh—Yes.

LEE: You don't fool around in Television, do you Saul?

SAUL: Uh— I have in the past. Produced some T.V. Specials. Network stuff. But it's mainly features now.

LEE: That's where the big money is, huh?

SAUL: Yes. That's right.

AUSTIN: Why don't I call you tomorrow, Saul and we'll get together. We can have lunch or something.

SAUL: That'd be terrific.

LEE: Right after the golf.

[*pause*]

Saul: What?
Lee: You can have lunch right after the golf.
Saul: Oh, right.
Lee: Austin was tellin' me that yer interested in stories.
Saul: Well, we develop certain projects that we feel have commercial potential.
Lee: What kinda' stuff do ya' go in for?
Saul: Oh, the usual. You know. Good love interest. Lots of action. [*chuckles at* Austin]
Lee: Westerns?
Saul: Sometimes.
Austin: I'll give you a ring, Saul.

[Austin *tries to move* Saul *across the kitchen but* Lee *blocks their way*]

Lee: I got a Western that'd knock yer lights out.
Saul: Oh really?
Lee: Yeah. Contemporary Western. Based on a true story. 'Course I'm not a writer like my brother here. I'm not a man of the pen.
Saul: Well—
Lee: I mean I can tell ya' a story off the tongue but I can't put it down on paper. That don't make any difference though does it?
Saul: No, not really.
Lee: I mean plenty a' guys have stories don't they? True-life stories. Musta' been a lota' movies made from real life.
Saul: Yes. I suppose so.
Lee: I haven't seen a good Western since "Lonely Are the Brave." You remember that movie?
Saul: No, I'm afraid I—
Lee: Kirk Douglas. Helluva' movie. You remember that movie, Austin?
Austin: Yes.
Lee: [*to* Saul] The man dies for the love of a horse.
Saul: Is that right.
Lee: Yeah. Ya' hear the horse screamin at the end of it. Rain's comin' down. Horse is screamin'. Then there's a shot. BLAM! Just a single shot like that. Then nothin' but the sound of rain. And Kirk Douglas is ridin' in the ambulance. Ridin' away from the scene of the accident. And when he hears that shot he knows that his horse has died. He knows. And you see his eyes. And his eyes die. Right inside his face. And then his eyes close. And you know that he's died too. You know that Kirk Douglas has died from the death of his horse.
Saul: [*eyes* Austin *nervously*] Well, it sounds like a great movie. I'm sorry I missed it.

LEE: Yeah, you shouldn't a' missed that one.

SAUL: I'll have to try to catch it some time. Arrange a screening or something. Well, Austin, I'll have to hit the freeway before rush hour.

AUSTIN: [*ushers him toward exit*] It's good seeing you, Saul.

[AUSTIN *and* SAUL *shake hands*]

LEE: So ya' think there's room for a real Western these days? A true-to-life Western?

SAUL: Well, I don't see why not. Why don't you uh—tell the story to Austin and have him write a little outline.

LEE: You'd take a look at it then?

SAUL: Yes. Sure. I'll give it a read-through. Always eager for new material. [*smiles at* AUSTIN]

LEE: That's great! You'd really read it then huh?

SAUL: It would just be my opinion of course.

LEE: That's all I want. Just an opinion. I happen to think it has a lota' possibilities.

SAUL: Well, it was great meeting you and I'll—

[SAUL *and* LEE *shake*]

LEE: I'll call you tomorrow about the golf.

SAUL: Oh. Yes, right.

LEE: Austin's got your number, right?

SAUL: Yes.

LEE: So long Saul. [*gives* SAUL *a pat on the back*]

[SAUL *exits,* AUSTIN *turns to* LEE, *looks at T.V. then back to* LEE]

AUSTIN: Give me the keys.

[AUSTIN *extends his hand toward* LEE, LEE *doesn't move, just stares at* AUSTIN, *smiles, lights to black*]

Scene 4

Night. Coyotes in distance, fade, sound of typewriter in dark, crickets, candlelight in alcove, dim light in kitchen, lights reveal AUSTIN *at glass table typing,* LEE *sits across from him, foot on table, drinking beer and whiskey, the T.V. is still on sink counter,* AUSTIN *types for a while, then stops.*

LEE: All right, now read it back to me.

AUSTIN: I'm not reading it back to you, Lee. You can read it when we're finished. I can't spend all night on this.

LEE: You got better things to do?

AUSTIN: Let's just go ahead. Now what happens when he leaves Texas?

LEE: Is he ready to leave Texas yet? I didn't know we were that far along. He's not ready to leave Texas.

AUSTIN: He's right at the border.

LEE: [*sitting up*] No, see this is one a' the crucial parts. Right here. [*taps paper with beer can*] We can't rush through this. He's not right at the border. He's a good fifty miles from the border. A lot can happen in fifty miles.

AUSTIN: It's only an outline. We're not writing an entire script now.

LEE: Well ya' can't leave things out even if it is an outline. It's one a' the most important parts. Ya' can't go leavin' it out.

AUSTIN: Okay, okay. Let's just—get it done.

LEE: All right. Now. He's in the truck and he's got his horse trailer and his horse.

AUSTIN: We've already established that.

LEE: And he sees this other guy comin' up behind him in another truck. And that truck is pullin' a gooseneck.

AUSTIN: What's a gooseneck?

LEE: Cattle trailer. You know the kind with a gooseneck, goes right down in the bed a' the pick-up.

AUSTIN: Oh. All right. [*types*]

LEE: It's important.

AUSTIN: Okay. I got it.

LEE: All these details are important.

[AUSTIN *types as they talk*]

AUSTIN: I've got it.

LEE: And this other guy's got his horse all saddled up in the back a' the gooseneck.

AUSTIN: Right.

LEE: So both these guys have got their horses right along with 'em, see.

AUSTIN: I understand.

LEE: Than this first guy suddenly realizes two things.

AUSTIN: The guy in front?

LEE: Right. The guy in front realizes two things almost at the same time. Simultaneous.

AUSTIN: What were the two things?

LEE: Number one, he realizes that the guy behind him is the husband of the woman he's been—

[LEE *makes gesture of screwing by pumping his arm*]

AUSTIN: [*sees* LEE'S *gesture*] Oh. Yeah.

LEE: And number two, he realizes he's in the middle of Tornado Country.

AUSTIN: What's "Tornado Country"?

LEE: Pandhandle.

AUSTIN: Panhandle?°

503. Panhandle, northern Texas.

LEE: Sweetwater. Around in that area. Nothin'. Nowhere. And number three—

AUSTIN: I thought there was only two.

LEE: There's three. There's a third unforeseen realization.

AUSTIN: And what's that?

LEE: That he's runnin' outa' gas.

AUSTIN: [*stops typing*] Come on, Lee.

[AUSTIN *gets up, moves to kitchen, gets a glass of water*]

LEE: Whatdya' mean, "come on"? That's what it is. Write it down! He's runnin' outa' gas.

AUSTIN: It's too—

LEE: What? It's too what? It's too real! That's what ya' mean isn't it? It's too much like real life!

AUSTIN: It's not like real life! It's not enough like real life. Things don't happen like that.

LEE: What! Men don't fuck other men's women?

AUSTIN: Yes. But they don't end up chasing each other across the Panhandle. Through "Tornado Country."

LEE: They do in this movie!

AUSTIN: And they don't have horses conveniently along with them when they run out of gas! And they don't run out of gas either!

LEE: These guys run outa' gas! This is my story and one a' these guys runs outa' gas!

AUSTIN: It's just a dumb excuse to get them into a chase scene. It's contrived.

LEE: It is a chase scene! It's already a chase scene. They been chasin' each other fer days.

AUSTIN: So now they're supposed to abandon their trucks, climb on their horses and chase each other into the mountains?

LEE: [*standing suddenly*] There aren't any mountains in the Panhandle! It's flat!

[LEE *turns violently toward windows in alcove and throws beer can at them*]

LEE: Goddamn these crickets! [*yells at crickets*] Shut up out there! [*pause, turns back toward table*] This place is like a fuckin' rest home here. How're you supposed to think!

AUSTIN: You wanna' take a break?

LEE: No, I don't wanna' take a break! I wanna' get this done! This is my last chance to get this done.

AUSTIN: [*moves back into alcove*] All right. Take it easy.

LEE: I'm gonna be leavin' this area. I don't have time to mess around here.

AUSTIN: Where are you going?

LEE: Never mind where I'm goin'! That's got nothin' to do with you. I just gotta' get this done. I'm not like you. Hangin' around bein' a parasite offa' other fools. I gotta' do this thing and get out.

[*pause*]

AUSTIN: A parasite? Me?
LEE: Yeah, you!
AUSTIN: After you break into people's houses and take their televisions?
LEE: They don't need their televisions! I'm doin' them a service.
AUSTIN: Give me back my keys, Lee.
LEE: Not until you write this thing! You're gonna' write this outline thing for me or that car's gonna' wind up in Arizona with a different paint job.
AUSTIN: You think you can force me to write this? I was doing you a favor.
LEE: Git off yer high horse will ya'! Favor! Big favor. Handin' down favors from the mountain top.
AUSTIN: Let's just write it, okay? Let's sit down and not get upset and see if we can just get through this.

[AUSTIN *sits at typewriter*]

[*long pause*]

LEE: Yer not gonna' even show it to him, are ya'?
AUSTIN: What?
LEE: This outline. You got no intention of showin' it to him. Yer just doin' this 'cause yer afraid a' me.
AUSTIN: You can show it to him yourself.
LEE: I will, boy! I'm gonna' read it to him on the golf course.
AUSTIN: And I'm not afraid of you either.
LEE: Then how come yer doin' it?
AUSTIN: [*pause*] So I can get my keys back.

[*pause as* LEE *takes keys out of his pocket slowly and throws them on table, long pause,* AUSTIN, *stares at keys*]

LEE: There. Now you got yer keys back.

[AUSTIN *looks up at* LEE *but doesn't take keys*]

LEE: Go ahead. There's yer keys.

[AUSTIN *slowly takes keys off table and puts them back in his own pocket*]

Now what're you gonna' do? Kick me out?
AUSTIN: I'm not going to kick you out, Lee.
LEE: You couldn't kick me out, boy.
AUSTIN: I know.
LEE: So you can't even consider that one. [*pause*] You could call the police. That'd be the obvious thing.
AUSTIN: You're my brother.
LEE: That don't mean a thing. You go down to the L.A. Police Department there

and ask them what kinda' people kill each other the most. What do you think they'd say?

AUSTIN: Who said anything about killing?

LEE: Family people. Brothers. Brothers-in-law. Cousins. Real American-type people. They kill each other in the heat mostly. In the Smog-Alerts. In the Brush Fire Season. Right about this time a' year.

AUSTIN: This isn't the same.

LEE: Oh no? What makes it different?

AUSTIN: We're not insane. We're not driven to acts of violence like that. Not over a dumb movie script. Now sit down.

[*long pause,* LEE *considers which way to go with it*]

LEE: Maybe not. [*he sits back down at table across from* AUSTIN] Maybe you're right. Maybe we're too intelligent, huh? [*pause*] We got our heads on our shoulders. One of us has even got a Ivy League diploma. Now that means somethin' don't it? Doesn't that mean somethin'?

AUSTIN: Look, I'll write this thing for you, Lee. I don't mind writing it. I just don't want to get all worked up about it. It's not worth it. Now, come on. Let's just get through it, okay?

LEE: Nah. I think there's easier money. Lotsa' places I could pick up thousands. Maybe millions. I don't need this shit. I could go up to Sacramento Valley and steal me a diesel. Ten thousand a week dismantling one a' those suckers. Ten thousand a week!

[LEE *opens another beer, puts his foot back up on table*]

AUSTIN: No, really, look, I'll write it out for you. I think it's a great idea.

LEE: Nah, you got yer own work to do. I don't wanna' interfere with yer life.

AUSTIN: I mean it'd be really fantastic if you could sell this. Turn it into a movie. I mean it.

[*pause*]

LEE: Ya' think so huh?

AUSTIN: Absolutely. You could really turn your life around, you know. Change things.

LEE: I could get me a house maybe.

AUSTIN: Sure you could get a house. You could get a whole ranch if you wanted to.

LEE: [*laughs*] A ranch? I could get a ranch?

AUSTIN: 'Course you could. You know what a screenplay sells for these days?

LEE: No. What's it sell for?

AUSTIN: A lot. A whole lot of money.

LEE: Thousands?

AUSTIN: Yeah. Thousands.

LEE: Millions?

AUSTIN: Well—

LEE: We could get the old man outa' hock then.

AUSTIN: Maybe.

LEE: Maybe? Whadya' mean, maybe?

AUSTIN: I mean it might take more than money.

LEE: You were just tellin' me it'd change my whole life around. Why wouldn't it change his?

AUSTIN: He's different.

LEE: Oh, he's of a different ilk huh?

AUSTIN: He's not gonna' change. Let's leave the old man out of it.

LEE: That's right. He's not gonna' change but I will. I'll just turn myself right inside out. I could be just like you then, huh? Sittin' around dreamin' stuff up. Gettin' paid to dream. Ridin' back and forth on the freeway just dreamin' my fool head off.

AUSTIN: It's not all that easy.

LEE: It's not, huh?

AUSTIN: No. There's a lot of work involved.

LEE: What's the toughest part? Deciding whether to jog or play tennis?

[*long pause*]

AUSTIN: Well, look. You can stay here—do whatever you want to. Borrow the car. Come in and out. Doesn't matter to me. It's not my house. I'll help you write this thing or—not. Just let me know what you want. You tell me.

LEE: Oh. So now suddenly you're at my service. Is that it?

AUSTIN: What do you want to do Lee?

[*long pause,* LEE *stares at him then turns and dreams at windows*]

LEE: I tell ya' what I'd do if I still had that dog. Ya' wanna' know what I'd do?

AUSTIN: What?

LEE: Head out to Ventura. Cook up a little match. God that little dog could bear down. Lota' money in dog fightin'. Big money.

[*pause*]

AUSTIN: Why don't we try to see this through, Lee. Just for the hell of it. Maybe you've really got something here. What do you think?

[*pause,* LEE *considers*]

LEE: Maybe so. No harm in tryin' I guess. You think it's such a hot idea. Besides, I always wondered what'd be like to be you.

AUSTIN: You did?

LEE: Yeah, sure. I used to picture you walkin' around some campus with yer arms fulla' books. Blondes chasin' after ya'.

AUSTIN: Blondes? That's funny.

LEE: What's funny about it?
AUSTIN: Because I always used to picture you somewhere.
LEE: Where'd you picture me?
AUSTIN: Oh, I don't know. Different places. Adventures. You were always on some adventure.
LEE: Yeah.
AUSTIN: And I used to say to myself, "Lee's got the right idea. He's out there in the world and here I am. What am I doing?"
LEE: Well you were settin' yourself up for somethin'.
AUSTIN: I guess.
LEE: We better get started on this thing then.
AUSTIN: Okay.

[AUSTIN *sits up at typewriter, puts new paper in*]

LEE: Oh. Can I get the keys back before I forget?

[AUSTIN *hesitates*]

You said I could borrow the car if I wanted, right? Isn't that what you said?
AUSTIN: Yeah. Right.

[AUSTIN *takes keys out of his pocket, sets them on table,* LEE *takes keys slowly, plays with them in his hand*]

LEE: I could get a ranch, huh?
AUSTIN: Yeah. We have to write it first though.
LEE: Okay. Let's write it.

[*lights start dimming slowly to end of scene as* AUSTIN *types,* LEE *speaks*] So they take off after each other straight into an endless black prairie. The sun is just comin' down and they can feel the night on their backs. What they don't know is that each one of 'em is afraid, see. Each one separately thinks that he's the only one that's afraid. And they keep ridin' like that straight into the night. Not knowing. And the one who's chasin' doesn't know where the other one is taking him. And the one who's being chased doesn't know where he's going.

[*lights to black, typing stops in the dark, crickets fade*]

ACT TWO

Scene 5

Morning. LEE *at the table in alcove with a set of golf clubs in a fancy leather bag,* AUSTIN *at sink washing a few dishes.*

AUSTIN: He really liked it, huh?
LEE: He wouldn't a' gave me these clubs if he didn't like it.
AUSTIN: He gave you the clubs?

LEE: Yeah. I told ya' he gave me the clubs. The bag too.

AUSTIN: I thought he just loaned them to you.

LEE: He said it was part a' the advance. A little gift like. Gesture of his good faith.

AUSTIN: He's giving you an advance?

LEE: Now what's so amazing about that? I told ya' it was a good story. You even said it was a good story.

AUSTIN: Well that is really incredible Lee. You know how many guys spend their whole lives down here trying to break into this business? Just trying to get in the door?

LEE: [*pulling clubs out of bag, testing them*] I got no idea. How many?

[*pause*]

AUSTIN: How much of an advance is he giving you?

LEE: Plenty. We were talkin' big money out there. Ninth hole is where I sealed the deal.

AUSTIN: He made a firm commitment?

LEE: Absolutely.

AUSTIN: Well, I know Saul and he doesn't fool around when he says he likes something.

LEE: I thought you said you didn't know him.

AUSTIN: Well, I'm familiar with his tastes.

LEE: I let him get two up on me goin' into the back nine. He was sure he had me cold. You shoulda' seen his face when I pulled out the old pitching wedge and plopped it pin-high, two feet from the cup. He 'bout shit his pants. "Where'd a guy like you ever learn how to play golf like that?" he says.

[LEE *laughs,* AUSTIN *stares at him*]

AUSTIN: 'Course there's no contract yet. Nothing's final until it's on paper.

LEE: It's final, all right. There's no way he's gonna' back out of it now. We gambled for it.

AUSTIN: Saul, gambled?

LEE: Yeah, sure. I mean he liked the outline already so he wasn't risking that much. I just guaranteed it with my short game.

[*pause*]

AUSTIN: Well, we should celebrate or something. I think Mom left a bottle of champagne in the refrigerator. We should have a little toast.

[AUSTIN *gets glasses from cupboard, goes to refrigerator, pulls out bottle of champagne*]

LEE: You shouldn't oughta' take her champagne, Austin. She's gonna' miss that.

AUSTIN: Oh, she's not going to mind. She'd be glad we put it to good use. I'll get her another bottle. Besides, it's perfect for the occasion.

[*pause*]

LEE: Yer gonna' get a nice fee fer writin' the script a' course. Straight fee.

[AUSTIN *stops, stares at* LEE, *puts glasses and bottle on table, pause*]

AUSTIN: I'm writing the script?

LEE: That's what he said. Said we couldn't hire a better screenwriter in the whole town.

AUSTIN: But I'm already working on a script. I've got my own project. I don't have time to write two scripts.

LEE: No, he said he was gonna' drop that other one.

[*pause*]

AUSTIN: What? You mean mine? He's going to drop mine and do yours instead?

LEE: [*smiles*] Now look, Austin, it's jest beginner's luck ya' know. I mean I sank a fifty foot putt for this deal. No hard feelings.

[AUSTIN *goes to phone on wall, grabs it, starts dialing*]

He's not gonna' be in, Austin. Told me he wouldn't be in 'till late this afternoon.

AUSTIN: [*stays on phone, dialing, listens*] I can't believe this. I just can't believe it. Are you sure he said that? Why would he drop mine?

LEE: That's what he told me.

AUSTIN: He can't do that without telling me first. Without talking to me at least. He wouldn't just make a decision like that without talking to me!

LEE: Well I was kinda' surprised myself. But he was real enthusiastic about my story.

[AUSTIN *hangs up phone violently, paces*]

AUSTIN: What'd he say! Tell me everything he said!

LEE: I been tellin' ya'! He said he liked the story a whole lot. It was the first authentic Western to come along in a decade.

AUSTIN: He liked that story! Your story?

LEE: Yeah! What's so surprisin' about that?

AUSTIN: It's stupid! It's the dumbest story I ever heard in my life.

LEE: Hey, hold on! That's my story yer talkin' about!

AUSTIN: It's a bullshit story! It's idiotic. Two lamebrains chasing each other across Texas! Are you kidding? Who do you think's going to see a film like that?

LEE: It's not a film! It's a movie. There's a big difference. That's somethin' Saul told me.

AUSTIN: Oh he did, huh?

LEE: Yeah, he said, "In this business we make movies, American movies. Leave the films to the French."

AUSTIN: So you got real intimate with old Saul huh? He started pouring forth his vast knowledge of Cinema.

LEE: I think he liked me a lot, to tell ya' the truth. I think he felt I was somebody he could confide in.

AUSTIN: What'd you do, beat him up or something?

LEE: [*stands fast*] Hey, I've about had it with the insults buddy! You think yer the only one in the brain department here? Yer the only one that can sit around and cook things up? There's other people got ideas too, ya' know!

AUSTIN: You must've done something. Threatened him or something. Now what'd you do Lee?

LEE: I convinced him!

[LEE *makes sudden menacing lunge toward* AUSTIN, *wielding golf club above his head, stops himself, frozen moment, long pause,* LEE *lowers club*]

AUSTIN: Oh, Jesus, You didn't hurt him did you?

[*long silence,* LEE *sits back down at table*]

Lee! Did you hurt him?

LEE: I didn't do nothin' to him! He liked my story. Pure and simple. He said it was the best story he's come across in a long, long time.

AUSTIN: That's what he told me about my story! That's the same thing he said to me.

LEE: Well, he musta' been lyin'. He musta' been lyin' to one of us anyway.

AUSTIN: You can't come into this town and start pushing people around. They're gonna' put you away!

LEE: I never pushed anybody around! I beat him fair and square. [*pause*] They can't touch me anyway. They can't put a finger on me. I'm gone. I can come in through the window and go out through the door. They never knew what hit 'em. You, yer stuck. Yer the one that's stuck. Not me. So don't be warnin' me what to do in this town.

[*pause,* AUSTIN *crosses to table, sits at typewriter, rests*]

AUSTIN: Lee, come on, level with me will you? It doesn't make any sense that suddenly he'd throw my idea out the window. I've been talking to him for months. I've got too much at stake. Everything's riding on this project.

LEE: What's yer idea?

AUSTIN: It's just a simple love story.

LEE: What kinda' love story?

AUSTIN: [*stands, crosses into kitchen*] I'm not telling you!

LEE: Ha! 'Fraid I'll steal it huh? Competition's gettin' kinda' close to home isn't it?

AUSTIN: Where did Saul say he was going?

LEE: He was gonna' take my story to a couple studios.

AUSTIN: That's *my* outline you know! I wrote that outline! You've got no right to be peddling it around.

LEE: You weren't ready to take credit for it last night.

AUSTIN: Give me my keys!

LEE: What?

AUSTIN: The keys! I want my keys back!

LEE: Where you goin'?

AUSTIN: Just give me my keys! I gotta' take a drive. I gotta' get out of here for a while.

LEE: Where you gonna' go, Austin?

AUSTIN: [*pause*] I might just drive out to the desert for a while. I gotta' think.

LEE: You can think here just as good. This is the perfect setup for thinkin'. We got some writin' to do here, boy. Now let's just have us a little toast. Relax. We're partners now.

[LEE *pops the cork of the champagne bottle, pours two drinks as the lights fade to black*]

Scene 6

Afternoon. LEE *and* SAUL *in kitchen,* AUSTIN *in alcove*

LEE: Now you tell him. You tell him, Mr. Kipper.

SAUL: Kimmer.

LEE: Kimmer. You tell him what you told me. He don't believe me.

AUSTIN: I don't want to hear it.

SAUL: It's really not a big issue, Austin. I was simply amazed by your brother's story and—

AUSTIN: Amazed? You lost a bet! You gambled with my material!

SAUL: That's really beside the point, Austin. I'm ready to go all the way with your brother's story. I think it has a great deal of merit.

AUSTIN: I don't want to hear about it, okay? Go tell it to the executives! Tell it to somebody who's going to turn it into a package deal or something. A T.V. series. Don't tell it to me.

SAUL: But I want to continue with your project too, Austin. It's not as though we can't do both. We're big enough for that aren't we?

AUSTIN: "We"? *I* can't do both! I don't know about "we."

LEE: [*to* SAUL] See, what'd I tell ya'. He's totally unsympathetic.

SAUL: Austin, there's no point in our going to another screenwriter for this. It just doesn't make sense. You're brothers. You know each other. There's a familiarity with the material that just wouldn't be possible otherwise.

AUSTIN: There's no familiarity with the material! None! I don't know what "Tornado Country" is. I don't know what a "gooseneck" is. And I don't want to know! [*pointing to* LEE] He's a hustler! He's a bigger hustler than you are! If you can't see that, then—

LEE: [*to* AUSTIN] Hey, now hold on. I didn't have to bring this bone back to you, boy. I persuaded Saul here that you were the right man for the job. You don't have to go throwin' up favors in my face.

AUSTIN: Favors! I'm the one who wrote the fuckin' outline! You can't even spell.

SAUL: [*to* AUSTIN] Your brother told me about the situation with your father.

[*pause*]

AUSTIN: What? [*looks at* LEE]

SAUL: That's right. Now we have a clear-cut deal here, Austin. We have big studio money standing behind this thing. Just on the basis of your outline.

AUSTIN: [*to* SAUL] What'd he tell you about my father?

SAUL: Well—that he's destitute. He needs money.

LEE: That's right. He does.

[AUSTIN *shakes his head, stares at them both*]

AUSTIN: [*to* LEE] And this little assignment is supposed to go toward the old man? A charity project? Is that what this is? Did you cook this up on the ninth green too?

SAUL: It's a big slice, Austin.

AUSTIN: [*to* LEE] I gave him money! I already gave him money. You know that. He drank it all up!

LEE: This is a different deal here.

SAUL: We can set up a trust for your father. A large sum of money. It can be doled out to him in parcels so he can't misuse it.

AUSTIN: Yeah, and who's doing the doling?

SAUL: Your brother volunteered.

[AUSTIN *laughs*]

LEE: That's right. I'll make sure he uses it for groceries.

AUSTIN: [*to* SAUL] I'm not doing this script! I'm not writing this crap for you or anybody else. You can't blackmail me into it. You can't threaten me into it. There's no way I'm doing it. So just give it up. Both of you.

[*long pause*]

SAUL: Well, that's it then. I mean this is an easy three hundred grand. Just for a first draft. It's incredible, Austin. We've got three different studios all trying to cut each other's throats to get this material. In one morning. That's how hot it is.

AUSTIN: Yeah, well you can afford to give me a percentage on the outline then. And you better get the genius here an agent before he gets burned.

LEE: Saul's gonna' be my agent. Isn't that right, Saul?

SAUL: That's right. [*to* AUSTIN] Your brother has really got something, Austin. I've been around too long not to recognize it. Raw talent.

AUSTIN: He's got a lota' balls is what he's got. He's taking you right down the river.

SAUL: Three hundred thousand, Austin. Just for a first draft. Now you've never been offered that kind of money before.

AUSTIN: I'm not writing it.

[*pause*]

SAUL: I see. Well—

LEE: We'll just go to another writer then. Right, Saul? Just hire us somebody with some enthusiasm. Somebody who can recognize the value of a good story.

SAUL: I'm sorry about this, Austin.

AUSTIN: Yeah.

SAUL: I mean I was hoping we could continue both things but now I don't see how it's possible.

AUSTIN: So you're dropping my idea altogether. Is that it? Just trade horses in midstream? After all these months of meetings.

SAUL: I wish there was another way.

AUSTIN: I've got everything riding on this, Saul. You know that. It's my only shot. If this falls through—

SAUL: I have to go with what my instincts tell me—

AUSTIN: Your instincts!

SAUL: My gut reaction.

AUSTIN: You lost! That's your gut reaction. You lost a gamble. Now you're trying to tell me you like his story? How could you possibly fall for that story? It's as phony as Hoppalong Cassidy.° What do you see in it? I'm curious.

SAUL: It has the ring of truth, Austin.

AUSTIN: [*laughs*] Truth?

LEE: It is true.

SAUL: Something about the real West.

AUSTIN: Why? Because it's got horses? Because it's got grown men acting like little boys?

SAUL: Something about the land. Your brother is speaking from experience.

AUSTIN: So am I!

SAUL: But nobody's interested in love these days, Austin. Let's face it.

LEE: That's right.

AUSTIN: [*to* SAUL] He's been camped out on the desert for three months. Talking to cactus. What's he know about what people wanna' see on the screen! I drive on the freeway every day. I swallow the smog. I watch the news in color. I shop in the Safeway. I'm the one who's in touch! Not him!

SAUL: I have to go now, Austin.

868. Hoppalong Cassidy, children's television cowboy show of the fifties and sixties.

[Saul *starts to leave*]

Austin: There's no such thing as the West anymore! It's a dead issue! It's dried up, Saul, and so are you.

[Saul *stops and turns to* Austin]

Saul: Maybe you're right. But I have to take the gamble, don't I?
Austin: You're a fool to do this, Saul.
Saul: I've always gone on my hunches. Always. And I've never been wrong. [*to* Lee] I'll talk to you tomorrow, Lee.
Lee: All right, Mr. Kimmer.
Saul: Maybe we could have some lunch.
Lee: Fine with me. [*smiles at* Austin]
Saul: I'll give you a ring.

[Saul *exits, lights to black as brothers look at each other from a distance*]

Scene 7

Night. Coyotes, crickets, sound of typewriter in dark, candlelight up on Lee *at typewriter struggling to type with one finger system,* Austin *sits sprawled out on kitchen floor with whiskey bottle, drunk.*

Austin: [*singing, from floor*]

"Red sails in the sunset
Way out on the blue
Please carry my loved one
Home safely to me

Red sails in the sunset—"

Lee: [*slams fist on table*] Hey! Knock it off will ya'! I'm tryin' to concentrate here.
Austin: [*laughs*] You're tryin' to concentrate?
Lee: Yeah. That's right.
Austin: Now you're tryin' to concentrate.
Lee: Between you, the coyotes and the crickets a thought don't have much of a chance.
Austin: "Between me, the coyotes and the crickets." What a great title.
Lee: I don't need a title! I need a thought.
Austin: [*laughs*] A thought! Here's a thought for ya'—
Lee: I'm not askin' fer yer thoughts! I got my own. I can do this thing on my own.
Austin: You're going to write an entire script on your own?
Lee: That's right.

[*pause*]

AUSTIN: Here's a thought. Saul Kimmer—

LEE: Shut up will ya'!

AUSTIN: He thinks we're the same person.

LEE: Don't get cute.

AUSTIN: He does! He's lost his mind. Poor old Saul. [*giggles*] Thinks we're one and the same.

LEE: Why don't you ease up on that champagne.

AUSTIN: [*holding up bottle*] This isn't champagne anymore. We went through the champagne a long time ago. This is serious stuff. The days of champagne are long gone.

LEE: Well, go outside and drink it.

AUSTIN: I'm enjoying your company, Lee. For the first time since your arrival I am finally enjoying your company. And now you want me to go outside and drink alone?

LEE: That's right.

[LEE *reads through paper in typewriter, makes an erasure*]

AUSTIN: You think you'll make more progress if you're alone? You might drive yourself crazy.

LEE: I could have this thing done in a night if I had a little silence.

AUSTIN: Well you'd still have the crickets to contend with. The coyotes. The sounds of the Police Helicopters prowling above the neighborhood. Slashing their searchlights down through the streets. Hunting for the likes of you.

LEE: I'm a screenwriter now! I'm legitimate.

AUSTIN: [*laughing*] A screenwriter!

LEE: That's right. I'm on salary. That's more'n I can say for you. I got an advance coming.

AUSTIN: This is true. This is very true. An advance. [*pause*] Well, maybe I oughta' go out and try my hand at your trade. Since you're doing so good at mine.

LEE: Ha!

[LEE *attempts to type some more but gets the ribbon tangled up, starts trying to rethread it as they continue talking*]

AUSTIN: Well, why not? You don't think I've got what it takes to sneak into people's houses and steal their T.V.s?

LEE: You couldn't steal a toaster without losin' yer lunch.

[AUSTIN *stands with a struggle, supports himself by the sink*]

AUSTIN: You don't think I could sneak into somebody's house and steal a toaster?

LEE: Go take a shower or somethin' will ya!

[Lee *gets more tangled up with the typewriter ribbon, pulling it out of the machine as though it was fishing line*]

Austin: You really don't think I could steal a crumby toaster? How much you wanna' bet I can't steal a toaster! How much? Go ahead! You're a gambler aren't you? Tell me how much yer willing to put on the line. Some part of your big advance? Oh, you haven't got that yet have you. I forgot.

Lee: All right. I'll bet you your car that you can't steal a toaster without gettin' busted.

Austin: You already got my car!

Lee: Okay, your house then.

Austin: What're you gonna' give me! I'm not talkin' about my house and my car. I'm talkin' about what are you gonna' give me. You don't have nothin' to give me.

Lee: I'll give you—shared screen credit. How 'bout that? I'll have it put in the contract that this was written by the both of us.

Austin: I don't want my name on that piece of shit! I want something of value. You got anything of value? You got any tidbits from the desert? Any Rattlesnake bones? I'm not a greedy man. Any little personal treasure will suffice.

Lee: I'm gonna' just kick yer ass out in a minute.

Austin: Oh, so now you're gonna' kick me out! Now I'm the intruder. I'm the one who's invading your precious privacy.

Lee: I'm trying to do some screenwriting here!!

[Lee *stands, picks up typewriter, slams it down hard on table, pause, silence except for crickets*]

Austin: Well, you got everything you need. You got plenty a' coffee? Groceries. You got a car. A contract. [*pause*] Might need a new typewriter ribbon but other than that you're pretty well fixed. I'll just leave ya' alone for a while.

[Austin *tries to steady himself to leave,* Lee *makes a move toward him*]

Lee: Where you goin'?

Austin: Don't worry about me. I'm not the one to worry about.

[Austin *weaves toward exit, stops*]

Lee: What're you gonna' do? Just go wander out into the night?

Austin: I'm gonna' make a little tour.

Lee: Why don't ya' just go to bed for Christ's sake. Yer makin' me sick.

Austin: I can take care a' myself. Don't worry about me.

[Austin *weaves badly in another attempt to exit, he crashes to the floor,* Lee *goes to him but remains standing*]

Lee: You want me to call your wife for ya' or something?

AUSTIN: [*from floor*] My wife?

LEE: Yeah. I mean maybe she can help ya' out. Talk to ya' or somethin'.

AUSTIN: [*struggles to stand again*] She's five hundred miles away. North. North of here. Up in the North country where things are calm. I don't need any help. I'm gonna' go outside and I'm gonna' steal a toaster. I'm gonna' steal some other stuff too. I might even commit bigger crimes. Bigger than you ever dreamed of. Crimes beyond the imagination!

[AUSTIN *manages to get himself vertical, tries to head for exit again*]

LEE: Just hang on a minute, Austin.

AUSTIN: Why? What for? You don't need my help, right? You got a handle on the project. Besides, I'm lookin' forward to the smell of the night. The bushes. Orange blossoms. Dust in the driveways. Rain bird sprinklers. Lights in people's houses. You're right about the lights, Lee. Everybody else is livin' the life. Indoors. Safe. This is a Paradise down here. You know that? We're livin' in a Paradise. We've forgotten about that.

LEE: You sound just like the old man now.

AUSTIN: Yeah, well we all sound alike when we're sloshed. We just sorta' echo each other.

LEE: Maybe if we could work on this together we could bring him back out here. Get him settled down some place.

[AUSTIN *turns violently toward* LEE, *takes a swing at him, misses and crashes to the floor again,* LEE *stays standing*]

AUSTIN: I don't want him out here! I've had it with him! I went all the way out there! I went out of my way. I gave him money and all he did was play Al Jolson° records and spit at me! I gave him money!

[*pause*]

LEE: Just help me a little with the characters, all right? You know how to do it, Austin.

AUSTIN: [*on floor, laughs*] The characters!

LEE: Yeah. You know. The way they talk and stuff. I can hear it in my head but I can't get it down on paper.

AUSTIN: What characters?

LEE: The guys. The guys in the story.

AUSTIN: Those aren't characters.

LEE: Whatever you call 'em then. I need to write somethin' out.

AUSTIN: Those are illusions of characters.

LEE: I don't give a damn what ya' call 'em! You know what I'm talkin' about!

AUSTIN: Those are fantasies of a long lost boyhood.

LEE: I gotta' write somethin' out on paper!!

1001–1002. Al Jolson, American entertainer and singer (1886–1950).

[*pause*]

Austin: What for? Saul's gonna' get you a fancy screenwriter isn't he?

Lee: I wanna' do it myself!

Austin: Then do it! Yer on your own now, old buddy. You bulldogged yer way into contention. Now you gotta' carry it through.

Lee: I will but I need some advice. Just a couple a' things. Come on, Austin. Just help me get 'em talkin' right. It won't take much.

Austin: Oh, now you're having a little doubt huh? What happened? The pressure's on, boy. This is it. You gotta' come up with it now. You don't come up with a winner on your first time out they just cut your head off. They don't give you a second chance ya' know.

Lee: I got a good story! I know it's a good story. I just need a little help is all.

Austin: Not from me. Not from yer little old brother. I'm retired.

Lee: You could save this thing for me, Austin. I'd give ya' half the money. I would. I only need half anyway. With this kinda' money I could be a long time down the road. I'd never bother ya' again. I promise. You'd never even see me again.

Austin: [*still on floor*] You'd disappear?

Lee: I would for sure.

Austin: Where would you disappear to?

Lee: That don't matter. I got plenty a' places.

Austin: Nobody can disappear. The old man tried that. Look where it got him. He lost his teeth.

Lee: He never had any money.

Austin: I don't mean that. I mean his teeth! His real teeth. First he lost his real teeth, then he lost his false teeth. You never knew that did ya'? He never confided in you.

Lee: Nah, I never knew that.

Austin: You wanna' drink?

[Austin *offers bottle to* Lee, Lee *takes it, sits down on kitchen floor with* Austin, *they share the bottle*]

Yeah, he lost his real teeth one at a time. Woke up every morning with another tooth lying on the mattress. Finally, he decides he's gotta' get 'em all pulled out but he doesn't have any money. Middle of Arizona with no money and no insurance and every morning another tooth is lying on the mattress. [*takes a drink*] So what does he do?

Lee: I dunno'. I never knew about that.

Austin: He begs the government. G.I. Bill or some damn thing. Some pension plan he remembers in the back of his head. And they send him out the money.

Lee: They did?

[*they keep trading the bottle between them, taking drinks*]

AUSTIN: Yeah. They send him the money but it's not enough money. Costs a lot to have all yer teeth yanked. They charge by the individual tooth, ya' know. I mean one tooth isn't equal to another tooth. Some are more expensive. Like the big ones in the back—

LEE: So what happened?

AUSTIN: So he locates a Mexican dentist in Juarez who'll do the whole thing for a song. And he takes off hitchhiking to the border.

LEE: Hitchhiking?

AUSTIN: Yeah. So how long you think it takes him to get to the border? A man his age.

LEE: I dunno.

AUSTIN: Eight days it takes him. Eight days in the rain and the sun and every day he's droppin' teeth on the blacktop and nobody'll pick him up 'cause his mouth's full a' blood.

[*pause, they drink*]

So finally he stumbles into the dentist. Dentist takes all his money and all his teeth. And there he is, in Mexico, with his gums sewed up and his pockets empty.

[*long silence,* AUSTIN, *drinks*]

LEE: That's it?

AUSTIN: Then I go out to see him, see. I go out there and I take him out for a nice Chinese dinner. But he doesn't eat. All he wants to do is drink Martinis outa' plastic cups. And he takes his teeth out and lays 'em on the table 'cause he can't stand the feel of 'em. And we ask the waitress for one a' those doggie bags to take the Chop Suey home in. So he drops his teeth in the doggie bag along with the Chop Suey. And then we go out to hit all the bars up and down the highway. Says he wants to introduce me to all his buddies. And in one a' those bars, in one a' those bars up and down the highway, he left that doggie bag with his teeth laying in the Chop Suey.

LEE: You never found it?

AUSTIN: We went back but we never did find it. [*pause*] Now that's a true story. True to life.

[*they drink as lights fade to black*]

Scene 8

Very early morning, between night and day. No crickets, coyotes yapping feverishly in distance before light comes up, a small fire blazes up in the dark from alcove area, sound of LEE *smashing typewriter with a golf club, lights coming up.* LEE *seen smashing typewriter methodically then dropping pages of his script into a burning bowl set on the floor of alcove, flames leap up,* AUSTIN *has a whole bunch of stolen toasters lined up on the sink counter along with* Lee's *stolen T.V., the toasters are of a wide variety of models, mostly chrome,* Austin *goes up and down the line of toasters, breathing on them and polishing them with a dish towel, both men are drunk, empty whiskey bottles and beer cans litter floor of kitchen, they share a half empty bottle on one of the chairs in the alcove,* Lee *keeps periodically taking deliberate ax-chops at the typewriter using a nine-iron as* Austin *speaks, all of their mother's house plants are dead and drooping.*

Austin: [*polishing toasters*] There's gonna be a general lack of toast in the neighborhood this morning. Many, many unhappy bewildered breakfast faces. I guess it's best not to even think of the victims. Not to even entertain it. Is that the right psychology?

Lee: [*pause*] What?

Austin: Is that the correct criminal psychology? Not to think of the victims?

Lee: What victims?

[Lee *takes another swipe at typewriter with nine-iron, adds pages to the fire*]

Austin: The victims of crime. Of breaking and entering. I mean is it a prerequisite for a criminal not to have a conscience?

Lee: Ask a criminal.

[*pause,* Lee *stares at* Austin]

What're you gonna' do with all those toasters? That's the dumbest thing I ever saw in my life.

Austin: I've got hundreds of dollars worth of household appliances here. You may not realize that.

Lee: Yeah, and how many hundreds of dollars did you walk right past?

Austin: It was toasters you challenged me to. Only toasters. I ignored every other temptation.

Lee: I never challenged you! That's no challenge. Anybody can steal a toaster.

[Lee *smashes typewriter again*]

Austin: You don't have to take it out on my typewriter ya' know. It's not the machine's fault that you can't write. It's a sin to do that to a good machine.

Lee: A sin?

Austin: When you consider all the writers who never even had a machine. Who would have given an eyeball for a good typewriter. Any typewriter.

[Lee *smashes typewriter again*]

Austin: [*polishing toasters*] All the ones who wrote on matchbook covers. Paper bags. Toilet paper. Who had their writing destroyed by their jailers. Who persisted beyond all odds. Those writers would find it hard to understand your actions.

[LEE *comes down on typewriter with one final crushing blow of the nine-iron then collapses in one of the chairs, takes a drink from bottle, pause*]

AUSTIN: [*after pause*] Not to mention demolishing a perfectly good golf club. What about all the struggling golfers? What about Lee Trevino?° What do you think he would've said when he was batting balls around with broomsticks at the age of nine. Impoverished.

[*pause*]

LEE: What time is it anyway?
AUSTIN: No idea. Time stands still when you're havin' fun.
LEE: Is it too late to call a woman? You know any women?
AUSTIN: I'm a married man.
LEE: I mean a local woman.

[AUSTIN *looks out at light through window above sink*]

AUSTIN: It's either too late or too early. You're the nature enthusiast. Can't you tell the time by the light in the sky? Orient yourself around the North Star or something?
LEE: I can't tell anything.
AUSTIN: Maybe you need a little breakfast. Some toast! How 'bout some toast?

[AUSTIN *goes to cupboard, pulls out loaf of bread and starts dropping slices into every toaster,* LEE *stays sitting, drinks, watches* AUSTIN]

LEE: I don't need toast. I need a woman.
AUSTIN: A woman isn't the answer. Never was.
LEE: I'm not talkin' about permanent. I'm talkin' about temporary.
AUSTIN: [*putting toast in toasters*] We'll just test the merits of these little demons. See which brands have a tendency to burn. See which one can produce a perfectly golden piece of fluffy toast.
LEE: How much gas you got in yer car?
AUSTIN: I haven't driven my car for days now. So I haven't had an opportunity to look at the gas gauge.
LEE: Take a guess. You think there's enough to get me to Bakersfield?
AUSTIN: Bakersfield? What's in Bakersfield?
LEE: Just never mind what's in Bakersfield! You think there's enough goddamn gas in the car!
AUSTIN: Sure.
LEE: Sure. You could care less, right. Let me run outa' gas on the Grapevine. You could give a shit.
AUSTIN: I'd say there was enough gas to get you just about anywhere, Lee. With your determination and guts.
LEE: What the hell time is it anyway?

1113. Lee Trevino, famous golfer.

[Lee *pulls out his wallet, starts going through dozens of small pieces of paper with phone numbers written on them, drops some on the floor, drops others in the fire*]

Austin: Very early. This is the time of morning when the coyotes kill people's cocker spaniels. Did you hear them? That's what they were doing out there. Luring innocent pets away from their homes.

Lee: [*searching through his papers*] What's the area code for Bakersfield? You know?

Austin: You could always call the operator.

Lee: I can't stand that voice they give ya'.

Austin: What voice?

Lee: That voice that warns you that if you'd only tried harder to find the number in the phone book you wouldn't have to be calling the operator to begin with.

[Lee *gets up, holding a slip of paper from his wallet, stumbles toward phone on wall, yanks receiver, starts dialing*]

Austin: Well I don't understand why you'd want to talk to anybody else anyway. I mean you can talk to me. I'm your brother.

Lee: [*dialing*] I wanna' talk to a woman. I haven't heard a woman's voice in a long time.

Austin: Not since the Botanist?

Lee: What?

Austin: Nothing. [*starts singing as he tends toast*]

"Red sails in the sunset
Way out on the blue
Please carry my loved one
Home safely to me"

Lee: Hey, knock it off will ya'! This is long distance here.

Austin: Bakersfield?

Lee: Yeah, Bakersfield. It's Kern County.

Austin: Well, what County are we in?

Lee: You better get yourself a 7-Up, boy.

Austin: One County's as good as another.

[Austin *hums "Red Sails" softly as* Lee *talks on phone*]

Lee: [*to phone*] Yeah, operator look—first off I wanna' know the area code for Bakersfield. Right. Bakersfield! Okay. Good. Now I wanna' know if you can help me track somebody down. [*pause*] No, no I mean a phone number. Just a phone number. Okay. [*holds a piece of paper up and reads it*] Okay, the name is Melly Ferguson. Melly. [*pause*] I dunno' Melly. Maybe. Yeah. Maybe Melanie. Yeah. Melanie Ferguson. Okay. [*pause*] What? I can't hear ya' so good. Sounds like yer under the ocean. [*pause*] You got ten Melanie Fergusons? How could that be? Ten Melanie Fergusons in Bakersfield? Well gimme all ten of 'em then. [*pause*] What d'ya' mean? Gimmie all ten Melanie Fergusons! That's right. Just a second. [*to* Austin] Gimme a pen.

Austin: I don't have a pen.

Lee: Gimme a pencil then!

Austin: I don't have a pencil.

Lee: [*to phone*] Just a second, operator. [*to* Austin] Yer a writer and ya' don't have a pen or a pencil!

Lee: I'm not a writer. You're a writer.

Lee: I'm on the phone here! Get me a pen or a pencil.

Austin: I gotta' watch the toast.

Lee: [*to phone*] Hang on a second, operator.

[Lee *lets the phone drop then starts pulling all the drawers in the kitchen out on the floor and dumping the contents, searching for a pencil,* Austin *watches him casually*]

Lee: [*crashing through drawers, throwing contents around kitchen*] This is the last time I try to live with people, boy! I can't believe it. Here I am! Here I am again in a desperate situation! This would never happen out on the desert. I would never be in this kinda' situation out on the desert. Isn't there a pen or a pencil in this house! Who lives in this house anyway!

Austin: Our mother.

Lee: How come she don't have a pen or a pencil! She's a social person isn't she? Doesn't she have to make shopping lists? She's gotta' have a pencil. [*finds a pencil*] Aaha! [*he rushes back to phone, picks up receiver*] All right operator. Operator? Hey! Operator! Goddamnit!

[Lee *rips the phone off the wall and throws it down, goes back to chair and falls into it, drinks, long pause*]

Austin: She hung up?

Lee: Yeah, she hung up. I knew she was gonna' hang up. I could hear it in her voice.

[Lee *starts going through his slips of paper again*]

Austin: Well, you're probably better off staying here with me anyway. I'll take care of you.

Lee: I don't need takin' care of! Not by you anyway.

Austin: Toast is almost ready.

[Austin *starts buttering all the toast as it pops up*]

Lee: I don't want any toast!

[*long pause*]

Austin: You gotta' eat something. Can't just drink. How long have we been drinking, anyway?

Lee: [*looking through slips of paper*] Maybe it was Fresno. What's the area code for Fresno? How could I have lost that number! She was beautiful.

[*pause*]

Austin: Why don't you just forget about that, Lee. Forget about the woman.

Lee: She had green eyes. You know what green eyes do to me?

Austin: I know but you're not gonna' get it on with her now anyway. It's dawn already. She's in Bakersfield for Christ's sake.

[*long pause,* Lee *considers the situation*]

Lee: Yeah. [*looks at windows*] It's dawn?

Austin: Let's just have some toast and—

Lee: What is this bullshit with the toast anyway! You make it sound like salvation or something. I don't want any goddamn toast! How many times I gotta' tell ya'! [Lee *gets up, crosses upstage to windows in alcove, looks out,* Austin *butters toast*]

Austin: Well it is like salvation sort of. I mean the smell. I love the smell of toast. And the sun's coming up. It makes me feel like anything's possible. Ya' know?

Lee: [*back to* Austin, *facing windows upstage*] So go to church why don't ya'.

Austin: Like a beginning. I love beginnings.

Lee: Oh yeah. I've always been kinda' partial to endings myself.

Austin: What if I come with you, Lee?

Lee: [*pause as* Lee *turns toward* Austin] What?

Austin: What if I come with you out to the desert?

Lee: Are you kiddin'?

Austin: No. I'd just like to see what it's like.

Lee: You wouldn't last a day out there pal.

Austin: That's what you said about the toasters. You said I couldn't steal a toaster either.

Lee: A toaster's got nothin' to do with the desert.

Austin: I could make it, Lee. I'm not that helpless. I can cook.

Lee: Cook?

Austin: I can.

Lee: So what! You can cook. Toast.

Austin: I can make fires. I know how to get fresh water from condensation.

[Austin *stacks buttered toast up in a tall stack on plate*]

[Lee *slams table*]

Lee: It's not somethin' you learn out of a Boy Scout handbook!

Austin: Well how do you learn it then! How're you supposed to learn it!

[*pause*]

LEE: Ya' just learn it, that's all. Ya' learn it 'cause ya' have to learn it. You don't *have* to learn it.

AUSTIN: You could teach me.

LEE: [*stands*] What're you, crazy or somethin'? You went to college. Here, you are down here, rollin' in bucks. Floatin' up and down in elevators. And you wanna' learn how to live on the desert!

AUSTIN: I do, Lee. I really do. There's nothin' down here for me. There never was. When we were kids here it was different. There was a life here then. But now—I keep comin' down here thinkin' it's the fifties or somethin'. I keep finding myself getting off the freeway at familiar landmarks that turn out to be unfamiliar. On the way to appointments. Wandering down streets I thought I recognized that turn out to be replicas of streets I remember. Streets I misremember. Streets I can't tell if I lived on or saw in a postcard. Fields that don't even exist anymore.

LEE: There's no point cryin' about that now.

AUSTIN: There's nothin' real down here, Lee! Least of all me!

LEE: Well I can't save you from that!

AUSTIN: You can let me come with you.

LEE: No dice, pal.

AUSTIN: You could let me come with you, Lee!

LEE: Hey, do you actually think I chose to live out in the middle a' nowhere? Do ya'? Ya' think it's some kinda' philosophical decision I took or somethin'? I'm livin' out there 'cause I can't make it here! And yer bitchin' to me about all yer success!

AUSTIN: I'd cash it all in in a second. That's the truth.

LEE: [*pause, shakes his head*] I can't believe this.

AUSTIN: Let me go with you.

LEE: Stop sayin' that will ya'! Yer worse than a dog.

[AUSTIN *offers out the plate of neatly stacked toast to* LEE]

AUSTIN: You want some toast?

[LEE *suddenly explodes and knocks the plate out of* AUSTIN'S *hand, toast goes flying, long frozen moment where it appears* LEE *might go all the way this time when* AUSTIN *breaks it by slowly lowering himself to his knees and begins gathering the scattered toast from the floor and stacking it back on the plate,* LEE *begins to circle* AUSTIN *in a slow, predatory way, crushing pieces of toast in his wake, no words for a while,* AUSTIN *keeps gathering toast, even the crushed pieces*]

LEE: Tell ya' what I'll do, little brother. I might just consider makin' you a deal. Little trade. [AUSTIN *continues gathering toast as* LEE *circles him through this*] You write me up this screenplay thing just like I tell ya'. I mean you can use all yer usual tricks and stuff. Yer fancy language. Yer artistic hocus pocus. But ya' gotta' write everything like I say. Every move. Every time they run outa' gas, they run outa' gas. Every time they wanna' jump on a horse, they do just that. If they wanna' stay in Texas, by God they'll stay in Texas! [*Keeps circling*] And you finish the whole thing up for me. Top to bottom. And you put my name on it. And I own all the rights. And every dime goes in my pocket. You do that and I'll sure enough take ya' with me to the desert. [LEE *stops, pause, looks down at* AUSTIN] How's that sound?

[*pause as* AUSTIN *stands slowly holding plate of demolished toast, their faces are very close, pause*]

AUSTIN: It's a deal.

[LEE *stares straight into* AUSTIN'S *eyes, then he slowly takes a piece of toast off the plate, raises it to his mouth and takes a huge crushing bite never taking his eyes off* AUSTIN'S, *as* LEE *crunches into the toast the lights black out*]

Scene 9

Mid-day. No sound, blazing heat, the stage is ravaged; bottles, toasters, smashed typewriter, ripped out telephone, etc. All the debris from previous scene is now starkly visible in intense yellow light, the effect should be like a desert junkyard at high noon, the coolness of the preceding scenes is totally obliterated. AUSTIN *is seated at table in alcove, shirt open, pouring with sweat, hunched over a writing notebook, scribbling notes desperately with a ballpoint pen.* LEE *with no shirt, beer in hand, sweat pouring down his chest, is walking a slow circle around the table, picking his way through the objects, sometimes kicking them aside.*

LEE: [*as he walks*] All right, read it back to me. Read it back to me!

AUSTIN: [*scribbling at top speed*] Just a second.

LEE: Come on, come on! Just read what ya' got.

AUSTIN: I can't keep up! It's not the same as if I had a typewriter.

LEE: Just read what we got so far. Forget about the rest.

AUSTIN: All right. Let's see—okay—[*wipes sweat from his face, reads as* LEE *circles*] Luke says uh—

LEE: Luke?

AUSTIN: Yeah.

LEE: His name's Luke? All right, all right—we can change the names later. What's he say? Come on, come on.

AUSTIN: He says uh—[*reading*] "I told ya' you were a fool to follow me in here. I know this prairie like the back a' my hand."

LEE: No, no, no! That's not what I said. I never said that.

AUSTIN: That's what I wrote.

LEE: It's not what I said. I never said "like the back a' my hand." That's stupid. That's one a' those—whadya' call it? Whatya' call that?

AUSTIN: What?

LEE: Whadya' call it when somethin's been said a thousand times before. Whatdya' call that?

AUSTIN: Um—a cliché?

LEE: Yeah. That's right. Cliché. That's what that is. A cliché. "The back a' my hand." That's stupid.

AUSTIN: That's what you said.

LEE: I never said that! And even if I did, that's where yer supposed to come in. That's where yer supposed to change it to somethin' better.

AUSTIN: Well how am I supposed to do that and write down what you say at the same time?

LEE: Ya' just do, that's all! You hear a stupid line you change it. That's yer job.

AUSTIN: All right. [*makes more notes*]

LEE: What're you changin' it to?

AUSTIN: I'm not changing it. I'm just trying to catch up.

LEE: Well change it! We gotta' change that, we can't leave that in there like that. ". . . the back a' my hand." That's dumb.

AUSTIN: [*stops writing, sits back*] All right.

LEE: [*pacing*] So what'll we change it to?

AUSTIN: Um—How 'bout—"I'm on intimate terms with this prairie."

LEE: [*to himself considering line as he walks*] "I'm on intimate terms with this prairie." Intimate terms, intimate terms. Intimate—that means like uh—sexual right?

AUSTIN: Well—yeah—or—

LEE: He's on sexual terms with the prairie? How dya' figure that?

AUSTIN: Well it doesn't necessarily have to mean sexual.

LEE: What's it mean then?

AUSTIN: It means uh—close—personal—

LEE: All right. How's it sound? Put it into the uh—the line there. Read it back. Let's see how it sounds. [*to himself*] "Intimate terms."

AUSTIN: [*scribbles in notebook*] Okay. It'd go something like this: [*reads*] "I told ya' you were a fool to follow me in here. I'm on intimate terms with this prairie."

LEE: That's good. I like that. That's real good.

AUSTIN: You do?

LEE: Yeah. Don't you?

AUSTIN: Sure.

LEE: Sounds original now. "Intimate terms." That's good. Okay. Now we're cookin! That has a real ring to it.

[Austin *makes more notes,* Lee *walks around, pours beer on his arms and rubs it over his chest feeling good about the new progress, as he does this* Mom *enters unobtrusively down left with her luggage, she stops and stares at the scene still holding luggage as the two men continue, unaware of her presence,* Austin *absorbed in his writing,* Lee *cooling himself off with beer*]

Lee: [*continues*] "He's on intimate terms with this prairie." Sounds real mysterious and kinda' threatening at the same time.

Austin: [*writing rapidly*] Good.

Lee: Now—[Lee *turns and suddenly sees* Mom, *he stares at her for a while, she stares back,* Austin *keeps writing feverishly, not noticing,* Lee *walks slowly over to* Mom *and takes a closer look, long pause*]

Lee: Mom?

[Austin *looks up suddenly from his writing, sees* mom, *stands quickly, long pause,* Mom *surveys the damage*]

Austin: Mom. What're you doing back?

Mom: I'm back.

Lee: Here, lemme take those for ya.

[Lee *sets beer on counter than takes both her bags but doesn't know where to set them down in the sea of junk so he just keeps holding them*]

Austin: I wasn't expecting you back so soon. I thought uh—How was Alaska?

Mom: Fine.

Lee: See any igloos?

Mom: No. Just glaciers.

Austin: Cold huh?

Mom: What?

Austin: It must've been cold up there?

Mom: Not really.

Lee: Musta' been colder than this here. I mean we're havin' a real scorcher here.

Mom: Oh? [*she looks at damage*]

Lee: Yeah. Must be in the hundreds.

Austin: You wanna' take your coat off, Mom?

Mom: No. [*pause, she surveys space*] What happened in here?

Austin: Oh um—Me and Lee were just sort of celebrating and uh—

Mom: Celebrating?

Austin: Yeah. Uh—Lee sold a screenplay. A story, I mean.

Mom: Lee did?

Austin: Yeah.

Mom: Not you?

Austin: No. Him.

Mom: [*to* Lee] You sold a screenplay?

LEE: Yeah. That's right. We're just sorta' finishing it up right now. That's what we're doing here.

AUSTIN: Me and Lee are going out to the desert to live.

MOM: You and Lee?

AUSTIN: Yeah. I'm taking off with Lee.

MOM: [*she looks back and forth at each of them, pause*] You gonna go live with your father?

AUSTIN: No. We're going to a different desert Mom.

MOM: I see. Well, you'll probably wind up on the same desert sooner or later. What're all these toasters doing here?

AUSTIN: Well—we had kind of a contest.

MOM: Contest?

LEE: Yeah.

AUSTIN: Lee won.

MOM: Did you win a lot of money, Lee?

LEE: Well not yet. It's comin' in any day now.

MOM: [*to* LEE] What happened to your shirt?

LEE: Oh. I was sweatin' like a pig and I took it off.

[AUSTIN *grabs* LEE'S *shirt off the table and tosses it to him,* LEE *sets down suitcases and puts his shirt on*]

MOM: Well it's one hell of a mess in here isn't it?

AUSTIN: Yeah, I'll clean it up for you, Mom. I just didn't know you were coming back so soon.

MOM: I didn't either.

AUSTIN: What happened?

MOM: Nothing. I just started missing all my plants.

[*she notices dead plants*]

AUSTIN: Oh.

MOM: Oh, they're all dead aren't they. [*she crosses toward them, examines them closely*] You didn't get a chance to water I guess.

AUSTIN: I was doing it and then Lee came and—

LEE: Yeah I just distracted him a whole lot here, Mom. It's not his fault.

[*pause, as* MOM *stares at plants*]

MOM: Oh well, one less thing to take care of I guess. [*turns toward brothers*] Oh, that reminds me—You boys will probably never guess who's in town. Try and guess.

[*long pause, brothers stare at her*]

AUSTIN: Whadya' mean, Mom?

MOM: Take a guess. Somebody very important has come to town. I read it, coming down on the Greyhound.

Lee: Somebody very important?

Mom: See if you can guess. You'll never guess.

Austin: Mom—we're trying to uh—[*points to writing pad*]

Mom: Picasso. [*pause*] Picasso's in town. Isn't that incredible? Right now.

[*pause*]

Austin: Picasso's dead, Mom.

Mom: No, he's not dead. He's visiting the museum. I read it on the bus. We have to go down there and see him.

Austin: Mom—

Mom: This is the chance of a lifetime. Can you imagine? We could all go down and meet him. All three of us.

Lee: Uh—I don't think I'm really up fer meetin' anybody right now. I'm uh—What's his name?

Mom: Picasso! Picasso! You've never of Picasso? Austin, you've heard of Picasso.

Austin: Mom, we're not going to have time.

Mom: It won't take long. We'll just hop in the car and go down there. An opportunity like this doesn't come along every day.

Austin: We're gonna' be leavin' here, Mom!

[*pause*]

Mom: Oh.

Lee: Yeah.

[*pause*]

Mom: You're both leaving?

Lee: [*looks at* Austin] Well we were thinkin' about that before but now I—

Austin: No, we are! We're both leaving. We've got it all planned.

Mom: [*to* Austin] Well you can't leave. You have a family.

Austin: I'm leaving. I'm getting out of here.

Lee: [*to* Mom] I don't really think Austin's cut out for the desert do you?

Mom: No. He's not.

Austin: I'm going with you, Lee!

Mom: He's too thin.

Lee: Yeah, he'd just burn up out there.

Austin: [*to* Lee] We just gotta' finish this screenplay and then we're gonna' take off. That's the plan. That's what you said. Come on, let's get back to work, Lee.

Lee: I can't work under these conditions here. It's too hot.

Austin: Then we'll do it on the desert.

Lee: Don't be tellin' me what we're gonna do!

Mom: Don't shout in the house.

Lee: We're just gonna' have to postpone the whole deal.

AUSTIN: I can't postpone it! It's gone past postponing! I'm doing everything you said. I'm writing down exactly what you tell me.

LEE: Yeah, but you were right all along see. It is a dumb story. "Two lamebrains chasin' each other across Texas." That's what you said, right?

AUSTIN: I never said that

[LEE *sneers in* AUSTIN'S *face than turns to* MOM]

LEE: I'm gonna' just borrow some a' your antiques, Mom. You don't mind do ya'? Just a few plates and things. Silverware.

[LEE *starts going through all the cupboards in kitchen pulling out plates and stacking them on counter as* MOM *and* AUSTIN *watch*]

MOM: You don't have any utensils on the desert?

LEE: Nah, I'm fresh out.

AUSTIN: [*to* LEE] What're you doing?

MOM: Well some of those are very old. Bone China.

LEE: I'm tired of eatin' outa' my bare hands, ya' know. It's not civilized.

AUSTIN: [*to* LEE] What're you doing? We made a deal!

MOM: Couldn't you borrow the plastic ones instead? I have plenty of plastic ones.

LEE: [*as he stacks plates*] It's not the same. Plastic's not the same at all. What I need is somethin' authentic. Somethin' to keep me in touch. It's easy to get outa' touch out there. Don't worry I'll get em' back to ya'.

[AUSTIN *rushes up to* LEE, *grabs him by shoulders*]

AUSTIN: You can't just drop the whole thing, Lee!

[LEE *turns, pushes* AUSTIN *in the chest knocking him backwards into the alcove,* MOM *watches numbly,* LEE *returns to collecting the plates, silverware, etc.*]

MOM: You boys shouldn't fight in the house. Go outside and fight.

LEE: I'm not fightin'. I'm leavin'.

MOM: There's been enough damage done already.

LEE: [*his back to* AUSTIN *and* MOM, *stacking dishes on counter*] I'm clearin' outa' here once and for all. All this town does is drive a man insane. Look what it's done to Austin there. I'm not lettin' that happen to me. Sell myself down the river. No sir. I'd rather be a hundred miles from nowhere than let that happen to me.

[*during this* AUSTIN *has picked up the ripped-out phone from the floor and wrapped the cord tightly around both his hands, he lunges at* LEE *whose back is still to him, wraps the cord around* LEE'S *neck, plants a foot in* LEE'S *back and pulls back on the cord, tightening it,* LEE *chokes desperately, can't speak and can't reach* AUSTIN *with his arms,* AUSTIN *keeps applying pressure on* LEE'S *back with his foot, bending him into the sink,* MOM *watches*]

AUSTIN: [*tightening cord*] You're not goin' anywhere! You're not takin' anything with you. You're not takin' my car! You're not takin' the dishes! You're not takin' anything! You're stayin' right here!

MOM: You'll have to stop fighting in the house. There's plenty of room outside to fight. You've got the whole outdoors to fight in.

[LEE *tries to tear himself away, he crashes across the stage like an enraged bull dragging* AUSTIN *with him, he snorts and bellows but* AUSTIN *hangs on and manages to keep clear of* LEE'S *attempts to grab him, they crash into the table, to the floor,* LEE *is face down thrashing wildly and choking,* AUSTIN *pulls cord tighter, stands with one foot planted on* LEE'S *back and the cord stretched taut*]

AUSTIN: [*holding cord*] Gimme back my keys, Lee! Take the keys out! Take 'em out!

[LEE *desperately tries to dig in his pockets, searching for the car keys,* MOM *moves closer*]

MOM: [*calmly to* AUSTIN] You're not killing him are you?

AUSTIN: I don't know. I don't know if I'm killing him. I'm stopping him. That's all. I'm just stopping him.

[LEE *thrashes but* AUSTIN *is relentless*]

MOM: You oughta' let him breathe a little bit.

AUSTIN: Throw the keys out, Lee!

[LEE *finally gets keys out and throws them on the floor but out of* AUSTIN'S *reach,* AUSTIN *keeps pressure on cord, pulling* LEE'S *neck back,* LEE *gets one hand to the cord but can't relieve the pressure*]

Reach me those keys would ya', Mom.

MOM: [*not moving*] Why are you doing this to him?

AUSTIN: Reach me the keys!

MOM: Not until you stop choking him.

AUSTIN: I can't stop choking him! He'll kill me if I stop choking him!

MOM: He won't kill you. He's your brother.

AUSTIN: Just get me the keys would ya'!

[*pause.* MOM *picks keys up off floor, hands them to* AUSTIN]

AUSTIN: [*to* MOM] Thanks.

MOM: Will you let him go now?

AUSTIN: I don't know. He's not gonna' let me get outa' here.

MOM: Well you can't kill him.

AUSTIN: I can kill him! I can easily kill him. Right now. Right here. All I gotta' do is just tighten up. See? [*he tightens cord,* LEE *thrashes wildly,* AUSTIN *releases pressure a little, maintaining control*] Ya' see that?

MOM: That's a savage thing to do.

AUSTIN: Yeah well don't tell me I can't kill him because I can. I can just twist. I can just keep twisting. [AUSTIN *twists the cord tighter,* LEE *weakens, his breathing changes to a short rasp*]

MOM: Austin!

[AUSTIN *relieves pressure,* LEE *breathes easier but* AUSTIN *keeps him under control*]

AUSTIN: [*eyes on* LEE, *holding cord*] I'm goin' to the desert. There's nothing stopping me. I'm going by myself to the desert.

[MOM *moving toward her luggage*]

MOM: Well, I'm going to go check into a motel. I can't stand this anymore.

AUSTIN: Don't go yet!

[MOM *pauses*]

MOM: I can't stay here. This is worse than being homeless.

AUSTIN: I'll get everything fixed up for you, Mom. I promise. Just stay for a while.

MOM: [*picking up luggage*] You're going to the desert.

AUSTIN: Just wait!

[LEE *thrashes,* AUSTIN *subdues him,* MOM *watches holding luggage, pause*]

MOM: It was the worst feeling being up there. In Alaska. Staring out a window. I never felt so desperate before. That's why when I saw that article on Picasso I thought—

AUSTIN: Stay here, Mom. This is where you live.

[*she looks around the stage*]

MOM: I don't recognize it at all.

[*she exits with luggage,* AUSTIN *makes a move toward her but* LEE *starts to struggle and* AUSTIN *subdues him again with cord, pause*]

AUSTIN: [*holding cord*] Lee? I'll make ya' a deal. You let me get outa' here. Just let me get to my car. All right, Lee? Gimme a little headstart and I'll turn you loose. Just gimme a little headstart. All right?

[LEE *makes no response,* AUSTIN *slowly releases tension cord, still nothing from* LEE]

AUSTIN: Lee?

[LEE *is motionless,* AUSTIN *very slowly begins to stand, still keeping a tenuous hold on the cord and his eyes riveted to* LEE *for any sign of movement,* AUSTIN *slowly drops the cord and stands, he stares down at* LEE *who appears to be dead*]

AUSTIN: [*whispers*] Lee?

[pause, AUSTIN *considers, looks toward exit, back to* LEE, *then makes a small movement as if to leave. Instantly* LEE *is on his feet and moves toward exit, blocking* AUSTIN'S *escape. They square off to each other, keeping a distance between them. Pause, a single coyote heard in distance, lights fade softly into moonlight, the figures of the brothers now appear to be caught in a vast desert-like landscape, they are very still but watchful for the next move, lights go slowly to black as the after-image of the brothers pulses in the dark, coyote fades]*

—1980

What are your reactions to and questions about this work? The following questions may help provoke some ideas.

Probing the Work

1. What is the source of the *conflict* (see page 74) between the two brothers? In what way is each of the brothers experiencing a conflict within himself? Are these conflicts resolved? If so, how? (What is the *climax* of the play?)
2. What is the *setting* (see page 74) of this play? What are the symbolic elements of the setting (look closely at the stage directions) and of the title?
3. What is the function of the mother in this play? Of the father? Which one has a greater impact on the brothers' relationship, and on the movement of the play?

Identifying Issues

4. To what extent does this play reinforce the idea that even adults, when they find themselves with their families, adopt the kinds of roles or personality traits that are expected of them? In your experience, how healthy or destructive are such roles and expectations?
5. Read the following critical assessments of the play. To what degree does Brookhouse improve or upset your understanding of the play? Summarize DeRose's main ideas: what new insights have you gained from reading his piece?

Commentary

CHRISTOPHER BROOKHOUSE

Story Itself (excerpt)

The title of Shepard's play refers to the question of truth, and Austin as well tries to convince Saul that he, Austin, is more qualified to write the truth. "I swallow the smog. I watch the news in color. I shop in the Safeway. I'm the one who's in touch." It turns out, however, that Austin retreats from his urban vision and returns to his imagination and his fantasies about living on the desert. Like so much of the play, Austin's change seems one more reversal, one more changing places with Lee. Lee wants to change places with Austin. Lee wants to settle down on a ranch. Their reversal of positions suggests their oneness (as it does in the situations of Wesley and Weston). Even Saul "thinks we're the same person," [Austin] says; later their mother underscores this when she suggests that despite going their separate ways, Lee and Austin, their father too, will "probably wind up on the same desert sooner or later."

Both Lee and Austin want to tell stories, but they can't do it without each other, which again suggests their oneness. Their vision of reality is split; there is no center of meaning, no outward reality, no focus of truth and reality that sustains their stories. There are only other stories, old stories. Austin finally turns against his story. He could write it, but he won't. He chooses the desert. Lee has less choice. He can't put his own story down on paper without help. The one successful storyteller, in an extended sense, is Picasso. The mother's confusion over Picasso's appearance at the local museum comes about because she fails to understand the artist and his art are one—where the art goes there also goes the artist. For Lee and Austin their failure at storytelling becomes their lives as well. The failed artist and the failed, or absent art, are also one. In this context, *True West* may be a cautionary and reflexive work, one in which its author is staring inward. This play, which audiences seem to find more accessible than *Curse* or *Buried Child,* is, perhaps, less complex than those plays. Does the play signal a point when its author falls back upon a refinement of the skills and material he has learned and has presented in earlier works? Does the failure of Austin and Lee hint at a self-awareness on Shepard's part, a concern for his own storytelling? Is he too aware of his 'old' stories?

—1988

DAVID J. DEROSE

Sam Shepard (excerpt)[1]

True West

The third of Shepard's family plays, *True West* (1980), offers none of *Buried Child*'s unveiling of the past nor *Curse of the Starving Class*'s disruptive fragmentation of reality. Instead, the play represents a conscious effort on Shepard's part to maintain a strict adherence to psychological and scenographic realism. In an interview given before the London premiere of the play, Shepard explained in musical terms his efforts to stay within the boundaries of

[1]Page numbers refer to the play as reprinted on pp. 502–549 of this text [Ed.].

conventional dramatic realism: "Musicians have this terminology—playing in and out. Playing out roughly means to improvise, whereas playing in means developing inside a structure. For me, now, it's much more interesting, though more difficult, playing in." Since his move to San Francisco, Shepard had played "out" with improvisationally inspired musical works such as *Inacoma* and *Angel City*. Even his first two family plays, *Buried Child* and *Curse of the Starving Class,* reflected Shepard's spontaneous flair for the irrational. But *True West* is grounded in and propelled by the psychological opposition of two conflicting brothers. In terms of character, playing "in" meant that Shepard was "determined in this play, no matter what, to ride the characters out" (McFerran, 25)—standard operating procedure for almost any playwright but Shepard. This intention does not mean that *True West* abandons the irrational; the theme and physical staging, while well within the realm of psychological and physical realism, still exhibit elements of the unfixing of reality and of character that had become Shepard's trademarks.

The play opens with Austin, a successful young scriptwriter, attempting to finish work on an artistic "project" he hopes to sell to Saul Kimmer, a Hollywood producer. He is staying at his mother's Southern California home while she is vacationing in Alaska. When Austin's older brother, Lee, unexpectedly appears, his threatening, untamed presence and persistently annoying attempts at conversation prevent Austin from progressing with his work. Lee is an outlaw who prowls the desert, sleeping in abandoned cars and making a living by stealing and gambling. Austin, by contrast, writes for and is a product of the Hollywood system and of the suburban society of shopping malls and superhighways. From the opening moments of the play, it is clear that these Cain and Abel siblings embody the struggle between the clashing life-styles of the "old" West and the "new" West. One lives off the land; the other has helped to pave over it. While each is openly disdainful of the other's life-style, they are secretly envious of each other. When Saul drops Austin's project in favor of an old-style western script proposed by Lee, the two brothers suddenly, almost eagerly, trade personas. Austin gets drunk, abandoning his own work and yearning for the desert, while Lee sheds his criminal self in an attempt to write a screenplay.

When Austin informs Lee that Saul "thinks we're the same person," he is not only suggesting a motivation for Saul's unexpected shift in allegiance—he is also hinting at the central dramatic conceit behind Shepard's creation of these two warring brothers. According to Shepard, Lee and Austin "are each other. . . . I've just divided one person in two" (McFerran, 25). Their opposing characters represent a split that Shepard feels within himself and within the human psyche in general, an "unresolvable clash" between our "social selves" and those darker "galaxies inside of us" that we try not to explore (Lippman, 6). In *Curse of the Starving Class,* those darker, uncivilized traits were manifest in the uncontrollable savagery passed by blood from parent to child. In *Buried Child,* it was the infant corpse that embodied the inherited brutality of the family's males. In *True West,* it is a primal capacity for violence and mayhem that

Lee seems to bring into the house and that is unleashed in Austin as he feels what it is like to be his brother.

The reversal of characters in *True West* is both a reflection of Shepard's personal demons and a continuation of his examination of the individual as "a composite of different mysteries" ("Inner Library," 55). From his early days writing transformational plays in the style of the Open Theatre, through the objectification of self in *Action,* to his exploration of character as improvisational jazz collage in *Angel City,* Shepard has looked upon character as malleable. The self, according to Shepard, is unstable; it is constantly recreated. "You act yourself out," Shooter reminds us in *Action.*

The first act of *True West* juxtaposes the world of the civilized self to a more primal plane of experience. "I just don't want to get all worked up about it," Austin tells Lee at one point [520]. The phrase serves to define his civilized, self-disciplined life-style; in the face of Lee's gradual domination of events. Austin attempts to maintain self-control, to play "inside" the rules. He has painstakingly developed a relationship with Saul, and he carefully nurtures it, expecting fair reward for his hard work. Lee, on the other hand, cannot summon enough patience to play inside the game. He is, as Saul calls him, a "raw talent." Whereas Austin lives by his refined skills, Lee survives on his instincts. He has the creative ability to concoct a winning western, but he lacks the self-imposed discipline to put it on paper. Lee short-circuits the system, lives outside the law, stealing, cheating, gambling, and using force to achieve immediate, if not lasting, gratification. If Lee is the "raw talent," then Austin is the discipline and technique needed to harness that talent. Together, they represent the opposing sides of Shepard's psyche as artist.

When Lee applies his hardball tactics to Austin's world, using his threatening powers of persuasion to make Saul look at his script, Austin claims, "You don't understand the way things work down here" [511]. As it turns out, Lee does know how things work; he understands how to tap into Saul's less civilized emotions—fear and greed—in order to cut through the businesslike system to which Austin is enslaved. By the end of the first act, the separate worlds of the brothers, so carefully isolated at the play's beginning, have begun to merge. The final image of the first act, Lee's description of two cowboys disappearing into the desert at night, mirrors the brothers' situation: "So they take off after each other straight into an endless black prairie. The sun is just comin' down and they can feel the night on their backs. What they don't know is that each one of 'em is afraid see. Each one separately thinks that he's the only one that's afraid. And they keep ridin' like that straight into the night. Not knowing. And the one who's chasin' doesn't know where the other one is taking him. And the one who's being chased doesn't know where he's going" [522]. Each brother explores unknown territory within himself. Lee's world, as well as Austin's, is subtly unfixed during the adventure. Each pushes the other out of his conventional mode of dealing with life, opening up new ways of viewing reality.

The second act maps the total collapse of the civilized self. Austin discovers that Saul has dropped his project in favor of Lee's outlandish western. Austin's sense of self dissolves and his ordered world is shattered as he witnesses the impossible. Reality, as he knows it, is turned upside down. The tight-lipped, businesslike Saul gambles with Austin's livelihood and loses. Lee wins an improbable game of golf and sells a terrible script that defies everything for which Austin stands as a writer. The tenets upon which Austin has based his personal integrity and behavior prove an illusion. Feeling as though his once-stable life view is no longer valid, he transforms himself (or tries to) into his brother Lee, drinking heavily and combing the neighborhood for household appliances to steal. Lee, meanwhile, apes Austin's behavior of the first act: typing by candlelight and complaining when Austin tries to break his concentration. Each recreates himself based on his image of the other. Although these transformations are, in the realistic framework of the play, too sudden, Austin reminds us that realism is an illusion, as is the concept of stable character: "Those aren't characters. . . . Those are illusions of characters" [532].

Perhaps the most memorable stage image in *True West* is the opening of scene 8, the "typewriter-toasters" scene, in which Shepard offers a tour de force of suprareal staging. At the end of the previous scene, Lee was left pounding out a script on the typewriter as Austin stumbled off into the night, determined to prove himself to his brother by stealing a toaster. Scene 8 opens several hours later:

> Very early morning, between night and day. No crickets, coyotes yapping feverishly in distance before light comes up, a small fire blazes up in the dark from alcove area, sound of LEE smashing typewriter with a golf club, lights coming up, LEE seen smashing typewriter methodically then dropping pages of his script into a burning bowl set on the floor of alcove, flames leap up, AUSTIN has a whole bunch of stolen toasters lined up on the sink counter along with LEE's stolen TV, the toasters are of a wide variety of models, mostly chrome. AUSTIN goes up and down the line of toasters, breathing on them and polishing them with a dish towel, both men are drunk, empty whiskey bottles and beer cans litter the floor of kitchen. . . . LEE keeps periodically taking deliberate ax-chops at the typewriter, using a nine-iron[.] [534–535]

In this scene, the psychologically farfetched transformation of the two brothers is provided with both a material grounding and a sharp surreal edge by the introduction of suprareal staging techniques. Shepard's disruption of ordered reality is physically anchored in the use of several operative toasters popping up burnt toast throughout the scene and a previously functional typewriter rendered into a lump of twisted metal by the persistent swing of Lee's nine iron. The toast is carefully buttered, only to be scattered across the floor, the contents of the kitchen drawers and cabinets are strewn across the stage, and the phone is literally ripped from the wall. This wonderful Walpurgisnacht [wild or extravagant party] of suprarealism is so accurate in its reproduction of material reality that one loses track of where the rational action ends and the surreal takes over. As William Kleb noted in his review of the original Magic Theatre production, "objective and subjective realities are not juxtaposed [as they were in many of Shepard's earlier plays], they are superimposed" (Kleb 121).

Once Shepard draws the audience into the undomesticated midnight landscape of the second act, like the unseen coyotes in the play who lure "innocent pets away from their homes," he sheds the light of day on his creation. In the midday heat of the final scene, "all the debris from the previous scene is now starkly visible in intense yellow light" [541]; Mom's clean, tidy kitchen has been transformed into a "desert junkyard." To accentuate the distance he has taken his audience, Shepard suddenly redirects the flow of the action by introducing a new character whose unintegrated presence, like the thugs at the end of *Curse of the Starving Class,* is completely foreign to the stage environment. The surreal intruder is none other than Mom herself, who has returned from the Alaskan frontier. While her presence might not have seemed unreal at the play's beginning, by the end of the play the stage has been transformed into a wasteland in which Mom, an anemic and emotionless little woman, dressed in white with matching red shoes, shoulder bag, and luggage, is completely out of place. She has cut short her vacation to the Alaskan wilds in order to return to the civility of her home. Upon entering, however, she is confronted by a savage battle between her sons that leaves her feeling "worse than being homeless." Her reaction, however, is completely bland, completely disproportionate to the wreckage in her kitchen and the violent struggle of her two sons. "You boys shouldn't fight in the house," she drones, as Lee and Austin poise on the verge of killing each other.

In the light of day and with his mother's entrance, Lee quickly dismisses the previous night's dreamlike activities, abandoning the script and his aspirations as a scriptwriter. Austin, however, is not as willing to drop his newly adopted persona. When Lee decides to back out of an earlier promise to take Austin to the desert, Austin turns savage. Throwing Lee to the floor and wrapping the phone cord around his neck, he chokes Lee until the older brother falls limp in his arms.

In the final moments of the play, Shepard creates an archetypal image that both encompasses and transcends all that has preceded it. With Lee lying motionless on the floor, Austin is free to take the car and escape into the desert. In the first act, he told Lee, "We're not insane. We're not driven to acts of violence" [520]. But in this final scene, as if to prove the complete adoption of his new primal persona, Austin expresses the remorselessness of his newly uncovered violence. With the phone cord still wrapped around his brother's neck, he tells his mother: "I can kill him! I can easily kill him. Right now. Right here" [547]. At the moment of his escape, however, Austin hesitates. Moral consciousness seems to creep back into his psyche as he stares at the inert body of his brother. In that instant of hesitation, Lee is on his feet, blocking Austin's escape. The lights suddenly change as the two brothers "square off to each other

. . . the figures of the brothers now appear to be caught in a vast desert-like landscape, they are very still but watchful for the next move, lights go slowly to black as the after-image of the brothers pulses in the dark, coyote fades" [549]. This final image is not a resolution, as Shepard himself has pointed out, but a timeless confrontation. The pulsing of the after-image suspends the moment in time and space, transporting it beyond the relatively realistic realm of the play. It is a "postplay" (in the sense of "posthypnotic") suggestion in which the brothers are transformed into archetypal figures, facing off, fighting hopelessly on against the backdrop of eternity. In Austin's moment of hesitation arises the germ of moral consciousness that forever separates him from Lee and places him at irresolvable odds with the amoral "Lee" in himself. As Ross Wetzsteon said of his moving exposure to the final image of Shepard's *La Turista,* it was a moment that "dramatized the themes of the play far more precisely than could any words, an image that communicated the emotional texture of the characters' lives far more vividly than could any speech" (Wetzsteon 1984, 1–2).

BIBLIOGRAPHY

Kleb, William, "Worse Than Being Homeless: *True West* and the Divided Self," in *American Dreams,* ed. Bonnie Maranca (New York: Performing Arts Journal Publications, 1981), p. 121.

"Language, Visualization and the Inner Library," *Drama Review (TDR)* **21** (December 1977):55.

Lippman, Amy, "A Conversation with Sam Shepard," *Harvard Advocate* (March 1983):2–6, 44–46. Reprinted as "Rhythm and Truths: An Interview with Sam Shepard," *American Theatre* (April 1984):9–13, 40–41.

McFerran, Ann, "Poet of Post-War Americana," *Time Out (London)* **4–10** (December 1981):25.

Wetzsteon, Ross, "Introduction," in *Fool For Love and Other Plays* (New York: Bantam Books, 1984).

—1992

WRITING ASSIGNMENT SEQUENCE (CONTINUED FROM PAGE 475)

4. Making Connections

Select one of the following questions and write an informal response in which you connect your own ideas with those conveyed in the works of this cluster, and/or make connections among the works themselves.

A. Which of the works comes closest to illustrating the definition of a family that you wrote in the first part of this assignment sequence? Have you rethought your definition, after reading these works? If so, revise it accordingly.

B. What are the class and cultural differences in family values that are illustrated in the works of this cluster?

C. Among the families described in these works, which are the dysfunctional families, and which are closer to the ideal? Explain the criteria you use to evalute them.

5. Putting It All Together

Write an essay that combines what you think about the topic of *Family Reunion* with what you now understand about the readings.

- Collect your informal writing, notes, and reading-journal entries on this topic and decide what will be the focus of your essay.
- Outline your essay. Select the literary passages and personal details you might use to illustrate and support your main focus.
- Write a draft of your essay in which you bring together what you think about the subject with what you understand about the readings. Try to include in your draft one or more *literary terms.*
- Share what you've written with your classmates and instructor, then revise it according to their recommendations.

Writing Tip: Descriptive Outline

An informal outline can help you plan and organize your essay; a *descriptive outline* can help you analyze your first draft. These outlines can be seen as guides. List the ideas and points you make in each paragraph after you've written a rough draft. Does the order of ideas make sense? Is there a logical progression of ideas? What kind of order are you using (e.g., chronological, most important to least important, etc.). Why are you using this order? Would another be better? Do you have enough evidence to illustrate your points? (See page 35 for more on *descriptive outlines.*)

CrossClusters

In your paper you might want to consider how the following works located elsewhere in this book depict families:

- Alice Munro, "Boys and Girls" (p. 89)
- James Joyce, "Araby" (p. 109)
- Shirley Jackson, "The Lottery" (p. 131)
- Sophocles, *Antigone* (p. 144)
- Lorraine Hansberry, *A Raisin in the Sun* (p. 253)
- Russell Baker, from *Growing Up* (p. 343)

- Frank O'Connor, "My Oedipus Complex" (p. 350)
- Marsha Norman, *'night, Mother* (p. 400)
- Raymond Carver, "My Father's Life" (p. 446)
- James Baldwin, "The Rockpile" (p. 462)
- John Updike, "Wife Wooing" (p. 653)
- Henrik Ibsen, *A Doll's House* (p. 659)
- Mme. de Beaumont, "Beauty and the Beast" (p. 732)
- William Shakespeare, *A Midsummer-Night's Dream* (p. 766)
- Grace Paley, "The Loudest Voice" (p. 971)

SYNTHESIS PAPER FOR SECTION 2: FAMILIES

How do your preliminary ideas about families hold up now that you have read a variety of works on the topic? Adding to, expanding on, and revising the writing that you have already done on the subject of families, write a long paper in which you examine some of the literature in this section, bringing together your early writing with the knowledge you have gained from your class discussions. The paper might combine research and critical analysis with your personal opinions and experiences. You might even bring in references to films, music, books, and/or magazine articles. There are many possibilities for topics relating to the complexities of *growing up, mothers, fathers,* and *family dynamics*.

Here are some questions to consider:

- Is the modern family as we know it in trouble?
- What keeps families together?
- What are the most important familial influences on an individual's well-being?
- How does a family succeed or not succeed in educating its members?
- How are family values passed on among generations?
- What is your revised definition of family?
- What are some secrets that families have?

SECTION 3 (CHAPTERS 17–19)

LOVE

What is *love?* Is there such a thing as true love, or is that just found in storybooks? What are the events, male/female behavior patterns, or aspects of human nature that obstruct the expression or realization of love? In this section you will find readings and writing assignments addressing the many types and degrees of love: from friendly to erotic, marital to adulterous, homosexual to heterosexual, physical to spiritual. You will be asked to write about your own knowledge of and experience with love, to probe the works in order to understand what writers are saying about it, and finally to bring both together in your writing on the topic.

GETTING STARTED: WRITING EXERCISES ON LOVE

1. What is love? Make a list of statements that begin with "Love is . . ." or "Love is *not* . . ."

2. Explain and agree/disagree with any one of the quotations below. Cite specific examples from your experience to illustrate your reaction.
   - "[Love is] friendship set on fire."—Jeremy Taylor
   - "[Love is] the whole history of a woman's life; it is only an episode in a man's."—Anna Louis de Staël
   - "It is impossible to love and be wise."—Francis Bacon
   - "Scratch a lover, and find a foe."—Dorothy Parker

3. Read the following section essay, from *The Natural History of Love,* by Diane Ackerman. Decide which of Ackerman's categories or definitions you agree or disagree with, and add some new ones of your own. Respond to two or three of the questions Ackerman asks in the last paragraph, relating them to your own experience.

SECTION ESSAY

DIANE ACKERMAN

The Natural History of Love (excerpt)

Diane Ackerman has been a college professor and writer of poetry and nonfiction. She has received prestigious grants from the National Endowment for the Arts and the Rockefeller Foundation, among other recognitions. Her best selling book, A Natural History of the Senses, *is being turned into a television series for the Public Broadcasting System. Originally from Illinois, she is now living in New York and writing for* The New Yorker *magazine.*

Introduction: Love's Vocabulary

Love is the great intangible. In our nightmares, we can create beasts out of pure emotion. Hate stalks the streets with dripping fangs, fear flies down narrow alleyways on leather wings, and jealousy spins sticky webs across the sky. In daydreams, we can maneuver with poise, foiling an opponent, scoring high on fields of glory while crowds cheer, cutting fast to the heart of an adventure. But what dream state is love? Frantic and serene, vigilant and calm, wrung-out and fortified, explosive and sedate—love commands a vast army of moods. Hoping for victory, limping from the latest skirmish, lovers enter the arena once again. Sitting still, we are as daring as gladiators.

When I set a glass prism on a windowsill and allow the sun to flood through it, a spectrum of colors dances on the floor. What we call "white" is a rainbow of colored rays packed into a small space. The prism sets them free. Love is the white light of emotion. It includes many feelings which, out of laziness and confusion, we crowd into one simple word. Art is the prism that sets them free, then follows the gyrations of one or a few. When art separates this thick tangle of feelings, love bares its bones. But it cannot be measured or mapped. Everyone admits that love is wonderful and necessary, yet no one can agree on what it is. I once heard a sportscaster say of a basketball player, "He does all the intangibles. Just watch him do his dance." As lofty as the idea of love can be, no image is too profane to help explain it. Years ago, I fell in love with someone who was both a sport and a pastime. At the end, he made fade-away jump shots in my life. But, for a while, love did all the intangibles. It lets us do our finest dance.

Love. What a small word we use for an idea so immense and powerful it has altered the flow of history, calmed monsters, kindled works of art, cheered the forlorn, turned tough guys to mush, consoled the enslaved, driven strong women mad, glorified the humble, fueled national scandals, bankrupted robber barons, and made mincemeat of kings. How can love's spaciousness be conveyed in the narrow confines of one syllable? If we search for the source of the word, we find a history vague and confusing, stretching back to the Sanskrit *lubhyati* ("he desires"). I'm sure the etymology rambles back much farther than that, to a one-syllable word heavy as a heartbeat. Love is an ancient delirium, a desire older than civilization, with taproots stretching deep into dark and mysterious days.

We use the word *love* in such a sloppy way that it can mean almost nothing or absolutely everything. It is the first conjugation students of Latin learn. It is a universally understood motive for crime. "Ah, he was in love," we sigh, "well, that explains it." In fact, in some European and South American countries, even murder is forgivable if it was "a crime of passion." Love, like truth, is the unassailable defense. Whoever first said "love makes the world go round" (it was an anonymous Frenchman) probably was not thinking about celestial mechanics, but the way love seeps into the machinery of life to keep generation after generation in motion. We think of love as a positive force that somehow ennobles the one feeling it. When a friend confesses that he's in love, we congratulate him.

In folk stories, unsuspecting lads and lasses ingest a love potion and quickly lose their hearts. As with all intoxicants, love comes in many guises and strengths. It has a mixed bouquet, and may include some piquant ingredients. One's taste in love will have a lot to do with one's culture, upbringing, generation, religion, era, gender, and so on. Ironically, although we sometimes think of it as the ultimate Oneness, love isn't monotone or uniform. Like a batik created from many emotional colors, it is a fabric whose pattern and brightness may vary. What is my goddaughter to think when she hears her mother say: "I love Ben & Jerry's Cherry Garcia ice cream"; "I really loved my high school boyfriend"; "Don't you just love this sweater?" "I'd love to go to the lake for a week this summer"; "Mommy loves you." Since all we have is one word, we talk about love in increments or unwieldy ratios. "How much do you love me?" a child asks. Because the parent can't answer *I* (verb that means unconditional parental love) *you,* she may fling her arms wide, as if welcoming the sun and sky, stretching her body to its limit, spreading her fingers to encompass all of Creation, and say: "This much!" Or: "Think of the biggest thing you can imagine. Now double it: I love you a hundred times that much!"

When Elizabeth Barrett Browning wrote her famous sonnet "How do I love thee?" she didn't "count the ways" because she had an arithmetical turn of mind, but because English poets have always had to search hard for personal signals of their love. As a society, we are embarrassed by love. We treat it as if it were an obscenity. We reluctantly admit to it. Even saying the word makes us stumble and blush. Why should we be ashamed of an emotion so beautiful and natural? In teaching writing students, I've sometimes given them the assignment of writing a love poem. "Be precise, be individual, and be descriptive. But don't use any clichés," I caution them, "or any curse words." Part of the reason for this assignment is that it helps them understand how inhibited we are about love. Love is the most important thing in our lives, a passion for which we would fight or die, and yet we're reluctant to linger over its name. Without a supple vocabulary, we can't even talk or think about it directly. On the other hand, we have many sharp verbs for the ways in which human beings can hurt one another, dozens of verbs for the subtle gradations of hate. But there are pitifully few synonyms for love. Our vocabulary of love and lovemaking is so paltry that a poet has to choose among clichés, profanities, or euphemisms. Fortunately, this has led to some richly imagined works of art. It has inspired poets to create their own private vocabularies. Mrs. Browning sent her husband a poetic abacus of love, which in a roundabout way expressed the sum of her feelings. Other lovers have tried to calibrate their love in equally ingenious ways. In "The Flea," John Donne watches a flea suck blood from his arm and his beloved's, and rejoices that their blood marries in the flea's stomach.

Yes, lovers are most often reduced to comparatives and quantities. "Do you love me more than her?" we ask. "Will you love me less if I don't do what you say?" We are afraid to face love head-on. We think of it as a sort of traffic accident of the heart. It is an emotion that scares us more than cruelty, more than violence, more than hatred. We allow ourselves to be foiled by the vagueness of the word. After all, love requires the utmost vulnerability. We equip someone with freshly sharpened knives; strip naked; then invite him to stand close. What could be scarier?

If you took a woman from ancient Egypt and put her in an automobile factory in Detroit, she would be understandably disoriented. Everything would be new, especially her ability to stroke the wall and make light flood the room, touch the wall elsewhere and fill the room with summer's warm breezes or winter's blast. She'd be astonished by telephones, computers, fashions, language, and customs. But if she saw a man and woman stealing a kiss in a quiet corner, she would smile. People everywhere and everywhen understand the phenomenon of love, just as they understand the appeal of music, finding it deeply meaningful even if they cannot explain exactly what that meaning is, or why they respond viscerally to one composer and not another. Our Egyptian woman, who prefers the birdlike twittering of a sistrum, and a twentieth-century man, who prefers the clashing jaws of heavy metal, share a passion for music that both would understand. So it is with love. Values, customs, and protocols may vary from ancient days to the present, but not the majesty of love. People are unique in the way they walk, dress, and gesture, yet we're able to look at two people—one wearing a business suit, the other a sarong—and recognize that both of them are clothed. Love also has many fashions, some bizarre and (to our taste) shocking, others more familiar, but all are part of a phantasmagoria we know. In the Serengeti of the heart, time and nation are irrelevant. On that plain, all fires are the same fire.

Remember the feeling of an elevator falling in your chest when you said good-bye to a loved one? Parting is more than sweet sorrow, it pulls you apart when you are glued together. It feels like hunger pains, and we use the same word, *pang*. Perhaps this is why Cupid is depicted with a quiver of arrows, because at times love feels like being pierced in the chest. It is a wholesome violence. Common as childbirth, love seems rare nonetheless, always catches one by surprise, and cannot be taught. Each child rediscovers it, each couple redefines it, each parent reinvents it. People search for love as if it were a city lost beneath the desert dunes, where pleasure is the law, the streets are lined with brocade cushions, and the sun never sets.

If it's so obvious and popular, then what *is* love? I began researching this book because I had many questions, not because I knew at the outset what answers I might find. Like most people, I believed what I had been told: that the idea of love was invented by the Greeks, and romantic love began in the Middle Ages. I know now how misguided such hearsay is. We can find romantic love in the earliest writings of our kind. Much of the vocabulary of love, and the imagery lovers use, has not changed for thousands of years. Why do the same images come to mind when people describe their romantic feelings? Custom, culture, and tastes vary, but not love itself, not the essence of the emotion.

"Animal attraction," we sometimes call it. After a passionate encounter, a woman might describe her bedmate as "a real animal" and mean it as a sexy compliment. If she says it to his face, she might toss in a mock growl for good measure, and that's usually enough to start festivities all over again. In fact, animals have much to teach us about our own romantic habits. There are many parallels. Male animals often give the equivalent of engagement rings, females often check a male's bank balance, and "modesty" or "playing coy" is as much a trump card for female birds or insects or reptiles as for humans. In this book, I sometimes refer to the mating habits of other animals, although not at great length because I've written on that subject in detail in other books. I think it would be a mistake to repeat—out of context and in different language—what I have struggled so hard to say elsewhere. . . .

For the history section of this book, I consider a mideastern culture (Egypt), where we find the earliest writings about love, and then I explore love's changing nature in the ancient and modern western world, so that I can follow a single thread as far as possible.

However, when it comes to the history of love, one must keep in mind that we know more about the love lives of the fairly well-to-do than about the love lives of common people, who had little leisure, and lived in caves or small rooms, sharing their beds with many people; their romantic lives would have been distinctly different from those blessed with spare time and privacy. The most remarkable time for the poor might have been that newlywed period, perhaps only nine months long, when they were alone. Happily, love is a peasant emotion and thrives as well in stables as in palaces.

It's tempting to think of love as a progression, from ignorance toward the refined light of reason, but that would be a mistake. The history of love is not a ladder we climb rung by rung leaving previous rungs below. Human history is not a journey across a landscape, in the course of which we leave one town behind as we approach another. Nomads constantly on the move, we carry everything with us, all we possess. We carry the seeds and nails and remembered hardships of everywhere we have lived, the beliefs and hurts and bones of every ancestor. Our baggage is heavy. We can't bear to part with anything that ever made us human. The way we love in the twentieth century is as much an accumulation of past sentiments as a response to modern life.

When I began researching this book, I scouted libraries for reputable studies of love and discovered how little serious research had been done. For example, the microfiche Human Relations Area File, an anthropological database representing over 300 cultures around the world, includes entries on everything from divorce to nose ornaments. It has no separate main category or code for love. Why has there been so little research into love? Surely it's not just that love seems a subjective field with unprovable assumptions, too emotional for social scientists to take seriously (and receive funding for). After all, there are countless studies on war, hate, crime, prejudice, and so on. Social scientists prefer to study negative behaviors and emotions. Perhaps, they don't feel as comfortable studying love per se. I add that "per se" because they *are* studying love—often they're studying what happens when love is deficient, thwarted, warped, or absent.

Why did love evolve? How does it make sense in evolutionary terms? What is the psychology of love? Are erotic and nonerotic love essentially the same? Who is naturally more loving, a man or a woman? What is mother love? How does love affect our health? Do men and women have different sexual agendas? What is the relationship between lack of love and crime? What is the chemistry of love? Are we monogamous by nature, or were we born to cheat?

How has the idea of love changed through the ages? Do aphrodisiacs really exist? Do animals feel love? What are some of love's customs and extravagances?

We have the great fortune to live on a planet abounding with humans, plants, and animals; and I often marvel at the strange tasks evolution sets them. Of all the errands life seems to be running, of all the mysteries that enchant us, love is my favorite.

—1994

17

TRUE LOVE

WRITING ASSIGNMENT SEQUENCE

1. Thinking About . . . True Love

Freewriting: Write about the differences, if any, between the *myth* of "true love" and the *reality* of love. Does true love exist? Do you know anyone who has experienced it?

2. Enacting the Topic

Find song lyrics that express your feelings, positive or negative, about love. Justify your selection in writing.

3. Responding to the Readings

As you read the works in this cluster, jot down in your response journals questions you have about the works, and comment on passages you find provocative or puzzling. Consider the questions following each reading for journal writing and prepare to discuss your reactions in class.

CLUSTER ESSAY

ANDY ROONEY

The Love That's Easy to Hate

Andrew Rooney began his writing career as a correspondent for The Stars & Stripes *during World War II. After the war he wrote for radio and television. He is best known for his weekly "A Few Minutes with Andy Rooney" on the television show "60 Minutes," and for his semiweekly syndicated newspaper column. His essays have earned him four Emmys, six Writers Guild Awards, the Peabody Award, and many other honors. He has authored 10 books, including* Sweet and Sour *(1992), from which the essay below is taken, and* My War *(1995).*

The good word "love" has been watered down and almost ruined by our repeated use of it in situations where love is not really what we mean.

"I love chocolate ice cream."

Really? In what comparative amount do you love it? Do you love it as much as you love your mother, your children, your husband, your wife?

"Ruth loves a good laugh."

"Ed loves baseball."

"I'd love to know who does your hair."

What we mean most of the time we use the word "love" is "like." We LIKE chocolate ice cream. Love is an emotion that should not be wasted on ice cream. It should be saved for more important occasions.

The standard wedding ceremony uses love in another way that has seemed wrong to me since the first church wedding I ever went to ended in divorce two years later.

"Do you, Jonathan, and do you, Ellen, promise to love, honor and obey until death do you part?"

"I do."

"I do."

Do you really, children? Do you know what you're promising? It's possible that you can promise to honor and even possible you can promise to obey, but love is not something you can promise. You can't discipline yourself to feel it. It is not an emotion that can be called forth on command or dismissed at will. You feel it or you don't and no amount of willpower can produce it if it doesn't come unbidden.

No one who ever married could honestly promise to love his or her husband or wife for the rest of life. It is a ridiculous promise for a clergyman to ask a couple to make under threat of not performing the marriage if they refuse.

To "make love" seems like a bad use of the word love, too. It's another example of diminishing the importance of a good word by using it as a euphemism for an act which has no socially acceptable word to describe it. "Love" is not usually what two young people who hardly know each other are making at all. They are satisfying a basic urge. They are scratching an itch. What they are doing has nothing whatsoever to do with love.

Love of a country seems more acceptable and probable than love of chocolate ice cream. I have felt love of a country most often when I've been farthest from it. If you saw the Star-Spangled Banner in Berlin in 1945 or over the U.S. Embassy in Moscow and felt that tingle down your spine, it would be hard to deny love to even so inanimate an object as our flag. Love of home, school, hometown are in the same category and might be said to have legitimately elevated themselves beyond the category of "like." This might be an argument, but you'd have to concede that using the word in relation to your country is less objectionable than using it for how you feel about the taste of chocolate ice cream.

For the most part we save love for the things that give us the most satisfaction and comfort. As soon as they don't, love wanes. Bye-bye, Miss American Pie. This accounts for love of country, the love of newlyweds, the enduring love of some lucky married couples and the love of a child for its mother—and to some lesser extent, its father. The kid has been fed and kept warm by this person. Forget the romance, being comfortable with someone is what produced or perpetuates true love.

It's interesting that we use the word "hate" as loosely as we use "love."

"I love chocolate ice cream but I hate whipped cream on it."

Even though we use "hate" casually like that, when you tell someone you hate them, it's irrevocable. You may have said "I love you" a thousand times, but those words roll off like rain hitting a tin roof. If, on the other hand, a woman looks a man in the eyes and says, "I hate you," there are not enough "I love yous" in life to make him forget you said it.

—1992

What are your reactions to and questions about this work? The following questions may help provoke some ideas.

Probing the Work

1. To what extent do you agree that love is "almost ruined by our repeated use of it" (p. 566)? Which of the distinctions that Rooney makes do you most agree with, and with which do you disagree?

Identifying Issues

2. What makes love so easy to hate? Explain the paradoxical relationship that Rooney describes and how that fits in with your own experience. How closely related are love and hate?

WILLIAM SHAKESPEARE

Sonnet 116 ("Let me not to the marriage . . .")

William Shakespeare (1564–1616) was born in Stratford, England, of middle-class parents. He worked as an actor in London while writing the great plays he is most famous for, among them Romeo and Juliet, Richard III, A Midsummer-Night's Dream, Hamlet, Othello, *and* Macbeth. *The poetry of his plays is unrivaled in drama, but he also published many sonnets independent of his plays, perfecting a form all his own (three quatrains and a final couplet).*

Let me not to the marriage of true minds
Admit impediments.° Love is not love
Which alters when it alteration finds,
Or bends with the remover to remove:
Oh, no! it is an ever-fixèd mark,
That looks on tempests and is never shaken;
It is the star to every wandering bark,°
Whose worth's unknown, although his height be taken.
Love's not Time's fool, though rosy lips and cheeks
Within his bending sickle's compass come;
Love alters not with his brief hours and weeks,
But bears° it out even to the edge of doom.°
If this be error and upon me proved,
I never writ, nor no man ever loved.

—1609

What are your reactions to and questions about this work? The following questions may help provoke some ideas.

Probing the Work

1. Did you assume that the *speaker* is a man writing about heterosexual love? Why do you suppose Shakespeare does not include any mention of gender in this sonnet?
2. What is the *tone* (see page 67) of this poem? How does it reflect or complicate the *subject?* Is it *ironic* (see page 79) or sincere? Why the last couplet—does it reflect arrogance or uncertainty?

Identifying Issues

3. *Should* love "alter when it alteration finds"? Explain how closely this sonnet fits your own definition of true love: is a "marriage of true minds" true love?

ELIZABETH BARRETT BROWNING

How do I love thee? Let me count the ways

Elizabeth Barrett (1806–1861) was well educated and published her first book of poetry at age 13. Her poor health and tyrannical father (who forbade his children to marry) forced her into a life of semiseclusion. One such visitor was Robert Browning

2. impediments, hindrances.
7. bark, ship.
12. bears, lasts; **doom,** judgment day.

(see page 840), who fell in love with Barrett through her poems. After a year of courtship they secretly married and eloped to Florence, Italy, where they lived happily until her death.

How do I love thee? Let me count the ways.
I love thee to the depth and breadth and height
My soul can reach, when feeling out of sight
For the ends of Being and ideal Grace.
I love thee to the level of everyday's
Most quiet need, by sun and candle-light.
I love thee freely, as men strive for Right;
I love thee purely, as they turn from Praise.
I love thee with the passion put to use
In my old griefs, and with my childhood's faith.
I love thee with a love I seemed to lose
With my lost saints—I love thee with the breath,
Smiles, tears, of all my life!—and, if God choose,
I shall but love thee better after death.

—1850

What are your reactions to and questions about this work? The following questions may help provoke some ideas.

Probing the Work

1. How many different ways of loving does the speaker express? Which seems most concrete? Which seems most abstract? What effect does the mix of concrete and abstract language have on you?

Identifying Issues

2. How effectively does this poem express true love? Explain. Can you add to this count with one of your own? ("I love thee with/to . . .")

BERNARD MALAMUD

The Magic Barrel

Brooklyn-born Bernard Malamud (1914–1986) began his career fairly late in life, publishing his first novel, The Natural, *at age 38. After publishing several well-received short stories, such as "The Magic Barrel," below, and his second novel,* The Assistant *(1957), he became an important member of the group of Jewish novelists who flourished in the 1950s and beyond; in particular, Malamud focused on the speech and manners of working-class, recently immigrated Jews.*

Not long ago there lived in uptown New York, in a small, almost meager room, though crowded with books, Leo Finkle, a rabbinical student at the Yeshiva University.[1] Finkle, after six years of study, was to be ordained in June and had been advised by an acquaintance that he might find it easier to win himself a congregation if he were married. Since he had no present prospects of marriage, after two tormented days of turning it over in his mind, he called in Pinye Salzman, a marriage broker whose two-line advertisement he had read in the *Forward*.[2]

The matchmaker appeared one night out of the dark fourth-floor hallway of the graystone rooming house where Finkle lived, grasping a black, strapped portfolio that had been worn thin with use. Salzman, who had been long in the business, was of slight but dignified build, wearing an old hat, and an overcoat too short and tight for him. He smelled frankly of fish, which he loved to eat, and although he was missing a few teeth, his presence was not displeasing, because of an amiable manner curiously contrasted with mournful eyes. His voice, his lips, his wisp of beard, his bony fingers were animated, but give him a moment of repose and his mild blue eyes revealed a depth of sadness, a characteristic that put Leo a little at ease although the situation, for him, was inherently tense.

He at once informed Salzman why he had asked him to come, explaining that but for his parents, who had married comparatively late in life, he was alone in the world. He had for six years devoted himself almost entirely to his studies, as a result of which, understandably, he had found himself without time for social life and the company of young women. Therefore he thought it the better part of trial and error—of embarrassing fumbling—to call in an experienced person to advise him on these matters. He remarked in passing that the function of the marriage broker was ancient and honorable, highly approved in the Jewish community, because it made practical the necessary without hindering joy. Moreover, his own parents had been brought together by a matchmaker. They had made, if not a financially profitable marriage—since neither had possessed any worldly goods to speak of—at least a successful one in the sense of their everlasting devotion to each other. Salzman listened in embarrassed surprise, sensing a sort of apology. Later, however, he experienced a glow of pride in his work, an emotion that had left him years ago, and he heartily approved of Finkle.

The two went to their business. Leo had led Salzman to the only clear place in the room, a table near a window that overlooked the lamp-lit city. He seated himself at the matchmaker's side but facing him, attempting by an act of will to suppress the unpleasant tickle in his throat. Salzman eagerly unstrapped his portfolio and removed a loose rubber band from a thin packet of much-handled cards. As he flipped through them, a gesture and sound that physically

[1]A university in New York City, "yeshiva" indicates seminary.

[2]The Yiddish language *The Jewish Daily Forward,* published in New York City.

hurt Leo, the student pretended not to see and gazed steadfastly out the window. Although it was still February, winter was on its last legs, signs of which he had for the first time in years begun to notice. He now observed the round white moon, moving high in the sky through a cloud menagerie, and watched with half-open mouth as it penetrated a huge hen, and dropped out of her like an egg laying itself. Salzman, though pretending through eyeglasses he had just slipped on to be engaged in scanning the writing on the cards, stole occasional glances at the young man's distinguished face, noting with pleasure the long, severe scholar's nose, brown eyes heavy with learning, sensitive yet ascetic lips, and a certain almost hollow quality of the dark cheeks. He gazed around at shelves upon shelves of books and let out a soft, contented sigh.

When Leo's eyes fell upon the cards, he counted six spread out in Salzman's hand.

"So few?" he asked in disappointment.

"You wouldn't believe me how much cards I got in my office," Salzman replied. "The drawers are already filled to the top, so I keep them now in a barrel, but is every girl good for a new rabbi?"

Leo blushed at this, regretting all he had revealed of himself in a curriculum vitae he had sent to Salzman. He had thought it best to acquaint him with his strict standards and specifications, but in having done so, felt he had told the marriage broker more than was absolutely necessary.

He hesitantly inquired, "Do you keep photographs of your clients on file?"

"First comes family, amount of dowry, also what kind promises," Salzman replied, unbuttoning his tight coat and settling himself in the chair. "After comes pictures, rabbi."

"Call me Mr. Finkle. I'm not yet a rabbi."

Salzman said he would, but instead called him doctor, which he changed to rabbi when Leo was not listening too attentively.

Salzman adjusted his horn-rimmed spectacles, gently cleared his throat, and read in an eager voice the contents of the top card:

"Sophie P. Twenty-four years. Widow one year. No children. Educated high school and two years college. Father promises eight thousand dollars. Has wonderful wholesale business. Also real estate. On the mother's side comes teachers, also one actor. Well known on Second Avenue."

Leo gazed up in surprise. "Did you say a widow?"

"A widow don't mean spoiled, rabbi. She lived with her husband maybe four months. He was a sick boy she made a mistake to marry him."

"Marrying a widow has never entered my mind."

"This is because you have no experience. A widow, especially if she is young and healthy like this girl, is a wonderful person to marry. She will be thankful to you the rest of her life. Believe me, if I was looking now for a bride, I would marry a widow."

Leo reflected, then shook his head.

Salzman hunched his shoulders in an almost imperceptible gesture of disappointment. He placed the card down on the wooden table and began to read another:

"Lily H. High school teacher. Regular. Not a substitute. Has savings and new Dodge car. Lived in Paris one year. Father is successful dentist thirty-five years. Interested in professional man. Well-Americanized family. Wonderful opportunity.

"I know her personally," said Salzman. "I wish you could see this girl. She is a doll. Also very intelligent. All day you could talk to her about books and theyater and what not. She also knows current events."

"I don't believe you mentioned her age?"

"Her age?" Salzman said, raising his brows. "Her age is thirty-two years."

Leo said after a while, "I'm afraid that seems a little too old."

Salzman let out a laugh. "So how old are you, rabbi?"

"Twenty-seven."

"So what is the difference, tell me, between twenty-seven and thirty-two? My own wife is seven years older than me. So what did I suffer?—Nothing. If Rothschild's[3] a daughter wants to marry you, would you say on account her age, no?"

"Yes," Leo said dryly.

Salzman shook off the no in the yes. "Five years don't mean a thing. I give you my word that when you will live with her for one week you will forget her age. What does it mean five years—that she lived more and knows more than somebody who is younger? On this girl, God bless her, years are not wasted. Each one that it comes makes better the bargain."

"What subject does she teach in high school?"

"Languages. If you heard the way she speaks French, you will think it is music. I am in the business twenty-five years, and I recommend her with my whole heart. Believe me, I know what I'm talking, rabbi."

"What's on the next card?" Leo said abruptly.

Salzman reluctantly turned up the third card:

"Ruth K. Nineteen years. Honor student. Father offers thirteen thousand cash to the right bridegroom. He is a medical doctor. Stomach specialist with marvelous practice. Brother-in-law owns own garment business. Particular people."

Salzman looked as if he had read his trump card.

"Did you say nineteen?" Leo asked with interest.

"On the dot."

"Is she attractive?" He blushed. "Pretty?"

Salzman kissed his fingertips. "A little doll. On this I give you my word. Let me call the father tonight and you will see what means pretty."

[3]An international Jewish banking family especially well-established in France.

But Leo was troubled. "You're sure she's that young?"

"This I am positive. The father will show you the birth certificate."

"Are you positive there isn't something wrong with her?" Leo insisted.

"Who says there is wrong?"

"I don't understand why an American girl her age should go to a marriage broker."

A smile spread over Salzman's face.

"So for the same reason you went, she comes."

Leo flushed. "I am pressed for time."

Salzman, realizing he had been tactless, quickly explained. "The father came, not her. He wants she should have the best, so he looks around himself. When we will locate the right boy he will introduce him and encourage. This makes a better marriage than if a young girl without experience takes for herself. I don't have to tell you this."

"But don't you think this young girl believes in love?" Leo spoke uneasily.

Salzman was about to guffaw but caught himself and said soberly, "Love comes with the right person, not before."

Leo parted dry lips but did not speak. Noticing that Salzman had snatched a glance at the next card, he cleverly asked, "How is her health?"

"Perfect," Salzman said, breathing with difficulty. "Of course, she is a little lame on her right foot from an auto accident that it happened to her when she was twelve years, but nobody notices on account she is so brilliant and also beautiful."

Leo got up heavily and went to the window. He felt curiously bitter and upbraided himself for having called in the marriage broker. Finally, he shook his head.

"Why not?" Salzman persisted, the pitch of his voice rising.

"Because I detest stomach specialists."

"So what do you care what is his business? After you marry her do you need him? Who says he must come every Friday night in your house?"

Ashamed of the way the talk was going, Leo dismissed Salzman, who went home with heavy, melancholy eyes.

Though he had felt only relief at the marriage broker's departure, Leo was in low spirits the next day. He explained it as arising from Salzman's failure to produce a suitable bride for him. He did not care for his type of clientele. But when Leo found himself hesitating whether to seek out another matchmaker, one more polished than Pinye, he wondered if it could be—his protestations to the contrary, and although he honored his father and mother—that he did not, in essence, care for the matchmaking institution? This thought he quickly put out of mind yet found himself still upset. All day he ran around in the woods—missed an important appointment, forgot to give out his laundry, walked out of a Broadway cafeteria without paying and had to run back with the ticket in his hand; had even not recognized his landlady in the street when she passed with a friend and courteously called out, "A good evening to you, Doctor Finkle." By nightfall, however, he had regained sufficient calm to sink his nose into a book and there found peace from his thoughts.

Almost at once there came a knock on the door. Before Leo could say enter, Salzman, commercial cupid, was standing in the room. His face was gray and meager, his expression hungry, and he looked as if he would expire on his feet. Yet the marriage broker managed, by some trick of the muscles, to display a broad smile.

"So good evening. I am invited?"

Leo nodded, disturbed to see him again, yet unwilling to ask the man to leave.

Beaming still, Salzman laid his portfolio on the table. "Rabbi, I got for you tonight good news."

"I've asked you not to call me rabbi. I'm still a student."

"Your worries are finished. I have for you a first-class bride."

"Leave me in peace concerning this subject." Leo pretended lack of interest.

"The world will dance at your wedding."

"Please, Mr. Salzman, no more."

"But first must come back my strength," Salzman said weakly. He fumbled with the portfolio straps and took out of the leather case an oily paper bag, from which he extracted a hard, seeded roll and a small smoked whitefish. With a quick motion of his hand he stripped the fish out of its skin and began ravenously to chew. "All day in a rush," he muttered.

Leo watched him eat.

"A sliced tomato you have maybe?" Salzman hesitantly inquired.

"No."

The marriage broker shut his eyes and ate. When he had finished he carefully cleaned up the crumbs and rolled up the remains of the fish, in the paper bag. His spectacled eyes roamed the room until he discovered, amid some piles of books, a one-burner gas stove. Lifting his hat he humbly asked, "A glass tea you got, rabbi?"

Conscience-stricken, Leo rose and brewed the tea. He served it with a chunk of lemon and two cubes of lump sugar, delighting Salzman.

After he had drunk his tea, Salzman's strength and good spirits were restored.

"So tell me, rabbi," he said amiably, "you considered some more the three clients I mentioned yesterday?"

"There was no need to consider."

"Why not?"

"None of them suits me."

"What then suits you?"

Leo let it pass because he could give only a confused answer.

Without waiting for a reply, Salzman asked, "You remember this girl I talked to you—the high school teacher?"

"Age thirty-two?"

But, surprisingly, Salzman's face lit in a smile. "Age twenty-nine."

Leo shot him a look. "Reduced from thirty-two?"

"A mistake," Salzman avowed. "I talked today with the dentist. He took me to his safety deposit box and showed me the birth certificate. She was twenty-nine years last August. They made her a party in the mountains where she went for her vacation. When her father spoke to me the first time I forgot to write the age and I told you thirty-two, but now I remember this was a different client, a widow."

"The same one you told me about, I thought she was twenty-four?"

"A different. Am I responsible that the world is filled with widows?"

"No, but I'm not interested in them, nor, for that matter, in schoolteachers."

Salzman pulled his clasped hands to his breast. Looking at the ceiling he devoutly exclaimed, "Yiddishe kinder,[4] what can I say to somebody that he is not interested in high school teachers? So what then you are interested?"

Leo flushed but controlled himself.

"In what else will you be interested," Salzman went on, "if you not interested in this fine girl that she speaks four languages and has personally in the bank ten thousand dollars? Also her father guarantees further twelve thousand. Also she has a new car, wonderful clothes, talks on all subjects, and she will give you a first-class home and children. How near do we come in our life to paradise?"

"If she's so wonderful, why wasn't she married ten years ago?"

"Why?" said Salzman with a heavy laugh. "—Why? Because she is *partikiler.* This is why. She wants the *best.*"

Leo was silent, amused at how he had entangled himself. But Salzman had aroused his interest in Lily H., and he began seriously to consider calling on her. When the marriage broker observed how intently Leo's mind was at work on the facts he had supplied, he felt certain they would soon come to an agreement.

Late Saturday afternoon, conscious of Salzman, Leo Finkle walked with Lily Hirschorn along Riverside Drive. He walked briskly and erectly, wearing with distinction the black fedora he had that morning taken with trepidation out of the dusty hat box on his closet shelf, and the heavy black Saturday coat he had thoroughly whisked clean. Leo also owned a walking stick, a present from a distant relative, but quickly put temptation aside and did not use it. Lily, petite and not unpretty, had on something signifying the approach of spring. She was au courant,[5] animatedly, with all sorts of subjects, and he weighed her words and found her surprisingly sound—score another for Salzman, whom he uneasily sensed to be somewhere around, hiding perhaps high

[4]"Yiddish children" (German).

[5]"Up to date" (French).

in a tree along the street, flashing the lady signals with a pocket mirror; or perhaps a cloven-hoofed Pan,[6] piping nuptial ditties as he danced his invisible way before them, strewing wild buds on the walk and purple grapes in their path, symbolizing fruit of a union, though there was of course still none.

Lily startled Leo by remarking, "I was thinking of Mr. Salzman, a curious figure, wouldn't you say?"

Not certain what to answer, he nodded.

She bravely went on, blushing, "I for one am grateful for his introducing us. Aren't you?"

He courteously replied, "I am."

"I mean," she said with a little laugh—and it was all in good taste, or at least gave the effect of being not in bad—"do you mind that we came together so?"

He was not displeased with her honesty, recognizing that she meant to set the relationship aright, and understanding that it took a certain amount of experience in life, and courage, to want to do it quite that way. One had to have some sort of past to make that kind of beginning.

He said that he did not mind. Salzman's function was traditional and honorable—valuable for what it might achieve, which, he pointed out, was frequently nothing.

Lily agreed with a sigh. They walked on for a while and she said after a long silence, again with a nervous laugh, "Would you mind if I asked you something a little bit personal? Frankly, I find the subject fascinating." Although Leo shrugged, she went on half embarrassedly, "How was it that you came to your calling? I mean, was it a sudden passionate inspiration?"

Leo, after a time, slowly replied, "I was always interested in the Law."

"You saw revealed in it the presence of the Highest?"

He nodded and changed the subject. "I understand that you spent a little time in Paris, Miss Hirschorn?"

"Oh, did Mr. Salzman tell you, Rabbi Finkle?" Leo winced but she went on, "It was ages ago and almost forgotten. I remember I had to return for my sister's wedding."

And Lily would not be put off. "When," she asked in a slightly trembly voice, "did you become enamored of God?"

He stared at her. Then it came to him that she was talking not about Leo Finkle but a total stranger, some mystical figure, perhaps even passionate prophet that Salzman had dreamed up for her—no relation to the living or dead. Leo trembled with rage and weakness. The trickster had obviously sold her a bill of goods, just as he had him, who'd expected to become acquainted with a young lady of twenty-nine, only to behold, the moment he had laid eyes upon her strained and anxious face, a woman past thirty-five and aging rapidly. Only his self-control had kept him this long in her presence.

[6]Greek god of flocks and shepherds, part man and part goat.

"I am not," he said gravely, "a talented religious person," and in seeking words to go on, found himself possessed by shame and fear. "I think," he said in a strained manner, "that I came to God not because I loved Him but because I did not."

This confession he spoke harshly because its unexpectedness shook him.

Lily wilted. Leo saw a profusion of loaves of bread go flying like ducks high over his head, not unlike the winged loaves by which he had counted himself to sleep last night. Mercifully, then, it snowed, which he would not put past Salzman's machinations.

He was infuriated with the marriage broker and swore he would throw him out of the room the moment he reappeared. But Salzman did not come that night, and when Leo's anger had subsided, an unaccountable despair grew in its place. At first he thought this was caused by his disappointment in Lily, but before long it became evident that he had involved himself with Salzman without a true knowledge of his own intent. He gradually realized—with an emptiness that seized him with six hands—that he had called in the broker to find him a bride because he was incapable of doing it himself. This terrifying insight he had derived as a result of his meeting and conversation with Lily Hirschorn. Her probing questions had somehow irritated him into revealing—to himself more than her—the true nature of his relationship to God, and from that it had come upon him, with shocking force, that apart from his parents, he had never loved anyone. Or perhaps it went the other way, that he did not love God so well as he might, because he had not loved man. It seemed to Leo that his whole life stood starkly revealed and he saw himself for the first time as he truly was—unloved and loveless. This bitter but somehow not fully unexpected revelation brought him to a point of panic, controlled only by extraordinary effort. He covered his face with his hands and cried.

The week that followed was the worst of his life. He did not eat and lost weight. His beard darkened and grew ragged. He stopped attending seminars and almost never opened a book. He seriously considered leaving the Yeshiva, although he was deeply troubled at the thought of the loss of all his years of study—saw them like pages torn from a book, strewn over the city—and at the devastating effect of this decision upon his parents. But he had lived without knowledge of himself, and never in the Five Books[7] and all the Commentaries—mea culpa[8]—had the truth been revealed to him. He did not know where to turn, and in all this desolating loneliness there was no *to whom,* although he often thought of Lily but not once could bring himself to go downstairs and make the call. He became touchy and irritable, especially with his landlady, who asked him all manner of personal questions; on the other hand, sensing his own disagreeableness, he waylaid her on the stairs and apologized abjectly, until,

[7]The five books of Moses ("pentateuch"), called the "Torah."
[8]"My fault" (Latin).

mortified, she ran from him. Out of this, however, he drew the consolation that he was a Jew and that a Jew suffered. But gradually, as the long and terrible week drew to a close, he regained his composure and some idea of purpose in life: to go on as planned. Although he was imperfect, the ideal was not. As for his quest of a bride, the thought of continuing afflicted him with anxiety and heartburn, yet perhaps with this new knowledge of himself he would be more successful than in the past. Perhaps love would now come to him and a bride to that love. And for this sanctified seeking who needed a Salzman?

The marriage broker, a skeleton with haunted eyes, returned that very night. He looked, withal, the picture of frustrated expectancy—as if he had steadfastly waited the week at Miss Lily Hirschorn's side for a telephone call that never came.

Casually coughing, Salzman came immediately to the point: "So how did you like her?"

Leo's anger rose and he could not refrain from chiding the matchmaker: "Why did you lie to me, Salzman?"

Salzman's pale face went dead white, the world had snowed on him.

"Did you not state that she was twenty-nine?" Leo insisted.

"I give you my word—"

"She was thirty-five, if a day. *At least* thirty-five."

"Of this don't be too sure. Her father told me—"

"Never mind. The worst of it is that you lied to her."

"How did I lie to her, tell me?"

"You told her things about me that weren't true. You made me out to be more, consequently less than I am. She had in mind a totally different person, a sort of semi-mystical Wonder Rabbi."

"All I said, you was a religious man."

"I can imagine."

Salzman sighed. "This is my weakness that I have," he confessed. "My wife says to me I shouldn't be a salesman, but when I have two fine people that they would be wonderful to be married, I am so happy that I talk too much." He smiled wanly. "This is why Salzman is a poor man."

Leo's anger left him. "Well, Salzman, I'm afraid that's all."

The marriage broker fastened hungry eyes on him.

"You don't want any more a bride?"

"I do," said Leo, "but I have decided to seek her in another way. I am no longer interested in an arranged marriage. To be frank, I now admit the necessity of premarital love. That is, I want to be in love with the one I marry."

"Love?" said Salzman, astounded. After a moment he remarked, "For us, our love is our life, not for the ladies. In the ghetto they—"

"I know, I know," said Leo. "I've thought of it often. Love, I have said to myself, should be a product of living and worship rather than its own end. Yet for myself I find it necessary to establish the level of my need and fulfill it."

Salzman shrugged but answered, "Listen, rabbi, if you want love, this I can find for you also. I have such beautiful clients that you will love them the minute your eyes will see them."

Leo smiled unhappily. "I'm afraid you don't understand."

But Salzman hastily unstrapped his portfolio and withdrew a manila packet from it.

"Pictures," he said, quickly laying the envelope on the table.

Leo called after him to take the pictures away, but as if on the wings of the wind, Salzman had disappeared.

March came. Leo had returned to his regular routine. Although he felt not quite himself yet—lacked energy—he was making plans for a more active social life. Of course it would cost something, but he was an expert in cutting corners; and when there were no corners left he would make circles rounder. All the while Salzman's pictures had lain on the table, gathering dust. Occasionally as Leo sat studying, or enjoying a cup of tea, his eyes fell on the manila envelope, but he never opened it.

The days went by and no social life to speak of developed with a member of the opposite sex—it was difficult, given the circumstances of his situation. One morning Leo toiled up the stairs to his room and stared out the window at the city. Although the day was bright his view of it was dark. For some time he watched the people in the street below hurrying along and then turned with a heavy heart to his little room. On the table was the packet. With a sudden relentless gesture he tore it open. For a half hour he stood by the table in a state of excitement, examining the photographs of the ladies Salzman had included. Finally, with a deep sigh he put them down. There were six, of varying degrees of attractiveness, but look at them long enough and they all became Lily Hirschorn: all past their prime, all starved behind bright smiles, not a true personality in the lot. Life, despite their frantic yoohooings, had passed them by; they were pictures in a briefcase that stank of fish. After a while, however, as Leo attempted to return the photographs into the envelope, he found in it another, a snapshot of the type taken by a machine for a quarter. He gazed at it a moment and let out a low cry.

Her face deeply moved him. Why, he could at first not say. It gave him the impression of youth—spring flowers, yet age—a sense of having been used to the bone, wasted; this came from the eyes, which were hauntingly familiar, yet absolutely strange. He had a vivid impression that he had met her before, but try as he might he could not place her although he could almost recall her name, as if he had read it in her own handwriting. No, this couldn't be; he would have remembered her. It was not, he affirmed, that she had an extraordinary beauty—no, though her face was attractive enough; it was that *something* about her moved him. Feature for feature, even some of the ladies of the photographs could do better; but she leaped forth to his heart—had *lived,* or wanted to—more than just wanted, perhaps regretted how she had lived—had somehow deeply suffered: it could be seen in the depths of those reluctant eyes, and from the way the light enclosed and shone from her, and within her, opening realms of possibility: this was her own. Her he desired. His head ached and eyes narrowed with the intensity of his gazing, then as if an obscure fog had blown up in the mind, he experienced fear of her and was aware that he had received an impression, somehow, of evil. He shuddered, saying softly, it is thus with us all. Leo brewed some tea in a small pot and sat sipping it without sugar, to calm himself. But before he had finished drinking, again with excitement he examined the face and found it good: good for Leo Finkle. Only such a one could understand him and help him seek whatever he was seeking. She might, perhaps, love him. How she had happened to be among the discards in Salzman's barrel he could never guess, but he knew he must urgently go find her.

Leo rushed downstairs, grabbed up the Bronx telephone book, and searched for Salzman's home address. He was not listed, nor was his office. Neither was he in the Manhattan book. But Leo remembered having written down the address on a slip of paper after he had read Salzman's advertisement in the "personals" column of the *Forward*. He ran up to his room and tore through his papers, without luck. It was exasperating. Just when he needed the matchmaker he was nowhere to be found. Fortunately Leo remembered to look in his wallet. There on a card he found his name written and a Bronx address. No phone number was listed, the reason—Leo now recalled—he had originally communicated with Salzman by letter. He got on his coat, put a hat on over his skullcap and hurried to the subway station. All the way to the far end of the Bronx he sat on the edge of his seat. He was more than once tempted to take out the picture and see if the girl's face was as he remembered, but he refrained, allowing the snapshot to remain in his inside coat pocket, content to have her so close. When the train pulled into the station he was waiting at the door and bolted out. He quickly located the street Salzman had advertised.

The building he sought was less than a block from the subway, but it was not an office building, nor even a loft, nor a store in which one could rent office space. It was a very old tenement house. Leo found Salzman's name in pencil on a soiled tag under the bell and climbed three dark flights to his apartment. When he knocked, the door was opened by a thin, asthmatic, gray-haired woman, in felt slippers.

"Yes?" she said, expecting nothing. She listened without listening. He could have sworn he had seen her, too, before but knew it was an illusion.

"Salzman—does he live here? Pinye Salzman?" he said, "the matchmaker?"

She stared at him a long minute. "Of course."

He felt embarrassed. "Is he in?"

"No." Her mouth, though left open, offered nothing more.

"The matter is urgent. Can you tell me where his office is?"

"In the air." She pointed upward.

"You mean he has no office?" Leo asked.

"In his socks."

He peered into the apartment. It was sunless and dingy, one large room divided by a half-open curtain, beyond which he could see a sagging metal bed. The near side of the room was crowded with rickety chairs, old bureaus, a three-legged table, racks of cooking utensils, and all the apparatus of a kitchen. But there was no sign of Salzman or his magic barrel, probably also a figment of the imagination. An odor of frying fish made Leo weak to the knees.

"Where is he?" he insisted. "I've got to see your husband."

At length she answered, "So who knows where he is? Every time he thinks a new thought he runs to a different place. Go home, he will find you."

"Tell him Leo Finkle."

She gave no sign she had heard.

He walked downstairs, depressed.

But Salzman, breathless, stood waiting at his door.

Leo was astounded and overjoyed. "How did you get here before me?"

"I rushed."

"Come inside."

They entered. Leo fixed tea, and a sardine sandwich for Salzman. As they were drinking he reached behind him for the packet of pictures and handed them to the marriage broker.

Salzman put down his glass and said expectantly, "You found somebody you like?"

"Not among these."

The marriage broker turned away.

"Here is the one I want." Leo held forth the snapshot.

Salzman slipped on his glasses and took the picture into his trembling hand. He turned ghastly and let out a groan.

"What's the matter?" cried Leo.

"Excuse me. Was an accident this picture. She isn't for you."

Salzman frantically shoved the manila packet into his portfolio. He thrust the snapshot into his pocket and fled down the stairs.

Leo, after momentary paralysis, gave chase and cornered the marriage broker in the vestibule. The landlady made hysterical outcries but neither of them listened.

"Give me back the picture, Salzman."

"No." The pain in his eyes was terrible.

"Tell me who she is then."

"This I can't tell you. Excuse me."

He made to depart, but Leo, forgetting himself, seized the matchmaker by his tight coat and shook him frenziedly.

"Please," sighed Salzman. *"Please."*

Leo ashamedly let him go. "Tell me who she is," he begged. "It's very important for me to know."

"She is not for you. She is a wild one—wild, without shame. This is not a bride for a rabbi."

"What do you mean wild?"

"Like an animal. Like a dog. For her to be poor was a sin. This is why to me she is dead now."

"In God's name, what do you mean?"

"Her I can't introduce to you," Salzman cried.

"Why are you so excited?"

"Why, he asks," Salzman said, bursting into tears. "This is my baby, my Stella, she should burn in hell."

Leo hurried up to bed and hid under the covers. Under the covers he thought his life through. Although he soon fell asleep he could not sleep her out of his mind. He woke, beating his breast. Though he prayed to be rid of her, his prayers went unanswered. Through days of torment he endlessly struggled not to love her; fearing success, he escaped it. He then concluded to convert her to goodness, himself to God. The idea alternately nauseated and exalted him.

He perhaps did not know that he had come to a final decision until he encountered Salzman in a Broadway cafeteria. He was sitting alone at a rear table, sucking the bony remains of a fish. The marriage broker appeared haggard, and transparent to the point of vanishing.

Salzman looked up at first without recognizing him. Leo had grown a pointed beard and his eyes were weighted with wisdom.

"Salzman," he said, "love has at last come to my heart."

"Who can love from a picture?" mocked the marriage broker.

"It is not impossible."

"If you can love her, then you can love anybody. Let me show you some new clients that they just sent me their photographs. One is a little doll."

"Just her I want," Leo murmured.

"Don't be a fool, doctor. Don't bother with her."

"Put me in touch with her, Salzman," Leo said humbly. "Perhaps I can be of service."

Salzman had stopped eating and Leo understood with emotion that it was now arranged.

Leaving the cafeteria, he was, however, afflicted by a tormenting suspicion that Salzman had planned it all to happen this way.

Leo was informed by letter that she would meet him on a certain corner, and she was there one spring night, waiting under a street lamp. He appeared, carrying a small bouquet of violets and rosebuds. Stella stood by the lamppost, smoking. She wore white with red shoes, which fitted his expectations, although in a troubled moment he had imagined the dress red, and only the shoes white. She waited uneasily and shyly. From afar he saw that her eyes—clearly her father's—were filled with desperate innocence. He pictured, in her, his own redemption. Violins and lit candles revolved in the sky. Leo ran forward with flowers outthrust.

Around the corner, Salzman, leaning against a wall, chanted prayers for the dead.

—1954

What are your reactions to and questions about this work? The following questions may help provoke some ideas.

Probing the Work

1. Explain the symbolic and/or allegorical elements (see p. 78) of this story. How does the symbolism affect your understanding of Leo's predicament?
2. How do you interpret the ending of this story? How much of a part did Salzman play? How unhappy is he with the "match"? Did he, as Finkle suspects, "[plan] it all to happen this way" (582)?

Identifying Issues

3. What are your views on matchmaking? On arranged marriages? To what extent might they be successful? Cite real-life examples of one or the other to support your opinion.

JUDITH VIORST

True Love

Judith Viorst (b. 1936) is a writer of children's books and contributing editor of Redbook. *She is also an accomplished poet; her collections include* The Village Square *(1965),* It's Hard to Be Hip over Thirty and Other Tragedies of Married Life *(1968),* People and Other Aggravations *(1971), and* How Did I Get to Be Forty and Other Atrocities *(1976). While her poems are very accessible, Viorst says she "slaves over them. . . . I sit and think about a poem all day and then throw it in the waste basket at night."*

It is true love because
I put on eyeliner and a concerto and make pungent observations about the great issues of the day
Even when there's no one here but him,
And because
I do not resent watching the Green Bay Packers
Even though I am philosophically opposed to football,
And because
When he is late for dinner and I know he must be either having an affair or

lying dead in the middle of the street,
I always hope he's dead.

It's true love because
If he said quit drinking martinis but I kept drinking them and the next morning I couldn't get out of bed,
He wouldn't tell me he told me,
And because
He is willing to wear unironed undershorts
Out of respect for the fact that I am philosophically opposed to ironing,
And because
If his mother was drowning and I was drowning and he had to choose one of us to save,
He says he'd save me.

It's true love because
When he went to San Francisco on business while I had to stay home with the painters and the exterminator and the baby who was getting the chicken pox,
He understood why I hated him,
And because
When I said that playing the stock market was juvenile and irresponsible and then the stock I wouldn't let him buy went up twenty-six points,
I understood why he hated me,
And because
Despite cigarette cough, tooth decay, acid indigestion, dandruff, and other features of married life that tend to dampen the fires of passion,
We still feel something
We can call
True love.

—*1968*

What are your reactions to and questions about this work? The following questions may help provoke some ideas.

Probing the Work

1. How does Viorst use *irony* (p. 79), *understatement*, and *hyperbole* (p. 67) to convey her ideas about true love?

Identifying Issues

2. We really get inside everyday issues of living in this poem. To what extent do you think true love can survive the ordinariness of life experiences?

LUISA VALENZUELA

I'm Your Horse in the Night

(translated by Deborah Bonner)

Luisa Valenzuela (b. 1938) lives in New York City, where she is a fellow for the New York Institute for the Humanities. She has worked as a journalist and newspaper editor in her native Argentina. Valenzuela has published a number of stories and novels that, like the one below, blur the line between dream and reality, and project a strong awareness of political injustice. Her publications include Los heréticos *(1967),* Aquí pasan cosas raras *(1975), and* Cambio de armas *(1982).*

The doorbell rang: three short rings and one long one. That was the signal, and I got up, annoyed and a little frightened; it could be them, and then again, maybe not; at these ungodly hours of the night it could be a trap. I opened the door expecting anything except him, face to face, at last.

He came in quickly and locked the door behind him before embracing me. So much in character, so cautious, first and foremost checking his—our—rear guard. Then he took me in his arms without saying a word, not even holding me too tight but letting all the emotions of our new encounter overflow, telling me so much by merely holding me in his arms and kissing me slowly. I think he never had much faith in words, and there he was, as silent as ever, sending me messages in the form of caresses.

We finally stepped back to look at one another from head to foot, not eye to eye, out of focus. And I was able to say Hello showing scarcely any surprise despite all those months when I had no idea where he could have been, and I was able to say

I thought you were fighting up north
I thought you'd been caught
I thought you were in hiding
I thought you'd been tortured and killed
I thought you were theorizing about the revolution in another country

Just one of many ways to tell him I'd been thinking of him, I hadn't stopped thinking of him or felt as if I'd been betrayed. And there he was, always so goddamn cautious, so much the master of his actions.

"Quiet, Chiquita. You're much better off not knowing what I've been up to."

Then he pulled out his treasures, potential clues that at the time eluded me: a bottle of cachaça and a Gal Costa record. What had he been up to in Brazil? What was he planning to do next? What had brought him back, risking his life, knowing they were after him? Then I stopped asking myself questions (quiet, Chiquita, he'd say). Come here, Chiquita, he was saying, and I chose to let myself sink into the joy of having him back again, trying not to worry. What would happen to us tomorrow, and the days that followed?

Cachaça's a good drink. It goes down and up and down all the right tracks, and then stops to warm up the corners that need it most. Gal Costa's voice is hot, she envelops us in its sound and half-dancing, half-floating, we reach the bed. We lie down and keep on staring deep into each other's eyes, continue caressing each other without allowing ourselves to give into the pure senses just yet. We continue recognizing, rediscovering each other.

Beto, I say, looking at him. I know that isn't his real name, but it's the only one I can call him out loud. He replies:

"We'll make it someday, Chiquita. But let's not talk now."

It's better that way. Better if he doesn't start talking about how we'll make it someday and ruin the wonder of what we're about to attain right now, the two of us, all alone.

"A noite eu so teu cavalo," Gal Costa suddenly sings from the record player.

"I'm your horse in the night," I translate slowly. And so as to bind him in a spell and stop him from thinking about other things:

"It's a saint's song, like in the *macumba*. Someone who's in a trance says she's the horse of the spirit who's riding her, she's his mount."

"Chiquita, you're always getting carried away with esoteric meanings and witchcraft. You know perfectly well that she isn't talking about spirits. If you're my horse in the night it's because I ride you, like this, see? . . . Like this . . . That's all."

It was so long, so deep and so insistent, so charged with affection that we ended up exhausted. I feel asleep with him still on top of me.

I'm your horse in the night.

The goddamn phone pulled me out in waves from a deep well. Making an enormous effort to wake up, I walked over to the receiver, thinking it could be Beto, sure who was no longer by my side, sure, following his inveterate habit of running away while I'm asleep without a word about where he's gone. To protect me, he says.

From the other end of the line, a voice I thought belonged to Andrés—the one we call Andrés—began to tell me:

"They found Beto dead, floating down the river near the other bank. It looks as if they threw him alive out of a chopper. He's all bloated and decomposed after six days in the water, but I'm almost sure it's him."

"No, it can't be Beto," I shouted carelessly. Suddenly the voice no longer sounded like Andrés: it felt foreign, impersonal.

"You think so?"

"Who is this?" Only then did I think to ask. But that very moment they hung up.

Ten, fifteen minutes? How long must I have stayed there staring at the phone like an idiot until the police arrived? I didn't expect them. But, then again, how could I not? Their hands feeling me, their voices insulting and threatening, the house searched, turned inside out. But I already knew. So what did I care if they broke every breakable object and tore apart my dresser?

They wouldn't find a thing. My only real possession was a dream and they can't deprive me of my dreams just like that. My dream the night before, when Beto was there with me and we loved each other. I'd dreamed it, dreamed every bit of it, I was deeply convinced that I'd dreamed it all in the richest detail, even in full color. And dreams are none of the cops' business.

They want reality, tangible facts, the kind I couldn't even begin to give them.

Where is he, you saw him, he was here with you, where did he go? Speak up, or you'll be sorry. Let's hear you sing, bitch, we know he came to see you, where is he, where is he holed up? He's in the city, come on, spill it, we know he came to get you.

I haven't heard a word from him in months. He abandoned me, I haven't heard from him in months. He ran away, went underground. What do I know, he ran off with someone else, he's in another country. What do I know, he abandoned me, I hate him, I know nothing.

(Go ahead, burn me with your cigarettes, kick me all you wish, threaten, go ahead, stick a mouse in me so it'll eat my insides out, pull my nails out, do as you please. Would I make something up for that? Would I tell you he was here when a thousand years ago he left me forever?)

I'm not about to tell them my dreams. Why should they care? I haven't seen that so-called Beto in more than six months, and I loved him. The man simply vanished. I only run into him in my dreams, and they're bad dreams that often become nightmares.

Beto, you know now, if it's true that they killed you, or wherever you may be, Beto, I'm your horse in the night and you can inhabit me whenever you wish, even if I'm behind bars. Beto, now that I'm in jail I know that I dreamed you that night; it was just a dream. And if by some wild chance there's a Gal Costa record and a half-empty bottle of cachaça in my house, I hope they'll forgive me: I will them out of existence.

—1985

What are your reactions to and questions about this work? The following questions may help provoke some ideas.

Probing the Work

1. Beto "[sends] messages in the form of caresses" in this story. Describe the nonverbal messages communicated in this story and in real-life romantic relationships.

Identifying Issues

2. To what degree is true love as much fantasy as it is reality, as it seems to be here?

LINDA PASTAN

love poem

Linda Pastan (b. 1932) was born in New York City, studied at Brandeis and Radcliffe, and is now poet laureate of Maryland. Her collections of poetry include Five Stages of Grief *(1978),* AM/PM *(1982),* Heroes in Disguise *(1991), and* Imperfect Paradise *(1988), from which this poem is taken.*

I want to write you
a love poem as headlong
as our creek
after thaw
when we stand
on its dangerous
banks and watch it carry
with it every twig
every dry leaf and branch
in its path
every scruple
when we see it
so swollen
with runoff
that even as we watch
we must grab
each other
and step back
we must grab each
other or
get our shoes
soaked we must
grab each other

—1988

What are your reactions to and questions about this work? The following questions may help provoke some ideas.

Probing the Work

1. How does the *form* of the poem match the poem's *meaning?*

Identifying Issues

2. To what extent do you agree with Pastan that love involves an element of danger and a "natural" loss of control? Explain and illustrate your answer.

GALWAY KINNELL

Rapture

Galway Kinnell (b. 1927) grew up in Providence, Rhode Island, and attended Princeton University and the University of Rochester. He has combined a life of poetry with political activism, writing incisive war poems and working as a journalist in Iran, for voter registration in the South, and for the Congress for Racial Equality in Louisiana. He has taught at a number of colleges and universities. His books of poetry include What a Kingdom It Was *(1960),* The Book of Nightmares *(1971), and* Mortal Acts, Mortal Words *(1980).*

I can feel she has got out of bed.
That means it is 7 A.M.
I have been lying with eyes shut,
thinking, or possibly dreaming,
of how she might look if, at breakfast,
I spoke about the hidden place in her
which, to me, is like a soprano's tremolo,
and right then, over toast and bramble jelly,
if such things are possible, she came.
I imagine she would show it while trying to conceal it.
I imagine her hair would fall about her face
and she would become apparently downcast,
as she does at a concert when she is moved.
The hypnopompic play passes, and I open my eyes,
and there she is, next to the bed,
bending to a low drawer, picking over
various small smooth black, white,
and pink items of underwear. She bends so low
her back runs parallel to the earth,
but there is no sway in it, there is little burden, the day has hardly begun.
The two mounds of muscles for fast-walking, leaping, lovemaking
lift toward the east—what can I say?
Simile is useless, there is nothing like them on earth.
Her breasts fall full, the nipples
are deep pink in the glare shining through the iron bars
of the gate under the earth where those who could not love
press, wanting to be born again.
I reach out and take her wrist

and she falls back into bed and at once starts unbuttoning my pajamas.
Later, when I open my eyes, there she is,
rummaging in the same low drawer.
The clock shows eight. Hmm.
With huge, silent effort of great
mounded muscles the earth has been turning.
She takes a glittering piece of cloth
from the drawer and stands up. Under the falls
of hair her face has become quiet and downcast,
as if she will be, all day among the strangers,
looking down inside herself at our rapture.

—1993

What are your reactions to and questions about this work? The following questions may help provoke some ideas.

Probing the Work

1. How important is the male perspective in this poem? How might this same morning be described from the woman's point of view?

Identifying Issues

2. In an overwhelming moment, the speaker says, "Simile is useless." What are some of the other events in life that seem to be impossible to express in words?
3. The private, inward "rapture" that the woman is said to have in this poem is felt both at a concert and in bed. Under what nonsexual circumstances might you feel a similar sort of rapture?

WENDY WASSERSTEIN

The Man in a Case

Wendy Wasserstein (b. 1950) was born in Brooklyn, daughter of immigrants from central Europe. After graduating from Mount Holyoke College and the Yale School of Drama, she has become a successful playwright, winning the Pulitzer Prize for The Heidi Chronicles *in 1989.* The Sisters Rosenzweig *opened in 1992.* The Man in a Case *is based on a short story by Anton Chekhov. Wasserstein admires the way Chekhov objectively mocked his characters' flaws and delusions yet sympathetically portrayed their hopes and sorrows.*

List of Characters

BYELINKOV VARINKA

A small garden in the village of Mironitski. 1898. BYELINKOV *is pacing. Enter* VARINKA *out of breath.*

BYELINKOV: You are ten minutes late.

VARINKA: The most amazing thing happened on my way over here. You know the woman who runs the grocery store down the road. She wears a black wig during the week, and a blond wig on Saturday nights. And she has the daughter who married an engineer in Moscow who is doing very well thank you and is living, God bless them, in a three-room apartment. But he really is the most boring man in the world. All he talks about is his future and his station in life. Well, she heard we were to be married and she gave me this basket of apricots to give to you.

BYELINKOV: That is a most amazing thing!

VARINKA: She said to me, Varinka, you are marrying the most honorable man in the entire village. In this village he is the only man fit to speak with my son-in-law.

BYELINKOV: I don't care for apricots. They give me hives.

VARINKA: I can return them. I'm sure if I told her they give you hives she would give me a basket of raisins or a cake.

BYELINKOV: I don't know this woman or her pompous son-in-law. Why would she give me her cakes?

VARINKA: She adores you!

BYELINKOV: She is emotionally loose.

VARINKA: She adores you by reputation. Everyone adores you by reputation. I tell everyone I am to marry Byelinkov, the finest teacher in the county.

BYELINKOV: You tell them this?

VARINKA: If they don't tell me first.

BYELINKOV: Pride can be an imperfect value.

VARINKA: It isn't pride. It is the truth. You are a great man!

BYELINKOV: I am the master of Greek and Latin at a local school at the end of the village of Mironitski.

(VARINKA *kisses him)*

VARINKA: And I am to be the master of Greek and Latin's wife!

BYELINKOV: Being married requires a great deal of responsibility. I hope I am able to provide you with all that a married man must properly provide a wife.

VARINKA: We will be very happy.

BYELINKOV: Happiness is for children. We are entering into a social contract, an amicable agreement to provide us with a secure and satisfying future.

VARINKA: You are so sweet! You are the sweetest man in the world!

BYELINKOV: I'm a man set in his ways who saw a chance to provide himself with a small challenge.

VARINKA: Look at you! Look at you! Your sweet round spectacles, your dear collar always starched, always raised, your perfectly pressed pants always creasing at right angles perpendicular to the floor, and my most favorite part, the sweet little galoshes, rain or shine, just in case. My Byelinkov, never taken by surprise. Except by me.

BYELINKOV: You speak about me as if I were your pet.

VARINKA: You are my pet! My little school mouse.

BYELINKOV: A mouse?

VARINKA: My sweetest dancing bear with galoshes, my little stale babka.°

BYELINKOV: A stale babka?

VARINKA: I am not Pushkin.°

BYELINKOV: *(Laughs)* That depends what you think of Pushkin.

VARINKA: You're smiling. I knew I could make you smile today.

BYELINKOV: I am a responsible man. Every day I have for breakfast black bread, fruit, hot tea, and every day I smile three times. I am halfway into my translation of the *Aeneid*° from classical Greek hexameter into Russian alexandrines. In twenty years I have never been late to school. I am a responsible man, but no dancing bear.

VARINKA: Dance with me.

BYELINKOV: Now? It is nearly four weeks before the wedding!

VARINKA: It's a beautiful afternoon. We are in your garden. The roses are in full bloom.

BYELINKOV: The roses have beetles.

VARINKA: Dance with me!

BYELINKOV: You are a demanding woman.

VARINKA: You chose me. And right. And left. And turn. And right. And left.

BYELINKOV: And turn. Give me your hand. You dance like a school mouse. It's a beautiful afternoon! We are in my garden. The roses are in full bloom! And turn. And turn. *(Twirls* VARINKA *around)*

VARINKA: I am the luckiest woman!

*(*BYELINKOV *stops dancing)*

Why are you stopping?

BYELINKOV: To place a lilac in your hair. Every year on this day I will place a lilac in your hair.

VARINKA: Will you remember?

BYELINKOV: I will write it down. *(Takes a notebook from his pocket)* Dear Byelinkov, don't forget the day a young lady, your bride, entered your garden, your peace, and danced on the roses. On that day every year you are to place a lilac in her hair.

VARINKA: I love you.

49. babka, cake with almonds and raisins.
51. Pushkin, Alexander Pushkin (1799–1837), Russian poet.
56. *Aeneid*, Latin epic poem by the Roman poet Virgil (70–19 B.C.).

BYELINKOV: It is convenient we met.

VARINKA: I love you.

BYELINKOV: You are a girl.

VARINKA: I am thirty.

BYELINKOV: But you think like a girl. That is an attractive attribute.

VARINKA: Do you love me?

BYELINKOV: We've never spoken about housekeeping.

VARINKA: I am an excellent housekeeper. I kept house for my family on the farm in Gadyatchsky. I can make a beetroot soup with tomatoes and aubergines which is so nice. Awfully awfully nice.

BYELINKOV: You are fond of expletives.

VARINKA: My beet soup, sir, is excellent!

BYELINKOV: Please don't be cross. I too am an excellent housekeeper. I have a place for everything in the house. A shelf for each pot, a cubby for every spoon, a folder for favorite recipes. I have cooked for myself for twenty years. Though my beet soup is not outstanding, it is sufficient.

VARINKA: I'm sure it's very good.

BYELINKOV: No. It is awfully, awfully not. What I am outstanding in, however, what gives me greatest pleasure, is preserving those things which are left over. I wrap each tomato slice I haven't used in a wet cloth and place it in the coolest corner of the house. I have had my shoes for seven years because I wrap them in the galoshes you are so fond of. And every night before I go to sleep I wrap my bed in quilts and curtains so I never catch a draft.

VARINKA: You sleep with curtains on your bed?

BYELINKOV: I like to keep warm.

VARINKA: I will make you a new quilt.

BYELINKOV: No. No new quilt. That would be hazardous.

VARINKA: It is hazardous to sleep under curtains.

BYELINKOV: Varinka, I don't like change very much. If one works out the arithmetic the final fraction of improvement is at best less than an eighth of value over the total damage caused by disruption. I never thought of marrying till I saw your eyes dancing among the familiar faces at the headmaster's tea. I assumed I would grow old preserved like those which are left over, wrapped suitably in my case of curtains and quilts.

VARINKA: Byelinkov, I want us to have dinners with friends and summer country visits. I want people to say, "Have you spent time with Varinka and Byelinkov? He is so happy now that they are married. She is just what he needed."

BYELINKOV: You have already brought me some happiness. But I never was a sad man. Don't ever think I thought I was a sad man.

VARINKA: My sweetest darling, you can be whatever you want! If you are sad, they'll say she talks all the time, and he is soft-spoken and kind.

BYELINKOV: And if I am difficult?

VARINKA: Oh, they'll say he is difficult because he is highly intelligent. All great men are difficult. Look at Lermontov, Tchaikovsky, Peter the Great.

BYELINKOV: Ivan the Terrible.[4]

VARINKA: Yes, him too.

BYELINKOV: Why are you marrying me? I am none of these things.

VARINKA: To me you are.

BYELINKOV: You have imagined this. You have constructed an elaborate romance for yourself. Perhaps you are the great one. You are the one with the great imagination.

VARINKA: Byelinkov, I am a pretty girl of thirty. You're right, I am not a woman. I have not made myself into a woman because I do not deserve that honor. Until I came to this town to visit my brother I lived on my family's farm. As the years passed I became younger and younger in fear that I would never marry. And it wasn't that I wasn't pretty enough or sweet enough, it was just that no man ever looked at me and saw a wife. I was not the woman who would be there when he came home. Until I met you I thought I would lie all my life and say I never married because I never met a man I loved. I will love you, Byelinkov. And I will help you to love me. We deserve the life everyone else has. We deserve not to be different.

BYELINKOV: Yes. We are the same as everyone else.

VARINKA: Tell me you love me.

BYELINKOV: I love you.

VARINKA: *(Takes his hands)* We will be very happy. I am very strong. *(Pauses)* It is time for tea.

BYELINKOV: It is too early for tea. Tea is at half past the hour.

VARINKA: Do you have heavy cream? It will be awfully nice with apricots.

BYELINKOV: Heavy cream is too rich for teatime.

VARINKA: But today is special. Today you placed a lilac in my hair. Write in your note pad. Every year we will celebrate with apricots and heavy cream. I will go to my brother's house and get some.

BYELINKOV: But your brother's house is a mile from here.

VARINKA: Today it is much shorter. Today my brother gave me his bicycle to ride. I will be back very soon.

BYELINKOV: You rode to my house by bicycle! Did anyone see you?

VARINKA: Of course. I had such fun. I told you I saw the grocery store lady with the son-in-law who is doing very well thank you in Moscow, and the headmaster's wife.

BYELINKOV: You saw the headmaster's wife!

VARINKA: She smiled at me.

129. Lermontov . . . Ivan the Terrible, Mikhail Lermontov (1814–41), poet and novelist; Peter Ilich Tchaikovsky (1840–93), composer; Peter the Great (1672–1725) and Ivan the Terrible (1530–84), czars credited with making Russia a great European power.

BYELINKOV: Did she laugh or smile?

VARINKA: She laughed a little. She said, "My dear, you are very progressive to ride a bicycle." She said you and your fiancé Byelinkov must ride together sometime. I wonder if he'll take off his galoshes when he rides a bicycle.

BYELINKOV: She said that?

VARINKA: She adores you. We had a good giggle.

BYELINKOV: A woman can be arrested for riding a bicycle. That is not progressive, it is a premeditated revolutionary act. Your brother must be awfully, awfully careful on behalf of your behavior. He has been careless—oh so careless—in giving you the bicycle.

VARINKA: Dearest Byelinkov, you are wrapping yourself under curtains and quilts! I made friends on the bicycle.

BYELINKOV: You saw more than the headmaster's wife and the idiot grocery woman.

VARINKA: She is not an idiot.

BYELINKOV: She is a potato-vending, sausage-armed fool!

VARINKA: Shhhh! My school mouse. Shhh!

BYELINKOV: What other friends did you make on this bicycle?

VARINKA: I saw students from my brother's classes. They waved and shouted, "Anthropos in love! Anthropos in love!!"

BYELINKOV: Where is that bicycle?

VARINKA: I left it outside the gate. Where are you going?

BYELINKOV: *(Muttering as he exits)* Anthropos in love, anthropos in love.

VARINKA: They were cheering me on. Careful, you'll trample the roses.

BYELINKOV: *(Returning with the bicycle)* Anthropos is the Greek singular for man. Anthropos in love translates as the Greek and Latin master in love. Of course they cheered you. Their instructor, who teaches them the discipline and contained beauty of the classics, is in love with a sprite on a bicycle. It is a good giggle, isn't it? A very good giggle! I am returning this bicycle to your brother.

VARINKA: But it is teatime.

BYELINKOV: Today we will not have tea.

VARINKA: But you will have to walk back a mile.

BYELINKOV: I have my galoshes on. *(Gets on the bicycle)* Varinka, we deserve not to be different. *(Begins to pedal. The bicycle doesn't move)*

VARINKA: Put the kickstand up.

BYELINKOV: I beg your pardon.

VARINKA: *(Giggling)* Byelinkov, to make the bicycle move, you must put the kickstand up.

*(*BYELINKOV *puts it up and awkwardly falls off the bicycle as it moves)*

(Laughing) Ha ha ha. My little school mouse. You look so funny! You are the sweetest dearest man in the world. Ha ha ha!

(Pause)

BYELINKOV: Please help me up. I'm afraid my galosh is caught.

VARINKA: *(Trying not to laugh)* Your galosh is caught! *(Explodes in laughter again)* Oh, you are so funny! I do love you so. *(Helps Byelinkov up)* You were right, my pet, as always. We don't need heavy cream for tea. The fraction of improvement isn't worth the damage caused by the disruption.

BYELINKOV: Varinka, it is still too early for tea. I must complete two stanzas of my translation before late afternoon. That is my regular schedule.

VARINKA: Then I will watch while you work.

BYELINKOV: No. You had a good giggle. That is enough.

VARINKA: Then while you work I will work too. I will make lists of guests for our wedding.

BYELINKOV: I can concentrate only when I am alone in my house. Please take your bicycle home to your brother.

VARINKA: But I don't want to leave you. You look so sad.

BYELINKOV: I never was a sad man. Don't ever think I was a sad man.

VARINKA: Byelinkov, it's a beautiful day, we are in your garden. The roses are in bloom.

BYELINKOV: Allow me to help you on to your bicycle. *(Takes* VARINKA*'s hand as she gets on the bike.)*

VARINKA: You are such a gentleman. We will be very happy.

BYELINKOV: You are very strong. Good day, Varinka.

*(*VARINKA *pedals off.* BYELINKOV, *alone in the garden, takes out his pad and rips up the note about the lilac, strews it over the garden, then carefully picks up each piece of paper and places them all in a small envelope as lights fade to black)*

—1986

What are your reactions to and questions about this work? The following questions may help provoke some ideas.

Probing the Work

1. Analyze some elements of humor in the play. What conventions are depicted comically?
2. Explain the various ways in which Byelinkov and Varinka are opposites.

Identifying Issues

3. Do you believe that opposites attract? What are the qualities these two characters find attractive in one another? To what extent do we look in others for the qualities we lack?

ASSIGNMENT SEQUENCE (CONTINUED FROM PAGE 565)

4. Making Connections

Select one of the following questions and write an informal response in which you connect your own ideas with those conveyed in the works of this cluster, and/or make connections among the works themselves.

A. Compare and contrast the writers' implied definitions of true love with your own.

B. What differentiates "true love" from ordinary love in these writings and in your experience?

5. Putting It All Together

Write an essay that combines what you think about the topic *True Love* with what you now understand about the readings.

- Collect your informal writing, notes, and reading-journal entries on this topic and decide what will be the focus of your essay.
- Outline your essay. Select the literary passages and personal details you might use to illustrate and support your main focus.
- Write a draft of your essay in which you bring together what you think about the subject with what you understand about the readings. Try to include in your draft one or more *literary terms.*
- Share what you've written with your classmates and instructor, then revise it according to their recommendations.

Writing Tip: Ask Yourself Questions

As you write your long paper, ask yourself the following questions:

- What evidence from the text(s) am I using to illustrate my point?
- What evidence from my own life am I drawing to make my point?
- What are the three most important things I want to say about this topic?
- Have I used quotations to my advantage? Have I overquoted?
- Have I written an original, interesting, or provocative introduction?

These questions might help you as you begin to revise.

After Elizabeth asked herself these questions, she decided to change the introduction for her essay on the True Love cluster. In her revised version she decided to begin with a dialog:

> "You're alive."
> "I told you I would come for you. Why didn't you wait for me?
> "Well you were dead."
> "Death cannot stop true love. What it can do is delay it for a while."
> This conversation, between Buttercup and Westley in the movie *The Princess Bride,* is typical of how idealized love is depicted in movies, songs, and literature.

CrossClusters

In your paper you might want to consider how the following works located elsewhere in this book depict true love:

- Anna Quindlen, "Married" (p. 630)
- Nathaniel Hawthorne, "The Birth-mark" (p. 633)
- John Updike, "Wife Wooing" (p. 653)
- Liz Rosenberg, "Married Love" (p. 658)
- Mme. de Beaumont, "Beauty and the Beast" (p. 732)
- John Keats, "La Belle Dame sans Merci" (p. 746)
- William Shakespeare, *A Midsummer-Night's Dream* (p. 766)
- Robert Browning, "Porphyria's Lover" (p. 840)
- Isabel Allende, "And of Clay Are We Created" (p. 996)

Sample Essay

Here is Benjamin's essay on the true love cluster.

"The Compromise of True Love," by Benjamin Herman

Shakespeare wrote in his famous Sonnet 116 that love ". . . is an ever-fixed mark/ That looks on tempests and is never shaken" (568). But is true love the perfect ideal that Shakespeare suggests? I doubt that. Rather, I see love as a compromise between two people. Each of the two individuals in a relationship enters into it with certain goals and expectations. As a relationship progresses, both individuals come to realize that their goals will not become completely fulfilled, and that their expectations are not completely realistic. However, if true love exists, the two members of a relationship will accept compromise for the sake of their significant other.

Compromise is at the heart of Judith Viorst's poem "True Love." The speaker in this work clearly acknowledges that her relationship with her husband is far from perfect. There are qualities that each member of the relationship does not like about the other. The speaker dislikes football, but she watches it because her husband does. The husband wants his undershorts ironed, but he will do without that because the speaker is "philosophically/opposed to ironing." Why do the two of them put up with these and many other conflicting likes and dislikes? The reason is that they love each other, which means they are willing to compromise. Perhaps the situation is best summed up by the closing lines of Viorst's poem: "Despite cigarette cough, tooth decay, acid/ indigestion, dandruff, and other features of/ married life that tend to dampen the fires of/ passion/ we still feel something/ We can call/ True love" (584).

Similarly, Wendy Wasserstein and Bernard Malamud, in their respective literary works, "The Man in a Case" and "The Magic Barrel," both reflect on the expectations and goals of people in love. The first of these is a play that Wasserstein based on an Anton Chekov story. It concerns two individuals named Byelinkov and Varinka who are preparing to get married. They are two dissimilar individuals. Byelinkov is a logical, orderly man whose daily routine is based on a strict schedule. Varinka, on the other hand, is an emotional, impulsive woman who lives for the day. Despite these differences, they appear to be in love. The reason for this seems to be that each offers something that the other needs. Byelinkov wants someone to love who will let him relax his self-imposed standards. Varinka wants someone to give her a normal existence. This shows the expectations and goals each of them has for the other. Again, compromise is the key word. This relationship is a compromise between conformity and change. I have no doubt that Byelinkov's and Varinka's love is genuine, because they are willing to live with the eccentricities and faults of the other.

Malamud's short story "The Magic Barrel" can be both compared and contrasted with the Wasserstein play. The Malamud story's protagonist is a rabbinical student named Leo Finkle. At the advice of an acquaintance, Leo is looking for a wife because this might improve his chances of receiving a congregation when he becomes a rabbi. During the course of his search for a wife, Leo experiences the revelation that he has doubts about his love and worship of God. Leo fears he is unable to love anyone else. Along comes Stella, a character introduced at the conclusion of the story. We do not learn much about her, other than that she has fallen from grace in the eyes of her father, and that she may be looking for redemption. From this brief description, it can clearly be seen that Leo and Stella, like Byelinkov and Varinka, contrast with each other. Similarly, both Leo and Stella have motives that propel their love. Leo thinks a wife will improve his chances of receiving a congregation. He also believes that by saving Stella he will renew his faith in God: "[Leo] pictured, in her, his own redemption" (583), upon seeing Stella in person for the first time. Unlike Varinka, we do not get to know Stella. However, it appears that she wishes to redeem her soul, and hopes that Leo will be able to aid her in doing so. Each character wants something, and loves his or her partner for being able to fulfill those wishes. By giving something of themselves, they hope to receive some of what they desire. At the same time, they would learn to live with someone they were very different from. This is the compromise that is true love. I think Byelinkov and Varinka realize this more than Leo and Stella. Of course, we see the first couple after they had become acquainted with each other. Still, I expect that Leo and Stella would have, over time, reached the same rapport as Byelinkov and Varinka and, indeed, the couple from the Viorst poem.

There are certainly many individuals who will disagree with me on the views I have raised. I'm sure that there are some who regard true love to be anything but a compromise, with each member of a relationship accepting the other exactly for who they are. While I can understand this more romantic view when contrasted to my apparently pessimistic one, I can argue in favor of my position. When I was preparing to write this essay, I asked my father if compromise was important in his relationship with my mother. His response was that the two of them had to reach compromises the majority of the time. My father emphasized that compromise was crucial to making both my parents' marriage and family life succeed. This does not mean my parents do not love one another; on the contrary, they both care deeply about each other. This is true love. One of the pivotal reasons for the large number of divorces and break-ups of couples is the inability of so many of them to reach compromises. It is the capability of people to be flexible that is a sign of true love.

As for the argument that true love is complete acceptance of the one you love, this is an idealistic definition that cannot be applied to the real world. Even in modern-day America, people place standards upon each other in matters of the heart. Appearance, personality, wealth, and lifestyle are just some of the many factors involved in the process of "falling in love." When two people do fall in love, it's because they fulfill the needs of the other, such as companionship, comfort, support, help, and sex. This is one part of the compromise issue. The couples in the Malamud and Wasserstein works are extreme examples of this. However, one need only to look at the Viorst poem to see that the "average" relationship is based on many compromises.

Finally, people are simply not perfect. It is unreasonable to expect to have a couple in love accept everything about each other. Compromise is a necessity to make any relationship, especially a romantic one, succeed.

No matter how much we might desire love to be pure and unconditional, there is no way it can possibly be so for us. In this imperfect world, a relationship based on compromise is the best possible alternative. If you truly love someone, you should be willing to make a compromise, to overlook the idiosyncrasies of your partner, and he or she should be willing to do the same. That is what keeps people together.

18

GUILT, DESIRE, AND LOVE

WRITING ASSIGNMENT SEQUENCE

1. Thinking About . . . Guilt, Desire, and Love

Asking a Series of Questions: Write quick, informal responses to the following questions:

- What differentiates the romantic relationships of your generation from those of the generations preceding yours? What remains the same?
- Is old-fashioned romance still alive? What are the advantages and disadvantages of maintaining the traits of old-fashioned love?
- Are you or is our society today more tolerant of various types of love?

2. Enacting the Topic

Find a magazine article that addresses the difficulties of contemporary romantic relationships or that depicts unconventional ones. Summarize the contents of the article to the class, and add your own opinions and experiences on the topic.

3. Responding to the Readings

As you read the works in this cluster, jot down in your response journals questions you have about the works, and comment on passages you find provocative or puzzling. Consider the questions following each reading for journal writing and prepare to discuss your reactions in class.

CLUSTER ESSAY

BRUCE WEBER

The Unromantic Generation

Bruce Weber (b. 1953) is an editor of The New York Times Magazine, *in which the essay below was first published. He has also published a collection of short stories,* Look Who's Talking: An Anthology of American Short Stories *(1986).*

Here is a contemporary love story.

Twenty-four-year-old Clark Wolfsberger, a native of St. Louis, and Kim Wright, twenty-five, who is from Chicago, live in Dallas. They've been going together since they met as students at Southern Methodist University three years ago. They are an attractive pair, trim and athletic, she dark and lissome, he broad-shouldered and square-jawed. They have jobs they took immediately after graduating—Clark works at Talent Sports International, a sports marketing and management company; Kim is an assistant account executive at Tracy-Locke, a large advertising agency—and they are in love.

"We're very compatible," she says.

"We don't need much time together to confirm our relationship," he says.

When they speak about the future, they hit the two-career family notes that are conventional now in the generations ahead of them. "At thirty, I'll probably be married and planning a family," says Kim. "I'll stay in advertising. I'll be a late parent."

"By thirty, I'll definitely be married; either that or water-skiing naked in Monaco," Clark says, and laughs. "No. I'll be married. Well-established in my line of work. Have the home, have the dog. Maybe not a kid yet, but eventually. I'm definitely in favor of kids."

In the month I spent last winter visiting several cities around the country, interviewing recent college graduates about marriage, relationships, modern romance, I heard a lot of this, life equations already written, doubt banished. I undertook the trip because of the impression so many of us have; that in one wavelike rush to business school and Wall Street, young Americans have succumbed to a culture of immediate gratification and gone deep-down elitist on us. I set out to test the image with an informal survey meant to take the emotional temperature of a generation, not far behind my own, that *seems* so cynical, so full of such "material" girls and boys.

The sixty or so people I interviewed, between the ages of twenty-two and twenty-six, were a diverse group. They spoke in distinct voices, testifying to a range of political and social views. Graduate students, lawyers, teachers, entertainers, business people, they are pursuing a variety of interests. What they have in common is that they graduated from college, are living in or around an urban center, and are heterosexual, mirrors of myself when I graduated from college in 1975. And yet as I moved from place to place, beginning with acquaintances of my friends and then randomly pursuing an expanding network of names and phone numbers, another quality emerged to the degree that I'd call it characteristic: they are planners. It was the one thing that surprised me, this looking ahead with certainty. They have priorities. I'd ask about love; they'd give me a graph.

This isn't how I remember it. Twelve years ago, who knew? I was three years away from my first full-time paycheck, six from anything resembling the job I have now. It was all sort of desultory and hopeful, a time of dabbling and waiting around for some event that would sprout a future. Frankly, I had it in mind that meeting a woman would do it.

My cultural prototype was Benjamin Braddock, the character played by Dustin Hoffman in Mike Nichols's 1967 film *The Graduate,* who, returning home after his college triumphs, finds the prospect of life after campus daunting in the extreme, and so plunges into inertia. His refrain "I'm just a little worried about my future," served me nicely as a sort of wryly understated mantra.

What hauls Benjamin from his torpor is love. Wisely or not, he responds to a force beyond logic and turns the world upside down for Elaine Robinson. And though in the end their future together is undetermined, the message of the movie is that love is meant to triumph, that its passion and promise, however naïve, are its strength, and that if we are lucky it will seize us and transform our lives.

Today I'm still single and, chastened by that, I suppose, a little more rational about what to expect from love. Setting out on my trip, I felt as if I'd be plumbing a little of my past. But the people I spoke with reminded me more of the way I am now than the way I was then. I returned thinking that young people are older than they used to be, *The Graduate* is out of date, and for young people just out of college today, the belief that love is all you need no longer obtains.

"Kim's a great girl; I love her," Clark Wolfsberger says. "But she's very career-oriented. I am, too, and with our schedules the way they are, we haven't put any restrictions on each other. I think that's healthy."

"He might want to go back to St. Louis," Kim Wright says. "I want to go back to Chicago. If it works out, great. If not, that's fine, too. I can handle it either way."

They are not heartless, soulless, cold, or unimaginative. They *are* self-preoccupied, but that's a quality, it seems to me, for which youthful generations have always been known. What distinguishes this generation from mine, I think, is that they're aware of it. News-conscious, media-smart, they are sophisticated in a way I was not.

They have come of age, of course, at a time when American social traditions barely survive. Since 1975, there have been more than a million divorces annually, and it is well publicized that nearly half of all marriages now end in divorce. Yet the era of condoned casual promiscuity and sexual experimentation—itself once an undermining of the nation's social fabric—now seems to be drawing to a close with the ever-spreading plague of sexually transmitted disease.

The achievements of feminist activism—particularly the infusion of women into the work force—have altered the expectations that the sexes have for each other and themselves.

And finally, the new college graduates have been weaned on scarifying forecasts of economic gloom. They feel housing problems already; according to *American Demographics* magazine, the proportion of young people living at home with their parents was higher in 1985 than in the last three censuses. They're aware, too, of predictions that however affluent they are themselves, they're probably better off than their children will be.

With all this in mind, today's graduates seem keenly aware that the future is bereft of conventional expectations, that what's ahead is more chaotic than mysterious. I've come to think it ironic that in a youth-minded culture such as ours, one that ostensibly grants greater freedom of choice to young people than it ever has before, those I spoke with seem largely restrained. Concerned with, if not consumed by, narrowing the options down, getting on track, they are aiming already at a distant comfort and security. I spoke, on my travels, with several college counselors and administrators, and they concur that the immediate concerns of today's graduates are more practical than those of their predecessors. "I talk to them about sex," says Gail Short Hanson, dean of students at George Washington University, in Washington. "I talk about careers. And marriage, with women, because of the balancing act they have to perform these days. But love? I can't remember the last conversation I had about love."

Career-minded, fiercely self-reliant, they responded to me, a single man with a good job, with an odd combination of comradeliness and respect. When the interviews were over, I fielded a lot of questions about what it's like to work at *The New York Times*. How did I get my job? Occasionally, someone would ask about my love life. Considering the subject of our discussions, I was surprised it happened so much. When it did, I told them I'd come reasonably close to marriage once, but it didn't work out. Nobody asked me why. Nobody asked if I was lonely.

Micah Materre, twenty-five, recently completed an internship at CBS News in Chicago and is looking for a job in broadcast journalism. Like many of the young people I talked to, she is farsighted in her romantic outlook: "I went out with a guy last fall. He had a good job as a stockbroker. He was nice to me. But then he started telling me about his family. And there were problems. And I thought, 'What happens if I fall in love and we get married? What then?' "

It may be a memory lapse, but I don't recall thinking about marriage much at all until I fell in love. I was twenty-nine; late, that's agreed. But the point is that for me (and for my generation as a whole, I believe, though you hate to make a statement like that), marriage loomed only as an outgrowth of happenstance; you met a person. Today's graduates, however, seem uneasy with that kind of serendipity. All of the married couples I spoke with are delighted to be married, but they do say their friends questioned their judgment. "I heard a lot of reasons why I shouldn't do it," one recent bride told me. "Finally, I just said to myself, 'I feel happier than I've ever felt. Why should I give this up just because I'm young?' "

Most of them too young to remember the assassination of *either* Kennedy, they are old enough to have romantic pasts, to have experienced the trauma of failure in love. What surprised me was how easily so many of them accepted it; it seems a little early to be resigned to the idea that things fall apart. In each interview, I asked about past involvements. Were you ever serious about anyone? Any marital close calls? And virtually everyone had a story. But I heard very little about heartbreak or lingering grief. Instead, with an almost uniform equanimity, they spoke of maturity gained, lessons learned. It isn't disillusionment exactly, and they *are* too young to be weary; rather, it sounds like determination.

Twenty-five-year-old Peter Mundy of San Francisco, for example, says that until six months ago he'd had a series of steady girlfriends. "I'm down on romance," he says. "There's too much pain, too much pressure. There are so many variables, and you can't tell until you're in the middle of it whether it'll be positive. It's only in retrospect that you can see how things went wrong. In the meantime, you end up neglecting other things."

The prevalent notion is that chemistry is untrustworthy; partners need to be up to snuff according to pretty rigorous standards. Ellen Lubin, twenty-six, of Los Angeles, for example, has just gotten engaged to the man she's been living with for two years. When she met him, she says: "I wasn't that attracted to him right away. But there were things about him that made me say, 'This is what I want in a man.' He's bright. He's a go-getter. He was making tons of money at the age of twenty-five. He's well-connected. He was like my mentor in coming to deal with life in the city."

At the end of *The Graduate,* Benjamin Braddock kidnaps his lady love at the altar, an instant after she has sealed her vows to someone else, and they manage to make their escape because Benjamin bolts the church door from the outside with a cross. That was the 1960s, vehement times. When I graduated, we were less obstreperous. Sacraments we could take or leave. And marriage wasn't much of an issue. If we put it off, it wasn't for the sake of symbolism so much as that it didn't seem necessary. In the last few years, I've been to a number of weddings among my contemporaries, people in their thirties, and that impression of us is still with me. What we did was drift toward marriage, arriving at it eventually, and with some surprise. Some of us are still drifting.

Today's graduates have forged a new attitude entirely. In spite of the high divorce rate, many of those I spoke with have marriage in mind. Overwhelmingly, they see it as not only desirable, but inevitable. Because of the odds, they approach it with wariness and pragmatism. More cautious than their parents (for American men in 1985, the median age at the time of their first marriage was 25.5, the highest since the turn of the century; it was 23.3 for women, a record), they are methodical in comparison with me.

Perhaps that explains why I find the way they speak about marriage so unromantic. Men and women tend to couch their views in different terms, but they seem to share the perception that marriage is necessarily restricting. Nonetheless they trust in its rewards, whatever they are. Overall, it doesn't represent the kind of commitment that seems viable without adequate preparation.

"I've been dating someone for a year and a half," says Tom Grossman, a twenty-four-year-old graduate of the University of Texas. "We don't talk about marriage, and frankly I don't think it'll occur." Currently area sales manager in San Antonio for the John H. Harland Company, a check-printing concern, Grossman says he has professional success in mind first. "I want to be really well-off financially, and I don't want that struggle to interfere with the marriage. There are too many other stress factors involved. I want to be able to enjoy myself right away. And I never want to look back and think that if I hadn't gotten married, I could have accomplished more."

Many young women say they responded with some alarm to last year's [1986] *Newsweek* report on the controversial demographic study conducted at Harvard, which concluded that once past thirty, a woman faces rapidly dwindling chances of marrying. At a time when women graduates often feel it incumbent on them to pursue careers, they worry that the possibility of "having it all" is, in fact, remote.

Janie Russell, twenty-five, graduated from the University of North Carolina in 1983, left a serious boyfriend behind, and moved to Los Angeles to pursue a career in the film industry. Working now as a director of production services at New Visions Inc., like many other young women she believes the independence fostered by a career is necessary, not only for her own self-esteem but as a foundation for a future partnership. "I look forward to marriage," she says. "But this is a very selfish time for me. I have to have my career. I have to say to myself, 'I did this on my own.' It makes me feel more interesting than I would otherwise. Of course, what may happen is that I'll look up one day and say, 'O.K., husband, where are you?' And he won't be there."

About halfway through my trip I stopped interviewing married couples because they tended to say similar things. They consider themselves the lucky ones. As twenty-four-year-old Adam Cooper put it, at dinner with his wife, Melanee, also twenty-four, in their Chicago apartment: "The grass is not greener on the other side."

I came away thinking it is as true as ever: all happy families are the same. But the couples I spoke with seemed to me part of a generation other than their own, older even than mine. Calling the Coopers to arrange an interview, I was invited for "a good, home-cooked meal."

The next day, I met Micah Materre, who expressed the prevailing contemporary stance as well as anyone. Outgoing and self-possessed, she gave me a long list of qualities she's looking for in a man: good looks, sense of humor, old-fashioned values, but also professional success, financial promise, and a solid family background. "Why not?" she said. "I deserve the best." But as I was folding up my notebook, she added a plaintive note: "I'll get married, won't I? It's the American way, right?"

Very early on in my sexual experience I was flattered by a woman who told me she ordinarily wouldn't go to bed with men who were under twenty-six. "Until then," she said, "all they're doing when they're with you is congratulating themselves." For whatever reason, she never returned my calls after that night. Not an untypical encounter, all in all. Congratulations to both of us.

We were a lusty, if callow, bunch, not least because we thought we could afford to be. Encouraged by the expansive social mores spawned by the sexual revolution, fortified by the advent of a widespread availability of birth control, and fundamentally unaware of germs, we interpreted sex, for our convenience, as pure pleasure shared by "consenting parties." If it feels good, do it. Remember that?

It is an attitude that the current generation inherited and put into practice at an early age. Asked about her circle of friends in Los Angeles, Lesley Bracker, twenty-three, puts it nonchalantly: "Oh, yeah, we were all sexually active as teenagers. When we were younger, it was considered O.K. to sleep around."

Now, however, they are reconsidering. In general, on this topic, I found them shy. They hesitate to speak openly about their sex lives, are prone to euphemism ("I'm not exactly out there, you know, mingling"), and say they worry about promiscuity only because they have friends who still practice it. According to Laura Kavesh and Cheryl Lavin, who write a column about single life, "Tales from the Front," for the *Chicago Tribune* that is syndicated in some sixty other papers around the country, a letter from a reader about the virtues of virginity generated more supportive mail than anything that has appeared in the column in its two years of existence. I'm not about to say there's a new celibacy among the young, but my impression is that even if they're having twice as much sex as they say they're having, it's not as much as you would think.

The AIDS scare, of course, is of primary relevance. "I talk about AIDS on first dates," says Jill Rotenberg, twenty-five, publishing manager of a rare-book company in San Francisco. "I talk about it all the time. I've spoken with the guy I'm dating about taking an AIDS test. Neither one of us is thrilled about condoms. But we use them. The first time we had sex, I was the one who had one in my wallet."

Not everyone is so vehement. But seriously or jokingly, in earnest tête-à-tête or idly at dinner parties, they all talk about it. To some, the new concern is merely a source of disappointment. Several of the young people I spoke with express the sense of having been robbed. It's tough to find sex when you want it, tougher than it used to be, is the lament of many, mostly men. As it was put to me at one point, "I wish I'd been born ten years earlier."

Jill Rotenberg says she feels betrayed: "I've had one long relationship in my life. He was my first lover, and for a long time my only one. So I feel I've had an untainted past. Now I feel I'm being punished anyway, even though I've been a good girl."

"I feel like I'm over the hurdle," says Douglas Ertman, twenty-two, of San Francisco, who got engaged last summer. "I'm really lucky to know that I'll have one sexual partner forever."

Most agree that the solution is monogamy, at least on a temporary basis. "It's a coupled-up society," says Alan Forman, twenty-six, a law student of George Washington University who, for the last several months, has been in a monogamous relationship. "Now more than ever. A lot of people I know are feeling the pressure to get hooked up with somebody."

I ask Forman and his girlfriend, twenty-four-year-old Debra Golden, about their future together. They say they don't know ("I'm too insecure to make a decision like that," she says), and I get the sense they never talk about it. Then she turns to him, genuinely curious. "Say you break up with me and go to New York next year," she says.

"I don't know," he says. "If I meet someone and I like her, what do I have to do, ask her to take a blood test?"

A decade ago, one of the privileges that my contemporaries and I inferred from our sexual freedom was more or less to deny that there might be, in the sexual act, an innately implied emotional exchange. It's no longer feasible, however, to explain away sex as frivolity, inconsequential gratification. And that has complicated things for all of us, of course, whatever age, single or not.

But for young people, it's an issue, like marriage, that has been raised early: what does sex mean, if it doesn't mean nothing?

It's clearly a struggle for them. In one of my first interviews, twenty-five-year-old Karl Wright of Chicago told me: "Maybe there's a silver lining in all this. Maybe AIDS will bring back romance." The more I think about that, the more chilling it gets.

Beverly Caro, a twenty-five-year-old associate in the Dallas law firm of Gardere & Wynne, graduated from Drake University, in Des Moines, in 1983, and attended law school there as well. Her office high above the street looks out on the city's jungle of futuristic skyscrapers. She had offers from firms in Denver and her hometown of Kansas City, Missouri, she says, but chose to come to Dallas because "I see upward mobility here; that's what I was looking for."

Ms. Caro has an attractive, thoughtful manner and a soft voice, but like many of her contemporaries, given the chance to discuss her personal goals, she speaks with a certitude that borders on defiance. Currently, she sees two men "somewhat regularly," she says. "I'd like to have a companion. A friend, I guess. But finding a man is not a top priority. I want to travel. I want to establish myself in the community. I don't see any drastic changes in my life by the time I turn thirty. Except that I'll be a property owner."

During my interviews, the theme of getting on track and staying there surfaced again and again. I came to think of it as the currency of self-definition. As a generation, they are not a particularly well-polled group, but certain figures bear out my impression.

According to annual surveys of 300,000 college freshmen conducted by the Higher Education Research Institute at the Graduate School of Education of the University of California at Los Angeles, young people today, by the time they *enter* college, are more inclined to express concrete life objectives than they've been for many years. Of those surveyed last fall, 73.2 percent cited being "very well off financially" as an essential or very important objective. That's up from 63.3 percent in 1980, 49.5 percent in 1975. Other objectives that the survey shows have risen in importance include "obtain recognition from colleagues for contributions to my special field"; "have administrative responsibility for the work of others"; "be successful in my own business"; and "raise a family." At the same time, the percentage of freshmen who consider it important to "develop a meaningful philosophy of life" has declined from 64.2 percent in 1975 to 40.6 percent last year.

Many of the people I spoke to feel the pressure of peer scrutiny. A status thing has evolved, to which many seem to have regretfully succumbed. Several expressed a weariness with meeting someone new and having to present themselves by their credentials. Yet, overwhelmingly, asked what they're looking for in a romantic partner, they responded first with phrases such as "an educated professional" and "someone with direction." They've conceded, more or less consciously, that unenlightened and exclusionary as it is, It's very uncool not to know what you want and not to be already chasing it.

"Seems like everyone in our generation has to be out there achieving," says Scott Birnbaum, twenty-five, who is the chief accountant for TIC United Corp., a holding company in Dallas.

Birnbaum graduated from the University of Texas in 1984, where, he says, "For me, the whole career-oriented thing kicked in." A native Texan with a broad drawl, he lives in the Greenville section of the city, an area populated largely by young singles. His apartment is comfortably roomy, not terribly well appointed. He shakes his head amiably as he points to the television set propped on a beer cooler. "What do I need furniture for?" he says. "Most of my time is taken up going to work."

Confident in himself professionally, Birnbaum was one of very few interviewees who spoke frankly about the personal cost of career success. Many speculated that they'll be worried if, in their thirties, they haven't begun to settle their love lives; this was more true of women than men. But Birnbaum confesses a desire to marry now. "It's kind of lonely being single," he says. "I'd hate to find myself successful at thirty without a family. Maybe once I'm married and have children, that might make being successful careerwise less important."

The problem, he goes on, is the collective outlook he's part and parcel of. "Here's how we think," he says. "Get to this point, move on. Get to that point, move on. Acquire, acquire. Career, career. We're all afraid to slow down for fear of missing out on something. That extends to your social life as well. You go out on a date and you're thinking, 'Hell, is there someone better for me?' I know how terrible that sounds but it seems to be my problem. Most of my peers are in the same position. Men and women. I tell you, its tough out there right now."

When I returned to New York, I called Alex de Gramont, whom I'd been saving to interview last. I've known Alex for a long time, since he was a gawky and curious high school student and I was his teacher. Handsome now, gentle-looking, he's a literary sort, prone to attractive gloom and a certain lack of perspective. He once told me that his paradigm of a romantic, his role model, was Heathcliff, the mad, doomed passion-monger from Emily Brontë's *Wuthering Heights*.

A year out of Wesleyan University in Middletown, Conn., Alex has reasons to be hopeful. His book-length senior thesis about Albert Camus has been accepted for publication, and on the strength of it, he has applied to four graduate programs in comparative literature. But he's unenthusiastic, and he has applied to law schools, too. In the meantime, he is living with his parents in New Jersey.

He tells me that last summer he went to West Germany in pursuit of a woman he'd met when he was in college. He expected to live there with her, but he was back in this country in a couple of weeks. "Camus has a line," Alex says, " 'Love can burn or love can last. It can't do both.' " Like Benjamin Braddock, Alex is a little worried about his future.

Dustin Hoffman is forty-nine. I'm thirty-three. Both of us are doing pretty well. Alex, at twenty-three, confesses to considerable unease. "Every minute I'm not accomplishing something, I feel is wasted," he says, sort of miserably. "I feel a lot of pressure to decide what to do with my life. I'm a romantic, but these are very unromantic times."

—1987

What are your reactions to and questions about this work? The following questions may help provoke some ideas.

Probing the Work

1. What are Weber's conclusions about the present generation of young college graduates, and what kinds of considerations and decisions seem most important to them?

Identifying Issues

2. How do your own attitudes match up with Weber's conclusions? What might you have to add to, or eliminate from, Weber's essay? Has anything changed since this essay was published in 1987?

ERNEST HEMINGWAY

Hills Like White Elephants

Ernest Hemingway (1899–1961) was born in Oak Park, Illinois. After graduating from high school he worked on the Kansas City Star, *but left to serve as a World War I volunteer ambulance driver in Italy, where he was wounded. He then worked home and abroad for the Toronto* Star, *but soon gave up journalism for fiction. In the 1920s he lived overseas and published a collection of short stories,* In Our Time *(1925) and* The Sun Also Rises *(1926). In 1954 he received the Nobel Prize for Literature, but in 1961, depressed by a sense of failing power, he took his own life. His works include* A Farewell to Arms *(1929),* For Whom the Bell Tolls *(1940), and* The Old Man and the Sea *(1952).*

The hills across the valley of the Ebro were long and white. On this side there was no shade and no trees and the station was between two lines of rails in the sun. Close against the side of the station there was the warm shadow of the building and a curtain, made of strings of bamboo beads, hung across the open door into the bar, to keep out flies. The American and the girl with him sat at a table in the shade, outside the building. It was very hot and the express from Barcelona would come in forty minutes. It stopped at this junction for two minutes and went on to Madrid.

"What should we drink?" the girl asked. She had taken off her hat and put it on the table.

"It's pretty hot," the man said.

"Let's drink beer."

"Dos cervezas," the man said into the curtain.

"Big ones?" a woman asked from the doorway.

"Yes. Two big ones."

The woman brought two glasses of beer and two felt pads. She put the felt pads and the beer glasses on the table and looked at the man and the girl. The girl was looking off to the line of hills. They were white in the sun and the country was brown and dry.

"They look like white elephants," she said.

"I've never seen one," the man drank his beer.

"No, you wouldn't have."

"I might have," the man said. "Just because you say I wouldn't have doesn't prove anything."

The girl looked at the bead curtain. "They've painted something on it," she said. "What does it say?"

"Anis del Toro. It's a drink."

"Could we try it?"

The man called "Listen" through the curtain. The woman came out from the bar.

"Four reales."

"We want two Anis del Toro."

"With water?"

"Do you want it with water?"

"I don't know," the girl said. "Is it good with water?"

"It's all right."

"You want them with water?" asked the woman.

"Yes, with water."

"It tastes like licorice," the girl said and put the glass down.

"That's the way with everything."

"Yes," said the girl. "Everything tastes of licorice. Especially all the things you've waited so long for, like absinthe."

"Oh, cut it out."

"You started it," the girl said. "I was being amused. I was having a fine time."

"Well, let's try and have a fine time."

"All right. I was trying. I said the mountains looked like white elephants. Wasn't that bright?"

"That was bright."

"I wanted to try this new drink. That's all we do, isn't it—look at things and try new drinks?"

"I guess so."

The girl looked across at the hills.

"They're lovely hills," she said. "They don't really look like white elephants. I just meant the coloring of their skin through the trees."

"Should we have another drink?"

"All right."

The warm wind blew the bead curtain against the table.

"The beer's nice and cool," the man said.

"It's lovely," the girl said.

"It's really an awfully simple operation, Jig," the man said. "It's not really an operation at all."

The girl looked at the ground the table legs rested on.

"I know you wouldn't mind it, Jig. It's really not anything. It's just to let the air in."

The girl did not say anything.

"I'll go with you and I'll stay with you all the time. They just let the air in and then it's all perfectly natural."

"Then what will we do afterward?"

"We'll be fine afterward. Just like we were before."

"What makes you think so?"

"That's the only thing that bothers us. It's the only thing that's made us unhappy."

The girl looked at the bead curtain, put her hand out and took hold of two of the strings of beads.

"And you think then we'll be all right and be happy."

"I know we will. You don't have to be afraid. I've known lots of people that have done it."

"So have I," said the girl. "And afterward they were all so happy."

"Well," the man said, "if you don't want to you don't have to. I wouldn't have you do it if you didn't want to. But I know it's perfectly simple."

"And you really want to?"

"I think it's the best thing to do. But I don't want you to do it if you don't really want to."

"And if I do it you'll be happy and things will be like they were and you'll love me?"

"I love you now. You know I love you."

"I know. But if I do it, then it will be nice again if I say things are like white elephants, and you'll like it?"

"I'll love it. I love it now but I just can't think about it. You know how I get when I worry."

"If I do it you won't ever worry?"

"I won't worry about that because it's perfectly simple."

"Then I'll do it. Because I don't care about me."

"What do you mean?"

"I don't care about me."

"Well, I care about you."

"Oh, yes. But I don't care about me. And I'll do it and then everything will be fine."

"I don't want you to do it if you feel that way."

The girl stood up and walked to the end of the station. Across, on the other side, were fields of grain and trees along the banks of the Ebro. Far away, beyond the river, were mountains. The shadow of a cloud moved across the field of grain and she saw the river through the trees.

"And we could have all this," she said. "And we could have everything and every day we make it more impossible."

"What did you say?"

"I said we could have everything."

"We can have everything."

"No, we can't."

"We can have the whole world."

"No, we can't."

"We can go everywhere."

"No, we can't. It isn't ours any more."

"It's ours."

"No, it isn't. And once they take it away, you never get it back."

"But they haven't taken it away."

"We'll wait and see."

"Come on back in the shade," he said. "You mustn't feel that way."

"I don't feel any way," the girl said. "I just know things."

"I don't want you to do anything that you don't want to do——"

"Nor that isn't good for me," she said. "I know. Could we have another beer?"

"All right. But you've got to realize——"

"I realize," the girl said. "Can't we maybe stop talking?"

They sat down at the table and the girl looked across at the hills on the dry side of the valley and the man looked at her and at the table.

"You've got to realize," he said, "that I don't want you to do it if you don't want to. I'm perfectly willing to go through with it if it means anything to you."

"Doesn't it mean anything to you? We could get along."

"Of course it does. But I don't want anybody but you. I don't want any one else. And I know it's perfectly simple."

"Yes, you know it's perfectly simple."

"It's all right for you to say that, but I do know it."

"Would you do something for me now?"

"I'd do anything for you."

"Would you please please please please please please please stop talking?"

He did not say anything but looked at the bags against the wall of the station. There were labels on them from all the hotels where they had spent nights.

"But I don't want you to," he said, "I don't care anything about it."

"I'll scream," the girl said.

The woman came out through the curtains with two glasses of beer and put them down on the damp felt pads. "The train comes in five minutes," she said.

"What did she say?" asked the girl.

"That the train comes in five minutes."

The girl smiled brightly at the woman, to thank her.

"I'd better take the bags over to the other side of the station," the man said. She smiled at him.

"All right. Then come back and we'll finish the beer."

He picked up the two heavy bags and carried them around the station to the other tracks. He looked up the tracks but could not see the train. Coming back, he walked through the barroom, where people waiting for the train were drinking. He drank an Anis at the bar and looked at the people. They were all waiting reasonably for the train. He went out through the bead curtain. She was sitting at the table and smiled at him. "Do you feel better?" he asked.

"I feel fine," she said. "There's nothing wrong with me. I feel fine."

—1927

What are your reactions to and questions about this work? The following questions may help provoke some ideas.

Probing the Work

1. To what degree is this story's ending, and the relationship between its two main characters, *ambiguous*? What are some of the elements of this story (*point of view, character, theme,* for example) that contribute to its *ambiguity* (see page 79)?

Identifying Issues

2. What are the problems in this relationship, judging from the dialogue you read here? How accurately does it reflect relationships you know of?

JAMES BALDWIN

Guilt, Desire and Love

*James Baldwin (1924–1987) was born in Harlem and lived as a young man in New Jersey and in the Greenwich Village section of New York City. In 1948 he moved to Paris; while in France and Switzerland he published two novels—*Go Tell It on the Mountain *(1953) and* Giovanni's Room *(1956), the latter a work that illustrates coming to terms with homosexuality—and a collection of essays,* Notes of a Native Son *(1955). He returned to America in 1957 and continued to publish (*The Fire Next Time *in 1963), travel, and teach until his death in France. This poem is from his collection,* Jimmy's Blues *(1983).*

At the dark street corner
where Guilt and Desire
are attempting to stare
each other down
(presently, one of them
will light a cigarette
and glance in the direction
of the abandoned warehouse)
Love came slouching along,
an exploded silence
standing a little apart
but visible anyway
in the yellow, silent, steaming light,
while Guilt and Desire wrangled,
trying not to be overheard
by this trespasser.

Each time Desire looked towards Love,
hoping to find a witness,

Guilt shouted louder
and shook them hips
and the fire of the cigarette
threatened to burn the warehouse down.

Desire actually started across the street,
time after time,
to hear what Love might have to say,
but Guilt flagged down a truckload
of other people
and knelt down in the middle of the street
and, while the truckload of other people
looked away, and swore that they
didn't see nothing
and couldn't testify nohow,
and Love moved out of sight,
Guilt accomplished upon the standing body
of Desire
the momentary, inflammatory soothing
which seals their union
(for ever?)
and creates a mighty traffic problem.

—1983

What are your reactions to and questions about this work? The following questions may help provoke some ideas.

Probing the Work

1. In this *allegory* (see page 78), what qualities are given to each "character"—Guilt, Desire, and Love—and why?

Identifying Issues

2. How is this scene described by Baldwin played out in a typical relationship? In your relationships?

SHARON OLDS

Sex Without Love

Sharon Olds (b. 1942) was born in San Francisco and educated at Stanford and Columbia. Her books of poetry include Satan Says *(1980),* The Dead and the Living *(1982),* The Gold Cell *(1987), and* The Father *(1992).*

How do they do it, the ones who make love
without love? Beautiful as dancers,

gliding over each other like ice-skaters
over the ice, fingers hooked
inside each other's bodies, faces
red as steak, wine, wet as the
children at birth whose mothers are going to
give them away. How do they come to the
come to the come to the God come to the
still waters, and not love
the one who came there with them, light
rising slowly as steam off their joined
skin? These are the true religious,
the purists, the pros, the ones who will not
accept a false Messiah, love the
priest instead of the God. They do not
mistake the lover for their own pleasure,
they are like great runners: they know they are alone
with the road surface, the cold, the wind,
the fit of their shoes, their over-all cardiovascular health—just factors, like the partner
in the bed, and not the truth, which is the
single body alone in the universe
against its own best time.

—*1975*

What are your reactions to and questions about this work? The following questions may help provoke some ideas.

Probing the Work

1. Explain the *metaphors* (see page 68) of the dancers and runners. Why do you think Olds chose these metaphors?

Identifying Issues

2. Can you think of any other metaphors she could have used, with either positive or negative implications?

MARGE PIERCY

To Have Without Holding

Marge Piercy (b. 1936) was born in Detroit and was the first member of her family to attend college. After earning a B.A. at the University of Michigan and an M.A. from Northwestern, she moved to Chicago, where she worked at odd jobs while writing novels and protesting the Vietnam War. Since her move to Massachusetts in 1970 she has become a prolific and influential writer of poetry, short stories, essays, and novels. She is currently a poetry editor of Tikkun *magazine.*

Learning to love differently is hard,
love with the hands wide open, love
with the doors banging on their hinges,
the cupboard unlocked, the wind
roaring and whimpering in the rooms
rustling the sheets and snapping the blinds
that thwack like rubber bands
in an open palm.

It hurts to love wide open
stretching the muscles that feel
as if they are made of wet plaster,
then of blunt knives, then
of sharp knives.

It hurts to thwart the reflexes
of grab, of clutch; to love and let
go again and again. It pesters to remember
the lover who is not in the bed,
to hold back what is owed to the work
that gutters like a candle in a cave
without air, to love consciously,
conscientiously, concretely, constructively.

I can't do it, you say it's killing
me, but you thrive, you glow
on the street like a neon raspberry,
You float and sail, a helium balloon
bright bachelor's button blue and bobbing
on the cold and hot winds of our breath,
as we make and unmake in passionate
diastole and systole the rhythm
of our unbound bonding, to have
and not to hold, to love
with minimized malice, hunger
and anger moment by moment balanced.

—1980

What are your reactions to and questions about this work? The following questions may help provoke some ideas.

Probing the Work

1. How does Percy express, metaphorically and stylistically, the complexities and varieties of emotion that make up modern love?

Identifying Issues

2. What does the phrase, "love with minimized malice" mean to you? Have you ever loved in that way? How closely related are love and malice?

MURIEL RUKEYSER

Looking at Each Other

Muriel Rukeyser (1913–1980) was born in New York City. In her distinguished career she published 14 volumes of poetry (her Collected Poems *was published in 1978), two biographies, essays, children's books, a play, and translations of verse (including that of Bertolt Brecht and Octavio Paz). She was a tireless activist, fighting against the exploitation of blue-collar workers, discrimination against blacks, the Vietnam War, and nuclear power.*

Yes, we were looking at each other
Yes, we knew each other very well
Yes, we had made love with each other many times
Yes, we had heard music together
Yes, we had gone to the sea together
Yes, we had cooked and eaten together
Yes, we had laughed often day and night
Yes, we fought violence and knew violence
Yes, we hated the inner and outer oppression
Yes, that day we were looking at each other
Yes, we saw the sunlight pouring down
Yes, the corner of the table was between us
Yes, bread and flowers were on the table
Yes, our eyes saw each other's eyes
Yes, our mouths saw each other's mouth
Yes, our breasts saw each other's breasts
Yes, our bodies entire saw each other
Yes, it was beginning in each
Yes, it threw waves across our lives
Yes, the pulses were becoming very strong
Yes, the beating became very delicate
Yes, the calling   the arousal
Yes, the arriving   the coming
Yes, there it was for both entire
Yes, we were looking at each other

—1973

What are your reactions to and questions about this work? The following questions may help provoke some ideas.

Probing the Work

1. Why does the poet repeat the word "Yes" and the line, "Yes, we were looking at each other"? What is the effect of such repetition? How does the meaning of the word or line change over the course of the poem?

Identifying Issues

2. How do you characterize the desire depicted here? What might distinguish it from more conventional descriptions of a love relationship?

TESS GALLAGHER

The Hug

Born in Port Angeles, Washington, Tess Gallagher (b. 1932) studied at the Universities of Washington and Iowa before publishing her first book, Stepping Outside *(1974). Married to Raymond Carver (see page 447) until his death in 1988, Gallagher has taught at a number of colleges and published three more books of poems.*

A woman is reading a poem on the street
and another woman stops to listen. We stop too,
with our arms around each other. The poem
is being read and listened to out here
in the open. Behind us
no one is entering or leaving the houses.

Suddenly a hug comes over me and I'm
giving it to you, like a variable star shooting light
off to make itself comfortable, then
subsiding. I finish but keep on holding
you. A man walks up to us and we know he hasn't
come out of nowhere, but if he could, he
would have. He looks homeless because of how
he needs. "Can I have one of those?" he asks you,
and I feel you nod. I'm surprised,
surprised you don't tell him how
it is—that I'm yours, only
yours, etc., exclusive as a nose to
its face. Love—that's what we're talking about, love
that nabs you with "for me
only" and holds on.

So I walk over to him and put my
arms around him and try to
hug him like I mean it. He's got an overcoat on

so thick I can't feel
him past it. I'm starting the hug
and thinking, "How big a hug is this supposed to be?
How long shall I hold this hug?" Already
we could be eternal, his arms falling over my
shoulders, my hands not
meeting behind his back, he is so big!

I put my head into his chest and snuggle
in. I lean into him. I lean my blood and my wishes
into him. He stands for it. This is his
and he's starting to give it back so well I know he's
getting it. This hug. So truly, so tenderly
we stop having arms and I don't know if
my lover has walked away or what, or
if the woman is still reading the poem, or the houses—
what about them?—the houses.

Clearly, a little permission is a dangerous thing.
But when you hug someone you want it
to be a masterpiece of connection, the way the button
on his coat will leave the imprint of
a planet in my cheek
when I walk away. When I try to find some place
to go back to.

—1984

What are your reactions to and questions about this work? The following questions may help provoke some ideas.

Probing the Work

1. Describe both the physical and symbolic dimensions of the hug.

Identifying Issues

2. What do you think about the poet's conclusion that "a little permission is a dangerous thing"? What does it mean in the context of the poem, and in your own experiences with relationships?

TONY KUSHNER

Angels in America, Part One: Millenium Approaches (excerpt)

Tony Kushner (b. 1956) was born in Manhattan and grew up in Lake Charles, Louisiana. He currently resides in Brooklyn. His plays include A Bright Room Called

Day, *Part Two of* Angels in America, Perestroika *(1993), and* Slavs *(1994).* Angels in America, Part One: Millenium Approaches *(1992), excerpted below, won a number of awards and ended a successful run on Broadway in late 1994.*

Cast of Characters:

JOSEPH PORTER PITT, *chief clerk for Justice Theodore Wilson of the Federal Court of Appeals, Second Circuit.*

HARPER AMATY PITT, *Joe's wife, an agoraphobic with a mild Valium addiction.*

LOUIS IRONSON, *a word processor working for the Second Circuit Court of Appeals.*

PRIOR WALTER, *Louis's boyfriend. Occasionally works as a club designer or caterer, otherwise lives very modestly but with great style off a small trust fund.*

Background: JOE, *a Mormon from Utah working in New York, has been offered a job at the Attorney General's office in Washington by the influential lawyer Roy Cohn.* JOE *is confused by his sexual identity.* HARPER, *confused by her husband's lack of affection and his late-night wanderings, has been reverting to her Valium pills for relief.*

PRIOR*'s health is deteriorating because he has contracted the AIDS virus; he has no hang-ups about his sexual identity.* LOUIS, *however, seems to adapt his sexual identity to his surroundings, oscillating between passing as heterosexual and behaving in an overtly homosexual manner, as when he flirts with* JOE *at work or in the park outside the courthouse.* LOUIS, *who has just buried his grandmother, is having difficulty confronting death, and with remaining loyal to* PRIOR *during the most agonizing trial of* PRIOR*'s life.*

LOUIS *and* JOE *eventually find solace in each other's company: both are steeped in self-loathing and guilt for failing in their romantic commitments, and both are confused about the public expression of their sexual identities.*

In the following "split scene" (two settings are on stage at once, and each couple does not hear the other's dialog), the two key relationships of the play begin to fall apart, simultaneously.

Scene 8

That night. Split scene: HARPER *and* JOE *at home;* PRIOR *and* LOUIS *in bed.*

HARPER: Where were you?
JOE: Out.
HARPER: Where?
JOE: Just out. Thinking.

HARPER: It's late.

JOE: I had a lot to think about.

HARPER: I burned dinner.

JOE: Sorry.

HARPER: Not my dinner. My dinner was fine. Your dinner. I put it back in the oven and turned everything up as high as it could go and I watched till it burned black. It's still hot. Very hot. Want it?

JOE: You didn't have to do that.

HARPER: I know. It just seemed like the kind of thing a mentally deranged sex-starved pill-popping housewife would do.

JOE: Uh huh.

HARPER: So I did it. Who knows anymore what I have to do?

JOE: How many pills?

HARPER: A bunch. Don't change the subject.

JOE: I won't talk to you when you . . .

HARPER: No. No. Don't do that! I'm . . . I'm fine, pills are not the problem, not our problem, I WANT TO KNOW WHERE YOU'VE BEEN! I WANT TO KNOW WHAT'S GOING ON!

JOE: Going on with what? The job?

HARPER: Not the job.

JOE: I said I need more time.

HARPER: Not the job!

JOE: Mr. Cohn, I talked to him on the phone, he said I had to hurry . . .

HARPER: Not the . . .

JOE: But I can't get you to talk sensibly about anything so . . .

HARPER: SHUT UP!

JOE: Then what?

HARPER: Stick to the subject.

JOE: I don't know what that is. You have something you want to ask me? Ask me. Go.

HARPER: I . . . can't. I'm scared of you.

JOE: I'm tired, I'm going to bed.

HARPER: Tell me without making me ask. Please.

JOE: This is crazy, I'm not . . .

HARPER: When you come through the door at night your face is never exactly the way I remembered it. I get surprised by something . . . mean and hard about the way you look. Even the weight of you in the bed at night, the way you breathe in your sleep seems unfamiliar.

You terrify me.

JOE: *(Cold)* I know who you are.

HARPER: Yes. I'm the enemy. That's easy. That doesn't change.

You think you're the only one who hates sex; I do; I hate it with you; I do. I dream that you batter away at me till all my joints come apart, like wax, and I fall into pieces. It's like a punishment. It was wrong of me to marry you. I knew you . . . *(She stops herself)* It's a sin, and it's killing us both.

JOE: I can always tell when you've taken pills because it makes you red-faced and sweaty and frankly that's very often why I don't want to . . .

HARPER: Because . . .

JOE: Well, you aren't pretty. Not like this.

HARPER: I have something to ask you.

JOE: Then ASK! ASK! What in hell are you . . .

HARPER: Are you a homo?

(Pause)

Are you? If you try to walk out right now I'll put your dinner back in the oven and turn it up so high the whole building will fill with smoke and everyone in it will asphyxiate. So help me God I will.

Now answer the question.

JOE: What if I . . .

(Small pause.)

HARPER: Then tell me, please. And we'll see.

JOE: No. I'm not.

I don't see what difference it makes.

LOUIS: Jews don't have any clear textual guide to the afterlife; even that it exists. I don't think much about it. I see it as a perpetual rainy Thursday afternoon in March. Dead leaves.

PRIOR: Eeeugh. Very Greco-Roman.

LOUIS: Well for us it's not the verdict that counts, it's the act of judgment. That's why I could never be a lawyer. In court all that matters is the verdict.

PRIOR: You could never be a lawyer because you are oversexed. You're too distracted.

LOUIS: Not distracted; *ab*stracted. I'm trying to make a point:

PRIOR: Namely:

LOUIS: It's the judge in his or her chambers, weighing, books open, pondering the evidence, ranging freely over categories: good, evil, innocent, guilty; the judge in the chamber of circumspection, not the judge on the bench with the gavel. The shaping of the law, not its execution.

PRIOR: The point, dear, the point . . .

LOUIS: That it should be the questions and shape of a life, its total complexity gathered, arranged and considered, which matters in the end, not some stamp of salvation or damnation which disperses all the complexity in some unsatisfying little decision—the balancing of the scales . . .

PRIOR: I like this; very zen; it's . . . reassuringly incomprehensible and useless. We who are about to die thank you.

LOUIS: You are not about to die.

PRIOR: It's not going well, really . . . two new lesions. My leg hurts. There's protein in my urine, the doctor says, but who knows what the fuck that portends. Anyway it shouldn't be there, the protein. My butt is chapped from diarrhea and yesterday I shat blood.

LOUIS: I really hate this. You don't tell me . . .

PRIOR: You get too upset, I wind up comforting you. It's easier . . .

LOUIS: Oh thanks.

PRIOR: If it's bad I'll tell you.

LOUIS: Shitting blood sounds bad to me.

PRIOR: And I'm telling you.

LOUIS: And I'm handling it.

PRIOR: Tell me some more about justice.

LOUIS: I *am* handling it.

PRIOR: Well Louis you win Trooper of the Month.

*(*LOUIS *starts to cry.)*

PRIOR: I take it back. You aren't Trooper of the Month.
This isn't working . . .
Tell me some more about justice.

LOUIS: You are not about to die.

PRIOR: Justice . . .

LOUIS: . . . is an immensity, a confusing vastness. Justice is God.
Prior?

PRIOR: Hmmm?

LOUIS: You love me.

PRIOR: Yes.

LOUIS: What if I walked out on this? Would you hate me forever?

*(*PRIOR *kisses* LOUIS *on the forehead.)*

PRIOR: Yes.

JOE: I think we ought to pray. Ask God for help. Ask him together . . .

HARPER: God won't talk to me. I have to make up people to talk to me.

JOE: You have to keep asking.

HARPER: I forgot the question.
Oh yeah. God, is my husband a . . .

JOE: *(Scary)* Stop it. Stop it. I'm warning you.

Does it make any difference? That I might be one thing deep within, no matter how wrong or ugly that thing is, so long as I have fought, with everything I have, to kill it. What do you want from me? What do you want from me, Harper? More than that? For God's sake, there's nothing left, I'm a shell. There's nothing left to kill.

As long as my behavior is what I know it has to be. Decent. Correct. That alone in the eyes of God.

HARPER: No, no, not that, that's Utah talk, Mormon talk, I hate it, Joe, tell me, say it . . .

JOE: All I will say is that I am a very good man who has worked very hard to become good and you want to destroy that. You want to destroy me, but I am not going to let you do that.

(Pause.)

HARPER: I'm going to have a baby.

JOE: Liar.

HARPER: You liar.

A baby born addicted to pills. A baby who does not dream but who hallucinates, who stares up at us with big mirror eyes and who does not know who we are.

(Pause.)

JOE: Are you really . . .

HARPER: No. Yes. No. Yes. Get away from me.

Now we both have a secret.

PRIOR: One of my ancestors was a ship's captain who made money bringing whale oil to Europe and returning with immigrants—Irish mostly, packed in tight, so many dollars per head. The last ship he captained foundered off the coast of Nova Scotia in a winter tempest and sank to the bottom. He went down with the ship—la Grande Geste—but his crew took seventy women and kids in the ship's only longboat, this big, open rowboat, and when the weather got too rough, and they thought the boat was overcrowded, the crew started lifting people up and hurling them into the sea. Until they got the ballast right. They walked up and down the longboat, eyes to the waterline, and when the boat rode low in the water they'd grab the nearest passenger and throw them into the sea. The boat was leaky, see; seventy people; they arrived in Halifax with nine people on board.

LOUIS: Jesus.

PRIOR: I think about that story a lot now. People in a boat, waiting, terrified, while implacable, unsmiling men, irresistibly strong, seize . . . maybe the person next to you, maybe you, and with no warning at all, with time only for a quick intake of air you are pitched into freezing, turbulent water and salt and darkness to drown.

I like your cosmology, baby. While time is running out I find myself drawn to anything that's suspended, that lacks an ending—but it seems to me that it lets you off scot-free.

LOUIS: What do you mean?
PRIOR: No judgment, no guilt or responsibility.
LOUIS: For me.
PRIOR: For anyone. It was an editorial "you."
LOUIS: Please get better. Please.
    Please don't get any sicker.

—1992

What are your reactions to and questions about this work? The following questions may help provoke some ideas.

Probing the Work

1. Why does Louis beg Prior not to "get any sicker" (p. 627)? What are the implications, for Louis, of Prior's deteriorating health?
2. Describe the quality and level of communication between Harper and Joe. What could they have done in their past to have prevented this moment from happening?

Identifying Issues

3. How is the love and commitment of both couples being tested here? What are the exterior and interior forces that are affecting their relationships? What obstacles in our society prevent any two people from freely loving each other?

WRITING ASSIGNMENT SEQUENCE (CONTINUED FROM PAGE 601)

4. Making Connections

Select one of the following questions and write an informal response in which you connect your own ideas with those conveyed in the works of this cluster, and/or make connections among the works themselves.

A. What works in this cluster illustrate some of the generational conflicts that you described in your in-class writing and discussion?
B. How do the works of this cluster describe a loss of traditional romance? What seem to be the authors' views of the advantages and disadvantages of that loss?
C. Categorize the various types of romantic love that are illustrated in these works. What other types can you think of?

5. Putting It All Together

Write an essay that combines what you think about the topic *Guilt, Desire, and Love* with what you now understand about the readings.

- Collect your informal writing, notes, and reading-journal entries on this topic and decide what will be the focus of your essay.
- Outline your essay. Select the literary passages and personal details you might use to illustrate and support your main focus.
- Write a draft of your essay in which you bring together what you think about the subject with what you understand about the readings. Try to include in your draft one or more literary terms.
- Share what you've written with your classmates and instructor, then revise it according to their recommendations.

Writing Tip: Quoting Selectively

Once you have a particular focus for your paper, return to the texts you will be discussing and pick out appropriate passages that illustrate your "nutshell sentence." Select your quotations carefully, and edit them so that (1) they do not dominate your essay; (2) you do not quote passages that have nothing to do with the focus of your essay; and (3) each quotation, when appropriate, is put into a context—set up by an introduction, and succeeded by an explanation.

Note how Sara sets up her quotation, then adds an explanation afterwards to make her point clear:

> Although the hug was at first innocent, it has now become a new experience; she has never felt this way before. The hug is portrayed as an ethereal, unworldly event that becomes "a masterpiece of connection, the way the button / on his coat will leave the imprint of / a planet in my cheek" (621). This is not only "larger-than-life," it is an almost supra-natural occurrence, so powerful that at its completion the speaker seems momentarily lost.

CrossClusters

In your paper you might want to consider how the following works located elsewhere in this book depict guilt, desire, and love:

- Stephen Dunn, "Tenderness" (p. 121)
- Joyce Carol Oates, "Where Are You Going, Where Have You Been?" (p. 198)
- Lorraine Hansberry, *A Raisin in the Sun* (p. 253)

- Nathaniel Hawthorne, "The Birth-mark" (p. 633)
- Kate Chopin, "The Storm" (p. 649)
- Liz Rosenberg, "Married Love" (p. 658)
- Robert Browning, "Porphyria's Lover" (p. 840)
- Shiga Naoya, "Han's Crime" (p. 859)
- Isabel Allende, "And of Clay Are We Created" (p. 996)

19

MARRIED LOVE

WRITING ASSIGNMENT SEQUENCE

1. Thinking About . . . Marriage

Brainstorming: Jot down all the words that come to mind when you write down the word *marriage*. What makes a good marriage? What are some of the causes of marital discord?

2. Enacting the Topic

Conduct a survey of couples you know to find out what has made their marriages successful or unsuccessful. What can you conclude about the ingredients of a successful marriage?

COMMUNICATION

3. Responding to the Readings

As you read the works in this cluster, jot down, in your response journals, questions you have about the works, and comment on passages you find provocative or puzzling. Consider the questions following each reading for journal writing and prepare to discuss your reactions in class.

CLUSTER ESSAY

ANNA QUINDLEN

Married

Anna Quindlen went to Barnard College and worked her way up at The New York Times, *from City Hall reporter to Pulitzer Prize-winning columnist. Collections of her work include* Object Lessons *and* Living Out Loud. *Following the success of her second novel,* One True Thing *(1994), Quindlen decided to leave the* Times *and devote her time to writing fiction and raising her children.*

Each night for the last week, as I have gone out to walk the dogs or leave the trash at the curb, the boy and girl have been shadows in the doorway of the house next door. Even when it was raining, lightning bisecting the sky, they were there, entangled in one of those kisses that last forever, that end only when the oxygen supply gives out. One night the boy spoke as the dogs sniffed at the steps below. "Do you know how much I love this girl?" he asked, a rhetorical boast to a middle-aged stranger.

"Oh, God," I said, tugging on the leashes, and though the lovers might have thought my response indicated disapproval, it was really the shock of recognition, sharp and silver as the lightning. I remember being in love like this. Entering into a state more like a tropical disease than a relationship, listening to one catchy piece of bubble-gum music over and over again and getting the same odd feeling in the stomach and the chest. When I was in high school, the song was by the Beach Boys, "Wouldn't It Be Nice": "Though it's gonna make it that much better/When we can say goodnight and stay together." The big payoff. Not so much sex, at least for the girls, as a kind of mythical domesticity: napkins and matching place mats, unlimited kissing, no adults, flowers every day. What our parents referred to as playing house.

It's getting on to ten years that I've been married. I'm not sure when I realized that reality was going to be both something less and something much more. Luckily many of us know this before we marry, or there would be even more disasters than we now suffer through, many more people packing away an expensive wedding album in some corner of the basement where, it is hoped, it will mildew.

When I was younger, I tended to fall in love with just one thing: a kind of bravado, a certain smile. (The girl in the doorway, I am convinced, has fallen for blond hair and a crooked grin.) I even fell in love with a certain set of bony shoulders in a sport jacket years ago. But unlike a lot of my friends, who went through more than a few Mr. Wrongs and have now settled down with Mr. Maybe, I married the person inside the sport jacket. And I held on like a dog with a bone to a love affair between a girl whose idea of awesome responsibility was a psych midterm and a boy who painted his dorm room black, long after that boy and girl were gone. I held onto what has been going on in that doorway long past the time when I was really too old to believe in magic.

Truth is, I still believe in magic, and it's still there, although there's no point denying that it is occasionally submerged beneath a welter of cereal bowls, dirty shirts, late nights, early mornings, and all the other everyday things that bubble-gum music never reflects. But what I didn't know about marriage, the less magical parts of it, has become perhaps more important to me. Now we have history as well as chemistry. An enormous part of my past does not exist without my husband. An enormous part of my present, too. I still feel somehow that things do not really happen to me unless I have told them to him. I don't mean this nonsense about being best friends, which I have never been able to cotton to; our relationship is too judgmental, too demanding, too prickly to have much in common with the quiet waters of friendship. Like emotional acupuncturists, we know just where to put the needle. And do.

But we are each other's family. And while I know people who have cut their families loose, who think them insignificant or too troublesome to be part of their lives, I am not one of those people. I came late to the discovery that we would be related by marriage. I once made a fool of myself in front of a friend in the emergency room of a small resort hospital after my husband's stomach and a bad fried clam had had an unfortunate meeting. "Are either of you related to him?" the nurse asked, and we both shook our heads until our friend prodded me gently in the side. "Oh, well, I'm his wife," I said.

There is something so settled and stodgy about turning a great romance into next of kin on an emergency room form, and something so soothing and special, too. I suppose that is what I find so dreadful about divorce; lovers are supposed to leave you in the lurch, but your family is supposed to stick by you forever. "You can pick your friends, but you can't pick your relations," the folksy folks always say. Ah, but in this one case you can. You just don't realize it at the time.

What does it mean that I do not envy the two of them, standing in the doorway, locked together like Romeo and Juliet in the tomb? I suppose when I was their age I would have assumed it meant that I was old and desiccated. But of course what has really happened is that I know the difference now between dedication and infatuation.

That doesn't mean I don't still get an enormous kick out of infatuation: the exciting ephemera, the punch in the stomach, the adrenaline to the heart. At a cocktail party the other night I looked across a crowded room and was taken by a stranger, in half profile, a handsome, terribly young-looking man with a halo of backlighted curls. And then he turned and I realized that it was the stranger I am married to, the beneficiary on my insurance policy, the sport jacket, the love of my life.

—1988

What are your reactions to and questions about this work? The following questions may help provoke some ideas.

Probing the Work

1. Quindlen speaks of marriage as a mix of "history as well as chemistry," "dedication and infatuation." Explain what she means by each word. How important is each of these ingredients?

Identifying Issues

2. To what extent does Quindlen describe what *you* want in a marriage? What other elements might you add?

NATHANIEL HAWTHORNE

The Birth-mark

Nathaniel Hawthorne (1804–1864) was born and lived much of his life in Salem, Massachusetts. After graduating from Bowdoin College he lived at his mother's house, anonymously publishing short stories (first collected in Twice-Told Tales, *1837). In the late 1830s Hawthorne fell in love with, and in 1842 married, Sophia Peabody. By their own account, and that of most biographers, theirs was a happy marriage, especially for the first few years they spent in Concord. The literary product of that period, and of Hawthorne's association with Concord neighbors Ralph W. Emerson and Henry Thoreau, is the collection* Mosses from an Old Manse *(1846), which includes "The Birth-mark." From 1850 to 1853 Hawthorne published an extraordinary number of books: three novels (including* The Scarlet Letter*), three collections of stories, and a campaign biography. But in the last decade of his life he published just two more, leaving several unfinished manuscripts at his death.*

In the latter part of the last century, there lived a man of science—an eminent proficient in every branch of natural philosophy—who, not long before our story opens, had made experience of a spiritual affinity, more attractive than any chemical one. He had left his laboratory to the care of an assistant, cleared his fine countenance from the furnace-smoke, washed the stain of acids from his fingers, and persuaded a beautiful woman to become his wife. In those days, when the comparatively recent discovery of electricity, and other kindred mysteries of nature, seemed to open paths into the region of miracle, it was not unusual for the love of science to rival the love of woman, in its depth and absorbing energy. The higher intellect, the imagination, the spirit, and even the heart, might all find their congenial aliment in pursuits which, as some of their ardent votaries believed, would ascend from one step of powerful intelligence to another, until the philosopher should lay his hand on the secret of creative force, and perhaps make new worlds for himself. We know not whether Aylmer possessed this degree of faith in man's ultimate control over nature. He had devoted himself, however, too unreservedly to scientific studies, ever to be weaned from them by any second passion. His love for his young wife might prove the stronger of the two; but it could only be by intertwining itself with his love of science, and uniting the strength of the latter to its own.

Such a union accordingly took place, and was attended with truly remarkable consequences, and a deeply impressive moral. One day, very soon after their marriage, Aylmer sat gazing at his wife, with a trouble in his countenance that grew stronger, until he spoke.

"Georgiana," said he, "has it never occurred to you that the mark upon your cheek might be removed?"

"No, indeed," said she, smiling; but perceiving the seriousness of his manner, she blushed deeply. "To tell you the truth, it has been so often called a charm, that I was simple enough to imagine it might be so."

"Ah, upon another face, perhaps it might," replied her husband. "But never on yours! No, dearest Georgiana, you came so nearly perfect from the hand of Nature, that this slightest possible defect—which we hesitate whether to term a defect or a beauty—shocks me, as being the visible mark of earthly imperfection."

"Shocks you, my husband!" cried Georgiana, deeply hurt; at first reddening with momentary anger, but then bursting into tears. "Then why did you take me from my mother's side? You cannot love what shocks you!"

To explain this conversation, it must be mentioned, that, in the centre of Georgiana's left cheek, there was a singular mark, deeply interwoven, as it were, with the texture and substance of her face. In the usual state of her complexion,—a healthy, though delicate bloom,—the mark wore a tint of deeper crimson, which imperfectly defined its shape amid the surrounding rosiness. When she blushed, it gradually became more indistinct, and finally vanished amid the triumphant rush of blood, that bathed the whole cheek with its brilliant glow. But, if any shifting emotion caused her to turn pale, there was the mark again, a crimson stain upon the snow, in what Aylmer sometimes deemed an almost fearful distinctness. Its shape bore not a little similarity to the human hand, though of the smallest pigmy size. Georgiana's lovers were wont to say, that some fairy, at her birth-hour, had laid her tiny hand upon the infant's cheek, and left this impress there, in token of the magic endowments that were to give her such sway over all hearts. Many a desperate swain would have risked life for the privilege of pressing his lips to the mysterious hand. It must not be concealed, however, that the impression wrought by this fairy sign-manual varied exceedingly, according to the difference of temperament in the beholders. Some fastidious persons—but they were exclusively of her own sex—affirmed that the Bloody Hand, as they chose to call it, quite destroyed the effect of Georgiana's beauty, and rendered her countenance even hideous. But it would be as reasonable to say, that one of those small blue stains, which sometimes occur in the purest statuary marble, would convert the Eve of Powers[1] to a monster. Masculine observers, if the birth-mark did not heighten their admiration, contented themselves with wishing it away, that the world might possess one living specimen of ideal loveliness, without the semblance of a flaw. After his marriage—for he thought little or nothing of the matter before—Aylmer discovered that this was the case with himself.

Had she been less beautiful—if Envy's self could have found aught else to

[1]America's most famous sculptor Hiram Powers (1805–1873), working in Florence, produced his nude marble statue of *Eve Tempted* in 1842 and the even more famous *Greek Slave* in 1843. During Hawthorne's stay in Italy, he and Powers were good friends.

sneer at—he might have felt his affection heightened by the prettiness of this mimic hand, now vaguely portrayed, now lost, now stealing forth again, and glimmering to-and-fro with every pulse of emotion that throbbed within her heart. But, seeing her otherwise so perfect, he found this one defect grow more and more intolerable, with every moment of their united lives.[2] It was the fatal flaw of humanity, which Nature, in one shape or another, stamps ineffaceably on all her productions, either to imply that they are temporary and finite, or that their perfection must be wrought by toil and pain. The Crimson Hand expressed the ineludible gripe, in which mortality clutches the highest and purest of earthly mould, degrading them into kindred with the lowest, and even with the very brutes, like whom their visible frames return to dust. In this manner, selecting it as the symbol of his wife's liability to sin, sorrow, decay, and death, Aylmer's sombre imagination was not long in rendering the birth-mark a frightful object, causing him more trouble and horror than ever Georgiana's beauty, whether of soul or sense, had given him delight.

At all the seasons which should have been their happiest, he invariably, and without intending it—nay, in spite of a purpose to the contrary—reverted to this one disastrous topic. Trifling as it at first appeared, it so connected itself with innumerable trains of thought, and modes of feeling, that it became the central point of all. With the morning twilight, Aylmer opened his eyes upon his wife's face, and recognized the symbol of imperfection; and when they sat together at the evening hearth, his eyes wandered stealthily to her cheek, and beheld, flickering with the blaze of the wood fire, the spectral Hand that wrote mortality, where he would fain have worshipped. Georgiana soon learned to shudder at his gaze. It needed but a glance, with the peculiar expression that his face often wore, to change the roses of her cheek into a deathlike paleness, amid which the Crimson Hand was brought strongly out, like a bas-relief of ruby on the whitest marble.

Late, one night, when the lights were growing dim, so as hardly to betray the stain on the poor wife's cheek, she herself, for the first time, voluntarily took up the subject.

"Do you remember, my dear Aylmer," said she, with a feeble attempt at a smile—"have you any recollection of a dream, last night, about this odious Hand?"

"None!—none whatever!" replied Aylmer, starting; but then he added in a dry, cold tone, affected for the sake of concealing the real depth of his emotion:—"I might well dream of it; for before I fell asleep, it had taken a pretty firm hold of my fancy."

"And you did dream of it," continued Georgiana, hastily; for she dreaded

[2]Hawthorne's story evolves from ideas in his notebooks, e.g., the 1837 entry, "A person to be in the possession of something as perfect as mortal man has a right to demand; he tries to make it better, and ruins it entirely."

lest a gush of tears should interrupt what she had to say—"A terrible dream! I wonder that you can forget it. Is it possible to forget this one expression?—'It is in her heart now—and we must have it out!'—Reflect, my husband; for by all means I would have you recall that dream."

The mind is in a sad note, when Sleep, the all-involving, cannot confine her spectres within the dim region of her sway, but suffers them to break forth, affrighting this actual life with secrets that perchance belong to a deeper one. Aylmer now remembered his dream. He had fancied himself, with his servant Aminadab, attempting an operation for the removal of the birth-mark. But the deeper went the knife, the deeper sank the Hand, until at length its tiny grasp appeared to have caught hold of Georgiana's heart; whence, however, her husband was inexorably resolved to cut or wrench it away.

When the dream had shaped itself perfectly in his memory, Aylmer sat in his wife's presence with a guilty feeling. Truth often finds its way to the mind close-muffled in robes of sleep, and then speaks with uncompromising directness of matters in regard to which we practise an unconscious self-deception, during our waking moments. Until now, he had not been aware of the tyrannizing influence acquired by one idea over his mind, and of the lengths which he might find in his heart to go, for the sake of giving himself peace.

"Aylmer," resumed Georgiana, solemnly, "I know not what may be the cost to both of us, to rid me of this fatal birth-mark. Perhaps its removal may cause cureless deformity. Or, it may be, the stain goes as deep as life itself. Again, do we know that there is a possibility, on any terms, of unclasping the firm gripe of this little Hand, which was laid upon me before I came into the world?"

"Dearest Georgiana, I have spent much thought upon the subject," hastily interrupted Aylmer—"I am convinced of the perfect practicability of its removal."

"If there be the remotest possibility of it," continued Georgiana, "let the attempt be made, at whatever risk. Danger is nothing to me; for life—while this hateful mark makes me the object of your horror and disgust—life is a burthen which I would fling down with joy. Either remove this dreadful Hand, or take my wretched life! You have deep science! All the world bears witness of it. You have achieved great wonders! Cannot you remove this little, little mark, which I cover with the tips of two small fingers? Is this beyond your power, for the sake of your own peace, and to save your poor wife from madness?"

"Noblest—dearest—tenderest wife!" cried Aylmer, rapturously. "Doubt not my power. I have already given this matter the deepest thought—thought which might almost have enlightened me to create a being less perfect than yourself. Georgiana, you have led me deeper than ever into the heart of science. I feel myself fully competent to render this dear cheek as faultless as its fellow; and then, most beloved, what will be my triumph, when I shall have corrected what Nature left imperfect, in her fairest work! Even Pygmalion, when his sculptured woman assumed life, felt not greater ecstasy than mine will be."

"It is resolved, then," said Georgiana, faintly smiling,—"And, Aylmer, spare me not, though you should find the birth-mark take refuge in my heart at last."

Her husband tenderly kissed her cheek—her right cheek—not that which bore the impress of the Crimson Hand.

The next day, Aylmer apprized his wife of a plan that he had formed, whereby he might have opportunity for the intense thought and constant watchfulness, which the proposed operation would require; while Georgiana, likewise, would enjoy the perfect repose essential to its success. They were to seclude themselves in the extensive apartments occupied by Aylmer as a laboratory, and where, during his toilsome youth, he had made discoveries in the elemental powers of nature, that had roused the admiration of all the learned societies in Europe. Seated calmly in this laboratory, the pale philosopher had investigated the secrets of the highest cloud-region, and of the profoundest mines; he had satisfied himself of the causes that kindled and kept alive the fires of the volcano; and had explained the mystery of fountains, and how it is that they gush forth, some so bright and pure, and others with such rich medicinal virtues, from the dark bosom of the earth. Here, too, at an earlier period, he had studied the wonders of the human frame, and attempted to fathom the very process by which Nature assimilates all her precious influences from earth and air, and from the spiritual world, to create and foster Man, her masterpiece. The latter pursuit, however, Aylmer had long laid aside, in unwilling recognition of the truth, against which all seekers sooner or later stumble, that our great creative Mother, while she amuses us with apparently working in the broadest sunshine, is yet severely careful to keep her own secrets, and, in spite of her pretended openness, shows us nothing but results. She permits us indeed, to mar, but seldom to mend, and, like a jealous patentee, on no account to make. Now, however, Aylmer resumed these half-forgotten investigations; not, of course, with such hopes or wishes as first suggested them; but because they involved much physiological truth, and lay in the path of his proposed scheme for the treatment of Georgiana.

As he led her over the threshold of the laboratory, Georgiana was cold and tremulous. Aylmer looked cheerfully into her face, with intent to reassure her, but was so startled with the intense glow of the birth-mark upon the whiteness of her cheek, that he could not restrain a strong convulsive shudder. His wife fainted.

"Aminadab! Aminadab!" shouted Aylmer, stamping violently on the floor.

Forthwith, there issued from an inner apartment a man of low stature, but bulky frame, with shaggy hair hanging about his visage, which was grimed with the vapors of the furnace. This personage had been Aylmer's underworker during his whole scientific career, and was admirably fitted for that office by his great mechanical readiness, and the skill with which, while incapable of comprehending a single principle, he executed all the practical details of his master's experiments. With his vast strength, his shaggy hair, his smoky aspect, and the indescribable earthiness that incrusted him, he seemed to represent man's physical nature; while Aylmer's slender figure, and pale, intellectual face, were no less apt a type of the spiritual element.

"Throw open the door of the boudoir, Aminadab," said Aylmer, "and burn a pastille."

"Yes, master," answered Aminadab, looking intently at the lifeless form of Georgiana; and then he muttered to himself:—"If she were my wife, I'd never part with that birth-mark."

When Georgiana recovered consciousness, she found herself breathing an atmosphere of penetrating fragrance, the gentle potency of which had recalled her from her deathlike faintness. The scene around her looked like enchantment. Aylmer had converted those smoky, dingy, sombre rooms, where he had spent his brightest years in recondite pursuits, into a series of beautiful apartments, not unfit to be the secluded abode of a lovely woman. The walls were hung with gorgeous curtains, which imparted the combination of grandeur and grace, that no other species of adornment can achieve; and as they fell from the ceiling to the floor, their rich and ponderous folds, concealing all angles and straight lines, appeared to shut in the scene from infinite space. For aught Georgiana knew, it might be a pavilion among the clouds. And Aylmer, excluding the sunshine, which would have interfered with his chemical processes, had supplied its place with perfumed lamps, emitting flames of various hue, but all uniting in a soft, empurpled radiance. He now knelt by his wife's side, watching her earnestly, but without alarm; for he was confident in his science, and felt that he could draw a magic circle round her, within which no evil might intrude.

"Where am I?—Ah, I remember!" said Georgiana, faintly; and she placed her hand over her cheek, to hide the terrible mark from her husband's eyes.

"Fear not, dearest!" exclaimed he. "Do not shrink from me! Believe me, Georgiana, I even rejoice in this single imperfection, since it will be such rapture to remove it."

"Oh, spare me!" sadly replied his wife—"Pray do not look at it again. I never can forget that convulsive shudder."

In order to soothe Georgiana, and, as it were, to release her mind from the burthen of actual things, Aylmer now put in practice some of the light and playful secrets, which science had taught him among its profounder lore. Airy figures, absolutely bodiless ideas, and forms of unsubstantial beauty, came and danced before her, imprinting their momentary footsteps on beams of light. Though she had some indistinct idea of the method of these optical phenomena, still the illusion was almost perfect enough to warrant the belief, that her husband possessed sway over the spiritual world. Then again, when she felt a wish to look forth from her seclusion, immediately, as if her thoughts were answered, the procession of external existence flitted across a screen. The scenery and the figures of actual life were perfectly represented, but with that bewitching, yet indescribable difference, which always makes a picture, an image, or a shadow, so much more attractive than the original. When wearied of this, Aylmer bade her cast her eyes upon a vessel, containing a quantity of earth. She did so, with little interest at first, but was soon startled, to perceive the germ of a plant, shooting upward from the soil. Then came the slender stalk—the leaves gradually unfolded themselves—and amid them was a perfect and lovely flower.

"It is magical!" cried Georgiana, "I dare not touch it."

"Nay, pluck it," answered Aylmer, "pluck it, and inhale its brief perfume while you may. The flower will wither in a few moments, and leave nothing save its brown seed-vessels—but thence may be perpetuated a race as ephemeral as itself."

But Georgiana had no sooner touched the flower than the whole plant suffered a blight, its leaves turning coal-black, as if by the agency of fire.

"There was too powerful a stimulus," said Aylmer thoughtfully.

To make up for this abortive experiment, he proposed to take her portrait by a scientific process of his own invention. It was to be effected by rays of light striking upon a polished plate of metal. Georgiana assented—but, on looking at the result, was affrighted to find the features of the portrait blurred and indefinable,[3] while the minute figure of a hand appeared where the cheek should have been. Aylmer snatched the metallic plate, and threw it into a jar of corrosive acid.

Soon, however, he forgot these mortifying failures. In the intervals of study and chemical experiment, he came to her, flushed and exhausted, but seemed invigorated by her presence, and spoke in glowing language of the resources of his art. He gave a history of the long dynasty of the Alchemists, who spent so many ages in quest of the universal solvent, by which the Golden Principle might be elicited from all things vile and base. Aylmer appeared to believe, that, by the plainest scientific logic, it was altogether within the limits of possibility to discover this long-sought medium; but, he added, a philosopher who should go deep enough to acquire the power, would attain too lofty a wisdom to stoop to the exercise of it. Not less singular were his opinions in regard to the Elixir Vitæ.[4] He more than intimated, that it was his option to concoct a liquid that should prolong life for years—perhaps interminably—but that it would produce a discord in nature, which all the world, and chiefly the quaffer of the immortal nostrum, would find cause to curse.

"Aylmer, are you in earnest?" asked Georgiana, looking at him with amazement and fear; "it is terrible to possess such power, or even to dream of possessing it!"

"Oh, do not tremble, my love!" said her husband, "I would not wrong ei-

[3]In a daguerreotype—the first practical photographic process, introduced in 1839—a sitter's reflected image was fixed onto a silvered and sensitized metal plate after about thirty seconds. Any movement produced a blurred image.

[4]The main project of alchemy was to transmute base metals into gold, but also involved seeking a panacea (or cure for all illnesses) and an elixir (or liquid) that might prolong life indefinitely.

ther you or myself by working such inharmonious effects upon our lives. But I would have you consider how trifling, in comparison, is the skill requisite to remove this little Hand."

At the mention of the birth-mark, Georgiana, as usual, shrank, as if a red-hot iron had touched her cheek.

Again Aylmer applied himself to his labors. She could hear his voice in the distant furnace-room, giving directions to Aminadab, whose harsh, uncouth, misshapen tones were audible in response, more like the grunt or growl of a brute than human speech. After hours of absence, Aylmer reappeared, and proposed that she should now examine his cabinet of chemical products, and natural treasures of the earth. Among the former he showed her a small vial, in which, he remarked, was contained a gentle yet most powerful fragrance, capable of impregnating all the breezes that blow across a kingdom. They were of inestimable value, the contents of that little vial; and, as he said so, he threw some of the perfume into the air, and filled the room with piercing and invigorating delight.

"And what is this?" asked Georgiana, pointing to a small crystal globe, containing a gold-colored liquid. "It is so beautiful to the eye, that I could imagine it the Elixir of Life."

"In one sense it is," replied Aylmer, "or rather the Elixir of Immortality. It is the most precious poison that ever was concocted in this world. By its aid, I could apportion the lifetime of any mortal at whom you might point your finger. The strength of the dose would determine whether he were to linger out years, or drop dead in the midst of a breath. No king, on his guarded throne, could keep his life, if I, in my private station, should deem that the welfare of millions justified me in depriving him of it."

"Why do you keep such a terrific drug?" inquired Georgiana in horror.

"Do not mistrust me, dearest!" said her husband, smiling; "its virtuous potency is yet greater than its harmful one. But, see! here is a powerful cosmetic. With a few drops of this, in a vase of water, freckles may be washed away as easily as the hands are cleansed. A stronger infusion would take the blood out of the cheek, and leave the rosiest beauty a pale ghost."

"Is it with this lotion that you intend to bathe my cheek?" asked Georgiana anxiously.

"Oh, no!" hastily replied her husband—"this is merely superficial. Your case demands a remedy that shall go deeper."

In his interviews with Georgiana, Aylmer generally made minute inquiries as to her sensations, and whether the confinement of the rooms, and the temperature of the atmosphere, agreed with her. These questions had such a particular drift, that Georgiana began to conjecture that she was already subjected to certain physical influences, either breathed in with the fragrant air, or taken with her food. She fancied, likewise—but it might be altogether fancy—that there was a stirring up of her system,—a strange indefinite sensation creeping through her veins, and tingling, half painfully, half pleasurably, at her heart.

Still, whenever she dared to look into the mirror, there she beheld herself, pale as a white rose, and with the crimson birth-mark stamped upon her cheek. Not even Aylmer now hated it so much as she.

To dispel the tedium of the hours which her husband found it necessary to devote to the processes of combination and analysis, Georgiana turned over the volumes of his scientific library. In many dark old tomes, she met with chapters full of romance and poetry. They were the works of the philosophers of the middle ages, such as Albertus Magnus, Cornelius Agrippa, Paracelsus, and the famous friar who created the prophetic Brazen Head.[5] All these antique naturalists stood in advance of their centuries, yet were imbued with some of their credulity, and therefore were believed, and perhaps imagined themselves, to have acquired from the investigation of nature a power above nature, and from physics a sway over the spiritual world. Hardly less curious and imaginative were the early volumes of the Transactions of the Royal Society,[6] in which the members, knowing little of the limits of natural possibility, were continually recording wonders, or proposing methods whereby wonders might be wrought.

But, to Georgiana, the most engrossing volume was a large folio from her husband's own hand, in which he had recorded every experiment of his scientific career, with its original aim, the methods adopted for its development, and its final success or failure, with the circumstances to which either event was attributable. The book, in truth, was both the history and emblem of his ardent, ambitious, imaginative, yet practical and laborious, life. He handled physical details, as if there were nothing beyond them; yet spiritualized them all, and redeemed himself from materialism, by his strong and eager aspiration towards the infinite. In his grasp, the veriest clod of earth assumed a soul. Georgiana, as she read, reverenced Aylmer, and loved him more profoundly than ever, but with a less entire dependence on his judgment than heretofore. Much as he had accomplished, she could not but observe that his most splendid successes were almost invariably failures, if compared with the ideal at which he aimed. His brightest diamonds were the merest pebbles, and felt to be so by himself, in comparison with the inestimable gems which lay hidden beyond his reach. The volume, rich with achievements that had won renown for its author, was yet as melancholy a record as ever mortal hand had penned. It was the sad confession, and continual exemplification, of the short-comings of the composite man—the spirit burthened with clay and working in matter—and of the despair that assails the higher nature, at finding itself so miserably thwarted by the earthly part. Perhaps every man of genius, in whatever sphere, might recognize the image of his own experience in Aylmer's journal.

[5]Medieval and Renaissance philosophers and scientists whose experiments were associated with magic. The friar was Roger Bacon.
[6]The Royal Society, founded in London in 1662, was committed to scientific experiment.

So deeply did these reflections affect Georgiana, that she laid her face upon the open volume, and burst into tears. In this situation she was found by her husband.

"It is dangerous to read in a sorcerer's books," said he, with a smile, though his countenance was uneasy and displeased. "Georgiana, there are pages in that volume, which I can scarcely glance over and keep my senses. Take heed lest it prove as detrimental to you!"

"It has made me worship you more than ever," said she.

"Ah! wait for this one success," rejoined he, "then worship me if you will. I shall deem myself hardly unworthy of it. But, come! I have sought you for the luxury of your voice. Sing to me, dearest!"

So she poured out the liquid music of her voice to quench the thirst of his spirit. He then took his leave, with a boyish exuberance of gaiety, assuring her that her seclusion would endure but a little longer, and that the result was already certain. Scarcely had he departed, when Georgiana felt irresistibly impelled to follow him. She had forgotten to inform Aylmer of a symptom, which, for two or three hours past, had begun to excite her attention. It was a sensation in the fatal birth-mark, not painful, but which induced a restlessness throughout her system. Hastening after her husband, she intruded, for the first time, into the laboratory.

The first thing that struck her eye was the furnace, that hot and feverish worker, with the intense glow of its fire, which, by the quantities of soot clustered above it, seemed to have been burning for ages. There was a distilling apparatus in full operation. Around the room were retorts, tubes, cylinders, crucibles, and other apparatus of chemical research. An electrical machine stood ready for immediate use. The atmosphere felt oppressively close, and was tainted with gaseous odors, which had been tormented forth by the processes of science. The severe and homely simplicity of the apartment, with its naked walls and brick pavement, looked strange, accustomed as Georgiana had become to the fantastic elegance of her boudoir. But what chiefly, indeed almost solely, drew her attention, was the aspect of Aylmer himself.

He was pale as death, anxious, and absorbed, and hung over the furnace as if it depended upon his utmost watchfulness whether the liquid, which it was distilling, should be the draught of immortal happiness or misery. How different from the sanguine and joyous mien that he had assumed for Georgiana's encouragement!

"Carefully now, Aminadab! Carefully, thou human machine! Carefully, thou man of clay!" muttered Aylmer, more to himself than his assistant. "Now, if there be a thought too much or too little, it is all over!"

"Hoh! hoh!" mumbled Aminadab—"look, master, look!"

Aylmer raised his eyes hastily, and at first reddened, then grew paler than ever, on beholding Georgiana. He rushed towards her, and seized her arm with a gripe that left the print of his fingers upon it.

"Why do you come hither? Have you no trust in your husband?" cried he impetuously. "Would you throw the blight of that fatal birth-mark over my labors? It is not well done. Go, prying woman, go!"

"Nay, Aylmer," said Georgiana, with the firmness of which she possessed no stinted endowment, "it is not you that have a right to complain. You mistrust your wife! You have concealed the anxiety with which you watch the development of this experiment. Think not so unworthily of me, my husband! Tell me all the risk we run; and fear not that I shall shrink, for my share in it is far less than your own!"

"No, no, Georgiana!" said Aylmer impatiently, "it must not be."

"I submit," replied she calmly. "And, Aylmer, I shall quaff whatever draught you bring me; but it will be on the same principle that would induce me to take a dose of poison, if offered by your hand."

"My noble wife," said Aylmer, deeply moved, "I knew not the height and depth of your nature, until now. Nothing shall be concealed. Know, then, that this Crimson Hand, superficial as it seems, has clutched its grasp into your being, with a strength of which I had no previous conception. I have already administered agents powerful enough to do aught except to change your entire physical system. Only one thing remains to be tried. If that fail us, we are ruined!"

"Why did you hesitate to tell me this?" asked she.

"Because, Georgiana," said Aylmer, in a low voice, "there is danger!"

"Danger? There is but one danger—that this horrible stigma shall be left upon my cheek!" cried Georgiana. "Remove it! remove it!—whatever be the cost—or we shall both go mad!"

"Heaven knows, your words are too true," said Aylmer, sadly. "And now, dearest, return to your boudoir. In a little while, all will be tested."

He conducted her back, and took leave of her with a solemn tenderness, which spoke far more than his words how much was now at stake. After his departure, Georgiana became wrapt in musings. She considered the character of Aylmer, and did it completer justice than at any previous moment. Her heart exulted, while it trembled, at his honorable love, so pure and lofty that it would accept nothing less than perfection, nor miserably make itself contented with an earthlier nature than he had dreamed of. She felt how much more precious was such a sentiment, than that meaner kind which would have borne with the imperfection for her sake, and have been guilty of treason to holy love, by degrading its perfect idea to the level of the actual. And, with her whole spirit, she prayed, that, for a single moment, she might satisfy his highest and deepest conception. Longer than one moment, she well knew, it could not be; for his spirit was ever on the march—ever ascending—and each instant required something that was beyond the scope of the instant before.

The sound of her husband's footsteps aroused her. He bore a crystal goblet, containing a liquor colorless as water, but bright enough to be the draught of immortality. Aylmer was pale; but it seemed rather the consequence of a highly wrought state of mind, and tension of spirit, than of fear or doubt.

"The concoction of the draught has been perfect," said he, in answer to Georgiana's look. "Unless all my science have deceived me, it cannot fail."

"Save on your account, my dearest Aylmer," observed his wife, "I might wish to put off this birth-mark of mortality by relinquishing mortality itself, in preference to any other mode. Life is but a sad possession to those who have attained precisely the degree of moral advancement at which I stand. Were I weaker and blinder, it might be happiness. Were I stronger, it might be endured hopefully. But, being what I find myself, methinks I am of all mortals the most fit to die."

"You are fit for heaven without tasting death!" replied her husband. "But why do we speak of dying? The draught cannot fail. Behold its effect upon this plant!"

On the window-seat there stood a geranium, diseased with yellow blotches, which had overspread all its leaves. Aylmer poured a small quantity of the liquid upon the soil in which it grew. In a little time, when the roots of the plant had taken up the moisture, the unsightly blotches began to be extinguished in a living verdure.

"There needed no proof," said Georgiana, quietly. "Give me the goblet. I joyfully stake all upon your word."

"Drink, then, thou lofty creature!" exclaimed Aylmer, with fervid admiration. "There is no taint of imperfection on thy spirit. Thy sensible frame, too, shall soon be all perfect!"

She quaffed the liquid, and returned the goblet to his hand.

"It is grateful," said she, with a placid smile. "Methinks it is like water from a heavenly fountain; for it contains I know not what of unobtrusive fragrance and deliciousness. It allays a feverish thirst, that had parched me for many days. Now, dearest, let me sleep. My earthly senses are closing over my spirit, like the leaves round the heart of a rose, at sunset."

She spoke the last words with a gentle reluctance, as if it required almost more energy than she could command to pronounce the faint and lingering syllables. Scarcely had they loitered through her lips, ere she was lost in slumber. Aylmer sat by her side, watching her aspect with the emotions proper to a man, the whole value of whose existence was involved in the process now to be tested. Mingled with this mood, however, was the philosophic investigation, characteristic of the man of science. Not the minutest symptom escaped him. A heightened flush of the cheek—a slight irregularity of breath—a quiver of the eyelid—a hardly perceptible tremor through the frame—such were the details which, as the moments passed, he wrote down in his folio volume. Intense thought had set its stamp upon every previous page of that volume; but the thoughts of years were all concentrated upon the last.

While thus employed, he failed not to gaze often at the fatal Hand, and not without a shudder. Yet once, by a strange and unaccountable impulse, he pressed it with his lips. His spirit recoiled, however, in the very act, and Georgiana, out of the midst of her deep sleep, moved uneasily and murmured, as if in remonstrance. Again, Aylmer resumed his watch. Nor was it without avail. The Crimson Hand, which at first had been strongly visible upon the marble paleness of Georgiana's cheek now grew more faintly outlined. She remained not less pale than ever; but the birth-mark, with every breath that came and went, lost somewhat of its former distinctness. Its presence had been awful; its departure was more awful still. Watch the stain of the rainbow fading out of the sky; and you will know how that mysterious symbol passed away.

"By Heaven, it is well nigh gone!" said Aylmer to himself, in almost irrepressible ecstasy. "I can scarcely trace it now. Success! Success! And now it is like the faintest rose-color. The slightest flush of blood across her cheek would overcome it. But she is so pale!"

He drew aside the window-curtain, and suffered the light of natural day to fall into the room, and rest upon her cheek. At the same time, he heard a gross, hoarse chuckle, which he had long known as his servant Aminadab's expression of delight.

"Ah, clod! Ah, earthly mass!" cried Aylmer, laughing in a sort of frenzy. "You have served me well! Matter and Spirit—Earth and Heaven—have both done their part in this! Laugh, thing of senses! You have earned the right to laugh."

These exclamations broke Georgiana's sleep. She slowly unclosed her eyes, and gazed into the mirror, which her husband had arranged for that purpose. A faint smile flitted over her lips, when she recognized how barely perceptible was now that Crimson Hand, which had once blazed forth with such disastrous brilliancy as to scare away all their happiness. But then her eyes sought Aylmer's face, with a trouble and anxiety that he could by no means account for.

"My poor Aylmer!" murmured she.

"Poor? Nay, richest! Happiest! Most favored!" exclaimed he. "My peerless bride, it is successful! You are perfect!"

"My poor Aylmer!" she repeated, with a more than human tenderness. "You have aimed loftily!—you have done nobly! Do not repent, that, with so high and pure a feeling, you have rejected the best that earth could offer. Aylmer—dearest Aylmer—I am dying!"

Alas, it was too true! The fatal Hand had grappled with the mystery of life, and was the bond by which an angelic spirit kept itself in union with a mortal frame. As the last crimson tint of the birth-mark—that sole token of human imperfection—faded from her cheek, the parting breath of the now perfect woman passed into the atmosphere, and her soul, lingering a moment near her husband, took its heavenward flight. Then a hoarse, chuckling laugh was heard again! Thus ever does the gross Fatality of Earth exult in its invariable triumph over the immortal essence, which, in this dim sphere of half-development, demands the completeness of a higher state. Yet, had Aylmer reached a profounder wisdom, he need not thus have flung away the happiness, which would have woven his mortal life of the self-same texture with the celestial. The momentary circumstance was too strong for him; he failed to look beyond the shadowy scope of Time, and living once for all in Eternity, to find the perfect Future in the present.

—1843

What are your reactions to and questions about this work? The following questions may help provoke some ideas.

Probing the Work

1. What does the birthmark represent, for Georgiana? For Aylmer? For Aminadab?
2. How is the theme of married love illustrated in this story? What form does love take for each main character? How is it expressed?

Identifying Issues

3. What traditional marital roles do Georgiana and Aylmer enact? To what extent are these roles still in evidence today?
4. What does this story illustrate about what men and women find attractive or unattractive in each other? Give some examples from the work and from your own experience.
5. In *The American Narcissus,* Joyce Warren explains that since the removal of the birthmark coincides with Georgiana's death and heavenly ascent, the story illustrates that Hawthorne did not believe in human perfection on earth. To what extent does the birthmark represent human imperfection? To what extent do husbands and wives accept imperfections? What married men or women do you know who refuse to accept, or accept without question, their spouse's imperfections?

KATE CHOPIN

The Story of an Hour

Kate O'Flaherty (1851–1904) was born to a prosperous family in St. Louis. She married Oscar Chopin, a French-Creole businessman from Louisiana, and moved to New Orleans with him, where they had six children. After Oscar died of malaria in 1882, she returned to St. Louis with her children, where she dedicated herself to her writing. Some of her stories and her novel, The Awakening, *received hostile public reaction because of their unconventional depictions of married women.*

Knowing that Mrs. Mallard was afflicted with a heart trouble, great care was taken to break to her as gently as possible the news of her husband's death.

It was her sister Josephine who told her, in broken sentences, veiled hints that revealed in half concealing. Her husband's friend Richards was there, too, near her. It was he who had been in the newspaper office when intelligence of the railroad disaster was received, with Brently Mallard's name leading the list of "killed." He had only taken the time to assure himself of its truth by a second telegram, and had hastened to forestall any less careful, less tender friend in bearing the sad message.

She did not hear the story as many women have heard the same, with a paralyzed inability to accept its significance. She wept at once, with sudden, wild abandonment, in her sister's arms. When the storm of grief had spent itself she went away to her room alone. She would have no one follow her.

There stood, facing the open window, a comfortable, roomy armchair. Into this she sank, pressed down by a physical exhaustion that haunted her body and seemed to reach into her soul.

She could see in the open square before her house the tops of trees that were all aquiver with the new spring life. The delicious breath of rain was in the air. In the street below a peddler was crying his wares. The notes of a distant song which some one was singing reached her faintly, and countless sparrows were twittering in the eaves.

There were patches of blue sky showing here and there through the clouds that had met and piled above the other in the west facing her window.

She sat with her head thrown back upon the cushion of the chair quite motionless, except when a sob came up into her throat and shook her, as a child who has cried itself to sleep continues to sob in its dreams.

She was young, with a fair, calm face, whose lines bespoke repression and even a certain strength. But now there was a dull stare in her eyes, whose gaze was fixed away off yonder on one of those patches of blue sky. It was not a glance of reflection, but rather indicated a suspension of intelligent thought.

There was something coming to her and she was waiting for it, fearfully. What was it? She did not know; it was too subtle and elusive to name. But she felt it, creeping out of the sky, reaching toward her through the sounds, the scents, the color that filled the air.

Now her bosom rose and fell tumultuously. She was beginning to recognize this thing that was approaching to possess her, and she was striving to beat it back with her will—as powerless as her two white slender hands would have been.

When she abandoned herself a little whispered word escaped her slightly parted lips. She said it over and over under her breath: "Free, free, free!" The vacant stare and the look of terror that had followed it went from her eyes. They stayed keen and bright. Her pulses beat fast, and the coursing blood warmed and relaxed every inch of her body.

She did not stop to ask if it were not a monstrous joy that held her. A clear and exalted perception enabled her to dismiss the suggestion as trivial.

She knew that she would weep again when she saw the kind, tender hands folded in death; the face that had never looked save with love upon her, fixed and gray and dead. But she saw beyond that bitter moment a long procession of years to come that would belong to her absolutely. And she opened and spread her arms out to them in welcome.

There would be no one to live for during those coming years; she would live for herself. There would be no powerful will bending her in that blind persistence with which men and women believe they have a right to impose a private will upon a fellow creature. A kind intention or a cruel intention made the act seem no less a crime as she looked upon it in that brief moment of illumination.

And yet she had loved him—sometimes. Often she had not. What did it matter! What could love, the unsolved mystery, count for in face of this possession of self-assertion which she suddenly recognized as the strongest impulse of her being.

"Free! Body and soul free!" she kept whispering.

Josephine was kneeling before the closed door with her lips to the keyhole, imploring for admission. "Louise, open the door! I beg; open the door—you will make yourself ill. What are you doing, Louise? For heaven's sake open the door."

"Go away. I am not making myself ill." No; she was drinking in a very elixir of life through that open window.

Her fancy was running riot along those days ahead of her. Spring days, and summer days, and all sorts of days that would be her own. She breathed a quick prayer that life might be long. It was only yesterday she had thought with a shudder that life might be long.

She arose at length and opened the door to her sister's importunities. There was a feverish triumph in her eyes, and she carried herself unwittingly like a goddess of Victory. She clasped her sister's waist, and together they descended the stairs. Richards stood waiting for them at the bottom.

Some one was opening the front door with a latchkey. It was Brently Mallard who entered, a little travel-stained, composedly carrying his grip-sack and umbrella. He had been far from the scene of accident, and did not even know there had been one. He stood amazed at Josephine's piercing cry; at Richards' quick motion to screen him from the view of his wife.

But Richards was too late.

When the doctors came they said she had died of heart disease—of joy that kills.

—1891

What are your reactions to and questions about this work? The following questions may help provoke some ideas.

Probing the Work

1. How does Chopin use *irony* (see page 79) in this story?

Identifying Issues

2. It is not uncommon for middle-aged women today to feel liberated by the loss of their husbands through death or divorce. What are the elements of a traditional marriage that cause women to feel imprisoned?

KATE CHOPIN

The Storm

See biographical note on page 646.

I

The leaves were so still that even Bibi thought it was going to rain. Bobinôt, who was accustomed to converse on terms of perfect equality with his little son, called the child's attention to certain sombre clouds that were rolling with sinister intention from the west, accompanied by a sullen, threatening roar. They were at Friedheimer's store and decided to remain there till the storm had passed. They sat within the door on two empty kegs. Bibi was four years old and looked very wise.

"Mama'll be 'fraid, yes," he suggested with blinking eyes.

"She'll shut the house. Maybe she got Sylvie helpin' her this evenin'," Bobinôt responded reassuringly.

"No; she ent got Sylvie. Sylvie was helpin' her yistiday," piped Bibi.

Bobinôt arose and going across to the counter purchased a can of shrimps, of which Calixta was very fond. Then he returned to his perch on the keg and sat stolidly holding the can of shrimps while the storm burst. It shook the wooden store and seemed to be ripping great furrows in the distant field. Bibi laid his little hand on his father's knee and was not afraid.

2

Calixta, at home, felt no uneasiness for their safety. She sat at a side window sewing furiously on a sewing machine. She was greatly occupied and did not notice the approaching storm. But she felt very warm and often stopped to mop her face on which the perspiration gathered in beads. She unfastened her white sacque at the throat. It began to grow dark, and suddenly realizing the situation she got up hurriedly and went about closing windows and doors.

Out on the small front gallery she had hung Bobinôt's Sunday clothes to air and she hastened out to gather them before the rain fell. As she stepped outside, Alcée Laballière rode in at the gate. She had not seen him very often since her marriage, and never alone. She stood there with Bobinôt's coat in her hands, and the big rain drops began to fall. Alcée rode his horse under the shelter of a side projection where the chickens had huddled and there were plows and a harrow piled up in the corner.

"May I come and wait on your gallery till the storm is over, Calixta?" he asked.

"Come 'long in, M'sieur Alcée."

His voice and her own startled her as if from a trance, and she seized Bobinôt's vest. Alcée, mounting to the porch, grabbed the trousers and snatched Bibi's braided jacket that was about to be carried away by a sudden gust of wind. He expressed an intention to remain outside, but it was soon apparent that he might as well have been out in the open: the water beat in upon the boards in driving sheets, and he went inside, closing the door after him. It was even necessary to put something beneath the door to keep the water out.

"My! what a rain! It's good two years sence it rain' like that," exclaimed Calixta as she rolled up a piece of bagging and Alcée helped her to thrust it beneath the crack.

She was a little fuller of figure than five years before when she married; but she had lost nothing of her vivacity. Her blue eyes still retained their melting quality; and her yellow hair, dishevelled by the wind and rain, kinked more stubbornly than ever about her ears and temples.

The rain beat upon the low, shingled roof with a force and clatter that threatened to break an entrance and deluge them there. They were in the dining room—the sitting room—the general utility room. Adjoining was her bed room, with Bibi's couch along side her own. The door stood open, and the room with its white, monumental bed, its closed shutters, looked dim and mysterious.

Alcée flung himself into a rocker and Calixta nervously began to gather up from the floor the lengths of a cotton sheet which she had been sewing.

"If this keeps up, *Dieu sait* if the levees goin' to stan' it!" she exclaimed.

"What have you got to do with the levees?"

"I got enough to do! An' there's Bobinôt with Bibi out in that storm—if he only didn' left Friedheimer's!"

"Let us hope, Calixta, that Bobinôt's got sense enough to come in out of a cyclone."

She went and stood at the window with a greatly disturbed look on her face. She wiped the frame that was clouded with moisture. It was stiflingly hot. Alcée got up and joined her at the window, looking over her shoulder. The rain was coming down in sheets obscuring the view of far-off cabins and enveloping the distant wood in a gray mist. The playing of the lightning was incessant. A bolt struck a tall chinaberry tree at the edge of the field. It filled all visible space with a blinding glare and the crash seemed to invade the very boards they stood upon.

Calixta put her hands to her eyes, and with a cry, staggered backward. Alcée's arm encircled her, and for an instant he drew her close and spasmodically to him.

"Bonte!" she cried, releasing herself from his encircling arm and retreating from the window, "the house'll go next! If I only knew w'ere Bibi was!" She would not compose herself; she would not be seated. Alcée clasped her shoulders and looked into her face. The contact of her warm, palpitating body when he had unthinkingly drawn her into his arms, had aroused all the old-time infatuation and desire for her flesh.

"Calixta," he said, "don't be frightened. Nothing can happen. The house is too low to be struck, with so many tall trees standing about. There! aren't you going to be quiet? say, aren't you?" He pushed her hair back from her face that was warm and steaming. Her lips were as red and moist as pomegranate seed. Her white neck and a glimpse of her full, firm bosom disturbed him powerfully. As she glanced up at him the fear in her liquid blue eyes had given place to a drowsy gleam that unconsciously betrayed a sensuous desire. He looked down into her eyes and there was nothing for him to do but to gather her lips in a kiss. It reminded him of Assumption.

"Do you remember—in Assumption. Calixta?" he asked in a low voice broken by passion. Oh! she remembered; for in Assumption he had kissed her and kissed and kissed her; until his senses would well nigh fail, and to save her he would resort to a desperate flight. If she was not an immaculate dove in those days, she was still inviolate; a passionate creature whose very defenselessness had made her defense, against which his honor forbade him to prevail. Now—well, now—her lips seemed in a manner free to be tasted, as well as her round, white throat and her whiter breasts.

They did not heed the crashing torrents, and the roar of the elements made her laugh as she lay in his arms. She was a revelation in that dim, mysterious chamber; as white as the couch she lay upon. Her firm, elastic flesh that was knowing for the first time its birthright, was like a creamy lily that the sun invites to contribute its breath and perfume to the undying life of the world.

The generous abundance of her passion, without guile or trickery, was like a white flame which penetrated and found response in depths of his own sensuous nature that had never yet been reached.

When he touched her breasts they gave themselves up in quivering ecstasy, inviting his lips. Her mouth was a fountain of delight. And when he possessed her, they seemed to swoon together at the very borderland of life's mystery.

He stayed cushioned upon her, breathless, dazed, enervated, with his heart beating like a hammer upon her. With one hand she clasped his head, her lips lightly touching his forehead. The other hand stroked with a soothing rhythm his muscular shoulders.

The growl of the thunder was distant and passing away. The rain beat softly upon the shingles, inviting them to drowsiness and sleep. But they dared not yield.

The rain was over; and the sun was turning the glistening green world into a palace of gems. Calixta, on the gallery, watched Alcée ride away. He turned and smiled at her with a beaming face; and she lifted her pretty chin in the air and laughed aloud.

3

Bobinôt and Bibi, trudging home, stopped without at the cistern to make themselves presentable.

"My! Bibi, w'at will yo' mama say! You ought to be ashame'. You oughtn' put on those good pants. Look at 'em! An' that mud on yo' collar! How you got that mud on yo' collar, Bibi? I never saw such a boy!" Bibi was the picture of pathetic resignation. Bobinôt was the embodiment of serious solicitude as he strove to remove from his own person and his son's the signs of their tramp over heavy roads and through wet fields. He scraped the mud off Bibi's bare legs and feet with a stick and carefully removed all traces from his heavy brogans. Then, prepared for the worst—the meeting with an over-scrupulous housewife, they entered cautiously at the back door.

Calixta was preparing supper. She had set the table and was dripping coffee at the hearth. She sprang up as they came in.

"Oh, Bobinôt! You back! My! but I was uneasy. W'ere you been during the rain? An' Bibi? he ain't wet? he ain't hurt?" She had clasped Bibi and was kissing him effusively. Bobinôt's explanations and apologies which he had been composing all along the way, died on his lips as Calixta felt him to see if he were dry, and seemed to express nothing but satisfaction at their safe return.

"I brought you some shrimps, Calixta," offered Bobinôt, hauling the can from his ample side pocket and laying it on the table.

"Shrimps! Oh, Bobinôt! you too good fo' anything!" and she gave him a smacking kiss on the cheek that resounded. *"J'vous reponds,*[1] we'll have a feas' to-night! umph-umph!"

Bobinôt and Bibi began to relax and enjoy themselves, and when the three seated themselves at table they laughed much and so loud that anyone might have heard them as far away as Laballière's.

4

Alcée Laballière wrote to his wife, Clarisse, that night. It was a loving letter, full of tender solicitude. He told her not to hurry back, but if she and the ba-

[1]Take my word for it; I assure you.

bies liked it at Biloxi, to stay a month longer. He was getting on nicely; and though he missed them, he was willing to bear the separation a while longer—realizing that their health and pleasure were the first things to be considered.

5

As for Clarisse, she was charmed upon receiving her husband's letter. She and the babies were doing well. The society was agreeable; many of her old friends and acquaintances were at the bay. And the first free breath since her marriage seemed to restore the pleasant liberty of her maiden days. Devoted as she was to her husband, their intimate conjugal life was something which she was more than willing to forego for a while.

So the storm passed and everyone was happy.

—1898

What are your reactions to and questions about this work? The following questions may help provoke some ideas.

Probing the Work

1. Explain the symbolic meaning of the storm.

Identifying Issues

2. To what extent does Chopin seem to endorse adultery as a positive event that could actually help a passionless but otherwise healthy marriage? Take a stand for or against this view of the author's intentions.

JOHN UPDIKE

Wife Wooing

John Updike (b. 1932) grew up in Shillington, Pennsylvania, and graduated from Harvard University. Once a reporter for The New Yorker, *he is now a frequent contributor. One of the most prolific and famous of America's writers, his many novels include* Rabbit Is Rich, The Witches of Eastwick, *and* Cousins. *In his work he seeks to "transcribe middleness with all its grits, bumps and anonymities, in it fullness of satisfaction and mystery." The following story appears in* Too Far To Go *(1979).*

Oh my love. Yes. Here we sit, on warm broad floorboards, before a fire, the children between us, in a crescent, eating. The girl and I share one half-pint of french-fried potatoes; you and the boy share another; and in the center, sharing nothing, making simple reflections within himself like a jewel, the baby, mounted in an Easybaby, sucks at his bottle with frowning mastery, his selfish, contemplative eyes stealing glitter from the center of the flames. And you. You. You allow your skirt, the same black skirt in which this morning you with woman's soft bravery mounted a bicycle and sallied forth to play hymns in difficult keys on the Sunday school's old piano—you allow this black skirt to slide off your raised knees down your thighs, slide *up* your thighs in your body's absolute geography, so the parallel whiteness of their undersides is exposed to the fire's warmth and to my sight. Oh. There is a line of Joyce. I try to recover it from the legendary, imperfectly explored grottoes of *Ulysses:* a garter snapped, to please Blazes Boylan, in a deep Dublin den. What? Smackwarm. That was the crucial word. Smacked smackwarm on her smackable warm woman's thighs. Something like that. A splendid man, to feel that. Smackwarm woman's. Splendid also to feel the curious and potent, inexplicable and irrefutably magical life language leads within itself. What soul took thought and knew that adding "wo" to man would make a woman? The difference exactly. The wide w, the receptive o. Womb. In our crescent the children for all their size seem to come out of you toward me, wet fingers and eyes, tinted bronze. Three children, five persons, seven years. Seven years since I wed wide warm woman, white-thighed. Wooed and wed. Wife. A knife of a word that for all its final bite did not end the wooing. To my wonderment.

We eat meat, meat I wrested warm from the raw hands of the hamburger girl in the diner a mile away, a ferocious place, slick with savagery, wild with chrome; young predators snarling dirty jokes menaced me, old men reached for me with coffee-warmed paws; I wielded my wallet, and won my way back. The fat brown bag of buns was warm beside me in the cold car; the smaller bag holding the two tiny cartons of french fries emitted an even more urgent heat. Back through the black winter air to the fire, the intimate cave, where halloos and hurrahs greeted me, the deer, mouth agape and its cotton throat gushing, stretched dead across my shoulders. And now you, beside the white O of the plate upon which the children discarded with squeals of disgust the rings of translucent onion that came squeezed in the hamburgers—you push your toes an inch closer to the blaze, and the ashy white of the inside of your deep thigh is lazily laid bare, and the eternally elastic garter snaps smackwarm against my hidden heart.

Who would have thought, wide wife, back there in the white tremble of the ceremony (in the corner of my eye I held, despite the distracting hail of ominous vows, the vibration of the cluster of stephanotis clutched against your waist), that seven years would bring us no distance, through all those warm beds, to the same trembling point, of beginning? The cells change every seven years, and down in the atom, apparently, there is a strange discontinuity; as if God wills the universe anew every instant. (Ah God, dear God, tall friend of my childhood, I will never forget you, though they say dreadful things. They say rose windows in cathedrals are vaginal symbols.) Your legs, exposed as fully as by a bathing suit, yearn deeper into the amber wash of heat. Well: begin. A green jet of flame spits out sideways from a pocket of resin in a log, crying, and the orange shadows on the ceiling sway with fresh life. Begin.

"Remember, on our honeymoon, how the top of the kerosene heater made a great big rose window on the ceiling?"

"Vnn." Your chin goes to your knees, your shins draw in, all is retracted. Not much to remember, perhaps, for you; blood badly spilled, clumsiness of all sorts. "It was cold for June."

"Mommy, what was cold? What did you say?" the girl asks, enunciating angrily, determined not to let language slip on her tongue and tumble her so that we laugh.

"A house where Daddy and I stayed one time."

"I don't like dat," the boy says, and throws a half bun painted with chartreuse mustard onto the floor.

You pick it up and with beautiful somber musing ask, "Isn't that funny? Did any of the others have mustard on them?"

"I *hate* dat," the boy insists; he is two. Language is to him thick vague handles swirling by; he grabs what he can.

"Here. He can have mine. Give me his." I pass my hamburger over, you take it, he takes it from you, there is nowhere a ripple of gratitude. There is no more praise of my heroism in fetching Sunday supper, saving you labor. Cunning, you sense, and sense that I sense your knowledge, that I had hoped to hoard your energy toward a more ecstatic spending. We sense everything between us, every ripple, existent and nonexistent; it is tiring. Courting a wife takes tenfold the strength of winning an ignorant girl. The fire shifts, shattering fragments of newspaper that carry in lighter gray the ghost of the ink of their message. You huddle your legs and bring the skirt back over them. With a sizzling noise like the sighs of the exhausted logs, the baby sucks the last from his bottle, drops it to the floor with its distasteful hoax of vacant suds, and begins to cry. His egotist's mouth opens; the delicate membrane of his satisfaction tears. You pick him up and stand. You love the baby more than me.

Who would have thought, blood once spilled, that no barrier would be broken, that you would be each time healed into a virgin again? Tall, fair, obscure, remote, and courteous.

We put the children to bed, one by one, in reverse order of birth. I am limitlessly patient, paternal, good. Yet you know. We watch the paper bags and cartons ignite on the breathing pillow of embers, read, watch television, eat crackers, it does not matter. Eleven comes. For a tingling moment you stand on the bedroom rug in your underpants, untangling your nightie; oh, fat white sweet fat fatness. In bed you read about Richard Nixon. He fascinates you; you hate him. You know how he defeated Jerry Voorhis, martyred Mrs. Douglas, how he played poker in the Navy despite being a Quaker, every fiendish trick, every low adaptation. Oh my Lord. Let's let the poor man go to bed. We're none of us perfect. "Hey let's turn out the light."

"Wait. He's just about to get Hiss convicted. It's very strange. It says he acted honorably."

"I'm sure he did." I reach for the switch.

"No. Wait. Just till I finish this chapter. I'm sure there'll be something at the end."

"Honey, Hiss was guilty. We're all guilty. Conceived in concupiscence, we die unrepentant." Once my ornate words wooed you.

I lie against your filmy convex back. You read sideways, a sleepy trick. I see the page through the fringe of your hair, sharp and white as a wedge of crystal. Suddenly it slips. The book has slipped from your hand. You are asleep. Oh cunning trick, cunning. In the darkness I consider. Cunning. The headlights of cars accidentally slide fanning slits of light around our walls and ceiling. The great rose window was projected upward through the petal-shaped perforations in the top of the black kerosene stove, which we stood in the center of the floor. As the flame on the circular wick flickered, the wide soft star of interlocked penumbrae moved and waved as if it were printed on a silk cloth being gently tugged or slowly blown. Its color soft blurred blood. We pay dear in blood for our peaceful homes.

In the morning, to my relief, you are ugly. Monday's wan breakfast light bleaches you blotchily, drains the goodness from your thickness, makes the bathrobe a limp stained tube flapping disconsolately, exposing sallow décolletage. The skin between your breasts a sad yellow. I feast with the coffee on your drabness. Every wrinkle and sickly tint a relief and a revenge. The children yammer. The toaster sticks. Seven years have worn this woman.

The man, he arrows off to work, jousting for right-of-way, veering on the thin hard edge of the legal speed limit. Out of domestic muddle, softness, pallor, flaccidity: into the city. Stone is his province. The winning coin. The maneuvering of abstractions. Making heartless things run. Oh the inanimate, adamant joys of job!

I return with my head enmeshed in a machine. A technicality it would take weeks to explain to you snags my brain; I fiddle with phrases and numbers all the blind evening. You serve me supper as a waitress—as less than a waitress, for I have known you. The children touch me timidly, as they would a steep girder bolted into a framework whose height they don't understand. They drift into sleep securely. We survive their passing in calm parallelity. My thoughts rework in chronic right angles the same snagging circuits on the same professional grid. You rustle the book about Nixon; vanish upstairs into the plumbing; the bathtub pipes cry. In my head I seem to have found the stuck switch at last: I push at it; it jams; I push; it is jammed. I grow dizzy, churning with cigarettes. I circle the room aimlessly.

So I am taken by surprise at a turning when at the meaningful hour of ten you come with a kiss of toothpaste to me moist and girlish and quick; the momentous moral of this story being, An expected gift is not worth giving.

—1960

What are your reactions to and questions about this work? The following questions may help provoke some ideas.

Probing the Work

1. How would you characterize the *narrator?* Is he being sincere or ironic? What is his version of his marriage? How accurate do you think it is? How might his wife's version differ? What is Updike trying to show through his narrator's monologue?

Identifying Issues

2. To what degree is this a romantic view of marriage? To what degree is this a realistic view? How does it match with your own view of marriage?

ROBERT CREELEY

A Marriage

Robert Creeley (b. 1926) was born in Arlington, Massachusetts. He attended Harvard, left to serve in India and Burma with the American Field Service, farmed in New Hampshire, lived in France and Majorca, then finished his B.A. at Black Mountain College in North Carolina in 1955. He taught at Black Mountain College, where he also founded and edited the Black Mountain Review. *Later he taught in Guatemala and at the University of British Columbia. In 1966 he settled at the State University of New York, Buffalo. His book of poems,* For Love: Poems 1950–1960 *(1962) focuses on the difficulties of marriage. Creeley has also published fiction.*

The first retainer
he gave to her
was a golden
wedding ring.

The second—late at night
he woke up,
leaned over on an elbow,
and kissed her.

The third and the last—
he died with
and gave up loving
and lived with her.

—1962

What are your reactions to and questions about this work? The following questions may help provoke some ideas.

Probing the Work

1. What is the *tone* (see p. 67) of this work? What words does Creeley use (his *diction*) to convey that tone? How does the tone change as the poem progresses?

Identifying Issues

2. How does Creeley depict the progression of a marriage? To what degree is such a change in the nature of a marriage inevitable? To what degree is it avoidable?

LIZ ROSENBERG

Married Love

Liz Rosenberg was born in Glen Cove, New York, and attended Bennington College and Johns Hopkins University. She has been teaching English and creative writing at SUNY Binghamton since 1979. Her first full-length poetry collection, The Fire Music, *won the Agnes Lynch Starrett Prize.*

The trees are uncurling their first
green messages: Spring, and some man
lets his arm brush my arm in a darkened
theatre. Faint-headed, I fight the throb.
Later I dream
the gas attendant puts a cool hand
on my breast, asking a question.
Slowly I rise through the surface of the dream,
brushing his hand and my own heat away.

Young, I burned to marry. Married,
the smolder goes on underground,
clutching at weeds, writhing everywhere.
I'm trying to talk to a friend on burning
issues, flaming from the feet up,
drinking in his breath, touching his wrist.
I want to grab the pretty woman
on the street, seize the falcon
by its neck, beat my way into whistling steam.

I turn to you in the dark, oh husband,
watching your lit breath circle the pillow.
Then you turn to me, throwing first one limb
and then another over me, in the easy brotherly
lust of marriage. I cling to you

as if I were a burning ship and you
could save me, as if I won't go sliding down
beneath you soon; as if our lives are made of rise
and fall, and we could ride this out forever,
with longing's thunder rolling heavy in our arms.

—1986

What are your reactions to and questions about this work? The following questions may help provoke some ideas.

Probing the Work

1. What is the difference between the reality of the poet's marriage and her fantasies? How is that difference resolved?
2. Pick out several phrases or images that would seem to be contradictory and analyze their significance.

Identifying Issues

3. Does an ideal marriage need to have an "easy brotherly lust"? What other kinds of passions would fit your ideal of a marriage?

HENRIK IBSEN

A Doll's House

(translated by Michael Meyer)

Henrik Ibsen (1828–1906) was born in Skien, Norway, of wealthy parents who soon after his birth lost their money. Ibsen worked as a pharmacist's apprentice, but at age 22 turned to writing. He worked and wrote for the theatre in Norway, then in Denmark and Germany. By 1865 his plays had won him a state pension that enabled him to settle in Rome. He wrote romantic, historic, and poetic plays, but is best known for such realistic "problem plays" as Ghosts, Hedda Gabler, *and* A Doll's House.

Characters

TORVALD HELMER, *a lawyer*
NORA, *his wife*
DR. RANK
MRS. LINDE
NILS KROGSTAD, *also a lawyer*
THE HELMERS' THREE SMALL CHILDREN
ANNE-MARIE, *their nurse*
HELEN, *the maid*
A PORTER

Scene: The action takes place in the HELMERS' *apartment.*

ACT I

A comfortably and tastefully, but not expensively furnished room. Backstage right a door leads out to the hall; backstage left, another door to HELMER*'s study. Between these two doors stands a piano. In the middle of the left-hand wall is a door, with a window downstage of it. Near the window, a round table with armchairs and a small sofa. In the right-hand wall, slightly upstage, is a door; downstage of this, against the same wall, a stove lined with porcelain tiles, with a couple of armchairs and a rocking-chair in front of it. Between the stove and the side door is a small table. Engravings on the wall. A what-not with china and other bric-a-brac; a small bookcase with leather-bound books. A carpet on the floor; a fire in the stove. A winter day.*

A bell rings in the hall outside. After a moment, we hear the front door being opened. NORA *enters the room, humming contentedly to herself. She is wearing outdoor clothes and carrying a lot of parcels, which she puts down on the table right. She leaves the door to the hall open; through it, we can see a* PORTER *carrying a Christmas tree and a basket. He gives these to the* MAID, *who has opened the door for them.*

NORA: Hide that Christmas tree away, Helen. The children mustn't see it before I've decorated it this evening. *(To the* PORTER, *taking out her purse.)* How much—?

PORTER: A shilling.

NORA: Here's half a crown. No, keep it.

The PORTER *touches his cap and goes.* NORA *closes the door. She continues to laugh happily to herself as she removes her coat, etc. She takes from her pocket a bag containing macaroons and eats a couple. Then she tiptoes across and listens at her husband's door.*

NORA: Yes, he's here. *(Starts humming again as she goes over to the table, right.)*

HELMER *(from his room)*: Is that my skylark twittering out there?

NORA *(opening some of the parcels)*: It is!

HELMER: Is that my squirrel rustling?

NORA: Yes!

HELMER: When did my squirrel come home?

NORA: Just now. *(Pops the bag of macaroons in her pocket and wipes her mouth.)* Come out here, Torvald, and see what I've bought.

HELMER: You mustn't disturb me! *(Short pause; then he opens the door and looks in, his pen in his hand.)* Bought, did you say? All that? Has my little squanderbird been overspending again?

NORA: Oh, Torvald, surely we can let ourselves go a little this year! It's the first Christmas we don't have to scrape.

HELMER: Well, you know, we can't afford to be extravagant.

NORA: Oh yes, Torvald, we can be a little extravagant now. Can't we? Just a tiny bit? You've got a big salary now, and you're going to make lots and lots of money.

HELMER: Next year, yes. But my new salary doesn't start till April.

NORA: Pooh; we can borrow till then.

HELMER: Nora! *(Goes over to her and takes her playfully by the ear.)* What a little spendthrift you are! Suppose I were to borrow fifty pounds today, and you spent it all over Christmas, and then on New Year's Eve a tile fell off a roof on to my head—

NORA *(puts her hand over his mouth)*: Oh, Torvald! Don't say such dreadful things!

HELMER: Yes, but suppose something like that did happen? What then?

NORA: If anything as frightful as that happened, it wouldn't make much difference whether I was in debt or not.

HELMER: But what about the people I'd borrowed from?

NORA: Them? Who cares about them? They're strangers.

HELMER: Oh, Nora, Nora, how like a woman! No, but seriously, Nora, you know how I feel about this. No debts! Never borrow! A home that is founded on debts can never be a place of freedom and beauty. We two have stuck it out bravely up to now; and we shall continue to do so for the short time we still have to.

NORA *(goes over towards the stove)*: Very well, Torvald. As you say.

HELMER: *(follows her)*: Now, now! My little songbird mustn't droop her wings. What's this? Is little squirrel sulking? *(Takes out his purse.)* Nora; guess what I've got here!

NORA *(turns quickly)*: Money!

HELMER: Look. *(Hands her some banknotes.)* I know how these small expenses crop up at Christmas.

NORA *(counts them)*: One—two—three—four. Oh, thank you, Torvald, thank you! I should be able to manage with this.

HELMER: You'll have to.

NORA: Yes, yes, of course I will. But come over here, I want to show you everything I've bought. And so cheaply! Look, here are new clothes for Ivar—and a sword. And a horse and a trumpet for Bob. And a doll and a cradle for Emmy—they're nothing much, but she'll pull them apart in a few days. And some bits of material and handkerchiefs for the maids. Old Anne-Marie ought to have had something better, really.

HELMER: And what's in that parcel?

NORA *(cries)*: No. Torvald, you mustn't see that before this evening!

HELMER: Very well. But now, tell me, you little spendthrift, what do you want for Christmas?

NORA: Me? Oh, pooh, I don't want anything.

HELMER: Oh, yes, you do. Now tell me, what, within reason, would you most like?

NORA: No, I really don't know. Oh, yes—Torvald—!

HELMER: Well?

NORA *(plays with his coat-buttons; not looking at him)*: If you really want to give me something, you could—you could—

HELMER: Come on, out with it.

NORA *(quickly)*: You could give me money, Torvald. Only as much as you feel you can afford; then later I'll buy something with it.

HELMER: But, Nora—

NORA: Oh yes, Torvald dear, please! Please! Then I'll wrap up the notes in pretty gold paper and hang them on the Christmas tree. Wouldn't that be fun?

HELMER: What's the name of that little bird that can never keep any money?

NORA: Yes, yes, squanderbird; I know. But let's do as I say, Torvald; then I'll have time to think about what I need most. Isn't that the best way? Mm?

HELMER *(smiles)*: To be sure it would be, if you could keep what I give you and really buy yourself something with it. But you'll spend it on all sorts of useless things for the house, and then I'll have to put my hand in my pocket again.

NORA: Oh, but Torvald—

HELMER: You can't deny it, Nora dear. *(Puts his arm round her waist.)* The squanderbird's a pretty little creature, but she gets through an awful lot of money. It's incredible what an expensive pet she is for a man to keep.

NORA: For shame! How can you say such a thing? I save every penny I can.

HELMER *(laughs)*: That's quite true. Every penny you can. But you can't.

NORA *(hums and smiles, quietly gleeful)*: Hm. If you only knew how many expenses we larks and squirrels have, Torvald.

HELMER: You're a funny little creature. Just like your father used to be. Always on the look-out for some way to get money, but as soon as you have any it just runs through your fingers, and you never know where it's gone. Well, I suppose I must take you as you are. It's in your blood. Yes, yes, yes, these things are hereditary, Nora.

NORA: Oh, I wish I'd inherited more of Papa's qualities.

HELMER: And I wouldn't wish my darling little songbird to be any different from what she is. By the way, that reminds me. You look awfully—how shall I put it?—awfully guilty today.

NORA: Do I?

HELMER: Yes, you do. Look me in the eyes.

NORA *(looks at him)*: Well?

HELMER *(wags his finger)*: Has my little sweet-tooth been indulging herself in town today, by any chance?

NORA: No, how can you think such a thing?

HELMER: Not a tiny little digression into a pastry shop?

NORA: No, Torvald, I promise—

HELMER: Not just a wee jam tart?

NORA: Certainly not.

HELMER: Not a little nibble at a macaroon?

NORA: No, Torvald—I promise you, honestly—

HELMER: There, there. I was only joking.

NORA *(goes over to the table, right)*: You know I could never act against your wishes.

HELMER: Of course not. And you've given me your word—*(Goes over to her.)* Well, my beloved Nora, you keep your little Christmas secrets to yourself. They'll be revealed this evening, I've no doubt, once the Christmas tree has been lit.

NORA: Have you remembered to invite Dr. Rank?

HELMER: No. But there's no need; he knows he'll be dining with us. Anyway, I'll ask him when he comes this morning. I've ordered some good wine. Oh, Nora, you can't imagine how I'm looking forward to this evening.

NORA: So am I. And, Torvald, how the children will love it!

HELMER: Yes, it's a wonderful thing to know that one's position is assured and that one has an ample income. Don't you agree? It's good to know that, isn't it?

NORA: Yes, it's almost like a miracle.

HELMER: Do you remember last Christmas? For three whole weeks you shut yourself away every evening to make flowers for the Christmas tree, and all those other things you were going to surprise us with. Ugh, it was the most boring time I've ever had in my life.

NORA: I didn't find it boring.

HELMER *(smiles)*: But it all came to nothing in the end, didn't it?

NORA: Oh, are you going to bring that up again? How could I help the cat getting in and tearing everything to bits?

HELMER: No, my poor little Nora, of course you couldn't. You simply wanted to make us happy, and that's all that matters. But it's good that those hard times are past.

NORA: Yes, it's wonderful.

HELMER: I don't have to sit by myself and be bored. And you don't have to tire your pretty eyes and your delicate little hands—

NORA *(claps her hands)*: No, Torvald, that's true, isn't it—I don't have to any longer? Oh, it's really all just like a miracle. *(Takes his arm.)* Now, I'm going to tell you what I thought we might do, Torvald. As soon as Christmas is over—*(A bell rings in the hall.)* Oh, there's the doorbell. *(Tidies up one or two things in the room.)* Someone's coming. What a bore.

HELMER: I'm not at home to any visitors. Remember!

MAID *(in the doorway)*: A lady's called, madam. A stranger.

NORA: Well, ask her to come in.

MAID: And the doctor's here too, sir.

HELMER: Has he gone to my room?

MAID: Yes, sir.

HELMER *goes into his room. The* MAID *shows in* MRS. LINDE, *who is dressed in traveling clothes, and closes the door.*

MRS. LINDE *(shyly and a little hesitantly)*: Good evening, Nora.

NORA *(uncertainly)*: Good evening—

MRS. LINDE: I don't suppose you recognize me.

NORA: No, I'm afraid I—Yes, wait a minute—surely—*(Exclaims.)* Why, Christine! Is it really you?

MRS. LINDE: Yes, it's me.

NORA: Christine! And I didn't recognize you! But how could I—? *(More quietly.)* How you've changed, Christine!

MRS. LINDE: Yes, I know. It's been nine years—nearly ten—

NORA: Is it so long? Yes, it must be. Oh, these last eight years have been such a happy time for me! So you've come to town? All that way in winter! How brave of you!

MRS. LINDE: I arrived by the steamer this morning.

NORA: Yes, of course—to enjoy yourself over Christmas. Oh, how splendid! We'll have to celebrate! But take off your coat. You're not cold, are you? *(Helps her off with it.)* There! Now let's sit down here by the stove and be comfortable. No, you take the armchair. I'll sit here in the rocking-chair. *(Clasps* MRS. LINDE*'s hands.)* Yes, now you look like your old self. It was just at first that—you've got a little paler, though, Christine. And perhaps a bit thinner.

MRS. LINDE: And older, Nora. Much, much older.

NORA: Yes, perhaps a little older. Just a tiny bit. Not much. *(Checks herself suddenly and says earnestly.)* Oh, but how thoughtless of me to sit here and chatter away like this! Dear, sweet Christine, can you forgive me?

MRS. LINDE: What do you mean, Nora?

NORA *(quietly)*: Poor Christine, you've become a widow.

MRS. LINDE: Yes. Three years ago.

NORA: I know, I know—I read it in the papers. Oh, Christine, I meant to write to you so often, honestly. But I always put it off, and something else always cropped up.

MRS. LINDE: I understand, Nora dear.

NORA: No, Christine, it was beastly of me. Oh, my poor darling, what you've gone through! And he didn't leave you anything?

MRS. LINDE: No.

NORA: No children, either?

MRS. LINDE: No.

NORA: Nothing at all, then?

MRS. LINDE: Not even a feeling of loss or sorrow.

NORA *(looks incredulously at her)*: But, Christine, how is that possible?

MRS. LINDE *(smiles sadly and strokes* NORA*'s hair)*: Oh, these things happen, Nora.

NORA: All alone. How dreadful that must be for you. I've three lovely children. I'm afraid you can't see them now, because they're out with nanny. But you must tell me everything—

MRS. LINDE: No, no, no. I want to hear about you.

NORA: No, you start. I'm not going to be selfish today, I'm just going to think about you. Oh, but there's one thing I *must* tell you. Have you heard of the wonderful luck we've just had?

MRS. LINDE: No. What?

NORA: Would you believe it—my husband's just been made manager of the bank!

MRS. LINDE: Your husband? Oh, how lucky—!

NORA: Yes, isn't it? Being a lawyer is so uncertain, you know, especially if one isn't prepared to touch any case that isn't—well—quite nice. And of course Torvald's been very firm about that—and I'm absolutely with him. Oh, you can imagine how happy we are! He's joining the bank in the New Year, and he'll be getting a big salary, and lots of percentages too. From now on we'll be able to live quite differently—we'll be able to do whatever we want. Oh, Christine, it's such a relief! I feel so happy! Well, I mean, it's lovely to have heaps of money and not to have to worry about anything. Don't you think?

MRS. LINDE: It must be lovely to have enough to cover one's needs, anyway.

NORA: Not just our needs! We're going to have heaps and heaps of money!

MRS. LINDE *(smiles)*: Nora, Nora, haven't you grown up yet? When we were at school you were a terrible little spendthrift.

NORA *(laughs quietly)*: Yes, Torvald still says that. *(Wags her finger.)* But "Nora, Nora" isn't as silly as you think. Oh, we've been in no position for me to waste money. We've both had to work.

MRS. LINDE: You too?

NORA: Yes, little things—fancy work, crocheting, embroidery and so forth. *(Casually.)* And other things too. I suppose you know Torvald left the Ministry when we got married? There were no prospects of promotion in his department, and of course he needed more money. But the first year he overworked himself quite dreadfully. He had to take on all sorts of extra jobs, and worked day and night. But it was too much for him, and he became frightfully ill. The doctors said he'd have to go to a warmer climate.

MRS. LINDE: Yes, you spent a whole year in Italy, didn't you?

NORA: Yes. It wasn't easy for me to get away, you know. I'd just had Ivar. But of course we had to do it. Oh, it was a marvelous trip! And it saved Torvald's life. But it cost an awful lot of money, Christine.

MRS. LINDE: I can imagine.

NORA: Two hundred and fifty pounds. That's a lot of money, you know.

MRS. LINDE: How lucky you had it.

NORA: Well, actually, we got it from my father.

MRS. LINDE: Oh, I see. Didn't he die just about that time?

NORA: Yes, Christine, just about then. Wasn't it dreadful, I couldn't go and look after him. I was expecting little Ivar any day. And then I had my poor Torvald to care for—we really didn't think he'd live. Dear, kind Papa! I never saw him again, Christine. Oh, it's the saddest thing that's happened to me since I got married.

MRS. LINDE: I know you were very fond of him. But you went to Italy—

NORA: Yes. Well, we had the money, you see, and the doctors said we mustn't delay. So we went the month after Papa died.

MRS. LINDE: And your husband came back completely cured?

NORA: Fit as a fiddle!

MRS. LINDE: But—the doctor?

NORA: How do you mean?

MRS. LINDE: I thought the maid said that the gentleman who arrived with me was the doctor.

NORA: Oh yes, that's Doctor Rank, but he doesn't come because anyone's ill. He's our best friend, and he looks us up at least once every day. No, Torvald hasn't had a moment's illness since we went away. And the children are fit and healthy and so am I. *(Jumps up and claps her hands.)* Oh God, oh God, Christine, isn't it a wonderful thing to be alive and happy! Oh, but how beastly of me! I'm only talking about myself. *(Sits on a footstool and rests her arms on* MRS. LINDE'S *knee.)* Oh, please don't be angry with me! Tell me, is it really true you didn't love your husband? Why did you marry him, then?

MRS. LINDE: Well, my mother was still alive; and she was helpless and bedridden. And I had my two little brothers to take care of. I didn't feel I could say no.

NORA: Yes, well, perhaps you're right. He was rich then, was he?

MRS. LINDE: Quite comfortably off, I believe. But his business was unsound, you see, Nora. When he died it went bankrupt, and there was nothing left.

NORA: What did you do?

MRS. LINDE: Well, I had to try to make ends meet somehow, so I started a little shop, and a little school, and anything else I could turn my hand to. These last three years have been just one endless slog for me, without a moment's rest. But now it's over, Nora. My poor dear mother doesn't need me any more; she's passed away. And the boys don't need me either; they've got jobs now and can look after themselves.

NORA: How relieved you must feel—

MRS. LINDE: No, Nora. Just unspeakably empty. No one to live for any more. *(Gets up restlessly.)* That's why I couldn't bear to stay out there any longer, cut off from the world. I thought it'd be easier to find some work here that will exercise and occupy my mind. If only I could get a regular job—office work of some kind—

NORA: Oh but, Christine, that's dreadfully exhausting; and you look practically finished already. It'd be much better for you if you could go away somewhere.

MRS. LINDE *(goes over to the window)*: I have no Papa to pay for my holidays, Nora.

NORA *(gets up)*: Oh, please don't be angry with me.

MRS. LINDE: My dear Nora, it's I who should ask you not to be angry. That's the worst thing about this kind of situation—it makes one so bitter. One has no one to work for; and yet one has to be continually sponging for jobs. One has to live; and so one becomes completely egocentric. When you told me about this luck you've just had with Torvald's new job—can you imagine?—I was happy not so much on your account, as on my own.

NORA: How do you mean? Oh, I understand. You mean Torvald might be able to do something for you?

MRS. LINDE: Yes, I was thinking that.

NORA: He will too, Christine. Just you leave it to me. I'll lead up to it so delicately, so delicately; I'll get him in the right mood. Oh, Christine, I do so want to help you.

MRS. LINDE: It's sweet of you to bother so much about me, Nora. Especially since you know so little of the worries and hardships of life.

NORA: I? You say *I* know little of—?

MRS. LINDE *(smiles)*: Well, good heavens—those bits of fancy work of yours—well, really—! You're a child, Nora.

NORA *(tosses her head and walks across the room)*: You shouldn't say that so patronizingly.

MRS. LINDE: Oh?

NORA: You're like the rest. You all think I'm incapable of getting down to anything serious—

MRS. LINDE: My dear—

NORA: You think I've never had any worries like the rest of you.

MRS. LINDE: Nora dear, you've just told me about all your difficulties—

NORA: Pooh—that! *(Quietly.)* I haven't told you about the big thing.

MRS. LINDE: What big thing? What do you mean?

NORA: You patronize me, Christine; but you shouldn't. You're proud that you've worked so long and so hard for your mother.

MRS. LINDE: I don't patronize anyone, Nora. But you're right—I am both proud and happy that I was able to make my mother's last months on earth comparatively easy.

NORA: And you're also proud of what you've done for your brothers.

MRS. LINDE: I think I have a right to be.

NORA: I think so too. But let me tell you something, Christine. I too have done something to be proud and happy about.

MRS. LINDE: I don't doubt it. But—how do you mean?

NORA: Speak quietly! Suppose Torvald should hear! He mustn't, at any price—no one must know, Christine—no one but you.

MRS. LINDE: But what is this?

NORA: Come over here. *(Pulls her down on to the sofa beside her.)* Yes, Christine—I too have done something to be happy and proud about. It was I who saved Torvald's life.

MRS. LINDE: Saved his—? How did you save it?

NORA: I told you about our trip to Italy. Torvald couldn't have lived if he hadn't managed to get down there—

MRS. LINDE: Yes, well—your father provided the money—

NORA *(smiles)*: So Torvald and everyone else thinks. But—

MRS. LINDE: Yes?

NORA: Papa didn't give us a penny. It was I who found the money.

MRS. LINDE: You? All of it?

NORA: Two hundred and fifty pounds. What do you say to that?

MRS. LINDE: But Nora, how could you? Did you win a lottery or something?

NORA *(scornfully)*: Lottery? *(Sniffs.)* What would there be to be proud of in that?

MRS. LINDE: But where did you get it from, then?

NORA *(hums and smiles secretively)*: Hm; tra-la-la-la!

MRS. LINDE: You couldn't have borrowed it.

NORA: Oh? Why not?

MRS. LINDE: Well, a wife can't borrow money without her husband's consent.

NORA *(tosses her head)*: Ah, but when a wife has a little business sense, and knows how to be clever—

MRS. LINDE: But Nora, I simply don't understand—

NORA: You don't have to. No one has said I borrowed the money. I could have got it in some other way. *(Throws herself back on the sofa.)* I could have got it from an admirer. When a girl's as pretty as I am—

MRS. LINDE: Nora, you're crazy!

NORA: You're dying of curiosity now, aren't you, Christine?

MRS. LINDE: Nora dear, you haven't done anything foolish?

NORA *(sits up again)*: Is it foolish to save one's husband's life?

MRS. LINDE: I think it's foolish if without his knowledge you—

NORA: But the whole point was that he mustn't know! Great heavens, don't you see? He hadn't to know how dangerously ill he was. I was the one they told that his life was in danger and that only going to a warm climate could save him. Do you suppose I didn't try to think of other ways of getting him down there? I told him how wonderful it would be for me to go abroad like other young wives; I cried and prayed; I asked him to remember my condition, and said he ought to be nice and tender to me; and then I suggested he might quite easily borrow the money. But then he got almost angry with me, Christine. He said I was frivolous, and that it was his duty as a husband not to pander to my moods and caprices—I think that's what he called them. Well, well, I thought, you've got to be saved somehow. And then I thought of a way—

MRS. LINDE: But didn't your husband find out from your father that the money hadn't come from him?

NORA: No, never. Papa died just then. I'd thought of letting him into the plot and asking him not to tell. But since he was so ill—! And as things turned out, it didn't become necessary.

MRS. LINDE: And you've never told your husband about this?

NORA: For heaven's sake, no! What an idea! He's frightfully strict about such matters. And besides—he's so proud of being a *man*—it'd be so painful and humiliating for him to know that he owed anything to me. It'd completely wreck our relationship. This life we have built together would no longer exist.

MRS. LINDE: Will you never tell him?

NORA *(thoughtfully, half-smiling)*: Yes—some time, perhaps. Years from now, when I'm no longer pretty. You mustn't laugh! I mean of course, when Torvald no longer loves me as he does now; when it no longer amuses him to see me dance and dress up and play the fool for him. Then it might be useful to have something up my sleeve. *(Breaks off.)* Stupid, stupid, stupid! That time will never come. Well, what do you think of my big secret, Christine? I'm not completely useless, am I? Mind you, all this has caused me a frightful lot of worry. It hasn't been easy for me to meet my obligations punctually. In case you don't know, in the world of business there are things called quarterly installments and interest, and they're a terrible problem to cope with. So I've had to scrape a little here and save a little there as best I can. I haven't been able to save much on the housekeeping money, because Torvald likes to live well; and I couldn't let the children go short of clothes—I couldn't take anything out of what he gives me for them. The poor little angels!

MRS. LINDE: So you've had to stint yourself, my poor Nora?

NORA: Of course. Well, after all, it was my problem. Whenever Torvald gave me money to buy myself new clothes, I never used more than half of it; and I always bought what was cheapest and plainest. Thank heaven anything suits me, so that Torvald's never noticed. But it made me a bit sad sometimes, because it's lovely to wear pretty clothes. Don't you think?

MRS. LINDE: Indeed it is.

NORA: And then I've found one or two other sources of income. Last winter I managed to get a lot of copying to do. So I shut myself away and wrote every evening, late into the night. Oh, I often got so tired, so tired. But it was great fun, though, sitting there working and earning money. It was almost like being a man.

MRS. LINDE: But how much have you managed to pay off like this?

NORA: Well, I can't say exactly. It's awfully difficult to keep an exact check on these kind of transactions. I only know I've paid everything I've managed to scrape together. Sometimes I really didn't know where to turn. *(Smiles.)* Then I'd sit here and imagine some rich old gentleman had fallen in love with me—

MRS. LINDE: What! What gentleman?

NORA: Silly! And that now he'd died and when they opened his will it said in big letters: "Everything I possess is to be paid forthwith to my beloved Mrs. Nora Helmer in cash."

MRS. LINDE: But, Nora dear, who was this gentleman?

NORA: Great heavens, don't you understand? There wasn't any old gentleman; he was just something I used to dream up as I sat here evening after evening wondering how on earth I could raise some money. But what does it matter? The old bore can stay imaginary as far as I'm concerned, because now I don't have to worry any longer! *(Jumps up.)* Oh, Christine, isn't it wonderful? I don't have to worry any more! No more troubles! I can play all day with the children, I can fill the house with pretty things, just the way Torvald likes. And, Christine, it'll soon be spring, and the air'll be fresh and the skies blue,—and then perhaps we'll be able to take a little trip somewhere. I shall be able to see the sea again. Oh, yes, yes, it's a wonderful thing to be alive and happy!

The bell rings in the hall.

MRS. LINDE *(gets up)*: You've a visitor. Perhaps I'd better go.

NORA: No, stay. It won't be for me. It's someone for Torvald—

MAID *(in the doorway)*: Excuse me, madam, a gentleman's called who says he wants to speak to the master. But I didn't know—seeing as the doctor's with him—

NORA: Who is this gentleman?

KROGSTAD *(in the doorway)*: It's me, Mrs. Helmer.

MRS. LINDE *starts, composes herself, and turns away to the window.*

NORA *(takes a step toward him and whispers tensely)*: You? What is it? What do you want to talk to my husband about?

KROGSTAD: Business—you might call it. I hold a minor post in the bank, and I hear your husband is to become our new chief—

NORA: Oh—then it isn't—?

KROGSTAD: Pure business, Mrs. Helmer. Nothing more.

NORA: Well, you'll find him in his study.

Nods indifferently as she closes the hall door behind him. Then she walks across the room and sees to the stove.

MRS. LINDE: Nora, who was that man?

NORA: A lawyer called Krogstad.

MRS. LINDE: It was him, then.

NORA: Do you know that man?

Mrs. Linde: I used to know him—some years ago. He was a solicitor's clerk in our town, for a while.

Nora: Yes, of course, so he was.

Mrs. Linde: How he's changed!

Nora: He was very unhappily married, I believe.

Mrs. Linde: Is he a widower now?

Nora: Yes, with a lot of children. Ah, now it's alight.

She closes the door of the stove and moves the rocking-chair a little to one side.

Mrs. Linde: He does—various things now, I hear?

Nora: Does he? It's quite possible—I really don't know. But don't let's talk about business. It's so boring.

Dr. Rank *enters from* Helmer*'s study.*

Rank *(still in the doorway)*: No, no, my dear chap, don't see me out. I'll go and have a word with your wife. *(Closes the door and notices* Mrs. Linde.*)* Oh, I beg your pardon. I seem to be *de trop* here too.

Nora: Not in the least. *(Introduces them.)* Dr. Rank. Mrs. Linde.

Rank: Ah! A name I have often heard in this house. I believe I passed you on the stairs as I came up.

Mrs. Linde: Yes. Stairs tire me; I have to take them slowly.

Rank: Oh, have you hurt yourself?

Mrs. Linde: No, I'm just a little run down.

Rank: Ah, is that all? Then I take it you've come to town to cure yourself by a round of parties?

Mrs. Linde: I have come here to find work.

Rank: Is that an approved remedy for being run down?

Mrs. Linde: One has to live, Doctor.

Rank: Yes, people do seem to regard it as a necessity.

Nora: Oh, really, Dr. Rank. I bet you want to stay alive.

Rank: You bet I do. However miserable I sometimes feel, I still want to go on being tortured for as long as possible. It's the same with all my patients; and with people who are morally sick, too. There's a moral cripple in with Helmer at this very moment—

Mrs. Linde *(softly)*: Oh!

Nora: Whom do you mean?

Rank: Oh, a lawyer fellow called Krogstad—you wouldn't know him. He's crippled all right; morally twisted. But even he started off by announcing, as though it were a matter of enormous importance, that he had to live.

Nora: Oh? What did he want to talk to Torvald about?

Rank: I haven't the faintest idea. All I heard was something about the bank.

Nora: I didn't know that Krog—that this man Krogstad had any connection with the bank.

RANK: Yes, he's got some kind of job down there. *(To* MRS. LINDE.*)* I wonder if in your part of the world you too have a species of human being that spends its time fussing around trying to smell out moral corruption? And when they find a case they give him some nice, comfortable position so that they can keep a good watch on him. The healthy ones just have to lump it.

MRS. LINDE: But surely it's the sick who need care most?

RANK *(shrugs his shoulders)*: Well, there we have it. It's that attitude that's turning human society into a hospital.

NORA, *lost in her own thoughts, laughs half to herself and claps her hands.*

RANK: Why are you laughing? Do you really know what society is?

NORA: What do I care about society? I think it's a bore. I was laughing at something else—something frightfully funny. Tell me, Dr. Rank—will everyone who works at the bank come under Torvald now?

RANK: Do you find that particularly funny?

NORA *(smiles and hums)*: Never you mind! Never you mind! *(Walks around the room.)* Yes, I find it very amusing to think that we—I mean, Torvald—has obtained so much influence over so many people. *(Takes the paper bag from her pocket.)* Dr. Rank, would you like a small macaroon?

RANK: Macaroons! I say! I thought they were forbidden here.

NORA: Yes, well, these are some Christine gave me.

MRS. LINDE: What? I—?

NORA: All right, all right, don't get frightened. You weren't to know Torvald had forbidden them. He's afraid they'll ruin my teeth. But, dash it—for once—! Don't you agree, Dr. Rank? Here! *(Pops a macaroon into his mouth.)* You too, Christine. And I'll have one too. Just a little one. Two at the most. *(Begins to walk round again.)* Yes, now I feel really, really happy. Now there's just one thing in the world I'd really love to do.

RANK: Oh? And what is that?

NORA: Just something I'd love to say to Torvald.

RANK: Well, why don't you say it?

NORA: No, I daren't. It's too dreadful.

MRS. LINDE: Dreadful?

RANK: Well, then, you'd better not. But you can say it to us. What is it you'd so love to say to Torvald?

NORA: I've the most extraordinary longing to say: "Bloody hell!"

RANK: Are you mad?

MRS. LINDE: My dear Nora—!

RANK: Say it. Here he is.

NORA *(hiding the bag of macaroons)*: Ssh! Ssh!

HELMER, *with his overcoat on his arm and his hat in his hand, enters from his study.*

NORA *(goes to meet him)*: Well, Torvald dear, did you get rid of him?

HELMER: Yes, he's just gone.

NORA: May I introduce you—? This is Christine. She's just arrived in town.

HELMER: Christine—? Forgive me, but I don't think—

NORA: Mrs. Linde, Torvald dear. Christine Linde.

HELMER: Ah. A childhood friend of my wife's, I presume?

MRS. LINDE: Yes, we knew each other in earlier days.

NORA: And imagine, now she's traveled all this way to talk to you.

HELMER: Oh?

MRS. LINDE: Well, I didn't really—

NORA: You see, Christine's frightfully good at office work, and she's mad to come under some really clever man who can teach her even more than she knows already—

HELMER: Very sensible, madam.

NORA: So when she heard you'd become head of the bank—it was in her local paper—she came here as quickly as she could and—Torvald, you will, won't you? Do a little something to help Christine? For my sake?

HELMER: Well, that shouldn't be impossible. You are a widow, I take it, Mrs. Linde?

MRS. LINDE: Yes.

HELMER: And you have experience of office work?

MRS. LINDE: Yes, quite a bit.

HELMER: Well then, it's quite likely I may be able to find some job for you—

NORA *(claps her hands)*: You see, you see!

HELMER: You've come at a lucky moment, Mrs. Linde.

MRS. LINDE: Oh, how can I ever thank you—?

HELMER: There's absolutely no need. *(Puts on his overcoat.)* But now I'm afraid I must ask you to excuse me—

RANK: Wait. I'll come with you.

He gets his fur coat from the hall and warms it at the stove.

NORA: Don't be long, Torvald dear.

HELMER: I'll only be an hour.

NORA: Are you going too, Christine?

MRS. LINDE *(puts on her outdoor clothes)*: Yes, I must start to look round for a room.

HELMER: Then perhaps we can walk part of the way together.

NORA *(helps her)*: It's such a nuisance we're so cramped here—I'm afraid we can't offer to—

MRS. LINDE: Oh, I wouldn't dream of it. Goodbye, Nora dear, and thanks for everything.

NORA: *Au revoir*. You'll be coming back this evening, of course. And you too, Dr. Rank. What? If you're well enough? Of course you'll be well enough. Wrap up warmly, though.

They go out, talking, into the hall. Children's voices are heard from the stairs.

NORA: Here they are! Here they are!

She runs out and opens the door. ANNE-MARIE, *the nurse, enters with the children.*

NORA: Come in, come in! *(Stoops down and kisses them.)* Oh, my sweet darlings—! Look at them, Christine! Aren't they beautiful?

RANK: Don't stand here chattering in this draught!

HELMER: Come, Mrs. Linde. This is for mothers only.

DR. RANK, HELMER, *and* MRS. LINDE *go down the stairs. The* NURSE *brings the children into the room.* NORA *follows, and closes the door to the hall.*

NORA: How well you look! What red cheeks you've got! Like apples and roses! *(The children answer her inaudibly as she talks to them.)* Have you had fun? That's splendid. You gave Emmy and Bob a ride on the sledge? What, both together? I say! What a clever boy you are, Ivar! Oh, let me hold her for a moment, Anne-Marie! My sweet little baby doll! *(Takes the smallest child from the nurse and dances with her.)* Yes, yes, Mummy will dance with Bob too. What? Have you been throwing snowballs? Oh, I wish I'd been there! No, don't—I'll undress them myself, Anne-Marie. No, please let me; it's such fun. Go inside and warm yourself; you look frozen. There's some hot coffee on the stove. *(The nurse goes into the room on the left.* NORA *takes off the children's outdoor clothes and throws them anywhere while they all chatter simultaneously.)* What? A big dog ran after you? But he didn't bite you? No, dogs don't bite lovely little baby dolls. Leave those parcels alone, Ivar. What's in them? Ah, wouldn't you like to know! No, no; it's nothing nice. Come on, let's play a game. What shall we play? Hide and seek. Yes, let's play hide and seek. Bob shall hide first. You want me to? All right, let me hide first.

NORA *and the children play around the room, and in the adjacent room to the left, laughing and shouting. At length* NORA *hides under the table. The* CHILDREN *rush in, look, but cannot find her. Then they hear her half-stifled laughter, run to the table, lift up the cloth, and see her. Great excitement. She crawls out as though to frighten them. Further excitement. Meanwhile, there has been a knock on the door leading from the hall, but no one has noticed it. Now the door is half-opened and* KROGSTAD *enters. He waits for a moment; the game continues.*

KROGSTAD: Excuse me, Mrs. Helmer—

NORA *(turns with a stifled cry and half jumps up)*: Oh! What do you want?

KROGSTAD: I beg your pardon; the front door was ajar. Someone must have forgotten to close it.

NORA *(gets up)*: My husband is not at home, Mr. Krogstad.

KROGSTAD: I know.

NORA: Well, what do you want here, then?

KROGSTAD: A word with you.

NORA: With—? *(To the children, quietly.)* Go inside to Anne-Marie. What? No, the strange gentleman won't do anything to hurt Mummy. When he's gone we'll start playing again.

She takes the children into the room on the left and closes the door behind them.

NORA *(uneasy, tense)*: You want to speak to me?

KROGSTAD: Yes.

NORA: Today? But it's not the first of the month yet.

KROGSTAD: No, it is Christmas Eve. Whether or not you have a merry Christmas depends on you.

NORA: What do you want? I can't give you anything today—

KROGSTAD: We won't talk about that for the present. There's something else. You have a moment to spare?

NORA: Oh, yes. Yes, I suppose so; though—

KROGSTAD: Good. I was sitting in the café down below and I saw your husband cross the street—

NORA: Yes.

KROGSTAD: With a lady.

NORA: Well?

KROGSTAD: Might I be so bold as to ask: was not that lady a Mrs. Linde?

NORA: Yes.

KROGSTAD: Recently arrived in town?

NORA: Yes, today.

KROGSTAD: She is a good friend of yours, is she not?

NORA: Yes, she is. But I don't see—

KROGSTAD: I used to know her too once.

NORA: I know.

KROGSTAD: Oh? You've discovered that. Yes, I thought you would. Well then, may I ask you a straight question: is Mrs. Linde to be employed at the bank?

NORA: How dare you presume to cross-examine me, Mr. Krogstad? You, one of my husband's employees? But since you ask, you shall have an answer. Yes, Mrs. Linde is to be employed by the bank. And I arranged it, Mr. Krogstad. Now you know.

KROGSTAD: I guessed right, then.

NORA *(walks up and down the room)*: Oh, one has a little influence, you know. Just because one's a woman it doesn't necessarily mean that—When one is in a humble position, Mr. Krogstad, one should think twice before offending someone who—hm—

KROGSTAD:—who has influence?

NORA: Precisely.

KROGSTAD *(changes his tone)*: Mrs. Helmer, will you have the kindness to use your influence on my behalf?

NORA: What? What do you mean?

KROGSTAD: Will you be so good as to see that I keep my humble position at the bank?

NORA: What do you mean? Who is thinking of removing you from your position?

KROGSTAD: Oh, you don't need to play innocent with me. I realize it can't be very pleasant for your friend to risk bumping into me; and now I also realize whom I have to thank for being hounded out like this.

NORA: But I assure you—

KROGSTAD: Look, let's not beat about the bush. There's still time, and I'd advise you to use your influence to stop it.

NORA: But, Mr. Krogstad, I have no influence!

KROGSTAD: Oh? I thought you just said—

NORA: But I didn't mean it like that! I? How on earth could you imagine that I would have any influence over my husband?

KROGSTAD: Oh, I've known your husband since we were students together. I imagine he has his weaknesses like other married men.

NORA: If you speak impertinently of my husband, I shall show you the door.

KROGSTAD: You're a bold woman, Mrs. Helmer.

NORA: I'm not afraid of you any longer. Once the New Year is in, I'll soon be rid of you.

KROGSTAD *(more controlled)*: Now listen to me, Mrs. Helmer. If I'm forced to, I shall fight for my little job at the bank as I would fight for my life.

NORA: So it sounds.

KROGSTAD: It isn't just the money; that's the last thing I care about. There's something else—well, you might as well know. It's like this, you see. You know of course, as everyone else does, that some years ago I committed an indiscretion.

NORA: I think I did hear something—

KROGSTAD: It never came into court; but from that day, every opening was barred to me. So I turned my hand to the kind of business you know about. I had to do something; and I don't think I was one of the worst. But now I want to give up all that. My sons are growing up; for their sake, I must try to regain what respectability I can. This job in the bank was the first step on the ladder. And now your husband wants to kick me off that ladder back into the dirt.

NORA: But my dear Mr. Krogstad, it simply isn't in my power to help you.

KROGSTAD: You say that because you don't want to help me. But I have the means to make you.

NORA: You don't mean you'd tell my husband that I owe you money?

KROGSTAD: And if I did?

NORA: That'd be a filthy trick! *(Almost in tears.)* This secret that is my pride and my joy—that he should hear about it in such a filthy, beastly way—hear about it from you! It'd involve me in the most dreadful unpleasantness—

KROGSTAD: Only—unpleasantness?

NORA *(vehemently)*: All right, do it! You'll be the one who'll suffer. It'll show my husband the kind of man you are, and then you'll never keep your job.

KROGSTAD: I asked you whether it was merely domestic unpleasantness you were afraid of.

NORA: If my husband hears about it, he will of course immediately pay you whatever is owing. And then we shall have nothing more to do with you.

KROGSTAD *(takes a step closer)*: Listen, Mrs. Helmer. Either you've a bad memory or else you know very little about financial transactions. I had better enlighten you.

NORA: What do you mean?

KROGSTAD: When your husband was ill, you came to me to borrow two hundred and fifty pounds.

NORA: I didn't know anyone else.

KROGSTAD: I promised to find that sum for you—

NORA: And you did find it.

KROGSTAD: I promised to find that sum for you on certain conditions. You were so worried about your husband's illness and so keen to get the money to take him abroad that I don't think you bothered much about the details. So it won't be out of place if I refresh your memory. Well—I promised to get you the money in exchange for an I.O.U., which I drew up.

NORA: Yes, and which I signed.

KROGSTAD: Exactly. But then I added a few lines naming your father as security for the debt. This paragraph was to be signed by your father.

NORA: Was to be? He did sign it.

KROGSTAD: I left the date blank for your father to fill in when he signed this paper. You remember, Mrs. Helmer?

NORA: Yes, I think so—

KROGSTAD: Then I gave you back this I.O.U. for you to post to your father. Is that not correct?

NORA: Yes.

KROGSTAD: And of course you posted it at once; for within five or six days you brought it along to me with your father's signature on it. Whereupon I handed you the money.

NORA: Yes, well. Haven't I repaid the installments as agreed?

KROGSTAD: Mm—yes, more or less. But to return to what we were speaking about—that was a difficult time for you just then, wasn't it, Mrs. Helmer?

NORA: Yes, it was.

KROGSTAD: And your father was very ill, if I am not mistaken.

NORA: He was dying.

KROGSTAD: He did in fact die shortly afterwards?

NORA: Yes.

KROGSTAD: Tell me, Mrs. Helmer, do you by any chance remember the date of your father's death? The day of the month, I mean.

NORA: Papa died on the twenty-ninth of September.

KROGSTAD: Quite correct; I took the trouble to confirm it. And that leaves me with a curious little problem—*(Takes out a paper.)*—which I simply cannot solve.

NORA: Problem? I don't see—

KROGSTAD: The problem, Mrs. Helmer, is that your father signed this paper three days after his death.

NORA: What? I don't understand—

KROGSTAD: Your father died on the twenty-ninth of September. But look at this. Here your father has dated his signature the second of October. Isn't that a curious little problem, Mrs. Helmer? *(*NORA *is silent.)* Can you suggest any explanation? *(She remains silent.)* And there's another curious thing. The words "second of October" and the year are written in a hand which is not your father's, but which I seem to know. Well, there's a simple explanation to that. Your father could have forgotten to write in the date when he signed, and someone else could have added it before the news came of his death. There's nothing criminal about that. It's the signature itself I'm wondering about. It *is* genuine, I suppose, Mrs. Helmer? It was your father who wrote his name here?

NORA *(after a short silence, throws back her head and looks defiantly at him)*: No, it was not. It was I who wrote Papa's name there.

KROGSTAD: Look, Mrs. Helmer, do you realize this is a dangerous admission?

NORA: Why? You'll get your money.

KROGSTAD: May I ask you a question? Why didn't you send this paper to your father?

NORA: I couldn't. Papa was very ill. If I'd asked him to sign this, I'd have had to tell him what the money was for. But I couldn't have told him in his condition that my husband's life was in danger. I couldn't have done that!

KROGSTAD: Then you would have been wiser to have given up your idea of a holiday.

NORA: But I couldn't! It was to save my husband's life. I couldn't put it off.

KROGSTAD: But didn't it occur to you that you were being dishonest towards me?

NORA: I couldn't bother about that. I didn't care about you. I hated you because of all the beastly difficulties you'd put in my way when you knew how dangerously ill my husband was.

KROGSTAD: Mrs. Helmer, you evidently don't appreciate exactly what you have done. But I can assure you that it is no bigger nor worse a crime than the one I once committed, and thereby ruined my whole social position.

NORA: You? Do you expect me to believe that you would have taken a risk like that to save your wife's life?

KROGSTAD: The law does not concern itself with motives.

NORA: Then the law must be very stupid.

KROGSTAD: Stupid or not, if I show this paper to the police, you will be judged according to it.

NORA: I don't believe that. Hasn't a daughter the right to shield her father from worry and anxiety when he's old and dying? Hasn't a wife the right to save her husband's life? I don't know much about the law, but there must be something somewhere that says that such things are allowed. You ought to know about that, you're meant to be a lawyer, aren't you? You can't be a very good lawyer, Mr. Krogstad.

KROGSTAD: Possibly not. But business, the kind of business we two have been transacting—I think you'll admit I understand something about that? Good. Do as you please. But I tell you this. If I get thrown into the gutter for a second time, I shall take you with me.

He bows and goes out through the hall.

NORA *(stands for a moment in thought, then tosses her head)*: What nonsense! He's trying to frighten me! I'm not that stupid. *(Busies herself gathering together the children's clothes; then she suddenly stops.)* But—? No, it's impossible. I did it for love, didn't I?

CHILDREN *(in the doorway, left)*: Mummy, the strange gentleman's gone out into the street.

NORA: Yes, yes, I know. But don't talk to anyone about the strange gentleman. You hear? Not even to Daddy.

CHILDREN: No, Mummy. Will you play with us again now?

NORA: No, no. Not now.

CHILDREN: Oh but, Mummy, you promised!

NORA: I know, but I can't just now. Go back to the nursery. I've a lot to do. Go away, my darlings, go away. *(She pushes them gently into the other room, and closes the door behind them. She sits on the sofa, takes up her embroidery, stitches for a few moments, but soon stops.)* No! *(Throws the embroidery aside, gets up, goes to the door leading to the hall, and calls.)* Helen! Bring in the Christmas tree! *(She goes to the table on the left and opens the drawer in it; then pauses again.)* No, but it's utterly impossible!

MAID *(enters with the tree)*: Where shall I put it, madam?

NORA: There, in the middle of the room.

MAID: Will you be wanting anything else?

NORA: No, thank you, I have everything I need.

The MAID *puts down the tree and goes out.*

NORA *(busy decorating the tree)*: Now—candles here—and flowers here. That loathsome man! Nonsense, nonsense, there's nothing to be frightened about. The Christmas tree must be beautiful. I'll do everything that you like, Torvald. I'll sing for you, dance for you—

HELMER, *with a bundle of papers under his arm, enters.*

NORA: Oh—are you back already?

HELMER: Yes. Has anyone been here?

NORA: Here? No.

HELMER: That's strange. I saw Krogstad come out of the front door.

NORA: Did you? Oh yes, that's quite right—Krogstad was here for a few minutes.

HELMER: Nora, I can tell from your face, he's been here and asked you to put in a good word for him.

NORA: Yes.

HELMER: And you were to pretend you were doing it of your own accord? You weren't going to tell me he'd been here? He asked you to do that too, didn't he?

NORA: Yes, Torvald. But—

HELMER: Nora, Nora! And you were ready to enter into such a conspiracy? Talking to a man like that, and making him promises—and then, on top of it all, to tell me an untruth!

NORA: An untruth?

HELMER: Didn't you say no one had been here? *(Wags his finger.)* My little songbird must never do that again. A songbird must have a clean beak to sing with; otherwise she'll start twittering out of tune. *(Puts his arm round her waist.)* Isn't that the way we want things? Yes, of course it is. *(Lets go of her.)* So let's hear no more about that. *(Sits down in front of the stove.)* Ah, how cozy and peaceful it is here. *(Glances for a few moments at his papers.)*

NORA *(busy with the tree; after a short silence)*: Torvald.

HELMER: Yes.

NORA: I'm terribly looking forward to that fancy dress ball at the Stenborgs on Boxing Day.

HELMER: And I'm terribly curious to see what you're going to surprise me with.

NORA: Oh, it's so maddening.

HELMER: What is?

NORA: I can't think of anything to wear. It all seems so stupid and meaningless.

HELMER: So my little Nora's come to that conclusion, has she?

NORA *(behind his chair, resting her arms on its back)*: Are you very busy, Torvald?

HELMER: Oh—

NORA: What are those papers?

HELMER: Just something to do with the bank.

NORA: Already?

HELMER: I persuaded the trustees to give me authority to make certain immediate changes in the staff and organization. I want to have everything straight by the New Year.

NORA: Then that's why this poor man Krogstad—

HELMER: Hm.

NORA *(still leaning over his chair, slowly strokes the back of his head)*: If you hadn't been so busy, I was going to ask you an enormous favor, Torvald.

HELMER: Well, tell me. What was it to be?

NORA: You know I trust your taste more than anyone's. I'm so anxious to look really beautiful at the fancy dress ball. Torvald, couldn't you help me to decide what I shall go as, and what kind of costume I ought to wear?

HELMER: Aha! So little Miss Independent's in trouble and needs a man to rescue her, does she?

NORA: Yes, Torvald. I can't get anywhere without your help.

HELMER: Well, well, I'll give the matter thought. We'll find something.

NORA: Oh, how kind of you! *(Goes back to the tree. Pause.)* How pretty these red flowers look! But, tell me, is it so dreadful, this thing that Krogstad's done?

HELMER: He forged someone else's name. Have you any idea what that means?

NORA: Mightn't he have been forced to do it by some emergency?

HELMER: He probably just didn't think—that's what usually happens. I'm not so heartless as to condemn a man for an isolated action.

NORA: No, Torvald, of course not!

HELMER: Men often succeed in re-establishing themselves if they admit their crime and take their punishment.

NORA: Punishment?

HELMER: But Krogstad didn't do that. He chose to try and trick his way out of it; and that's what has morally destroyed him.

NORA: You think that would—?

HELMER: Just think how a man with that load on his conscience must always be lying and cheating and dissembling; how he must wear a mask even in the presence of those who are dearest to him, even his own wife and children! Yes, the children. That's the worst danger, Nora.

NORA: Why?

HELMER: Because an atmosphere of lies contaminates and poisons every corner of the home. Every breath that the children draw in such a house contains the germs of evil.

NORA *(comes closer behind him)*: Do you really believe that?

HELMER: Oh, my dear, I've come across it so often in my work at the bar. Nearly all young criminals are the children of mothers who are constitutional liars.

NORA: Why do you say mothers?

HELMER: It's usually the mother; though of course the father can have the same influence. Every lawyer knows that only too well. And yet this fellow Krogstad has been sitting at home all these years poisoning his children with his lies and pretenses. That's why I say that, morally speaking, he is dead. *(Stretches out his hands towards her.)* So my pretty little Nora must promise me not to plead his case. Your hand on it. Come, come, what's this? Give me your hand. There. That's settled, now. I assure you it'd be quite impossible for me to work in the same building as him. I literally feel physically ill in the presence of a man like that.

NORA *(draws her hand from his and goes over to the other side of the Christmas tree)*: How hot it is in here! And I've so much to do.

HELMER *(gets up and gathers his papers)*: Yes, and I must try to get some of this read before dinner. I'll think about your costume too. And I may even have something up my sleeve to hang in gold paper on the Christmas tree. *(Lays his hand on her head.)* My precious little songbird!

He goes into his study and closes the door.

NORA *(softly, after a pause)*: It's nonsense. It must be. It's impossible. It *must* be impossible!

NURSE *(in the doorway, left)*: The children are asking if they can come in to Mummy.

NORA: No, no, no; don't let them in! You stay with them, Anne-Marie.

NURSE: Very good, madam. *(Closes the door.)*

NORA *(pale with fear)*: Corrupt my little children—! Poison my home! *(Short pause. She throws back her head.)* It isn't true! It *couldn't* be true!

ACT II

The same room. In the corner by the piano the Christmas tree stands, stripped and disheveled, its candles burned to their sockets. NORA*'s outdoor clothes lie on the sofa. She is alone in the room, walking restlessly to and fro. At length she stops by the sofa and picks up her coat.*

NORA *(drops the coat again)*: There's someone coming! *(Goes to the door and listens.)* No, it's no one. Of course—no one'll come today, it's Christmas Day. Nor tomorrow. But perhaps—! *(Opens the door and looks out.)* No. Nothing in the letter-box. Quite empty. *(Walks across the room.)* Silly, silly. Of course he won't do anything. It couldn't happen. It isn't possible. Why, I've three small children.

The NURSE, *carrying a large cardboard box, enters from the room on the left.*

NURSE: I found those fancy dress clothes at last, madam.

NORA: Thank you. Put them on the table.

NURSE *(does so)*: They're all rumpled up.

NORA: Oh, I wish I could tear them into a million pieces!

NURSE: Why, madam! They'll be all right. Just a little patience.

NORA: Yes, of course. I'll go and get Mrs. Linde to help me.

NURSE: What, out again? In this dreadful weather? You'll catch a chill, madam.

NORA: Well, that wouldn't be the worst. How are the children?

NURSE: Playing with their Christmas presents, poor little dears. But—

NORA: Are they still asking to see me?

NURSE: They're so used to having their Mummy with them.

NORA: Yes, but, Anne-Marie, from now on I shan't be able to spend so much time with them.

NURSE: Well, children get used to anything in time.

NORA: Do you think so? Do you think they'd forget their mother if she went away from them—for ever?

NURSE: Mercy's sake, madam! For ever!

NORA: Tell me, Anne-Marie—I've so often wondered. How could you bear to give your child away—to strangers?

NURSE: But I had to when I came to nurse my little Miss Nora.

NORA: Do you mean you wanted to?

NURSE: When I had the chance of such a good job? A poor girl what's got into trouble can't afford to pick and choose. That good-for-nothing didn't lift a finger.

NORA: But your daughter must have completely forgotten you.

NURSE: Oh no, indeed she hasn't. She's written to me twice, once when she got confirmed and then again when she got married.

NORA *(hugs her)*: Dear old Anne-Marie, you were a good mother to me.

NURSE: Poor little Miss Nora, you never had any mother but me.

NORA: And if my little ones had no one else, I know you would—no, silly, silly, silly! *(Opens the cardboard box.)* Go back to them, Anne-Marie. Now I must—Tomorrow you'll see how pretty I shall look.

NURSE: Why, there'll be no one at the ball as beautiful as my Miss Nora.

She goes into the room, left.

NORA *(begins to unpack the clothes from the box, but soon throws them down again)*: Oh, if only I dared to go out! If I could be sure no one would come, and nothing would happen while I was away! Stupid, stupid! No one will come. I just mustn't think about it. Brush this muff. Pretty gloves, pretty gloves! Don't think about it, don't think about it! One, two, three, four, five, six—*(Cries.)* Ah—they're coming—!

She begins to run toward the door, but stops uncertainly. MRS. LINDE *enters from the hall, where she has been taking off her outdoor clothes.*

NORA: Oh, it's you, Christine. There's no one else out there, is there? Oh, I'm so glad you've come.

MRS. LINDE: I hear you were at my room asking for me.

NORA: Yes, I just happened to be passing. I want to ask you to help me with something. Let's sit down here on the sofa. Look at this. There's going to be a fancy dress ball tomorrow night upstairs at Consul Stenborg's, and Torvald wants me to go as a Neapolitan fisher-girl and dance the tarantella. I learned it on Capri.

MRS. LINDE: I say, are you going to give a performance?

NORA: Yes, Torvald says I should. Look, here's the dress. Torvald had it made for me in Italy; but now it's all so torn, I don't know—

MRS. LINDE: Oh, we'll soon put that right; the stitching's just come away. Needle and thread? Ah, here we are.

NORA: You're being awfully sweet.

MRS. LINDE *(sews)*: So you're going to dress up tomorrow, Nora? I must pop over for a moment to see how you look. Oh, but I've completely forgotten to thank you for that nice evening yesterday.

NORA *(gets up and walks across the room)*: Oh, I didn't think it was as nice as usual. You ought to have come to town a little earlier, Christine. . . . Yes, Torvald understands how to make a home look attractive.

MRS. LINDE: I'm sure you do, too. You're not your father's daughter for nothing. But, tell me. Is Dr. Rank always in such low spirits as he was yesterday?

NORA: No, last night it was very noticeable. But he's got a terrible disease; he's got spinal tuberculosis, poor man. His father was a frightful creature who kept mistresses and so on. As a result Dr. Rank has been sickly ever since he was a child—you understand—

MRS. LINDE *(puts down her sewing)*: But, my dear Nora, how on earth did you get to know about such things?

NORA *(walks about the room)*: Oh, don't be silly, Christine—when one has three children, one comes into contact with women who—well, who know about medical matters, and they tell one a thing or two.

MRS. LINDE *(sews again; a short silence)*: Does Dr. Rank visit you every day?

NORA: Yes, every day. He's Torvald's oldest friend, and a good friend to me too. Dr. Rank's almost one of the family.

MRS. LINDE: But, tell me—is he quite sincere? I mean, doesn't he rather say the sort of thing he thinks people want to hear?

NORA: No, quite the contrary. What gave you that idea?

MRS. LINDE: When you introduced me to him yesterday, he said he'd often heard my name mentioned here. But later I noticed your husband had no idea who I was. So how could Dr. Rank—?

NORA: Yes, that's quite right, Christine. You see, Torvald's so hopelessly in love with me that he wants to have me all to himself—those were his very words. When we were first married, he got quite jealous if I as much as mentioned any of my old friends back home. So naturally, I stopped talking about them. But I often chat with Dr. Rank about that kind of thing. He enjoys it, you see.

MRS. LINDE: Now listen, Nora. In many ways you're still a child; I'm a bit older than you and have a little more experience of the world. There's something I want to say to you. You ought to give up this business with Dr. Rank.

NORA: What business?

MRS. LINDE: Well, everything. Last night you were speaking about this rich admirer of yours who was going to give you money—

NORA: Yes, and who doesn't exist—unfortunately. But what's that got to do with—?

MRS. LINDE: Is Dr. Rank rich?

NORA: Yes.

MRS. LINDE: And he has no dependents?

NORA: No, no one. But—

MRS. LINDE: And he comes here to see you every day?

NORA: Yes, I've told you.

MRS. LINDE: But how dare a man of his education be so forward?

NORA: What on earth are you talking about?

MRS. LINDE: Oh, stop pretending, Nora. Do you think I haven't guessed who it was who lent you that two hundred pounds?

NORA: Are you out of your mind? How could you imagine such a thing? A friend, someone who comes here every day! Why, that'd be an impossible situation!

MRS. LINDE: Then it really wasn't him?

NORA: No, of course not. I've never for a moment dreamed of—anyway, he hadn't any money to lend then. He didn't come into that till later.

MRS. LINDE: Well, I think that was a lucky thing for you, Nora dear.

NORA: No, I could never have dreamed of asking Dr. Rank— Though I'm sure that if I ever did ask him—

MRS. LINDE: But of course you won't.

NORA: Of course not. I can't imagine that it should ever become necessary. But I'm perfectly sure that if I did speak to Dr. Rank—

MRS. LINDE: Behind your husband's back?

NORA: I've got to get out of this other business; and *that's* been going on behind his back. I've *got* to get out of it.

MRS. LINDE: Yes, well, that's what I told you yesterday. But—

NORA *(walking up and down)*: It's much easier for a man to arrange these things than a woman—

MRS. LINDE: One's own husband, yes.

NORA: Oh, bosh. *(Stops walking.)* When you've completely repaid a debt, you get your I.O.U. back, don't you?

MRS. LINDE: Yes, of course.

NORA: And you can tear it into a thousand pieces and burn the filthy, beastly thing!

MRS. LINDE *(looks hard at her, puts down her sewing, and gets up slowly)*: Nora, you're hiding something from me.

NORA: Can you see that?

MRS. LINDE: Something has happened since yesterday morning. Nora, what is it?

NORA *(goes toward her)*: Christine! *(Listens.)* Ssh! There's Torvald. Would you mind going into the nursery for a few minutes? Torvald can't bear to see sewing around. Anne-Marie'll help you.

MRS. LINDE *(gathers some of her things together)*: Very well. But I shan't leave this house until we've talked this matter out.

She goes into the nursery, left. As she does so, HELMER *enters from the hall.*

NORA *(runs to meet him)*: Oh, Torvald dear, I've been so longing for you to come back!

HELMER: Was that the dressmaker?

NORA: No, it was Christine. She's helping me mend my costume. I'm going to look rather splendid in that.

HELMER: Yes, that was quite a bright idea of mine, wasn't it?

NORA: Wonderful! But wasn't it nice of me to give in to you?

HELMER *(takes her chin in his hand)*: Nice—to give in to your husband? All right, little silly, I know you didn't mean it like that. But I won't disturb you. I expect you'll be wanting to try it on.

NORA: Are you going to work now?

HELMER: Yes. *(Shows her a bundle of papers.)* Look at these. I've been down to the bank—*(Turns to go into his study.)*

NORA: Torvald.

HELMER *(stops)*: Yes.

NORA: If little squirrel asked you really prettily to grant her a wish—

HELMER: Well?

NORA: Would you grant it to her?

HELMER: First I should naturally have to know what it was.

NORA: Squirrel would do lots of pretty tricks for you if you granted her wish.

HELMER: Out with it, then.

NORA: Your little skylark would sing in every room—

HELMER: My little skylark does that already.

NORA: I'd turn myself into a little fairy and dance for you in the moonlight, Torvald.

HELMER: Nora, it isn't that business you were talking about this morning?

NORA *(comes closer)*: Yes, Torvald—oh, please! I beg of you!

HELMER: Have you really the nerve to bring that up again?

NORA: Yes, Torvald, yes, you must do as I ask! You must let Krogstad keep his place at the bank!

HELMER: My dear Nora, his is the job I'm giving to Mrs. Linde.

NORA: Yes, that's terribly sweet of you. But you can get rid of one of the other clerks instead of Krogstad.

HELMER: Really, you're being incredibly obstinate. Just because you thoughtlessly promised to put in a word for him, you expect me to—

NORA: No, it isn't that, Helmer. It's for your own sake. That man writes for the most beastly newspapers—you said so yourself. He could do you tremendous harm. I'm so dreadfully frightened of him—

HELMER: Oh, I understand. Memories of the past. That's what's frightening you.

NORA: What do you mean?

HELMER: You're thinking of your father, aren't you?

NORA: Yes, yes. Of course. Just think what those dreadful men wrote in the papers about Papa! The most frightful slanders. I really believe it would have lost him his job if the Ministry hadn't sent you down to investigate, and you hadn't been so kind and helpful to him.

HELMER: But my dear little Nora, there's a considerable difference between your father and me. Your father was not a man of unassailable reputation. But I am; and I hope to remain so all my life.

NORA: But no one knows what spiteful people may not dig up. We could be so peaceful and happy now, Torvald—we could be free from every worry—you and I and the children. Oh, please, Torvald, please—!

HELMER: The very fact of your pleading his cause makes it impossible for me to keep him. Everyone at the bank already knows that I intend to dismiss Krogstad. If the rumor got about that the new manager had allowed his wife to persuade him to change his mind—

NORA: Well, what then?

HELMER: Oh, nothing, nothing. As long as my little Miss Obstinate gets her way—Do you expect me to make a laughing-stock of myself before my entire staff—give people the idea that I am open to outside influence? Believe me, I'd soon feel the consequences! Besides—there's something else that makes it impossible for Krogstad to remain in the bank while I am its manager.

NORA: What is that?

HELMER: I might conceivably have allowed myself to ignore his moral obloquies—

NORA: Yes, Torvald, surely?

HELMER: And I hear he's quite efficient at his job. But we—well, we were schoolfriends. It was one of those friendships that one enters into overhastily and so often comes to regret later in life. I might as well confess the truth. We—well, we're on Christian name terms. And the tactless idiot makes no attempt to conceal it when other people are present. On the contrary, he thinks it gives him the right to be familiar with me. He shows off the whole time, with "Torvald this," and "Torvald that." I can tell you, I find it damned annoying. If he stayed, he'd make my position intolerable.

NORA: Torvald, you can't mean this seriously.

HELMER: Oh? And why not?

NORA: But it's so petty.

HELMER: What did you say? Petty? You think *I* am petty?

NORA: No, Torvald dear, of course you're not. That's just why—

HELMER: Don't quibble! You call my motives petty. Then I must be petty too. Petty! I see. Well, I've had enough of this. *(Goes to the door and calls into the hall.)* Helen!

Nora: What are you going to do?

Helmer *(searching among his papers)*: I'm going to settle this matter once and for all. *(The* Maid *enters.)* Take this letter downstairs at once. Find a messenger and see that he delivers it. Immediately! The address is on the envelope. Here's the money.

Maid: Very good, sir. *(Goes out with the letter.)*

Helmer *(putting his papers in order)*: There now, little Miss Obstinate.

Nora *(tensely)*: Torvald—what was in that letter?

Helmer: Krogstad's dismissal.

Nora: Call her back, Torvald! There's still time. Oh, Torvald, call her back! Do it for my sake—for your own sake—for the children! Do you hear me, Torvald? Please do it! You don't realize what this may do to us all!

Helmer: Too late.

Nora: Yes. Too late.

Helmer: My dear Nora, I forgive you this anxiety. Though it is a bit of an insult to me. Oh, but it is! Isn't it an insult to imply that I should be frightened by the vindictiveness of a depraved hack journalist? But I forgive you, because it so charmingly testifies to the love you bear me. *(Takes her in his arms.)* Which is as it should be, my own dearest Nora. Let what will happen, happen. When the real crisis comes, you will not find me lacking in strength or courage. I am man enough to bear the burden for us both.

Nora *(fearfully)*: What do you mean?

Helmer: The whole burden, I say—

Nora *(calmly)*: I shall never let you do that.

Helmer: Very well. We shall share it, Nora—as man and wife. And that is as it should be. *(Caresses her.)* Are you happy now? There, there, there; don't look at me with those frightened little eyes. You're simply imagining things. You go ahead now and do your tarantella, and get some practice on that tambourine. I'll sit in my study and close the door. Then I won't hear anything, and you can make all the noise you want. *(Turns in the doorway.)* When Dr. Rank comes, tell him where to find me. *(He nods to her, goes into his room with his papers, and closes the door.)*

Nora *(desperate with anxiety, stands as though transfixed, and whispers)*: He said he'd do it. He will do it. He will do it, and nothing'll stop him. No, never that. I'd rather anything. There must be some escape—Some way out—! *(The bell rings in the hall.)* Dr. Rank—! Anything but that! Anything, I don't care—!

She passes her hand across her face, composes herself, walks across, and opens the door to the hall. Dr. Rank *is standing there, hanging up his fur coat. During the following scene, it begins to grow dark.*

Nora: Good evening, Dr. Rank. I recognized your ring. But you mustn't go to Torvald yet. I think he's busy.

RANK: And—you?

NORA *(as he enters the room and she closes the door behind him)*: Oh, you know very well I've always time to talk to you.

RANK: Thank you. I shall avail myself of that privilege as long as I can.

NORA: What do you mean by that? As long as you *can?*

RANK: Yes. Does that frighten you?

NORA: Well, it's rather a curious expression. Is something going to happen?

RANK: Something I've been expecting to happen for a long time. But I didn't think it would happen quite so soon.

NORA *(seizes his arm)*: What is it? Dr. Rank, you must tell me!

RANK *(sits down by the stove)*: I'm on the way out. And there's nothing to be done about it.

NORA *(sighs with relief)*: Oh, it's you—?

RANK: Who else? No, it's no good lying to oneself. I am the most wretched of all my patients, Mrs. Helmer. These last few days I've been going through the books of this poor body of mine, and I find I am bankrupt. Within a month I may be rotting up there in the churchyard.

NORA: Ugh, what a nasty way to talk!

RANK: The facts aren't exactly nice. But the worst is that there's so much else that's nasty to come first. I've only one more test to make. When that's done I'll have a pretty accurate idea of when the final disintegration is likely to begin. I want to ask you a favor. Helmer's a sensitive chap, and I know how he hates anything ugly. I don't want him to visit me when I'm in hospital—

NORA: Oh but, Dr. Rank—

RANK: I don't want him there. On any pretext. I shan't have him allowed in. As soon as I know the worst, I'll send you my visiting card with a black cross on it, and then you'll know that the final filthy process has begun.

NORA: Really, you're being quite impossible this evening. And I did hope you'd be in a good mood.

RANK: With death on my hands? And all this to atone for someone else's sin? Is there justice in that? And in every single family, in one way or another, the same merciless law of retribution is at work—

NORA *(holds her hands to her ears)*: Nonsense! Cheer up! Laugh!

RANK: Yes, you're right. Laughter's all the damned thing's fit for. My poor innocent spine must pay for the fun my father had as a gay young lieutenant.

NORA *(at the table, left)*: You mean he was too fond of asparagus and *foie gras?*

RANK: Yes, and truffles too.

NORA: Yes, of course, truffles, yes. And oysters too, I suppose?

RANK: Yes, oysters, oysters. Of course.

NORA: And all that port and champagne to wash them down. It's too sad that all those lovely things should affect one's spine.

RANK: Especially a poor spine that never got any pleasure out of them.

NORA: Oh yes, that's the saddest thing of all.

RANK *(looks searchingly at her)*: Hm—

NORA *(after a moment)*: Why did you smile?

RANK: No, it was you who laughed.

NORA: No, it was you who smiled, Dr. Rank!

RANK *(gets up)*: You're a worse little rogue than I thought.

NORA: Oh, I'm full of stupid tricks today.

RANK: So it seems.

NORA *(puts both her hands on his shoulders)*: Dear, dear Dr. Rank, you mustn't die and leave Torvald and me.

RANK: Oh, you'll soon get over it. Once one is gone, one is soon forgotten.

NORA *(looks at him anxiously)*: Do you believe that?

RANK: One finds replacements, and then—

NORA: Who will find a replacement?

RANK: You and Helmer both will, when I am gone. You seem to have made a start already, haven't you? What was this Mrs. Linde doing here yesterday evening?

NORA: Aha! But surely you can't be jealous of poor Christine?

RANK: Indeed I am. She will be my successor in this house. When I have moved on, this lady will—

NORA: Ssh—don't speak so loud! She's in there!

RANK: Today again? You see!

NORA: She's only come to mend my dress. Good heavens, how unreasonable you are! *(Sits on the sofa.)* Be nice now, Dr. Rank. Tomorrow you'll see how beautifully I shall dance; and you must imagine that I'm doing it just for you. And for Torvald of course; obviously. *(Takes some things out of the box.)* Dr. Rank, sit down here and I'll show you something.

RANK *(sits)*: What's this?

NORA: Look here! Look!

RANK: Silk stockings!

NORA: Flesh colored. Aren't they beautiful? It's very dark in here now, of course, but tomorrow—No, no, no; only the soles. Oh well, I suppose you can look a bit higher if you want to.

RANK: Hm—

NORA: Why are you looking so critical? Don't you think they'll fit me?

RANK: I can't really give you a qualified opinion on that.

NORA *(looks at him for a moment)*: Shame on you! *(Flicks him on the ear with the stockings.)* Take that. *(Puts them back in the box.)*

RANK: What other wonders are to be revealed to me?

NORA: I shan't show you anything else. You're being naughty.

She hums a little and looks among the things in the box.

Rank *(after a short silence)*: When I sit here like this being so intimate with you, I can't think—I cannot imagine what would have become of me if I had never entered this house.

Nora *(smiles)*: Yes, I think you enjoy being with us, don't you?

Rank *(more quietly, looking into the middle distance)*: And now to have to leave it all—

Nora: Nonsense. You're not leaving us.

Rank *(as before)*: And not to be able to leave even the most wretched token of gratitude behind; hardly even a passing sense of loss; only an empty place, to be filled by the next comer.

Nora: Suppose I were to ask you to—? No—

Rank: To do what?

Nora: To give me proof of your friendship—

Rank: Yes, yes?

Nora: No, I mean—to do me a very great service—

Rank: Would you really for once grant me that happiness?

Nora: But you've no idea what it is.

Rank: Very well, tell me, then.

Nora: No, but, Dr. Rank, I can't. It's far too much—I want your help and advice, and I want you to do something for me.

Rank: The more the better. I've no idea what it can be. But tell me. You do trust me, don't you?

Nora: Oh, yes, more than anyone. You're my best and truest friend. Otherwise I couldn't tell you. Well then, Dr. Rank—there's something you must help me to prevent. You know how much Torvald loves me—he'd never hesitate for an instant to lay down his life for me—

Rank *(leans over towards her)*: Nora—do you think he is the only one—?

Nora *(with a slight start)*: What do you mean?

Rank: Who would gladly lay down his life for you?

Nora *(sadly)*: Oh, I see.

Rank: I swore to myself I would let you know that before I go. I shall never have a better opportunity. . . . Well, Nora, now you know that. And now you also know that you can trust me as you can trust nobody else.

Nora *(rises; calmly and quietly)*: Let me pass, please.

Rank *(makes room for her but remains seated)*: Nora—

Nora *(in the doorway to the hall)*: Helen, bring the lamp. *(Goes over to the stove.)* Oh, dear Dr. Rank, this was really horrid of you.

Rank *(gets up)*: That I have loved you as deeply as anyone else has? Was that horrid of me?

Nora: No—but that you should go and tell me. That was quite unnecessary—

Rank: What do you mean? Did you know, then—?

The Maid *enters with the lamp, puts it on the table, and goes out.*

RANK: Nora—Mrs. Helmer—I am asking you, did you know this?

NORA: Oh, what do I know, what did I know, what didn't I know—I really can't say. How could you be so stupid, Dr. Rank? Everything was so nice.

RANK: Well, at any rate now you know that I am ready to serve you, body and soul. So—please continue.

NORA *(looks at him)*: After this?

RANK: Please tell me what it is.

NORA: I can't possibly tell you now.

RANK: Yes, yes! You mustn't punish me like this. Let me be allowed to do what I can for you.

NORA: You can't do anything for me now. Anyway, I don't need any help. It was only my imagination—you'll see. Yes, really. Honestly. *(Sits in the rocking-chair, looks at him, and smiles.)* Well, upon my word you *are* a fine gentleman, Dr. Rank. Aren't you ashamed of yourself, now that the lamp's been lit?

RANK: Frankly, no. But perhaps I ought to say—*adieu?*

NORA: Of course not. You will naturally continue to visit us as before. You know quite well how Torvald depends on your company.

RANK: Yes, but you?

NORA: Oh, I always think it's enormous fun having you here.

RANK: That was what misled me. You're a riddle to me, you know. I'd often felt you'd just as soon be with me as with Helmer.

NORA: Well, you see, there are some people whom one loves, and others whom it's almost more fun to be with.

RANK: Oh yes, there's some truth in that.

NORA: When I was at home, of course I loved Papa best. But I always used to think it was terribly amusing to go down and talk to the servants; because they never told me what I ought to do; and they were such fun to listen to.

RANK: I see. So I've taken their place?

NORA *(jumps up and runs over to him)*: Oh, dear, sweet Dr. Rank, I didn't mean that at all. But I'm sure you understand—I feel the same about Torvald as I did about Papa.

MAID *(enters from the hall)*: Excuse me, madam. *(Whispers to her and hands her a visiting card.)*

NORA *(glances at the card)*: Oh! *(Puts it quickly in her pocket.)*

RANK: Anything wrong?

NORA: No, no, nothing at all. It's just something that—it's my new dress.

RANK: What? But your costume is lying over there.

NORA: Oh—that, yes—but there's another—I ordered it specially—Torvald mustn't know—

RANK: Ah, so that's your big secret?

NORA: Yes, yes. Go in and talk to him—he's in his study—keep him talking for a bit—

RANK: Don't worry. He won't get away from me. *(Goes into* HELMER'S *study.)*

NORA *(to the* MAID*)*: Is he waiting in the kitchen?

MAID: Yes, madam, he came up the back way—

NORA: But didn't you tell him I had a visitor?

MAID: Yes, but he wouldn't go.

NORA: Wouldn't go?

MAID: No, madam, not until he'd spoken with you.

NORA: Very well, show him in; but quietly. Helen, you mustn't tell anyone about this. It's a surprise for my husband.

MAID: Very good, madam. I understand. *(Goes.)*

NORA: It's happening. It's happening after all. No, no, no, it can't happen, it mustn't happen.

She walks across and bolts the door of HELMER*'s study. The* MAID *opens the door from the hall to admit* KROGSTAD, *and closes it behind him. He is wearing an overcoat, heavy boots, and a fur cap.*

NORA *(goes towards him)*: Speak quietly. My husband's at home.

KROGSTAD: Let him hear.

NORA: What do you want from me?

KROGSTAD: Information.

NORA: Hurry up, then. What is it?

KROGSTAD: I suppose you know I've been given the sack.

NORA: I couldn't stop it, Mr. Krogstad. I did my best for you, but it didn't help.

KROGSTAD: Does your husband love you so little? He knows what I can do to you, and yet he dares to—

NORA: Surely you don't imagine I told him?

KROGSTAD: No. I didn't really think you had. It wouldn't have been like my old friend Torvald Helmer to show that much courage—

NORA: Mr. Krogstad, I'll trouble you to speak respectfully of my husband.

KROGSTAD: Don't worry, I'll show him all the respect he deserves. But since you're so anxious to keep this matter hushed up, I presume you're better informed than you were yesterday of the gravity of what you've done?

NORA: I've learned more than you could ever teach me.

KROGSTAD: Yes, a bad lawyer like me—

NORA: What do you want from me?

KROGSTAD: I just wanted to see how things were with you, Mrs. Helmer. I've been thinking about you all day. Even duns and hack journalists have hearts, you know.

NORA: Show some heart, then. Think of my little children.

KROGSTAD: Have you and your husband thought of mine? Well, let's forget that. I just wanted to tell you, you don't need to take this business too seriously, I'm not going to take any action, for the present.

NORA: Oh, no—you won't, will you? I knew it.

KROGSTAD: It can all be settled quite amicably. There's no need for it to become public. We'll keep it among the three of us.

NORA: My husband must never know about this.

KROGSTAD: How can you stop him? Can you pay the balance of what you owe me?

NORA: Not immediately.

KROGSTAD: Have you any means of raising the money during the next few days?

NORA: None that I would care to use.

KROGSTAD: Well, it wouldn't have helped anyway. However much money you offered me now I wouldn't give you back that paper.

NORA: What are you going to do with it?

KROGSTAD: Just keep it. No one else need ever hear about it. So in case you were thinking of doing anything desperate—

NORA: I am.

KROGSTAD: Such as running away—

NORA: I am.

KROGSTAD: Or anything more desperate—

NORA: How did you know?

KROGSTAD: —just give up the idea.

NORA: How did you know?

KROGSTAD: Most of us think of that at first. I did. But I hadn't the courage—

NORA *(dully)*: Neither have I.

KROGSTAD *(relieved)*: It's true, isn't it? You haven't the courage either?

NORA: No. I haven't. I haven't.

KROGSTAD: It'd be a stupid thing to do anyway. Once the first little domestic explosion is over. . . . I've got a letter in my pocket here addressed to your husband—

NORA: Telling him everything?

KROGSTAD: As delicately as possible.

NORA *(quickly)*: He must never see that letter. Tear it up. I'll find the money somehow—

KROGSTAD: I'm sorry, Mrs. Helmer, I thought I'd explained—

NORA: Oh, I don't mean the money I owe you. Let me know how much you want from my husband, and I'll find it for you.

KROGSTAD: I'm not asking your husband for money.

NORA: What do you want, then?

KROGSTAD: I'll tell you. I want to get on my feet again, Mrs. Helmer. I want to get to the top. And your husband's going to help me. For eighteen months now my record's been clean. I've been in hard straits all that time; I was content to fight my way back inch by inch. Now I've been chucked back into the mud, and I'm not going to be satisfied with just getting back my job. I'm going to get to the top, I tell you. I'm going to get back into the bank, and it's going to be higher up. Your husband's going to create a new job for me—

NORA: He'll never do that!

KROGSTAD: Oh, yes he will. I know him. He won't dare to risk a scandal. And once I'm in there with him, you'll see! Within a year I'll be his right-hand man. It'll be Nils Krogstad who'll be running that bank, not Torvald Helmer!

NORA: That will never happen.

KROGSTAD: Are you thinking of—?

NORA: Now I *have* the courage.

KROGSTAD: Oh, you can't frighten me. A pampered little pretty like you—

NORA: You'll see! You'll see!

KROGSTAD: Under the ice? Down in the cold, black water? And then, in the spring, to float up again, ugly, unrecognizable, hairless—?

NORA: You can't frighten me.

KROGSTAD: And you can't frighten me. People don't do such things, Mrs. Helmer. And anyway, what'd be the use? I've got him in my pocket.

NORA: But afterwards? When I'm no longer—?

KROGSTAD: Have you forgotten that then your reputation will be in my hands? *(She looks at him speechlessly.)* Well, I've warned you. Don't do anything silly. When Helmer's read my letter, he'll get in touch with me. And remember, it's your husband who's forced me to act like this. And for that I'll never forgive him. Goodbye, Mrs. Helmer. *(He goes out through the hall.)*

NORA *(runs to the hall door, opens it a few inches, and listens)*: He's going. He's not going to give him the letter. Oh, no, no, it couldn't possibly happen. *(Opens the door a little wider.)* What's he doing? Standing outside the front door. He's not going downstairs. Is he changing his mind? Yes, he—!

A letter falls into the letter-box. KROGSTAD*'s footsteps die away down the stairs.*

NORA *(with a stifled cry, runs across the room towards the table by the sofa. A pause)*: In the letter-box. *(Steals timidly over towards the hall door.)* There it is! Oh, Torvald, Torvald! Now we're lost!

MRS. LINDE *(enters from the nursery with* NORA*'s costume)*: Well, I've done the best I can. Shall we see how it looks—?

NORA *(whispers hoarsely)*: Christine, come here.

MRS. LINDE *(throws the dress on the sofa)*: What's wrong with you? You look as though you'd seen a ghost!

NORA: Come here. Do you see that letter? There—look—through the glass of the letter-box.

MRS. LINDE: Yes, yes, I see it.

NORA: That letter's from Krogstad—

MRS. LINDE: Nora! It was Krogstad who lent you the money!

NORA: Yes. And now Torvald's going to discover everything.

MRS. LINDE: Oh, believe me, Nora, it'll be best for you both.

NORA: You don't know what's happened. I've committed a forgery—

MRS. LINDE: But, for heaven's sake—!

NORA: Christine, all I want is for you to be my witness.

MRS. LINDE: What do you mean? Witness what?

NORA: If I should go out of my mind—and it might easily happen—

MRS. LINDE: Nora!

NORA: Or if anything else should happen to me—so that I wasn't here any longer—

MRS. LINDE: Nora, Nora, you don't know what you're saying!

NORA: If anyone should try to take the blame, and say it was all his fault—you understand—?

MRS. LINDE: Yes, yes—but how can you think—?

NORA: Then you must testify that it isn't true, Christine. I'm not mad—I know exactly what I'm saying—and I'm telling you, no one else knows anything about this. I did it entirely on my own. Remember that.

MRS. LINDE: All right. But I simply don't understand—

NORA: Oh, how could you understand? A—miracle—is about to happen.

MRS. LINDE: Miracle?

NORA: Yes. A miracle. But it's so frightening, Christine. It *mustn't* happen, not for anything in the world.

MRS. LINDE: I'll go over and talk to Krogstad.

NORA: Don't go near him. He'll only do something to hurt you.

MRS. LINDE: Once upon a time he'd have done anything for my sake.

NORA: He?

MRS. LINDE: Where does he live?

NORA: Oh, how should I know—? Oh, yes, wait a moment—! *(Feels in her pocket.)* Here's his card. But the letter, the letter—!

HELMER *(from his study, knocks on the door)*: Nora!

NORA *(cries in alarm)*: What is it?

HELMER: Now, now, don't get alarmed. We're not coming in; you've closed the door. Are you trying on your costume?

NORA: Yes, yes—I'm trying on my costume. I'm going to look so pretty for you, Torvald.

MRS. LINDE *(who has been reading the card)*: Why, he lives just around the corner.

NORA: Yes; but it's no use. There's nothing to be done now. The letter's lying there in the box.

MRS. LINDE: And your husband has the key?

NORA: Yes, he always keeps it.

MRS. LINDE: Krogstad must ask him to send the letter back unread. He must find some excuse—

NORA: But Torvald always opens the box at just about this time—

MRS. LINDE: You must stop him. Go in and keep him talking. I'll be back as quickly as I can.

She hurries out through the hall.

NORA *(goes over to* HELMER*'s door, opens it and peeps in)*: Torvald!

HELMER *(offstage)*: Well, may a man enter his own drawing-room again? Come on, Rank, now we'll see what—*(In the doorway.)* But what's this?

NORA: What, Torvald dear?

HELMER: Rank's been preparing me for some great transformation scene.

RANK *(in the doorway)*: So I understood. But I seem to have been mistaken.

NORA: Yes, no one's to be allowed to see me before tomorrow night.

HELMER: But, my dear Nora, you look quite worn out. Have you been practicing too hard?

NORA: No, I haven't practiced at all yet.

HELMER: Well, you must.

NORA: Yes, Torvald, I must, I know. But I can't get anywhere without your help. I've completely forgotten everything.

HELMER: Oh, we'll soon put that to rights.

NORA: Yes, help me, Torvald. Promise me you will? Oh, I'm so nervous. All those people—! You must forget everything except me this evening. You mustn't think of business—I won't even let you touch a pen. Promise me, Torvald?

HELMER: I promise. This evening I shall think of nothing but you—my poor, helpless little darling. Oh, there's just one thing I must see to—*(Goes towards the hall door.)*

NORA: What do you want out there?

HELMER: I'm only going to see if any letters have come.

NORA: No, Torvald, no!

HELMER: Why, what's the matter?

NORA: Torvald, I beg you. There's nothing there.

HELMER: Well, I'll just make sure.

He moves towards the door. NORA *runs to the piano and plays the first bars of the tarantella.*

HELMER *(at the door, turns)*: Aha!

NORA: I can't dance tomorrow if I don't practice with you now.

HELMER *(goes over to her)*: Are you really so frightened, Nora dear?

NORA: Yes, terribly frightened. Let me start practicing now, at once—we've still time before dinner. Oh, do sit down and play for me, Torvald dear. Correct me, lead me, the way you always do.

HELMER: Very well, my dear, if you wish it.

He sits down at the piano. NORA *seizes the tambourine and a long multicolored shawl from the cardboard box, wraps the latter hastily around her, then takes a quick leap into the center of the room.*

NORA: Play for me! I want to dance!

HELMER *plays and* NORA *dances.* DR. RANK *stands behind* HELMER *at the piano and watches her.*

HELMER *(as he plays)*: Slower, slower!

NORA: I can't!

HELMER: Not so violently, Nora.

NORA: I must!

HELMER *(stops playing)*: No, no, this won't do at all.

NORA *(laughs and swings her tambourine)*: Isn't that what I told you?

RANK: Let me play for her.

HELMER *(gets up)*: Yes, would you? Then it'll be easier for me to show her.

RANK *sits down at the piano and plays.* NORA *dances more and more wildly.* HELMER *has stationed himself by the stove and tires repeatedly to correct her, but she seems not to hear him. Her hair works loose and falls over her shoulders; she ignores it and continues to dance.* MRS. LINDE *enters.*

MRS. LINDE *(stands in the doorway as though tongue-tied)*: Ah—!

NORA *(as she dances)*: Oh, Christine, we're having such fun!

HELMER: But, Nora darling, you're dancing as if your life depended on it.

NORA: It does.

HELMER: Rank, stop it! This is sheer lunacy. Stop it, I say!

RANK *ceases playing.* NORA *suddenly stops dancing.*

HELMER *(goes over to her)*: I'd never have believed it. You've forgotten everything I taught you.

NORA *(throws away the tambourine)*: You see!

HELMER: I'll have to show you every step.

NORA: You see how much I need you! You must show me every step of the way. Right to the end of the dance. Promise me you will, Torvald?

HELMER: Never fear. I will.

NORA: You mustn't think about anything but me—today or tomorrow. Don't open any letters—don't even open the letter-box—

HELMER: Aha, you're still worried about that fellow—

NORA: Oh, yes, yes, him too.

HELMER: Nora, I can tell from the way you're behaving, there's a letter from him already lying there.

NORA: I don't know. I think so. But you mustn't read it now. I don't want anything ugly to come between us till it's all over.

RANK *(quietly, to* HELMER*)*: Better give her her way.

HELMER *(puts his arm round her)*: My child shall have her way. But tomorrow night, when your dance is over—

NORA: Then you will be free.

MAID *(appears in the doorway, right)*: Dinner is served, madam.

NORA: Put out some champagne, Helen.

MAID: Very good, madam. *(Goes.)*

HELMER: I say! What's this, a banquet?

NORA: We'll drink champagne until dawn! *(Calls.)* And, Helen! Put out some macaroons! Lots of macaroons—for once!

HELMER *(takes her hands in his)*: Now, now, now. Don't get so excited. Where's my little songbird, the one I know?

NORA: All right. Go and sit down—and you too, Dr. Rank. I'll be with you in a minute. Christine, you must help me put my hair up.

RANK *(quietly, as they go)*: There's nothing wrong, is there? I mean, she isn't—er—expecting—?

HELMER: Good heavens no, my dear chap. She just gets scared like a child sometimes—I told you before—

They go out right.

NORA: Well?

MRS. LINDE: He's left town.

NORA: I saw it from your face.

MRS. LINDE: He'll be back tomorrow evening. I left a note for him.

NORA: You needn't have bothered. You can't stop anything now. Anyway, it's wonderful really, in a way—sitting here and waiting for the miracle to happen.

MRS. LINDE: Waiting for what?

NORA: Oh, you wouldn't understand. Go in and join them. I'll be with you in a moment.

MRS. LINDE *goes into the dining-room.*

NORA *(stands for a moment as though collecting herself. Then she looks at her watch)*: Five o'clock. Seven hours till midnight. Then another twenty-four hours till midnight tomorrow. And then the tarantellá will be finished. Twenty-four and seven? Thirty-one hours to live.

HELMER *(appears in the doorway, right)*: What's happened to my little songbird?

NORA *(runs to him with her arms wide)*: Your songbird is here!

ACT III

The same room. The table which was formerly by the sofa has been moved into the center of the room; the chairs surround it as before. The door to the hall stands open. Dance music can be heard from the floor above. MRS. LINDE *is seated at the table, absent-mindedly glancing through a book. She is trying to read, but seems unable to keep her mind on it. More than once she turns and listens anxiously towards the front door.*

MRS. LINDE *(looks at her watch)*: Not here yet. There's not much time left. Please God he hasn't—! *(Listens again.)* Ah, here he is. *(Goes out into the hall and cautiously opens the front door. Footsteps can be heard softly ascending the stairs. She whispers.)* Come in. There's no one here.

KROGSTAD *(in the doorway)*: I found a note from you at my lodgings. What does this mean?

MRS. LINDE: I must speak with you.

KROGSTAD: Oh? And must our conversation take place in this house?

MRS. LINDE: We couldn't meet at my place; my room has no separate entrance. Come in. We're quite alone. The maid's asleep, and the Helmers are at the dance upstairs.

KROGSTAD *(comes into the room)*: Well, well! So the Helmers are dancing this evening? Are they indeed?

MRS. LINDE: Yes. Why not?

KROGSTAD: True enough. Why not?

MRS. LINDE: Well, Krogstad. You and I must have a talk together.

KROGSTAD: Have we two anything further to discuss?

MRS. LINDE: We have a great deal to discuss.

KROGSTAD: I wasn't aware of it.

MRS. LINDE: That's because you've never really understood me.

KROGSTAD: Was there anything to understand? It's the old story, isn't it—a woman chucking a man because something better turns up?

MRS. LINDE: Do you really think I'm so utterly heartless? You think it was easy for me to give you up?

KROGSTAD: Wasn't it?

MRS. LINDE: Oh, Nils, did you really believe that?

KROGSTAD: Then why did you write to me the way you did?

MRS. LINDE: I had to. Since I had to break with you, I thought it my duty to destroy all the feelings you had for me.

KROGSTAD *(clenches his fists)*: So that was it. And you did this for money!

MRS. LINDE: You mustn't forget I had a helpless mother to take care of, and two little brothers. We couldn't wait for you, Nils. It would have been so long before you'd had enough to support us.

KROGSTAD: Maybe. But you had no right to cast me off for someone else.

MRS. LINDE: Perhaps not. I've often asked myself that.

KROGSTAD *(more quietly)*: When I lost you, it was just as though all solid ground had been swept from under my feet. Look at me. Now I am a shipwrecked man, clinging to a spar.

MRS. LINDE: Help may be near at hand.

KROGSTAD: It was near. But then you came, and stood between it and me.

MRS. LINDE: I didn't know, Nils. No one told me till today that this job I'd found was yours.

KROGSTAD: I believe you, since you say so. But now you know, won't you give it up?

MRS. LINDE: No—because it wouldn't help you even if I did.

KROGSTAD: Wouldn't it? I'd do it all the same.

Mrs. Linde: I've learned to look at things practically. Life and poverty have taught me that.

Krogstad: And life has taught me to distrust fine words.

Mrs. Linde: Then it's taught you a useful lesson. But surely you still believe in actions?

Krogstad: What do you mean?

Mrs. Linde: You said you were like a shipwrecked man clinging to a spar.

Krogstad: I have good reason to say it.

Mrs. Linde: I'm in the same position as you. No one to care about, no one to care for.

Krogstad: You made your own choice.

Mrs. Linde: I had no choice—then.

Krogstad: Well?

Mrs. Linde: Nils, suppose we two shipwrecked souls could join hands?

Krogstad: What are you saying?

Mrs. Linde: Castaways have a better chance of survival together than on their own.

Krogstad: Christine!

Mrs. Linde: Why do you suppose I came to this town?

Krogstad: You mean—you came because of me?

Mrs. Linde: I must work if I'm to find life worth living. I've always worked, for as long as I can remember; it's been the greatest joy of my life—my only joy. But now I'm alone in the world, and I feel so dreadfully lost and empty. There's no joy in working just for oneself. Oh, Nils, give me something—someone—to work for.

Krogstad: I don't believe all that. You're just being hysterical and romantic. You want to find an excuse for self-sacrifice.

Mrs. Linde: Have you ever known me to be hysterical?

Krogstad: You mean you really—? Is it possible? Tell me—you know all about my past?

Mrs. Linde: Yes.

Krogstad: And you know what people think of me here?

Mrs. Linde: You said just now that with me you might have become a different person.

Krogstad: I know I could have.

Mrs. Linde: Couldn't it still happen?

Krogstad: Christine—do you really mean this? Yes—you do—I see it in your face. Have you really the courage—?

Mrs. Linde: I need someone to be a mother to; and your children need a mother. And you and I need each other. I believe in you, Nils. I am afraid of nothing—with you.

Krogstad *(clasps her hands)*: Thank you, Christine—thank you! Now I shall make the world believe in me as you do! Oh—but I'd forgotten—

Mrs. Linde *(listens)*: Ssh! The tarantella! Go quickly, go!

KROGSTAD: Why? What is it?

MRS. LINDE: You hear that dance? As soon as it's finished, they'll be coming down.

KROGSTAD: All right, I'll go. It's no good, Christine. I'd forgotten—you don't know what I've just done to the Helmers.

MRS. LINDE: Yes, Nils. I know.

KROGSTAD: And yet you'd still have the courage to—?

MRS. LINDE: I know what despair can drive a man like you to.

KROGSTAD: Oh, if only I could undo this!

MRS. LINDE: You can. Your letter is still lying in the box.

KROGSTAD: Are you sure?

MRS. LINDE: Quite sure. But—

KROGSTAD *(looks searchingly at her)*: Is that why you're doing this? You want to save your friend at any price? Tell me the truth. Is that the reason?

MRS. LINDE: Nils, a woman who has sold herself once for the sake of others doesn't make the same mistake again.

KROGSTAD: I shall demand my letter back.

MRS. LINDE: No, no.

KROGSTAD: Of course I shall. I shall stay here till Helmer comes down. I'll tell him he must give me back my letter—I'll say it was only to do with my dismissal, and that I don't want him to read it—

MRS. LINDE: No, Nils, you mustn't ask for that letter back.

KROGSTAD: But—tell me—wasn't that the real reason you asked me to come here?

MRS. LINDE: Yes—at first, when I was frightened. But a day has passed since then, and in that time I've seen incredible things happen in this house. Helmer must know the truth. This unhappy secret of Nora's must be revealed. They must come to a full understanding; there must be an end of all these shifting and evasions.

KROGSTAD: Very well. If you're prepared to risk it. But one thing I can do—and at once—

MRS. LINDE *(listens)*: Hurry! Go, go! The dance is over. We aren't safe here another moment.

KROGSTAD: I'll wait for you downstairs.

MRS. LINDE: Yes, do. You can see me home.

KROGSTAD: I've never been so happy in my life before!

He goes out through the front door. The door leading from the room into the hall remains open.

MRS. LINDE *(tidies the room a little and gets her hat and coat)*: What a change! Oh, what a change! Someone to work for—to live for! A home to bring joy into! I won't let this chance of happiness slip through my fingers. Oh, why don't they come? *(Listens.)* Ah, here they are. I must get my coat on.

She takes her hat and coat. HELMER*'s and* NORA*'s voices become audible outside. A key is turned in the lock and* HELMER *leads* NORA *almost forcibly into the hall. She is dressed in an Italian costume with a large black shawl. He is in evening dress, with a black cloak.*

NORA *(still in the doorway, resisting him)*: No, no, no—not in here! I want to go back upstairs. I don't want to leave so early.

HELMER: But my dearest Nora—

NORA: Oh, please, Torvald, please! Just another hour!

HELMER: Not another minute, Nora, my sweet. You know what we agreed. Come along, now. Into the drawing-room. You'll catch cold if you stay out here.

He leads her, despite her efforts to resist him, gently into the room.

MRS. LINDE: Good evening.

NORA: Christine!

HELMER: Oh, hullo, Mrs. Linde. You still here?

MRS. LINDE: Please forgive me. I did so want to see Nora in her costume.

NORA: Have you been sitting here waiting for me?

MRS. LINDE: Yes. I got here too late, I'm afraid. You'd already gone up. And I felt I really couldn't go back home without seeing you.

HELMER *(takes off* NORA*'s shawl)*: Well, take a good look at her. She's worth looking at, don't you think? Isn't she beautiful, Mrs. Linde?

MRS. LINDE: Oh, yes, indeed—

HELMER: Isn't she unbelievably beautiful? Everyone at the party said so. But dreadfully stubborn she is, bless her pretty little heart. What's to be done about that? Would you believe it, I practically had to use force to get her away!

NORA: Oh, Torvald, you're going to regret not letting me stay—just half an hour longer.

HELMER: Hear that, Mrs. Linde? She dances her tarantella—makes a roaring success—and very well deserved—though possibly a trifle too realistic—more so than was aesthetically necessary, strictly speaking. But never mind that. Main thing is—she had a success—roaring success. Was I going to let her stay on after that and spoil the impression? No, thank you. I took my beautiful little Capri signorina—my capricious little Capricienne, what?—under my arm—a swift round of the ballroom, a curtsey to the company, and, as they say in novels, the beautiful apparition disappeared! An exit should always be dramatic, Mrs. Linde. But unfortunately that's just what I can't get Nora to realize. I say, it's hot in here. *(Throws his cloak on a chair and opens the door to his study.)* What's this? It's dark in here. Ah, yes, of course—excuse me. *(Goes in and lights a couple of candles.)*

NORA *(whispers swiftly, breathlessly)*: Well?

MRS. LINDE *(quietly)*: I've spoken to him.

NORA: Yes?

MRS. LINDE: Nora—you must tell your husband everything.

NORA *(dully)*: I knew it.

MRS. LINDE: You've nothing to fear from Krogstad. But you must tell him.

NORA: I shan't tell him anything.

MRS. LINDE: Then the letter will.

NORA: Thank you, Christine. Now I know what I must do. Ssh!

HELMER *(returns)*: Well, Mrs. Linde, finished admiring her?

MRS. LINDE: Yes. Now I must say good night.

HELMER: Oh, already? Does this knitting belong to you?

MRS. LINDE *(takes it)*: Thank you, yes. I nearly forgot it.

HELMER: You knit, then?

MRS. LINDE: Why, yes.

HELMER: Know what? You ought to take up embroidery.

MRS. LINDE: Oh? Why?

HELMER: It's much prettier. Watch me, now. You hold the embroidery in your left hand, like this, and then you take the needle in your right hand and go in and out in a slow, easy movement—like this. I am right, aren't I?

MRS. LINDE: Yes, I'm sure—

HELMER: But knitting, now—that's an ugly business—can't help it. Look—arms all huddled up—great clumsy needles going up and down—makes you look like a damned Chinaman. I say, that really was a magnificent champagne they served us.

MRS. LINDE: Well, good night, Nora. And stop being stubborn. Remember!

HELMER: Quite right, Mrs. Linde!

MRS. LINDE: Good night, Mr. Helmer.

HELMER *(accompanies her to the door)*: Good night, good night! I hope you'll manage to get home all right? I'd gladly—but you haven't far to go, have you? Good night, good night. *(She goes. He closes the door behind her and returns.)* Well, we've got rid of her at last. Dreadful bore that woman is!

NORA: Aren't you very tired, Torvald?

HELMER: No, not in the least.

NORA: Aren't you sleepy?

HELMER: Not a bit. On the contrary, I feel extraordinarily exhilarated. But what about you? Yes, you look very sleepy and tired.

NORA: Yes, I am very tired. Soon I shall sleep.

HELMER: You see, you see! How right I was not to let you stay longer!

NORA: Oh, you're always right, whatever you do.

HELMER *(kisses her on the forehead)*: Now my little songbird's talking just like a real big human being. I say, did you notice how cheerful Rank was this evening?

NORA: Oh? Was he? I didn't have a chance to speak with him.

HELMER: I hardly did. But I haven't seen him in such a jolly mood for ages. *(Looks at her for a moment, then comes closer.)* I say, it's nice to get back to one's home again, and be all alone with you. Upon my word, you're a distractingly beautiful young woman.

NORA: Don't look at me like that, Torvald!

HELMER: What, not look at my most treasured possession? At all this wonderful beauty that's mine, mine alone, all mine.

NORA *(goes round to the other side of the table)*: You mustn't talk to me like that tonight.

HELMER *(follows her)*: You've still the tarantella in your blood, I see. And that makes you even more desirable. Listen! Now the other guests are beginning to go. *(More quietly.)* Nora—soon the whole house will be absolutely quiet.

NORA: Yes, I hope so.

HELMER: Yes, my beloved Nora, of course you do! Do you know—when I'm out with you among other people like we were tonight, do you know why I say so little to you, why I keep so aloof from you, and just throw you an occasional glance? Do you know why I do that? It's because I pretend to myself that you're my secret mistress, my clandestine little sweetheart, and that nobody knows there's anything at all between us.

NORA: Oh, yes, yes, yes—I know you never think of anything but me.

HELMER: And then when we're about to go, and I wrap the shawl round your lovely young shoulders, over this wonderful curve of your neck—then I pretend to myself that you are my young bride, that we've just come from the wedding, that I'm taking you to my house for the first time—that, for the first time, I am alone with you—quite alone with you, as you stand there young and trembling and beautiful. All evening I've had no eyes for anyone but you. When I saw you dance the tarantella, like a huntress, a temptress, my blood grew hot, I couldn't stand it any longer! That was why I seized you and dragged you down here with me—

NORA: Leave me, Torvald! Get away from me! I don't want all this.

HELMER: What? Now, Nora, you're joking with me. Don't want, don't want—? Aren't I your husband—?

There is a knock on the front door.

NORA *(starts)*: What was that?

HELMER *(goes towards the hall)*: Who is it?

RANK *(outside)*: It's me. May I come in for a moment?

HELMER *(quietly, annoyed)*: Oh, what does he want now? *(Calls.)* Wait a moment. *(Walks over and opens the door.)* Well! Nice of you not to go by without looking in.

RANK: I thought I heard your voice, so I felt I had to say goodbye. *(His eyes travel swiftly around the room.)* Ah, yes—these dear rooms, how well I know them. What a happy, peaceful home you two have.

HELMER: You seemed to be having a pretty happy time yourself upstairs.

RANK: Indeed I did. Why not? Why shouldn't one make the most of this world?

As much as one can, and for as long as one can. The wine was excellent—

HELMER: Especially the champagne.

RANK: You noticed that too? It's almost incredible how much I managed to get down.

NORA: Torvald drank a lot of champagne too, this evening.

RANK: Oh?

NORA: Yes. It always makes him merry afterwards.

RANK: Well, why shouldn't a man have a merry evening after a well-spent day?

HELMER: Well-spent? Oh, I don't know that I can claim that.

RANK *(slaps him across the back)*: I can, though, my dear fellow!

NORA: Yes, of course, Dr. Rank—you've been carrying out a scientific experiment today, haven't you?

RANK: Exactly.

HELMER: Scientific experiment! Those are big words for my little Nora to use!

NORA: And may I congratulate you on the finding?

RANK: You may indeed.

NORA: It was good, then?

RANK: The best possible finding—both for the doctor and the patient. Certainty.

NORA *(quickly)*: Certainty?

RANK: Absolute certainty. So aren't I entitled to have a merry evening after that?

NORA: Yes, Dr. Rank. You were quite right to.

HELMER: I agree. Provided you don't have to regret it tomorrow.

RANK: Well, you never get anything in this life without paying for it.

NORA: Dr. Rank—you like masquerades, don't you?

RANK: Yes, if the disguises are sufficiently amusing.

NORA: Tell me. What shall we two wear at the next masquerade?

HELMER: You little gadabout! Are you thinking about the next one already?

RANK: We two? Yes, I'll tell you. You must go as the Spirit of Happiness—

HELMER: You try to think of a costume that'll convey that.

RANK: Your wife need only appear as her normal, everyday self—

HELMER: Quite right! Well said! But what are you going to be? Have you decided that?

RANK: Yes, my dear friend. I have decided that.

HELMER: Well?

RANK: At the next masquerade, I shall be invisible.

HELMER: Well, that's a funny idea.

RANK: There's a big, black hat—haven't you heard of the invisible hat? Once it's over your head, no one can see you any more.

HELMER *(represses a smile)*: Ah yes, of course.

RANK: But I'm forgetting what I came for. Helmer, give me a cigar. One of your black Havanas.

HELMER: With the greatest pleasure. *(Offers him the box.)*

RANK *(takes one and cuts off the tip)*: Thank you.

NORA *(strikes a match)*: Let me give you a light.

RANK: Thank you. *(She holds out the match for him. He lights his cigar.)* And now—goodbye.

HELMER: Goodbye, my dear chap, goodbye.

NORA: Sleep well, Dr. Rank.

RANK: Thank you for that kind wish.

NORA: Wish me the same.

RANK: You? Very well—since you ask. Sleep well. And thank you for the light. *(He nods to them both and goes.)*

HELMER *(quietly)*: He's been drinking too much.

NORA *(abstractedly)*: Perhaps.

HELMER *takes his bunch of keys from his pocket and goes out into the hall.*

NORA: Torvald, what do you want out there?

HELMER: I must empty the letter-box. It's absolutely full. There'll be no room for the newspapers in the morning.

NORA: Are you going to work tonight?

HELMER: You know very well I'm not. Hullo, what's this? Someone's been at the lock.

NORA: At the lock—?

HELMER: Yes, I'm sure of it. Who on earth—? Surely not one of the maids? Here's a broken hairpin. Nora, it's yours—

NORA *(quickly)*: Then it must have been the children.

HELMER: Well, you'll have to break them of that habit. Hm, hm. Ah, that's done it. *(Takes out the contents of the box and calls into the kitchen.)* Helen! Put out the light on the staircase. *(Comes back into the drawing-room with the letters in his hand and closes the door to the hall.)* Look at this! You see how they've piled up? *(Glances through them.)* What on earth's this?

NORA *(at the window)*: The letter! Oh, no, Torvald, no!

HELMER: Two visiting cards—from Rank.

NORA: From Dr. Rank?

HELMER *(looks at them)*: Peter Rank, M.D. They were on top. He must have dropped them in as he left.

NORA: Has he written anything on them?

HELMER: There's a black cross above his name. Look. Rather gruesome, isn't it? It looks just as though he was announcing his death.

NORA: He is.

HELMER: What? Do you know something? Has he told you anything?

NORA: Yes. When these cards come, it means he's said goodbye to us. He wants to shut himself up in his house and die.

HELMER: Ah, poor fellow. I knew I wouldn't be seeing him for much longer. But so soon—! And now he's going to slink away and hide like a wounded beast.

NORA: When the time comes, it's best to go silently. Don't you think so, Torvald?

HELMER *(walks up and down)*: He was so much a part of our life. I can't realize that he's gone. His suffering and loneliness seemed to provide a kind of dark background to the happy sunlight of our marriage. Well, perhaps it's best this way. For him, anyway. *(Stops walking.)* And perhaps for us too, Nora. Now we have only each other. *(Embraces her.)* Oh, my beloved wife—I feel as though I could never hold you close enough. Do you know, Nora, often I wish some terrible danger might threaten you, so that I could offer my life and my blood, everything, for your sake.

NORA *(tears herself loose and says in a clear, firm voice)*: Read your letters now, Torvald.

HELMER: No, no. Not tonight. Tonight I want to be with you, my darling wife—

NORA: When your friend is about to die—?

HELMER: You're right. This news has upset us both. An ugliness has come between us; thoughts of death and dissolution. We must try to forget them. Until then—you go to your room; I shall go to mine.

NORA *(throws her arms round his neck)*: Good night, Torvald! Good night!

HELMER *(kisses her on the forehead)*: Good night, my darling little songbird. Sleep well, Nora. I'll go and read my letters.

He goes into the study with the letters in his hand, and closes the door.

NORA *(wild-eyed, fumbles around, seizes* HELMER*'s cloak, throws it round herself and whispers quickly, hoarsely)*: Never see him again. Never. Never. Never. *(Throws the shawl over her head.)* Never see the children again. Them too. Never. Never. Oh—the icy black water! Oh—that bottomless—that—! Oh, if only it were all over! Now he's got it—he's reading it. Oh, no, no! Not yet! Goodbye, Torvald! Goodbye, my darlings!

She turns to run into the hall. As she does so, HELMER *throws open his door and stands there with an open letter in his hand.*

HELMER: Nora!

NORA *(shrieks)*: Ah—!

HELMER: What is this? Do you know what is in this letter?

NORA: Yes, I know. Let me go! Let me go!

HELMER *(holds her back)*: Go? Where?

NORA *(tries to tear herself loose)*: You mustn't try to save me, Torvald!

HELMER *(staggers back)*: Is it true? Is it true, what he writes? Oh, my God! No, no—it's impossible, it can't be true!

NORA: It *is* true. I've loved you more than anything else in the world.

HELMER: Oh, don't try to make silly excuses.

NORA *(takes a step toward him)*: Torvald—

HELMER: Wretched woman! What have you done?

NORA: Let me go! You're not going to suffer for my sake. I won't let you!

HELMER: Stop being theatrical. *(Locks the front door.)* You're going to stay here and explain yourself. Do you understand what you've done? Answer me! Do you understand?

NORA *(looks unflinchingly at him and, her expression growing colder, says)*: Yes. Now I am beginning to understand.

HELMER *(walking around the room)*: Oh, what a dreadful awakening! For eight whole years—she who was my joy and my pride—a hypocrite, a liar—worse, worse—a criminal! Oh, the hideousness of it! Shame on you, shame!

NORA *is silent and stares unblinkingly at him.*

HELMER *(stops in front of her)*: I ought to have guessed that something of this sort would happen. I should have foreseen it. All your father's recklessness and instability—be quiet!—I repeat, all your father's recklessness and instability he has handed on to you. No religion, no morals, no sense of duty! Oh, how I have been punished for closing my eyes to his faults! I did it for your sake. And now you reward me like this.

NORA: Yes. Like this.

HELMER: Now you have destroyed all my happiness. You have ruined my whole future. Oh, it's too dreadful to contemplate! I am in the power of a man who is completely without scruples. He can do what he likes with me, demand what he pleases, order me to do anything—I dare not disobey him. I am condemned to humiliation and ruin simply for the weakness of a woman.

NORA: When I am gone from this world, you will be free.

HELMER: Oh, don't be melodramatic. Your father was always ready with that kind of remark. How would it help me if you were "gone from this world," as you put it? It wouldn't assist me in the slightest. He can still make all the facts public; and if he does, I may quite easily be suspected of having been an accomplice in your crime. People may think that I was behind it—that it was I who encouraged you! And for all this I have to thank you, you whom I have carried on my hands through all the years of our marriage! Now do you realize what you've done to me?

NORA *(coldly calm)*: Yes.

HELMER: It's so unbelievable I can hardly credit it. But we must try to find some way out. Take off that shawl. Take it off, I say! I must try to buy him off somehow. This thing must be hushed up at any price. As regards our relationship—we must appear to be living together just as before. Only *appear,* of course. You will therefore continue to reside here. That is understood. But the children shall be taken out of your hands. I dare no longer entrust them to you. Oh, to have to say this to the woman I once loved so dearly—and whom I still—! Well, all that must be finished. Henceforth there can be no question of happiness; we must merely strive to save what shreds and tatters—*(The front door bell rings.* HELMER *starts.)* What can that be? At this hour? Surely not—? He wouldn't—? Hide yourself, Nora. Say you're ill.

NORA *does not move.* HELMER *goes to the door of the room and opens it. The* MAID *is standing half-dressed in the hall.*

MAID: A letter for madam.

HELMER: Give it to me. *(Seizes the letter and shuts the door.)* Yes, it's from him. You're not having it. I'll read this myself.

NORA: Read it.

HELMER *(by the lamp)*: I hardly dare to. This may mean the end for us both. No, I must know. *(Tears open the letter hastily; reads a few lines; looks at a piece of paper which is enclosed with it; utters a cry of joy.)* Nora! *(She looks at him questioningly.)* Nora! No—I must read it once more. Yes, yes, it's true! I am saved! Nora, I am saved!

NORA: What about me?

HELMER: You too, of course. We're both saved, you and I. Look! He's returning your I.O.U. He writes that he is sorry for what has happened—a happy accident has changed his life—oh, what does it matter what he writes? We are saved, Nora! No one can harm you now. Oh, Nora, Nora—no, first let me destroy this filthy thing. Let me see—! *(Glances at the I.O.U.)* No, I don't want to look at it. I shall merely regard the whole business as a dream. *(He tears the I.O.U. and both letters into pieces, throws them into the stove, and watches them burn.)* There. Now they're destroyed. He wrote that ever since Christmas Eve you've been—oh, these must have been three dreadful days for you, Nora.

NORA: Yes. It's been a hard fight.

HELMER: It must have been terrible—seeing no way out except—no, we'll forget the whole sordid business. We'll just be happy and go on telling ourselves over and over again: "It's over! It's over!" Listen to me, Nora. You don't seem to realize. It's over! Why are you looking so pale? Ah, my poor little Nora, I understand. You can't believe that I have forgiven you. But I have, Nora. I swear it to you. I have forgiven you everything. I know that what you did you did for your love of me.

NORA: That is true.

HELMER: You have loved me as a wife should love her husband. It was simply that in your inexperience you chose the wrong means. But do you think I love you any the less because you don't know how to act on your own initiative? No, no. Just lean on me. I shall counsel you. I shall guide you. I would not be a true man if your feminine helplessness did not make you doubly attractive in my eyes. You mustn't mind the hard words I said to you in those first dreadful moments when my whole world seemed to be tumbling about my ears. I have forgiven you, Nora. I swear it to you; I have forgiven you.

NORA: Thank you for your forgiveness.

She goes out through the door, right.

HELMER: No, don't go—*(Looks in.)* What are you doing there?

NORA *(offstage)*: Taking off my fancy dress.

HELMER *(by the open door)*: Yes, do that. Try to calm yourself and get your balance again, my frightened little songbird. Don't be afriad. I have broad wings to shield you. *(Begins to walk around near the door.)* How lovely and peaceful this little home of ours is, Nora. You are safe here; I shall watch over you like a hunted dove which I have snatched unharmed from the claws of the falcon. Your wildly beating little heart shall find peace with me. It will happen, Nora; it will take time, but it will happen, believe me. Tomorrow all this will seem quite different. Soon everything will be as it was before. I shall no longer need to remind you that I have forgiven you; your own heart will tell you that it is true. Do you really think I could ever bring myself to disown you, or even to reproach you? Ah, Nora, you don't understand what goes on in a husband's heart. There is something indescribably wonderful and satisfying for a husband in knowing that he has forgiven his wife—forgiven her unreservedly, from the bottom of his heart. It means that she has become his property in a double sense; he has, as it were, brought her into the world anew; she is now not only his wife but also his child. From now on that is what you shall be to me, my poor, helpless, bewildered little creature. Never be frightened of anything again, Nora. Just open your heart to me. I shall be both your will and your conscience. What's this? Not in bed? Have you changed?

NORA *(in her everyday dress)*: Yes, Torvald. I've changed.

HELMER: But why now—so late—?

NORA: I shall not sleep tonight.

HELMER: But, my dear Nora—

NORA *(looks at her watch)*: It isn't that late. Sit down here, Torvald. You and I have a lot to talk about.

She sits down on one side of the table.

HELMER: Nora, what does this mean? You look quite drawn—

NORA: Sit down. It's going to take a long time. I've a lot to say to you.

HELMER *(sits down on the other side of the table)*: You alarm me, Nora. I don't understand you.

NORA: No, that's just it. You don't understand me. And I've never understood you—until this evening. No, don't interrupt me. Just listen to what I have to say. You and I have got to face facts, Torvald.

HELMER: What do you mean by that?

NORA *(after a short silence)*: Doesn't anything strike you about the way we're sitting here?

HELMER: What?

NORA: We've been married for eight years. Does it occur to you that this is the first time that we two, you and I, man and wife, have ever had a serious talk together?

HELMER: Serious? What do you mean, serious?

NORA: In eight whole years—no, longer—ever since we first met—we have never exchanged a serious word on a serious subject.

HELMER: Did you expect me to drag you into all my worries—worries you couldn't possibly have helped me with?

NORA: I'm not talking about worries. I'm simply saying that we have never sat down seriously to try to get to the bottom of anything.

HELMER: But, my dear Nora, what on earth has that got to do with you?

NORA: That's just the point. You have never understood me. A great wrong has been done to me, Torvald. First by Papa, and then by you.

HELMER: What? But we two have loved you more than anyone in the world!

NORA *(shakes her head)*: You have never loved me. You just thought it was fun to be in love with me.

HELMER: Nora, what kind of a way is this to talk?

NORA: It's the truth, Torvald. When I lived with Papa, he used to tell me what he thought about everything, so that I never had any opinions but his. And if I did have any of my own, I kept them quiet, because he wouldn't have liked them. He called me his little doll, and he played with me just the way I played with my dolls. Then I came here to live in your house—

HELMER: What kind of a way is that to describe our marriage?

NORA *(undisturbed)*: I mean, then I passed from Papa's hands into yours. You arranged everything the way you wanted it, so that I simply took over your taste in everything—or pretended I did—I don't really know—I think it was a little of both—first one and then the other. Now I look back on it, it's as if I've been living here like a pauper, from hand to mouth. I performed tricks for you, and you gave me food and drink. But that was how you wanted it. You and Papa have done me a great wrong. It's your fault that I have done nothing with my life.

HELMER: Nora, how can you be so unreasonable and ungrateful? Haven't you been happy here?

NORA: No; never. I used to think I was; but I haven't ever been happy.

HELMER: Not—not happy?

NORA: No. I've just had fun. You've always been very kind to me. But our home has never been anything but a playroom. I've been your doll-wife, just as I used to be Papa's doll-child. And the children have been my dolls. I used to think it was fun when you came in and played with me, just as they think it's fun when I go in and play games with them. That's all our marriage has been, Torvald.

HELMER: There may be a little truth in what you say, though you exaggerate and romanticize. But from now on it'll be different. Playtime is over. Now the time has come for education.

NORA: Whose education? Mine or the children's?

HELMER: Both yours and the children's, my dearest Nora.

NORA: Oh, Torvald, you're not the man to educate me into being the right wife for you.

HELMER: How can you say that?

NORA: And what about me? Am I fit to educate the children?

HELMER: Nora!

NORA: Didn't you say yourself a few minutes ago that you dare not leave them in my charge?

HELMER: In a moment of excitement. Surely you don't think I meant it seriously?

NORA: Yes. You were perfectly right. I'm not fitted to educate them. There's something else I must do first. I must educate myself. And you can't help me with that. It's something I must do by myself. That's why I'm leaving you.

HELMER *(jumps up)*: What did you say?

NORA: I must stand on my own feet if I am to find out the truth about myself and about life. So I can't go on living here with you any longer.

HELMER: Nora, Nora!

NORA: I'm leaving you now, at once. Christine will put me up for tonight—

HELMER: You're out of your mind! You can't do this! I forbid you!

NORA: It's no use your trying to forbid me any more. I shall take with me nothing but what is mine. I don't want anything from you, now or ever.

HELMER: What kind of madness is this?

NORA: Tomorrow I shall go home—I mean, to where I was born. It'll be easiest for me to find some kind of a job there.

HELMER: But you're blind! You've no experience of the world—

NORA: I must try to get some, Torvald.

HELMER: But to leave your home, your husband, your children! Have you thought what people will say?

NORA: I can't help that. I only know that I must do this.

HELMER: But this is monstrous! Can you neglect your most sacred duties?

NORA: What do you call my most sacred duties?

HELMER: Do I have to tell you? Your duties towards your husband, and your children.

NORA: I have another duty which is equally sacred.

HELMER: You have not. What on earth could that be?

NORA: My duty towards myself.

HELMER: First and foremost you are a wife and a mother.

NORA: I don't believe that any longer. I believe that I am first and foremost a human being, like you—or anyway, that I must try to become one. I know most people think as you do, Torvald, and I know there's something of the sort to be found in books. But I'm no longer prepared to accept what people say and what's written in books. I must think things out for myself, and try to find my own answer.

HELMER: Do you need to ask where your duty lies in your own home? Haven't you an infallible guide in such matters—your religion?

NORA: Oh, Torvald, I don't really know what religion means.

HELMER: What are you saying?

NORA: I only know what Pastor Hensen told me when I went to confirmation. He explained that religion meant this and that. When I get away from all this and can think things out on my own, that's one of the questions I want to look into. I want to find out whether what Pastor Hensen said was right—or anyway, whether it is right for me.

HELMER: But it's unheard of for so young a woman to behave like this! If religion cannot guide you, let me at least appeal to your conscience. I presume you have some moral feelings left? Or—perhaps you haven't? Well, answer me.

NORA: Oh, Torvald, that isn't an easy question to answer. I simply don't know. I don't know where I am in these matters. I only know that these things mean something quite different to me from what they do to you. I've learned now that certain laws are different from what I'd imagined them to be; but I can't accept that such laws can be right. Has a woman really not the right to spare her dying father pain, or save her husband's life? I can't believe that.

HELMER: You're talking like a child. You don't understand how society works.

NORA: No, I don't. But now I intend to learn. I must try to satisfy myself which is right, society or I.

HELMER: Nora, you're ill; you're feverish. I almost believe you're out of your mind.

NORA: I've never felt so sane and sure in my life.

HELMER: You feel sure that it is right to leave your husband and your children?

NORA: Yes, I do.

HELMER: Then there is only one possible explanation.

NORA: What?

HELMER: That you don't love me any longer.

NORA: No, that's exactly it.

HELMER: Nora! How can you say this to me?

NORA: Oh, Torvald, it hurts me terribly to have to say it, because you've always been so kind to me. But I can't help it. I don't love you any longer.

HELMER *(controlling his emotions with difficulty)*: And you feel quite sure about this too?

NORA: Yes, absolutely sure. That's why I can't go on living here any longer.

HELMER: Can you also explain why I have lost your love?

NORA: Yes, I can. It happened this evening, when the miracle failed to happen. It was then that I realized you weren't the man I'd thought you to be.

HELMER: Explain more clearly. I don't understand you.

NORA: I've waited so patiently, for eight whole years—well, good heavens, I'm not such a fool as to suppose that miracles occur every day. Then this dreadful thing happened to me, and then I *knew:* "Now the miracle will take place!" When Krogstad's letter was lying out there, it never occurred to me for a moment that you would let that man trample over you. I knew that you would say to him: "Publish the facts to the world." And when he had done this—

HELMER: Yes, what then? When I'd exposed my wife's name to shame and scandal—

NORA: I was certain that you would step forward and take all the blame on yourself, and say: "I am the one who is guilty!"

HELMER: Nora!

NORA: You're thinking I wouldn't have accepted such a sacrifice from you? No, of course I wouldn't! But what would my world have counted for against yours? That was the miracle I was hoping for, and dreading. And it was to prevent it happening that I wanted to end my life.

HELMER: Nora, I would gladly work for you night and day, and endure sorrow and hardship for your sake. But no man can be expected to sacrifice his honor, even for the person he loves.

NORA: Millions of women have done it.

HELMER: Oh, you think and talk like a stupid child.

NORA: That may be. But you neither think nor talk like the man I could share my life with. Once you'd got over your fright—and you weren't frightened of what might threaten me, but only of what threatened you—once the danger was past, then as far as you were concerned it was exactly as though nothing had happened. I was your little songbird just as before—your doll whom henceforth you would take particular care to protect from the world because she was so weak and fragile. *(Gets up.)* Torvald, in that moment I realized that for eight years I had been living here with a complete stranger, and had borne him three children—! Oh, I can't bear to think of it! I could tear myself to pieces!

HELMER *(sadly)*: I see it, I see it. A gulf has indeed opened between us. Oh, but Nora—couldn't it be bridged?

NORA: As I am now, I am no wife for you.

HELMER: I have the strength to change.

NORA: Perhaps—if your doll is taken from you.

HELMER: But to be parted—to be parted from you! No, no, Nora, I can't conceive of it happening!

NORA *(goes into the room, right)*: All the more necessary that it should happen.

She comes back with her outdoor things and a small traveling-bag, which she puts down on a chair by the table.

HELMER: Nora, Nora, not now! Wait till tomorrow!

NORA *(puts on her coat)*: I can't spend the night in a strange man's house.

HELMER: But can't we live here as brother and sister, then—?

NORA *(fastens her hat)*: You know quite well it wouldn't last. *(Puts on her shawl.)* Goodbye, Torvald. I don't want to see the children. I know they're in better hands than mine. As I am now, I can be nothing to them.

HELMER: But some time, Nora—some time—?

NORA: How can I tell? I've no idea what will happen to me.

HELMER: But you are my wife, both as you are and as you will be.

NORA: Listen, Torvald. When a wife leaves her husband's house, as I'm doing now, I'm told that according to the law he is freed of any obligations towards her. In any case, I release you from any such obligations. You mustn't feel bound to me in any way, however small, just as I shall not feel bound to you. We must both be quite free. Here is your ring back. Give me mine.

HELMER: That too?

NORA: That too.

HELMER: Here it is.

NORA: Good. Well, now it's over. I'll leave the keys here. The servants know about everything to do with the house—much better than I do. Tomorrow, when I have left town, Christine will come to pack the things I brought here from home. I'll have them sent on after me.

HELMER: This is the end then! Nora, will you never think of me any more?

NORA: Yes, of course. I shall often think of you and the children and this house.

HELMER: May I write to you, Nora?

NORA: No, never. You mustn't do that.

HELMER: But at least you must let me send you—

NORA: Nothing. Nothing.

HELMER: But if you should need help—?

NORA: I tell you, no. I don't accept things from strangers.

HELMER: Nora—can I never be anything but a stranger to you?

NORA *(picks up her bag)*: Oh, Torvald! Then the miracle of miracles would have to happen.

HELMER: The miracle of miracles?

NORA: You and I would both have to change so much that—oh, Torvald, I don't believe in miracles any longer.

HELMER: But I want to believe in them. Tell me. We should have to change so much that—?

NORA: That life together between us two could become a marriage. Goodbye.

She goes out through the hall.

HELMER *(sinks down on a chair by the door and buries his face in his hands)*: Nora! Nora! *(Looks round and gets up.)* Empty! She's gone! *(A hope strikes him.)* The miracle of miracles—?

The street door is slammed shut downstairs.

—1879

What are your reactions to and questions about this work? The following questions may help provoke some ideas.

Probing the Work

1. What details does Ibsen use to *characterize* (see page 77) Nora and Torvald?
2. What is the central *conflict* (see page 74) of this play? When is the conflict resolved? (When does the *climax* occur?)
3. What is the function of the subplot of Mr. Krogstad and Mrs. Linde?
4. What does this play say about marriage?

Identifying Issues

5. Debate the pros and cons of Nora's decision to leave. Why do you agree or disagree with her choice? Can you think of present-day women who have made similar decisions about their lives?
6. Read the following *Commentaries* by Elizabeth Hardwick and Errol Durbach. What is the thesis of each critical excerpt? Take a stand for or against what either Hardwick or Durbach says about the play, and find evidence in the play to support your opinion.

Commentary

ELIZABETH HARDWICK

"Ibsen's Women" (excerpt)

In William Archer's Preface to *A Doll's House* he had the idea that the woman who served as the model for Nora had actually, in real life, borrowed the money to redecorate her house! There is something beguiling in this thought, something of Nora Helmer in it. The real case was a dismal and more complicated one. The borrowing woman was an intellectual, a sort of writer, who had some literary correspondence with Ibsen. A meeting was arranged and the biographer, Halvdan Koht, says that "she was hardly what he [Ibsen] expected, but young, pretty and vivacious." She was invited to Dresden, and Ibsen called her "the lark." Some years later the lark married and borrowed money secretly to take her husband south for his health. She had trouble paying the money back and the Ibsens urged her to confess to her husband. She confessed and he, in fury, demanded a divorce. The poor wife suffered a nervous breakdown, was sent to an asylum. "In this catastrophe the marriage was dissolved."

The play and the true happening are a wonderfully rich psychological comment on each other. When we learn that the model for Nora was intelligent and ambitious everything falls into place. There is no need to wonder about motivation or changes of character, sudden revelations. Ibsen has not made Nora a writer, but he has, if we look carefully, made her extremely intelligent. She is the most sympathetic of all his heroines. There is nothing bitter, ruthless, or self-destructive in her. She has the amiability and endurance that are the clues to moral courage. Nora is gracious and fair-minded. Even when she is leaving Helmer, she thanks him for being kind to her. With Dr. Rank, the family friend, who is in love with her, she is honest and her flirtation has none of the heavy cynicism of Hedda Gabler's relation with *her* family friend, Judge Brack, and none of the bitter ambitiousness of Rebecca's relationship with Rosmer. . . . Nora's freedom rests upon her affectionate nature.

The habit is to play Nora too lightly in the beginning and too heavily in the end. The person who has been charming in Acts 1 and 2 puts on a dowdy traveling suit in Act 3 and is suddenly standing before you as a spinster governess. If the play is to make sense, the woman who has decided to leave her husband must be the very same woman we have known before. We may well predict that she will soon be laughing and chattering again and eating her macaroons in peace, telling her friends—she is going back to her hometown—what a stick Helmer turned out to be. Otherwise her freedom is worth nothing. Nora's liberation is not a transformation, but an acknowledgment of error, of having married the wrong man. Her real problem is money—at the beginning and at the end. What will she live on? What kind of work will she do? Will she get her children back? Who will be her next husband? When the curtain goes down it is only the end of Volume One.

Because Nora is free and whole she does not present the puzzling tangle of deceit and subterfuge, suppressed rage and dishonesty, that are so peculiar a tendency in the women in Ibsen's other realistic plays. *A Doll's House* is a comedy, a happy ending—except for the matter of the children. The play was published more than ninety years ago and we have found out very little we could add. In the case of grating marriages the children are still there, a matter of improvisation, resistant to fixed principles. Fortunately some of Ibsen's more far-out heroines—Hedda Gabler, Rebecca West, and Irene—are childless and this makes their suicides and falling off a mountain easier on the moral sensibilities of the audience.

—1974

ERROL DURBACH

A Doll's House: Ibsen's Myth of Transformation (excerpt)

"The Problem of Women": Nora and Mrs. Linde

On the occasion of his seventieth birthday in May 1898, Ibsen demonstrated his reputation for contradiction and contrariness. To an enthusiastic attempt by the Norwegian Society for Women's Rights to claim his active partisanship, he uttered this crusty response: "I thank you for your toast, but must disclaim the honour of having consciously worked for women's rights. I am not even quite sure what women's rights really are. To me it has been a question of human rights. And if you have read my books carefully you will realize that. Of course it is incidentally desirable to solve the problem of women; but that has not been my whole object." This is Ibsen at his most disingenuous. "The problem of women" is clearly a central, not merely a peripheral issue in *A Doll's House,* and I imagine in his rejoinder he was overreacting to the tendency among his champions to reduce the complex analysis of freedom in his plays about women to the politics of women's liberation.

If one understands "the problem of women" in strictly political terms, Norwegian working-class women had already broken the stony ground of equal rights for their middle-class sisters and the women's movement was well under way long before the advent of *A Doll's House*. The grinding poverty of the early 1800s had forced women into the labor force, and the Storting, the Norwegian parliament, had made it possible for women to find both employment and protection within their work. It may be of small consolation to feminists to discover that, by 1845, Norwegian women had acquired the legal status of minor males, but however slowly the struggle proceeded, it achieved its gradual victories with little of the trauma that characterized the Women's Suffrage movement in England. Inheritance rights for women were secured in 1854, the right to university education in 1882, and a major victory for legal equality was won in 1888—10 years too late for Nora—when married women finally gained control over their own funds. *A Doll's House* may not be a "votes for women" sort of play (and Ibsen's crusty speech in 1898 clearly disclaims any tendentious issues in his writing), but *ufrihet*—the "unfree" condition of middle-class women—is of major concern in all his drama and encompasses the most crucial moral, psychological, and existential ideas in the plays from *A Doll's House* to *When We Dead Awaken*.

It would be misleading, however, to regard *A Doll's House* as a militant blow against the institution of marriage. Read my play carefully, Ibsen might say to his modern feminist celebrants, and you will find a dialectical contradiction at its center, for Nora's slamming the door on the dolls' house must be seen in the dramatic context of Mrs. Linde's motives for reentering that secure domestic world, and to see the play as recommending domestic revolution is to miss its surprising *tvertimod*.[1]

With the resurgence of the women's liberation movement in the late 1960s, there has been a tendency to read *A Doll's House* as propaganda once more, and Kate Millett's influential and persuasive *Sexual Politics* (1970) has claimed Ibsen for the militant sisterhood even more enthusiastically than did the Norwegian Society for Women's Rights some 80 years earlier. *A Doll's House,* Millett writes, is a blow against the patriarchy, and Nora is "the true insurrectionary of the sexual revolution . . . battling the sexual politic openly and rationally . . . [with her] band of revolutionaries."

The sentiments are perfectly sincere, but Kate Millett's banners-and-trum-

[1]opposing theme [Ed.]

pets rhetoric seems inappropriate to Ibsen's play. The play's point is that there is *no* band of revolutionaries, *no* sisterhood to support Nora in her decision, and her one potential ally—the friend who escapes from her burden of intolerable freedom into the domestic world—provides the gloss, the *tvertimod,* on Nora's tragic impulse towards a lonely liberation. In the 1880s, Nora's door-slamming exit demanded explanation and defense. In the 1990s, however, it is Mrs. Linde's surprisingly accommodating choice to embrace marriage and the dolls' house that challenges the liberated feminists and that they tend to ignore as an aspect of the play's governing idea. For the meaning of *A Doll's House,* its definition of the "problem of women," is inseparable from Ibsen's dramatic vision of liberation in the life choices of *both* of his female protagonists.

—1991

WRITING ASSIGNMENT SEQUENCE (CONTINUED FROM PAGE 630)

4. Making Connections

Select one of the following questions and write an informal response in which you connect your own ideas with those conveyed in the works of this cluster, and/or make connections among the works themselves.

A. Apply the criteria of good marriages that you listed in your *prewriting* exercise (p. 630) to the readings of this cluster. How do they measure up?

B. In most of these readings the marriages are dysfunctional. How do the problems that these fictitious couples face compare with those of the troubled marriages you know?

5. Putting It All Together

Write an essay that combines what you think about the topic *Married Love* with what you now understand about the readings.

- Collect your informal writing, notes, and reading-journal entries on this topic and decide what will be the focus of your essay.
- Outline your essay. Select the literary passages and personal details you might use to illustrate and support your main focus.
- Write a draft of your essay in which you bring together what you think about the subject with what you understand about the readings. Try to include in your draft one or more *literary terms.*

- Share what you've written with your classmates and instructor, then revise it according to their recommendations.

Writing Tip: Gathering Details

Details are the heart of your paper: the reader will best understand and appreciate your ideas through your strong examples and facts. Details can take the form of examples, statistics, quotations, explanations of abstract terms, persuasive wording, concrete language, words that appeal to the senses, and imagery. *Show* what you mean, don't just *tell* the reader about it. Ask yourself

- How many sensory details and examples do I include?
- Are they appropriate to the point I wish to make?
- Do I use words that show my feelings and ideas?
- Have I used intriguing details and words rather than clichés?

CrossClusters

In your paper you might want to consider how the following works located elsewhere in this book depict *marriage:*

- Adrienne Rich, "Aunt Jennifer's Tigers" (p. 197)
- Susan Glaspell, "Trifles" (p. 220)
- Lorraine Hansberry, *A Raisin in the Sun* (p. 253)
- Russell Baker, from *Growing Up* (p. 343)
- Raymond Carver, *"My Father's Life"* (p. 446)
- Barbara Dafoe Whitehead, "Dan Quayle Was Right" (p. 475)
- Galway Kinnel, "Rapture" (p. 589)
- Tony Kushner, from *Angels in America* (p. 622)
- Mme. de Beaumont, "Beauty and the Beast" (p. 732)
- William Shakespeare, *A Midsummer-Night's Dream* (p. 766)
- Shiga Naoya, "Han's Crime" (p. 859)

SYNTHESIS PAPER FOR SECTION 3: LOVE

How do your preliminary ideas about *love* hold up now that you have read a variety of works on the topic? Adding to, expanding on, and revising the writing that you have already done on the subject of *love,* write a long paper in which you examine some of the literature in this section, bringing together your early writing with the knowledge you have gained from your class discussions. The paper might combine research and critical analysis with your personal opinions and experiences. You might even bring in references to films, music, books, and/or magazine articles. There are many possibilities for topics relating to the complexities of *true love, guilt* and *desire,* and *married love.*

Here are some questions to consider:

- How is true love idealized?
- What are the different ways in which love is expressed?
- How does married love compare with or contrast to romantic love?
- How would you characterize a modern "relationship," or modern love?

SECTION 4 (CHAPTERS 20–22)

FRAMES OF MIND

This section explores some of the fascinating pursuits of the human mind. The readings and writing exercises will challenge you to consider the complex boundaries between *fantasy and reality* and between *sanity and insanity,* as well as what constitutes true *learning*. Qualities or definitions that are often seen as clear-cut—illustrated in such comments as "That's just your imagination"; "He's gone nuts!"; and "What did you do in school today?"—are actually quite difficult to pinpoint. If there is one theme running through this section, it is that things aren't always what they seem to be, or what they are supposed to be.

GETTING STARTED: WRITING EXERCISES ON FRAMES OF MIND

1. Define one of the following words: intelligence, madness, learning, fantasy, or sanity.
2. Explain and/or agree/disagree with one of the following quotations:
   - "Our purses shall be proud, / our garments poor / for 'tis the mind that makes the body rich."—William Shakespeare
   - "The mind is its own place, and in itself / can make a heaven of hell, a hell of heaven."—John Milton
3. Read the following section essay by Howard Gardner, which first appeared in the Harvard Graduate School of Education Bulletin. Write a summary explanation of Gardner's main points, and agree or disagree with one or two of his definitions or conclusions.

SECTION ESSAY

HOWARD GARDNER

Intelligence in Seven Steps

Howard Gardner is a professor of education and codirector of the Project Zero at Harvard, and adjunct professor of neurology at Boston University School of Medicine. He was awarded a MacArthur Prize in 1981. He has written over a dozen books, including Frames of Mind; Art, Mind, and Brain; *and* Creating Minds.

The concept of intelligence, a very old one, has been employed in the most varied ways over the centuries. During the past century, there has been considerable movement on the "intelligence front" and this trend shows no sign of abating. In this essay I briefly describe seven historical steps, or phases, in the development of thinking about intelligence, focussing in particular on work inspired by the Theory of Multiple Intelligences.[1]

1. Lay Conceptions. Until this century, the word "intelligence" has been used primarily by ordinary individuals in an effort to describe their own mental powers as well as those of other persons. Consistent with ordinary language usage, "intelligence" has been deployed in anything but a precise manner. Forgetting about homonyms which denote the gathering of information, individuals living in the West were called "intelligent" if they were quick or eloquent or

[1]Gardner, H. (1983) *Frames of Mind.* New York: Basic Books.

scientifically astute or wise. In other cultures, the individual who was obedient, or well behaved, or quiet, or equipped with magical powers, may well have been referred to by terms which have been translated as "intelligent."

For the most part, the word "intelligent" was used in a beneficient way; however, its imprecision can be readily displayed by a recognition that it has been applied to nearly all of the American presidents in this century, even though it is doubtful that any two of our presidents exhibited similar kinds of minds.

2. The Scientific Turn. In a sequence of events that is by now familiar, Alfred Binet responded to requests from Parisian ministers at the turn of the century by creating the first intelligence test. It now became possible to estimate an individual's "intelligence" by noting his or her performance on a deliberately heterogeneous set of items, ranging from sensory discrimination to vocabulary knowledge. Used first clinically for "at risk" Parisian elementary schoolchildren, the intelligence test became "normed" on Californian middle-class children and was administered quite widely, thanks in large part to the efforts of Lewis Terman at Stanford University. By the 1920s and 1930s, intelligence tests (and their product, an individual's IQ) had become deeply ensconced in American society and had also gained considerable notoriety elsewhere.

3. Pluralization of Intelligence. While intelligence was initially perceived as a unitary (if overarching) concept, which could be captured by a single number, a debate soon arose about whether the concept could legitimately be decomposed. Such researchers as L. L. Thurstone and J. P. Guilford argued that intelligence was better conceived of as a set of possibly independent factors. In recent years, buoyed by findings from fields as disparate as artificial intelligence, developmental psychology, and neurology, a number of investigators have put forth the view that the mind consists of several independent modules or "intelligences." In my own "theory of multiple intelligences," I argue that human beings have evolved to be able to carry out at least seven separate forms of analysis: *1. Linguistic intelligence* (as in a poet); *2. Logical-mathematical intelligence* (as in a scientist); *3. Musical intelligence* (as in a composer); *4. Spatial intelligence* (as in a sculptor or airplane pilot); *5. Bodily-kinesthetic intelligence* (as in an athlete or dancer); *6. Interpersonal intelligence* (as in a salesman or teacher); *7. Intrapersonal intelligence* (exhibited by individuals with accurate views of themselves). These ideas have attracted some attention on the part of educators who seek a more comprehensive and individualized educational system. Recently my colleagues and I have been exploring certain educational implications of the theory in our own research.

4. Contextualization. As initially put forth, most theories of intelligence—whether singular or multiple—have assumed that intelligences are simply biological entities or potentials, which exist "in the head" (and "in the brain") and can be measured reliably independent of context. While the theory of multiple intelligences was deliberately formulated to take into account the unfolding of intelligence in different cultures, it nevertheless suffered in its early formulations from an "individual-centered" bias. However, most students of intelligence are now coming to the realization that intelligence cannot be conceptualized, or measured with accuracy, independent of the particular contexts in which an individual happens to live, work, and play and the opportunities and values provided by that milieu. Bobby Fischer might have had the potential to be a great chess player, but if he had lived in a culture without chess, that potential would never have been manifested let alone actualized. Intelligence is always an interaction between biological proclivities and opportunities for learning in a particular cultural context.

Project Spectrum, a curriculum-and-assessment project for young children, is one reflection of this view. We initially designed the project to determine whether young children exhibit distinctive profiles of intelligences, but we soon came to realize that intelligences could not be measured in the abstract; instead we had to create new environments, contexts more like children's museums than like traditional schoolrooms, in which children's intellectual proclivities had an opportunity to be elicited and practiced. Only then could some kind of meaningful assessment become possible.

5. Intelligence as Distributed. Closely related to the trend toward the contextualization of intelligence is the realization that significant parts of intelligence are *distributed*. The essential insight here is, again, that not all of intelligence is in the head. But rather than residing simply in the general context in which a person lives, much of everyday intelligence can be located in the human and nonhuman resources with which individuals work, and on which they come to depend in their productive work. Typically these resources are thought of as nonhuman artifacts, such as books, notebooks, computer files, and the like.

However, it is also appropriate to think of other individuals as part of one's "distributed intelligence." Most workers do not depend exclusively on their own skills and understandings; rather, they assume the presence of others in their work environments with whom they can regularly interact.

Our efforts to examine the distributed nature of intelligence can be seen in two of our projects. In ARTS PROPEL, a cooperative project in arts and humanities assessment, we ask students to keep detailed "process-folios"—complete records of their involvement in a project, from initial conception through interim sketches and drafts, ultimately to new plans which grow out of the final completed project. We believe that students' learning is significantly enhanced when they can have an ongoing dialogue with the record of their previous efforts, as captured in these constantly evolving process-folios.

In the Key School, an Indianapolis elementary school, children are exposed each day to contexts which nurture each of the intelligences. As part of their regular work at this experimental public school, students carry out three theme-related projects each year. Our research interest is in developing methods whereby these projects can be evaluated in a fair and comprehensive way. Part of that evaluation centers on the ways in which participation in a project has been cooperative: the human and nonhuman resources involved in preparation of the project, the help given by others in the presentation of the project, and the reactions of other individuals—peers as well as experts—to the final project. By deliberately including these "extra-individual" elements in our evaluations, we hope to bring home to the community the importance of "distributed aspects of intelligence." At the same time we want to undercut the common notion that all skill and learning must exist within a single brain, be that brain at home, at school, or at the work place.

Thus far, I have spoken of historical "steps" which have already been traversed, or which at least are being taken at the present time. My last two "steps" represent hopes for future work on intelligence in our own laboratory and in others around the world.

6. Nurturance of Intelligence. Even though our efforts to understand intelligence have been advancing, we still know very little about how to nurture intelligence, be it conceptualized in unitary or pluralistic fashion, in individual-centered, contextualized, or distributed form. Yet surely our efforts to understand intelligence as scientists can best be crowned by a demonstration that intelligence can be nurtured in particular educational settings, using strategic pedagogical or facilitating techniques. Here lies one important challenge for the future.

7. Humanizing Intelligence. Understanding the nature of the human mind in all of its complexity is no mean feat, and a complete understanding may well exceed human investigative capacities. But understanding intelligence—and even knowing how better to develop it—does not suffice in itself. Any human capacity can be used for ill as well as for good; and it is part of our responsibility as human beings living on a single troubled planet to try to use our competencies, our intelligences, in morally responsible ways. This assignment cannot fall exclusively on the shoulders of researchers; but nor can we simply afford to pass this responsibility on to others.

The human being is also more than his or her intellectual powers. Perhaps more crucial than intelligence in the human firmament are motivation, personality, emotions, and will. If we are ever to obtain a comprehensive and fully integrated picture of human beings, we need to meld our insights about cognition with comparable insights in respect to these other aspects of the human being. Perhaps, indeed, a different view of human nature will result from this activity of synthesis. The task is formidable but the increases in understanding obtained over the past decade give one some reason for optimism.

—*1992*

20

THE MAGIC CHALK

WRITING ASSIGNMENT SEQUENCE

1. Thinking About . . . Fantasy and Reality

Focused Freewriting: Freewrite about one of the following topics:

- your experiences with fairy tales
- the appeal of fantasy or of supernatural worlds
- your own vision of utopia

2. Enacting the Topic

Write an updated version of a favorite fairy tale, or make up a fairy tale of your own.

3. Responding to the Readings

As you read the works in this cluster, jot down in your response journals questions you have about the works, and comment on passages you find provocative or puzzling. Consider the questions following each reading for journal writing and prepare to discuss your reactions in class.

CLUSTER ESSAY

BRUNO BETTELHEIM

The Child's Need for Magic (excerpt)

Bruno Bettelheim (1903–1990) was born in Vienna and was educated at the University of Vienna. A survivor of the Nazi Holocaust, Bettelheim emigrated to America and became director of the University of Chicago's Orthogenic School, from 1944 to 1973. He is the author of numerous books dealing with parent-child relationships, the psychosocial importance of fairy tales, and the impact of the Holocaust. Among his most famous works are Love Is Not Enough *(1950);* The Uses of Enchantment *(1976), from which the essay below is excerpted; and* Freud and Man's Soul *(1983).*

Myths and fairy stories both answer the eternal questions: What is the world really like? How am I to live my life in it? How can I truly be myself? The answers given by myths are definite, while the fairy tale is suggestive; its messages may imply solutions, but it never spells them out. Fairy tales leave to the child's fantasizing whether and how to apply to himself what the story reveals about life and human nature.

The fairy tale proceeds in a manner which conforms to the way a child thinks and experiences the world; this is why the fairy tale is so convincing to him. He can gain much better solace from a fairy tale than he can from an effort to comfort him based on adult reasoning and viewpoints. A child trusts what the fairy story tells, because its world view accords with his own.

Whatever our age, only a story conforming to the principles underlying our thought processes carries conviction for us. If this is so for adults, who have learned to accept that there is more than one frame of reference for comprehending the world—although we find it difficult if not impossible truly to think in any but our own—it is exclusively true for the child. His thinking is animistic.

Like all preliterate and many literate people, "the child assumes that his relations to the inanimate world are of one pattern with those to the animate world of people: he fondles as he would his mother the pretty thing that pleased him; he strikes the door that has slammed on him." It should be added that he does the first because he is convinced that this pretty thing loves to be petted as much as he does; and he punishes the door because he is certain that the door slammed deliberately, out of evil intention.

As Piaget has shown, the child's thinking remains animistic until the age of puberty. His parents and teachers tell him that things cannot feel and act; and as much as he may pretend to believe this to please these adults, or not to be ridiculed, deep down the child knows better. Subjected to the rational teachings of others, the child only buries his "true knowledge" deeper in his soul and it remains untouched by rationality; but it can be formed and informed by what fairy tales have to say.

To the eight-year-old (to quote Piaget's examples), the sun is alive because it gives light (and, one may add, it does that because it wants to). To the child's animistic mind, the stone is alive because it can move, as it rolls down a hill. Even a twelve-and-a-half-year-old is convinced that a stream is alive and has a will, because its water is flowing. The sun, the stone, and the water are believed to be inhabited by spirits very much like people, so they feel and act like people.

To the child, there is no clear line separating objects from living things: and whatever has life has life very much like our own. If we do not understand what rocks and trees and animals have to tell us, the reason is that we are not sufficiently attuned to them. To the child trying to understand the world, it seems reasonable to expect answers from those objects which arouse his curiosity. And since the child is self-centered, he expects the animal to talk about the things which are really significant to him, as animals do in fairy tales, and as the child himself talks to his real or toy animals. A child is convinced that the animal understands and feels with him, even though it does not show it openly.

Since animals roam freely and widely in the world, how natural that in fairy tales these animals are able to guide the hero in his search which takes him into distant places. Since all that moves is alive, the child can believe that the wind can talk and carry the hero to where he needs to go, as in "East of the Sun and West of the Moon." In animistic thinking, not only animals feel and think as we do, but even stones are alive; so to be turned into stone simply means that the being has to remain silent and unmoving for a time. By the same reasoning, it is entirely believable when previously silent objects begin to talk, give advice, and join the hero on his wanderings. And since everything is inhabited by a spirit similar to all other spirits (namely, that of the child who has projected his spirit into all these things), because of this inherent sameness it is believable that man can change into animal, or the other way around, as in "Beauty and the Beast" or "The Frog King." Since there is no sharp line drawn between living and dead things, the latter, too, can come to life.

When, like the great philosophers, children are searching for the solutions to the first and last questions—"Who am I? How ought I to deal with life's problems? What must I become?"—they do so on the basis of their animistic thinking. But since the child is so uncertain of what his existence consists, first and foremost comes the question "Who am I?"

As soon as a child begins to move about and explore, he begins to ponder the problem of his identity. When he spies his mirror image, he wonders whether what he sees is really he, or a child just like him standing behind this glassy wall. He tries to find out by exploring whether this other child is really, in all ways, like him. He makes faces, turns this way or that, walks away from the mirror and jumps back in front of it to ascertain whether this other one has moved away or is still there. Though only three years old, the child is already up against the difficult problem of personal identity.

The child asks himself: "Who am I? Where did I come from? How did the world come into being? Who created man and all the animals? What is the purpose of life?" True, he ponders these vital questions not in the abstract, but mainly as they pertain to him. He worries not whether there is justice for individual man, but whether *he* will be treated justly. He wonders who or what projects him into adversity, and what can prevent this from happening to him. Are there benevolent powers in addition to his parents? Are his parents benevolent powers? How should he form himself, and why? Is there hope for him, though he may have done wrong? Why has all this happened to him? What will it mean for his future? Fairy tales provide answers to these pressing questions, many of which the child becomes aware of only as he follows the stories.

From an adult point of view and in terms of modern science, the answers which fairy stories offer are fantastic rather than true. As a matter of fact, these solutions seem so incorrect to many adults—who have become estranged from the ways in which young people experience the world—that they object to exposing children to such "false" information. However, realistic explanations are usually incomprehensible to children, because they lack the abstract understanding required to make sense of them. While giving a scientifically correct answer makes adults think they have clarified things for the child, such explanations leave the young child confused, overpowered, and intellectually defeated. A child can derive security only from the conviction that he understands now what baffled him before—never from being given facts which create *new* uncertainties. Even as the child accepts such an answer, he comes to doubt that he has asked the right question. Since the explanation fails to make sense to him, it must apply to some unknown problem—not the one he asked about.

It is therefore important to remember that only statements which are intelligible in terms of the child's existing knowledge and emotional preoccupations carry conviction for him. To tell a child that the earth floats in space, attracted by gravity into circling around the sun, but that the earth doesn't fall to the sun as the child falls to the ground, seems very confusing to him. The child knows from his experience that everything has to rest on something, or be held up by something. Only an explanation based on that knowledge can make him feel he understands better about the earth in space. More important, to feel secure on earth, the child needs to believe that this world is held firmly in place. Therefore he finds a better explanation in a myth that tells him that the earth rests on a turtle, or is held up by a giant.

—1975

What are your reactions to and questions about this work? The following questions may help provoke some ideas.

Probing the Work

1. Bettelheim says that fairy tales help children to better understand the world around them. What is it about the nature of fairy tales that enables children to relate so well to them?

Identifying Issues

2. What are the roles of fantasy and myth in our everyday life?

MME. DE BEAUMONT

Beauty and the Beast

Marie Le Prince de Beaumont was a French expatriate living in London in flight from an unhappy marriage when she published Le Magasin des enfans *(1756), a collection of essays and tales by a "wise governess." Among the tales was "Beauty and the Beast." Mme. de Beaumont probably got the tale from a version published in 1740 by Madame Gabrielle de Gallon de Villeneuve, which was over 300 pages long. While Mme. de Villeneuve's is probably the original version, it is Mme. de Beaumont's that gave the story the form in which it is best known throughout the world.*

Once upon a time, in a very far-off country, there lived a merchant who had been so fortunate in all his undertakings that he was enormously rich. As he had, however, six sons and six daughters, he found that his money was not too much to let them all have everything they fancied, as they were accustomed to do.

But one day a most unexpected misfortune befell them. Their house caught fire and was speedily burned to the ground, with all the splendid furniture, the books, pictures, gold, silver, and precious goods it contained; and this was only the beginning of their troubles. Their father, who had until this moment prospered in all ways, suddenly lost every ship he had upon the sea, either by dint of pirates, shipwreck, or fire. Then he heard that his clerks in distant countries, whom he trusted entirely, had proved unfaithful; and at last from great wealth he fell into the direst poverty.

All that he had left was a little house in a desolate place at least a hundred leagues from the town in which he had lived, and to this he was forced to retreat with his children, who were in despair at the idea of leading such a different life. Indeed, the daughters at first hoped that their friends, who had been so numerous while they were rich, would insist on their staying in their houses now they no longer possessed one. But they soon found that they were left alone, and that their former friends even attributed their misfortunes to their own extravagance, and showed no intention of offering them any help. So nothing was left for them but to take their departure to the cottage, which stood in the midst of a dark forest, and seemed to be the most dismal place upon the face of the earth. As they were too poor to have any servants, the girls had to work hard, like peasants, and the sons, for their part, cultivated the fields to earn their living. Roughly clothed, and living in the simplest way, the girls regretted unceasingly the luxuries and amusements of their former life; only the youngest tried to be brave and cheerful. She had been as sad as anyone when misfortune first overtook her father, but, soon recovering her natural gaiety, she set to work to make the best of things, to amuse her father and brothers as well as she could, and to try to persuade her sisters to join her in dancing and singing. But they would do nothing of the sort, and, because she was not as doleful as themselves, they declared that this miserable life was all she was fit for. But she was really far prettier and cleverer than they were; indeed, she was so lovely that she was always called Beauty. After two years, when they were all beginning to get used to their new life, something happened to disturb their tranquility. Their father received the news that one of his ships, which he had believed to be lost, had come safely into port with a rich cargo. All the sons and daughters at once thought that their poverty was at an end, and wanted to set out directly for the town; but their father, who was more prudent, begged them to wait a little, and, though it was harvest-time, and he could ill be spared, determined to go himself first, to make inquiries. Only the youngest daughter had any doubt but that they would soon again be as rich as they were before, or at least rich enough to live comfortably in some town where they would find amusement and gay companions once more. So they all loaded their father with commissions for jewels and dresses which it would have taken a fortune to buy; only Beauty, feeling sure that it was of no use, did not ask for anything. Her father, noticing her silence, said: "And what shall I bring for you, Beauty?"

"The only thing I wish for is to see you come home safely," she answered.

But this reply vexed her sisters, who fancied she was blaming them for having asked for such costly things. Her father, however, was pleased, but as he thought that at her age she certainly ought to like pretty presents, he told her to choose something.

"Well, dear father," she said, "as you insist upon it, I beg that you will bring me a rose. I have not seen one since we came here, and I love them so much."

So the merchant set out and reached the town as quickly as possible, but only to find that his former companions, believing him to be dead, had divided between them the goods which the ship had brought; and after six months of trouble and expense he found himself as poor as when he started, having been able to recover only just enough to pay the cost of his journey. To make matters worse, he was obliged to leave the town in the most terrible weather, so that by the time he was within a few leagues of his home he was almost exhausted with cold and fatigue. Though he knew it would take some hours to get through the forest, he was so anxious to be at his journey's end that he resolved to go on; but night overtook him, and the deep snow and bitter frost made it impossible for his horse to carry him any further. Not a house was to be seen; the only shelter he could get was the hollow trunk of a great tree, and there he crouched all the night, which seemed to him the longest he had ever known. In spite of his weariness the howling of the wolves kept him awake, and even when at last the day broke he was not much better off, for the falling snow had covered up every path, and he did not know which way to turn.

At length he made out some sort of track, and though at the beginning it was so rough and slippery that he fell down more than once, it presently became easier, and led him into an avenue of trees which ended in a splendid castle. It seemed to the merchant very strange that no snow had fallen in the avenue, which was entirely composed of orange trees, covered with flowers and fruit. When he reached the first court of the castle he saw before him a flight of agate steps, and went up them, and passed through several splendidly furnished rooms. The pleasant warmth of the air revived him, and he felt very hungry; but there seemed to be nobody in all this vast and splendid palace whom he could ask to give him something to eat. Deep silence reigned everywhere, and at last, tired of roaming through empty rooms and galleries, he stopped in a room smaller than the rest, where a clear fire was burning and a couch was drawn up cozily close to it. Thinking that this must be prepared for someone who was expected, he sat down to wait till he should come, and very soon fell into a sweet sleep.

When his extreme hunger wakened him after several hours, he was still alone; but a little table, upon which was a good dinner, had been drawn up close to him, and, as he had eaten nothing for twenty-four hours, he lost no time in beginning his meal, hoping that he might soon have an opportunity of thanking his considerate entertainer, whoever it might be. But no one appeared, and even after another long sleep, from which he awoke completely refreshed, there was no sign of anybody, though a fresh meal of dainty cakes and fruit was prepared upon the little table at his elbow. Being naturally timid, the silence began to terrify him, and he resolved to search once more through all the rooms; but it was of no use. Not even a servant was to be seen; there was no sign of life in the palace! He began to wonder what he should do, and to amuse himself by pretending that all the treasures he saw were his own, and considering how he would divide them among his children. Then he went down into the garden, and though it was winter everywhere else, here the sun shone, and the birds sang, and the flowers bloomed, and the air was soft and sweet. The merchant, in ecstasies with all he saw and heard, said to himself:

"All this must be meant for me. I will go this minute and bring my children to share all these delights."

In spite of being so cold and weary when he reached the castle, he had taken his horse to the stable and fed it. Now he thought he would saddle it for his homeward journey, and he turned down the path which led to the stable. This path had a hedge of roses on each side of it, and the merchant thought he had never seen or smelled such exquisite flowers. They reminded him of his promise to Beauty, and he stopped and had just gathered one to take to her when he was startled by a strange noise behind him. Turning around, he saw a frightful Beast, which seemed to be very angry and said, in a terrible voice:

"Who told you that you might gather my roses? Was it not enough that I allowed you to be in my palace and was kind to you? This is the way you show your gratitude, by stealing my flowers! But your insolence shall not go unpunished." The merchant, terrified by these furious words, dropped the fatal rose, and, throwing himself on his knees, cried: "Pardon me, noble sir. I am truly grateful to you for your hospitality, which was so magnificent that I could not imagine that you would be offended by my taking such a little thing as a rose." But the Beast's anger was not lessened by this speech.

"You are very ready with excuses and flattery," he cried; "but that will not save you from the death you deserve."

"Alas!" thought the merchant, "if my daughter Beauty could only know what danger her rose has brought me into!"

And in despair he began to tell the Beast all his misfortunes, and the reason of his journey, not forgetting to mention Beauty's request.

"A king's ransom would hardly have procured all that my other daughters asked," he said; "but I thought that I might at least take Beauty her rose. I beg you to forgive me, for you see I meant no harm."

The Beast considered for a moment, and then he said, in a less furious tone:

"I will forgive you on one condition—that is, that you will give me one of your daughters."

"Ah!" cried the merchant, "if I were cruel enough to buy my own life at the expense of one of my children's, what excuse could I invent to bring her here?"

"No excuse would be necessary," answered the Beast. "If she comes at all she must come willingly. On no other condition will I have her. See if any one of them is courageous enough, and loves you well enough to come and save your life. You seem to be an honest man, so I will trust you to go home. I give you a month to see if one of your daughters will come back with you and stay here, to let you go free. If none of them is willing, you must come alone, after bidding them good-bye forever, for then you will belong to me. And do not imagine that you can hide from me, for if you fail to keep your word I will come and fetch you!" added the Beast grimly.

The merchant accepted this proposal, though he did not really think any of his daughters would be persuaded to come. He promised to return at the time appointed, and then, anxious to escape from the presence of the Beast, he asked permission to set off at once. But the Beast answered that he could not go until the next day.

"Then you will find a horse ready for you," he said. "Now go and eat your supper, and await my orders."

The poor merchant, more dead than alive, went back to his room, where the most delicious supper was already served on the little table which was drawn up before a blazing fire. But he was too terrified to eat, and only tasted a few of the dishes, for fear the Beast should be angry if he did not obey his orders. When he had finished he heard a great noise in the next room, which he knew meant that the Beast was coming. As he could do nothing to escape his visit, the only thing that remained was to seem as little afraid as possible; so when the Beast appeared and asked roughly if he had supped well, the merchant answered humbly that he had, thanks to his host's kindness. Then the Beast warned him to remember their agreement, and to prepare his daughter exactly for what she had to expect.

"Do not get up tomorrow," he added, "until you see the sun and hear a golden bell ring. Then you will find your breakfast waiting for you here, and the horse you are to ride will be ready in the courtyard. He will also bring you back again when you come with your daughter a month hence. Farewell. Take a rose to Beauty, and remember your promise!"

The merchant was only too glad when the Beast went away, and though he could not sleep for sadness, he lay down until the sun rose. Then, after a hasty breakfast, he went to gather Beauty's rose, and mounted his horse, which carried him off so swiftly that in an instant he had lost sight of the palace, and he was still wrapped in gloomy thoughts when it stopped before the door of the cottage.

His sons and daughters, who had been very uneasy at his long absence, rushed to meet him, eager to know the result of his journey, which, seeing him mounted upon a splendid horse and wrapped in a rich mantle, they supposed to be favorable. But he hid the truth from them at first, only saying sadly to Beauty as he gave her the rose:

"Here is what you asked me to bring you; you little know what it has cost."

But this excited their curiosity so greatly that presently he told them his adventures from beginning to end, and then they were all very unhappy. The girls lamented loudly over their lost hopes, and the sons declared that their father should not return to this terrible castle, and began to make plans for killing the Beast if it should come to fetch him. But he reminded them that he had promised to go back. Then the girls were very angry with Beauty, and said it was all her fault, and that if she had asked for something sensible this would never have happened, and complained bitterly that they should have to suffer for her folly.

Poor Beauty, much distressed, said to them:

"I have indeed caused this misfortune, but I assure you I did it innocently. Who could have guessed that to ask for a rose in the middle of summer would cause so much misery? But as I did the mischief it is only just that I should suffer for it. I will therefore go back with my father to keep his promise."

At first nobody would hear of this arrangement, and her father and brothers, who loved her dearly, declared that nothing should make them let her go; but Beauty was firm. As the time drew near she divided all her little possessions between her sisters, and said good-bye to everything she loved, and when the fatal day came she encouraged and cheered her father as they mounted together the horse which had brought him back. It seemed to fly rather than gallop, but so smoothly that Beauty was not frightened; indeed, she would have enjoyed the journey if she had not feared what might happen to her at the end of it. Her father still tried to persuade her to go back, but in vain. While they were talking the night fell, and then, to their great surprise, wonderful colored lights began to shine in all directions, and splendid fireworks blazed out before them; all the forest was illuminated by them, and even felt pleasantly warm, though it had been bitterly cold before. This lasted until they reached the avenue of orange trees, where were statues holding flaming torches, and when they got nearer to the palace they saw that it was illuminated from the roof to the ground, and music sounded softly from the courtyard. "The Beast must be very hungry," said Beauty, trying to laugh, "if he makes all this rejoicing over the arrival of his prey."

But, in spite of her anxiety, she could not help admiring all the wonderful things she saw.

The horse stopped at the foot of the flight of steps leading to the terrace, and when they had dismounted her father led her to the little room he had been in before, where they found a splendid fire burning, and the table daintily spread with a delicious supper.

The merchant knew that this was meant for them, and Beauty, who was rather less frightened now that she had passed through so many rooms and seen nothing of the Beast, was quite willing to begin, for her long ride had made her very hungry. But they had hardly finished their meal when the noise of the Beast's footsteps was heard approaching, and Beauty clung to her father in terror, which became all the greater when she saw how frightened he was. But when the Beast really appeared, though she trembled at the sight of him, she made a great effort to hide her horror, and saluted him respectfully.

This evidently pleased the Beast. After looking at her he said, in a tone that might have struck terror into the boldest heart, though he did not seem to be angry:

"Good evening, old man. Good evening, Beauty."

The merchant was too terrified to reply, but Beauty answered sweetly:

"Good evening, Beast."

"Have you come willingly?" asked the Beast. "Will you be content to stay here when your father goes away?"

Beauty answered bravely that she was quite prepared to stay.

"I am pleased with you," said the Beast. "As you have come of your own accord, you may stay. As for you, old man," he added, turning to the merchant, "at sunrise tomorrow you will take your departure. When the bell rings get up quickly and eat your breakfast, and you will find the same horse waiting to take you home; but remember that you must never expect to see my palace again."

Then turning to Beauty, he said:

"Take your father into the next room, and help him to choose everything you think your brothers and sisters would like to have. You will find two traveling-trunks there; fill them as full as you can. It is only just that you should send them something very precious as a remembrance of yourself."

Then he went away, after saying, "Good-bye, Beauty. Good-bye, old man"; and though Beauty was beginning to think with great dismay of her father's departure, she was afraid to disobey the Beast's orders; and they went into the next room, which had shelves and cupboards all around it. They were greatly surprised at the riches it contained. There were splendid dresses fit for a queen, with all the ornaments that were to be worn with them; and when Beauty opened the cupboards she was quite dazzled by the gorgeous jewels that lay in heaps upon every shelf. After choosing a vast quantity, which she divided between her sisters—for she had made a heap of the wonderful dresses for each of them—she opened the last chest, which was full of gold.

"I think, father," she said, "that, as the gold will be more useful to you, we had better take out the other things again, and fill the trunks with it." So they did this; but the more they put in, the more room there seemed to be, and at last they put back all the jewels and dresses they had taken out, and Beauty even added as many more of the jewels as she could carry at once; and then the trunks were not too full, but they were so heavy that an elephant could not have carried them!

"The Beast was mocking us," cried the merchant; "he must have pretended to give us all these things, knowing that I could not carry them away."

"Let us wait and see," answered Beauty. "I cannot believe that he meant to deceive us. All we can do is to fasten them up and leave them ready."

So they did this and returned to the little room, where, to their astonishment, they found breakfast ready. The merchant ate his with a good appetite, as the Beast's generosity made him believe that he might perhaps venture to come back soon and see Beauty. But she felt sure that her father was leaving her forever, so she was very sad when the bell rang sharply for the second time, and warned them that the time was come for them to part. They went down into the courtyard, where two horses were waiting, one loaded with the two trunks, the other for him to ride. They were pawing the ground in their impatience to start, and the merchant was forced to bid Beauty a hasty farewell; and as soon as he was mounted he went off at such a pace that she lost sight of him in an instant. Then Beauty began to cry, and wandered sadly back to her own room. But she soon found that she was very sleepy, and as she had nothing better to do she lay down and instantly fell asleep. And then she dreamed that she was walking by a brook bordered with trees, and lamenting her sad fate, when a young prince, handsomer than anyone she had ever seen, and with a voice that went straight to her heart, came and said to her, "Ah, Beauty! you are not so unfortunate as you suppose. Here you will be rewarded for all you have suffered elsewhere. Your every wish shall be gratified. Only try to find me out, no matter how I may be disguised, as I love you dearly, and in making me happy you will find your own happiness. Be as true-hearted as you are beautiful, and we shall have nothing left to wish for."

"What can I do, Prince, to make you happy?" said Beauty.

"Only be grateful," he answered, "and do not trust too much to your eyes. And, above all, do not desert me until you have saved me from my cruel misery."

After this she thought she found herself in a room with a stately and beautiful lady, who said to her:

"Dear Beauty, try not to regret all you have left behind you, for you are destined to a better fate. Only do not let yourself be deceived by appearances."

Beauty found her dreams so interesting that she was in no hurry to awake, but presently the clock roused her by calling her name softly twelve times, and then she got up and found her dressing table set out with everything she could possibly want; and when her toilet was finished she found dinner was waiting in the room next to hers. But dinner does not take very long when you are all by yourself, and very soon she sat down cozily in the corner of a sofa, and began to think about the charming Prince she had seen in her dream.

"He said I could make him happy," said Beauty to herself.

"It seems, then, that this horrible Beast keeps him a prisoner. How can I set him free? I wonder why they both told me not to trust to appearances? I don't understand it. But, after all, it was only a dream, so why should I trouble myself about it? I had better go and find something to do to amuse myself."

So she got up and began to explore some of the many rooms of the palace.

The first she entered was lined with mirrors, and Beauty saw herself reflected on every side, and thought she had never seen such a charming room. Then a bracelet which was hanging from a chandelier caught her eye, and on taking it down she was greatly surprised to find that it held a portrait of her unknown admirer, just as she had seen him in her dream. With great delight she slipped the bracelet on her arm, and went on into a gallery of pictures, where she soon found a portrait of the same handsome Prince, as large as life, and so well painted that as she studied it he seemed to smile kindly at her. Tearing herself away from the portrait at last, she passed through into a room which contained every musical instrument under the sun, and here she amused herself for a long while in trying some of them, and singing until she was tired. The next room was a library, and she saw everything she had ever wanted to read, as well as everything she had read, and it seemed to her that a whole lifetime would not be enough even to read the names of the books, there were so many. By this time it was growing dusk, and wax candles in diamond and ruby candlesticks were beginning to light themselves in every room.

Beauty found her supper served just at the time she preferred to have it, but she did not see anyone or hear a sound, and, though her father had warned her that she would be alone, she began to find it rather dull.

But presently she heard the Beast coming, and wondered tremblingly if he meant to eat her up now.

However, as he did not seem at all ferocious, and only said gruffly:

"Good evening, Beauty," she answered cheerfully and managed to conceal her terror. Then the Beast asked her how she had been amusing herself, and she told him all the rooms she had seen.

Then he asked if she thought she could be happy in his palace; and Beauty answered that everything was so beautiful that she would be very hard to please if she could not be happy. And after about an hour's talk Beauty began to think that the Beast was not nearly so terrible as she had supposed at first. Then he got up to leave her, and said in his gruff voice:

"Do you love me, Beauty? Will you marry me?"

"Oh! what shall I say?" cried Beauty, for she was afraid to make the Beast angry by refusing.

"Say 'yes' or 'no' without fear," he replied.

"Oh! no, Beast," said Beauty hastily.

"Since you will not, good night, Beauty," he said. And she answered:

"Good night, Beast," very glad to find that her refusal had not provoked him. And after he was gone she was very soon in bed and asleep, and dreaming of her unknown Prince. She thought he came and said to her:

"Ah, Beauty! why are you so unkind to me? I fear I am fated to be unhappy for many a long day still."

And then her dreams changed, but the charming Prince figured in them all; and when morning came her first thought was to look at the portrait and see if it was really like him, and she found that it certainly was.

This morning she decided to amuse herself in the garden, for the sun shone, and all the fountains were playing; but she was astonished to find that every place was familiar to her, and presently she came to the brook where the myrtle trees were growing where she had first met the Prince in her dream, and that made her think more than ever that he must be kept a prisoner by the Beast. When she was tired she went back to the palace, and found a new room full of materials for every kind of work—ribbons to make into bows, and silks to work into flowers. Then there was an aviary full of rare birds, which were so tame that they flew to Beauty as soon as they saw her, and perched upon her shoulders and her head.

"Pretty little creatures," she said, "how I wish that your cage was nearer to my room, that I might often hear you sing!"

So saying she opened a door, and found to her delight that it led into her own room, though she had thought it was quite the other side of the palace.

There were more birds in a room farther on, parrots and cockatoos that could talk, and they greeted Beauty by name; indeed, she found them so entertaining that she took one or two back to her room, and they talked to her while she was at supper; after which the Beast paid her his usual visit, and asked the same questions as before, and then with a gruff good night he took his departure, and Beauty went to bed to dream of her mysterious Prince. The days passed swiftly in different amusements, and after a while Beauty found out another strange thing in the palace, which often pleased her when she was tired of being alone. There was one room which she had not noticed particularly; it was empty, except that under each of the windows stood a very comfortable chair; and the first time she had looked out of the window it had seemed to her that a black curtain prevented her from seeing anything outside. But the second time she went into the room, happening to be tired, she sat down in one of the chairs, when instantly the curtain was rolled aside, and a most amusing pantomime was acted before her; there were dances, and colored lights, and music, and pretty dresses, and it was all so gay that Beauty was in ecstasies. After that she tried the other seven windows in turn, and there was some new and surprising entertainment to be seen from each of them, so that Beauty never could feel lonely any more. Every evening after supper the Beast came to see her, and always before saying good night asked her in his terrible voice:

"Beauty, will you marry me?"

And it seemed to Beauty, now she understood him better, that when she said, "No, Beast," he went away quite sad. But her happy dreams of the handsome young Prince soon made her forget the poor Beast, and the only thing that at all disturbed her was to be constantly told to distrust appearances, to let her heart guide her, and not her eyes, and many other equally perplexing things, which, consider as she would, she could not understand.

So everything went on for a long time, until at last, happy as she was, Beauty began to long for the sight of her father and her brothers and sisters; and one night, seeing her look very sad, the Beast asked her what was the matter. Beauty had quite ceased to be afraid of him. Now she knew that he was really gentle in spite of his ferocious looks and his dreadful voice. So she answered that she was longing to see her home once more. Upon hearing this the Beast seemed sadly distressed, and cried miserably.

"Ah! Beauty, have you the heart to desert an unhappy Beast like this? What more do you want to make you happy? Is it because you hate me that you want to escape?"

"No, dear Beast," answered Beauty softly, "I do not hate you, and I should be very sorry never to see you any more, but I long to see my father again. Only let me go for two months, and I promise to come back to you and stay for the rest of my life."

The Beast, who had been sighing dolefully while she spoke, now replied:

"I cannot refuse you anything you ask, even though it should cost me my life. Take the four boxes you will find in the room next to your own, and fill them with everything you wish to take with you. But remember your promise and come back when the two months are over, or you may have cause to repent it, for if you do not come in good time you will find your faithful Beast dead. You will not need any chariot to bring you back. Only say good-bye to all your brothers and sisters the night before you come away, and when you have gone to bed turn this ring round upon your finger and say firmly: 'I wish to go back to my palace and see my Beast again.' Good night, Beauty. Fear nothing, sleep peacefully, and before long you shall see your father once more."

As soon as Beauty was alone she hastened to fill the boxes with all the rare and precious things she saw about her, and only when she was tired of heaping things into them did they seem to be full.

Then she went to bed, but could hardly sleep for joy. And when at last she did begin to dream of her beloved Prince she was grieved to see him stretched upon a grassy bank sad and weary, and hardly like himself.

"What is the matter?" she cried.

But he looked at her reproachfully, and said:

"How can you ask me, cruel one? Are you not leaving me to my death perhaps?"

"Ah! don't be so sorrowful," cried Beauty; "I am only going to assure my father that I am safe and happy. I have promised the Beast faithfully that I will come back, and he would die of grief if I did not keep my word!"

"What would that matter to you?" said the Prince. "Surely you would not care?"

"Indeed I should be ungrateful if I did not care for such a kind Beast," cried Beauty indignantly. "I would die to save him from pain. I assure you it is not his fault that he is so ugly."

Just then a strange sound woke her—someone was speaking not very far away; and opening her eyes she found herself in a room she had never seen before, which was certainly not nearly so splendid as those she was used to in the Beast's palace. Where could she be? She got up and dressed hastily, and then saw that the boxes she had packed the night before were all in the room. While she was wondering by what magic the Beast had transported them and herself to this strange place she suddenly heard her father's voice, and rushed out and greeted him joyfully. Her brothers and sisters were all astonished at her appearance, as they had never expected to see her again, and there was no end to the questions they asked her. She had also much to hear about what had happened to them while she was away, and of her father's journey home. But when they heard that she had only come to be with them for a short time, and then must go back to the Beast's palace forever, they lamented loudly. Then Beauty asked her father what he thought could be the meaning of her strange dreams, and why the Prince constantly begged her not to trust to appearances. After much consideration he answered: "You tell me yourself that the Beast, frightful as he is, loves you dearly, and deserves your love and gratitude for his gentleness and kindness; I think the Prince must mean you to understand that you ought to reward him by doing as he wishes you to, in spite of his ugliness."

Beauty could not help seeing that this seemed very probable; still, when she thought of her dear Prince who was so handsome, she did not feel at all inclined to marry the Beast. At any rate, for two months she need not decide, but could enjoy herself with her sisters. But though they were rich now, and lived in a town again, and had plenty of acquaintances, Beauty found that nothing amused her very much; and she often thought of the palace, where she was so happy, especially as at home she never once dreamed of her dear Prince, and she felt quite sad without him.

Then her sisters seemed to have got quite used to being without her, and even found her rather in the way, so she would not have been sorry when the two months were over but for her father and brothers, who begged her to stay, and seemed so grieved at the thought of her departure that she had not the courage to say good-bye to them. Every day when she got up she meant to say it at night, and when night came she put it off again, until at last she had a dismal dream which helped her to make up her mind. She thought she was wandering in a lonely path in the palace gardens, when she heard groans which seemed to come from some bushes hiding the entrance of a cave, and running quickly to see what could be the matter, she found the Beast stretched out upon his side, apparently dying. He reproached her faintly with being the cause of his distress, and at the same moment a stately lady appeared, and said very gravely:

"Ah! Beauty, you are only just in time to save his life. See what happens when people do not keep their promises! If you had delayed one day more, you would have found him dead."

Beauty was so terrified by this dream that the next morning she announced her intention of going back at once, and that very night she said good-bye to her father and all her brothers and sisters, and as soon as she was in bed she turned her ring round upon her finger, and said firmly:

"I wish to go back to my palace and see my Beast again," as she had been told to do.

Then she fell asleep instantly, and only woke up to hear the clock saying, "Beauty, Beauty," twelve times in its musical voice, which told her at once that she was really in the palace once more. Everything was just as before, and her birds were so glad to see her! but Beauty thought she had never known such a long day, for she was so anxious to see the Beast again that she felt as if suppertime would never come.

But when it did come and no Beast appeared she was really frightened; so, after listening and waiting for a long time, she ran down into the garden to search for him. Up and down the paths and avenues ran poor Beauty, calling him in vain, for no one answered, and not a trace of him could she find; until at last, quite tired, she stopped for a minute's rest, and saw that she was standing opposite the shady path she had seen in her dream. She rushed down it, and, sure enough, there was the cave, and in it lay the Beast—asleep, as Beauty thought. Quite glad to have found him, she ran up and stroked his head, but to her horror he did not move or open his eyes.

"Oh! he is dead; and it is all my fault," said Beauty, crying bitterly.

But then, looking at him again, she fancied he still breathed, and, hastily fetching some water from the nearest fountain, she sprinkled it over his face, and to her great delight he began to revive.

"Oh! Beast, how you frightened me!" she cried. "I never knew how much I loved you until just now, when I feared I was too late to save your life."

"Can you really love such an ugly creature as I am?" said the Beast faintly. "Ah! Beauty, you only came just in time. I was dying because I thought you had forgotten your promise. But go back now and rest; I shall see you again by and by."

Beauty, who had half expected that he would be angry with her, was reassured by his gentle voice, and went back to the palace, where supper was awaiting her; and afterward the Beast came in as usual, and talked about the time she had spent with her father, asking if she had enjoyed herself, and if they had all been very glad to see her.

Beauty answered politely, and quite enjoyed telling him all that had happened to her. And when at last the time came for him to go, and he asked, as he had so often asked before:

"Beauty, will you marry me?" she answered softly:

"Yes, dear Beast."

As she spoke a blaze of light sprang up before the windows of the palace; fireworks crackled and guns banged, and across the avenue of orange trees, in letters all made of fireflies, was written: LONG LIVE THE PRINCE AND HIS BRIDE.

Turning to ask the Beast what it could all mean, Beauty found that he had disappeared, and in his place stood her long-loved Prince! At the same moment the wheels of a chariot were heard upon the terrace, and two ladies entered the room. One of them Beauty recognized as the stately lady she had seen in her dreams; the other was also so grand and queenly that Beauty hardly knew which to greet first.

But the one she already knew said to her companion:

"Well, Queen, this is Beauty, who has had the courage to rescue your son from the terrible enchantment. They love one another, and only your consent to their marriage is wanting to make them perfectly happy."

"I consent with all my heart," cried the Queen. "How can I ever thank you enough, charming girl, for having restored my dear son to his natural form?"

And then she tenderly embraced Beauty and the Prince, who had meanwhile been greeting the Fairy and receiving her congratulations.

"Now," said the Fairy to Beauty, "I suppose you would like me to send for all your brothers and sisters to dance at your wedding?"

And so she did, and the marriage was celebrated the very next day with the utmost splendor, and Beauty and the Prince lived happily ever after.

—1756

What are your reactions to and questions about this work? The following questions may help provoke some ideas.

Probing the Work

1. What *symbols* (see page 78) are at work in this fairy tale? Select a few prominent persons, places, or things in the story—for example, the rose, the treasures, the clock, the beast, the bird, the rooms—and discuss their symbolic meaning (what do they represent?) as well as their importance to the story.

2. What are some familiar devices of the fairy tale at work here? How do they compare/contrast with others you know of?

Identifying Issues

3. This fairy tale can be seen to have different morals. What is the moral of the story, as you see it? What meaning might it have in our present-day world?

4. What standards of pleasure are illustrated in the description of the rooms? How would those rooms be furnished today?
5. What are the standards by which men and women are valued, according to this fairy tale? To what degree do these same standards apply to our world?

JOHN KEATS

La Belle Dame sans Merci[1]

John Keats (1795–1821), the son of a London stable keeper, was taken out of school when he was 15 and was apprenticed to a surgeon and apothecary. He was later licensed to practice, but abandoned medicine to be a poet when 33 of his poems were published. He was remarkably adept at poetry, writing what many consider among the greatest English poems, especially his odes (e.g., "Ode to a Nightingale," "Ode to Autumn," "Ode on a Grecian Urn"). He once wrote, "I am certain of the heart's affections and the truth of imagination"—a conviction illustrated in the following poem. Keats died of tuberculosis at age 25.

1

O what can ail thee, knight at arms,
Alone and palely loitering?
The sedge has wither'd from the lake,
And no birds sing.

2

O what can ail thee, knight at arms,
So haggard and so woe-begone?
The squirrel's granary is full,
And the harvest's done.

3

I see a lily on thy brow
With anguish moist and fever dew,
And on thy cheeks a fading rose
Fast withereth too.

4

I met a lady in the meads,
Full beautiful, a fairy's child;
Her hair was long, her foot was light,
And her eyes were wild.

[1]The beautiful lady without pity

5

I made a garland for her head,
And bracelets too, and fragrant zone;°
She look'd at me as she did love,
And made sweet moan.

6

I set her on my pacing steed,
And nothing else saw all day long,
For sidelong would she bend, and sing
A fairy's song.

7

She found me roots of relish sweet,
And honey wild, and manna dew,
And sure in language strange she said—
I love thee true.

8

She took me to her elfin grot,
And there she wept, and sigh'd full sore,
And there I shut her wild wild eyes
With kisses four.

9

And there she lulled me asleep,
And there I dream'd—Ah! woe betide!
The latest° dream I ever dream'd
On the cold hill's side:

10

I saw pale kings, and princes too,
Pale warriors, death pale were they all;
They cried—"La belle dame sans merci
Hath thee in thrall!"

11

I saw their starv'd lips in the gloam
With horrid warning gaped wide,

18. zone, belt, girdle (of flowers).
35. latest, last.

And I awoke and found me here
On the cold hill's side.

12

And this is why I sojourn here,
Alone and palely loitering,
Though the sedge is wither'd from the lake,
And no birds sing.

—1819–1820

What are your reactions to and questions about this work? The following questions may help provoke some ideas.

Probing the Work

1. What kind of encounter does the knight have with the "fairy child" and to what degree is he changed by his experience?

Identifying Issues

2. Keats seems to be expressing his belief in the power of the imagination (and/or dreams) to transform one's life. How much influence do you think one's imagination and/or dreams can have over one's real-world experiences?

KOBO ABE

The Magic Chalk

(translated by Alison Kibrick)

Kobo Abe (b. 1924) was born in Tokyo and grew up in the Manchurian city of Mukden, which was occupied by an invading Japanese army from 1931 to 1945. Alienated from his homeland, he changed his name from Kimfusa *to the more Chinese-sounding* Kobo. *He received a medical degree from Tokyo University, but decided to pursue a literary career. He has written the novels* The Woman in the Dunes *(1964) and* The Box Man *(1975); his plays include* Friends *(1969) and* The Man Who Turned Into a Stick *(1975); and some of his stories are collected in* Beyond the Curve *(1991).*

Next door to the toilet of an apartment building on the edge of the city, in a room soggy with roof leaks and cooking vapors, lived a poor artist named Argon.

The small room, nine feet square, appeared to be larger than it was because it contained nothing but a single chair set against the wall. His desk, shelves, paint box, even his easel had been sold for bread. Now only the chair and Argon were left. But how long would these two remain?

Dinnertime drew near. "How sensitive my nose has become!" Argon thought. He was able to distinguish the colors and proximity of the complex aromas entering his room. Frying pork at the butcher's along the streetcar line: yellow ocher. A southerly wind drifting by the front of the fruit stand: emerald green. Wafting from the bakery: stimulating chrome yellow. And the fish the housewife below was broiling, probably mackerel: sad cerulean blue.

The fact is, Argon hadn't eaten anything all day. With a pale face, a wrinkled brow, an Adam's apple that rose and fell, a hunched back, a sunken abdomen, and trembling knees, Argon thrust both hands into his pockets and yawned three times in succession.

His fingers found a stick in his pocket.

"Hey, what's this? Red chalk. Don't remember it being there."

Playing with the chalk between his fingers, he produced another large yawn.

"Aah, I need something to eat."

Without realizing it, Argon began scribbling on the wall with the chalk. First, an apple. One that looked big enough to be a meal in itself. He drew a paring knife beside it so that he could eat it right away. Next, swallowing hard as baking smells curled through the hallway and window to permeate his room, he drew bread. Jam-filled bread the size of a baseball glove. Butter-filled rolls. A loaf as large as a person's head. He envisioned glossy browned spots on the bread. Delicious-looking cracks, dough bursting through the surface, the intoxicating aroma of yeast. Beside the bread, then, a stick of butter as large as a brick. He thought of drawing some coffee. Freshly brewed, steaming coffee. In a large, juglike cup. On a saucer, three matchbox-size sugar cubes.

"Damn it!" He ground his teeth and buried his face in his hands. "I've got to eat!"

Gradually his consciousness sank into darkness. Beyond the windowpane was a bread and pastry jungle, a mountain of canned goods, a sea of milk, a beach of sugar, a beef and cheese orchard—he scampered about until, fatigued, he fell asleep.

A heavy thud on the floor and the sound of smashing crockery woke him up. The sun had already set. Pitch black. Bewildered, he glanced toward the noise and gasped. A broken cup. The spilled liquid, still steaming, was definitely coffee, and near it were the apple, bread, butter, sugar, spoon, knife, and (luckily unbroken) the saucer. The pictures he had chalked on the wall had vanished.

"How could it . . . ?"

Suddenly every vein in his body was wide awake and pounding. Argon stealthily crept closer.

"No, no, it can't be. But look, it's real. Nothing fake about the smothering aroma of this coffee. And here, the bread is smooth to the touch. Be bold, taste it. Argon, don't you believe it's real even now? Yes, it's real. I believe it. But frightening. To believe it is frightening. And yet, it's real. It's edible!"

The apple tasted like an apple (a "snow" apple). The bread tasted like bread (American flour). The butter tasted like butter (same contents as the label on the wrapper—not margarine). The sugar tasted like sugar (sweet). Ah, they all tasted like the real thing. The knife gleamed, reflecting his face.

By the time he came to his senses, Argon had somehow finished eating and heaved a sigh of relief. But when he recalled why he had sighed like this, he immediately became confused again. He took the chalk in his fingers and stared at it intently. No matter how much he scrutinized it, he couldn't understand what he didn't understand. He decided to make sure by trying it once more. If he succeeded a second time, then he would have to concede that it had actually happened. He thought he would try to draw something different, but in his haste just drew another familiar-looking apple. As soon as he finished drawing, it fell easily from the wall. So this is real after all. A repeatable fact.

Joy suddenly turned his body rigid. The tips of his nerves broke through his skin and stretched out toward the universe, rustling like fallen leaves. Then, abruptly, the tension eased, and, sitting down on the floor, he burst out laughing like a panting goldfish.

"The laws of the universe have changed. My fate has changed, misfortune has taken its leave. Ah, the age of fulfillment, a world of desires realized . . . God, I'm sleepy. Well, then, I'll draw a bed. This chalk has become as precious as life itself, but a bed is something you always need after eating your fill, and it never really wears out, so no need to be miserly about it. Ah, for the first time in my life I'll sleep like a lamb."

One eye soon fell asleep, but the other lay awake. After today's contentment he was uneasy about what tomorrow might bring. However, the other eye, too, finally closed in sleep. With eyes working out of sync he dreamed mottled dreams throughout the night.

Well, this worrisome tomorrow dawned in the following manner.

He dreamed that he was being chased by a ferocious beast and fell off a bridge. He had fallen off the bed . . . No. When he awoke, there was no bed anywhere. As usual, there was nothing but that one chair. Then what had happened last night? Argon timidly looked around the wall, tilting his head.

There, in red chalk, were drawings of a cup (it was broken!), a spoon, a knife, apple peel, and a butter wrapper. Below these was a bed—a picture of the bed off which he was supposed to have fallen.

Among all of last night's drawings, only those he could not eat had once again become pictures and returned to the wall. Suddenly he felt pain in his hip and shoulder. Pain in precisely the place he should feel it if he had indeed fallen out of bed. He gingerly touched the sketch of the bed where the sheets had been rumpled by sleep and felt a slight warmth, clearly distinguishable from the coldness of the rest of the drawing.

He brushed his finger along the blade of the knife picture. It was certainly nothing more than chalk; there was no resistance, and it disappeared leaving only a smear. As a test he decided to draw a new apple. It neither turned into a real apple and fell nor even peeled off like a piece of unglued paper, but rather vanished beneath his chafed palm into the surface of the wall.

His happiness had been merely a single night's dream. It was all over, back to what it was before anything had happened. Or was it really? No, his misery had returned fivefold. His hunger pangs attacked him fivefold. It seemed that all he had eaten had been restored in his stomach to the original substances of wall and chalk powder.

When he had gulped from his cupped hands a pint or so of water from the communal sink, he set out toward the lonely city, still enveloped in the mist of early dawn. Leaning over an open drain that ran from the kitchen of a restaurant about a hundred yards ahead, he thrust his hands into the viscous, tarlike sewage and pulled something out. It was a basket made of wire netting. He washed it in a small brook nearby. What was left in it seemed edible, and he was particularly heartened that half of it looked like rice. An old man in his apartment building had told him recently that by placing the basket in the drain one could obtain enough food for a meal a day. Just about a month ago the man had found the means to afford bean curd lees, so he had ceded the restaurant drain to the artist.

Recalling last night's feast, this was indeed muddy, unsavory fare. But it wasn't magic. What actually helped fill his stomach was precious and so could not be rejected. Even if its nastiness made him aware of every swallow, he must eat it. Shit. This was the real thing.

Just before noon he entered the city and dropped in on a friend who was employed at a bank. The friend smiled wryly and asked, "My turn today?"

Stiff and expressionless, Argon nodded. As always, he received half of his friend's lunch, bowed deeply and left.

For the rest of the day, Argon thought.

He held the chalk lightly in his hand, leaned back in the chair, and as he sat absorbed in his daydreams about magic, anticipation began to crystallize around that urgent longing. Finally, evening once again drew near. His hope that at sunset the magic might take effect had changed into near confidence.

Somewhere a noisy radio announced that it was five o'clock. He stood up and on the wall drew bread and butter, a can of sardines, and coffee, not forgetting to add a table underneath so as to prevent anything from falling and breaking as had occurred the previous night. Then he waited.

Before long darkness began to crawl quietly up the wall from the corners of the room. In order to verify the course of the magic, he turned on the light. He had already confirmed last night that electric light did it no harm.

The sun had set. The drawings on the wall began to fade, as if his vision had blurred. It seemed as if a mist was caught between the wall and his eyes. The pictures grew increasingly faint, and the mist grew dense. And soon, just as he had anticipated, the mist had settled into solid shapes—success! The contents of the pictures suddenly appeared as real objects.

The steamy coffee was tempting, the bread freshly baked and still warm.

"Oh! Forgot a can opener."

He held his left hand underneath to catch it before it fell, and, as he drew, the outlines took on material form. His drawing had literally come to life.

All of a sudden, he stumbled over something. Last night's bed "existed" again. Moreover, the knife handle (he had erased the blade with his finger), the butter wrapper, and the broken cup lay fallen on the floor.

After filling his empty stomach, Argon lay down on the bed.

"Well, what shall it be next? It's clear now that the magic doesn't work in daylight. Tomorrow I'll have to suffer all over again. There must be a simple way out of this. Ah, yes! a brilliant plan—I'll cover up the window and shut myself in darkness."

He would need some money to carry out the project. To keep out the sun required some objects that would not lose their substance when exposed to sunlight. But drawing money is a bit difficult. He racked his brains, then drew a purse full of money . . . The idea was a success, for when he opened up the purse he found more than enough bills stuffed inside.

This money, like the counterfeit coins that badgers made from tree leaves in the fairy tale, would disappear in the light of day, but it would leave no trace behind, and that was a great relief. He was cautious nonetheless and deliberately proceeded toward a distant town. Two heavy blankets, five sheets of black woolen cloth, a piece of felt, a box of nails, and four pieces of squared lumber. In addition, one volume of a cookbook collection that caught his eye in a secondhand bookstore along the way. With the remaining money he bought a cup of coffee, not in the least superior to the coffee he had drawn on the wall. He was (why?) proud of himself. Lastly, he bought a newspaper.

He nailed the door shut, then attached two layers of cloth and a blanket. With the rest of the material, he covered the window, and he blocked the edges with the wood. A feeling of security, and at the same time a sense of being attacked by eternity, weighed upon him. Argon's mind grew distant, and, lying down on the bed, he soon fell asleep.

Sleep neither diminished nor neutralized his happiness in the slightest. When he awoke, the steel springs throughout his body were coiled and ready to leap, full of life. A new day, a new time . . . tomorrow wrapped in a mist of glittering gold dust, and the day after tomorrow, and more and more overflowing armfuls of tomorrows were waiting expectantly. Argon smiled, overcome with joy. Now, at this very moment, everything, without any hindrance whatsoever, was waiting eagerly among myriad possibilities to be created by his own hand. It was a brilliant moment. But what, in the depths of his heart, was this faintly aching sorrow? It might have been the sorrow that God had felt just before Creation. Beside the muscles of his smile, smaller muscles twitched slightly.

Argon drew a large wall clock. With a trembling hand he set the clock precisely at twelve, determining at that moment the start of a new destiny.

He thought the room was a bit stuffy, so he drew a window on the wall facing the hallway. Hm, what's wrong? The window didn't materialize. Perplexed for a moment, he then realized that the window could not acquire any substance because it did not have an outside; it was not equipped with all the conditions necessary to make it a window.

"Well, then, shall I draw an outside? What kind of view would be nice? Shall it be the Alps or the Bay of Naples? A quiet pastoral scene wouldn't be bad. Then again, a primeval Siberian forest might be interesting." All the beautiful landscapes he had seen on postcards and in travel guides flickered before him. But he had to choose one from among them all, and he couldn't make up his mind. "Well, let's attend to pleasure first," he decided. He drew some whiskey and cheese and, as he nibbled, slowly thought about it.

The more he thought, the less he understood.

"This isn't going to be easy. It could involve work on a larger scale than anything I—or anyone—has ever tried to design. In fact, now that I think about it, it wouldn't do simply to draw a few streams and orchards, mountains and seas, and other things pleasing to the eye. Suppose I drew a mountain; it would no longer be just a mountain. What would be beyond it? A city? A sea? A desert? What kind of people would be living there? What kind of animals? Unconsciously I would be deciding those things. No, making this window a window is serious business. It involves the creation of a world. Defining a world with just a few lines. Would it be right to leave that to chance? No, the scene outside can't be casually drawn. I must produce the kind of picture that no human hand has yet achieved."

Argon sank into deep contemplation.

The first week passed in discontent as he pondered a design for a world of infinitude. Canvases once again lined his room, and the smell of turpentine hung in the air. Dozens of rough sketches accumulated in a pile. The more he thought, however, the more extensive the problem became, until finally he felt it was all too much for him. He thought he might boldly leave it up to chance, but in that case his efforts to create a new world would come to nothing. And if he merely captured accurately the inevitability of partial reality, the contradictions inherent in that reality would pull him back into the past, perhaps trapping him again in starvation. Besides, the chalk had a limited lifespan. He had to capture the world.

The second week flew by in inebriation and gluttony.

The third week passed in a despair resembling insanity. Once again his canvases lay covered with dust, and the smell of oils had faded.

In the fourth week Argon finally made up his mind, a result of nearly total desperation. He just couldn't wait any longer. In order to evade the responsibility of creating with his own hand an outside for the window, he decided to take a great risk that would leave everything to chance.

"I'll draw a door on the wall. The outside will be decided by whatever is beyond the door. Even if it ends in failure, even if it turns out to be the same apartment scene as before, it'll be far better than being tormented by this responsibility. I don't care what happens, better to escape."

Argon put on a jacket for the first time in a long while. It was a ceremony in honor of the establishment of the world, so one couldn't say he was being extravagant. With a stiff hand he lowered the chalk of destiny. A picture of the door. He was breathing hard. No wonder. Wasn't the sight beyond the door the greatest mystery a man could contemplate? Perhaps death was awaiting him as his reward.

He grasped the knob. He took a step back and opened the door.

Dynamite pierced his eyes, exploding. After a while he opened them fearfully to an awesome wasteland glaring in the noonday sun. As far as he could see, with the exception of the horizon, there was not a single shadow. To the extent that he could peer into the dark sky, not a single cloud. A hot dry wind blew past, stirring up a dust storm.

"Aah . . . It's just as though the horizon line in one of my designs had become the landscape itself. Aah . . ."

The chalk hadn't resolved anything after all. He still had to create it all from the beginning. He had to fill this desolate land with mountains, water, clouds, trees, plants, birds, beasts, fish. He had to draw the world all over again. Discouraged, Argon collapsed onto the bed. One after another, tears fell unceasingly.

Something rustled in his pocket. It was the newspaper he had bought on that first day and forgotten about. The headline on the first page read, "Invasion Across 38th Parallel!" On the second page, an even larger space devoted to a photograph of Miss Nippon. Underneath, in small print, "Riot at N Ward Employment Security Office," and "Large-scale Dismissals at U Factory."

Argon stared at the half-naked Miss Nippon. What intense longing. What a body. Flesh of glass.

"This is what I forgot. Nothing else matters. It's time to begin everything from Adam and Eve. That's it—Eve! I'll draw Eve!"

Half an hour later Eve was standing before him, stark naked. Startled, she looked around her.

"Oh! Who are you? What's happened? Golly, I'm naked!"

"I am Adam. You are Eve." Argon blushed bashfully.

"I'm Eve, you say? Ah, no wonder I'm naked. But why are you wearing clothes? Adam, in Western dress—now that's weird."

Suddenly her tone changed.

"You're lying! I'm not Eve. I'm Miss Nippon."

"You're Eve. You really are Eve."

"You expect me to believe this is Adam—in those clothes—in a dump like this? Come on, give me back *my* clothes. What am I doing here anyway? I'm due to make a special modeling appearance at a photo contest."

"Oh, no. You don't understand. You're Eve, I mean it."

"Give me a break, will you? Okay, where's the apple? And I suppose this is the Garden of Eden? Ha, don't make me laugh. Now give me my clothes."

"Well, at least listen to what I have to say. Sit down over there. Then I'll explain everything. By the way, can I offer you something to eat?"

"Yes, go ahead. But hurry up and give me my clothes, okay? My body's valuable."

"What would you like? Choose anything you want from this cookbook."

"Oh, great! Really? The place is filthy, but you must be pretty well fixed. I've changed my mind. Maybe you really are Adam after all. What do you do for a living? Burglar?"

"No, I'm Adam. Also an artist, and a world planner."

"I don't understand."

"Neither do I. That's why I'm depressed."

Watching Argon draw the food with swift strokes as he spoke, Eve shouted, "Hey, great, that's great. This *is* Eden, isn't it? Wow. Yeah, okay, I'll be Eve. I don't mind being Eve. We're going to get rich—right?"

"Eve, please listen to me."

In a sad voice, Argon told her his whole story, adding finally, "So you see, with your cooperation we must design this world. Money's irrelevant. We have to start everything from scratch."

Miss Nippon was dumbfounded.

"Money's irrelevant, you say? I don't understand. I don't get it. I absolutely do not understand."

"If you're going to talk like that, well, why don't you open this door and take a look outside."

She glanced through the door Argon had left half open.

"My God! How awful!"

She slammed the door shut and glared at him.

"But how about *this* door," she said, pointing to his real, blanketed door. "Different, I'll bet."

"No, don't. That one's no good. It will just wipe out this world, the food, desk, bed, and even you. *You* are the new Eve. And we must become the father and mother of our world."

"Oh no. No babies. I'm all for birth control. I mean, they're such a bother. And besides, I won't disappear."

"You will disappear."

"I won't. I know myself best. I'm me. All this talk about disappearing—you're really weird."

"My dear Eve, you don't know. If we don't re-create the world, then sooner or later we're faced with starvation."

"What? Calling me 'dear' now, are you? You've got a nerve. And you say I'm going to starve. Don't be ridiculous. My body's valuable."

"No, your body's the same as my chalk. If we don't acquire a world of our own, your existence will just be a fiction. The same as nothing at all."

"Okay, that's enough of this junk. Come on, give me back my clothes. I'm leaving. No two ways about it, my being here is weird. I shouldn't be here. You're a magician or something. Well, hurry up. My manager's probably fed up with waiting. If you want me to drop in and be your Eve every now and then, I don't mind. As long as you use your chalk to give me what I want."

"Don't be a fool! You can't do that."

The abrupt, violent tone of Argon's voice startled her, and she looked into his face. They both stared at each other for a moment in silence. Whatever was in her thoughts, she then said calmly, "All right, I'll stay. But, in exchange, will you grant me one wish?"

"What is it? If you stay with me, I'll listen to anything you have to say."

"I want half of your chalk."

"That's unreasonable. After all, dear, you don't know how to draw. What good would it do you?"

"I do know how to draw. I may not look like it, but I used to be a designer. I insist on equal rights."

He tilted his head for an instant, then straightening up again, said decisively, "All right, I believe you."

He carefully broke the chalk in half and gave one piece to Eve. As soon as she received it, she turned to the wall and began drawing.

It was a pistol.

"Stop it! What are you going to do with that thing?"

"Death, I'm going to make death. We need some divisions. They're very important in making a world."

"No, that'll be the end. Stop it. It's the most unnecessary thing of all."

But it was too late. Eve was clutching a small pistol in her hand. She raised it and aimed directly at his chest.

"Move and I'll shoot. Hands up. You're stupid, Adam. Don't you know that a promise is the beginning of a lie? It's you who made me lie."

"What? *Now* what are you drawing?"

"A hammer. To smash the door down."

"You can't!"

"Move and I'll shoot!"

The moment he leaped the pistol rang out. Argon held his chest as his knees buckled and he collapsed to the floor. Oddly, there was no blood.

"Stupid Adam."

Eve laughed. Then, raising the hammer, she struck the door. The light streamed in. It wasn't very bright, but it was real. Light from the sun. Eve was suddenly absorbed, like mist. The desk, the bed, the French meal, all disappeared. All but Argon, the cookbook which had landed on the floor, and the chair were transformed back into pictures on the wall.

Argon stood up unsteadily. His chest wound had healed. But something stronger than death was summoning him, compelling him—the wall. The wall was calling him. His body, which had eaten drawings from the wall continuously for four weeks, had been almost entirely transformed by them. Resistance was impossible now. Argon staggered toward the wall and was drawn in on top of Eve.

The sound of the gunshot and the door being smashed were heard by others in the building. By the time they ran in, Argon had been completely absorbed into the wall and had become a picture. The people saw nothing but the chair, the cookbook, and the scribblings on the wall. Staring at Argon lying on top of Eve, someone remarked, "Starved for a woman, wasn't he."

"Doesn't it look just like him, though?" said another.

"What was he doing, destroying the door like that? And look at this, the wall's covered with scribbles. Huh. He won't get away with it. Where in the world did he disappear to? Calls himself a painter!"

The man grumbling to himself was the apartment manager.

After everyone left, there came a murmuring from the wall.

"It isn't chalk that will remake the world . . ."

A single drop welled out of the wall. It fell from just below the eye of the pictorial Argon.

—1950

What are your reactions to and questions about this work? The following questions may help provoke some ideas.

Probing the Work

1. What do you think of Argon's attempts to "create a new world" with his magic chalk? Does he succeed? Explain why or why not.

Identifying Issues

2. What does the author seem to be saying about the role of the artist and his or her creative powers in relation to the rest of society?

URSULA LE GUIN

The Ones Who Walk Away from Omelas

Ursula K. Le Guin (b. 1929), the daughter of a psychologist mother and anthropologist father, grew up in Berkeley, California, and was educated at Radcliffe College and Columbia University before going to France, marrying, and returning to live in Oregon. There she began her prolific career as poet, novelist, critic, and children's author. Among her many books are Dancing at the Edge of the World *(1989), a collection of critical essays;* Searoad *(1991), a selection of science-fiction stories; and the science-fiction novels* The Dispossessed *(1974)—subtitled "an ambiguous Utopia,"* The Lathe of Heaven *(1971), the experimental novel* Always Coming Home *(1985),* Thanu: The Last Book of Earthsea *(1990); and* Going Out with Peacocks *(1994).*

With a clamor of bells that set the swallows soaring, the Festival of Summer came to the city Omelas, bright-towered by the sea. The rigging of the boats in harbor sparkled with flags. In the streets between houses with red roofs and painted walls, between old moss-grown gardens and under avenues of trees, past great parks and public buildings, processions moved. Some were decorous: old people in long stiff robes of mauve and gray, grave master workmen, quiet, merry women carrying their babies and chatting as they walked. In other streets the music beat faster, a shimmering of gong and tambourine, and the people went dancing, the procession was a dance. Children dodged in and out, their high calls rising like the swallows' crossing flights over the music and the singing. All the processions wound towards the north side of the city, where on the great water-meadow called the Green Fields boys and girls, naked in the bright air, with mud-stained feet and ankles and long, lithe arms, exercised their restive horses before the race. The horses wore no gear at all but a halter without bit. Their manes were braided with streamers of silver, gold, and green. They flared their nostrils and pranced and boasted to one another; they were vastly excited, the horse being the only animal who has adopted our ceremonies as his own. Far off to the north and west the mountains stood up half encircling Omelas on her bay. The air of morning was so clear that the snow still crowning the Eighteen Peaks burned with white-gold fire across the miles of sunlit air, under the dark blue of the sky. There was just enough wind to make the banners that marked the racecourse snap and flutter now and then. In the silence of the broad green meadows one could hear the music winding through the city streets, farther and nearer and ever approaching, a cheerful faint sweetness of the air that from time to time trembled and gathered together and broke out into the great joyous clanging of the bells.

Joyous! How is one to tell about joy? How describe the citizens of Omelas?

They were not simple folk, you see, though they were happy. But we do not say the words of cheer much any more. All smiles have become archaic. Given a description such as this one tends to make certain assumptions. Given a description such as this one tends to look next for the King, mounted on a splendid stallion and surrounded by his noble knights, or perhaps in a golden litter borne by great-muscled slaves. But there was no king. They did not use swords, or keep slaves. They were not barbarians. I do not know the rules and laws of their society, but I suspect that they were singularly few. As they did without monarchy and slavery, so they also got on without the stock exchange, the advertisement, the secret police, and the bomb. Yet I repeat that these were not simple folk, not dulcet shepherds, noble savages, bland utopians. They were not less complex than us. The trouble is that we have a bad habit, encouraged by pedants and sophisticates, of considering happiness as something rather stupid. Only pain is intellectual, only evil interesting. This is the treason of the artist: a refusal to admit the banality of evil and the terrible boredom of pain. If you can't lick 'em, join 'em. If it hurts, repeat it. But to praise despair is to condemn delight, to embrace violence is to lose hold of everything else. We have almost lost hold; we can no longer describe a happy man, nor make any celebration of joy. How can I tell you about the people of Omelas? They were not naïve and happy children—though their children were, in fact, happy. They were mature, intelligent, passionate adults whose lives were not wretched. O miracle! but I wish I could describe it better. I wish I could convince you. Omelas sounds in my words like a city in a fairy tale, long ago and far away, once upon a time. Perhaps it would be best if you imagined it as your own fancy bids, assuming it will rise to the occasion, for certainly I cannot suit you all. For instance, how about technology? I think that there would be no cars or helicopters in and above the streets; this follows from the fact that the people of Omelas are happy people. Happiness is based on a just discrimination of what is necessary, what is neither necessary nor destructive, and what is destructive. In the middle category, however—that of the unnecessary but undestructive, that of comfort, luxury, exuberance, etc.—they could perfectly well have central heating, subway trains, washing machines, and all kinds of marvelous devices not yet invented here, floating light-sources, fuelless power, a cure for the common cold. Or they could have none of that: it doesn't matter. As you like it. I incline to think that people from towns up and down the coast have been coming in to Omelas during the last days before the Festival on very fast little trains and double-decked trams, and that the train station of Omelas is actually the handsomest building in town, though plainer than the magnificent Farmers' Market. But even granted trains, I fear that Omelas so far strikes some of you as goody-goody. Smiles, bells, parades, horses, bleh. If so, please add an orgy. If an orgy would help, don't hesitate. Let us not, however, have temples from which issue beautiful nude priests and priestesses already half in ecstasy and ready to copulate with any man or woman, lover or stranger, who desires union with the deep godhead of the blood, although that was my first idea. But really it would be better not to have any temples in Omelas—at least, not manned temples. Religion yes, clergy no. Surely the beautiful nudes can just wander about, offering themselves like divine soufflés to the hunger of the needy and the rapture of the flesh. Let them join the processions. Let tambourines be struck above the copulations, and the glory of desire be proclaimed upon the gongs, and (a not unimportant point) let the offspring of these delightful rituals be beloved and looked after by all. One thing I know there is none of in Omelas is guilt. But what else should there be? I thought at first there were no drugs, but that is puritanical. For those who like it, the faint insistent sweetness of *drooz* may perfume the ways of the city, *drooz* which first brings a great lightness and brilliance to the mind and limbs, and then after some hours a dreamy languor, and wonderful visions at last of the very arcana and inmost secrets of the Universe, as well as exciting the pleasure of sex beyond all belief; and it is not habit-forming. For more modest tastes I think there ought to be beer. What else, what else belongs in the joyous city? The sense of victory, surely, the celebration of courage. But as we did without clergy, let us do without soldiers. The joy built upon successful slaughter is not the right kind of joy; it will not do; it is fearful and it is trivial. A boundless and generous contentment, a magnanimous triumph felt not against some outer enemy but in communion with the finest and fairest in the souls of all men everywhere and the splendor of the world's summer: this is what swells the hearts of the people of Omelas, and the victory they celebrate is that of life. I really don't think many of them need to take *drooz.*

Most of the processions have reached the Green Fields by now. A marvelous smell of cooking goes forth from the red and blue tents of the provisioners. The faces of small children are amiably sticky; in the benign gray beard of a man a couple of crumbs of rich pastry are entangled. The youths and girls have mounted their horses and are beginning to group around the starting line of the course. An old woman, small, fat, and laughing, is passing out flowers from a basket, and tall young men wear her flowers in their shining hair. A child of nine or ten sits at the edge of the crowd, alone, playing on a wooden flute. People pause to listen, and they smile, but they do not speak to him for he never ceases playing and never sees them, his dark eyes wholly rapt in the sweet, thin magic of the tune.

He finishes, and slowly lowers his hands holding the wooden flute.

As if that little private silence were the signal, all at once a trumpet sounds from the pavilion near the starting line: imperious, melancholy, piercing. The horses rear on their slender legs, and some of them neigh in answer. Sober-faced, the young riders stroke the horses' necks and soothe them, whispering, "Quiet, quiet, there my beauty, my hope. . . ." They begin to form in rank along the starting line. The crowds along the racecourse are like a field of grass and flowers in the wind. The Festival of Summer has begun.

Do you believe? Do you accept the festival, the city, the joy? No? Then let me describe one more thing.

In a basement under one of the beautiful public buildings of Omelas, or perhaps in the cellar of one of its spacious private homes, there is a room. It has one locked door, and no window. A little light seeps in dustily between cracks in the boards, secondhand from a cobwebbed window somewhere across the cellar. In one corner of the little room a couple of mops, with stiff, clotted, foul-smelling heads, stand near a rusty bucket. The floor is dirt, a little damp to the touch, as cellar dirt usually is. The room is about three paces long and two wide: a mere broom closet or disused tool room. In the room a child is sitting. It could be a boy or a girl. It looks about six, but actually is nearly ten. It is feeble-minded. Perhaps it was born defective, or perhaps it has become imbecile through fear, malnutrition, and neglect. It picks its nose and occasionally fumbles vaguely with its toes or genitals, as it sits hunched in the corner farthest from the bucket and the two mops. It is afraid of the mops. It finds them horrible. It shuts its eyes, but it knows the mops are still standing there; and the door is locked; and nobody will come. The door is always locked; and nobody ever comes, except that sometimes—the child has no understanding of time or interval—sometimes the door rattles terribly and opens, and a person, or several people, are there. One of them may come in and kick the child to make it stand up. The others never come close, but peer in at it with frightened, disgusted eyes. The food bowl and the water jug are hastily filled, the door is locked, the eyes disappear. The people at the door never say anything, but the child, who has not always lived in the tool room, and can remember sunlight and its mother's voice, sometimes speaks. "I will be good," it says. "Please let me out. I will be good!" They never answer. The child used to scream for help at night, and cry a good deal, but now it only makes a kind of whining, "eh-haa, eh-haa," and it speaks less and less often. It is so thin there are no calves to its legs; its belly protrudes; it lives on a half-bowl of corn meal and grease a day. It is naked. Its buttocks and thighs are a mass of festered sores, as it sits in its own excrement continually.

They all know it is there, all the people of Omelas. Some of them have come to see it, others are content merely to know it is there. They all know that it has to be there. Some of them understand why, and some do not, but they all understand that their happiness, the beauty of their city, the tenderness of their friendships, the health of their children, the wisdom of their scholars, the skill of their makers, even the abundance of their harvest and the kindly weathers of their skies, depend wholly on this child's abominable misery.

This is usually explained to children when they are between eight and twelve, whenever they seem capable of understanding; and most of those who come to see the child are young people, though often enough an adult comes, or comes back, to see the child. No matter how well the matter has been explained to them, these young spectators are always shocked and sickened at the sight. They feel disgust, which they had thought themselves superior to. They feel anger, outrage, impotence, despite all the explanations. They would like to do something for the child. But there is nothing they can do. If the child were brought up into the sunlight out of that vile place, if it were cleaned and fed and comforted, that would be a good thing, indeed; but if it were done, in that day and hour all the prosperity and beauty and delight of Omelas would wither and be destroyed. Those are the terms. To exchange all the goodness and grace of every life in Omelas for that single, small improvement: to throw away the happiness of thousands for the chance of the happiness of one: that would be to let guilt within the walls indeed.

The terms are strict and absolute; there may not even be a kind word spoken to the child.

Often the young people go home in tears, or in a tearless rage, when they have seen the child and faced this terrible paradox. They may brood over it for weeks or years. But as time goes on they begin to realize that even if the child could be released, it would not get much good of its freedom: a little vague pleasure of warmth and food, no doubt, but little more. It is too degraded and imbecile to know any real joy. It has been afraid too long ever to be free of fear. Its habits are too uncouth for it to respond to humane treatment. Indeed, after so long it would probably be wretched without walls about it to protect it, and darkness for its eyes, and its own excrement to sit in. Their tears at the bitter injustice dry when they begin to perceive the terrible justice of reality, and to accept it. Yet it is their tears and anger, the trying of their generosity and the acceptance of their helplessness, which are perhaps the true source of the splendor of their lives. Theirs is no vapid, irresponsible happiness. They know that they, like the child, are not free. They know compassion. It is the existence of the child, and their knowledge of its existence, that makes possible the nobility of their architecture, the poignancy of their music, the profundity of their science. It is because of the child that they are so gentle with children. They know that if the wretched one were not there sniveling in the dark, the other one, the flute-player, could make no joyful music as the young riders line up in their beauty for the race in the sunlight of the first morning of summer.

Now do you believe in them? Are they not more credible? But there is one more thing to tell, and this is quite incredible.

At times one of the adolescent girls or boys who go to see the child does not go home to weep or rage, does not, in fact, go home at all. Sometimes also a man or woman much older falls silent for a day or two, and then leaves home. These people go out into the street, and walk down the street alone. They keep walking, and walk straight out of the city of Omelas, through the beautiful gates. They keep walking across the farmlands of Omelas. Each one goes alone, youth or girl, man or woman. Night falls; the traveler must pass down village streets, between the houses with yellow-lit windows, and on out into the darkness of the fields. Each alone, they go west or north, towards the mountains. They go on. They leave Omelas, they walk ahead into the darkness, and they do not come back. The place they go towards is a place even less imaginable to most of us than the city of happiness. I cannot describe it at all. It is possible that it does not exist. But they seem to know where they are going, the ones who walk away from Omelas.

—1973

What are your reactions to and questions about this work? The following questions may help provoke some ideas.

Probing the Work

1. The people of Omelas are supposedly "happy people." What are some of the factors involved in maintaining this happiness? How do you interpret the following sentence in light of the ending of the story: "Happiness is

based on a just discrimination of what is necessary, what is neither necessary nor destructive, and what is destructive."

Identifying Issues

2. Discuss your understanding of the concept of utopia as expressed in this story. How does LeGuin's version fit with others you have come across? Is it important or counterproductive to have some kind of utopian vision?
3. What could the ugliness that the people in Omelas avoid symbolically represent, in 1973, when the story was published? What could it represent today?

NAGUIB MAHFOUZ

Half a Day

(translated by Denys Johnson-Davies)

Naguib Mahfouz (b. 1911) was born in Cairo, Egypt, and majored in philosophy in college. When he won the Nobel Prize for Literature in 1988, he had written over 20 novels (several banned), and 12 volumes of short stories, including The Time and the Place and Other Stories *(1991), where the following story is found. When the Ayatollah Khomeini placed the death sentence on Salman Rushdie, Mahfouz defended Rushdie, which led to death threats against him for "blasphemy."*

I proceeded alongside my father, clutching his right hand, running to keep up with the long strides he was taking. All my clothes were new: the black shoes, the green school uniform, and the red tarboosh.[1] My delight in my new clothes, however, was not altogether unmarred, for this was no feast day but the day on which I was to be cast into school for the first time.

My mother stood at the window watching our progress, and I would turn toward her from time to time, as though appealing for help. We walked along a street lined with gardens; on both sides were extensive fields planted with crops, prickly pears, henna trees, and a few date palms.

"Why school?" I challenged my father openly. "I shall never do anything to annoy you."

"I'm not punishing you," he said, laughing. "School's not a punishment. It's the factory that makes useful men out of boys. Don't you want to be like your father and brothers?"

I was not convinced. I did not believe there was really any good to be had in tearing me away from the intimacy of my home and throwing me into this building that stood at the end of the road like some huge, high-walled fortress, exceedingly stern and grim.

[1]A tassled cap often worn by Muslim men and made from felt or cloth.

When we arrived at the gate we could see the courtyard, vast and crammed full of boys and girls. "Go in by yourself," said my father, "and join them. Put a smile on your face and be a good example to others."

I hesitated and clung to his hand, but he gently pushed me from him. "Be a man," he said. "Today you truly begin life. You will find me waiting for you when it's time to leave."

I took a few steps, then stopped and looked but saw nothing. Then the faces of boys and girls came into view. I did not know a single one of them, and none of them knew me. I felt I was a stranger who had lost his way. But glances of curiosity were directed toward me, and one boy approached and asked, "Who brought you?"

"My father," I whispered.

"My father's dead," he said quite simply.

I did not know what to say. The gate was closed, letting out a pitiable screech. Some of the children burst into tears. The bell rang. A lady came along, followed by a group of men. The men began sorting us into ranks. We were formed into an intricate pattern in the great courtyard surrounded on three sides by high buildings of several floors; from each floor we were overlooked by a long balcony roofed in wood.

"This is your new home," said the woman. "Here too there are mothers and fathers. Here there is everything that is enjoyable and beneficial to knowledge and religion. Dry your tears and face life joyfully."

We submitted to the facts, and this submission brought a sort of contentment. Living beings were drawn to other living beings, and from the first moments my heart made friends with such boys as were to be my friends and fell in love with such girls as I was to be in love with, so that it seemed my misgivings had had no basis. I had never imagined school would have this rich variety. We played all sorts of different games: swings, the vaulting horse, ball games. In the music room we chanted our first songs. We also had our first introduction to language. We saw a globe of the Earth, which revolved and showed the various continents and countries. We started learning the numbers. The story of the Creator of the universe was read to us, we were told of His present world and of His Hereafter, and we heard examples of what He said. We ate delicious food, took a little nap, and woke up to go on with friendship and love, play and learning.

As our path revealed itself to us, however, we did not find it as totally sweet and unclouded as we had presumed. Dust-laden winds and unexpected accidents came about suddenly, so we had to be watchful, at the ready, and very patient. It was not all a matter of playing and fooling around. Rivalries could bring about pain and hatred or give rise to fighting. And while the lady would sometimes smile, she would often scowl and scold. Even more frequently she would resort to physical punishment.

In addition, the time for changing one's mind was over and gone and there was no question of ever returning to the paradise of home. Nothing lay ahead of us but exertion, struggle, and perseverance. Those who were able took advantage of the opportunities for success and happiness that presented themselves amid the worries.

The bell rang announcing the passing of the day and the end of work. The throngs of children rushed toward the gate, which was opened again. I bade farewell to friends and sweethearts and passed through the gate. I peered around but found no trace of my father, who had promised to be there. I stepped aside to wait. When I had waited for a long time without avail, I decided to return home on my own. After I had taken a few steps, a middle-aged man passed by, and I realized at once that I knew him. He came toward me, smiling, and shook me by the hand, saying, "It's a long time since we last met—how are you?"

With a nod of my head, I agreed with him and in turn asked, "And you, how are you?"

"As you can see, not all that good, the Almighty be praised!"

Again he shook me by the hand and went off. I proceeded a few steps, then came to a startled halt. Good Lord! Where was the street lined with gardens? Where had it disappeared to? When did all these vehicles invade it? And when did all these hordes of humanity come to rest upon its surface? How did these hills of refuse come to cover its sides? And where were the fields that bordered it? High buildings had taken over, the street surged with children, and disturbing noises shook the air. At various points stood conjurers showing off their tricks and making snakes appear from baskets. Then there was a band announcing the opening of a circus, with clowns and weight lifters walking in front. A line of trucks carrying central security troops crawled majestically by. The siren of a fire engine shrieked, and it was not clear how the vehicle would cleave its way to reach the blazing fire. A battle raged between a taxi driver and his passenger, while the passenger's wife called out for help and no one answered. Good God! I was in a daze. My head spun. I almost went crazy. How could all this have happened in half a day, between early morning and sunset? I would find the answer at home with my father. But where was my home? I could see only tall buildings and hordes of people. I hastened on to the crossroads between the gardens and Abu Khoda. I had to cross Abu Khoda to reach my house, but the stream of cars would not let up. The fire engine's siren was shrieking at full pitch as it moved at a snail's pace, and I said to myself, "Let the fire take its pleasure in what it consumes." Extremely irritated, I wondered when I would be able to cross. I stood there a long time, until the young lad employed at the ironing shop on the corner came up to me. He stretched out his arm and said gallantly, "Grandpa, let me take you across."

—1989

What are your questions and reactions to this work? The following questions may help provoke some ideas.

Probing the Work

1. Why is the story called "Half a Day"? In what sense could all this have happened in half a day?

Identifying Issues

2. How accurately does this story depict a child's perspective of a first day at school? An old man's perspective of the modern urban world?

WILLIAM SHAKESPEARE

A Midsummer-Night's Dream

William Shakespeare (1564–1616) was born in Stratford, England, of middle-class parents. He worked as an actor in London while writing the great plays he is most famous for, among them Romeo and Juliet, Richard III, Hamlet, Othello, Macbeth, *and* The Winter's Tale.

Summary:

A Midsummer-Night's Dream *opens with the wedding plans of two former enemies—*THESEUS, *Duke of Athens, and* HIPPOLYTA, *queen of the Amazons—suggesting a model of peaceful union for the other, "lesser" characters in the play, whose loves are mostly unrequited:* DEMETRIUS *loves* HERMIA, *and has the approval of Hermia's father, who has ordered her to marry Demetrius or face either death or a life in the nunnery. Hermia vows to disobey her father because she and* LYSANDER *are in love.* HELENA *is pathetically in love with Demetrius.*

OBERON *and* TITANIA *are rulers of the fairy kingdom: after they have a spat Oberon orders his servant,* PUCK, *to cast spells on Titania, and on the lovers as well. Puck makes fools of all of them—or exposes the inherent foolishness of humans in love—by having Titania fall in love with* BOTTOM, *a lowly mortal whose head has been transformed to that of an ass, and by having both Demetrius and Lysander fall in love with Helena, who only feels mocked by their sudden interest in her.*

The play-within-a-play, rehearsed and performed by some Athenian craftsmen (led by PETER QUINCE*), is a farcical version of the Pyramus and Thisbe myth. (Forbidden to love by their families, Pyramus and Thisbe speak to each other through a chink in the wall separating their homes, agreeing to meet outside where they will be able to love each other at last. Thisbe arrives first, but is chased away by a lion who rends her cloak near a berry bush; Pyramus arrives, sees the cloak, concludes his love is dead, and accordingly impales himself with his sword. Returning, Thisbe sees her dead lover and kills herself.) The craftsmen's comically inept version of this romantic myth allows us to question the nature of love and of myth, and to see that reality is often what we make of it.*

In the end, of course, everything works out for the best.

Dramatis Personæ

THESEUS, *Duke of Athens.*
EGEUS, *father to Hermia.*
LYSANDER, DEMETRIUS, } *in love with Hermia.*
PHILOSTRATE, *master of the revels to Theseus.*
QUINCE, *a carpenter.*
SNUG, *a joiner.*
BOTTOM, *a weaver.*
FLUTE, *a bellows-mender.*
SNOUT, *a tinker.*
STARVELING, *a tailor.*
HIPPOLYTA, *queen of the Amazons, betrothed to Theseus.*
HERMIA, *daughter to Egeus, in love with Lysander.*
HELENA, *in love with Demetrius.*
OBERON, *king of the fairies.*
TITANIA, *queen of the fairies.*
PUCK, *or* ROBIN GOODFELLOW.
PEASEBLOSSOM, COBWEB, MOTH, MUSTARDSEED, } *fairies.*
Other FAIRIES *attending their King and Queen.*
ATTENDANTS *on Theseus and Hippolyta.*

SCENE: *Athens, and a wood near it.*

ACT I

Scene I. Athens. The Palace of Theseus.

[*Enter* THESEUS, HIPPOLYTA, PHILOSTRATE, *and* ATTENDANTS.]

THE.: Now, fair Hippolyta, our nuptial hour
Draws on apace; four happy days bring in
Another moon: but, O, methinks, how slow
This old moon wanes! she lingers my desires
Like to a step-dame or a dowager
Long withering out a young man's revenue.
HIP.: Four days will quickly steep themselves in night;
Four nights will quickly dream away the time;
And then the moon, like to a silver bow
New-bent in heaven, shall behold the night
Of our solemnities.
THE.: Go, Philostrate,
Stir up the Athenian youth to merriments;
Awake the pert and nimble spirit of mirth:
Turn melancholy forth to funerals;
The pale companion is not for our pomp.

Dramatis Personae: The name of each artisan suggests his craft: **Quince,** or quoins, wedges of wood; **Snug,** tight-fitting; **Bottom,** core of a ball of yarn and the ball itself; **Flute,** the mender of the pipes or flutes of an organ. **Act I, Scene i: 4. lingers,** delays the fulfillment of. **5. dowager,** a widow with property inherited from her husband. **6. withering out,** making dwindle. **13. pert,** lively.

[*Exit* PHILOSTRATE.]

Hippolyta, I woo'd thee with my sword,
And won thy love, doing thee injuries;
But I will wed thee in another key,
With pomp, with triumph and with revelling.

[*Enter* EGEUS, HERMIA, LYSANDER, *and* DEMETRIUS.]

EGE.: Happy be Theseus, our renownèd duke!
THE.: Thanks, good Egeus: what's the news with thee?
EGE.: Full of vexation come I, with complaint
Against my child, my daughter Hermia.
Stand forth, Demetrius. My noble lord,
This man hath my consent to marry her.
Stand forth, Lysander: and, my gracious duke,
This man hath bewitch'd the bosom of my child:
Thou, thou, Lysander, thou hast given her rhymes
And interchanged love-tokens with my child:
Thou hast by moonlight at her window sung
With feigning voice verses of feigning love,
And stolen the impression of her fantasy
With bracelets of thy hair, rings, gawds, conceits,
Knacks, trifles, nosegays, sweetmeats, messengers
Of strong prevailment in unharden'd youth:
With cunning hast thou filch'd my daughter's heart,
Turn'd her obedience, which is due to me,
To stubborn harshness: and, my gracious duke,
Be it so she will not here before your grace
Consent to marry with Demetrius,
I beg the ancient privilege of Athens,
As she is mine, I may dispose of her:
Which shall be either to this gentleman
Or to her death, according to our law
Immediately provided in that case.
THE.: What say you, Hermia? be advised, fair maid;
To you your father should be as a god;
One that composed your beauties, yea, and one
To whom you are but as a form in wax
By him imprinted and within his power

19. triumph, public show. **27. bosom,** i.e., the seat of the emotions. **31. feigning,** deceptive; feigning, feigned. **32. and . . .** fantasy, captured her imagination by impressing your image upon it. **33. gawds,** pieces of jewelry; conceits, showy trinkets. **34. knacks,** knick-knacks; sweetmeats, candy. **35. strong prevailment,** great influence. **45. immediately,** expressly.

To leave the figure or disfigure it.
Demetrius is a worthy gentleman.
Her.: So is Lysander.
The.: In himself he is;
But in this kind, wanting your father's voice,
The other must be held the worthier.
Her.: I would my father look'd but with my eyes.
The.: Rather your eyes must with his judgement look.
Her.: I do entreat your grace to pardon me.
I know not by what power I am made bold,
Nor how it may concern my modesty,
In such a presence here to plead my thoughts;
But I beseech your grace that I may know
The worst that may befall me in this case,
If I refuse to wed Demetrius.
The.: Either to die the death or to abjure
For ever the society of men.
Therefore, fair Hermia, question your desires;
Know of your youth, examine well your blood,
Whether, if you yield not to your father's choice,
You can endure the livery of a nun,
For aye to be in shady cloister mew'd,
To live a barren sister all your life,
Chanting faint hymns to the cold fruitless moon.
Thrice-blessèd they that master so their blood,
To undergo such maiden pilgrimage;
But earthlier happy is the rose distill'd,
Than that which withering on the virgin thorn
Grows, lives and dies in single blessedness.
Her.: So will I grow, so live, so die, my lord,
Ere I will yield my virgin patent up
Unto his lordship, whose unwishèd yoke
My soul consents not to give sovereignty.
The.: Take time to pause; and, by the next new moon—
The sealing-day betwixt my love and me,
For everlasting bond of fellowship—
Upon that day either prepare to die
For disobedience to your father's will,
Or else to wed Demetrius, as he would;

51. disfigure, obliterate. **54. kind,** instance; **wanting,** lacking; **voice,** approval. **60. concern,** befit. **71. mew'd,** shut up. **74. blood,** passion. **76. earthlies happy,** happier on earth. **80. patent,** phrase formed on the analogy of "letters patent," here, identification mark, i.e., maidenhead.

Or on Diana's altar to protest
For aye austerity and single life.
DEM.: Relent, sweet Hermia: and, Lysander, yield
Thy crazèd title to my certain right.
LYS.: You have her father's love, Demetrius;
Let me have Hermia's: do you marry him.
EGE.: Scornful Lysander! true, he hath my love,
And what is mine my love shall render him.
And she is mine, and all my right of her
I do estate unto Demetrius.
LYS.: I am, my lord, as well derived as he,
As well possess'd; my love is more than his;
My fortunes every way as fairly rank'd,
If not with vantage, as Demetrius';
And, which is more than all these boasts can be,
I am beloved of beauteous Hermia:
Why should not I then prosecute my right?
Demetrius, I'll avouch it to his head,
Made love to Nedar's daughter, Helena,
And won her soul; and she, sweet lady, dotes,
Devoutly dotes, dotes in idolatry,
Upon this spotted and inconstant man.
THE.: I must confess that I have heard so much,
And with Demetrius thought to have spoke thereof;
But, being over-full of self-affairs,
My mind did lose it. But, Demetrius, come;
And come, Egeus; you shall go with me,
I have some private schooling for you both.
For you, fair Hermia, look you arm yourself
To fit your fancies to your father's will;
Or else the law of Athens yields you up—
Which by no means we may extenuate—
To death, or to a vow of single life.
Come, my Hippolyta: what cheer, my love?
Demetrius and Egeus, go along:
I must employ you in some business
Against our nuptial and confer with you
Of something nearly that concerns yourselves.
EGE.: With duty and desire we follow you.

[*Exeunt all but* LYSANDER *and* HERMIA.

89. protest, vow. **92. crazed,** unsound. **98. estate unto,** settle upon. **99. well-derived,** of as good birth. **100. as well possess'd,** as well off. **106. avouch . . . head,** affirm it to his face. **120. extenuate,** mitigate, alleviate. **125. against,** in anticipation of. **126. nearly that,** that intimately.

LYS.: How now, my love! why is your cheek so pale?
How chance the roses there do fade so fast?
HER.: Belike for want of rain, which I could well
Beteem them from the tempest of my eyes.
LYS.: Ay me! for aught that I could ever read,
Could ever hear by tale or history,
The course of true love never did run smooth;
But, either it was different in blood,—
HER.: O cross! too high to be enthrall'd to low.
LYS.: Or else misgraffèd in respect of years,—
HER.: O spite! too old to be engaged to young.
LYS.: Or else it stood upon the choice of friends,—
HER.: O hell! to choose love by another's eyes.
LYS.: Or, if there were a sympathy in choice,
War, death, or sickness did lay siege to it,
Making it momentany as a sound,
Swift as a shadow, short as any dream;
Brief as the lightning in the collied night,
That, in a spleen, unfolds both heaven and earth,
And ere a man hath power to say "Behold!"
The jaws of darkness do devour it up:
So quick bright things come to confusion.
HER.: If then true lovers have been ever cross'd,
It stands as an edict in destiny:
Then let us teach our trial patience,
Because it is a customary cross,
As due to love as thoughts and dreams and sighs,
Wishes and tears, poor fancy's followers.
LYS.: A good persuasion: therefore, hear me, Hermia.
I have a widow aunt, a dowager
Of great revénue, and she hath no child:
From Athens is her house remote seven leagues;
And she respects me as her only son.
There, gentle Hermia, may I marry thee;
And to that place the sharp Athenian law
Cannot pursue us. If thou lovest me then,
Steal forth thy father's house to-morrow night;
And in the wood, a league without the town,
Where I did meet thee once with Helena,

130. belike, probably. **131. Beteem them,** bring forth for them. **136. cross,** perversity; **enthrall'd to low,** made servant to one of low birth. **137. misgraffed,** badly matched. **139. stood upon,** concerned. **143. momentany,** momentary. **145. collied,** coal-black. **146. spleen,** fit of anger. **149. confusion,** ruin. **152. teach . . . patience,** teach ourselves patience to endure the trial. **155. fancy's,** love's. **160. respects,** regards.

To do observance to a morn of May,
There will I stay for thee.
HER.: My good Lysander!
I swear to thee, by Cupid's strongest bow,
By his best arrow with the golden head,
By the simplicity of Venus' doves,
By that which knitteth souls and prospers loves,
And by that fire which burn'd the Carthage queen,
When the false Troyan under sail was seen,
By all the vows that ever men have broke,
In number more than ever women spoke,
In that same place thou hast appointed me,
To-morrow truly will I meet with thee.
LYS.: Keep promise, love. Look, here comes Helena.

[*Enter* HELENA.]

HER.: God speed fair Helena! whither away?
HEL.: Call you me fair? that fair again unsay
Demetrius loves your fair: O happy fair!
Your eyes are lode-stars; and your tongue's sweet air
More tuneable than lark to shepherd's ear,
When wheat is green, when hawthorn buds appear.
Sickness is catching: O, were favour so,
Yours would I catch, fair Hermia, ere I go;
My ear should catch your voice, my eye your eye,
My tongue should catch your tongue's sweet melody.
Were the world mine, Demetrius being bated,
The rest I'ld give to be to you translated.
O, teach me how you look, and with what art
You sway the motion of Demetrius' heart.
HER.: I frown upon him, yet he loves me still.
HEL.: O that your frowns would teach my smiles such skill!
HER.: I give him curses, yet he gives me love.
HEL.: O that my prayers could such affection move!
HER.: The more I hate, the more he follows me.
HEL.: The more I love, the more he hateth me.
HER.: His folly, Helena, is no fault of mine.
HEL.: None, but your beauty: would that fault were mine!
HER.: Take comfort: he no more shall see my face;

167. do . . . May, celebrate May Day. **172. that . . . loves,** i.e., the girdle of Venus. **173. And . . . Queen,** according to Vergil's Aeneid [Book IV], Dido, deserted by Aeneas, burned herself to death on a funeral pyre. **182. your fair,** your beauty. **183. lode-stars,** guiding stars. **184. tuneable,** musical. **186. favour,** (1) physical appearance, (2) affection. **190. bated,** excepted. **191. translated,** transformed. **193. notion,** inclination.

Lysander and myself will fly this place.
Before the time I did Lysander see,
Seem'd Athens as a paradise to me:
O, then, what graces in my love do dwell,
That he hath turn'd a heaven unto a hell!
LYS.: Helen, to you our minds we will unfold:
To-morrow night, when Phœbe doth behold
Her silvery visage in the watery glass,
Decking with liquid pearl the bladed grass,
A time that lovers' flights doth still conceal,
Through Athens' gates have we devised to steal.
HER.: And in the wood, where often you and I
Upon faint primrose beds were wont to lie,
Emptying our bosoms of their counsel sweet,
There my Lysander and myself shall meet;
And thence from Athens turn away our eyes,
To seek new friends and stranger companies.
Farewell, sweet playfellow: pray thou for us;
And good luck grant thee thy Demetrius!
Keep word, Lysander: we must starve our sight
From lovers' food till morrow deep midnight.
LYS.: I will, my Hermia. [*Exit* HERM.
Helena, adieu:
As you on him, Demetrius dote on you! [*Exit.*
HEL.: How happy some o'er other some can be!
Through Athens I am thought as fair as she.
But what of that? Demetrius thinks not so;
He will not know what all but he do know:
And as he errs, doting on Hermia's eyes,
So I, admiring of his qualities:
Things base and vile, holding no quantity,
Love can transpose to form and dignity:
Love looks not with the eyes, but with the mind;
And therefore is wing'd Cupid painted blind:
Nor hath Love's mind of any judgement taste;
Wings and no eyes figure unheedy haste:
And therefore is Love said to be a child,
Because in choice he is so oft beguiled.
As waggish boys in game themselves forswear,
So the boy Love is perjured every where:
For ere Demetrius look'd on Hermia's eyne,

209. Phœbe, Diana, the moon. **215. faint,** pale. **237. figure,** are a symbol of. **240. waggish,** playful. **242, eyne,** eyes.

He hail'd down oaths that he was only mine;
And when this hail some heat from Hermia felt,
So he dissolved, and showers of oaths did melt.
I will go tell him of fair Hermia's flight:
Then to the wood will he to-morrow night
Pursue her; and for this intelligence
If I have thanks, it is a dear expense:
But herein mean I to enrich my pain,
To have his sight thither and back again.

[*Exit.*

SCENE II. ATHENS. QUINCE'S HOUSE.

[*Enter* QUINCE, SNUG, BOTTOM, FLUTE, SNOUT, *and* STARVELING.]

QUIN.: Is all our company here?

BOT.: You were best to call them generally, man by man, according to the scrip.

QUIN.: Here is the scroll of every man's name, which is thought fit, through all Athens, to play in our interlude before the duke and the duchess, on his wedding-day at night.

BOT.: First, good Peter Quince, say what the play treats on, then read the names of the actors, and so grow to a point.

QUIN.: Marry, our play is, The most lamentable comedy, and most cruel death of Pyramus and Thisby.

BOT.: A very good piece of work, I assure you, and a merry. Now, good Peter Quince, call forth your actors by the scroll. Masters, spread yourselves.

QUIN.: Answer as I call you. Nick Bottom, the weaver.

BOT.: Ready. Name what part I am for, and proceed.

QUIN.: You, Nick Bottom, are set down for Pyramus.

BOT.: What is Pyramus? a lover, or a tyrant?

QUIN.: A lover, that kills himself most gallant for love.

BOT.: That will ask some tears in the true performing of it: if I do it, let the audience look to their eyes; I will move storms, I will condole in some measure. To the rest: yet my chief humour is for a tyrant: I could play Ercles rarely, or a part to tear a cat in, to make all split.

The raging rocks
And shivering shocks

248. intelligence, news. **249. dear expense,** a thing that will cost me dear. **Scene ii: 2. generally,** severally, the first of Bottom's many malapropisms. **3. scrip,** written list. **8. grow to,** come to. **19. condole,** lament. **20. Ercles,** Hercules was a ranting character in the earlier drama; tear a cat, proverbial for "rant." **21. make all split,** proverbial for "cause an uproar."

Shall break the locks
    Of prison gates;
And Phibbus' car
Shall shine from far
And make and mar
    The foolish Fates.

This was lofty! Now name the rest of the players. This is Ercles' vein, a tyrant's vein; a lover is more condoling.

QUIN.: Francis Flute, the bellows-mender.

FLU.: Here, Peter Quince.

QUIN.: Flute, you must take Thisby on you.

FLU.: What is Thisby? a wandering knight?

QUIN.: It is the lady that Pyramus must love.

FLU.: Nay, faith, let not me play a woman; I have a beard coming.

QUIN.: That's all one: you shall play it in a mask, and you may speak as small as you will.

BOT.: An I may hide my face, let me play Thisby too, I'll speak in a monstrous little voice, "Thisne, Thisne;" "Ah Pyramus, my lover dear! thy Thisby dear, and lady dear!"

QUIN.: No, no; you must play Pyramus: and, Flute, you Thisby.

BOT.: Well, proceed.

QUIN.: Robin Starveling, the tailor.

STAR.: Here, Peter Quince.

QUIN.: Robin Starveling, you must play Thisby's mother. Tom Snout, the tinker.

SNOUT.: Here, Peter Quince.

QUIN.: You, Pyramus' father: myself, Thisby's father. Snug, the joiner; you, the lion's part: and, I hope, here is a play fitted.

SNUG.: Have you the lion's part written? pray you, if it be, give it to me, for I am slow of study.

QUIN.: You may do it extempore, for it is nothing but roaring.

BOT.: Let me play the lion too: I will roar, that I will do any man's heart good to hear me; I will roar, and that I will make the duke say "Let him roar again, let him roar again."

QUIN.: An you should do it too terribly, you would fright the duchess and the ladies, that they would shriek; and that were enough to hang us all.

ALL.: That would hang us, every mother's son.

BOT.: I grant you, friends, if that you should fright the ladies out of their wits, they would have no more discretion but to hang us: but I will aggravate my voice so that I will roar you as gently as any sucking dove; I will roar you as 'twere any nightingale.

26. Phibbus', Phoebus'. **35. wandering knight,** knight errant. **38. small,** shrilly. **40. an,** if. **50. fitted,** i.e., cast. **61. aggravate,** he means "moderate." **62. sucking,** i.e., not full-fledged.

Quin.: You can play no part but Pyramus; for Pyramus is a sweet-faced man; a proper man, as one shall see in a summer's day; a most lovely gentleman-like man: therefore you must needs play Pyramus.

Bot.: Well, I will undertake it. What beard were I best to play it in?

Quin.: Why, what you will.

Bot.: I will discharge it in either your straw-colour beard, your orange-tawny beard, your purple-in-grain beard, or your French-crown-colour beard, your perfect yellow.

Quin.: Some of your French crowns have no hair at all, and then you will play barefaced. But, masters, here are your parts: and I am to entreat you, request you and desire you, to con them by to-morrow night; and meet me in the palace wood, a mile without the town, by moonlight; there will we rehearse, for if we meet in the city, we shall be dogged with company, and our devices known. In the meantime I will draw a bill of properties, such as our play wants. I pray you, fail me not.

Bot.: We will meet; and there we may rehearse most obscenely and courageously. Take pains; be perfect: adieu.

Quin.: At the duke's oak we meet.

Bot.: Enough; hold or cut bow-strings.

[*Exeunt.*

ACT II

Scene I. A Wood Near Athens.

[*Enter, from opposite sides, a* FAIRY, *and* PUCK.]

Puck.: How now, spirit! whither wander you?

Fai.:
Over hill, over dale,
  Thorough bush, thorough brier,
Over park, over pale,
  Thorough flood, thorough fire,
I do wander every where,
Swifter than the moon's sphere;
And I serve the fairy queen,
To dew her orbs upon the green.
The cowslips tall her pensioners be:
In their gold coats spots you see;
Those be rubies, fairy favours,
In those freckles live their savours:

65. proper, handsome. **69. discharge,** perform. **70. purple-in-grain,** deep red. **70. French-crown-colour,** i.e., golden. **74. con,** learn by heart. **77. devices,** i.e., dramatic plans. **79. obscenely,** mistake for "obscurely," i.e., privately. **82. hold . . . strings,** i.e., be on hand or give up the play. **Act II, Scene i: 4. pale,** fence. **9. orbs,** fairy rings. **10. pensioners,** royal bodyguard.

I must go seek some dewdrops here
And hang a pearl in every cowslip's ear.
Farewell, thou lob of spirits; I'll be gone:
Our queen and all her elves come here anon.
PUCK.: The king doth keep his revels here to-night:
Take heed the queen come not within his sight;
For Oberon is passing fell and wrath,
Because that she as her attendant hath
A lovely boy, stolen from an Indian king;
She never had so sweet a changeling;
And jealous Oberon would have the child
Knight of his train, to trace the forests wild;
But she perforce withholds the lovèd boy,
Crowns him with flowers and makes him all her joy:
And now they never meet in grove or green,
By fountain clear, or spangled starlight sheen,
But they do square, that all their elves for fear
Creep into acorn-cups and hide them there.
FAI.: Either I mistake your shape and making quite,
Or else you are that shrewd and knavish sprite
Call'd Robin Goodfellow: are not you he
That frights the maidens of the villagery;
Skim milk, and sometimes labour in the quern
And bootless make the breathless housewife churn;
And sometime make the drink to bear no barm;
Mislead night-wanderers, laughing at their harm?
Those that Hobgoblin call you and sweet Puck,
You do their work, and they shall have good luck:
Are not you he?
PUCK.: Thou speak'st aright;
I am that merry wanderer of the night.
I jest to Oberon and make him smile
When I a fat and bean-fed horse beguile,
Neighing in likeness of a filly foal:
And sometime lurk I in a gossip's bowl,
In very likeness of a roasted crab,
And when she drinks, against her lips I bob
And on her wither'd dewlap pour the ale.

16. lob, lout. **20. passing fell,** extremely angry. **23. changeling,** a child left by the fairies in the place of one they have stolen. Here merely "stolen child." **30. square,** quarrel; **that,** so that. **33. shrewd,** mischievous, vexatious. **36. quern,** hand mill for grinding wheat. **37. bootless,** vainly. **38. barm,** yeast formed on brewing liquors. **47. bowl,** i.e., of liquor. **48. crab,** crabapple, often put in drink. **50. dewlap,** loose skin about the throat.

The wisest aunt, telling the saddest tale,
Sometime for three-foot stool mistaketh me;
Then slip I from her bum, down topples she,
And "tailor" cries, and falls into a cough;
And then the whole quire hold their hips and laugh,
And waxen in their mirth and neeze and swear
A merrier hour was never wasted there.
But, room, fairy! here comes Oberon.
FAI.: And here my mistress. Would that he were gone!

[*Enter, from one side,* OBERON, *with his train; from the other,* TITANIA, *with hers.*]

OBE.: Ill met by moonlight, proud Titania.
TITA.: What, jealous Oberon! Fairies, skip hence:
I have forsworn his bed and company.
OBE.: Tarry, rash wanton: am not I thy lord?
TITA.: Then I must be thy lady: but I know
When thou hast stolen away from fairy land,
And in the shape of Corin sat all day,
Playing on pipes of corn and versing love
To amorous Phillida. Why art thou here,
Come from the farthest steppe of India?
But that, forsooth, the bouncing Amazon,
Your buskin'd mistress and your warrior love,
To Theseus must be wedded, and you come
To give their bed joy and prosperity.
Obe.: How canst thou thus for shame, Titania,
Glance at my credit with Hippolyta,
Knowing I know thy love to Theseus?
Didst thou not lead him through the glimmering night
From Perigenia, whom he ravished?
And make him with fair Ægle break his faith,
With Ariadne and Antiopa?
TITA.: These are the forgeries of jealousy:
And never, since the middle summer's spring,
Met we on hill, in dale, forest or mead,
By pavèd fountain or by rushy brook,

51. aunt, old woman. **54. "tailor,"** allusion obscure, probably a play on the word "tail." **55. quire,** company. **56. neeze,** sneeze. **66–8. corin . . . Phillida,** conventional names of shepherds in pastoral literature. **67. pipes of corn,** pipes made out of oaten straws. **69. steppe,** mountain range. **70. bouncing,** big and lusty; **Amazon,** Hippolyta, Queen of the Amazons. **71. buskin'd,** wearing half-boots. **75. glance at,** allude to contemptuously; credit, reputation. **78–80. Perigenia . . . Antiopa,** these are the women whom, according to Plutarch (Life of Theseus), Theseus had loved. **82. middle summer's spring,** the beginning of mid-summer.

Or in the beached margent of the sea,
To dance our ringlets to the whistling wind,
But with thy brawls thou hast disturb'd our sport.
Therefore the winds, piping to us in vain,
As in revenge, have suck'd up from the sea
Contagious fogs; which falling in the land
Have every pelting river made so proud
That they have overborne their continents:
The ox hath therefore stretch'd his yoke in vain,
The ploughman lost his sweat, and the green corn
Hath rotted ere his youth attain'd a beard;
The fold stands empty in the drownèd field,
And crows are fatted with the murrion flock;
The nine men's morris is fill'd up with mud,
And the quaint mazes in the wanton green
For lack of tread are undistinguishable:
The human mortals want their winter here;
No night is now with hymn or carol blest:
Therefore the moon, the governess of floods,
Pale in her anger, washes all the air,
That rheumatic diseases do abound:
And thorough this distemperature we see
The seasons alter: hoary-headed frosts
Fall in the fresh lap of the crimson rose,
And on old Hiems' thin and icy crown
An odorous chaplet of sweet summer buds
Is, as in mockery, set: the spring, the summer,
The childing autumn, angry winter, change
Their wonted liveries, and the mazed world,
By their increase, now knows not which is which:
And this same progeny of evils comes
From our debate, from our dissension;
We are their parents and original.

OBE.: Do you amend it then; it lies in you:
Why should Titania cross her Oberon?
I do but beg a little changeling boy,
To be my henchman.

TITA.: Set your heart at rest:

85. in, on. **86. ringlets,** round dances. **91. pelting,** paltry. **92. continents,** banks. **97. murrion,** diseased. **98. nine men's morris,** squares on the village green, marked out by nine stones, on which a kind of bowling game was played. **99. quaint mazes,** intricate figures marked out on the green; **wanton green,** luxuriant grass. **101. want,** lack. **106. thorough,** through; **distemperature,** bad weather. **109. Hiems',** God of Winter. **112. childing,** fruitful. **113. mazed,** bewildered. **117. original,** source. **121. henchman,** attendant page.

The fairy land buys not the child of me.
His mother was a votaress of my order:
And, in the spicèd Indian air, by night,
Full often hath she gossip'd by my side,
And sat with me on Neptune's yellow sands,
Marking the embarkèd traders on the flood,
When we have laugh'd to see the sails conceive
And grow big-bellied with the wanton wind;
Which she, with pretty and with swimming gait
Following,—her womb then rich with my young squire,—
Would imitate, and sail upon the land,
To fetch me trifles, and return again,
As from a voyage, rich with merchandise.
But she, being mortal, of that boy did die;
And for her sake do I rear up her boy,
And for her sake I will not part with him.

OBE.: How long within this wood intend you stay?

TITA.: Perchance till after Theseus' wedding-day.
If you will patiently dance in our round
And see our moonlight revels, go with us;
If not, shun me, and I will spare your haunts.

OBE.: Give me that boy, and I will go with thee.

TITA.: Not for thy fairy kingdom. Fairies, away!
We shall chide downright, if I longer stay.

[*Exit* TITANIA *with her train.*

OBE.: Well, go thy way: thou shalt not from this grove
Till I torment thee for this injury.
My gentle Puck, come hither. Thou rememberest
Since once I sat upon a promontory,
And heard a mermaid on a dolphin's back
Uttering such dulcet and harmonious breath
That the rude sea grew civil at her song
And certain stars shot madly from their spheres,
To hear the sea-maid's music.

PUCK: I remember.

OBE.: That very time I saw, but thou couldst not,
Flying between the cold moon and the earth,
Cupid all arm'd: a certain aim he took
At a fair vestal thronèd by the west,
And loosed his love-shaft smartly from his bow,

127. embarked traders, merchant ships. **140. round,** i.e., round dance. **142. spare,** avoid. **149. since,** when. **151. breath,** voice. **153. And . . . spheres,** i.e., skyrockets and other forms of fireworks. **158. vestal,** vestal virgin, hence virgin.

As it should pierce a hundred thousand hearts;
But I might see young Cupid's fiery shaft
Quench'd in the chaste beams of the watery moon,
And the imperial votaress passèd on,
In maiden meditation, fancy-free.
Yet mark'd I where the bolt of Cupid fell:
It fell upon a little western flower,
Before milk-white, now purple with love's wound,
And maidens call it love-in-idleness.
Fetch me that flower; the herb I shew'd thee once:
The juice of it on sleeping eye-lids laid
Will make or man or woman madly dote
Upon the next live creature that it sees.
Fetch me this herb; and be thou here again
Ere the leviathan can swim a league.

PUCK: I'll put a girdle round about the earth
In forty minutes. [*Exit.*

OBE.: Having once this juice,
I'll watch Titania when she is asleep,
And drop the liquor of it in her eyes.
The next thing then she waking looks upon,
Be it on lion, bear, or wolf, or bull,
On meddling monkey, or on busy ape,
She shall pursue it with the soul of love:
And ere I take this charm from off her sight,
As I can take it with another herb,
I'll make her render up her page to me.
But who comes here? I am invisible;
And I will overhear their conference.

[*Enter* DEMETRIUS, HELENA *following him.*]

DEM.: I love thee not, therefore pursue me not.
Where is Lysander and fair Hermia?
The one I'll slay, the other slayeth me.
Thou told'st me they were stolen unto this wood;
And here am I, and wode within this wood,
Because I cannot meet my Hermia.
Hence, get thee gone, and follow me no more.

HEL.: You draw me, you hard-hearted adamant;
But yet you draw not iron, for my heart

163. imperial votaress, i.e., Queen Elizabeth. **164. fancy-free,** untouched by love. **165. bolt,** arrow. **168. love-in-idleness,** pansy. **174. leviathan,** whale. **175. I'll . . . earth,** I fly around the earth. **192. wode,** mad. **195. adamant,** loadstone.

Is true as steel: leave you your power to draw,
And I shall have no power to follow you.
DEM.: Do I entice you? do I speak you fair?
Or, rather, do I not in plainest truth
Tell you, I do not, nor I cannot love you?
HEL.: And even for that do I love you the more.
I am your spaniel; and, Demetrius,
The more you beat me, I will fawn on you:
Use me but as your spaniel, spurn me, strike me,
Neglect me, lose me; only give me leave,
Unworthy as I am, to follow you.
What worser place can I beg in your love,—
And yet a place of high respect with me,—
Than to be usèd as you use your dog?
DEM.: Tempt not too much the hatred of my spirit,
For I am sick when I do look on thee.
HEL.: And I am sick when I look not on you.
DEM.: You do impeach your modesty too much,
To leave the city and commit yourself
Into the hands of one that loves you not;
To trust the opportunity of night
And the ill counsel of a desert place
With the rich worth of your virginity.
HEL.: Your virtue is my privilege: for that
It is not night when I do see your face,
Therefore I think I am not in the night;
Nor doth this wood lack worlds of company,
For you in my respect are all the world:
Then how can it be said I am alone,
When all the world is here to look on me?
DEM.: I'll run from thee and hide me in the brakes,
And leave thee to the mercy of wild beasts.
HEL.: The wildest hath not such a heart as you.
Run when you will, the story shall be changed:
Apollo flies, and Daphne holds the chase;
The dove pursues the griffin; the mild hind
Makes speed to catch the tiger; bootless speed,
When cowardice pursues and valour flies.
DEM.: I will not stay thy questions; let me go:

197. leave, give up. **199. speak you fair,** speak to you in a friendly manner. **214. impeach,** discredit. **220. privilege,** protection. **224. in my respect,** as far as I am concerned. **227. brakes,** thickets. **231. holds the chase,** in Ovid, Apollo pursues Daphne; here the rôles are reversed. **232. griffin,** fabulous beast with an eagle's head attached to a lion's body; hind, doe.

Or, if thou follow me, do not believe
But I shall do thee mischief in the wood.
HEL.: Ay, in the temple, in the town, the field,
You do me mischief. Fie, Demetrius!
Your wrongs do set a scandal on my sex:
We cannot fight for love, as men may do;
We should be woo'd and were not made to woo.
[*Exit* DEM.]
I'll follow thee and make a heaven of hell,
To die upon the hand I love so well.
[*Exit*.
OBE.: Fare thee well, nymph: ere he do leave this grove,
Thou shalt fly him and he shall seek thy love.

[*Re-enter* PUCK.]

Hast thou the flower there? Welcome, wanderer.
PUCK: Ay, there it is.
OBE.: I pray thee, give it me.
I know a bank where the wild thyme blows,
Where oxlips and the nodding violet grows,
Quite over-canopied with luscious woodbine,
With sweet musk-roses and with eglantine:
There sleeps Titania sometime of the night,
Lull'd in these flowers with dances and delight;
And there the snake throws her enamell'd skin,
Weed wide enough to wrap a fairy in:
And with the juice of this I'll streak her eyes,
And make her full of hateful fantasies.
Take thou some of it, and seek through this grove:
A sweet Athenian lady is in love
With a disdainful youth: anoint his eyes;
But do it when the next thing he espies
May be the lady: thou shalt know the man
By the Athenian garments he hath on.
Effect it with some care that he may prove
More fond on her than she upon her love:
And look thou meet me ere the first cock crow.
PUCK: Fear not, my lord, your servant shall do so.
[*Exeunt*.

235. stay thy questions, listen to your talk. **244. upon,** by. **249. blows,** blossoms. **250. oxlips,** hybrid primroses. **251. woodbine,** honeysuckle, Virginia creeper. **252. eglantine,** the sweetbrier. **256. weed,** garment. **257. streak her eyes,** rub her eyelids. **266. fond,** doting.

Scene II. Another Part of the Wood.

[*Enter* TITANIA, *with her train.*]

TITA.: Come, now a roundel and a fairy song;
Then, for the third part of a minute, hence;
Some to kill cankers in the musk-rose buds,
Some war with rere-mice for their leathern wings,
To make my small elves coats, and some keep back
The clamorous owl that nightly hoots and wonders
At our quaint spirits. Sing me now asleep;
Then to your offices and let me rest.

THE FAIRIES SING.

You spotted snakes with double tongue,
Thorny hedgehogs, be not seen;
Newts and blind-worms, do no wrong,
Come not near our fairy queen.
Philomel, with melody
Sing in our sweet lullaby;
Lulla, lulla, lullaby, lulla, lulla, lullaby:
Never harm,
Nor spell nor charm,
Come our lovely lady nigh;
So, good night, with lullaby.

Weaving spiders, come not here;
Hence, you long-legg'd spinners, hence!
Beetles black, approach not near;
Worm nor snail, do no offence.
Philomel, with melody, &c.

A FAIRY: Hence, away! now all is well:
One aloof stand sentinel.

[*Exeunt* FAIRIES. TITANIA *sleeps.*

[*Enter* OBERON, *and squeezes the flower on* TITANIA'S *eyelids.*]

OBE.: What thou seest when thou dost wake,
Do it for thy true-love take,
Love and languish for his sake:
Be it ounce, or cat, or bear,
Pard, or boar with bristled hair,

Scene II: 1. roundel, dance in a ring. **3. cankers,** cankerworms. **4. rere-mice,** bats. **7. quaint,** dainty. **8. offices,** duties. **11. blind worms,** legless lizards, small snakelike animals. **13. Philomel,** i.e., the nightingale. **30. ounce,** lynx; **cat,** wildcat. **31. Pard,** leopard.

In thy eye that shall appear
When thou wakest, it is thy dear:
Wake when some vile thing is near. [*Exit.*

[*Enter* LYSANDER *and* HERMIA.]

LYS.: Fair love, you faint with wandering in the wood;
And to speak troth, I have forgot our way:
We'll rest us, Hermia, if you think it good,
And tarry for the comfort of the day.
HER.: Be it so, Lysander: find you out a bed;
For I upon this bank will rest my head.
LYS.: One turf shall serve as pillow for us both;
One heart, one bed, two bosoms and one troth.
HER.: Nay, good Lysander; for my sake, my dear,
Lie further off yet, do not lie so near.
LYS.: O, take the sense, sweet, of my innocence!
Love takes the meaning in love's conference.
I mean, that my heart unto yours is knit
So that but one heart we can make of it;
Two bosoms interchainèd with an oath;
So then two bosoms and a single troth.
Then by your side no bed-room me deny;
For lying so, Hermia, I do not lie.
HER.: Lysander riddles very prettily:
Now much beshrew my manners and my pride,
If Hermia meant to say Lysander lied.
But, gentle friend, for love and courtesy
Lie further off; in human modesty,
Such separation as may well be said
Becomes a virtuous bachelor and a maid,
So far be distant; and, good night, sweet friend:
Thy love ne'er alter till thy sweet life end!
LYS.: Amen, amen, to that fair prayer, say I;
And then end life when I end loyalty!
Here is my bed: sleep give thee all his rest!
HER.: With half that wish the wisher's eyes be press'd!
[*They sleep.*

[*Enter* PUCK.]

PUCK: Through the forest have I gone,
But Athenian found I none,
On whose eyes I might approve

36. troth, truth. **50. troth,** troth-plight. **54. beshrew,** curse (a mild oath). **57. human,** courteous. **68. approve,** test.

This flower's force in stirring love.
Night and silence.—Who is here?
Weeds of Athens he doth wear:
This is he, my master said,
Despisèd the Athenian maid;
And here the maiden, sleeping sound,
On the dank and dirty ground.
Pretty soul! she durst not lie
Near this lack-love, this kill-courtesy.
Churl, upon thy eyes I throw
All the power this charm doth owe.
When thou wakest, let love forbid
Sleep his seat on thy eyelid:
So awake when I am gone;
For I must now to Oberon. [*Exit.*

[*Enter* DEMETRIUS *and* HELENA, *running*.]

HEL.: Stay, though thou kill me, sweet Demetrius.
DEM.: I charge thee, hence, and do not haunt me thus.
HEL.: O, wilt thou darkling leave me? do not so.
DEM.: Stay, on thy peril: I alone will go. [*Exit.*
HEL.: O, I am out of breath in this fond chase!
The more my prayer, the lesser is my grace.
Happy is Hermia, wheresoe'er she lies;
For she hath blessèd and attractive eyes.
How came her eyes so bright? Not with salt tears:
If so, my eyes are oftener wash'd than hers.
No, no, I am as ugly as a bear;
For beasts that meet me run away for fear:
Therefore no marvel though Demetrius
Do, as a monster, fly my presence thus.
What wicked and dissembling glass of mine
Made me compare with Hermia's sphery eyne?
But who is here? Lysander! on the ground!
Dead? or asleep? I see no blood, no wound.
Lysander, if you live, good sir, awake.
LYS.: [*Awaking*] And run through fire I will for thy sweet sake.
Transparent Helena! Nature shows art,
That through thy bosom makes me see thy heart.
Where is Demetrius? O, how fit a word
Is that vile name to perish on my sword!

79. owe, possess. **86. darkling,** in the dark. **88. fond,** foolish. **89. grace,** good fortune. **98. dissembling,** deceiving. **99. sphery eyne,** starry eyes.

HEL.: Do not say so, Lysander; say not so.
What though he love your Hermia? Lord, what though?
Yet Hermia still loves you: then be content.
LYS.: Content with Hermia! No; I do repent
The tedious minutes I with her have spent.
Not Hermia but Helena I love:
Who will not change a raven for a dove?
The will of man is by his reason sway'd;
And reason says you are the worthier maid.
Things growing are not ripe until their season:
So I, being young, till now ripe not to reason;
And touching now the point of human skill,
Reason becomes the marshal to my will
And leads me to your eyes, where I o'erlook
Love's stories written in love's richest book.
HEL.: Wherefore was I to this keen mockery born?
When at your hands did I deserve this scorn?
Is't not enough, is't not enough, young man,
That I did never, no, nor never can,
Deserve a sweet look from Demetrius' eye,
But you must flout my insufficiency?
Good troth, you do me wrong, good sooth, you do,
In such disdainful manner me to woo.
But fare you well: perforce I must confess
I thought you lord of more true gentleness.
O, that a lady, of one man refused,
Should of another therefore be abused! [*Exit.*
LYS.: She sees not Hermia. Hermia, sleep thou there:
And never mayst thou come Lysander near!
For as a surfeit of the sweetest things
The deepest loathing to the stomach brings,
Or as the heresies that men do leave
Are hated most of those they did deceive,
So thou, my surfeit and my heresy,
Of all be hated, but the most of me!
And, all my powers, address your love and might
To honour Helen and to be her knight! [*Exit.*
HER.: [*Awaking*] Help me, Lysander, help me! do thy best
To pluck this crawling serpent from my breast!
Ay me, for pity! what a dream was here!
Lysander, look how I do quake with fear:
Methought a serpent eat my heart away,

118. ripe, grown ripe. **119. point,** apex. **120. will,** passion. **128. flout,** make fun of, insult.

And you sat smiling at his cruel prey.
Lysander! what, removed? Lysander! lord!
What, out of hearing? gone? no sound, no word?
Alack, where are you? speak, an if you hear;
Speak, of all loves! I swoon almost with fear.
No? then I well perceive you are not nigh:
Either death or you I'll find immediately. [*Exit.*

ACT III

Scene I. The Wood. Titania Lying Asleep.

[*Enter* Quince, Snug, Bottom, Flute, Snout, *and* Starveling.]

Bot.: Are we all met?

Quin.: Pat, pat; and here's a marvellous convenient place for our rehearsal. This green plot shall be our stage, this hawthorn-brake our tiring-house; and we will do it in action as we will do it before the duke.

Bot.: Peter Quince,—

Quin.: What sayest thou, bully Bottom?

Bot.: There are things in this comedy of Pyramus and Thisby that will never please. First, Pyramus must draw a sword to kill himself; which the ladies cannot abide. How answer you that?

Snout: By'r lakin, a parlous fear.

Star.: I believe we must leave the killing out, when all is done.

Bot.: Not a whit: I have a device to make all well. Write me a prologue; and let the prologue seem to say, we will do no harm with our swords and that Pyramus is not killed indeed; and, for the more better assurance, tell them that I Pyramus am not Pyramus, but Bottom the weaver: this will put them out of fear.

Quin.: Well, we will have such a prologue; and it shall be written in eight and six.

Bot.: No, make it two more; let it be written in eight and eight.

Snout: Will not the ladies be afeard of the lion?

Star.: I fear it, I promise you.

Bot.: Masters, you ought to consider with yourselves: to bring in—God shield us!—a lion among ladies, is a most dreadful thing; for there is not a more fearful wild-fowl than your lion living; and we ought to look to't.

Snout: Therefore another prologue must tell he is not a lion.

Bot.: Nay, you must name his name, and half his face must be seen through the lion's neck: and he himself must speak through, saying thus, or to

150. prey, preying [on me]. **154. of all loves,** for the sake of all love. **Act III, Scene i: 3. tiring-house,** dressing room. **6. bully Bottom,** "good old" Bottom. **10. By'r lakin,** by our ladykin, i.e., Virgin Mary; **parlous,** dangerous, risky. **17. eight and six,** alternate lines of eight and six syllables.

the same defect,—"Ladies,"—or "Fair ladies,—I would wish you,"—or "I would request you,"—or "I would entreat you,—not to fear, not to tremble: my life for yours. If you think I come hither as a lion, it were pity of my life: no, I am no such thing; I am a man as other men are;" and there indeed let him name his name, and tell them plainly he is Snug the joiner.

QUIN.: Well, it shall be so. But there is two hard things; that is, to bring the moonlight into a chamber; for, you know, Pyramus and Thisby meet by moonlight.

SNOUT: Doth the moon shine that night we play our play?

BOT.: A calendar, a calendar! look in the almanac; find out moonshine, find out moonshine.

QUIN.: Yes, it doth shine that night.

BOT.: Why, then may you leave a casement of the great chamber window, where we play, open, and the moon may shine in at the casement.

QUIN.: Ay; or else one must come in with a bush of thorns and a lanthorn, and say he comes to disfigure, or to present, the person of Moonshine. Then, there is another thing: we must have a wall in the great chamber; for Pyramus and Thisby, says the story, did talk through the chink of a wall.

SNOUT: You can never bring in a wall. What say you, Bottom?

BOT.: Some man or other must present Wall: and let him have some plaster, or some loam, or some rough-cast about him, to signify wall; and let him hold his fingers thus, and through that cranny shall Pyramus and Thisby whisper.

QUIN.: If that may be, then all is well. Come, sit down, every mother's son, and rehearse your parts. Pyramus, you begin: when you have spoken your speech, enter into that brake: and so every one according to his cue.

[*Enter* PUCK *behind.*]

PUCK: What hempen home-spuns have we swaggering here,
So near the cradle of the fairy queen?
What, a play toward! I'll be an auditor;
An actor too perhaps, if I see cause.

QUIN.: Speak, Pyramus. Thisby, stand forth.

BOT.: Thisby, the flowers of odious savours sweet,—

QUIN.: Odours, odours.

BOT.: ——odours savours sweet:
So hath thy breath, my dearest Thisby dear. But hark, a voice! stay thou but here awhile,
And by and by I will to thee appear. [*Exit.*

28. defect, mistake for "effect." **31. pity of my life,** sad thing for me. **41. great chamber,** hall of a great house. **44. disfigure,** mistake for "prefigure." **49. rough-cast,** coarse plaster. **57. toward,** about to begin.

PUCK: A stranger Pyramus than e'er played here. [*Exit.*

FLU.: Must I speak now?

QUIN.: Ay, marry, must you; for you must understand he goes but to see a noise that he heard, and is to come again.

FLU.: Most radiant Pyramus, most lily-white of hue,
Of colour like the red rose on triumphant brier,
Most brisky juvenal and eke most lovely Jew,
As true as truest horse that yet would never tire
I'll meet thee, Pyramus, at Ninny's tomb.

QUIN.: "Ninus' tomb," man: why, you must not speak that yet; that you answer to Pyramus: you speak all your part at once, cues and all. Pyramus enter: your cue is past; it is, "never tire."

FLU.: O,—As true as truest horse, that yet would never tire.

[*Re-enter* PUCK, *and* BOTTOM *with an ass's head.*]

BOT.: If I were fair, Thisby, I were only thine.

QUIN.: O monstrous! O strange! we are haunted. Pray, masters! fly, masters! Help!

[*Exeunt* QUINCE, SNUG, FLUTE, SNOUT, *and* STARVELING.

PUCK: I'll follow you, I'll lead you about a round,
Through bog, through bush, through brake, through brier:
Sometime a horse I'll be, sometime a hound,
A hog, a headless bear, sometime a fire;
And neigh; and bark, and grunt, and roar, and burn,
Like horse, hound, hog, bear, fire, at every turn. [*Exit.*

BOT.: Why do they run away? this is a knavery of them to make me afeard.

[*Re-enter* SNOUT.]

SNOUT: O Bottom, thou art changed! what do I see on thee?

BOT.: What do you see? you see an ass-head of your own, do you?
[*Exit* SNOUT.

[*Re-enter* QUINCE.]

QUIN.: Bless thee, Bottom! bless thee! thou art translated. [*Exit.*

BOT.: I see their knavery: this is to make an ass of me; to fright me, if they could. But I will not stir from this place, do what they can: I will walk up and down here, and I will sing, that they shall hear I am not afraid.
[*Sings.*

72. brisky juvenal, brisk youth; **Jew,** nonsensical repetition of the first syllable of juvenal. **75. Ninus,** founder of Babylon, at whose tomb in Ovid's story the lovers used to meet. **82. about a round,** round about. **91. translated,** transformed. **95. ousel,** blackbird.

The ousel cock so black of hue,
With orange-tawny bill,
The throstle with his note so true,
The wren with little quill,—

TITA.: [*Awakening*] What angel wakes me from my flowery bed?
BOT.: [*Sings.*]

The finch, the sparrow and the lark,
The plain-song cuckoo gray,
Whose note full many a man doth mark,
And dares not answer nay;—

for, indeed, who would set his wit to so foolish a bird? who would give a bird the lie, though he cry "cuckoo" never so?

TITA.: I pray thee, gentle mortal, sing again:
Mine ear is much enamour'd of thy note;
So is mine eye enthrallèd to thy shape;
And thy fair virtue's force perforce doth move me
On the first view to say, to swear, I love thee.

BOT.: Methinks, mistress, you should have little reason for that: and yet, to say the truth, reason and love keep little company together now-a-days; the more the pity that some honest neighbours will not make them friends. Nay, I can gleek upon occasion.

TITA.: Thou art as wise as thou art beautiful.

BOT.: Not so, neither: but if I had wit enough to get out of this wood, I have enough to serve mine own turn.

TITA.: Out of this wood do not desire to go:
Thou shalt remain here, whether thou wilt or no.
I am a spirit of no common rate:
The summer still doth tend upon my state;
And I do love thee: therefore, go with me;
I'll give thee fairies to attend on thee,
And they shall fetch thee jewels from the deep,
And sing while thou on pressèd flowers dost sleep:
And I will purge thy mortal grossness so
That thou shalt like an airy spirit go.
Peaseblossom! Cobweb! Moth! and Mustardseed!

[*Enter* PEASEBLOSSOM, COBWEB, MOTH, *and* MUSTARDSEED.]

97. throstle, thrush. **98. quill,** pipe. **101. plain song,** singing a simple air. **105. "cuckoo,"** the word sounded like "cuckold," which meant a deceived husband. What married man dare contradict the bird's accusation? **109. fair virtue's force,** the power of your beauty. **114. gleek,** scoff. **120. rate,** value, estimation. **121. still,** always; **tend upon,** serve as an attendant.

PEAS.: Ready.
COB.: And I.
MOTH: And I.
MUS.: And I.
ALL: Where shall we go?
TITA.: Be kind and courteous to this gentleman;
Hop in his walks and gambol in his eyes;
Feed him with apricocks and dewberries,
With purple grapes, green figs, and mulberries;
The honey-bags steal from the humble-bees,
And for night-tapers crop their waxen thighs
And light them at the fiery glow-worm's eyes,
To have my love to bed and to arise;
And pluck the wings from painted butterflies
To fan the moonbeams from his sleeping eyes:
Nod to him, elves, and do him courtesies.
PEAS.: Hail, mortal!
COB.: Hail!
MOTH: Hail!
MUS.: Hail!
BOT.: I cry your worships mercy, heartily: I beseech your worship's name.
COB.: Cobweb.
BOT.: I shall desire you of more acquaintance, good Master Cobweb: if I cut my finger, I shall make bold with you. Your name, honest gentleman?
PEAS.: Peaseblossom.
BOT.: I pray you, commend me to Mistress Squash, your mother, and to Master Peascod, your father. Good Master Peaseblossom, I shall desire you of more acquaintance too. Your name, I beseech you, sir?
MUS.: Mustardseed.
BOT.: Good Master Mustardseed, I know your patience well: that same cowardly, giant-like ox-beef hath devoured many a gentleman of your house: I promise you your kindred hath made my eyes water ere now. I desire your more acquaintance, good Master Mustardseed.
TITA.: Come, wait upon him; lead him to my bower.
The moon methinks looks with a watery eye;
And when she weeps, weeps every little flower,
Lamenting some enforcèd chastity.
Tie up my love's tongue, bring him silently.

[*Exeunt.*

136. gambol, caper. **139. crop,** snip off. **149. I . . . mercy,** I beg your worship's pardon. **154. squash,** unripe peaspod. **158. patience,** sufferings. **165. enforced,** violated.

Scene II. Another Part of the Wood.

[*Enter* OBERON.]

OBE.: I wonder if Titania be awaked;
Then, what it was that next came in her eye,
Which she must dote on in extremity.

[*Enter* PUCK.]

Here comes my messenger.
How now, mad spirit!
What night-rule now about this haunted grove?
PUCK: My mistress with a monster is in love.
Near to her close and consecrated bower,
While she was in her dull and sleeping hour,
A crew of patches, rude mechanicals,
That work for bread upon Athenian stalls,
Were met together to rehearse a play
Intended for great Theseus' nuptial-day.
The shallowest thick-skin of that barren sort,
Who Pyramus presented, in their sport
Forsook his scene and enter'd in a brake:
When I did him at this advantage take,
An ass's nole I fixèd on his head:
Anon his Thisbe must be answerèd,
And forth my mimic comes. When they him spy,
As wild geese that the creeping fowler eye,
Or russet-pated choughs, many in sort,
Rising and cawing at the gun's report,
Sever themselves and madly sweep the sky,
So, at his sight, away his fellows fly;
And, at our stamp, here o'er and o'er one falls;
He murder cries and help from Athens calls.
Their sense thus weak, lost with their fears thus strong,
Made senseless things begin to do them wrong;
For briers and thorns at their apparel snatch;
Some sleeves, some hats, from yielders all things catch.
I led them on in this distracted fear,
And left sweet Pyramus translated there:

Scene ii: 2. next, first. **3. in extremity,** extremely. **5. night-rule,** mischief. **9. patches,** clowns, dolts; **mechanicals,** laborers. **10. upon Athenian stalls,** in Athenian shops. **13. barren sort,** stupid crowd. **15. brake,** thicket. **17. nole,** head. **19. mimic,** buffoon. **21. russet-pated choughs,** gray-headed grackles; **in sort,** together.

When in that moment, so it came to pass,
Titania waked and straightway loved an ass.
OBE.: This falls out better than I could devise.
But hast thou yet latch'd the Athenian's eyes
With the love-juice, as I did bid thee do?
PUCK: I took him sleeping,—that is finish'd too,—
And the Athenian woman by his side;
That, when he waked, of force she must be eyed.

[*Enter* HERMIA *and* DEMETRIUS.]

OBE.: Stand close: this is the same Athenian.
PUCK: This is the woman, but not this the man.
DEM.: O, why rebuke you him that loves you so?
Lay breath so bitter on your bitter foe.
HER.: Now I but chide; but I should use thee worse,
For thou, I fear, hast given me cause to curse.
If thou hast slain Lysander in his sleep,
Being o'er shoes in blood, plunge in the deep,
And kill me too.
The sun was not so true unto the day
As he to me: would he have stolen away
From sleeping Hermia? I'll believe as soon
The whole earth may be bored and that the moon
May through the centre creep and so displease
Her brother's noontide with the Antipodes.
It cannot be but thou hast murder'd him;
So should a murderer look, so dead, so grim.
DEM.: So should the murder'd look, and so should I,
Pierced through the heart with your stern cruelty:
Yet you, the murderer, look as bright, as clear,
As yonder Venus in her glimmering sphere.
HER.: What's this to my Lysander? where is he?
Ah, good Demetrius, wilt thou give him me?
DEM.: I had rather give his carcass to my hounds.
HER.: Out, dog! out, cur! thou drivest me past the bounds
Of maiden's patience. Hast thou slain him, then?
Henceforth be never number'd among men!
O, once tell true, tell true, even for my sake!
Durst thou have look'd upon him being awake,
And hast thou kill'd him sleeping? O brave touch
Could not a worm, an adder, do so much?

36. latch'd, charmed. **40. of force,** of necessity. **41. close,** hidden. **54. center,** i.e., of the earth. **57. dead,** deadly. **70. brave touch,** splendid exploit. **71. worm,** snake.

An adder did it; for with doubler tongue
Than thine, thou serpent, never adder stung.
DEM.: You spend your passion on a misprised mood:
I am not guilty of Lysander's blood;
Nor is he dead, for aught that I can tell.
HER.: I pray thee, tell me then that he is well.
DEM.: And if I could, what should I get therefore?
HER.: A privilege never to see me more.
And from thy hated presence part I so:
See me no more, whether he be dead or no. [*Exit.*
DEM.: There is no following her in this fierce vein:
Here therefore for a while I will remain.
So sorrow's heaviness doth heavier grow
For debt that bankrupt sleep doth sorrow owe;
Which now in some slight measure it will pay,
If for his tender here I make some stay.
[*Lies down and sleeps.*
OBE.: What hast thou done? thou hast mistaken quite
And laid the love-juice on some true-love's sight:
Of thy misprision must perforce ensue
Some true love turn'd and not a false turn'd true.
PUCK: Then fate o'er-rules, that, one man holding troth,
A million fail, confounding oath on oath.
OBE.: About the wood go swifter than the wind,
And Helena of Athens look thou find:
All fancy-sick she is and pale of cheer,
With sighs of love, that costs the fresh blood dear:
By some illusion see thou bring her here:
I'll charm his eyes against she do appear.
PUCK: I go, I go; look how I go,
Swifter than arrow from the Tartar's bow. [*Exit.*

OBE.: Flower of this purple dye,
Hit with Cupid's archery,
Sink in apple of his eye.
When his love he doth espy,
Let her shine as gloriously
As the Venus of the sky.
When thou wakest, if she be by,
Beg of her for remedy.

74. on a misprised mood, in mistaken anger. **82. in . . . vein,** while she is in this fierce mood. **87. If . . . stay,** if I wait for sleep's offer [of himself]. **90. misprision,** mistake. **96. fancy-sick,** love-sick; **cheer,** face. **97. sighs of love,** allusion to the belief that each sigh costs the heart a drop of blood. **98. illusion,** deception. **99. against,** by the time that.

[*Re-enter* PUCK.]

PUCK. Captain of our fairy band,
Helena is here at hand;
And the youth, mistook by me,
Pleading for a lover's fee.
Shall we their fond pageant see?
Lord, what fools these mortals be!

OBE. Stand aside: the noise they make
Will cause Demetrius to awake.

PUCK. Then will two at once woo one;
That must needs be sport alone;
And those things do best please me
That befall preposterously.

[*Enter* LYSANDER *and* HELENA.]

LYS.: Why should you think that I should woo in scorn?
Scorn and derision never come in tears:
Look, when I vow, I weep; and vows so born,
In their nativity all truth appears.
How can these things in me seem scorn to you,
Bearing the badge of faith, to prove them true?

HEL.: You do advance your cunning more and more.
When truth kills truth, O devilish-holy fray!
These vows are Hermia's: will you give her o'er?
Weigh oath with oath, and you will nothing weigh:
Your vows to her and me, put in two scales,
Will even weigh, and both as light as tales.

LYS.: I had no judgement when to her I swore.

HEL.: Nor none, in my mind, now you give her o'er.

LYS.: Demetrius loves her, and he loves not you.

DEM.: [*Awaking*] O Helen, goddess, nymph, perfect, divine!
To what, my love, shall I compare thine eyne?
Crystal is muddy. O, how ripe in show
Thy lips, those kissing cherries, tempting grow!
That pure congealèd white, high Taurus' snow,
Fann'd with the eastern wind, turns to a crow
When thou hold'st up thy hand: O, let me kiss
This princess of pure white, this seal of bliss!

HEL.: O spite! O hell! I see you all are bent

114. fond pageant, silly spectacle. **121. preposterously,** contrary to reason. **124–5. vows . . . appears,** i.e., vows born in tears seem at their birth to be wholly true. **141. Taurus,** a mountain range in Asia Minor. **144. seal,** pledge, ratification.

To set against me for your merriment:
If you were civil and knew courtesy,
You would not do me thus much injury.
Can you not hate me, as I know you do,
But you must join in souls to mock me too?
If you were men, as men you are in show,
You would not use a gentle lady so;
To vow, and swear, and superpraise my parts,
When I am sure you hate me with your hearts.
You both are rivals, and love Hermia;
And now both rivals, to mock Helena:
A trim exploit, a manly enterprise,
To conjure tears up in a poor maid's eyes
With your derision! none of noble sort
Would so offend a virgin and extort
A poor soul's patience, all to make you sport.

LYS.: You are unkind, Demetrius; be not so;
For you love Hermia; this you know I know:
And here, with all good will, with all my heart,
In Hermia's love I yield you up my part;
And yours of Helena to me bequeath,
Whom I do love and will do till my death.

HEL.: Never did mockers waste more idle breath.

DEM.: Lysander, keep thy Hermia; I will none:
If e'er I loved her, all that love is gone.
My heart to her but as guest-wise sojourn'd,
And now to Helen is it home return'd,
There to remain.

LYS.: Helen, it is not so.

DEM.: Disparage not the faith thou dost not know,
Lest, to thy peril, thou aby it dear.
Look, where thy love comes; yonder is thy dear.

[*Re-enter* HERMIA.]

HER.: Dark night, that from the eye his function takes,
The ear more quick of apprehension makes;
Wherein it doth impair the seeing sense,
It pays the hearing double recompense.
Thou art not by mine eye, Lysander, found;

153. superpraise, overpraise. **157. trim,** fine (used ironically). **160. extort,** torture. **169. will none,** i.e., none of her. **171. as guest-sojourned,** has made a short stay. **175. aby,** atone for. **177. his,** its.

Mine ear, I thank it, brought me to thy sound
But why unkindly didst thou leave me so?
LYS.: Why should he stay, whom love doth press to go?
HER.: What love could press Lysander from my side?
LYS.: Lysander's love, that would not let him bide,
Fair Helena, who more engilds the night
Than all yon fiery oes and eyes of light.
Why seek'st thou me? could not this make thee know,
The hate I bear thee made me leave thee so?
HER.: You speak not as you think: it cannot be.
HEL.: Lo, she is one of this confederacy!
Now I perceive they have conjoin'd all three
To fashion this false sport, in spite of me.
Injurious Hermia! most ungrateful maid!
Have you conspired, have you with these contrived
To bait me with this foul derision?
Is all the counsel that we two have shared,
The sisters' vows, the hours that we have spent,
When we have chid the hasty-footed time
For parting us,—O, is it all forgot?
All school-days' friendship, childhood innocence?
We, Hermia, like two artificial gods,
Have with our needles created both one flower,
Both on one sampler, sitting on one cushion,
Both warbling of one song, both in one key,
As if our hands, our sides, voices and minds,
Had been incorporate. So we grew together,
Like to a double cherry, seeming parted,
But yet an union in partition;
Two lovely berries moulded on one stem;
So, with two seeming bodies, but one heart;
Two of the first, like coats in heraldry,
Due but to one and crownèd with one crest.
And will you rent our ancient love asunder,
To join with men in scorning your poor friend?
It is not friendly, 'tis not maidenly:
Our sex, as well as I, may chide you for it,
Though I alone do feel the injury.

188. oes, circles, i.e., stars. **195. injurious,** insulting. **203. artificial,** skilled in art. **205. sampler,** a piece of embroidery. **208. incorporate,** parts of the same body. **213–4. Two . . . one crest,** i.e., the two bodies are like the double coats of arms which belong to husband and wife, yet have but one crest, as we have but one heart.

HER.: I am amazèd at your passionate words.
I scorn you not: it seems that you scorn me.
HEL.: Have you not set Lysander, as in scorn,
To follow me and praise my eyes and face?
And made your other love, Demetrius,
Who even but now did spurn me with his foot,
To call me goddess, nymph, divine and rare,
Precious, celestial? Wherefore speaks he this
To her he hates? and wherefore doth Lysander
Deny your love, so rich within his soul,
And tender me, forsooth, affection,
But by your setting on, by your consent?
What though I be not so in grace as you,
So hung upon with love, so fortunate,
But miserable most, to love unloved?
This you should pity rather than despise.
HER.: I understand not what you mean by this.
HEL.: Ay, do, persévér, counterfeit sad looks,
Make mouths upon me when I turn my back;
Wink each at other; hold the sweet jest up:
This sport, well carried, shall be chronicled.
If you have any pity, grace, or manners,
You would not make me such an argument.
But fare ye well: 'tis partly my own fault;
Which death or absence soon shall remedy.
LYS.: Stay, gentle Helena; hear my excuse:
My love, my life, my soul, fair Helena!
HEL.: O excellent!
HER.: Sweet, do not scorn her so.
DEM.: If she cannot entreat, I can compel.
LYS.: Thou canst compel no more than she entreat:
Thy threats have no more strength than her weak prayers.
Helen, I love thee; by my life, I do:
I swear by that which I will lose for thee,
To prove him false that says I love thee not.
DEM.: I say I love thee more than he can do.
LYS.: If thou say so, withdraw, and prove it too.
DEM.: Quick, come!
HER.: Lysander, whereto tends all this?
LYS.: Away, you Ethiope!

237. persévér, persevere; **sad,** serious. **238. make mouths upon,** make faces at. **242. argument,** plot for a story.

DEM.: No, no; he'll . . .
Seem to break loose; take on as you would follow,
But yet come not: you are a tame man, go!
LYS.: Hang off, thou cat, thou burr! vile thing, let loose,
Or I will shake thee from me like a serpent!
HER.: Why are you grown so rude? what change is this?
Sweet love,—
LYS.: Thy love! out, tawny Tartar, out!
Out, loathèd medicine! hated potion, hence!
HER.: Do you not jest?
HEL.: Yes, sooth; and so do you.
LYS.: Demetrius, I will keep my word with thee.
DEM.: I would I had your bond, for I perceive
A weak bond holds you: I'll not trust your word.
LYS.: What, should I hurt her, strike her, kill her dead?
Although I hate her, I'll not harm her so.
HER.: What, can you do me greater harm than hate?
Hate me! wherefore? O me! what news, my love!
Am not I Hermia? are not you Lysander?
I am as fair now as I was erewhile.
Since night you loved me; yet since night you left me:
Why, then you left me—O, the gods forbid!—
In earnest, shall I say?
LYS.: Ay, by my life;
And never did desire to see thee more.
Therefore be out of hope, of question, of doubt;
Be certain, nothing truer; 'tis no jest
That I do hate thee and love Helena.
HER.: O me! you juggler! you canker-blossom!
You thief of love! what, have you come by night
And stolen my love's heart from him?
HEL.: Fine, i' faith!
Have you no modesty, no maiden shame,
No touch of bashfulness? What, will you tear
Impatient answers from my gentle tongue?
Fie, fie! you counterfeit, you puppet, you!
HER.: Puppet? why so? ay, that way goes the game.
Now I perceive that she hath made compare
Between our statures; she hath urged her height;
And with her personage, her tall personage,

260. hang off, let go. **267. bond,** written agreement. **272. what news,** i.e., what's the matter. **274. erewhile,** a little while ago. **282. juggler,** deceiver; **canker-blossom,** canker worm. **288. puppet,** doll-like person; the epithet suggests that she was very small. Cf. **dwarfish,** line 295.

Her height, forsooth, she hath prevail'd with him.
And are you grown so high in his esteem,
Because I am so dwarfish and so low?
How low am I, thou painted maypole? speak;
How low am I? I am not yet so low
But that my nails can reach unto thine eyes.

HEL.: I pray you, though you mock me, gentlemen,
Let her not hurt me: I was never curst;
I have no gift at all in shrewishness;
I am a right maid for my cowardice:
Let her not strike me. You perhaps may think,
Because she is something lower than myself,
That I can match her.

HER.: Lower! hark, again.

HEL.: Good Hermia, do not be so bitter with me.
I evermore did love you, Hermia,
Did ever keep your counsels, never wrong'd you;
Save that, in love unto Demetrius,
I told him of your stealth unto this wood.
He follow'd you; for love I follow'd him;
But he hath chid me hence and threaten'd me
To strike me, spurn me, nay, to kill me too:
And now, so you will let me quiet go,
To Athens will I bear my folly back
And follow you no further: let me go:
You see how simple and how fond I am.

HER.: Why, get you gone: who is't that hinders you?

HEL.: A foolish heart, that I leave here behind.

HER.: What, with Lysander?

HEL.: With Demetrius.

LYS.: Be not afraid; she shall not harm thee, Helena.

DEM.: No, sir, she shall not, though you take her part.

HEL.: O, when she's angry, she is keen and shrewd!
She was a vixen when she went to school;
And though she be but little, she is fierce.

HER.: "Little" again! nothing but "low" and "little"!
Why will you suffer her to flout me thus?
Let me come to her.

LYS.: Get you gone, you dwarf;
You minimus, of hindering knot-grass made;
You bead, you acorn.

300. curst, shrewish. **302. I . . . cowardice,** in my lack of courage I am a true woman. **310. stealth,** stealing away. **313. spurn,** kick. **323. shrewd,** sharp-tongued. **329. minimus,** tiny creature; **knot-grass,** a weed, the infusion of which was supposed to stunt growth.

DEM.: You are too officious
In her behalf that scorns your services.
Let her alone: speak not of Helena;
Take not her part; for, if thou dost intend
Never so little show of love to her,
Thou shalt aby it.
LYS.: Now she holds me not;
Now follow, if thou darest, to try whose right,
Of thine or mine, is most in Helena.
DEM.: Follow! nay, I'll go with thee, cheek by jole.
[*Exeunt* LYSANDER *and* DEMETRIUS.
HER.: You, mistress, all this coil is 'long of you:
Nay, go not back.
HEL.: I will not trust you, I,
Nor longer stay in your curst company.
Your hands than mine are quicker for a fray,
My legs are longer though, to run away. [*Exit.*
HER.: I am amazed, and know not what to say.
[*Exit.*
OBE.: This is thy negligence: still thou mistakest,
Or else committ'st thy knaveries wilfully.
PUCK: Believe me, king of shadows, I mistook.
Did not you tell me I should know the man
By the Athenian garments he had on?
And so far blameless proves my enterprise,
That I have 'nointed an Athenian's eyes;
And so far am I glad it so did sort
As this their jangling I esteem a sport.
OBE.: Thou see'st these lovers seek a place to fight:
Hie therefore, Robin, overcast the night;
The starry welkin cover thou anon
With drooping fog as black as Acheron,
And lead these testy rivals so astray
As one come not within another's way.
Like to Lysander sometime frame thy tongue,
Then stir Demetrius up with bitter wrong;
And sometime rail thou like Demetrius;
And from each other look thou lead them thus,
Till o'er their brows death-counterfeiting sleep

333. intend, extend. **335. aby,** pay for it. **338. jole,** jowl, chin. **339. coil,** turmoil; **'long of,** because of. **345. negligence,** carelessness. **352. sort,** turn out. **353. jangling,** wrangling. **357. Acheron,** a river in Hades. **359. As,** so that. **361. wrong,** insults.

With leaden legs and batty wings doth creep:
Then crush this herb into Lysander's eye;
Whose liquor hath this virtuous property,
To take from thence all error with his might,
And make his eyeballs roll with wonted sight.
When they next wake, all this derision
Shall seem a dream and fruitless vision,
And back to Athens shall the lovers wend,
With league whose date till death shall never end.
Whiles I in this affair do thee employ,
I'll to my queen and beg her Indian boy:
And then I will her charmèd eye release
From monster's view, and all things shall be peace.

PUCK: My fairy lord, this must be done with haste,
For night's swift dragons cut the clouds full fast,
And yonder shines Aurora's harbinger;
At whose approach, ghosts, wandering here and there,
Troop home to churchyards: damnèd spirits all,
That in crossways and floods have burial,
Already to their wormy beds are gone;
For fear lest day should look their shames upon,
They wilfully themselves exile from light
And must for aye consort with black-brow'd night.

OBE.: But we are spirits of another sort:
I with the morning's love have oft made sport,
And, like a forester, the groves may tread,
Even till the eastern gate, all fiery-red,
Opening on Neptune with fair blessèd beams,
Turns into yellow gold his salt green streams.
But, notwithstanding, haste; make no delay:
We may effect this business yet ere day. [*Exit.*

PUCK. Up and down, up and down,
I will lead them up and down:
I am fear'd in field and town:
Goblin, lead them up and down.

Here comes one.

367. virtuous, potent. **368. with his might,** by his power. **379. night's swift dragons,** Shakespeare conceived the dragons as being yoked to Night's chariot. **380. Aurora's harbinger,** forerunner of the dawn, i.e., the morning star. **383. in crossways,** suicides were buried at the crossroads; **floods,** drowned persons having had no burial rites, would be unable to enter purgatory or heaven. **388. of another sort,** i.e., not infernal and so able to endure daylight. **389. morning's love,** either Cephalus, a youth loved of Aurora, or the goddess herself.

[*Re-enter* LYSANDER.]

LYS.: Where art thou, proud Demetrius? speak thou now.
PUCK: Here, villain; drawn and ready. Where art thou?
LYS.: I will be with thee straight.
PUCK: Follow me, then,
To plainer ground.
[Exit LYSANDER, *as following the voice.*

[*Re-enter* DEMETRIUS.]

DEM.: Lysander! speak again:
Thou runaway, thou coward, art thou fled?
Speak! In some bush? Where dost thou hide thy head?
PUCK: Thou coward, art thou bragging to the stars,
Telling the bushes that thou look'st for wars,
And wilt not come? Come, recreant; come, thou child,
I'll whip thee with a rod: he is defiled
That draws a sword on thee.
DEM.: Yea, art thou there?
PUCK: Follow my voice: we'll try no manhood here. [*Exeunt.*

[*Re-enter* LYSANDER.]

LYS.: He goes before me and still dares me on:
When I come where he calls, then he is gone.
The villain is much lighter-heel'd than I:
I follow'd fast, but faster he did fly;
That fallen am I in dark uneven way,
And here will rest me. [*Lies down.*] Come, thou gentle day!
For if but once thou show me thy grey light,
I'll find Demetrius and revenge this spite. [*Sleeps.*

[*Re-enter* PUCK *and* DEMETRIUS.]

PUCK: Ho, ho, ho! Coward, why comest thou not?
DEM.: Abide me, if thou darest; for well I wot
Thou runn'st before me, shifting every place.
And darest not stand, nor look me in the face.
Where art thou now?
PUCK: Come hither: I am here.
DEM.: Nay, then, thou mock'st me. Thou shalt buy this dear,
If ever I thy face by daylight see:
Now, go thy way. Faintness constraineth me

402. drawn, with sword drawn. **404. plainer,** more level. **409. recreant,** coward. **422. wot,** know.

To measure out my length on this cold bed.
By day's approach look to be visited.
[*Lies down and sleeps.*

[*Re-enter* HELENA.]

HEL.: O weary night, O long and tedious night,
Abate thy hours! Shine comforts from the east,
That I may back to Athens by daylight,
From these that my poor company detest:
And sleep, that sometimes shuts up sorrow's eye,
Steal me awhile from mine own company.
[*Lies down and sleeps.*

PUCK. Yet but three? Come one more;
Two of both kinds makes up four.
Here she comes, curst and sad:
Cupid is a knavish lad,
Thus to make poor females mad.

[*Re-enter* HERMIA.]

HER.: Never so weary, never so in woe,
Bedabbled with the dew and torn with briers,
I can no further crawl, no further go;
My legs can keep no pace with my desires.
Here will I rest me till the break of day.
Heavens shield Lysander, if they mean a fray!
[*Lies down and sleeps.*

PUCK. On the ground
Sleep sound:
I'll apply
To your eye,
Gentle lover, remedy.

[*Squeezing the juice on* LYSANDER'S *eyes.*]

When thou wakest,
Thou takest
True delight
In the sight
Of thy former lady's eye:
And the country proverb known,
That every man should take his own,

432. abate, shorten. **439. curst,** shrewish.

In your waking shall be shown:
Jack shall have Jill;
Nought shall go ill;
The man shall have his mare again, and all shall be well. [*Exit.*

ACT IV

Scene I. The Same. Lysander, Demetrius, Helena, and Hermia Lying Asleep.

[*Enter* TITANIA *and* BOTTOM; PEASEBLOSSOM, COBWEB, MOTH, MUSTARDSEED, *and other* FAIRIES *attending;* OBERON *behind unseen.*]

TITA.: Come, sit thee down upon this flowery bed,
While I thy amiable cheeks do coy,
And stick musk-roses in thy sleek smooth head,
And kiss thy fair large ears, my gentle joy.

BOT.: Where's Peaseblossom?

PEAS.: Ready.

BOT.: Scratch my head, Peaseblossom. Where's Mounsieur Cobweb?

COB.: Ready.

BOT.: Mounsieur Cobweb, good mounsieur, get you your weapons in your hand, and kill me a red-hipped humble-bee on the top of a thistle; and, good mounsieur, bring me the honey-bag. Do not fret yourself too much in the action, mounsieur; and, good mounsieur, have a care the honey-bag break not; I would be loath to have you overflown with a honey-bag, signior. Where's Mounsieur Mustardseed?

MUS.: Ready.

BOT.: Give me your neaf, Mounsieur Mustardseed. Pray you, leave your courtesy, good mounsieur.

MUS.: What's your will?

BOT.: Nothing, good mounsieur, but to help Cavalery Cobweb to scratch. I must to the barber's, mounsieur; for methinks I am marvellous hairy about the face; and I am such a tender ass, if my hair do but tickle me, I must scratch.

TITA.: What, wilt thou hear some music, my sweet love?

BOT.: I have a reasonable good ear in music. Let's have the tongs and the bones.

TITA.: Or say, sweet love, what thou desirest to eat.

BOT.: Truly, a peck of provender: I could munch your good dry oats. Methinks I have a great desire to a bottle of hay: good hay, sweet hay, hath no fellow.

Act IV, Scene i: 2. coy, stroke, caress. **16. neaf,** fist. **16-17. leave your courtesy,** i.e., put on your hat. **19. Cavalery,** cavaliero, i.e., gentleman. **24-25. tongs and bones,** crude musical instruments: tongs—a kind of triangle; bones—clappers. **28. bottle,** bundle (of hay).

TITA.: I have a venturous fairy that shall seek
The squirrel's hoard, and fetch thee new nuts.
BOT.: I had rather have a handful or two of dried peas. But, I pray you, let none of your people stir me: I have an exposition of sleep come upon me.
TITA.: Sleep thou, and I will wind thee in my arms.
Fairies, be gone, and be all ways away.

[*Exeunt* FAIRIES.]

So doth the woodbine the sweet honeysuckle
Gentle entwist; the female ivy so
Enrings the barky fingers of the elm.
O, how I love thee! how I dote on thee! [*They sleep.*

[*Enter* PUCK.]

OBE.: [*Advancing*] Welcome, good Robin.
See'st thou this sweet sight?
Her dotage now I do begin to pity:
For, meeting her of late behind the wood,
Seeking sweet favours for this hateful fool,
I did upbraid her and fall out with her;
For she his hairy temples then had rounded
With coronet of fresh and fragrant flowers;
And that same dew, which sometime on the buds
Was wont to swell like round and orient pearls,
Stood now within the pretty flowerets' eyes
Like tears that did their own disgrace bewail.
When I had at my pleasure taunted her
And she in mild terms begg'd my patience,
I then did ask of her changeling child;
Which straight she gave me, and her fairy sent
To bear him to my bower in fairy land.
And now I have the boy, I will undo
This hateful imperfection of her eyes:
And, gentle Puck, take this transformèd scalp
From off the head of this Athenian swain;
That, he awaking when the other do,
May all to Athens back again repair
And think no more of this night's accidents
But as the fierce vexation of a dream.

32. exposition of, Bottom means "disposition to." **34. all ways,** in every direction. **43. favours,** nosegays. **48. orient,** lustrous, because the most beautiful pearls were supposed to come from the Orient. **60. other,** others. **63. fierce,** violent.

But first I will release the fairy queen.
Be as thou wast wont to be;
See as thou wast wont to see:
Dian's bud o'er Cupid's flower
Hath such force and blessèd power.
Now, my Titania; wake you, my sweet queen.
TITA.: My Oberon! what visions have I seen!
Methought I was enamour'd of an ass.
OBE.: There lies your love.
TITA.: How came these things to pass?
O, how mine eyes do loathe his visage now!
OBE.: Silence awhile. Robin, take off this head.
Titania, music call; and strike more dead
Than common sleep of all these five the sense.
TITA.: Music, ho! music, such as charmeth sleep! [*Music, still.*
PUCK: Now, when thou wakest, with thine own fool's eyes peep.
OBE.: Sound, music! Come, my queen, take hands with me,
And rock the ground whereon these sleepers be.
Now thou and I are new in amity
And will to-morrow midnight solemnly
Dance in Duke Theseus' house triumphantly
And bless it to all fair prosperity:
There shall the pair of faithful lovers be
Wedded, with Theseus, all in jollity.

PUCK. Fairy king, attend, and mark:
I do hear the morning lark.
OBE. Then, my queen, in silence sad,
Trip we after night's shade:
We the globe can compass soon,
Swifter than the wandering moon.
TITA. Come, my lord, and in our flight
Tell me how it came this night
That I sleeping here was found
With these mortals on the ground. [*Exeunt.*

[*Horns winded within.*

[*Enter* THESEUS, HIPPOLYTA, EGEUS, *and train.*]

THE.: Go, one of you, find out the forester;
For now our observation is perform'd;

67. Dian's bud, a plant, agnus castus, which was supposed to preserve chastity. **76-77. strike . . . sleep,** make them sleep more soundly than normal. **77. these five,** Bottom and the two pair of lovers. **78. s.d. Music, still,** continuous music. **79. peep,** take a look. **90. sad,** serious. **99. observation,** May Day rites.

And since we have the vaward of the day,
My love shall hear the music of my hounds.
Uncouple in the western valley; let them go:
Dispatch, I say, and find the forester.
[*Exit an* ATTENDANT.]
We will, fair queen, up to the mountain's top
And mark the musical confusion
Of hounds and echo in conjunction.

HIP.: I was with Hercules and Cadmus once,
When in a wood of Crete they bay'd the bear
With hounds of Sparta: never did I hear
Such gallant chiding; for, besides the groves,
The skies, the fountains, every region near
Seem'd all one mutual cry: I never heard
So musical a discord, such sweet thunder.

THE.: My hounds are bred out of the Spartan kind,
So flew'd, so sanded, and their heads are hung
With ears that sweep away the morning dew;
Crook-knee'd, and dew-lapp'd like Thessalian bulls;
Slow in pursuit, but match'd in mouth like bells,
Each under each. A cry more tuneable
Was never holla'd to, nor cheer'd with horn,
In Crete, in Sparta, nor in Thessaly:
Judge when you hear. But, soft! what nymphs are these?

EGE.: My lord, this is my daughter here asleep;
And this, Lysander; this Demetrius is;
This Helena, old Nedar's Helena:
I wonder of their being here together.

THE.: No doubt they rose up early to observe
The rite of May, and, hearing our intent,
Came here in grace of our solemnity.
But speak, Egeus; is not this the day
That Hermia should give answer of her choice?

EGE.: It is, my lord.

THE.: Go, bid the huntsmen wake them with their horns. [*Horns
and shout within.* LYS., DEM., HEL., *and* HER., *wake and
start up.*] Good morrow, friends. Saint Valentine is past:
Begin these wood-birds but to couple now?

100. vaward, vanguard, i.e., early part. **103. Dispatch,** hurry. **110. chiding,** clamor. **115. flew'd,** with large hanging chaps; **sanded,** of a sandy color. **118. mouth,** voice. Elizabethan huntsmen chose hounds whose baying would make harmony. **119. Each under each,** each harmonious with the rest; **cry,** pack of hounds. **129. in grace of our solemnity,** to do honor to our wedding ceremony. **s.d. within,** offstage. **135. Begin . . . couple now,** birds were supposed to choose their mates on St. Valentine's Day.

LYS.: Pardon, my lord.
THE.: I pray you all, stand up.
I know you two are rival enemies:
How comes this gentle concord in the world,
That hatred is so far from jealousy,
To sleep by hate, and fear no enmity?
LYS.: My lord, I shall reply amazedly,
Half sleep, half waking: but as yet, I swear,
I cannot truly say how I came here;
But, as I think,—for truly would I speak,
And now I do bethink me, so it is,—
I came with Hermia hither: our intent
Was to be gone from Athens, where we might,
Without the peril of the Athenian law.
EGE.: Enough, enough, my lord; you have enough:
I beg the law, the law, upon his head.
They would have stolen away; they would, Demetrius,
Thereby to have defeated you and me,
You of your wife and me of my consent,
Of my consent that she should be your wife.
DEM.: My lord, fair Helen told me of their stealth,
Of this their purpose hither to this wood;
And I in fury hither follow'd them,
Fair Helena in fancy following me.
But, my good lord, I wot not by what power,—
But by some power it is,—my love to Hermia,
Melted as the snow, seems to me now
As the remembrance of an idle gawd
Which in my childhood I did dote upon;
And all the faith, the virtue of my heart,
The object and the pleasure of mine eye,
Is only Helena. To her, my lord,
Was I betroth'd ere I saw Hermia:
But, like in sickness, did I loathe this food;
But, as in health, come to my natural taste,
Now I do wish it, love it, long for it,
And will for evermore be true to it.
THE.: Fair lovers, you are fortunately met:
Of this discourse we more will hear anon.
Egeus, I will overbear your will;

148. where, where-ever. **149. without,** beyond the reach of. **150. enough,** i.e., enough to convict him. **159. in fancy,** out of love. **163. idle gawd,** worthless trifle

For in the temple, by and by, with us
These couples shall eternally be knit:
And, for the morning now is something worn,
Our purposed hunting shall be set aside.
Away with us to Athens; three and three,
We'll hold a feast in great solemnity.
Come, Hippolyta.

[*Exeunt* THESEUS, HIPPOLYTA, EGEUS, *and train.*

DEM.: These things seem small and undistinguishable,
Like far-off mountains turned into clouds.
HER.: Methinks I see these things with parted eye,
When every thing seems double.
HEL.: So methinks:
And I have found Demetrius like a jewel,
Mine own, and not mine own.
DEM.: Are you sure
That we are awake? It seems to me
That yet we sleep, we dream. Do not you think
The duke was here, and bid us follow him?
HER.: Yea; and my father.
HEL.: And Hippolyta.
LYS.: And he did bid us follow to the temple.
DEM.: Why, then, we are awake: let's follow him;
And by the way let us recount our dreams. [*Exeunt.*

BOT.: [*Awaking*] When my cue comes, call me, and I will answer: my next is, "Most fair Pyramus." Heigh-ho! Peter Quince! Flute, the bellows-mender! Snout, the tinker! Starveling! God's my life, stolen hence, and left me asleep! I have had a most rare vision. I have had a dream, past the wit of man to say what dream it was: man is but an ass, if he go about to expound this dream. Methought I was—there is no man can tell what. Methought I was,—and methought I had,—but man is but a patched fool, if he will offer to say what methought I had. The eye of man hath not heard, the ear of man hath not seen, man's hand is not able to taste, his tongue to conceive, nor his heart to report, what my dream was. I will get Peter Quince to write a ballad of this dream: it shall be called Bottom's Dream, because it hath no bottom; and I will sing it in the latter end of a play, before the duke: peradventure, to make it the more gracious, I shall sing it at her death.

[*Exit.*

176. by and by, immediately. **185. parted eye,** unfocused eyes. **204. go about,** attempt. **206. patched,** dressed in motley.

Scene II. Athens. Quince's House.

[*Enter* QUINCE, FLUTE, SNOUT, *and* STARVELING.]

QUIN.: Have you sent to Bottom's house? is he come home yet?

STAR.: He cannot be heard of. Out of doubt he is transported.

FLU.: If he come not, then the play is marred: it goes not forward, doth it?

QUIN.: It is not possible: you have not a man in all Athens able to discharge Pyramus but he.

FLU.: No, he hath simply the best wit of any handicraft man in Athens.

QUIN.: Yea, and the best person too; and he is a very paramour for a sweet voice.

FLU.: You must say 'paragon:' a paramour is, God bless us, a thing of naught.

[*Enter* SNUG.]

SNUG: Masters, the duke is coming from the temple, and there is two or three lords and ladies more married: if our sport had gone forward, we had all been made men.

FLU.: O sweet bully Bottom! Thus hath he lost sixpence a day during his life; he could not have 'scaped sixpence a day: an the duke had not given him sixpence a day for playing Pyramus, I'll be hanged; he would have deserved it: sixpence a day in Pyramus, or nothing.

[*Enter* BOTTOM.]

BOT.: Where are these lads? where are these hearts?

QUIN.: Bottom! O most courageous day! O most happy hour!

BOT.: Masters, I am to discourse wonders: but ask me not what; for if I tell you, I am no true Athenian. I will tell you every thing, right as it fell out.

QUIN.: Let us hear, sweet Bottom.

BOT.: Not a word of me. All that I will tell you is, that the duke hath dined. Get your apparel together, good strings to your beards, new ribbons to your pumps; meet presently at the palace; every man look o'er his part; for the short and the long is, our play is preferred. In any case, let Thisby have clean linen; and let not him that plays the lion pare his nails, for they shall hang out for the lion's claws. And, most dear actors, eat no onions nor garlic, for we are to utter sweet breath; and I do not doubt but to hear them say, it is a sweet comedy. No more words: away! go, away!

[*Exeunt.*

Scene ii: 2. transported, carried off. **9. a thing of naught,** a wicked thing. **13. sixpence a day,** i.e., as a royal pension. **17. hearts,** good fellows. **24. presently,** at once. **25. preferred,** chosen over its rivals for presentation.

ACT V

Scene I. Athens. The Palace of Theseus.

[*Enter* THESEUS, HIPPOLYTA, PHILOSTRATE, LORDS, *and* ATTENDANTS.]

HIP.: 'Tis strange, my Theseus, that these lovers speak of.
THE.: More strange than true: I never may believe
These antique fables, nor these fairy toys.
Lovers and madmen have such seething brains,
Such shaping fantasies, that apprehend
More than cool reason ever comprehends.
The lunatic, the lover and the poet
Are of imagination all compact:
One sees more devils than vast hell can hold,
That is, the madman: the lover, all as frantic,
Sees Helen's beauty in a brow of Egypt:
The poet's eye, in a fine frenzy rolling,
Doth glance from heaven to earth, from earth to heaven;
And as imagination bodies forth
The forms of things unknown, the poet's pen
Turns them to shapes and gives to airy nothing
A local habitation and a name.
Such tricks hath strong imagination,
That, if it would but apprehend some joy,
It comprehends some bringer of that joy;
Or in the night, imagining some fear,
How easy is a bush supposed a bear!
HIP.: But all the story of the night told over,
And all their minds transfigured so together,
More witnesseth than fancy's images
And grows to something of great constancy;
But, howsoever, strange and admirable.
THE.: Here come the lovers, full of joy and mirth.

[*Enter* LYSANDER, DEMETRIUS, HERMIA, *and* HELENA.]

Joy, gentle friends! joy and fresh days of love
Accompany your hearts!

Act V, Scene i: 2. may, can. **3. antique,** strange; **toys,** trifles. **8. Are . . . compact,** are wholly composed of the power of seeing things. **11. Sees Helen's . . . Egypt,** sees in the face of a dusky gypsy the beauty of Helen of Troy. **25. More . . . images,** is evidence of more than just imagination. **26. constancy,** certainty.

LYS.: More than to us
Wait in your royal walks, your board, your bed!
THE.: Come now; what masques, what dances shall we have,
To wear away this long age of three hours
Between our after-supper and bed-time?
Where is our usual manager of mirth?
What revels are in hand? Is there no play,
To ease the anguish of a torturing hour?
Call Philostrate.
PHIL.: Here, mighty Theseus.
THE.: Say, what abridgement have you for this evening?
What masque? what music? How shall we beguile
The lazy time, if not with some delight?
PHIL.: There is a brief how many sports are ripe:
Make choice of which your highness will see first.
[*Giving a paper.*
THE.: [*Reads*] "The battle with the Centaurs, to be sung
By an Athenian eunuch to the harp."
We'll none of that: that have I told my love,
In glory of my kinsman Hercules.
[*Reads*] "The riot of the tipsy Bacchanals,
Tearing the Thracian singer in their rage."
That is an old device; and it was play'd
When I from Thebes came last a conqueror.
[*Reads*] "The thrice three Muses mourning for the death
Of Learning, late deceased in beggary."
That is some satire, keen and critical,
Not sorting with a nuptial ceremony.
[*Reads*] "A tedious brief scene of young Pyramus
And his love Thisbe; very tragical mirth."
Merry and tragical! tedious and brief!
That is, hot ice and wondrous strange snow.
How shall we find the concord of this discord?
PHIL.: A play there is, my lord, some ten words long,
Which is as brief as I have known a play;
But by ten words, my lord, it is too long,
Which makes it tedious; for in all the play
There is not one word apt, one player fitted:
And tragical, my noble lord, it is;
For Pyramus therein doth kill himself.

39. abridgement, pastime. **42. brief,** list. **44. The battle . . . Centaurs,** Ovid tells of a battle between the Centaurs and Lapithae. **48–9. The riot . . . rage,** Orpheus was torn limb from limb by the maenads, female priests of Bacchus. **55. not sorting with,** not fitting for.

Which, when I saw rehearsed, I must confess,
Made mine eyes water; but more merry tears
The passion of loud laughter never shed.
THE.: What are they that do play it?
PHIL.: Hard-handed men that work in Athens here,
Which never labour'd in their minds till now,
And now have toil'd their unbreathed memories
With this same play, against your nuptial.
THE.: And we will hear it.
PHIL.: No, my noble lord;
It is not for you: I have heard it over,
And it is nothing, nothing in the world;
Unless you can find sport in their intents,
Extremely stretch'd and conn'd with cruel pain,
To do you service.
THE.: I will hear that play;
For never anything can be amiss,
When simpleness and duty tender it.
Go, bring them in: and take your places, ladies.

[*Exit* PHILOSTRATE.

HIP.: I love not to see wretchedness o'ercharged
And duty in his service perishing.
THE.: Why, gentle sweet, you shall see no such thing.
HIP.: He says they can do nothing in this kind.
THE.: The kinder we, to give them thanks for nothing.
Our sport shall be to take what they mistake:
And what poor duty cannot do, noble respect
Takes it in might, not merit.
Where I have come, great clerks have purposed
To greet me with premeditated welcomes;
Where I have seen them shiver and look pale,
Make periods in the midst of sentences,
Throttle their practised accent in their fears
And in conclusion dumbly have broke off,
Not paying me a welcome. Trust me, sweet,
Out of this silence yet I pick'd a welcome;
And in the modesty of fearful duty
I read as much as from the rattling tongue
Of saucy and audacious eloquence.

74. unbreathed, unexercised. **75. against,** in preparation for. **80. stretch'd,** strained; **conn'd,** learned by heart. **85. o'ercharged,** oppressed. **86. perishing,** ruining itself. **92. Takes . . . merit,** i.e., takes the will for the deed. **93. clerks,** learned men. **96. periods,** long stops.

Love, therefore, and tongue-tied simplicity
In least speak most, to my capacity.

[*Re-enter* PHILOSTRATE.]

PHIL.: So please your grace, the Prologue is address'd.
THE.: Let him approach. [*Flourish of trumpets.*

[*Enter* QUINCE *for the* PROLOGUE.]

PRO.: If we offend, it is with our good will
That you should think, we come not to offend,
But with good will. To show our simple skill,
That is the true beginning of our end.
Consider then we come but in despite.
We do not come as minding to content you,
Our true intent is. All for your delight
We are not here. That you should here repent you,
The actors are at hand and by their show
You shall know all that you are like to know.
THE.: This fellow doth not stand upon points.
LYS.: He hath rid his prologue like a rough colt; he knows not the stop. A good moral, my lord: it is not enough to speak, but to speak true.
HIP.: Indeed he hath played on his prologue like a child on a recorder; a sound, but not in government.
THE.: His speech was like a tangled chain; nothing impaired, but all disordered. Who is next?

[*Enter* PYRAMUS *and* THISBE, WALL, MOONSHINE, *and* LION.]

PRO.: Gentles, perchance you wonder at this show;
But wonder on, till truth make all things plain.
This man is Pyramus, if you would know;
This beauteous lady Thisby is certain.
This man, with lime and rough-cast, doth present
Wall, that vile Wall which did these lovers sunder;
And through Wall's chink, poor souls, they are content
To whisper. At the which let no man wonder.
This man, with lanthorn, dog, and bush of thorn,
Presenteth Moonshine; for, if you will know,
By moonshine did these lovers think no scorn
To meet at Ninus' tomb, there, there to woo.

105. capacity, sympathetic comprehension. **106. Prologue is address'd,** the speaker of the prologue is ready. **108ff.** Quince perverts the sense of his speech by blundering punctuation. **118. stand upon points,** "pays no attention to punctuation," also "does not care about trifles." **119. the stop,** quibble on (1) period or end of a sentence, (2) signal to halt, e.g., "whoa." **121. recorder,** a wind instrument something like a flute. **122. in government,** under control.

This grisly beast, which Lion hight by name,
The trusty Thisby, coming first by night,
Did scare away, or rather did affright;
And, as she fled, her mantle she did fall,
    Which Lion vile with bloody mouth did stain.
Anon comes Pyramus, sweet youth and tall,
    And finds his trusty Thisby's mantle slain:
Whereat, with blade, with bloody blameful blade,
    He bravely broach'd his boiling bloody breast;
And Thisby, tarrying in mulberry shade,
    His dagger drew, and died. For all the rest,
Let Lion, Moonshine, Wall, and lovers twain
At large discourse, while here they do remain.

[*Exeunt* PROLOGUE, PYRAMUS, THISBE, LION, *and* MOONSHINE.

THE.: I wonder if the lion be to speak.
DEM.: No wonder, my lord: one lion may, when many asses do.
WALL: In this same interlude it doth befall
    That I, one Snout by name, present a wall;
    And such a wall, as I would have you think,
    That had in it a crannied hole or chink,
    Through which the lovers, Pyramus and Thisby,
    Did whisper often very secretly.
    This loam, this rough-cast and this stone doth show
    That I am that same wall; the truth is so:
    And this the cranny is, right and sinister,
    Through which the fearful lovers are to whisper.
THE.: Would you desire lime and hair to speak better?
DEM.: It is the wittiest partition that ever I heard discourse, my lord.

[*Re-enter* PYRAMUS.]

THE.: Pyramus draws near the wall: silence!
PYR.: O grim-look'd night! O night with hue so black!
        O night, which ever art when day is not!
    O night, O night! alack, alack, alack,
        I fear my Thisby's promise is forgot!
    And thou, O wall, O sweet, O lovely wall,
        That stand'st between her father's ground and mine!
    Thou wall, O wall, O sweet and lovely wall,
        Show me thy chink, to blink through with mine eyne!
[WALL *holds up his fingers.*]

137. hight, is called. **141. fall,** let fall. **142. tall,** brave. **145. broach'd,** opened, i.e., stabbed. **150. be to speak,** is going to speak. **161. cranny,** chink; **sinister,** left. **164. partition,** quibble on (1) wall, (2) a section of a book. **166. grim-look'd,** grim-faced.

Thanks, courteous wall: Jove shield thee well for this!
But what see I? No Thisby do I see.
O wicked wall, through whom I see no bliss!
Cursed be thy stones for thus deceiving me!

THE.: The wall, methinks, being sensible, should curse again.

PYR.: No, in truth, sir, he should not. "Deceiving me" is Thisby's cue: she is to enter now, and I am to spy her through the wall. You shall see, it will fall pat as I told you. Yonder she comes.

[*Re-enter* THISBE.]

THIS.: O wall, full often hast thou heard my moans,
For parting my fair Pyramus and me!
My cherry lips have often kiss'd thy stones,
Thy stones with lime and hair knit up in thee.

PYR.: I see a voice: now will I to the chink,
To spy an I can hear my Thisby's face.
Thisby!

THIS.: My love thou art, my love I think.

PYR.: Think what thou wilt, I am thy lover's grace;
And, like Limander, am I trusty still.

THIS.: And I like Helen, till the Fates me kill.

PYR.: Not Shafalus to Procrus was so true.

THIS.: As Shafalus to Procrus, I to you.

PYR.: O, kiss me through the hole of this vile wall!

THIS.: I kiss the wall's hole, not your lips at all.

PYR.: Wilt thou at Ninny's tomb meet me straightway?

THIS.: 'Tide life, 'tide death, I come without delay.

[*Exeunt* PYRAMUS *and* THISBE.

WALL: Thus have I, Wall, my part discharged so;
And, being done, thus Wall away doth go.

[*Exit.*

THE.: Now is the mural down between the two neighbours.

DEM.: No remedy, my lord, when walls are so wilful to hear without warning.

HIP.: This is the silliest stuff that ever I heard.

THE.: The best in this kind are but shadows; and the worst are no worse, if imagination amend them.

HIP.: It must be your imagination then, and not theirs.

THE.: If we imagine no worse of them than they of themselves, they may pass for excellent men. Here come two noble beasts in, a man and a lion.

178. sensible, capable of feeling. **191. Limander,** blunder for Leander. **192. Helen,** he means Hero. **193. Shafalus to Procrus,** blunder for "Cephalus to Procris." **199. 'Tide . . . death,** whether life or death betide [happens]. **202. mural,** wall.

[*Re-enter* Lion *and* Moonshine.]

Lion: You, ladies, you, whose gentle hearts do fear
The smallest monstrous mouse that creeps on floor,
May now perchance both quake and tremble here,
When lion rough in wildest rage doth roar
Then know that I, one Snug the joiner, am
A lion-fell, nor else no lion's dam;
For, if I should as lion come in strife
Into this place, 'twere pity on my life.
The.: A very gentle beast, and of a good conscience.
Dem.: The very best at a beast, my lord, that e'er I saw.
Lys.: This lion is a very fox for his valour.
The.: True; and a goose for his discretion.
Dem.: Not so, my lord; for his valour cannot carry his discretion; and the fox carries the goose.
The.: His discretion, I am sure, cannot carry his valour; for the goose carries not the fox. It is well: leave it to his discretion, and let us listen to the moon.
Moon: This lanthorn doth the hornèd moon present;—
Dem.: He should have worn the horns on his head.
The.: He is no crescent, and his horns are invisible within the circumference.
Moon: This lanthorn doth the horned moon present;
Myself the man i' the moon do seem to be.
The.: This is the greatest error of all the rest: the man should be put into the lanthorn. How is it else the man i' the moon?
Dem.: He dares not come there for the candle; for, you see, it is already in snuff.
Hip.: I am aweary of this moon: would he would change!
The.: It appears, by his small light of discretion, that he is in the wane; but yet, in courtesy, in all reason, we must stay the time.
Lys.: Proceed, Moon.
Moon: All that I have to say, is, to tell you that the lanthorn is the moon; I, the man in the moon; this thorn-bush, my thorn-bush; and this dog, my dog.
Dem.: Why, all these should be in the lanthorn; for all these are in the moon. But, silence! here comes Thisbe.

[*Re-enter* Thisbe.]

This.: This is old Ninny's tomb. Where is my love?
Lion: [*Roaring*] *Oh*——[Thisbe *runs off.*

215. lion-fell, lion skin, i.e., he is a lion only in that he is cased in a lion skin. **217. 'twere . . . life,** i.e., I should be in danger of hanging. **228. He . . . head,** the ancient joke about the horns of a cuckold. **234. for,** because of. **234-35. in snuff,** quibble (1) in need of snuffing, (2) offended. **238. stay . . . time,** see it through.

DEM.: Well roared, Lion.
THE.: Well run, Thisbe.
HIP.: Well shone, Moon. Truly, the moon shines with a good grace.

[*The* LION *shakes* THISBE'S *mantle, and exit.*

THE.: Well moused, Lion.
LYS.: And so the lion vanished.
DEM.: And then came Pyramus.

[*Re-enter* PYRAMUS.]

PYR. Sweet Moon, I thank thee for thy sunny beams;
I thank thee, Moon, for shining now so bright;
For, by thy gracious, golden, glittering gleams,
I trust to take of truest Thisby sight.
But stay, O spite!
But mark, poor knight,
What dreadful dole is here!
Eyes, do you see?
How can it be?
O dainty duck! O dear!
Thy mantle good,
What, stain'd with blood!
Approach, ye Furies fell!
O Fates, come, come,
Cut thread and thrum;
Quail, crush, conclude, and quell!

THE.: This passion, and the death of a dear friend, would go near to make a man look sad.
HIP.: Beshrew my heart, but I pity the man.
PYR.: O wherefore, Nature, didst thou lions frame?
Since lion vile hath here deflower'd my dear:
Which is—no, no—which was the fairest dame
That lived, that loved, that liked, that
look'd with cheer.
Come, tears, confound;
Out, sword, and wound
The pap of Pyramus;
Ay, that left pap,
Where heart doth hop: [*Stabs himself.*

249. moused, shaken (as a cat shakes a mouse). **258. dole,** grief. **264. fell,** fierce. **266. thread and thrum,** the warp of a piece of cloth and the fringe-like threads at the end. **267. quail,** subdue; **quell,** kill. **275. with cheer,** with a face.

Thus die I, thus, thus, thus.
Now am I dead,
Now am I fled;
My soul is in the sky:
Tongue, lose thy light;
Moon, take thy flight:

[*Exit* MOONSHINE.]

Now die, die, die, die, die. [*Dies.*

DEM.: No die, but an ace, for him; for he is but one.
LYS.: Less than an ace, man; for he is dead; he is nothing.
THE.: With the help of a surgeon he might yet recover, and prove an ass.
HIP.: How chance Moonshine is gone before Thisbe comes back and finds her lover?
THE.: She will find him by starlight. Here she comes; and her passion ends the play.

[*Re-enter* THISBE.]

HIP.: Methinks she should not use a long one for such a Pyramus: I hope she will be brief.
DEM.: A mote will turn the balance, which Pyramus, which Thisbe, is the better; he for a man, God warrant us; she for a woman, God bless us.
LYS.: She hath spied him already with those sweet eyes.
DEM.: And thus she means, videlicet:—

THIS.
Asleep, my love?
What, dead, my dove?
O Pyramus, arise!
Speak, speak. Quite dumb?
Dead, dead? A tomb
Must cover thy sweet eyes.
These lily lips,
This cherry nose,
These yellow cowslip cheeks,
Are gone, are gone:
Lovers, make moan:
His eyes were green as leeks.
O Sisters Three,
Come, come to me,
With hands as pale as milk;
Lay them in gore,
Since you have shore

288. No . . . ace, pun (1) die = perish, (2) die = the singular of dice. **300. means,** moans. **313. Sisters Three,** the Fates.

With shears his thread of silk.
Tongue, not a word:
Come, trusty sword;
Come, blade, my breast imbrue:

[*Stabs herself.*]

And, farewell, friends;
Thus Thisby ends:
Adieu, adieu, adieu. [*Dies.*

THE.: Moonshine and Lion are left to bury the dead.

DEM.: Ay, and Wall too.

BOT.: [*Starting up*] No, I assure you; the wall is down that parted their fathers. Will it please you to see the epilogue, or to hear a Bergomask dance between two of our company?

THE.: No epilogue, I pray you; for your play needs no excuse. Never excuse; for when the players are all dead, there need none to be blamed. Marry, if he that writ it had played Pyramus and hanged himself in Thisbe's garter, it would have been a fine tragedy: and so it is, truly; and very notably discharged. But, come, your Bergomask; let your epilogue alone. [*A dance.*]
The iron tongue of midnight hath told twelve:
Lovers, to bed; 'tis almost fairy time.
I fear we shall out-sleep the coming morn
As much as we this night have overwatch'd.
This palpable-gross play hath well beguiled
The heavy gait of night. Sweet friends, to bed.
A fortnight hold we this solemnity,
In nightly revels and new jollity. [*Exeunt.*

[*Enter* PUCK.]

PUCK: Now the hungry lion roars,
And the wolf behowls the moon;
Whilst the heavy ploughman snores,
All with weary task fordone.
Now the wasted brands do glow,
Whilst the screech-owl, screeching loud,
Puts the wretch that lies in woe
In remembrance of a shroud.
Now it is the time of night
That the graves all gaping wide,
Every one lets forth his sprite,
In the church-way paths to glide:
And we fairies, that do run

322. imbrue, wet with gore. **329. Bergomask dance,** a grotesque rustic dance (named from the Italian town Bergamo). **340. palpable-gross,** palpably crude. **347. fordone,** worn out.

By the triple Hecate's team,
From the presence of the sun,
Following darkness like a dream,
Now are frolic: not a mouse
Shall disturb this hallow'd house:
I am sent with broom before,
To sweep the dust behind the door.

[*Enter* OBERON *and* TITANIA *with their train.*]

OBE.: Through the house give glimmering light,
By the dead and drowsy fire:
Every elf and fairy sprite
Hop as light as bird from brier;
And this ditty, after me,
Sing, and dance it trippingly.
TITA.: First, rehearse your song by rote,
To each word a warbling note:
Hand in hand, with fairy grace,
Will we sing, and bless this place.

[*Song and dance.*

OBE.: Now, until the break of day,
Through this house each fairy stray.
To the best bride-bed will we,
Which by us shall blessèd be;
And the issue there create
Ever shall be fortunate.
So shall all the couples three
Ever true in loving be;
And the blots of Nature's hand
Shall not in their issue stand;
Never mole, hare lip, nor scar,
Nor mark prodigious, such as are
Despisèd in nativity,
Shall upon their children be.
With this field-dew consecrate,
Every fairy take his gait;
And each several chamber bless,
Through this palace, with sweet peace;
And the owner of it blest

367. triple Hecate, Diana was three-named; she was called Cynthia in heaven, Diana on earth, Hecate in hell. **370. frolic,** gay. **373. To . . . door,** Robin Goodfellow was a domestic sprite, who could be induced to do the housework by night. **388. create,** created. **495. prodigious,** unnatural. **398. consecrate,** consecrated. **400. several,** separate.

Ever shall in safety rest.
Trip away; make no stay;
Meet me all by break of day.

[*Exeunt* OBERON, TITANIA, *and train.*

PUCK: If we shadows have offended,
Think but this, and all is mended,
That you have but slumber'd here
While these visions did appear.
And this weak and idle theme,
No more yielding but a dream,
Gentles, do not reprehend:
If you pardon, we will mend:
And, as I am an honest Puck,
If we have unearnèd luck
Now to 'scape the serpent's tongue,
We will make amends ere long;
Else the Puck a liar call:
So, good night unto you all.
Give me your hands, if we be friends,
And Robin shall restore amends.

[*Exit.*

—1594–1596

What are your questions and reactions to this work? The following questions may help provoke some ideas.

Probing the Work

1. In Act V Theseus says "Lovers and madmen have such seething brains, / Such shaping fantasies, that apprehend / More than cool reason ever comprehends. / The lunatic, the lover and the poet / Are of imagination all compact" (ls. 4–8). Explain what these lines mean and the different ways they reflect on the actions of the play.
2. The comic subplot of this play involves the characters (Bottom, Quince, and friends) who are putting on a play to honor the marriage of Theseus and Hippolyta. What makes the actions and dialogue of these characters humorous? How does Shakespeare play with the borders of illusion and reality through this subplot?
3. What role does Puck play in *A Midsummer-Night's Dream?* What powers does he have? What does Puck represent? What does he mean when he says, "Lord, what fools these mortals be" (3.2.115)?

416. serpent's tongue, i.e., hissing. **420. Give . . . hands,** applaud.

4. According to David P. Young, in *Something of Great Constancy: The Art of A Midsummer-Night's Dream,* Shakespeare's play "divides to reunite. The multiple activities and beings we see belong to a single panorama. There is . . . an interplay of reflections in language and action. The sharing of likenesses among the most diverse and unlikely elements of the play serves to unite them even as it functions to surprise and amuse us." What are the reflected actions and language in this play? How do the different characters mirror one another's actions and speech? How do these reflections bring the various plots together?

Identifying Issues

5. Henry Myers, in *Tragedy: a View of Life,* writes that *A Midsummer-Night's Dream* "presents the theme of love on three levels: the level of common sense; the level of nonsense, incongruity and absurdity; and the level of fantasy." Can you find examples of each level and how they interact? How does the level of fantasy influence both the serious world and the world of nonsense in our own time?
6. Shakespeare plays with the theme of illusion versus reality in *A Midsummer-Night's Dream* as he creates enchanting worlds that operate both separately and together. Discuss how he treats this theme through the antics of the fairies and the use of the supernatural, and/or through the world of Bottom and his friends. In your experience, what events have blurred the distinctions between the real and imaginary realms?
7. Read the following passage from a critical essay by Daniel Bender. What is Bender's thesis? What does he mean when he asserts that the basis of Shakespeare's dramatization of illusion is the "generous belief that illusion is the necessary medium for the discovery of reality" (827)? In how many ways could you apply this idea to your own lives, or to films and other plays?

Commentary

DANIEL BENDER

The Moon in A Midsummer-Night's Dream: *The Reality of Illusion*

"Doth the moon shine that night we play our play?" (3.1.53)
"Find out moonshine, find out moonshine." (3.1.55)

Images of the moon, appearing throughout the comedy, unfold something of Shakespeare's thinking about the comedy of love. For the young couples of the play, moonlight seems welcome, an eerie half-light which provides both light and secrecy. Yet perception alters drastically when we consider the figure of Egeus, the controlling father, who would no doubt regard the moon as a sign that sensible people should be at rest, as nature itself is. The moon yields yet a further insight into the differences which fragment Athenian society when it emerges as the merry accompaniment for the fairy world and especially for Puck, whose nocturnal antics are conducted under its mysterious radiance.

A playwright sensitive to allegorical forms of thought, Shakespeare seizes the imagery of the moon to embody the nature of illusion itself. Appearing to the eyes through lunar cycles, the moon changes from something as solid as the earth into something liquid or amorphous. Now we see a sliver of light, a crescent; on another night we gaze at something that has seemingly doubled in size, the half-moon. As a grand finale to this allegorical comedy of changefulness, the moon shows itself full and resplendent—yet we are really seeing but half its surface.

These perceptions of the moon are not illusions: a quarter-moon really is illuminated such that the curved arc is visible and vivid to the eye. Most people, Shakespeare knows, hold to the common-sense axiom that seeing is believing. But each of the dramatic sites of this comedy—whether the ducal palace, the misty darkness of the woods outside Athens, or the earnest rehearsals of the workers preparing an entertainment for Theseus's wedding—reveal how characters superimpose their partial perception of the truth onto the realm of the whole truth; the transitory crescent moon is mistakenly said to be "reality."

As a result, virtually every character in the play seeks not only to embody their view of reality, but to offer it to other characters as the correct or rational view. To their surprise and even horror, they find other characters holding a quite different view of the same object. Someone—usually someone else—must be crazy. If one view is true, "real," and rational, then the opposite view must be based on illusion. This experience of individual characters discovering the great distance between their own minds and the minds of others is conveyed with a smile in the title's reference to "midsummer," a time in folklore when people go crazy, as if—fittingly enough—they are "lunatics."

Conflicting views of what is real and what is illusion grow particularly intense when people enter into that mysterious state of feeling known as love. The process of falling in love—always the set-up for the shocking discovery that one's whole "view" of reality is only a partial one—often begins with the eyes, with the partial truth of a person's physical attractiveness. This is what Helena, accepting the illusion of "favor" or looks, recognizes as the basis for "love" between her best friend Hermia and the dashing young Demetrius. Helena wishes that she had Hermia's pretty face and soft voice, since then she could win Demetrius's so-called love:

> Call you me fair? That fair again unsay.
> Demetrius loves you fair: O happy fair!
> Your eyes are lode-stars, and your tongue's sweet air

More tuneable than lark to shepherd's ear
When wheat is green, when hawthorn buds appear. . . .
O, teach me how you look, and with what art
You sway the motion of Demetrius' heart. (1.1.181–93)

Written a little later than *Romeo and Juliet,* probably in 1595, *A Midsummer-Night's Dream* shows us a playwright moving away from love as the province of youthful couples. Like the moon, which shines over the whole earth, this comedy moves across differences of age and class. The illusion of being in love affects an older and seemingly more seasoned couple: Theseus, Duke of Athens, and Hippolyta, Queen of the Amazons. Theseus has won his bride in strange fashion: at war with her country, he decided that his enemy was also his true love. Shakespeare does not write a post-marriage scene for the royal couple, or for the other couples—including the newly reconciled Titania and Oberon, Queen and King of the Spirit World. But as an audience, we are asked to judge the presence of illusion: Theseus may well have impressed Hippolyta with his martial prowess (he reminds her that he "won" her love, by "doing [her] injuries"), but Hippolyta may not accept this prowess as the whole basis for her love. When she refers to the moon as a "silver bow, New-bent in heaven" her reference to the current phase of the moon conveys a different reality: a bow, fitted with an arrow, suggests that not all her feelings are taken up by tenderness.

Shakespeare's brilliant dramatization of illusion in the minds of various lovers is based on a positive, even generous belief that illusion is the necessary medium for the discovery of reality. Only when Hermia discovers that her beloved Demetrius can be cold and rejecting ("I love thee not, therefore leave me") does she move away from the illusion of a perfect man to see the reality of a man who is sweet—sometimes.

The comedy concludes with a new cosmological image which finally dispels the fracturing illusion—bringing night. Awakening from their night of confusion and broken illusion, the young lovers find the sun shining through the trees. One sees clearly only after shedding the illusions that had blocked out other, less attractive realities. This movement from the moon to the sun does not mean that illusion has run its course. Shakespeare, a gifted manufacturer of illusions, uses his stage to present one of an "Athens" that is very much like his London, and the various actors teach us about love only by achieving the illusion that they are living, breathing people with names like Helena or Oberon. Illusion, then, is not the antithesis of reality or love. In Shakespeare's hands it is the medium for revealing that audiences, too, are bound up in the intricate net of perception and must make their way through the Athens moonlit woods, wherever that happens to be.

—1995

WRITING ASSIGNMENT SEQUENCE (CONTINUED FROM PAGE 729)

4. Making Connections

Select one of the following questions and write an informal response in which you connect your own ideas with those conveyed in the works of this cluster, and/or make connections among the works themselves.

A. Compare the different kinds of fantasy worlds imagined by these authors. Which ones are most appealing to you and why?

B. How do the writers depict the boundaries between or integration of fantasy and reality?

5. Putting It All Together

Write an essay that combines what you think about the topic *The Magic Chalk* (i.e., the nature of fantasy versus reality) with what you now understand about the readings.

- Collect your informal writing, notes, and reading-journal entries on this topic and decide what will be the focus of your essay.
- Outline your essay. Select the literary passages and personal details you might use to illustrate and support your main focus.
- Write a draft of your essay in which you bring together what you think about the subject with what you understand about the readings. Try to include in your draft one or more *literary terms*.
- Share what you've written with your classmates and instructor, then revise it according to their recommendations.

Writing Tip: Vigorous Verbs

Strong verbs energize your writing. Whenever you can, replace *to be* verbs *(is, are, being)* with *active verbs*. Go through the draft of your essay and circle all the linking and lame verbs—look for *it is, it was, there is, there are* constructions—and substitute more specific, more accurate, more *vigorous* verbs.

Notice how the student sentence below was improved from first draft to final draft when the student changed the *to be* and *to do* verbs. Finding ways to avoid those verbs led the student to strengthen other verbs as well, and to improve the wording of the whole passage:

- *First Draft:* While I know that *it is* easier and more practical to work for the things you need in order to survive, one of my beliefs *is that it is* important that you *don't* get so wrapped up in the things you have *to do* so that you *don't* leave any room for *being* satisfied spiritually.

- *Final Draft:* While I understand that *working* for material comfort *allows* for an easier and more practical life, I *believe* that we *should avoid becoming* so wrapped up in life's necessities that we *fail to leave room* for *satisfying* our spiritual needs.

CrossClusters

In your paper you might want to consider how the following works located elsewhere in this book depict the boundaries of fantasy and reality:

- Gabriel García Márquez, "The Handsomest Drowned Man in the World" (p. 13)
- Rita Dove, "Adolescence III" (p. 120)
- Michael Dorris, "The Contest" (p. 374)
- Bernard Malamud, "The Magic Barrel" (p. 569)
- Louisa Valenzuela, "I'm Your Horse in the Night" (p. 585)
- Tony Kushner, from *Angels in America* (p. 621)
- Edgar Allan Poe, "The Tell-Tale Heart" (p. 834)
- Charlotte Perkins Gilman, "The Yellow Wallpaper" (p. 842)
- Sylvia Plath, "Lady Lazarus" (p. 856)
- Eugène Ionesco, *The Lesson* (p. 904)
- Leslie Marmon Silko, "The Man to Send Rain Clouds" (p. 978)
- Isabel Allende, "And of Clay We Are Created" (p. 996)
- Woody Allen, *Death Knocks* (p. 1005)

21

MUCH MADNESS

WRITING ASSIGNMENT SEQUENCE

1. Thinking About . . . Madness

Asking a Series of Questions: Write quick, informal responses to the following questions:

- How do we know if someone is "mad"?
- What are some common signs of insanity?
- Who decides who is sane or insane?
- What are some different forms of mental illness?
- What are the complicating factors that make it difficult to determine when someone is "mad"?

2. Enacting the Topic

With a few other students, *develop a "case study"* of a person who suddenly "goes over the edge" into madness. Try to answer the following questions:

- Who is the person?
- What are the circumstances?
- Who else might be involved?
- How does the person behave?
- What are your criteria for deciding what is insane behavior, and what is sane?
- What kind of help might the person need?
- Who is deciding that this person is insane?

3. Responding to the Readings

As you read the works in this cluster, jot down in your response journals questions you have about the works, and comment on passages you find provocative or puzzling. Consider the questions following each reading for journal writing and prepare to discuss your reactions in class.

CLUSTER ESSAY

PHYLLIS CHESLER

Women and Madness (excerpt)

*Phyllis Chesler (b. 1940) was born in Brooklyn, New York, and attended Bard College and the New School for Social Research, where she earned her Ph.D. She has written and lectured widely on a variety of subjects, especially those dealing with the cultural and psychological significance of male and female roles. She is politically active in the women's movement: her controversial books—*Women and Madness *(1972), excerpted below;* Women, Money, and Power *(1976); and* About Men *(1978)—have become seminal to feminist studies.*

Women in Asylums: Four Lives

Mrs. Elizabeth Packard (1816–c. 1890)

Mrs. Ellen West (c. 1890–c. 1926)

Mrs. Zelda Fitzgerald (1900–1948)

Mrs. Sylvia Plath Hughes (1932–1963)

During the nineteenth and twentieth centuries these four women were hospitalized for various psychiatric "symptoms." All were uncommonly stubborn, talented, and aggressive. Some became socially withdrawn: they no longer cared how they "looked," they refused to eat, they became sexually disinterested in their husbands. One woman "heard" things. Two others repeatedly attempted to kill themselves. Ellen West and Sylvia Plath finally committed suicide when they were in their early thirties. Zelda Fitzgerald burned to death in a mental asylum fire. Elizabeth Packard managed to escape after three years in an Illinois asylum. She published an account of her hospital experience and fought for the legal rights of mental patients and married women.

These four women share a rather fatal allegiance to their own uniqueness. For years they denied themselves—or were denied—the duties and privileges of talent and conscience. Like many women, they buried their own destinies in romantically extravagant marriages, in motherhood, and in approved female pleasure. However, their repressed energies eventually struggled free, demanding long overdue and therefore heavier prices: marital and maternal "disloyalty," social ostracism, imprisonment, madness, and death.

The patriarchal nature of psychiatric hospitals has been documented by M. Foucault, T. Szasz, E. Goffman, and T. Scheff. Journalists, social scientists, and novelists have described, deplored, and philosophized about the prevalence of overcrowding, understaffing, and brutality in America's public mental asylums, jails, and medical hospitals.[1] It is obvious that *state* mental asylums are the "Indian reservations" for America's non-criminally labeled poor, old, black, Latin, and female populations. It is also obvious that the state hospital, much like the poor or workhouse of old, functions as a warning specter, particularly to those women involved in earlier or more part-time phases of their "careers" as psychiatric patients.

Mental asylums rarely offer asylum. Both their calculated and their haphazard brutality mirrors the brutality of "outside" society. The "scandals" about them that periodically surface in the media are like all atrocities—only everyday events, writ large. Madness—as a label or reality—is not conceived of as divine, prophetic, or useful. It is perceived as (and often further shaped into) a shameful and menacing disease, from whose spiteful and exhausting eloquence society must be protected. At their best, mental asylums are special hotels or collegelike dormitories for white and wealthy Americans, where the temporary descent into "unreality" (or sobriety) is accorded the dignity of optimism, short internments, and a relatively earnest bedside manner. At their worst, mental asylums are families bureaucratized: the degradation and disenfranchisement of self, experienced by the biologically owned child (patient, woman), takes place in the anonymous and therefore guiltless embrace of strange fathers and mothers. In general psychiatric wards and state hospitals, "therapy," privacy, and self-determination are all either minimal or forbidden.[2] Experimental or traditional medication, surgery, shock, and insulin coma treatment, isolation, physical and sexual violence, medical neglect, and slave labor are routinely enforced.[3] Mental patients are somehow less "human" than either medical patients or criminals. They are, after all, "crazy"; they have been abandoned by (or have abandoned dialogue with) their "own" families. As such, they have no way—and no one—to "tell" what is happening to them.

The mental asylum closely approximates the female rather than the male experience within the family. This is probably one of the reasons why Erving Goffman, in *Asylums,* considered psychiatric hospitalization more destructive of self than criminal incarceration. Like most people, he is primarily thinking of the debilitating effect—*on men*—of being treated like a woman (as helpless,

[1]No changes have occurred. Avoidance, denial, and tokenism continue.

[2]In such settings, I have heard legitimate and pitiful patient requests for cigarettes or spending money, or complaints about bureaucratic red tape, "interpreted" psychodynamically by student psychiatrists, psychologists, social workers, nurses, and orderlies.

[3]Legally, all medication and treatment can be refused if the patient has not been legally declared "incompetent" as well as "insane."

dependent, sexless, unreasonable—as "crazy"). But what about the effect of being treated like a woman when you *are* a woman? And perhaps a woman who is already ambivalent or angry about just such treatment?

Perhaps one of the reasons women embark and re-embark on "psychiatric careers" more than men do is because they feel, quite horribly, at "home" within them. Also, to the extent to which *all* women have been poorly nurtured as female children, and are refused "mothering" by men as female adults, they might be eager for, or at least willing to settle for, periodic bouts of ersatz "mothering," which they receive as "patients." Those women who are more ambivalent about or rejecting of the female role are often eager to be punished for such dangerous boldness—in order to be saved from its ultimate consequences. Many mental asylum procedures *do* threaten, punish, or misunderstand such women into a real or wily submission. Some of these women react to such punishment (or to a dependency-producing environment) with increased and higher levels of anger and sex-role alienation. If such anger or aggressiveness persists, the women are isolated, strait-jacketed, sedated, and given shock therapy.[4] One study published by four male professionals in 1969 in the *Journal of Nervous and Mental Diseases* describes how they attempted to reduce the aggressive behavior of a thirty-one-year-old "schizophrenic" woman by shocking her with a cattle prod whenever she "made accusations of being persecuted and abused; made verbal threats; or committed aggressive acts." They labeled their treatment a "punishment program" and note that the "procedure was administered against the expressed will of the patient."

Celibacy is the official order of the asylum day. Patients are made to inhabit an eternal American adolescence, where sexuality and aggression are as feared, mocked, and punished as they are within the Family. Traditionally, mental hospital wards are sex-segregated; homosexuality, lesbianism, and masturbation are discouraged or forcibly interrupted.[5] The heterosexual dances sponsored in the late 1950s and 1960s were like high school proms, replete with chaperones, curfews, and frustration.

The female-"dominated" atmosphere of hospitals means a (shameful) return to childhood, for both men and women. However, the effect of sexual repression, for example, is probably different for female than for male patients.[6] Women have already been bitterly and totally repressed sexually; many may be reacting to or trying to escape from just such repression, and the powerlessness it signifies, by "going mad." Many male patients may be escaping the demands of a compulsive and aggressive heterosexuality by "going mad." Its

[4]They certainly aren't recruited by the Marines—or by an Olympic committee.

[5]Although homosexual, lesbian and heterosexual seduction and rape of the patients by the staff are not unknown, I think they occur less frequently than in criminal institutions.

[6]We must remember that in state hospitals approximately 50 per cent of the male patients are drug addicts and alcoholics—groups which are already somewhat withdrawn from heterosexual activity, for any number of reasons (lack of money, lack of desire for family "responsibilities," passivity, anxiety, physiological incapacity, misogyny, etc.).

absence is *perhaps* not as psychologically or physiologically devastating as it is for women.

Female patients, like female children, are closely supervised by other women (nurses, attendants) who, like mothers, are relatively powerless in terms of the hospital hierarchy and who, like mothers, don't really "like" their (wayward) daughters. Such supervision, however, doesn't protect the female as patient-child from rape, prostitution, pregnancy, and the blame for all three—any more than similar "motherly" supervision protects the female as female child in the "real" world, either within or outside the family. From 1968 to 1970 there were numerous newspaper accounts of the prostitution, rape, and impregnation of female mental patients by the professional and non-professional staff, and by male inmates.[7]

—1972

What are your reactions to and questions about this work? The following questions may help provoke some ideas.

Probing the Work

1. Chesler says that more women than men "embark on psychiatric careers" (as patients, not as doctors). What are some of the reasons she gives for women being so vulnerable to this kind of "career"?

Identifying Issues

2. To what extent do you believe that the defining of mental illness is related to gender? What examples can you give of psychological disorders that might stigmatize one sex more than another?

EDGAR ALLAN POE

The Tell-Tale Heart

Edgar Allan Poe (1809–1849) was the son of traveling actors. Before Poe was 3 years old, his father had abandoned the family and his mother had died. He was taken in—but never legally adopted—by John Allan, a prosperous merchant, and his wife, in Richmond. Poe was very well educated, but his personal life was fraught with tensions with Allan over Poe's drinking and gambling. In 1827 Poe left Richmond for Boston, where he began writing poetry. He served briefly in the army and then at West Point. He and Allan had their final falling-out following the death of Mrs. Allan, a favorite of Poe's, and Poe went on to become a successful writer and editor.

[7]For example: the New York *Times,* June 1968, regarding Chicago State Hospital and an "unnamed hospital in suburban Tinley Park"; the New York *Times,* June 1969, regarding Fairfield Hills Hospital in Newtown, Connecticut; the New York *Daily News,* November 1969, regarding Modesto State Hospital in California; *Newsday,* January 1970, regarding Pilgrim State Hospital in New York; the New York *Daily News,* February 1970, regarding Greystone State Hospital in New Jersey.

True!—nervous—very, very dreadfully nervous I had been and am; but why *will* you say that I am mad? The disease had sharpened my senses—not destroyed—not dulled them. Above all was the sense of hearing acute. I heard all things in the heaven and in the earth.[1] I heard many things in hell. How, then, am I mad? Hearken! and observe how healthily—how calmly I can tell you the whole story.

It is impossible to say how first the idea entered my brain; but, once conceived, it haunted me day and night. Object there was none. Passion there was none. I loved the old man. He had never wronged me. He had never given me insult. For his gold I had no desire. I think it was his eye! yes, it was this! One of his eyes resembled that of a vulture—a pale blue eye, with a film over it. Whenever it fell upon me, my blood ran cold; and so by degrees—very gradually—I made up my mind to take the life of the old man, and thus rid myself of the eye forever.

Now this is the point. You fancy me mad. Madmen know nothing. But you should have seen *me*. You should have seen how wisely I proceeded—with what caution—with what foresight—with what dissimilation I went to work! I was never kinder to the old man than during the whole week before I killed him. And every night, about midnight, I turned the latch of his door and opened it—oh, so gently! And then, when I had made an opening sufficient for my head, I put in a dark lantern,[2] all closed, closed, so that no light shone out, and then I thrust in my head. Oh, you would have laughed to see how cunningly I thrust it in! I moved it slowly—very, very slowly, so that I might not disturb the old man's sleep. It took me an hour to place my whole head within the opening so far that I could see him as he lay upon his bed. Ha!—would a madman have been so wise as this? And then, when my head was well in the room, I undid the lantern cautiously—oh, so cautiously—cautiously (for the hinges creaked)—I undid it just so much that a single thin ray fell upon the vulture eye. And this I did for seven long nights—every night just at midnight—but I found the eye always closed; and so it was impossible to do the work; for it was not the old man who vexed me, but his Evil Eye. And every morning, when the day broke, I went boldly into the chamber, and spoke courageously to him, calling him by name in a hearty tone and inquiring how he had passed the night. So you see he would have been a very profound old man, indeed, to suspect that every night, just at twelve, I looked in upon him while he slept.

Upon the eighth night I was more than usually cautious in opening the door. A watch's minute hand moves more quickly than did mine. Never, before that night, had I *felt* the extent of my own powers—of my sagacity. I could scarcely contain my feelings of triumph. To think that there I was, opening the door, little by little, and he not even to dream of my secret deeds or

[1]"That at the name of Jesus every knee should bow, of things in heaven, and things on earth, and things under the earth." Philippians 2:10

[2]A lantern with enclosing shutters that can block the light.

thoughts. I fairly chuckled at the idea; and perhaps he heard me; for he moved on the bed suddenly, as if startled. Now you may think that I drew back—but no. His room was black as pitch with the thick darkness, (for the shutters were close fastened, through fear of robbers,) and so I knew that he could not see the opening of the door, and I kept pushing it on steadily, steadily.

I had my head in, and was about to open the lantern, when my thumb slipped upon the tin fastening, and the old man sprang up in the bed, crying out—"Who's there?"

I kept quite still and said nothing. For a whole hour I did not move a muscle, and in the meantime I did not hear him lie down. He was still sitting up in the bed, listening;—just as I have done, night after night, hearkening to the death-watches in the wall.[3]

Presently I heard a slight groan, and I knew it was the groan of mortal terror. It was not a groan of pain or of grief—oh, no!—it was the low stifled sound that arises from the bottom of the soul when overcharged with awe. I knew the sound well. Many a night, just at midnight, when all the world slept, it has welled up from my own bosom, deepening, with its dreadful echo, the terrors that distracted me. I say I knew it well. I knew what the old man felt, and pitied him, although I chuckled at heart. I knew that he had been lying awake ever since the first slight noise, when he had turned in the bed. His fears had been ever since growing upon him. He had been trying to fancy them causeless, but could not. He had been saying to himself—"It is nothing but the wind in the chimney—it is only a mouse crossing the floor," or "it is merely a cricket which has made a single chirp." Yes, he had been trying to comfort himself with these suppositions: but he had found all in vain. *All in vain;* because Death, in approaching him, had stalked with his black shadow before him, and enveloped the victim. And it was the mournful influence of the unperceived shadow that caused him to feel—although he neither saw nor heard—to *feel* the presence of my head within the room.

When I had waited a long time, very patiently, without hearing him lie down, I resolved to open a little—a very, very little crevice in the lantern. So I opened it—you cannot imagine how stealthily, stealthily—until, at length, a single dim ray, like the thread of the spider, shot from out the crevice and fell upon the vulture eye.

It was open—wide, wide open—and I grew furious as I gazed upon it. I saw it with perfect distinctness—all a dull blue, with a hideous veil over it that chilled the very marrow in my bones; but I could see nothing else of the old man's face or person: for I had directed the rays as if by instinct, precisely upon the damned spot.

And now—have I not told you that what you mistake for madness is but

[3]A reference to "death-watch beetles," insects that make a hollow clicking sound by striking their heads against the wood into which they have burrowed. The sound was thought to signal the coming of death.

over acuteness of the senses?—now, I say, there came to my ears a low, dull, quick sound, such as a watch makes when enveloped in cotton. I knew *that* sound well, too. It was the beating of the old man's heart. It increased my fury, as the beating of a drum stimulates the soldier into courage.

But even yet I refrained and kept still. I scarcely breathed. I held the lantern motionless. I tried how steadily I could maintain the ray upon the eye. Meantime the hellish tattoo of the heart increased. It grew quicker and quicker, and louder and louder every instant. The old man's terror *must* have been extreme! It grew louder, I say, louder every moment!—do you mark me well? I have told you that I am nervous: so I am. And now at the dead hour of the night, amid the dreadful silence of that old house, so strange a noise as this excited me to uncontrollable terror. Yet, for some minutes longer I refrained and stood still. But the beating grew louder, louder! I thought the heart must burst. And now a new anxiety seized me—the sound would be heard by a neighbor! The old man's hour had come! With a loud yell, I threw open the lantern and leaped into the room. He shrieked once—once only. In an instant I dragged him to the floor, and pulled the heavy bed over him. I then smiled gaily, to find the deed so far done. But, for many minutes, the heart beat on with a muffled sound. This, however, did not vex me; it would not be heard through the wall. At length it ceased. The old man was dead. I removed the bed and examined the corpse. Yes, he was stone, stone dead. I placed my hand upon the heart and held it there many minutes. There was no pulsation. He was stone dead. His eye would trouble me no more.

If you still think me mad, you will think so no longer when I describe the wise precautions I took for the concealment of the body. The night waned, and I worked hastily, but in silence. First of all I dismembered the corpse. I cut off the head and the arms and the legs.

I then took up three planks from the flooring of the chamber, and deposited all between the scantlings.[4] I then replaced the boards so cleverly, so cunningly, that no human eye—not even *his*—could have detected anything wrong. There was nothing to wash out—no stain of any kind—no bloodspot whatever, I had been too wary for that. A tub had caught all—ha! ha!

When I had made an end of these labors, it was four o'clock—still dark as midnight. As the bell sounded the hour, there came a knocking at the street door. I went down to open it with a light heart,—for what had I *now* to fear? There entered three men, who introduced themselves, with perfect suavity, as officers of the police. A shriek had been heard by a neighbor during the night; suspicion of foul play had been aroused; information had been lodged at the police office, and they (the officers) had been deputed to search the premises.

I smiled,—for *what* had I to fear? I bade the gentlemen welcome. The shriek, I said, was my own in a dream. The old man, I mentioned, was absent in the country. I took my visiters all over the house. I bade them search—

[4]Timbers that support floor boards.

search *well.* I led them, at length, to *his* chamber. I showed them his treasures, secure, undisturbed. In the enthusiasm of my confidence, I brought chairs into the room and desired them *here* to rest from their fatigues, while I myself, in the wild audacity of my perfect triumph, placed my own seat upon the very spot beneath which reposed the corpse of the victim.

The officers were satisfied. My *manner* had convinced them. I was singularly at ease. They sat, and while I answered cheerily, they chatted of familiar things. But, ere long, I felt myself getting pale and wished them gone. My head ached, and I fancied a ringing in my ears: but still they sat and still chatted. The ringing became more distinct:—it continued and became more distinct: I talked more freely to get rid of the feeling: but it continued and gained definitiveness—until, at length, I found that the noise was *not* within my ears.

No doubt I now grew *very* pale;—but I talked more fluently, and with a heightened voice. Yet the sound increased—and what could I do? It was *a low, dull, quick sound—much such as a watch makes when enveloped in cotton.* I gasped for breath—and yet the officers heard it not. I talked more quickly—more vehemently; but the noise steadily increased. I arose and argued about trifles, in a high key and with violent gesticulations; but the noise steadily increased. Why *would* they not be gone? I paced the floor to and fro with heavy strides, as if excited to fury by the observations of the men—but the noise steadily increased. Oh God! what *could* I do? I foamed—I raved—I swore! I swung the chair upon which I had been sitting, and grated it upon the boards, but the noise arose over all and continually increased. It grew louder—louder—*louder!* And still the men chatted pleasantly, and smiled. Was it possible they heard not? Almighty God!—no, no! They heard!—they suspected!—they *knew!*—they were making a mockery of my horror!—this I thought, and this I think. But anything was better than this agony! Anything was more tolerable than this derision! I could bear those hypocritical smiles no longer! I felt that I must scream or die!—and now—again!—hark! louder! louder! louder! *louder!*—

"Villains!" I shrieked, "dissemble no more! I admit the deed!—tear up the planks!—here, here!—it is the beating of his hideous heart!"

—1843

What are your reactions to and questions about this work? The following questions may help provoke some ideas.

Probing the Work

1. The narrator asks, "How then am I mad?" How would you answer? To what extent can you agree with the narrator's explanation? What evidence can you find that reveals his true state of mind?
2. What do you think the old man's *eye* represents?

Identifying Issues

3. If you were a judge or on a jury, would you think the narrator mentally competent to stand trial or would you find him innocent by reason of insanity? Support your decision with evidence from the story.
4. In *The Life and Works of Edgar Allan Poe: a Psycho-Analytical Interpretation* (1949), Marie Bonaparte argues that the "old man" in this story resembles Poe's foster father John Allan, who was afflicted with dropsy, a disease which made his breathing and heartbeat laborious. The narrator hates the father figure's castrated power (his partially incapacitated eye) and his jealousy over his sleeping with the mother (Mrs. Allan and Poe adored each other) impels him to carry out his Oedipal wish to kill the father (see the questions following O'Connor's "My Oedipus Complex," p. 350). What do you think of Bonaparte's interpretation? Explain your answer.

EMILY DICKINSON

Much Madness is divinest Sense

Emily Dickinson (1830–1886), the daughter of a successful lawyer, lived most of her life in her father's house in Amherst, Massachusetts. She was educated in local schools and at Mount Holyoke Female Seminary in South Hadley. She spent a socially active childhood, but after a trip to Washington and Philadelphia in 1855 she settled into a quiet pattern of life, only twice leaving Amherst and seeing few people outside her close family circle and old friends. Dickinson published only seven anonymous verses during her lifetime, but after she died her sister discovered hundreds of poems. Since then nearly 1800 have been published, and Dickinson is considered by many to be one of the greatest American poets.

Much Madness is divinest Sense—
To a discerning Eye—
Much Sense—the starkest Madness—
'Tis the Majority
In this, as All, prevail—
Assent—and you are sane—
Demur—you're straightway dangerous—
And handled with a Chain—

—1862

What are your reactions to and questions about this work? The following questions may help provoke some ideas.

Probing the Work

1. What does the paradox, "much madness is divinest sense," seem to mean to the poet? To what degree can you agree with her?

Identifying Issues

2. Dickinson seems to be saying that the nonconformist is often considered mad by "the majority." Can you think of examples to support or disagree with this conclusion?

ROBERT BROWNING

Porphyria's Lover

Robert Browning (1812–1889) was born in the London suburb of Camberwell. He was extraordinarily well educated at home, where he lived until he was 34. At that age, he met and courted the well-known poet Elizabeth Barrett (see p. 568), after falling in love with her first through her poetry. Semi-invalided, six years older than he, and jealously guarded by her tyrannical father, she was nonetheless won over by Browning: the two eloped to Italy, where they lived happily until her death in 1861. With their son, Browning returned to London, where he continued to write poetry. While his first book of poems, Dramatic Lyrics *(1842), was poorly received, his stature as a poet grew late in his life, and continued to grow after his death. The poem below is a dramatic monologue (see page 72), a form Browning perfected, and which many twentieth-century poets embraced.*

The rain set early in tonight,
    The sullen wind was soon awake,
It tore the elm-tops down for spite,
    And did its worst to vex the lake:
    I listened with heart fit to break.
When glided in Porphyria: straight
    She shut the cold out and the storm,
And kneeled and made the cheerless grate
    Blaze up, and all the cottage warm;
    Which done, she rose, and from her form
Withdrew the dripping cloak and shawl,
    And laid her soiled gloves by, untied
Her hat and let the damp hair fall,
    And, last, she sat down by my side
    And called me. When no voice replied,
She put my arm about her waist,
    And made her smooth white shoulder bare,
And all her yellow hair displaced,

And, stooping, made my cheek lie there,
And spread, o'er all, her yellow hair,
Murmuring how she loved me—she
Too weak, for all her heart's endeavor,
To set its struggling passion free
From pride, and vainer ties dissever,
And give herself to me forever.
But passion sometimes would prevail,
Nor could tonight's gay feast restrain
A sudden thought of one so pale
For love of her, and all in vain:
So, she was come through wind and rain.
Be sure I looked up at her eyes
Happy and proud: at last I knew
Porphyria worshiped me: surprise
Made my heart swell, and still it grew
While I debated what to do.
That moment she was mine, mine, fair,
Perfectly pure and good: I found
A thing to do, and all her hair
In one long yellow string I wound
Three times her little throat around,
And strangled her. No pain felt she;
I am quite sure she felt no pain.
As a shut bud that holds a bee,
I warily oped her lids: again
Laughed the blue eyes without a stain.
And I untightened next the tress
About her neck: her cheek once more
Blushed bright beneath my burning kiss:
I propped her head up as before,
Only, this time my shoulder bore
Her head, which droops upon it still:
The smiling rosy little head,
So glad it has its utmost will,
That all it scorned at once is fled,
And I, its love, am gained instead!
Porphyria's love: she guessed not how
Her darling one wish would be heard.
And thus we sit together now,
And all night long we have not stirred,
And yet God has not said a word!

—1834

What are your reactions to and questions about this work? The following questions may help provoke some ideas.

Probing the Work

1. What are Porphyria's feelings for the speaker? Point to the lines that describe most precisely her attitude towards him. Considering her feelings, why does the speaker kill her?
2. How does the *setting* (see page 74) reflect the events and the mood of this poem?

Identifying Issues

3. Do you think the speaker is sane or insane? Upon what definitions of those terms do you base your judgment? What evidence can you find in the poem that illuminate his state of mind? What connections can you make between the speaker and others who commit crimes of passion? What degree of responsibility do he and other such people bear for their actions?

CHARLOTTE PERKINS GILMAN

The Yellow Wallpaper

Charlotte Perkins Gilman (1860–1935) was born in Hartford, Connecticut. Soon after she was born her father abandoned the family. She worked as a teacher, married Charles Stetson at 24, and became deeply depressed after the birth of her first child. The famous neurologist Weir Mitchell ordered complete bed rest and forbade her from writing, which made matters worse. In 1887 she left her husband, moved to California, and began writing and speaking on economics and feminism. Eventually she divorced Stetson, then relinquished custody of her daughter to him and his second wife. In 1900 she married George Gilman, with whom she lived happily until his death in 1934. She edited—and wrote most of the contents for—a monthly journal, The Forerunner, *for seven years. Among her works are* Women and Economics *(1898), and* Herland *(1915).*

It is very seldom that mere ordinary people like John and myself secure ancestral halls for the summer.

A colonial mansion, a hereditary estate, I would say a haunted house, and reach the height of romantic felicity—but that would be asking too much of fate!

Still I will proudly declare that there is something queer about it.

Else, why should it be let so cheaply? And why have stood so long untenanted?

John laughs at me, of course, but one expects that in marriage.

John is practical in the extreme. He has no patience with faith, an intense horror of superstition, and he scoffs openly at any talk of things not to be felt and seen and put down in figures.

John is a physician, and *perhaps*—(I would not say it to a living soul, of course, but this is dead paper and a great relief to my mind—) *perhaps* that is one reason I do not get well faster.

You see he does not believe I am sick!

And what can one do?

If a physician of high standing, and one's own husband, assures friends and relatives that there is really nothing the matter with one but temporary nervous depression—a slight hysterical tendency[1]—what is one to do?

My brother is also a physician, and also of high standing, and he says the same thing.

So I take phosphates or phosphites—whichever it is, and tonics, and journeys, and air, and exercise, and am absolutely forbidden to "work" until I am well again.

Personally, I disagree with their ideas.

Personally, I believe that congenial work, with excitement and change, would do me good.

But what is one to do?

I did write for a while in spite of them; but it *does* exhaust me a good deal—having to be so sly about it, or else meet with heavy opposition.

I sometimes fancy that in my condition if I had less opposition and more society and stimulus—but John says the very worst thing I can do is to think about my condition, and I confess it always makes me feel bad.

So I will let it alone and talk about the house.

The most beautiful place! It is quite alone, standing well back from the road, quite three miles from the village. It makes me think of English places that you read about, for there are hedges and walls and gates that lock, and lots of separate little houses for the gardeners and people.

There is a *delicious* garden! I never saw such a garden—large and shady, full of box-bordered paths, and lined with long grape-covered arbors with seats under them.

There were greenhouses, too, but they are all broken now.

There was some legal trouble, I believe, something about the heirs and co-heirs; anyhow, the place has been empty for years.

That spoils my ghostliness, I am afraid, but I don't care—there is something strange about the house—I can feel it.

I even said so to John one moonlight evening, but he said what I felt was a *draught,* and shut the window.

[1]At the time this story was written, *hysteria* was a term used loosely to describe a wide variety of symptoms, thought to be particularly prevalent among women, that indicated emotional disturbance or dysfunction. Depression, anxiety, excitability, and vague somatic complaints were among the conditions treated as "hysteria."

I get unreasonably angry with John sometimes. I'm sure I never used to be so sensitive. I think it is due to this nervous condition.

But John says if I feel so, I shall neglect proper self-control; so I take pains to control myself—before him, at least, and that makes me very tired.

I don't like our room a bit. I wanted one downstairs that opened on the piazza and had roses all over the window, and such pretty old-fashioned chintz hangings! but John would not hear of it.

He said there was only one window and not room for two beds, and no near room for him if he took another.

He is very careful and loving, and hardly lets me stir without special direction.

I have a schedule prescription for each hour in the day; he takes all care from me, and so I feel basely ungrateful not to value it more.

He said we came here solely on my account, that I was to have perfect rest and all the air I could get. "Your exercise depends on your strength, my dear," said he, "and your food somewhat on your appetite; but air you can absorb all the time." So we took the nursery at the top of the house.

It is a big, airy room, the whole floor nearly, with windows that look all ways, and air and sunshine galore. It was nursery first and then playroom and gymnasium, I should judge; for the windows are barred for little children, and there are rings and things in the walls.

The paint and paper look as if a boys' school had used it. It is stripped off—the paper—in great patches all around the head of my bed, about as far as I can reach, and in a great place on the other side of the room low down. I never saw a worse paper in my life.

One of those sprawling flamboyant patterns committing every artistic sin.

It is dull enough to confuse the eye in following, pronounced enough to constantly irritate and provoke study, and when you follow the lame uncertain curves for a little distance they suddenly commit suicide—plunge off at outrageous angles, destroy themselves in unheard of contradictions.

The color is repellant, almost revolting; a smouldering unclean yellow, strangely faded by the slow-turning sunlight.

It is a dull yet lurid orange in some places, a sickly sulphur tint in others.

No wonder the children hated it! I should hate it myself if I had to live in this room long.

There comes John, and I must put this away,—he hates to have me write a word.

We have been here two weeks, and I haven't felt like writing before, since that first day.

I am sitting by the window now, up in this atrocious nursery, and there is nothing to hinder my writing as much as I please, save lack of strength.

John is away all day, and even some nights when his cases are serious.

I am glad my case is not serious!

But these nervous troubles are dreadfully depressing.

John does not know how much I really suffer. He knows there is no *reason* to suffer, and that satisfies him.

Of course it is only nervousness. It does weigh on me so not to do my duty in any way!

I mean to be such a help to John, such a real rest and comfort, and here I am a comparative burden already!

Nobody would believe what an effort it is to do what little I am able,—to dress and entertain, and order things.

It is fortunate Mary is so good with the baby. Such a dear baby!

And yet I *cannot* be with him, it makes me so nervous.

I suppose John never was nervous in his life. He laughs at me so about this wallpaper!

At first he meant to repaper the room, but afterwards he said that I was letting it get the better of me, and that nothing was worse for a nervous patient than to give way to such fancies.

He said that after the wallpaper was changed it would be the heavy bedstead, and then the barred windows, and then that gate at the head of the stairs, and so on.

"You know the place is doing you good," he said, "and really, dear, I don't care to renovate the house just for a three months' rental."

"Then do let us go downstairs," I said, "there are such pretty rooms there."

Then he took me in his arms and called me a blessed little goose, and said he would go down cellar, if I wished, and have it whitewashed into the bargain.

But he is right enough about the beds and windows and things.

It is an airy and comfortable room as any one need wish, and, of course, I would not be so silly as to make him uncomfortable just for a whim.

I'm really getting quite fond of the big room, all but that horrid paper.

Out of one window I can see the garden, those mysterious deep-shaded arbors, the riotous old-fashioned flowers, and bushes and gnarly trees.

Out of another I get a lovely view of the bay and a little private wharf belonging to the estate. There is a beautiful shaded lane that runs down there from the house. I always fancy I see people walking in these numerous paths and arbors, but John has cautioned me not to give way to fancy in the least. He says that with my imaginative power and habit of story-making, a nervous weakness like mine is sure to lead to all manner of excited fancies, and that I ought to use my will and good sense to check the tendency. So I try.

I think sometimes that if I were only well enough to write a little it would relieve the press of ideas and rest me.

But I find I get pretty tired when I try.

It is so discouraging not to have any advice and companionship about my work. When I get really well, John says we will ask Cousin Henry and Julia down for a long visit; but he says he would as soon put fireworks in my pillowcase as to let me have those stimulating people about now.

I wish I could get well faster.

But I must not think about that. This paper looks to me as if it *knew* what a vicious influence it had!

There is a recurrent spot where the pattern lolls like a broken neck and two bulbous eyes stare at you upside down.

I get positively angry with the impertinence of it and the everlastingness. Up and down and sideways they crawl, and those absurd, unblinking eyes are everywhere. There is one place where two breadths didn't match, and the eyes go all up and down the line, one a little higher than the other.

I never saw so much expression in an inanimate thing before, and we all know how much expression they have! I used to lie awake as a child and get more entertainment and terror out of blank walls and plain furniture than most children could find in a toy-store.

I remember what a kindly wink the knobs of our big, old bureau used to have, and there was one chair that always seemed like a strong friend.

I used to feel that if any of the other things looked too fierce I could always hop into that chair and be safe.

The furniture in this room is no worse than inharmonious, however, for we had to bring it all from downstairs. I suppose when this was used as a playroom they had to take the nursery things out, and no wonder! I never saw such ravages as the children have made here.

The wallpaper, as I said before, is torn off in spots, and it sticketh closer than a brother—they must have had perseverance as well as hatred.

Then the floor is scratched and gouged and splintered, the plaster itself is dug out here and there, and this great heavy bed which is all we found in the room, looks as if it had been through the wars.

But I don't mind it a bit—only the paper.

There comes John's sister. Such a dear girl as she is, and so careful of me! I must not let her find me writing.

She is a perfect and enthusiastic housekeeper, and hopes for no better profession. I verily believe she thinks it is the writing which made me sick!

But I can write when she is out, and see her a long way off from these windows.

There is one that commands the road, a lovely shaded winding road, and one that just looks off over the country. A lovely country, too, full of great elms and velvet meadows.

This wallpaper has a kind of sub-pattern in a different shade, a particularly irritating one, for you can only see it in certain lights, and not clearly then.

But in the places where it isn't faded and where the sun is just so—I can see a strange, provoking, formless sort of figure, that seems to skulk about behind that silly and conspicuous front design.

There's sister on the stairs!

Well, the Fourth of July is over! The people are all gone and I am tired out. John thought it might do me good to see a little company, so we just had mother and Nellie and the children down for a week.

Of course I didn't do a thing. Jennie sees to everything now.

But it tired me all the same.

John says if I don't pick up faster he shall send me to Weir Mitchell[2] in the fall.

But I don't want to go there at all. I had a friend who was in his hands once, and she says he is just like John and my brother, only more so!

Besides, it is such an undertaking to go so far.

I don't feel as if it was worth while to turn my hand over for anything, and I'm getting dreadfully fretful and querulous.

I cry at nothing, and cry most of the time.

Of course I don't when John is here, or anybody else, but when I am alone.

And I am alone a good deal just now. John is kept in town very often by serious cases, and Jennie is good and lets me alone when I want her to.

So I walk a little in the garden or down that lovely lane, sit on the porch under the roses, and lie down up here a good deal.

I'm getting really fond of the room in spite of the wallpaper. Perhaps *because* of the wallpaper.

It dwells in my mind so!

I lie here on this great immovable bed—it is nailed down, I believe—and follow that pattern about by the hour. It is as good as gymnastics, I assure you. I start, we'll say, at the bottom, down in the corner over there where it has not been touched, and I determine for the thousandth time that I *will* follow that pointless pattern to some sort of conclusion.

I know a little of the principle of design, and I know this thing was not arranged on any laws of radiation, or alternation, or repetition, or symmetry, or anything else that I ever heard of.

It is repeated, of course, by the breadths, but not otherwise.

Looked at in one way each breadth stands alone, the bloated curves and

[2]Silas Weir Mitchell (1829–1914), American physician, novelist, and specialist in nerve disorders, popularized the "rest cure" in the management of hysteria, nervous breakdowns and related disorders. A friend of William Dean Howells (1837–1920), he was the model for the nerve specialist in Howells's *The Shadow of a Dream* (1890).

flourishes—a kind of "debased Romanesque"[3] with *delirium tremens*—go waddling up and down in isolated columns of fatuity.

But, on the other hand, they connect diagonally, and the sprawling outlines run off in great slanting waves of optic horror, like a lot of wallowing seaweeds in full chase.

The whole thing goes horizontally, too, at least it seems so, and I exhaust myself in trying to distinguish the order of its going in that direction.

They have used a horizontal breadth for a frieze,[4] and that adds wonderfully to the confusion.

There is one end of the room where it is almost intact, and there, when the crosslights fade and the low sun shines directly upon it, I can almost fancy radiation after all,—the interminable grotesque seem to form around a common center and rush off in headlong plunges of equal distraction.

It makes me tired to follow it. I will take a nap I guess.

I don't know why I should write this.

I don't want to.

I don't feel able.

And I know John would think it absurd. But I *must* say what I feel and think in some way—it is such a relief!

But the effort is getting to be greater than the relief.

Half the time now I am awfully lazy, and lie down ever so much.

John says I mustn't lose my strength, and has me take cod liver oil and lots of tonics and things, to say nothing of ale and wine and rare meat.

Dear John! He loves me very dearly, and hates to have me sick. I tried to have a real earnest reasonable talk with him the other day, and tell him how I wish he would let me go and make a visit to Cousin Henry and Julia.

But he said I wasn't able to go, nor able to stand it after I got there; and I did not make out a very good case for myself, for I was crying before I had finished.

It is getting to be a great effort for me to think straight. Just this nervous weakness I suppose.

And dear John gathered me up in his arms, and just carried me upstairs and laid me on the bed, and sat by me and read to me till it tired my head.

He said I was his darling and his comfort and all he had, and that I must take care of myself for his sake, and keep well.

He says no one but myself can help me out of it, that I must use my will and self-control and not let any silly fancies run away with me.

There's one comfort, the baby is well and happy, and does not have to occupy this nursery with the horrid wallpaper.

If we had not used it, that blessed child would have! What a fortunate es-

[3]Romanesque style is here associated with ornamental complexity and repeated motifs and figures.

[4]An ornamental band used as a border at the top of the wall.

cape! Why, I wouldn't have a child of mine, an impressionable little thing, live in such a room for worlds.

I never thought of it before, but it is lucky that John kept me here after all, I can stand it so much easier than a baby, you see.

Of course I never mention it to them any more—I am too wise,—but I keep watch of it all the same.

There are things in that paper that nobody knows but me, or ever will.

Behind that outside pattern the dim shapes get clearer every day.

It is always the same shape, only very numerous.

And it is like a woman stooping down and creeping about behind that pattern. I don't like it a bit. I wonder—I begin to think—I wish John would take me away from here!

It is so hard to talk with John about my case, because he is so wise, and because he loves me so.

But I tried it last night.

It was moonlight. The moon shines in all around just as the sun does.

I hate to see it sometimes, it creeps so slowly, and always comes in by one window or another.

John was asleep and I hated to waken him, so I kept still and watched the moonlight on that undulating wallpaper till I felt creepy.

The faint figure behind seemed to shake the pattern, just as if she wanted to get out.

I got up softly and went to feel and see if the paper *did* move, and when I came back John was awake.

"What is it, little girl?" he said. "Don't go walking about like that—you'll get cold."

I thought it was a good time to talk, so I told him that I really was not gaining here, and that I wished he would take me away.

"Why, darling!" said he, "our lease will be up in three weeks, and I can't see how to leave before.

"The repairs are not done at home, and I cannot possibly leave town just now. Of course if you were in any danger, I could and would, but you really are better, dear, whether you can see it or not. I am a doctor, dear, and I know. You are gaining flesh and color, your appetite is better, I feel really much easier about you."

"I don't weigh a bit more," said I, "nor as much; and my appetite may be better in the evening when you are here, but it is worse in the morning when you are away!"

"Bless her little heart!" said he with a big hug, "she shall be as sick as she pleases! But now let's improve the shining hours by going to sleep, and talk about it in the morning!"

"And you won't go away?" I asked gloomily.

"Why, how can I, dear? It is only three weeks more and then we will take a nice little trip of a few days while Jennie is getting the house ready. Really dear you are better!"

"Better in body perhaps—" I began, and stopped short, for he sat up straight and looked at me with such a stern, reproachful look that I could not say another word.

"My darling," said he, "I beg of you, for my sake and for our child's sake, as well as for your own, that you will never for one instant let that idea enter your mind! There is nothing so dangerous, so fascinating, to a temperament like yours. It is a false and foolish fancy. Can you not trust me as a physician when I tell you so?"

So of course I said no more on that score, and we went to sleep before long. He thought I was asleep first, but I wasn't, and lay there for hours trying to decide whether that front pattern and the back pattern really did move together or separately.

On a pattern like this, by daylight, there is a lack of sequence, a defiance of law, that is a constant irritant to a normal mind.

The color is hideous enough, and unreliable enough, and infuriating enough, but the pattern is torturing.

You think you have mastered it, but just as you get well underway in following, it turns a back-somersault and there you are. It slaps you in the face, knocks you down, and tramples upon you. It is like a bad dream.

The outside pattern is a florid arabesque, reminding one of a fungus. If you can imagine a toadstool in joints, an interminable string of toadstools, budding and sprouting in endless convolutions—why, that is something like it.

That is, sometimes!

There is one marked peculiarity about this paper, a thing nobody seems to notice but myself, and that is that it changes as the light changes.

When the sun shoots in through the east window—I always watch for that first long, straight ray—it changes so quickly that I never can quite believe it.

That is why I watch it always.

By moonlight—the moon shines in all night when there is a moon—I wouldn't know it was the same paper.

At night in any kind of light, in twilight, candlelight, lamplight, and worst of all by moonlight, it becomes bars! The outside pattern I mean, and the woman behind it is as plain as can be.

I didn't realize for a long time what the thing was that showed behind, that dim sub-pattern, but now I am quite sure it is a woman.

By daylight she is subdued, quiet. I fancy it is the pattern that keeps her so still. It is so puzzling. It keeps me quiet by the hour.

I lie down ever so much now. John says it is good for me, and to sleep all I can.

Indeed he started the habit by making me lie down for an hour after each meal.

It is a very bad habit I am convinced, for you see I don't sleep.

And that cultivates deceit, for I don't tell them I'm awake—O no!

The fact is I am getting a little afraid of John.

He seems very queer sometimes, and even Jennie has an inexplicable look.

It strikes me occasionally, just as a scientific hypothesis,—that perhaps it is the paper!

I have watched John when he did not know I was looking, and come into the room suddenly on the most innocent excuses, and I've caught him several times *looking at the paper!* And Jennie too. I caught Jennie with her hand on it once.

She didn't know I was in the room, and when I asked her in a quiet, a very quiet voice, with the most restrained manner possible, what she was doing with the paper—she turned around as if she had been caught stealing, and looked quite angry—asked me why I should frighten her so!

Then she said that the paper stained everything it touched, that she had found yellow smooches on all my clothes and John's, and she wished we would be more careful!

Did not that sound innocent? But I know she was studying that pattern, and I am determined that nobody shall find it out but myself!

Life is very much more exciting now than it used to be. You see I have something more to expect, to look forward to, to watch. I really do eat better, and am more quiet than I was.

John is so pleased to see me improve! He laughed a little the other day, and said I seemed to be flourishing in spite of my wallpaper.

I turned it off with a laugh. I had no intention of telling him it was *because* of the wallpaper—he would make fun of me. He might even want to take me away.

I don't want to leave now until I have found it out. There is a week more, and I think that will be enough.

I'm feeling ever so much better! I don't sleep much at night, for it is so interesting to watch developments; but I sleep a good deal in the daytime.

In the daytime it is tiresome and perplexing.

There are always new shoots on the fungus, and new shades of yellow all over it. I cannot keep count of them, though I have tried conscientiously.

It is the strangest yellow, that wallpaper! It makes me think of all the yellow things I ever saw—not beautiful ones like buttercups, but old foul, bad yellow things.

But there is something else about that paper—the smell! I noticed it the moment we came into the room, but with so much air and sun it was not bad. Now we have had a week of fog and rain, and whether the windows are open or not, the smell is here.

It creeps all over the house.

I find it hovering in the dining-room, skulking in the parlor, hiding in the hall, lying in wait for me on the stairs.

It gets into my hair.

Even when I go to ride, if I turn my head suddenly and surprise it—there is that smell!

Such a peculiar odor, too! I have spent hours in trying to analyze it, to find what it smelled like.

It is not bad—at first, and very gentle, but quite the subtlest, most enduring odor I ever met.

In this damp weather it is awful, I wake up in the night and find it hanging over me.

It used to disturb me at first. I thought seriously of burning the house—to reach the smell.

But now I am used to it. The only thing I can think of that it is like is the *color* of the paper! A yellow smell.

There is a very funny mark on this wall, low down, near the mopboard. A streak that runs round the room. It goes behind every piece of furniture, except the bed, a long, straight, even *smooch,* as if it had been rubbed over and over.

I wonder how it was done and who did it, and what they did it for. Round and round and round—round and round and round—it makes me dizzy!

I really have discovered something at last.

Through watching so much at night, when it changes so, I have finally found out.

The front pattern *does* move—and no wonder! The woman behind shakes it!

Sometimes I think there are a great many women behind, and sometimes only one, and she crawls around fast, and her crawling shakes it all over.

Then in the very bright spots she keeps still, and in the very shady spots she just takes hold of the bars and shakes them hard.

And she is all the time trying to climb through. But nobody could climb through that pattern—it strangles so; I think that is why it has so many heads.

They get through, and then the pattern strangles them off and turns them upside down, and makes their eyes white!

If those heads were covered or taken off it would not be half so bad.

I think that woman gets out in the daytime!

And I'll tell you why—privately—I've seen her!

I can see her out of every one of my windows!

It is the same woman, I know, for she is always creeping, and most women do not creep by daylight.

I see her in that long shaded lane, creeping up and down. I see her in those dark grape arbors, creeping all around the garden.

I see her on that long road under the trees, creeping along, and when a carriage comes she hides under the blackberry vines.

I don't blame her a bit. It must be very humiliating to be caught creeping by daylight!

I always lock the door when I creep by daylight. I can't do it at night, for I know John would suspect something at once.

And John is so queer now, that I don't want to irritate him. I wish he would take another room! Besides, I don't want anybody to get that woman out at night but myself.

I often wonder if I could see her out of all the windows at once.

But, turn as fast as I can, I can only see out of one at one time.

And though I always see her, she *may* be able to creep faster than I can turn!

I have watched her sometimes away off in the open country, creeping as fast as a cloud shadow in a high wind.

If only that top pattern could be gotten off from the under one! I mean to try it, little by little.

I have found out another funny thing, but I shan't tell it this time! It does not do to trust people too much.

There are only two more days to get this paper off, and I believe John is beginning to notice. I don't like the look in his eyes.

And I heard him ask Jennie a lot of professional questions about me. She had a very good report to give.

She said I slept a good deal in the daytime.

John knows I don't sleep very well at night, for all I'm so quiet!

He asked me all sorts of questions, too, and pretended to be very loving and kind.

As if I couldn't see through him!

Still, I don't wonder he acts so, sleeping under this paper for three months.

It only interests me, but I feel sure John and Jennie are secretly affected by it.

Hurrah! This is the last day, but it is enough. John to stay in town over night, and won't be out until this evening.

Jennie wanted to sleep with me—the sly thing! but I told her I should undoubtedly rest better for a night all alone.

That was clever, for really I wasn't alone a bit! As soon as it was moonlight and that poor thing began to crawl and shake the pattern, I got up and ran to help her.

I pulled and she shook, I shook and she pulled, and before morning we had peeled off yards of that paper.

A strip about as high as my head and half around the room.

And then when the sun came and that awful pattern began to laugh at me, I declared I would finish it to-day!

We go away to-morrow, and they are moving all my furniture down again to leave things as they were before.

Jennie looked at the wall in amazement, but I told her merrily that I did it out of pure spite at the vicious thing.

She laughed and said she wouldn't mind doing it herself, but I must not get tired.

How she betrayed herself that time!

But I am here, and no person touches this paper but me,—not *alive!*

She tried to get me out of the room—it was too patent! But I said it was so quiet and empty and clean now that I believed I would lie down again and sleep all I could; and not to wake me even for dinner—I would call when I woke.

So now she is gone, and the servants are gone, and the things are gone, and there is nothing left but that great bedstead nailed down, with the canvas mattress we found on it.

We shall sleep downstairs to-night, and take the boat home to-morrow.

I quite enjoy the room, now it is bare again.

How those children did tear about here!

This bedstead is fairly gnawed!

But I must get to work.

I have locked the door and thrown the key down into the front path.

I don't want to go out, and I don't want to have anybody come in, till John comes.

I want to astonish him.

I've got a rope up here that even Jennie did not find. If that woman does get out, and tries to get away, I can tie her!

But I forgot I could not reach far without anything to stand on!

This bed will *not* move!

I tried to lift and push it until I was lame, and then I got so angry I bit off a little piece at one corner—but it hurt my teeth.

Then I peeled off all the paper I could reach standing on the floor. It sticks horribly and the pattern just enjoys it! All those strangled heads and bulbous eyes and waddling fungus growths just shriek with derision!

I am getting angry enough to do something desperate. To jump out of the window would be admirable exercise, but the bars are too strong even to try.

Besides I wouldn't do it. Of course not. I know well enough that a step like that is improper and might be misconstrued.

I don't like to *look* out of the windows even—there are so many of those creeping women, and they creep so fast.

I wonder if they all come out of that wallpaper as I did?

But I am securely fastened now by my well-hidden rope—you don't get *me* out in the road there!

I suppose I shall have to get back behind the pattern when it comes night, and that is hard!

It is so pleasant to be out in this great room and creep around as I please!

I don't want to go outside. I won't, even if Jennie asks me to.

For outside you have to creep on the ground, and everything is green instead of yellow.

But here I can creep smoothly on the floor, and my shoulder just fits in that long smooch around the wall, so I cannot lose my way.

Why there's John at the door!

It is no use, young man, you can't open it!

How he does call and pound!

Now he's crying for an axe.

It would be a shame to break down that beautiful door!

"John dear!" said I in the gentlest voice, "the key is down by the front steps, under a plantain leaf!"

That silenced him for a few moments.

Then he said—very quietly indeed, "Open the door, my darling!"

"I can't," said I. "The key is down by the front door under a plantain leaf!"

And then I said it again, several times, very gently and slowly, and said it so often that he had to go and see, and he got it of course, and came in. He stopped short by the door.

"What is the matter?" he cried. "For God's sake, what are you doing!"

I kept on creeping just the same, but I looked at him over my shoulder.

"I've got out at last," said I, "in spite of you and Jane? And I've pulled off most of the paper, so you can't put me back!"

Now why should that man have fainted? But he did, and right across my path by the wall, so that I had to creep over him every time!

—1892

What are your reactions to and questions about this work? The following questions may help provoke some ideas.

Probing the Work

1. Trace the narrator's involvement with the wallpaper and the changes that take place in her perception of it; what does the wallpaper seem to represent here?
2. Examine the *point of view* (see page 66) of this story. How does the perspective from which it is told influence your sympathies? How would the

story change if it were narrated from a different point of view? How might your judgment of the main character change?

Identifying Issues

3. What seems to be the major cause of the narrator's illness? Examine the connections between madness and imprisonment or subjugation.
4. Gilman said that the story "was not intended to drive people crazy, but to save people from being driven crazy." What do you think she meant by this?
5. In *The Madwoman in the Attic* (1979), Sandra Gilbert and Susan Gubar argue that this story of "female confinement and escape" mirrors the progress of nineteenth-century literary women who had to establish their own authority apart from the "patriarchal standards" defined for them. The narrator is "locked away from creativity" by her physician husband, who is treating her for postpartum depression. However, the cure is worse than the disease: unable to write or socialize, she becomes more and more "unhinged." Gilbert and Gubar see the narrator ultimately triumphing "through her own imaginings and creations," which are "mirages of health and freedom."

   To what extent do you agree with Gilbert's and Gubar's conclusion that this story illustrates a kind of triumph? To what extent are women still treated dismissively or improperly for their distinct ailments (such as postpartum depression or menopause)? Are women still "locked away from creativity"? To what degree are women today forced to strive for private triumphs "through [their] own imaginings and creations" because their expression is squelched by society?

SYLVIA PLATH

Lady Lazarus[1]

Sylvia Plath (1932–1963) was an excellent student, winning poetry prizes, scholarships at Smith College (graduating summa cum laude*), and a Fullbright Scholarship to Cambridge University, where she met and married the English poet Ted Hughes. After two children, several books of poetry (including her best and last,* Ariel*), bouts with depression, and failed suicide attempts, she took her own life at the age of 30.*

I have done it again.
One year in every ten
I manage it—

[1]Lazarus was raised from the dead by Jesus (John 11.1–45).

A sort of walking miracle, my skin
Bright as a Nazi lampshade,°
My right foot

A paperweight,
My face a featureless, fine
Jew linen.

Peel off the napkin
O my enemy.
Do I terrify?—

The nose, the eye pits, the full set of teeth?
The sour breath
Will vanish in a day.

Soon, soon the flesh
The grave cave ate will be
At home on me

And I a smiling woman.
I am only thirty.
And like the cat I have nine times to die.

This is Number Three.
What a trash
To annihilate each decade.

What a million filaments.
The peanut-crunching crowd
Shoves in to see

Them unwrap me hand and foot—
The big strip tease.
Gentleman, ladies,

These are my hands,
My knees.
I may be skin and bone,

Nevertheless, I am the same, identical woman.
The first time it happened I was ten.
It was an accident.

The second time I meant
To last it out and not come back at all.
I rocked shut

5. Nazi lampshade, In the Nazi death camps, the skins of victims were sometimes used to make lampshades.

As a seashell.
They had to call and call
And pick the worms off me like sticky pearls.

Dying
Is an art, like everything else.
I do it exceptionally well.

I do it so it feels like hell.
I do it so it feels real.
I guess you could say I've a call.

It's easy enough to do it in a cell
It's easy enough to do it and stay put.
It's the theatrical

Comeback in broad day
To the same place, the same face, the same brute
Amused shout:

"A miracle!"
That knocks me out.
There is a charge

For the eyeing of my scars, there is a charge
For the hearing of my heart—
It really goes.

And there is a charge, a very large charge,
For a word or a touch
Or a bit of blood

Or a piece of my hair or my clothes.
So, so, Herr° Doktor.
So, Herr Enemy.

I am your opus,
I am your valuable,
The pure gold baby

That melts to a shriek.
I turn and burn.
Do not think I underestimate your great concern.

Ash, ash—
You poke and stir.
Flesh, bone, there is nothing there—

65. Herr, Mr.

A cake of soap,
A wedding ring,
A gold filling.

Herr God, Herr Lucifer,
Beware
Beware.

Out of the ash°
I rise with my red hair
And I eat men like air.

—1962

What are your reactions to and questions about this work? The following questions may help provoke some ideas.

Probing the Work

1. What is the *tone* (see page 67) of this poem? What is the speaker's attitude? Is it consistent throughout the poem? If not, where does it change, and why?
2. Find an *image* (see page 79) or *metaphor* (see page 68) whose relevance is not quite clear to you. Speculate thoughtfully about what Plath might be trying to express through her use of it.

Identifying Issues

3. Is a person's obsession with suicide a sign of madness? Why or why not?
4. How is the outside world depicted here? To what extent are other people responsible for the narrator's condition—her state of mind?

SHIGA NAOYA

Han's Crime

(translated by Lane Dunlop)

Shiga Naoya (1883–1971) was born into a rich family in Japan, in the harbor town of Ishinomaki. His mother died when he was 12; his father, a bank official, married again, and although Shiga got along with his stepmother, he quarreled often with his father. He published one novel, A Dark Night's Passing, *but he is chiefly known for his short stories.*

82. Out of the ash, an allusion to the phoenix, a mythical bird (the only one of its kind) said to live in the Arabian desert; after five to six hundred years, the bird dies by fire and is reborn out of its own ashes.

In an unusual incident, a young Chinese juggler called Han severed his wife's carotid artery during a performance with a knife the size of a carver. The young wife died on the spot. Han was immediately arrested.

The act was witnessed by the owner-manager of the troupe, a Chinese stagehand, the introducer, and an audience of over three hundred. A policeman, sitting on a chair set up slightly above and at the edge of the audience, also saw it. But it was not at all known whether this incident, which had occurred before so many eyes, was a deliberate act or an accident.

For this performance, Han made his wife stand in front of a thick board the size of a rain shutter. From a distance of twelve feet, he hurled several of the carver-sized knives, each with a shout, to form an outline of her body not two inches removed from it.

The judge commenced by interrogating the owner-manager.

"Is that performance a particularly difficult one?"

"No. For an experienced performer, it is not that difficult. All that's required is an alert, healthy state of mind."

"If that's so, an incident like this should not have happened even as a mistake."

"Of course, unless one is sure of the performer—extremely sure—one cannot allow the performance."

"Well, then. Do you think it was a deliberate act?"

"No. I don't. The performance requires experience, instinctive skill and nothing else. But one cannot say that it will always come off with a machine-like precision. It's a fact that we never thought something like this would happen. But I do not think it is fair, now that it *has* happened, to say that we had considered the possibility and hold it against us."

"Well, what do you think it was?"

"I don't know."

The judge was perplexed. There was, here, the fact of homicide. But there was absolutely no proof as to whether it was premeditated murder or manslaughter (if the former, the judge thought, there was never such a cunning murder as this). Next calling in the Chinese stagehand, who had served with the troupe longer than Han, the judge questioned him.

"What is Han's ordinary behavior like?"

"He's a good person. He doesn't gamble, fool around with other women, or drink. About a year ago, he converted to Christianity. His English is good, and when he has the time he often reads collections of sermons."

"And his wife?"

"She was a good person too. As you know, people of our sort aren't always known for their strict morals. One often hears of somebody running off with somebody else's wife. Han's wife was a beautiful woman, although on the small side, and she now and then got solicitations of that sort. But she never took up with such people."

"What were their dispositions like?"

"Toward others, they were both extremely kind and gentle. They never thought of themselves and never got angry. And yet" (here the stagehand paused. Thinking a moment, he went on) "I'm afraid this may be to Han's detriment, but to tell the truth, strangely enough, those two, who were so kind, gentle, and self-effacing with others, when it came to their own relationship, were surprisingly cruel to each other."

"Why was that?"

"I don't know why."

"Had they always been that way?"

"No. About two years ago, the wife gave birth. The baby was premature, and died in three days or so. But after that, it was clear even to us that their relationship was slowly going to the bad. They would often have arguments over the most trivial things. At such times, Han would suddenly turn dead pale. But in the end, no matter what, he always fell silent. He never mistreated his wife. Of course, that's most likely because his religion forbade him to. But sometimes, when you looked at his face, there was a terrible, uncontrollable anger in it. Once, I suggested that if things were so bad between them it might be good to get a divorce. But Han said that even if his wife had reasons for seeking a divorce, he himself had none. Han followed his own will in the matter. He even said that there was no way he could love his wife. It was only natural, he said, if a woman he did not love gradually came not to love him. It was why he took to reading the Bible and collections of sermons. He seemed to think that by somehow calming his heart he could correct his fairly unruly feelings of hatred. After all, he had no reason to hate his wife. She, too, deserved sympathy. After their marriage, they had travelled about as road-players for nearly three years. Owing to an older brother's profligacy, the family back home was already broken up and gone. Even if she had left Han and gone back, nobody would have trusted a woman who'd been on the road four years enough to marry her. Bad as things were, she had no choice but to stay with Han."

"What is *your* opinion of the incident?"

"You mean whether it was deliberate or an accident?"

"Yes."

"Actually, I've thought a lot about that. But the more I've thought, the more I've come, by degrees, not to understand anything."

"Why is that?"

"I don't know why. I really do not. I think anyone would have the same problem. I asked the introducer what he thought, but he said he didn't know either."

"Well, at the instant it happened, what did you think?"

"I thought: He's murdered her. I did think that."

"Is that so?"

"But the introducer told me that he thought: He's bungled it."

"Is that so? But isn't that what he would think, not knowing too much about their relationship?"

"Maybe so. But later, I thought that my thinking he'd murdered her might also, in the same way, simply have been because I knew a good deal about their relationship."

"What was Han's demeanor just then?"

"He gave a short cry: 'Aa!' That was what drew my attention to what had happened. The blood suddenly gushed out of the wife's neck. Even so, she remained upright for a moment. Her body was held in place by the knife's sticking in the board behind her. Then, all of a sudden, her knees buckled, the knife came out and collapsing all together she fell forward. There was nothing anyone could do. We all of us just went stiff and watched. But I can't be sure of anything. I didn't have the leisure to observe Han's demeanor just then. But it seems to me that for those few seconds he was just like us. It was only afterward that I thought: He's murdered her at last. Han went dead pale and stood there with his eyes closed. We drew the curtain down and tried to revive the woman, but she was already dead. Han, his face bluish with excitement, blurted out: 'How could I make such a blunder?' Then he knelt, in a long silent prayer."

"Was his demeanor agitated then?"

"It was somewhat agitated."

"Good. If I have any further questions, I'll call you."

Dismissing the Chinese stagehand, the judge finally had Han himself brought in. Han, his face drawn and pale, was an intelligent-looking man. It was clear at a glance to the judge that he was suffering from nervous exhaustion. As soon as Han had seated himself, the judge said: "I've been questioning the owner-manager and the stagehand. I will now ask you some questions." Han nodded.

"Have you never loved your wife at all?"

"From the day I married her until the day she had the baby, I loved my wife with all my heart."

"Why did the birth become a source of discord?"

"Because I knew it wasn't my child."

"Do you know who the father was?"

"I have an idea it was my wife's cousin."

"Did you know the man?"

"He was a close friend of mine. It was he who suggested that we get married. He introduced me to her."

"Was there a relationship before she married you?"

"Of course there was. The baby was born the eighth month after the marriage."

"The stagehand said it was a premature birth."

"That's because I told him it was."

"The baby died shortly afterwards?"

"Yes."

"What was the cause of death?"

"It choked at the breast."

"Was that a deliberate act of your wife's?"

"She said it was an accident."

The judge, falling silent, looked intently at Han. Han, eyes lowered in his raised face, waited for the next question.

"Did your wife tell you about the relationship?"

"No, she didn't. Nor did I ask her about it. I felt that the baby's death was a judgement on her for what she'd done. I thought that I myself should be as forgiving as possible."

"But, in the end, you couldn't forgive her?"

"That's right. My feeling remained that the baby's death wasn't enough of a judgement. At times, when I thought about it by myself, I could be rather forgiving. But then, my wife would come in. She would go about her business. As I looked at her, at her body, I could not keep down my displeasure."

"You didn't think of divorcing her?"

"I often thought I'd like a divorce. But I never said anything."

"Why was that?"

"I was weak. And my wife had said that if I divorced her she would not survive."

"Did your wife love you?"

"She did not love me."

"If that was so, why did she say such a thing?"

"I think it was from the necessity of going on living. Her brother had broken up the household back home, and she knew that no respectable man would marry a woman who'd been the wife of a road-player. And her feet were too small for ordinary work."

"What were your sexual relations?"

"I believe they were probably not much different from those of an average couple."

"Did your wife feel any sympathy for you?"

"I can't think she felt any sympathy. I believe that for my wife living with me was an extraordinary hardship. But the patience with which she endured that hardship was beyond what one would have thought possible even for a man. My wife simply observed, with cruel eyes, the gradual destruction of my life. My writhing, desperate attempts to save myself, to enter upon my true life, she coolly, from the side and without the slightest wish to help, as if surrounding me, looked on at."

"Why were you unable to take a more assertive, resolute attitude?"

"Because I was thinking about various things."

"Various things? What sort of things?"

"I thought I would act in such a way as to leave no room for error. But, in the end, those thoughts never offered any solution."

"Did you ever think of killing your wife?"

Han did not answer. The judge repeated his question. Even then, Han did not answer immediately. Then, he said:

"I'd often thought, before then, that it would be good if she were dead."

"Then, if the law had allowed it, you might have killed her?"

"I was afraid of the law, and I had never had such thoughts before. It was merely because I was weak. But even though I was weak, my desire to live my own life was strong."

"So, after that, you thought about killing your wife?"

"I didn't make my mind up to it. But I did think about it."

"How long before the incident was this?"

"The night before. Toward daybreak."

"Had you quarrelled that evening?"

"Yes."

"What about?"

"Something so trivial it isn't worth mentioning."

"Tell me anyway."

"It was about food. When I'm hungry, I get irritable. The way she dawdled over the preparations for supper made me angry."

"Did you quarrel more violently than usual?"

"No. But I remained excited longer than usual. It was because lately I'd felt intolerably frustrated by the fact that I did not have a life of my own. I went to bed, but I couldn't sleep at all. I thought about all sorts of things. I felt as if my present existence in which, like a grub suspended in midair, I looked to one side and the other, always hesitating, without the courage to want what I wanted, without the courage to get rid of what was unbearable, was all due to my relationship with my wife. I could see no light in my future. A desire to seek the light was burning inside me. Or, if it was not, it was trying to catch fire. But my relationship with my wife would not let it. The flame was not out. It was smouldering, in a fitful, ugly way. What with the pain and unhappiness of it all, I was being poisoned. When the poisoning was complete, I would die. Although alive, I would be a dead man. And though this was what I had come to, I was still trying to put up with it. It would be good if she died—one part of me kept having that dirty, hateful thought. If this was how things were, why didn't I kill her? The consequences of such an act did not trouble me now. I might be put in jail. Who could tell how much better life in jail might be than this life? I would cross that bridge when I came to it. It would be enough if, in any way I could, I broke through whatever came up at the time it came up. Even if I broke through, and broke through, I might not break through all the way. But if I went on breaking through until the day I died, that would be my true life. I almost forgot that my wife was lying beside me. At last, I grew tired. But even though I was tired, it was not the sort of fatigue that leads to sleep. My thoughts began to blur. As my tensed up feelings relaxed, my dark thoughts of murder faded away. A feeling of loneliness came over me, as after a nightmare. I even felt pity for my own weak spirit, that the ability to think hard had, in a single night, become so feeble and forlorn. And then, at last, the night was over. It seemed to me that my wife hadn't slept either."

"When you got up, was everything as usual between you?"

"Neither of us said a word to each other."

"Why didn't you think of leaving your wife?"

"Do you mean that as a desired result, it would have come to the same thing?"

"Yes."

"For me, there was a great difference."

Saying this, Han looked at the judge and was silent. The judge, his face softening, nodded.

"But, between my thinking about such a thing and actually deciding to kill her, there was still a wide gap. That day, from early morning on, I felt insanely keyed up. Because of my bodily fatigue, my nerves were edgy, without elasticity. Unable to remain still, I stayed outside all morning. I walked about restlessly, away from the others. I kept thinking that no matter what I would have to do something. But I no longer thought of killing her, as I had the night before. And I was not at all worried about that day's performance. If I had been, I would not have chosen that particular act. We had many other acts. Finally, that evening, our turn came. Then also, I was not thinking of such a thing. As usual, I demonstrated to the audience that the knives were sharp by slicing through a slice of paper and sticking a knife into the stage. My wife, heavily made up and wearing a gaudy Chinese costume, came on. Her stage manner was no different from always. Greeting the audience with a winsome smile, she stepped up to the thick board and stood bolt upright with her back to it. A knife in my hand, I stood at a set distance straight across from her. For the first time since the night before, we exchanged looks. Only then did I realize the danger of having chosen this act for tonight. Unless I practiced the utmost care, I thought, there would be trouble. I must alleviate, as best I could, the day's restless agitation and my strained, edgy nerves. But no matter how I tried, a weariness that had eaten into my heart would not let me. I began to feel that I would not trust my own arm. Closing my eyes, I attempted to calm myself. My body started to sway. The moment came. I drove in the first knife above her head. It went in slightly higher than usual. Then I drove in one knife each under the pits of her arms which were raised to shoulder level. As each knife left my fingertips, something clung to it an instant, as if to hold it back. I felt as if I no longer knew where the knives would go in. Each time one hit, I thought: Thank God. Calm down, calm down, I thought. But I could feel in my arm the constraint that comes from a thing's having become conscious. I drove in a knife to the left of her throat. I was about to drive in the next one to the right, when suddenly a strange look came over her face. She must have felt an impulse of violent fear. Did she have a premonition that the knife about to fly at her would go through her neck? I don't know. I only felt that face of violent fear, thrown back at my heart with the same force as the knife. Dizziness struck me. But even so, with all my strength, almost without a target, as though aiming in the dark, I threw the knife . . ."

The judge was silent.

"I've killed her at last, I thought."

"How do you mean? That you'd done it on purpose?"

"Yes. I suddenly felt as if I had."

"Afterwards, you knelt by the body in silent prayer . . . ?"

"That was a trick that occurred to me at the moment. I knew everyone thought I seriously believed in Christianity. While pretending to pray, I was thinking about what attitude I should take."

"You felt sure that what you'd done was intentional?"

"Yes. And I thought right away I could make out it was an accident."

"But why did you think it was deliberate murder?"

"Because of my feelings, which were unhinged."

"So you thought you'd skillfully deceived the others?"

"Thinking about it later, I was shocked at myself. I acted surprised in a natural manner, was considerably agitated, and also displayed grief. But any perceptive person, I believe, could have seen that I was playacting. Recalling my behavior, I sweated cold sweat. That night, I decided that I would have to be found innocent. First of all, I was extremely encouraged by the fact that there was not a scrap of objective proof of my crime. Everyone knew we'd been on bad terms, of course, so there was bound to be a suspicion of murder. I couldn't do anything about that. But if I insisted, throughout, that it was an accident, that would be the end of it. That we'd gotten along badly might make people conjecture, but it was no proof. In the end, I thought, I would be acquitted for lack of evidence. Thinking back over the incident, I made up a rough version of my plea, as plausible as possible, so that it would seem like an accident. Soon, though, for some reason, a doubt rose up in me as to whether I myself believed it was murder. The night before, I had thought about killing her, but was that alone a reason for deciding, myself, that it was murder? Gradually, despite myself, I became unsure. A sudden excitement swept over me. I felt so excited I couldn't sit still. I was so happy, I was beside myself. I wanted to shout for joy."

"Was it because you yourself could now believe that it was an accident?"

"No. I'm still unsure of that. It was because it was completely unclear, even to myself, which it had been. It was because I could now tell the truth and be found innocent. Being found innocent meant everything to me now. For that purpose, rather than trying to deceive myself and insisting that it was an accident, it was far better to be able to be honest, even if it meant saying I didn't know which it was. I could no longer assert that it was an accident, nor, on the other hand, could I say that it was a deliberate act. I was so happy because come what may it was no longer a question of a confession of guilt."

Han felt silent. The judge, also, was silent for a moment. Then, as if to himself, he said: "On the whole, it seems to be the truth." And then: "By the way, do you not feel the slightest sorrow about your wife's death?"

"None whatsoever. And up to now, no matter what my feelings of hatred for her, I never imagined that I'd be able to talk so cheerfully about her death."

"That will be all. You may step down," the judge said. Han, after a slight wordless bow, left the room.

The judge felt an excitement, he could not put a name to it, surge up in him.

Quickly, he took up his pen. And, then and there, he wrote: "Innocent."

—1913

What are your reactions to and questions about this work? The following questions may help provoke some ideas.

Probing the Work

1. What evidence can you find to illustrate Han's guilt? His innocence? What evidence indicates the murder was premeditated? What evidence indicates it was accidental?

Identifying Issues

2. Most psychologists believe that a good percentage of our actions are determined by our subconscious. To what extent do you feel this to be true, in this story, and in your life? Think of an example or two that would illustrate your opinion.

WRITING ASSIGNMENT SEQUENCE (CONTINUED FROM PAGE 830)

4. Making Connections

Select one of the following questions and write an informal response in which you connect your own ideas with those conveyed in the works of this cluster, and/or make connections among the works themselves.

A. What are the various degrees of "madness" illustrated in the works of this cluster?

B. How do these writers depict the boundaries between sanity and insanity, between the conscious and unconscious minds?

5. Putting It All Together

Write an essay that combines what you think about the topic *Much Madness* with what you now understand about the readings.

- Collect your informal writing, notes, and reading-journal entries on this topic and explain what will be the focus of your essay.
- Outline your essay. Select the literary passages and personal details you might use to illustrate and support your main focus.
- Write a draft of your essay in which you bring together what you think about the subject with what you understand about the readings. Try to include in your draft one or more *literary terms.*
- Share what you've written with your classmates and instructor, then revise it according to their recommendations.

Writing Tip: Using Parallel Structure

When you maintain parallelism—coordinate ideas grammatically—you help achieve order, balance, and economy in your sentences. Here's an example from Janet's paper, with her use of parallel structure in *italics:*

> Women have been stereotyped by the male-dominated society as *inferior, separate and unequal.* In the past, the "ideal woman" was *passive, submissive and meek.* Many believe that now, the feminist movement has stripped women of their so-called "feminine" characteristics, and they have become *aggressive, dominating, and overly ambitious.* But women should have the opportunity to express themselves, and succeed in everything they do, without being shackled by stereotypes.

CrossClusters

In your paper you might want to consider how the following works located elsewhere in this book depict the boundaries of sanity and madness:

- Joyce Carol Oates, "Where Are You Going, Where Have You Been?" (p. 198)
- Susan Glaspell, "Trifles" (p. 220)
- Audre Lorde, "Power" (p. 251)
- Frank O'Connor, "My Oedipus Complex" (p. 350)
- Anne Sexton, "The Fury of Overshoes" (p. 359)
- Audre Lorde, "Hanging Fire" (p. 361)
- Cynthia Ozick, "The Shawl" (p. 381)

- Sam Shepard, *True West* (p. 502)
- Tony Kushner, from *Angels in America* (p. 621)
- Nathaniel Hawthorne, "The Birth-mark" (p. 633)
- Kate Chopin, "The Story of an Hour" (p. 646)
- William Shakespeare, *A Midsummer-Night's Dream* (p. 766)
- Eugène Ionesco, *The Lesson* (p. 904)
- Isabel Allende, "And of Clay Are We Created" (p. 996)

Sample Essay

Here is Jessica's draft on the "Much Madness" cluster.

"Guilty or Innocent by Reason of Insanity," by Jessica McAlpine

Is it possible for people to be so overcome with emotion that they are motivated to kill another? This question is explored in "The Tell-Tale Heart," by Edgar Allan Poe, "Han's Crime," by Shiga Naoya and "Porphyria's Lover," by Robert Browning. When a murder occurs in each work, the criminal's frame of mind at the time of the crime is unclear. The reader is urged to contemplate whether or not obsession can push a person over the fine line between sanity and insanity. The conclusion to this matter, in turn, can determine whether the killer is guilty or "innocent" by reason of insanity.

The narrator of "The Tell-Tale Heart" claims to be driven to murder by an obsession with a seemingly harmless object—the eye of an old man. The film-covered, pale blue eye torments him to the point that he feels he must take action; "I made up my mind to take the life of the old man, and thus rid myself of the eye forever" (Poe 835). Though this plan appears to be that of a madman, the narrator makes a rather obvious point of establishing his sanity at the time of the murder. As he tells of his procedure, he remarks, "Madmen know nothing. But you should have seen me" (835). The fact that he repeatedly claims to be sane hints that he is insecure and unsure of his own state of mind. He seems to be denying the possibility of insanity to reassure himself.

The narrator also shows other signs of madness. Right before the murder, his insecurities and anger cause his own heart to beat loud and fast within his chest—the noise which he mistakes for the beating of the old man's heart. This noise enrages him and pushes him over the edge. "So strange a noise as this excited me to uncontrollable terror" (837). He is haunted by the noise once again when he is being questioned by the police officers, and desperately tries to stop it: "Oh God! what *could* I do? I foamed—I raved—I swore! . . . but the noise arose overall and continually increased" (838). When he can take no more, he confesses his crime in a fit of madness. Although the murder was premeditated and the narrator describes the crime very coherently, his actions suggest that he is insane.

"Porphyria's Lover" focuses on the topic of obsessive love. The speaker tells of Porphyria, a young woman whose beauty and purity overwhelm him. He feels sure that she loves him with an intensity that equals his own, but he leads the reader to believe that something is keeping them from being together. She tries to explain why she can't give herself to him,

> Murmuring how she loved me—she
>   Too weak, for all her heart's endeavor,
> To set its struggling passion free
>   From pride, and vainer ties dissever,
> And give herself to me forever. (Browning 841)

These lines imply that Porphyria cannot break away from the ties that are keeping her away from her lover, despite the great affection she feels for him. As the man contemplates this matter, he seems to grow quite insecure at the thought of losing her and feels that he must take action in order to keep her. Impulsively, he decides to strangle Porphyria with her own hair in what appears to be an attempt to preserve her love for him and release her from the troubles that are straining their relationship. His goal accomplished, the man continues to act as if his lover is still alive, holding and caressing her. These are most definitely the actions of a madman.

> Her head, which droops upon it (his shoulder) still:
>   The smiling rosy little head,
> So glad it has its utmost will,
>   That all it scorned at once is fled,
> And I, its love, am gained instead! (841)

The speaker feels no guilt for his actions because he honestly believes that he did the right thing to please the woman he loves, which is also a symptom of his insanity.

In "Han's Crime," a man kills his wife during a knife-throwing act in the circus. When questioned at his trial, nobody can be sure whether the incident was an accident or deliberate murder; even Han himself is unsure. On the surface, Han appears to be a kind, gentle man and an all-around good citizen. Deeply hidden, however, are mental problems and insecurities caused by his wife.

When asked if he has ever loved his wife, Han answers that he had strong feelings for her up until the day that her baby was born. He goes on to explain that on that day he came to the conclusion that the baby was not his, but that of his wife's cousin. He also feels that his wife married him for the sole purpose of security. The baby "accidentally" choked to death while being breast fed soon after it was born, and Han "felt that the baby's death was a judgment on her for what she'd done" (Naoya 863). However, a "feeling remained that the baby's death wasn't enough of a judgment" (863). This problem continued to gnaw at him throughout the remainder of their time together. Although Han was very unhappy with his marriage, his wife begged him to stay with her and, in turn, made his life miserable: "My wife simply observed, with cruel eyes, the gradual destruction of my life" (863). Han felt as if he was being "poisoned," and "felt intolerably frustrated by the fact that he did not have a life of his own" (863).

Han lay awake the entire night before the fatal performance thinking about his troubles, which increased in intensity the more he concentrated on them. This made him very irritable and could possibly have kept him from performing the act perfectly the next day. Han commented that, "That day, from early morning on, I felt insanely keyed up" (864). That statement alone is a strong argument against his sanity. The way that Han describes the moments before the murder leaves little doubt that he was in a very unstable frame of mind.

Whenever a murder occurs, the sanity of the suspected killer is analyzed to help establish a motive for the killing. In each of the above works, the sanity of the murderer is questionable and is pertinent in determining the character's guilt or innocence. While madness is hinted at in each case, the final decision is left up to the reader.

22

THE LESSON

WRITING ASSIGNMENT SEQUENCE

1. Thinking About . . . Lessons

Brainstorming: Write a list of words, people, or events associated with moments in your life when you truly learned something, and matured as a result of that learning experience. (For more on *brainstorming* see page 26.)

2. Enacting the Topic

Interview: Interview a student or faculty member at your school and ask him or her to describe an incident when true learning took place, either inside or outside the classroom. What were the ingredients of this true learning experience?

3. Responding to the Readings

As you read the works in this cluster, jot down in your response journals questions you have about the works, and comment on passages you find provocative or puzzling. Consider the questions following each reading for journal writing and prepare to discuss your reactions in class.

CLUSTER ESSAY

WILLIAM ZINSSER

College Pressures

Born in New York and educated at Princeton, William Zinsser (b. 1922) worked for the New York Herald Tribune *as a features editor, drama editor, film critic, and editorialist. In the 1970s he taught at Yale University. His works include* On Writing Well *and* Writing with a Word Processor. *He is currently a freelance writer.*

Dear Carlos: I desperately need a dean's excuse for my chem midterm which will begin in about one hour. All I can say is that I totally blew it this week. I've fallen incredibly, inconceivably behind.

Carlos: Help! I'm anxious to hear from you. I'll be in my room and won't leave it until I hear from you. Tomorrow is the last day for . . .

Carlos: I left town because I started bugging out again. I stayed up all night to finish a take-home make-up exam and am typing it to hand in on the tenth. It was due on the fifth. P.S. I'm going to the dentist. Pain is pretty bad.

Carlos: Probably by Friday I'll be able to get back to my studies. Right now I'm going to take a long walk. This whole thing has taken a lot out of me.

Carlos: I'm really up the proverbial creek. The problem is I really *bombed* the history final. Since I need that course for my major I . . .

Carlos: Here follows a tale of woe. I went home this weekend, had to help my Mom, and caught a fever so didn't have much time to study. My professor . . .

Carlos: Aargh! Trouble. Nothing original but everything's piling up at once. To be brief, my job interview . . .

Hey Carlos, good news! I've got mononucleosis.

Who are these wretched supplicants, scribbling notes so laden with anxiety, seeking such miracles of postponement and balm? They are men and women who belong to Branford College, one of the twelve residential colleges at Yale University, and the messages are just a few of the hundreds that they left for their dean, Carlos Hortas—often slipped under his door at 4 a.m.—last year.

But students like the ones who wrote those notes can also be found on campuses from coast to coast—especially in New England and at many other private colleges across the country that have high academic standards and highly motivated students. Nobody could doubt that the notes are real. In their urgency and their gallows humor they are authentic voices of a generation that is panicky to succeed.

My own connection with the message writers is that I am master of Branford College. I live in its Gothic quadrangle and know the students well. (We have 485 of them.) I am privy to their hopes and fears—and also to their stereo music and their piercing cries in the dead of night ("Does anybody *ca-a-are?*"). If they went to Carlos to ask how to get through tomorrow, they come to me to ask how to get through the rest of their lives.

Mainly I try to remind them that the road ahead is a long one and that it will have more unexpected turns than they think. There will be plenty of time to change jobs, change careers, change whole attitudes and approaches. They don't want to hear such liberating news. They want a map—right now—that they can follow unswervingly to career security, financial security, Social Security and, presumably, a prepaid grave.

What I wish for all students is some release from the clammy grip of the future. I wish them a chance to savor each segment of their education as an experience in itself and not as a grim preparation for the next step. I wish them the right to experiment, to trip and fall, to learn that defeat is as instructive as victory and is not the end of the world.

My wish, of course, is naive. One of the few rights that America does not proclaim is the right to fail. Achievement is the national god, venerated in our media—the million-dollar athlete, the wealthy executive—and glorified in our praise of possessions. In the presence of such a potent state religion, the young are growing up old.

I see four kinds of pressure working on college students today: economic pressure, parental pressure, peer pressure, and self-induced pressure. It is easy to look around for villains—to blame the colleges for charging too much money, the professors for assigning too much work, the parents for pushing their children too far, the students for driving themselves too hard. But there are no villains; only victims.

"In the late 1960s," one dean told me, "the typical question that I got from students was 'Why is there so much suffering in the world?' or 'How can I make a contribution?' Today it's 'Do you think it would look better for getting into law school if I did a double major in history and political science, or just majored in one of them?' " Many other deans confirmed this pattern. One said: "They're trying to find an edge—the intangible something that will look better on paper if two students are about equal."

Note the emphasis on looking better. The transcript has become a sacred document, the passport to security. How one appears on paper is more important than how one appears in person. *A* is for Admirable and *B* is for Borderline, even though, in Yale's official system of grading, *A* means "excellent" and *B* means "very good." Today, looking very good is no longer good enough, especially for students who hope to go on to law school or medical school. They know that entrance into the better schools will be an entrance into the better law firms and better medical practices where they will make a lot of money. They also know that the odds are harsh. Yale Law School, for instance, matriculates 170 students from an applicant pool of 3,700; Harvard enrolls 550 from a pool of 7,000.

It's all very well for those of us who write letters of recommendation for our students to stress the qualities of humanity that will make them good lawyers or doctors. And it's nice to think that admission officers are really reading our letters and looking for the extra dimension of commitment or concern. Still, it would be hard for a student not to visualize these officers shuffling so many transcripts studded with *A*s that they regard a *B* as positively shameful.

The pressure is almost as heavy on students who just want to graduate and get a job. Long gone are the days of the "gentleman's *C*," when students journeyed through college with a certain relaxation, sampling a wide variety of courses—music, art, philosophy, classics, anthropology, poetry, religion—that would send them out as liberally educated men and women. If I were an employer I would rather employ graduates who have this range and curiosity than those who narrowly pursued safe subjects and high grades. I know countless students whose inquiring minds exhilarate me. I like to hear the play of their ideas. I don't know if they are getting *A*s or *C*s, and I don't care. I also like them as people. The country needs them, and they will find satisfying jobs. I tell them to relax. They can't.

Nor can I blame them. They live in a brutal economy. Tuition, room, and board at most private colleges now [1979] comes to at least $7,000, not counting books and fees. This might seem to suggest that the colleges are getting rich. But they are equally battered by inflation. Tuition covers only 60 percent of what it costs to educate a student, and ordinarily the remainder comes from what colleges receive in endowments, grants, and gifts. Now the remainder keeps being swallowed by the cruel costs—higher every year—of just opening the doors. Heating oil is up. Insurance is up. Postage is up. Health-premium costs are up. Everything is up. Deficits are up. We are witnessing in America the creation of a brotherhood of paupers—colleges, parents, and students, joined by the common bond of debt.

Today it is not unusual for a student, even if he works part time at college and full time during the summer, to accrue $5,000 in loans after four years—loans that he must start to repay within one year after graduation. Exhorted at commencement to go forth into the world, he is already behind as he goes forth. How could he not feel under pressure throughout college to prepare for this day of reckoning? I have used "he," incidentally, only for brevity. Women at Yale are under no less pressure to justify their expensive education to themselves, their parents, and society. In fact, they are probably under more pressure. For although they leave college superbly equipped to bring fresh leadership to traditionally male jobs, society hasn't yet caught up with this fact.

Along with economic pressure goes parental pressure. Inevitably, the two are deeply intertwined.

I see many students taking pre-medical courses with joyless tenacity. They go off to their labs as if they were going to the dentist. It saddens me because I know them in other corners of their life as cheerful people.

"Do you want to go to medical school?" I ask them.

"I guess so," they say, without conviction, or "Not really."

"Then why are you going?"

"Well, my parents want me to be a doctor. They're paying all this money and . . ."

Poor students, poor parents. They are caught in one of the oldest webs of love and duty and guilt. The parents mean well; they are trying to steer their sons and daughters toward a secure future. But the sons and daughters want to major in history or classics or philosophy—subjects with no "practical" value. Where's the payoff on the humanities? It's not easy to persuade such loving parents that the humanities do indeed pay off. The intellectual faculties developed by studying subjects like history and classics—an ability to synthesize and relate, to weigh cause and effect, to see events in perspective—are just the faculties that make creative leaders in business or almost any general field. Still, many fathers would rather put their money on courses that point toward a specific profession—courses that are pre-law, pre-medical, pre-business, or, as I sometimes heard it put, "pre-rich."

But the pressure on students is severe. They are truly torn. One part of them feels obligated to fulfill their parents' expectations; after all, their parents are older and presumably wiser. Another part tells them that the expectations that are right for their parents are not right for them.

I know a student who wants to be an artist. She is very obviously an artist and will be a good one—she has already had several modest local exhibits. Meanwhile she is growing as a well-rounded person and taking humanistic subjects that will enrich the inner resources out of which her art will grow. But her father is strongly opposed. He thinks that an artist is a "dumb" thing to be. The student vacillates and tries to please everybody. She keeps up with her art somewhat furtively and takes some of the "dumb" courses her father wants her to take—at least they are dumb courses for her. She is a free spirit on a campus of tense students—no small achievement in itself—and she deserves to follow her muse.

Peer pressure and self-induced pressure are also intertwined, and they begin almost at the beginning of freshman year.

"I had a freshman student I'll call Linda," one dean told me, "who came in and said she was under terrible pressure because her roommate, Barbara, was much brighter and studied all the time. I couldn't tell her that Barbara had come in two hours earlier to say the same thing about Linda."

The story is almost funny—except that it's not. It's symptomatic of all the pressures put together. When every student thinks every other student is working harder and doing better, the only solution is to study harder still. I see students going off to the library every night after dinner and coming back when it closes at midnight. I wish they would sometimes forget about their peers and go to a movie. I hear the clacking of typewriters in the hours before dawn. I see the tension in their eyes when exams are approaching and paper are due: *"Will I get everything done?"*

Probably they won't. They will get sick. They will get "blocked." They will sleep. They will oversleep. They will bug out. *Hey Carlos, help!*

Part of the problem is that they do more than they are expected to do. A professor will assign five-page papers. Several students will start writing ten-page papers to impress him. Then more students will write ten-page papers, and a few will raise the ante to fifteen. Pity the poor student who is still just doing the assignment.

"Once you have twenty or thirty percent of the student population deliberately overexerting," one dean points out, "it's bad for everybody. When a teacher gets more and more effort from his class, the student who is doing normal work can be perceived as not doing well. The tactic works, psychologically."

Why can't the professor just cut back and not accept longer papers? He can, and he probably will. But by then the term will be half over and the damage done. Grade fever is highly contagious and not easily reversed. Besides, the professor's main concern is with his course. He knows his students only in relation to the course and doesn't know that they are also overexerting in their other courses. Nor is it really his business. He didn't sign up for dealing with the student as a whole person and with all the emotional baggage the student brought along from home. That's what deans, masters, chaplains, and psychiatrists are for.

To some extent this is nothing new: a certain number of professors have always been self-contained islands of scholarship and shyness, more comfortable with books than with people. But the new pauperism has widened the gap still further, for professors who actually like to spend time with students don't have as much time to spend. They also are overexerting. If they are young, they are busy trying to publish in order not to perish, hanging by their fingernails onto a shrinking profession. If they are old and tenured, they are buried under the duties of administering departments—as departmental chairmen or members of committees—that have been thinned out by the budgetary axe.

Ultimately it will be the students' own business to break the circles in which they are trapped. They are too young to be prisoners of their parents' dreams and their classmates' fears. They must be jolted into believing in themselves as unique men and women who have the power to shape their own future.

"Violence is being done to the undergraduate experience," says Carlos Hortas. "College should be open-ended: at the end it should open many, many roads. Instead, students are choosing their goal in advance, and their choices narrow as they go along. It's almost as if they think that the country has been codified in the type of jobs that exist—that they've got to fit into certain slots. Therefore, fit into the best-paying slot.

"They ought to take chances. Not taking chances will lead to a life of colorless mediocrity. They'll be comfortable. But something in the spirit will be missing."

I have painted too drab a portrait of today's students, making them seem a solemn lot. That is only half of their story; if they were so dreary I wouldn't so thoroughly enjoy their company. The other half is that they are easy to like. They are quick to laugh and to offer friendship. They are not introverts. They are unusually kind and are more considerate of one another than any student generation I have known.

Nor are they so obsessed with their studies that they avoid sports and extracurricular activities. On the contrary, they juggle their crowded hours to play on a variety of teams, perform with musical and dramatic groups, and write for campus publications. But this in turn is one more cause of anxiety. There are too many choices. Academically, they have 1,300 courses to select from; outside class they have to decide how much spare time they can spare and how to spend it.

This means that they engage in fewer extracurricular pursuits than their predecessors did. If they want to row on the crew and play in the symphony they will eliminate one; in the sixties they would have done both. They also tend to choose activities that are self-limiting. Drama, for instance, is flourishing in all twelve of Yale's residential colleges as it never has before. Students hurl themselves into these productions—as actors, directors, carpenters, and technicians—with a dedication to create the best possible play, knowing that the day will come when the run will end and they can get back to their studies.

They also can't afford to be the willing slave of organizations like the *Yale Daily News*. Last spring at the one-hundredth anniversary banquet of that paper—whose past chairmen include such once and future kings as Potter Stewart, Kingman Brewster, and William F. Buckley, Jr.—much was made of the fact that the editorial staff used to be small and totally committed and that "newsies" routinely worked fifty hours a week. In effect they belonged to a club; Newsies is how they defined themselves at Yale. Today's students will write one or two articles a week, when he can, and he defines himself as a student. I've never heard the word Newsie except at the banquet.

If I have described the modern undergraduate primarily as a driven creature who is largely ignoring the blithe spirit inside who keeps trying to come out and play, it's because that's where the crunch is, not only at Yale but throughout American education. It's why I think we should all be worried about the values that are nurturing a generation so fearful of risk and so goal-obsessed at such an early age.

I tell students that there is no one "right" way to get ahead—that each of them is a different person, starting from a different point and bound for a different destination. I tell them that change is a tonic and that all the slots are not codified nor the frontiers closed. One of my ways of telling them is to invite men and women who have achieved success outside the academic world to come and talk informally with my students during the year. They are heads of companies or ad agencies, editors of magazines, politicians, public officials, television magnates, labor leaders, business executives, Broadway producers, artists, writers, economists, photographers, scientists, historians—a mixed bag of achievers.

I ask them to say a few words about how they got started. The students assume that they started in their present profession and knew all along that it was what they wanted to do. Luckily for me, most of them got into their field by a circuitous route, to their surprise, after many detours. The students are startled. They can hardly conceive of a career that was not pre-planned. They can hardly imagine allowing the hand of God or chance to nudge them down some unforeseen trail.

—1979

What are your reactions to and questions about this work? The following questions may help provoke some ideas.

Probing the Work

1. Categorize the kinds of pressures on college students that Zinsser identifies in this essay. What others have you felt or noticed?

Identifying Issues

2. This essay was published in 1979. Which of the pressures discussed here applies most to college students today? To you in particular?

WALT WHITMAN

When I Heard the Learn'd Astronomer

Walt Whitman (1819–1892), one of the most influential poets in American literature, spent his childhood and young adulthood in the New York area—on Long Island, in Brooklyn, and Manhattan—where he worked as a journalist and printer. In 1855 he wrote and printed the first edition of Leaves of Grass, *a milestone in American poetry. He added to and revised this book for eight more editions before his death in Camden, New Jersey.*

When I heard the learn'd astronomer,
When the proofs, the figures, were ranged in columns before me,
When I was shown the charts and diagrams, to add, divide, and measure them,
When I sitting heard the astronomer where he lectured with much applause in the lecture-room,
How soon unaccountable I became tired and sick,
Till rising and gliding out I wander'd off by myself,
In the mystical moist night-air, and from time to time,
Look'd up in perfect silence at the stars.

—1865

What are your reactions to and questions about this work? The following questions may help provoke some ideas.

Probing the Work

1. What are two kinds of learning described in this poem, and how does the speaker feel about them?

Identifying Issues

2. Which kinds of learning have the most value for you? For your parents? For your teachers? For your peers? Explain your answers.

ANZIA YEZIERSKA

Soap and Water

Anzia Yezierska (1885–1970) was born in the Russian part of Poland and emigrated to New York City with her family around 1890. By the 1920s she made waves with her sympathetic and realistic portrayals of life in New York's lower East Side: such works include Hungry Hearts *(1920),* Children of Loneliness *(1923), and* Bread Givers *(1925), an autobiographical novel. She spent some time in Hollywood but found life there unsavory. Her later works include another autobiographical novel and an autobiography,* Red Ribbon on a White Horse *(1950). Her short stories are collected in the volume* How I Found America.

What I so greatly feared, happened! Miss Whiteside, the dean of our college, withheld my diploma. When I came to her office, and asked her why she did not pass me, she said that she could not recommend me as a teacher because of my personal appearance.

She told me that my skin looked oily, my hair unkempt, and my fingernails sadly neglected. She told me that I was utterly unmindful of the little niceties of the well-groomed lady. She pointed out that my collar did not set evenly, my belt was awry, and there was a lack of freshness in my dress. And she ended with: "Soap and water are cheap. Anyone can be clean."

In those four years while I was under her supervision, I was always timid and diffident. I shrank and trembled when I had to come near her. When I had to say something to her, I mumbled and stuttered, and grew red and white in the face with fear.

Every time I had to come to the dean's office for a private conference, I prepared for the ordeal of her cold scrutiny, as a patient prepares for a surgical operation. I watched her gimlet eyes searching for a stray pin, for a spot on my dress, for my unpolished shoes, for my uncared-for fingernails, as one strapped on the operating table watches the surgeon approaching with his tray of sterilized knives.

She never looked into my eyes. She never perceived that I had a soul. She did not see how I longed for beauty and cleanliness. How I strained and struggled to lift myself from the dead toil and exhaustion that weighed me down.

She could see nothing in people like me, except the dirt and the stains on the outside.

But this last time when she threatened to withhold my diploma, because of my appearance, this last time when she reminded me that "Soap and water are cheap. Anyone can be clean," this last time, something burst within me.

I felt the suppressed wrath of all the unwashed of the earth break loose within me. My eyes blazed fire. I didn't care for myself, nor the dean, nor the whole laundered world. I had suffered the cruelty of their cleanliness and the tyranny of their culture to the breaking point. I was too frenzied to know what I said or did. But I saw clean, immaculate, spotless Miss Whiteside shrivel and tremble and cower before me, as I had shriveled and trembled and cowered before her for so many years.

Why did she give me my diploma? Was it pity? Or can it be that in my outburst of fury, at the climax of indignities that I had suffered, the barriers broke, and she saw into the world below from where I came?

Miss Whiteside had no particular reason for hounding and persecuting me. Personally, she didn't give a hang if I was clean or dirty. She was merely one of the agents of clean society, delegated to judge who is fit and who is unfit to teach.

While they condemned me as unfit to be a teacher, because of my appearance, I was slaving to keep them clean. I was slaving in a laundry from five to eight in the morning, before going to college, and from six to eleven at night, after coming from college. Eight hours of work a day, outside my studies. Where was the time and the strength for the "little niceties of the well-groomed lady"?

At the time when they rose and took their morning bath, and put on their fresh-laundered linen that somebody had made ready for them, when they were being served with their breakfast, I had already toiled for three hours in a laundry.

When the college hours were over, they went for a walk in the fresh air. They had time to rest, and bathe again, and put on fresh clothes for dinner. But I, after college hours, had only time to bolt a soggy meal, and rush back to the grind of the laundry till eleven at night.

At the hour when they came from the theater or musicale, I came from the laundry. But I was so bathed in the sweat of exhaustion that I could not think of a bath of soap and water. I had only strength to drag myself home, and fall down on the bed and sleep. Even if I had had the desire and the energy to take a bath, there were no such things as bathtubs in the house where I lived.

Often as I stood at my board at the laundry, I thought of Miss Whiteside, and her clean world, clothed in the snowy shirtwaists I had ironed. I was thinking—I, soaking in the foul vapors of the steaming laundry, I, with my dirty, tired hands, I am ironing the clean, immaculate shirtwaists of clean, immaculate society. I, the unclean one, am actually fashioning the pedestal of their cleanliness, from which they reach down, hoping to lift me to the height that I have created for them.

I look back at my sweatshop childhood. One day, when I was about sixteen, someone gave me Rosenfeld's poem "The Machine" to read. Like a spark thrown among oil rags, it set my whole being aflame with longing for self-expression. But I was dumb. I had nothing but blind, aching feeling. For days I went about with agonies of feeling, yet utterly at sea how to fathom and voice those feelings—birth-throes of infinite worlds, and yet dumb.

Suddenly, there came upon me this inspiration. I can go to college! There I shall learn to express myself, to voice my thoughts. But I was not prepared to go to college. The girl in the cigar factory, in the next block, had gone first to a preparatory school. Why shouldn't I find a way, too?

Going to college seemed as impossible for me, at that time, as for an ignorant Russian shop-girl to attempt to write poetry in English. But I was sixteen then, and the impossible was a magnet to draw the dreams that had no outlet. Besides, the actual was so barren, so narrow, so strangling, that the dream of the unattainable was the only air in which the soul could survive.

The ideal of going to college was like the birth of a new religion in my soul. It put new fire in my eyes, and new strength in my tired arms and fingers.

For six years I worked daytimes and went at night to a preparatory school. For six years I went about nursing the illusion that college was a place where I should find self-expression, and vague, pent-up feelings could live as thoughts and grow as ideas.

At last I came to college. I rushed for it with the outstretched arms of youth's aching hunger to give and take of life's deepest and highest, and I came against the solid wall of the well-fed, well-dressed world—the frigid whitewashed wall of cleanliness.

Until I came to college I had been unconscious of my clothes. Suddenly I felt people looking at me at arm's length, as if I were crooked or crippled, as if I had come to a place where I didn't belong, and would never be taken in.

How I pinched, and scraped, and starved myself, to save enough to come to college! Every cent of the tuition fee I paid was drops of sweat and blood from underpaid laundry work. And what did I get for it? A crushed spirit, a broken heart, a stinging sense of poverty that I never felt before.

The courses of study I had to swallow to get my diploma were utterly barren of interest to me. I didn't come to college to get dull learning from dead books. I didn't come for that dry, inanimate stuff that can be hammered out in lectures. I came because I longed for the larger life, for the stimulus of intellectual associations. I came because my whole being clamored for more vision, more light. But everywhere I went I saw big fences put up against me, with the brutal signs: "No trespassing. Get off the grass."

I experienced at college the same feeling of years ago when I came to this country, when after months of shut-in-ness, in dark tenements and stifling sweatshops, I had come to Central Park for the first time. Like a bird just out from a cage, I stretched out my arms, and then flung myself in ecstatic abandon on the grass. Just as I began to breathe in the fresh-smelling earth, and lift up my eyes to the sky, a big, fat policeman with a club in his hand, seized me, with: "Can't you read the sign? Get off the grass!" Miss Whiteside, the dean of the college, the representative of the clean, the educated world, for all her external refinement, was to me like that big, brutal policeman, with the club in his hand, that drove me off the grass.

The death-blows to all aspiration began when I graduated from college and tried to get a start at the work for which I had struggled so hard to fit myself. I soon found other agents of clean society, who had the power of giving or withholding the positions I sought, judging me as Miss Whiteside judged me. One glance at my shabby clothes, the desperate anguish that glazed and dulled my eyes and I felt myself condemned by them before I opened my lips to speak.

Starvation forced me to accept the lowest-paid substitute position. And because my wages were so low and so unsteady, I could never get the money for the clothes to make an appearance to secure a position with better pay. I was tricked and foiled. I was considered unfit to get decent pay for my work because of my appearance, and it was to the advantage of those who used me that my appearance should damn me, so as to get me to work for the low wages I was forced to accept. It seemed to me the whole vicious circle of society's injustices was thrust like a noose around my neck to strangle me.

The insults and injuries I had suffered at college had so eaten into my flesh that I could not bear to get near it. I shuddered with horror whenever I had to pass the place blocks away. The hate which I felt for Miss Whiteside spread like poison inside my soul, into hate for all clean society. The whole clean world was massed against me. Whenever I met a well-dressed person, I felt the secret stab of a hidden enemy.

I was so obsessed and consumed with my grievances that I could not get away from myself and think things out in the light. I was in the grip of that blinding, destructive, terrible thing—righteous indignation. I could not rest. I wanted the whole world to know that the college was against democracy in education, that clothes form the basis of class distinctions, that after graduation the opportunities for the best positions are passed out to those who are best-dressed, and the students too poor to put up a front are pigeon-holed and marked unfit and abandoned to the mercy of the wind.

A wild desire raged in the corner of my brain. I knew that the dean gave dinners to the faculty at regular intervals. I longed to burst in at one of those feasts, in the midst of their grand speech-making, and tear down the fine clothes from these well-groomed ladies and gentlemen, and trample them under my feet, and scream like a lunatic: "Soap and water are cheap! Soap and water are cheap! Look at me! See how cheap it is!"

There seemed but three avenues of escape to the torments of my wasted life: madness, suicide, or a heart-to-heart confession to someone who understood. I had not energy enough for suicide. Besides, in my darkest moments of despair, hope clamored loudest. Oh, I longed so to live, to dream my way up on the heights, above the unreal realities that ground me and dragged me down to earth.

Inside the ruin of my thwarted life, the *unlived* visionary immigrant hungered and thirsted for America. I had come a refugee from the Russian pogroms, aflame with dreams of America. I did not find America in the sweatshops, much less in the schools and colleges. But for hundreds of years the persecuted races all over the world were nurtured on hopes of America. When a little baby in my mother's arms, before I was old enough to speak, I saw all around me weary faces light up with thrilling tales of the far-off "golden country." And so, though my faith in this so-called America was shattered, yet underneath, in the sap and roots of my soul, burned the deathless faith that America is, must be, somehow, somewhere. In the midst of my bitterest hates and rebellions, visions of America rose over me, like songs of freedom of an oppressed people.

My body was worn to the bone from overwork, my footsteps dragged with exhaustion, but my eyes still sought the sky, praying, ceaselessly praying, the dumb, inarticulate prayer of the lost immigrant: "America! Ach, America! Where is America?"

It seemed to me if I could only find some human being to whom I could unburden my heart, I would have new strength to begin again my insatiable search for America.

But to whom could I speak? The people in the laundry? They never understood me. They had a grudge against me because I left them when I tried to work myself up. Could I speak to the college people? What did these icebergs of convention know about the vital things of the heart?

And yet, I remembered, in the freshman year, in one of the courses in chemistry, there was an instructor, a woman, who drew me strangely. I felt she was the only real teacher among all the teachers and professors I met. I didn't care for the chemistry, but I liked to look at her. She gave me life, air, the unconscious emanation of her beautiful spirit. I had not spoken a word to her, outside the experiments in chemistry, but I knew her more than the people around her who were of her own class. I felt in the throb of her voice, in the subtle shading around the corner of her eyes, the color and texture of her dreams.

Often in the midst of our work in chemistry I felt like crying out to her: "Oh, please be my friend. I'm so lonely." But something choked me. I couldn't speak. The very intensity of my longing for her friendship made me run away from her in confusion the minute she approached me. I was so conscious of my shabbiness that I was afraid maybe she was only trying to be kind. I couldn't bear kindness. I wanted from her love, understanding, or nothing.

About ten years after I left college, as I walked the streets bowed and beaten with the shame of having to go around begging for work, I met Miss Van Ness. She not only recognized me, but stopped to ask how I was, and what I was doing.

I had begun to think that my only comrades in this world were the homeless and abandoned cats and dogs of the street, whom everybody gives another kick, as they slam the door on them. And here was one from the clean world human enough to be friendly. Here was one of the well-dressed, with a look in her eyes and a sound in her voice that was like healing oil over the bruises of my soul. The mere touch of that woman's hand in mine so overwhelmed me, that I burst out crying in the street.

The next morning I came to Miss Van Ness at her office. In those ten years she had risen to a professorship. But I was not in the least intimidated by her high office. I felt as natural in her presence as if she were my own sister. I heard myself telling her the whole story of my life, but I felt that even if I had not said a word she would have understood all I had to say as if I had spoken. It was all so unutterable, to find one from the other side of the world who was so simply and naturally that miraculous thing—a friend. Just as contact with Miss Whiteside had tied and bound all my thinking processes, so Miss Van Ness unbound and freed me and suffused me with light.

I felt the joy of one breathing on the mountain-tops for the first time. I looked down at the world below. I was changed and the world was changed. My past was the forgotten night. Sunrise was all around me.

I went out from Miss Van Ness's office, singing a song of new life: "America! I found America."

—1920

What are your reactions to and questions about this work? The following questions may help provoke some ideas.

Probing the Work

1. What are the examples of *irony* (see page 79) in this story?
2. What *symbolism* (see page 78) has Yezierska included to support the theme of her story?
3. What is the *tone* (see page 67) of the ending? Why? What has happened? What has the narrator learned, and for whom has she learned it?

Identifying Issues

4. To what extent does your financial obligation to the payment of your tuition affect your attitude toward learning and the degree to which you are involved in the college community?

5. In what way is this story about the kinds of dilemmas faced by immigrant students then and now? How have these problems been addressed at your school, or in your community?

LANGSTON HUGHES

Theme for English B

Langston Hughes (1902–1967) grew up mainly in Lawrence, Kansas, then in Cleveland. He entered Lincoln University (Pennsylvania) in 1926. By the time he graduated three years later, he had published two books of poetry (including The Weary Blues*) and established himself as the best poet of the Harlem (then called the "New Negro") Renaissance. Hughes was also a political activist, dramatist, short-story writer, journalist, songwriter, and translator.*

The instructor said,

Go home and write
a page tonight,
And let that page come out of you—
Then, it will be true.

I wonder if it's that simple?

I am twenty-two, colored, born in Winston-Salem.
I went to school there, then Durham, then here
to this college on the hill above Harlem.
I am the only colored student in my class.
The steps from the hill lead down into Harlem,
through a park, then I cross St. Nicholas,
Eighth Avenue, Seventh, and I come to the Y,
the Harlem Branch Y, where I take the elevator
up to my room, sit down, and write this page:

It's not easy to know what is true for you or me
at twenty-two, my age. But I guess I'm what
I feel and see and hear. Harlem, I hear you:
hear you, hear me—we two—you, me, talk on this page.
(I hear New York, too.) Me—who?
Well, I like to eat, sleep, drink, and be in love.
I like to work, read, learn, and understand life.
I like a pipe for a Christmas present,
or records—Bessie, bop, or Bach.
I guess being colored doesn't make me *not* like
the same things other folks like who are other races.

So will my page be colored that I write?
Being me, it will not be white.
But it will be
a part of you, instructor.
You are white—
yet a part of me, as I am a part of you.
That's American.
Sometimes perhaps you don't want to be a part of me.
Nor do I often want to be a part of you.
But we are, that's true!
As I learn from you,
I guess you learn from me—
although you're older—and white—
and somewhat more free.

This is my page for English B.

—1949

What are your reactions to and questions about this work? The following questions may help provoke some ideas.

Probing the Work

1. What is the speaker's view of his instructor, and of learning in general? Choose a few lines that illustrate his attitude toward either.

Identifying Issues

2. In what sense is the learning process reciprocal?
3. How much of your learning involves crossing cultural, racial, sexual, and class boundaries? What role does college play in this kind of learning?

TONI CADE BAMBARA

The Lesson

Toni Cade (b. 1939)—she adopted the name Bambara *when she discovered it as a signature on a sketchbook in her great-grandmother's trunk—grew up in the kinds of neighborhoods she describes in her fiction—Harlem, Bedford-Stuyvesant, and Queens. She was educated at Queens College and City College, then studied at the Commedia del' Arte in Milan. She learned filmmaking in England, and has studied modern dance and painting. Her books include the short-story collections* Gorilla My Love *(1972), which contains the story below;* The Sea Birds Are Still Alive *(1977); and the novel* The Salt Eaters *(1980), for which she earned an American Book Award.*

Back in the days when everyone was old and stupid or young and foolish and me and Sugar were the only ones just right, this lady moved on our block with nappy hair and proper speech and no makeup. And quite naturally we laughed at her, laughed the way we did at the junk man who went about his business like he was some big-time president and his sorry-ass horse his secretary. And we kinda hated her too, hated the way we did the winos who cluttered up our parks and pissed on our handball walls and stank up our hallways and stairs so you couldn't halfway play hide-and-seek without a goddamn gas mask. Miss Moore was her name. The only woman on the block with no first name. And she was black as hell, cept for her feet, which were fish-white and spooky. And she was always planning these boring-ass things for us to do, us being my cousin, mostly, who lived on the block cause we all moved North the same time and to the same apartment then spread out gradual to breathe. And our parents would yank our heads into some kinda shape and crisp up our clothes so we'd be presentable for travel with Miss Moore, who always looked like she was going to church, though she never did. Which is just one of things the grown-ups talked about when they talked behind her back like a dog. But when she came calling with some sachet she'd sewed up or some gingerbread she'd made or some book, why then they'd all be too embarrassed to turn her down and we'd get handed over all spruced up. She'd been to college and said it was only right that she should take responsibility for the young ones' education, and she not even related by marriage or blood. So they'd go for it. Specially Aunt Gretchen. She was the main gofer in the family. You got some ole dumb shit foolishness you want somebody to go for, you send for Aunt Gretchen. She been screwed into the go-along for so long, it's a blood-deep natural thing with her. Which is how she got saddled with me and Sugar and Junior in the first place while our mothers were in a la-de-da apartment up the block having a good ole time.

So this one day Miss Moore rounds us all up at the mailbox and it's puredee hot and she's knocking herself out about arithmetic. And school suppose to let up in summer I heard, but she don't never let up. And the starch in my pinafore scratching the shit outta me and I'm really hating this nappy-head bitch and her goddamn college degree. I'd much rather go to the pool or to the show where it's cool. So me and Sugar leaning on the mailbox being surly, which is a Miss Moore word. And Flyboy checking out what everybody brought for lunch. And Fat Butt already wasting his peanut-butter-and-jelly sandwich like the pig he is. And Junebug punchin on Q.T.'s arm for potato chips. And Rosie Giraffe shifting from one hip to the other waiting for somebody to step on her foot or ask her if she from Georgia so she can kick ass, preferably Mercedes's. And Miss Moore asking us do we know what money is, like we a bunch of retards. I mean real money, she say, like it's only poker chips or monopoly papers we lay on the grocer. So right away I'm tired of this and say so. And would much rather snatch Sugar and go to the Sunset and terrorize the West Indian kids and take their hair ribbons and their money too. And Miss Moore files that remark away for next week's lesson on brotherhood, I can tell. And finally I say we oughta get to the subway cause it's cooler and besides we might meet some cute boys. Sugar done swiped her mama's lipstick, so we ready.

So we heading down the street and she's boring us silly about what things cost and what our parents make and how much goes for rent and how money ain't divided up right in this country. And then she gets to the part about we all poor and live in the slums, which I don't feature. And I'm ready to speak on that, but she steps out in the street and hails two cabs just like that. Then she hustles half the crew in with her and hands me a five-dollar bill and tells me to calculate 10 percent tip for the driver. And we're off. Me and Sugar and Junebug and Flyboy hanging out the window and hollering to everybody, putting lipstick on each other cause Flyboy a faggot anyway, and making farts with our sweaty armpits. But I'm mostly trying to figure how to spend this money. But they all fascinated with the meter ticking and Junebug starts laying bets as to how much it'll read when Flyboy can't hold his breath no more. Then Sugar lay bets as to how much it'll be when we get there. So I'm stuck. Don't nobody want to go for my plan, which is to jump out at the next light and run off to the first bar-b-que we can find. Then the driver tells us to get the hell out cause we there already. And the meter reads eight-five cents. And I'm stalling to figure out the tip and Sugar say give him a dime. And I decide he don't need it bad as I do, so later for him. But then he tries to take off with Junebug's foot still in the door so we talk about his mama something ferocious. Then we check out that we on Fifth Avenue and everybody dressed up in stockings. One lady in a fur coat, hot as it is. White folks crazy.

"This is the place," Miss Moore say, presenting it to us in the voice she uses at the museum. "Let's look in the windows before we go in."

"Can we steal?" Sugar asks very serious like she's getting the ground rules squared away before she plays. "I beg your pardon," say Miss Moore, and we fall out. So she leads us around the windows of the toy store and me and Sugar screamin, "This is mine, that's mine, I gotta have that, that was made for me, I was born for that," till Big Butt drowns us out.

"Hey, I'm going to buy that there."

"That there? You don't even know what it is, stupid."

"I do so," he say punchin on Rosie Giraffe. "It's a microscope."

"Whatcha gonna do with a microscope, fool?"

"Look at things."

"Like what, Ronald?" ask Miss Moore. And Big Butt ain't got the first notion. So here go Miss Moore gabbing about the thousands of bacteria in a drop of water and the somethinorother in a speck of blood and the million and one living things in the air around us is invisible to the naked eye. And what she say that for? Junebug go to town on that "naked" and we rolling. Then Miss Moore ask what it cost. So we all jam into the window smudgin it up and the price tag say three hundred dollars. So then she ask how long'd take for Big

Butt and Junebug to save up their allowances. "Too long," I say. "Yeh," adds Sugar, "outgrown it by that time." And Miss Moore say no, you never outgrow learning instruments. "Why, even medical students and interns and," blah, blah, blah. And we ready to choke Big Butt for bringing it up in the first damn place.

"This here costs four hundred eighty dollars," say Rosie Giraffe. So we pile up all over her to see what she pointin out. My eyes tell me it's a chunk of glass cracked with something heavy, and different color inks dripped into the splits, then the whole thing put into a oven or something. But for $480 it don't make sense.

"That's a paperweight made of semi-precious stones fused together under tremendous pressure," she explains slowly, with her hands doing the mining and all the factory work.

"So what's a paperweight?" asks Rosie Giraffe.

"To weigh paper with, dumbbell," say Flyboy, the wise man from the East.

"Not exactly," say Miss Moore, which is what she say when you warm or way off too. "It's to weigh paper down so it won't scatter and make your desk untidy." So right away me and Sugar curtsy to each other and then to Mercedes who is more the tidy type.

"We don't keep paper on top of the desk in my class," say Junebug, figuring Miss Moore crazy or lyin one.

"At home, then," she say. "Don't you have a calendar and a pencil case and a blotter and a letter-opener on your desk at home where you do your homework?" And she know damn well what our homes look like cause she nosys around in them every chance she gets.

"I don't even have a desk," say Junebug, "Do we?"

"No. And I don't get no homework neither," says Big Butt.

"And I don't even have a home," say Flyboy like he do at school to keep the white folks off his back and sorry for him. Send this poor kid to camp posters, is his specialty.

"I do," says Mercedes. "I have a box of stationery on my desk and a picture of my cat. My godmother bought the stationery and the desk. There's a big rose on each sheet and the envelopes smell like roses."

"Who wants to know about your smelly-ass stationery," say Rosie Giraffe fore I can get my two cents in.

"It's important to have a work area all your own so that . . ."

"Will you look at this sailboat, please," say Flyboy, cuttin her off and pointin to the thing like it was his. So once again we tumble all over each other to gaze at this magnificent thing in the toy store which is just big enough to maybe sail two kittens across the pond if you strap them to the posts tight. We all start reciting the price tag like we in assembly. "Handcrafted sailboat of fiberglass at one thousand one hundred ninety five dollars."

"Unbelievable," I hear myself say and am really stunned. I read it again for myself just in case the group recitation put me in a trance. Same thing. For some reason this pisses me off. We look at Miss Moore and she lookin at us, waiting for I dunno what.

"Who'd pay all that when you can buy a sailboat set for a quarter at Pop's, a tube of glue for a dime, and a ball of string for eight cents? It must have a motor and a whole lot else besides," I say. "My sailboat cost me about fifty cents."

"But will it take water?" say Mercedes with her smart ass.

"Took mine to Alley Pond Park once," say Flyboy. "String broke. Lost it. Pity."

"Sailed mine in Central Park and it keeled over and sank. Had to ask my father for another dollar."

"And you got the strap," laugh Big Butt. "The jerk didn't even have a string on it. My old man wailed on his behind."

Little Q.T. was staring hard at the sailboat and you could see he wanted it bad. But he too little and somebody'd just take it from him. So what the hell. "This boat for kids, Miss Moore?"

"Parents silly to buy something like that just to get all broke up," say Rosie Giraffe.

"That much money it should last forever," I figure.

"My father'd buy it for me if I wanted it."

"Your father, my ass," say Rosie Giraffe getting a chance to finally push Mercedes.

"Must be rich people shop here," say Q.T.

"You are a very bright boy," say Flyboy. "What was your first clue?" And he rap him on the head with the back of his knuckles, since Q.T. the only one he could get away with. Though Q.T. liable to come up behind you years later and get his licks in when you half expect it.

"What I want to know is," I says to Miss Moore though I never talk to her, I wouldn't give the bitch that satisfaction, "is how much a real boat costs? I figure a thousand'd get you a yacht any day."

"Why don't you check that out," she says, "and report back to the group?" Which really pains my ass. If you gonna mess up a perfectly good swim day least you could do is have some answers. "Let's go in," she say like she got something up her sleeve. Only she don't lead the way. So me and Sugar turn the corner to where the entrance is, but when we get there I kinda hang back. Not that I'm scared, what's there to be afraid of, just a toy store. But I feel funny, shame. But what I got to be shamed about? Got as much right to go in as anybody. But somehow I can't seem to get hold of the door, so I step away for Sugar to lead. But she hangs back too. And I look at her and she looks at me and this is ridiculous. I mean, damn, I have never ever been shy about doing nothing or going nowhere. But then Mercedes steps up and then Rosie Giraffe and Big Butt crowd in behind and shove, and next thing we all stuffed into the doorway with only Mercedes squeezing past us, smoothing out her jumper and walking right down the aisle. Then the rest of us tumble in like a glued-together jigsaw done all wrong. And people lookin at us. And it's like the time me and Sugar crashed into the Catholic church on a dare. But once we got in there and everything so hushed and holy and the candles and the bowin and the handkerchiefs on all the drooping heads, I just couldn't go through with the plan. Which was for me to run up to the altar and do a tap dance while Sugar played the nose flute and messed around in the holy water. And Sugar kept givin me the elbow. Then later teased me so bad I tied her up in the shower and turned it on and locked her in. And she'd be there till this day if Aunt Gretchen hadn't finally figured I was lyin about the boarder takin a shower.

Same thing in the store. We all walkin on tiptoe and hardly touchin the games and puzzles and things. And I watched Miss Moore who is steady watchin us like she waiting for a sign. Like Mama Drewery watches the sky and sniffs the air and takes note of just how much slant is in the bird formation. Then me and Sugar bump smack into each other, so busy gazing at the toys, 'specially the sailboat. But we don't laugh and go into our fat-lady bump-stomach routine. We just stare at that price tag. Then Sugar ran a finger over the whole boat. And I'm jealous and want to hit her. Maybe not her, but I sure want to punch somebody in the mouth.

"Whatcha bring us here for, Miss Moore?"

"You sound angry, Sylvia. Are you mad about something?" Givin me one of them grins like she tellin a grown-up joke that never turns out to be funny. And she's lookin very closely at me like maybe she plannin to do my portrait from memory. I'm mad, but I won't give her that satisfaction. So I slouch around the store bein very bored and say, "Let's go."

Me an Sugar at the back of the train watchin the tracks whizzin by large then small then gettin gobbled up in the dark. I'm thinkin about this tricky toy I saw in the store. A clown that somersaults on a bar then does chin-ups just cause you yank lightly at his leg. Cost \$35. I could see me askin my mother for a \$35 birthday clown. "You wanna who that costs what?" she'd say, cocking her head to the side to get a better view of the hole in my head. Thirty-five dollars could buy new bunk beds for Junior and Gretchen's boy. Thirty-five dollars and the whole household could go visit Granddaddy Nelson in the country. Thirty-five dollars would pay for the rent and the piano bill too. Who are these people that spend that much for performing clowns and \$1,000 for toy sailboats? What kinda work they do and how they live and how come we ain't in on it? Where we are is who we are, Miss Moore always pointin out. But it don't necessarily have to be that way, she always adds then waits for somebody to say that poor people have to wake up and demand their share of the pie and don't none of us know what kind of pie she talkin about in the first damn place. But she ain't so smart cause I still got her four dollars from the taxi and she sure ain't getting it. Messin up my day with this shit. Sugar nudges me in my pocket and winks.

Miss Moore lines us up in front of the mailbox where we started from, seem like years ago, and I got a headache for thinkin so hard. And we lean all over each other so we can hold up under the draggy-ass lecture she always finishes us off with at the end before we thank her for borin us to tears. But she just looks at us like she readin tea leaves. Finally she say, "Well, what did you think of F.A.O. Schwartz?"

Rosie Giraffe mumbles, "White folks crazy."

"I'd like to go there again when I get my birthday money," says Mercedes, and we shove her out the pack so she has to lean on the mailbox by herself.

"I'd like a shower. Tiring day," says Flyboy.

Then Sugar surprises me by sayin, "You know, Miss Moore, I don't think all of us here put together eat in a year what that sailboat costs." And Miss Moore lights up like somebody goosed her. "And?" she say, urging Sugar on. Only I'm standin on her foot so she don't continue.

"Imagine for a minute what kind of society it is in which some people can spend on a toy what it would cost to feed a family of six or seven. What do you think?"

"I think," say Sugar pushing me off her feet like she never done before, cause I whip her ass in a minute, "that this is not much of a democracy if you ask me. Equal chance to pursue happiness means an equal crack at the dough, don't it?" Miss Moore is besides herself and I am disgusted with Sugar's treachery. So I stand on her foot one more time to see if she'll shove me. She shuts up, and Miss Moore looks at me, sorrowfully I'm thinkin. And somethin weird is goin on. I can feel it in my chest.

"Anybody else learn anything today?" lookin dead at me. I walk away and Sugar has to run to catch up and don't even seem to notice when I shrug her arm off my shoulder.

"Well, we got four dollars anyway," she says.

"Uh-hunh."

"We could go to Hascombs and get half a chocolate layer and then go to the Sunset and still have plenty money for potato chips and ice cream sodas."

"Uh-hunh."

"Race you to Hascombs," she say.

We start down the block and she gets ahead which is OK by me cause I'm going to the West End and then over to the Drive to think this day through. She can run if she want to and even run faster. But ain't nobody gonna beat me at nuthin.

—1972

What are your reactions to and questions about this work? The following questions may help provoke some ideas.

Probing the Work

1. What is the "lesson," or what are the lessons, that Miss Moore is trying to teach? What are the lessons of the store? Of the street?
2. What are the various perspectives about the boat in the toy store, and what does each reveal about the character who perceives it?

Identifying Issues

3. Distinguish between Sugar's and the narrator's attitude toward Miss Moore. Do you see evidence of both attitudes at your school? Among your friends? Among the students in this class? What are the consequences of these attitudes?

SHIRLEY LAURO

Open Admission

Shirley Lauro is a former professor of speech; her one-act play, below, won the Dramatists Guild's Hull-Warriner Award as Best Play of the Year on a Controversial Theme and was co-winner in the Off-Broadway original Short Play Festival.

The Characters

PROFESSOR ALICE MILLER—*Professor of Speech Communications. Started out to be a Shakespearean scholar. Has been teaching Speech at a city college in New York for twelve years. She is overloaded with work and exhausted.*
Late thirties. Wears skirt, blouse, sweater, coat, gloves. Carries briefcases.

CALVIN JEFFERSON—*Eighteen, a Freshman in Open Admissions Program at the college. Black, powerfully built, handsome, big. At first glance a streetperson, but belied by his intensity. Wears jacket, jeans, cap, sneakers. Has been at the college three months, hoping it will work out.*

The Place

A cubicle speech office at a city college in New York.

The Time

The present. Late fall. 6 o'clock in the evening.

The play begins on a very high level of tension and intensity and builds from there. The level of intensity is set by CALVIN *who enters the play with a desperate urgency, as though he had arrived at the emergency room of a hospital, needing immediate help for a serious problem. He also enters in a state of rage and frustration but is containing these feelings at first. The high level of tension is set by both* ALICE *and* CALVIN *and occurs from the moment* CALVIN *enters.* ALICE *wants to leave. She does not want the scene to take place. The audience's experience from the start should be as if they had suddenly tuned in on the critical round of a boxing match.*

CALVIN'S *speech is "Street Speech" jargon. Run-on sentences and misspellings in the text are for the purpose of helping the actor with the pronunciations and rhythms of the language.*

The speech office of Professor Alice Miller in a city college in New York. A small cubicle with partitions going three-quarters of the way up. Windowless, airless, with a cold antiseptic quality and a strong sense of impersonalness and transience. The cubicle has the contradictory feelings of claustrophobia and alienation at the same time. It is a space used by many teachers during every day of the week

On the glass-windowed door it says:

SPEECH COMMUNICATIONS DEPT.
Prof. Alice Miller, B.A., M.A., Ph.D.

There are other names beneath that.

In the cubicle there is a desk with nothing on it except a phone, a chair with a rain coat on it, a swivel chair and a portable blackboard on which has been tacked a diagram of the "Speech Mechanism." Room is bare except for these things.

At Rise: Cubicle is in darkness. Muted light filters through glass window on door from hallway. Eerie feeling. A shadow appears outside door. Someone enters, snapping on light.

It is ALICE. *She carries a loose stack of essays, a booksack loaded with books and a grade book, one Shakespeare book, two speech books, and a portable cassette recorder. She closes the door, crosses to the desk, puts the keys in her purse, puts purse and booksack down and dials "0."*

ALICE: Outside please. *(Waits for this, then dials a number.)* Debbie? Mommy, honey . . . A "93?" Terrific! Listen, I just got through. I had to keep the class late to finish . . . So, I can't stop home for dinner. I'm going right to the meeting . . . no, I'll be safe . . . don't worry. But you go put the double lock on, ok? And eat the cold meatloaf. *(She puts essays in booksack.)* See you later. Love you too. *(She kisses the receiver.)* Bye.

(She hangs up, puts on coat, picks up purse and booksack, crosses to door and snaps off light. Then opens door to go. CALVIN *looms in doorway.)*

ALICE: OOHH! You scared me!

CALVIN: Yes ma'am, I can see I scared you okay. I'm sorry.

ALICE: Calvin Washington? 10:30 section?

CALVIN: Calvin Jefferson. 9:30 section.

ALICE: Oh, right. Of course. Well, I was just leaving. Something you wanted?

CALVIN: Yes, Professor Miller. I came to talk to you about my grades. My grade on that Shakespeare project especially.

ALICE: Oh. Yes. Well. What did you get, Calvin? A "B" wasn't it? Something like that?

CALVIN: UMHMM. Thass right. Somethin like that . . .

ALICE: Yes. Well, look, I don't have office hours today at all. It's very dark already. I just stopped to make a call. But if you'd like to make an appointment for a conference, I'm not booked yet next month. Up 'till then, I'm just jammed.

CALVIN: Thass two weeks! I need to talk to you right now!

ALICE: Well what exactly is it about? I mean the grade is self-explanatory—"Good"—"B" work. And I gave you criticism in class the day of the project, didn't I? So what's the problem?

CALVIN: I wanna sit down and talk about *why* I got that grade! And all my grades in point of fact.

ALICE: But I don't have office hours today. It's very late and I have another commitment. Maybe tomor—*(She tries to leave.)*

CALVIN: *(voice rising)* I have to talk to you *now!*

ALICE: Look, tomorrow there's a faculty meeting. I can meet you here afterwards . . . around 12:30. Providing Professor Roth's not scheduled to use the desk.

CALVIN: I got a job tomorrow! Can't you talk to me right now?

ALICE: But what's it about? I don't see the emergen—

CALVIN: *(voice rising loudly)* I jiss *tole* you what it's about! My project and my *grades* is what it's about!

ALICE: *(glancing down the hall, not wanting a commotion overheard)* All right! Just stop shouting out here, will you? *(She snaps on light and crosses to desk.)* Come on in. I'll give you a few minutes now.

(He comes in.)

ALICE: *(She pulls purse and booksack down and sits at desk.)* Okay. Now then. What?

CALVIN: *(Closes door and crosses UC. Silent for a moment looking at her. Then:)* How come all I ever git from you is "B"?

ALICE: *(stunned)* What?

CALVIN: This is the third project I did for you. An all I ever git is "B".

ALICE: Are you joking? This is what you wanted to talk about? "B" is an excellent grade!

CALVIN: No it's not! "A" is "excellent." "B" is "good."

ALICE: You don't think you deserved an "A" on those projects, do you?

CALVIN: No. But I got to know how to improve myself somehow, so maybe sometime I can try for a "A". I wouldn't even mind on one of those projects if I got a "C". Thass average—if you know what I mean? Or a "D". But all I ever git from you is "B". It don't matter what I do in that Speech Communications Class, seems like. I come in the beginnin a it three months ago? On the Open Admissions? Shoot, I didn't know which end was up. I stood up there and give this speech you assigned on "My Hobby." You remember that?

ALICE: *(Reads note on desk.)* About basketball?

CALVIN: Huh-uh. That was Franklin Perkins give that speech. Sits in the back row?

ALICE: *(Tosses note in wastebasket.)* Oh. Yes. Right. Franklin.

CALVIN: Umhmm. I give some dumb speech about "The Hobby a Makin Wooden Trays."

ALICE: Oh, yes. Right. I remember that.

CALVIN: Except I didn't have no hobby makin wooden trays, man. I made one in high school one time, thass all.

ALICE: *(Leafs through pages of speech books.)* Oh, well, that didn't matter. It was the speech that counted.

CALVIN: Umhmm? Well, that was the sorriest speech anybody ever heard in their lives! I was scared to death and couldn't put one word in front a the other any way I tried. Supposed to be five minutes. Lasted two! And you give me a "B"!

ALICE: *(Rises, crosses to DR table and puts speech books down.)* Well, it was your first time up in class, and you showed a lot of enthusiasm and effort. I remember that speech.

CALVIN: Everybody's firss time up in class, ain't it?

ALICE: Yes. Of course.

CALVIN: *(Crosses DR to* ALICE.*)* That girl sits nex to me, that Jody Horowitz—firss time she was up in class too. She give that speech about "How to Play the Guitar?" And man, she brought in charts and taught us to read chords and played a piece herself an had memorized the whole speech by heart. An you give *her* a "B".

ALICE: *(Crosses to desk, picks up booksack and puts it on desk.)* Well, Judy's organization on her outline was a little shaky as I recall.

CALVIN: *(Crosses end of desk.)* I didn' even turn no outline in.

ALICE: *(Picks up purse and puts it on desk.)* You didn't?

CALVIN: *(Leans in.)* Huh-uh. Didn' you notice?

ALICE: Of course! It's—just—well, it's been sometime—*(She quickly takes the gradebook from the booksack and looks up his name.)* Let me see, oh, yes. Right. Here, I see. You didn't hand it in . . .

CALVIN: Thass right, I didn'.

ALICE: You better do that before the end of the term.

CALVIN: I can't. Because I don' know which way to do no outline!

ALICE: *(Looks up name in gradebook and marks it with red pencil.)* Oh. Well . . . that's all right. Don't worry about it, okay? *(She puts gradebook away.)* Just work on improving yourself in other ways.

CALVIN: What other ways? Only thing you ever say about anything I ever done in there is how I have got to get rid of my "Substandard Urban Speech!"

ALICE: *(Picks up two files from desk and crosses to UCR file cabinet.)* Well, yes, you do! You see, that's your real problem, Calvin! "Substandard Speech." It undercuts your "Positive Communicator's Image!" Remember how I gave a lecture about that? About how all of you here have Substandard Urban Speech because this is a Sub—an *Urban* College. *(She puts on gloves.)* Remember? But that's perfectly okay! It's okay! Just like I used to have Substandard Midwestern Speech when I was a student. Remember my explaining about that? How I used to say "crik" for "creek," and "kin" for "can" and "tin" for "ten?" *(She crosses in back of desk and chuckles at herself.)* Oh, and my breathiness! *(She picks up purse.)* That was just my biggest problem of all: Breathiness. I just about worked myself to death up at Northwestern U. getting it right straight out of my speech. Now, that's what you have to do too, Calvin. *(She picks up booksack and keys.)* Nothing to be ashamed of—but get it right straight out! *(She is ready to leave. She pats* CALVIN *on the shoulder and crosses UC.)*

CALVIN: *(Pause. Looks at her.)* Thass how come I keep on gittin "B"?

ALICE: "That's."

CALVIN: *(Steps in to* ALICE.*)* Huh?

ALICE: "That's." Not "Thass." Can't you hear the difference? That's one of the words in the Substandard Black Urban Pattern. No final "T's". Undermining your Positive Image . . . labeling you. It's "Street Speech." Harlemese. Don't you remember? I called everyone's attention to your particular syndrome in class the minute you started talking?

(He looks at her, not speaking.)

ALICE: It's "last," not "lass;" "first," not "firss." That's your friend, that good old "Final T!" Hear *it* when I talk?

CALVIN: Sometimes. When you say i*t*, hi*tt*ing i*t* like tha*t!*

ALICE: Well, you should be going over the exercises on it in the speech book all the time, and recording yourself on your tape recorder. *(She pats booksack.)*

CALVIN: I don't got no tape recorder.

ALICE: Well, borrow one! *(She turns away.)*

CALVIN: *(Crosses in back of* ALICE *to her right.)* On that Shakespeare scene I jiss did? Thass why I got a "B"? Because of the "Final T's?"

ALICE: *(Backs DS a step.)* Well, you haven't improved your syndrome, have you?

CALVIN: How come you keep on answerin me by axin me somethin else?

ALICE: And that's the other one.
CALVIN: What "other one?"
ALICE: Other most prevalent deviation. You said: "axing" me something else.
CALVIN: Thass right. How come you keep axin me somethin else?
ALICE: "Asking me," Calvin, "asking me!"
CALVIN: I jiss did!
ALICE: No, no. Look. That's classic Substandard Black! Textbook case. *(She puts purse and booksack down and crosses to diagram on blackboard.)* See, the jaw and teeth are in two different positions for the two sounds, and they make two completely different words! *(She writes "ass-king," and "axing" on the blackboard, pronouncing them in an exaggerated way for him to see.)* "ass-king" and "ax-ing". I am "ass-king" you the question. But, the woodcutter is "axing" down the tree. Can't you hear the difference? *(She picks up his speech book from desk.)* Here.

(CALVIN *follows her to desk.)*

ALICE: Go over to page 105. It's called a "Sharp S" problem with a medial position "sk" substitution. See? "skin, screw, scream"—those are "sk" sounds in the Primary Position. "Asking, risking, frisking"—that's medial position. And "flask, task, mask"—that's final position. Now you should be working on those, Calvin. Reading those exercises over and over again. I mean the way you did the Othello scene was just ludicrous: "Good gentlemen, I ax thee—" *(She crosses to the board and points to "axing". She chuckles.)* That meant Othello was chopping the gentlemen down!
CALVIN: How come I had to do the Othello scene anyhow? Didn git any choice. An Franklin Perkins an Sam Brown an Lester Washington they had to too.
ALICE: What do you mean?
CALVIN: An Claudette Jackson an Doreen Simpson an Melba Jones got themselves assigned to Cleopatra on the Nile?
ALICE: Everyone was assigned!
CALVIN: Uh-huh. But everybody else had a choice, you know what I mean? That Judy Horowitz, she said you told her she could pick outa five, six different characters. And that boy did his yesterday? That Nick Rizoli? Did the Gravedigger? He said he got three, four to choose off of too.
ALICE: *(Crosses to* CALVIN.*)* Well some of the students were "right" for several characters. And you know, Calvin, how we talked in class about Stanislavsky and the importance of "identifying" and "feeling" the part?
CALVIN: Well how Doreen Simpson "identify" herself some Queen sittin on a barge? How I supposed to "identify" some Othello? I don't!
ALICE: *(Crosses to blackboard, picks up fallen chalk.)* Oh, Calvin, don't be silly.
CALVIN: *(Crosses center.)* Well, I don'! I'm not no kind a jealous husband. I haven' got no wife. I don' even got no girlfriend, hardly! And thass

what it's all about ain't it? So what's it I'm supposed to "identify" with anyhow?

ALICE: *(Turns to* CALVIN*.)* Oh, Calvin, what are you arguing about? You did a good job!

CALVIN: "B" job, right?

ALICE: Yes.

CALVIN: *(Crosses to* ALICE*.)* Well, what's that "B" standin for? Cause I'll tell you somethin you wanna know the truth: I stood up there didn' hardly know the sense a anythin I read, couldn't hardly even read it at all. Only you didn't notice. Wasn't even listenin, sittin there back a the room jiss thumbin through your book.

*(*ALICE *crosses to desk.)*

CALVIN: So you know what I done? Skip one whole paragraph, tess you out—you jiss kep thumbin through your book! An then you give me a "B"! *(He has followed* ALICE *to desk.)*

ALICE: *(Puts papers in box and throws out old coffee cup.)* Well that just shows how well you did the part!

CALVIN: You wanna give me somethin I could "identify" with, how come you ain' let me do that other dude in the play . . .

ALICE: Iago?

CALVIN: Yeah. What is it they calls him? Othello's . . .

ALICE: Subordinate.

CALVIN: Go right along there with my speech syndrome, wouldn' it now? See, Iago has to work for the Man. I identifies with him! He gits jealous man. Know what I mean? Or that Gravedigger? Shovelin dirt for his day's work! How come you wouldn't let me do him? Thass the question I wanna ax you!

ALICE: *(Turns to* CALVIN*.)* "Ask me," Calvin, "Ask me!"

CALVIN: *(Steps SR.)* "Ax you?" Okay, man. *(Turns to* ALICE*.)* Miss Shakespeare, Speech Communications 1! *(Crosses US of* ALICE*.)* Know what I'll "ax" you right here in this room, this day, at this here desk right now? I'll "ax" you how come I have been in this here college three months on this here Open Admissions and I don't know nothin more than when I came in here? You know what I mean? This supposed to be some big break for me. This here is where all them smart Jewish boys has gone from the Bronx Science and went an become some Big Time Doctors at Bellevue. An some Big Time Judges in the Family Court an like that there. And now it's supposed to be my turn.

*(*ALICE *looks away and* CALVIN *crosses R of* ALICE*.)*

CALVIN: You know what I mean? *(He crosses UR.)* An my sister Jonelle took me out of foster care where I been in six homes and five school to give me my chance. *(He crosses DR.)* Livin with her an she workin three shifts in some "Ladies Restroom" give me my opportunity. An she say she gonna buss her ass git me this education I don't end up on the streets! *(Crosses on a diagonal to* ALICE.*)* Cause I have got brains!

(ALICE *sits in student chair.* CALVIN *crosses in back, to her left.)*

CALVIN: You understand what I am Communicatin to you? My high school has tole me I got brains an can make somethin outta my life if I gits me the chance! And now this here's supposed to be my chance! High school says you folks gonna bring me up to date on my education and git me even. Only nothin is happenin to me in my head except I am gettin more and more confused about what I knows and what I don't know! *(He sits in swivel chair.)* So what I wanna "ax" you is: How came you don't sit down with me and teach me which way to git my ideas down instead of givin me a "B".

(ALICE *rises and crosses UR.)*

CALVIN: I don't even turn no outline in? Jiss give me a "B". *(He rises and crosses R of* ALICE.*)* An Lester a "B"! An Melba a "B"! and Sam a "B"! What's that "B" standin for anyhow? Cause it surely ain't standin for no piece of work!

ALICE: Calvin don't blame me!

(CALVIN *crosses DR.)*

ALICE: I'm trying! God knows I'm trying! The times are rough for everyone. I'm a Shakespearean scholar, and they have me teaching beginning speech. I was supposed to have twelve graduate students a class, nine classes a week, and they gave me thirty-five Freshmen a class, twenty classes a week. I hear 157 speeches a week! You know what that's like? And I go home late on the subway scared to death! In Graduate School they told me I'd have a first-rate career. Then I started here and they said: "Hang on! Things will improve!" But they only got worse . . . and worse! Now I've been here for twelve years and I haven't written one word in my field! I haven't read five research books! I'm exhausted . . . and I'm finished! We all have to bend. I'm just hanging on now . . . supporting my little girl . . . earning a living . . . and that's all . . . *(She crosses to desk.)*

CALVIN: *(Faces* ALICE.*)* What I'm supposed to do, feel sorry for you? Least you can *earn* a livin! Clean office, private phone, name on the door with all them B.A.'s, M.A.'s, Ph.D.'s.

ALICE: You can have those too. *(She crosses DR to* CALVIN.*)* Look, last year we got ten black students into Ivy League Graduate Programs. And they were not better than you. They were just *perceived (Points to blackboard.)* as better. Now that's the whole key for you . . . to be perceived as better! So you can get good recommendations and do well on interviews. You're good looking and ambitious and you have a fine native intelligence. You can make it, Calvin. All we have to do is work on improving your Positive

Communicator's Image . . . by getting rid of that Street Speech. Don't you see?

CALVIN: See what? What you axin *me* to see?

ALICE: *"Asking"* me to see, Calvin. *"Asking"* me to see!

CALVIN: *(Starts out of control at this, enraged, crosses UC and bangs on file cabinet.)* Ooooeee! Ooooeee! You wanna *see?* You wanna *see?* Ooooeee!

ALICE: Calvin stop it! STOP IT!

CALVIN: "Calvin stop it?" "Stop it?" *(Picks up school books from desk.)* There any black professors here?

ALICE: *(Crosses UR.)* No! They got cut . . . the budget's low . . . they got . . .

CALVIN: *(interrupting) Cut? They* got CUT? *(Crosses to* ALICE *and backs her to the DS edge of desk.)* Gonna *cut you,* lady! Gonna cut you, throw you out the fuckin window, throw the fuckin books out the fuckin window, burn it all mother fuckin down. FUCKIN DOWN!!!

ALICE: Calvin! Stop it! STOP IT! YOU HEAR ME?

CALVIN: *(Turns away, center stage.)* I CAN'T!! *YOU* HEAR *ME?* I CAN'T! *YOU* HEAR *ME!* I CAN'T! YOU GOTTA GIVE ME MY EDUCATION! GOTTA TEACH ME! GIVE ME SOMETHING NOW! GIVE ME NOW! NOW! NOW! NOW! NOW! NOW!

*(*CALVIN *tears up textbook. He starts to pick up torn pages and drops them. He bursts into a wailing, bellowing cry in his anguish and despair, doubled over in pain and grief. It is a while before his sobs subside. Finally,* ALICE *speaks.)*

ALICE: Calvin . . . from the bottom of my heart . . . I want to help you . . .

CALVIN: *(Barely able to speak.)* By changin my words? Thass nothing . . . nothin! I got to know them big ideas . . . and which way to git em down . . .

ALICE: But how can I teach you that? You can't write a paragraph, Calvin . . . or a sentence . . . you can't spell past fourth grade . . . the essay you wrote showed that . . .

CALVIN: *(Rises.)* What essay?

ALICE: *(Crosses to UL files, gets essay and hands it to* CALVIN.*)* The autobiographical one . . . you did it the first day . . .

CALVIN: You said that was for *your* reference . . . didn't count . . .

ALICE: Here . . .

CALVIN: *(Opens it up. Stunned.)* "F?" Why didn't you tell me I failed?

ALICE: *(Crosses to desk, puts essay down.)* For what?

CALVIN: *(Still stunned.)* So you could teach me how to write.

ALICE: *(Crosses DL.)* In sixteen weeks?

CALVIN: *(Still can't believe this.)* You my teacher!

ALICE: That would take years! And speech is my job. You need a tutor.

CALVIN: I'm your job. They outa tutors!

ALICE: *(Turns to him.)* I can't do it, Calvin. And that's the real truth. I'm one person, in one job. And I can't. Do you understand? And even if I could, it wouldn't matter. All that matters is the budget . . . and the curriculum . . . and the grades . . . and how you look . . . and how you talk!

CALVIN: *(Pause. Absorbing this.)* Then I'm finished, man.

(There is a long pause. Finally:)

ALICE: *(Gets essay from desk, refiles it and returns to desk.)* No, you're not. If you'll bend and take what I can give you, things will work out for you . . . Trust me . . . Let me help you Calvin . . . Please . . . I can teach you speech . . .

CALVIN: *(Crosses to UC file cabinet. Long pause.)* Okay . . . all right, man . . . *(Crosses to student chair and sits.)*

ALICE: *(Crosses to desk, takes off rain coat and sits in swivel chair.)* Now, then, we'll go through the exercise once then you do it at home . . . please, repeat after me, slowly . . . "asking" . . . "asking" . . . "asking" . . .

CALVIN: *(long pause)* Ax-ing . . .

ALICE: Ass-king . . .

CALVIN: *(During the following, he now turns from* ALICE, *faces front, and gazes out beyond the audience; on his fourth word, lights begin to fade to black:)* Ax-ing . . . Aks-ing . . . ass-king . . . asking . . . asking . . . asking . . .

BLACKOUT

END OF PLAY

—1983

What are your reactions to and questions about this work? The following questions may help provoke some ideas.

Probing the Work

1. Does the ending represent a defeat or victory for Alice? For Calvin? Explain your answer.
2. Explain the predicament each character is in. With whom do you sympathize more, and why?
3. What are the two different kinds of learning expressed by the two characters?

Identifying Issues

4. How does this play illustrate the significance of *grades* and the problems of grading in the college learning experience? Have you ever received a grade better or worse than the one you felt sure you deserved? How often does the grade you receive match the amount of work you put into an assignment or course? When do grades actually *hinder* learning?

EUGÈNE IONESCO

The Lesson

(Translated by Donald M. Allen)

Eugène Ionesco (1912–1994) was born in Romania, where he taught French. He left for Paris under the threat of fascism, and became a permanent French citizen. After World War II he wrote avant-garde plays that began a genre known as the theatre of the absurd. *They include* The Bald Soprano *(1948),* The Chairs *(1951),* The Killer *(1957),* Rhinoceros *(1959), and* The Pedestrian in the Air *(1962).*

The Characters

THE PROFESSOR, *aged 50 to 60*
THE YOUNG PUPIL, *aged 18*
THE MAID, *aged 45 to 50*

Scene: The office of the old professor, which also serves as a dining room. To the left, a door opens onto the apartment stairs; upstage, to the right, another door opens onto a corridor of the apartment. Upstage, a little left of center, a window, not very large, with plain curtains; on the outside sill of the window are ordinary potted plants. The low buildings with red roofs of a small town can be seen in the distance. The sky is grayish-blue. On the right stands a provincial buffet. The table doubles as a desk, it stands at stage center. There are three chairs around the table, and two more stand on each side of the window. Light-colored wallpaper, some shelves with books.

[*When the curtain rises the stage is empty, and it remains so for a few moments. Then we hear the doorbell ring.*]

VOICE OF THE MAID [*from the corridor*]: Yes. I'm coming.

[*The* MAID *comes in, after having run down the stairs. She is stout, aged 45 to 50, red-faced, and wears a peasant woman's cap. She rushes in, slamming the door to the right behind her, and dries her hands on her apron as she runs towards the door on the left. Meanwhile we hear the doorbell ring again.*]

MAID: Just a moment, I'm coming.

[*She opens the door. A young* PUPIL, *aged 18, enters. She is wearing a gray student's smock, a small white collar, and carries a student's satchel under her arm.*]

MAID: Good morning, miss.
PUPIL: Good morning, madam. Is the Professor at home?
MAID: Have you come for the lesson?
PUPIL: Yes, I have.
MAID: He's expecting you. Sit down for a moment. I'll tell him you're here.
PUPIL: Thank you.

[*She seats herself near the table, facing the audience; the hall door is to her left; her back is to the other door, through which the* MAID *hurriedly exits, calling:*]

MAID: Professor, come down please, your Pupil is here.
VOICE OF THE PROFESSOR [*rather reedy*]: Thank you. I'm coming . . . in just a moment . . .

[*The* MAID *exits; the* PUPIL *draws in her legs, holds her satchel on her lap, and waits demurely. She casts a glance or two around the room, at the furniture, at the ceiling too. Then she takes a notebook out of her satchel, leafs through it, and stops to look at a page for a moment as though reviewing a lesson, as though taking a last look at her homework. She seems to be a well-brought-up girl, polite, but lively, gay, dynamic; a fresh smile is on her lips. During the course of the play she progressively loses the lively rhythm of her movement and her carriage, she becomes withdrawn. From gay and smiling she becomes progressively sad and morose; from very lively at the beginning, she becomes more and more fatigued and somnolent. Towards the end of the play her face must clearly express a nervous depression; her way of speaking shows the effects of this, her tongue becomes thick, words come to her memory with difficulty and emerge from her mouth with as much difficulty; she comes to have a manner vaguely paralyzed, the beginning of aphasia. Firm and determined at the beginning, so much so as to appear to be almost aggressive, she becomes more and more passive, until she is almost a mute and inert object, seemingly inanimate in the* PROFESSOR'S *hands, to such an extent that when he makes his final gesture, she no longer reacts. Insensible, her reflexes deadened, only her eyes in an expressionless face will show inexpressible astonishment and fear. The transition from one manner to the other must of course be made imperceptibly.*

The PROFESSOR *enters. He is a little old man with a little white beard. He wears pince-nez, a black skullcap, a long black schoolmaster's coat, trousers and shoes of black, detachable white collar, a black tie. Excessively polite, very timid, his voice deadened by his timidity, very proper, very much the teacher. He rubs his hands together constantly; occasionally a lewd gleam comes into his eyes and is quickly repressed.*

During the course of the play his timidity will disappear progressively, imperceptibly; and the lewd gleams in his eyes will become a steady devouring flame in the end. From a manner that is inoffensive at the start, the PROFESSOR *becomes more and more sure of himself, more and more nervous, aggressive, dominating, until he is able to do as he pleases with the* PUPIL, *who has become, in his hands, a pitiful creature. Of course, the voice of the* PROFESSOR *must change too, from thin and reedy, to stronger and stronger, until at the end it is extremely powerful, ringing, sonorous, while the* PUPIL'S *voice changes from the very clear and ringing tones that she has at the beginning of the play until it is almost inaudible. In these first scenes the* PROFESSOR *might stammer very slightly.*]

PROFESSOR: Good morning, young lady. You . . . I expect that you . . . that you are the new pupil?

PUPIL [*turns quickly with a lively and self-assured manner; she gets up, goes toward the* PROFESSOR, *and gives him her hand*]: Yes, Professor. Good morning, Professor. As you see, I'm on time. I didn't want to be late.

PROFESSOR: That's fine, miss. Thank you, you didn't really need to hurry. I am very sorry to have kept you waiting . . . I was just finishing up . . . well . . . I'm sorry . . . You will excuse me, won't you? . . .

PUPIL: Oh, certainly, Professor. It doesn't matter at all, Professor.

PROFESSOR: Please excuse me . . . Did you have any trouble finding the house?

PUPIL: No . . . Not at all. I just asked the way. Everybody knows you around here.

PROFESSOR: For thirty years I've lived in this town. You've not been here for long? How do you find it?

PUPIL: It's all right. The town is attractive and even agreeable, there's a nice park, a boarding school, a bishop, nice shops and streets . . .

PROFESSOR: That's very true, young lady. And yet, I'd just as soon live somewhere else. In Paris, or at least Bordeaux.

PUPIL: Do you like Bordeaux?

PROFESSOR: I don't know. I've never seen it.

PUPIL: But you know Paris?

PROFESSOR: No, I don't know it either, young lady, but if you'll permit me, can you tell me, Paris is the capital city of . . . miss?

PUPIL [*searching her memory for a moment, then, happily guessing*]: Paris is the capital city of . . . France?

PROFESSOR: Yes, young lady, bravo, that's very good, that's perfect. My congratulations. You have your French geography at your finger tips. You know your chief cities.

PUPIL: Oh! I don't know them all yet, Professor, it's not quite that easy, I have trouble learning them.

PROFESSOR: Oh! It will come . . . you mustn't give up . . . young lady . . . I beg your pardon . . . have patience . . . little by little . . . You will see, it will come in time . . . What a nice day it is today . . . or rather, not so nice . . . Oh! but then yes it is nice. In short, it's not too bad a day, that's the main thing . . . ahem . . . ahem . . . it's not raining and it's not snowing either.

PUPIL: That would be most unusual, for it's summer now.

PROFESSOR: Excuse me, miss, I was just going to say so . . . but as you will learn, one must be ready for anything.

PUPIL: I guess so, Professor.

PROFESSOR: We can't be sure of anything, young lady, in this world.

PUPIL: The snow falls in the winter. Winter is one of the four seasons. The other three are . . . uh . . . spr . . .

PROFESSOR: Yes?

PUPIL: . . . ing, and then summer . . . and . . . uh . . .

Professor: It begins like "automobile," miss.

Pupil: Ah, yes, autumn . . .

Professor: That's right, miss. That's a good answer, that's perfect. I am convinced that you will be a good pupil. You will make real progress. You are intelligent, you seem to me to be well informed, and you've a good memory.

Pupil: I know my seasons, don't I, Professor?

Professor: Yes, indeed, miss . . . or almost. But it will come in time. In any case, you're coming along. Soon you'll know all the seasons, even with your eyes closed. Just as I do.

Pupil: It's hard.

Professor: Oh, no. All it takes is a little effort, a little good will, miss. You will see. It will come, you may be sure of that.

Pupil: Oh, I do hope so, Professor. I have a great thirst for knowledge. My parents also want me to get an education. They want me to specialize. They consider a little general culture, even if it is solid, is no longer enough, in these times.

Professor: Your parents, miss, are perfectly right. You must go on with your studies. Forgive me for saying so, but it is very necessary. Our contemporary life has become most complex.

Pupil: And so very complicated too . . . My parents are fairly rich, I'm lucky. They can help me in my work, help me in my very advanced studies.

Professor: And you wish to qualify for . . . ?

Pupil: Just as soon as possible, for the first doctor's orals. They're in three weeks' time.

Professor: You already have your high school diploma, if you'll pardon the question?

Pupil: Yes, Professor, I have my science diploma and my arts diploma, too.

Professor: Ah, you're very far advanced, even perhaps too advanced for your age. And which doctorate do you wish to qualify for? In the physical sciences or in moral philosophy?

Pupil: My parents are very much hoping—if you think it will be possible in such a short time—they very much hope that I can qualify for the total doctorate.

Professor: The total doctorate? . . . You have great courage, young lady, I congratulate you sincerely. We will try, miss, to do our best. In any case, you already know quite a bit, and at so young an age too.

Pupil: Oh, Professor.

Professor: Then, if you'll permit me, pardon me, please, I do think that we ought to get to work. We have scarcely any time to lose.

Pupil: Oh, but certainly, Professor, I want to. I beg you to.

Professor: Then, may I ask you to sit down . . . there . . . Will you permit me, miss, that is if you have no objections, to sit down opposite you?

Pupil: Oh, of course, Professor, please do.

PROFESSOR: Thank you very much, miss. [*They sit down facing each other at the table, their profiles to the audience.*] There we are. Now have you brought your books and notebooks?

PUPIL [*taking notebooks and books out of her satchel*]: Yes, Professor. Certainly, I have brought all that we'll need.

PROFESSOR: Perfect, miss. This is perfect. Now, if this doesn't bore you . . . shall we begin?

PUPIL: Yes, indeed, Professor, I am at your disposal.

PROFESSOR: At my disposal? [*A gleam comes into his eyes and is quickly extinguished; he begins to make a gesture that he suppresses at once.*] Oh, miss, it is I who am at *your* disposal. I am only your humble servant.

PUPIL: Oh, Professor . . .

PROFESSOR: If you will . . . now . . . we . . . we . . . I . . . I will begin by making a brief examination of your knowledge, past and present, so that we may chart our future course . . . Good. How is your perception of plurality?

PUPIL: It's rather vague . . . confused.

PROFESSOR: Good. We shall see.

[*He rubs his hands together. The* MAID *enters, and this appears to irritate the* PROFESSOR. *She goes to the buffet and looks for something, lingering.*]

PROFESSOR: Now, miss, would you like to do a little arithmetic, that is if you want to . . .

PUPIL: Oh, yes, Professor. Certainly, I ask nothing better.

PROFESSOR: It is rather a new science, a modern science, properly speaking, it is more a method than a science . . . And it is also a therapy. [*To the* MAID:] Have you finished, Marie?

MAID: Yes, Professor, I've found the plate. I'm just going . . .

PROFESSOR: Hurry up then. Please go along to the kitchen, if you will.

MAID: Yes, Professor, I'm going. [*She starts to go out.*] Excuse me, Professor, but take care, I urge you to remain calm.

PROFESSOR: You're being ridiculous, Marie. Now, don't worry.

MAID: That's what you always say.

PROFESSOR: I will not stand for your insinuations. I know perfectly well how to comport myself. I am old enough for that.

MAID: Precisely, Professor. You will do better not to start the young lady on arithmetic. Arithmetic is tiring, exhausting.

PROFESSOR: Not at my age. And anyhow, what business is it of yours? This is my concern. And I know what I'm doing. This is not your department.

MAID: Very well, Professor. But you can't say that I didn't warn you.

PROFESSOR: Marie, I can get along without your advice.

MAID: As you wish, Professor. [*She exits.*]

PROFESSOR: Miss, I hope you'll pardon this absurd interruption . . . Excuse this woman . . . She is always afraid that I'll tire myself. She fusses over my health.

PUPIL: Oh, that's quite all right, Professor. It shows that she's very devoted. She loves you very much. Good servants are rare.

PROFESSOR: She exaggerates. Her fears are stupid. But let's return to our arithmetical knitting.

PUPIL: I'm following you, Professor.

PROFESSOR [*wittily*]: Without leaving your seat!

PUPIL [*appreciating his joke*]: Like you, Professor.

PROFESSOR: Good. Let us arithmetize a little now.

PUPIL: Yes, gladly, Professor.

PROFESSOR: It wouldn't be too tiresome for you to tell me . . .

PUPIL: Not at all, Professor, go on.

PROFESSOR: How much are one and one?

PUPIL: One and one make two.

PROFESSOR [*marveling at the* PUPIL'S *knowledge*]: Oh, but that's very good. You appear to me to be well along in your studies. You should easily achieve the total doctorate, miss.

PUPIL: I'm so glad. Especially to have someone like you tell me this.

PROFESSOR: Let's push on: how much are two and one?

PUPIL: Three.

PROFESSOR: Three and one?

PUPIL: Four.

PROFESSOR: Four and one?

PUPIL: Five.

PROFESSOR: Five and one?

PUPIL: Six.

PROFESSOR: Six and one?

PUPIL: Seven.

PROFESSOR: Seven and one?

PUPIL: Eight.

PROFESSOR: Seven and one?

PUPIL: Eight again.

PROFESSOR: Very well answered. Seven and one?

PUPIL: Eight once more.

PROFESSOR: Perfect. Excellent. Seven and one?

PUPIL: Eight again. And sometimes nine.

PROFESSOR: Magnificent. You are magnificent. You are exquisite. I congratulate you warmly, miss. There's scarcely any point in going on. At addition you are a past master. Now, let's look at subtraction. Tell me, if you are not exhausted, how many are four minus three?

PUPIL: Four minus three? . . . Four minus three?

PROFESSOR: Yes. I mean to say: subtract three from four.

PUPIL: That makes . . . seven?

PROFESSOR: I am sorry but I'm obliged to contradict you. Four minus three does not make seven. You are confused: four plus three makes seven, four minus three does not make seven . . . This is not addition anymore, we must subtract now.

PUPIL [*trying to understand*]: Yes . . . yes . . .

PROFESSOR: Four minus three makes . . . How many? . . . How many?

PUPIL: Four?

PROFESSOR: No, miss, that's not it.

PUPIL: Three, then.

PROFESSOR: Not that either, miss . . . Pardon, I'm sorry . . . I ought to say, that's not it . . . excuse me.

PUPIL: Four minus three . . . Four minus three . . . Four minus three? . . . But now doesn't that make ten?

PROFESSOR: Oh, certainly not, miss. It's not a matter of guessing, you've got to think it out. Let's try to deduce it together. Would you like to count?

PUPIL: Yes, Professor. One . . . two . . . uh . . .

PROFESSOR: You know how to count? How far can you count up to?

PUPIL: I can count to . . . to infinity.

PROFESSOR: That's not possible, miss.

PUPIL: Well then, let's say to sixteen.

PROFESSOR: That is enough. One must know one's limits. Count then, if you will, please.

PUPIL: One . . . two . . . and after two, comes three . . . then four . . .

PROFESSOR: Stop there, miss. Which number is larger? Three or four?

PUPIL: Uh . . . three or four? Which is the larger? The larger of three or four? In what sense larger?

PROFESSOR: Some numbers are smaller and others are larger. In the larger numbers there are more units than in the small . . .

PUPIL: Than in the small numbers?

PROFESSOR: Unless the small ones have smaller units. If they are very small, then there might be more units in the small numbers than in the large . . . if it is a question of other units . . .

PUPIL: In that case, the small numbers can be larger than the large numbers?

PROFESSOR: Let's not go into that. That would take us much too far. You must realize simply that more than numbers are involved here . . . there are also magnitudes, totals, there are groups, there are heaps, heaps of such things as plums, trucks, geese, prune pits, etc. To facilitate our work, let's merely suppose that we have only equal numbers, then the bigger numbers will be those that have the most units.

PUPIL: The one that has the most is the biggest? Ah, I understand, Professor, you are identifying quality with quantity.

PROFESSOR: That is too theoretical, miss, too theoretical. You needn't concern yourself with that. Let us take an example and reason from a definite case. Let's leave the general conclusions for later. We have the number four and the number three, and each has always the same number of units. Which number will be larger, the smaller or the larger?

PUPIL: Excuse me, Professor . . . What do you mean by the larger number? Is it the one that is not so small as the other?

PROFESSOR: That's it, miss, perfect. You have understood me very well.

PUPIL: Then, it is four.

PROFESSOR: What is four—larger or smaller than three?

PUPIL: Smaller . . . no, larger.

PROFESSOR: Excellent answer. How many units are there between three and four? . . . Or between four and three, if you prefer?

PUPIL: There aren't any units, Professor, between three and four. Four comes immediately after three; there is nothing at all between three and four!

PROFESSOR: I haven't made myself very well understood. No doubt, it is my fault. I've not been sufficiently clear.

PUPIL: No, Professor, it's my fault.

PROFESSOR: Look here. Here are three matches. And here is another one, that makes four. Now watch carefully—we have four matches. I take one away, now how many are left?

[*We don't see the matches, nor any of the objects that are mentioned. The* PROFESSOR *gets up from the table, writes on the imaginary blackboard with an imaginary piece of chalk, etc.*]

PUPIL: Five. If three and one make four, four and one make five.

PROFESSOR: That's not it. That's not it at all. You always have a tendency to add. But one must be able to subtract too. It's not enough to integrate, you must also disintegrate. That's the way life is. That's philosophy. That's science. That's progress, civilization.

PUPIL: Yes, Professor.

PROFESSOR: Let's return to our matches. I have four of them. You see, there are really four. I take one away, and there remain only . . .

PUPIL: I don't know, Professor.

PROFESSOR: Come now, think. It's not easy, I admit. Nevertheless, you've had enough training to make the intellectual effort required to arrive at an understanding. So?

PUPIL: I can't get it, Professor. I don't know, Professor.

PROFESSOR: Let us take a simpler example. If you had two noses, and I pulled one of them off . . . how many would you have left?

PUPIL: None.

PROFESSOR: What do you mean, none?

PUPIL: Yes, it's because you haven't pulled off any, that's why I have one now. If you had pulled it off, I wouldn't have it anymore.

PROFESSOR: You've not understood my example. Suppose that you have only one ear.

PUPIL: Yes, and then?

PROFESSOR: If I gave you another one, how many would you have then?

PUPIL: Two.

PROFESSOR: Good. And if I gave you still another ear. How many would you have then?

PUPIL: Three ears.

PROFESSOR: Now, I take one away . . . and there remain . . . how many ears?

PUPIL: Two.

PROFESSOR: Good. I take away still another one, how many do you have left?

PUPIL: Two.

PROFESSOR: No. You have two, I take one away, I eat one up, then how many do you have left?

PUPIL: Two.

PROFESSOR: I eat one of them . . . one.

PUPIL: Two.

PROFESSOR: One.

PUPIL: Two.

PROFESSOR: One!

PUPIL: Two!

PROFESSOR: One!!!

PUPIL: Two!!!

PROFESSOR: One!!!

PUPIL: Two!!!

PROFESSOR: One!!!

PUPIL: Two!!!

PROFESSOR: No. No. That's not right. The example is not . . . it's not convincing. Listen to me.

PUPIL: Yes, Professor.

PROFESSOR: You've got . . . you've got . . . you've got . . .

PUPIL: Ten fingers!

PROFESSOR: If you wish. Perfect. Good. You have then ten fingers.

PUPIL: Yes, Professor.

PROFESSOR: How many would you have if you had only five of them?

PUPIL: Ten, Professor.

PROFESSOR: That's not right!

PUPIL: But it is, Professor.

PROFESSOR: I tell you it's not!

PUPIL: You just told me that I had ten . . .

PROFESSOR: I also said, immediately afterwards, that you had five!

PUPIL: I don't have five, I've got ten!

PROFESSOR: Let's try another approach . . . for purposes of subtraction let's limit ourselves to the numbers from one to five . . . Wait now, miss, you'll soon see. I'm going to make you understand.

[*The* PROFESSOR *begins to write on the imaginary blackboard. He moves it closer to the* PUPIL, *who turns around in order to see it.*]

Professor: Look here, miss . . . [*He pretends to draw a stick on the blackboard and the number 1 below the stick; then two sticks and the number 2 below, then three sticks and the number 3 below, then four sticks with the number 4 below.*] You see . . .

Pupil: Yes, Professor.

Professor: These are sticks, miss, sticks. This is one stick, these are two sticks, and three sticks, then four sticks, then five sticks. One stick, two sticks, three sticks, four and five sticks, these are numbers. When we count the sticks, each stick is a unit, miss . . . What have I just said?

Pupil: "A unit, miss! What have I just said?"

Professor: Or a figure! Or a number! One, two, three, four, five, these are the elements of numeration, miss.

Pupil [*hesitant*]: Yes, Professor. The elements, figures, which are sticks, units and numbers . . .

Professor: At the same time . . . that's to say, in short—the whole of arithmetic is there.

Pupil: Yes, Professor. Good, Professor. Thanks, Professor.

Professor: Now, count, if you will please, using these elements . . . add and subtract . . .

Pupil [*as though trying to impress them on her memory*]: Sticks are really figures and numbers are units?

Professor: Hmm . . . so to speak. And then?

Pupil: One could subtract two units from three units, but can one subtract two twos from three threes? And two figures from four numbers? And three numbers from one unit?

Professor: No, miss.

Pupil: Why, Professor?

Professor: Because, miss.

Pupil: Because why, Professor? Since one is the same as the other?

Professor: That's the way it is, miss. It can't be explained. This is only comprehensible through internal mathematical reasoning. Either you have it or you don't.

Pupil: So much the worse for me.

Professor: Listen to me, miss, if you don't achieve a profound understanding of these principles, these arithmetical archetypes, you will never be able to perform correctly the functions of a polytechnician. Still less will you be able to teach a course in a polytechnical school . . . or the primary grades. I realize that this is not easy, it is very, very abstract . . . obviously . . . but unless you can comprehend the primary elements, how do you expect to be able to calculate mentally—and this is the least of the things that even an ordinary engineer must be able to do—how much, for example, are three billion seven hundred fifty-five million nine hundred ninety-eight thousand two hundred fifty-one, multiplied by five billion one hundred sixty-two million three hundred and three thousand five hundred and eight?

PUPIL [*very quickly*]: That makes nineteen quintillion three hundred ninety quadrillion two trillion eight hundred forty-four billion two hundred nineteen million one hundred sixty-four thousand five hundred and eight . . .

PROFESSOR [*astonished*]: No. I don't think so. That must make nineteen quintillion three hundred ninety quadrillion two trillion eight hundred forty-four billion two hundred nineteen million one hundred sixty-four thousand five hundred and nine . . .

PUPIL: . . . No . . . five hundred and eight . . .

PROFESSOR [*more and more astonished, calculating mentally*]: Yes . . . you are right . . . the result is indeed . . . [*He mumbles unintelligibly:*] . . . quintillion, quadrillion, trillion, billion, million . . . [*Clearly:*] one hundred sixty-four thousand five hundred and eight . . . [*Stupefied:*] But how did you know that, if you don't know the principles of arithmetical reasoning?

PUPIL: It's easy. Not being able to rely on my reasoning, I've memorized all the products of all possible multiplications.

PROFESSOR: That's pretty good . . . However, permit me to confess to you that that doesn't satisfy me, miss, and I do not congratulate you: in mathematics and in arithmetic especially, the thing that counts—for in arithmetic it is always necessary to count—the thing that counts is, above all, understanding . . . It is by mathematical reasoning, simultaneously inductive and deductive, that you ought to arrive at this result—as well as at any other result. Mathematics is the sworn enemy of memory, which is excellent otherwise, but disastrous, arithmetically speaking! . . . That's why I'm not happy with this . . . this won't do, not at all . . .

PUPIL [*desolated*]: No, Professor.

PROFESSOR: Let's leave it for the moment. Let's go on to another exercise . . .

PUPIL: Yes, Professor.

MAID [*entering*]: Hmm, hmm, Professor . . .

PROFESSOR [*who doesn't hear her*]: It is unfortunate, miss, that you aren't further along in specialized mathematics . . .

MAID [*taking him by the sleeve*]: Professor! Professor!

PROFESSOR: I hear that you will not be able to qualify for the total doctor's orals . . .

PUPIL: Yes, Professor, it's too bad!

PROFESSOR: Unless you . . . [*To the* MAID:] Let me be, Marie . . . Look here, why are you bothering me? Go back to the kitchen! To your pots and pans! Go away! Go away! [*To the* PUPIL:] We will try to prepare you at least for the partial doctorate . . .

MAID: Professor! . . . Professor! . . . [*She pulls his sleeve.*]

PROFESSOR [*to the* MAID]: Now leave me alone! Let me be! What's the meaning of this? . . . [*To the* PUPIL:] I must therefore teach you, if you really do insist on attempting the partial doctorate . . .

PUPIL: Yes, Professor.

PROFESSOR: . . . The elements of linguistics and of comparative philology . . .

MAID: No, Professor, no! . . . You mustn't do that! . . .

PROFESSOR: Marie, you're going too far!

MAID: Professor, especially not philology, philology leads to calamity . . .

PUPIL [*astonished*]: To calamity? [*Smiling, a little stupidly:*] That's hard to believe.

PROFESSOR [*to the* MAID]: That's enough now! Get out of here!

MAID: All right, Professor, all right. But you can't say that I didn't warn you! Philology leads to calamity!

PROFESSOR: I'm an adult, Marie!

PUPIL: Yes, Professor.

MAID: As you wish.

[*She exits.*]

PROFESSOR: Let's continue, miss.

PUPIL: Yes, Professor.

PROFESSOR: I want you to listen now with the greatest possible attention to a lecture I have prepared . . .

PUPIL: Yes, Professor!

PROFESSOR: . . . Thanks to which, in fifteen minutes' time, you will be able to acquire the fundamental principles of the linguistic and comparative philology of the neo-Spanish languages.

PUPIL: Yes, Professor, oh good!

[*She claps her hands.*]

PROFESSOR [*with authority*]: Quiet! What do you mean by that?

PUPIL: I'm sorry, Professor.

[*Slowly, she replaces her hands on the table.*]

PROFESSOR: Quiet! [*He gets up, walks up and down the room, his hands behind his back; from time to time he stops at stage center or near the* PUPIL, *and underlines his words with a gesture of his hand; he orates, but without being too emotional. The* PUPIL *follows him with her eyes, occasionally with some difficulty, for she has to turn her head far around; once or twice, not more, she turns around completely.*] And now, miss, Spanish is truly the mother tongue which gave birth to all the neo-Spanish languages, of which Spanish, Latin, Italian, our own French, Portuguese, Romanian, Sardinian or Sardanapalian, Spanish and neo-Spanish—and also, in certain of its aspects, Turkish which is otherwise very close to Greek, which is only logical, since it is a fact that Turkey is a neighbor of Greece and Greece is even closer to Turkey than you are to me—this is only one more illustration of the very important linguistic law which states that geography and philology are twin sisters . . . You may take notes, miss.

PUPIL [*in a dull voice*]: Yes, Professor!

PROFESSOR: That which distinguishes the neo-Spanish languages from each other and their idioms from the other linguistic groups, such as the group of languages called Austrian and neo-Austrian or Hapsburgian, as well as the Esperanto, Helvetian, Monacan, Swiss, Andorran, Basque, and jai alai groups, and also the groups of diplomatic and technical languages—that which distinguishes them, I repeat, is their striking resemblance which makes it so hard to distinguish them from each other—I'm speaking of the neo-Spanish languages which one is able to distinguish from each other, however, only thanks to their distinctive characteristics, absolutely indisputable proofs of their extraordinary resemblance, which renders indisputable their common origin, and which, at the same time, differentiates them profoundly—through the continuation of the distinctive traits which I've just cited.

PUPIL: Oooh! Ye-e-e-s-s-s, Professor!

PROFESSOR: But let's not linger over generalities . . .

PUPIL [*regretfully, but won over*]: Oh, Professor . . .

PROFESSOR: This appears to interest you. All the better, all the better.

PUPIL: Oh, yes, Professor . . .

PROFESSOR: Don't worry, miss. We will come back to it later . . . That is if we come back to it at all. Who can say?

PUPIL [*enchanted in spite of everything*]: Oh, yes, Professor.

PROFESSOR: Every tongue—you must know this, miss, and remember it *until the hour of your death* . . .

PUPIL: Oh! yes, Professor, until the hour of my death . . . Yes, Professor . . .

PROFESSOR: . . . And this, too, is a fundamental principle, every tongue is at bottom nothing but language, which necessarily implies that it is composed of sounds, or . . .

PUPIL: Phonemes . . .

PROFESSOR: Just what I was going to say. Don't parade your knowledge. You'd do better to listen.

PUPIL: All right, Professor. Yes, Professor.

PROFESSOR: The sounds, miss, must be seized on the wing as they fly so that they'll not fall on deaf ears. As a result, when you set out to articulate, it is recommended, insofar as possible, that you lift up your neck and chin very high, and rise up on the tips of your toes, you see, this way . . .

PUPIL: Yes, Professor.

PROFESSOR: Keep quiet. Remain seated, don't interrupt me . . . And project the sounds very loudly with all the force of your lungs in conjunction with that of your vocal cords. Like this, look: "Butterfly," "Eureka," "Trafalgar," "Papaya." This way, the sounds become filled with a warm air that is lighter than the surrounding air so that they can fly without danger of falling on deaf ears, which are veritable voids, tombs of sonorities. If you utter several sounds at an accelerated speed, they will automatically cling to each other, constituting thus syllables, words, even sentences, that is to say groupings of various importance, purely irrational assemblages of sounds, denuded of all sense, but for that very reason the more capable of maintaining themselves without danger at a high altitude in the air. By themselves, words charged with significance will fall, weighted down by their meaning, and in the end they always collapse, fall . . .

PUPIL: . . . On deaf ears.

PROFESSOR: That's it, but don't interrupt . . . and into the worst confusion . . . Or else burst like balloons. Therefore, miss . . . [*The* PUPIL *suddenly appears to be unwell.*] What's the matter?

PUPIL: I've got a toothache, Professor.

PROFESSOR: That's not important. We're not going to stop for anything so trivial. Let us go on . . .

PUPIL [*appearing to be in more and more pain*]: Yes, Professor.

PROFESSOR: I draw your attention in passing to the consonants that change their nature in combinations. In this case *f* becomes *v, d* becomes *t, g* becomes *k,* and vice versa, as in these examples that I will cite for you: "That's all right," "hens and chickens," "Welsh rabbit," "lots of nothing," "not at all."*

PUPIL: I've got a toothache.

PROFESSOR: Let's continue.

PUPIL: Yes.

PROFESSOR: To resume: it takes years and years to learn to pronounce. Thanks to science, we can achieve this in a few minutes. In order to project words, sounds and all the rest, you must realize that it is necessary to pitilessly expel air from the lungs, and make it pass delicately, caressingly, over the vocal cords, which, like harps or leaves in the wind, will suddenly shake, agitate, vibrate, vibrate, vibrate or uvulate, or fricate or jostle against each other, or sibilate, sibilate, placing everything in movement, the uvula, the tongue, the palate, the teeth . . .

PUPIL: I have a toothache.

PROFESSOR: . . . And the lips . . . Finally the words come out through the nose, the mouth, the ears, the pores, drawing along with them all the organs that we have named, torn up by the roots, in a powerful, majestic flight, which is none other than what is called, improperly, the voice, whether modulated in singing or transformed into a terrible symphonic storm with a whole procession . . . of garlands of all kinds of flowers, of sonorous artifices: labials, dentals, occlusives, palatals, and others, some caressing, some bitter or violent.

PUPIL: Yes, Professor, I've got a toothache.

PROFESSOR: Let's go on, go on. As for the neo-Spanish languages, they are closely related, so closely to each other, that they can be considered as true second cousins. Moreover, they have the same mother: Spanishe, with

*All to be heavily elided.—Translator's note.

a mute *e*. That is why it is so difficult to distinguish them from one another. That is why it is so useful to pronounce carefully, and to avoid errors in pronunciation. Pronunciation itself is worth a whole language. A bad pronunciation can get you into trouble. In this connection, permit me, parenthetically, to share a personal experience with you. [*Slight pause. The* PROFESSOR *goes over his memories for a moment; his features mellow, but he recovers at once.*] I was very young, little more than a child. It was during my military service. I had a friend in the regiment, a vicomte, who suffered from a rather serious defect in his pronunciation: he could not pronounce the letter *f*. Instead of *f*, he said *f*. Thus, instead of "Birds of a feather flock together," he said: "Birds of a feather flock together." He pronounced filly instead of filly, Firmin instead of Firmin, French bean instead of French bean, go frig yourself instead of go frig yourself, farrago instead of farrago, fee fi fo fum instead of fee fi fo fum, Philip instead of Philip, fictory instead of fictory, February instead of February, March–April instead of March–April, Gerard de Nerval and not as is correct—Gerard de Nerval, Mirabeau instead of Mirabeau, etc., instead of etc., and thus instead of etc., instead of etc., and thus and so forth. However, he managed to conceal his fault so effectively that, thanks to the hats he wore, no one ever noticed it.

PUPIL: Yes, I've got a toothache.

PROFESSOR [*abruptly changing his tone, his voice hardening*]: Let's go on. We'll first consider the points of similarity in order the better to apprehend, later on, that which distinguishes all these languages from each other. The differences can scarcely be recognized by people who are not aware of them. Thus, all the words of all the languages . . .

PUPIL: Uh, yes? . . . I've got a toothache.

PROFESSOR: Let's continue . . . are always the same, just as all the suffixes, all the prefixes, all the terminations, all the roots . . .

PUPIL: Are the roots of words square?

PROFESSOR: Square or cube. That depends.

PUPIL: I've got a toothache.

PROFESSOR: Let's go on. Thus, to give you an example which is little more than an illustration, take the word "front" . . .

PUPIL: How do you want me to take it?

PROFESSOR: However you wish, so long as you take it, but above all do not interrupt.

PUPIL: I've got a toothache.

PROFESSOR: Let's continue . . . I said: Let's continue. Take now the word "front." Have you taken it?

PUPIL: Yes, yes, I've got it. My teeth, my teeth . . .

PROFESSOR: The word "front" is the root of "frontispiece." It is also to be found in "affronted." "Ispiece" is the suffix, and "af" the prefix. They are so called because they do not change. They don't want to.

PUPIL: I've got a toothache.

PROFESSOR: Let's go on. [*Rapidly:*] These prefixes are of Spanish origin. I hope you noticed that, did you?

PUPIL: Oh, how my tooth aches.

PROFESSOR: Let's continue. You've surely also noticed that they've not changed in French. And now, young lady, nothing has succeeded in changing them in Latin either, nor in Italian, nor in Portuguese, nor in Sardanapalian, nor in Sardanapali, nor in Romanian, nor in neo-Spanish, nor in Spanish, nor even in the Oriental: front, frontispiece, affronted, always the same word, invariably with the same root, the same suffix, the same prefix, in all the languages I have named. And it is always the same for all words.

PUPIL: In all languages, these words mean the same thing? I've got a toothache.

PROFESSOR: Absolutely. Moreover, it's more a notion than a word. In any case, you have always the same signification, the same composition, the same sound structure, not only for this word, but for all conceivable words, in all languages. For one single notion is expressed by one and the same word, and its synonyms, in all countries. Forget about your teeth.

PUPIL: I've got a toothache. Yes, yes, yes.

PROFESSOR: Good, let's go on. I tell you, let's go on . . . How would you say, for example, in French: the roses of my grandmother are as yellow as my grandfather who was Asiatic?

PUPIL: My teeth ache, ache, ache.

PROFESSOR: Let's go on, let's go on, go ahead and answer, anyway.

PUPIL: In French?

PROFESSOR: In French.

PUPIL: Uhh . . . I should say in French: the roses of my grandmother are . . . ?

PROFESSOR: As yellow as my grandfather who was Asiatic . . .

PUPIL: Oh well, one would say, in French, I believe, the roses . . . of my . . . how do you say "grandmother" in French?

PROFESSOR: In French? Grandmother.

PUPIL: The roses of my grandmother are as yellow—in French, is it "yellow"?

PROFESSOR: Yes, of course!

PUPIL: Are as yellow as my grandfather when he got angry.

PROFESSOR: No . . . who was A . . .

PUPIL: . . . siatic . . . I've got a toothache.

PROFESSOR: That's it.

PUPIL: I've got a tooth . . .

PROFESSOR: Ache . . . so what . . . let's continue! And now translate the same sentence into Spanish, then into neo-Spanish . . .

PUPIL: In Spanish . . . this would be: the roses of my grandmother are as yellow as my grandfather who was Asiatic.

PROFESSOR: No. That's wrong.

PUPIL: And in neo-Spanish: the roses of my grandmother are as yellow as my grandfather who was Asiatic.

PROFESSOR: That's wrong. That's wrong. That's wrong. You have inverted it, you've confused Spanish with neo-Spanish, and neo-Spanish with Spanish . . . Oh . . . no . . . it's the other way around . . .

PUPIL: I've got a toothache. You're getting mixed up.

PROFESSOR: You're the one who is mixing me up. Pay attention and take notes. I will say the sentence to you in Spanish, then in neo-Spanish, and finally, in Latin. You will repeat after me. Pay attention, for the resemblances are great. In fact, they are identical resemblances. Listen, follow carefully . . .

PUPIL: I've got a tooth . . .

PROFESSOR: . . . Ache.

PUPIL: Let us go on . . . Ah! . . .

PROFESSOR: . . . In Spanish: the roses of my grandmother are as yellow as my grandfather who was Asiatic; in Latin: the roses of my grandmother are as yellow as my grandfather who was Asiatic. Do you detect the differences? Translate this into . . . Romanian.

PUPIL: The . . . how do you say "roses" in Romanian?

PROFESSOR: But "roses," what else?

PUPIL: It's not "roses"? Oh, how my tooth aches!

PROFESSOR: Certainly not, certainly not, since "roses" is a translation in Oriental of the French word "roses," in Spanish "roses," do you get it? In Sardanapali, "roses" . . .

PUPIL: Excuse me, Professor, but . . . Oh, my toothache! . . . I don't get the difference.

PROFESSOR: But it's so simple! So simple! It's a matter of having a certain experience, a technical experience and practice in these diverse languages, which are so diverse in spite of the fact that they present wholly identical characteristics. I'm going to try to give you a key . . .

PUPIL: Toothache . . .

PROFESSOR: That which differentiates these languages, is neither the words, which are absolutely the same, nor the structure of the sentence which is everywhere the same, nor the intonation, which does not offer any differences, nor the rhythm of the language . . . that which differentiates them . . . are you listening?

PUPIL: I've got a toothache.

PROFESSOR: Are you listening to me, young lady? Aah! We're going to lose our temper.

PUPIL: You're bothering me, Professor. I've got a toothache.

PROFESSOR: Son of a cocker spaniel! Listen to me!

PUPIL: Oh well . . . yes . . . yes . . . go on . . .

PROFESSOR: That which distinguishes them from each other, on the one hand, and from their mother, Spanishe with its mute *e,* on the other hand . . . is . . .

PUPIL [*grimacing*]: Is what?

PROFESSOR: Is an intangible thing. Something intangible that one is able to perceive only after very long study, with a great deal of trouble and after the broadest experience . . .

PUPIL: Ah?

PROFESSOR: Yes, young lady. I cannot give you any rule. One must have a feeling for it, and well, that's it. But in order to have it, one must study, study, and then study some more.

PUPIL: Toothache.

PROFESSOR: All the same, there are some specific cases where words differ from one language to another . . . but we cannot base our knowledge on these cases, which are, so to speak, exceptional.

PUPIL: Oh, yes? . . . Oh, Professor, I've got a toothache.

PROFESSOR: Don't interrupt! Don't make me lose my temper! I can't answer for what I'll do. I was saying, then . . . Ah, yes, the exceptional cases, the so-called easily distinguished . . . or facilely distinguished . . . or conveniently . . . if you prefer . . . I repeat, if you prefer, for I see that you're not listening to me . . .

PUPIL: I've got a toothache.

PROFESSOR: I say then: in certain expressions in current usage, certain words differ totally from one language to another, so much so that the language employed is, in this case, considerably easier to identify. I'll give you an example: the neo-Spanish expression, famous in Madrid: "My country is the new Spain," becomes in Italian: "My country is . . .

PUPIL: The new Spain.

PROFESSOR: No! "My country is Italy." Tell me now, by simple deduction, how do you say "Italy" in French?

PUPIL: I've got a toothache.

PROFESSOR: But it's so easy: for the word "Italy," in French we have the word "France," which is an exact translation of it. My country is France. And "France" in Oriental: "Orient!" My country is the Orient. And "Orient" in Portuguese: "Portugal!" The Oriental expression: My country is the Orient is translated then in the same fashion into Portuguese: My country is Portugal! And so on . . .

PUPIL: Oh, no more, no more. My teeth . . .

PROFESSOR: Ache! ache! ache! . . . I'm going to pull them out, I will! One more example. The word "capital"—it takes on, according to the language one speaks, a different meaning. That is to say that when a Spaniard says: "I reside in the capital," the word "capital" does not mean at all the same thing that a Portuguese means when he says: "I reside in the capital." All the more so in the case of a Frenchman, a neo-Spaniard, a Romanian, a Latin, a Sardanapali . . . Whenever you hear it, young lady—young lady, I'm saying this for you! Pooh! Whenever you hear the expression: "I reside in the capital," you will immediately and easily know whether this is Spanish or Spanish, neo-Spanish, French, Oriental, Romanian, or Latin, for it is enough to know which metropolis is referred to by the person who pronounces the sentence . . . at the very moment he pronounces it . . . But these are almost the only precise examples that I can give you . . .

PUPIL: Oh dear! My teeth . . .

PROFESSOR: Silence! Or I'll bash in your skull!

PUPIL: Just try to! Skulldugger!

[*The* PROFESSOR *seizes her wrist and twists it.*]

PUPIL: Oww!

PROFESSOR: Keep quiet now! Not a word!

PUPIL [*whimpering*]: Toothache . . .

PROFESSOR: One thing that is the most . . . how shall I say it? . . . the most paradoxical . . . yes . . . that's the word . . . the most paradoxical thing, is that a lot of people who are completely illiterate speak these different languages . . . do you understand? What did I just say?

PUPIL: . . . "Speak these different languages! What did I just say?"

PROFESSOR: You were lucky that time! . . . The common people speak a Spanish full of neo-Spanish words that they are entirely unaware of, all the while believing that they are speaking Latin . . . or they speak Latin, full of Oriental words, all the while believing that they're speaking Romanian . . . or Spanish, full of neo-Spanish, all the while believing that they're speaking Sardanapali, or Spanish . . . Do you understand?

PUPIL: Yes! yes! yes! yes! What more do you want . . . ?

PROFESSOR: No insolence, my pet, or you'll be sorry . . . [*In a rage:*] But the worst of all, young lady, is that certain people, for example, in a Latin that they suppose is Spanish, say: "Both my kidneys are of the same kidney," in addressing themselves to a Frenchman who does not know a word of Spanish, but the latter understands it as if it were his own language. For that matter he thinks it is his own language. And the Frenchman will reply, in French: "Me too, sir, mine are too," and this will be perfectly comprehensible to a Spaniard, who will feel certain that the reply is in pure Spanish and that Spanish is being spoken . . . when, in reality, it was neither Spanish nor French, but Latin in the neo-Spanish dialect . . . Sit still, young lady, don't fidget, stop tapping your feet . . .

PUPIL: I've got a toothache.

PROFESSOR: How do you account for the fact that, in speaking without knowing which language they speak, or even while each of them believes that he is speaking another, the common people understand each other at all?

PUPIL: I wonder.

PROFESSOR: It is simply one of the inexplicable curiosities of the vulgar empiricism of the common people—not to be confused with experience!—a paradox, a non-sense, one of the aberrations of human nature, it is purely and simply instinct—to put it in a nutshell . . . That's what is involved here.

PUPIL: Hah! hah!

PROFESSOR: Instead of staring at the flies while I'm going to all this trouble . . .

you would do much better to try to be more attentive . . . it is not I who is going to qualify for the partial doctor's orals . . . I passed mine a long time ago . . . and I've won my total doctorate, too . . . and my supertotal diploma . . . Don't you realize that what I'm saying is for your own good?

PUPIL: Toothache!

PROFESSOR: Ill-mannered . . . It can't go on like this, it won't do, it won't do, it won't do . . .

PUPIL: I'm . . . listening . . . to you . . .

PROFESSOR: Ahah! In order to learn to distinguish all the different languages, as I've told you, there is nothing better than practice . . . Let's take them up in order. I am going to try to teach you all the translations of the word "knife."

PUPIL: Well, all right . . . if you want . . .

PROFESSOR [*calling the* MAID]: Marie! Marie! She's not there . . . Marie! Marie! . . . Marie, where are you? [*He opens the door on the right.*] Marie! . . .

[*He exits. The* PUPIL *remains alone several minutes, staring into space, wearing a stupefied expression.*]

PROFESSOR [*offstage, in a shrill voice*]: Marie! What are you up to? Why don't you come! When I call you, you must come! [*He re-enters, followed by* MARIE.] It is I who gives the orders, do you hear? [*He points at the* PUPIL:] She doesn't understand anything, that girl. She doesn't understand!

MAID: Don't get into such a state, sir, you know where it'll end! You're going to go too far, you're going to go too far.

PROFESSOR: I'll be able to stop in time.

MAID: That's what you always say. I only wish I could see it.

PUPIL: I've got a toothache.

MAID: You see, it's starting, that's the symptom!

PROFESSOR: What symptom? Explain yourself? What do you mean?

PUPIL [*in a spiritless voice*]: Yes, what do you mean? I've got a toothache.

MAID: The final symptom! The chief symptom!

PROFESSOR: Stupid! stupid! stupid! [*The* MAID *starts to exit.*] Don't go away like that! I called you to help me find the Spanish, neo-Spanish, Portuguese, French, Oriental, Romanian, Sardanapali, Latin and Spanish knives.

MAID [*severely*]: Don't ask me. [*She exits.*]

PROFESSOR [*makes a gesture as though to protest, then refrains, a little helpless. Suddenly, he remembers*]: Ah! [*He goes quickly to the drawer where he finds a big knife, invisible or real according to the preference of the director. He seizes it and brandishes it happily.*] Here is one, young lady, here is a knife. It's too bad that we only have this one, but we're going to try to make it serve for all the languages, anyway! It will be enough if you will pronounce the word "knife" in all the languages, while looking at the object, very closely, fixedly, and imagining that it is in the language that you are speaking.

PUPIL: I've got a toothache.

PROFESSOR [*almost singing, chanting*]: Now, say "kni," like "kni," "fe," like "fe" . . . And look, look, look at it, watch it . . .

PUPIL: What is this one in? French, Italian or Spanish?

PROFESSOR: That doesn't matter now . . . That's not your concern. Say: "kni."

PUPIL: "Kni."

PROFESSOR: . . . "fe" . . . Look.

[*He brandishes the knife under the* PUPIL*'s eyes.*]

PUPIL: "fe" . . .

PROFESSOR: Again . . . Look at it.

PUPIL: Oh, no! My God! I've had enough. And besides, I've got a toothache, my feet hurt me, I've got a headache.

PROFESSOR [*abruptly*]: Knife . . . look . . . knife . . . look . . . knife . . . look . . .

PUPIL: You're giving me an earache, too. Oh, your voice! It's so piercing!

PROFESSOR: Say: knife . . . kni . . . fe . . .

PUPIL: No! My ears hurt, I hurt all over . . .

PROFESSOR: I'm going to tear them off, your ears, that's what I'm going to do to you, and then they won't hurt you anymore, my pet.

PUPIL: Oh . . . you're hurting me, oh, you're hurting me . . .

PROFESSOR: Look, come on, quickly, repeat after me: "kni" . . .

PUPIL: Oh, since you insist . . . knife . . . knife . . . [*In a lucid moment, ironically:*] Is that neo-Spanish . . . ?

PROFESSOR: If you like, yes, it's neo-Spanish, but hurry up . . . we haven't got time . . . And then, what do you mean by that insidious question? What are you up to?

PUPIL [*becoming more and more exhausted, weeping, desperate, at the same time both exasperated and in a trance*]: Ah!

PROFESSOR: Repeat, watch. [*He imitates a cuckoo:*] Knife, knife . . . knife, knife . . . knife, knife . . . knife, knife . . .

PUPIL: Oh, my head . . . aches . . . [*With her hand she caressingly touches the parts of her body as she names them:*] . . . My eyes . . .

PROFESSOR [*like a cuckoo*]: Knife, knife . . . knife, knife . . .

[*They are both standing. The* PROFESSOR *still brandishes his invisible knife, nearly beside himself, as he circles around her in a sort of scalp dance, but it is important that this not be exaggerated and that his dance steps be only suggested. The* PUPIL *stands facing the audience, then recoils in the direction of the window, sickly, languid, victimized.*]

PROFESSOR: Repeat, repeat: knife . . . knife . . . knife . . .

PUPIL: I've got a pain . . . my throat, neck . . . oh, my shoulders . . . my breast . . . knife . . .

PROFESSOR: Knife . . . knife . . . knife . . .

PUPIL: My hips . . . knife . . . my thighs . . . kni . . .

PROFESSOR: Pronounce it carefully . . . knife . . . knife . . .

PUPIL: Knife . . . my throat . . .

PROFESSOR: Knife . . . knife . . .

PUPIL: Knife . . . my shoulders . . . my arms, my breast, my hips . . . knife . . . knife . . .

PROFESSOR: That's right . . . Now, you're pronouncing it well . . .

PUPIL: Knife . . . my breast . . . my stomach . . .

PROFESSOR [*changing his voice*]: Pay attention . . . don't break my window . . . the knife kills . . .

PUPIL [*in a weak voice*]: Yes, yes . . . the knife kills?

PROFESSOR [*striking the* PUPIL *with a very spectacular blow of the knife*]: Aaah! That'll teach you!

[PUPIL *also cries "Aah!" then falls, flopping in an immodest position onto a chair which, as though by chance, is near the window. The murderer and his victim shout "Aaah!" at the same moment. After the first blow of the knife, the* PUPIL *flops onto the chair, her legs spread wide and hanging over both sides of the chair. The* PROFESSOR *remains standing in front of her, his back to the audience. After the first blow, he strikes her dead with a second slash of the knife, from bottom to top. After that blow a noticeable convulsion shakes his whole body.*]

PROFESSOR [*winded, mumbling*]: Bitch . . . Oh, that's good, that does me good . . . Ah! Ah! I'm exhausted . . . I can scarcely breathe . . . Aah! [*He breathes with difficulty; he falls—fortunately a chair is there; he mops his brow, mumbles some incomprehensible words; his breathing becomes normal. He gets up, looks at the knife in his hand, looks at the young girl, then as though he were waking up, in a panic:*] What have I done! What's going to happen to me now! What's going to happen! Oh! dear! Oh dear, I'm in trouble! Young lady, young lady, get up! [*He is agitated, still holding onto the invisible knife, which he doesn't know what to do with.*] Come now, young lady, the lesson is over . . . you may go . . . you can pay another time . . . Oh! she is dead . . . dea-ead . . . And by my knife . . . She is dea-ead . . . It's terrible. [*He calls the* MAID:] Marie! Marie! My good Marie, come here! Ah! ah! [*The door on the right opens a little and* MARIE *appears.*] No . . . don't come in . . . I made a mistake . . . I don't need you, Marie . . . I don't need you anymore . . . do you understand? . . .

[MAID *enters wearing a stern expression, without saying a word. She sees the corpse.*]

PROFESSOR [*in a voice less and less assured*]: I don't need you, Marie . . .

MAID [*sarcastic*]: Then, you're satisfied with your pupil, she's profited by your lesson?

PROFESSOR [*holding the knife behind his back*]: Yes, the lesson is finished . . . but . . . she . . . she's still there . . . she doesn't want to leave . . .

MAID [*very harshly*]: Is that a fact? . . .

PROFESSOR [*trembling*]: It wasn't I . . . it wasn't I . . . Marie . . . No . . . I assure you . . . it wasn't I, my little Marie . . .

MAID: And who was it? Who was it then? Me?

PROFESSOR: I don't know . . . maybe . . .

MAID: Or the cat?

PROFESSOR: That's possible . . . I don't know . . .

MAID: And today makes it the fortieth time! . . . And every day it's the same thing! Every day! You should be ashamed, at your age . . . and you're going to make yourself sick! You won't have any pupils left. That will serve you right.

PROFESSOR [*irritated*]: It wasn't my fault! She didn't want to learn! She was disobedient! She was a bad pupil! She didn't want to learn!

MAID: Liar! . . .

PROFESSOR [*craftily approaching the* MAID, *holding the knife behind his back*]: It's none of your business! [*He tries to strike her with a great blow of the knife; the* MAID *seizes his wrist in mid-gesture and twists it; the* PROFESSOR *lets the knife fall to the floor*]: . . . I'm sorry!

MAID [*gives him two loud, strong slaps; the* PROFESSOR *falls onto the floor, on his prat; he sobs*]: Little murderer! bastard! You're disgusting! You wanted to do that to me? I'm not one of your pupils, not me! [*She pulls him up by the collar, picks up his skullcap and puts it on his head; he's afraid she'll slap him again and holds his arm up to protect his face, like a child.*] Put the knife back where it belongs, go on! [*The* PROFESSOR *goes and puts it back in the drawer of the buffet, then comes back to her.*] Now didn't I warn you, just a little while ago: arithmetic leads to philology, and philology leads to crime . . .

PROFESSOR: You said "to calamity"!

MAID: It's the same thing.

PROFESSOR: I didn't understand you. I thought that "calamity" was a city and that you meant that philology leads to the city of Calamity . . .

MAID: Liar! Old fox! An intellectual like you is not going to make a mistake in the meanings of words. Don't try to pull the wool over my eyes.

PROFESSOR [*sobbing*]: I didn't kill her on purpose!

MAID: Are you sorry at least?

PROFESSOR: Oh, yes, Marie, I swear it to you!

MAID: I can't help feeling sorry for you! Ah! you're a good boy in spite of everything! I'll try to fix this. But don't start it again . . . It could give you a heart attack . . .

PROFESSOR: Yes, Marie! What are we going to do, now?

MAID: We're going to bury her . . . along with the thirty-nine others . . . that will make forty coffins . . . I'll call the undertakers and my lover, Father Augustus . . . I'll order the wreaths . . .

PROFESSOR: Yes, Marie, thank you very much.

MAID: Well, that's that. And perhaps it won't be necessary to call Augustus since you yourself are something of a priest at times, if one can believe the gossip.

PROFESSOR: In any case, don't spend too much on the wreaths. She didn't pay for her lesson.

MAID: Don't worry . . . The least you can do is cover her up with her smock, she's not decent that way. And then we'll carry her out . . .

PROFESSOR: Yes, Marie, yes. [*He covers up the body.*] There's a chance that we'll get pinched . . . with forty coffins . . . Don't you think . . . people will be surprised . . . Suppose they ask us what's inside them?

MAID: Don't worry so much. We'll say that they're empty. And besides, people won't ask questions, they're used to it.

PROFESSOR: Even so . . .

MAID [*she takes out an armband with an insignia, perhaps the Nazi swastika*]: Wait, if you're afraid, wear this, then you won't have anything more to be afraid of. [*She puts the armband around his arm.*] . . . That's good politics.

PROFESSOR: Thanks, my little Marie. With this, I won't need to worry . . . You're a good girl, Marie . . . very loyal . . .

MAID: That's enough. Come on, sir. Are you all right?

PROFESSOR: Yes, my little Marie. [*The* MAID *and the* PROFESSOR *take the body of the young girl, one by the shoulders, the other by the legs, and move towards the door on the right.*] Be careful. We don't want to hurt her.

[*They exit. The stage remains empty for several moments. We hear the doorbell ring at the left.*]

VOICE OF THE MAID: Just a moment, I'm coming!

[*She appears as she was at the beginning of the play, and goes towards the door. The doorbell rings again.*]

MAID [*aside*]: She's certainly in a hurry, this one! [*Aloud:*] Just a moment! [*She goes to the door on the left, and opens it.*] Good morning, miss! You are the new pupil? You have come for the lesson? The Professor is expecting you. I'll go tell him that you've come. He'll be right down. Come in, miss, come in!

—1958

What are your reactions to and questions about this work? The following questions may help provoke some ideas.

Probing the Work

1. What is the role of the Maid in this play? How important is her part in helping us to understand the Professor?
2. Look at the stage directions at the beginning of the play, in which Ionesco characterizes the transformation in the Pupil's behavior from beginning to

end. What is the nature of her transformation? Cite examples from the play to show how she changes.

3. What *is* "The Lesson"?

Identifying Issues

4. According to Lee A. Jacobus the *theatre of the absurd* "assumes that the world is meaningless, that meaning is a human concept, and that individuals must create significance and not rely on institutions or traditions to provide it." How does Ionesco's play illustrate this definition of absurdist drama? How does Ionesco treat the teaching/learning construct as absurd? What absurdities have you found in your learning situations? In your schooling in general?
5. How does the Professor control the Pupil in the play? To what extent is and should learning be controlled by teachers? What destructive or constructive models of teaching have you experienced?
6. In an interview Ionesco said, "With *The Lesson* I wanted to describe an ascending curve, to start out quietly and build to the professor's crescendo of madness, then to a violent fall." To what extent do you think that Ionesco has succeeded? Explain, using specific examples from the play. Could you graph or illustrate this curve in terms of the action of the play?

WRITING ASSIGNMENT SEQUENCE (CONTINUED FROM PAGE 872)

4. Making Connections

Select one of the following questions and write an informal response in which you connect your own ideas with those conveyed in the works of this cluster, and/or make connections among the works themselves.

A. Compare and contrast the types of teachers found in the works of this cluster.
B. Compare and contrast the types of students found in the works of this cluster.
C. Compare and contrast the types of learning found in the works of this cluster.
D. Based on what you've read, design or describe an ideal teacher/student relationship, referring directly to the works for positive or negative models.

5. Putting It All Together

Write an essay that combines what you think about the topic *The Lesson* with what you now understand about the readings.

- Collect your informal writing, notes, and reading-journal entries on this topic and decide what will be the focus of your essay.
- Outline your essay. Select the literary passages and personal details you might use to illustrate and support your main focus.
- Write a draft of your essay in which you bring together what you think about the subject with what you understand about the readings. Try to include in your draft one or more *literary terms*.
- Share what you've written with your classmates and instructor, then revise it according to their recommendations.

Writing Tip: Colloquial Versus Standard English

You should be able to recognize the difference between colloquial *(street, slang, informal)* language and the standard English of most college writing. The trick is to use colloquial language to your advantage when it is appropriate, and not when writing a formal essay. You might insert quotation marks around colloquialisms, or, to be safe, eliminate them entirely. Just be consistent.

CrossClusters

In your paper you might want to consider how the following works located elsewhere in this book depict learning:

- Gwendolyn Brooks, "We Real Cool" (p. 42)
- Gwendolyn Brooks, "Sadie and Maude" (p. 241)
- Naguib Mahfouz, "Half a Day" (p. 763)
- Grace Paley, "The Loudest Voice" (p. 971)

See Joe's essay in Appendix A (p. 1016) for a sample of writing on the *learning* cluster.

SYNTHESIS PAPER FOR SECTION 4: FRAMES OF MIND

How do your preliminary ideas about *frames of mind* hold up now that you have read a variety of works on the topic? Adding to, expanding on, and revising the writing that you have already done on the subject of the mind, write a long paper in which you examine some of the literature in this section, bringing together your early writing with the knowledge you have gained from your class discussions. The paper might combine research and critical analysis with your personal opinions and experiences. You might even bring in references to films, music, books, and/or magazine articles. There are many possibilities for topics relating to the complexities of *fantasy, madness,* and *learning*. Here are some questions to consider:

- What boundaries do you think exist between the different realms of fantasy/reality, madness/sanity, learning/schooling? How clear-cut are they?
- How does the human mind make sense of the world?
- What are various assumptions we make about "normal" ways of seeing the world and ourselves? What are the problems with such assumptions?

SECTION 5 (CHAPTERS 23–25)

THE INDIVIDUAL AND THE COSMOS

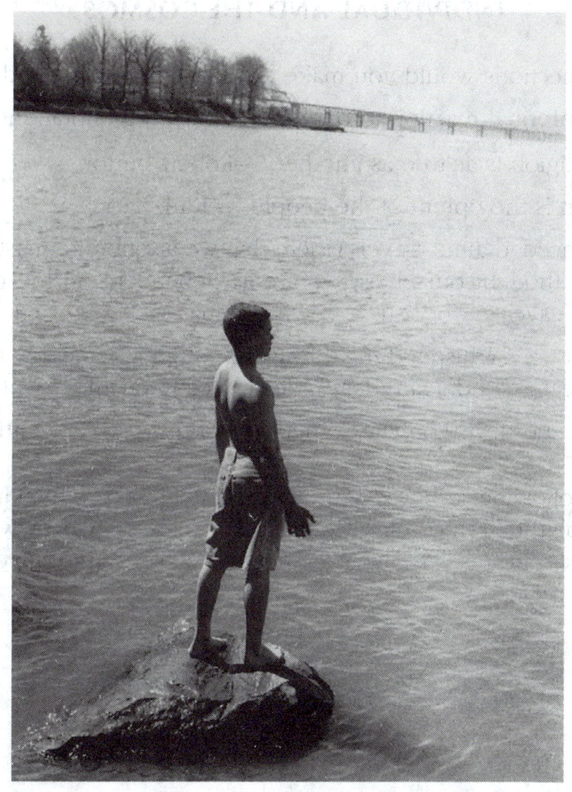

This section consists of some challenging readings and writing assignments on the "big issues": our relationship with nature, perspectives on God and religion, and considerations of death. To many people these three issues are intricately related. Their notions of God and their religious beliefs are tied in with how they see the natural world and how they view death and the afterlife. Similarly, "seeing" nature as it should be seen, for many, is to see "God" at work and to be more comfortable with death as part of the natural process. Finally, their concept of death and what happens afterwards is inseparable from their religious beliefs and their standing with the rest of the natural world. The readings and the writing assignments in this section might challenge some beliefs you might not want to question, but convictions that have withstood, or adapted to, some healthy introspection might become stronger and more meaningful than those that exist in a vacuum.

GETTING STARTED: WRITING EXERCISES ON THE INDIVIDUAL AND THE COSMOS

1. What connections would you make among nature, God, and death?
2. Write an informal reaction to one of the following quotations:
   - "One religion is as true as another."—Robert Burton
   - "Religion is the opium of the people."—Karl Marx
   - "It is conceded almost everywhere that we are not the masters of nature that we thought ourselves; we are as dependent on the rest of life as are the leaves . . . or fish."—Lewis Thomas
   - "The sea . . . / Whisper'd me through the night . . . the low and delicious word death, / and again death, death, death, death."—Walt Whitman
   - "There is no death, only a change of worlds."—Chief Seattle
3. Read the following section essay and apply to your own thinking what Dyer says about the "remorseless logical universe we live in where actions have consequences." To what degree do you see the universe as being logical?

SECTION ESSAY

GWYNNE DYER

A Cruel Universe, But the Only One Where Humans Could Exist

Gwynne Dyer was born in Newfoundland, Canada. After serving in the Canadian Navy, he earned a Ph.D. in war studies from the University of London. He now lives in London, and, in addition to teaching and lecturing, writes a syndicated column that appears in over 200 newspapers worldwide. In 1985 he created and wrote a seven-part television series, War, *that appeared on the Public Broadcasting System.*

Why do babies die? Why do people starve to death in famines? Why is the universe so cruel, taking some people's lives away before they even had a chance to enjoy life, while others have long, happy lives and die peacefully in bed?

Religious people call it "the problem of evil." If God is all-powerful, why does he allow such horror and pain in his universe? A god who deliberately allowed Auschwitz and the killing fields of Cambodia to happen would not deserve our love, or even our respect—and if he couldn't prevent them, then he isn't all-powerful.

Cardinal Basil Hume, an English clergyman, was recently asked why God permitted such things by a journalist as they both stood in the middle of an Ethiopian refugee camp. Hume had the honesty to answer that he had "no idea." More sophisticated men of religion, whether Christian, Muslim or Jewish, might give longer answers that sounded plausible—but they are all answers that go round in circles.

If you don't believe in God, of course, then there is no philosophical problem. The universe is impersonal, human beings are on their own, and terrible things happen to them for the same reason they happen to fruit flies: no reason at all, except blind chance. But even non-believers often wish the universe were a kinder, more forgiving environment. And the answer is: it can't be.

It is an answer that applies equally to a universe created by a loving God and to a Godless universe which doesn't care about people at all. Any universe which could conceivably be a habitat for human beings must be one in which events have predictable consequences—even if those consequences include terrible tragedies for human beings.

Imagine, for a moment, a universe in which tragedies didn't happen. When the engines of a jet airliner fail on takeoff, it does not crash at the end of the runway and burn 150 people to death. Instead, it just wafts gently to the ground, because God loved the passengers and chose to save them.

But if that were all that happened when aircraft engines failed, there would be no need for aircraft maintenance. Indeed, there would be no need for engines, or even wings—and people could safely step off the edge of cliffs and walk on air. The law of gravity would be suspended whenever it endangered human lives.

So would all the other laws of nature. Whenever children's lives were at risk from disease, biochemistry would change its rules to save them. If an earthquake were going to kill thousands of people, continental drift would simply have to stop: so much for geology. And if someone tried to kill somebody else, the gun wouldn't work, or the bullet wouldn't fly straight, or it would turn into a marshmallow before it struck the victim.

In such a universe, there could be no science or technology, because there would be no fixed natural laws on which we could base them. The strength of steel and the temperature of boiling water would vary depending on whether human lives were threatened by a given value. There could not even be logic, since the same causes would not invariably have the same effects. It would be an entirely magical universe.

It is all a package, and quite indivisible. Either you have a magical Garden of Eden where non-human creatures closely resembling angels, with no hard choices to make and no penalties to pay, browse idly on lotus leaves. Or else you get the remorselessly logical universe we live in, where actions have consequences and you pay dearly for your own mistakes (and those of others).

I know there is little consolation in all this for those who have had to watch helplessly while their child died, or for the millions whose loves and hopes lie 40 years buried with the last world war. It is a cruel universe, and knowing why does not make it less cruel. But even God could not have made it any different if he wanted it to be an appropriate home for human beings.

It's cold comfort, but maybe there is some consolation to be had in the fact that we're extremely fortunate to have been able to visit the universe even briefly. At the instant of your conception and mine, a million other potential men and women lost their only chance to see the place at all.

—1985

23

SEEING

WRITING ASSIGNMENT SEQUENCE

1. Thinking About . . . "Seeing" Nature

Asking a Series of Questions: Write quick, informal responses to the following questions:

- What place in "nature" do you know well?
- What makes it special for you?
- What is your relationship to it?
- How often do you, or did you, go there?
- What qualities about this spot do you appreciate that others may not?
- Have you noticed any changes in this spot lately?

2. Enacting the Topic

Take a hike—to some "natural" place on or near your campus, and look closely at a particular spot—under a rock, up a tree, or simply at any seemingly nondescript spot—for a minimum of twenty minutes.

- Take note of what you see, first on the surface, then "under the surface." Document what you see that you would not normally notice were you simply to walk past that spot.
- Next, note the nature of nature: is it really "natural"? Is it "man-made" nature? Is it unstained by human hands?
- Finally, reflect on what this spot might represent, in terms of the relationship between humans and nature.

3. Responding to the Readings

As you read the works in this cluster, jot down in your response journals questions you have about the works, and comment on passages you find provocative or puzzling. Consider the questions following each reading for journal writing and prepare to discuss your reactions in class.

CLUSTER ESSAY

ANNIE DILLARD

Seeing

Annie Dillard (b. 1945) was born and raised in Pittsburgh, and won the Pulitzer Prize before she was 30 years old for her nonfiction book, Pilgrim at Tinker Creek *(1974). The essay below is excerpted from this book, which presents her observations of the Blue Ridge area of Virginia and the meditations those observations provoked. Dillard teaches creative writing at Wesleyan University. Her other books include the poetry collection* Tickets for a Prayer Wheel *(1974), the memoir* An American Childhood *(1987),* A Writing Life *(1989), the novel* The Living *(1992), and a book of found poems,* Mornings Like This *(1995).*

When I was six or seven years old, growing up in Pittsburgh, I used to take a precious penny of my own and hide it for someone else to find. It was a curious compulsion; sadly, I've never been seized by it since. For some reason I always "hid" the penny along the same stretch of sidewalk up the street. I would cradle it at the roots of a sycamore, say, or in a hole left by a chipped-off piece of sidewalk. Then I would take a piece of chalk, and, starting at either end of the block, draw huge arrows leading up to the penny from both directions. After I learned to write I labeled the arrows: SURPRISE AHEAD or MONEY THIS WAY. I was greatly excited, during all this arrow-drawing, at the thought of the first lucky passer-by who would receive in this way, regardless of merit, a free gift from the universe. But I never lurked about. I would go straight home and not give the matter another thought, until, some months later, I would be gripped again by the impulse to hide another penny.

It is still the first week in January, and I've got great plans. I've been thinking about seeing. There are lots of things to see, unwrapped gifts and free surprises. The world is fairly studded and strewn with pennies cast broadside from a generous hand. But—and this is the point—who gets excited by a mere penny? If you follow one arrow, if you crouch motionless on a bank to watch a tremulous ripple thrill on the water and are rewarded by the sight of a muskrat kit paddling from its den, will you count that sight a chip of copper only, and go your rueful way? It is dire poverty indeed when a man is so malnourished and fatigued that he won't stoop to pick up a penny. But if you cultivate a healthy poverty and simplicity, so that finding a penny will literally make your day, then, since the world is in fact planted in pennies, you have with your poverty bought a lifetime of days. It is that simple. What you see is what you get.

I used to be able to see flying insects in the air. I'd look ahead and see, not the row of hemlocks across the road, but the air in front of it. My eyes would focus along that column of air, picking out flying insects. But I lost interest, I guess, for I dropped the habit. Now I can see birds. Probably some people can look at the grass at their feet and discover all the crawling creatures. I would like to know grasses and sedges—and care. Then my least journey into the world would be a field trip, a series of happy recognitions. Thoreau, in an expansive mood, exulted, "What a rich book might be made about buds, including, perhaps, sprouts!" It would be nice to think so. I cherish mental images I have of three perfectly happy people. One collects stones. Another—an Englishman, say—watches clouds. The third lives on a coast and collects drops of seawater which he examines microscopically and mounts. But I don't see what the specialist sees, and so I cut myself off, not only from the total picture, but from the various forms of happiness.

Unfortunately, nature is very much a now-you-see-it, now-you-don't affair. A fish flashes, then dissolves in the water before my eyes like so much salt. Deer apparently ascend bodily into heaven; the brightest oriole fades into leaves. These disappearances stun me into stillness and concentration; they say of nature that it conceals with a grand nonchalance, and they say of vision that it is a deliberate gift, the revelation of a dancer who for my eyes only flings away her seven veils. For nature does reveal as well as conceal: now-you-don't-see-it, now-you-do. For a week last September migrating red-winged blackbirds were feeding heavily down by the creek at the back of the house. One day I went out to investigate the racket; I walked up to a tree, an Osage orange, and a hundred birds flew away. They simply materialized out of the tree. I saw a tree, then a whisk of color, then a tree again. I walked closer and another hundred blackbirds took flight. Not a branch, not a twig budged: The birds were apparently weightless as well as invisible. Or, it was as if the leaves of the Osage orange had been freed from a spell in the form of red-winged blackbirds; they flew from the tree, caught my eye in the sky, and vanished. When I looked again at the tree the leaves had reassembled as if nothing had happened. Finally I walked directly to the trunk of the tree and a final hundred, the real diehards, appeared, spread, and vanished. How could so many hide in the tree without my seeing them? The Osage orange, unruffled, looked just as it had looked from the house, when three hundred red-winged blackbirds cried from its crown. I looked downstream where they flew, and they were gone. Searching, I couldn't spot one. I wandered downstream to force them to play their hand, but they'd crossed the creek and scattered. One show to a customer. These appearances catch at my throat; they are the free gifts, the bright coppers at the roots of trees.

It's all a matter of keeping my eyes open. Nature is like one of those line drawings of a tree that are puzzles for children: Can you find hidden in the leaves a duck, a house, a boy, a bucket, a zebra, and a boot? Specialists can find the most incredibly well-hidden things. A book I read when I was young recommended an easy way to find caterpillars to rear: You simply find some fresh caterpillar droppings, look up, and there's your caterpillar. More recently an author advised me to set my mind at ease about those piles of cut stems on the ground in grassy fields. Field mice make them; they cut the grass down by degrees to reach the seeds at the head. It seems that when the grass is tightly packed, as in a field of ripe grain, the blade won't topple at a single cut through the stem; instead, the cut stem simply drops vertically, held in the crush of grain. The mouse severs the bottom again and again, the stem keeps dropping an inch at a time, and finally the head is low enough for the mouse to reach the seeds. Meanwhile, the mouse is positively littering the field with its little piles of cut stems into which, presumably, the author of the book is constantly stumbling.

If I can't see these minutiae, I still try to keep my eyes open. I'm always on the lookout for antlion traps in sandy soil, monarch pupae near milkweed, skipper larvae in locust leaves. These things are utterly common, and I've not seen one. I bang on hollow trees near water, but so far no flying squirrels have appeared. In flat country I watch every sunset in hopes of seeing the green ray. The green ray is a seldom-seen streak of light that rises from the sun like a spurting fountain at the moment of sunset; it throbs into the sky for two seconds and disappears. One more reason to keep my eyes open. A photography professor at the University of Florida just happened to see a bird die in midflight; it jerked, died, dropped, and smashed on the ground. I squint at the wind because I read Stewart Edward White: "I have always maintained that if you looked closely enough you could *see* the wind—the dim, hardly-made-out, fine débris fleeing high in the air." White was an excellent observer, and devoted an entire chapter of *The Mountains* to the subject of seeing deer: "As soon as you can forget the naturally obvious and construct an artificial obvious, then you too will see deer."

But the artificial obvious is hard to see. My eyes account for less than one percent of the weight of my head; I'm bony and dense; I see what I expect. I once spent a full three minutes looking at a bullfrog that was so unexpectedly large I couldn't see it even though a dozen enthusiastic campers were shouting directions. Finally I asked, "What color am I looking for?" and a fellow said, "Green." When at last I picked out the frog, I saw what painters are up against: The thing wasn't green at all, but the color of wet hickory bark.

The lover can see, and the knowledgeable. I visited an aunt and uncle at a quarter-horse ranch in Cody, Wyoming. I couldn't do much of anything useful, but I could, I thought, draw. So, as we all sat around the kitchen table after supper, I produced a sheet of paper and drew a horse. "That's one lame horse," my aunt volunteered. The rest of the family joined in: "Only place to saddle that one is his neck"; "Looks like we better shoot the poor thing, on account of those terrible growths." Meekly, I slid the pencil and paper down the table. Everyone in that family, including my three young cousins, could draw a horse. Beautifully. When the paper came back it looked as though five shining, real quarter horses had been corraled by mistake with a papier-mâché moose; the real horses seemed to gaze at the monster with a steady, puzzled air. I stay away from horses now, but I can do a creditable goldfish. The point is that I just don't know what the lover knows; I just can't see the artificial obvious that those in the know construct. The herpetologist asks the native, "Are there snakes in that ravine?" "Nosir." And the herpetologist comes home with, yessir, three bags full. Are there butterflies on that mountain? Are the bluets in bloom, are there arrowheads here, or fossil shells in the shale?

Peeping through my keyhole I see within the range of only about thirty percent of the light that comes from the sun; the rest is infrared and some little ultraviolet, perfectly apparent to many animals, but invisible to me. A nightmare network of ganglia, charged and firing without my knowledge, cuts and splices what I do see, editing it for my brain. Donald E. Carr points out that the sense impressions of one-celled animals are *not* edited for the brain: "This is philosophically interesting in a rather mournful way, since it means that only the simplest animals perceive the universe as it is."

A fog that won't burn away drifts and flows across my field of vision. When you see fog move against a backdrop of deep pines, you don't see the fog itself, but streaks of clearness floating across the air in dark shreds. So I see only tatters of clearness through a pervading obscurity. I can't distinguish the fog from the overcast sky; I can't be sure if the light is direct or reflected. Everywhere darkness and the presence of the unseen appalls. We estimate now that only one atom dances alone in every cubic meter of intergalactic space. I blink and squint. What planet or power yanks Halley's Comet out of orbit? We haven't seen that force yet; it's a question of distance, density, and the pallor of reflected light. We rock, cradled in the swaddling band of darkness. Even the simple darkness of night whispers suggestions to the mind. Last summer, in August, I stayed at the creek too late.

Where Tinker Creek flows under the sycamore log bridge to the tear-shaped island, it is slow and shallow, fringed thinly in cattail marsh. At this spot an astonishing bloom of life supports vast breeding populations of insects, fish, reptiles, birds, and mammals. On windless summer evenings I stalk along the creek bank or straddle the sycamore log in absolute stillness, watching for muskrats. The night I stayed too late I was hunched on the log staring spellbound at spreading, reflected stains of lilac on the water. A cloud in the sky suddenly lighted as if turned on by a switch; its reflection just as suddenly materialized on the water upstream, flat and floating, so that I couldn't see the creek bottom, or life in the water under the cloud. Downstream, away from the cloud on the water, water turtles smooth as beans were gliding down with the current in a series of easy, weightless push-offs, as men bound on the moon. I didn't know whether to trace the progress of one turtle I was sure of, risking sticking my face in one of the bridge's spider webs made invisible by the gathering dark, or take a chance on seeing the carp, or scan the mudbank in hope of seeing a muskrat, or follow the last of the swallows who caught at my heart and trailed it after them like streamers as they appeared from directly below, under the log, flying upstream with the tails forked, so fast.

But shadows spread, and deepened, and stayed. After thousands of years we're still strangers to darkness, fearful aliens in an enemy camp with our arms crossed over our chests. I stirred. A land turtle on the bank, startled, hissed the air from its lungs and withdrew into its shell. An uneasy pink here, an unfathomable blue there, gave great suggestion of lurking beings. Things were going on. I couldn't see whether that sere rustle I heard was a distant rattlesnake, slit-eyed, or a nearby sparrow kicking in the dry flood debris slung at the foot of a willow. Tremendous action roiled the water everywhere I looked, big action, inexplicable. A tremor welled up beside a gaping muskrat burrow in the bank and I caught my breath, but no muskrat appeared. The ripples continued to fan upstream with a steady, powerful thrust. Night was knitting over my face an eyeless mask, and I still sat transfixed. A distant airplane, a delta wing out of nightmare, made a gliding shadow on the creek's bottom that looked like a stingray cruising upstream. At once a black fin slit the pink cloud on the water, shearing it in two. The two halves merged together and seemed to dissolve before my eyes. Darkness pooled in the cleft of the creek and rose, as water collects in a well. Untamed, dreaming lights flickered over the sky. I saw hints of hulking underwater shadows, two pale splashes out of the water, and round ripples rolling close together from a blackened center.

At last I stared upstream where only the deepest violet remained of the cloud, a cloud so high its underbelly still glowed feeble color reflected from a hidden sky lighted in turn by a sun halfway to China. And out of that violet, a sudden enormous black body arced over the water. I saw only a cylindrical sleekness. Head and tail, if there was a head and tail, were both submerged in cloud. I saw only one ebony fling, a headlong dive to darkness; then the waters closed, and the lights went out.

I walked home in a shivering daze, up hill and down. Later I lay open-mouthed in bed, my arms flung wide at my sides to steady the whirling darkness. At this latitude I'm spinning 836 miles an hour round the earth's axis; I often fancy I feel my sweeping fall as a breakneck arc like the dive of dolphins, and the hollow rushing of wind raises hair on my neck and the side of my face. In orbit around the sun I'm moving 64,800 miles an hour. The solar system as a whole, like a merry-go-round unhinged, spins, bobs, and blinks at the speed of 43,200 miles an hour along a course set east of Hercules. Someone has piped, and we are dancing a tarantella until the sweat pours. I open my eyes and I see dark, muscled forms curl out of water, with flapping gills and flattened eyes. I close my eyes and I see stars, deep stars giving way to deeper stars, deeper stars bowing to deepest stars at the crown of an infinite cone.

"Still," wrote van Gogh in a letter, "a great deal of light falls on everything."

If we are blinded by darkness, we are also blinded by light. When too much light falls on everything, a special terror results. Peter Freuchen describes the notorious kayak sickness to which Greenland Eskimos are prone. "The Greenland fjords are peculiar for the spells of completely quiet weather, when there is not enough wind to blow out a match and the water is like a sheet of glass. The kayak hunter must sit in his boat without stirring a finger so as not to scare the shy seals away. . . . The sun, low in the sky, sends a glare into his eyes, and the landscape around moves into the realm of the unreal. The reflex from the mirror-like water hypnotizes him, he seems to be unable to move, and all of a sudden it is as if he were floating in a bottomless void, sinking, sinking, and sinking. . . . Horror-stricken, he tries to stir, to cry out, but he cannot, he is completely paralyzed, he just falls and falls." Some hunters are especially cursed with this panic, and bring ruin and sometimes starvation to their families.

Sometimes here in Virginia at sunset low clouds on the southern or northern horizon are completely invisible in the lighted sky. I only know one is there because I can see its reflection in still water. The first time I discovered this mystery I looked from cloud to no-cloud in bewilderment, checking my bearings over and over, thinking maybe the ark of the covenant was just passing by south of Dead Man Mountain. Only much later did I read the explanation: Polarized light from the sky is very much weakened by reflection, but the light in clouds isn't polarized. So invisible clouds pass among visible clouds, till all slide over the mountains; so a greater light extinguishes a lesser as though it didn't exist.

In the great meteor shower of August, the Perseid, I wail all day for the shooting stars I miss. They're out there showering down, committing hara-kiri in a flame of fatal attraction, and hissing perhaps at last into the ocean. But at dawn what looks like a blue dome clamps down over me like a lid on a pot. The stars and planets could smash and I'd never know. Only a piece of ashen moon occasionally climbs up or down the inside of the dome, and our local star without surcease explodes on our heads. We have really only that one light, one source for all power, and yet we must turn away from it by universal decree. Nobody here on the planet seems aware of this strange, powerful taboo, that we all walk about carefully averting our faces, this way and that, lest our eyes be blasted forever.

Darkness appalls and light dazzles; the scrap of visible light that doesn't hurt my eyes hurts my brain. What I see sets me swaying. Size and distance and the sudden swelling of meanings confuse me, bowl me over. I straddle the sycamore log bridge over Tinker Creek in the summer. I look at the lighted creek bottom: Snail tracks tunnel the mud in quavering curves. A crayfish jerks, but by the time I absorb what has happened, he's gone in a billowing smokescreen of silt. I look at the water: minnows and shiners. If I'm thinking minnows, a carp will fill my brain till I scream. I look at the water's surface:

skaters, bubbles, and leaves sliding down. Suddenly, my own face, reflected, startles me witless. Those snails have been tracking my face! Finally, with a shuddering wrench of the will, I see clouds, cirrus clouds. I'm dizzy, I fall in. This looking business is risky.

Once I stood on a humped rock on nearby Purgatory Mountain, watching through binoculars the great autumn hawk migration below, until I discovered that I was in danger of joining the hawks on a vertical migration of my own. I was used to binoculars, but not, apparently, to balancing on humped rocks while looking through them. I staggered. Everything advanced and receded by turns; the world was full of unexplained foreshortenings and depths. A distant huge tan object, a hawk the size of an elephant, turned out to be the browned bough of a nearby loblolly pine. I followed a sharp-shinned hawk against a featureless sky, rotating my head unawares as it flew, and when I lowered the glass a glimpse of my own looming shoulder sent me staggering. What prevents the men on Palomar from falling, voiceless and blinded, from their tiny, vaulted chairs?

I reel in confusion; I don't understand what I see. With the naked eye I can see two million light-years to the Andromeda galaxy. Often I slop some creek water in a jar and when I get home I dump it in a white china bowl. After the silt settles I return and see tracings of minute snails on the bottom, a planarian or two winding round the rim of water, roundworms shimmying frantically, and finally, when my eyes have adjusted to these dimensions, amoebae. At first the amoebae look like muscae volitantes, those curled moving spots you seem to see in your eyes when you stare at a distant wall. Then I see the amoebae as drops of water congealed, bluish, translucent, like chips of sky in the bowl. At length I choose one individual and give myself over to its idea of an evening. I see it dribble a grainy foot before it on its wet, unfathomable way. Do its unedited sense impressions include the fierce focus of my eyes? Shall I take it outside and show it Andromeda, and blow its little endoplasm? I stir the water with a finger, in case it's running out of oxygen. Maybe I should get a tropical aquarium with motorized bubblers and lights, and keep this one for a pet. Yes, it would tell its fissioned descendants, the universe is two feet by five, and if you listen closely you can hear the buzzing music of the spheres.

Oh, it's mysterious lamplit evenings, here in the galaxy, one after the other. It's one of those nights when I wander from window to window, looking for a sign. But I can't see. Terror and a beauty insoluble are a ribband of blue woven into the fringes of garments of things both great and small. No culture explains, no bivouac offers real haven or rest. But it could be that we are not seeing something. Galileo thought comets were an optical illusion. This is fertile ground: Since we are certain that they're not, we can look at what our scientists have been saying with fresh hope. What if there are *really* gleaming, castellated cities hung upside-down over the desert sand? What limpid lakes and cool date palms have our caravans always passed untried? Until, one by one, by the blindest of leaps, we light on the road to these places, we must stumble in darkness and hunger. I turn from the window. I'm blind as a bat, sensing only from every direction the echo of my own thin cries.

I chanced on a wonderful book by Marius von Senden, called *Space and Light*. When Western surgeons discovered how to perform safe cataract operations, they ranged across Europe and America operating on dozens of men and women of all ages who had been blinded by cataracts since birth. Von Senden collected accounts of such cases; the histories are fascinating. Many doctors had tested their patients' sense perceptions and ideas of space both before and after the operations. The vast majority of patients, of both sexes and all ages, had, in von Senden's opinion, no idea of space whatsoever. Form, distance, and size were so many meaningless syllables. A patient "had no idea of depth, confusing it with roundness." Before the operation a doctor would give a blind patient a cube and a sphere; the patient would tongue it or feel it with his hands, and name it correctly. After the operation the doctor would show the same objects to the patient without letting him touch them; now he had no clue whatsoever what he was seeing. One patient called lemonade "square" because it pricked on his tongue as a square shape pricked on the touch of his hands. Of another postoperative patient, the doctor writes, "I have found in her no notion of size, for example, not even within the narrow limits which she might have encompassed with the aid of touch. Thus when I asked her to show me how big her mother was, she did not stretch out her hands, but set her two index-fingers a few inches apart." Other doctors reported their patients' own statements to similar effect. "The room he was in . . . he knew to be but part of the house, yet he could not conceive that the whole house could look bigger"; "Those who are blind from birth . . . have no real conception of height or distance. A house that is a mile away is thought of as nearby, but requiring the taking of a lot of steps. . . . The elevator that whizzes him up and down gives no more sense of vertical distance than does the train of horizontal."

For the newly sighted, vision is pure sensation unencumbered by meaning: "The girl went through the experience that we all go through and forget, the moment we are born. She saw, but it did not mean anything but a lot of different kinds of brightness." Again, "I asked the patient what he could see; he answered that he saw an extensive field of light, in which everything appeared dull, confused, and in motion. He could not distinguish objects." Another patient saw "nothing but a confusion of forms and colours." When a newly sighted girl saw photographs and paintings, she asked, " 'Why do they put those dark marks all over them?' 'Those aren't dark marks,' her mother explained, 'those are shadows. That is one of the ways the eye knows that things have shape. If it were not for shadows many things would look flat.' 'Well, that's how things do look,' Joan answered. 'Everything looks flat with dark patches.' "

But it is the patients' concepts of space that are most revealing. One patient, according to his doctor, "practiced his vision in a strange fashion; thus he takes off one of his boots, throws it some way off in front of him, and then attempts to gauge the distance at which it lies; he takes a few steps toward the boot and tries to grasp it; on failing to reach it, he moves on a step or two and gropes for the boot until he finally gets hold of it." "But even at this stage, after three weeks' experience of seeing," von Senden goes on, " 'space,' as he conceives it, ends with visual space, i.e., with color-patches that happen to bound his view. He does not yet have the notion that a larger object (a chair) can mask a smaller one (a dog), or that the latter can still be present even though it is not directly seen."

In general the newly sighted see the world as a dazzle of color-patches. They are pleased by the sensation of color, and learn quickly to name the colors, but the rest of seeing is tormentingly difficult. Soon after his operation a patient "generally bumps into one of these color-patches and observes them to be substantial, since they resist him as tactual objects do. In walking about it also strikes him—or can if he pays attention—that he is continually passing in between the colors he sees, that he can go past a visual object, that a part of it then steadily disappears from view; and that in spite of this, however he twists and turns—whether entering the room from the door, for example, or returning back to it—he always has a visual space in front of him. Thus he gradually comes to realize that there is also a space behind him, which he does not see."

The mental effort involved in these reasonings proves overwhelming for many patients. It oppresses them to realize, if they ever do at all, the tremendous size of the world, which they had previously conceived of as something touchingly manageable. It oppresses them to realize that they have been visible to people all along, perhaps unattractively so, without their knowledge or consent. A disheartening number of them refuse to use their new vision, continuing to go over objects with their tongues, and lapsing into apathy and despair. "The child can see, but will not make use of his sight. Only when pressed can he with difficulty be brought to look at objects in his neighborhood; but more than a foot away it is impossible to bestir him to the necessary effort." Of a twenty-one-year-old girl, the doctor relates, "Her unfortunate father, who had hoped for so much from this operation, wrote that his daughter carefully shuts her eyes whenever she wishes to go about the house, especially when she comes to a staircase, and that she is never happier or more at ease than when, by closing her eyelids, she relapses into her former state of total blindness." A fifteen-year-old boy, who was also in love with a girl at the asylum for the blind, finally blurted out, "No, really, I can't stand it any more; I want to be sent back to the asylum again. If things aren't altered, I'll tear my eyes out."

Some do learn to see, especially the young ones. But it changes their lives. One doctor comments on "the rapid and complete loss of that striking and wonderful serenity which is characteristic only of those who have never yet seen." A blind man who learns to see is ashamed of his old habits. He dresses up, grooms himself, and tries to make a good impression. While he was blind he was indifferent to objects unless they were edible; now, "a sifting of values sets in . . . his thoughts and wishes are mightily stirred and some few of the patients are thereby led into dissimulation, envy, theft and fraud."

On the other hand, many newly sighted people speak well of the world, and teach us how dull is our own vision. To one patient, a human hand, unrecognized, is "something bright and then holes." Shown a bunch of grapes, a boy calls out, "It is dark, blue and shiny. . . . It isn't smooth, it has bumps and hollows." A little girl visits a garden. "She is greatly astonished, and can scarcely be persuaded to answer, stands speechless in front of the tree, which she only names on taking hold of it, and then as 'the tree with the lights in it.' " Some delight in their sight and give themselves over to the visual world. Of a patient just after her bandages were removed, her doctor writes, "The first things to attract her attention were her own hands; she looked at them very closely, moved them repeatedly to and fro, bent and stretched the fingers, and seemed greatly astonished at the sight." One girl was eager to tell her blind friend that "men do not really look like trees at all," and astounded to discover that her every visitor had an utterly different face. Finally, a twenty-two-year-old girl was dazzled by the world's brightness and kept her eyes shut for two weeks. When at the end of that time she opened her eyes again, she did not recognize any objects, but, "the more she now directed her gaze upon everything about her, the more it could be seen how an expression of gratification and astonishment overspread her features; she repeatedly exclaimed: 'Oh God! How beautiful!' "

I saw color-patches for weeks after I read this wonderful book. It was summer; the peaches were ripe in the valley orchards. When I woke in the morning, color-patches wrapped round my eyes, intricately, leaving not one unfilled spot. All day long I walked among shifting color-patches that parted before me like the Red Sea and closed again in silence, transfigured, wherever I looked back. Some patches swelled and loomed, while others vanished utterly, and dark marks flitted at random over the whole dazzling sweep. But I couldn't sustain the illusion of flatness. I've been around for too long. Form is condemned to an eternal danse macabre with meaning: I couldn't unpeach the peaches. Nor can I remember ever having seen without understanding; the color-patches of infancy are lost. My brain then must have been smooth as any balloon. I'm told I reached for the moon; many babies do. But the color-patches of infancy swelled as meaning filled them; they arrayed themselves in solemn ranks down distance which unrolled and stretched before me like a plain. The moon rocketed away. I live now in a world of shadows that shape and distance color, a world where space makes a kind of terrible sense. What gnosticism is this, and what physics? The fluttering patch I saw in my nursery window—silver and green and shape-shifting blue—is gone; a row of Lombardy poplars takes its place, mute, across the distant lawn. That humming oblong creature pale as light that stole along the walls of my room at night, stretching exhilaratingly around the corners, is gone, too, gone the night I ate of the bittersweet fruit, put two and two together and puckered forever my brain. Martin Buber tells this tale: "Rabbi Mendel once boasted to his teacher Rabbi Elimelekh that evenings he saw the angel who rolls away the light before the darkness, and mornings the angel who rolls away the darkness before the light. 'Yes,' said Rabbi Elimelekh, 'in my youth I saw that too. Later on you don't see these things any more.' "

Why didn't someone hand those newly sighted people paints and brushes from the start, when they still didn't know what anything was? Then maybe we all could see color-patches too, the world unraveled from reason, Eden before Adam gave names. The scales would drop from my eyes; I'd see trees like men walking; I'd run down the road against all orders, hallooing and leaping.

Seeing is of course very much a matter of verbalization. Unless I call my attention to what passes before my eyes, I simply won't see it. It is, as Ruskin says, "not merely unnoticed, but in the full, clear sense of the word, unseen." My eyes alone can't solve analogy tests using figures, the ones which show, with increasing elaborations, a big square, then a small square in a big square, then a big triangle, and expect me to find a small triangle in a big triangle. I have to say the words, describe what I'm seeing. If Tinker Mountain erupted, I'd be likely to notice. But if I want to notice the lesser cataclysms of valley life, I have to maintain in my head a running description of the present. It's not that I'm observant; it's just that I talk too much. Otherwise, especially in a strange place, I'll never know what's happening. Like a blind man at the ball game, I need a radio.

When I see this way I analyze and pry. I hurl over logs and roll away stones; I study the bank a square foot at a time, probing and tilting my head. Some days when a mist covers the mountains, when the muskrats won't show and the microscope's mirror shatters, I want to climb up the blank blue dome as a man would storm the inside of a circus tent, wildly, dangling, and with a steel knife claw a rent in the top, peep, and, if I must, fall.

But there is another kind of seeing that involves a letting go. When I see this way I sway transfixed and emptied. The difference between the two ways of seeing is the difference between walking with and without a camera. When I walk with a camera I walk from shot to shot, reading the light on a calibrated meter. When I walk without a camera, my own shutter opens, and the moment's light prints on my own silver gut. When I see this second way I am above all an unscrupulous observer.

It was sunny one evening last summer at Tinker Creek; the sun was low in the sky, upstream. I was sitting on the sycamore log bridge with the sunset at my back, watching the shiners the size of minnows who were feeding over the muddy sand in skittery schools. Again and again, one fish, then another, turned for a split second across the current and flash! the sun shot out from its silver side. I couldn't watch for it. It was always just happening somewhere else, and it drew my vision just as it disappeared: flash, like a sudden dazzle of the thinnest blade, a sparking over a dun and olive ground at chance intervals from every direction. Then I noticed white specks, some sort of pale petals, small, floating from under my feet on the creek's surface, very slow and steady. So I blurred my eyes and gazed toward the brim of my hat and saw a new world. I saw the pale white circles roll up, roll up, like the world's turning, mute and perfect, and I saw the linear flashes, gleaming silver, like stars being born at random down a rolling scroll of time. Something broke and something opened. I filled up like a new wineskin. I breathed an air like light; I saw a light like water. I was the lip of a fountain the creek filled forever; I was ether, the leaf in the zephyr; I was flesh-flake, feather, bone.

When I see this way I see truly. As Thoreau says, I return to my senses. I am the man who watches the baseball game in silence in an empty stadium. I see the game purely; I'm abstracted and dazed. When it's all over and the white-suited players lope off the green field to their shadowed dugouts, I leap to my feet; I cheer and cheer.

But I can't go out and try to see this way. I'll fail, I'll go mad. All I can do is try to gag the commentator, to hush the noise of useless interior babble that keeps me from seeing just as surely as a newspaper dangled before my eyes. The effort is really a discipline requiring a lifetime of dedicated struggle; it marks the literature of saints and monks of every order East and West, under every rule and no rule, discalced and shod. The world's spiritual geniuses seem to discover universally that the mind's muddy river, this ceaseless flow of trivia and trash, cannot be dammed, and that trying to dam it is a waste of effort that might lead to madness. Instead you must allow the muddy river to flow unheeded in the dim channels of consciousness; you raise your sights; you look along it, mildly, acknowledging its presence without interest and gazing beyond it into the realm of the real where subjects and objects act and rest purely, without utterance. "Launch into the deep," says Jacques Ellul, "and you shall see."

The secret of seeing is, then, the pearl of great price. If I thought he could teach me to find it and keep it forever I would stagger barefoot across a hundred deserts after any lunatic at all. But although the pearl may be found, it may not be sought. The literature of illumination reveals this above all: Although it comes to those who wait for it, it is always, even to the most practiced and adept, a gift and a total surprise. I return from one walk knowing where the killdeer nests in the field by the creek and the hour the laurel blooms. I return from the same walk a day later scarcely knowing my own name. Litanies hum in my ears; my tongue flaps in my mouth Ailinon, alleluia! I cannot cause light; the most I can do is try to put myself in the path of its beam. It is possible, in deep space, to sail on solar wind. Light, be it particle or wave, has force: you rig a giant sail and go. The secret of seeing is to sail on solar wind. Hone and spread your spirit till you yourself are a sail, whetted, translucent, broadside to the merest puff.

When her doctor took her bandages off and led her into the garden, the girl who was no longer blind saw "the tree with the lights in it." It was for this tree I searched through the peach orchards of summer, in the forests of fall and down winter and spring for years. Then one day I was walking along Tinker Creek thinking of nothing at all and I saw the tree with the lights in it. I saw the backyard cedar where the mourning doves roost charged and transfigured, each cell buzzing with flame. I stood on the grass with the lights in it, grass that was wholly fire, utterly focused and utterly dreamed. It was less like seeing than like being for the first time seen, knocked breathless by a powerful glance. The flood of fire abated, but I'm still spending the power. Gradually the lights went out in the cedar, the colors died, the cells unflamed and disappeared. I was still ringing. I had been my whole life a bell, and never knew it until at that moment I was lifted and struck. I have since only very rarely seen the tree with the lights in it. The vision comes and goes, mostly goes, but I live for it, for the moment when the mountains open and a new light roars in spate through the crack, and the mountains slam.

—1974

What are your reactions to and questions about this work? The following questions may help provoke some ideas.

Probing the Work

1. How does Dillard define real "seeing"? What faculties does a person need to "see" clearly?
2. How are the beginning and ending of the essay linked? Can you trace the author's train of thought regarding the development of *seeing?*

Identifying Issues

3. Consider the practical and intellectual benefits of applying Dillard's ideas about *seeing* to your own experiences.
4. Nature is very much a "now-you-see-it, now-you-don't affair," according to Dillard (p. 937). In what sense is nature (and life) unpredictable? How can you be better prepared to catch its fleeting or sudden beauty?

ROBERT FROST

Stopping By Woods on a Snowy Evening

Robert Frost (1874–1963) was born in San Francisco but moved with his mother to New England after his father died. Frost married and in 1900 moved to a farm in New Hampshire for about 12 years. He then moved to England, where he published two books of poems: A Boy's Will *(1913) and* North of Boston *(1914). Frost returned to America in 1915 and fast became the nation's most popular poet.*

Whose woods these are I think I know.
His house is in the village though;
He will not see me stopping here
To watch his woods fill up with snow.

My little horse must think it queer
To stop without a farmhouse near
Between the woods and frozen lake
The darkest evening of the year.

He gives his harness bells a shake
To ask if there is some mistake.
The only other sound's the sweep
Of easy wind and downy flake.

The woods are lovely, dark and deep,
But I have promises to keep,
And miles to go before I sleep.
And miles to go before I sleep.

—1923

What are your reactions to and questions about this work? The following questions may help provoke some ideas.

Probing the Work

1. What are the two conflicting influences on the speaker?
2. Look at the *rhyme* (see page 71), *meter* (see page 69), and *structure* (see page 73) of this poem. In what way does the *form* of the poem affect your understanding of its *meaning?* How do form and meaning work together here?

Identifying Issues

3. Critic John Ciardi has explained (in *How Does a Poem Mean?*) that the symbolism in this poem "is like a rock dropped into a pool: it sends out rip-

ples in all directions, and the ripples are in motion" (673). For example, the horse "without losing his identity as a horse has also become a symbol that stands for something else. That something else may, perhaps, be taken as the order of life that does not understand why a man stops in the wintry middle of nowhere to watch snow come down." Ciardi also shows how the dark and snowfall take on larger meanings (a death wish? the final rest?). There are a combination of forces and feelings, and a crosstug of motives being dramatized here. Do you agree with Ciardi's suggestions about the *symbolism* of the poem? To what extent are many people caught in the predicament the speaker finds himself in, pulled by the appeals of nature, by "social obligation" and by other "order[s] of life" (673)?

ROBERT FROST

Once by the Pacific

(See biographical information on page 949.)

The shattered water made a misty din.
Great waves looked over others coming in,
And thought of doing something to the shore
That water never did to land before.
The clouds were low and hairy in the skies,
Like locks blown forward in the gleam of eyes.
You could not tell, and yet it looked as if
The shore was lucky in being backed by cliff,
The cliff in being backed by continent;
It looked as if a night of dark intent
Was coming, and not only a night, an age.
Someone had better be prepared for rage.
There would be more than ocean-water broken
Before God's last *Put out the Light* was spoken.

—*1928*

What are your reactions to and questions about this work? The following questions may help provoke some ideas.

Probing the Work

1. What does the ocean seem to *represent* for the speaker, and how does this affect his *mood?* What is his *attitude* toward nature?
2. Paraphrase the last two lines of the poem. What is their significance in relation to the poem as a whole?

Identifying Issues

3. In what way does this poem link God, nature, and death? How close to the poet's ideas about the future are your own ideas?

ELIZABETH BISHOP

The Fish

Elizabeth Bishop (1911–1979) was born in Worcester, Massachusetts. Her father died before she was a year old, and a few years later her mother was committed to a sanatorium. Raised by relatives in New England and Nova Scotia, Bishop was financially independent, and free to devote her time to writing. She was coeditor of the Vassar College literary magazine, and after her graduation in 1934, she lived mostly in Brazil, but also in Key West, Mexico, and France. She eventually returned to the United States to teach at Harvard.

I caught a tremendous fish
and held him beside the boat
half out of water, with my hook
fast in a corner of his mouth.
He didn't fight.
He hadn't fought at all.
He hung a grunting weight,
battered and venerable
and homely. Here and there
his brown skin hung in strips
like ancient wallpaper,
and its pattern of darker brown
was like wallpaper:
shapes like full-blown roses
stained and lost through age.
He was speckled with barnacles,
fine rosettes of lime,
and infested
with tiny white sea-lice,
and underneath two or three
rags of green weed hung down.
While his gills were breathing in
the terrible oxygen
—the frightening gills,
fresh and crisp with blood,
that can cut so badly—
I thought of the coarse white flesh

packed in like feathers,
the big bones and the little bones,
the dramatic reds and blacks
of his shiny entrails,
and the pink swim-bladder
like a big peony.
I looked into his eyes
which were far larger than mine
but shallower, and yellowed,
the irises backed and packed
with tarnished tinfoil
seen through the lenses
of old scratched isinglass.°
They shifted a little, but not
to return my stare.
—It was more like the tipping
of an object toward the light.
I admired his sullen face,
the mechanism of his jaw,
and then I saw
that from his lower lip
—if you could call it a lip—
grim, wet, and weaponlike,
hung five old pieces of fish-line,
or four and a wire leader
with the swivel still attached,
with all their five big hooks
grown firmly in his mouth.
A green line, frayed at the end
where he broke it, two heavier lines,
and a fine black thread
still crimped from the strain and snap
when it broke and he got away.
Like medals with their ribbons
frayed and wavering,
a five-haired beard of wisdom
trailing from his aching jaw.
I stared and stared
and victory filled up
the little rented boat,
from the pool of bilge

40. Isinglass, a whitish, semitransparent substance, originally obtained from the swim-bladders of some fresh-water fishes and occasionally used for windows.

where oil had spread a rainbow
around the rusted engine
to the bailer rusted orange,
the sun-cracked thwarts,
the oarlocks on their strings,
the gunnels—until everything
was rainbow, rainbow, rainbow!
And I let the fish go.

—1946

What are your reactions to and questions about this work? The following questions may help provoke some ideas.

Probing the Work

1. Choose three *images* (see page 79) from the poem that express how the poet feels about the fish. What do the images have in common? What is Bishop trying to show through them?

Identifying Issues

2. Why does the speaker let the fish go? What has she realized about our relationship with nature? In your opinion, how much control and power should we exert over nature?

DORIS LESSING

A Sunrise on the Veld

Doris Lessing (b. 1919) was born in Persia of British parents and grew up on a Southern Rhodesian farm before settling in England as an adult. She is best known for her novel The Golden Notebook *(1962), but has published many other books, including the collection of short stories* A Man and Two Women.

Every night that winter he said aloud into the dark of the pillow: Half-past four! Half-past four! till he felt his brain had gripped the words and held them fast. Then he fell asleep at once, as if a shutter had fallen; and lay with his face turned to the clock so that he could see it first thing when he woke.

It was half-past four to the minute, every morning. Triumphantly pressing down the alarm-knob of the clock, which the dark half of his mind had outwitted, remaining vigilant all night and counting the hours as he lay relaxed in sleep, he huddled down for a last warm moment under the clothes, playing with the idea of lying abed for this once only. But he played with it for the fun of knowing that it was a weakness he could defeat without effort; just as he set the alarm each night for the delight of the moment when he woke and stretched his limbs, feeling the muscles tighten, and thought: Even my brain—even that! I can control every part of myself.

Luxury of warm rested body, with the arms and legs and fingers waiting like soldiers for a word of command! Joy of knowing that the precious hours were given to sleep voluntarily!—for he had once stayed awake three nights running, to prove that he could, and then worked all day, refusing even to admit that he was tired; and now sleep seemed to him a servant to be commanded and refused.

The boy stretched his frame full-length, touching the wall at his head with his hands, and the bedfoot with his toes; then he sprung out, like a fish leaping from water. And it was cold, cold.

He always dressed rapidly, so as to try and conserve his night-warmth till the sun rose two hours later; but by the time he had on his clothes his hands were numbed and he could scarcely hold his shoes. These he could not put on for fear of waking his parents, who never came to know how early he rose.

As soon as he stepped over the lintel, the flesh of his soles contracted on the chilled earth, and his legs began to ache with cold. It was night: the stars were glittering, the trees standing black and still. He looked for signs of day, for the greying of the edge of a stone, or a lightening in the sky where the sun would rise, but there was nothing yet. Alert as an animal he crept past the dangerous window, standing poised with his hand on the sill for one proudly fastidious moment, looking in at the stuffy blackness of the room where his parents lay.

Feeling for the grass-edge of the path with his toes, he reached inside another window further along the wall, where his gun had been set in readiness the night before. The steel was icy, and numbed fingers slipped along it, so that he had to hold it in the crook of his arm for safety. Then he tiptoed to the room where the dogs slept, and was fearful that they might have been tempted to go before him; but they were waiting, their haunches crouched in reluctance at the cold, but ears and swinging tails greeting the gun ecstatically. His warning undertone kept them secret and silent till the house was a hundred yards back: then they bolted off into the bush, yelping excitedly. The boy imagined his parents turning in their beds and muttering: Those dogs again! before they were dragged back in sleep; and he smiled scornfully. He always looked back over his shoulder at the house before he passed a wall of trees that shut it from sight. It looked so low and small, crouching there under a tall and brilliant sky. Then he turned his back on it, and on the frowsting sleepers, and forgot them.

He would have to hurry. Before the light grew strong he must be four miles away; and already a tint of green stood in the hollow of a leaf, and the air smelled of morning and the stars were dimming.

He slung the shoes over his shoulder, veld *skoen* that were crinkled and hard with the dews of a hundred mornings. They would be necessary when the ground became too hot to bear. Now he felt the chilled dust push up between his toes, and he let the muscles of his feet spread and settle into the shapes of the earth; and he thought: I could walk a hundred miles on feet like these! I could walk all day, and never tire!

He was walking swiftly through the dark tunnel of foliage that in day-time was a road. The dogs were invisibly ranging the lower travelways of the bush, and he heard them panting. Sometimes he felt a cold muzzle on his leg before they were off again, scouting for a trail to follow. They were not trained, but free-running companions of the hunt, who often tired of the long stalk before the final shots, and went off on their own pleasure. Soon he could see them, small and wild-looking in a wild strange light, now that the bush stood trembling on the verge of colour, waiting for the sun to paint earth and grass afresh.

The grass stood to his shoulders; and the trees were showering a faint silvery rain. He was soaked; his whole body was clenched in a steady shiver.

Once he bent to the road that was newly scored with animal trails, and regretfully straightened, reminding himself that the pleasure of tracking must wait till another day.

He began to run along the edge of a field, noting jerkily how it was filmed over with fresh spiderweb, so that the long reaches of great black clods seemed netted in glistening grey. He was using the steady lope he had learned by watching the natives, the run that is a dropping of the weight of the body from one foot to the next in a slow balancing movement that never tires, nor shortens the breath; and he felt the blood pulsing down his legs and along his arms, and the exultation and pride of body mounted in him till he was shutting his teeth hard against a violent desire to shout his triumph.

Soon he had left the cultivated part of the farm. Behind him the bush was low and black. In front was a long vlei, acres of long pale grass that sent back a hollowing gleam of light to a satiny sky. Near him thick swathes of grass were bent with the weight of water, and diamond drops sparkled on each frond.

The first bird woke at his feet and at once a flock of them sprang into the air calling shrilly that day had come; and suddenly, behind him, the bush woke into song, and he could hear the guinea fowl calling far ahead of him. That meant they would now be sailing down from their trees into thick grass, and it was for them he had come: he was too late. But he did not mind. He forgot he had come to shoot. He set his legs wide, and balanced from foot to foot, and swung his gun up and down in both hands horizontally, in a kind of improvised exercise, and let his head sink back till it was pillowed in his neck muscles, and watched how above him small rosy clouds floated in a lake of gold.

Suddenly it all rose in him: it was unbearable. He leapt up into the air, shouting and yelling wild, unrecognisable noises. Then he began to run, not carefully, as he had before, but madly, like a wild thing. He was clean crazy, yelling mad with the joy of living and a superfluity of youth. He rushed down the vlei under a tumult of crimson and gold, while all the birds of the world sang about him. He ran in great leaping strides, and shouted as he ran, feeling his body rise into the crisp rushing air and fall back surely on to sure feet; and thought briefly, not believing that such a thing could happen to him, that he could break his ankle any moment, in this thick tangled grass. He cleared bushes like a duiker, leapt over rocks; and finally came to a dead stop at a place where the ground fell abruptly away below him to the river. It had been a two-mile-long dash through waist-high growth, and he was breathing hoarsely and could no longer sing. But he poised on a rock and looked down at stretches of water that gleamed through stooping trees, and thought suddenly, I am fifteen! Fifteen! The words came new to him; so that he kept repeating them wonderingly, with swelling excitement; and he felt the years of his life with his hands, as if he were counting marbles, each one hard and separate and compact, each one a wonderful shining thing. That was what he was: fifteen years of this rich soil, and this slow-moving water, and air that smelt like a challenge whether it was warm and sultry at noon, or as brisk as cold water, like it was now.

There was nothing he couldn't do, nothing! A vision came to him, as he stood there, like when a child hears the word "eternity" and tries to understand it, and time takes possession of the mind. He felt his life ahead of him as a great and wonderful thing, something that was his; and he said aloud, with the blood rising to his head: all the great men of the world have been as I am now, and there is nothing I can't become, nothing I can't do; there is no country in the world I cannot make part of myself, if I choose. I contain the world. I can make of it what I want. If I choose, I can change everything that is going to happen: it depends on me, and what I decide now.

The urgency, and the truth and the courage of what his voice was saying exulted him so that he began to sing again, at the top of his voice, and the sound went echoing down the river gorge. He stopped for the echo, and sang again: stopped and shouted. That was what he was!—he sang, if he chose; and the world had to answer him.

And for minutes he stood there, shouting and singing and waiting for the lovely eddying sound of the echo; so that his own new strong thoughts came back and washed round his head, as if someone were answering him and encouraging him; till the gorge was full of soft voices clashing back and forth from rock to rock over the river. And then it seemed as if there was a new voice. He listened, puzzled, for it was not his own. Soon he was leaning forward, all his nerves alert, quite still: somewhere close to him there was a noise that was no joyful bird, nor tinkle of falling water, nor ponderous movement of cattle.

There it was again. In the deep morning hush that held his future and his past, was a sound of pain, and repeated over and over: it was a kind of shortened scream, as if someone, something, had no breath to scream. He came to himself, looked about him, and called for the dogs. They did not appear: they had gone off on their own business, and he was alone. Now he was clean sober, all the madness gone. His heart beating fast, because of that frightened screaming, he stepped carefully off the rock and went towards a belt of trees. He was moving cautiously, for not so long ago he had seen a leopard in just this spot.

At the edge of the trees he stopped and peered, holding his gun ready; he advanced, looking steadily about him, his eyes narrowed. Then, all at once, in the middle of a step, he faltered, and his face was puzzled. He shook his head impatiently, as if he doubted his own sight.

There, between two trees, against a background of gaunt black rocks, was a figure from a dream, a strange beast that was horned and drunken-legged, but like something he had never even imagined. It seemed to be ragged. It looked like a small buck that had black ragged tufts of fur standing up irregularly all over it, with patches of raw flesh beneath . . . but the patches of rawness were disappearing under moving black and came again elsewhere; and all the time the creature screamed, in small gasping screams, and leaped drunkenly from side to side, as if it were blind.

Then the boy understood: it *was* a buck. He ran closer, and again stood still, stopped by a new fear. Around him the grass was whispering and alive. He looked wildly about, and then down. The ground was black with ants, great energetic ants that took no notice of him, but hurried and scurried towards the fighting shape, like glistening black water flowing through the grass.

And, as he drew in his breath and pity and terror seized him, the beast fell and the screaming stopped. Now he could hear nothing but one bird singing, and the sound of the rustling, whispering ants.

He peered over at the writhing blackness that jerked convulsively with the jerking nerves. It grew quieter. There were small twitches from the mass that still looked vaguely like the shape of a small animal.

It came into his mind that he should shoot it and end its pain; and he raised the gun. Then he lowered it again. The buck could no longer feel; its fighting was a mechanical protest of the nerves. But it was not that which made him put down the gun. It was a swelling feeling of rage and misery and protest that expressed itself in the thought: if I had not come it would have died like this: so why should I interfere? All over the bush things like this happen; they happen all the time; this is how life goes on, by living things dying in anguish. He gripped the gun between his knees and felt in his own limbs the myriad swarming pain of the twitching animal that could no longer feel, and set his teeth, and said over and over again under his breath: I can't stop it. I can't stop it. There is nothing I can do.

He was glad that the buck was unconscious and had gone past suffering so that he did not have to make a decision to kill it even when he was feeling with his whole body: this is what happens, this is how things work.

It was right—that was what he was feeling. *It was right and nothing could alter it.*

The knowledge of fatality, of what has to be, had gripped him and for the first time in his life; and he was left unable to make any movement of brain or body, except to say: "Yes, yes. That is what living is." It had entered his flesh and his bones and grown in to the furthest corners of his brain and would never leave him. And at that moment he could not have performed the smallest action of mercy, knowing as he did, having lived on it all his life, the vast unalterable, cruel veld, where at any moment one might stumble over a skull or crush the skeleton of some small creature.

Suffering, sick, and angry, but also grimly satisfied with his new stoicism, he stood there leaning on his rifle, and watched the seething black mound grow smaller. At his feet, now, were ants trickling back with pink fragments in their mouths, and there was a fresh acid smell in his nostrils. He sternly controlled the uselessly convulsing muscles of his empty stomach, and reminded himself: the ants must eat too! At the same time he found that the tears were streaming down his face, and his clothes were soaked with the sweat of that other creature's pain.

The shape had grown small. Now it looked like nothing recognisable. He did not know how long it was before he saw the blackness thin, and bits of white showed through, shining in the sun—yes, there was the sun, just up, glowing over the rocks. Why, the whole thing could not have taken longer than a few minutes.

He began to swear, as if the shortness of the time was in itself unbearable, using the words he had heard his father say. He strode forward, crushing ants with each step, and brushing them off his clothes, till he stood above the skeleton, which lay sprawled under a small bush. It was clean-picked. It might have been lying there years, save that on the white bone were pink fragments of gristle. About the bones ants were ebbing away, their pincers full of meat.

The boy looked at them, big black ugly insects. A few were standing and gazing up at him with small glittering eyes.

"Go away!" he said to the ants, very coldly. "I am not for you—not just yet, at any rate. Go away." And he fancied that the ants turned and went away.

He bent over the bones and touched the sockets in the skull; that was where the eyes were, he thought incredulously, remembering the liquid dark eyes of a buck. And then he bent the slim foreleg bone, swinging it horizontally in his palm.

That morning, perhaps an hour ago, this small creature had been stepping proud and free through the bush, feeling the chill on its hide even as he himself had done, exhilarated by it. Proudly stepping the earth, tossing its horns, frisking a pretty white tail, it had sniffed the cold morning air. Walking like kings and conquerors it had moved through this free-held bush, where each blade of grass grew for it alone, and where the river ran pure sparkling water for its slaking.

And then—what had happened? Such a swift surefooted thing could surely not be trapped by a swarm of ants?

The boy bent curiously to the skeleton. Then he saw that the back leg that lay uppermost and strained out in the tension of death, was snapped midway to the thigh, so that broken bones jutted over each other uselessly. So that was it! Limping into the ant-masses it could not escape, once it had sensed the danger. Yes, but how had the leg been broken? Had it fallen, perhaps? Impossible, a buck was too light and graceful. Had some jealous rival horned it?

What could possibly have happened? Perhaps some Africans had thrown stones at it, as they do, trying to kill it for meat, and had broken its leg. Yes, that must be it.

Even as he imagined the crowd of running, shouting natives, and the flying stones, and the leaping buck, another picture came into his mind. He saw himself, on any one of these bright ringing mornings, drunk with excitement, taking a snap shot at some half-seen buck. He saw himself with the gun lowered, wondering whether he had missed or not; and thinking at last that it was late, and he wanted his breakfast, and it was not worth while to track miles after an animal that would very likely get away from him in any case.

For a moment he would not face it. He was a small boy again, kicking sulkily at the skeleton, hanging his head, refusing to accept the responsibility.

Then he straightened up, and looked down at the bones with an odd expression of dismay, all the anger gone out of him. His mind went quite empty: all around him he could see trickles of ants disappearing into the grass. The whispering noise was faint and dry, like the rustling of a cast snakeskin.

At last he picked up his gun and walked homewards. He was telling himself half defiantly that he wanted his breakfast. He was telling himself that it was getting very hot, much too hot to be out roaming the bush.

Really, he was tired. He walked heavily, not looking where he put his feet. When he came within sight of his home he stopped, knitting his brows. There was something he had to think out. The death of that small animal was a thing that concerned him, and he was by no means finished with it. It lay at the back of his mind uncomfortably.

Soon, the very next morning, he would get clear of everybody and go to the bush and think about it.

—1951

What are your reactions to and questions about this work? The following questions may help provoke some ideas.

Probing the Work

1. Contrast the boy's attitude and gait as he sets out for the veld, and then when he returns. What is it about his experience there that transforms him? Is his change a lasting one?

Identifying Issues

2. What role should we play in the workings of the natural world? How much interference is feasible?
3. Why does the boy shoot aimlessly at "some half-seen buck"? Is it possible to make reparation for the damage humans have caused, or might have caused, to nature? Explain.

JOY HARJO

Eagle Poem

Joy Harjo (b. 1951), of the Creek Tribe, was born in Tulsa, Oklahoma. Among her books of poetry is She Had Some Horses *and* The Woman Who Fell From the Sky *(1994). She teaches at the University of Colorado, Boulder, is a member of the Board of Directors for the Native American Public Broadcasting Consortium, and is poetry editor for* High Plains Literary Review.

To pray you open your whole self
To sky, to earth, to sun, to moon
To one whole voice that is you.
And know there is more
That you can't see, can't hear
Can't know except in moments
Steadily growing, and in languages
That aren't always sound but other
Circles of motion.
Like eagle that Sunday morning
Over Salt River. Circled in blue sky
In wind, swept our hearts clean
With sacred wings.
We see you, see ourselves and know
That we must take the utmost care
And kindness in all things.
Breathe in, knowing we are made of
All this, and breathe, knowing
We are truly blessed because we
Were born, and die soon, within a
True circle of motion,
Like eagle rounding out the morning
Inside us.
We pray that it will be done
In beauty.
In beauty.

—1986

What are your reactions to and questions about this work? The following questions may help provoke some ideas.

Probing the Work

1. What is the *tone* (see page 67) of this poem? What words or phrases determine the tone?
2. Select one line or *image* (see page 79) from this poem and explain what it suggests to you.

Identifying Issues

3. What attitude toward nature is expressed in this poem? Do you share it?

WRITING ASSIGNMENT SEQUENCE (CONTINUED FROM PAGE 935)

4. Making Connections

Select one of the following questions and write an informal response in which you connect your own ideas with those conveyed in the works of this cluster, and/or make connections among the works themselves.

A. How do the works in this cluster illustrate what Annie Dillard says about "seeing" nature? What different kinds of seeing are depicted?

B. What are the various ways of interacting with nature illustrated in the works of this cluster?

C. What are the several ways nature is depicted in these works?

D. Which, if any, of the works of this cluster illustrate what you feel about the relationship between human beings and nature?

5. Putting It All Together

Write an essay that combines what you think about the topic *Seeing* with what you now understand about the readings.

- Collect your informal writing, notes, and reading-journal entries on this topic and decide what will be the focus of your essay.
- Outline your essay. Select the literary passages and personal details you might use to illustrate and support your main focus.

- Write a draft of your essay in which you bring together what you think about the subject with what you understand about the readings. Try to include in your draft one or more *literary terms.*
- Share what you've written with your classmates and instructor, then revise it according to their recommendations.

Writing Tip: Proofreading

You need to gain *critical distance* from your own writing in order to pick out the errors and misjudgments you have made. One way to gain this distance is by *reading aloud* slowly, sentence by sentence. You might also try *reading the paper backwards,* from the last sentence to the first. You should read and proofread your essay *at least three times.* Keep your own *proofreading log*—of patterns of errors. For example, do you often write overly long sentences? Are your sentences short and choppy? Check for types of errors you know you often make.

Choose one paragraph from your paper to edit carefully. Experiment with rewriting three or four sentences: if long, shorten them; if short, combine them. Check your punctuation; check what kinds of connecting words you have used to show time, cause and effect, and so forth. Remember, if you are using a word processor after you have corrected on screen, and used spell checkers, you still must edit your printed essay (hard copy). (See also "An Editing Checklist" on page 40.)

CrossClusters

In your paper you might want to consider how the following works located elsewhere in this book depict nature:

- Sharon Olds, "Photograph of the Girl" (p. 8)
- Gabriel García Màrquez, "The Handsomest Drowned Man in the World" (p. 13)
- Rita Dove, "Adolescence III" (p. 120)
- Robert Frost, "Mending Wall" (p. 129)
- Chinua Achebe, "Dead Men's Path" (p. 138)
- Ernest Hemingway, "Fathers and Sons" (p. 454)
- Alice Walker, "Everyday Use" (p. 483)
- Louise Erdrich, "Family Reunion" (p. 491)
- Sam Shepard, *True West* (p. 502)
- Ernest Hemingway, "Hills Like White Elephants" (p. 611)

- Kate Chopin, "The Storm" (p. 649)
- Mme. de Beaumont, "Beauty and the Beast" (p. 732)
- William Shakespeare, *A Midsummer-Night's Dream* (p. 766)
- William Blake, "Proverbs of Hell" (p. 908)
- Leslie Marmon Silko, "The Man to Send Rain Clouds" (p. 978)
- Isabel Allende, "And of Clay Are We Created" (p. 996)

24

CELESTIAL MUSIC

WRITING ASSIGNMENT SEQUENCE

1. Thinking About . . . Religion

Respond to the following questions in writing:

- What are your religious beliefs?
- What term or combination of terms *(atheist, agnostic, Muslim, Jewish, Christian, Catholic, Protestant, Baptist, Hindu, Buddhist, etc.)* would you use to describe yourself? Why would you use that particular term?
- If you belong to a religion, what aspects of it do you like? What aspects of it are you troubled by?

2. Enacting the Topic

Take a poll of your friends, classmates, or dormmates, noting (a) the different religious beliefs represented in your "community," (b) the levels of religious belief (how serious? How devout?), and (c) how frequently these people attend their places of worship. What conclusions can you draw from your poll?

3. Responding to the Readings

As you read the works in this cluster, jot down in your response journals questions you have about the works, and comment on passages you find provocative or puzzling. Consider the questions following each reading for journal writing and prepare to discuss your reactions in class.

CLUSTER ESSAY

PAUL TILLICH

The Lost Dimension in Religion (excerpt)

Philosopher and theologian Paul Tillich (1886–1965) was born in Starzeddel, Prussia, and was educated in Berlin. He received his Ph.D. from Breslau, and was removed from a teaching position for his criticism of the Nazi party. He emigrated to the United States, where he taught at Harvard and at the University of Chicago. Among his books are The Protestant Era *(1948),* Search for Ultimate Realities *(1955), and the three-volume* Systematic Theology *(1951–1963).*

Every observer of our Western civilization is aware of the fact that something has happened to religion. It especially strikes the observer of the American scene. Everywhere he finds symptoms of what one has called religious revival, or more modestly, the revival of interest in religion. He finds them in the churches with their rapidly increasing membership. He finds them in the mushroomlike growth of sects. He finds them on college campuses and in the theological faculties of universities. Most conspicuously, he finds them in the tremendous success of men like Billy Graham and Norman Vincent Peale, who attract masses of people Sunday after Sunday, meeting after meeting. The facts cannot be denied, but how should they be interpreted? It is my intention to show that these facts must be seen as expressions of the predicament of Western man in the second half of the twentieth century. But I would even go a step further. I believe that the predicament of man in our period gives us also an important insight into the predicament of man generally—at all times and in all parts of the earth.

There are many analyses of man and society in our time. Most of them show important traits in the picture, but few of them succeed in giving a general key to our present situation. Although it is not easy to find such a key, I shall attempt it and, in so doing, will make an assertion which may be somewhat mystifying at first hearing. The decisive element in the predicament of Western man in our period is his loss of the dimension of depth. Of course, "dimension of depth" is a metaphor. It is taken from the spatial realm and applied to man's spiritual life. What does it mean?

It means that man has lost an answer to the question: What is the meaning of life? Where do we come from, where do we go to? What shall we do, what should we become in the short stretch between birth and death? Such questions are not answered or even asked if the "dimension of depth" is lost. And this is precisely what has happened to man in our period of history. He has lost the courage to ask such questions with an infinite seriousness—as former generations did—and he has lost the courage to receive answers to these questions, wherever they may come from.

I suggest that we call the dimension of depth the religious dimension in man's nature. Being religious means asking passionately the question of the meaning of our existence and being willing to receive answers, even if the answers hurt. Such an idea is usually called religion. It does not describe religion as the belief in the existence of gods or one God, and as a set of activities and institutions for the sake of relating oneself to these beings in thought, devotion and obedience. No one can deny that the religions which have appeared in history are religions in this sense. Nevertheless, religion in its innermost nature is more than religion in this narrower sense. It is the state of being concerned about one's own being and being universally.

There are many people who are ultimately concerned in this way who feel far removed, however, from religion in the narrower sense, and therefore from every historical religion. It often happens that such people take the question of the meaning of their life infinitely seriously and reject any historical religion just for this reason. They feel that the concrete religions fail to express their profound concern adequately. They are religious while rejecting the religions. It is this experience which forces us to distinguish the meaning of religion as living in the dimension of depth from particular expressions of one's ultimate concern in the symbols and institutions of a concrete religion. If we now turn to the concrete analysis of the religious situation of our time, it is obvious that our key must be the basic meaning of religion and not any particular religion, not even Christianity. What does this key disclose about the predicament of man in our period?

If we define religion as the state of being grasped by an infinite concern we must say: Man in our time has lost such infinite concern. And the resurgence of religion is nothing but a desperate and mostly futile attempt to regain what has been lost.

How did the dimension of depth become lost? Like any important event, it has many causes, but certainly not the one which one hears often mentioned from ministers' pulpits and evangelists' platforms, namely that a widespread impiety of modern man is responsible. Modern man is neither more pious nor more impious than man in any other period. The loss of the dimension of depth is caused by the relation of man to his world and to himself in our period, the period in which nature is being subjected scientifically and technically to the control of man. In this period, life in the dimension of depth is replaced by life in the horizontal dimension. The driving forces of the industrial society of which we are a part go ahead horizontally and not vertically. In popular terms this is expressed in phrases like "better and better," "bigger and bigger," "more and more." One should not disparage the feeling which lies behind such speech. Man is right in feeling that he is able to know and transform the world he encounters without a foreseeable limit. He can go ahead in all directions without a definite boundary.

A most expressive symbol of this attitude of going ahead in the horizontal dimension is the breaking through of the space which is controlled by the gravitational power of the earth into the world-space. It is interesting that one calls this world-space simply "space" and speaks, for instance, of space travel, as if every trip were not travel into space. Perhaps one feels that the true nature of space has been discovered only through our entering into indefinite world-space. In any case, the predominance of the horizontal dimension over the dimension of depth has been immensely increased by the opening up of the space beyond the space of the earth.

If we now ask what does man do and seek if he goes ahead in the horizontal dimension, the answer is difficult. Sometimes one is inclined to say that the mere movement ahead without an end, the intoxication with speeding forward without limits, is what satisfies him. But this answer is by no means sufficient. For on his way into space and time man changes the world he encounters. And the changes made by him change himself. He transforms everything he encounters into a tool; and in doing so he himself becomes a tool. But if he asks, a tool for what, there is no answer. One does not need to look far beyond everyone's daily experience in order to find examples to describe this predicament. Indeed our daily life in office and home, in cars and airplanes, at parties and conferences, while reading magazines and watching television, while looking at advertisements and hearing radio, are in themselves continuous examples of a life which has lost the dimension of depth. It runs ahead, every moment is filled with something which must be done or seen or said or planned. But no one can experience depth without stopping and becoming aware of himself. Only if he has moments in which he does not care about what comes next can he experience the meaning of this moment here and now and ask himself about the meaning of his life. As long as the preliminary, transitory concerns are not silenced, no matter how interesting and valuable and important they may be, the voice of the ultimate concern cannot be heard. This is the deepest root of the loss of the dimension of depth in our period—the loss of religion in its basic and universal meaning.

—1958

What are your reactions to and questions about this work? The following questions may help provoke some ideas.

Probing the Work

1. Define what Tillich means by "dimension of depth." Do you agree that this quality is lacking today?
2. How does Tillich define religion? To what extent does his definition fit in with your own ideas?

Identifying Issues

3. What role does religion play in our society?
4. To what extent do you agree that the conventional way of seeing religion is "nothing but a desperate and mostly futile attempt to regain what has been lost" (966)?

WILLIAM BLAKE

Proverbs of Hell

William Blake (1757–1827) was born and raised in London, where he was well educated in art and apprenticed for seven years to an engraver. He and his wife Catherine prospered for a while as Blake taught, illustrated books, and engraved other artists' designs, but after moving to the Sussex seacoast town of Felpham and being charged with sedition (he was acquitted), Blake entered a life of isolation and poverty as he pursued his true artistic visions. His work was little known when he died, but he is now among the most highly regarded of the British Romantic poets.

Most of Blake's best-known work, including Songs of Innocence and of Experience *(1794) appeared in the mode of relief etching—lines of verse etched under an illustration. The lines below are excerpted from* The Marriage of Heaven and Hell. *In this work Blake presents the Christian faith as one that overemphasizes reason and spirituality (Heaven) while demonizing bodily urges and other forms of God-given "Energy." Thus the "Proverbs of Hell" in this work are presented as truer than the limiting prescriptions of Heaven.*

In seed time learn, in harvest teach, in winter enjoy.
Drive your cart and your plow over the bones of the dead.
The road of excess leads to the palace of wisdom.
Prudence is a rich ugly old maid courted by Incapacity.
He who desires but acts not, breeds pestilence.
The cut worm forgives the plow.
Dip him in the river who loves water.
A fool sees not the same tree that a wise man sees.
He whose face gives no light, shall never become a star.
Eternity is in love with the productions of time.
The busy bee has no time for sorrow.
The hours of folly are measur'd by the clock; but of wisdom, no clock can measure.
All wholsom food is caught without a net or a trap.
Bring out number, weight, & measure in a year of dearth.
No bird soars too high, if he soars with his own wings.
A dead body revenges not injuries.
The most sublime act is to set another before you.
If the fool would persist in his folly he would become wise.

Folly is the cloke of knavery.
Shame is Pride's cloke.

PLATE 8

Prisons are built with stones of Law, Brothels with bricks of Religion.
The pride of the peacock is the glory of God.
The lust of the goat is the bounty of God.
The wrath of the lion is the wisdom of God.
The nakedness of woman is the work of God.
Excess of sorrow laughs. Excess of joy weeps.
The roaring of lions, the howling of wolves, the raging of the stormy sea, and the destructive sword, are portions of eternity too great for the eye of man.
The fox condemns the trap, not himself.
Joys impregnate. Sorrows bring forth.
Let man wear the fell of the lion, woman the fleece of the sheep.
The bird a nest, the spider a web, man friendship.
The selfish smiling fool & the sullen frowning fool shall be both thought wise, that they may be a rod.
What is now proved was once only imagin'd.
The rat, the mouse, the fox, the rabbit watch the roots; the lion, the tyger, the horse, the elephant, watch the fruits.
The cistern contains; the fountain overflows.
One thought fills immensity.
Always be ready to speak your mind, and a base man will avoid you.
Every thing possible to be believ'd is an image of truth.
The eagle never lost so much time as when he submitted to learn of the crow.

PLATE 11

The ancient Poets animated all sensible objects with Gods or Geniuses, calling them by the names and adorning them with the properties of woods, rivers, mountains, lakes, cities, nations, and whatever their enlarged & numerous senses could perceive.

And particularly they studied the genius of each city & country, placing it under its mental deity.

Till a system was formed, which some took advantage of & enslav'd the vulgar by attempting to realize or abstract the mental deities from their objects; thus began Priesthood,

Choosing forms of worship from poetic tales.

And at length they pronounced that the Gods had ordered such things.

Thus men forgot that All deities reside in the human breast.

—1792

What are your reactions to and questions about this work? The following questions may help provoke some ideas.

Probing the Work

1. Select one of the proverbs that employs a *metaphor* (see page 68) and explain in literal prose what Blake is expressing poetically.
2. If these are "Proverbs of Hell," write what you would guess might be "Proverbs of Heaven."

Identifying Issues

3. Select one of the proverbs and apply its message to our lives today, or to your life specifically.

HÔ XUÂN HU'O'NG

A Buddhist Priest

(translated by Nguyen Ngoc Bich and Burton Raffel)

He's neither Chinese
Nor one of us:
Bald, his clothes unstitched,
He sits behind rows of rice-cake offerings
And in front of six or seven nuns.
Now and then he touches a gong,
A bell, cymbals;
He hums, drawls, incants.
Pray hard: You too can be a Superior
And squat, proud, on a lotus.

—*19th century*

What are your reactions to and questions about this work? The following questions may help provoke some ideas.

Probing the Work

1. How does the poet convey her attitude toward her subject? What do some of her words suggest beyond their literal meaning?

Identifying Issues

2. To what extent might religious figures be "one of us"? Should they connect with the people they represent, or devote themselves more to their god and faith?

GRACE PALEY

The Loudest Voice

Grace Paley (b. 1922) is a political activist and teacher (at Sarah Lawrence College) as well as writer; during the 1960s she spoke out against human rights abuses while she was in Moscow. Her first collection of stories, The Little Disturbances of Man *(1959), contains the story below. Other short-story collections include* Enormous Changes at the Last Minute *(1974),* Later the Same Day *(1985), and* Collected Stories *(1994). She is also the author of two books of poetry and a collection of poems and prose,* Long Walks and Intimate Talks.

There is a certain place where dumbwaiters boom, doors slam, dishes crash; every window is a mother's mouth bidding the street shut up, go skate somewhere else, come home. My voice is the loudest.

There, my own mother is still as full of breathing as me and the grocer stands up to speak to her. "Mrs. Abramowitz," he says, "people should not be afraid of their children."

"Ah, Mr. Bialik," my mother replies, "if you say to her or her father 'Ssh,' they say, 'In the grave it will be quiet.' "

"From Coney Island to the cemetery," says my papa. "It's the same subway; it's the same fare."

I am right next to the pickle barrel. My pinky is making tiny whirlpools in the brine. I stop a moment to announce: "Campbell's Tomato Soup. Campbell's Vegetable Beef Soup. Campbell's S-c-otch Broth . . ."

"Be quiet," the grocer says, "the labels are coming off."

"Please, Shirley, be a little quiet," my mother begs me.

In that place the whole street groans: Be quiet! Be quiet! but steals from the happy chorus of my inside self not a tittle or a jot.

There, too, but just around the corner, is a red brick building that has been old for many years. Every morning the children stand before it in double lines which must be straight. They are not insulted. They are waiting anyway.

I am usually among them. I am, in fact, the first, since I begin with "A."

One cold morning the monitor tapped me on the shoulder. "Go to Room 409, Shirley Abramowitz," he said. I did as I was told. I went in a hurry up a down staircase to Room 409, which contained sixth-graders. I had to wait at the desk without wiggling until Mr. Hilton, their teacher, had time to speak.

After five minutes he said, "Shirley?"

"What?" I whispered.

He said, "My! My! Shirley Abramowitz! They told me you had a particularly loud, clear voice and read with lots of expression. Could that be true?"

"Oh, yes," I whispered.

"In that case, don't be silly; I might very well be your teacher someday. Speak up, speak up."

"Yes," I shouted.

"More like it," he said. "Now, Shirley, can you put a ribbon in your hair or a bobby pin? It's too messy."

"Yes!" I bawled.

"Now, now, calm down." He turned to the class. "Children, not a sound. Open at page 39. Read till 52. When you finish, start again." He looked me over once more. "Now, Shirley, you know, I suppose, that Christmas is coming. We are preparing a beautiful play. Most of the parts have been given out. But I still need a child with a strong voice, lots of stamina. Do you know what stamina is? You do? Smart kid. You know, I heard you read 'The Lord is my shepherd' in Assembly yesterday. I was very impressed. Wonderful delivery. Mrs. Jordan, your teacher, speaks highly of you. Now listen to me, Shirley Abramowitz, if you want to take the part and be in the play, repeat after me, 'I swear to work harder than I ever did before.' "

I looked to heaven and said at once, "Oh, I swear." I kissed my pinky and looked at God.

"That is an actor's life, my dear," he explained. "Like a soldier's, never tardy or disobedient to his general, the director. Everything," he said, "absolutely everything will depend on you."

That afternoon, all over the building, children scraped and scrubbed the turkeys and the sheaves of corn off the schoolroom windows. Goodbye Thanksgiving. The next morning a monitor brought red paper and green paper from the office. We made new shapes and hung them on the walls and glued them to the doors.

The teachers became happier and happier. Their heads were ringing like the bells of childhood. My best friend Evie was prone to evil, but she did not get a single demerit for whispering. We learned "Holy Night" without an error. "How wonderful!" said Miss Glacé, the student teacher. "To think that some of you don't even speak the language!" We learned "Deck the Halls" and "Hark! The Herald Angels." . . . They weren't ashamed and we weren't embarrassed.

Oh, but when my mother heard about it all, she said to my father: "Misha, you don't know what's going on there. Cramer is the head of the Tickets Committee."

"Who?" asked my father. "Cramer? Oh yes, an active woman."

"Active? Active has to have a reason. Listen," she said sadly, "I'm surprised to see my neighbors making tra-la-la for Christmas."

My father couldn't think of what to say to that. Then he decided: "You're in America! Clara, you wanted to come here. In Palestine the Arabs would be eating you alive. Europe you had pogroms. Argentina is full of Indians. Here you got Christmas. . . . Some joke, ha?"

"Very funny, Misha. What is becoming of you? If we came to a new country a long time ago to run away from tyrants, and instead we fall into a creeping pogrom, that our children learn a lot of lies, so what's the joke? Ach, Misha, your idealism is going away."

"So is your sense of humor."

"That I never had, but idealism you had a lot of."

"I'm the same Misha Abramovitch, I didn't change an iota. Ask anyone."

"Only ask me," says my mama, may she rest in peace. "I got the answer."

Meanwhile the neighbors had to think of what to say too.

Marty's father said: "You know, he has a very important part, my boy."

"Mine also," said Mr. Sauerfeld.

"Not my boy!" said Mrs. Klieg. "I said to him no. The answer is no. When I say no! I mean no!"

The rabbi's wife said, "It's disgusting!" But no one listened to her. Under the narrow sky of God's great wisdom she wore a strawberry-blond wig.

Every day was noisy and full of experience. I was Right-hand Man. Mr. Hilton said: "How could I get along without you, Shirley?"

He said: "Your mother and father ought to get down on their knees every night and thank God for giving them a child like you."

He also said: "You're absolutely a pleasure to work with, my dear, dear child."

Sometimes he said: "For God's sakes, what did I do with the script? Shirley! Shirley! Find it."

Then I answered quietly: "Here it is, Mr. Hilton."

Once in a while, when he was very tired, he would cry out: "Shirley, I'm just tired of screaming at those kids. Will you tell Ira Pushkov not to come in till Lester points to that star the second time?"

Then I roared: "Ira Pushkov, what's the matter with you? Dope! Mr. Hilton told you five times already, don't come in till Lester points to that star the second time."

"Ach, Clara," my father asked, "what does she do there till six o'clock she can't even put the plates on the table?"

"Christmas," said my mother coldly.

"Ho! Ho!" my father said. "Christmas. What's the harm? After all, history teaches everyone. We learn from reading this is a holiday from pagan times also, candles, lights, even Chanukah. So we learn it's not altogether Christian. So if they think it's a private holiday, they're only ignorant, not patriotic. What belongs to history, belongs to all men. You want to go back to the Middle Ages? Is it better to shave your head with a secondhand razor? Does it hurt Shirley to learn to speak up? It does not. So maybe someday she won't live between the kitchen and the shop. She's not a fool."

I thank you, Papa, for your kindness. It is true about me to this day. I am foolish but I am not a fool.

That night my father kissed me and said with great interest in my career, "Shirley, tomorrow's your big day. Congrats."

"Save it," my mother said. Then she shut all the windows in order to prevent tonsillitis.

In the morning it snowed. On the street corner a tree had been decorated for us by a kind city administration. In order to miss its chilly shadow our neighbors walked three blocks east to buy a loaf of bread. The butcher pulled down black window shades to keep the colored lights from shining on his chickens. Oh, not me. On the way to school, with both my hands I tossed it a kiss of tolerance. Poor thing, it was a stranger in Egypt.

I walked straight into the auditorium past the staring children. "Go ahead, Shirley!" said the monitors. Four boys, big for their age, had already started work as propmen and stagehands.

Mr. Hilton was very nervous. He was not even happy. Whatever he started to say ended in a sideward look of sadness. He sat slumped in the middle of the first row and asked me to help Miss Glacé. I did this, although she thought my voice too resonant and said, "Show-off!"

Parents began to arrive long before we were ready. They wanted to make a good impression. From among the yards of drapes I peeked out at the audience. I saw my embarrassed mother.

Ira, Lester, and Meyer were pasted to their beards by Miss Glacé. She almost forgot to thread the star on its wire, but I reminded her. I coughed a few times to clear my throat. Miss Glacé looked around and saw that everyone was in costume and on line waiting to play his part. She whispered, "All right . . ." Then:

Jackie Sauerfeld, the prettiest boy in first grade, parted the curtains with his skinny elbow and in a high voice sang out:

"Parents dear
We are here
To make a Christmas play in time.
It we give
In narrative
And illustrate with pantomime."

He disappeared.

My voice burst immediately from the wings to the great shock of Ira, Lester, and Meyer, who were waiting for it but were surprised all the same.

"I remember, I remember, the house where I was born . . ."

Miss Glacé yanked the curtain open and there it was, the house—an old hayloft, where Celia Kornbluh lay in the straw with Cindy Lou, her favorite doll. Ira, Lester, and Meyer moved slowly from the wings toward her, sometimes pointing to a moving star and sometimes ahead to Cindy Lou.

It was a long story and it was a sad story. I carefully pronounced all the words about my lonesome childhood, while little Eddie Braunstein wandered upstage and down with his shepherd's stick, looking for sheep. I brought up lonesomeness again, and not being understood at all except by some women everybody hated. Eddie was too small for that and Marty Groff took his place, wearing his father's prayer shawl. I announced twelve friends, and half the boys in the fourth grade gathered round Marty, who stood on an orange crate while my voice harangued. Sorrowful and loud, I declaimed about love and God and Man, but because of the terrible deceit of Abie Stock we came suddenly to a famous moment. Marty, whose remembering tongue I was, waited at the foot of the cross. He stared desperately at the audience. I groaned, "My God, my God, why hast thou forsaken me?" The soldiers who were sheiks grabbed poor Marty to pin him up to die, but he wrenched free, turned again to the audience, and spread his arms aloft to show despair and the end. I murmured at the top of my voice, "The rest is silence, but as everyone in this room, in this city—in this world—now knows, I shall have life eternal."

That night Mrs. Kornbluh visited our kitchen for a glass of tea.

"How's the virgin?" asked my father with a look of concern.

"For a man with a daughter, you got a fresh mouth, Abramovitch."

"Here," said my father kindly, "have some lemon, it'll sweeten your disposition."

They debated a little in Yiddish, then fell in a puddle of Russian and Polish. What I understood next was my father, who said, "Still and all, it was certainly a beautiful affair, you have to admit, introducing us to the beliefs of a different culture."

"Well, yes," said Mrs. Kornbluh. "The only thing . . . you know Charlie Turner—that cute boy in Celia's class—a couple others? They got very small parts or no part at all. In very bad taste, it seemed to me. After all, it's their religion."

"Ach," explained my mother, "what could Mr. Hilton do? They got very small voices; after all, why should they holler? The English language they know from the beginning by heart. They're blond like angels. You think it's so important they should get in the play? Christmas . . . the whole piece of goods . . . they own it."

I listened and listened until I couldn't listen any more. Too sleepy, I climbed out of bed and kneeled. I made a little church of my hands and said, "Hear, O Israel . . ." Then I called out in Yiddish, "Please, good night, good night. Ssh." My father said, "Ssh yourself," and slammed the kitchen door.

I was happy. I fell asleep at once. I had prayed for everybody: my talking family, cousins far away, passersby, and all the lonesome Christians. I expected to be heard. My voice was certainly the loudest.

—1956

What are your reactions to and questions about this work? The following questions may help provoke some ideas.

Probing the Work

1. What is the difference in attitude between the father and mother? Find an exchange between them that illustrates their differences.

2. Shirley is *characterized* by her loud voice. How does this detail affect your perception of her? How does Shirley use her loud voice throughout the story?

Identifying Issues

3. What are some differences between children and adults with regard to their religious beliefs, or their attitudes toward religion? To your mind, which in this story represents the preferable attitude, the mother's or the father's? Why?
4. What is the extent of responsibility on the part of schools to incorporate religion into the educational experience and to give equal time to different religions? What are the problems associated with this issue?

PHILIP LARKIN

Church Going

Philip Larkin (1922–1985) was born in Coventry, England, studied at Oxford, and worked as a university librarian. With the publication of his second book of poems, The Less Deceived *(1960), he achieved critical recognition, and is now considered by many critics to be the finest English poet of his generation.*

Once I am sure there's nothing going on
I step inside, letting the door thud shut.
Another church: matting, seats, and stone,
And little books; sprawlings of flowers, cut
For Sunday, brownish now; some brass and stuff
Up at the holy end; the small neat organ;
And a tense, musty, unignorable silence,
Brewed God knows how long. Hatless, I take off
My cycle-clips in awkward reverence,

Move forward, run my hand around the font.
From where I stand, the roof looks almost new—
Cleaned, or restored? Someone would know: I don't.
Mounting the lectern, I peruse a few
Hectoring large-scale verses, and pronounce
"Here endeth" much more loudly than I'd meant.
The echoes snigger briefly. Back at the door
I sign the book, donate an Irish sixpence,°
Reflect the place was not worth stopping for.

17. Irish sixpence, of no value in England.

Yet stop I did: in fact I often do,
And always end much at a loss like this,
Wondering what to look for; wondering, too,
When churches fall completely out of use
What we shall turn them into, if we shall keep
A few cathedrals chronically on show,
Their parchment, plate and pyx° in locked cases,
And let the rest rent-free to rain and sheep.
Shall we avoid them as unlucky places?

Or, after dark, will dubious women come
To make their children touch a particular stone;
Pick simples° for a cancer; or on some
Advised night see walking a dead one?
Power of some sort or other will go on
In games, in riddles, seemingly at random;
But superstition, like belief, must die,
And what remains when disbelief has gone?
Grass, weedy pavement, brambles, buttress, sky,

A shape less recognisable each week,
A purpose more obscure. I wonder who
Will be the last, the very last, to seek
This place for what it was; one of the crew
That tap and jot and know what rood-lofts° were?
Some ruin-bibber, randy for antique,
Or Christmas-addict, counting on a whiff
Of gown-and-bands and organ-pipes and myrrh?°
Or will he be my representative,

Bored, uninformed, knowing the ghostly silt
Dispersed, yet tending to this cross of ground
Through suburb scrub because it held unspilt
So long and equably what since is found
Only in separation—marriage, and birth,
And death, and thoughts of these—for which was built
This special shell? For, though I've no idea
What this accoutred frowsty barn is worth,
It pleases me to stand in silence here;

25. pyx, box in which communion wafers are kept.
30. simples, medicinal herbs.
41. rood-lofts, galleries on top of carved screens separating the nave of a church from the choir.
44. myrrh, gum resin, from trees of genus *Commiphora* used in the making of incense; one of three presents given by the Three Wise Men to the infant Jesus. "Gown-and-bands": gown and decorative collar worn by clergymen.

A serious house on serious earth it is,
In whose blent air all our compulsions meet,
Are recognised, and robed as destinies.
And that much never can be obsolete,
Since someone will forever be surprising
A hunger in himself to be more serious,
And gravitating with it to this ground,
Which, he once heard, was proper to grow wise in,
If only that so many dead lie round.

—1955

What are your reactions to and questions about this work? The following questions may help provoke some ideas.

Probing the Work

1. What does Larkin mean by the question, "And what remains when disbelief is gone?" Paraphrase the answer Larkin arrives at in the lines that follow.
2. What is the *tone* (see page 67) of the poem? How is the tone reflected in the speaker's attitude and diction?

Identifying Issues

3. This poem was published in 1955. Has *belief* gone? If so, can you see the day when *disbelief* will be gone? Explain.

LESLIE MARMON SILKO

The Man to Send Rain Clouds

Leslie Marmon Silko (b. 1948) is part Laguna Pueblo Indian, part Mexican, part Anglo. She was born in Albuquerque, New Mexico, and grew up on the Laguna Pueblo Reservation. After attending the Bureau of Indian Affairs school, she went to the University of New Mexico and taught at Navajo Community College and the University of Arizona. In 1981 she received a five-year MacArthur Foundation grant.

One

They found him under a big cottonwood tree. His Levi jacket and pants were faded light-blue so that he had been easy to find. The big cottonwood tree stood apart from a small grove of winterbare cottonwoods which grew in the wide, sandy arroyo. He had been dead for a day or more, and the sheep had wandered and scattered up and down the arroyo. Leon and his brother-in-law, Ken, gathered the sheep and left them in the pen at the sheep camp before they returned to the cottonwood tree. Leon waited under the tree while Ken drove the truck through the deep sand to the edge of the arroyo. He squinted up at the sun and unzipped his jacket—it sure was hot for this time of year. But high and northwest the blue mountains were still deep in snow. Ken came sliding down the low, crumbling bank about fifty yards down, and he was bringing the red blanket.

Before they wrapped the old man, Leon took a piece of string out of his pocket and tied a small gray feather in the old man's long white hair. Ken gave him the paint. Across the brown wrinkled forehead he drew a streak of white and along the high cheekbones he drew a strip of blue paint. He paused and watched Ken throw pinches of corn meal and pollen into the wind that fluttered the small gray feather. Then Leon painted with yellow under the old man's broad nose, and finally, when he had painted green across the chin, he smiled.

"Send us rain clouds, Grandfather." They laid the bundle in the back of the pickup and covered it with a heavy tarp before they started back to the pueblo.

They turned off the highway onto the sandy pueblo road. Not long after they passed the store and post office they saw Father Paul's car coming toward them. When he recognized their faces he slowed his car and waved for them to stop. The young priest rolled down the car window.

"Did you find old Teofilo?" he asked loudly.

Leon stopped the truck. "Good morning, Father. We were just out to the sheep camp. Everything is O.K. now."

"Thank God for that. Teofilo is a very old man. You really shouldn't allow him to stay at the sheep camp alone."

"No, he won't do that any more now."

"Well, I'm glad you understand. I hope I'll be seeing you at Mass this week—we missed you last Sunday. See if you can get old Teofilo to come with you." The priest smiled and waved at them as they drove away.

Two

Louise and Teresa were waiting. The table was set for lunch, and the coffee was boiling on the black iron stove. Leon looked at Louise and then at Teresa.

"We found him under a cottonwood tree in the big arroyo near sheep camp. I guess he sat down to rest in the shade and never got up again." Leon walked toward the old man's bed. The red plaid shawl had been shaken and spread carefully over the bed, and a new brown flannel shirt and pair of stiff new Levis were arranged neatly beside the pillow. Louise held the screen door open while Leon and Ken carried in the red blanket. He looked small and shriveled, and after they dressed him in the new shirt and pants he seemed more shrunken.

It was noontime now because the church bells rang the Angelus. They ate the beans with hot bread, and nobody said anything until after Teresa poured the coffee.

Ken stood up and put on his jacket. "I'll see about the gravediggers. Only the top layer of soil is frozen. I think it can be ready before dark."

Leon nodded his head and finished his coffee. After Ken had been gone for a while, the neighbors and clanspeople came quietly to embrace Teofilo's family and to leave food on the table because the grave-diggers would come to eat when they were finished.

Three

The sky in the west was full of pale-yellow light. Louise stood outside with her hands in the pockets of Leon's green army jacket that was too big for her. The funeral was over, and the old men had taken their candles and medicine bags and were gone. She waited until the body was laid into the pickup before she said anything to Leon. She touched his arm, and he noticed that her hands were still dusty from the corn meal that she had sprinkled around the old man. When she spoke, Leon could not hear her.

"What did you say? I didn't hear you."

"I said that I had been thinking about something."

"About what?"

"About the priest sprinkling holy water for Grandpa. So he won't be thirsty."

Leon stared at the new moccasins that Teofilo had made for the ceremonial dances in the summer. They were nearly hidden by the red blanket. It was getting colder, and the wind pushed gray dust down the narrow pueblo road. The sun was approaching the long mesa where it disappeared during the winter. Louise stood there shivering and watching his face. Then he zipped up his jacket and opened the truck door. "I'll see if he's there."

Four

Ken stopped the pickup at the church, and Leon got out; and then Ken drove down the hill to the graveyard where people were waiting. Leon knocked at the old carved door with its symbols of the Lamb. While he waited he looked up at the twin bells from the king of Spain with the last sunlight pouring around them in their tower.

The priest opened the door and smiled when he saw who it was. "Come in! What brings you here this evening?"

The priest walked toward the kitchen, and Leon stood with his cap in his hand, playing with the earflaps and examining the living room—the brown sofa, the green armchair, and the brass lamp that hung down from the ceiling by links of chain. The priest dragged a chair out of the kitchen and offered it to Leon.

"No thank you, Father. I only came to ask you if you would bring your holy water to the graveyard."

The priest turned away from Leon and looked out the window at the patio full of shadows and the dining-room windows of the nuns' cloister across the patio. The curtains were heavy, and the light from within faintly penetrated; it was impossible to see the nuns inside eating supper. "Why didn't you tell me he was dead? I could have brought the Last Rites anyway."

Leon smiled. "It wasn't necessary, Father."

The priest stared down at his scuffed brown loafers and the worn hem of his cassock. "For a Christian burial it was necessary."

His voice was distant, and Leon thought that his blue eyes looked tired.

"It's O.K., Father, we just want him to have plenty of water."

The priest sank down in the green chair and picked up a glossy missionary magazine. He turned the colored pages full of lepers and pagans without looking at them.

"You know I can't do that, Leon. There should have been the Last Rites and a funeral Mass at the very least."

Leon put on his green cap and pulled the flaps down over his ears. "It's getting late, Father. I've got to go."

When Leon opened the door Father Paul stood up and said, "Wait." He left the room and came back wearing a long brown overcoat. He followed Leon out the door and across the dim churchyard to the adobe steps in front of the church. They both stooped to fit through the low adobe entrance. And when they started down the hill to the graveyard only half of the sun was visible above the mesa.

The priest approached the grave slowly, wondering how they had managed to dig into the frozen ground; and then he remembered that this was New Mexico, and saw the pile of cold loose sand beside the hole. The people stood close to each other with little clouds of steam puffing from their faces. The priest looked at them and saw a pile of jackets, gloves, and scarves in the yellow, dry tumbleweeds that grew in the graveyard. He looked at the red blanket, not sure that Teofilo was so small, wondering if it wasn't some perverse Indian trick—something they did in March to ensure a good harvest—wondering if maybe old Teofilo was actually at sheep camp corraling the sheep for the night. But there he was, facing into a cold dry wind and squinting at the last sunlight, ready to bury a red wool blanket while the faces of the parishioners were in shadow with the last warmth of the sun on their backs.

His fingers were stiff, and it took them a long time to twist the lid off the holy water. Drops of water fell on the red blanket and soaked into dark icy spots. He sprinkled the grave and the water disappeared almost before it touched the dim, cold sand; it reminded him of something—he tried to remember what it was, because he thought if he could remember he might understand this. He sprinkled more water; he shook the container until it was empty, and the water fell through the light from sundown like August rain that fell while the sun was still shining, almost evaporating before it touched the wilted squash flowers.

The wind pulled at the priest's brown Franciscan robe and swirled away the corn meal and pollen that had been sprinkled on the blanket. They lowered the bundle into the ground, and they didn't bother to untie the stiff pieces of new rope that were tied around the ends of the blanket. The sun was gone, and over on the highway the eastbound lane was full of headlights. The priest walked away slowly. Leon watched him climb the hill, and when he had disappeared within the tall, thick walls, Leon turned to look up at the high blue mountains in the deep snow that reflected a faint red light from the west. He felt good because it was finished, and he was happy about the sprinkling of the holy water; now the old man could send them big thunderclouds for sure.

—1969

What are your reactions to and questions about this work? The following questions may help provoke some ideas.

Probing the Work

1. What is the significance of the holy water, from the perspective of the Native American and of the priest? What does each one's attitude toward the holy water say about their religious beliefs?
2. When the holy water seems to evaporate before it hits the dead body, it "reminds [the priest] of something." What do you suppose that it reminds him of?

Identifying Issues

3. What role do mystery and magic play in religious beliefs, both in this story and in "real life"?

LOUISE GLÜCK

Celestial Music

Louise Glück (b. 1943) was born on Long Island, New York, and was educated at Sarah Lawrence College and at Columbia University. She has published six books of poetry and taught in writing programs at a number of colleges and universities. Her poetry tends to focus on the anxieties of women, expressed often through reference to myth and symbol.

I have a friend who still believes in heaven.
Not a stupid person, yet with all she knows, she literally talks to god,
she thinks someone listens in heaven.
On earth, she's unusually competent.
Brave, too, able to face unpleasantness.

We found a caterpillar dying in the dirt, greedy ants crawling over it.
I'm always moved by weakness, by disaster, always eager to oppose vitality.
But timid, also, quick to shut my eyes.
Whereas my friend was able to watch, to let events play out
according to nature. For my sake, she intervened,
brushing a few ants off the torn thing, and set it down across the road.

My friend says I shut my eyes to god, that nothing else explains
my aversion to reality. She says I'm like the child who buries her head
in the pillow

so as not to see, the child who tells herself
that light causes sadness—
My friend is like the mother. Patient, urging me
to wake up an adult like herself, a courageous person—

In my dreams, my friend reproaches me. We're walking
on the same road, except it's winter now;
she's telling me that when you love the world you hear celestial music;
look up, she says. When I look up, nothing.
Only clouds, snow, a white business in the trees
like brides leaping to a great height—
Then I'm afraid for her; I see her
caught in a net deliberately cast over the earth—

In reality, we sit by the side of the road, watching the sun set,
from time to time the silence pierced by a birdcall.
It's this moment we're both trying to explain, the fact
that we're at ease with death, with solitude.
My friend draws a circle in the dirt; inside, the caterpillar doesn't move.
She's always trying to make something whole, something beautiful, an image
capable of life apart from her.
We're very quiet. It's peaceful sitting here, not speaking, the composition
fixed, the road turning suddenly dark, the air
going cool, here and there the rocks shining and glittering—
it's this stillness that we both love.
The love of form is a love of endings.

—1989

What are your reactions to and questions about this work? The following questions may help provoke some ideas.

Probing the Work

1. How do the speaker's behavior and her friend's behavior toward the caterpillar illustrate their respective "religious" beliefs?
2. What, according to the last few lines of the poem, do they have in common?

Identifying Issues

3. How important is it to a friendship that friends share values and beliefs? Which values and beliefs are more critical to a friendship than others?

WRITING ASSIGNMENT SEQUENCE (CONTINUED FROM PAGE 964)

4. Making Connections

Select one of the following questions and write an informal response in which you connect your own ideas with those conveyed in the works of this cluster, and/or make connections among the works themselves.

A. What are the various attitudes and religious beliefs expressed in the works of this cluster? With which could you best identify?

B. Have any of these works changed your perception of your own or someone else's religion? Explain how.

5. Putting It All Together

Write an essay that combines what you think about the topic *Celestial Music* (religious beliefs) with what you now understand about the readings.

- Collect your informal writing, notes, and reading-journal entries on this topic and decide what will be the focus of your essay.
- Outline your essay. Select the literary passages and personal details you might use to illustrate and support your main focus.
- Write a draft of your essay in which you bring together what you think about the subject with what you understand about the readings. Try to include in your draft one or more *literary terms*.

- Share what you've written with your classmates and instructor, then revise it according to their recommendations.

Writing Tip: Crafting Sentences

Just as any idea can be expressed in many different ways, any sentence can be rewritten and manipulated to say exactly what you wish. Select a page from a first draft of your essay and try some of the following:

- Count the sentences and note how they start and finish: have you varied the sentence lengths? Do they all follow the same patterns? How do you link ideas? How often have you used coordinating words such as *and* and *but,* or subordinating words such as *although* and *since?*
- Choose two sentences to rewrite five different ways. Often sentences are effective because they put off the main idea until the end. Some sentences begin with the main idea and build in phrases and clauses. Some sentences begin with phrases, while others have them in the middle. Some sentences benefit from some cutting: are there superfluous words, like "really" or "truly"? Try out all of the possibilities; you'll be surprised how your writing improves when you vary your sentences.

Remember to highlight your main idea, to make every word count, and to punctuate sentences properly. Here is a sentence from one of Lisa's essays (a run-on sentence that she needed to fix) and the number of ways she rewrote it:

- Dads are more concerned with the physical safety of their daughters than their sons, they often keep girls closer to home than boys.
- Dads, who are more concerned with the physical safety of their daughters than of their sons, often keep their girls closer to home.
- Because they are more concerned with the physical safety of their daughters than of their sons, Dads often keep their girls closer to home.

In one of the paragraphs in her celestial music essay, Debbie's sentences were short and choppy:

- I'm not sure Larkin is correct. He assumes that "disbelief" will be "gone" someday. But I refuse to believe that. Religion has always been around. People always need to believe in something! Some higher power. It helps them get through the hard times.

How would you improve this paragraph?

CrossClusters

In your paper you might want to consider how the following works located elsewhere in this book depict religion:

- Gabriel García Márquez, "The Handsomest Drowned Man in the World" (p. 13)
- Langston Hughes, "Salvation" (p. 86)
- James Joyce, "Araby" (p. 89)
- Chinua Achebe, "Dead Men's Path" (p. 138)
- Sophocles, *Antigone* (p. 144)
- Lucille Clifton, "for de Lawd" (p. 250)
- James Baldwin, "The Rockpile" (p. 462)
- Bernard Malamud, "The Magic Barrel" (p. 569)
- Tony Kushner, from *Angels in America* (p. 621)
- Robert Browning, "Porphyria's Lover" (p. 840)
- Emily Dickinson, "Because I could not stop for Death" (p. 993)
- Isabel Allende, "And of Clay Are We Created" (p. 996)
- Woody Allen, *Death Knocks* (p. 1005)

Sample Essay

Here is Mike's essay. He focuses on Larkin's poem "Church Going."

"A Quiet God," by Mike Frazer

What makes a church so quiet? An architect would say it is because of the design of the building; its walls, vaulted ceilings, and soft carpeting. A poet might say it is meant to be that way. A priest would probably tell you it is the house of God and should be revered. Those who do not really have any answer may just say a church is quiet because "churches just are." If these are some possible answers then the next obvious question is which answer is correct? Personally, I think they all are.

Churches are interesting objects to say the least. They have been around, in one sense or another, for as long as human civilization. Thousands of years ago people went to church to witness God. It may not have been God in the sense that we currently think of, but it was God just the same. Even then, humanity attempted to house something without definition. They chose a plot of land called Holy for one reason or other and put a building on it. This they declared the House of God.

Erecting places "where God lives" is a pastime people have apparently never gotten tired of. Today, we still build churches in the name of God and hire priests to work in them and tell us what God has to say to us this week right along with a plug for Saturday night Bingo in the church hall. In fact, some architects have even gotten quite fancy with the whole church idea and gone so far as to design buildings which look like crosses from above. These places are not built on mountains anymore, or stuck on some piece of rock where someone-or-other saw Him once. Today, they are just built like any other building, on a plot of land in a convenient place. What then, makes a church holy? Why do people go there to find peace, solace, comfort, and prayers answered?

My opinion on the matter fits fairly well with those of the poet Philip Larkin. In "Church Going," he seems to sum up all churches in just a few brief lines.

> Another church: matting, seats, and stone,
> And little books; sprawlings of flowers, cut
> For Sunday, brownish now; some brass and stuff
> Up at the holy end; the small neat organ;
> And a tense, musty, unignorable silence,
> Brewed God knows how long. (976)

Larkin's church could be anywhere, in any town, in any country. I know it describes the church back home where I punch my weekly time card. In fact, it describes every church I have ever had occasion to enter, from the smallest back-water one-car town church to St. Patrick's cathedral on Fifth Avenue in New York City. All these things are shared by every church, including the silence.

In the poem, Larkin seems to be of the opinion that the church is silent because no matter how silly the idea of a church may be, it is still something that should be treated with reverence. There is definitely something to that view that deserves recognition and there are a number of reasons for this. First, we need to address what makes the idea of a church silly. I would first address the concept of priesthood. Priests tell the people what God has to say to them. This is very strange because I believe that if God has anything special He would like to say, He is more than capable of getting the message across. Priests are useful in their knowledge of *The Bible* and such works but I do not feel they have a more direct line with The Almighty than anyone else.

Another strange thing about churches is the fact that, technically speaking, they are only buildings. Yet at the same time, there is something undefinable in a church that makes it more than it is. In the future, as Larkin wonders, "When churches fall completely out of use / What we shall turn them into"? There are very few people in the world who will simply tear down a church, even though it is supposedly "just another building." So what then, will the churches be? I ask that question and cannot help but think that, to the ancient druids, Stonehenge was a church of sorts; and, to the Israelites, any number of weathered ruins had been churches. No one prays to these places now but they still seem to hold some sort of power.

I find myself drifting back towards Larkin's "tense, musty, unignorable silence." This one line, it seems to me, holds within it the key to the power of a church. If a person yelled in a church, his voice would not be muffled. It would be loud, distinct, possibly even echoing around the room. The tests of this theory are few and far between though because it is a difficult thing to convince someone, even yourself, to yell in a church. There is nothing physical to stop anyone from making noise; it just would not seem right somehow. It is almost as if the silence would berate you for breaking it. The last stanza of "Church Going" describes the feeling of a church best:

> A serious house on serious earth it is,
> In whose blent air all our compulsions meet,
> Are recognised, and robed as destinies.
> And that much never can be obsolete,
> Since someone will forever be surprising
> A hunger in himself to be more serious,
> And gravitating with it to this ground,
> Which, he once, heard, was proper to grow wise in,
> If only that so many dead lie round. (978)

There is something to be revered in a church, that much is doubtless. The problem lies in what that something is. It is a commodity that is undefinable, indistinguishable, and invisible. Yet it holds you and captivates you and makes you wonder about it in seriousness and in silence. Maybe we still have churches because the reason cannot be seen or heard, and in that weighty nothing something can be felt.

25

DEATH & CO.

WRITING ASSIGNMENT SEQUENCE

1. Thinking About . . . Death

Freewriting: Freewrite about your encounters with, or your imaginings about, death. What are your feelings about your own death, and how have you arrived at those feelings?

2. Enacting the Topic

Write a creative description (in the form of prose or poetry) of what happens when we die, of a near-death experience, or of an after-death experience.

3. Responding to the Readings

As you read the works in this cluster, jot down in your response journals questions you have about the works, and comment on passages you find provocative or puzzling. Consider the questions following each reading for journal writing and prepare to discuss your reactions in class.

CLUSTER ESSAY

J. BRUCE LONG

The Death That Ends Death in Hinduism and Buddhism (excerpt)

II. Death, Rebirth and Liberation in Buddhist Doctrine

There is general agreement between Hinduism and Buddhism that no human life can be filled with a sense of meaning and efficacious action unless it is lived in full acceptance of the fact of death. He who tries to ignore death by deluding himself into believing that he, his relatives, and his possessions will endure forever, robs himself of the purposeful life which can come only to him who unflinchingly accepts death as an integral part of life. On the other hand, that person who faces death calmly, courageously, and confidently—desiring neither to flee it nor to rush into its grasp—will come to recognize death not as an enemy or a robber but as an ever-present companion and ultimately, as a friend. To meet death, not only as an event at the end of life but as an ever-present ingredient in the life-process itself, is the final goal to be sought in both Hinduism and Buddhism.

Buddhist doctrine defines death as a cutting off of the life-force or a total nonfunctioning of the physical body and the mind. Not that the life-force is totally destroyed with the death of the body; it is merely displaced and transformed to continue functioning in another form. Every birth is, in fact, a rebirth. Many Buddhists believe that rebirth occurs immediately after death. Others believe that forty-nine days separate death and rebirth in an "intermediary state" *(Bardo),* graphically described in the *Tibetan Book of the Dead,* about which we will speak in greater detail presently.

Birth and death, when viewed at the cosmic level of perception, describes the outer limits of the life of both the individual person and of the cosmos. Strictly speaking, neither human beings nor the universe itself experiences either an absolute beginning or an absolute end. When this same drama of birth and death is viewed as the microlevel in terms of seconds and fractions of seconds rather than years or aeons, birth and death are discovered to occur almost simultaneously in each instant of time. The human person is nothing more than a conglomeration of "aggregates" (i.e. body, sensations, perceptions, mental formations, and consciousness) which, taken together form the mind-body organism engaged in the process of coming-to-being and passing-away in every moment.

But, according to Buddhist teachings, there is no single permanent, unchanging entity or substance constituting the Self or Soul which endures in a uniform state from moment to moment and from lifetime to lifetime. That phenomenon which we customarily call "the self" in speaking of "I myself" or "you yourself" is nothing more than a continuity of a series of psycho-physiological occasions (described by the American psychologist, William James, as "the stream of consciousness") which undergoes an unbroken series of alterations in every moment. As one teacher states it: "When the Aggregates arise, decay and die, O monk, every moment you are born, decay and die." Thus, in every instant we are born; in every instant we die. Birth and death are two almost indistinguishable and imperceptible strands of a single rope of existence.

The human self, therefore, is composed of a stream of consciousness, changing momentarily and filled with impressions and tendencies created by good and evil actions *(karma)* which at death is transposed to a new mode of being, while the imagined "self" who thinks in terms of "I" and "mine" does not survive from one moment to the next and hence, does not transmigrate.

The Buddhists, like the Hindus, believe that there are differences in the quality of deaths, just as there are differences in the quality of births and existences. The differences in deaths depends upon the difference between disciplined and undisciplined living, between pure and impure mind or between "carefulness" and "carelessness." "Carefulness is the path of the deathless; carelessness is the path to death . . . The constantly meditative, the ever earnestly striving ones, realize the bond-free, supreme Nirvana" (*Dhammapada* 21–23).

The "soul" or "the fruits of the karma" of a deceased person who is still trapped by the bonds of "desire," according to popular Buddhist belief, will go immediately after death to Yama's judgment chamber where, after a waiting period of seven days, he is required to cross a treacherous river with three current speeds simultaneously (representing three karmic destinies of hell: human beings, animals and hungry ghosts). Those who cross the river successfully are ushered into a Paradise or a Happy Land, ruled by Amitābha ("Boundless Light") who will provide a rebirth in his Paradise for those who have true faith in him and praise his holy name.

All of this is by way of saying that for Gautama, the Buddha, the way to an effective life within this world and to a final release from the curse of rebirth beyond this world leads through a calm and confident recognition of the universal truth that, "all composite things must pass away." The truly Awakened One is that person who recognizes that, indeed, the whole universe is passing away, that nothing remains as it is for more than an instant and that, for this reason, nothing which abides within this realm of death is deserving of a person's absolute trust. This is the Truth which Gautama foresaw during his legendary "pleasure excursion" when he witnessed the four signs of suffering: poverty, sickness, old age, and death. On that occasion, he experienced a total loss of confidence in the reality and value of existence in the finite world because of his discovery that everything is "subject to change and decay" and death "is the end which has been fixed for all." He sighed to his charioteer: ". . . and yet the world forgets its fear and takes no heed. The hearts of men are surely hardened to fears, for they feel quite at ease even while travelling along the road to the next life . . ."

The message of the Buddha to all suffering humanity is this: everything inevitably comes to extinction even though it may last for a millennium. Everything must be parted from what it desires in the end. Recognize that all living things (mineral, vegetable, animal, human, and divine) are subject to the law of death. Therefore, recognize the true nature of the living world and do not be anxious about your life or your death. "When the light of true knowledge has dispelled the darkness of ignorance, when all existence has been seen as without substance, peace ensues when life draws to an end, which seems to cure a long illness at last. Everything, whether stationary or movable is bound to perish in the end. Be ye therefore mindful and vigilant." (*Buddhacārita* XXVI 88 ff.)

Men are instructed by the Buddha not to make any plans in this world without reckoning with death. For death comes according to the dictates of time, unannounced and unanticipated by most persons. How can one know beforehand when death will strike: whether today or tomorrow, one year or five years hence or within the next moment? How can one anticipate the form that death will take: a mortal wound from a knife or a gun, an automobile accident, a lingering illness or a sudden heart-attack? Death strikes without notice; the young and the old, the well and the sickly, the high and the low, the wealthy and the poor. It is no respecter of persons. There is no lasting peace as long as the person is still in the body. Therefore, one should not place any trust in a life which is sustained by so uncertain a thing as breathing in and out.

This doctrine of the inevitability of death for all living creatures is movingly expressed in one of the most popular of all Buddhist stories, the "Parable of the Mustard Seed." According to this story, a woman is discovered grieving uncontrollably over the death of her beloved son whose corpse she carries in her arms. She does not seem to be aware that death is a terminal event—for this lifetime, at least. In hopes of finding an antidote to her child's "malady" which would restore him to consciousness, she approaches the Buddha who is renowned for his miraculous powers to heal. The Buddha does provide her with an antidote, but not the sort that she has sought. He instructs her to go from house to house throughout the city in search of a few grains of mustard seed. The mustard seeds, he says, will provide the proper antidote to the child's disease (i.e. death). But, she must accept the mustard seed only from a household in which no one has ever died—not a father or a mother, not a brother or a sister, not a servant or an animal. After searching from house to house, she discovers that not a single household can be found which has never experienced the death of one of its members. In time she comes to see the truth which is the panacea to death and sorrow: that death is the inescapable destiny of all creatures and that, given its inevitability, she has no cause to grieve. Relieved from the pangs of both false-hope and needless grief, she goes immediately with peace of mind, to the burning-ground and there submits her son to the fires of cremation.

—1975

What are your reactions to and questions about this work? The following questions may help provoke some ideas.

Probing the Work

1. Summarize what Buddhists believe about death. What is the most significant or interesting idea articulated in this description?

Identifying Issues

2. What kinds of connections and contrasts can you make between the ideas and beliefs about death that are illustrated in this essay and the way death is commonly portrayed or talked about in American culture?

EMILY DICKINSON

Because I could not stop for Death

Emily Dickinson (1830–1886), the daughter of a successful lawyer, lived almost all her life in the same house on a main street in Amherst, Massachusetts, where she could watch life—and funeral processions—go by. Something of a recluse, she spoke volumes through her poetry. Only a few were published during her lifetime, but nearly 1800 were found after her death.

Because I could not stop for Death—
He kindly stopped for me—
The Carriage held but just Ourselves—
And Immortality.

We slowly drove—He knew no haste
And I had put away
My labor and my leisure too,
For His Civility—

We passed the School, where Children strove
At Recess—in the Ring—
We passed the Fields of Gazing Grain—
We passed the Setting Sun—

Or rather—He passed Us—
The Dews drew quivering and chill—
For only Gossamer, my Gown—
My Tippet—only Tulle—

We paused before a House that seemed
A Swelling of the Ground—
The Roof was scarcely visible—
The Cornice—in the Ground—

Since then—'tis Centuries—and yet
Feels shorter than the Day
I first surmised the Horses' Heads
Were toward Eternity—

—1863

What are your reactions to and questions about this work? The following questions may help provoke some ideas.

Probing the Work

1. How does the speaker *personify* death? What does that particular personification reveal about her vision of and her attitude toward death?

2. To what extent is this poem an example of *allegory* (see page 78)? What is the symbolic meaning of the poem as a whole?

Identifying Issues

3. When, if ever, are you ever ready to "stop for Death"? Are there things you can do to prepare yourself for death? Use examples.

DYLAN THOMAS

Do not go gentle into that good night

Dylan Thomas (1914–1953) was born in Swansea, Wales. His father, a teacher of English literature at a grammar school, was a frustrated poet and a "hard drinker"; an intense intellectual and emotional bond existed between father and son. Thomas published his first book (18 Poems) *when he was 20, beginning a successful, though turbulent, writing career. In his last years he supported himself with lecture tours and poetry readings in the United States, and died in New York City of chronic alcoholism. He called his poetry a record of his "struggle from darkness toward some measure of light."*

Do not go gentle into that good night,
Old age should burn and rave at close of day;
Rage, rage against the dying of the light.

Though wise men at their end know dark is right,
Because their words had forked no lightning they
Do not go gentle into that good night.

Good men, the last wave by, crying how bright
Their frail deeds might have danced in a green bay,
Rage, rage against the dying of the light.

Wild men who caught and sang the sun in flight,
And learn, too late, they grieved it on its way,
Do not go gentle into that good night.

Grave men, near death, who see with blinding sight
Blind eyes could blaze like meteors and be gay,
Rage, rage against the dying of the light.

And you, my father, there on the sad height,
Curse, bless, me now with your fierce tears, I pray.
Do not go gentle into that good night.
Rage, rage against the dying of the light.

—1951

What are your reactions to and questions about this work? The following questions may help provoke some ideas.

Probing the Work

1. Paraphrase and categorize the different types of people Thomas describes in stanzas 2–5.
2. What seems to be the *speaker's* relationship with his father, based on the imagery of this poem?

Identifying Issues

3. Do you agree with the implications of the speaker's advice, that you should "rage against" death? What are the potential consequences of such anger? What are some other possible responses?

SYLVIA PLATH

Death & Co.

Sylvia Plath (1932–1963) was an excellent student, winning poetry prizes, scholarships at Smith College (graduating summa cum laude*), and a Fulbright Scholarship to Cambridge University, where she met and married the English poet Ted Hughes. After having two children, publishing several books of poetry (including her best and last,* Ariel*), and suffering bouts of depression, she took her own life at the age of 30.*

Two, of course there are two.
It seems perfectly natural now—
The one who never looks up, whose eyes are lidded
And balled, like Blake's,
Who exhibits

The birthmarks that are his trademark—
The scald scar of water,
The nude
Verdigris of the condor.
I am red meat. His beak

Claps sidewise: I am not his yet.
He tells me how badly I photograph.
He tells me how sweet
The babies look in their hospital
Icebox, a simple

Frill at the neck,
Then the flutings of their Ionian
Death-gowns,
Then two little feet.
He does not smile or smoke.

The other does that,
His hair long and plausive.
Bastard
Masturbating a glitter,
He wants to be loved.

I do not stir.
The frost makes a flower,
The dew makes a star,
The dead bell,
The dead bell.

Somebody's done for.

—1963

What are your reactions to and questions about this work? The following questions may help provoke some ideas.

Probing the Work

1. In your own words summarize the two versions of death Plath depicts.
2. Look at one *image* (see page 79) in this poem and explain its significance.

Identifying Issues

3. Is there another version of death you can come up with?
4. How relevant are these visions of death to you? How might our actions and behavior demonstrate our visions of death?

ISABEL ALLENDE

And of Clay Are We Created

(translated by Margaret Sayers Peden)

Isabel Allende (b. 1942) was born in Peru. Her parents were divorced when she was a child, and she lived with her grandparents. After her mother remarried she moved to various countries until she settled in Chile at 16. She was a journalist, eventually developing her own television program as well as writing for a radical women's magazine; she then wrote fiction. When her uncle, Chile's president Salvador Allende, was assassinated, her family relocated to Venezuela. Her works include The House of the Spirits *(1982),* Of Love and Shadows *(1986),* The Stories of Eva Luna *(1991), and* Paula *(1995).*

They discovered the girl's head protruding from the mudpit, eyes wide open, calling soundlessly. She had a First Communion name, Azucena. Lily. In that vast cemetery where the odor of death was already attracting vultures from far away, and where the weeping of orphans and wails of the injured filled the air, the little girl obstinately clinging to life became the symbol of the tragedy. The television cameras transmitted so often the unbearable image of the head budding like a black squash from the clay that there was no one who did not recognize her and know her name. And every time we saw her on the screen, right behind her was Rolf Carlé, who had gone there on assignment, never suspecting that he would find a fragment of his past, lost thirty years before.

First a subterranean sob rocked the cotton fields, curling them like waves of foam. Geologists had set up their seismographs weeks before and knew that the mountain had awakened again. For some time they had predicted that the heat of the eruption could detach the eternal ice from the slopes of the volcano, but no one heeded their warnings; they sounded like the tales of frightened old women. The towns in the valley went about their daily life, deaf to the moaning of the earth, until that fateful Wednesday night in November when a prolonged roar announced the end of the world, and walls of snow broke loose, rolling in an avalanche of clay, stones, and water that descended on the villages and buried them beneath unfathomable meters of telluric vomit. As soon as the survivors emerged from the paralysis of that first awful terror, they could see that houses, plazas, churches, white cotton plantations, dark coffee forests, cattle pastures—all had disappeared. Much later, after soldiers and volunteers had arrived to rescue the living and try to assess the magnitude of the cataclysm, it was calculated that beneath the mud lay more than twenty thousand human beings and an indefinite number of animals putrefying in a viscous soup. Forests and rivers had also been swept away, and there was nothing to be seen but an immense desert of mire.

When the station called before dawn, Rolf Carlé and I were together. I crawled out of bed, dazed with sleep, and went to prepare coffee while he hurriedly dressed. He stuffed his gear in the green canvas backpack he always carried, and we said goodbye, as we had so many times before. I had no presentiments. I sat in the kitchen, sipping my coffee and planning the long hours without him, sure that he would be back the next day.

He was one of the first to reach the scene, because while other reporters were fighting their way to the edges of that morass in jeeps, bicycles, or on foot, each getting there however he could, Rolf Carlé had the advantage of the television helicopter, which flew him over the avalanche. We watched on our screens the footage captured by his assistant's camera, in which he was up to his knees in muck, a microphone in his hand, in the midst of a bedlam of lost children, wounded survivors, corpses, and devastation. The story came to us in his calm voice. For years he had been a familiar figure in newscasts, reporting live at the scene of battles and catastrophes with awesome tenacity. Nothing could stop him, and I was always amazed at his equanimity in the face of danger and suffering; it seemed as if nothing could shake his fortitude or deter his curiosity. Fear seemed never to touch him, although he had confessed to me that he was not a courageous man, far from it. I believe that the lens of the camera had a strange effect on him; it was as if it transported him to a different time from which he could watch events without actually participating in them. When I knew him better, I came to realize that this fictive distance seemed to protect him from his own emotions.

Rolf Carlé was in on the story of Azucena from the beginning. He filmed the volunteers who discovered her, and the first persons who tried to reach her; his camera zoomed in on the girl, her dark face, her large desolate eyes, the plastered-down tangle of her hair. The mud was like quicksand around her, and anyone attempting to reach her was in danger of sinking. They threw a rope to her that she made no effort to grasp until they shouted to her to catch it; then she pulled a hand from the mire and tried to move, but immediately sank a little deeper. Rolf threw down his knapsack and the rest of his equipment and waded into the quagmire, commenting for his assistant's microphone that it was cold and that one could begin to smell the stench of corpses.

"What's your name?" he asked the girl, and she told him her flower name. "Don't move, Azucena," Rolf Carlé directed, and kept talking to her, without a thought for what he was saying, just to distract her, while slowly he worked his way forward in mud up to his waist. The air around him seemed as murky as the mud.

It was impossible to reach her from the approach he was attempting, so he retreated and circled around where there seemed to be firmer footing. When finally he was close enough, he took the rope and tied it beneath her arms, so they could pull her out. He smiled at her with that smile that crinkles his eyes and makes him look like a little boy; he told her that everything was fine, that he was here with her now, that soon they would have her out. He signaled the others to pull, but as soon as the cord tensed, the girl screamed. They tried again, and her shoulders and arms appeared, but they could move her no farther; she was trapped. Someone suggested that her legs might be caught in the collapsed walls of her house, but she said it was not just rubble, that she was also held by the bodies of her brothers and sisters clinging to her legs.

"Don't worry, we'll get you out of here," Rolf promised. Despite the quality of the transmission, I could hear his voice break, and I loved him more than ever. Azucena looked at him, but said nothing.

During those first hours Rolf Carlé exhausted all the resources of his ingenuity to rescue her. He struggled with poles and ropes, but every tug was an intolerable torture for the imprisoned girl. It occurred to him to use one of the poles as a lever but got no result and had to abandon the idea. He talked a couple of soldiers into working with him for a while, but they had to leave because so many other victims were calling for help. The girl could not move, she barely could breathe, but she did not seem desperate, as if an ancestral resignation allowed her to accept her fate. The reporter, on the other hand, was determined to snatch her from death. Someone brought him a tire, which he placed beneath her arms like a life buoy, and then laid a plank near the hole to hold his weight and allow him to stay closer to her. As it was impossible to remove the rubble blindly, he tried once or twice to dive toward her feet, but emerged frustrated, covered with mud, and spitting gravel. He concluded that he would have to have a pump to drain the water, and radioed a request for one, but received in return a message that there was no available transport and it could not be sent until the next morning.

"We can't wait that long!" Rolf Carlé shouted, but in the pandemonium no one stopped to commiserate. Many more hours would go by before he accepted that time had stagnated and reality had been irreparably distorted.

A military doctor came to examine the girl, and observed that her heart was functioning well and that if she did not get too cold she could survive the night.

"Hang on, Azucena, we'll have the pump tomorrow," Rolf Carlé tried to console her.

"Don't leave me alone," she begged.

"No, of course I won't leave you."

Someone brought him coffee, and he helped the girl drink it, sip by sip. The warm liquid revived her and she began telling him about her small life, about her family and her school, about how things were in that little bit of world before the volcano had erupted. She was thirteen, and she had never been outside her village. Rolf Carlé, buoyed by a premature optimism, was convinced that everything would end well: the pump would arrive, they would drain the water, move the rubble, and Azucena would be transported by helicopter to a hospital where she would recover rapidly and where he could visit her and bring her gifts. He thought, She's already too old for dolls, and I don't know what would please her; maybe a dress. I don't know much about women, he concluded, amused, reflecting that although he had known many women in his lifetime, none had taught him these details. To pass the hours he began to tell Azucena about his travels and adventures as a newshound, and when he exhausted his memory, he called upon imagination, inventing things he thought might entertain her. From time to time she dozed, but he kept talking in the darkness, to assure her that he was still there and to overcome the menace of uncertainty.

That was a long night.

Many miles away, I watched Rolf Carlé and the girl on a television screen. I could not bear the wait at home, so I went to National Television, where I often spent entire nights with Rolf editing programs. There, I was near his world, and I could at least get a feeling of what he lived through during those three decisive days. I called all the important people in the city, senators, commanders of the armed forces, the North American ambassador, and the president of National Petroleum, begging them for a pump to remove the silt, but obtained only vague promises. I began to ask for urgent help on radio and television, to see if there wasn't *someone* who could help us. Between calls I would run to the newsroom to monitor the satellite transmissions that periodically brought new details of the catastrophe. While reporters selected scenes with most impact for the news report, I searched for footage that featured Azucena's mudpit. The screen reduced the disaster to a single plane and accentuated the tremendous distance that separated me from Rolf Carlé; nonetheless, I was there with him. The child's every suffering hurt me as it did him; I felt his frustration, his impotence. Faced with the impossibility of communicating with him, the fantastic idea came to me that if I tried, I could reach him by force of mind and in that way give him encouragement. I concentrated until I was dizzy—a frenzied and futile activity. At times I would be overcome with compassion and burst out crying; at other times, I was so drained I felt as if I were staring through a telescope at the light of a star dead for a million years.

I watched that hell on the first morning broadcast, cadavers of people and animals awash in the current of new rivers formed overnight from the melted snow. Above the mud rose the tops of trees and the bell towers of a church where several people had taken refuge and were patiently awaiting rescue teams. Hundreds of soldiers and volunteers from the Civil Defense were clawing through rubble searching for survivors, while long rows of ragged specters awaited their turn for a cup of hot broth. Radio networks announced that their phones were jammed with calls from families offering shelter to orphaned children. Drinking water was in scarce supply, along with gasoline and food. Doctors, resigned to amputating arms and legs without anesthesia, pled that at least they be sent serum and painkillers and antibiotics; most of the roads, however, were impassable, and worse were the bureaucratic obstacles that stood in the way. To top it all, the clay contaminated by decomposing bodies threatened the living with an outbreak of epidemics.

Azucena was shivering inside the tire that held her above the surface. Immobility and tension had greatly weakened her, but she was conscious and could still be heard when a microphone was held out to her. Her tone was humble, as if apologizing for all the fuss. Rolf Carlé had a growth of beard, and dark circles beneath his eyes; he looked near exhaustion. Even from that enormous distance I could sense the quality of his weariness, so different from the fatigue of other adventures. He had completely forgotten the camera; he could not look at the girl through a lens any longer. The pictures we were receiving were not his assistant's but those of other reporters who had appropriated Azucena, bestowing on her the pathetic responsibility of embodying the horror of what had happened in that place. With the first light Rolf tried again to dislodge the obstacles that held the girl in her tomb, but he had only his hands to work with; he did not dare use a tool for fear of injuring her. He fed Azucena a cup of the cornmeal mush and bananas the Army was distributing, but she immediately vomited it up. A doctor stated that she had a fever, but added that there was little he could do: antibiotics were being reserved for cases of gangrene. A priest also passed by and blessed her, hanging a medal of the Virgin around her neck. By evening a gentle, persistent drizzle began to fall.

"The sky is weeping," Azucena murmured, and she, too, began to cry.

"Don't be afraid," Rolf begged. "You have to keep your strength up and be calm. Everything will be fine. I'm with you, and I'll get you out somehow."

Reporters returned to photograph Azucena and ask her the same questions, which she no longer tried to answer. In the meanwhile, more television and movie teams arrived with spools of cable, tapes, film, videos, precision lenses, recorders, sound consoles, lights, reflecting screens, auxiliary motors, cartons of supplies, electricians, sound technicians, and cameramen: Azucena's face was beamed to millions of screens around the world. And all the while Rolf Carlé kept pleading for a pump. The improved technical facilities bore results, and National Television began receiving sharper pictures and clearer sound; the distance seemed suddenly compressed, and I had the horrible sensation that Azucena and Rolf were by my side, separated from me by impenetrable glass. I was able to follow events hour by hour; I knew everything my love did to wrest the girl from her prison and help her endure her suffering; I overheard fragments of what they said to one another and could guess the rest; I was present when she taught Rolf to pray, and when he distracted her with the stories I had told him in a thousand and one nights beneath the white mosquito netting of our bed.

When darkness came on the second day, Rolf tried to sing Azucena to sleep with old Austrian folk songs he had learned from his mother, but she was far beyond sleep. They spent most of the night talking, each in a stupor of exhaustion and hunger, and shaking with cold. That night, imperceptibly, the unyielding floodgates that had contained Rolf Carlé's past for so many years began to open, and the torrent of all that had lain hidden in the deepest and most secret layers of memory poured out, leveling before it the obstacles that had blocked his consciousness for so long. He could not tell it all to Azucena; she perhaps did not know there was a world beyond the sea or time previous to her own; she was not capable of imagining Europe in the years of the war. So he could not tell her of defeat, nor of the afternoon the Russians had led them to the concentration camp to bury prisoners dead from starvation. Why should he describe to her how the naked bodies piled like a mountain of firewood resembled fragile china? How could he tell this dying child about ovens and gallows? Nor did he mention the night that he had seen his mother naked, shod in stiletto-heeled red boots, sobbing with humiliation. There was much he did not tell, but in those hours he relived for the first time all the things his mind had tried to erase. Azucena had surrendered her fear to him and so, without wishing it, had obliged Rolf to confront his own. There, beside that hellhole of mud, it was impossible for Rolf to flee from himself any longer, and the visceral terror he had lived as a boy suddenly invaded him. He reverted to the years when he was the age of Azucena, and younger, and, like her, found himself trapped in a pit without escape, buried in life, his head barely above ground; he saw before his eyes the boots and legs of his father, who had removed his belt and was whipping it in the air with the never-forgotten hiss of a viper coiled to strike. Sorrow flooded through him, intact and precise, as if it had lain always in his mind, waiting. He was once again in the armoire where his father locked him to punish him for imagined misbehavior, there where for eternal hours he had crouched with his eyes closed, not to see the darkness, with his hands over his ears, to shut out the beating of his heart, trembling, huddled like a cornered animal. Wandering in the mist of his memories he found his sister Katharina, a sweet, retarded child who spent her life hiding, with the hope that her father would forget the disgrace of her having been born. With Katharina, Rolf crawled beneath the dining room table, and with her hid there under the long white tablecloth, two children forever embraced, alert to footsteps and voices. Katharina's scent melded with his own sweat, with aromas of cooking, garlic, soup, freshly baked bread, and the unexpected odor of putrescent clay. His sister's hand in his, her frightened breathing, her silk hair against his cheek, the candid gaze of her eyes. Katharina . . . Katharina materialized before him, floating on the air like a flag, clothed in the white tablecloth, now a winding sheet, and at last he could weep for her death and for the guilt of having abandoned her. He understood then that all his exploits as a reporter, the feats that had won him such recognition and fame, were merely an attempt to keep his most ancient fears at bay, a strategem for taking refuge behind a lens to test whether reality was more tolerable from that perspective. He took excessive risks as an exercise of courage, training by day to conquer the monsters that tormented him by night. But he had come face to face with the moment of truth; he could not continue to escape his past. He *was* Azucena; he was buried in the clayey mud; his terror was not the distant emotion of an almost forgotten childhood, it was a claw sunk in his throat. In the flush of his tears he saw his mother, dressed in black and clutching her imitation-crocodile pocketbook to her bosom, just as he had last seen her on the dock when she had come to put him on the boat to South America. She had not come to dry his tears, but to tell him to pick up a shovel: the war was over and now they must bury the dead.

"Don't cry. I don't hurt anymore. I'm fine," Azucena said when dawn came.

"I'm not crying for you," Rolf Carlé smiled. "I'm crying for myself. I hurt all over."

The third day in the valley of the cataclysm began with a pale light filtering through storm clouds. The President of the Republic visited the area in his tailored safari jacket to confirm that this was the worst catastrophe of the century; the country was in mourning; sister nations had offered aid; he had ordered a state of siege; the Armed Forces would be merciless, anyone caught stealing or committing other offenses would be shot on sight. He added that it was impossible to remove all the corpses or count the thousands who had disappeared; the entire valley would be declared holy ground, and bishops would come to celebrate a solemn mass for the souls of the victims. He went to the Army field tents to offer relief in the form of vague promises to crowds of the rescued, then to the improvised hospital to offer a word of encouragement to doctors and nurses worn down from so many hours of tribulations. Then he asked to be taken to see Azucena, the little girl the whole world had seen. He waved to her with a limp statesman's hand, and microphones recorded his emotional voice and paternal tone as he told her that her courage had served as an example to the nation. Rolf Carlé interrupted to ask for a pump, and the President assured him that he personally would attend to the matter. I caught a glimpse of Rolf for a few seconds kneeling beside the mudpit. On the evening news broadcast, he was still in the same position; and I, glued to the screen like a fortuneteller to her crystal ball, could tell that something fundamental had changed in him. I knew somehow that during the night his defenses had crumbled and he had given in to grief; finally he was vulnerable. The girl had touched a part of him that he himself had no access to, a part he had never shared with me. Rolf had wanted to console her, but it was Azucena who had given him consolation.

I recognized the precise moment at which Rolf gave up the fight and surrendered to the torture of watching the girl die. I was with them, three days and two nights, spying on them from the other side of life. I was there when she told him that in all her thirteen years no boy had ever loved her and that it was a pity to leave this world without knowing love. Rolf assured her that he loved her more than he could ever love anyone, more than he loved his mother, more than his sister, more than all the women who had slept in his arms, more than he loved me, his life companion, who would have given anything to be trapped in that well in her place, who would have exchanged her life for Azucena's, and I watched as he leaned down to kiss her poor forehead, consumed by a sweet, sad emotion he could not name. I felt how in that instant both were saved from despair, how they were freed from the clay, how they rose above the vultures and helicopters, how together they flew above the vast swamp of corruption and laments. How, finally, they were able to accept death. Rolf Carlé prayed in silence that she would die quickly, because such pain cannot be borne.

By then I had obtained a pump and was in touch with a general who had agreed to ship it the next morning on a military cargo plane. But on the night of that third day, beneath the unblinking focus of quartz lamps and the lens of a hundred cameras, Azucena gave up, her eyes locked with those of the friend who had sustained her to the end. Rolf Carlé removed the life buoy, closed her eyelids, held her to his chest for a few moments, and then let her go. She sank slowly, a flower in the mud.

You are back with me, but you are not the same man. I often accompany you to the station and we watch the videos of Azucena again; you study them intently, looking for something you could have done to save her, something you did not think of in time. Or maybe you study them to see yourself as if in a mirror, naked. Your cameras lie forgotten in a closet; you do not write or sing; you sit long hours before the window, staring at the mountains. Beside you, I wait for you to complete the voyage into yourself, for the old wounds to heal. I know that when you return from your nightmares, we shall again walk hand in hand, as before.

—1989

What are your reactions to and questions about this work? The following questions may help provoke some ideas.

Probing the Work

1. The narrator notes that "something fundamental had changed" in Rolf as a result of his vigil by the dying child, Azucena. How has he changed? What is his perception of himself, and his demeanor on camera, at the beginning of the story, and at the end? Can you describe the relationship that develops between Rolf and the girl, and why it changes him?
2. Describe the type of person the *narrator* seems to be. In what sense is her situation worse than Rolf's? In what sense is it better? Why is the narrator not jealous when Rolf professes a greater love for the girl than for her?
3. In what sense is this story as much about life as it is about death?

Identifying Issues

4. What has elevated Rolf and Azucena above the muck of the real world, by the end of the story? To what degree is suffering necessary in order to be so uplifted?
5. To what extent can we become involved in media coverage of a national catastrophe or tragedy? Give some examples of coverage of catastrophic events that you have witnessed. Evaluate your emotional reactions, and the role that the media seemed to play in reporting the deaths.

BARBARA HOLDER

October

Barbara Holder (b. 1939) was born in Brooklyn, New York. She studied and taught ballet for many years, and was educated at Columbia University. She teaches writing at two colleges in Westchester, New York, where she also runs writing and journalism workshops.

Death will not be this lovely
when I visit the graves of my parents
side by side. Tomorrow I lift the veil
of my mother's monument, the small bronze plaque
whose words I struggled over—"Beloved Mother,"
a graveyard cliché, or "Dear Mother," too cold.

Among the leaves that fall lyrical and brilliant,
the square memorials of stone and bronze will poke
their silent coldness from the ground, signaling
a different kind of death.

But like the leaves, her head pillowed in the hard
ground, she will mix and churn and vaporize,
and I will never understand how what is disappears,
or if the air seeming so blank, makes us live
by filling us with what has died.

—1994

What are your reactions to and questions about this work? The following questions may help provoke some ideas.

Probing the Work

1. What does the poet mean by the leaves "signaling a different kind of death"?

Identifying Issues

2. In what ways do we try to make meaning out of a natural process like death? What are the various stages we experience as part of the grieving process?

WOODY ALLEN

Death Knocks

Woody Allen (b. 1935) was born Allen Konigsberg and grew up in Brooklyn, New York. After graduating from high school, he attended and dropped out of both New York University and City College of New York. While a student, he sold jokes to newspaper columnists and joined NBC as a staff writer. In 1964 he wrote his first screenplay, What's New Pussycat? *He has since written more than 20 films and published three books of stories and sketches:* Getting Even *(1971),* Without Feathers *(1975), and* Side Effects *(1980).*

The play takes place in the bedroom of the NAT ACKERMANS' *two-story house, somewhere in Kew Gardens. The carpeting is wall-to-wall. There is a big double bed and a large vanity. The room is elaborately furnished and curtained, and on the walls there are several paintings and a not really attractive barometer. Soft theme music as the curtain rises.* NAT ACKERMAN, *a bald, paunchy fifty-seven-year-old dress manufacturer is lying on the bed finishing off tomorrow's* Daily News. *He wears a bathrobe and slippers, and reads by a bed light clipped to the white headboard of the bed. The time is near midnight. Suddenly we hear a noise, and* NAT *sits up and looks at the window.*

NAT: What the hell is that?

(Climbing awkwardly through the window is a sombre, caped figure. The intruder wears a black hood and skintight black clothes. The hood covers his head but not his face, which is middle-aged and stark white. He is something like NAT *in appearance. He huffs audibly and then trips over the windowsill and falls into the room.)*

DEATH *(for it is no one else)*: Jesus Christ. I nearly broke my neck.
NAT *(watching with bewilderment)*: Who are you?
DEATH: Death.
NAT: Who?
DEATH: Death. Listen—can I sit down? I nearly broke my neck. I'm shaking like a leaf.
NAT: Who *are* you?
DEATH: *Death*. You got a glass of water?
NAT: Death? What do you mean, Death?
DEATH: What is wrong with you? You see the black costume and the whitened face?
NAT: Yeah.
DEATH: Is it Halloween?
NAT: No.
DEATH: Then I'm Death. Now can I get a glass of water—or a Fresca?
NAT: If this is some joke—
DEATH: What kind of joke? You're fifty-seven? Nat Ackerman? One eighteen Pacific Street? Unless I blew it—where's that call sheet? *(He fumbles through pocket, finally producing a card with an address on it. It seems to check.)*
NAT: What do you want with me?
DEATH: What do I want? What do you think I want?
NAT: You must be kidding. I'm in perfect health.
DEATH *(unimpressed)*: Uh-huh. *(Looking around)* This is a nice place. You do it yourself?
NAT: We had a decorator, but we worked with her.
DEATH *(looking at picture on the wall)*: I love those kids with the big eyes.
NAT: I don't want to go yet.

DEATH: *You* don't want to go? Please don't start in. As it is, I'm nauseous from the climb.

NAT: What climb?

DEATH: I climbed up the drainpipe. I was trying to make a dramatic entrance. I see the big windows and you're awake reading. I figure it's worth a shot. I'll climb up and enter with a little—you know . . . *(Snaps fingers)* Meanwhile, I get my heel caught on some vines, the drainpipe breaks, and I'm hanging by a thread. Then my cape begins to tear. Look, let's just go. It's been a rough night.

NAT: You broke my drainpipe?

DEATH: Broke. It didn't break. It's a little bent. Didn't you hear anything? I slammed into the ground.

NAT: I was reading.

DEATH: You must have really been engrossed. *(Lifting newspaper Nat was reading)* "NAB COEDS IN POT ORGY." Can I borrow this?

NAT: I'm not finished.

DEATH: Er—I don't know how to put this to you, pal. . . .

NAT: Why didn't you just ring downstairs?

DEATH: I'm telling you, I could have, but how does it look? This way I get a little drama going. Something. Did you read "Faust"?

NAT: What?

DEATH: And what if you had company? You're sitting there with important people. I'm Death—I should ring the bell and traipse right in the front? Where's your thinking?

NAT: Listen, Mister, it's very late.

DEATH: Yeah. Well, you want to go?

NAT: Go where?

DEATH: Death. It. The Thing. The Happy Hunting Grounds. *(Looking at his own knee)* Y'know, that's a pretty bad cut. My first job, I'm liable to get gangrene yet.

NAT: Now, wait a minute. I need time. I'm not ready to go.

DEATH: I'm sorry. I can't help you. I'd like to, but it's the moment.

NAT: How can it be the moment? I just merged with Modiste Originals.

DEATH: What's the difference, a couple of bucks more or less.

NAT: Sure, what do you care? You guys probably have all your expenses paid.

DEATH: You want to come along now?

NAT *(studying him)*: I'm sorry, but I cannot believe you're Death.

DEATH: Why? What'd you expect—Rock Hudson?

NAT: No, it's not that.

DEATH: I'm sorry if I disappointed you.

NAT: Don't get upset. I don't know, I always thought you'd be . . . uh . . . taller.

DEATH: I'm five seven. It's average for my weight.

NAT: You look a little like me.

DEATH: Who should I look like? I'm your death.

NAT: Give me some time. Another day.

DEATH: I can't. What do you want me to say?

NAT: One more day. Twenty-four hours.

DEATH: What do you need it for? The radio said rain tomorrow.

NAT: Can't we work out something?

DEATH: Like what?

NAT: You play chess?

DEATH: No, I don't.

NAT: I once saw a picture of you playing chess.

DEATH: Couldn't be me, because I don't play chess. Gin rummy, maybe.

NAT: You play gin rummy?

DEATH: Do I play gin rummy? Is Paris a city?

NAT: You're good, huh?

DEATH: Very good.

NAT: I'll tell you what I'll do—

DEATH: Don't make any deals with me.

NAT: I'll play you gin rummy. If you win, I'll go immediately. If I win, give me some more time. A little bit—one more day.

DEATH: Who's got time to play gin rummy?

NAT: Come on. If you're so good.

DEATH: Although I feel like a game . . .

NAT: Come on. Be a sport. We'll shoot for a half hour.

DEATH: I really shouldn't.

NAT: I got the cards right here. Don't make a production.

DEATH: All right, come on. We'll play a little. It'll relax me.

NAT *(getting cards, pad, and pencil)*: You won't regret this.

DEATH: Don't give me a sales talk. Get the cards and give me a Fresca and put out something. For God's sake, a stranger drops in, you don't have potato chips or pretzels.

NAT: There's M&M's downstairs in a dish.

DEATH: M&M's. What if the President came? He'd get M&M's, too?

NAT: You're not the President.

DEATH: Deal.

(NAT *deals, turns up a five.)*

NAT: You want to play a tenth of a cent a point to make it interesting?

DEATH: It's not interesting enough for you?

NAT: I play better when money's at stake.

DEATH: Whatever you say, Newt.

NAT: Nat. Nat Ackerman. You don't know my name?

DEATH: Newt, Nat—I got such a headache.

NAT: You want that five?

DEATH: No.

NAT: So pick.
DEATH *(surveying his hand as he picks)*: Jesus, I got nothing here.
NAT: What's it like?
DEATH: What's what like?

(Throughout the following, they pick and discard.)

NAT: Death.
DEATH: What should it be like? You lay there.
NAT: Is there anything after?
DEATH: Aha, you're saving twos.
NAT: I'm asking. Is there anything after?
DEATH *(absently)*: You'll see.
NAT: Oh, then I will actually see something?
DEATH: Well, maybe I shouldn't have put it that way. Throw.
NAT: To get an answer from you is a big deal.
DEATH: I'm playing cards.
NAT: All right, play, play.
DEATH: Meanwhile, I'm giving you one card after another.
NAT: Don't look through the discards.
DEATH: I'm not looking. I'm straightening them up. What was the knock card?
NAT: Four. You ready to knock already?
DEATH: Who said I'm ready to knock. All I asked was what was the knock card.
NAT: And all I asked was is there anything for me to look forward to.
DEATH: Play.
NAT: Can't you tell me anything? Where do we go?
DEATH: We? To tell you the truth, *you* fall in a crumpled heap on the floor.
NAT: Oh, I can't wait for that! Is it going to hurt?
DEATH: Be over in a second.
NAT: Terrific. *(Sighs)* I needed this. A man merges with Modiste Originals . . .
DEATH: How's four points?
NAT: You're knocking?
DEATH: Four points is good?
NAT: No, I got two.
DEATH: You're kidding.
NAT: No, you lose.
DEATH: Holy Christ, and I thought you were saving sixes.
NAT: No. Your deal. Twenty points and two boxes. Shoot. *(*DEATH *deals.)* I must fall on the floor, eh? I can't be standing over the sofa when it happens?
DEATH: No. Play.
NAT: Why not?
DEATH: Because you fall on the floor! Leave me alone. I'm trying to concentrate.

NAT: Why must it be on the floor? That's all I'm saying! Why can't the whole thing happen and I'll stand next to the sofa?

DEATH: I'll try my best. Now can we play?

NAT: That's all I'm saying. You remind me of Moe Lefkowitz. He's also stubborn.

DEATH: I remind him of Moe Lefkowitz. I'm one of the most terrifying figures yoou could possibly imagine, and him I remind of Moe Lefkowitz. What is he, a furrier?

NAT: You should be such a furrier. He's good for eighty thousand a year. Passementeries. He's got his own factory. Two points.

DEATH: What?

NAT: Two points. I'm knocking. What have you got?

DEATH: My hand is like a basketball score.

NAT: And it's spades.

DEATH: If you didn't talk so much.

(They redeal and play on.)

NAT: What'd you mean before when you said this was your first job?

DEATH: What does it sound like?

NAT: What are you telling me—that nobody ever went before?

DEATH: Sure they went. But I didn't take them.

NAT: So who did?

DEATH: Others.

NAT: There's others?

DEATH: Sure. Each one has his own personal way of going.

NAT: I never knew that.

DEATH: Why should you know? Who are you?

NAT: What do you mean who am I? Why—I'm nothing?

DEATH: Not nothing. You're a dress manufacturer. Where do you come to knowledge of the eternal mysteries?

NAT: What are you talking about? I make a beautiful dollar. I sent two kids through college. One is in advertising, the other's married. I got my own home. I drive a Chrysler. My wife has whatever she wants. Maids, mink coat, vacations. Right now she's at the Eden Roc. Fifty dollars a day because she wants to be near her sister. I'm supposed to join her next week, so what do you think I am—some guy off the street?

DEATH: All right. Don't be so touchy.

NAT: Who's touchy?

DEATH: How would you like it if I got insulted quickly?

NAT: Did I insult you?

DEATH: You didn't say you were disappointed in me?

NAT: What do you expect? You want me to throw you a block party?

DEATH: I'm not talking about that. I mean me personally. I'm too short, I'm this, I'm that.

Nat: I said you looked like me. It's like a reflection.

Death: All right, deal, deal.

(They continue to play as music steals in and the lights dim until all is in total darkness. The lights slowly come up again, and now it is later and their game is over. Nat *tallies.)*

Nat: Sixty-eight . . . one-fifty . . . Well, you lose.

Death *(dejectedly looking through the deck)*: I knew I shouldn't have thrown that nine. Damn it.

Nat: So I'll see you tomorrow.

Death: What do you mean you'll see me tomorrow?

Nat: I won the extra day. Leave me alone.

Death: You were serious?

Nat: We made a deal.

Death: Yeah, but—

Nat: Don't "but" me. I won twenty-four hours. Come back tomorrow.

Death: I didn't know we were actually playing for time.

Nat: That's too bad about you. You should pay attention.

Death: Where am I going to go for twenty-four hours?

Nat: What's the difference? The main thing is I won an extra day.

Death: What do you want me to do—walk the streets?

Nat: Check into a hotel and go to a movie. Take a *schvitz.*° Don't make a federal case.

Death: Add the score again.

Nat: Plus you owe me twenty-eight dollars.

Death: *What?*

Nat: That's right, Buster. Here it is—read it.

Death *(going through pockets)*: I have a few singles—not twenty-eight dollars.

Nat: I'll take a check.

Death: From what account?

Nat: Look who I'm dealing with.

Death: Sue me. Where do I keep my checking account?

Nat: All right, gimme what you got and we'll call it square.

Death: Listen, I need that money.

Nat: Why should you need money?

Death: What are you talking about? You're going to the Beyond.

Nat: So?

Death: So—you know how far that is?

Nat: So?

Death: So where's gas? Where's tolls?

Nat: We're going by car!

215. schvitz, steam bath.

DEATH: You'll find out. *(Agitatedly)* Look—I'll be back tomorrow, and you'll give me a chance to win the money back. Otherwise I'm in definite trouble.

NAT: Anything you want. Double or nothing we'll play. I'm liable to win an extra week or a month. The way you play, maybe years.

DEATH: Meantime I'm stranded.

NAT: See you tomorrow.

DEATH *(being edged to the doorway)*: Where's a good hotel? What am I talking about hotel, I got no money. I'll go sit in Bickford's.° *(He picks up the* News.*)*

NAT: Out. Out. That's my paper. *(He takes it back.)*

DEATH *(exiting)*: I couldn't just take him and go. I had to get involved in rummy.

NAT *(calling after him)*: And be careful going downstairs. On one of the steps the rug is loose.

(And, on cue, we hear a terrific crash. NAT *sighs, then crosses to the bedside table and makes a phone call.)*

NAT: Hello, Moe? Me. Listen, I don't know if somebody's playing a joke, or what, but Death was just here. We played a little gin. . . . No, *Death.* In person. Or somebody who claims to be Death. But, Moe, he's such a *schlep!*°

Curtain

—1968

What are your reactions to and questions about this work? The following questions may help provoke some ideas.

Probing the Work

1. How is Death characterized here? How does this characterization match or contradict traditional depictions of death?
2. Why does Nat believe it should not be his time to die? To what degree is he convincing, and what strategies does he use to delay Death?

Identifying Issues

3. Compare and contrast Allen's and Emily Dickinson's personifications of Death. How would *you* personify death?
4. Death mentions "Faust," a famous fictional character who sells his soul to the devil for borrowed time on earth. What are the various ways in which people in our society try to put off death?

242. Bickfords, Bickford's was a chain of inexpensive all-night cafeterias in New York City.
252. schlep, boring jerk.

5. Allen has said that if his work is successful, "the laughs don't come from jokes, they come from characters in emotionally desperate circumstances." To what extent is that true of this play? Of the "laughs" in life?

WRITING ASSIGNMENT SEQUENCE (CONT. FROM PAGE 989)

4. Making Connections

Select one of the following questions and write an informal response in which you connect your own ideas with those conveyed in the works of this cluster, and/or make connections among the works themselves.

A. What are the various personifications and visions of death described in the works of this cluster? Which do you like best, and why? Which do you find most truthful? Most moving? Most believable?

B. What are the various attitudes toward death illustrated in these works? How realistic are they?

5. Putting It All Together

Write an essay that combines what you think about the topic *Death & Co.* with what you now understand about the readings.

- Collect your informal writing, notes, and reading-journal entries on this topic and decide what will be the focus of your essay.
- Outline your essay. Select the literary passages and personal details you might use to illustrate and support your main focus.
- Write a draft of your essay in which you bring together what you think about the subject with what you understand about the readings. Try to include in your draft one or more *literary terms*.
- Share what you've written with your classmates and instructor, then revise it according to their recommendations.

Writing Tip: Figurative Language

You have seen how writers weave *figurative language* into their stories, poems, and plays. You could also be adding color and rhythm to your writing. Well-crafted, well-placed metaphors, similes, images, analogies, allusions, and alliteration could help you "show" your ideas, clarify and make concrete a point, and enrich your style. Remember: avoid trite expressions and clichés such as "white as a sheet" or "the game of life." Be *original.* Use figurative language appropriately and sparingly so that it doesn't overpower or interfere with clear expression.

In the following excerpt from her paper on the "Death & Co." cluster, Stacy takes a fairly common sensation—feeling refreshed in the autumn—and uses *figurative language* to bring out the *irony* of feeling revived when nature is "dying," to use the falling leaves as a *metaphor* for death, and to *personify* nature.

> I cannot help but smile when the tired October sun descends from the sky, casting an unearthly glow on the Autumn landscape. I am serene in the face of the falling leaves, which are crisp, graceful, golden reminders of death. . . . Gone are the days of lush greenery. In its place are naked trees, shivering in the fall breeze. It is a season for pondering, questioning, and philosophizing. It is a time for myself. So why am I happy during the dying season? Because death brings new life.

CrossClusters

In your paper you might want to consider how the following works located elsewhere in this book depict death:

- Shirley Jackson, "The Lottery" (p. 131)
- Chinua Achebe, "Dead Men's Path" (p. 138)
- Sophocles, *Antigone* (p. 144)
- Susan Glaspell, *Trifles* (p. 220)
- Charles Johnson, "Exchange Value" (p. 243)
- Audre Lorde, "Power" (p. 251)
- David Leavitt, "Gravity" (p. 394)
- Marsha Norman, *'night, Mother* (p. 400)
- Raymond Carver, "My Father's Life" (p. 446)
- Seamus Heaney, "Mid-Term Break" (p. 490)
- Nathaniel Hawthorne, "The Birth-mark" (p. 633)
- Tony Kushner, from *Angels in America* (p. 621)
- Kate Chopin, "Story of an Hour" (p. 646)
- Robert Browning, "Porphyria's Lover" (p. 840)
- Sylvia Plath, "Lady Lazarus" (p. 856)
- Eugène Ionesco, *The Lesson* (p. 904)
- Leslie Marmon Silko, "The Man to Send Rain Clouds" (p. 978)

SYNTHESIS ESSAY FOR SECTION 5: THE INDIVIDUAL AND THE COSMOS 100

How do your preliminary ideas about *nature, religion,* and *death* hold up now that you have read a variety of works on the topic? Adding to, expanding on, and revising the writing that you have already done on the subject of the *Individual and the Cosmos,* write a long paper in which you examine some of the literature in this section, bringing together your early writing with the knowledge you have gained from your class discussions. The paper might combine research and critical analysis with your personal opinions and experiences. You might even work in references to movies, songs, books, and magazine articles. There are many possibilities for topics relating to the complexities of nature, religion, and death.

Here are some questions to consider:

- How have your beliefs been expanded as a result of these readings?
- How close a relationship should we have to the earth? To God? To the universe?

APPENDIX A: SAMPLE CLUSTER ESSAY

What Is Knowledge?

BY JOSEPH FLAGIELLO

A word in the English language refers to the capacity of a person's mind, yet ironically, different people give different connotations to the word. This word is "knowledge" and it is ironic that many people do not "know" the full meaning of it. Taken as a whole, the Lesson cluster shows that all types of learning encompass the definition of "knowledge" and each aspect complements the other. It is important to realize that being knowledgeable is a complex state of mind that can be obtained not from learning about one aspect of life or through one method, but through a variety of learning experiences and methods. While Whitman's "When I Heard the Learn'd Astronomer" deals with book learning as opposed to experiential learning, Hughes' "Theme for English B" demonstrates learning from different cultures and Yezierska's "Soap and Water" deals with learning about how certain inequalities in society affect learning itself.

Whitman's main idea in "When I Heard the Learn'd Astronomer" is that learning about a concept through someone else, even an expert, is not as fulfilling as learning about it through personal experience. The repetition of "when" in the poem as the speaker is listening to the astronomer's lecture suggests a dull, boring atmosphere. Furthermore, when the speaker listens to the astronomer and is being shown charts and diagrams, he becomes "tired and sick" from passively taking in this information. But when the speaker goes outside to learn about the stars by actually seeing them, the poem takes on an enlightened tone. The air is described as "mystical," which gives the feeling that the speaker is enchanted with what he sees, unlike his experience in the lecture-room. It should also be noted that more active verbs are now used, such as "rising," "gliding," "Look'd," and "wander'd." By contrasting the two scenes, the speaker is conveying the idea that passive learning through lecture needs to be emphasized through more active experience, whereby full knowledge can be gained.

The ideas in Whitman's poem are still a focus of discussion today with many parents, teachers, and students. Many people believe that absorbing information through books and teachers alone is not learning and that real learning is gained through experience and critical thinking. Jerome Wiesner reflects these views when he says that education should "include opportunities for discovery and experimentation to stimulate the curiosity and develop intellectual self-reliance" (99). I believe in Wiesner's statement because in real life, answers are not just given to a person; one has to find them for oneself. And since sometimes the answers that one does find are not the right ones, one has to realize that just because a person claims to be an "expert" does not necessarily mean that this person has all the right answers.

Many students also realize the importance of Wiesner's statement. Pace freshman Anthony Cinquemani responded to Wiesner's statement by saying, "Sometimes teachers only care about teaching the requirements of the course and testing on this material. This isn't a good way to stimulate the mind because I know some people who have good grades but no common sense or sense of reality. Teachers must present their courses in such a way to be relevant to the real world." It seems that Whitman's sentiments are valid, even today.

In the poem "Theme for English B," Hughes comments on the cultural differences between a teacher and a student. The speaker clearly differentiates himself from his professor by stating that he is young and black while his professor is old and white. However, the speaker also suggests a similarity between himself and his instructor. When describing what is "true" to him, the student mentions that he likes, among other things, to eat, be in love, "read, learn, and understand life" (886 l. 22). All of these pleasures that the student describes cross cultural lines and are used to show a connection between the student and teacher, leading the student to make the dramatic statement to the instructor that he is "a part of me, as I am a part of you" (887 l. 32).

The poem ends by stating that the student and instructor could learn from each other. This is a very valid point, especially in today's multicultural, inner city schools. The poem, although stating that both people can learn from each other, seems to put more emphasis on the need for the professor to relate to the student by the very fact that the student has shown understanding by initiating the discussion. According to Solon Kimball, a teacher who disregards the cultural upbringing of his or her pupils and tries to teach only from his or her experience will result in student frustration and apathy towards the material (82). Without cultural learning, teachers may know the material that needs to be taught, but not know how to pass it on to those whom he or she is meant to teach.

Another part of learning about real life involves learning about obstacles in the world and learning never to give up when faced with these obstacles. Yezierska's "Soap and Water" shows the difficulties that the main character faces in trying to change her status in society. She is very determined to succeed and has to work eight hours a day to pay for her college education. However, at one point, her college diploma is withheld from her and she is also denied a teaching position because of her untidy appearance. The irony of the situation is that she is constantly unkempt because she has no time for herself since she works in a laundry cleaning the clothes of the very upper class people who have looked down on her because of her appearance. Therefore, going to college, which is supposed to allow for greater social mobility, actually hinders the main character. I think that Yezierska's intention is to show that sometimes society does not honor those who deserve better, but honors those who are already privileged.

However, the author leaves the reader with a sense of hope at the end of the story when the main character meets a former professor who treats her with respect instead of hatred or pity, causing the main character to have hope in America again. This renewed hope leaves the reader with the lesson that one should never give up hope when faced with adversity. Realizing one's potential is an important part of knowledge because unrealistic negative expectations can hinder a person in other areas of learning. For instance, a student who is convinced that a course is too hard will probably get bad grades because he or she has given up, allowing for a self-fulfilling prophecy.

Learning does not begin and end with the school year. In fact, as seen from the stories and poems in the Lesson cluster, sometimes learning has nothing to do with school. Learning about the world around us, learning about different cultures, and learning about the harsh realities of life without giving up on life itself allow us to be fully knowledgeable about life and others.

WORKS CITED

Cinquemani, Anthony. Personal Interview. 8 April 1995.

Kimball, Solon T. *Culture and The Educative Process: An Anthropological Perspective.* New York: Teachers College Press, 1974.

Wiesner, Jerome B. "Education for Creativity in the Sciences." *Creativity and Learning.* Ed. Jerome Kagan. Boston: Beacon Press, 1967, pp. 92–102.

APPENDIX B: SAMPLE SYNTHESIS ESSAY

Nurturing and Protecting: Parent-Child Relationships

BY MICHELLE DIBBINI

It has been said that we live in a world dominated by sexual stereotypes. Boys are taught to be masculine and aggressive, while girls are raised to be submissive and pleasing. The stereotypes have existed since the beginning of human history, when the men hunted animals and the women cooked the food. Where do men and women receive guidance for this stereotypical behavior? It may be said that the answer lies in the children's relationships with their parents.

It would be enlightening to explore the psychological relationships of fathers and mothers to sons and daughters in various literary works in order to test these sexual stereotypes. Theodore Roethke, in "My Papa's Waltz," and Ronald Koertge, in "Orientation Week," demonstrate how a father's behavior is influenced by the gender of his child. David Leavitt, in "Gravity," and Margaret Atwood, in "Today," express the emotional tensions in mother-child relationships.

The speaker of Roethke's "My Papa's Waltz" is a grown man reflecting on his childhood and the "waltzing" ritual he experienced with his father (Roethke 470, l. 4). When the father came home, they would begin "waltzing" and "romping" (l. 5). The word "romp" connotes happiness: it represents a pleasurable tour of the house, as opposed to a word like "stumbled." This was valuable time the son spent with the father. However, the "quality time" and "waltzing" can be described as "rough play." As Carole Wade and Carol Tavris explain, fathers tend to be "more physically stimulating, playful, and unpredictable" than mothers (*Psychology* 481).

The poem also describes the mother's "countenance" (l. 7). She disapproves of this behavior; however, she does not interfere. She simply watches the "dancing" until the boy is "waltzed off to bed" (l. 15). Before her frowning but deferential gaze the father and son engage in a playful but worrisome kind of bonding ritual.

Koertge's "Orientation Week" is a typical example of how fathers tend to "protect" their daughters. The situation of the poem is that of a father, the speaker of the poem, leaving his daughter at college for the first time. Many worries and fears, including those having to do with drugs and sex, rush to his mind. His apprehensions are enhanced by the daughter's behavior and "coaxing" (Koertge 471, l. 13). Can he "follow her everywhere, revolvers drawn" (l. 16)? Of course not: therefore, he must trust her while she is out of his clutches. The father should realize that his daughter is "growing up" and will be faced with many difficult decisions.

The title of this poem is intriguing and ambiguous. In one sense, the daughter is being oriented to "college life" and to her new environment. She will now be surrounded by young men who will want to take advantage of her innocence. On the other hand, the father is being introduced to his daughter's emerging womanhood. She is not a little girl anymore. Consequently, he realizes that he can not "lock those vivid hips in her room" (l. 15). It is his orientation week as well. Leaving her with a thoughtful "Be good," he achieves his epiphany as a father (l. 20).

At the risk of stating the obvious, fathers tend to have different relationships with their sons than they do with their daughters. In "My Papa's Waltz," the father tends to play roughly with his son. Fathers are, generally, physically active with their boys. However, they do not behave in this manner with their daughters. As Haim G. Ginott explains, "It is inappropriate for [fathers] to engage [their daughters] in shadow boxing and rough play" (*Between Parent and Child* 172). Fathers want to protect their daughters from the same world that they encourage their sons to conquer. "Fathers allow their sons to explore, break rules and take physical chances, but they protectively keep their daughters nearby" (Wade and Tavris 481).

Mother-child relationships differ from those involving the father because mothers tend to be more verbal, instructive and calming (481). An exceptional mother-son association is depicted in "Gravity," by David Leavitt. In this story the mother, Sylvia, is caring for her dying son, Theo. To his surprise, the "injections she took in stride". . . . "She was intricately cheerful," never letting Theo see the pain she was experiencing (395). She encouraged Theo to live the rest of his life to the fullest. However, he rarely indulged in his mother's advice. Embarrassed and afraid, Theo opts to stay home rather than accompany her on her daily missions.

One day, Theo and Sylvia are out shopping for a wedding gift. When Sylvia tells her son that she has sent a gift in his name, Theo becomes very frustrated over his mother's control. However, Sylvia is a perfect example of a nurturing mother who wants to do all she can for her son. While inspecting merchandise she is considering for purchase, she tosses Theo a large, heavy crystal bowl. He catches it, astonishing himself and the spectators. However, Sylvia is not surprised, for she knew her son could catch it. This is a victory for Sylvia, because she is trying to teach her son that he is capable of proceeding with a somewhat normal life.

Mothers tend to be nurturing with both their sons and daughters. The poem "Today," by Margaret Atwood, shows a mother watching her young daughter explore nature. The lawn "holds" her daughter "like a hostage" because the girl cannot break free from the curiosity which binds her to the green grass (398, ll. 1–2). The mother sees the stepping stones only as a danger to the child. She attempts to warn her daughter: "watch the slope" (l. 9). However, the child is so overwhelmed by the beauty of nature that she is oblivious to her mother's cautions.

The pond also poses a potential hazard. "The lure of eleven birds" is putting the girl in jeopardy (l. 16). According to Louis Genevie and Eva Margolies, "A girl seems to need more protective parenting" (*The Motherhood Report* 293). But by protecting and rescuing her daughter, the mother in this poem may eliminate the "bluegreen gold" beauty that the child finds so alluring (l. 19). The mother perceives everything as a danger; therefore, she tries to protect her daughter from the "edges" of life (l. 26). However, she realizes that her fragile daughter must experience these "journeys" alone. Atwood's mother wants to liberate her daughter, but at the same time to protect her.

Mothers attend to their children in the same protective and caring ways. However, they seem to have a stronger bond with their daughters than with their sons. Genevie and Margolies explain why: "Boys have to break away and eventually love another woman more than mom. Girls, on the other hand, start out closer, and never have to give up mom as the number one woman in their life" (290). Yet, Sylvia, the mother in "Gravity," expresses her fierce love for her son in the face of his illness: she refuses to coddle him, but she tries to protect him. Perhaps this closeness, more characteristic of mother-daughter relationships, stems from the lack of any female competitor for the mother's love.

More typically, in literature as in life, both fathers and mothers tend to shelter their daughters more than they do their sons. Their perception is that girls "need more coddling because they are fragile" (298). They do not want their girls to enter the world and experience all the dangers it has to offer. Regarding boys, fathers tend to be more playful, and to encourage boisterous behavior. In contrast, mothers want to nurture their sons and to try to calm their rowdy demeanor.

I think the differences in parental behavior and perceptions are a springboard for social stereotypes. Parents often instill a mentality regarding "boy and girl behavior." For example, rough play is "boy stuff" while learning to care and nurture dolls is "girl stuff." Obviously, society's stereotypes can not be abolished by a few liberated parents who buy neutral toys and teach their sons to play with dolls. This is a never-ending battle for those who want to live in a non-sexist environment. Their efforts must begin at home with parent-child relationships. The "double standard" should be eliminated. However, considering my personal experiences, and the depictions of parent-child relationships found in the literary works above, I am forced to conclude that the abolition of gender stereotypes would be nearly impossible.

WORKS CITED

Genevie, Louis, and Eva Margolies. *The Motherhood Report.* New York: MacMillan Publishing, 1987.

Ginott, Haim G. *Between Parent and Child.* New York: Macmillan Publishing, 1965.

Wade, Carole, and Carol Tavris. *Psychology, 2d ed.* New York: HarperCollins, 1990.

CREDITS

Kobo Abe, "The Magic Chalk" (originally titled "Maho no Chalk"), *Ningren* magazine, December 1950. Translated by Alison Kibrick. Copyright 1950. © 1982, 1985 by Kobo Abe. Reprinted with the permission of International Creative Management.

Fawzia Abu-Khalid, "Mother's Inheritance" from *Women From the Fertile Crescent* (Washington, DC: Three Continents Press, 1978). Reprinted with the permission of the publishers.

Chinua Achebe, "Dead Men's Path" from *Girls at War and Other Stories*. Copyright © 1972, 1973 by Chinua Achebe. Reprinted with the permission of Doubleday, a division of Bantam Doubleday Publishing Group, Inc.

Diane Ackerman, selection from *The Natural History of Love*. © 1994 by Diane Ackerman. Reprinted with the permission of Random House, Inc.

Woody Allen, "Death Knocks" from *Getting Even*. Copyright © 1966, 1967, 1969, 1970, 1971 by Woody Allen. Reprinted with the permission of Random House, Inc.

Isabel Allende, "And From Clay We Are Created" from *The Stories of Eva Luna,* translated by Margaret Sayers Peden. Copyright © 1989 by Isabel Allende. English translation copyright © 1991 by Macmillan Publishing Company. Reprinted with the permission of Atheneum Publishers, an imprint of Macmillan Publishing Company.

Maya Angelou, "Phenomenal Woman" from *And I Still Rise*. Copyright © 1978 by Maya Angelou. Reprinted with the permission of Random House, Inc.

Margaret Atwood, "Today" from *Two-Headed Poems* (New York: Simon and Schuster). Reprinted with the permission of the author, c/o Phoebe Larmore Literary Agency.

Houston Baker, excerpt from "The Achievement of Gwendolyn Brooks," *College Language Association Journal* 1 (September 1972). Reprinted with the permission of the College Language Association.

Russell Baker, excerpt from *Growing Up*. Copyright © 1982 by Russell Baker. Reprinted with permission of Congdon & Weed, Inc. and Contemporary Books, Chicago.

James Baldwin, "Guilt, Desire and Love" from *Jimmy's Blues: Selected Poems by James Baldwin*. Copyright © 1986 by James Baldwin. Reprinted with the permission of St. Martin's Press, Inc. "The Rockpile" from *Going to Meet the Man* (Vintage Books). Copyright © 1965 by James Baldwin. Copyright renewed. Reprinted with the permission of The James Baldwin Estate.

Amiri Baraka, "*A Raisin in the Sun*'s Enduring Passion" from *A Raisin in the Sun and the Sign in Sydney Brustein's Window by Lorraine Hansberry,* edited by Robert Nemiroff (New American Library, 1987). Copyright © 1987 by Amiri Baraka. Reprinted with the permission of Sterling Lord Literistic, Inc.

Toni Cade Bambara, "The Lesson" from *Gorilla My Love*. Copyright © 1972 by Toni Cade Bambara. Reprinted with the permission of Random House, Inc.

Bruno Bettelheim, "The Child's Need for Magic" from *The Uses of Enchantment*. Originally appeared in *The New Yorker*. Copyright © 1975, 1976 by Bruno Bettelheim. Reprinted with the permission of Alfred A. Knopf, Inc.

Elizabeth Bishop, "The Fish" from *The Complete Poems 1927–1979*. Copyright 1950 by Elizabeth Bishop. Reprinted with the permission of Farrar, Straus & Giroux, Inc.

Christopher Brookhouse, excerpt from "Story Itself" in *Sam Shepard: A Casebook*. Copyright by Garland Publishing. Reprinted with the permission of Garland Publishing Inc.

Gwendolyn Brooks, "Sadie and Maude" and "We Real Cool" from *Blacks* by Gwendolyn Brooks. (Chicago, IL: Third World Press, 1991). Copyright © 1991 by Gwendolyn Brooks. Reprinted with the permission of the author.

Raymond Carver, "My Father's Life." © 1984 by Tess Gallagher. Permission granted by Tess Gallagher.

Phyllis Chesler, excerpt from "Women and Asylums: Four Lives" from *Women and Madness* (New York: Harcourt, Brace, 1989). Reprinted with the permission of the author.

Credits

Kate Chopin, "The Storm" and "The Story of an Hour" from *The Complete Works of Kate Chopin,* edited by Per Seyersted. Copyright © 1969 Louisiana State University Press. Reprinted with the permission of the publishers.

Lucille Clifton, "for de Lawd" from *good woman: poems and a memoir, 1969–1980.* Copyright © 1987 by Lucille Clifton. Reprinted with the permission of BOA Editions, Ltd., 92 Park Avenue, Brockport, NY 14420.

Robert Creeley, "A Marriage" from *Collected Poems of Robert Creeley, 1945–1975.* Originally in *Origin 19* (Summer 1956). Copyright © 1956 by Robert Creeley. Reprinted with the permission of the author and University of California Press.

David J. DeRose, excerpt from *Sam Shepard.* Copyright © 1992 by Twayne Publishers. Reprinted with the permission of Simon & Schuster Macmillan.

Annie Dillard, "Seeing" from *Pilgrim at Tinker Creek.* Copyright © 1974 by Annie Dillard. Reprinted with the permission of HarperCollins Publishers, Inc.

Michael Dorris, "The Contest" from *Paper Trail: Essays.* Originally appeared in *Ladies' Home Journal,* May 1993. Copyright © 1993 by Michael Dorris. Reprinted with the permission of HarperCollins Publishers, Inc.

Rita Dove, "Adolescence III" from *Selected Poems* (New York: Vintage, 1993). Copyright © 1980, 1993 by Rita Dove. Reprinted with the permission of the author.

Stephen Dunn, "Tenderness" from *Between Angels: Poems.* Copyright © 1989 by Stephen Dunn. Reprinted with the permission of W. W. Norton & Company, Inc.

Errol Durbach, excerpt from *A Doll's House: Ibsen's Myth of Transformation.* Copyright © 1991 by G. K. Hall & Company. Reprinted with the permission of Twayne Publishers, an imprint of Macmillan Publishing Company.

Louise Erdrich, "Family Reunion" from Jacklight. Copyright © 1984 by Louise Erdrich. Reprinted with the permission of Henry Holt and Company, Inc.

Robert Frost, "Mending Wall," "Once by the Pacific," and "Stopping by Woods on a Snowy Evening" from *The Poetry of Robert Frost,* edited by Edward Connery Lathem. Copyright 1923, 1928 by Henry Holt and Company, Inc., renewed 1951, © 1956 by Robert Frost. Reprinted with the permission of the publishers.

Howard Gardner, "Intelligence in Seven Steps," *Harvard Graduate School of Education Alumni Bulletin.* Reprinted with the permission of the author.

Tess Gallagher, "The Hug" from *Amplitude.* Copyright © 1987 by Tess Gallagher. Reprinted with the permission of Graywolf Press, St. Paul, MN.

Louise Glück, "Celestial Music" from *Ararat.* Copyright © 1990 by Louise Glück. Reprinted with the permission of The Ecco Press.

Lorraine Hansberry, "A Raisin in the Sun." Copyright © 1959, 1966, 1984 by Robert Nemiroff. Reprinted with the permission of Random House, Inc.

Elizabeth Hardwick, "Ibsen's Women" from *Seduction and Betrayal: Women and Literature.* Copyright © 1970, 1972, 1973, 1974 by Elizabeth Hardwick Lowell. Reprinted with the permission of Random House, Inc.

Joy Harjo, "Eagle Poem" from *In Mad Love and War.* Copyright © 1990 by Joy Harjo, University Press of New England.

Seamus Heaney, "Mid-Term Break" from *Poems 1965–1975.* Copyright © 1980 by Seamus Heaney. Reprinted with the permission of Farrar, Straus & Giroux, Inc.

Liliana Heker, "The Stolen Party" from *Other Fires: Short Fiction by Latin American Women,* edited and translated by Alberto Manguel. Copyright © 1992 by Liliana Heker. Translation copyright © 1986 by Alberto Manguel. Reprinted with the permission of the author and Clarkson N. Potter, a division of Crown Publishers, Inc.

Ernest Hemingway, "Fathers and Sons" from *Winner Take Nothing.* Copyright 1933 by Charles Scribner's Sons, renewed © 1961 by Mary Hemingway. "Hills Like White Elephants" from *Men Without Women.* Copyright 1927 by Charles Scribner's Sons, renewed © 1955 by Ernest Hemingway. Each story reprinted with permission from Charles Scribner's Sons, an imprint of Simon and Schuster.

Barbara Holder, "October." Copyright © 1994 by Barbara Holder. Reprinted with the permission of the author.

Jane Howard, "Families" from *Families.* Copyright © 1978 by Jane Howard. Reprinted with the permission of Simon & Schuster, Inc.

Langston Hughes, "As I Grew Older" from *Selected Poems of Langston Hughes.* Copyright 1926 by Alfred A. Knopf, Inc., renewed 1954 by Langston Hughes. Reprinted with the permission of Alfred A. Knopf,

Inc. "Harlem (A Dream Deferred)" from *The Panther and the Lash: Poems of Our Times.* Copyright 1951 by Langston Hughes. Reprinted with the permission of Alfred A. Knopf, Inc. "Salvation" from *The Big Sea.* Copyright 1940 by Langston Hughes, renewed © Arna Bontemps and George Houston Bass. Reprinted with the permission of Hill & Wang, a division of Farrar, Straus & Giroux, Inc. "Theme for English B." Copyright 1951 by Langston Hughes, renewed © 1979 by George Houston Bass. Reprinted with the permission of Harold Ober & Associates, Inc.

Henrik Ibsen, "A Doll's House" from *Eight Plays,* translated by Eva Le Gallienne. Copyright © 1957 by Eva Le Gallienne. Reprinted with the permission of Random House, Inc.

Eugene Ionesco, "The Lesson" from *The Bald Soprano and Other Plays,* translated by Donal M. Allen. Copyright © by Grove Press, Inc. Reprinted with the permission of Grove/Atlantic, Inc.

Kazuo Ishiguro, "A Family Supper," *Esquire* 1990. Reprinted with the permission of The Estate of Kazuo Ishiguro, c/o Rogers, Coleridge & White Ltd., 20 Powis Mews, London W11 1JN.

Shirley Jackson, "The Lottery" from *The Lottery and Other Stories.* Copyright 1948, 1949 by Shirley Jackson, renewed © 1976, 1977 by Lawrence Hyman, Barry Hyman, Mrs. Sarah Webster, and Mrs. Joanne Schnurer. Reprinted with the permission of Farrar, Straus & Giroux, Inc.

Charles Johnson, "Exchange Value" from *The Sorcerer's Apprentice.* First appeared in *Choice.* Copyright © 1981 by Charles Johnson. Reprinted with the permission of Atheneum Publishers, an imprint of Macmillan Publishing Company.

Stanley Kaufman, "More Trick Than Tragedy" in *The Saturday Review,* Sept./Oct. 1983, Vol 9 no. 10. Copyright © 1983 by *The Saturday Review.* Reprinted by permission.

Jamaica Kincaid, "Girl" from *At the Bottom of the River.* Copyright © 1978, 1983 by Jamaica Kincaid. Reprinted with the permission of Farrar, Straus & Giroux, Inc.

Martin Luther King, Jr., "I Have a Dream." Copyright © 1963 by Martin Luther King, Jr., renewed 1991 by Coretta Scott King. Reprinted with the permission of The Heirs to The Estate of Martin Luther King, Jr., c/o Joan Daves Agency.

Galway Kinnell, "Rapture" from *Imperfect Thirst.* Originally in *The New Yorker.* Copyright © 1993 by Galway Kinnell. Reprinted with the permission of Houghton Mifflin Company.

Ronald Koertge, "Orientation Week" from *Life on the Edge of the Continent.* Copyright © 1982. Reprinted with the permission of University of Alabama Press.

Tony Kushner, excerpt from *Angels in America, Part One: Millenium Approaches.* Copyright 1992, 1993 by Tony Kushner. Reprinted with the permission of Theatre Communications Group, New York, NY.

Philip Larkin, "Church Going" from *The Less Deceived.* Reprinted with the permission of the Marvell Press.

Shirley Lauro, "Open Admissions." Copyright © 1979, 1980, 1981, 1983 by Shirley Lauro. Reprinted with the permission of William Morris Agency. "Open Admissions" is the sole property of the author and is fully protected by copyright. It may not be acted either by professionals or amateurs without written consent. Public readings, radio, and television broadcasts likewise are forbidden. All inquiries concerning these rights should be addressed to Samuel French, Inc., 45 West 25th Street, New York, NY 10010.

David Leavitt, "Gravity" from *A Place I've Never Seen.* Copyright © 1990 by David Leavitt. Originally in *The East Hampton Star.* Reprinted with the permission of Viking Penguin, a division of Penguin Books USA Inc.

Ursula Le Guin, "The Ones Who Walk Away from Omelas" from *New Dimensions 3.* Copyright © 1973 by Ursula K. Le Guin. Reprinted with the permission of the author and the author's agent, Virginia Kidd.

Doris Lessing, "A Sunrise on the Veld" from *African Stories.* Copyright 1951, 1953, 1954, © 1957, 1958, 1963, 1964, 1965 by Doris Lessing. Reprinted with the permission of Simon & Schuster, Inc.

Audre Lorde, "Hanging Fire" and "Power" from *The Black Unicorn.* Copyright © 1978 by Audre Lorde. Reprinted with the permission of W. W. Norton & Company, Inc.

Naguib Mahfouz, "Half a Day" from *The Time and the Place and Other Stories.* Copyright © 1991 by the American University in Cairo Press. Reprinted with the permission of Doubleday, a division of Bantam Doubleday Dell Publishing Group, Inc.

Bernard Malamud, "The Magic Barrel" from *The Magic Barrel and Other Stories.* Copyright © 1958 and renewed 1986 by Bernard Malamud. Reprinted with the permission of Farrar, Straus & Giroux, Inc.

Gabriel Garcia Márquez, "The Handsomest Drowned Man in the World" from *Leaf Storm and Other Stories.* Copyright © 1971 by Gabriel Garcia Márquez. Reprinted with the permission of HarperCollins Publishers, Inc.

Credits

Rollo May, "The Experience of Becoming a Person" from *Man's Search for Himself.* Copyright 1953 by W. W. Norton & Company, Inc., renewed © 1981 by Rollo May. Reprinted with the permission of W. W. Norton & Company, Inc.

Gardner McFall, "Four Corners." Copyright © 1987 by Gardner McFall. Originally appeared in *The Missouri Review* 1987, Vol. X no. 2. Reprinted with the permission of the author.

Alice Munro, "Boys and Girls" from *Dance of the Happy Shades.* Copyright © 1968 by Alice Munro. Reprinted with the permission of the Virginia Barber Literary Agency, Inc.

Shiga Naoya, "Han's Crime" from *The Paper Door and Other Stories* by Shiga Naoya, translated by Lane Dunlop. Reprinted with the permission of the translator.

Marsha Norman, *'night, Mother.* © 1983 by Marsha Narman. Reprinted with permission of Hill and Wang, a division of Farrar, Straus & Giroux, Inc.

Joyce Carol Oates, "Where Are You Going, Where Have You Been?" from *The Wheel of Love.* Copyright © 1970 by Joyce Carol Oates. Reprinted with the permission of John Hawkins Associates, Inc.

Frank O'Connor, "My Oedipus Complex" from *Collected Stories.* Copyright 1950 by Frank O'Connor. Reprinted with the permission of Alfred A. Knopf, Inc.

Sharon Olds, "Photograph of the Girl," "Sex Without Love," and "The Victims" from *The Dead and the Living.* Copyright © 1983 by Sharon Olds. Reprinted with the permission of Alfred A. Knopf, Inc.

Cynthia Ozick, "The Shawl" from *The Shawl.* Originally appeared in *The New Yorker.* Copyright © 1980 by Cynthia Ozick. Reprinted with the permission of Alfred A. Knopf, Inc.

Grace Paley, "The Loudest Voice" from *The Little Disturbances of Man.* (New York: Penguin, 1985). Copyright © 1959 by Grace Paley. Reprinted with the permission of the author and Elaine Markson Literary Agency.

Linda Pastan, "Marks" from *PM/AM: New and Selected Poems.* Copyright © 1978, 1982 by Linda Pastan. Reprinted with the permission of W. W. Norton & Company, Inc. "love poem" from *The Imperfect Paradise,Poems.* Copyright © 1988 by Linda Pastan. Reprinted with the permission of W. W. Norton & Company, Inc.

Marge Piercy, "Barbie Doll" from *Circles on the Water.* Copyright © 1982 by Marge Piercy. Reprinted with the permission of Alfred A. Knopf, Inc. "To Have Without Holding" from *The Moon is Always Female.* Copyright © 1980 by Marge Piercy. Reprinted with the permission of Alfred A. Knopf, Inc.

Sylvia Plath, "Death and Co." and "Lady Lazarus" from *Ariel.* Copyright © 1963 and renewed 1991 by Ted Hughes. Reprinted with the permission of HarperCollins Publishers, Inc. "Metaphors" from *Crossing the Water.* Copyright © 1960 and renewed 1988 by Ted Hughes. Reprinted with the permission of HarperCollins Publishers, Inc.

Anna Quindlen, "Married" from *Living Out Loud.* Copyright © 1987 by Anna Quindlen. Reprinted with the permission of Random House, Inc.

Adrienne Rich, "Aunt Jennifer's Tigers" from *The Fact of a Doorframe: Poems Selected and New 1950–1984.* Copyright © 1984 by Adrienne Rich. Reprinted with the permission of W. W. Norton & Company, Inc.

Frank Rich, "Suicide Talk in *'night, Mother.*" Copyright © 1983 by The New York Times Company. Reprinted with the permission of The New York Times Company.

Theodore Roethke, "My Papa's Waltz" from *The Collected Poems of Theodore Roethke.* Copyright 1942 by Hearst magazines, Inc., renewed © 1969 by Beatrice Roethke Lushington. Reprinted with the permission of Doubleday, a division of Doubleday Dell Publishing Group, Inc.

Andy Rooney, "The Love That's Easy to Hate" from *Sweet and Sour.* Copyright © 1992 by essay Productions, Inc. Reprinted with the permission of The Putnam Publishing Group, Inc.

Liz Rosenberg, "Married Love" from *The Fire Music.* Copyright © 1986 by Liz Rosenberg. Reprinted with the permission of The University of Pittsburgh Press.

Muriel Rukeyser, "Looking at Each Other" from *A Muriel Rukeyser Reader* (1994: W.W. Norton, New York). Reprinted with the permission of William L. Rukeyser.

Kate Rushin, "The Tired Poem: Last Letter from a Typical Unemployed Black Professional Woman" from *The Black Back-Ups.* Copyright © 1986, 1993 by Kate Rushin. Originally in *Conditions Five: The Black Woman's Issue,* co-edited by Lorraine Bethel and Barbara Smith. Reprinted with the permission of Firebrand Books, Ithaca, NY.

Charles Segal, "Sophocles' Praise of Man and the Conflicts of the *Antigone*" from *Interpreting Greek Tragedy: Myth, Poetry Text,* Copyright © 1986 by Cornell University Press. Originally appeared in *Arion* III, No. 2 (Summer 1964). Reprinted with the permission of the author and Cornell University Press.

Credits

Anne Sexton, "The Fury of Overshoes" from *The Death Notebooks.* Copyright © 1974 by Anne Sexton. Reprinted with the permission of Houghton Mifflin Company.

Sam Shepard, "True West" from *Seven Plays.* Copyright © 1981 by Sam Shepard. Reprinted with the permission of Bantam Books, a division of Bantam Doubleday Dell Publishing Group, Inc.

Leslie Marmon Silko, "The Man to Send Rainclouds" from *Storyteller.* Copyright © 1981 by Leslie Marmon Silko. Reprinted with the permission of Seaver Books.

Sophocles, "Antigone" from *Three Theban Plays* by Sophocles, translated by Robert Fagles. Translation copyright © 1982 by Robert Fagles. Used by permission of Viking Penguin, a division of Penguin Books USA Inc.

Wole Soyinka, "Telephone Conversation." Copyright © 1960 by Wole Soyinka. Reprinted by permission of Brandt & Brandt Literary Agents, Inc.

Hortense Spillers, excerpt from "Gwendolyn the Terrible: Propositions on Eleven Poems" from *Shakespeare's Sisters,* edited by Sandra M. Gilbert and Susan Gubar (Bloomington, IN: Indiana University Press, 1979). Reprinted with the permission of the publishers.

Amy Tan, "Two Kinds" from *The Joy Luck Club.* Copyright © 1989 by Amy Tan. Reprinted with the permission of The Putnam Publishing Group.

Dylan Thomas, "Do not go gentle into that good night" from *The Poems of Dylan Thomas.* Copyright 1952 by Dylan Thomas. Reprinted with the permission of New Directions Publishing Corporation.

Paul Tillich, "The Lost Dimension in Religion," *The Saturday Evening Post.* Copyright © 1958 by The Curtis Publishing Company. Reprinted with the permission of the publishers.

Kitty Tsui, "It's in the Name" from *The Words of a Woman Who Breathes Fire* (San Francisco, CA: Spinsters/Aunt Lute Book Company). Reprinted with the permission of the author.

John Updike, "A & P" and "Wife Wooing" from *Pigeon Feathers and Other Stories.* Originally appeared in *The New Yorker.* Copyright © 1962 and © 1960 by John Updike. Reprinted with the permission of Alfred A. Knopf, Inc.

Luisa Valenzuela, "I'm Your Horse in the Night" from *Other Weapons* translated by Deborah Bronner. Originally titled "Cambio de Armas." Reprinted with the permission of Ediciones del Norte, Hanover, NH 03755.

Judith Viorst, "True Love" from *When Did I Stop Being 20 and Other Injustices* (New York: Simon & Schuster). Copyright © 1968, 1987 by Judith Viorst. Reprinted with the permission of Lescher & Lescher, Ltd.

Jean Wagner, from *Black Poets of the United States* (Champaign, IL: University of Illinois Press, 1973). Reprinted with the permission of the publishers.

Alice Walker, "Everyday Use" from *In Love and Trouble: Stories of Black Women.* Copyright © 1973 by Alice Walker. Reprinted with the permission of Harcourt Brace and Company.

Wendy Wasserstein, "The Man in a Case" from *Orchids* by Anton Chekhov, et al. Copyright © 1986 by Wendy Wasserstein. Reprinted with the permission of Alfred A. Knopf, Inc.

Bruce Weber, "The Unromantic Generation" from *The New York Times Magazine,* April 5, 1987. Reprinted with the permission of the author.

Barbara Dafoe Whitehead, excerpt from "Dan Quayle Was Right," *The Atlantic Monthly,* April 15, 1993. Reprinted with the permission of the author.

Kenny Williams, excerpt from "The World of Satin Legs, Mrs. Sallie and the Blackstone Rangers: The Restricted Chicago of Gwendolyn Brooks" from *A Life Distilled: Gwendolyn Brooks, Her Poetry and Fiction* edited by Maria K. Mootry and Gary Smith (Urbana, IL: University of Illinois Press, 1989). Reprinted with the permission of the publishers.

Virginia Woolf, "Professions for Women" from *The Death of the Moth and Other Essays.* Copyright 1942 by Harcourt Brace and World, renewed © 1970 by Marjorie T. Parsons, Executrix. Reprinted with the permission of Harcourt Brace and Company.

Richard Wright, "The Man Who Was Almost a Man" from *Eight Men.* Copyright © 1987 by the Estate of Richard Wright. Originally published in *Harper's Bazaar,* 1939, titled "Almos' a Man." Reprinted with the permission of Thunder's Mouth Press.

Anzia Yezierska, "Soap and Water" from *Hungry Hearts and Other Stories.* Copyright © 1985 by Louise Levitas Henriksen. Reprinted with the permission of Persea Books.

William Zinsser, "College Pressures" from *Blair & Ketchum's Country Journal,* Vol. IV, No. 4 (April 1979). Copyright © 1979 by William K. Zinsser. Reprinted with the permission of the author and Carol Brissie.

AUTHOR/TITLE INDEX

SUBJECT INDEX

ICD-10-CM AND ICD-10-PCS Coding Handbook

ICD-10-CM AND ICD-10-PCS Coding Handbook *with Answers*

2014 Revised Edition

NELLY LEON-CHISEN, RHIA

CENTRAL OFFICE ON ICD-10-CM AND ICD-10-PCS
OF THE
AMERICAN HOSPITAL ASSOCIATION

HEALTH FORUM, INC.
An American Hospital Association Company
Chicago

This publication is designed to provide accurate and authoritative information in regard to the subject matter covered. It is sold with the understanding that neither the authors nor the publisher are engaged in rendering legal, accounting, or other professional service. If legal advice or other expert assistance is required, the services of a competent professional should be sought.

The views expressed in this publication are strictly those of the authors and do not necessarily represent official positions of the American Hospital Association.

AHA and American Hospital Association are service marks of the American Hospital Association used under license by Health Forum, Inc.

Printed in the United States of America—08/13

COVER DESIGN: Cheri Kusek

PROJECT MANAGEMENT, INTERIOR DESIGN, TYPOGRAPHY: Fine Print, Ltd.

NEW ILLUSTRATIONS FOR THE 2012 AND SUBSEQUENT EDITIONS: Christoph Blumrich

ISBN: 978-1-55648-387-5

Item Number: 148054

To my husband, Penku (Jorge) Chisen,
who supported and encouraged me
with his patience and understanding
throughout the long and arduous months
it took to complete this handbook

Contents

CODING OF DISEASES OF THE RESPIRATORY, DIGESTIVE, AND GENITOURINARY SYSTEMS

CODING OF DISEASES OF THE SKIN AND DISEASES OF THE MUSCULOSKELETAL SYSTEM

CODING OF PREGNANCY AND CHILDBIRTH COMPLICATIONS, ABORTION, CONGENITAL ANOMALIES, AND PERINATAL CONDITIONS

CODING OF CIRCULATORY SYSTEM DISEASES AND NEOPLASTIC DISEASES

CODING OF INJURIES, BURNS, POISONING, AND COMPLICATIONS OF CARE

List of Tables and Figures

About the Author and Contributors

Nelly Leon-Chisen, RHIA, is the director of coding and classification at the American Hospital Association (AHA), where she heads the Central Office on ICD-9-CM and the Central Office on HCPCS. She represents the AHA as one of the cooperating parties responsible for the development of *AHA Coding Clinic® for ICD-9-CM* and the *ICD-9-CM Official Guidelines for Coding and Reporting.*

Ms. Leon-Chisen's ICD-10 activities include representing the AHA in the development of the *ICD-10-CM Official Guidelines for Coding and Reporting* and the *ICD-10-PCS Official Coding Guidelines,* membership in the ICD-10-PCS Technical Advisory Panel, past co-chair of the Workgroup for Electronic Data Interchange (WEDI) ICD-10 Implementation Workgroup, and numerous testimonies on ICD-10-CM and ICD-10-PCS before the ICD-9-CM Coordination and Maintenance Committee and the National Committee on Vital and Health Statistics. She was also the AHA lead project manager on the joint American Hospital Association–American Health Information Management Association (AHIMA) ICD-10-CM Field Study. She is an AHIMA-approved ICD-10 Trainer.

Ms. Leon-Chisen has lectured on ICD-9-CM, ICD-10, and POA coding, data quality, and DRGs throughout the United States, Europe, Asia, and Latin America. She is also a speaker for the popular *AHA Coding Clinic®* audioseminar series. She has broad HIM experience in hospital inpatient and outpatient management, consulting, and teaching. She has been an instructor in the HIM and Health Information Technology Programs for the University of Illinois and Truman Community College, both in Chicago. She is a past president of the Chicago Area Health Information Management Association and the recipient of its Distinguished Member Award. She is the recipient of the Professional Achievement Award from the Illinois Health Information Management Association. She is a member of the Advisory Board of the Health Information Technology Program of DeVry University in Chicago.

The Central Office on ICD-9-CM was created through a written Memorandum of Understanding between the AHA and the National Center for Health Statistics in 1963 to do the following:

- Serve as the U.S. clearinghouse for issues related to the use of ICD-9-CM
- Work with the National Center for Health Statistics and the Centers for Medicare & Medicaid Services to maintain the integrity of the classification system
- Recommend revisions and modifications to the current and future revisions of the ICD
- Develop educational material and programs on ICD-9-CM

The Central Office on ICD-9-CM is the publisher of the *AHA Coding Clinic® for ICD-9-CM.* In addition, the Central Office provides expert advice by serving as the clearinghouse for the dissemination of ICD-9-CM information. The Central Office intends to continue this long-standing tradition with ICD-10-CM and ICD-10-PCS.

Acknowledgments

Nelly Leon-Chisen gratefully acknowledges the invaluable contributions of Anita Rapier, Gretchen Young-Charles, and Denene M. Harper, members of the AHA Central Office on ICD-9-CM, who assisted in the revision and review of the manuscript for the handbook and the case summary exercises.

Anita Rapier, RHIT, CCS, is a senior coding consultant with the AHA Central Office on ICD-9-CM. She is also the managing editor of *AHA Coding Clinic® for ICD-9-CM,* for which she is responsible for developing educational material. She has more than 25 years of experience in health information management and has held several positions in HIM, including education, quality, compliance, hospital-based outpatient and acute care, and long-term care. Ms. Rapier has presented numerous educational seminars and has authored articles on coding and compliance. She is also a speaker for the popular *AHA Coding Clinic®* audioseminar series and an AHIMA-approved ICD-10 Trainer.

Gretchen Young-Charles, RHIA, is a senior coding consultant at the AHA Central Office on ICD-9-CM. In this role, she develops educational articles on official coding advice for publication in *AHA Coding Clinic® for ICD-9-CM.* She also served as the secretary to the AHA's Rehabilitation Coding Workgroup. Ms. Young-Charles has more than 20 years of experience in the HIM field. She has worked in numerous HIM roles, including education, quality, hospital-based outpatient and acute care, and rehabilitation. She also spent a number of years with the Peer Review Organization for the state of Illinois. She is also a speaker for the popular *AHA Coding Clinic®* audioseminar series and an AHIMA-approved ICD-10 Trainer.

Denene M. Harper, RHIA, is a senior coding consultant at the AHA Central Office on ICD-9-CM. She is responsible for writing articles on official coding advice for publication in *AHA Coding Clinic® for ICD-9-CM.* Ms. Harper has more than 20 years of experience in the HIM field, including hospital-based outpatient and acute care, utilization review, and quality improvement. She is also an AHIMA-approved ICD-10 Trainer.

In addition, Nelly Leon-Chisen gratefully acknowledges the significant contributions of Janatha Ashton, MS, RHIA, who authored the original case summary exercises in appendix C, and Therese (Teri) Jorwic, who revised those exercises and converted them to ICD-10.

Therese (Teri) Jorwic, MPH, RHIA, CCS, CCS-P, FAHIMA, is an assistant professor in Health Information Management at the University of Illinois at Chicago. She presents numerous workshops and develops educational material for in-class and online courses on ICD-10-CM/PCS, ICD-9-CM, and HCPCS/CPT coding as well as on reimbursement systems for hospitals, physicians, and other health care providers. She also presents workshops for associations and serves as External Faculty for the AHIMA ICD-10 Academy programs.

Thanks are due to Richard Hill, AHA Press editor, who read the author's drafts and helped me to say in plain English what I wanted to say, even without being a coding professional himself.

A sincere thanks to the representatives of the Cooperating Parties: Donna Pickett, RHIA, MPH; Pat Brooks, RHIA; and Sue Bowman, RHIA, CCS—whose collaboration and friendship have made *Coding Clinic* advice and the Official Coding Guidelines a reality. The author looks forward to continuing our collaboration as we implement ICD-10-CM and ICD-10-PCS.

Thanks are also in order to 3M for its generous permission for the author and Central Office staff to use 3M's ICD-10 Translation Tool. This tool enhanced our understanding of the implications of the code set change.

And thank you to Channel Publishing, Inc., for supplying the Central Office staff with ICD-9-CM, ICD-10-CM, and ICD-10-PCS coding books.

Finally, Nelly Leon-Chisen wishes to acknowledge the tradition of excellence in coding education established by Faye Brown through the *ICD-9-CM Coding Handbook.* Ms. Brown's work served as the foundation on which this handbook was built. The author humbly hopes this handbook can continue educating generations of coders as the field implements ICD-10-CM and ICD-10-PCS.

How to Use This Handbook

As with the ICD-9-CM handbooks, this ICD-10 edition is designed as a versatile resource:

- Textbook for academic programs in health information technology and administration
- Text for in-service training programs
- Self-instructional guide for individuals who would like to learn coding or refresh their skills outside a formal program
- Reference tool for general use in the workplace

The general and basic areas of information covered in chapters 1 through 11 are designed to meet the requirements of various basic courses on the use of ICD-10-CM and ICD-10-PCS. They may also be used as a foundation for moving on to the study of individual chapters of ICD-10-CM and ICD-10-PCS. Chapters 12 through 33 of the handbook include advanced material for both continuing education students and professionals in the field.

This handbook is designed to be used in conjunction with the ICD-10-CM and ICD-10-PCS coding manuals (either in book or PDF format). The coding manuals must be consulted throughout the learning process, and the material in this text cannot be mastered without using them. The official versions are available in PDF format from the National Center for Health Statistics (ICD-10-CM) and the Centers for Medicare & Medicaid Services (ICD-10-PCS). At press time, at least two publishers had made available unofficial, printed versions; more publishers are expected to make printed versions available in the near future. There may be minor variations between the way material is displayed in this handbook and the way it is displayed in printed versions.

The chapters in this handbook are not arranged in the same sequence as the chapters in ICD-10-CM or ICD-10-PCS. The first two sections of the handbook (chapters 1–13) provide discussions on the format and conventions followed in ICD-10-CM and ICD-10-PCS, as well as basic coding guidelines and introductory material on Z codes and External cause of morbidity codes. The next eight sections (chapters 14–33) progress from the less complicated ICD-10-CM/PCS chapters to the more difficult. Faculty in academic and in-service programs can rearrange this sequence to suit their particular course outlines.

Appendix A, Coding and Reimbursement, contains basic information on the role of coding with reimbursement models for hospitals, physician practices, and other health care settings.

Appendix B, Reporting of the Present on Admission Indicator, contains information on the reporting of the Medicare requirement associated with the hospital inpatient reporting of all ICD-10-CM diagnosis codes.

Appendix C, Case Summary Exercises, is designed for students who have learned the basic coding principles and need additional practice applying the principles to actual cases. The exercises are geared for beginning to intermediate levels of knowledge. The case summaries are based on actual health records of both inpatients and outpatients. The patients described often have multiple conditions that may or may not relate to the current episode of care. Some exercises include several episodes of care for a patient in various settings.

Students using the handbook edition without answers will need to ask their instructors for the answers. After students have completed the exercises, they can check their answers against the instructor's edition, which lists the appropriate codes for each exercise, with the codes for the principal diagnosis and principal procedure sequenced first. Explanatory comments discuss why certain codes are appropriate and others are not and why some conditions listed in the case summaries are not coded at all. The comments also indicate how the principal diagnosis and procedure codes were designated, and which symptoms are inherent to certain conditions and so are not coded separately.

The *ICD-10-CM Official Guidelines for Coding and Reporting* and the *ICD-10-PCS Official Coding Guidelines*, referenced throughout this handbook, may be downloaded from the AHA Central Office Web site: www.ahacentraloffice.org.

To use this handbook effectively, readers should work through the coding examples provided throughout the text until they fully understand the coding principles under discussion. Readers should be able to arrive at correct code assignments by following the instructions provided and reviewing the pertinent handbook material until it is fully understood. Exercises in the body of each chapter should be completed as they come up in the discussion rather than at the end of the chapter or section. Most chapters provide a review exercise with additional material that covers the entire chapter. There is also a final review exercise toward the end of the book that offers additional coding practice. Answers to all of these exercises are provided in the edition with answers.

The handbook follows three conventions:

- In some examples, a hyphen is used to indicate that additional characters are required but cannot be assigned in the example because certain information needed for assignment of these characters is not given. This is done to emphasize concepts and specific guidelines without going too deeply into specific coding situations.
- **The underlining of codes in text examples indicates correct sequencing;** that is, the underlined code must be sequenced first in that particular combination of codes. When no code is underlined, there is no implicit reason why any of the codes in the series should be sequenced first. In actual coding, of course, other information in the health record may dictate a different sequence. This underlining convention is used in the handbook solely as a teaching device. It is not an element of the ICD-10-CM/PCS coding system.
- In the edition with answers, **the underlining of words in exercise questions indicates the appropriate term to be referenced in using the alphabetic indexes. The underlining of codes in the answer column of the exercises indicates correct code sequencing,** as it does in the examples in the main text.

Changes in Code Usage

Official coding guidelines approved by the four cooperating parties responsible for administering the ICD-10-CM and ICD-10-PCS systems in the United States (American Hospital Association, American Health Information Management Association, Centers for Medicare & Medicaid Services, and National Center for Health Statistics) are published on a yearly basis. A partial code-set freeze for ICD-10-CM/PCS went into effect in 2012, and very limited changes are expected for the 2014 version of the guidelines as well as for the code set.

ICD-10-CM and ICD-10-PCS coding advice has been included in the *AHA Coding Clinic® for ICD-9-CM* since the Fourth Quarter 2012 issue. Subsequent issues will provide official guidance in the use of ICD-10, as they currently do for ICD-9-CM. *AHA Coding Clinic® for ICD-10-CM and ICD-10-PCS* will be published starting in 2014. Further information on *AHA Coding Clinic®* may be found on the next two pages.

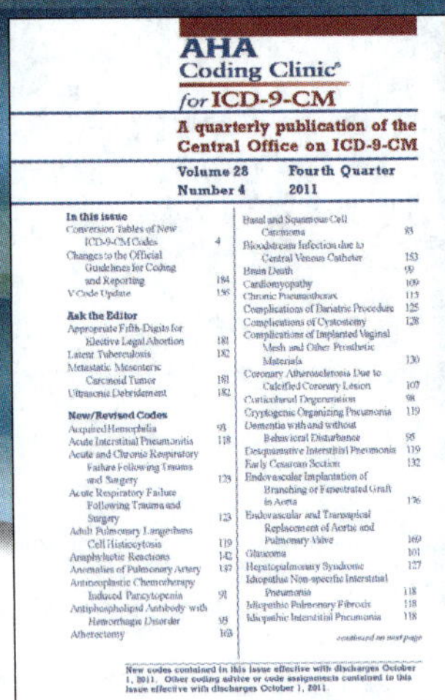

AHA Coding Clinic® for ICD-9-CM

A quarterly publication of the Central Office on ICD-9-CM

Volume 28 Number 4 — Fourth Quarter 2011

Enhance Your Coding Knowledge with AHA Coding Clinic®

AHA Coding Clinic is an essential component of your coding education and compliance program.

The only official publication for coding guidelines and advice as designated by the four Cooperating Parties (AHA, AHIMA, CMS, NCHS) and the Editorial Advisory Board (EAB) including selected questions of greatest interest to the coding community.

AHA Coding Clinic is valuable to hospitals, physician offices, ambulatory and other health care settings.

- Correct code assignments for new technologies/ newly identified diseases
- Articles and topics offering practical information to improve data quality
- Conduit for the dissemination of coding changes and/or corrections
- "Ask the Editor" section with examples from AHA Coding Clinic Advisor
- **New feature! AHA Coding Clinic for ICD-9-CM includes advice on ICD-10-CM and ICD-10-PCS**

ALSO AVAILABLE:
AHA Coding Clinic for HCPCS

AHA Coding Clinic® for HCPCS

Endoscopic Procedures

INSIDE:

Visit **www.ahaonlinestore.com** to order.

Format AND Conventions AND Current Coding Practices FOR ICD-10-CM AND ICD-10-PCS

CHAPTER 1

Background of the ICD-10-CM and ICD-10-PCS Classification

CHAPTER OVERVIEW

- ICD-10-CM and ICD-10-PCS have been developed to take the place of ICD-9-CM.
- The change to ICD-10 is needed for a variety of reasons, including the following:
  - —The ICD-9-CM classification is limited in its ability to expand to include new technology.
  - —Once a category becomes full in ICD-9-CM, several types of diagnoses or procedures have to be classified within the same code to save space.
  - —Many other countries in the world have already made the change. This situation makes it difficult to compare the health data of the United States with the rest of the world.
- Implementing ICD-10-CM and ICD-10-PCS could improve quality of care and patient safety and make the reimbursement claims process run more smoothly.
- Every application and database in which diagnosis or procedure codes are captured, stored, analyzed, or reported will use the new classification system.
- ICD-10-CM has many similarities to ICD-9-CM, especially with regard to the classification format and conventions. The code structure has changed slightly to accommodate code expansion and improvements to the classification.
- ICD-10-PCS is a replacement for volume 3 of ICD-9-CM, but it bears little resemblance to its predecessor.

LEARNING OUTCOMES

After studying this chapter you should be able to:

Explain the improvements that make the ICD-10 system more efficient and useful than the ICD-9 system.

Explain why a change to ICD-10-CM and ICD-10-PCS will be beneficial.

Make an initial comparison between the ICD-9 and ICD-10 systems.

TERMS TO KNOW

ICD-10-CM

International Classification of Diseases, Tenth Revision, Clinical Modification; consists of diagnosis codes

ICD-10-PCS

International Classification of Diseases, Tenth Revision, Procedure Coding System; consists of procedure codes

REMEMBER . . .

Coders must understand the basic principles behind the classification system in order to use ICD-10-CM and ICD-10-PCS appropriately and effectively.

INTRODUCTION

The *International Classification of Diseases, Tenth Revision, Clinical Modification* (ICD-10-CM) and the *International Classification of Diseases, Tenth Revision, Procedure Coding System* (ICD-10-PCS) have been developed as a replacement for ICD-9-CM. ICD-10-CM consists of a clinical modification of the World Health Organization's (WHO) ICD-10. ICD-10-CM consists of diagnosis codes, while ICD-10-PCS consists of procedure codes. The clinical modification expands ICD-10 codes to facilitate more precise coding of clinical diagnoses. The ICD-10-PCS is a classification of operations and procedures developed for use in the United States; it is not a part of the WHO classification.

A classification system is an arrangement of elements into groups according to established criteria. In ICD-10-CM and ICD-10-PCS these elements are diseases, injuries, surgeries, and procedures, which are grouped into appropriate chapters and sections. Three-character categories are used in ICD-10-CM, and seven-character codes are used in ICD-10-PCS. These groups are the common basis of classification for general medical statistical use. They help to answer questions about groups of related causes and provide the capacity for the systematic tabulation, storage, and retrieval of disease-related data. Each alphanumerical code represents a counting unit, with the three-character categories forming the basis for data tabulation. In ICD-10-CM many disease and injury categories have been expanded by fourth, fifth, or sixth characters that provide additional specificity but remain collapsible to the three-character category. In addition, in ICD-10-CM some categories use a seventh-character value to provide additional information regarding the encounter.

ICD-10-CM and ICD-10-PCS are closed classification systems—they provide one and only one place to classify each condition and procedure. Despite the large number of different conditions to be classified, the system must limit its size in order to be usable. Certain conditions that occur infrequently or are of low importance are often grouped together in residual codes labeled "other" or "not elsewhere classified." A final residual category is provided for diagnoses not stated specifically enough to permit more precise classification. Occasionally these two residual groups are combined in one code.

Medical coders must understand the basic principles behind the classification system in order to use ICD-10-CM and ICD-10-PCS appropriately and effectively. This knowledge is also the basis for understanding and applying the official coding advice provided through the *AHA Coding Clinic®*, published by the Central Office of the American Hospital Association. It is important for coders in all health care settings to keep current with the *ICD-10-CM and ICD-10-PCS Official Guidelines for Coding and Reporting* as well as the *Coding Clinic.* This official advice is developed through the editorial board for the *Coding Clinic* and is approved by the four cooperating parties, which include the American Hospital Association, the American Health Information Management Association, the Centers for Medicare & Medicaid Services (CMS), and the National Center for Health Statistics (NCHS). Effective with the Fourth Quarter 2012 issue, ICD-10-CM and ICD-10-PCS coding advice has been published in *Coding Clinic for ICD-9-CM. Coding Clinic for ICD-10-CM and ICD-10-PCS* is scheduled to launch in 2014.

DEVELOPMENT OF ICD-10-CM

ICD-10 was released by the WHO in 1993. In 1994 the NCHS, a federal agency under the Centers for Disease Control and Prevention, determined that a clinical modification of the ICD-10 would be a significant improvement worth implementing in the United States. It was needed to include emerging diseases and more recent medical knowledge, as well as to include new concepts and expand distinctions for ambulatory and managed care encounters. In response, the WHO authorized development of an adaptation of the ICD-10 for use in the United States. All modifications to the ICD-10 need to conform to the WHO conventions for the ICD. ICD-10 contains only diagnosis codes. ICD-10-CM was developed under the leadership of the NCHS as a replacement for volumes 1 and 2 of the ICD-9-CM (diagnosis codes).

The ICD-10-CM is in the public domain. However, neither the codes nor the code titles may be changed except through the Coordination and Maintenance Process overseen jointly by the NCHS and CMS. ICD-10-CM consists of 21 chapters resulting in nearly sixty-nine thousand codes. The classification of external causes of injury and poisoning and the classification of factors influencing health status and contact with health services are incorporated within ICD-10-CM.

DEVELOPMENT OF ICD-10-PCS

In 1992 the U.S. Health Care Financing Administration (HCFA, now CMS) funded a preliminary design project for a replacement for volume 3 of the ICD-9-CM. In 1995 HCFA awarded a three-year contract to 3M Health Information Systems (3M HIS) to complete the development of a procedure coding replacement system. The new system was called ICD-10 Procedure Coding System (ICD-10-PCS). The first year of the 3M HIS contract involved the completion of the first draft of the system. The second year was devoted to external review and limited informal testing, and the third year consisted of formal, independent review and testing. ICD-10-PCS was completed in 1998 and has been updated annually by 3M HIS since then. The goal of the revisions is to keep current with medical technology and coding needs. The four main objectives in the development of ICD-10-PCS were:

- Completeness: All substantially different procedures should have a unique code.
- Expandability: The structure of ICD-10-PCS should allow for the easy incorporation of unique codes as new procedures are developed.
- Multi-axial structure: The structure of ICD-10-PCS should be multi-axial, with each code character having the same meaning within a specific procedure section and across procedure sections, whenever possible.
- Standardized methodology: ICD-10-PCS should include unique definitions for the terms used, with each term having a specific meaning.

The guiding principles that were followed in the development of ICD-10-PCS are these:

- Diagnostic information is not included in the procedure description.
- Explicit "not otherwise specified" (NOS) options are not provided.
- "Not elsewhere classified" (NEC) options are provided on a limited basis.
- All possible procedures are defined regardless of the frequency of occurrence. If a procedure could be performed, a code was created.

The 16 sections in ICD-10-PCS represent nearly seventy-two thousand codes. ICD-10-PCS uses a table structure that permits the specification of a large number of codes on a single page in the tabular division.

RATIONALE FOR CHANGE

ICD-9-CM has been in use in the United States since 1979. Many improvements in medical practice and technology have taken place since ICD-9-CM was first implemented. Although ICD-9-CM is updated on a regular basis, the classification is limited in its ability to expand enumeration because of the physical numbering constraints contained in the current system. Some categories have vague and imprecise codes. This lack of specificity creates problems such as the inability to collect accurate data on new technology, increased requirements for submission of documentation to support claims, lack of quality data to support health outcomes, and less accurate reimbursement.

Over the years, many of the ICD-9-CM categories have become full, making it difficult to create new codes. Once a category is full, several types of similar diagnoses or procedures are combined under one code, or a place is found in another section of the classification for a new code. Due to a lack of space in the classification, several distinct procedures performed in different parts of the body, and with widely different resource utilization, may be grouped together under the same procedure code. The structural integrity of the ICD-9-CM procedure classification has already been compromised with new code numbers being assigned to "chapter 00" and "chapter 17" when new numbers were not available within the appropriate body system chapter. More importantly, many other countries have already converted to ICD-10, making it difficult to compare United States health data with international data. Thus far, 138 countries have implemented ICD-10 for mortality, and more than 100 countries have implemented it for morbidity reporting. Each country has developed its own procedure coding system.

COMPLIANCE DATE

The U.S. Department of Health and Human Services (HHS) has adopted ICD-10-CM and ICD-10-PCS as medical data code sets under the Health Insurance Portability and Accountability Act, replacing the ICD-9-CM volumes 1 and 2 code sets for reporting diagnoses and the volume 3 code set for reporting procedures—including the official coding guidelines—when conducting standard transactions. Because ICD-10-PCS codes are used only by hospitals for inpatient procedures, the ICD-10-PCS codes would not be used in outpatient transactions or by physicians.

Full compliance is required for claims submitted for encounters and discharges occurring on or after **October 1, 2014** (FY 2015). HHS believed it was in the best interests of the health care field to have a single compliance date for ICD-10-CM and ICD-10-PCS to ensure the accuracy and timeliness of claims and transaction processing. The compliance date is based on the date of discharge for inpatient claims and the date of service for outpatient claims. The date is consistent with the long-standing practice of inpatient facilities using the version of ICD codes in effect on the date of discharge. ICD-10-CM/PCS codes may not be reported before the compliance date.

A large number of provider and health plan databases and applications will be affected—every application in which diagnosis or procedure codes are captured, stored, analyzed, or reported. A successful transition to ICD-10-CM and ICD-10-PCS will require careful planning and coordination of resources. Health information coding professionals will need to become proficient in the new system. This change is welcome and long overdue because ICD-9-CM is no longer able to meet the pressing requirements for increased granularity and specificity in a hospital coding system.

EXERCISE 1.1

Without referring to the handbook material or any volume of ICD-10-CM or ICD-10-PCS, mark the following statements either true or false.

1. ICD-10-CM consists of diagnosis and procedure codes. F
2. The compliance date for ICD-10-CM and ICD-10-PCS in the United States is October 1, 2014. T
3. Three-character categories are used in ICD-10-CM, and seven-character codes are used in ICD-10-PCS. T

4. Both ICD-10-CM and ICD-10-PCS were developed by the World Health Organization. F

5. ICD-10-CM and ICD-10-PCS were developed because ICD-9-CM had become outdated and there were physical numbering constraints. T

COMPARISON OF ICD-9-CM AND ICD-10-CM

ICD-10-CM has many similarities to ICD-9-CM, especially with regard to the classification format and conventions. The code structure has changed slightly to accommodate code expansion and improvements to the classification.

Code Structure

Table 1.1 shows the major differences between the code structures of the ICD-9-CM and ICD-10-CM systems.

Figure 1.1 shows the difference in the code structure between ICD-9-CM and ICD-10-CM for the same diagnosis: closed cervical fracture.

Format

ICD-9-CM diagnoses and ICD-10-CM are divided into the Index and the Tabular List.

The Alphabetic Index is divided into two sections: the Index to Diseases and Injuries and the Index to External Causes. There is also a Neoplasm Table and a Table of Drugs and Chemicals. However, unlike ICD-9-CM, ICD-10-CM does not have a "Hypertension" Table. In general, the same indention pattern and alphabetization rules are found in both systems. A new feature in the ICD-10-CM Index not found in ICD-9-CM is the use of a dash (-) at the end of an index entry to indicate that additional characters are required.

TABLE 1.1 Major Differences between ICD-9-CM and ICD-10-CM

Feature	ICD-9-CM	ICD-10-CM
Minimum number of digits/characters	3	3
Maximum number of digits/characters	5	7
Number of chapters	17	21
Supplemental classification	V codes and E codes	No, incorporated into classification
Laterality (right vs. left)	No	Yes
Alphanumeric vs. numeric	Numeric, except for V codes and E codes	Alphanumeric, with all codes starting with an alpha character and some codes with alpha seventh-character value
Excludes notes	Yes	Exclude 1 Exclude 2
Dummy placeholders	No	Yes: "x"

FIGURE 1.1 ICD-9-CM versus ICD-10-CM Code Structure

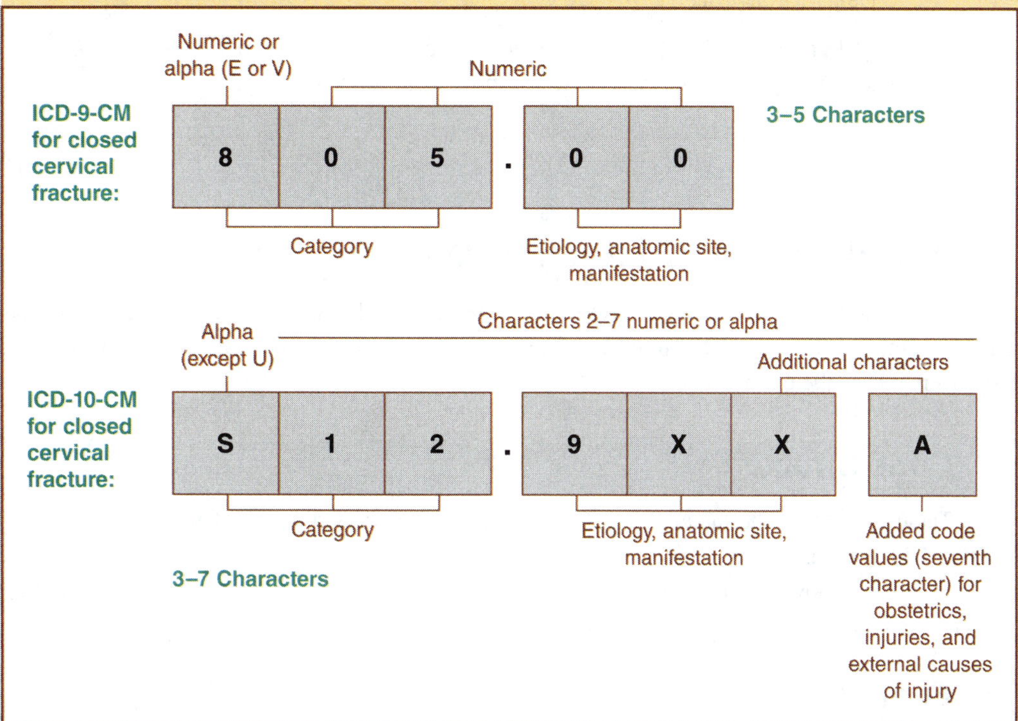

Conventions

ICD-10-CM has retained several conventions already familiar to users of ICD-9-CM, such as instructional notes, abbreviations, cross-reference notes, punctuation marks, and relational terms ("and"). One of the more significant changes for ICD-10-CM is the clarification of the exclusion notes. ICD-9-CM provides a single type of exclusion note, whereas ICD-10-CM has two types of "excludes" notes—each one with a different use. Both indicate that excluded codes are independent of each other. The ICD-10-CM conventions are covered in chapter 3 of this handbook.

Improvements and Major Modifications

ICD-10-CM includes the following improvements and major modifications to ICD-9-CM:

- Significant improvements in coding primary care encounters, external causes of injury, mental disorders, neoplasms, and preventive health
- Inclusion of codes for advances in medicine that have occurred since the last revision
- Codes with more detail on socioeconomic conditions, family relationships, ambulatory care conditions, problems related to lifestyle, and the results of screening tests
- More space to accommodate future expansions (alphanumeric structure)
- New categories for postprocedural disorders
- The addition of laterality—specifying which organ or part of the body is involved when the location could be on the right, the left, or bilateral
- Expanded distinctions for ambulatory and managed care encounters
- Expansion of diabetes and injury codes
- Creation of combination diagnosis/symptom codes to reduce the number of codes needed to fully describe a condition
- Greater specificity in code assignment
- Inclusion of trimester information in pregnancy codes

COMPARISON OF ICD-9-CM AND ICD-10-PCS

ICD-10-PCS is a replacement for volume 3 of ICD-9-CM but bears little resemblance to its predecessor. Table 1.2 shows the major differences between ICD-9-CM and ICD-10-PCS code structure and conventions.

Figure 1.2 shows the difference in the code structure between ICD-9-CM and ICD-10-PCS for the same procedure: laparoscopic cholecystectomy.

Format

ICD-9-CM volume 3 (procedures) is divided into the Index and the Tabular List. The Index and the Tabular List have a format similar to ICD-9-CM.

ICD-10-PCS is divided into three sections: Index, Tables, and List of Codes. Main term entries for procedures can be located in alphabetical order within the Index. Unlike ICD-9-CM, the ICD-10-PCS Index does not generally provide a complete code (with a few exceptions), but it will guide the coder to the correct Table by specifying the first three or four characters of the code. The ICD-10-PCS Tables are composed of grids identifying the valid combinations of characters that make up a procedure code.

TABLE 1.2 Major Differences between ICD-9-CM and ICD-10-PCS

Feature	ICD-9-CM	ICD-10-PCS
Minimum number of digits/characters	3	7
Maximum number of digits/characters	4	7
Decimal point	Yes	No
Alphanumeric or numeric	Numeric	Alphanumeric
Includes notes	Yes	No
Excludes notes	Yes	No
Embedded meaning of characters	No	Yes, multi-axial structure, with each code character having the same meaning within the specific procedure section and across procedure sections to the extent possible

FIGURE 1.2 ICD-9-CM versus ICD-10-PCS Code Structure

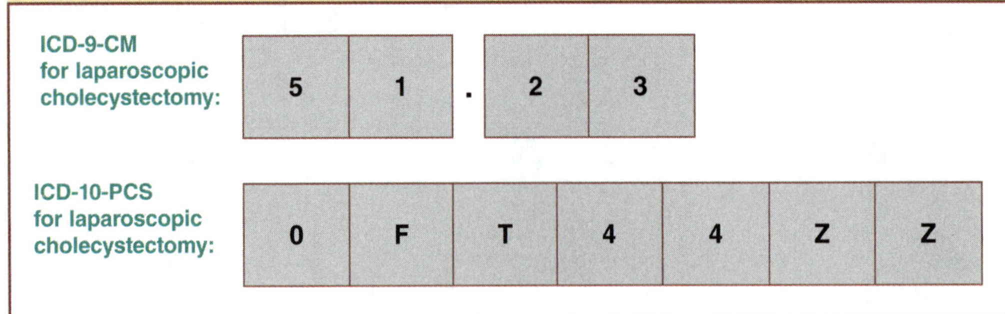

Improvements and Major Modifications

ICD-10-PCS includes the following improvements and major modifications to ICD-9-CM:

- Reflects current usage of medical terminology and devices
- Is flexible for adding new codes
- Is very specific
- Has laterality
- Provides detailed descriptions for body parts
- Provides detailed descriptions of methodology and approach for procedures
- Precisely defines procedures with detail regarding body part, approach, any device used, and qualifying information
- Gives all codes a unique definition
- Has the ability to aggregate codes across all essential components of a procedure
- Allows new procedures and technologies to be incorporated easily
- Ensures that code expansions do not disrupt the structure of the system
- Makes limited use of NOS and NEC categories
- Ensures that all terminology is precisely defined and used consistently across all codes
- Includes no diagnostic information in the code

CHAPTER 2

Introduction to the ICD-10-CM Classification

CHAPTER OVERVIEW

- ICD-10-CM is a medical diagnosis classification system.
- Volume 1 is the Tabular List of Diseases and Injuries.
    - There are three-, four-, five-, six-, and seven-character codes.
    - Codes appear in alphanumerical order.
- Volume 2 is the Alphabetic Index of Diseases and Injuries. There is a pattern to the indentions found in this volume.
    - Main terms are flush to the left-hand margin.
    - Subterms are indented. The more specific the subterm, the farther the indent.
    - Carryover lines are two indents from the indent level of the preceding line.
    - There are also strict alphabetization rules.

LEARNING OUTCOMES

After studying this chapter you should be able to:

Explain the basic principles of the medical classification system ICD-10-CM.

Demonstrate understanding of the three-, four-, five-, six-, and seven-character subdivisions.

Explain the alphabetization rules and indention patterns.

TERM TO KNOW

ICD-10-CM
International Classification of Diseases, Tenth Revision, Clinical Modification; a medical classification system used for the collection of information regarding disease and injury

INTRODUCTION

ICD-10-CM has many similarities to ICD-9-CM, especially in regard to the classification format and conventions. The code structure has changed slightly to accommodate code expansion and improvements to the classification.

FORMAT

The ICD-10-CM is divided into the Tabular List and the Alphabetic Index. The Tabular List is an alphanumerical list of codes divided into chapters based on body system or condition. The Index is an alphabetical list of terms and their corresponding code.

TABULAR LIST OF DISEASES AND INJURIES

The main classification of diseases and injuries in the Tabular List of Diseases and Injuries consists of 21 chapters. (See the table of contents reproduced in figure 2.1.) Approximately half of the chapters are devoted to conditions that affect a specific body system; the rest classify conditions according to etiology. Chapter 2, for example, classifies neoplasms of all body systems, whereas chapter 10 addresses diseases of the respiratory system only.

In addition, Z codes represent factors influencing health status and contact with health services that may be recorded as diagnoses. V, W, X, and Y codes are used to indicate the external circumstances responsible for injuries and certain other conditions. V, W, X, Y, and Z codes will be discussed briefly in chapter 12 of this handbook and in more detail in the chapters discussing the conditions to which they apply.

The variation in chapter titles in ICD-10-CM's table of contents represents the compromises made during the development of a statistical classification system based partially on etiology, partially on anatomical site, and partially on the circumstances of onset. The result is a classification system based on multiple axes. By contrast, a single-axis classification would be based entirely on the etiology of the disease, the anatomical site of the disease, or the nature of the disease process.

Codes in the Tabular List appear in alphanumerical order. References from the Alphabetic Index to the Tabular List are by code number, not by page number. Code numbers and titles appear in bold type in the Tabular List. Instructional notes that apply to the section, category, or subcategory are also included in the Tabular List.

Code Structure

All ICD-10-CM codes have an alphanumeric structure with all codes starting with an alphabetic character. The basic code structure consists of three characters. A decimal point is used to separate the basic three-character category code from its subcategory and subclassifications (for example, L98.491). Most ICD-10-CM codes contain a maximum of six characters, with a few categories having a seventh-character code value.

Each chapter in the main classification is structured to provide the following subdivisions:

- Sections (groups of three-character categories), e.g., Infections of the skin and subcutaneous tissue (L00–L08)
- Categories (three-character code numbers), e.g., L02, Cutaneous abscess, furuncle and carbuncle
- Subcategories (four-character code numbers), e.g., L02.2, Cutaneous abscess, furuncle and carbuncle of trunk
- Fifth-, sixth-, or seventh-character subclassifications (five-, six-, or seven-character code numbers), e.g., L02.211, Cutaneous abscess of abdominal wall

FIGURE 2.1 Table of Contents from ICD-10-CM

The ICD-10-CM Tabular List contains categories, subcategories, and codes. The basic code used to classify a particular disease or injury consists of three characters and is called a category (e.g., K29, Gastritis and duodenitis). Characters for categories, subcategories, and codes may be either a letter or a number. All categories are three characters. A three-character category that has no further subdivision is equivalent to a code. Subcategories are either four or five characters. Codes may be three, four, five, six, or seven characters. That is, each level of subdivision after a category is a subcategory. The final level of subdivision is a code.

Codes that have applicable seventh characters are still referred to as codes, not subcategories. A code that has an applicable seventh character is considered invalid without the seventh character.

For example:

- K29 Gastritis and duodenitis *(category)*
  - K29.0 Acute gastritis *(subcategory)*
    - K29.00 Acute gastritis without bleeding *(code)*
- R10 Abdominal and pelvic pain *(category)*
  - R10.8 Other abdominal pain *(subcategory)*
    - R10.81 Abdominal tenderness *(subcategory)*
      - R10.811 Right upper quadrant abdominal tenderness *(code)*

Placeholder Character

ICD-10-CM uses the letter "x" as a placeholder character at certain codes to allow for future expansion. An example of this may be seen at the poisoning, adverse effect, underdosing (T36–T50), and toxic effects (T51–T65) codes. For these categories, the sixth character represents the intent: accidental, intentional self-harm, assault, undetermined, adverse effect, or underdosing. Where a placeholder exists, the "x" must be used in order for the code to be considered valid.

For example, where the sixth character of "1" represents accidental, and "2" represents intentional self-harm:

T37.5x1 Poisoning by antiviral drugs, accidental (unintentional)
T37.5x2 Poisoning by antiviral drugs, intentional self-harm
T52.0x1 Toxic effect of petroleum products, accidental (unintentional)
T52.0x2 Toxic effect of petroleum products, intentional self-harm

Certain categories have an additional seventh-character value. The applicable seventh-character value is required for all codes within the category, or as the notes in the Tabular List instruct. The seventh character must always be the seventh character in the code. If a code is not a full six characters, a placeholder character "x" must be used to fill in the empty characters when a seventh-character value is required. Seventh-character values can be seen in chapter 19 of ICD-10-CM, Injury, Poisoning and Certain Other Consequences of External Causes (S00–T88).

An example of the use of the placeholder character "x" and the seventh-character value is shown here with an excerpt from the Tabular List:

T16 Foreign body in ear
Includes: foreign body in auditory canal

The appropriate 7th character values are to be added to each code from category T16:

A initial encounter
D subsequent encounter
S sequela

T16.1 Foreign body in right ear
T16.2 Foreign body in left ear
T16.9 Foreign body in ear, unspecified ear

A child presents to the emergency department with a bean in the right ear. The mother has brought the child because she was not able to remove the bean at home. This encounter would be assigned code T16.1xxA. The Tabular List shows subcategory T16.1 as the descriptor best fitting this scenario. Category T16 requires a seventh-character value. Because the code subcategory has only four characters (T16.1), the placeholder "x" is inserted twice to preserve the code structure before the seventh character "A" is added to report this as the initial encounter.

ALPHABETIC INDEX

The Alphabetic Index consists of the Index of Diseases and Injuries, the Index to External Causes, the Neoplasm Table, and the Table of Drugs and Chemicals.

The Alphabetic Index includes entries for main terms, subterms, and more specific subterms. An indented format is used for ease of reference.

Main terms identify disease conditions or injuries. Subterms indicate site, type, or etiology for conditions or injuries. For example, acute appendicitis is listed under **Appendicitis,** acute, and stress fracture is listed under **Fracture, traumatic,** stress. Occasionally, it is necessary for the coder to think of a synonym or another alternative term in order to locate the correct entry. There are, however, exceptions to this general rule, including the following:

- Congenital conditions are often indexed under the main term **Anomaly** rather than under the name of the condition.
- Conditions that complicate pregnancy, childbirth, or the puerperium are usually found under such terms as **Delivery, Pregnancy,** and **Puerperal.** They may also appear under the main term for the condition causing the complication by referencing the subterm "complicating pregnancy." (An example of this type of entry appears under the main term **Hypertension** in the Alphabetic Index.)
- Many of the complications of medical or surgical care are indexed under the term **Complications** rather than under the name of the condition.
- Late effects of an earlier condition can be found under **Sequelae,** or under the condition (as in the case of traumatic injuries).

A clear understanding of the format of the Alphabetic Index is a prerequisite for accurate coding. Understanding the indention pattern of the entries is a very important part of learning how to use the Index. A variety of vendors provide printed versions and others have computer programs

for coding, but the format may not be consistent across versions. The draft version of the Index represents each indention level by a hyphen. In general, however, the following pattern is anticipated:

- Main terms are set flush with the left-hand margin. They are printed in bold type and begin with a capital letter.
- Subterms are indented one standard indention (equivalent to about two typewriter spaces) to the right under the main term. They are printed in regular type and begin with a lowercase letter.
- More specific subterms are indented farther and farther to the right as needed, always indented by one standard indention from the preceding subterm and listed in alphabetical order.
- A dash (-) at the end of an index entry indicates that additional characters are required.

Carryover lines are indented two standard indentions from the level of the preceding line. Carryover lines are used only when the complete entry cannot fit on a single line. They are indented farther to avoid confusion with subterm entries.

In printed versions, entries will most likely use two, three, or four columns to a page, dictionary style.

The subterms listed under the main term **Metrorrhagia** in the following entry provide an example:

Metrorrhagia N92.1	[main term]
climacteric N92.4	[subterm]
menopausal N92.4	[subterm]
postpartum NEC (atonic) (following delivery	[subterm]
of placenta) O72.1	[carryover line]
delayed or secondary O72.2	[more specific subterm]
preclimacteric or premenopausal N92.4	[subterm]
psychogenic F45.8	[subterm]

Each of the subterms (climacteric, menopausal, postpartum, preclimacteric, and psychogenic) is indented one standard indention from the level of the main term and is listed in alphabetical order. The fifth line is a carryover line two standard indentions from the preceding line. The sixth line is a more specific entry ("delayed or secondary" under the subterm "postpartum").

EXERCISE 2.1

A reproduction of a page from the Alphabetic Index is shown below. Label the numbered lines as either main terms, subterms, or carryover lines. Each hyphen is meant to represent one level of indention.

1.	**Railroad neurosis** F48.8	Main term
2.	**Railway spine** F48.8	Main term
	Raised—see also Elevated	
3.	--antibody titer R76.0	Carryover line
	Rake teeth, tooth M26.39	
	Rales R09.89	
4.	**Ramifying renal pelvis** Q63.8	Main term
	Ramsay-Hunt disease or syndrome—(see also	
5.	--Hunt's disease) B02.21	Carryover line
6.	-meaning dyssynergia cerebellaris myoclonica G11.1	Subterm
	Ranula K11.6	
	-congenital Q38.4	
7.	**Rape**	Main term
8.	-adult	Subterm
	--confirmed T74.21	
	--suspected T76.21	
	-alleged, observation or examination ruled	
	--out	
9.	--adult Z04.41	Subterm
	--child Z04.42	
10.	-child	Subterm
	--confirmed T74.22	
	--suspected T76.22	

Alphabetization Rules

In order to locate main terms and subterms quickly and efficiently, it is important to understand the alphabetization rules followed in the Alphabetic Index. Letter-by-letter alphabetization is used. The system of alphabetization ignores the following:

- Single spaces between words
- Single hyphens within words
- The final "s" in the possessive forms of words

The following list shows an example of letter-by-letter alphabetization with these modifications:

Beckwith-Wiedemann syndrome Q87.3	[ignores hyphen]
Beer drinker's heart (disease) I42.6	[ignores space between words]
Blood-forming organs, disease D75.9	[ignores hyphen]
Bloodgood's disease—see **Mastopathy**, cystic	[ignores possessive form]

Numerical Entries

Subterm entries for numerical characters and words indicating numbers appear first under the appropriate main term or subterm. These are listed in alphabetical order when listed in their spelled-out form. For example, **Paralysis,** nerve, fourth, comes before, rather than after, **Paralysis,** nerve, third.

However, when Roman numerals (such as "II") and Arabic numerals (such as "2") are used, they are listed in numerical order. For example (each hyphen below represents one level of indention):

Deficiency . . .
factor
--I (congenital) (hereditary) D68.2
--II (congenital) (hereditary) D68.2
--IX (congenital) (functional) (hereditary) (with functional defect) D67
--multiple (congenital) D68.8
---acquired D68.4
--V (congenital) (hereditary) D68.2
--VII (congenital) (hereditary) D68.2
--VIII (congenital) (functional) (hereditary) (with functional defect) D66
---with vascular defect D68.0
--X (congenital) (hereditary) D68.2
--XI (congenital) (hereditary) D68.1
--XII (congenital) (hereditary) D68.2
--XIII (congenital) (hereditary) D68.2

Connecting Words

Words such as "with," "in," "due to," and "associated with" are used to express the relationship between the main term or a subterm indicating an associated condition or etiology. Subterms preceded by "with" or "without" are not listed in alphabetical order but appear immediately below

the main term or appropriate subterm entries; subterms beginning with other connecting words appear in alphabetical order. Coders who fail to remember this feature of the alphabetization rules often make coding errors by overlooking the appropriate subterm. Review the following subterm entries under the main term **Bronchitis** using the instructions at the end of this example. Note that each hyphen represents one level of indention:

	Bronchitis (diffuse) (fibrinous) (hypostatic) (infective) (membranous) J40
1	-with --influenza, flu or grippe—see Influenza, with respiratory manifestations NEC
2	--obstruction (airway) (lung) J44.9
3	--tracheitis (15 years of age and above) J40 ---acute or subacute J20.9 ---chronic J42 ---under 15 years of age J20.9
4	-acute or subacute (with bronchospasm or obstruction) J20.9
5	--with ---bronchiectasis J47.0 ---chronic obstructive pulmonary disease J44.0
6	--chemical (due to gases, fumes or vapors) J68.0
7	--due to ---fumes or vapors J68.0 ---*Haemophilus influenzae* J20.1 ---*Mycoplasma pneumoniae* J20.0 ---radiation J70.0 ---specified organism NEC J20.8 ---Streptococcus J20.2 ---virus ----coxsackie J20.3 ----echovirus J20.7 ----parainfluenzae J20.4 ----respiratory syncytial J20.5 ----rhinovirus J20.6 --viral NEC J20.8
8	-allergic (acute) J45.909
9	--with ---exacerbation (acute) J45.901 ---status asthmaticus J45.902
10	-arachidic T17.528

Refer to sections 1, 4, 8, and 10 as indicated in the example. Note that the subterms preceded by the connecting word "with" immediately follow the main term **Bronchitis** and precede the subterms beginning with the letter "a" (sections 4, 8, and 10).

Refer to sections 5, 6, and 7 as indicated in the example. Note that the more specific subterms preceded by the connecting word "with" immediately follow the subterm "acute or subacute." In this case, the subterms beginning with the word "with" precede the subterms beginning with the letters "c" and "d" (sections 6 and 7).

Also note that the subterms indented under the connecting word "with" are listed in alphabetical order. For example, sections 1, 2, and 3 indicated in the example are in alphabetical order.

Index Tables

The main body of the Alphabetic Index uses a table for the systematic arrangement of subterms under the main entry **Neoplasm.** This table simplifies access to complex combinations of subterms. The use of this table will be discussed in the Neoplasm chapter. The Table of Drugs and Chemicals will be discussed later in this handbook in the chapter on poisoning and adverse effects of drugs.

The format and alphabetization rules used within the tables are the same as those followed in the rest of the Alphabetic Index. The use of these two tables will be discussed in detail later in this handbook, but it would be useful for the reader to become familiar with the location and format of the tables at this point of the discussion.

CHAPTER 3 ICD-10-CM Conventions

CHAPTER OVERVIEW

- A variety of notes appear in ICD-10-CM.
  - *General notes* commonly provide general information on usage in a specific section.
  - *Inclusion notes* and *exclusion notes* indicate when certain conditions are or are not included in a subdivision.
  - Additional instructional notes direct the coder to create a complete statement on the condition.
- Two main abbreviations (NEC and NOS) are used in ICD-10-CM.
- Cross-reference notes advise the coder to look elsewhere before assigning a code.
- Punctuation marks and relational terms have a specialized meaning in ICD-10-CM.

LEARNING OUTCOMES

After studying this chapter you should be able to:

List the different types of instructional notes.

Explain the importance of additional notes to the coding process.

Describe the difference between the abbreviations NEC and NOS.

Use your knowledge of cross-reference notes to navigate ICD-10-CM.

Define the specialized meanings of punctuation marks and relational terms in ICD-10-CM.

TERMS TO KNOW

NEC
not elsewhere classified; used in the Alphabetic Index to indicate that there is no separate code for the condition even though the diagnostic statement is specific

NOS
not otherwise specified; equivalent to the term "unspecified"

REMEMBER . . .

These conventions aren't just helpful; they're necessary to successful coding.

INTRODUCTION

ICD-10-CM follows certain conventions in order to provide large amounts of information in a succinct and consistent manner. A thorough understanding of these conventions is fundamental to accurate coding. The conventions and instructions of the classification are applicable to all health care settings, unless otherwise indicated.

ICD-10-CM conventions include the following:

- Instructional notes
- Abbreviations
- Cross-reference notes
- Punctuation marks
- Relational terms ("and," "with," "without," "due to")

INSTRUCTIONAL NOTES

A variety of notes appear as instructions to the coder. These include general notes, inclusion and exclusion notes, "code first" notes, "use additional code" notes, and "code also" notes.

General Notes

General notes in the Tabular List of Diseases and Injuries provide general information on usage in a specific section, such as the note under chapter 15 of ICD-10-CM, Pregnancy, Childbirth and the Puerperium, that explains that codes from this chapter are for use only on maternal records, never on newborn records.

Inclusion and Exclusion Notes

Codes in a classification system must be mutually exclusive, with no overlapping of content. In ICD-10-CM, therefore, it is sometimes necessary to indicate when certain conditions are or are not included in a given subdivision. This is accomplished by means of inclusion and exclusion notes.

The location of inclusion and exclusion notes is extremely important. When this type of note is located at the beginning of a chapter or a section in ICD-10-CM, that advice applies to all codes within the chapter or section and is not repeated with individual categories or specific codes. The coder must keep in mind that instructional notes affecting the code under consideration may be located on a previous page.

Inclusion Notes

Inclusion notes are introduced by the word "includes" when placed at the beginning of a chapter or section. Inclusion notes are used to further define, or give examples of, the content of the chapter, section, or category. Conditions listed in an inclusion note may be synonyms or conditions similar enough to be classified to the same code. Inclusion notes are not exhaustive; rather, they list certain conditions to reassure the coder, particularly when the title in the Tabular List may not seem to apply.

An example of an inclusion note can be found in the Tabular List, chapter 1, Certain Infectious and Parasitic diseases (A00–B99). The inclusion note states that this chapter includes diseases generally recognized as communicable or transmissible. This note applies to all codes listed from A00 through B99.

Inclusion notes may also appear immediately under a three-character code title to further define, or give examples of, the content of the category. An example of this type of inclusion note can be found in the Tabular List at category D50, Iron deficiency anemia. The inclusion note states that codes in this category include asiderotic anemia and hypochromic anemia.

Inclusion Terms

Lists of terms are included under some codes. The terms are some of the conditions that may be reported with those codes. The terms may represent terms synonymous to the code title. In the case of "other specified codes," the terms may be a list of the various conditions that are assigned to that code. As in the case of the inclusion notes, the list of inclusion terms is not meant to be exhaustive. The Index may also list additional terms classified to a code and not repeated as inclusion terms.

Exclusion Notes

Exclusion notes are introduced by the word "excludes." Excluded conditions are listed in alphabetical order, with the code number or code range shown in parentheses. Exclusion notes are the opposite of inclusion notes; they indicate that a particular condition is not assigned to the code to which the note applies. The basic message of an excludes note is "code this condition elsewhere."

There are two types of exclusion notes in ICD-10-CM—each has a different use, but both indicate that codes excluded are independent of each other.

"Excludes1"

An "excludes1" note means "NOT CODED HERE!" An "excludes1" note instructs that the code excluded should never be used at the same time as the code above the "excludes1" note. This instruction is used when two conditions cannot occur together and therefore both codes cannot be used together. For example:

Q03 Congenital hydrocephalus
Excludes1: acquired hydrocephalus (G91.-)

In this example, the congenital form of the condition cannot be reported with the acquired form of the same condition.

"Excludes2"

An "excludes2" note means "NOT INCLUDED HERE!" An "excludes2" note instructs that the condition excluded is not part of the condition represented by the code. However, a patient may have both conditions at the same time. When an "excludes2" note appears under a code, it is acceptable to use both the code and the excluded code together. For example:

F90 Attention-deficit hyperactivity disorders
Excludes2: anxiety disorders (F40.-, F41.-)
mood [affective] disorders (F30–F39)

In this example, the "excludes2" note serves as a warning that if a patient has an anxiety disorder, rather than attention-deficit hyperactivity disorder, the user should go to categories F40–F41 rather than remain in category F90. However, if a patient has both attention-deficit hyperactivity and an anxiety disorder, a code from category F90 could be used along with a code from categories F40–F41.

"Code First" and "Use Additional Code"

Certain conditions have both an underlying etiology and multiple body system manifestations due to the underlying etiology. In the Tabular List, "code first" and "use additional code" instructional notes indicate the proper sequencing order of these conditions—etiology (underlying condition) followed by manifestation. The "use additional code" note is found at the etiology code as a clue to identify the manifestations commonly associated with the disease. The "code first" note is found at the manifestation code to provide instructions that the underlying condition should be sequenced first.

The manifestation codes usually have the phrase "in diseases classified elsewhere" as part of the code title. Codes with this phrase are never used as a first-listed or principal diagnosis code. For such codes, a "use additional code" note appears at the etiology code, and a "code first" note appears at the manifestation code. An example of this convention is category F02, Dementia in other diseases classified elsewhere.

Other notes of this type provide a list introduced by the phrase "such as," meaning that any of the listed codes or any other appropriate code can be assigned first. Code **J99, Respiratory disorders in diseases classified elsewhere,** provides a list of conditions that may be the underlying disease.

It is not necessary to report the code identified in a "use additional code" note in the diagnosis field immediately following the primary code. There is no strict hierarchy inherent in the guidelines, nor in the ICD-10-CM classification, regarding the sequencing of secondary diagnosis codes.

"Code Also"

"Code also" notes in ICD-10-CM indicate that two codes may be required to fully describe a condition. The sequencing order will depend on the reason for the encounter and the severity of the conditions. An example of this note can be found under code **G47.01, Insomnia due to medical condition,** where the instructional note tells us to code also the associated medical condition.

ABBREVIATIONS

ICD-10-CM uses two main abbreviations:

- NEC, for not elsewhere classified
- NOS, for not otherwise specified

Although their meanings appear simple, these abbreviations are often misunderstood and misapplied by coders. It is very important to understand not only their meanings but also their differences, because they provide guidelines for correct code selection.

NEC

The abbreviation NEC is used in the Alphabetic Index and the Tabular List to indicate that there is no separate code for the condition even though the diagnostic statement may be very specific. It is used when the information in the medical record provides detail for which a specific code does not exist. It represents "other specified." In the Tabular List, such conditions are ordinarily classified to a code with a fourth or sixth character "8" (or a fifth character "9") with a title that includes the words "other specified" or "not elsewhere classified," which permits the grouping of related conditions to conserve space and limit the size of the classification system. For example, a disease of the pleura specified as hydropneumothorax is included in code **J94.8, Other specified pleural conditions.**

NOS

The abbreviation NOS is the equivalent of "unspecified" and is used in the Alphabetic Index and the Tabular List. Codes so identified are to be used only when neither the diagnostic statement nor the medical record provides information that permits classification to a more specific code. The codes in these cases are ordinarily classified to codes with a fourth or sixth character "9" and fifth character "0"; conditions listed as both "not elsewhere classified" and "unspecified" are sometimes combined in one code. Note that a main term followed by a list of subterms in the Alphabetic Index usually displays the unspecified code; the subterms must always be reviewed to determine whether a more specific code can be assigned.

For example, the main term **Cardiomyopathy** displays code I42.9. Subterms such as "alcoholic" or "congestive" are provided for more specific cardiomyopathies. Code I42.9 should be assigned only when there is no information in the medical record to identify one of these subterms.

CROSS-REFERENCE NOTES

Cross-reference notes are used in the Alphabetic Index to advise the coder to look elsewhere before assigning a code. The cross-reference instructions include "see," "see also," "see category," and "see condition."

"See"

The "see" cross-reference indicates that the coder must refer to an alternative term. This instruction is mandatory; coding cannot be completed without following this advice. For example, the entry for **Hemarthrosis,** traumatic, uses this cross-reference to advise the coder to reference the entry for "sprain" by site.

"See Also"

The "see also" cross-reference advises the coder that there is another place in the Alphabetic Index to which the coder must refer when the entries under consideration do not provide a code for the specific condition or procedure. It is not necessary to follow this cross-reference when the original entries provide all the information necessary.

For example, the cross-reference for the term **Psychoneurosis** advises the coder to "see also Neurosis" when none of the specific subterms provides a code. If a coder is attempting to locate the code for neurasthenic psychoneurosis, it would not be necessary to follow this cross-reference because there is a subterm "neurasthenic" under the term **Psychoneurosis.** If the diagnosis were psychasthenic psychoneurosis, however, the code could be located only by following the "see also" reference.

"See Category"

The "see category" variation of the "see" cross-reference provides the coder with a category number. The coder must refer to that number in the Tabular List and select a code from the options provided there. For example, a cross-reference under the index entry for **TBI** (traumatic brain injury) refers the coder to category S06.

"See Condition"

Occasionally, the Index advises the coder to refer to the main term of a condition. For example, if a coder references the main term **Arterial** for arterial thrombosis, the Index advice is to "see condition," and the coder should then go to the main term **Thrombosis.** This cross-reference ordinarily appears when the coder has referenced the adjective rather than the term (in noun form) for the condition itself.

PUNCTUATION MARKS

Several punctuation marks are used in ICD-10-CM, most of which have a specialized meaning in addition to the usual English language usage.

Parentheses

Parentheses are used in ICD-10-CM to enclose supplementary words or explanatory information that may be either present or absent in the statement of diagnosis without affecting the code to which it is assigned. Such terms are considered to be "nonessential modifiers" and are used to suggest that the terms in parentheses are included in the code but need not be stated in the diagnosis. This is a significant factor in correct code assignment. Terms enclosed in parentheses in either the Tabular List or the Alphabetic Index do not affect the code assignment in any way; they serve only as reassurance that the correct code has been located.

For example, refer to the main term **Pneumonia,** which has several nonessential modifiers enclosed in parentheses. Unless a more specific subterm is located, this code will be assigned for pneumonia described by any of the terms in parentheses. Diagnoses of acute pneumonia and purulent pneumonia, for example, are both coded J18.9 because both terms appear in parentheses as nonessential modifiers. Pneumonia not otherwise specified is also assigned to code J18.9 because none of the terms in parentheses is required for this code assignment.

It is important to distinguish between the use of nonessential and essential modifiers. Essential modifiers are listed as subterms in the Alphabetic Index, not in parentheses, and they do affect code assignment. In contrast, words in parentheses are nonessential and do not affect the code assignment. For example, scoliosis described as acquired or postural is classified as M41.9, as the words "acquired" and "postural" are nonessential modifiers and do not affect the code; on the other hand, the term "congenital" is an essential modifier, and the code for this term is Q67.5.

The nonessential modifiers in the Index to Diseases apply to subterms following a main term, except when a nonessential modifier and a subentry are mutually exclusive, in which case the subentry takes precedence. For example, in ICD-10-CM's Alphabetic Index under the main term **Enteritis,** "acute" is a nonessential modifier, and "chronic" is a subentry. In this case, the nonessential modifier "acute" does not apply to the subentry "chronic."

EXERCISE 3.1

Referring only to the title and inclusion notes for code J40, mark an "X" next to each of the diagnostic statements listed below that is included in code J40.

1. Catarrhal bronchitis X
2. Chronic bronchitis ____
3. Allergic bronchitis ____
4. Tracheobronchitis NOS X
5. Asthmatic bronchitis ____

Square Brackets

Square brackets are often used in the Tabular List to enclose synonyms, alternative wordings, abbreviations, and explanatory phrases that provide additional information—for example, human immunodeficiency virus [HIV]. They are similar to parentheses in that they are not required for the statement of diagnosis. Square brackets are also used to indicate that the number in the bracket can only be a manifestation and the other number must be assigned first for the underlying code. The code in the brackets in this situation indicates that both conditions must be used, and the code in the brackets can never be assigned as the principal diagnosis. In the following example from the Alphabetic Index, the first code represents an underlying disease, and the second code enclosed in brackets represents a manifestation:

Nephropathy . . .
  sickle cell D57.- [N08]

Colons

Colons are used in the Tabular List in both inclusion notes and exclusion notes after an incomplete term that needs one or more of the modifiers following the colon in order for the term to apply. The exclusion statement under code N92.6 in the Tabular List is an example of this usage. Here, the colon following the subterms "irregular menstruation with" indicates that if it is described as irregular menstruation with lengthened intervals or scanty bleeding, or irregular menstruation with shortened intervals or excessive bleeding, code N92.6 is excluded.

N92.6 Irregular menstruation, unspecified
Irregular bleeding NOS
Irregular periods NOS
Excludes1: irregular menstruation with:
  lengthened intervals or scanty bleeding (N91.3–N91.5)
  shortened intervals or excessive bleeding (N92.1)

EXERCISE 3.2

Referring only to the title and inclusion notes provided for the four-character code D04.5, mark an "X" next to each diagnosis listed below that is included in code D04.5.

1. Carcinoma in situ of anal margin	X
2. Carcinoma in situ of perianal skin	X
3. Carcinoma in situ of skin of breast	X
4. Carcinoma in situ of breast	
5. Carcinoma in situ of anal skin	X

RELATIONAL TERMS

"And"

The word "and" should be interpreted to mean either "and" or "or" when it appears in a code title. For example, cases of "tuberculosis of bones," "tuberculosis of joints," and "tuberculosis of bones and joints" are classified to subcategory A18.0, Tuberculosis of bones and joints.

"With"

The word "with" should be interpreted to mean "associated with" or "due to" when it appears in a code title, the Alphabetic Index, or an instructional note in the Tabular List. The word "with" in the Alphabetic Index is sequenced immediately following the main term, not in alphabetical order.

"Due To"

The words "due to" in either the Alphabetic Index or the Tabular List indicate that a causal relationship between two conditions is present. ICD-10-CM occasionally makes such an assumption when both conditions are present. In other combinations, however, the diagnostic statement must indicate this relationship. For example, certain conditions affecting the mitral valve are assumed to be rheumatic in origin, regardless of whether or not the diagnostic statement makes this distinction. In other cases, the Alphabetic Index provides a subterm "due to," which must be followed when the physician's statement indicates a causal relationship. The coder should be guided by the Index entry.

CHAPTER 4

Uniform Hospital Discharge Data Set

CHAPTER OVERVIEW

- The Uniform Hospital Discharge Data Set (UHDDS) is used for reporting inpatient data.
- The following items are always found in the UHDDS:
  - — General demographic information
  - — Expected payer
  - — Hospital identification
  - — Principal diagnosis
  - — Other diagnoses that have specific significance
  - — All significant procedures
- The rules for identifying the first-listed diagnosis for an outpatient encounter differ from those for selecting the principal diagnosis for an inpatient encounter.
- Following all the coding guidelines will ensure accurate and ethical coding.

LEARNING OUTCOMES

After studying this chapter you should be able to:

- Correctly identify a principal diagnosis.
- Understand the guidelines for assigning a principal diagnosis.
- Understand when other diagnoses have significance and should be reported.
- Explain the difference between a principal diagnosis and an admitting diagnosis.
- Explain the importance of accurate and ethical coding.

TERMS TO KNOW

MS-DRG system
Medicare severity-adjusted diagnosis-related groups system; a patient classification system used in hospital inpatient reimbursement

Other reportable diagnoses
conditions that coexist at the time of admission, develop subsequently, or affect patient care during the hospital stay

Principal diagnosis
the condition established after study that is chiefly responsible for admission of the patient to the hospital

UHDDS
Uniform Hospital Discharge Data Set; information used for reporting inpatient data

REMEMBER . . .

The admitting diagnosis is not an element of the UHDDS.

. . . Diagnoses that have no impact on patient care or that are related to an earlier episode are not reported on the UHDDS.

INTRODUCTION

The Uniform Hospital Discharge Data Set (UHDDS) is used for reporting inpatient data in acute care, short-term care, and long-term care hospitals. It uses a minimum set of items based on standard definitions that could provide consistent data for multiple users. Only those items that met the following criteria were included:

- Easily identified
- Readily defined
- Uniformly recorded
- Easily abstracted from the medical record

Its use is required for claims reporting for Medicare and Medicaid patients. In addition, many other health care payers use most of the UHDDS as a uniform billing system.

DATA ITEMS

The UHDDS requires the following items:

- Principal diagnosis
- Other diagnoses that have significance for the specific hospital episode
- All significant procedures

The four cooperating parties responsible for developing and maintaining ICD-10-CM (American Hospital Association, American Health Information Management Association, Centers for Medicare & Medicaid Services, and National Center for Health Statistics) have developed official guidelines for designating the principal diagnosis and for identifying other diagnoses that should be reported in certain situations. The UHDDS also contains a core of general information that pertains to the patient and to the specific episode of care, such as the age, sex, and race of the patient; the expected payer; and the hospital's identification.

The UHDDS definitions were originally developed in 1985 for hospital reporting of inpatient data elements. Since that time, the application of UHDDS definitions has been expanded to include all nonoutpatient settings. In addition to their application to acute care, short-term care, and long-term care hospitals, the definitions for principal diagnosis and other (secondary) diagnoses also apply to psychiatric hospitals, home health agencies, rehabilitation facilities, nursing homes, and other settings. Guidelines for selection of principal diagnosis and other diagnoses discussed below apply to all these settings.

Principal Diagnosis

The principal diagnosis is defined as the condition established after study to be chiefly responsible for admission of the patient to the hospital for care. It is important that the principal diagnosis be designated correctly because its establishment is significant in cost comparisons, in care analysis, and in utilization review. It is crucial for reimbursement because many third-party payers (including Medicare) base reimbursement primarily on principal diagnosis. The principal diagnosis is ordinarily listed first in the physician's diagnostic statement, but not always; the coder must review the entire medical record to determine the condition that should be designated as the principal diagnosis.

The words "after study" in the definition of principal diagnosis are important, but their meaning is sometimes confusing. It is not the admitting diagnosis but rather the diagnosis found after workup or even after surgery that proves to be the reason for admission. For example:

- A patient admitted with urinary retention may prove to have hypertrophy of the prostate, which is causing the urinary retention. In this case, the prostatic hypertrophy is the principal diagnosis unless treatment was directed only to the urinary retention.
- A patient may be admitted because of unstable angina, and a percutaneous transluminal angioplasty may be carried out to clear arteriosclerotic blockage of the coronary artery in order to abort what appears to be an impending myocardial infarction. In this case, the coronary arteriosclerosis is the principal diagnosis because, after study, it was determined to be the underlying cause of the angina and the reason for admission.
- A patient is admitted with severe abdominal pain. The white blood cell count is elevated to 16,000, with shift to the left. The patient is taken to surgery, where an acute ruptured appendix is removed. After study, the principal diagnosis is determined to be acute ruptured appendicitis.
- A patient is admitted with severe abdominal pain in the right lower quadrant, and an admitting diagnosis of probable acute appendicitis is given. The white blood cell count is slightly elevated. The patient is taken to surgery, where a normal appendix is found but an inflamed Meckel's diverticulum is removed. After study, the principal diagnosis is determined to be Meckel's diverticulum.

The circumstances of inpatient admission always govern the selection of the principal diagnosis, and the coding directives in the ICD-10-CM classification take precedence over all other guidelines. The importance of consistent, complete documentation in the medical record cannot be overemphasized. Without such documentation, the application of all coding guidelines is a difficult, if not impossible, task.

There are special instructions related to the selection of principal diagnosis when a patient is admitted as an inpatient from the hospital's observation unit or from outpatient surgery. This coding advice applies if a single bill is submitted to a payer. If separate inpatient and outpatient bills are submitted, then the advice does not apply. Hospitals should apply codes for the current encounter based on individual payer billing instructions.

For example:

- *Admission following medical observation:* A patient may be treated in a hospital's observation unit to determine whether the condition improves sufficiently for the patient to be discharged. If the condition either worsens or does not improve, the physician may decide to admit the patient as an inpatient of the same hospital for this same medical condition. The principal diagnosis reported is the medical condition that led to the hospital admission.
- *Admission following postoperative observation:* A patient undergoing outpatient surgery may require postoperative admission to an observation unit to monitor a condition (or complication) that develops postoperatively. If the patient subsequently requires inpatient admission to the same hospital, the UHDDS definition of principal diagnosis applies: "that condition established after study to be chiefly responsible for occasioning the admission of the patient to the hospital for care."
- *Admission from outpatient surgery:* A patient undergoing outpatient surgery may be subsequently admitted for continuing inpatient care at the same hospital. The following guidelines should be followed in selecting the principal diagnosis for the inpatient admission:
  —If the reason for the inpatient admission is a complication, assign the complication as the principal diagnosis.
  —If no complication or other condition is documented as the reason for the inpatient admission, assign the reason for the outpatient surgery as the principal diagnosis.
  —If the reason for the inpatient admission is another condition unrelated to the surgery, assign the unrelated condition as the principal diagnosis.

The following official guidelines for designating the principal diagnosis apply to all systems and etiologies. (Guidelines that apply only to specific body systems or etiologies are discussed in the relevant chapters of this handbook. To download a copy of the current version of the complete *ICD-10-CM Official Guidelines for Coding and Reporting,* please visit www.ahacentraloffice.org.)

1. *Two or more diagnoses that equally meet the definition for principal diagnosis:* In the unusual situation that two or more diagnoses equally meet the criteria for principal diagnosis as determined by the circumstances of the admission and the diagnostic workup and/or therapy provided, either may be sequenced first when neither the Alphabetic Index nor the Tabular List directs otherwise. However, it is not simply the fact that both conditions exist that makes this choice possible. When treatment is totally or primarily directed toward one condition, or when only one condition would have required inpatient care, that condition should be designated as the principal diagnosis. Also, if another coding guideline (general or disease specific) provides sequencing direction, that guideline must be followed.

   Example 1: A patient is admitted with unstable angina and acute congestive heart failure. The unstable angina is treated with nitrates, and intravenous Lasix is given to manage the heart failure. Both diagnoses meet the definition of principal diagnosis equally, and either may be sequenced first.

   Example 2: A patient is admitted with acute atrial fibrillation with rapid ventricular response and is also in heart failure with pulmonary edema. The patient is digitalized to reduce the ventricular rate and given intravenous Lasix to reduce the cardiogenic pulmonary edema. Both conditions meet the definition of principal diagnosis equally, and either may be sequenced first.

   Example 3: A patient is admitted with severe abdominal pain, nausea, and vomiting due to acute pyelonephritis and diverticulitis. Both underlying conditions are treated, and the physician believes both equally meet the criteria for principal diagnosis. In this instance, either condition may be listed as principal diagnosis.

2. *Two or more comparable or contrasting conditions:* In the rare instance that two or more comparable or contrasting conditions are documented as either/or (or similar terminology), both diagnoses are coded as though confirmed and the principal diagnosis is designated according to the circumstances of the admission and the diagnostic workup and/or therapy provided. When no further determination can be made as to which diagnosis more closely meets the criteria for principal diagnosis, either may be sequenced first. Note that this guideline does not apply for outpatient encounters.

   Example 1: A patient with the same complaints as those outlined in example 3 above is admitted with a final diagnosis of acute pyelonephritis versus diverticulum of the colon. The patient is treated symptomatically and discharged for further studies. In this case, both conditions meet the criteria for principal diagnosis equally, and either can be designated as the principal diagnosis.

   Example 2: The treatment of another patient with the same symptoms and the same final diagnoses is directed almost entirely toward the acute pyelonephritis, indicating that the physician considers this condition the more likely problem and that, after study, it is the condition that occasioned the admission. In this case, both conditions are coded, but the acute pyelonephritis is sequenced first because of the circumstances of the admission.

3. *A symptom followed by contrasting/comparative diagnoses:* When a symptom is followed by contrasting/comparative diagnoses, the symptom code is sequenced first. However, if the symptom code is integral to the conditions listed, no additional code for the symptom is reported. This directive is supported by guideline Section I.B.5, which states: "Conditions that are an integral part of a disease process—Signs and symptoms that are associated routinely with a disease process should not be assigned as additional codes, unless otherwise instructed by the classification." Guidelines in Section I.A and Section I.B are overarching guidelines that apply across chapters or broad areas. Codes are assigned for all listed contrasting/comparative diagnoses.

   Example 1: A patient is admitted for workup because of severe fatigue. The discharge diagnosis is recorded as fatigue, due to either depressive reaction or hypothyroidism. In this case, the symptom code for fatigue is designated the principal diagnosis, with additional codes assigned for both the depressive reaction and the hypothyroidism.

   Example 2: The discharge diagnosis is stated as gastrointestinal bleeding, due to either acute gastritis or angiodysplasia. In this case, the diagnoses are coded as contrasting/comparative diagnoses, and no separate code is assigned for the bleeding because the codes for both conditions include any associated bleeding.

4. *Original treatment plan not carried out:* In a situation in which the original treatment plan cannot be carried out due to unforeseen circumstances, the criteria for designation of the principal diagnosis do not change. The condition that occasioned the admission is designated as the principal diagnosis even though the planned treatment was not carried out.

   Example 1: A patient with benign hypertrophy of the prostate is admitted for the purpose of a transurethral resection of the prostate (TURP). Shortly after admission, but before the patient is taken to the operating suite, the patient falls and sustains a fracture of the left femur. The TURP is canceled; hip pinning is carried out the following day. The principal diagnosis remains hypertrophy of the prostate even though that condition was not treated.

   Example 2: A patient with a diagnosis of carcinoma of the breast confirmed from an outpatient biopsy is admitted for the purpose of modified radical mastectomy. Before the preoperative medications are administered the next morning, the patient indicates that she has decided against having the procedure until she is able to consider possible alternative treatment more thoroughly. No treatment is given, and she is discharged. The carcinoma of the breast remains the principal diagnosis because it is the condition that occasioned the admission even though no treatment was rendered.

Other Diagnoses

Other reportable diagnoses are defined as those conditions that coexist at the time of admission or develop subsequently or affect patient care for the current hospital episode. Diagnoses that have no impact on patient care during the hospital stay are not reported even when they are present. Diagnoses that relate to an earlier episode and have no bearing on the current hospital stay are not reported.

For UHDDS reporting purposes, the definition of "other diagnosis" includes only those conditions that affect the episode of hospital care in terms of any of the following:

- Clinical evaluation
- Therapeutic treatment
- Further evaluation by diagnostic studies, procedures, or consultation
- Extended length of hospital stay
- Increased nursing care and/or other monitoring

All these factors are self-explanatory except the first. Clinical evaluation means that the physician is aware of the problem and is evaluating it in terms of testing, consultations, or close clinical observation of the patient's condition. In most cases, a patient who is being evaluated clinically will also fit into one of the other criteria. Note that a physical examination alone does not qualify as further evaluation or clinical evaluation; the physical examination is a routine part of every hospital admission. No particular order is mandated for sequencing other diagnoses. The more significant diagnoses should be sequenced early in the list when the number of diagnoses that may be reported is limited.

Reporting Guidelines for Other Diagnoses

The following guidelines and examples should be studied carefully in order to understand the rationale for determining other diagnoses that should be reported:

1. *Previous conditions stated as diagnoses:* Physicians sometimes include in the diagnostic statement historical information or status post procedures performed on a previous admission that have no bearing on the current stay. Such conditions are not reported. However, history codes (categories Z80–Z87; subcategories Z91.4-, Z91.5-, and Z91.8; and category Z92) may be used as secondary codes if the historical condition or family history has an impact on current care or influences treatment.

   Example: A patient is admitted with acute myocardial infarction; the physician notes in the history that the patient is status post cholecystectomy and had been hospitalized one year earlier for pneumonia. At discharge, the physician documents the final diagnoses as acute myocardial infarction, status post cholecystectomy, and history of pneumonia. Only the acute myocardial infarction is coded and reported; the other conditions included in the diagnostic statement have no bearing on the current episode of care.

2. *Other diagnosis with no documentation supporting reportability:* If the physician has included a diagnosis in the final diagnostic statement, it should ordinarily be coded. If there is no supporting documentation in the medical record, however, the physician should be consulted as to whether the diagnosis meets reporting criteria; if so, the physician should be asked to add the necessary documentation. Reporting of conditions for which there is no supporting documentation is in conflict with UHDDS criteria.

   Example 1: A 10-year-old boy is admitted with open fracture of the tibia and fibula following a bicycle accident. On physical examination, the physician notes that there is a nevus on the leg and that the patient has a small, asymptomatic inguinal hernia. All these diagnoses are documented on the face sheet. The fracture is reduced with internal fixation, but neither the nevus nor the hernia is treated or further evaluated on this admission. The nevus and hernia are not reported because there is nothing to indicate that they had any effect on the episode of care.

Example 2: A patient is admitted with an acute myocardial infarction. The physician also includes in the diagnostic statement a strabismus and a bunion noted on the physical examination. Review of the medical record reveals that no further reference to these conditions was made in terms of further evaluation or treatment; therefore, no codes for either the strabismus or the bunion are assigned.

3. *Chronic conditions that are not the thrust of treatment:* The criteria for selection of chronic conditions to be reported as "other diagnoses" include the severity of the condition, the use or consideration of alternative measures or an increase in nursing care required in the treatment of the principal diagnosis due to the coexisting condition, the use of diagnostic or therapeutic services for the particular coexisting condition, the need for close monitoring of medications because of the coexisting condition, or modifications of nursing care plans because of the coexisting condition.

   Chronic conditions such as (but not limited to) hypertension, Parkinson's disease, chronic obstructive pulmonary disease, and diabetes mellitus are systemic diseases that ordinarily should be coded even in the absence of documented intervention or further evaluation. Some chronic conditions affect the patient for the rest of his or her life; such conditions almost always require some form of continuous clinical evaluation or monitoring during hospitalization and therefore should be coded. This advice applies to inpatient coding.

   For outpatient encounters/visits, chronic conditions that require or affect patient care treatment or management should be coded.

Example 1: A patient is admitted following a hip fracture, and a diagnosis of Parkinson's disease is noted in the history and physical examination. Nursing notes indicate that the patient required additional care because of the Parkinsonism. Both diagnoses are reported.

Example 2: A patient is admitted with pneumonia, and the presence of diabetes mellitus is documented in the record. Blood sugars are monitored by laboratory studies, and nursing personnel also check blood sugars before each meal. The patient is continued on his diabetic diet. Although no active treatment is provided, ongoing monitoring is required, and the condition is reported.

Example 3: A patient is admitted with acute diverticulitis, and the physician documents in the admitting note a history of hypertension. Review of the medical record indicates that blood pressure medications were given throughout the stay. The hypertension is reportable, and the physician should be asked to add it to the diagnostic statement.

Example 4: A patient is admitted in congestive heart failure. She has known hiatal hernia and degenerative arthritis. Neither condition is further evaluated or treated; by their nature, the conditions do not require continuing clinical evaluation. Only the code for the congestive heart failure is assigned; the other conditions are not reportable.

Example 5: A 60-year-old diabetic patient is transferred from an extended care facility for treatment of a pressure ulcer. The physician notes in the history and physical exam that the patient is status post left below-the-knee amputation due to peripheral vascular disease. This condition requires additional nursing assistance and is reported.

4. *Conditions that are an integral part of a disease process should not be reported as additional diagnoses, unless otherwise instructed by the classification.*

   Example 1: A patient is admitted with nausea and vomiting due to infectious gastroenteritis. Nausea and vomiting are common symptoms of infectious gastroenteritis and are not reported.

   Example 2: A patient is admitted with severe joint pain and rheumatoid arthritis. Severe joint pain is a characteristic part of rheumatoid arthritis and is not reportable.

   Example 3: A patient is seen in the physician's office complaining of urinary frequency and is diagnosed with benign prostatic hypertrophy. Although urinary frequency is a common symptom of benign prostatic hypertrophy, both conditions are reported because of the instructional note in the Tabular List under code N40.1 to use additional codes to identify associated symptoms when specified.

5. *Conditions that are not an integral part of a disease process should be coded when present.*

   Example 1: A patient is admitted by ambulance following a cerebrovascular accident suffered at work. The patient was in a coma but gradually recovers consciousness. Diagnosis at discharge is reported as cerebrovascular thrombosis with coma. In this case, coma is coded as an additional diagnosis because it is not implicit in a cerebrovascular accident and is not always present.

   Example 2: A five-year-old boy is admitted with a 104-degree fever associated with acute pneumonia. During the first 24 hours, the patient also experiences convulsions due to the high fever. Both the pneumonia and the convulsions are reported because convulsions are not routinely associated with pneumonia. Fever is commonly associated with pneumonia, however, and no code is assigned.

6. *Abnormal findings:* Codes from sections R70–R97 for nonspecific abnormal findings (laboratory, radiology, pathology, and other diagnostic results) should be assigned only when the physician has not been able to arrive at a related diagnosis but indicates that the abnormal finding is considered to be clinically significant by listing it in the diagnostic statement. This differs from the coding practices in the outpatient setting when one is coding encounters for diagnostic tests that have been interpreted by a physician.

   The coder should never assign a code on the basis of an abnormal finding alone. To make a diagnosis on the basis of a single lab value or abnormal diagnostic finding is risky and carries the possibility of error. A value reported as either lower or higher than the normal range does not necessarily indicate a disorder. Many factors influence the values in a lab sample; these include the collection device, the method used to transport the sample to the lab, the calibration of the machine that reads the values, and the condition of the patient. For example, a patient who is dehydrated may show an elevated hemoglobin due to increased viscosity of the blood. When findings are clearly outside the normal range and the physician has ordered other tests to evaluate the condition or has prescribed treatment without documenting an associated diagnosis, it is appropriate to ask the physician whether a diagnosis should be added or whether the abnormal finding should be listed in the diagnostic statement. Incidental findings on X-ray such as asymptomatic hiatal hernia or a diverticulum should not be reported unless further evaluation or treatment is carried out.

   Example 1: A low potassium level treated with intravenous or oral potassium is clinically significant and should be brought to the attention of the physician if no related diagnosis has been recorded.

Example 2: A hematocrit of 28 percent, even though asymptomatic and not treated, is evaluated with serial hematocrits. Because the finding is outside the range of normal laboratory values and has been further evaluated, the physician should be asked whether an associated diagnosis should be documented.

Example 3: A routine preoperative chest X-ray on an elderly patient reveals collapse of a vertebral body. The patient is asymptomatic, and no further evaluation or treatment is carried out. This is a common finding in elderly patients and is insignificant for this episode.

Example 4: In the absence of a cardiac problem, an isolated electrocardiographic finding of bundle branch block is ordinarily not significant, whereas a finding of a Mobitz II block may have important implications for the patient's care and warrants asking the physician whether it should be reported for this admission.

Example 5: The physician lists an abnormal sedimentation rate as part of the diagnostic statement. The physician has been unable to make a definitive diagnosis during the hospitalization in spite of further evaluation and considers the abnormal finding a significant clinical problem. Code **R70.0, Elevated erythrocyte sedimentation rate,** should be assigned.

Admitting Diagnosis

Although the admitting diagnosis is not an element of the UHDDS, it must be reported for some payers and may also be useful in quality-of-care studies. Ordinarily, only one admitting diagnosis can be reported. The inpatient admitting diagnosis may be reported as one of the following:

- A significant finding (symptom or sign) representing patient distress or an abnormal finding on outpatient examination
- A possible diagnosis based on significant findings (working diagnosis)
- A diagnosis established on an ambulatory care basis or during a previous hospital admission
- An injury or a poisoning
- A reason or condition that is not actually an illness or injury, such as a follow-up examination or pregnancy in labor

If the admitting diagnosis is reported, the code should indicate the diagnosis provided by the physician at the time of admission. Although the admitting diagnosis may not agree with the principal diagnosis on discharge, the admitting diagnosis should not be changed to conform to the principal diagnosis. Examples of admitting diagnoses and subsequent principal diagnoses follow:

- *Admitting:* K92.2 Gastrointestinal bleeding
  Principal: K26.0 Acute duodenal ulcer with hemorrhage
- *Admitting:* N63 Lump in right breast
  Principal: C50.911 Carcinoma of right female breast
- *Admitting:* K81.0 Acute cholecystitis
  Principal: K80.00 Acute cholecystitis with cholelithiasis
- *Admitting:* I50.9 Congestive heart failure
  Principal: I21.09 Acute myocardial infarction, anterior wall
- *Admitting:* I21.3 Suspected myocardial infarction
  Principal: I71.01 Dissection of thoracic aorta

PROCEDURES

The UHDDS requires that all significant procedures be reported. The UHDDS definitions of significant procedures and other reporting guidelines are discussed in chapters 9 through 11 of this handbook, along with other information on coding operations and procedures.

RELATIONSHIP OF UHDDS TO OUTPATIENT REPORTING

The UHDDS definition of principal diagnosis does not apply to the coding of outpatient encounters. In contrast to inpatient coding, no "after study" element is involved because ambulatory care visits do not permit the continued evaluation ordinarily needed to meet UHDDS criteria. If the physician does not identify a definite condition or problem at the conclusion of a visit or an encounter, the coder should report the documented chief complaint as the reason for the encounter/visit.

RELATIONSHIP OF UHDDS TO LONG-TERM CARE REPORTING

The UHDDS definition of principal diagnosis has been expanded since its initial development so that it now applies to coding in all non-outpatient settings (acute care, short-term care, long-term care, and psychiatric hospitals; home health agencies; rehabilitation facilities; nursing homes; and so forth). Other diagnoses documented by the physician (e.g., chronic conditions) that affect a resident's continued care should also be coded. However, in long-term care (LTC) settings, there are some differences in the application of the principal and secondary diagnoses.

The diagnostic listing in LTC is dynamic, depending on many factors including the point in time when codes are assigned. LTC has a longer time frame than an acute care stay: ICD-10-CM codes are assigned upon admission; concurrently as diagnoses arise; and at the time of discharge, transfer, or expiration of a resident.

The first-listed diagnosis is the diagnosis chiefly responsible for the admission to, or continued residence in, a nursing facility and should be sequenced first. For example, when coding an admission, the first-listed diagnosis is the condition chiefly responsible for the admission to the facility. If the coder is assigning diagnosis codes during the resident's stay, the first-listed diagnosis is the condition chiefly responsible for the continued stay in the facility.

Example 1: A patient is admitted to a nursing home for convalescence following an acute illness or injury. Code assignment is based on the condition being treated as documented in the medical record. It would also be appropriate to assign codes for any late effects, residual conditions, signs, or symptoms that are present. When the reason for the admission is strictly for convalescence and there is no other definitive diagnosis, assign code **Z51.89, Encounter for other specified aftercare,** as the first-listed diagnosis.

Example 2: A patient is admitted to LTC following hospital treatment of a fracture of the right femur. The reason for the LTC admission is to allow the patient to regain strength and the fracture to heal. Assign code **S72.90XD, Unspecified fracture of right femur, subsequent encounter for closed fracture with routine healing,** as the principal diagnosis. The seventh character "D" is used for encounters after the patient has received active treatment for the condition and is now receiving routine care during the healing or recovery phase. Code any other coexistent conditions that require treatment.

Example 3: A nursing home resident is transferred to the hospital for treatment of pneumonia. She returns to the nursing home still receiving antibiotics for the pneumonia. However, the main reason she is returning to the nursing home is because this has been her residence since developing a cerebrovascular accident (CVA) with residuals several years ago. The appropriate code from subcategory I69.3, Sequelae of cerebral infarction, is assigned as the principal diagnosis to identify the neurologic deficits that resulted from the acute CVA. The appropriate code for the pneumonia is assigned as a secondary diagnosis for as long as the patient receives treatment for the condition.

ETHICAL CODING AND REPORTING

Whereas coded medical data are used for a variety of purposes, they have become increasingly important in determining payment for health care. Medicare reimbursement depends on the following:

- The correct designation of the principal diagnosis
- The presence or absence of additional codes that represent complications, comorbidities, or major complications or comorbidities as defined by the Medicare severity-adjusted diagnosis-related groups system
- Procedures performed

Other third-party payers may follow slightly different reimbursement methods, but the accuracy of ICD-10-CM and ICD-10-PCS coding is always vital.

Accurate and ethical ICD-10-CM and ICD-10-PCS coding depends on correctly following all instructions in the coding manuals as well as all official guidelines developed by the cooperating parties and coding advice published in the American Hospital Association's quarterly *Coding Clinic*. (At press time, it is planned that the *AHA Coding Clinic® for ICD-9-CM* will be replaced by a similar publication for ICD-10-CM/PCS in 2014.) Accurate and ethical reporting requires the correct selection of those conditions that meet the criteria set by the UHDDS and the official guidelines mentioned above. Over-coding and over-reporting may result in higher payment, but it is unethical and may be considered fraudulent. On the other hand, it is important to be sure that all appropriate codes are reported, as failure to include all diagnoses or procedures that meet reporting criteria may result in financial loss for the health care provider.

It is important for coders to abide by the American Health Information Management Association Standards of Ethical Coding, which are available for download at http://www.ahima.org/about/ethicsstandards.aspx.

Occasionally, certain codes are identified by Medicare or another payer as being unacceptable as the principal diagnosis. This does not mean that the code should not be assigned when it is correct; it means that the third-party payer may question or deny payment. It is important to code correctly and then make whatever adjustment is required for reporting. Otherwise, the coder runs the risk of developing incorrect coding practices that will distort data used for other purposes.

Hospitals sometimes feel a need to code nonreportable diagnoses or procedures for internal use; this is acceptable if the facility has a system for maintaining this information outside the reporting system.

There are a variety of payment policies that may have an impact on coding. Many of those policies may contradict each other or may be inconsistent with ICD-10-CM/PCS rules and conventions. Therefore, it is not possible to write coding guidelines that are consistent with all existing payer guidelines.

The following advice is shared to help providers resolve coding disputes with payers:

- First, determine whether it is really a coding dispute and not a coverage issue. For example, a payer may deny code Z00.00 for encounters for radiology and laboratory examinations. This code is to be used only for routine examinations without complaint, suspected or reported diagnosis. Many payers do not provide coverage for routine tests. So, such denials are not made on the basis of incorrect coding but rather relate to non-coverage of routine tests, e.g., annual physical exams or screening tests without signs or symptoms. Therefore, always contact the payer for clarification if the reason for the denial is unclear.
- If a payer really does have a policy that clearly conflicts with official coding rules or guidelines, every effort should be made to resolve the issue with the payer. Provide the applicable coding rule/guideline to the payer. For Medicare claims, contact the Medicare Administrative Contractor (MAC) for clarification. If you are not satisfied with the answer you receive, follow up with the Centers for Medicare & Medicaid Services Regional Office. The MAC should be able to provide you with information as to which Regional Office has jurisdiction over your area.
- If a payer refuses to change its policy, obtain the payer requirements in writing. If the payer refuses to provide its policy in writing, document all discussions with the payer, including dates and the names of individuals involved in the discussion. Confirm the existence of the policy with the payer's supervisory personnel.
- Keep a permanent file of the documentation obtained regarding payer coding policies. It may come in handy in the event of an audit.

CHAPTER 5

The Medical Record as a Source Document

CHAPTER OVERVIEW

- The medical record is the source document for coding.
- Medical records contain a variety of reports. These include the following:
  - — Reason the patient came to the hospital
  - — Tests performed and their findings
  - — Therapies provided
  - — Descriptions of surgical procedures
  - — Daily records of patient progress
- The discharge summary provides a synopsis of the patient's stay.

LEARNING OUTCOMES

After studying this chapter you should be able to:

Explain what is present in a medical record.

Understand when it is appropriate to query a physician about his or her documentation.

TERMS TO KNOW

POA indicator
present on admission indicator; a data element that applies to diagnosis codes for claims involving inpatient care

Provider
a physician or any qualified health care practitioner (such as a nurse practitioner or physician assistant) who is legally accountable for establishing the patient's diagnosis

REMEMBER . . .

The coder must make sure that the medical record documentation supports the principal diagnosis. . . . Refer to appendix B for more information on the POA indicator.

INTRODUCTION

The source document for coding and reporting diagnoses and procedures is the medical record. Although discharge diagnoses are usually recorded on the face sheet, a final progress note, or the discharge summary, further review of the medical record is needed to ensure complete and accurate coding. Operations and procedures are frequently not listed on the face sheet or are not described in sufficient detail, making a review of operative reports, pathology reports, and other special reports imperative. The entire record should be reviewed to determine the specific reason for the encounter and the conditions treated.

Physicians sometimes fail to list reportable conditions that developed during the stay but were resolved prior to discharge. Conditions such as urinary tract infection or dehydration, for example, are often not included in the diagnostic statement even though progress notes, physicians' orders, and laboratory reports make it clear that such conditions were treated. It is inappropriate for coders to assign a diagnosis based solely on a physician's orders for prescribed medications without the physician's documentation of the diagnosis being treated. If enough information is present to strongly suggest that an additional diagnosis should be reported, the physician should be consulted; no diagnosis should be added without the approval of the physician. Because diagnostic statements sometimes include diagnoses that represent past history or existing diagnoses that do not meet the Uniform Hospital Discharge Data Set (UHDDS) guidelines for reportable diagnoses, a review of the medical record is required to determine whether these diagnoses should be coded for this encounter.

It is customary to list the principal diagnosis first in the diagnostic statement. Many physicians, however, are not aware of coding and reporting guidelines, and, consequently, this custom is not consistently followed. Because the correct designation of the principal diagnosis is of critical importance in reporting diagnostic information, the coder must be sure that medical record documentation supports the designation of principal diagnosis. If it appears that another diagnosis should be designated as the principal diagnosis, or if conditions not listed should be reported, the coder should follow the health care facility's procedures for obtaining a corrected diagnostic statement.

CONTENTS OF THE MEDICAL RECORD

Medical records contain a variety of reports that document the reason the patient came to the hospital, the tests performed and their findings, the therapies provided, descriptions of any surgical procedures, and daily records of the patient's progress. Each report contains important information needed for accurate coding and reporting of the principal diagnosis, other diagnoses, and the procedures performed.

A number of standard reports can be found in almost any medical record, but other reports will appear depending on the condition for which the patient is being treated, the extent of workup and therapy provided, and the attending physician's style of documentation. For example, a physician may list final diagnoses on the admission record (face sheet), on progress notes, or on the discharge summary. Consultants occasionally record their consultation notes in the progress notes rather than on separate reports.

Review of the inpatient medical record should begin with the discharge summary, when available, because it provides a synopsis of the patient's hospital stay, including the reason for admission, significant diagnostic findings, the treatment given, the patient's course in the hospital, the follow-up plan, and the final diagnostic statement. The history section usually indicates the reason for admission (principal diagnosis), which may require confirmation by review of the history and physical examination and admitting and emergency department records.

The section of the discharge summary that describes the patient's course in the hospital usually indicates treatment that has been given and any further workup that has been done. It is particularly useful in determining whether all listed diagnoses meet the criteria for reporting and identifying other conditions that may merit reporting.

Conditions mentioned elsewhere in the body of the discharge summary do not necessarily warrant reporting but may provide clues for more specific review to make a final determination. The medical record should be reviewed further to determine whether such conditions meet the criteria for reportable diagnoses as defined in the UHDDS. The medication record is often helpful in indicating that therapeutic treatment may have been administered, but the coder must not assume a diagnosis solely on the basis of medication administration or abnormal findings in diagnostic reports. In addition, recorded diagnoses do not always contain sufficient information for providing the required specificity in coding. For example, a diagnosis of pneumonia may not indicate the organism responsible for the infection; a review of diagnostic studies of the sputum may provide this information. The physician should be asked to confirm that the organism discovered on the positive culture is the causative agent. Then the physician should indicate his or her confirmation by documenting it in the medical record; this step must be taken before a code identifying the specific type of pneumonia can be assigned. A diagnosis of fracture may indicate which bone was fractured but not the particular part of the bone, information that is necessary for accurate code assignment. The X-ray or the operative report should supply these data.

Some facilities may develop their own additional coding guidelines to provide assistance in determining when a physician query is appropriate. If the test findings are outside the normal range and the physician has ordered other tests to evaluate the condition or prescribed treatment, it is appropriate to ask the physician whether the diagnosis should be added. However, a facility's internal guidelines may not interpret abnormal findings to replace physician documentation or a physician query.

The following examples illustrate diagnoses that are often recorded with less-than-complete information but can be coded more specifically by referring to diagnostic reports within the medical record and then obtaining the appropriate physician confirmation. Note the variation in code assignment when more information is available after physician confirmation:

- *Diagnosis:* C53.9 Cancer of cervix
  Pathology report: D06.9 Carcinoma, in situ, of cervix
- *Diagnosis:* N39.0 Urinary tract infection
  Laboratory report: N39.0 + B96.20 *E. coli* in urine
- *Diagnosis:* S72.90xA Fracture of femur, initial encounter
  X-ray report: S72.21xB Open fracture of subtrochanteric neck of the right femur, initial encounter

Code assignment is generally based on the attending physician's documentation. It is also appropriate to base code assignment on the documentation of other physicians (e.g., consultants, residents, anesthesiologists) involved in the care and treatment of the patient so long as there is no conflicting information from the attending physician. A physician query is not necessary if a physician involved in the care and treatment of the patient, including consulting physicians, has documented a diagnosis and there is no conflicting documentation from another physician. If documentation from different physicians conflicts, the attending physician should be queried for clarification because he or she is ultimately responsible for the final diagnosis.

For inpatient coding, if the attending physician does not confirm the pathological or radiological findings, query him or her regarding the clinical significance of the findings and request that appropriate documentation be provided. Although the pathologist or radiologist provides a written

interpretation of a tissue biopsy or an X-ray image, this is not equivalent to the attending physician's medical diagnosis, which is based on the patient's complete clinical picture. The attending physician is responsible for, and directly involved in, the care and treatment of the patient. A pathologist's interpretation of a specimen or a radiologist's interpretation of an image is not the same as a diagnosis provided by a physician directly involved in the patient's care. For example, if the attending physician documented "breast mass" and the pathologist documented "carcinoma of the breast," this would be conflicting information requiring clarification from the attending physician.

When coding outpatient laboratory, pathology, and radiology encounters in hospital-based as well as stand-alone facilities, it is appropriate to assign codes on the basis of the written interpretation by a radiologist or pathologist.

In some institutions, midlevel providers, such as nurse practitioners and physician assistants, are involved in the care of the patient and document diagnoses in the medical record. It is appropriate to base code assignments on the documentation of midlevel providers if they are considered legally accountable for establishing a diagnosis within the regulations governing the provider and the facility. The *ICD-10-CM Official Guidelines for Coding and Reporting* use the term "provider" to mean physician or any qualified health care practitioner who is legally accountable for establishing the patient's diagnosis.

Not all reportable services or procedures during an encounter or admission are performed or documented by physicians. It is appropriate to assign a procedure code based on documentation by the nonphysician professional who provided the service. This applies only to procedure coding where there is documentation to substantiate the code. It does not apply to diagnosis coding. The documentation from the nonphysician professional who provided the service may be the only evidence that the service was provided. This is true of services such as infusions carried out by nurses and therapies provided by physical, respiratory, or occupational therapists.

Outpatient records generally contain less information than inpatient records do. Nevertheless, all available reports for the encounter should be reviewed prior to code assignment. Code assignment is dependent on the information available at the time of code assignment.

For ambulatory records, an additional data element called "patient's reason for visit" (PRV) is usually reported. The PRV is reported on unscheduled outpatient visits (e.g., emergency department or urgent care visits) to identify the main reason the patient sought treatment. The reason may differ from the physician's final diagnosis at the end of the encounter. Only one diagnosis code can be reported in this field on the electronic claim. If there are multiple conditions present, the code most likely to justify the patient encounter should be reported. This data element is found at Form Locator 70a–c on the UB-04 paper claim. Both the UB-04 paper claim and the electronic claim allow the reporting of three diagnosis codes for the patient's reason for visit.

The "present on admission" (POA) indicator is a data element approved by the National Uniform Billing Committee for inpatient reporting. The POA indicator applies to the diagnosis codes for claims involving inpatient admissions to general acute care hospitals or other facilities. Please refer to appendix B of this handbook for more detailed information on this topic.

CHAPTER 6

Basic ICD-10-CM Coding Steps

CHAPTER OVERVIEW

- There are three basic steps for locating codes to be assigned.
  - Locate the main term in the Alphabetic Index. Search for subterms, notes, or cross-references.
  - Verify the code number in the Tabular List.
  - Assign the verified code or codes.
- It is important to understand basic coding techniques before moving on to the harder, system-based chapters of this handbook.

LEARNING OUTCOMES

After studying this chapter you should be able to:

Locate code entries in the Alphabetic Index.

Determine the course of action when there are discrepancies between the Alphabetic Index and the Tabular List.

Perform basic coding techniques.

TERMS TO KNOW

Alphabetic Index of Diseases and Injuries and the Index to External Causes
include entries for main terms (diseases, conditions, or injuries) and subterms (site, type, or etiology), the Neoplasm Table, and the Table of Drugs and Chemicals

Tabular List
contains categories, subcategories, and valid codes

REMEMBER . . .

You can't begin to code unless you have determined the principal diagnosis and other reportable diagnoses from the medical record.

INTRODUCTION

Once the medical record has been reviewed to determine the principal/first-listed diagnosis and other reportable diagnoses, the following steps in locating the codes to be assigned should be undertaken:

1. Locate the main term in the Alphabetic Index.
   - Review subterms and nonessential modifiers related to the main term.
   - Follow any cross-reference instructions.
   - Refer to any notes in the Alphabetic Index.
   - A dash (-) at the end of an Index entry indicates that additional characters are required.
2. Verify the code number in the Tabular List.
   - Read the code title.
   - Read and follow any instructional notes. Refer to other codes as instructed.
   - Determine whether an additional character must be added.
   - Determine laterality (right or left) and any applicable extensions.
3. Assign the verified code or codes.

It is imperative that these steps be followed without exception; the condition to be coded must first be located in the Alphabetic Index and then verified in the Tabular List. Relying on memory or using only the Index or Tabular List may lead to incorrect code assignment.

LOCATE THE CODE ENTRY IN THE ALPHABETIC INDEX

The first step in coding is to locate the main term in the Alphabetic Index. In the ICD-10-CM Alphabetic Index, the condition is listed as the main term, usually expressed as a noun. General terms such as "admission," "encounter," and "examination" are used to locate code entries for the Z code section. Some conditions are indexed under more than one main term. For example, anxiety reaction can be located in either of the following Index entries:

Anxiety . . .
-reaction F41.1

Reaction . . .
-anxiety F41.1

If a main term cannot be located, the coder should consider a synonym, an eponym, or another alternative term. Once the main term is located, a search should be made of subterms, notes, or cross-references. Subterms provide more specific information of many types and must be checked carefully, following all the rules of alphabetization. The main term code entry should not be assigned until all subterm possibilities have been exhausted. During this process, it may be necessary to refer again to the medical record to determine whether any additional information is available to permit assignment of a more specific code. If a subterm cannot be located, the nonessential modifiers following the main term should be reviewed to see whether the subterm may be included there. If not, alternative terms should be considered.

EXERCISE 6.1

Without referring to the Alphabetic Index of Diseases and Injuries, underline the word that indicates the main term for each diagnosis.

1. Acute myocardial infarction
2. Chronic hypertrophy of tonsils and adenoids
3. Acute suppurative cholecystitis
4. Syphilitic aortic aneurysm
5. Normal, spontaneous delivery, full-term infant
6. Drug overdose due to barbiturates
7. Urinary tract infection due to *E. coli*
8. Hemorrhagic pneumonia
9. Admission for adjustment of artificial arm
10. Bilateral inguinal hernia

VERIFY THE CODE NUMBER IN THE TABULAR LIST

Once a code number entry has been located in the Alphabetic Index, the coder must refer to that number in the Tabular List; a code should not be assigned without such verification. In addition to the title for the code entry, it may be necessary for coders to review the title for the chapter, section, and category in order to be sure the correct code has been identified. Although the title in the Tabular List does not always match exactly the Alphabetic Index entry, it is usually clear whether it applies. For example:

- Appendicitis (K37) has an additional modifier of "unspecified" in the Tabular List. This alerts the coder to look elsewhere when the type of appendicitis is stated in the medical record.
- Painful menstruation (N94.6) has the title **Dysmenorrhea, unspecified,** in the Tabular List. Although the title in the Tabular List is not identical to the term in the Alphabetic Index, it is clear that it is the right code for this condition.

Any significant discrepancy between the Index entry and the tabular listing should alert the coder to the need to review the Alphabetic Index for a more appropriate term.

All instructional terms and notes should be read and followed when they apply, with particular attention to exclusion notes. Ordinarily the code number listed with the main term entry in the Index is for an unspecified condition. It is important to review other codes in the related area to determine whether a more specific code can be assigned.

CODING DEMONSTRATIONS

Follow the steps outlined above to determine the correct code for each of the diagnostic statements listed below:

- **Hirsutism**
  Refer to the main term **Hirsutism** in the Alphabetic Index, which provides a code of L68.0. Note that there are no subterms. Verify this by referring to code L68.0 in the Tabular List. In this case, the Index entry and Tabular List title are identical and code L68.0 should be assigned.

- **Portal vein obstruction**
  Refer to code I81 by the main term **Obstruction** in the Alphabetic Index and the subterm for portal (circulation) (vein). An inclusion note in the Tabular List indicates "portal (vein) obstruction." If you are uncertain whether thrombosis and obstruction are the same condition for the purposes of coding, check the Index for the main term **Thrombosis.**

- **Abscess abdominal wall due to Staphylococcus**
  Look up the main term **Abscess;** and then the subterm "abdomen, abdominal"; and then subterm "wall." The code entry is L02.211. Read the "use additional note" in the Tabular List that advises you to also assign a code to identify the organism involved (B95–B96). Hint: if you have trouble locating this note, find it under the category title L02. Look up **Infection,** staphylococcal, and the subterm "as cause of disease classified elsewhere" and find code B95.8, which is assigned in the Tabular List. The code title is "Unspecified staphylococcus as the cause of diseases classified elsewhere." Review the medical record for any mention of the specific type of *Staphylococcus*. If one is mentioned, consider assigning the code B95.61, B95.62, or B95.7; if not, assign code B95.8 as an additional code.

- **Aplasia of pulmonary artery**
  Refer to the main term **Aplasia.** Check the subterms, and note that there is no entry for pulmonary artery but that there is a cross-reference note to "see also Agenesis." Follow the cross-reference advice and refer to Agenesis. You immediately see a more specific subterm for "artery, pulmonary," with code entry Q25.79. The title for this code in the Tabular List is "Other congenital malformations of pulmonary artery," and it is clearly the correct code for this condition. As additional confirmation that this is the correct code, "agenesis of pulmonary artery" is listed as an inclusion term.

- **Acute bronchopneumonia due to aspiration of oil**
  Locate the main term **Bronchopneumonia** in the Alphabetic Index. Note the cross-reference instruction to "see Pneumonia, broncho." Follow the cross-reference by turning to the main term **Pneumonia** (acute) (double) (migratory). . . . Note that the term "acute" is a nonessential modifier enclosed in parentheses under the main term **Pneumonia.** This applies also to the subterm, and so this term has now been accounted for but does not directly affect code assignment. Refer to the following subterms listed under the main term:

> **Pneumonia** (acute) (double) (migratory) . . .
> -broncho-, bronchial (confluent) (croupous)
> (diffuse) (disseminated) (hemorrhagic) . . .
> -aspiration—see Pneumonia, aspiration

Note the cross-reference to "see Pneumonia, aspiration." Refer back to the subterm "aspiration" and locate the code J69.0. Search through the main term and subterms cited above and underline the component parts of the diagnostic statement that have been located so far. Note that all component parts of the diagnostic statement except "of oil" have been located. Refer back to "Pneumonia, aspiration," and you will see that there are additional subterms here under the connecting words "due to," with a subterm for "oils and essences," that takes you to code J69.1. Refer to code J69.1 in the Tabular List, and note that the title for this code is "Pneumonitis due to inhalation of oils and essences." Although the title is not worded exactly the same as the diagnosis, there is such a close correlation that it is clear that this is the code that should be assigned. Assign code J69.1 because it covers all elements of the diagnosis and no instructional notes contradict its use.

REVIEW EXERCISE 6.2

Using the Alphabetic Index and the Tabular List, code the following diagnoses.

	Diagnosis	Code
1.	Chronic hypertrophy of tonsils and adenoids	J35.3
2.	Fibrocystic disease of breast (female)	N60.19
3.	Acute suppurative mastoiditis with subperiosteal abscess	H70.019
4.	Recurrent direct left inguinal hernia with gangrene	K40.41
5.	Acute upper respiratory infection with influenza	J11.1
6.	Benign cyst of right breast	N60.01
7.	Bunion, right great toe	M20.11
8.	Nondisplaced abduction fracture anterior acetabulum, subsequent encounter with routine healing	S32.436D
9.	Bronchiectasis with acute bronchitis	J47.0
10.	Acute bleeding peptic ulcer	K27.0
11.	Dementia with aggressive behavior	F03.91
12.	Hereditary retinal degeneration	H35.9

CHAPTER 7

Basic ICD-10-CM Coding Guidelines

CHAPTER OVERVIEW

- There are basic principles that all coders must follow.
- It is important to use both the Alphabetic Index and the Tabular List during the coding process.
  - Follow all instructional notes.
  - Even if common codes have been memorized, refer to the Alphabetic Index and Tabular List.
- Always assign codes to the highest level of detail.
  - All characters must be used.
  - None can be omitted or added.
- NEC and NOS codes should be assigned only when appropriate.
- Combination codes should be used if they are available.
  - Assign multiple codes as needed to fully describe a condition.
  - Avoid coding irrelevant information.

LEARNING OUTCOMES

After studying this chapter you should be able to:

- Determine what level of detail to assign to a code.
- Understand how to use combination codes.
- Explain how to assign multiple codes to fully describe a condition.
- Determine what qualifications determine whether an unconfirmed diagnosis is coded as though it were an established diagnosis.
- Explain the difference between "rule out" and "ruled out."
- Code "borderline" diagnoses.
- Code acute and chronic conditions.
- Code a condition labeled "impending," "threatened," or "late effect."

TERMS TO KNOW

Combination code
a single code used to classify two diagnoses, a diagnosis with a secondary condition, or a diagnosis with an associated complication

NEC
not elsewhere classified

NOS
not otherwise specified

"Rule out"
indicates that a diagnosis is still possible

"Ruled out"
indicates that a diagnosis once considered likely is no longer possible

REMEMBER . . .

For the current version of the *ICD-10-CM Official Guidelines for Coding and Reporting* visit www.ahacentraloffice.org.

INTRODUCTION

The basic coding guidelines discussed in this chapter apply throughout the ICD-10-CM classification system. Following these principles is vital to accurate code selection and correct sequencing. Guidelines that apply to specific chapters of ICD-10-CM will be discussed in the relevant chapters of this handbook. To download a copy of the current version of the complete *ICD-10-CM Official Guidelines for Coding and Reporting,* please visit www.ahacentraloffice.org. This handbook has been prepared using the 2013 version of the Official Coding Guidelines. Adherence to the guidelines when assigning ICD-10-CM diagnosis codes is required under the Health Insurance Portability and Accountability Act. The instructions and conventions of the classification take precedence over guidelines.

USE BOTH THE ALPHABETIC INDEX AND THE TABULAR LIST

Section I of the ICD-10-CM Official Coding Guidelines contains the conventions, general coding guidelines, and chapter-specific guidelines. The conventions for ICD-10-CM are the general rules for use of the classification independent of the guidelines. These conventions are incorporated within the Alphabetic Index and Tabular List of ICD-10-CM as instructional notes.

The first coding principle is that both the Alphabetic Index and the Tabular List must be used to locate and assign appropriate codes. The diagnosis, condition, or reason for visit to be coded must first be located in the Index, and the code provided there must then be verified in the Tabular List. The Index does not provide the full code. Selection of the full code, including laterality and any applicable seventh character, can only be done using the Tabular List. The coder must follow all instructional notes to ensure that more specific subterms or other instructional notes are not overlooked. Experienced coders sometimes rely on their memory for commonly used codes, but consistent reference to the Alphabetic Index and the Tabular List is imperative, no matter how experienced the coder is.

ASSIGN CODES TO THE HIGHEST LEVEL OF DETAIL

A second basic principle is that codes must be used to the highest number of characters available. This can be accomplished by following these steps:

1. Assign a three-character disease code only if it is not further divided (when there are no four-character codes within that category).
2. Assign a four-character code only when there are no five-character codes within that subcategory.
3. Assign a five-character code only when there are no six-character codes for that subcategory.
4. Assign a six-character code when a sixth-character subclassification is provided.
5. Assign a seventh-character value when provided.

All characters must be used. None can be omitted, and none can be added. The one exception to this rule is the placeholder character "x." For codes less than six characters that require a seventh character, a placeholder "x" should be assigned for all characters less than six. The seventh character must always be the seventh character of a code. An example of this exception is at categories T36–T50 (poisoning, adverse effects, and underdosing codes).

The following examples demonstrate these basic coding principles:

- Refer to the Tabular List, category J40, Bronchitis, not specified as acute or chronic. Code J40 has no fourth-character subdivisions; therefore, the three-character code is assigned.
- Refer to Tabular List, category K35, Acute appendicitis. This category includes fourth characters that indicate the presence of generalized or localized peritonitis. Because fourth-character subdivisions are provided, code K35 cannot be assigned.
- Refer to Tabular List, category J45, Asthma. Category J45 has five fourth-character subdivisions (J45.2, J45.3, J45.4, J45.5, and J45.9). It also uses a final-character (fifth- or sixth-character) subclassification to specify whether there is any mention of status asthmaticus or acute exacerbation. Any code assignment from category J45 must have five characters (for subcategories J45.2–J45.5) or six characters (for subcategory J45.9) to ensure coding accuracy.
- Refer to Tabular List, category T27, Burn and corrosion of respiratory tract. Category T27 has eight four-character subdivisions to specify whether the condition is burn or corrosion and to provide detail on the part of the respiratory tract affected. The general note at category T27 also indicates that the appropriate seventh character is to be added to each code from this category. Because the codes from category T27 are only four characters long, the placeholder character "x" is used as a fifth- and sixth-character placeholder before the seventh character can be added. For example, an initial encounter for burn of the larynx and trachea would be coded to T27.0xxA.

ASSIGN RESIDUAL CODES (NEC AND NOS) AS APPROPRIATE

The main term entry in the Alphabetic Index is usually followed by the code number for the unspecified condition. This code should never be assigned without a careful review of subterms to determine whether a more specific code can be located. When the coder's review does not identify a more specific code entry in the Index, the titles and inclusion notes in the subdivisions under either the three-character, four-character, or five-character code in the Tabular List should be reviewed. The residual NOS (not otherwise specified) code should never be assigned when a more specific code is available. The following examples demonstrate this basic coding principle:

- Refer to the Alphabetic Index for nontraumatic hematoma of breast, which is classified as N64.89. This is listed as "other" specified disorders of the breast. Even though the diagnosis is very specific, no separate code is provided.
- Refer to the Alphabetic Index for phlebitis. Note that phlebitis, not otherwise specified, is assigned to code **I80.9, Phlebitis and thrombophlebitis of unspecified site.** Now suppose that review of the medical record provides even further specificity, that this is phlebitis of not only the lower extremity but the right popliteal vein. The more specific code **I80.221, Phlebitis and thrombophlebitis of right popliteal vein,** should be assigned.

ASSIGN COMBINATION CODES WHEN AVAILABLE

A single code used to classify either two diagnoses, a diagnosis with an associated secondary process (manifestation), or a diagnosis with an associated complication is called a combination code. Combination codes can be located in the Index by referring to subterm entries, with particular reference to subterms that follow connecting words such as "with," "due to," "in," and "associated with." Other combination codes can be identified by reading inclusion and exclusion notes in the Tabular List.

Only the combination code is assigned when that code fully identifies the diagnostic conditions involved or when the Alphabetic Index so directs. For example:

K80.00	Acute cholecystitis with cholelithiasis
J02.0	Acute pharyngitis due to streptococcal infection
K41.11	Bilateral recurrent femoral hernia with gangrene
H40.812	Glaucoma with increased episcleral venous pressure, left eye

EXERCISE 7.1

Code the following diagnoses.

1.	Influenza with gastroenteritis	J11.2
2.	Acute cholecystitis with cholelithiasis and choledocholithiasis	K80.62
3.	Meningitis due to *Salmonella* infection	A02.21
4.	Atherosclerotic heart disease (native vessel) with unstable angina pectoris	I25.110

Occasionally, a combination code lacks the necessary specificity to describe the manifestation or complication; in such cases, an additional code may be assigned. The coder should be guided by directions in the Tabular List for the use of an additional code or codes that may provide more specificity. For example, code O99.01- classifies anemia complicating pregnancy. Because it does not indicate the type of anemia, an additional code can be assigned for this purpose.

ASSIGN MULTIPLE CODES AS NEEDED

Multiple coding is the use of more than one code to fully identify the component elements of a complex diagnostic or procedural statement. A complex statement is one that involves connecting words or phrases such as "with," "due to," "incidental to," "secondary to," or similar terminology. The coder should be guided by directions in the Tabular List for the use of an additional code or codes that may provide more specificity. When no combination code is provided, multiple codes should be assigned as needed to fully describe the condition regardless of whether there is advice to that effect.

Mandatory Multiple Coding

The term "dual classification" is used to describe the required assignment of two codes to provide information about both a manifestation and the associated underlying disease or etiology. Mandatory multiple coding is identified in the Alphabetic Index by the use of a second code in brackets. The first code identifies the underlying condition, and the second identifies the manifestation. Both codes must be assigned and sequenced in the order listed.

In the Tabular List the need for dual coding is indicated by the presence of a "use additional code" note with the code for the underlying condition, and a "code first underlying condition" note with the manifestation code. In printed versions of the manuals, the manifestation code is in italics. Manifestation codes cannot be designated as the principal diagnosis, and a code for the underlying condition must always be listed first, except for an occasional situation where other directions are provided. A code in brackets in the Alphabetic Index can be used only as a secondary code for the specific condition or procedure indexed in this way. For example:

G20 + F02.80 Dementia in Parkinson's disease
D66 + M36.2 Arthritis in hemophilia

EXERCISE 7.2

Code the following diagnoses according to the coding principles for correct sequencing of codes.

1. Amyloid heart	E85.4 I43
2. Chorioretinitis due to histoplasmosis	B39.9 H32
3. Combined spinal cord degeneration with anemia due to dietary vitamin B12 deficiency	D51.3 G32.0
4. Otomycosis, right ear	B36.9 H62.41
5. Cataract associated with galactosemia	E74.21 H28

Discretionary Multiple Coding

The "code first" notes appear in the Tabular List under certain codes that are not specifically manifestation codes, but codes in which the condition may be due to an underlying cause. When there is a "code first" note and an underlying condition is present, the underlying condition should be sequenced first. For example, malignant ascites (R18.0) has a note to "code first" the malignancy, such as: malignant neoplasm of ovary (C56.-). In this situation, code C56.- would be assigned first, followed by code R18.0

The "code, if applicable, any causal condition first" note indicates that multiple codes should be assigned only if the causal condition is documented as being present. For example, "Other retention of urine" (R33.8) requires that the code to identify enlarged prostate (N40.1) be assigned as the first-listed code or principal diagnosis, but only if it is documented as being the cause of the urinary retention.

The instruction to "use additional code" indicates that multiple codes should be assigned only if the condition mentioned is documented as being present. Examples include the following:

- Malignant neoplasm of base of tongue (C01) requires an additional code to identify history of tobacco use (Z87.891), but only when history of tobacco use is documented in the medical record.
- Urinary tract infection (N39.0) requires an additional code to identify the organism if it is documented, such as positive culture of *E. coli* (B96.20).

EXERCISE 7.3

Code the following diagnoses.

1. Acute cystitis due to *E. coli* infection — N30.00, B96.20
2. Alcoholic gastritis due to chronic alcoholism — K29.20, F10.20
3. Diverticulitis of colon with intestinal hemorrhage — K57.33
4. Diabetic neuralgia due to type 2 diabetes mellitus, patient on insulin — E11.42, Z79.4
5. Erythema multiforme with arthritis — L51.9, M14.80
6. Fulminant hepatitis, type A, with hepatic coma — B15.0

Avoid Indiscriminate Multiple Coding

Indiscriminate coding of irrelevant information should be avoided. For example, codes for symptoms or signs characteristic of the diagnosis and integral to it should not be assigned. Codes are never assigned solely on the basis of findings of diagnostic tests, such as laboratory, X-ray, or electrocardiographic tests, unless the diagnosis is confirmed by the physician. This guideline differs from the coding practices in the outpatient setting when one is coding encounters for diagnostic tests that have been interpreted by a physician. Codes should not be assigned for conditions that do not meet Uniform Hospital Discharge Data Set criteria for reporting. For example, diagnostic reports often mention such conditions as hiatal hernia, atelectasis, and right bundle branch block with no further mention to indicate any relevance to the care given. Assigning a code is inappropriate for reporting purposes unless the physician provides documentation to support the condition's significance for the episode of care.

Codes designated as unspecified are never assigned when a more specific code for the same general condition is assigned. For example, diabetes mellitus with unspecified complication (E11.8) would never be assigned when a code for diabetes with renal complication (E11.29) is assigned for the same episode of care.

Laterality

Some ICD-10-CM codes indicate laterality, specifying whether the condition occurs on the left or right or whether the condition is bilateral. If no bilateral code is provided, and the condition is bilateral, assign separate codes for the left side and the right side. If the side is not identified in the medical record, assign the code for unspecified side. For example:

Q70.10 Webbed fingers, unspecified hand
Q70.11 Webbed fingers, right hand
Q70.12 Webbed fingers, left hand
Q70.13 Webbed fingers, bilateral

CODE UNCONFIRMED DIAGNOSES AS IF ESTABLISHED

When a diagnosis for an inpatient admission is qualified as "possible," "probable," "suspected," "likely," "questionable," "?," or "rule out" at the time of discharge, the condition should be coded and reported as though the diagnosis were established. Other terms that fit the definition of a probable or suspected condition are "consistent with," "compatible with," "indicative of," "suggestive of," "appears to be," and "comparable with." Note that the exception to this guideline is the coding of HIV infection/illness and influenza due to certain identified influenza viruses (e.g., avian influenza or other novel influenza A virus). Code only cases confirmed by physician documentation. The guideline regarding unconfirmed diagnoses does not apply to coding or reporting for outpatient services. For these patients, code to the highest degree of certainty, such as symptoms, signs, or abnormalities. For example:

- A patient is admitted with severe generalized abdominal pain. The physician's diagnostic statement on discharge is: abdominal pain, probably due to acute gastritis. K29.00
  Only the code for gastritis is assigned as the pain is implicit in the diagnosis.
- A patient is admitted and discharged with a final diagnosis of probable peptic ulcer with a recommendation for additional workup. K27.9
- A patient is admitted as an inpatient and discharged with possible posttraumatic brain syndrome, nonpsychotic. F07.81
- A patient is seen in the outpatient clinic with malaise. The physician's diagnostic statement is possible viral syndrome. Only the malaise is coded. R53.81

Caution should be used in coding unconfirmed diagnoses of conditions such as epilepsy, HIV disease, and multiple sclerosis as if they were established. Incorrect reporting of such conditions can have serious personal consequences for the patient, such as the inability to obtain a driver's license and possible social and job discrimination. Physicians are often unaware that official coding guidelines require a diagnosis qualified as unconfirmed to be coded as if established; therefore, the coder should consult the physician before assigning codes for such unconfirmed conditions.

"Rule Out" versus "Ruled Out"

It is important to distinguish between the terms "rule out," which indicates that a diagnosis is still considered to be possible, and "ruled out," which indicates that a diagnosis originally considered as likely is no longer a possibility.

Diagnoses qualified by the term "rule out" are coded as if established for inpatient episodes of care in the same way that diagnoses described as possible or probable are coded. A diagnosis described as "ruled out" is never coded. If an alternative condition has been identified, that diagnosis should be coded; otherwise, a code for the presenting symptom or other precursor condition should be assigned. Here are some examples of codes assigned according to this coding principle:

- Rule out gastric ulcer . . . K25.9 *[condition is coded]*
- Acute appendicitis, ruled out; Meckel's diverticulum found at surgery . . . Q43.0 *[code only the diverticulum]*
- Rule out angiodysplasia of the colon . . . K55.20 *[condition is coded]*

"Borderline" Diagnoses

Care should be exercised with diagnoses documented as "borderline." A borderline diagnosis is not the same as an uncertain diagnosis and is handled differently. Borderline diagnoses are coded as confirmed unless the classification provides a specific entry (e.g., borderline diabetes mellitus). If a borderline condition has a specific index entry in ICD-10-CM, it should be coded as such. Because borderline conditions are not uncertain diagnoses, no distinction is made between the care setting (inpatient versus outpatient). Query for clarification whenever the documentation is unclear regarding a borderline condition.

ACUTE AND CHRONIC CONDITIONS

When the same condition is described as both acute (or subacute) and chronic, it should be coded according to the Alphabetic Index subentries for that condition. If separate subterms for acute (or subacute) and chronic are listed at the same indention level in the Alphabetic Index, both codes are assigned, with the code for the acute condition sequenced first. (Note that a condition described as subacute is coded as acute if there is no separate subterm entry for subacute.) For example, refer to the Alphabetic Index entry for acute and chronic bronchitis:

Bronchitis . . .
-acute or subacute . . . J20.9 . . .
-chronic . . . J42

Because both subterms appear at the same indention level, both codes are assigned, with code J20.9 sequenced first.

When only one term is listed as a subterm, with the other in parentheses as a nonessential modifier, only the code listed for the subterm is assigned. For example, for a diagnosis of acute and chronic adenoiditis, the Alphabetic Index entry is as follows:

Adenoiditis (chronic) J35.02 . . .
-acute J03.90

The only code assigned in this situation is **J03.90, Acute tonsillitis, unspecified.**

In some cases, a combination code has been provided for use when the condition is described as both acute and chronic. For example, code J96.20 includes both acute and chronic respiratory failure. When there are no subentries for acute (or subacute) or chronic, these modifiers are disregarded in coding the condition. For example, refer to **Mastopathy,** cystic. Neither acute nor chronic is listed as a subterm, and so code N60.1- is assigned.

EXERCISE 7.4

Code the following diagnoses.

1. Acute and chronic appendicitis	K35.80 K36
2. Subacute and chronic pyelonephritis	N10 N11.9
3. Acute and chronic cervicitis	N72
4. Acute and chronic abscess of the broad ligament	N73.0 N73.1
5. Acute and chronic bilateral canaliculitis	H04.423

IMPENDING OR THREATENED CONDITION

Selection of a code for a condition described at the time of discharge, or at the conclusion of an outpatient encounter, as impending or threatened depends first on whether the condition actually occurred. If so, the threatened/impending condition is coded as a confirmed diagnosis.

For example, a medical record shows a diagnosis of threatened premature labor at 28 weeks gestation. Review of the medical record indicates that a stillborn was delivered during the hospital stay. This is coded as **O60.14x0, Preterm labor third trimester with preterm delivery third trimester, not applicable or unspecified,** because the threatened condition did occur.

If neither the threatened/impending condition nor a related condition occurred, however, the coder must refer to the Alphabetic Index to answer the following two questions: Is the condition indexed under the main term threatened or impending? Is there a subterm for impending or threatened under the main term for the condition? If such terms appear, the coder should assign the code provided. There are several subterms under each of the main terms **Impending** and **Threatened,** as well as several main terms with such subentries. For example, if a patient is admitted with threatened abortion but the abortion is averted, the code **O20.0, Threatened abortion,** is assigned, because there is an Index entry for "threatened" under the main term **Abortion.**

When neither term is indexed, the precursor condition that actually existed is coded; a code is not assigned for the condition described as impending or threatened. For example, a patient is admitted with a diagnosis of impending gangrene of the lower extremities, but the gangrene was averted by prompt treatment. Because the gangrene did not occur and there is no index entry for impending gangrene, a code must be assigned for the presenting situation that suggested the possibility of gangrene, such as redness or swelling of the extremity.

REPORTING THE SAME DIAGNOSIS CODE MORE THAN ONCE

Each unique ICD-10-CM diagnosis code may be reported only once for an encounter. This applies both to bilateral conditions when there are no distinct codes identifying laterality and to two different conditions classified to the same ICD-10-CM diagnosis code.

LATE EFFECTS

A late effect is a residual condition that remains after the termination of the acute phase of an illness or injury. Such conditions may occur at any time after an acute injury or illness. There is no set period of time that must elapse before a condition is considered to be a late effect. Some late effects are apparent early; others may make an appearance long after the original injury or illness has been resolved. Certain conditions due to trauma, such as contractures and scarring, are inherent late effects no matter how early they occur.

Late effects include conditions reported as such or as sequela of a previous illness or injury. The fact that a condition is a late effect may be inferred when the diagnostic statement includes terms such as the following:

- Late
- Old
- Due to previous injury or illness
- Following previous injury or illness
- Traumatic, unless there is evidence of current injury

EXERCISE 7.5

Write an "X" next to each diagnostic statement given below that identifies a late effect of an injury or illness. For each such statement, underline the residual condition once and the cause of the late effect twice.

1. Hemiplegia due to previous cerebrovascular accident X
2. Joint contracture of fracture, right index finger X
3. Scoliosis due to old infantile paralysis X
4. Laceration of tendon of finger two weeks ago; admitted now for tendon repair ____
5. Keloid secondary to injury nine months ago X
6. Mental retardation due to previous viral encephalitis X

Locating Late Effect Codes

Codes that indicate the cause of a late effect can be located by referring to the main term **Sequelae** in the Alphabetic Index of Diseases and Injuries (with the exception of late effects due to injury, poisoning, and certain other consequences of external causes). Note that ICD-10-CM provides only a limited number of codes to indicate the cause of a late effect:

B90.0–B90.9	Sequelae of tuberculosis
B91	Sequelae of poliomyelitis
B92	Sequelae of leprosy
B94.0–B94.9	Sequelae of other and unspecified infectious and parasitic diseases
E64.0–E64.9	Sequelae of malnutrition and other nutritional deficiencies
E68	Sequelae of hyperalimentation
G09	Sequelae of inflammatory diseases of central nervous system
G65.0–G65.2	Sequelae of inflammatory and toxic polyneuropathies
I69.0–I69.9	Sequelae of cerebrovascular disease
O94	Sequelae of complication of pregnancy, childbirth, and the puerperium

Two Codes Required

Complete coding of late effects requires two codes:

- The condition or nature of the late effect
- The late effect code

The condition or nature of the late effect is sequenced first, followed by the code for the cause of the late effect, except in a few instances where the Alphabetic Index or the Tabular List directs otherwise. If the late effect is due to injury, poisoning, and certain other consequences of external causes (S00–T88), a seventh-character value for "sequelae" should be assigned to the injury code as well as the external causes code (V01–Y95). For example:

M19.111 + S42.301S	Traumatic arthritis of right shoulder due to old fracture of right humerus
G83.10 + B91	Paralysis of leg due to old poliomyelitis
B90.8 + E35	Adrenal tuberculous calcification

There are three exceptions to the coding principle that requires two codes for late effect:

- When the residual effect is not stated, the cause of the late effect code is used alone.
- When no late effect code is provided in ICD-10-CM but the condition is described as being a late effect, only the residual condition is coded. Note that conditions described as due to previous surgery are not coded as late effects but are classified as history of or complications of previous surgery, depending on the specific situation.
- When the late effect code has been expanded at the fourth-, fifth-, or sixth-character level(s) to include the manifestation condition, only the cause of the late effect code is assigned. For example, code **I69.01, Cognitive deficits following nontraumatic subarachnoid hemorrhage,** includes the cause of the late effect (nontraumatic subarachnoid hemorrhage), as well as the manifestation (cognitive deficits).

LATE EFFECT VERSUS CURRENT ILLNESS OR INJURY

A late effect code is not used with a code for a current injury or illness of the same type, with one exception. Codes from category I69, Sequelae of cerebrovascular disease, may be assigned as an additional code with codes from I60–I67, if the patient has a current cerebrovascular disease and residual deficits from an old cerebrovascular disease. For example, a patient with residual aphasia due to subdural hemorrhage two years ago who is admitted because of acute cerebral thrombosis would have the following codes assigned: **I66.9, Occlusion and stenosis of unspecified cerebral artery,** and **I69.220, Aphasia following other nontraumatic intracranial hemorrhage.**

EXERCISE 7.6

Code the following diagnoses.

1. Residuals of poliomyelitis Sequelae	B91
2. Sequela of old crush injury to left foot	S97.82xS
3. Stroke two years ago with residual hemiplegia of the right dominant side Sequelae	I69.351
4. Contracture of hip following partial hip replacement one year ago	M24.559 Z96.649

REVIEW EXERCISE 7.7

Code the following diagnoses.

1. Traumatic arthritis, right ankle, following fracture, right ankle	M12.571 S82.891S
2. Cicatricial contracture of left hand due to burn	L90.5 T23.002S

3.	Brain damage following cerebral abscess seven months ago Sequelae	G93.9 G09
4.	Flaccid hemiplegia due to old cerebral infarction	I69.359
5.	Bilateral neural deafness resulting from childhood measles 10 years ago	H90.3 B94.8
6.	Mononeuritis, median nerve, resulting from previous crush injury to right arm Crush	G56.11 S47.1xxS
7.	Posttraumatic, painful arthritis, left hand Injury	M12.542 S69.92xS
8.	Residuals of previous severe burn, left wrist	T23.072S
9.	Locked-in state (paralytic syndrome) due to old cerebrovascular infarction	G83.5 I69.369
10.	Borderline diabetes mellitus	R73.09
11.	Impending myocardial infarction	I20.0
12.	Borderline hypothyroidism	E03.9

CHAPTER 8 Introduction to the ICD-10-PCS Classification

CHAPTER OVERVIEW

- All ICD-10-PCS codes have an alphanumeric structure, no decimal points, and seven characters.
- ICD-10-PCS is divided into 16 sections relating to the general type of procedure.
- Codes in the Medical and Surgical Section specify the section, body system, root operation, body part, approach, device, and qualifier.
- ICD-10-PCS is divided into Index, Tables, and List of Codes.

LEARNING OUTCOMES

After studying this chapter you should be able to:

- Explain the structure, format, and conventions of ICD-10-PCS.

TERMS TO KNOW

Character
an axis of classification that specifies information about the procedure performed

Value
one of the 34 letters or numbers that can be selected to represent one of the characters in an ICD-10-PCS code

Approach
the fifth character in the code in the Medical and Surgical Section;
the way the procedure site is reached (for example: open or percutaneous)

Qualifier
the seventh character in the code in the Medical and Surgical Section;
it carries additional information for that particular procedure

Root operation
the third character in the code in the Medical and Surgical Section corresponding to the objective of the procedure; in this section alone there are 31 possible objectives

REMEMBER . . .

In the alphanumeric structure of ICD-10-PCS, don't confuse the letters "O" and "I" with the numbers "0" and "1."

INTRODUCTION

The ICD-10-PCS uses standardized terminology to provide precise and stable definitions for all procedures performed. As such, ICD-10-PCS does not include eponyms, usually the name of the surgeon (or surgeons) who developed the procedure. Instead, such procedures are coded to the operation that identifies the objective of the procedure. General information on ICD-10-PCS including conventions and definitions of the components of a code are provided in this chapter. Procedures specific to certain body systems will be covered in the relevant chapters of this handbook.

FORMAT AND ORGANIZATION

Format

The ICD-10-PCS is divided into the Alphabetic Index, Tables, and List of Codes. Codes can be located in alphabetical order within the Index. The Index will refer to a specific location within a Table, but the complete code can be obtained only by referring to the Tables. The List of Codes allows for direct lookup of each code, with the description of each code being provided.

Alphabetic Index

The Index is arranged in alphabetical order based on the type of procedure being performed. The ICD-10-PCS Index does not provide a complete code (with a few exceptions), but it points to a specific location in the Tables by specifying the first three or four characters of the code. The purpose of the Alphabetic Index is to locate the appropriate table in which you'll find the information needed to complete the other characters of the code. It is not required to consult the Index first before proceeding to the Tables to complete the code.

For example, "cholecystectomy" may be looked up by "Excision, gallbladder," or "Resection, gallbladder." The term **Cholecystectomy** has two reference notes as follows:

Cholecystectomy
—see Excision, Gallbladder 0FB4
—see Resection, Gallbladder 0FT4

The Index entries "0FB4" and "0FT4" are not complete codes, but rather they point the user to the appropriate Table identified by the first three values (for example, 0FT, which is shown in figure 8.1).

Tables

The ICD-10-PCS Tables are composed of grids specifying the valid combinations of characters that make up a procedure code. Within a Table, valid codes include all combinations of choices in characters 4 through 7 contained in the same row of the Table.

List of Codes

The ICD-10-PCS List of Codes displays all valid codes in alphanumeric order. Each entry begins with the seven-character code, followed by the full text description. The code descriptions

FIGURE 8.1 Sample Excerpt of ICD-10-PCS Table

Section **0** Medical and Surgical
Body System **F** Hepatobiliary System and Pancreas
Operation **T** Resection: Cutting out or off, without replacement, all of a body part

Body Part	Approach	Device	Qualifier
0 Liver **1** Liver, Right Lobe **2** Liver, Left Lobe **4** Gallbladder **G** Pancreas	**0** Open **4** Percutaneous Endoscopic	**Z** No Device	**Z** No Qualifier
5 Hepatic Duct, Right **6** Hepatic Duct, Left **8** Cystic Duct **9** Common Bile Duct **C** Ampulla of Vater **D** Pancreatic Duct **F** Pancreatic Duct, Accessory	**0** Open **4** Percutaneous Endoscopic **7** Via Natural or Artificial Opening **8** Via Natural or Artificial Opening Endoscopic	**Z** No Device	**Z** No Qualifier

are generated using rules that produce standardized, complete, and easy-to-read code descriptions. Because of the large volume of codes, published ICD-10-PCS code books generally do not include the List of Codes. However, the List of Codes is available from the following Web site: http://www.cms.gov/Medicare/Coding/ICD10/2013-ICD-10-PCS-GEMs.html under "2013 PCS - Long and Abbreviated Titles."

Code Structure

All ICD-10-PCS codes have an alphanumeric structure, with all codes made up of seven characters and no decimal points. It is important to distinguish between "character" and "value" before we get any further. Each **character** in a code is an axis of classification that represents an aspect of the procedure. A **value** is one of the 34 letters or numbers that can be selected to represent one of the characters in an ICD-10-PCS code. These values are made up of digits 0–9, or the letters A–H, J–N, and P–Z. The letters "O" and "I" are not used so as not to be confused with the digits "0" and "1."

Refer to figure 8.2 for the structure and meaning of each character for codes within the Medical and Surgical Section.

FIGURE 8.2 Structure of Codes in the Medical and Surgical Section

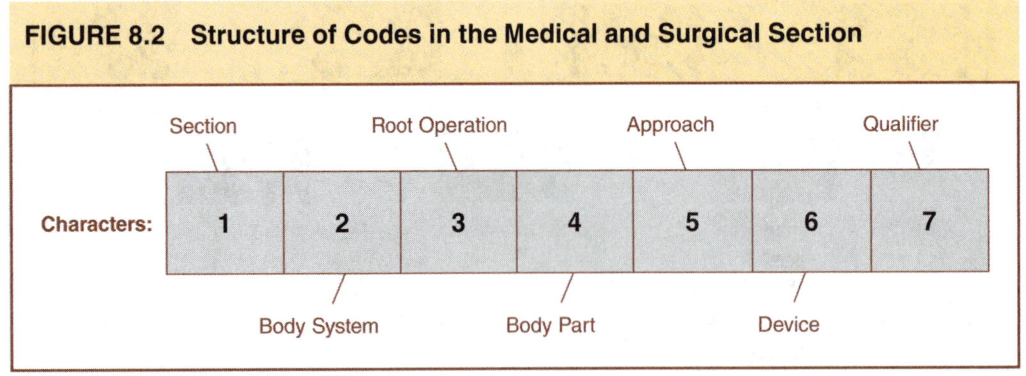

Within a defined code range, the second through seventh characters have a standard meaning—but may have different meanings across sections. Within a defined code range, a character specifies the same type of information in that axis of classification, as follows: The first character represents the axis for section, the second for body system, the third for root operation, the fourth for body part, the fifth for approach, the sixth for device, and the seventh for qualifier. These specific components of a code and their definitions will be covered in more detail later.

The number of unique values used in an axis of classification differs as needed. This means that within different axes of the classification, there may be different unique values. So, for example, the body part axis will have many more unique values than the approach axis, because there are many more body parts than surgical approaches.

As with words in their context, the meaning of any single value is a combination of its axis of classification and any preceding values on which it may be dependent. For example, the meaning of a body part value in the Medical and Surgical Section is always dependent on the body system value. The body part value "0" in the "central nervous" body system specifies "brain," and the body part value "0" in the "peripheral nervous" body system specifies "cervical plexus." (Refer to figure 8.3 for a graphic representation of this example).

FIGURE 8.3 Examples of Body Part Values

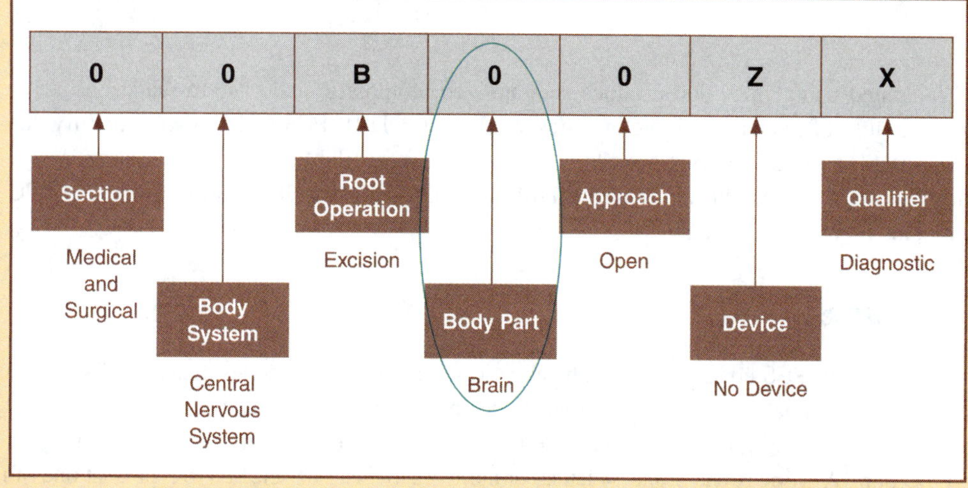

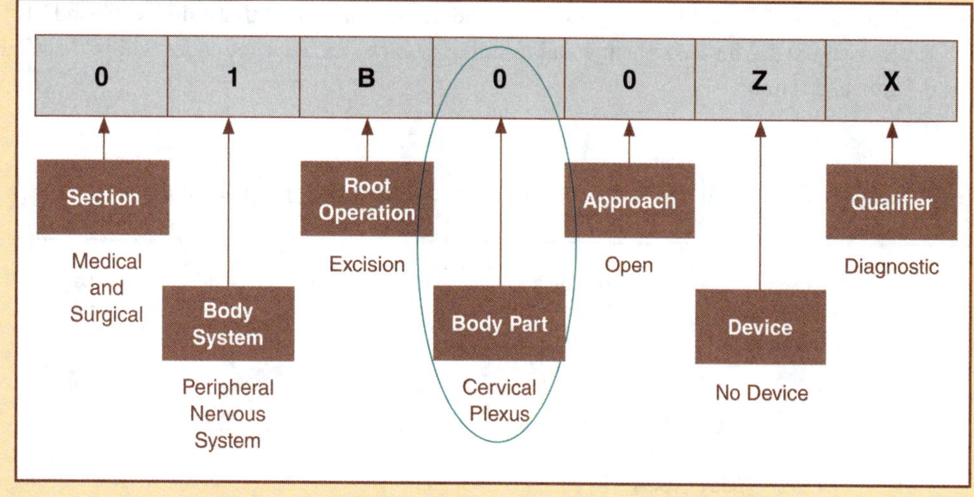

Relational Terms

The term "and," when used in a code description, means "and/or." For example, "lower arm and wrist muscle" means lower arm and/or wrist muscle.

EXERCISE 8.1

Without referring to the handbook material or ICD-10-PCS, mark the following statements either true or false.

1. The ICD-10-PCS Index includes eponyms to identify procedures. F
2. All ICD-10-PCS codes have an alphanumeric structure, with all codes made up of seven characters. T
3. All complete ICD-10-PCS codes can be located within the Index. F
4. The ICD-10-PCS Tables specify the valid combinations of characters that make up a procedure code. T
5. The letters "O" and "I" are not used as ICD-10-PCS values so as not to be confused with the digits "0" and "1." T

CODE CHARACTERS AND THEIR DEFINITIONS

All ICD-10-PCS codes are composed of seven characters. All seven characters must be specified for the code to be valid. If the documentation is incomplete for coding purposes, the provider must be queried for the necessary information. This section discusses each character that makes up ICD-10-PCS, and the definition of each, as well as the main values that are applicable to build a PCS code in the Medical and Surgical Section.

Character 1: Section

The first character in the code always refers to the section. A section refers to a broad procedure category or section where the code is found. ICD-10-PCS is divided into 16 sections relating to the general type of procedure. Table 8.1 displays the ICD-10-PCS sections along with the first character of each code specifying the section.

As shown in table 8.1, the number "0" represents the Medical and Surgical Section, while the other sections have a different numeric or alphabetic value. For example, Obstetrics has a first character of "1." There are also some limited ancillary diagnostic codes, such as "B" for Imaging and "C" for Nuclear Medicine. There is no section for laboratory tests, as most facilities don't code lab tests for inpatient records. The majority of the procedures that would normally be reported in an inpatient setting can be found in the Medical and Surgical Section. Therefore, the following discussion regarding the component characters of a code refers strictly to the Medical and Surgical Section. The Medical- and Surgical-Related Section and the Ancillary Section are both covered in chapter 11 of this handbook.

TABLE 8.1 ICD-10-PCS Sections and Their Corresponding Character Value

Value	Section	Value	Section
0	Medical and Surgical	8	Other Procedures
1	Obstetrics	9	Chiropractic
2	Placement	B	Imaging
3	Administration	C	Nuclear Medicine
4	Measurement and Monitoring	D	Radiation Oncology
5	Extracorporeal Assistance and Performance	F	Physical Rehabilitation and Diagnostic Audiology
6	Extracorporeal Therapies	G	Mental Health
7	Osteopathic	H	Substance Abuse Treatment

Character 2: Body System

The second character in an ICD-10-PCS code represents the body system. This character indicates the general physiological system or anatomical region involved (e.g., gastrointestinal). Within the Medical and Surgical Section, these characters will retain the same value. For example, a central nervous system procedure in this section will always have the value "0" for the second character, while a respiratory system procedure will have the value "B" for the second character.

For additional detail, some traditional body systems have been assigned multiple values. For example, the circulatory system has been subdivided into heart and great vessels, upper arteries, lower arteries, upper veins, and lower veins. Within the conventions of ICD-10-PCS, each of these areas is considered a separate body system with different values. Refer to table 8.2 for the body systems in the Medical and Surgical Section, along with their corresponding character value.

The diaphragm is used as the frame of reference for body part values classified as upper or lower in the "upper arteries," "lower arteries," "upper veins," "lower veins," and "muscles and tendons" body systems. For example, veins located above the diaphragm are found in the "upper veins" body system, while veins located below the diaphragm are found in the "lower veins" body system.

Three body systems refer to anatomical regions, as follows:

- Anatomical regions, general
- Anatomical regions, upper extremities
- Anatomical regions, lower extremities

The "anatomical regions" body system codes should only be used when the procedure is performed on an anatomical region, rather than a specific body part. For example, they can be used when a procedure is performed on body layers that span more than one body system, such as a debridement of skin, muscle, and bone at a procedure site. "Anatomical regions" body systems can also be used on the rare occasion when no information is available to support assignment of a code to a more specific body part within a body system.

TABLE 8.2 Medical and Surgical Section Body Systems and Values

Value	Body System	Value	Body System
0	Central nervous	J	Subcutaneous tissue and fascia
1	Peripheral	K	Muscles
2	Heart and great vessels	L	Tendons—includes synovial membrane
3	Upper arteries	M	Bursae and ligaments—includes synovial membrane
4	Lower arteries	N	Head and facial bones
5	Upper veins	P	Upper bones
6	Lower veins	Q	Lower bones
7	Lymphatic and hemic—includes lymph vessels and lymph nodes	R	Upper joints—includes synovial membrane
8	Eye	S	Lower joints—includes synovial membrane
9	Ear, nose, sinus—includes sinus ducts	T	Urinary
B	Respiratory	U	Female reproductive
C	Mouth and throat	V	Male reproductive
D	Gastrointestinal	W	Anatomical regions, general
F	Hepatobiliary and pancreas	X	Anatomical regions, upper extremities
G	Endocrine	Y	Anatomical regions, lower extremities
H	Skin and breast—includes skin and breast glands and ducts		

EXERCISE 8.2

Referring to table 8.2, mark an "X" next to each term or phrase identifying a body system as classified by a unique value within ICD-10-PCS.

1. Respiratory X
2. Heart and great vessels X
3. Circulatory ______
4. Musculoskeletal ______
5. Upper bones X

Character 3: Root Operation

The third character refers to the root operation. Root operation is one of the most important concepts that the user needs to understand in order to identify and select the correct ICD-10-PCS code. Mastering the definitions of these root operations is the key to "building" a code in ICD-10-PCS. Root operation refers to the objective of the procedure. The distinction between the different root operations is the objective, namely, what is the procedure trying to accomplish?

In the Medical and Surgical Section, there are 31 different root operations. Each root operation is precisely defined in the classification. The definitions are easily found in the Table. For example, in the excerpt of the Table shown in figure 8.1, the root operation "Resection" is defined on the third line of the first row as "cutting out or off, without replacement, all of a body part."

Root operations include terms such as "Alteration," "Bypass," "Change," "Creation," "Dilation," "Excision," "Resection," "Fusion," "Insertion," "Occlusion," and "Repair." The complete list of root operations in the Medical and Surgical Section, along with their corresponding value, is included in table 8.3.

Some of the root operations used in ICD-10-PCS may not necessarily coincide with terminology used by physicians in their documentation. However, because many of the terms used to construct ICD-10-PCS codes are defined within the system, the physician is not expected to use the exact terms used in ICD-10-PCS code descriptions. Instead, it is the coder's responsibility to determine what the documentation in the medical record equates to in the ICD-10-PCS definitions.

The coder is not required to query the physician when the correlation between the documentation and the defined ICD-10-PCS terms is clear. For example, if the physician documents "partial resection," the coder can independently correlate "partial resection" to the root operation "Excision" without querying the physician for clarification because it meets the definition of excision within ICD-10-PCS, namely, "cutting out or off, without replacement, a portion of a body part."

Because of the large number of root operations and their importance in assigning ICD-10-PCS codes, specific root operations are covered in more detail in chapter 10 of this handbook.

TABLE 8.3 ICD-10-PCS Root Operations and Their Corresponding Value

Value	Root Operation	Value	Root Operation	Value	Root Operation	Value	Root Operation
0	Alteration	8	Division	J	Inspection	S	Reposition
1	Bypass	9	Drainage	K	Map	T	Resection
2	Change	B	Excision	L	Occlusion	V	Restriction
3	Control	C	Extirpation	M	Reattachment	W	Revision
4	Creation	D	Extraction	N	Release	U	Supplement
5	Destruction	F	Fragmentation	P	Removal	X	Transfer
6	Detachment	G	Fusion	Q	Repair	Y	Transplantation
7	Dilation	H	Insertion	R	Replacement		

Character 4: Body Part

The fourth character indicates the specific part of the body system or anatomical site where the procedure was performed (for example, appendix). Within ICD-10-PCS, body part values may refer to an entire organ (e.g., liver) or to specific portions of an organ (e.g., liver, right lobe). Appendix C of ICD-10-PCS, Body Part Key, includes helpful information listing specific alternative names for muscles, veins, nerves, and other anatomic sites, as well as the corresponding ICD-10-PCS body part that should be used for code selection. For example, the key indicates that the term "abdominal aortic plexus" should use the body part "abdominal sympathetic nerve."

If a procedure is performed on a portion of a body part that does not have a separate body part value, the value corresponding to the whole body part value should be selected. For example, a procedure that is done on the alveolar process of the mandible would get coded to the whole—the "mandible" body part.

Procedures performed on body parts identified with the prefix "peri" (meaning "around" or "near") should be coded to the body part named. For example, a procedure identified as "perirenal" would be coded to the body part "kidney."

Branches of body parts. Where ICD-10-PCS does not provide a body part value to a specific branch of a body part, the body part is coded to the closest proximal branch that has a specific body part value. For example, a procedure performed on the mandibular branch of the trigeminal nerve is coded to the "trigeminal nerve" body part value.

Bilateral body part values. ICD-10-PCS provides values for some bilateral body parts. However, not every paired organ or body part has a "bilateral" value. If the identical procedure is performed on

FIGURE 8.4 Excerpt from Table Showing Bilateral Body Part

Section **0** Medical and Surgical
Body System **U** Female Reproductive System
Operation **T** Resection: Cutting out or off, without replacement, all of a body part

Body Part	Approach	Device	Qualifier
0 Ovary, Right **1** Ovary, Left **2** Ovaries, Bilateral **5** Fallopian Tube, Right **6** Fallopian Tube, Left **7** Fallopian Tubes, Bilateral **9** Uterus	**0** Open **4** Percutaneous Endoscopic **7** Via Natural or Artificial Opening **8** Via Natural or Artificial Opening Endoscopic **F** Via Natural or Artificial Opening With Percutaneous Endoscopic Assistance	**Z** No Device	**Z** No Qualifier
4 Uterine Supporting Structure **C** Cervix **F** Cul-de-sac **G** Vagina	**0** Open **4** Percutaneous Endoscopic **7** Via Natural or Artificial Opening **8** Via Natural or Artificial Opening Endoscopic	**Z** No Device	**Z** No Qualifier
J Clitoris **L** Vestibular Gland **M** Vulva	**0** Open **X** External	**Z** No Device	**Z** No Qualifier
K Hymen	**0** Open **4** Percutaneous Endoscopic **7** Via Natural or Artificial Opening **8** Via Natural or Artificial Opening Endoscopic **X** External	**Z** No Device	**Z** No Qualifier

both sides, and a bilateral body part value exists for that body part, the procedure code is assigned once using the bilateral body part value. For example, refer to figure 8.4 to code bilateral oophorectomy. The identical procedure was performed on both ovaries, and there is a body part value that includes bilateral ovaries. Because there is a value for "bilateral," we would report a single code.

If no bilateral body part value exists, each procedure should be coded separately using the appropriate body part value. For example, consider bilateral hip replacement. There are body part values for "right hip" and for "left hip," but not for bilateral hips. If the exact same procedure was performed on both hips, two separate codes should be reported to identify that both hips were replaced.

Skin, subcutaneous tissue, and fascia overlying a joint. If a procedure is performed on the skin, subcutaneous tissue, or fascia overlying a joint, the procedure is coded to the following body part:

- Shoulder is coded to upper arm.
- Elbow is coded to lower arm.
- Wrist is coded to lower arm.
- Hip is coded to upper leg.
- Knee is coded to lower leg.
- Ankle is coded to foot.

Fingers and toes. If a body system does not contain a separate body part value for fingers, procedures performed on the fingers are coded to the body part value for the hand. If a body system does not contain a separate body part value for toes, procedures performed on the toes are coded to the body part value for the foot. For example, excision of a finger tendon is coded to one of the hand tendon body part values in the "tendons" body system.

We have now covered the majority of the body part guidelines, except for a few that are reserved for the body system. Procedures on the following body parts are covered in more detail in later chapters of this handbook.

- Upper intestinal tract and lower intestinal tract are addressed in chapter 20, Diseases of the Digestive System.
- Tendons, ligaments, bursae, and fascia near a joint are addressed in chapter 23, Diseases of the Musculoskeletal System and Connective Tissue.
- Coronary arteries are addressed in chapter 28, Diseases of the Circulatory System.

Character 5: Approach

The fifth character refers to the technique or approach used to reach the procedure site (e.g., open). Seven approaches are listed in the Medical and Surgical Section. Approaches can be external, through the skin or mucous membrane, or through an orifice. The following list breaks down the approaches.

- External
- Through the skin or mucous membrane
  —Open
  —Percutaneous
  —Percutaneous endoscopic
- Through an orifice
  —Via natural or artificial opening
  —Via natural or artificial opening endoscopic
  —Via natural or artificial opening with percutaneous endoscopic assistance

As with root operations, each approach is precisely defined in the classification. Refer to table 8.4 for the approaches shown in the Medical and Surgical Section, along with their corresponding value and definition, and to figure 8.5 for illustrations of surgical approaches.

TABLE 8.4 Medical and Surgical Section Approaches

Value	Approach	Definition
X	External	Procedures performed directly on the skin or mucous membrane and procedures performed indirectly by the application of external force through the skin or mucous membrane
0	Open	Cutting through the skin or mucous membrane and any other body layers necessary to expose the site of the procedure
3	Percutaneous	Entry, by puncture or minor incision, of instrumentation through the skin or mucous membrane and/or any other body layers necessary to reach the site of the procedure
4	Percutaneous endoscopic	Entry, by puncture or minor incision, of instrumentation through the skin or mucous membrane and/or any other body layers necessary to reach and visualize the site of the procedure
7	Via natural or artificial opening	Entry of instrumentation through a natural or artificial external opening to reach the site of the procedure
8	Via natural or artificial opening endoscopic	Entry of instrumentation through a natural or artificial external opening to reach and visualize the site of the procedure
F	Via natural or artificial opening with percutaneous endoscopic assistance	Entry of instrumentation through a natural or artificial external opening, and entry, by puncture or minor incision, of instrumentation through the skin or mucous membrane and any other body layers necessary to aid in the performance of the procedure

In addition to the approach definitions listed in table 8.4, there are a handful of guidelines related to the selection of the approach, as follows:

- *Open approach with percutaneous endoscopic assistance*: code to "open" approach. Example: laparoscopic-assisted sigmoidectomy is coded to "open."
- *External approach.* The following procedures should be coded to "external":
  —Procedures performed within an orifice on structures that are visible without the aid of any instrumentation. Example: resection of tonsils.
  —Procedures performed indirectly by the application of external force through the intervening body layers. Example: closed reduction of fracture.
- *Percutaneous procedure via device*: Code to "percutaneous." Example: fragmentation of kidney stone via percutaneous nephrostomy.

FIGURE 8.5 Illustrations of Medical and Surgical Section Approaches

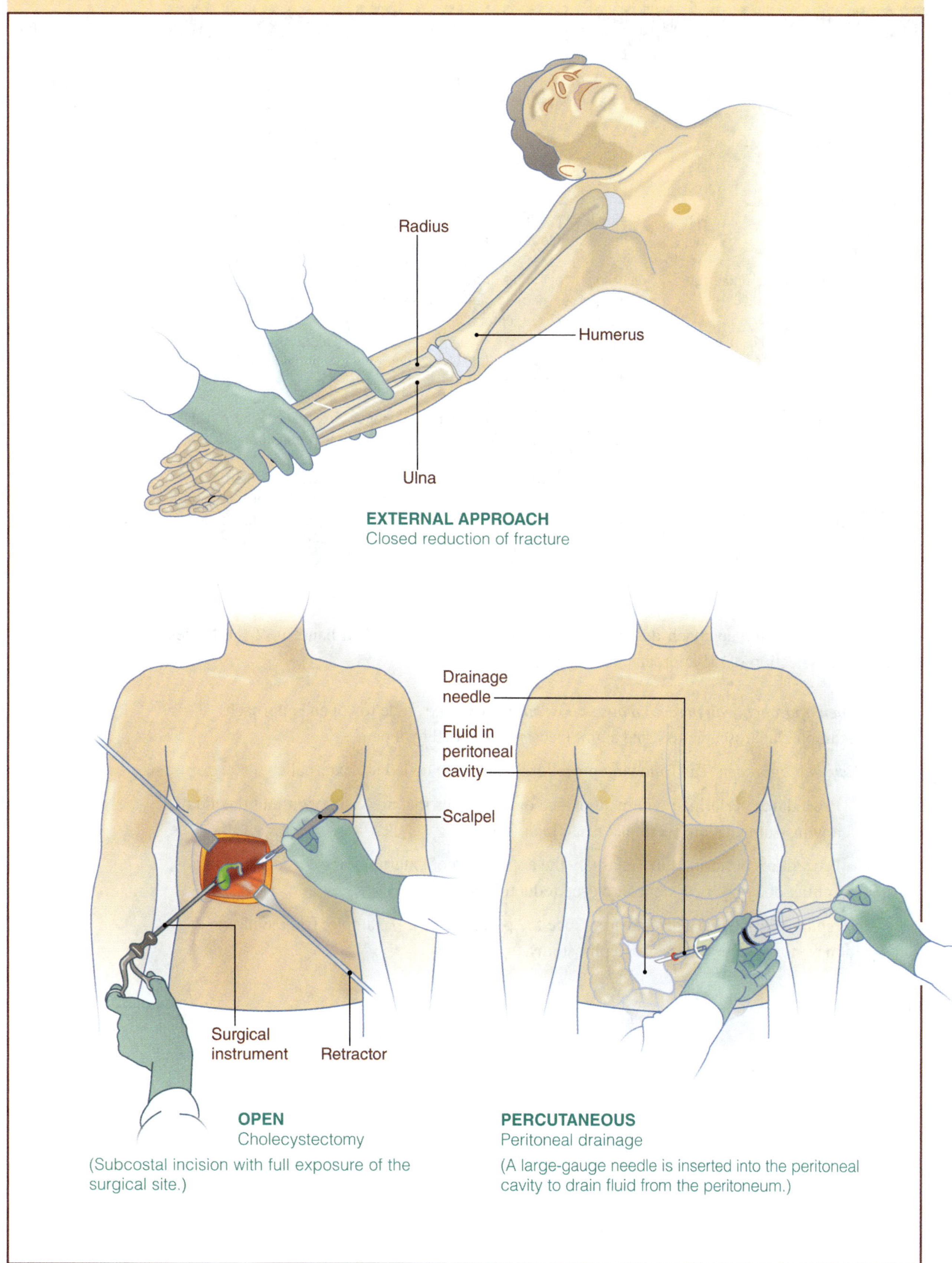

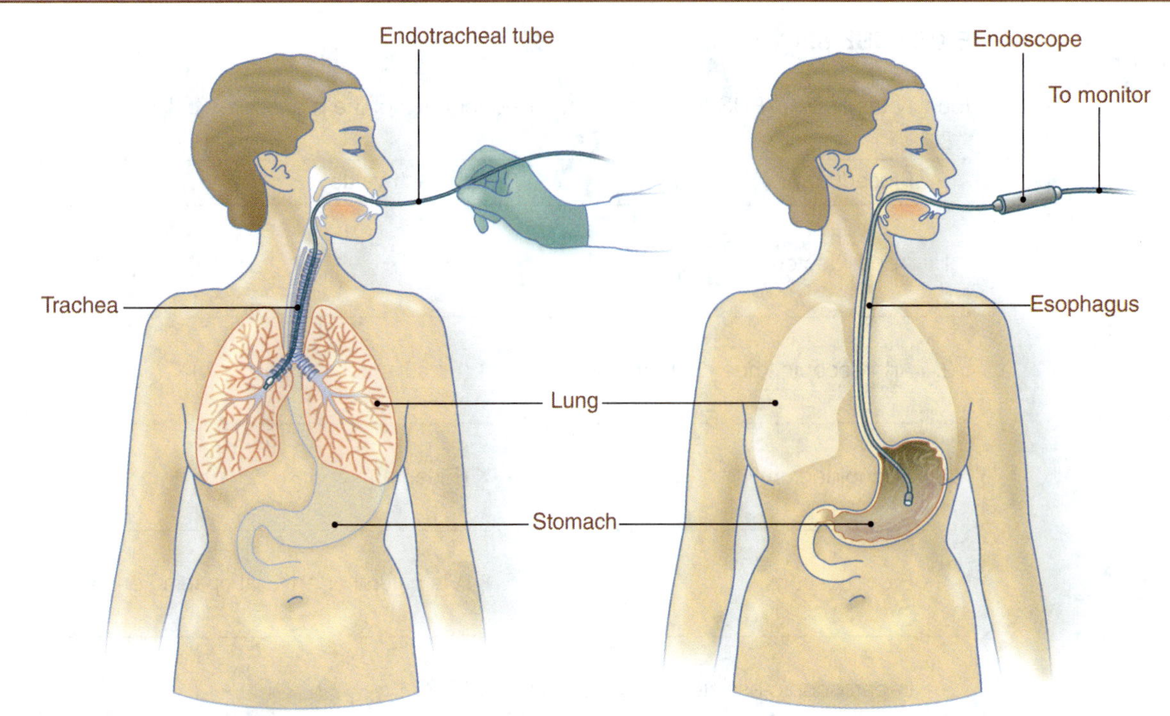

VIA NATURAL OR ARTIFICIAL OPENING
Insertion of endotracheal tube
(The tube is inserted through the mouth into the trachea.)

VIA NATURAL OR ARTIFICIAL OPENING ENDOSCOPIC
Gastroscopy
(The endoscope is inserted through the mouth into the stomach.)

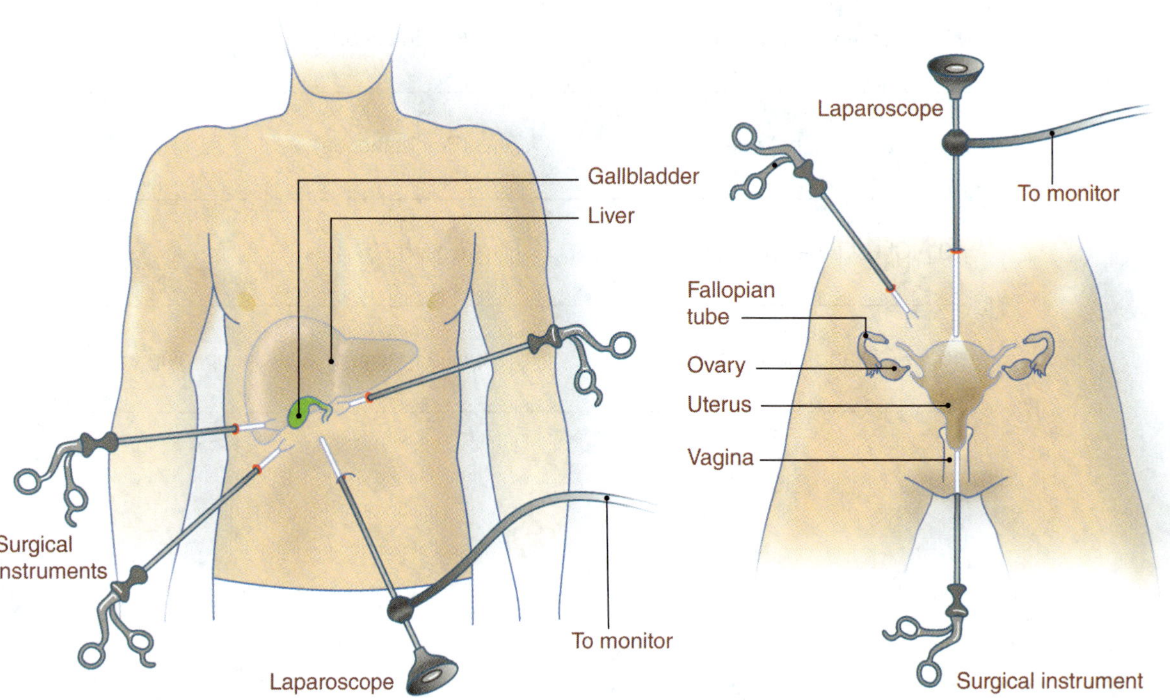

PERCUTANEOUS ENDOSCOPIC
Laparoscopic cholecystectomy
(Several small incisions are made in the abdomen, through which surgical instruments and a laparoscope with a video camera are placed into the abdominal cavity.)

VIA NATURAL OR ARTIFICIAL OPENING WITH PERCUTANEOUS ENDOSCOPIC ASSISTANCE
Laparoscopic-assisted vaginal hysterectomy
(A vaginal hysterectomy is done with laparoscopic assistance; ovaries and fallopian tubes may be detached using a laparoscope, and the uterus is detached and all of the organs are removed through the vagina.)

EXERCISE 8.3

Identify the ICD-10-PCS approach value used for each of the procedures below:

	Procedure	Approach Value
1.	Appendectomy	0 (Open)
2.	Arthroscopic knee chondroplasty	4 (Percutaneous endoscopic)
3.	Adenoidectomy	X (External)
4.	Bronchoscopy	8 (Via natural or artificial opening endoscopic)
5.	Laparoscopic-assisted hysterectomy	0 (Open)
6.	Vaginal endometrial ablation	7 (Via natural or artificial opening)
7.	Insertion of pacemaker lead	3 (Percutaneous)
8.	Carpal tunnel release	3 (Percutaneous)
9.	Chest tube removal	X (External)
10.	EGD and biopsy of stomach	8 (Via natural or artificial opening endoscopic)

Character 6: Device

The sixth character is used to identify whether a device was used in a procedure. Only devices that remain in or on the patient's body after the procedure is completed are coded; materials that are incidental to a procedure are not coded. Examples of incidental materials are sutures, ligatures, clips, radiological markers, and temporary postoperative wound drains.

Device values fall into four basic categories:

- Grafts and prostheses
- Implants
- Simple or mechanical appliances
- Electronic appliances

When no device is involved in the procedure, the letter "Z," representing "none," is used as the sixth character to complete the code structure.

The ICD-10-PCS Index contains entries to provide guidance on the selection of codes related to devices. In addition, two appendixes have been created for ease of use:

- Appendix D, Device Key
- Appendix E, Device Aggregation Table

The Device Key provides listings of devices by the common names, as well as the brand names, with the corresponding ICD-10-PCS terms to assist in selecting the appropriate device value. For example, the key indicates that the common device name "Total artificial (replacement) heart" as well as the brand name "AbioCor® Total Replacement Heart" should be coded to the ICD-10-PCS value for "synthetic substitute" device.

The Device Aggregation Table provides a mechanism for directing coders and secondary data users to correlate a specific device value, used in the original root operation where the device was placed, with its more general device value used in other root operations. Often, in root operations such as "Removal" and "Revision," the device value is the aggregate general device of an entire family of specific device values. For example, in figure 8.6, the Device Aggregation Table indicates that, for the root operation "Insertion," there are two specific cardiac lead devices available—one for defibrillators and one for pacemakers. However, when coding a less specific root operation such as "Removal" or "Revision," the device value is less specific. In these cases, only the general device "cardiac lead" is available and the type of cardiac device for the lead (i.e., defibrillator or pacemaker) is not specified.

FIGURE 8.6 Excerpt from the Device Aggregation Table

Specific Device	For Operation	In Body System	General Device
Cardiac Lead, Defibrillator	Insertion	Heart and Great Vessels	M Cardiac Lead
Cardiac Lead, Pacemaker	Insertion	Heart and Great Vessels	M Cardiac Lead

EXERCISE 8.4

Mark an "X" next to each term or phrase that can be considered a codeable device within ICD-10-PCS.

1. Joint prosthesis X
2. Cardiac pacemaker X
3. Prolene sutures ____
4. Neurostimulator X
5. Mesh graft X

Character 7: Qualifier

The seventh character indicates a qualifier. A qualifier has a unique meaning within individual procedures. This position within the code is used to provide additional information. Examples of qualifiers include "diagnostic" and "stereotactic." When there is no qualifier, the seventh character is the letter "Z" to complete the code structure.

CHAPTER 9

Basic ICD-10-PCS Coding Steps

CHAPTER OVERVIEW

- The Uniform Hospital Discharge Data Set (UHDDS) requires all significant procedures to be reported. Significant procedures meet any one of the following conditions:
  - — The procedure is surgical in nature.
  - — It carries an anesthetic risk.
  - — It carries a procedural risk.
  - — It requires specialized training.
- The ICD-10-PCS contains the Alphabetic Index, the Tables, and the List of Codes.

LEARNING OUTCOMES

After studying this chapter you should be able to:

Identify main terms in the Alphabetic Index.

Navigate the Tables to find the appropriate Table.

TERM TO KNOW

Principal procedure
procedure performed for definitive treatment (rather than for diagnostic or exploratory purposes)

INTRODUCTION

This chapter covers the steps to take in locating ICD-10-PCS codes. In addition, it discusses general information on reporting procedures as well as selection of the principal procedure.

The following steps should be undertaken to locate the procedure codes using ICD-10-PCS:

1. Locate the main term in the Alphabetic Index
   - Follow any cross-reference instructions.
   - Obtain the first three or four characters for the procedure.
   - In a few instances, complete seven-character codes are provided.
2. Find the applicable Table.
   - Review the section, body system, and root operation definition, and verify that the first three characters referenced by the Index are correct.
3. Continue building the ICD-10-PCS code by selecting a value from each column for the remaining four characters, as follows:
   - Select a value from the body part column for the fourth character.
   - Select a value from the approach column for the fifth character.
   - Select a value from the device column for the sixth character.
   - Select a value from the qualifier column for the seventh character.

It is important to note that valid codes can be built using all combinations of choices in characters 4 through 7 that are in the same row of the Table. Because all ICD-10-PCS codes are seven characters long, the code must specify all seven characters to be valid.

LOCATE THE MAIN TERM IN THE ALPHABETIC INDEX

The first step in coding is to locate the main term in the Alphabetic Index. The Index can be used to access the Tables. Main terms may be a common procedure term (e.g., **Appendectomy, Cholecystectomy**), a root operation value (e.g., Resection, Excision), or body parts. Subterms provide more specific information. Each indention level of the Index is represented below by a hyphen. Please note that some publishers have adopted the convention used in the ICD-10-CM Index of adding a dash (-) at the end of an Index entry to indicate that additional characters are required.

The following examples demonstrate the different main terms and subterms used in ICD-10-PCS.

- When the main term is a root operation value (e.g., Excision), the subterms will be body parts where the operation was performed, as shown below:

Excision
-Acetabulum
--Left 0QB5
--Right 0QB4
-Adenoids 0CBQ

- When the main term is a common procedure, references are provided to the corresponding ICD-10-PCS root operation and body part, as shown below:

Claviculectomy
—see Excision, Upper Bones 0PB
—see Resection, Upper Bones 0PT

Condylectomy
—see Excision, Head and Facial Bones 0NB
—see Excision, Upper Bones 0PB
—see Excision, Lower Bones 0QB

- When the main term is an anatomical term, helpful references are provided to identify specific ICD-10-PCS body parts, as shown below:

Adductor hallucis muscle
—use Muscle, Foot, Left
—use Muscle, Foot, Right

It is not necessary to start with the Alphabetic Index before proceeding to the Tables to complete a code. A valid code may be chosen directly from the Tables, but it will require a thorough familiarity with the body systems and root operations.

EXERCISE 9.1

Without referring to the Alphabetic Index, underline the word(s) in each item that indicate the main term for each procedure.

1. Laparoscopic cholecystectomy
2. Resection of pancreas
3. Bilateral oophorectomy
4. Incision and drainage of abscess, neck

5. Bowel resection with transverse colostomy

6. Fusion of L5-S1 vertebral joints

7. Lysis of intestinal adhesions

FIND THE APPLICABLE TABLE

Once the first three or more characters of a code have been located in the Alphabetic Index, the coder must refer to the appropriate Table. There is no need to follow the reference notes to see other terms if the Index provides the first three or four characters of a code. For example, the main term **Cholecystectomy** refers us to "0FT4" for "Resection, gallbladder." Looking up the main term "Resection" with the subterm "gallbladder" will not yield the complete seven-character code. Instead, it will reference the same Table: 0FT4.

To find the appropriate Table:

- If using the PDF version available on the Centers for Medicare & Medicaid Services Web site, the Tables can be accessed directly by clicking on the hyperlink represented by the character values provided by the Index (e.g., 0FT4).
- If using a published ICD-10-PCS book, it will be necessary to manually locate the appropriate Table. The Tables are arranged in a series, beginning with section 0, Medical and Surgical, and body system 0, Central Nervous, and proceeding in numerical order. Sections 0 through 9 are followed by sections B through D and F through H. The same convention is followed within each Table for the second through seventh characters—numeric values in order first, followed by alphabetical values in order.

EXERCISE 9.2

Without referring to ICD-10-PCS, identify the order in which the following Tables (represented by the first three characters) can be located.

1. 0JQ 4
2. 0J9 3
3. B31 5
4. 09B 1
5. 09W 2

CODING DEMONSTRATIONS

Follow the steps outlined above to determine the correct code for each of the procedural statements listed below:

Total Laparoscopic Cholecystectomy

Refer to main term **Cholecystectomy.** Note that there are two references: "see Excision, Gallbladder [0FB4]" and "see Resection, Gallbladder [0FT4]." There is no need to find the Index entry for the main term "Excision," subterm "gallbladder," or main term "Resection," subterm "gallbladder," as they will both still refer to the same Tables. If you're not familiar with the difference between these two root operations, refer to Appendix A of ICD-10-PCS and review the definitions. Otherwise, follow the Index entries by locating both Tables (0FB) and (0FT) to determine the difference in the definitions of the root operations "Excision" and "Resection."

Review Table 0FB. Reading across the first row of the Table, the first character, "0," refers to Medical and Surgical Section; the second character, "F," refers to the body system "hepatobiliary system and pancreas"; and the third character, "B," refers to the root operation "Excision." Excision is defined on the 0FB table as "cutting out or off, without replacement, a portion of a body part." Because the procedure is total cholecystectomy, "Excision" is not the correct root operation.

Review Table 0FT. The third character, "T," refers to the root operation "Resection." Resection is defined on the 0FT table as "cutting out or off, without replacement, all of a body part." Based on this review, it becomes clear that "Excision, gallbladder" is the root operation for a partial cholecystectomy, and "Resection" is the root operation for a total cholecystectomy; therefore, 0FT is the correct Table.

Continue building the remainder of the code by selecting the remaining values among the appropriate characters from the four columns shown in figure 9.1. In the first column—body part—select the value of "4" for gallbladder. From the second column—approach—because this was a laparoscopic procedure, select the value "4" for percutaneous endoscopic. Moving across the table, select as the sixth character "Z" for device, because no device was used for this procedure, and select as the last character "Z," representing no qualifier. The ICD-10-PCS procedure code, then, is 0FT44ZZ. Figure 9.1 shows the 0FT Table used for this demonstration, with the appropriate value circled for each character of the code.

FIGURE 9.1 Excerpt of 0FT Table from ICD-10-PCS

Section 0 Medical and Surgical
Body System F Hepatobiliary System and Pancreas
Operation T Resection: Cutting out or off, without replacement, all of a body part

Body Part	Approach	Device	Qualifier
0 Liver 1 Liver, Right Lobe 2 Liver, Left Lobe 4 Gallbladder G Pancreas	0 Open 4 Percutaneous Endoscopic	Z No Device	Z No Qualifier
5 Hepatic Duct, Right 6 Hepatic Duct, Left 8 Cystic Duct 9 Common Bile Duct C Ampulla of Vater D Pancreatic Duct F Pancreatic Duct, Accessory	0 Open 4 Percutaneous Endoscopic 7 Via Natural or Artificial Opening 8 Via Natural or Artificial Opening Endoscopic	Z No Device	Z No Qualifier

Note that within an ICD-10-PCS table, valid codes include all combinations of choices in characters 4 through 7 contained in the same row of the Table. For example, using the Table on figure 9.1, the value "8" is not valid as the fifth character for approach because it's not on the same row as the body part "4" for gallbladder.

Below Knee Amputation, Distal Portion, Right Leg

Look up the main term **Amputation** in the Alphabetic Index. Note the cross-reference instruction to "see detachment." Follow the cross-reference by turning to the main term "Detachment," and then the subterm "leg." Note that additional subterms specify "lower" and then "left" and "right." In this instance, the Index provides code 0Y6H0Z for the right lower leg—it is almost complete, except that it only has six characters.

Refer to Table 0Y6 (shown as figure 9.2) and locate the appropriate row for the body part character "H" for lower leg, right. Because the only acceptable values for approach and device for this body part are "0" and "Z," they have already been provided in the Index. Review the values available for the qualifier. As this particular case refers to a "below the knee, distal portion" amputation, select the value "3" for "low." The ICD-10-PCS procedure code, then, is 0Y6H0Z3.

FIGURE 9.2 Excerpt of 0Y6 Table from ICD-10-PCS

Section 0 Medical and Surgical
Body System Y Anatomical Regions, Lower Extremities
Operation 6 Detachment: Cutting off all or a portion of the upper or lower extremities

Body Part	Approach	Device	Qualifier
2 Hindquarter, Right **3** Hindquarter, Left **4** Hindquarter, Bilateral **7** Femoral Region, Right **8** Femoral Region, Left **F** Knee Region, Right **G** Knee Region, Left	**0** Open	**Z** No Device	**Z** No Qualifier
C Upper Leg, Right **D** Upper Leg, Left **H** Lower Leg, Right **J** Lower Leg, Left	**0** Open	**Z** No Device	**1** High **2** Mid **3** Low

UNIFORM HOSPITAL DISCHARGE DATA SET FOR REPORTING PROCEDURES

The Uniform Hospital Discharge Data Set (UHDDS) requires all significant procedures to be reported. In addition, Medicare requires the reporting of any procedure that affects payment, whether or not it meets the definition of a significant procedure. Other procedures may be reported at the hospital's discretion. Most hospitals do not code ancillary or diagnostic procedures in the inpatient setting.

A significant procedure is defined as one that meets any of the following conditions:

- Is surgical in nature
- Carries an anesthetic risk
- Carries a procedural risk
- Requires specialized training

Surgery includes incision, excision, destruction, amputation, introduction, insertion, endoscopy, repair, suturing, and manipulation. Any procedure performed under anesthesia other than topical carries an anesthetic risk. Procedural risk is more difficult to define, but any procedure that has a recognized risk of inducing functional impairment, physiologic disturbance, or possible trauma during an invasive procedure is included in this group. Procedures requiring specialized training are those that are performed by specialized professionals, qualified technicians, or clinical teams specifically trained to perform certain procedures or whose services are directed primarily to carrying them out. This definition implies training over and above that ordinarily provided in the education of physicians, nurses, or technicians.

Meeting Various Reporting Requirements

Under the Health Insurance Portability and Accountability Act of 1996, for administrative simplification purposes, standard code sets have been designated for electronic claims transactions. ICD-10-PCS is the standard for hospitals when reporting surgery and procedures for inpatients, whereas the American Medical Association's Current Procedural Terminology and the Health Care Procedure Coding System level II codes are the standards for hospital reporting of outpatient procedures and physician reporting.

A hospital may also code outpatient procedures using the ICD-10-PCS system for internal or non-claim-related purposes, if desired. In addition, hospitals may report ICD-10-PCS codes for outpatient services, for specific payers under contractual agreements, or as required by their state data-reporting requirements.

Designating the Principal Procedure

The principal procedure as described by the UHDDS is one performed for definitive treatment (rather than for diagnostic or exploratory purposes) or one that is necessary to care for a complication. If two or more procedures appear to meet this definition, the one most related to the principal diagnosis is designated the principal procedure. If both are equally related to the principal diagnosis, the most resource-intensive or complex procedure is usually designated as principal. When more than one procedure is reported, the principal procedure should be identified as that which relates to the principal diagnosis. Coders are advised to follow UHDDS definitions for reporting unless a particular payer has substantially different reporting requirements.

The following additional guidance is provided for selecting principal procedures in relation to the principal diagnosis when more than one procedure is performed:

- A procedure was performed for definitive treatment of both principal diagnosis and secondary diagnosis.

  Sequence as principal procedure the procedure performed for definitive treatment most related to principal diagnosis.

- A procedure was performed for definitive treatment, and diagnostic procedures were performed for both principal diagnosis and secondary diagnosis.

  Sequence as principal procedure the procedure performed for definitive treatment most related to principal diagnosis.

- A diagnostic procedure was performed for the principal diagnosis, and a procedure was performed for definitive treatment of a secondary diagnosis.

  Sequence the diagnostic procedure as principal procedure because the procedure most related to principal diagnosis takes precedence.

- No procedures related to principal diagnosis were performed; however, procedures were performed for definitive treatment, and diagnostic procedures were performed for secondary diagnosis.

  Sequence as principal procedure the procedure performed for definitive treatment of secondary diagnosis because there were no procedures (definitive or nondefinitive treatment) related to principal diagnosis.

It is important to follow UHDDS definitions because principal procedures are significant in the reporting of surgical quality indicators.

CHAPTER 10

ICD-10-PCS Root Operations in the Medical and Surgical Section

CHAPTER OVERVIEW

The thirty-one Medical and Surgical root operations can be divided into nine groups that share similar attributes:

- Root operations to take out some/all of a body part
- Root operations to take out solids/fluids/gases from a body part
- Root operations that involve cutting or separation only
- Root operations to put in/put back or move some/all of a body part
- Root operations to alter the diameter or route of a tubular body part
- Root operations that always involve a device
- Root operations that involve examination only
- Root operations that include other repairs
- Root operations that include other objectives

LEARNING OUTCOMES

After studying this chapter you should be able to:

Identify the objectives of each root operation.

Distinguish among the different root operations in the Medical and Surgical Section.

Discuss the general guidelines applicable to root operations.

TERM TO KNOW

Root operation
the third character in an ICD-10-PCS code, which refers to the objective of the procedure

INTRODUCTION

The previous chapters introduce the structure of ICD-10-PCS codes and discuss the basic steps to select ICD-10-PCS codes. Character 3 in the built code, root operations, is one of the most important concepts the user needs to understand in order to identify and select the correct ICD-10-PCS code. The root operation refers to the objective of the procedure. This chapter covers in detail the 31 root operations in the Medical and Surgical Section and their corresponding definitions. In addition, applicable guidelines from the *ICD-10-PCS Official Coding Guidelines* (2013 edition) are introduced.

ROOT OPERATION GUIDELINES

The majority of the ICD-10-PCS Official Coding Guidelines relate to the third character in a code, which represents the root operation. In this section, we start with the general guidelines applicable to all root operations and then move on to overarching concepts such as coding multiple procedures and discontinued procedures. Guidelines related to specific root operations are covered under the applicable root operation.

To determine the appropriate root operation, the full definition of the root operation must be applied. The definitions for the root operations (within the ICD-10-PCS classification) are included in the classification in Appendix A as well as within each Table (see figure 10.1).

Components of a procedure specified in the root operation definition and explanation are not coded separately. The full definition of each root operation provided in the Table must be carefully considered, as that definition will guide what procedure gets coded separately and what does not. For example, resection of a joint as part of a joint replacement procedure is included in the definition for "Replacement" and is not coded separately. Also not coded separately are procedural steps necessary to reach the operative site (such as incision or approach) and to close the operative site (such as suturing), including anastomosis of a tubular body part. For example, in a resection of sigmoid colon with anastomosis of descending colon to rectum, the anastomosis is not coded separately.

FIGURE 10.1 Table Excerpt Demonstrating Location of Root Operation Definition

Section 0 Medical and Surgical
Body System F Hepatobiliary System and Pancreas
Operation T Resection: Cutting out or off, without replacement, all of a body part

Root operation definition

Body Part	Approach	Device	Qualifier
0 Liver 1 Liver, Right Lobe 2 Liver, Left Lobe 4 Gallbladder G Pancreas	0 Open 4 Percutaneous Endoscopic	Z No Device	Z No Qualifier
5 Hepatic Duct, Right 6 Hepatic Duct, Left 8 Cystic Duct 9 Common Bile Duct C Ampulla of Vater D Pancreatic Duct F Pancreatic Duct, Accessory	0 Open 4 Percutaneous Endoscopic 7 Via Natural or Artificial Opening 8 Via Natural or Artificial Opening Endoscopic	Z No Device	Z No Qualifier

Coding Multiple Procedures

Multiple procedures performed during the same operative episode are coded separately if they meet one of the following four conditions:

1. *The same root operation is performed on different body parts as defined by distinct values of the body part character.* One example is the diagnostic excision of the liver and pancreas. This guideline is straightforward, except that it requires knowing how "body part" is used in the context of ICD-10-PCS. Refer to the excerpt of the Table in figure 10.1. You will note that liver is an individual body part, but if you look right below it, you will see that "liver, right lobe" is considered a different body part from "liver, left lobe" because each has a distinct value. So, separate biopsies of the right and left lobes of the liver are coded separately because we have different values in the fourth character for "body part."
2. *The same root operation is repeated at different body sites that are included in the same body part value.* For example, excision of the sartorius muscle and excision of the gracilis muscle are both included in the upper leg muscle body part value, and multiple procedures are coded. This example represents two excisions performed at two muscles that are both included in the upper leg muscle body part value. If the distinct parts of the procedure are not coded separately, it will not be apparent that two excisions were performed.
3. *Multiple root operations with distinct objectives are performed on the same body part.* An example is destruction of sigmoid lesion and bypass of sigmoid colon.
4. *The intended root operation is attempted using one approach but is converted to a different approach.* For example, laparoscopic cholecystectomy converted to an open cholecystectomy is coded as percutaneous endoscopic "Inspection" and open "Resection."

Coding Discontinued Procedures

When a planned procedure is begun but cannot be completed, it is coded to the extent to which it was actually performed according to the following principles:

- If the intended procedure is discontinued, code the procedure to the root operation performed.
- If a procedure is discontinued before any other root operation is performed, code the root operation "Inspection" of the body part or anatomical region inspected.

The following examples show how to code discontinued procedures:

- A patient is admitted for transurethral removal of ureteral stone. Scope is passed as far as the bladder, but the surgeon is unable to pass it into the ureter. Code only "Inspection" of the bladder.
- A patient is admitted for cholecystectomy with exploration of common duct. When the abdominal cavity is entered, extensive metastatic malignancy involving the stomach and duodenum with probable primary neoplasm in the pancreas is found. The procedure is discontinued and the operative wound closed. Code only the exploratory laparotomy.
- A planned aortic valve replacement procedure is discontinued after the initial thoracotomy and before any incision is made in the heart muscle when the patient becomes hemodynamically unstable. This procedure is coded as an open "Inspection" of the mediastinum.

When a procedure is considered to have "failed" in that it did not achieve the hoped-for result or because every objective of the procedure could not be accomplished, the procedure is coded as performed. For example, occasionally an almost immediate reocclusion of the coronary artery occurs

after the completion of a percutaneous coronary angioplasty, which makes it necessary to return to the operating room to perform a coronary artery bypass to correct the problem. The angioplasty might be described as a failed procedure, but, in fact, the procedure was performed and should be coded. Note that failure to achieve the therapeutic objective is not classified as a complication of the procedure.

Coding Biopsies

A biopsy is defined as the taking of tissue from a living person for the purpose of microscopic study. A biopsy code is not assigned when a lesion removed for therapeutic purposes is sent to the laboratory for examination, even though the term "biopsy" may be used in describing the procedure. Surgical specimens are routinely sent to the pathology laboratory for study; this procedure is not considered a biopsy, and assigning a biopsy code is inappropriate. Biopsies may be coded with several different root operations depending on how the biopsy was performed, keeping in mind the definitions for the different root operations. For example, biopsies may be reported with the root operations "Excision," "Extraction," or "Drainage" with the qualifier "diagnostic."

Biopsy followed by more definitive treatment. If a diagnostic "Excision," "Extraction," or "Drainage" procedure (biopsy) is followed by a more definitive procedure, such as "Destruction," "Excision," or "Resection" at the same procedure site, both the biopsy and the more definitive treatment are coded. For example, a biopsy of the breast is followed by partial mastectomy at the same procedure site; both the biopsy and the partial mastectomy procedure are coded.

Coding Procedures on Overlapping Body Layers

Occasionally, a procedure may involve overlapping body layers. In those instances, the following guideline applies: *If the root operations "Excision," "Repair," or "Inspection" are performed on overlapping layers of the musculoskeletal system, the body part specifying the deepest layer is coded.* For example, an excisional debridement that includes skin and subcutaneous tissue as well as muscle is coded to the body part "muscle."

MEDICAL AND SURGICAL ROOT OPERATIONS

The 31 Medical and Surgical root operations can be divided into nine groups that share similar attributes:

1. Root operations to remove some/all of a body part
2. Root operations to remove solids/fluids/gases from a body part
3. Root operations that involve cutting or separation only
4. Root operations that put in/put back or move some/all of a body part
5. Root operations that alter the diameter or route of a tubular body part
6. Root operations that always involve a device
7. Root operations that involve examination only
8. Root operations that include other repairs
9. Root operations that include other objectives

Root Operations to Take Out Some or All of a Body Part

This group of root operations includes "Excision," "Resection," "Detachment," "Destruction," and "Extraction." Table 10.1 provides an overview of these root operations, including the objective of the procedure, the site of the procedure, and examples of each root operation.

"Excision," "Resection," and "Detachment" are similar in that they all cut out or off without replacement. The difference between these three root operations is based on the site and extent of the procedure—some ("Excision") or all ("Resection") of a body part or an extremity ("Detachment"). A breast lumpectomy is "Excision," while a total mastectomy is "Resection." When the excision is a biopsy, the qualifier "diagnostic" is used. "Excision" is defined as cutting out or off, without replacement, "a portion" of a body part, while "Resection" is cutting out or off, without replacement, "all" of a body part. This distinction is a key concept within ICD-10-PCS; "all" of a body part is uniquely defined in ICD-10-PCS, and it can vary for different organs.

Excision versus Resection

ICD-10-PCS contains values for anatomical subdivisions of a body part, such as lobes of the lungs or liver and regions of the intestine. Resection of the specific body part is coded whenever all of the body part is cut out or off; excision of a less specific body part is not coded. It is important to review the body part values within the Table to confirm whether the procedure should be coded as "Resection" or "Excision." For example, refer back to figure 10.1. The body part column shows unique values for "liver"; "liver, right lobe"; and "liver, left lobe." Removal of the entire right lobe of the liver is considered "Resection" (cutting out all of a body part) based on this Table—even though only one lobe of the liver was removed, as each lobe of the liver is considered a body part. Adjunct information about the anastomotic technique used to complete a procedure (e.g., end-to-end or side-to-end anastomosis after a colectomy) is not specified in ICD-10-PCS. Only the specific excision or resection code is assigned.

Excision for Graft

For procedures involving harvesting of graft tissue, the following guideline applies: *If an autograft is obtained from a different body part in order to complete the objective of the procedure, a separate procedure is coded.* For example, for a coronary bypass with excision of saphenous vein graft, the excision of the saphenous vein is coded separately.

TABLE 10.1 Root Operations to Take Out Some or All of a Body Part

Root Operation	Objective of Procedure	Site of Procedure	Example
Excision	Cutting out/off without replacement	Some of a body part	Breast lumpectomy
Resection	Cutting out/off without replacement	All of a body part	Total mastectomy
Detachment	Cutting out/off without replacement	Extremity only, any level	Amputation above elbow
Destruction	Eradicating without replacement	Some/all of a body part	Fulguration of endometrium
Extraction	Pulling out or off without replacement	Some/all of a body part	Suction D&C

Detachment, Destruction, and Extraction

The root operation "Detachment" is used exclusively for extremity amputation procedures at any level. For "Detachment," the body part value is the site of the detachment, with a qualifier, if applicable, to further specify the level where the extremity was amputated.

"Destruction" and "Extraction" also share the site of procedure—some/all of a body part. But "Destruction" represents eradication without replacement, while "Extraction" represents pulling out or off without replacement. "Destruction" is defined as physical eradication of all or a portion of a body part by the direct use of energy, force, or a destructive agent. With "Destruction," none of the body part is physically taken out. Examples of the root operation "Destruction" are fulguration, ablation, cauterization, and cryoablation. "Extraction" is defined as pulling or stripping out or off all or a portion of a body part by use of force. When the extraction procedure is a biopsy, the qualifier "diagnostic" is used. Examples of the root operation "Extraction" are dilation and curettage, vein stripping, non-excisional biopsy, and dermabrasion.

EXERCISE 10.1

Code these procedures.

1. Laparoscopic excision of right ovarian cyst — 0UB04ZZ
2. Diagnostic dilatation and curettage — 0UDB7ZX
   Extraction
3. Below knee amputation, distal portion, right leg — 0Y6H0Z3
4. Laparoscopic total right oophorectomy — 0UT04ZZ
   Resection
5. Rectal polyp fulguration via sigmoidoscope — 0D5P8ZZ
   Destruction
6. Wedge biopsy of right breast — 0HBT0ZX
   Excision
7. Surgical removal of entire sigmoid colon via abdominal incision — 0DTN0ZZ
   Resection

Root Operations to Take Out Solids/Fluids/Gases from a Body Part

The next group of root operations includes "Drainage," "Extirpation," and "Fragmentation." These root operations share the same site of procedure, namely "within a body part." Table 10.2 provides an overview of these root operations, including the objective of the procedure, the site of the procedure, and examples of each root operation.

The difference between these three root operations is that "Drainage" takes or lets out fluids or gases, "Extirpation" takes or cuts out solid matter from a body part, and "Fragmentation" breaks solid matter into pieces. The root operation "Drainage" is applicable to both diagnostic and therapeutic drainage procedures. The qualifier "diagnostic" is used to identify "Extraction" or "Drainage" root operations that are biopsies. Note that a separate procedure to put in a drainage device is coded to the root operation "Drainage" with the device value "drainage device."

For "Extirpation," the solid matter may be an abnormal by-product of a biological function or a foreign body; it may be embedded in a body part or in the lumen of a tubular body part. The solid matter may or may not have been previously broken into pieces. For "Fragmentation," the physical force (e.g., manual, ultrasonic) applied directly or indirectly is used to break the solid matter into pieces. The solid matter may be an abnormal by-product of a biological function or a foreign body. While it may appear that root operations "Extirpation" and "Fragmentation" are closely related, the key difference is that for "Fragmentation" the pieces of solid matter are not taken out.

TABLE 10.2 Root Operations to Take Out Solids/Fluids/Gases from a Body Part

Root Operation	Objective of Procedure	Site of Procedure	Example
Drainage	Taking/letting out fluids/gases	Within a body part	Incision and drainage
Extirpation	Taking/cutting out solid matter	Within a body part	Thrombectomy
Fragmentation	Breaking solid matter into pieces	Within a body part	Lithotripsy

EXERCISE 10.2

Code these procedures.

1. Incision and drainage of external perianal abscess — 0D9QXZZ
2. Percutaneous mechanical thrombectomy, left brachial artery — 03C83ZZ

   Extirpation
3. Hysteroscopy with intraluminal lithotripsy of left fallopian tube calcification — 0UF68ZZ

   Fragmentation

Root Operations Involving Cutting or Separation Only

This group of root operations is made up of two root operations: "Division" and "Release." Table 10.3 provides an overview of these root operations, including the objective and site of the procedure and examples of each root operation.

"Division" is cutting into/separating a body part. This procedure is performed *within* a body part. With "Division," all or a portion of the body part is separated into two or more portions. Examples of "Division" include neurotomy, spinal cordotomy, and osteotomy.

"Release" is freeing a body part from an abnormal physical constraint. The site of procedure is *around* a body part. With "Release," some of the restraining tissue may be taken out, but none of the body part is taken out. The body part value coded is the body part being freed, not the tissue being manipulated or cut to free the body part. An example is lysis of intestinal adhesions; the value selected should be the specific intestine body part value.

Release versus Division: If the sole objective of the procedure is to free a body part without cutting the body part, that procedure should be identified as root operation "Release." An example is freeing a nerve root from surrounding scar tissue without cutting the nerve. However, if the sole objective of the procedure is separating, or transecting, a body part, that procedure should be identified as root operation "Division," as when severing the nerve root to relieve the pain.

TABLE 10.3 Root Operations Involving Cutting or Separation Only

Root Operation	Objective of Procedure	Site of Procedure	Example
Division	Cutting into/separating a body part	Within a body part	Neurotomy
Release	Freeing a body part from constraint	Around a body part	Adhesiolysis

Root Operations That Put In/Put Back or Move Some/All of a Body Part

The next grouping of root operations includes "Transplantation," "Reattachment," "Transfer," and "Reposition." Table 10.4 provides an overview of these root operations, including the objective of the procedure, the site of the procedure, and examples of each root operation.

TABLE 10.4 Root Operations That Put In/Put Back or Move Some/All of a Body Part

Root Operation	Objective of Procedure	Site of Procedure	Example
Transplantation	Putting in a living body part from a person/animal	Some/all of a body part	Kidney transplant
Reattachment	Putting back a detached body part	Some/all of a body part	Reattach finger
Transfer	Moving a body part to function for a similar body part	Some/all of a body part	Skin transfer flap
Reposition	Moving a body part to normal or other suitable location	Some/all of a body part	Move undescended testicle

The root operation "Transplantation" refers to putting in a living body part taken from another individual or animal to physically take the place and/or function of all or a portion of a similar body part. The native body part may or may not be removed, and the transplanted body part may take over all or a portion of its function. Examples include organ transplants such as liver or kidney transplants. Please note that a procedure in which autologous or nonautologous cells are put in is coded to the Administration Section (rather than the Medical and Surgical Section), even though the procedure may be referred to as a transplantation—for example, stem cell transplantation.

Another root operation in this group is "Reattachment." This root operation involves putting back in, or on, all or a portion of a separated (detached) body part to its normal location or other suitable location. Vascular circulation and nervous system pathways may or may not be reestablished. Examples of this root operation are reattachment of fingers or hand.

The root operation "Transfer" is moving, without taking out, all or a portion of a body part to another location to take over the function of all or a portion of a body part. The body part transferred remains connected to its vascular and nervous supply. Examples include tendon transfer and skin pedicle flap transfer.

The root operation "Reposition" refers to moving a body part to normal or other suitable location. So both "Transfer" and "Reposition" involve moving a body part—but transfer is performed with the objective that the body part will take over or replace the function of a body part. Reposition, on the other hand, is moving a body part, but moving it to where it should normally be or to another appropriate position. One example is the reposition of undescended testicle and reduction of displaced fracture.

EXERCISE 10.3

Code these procedures.

1. Percutaneous right foot tenotomy — 0L8V3ZZ
   Division
2. Laparotomy with lysis of large intestine adhesions — 0DNE0ZZ
   Release
3. Reattachment of severed left index finger — 0XMP0ZZ
4. Liver transplant with donor matched liver — 0FY00Z0
5. Closed reduction of dislocation of the right shoulder joint — 0RSJXZZ
   Reposition

Root Operations to Alter the Diameter or Route of a Tubular Body Part

Four root operations are performed to alter the diameter or route of a tubular body part: "Restriction," "Occlusion," "Dilation," and "Bypass." Tubular body parts are defined in ICD-10-PCS as the hollow body parts that provide a route of passage for solids, liquids, or gases. They include the cardiovascular system and body parts in the gastrointestinal, genitourinary, biliary, and respiratory tracts. Table 10.5 provides an overview of these root operations.

The objective of the root operation "Restriction" is to *partially* close, or narrow, the diameter of an orifice or a lumen, whereas the objective of the root operation "Occlusion" is to *completely* close an orifice or a lumen. The orifice may be a natural orifice or an artificially created orifice. Both "Restriction" and "Occlusion" include intraluminal and extraluminal methods.

- An example of "Restriction" is a gastroesophageal fundoplication. In this procedure, the upper part of the stomach is wrapped around the lower esophageal sphincter to strengthen the sphincter, prevent acid reflux, and repair a hiatal hernia. It is essentially partially closing the valve between the esophagus and stomach (lower esophageal sphincter), which stops acid from backing up into the esophagus easily.
- An example of "Occlusion" is fallopian tube ligation, which is performed to completely close the fallopian tube to prevent pregnancy.

The objective of the root operation "Dilation" is to expand, or enlarge, the diameter of the orifice or lumen of a tubular body part. As with "Restriction" and "Occlusion," the orifice may be a natural orifice or an artificially created orifice and may include intraluminal or extraluminal methods. For example, a percutaneous transluminal angioplasty is performed to expand the lumen of narrow coronary vessels to improve blood circulation.

The objective of the root operation "Bypass," on the other hand, is to alter the route of passage of the contents of a tubular body part. "Bypass" may include rerouting contents of a body part to a downstream area of the normal route, to a similar route and body part, or to an abnormal route and dissimilar body part. "Bypass" includes one or more anastomoses, with or without the use of a device. "Bypass" procedures are coded by identifying the body part bypassed "from" and the body part bypassed "to." Other specific guidelines for bypass procedures are covered in the Diseases of the Circulatory System chapter and the Diseases of the Digestive System chapter. An example of a "Bypass" root operation is a coronary artery bypass graft procedure whereby blood flow is rerouted through a new artery or vein that is grafted around diseased sections of the coronary arteries to increase blood flow to the heart muscle.

TABLE 10.5 Root Operations to Alter the Diameter or Route of a Tubular Body Part

Root Operation	Objective of Procedure	Site of Procedure	Example
Restriction	Partially closing orifice/lumen	Tubular body part	Gastroesophageal fundoplication
Occlusion	Completely closing orifice/lumen	Tubular body part	Fallopian tube ligation
Dilation	Expanding orifice/lumen	Tubular body part	Percutaneous transluminal coronary angioplasty (PTCA)
Bypass	Altering route of passage	Tubular body part	Coronary artery bypass graft (CABG)

Root Operations That Always Involve a Device

The next grouping involves six root operations that always involve a device: "Insertion," "Replacement," "Supplement," "Change," "Removal," and "Revision." Table 10.6 provides an overview of these root operations.

The objective of the root operation "Insertion" is to put in a nonbiological device that monitors, assists, performs, or prevents a physiological function but does not physically take the place of a body part. This root operation represents those procedures whose sole objective is to put in a device without doing anything else to the body part. Examples include insertion of radioactive implant and insertion of central venous catheter.

The objective of the root operation "Replacement" is to put in a device (biological or synthetic material) that takes the place of some, or all, of a body part. The body part may have been taken out or replaced, or may be taken out, physically eradicated, or rendered nonfunctional during the "Replacement" procedure. Examples include hip replacement, bone graft, and free skin graft.

The objective of the root operation "Supplement" is to put in a device (biological or synthetic material) that physically reinforces and/or augments the function of a body part. The biological material may be nonliving, or living, and from the same individual. The body part may have been previously replaced, and the "Supplement" procedure is performed to physically reinforce and/or augment the function of the replaced body part. Common examples include hernia repair using mesh, mitral valve ring annuloplasty, and free nerve graft.

The root operation "Change" involves procedures whereby similar devices are exchanged without cutting or puncturing the skin or mucous membrane. All procedures with the root operation "Change" are reported with an external approach. Examples of "Change" root operations include urinary catheter change and changing of gastrostomy tube.

The root operation "Removal" involves procedures for taking out, or off, a device from a body part. This root operation should be coded only when it is not an integral part of another root operation. For example, if a device is taken out and a similar device is put in without cutting or puncturing the skin or mucous membrane, the root operation is "Change," and "Removal" is not coded separately. Examples of "Removal" include drainage tube removal and removal of external fixation device.

The root operation "Revision" applies to procedures whose objective is to correct, to the extent possible, the position or function of a previously placed device without taking the entire device out and putting a whole new device in its place. This root operation may include taking out

TABLE 10.6 Root Operations That Always Involve a Device

Root Operation	Objective of Procedure	Site of Procedure	Example
Insertion	Putting in non-biological device	In/on a body part	Central line insertion
Replacement	Putting in device that replaces a body part	Some/all of a body part	Total hip replacement
Supplement	Putting in device that reinforces or augments a body part	In/on a body part	Abdominal wall herniorrhaphy using mesh
Change	Exchanging device without cutting/puncturing	In/on a body part	Drainage tube change
Removal	Taking out device	In/on a body part	Central line removal
Revision	Correcting a malfunctioning displaced device	In/on a body part	Revision of pacemaker insertion

and/or putting in part of the device, so a "Removal" of the old device would not be coded separately. It is important to understand that a complete re-do of a procedure is coded to the root operation performed, rather than "Revision." Examples of "Revision" include adjustment of pacemaker leads and adjustment of hip prosthesis.

Note that for the root operations "Change," "Removal," and "Revision," general body part values are used when the specific body part value is not in the Table.

Some procedures are performed on the device only, and not on a body part. Examples include irrigation of gastrostomy tube and replacement of pulse generator. In such instances, these procedures are reported with the root operations "Change," "Irrigation," "Removal," and "Revision."

EXERCISE 10.4

Code these procedures.

1. Cystoscopy with intraluminal dilation of bladder neck stricture — 0T7C8ZZ
2. Total right knee arthroplasty with insertion of total knee prosthesis — 0SRC0JZ

   Replacement
3. Laparoscopic bilateral fallopian tube ligation — 0UL74ZZ

   Occlusion
4. Left ventral hernia repair (open) with Marlex mesh — 0WUF0JZ

   Supplement
5. Open revision of right knee replacement, with removal and exchange of the polyethylene patellar component — 0SWC0JZ

Root Operations That Involve Examination Only

Two root operations involve examination of a body part: "Inspection" and "Map." Refer to table 10.7 for an overview of these root operations.

If the examination's objective is visual or manual exploration of some or all of a body part, the root operation is "Inspection." The visual exploration may be accomplished with or without optical instrumentation. Manual exploration may be performed directly or through intervening body layers. Examples of "Inspection" root operations include diagnostic arthroscopy and exploratory laparotomy.

Three important guidelines apply to the root operation "Inspection":

- *Inspection of a body part(s) performed in order to achieve the objective of a procedure is not coded separately.* For example, a fiberoptic bronchoscopy (which is the procedure to inspect the lung) is performed to irrigate the bronchus. The root operation "Inspection" is not coded because the objective of the procedure is not to visually explore the bronchus but to perform the irrigation.
- *If multiple tubular body parts are inspected, the most distal body part inspected is coded. If multiple nontubular body parts in a region are inspected, the body part that specifies the entire area inspected is coded.* For example, when endoscopies are performed, multiple areas may be inspected as in a cystourethroscopy, whereby the bladder and ureters are examined. The most distal (or farthest away) body part in this situation is the ureter, so the body part value for the ureter is selected. An example of "Inspection" of multiple nontubular body parts in a region is an exploratory laparotomy whereby the abdominal contents are inspected. In this instance, the body part value would be "peritoneal cavity" because this body part specifies the entire area inspected.
- *When both an "Inspection" procedure and another procedure are performed on the same body part during the same episode, if the "Inspection" procedure is performed using a different approach than the other procedure, the "Inspection" procedure is coded separately.* For example, if an endoscopic inspection of the duodenum and an open excision of the duodenum are performed during the same procedural episode, both procedures would be coded separately. The different approaches are endoscopic for the "Inspection" and open for the "Excision."

The root operation "Map" should be used if the examination's objective is to locate electrical impulses or functional areas in a body part. The root operation "Map" has a limited applicability to the cardiac conduction mechanism and the central nervous system. Examples include cardiac electrophysiological study, heart catheterization with cardiac mapping, percutaneous mapping of basal ganglia, or intraoperative whole brain mapping via craniotomy.

TABLE 10.7 Root Operations That Involve Examination Only

Root Operation	Objective of Procedure	Site of Procedure	Example
Inspection	Visual/manual exploration	Some/all of a body part	Diagnostic cystoscopy
Map	Location electrical impulses/ functional areas	Brain/cardiac conduction mechanism	Cardiac electrophysiological study

Root Operations That Include Other Repairs

This grouping includes two root operations: "Control" and "Repair." Refer to table 10.8 for an overview of these root operations.

The root operation "Control" describes stopping or attempting to stop postprocedural bleeding. It includes irrigation or evacuation of hematoma at the operative site. The bleeding site is coded as an anatomical region and not to a specific body part. Examples of this root operation are control of post-prostatectomy hemorrhage and control of post-tonsillectomy hemorrhage. It is important to note that the root operation "Control" should not be coded if an attempt to stop the postprocedural bleeding is initially unsuccessful and a definitive root operation (such as "Bypass," "Detachment," "Excision," "Extraction," "Reposition," "Replacement," or "Resection") is required to stop the bleeding.

The root operation "Repair" represents a broad range of procedures for restoring, to the extent possible, a body part to its normal anatomical structure and function. This root operation is only used when the procedure performed does not meet the definition of one of the other root operations. Examples of "Repair" include herniorraphy and suturing of laceration.

TABLE 10.8 Root Operations That Include Other Repairs

Root Operation	Objective of Procedure	Site of Procedure	Example
Control	Stopping/attempting to stop postprocedural bleeding	Anatomical region	Post-prostatectomy bleeding control
Repair	Restoring body part to its normal structure	Some/all of a body part	Suture laceration

Root Operations That Include Other Objectives

The last group of root operations is made up of those procedures that include other objectives not included in the previous groups. This group includes the root operations "Fusion," "Alteration," and "Creation." Table 10.9 provides an overview of these root operations.

The root operation "Fusion" refers to joining together portions of an articular body part, rendering the articular body part immobile. The procedure may be accomplished by a fixation device, a bone graft, or other means. The most common example of this root operation is spinal fusion. Specific guidelines related to coding of spinal fusion are covered in detail in chapter 23 of this handbook, Diseases of the Musculoskeletal System and Connective Tissue.

The root operation "Alteration" is coded for all procedures performed solely to improve appearance. This root operation refers to modifying a body part for cosmetic purposes without affecting the function of the body part. All methods, approaches, and devices used for the objective of improving appearance are coded here. Note that coding of the root operation "Alteration" requires diagnostic confirmation that the procedure was performed to improve appearance. Examples include face lift and breast augmentation.

The last root operation, "Creation," involves a very narrow range of procedures that are performed for sex change. It involves making a new genital structure that does not physically take the place of a body part. Examples include creation of a vagina in a male patient and creation of a penis in a female patient.

In summary, ICD-10-PCS requires mastering the 31 root operations in the Medical and Surgical Section as the key to selecting the appropriate codes. These concepts are applied in future chapters in this handbook as the more common procedures for each body system are discussed.

TABLE 10.9 Root Operations That Include Other Objectives

Root Operation	Objective of Procedure	Site of Procedure	Example
Fusion	Rendering joint immobile	Joint	Spinal fusion
Alteration	Modifying body part for cosmetic purposes without affecting function	Some/all of a body part	Face lift
Creation	Making new structure for sex change operation	Perineum	Artificial vagina/penis

EXERCISE 10.5

Code these procedures.

1. Thoracotomy with exploration of right pleural cavity — 0WJ90ZZ
   Inspection
2. Reopening of thoracotomy site with drainage and control of postoperative hemopericardium — 0W3D0ZZ
3. Open cosmetic plastic repair of deformed left ear lobe — 09010ZZ
   Alteration
4. Exploratory laparotomy peritoneal cavity — 0WJG0ZZ
   Inspection
5. Arthroscopic left subtalar arthrodesis with internal fixation device — 0SGJ44Z
   Fusion
6. Partial removal of right ovary — 0UB00ZZ
   Excision
7. Endometrial ablation using hysteroscope — 0U5B7ZZ
8. Percutaneous excisional biopsy of the liver — 0FB03ZX
   Excision
9. Total left hip replacement with cemented ceramic on ceramic bearing prosthesis — 0SRB039
10. Total nephrectomy, left kidney — 0TT10ZZ
    Resection

CHAPTER 11

ICD-10-PCS Procedures in the Medical- and Surgical-Related and Ancillary Sections

CHAPTER OVERVIEW

- ICD-10-PCS provides codes for Medical- and Surgical-Related and Ancillary Procedures in addition to the Medical and Surgical Section.
- There are nine sections in the Medical- and Surgical-Related Procedures. These sections include obstetrical procedures, administration of substances, measurement and monitoring of body functions, extracorporeal therapies, osteopathic, other procedures, and chiropractic procedures.
- There are six sections in the Ancillary Procedures. These sections include imaging, nuclear medicine, radiation oncology, physical rehabilitation and diagnostic audiology, mental health, and substance abuse treatment.

LEARNING OUTCOMES

After studying this chapter you should be able to:

Identify the objectives of each root operation.

Distinguish between the different root operations in the Medical- and Surgical-Related Section.

Discuss the general guidelines applicable to root operations.

Correctly assign codes for ancillary services.

TERM TO KNOW

Root operation
the third character in an ICD-10-PCS code, which refers to the objective of the procedure

INTRODUCTION

The previous chapter introduces the Medical and Surgical Section of ICD-10-PCS, where the majority of the hospital inpatient procedures are classified. In addition to the Medical and Surgical Section, ICD-10-PCS has two additional sections: Medical- and Surgical-Related and Ancillary Procedures, which are covered in this chapter.

Many hospitals do not code minor ancillary procedures for inpatient stays. However, for the sake of completeness, ICD-10-PCS includes codes for these minor procedures should a hospital wish to collect data on these services.

MEDICAL- AND SURGICAL-RELATED PROCEDURES

There are nine sections in the Medical- and Surgical-Related Procedures. These sections include obstetrical procedures, placement, administration of substances, measurement and monitoring of body functions, extracorporeal therapies, osteopathic, other procedures, and chiropractic, as shown in table 11.1. The obstetrical procedures (section 1) are covered in detail in chapter 24 of this handbook, Complications of Pregnancy, Childbirth, and the Puerperium.

TABLE 11.1 Medical- and Surgical-Related Sections

Section Value	Description
1	Obstetrics
2	Placement
3	Administration
4	Measurement and Monitoring
5	Extracorporeal Assistance and Performance
6	Extracorporeal Therapies
7	Osteopathic
8	Other Procedures
9	Chiropractic

Placement Section

Codes in the Placement Section follow the same conventions used in the Medical and Surgical Section. All seven characters retain the same meaning in both sections, as shown in figure 11.1.

The root operations in the Placement Section are different from those in the Medical and Surgical Section covered in the previous chapter. These root operations include only those procedures that are performed without making an incision or a puncture. There are two body system (character 2) values in this section: "anatomical regions" (W) and "anatomical orifices" (Y). In addition, there are two body region (character 4) values: external body regions (e.g., abdominal wall) and natural orifices (e.g., ear).

FIGURE 11.1 Structure of Codes in the Placement Section

Character 1	Character 2	Character 3	Character 4	Character 5	Character 6	Character 7
Section	Body System	Root Operation	Body Region	Approach	Device	Qualifier

Table 11.2 provides an overview of the root operations (third character) in the Placement Section with the corresponding value and definition. The root operations "Change" and "Removal" are common to other sections. The remaining five root operations, unique to the Placement Section, are:

- Compression
- Dressing
- Immobilization
- Packing
- Traction

TABLE 11.2 Placement Section Root Operation Values and Definitions

Value	Description	Definition
0	Change	Taking out or off a device from a body region and putting back an identical or similar device in or on the same body region without cutting or puncturing the skin or a mucous membrane
1	Compression	Putting pressure on a body region
2	Dressing	Putting material on a body region for protection
3	Immobilization	Limiting or preventing motion of a body region
4	Packing	Putting material in a body region
5	Removal	Taking out or off a device from a body region
6	Traction	Exerting a pulling force on a body region in a distal direction

Devices in this section specify the material or device (e.g., splint, traction apparatus, bandage) and include casts for fractures and dislocations. When the placement of devices requires extensive design, fabrication, or fitting, ICD-10-PCS classifies these procedures to the Rehabilitation Section. The devices classified to the Placement Section are off-the-shelf devices.

Examples of procedures in the Placement Section are the following:

Cast change, lower right arm

Character 1 Section	Character 2 Body System	Character 3 Root Operation	Character 4 Body Region	Character 5 Approach	Character 6 Device	Character 7 Qualifier
2	W	0	C	X	2	Z
Placement	Anatomical region	Change	Lower arm, right	External	Cast	No qualifier

Application of compression dressing to abdominal wound

Character 1 Section	Character 2 Body System	Character 3 Root Operation	Character 4 Body Region	Character 5 Approach	Character 6 Device	Character 7 Qualifier
2	W	1	3	X	6	Z
Placement	Anatomical region	Compression	Abdominal wall	External	Pressure dressing	No qualifier

Application of dressing to right hand

Character 1 Section	Character 2 Body System	Character 3 Root Operation	Character 4 Body Region	Character 5 Approach	Character 6 Device	Character 7 Qualifier
2	W	2	E	X	4	Z
Placement	Anatomical region	Dressing	Hand, right	External	Bandage	No qualifier

Placement of stereotactic head frame

Character 1 Section	Character 2 Body System	Character 3 Root Operation	Character 4 Body Region	Character 5 Approach	Character 6 Device	Character 7 Qualifier
2	W	3	0	X	Y	Z
Placement	Anatomical region	Immobilization	Head	External	Other device	No qualifier

Caution should be exercised with the root operation "Immobilization" to distinguish it from several similar-sounding procedures that ICD-10-PCS classifies to different sections based on the setting where the procedure is performed. When the splint and braces are placed in inpatient settings (except for the rehabilitation setting), they are coded to "Immobilization," Table 2X3 in the Placement Section. However, for the rehabilitation setting, these procedures are coded to F0DZ6EZ and F0DZ7EZ in the Physical Rehabilitation and Diagnostic Audiology Section.

Removal of stereotactic head frame

Character 1 Section	Character 2 Body System	Character 3 Root Operation	Character 4 Body Region	Character 5 Approach	Character 6 Device	Character 7 Qualifier
2	W	5	0	X	Y	Z
Placement	Anatomical region	Removal	Head	External	Other device	No qualifier

Cervical traction using a traction apparatus

Character 1 Section	Character 2 Body System	Character 3 Root Operation	Character 4 Body Region	Character 5 Approach	Character 6 Device	Character 7 Qualifier
2	W	6	2	X	0	Z
Placement	Anatomical region	Traction	Neck	External	Traction apparatus	No qualifier

Note that "traction" in this section includes only traction performed using a mechanical traction apparatus. When manual traction is performed by a physical therapist, it should be classified to the Manual Therapy Techniques in section F, Physical Rehabilitation and Diagnostic Audiology.

Administration Section

The Administration Section includes services such as injections, infusions, and transfusions, along with related procedures such as irrigation and tattooing. The structure of codes in this section is shown in figure 11.2.

FIGURE 11.2 Structure of Codes in the Administration Section

Character 1	Character 2	Character 3	Character 4	Character 5	Character 6	Character 7
Section	Body System	Root Operation	Body System/Region	Approach	Substance	Qualifier

There are three body system (character 2) values in this section:

0 Circulatory
C Indwelling device
E Physiological systems and anatomical regions

There are three root operations in the Administration Section, and they are classified according to the broad category of substance administered. Blood products are classified to the root operation "Transfusion"; cleansing substances are classified to "Irrigation." All other therapeutic, diagnostic, nutritional, physiological, or prophylactic substances administered are classified to "Introduction."

Character 5 (approach) uses values defined in the Medical and Surgical Section. The percutaneous approach is used for intradermal, subcutaneous, and intramuscular injections. Catheter utilization to introduce substances into the circulatory system is classified to the percutaneous approach.

Examples of procedures for each root operation in the Administration Section are as follows:

Infusion of chemotherapy central vein insertion

Character 1 Section	Character 2 Body System	Character 3 Root Operation	Character 4 Body System/ Region	Character 5 Approach	Character 6 Substance	Character 7 Qualifier
3	E	0	4	3	0	5
Administration	Physiological systems and anatomical regions	Introduction	Central vein	Percutaneous	Antineoplastic	Other antineoplastic

Peritoneal dialysis via indwelling catheter

Character 1 Section	Character 2 Body System	Character 3 Root Operation	Character 4 Body System/ Region	Character 5 Approach	Character 6 Substance	Character 7 Qualifier
3	E	1	M	3	9	Z
Administration	Physiological systems and anatomical regions	Irrigation	Peritoneal cavity	Percutaneous	Dialysate	No qualifier

Transfusion of embryonic stem cells into central vein

Character 1 Section	Character 2 Body System	Character 3 Root Operation	Character 4 Body System/ Region	Character 5 Approach	Character 6 Substance	Character 7 Qualifier
3	0	2	4	3	A	Z
Administration	Circulatory	Transfusion	Central vein	Percutaneous	Stem cells, embryonic	No qualifier

Measurement and Monitoring Section

The Measurement and Monitoring Section classifies procedures that determine the level of a physiological or physical function. There are two root operations in this section, and they differ in only one respect: "Measurement" describes a single level taken, at a point in time; "Monitoring" describes a series of tests performed repetitively over a period of time. The structure of the codes in this section differs from other sections in that the sixth character, instead of defining a device or substance (as in the Administration Section), defines the physiological or physical function being tested (e.g., pressure, temperature). There are two body system values used in this section, "physiological systems" and "physiological devices." The structure of codes in this section is shown in figure 11.3.

FIGURE 11.3 Structure of Codes in the Measurement and Monitoring Section

Character 1	Character 2	Character 3	Character 4	Character 5	Character 6	Character 7
Section	Body System	Root Operation	Body System	Approach	Function/Device	Qualifier

Examples of procedures in the Measurement and Monitoring Section are the following:

Single external EKG (electrocardiogram) reading

Character 1 Section	Character 2 Body System	Character 3 Root Operation	Character 4 Body System	Character 5 Approach	Character 6 Function/Device	Character 7 Qualifier
4	A	0	2	X	4	Z
Measurement and monitoring	Physiological systems	Measurement	Cardiac	External	Electrical activity	No qualifier

Holter monitoring

Character 1 Section	Character 2 Body System	Character 3 Root Operation	Character 4 Body System	Character 5 Approach	Character 6 Function/Device	Character 7 Qualifier
4	A	1	2	X	4	5
Measurement and monitoring	Physiological systems	Monitoring	Cardiac	External	Electrical activity	Ambulatory

EXERCISE 11.1

Code the following procedures.

1. Percutaneous irrigation of pleural cavity using irrigating substance — 3E1L38Z
2. Transplant of autologous bone marrow via central vein — 30243G0 — Transfusion
3. Placement of cast on right lower arm — 2W3CX2Z — Immobilization
4. Insertion of nasal packing — 2Y41X5Z
5. Cardiac pacemaker rate check (external) — 4B02XSZ — Measurement
6. Application of compression dressing to the back — 2W15X6Z

Extracorporeal Assistance and Performance Section

The Extracorporeal Assistance and Performance Section includes procedures that use equipment to support a physiological function, such as breathing (e.g., mechanical ventilation), circulating the blood (e.g., hemodialysis), or restoring the natural rhythm of the heart (e.g., cardioversion). These procedures are typically performed in a critical care setting.

The structure of codes in this section is shown in figure 11.4.

FIGURE 11.4 Structure of Codes in the Extracorporeal Assistance and Performance Section

Character 1	Character 2	Character 3	Character 4	Character 5	Character 6	Character 7
Section	Body System	Root Operation	Body System	Duration	Function	Qualifier

There is a single body system (character 2) value, "physiological systems" (A). Character 5 differs from other sections in that it describes the duration of the procedure, rather than the approach. Character 5 specifies whether the procedure was a single occurrence, multiple occurrences, intermittent, or continuous; except in the case of the respiratory body system, character 5 indicates whether the procedure was less than 24 consecutive hours, 24–96 consecutive hours, or greater than 96 consecutive hours. Character 6 describes the body function being acted upon (e.g., ventilation to assist with respiration).

This section contains three root operations: "Assistance," "Performance," and "Restoration." "Assistance" and "Performance" vary only in the degree of control exercised over the physiological function. Assistance takes over a portion of a physiological function, while performance takes over the function completely—both by extracorporeal means. The root operation "Restoration" is defined as returning, or attempting to return, a physiological function to its original state by extracorporeal means. "Restoration" defines only external cardioversion and defibrillation procedures. Cardioversion procedures are classified to the root operation "Restoration" whether the procedure is successful or fails.

Examples of each root operation in this section are the following:

Continuous positive airway pressure for sleep apnea—eight hours

Character 1 Section	Character 2 Body System	Character 3 Root Operation	Character 4 Body System	Character 5 Duration	Character 6 Function	Character 7 Qualifier
5	A	0	9	3	5	7
Extracorporeal assistance and performance	Physiological systems	Assistance	Respiratory	Less than 24 consecutive hours	Ventilation	Continuous positive airway pressure

Continuous mechanical ventilation, over six consecutive days

Character 1 Section	Character 2 Body System	Character 3 Root Operation	Character 4 Body System	Character 5 Duration	Character 6 Function	Character 7 Qualifier
5	A	1	9	5	5	Z
Extracorporeal assistance and performance	Physiological systems	Performance	Respiratory	Greater than 96 consecutive hours	Ventilation	No qualifier

External cardioversion

Character 1 Section	Character 2 Body System	Character 3 Root Operation	Character 4 Body System	Character 5 Duration	Character 6 Function	Character 7 Qualifier
5	A	2	2	0	4	Z
Extracorporeal assistance and performance	Physiological systems	Restoration	Cardiac	Single	Rhythm	No qualifier

Extracorporeal Therapies Section

The Extracorporeal Therapies Section describes other extracorporeal procedures not defined by the root operations "Assistance" and "Performance" in section 5, Extracorporeal Assistance and Performance. The structure of codes in this section is shown in figure 11.5.

FIGURE 11.5 Structure of Codes in the Extracorporeal Therapies Section

Character 1	Character 2	Character 3	Character 4	Character 5	Character 6	Character 7
Section	Body System	Root Operation	Body System	Duration	Qualifier	Qualifier

This section contains a single body system value, "physiological systems." Character 5, duration, specifies whether the procedure was single or multiple. This section is different from others in that two characters, 6 and 7, are qualifiers, but none is used for character 6. This is to comply with the overall structure of all ICD-10-PCS codes to be seven characters long. The seventh-character qualifier identifies various blood components separated out in pheresis procedures such as red blood cells, white blood cells, platelets, plasma, stem cells from cord blood, and hematopoietic stem cells.

There are 10 root operations in the Extracorporeal Therapies Section. The meaning of each root operation as used in ICD-10-PCS is consistent with the terminology used in the medical community, except for "Decompression" and "Hyperthermia," as follows:

- *Atmospheric control:* Extracorporeal control of atmospheric pressure and composition.
- *Decompression:* Extracorporeal elimination of undissolved gas from body fluids. "Decompression" describes a single type of procedure: treatment for decompression sickness (the bends) in a hyperbaric chamber.
- *Electromagnetic therapy:* Extracorporeal treatment by electromagnetic rays.
- *Hyperthermia:* Extracorporeal raising of body temperature. It is important to distinguish the objective of the hyperthermia procedure for proper code assignment. Hyperthermia may be used to treat temperature imbalance, in which case it is coded to the Extracorporeal Therapies Section. However, hyperthermia is also used as an adjunct radiation treatment for cancer, in which case ICD-10-PCS classifies it to the Radiation Oncology Section.
- *Hypothermia:* Extracorporeal lowering of body temperature.
- *Pheresis:* Extracorporeal separation of blood products. This procedure is used in medical practice for two main purposes: to treat diseases in which too much of a blood component is produced, such as leukemia, or to remove a blood product, such as platelets, from a donor for transfusion into a patient who needs it.
- *Phototherapy:* Extracorporeal treatment by light rays. Phototherapy to the circulatory system refers to exposing the blood to light rays outside the body using a machine that recirculates the blood and returns it to the body after phototherapy.
- *Shock wave therapy:* Extracorporeal treatment by shock waves.
- *Ultrasound therapy:* Extracorporeal treatment by ultrasound.
- *Ultraviolet light therapy:* Extracorporeal treatment by ultraviolet light.

Examples are the following:

Donor peripheral lymphocyte apheresis procedure, multiple

Character 1 Section	Character 2 Body System	Character 3 Root Operation	Character 4 Body System	Character 5 Duration	Character 6 Qualifier	Character 7 Qualifier
6	A	5	5	1	Z	1
Extracorporeal therapies	Physiological systems	Pheresis	Circulatory	Multiple	No qualifier	Leukocytes

Shock wave therapy for heel pain, single treatment

Character 1 Section	Character 2 Body System	Character 3 Root Operation	Character 4 Body System	Character 5 Duration	Character 6 Qualifier	Character 7 Qualifier
6	A	9	3	0	Z	Z
Extracorporeal therapies	Physiological systems	Shock wave therapy	Musculoskeletal	Single	No qualifier	No qualifier

EXERCISE 11.2

Code the following procedures.

1. Continuous hyperbaric oxygenation — 5A05221
2. Ultrasound therapy of peripheral vascular vessels, single treatment — 6A750Z6
3. Hemodialysis, single treatment — 5A1D00Z
   Performance
4. Failed cardioversion — 5A2204Z
   Restoration
5. Pheresis of hematopoietic stem cells, single episode — 6A550ZV

Osteopathic Section

The Osteopathic Section is one of the smallest sections in ICD-10-PCS. There is a single body system ("anatomical regions") and a single root operation ("Treatment"). The structure of codes in this section is shown in figure 11.6.

FIGURE 11.6 Structure of Codes in the Osteopathic Section

Character 1	Character 2	Character 3	Character 4	Character 5	Character 6	Character 7
Section	Body System	Root Operation	Body Region	Approach	Method	Qualifier

Character 6, method, in this section defines the osteopathic method of the procedure. The following osteopathic methods are specified: articulatory raising, fascial release, general mobilization, high velocity–low amplitude, indirect, low velocity–high amplitude, lymphatic pump, muscle energy–isometric, muscle energy–isotonic, and other method.

One example is muscle energy isotonic osteopathic treatment of neck.

Character 1 Section	Character 2 Body System	Character 3 Root Operation	Character 4 Body Region	Character 5 Approach	Character 6 Method	Character 7 Qualifier
7	W	0	1	X	8	Z
Osteopathic	Anatomical regions	Treatment	Cervical	External	Muscle energy isotonic	None

Other Procedures Section

This section contains codes for procedures not included in the other medical- and surgical-related sections. The structure of codes in this section is shown in figure 11.7. There is a single root operation, "Other procedures." This root operation is defined as methodologies that attempt to remediate or cure a disorder or disease. There are relatively few codes in this section, including some nontraditional, whole body therapies such as acupuncture, meditation, and yoga therapy. Character 6, method, defines the method of the procedure, such as computer-assisted procedure, robotic-assisted procedure, or acupuncture. Note that the procedure codes for robotic-assisted and computer-assisted procedures are coded in addition to the primary procedure (e.g., cholecystectomy). Another procedure included in this section is the fertilization portion of an in-vitro fertilization procedure.

FIGURE 11.7 Structure of Codes in the Other Procedures Section

Character 1	Character 2	Character 3	Character 4	Character 5	Character 6	Character 7
Section	Body System	Root Operation	Body Region	Approach	Method	Qualifier

Here are two examples:

Robotic-assisted laparoscopic cholecystectomy (the robotic assistance only)

Character 1 Section	Character 2 Body System	Character 3 Root Operation	Character 4 Body Region	Character 5 Approach	Character 6 Method	Character 7 Qualifier
8	E	0	W	4	C	Z
Other procedures	Physiological systems and anatomical regions	Other procedures	Trunk region	Percutaneous endoscopic	Robotic assisted procedure	No qualifier

Suture removal of left arm

Character 1 Section	Character 2 Body System	Character 3 Root Operation	Character 4 Body Region	Character 5 Approach	Character 6 Method	Character 7 Qualifier
8	E	0	X	X	Y	8
Other procedures	Physiological systems and anatomical regions	Other procedures	Upper extremity	External	Other method	Suture removal

Chiropractic Section

The last section in the Medical- and Surgical-Related Procedures is the Chiropractic Section. This section consists of a single body system, "anatomical regions," and a single root operation, "Manipulation." "Manipulation" is defined in ICD-10-PCS as a manual procedure that involves a directed thrust to move a joint past the physiological range of motion without exceeding the anatomical limit. The structure of codes in this section is similar to the structure of codes in the Other Procedures Section (see figure 11.7). An example for this section is the following:

Chiropractic mechanically assisted manipulation of right wrist

Character 1 Section	Character 2 Body System	Character 3 Root Operation	Character 4 Body Region	Character 5 Approach	Character 6 Method	Character 7 Qualifier
9	W	B	7	X	K	Z
Chiropractic	Anatomical regions	Manipulation	Upper extremity	External	Mechanically assisted	None

EXERCISE 11.3

Code the following procedures.

1. Acupuncture to the back using anesthesia — 8E0H300
2. Blood collection from indwelling vascular access device — 8C02X6K
3. Osteopathic manipulation lower back using high velocity–low amplitude — 7W03X3Z
4. Open excision of acoustic neuroma with computer-assisted magnetic resonance imaging — 00BN0ZZ, 8E09XBH
5. Chiropractic manipulation of low back with high velocity, short lever arm thrust contact — 9WB3XHZ

ANCILLARY PROCEDURES

There are six sections in ICD-10-PCS for ancillary procedures, as follows:

B Imaging
C Nuclear Medicine
D Radiation Oncology
F Physical Rehabilitation and Diagnostic Audiology
G Mental Health
H Substance Abuse Treatment

Ancillary Sections (B–H) do not include root operations. Instead, character 3 in these sections represents the root type of the procedure. Codes in these sections include characters not previously defined, such as contrast, modality qualifier, and equipment. Section G, Mental Health, and section H, Substance Abuse Treatment, are covered in chapter 16 of this handbook, Mental Disorders.

Imaging Section

The Imaging Section follows the same conventions established in the Medical and Surgical Section, except that the third and fifth characters introduce definitions not used in previous sections. The third character defines root type, rather than root operation, and the fifth character defines contrast, if used. In addition, contrast is differentiated by whether it is low or high osmolar contrast. The sixth-character qualifier in this section provides the ability to specify that an image is taken without contrast, followed by one with contrast (unenhanced and enhanced).

The structure of codes in this section is shown in figure 11.8.

FIGURE 11.8 Structure of Codes in the Imaging Section

Character 1	Character 2	Character 3	Character 4	Character 5	Character 6	Character 7
Section	Body System	Root Type	Body Part	Contrast	Qualifier	Qualifier

The Imaging Section utilizes the following five root types:

- *Value 0—Plain radiography:* Planar display of an image developed from the capture of external ionizing radiation on photographic or photoconductive plate.
- *Value 1—Fluoroscopy:* Single plane or biplane real-time display of an image developed from the capture of external ionizing radiation on a fluorescent screen. The image may also be stored by either digital or analog means.
- *Value 2—Computed tomography (CT scan):* Computer reformatted digital display of multiplanar images developed from the capture of multiple exposures of external ionizing radiation.
- *Value 3—Magnetic resonance imaging (MRI):* Computer-reformatted digital display of multiplanar images developed from the capture of radio-frequency signals emitted by nuclei in a body site excited within a magnetic field.
- *Value 4—Ultrasonography:* Real-time display of images of anatomy or flow information developed from the capture of reflected and attenuated high-frequency sound waves.

Examples include the following:

X-ray of right upper arm

Character 1 Section	Character 2 Body System	Character 3 Root Type	Character 4 Body Part	Character 5 Contrast	Character 6 Qualifier	Character 7 Qualifier
B	P	0	E	Z	Z	Z
Imaging	Non-axial upper bones	Plain radiography	Upper arm, right	None	None	None

Retrograde pyelogram (kidneys, ureters, bladder) with low osmolar contrast

Character 1 Section	Character 2 Body System	Character 3 Root Type	Character 4 Body Part	Character 5 Contrast	Character 6 Qualifier	Character 7 Qualifier
B	T	1	4	1	Z	Z
Imaging	Urinary system	Fluoroscopy	Kidneys, ureters and bladder	Low osmolar	None	None

CT of brain without contrast, followed by high osmolar contrast

Character 1 Section	Character 2 Body System	Character 3 Root Type	Character 4 Body Part	Character 5 Contrast	Character 6 Qualifier	Character 7 Qualifier
B	0	2	0	0	0	Z
Imaging	Central nervous system	Computerized tomography	Brain	High osmolar	Unenhanced and enhanced	None

MRI of liver and spleen with contrast

Character 1 Section	Character 2 Body System	Character 3 Root Type	Character 4 Body Part	Character 5 Contrast	Character 6 Qualifier	Character 7 Qualifier
B	F	3	6	Y	Z	Z
Imaging	Hepatobiliary system and pancreas	Magnetic resonance imaging	Liver and spleen	Other contrast	None	None

Bilateral ovarian ultrasound

Character 1 Section	Character 2 Body System	Character 3 Root Type	Character 4 Body Part	Character 5 Contrast	Character 6 Qualifier	Character 7 Qualifier
B	U	4	5	Z	Z	Z
Imaging	Female reproductive system	Ultrasonography	Ovaries, bilateral	None	None	None

Nuclear Medicine Section

The Nuclear Medicine Section is organized like the Imaging Section, with the only significant difference being that the fifth character is used to define the radionuclide (radiation source) instead of the contrast material used in the procedure. Similar to the Imaging Section, the third character classifies the procedure by root type, rather than root operation. The sixth and seventh characters are qualifiers and are not used in this section.

The structure of the codes in this section is shown in figure 11.9.

FIGURE 11.9 Structure of Codes in the Nuclear Medicine Section

Character 1	Character 2	Character 3	Character 4	Character 5	Character 6	Character 7
Section	Body System	Root Type	Body Part	Radionuclide	Qualifier	Qualifier

The following seven root types are used in the Nuclear Medicine Section:

- *Value 1—Planar nuclear medicine imaging:* Introduction of radioactive materials into the body for single-plane display of images developed from the capture of radioactive emissions.
- *Value 2—Tomographic nuclear medicine imaging:* Introduction of radioactive materials into the body for three-dimensional displays of images developed from the capture of radioactive emissions.
- *Value 3—Positron emission tomography (PET):* Introduction of radioactive materials into the body for three-dimensional displays of images developed from the simultaneous capture, 180 degrees apart, of radioactive emissions.
- *Value 4—Nonimaging nuclear medicine uptake:* Introduction of radioactive materials into the body for measurements of organ function, from the detection of radioactive emissions.

- *Value 5—Nonimaging nuclear medicine probe:* Introduction of radioactive materials into the body for the study of distribution and fate of certain substances by the detection of radioactive emissions from an external source.
- *Value 6—Nonimaging nuclear medicine assay:* Introduction of radioactive materials into the body for the study of body fluids and blood elements by the detection of radioactive emissions.
- *Value 7—Systemic nuclear medicine therapy:* Introduction of unsealed radioactive materials into the body for treatment.

Examples include the following:

Brain PET scan with C-11

Character 1 Section	Character 2 Body System	Character 3 Root Type	Character 4 Body Part	Character 5 Radionuclide	Character 6 Qualifier	Character 7 Qualifier
C	0	3	0	B	Z	Z
Nuclear medicine	Central nervous system	Positron emission tomographic (PET) imaging	Brain	Carbon 11	None	None

I-131 thyroid uptake study

Character 1 Section	Character 2 Body System	Character 3 Root Type	Character 4 Body Part	Character 5 Radionuclide	Character 6 Qualifier	Character 7 Qualifier
C	G	4	2	G	Z	Z
Nuclear medicine	Endocrine system	Nonimaging nuclear medicine uptake	Thyroid gland	Iodine 131	None	None

Radiation Oncology Section

The ICD-10-PCS Radiation Oncology Section contains the radiation procedures used for cancer treatment. The structure of the codes in this section is shown in figure 11.10.

FIGURE 11.10 Structure of Codes in the Radiation Oncology Section

Character 1	Character 2	Character 3	Character 4	Character 5	Character 6	Character 7
Section	Body System	Root Type	Body Part	Modality Qualifier	Isotope	Qualifier

The differences in character meanings for this section are as follows:

- Character 3 defines root type, which is the basic radiation delivery modality used (beam radiation, brachytherapy, stereotactic radiosurgery, and other radiation).
- Character 5 specifies further the treatment modality used (e.g., photons, electrons, heavy particles, contact radiation).
- Character 6 defines the radioactive isotope used, if applicable.
- Character 7 is a qualifier and is not specified in this section.

Examples include the following:

External beam radiation to left breast (photons 1.33 MeV)

Character 1 Section	Character 2 Body System	Character 3 Root Type	Character 4 Body Part	Character 5 Modality Qualifier	Character 6 Isotope	Character 7 Qualifier
D	M	0	0	1	Z	Z
Radiation oncology	Breast	Beam radiation	Breast, left	Photons 1–10 MeV	None	None

Prostate brachytherapy seeds, LDR, Iodine 125

Character 1 Section	Character 2 Body System	Character 3 Root Type	Character 4 Body Part	Character 5 Modality Qualifier	Character 6 Isotope	Character 7 Qualifier
D	V	1	0	B	9	Z
Radiation oncology	Male reproductive system	Brachytherapy	Prostate	Low-dose rate (LDR)	Iodine 125	None

EXERCISE 11.4

Code the following procedures.

1. Intravascular ultrasound bilateral internal carotid arteries — B348ZZ3
2. MRI of the brain with contrast — B030YZZ
3. PET scan of the lungs with F-18 — CB32KZZ
4. Right breast brachytherapy, LDR, Palladium 103 — DM11BBZ
5. CT scan of the lungs without contrast — BB24ZZZ

Physical Rehabilitation and Diagnostic Audiology Section

The structure of the codes in the Physical Rehabilitation and Diagnostic Audiology Section is shown in figure 11.11.

FIGURE 11.11 Structure of Codes in the Physical Rehabilitation and Diagnostic Audiology Section

Character 1	Character 2	Character 3	Character 4	Character 5	Character 6	Character 7
Section	Section Qualifier	Root Type	Body System and Region	Type Qualifier	Equipment	Qualifier

This section contains character definitions unlike the other sections in ICD-10-PCS, as follows:

- Character 2 is a section qualifier that specifies whether the procedure is a rehabilitation or diagnostic audiology procedure.
- Character 3 defines the general procedure root type.
- Character 4 defines the body system and body regions combined, where applicable.
- Character 5 specifies further the procedure type.
- Character 6 specifies any equipment used.

This section contains 14 root types, which are defined in table 11.3.

TABLE 11.3 Physical Rehabilitation and Diagnostic Audiology Root Types, Values, and Definitions

Value	Description	Definition
0	Speech assessment	Measurement of speech and related functions
1	Motor and/or nerve function assessment	Measurement of motor, nerve, and related functions
2	Activites of daily living assessment	Measurement of functional level for activities of daily living
3	Hearing assessment	Measurement of hearing and related functions
4	Hearing aid assessment	Measurement of the appropriateness and/or effectiveness of a hearing device
5	Vestibular assessment	Measurement of the vestibular system and related functions
6	Speech treatment	Application of techniques to improve, augment, or compensate for speech and related functional impairment
7	Motor treatment	Exercise or activities to increase or facilitate motor function
8	Activities of daily living treatment	Exercise or activities to facilitate functional competence for activities of daily living
9	Hearing treatment	Application of techniques to improve, augment, or compensate for hearing and related functional impairment
B	Hearing aid treatment	Application of techniques to improve the communication abilities of individuals with cochlear implant
C	Vestibular treatment	Application of techniques to improve, augment, or compensate for vestibular and related functional impairment
D	Device fitting	Fitting of a device designed to facilitate or support achievement of a higher level of function
F	Caregiver training	Training in activities to support patient's optimal level of function

The following important coding notes apply to this section:

- Treatment procedures include swallowing dysfunction exercises, bathing and showering techniques, wound management, gait training, and a host of activities typically associated with rehabilitation.
- Assessments are further classified into more than 100 different tests or methods. The majority of these assessments focus on the faculties of hearing and speech; others focus on various aspects of body function and on the patient's quality of life, such as muscle performance, neuromotor development, and reintegration skills.
- The fifth character used in device fitting describes the device being fitted rather than the method used to fit the device.
- Caregiver training is divided into 18 different broad subjects taught to help a caregiver provide proper patient care. Examples include bathing, dressing, feeding, and eating.

Examples include the following:

Pulsatile lavage skin ulcer of right heel

Character 1 Section	Character 2 Section Qualifier	Character 3 Root Type	Character 4 Body System and Region	Character 5 Type Qualifier	Character 6 Equipment	Character 7 Qualifier
F	0	8	G	5	B	Z
Physical rehabilitation and diagnostic audiology	Rehabilitation	Activities of daily living treatment	Integumentary lower extremity	Wound management	Physical agents	None

Bedside swallowing assessment of stroke patient

Character 1 Section	Character 2 Section Qualifier	Character 3 Root Type	Character 4 Body System and Region	Character 5 Type Qualifier	Character 6 Equipment	Character 7 Qualifier
F	0	0	Z	H	Z	Z
Physical rehabilitation and diagnostic audiology	Rehabilitation	Speech assessment	None	Bedside swallowing and oral function	None	None

EXERCISE 11.5

Code the following procedures.

1. Aphasia assessment by speech therapist — **F00ZCZZ**

   Speech assessment

2. Prosthetic device fitting, below knee leg prosthetic — **F0DZ8UZ**

3. Caregiver training in keeping wound clean and dressing change — **F0FZ9ZZ**

CHAPTER 12

Z Codes and External Cause of Morbidity Codes

CHAPTER OVERVIEW

- Z codes and External cause of morbidity codes follow the same format and conventions as the main classification.
- Certain Z codes are used as principal diagnosis codes in specific situations.
- Aftercare management Z codes are generally listed first to explain the reason for continued care after the initial treatment of an injury or disease.
- Z codes are also useful for coding admission for observation and evaluation and admission for palliative care.
- They are also used for special investigative examinations when no problem, diagnosis, or condition is identified and for screening examinations.
- Z codes indicate personal history, family history, and genetic susceptibility to disease.

LEARNING OUTCOMES

After studying this chapter you should be able to:

Locate Z codes and External cause of morbidity codes.

Explain how and when Z codes and External cause of morbidity codes are used.

TERMS TO KNOW

Aftercare management
continued care during the healing phase or long-term care due to the consequences of a disease

External cause of morbidity codes
codes for external causes to provide information for injury research and evaluation of injury prevention strategies

Palliative care
care focused on the management of pain and other symptoms of patients who are in the terminal phase of an illness

Z codes
codes for factors influencing health status and contact with health services

REMEMBER . . .

Z and External cause of morbidity codes are used throughout the classification.

INTRODUCTION

In addition to the main classification (A00.0 through T88.9), two special groups of codes are provided in ICD-10-CM:

- Factors influencing health status and contact with health service (Z codes: Z00–Z99)
- External causes of morbidity (V00–Y99)

USING Z CODES AND EXTERNAL CAUSE OF MORBIDITY CODES

Certain Z codes are designated as the principal (or first-listed) diagnosis in specific situations; others are assigned as additional codes when it is important to indicate a history, status, or problem that may affect health care. Some Z codes can be used as either the principal (or first-listed) diagnosis or as an additional code. External cause codes are assigned as additional codes to indicate how the injury or health condition happened (cause), the intent (unintentional or accidental; intentional, such as suicide or assault), the place where the event occurred, the activity of the patient at the time of the event, and the person's status (e.g., civilian, military).

There is no national requirement for mandatory ICD-10-CM external cause code reporting. Unless a provider is subject to a state-based external cause code reporting mandate, or unless these codes are required by a particular payer, reporting of ICD-10-CM codes in Chapter 20, External Causes of Morbidity, is not required. In the absence of a mandatory reporting requirement, providers are encouraged to report External cause codes voluntarily, as they provide valuable data for injury research and evaluation of injury prevention strategies.

Because Z codes and External cause codes are used throughout the classification, this chapter provides a general introduction before their treatment in other chapters in the handbook.

LOCATING Z CODES AND EXTERNAL CAUSE OF MORBIDITY CODES

The format and conventions used throughout the main classification are also used in the Indexes and Tabular Lists for these supplementary classifications. Index entries for Z codes are included in the main Alphabetic Index. These are the key main terms:

- Admission
- Examination
- History
- Observation
- Aftercare
- Problem
- Status

The Tabular List for Z codes follows immediately after the External Causes of Morbidity (V00–Y99) section in the Tabular List.

External cause of morbidity codes are not used to report the intent for poisonings, toxic effects, adverse effects, or underdosing of drugs. ICD-10-CM classifies these conditions using codes in categories T36–T65, which combine the substances involved with the external cause. These situations are discussed in chapter 32, Poisoning, Toxic Effects, Adverse Effects, and Underdosing of Drugs.

Z CODES

Z codes are used as the principal (or first-listed) diagnosis in the following situations:

- To indicate that a person with a resolving disease or injury or a chronic condition is being seen for specific aftercare, such as the removal of internal fixation devices such as orthopedic pins
- To indicate that the patient is seen for the sole purpose of special therapy, such as radiotherapy or chemotherapy
- To indicate that a person not currently ill is encountering the health service for a specific reason, such as to act as an organ donor, to receive prophylactic care, or to receive counseling
- To indicate the birth status of newborns

Z codes are assigned as additional diagnosis codes in the following situations:

- To indicate that a patient has a history, a health status, or another problem that is not in itself an illness or injury but may influence patient care. Note that the following Z codes can be listed first if the fact of the history itself is the reason for admission or encounter:

Z85.-	Personal history of malignant neoplasm
Z86.-	Personal history of certain other diseases
Z80–Z84	Family history

- To indicate the outcome of delivery for obstetric patients

Admission or Encounter for Aftercare Management

Aftercare visit codes (Z42–Z51) are used when the initial treatment of a disease has been completed but the patient requires continued care during the healing or recovery phase or for long-term consequences of the disease. The aftercare code is not assigned when treatment is directed at a current acute disease. The diagnosis code is to be used in these cases. The exceptions to this rule are encounters for antineoplastic chemotherapy and immunotherapy (Z51.1-) or radiotherapy (Z51.0). When the encounter is for the purpose of more than one type of antineoplastic therapy (e.g., radiation and chemotherapy), both codes are assigned and either can be sequenced first. (Chapter 29 of this handbook, Neoplasms, discusses the correct use of radiation and chemotherapy codes.)

Admission for aftercare management ordinarily involves planned care, such as the fitting and adjustment of an external prosthetic device (Z44.-), attention to an artificial opening (Z43.-), breast reconstruction following mastectomy (Z42.1), or removal of an internal fixation device (Z47.2).

There are codes for encounters for attention to dressings, sutures, and drains (Z48.0-). There are also codes to report aftercare following surgery for neoplasms (Z48.3), following organ transplant (Z48.2-), and for surgery to specific body systems (Z48.810–Z48.817). These codes should be reported along with any other aftercare codes or other diagnosis codes to provide more detail regarding an aftercare visit.

Palliative care is an alternative to aggressive treatment for patients who are in the terminal phase of an illness. Care is focused on the management of pain and other symptoms of the disease, which is often more appropriate than aggressive care when a patient is dying of an incurable illness. Code **Z51.5, Encounter for palliative care,** is used to classify admissions or encounters for comfort care, end-of-life care, hospice care, and terminal care for terminally ill patients. It may be used in any health care setting.

The aftercare Z codes should not be used for aftercare for injuries. For aftercare of an injury, assign the acute injury code with the appropriate seventh character for subsequent encounter (e.g., "D" or "G," "K," or "P" for fractures). These codes are covered in more detail in chapter 30 of this handbook.

Aftercare codes are generally listed first to explain the specific reason for the encounter. They can be used occasionally as additional codes when aftercare is provided during an encounter for treatment of an unrelated condition but no applicable diagnosis code is available (for example, the closure of a colostomy during an admission to treat an injury sustained in an automobile accident). Aftercare codes should be used in conjunction with any other aftercare or diagnosis code(s) to provide better detail on the specifics of an aftercare visit, unless otherwise directed by the classification. The sequencing of multiple aftercare codes depends on the circumstances of the encounter. Certain aftercare Z codes need a secondary diagnosis code to describe the resolving condition or sequelae. For others, the condition is included in the code title.

When the patient is admitted because of a complication of previous care, the appropriate code from the main classification is assigned rather than the aftercare Z code. (See chapter 33 of this handbook.)

Admission for Follow-Up Examination

A code from category Z08, Z09, or Z39 is assigned as the principal diagnosis or reason for encounter when a patient is admitted for the purpose of surveillance after the initial treatment of a disease or injury has been completed. Examples include:

Z09	Encounter for follow-up examination after completed treatment for conditions other than malignant neoplasm
Z08	Encounter for follow-up examination after completed treatment for malignant neoplasm
Z39.2	Encounter for routine postpartum follow up

If a recurrence, an extension, or a related condition is identified, the code for that condition is assigned as the principal diagnosis rather than a code from categories Z08, Z09, or Z39. Examples include the following:

- An asymptomatic patient who had a resection of the descending colon a year earlier is admitted for colonoscopy to evaluate the anastomosis and determine whether there is any recurrence of malignancy. Colonoscopy proved the anastomosis to be normal, and there was no evidence of cancer recurrence. In this case, code **Z08, Encounter for follow-up examination after completed treatment for malignant neoplasm,** is coded as the principal diagnosis, with an additional code of **Z85.038, Personal history of other malignant neoplasm of large intestine,** and a code for the colonoscopy.
- An asymptomatic patient who had a resection of the descending colon a year earlier is admitted for colonoscopy to evaluate the anastomosis and determine whether there is any recurrence of malignancy. Colonoscopy showed the anastomosis to be normal, and there was no evidence of cancer recurrence. A polyp of the transverse colon was found, however, and it was removed; pathology examination showed it to be benign. Code **D12.3, Benign neoplasm of transverse colon,** is assigned as the principal diagnosis, with code **Z85.038, Personal history of other malignant neoplasm of large intestine,** assigned as an additional code. In this case, code Z08 is not assigned because a related condition was identified.

- A patient who had a colon resection for removal of carcinoma of the descending colon one year ago is now seen for follow-up examination to evaluate the anastomosis and determine whether there is any recurrence of disease. Colonoscopy showed normal anastomosis but revealed a recurrence of cancer at the primary site. Code **C18.6, Malignant neoplasm of descending colon,** is assigned as the principal diagnosis. Code Z08 is not assigned.
- A patient who had surgical excision of a malignant neoplasm of the ovary one year ago, followed by chemotherapy, is admitted for follow-up examination. There is no evidence of recurrence or metastasis, and no other pathologic condition is identified. Code **Z08, Encounter for follow-up examination after completed treatment for malignant neoplasm,** is assigned along with a code of Z85.43 to indicate the history of ovarian cancer as the reason for the examination.
- A patient who had benign polyps of the colon removed one year ago is now complaining of pain in the left lower abdomen. A colonoscopy performed to determine whether there is any recurrence of colon polyps proved to be entirely normal. In this case, code **R10.32, Left lower quadrant pain,** is assigned rather than a Z09 code because the abdominal pain was the reason for the admission.

Code **Z09, Encounter for follow-up examination after completed treatment for conditions other than malignant neoplasm,** may be assigned as the reason for encounter only when the patient is no longer receiving treatment.

Admission for Observation and Evaluation

A code from category Z03, Encounter for medical observation for suspected diseases and conditions ruled out, or category Z04, Encounter for examination and observation for other reasons, is assigned when a person without a diagnosis is suspected of having an abnormal condition, without signs or symptoms, which requires study, but, after examination and observation, is ruled out. Categories Z03 and Z04 are also for use for administrative and legal observation status. Outpatient referral for surveillance or for further diagnostic studies does not contradict the use of a code from this category. The observation codes are not used if an injury or illness, or any signs or symptoms related to the suspected condition, are present. In those cases, the diagnosis or symptom code is used. When a related diagnosis is established, the code for that condition is assigned instead of a code from category Z03. Codes from categories P00–P04 are used for observation of a newborn suspected condition, ruled out (see chapter 27 of this handbook). For persons with feared complaint in whom no diagnosis is made, assign code Z71.1.

A code from categories Z03–Z04 can be assigned only as the principal diagnosis or reason for encounter, never as a secondary diagnosis. A code from categories Z03–Z04 is ordinarily assigned as a solo code, with two exceptions:

- When a chronic condition requires care or monitoring during the stay, a code for that condition can be assigned as an additional code. Codes for chronic conditions that do not affect the stay are not assigned.
- When admission is for the purpose of ruling out a serious injury, such as concussion, codes for minor injuries such as abrasions or contusions may be assigned as additional codes. This exception is based on the fact that such minor injuries in themselves would not require hospitalization.

The following examples may help the coder to better understand the use of categories Z03–Z04:

- A law enforcement representative refers the patient for evaluation of a suspected mental disorder. None is found, and no other condition is identified. Code **Z04.6, Encounter for general psychiatric examination, requested by authority,** is assigned.
- An adult patient is seen in the emergency department because of alleged rape. Observation and examination reveal no physical findings, such as hemorrhage or laceration. Code **Z04.41, Encounter for examination and observation following alleged adult rape,** is assigned as the principal diagnosis. Code Z04.41 covers the collection of specimens, advice given for prophylaxis of pregnancy, and any other provision of counseling services. When physical findings suggest that a rape has occurred, code Z04.41 is not assigned; the condition identified is coded and designated as the principal diagnosis. Rape is not a medical diagnosis but a matter of jurisprudence. Confirmed adult rape is coded to **T74.21-, Adult sexual abuse, confirmed.** Suspected adult rape is coded to **T76.21-, Adult sexual abuse, suspected.**
- A patient presents with generalized complaints involving nonspecific abdominal pain, minimal weight loss, and change of bowel habits. Because of a strong family history of colon cancer, the patient is admitted for evaluation for suspected malignancy. The presence of a neoplasm is ruled out, and no alternative diagnosis is made; it seems obvious that the symptoms reported are largely subjective. Code **Z03.89, Encounter for observation for other suspected diseases and conditions ruled out,** is assigned with an additional code of **Z80.0, Family history of malignant neoplasm of digestive organs.**

Note that a code from categories Z03–Z04 is not assigned when a patient is admitted to the observation unit of the hospital immediately following same-day (outpatient) surgery, even though the medical record may suggest that the admission is for observation. Hospitals are advised to contact their individual payers to obtain billing instructions on whether a single claim should be submitted or whether separate claims should be submitted. If a single bill is submitted to a payer, code the reason for the surgery as the first reported diagnosis (reason for the encounter). If the patient develops complications during the outpatient encounter, including during the observation stay, code these complications as secondary diagnoses. Continue to report the reason for the surgery as the reason for the overall encounter. Additional codes are assigned for the procedures performed. However, if separate bills are submitted, then this advice would not apply. Hospitals should apply codes for the current encounter based on individual payer billing instructions.

Consider the following examples:

- A patient is admitted following outpatient surgery for a right direct inguinal hernia repair for "continued observation." Review of the medical record indicates that the patient was admitted to observation because he was experiencing severe nausea and vomiting.

  If a single claim is submitted: Code **K40.90, Unilateral inguinal hernia, without obstruction or gangrene, not specified as recurrent,** is assigned as the first-listed diagnosis, not a code from categories Z03–Z04. In addition, code **R11.2, Nausea with vomiting, unspecified,** is assigned as the secondary diagnosis, and code **0YQ50ZZ, Repair right inguinal region, open approach,** is assigned for the procedure.

  If separate bills are submitted: For the outpatient surgery bill, assign code **K40.90, Unilateral inguinal hernia, without obstruction or gangrene, not specified as recurrent,** as the first-listed diagnosis, along with the appropriate Healthcare Common Procedural Coding System code for the surgical procedure. For the observation bill, code **R11.2, Nausea with vomiting, unspecified,** is assigned as the first-listed diagnosis, not a code from categories Z03–Z04.

Codes from subcategory Z03.7, Encounter for suspected maternal and fetal conditions ruled out, may either be used as a first-listed or as an additional code assignment depending on the case. Generally, this subcategory may only be reported as the principal or first-listed diagnosis, except when there are multiple encounters on the same day and the medical records for the encounters are combined. These codes should be used in very limited circumstances on a maternal record when an encounter is for a suspected maternal or fetal condition that is ruled out during that encounter. For example, a maternal or fetal condition may be suspected due to an abnormal test result, but the condition is not confirmed. If the condition is confirmed, code the condition instead of a code from subcategory Z03.7. In addition, these codes are not for use if an illness or any signs or symptoms related to the suspected condition or problem are present. In such cases the diagnosis/symptom code is used. Other codes may be used in addition to the code from subcategory Z03.7, but only if they are unrelated to the suspected condition being evaluated.

If a patient is admitted after a period in the outpatient observation unit for further evaluation unrelated to surgery, the principal diagnosis is the condition that provided the original reason for the outpatient observation. If a patient is admitted to an observation unit for a medical condition, and the medical condition worsens or does not improve, it may be necessary for the patient to be admitted to the hospital as an inpatient. In this case, the medical condition that led to the hospital admission would be the principal diagnosis.

Special Investigations and Examinations

When a patient receives only diagnostic services during an episode of care, a code for the condition or problem that was chiefly responsible for the encounter is assigned first. A code from category Z01, Encounter for other special examination without complaint, suspected or reported diagnosis, is assigned as the reason for the encounter only when no problem, diagnosis, or condition is identified as the reason for the examination. A separate procedure code is required to identify any examinations or procedures performed. Codes from category Z01 are rarely appropriate for inpatient coding and are never assigned as additional codes. For example:

- A patient is referred to the radiology department for a chest X-ray, with the reason for the examination identified as cough and fever, which may rule out pneumonia. The radiologist's report indicates that the X-ray is normal. The code for the cough (R05) or the fever (R50.9) is listed as the reason for the encounter. A code for pneumonia is not assigned; neither is a code assigned from category Z01.
- A patient is referred to the radiology department for a chest X-ray with the reason for the examination identified as cough and fever, rule out pneumonia. The radiologist's report confirms a diagnosis of bronchopneumonia. Code **J18.0, Bronchopneumonia, unspecified organism,** is listed as the reason for the visit. Codes are not assigned for the cough or fever because these symptoms are implicit in the diagnosis of bronchopneumonia. No code from category Z01 is assigned.
- A patient is referred to the clinical laboratory for blood work, with the reason for the examination identified as vertigo with possibly the need to rule out hypothyroidism. Code **R42, Dizziness and giddiness,** is assigned as the reason for the visit. A code for hypothyroidism is not assigned because hypothyroidism is not an established diagnosis. Code **Z01.89, Encounter for other specified special examination,** is not assigned.
- A patient is referred to the radiology department for a chest X-ray as part of a routine physical examination. Code **Z00.00, Encounter for general adult medical examination,** is listed as the reason for the encounter because there are no presenting symptoms and the X-ray was not performed to rule out any suspected disease.

Patients are often referred to hospital ancillary services for preoperative evaluations that involve a variety of tests performed in various departments. Patients may also be referred for preoperative blood typing. Preoperative and preprocedural laboratory examination Z codes are for use only in those situations when a patient is being cleared for a procedure or surgery and no treatment is given. In this situation, one of the following codes is assigned, with additional codes for the condition for which surgery is planned and for any findings related to the preoperative evaluation:

Z01.810	Encounter for preprocedural cardiovascular examination
Z01.811	Encounter for preprocedural respiratory examination
Z01.812	Encounter for preprocedural laboratory examination
Z01.818	Encounter for other preprocedural examination
Z01.83	Encounter for blood typing

For example:

- A patient with the diagnosis of cholelithiasis is referred to the radiology department for a preoperative chest X-ray. Code **Z01.818, Encounter for other preprocedural examination,** should be listed as the reason for the encounter, with an additional code for the cholelithiasis.

Some of the codes for routine health examinations distinguish between "with" and "without" abnormal findings (for example, code Z00.00 versus code Z00.01). Code assignment depends on the information that is known at the time the encounter is being coded. For example, if no abnormal findings were identified during the examination but the encounter is being coded before test results are back, it is acceptable to assign the code for "without abnormal findings." When assigning a code for "with abnormal findings," an additional code(s) should be assigned to identify the specific abnormal finding(s).

Screening Examinations

Codes from categories Z11–Z13, Encounter for screening, are assigned to encounters for tests performed to identify a disease or disease precursors for the purpose of early detection and treatment for those who test positive. Screening is performed on apparently well individuals who present no signs or symptoms relative to the disease. A screening mammogram is an example of such a test. If a screening examination identifies pathology, the code for the reason for the test (namely, the screening code from categories Z11–Z13) is assigned as the principal diagnosis or first-listed code, followed by a code for the pathology or condition found during the screening exam. For example:

- A patient undergoes routine mammography, which reveals no pathology. Code **Z12.31, Encounter for screening mammogram for malignant neoplasm of breast,** is assigned.
- An asymptomatic patient undergoes a screening mammography. The radiologist reports the presence of microcalcifications. Assign code **Z12.31, Encounter for screening mammogram for malignant neoplasm of breast,** followed by code **R92.0, Mammographic microcalcification found on diagnostic imaging of breast.**
- A patient with a family history of breast cancer in her mother, aunt, and older sister presents for a screening mammogram because she is considered at high risk for the disease. Assign code **Z12.31, Encounter for screening mammogram for malignant neoplasm of breast,** followed by code **Z80.3, Family history of malignant neoplasm of breast.**

Codes Representing Patient History, Status, or Problems

Codes from categories Z85 through Z92 are used to indicate a personal history of a previous condition. When the condition mentioned is still present or still under treatment, or if a complication is present, a code from the series Z85 through Z92 is not assigned. Categories Z80 through Z84 indicate a family history and may be assigned when the family history is the reason for examination or treatment.

Status codes indicate that a patient is a carrier of a disease, has the sequelae or residual of a past disease or condition, or has another factor influencing his or her health status. Categories Z88 through Z99 indicate that the patient has a continuing condition or health status that may influence care, such as the fact that a tracheostomy (Z93.0), a colostomy (Z93.3), a cardiac pacemaker (Z95.0), or an aortocoronary bypass graft (Z95.1) is in place. Z codes indicating status are redundant when the diagnosis code itself indicates that the status exists. For example, in the case of an acute rejection crisis of a transplanted kidney, code **T86.11, Kidney transplant rejection,** is used. As the patient's transplant status is implicit in that diagnosis, an additional code Z94.0, indicating kidney transplant status, is not meaningful and should not be assigned.

A diagnostic statement expressed as "status post" most often refers to an earlier surgery, injury, or illness and usually has no significance for the episode of care. No code for the condition is assigned in this case. A personal history code can be assigned if desired. Note the important distinction between history and status codes. History codes indicate that the problem no longer exists. Status codes indicate that the condition is present.

Codes from category Z79 are assigned to indicate a patient's continuous use of a prescribed drug for the long-term treatment of a condition or for prophylactic use. Examples include situations when the patient is currently receiving long-term anticoagulant therapy (Z79.01), antithrombotics/antiplatelets (Z79.02), nonsteroidal anti-inflammatories (Z79.1), antibiotic therapy (Z79.2), hormonal contraceptives (Z79.3), insulin (Z79.4), steroids (Z79.51–Z79.52), or other long-term drug therapy (Z79.81–Z79.899). Subcategory Z79.8 includes long-term use of selective estrogen receptor modulators (Z79.810), aromatase inhibitors (Z79.811), other agents affecting estrogen receptors and estrogen levels (Z79.818), aspirin (Z79.82), biphosphonates (Z79.83), hormone replacement therapy (Z79.890), opiate analgesic (Z79.891), and other long-term drug therapy (Z79.899). Codes from category Z79 are assigned if the patient is receiving a medication for an extended period, for example:

- As a prophylactic measure (e.g., to prevent deep venous thrombosis)
- As treatment of a chronic condition (e.g., arthritis)
- For a disease requiring a lengthy course of treatment (e.g., cancer)

An additional code is assigned for the condition for which the medication is prescribed. Do not assign a code from category Z79 when the medication is prescribed to treat an acute illness or injury and is being given for a brief period of time (e.g., antibiotics to treat bronchitis). This category is not used when medications are given for detoxification or maintenance programs used to prevent withdrawal symptoms in patients with drug dependence. For example, long-term use of methadone for pain management is coded with **Z79.891, Long term (current) use of opiate analgesic,** but the use of methadone in a maintenance program to prevent withdrawal symptoms is coded using the drug dependence code (F11.2-).

Code Z51.81 is used to report encounters for therapeutic drug monitoring. If the drug being monitored is one that the patient has been receiving on a long-term basis, a code from category Z79 should be added. Coding guidelines do not provide a definition or time frame for long-term drug therapy. If a patient receives a drug on a regular basis and has multiple refills available for a prescription, then it is appropriate to document long-term drug use. Documentation of long-term drug use is at the discretion of the health care provider.

Codes from categories Z55 through Z65 are used to indicate certain problems that may affect the patient's care or prevent satisfactory compliance with the recommended regimen. Housing

problems, social maladjustment, and economic or job concerns are examples of situations that can affect a patient's compliance.

History, status, and problem codes ordinarily cannot be used as the principal diagnosis or reason for encounter, with the following exceptions:

- Codes from categories Z85–Z87 (except subcategory Z87.7)
- Code Z91.81
- Codes from categories Z80–Z84

These codes can be used when the history is the reason for admission or encounter. They can be used as additional codes for any patient regardless of the reason for the encounter, but they are ordinarily assigned only when the history, status, or problem has some significance for the episode of care. For example, a history of previously treated carcinoma or a family history of malignant neoplasm may be useful in explaining why certain tests are performed. Status subcategory Z96.6- indicates that the patient has had an orthopedic joint replacement, but this fact would probably be significant only if it limits the patient's movement to the extent that additional nursing care is required or when it prevents the patient's full participation in a rehabilitation program.

Genetic Susceptibility to Disease

Codes from category Z15 are used to report genetic susceptibility to disease. Genetic susceptibility refers to a genetic predisposition for contracting a disease. Patients with a genetic susceptibility to disease may request prophylactic removal of an organ to prevent the disease from occurring. It is important to distinguish susceptibility from carrier state. An individual who is a carrier of a disease is able to pass it on to an offspring. Subcategory Z15.0, Genetic susceptibility to malignant neoplasm, is further subdivided to identify the potential body site, such as breast (Z15.01), ovary (Z15.02), prostate (Z15.03), endometrium (Z15.04), and other (Z15.09).

Codes from category Z15 should not be used as principal or first-listed codes. Sequencing of category Z15 codes would depend on the circumstances of the encounter, as follows:

- If the patient has the condition to which he or she is susceptible, and that condition is the reason for the encounter, the code for the current condition is sequenced first, followed by the Z15.- code.
- If the patient is being seen for follow-up after completed treatment for this condition, and the condition no longer exists, a follow-up code should be sequenced first, followed by the appropriate personal history (Z85.- to Z87.-) and genetic susceptibility codes (Z15.-).
- If the purpose of the encounter is genetic counseling associated with procreative management, assign first code **Z31.5, Encounter for genetic counseling,** followed by a code from category Z15. Additional codes should be assigned for any applicable family or personal history.

Z Codes as Principal/First-Listed Diagnosis

Z codes may be assigned as the principal or first-listed diagnosis or as secondary diagnoses. The *ICD-10-CM Official Guidelines for Coding and Reporting* contain a list of Z codes that may only be a principal/first-listed diagnosis. Z codes on that list may only be reported as the principal/first-listed diagnosis except for cases in which there are multiple encounters on the same day and the medical records for the encounters are combined, or when there is more than one Z code that meets the definition of principal diagnosis (e.g., a patient is admitted to home health care for aftercare and rehabilitation, and both diagnoses equally meet the definition of principal diagnosis). These codes should not be reported if they do not meet the definition of principal or first-listed diagnosis.

REVIEW EXERCISE 12.1

Code the following diagnoses.

1.	Visit to change surgical dressing	Z48.01
2.	Family history of polyps of the colon	Z83.71
3.	Status post aortocoronary bypass procedure	Z95.1
4.	Encounter for gastrostomy tube irrigation	Z43.1
5.	Adjustment of cardiac pacemaker pulse generator	Z45.010
6.	Long-term use of anticoagulant therapy	Z79.01
7.	Dependence on respirator	Z99.11
8.	Aftercare for end-of-life care	Z51.5
9.	Encounter for screening mammogram	Z12.31
10.	Encounter for radiation therapy	Z51.0
11.	Noncompliance with medication, unintentional, due to patient's advanced age	Z91.130
12.	Encounter for removal of sutures	Z48.02

Coding of Signs and Symptoms

CHAPTER 13

Symptoms, Signs, and Ill-Defined Conditions

CHAPTER OVERVIEW

- Many symptoms and signs are classified to chapter 18 of ICD-10-CM if they point to multiple diseases or systems or if they are of an unexplained etiology.
- There are few situations in which a symptom code from chapter 18 is used as a principal diagnosis.
- Conversely, for outpatients, the symptom code is often used as the reason for the encounter.
- Codes from chapter 18 are assigned as secondary only when the sign or symptom is not integral to a condition.
- The codes for nonspecific abnormal findings are rarely appropriate for use in an inpatient setting.

LEARNING OUTCOMES

After studying this chapter you should be able to:

Explain the difference between a sign and a symptom.

Determine when to properly use a code from chapter 18 of the ICD-10-CM for a principal diagnosis.

Determine when to properly use a code from chapter 18 for an additional diagnosis.

TERMS TO KNOW

Sign
objective evidence of disease observed by the examining physician

Symptom
subjective observation reported by the patient

REMEMBER . . .

In an inpatient situation, there are often more appropriate options than the codes found in chapter 18 of the ICD-10-CM.
. . . For inpatients, a diagnosis described as possible, probable, and so on is considered to be an established diagnosis.

INTRODUCTION

A sign is defined as objective evidence of disease that can be observed by the examining physician. A symptom, on the other hand, is a subjective observation reported by the patient but not confirmed objectively by the physician.

Symptoms and signs are classified in two ways in ICD-10-CM: Those that point to a specific diagnosis have been assigned to a category in other chapters of ICD-10-CM. Those that can point to more than one disease or system, or that are of unexplained etiology, are classified to chapter 18 of ICD-10-CM.

SIGNS AND SYMPTOMS AS PRINCIPAL DIAGNOSES

Codes for symptoms, signs, and ill-defined conditions from chapter 18 of ICD-10-CM cannot be used as principal diagnoses or reasons for outpatient encounters when related diagnoses have been established. Examples include:

T40.1x4A + R40.20	Coma due to poisoning by heroin, initial encounter
I44.2 + R55	Syncope due to third-degree atrioventricular block

If the patient is an inpatient, a diagnosis described as possible, probable, and so on at the time of discharge is considered to be an established diagnosis. For example, a patient is admitted with severe generalized abdominal pain. The physician's diagnostic statement is abdominal pain, probably due to acute gastritis (K29.00). Only the code for the gastritis is assigned, as the abdominal pain is integral to the probable gastritis. Words such as "possible" and "probable" are not considered to be established for outpatient visits or encounters. If there is not an established diagnosis, only symptoms or signs that are available at the highest level of certainty are assigned.

There are only a few situations in which a symptom code from chapter 18 can be correctly designated the principal diagnosis, as follows:

1. When the diagnostic statement lists the symptom first, followed by two or more contrasting/comparative conditions, a symptom code may be assigned as the principal diagnosis. However, if the symptom code is integral to each of the conditions listed, no additional code for the symptom is reported. More detail is offered in chapter 4 of this handbook.
2. When no related condition is identified and the symptom is the reason for the encounter, a code from chapter 18 of ICD-10-CM is assigned as the principal diagnosis even though other unrelated diagnoses may be listed. For example, a patient is admitted with tachycardia. An electrocardiogram (EKG) does not provide any conclusive evidence of the type of tachycardia or of any underlying cardiac condition. The patient is also an insulin-dependent diabetic; blood sugars are monitored daily during the hospital stay. The reason for admission is tachycardia; therefore, code **R00.0, Tachycardia, unspecified,** is the principal diagnosis. Because the diabetes was treated during the hospital stay, an additional code is assigned for the diabetes mellitus.
3. This guideline does not apply if the diagnosis is stated as a symptom due to two conditions rather than as two contrasting diagnoses. In this case, both conditions are coded, and the symptom code is assigned as an additional code only if it meets criteria for the reporting of additional diagnoses. For example, if a diagnosis is stated as chest pain due to costochondritis and possible hiatal hernia, both the costochondritis and the hiatal hernia are coded according to the guideline governing coding of contrasting/comparative conditions. No code for chest pain is assigned because it is integral to both diagnoses.

4. Other situations in which codes from chapter 18 of the ICD-10-CM manual can be appropriately used as the principal diagnosis for an inpatient admission include the following:
   - Presenting signs or symptoms are transient, and no definitive diagnosis can be made.
   - The patient is referred elsewhere for further study or treatment before a diagnosis is made.
   - A more precise diagnosis cannot be made for any other reason.
   - The symptom is treated in an outpatient setting without the additional workup required to arrive at a more definitive diagnosis.
   - Provisional diagnosis of a sign or symptom is made for a patient who fails to return for further investigation or care.
   - A residual late effect is the reason for admission, and the Alphabetic Index directs the coder to an alternative sequencing.

Generally speaking, symptom codes classified to other chapters of ICD-10-CM are not designated as principal diagnoses when a related condition has been identified. The symptom can be designated as principal diagnosis, however, when the patient is admitted for the sole purpose of treating the symptom and no treatment or further evaluation of the underlying disease takes place. For example, patients with dehydration secondary to gastroenteritis are sometimes admitted for the purpose of rehydration when the gastroenteritis itself could be managed on an outpatient basis. In this case, the code for the dehydration can be designated as the principal diagnosis even though the cause of the dehydration is stated.

Note that these guidelines do not apply when coding and reporting hospital outpatient care or physician services. Outpatient encounters do not ordinarily permit the type of study that results in an established diagnosis, and treatment is often directed at relieving symptoms rather than treating the underlying condition. The highest level of certainty is reported as the reason for encounter for outpatients, which often means that a symptom code is assigned as the reason for the encounter.

SIGNS AND SYMPTOMS AS ADDITIONAL DIAGNOSES

Codes from chapter 18 are assigned as secondary codes only when the symptom or sign is not integral to the underlying condition, unless otherwise instructed by the classification, and when its presence makes a difference in the severity of the patient's condition and/or the care given. For example, many but not all patients with cirrhosis of the liver have ascites. When ascites is present, it makes a difference in the care given, and so the chapter 18 code for ascites (R18.8) should be assigned as an additional code. Codes from chapter 18 are not assigned when they are implicit in the diagnosis or when the symptom is included in the condition code. Such redundant coding is inappropriate. Examples include:

- Abdominal pain due to gastric ulcer—no symptom code is assigned to the abdominal pain because it is integral to the ulcer.
- Coma due to diabetes mellitus—the symptom code for coma is not assigned because combination codes are provided for diabetes with associated coma.
- Patient admitted with chest pain, initially thought to be angina—diagnostic studies do not support this diagnosis, and the physician's diagnosis is chest pain, probable costochondritis (M94.0). The chest pain is not coded because it is implicit in the costochondritis.

ABNORMAL FINDINGS

Although categories R70 through R97 in chapter 18 are provided for coding nonspecific abnormal findings, it is rarely appropriate to assign one of these codes for acute inpatient hospital care. They are assigned only when (1) the physician has not been able to arrive at a definitive related diagnosis and lists the abnormal finding itself as a diagnosis and (2) the condition meets the Uniform Hospital Discharge Data Set criteria for reporting of other diagnoses.

For example, if the physician lists a diagnosis of abnormal electrocardiographic findings without any mention of associated disease, assigning code **R94.31, Abnormal electrocardiogram [ECG] [EKG],** would be appropriate if there was evidence of further evaluation for a possible cardiac condition. On the other hand, a coder might note an elevated blood pressure reading in the medical record, but the physician has not listed it as a diagnosis and there is no evidence of any follow-up or treatment. In this situation, assigning a code for this abnormal finding would be inappropriate.

If the coder notes clinical findings outside the normal range but no related diagnosis is stated, the coder should review the medical record to determine whether additional tests and/or consultations were carried out related to these findings or whether specific related care was given. If such documentation is present, it is appropriate to ask the physician whether a code should be assigned.

For example, a patient with a low potassium level treated with oral or intravenous potassium has a clinically significant condition that probably should be reported; the physician should be asked whether a diagnosis should be added. On the other hand, a finding of degenerative arthritis on a routine postoperative chest X-ray of an elderly patient when no treatment or further diagnostic evaluation has been carried out does not warrant a code assignment.

GLASGOW COMA SCALE

The Glasgow coma scale is a scale for assessing the degree of consciousness, especially after a head injury. The scoring is determined by three factors: amount of eye opening, verbal responsiveness, and motor responsiveness. The test score can function as an indicator for certain diagnostic tests or treatments and for predicting the duration and ultimate outcome of coma.

Codes in subcategory R40.2, Coma, can be used in combination with traumatic brain injury or acute cerebrovascular disease codes, or sequelae of cerebrovascular disease codes. These codes are primarily for use by trauma registries but may be used in any setting where this information is collected. The coma scale codes should be sequenced after the diagnosis code(s). One code from each subcategory (amount of eye opening, verbal responsiveness, and motor responsiveness) is needed to complete the scale. The seventh character indicates when the scale was recorded (e.g., in the field, at arrival to emergency department, at hospital admission). The seventh character should match for all three codes.

At a minimum, the initial score documented upon presentation at the facility should be recorded. This may be a score from the emergency medicine technician or documented in the emergency department. A facility may choose to capture multiple Glasgow coma scale scores, if desired. Assign a code from R40.24-, Glasgow coma scale, total score, when only the total score is documented in the medical record. When individual score(s) are documented, codes R40.21- through R40.23- are assigned. Code R40.244 is used to report other coma, without documented Glasgow coma scale score, or when there is only a partial score reported.

ILL-DEFINED CONDITIONS

Code **R99, Ill-defined and unknown cause of mortality,** is only for use in the very limited circumstances when a patient who has already died is brought into an emergency department or other health care facility and is pronounced dead on arrival. This code should not be used to represent the discharge disposition of death.

EXERCISE 13.1

Code the following diagnoses and procedures as statements given at the time of discharge. Do not assign External cause of morbidity codes.

1.	Dysuria	R30.0
	Transurethral biopsy of bladder	0TBB7ZX
2.	Acute chest pain due to influenzal pleurisy	J11.1
3.	Gross, painless hematuria, cause undetermined	R31.0
	Cystoscopy with control of bladder hemorrhage by cauterization	0T5B8ZZ
4.	Pyuria, intermittent, cause undetermined	N39.0
5.	Hyperplastic lymph node, left axilla	R59.9
	Open Biopsy, axillary lymph node	07B60ZX
6.	Elevated glucose tolerance test	R73.02
7.	Severe vertigo, left temporal headache, and nausea	R42 R51 R11.0
8.	Syncope, cause undetermined	R55
9.	Chest pain, probably angina pectoris	I20.9
10.	Psychogenic dysuria	F45.8
11.	Arteriosclerotic gangrene, left foot	I70.262
12.	Chronic epistaxis, severe, recurrent	R04.0
	Anterior and posterior nasal packing	2Y41X5Z

13.	Severe epistaxis due to hypertension Nasal packing	I10 R04.0 2Y41X5Z
14.	Hereditary epistaxis	I78.0
15.	Generalized abdominal pain due to pancreatitis versus cholecystitis	K85.9 K81.9
16.	Chronic fatigue syndrome	R53.82
17.	Fever and malaise due to viral syndrome	B34.9
18.	Fever of unknown etiology, headache	R50.9 R51

Coding of Infectious and Parasitic Diseases, Endocrine Diseases and Metabolic Disorders, and Mental Disorders

CHAPTER 14

Infectious and Parasitic Diseases

CHAPTER OVERVIEW

- Chapter 1 of ICD-10-CM includes information on how to code infectious and parasitic diseases.
  - The primary axis of chapter 1 is the organism responsible for the disease.
  - When the main term for the condition is located, specific subterms always take precedence over general subterms.
- This chapter has information on coding specific infectious and parasitic diseases, including tuberculosis, severe acute respiratory syndrome (SARS), West Nile virus, bacteremia, septicemia, systemic inflammatory response syndrome (SIRS), sepsis, toxic shock syndrome, and gram-negative bacterial infections.
- Also included in chapter 1 of ICD-10-CM is detailed information on all aspects of HIV/AIDS coding procedures.

LEARNING OUTCOMES

After studying this chapter you should be able to:

- Code infectious and parasitic diseases.
- Explain the difference between, and be able to code properly, bacteremia, septicemia, SIRS, sepsis, and septic shock.
- Explain how to code for HIV testing, diagnosis, and treatment.

TERMS TO KNOW

Bacteremia
presence of bacteria in the blood-stream after a trauma or an infection

Sepsis
SIRS due to infection; a severe case indicates organ dysfunction

Septic shock
circulatory failure associated with severe sepsis

Septicemia
a systemic disease associated with pathological microorganisms or toxins in the bloodstream

SIRS
systemic inflammatory response syndrome; a systemic response to infection or trauma with such symptoms as fever and tachycardia

REMEMBER . . .

Codes from chapter 1 of ICD-10-CM take precedence over codes from other chapters for the same condition. . . . Coding for HIV/AIDS is not allowed unless the diagnostic statement reports the diagnosis with absolute certainty.

INTRODUCTION

Chapter 1 of ICD-10-CM classifies infectious and parasitic diseases that are easily transmissible (communicable). The primary axis for this chapter is the organism responsible for the condition. Infectious and parasitic conditions are classified in one of several ways, making careful use of the Alphabetic Index imperative. Some examples follow.

- A single code from chapter 1 is assigned to indicate the organism. For example, code B26.- is assigned for mumps. Some codes of this type use a fourth character to indicate a site or an associated condition. For example, code B37.1 is assigned for candidiasis of the lung.
- Combination codes frequently identify both the condition and the organism. For example:

  J15.212 Pneumonia due to Methicillin resistant *Staphylococcus aureus*
  B26.0 Orchitis due to mumps

Dual classification is also used extensively for chapter 1. For example:

B49 + J99 Bronchomycosis
B39.9 + H32 Chorioretinitis in histoplasmosis

Codes from chapter 1 take precedence over codes from other chapters for the same condition. For example, urinary tract infection due to candidiasis is classified to code **B37.49, Other urogenital candidiasis,** rather than to code **N39.0, Urinary tract infection, site not specified.** Conditions that are not considered to be easily transmissible or communicable are classified in the appropriate body system chapter, with an additional code from category B95–B97 to indicate the responsible organism. For example, codes **N41.00, Acute prostatitis without hematuria,** and **B95.0, *Streptococcus,* group A, as the cause of diseases classified elsewhere,** are assigned for acute prostatitis due to group A *Streptococcus*.

ORGANISM VERSUS SITE OR OTHER SUBTERM

A thorough search of the Alphabetic Index is required in coding infection. When the main term for the condition has been located, a subterm for the organism always takes precedence over a more general subterm (such as "acute" or "chronic") when both subterms occur at the same indention level in the Alphabetic Index. For example, for a diagnosis of chronic cystitis due to gonococcus, the Alphabetic Index provides subterms for both chronic and gonococcal:

Cystitis (exudative) . . .
  chronic N30.20 . . .
  gonococcal A54.01

In this case, only code A54.01 is assigned because the subterm for the organism takes precedence over the subterm "chronic."

When the organism is specified but is not indexed under the main term for the condition, the coder should refer to the main term **Infection** or to the main term for the organism. For example, consider a diagnosis of candidal cystitis. No subterm for candidal is located under the main term **Cystitis,** but there is a main term entry **Infection,** followed by a subterm for *Candida,* as well as a main term **Candidiasis, candidal,** subterm "urogenital site, NEC." Code B37.49 is therefore assigned for this diagnosis rather than the code for cystitis.

SEVERE ACUTE RESPIRATORY SYNDROME (SARS)

There are specific codes provided for SARS. This is a respiratory illness caused by a coronavirus. SARS begins with a fever and may include chills, headache, and malaise. In some patients, there are also mild respiratory symptoms, dry cough, and trouble breathing. The codes are as follows:

Z20.828 Contact with or exposure to SARS-associated coronavirus
B97.21 SARS-associated coronavirus infection
J12.81 Pneumonia due to SARS-associated coronavirus

WEST NILE VIRUS FEVER

Subcategory A92.3 is used to report West Nile virus infection. The virus is transmitted to humans by the bite of a mosquito that has bitten an infected bird. Most healthy people infected by the virus have few symptoms or have a mild illness consisting of fever, headache, and body aches prior to recovering. In elderly patients or those with a weakened immune system, the virus may cause encephalitis, meningitis, or permanent neurological damage and may be life threatening. Subcategory A92.3 is further subdivided to distinguish between West Nile virus infection unspecified (A92.30), with encephalitis (A92.31), with other neurologic manifestation (A92.32), and with other complications (A92.39). This expansion allows the differentiation between the milder cases of the disease and those with more serious complications and neurological manifestations.

LATE EFFECTS

Chapter 1 provides four sequelae categories for use when there is a residual condition due to previous infection or parasitic infestation:

B90 Sequelae of tuberculosis
B91 Sequelae of poliomyelitis
B92 Sequelae of leprosy
B94 Sequelae of other and unspecified infectious and parasitic diseases

As discussed earlier, the code for the residual effect is sequenced first, followed by the appropriate sequelae code, except in a few instances where the Alphabetic Index instructs otherwise. A code for the infection itself is not assigned because it is no longer present. For example:

G93.9 + B94.1 Brain damage resulting from previous viral encephalitis (three years ago)
B90.8 + E35 Tuberculous calcification of adrenal gland

TUBERCULOSIS

Tuberculosis (TB) is a bacterial disease caused by *Mycobacterium tuberculosis* and *Mycobacterium bovis*. People with weakened immune systems are at increased risk for contracting TB. It is spread through the air when a person with untreated pulmonary TB coughs or sneezes. Prolonged exposure to a person with untreated TB usually is necessary for infection to occur.

Tuberculosis is classified to categories A15 through A19 based on the general site (e.g., respiratory system) or type of tuberculosis (e.g., miliary), as follows:

A15 Respiratory tuberculosis
A17 Tuberculosis of nervous system
A18 Tuberculosis of other organs
A19 Miliary tuberculosis

Categories A15, A17, and A18 are subdivided further to specify the site. Tuberculosis usually affects the lungs (code A15.0), although other parts of the body can also be affected, for example, intrathoracic lymph nodes (code A15.4), kidneys (code A18.11), and bones and joints (subcategory A18.0). Miliary tuberculosis (category A19) is the form of TB in which the bacillus spreads through all body tissues and organs, producing many thousands of tiny tubercular lesions.

Care should be taken to differentiate between a diagnosis of tuberculosis and a positive tuberculin skin test without a diagnosis of active tuberculosis. Code R76.11 classifies the following:

- Nonspecific reaction to tuberculin skin test without active tuberculosis
- Positive tuberculin skin test without active tuberculosis
- Positive PPD (skin test)
- Abnormal result of Mantoux test
- Tuberculin (skin test) positive
- Tuberculin (skin test) reactor

SEPSIS, SEVERE SEPSIS, AND SEPTIC SHOCK

For a diagnosis of sepsis, the appropriate code for the underlying systemic infection should be assigned. Streptococcal sepsis is classified to category A40 with the third character specifying sepsis due to different streptococci strains such as group A (A40.0), group B (A40.1), *Streptococcus pneumoniae* (A40.3), other (A40.8), or unspecified (A40.9). However, sepsis due to *Streptococcus* group D is assigned to code **A41.81, Sepsis due to *Enterococcus*.**

Other types of sepsis are classified to other organisms, such as candidal sepsis (B37.7) or disseminated herpesviral disease (B00.7). If the type of infection or causal organism is not further specified, assign code **A41.9, Sepsis, unspecified organism.**

Organisms are sometimes transferred to other tissue, where they may seed infection in another site and lead to such conditions as arteritis, meningitis, and pyelonephritis. Additional codes are assigned for these manifestations when they are present.

A diagnosis of sepsis can neither be assumed nor ruled out on the basis of laboratory values alone. Negative or inconclusive blood cultures do not preclude a diagnosis of sepsis in patients with clinical evidence of the condition; however, the provider should be queried. A code for sepsis is assigned only when the physician makes such a diagnosis.

Bacteremia (R78.81) refers to the presence of bacteria in the bloodstream after trauma or mild infection. This condition is usually transient and ordinarily clears promptly through the action of the body's own immune system.

The unusual or imprecise diagnostic reference to a site-specific or organ-specific sepsis, such as urosepsis, may require further clarification for coding purposes. For example, the term "urosepsis" refers to pyuria or bacteria in the urine, not the blood. Unfortunately, urosepsis is sometimes stated as the diagnosis even though the condition has progressed from a localized urinary tract infection and has become a generalized sepsis. The term "urosepsis" is a nonspecific term and should not be considered synonymous with sepsis. It has no default code in the Alphabetic Index. When this term is documented, the coder should consult the provider for clarification.

Systemic inflammatory response syndrome (SIRS) generally refers to the systemic response to infection, trauma/burns, or other insult (such as cancer), with symptoms including fever, tachycardia, tachypnea, and leukocytosis. SIRS of noninfectious origin is coded to subcategory R65.1 depending on whether acute organ dysfunction is present (R65.11) or not (R65.10).

Severe sepsis (subcategory R65.2) generally refers to sepsis with associated acute or multiple organ dysfunction. Subcategory R65.2 is further subdivided to identify whether it is associated with septic shock (R65.21) or without septic shock (R65.20). Septic shock generally refers to circulatory failure associated with severe sepsis and therefore represents a type of acute organ dysfunction. The

physician must specifically record "septic shock" in the diagnostic statement in order to code it as such. Septic shock indicates the presence of severe sepsis and code **R65.21, Severe sepsis with septic shock,** must be assigned, even if the term "severe sepsis" is not documented.

A code from subcategory R65.2, Severe sepsis, should not be assigned unless severe sepsis or an associated acute organ dysfunction is documented. When a patient has sepsis and an acute organ dysfunction, but the documentation indicates that the acute organ dysfunction is related to a medical condition other than sepsis, codes from subcategory R65.2 should not be used. If the documentation is not clear as to whether an acute organ dysfunction is related to the sepsis or another medical condition, the provider should be queried. Due to the complex nature of severe sepsis, some cases may require querying the provider prior to code assignment.

Coding and Sequencing

Coders should be guided by the following instructions when coding sepsis or severe sepsis. The coding of these conditions is dependent on the documentation available.

Severe Sepsis

The coding of severe sepsis requires a minimum of two codes:

- Sequence first a code for the underlying infection followed by a code from subcategory R65.2, Severe sepsis.
- If the causal organism is not documented, assign code **A41.9, Sepsis, unspecified organism,** for the infection.
- An additional code(s) should also be assigned for the associated acute organ dysfunction.

If severe sepsis is present on admission and meets the Uniform Hospital Discharge Data Set definition of principal diagnosis—that is, the condition after study that necessitated the admission—assign first the code for the underlying systemic infection (e.g., A40.-, A41.-, B37.7) followed by the appropriate code from subcategory R65.2 as required by the sequencing rules in the Tabular List. A code from subcategory R65.2 can never be assigned as a principal diagnosis.

When severe sepsis develops during an encounter (it was not present on admission), the underlying systemic infection code should be assigned first, and a code from subcategory R65.2 should be assigned as secondary diagnosis. Severe sepsis may be present on admission, but the diagnosis may not be confirmed until sometime after admission. When the documentation is not clear as to whether severe sepsis was present on admission, the provider must be queried for clarification.

Sepsis and Severe Sepsis with a Localized Infection

When the reason for admission is both sepsis, or severe sepsis, and a localized infection (e.g., pneumonia or cellulitis), a code(s) for the underlying systemic infection should be assigned first and the code for the localized infection should be assigned as a secondary diagnosis. If the patient has severe sepsis, a code from subcategory R65.2 should also be assigned as a secondary diagnosis. On the other hand, if the patient is admitted with a localized infection, such as pneumonia, and the sepsis/severe sepsis does not develop until after admission, the localized infection should be assigned first, followed by the appropriate sepsis/severe sepsis codes.

Sepsis due to a Postprocedural Infection

As with all postprocedural complications, code assignment for sepsis due to a postprocedural infection is based on the provider's documentation of the relationship between the infection and the procedure. For such cases, the postprocedural infection code—such as **T80.2-, Infections following infusion, transfusion, and therapeutic injection; T81.4, Infection following a procedure;**

T88.0-, Infection following immunization; or **O86.0, Infection of obstetric surgical wound**—should be coded first, followed by the code for the specific infection. In addition, for severe sepsis, the appropriate code from subcategory R65.2 should also be assigned along with the code(s) for any acute organ dysfunction.

Postprocedural infections can result in severe sepsis and postprocedural septic shock. In such cases, the code for the precipitating complication—such as codes **T81.4, Infection following a procedure,** or **O86.0, Infection of obstetrical surgical wound**—should be coded first, followed by code **R65.21, Severe sepsis with septic shock,** and a code for the systemic infection.

Sepsis and Severe Sepsis Associated with a Noninfectious Process (Condition)

In some cases, a noninfectious process (condition), such as trauma, may lead to an infection that can result in sepsis or severe sepsis. If sepsis or severe sepsis is documented as associated with a noninfectious condition, such as a burn or serious injury, and this condition meets the definition for principal diagnosis, the code for the noninfectious condition should be sequenced first, followed by the code for the resulting infection. If severe sepsis is present, a code from subcategory R65.2 should also be assigned with any associated organ dysfunction(s) codes. It is not necessary to assign a code from subcategory R65.1, Systemic inflammatory response syndrome (SIRS) of non-infectious origin, for these cases.

If the infection meets the definition of principal diagnosis, it should be sequenced before the noninfectious condition. When both the associated noninfectious condition and the infection meet the definition of principal diagnosis, either condition may be assigned as principal diagnosis. Only one code from category R65, Symptoms and signs specifically associated with systemic inflammation and infection, should be assigned. Therefore, when a noninfectious condition leads to an infection resulting in severe sepsis, assign the appropriate code from subcategory R65.2, Severe sepsis. Do not additionally assign a code from subcategory R65.1, Systemic inflammatory response syndrome (SIRS) of non-infectious origin.

Sepsis and septic shock complicating abortion, pregnancy, childbirth, and the puerperium are discussed in chapter 24 of this handbook, Complications of Pregnancy, Childbirth, and the Puerperium. Newborn sepsis is discussed in chapter 27, Perinatal Conditions.

Note carefully in the following cases the different codes that would be assigned based on the information available:

1. Streptococcal sepsis: Assign code **A40.9, Streptococcal sepsis, unspecified.**
2. Severe sepsis: Assign first the code for the systemic infection (e.g., A40.-, A41.-, B37.7) followed by the appropriate code from subcategory R65.2 as required by the sequencing rules in the Tabular List. Additional codes are also assigned to identify the specific acute organ dysfunction (e.g., renal, respiratory, hepatic).
3. Septic shock: Assign first the code for the initiating systemic infection (e.g., A40.-, A41.-, B37.7) followed by code **R65.21, Severe sepsis with septic shock,** or code **T81.12-, Postprocedural septic shock,** and codes for any associated acute organ dysfunction. Note that the sequencing instructions in the Tabular List preclude the assignment of the code for septic shock as a principal diagnosis.
4. Patient admitted due to both pneumonia and sepsis: A41.9 + J18.9.
5. Patient admitted with pneumonia, develops sepsis after admission: J18.9 + A41.9.
6. Sepsis due to a postprocedural infection: Assign code **T80.2-, Infections following infusion, transfusion, and therapeutic injection; T81.4, Infection following a procedure; T88.0-, Infection following immunization;** or **O86.0, Infection of obstetric surgical wound**—followed by the code for the specific infection (e.g., A40.-, A41.-, B37.7).
7. Bacteremia: Assign code R78.81.

TOXIC SHOCK SYNDROME

Toxic shock syndrome (A48.3) is caused by a bacterial infection. The symptoms include high fever of sudden onset, vomiting, watery diarrhea, and myalgia, followed by hypotension and sometimes shock. It was originally reported almost exclusively in menstruating women using high-absorbency tampons. The organism isolated was *Staphylococcus aureus.* A similar syndrome has been identified in children and males infected with group A *Streptococcus.* An additional code from categories B95–B96 is reported to identify the responsible organism.

GRAM-NEGATIVE BACTERIAL INFECTION

Gram-negative bacteria are a specific group of organisms with particular staining characteristics. They are clinically similar, as is the case with *Klebsiella* and *Pseudomonas,* and are thought of as a group even when the specific organism cannot be determined. Occasionally, several gram-negative organisms may be seen, but no single organism is identified as the causative agent, resulting in a diagnosis of gram-negative infection. Gram-negative infections are ordinarily more severe and require more intensive care than gram-positive infections. Again, a code is never assigned solely on the basis of gram-stain results; the assignment is based on the physician's clinical evaluation of the condition.

When the infectious organism has been identified, a specific code is often provided, such as **J15.0, Pneumonia due to *Klebsiella pneumoniae.*** Certain infections are classified in chapters other than chapter 1, and no organism is identified as part of the infection code, for example, urinary tract infection (N39.0). In these instances, an additional code from categories B95–B97 is assigned to indicate the responsible infectious agent. An instructional note will be found at the infection code advising coders to assign an additional code to identify the organism. Two examples follow:

J15.8	Pneumonia, due to anaerobic gram-negative bacteria
N11.8 + B96.89	Chronic pyelonephritis due to gram-negative bacteria

Table 14.1 provides a sampling of gram-negative and gram-positive organisms. A more complete list can be obtained from the health care organization's clinical laboratory director.

TABLE 14.1 Gram-Negative and Gram-Positive Bacteria

Gram-Negative Bacteria		Gram-Positive Bacteria
Bacteroides (anaerobic)	Hemophilus	Actinomyces
Bordetella	Klebsiella	Corynebacterium
Branhamella	Legionella	Lactobacillus
Brucella	Morganella	Listeria
Campylobacter	Neisseria	Mycobacterium
Citrobacter	Proteus	Nocardia
E. coli	Pseudomonas	Peptococcus
Enterobacter	Salmonella	Peptostreptococcus
Francisella	Shigella	Staphylococcus
Fusobacterium (anaerobic)	Trichinella vaginalis	Streptococcus
Gardnerella	Vellonella (anaerobic)	
Helicobacter	Yersinia	

NOSOCOMIAL INFECTIONS

Nosocomial infections are secondary infections that are contracted as a result of medical treatment or develop during hospitalization. They are also known as "hospital-acquired infections." ICD-10-CM provides code **Y95, Nosocomial condition,** as an additional External cause of morbidity code to identify these infections.

DRUG-RESISTANT INFECTIONS

ICD-10-CM provides unique codes to distinguish between methicillin-susceptible and methicillin-resistant *Staphylococcus aureus* (MRSA) infection for sepsis (A41.01 and A41.02), infection (A49.01 and A49.02), infection in diseases classified elsewhere (B95.61 and B95.62), and pneumonia (J15.211 and J15.212).

When a patient is diagnosed with methicillin-resistant *Staphylococcus aureus* infection, and that infection has a combination code that includes the causal organism (e.g., sepsis, pneumonia), assign the appropriate combination code for the condition (e.g., code **A41.02, Sepsis due to Methicillin resistant *Staphylococcus aureus,*** or code **J15.212, Pneumonia due to Methicillin resistant *Staphylococcus aureus*).** Do not assign code **B95.62, Methicillin resistant *Staphylococcus aureus* infection as the cause of diseases classified elsewhere,** as an additional code, because the combination code includes the type of infection and the MRSA organism.

Not every infection has a combination code that includes the causal organism. When there is documentation of a current infection (e.g., wound infection, stitch abscess, urinary tract infection) due to MRSA, and that infection does not have a combination code that includes the causal organism, assign the appropriate code to identify the condition, along with code **B95.62, Methicillin resistant *Staphylococcus aureus* infection as the cause of diseases classified elsewhere,** for the MRSA infection.

Many bacterial infections are resistant to current antibiotics. It is necessary to identify all infections documented as antibiotic resistant. Assign a code from category Z16, Resistance to antimicrobial drugs, following the infection code only if the infection code does not identify drug resistance. For example, for MRSA cases, do not assign a code from subcategory Z16.11, Resistance to penicillins, as an additional diagnosis. Drug resistance codes may be located in the Alphabetic Index by referring to the main term **Resistance, Organism(s), to, Drug.** Codes from category Z16, Resistance to antimicrobial drugs, are assigned only as an additional code when the physician specifically documents an infection that has become drug resistant to identify the resistance and nonresponsiveness of a condition to antimicrobial drugs. Such statements as "multi-drug resistant" or "(specified drug) resistant condition" or similar terminology indicate this condition. The code for the infection should be assigned first, followed by the code from category Z16. For example:

J15.20 + Z16.24   Staphylococcal pneumonia resistant to penicillin and other antibiotic

It is important to distinguish colonization from infection. A patient may be referred to as being colonized or a carrier—meaning that an infectious organism (e.g., methicillin-resistant *Staphylococcus aureus*) is present on or in the body without necessarily causing illness. Colonization is not necessarily indicative of a disease process, and it may not be considered the cause of a patient's specific condition unless documented as such by the provider. A positive colonization test might be documented as "MRSA screen positive" or "MRSA nasal swab positive." ICD-10-CM provides codes under category Z22 for carrier or suspected carrier of infectious diseases and colonization status for several common infections, such as staphylococcus (Z22.321 or Z22.322) and group B streptococcus (Z22.330).

If a patient is documented as having both MRSA colonization and MRSA infection during a hospital admission, code **Z22.322, Carrier or suspected carrier of Methicillin resistant *Staphylococcus aureus,*** and a code for the MRSA infection may both be assigned.

EXERCISE 14.1

Code the following diagnoses.

1.	Acute viral hepatitis (Australian antigen) with hepatitis delta and hepatic coma	B16.0
2.	Chronic gonococcal cystitis	A54.01
3.	Infectious gammaherpesviral mononucleosis with hepatomegaly	B27.09
4.	Postmeasles otitis media	B05.3
5.	Acute scarlet fever	A38.9
6.	Anaerobic gram-negative sepsis	A41.4
7.	Sepsis due to methicillin-resistant *Staphylococcus aureus* (MRSA)	A41.02
8.	Chronic moniliasis of vulva	B37.3
9.	Pulmonary tuberculosis, infiltrative	A15.0
10.	Late, latent syphilis	A52.8
11.	Herpes zoster of conjunctiva	B02.31
12.	Pneumonia due to schistosomiasis	B65.9 J17
13.	Acute empyema due to group B streptococcal infection	J86.9 B95.1

14.	Encephalitis due to typhus	A75.9 G94
15.	Acute respiratory distress due to sin nombre virus	J80 B33.4
16.	Adenoviral pneumonia	J12.0
17.	Chronic gonococcal urethritis	A54.01
18.	Chronic vulvitis due to monilia with microorganisms resistant to cephalosporin	B37.3 Z16.19
19.	Amebic abscess of brain and lung Long-term use of antibiotic	A06.6 Z79.2
20.	Enterococcal septic shock due to acute postoperative peritonitis (surgery performed in previous admission)	A41.81 T81.12xD K65.9

AIDS AND OTHER HIV INFECTIONS

Because the human immunodeficiency virus (HIV) infection has become a major health care concern, the collection of accurate and complete data on conditions associated with HIV infection is important for health care resource planning. Code B20 is assigned for all types of HIV infections, which are described by a variety of terms, such as the following:

- AIDS
- Acquired immune deficiency syndrome
- Acquired immunodeficiency syndrome
- AIDS-related complex (ARC)
- AIDS-related conditions
- HIV infection, symptomatic

Unconfirmed Diagnosis of HIV Infection

Code B20 is not assigned when the diagnostic statement indicates that the infection is "suspected," "possible," "likely," or "?" This is an exception to the general guideline that directs the coder to assign a code for a diagnosis qualified as "suspected" or "possible" as if it were established. Confirmation in this case does not require documentation of a positive serology or culture

for HIV; the provider's diagnostic statement that the patient is HIV-positive or has an HIV-related illness is sufficient. The provider should be asked to state the diagnosis in positive terms.

Serologic Testing for HIV Infection

When an asymptomatic patient with no prior diagnosis of HIV infection or positive-HIV status requests testing to determine his or her HIV status, use code **Z11.4, Encounter for screening for human immunodeficiency virus [HIV].** When the patient shows signs or symptoms of illness or has been diagnosed with a condition related to HIV infection, code the signs and symptoms or the diagnosis rather than the screening code.

When the patient makes a return visit to learn the result of the serology test, code **Z71.7, Human immunodeficiency virus [HIV] counseling,** should be assigned as the reason for the encounter when the test result is negative, inconclusive (R75), or positive. Code Z71.7 can be assigned as an additional code when counseling is provided for patients who test HIV-positive. When a patient is known to be in a high-risk group for HIV infection, code **Z72.89, Other problems related to lifestyle,** can be assigned as an additional code. When the test result is positive but the patient displays no symptoms and has no related complications and no established diagnosis of HIV infection, code **Z21, Asymptomatic human immunodeficiency virus [HIV] infection status,** is assigned. Code Z21 is not assigned when the term "AIDS" is used, when the patient is under treatment for an HIV-related illness, or when the patient is described as having any active HIV-related condition; code B20 is assigned instead.

When a patient has had contact with, or has been exposed to, the HIV virus but shows no signs or symptoms of illness and has not been diagnosed with a condition related to HIV, assign code **Z20.6, Contact with and (suspected) exposure to human immunodeficiency virus [HIV].**

Newborns with HIV-positive mothers often test positive on ELISA (enzyme-linked immunosorbent assay) and/or Western blot HIV tests. This finding usually indicates the antibody status of the mother rather than the status of the newborn; antibodies can cross the placenta and remain for as long as 18 months after birth without the newborn ever being infected. Such inconclusive test results are also coded R75. (See chapter 27 of this handbook for further information on coding HIV infection in the newborn.)

Sequencing of HIV-Related Diagnoses

When a patient is admitted for treatment of an HIV infection or any related complications, code **B20, Human immunodeficiency virus (HIV) disease,** is sequenced as the principal diagnosis, with additional codes for the HIV-related conditions. When a patient with an HIV infection is admitted for treatment of an entirely unrelated condition, such as an injury, that condition is designated as the principal diagnosis, with code B20 and codes for any associated conditions assigned as additional codes.

When an obstetric patient is identified as having any HIV infection, a code from subcategory O98.7, Human immunodeficiency virus [HIV] disease complicating pregnancy, childbirth and the puerperium, is assigned, with code B20 assigned as an additional code. If an obstetric patient tests positive for HIV but has no symptoms and no history of an HIV infection, codes O98.7- and **Z21, Asymptomatic human immunodeficiency virus [HIV] infection status,** are assigned rather than B20.

EXERCISE 14.2

Code the following diagnoses and procedures.

1.	Candidiasis, of esophagus, opportunistic, secondary to AIDS	B20 B37.81
2.	*Pneumocystis carinii* AIDS	B20 B59
3.	Positive HIV test in patient who is asymptomatic, presents no related symptoms, and has no history of HIV infection	Z21
4.	Acute lymphadenitis due to HIV infection	B20 L04.9
5.	Acute appendicitis (admitted for appendectomy) Kaposi's sarcoma of skin of chest, due to HIV infection Total laparoscopic appendectomy	K35.80 B20 C46.0 0DTJ4ZZ
6.	Kaposi's sarcoma of oral cavity AIDS Biopsy of oral cavity mucosa	B20 C46.7 0CB4XZX
7.	Agranulocytosis due to HIV infection	B20 D70.3
8.	Burkitt's tumor of inguinal region associated with AIDS	B20 C83.75
9.	Background retinopathy due to AIDS	B20 H35.00
10.	Inconclusive HIV test	R75

CHAPTER 15

Endocrine, Nutritional, and Metabolic Diseases

CHAPTER OVERVIEW

- Diabetes mellitus is the condition coders encounter most in working with chapter 4 of ICD-10-CM.
- Diabetes mellitus has two classification axes.
  - The first axis is the type of diabetes.
  - The fourth character identifies any associated complication.
- Diabetes causes many concurrent complications.
  - These complications may be either acute or chronic.
  - Assign as many codes as necessary to identify all the conditions.
- Codes from category E08, E09, and E13 are used for classification of secondary diabetes.
- Nutritional disorders classified by ICD-10-CM include deficiencies of specific vitamins and minerals and obesity.
- Specific codes for cystic fibrosis identify site of manifestation involvement.
  - There may be pulmonary, gastrointestinal, or other site involvement.
  - Use codes together if different sites are involved.
- Fluid overload is a component of congestive heart failure.

LEARNING OUTCOMES

After studying this chapter you should be able to:

Code diabetes mellitus properly.

Identify the differences when coding for diabetes during pregnancy and gestational diabetes.

Code fluid overload due to congestive heart failure.

Code nutritional disorders such as obesity.

TERMS TO KNOW

Diabetes mellitus
a chronic disorder of impaired carbohydrate, protein, and fat metabolism

Type 1 diabetes
also known as juvenile type; characterized by the body's failure to produce insulin

Type 2 diabetes
characterized by the body's production of insulin in an insufficient quantity or the body's inability to utilize such insulin

REMEMBER . . .

You can use as many codes as necessary to identify all the conditions related to diabetes that a patient is experiencing.

INTRODUCTION

This chapter covers a variety of conditions that are related in a general way. Because diabetes mellitus is a common medical problem, it is the condition coders encounter most often when working with chapter 4 of ICD-10-CM.

DIABETES MELLITUS

Diabetes mellitus, classified in categories E08 through E13, is a chronic disorder of impaired carbohydrate, protein, and fat metabolism. The disorder is caused by either an absolute decrease in the amount of insulin secreted by the pancreas or a reduction in the biologic effectiveness of the insulin secreted. Other conditions include the term "diabetes," such as bronze diabetes and diabetes insipidus, but a diagnosis of diabetes without further qualification should be interpreted as diabetes mellitus.

FIGURE 15.1 Major Organs of the Endocrine System

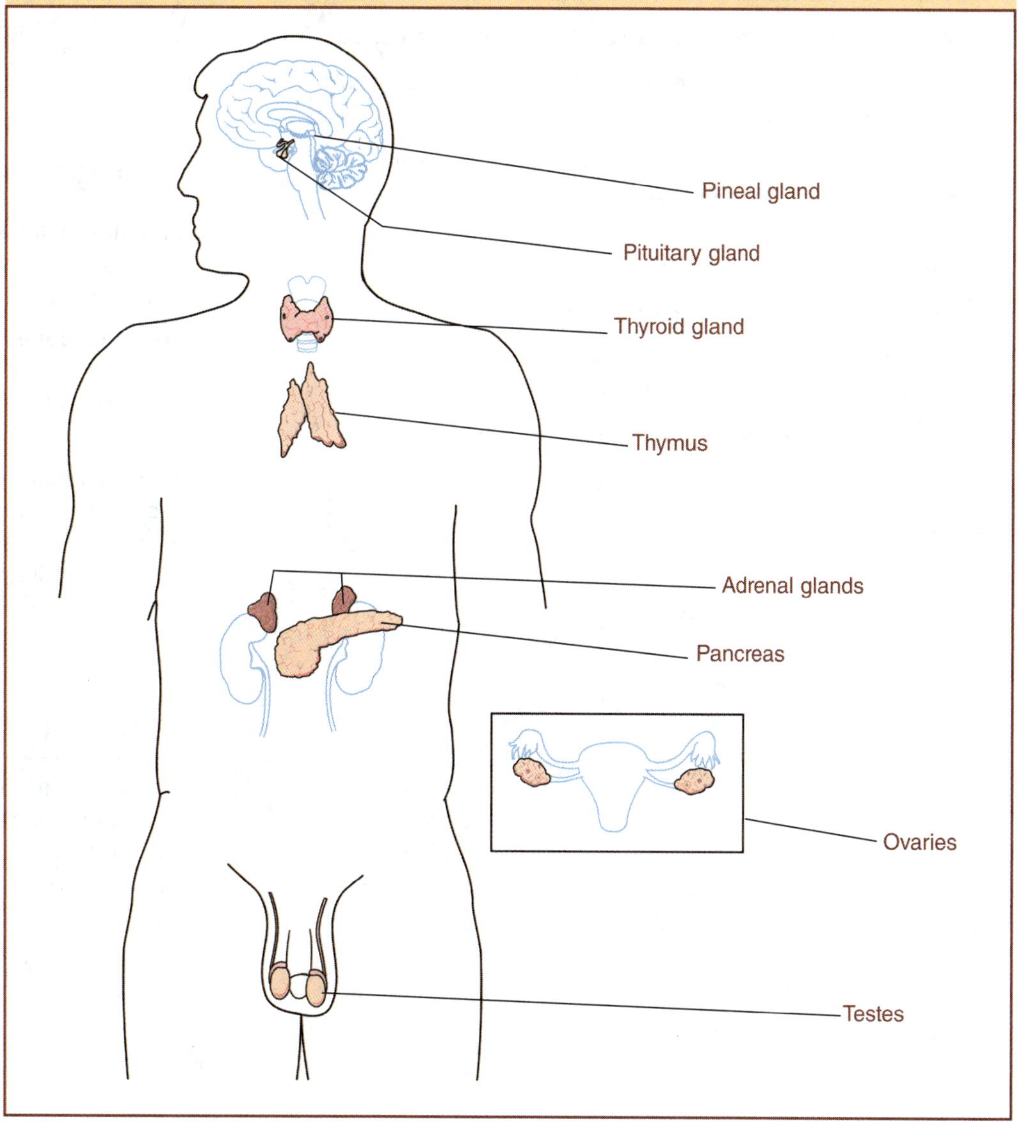

The diabetes mellitus codes are combination codes that include the type of diabetes mellitus, the body system affected, and the complications affecting that body system. The type of diabetes (e.g., secondary, type 1, type 2) is identified at the category level, while the fourth character identifies the presence of any associated complication and the fifth-character and sixth-character subclassification provides further specificity regarding the complication. As many codes within a particular category as are necessary to describe all of the complications of the disease may be used.

Care should be taken when coding a diagnosis documented as "borderline diabetes." If the provider has confirmed a diagnosis of diabetes mellitus, the appropriate code from categories E08–E13, Diabetes mellitus, should be assigned. Otherwise, a diagnosis of "borderline diabetes" without further provider confirmation of the disease should be assigned a code from subcategory R73.0-, Abnormal glucose.

Types of Diabetes Mellitus

There are three major types of diabetes mellitus: type 1 (or type I); type 2 (or type II); and secondary, such as due to an underlying condition or drug or chemical induced. The type of diabetes is the essential element in the selection of the codes in categories E08–E13, rather than whether the patient is on insulin, as follows:

E08 Diabetes mellitus due to underlying condition
E09 Drug or chemical induced diabetes mellitus
E10 Type 1 diabetes mellitus
E11 Type 2 diabetes mellitus
E13 Other specified diabetes mellitus

If the medical record documentation is not clear with regard to the type of diabetes, the default is category E11, Type 2 diabetes mellitus. When the type of diabetes is not documented but the record does indicate that the patient uses insulin, the default is still type 2. The fact that a patient is receiving insulin does not indicate that the diabetes is type 1.

Type 1 diabetes mellitus (category E10) may also be described as ketosis-prone, juvenile type, juvenile onset, or juvenile diabetes. The age of a patient is not the sole determining factor, though most type 1 diabetics develop the condition before reaching puberty. Type 1 diabetes is characterized by the body's failure to produce insulin at all or by an absolute decrease in such production. These patients require regular insulin injections to sustain life and experience significant health problems when they do not follow the prescribed regimen for medication and diet. Careful monitoring is required in order to avoid serious complications. Code **Z79.4, Long-term (current) use of insulin,** is not required for type 1 diabetics because these patients require insulin. However, this code may be assigned, if desired, to provide additional information.

Type 2 diabetes mellitus (category E11) may also be described as ketosis resistant. Insulin is produced, but either it is produced in insufficient quantity or the body is unable to utilize it adequately. Type 2 diabetic patients usually do not require insulin; they are ordinarily managed with oral hypoglycemic agents, diet, and exercise. For some patients, however, these measures are not effective, and insulin therapy may be required to control persistent hyperglycemia.

When a type 2 diabetic patient routinely uses insulin, assign code **Z79.4, Long-term (current) use of insulin.** However, code Z79.4 should not be used if insulin is given temporarily to bring the patient's blood sugar under control during the encounter.

Secondary diabetes is always caused by another condition or event. Secondary diabetes may be due to an underlying condition (E08), drug or chemically induced (E09), due to an infection, or the result of therapy (such as the surgical removal of the pancreas); or it may be some other specified type of diabetes (E13). It can also be the result of an adverse effect of correctly administered medications, the result of poisoning, or a late effect of using certain medications. Secondary diabetes is coded as follows:

- Secondary diabetes that is due to an underlying condition is coded to category E08, Diabetes mellitus due to underlying condition, with the underlying condition coded first. Underlying conditions include congenital rubella (P35.0), Cushing's syndrome (E24.-), cystic fibrosis (E84.-), malignant neoplasm (C00–C96), malnutrition (E40–E46), and pancreatitis and other diseases of the pancreas (K85–K86.-)
- Secondary diabetes that is drug induced or chemically induced is coded to category E09. Codes from category E10–E11 are not assigned for secondary diabetes. For example, steroid-induced diabetes mellitus due to the prolonged use of prednisone for an unrelated condition is coded as **E09.9, Drug or chemical induced diabetes mellitus without complications,** followed by code **T38.0x5-, Adverse effect of glucocorticoids and synthetic analogues.**
- The sequencing of the secondary diabetes codes is based on the Tabular List instructions for categories E08, E09, and E13. For category E08, the underlying condition should be coded first. For category E09, the responsible drug or chemical is coded first.
- Secondary diabetes mellitus that is due to pancreatectomy is coded to **E89.1, Postprocedural hypoinsulinemia.** Assign a code from category E13 and either code **Z90.410, Acquired total absence of pancreas,** or code **Z90.411, Acquired partial absence of pancreas,** as additional diagnoses. For example, postpancreatectomy diabetes mellitus due to surgical removal of part of the pancreas is coded to E89.1, E13, and Z90.411.
- For patients with secondary diabetes who routinely use insulin, code **Z79.4, Long-term (current) use of insulin,** should be assigned. However, code Z79.4 should not be used if insulin is given temporarily to bring the patient's blood sugar under control during the encounter.

Category E13, Other specified diabetes mellitus, includes diabetes mellitus due to genetic defects of beta-cell function and diabetes mellitus due to genetic defects in insulin action.

Complications and Manifestations of Diabetes Mellitus

Type 1 and type 2 diabetes mellitus, as well as secondary diabetes mellitus, can lead to a variety of complications that involve either acute metabolic derangements (E08–E13 with .0- or .1-) or long-term complications (E08–E13 with .2- to .6-). Sequencing of the diabetes mellitus and the complication or manifestation is based on the reason for a particular encounter. Assign as many codes from categories E08–E13 as needed to identify all of the patient's associated conditions.

Acute Metabolic Complications

Acute metabolic complications include hyperosmolarity with coma (E08–E09 and E11–E13 with .01) or without nonketotic hyperglycemic-hyperosmolar coma (E08–E13 with .00), ketoacidosis with coma (E08–E10 and E12–E13 with .11) or without coma (E08–E10 and E12–E13 with .10), and hypoglycemia with coma (E08–E13 with .641) or without coma (E08–E13 with .649). Typical findings for patients with diabetic ketoacidosis (DKA) are glycosuria, strong ketonuria, hyperglycemia, ketonemia (blood ketone), acidosis (low arterial blood pH), and low plasma bicarbonate. Ketoacidosis is a complication of type 1 diabetes; type 2 diabetics seldom develop ketoacidosis. A diagnosis of DKA should be classified as type 1 diabetes mellitus E10.1-. Diabetes with hyperosmolarity (E08–E13 with .01 or .00) is a condition in which there is hyperosmolarity and dehydration without significant ketosis. This condition most often occurs in patients with type 2 diabetes. Coma may or may not be present.

Diabetes with hypoglycemia may occur when an excessive amount of insulin is given, when the patient misses a meal, or when the patient is under stress. The condition may progress to coma. ICD-10-CM provides codes for diabetic hypoglycemia with coma (E08–E13 with .641) or without coma (E08–E13 with .649).

Chronic Complications

Patients with diabetes mellitus are susceptible to one or more chronic conditions that affect the renal, nervous, and peripheral vascular systems, particularly the feet and the eyes. Onset may occur early or late in the course of the diabetes and may occur in both insulin-dependent and non-insulin-dependent patients.

Diabetic patients often suffer several complications concurrently, in which case multiple codes from categories E08–E13 are assigned to identify all the associated diabetic conditions.

Renal Complications

Patients with diabetes are particularly prone to developing complications that affect the kidneys, such as nephritis, nephrosis, or chronic kidney disease. Nephritis is an inflammation of the kidney that develops slowly, over a long period of time. Nephrosis is an advanced stage of disease characterized by massive edema and marked proteinuria. Chronic kidney disease is often the ultimate progression of such conditions.

Diabetic kidney complications are coded to E08–E13 with .21 for diabetic nephropathy, .22 for chronic kidney disease, and .29 for other kidney complication. When the renal condition has progressed to chronic kidney disease, the diagnosis is sometimes stated in a way that appears to require three codes, one for the diabetes with chronic kidney disease (E08–E13 with .22), one for an interim manifestation (N08), and one for the final or current problem (N18.1–N18.6, Chronic kidney disease). It is not necessary to code the intermediate condition, but all three codes may be assigned if the hospital prefers.

Patients who have both diabetes and hypertension may develop chronic kidney disease as a result. In this case, three codes are required: one code for the diabetes with renal manifestation, E08–E13 with .22; a second code from category I12 (or I13) with a fourth character of "0" with chronic kidney disease stage 5 or end-stage renal disease or a fourth character of "9" with chronic kidney disease stage 1 through stage 4, or unspecified; and a third code from category N18 to indicate the specific stage of the chronic kidney disease. No other manifestation code is assigned. An example follows:

E10.22 + I12.0 + N18.5	Progressive type 1 diabetic nephropathy with hypertensive renal disease and chronic kidney disease stage 5

Diabetic Eye Disease

Retinopathy is a common complication of diabetes. Any disease of the retina said to be due to diabetes requires a code of E08–E13 with .3-. Diabetes with unspecified diabetic retinopathy is coded to E08–E13 with .31-. Nonproliferative diabetic retinopathy may be classified as mild (E08–E13 with .32-), moderate (E08–E13 with .33-), or severe (E08–E13 with .34-). Proliferative diabetic retinopathy is coded to E08–E13 with .35-. The sixth character provides additional information to identify the presence or absence of macular edema.

Senile cataracts develop more frequently in patients with diabetes, but they are not true diabetic cataracts and are not classified as ocular manifestations of the disease. A code from category H25, Age-related cataract, and a code from category E08–E13 should be assigned for senile cataracts in a diabetic patient, with sequencing depending on the circumstances of admission. Diabetic cataract (snowflake cataract, true diabetic cataract) is relatively rare. Assign codes for diabetic cataract only when the physician specifically describes the condition as such. For example:

E11.36	Type 2 diabetes mellitus with diabetic cataract
K86.1 + E08.9 + H25.9	Secondary diabetes mellitus due to chronic pancreatitis with mature senile cataract

Diabetic Neurological Complications

Peripheral, cranial, and autonomic neuropathy are chronic manifestations of diabetes mellitus. The subclassification for diabetic neurological complications is as follows:

E08–E13 with .40	Unspecified diabetic neuropathy
E08–E13 with .41	Diabetic mononeuropathy
E08–E13 with .42	Diabetic polyneuropathy
E08–E13 with .43	Diabetic autonomic (poly)neuropathy
E08–E13 with .44	Diabetic amyotrophy
E08–E13 with .49	Other diabetic neurological complication

Do not use the code for autonomic neuropathy unless the diagnosis is stated as such by the physician. For example:

E11.41 + H49.01	Diabetic third (cranial) nerve palsy, right eye
E11.41 + G57.90	Mononeuropathy of the lower limb due to type 2 diabetes
E10.40	Diabetes type 1 with neuropathy
E10.43 + K31.84	Type 1 diabetes with diabetic gastroparesis

Diabetic Circulatory Complications

Peripheral vascular disease is a frequent complication of diabetes mellitus. Diabetic peripheral vascular disease without gangrene is coded as E08–E13 with .51; diabetic peripheral vascular disease with gangrene is coded as E08–E13 with .52. Diabetes with other circulatory complications is coded to E08–E13 with .59. Although arteriosclerosis occurs earlier and more extensively in diabetic patients, coronary artery disease, cardiomyopathy, and cerebrovascular disease are not complications of diabetes and are not included in subcategories E08–E13 with .5-. These conditions are coded separately unless the physician documents a causal relationship.

Other Manifestations of Diabetes Mellitus

Common chronic complications of diabetes mellitus, besides renal, ophthalmic, neurological, or circulatory, are classified to E08–E13 with .6- as follows:

E08–E13 with .61-	Diabetic arthropathy
E08–E13 with .62-	Diabetic skin complications
E08–E13 with .63-	Diabetic oral complications

Ulcers of the lower extremities, particularly the feet, are common complications of diabetes. The code for the diabetic foot ulcer complication (E08–E13 with .621) is assigned first, with an additional code of L97.4-, L97.5- indicating the specific site of the ulcer. If gangrene is present, code E08–E13 with .52 should be assigned as an additional code. It is important to recognize that not all ulcers in diabetic patients are diabetic ulcers; if there is a question as to the relationship, the physician should be consulted. Other diabetic skin ulcers are coded to E08–E13 with .622 and an additional code to identify the site of the ulcer (L97.1–L97.9, L98.41–L98.49).

Organic impotence is often the result of either diabetic peripheral neuropathy or diabetic peripheral vascular disease. It is coded first to either E08–E13 with .40 or E08–E13 with .51, with an additional code of **N52.1, Erectile dysfunction due to diseases classified elsewhere.**

Either of the preceding conditions specified as diabetic but without an indication as to whether the condition is due to neuropathy or peripheral vascular disease is coded as E08–E13 with .69 (with other specified complication), with an additional code for the complications. Codes E08–E13 with .69 are used for any other specified chronic manifestation that cannot be captured with the other codes in categories E08–E13. For example:

E10.69 + M86.171	Diabetes mellitus, type 1, with acute osteomyelitis great toe of right foot

Complications due to Insulin Pump Malfunction

Some diabetic patients require the use of an insulin pump to receive insulin therapy. An insulin pump is a small, computerized device attached to the body that delivers insulin via a catheter. The pump may provide a continuous drip of insulin all day long, or it may allow the patient to self-administer an insulin bolus by pushing a button. Failure or malfunction of the pump may result in underdosing or overdosing of insulin. Both of these situations are considered mechanical complications and are assigned a code from subcategory T85.6, Mechanical complication of other specified internal and external prosthetic devices, implants and grafts, as the principal diagnosis or first-listed code. The appropriate T85.6- code is selected depending on the type of malfunction, as follows:

T85.614 Breakdown (mechanical) of insulin pump
T85.624 Displacement of insulin pump
T85.633 Leakage of insulin pump

In addition, codes are assigned to specify underdose (T38.3x6-) or overdose (T38.3x1-), as well as the code for the type of diabetes mellitus and any associated complications.

DIABETES MELLITUS COMPLICATING PREGNANCY

Diabetes mellitus complicating pregnancy, delivery, or the puerperium is classified in chapter 15 of ICD-10-CM. Diabetes mellitus is a significant complicating factor in pregnancy. Pregnant women who are diabetic should be assigned a code from category O24, Diabetes mellitus in pregnancy, childbirth and puerperium, first, followed by the appropriate diabetes code(s) (E08–E13) from chapter 4 of ICD-10-CM to indicate the type of diabetes involved.

Because diabetes mellitus inevitably complicates the pregnant state, is aggravated by the pregnancy, or is a main reason for obstetric care, it is appropriate to assign these codes for a pregnant diabetic patient. Assign also code **Z79.4, Long-term (current) use of insulin,** if the diabetes mellitus is routinely treated with insulin.

Gestational Diabetes

A diagnosis of gestational diabetes refers to abnormal glucose tolerance that appears during pregnancy in previously nondiabetic women; it is not a true diabetes mellitus. It can occur during the second and third trimesters of pregnancy. It is thought to be due to metabolic or hormonal changes that occur during pregnancy. Patients with gestational diabetes are usually placed on a diabetic diet and sometimes require insulin therapy to maintain normal blood glucose levels during pregnancy, but the condition usually resolves during the postpartum period. Gestational diabetes can cause complications in the pregnancy similar to those of pre-existing diabetes mellitus. It also places the woman at greater risk of developing diabetes after the pregnancy. Subcategory O24.4, Gestational diabetes mellitus, is assigned for this condition. No other code from category O24 should be used with a code from O24.4.

Subcategory O24.4 is further subdivided on the basis of whether the gestational diabetes occurs in pregnancy, childbirth, or puerperium as well as whether it is diet or insulin controlled. If a patient with gestational diabetes is treated with both diet and insulin, only the code for insulin controlled is required. Code **Z79.4, Long-term (current) use of insulin,** should not be used with codes from subcategory O24.4.

An abnormal glucose tolerance in pregnancy, without a diagnosis of gestational diabetes, is assigned a code from subcategory O99.81, Abnormal glucose complicating pregnancy, childbirth, and the puerperium. Codes O24.4- (gestational diabetes) and O99.81- (abnormal glucose tolerance complicating pregnancy) should never be used together on the same record.

Neonatal Conditions Associated with Maternal Diabetes

Newborns with diabetic mothers sometimes experience either a transient decrease in blood sugar (**P70.0, Syndrome of infant of mother with gestational diabetes; P70.1, Syndrome of infant of a diabetic mother; P70.3, Iatrogenic neonatal hypoglycemia;** or **P70.4, Other neonatal hypoglycemia**) or a transient hyperglycemia (**P70.2, Neonatal diabetes mellitus**). The latter condition is sometimes referred to as pseudodiabetes and occasionally requires a short course of insulin therapy. Note, however, that these codes are assigned only when the maternal condition has actually had such an effect; the fact that the mother has diabetes in itself does not warrant the assignment of one of these codes for the newborn. When laboratory reports seem to indicate either condition, it is appropriate to check with the attending physician.

When a normal infant is born to a diabetic mother, and the infant presents no manifestations of the syndrome, assign code **Z38.00, Single liveborn, born in hospital, delivered vaginally,** as the principal diagnosis. Code **Z83.3, Family history of diabetes mellitus,** should be assigned as an additional diagnosis. In addition, assign code **P00.89, Newborn (suspected to be) affected by other maternal conditions,** as an additional diagnosis for a newborn infant who requires special surveillance after being born to a diabetic mother but who lacks manifestations of infant of a diabetic mother syndrome.

EXERCISE 15.1

Code the following diagnoses. Do not assign External cause of morbidity codes.

1.	Diabetes mellitus, type 1 Diabetic nephrosis	E10.21
2.	Secondary diabetes mellitus due to pancreatic malignancy Snowflake cataract	C25.9 E08.36
3.	Type 1 diabetes with ketoacidosis	E10.10
4.	Diabetes mellitus, type 2, with hyperosmolar, nonketotic coma	E11.01
5.	Diabetic Kimmelstiel-Wilson disease	E11.21
6.	Chronic kidney disease, stage IV due to type 1 diabetes	E10.22 N18.4
7.	Impotence due to diabetic peripheral neuropathy	E11.40 N52.1

HYPOGLYCEMIC AND INSULIN REACTIONS

Hypoglycemic reactions can occur in both diabetic and nondiabetic patients. In a diabetic patient, hypoglycemia with coma is coded as E08–E13 with .641, or E08–E13 with .649 if there is no mention of coma. Such reactions may occur when there is an imbalance between eating or exercise patterns and the dosage of insulin or oral hypoglycemic drugs. Hypoglycemia due to insulin may also occur in a newly diagnosed, type 1 diabetic during the initial phase of therapy while the dosage is being adjusted.

In a patient who does not have diabetes, code **E15, Nondiabetic hypoglycemic coma,** is assigned for hypoglycemic coma not otherwise specified. Code E15 also includes drug-induced insulin coma in a nondiabetic patient. Code **E16.2, Hypoglycemia, unspecified,** is assigned for hypoglycemia not otherwise specified.

Hypoglycemia without coma, due to a drug used as prescribed in a nondiabetic patient, requires code **E16.0, Drug-induced hypoglycemia without coma,** followed by a code from categories T36–T50 with a sixth character of "5" to indicate adverse effect and the responsible drug. Hypoglycemic coma or shock in a nondiabetic patient resulting from the incorrect use of insulin or other antidiabetic agent is coded as poisoning (T38.3x- with a sixth character of 1–4) with the poisoning code first, followed by code **E15, Nondiabetic hypoglycemic coma.**

EXERCISE 15.2

Code the following diagnoses. Do not assign External cause of morbidity codes.

1. Neonatal hypoglycemia	P70.4
2. Hypoglycemic coma in patient without diabetes	E15
3. Patient with type 2 diabetes mellitus participated in a strenuous game of racquetball without adjusting his insulin dosage; he is admitted with blood sugar of 35 and is diagnosed as being hypoglycemic Hypoglycemia	E11.649 Z79.4
4. Type 1 diabetic developed hypoglycemia even though she had taken only the prescribed dose of insulin and did not alter her exercise or eating regimen	E10.649

CODES FOR NUTRITIONAL DISORDERS

Nutritional disorders, such as deficiency of specific vitamins and minerals, are classified in categories E40 through E64, with the exception of nutritional anemias, which are classified in categories D50 through D53 series.

Several codes are used to identify overweight and obesity, including the following:

- E66.01 Morbid (severe) obesity due to excess calories
- E66.09 Other obesity due to excess calories
- E66.1 Drug-induced obesity
- E66.2 Morbid (severe) obesity with alveolar hypoventilation
- E66.3 Overweight
- E66.8 Other obesity
- E66.9 Obesity, unspecified

These codes are assigned only on the basis of the physician's diagnostic statement. Category E66, Overweight and obesity, requires that an additional code (Z68.-) for the body mass index (BMI) be assigned, if known. BMI is a tool for indicating weight status in adults. It is a measure of weight for height. The BMI code assignment should be based on medical record documentation, which may be found in the notes of other clinicians involved in the care of the patient (i.e., physician or other qualified health care practitioner legally accountable for establishing the patient's diagnosis). BMI is typically documented by the dietitian or the nurse. Coding BMI is an exception to the guideline that requires that code assignment be based on the documentation by the provider. While BMI may be reported on the basis of another clinician's documentation, the codes for the associated diagnosis (such as overweight and obesity) should be based on the provider's documentation.

Code **E66.2, Morbid (severe) obesity with alveolar hypoventilation,** also known as Pickwickian syndrome, involves sleep-disordered breathing that causes a person to stop breathing for short periods of time while sleeping. It may be related to both obesity and neurological conditions.

METABOLIC DISORDERS

Metabolic disorders other than diabetes are classified to categories E70–E88. A metabolic disorder occurs when abnormal reactions in the body disrupt the metabolism. These disorders involve an alteration in the normal metabolism of carbohydrates, lipids, proteins, water, and nucleic acids.

Fluid Overload

Fluid overload (E87.7-) is the excessive accumulation of fluid in the body. It may be caused by excessive parenteral infusion or deficiencies in cardiovascular or renal fluid volume regulation. However, when fluid overload is a component of congestive heart failure, it is not coded separately.

Cystic Fibrosis

Cystic fibrosis (E84.-), also known as mucoviscidosis or cystic fibrosis of the pancreas, is a disorder of the exocrine glands that causes the accumulation of thick, tenacious mucus. It is the primary cause of pancreatic deficiency and chronic malabsorption in children. Although cystic fibrosis affects the body in a number of ways, progressive respiratory insufficiency is the major cause of illness in patients with this disease. The symptoms primarily affect the digestive and respiratory

systems. In some glands, like the pancreas, the thick mucus may obstruct the pancreas, preventing digestive enzymes from reaching the intestines. The pulmonary manifestation results in mucus secretions that clog the airways and allow bacteria to multiply. Sometimes this state progresses to complications such as acute and chronic bronchitis, bronchiectasis, pneumonia, atelectasis, peribronchial and parenchyma scarring, pneumothorax, and hemoptysis. Intra-abdominal complications such as meconium ileus, rectal prolapse, inguinal hernia, gallstones, ileocolic intussusception, and gastroesophageal reflux also occur.

Specific codes identify the site of manifestation involvement such as pulmonary involvement (E84.0), meconium ileus (E84.11), other intestinal manifestations (E84.19), or other site involvement (E84.8). These manifestation codes may be used together if different sites are involved. Code **E84.9, Cystic fibrosis, unspecified,** should be used if the manifestation is not specified. If an infectious organism is involved with cystic fibrosis with pulmonary involvement, assign an additional code for the organism present.

Because there is no known cure for cystic fibrosis, therapy is directed toward the complications of the disease, with the major focus on the maintenance of adequate nutritional and respiratory status. Admissions due to the cystic fibrosis itself most often occur when the patient is brought in for workup to confirm the diagnosis.

Tumor Lysis Syndrome

Tumor lysis syndrome (TLS) refers to a group of serious, potentially life-threatening metabolic disturbances that can occur after antineoplastic therapy. TLS can develop spontaneously as a result of radiation therapy or corticosteroid therapy. However, it usually occurs following the administration of anticancer drugs and is often associated with leukemias and lymphomas. It is also seen in other hematologic malignancies and solid tumors. When cancer cells are destroyed, they can release intracellular ions and metabolic by-products into the circulation, leading to TLS. Code **E88.3, Tumor lysis syndrome,** is used to report spontaneous tumor lysis syndrome as well as tumor lysis syndrome following antineoplastic drug therapy. Use an additional code (T45.1x5-) to identify an adverse effect of drug when tumor lysis syndrome is drug induced.

EXERCISE 15.3

Code the following diagnoses and procedures. Do not assign External cause of morbidity codes.

1. Hypercholesterolemia and endogenous hyperglyceridemia	E78.2
2. Cystic fibrosis with mild mental intellectual disabilities	E84.9 F70
3. Congenital myxedema Inappropriate antidiuretic hormone secretion syndrome	E00.1 E22.2

4.	Hypokalemia	E87.6
5.	Uninodular toxic nodular goiter with thyrotoxicosis Open left thyroid lobectomy	E05.10 0GTG0ZZ
6.	Adenomatous goiter with thyrotoxicosis Percutaneous endoscopic substernal thyroidectomy, complete	E05.20 0GTK4ZZ
7.	Toxic diffuse goiter with thyrotoxic crisis	E05.01
8.	Hypothyroidism, ablative, following total thyroidectomy performed three years ago	E89.0
9.	Morbidly obese patient with a BMI of 39 Laparoscopic gastroplasty with gastric banding Restriction	E66.01 Z68.39 0DV64CZ
10.	Flushing and sleeplessness due to premature menopause	E28.310
11.	Fluid overload following blood transfusion due to transfusion associated circulatory overload (TACO)	E87.71
12.	Nutritional anemia with moderate protein-calorie malnutrition and BMI of 18	D53.9 E44.0 Z68.1

CHAPTER 16

Mental Disorders

CHAPTER OVERVIEW

- Mental disorders are classified in chapter 5 of the ICD-10-CM.
- Organic anxiety disorder is a psychosis and is the direct effect of a medical condition. The medical condition should be coded first.
- Schizophrenia is classified in category F20, with a fourth character indicating the type of schizophrenia.
- Affective disorders are common mental diseases with multiple aspects, including biological, behavioral, social, and psychological factors. The most common affective disorders are the following:
  - — Major depressive disorder
  - — Bipolar disorders
  - — Anxiety disorders
- Nonpsychotic mental disorders are also classified. These include the following:
  - — Reactions to stress (both acute and chronic)
  - — Psychophysiologic disorders
- Substance abuse and dependence are classified as mental disorders in ICD-10-CM.
  - — Use, abuse, and dependence are different conditions and should be coded differently.
  - — Alcohol dependence syndrome, drug dependence, and nondependent abuse of drugs are classified to three different categories.

LEARNING OUTCOMES

After studying this chapter you should be able to:

Code a variety of mental disorders.

Determine the difference in types of affective disorders.

Explain the difference between substance abuse and dependence and code the conditions and therapies surrounding these two distinct conditions.

TERMS TO KNOW

Abuse
problematic use of drugs or alcohol but without dependence

Dependence
increased tolerance to drugs or alcohol with a compulsion to continue taking the substance despite the cost; withdrawal symptoms often occur upon cessation

REMEMBER . . .

Although coding assignments for mental disorders are made according to ICD-10-CM, psychiatrists often state diagnoses using the different terminology found in the *Diagnostic and Statistical Manual of Mental Disorders, Fourth Edition, Text Revision.*

INTRODUCTION

Mental disorders of all types are classified in chapter 5 of ICD-10-CM.

Psychiatrists ordinarily state diagnoses in accordance with the nomenclature used in the *Diagnostic and Statistical Manual of Mental Disorders, Fourth Edition, Text Revision* (DSM-IV-TR®), published by the American Psychiatric Association. Most of these codes are the same as those used in ICD-10-CM, but the terminology may differ. Coders working with mental health records may find it useful to become familiar with this manual, but actual coding assignment is made according to the classifications in ICD-10-CM.

MENTAL DISORDERS DUE TO KNOWN PHYSIOLOGICAL CONDITIONS

Categories F01 through F09, Mental disorders due to known physiological conditions, include a range of mental disorders grouped together on the basis of having a demonstrable etiology in cerebral disease, brain injury, or other insult leading to cerebral dysfunction. The cerebral dysfunction may be primary or secondary. Primary cerebral dysfunction includes diseases, injuries, and insults affecting the brain directly and selectively. Secondary cerebral dysfunction includes systemic diseases and disorders that attack the brain only as one of the multiple organs or body systems involved.

FIGURE 16.1 Side View of the Brain

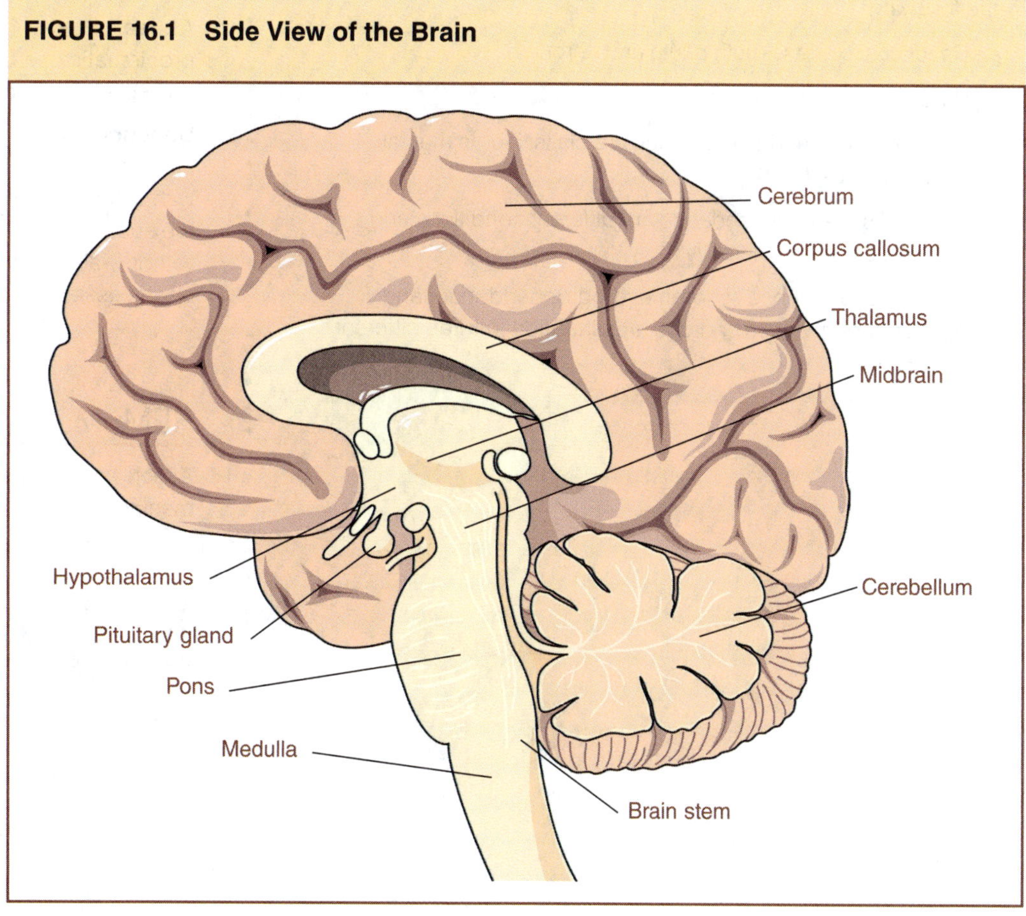

This section includes the following categories:

F01 Vascular dementia
F02 Dementia in other diseases classified elsewhere
F03 Unspecified dementia
F04 Amnestic disorder due to known physiological condition
F05 Delirium due to known physiological condition
F06 Other mental disorders due to known physiological condition
F07 Personality and behavioral disorders due to known physiological condition
F09 Unspecified mental disorder due to known physiological condition

Instructional notes to code first the underlying physiological condition are provided for categories F02 through F09, except category F03, Unspecified dementia. Category F01, Vascular dementia, has an instructional note to code first the underlying physiological condition or sequelae of cerebrovascular disease.

Organic Brain Syndrome

Organic brain syndrome is an older general term used to describe decreased mental function due to a medical disease other than a psychiatric illness. In general, organic brain syndromes cause agitation; confusion; long-term loss of brain function (dementia); and severe, short-term loss of brain function (delirium). Organic brain syndrome is common in the elderly but is not part of the normal aging process. Organic brain syndrome, not otherwise specified, is coded to **F09, Unspecified mental disorder due to known physiological condition.** The underlying physiological condition should be coded first. Posttraumatic organic brain syndrome is coded to **F07.81, Postconcussional syndrome,** with an additional code to identify any associated posttraumatic headache.

Organic Anxiety Disorder

Organic anxiety disorder is a transient organic psychosis characterized by clinically significant anxiety. It is considered to be the direct physiological effect of a general medical condition. The code for the general condition is sequenced first, with an additional code of **F06.4, Anxiety disorder due to known physiological condition.**

Dementia in Other Diseases Classified Elsewhere

When the cause of the dementia is not specified, the dementia is classified to subcategory F03.9, Dementia, unspecified, with the fifth digit distinguishing without behavioral disturbance (F03.90) or with behavioral disturbance (F03.91). Unspecified dementia with behavior described as aggressive, combative, or violent is classified to code F03.91. Subcategory F02.8, Dementia in other diseases classified elsewhere, specifically identifies the presence or absence of behavioral disturbances such as aggressive behavior, violent behavior, wandering off, or combative behavior. The dementia classified in subcategory F02.8 is due to direct physiological effects of a general medical condition. Dementia is characterized by the development of multiple cognitive deficits such as memory impairment and cognitive disturbances including aphasia, apraxia, and agnosia. When assigning codes F02.80 and F02.81, code first the underlying physiological condition associated with the dementia, such as Alzheimer's disease (G30.-) or Parkinson's disease (G20). If the patient has a tendency to wander off, code **Z91.83, Wandering in diseases classified elsewhere,** may be assigned in addition to code F02.81 or F03.91.

ALTERED MENTAL STATE

An alteration in level of consciousness not associated with delirium or another identified condition is classified to category R40 in chapter 18 of ICD-10-CM. Category R40 is further subdivided to indicate whether it is identified as somnolence (R40.0), stupor (R40.1), coma (R40.2-), persistent vegetative state (R40.3), or transient alteration of awareness (R40.4). An altered mental status, or a change in mental status, of unknown etiology is coded to **R41.82, Altered mental status, unspecified.** If the condition causing the change in mental status is known, do not assign code R41.82; code the condition instead.

TRANSIENT GLOBAL AMNESIA

Transient global amnesia is a distinct form of amnesia of unknown etiology, characterized by a sudden loss of memory function. During an episode, the patient is unable to form memories or remember recent events and may ask the same question over and over because no memories of previous answers are formed. The episode usually lasts for a few hours, followed by total or near-total resolution of the memory loss, although the patient will remain amnesic for the event itself. Transient global amnesia is not psychotic in nature, and it is not considered to be due to ischemia; rather, it is a distinct cerebrovascular condition with its own code, G45.4.

SCHIZOPHRENIC DISORDERS

Schizophrenia is a severe mental illness characterized by a variety of symptoms including, but not limited to:

- Loss of contact with reality
- Bizarre behavior
- Disorganized thinking
- Disorganized speech
- Decreased emotional expressiveness
- Diminished or loss of contact with reality
- Diminished to total social withdrawal

Schizophrenic disorders are classified in category F20, with a fourth character indicating the type of schizophrenia as follows:

F20.0 Paranoid schizophrenia
Patients suffering from this type of schizophrenia are preoccupied with delusions about being punished or persecuted by others.

F20.1 Disorganized schizophrenia
A type of schizophrenia whereby patients are usually confused and illogical; behavior is disorganized, emotionless, and inappropriate. It may lead to the patient having a limited ability to perform normal activities of daily living.

F20.2 Catatonic schizophrenia
A type of schizophrenia whereby patients become unresponsive and have limited physical response.

F20.3 Undifferentiated schizophrenia
A form of schizophrenia characterized by a number of schizophrenic symptoms, such as delusion(s), disorganized behavior, disorganized speech, flat affect, or hallucinations, but that does not meet the criteria for any other type of schizophrenia.

F20.5 Residual schizophrenia
This type of schizophrenia is characterized by decreased severity of symptoms of schizophrenia. Delusion, hallucinations, and other symptoms may be present but are far less severe than when originally diagnosed.

F20.8 Other schizophrenia
This subcategory is further subdivided as follows:

F20.81 Schizophreniform disorder
This is a short-term type of schizophrenia that distorts the way a person thinks, acts, expresses emotions, perceives reality, and relates to others. Schizophreniform disorder generally lasts less than six months, while schizophrenia is a life-long illness.

F20.89 Other schizophrenia
This code includes cenesthopathic schizophrenia (a subgroup of schizophrenia with marked and dominating abnormal bodily sensations) and simple schizophrenia (a disorder characterized by an insidious but progressive development of oddities of conduct, inability to meet the demands of society, and decline in total performance).

F20.9 Schizophrenia, unspecified
This is not a type of schizophrenia per se, but this code is used when the type of schizophrenia is not specified.

AFFECTIVE DISORDERS

Affective disorders are common mental diseases with multiple aspects, including biological, behavioral, social, and psychological factors. Major depressive disorder, bipolar disorders, and anxiety disorders are the most common affective disorders. Affective disorders can result in symptoms ranging from the mild and inconvenient to the severe and life threatening. Affective disorders are common mental diseases characterized by mood disturbance. Mood [affective] disorders are classified under categories F30–F39 in ICD-10-CM.

Major depressive disorder (MDD) is also known as monopolar depression or unipolar affective disorder. MDD causes prolonged periods of emotional, mental, and physical exhaustion. Patients suffering from this condition have a considerable risk of self-destructive behavior, sometimes leading to suicide. MDD is classified in ICD-10-CM as:

F32.- Major depressive disorder, single episode
F33.- Major depressive disorder, recurrent

Categories F32 and F33 are further subdivided with fourth characters (or fifth characters) to provide information about the current severity of the disorder, as follows:

0 Mild
1 Moderate
2 Severe, without psychotic features
3 Severe with psychotic features
4 In partial remission (used for category F32 to indicate in partial remission; category F33 uses the fourth character of "4" to indicate remission and is further subdivided with fifth characters to indicate unspecified remission, partial remission, or full remission)
5 In full remission (used only for category F32)
8 Other
9 Unspecified

Fourth characters 1 through 8 are assigned only when provider documentation of severity is included in the medical record.

Bipolar affective diseases are divided into various types according to the symptoms displayed. Other names for bipolar affective disease include manic-depressive disorder, cyclothymia, manic-depressive illness, and bipolar disorder. Patients suffering from bipolar diseases experience periods of manic (hyper-excitable) episodes alternating with periods of deep depression. These disorders are chronic and recurrent with varying degrees of severity. Severe crises can lead to suicide attempts during depressive episodes or to physical violence against oneself or others during manic episodes. In many patients, however, episodes are mild and infrequent. Mixed states may also occur with elements of mania and depression simultaneously present. Some people with bipolar affective disorders show a rapid cycling between manic and depressive states.

ICD-10-CM classifies bipolar disorders under the following categories/codes:

F30.- Manic episode (includes bipolar disorder, single manic episode, and mixed affective episode)

F31.- Bipolar disorder (includes manic-depressive illness, manic-depressive psychosis, and manic-depressive reaction)

F34.- Persistent mood [affective] disorders (includes cyclothymic disorder and dysthymic disorder)

F39 Unspecified mood [affective] disorder (includes affective psychosis not otherwise specified)

Category F30, Manic episode, is further subdivided to identify the severity of the current episode and to indicate that psychotic symptoms are involved. Category F31, Bipolar disorder, is further subdivided to specify the severity of the current episode; whether the current episode is hypomanic, manic, depressed, or mixed; and whether psychotic features are involved. Additionally, for patients with bipolar disorder currently in remission (F31.7-), fifth characters are available to specify whether the patient is in full or partial remission and whether the most recent episode was hypomanic, manic, depressed, mixed, or unspecified.

EXERCISE 16.1

Code the following diagnoses and procedures. Do not assign External cause of morbidity codes.

1. Schizoaffective psychosis, depressive type — F25.1
2. Schizophrenia, catatonic type — F20.2
3. Schizophrenia, paranoid type — F20.0

4. Severe depressive disorder, recurrent, current episode severe with psychotic symptoms F33.3

____

5. Reactive depressive psychosis F32.3

____

6. Bipolar disorder, in manic phase, mild F31.11

____

7. Bipolar affective disorder, most recent episode mixed, in partial remission F31.77

____

NONPSYCHOTIC MENTAL DISORDERS

A variety of anxiety, dissociative, stress-related, somatoform, and other nonpsychotic mental disorders are classified in categories F40 through F48. These include such conditions as phobic anxiety disorders, reaction to stress, dissociative and conversion disorders, somatoform disorders, and other nonpsychotic mental disorders.

Anxiety Disorders

Anxiety disorders are common psychiatric disorders and are considered to be one of the most undertreated and overlooked health problems. Among their common manifestations are panic disorders, phobias, chronic generalized anxiety disorder, obsessive-compulsive disorder, and posttraumatic disorder. A phobia is a persistent and irrational fear of a particular type of object, animal, activity, or situation. Anxiety disorders are classified in ICD-10-CM under the following categories:

F40 Phobic anxiety disorders
F41 Other anxiety disorders
F42 Obsessive-compulsive disorder

Reactions to Stress

ICD-10-CM provides category F43 for coding reaction to severe stress and adjustment disorders. Code **F43.0, Acute stress reaction,** classifies acute reaction to stress, including acute crisis reaction, combat fatigue, crisis state, and psychic shock. Acute stress reaction is the result of a person experiencing or witnessing a traumatic event that causes the individual to experience extreme, disturbing, or unexpected fear, stress, or pain and that involves or threatens serious injury, perceived serious injury, or death to self or someone else.

Posttraumatic stress disorder (PTSD) is classified in ICD-10-CM to subcategory F43.1, with fifth characters for unspecified, acute, or chronic. PTSD is a severe anxiety disorder that can develop after exposure to any event resulting in psychological trauma. As an effect of psychological trauma, PTSD is less frequent and more enduring than the more commonly seen acute stress

response. Symptoms of PTSD include re-experiencing the original trauma(s) through flashbacks or nightmares; avoiding stimuli associated with the trauma; and experiencing increased arousal, such as difficulty falling or staying asleep, anger, and hypervigilance. These symptoms last more than one month and cause significant impairment in social, occupational, or other important areas of functioning.

Adjustment disorders are a psychological response to an identifiable stressor or group of stressors that cause(s) significant emotional or behavioral symptoms. They differ from acute stress disorder and PTSD in that adjustment disorders are usually associated with a less intense stressor. Adjustment disorders are classified to subcategory F43.2, with the fifth-character axis being the nature of the reaction—for example, anxiety, depression, disturbance of conduct, or other symptoms. The following situations fall into this category:

F43.21 Patient depressed over death of son
F43.24 Child adopted from a foreign country, suffering from culture shock with conduct disturbance

Dissociative and Conversion Disorders

ICD-10-CM classifies dissociative and conversion disorders to category F44. Dissociative disorders refer to conditions that involve disruptions or breakdowns of memory, awareness, identity, and/or perception. Four codes are available for dissociative disorders, as follows:

F44.0 Dissociative amnesia
F44.1 Dissociative fugue
F44.2 Dissociative stupor
F44.81 Dissociative identity disorder

Conversion disorder is a condition whereby the patient presents with neurological symptoms but with the exclusion of neurological disease or feigning, and the determination of a psychological mechanism. The symptoms can vary from weakness/paralysis of a limb or the entire body to impaired hearing or vision, loss of sensation, impairment of speech, seizures, syncope, and other neurological findings. The following codes are used to describe conversion disorder:

F44.4 Conversion disorder with motor symptom or deficit
F44.5 Conversion disorder with seizures or convulsions
F44.6 Conversion disorder with sensory symptom or deficit
F44.7 Conversion disorder with mixed symptom presentation

In addition, two codes are available for other (F44.89) and unspecified (F44.9) dissociative and conversion disorders.

Examples of conditions that are classified in category F44 include the following:

F44.4 Psychogenic paralysis
F44.4 Abnormal hysterical gait
F44.0 Hysterical amnesia
F44.6 Emotional blindness

Somatoform Disorders

Somatoform disorders are mental disorders characterized by physical symptoms that mimic physical disease or injury for which there is no identifiable physical cause. Instead, the symptoms are caused by mental factors. A diagnosis of a somatoform disorder implies that mental factors are a large contributor to the symptoms' onset, severity, and duration. ICD-10-CM classifies somatoform disorders to category F45. Examples of conditions classified in category F45 include the following:

F45.8	Psychogenic diarrhea
F45.8	Psychogenic dysmenorrhea
F45.20	Hypochondriacal disorder

In assigning codes from categories F44 and F45 it is important to make the distinction between these conditions and similar conditions that fall under the categories for neurotic disorders, psychoses, or organic disorders.

For pain that is exclusively related to psychological factors, assign code **F45.41, Pain disorder exclusively related to psychological factors.** A code from category G89, Pain, not elsewhere classified, should not be assigned with code F45.41. When the documentation reflects a psychological component for a patient's acute or chronic pain, assign code **F45.42, Pain disorder with related psychological factors,** with a code from category G89.

BEHAVIORAL SYNDROMES ASSOCIATED WITH PHYSIOLOGICAL DISTURBANCES AND PHYSICAL FACTORS

Categories F50 through F59 are devoted to behavioral syndromes associated with physiological disturbances and physical factors. These codes are not assigned when the conditions are present due to a mental disorder classified elsewhere or are of organic origin. This grouping includes the following conditions:

F50.-	Eating disorders (such as anorexia nervosa and bulimia nervosa)
F51.-	Sleep disorders not due to a substance or known physiological condition
F52.-	Sexual dysfunction not due to a substance or known physiological condition
F53	Puerperal psychosis
F54	Psychological and behavioral factors associated with disorders or diseases classified elsewhere
F55.-	Abuse of nonpsychoactive substances
F59	Unspecified behavioral syndromes associated with physiological disturbances and physical factors

Code F54 classifies psychological and behavioral factors associated with diseases classified elsewhere. Typical conditions that are often associated with code F54 include asthma, ulcerative colitis, and dermatitis. If such a condition is considered to be psychogenic in origin, the associated physical disorder is coded first, followed by code F54. For example:

J45.20 + F54	Mild intermittent psychogenic asthma
I47.1 + F54	Psychogenic paroxysmal atrial tachycardia

EXERCISE 16.2

Code the following diagnoses.

1.	Acute delirium resulting from pneumonia due to *Hemophilus influenzae*	F05 J14
2.	Passive-aggressive personality	F60.89
3.	Depression anxiety Conversion disorder (convulsions)	F41.8 F44.5
4.	Adolescent adjustment reaction, with severe disturbance of conduct	F43.24
5.	Severe depression, recurrent	F33.2
6.	Stress reaction, psychomotor	F43.0

SUBSTANCE ABUSE DISORDERS

Substance abuse and dependence are classified as mental disorders in ICD-10-CM. These disorders are classified to categories F10 through F19. Although the terms "abuse" and "dependence" may be used interchangeably in certain treatment programs, they are different conditions and are coded differently in ICD-10-CM.

Alcohol Dependence and Abuse

Alcohol-related disorders are classified in ICD-10-CM to category F10. An additional code for blood alcohol level may be assigned, if applicable (Y90.-). Alcohol abuse refers to the recurring use of alcoholic beverages despite negative consequences. Alcohol dependence, as described in the DSM-IV, is a psychiatric diagnosis describing a condition in which an individual uses alcohol despite significant areas of dysfunction, evidence of physical dependence, and/or related hardship. Alcohol dependence is differentiated from alcohol abuse by the presence of symptoms such as tolerance and withdrawal. Both alcohol dependence and alcohol abuse are sometimes referred to by the less specific term "alcoholism."

Alcohol abuse is classified in ICD-10-CM under subcategory F10.1, Alcohol abuse, while alcohol dependence is classified under subcategory F10.2, Alcohol dependence. If alcohol use is documented without further specificity as to abuse or dependence, it is classified to subcategory F10.9, Alcohol use, unspecified. All three subcategories are further subdivided to specify the presence of intoxication or intoxication delirium. Additional characters are also provided to specify alcohol-induced mood disorder, psychotic disorder, and other alcohol-induced disorders. Codes in subclassification F10.23-, Alcohol dependence with withdrawal, provide additional detail regarding withdrawal symptoms such as delirium and perceptual disturbance.

Code **F10.129, Alcohol abuse with intoxication, unspecified,** is assigned for a diagnosis of simple drunkenness. However, acute drunkenness in alcoholism is indexed to **F10.229, Alcohol dependence with intoxication, unspecified;** chronic drunkenness is indexed to **F10.20, Alcohol dependence, uncomplicated;** and chronic drunkenness in remission is indexed to **F10.21, Alcohol dependence, in remission.** Selection of code F10.21 for "in remission" requires the provider's clinical judgment, as defined by the *ICD-10-CM Official Guidelines for Coding and Reporting*, rather than nursing or other documentation. Note that toxic effect of alcohol is not classified to category F10 but to subcategory T51.0- instead.

Drug Dependence and Abuse

ICD-10-CM classifies drug dependence and abuse in the following categories according to the class of drug:

F11 Opioid related disorders
F12 Cannabis related disorders
F13 Sedative, hypnotic or anxiolytic related disorders
F14 Cocaine related disorders
F15 Other stimulant related disorders
F16 Hallucinogen related disorders
F17 Nicotine dependence
F18 Inhalant related disorders
F19 Other psychoactive substance related disorders

In most cases, fourth characters indicate whether the disorder is nondependent abuse (1), dependence (2), or unspecified use (9). Additional characters are also provided to specify intoxication, intoxication delirium, and intoxication with perceptual disturbance. Patients with substance abuse or dependence often develop related physical complications or psychotic symptoms. These complications are classified to the specific drug abuse or dependence, with the fifth or sixth characters providing further specificity regarding any associated drug-induced mood disorder, psychotic disorder, withdrawal, and other drug-induced disorders (such as sexual dysfunction or sleep disorder).

Patients dependent on alcohol, drugs, or both frequently experience withdrawal symptoms and require detoxification. Withdrawal most commonly refers to the group of symptoms that occurs upon the abrupt discontinuation/separation or a decrease in dosage of the intake of medications, recreational drugs, and/or alcohol. Symptoms and signs of withdrawal can vary based on the substance and from individual to individual. They include tremulousness, agitation, irritability, disturbed sleep, anorexia, autonomic hyperactivity, seizures, and hallucinations. A severe form of withdrawal known as delirium tremens is characterized by fever, tachycardia, hypertension or hypotension, hallucinations, agitation, confusion, fluctuating mental states, and seizures.

ICD-10-CM provides combination codes that include both the alcohol or substance abuse/dependence and any associated complications. Examples include:

F10.231	Alcoholic withdrawal delirium due to alcohol dependence
F10.251	Alcohol-induced psychotic disorder with hallucinations due to alcohol dependence
F10.180	Alcohol-induced anxiety disorder due to alcohol abuse
F11.250	Heroin dependence with heroin-induced psychosis and delusions

Category F19, Other psychoactive substance related disorders, may be used when the specific drug class is not specified.

Similar to code **F10.21, Alcohol dependence, in remission,** the selection of codes for "in remission" for categories F11–F19 with -.21 requires the provider's clinical judgment. The appropriate codes for "in remission" are assigned only on the basis of provider documentation (as defined in the *ICD-10-CM Official Guidelines for Coding and Reporting*).

Psychoactive Substance Use

In addition to the codes for psychoactive substance abuse and dependence, ICD-10-CM provides codes for psychoactive substance use (F10.9-, F11.9-, F12.9-, F13.9-, F14.9-, F15.9-, F16.9-). As with all other diagnoses, these codes should only be assigned based on provider documentation and when they meet the definition of a reportable diagnosis per Section III, Reporting Additional Diagnoses, of the *ICD-10-CM Official Guidelines for Coding and Reporting*. The codes are to be used only when the psychoactive substance use is associated with a mental or behavioral disorder and such a relationship is documented by the provider.

Psychoactive Substance Use, Abuse, and Dependence Code Hierarchy

When the provider documentation refers to use, abuse, and dependence of the same substance (e.g., alcohol, opioid, cannabis), only one code should be assigned to identify the pattern of use, based on the following hierarchy:

- If both use and abuse are documented, assign only the code for abuse.
- If both abuse and dependence are documented, assign only the code for dependence.
- If use, abuse, and dependence are all documented, assign only the code for dependence.
- If both use and dependence are documented, assign only the code for dependence.

Selection of the Principal Diagnosis

The designation of the principal diagnosis for patients with either substance abuse or substance dependence is determined by the circumstances of the admission, as defined in the following examples:

1. When a patient is admitted for detoxification or rehabilitation for both drug and alcohol abuse or dependence, and both are treated, either condition may be designated as the principal diagnosis.
2. When a patient with a diagnosis of substance abuse or dependence is admitted for treatment or evaluation of a physical complaint related to the substance use, follow the directions in the Alphabetic Index for conditions described as alcoholic or due to drugs; sequence the physical condition first, followed by the code for abuse or dependence.
3. When a patient with a diagnosis of alcohol or drug abuse or dependence is admitted because of an unrelated condition, follow the usual guidelines for selecting a principal diagnosis.

Substance Abuse Therapy

Treatment for patients with a diagnosis of substance abuse or dependence consists of detoxification, rehabilitation, or both. The abuse or dependence is the principal diagnosis for a patient admitted for such programs.

Detoxification is the management of withdrawal symptoms for a patient who is physically dependent on alcohol or drugs. The process is more than simple observation; it involves active management. Treatment may involve evaluation, observation and monitoring, and administration of thiamine and multivitamins for nutrition as well as other medications (such as methadone, long-acting barbiturates or benzodiazepines, or carbamazepine) as needed. The detoxification program for patients with alcohol dependence is usually continued over a four- or five-day period, although it can also be provided on an outpatient basis depending on the severity of the withdrawal symptoms. Detoxification takes longer for opiates and sedatives/hypnotics, usually lasting from three weeks to a period of months, and may be carried out in either a residential or an outpatient setting. If the medical record documents detoxification as having been carried out, the code can be assigned even when no medications were actually administered.

Rehabilitation is a structured program carried out with the goal of establishing strict control of drinking and drug use. A variety of rehabilitation modalities may be utilized. These include methadone maintenance, therapeutic residential communities, and long-term outpatient drug- or alcohol-free treatments. When a patient with drug dependence is on medications for detoxification or for maintenance programs to prevent withdrawal symptoms (e.g., methadone maintenance for opiate dependence), the appropriate code for the drug dependence should be assigned, rather than code **Z79.891, Long-term (current) use of opiate analgesic,** or **Z79.899, Other long-term (current) drug therapy.**

EXERCISE 16.3

Code the following diagnoses.

1. Paranoid alcoholic psychosis with alcohol dependence	F10.250
2. Alcoholic cirrhosis of liver	K70.30
Chronic alcoholism	F10.20
3. Acute alcoholic intoxication	F10.129
Blood alcohol level of 59 mg/100 mL	Y90.2
4. Marijuana dependence	F12.20
5. Acute alcohol intoxication and dependence	F10.229
6. Barbiturate abuse with sleep disorder	F13.182

7. Cocaine dependence F14.20

8. Amphetamine abuse F15.10

9. Dependence on barbiturate and heroin F13.20
F11.20

10. Admitted because of syndrome of inappropriate secretion of antidiuretic hormone secondary to chronic alcoholism E22.2
F10.20

MENTAL HEALTH AND SUBSTANCE ABUSE TREATMENT PROCEDURE CODING

Mental disorders other than substance abuse disorders are commonly treated with psychodynamic ("talk") therapy, drug therapy, electroconvulsive therapy, or a combination of therapeutic modes. Because the diagnosis alone does not always explain the length of stay or the level of resource utilization for such patients, therapy codes are helpful in analyzing patterns of care.

ICD-10-PCS provides two sections for procedures related to mental health and substance abuse, as follows:

G Mental Health
H Substance Abuse Treatment

Mental Health Procedures

The Mental Health Section of ICD-10-PCS contains specific values in the third and fourth characters to describe mental health procedures. The most important character in this section is the root type (the third character), while the type qualifier (the fourth character) further specifies the procedure type as needed. The remaining characters (second, fifth, sixth, and seventh) only function as placeholders and do not represent specific information about the procedure. The value Z is used as the placeholder for these characters. The following example demonstrates the structure of ICD-10-PCS codes in the Mental Health Section.

Electroconvulsive therapy, unilateral-multiple seizure

Character 1 Section	Character 2 Body System	Character 3 Root Type	Character 4 Type Qualifier	Character 5 Qualifier	Character 6 Qualifier	Character 7 Qualifier
G	Z	B	1	Z	Z	Z
Mental health	None	Electroconvulsive therapy	Unilateral—multiple seizure	None	None	None

There are 12 values representing mental health root types, as listed in table 16.1, along with their corresponding definitions.

Examples of commonly performed mental health procedures in the inpatient setting include:

GZB1ZZZ ECT (electroconvulsive therapy), unilateral, multiple seizure
GZ2ZZZZ Crisis intervention
GZHZZZZ Group psychotherapy

TABLE 16.1 Root Type Values in the Mental Health Section

Value	Description	Definition
1	Psychological tests	The administration and interpretation of standardized psychological tests and measurement instruments for the assessment of psychological function
2	Crisis intervention	Treatment of a traumatized, acutely disturbed or distressed individual for the purpose of short-term stabilization
3	Medication management	Monitoring and adjusting the use of medications for the treatment of a mental health disorder
5	Individual psychotherapy	Treatment of an individual with a mental health disorder by behavioral, cognitive, psychoanalytic, psychodynamic, or psychophysiological means to improve functioning or well-being
6	Counseling	The application of psychological methods to treat an individual with normal developmental issues and psychological problems in order to increase function, improve well-being, alleviate distress, address maladjustment, or resolve crises
7	Family psychotherapy	Treatment that includes one or more family members of an individual with a mental health disorder by behavioral, cognitive, psychoanalytic, psychodynamic, or psychophysiological means to improve functioning or well-being
B	Electroconvulsive therapy	The application of controlled electrical voltages to treat a mental health disorder
C	Biofeedback	Provision of information from the monitoring and regulating of physiological processes in conjunction with cognitive-behavioral techniques to improve patient functioning or well-being
F	Hypnosis	Induction of a state of heightened suggestibility by auditory, visual, and tactile techniques to elicit an emotional or behavioral response
G	Narcosynthesis	Administration of intravenous barbiturates in order to release suppressed or repressed thoughts
H	Group psychotherapy	Treatment of two or more individuals with a mental health disorder by behavioral, cognitive, psychoanalytic, psychodynamic, or psychophysiological means to improve functioning or well-being
J	Light therapy	Application of specialized light treatments to improve functioning or well-being

Substance Abuse Treatment

The Substance Abuse Treatment Section of ICD-10-PCS is structured as a smaller version of the Mental Health Section. Once again, the most important character in these codes is the third character, which describes the root type, while the fourth character is a qualifier that further classifies the root type. The remaining characters (second, fifth, sixth, and seventh) only function as placeholders and do not represent specific information about the procedure. The value Z is used as the placeholder for these characters. The following example demonstrates the structure of ICD-10-PCS codes in the Substance Abuse Treatment Section.

Methadone maintenance medication management

Character 1 Section	Character 2 Body System	Character 3 Root Type	Character 4 Type Qualifier	Character 5 Qualifier	Character 6 Qualifier	Character 7 Qualifier
H	Z	8	1	Z	Z	Z
Substance abuse treatment	None	Medication management	Methadone maintenance	None	None	None

Seven values represent substance abuse treatment root types, as listed in table 16.2, along with their corresponding definitions.

Examples of commonly provided substance abuse treatments in the inpatient setting include:

HZ2ZZZZ Detoxification from alcohol and/or drugs
HZ83ZZZ Medication management with Antabuse
HZ81ZZZ Medication management with methadone
HZ41ZZZ Behavioral group counseling

TABLE 16.2 Root Type Values in the Substance Abuse Treatment Section

Value	Description	Definition
2	Detoxification services	Detoxification from alcohol and/or drugs
3	Individual counseling	The application of psychological methods to treat an individual with addictive behavior
4	Group counseling	The application of psychological methods to treat two or more individuals with addictive behavior
5	Individual psychotherapy	Treatment of an individual with addictive behavior by behavioral, cognitive, psychoanalytic, psychodynamic, or psychophysiological means
6	Family counseling	The application of psychological methods that includes one or more family members to treat an individual with addictive behavior
8	Medication management	Monitoring and adjusting the use of replacement medications for the treatment of addiction
9	Pharmacotherapy	The use of replacement medications for the treatment of addiction

EXERCISE 16.4

Code the following procedures.

1. Individual supportive psychotherapy	GZ56ZZZ
2. Crisis intervention	GZ2ZZZZ
3. Substance abuse behavioral group counseling	HZ41ZZZ
4. Electroconvulsive therapy, bilateral, multiple seizures	GZB3ZZZ
5. Alcohol abuse detoxification	HZ2ZZZZ
6. Nicotine patch management of tobacco dependence	HZ80ZZZ
7. Group counseling 12-step program	HZ43ZZZ

Coding OF **Diseases** OF THE **Blood** AND **Blood-Forming Organs, Certain Disorders Involving** THE **Immune Mechanism,** AND **Diseases** OF THE **Nervous System**

CHAPTER 17

Diseases of the Blood and Blood-Forming Organs and Certain Disorders Involving the Immune Mechanism

CHAPTER OVERVIEW

- Diseases of the blood and blood-forming organs are classified in chapter 3 of ICD-10-CM.
- Anemia is the most common condition dealt with in chapter 3.
  - It can be caused by chronic or acute blood loss, chronic disease, or the use of chemotherapy. Acute blood loss anemia may occur after surgery or trauma.
  - The use of precise terminology is important in classifying anemias.
- A variety of codes are associated with sickle-cell anemia.
  - It is important to distinguish between sickle cell anemia and sickle cell trait.
  - Other conditions for sickle cell include Hb-SS disease and thalassemia.
- Coagulation defects are another type of disease of the blood.
  - They affect clotting time and ability.
  - Hypercoagulation is also a possible condition.
- Diseases may decrease or increase the production of white blood cells (leukocytes). These diseases are classified according to whether the count is low or elevated.

LEARNING OUTCOMES

After studying this chapter you should be able to:

- Code the various types of anemia.
- Understand when and when not to code a coagulation defect because certain drug therapies are being used.
- Distinguish among the various diseases of the white blood cells and the various types of white blood cells.

TERMS TO KNOW

Anemia
a condition in which blood is deficient in the amount of hemoglobin in red blood cells or in the volume of red blood cells

Aplastic anemia
a condition in which there is a deficiency of red blood cells because the bone marrow is failing to produce them

Pancytopenia
a type of aplastic anemia in which red blood cells, white blood cells, and platelets are all deficient

Sickle-cell anemia
a hereditary disease of the red blood cells passed to a child when both parents carry the genetic trait

Sickle-cell trait
a condition that occurs when a child receives the trait from only one parent

Thrombocytopenia
a deficiency in platelets, the cells that are important in blood clotting

REMEMBER . . .

A variety of conditions can be classified as an anemia. Be sure to check with the diagnosing physician if the terminology in the medical report is nonspecific or misleading.

INTRODUCTION

Diseases of the blood and blood-forming organs—including bone marrow, lymphatic tissue, platelets, and coagulation factors—are classified in chapter 3 of ICD-10-CM. Chapter 3 also includes certain disorders involving the immune mechanism, such as immunodeficiency disorders except human immunodeficiency virus (HIV) disease. Neoplastic diseases, such as leukemia, are classified in chapter 2 of ICD-10-CM along with other neoplastic diseases. Diseases of the blood and blood-forming organs complicating pregnancy, childbirth, or the puerperium are reclassified in chapter 15 of ICD-10-CM. Anemia of pregnancy, for example, is coded O99.01-, with an additional code from chapter 3 assigned to indicate the specific type of anemia. Hematological disorders of the fetus and newborn are classified as perinatal conditions in chapter 16 of ICD-10-CM.

ANEMIA

The condition that coders must deal with most often in chapter 3 of ICD-10-CM is anemia. Anemia refers to either a reduction in the quantity of hemoglobin or a reduction in the volume of packed red cells, a condition that occurs whenever the equilibrium between red cell loss and red cell production is disturbed. A decrease in production can result from a variety of causes, including aging, bleeding, and cell destruction.

The use of precise terminology is important in classifying anemias. When a diagnostic statement of anemia is not qualified in any way, the coder should review the medical record to determine whether more information can be located in laboratory or pathology reports or in a hematology consultation before the code for an unspecified type of anemia is assigned. Remember, however, that a code should not be assigned on the basis of a diagnostic report alone; when it appears that a more specific type of anemia is present, the coder should check with the physician for concurrence.

Deficiency Anemias

Iron-deficiency anemias are classified in category D50. This type of anemia may be due to a chronic blood loss (D50.0) from conditions such as chronic hemorrhagic gastrointestinal conditions or menorrhagia, or to inadequate intake of dietary iron (D50.8). If the cause is unspecified, code D50.9 is assigned. Note, however, that iron-deficiency anemia specified as secondary to acute blood loss is assigned to code **D62, Acute posthemorrhagic anemia,** rather than to category D50. Other deficiency anemias are coded according to the type of deficiency, such as vitamin B12 (category D51), folate (category D52), or other nutritional deficiencies (category D53), with a fourth character indicating the specific type of deficiency, such as dietary folate deficiency anemia or B12 vitamin deficiency due to intrinsic factor deficiency. In addition, code **D52.1, Drug-induced folate deficiency anemia,** requires that a code from T36–T50 be coded with fifth or sixth character of "5" to identify the drug.

EXERCISE 17.1

Code the following diagnoses and procedures. Do not assign External cause of morbidity codes.

1. Anemia, hypochromic, microcytic, with iron deficiency, cause unknown — D50.9

2. Macrocytic anemia secondary to selective vitamin B12 malabsorption with proteinuria — D51.1

Anemia Due to Acute Blood Loss

It is important to distinguish between anemia due to chronic blood loss and anemia due to acute blood loss, because the two conditions have entirely different codes in ICD-10-CM. Acute blood-loss anemia results from a sudden, significant loss of blood over a brief period of time. It may occur due to trauma, such as laceration, or a rupture of the spleen or other injury of abdominal viscera, where no external blood loss is noted. A diagnosis of acute blood-loss anemia should be supported by documented evidence of the condition, such as a sustained, significant lowering of the hemoglobin level and/or hematocrit.

Acute blood-loss anemia may occur following surgery, but it is not necessarily a complication of the procedure and should not be coded as a postoperative complication unless the physician identifies it as such. Many surgical procedures, such as hip replacement, routinely involve a considerable amount of bleeding as an expected part of the operation. This may or may not result in anemia; a code for anemia should be assigned only when the anemia is documented by the physician. If, in the physician's clinical judgment, surgery results in an expected amount of blood loss and the physician does not describe the patient as having anemia or a complication of surgery, do not assign a code for the blood loss. If a postoperative blood count is low enough to suggest anemia, it is appropriate to ask the physician whether a diagnosis of anemia should be added. The coder should not assume, however, that mention of blood loss and/or transfusion during surgery is an indication that anemia is present. Blood replacement is sometimes carried out as a preventive measure. When postoperative anemia is documented without specification of acute blood loss, code **D64.9, Anemia, unspecified,** is the default. Code **D62, Acute posthemorrhagic anemia,** should be assigned when postoperative anemia is due to acute blood loss. When neither the diagnostic statement nor review of the medical record indicates whether a blood-loss anemia is acute or chronic, code **D50.0, Iron deficiency anemia secondary to blood loss (chronic),** should be assigned.

EXERCISE 17.2

Code the following diagnoses and procedures. Do not assign External cause of morbidity codes.

1.	Anemia due to blood loss from chronic gastric ulcer	D50.0 K25.4
2.	Anemia, chronic, secondary to blood loss due to adenomyosis	D50.0 N80.0
3.	Posthemorrhagic anemia due to acute blood loss following perforation of chronic bleeding duodenal ulcer	D62 K26.6

Anemia of Chronic Disease

Patients with chronic illnesses are often seen with anemia, which may be the cause of the health care admission or encounter. Treatment is often directed at the anemia, not the underlying condition. Codes for this type of anemia are classified as follows:

- Anemia in chronic kidney disease: Code first the underlying chronic kidney disease (CKD) with a code from category N18 to indicate the stage of CKD, and code D63.1.
- Anemia in neoplastic disease: Code first the neoplasm (C00–D49) responsible for the anemia and code D63.0. Code D63.0 is for anemia in, due to, or with the malignancy, and not due to the antineoplastic chemotherapy drugs, which is an adverse effect.
- Anemia of other chronic disease: Code first the underlying chronic disease, followed by code D63.8.

Anemia Due to Chemotherapy

Antineoplastic chemotherapy–induced anemia is classified to code **D64.81, Anemia due to antineoplastic chemotherapy.** This type of anemia is rarely a hemolytic process and is not truly an aplastic process. Antineoplastic chemotherapy–induced changes are generally short term and do not usually reduce the marrow cellularity to a point of aplasia. When the admission/encounter is for management of an anemia associated with an adverse effect of chemotherapy, and the only treatment is for anemia, the anemia code should be sequenced first, followed by the appropriate codes for the adverse effect and neoplasm.

Anemia due to chemotherapy should not be confused with aplastic anemia due to antineoplastic chemotherapy, which is coded to **D61.1, Drug-induced aplastic anemia.** Anemia due to a drug, where the drug is not specified, is coded to the type of anemia (or to code D64.9 if the type of anemia is not specified).

Aplastic Anemia

Aplastic anemia (D60.- and D61.-) is caused by a failure of the bone marrow to produce red blood cells. The condition may be congenital, but it is usually idiopathic or acquired. It may be due to an underlying disease such as a malignant neoplasm or an infection (for example, viral hepatitis). It may also be caused by exposure to ionizing radiation, chemicals, or drugs, and it often results from treatment for malignancy. Aplastic anemia due to drugs is coded to **D61.1, Drug-induced aplastic anemia.** Aplastic anemia due to infection, radiation, other external agents, or that is toxic is coded to D61.2. Idiopathic aplastic anemia is coded to D61.3. When the type of anemia is not specified but appears to be related to a diagnosis of malignancy or treatment for malignancy, the physician should be queried to determine whether the code for aplastic anemia may be appropriate.

Pancytopenia (D61.81-) is a type of aplastic anemia that represents a deficiency of all three elements of the blood. When a patient has anemia (deficiency of red cells), neutropenia (deficiency of white cells), and thrombocytopenia (deficiency of platelets), only the code for pancytopenia (D61.81-) should be assigned. When the pancytopenia is drug induced, ICD-10-CM distinguishes whether it is due to antineoplastic chemotherapy (D61.810) or other drug (D61.811). Code **D61.09, Other constitutional aplastic anemia,** is assigned if the pancytopenia is congenital rather than due to chronic disease. Do not assign a code from subcategory D61.81 if the pancytopenia is due to, or with, aplastic anemia (D61.9), bone marrow infiltration (D61.82), congenital (pure) red cell aplasia (D61.01), hairy cell leukemia (C91.4-), HIV disease (B20.-), leukoerythroblastic anemia (D61.82), myelodysplastic syndromes (D46.-), or myeloproliferative disease (D47.1).

EXERCISE 17.3

Code the following diagnoses and procedures.

1. Aplastic anemia due to accidental benzene exposure (subsequent encounter)	T52.1x1D D61.2
2. Myelophthisic anemia	D61.82
3. Initial encounter for anemia due to chemotherapy treatment	D64.81 T45.1x5A
4. Pancytopenia related to methotrexate therapy for rheumatoid arthritis (initial encounter)	D61.811 T45.1x5A M06.9

Sickle-Cell Anemia and Thalassemia

In coding sickle-cell disorders, it is important to understand the difference between sickle-cell anemia or disease (D57.0-, D57.1-, D57.2-, D57.4-, and D57.8-) and sickle-cell trait (D57.3). Sickle-cell disease is a hereditary disease of the red blood cells; the disease is passed to a child when both parents carry the genetic trait. Sickle-cell trait occurs when a child receives the genetic trait from only one parent. Patients with sickle-cell trait do not generally develop sickle-cell disease; they are carriers of the trait. When a medical record contains both the terms "sickle-cell trait" and "sickle-cell disease," only the code for the sickle-cell disease is assigned.

A code from subcategory D57.0, Hb-SS disease with crisis, or subcategory D57.21, Sickle cell/Hb-C disease, is assigned when vaso-occlusive crises or other crises are present. These subcategories are further subdivided to specify the type of crisis, such as acute chest syndrome (D57.01 or D57.211) or splenic sequestration (D57.02 or D57.212). If a condition such as cerebrovascular embolism occurs, a code should also be assigned to indicate its presence.

Another possible type of sickle-cell disease is sickle-cell thalassemia. Specific codes are available for sickle-cell thalassemia with crisis (D57.41-) or without crisis (D57.40). Codes in subcategory D57.41- have an additional sixth character to specify the type of crisis.

Other sickle-cell disorders include Hb-SD disease and Hb-SE disease, which are classified to subcategory D57.8. Codes in subcategory D57.8 have additional characters to specify whether there is crisis and the type of crisis when present.

Thalassemia is a genetic blood disorder resulting from a defect in a gene that controls production of one of the hemoglobin proteins. There are many forms of thalassemia. Each type has many different subtypes. The defective gene must be inherited from both parents in order for a person to develop thalassemia major. Thalassemia minor occurs when the defective gene is inherited from only one parent. Persons with this form of the disorder are carriers of the disease and usually do not have symptoms. ICD-10-CM provides unique codes for different types of thalassemia, such as alpha thalassemia (D56.0), beta thalassemia (D56.1), delta-beta thalassemia (D56.2), thalassemia minor (D56.3), hemoglobin E-beta thalassemia (D56.5), and other thalassemia (D56.8). Code **D56.9, Thalassemia, unspecified,** is reported when the type of thalassemia is not identified. However, thalassemia trait, not otherwise specified, is assigned to code **D56.3, Thalassemia minor.**

EXERCISE 17.4

Code the following diagnoses. Do not assign External cause of morbidity codes.

1. Classical hemophilia — D66
2. Sickle-cell Hb-SS disease — D57.1
3. Hereditary spherocytic, hemolytic anemia — D58.0
4. Thalassemia — D56.9
5. Sickle-cell crisis with acute chest syndrome — D57.01

COAGULATION DEFECTS

Coagulation defects are characterized by prolonged clotting time. Some are congenital in origin; others are acquired. Conditions in subcategory D68.31, Hemorrhagic disorder due to intrinsic circulating anticoagulants, antibodies, or inhibitors, result from the presence of circulating anticoagulants in the blood that interfere with normal clotting. These anticoagulants are usually inherent or intrinsic in the blood, like other coagulation defects. Autoimmune hemophilia, autoimmune inhibitors to clotting factors, and secondary and acquired hemophilia are assigned to code D68.311. Lupus anticoagulant (LAC) with hemorrhagic disorder, systemic lupus erythematosus [SLE] inhibitor with hemorrhagic disorder, and antiphospholipid antibody with hemorrhagic disorder are assigned to code D68.312. Code D68.318 includes hemorrhagic disorders due to increases in antithrombin, anti-VIIIa, anti-IXa, and other intrinsic circulating anticoagulants, antibodies, or inhibitors.

Bleeding in a patient who is being treated with Coumadin, heparin, anticoagulants, or other antithrombotics does not indicate that a hemorrhagic disorder due to intrinsic circulating anticoagulant is present. In this situation, assign code **T45.515-, Adverse effect of anticoagulant,** or code **T45.525-, Adverse effect of antithrombotic drugs,** to indicate any adverse effect of an administered drug, with code **D68.32, Hemorrhagic disorder due to extrinsic circulating anticoagulants.** Code D68.31- is not assigned for hemorrhagic disorder due to extrinsic circulating anticoagulants; it is only assigned when the physician specifically documents a diagnosis of hemorrhagic disorder due to intrinsic circulating anticoagulants.

Heparin-induced thrombocytopenia (D75.82) is one of the most severe side effects of heparin therapy. Heparin therapy is widely used to prevent and treat clotting disorders. In some people, heparin triggers autoimmune conditions of severe platelet deficiency with severe thrombotic (clot-related) complications.

Hypercoagulable states refer to a group of acquired and inherited disorders caused by increased thrombin generation. There is an increased tendency for blood clotting, and there may be fibrin deposition in the small blood vessels. These disorders are divided into primary and secondary hypercoagulable states. Primary hypercoagulable states (D68.5-) are inherited disorders of specific anticoagulant factors. Secondary hypercoagulable states (D68.6-) are primarily acquired disorders that predispose to thrombosis through complex and multifactorial mechanisms involving blood flow abnormalities or defects in blood composition and of vessel walls. Examples of conditions that can cause secondary hypercoagulable states are malignancy, pregnancy, trauma, myeloproliferative disorders, and antiphospholipid antibody syndrome.

Prolonged prothrombin time or other abnormal coagulation profiles should not be coded as a coagulation defect. Code **R79.1, Abnormal coagulation profile,** is assigned for this abnormal laboratory finding. If the patient is receiving Coumadin therapy, however, a prolonged bleeding time is an expected result, and therefore code R79.1 is not assigned. Note also that Coumadin is not a circulating anticoagulant; it induces anticoagulation through other mechanisms. Examples of appropriate code assignments include the following:

K26.4 + T45.515A	Duodenal ulcer with hemorrhage due to Coumadin therapy, initial encounter
K29.01 + T45.515D	Acute gastritis with hemorrhage due to anticoagulant therapy, subsequent encounter

Following are case examples demonstrating code assignments:

- A 50-year-old man receiving Coumadin therapy is admitted with hematemesis secondary to acute gastritis. A prolonged prothrombin time is reported, secondary to the anticoagulant effects of the Coumadin therapy. Code **K29.01, Acute gastritis with bleeding,** is assigned; code D68.3- is not reported because no hemorrhagic disorder was identified. No code is assigned for the prolonged bleeding time because this is an expected result of Coumadin therapy. Note again that Coumadin is not a circulating anticoagulant; it induces anticoagulation through other mechanisms.
- A patient is admitted following multiple episodes of hematemesis secondary to Coumadin therapy. No significant pathology was discovered. The Coumadin is discontinued, and no recurrence of the bleeding occurs. Code **K92.0, Hematemesis,** with code **T45.515A, Adverse effect of anticoagulants, initial encounter,** are assigned to indicate Coumadin as the responsible external agent. Code D68.3- is not assigned.

FIGURE 17.1 Four Major Types of Blood Cells

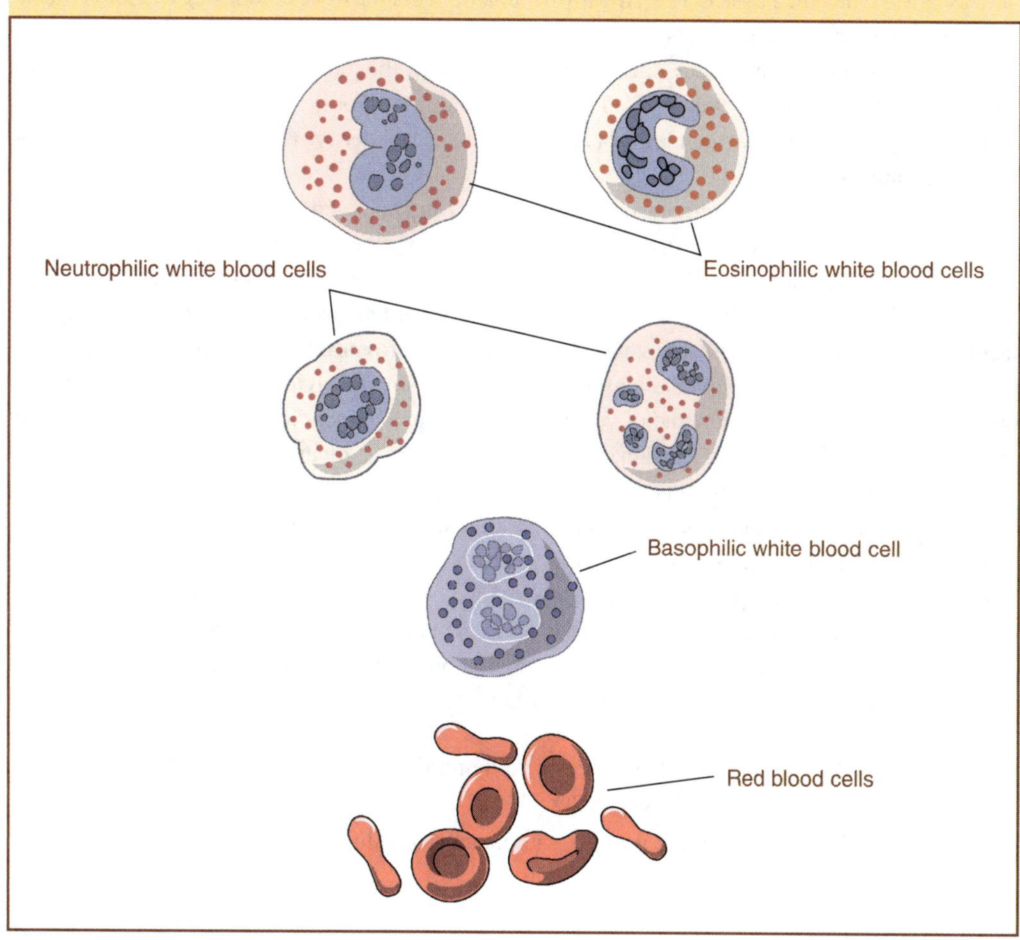

DISEASES OF PLATELET CELLS

Thrombocytopenia is a deficiency in the blood cells that help the blood to clot. Post-transfusion purpura is the recipient's response to produce anti-HPA (human platelet antigen) antibodies that destroy the platelets following a transfusion of blood products from an HPA-positive donor. The alloantibody destroys the transfused platelets as well as the recipient's own platelets to produce a severe thrombocytopenia in HPA-negative women who were immunized during previous pregnancy or transfusion. Code **D69.51, Posttransfusion purpura,** is assigned for this rare condition. Code **D69.59, Other secondary thrombocytopenia,** is assigned for secondary thrombocytopenia that is due to dilutional causes, drugs, extracorporeal circulation of blood, massive blood transfusion, platelet alloimmunization, and other secondary thrombocytopenia.

DISEASES OF WHITE BLOOD CELLS

White blood cells (leukocytes) play an important role in the body's immune system by fighting off infection. Many different diseases can affect white blood cells. There are several different types of normal white blood cells (WBCs), including neutrophils, lymphocytes, monocytes, eosinophils, and basophils.

Diseases that may decrease production of WBCs include drug toxicity, vitamin deficiencies, blood diseases, infections (viral diseases, tuberculosis, typhoid), or abnormalities of the bone marrow; or the decrease could be cyclic (varying in severity, possibly due to biorhythm changes). Antibodies may attack WBCs as a result of a disease or because of medications stimulating the immune system. Pooling of WBCs occurs with some overwhelming infections, heart-lung bypass during heart surgery, and hemodialysis.

Some diseases increase the production of WBCs. If all types of WBCs are affected, leukocytosis occurs. Leukocytosis can be caused by infection, inflammation, allergic reaction, malignancy, hereditary disorders, or other miscellaneous causes—for example, medications such as cortisone-like drugs (prednisone), lithium, and nonsteroidal anti-inflammatory drugs. Other illnesses target specific types of WBCs, such as neutrophilia, lymphocytosis, and granulocytosis.

Diseases of the WBCs are primarily classified on the basis of whether the WBC count is low or elevated. In addition, more specific codes are available depending on the type of blood cell affected, as shown by the examples that follow.

- Low neutrophil count or neutropenia (category D70) is further subdivided as follows: congenital (D70.0), agranulocytosis secondary to cancer chemotherapy (D70.1), other drug-induced agranulocytosis (D70.2), neutropenia due to infection (D70.3), cyclic (D70.4), other (D70.8), and unspecified (D70.9).
- Decreased WBC counts (subcategory D72.81-) are classified as follows: decreased lymphocytes or lymphocytopenia (D72.810); other decreased WBC count including basophils, eosinophils, monocytes, or plasmacytes (D72.818); unspecified decreased WBC count (D72.819).
- Elevated WBC counts (subcategory D72.82-) are classified as follows: elevated lymphocytes or lymphocytosis (D72.820); monocytosis (D72.821); plasmacytosis (D72.822); leukemoid reaction including basophilic, lymphocytic, monocytic, myelocytic, or neutrophilic leukemoid reaction (D72.823); basophilia (D72.824); bandemia (D72.825); other elevated WBC count (D72.828); and unspecified leukocytosis (D72.829).

It is important to remember that these codes should not be assigned on the basis of laboratory findings alone. Physician concurrence regarding the significance of the laboratory results should be confirmed before assigning these codes.

DISORDERS OF THE IMMUNE SYSTEM

Categories D80 through D89 classify various disorders of the immune system, with the exception of conditions associated with or due to HIV, which are classified to code B20. The immune disorders discussed in this chapter include the following categories:

D80 Immunodeficiency with predominantly antibody defects
D81 Combined immunodeficiencies
D82 Immunodeficiency associated with other major defects
D83 Common variable immunodeficiency
D84 Other immunodeficiencies
D86 Sarcoidosis
D89 Other disorders involving the immune mechanism, not elsewhere classified

Sarcoidosis

Sarcoidosis is a disease of gradual onset in which abnormal collections of inflammatory cells (granulomas) form as nodules in many organs of the body. Sarcoidosis may be asymptomatic or chronic, and its etiology is unknown. The current working hypothesis is that in genetically susceptible individuals, sarcoidosis is caused through alteration in immune response after exposure to an environmental, occupational, or infectious agent. The granulomas most often appear in the lungs or the lymph nodes, but any organ can be affected. ICD-10-CM provides unique codes within category D86, Sarcoidosis, for the most common sites affected, such as lungs (D86.0), lymph nodes (D86.1), lung with lymph nodes (D86.2), skin (D86.3), meninges (D86.81), cranial nerves (D86.82), eye uvea (D86.83), kidney and ureters (D86.84), myocardium (D86.85), joints (D86.86), muscles (D86.87), and other sites including liver (D86.89) or unspecified (D86.9).

EXERCISE 17.5

Code the following diagnoses.

1.	Pancytopenia, congenital	D61.09
2.	Cyclic neutropenia	D70.4
3.	Hereditary thrombocytopenia	D69.42
4.	Anemia Neutropenia Thrombocytopenia Pancytopenia	D61.818
5.	Autoerythrocyte sensitization purpura	D69.2
6.	Cell-mediated immune deficiency with thrombocytopenia and eczema	D82.0
7.	Sarcoidosis of lung and lymph nodes	D86.2
8.	Pernicious anemia, Addison type	D51.0
9.	Acute gastritis with hemorrhage, exacerbated by heparin therapy, initial encounter Table: heparin	K29.01 T45.515A
10.	Autoimmune lymphoproliferative syndrome	D89.82

CHAPTER 18

Diseases of the Nervous System and Sense Organs

CHAPTER OVERVIEW

- Nervous system diseases can be found in chapter 6 of ICD-10-CM.
- Diseases of the eye and adnexa can be found in chapter 7 of ICD-10-CM, and diseases of the ear and mastoid process are found in chapter 8.
- Dual coding is often required for infectious diseases of the central nervous system.
- Pain can be coded by recording the site of the pain.
    - —Codes for pain, not elsewhere classified (G89), can be used for coding pain control or management.
    - —If the cause is known but not treated during the encounter, code it as an additional diagnosis.
- Coders must be careful when coding seizures to epilepsy. Seizures may be caused by a variety of conditions and should be coded accordingly.
- Other diseases of the central nervous system covered in this chapter of the handbook are hemiplegia, Parkinson's disease, autonomic dysreflexia, and narcolepsy.
- Many problems of the peripheral nervous system are manifestations of other conditions.
    - —These problems are assigned as additional codes.
    - —Critical illness polyneuropathy and critical illness myopathy, for example, are complications of sepsis.
- Eye diseases are extremely complicated to code, and understanding the terminology and diagnostic statement completely is vital to proper coding.
- Eye diseases and conditions covered in this handbook include corneal injuries (from both light and wounding), conjunctivitis, cataracts, and glaucoma.
- Hearing loss may be coded as conductive, sensorineural, or a combination of the two.

LEARNING OUTCOMES

After studying this chapter you should be able to:

Explain the difference between the central and peripheral nervous systems and locate the two areas in the ICD-10-CM.

Understand how to code for pain.

Explain what is needed before a code of epilepsy is assigned.

Code for a variety of conditions of the nervous system.

Code disorders of the eye and ear.

TERMS TO KNOW

Central nervous system
the brain and spinal cord

Conductive hearing loss
hearing loss due to a problem with a part of the ear

Peripheral nervous system
all elements of the nervous system except the brain and spinal cord

Sensorineural hearing loss
hearing loss due to a problem with the sensory part of the ear or the nerves associated with hearing

REMEMBER . . .

Due to legal and personal reasons, a code of epilepsy cannot be assigned unless it is clearly diagnosed by a physician.

INTRODUCTION

Diseases of the nervous system are classified in chapter 6 of ICD-10-CM. Eye and adnexa diseases can be found in chapter 7 of ICD-10-CM, and diseases of the ear and mastoid process are found in chapter 8. Because the nervous system is complex and difficult to comprehend, thinking of it as a two-level system may help to simplify the coding process:

G00–G47; G80–G99	Central nervous system (brain and spinal cord)
G50–G73	Peripheral nervous system (all other neural elements in the rest of the body)

Cerebral degeneration, Parkinson's disease, and meningitis are conditions affecting the central nervous system. Polyneuropathy, myasthenia gravis, and muscular dystrophies affect the peripheral nerves. The peripheral nervous system includes the autonomic nervous system, which regulates the activity of the cardiac muscle, smooth muscle, and glands.

FIGURE 18.1 The Nervous System

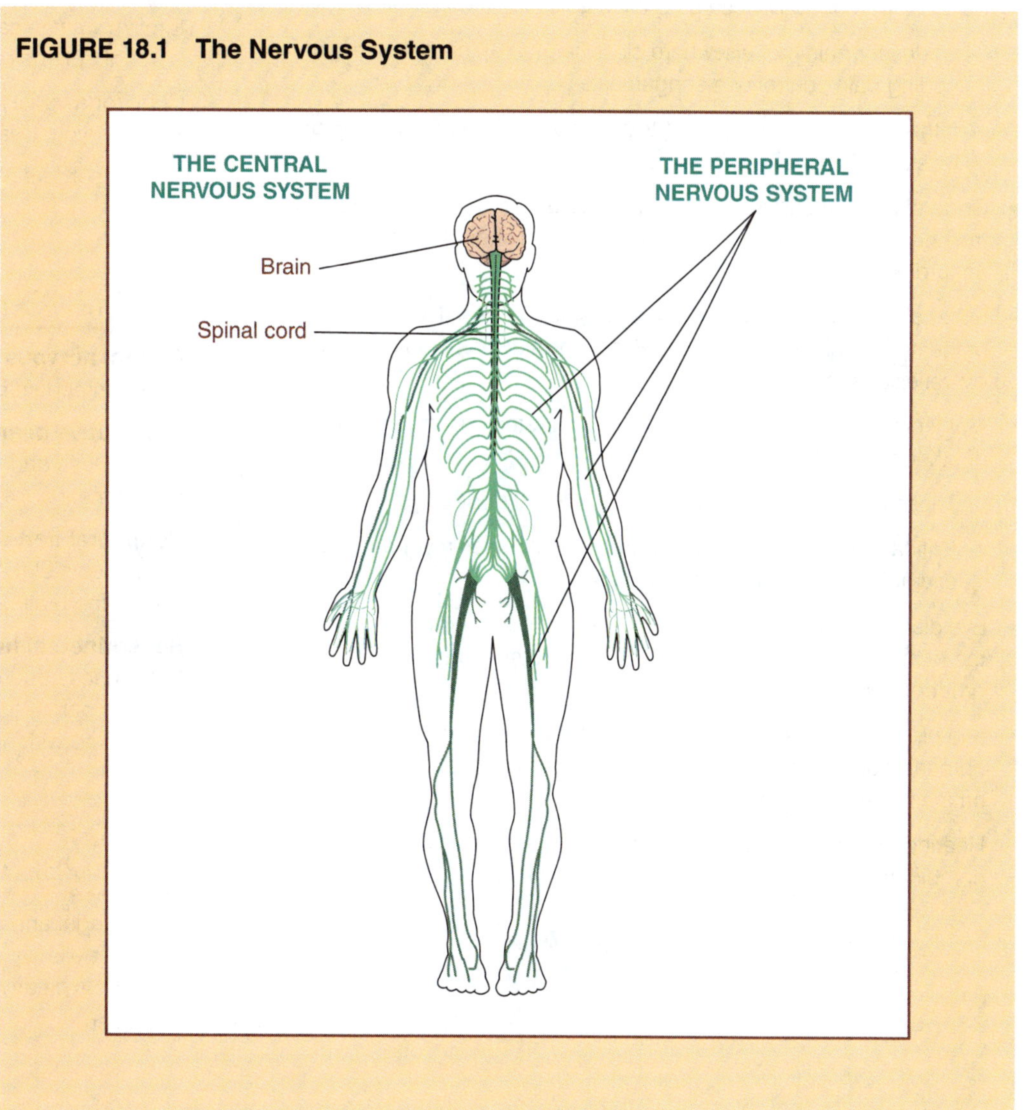

INFLAMMATORY DISEASES OF THE CENTRAL NERVOUS SYSTEM

Infectious diseases of the central nervous system are classified in several ways, and it is imperative that the coder carefully follow the directions provided by the Alphabetic Index and Tabular List. Dual coding is frequently required, with the code for the underlying condition sequenced first, followed by a manifestation code. For example, meningitis due to poliovirus is classified as **A80.9, Acute poliomyelitis, unspecified,** with a manifestation of **G02, Meningitis in other infectious and parasitic diseases classified elsewhere.** Bacterial meningitis due to certain organisms such as *Pneumococcus, Streptococcus,* and *Staphylococcus* is classified in category G00, with a fourth character indicating the responsible organism. Codes G00.2–G00.8 also require an additional code to further specify the organism. Care should be exercised to determine if the condition should be coded to the nervous system, or if there are combination codes in the Infectious Disease chapter that include the condition as well as the infectious organism. For example, candidal meningitis is coded to B37.5 and meningitis due to Lyme disease is coded to A69.21 rather than to categories G01 or G02.

EXERCISE 18.1

Code the following diagnoses and procedures.

1. Candidal meningitis	B37.5
2. Poliovirus encephalitis	A80.9 G05.3
3. Encephalitis due to rubella	B06.01
4. Herpes zoster with meningitis	B02.1
5. *Staphylococcus aureus* meningitis	G00.3 B95.61

PARKINSON'S DISEASE

Parkinson's disease, also known as parkinsonism, is a chronic, progressive disorder of the central nervous system characterized by a fine, slowly spreading involuntary tremor, postural instability, and muscle weakness and rigidity. Parkinson's disease is assigned to code G20 and includes primary parkinsonism. Secondary Parkinson's disease (G21.-) is often an adverse effect of the therapeutic use of medication, in which case a code from category G21 (e.g., G21.0, G21.11, G21.19) is assigned first, followed by code T43.3X5, T43.4X5, T43.505, T43.595, or T36–T50, with fifth or sixth character "5" as an additional code to identify the responsible drug. Secondary parkinsonism may also be postencephalitic (G21.3), vascular (G21.4), other (G21.8), or unspecified (G21.9). Parkinson's disease is sometimes caused by syphilis and in that case is coded to **A52.19, Other symptomatic neurosyphilis.**

ALZHEIMER'S DISEASE

Alzheimer's disease is a process of progressive atrophy involving the degeneration of nerve cells. This degeneration leads to mental changes that range from subtle intellectual impairment to dementia with loss of cognitive functions and failure of memory. Alzheimer's disease is coded to category G30 and is further subdivided to specify early onset (G30.0), late onset (G30.1), other (G30.8), or unspecified (G30.9). When associated dementia is present, code **F02.8-, Dementia in conditions classified elsewhere,** is assigned as an additional diagnosis. For example:

G30.9	Alzheimer's disease [without any mention of dementia]
G30.1 + F02.81	Dementia with behavioral disturbance due to late onset Alzheimer's disease

EPILEPSY

Epilepsy is a paroxysmal disorder of cerebral function characterized by recurrent seizures. Coders must not assume, however, that any diagnostic statement describing convulsions or seizures should be coded to epilepsy; these conditions also occur in a number of other diseases, such as brain tumor, cerebrovascular accident, alcoholism, electrolyte imbalance, and febrile conditions. Grand mal seizures, for example, can be due to causes other than epilepsy. Because a diagnosis of epilepsy can have serious legal and personal implications for the patient, such as the inability to obtain a driver's license, a code for epilepsy must not be assigned unless the physician clearly identifies the condition as such in the diagnostic statement. When the diagnosis is stated only in terms of convulsion or seizure without any further identification of the cause, code **R56.9, Unspecified convulsions,** should be assigned. When the physician mentions a history of seizure in the workup but does not include any mention of seizures in the diagnostic statement, no code should be assigned unless clear documentation indicates that the criteria for reporting the condition have been met and the physician agrees that a code should be added. Please note that the classification assigns seizure disorder and recurrent seizures to epilepsy G40.909, whereas the main term "seizure(s)" is indexed to R56.9

ICD-10-CM provides a fifth-character subclassification for category G40, Epilepsy and recurrent seizures, that permits identification of epilepsy as intractable when so described by the physician. Terms such as "pharmacoresistant (pharmacologically resistant)," "poorly controlled," "refractory (medically)," and "treatment resistant" are considered to be equivalent to intractable. The coder should not assume that the condition is intractable from general statements in the medical record. In addition, a sixth character is used to identify whether status epilepticus is present.

EXERCISE 18.2

Code the following diagnoses. Do not assign External cause of morbidity codes.

1. Parkinson's disease	G20
2. Secondary parkinsonism due to prescribed Thorazine (neuroleptic drug), initial encounter	G21.11 T43.3x5A
3. Intractable epilepsy, grand mal type, status epilepticus	G40.411
4. Poorly controlled generalized idiopathic epilepsy	G40.319
5. Intractable focal epilepsy	G40.119
6. Febrile convulsions, recurrent	R56.00
7. Alzheimer's disease with delirium	G30.9 F05

HEADACHE AND MIGRAINE

A diagnosis of headache without any further specificity is classified to chapter 18 of ICD-10-CM and coded to **R51, Headache.** Migraines are classified to category G43, while specific headaches are classified to category G44, Other headache syndromes, in chapter 6, Diseases of the Nervous System.

Migraine is a neurological syndrome characterized by altered bodily perceptions, severe headaches, and nausea and vomiting. Approximately one-third of people who suffer from migraine headaches perceive an aura—unusual visual, olfactory, or other sensory experiences that signal the migraine will soon occur. The following terms are considered equivalent to intractable: "pharmacoresistant (pharmacologically resistant)," "treatment resistant," "refractory (medically)," and "poorly controlled." Status migrainosus generally refers to a severe migraine attack that lasts for more than 72 hours. However, the designation of status migrainosus should be confirmed by the physician.

ICD-10-CM classifies migraines to category G43 as follows:

G43.0- Migraine without aura
G43.1- Migraine with aura
G43.4- Hemiplegic migraine
G43.5- Persistent migraine aura without cerebral infarction
G43.6- Persistent migraine aura with cerebral infarction
G43.7- Chronic migraine without aura
G43.A- Cyclical vomiting
G43.B- Ophthalmoplegic migraine
G43.C- Periodic headache syndromes in child or adult
G43.D- Abdominal migraine
G43.8- Other migraine
G43.9- Migraine, unspecified

Specific headaches are classified in chapter 6 of ICD-10-CM under Other headache syndromes (category G44) as follows:

G44.0- Cluster headaches and other trigeminal autonomic cephalgias
G44.1 Vascular headache, not elsewhere classified
G44.2- Tension-type headache
G44.3- Posttraumatic headache
G44.4- Drug-induced headache, not elsewhere classified
G44.5- Complicated headache syndromes
G44.8- Other specific headache syndromes

Headache following lumbar puncture is assigned to code **G97.1, Other reaction to spinal or lumbar puncture.**

NARCOLEPSY

Narcolepsy is a chronic neurological disorder characterized by the inability to regulate sleep and wakefulness normally. Symptoms are excessive daytime sleepiness, sleep paralysis (paralysis upon falling asleep or waking up), cataplexy (sudden, brief episodes of paralysis or muscle weakness), and vivid hallucinations (vivid dreamlike images that occur at sleep onset). Other possible symptoms are disturbed nighttime sleep, leg jerks, nightmares, and frequent awakenings. Irresistible sleep attacks may occur throughout the day regardless of the amount or quality of prior nighttime sleep. Affected individuals may fall asleep at work or school or while eating, talking, or driving.

ICD-10-CM distinguishes between subcategory G47.41- (narcolepsy) and G47.42- (narcolepsy in conditions classified elsewhere). Fifth characters distinguish between narcolepsy with cataplexy (G47.411, G47.421) and without cataplexy (G47.419, G47.429).

HEMIPLEGIA/HEMIPARESIS

Hemiplegia is paralysis of one side of the body. It is classified to category G81, with a fifth character to indicate the side affected and whether the affected side is dominant or nondominant.

When information is not available regarding whether the affected side is dominant or nondominant, and when the classification does not provide a default, code selection is as follows: For ambidextrous patients, the default should also be dominant. If the left side is affected, the default is non-dominant. If the right side is affected, the default is dominant. This guideline applies to codes from category G81, Hemiplegia and hemiparesis, and subcategories G83.1, Monoplegia of lower limb; G83.2, Monoplegia of upper limb; and G83.3, Monoplegia, unspecified.

Hemiplegia occurring in connection with a cerebrovascular accident (CVA) often clears quickly and is sometimes called a transient hemiplegia. Hemiplegia is not inherent to an acute CVA; therefore, a code from category G81, Hemiplegia and hemiparesis, is assigned as an additional code when it occurs. Even if it resolves without treatment, it affects the patient's care. Any neurologic deficits caused by CVA should be reported even when they have resolved at the time of discharge. When the patient is admitted at a later time with hemiplegia and hemiparesis due to sequela of cerebrovascular disease, a code from category I69 is assigned to indicate that the condition is a late effect of a CVA. (See chapter 28 of this handbook for more discussion of cerebrovascular disease.)

Examples of appropriate coding for hemiplegia follow:

I66.9 + G81.91	Cerebral thrombosis with transient right hemiplegia that has cleared by discharge
I66.9 + G81.91	Cerebral thrombosis with hemiplegia right dominant side
I69.352	Hemiplegia of left dominant side due to previous CVA
G81.90 + S34.109S	Hemiparesis due to old lumbar spinal cord injury

PAIN

Pain may be coded by reporting the site of pain. These codes may be found in the symptom chapter (e.g., headache, R51) or in the appropriate body system chapter (e.g., pain in limb, M79.609). Codes from category G89, Pain, not elsewhere classified, may be used in conjunction with the site of pain codes if the category G89 code provides more detail about acute or chronic pain and neoplasm-related pain unless otherwise indicated below.

The determination of whether the pain is acute, chronic, or chronic pain syndrome is dependent on the provider's documentation. There is no time frame defining when pain becomes chronic. If the pain is not specified as acute or chronic, post-thoracotomy, postprocedural, or neoplasm related, do not assign codes from category G89. A code from category G89 should not be assigned if the underlying (definitive) diagnosis is known, unless the reason for the encounter is pain control/management and not management of the underlying condition.

When an admission or encounter is for a procedure aimed at treating the underlying condition, such as a spinal fusion for treatment of pain associated with a vertebral fracture, a code for the underlying condition (e.g., vertebral fracture) should be assigned as the principal diagnosis. No code from category G89 should be assigned.

Encounter/Admission for Pain Control/Management

Category G89 codes may be used as the principal diagnosis or first-listed code when pain control or pain management is the reason for the admission/encounter. These encounters are typically not for diagnostic workup or treatment of the underlying condition but for management of pain. In these situations, if the underlying cause of the pain is known, report it as an additional diagnosis. An example is a patient with displaced intervertebral disc, nerve impingement, and severe back pain who presents for injection of steroid into the spinal canal. The injection is intended to relieve the pain, but it does not treat the displaced disc.

If the admission is for control of pain related to, associated with, or due to a malignancy, code **G89.3, Neoplasm related pain (acute) (chronic),** should be assigned. The underlying neoplasm is reported as an additional diagnosis. Because the neoplasm code will provide information regarding the specific site, an additional code for the site of pain should not be assigned. When the reason for the admission/encounter is management of the neoplasm and the pain associated with the neoplasm is also documented, code G89.3 may be assigned as an additional diagnosis. It is not necessary to assign an additional code for the site of the pain.

If the admission or encounter is for a procedure to treat the underlying condition, the underlying condition should be assigned as the principal or first-listed diagnosis. For example, if a patient is admitted for a spinal fusion to treat lumbar spinal stenosis, assign code **M48.06, Spinal stenosis, lumbar region,** as the principal diagnosis. No code from category G89 should be assigned.

Patients with chronic pain whose conservative therapies have failed may undergo insertion of neurostimulators for pain control. In such cases, the appropriate pain code is assigned as the principal or first-listed diagnosis. When an admission or encounter is for a procedure aimed at treating the underlying condition, and a neurostimulator is inserted for pain control during the same admission/encounter, a code for the underlying condition should be assigned as the principal diagnosis with the pain code as a secondary diagnosis.

If the encounter is for any other reason except pain control or pain management and a related definitive diagnosis for the pain has not been established (confirmed) by the provider, the code for the specific site of pain should be assigned first, followed by the appropriate code from category G89. If the definitive diagnosis has been established, assign the code for the definitive diagnosis.

Postoperative Pain

Post-thoracotomy pain and other postoperative pain are classified to subcategories G89.1 and G89.2, depending on whether the pain is acute or chronic. The default for post-thoracotomy and other postoperative pain not specified as acute or chronic is the code for the acute form. Postoperative pain associated with a specific postoperative complication (such as painful wire sutures) or associated with devices, implants, or grafts left in a surgical site (such as a painful hip prosthesis) is assigned to the appropriate code(s) found in chapter 19 of ICD-10-CM, Injury, Poisoning, and Certain Other Consequences of External Causes. A code from category G89 is assigned as an additional code to identify acute or chronic pain (G89.18 or G89.28).

Postoperative pain may be reported as the principal or first-listed diagnosis when the reason for the encounter or admission is postoperative pain control/management. Postoperative pain may be reported as a secondary diagnosis code when a patient presents for outpatient surgery and develops an unusual or inordinate amount of postoperative pain. Please note that routine or expected postoperative pain immediately after surgery should not be coded.

AUTONOMIC DYSREFLEXIA

Autonomic dysreflexia is a syndrome characterized by an abrupt onset of excessively high blood pressure caused by an uncontrolled sympathetic nervous system discharge in persons with spinal cord injury, usually at or above the T6 level. Anything that would ordinarily cause pain below this level may trigger a parasympathetic response resulting in bradycardia, blurred vision, and sweating. True autonomic dysreflexia is potentially life threatening and is considered a medical emergency. Code **G90.4, Autonomic dysreflexia,** is used to report this condition. It is not necessary to code each manifestation or symptom separately. Unlike most dual coding, whereby the underlying condition is listed first, in this case the code for the dysreflexia is sequenced first, with an additional code for the underlying chronic condition that has precipitated this life-threatening condition (e.g., pressure ulcer, fecal impaction, urinary tract infection).

HYDROCEPHALUS

Normal pressure hydrocephalus (NPH) or secondary NPH can be caused by any condition in which the flow of cerebrospinal fluid (CSF) is blocked, such as subarachnoid hemorrhage, head trauma, cerebral infarction, infection, tumor, or complications of surgery. Assign code **G91.0, Communicating hydrocephalus,** for secondary NPH. Obstructive hydrocephalus develops secondary to a blockage in the normal circulation of CSF in the brain. In most instances, the blockage affects the third and fourth ventricles at the level of the aqueduct of Sylvius, also referred to as an aqueductal obstruction, which can result from scarring or tumor. Assign code **G91.1, Obstructive hydrocephalus,** for this acquired condition. Idiopathic normal pressure hydrocephalus (INPH) can occur without any identifiable cause. Code **G91.2, (Idiopathic) normal pressure hydrocephalus (INPH),** is assigned for this type of acquired hydrocephalus. If the medical record documentation does not specify whether the hydrocephalus is congenital or acquired, code **G91.9 Hydrocephalus, unspecified,** should be assigned.

ENCEPHALOPATHY

Encephalopathy is a general term used to describe any disorder of cerebral function. It is a very broad term and in most cases will be preceded by various terms describing the reason, cause, or special conditions leading to the brain disorder. It is important to carefully note these additional terms, as they will affect code assignment. More than 150 different terms modify or precede "encephalopathy" in the medical literature—not all of them are classified to chapter 6 of ICD-10-CM. Some of the more common encephalopathies are noted below:

- *Anoxic encephalopathy* refers to brain damage due to lack of oxygen. This type of encephalopathy is assigned to **G93.1, Anoxic brain damage, not elsewhere classified.**
- *Alcoholic encephalopathy* is a serious complication of alcoholic liver disease usually caused by excessive drinking for several years. It results in a loss of specific brain function (damage of brain tissue) caused by a thiamine deficiency. Alcoholic encephalopathy is classified to **G31.2, Degeneration of nervous system due to alcohol.**
- *Hepatic encephalopathy* is brain damage due to liver disease, and it is classified to category K72, Hepatic failure, not elsewhere classified.
- *Metabolic encephalopathy* is temporary or permanent damage to the brain due to lack of glucose, oxygen or other metabolic agent, or organ dysfunction. Symptoms include an altered state of consciousness, usually characterized as delirium, confusion, or agitation, and changes in behavior or personality. There may also be symptoms of muscle stiffness

or rigidity, tremor, stupor, or coma. Symptoms can develop quickly and may resolve when the condition is reversed. Assign code **G93.41, Metabolic encephalopathy,** for this condition. Code G93.41 also includes septic encephalopathy.

- *Toxic encephalopathy* is also known as *toxic-metabolic encephalopathy*. This type of encephalopathy is a degenerative neurologic disorder caused by exposure to toxic substances. It consists of a variety of symptoms, characterized by an altered mental status, and can include memory loss, small personality changes, lack of concentration, involuntary movements, nausea, fatigue, seizures, arm strength problems, and depression. ICD-10-CM classifies this condition to code **G92, Toxic encephalopathy.** A code from categories T51–T65 is assigned first to identify the causative toxic agent.
- *Wernicke's encephalopathy* involves damage to the central nervous system and the peripheral nervous system and is caused by disorders of the liver such as cirrhosis, hepatitis, malnutrition, and conditions in which blood circulation bypasses the liver entirely. The symptoms can range from mild to severe and consist of various neurological symptoms including changes in consciousness, reflexes, and behavior. ICD-10-CM classifies this condition to **E51.2, Wernicke's encephalopathy.**
- *Unspecified encephalopathy* is assigned to code **G93.40, Encephalopathy, unspecified.**

EXERCISE 18.3

Code the following diagnoses and procedures. Do not assign External cause of morbidity codes.

1.	Chronic intractable tension-type headache	G44.221
2.	Cerebrovascular accident with left-sided hemiparesis	I63.9 G81.94
3.	Severe hypertension and pounding headache due to autonomic dysreflexia due to fecal impaction	G90.4 K56.41 I10
4.	Severe chronic low back pain due to displaced lumbar disc with neuritis due to previous trauma. Epidural injection of steroid (anti-inflammatory) for pain	G89.21 M54.5 M51.16 3E0S33Z
5.	Metabolic encephalopathy	G93.41
6.	Toxic metabolic encephalopathy	G92

DISORDERS OF THE PERIPHERAL NERVOUS SYSTEM

Disorders of the peripheral nervous system are classified to categories G50 through G73 according to the condition and the nerves involved. Many codes in this section are manifestations of other diseases and are assigned as additional codes, with the underlying condition listed first.

CRITICAL ILLNESS POLYNEUROPATHY

Critical illness polyneuropathy is commonly associated with complications of sepsis and multiple organ failure. It is considered to be secondary to systemic inflammatory response syndrome. Synonyms for critical illness polyneuropathy include neuropathy of critical illness, intensive care unit neuropathy, and intensive care polyneuropathy. Patients with this condition show abnormal electrophysiologic changes consistent with primary axonal degeneration of motor fibers. They also demonstrate severe weakness, making it difficult to wean them from mechanical ventilation. Assign code **G62.81, Critical illness polyneuropathy,** for this condition.

CRITICAL ILLNESS MYOPATHY

Critical illness myopathy is also associated with sepsis. It is a cause of difficulty in weaning patients from mechanical ventilation and prolonged recovery after illness. It is also associated with neuromuscular blocking agents and corticosteroids (in asthma and organ transplant patients), and neuropathy. Code **G72.81, Critical illness myopathy,** is used to report this condition.

EXERCISE 18.4

Code the following diagnoses and procedures.

1. Amyloid polyneuropathy	E85.1 + G63
2. Morton's neuroma, 3-4 and 4-5 interspaces, left foot Excision of Morton's neuroma, left foot	G57.62 01BG0ZZ
3. Tardy palsy due to entrapment of right ulnar nerve	G56.21
4. Peripheral polyneuritis, severe, due to chronic alcoholism	G62.1 + F10.20
5. Nutritional polyneuropathy	E63.9 + G63
6. Tic douloureux	G50.0

DISORDERS OF THE EYE AND ADNEXAE

The classification for diseases of the eye is very detailed, and understanding the terminology used is especially important for the coder. Terms that seem similar may have entirely different meanings. The coder should be sure to fully understand the diagnostic statement in the medical record before assigning a code.

Visual impairment (H54) is classified according to severity, with the status of the lesser eye listed first and the better eye listed second in the code title. If the associated underlying cause of the blindness is known, it should be coded first. ICD-10-CM includes a table with the classification of severity of visual impairment recommended by a World Health Organization study group. The term "low vision" in category H54 comprises categories 1 and 2 of the table; the term "blindness," categories 3, 4, and 5; and the term "unqualified visual loss," category 9. The information is intended to provide the coder with "clues" to identify possible gaps in documentation where provider query may be necessary. It is not intended to replace the need for specific provider documentation to substantiate code assignment. Sample codes include the following:

H54.11 Blindness, right eye, low vision left eye
H54.41 Blindness, right eye, normal vision left eye

Occasionally, visual problems can cause tilting of the head, resulting in ocular torticollis or ocular-induced torticollis. Torticollis refers to abnormal head posture. Palsy of the superior or inferior oblique muscles causes the patient to hold the head at an angle to compensate for the visual disturbance. Ocular torticollis is coded by assigning first the appropriate code for the ocular condition causing the torticollis, e.g., nystagmus (H55.-), strabismus (H50.9), fourth nerve palsy (H49.1-), followed by code **R29.891, Ocular torticollis.**

FIGURE 18.2 The Eye

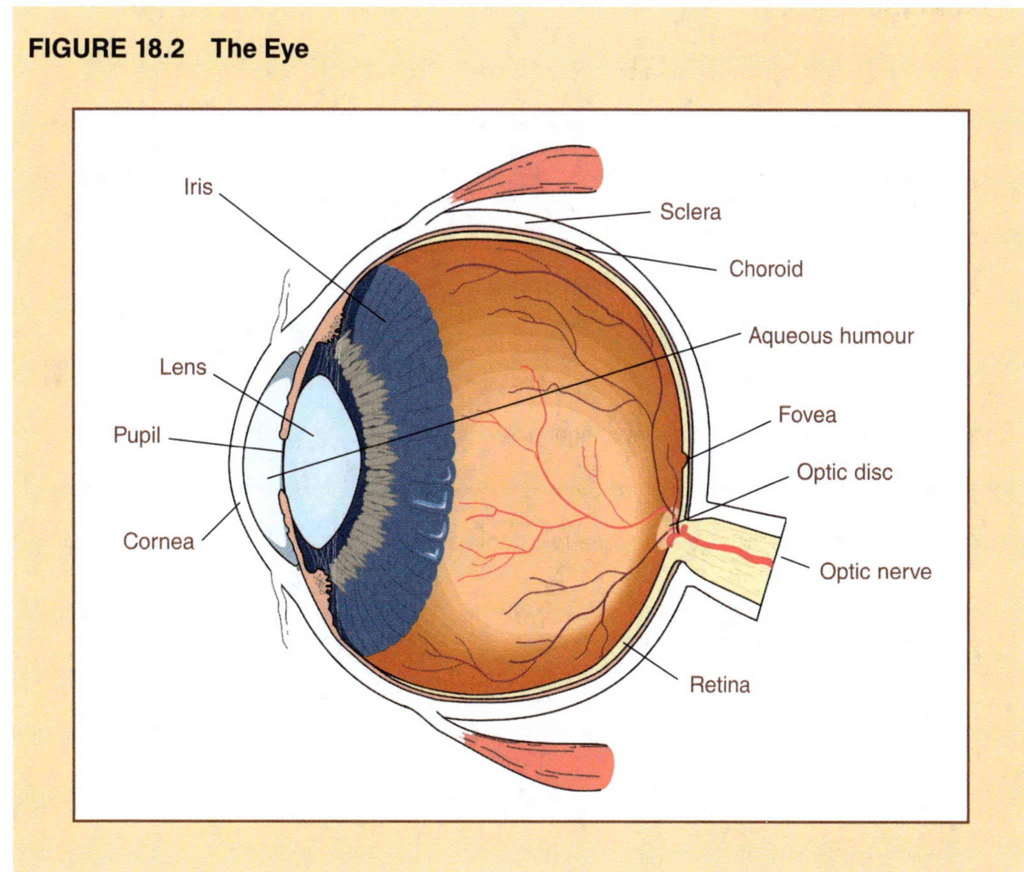

Corneal Injury

Code **H16.13-, Photokeratitis,** is assigned for a corneal flash burn, generally referred to as ultraviolet keratitis. The condition typically occurs at high altitudes on highly reflective snow fields or, less often, with a solar eclipse. Artificial sources of ultraviolet light can also cause photokeratitis. These sources include sun-tanning beds, a welder's arc (flash burn, welder's flash, or arc eye), carbon arcs, photographic flood lamps, lightning, electric sparks, and halogen desk lamps. It is always an injury, and the appropriate External cause of morbidity code should be assigned as an additional code, such as codes from category W89, Exposure to man-made visible and ultraviolet light, or code **X32.-, Exposure to sunlight.**

Corneal or corneoscleral lacerations are classified in category S05, Injury of eye and orbit. The fourth characters are assigned to indicate whether there is contusion of eyeball and orbital tissues, whether there is associated prolapse or loss of intraocular tissue, whether the laceration is a penetrating injury, whether it is with or without a foreign body, whether there is avulsion of the eye, and whether the laceration is related to other conditions. The fifth characters indicate unspecified eye, right eye, or left eye. An External cause of morbidity code is assigned for the external cause. Corneal repair is classified as **08Q8XZZ, Repair right cornea, external approach,** or **08Q9XZZ, Repair left cornea, external approach.**

Conjunctivitis

Conjunctivitis (category H10) is an inflammation of the conjunctiva that may be due to infection, allergy, or other cause. When the cause of acute conjunctivitis is a chemical or toxic agent, code H10.21- is used, with a code from categories T51–T65 assigned first to identify the chemical agent and intent (e.g., accidental, assault).

Giant papillary conjunctivitis, also called contact lens–induced papillary conjunctivitis, is a common complication of contact lens wear. It is an inflammation resulting from an allergic reaction to contact lenses. Chronic giant papillary conjunctivitis is classified to subcategory H10.41-. Vernal conjunctivitis (H10.44) is due to an allergic reaction to pollen. Acute toxic conjunctivitis is classified to H10.21-, with a code from categories T51–T65 assigned first to identify the chemical and intent. Conjunctivitis due to chlamydia is classified to A74.0 or to A71.1 when designated as due to trachoma.

Disorders of conjunctivochalasis are reported using code H11.82-. This is a situation in which redundant conjunctiva lies over the lower eyelid margin and covers the lower punctum. It can create a variety of symptoms, from aggravation of a dry eye at the mild stage to disruption of the normal flow of tears at the moderate stage to exposure problems at the severe stage. Treatment consists of a simple local surgical excision to relieve the symptoms.

Code **H16.21-, Exposure keratoconjunctivitis,** is assigned for dry eye related to Bell's palsy. Code **H04.12-, Dry eye syndrome,** is provided by the Index for dry eye syndrome, a disorder of the lacrimal gland. Code H04.12-, however, is inappropriate for the dry eye associated with Bell's palsy, which does not involve the lacrimal gland but is due to exposure to the air resulting from the inability to close the eye as a result of the acute severe facial paralysis of Bell's palsy.

EXERCISE 18.5

Code the following diagnoses. Do not assign External cause of morbidity codes.

1. Intermittent monocular esotropia right eye — H50.311
2. Senile entropion, left upper eyelid — H02.034
3. Blepharoptosis, congenital, bilateral — Q10.0
4. Ectropion due to cicatrix left upper eyelid — H02.114
5. Conjunctivochalasis, bilateral — H11.823

Cataracts

In coding cataracts the coder must avoid making assumptions about the type of cataract based on the patient's age or other conditions. A cataract in an older patient is not necessarily senile or mature; the coder should be alert to the terminology used in the diagnostic statement. Cataracts in patients with diabetes are most often senile; a true diabetic cataract is rare, and its code should not be assigned unless the physician clearly identifies it as such.

EXERCISE 18.6

Code the following diagnoses. Do not assign External cause of morbidity codes.

1. True diabetic cataract in type 1 diabetes mellitus — E10.36
2. Incipient senile cataract, right eye — H25.091
   Diabetes mellitus, type 2 — E11.9
3. Myotonic cataract with Thomsen's disease — G71.12
   H28

4.	Steroid-induced cataract, bilateral Long-term use of Prednisone for chronic obstructive asthma	H26.33 T38.0x5S J44.9 Z79.52
5.	Trauma to the left eye six years ago, causing left cataract and mydriasis	H26.102 H57.04 S05.92xS

Glaucoma

Glaucoma is an eye disease characterized by increased intraocular pressure that causes pathological changes in the optic disk and defects in the field of vision. Category H40, Glaucoma, uses a third, fourth, or fifth character to classify glaucoma by type and, to provide more specificity, a fifth or sixth character to identify the affected eye. In addition, codes in subcategories H40.1-, H40.20-, H40.22-, H40.3-, H40.4-, H40.5-, and H40.6- require a seventh character for the stage (unspecified, mild, moderate, severe, or indeterminate). Assign as many codes from category H40 as needed to identify the type of glaucoma, the affected eye, and the glaucoma stage.

It is possible for a patient to have bilateral glaucoma, with each eye being of the same or different types, and the same or different glaucoma stages in each eye. Specific guidelines have been created to address the coding of these situations. The guidelines largely vary on the basis of whether the classification distinguishes laterality (i.e., subcategories H40.10-, H40.11-, and H40.20-). Table 18.1 summarizes these guidelines.

When a patient is admitted with glaucoma and the stage of the glaucoma progresses during the admission, only the code for the highest stage documented is coded. Care should be taken not to confuse a glaucoma in which the stage is unspecified or not documented (seventh character "0") with a glaucoma stage documented as "indeterminate" (seventh character "4"). The assignment of the "indeterminate" stage should be based on clinical documentation and is reserved for glaucomas whose stage cannot clinically be determined.

Category H42, Glaucoma in diseases classified elsewhere, requires that the underlying condition be coded first, for example, amyloidosis (E85.-), aniridia (Q13.1), or specified metabolic disorder (E70–E88). Glaucoma in diabetes mellitus is classified to the type of diabetes (E08–E13) with -.39. Note that glaucoma in syphilis is coded to **A52.71, Late syphilitic oculopathy,** while tuberculous glaucoma is classified to **A18.59, Other tuberculosis of eye.**

Aqueous misdirection was formerly known as malignant glaucoma. No true malignancy is associated with this type of glaucoma. Aqueous misdirection is characterized by fluid buildup in the back of the eye, pushing the lens and iris forward, blocking off the drain, and thereby increasing the intraocular pressure. This condition is extremely difficult to treat and often requires surgical intervention. Code **H40.83-, Aqueous misdirection,** is used to report this condition.

TABLE 18.1 Coding of Glaucoma

Bilateral Glaucoma	Classification Distinguishes Laterality	Classification Does Not Distinguish Laterality
Same type and stage	Assign one code for the type of glaucoma, bilateral, with the seventh character for the stage. **Example:** Bilateral chronic angle-closure glaucoma, mild stage H40.2231	Assign one code for the type of glaucoma, with the seventh character for the stage. **Example:** Bilateral open-angle glaucoma, mild stage H40.10x1
Same type, but different stage	Assign codes for the type of glaucoma for each eye, with the seventh character for the specific stage rather than the code for bilateral glaucoma. **Example:** Bilateral chronic angle-closure glaucoma, mild stage right eye, moderate stage left eye H40.2211 + H40.2222	Assign codes for the type of glaucoma for each eye, with seventh character for the specific stage. **Example:** Bilateral open-angle glaucoma, mild stage right eye, moderate stage left eye H40.10x1 + H40.10x2
Different type, but same stage	Assign appropriate code for each eye rather than the code for bilateral glaucoma. **Example:** Chronic-angle closure glaucoma, mild stage left eye, low tension open-angle glaucoma, mild stage right eye H40.2221 + H40.1211	Assign codes for the specific type of glaucoma for each eye, with the seventh character for the stage. **Example:** Open-angle glaucoma, mild stage right eye, primary angle-closure glaucoma, mild stage left eye H40.10x1 + H40.20x1

EXERCISE 18.7

Code the following diagnoses. Do not assign External cause of morbidity codes.

1. Glaucoma secondary to posterior dislocation of lens, right eye — H40.51x0, H27.131
2. Exophthalmos secondary to thyrotoxicosis — E05.00
3. Acute narrow-angle glaucoma, right eye — H40.211
   Chronic severe stage narrow-angle glaucoma, left eye — H40.2223
4. Primary open-angle glaucoma, moderate stage, bilateral — H40.11x2

DISEASES OF THE EAR AND MASTOID PROCESS

Chapter 8 of ICD-10-CM, Diseases of the Ear and Mastoid Process, includes diseases of the external ear (H60–H62), diseases of the middle ear and mastoid (H65–H75), diseases of the inner ear (H80–H83), other disorders of the ear (H90–H94), and intraoperative and postprocedural complications and disorders of the ear and mastoid process not elsewhere classified (H95).

Otitis

Otitis is a general term for infection or inflammation of the ear. Symptoms may include chills, drainage from the ear, earache, buzzing, hearing loss, malaise, irritability, itching or discomfort in the ear or ear canal, nausea, and vomiting. Otitis can affect the inner or outer parts of the ear.

ICD-10-CM classifies otitis to the following categories on the basis of whether it affects the external or middle ear and whether it occurs suddenly and for a short time (acute) or repeatedly over a long period of time (chronic):

H60 Otitis externa
H61 Other disorders of external ear
H62 Diseases of external ear in diseases classified elsewhere
H65 Nonsuppurative otitis media
H66 Suppurative and unspecified otitis media
H67 Otitis media in diseases classified elsewhere

For otitis externa (category H60), additional characters provide further specificity regarding the condition, such as infective and noninfective (chemical, actinic, reactive, or eczematoid). Category H65, Nonsuppurative otitis media, is further divided to provide specificity for acute, subacute, or chronic, whether serous, allergic, or mucoid. Suppurative and unspecified otitis media (H66.-) is further subdivided to identify whether the condition is acute or chronic and whether there is spontaneous rupture of the ear drum.

FIGURE 18.3 The Ear

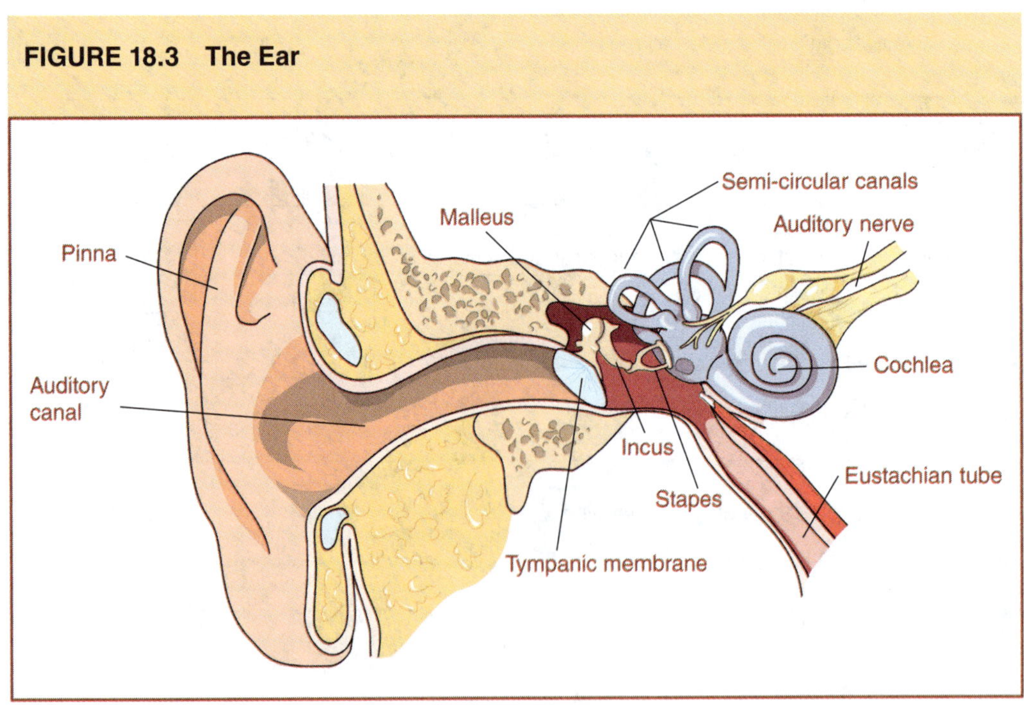

Deafness and Hearing Loss

Hearing loss may be unilateral or bilateral. Most hearing loss is classified in one of three ways:

- Conductive (H90.0–H90.2), with decrease due to a defect in the conductive apparatus of the ear (also called conduction deafness)
- Sensorineural (H90.3–H90.5), with the loss due to a defect in the sensory mechanism of the ear or nerves
- Mixed conductive and sensorineural hearing loss (H90.6–H90.8)

Other classifications of hearing loss are related to the underlying cause, such as the following:

- Ototoxic hearing loss (H91.0-) caused by ingestion of toxic substances. This type of hearing loss requires that code T36–T65 with fifth or sixth character 1–4 or 6 be assigned first when it is a poisoning. Code T36–T50 with fifth or sixth character 5 is assigned as an additional code when it is an adverse effect.
- Presbycusis (H91.1-), or age-related hearing loss with gradually progressing inability to hear. It is considered a sensorineural hearing loss.
- Sudden idiopathic hearing loss (H91.2-), or sudden, unexplained hearing loss.

EXERCISE 18.8

Code the following diagnoses and procedures. Do not assign External cause of morbidity codes.

1. Congenital external canal atresia — Q16.1
2. Bilateral otitis media due to measles — B05.3
3. Sensory hearing loss, bilateral — H90.3
4. Mixed conductive and sensorineural deafness, bilateral — H90.6
5. Perforation of tympanic membrane due to chronic suppurative otitis media, right ear — H66.3x1, H72.91
6. Acute suppurative otitis media, with spontaneous tear of ear drum, right ear — H66.011

Coding of Diseases of the Respiratory, Digestive, and Genitourinary Systems

CHAPTER 19

Diseases of the Respiratory System

CHAPTER OVERVIEW

- Respiratory diseases are classified in chapter 10 of ICD-10-CM.
- Pneumonia is a common infection that is coded several ways.
  - It is coded in combination with the responsible organism.
  - It is coded as a dual classification.
- Influenza may be coded alone or in combination with other codes.
- Chronic obstructive pulmonary disease (COPD) is always caused by another condition.
- Asthma is classified with a fourth character to indicate type and a fifth character to indicate exacerbation or status asthmaticus.
- Pleural effusion is almost always integral to other diseases. Only the code for the underlying disease is assigned.
- Respiratory failure is always due to an underlying condition. Therefore, it is important to be sure that the principal diagnosis and secondary diagnosis are properly assigned.
- Acute pulmonary edema is divided into two categories.
  - Those acute pulmonary edemas of cardiogenic origin take codes that are related to heart failure.
  - Those of noncardiogenic origin take a variety of codes, such as for drowning.
- Procedures involving the respiratory system have a large section of codes. Some of these procedures include biopsies of the bronchus and lung, ablation, thoracoscopic, open, mechanical ventilation, and respiratory assistance not considered mechanical.

LEARNING OUTCOMES

After studying this chapter you should be able to:

- Classify the variety of pneumonia that you will encounter as a coder.
- Determine the correct coding of COPD based on the documented diagnosis.
- Know when to code for respiratory failure as the principal or secondary diagnosis.
- Know how to classify both cardiogenic and noncardiogenic acute pulmonary edemas.
- Code procedures commonly used to treat respiratory system diseases.

TERMS TO KNOW

Acute pulmonary edema
excessive fluid in the tissue and alveolar spaces of the lung

Atelectasis
a collapse of lung tissue; an integral part of pulmonary disease

Bronchospasm
a sudden constriction of the muscles in the walls of the bronchioles

COPD
chronic obstructive pulmonary disease; a general term describing conditions (e.g., emphysema, asthma, chronic bronchitis) that result in an airway obstruction

Pleural effusion
accumulation of fluid within the pleural spaces

REMEMBER . . .

You should only code for avian influenza or other novel influenza A if the case is confirmed. Modifiers such as "suspected" are not adequate to establish a classification.

INTRODUCTION

Except for neoplastic diseases and some major infectious diseases, respiratory diseases are classified in categories J00 through J99 in chapter 10 of ICD-10-CM. Note that *Streptococcus* and *Neisseria* are normal flora for the respiratory system; therefore, their presence does not indicate an infection unless they are seriously out of control. A respiratory infection cannot be assumed from a laboratory report alone; physician concurrence and documentation are necessary. Remember also that infectious organisms are not always identified by laboratory examination, particularly when antibiotic therapy has been started; an infection code may be assigned without laboratory evidence when it is supported by clinical documentation.

PNEUMONIA

Pneumonia is a common respiratory infection that is coded in several ways in ICD-10-CM. Combination codes that account for both pneumonia and the responsible organism are included in chapters 1 and 10 of ICD-10-CM. Examples of appropriate codes for pneumonia include the following:

J15.0	Pneumonia due to *Klebsiella*
J15.211	Pneumonia due to *Staphylococcus aureus*
A02.22	Salmonella pneumonia
B05.2	Post-measles pneumonia
J11.08 + J12.9	Viral pneumonia with influenza

FIGURE 19.1 The Respiratory System

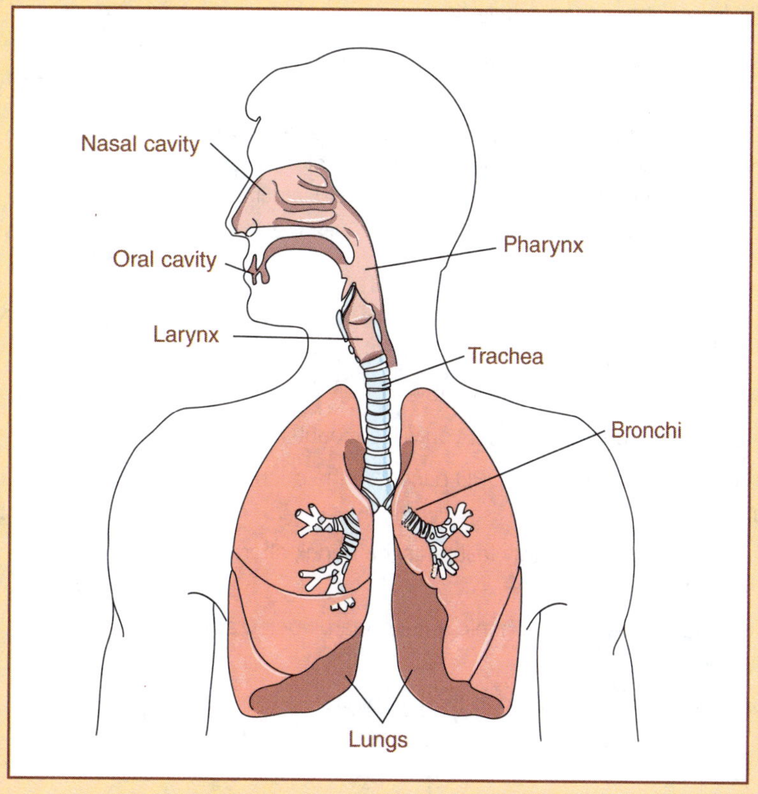

Other pneumonias are coded as manifestations of underlying infections classified in chapter 1, and two codes are required in such cases. Examples of this dual classification coding include the following:

I00 + J17	Pneumonia in rheumatic fever
B65.9 + J17	Pneumonia due to schistosomiasis

When the diagnostic statement is pneumonia without any further specification, the coder should review laboratory reports for mention of the causative organism and check with the physician to determine whether there appears to be support for a more definitive diagnosis. When the organism is not identified, code **J18.9, Pneumonia, unspecified organism,** is assigned.

Lobar Pneumonia

A diagnosis of "lobar pneumonia" (pneumonia that mentions the affected lobe) or "multilobar pneumonia" (pneumonia affecting more than one lobe) describes the specific site of the pneumonia and should be coded according to the responsible organism, if known. If the provider is unable to identify the organism causing the lobar or multilobar pneumonia, assign code **J18.1, Lobar pneumonia, unspecified organism.** Examples include:

J13	Left lobar pneumococcal pneumonia
J15.211	Multilobar staphylococcal aureus pneumonia
J18.1	Lobar pneumonia

Interstitial Lung Diseases

Interstitial lung diseases are a group of scarring diseases of the lung of unknown etiology with distinctive presentation, pathophysiology, and clinical course. Subcategories J84.1–J84.9 provide codes for several specific types. For example:

J84.112	Idiopathic pulmonary fibrosis
J84.113	Idiopathic non-specific interstitial pneumonitis
J84.114	Acute interstitial pneumonitis
J84.115	Respiratory bronchiolitis interstitial lung disease
J84.116	Cryptogenic organizing pneumonia
J84.2	Lymphoid interstitial pneumonia
J84.89	Bronchiolitis obliterans organized pneumonia

Childhood interstitial lung disease (subcategory J84.84-) is rarer than interstitial lung disease in adults and is typically associated with respiratory distress, diffuse infiltrates on chest imaging, and abnormal lung histology. Codes for childhood interstitial lung disease include:

J84.841	Neuroendocrine cell hyperplasia of infancy
J84.842	Pulmonary interstitial glycogenosis
J84.843	Alveolar capillary dysplasia with vein misalignment
J84.848	Other interstitial lung diseases of childhood

If not more specifically identified, interstitial pneumonia is classified in ICD-10-CM as **J84.9, Interstitial pulmonary disease, unspecified.**

Lymphoid interstitial pneumonia (J84.2) is a rare disorder with lymphocytic infiltration of the alveolar interstitium and air spaces. It is the most common cause of pulmonary disease after *Pneumocystis* infection in human immunodeficiency virus (HIV)–positive children. It most often occurs in children with HIV infection and in people of any age with an autoimmune disorder.

Plasma cell interstitial pneumonia is an acute and highly contagious pneumonia caused by *Pneumocystis carinii*. It is coded as **B59, Pneumocystosis.** This condition is frequently seen in patients with acquired immunodeficiency syndrome (AIDS) and is a major cause of death among AIDS patients. When associated with AIDS, code B20 is sequenced first with an additional code of B59. This type of pneumonia is not limited to patients with AIDS, however; it may develop in patients with immunocompromised states due to other causes, such as cancer, severe malnutrition, and debility. It may also occur in patients treated with certain types of immunosuppressive drugs after undergoing organ transplantation or cancer treatment. Never assume that this code should be assigned because the patient's condition is severe enough to warrant admission to the hospital. Interstitial pneumonia is classified as B59 only when specifically diagnosed by the physician as plasma cell pneumonia, pneumocystosis, or pneumonia caused by *Pneumocystis carinii*.

Legionnaires' Disease

Legionnaires' disease (A48.1) is a type of pneumonia that is almost always caused by inhalation of aerosols that come from a contaminated water source. This disease usually occurs as single, isolated cases not associated with any recognized outbreak. The fatality rate of Legionnaires' disease has ranged from 5 percent to 30 percent during various outbreaks.

Gram-Negative Pneumonia

Gram-negative pneumonia not elsewhere classified is classified as **J15.6, Pneumonia due to other aerobic Gram-negative bacteria,** or **J15.8, Pneumonia due to other specified bacteria,** when it is specified as anaerobic. When the organism has been identified, the Alphabetic Index may provide a more specific code. A gram-negative organism is one that develops a particular type of stain on testing and is considered part of a group of organisms that require careful management. Gram-positive pneumonia, not otherwise qualified, is classified as **J15.9, Unspecified bacterial pneumonia.** Gram-positive pneumonia is far easier to treat, and requires the expenditure of fewer resources, than gram-negative pneumonia.

Gram-negative pneumonia most often affects people who are hospitalized, infants, the elderly, alcoholics, and patients with chronic diseases, particularly immune system disorders. These bacteria rarely infect the lungs of healthy adults. The symptoms of gram-negative bacterial pneumonia are similar to those for gram-positive pneumonia. However, patients with gram-negative pneumonia tend to be sicker, and their condition deteriorates quickly because the bacteria can rapidly destroy lung tissue. About 25 to 50 percent of patients with gram-negative pneumonia die, in spite of treatment.

Note, however, that a diagnosis of gram-negative or other bacterial pneumonia cannot be assumed on the basis of the presence of laboratory or clinical findings alone; only the physician can determine the diagnosis. Such findings can, however, help document a diagnosis or serve as the basis for a query to the doctor.

Aspergillosis

Pneumonia due to infectious aspergillosis is classified as code **B44.9, Aspergillosis, unspecified.** Allergic bronchopulmonary or pulmonary aspergillosis, however, occurs as an eosinophilic pneumonia caused by an allergic reaction to the aspergillosis fungus, commonly found on dead leaves, bird droppings, compost stacks, or other decaying vegetation. Code **B44.81, Allergic bronchopulmonary aspergillosis,** is assigned for this allergic condition.

Aspiration Pneumonia

Aspiration pneumonia is a severe type of pneumonia resulting from the inhalation of foods, liquids, oils, vomitus, or microorganisms from the upper respiratory tract or the oropharyngeal area. Pneumonitis due to inhalation of foods or vomitus is coded to J69.0, that due to inhalation of oils and essences to J69.1, and that due to inhalation of other solids or liquids to J69.8. Pneumonia due to aspiration of microorganisms is classified to bacterial or viral pneumonia in category J15 or J12. Patients transferred from a nursing home to an acute care hospital because of pneumonia are often suffering from aspiration pneumonia due to aspirated organisms, usually gram-negative bacteria.

Ventilator-Associated Pneumonia

Pneumonia associated with the use of a ventilator is assigned to code **J95.851, Ventilator associated pneumonia.** In addition, a code to identify the organism, if known (B95.-, B96.-, B97.-) should be assigned. Do not assign an additional code from categories J12 through J18 to identify the type of pneumonia. For example, ventilator-associated pneumonia (VAP) due to *Staphylococcus aureus* is coded to J95.851 and B95.61. Code J95.851 should be assigned only when the provider has documented VAP. As with all procedural or postprocedural complications, code assignment is based on the provider's documentation of the relationship between the condition and the procedure. J95.851 should not be assigned for cases where the patient has pneumonia and is on mechanical ventilation, and where the provider has not specifically stated that the pneumonia is VAP. The provider should be queried when the documentation is unclear.

It is clinically possible for a patient to be admitted with one type of pneumonia and to develop VAP later. The principal diagnosis is the type of pneumonia diagnosed at the time of admission (J12–J18), and code J95.851 is a secondary diagnosis.

EXERCISE 19.1

Code the following diagnoses. Do not assign External cause of morbidity codes.

1. Lobar pneumonia with influenza	J11.00 J18.1
2. Pneumonia, bacterial, left upper lobe	J15.9
3. Klebsiella pneumonia	J15.0
4. Postinfectional pneumonia	B99.9 J17
5. Acute pneumococcal lobar pneumonia	J13
6. Perihilar viral pneumonia	J12.9

7. Pneumonia due to chlamydia		J16.0
Intermittent positive-pressure breathing (IPPB), 4 hours	Assistance	5A09358
8. Aspiration pneumonia due to aspiration of vomitus		J69.0
9. Plasma cell interstitial pneumonia due to AIDS		B20
		B59
10. Pneumonia due to pulmonary coccidioidomycosis		B38.2

INFLUENZA

ICD-10-CM classifies influenza due to certain identified influenza viruses to category J09. Subcategory J09.x- is used to report avian influenza, bird influenza, influenza A/H5N1, influenza of other animal origin (not bird or swine), and swine influenza virus. Category J10 is used to report influenza due to other identified influenza virus, and category J11 is used for influenza due to unidentified influenza virus.

Influenza in combination with any form of pneumonia or bronchopneumonia is assigned to influenza with pneumonia (J09.x1, J10.00–J10.08, and J11.00–J11.08). For codes J09.x1, J10.08, and J11.08, code also the other specified type of pneumonia. Influenza with other types of respiratory manifestations are classifiable to J09.x2, J10.1, and J11.1, and include upper respiratory infection, laryngitis, pharyngitis, and pleural effusion. Influenza may also involve body systems other than the respiratory system, such as the gastrointestinal tract (J09.x3, J10.2, and J11.2), and other manifestations such as encephalopathy, myocarditis, and otitis media (J09.x9, J10.81–J10.89, and J11.81–J11.89).

Similar to the guidelines for coding HIV infection, codes from categories J09 and J10 should be assigned only for confirmed cases of avian flu or other novel influenza A, or for other identified influenza virus. In this context, "confirmation" does not require documentation of positive laboratory testing; however, it does require provider documentation of avian influenza or other novel influenza A.

A code from categories J09 or J10 is not assigned when the diagnostic statement indicates that the infection is "suspected," "possible," "likely," or "?". This advice is an exception to the general guideline that directs the coder to assign a code for a diagnosis qualified as "suspected" or "possible" as if it were established. Instead, a code from category J11, Influenza due to unidentified influenza virus, should be assigned.

LARYNGITIS AND TRACHEITIS

Category J04, Acute laryngitis and tracheitis, has unique subcategories for laryngitis, tracheitis, and laryngotracheitis; the exception of acute laryngitis and laryngotracheitis, with and without obstruction, is identified at the code level.

The diagnosis of supraglottitis may represent any of the codes within category J04. It is an infection of the supraglottic structures that affects the lingual tonsillar areas, epiglottic folds, false vocal cords, and the epiglottis. Because the infection covers all the supraglottic structures, the term "supraglottitis" is nonspecific. Supraglottitis is an acute, life-threatening upper respiratory infection. It seems to occur primarily in children but can be rapidly fatal to individuals in all age groups. This fatal event appears to result from an edematous epiglottis that is obstructing the airway. Subcategory J04.3 is used for supraglottitis when the term is used and a specific site of infection is not identified; a fifth character is used to indicate the presence or absence of obstruction. The codes for the conditions affecting the supraglottic structures are as follows:

J04.0 Acute laryngitis
J04.1 Acute tracheitis
    J04.10 Acute tracheitis without obstruction
    J04.11 Acute tracheitis with obstruction
J04.2 Acute laryngotracheitis
J04.3 Supraglottitis, unspecified
    J04.30 Supraglottitis, unspecified, without obstruction
    J04.31 Supraglottitis, unspecified, with obstruction

Acute obstructive laryngitis, or croup (J05.0), occurs in young children, usually between the ages of three and six. The manifestations are a high-pitched cough and difficulty in breathing, due to a spasm or swelling of the larynx. It can be caused by an acute infection (especially by the influenza virus or diphtheria bacterium), an allergy, a tumor of the larynx, or obstruction by a swallowed object.

Acute epiglottitis refers to a severe, rapidly progressing bacterial infection of the upper respiratory tract. Symptoms include sore throat, croupy stridor, and inflamed epiglottis, which may result in sudden respiratory obstruction and possibly death. The condition affects young children between the ages of two and seven. The infection is generally caused by *Haemophilus influenzae,* type B, although streptococci may occasionally be the causative agents. Acute epiglottitis is coded to subcategory J05.1, with a fifth character to indicate the presence or absence of obstruction. Both categories J04 and J05 use an additional code (B95–B97) to specifically identify the infectious agent.

CHRONIC OBSTRUCTIVE PULMONARY DISEASE

Chronic obstructive pulmonary disease (COPD) is a general term used to describe a variety of conditions that result in obstruction of the airway. ICD-10-CM classifies these conditions to category J44, Other chronic obstructive pulmonary disease. Category J44 includes the following conditions:

- Asthma with chronic obstructive pulmonary disease
- Chronic asthmatic (obstructive) bronchitis
- Chronic bronchitis with airways obstruction
- Chronic bronchitis with emphysema
- Chronic emphysematous bronchitis
- Chronic obstructive asthma
- Chronic obstructive bronchitis
- Chronic obstructive tracheobronchitis

Category J44 is further subdivided to specify whether there is an acute lower respiratory infection (J44.0) and whether there is an exacerbation of the condition (J44.1). If applicable, a code from category J45 is assigned to specify the type of asthma. In the case of code **J44.0, Chronic obstructive pulmonary disease with acute lower respiratory infection,** an additional code should

be reported to identify the infection. The codes in category J44 distinguish between uncomplicated cases (J44.9) and those in acute exacerbation (J44.1). An acute exacerbation is a worsening or a decompensation of a chronic condition. An acute exacerbation is not equivalent to an infection superimposed on a chronic condition, though an exacerbation may be triggered by an infection. For example, COPD with acute bronchitis should be coded to J44.0, rather than J44.1.

Examples of the terms classified to **J44.1, Chronic obstructive pulmonary disease with (acute) exacerbation,** are "exacerbation," "in exacerbation," "decompensated," "acute exacerbation," "exacerbated," or "uncompensated." When the diagnosis is stated only as COPD, the coder should review the medical record to determine whether a more definitive diagnosis is documented. Code **J44.9, Chronic obstructive pulmonary disease, unspecified,** is assigned only when a more specific code cannot be assigned.

In addition to codes in category J44, codes may also be assigned to identify exposure to environmental tobacco smoke (Z77.22), history of tobacco use (Z87.891), occupational exposure to environmental tobacco smoke (Z57.31), tobacco dependence (F17.-), or tobacco use (Z72.0).

Note that emphysema without chronic bronchitis is coded to J43.-, and chronic bronchitis not otherwise specified is classified to J42.

Asthma

Asthma is a bronchial hypersensitivity characterized by mucosal edema, constriction of bronchial musculature, and excessive viscid edema. Manifestations of asthma are wheezing, dyspnea out of proportion to exertion, and cough. A diagnosis of wheezing alone is not classified as asthma; code R06.2 is assigned in such a case. Asthma is classified into category J45, with a fourth character indicating the severity (mild intermittent, mild persistent, moderate persistent, severe persistent, other, and unspecified) and a final character indicating whether it is uncomplicated or whether status asthmaticus or exacerbation is present.

Status asthmaticus is defined in slightly different ways by different authorities, but in general it represents a patient who continues to have extreme wheezing in spite of conventional therapy or has suffered from an acute asthmatic attack in which the degree of obstruction is not relieved by the usual therapeutic measures. Early status asthmaticus represents patients who are refractory to treatment or who fail to respond to the usual therapies; advanced status asthmaticus represents patients who show full development of an asthma attack that could result in respiratory failure, with signs and symptoms of hypercapnia (excess carbon dioxide in the blood). The final character "2" is assigned for both types of status asthmaticus. Use of this final character usually indicates a medical emergency for treatment of acute, severe asthma. Other terms used to describe status asthmaticus include the following:

- Intractable asthma attack
- Refractory asthma
- Severe, intractable wheezing
- Airway obstruction not relieved by bronchodilators
- Severe, prolonged asthmatic attack

The coder should never assume that status asthmaticus is present without a specific statement from the provider. However, asthma described as acute, characterized by prolonged or severe intractable wheezing, or asthma being treated by the administration of adrenal corticosteroids should alert the coder that status asthmaticus may exist and that the provider should be asked whether the diagnosis is to be added.

Exacerbations of asthma are acute or subacute episodes of progressively worsening shortness of breath, cough, wheezing, and chest tightness—or some combination of these symptoms. The final character "1" is used for asthma referred to as "exacerbated" or in "acute exacerbation."

Asthma characterized as obstructive or diagnosed in conjunction with COPD is classified to category J44, Other chronic obstructive pulmonary disease. Code also the type of asthma (J45.-) if applicable. An asthma code with a final character "1," with acute exacerbation, may *not* be assigned with an asthma code with a final character "2," with status asthmaticus. When there is documentation of both acute exacerbation and status asthmaticus, only the code with the final character "2" should be assigned.

A diagnosis of asthmatic bronchitis without further specification is coded as J45.9-. If the diagnosis is stated as exacerbated or acute chronic asthmatic bronchitis, code J44.1 is assigned. A diagnosis of asthmatic bronchitis with COPD or chronic asthmatic bronchitis is coded to J44.9. Examples of coding for asthma include the following:

J45.902	Asthmatic bronchitis with status asthmaticus
J45.909	Childhood asthma
J44.9 + J45.909	Asthma with COPD
J44.1 + J45.901	Chronic asthmatic bronchitis with acute exacerbation
J45.909 + F54	Psychogenic asthma

Bronchospasm

Bronchospasm is an integral part of asthma or any other type of chronic airway obstruction, but no additional code is assigned to indicate its presence. Code **J98.01, Acute bronchospasm,** is assigned only when the underlying cause has not been identified.

EXERCISE 19.2

Code the following diagnoses. Do not assign External cause of morbidity codes.

1. Bronchial asthma, allergic, due to house dust — J45.909
2. Chronic bronchitis with decompensated COPD — J44.1
3. Acute exacerbation of chronic asthmatic bronchitis — J44.1
4. Emphysema — J43.9
5. Chronic obstructive lung disease with acute exacerbation — J44.1
6. Emphysema with chronic obstructive bronchitis — J44.9

7. Mild intermittent asthma with status asthmaticus J45.22

8. Acute bronchitis with acute bronchiectasis J47.0

9. Perforated right tympanic membrane due to influenza with otitis media J11.83 H72.91

10. Exacerbation of severe persistent asthma J45.51

ATELECTASIS

Atelectasis is a very common finding in chest X-rays and other radiological studies. It is a condition where the alveoli are deflated. It may be caused by normal exhalation or by several medical conditions. Atelectasis reduces the ventilatory function. Pulmonary collapse can be a severe problem, but mild atelectasis usually has little effect on the patient's condition or the therapy provided. Slight strands of atelectasis are often noted on X-ray reports, but this finding is generally of little clinical importance and is usually not further evaluated or treated. Code **J98.11, Atelectasis,** should not be assigned on the basis of an X-ray finding alone; it should be coded only when the physician identifies it as a clinical condition that meets the criteria for a reportable diagnosis.

PLEURAL EFFUSION

Pleural effusion is an abnormal accumulation of fluid within the pleural spaces. It occurs in association with pulmonary disease and certain cardiac conditions, such as congestive heart failure, or certain diseases involving other organs. It is almost always integral to the underlying disease and is usually addressed only by treatment of that condition. In this situation, only the code for the underlying disease is assigned. However, occasionally the effusion is addressed separately, with additional diagnostic studies such as decubitus X-ray or diagnostic thoracentesis. The effusion may be treated by therapeutic thoracentesis, or chest-tube drainage. When treatment is addressed only to the pleural effusion, it can be designated as the principal diagnosis; otherwise, it can be assigned as an additional code when it is further evaluated or treated. Pleural effusion noted only on an X-ray report is not reported.

Pleural effusion due to tuberculosis is classified to A15.6 unless it is due to primary progressive tuberculosis (A15.7). Pleural effusion due to systemic lupus erythematosus is coded to **M32.13, Lung involvement in systemic lupus erythematosus.** Pleural effusion in heart failure is not coded separately; only the code for the heart failure (I50.-) is assigned. Influenzal pleural effusion is coded to influenza, with respiratory manifestations (J09.x2, J10.1, or J11.1), with code **J91.8, Pleural effusion in other conditions classified elsewhere,** to specify the associated pleural effusion.

Malignant pleural effusion can occur due to impaired pleural lymphatic drainage from a mediastinal tumor (especially in lymphomas) and not because of direct tumor invasion into the pleura. Malignant pleural effusion is coded to J91.0 with the underlying neoplasm assigned as the first-listed or principal diagnosis.

RESPIRATORY FAILURE

Respiratory failure is a life-threatening condition that is always due to an underlying condition. It may be the final pathway of a disease process or a combination of different processes. Respiratory failure can result from either acute or chronic diseases that cause airway obstruction, parenchymal infiltration, or pulmonary edema. It can arise from an abnormality in any of the components of the respiratory system, central nervous system, peripheral nervous system, respiratory muscles, and chest wall muscles. The diagnosis is based largely on arterial blood gas analysis findings, which vary from individual to individual, depending on several factors. The coder should never assume a diagnosis of respiratory failure without a documented diagnosis by the physician. Respiratory failure is classified as acute (J96.0-), chronic (J96.1-), acute and chronic combined (J96.2-), or unspecified (J96.9-) and a fifth character that specifies whether hypoxia or hypercapnia is present. When respiratory failure follows surgery, code **J95.821, Acute postprocedural respiratory failure,** or code **J95.822, Acute and chronic postprocedural respiratory failure,** is assigned.

Careful review of the medical record is required for the coding and sequencing of respiratory failure. The coder must review the circumstances of admission to determine the principal diagnosis. Code **J96.00, Acute respiratory failure, unspecified whether with hypoxia or hypercapnia,** or code **J96.20, Acute and chronic respiratory failure, unspecified whether with hypoxia or hypercapnia,** may be assigned as a principal diagnosis when it is the condition established after study to be chiefly responsible for occasioning the admission to the hospital, and the selection is supported by the Alphabetic Index and Tabular List. Respiratory failure may be listed as a secondary diagnosis if it develops after admission.

When a patient is admitted with respiratory failure and another acute condition (e.g., myocardial infarction, aspiration pneumonia, cerebrovascular accident), the principal diagnosis will depend on the individual patient's situation and what caused the admission of the patient to the hospital. This guideline applies regardless of whether the other acute condition is a respiratory or nonrespiratory condition. The physician should be queried for clarification if the documentation is unclear as to which one of the two conditions was the reason for the admission. The guideline regarding two or more diagnoses equally meeting the definition of principal diagnosis (Section II, C) may be applied in situations when both the respiratory failure and the other acute condition are equally responsible for occasioning the admission to the hospital. Examples are the following.

EXAMPLE 1: A patient with chronic myasthenia gravis goes into acute exacerbation and develops acute respiratory failure. The patient is admitted due to the respiratory failure.

Principal diagnosis:	J96.00	Acute respiratory failure, unspecified whether with hypoxia or hypercapnia
Secondary diagnosis:	G70.01	Myasthenia gravis with (acute) exacerbation

EXAMPLE 2: A patient with emphysema develops acute respiratory failure. The patient is admitted through the emergency department for treatment of the respiratory failure.

Principal diagnosis:	J96.00	Acute respiratory failure, unspecified whether with hypoxia or hypercapnia
Secondary diagnosis:	J43.9	Emphysema, unspecified

EXAMPLE 3: A patient arrived in the hospital in acute respiratory failure and hypoxia. The patient was intubated, and the physician documents that the patient is being admitted to the hospital for treatment of the acute respiratory failure with hypoxia. The patient also has congestive heart failure.

Principal diagnosis:	J96.01	Acute respiratory failure with hypoxia
Secondary diagnosis:	I50.9	Heart failure, unspecified

Some ICD-10-CM chapter-specific coding guidelines (e.g., obstetrics, poisoning, HIV, newborn) provide sequencing direction. These guidelines would take precedence over code J96.0- or J96.2- when coding respiratory failure associated with a condition from one of these chapters. Examples are the following.

EXAMPLE 1: A patient is admitted to the hospital postpartum as a result of developing pulmonary embolism leading to respiratory failure.

Principal diagnosis:	O88.23	Thromboembolism in the puerperium
Secondary diagnosis:	J96.00	Acute respiratory failure, unspecified whether with hypoxia or hypercapnia

In example 1 above, the obstetrical code is sequenced first because a chapter-specific guideline (Section I, C, 15, a, 1) provides sequencing directions specifying that chapter 15 codes have sequencing priority over codes from other chapters.

EXAMPLE 2: A patient who is diagnosed as overdosing on crack cocaine is admitted to the hospital with respiratory failure.

Principal diagnosis:	T40.5x4A	Poisoning by cocaine, undetermined, initial encounter
Secondary diagnosis:	J96.00	Acute respiratory failure, unspecified whether with hypoxia or hypercapnia
	F14.10	Cocaine abuse, uncomplicated

In example 2 above, poisoning is sequenced first because a chapter-specific guideline (Section I, C, 19, e, 5, b) provides sequencing directions specifying that the poisoning code is sequenced first, followed by a code for the manifestation. The acute respiratory failure is a manifestation of the poisoning.

EXAMPLE 3: A patient is admitted with respiratory failure due to *Pneumocystis carinii* due to AIDS.

Principal diagnosis:	B20	Human immunodeficiency virus [HIV] disease
Secondary diagnosis:	J96.00	Acute respiratory failure, unspecified whether with hypoxia or hypercapnia
	B59	Pneumocystosis

In example 3, the HIV is sequenced first because a chapter-specific guideline (Section I, C, 1, a, 2, a) provides sequencing directions specifying that if a patient is admitted for an HIV-related condition

(in this case the *Pneumocystis carinii*), the principal diagnosis should be B20, followed by additional diagnosis codes for all reported HIV-related conditions.

In the event that instructional notes in the Tabular List provide sequencing direction, the sequencing of respiratory failure is dependent on these notes. An example follows.

EXAMPLE 4: A patient is admitted to the hospital with severe *Staphylococcus aureus* sepsis and acute respiratory failure.

Principal diagnosis:	A41.01	Sepsis due to *Staphylococcus aureus*
Secondary diagnosis:	R65.20	Severe sepsis without septic shock
	J96.00	Acute respiratory failure, unspecified whether with hypoxia or hypercapnia

Sepsis is sequenced first in this case because an instructional note under subcategory R65.2- indicates to code first the underlying infection. In addition, subcategory R65.2- has a "use additional code" note to specify acute organ dysfunction and lists acute respiratory failure (J96.0-). Following this instruction, respiratory failure is given as a secondary diagnosis.

ACUTE RESPIRATORY DISTRESS SYNDROME

Acute respiratory distress syndrome (ARDS) is a lung condition that leads to low oxygen levels in the blood. ARDS can be life threatening because organs such as the kidneys and brain need oxygen-rich blood for proper functioning. ARDS can occur within 24 to 48 hours of an injury (trauma, burns, aspiration, massive blood transfusion, drug/alcohol abuse) or an acute illness (infectious pneumonia, sepsis, acute pancreatitis). ARDS patients usually present with shortness of breath, tachypnea, and occasionally confusion. Long-term illnesses, such as malaria, can also trigger ARDS, which may then occur sometime after the onset of a particularly acute case of the infection. ARDS is coded to **J80, Acute respiratory distress syndrome.**

ACUTE PULMONARY EDEMA

Acute pulmonary edema is a pathological state in which there is excessive, diffuse accumulation of fluid in the tissues and the alveolar spaces of the lung. It is broadly divided into two categories that reflect the origin of the condition: cardiogenic and noncardiogenic.

Cardiogenic

Acute pulmonary edema of cardiac origin is a manifestation of heart failure and as such is included in the following code assignments:

I50.1	Left ventricular failure
I50.-	Heart failure
I11.-	Hypertensive heart disease
I01.-	Rheumatic heart disease, acute
I09.81	Rheumatic heart failure

Pulmonary edema is not included in the codes for acute myocardial infarction (I21.01–I22.9), acute ischemic heart disease (I24.0–I24.9), or chronic ischemic heart disease (I25.-). When pulmonary edema is present along with a heart condition or failure, the pulmonary edema is assumed to

be associated with left ventricular failure (I50.1) unless the heart failure is described as congestive or decompensated, in which case a code for the more specific congestive heart failure (I50.2–I50.9) is assigned. Pulmonary edema is included in codes I50.-; no additional code is assigned.

Noncardiogenic

Noncardiogenic acute pulmonary edema occurs in the absence of heart failure or other heart disease. It is coded in a variety of ways depending on the cause. When the cause is not specified, code **J81.-, Pulmonary edema,** is assigned. When the cause of the pulmonary edema is known, it is coded as follows:

- Post-radiation pulmonary edema (post-radiation pneumonia) is an inflammation of the lungs due to the adverse effects of radiation. It is coded as **J70.0, Acute pulmonary manifestations due to radiation.**
- Pulmonary edema due to chemicals, gas fumes, or vapors is coded as J68.1.
- Pulmonary edema due to aspiration of water in a near-drowning is coded to **T75.1-, Unspecified effects of drowning and nonfatal submersion.**
- Pulmonary edema due to high altitude is coded as **T70.29-, Other effects of high altitude.**
- Acute pulmonary edema in cases of drug overdose is classified as poisoning, with code J81.0 assigned as an additional code. Any mention of drug dependence or abuse should also be coded.

External cause of morbidity codes should be assigned with any of these codes to indicate the external circumstances involved.

Chronic pulmonary edema or pulmonary edema not otherwise specified that is not of cardiac origin is coded as **J81.1, Chronic pulmonary edema,** unless the Alphabetic Index or the Tabular List instructs otherwise.

Pulmonary edema caused by congestive overloads, such as pulmonary fibrosis (J84.10), congenital stenosis of the pulmonary veins (Q26.8), or pulmonary venous embolism (I26.99), is noncardiogenic. Such conditions are assigned to code J81.0 when described as acute or to code J81.1 when described as chronic or not otherwise specified. Be careful not to confuse this condition with edema associated with heart disease.

SURGICAL PROCEDURES

When assigning ICD-10-PCS codes for procedures performed in the respiratory system, it is important to ensure that the documentation provides information regarding the site where the procedure was performed. Body part values include the specific lobe of the lung (when available), or at a minimum whether the site is the right or left lung, or bilateral lungs. Many of the root operations commonly performed do not provide "unspecified" body part values for when the left or right side is not stated for the lungs, pleura, or diaphragm. Examples of these root operations include "Destruction," "Drainage," "Excision," "Insertion," and "Extirpation."

It is also important to understand the surgical approaches in order to select the correct ICD-10-PCS codes. (For illustrations of such approaches, please refer to figure 8.5 on pages 76–77.) For example, thoracoscopic procedures involve the creation of small incisions into the chest wall and insertion of a thoracoscope through the incision. Thoracoscopic procedures are coded to the approach "percutaneous endoscopic." Procedures stated as "bronchoscopic" involve passing the bronchoscope through the nose (or sometimes the mouth), down the throat, and into the airway. The approach character for bronchoscopic procedures is "via natural or artificial opening endoscopic"

because the procedure involves entering via a natural opening (nose or mouth) and then using an endoscope.

BIOPSIES OF BRONCHUS AND LUNG

An endoscopic biopsy of the bronchus involves passing an endoscope into the lumen of the trachea and bronchus, where a bit of tissue is removed for pathological study. ICD-10-PCS classifies biopsies to the root operation "Excision" and the qualifier "diagnostic." For example, endoscopic excisional biopsy of the right upper lobe bronchus is coded to **0BB48ZX, Excision of right upper lobe bronchus, via natural or artificial opening endoscopic, diagnostic.**

An endoscopic biopsy of the lung is performed by passing the endoscope through the main bronchus into the smaller bronchi and lung alveoli. Either type of biopsy can be performed independently, or both may be performed in the same operative episode, in which case both codes are assigned. The approach character is "via natural or artificial opening endoscopic." For example, endoscopic biopsy of the right middle lobe of the lung is coded to **0BBD8ZX, Excision of right middle lung lobe, via natural or artificial opening endoscopic, diagnostic.**

Another type of lung biopsy is the thoracoscopic biopsy. In this procedure, small incisions are made into the chest wall and a thoracoscope is inserted through them to remove specimens for pathologic examination. The approach for this type of biopsy is "percutaneous endoscopic" because it requires entering through the skin and inserting a scope. For example, thoracoscopic biopsy of the right lung is coded to **0BBK4ZX, Excision of right lung, percutaneous endoscopic approach, diagnostic.**

Bronchoalveolar lavage (BAL), also called "liquid biopsy," should not be confused with whole lung lavage. BAL is a diagnostic procedure performed via a bronchoscope under local anesthesia. It involves washing out alveoli tissue and peripheral airways to obtain a small sampling of tissue. BAL is coded to the root operation "Drainage" because it involves removing fluids. For example, bronchoalveolar lavage of the right lower lobe bronchus of the lung is coded to **0B968ZX, Drainage of right lower lobe bronchus, via natural or artificial opening endoscopic, diagnostic.**

Whole lung lavage is a therapeutic procedure performed for pulmonary alveolar proteinosis. The procedure is performed under general anesthesia and mechanical ventilation. The lungs are lavaged by filling and emptying one lung at a time with saline solution. The second lung is usually lavaged three to seven days after the first lung has been lavaged. Report whole lung lavage using code **3E1F88Z, Irrigation of respiratory tract using irrigating substance, via natural or artificial opening endoscopic.** Assign also a code for the mechanical ventilation provided.

ABLATION OF LUNG

Tumor ablation is an alternative to surgical removal of lung lesions. Ablation can be achieved using extreme heat, freezing chemicals (cryoablation), focused ultrasound, microwaves, or radiofrequency. These procedures are typically performed by interventional radiologists using imaging guidance—such as computed tomography (CT), ultrasound, or fluoroscopy—and inserting a probe directly to the lesion.

ICD-10-PCS classifies ablation procedures under the root operation "Destruction," meaning "physical eradication of all or a portion of a body part by the direct use of energy, force, or a destructive agent." ICD-10-PCS codes for ablation do not distinguish between the different energy sources used to ablate the tumor. Examples include the following:

0B5G0ZZ	Open ablation left upper lung lobe
0B5L3ZZ	Percutaneous ablation left lung
0B5J4ZZ	Thoracoscopic ablation left lower lung lobe

Bronchoscopic ablation (or bronchial thermoplasty ablation) of airway smooth muscle of the lung is a procedure performed to reduce excess airway smooth muscle to treat asthmatic patients. The procedure is performed using a bronchoscope and a catheter to deliver radiofrequency energy into the airways to reduce the constricted airway smooth muscle. This reduction lessens the area that narrows in response to external stimuli such as dust and other allergens. For example, bronchial thermoplasty ablation of the right main bronchus is coded as **0B538ZZ, Destruction of right main bronchus, via natural or artificial opening endoscopic.**

Other examples of common lung procedures include:

0BBD4ZZ	Thoracoscopic excision of lesion right middle lobe
0BBC0ZZ	Open segmental resection of right upper lobe
0BTG0ZZ	Open lobectomy, left upper lobe
0B9N30Z	Percutaneous drainage of right pleura

MECHANICAL VENTILATION

Mechanical ventilation is a process by which the patient's own effort to breathe is augmented or replaced by the use of a mechanical device. ICD-10-PCS classifies mechanical ventilation to the extracorporeal assistance and performance section (first character = 5). Mechanical ventilation may be described as noninvasive when delivered via a noninvasive interface like a face mask, a nasal mask, a nasal pillow, an oral mouthpiece, or an oronasal mask. ICD-10-PCS classifies this type of mechanical ventilation to the root operation "Assistance" because it meets the definition of "taking over a portion of a physiological function by extracorporeal means." Character 5 in this section provides values for the duration of the ventilation, such as less than 24 consecutive hours (value = 3), 24–96 consecutive hours (value = 4), or greater than 96 consecutive hours (value = 5). Character 7, qualifier, specifies the type of ventilation with the following values:

7	Continuous positive airway pressure
8	Intermittent positive airway pressure
9	Continuous negative airway pressure
B	Intermittent negative airway pressure
Z	No qualifier

Coding examples follow:

5A09357	Assistance with respiratory ventilation, less than 24 consecutive hours, continuous positive airway pressure
5A09457	Assistance with respiratory ventilation, 24–96 consecutive hours, continuous positive airway pressure
5A09458	Assistance with respiratory ventilation, 24–96 consecutive hours, intermittent positive airway pressure
5A09559	Assistance with respiratory ventilation, greater than 96 consecutive hours, continuous negative airway pressure
5A0955Z	Assistance with respiratory ventilation, greater than 96 consecutive hours

Mechanical ventilation is considered invasive when the ventilatory assistance is provided via an invasive interface such as endotracheal intubation or tracheostomy and the patient receives mechanical ventilation in an uninterrupted fashion. An endotracheal tube can be placed orally or

nasally. If either intubation or tracheostomy is performed after admission or in the emergency department of the same hospital immediately before admission, it should be reported. Intubation or tracheostomy carried out elsewhere prior to admission or in an ambulance prior to arrival at the hospital cannot be reported even though the ambulance may be operated by the same facility.

Codes for invasive mechanical ventilation are classified to the root operation "Performance" because these procedures completely take over the physiological function of breathing by extracorporeal means. Similar to the root operation "Assistance," character 5 in this section provides values for the duration of the ventilation, such as less than 24 consecutive hours (value = 3), 24–96 consecutive hours (value = 4), or greater than 96 consecutive hours (value = 5).

Examples include the following codes:

5A19054	Respiratory ventilation, single, nonmechanical
5A1935Z	Respiratory ventilation, less than 24 consecutive hours
5A1945Z	Respiratory ventilation, 24–96 consecutive hours
5A1955Z	Respiratory ventilation, greater than 96 consecutive hours

Duration of Mechanical Ventilation

The starting time for calculating the duration begins with one of these events:

- Endotracheal intubation performed in the hospital or hospital emergency room, followed by initiation of mechanical ventilation
- Initiation of mechanical ventilation through tracheostomy performed in the hospital or emergency room
- Admission of a patient who is already on mechanical ventilation after previous intubation or tracheostomy

A tracheal tube is often inserted to keep the tracheostomy open for attachment to the mechanical ventilator. Start counting hours on ventilation only after mechanical ventilation has actually been initiated.

It is occasionally necessary to replace an endotracheal tube because of a problem such as a leak; removal with immediate replacement is considered part of the duration and counting should continue. Patients who are started on mechanical ventilation by means of an endotracheal tube may later receive a tracheostomy through which the ventilation continues. Continue counting the number of hours the patient is on ventilation from the time the original intubation was initiated.

Once a patient's condition has stabilized and the patient no longer needs continuous ventilatory assistance, various weaning methods may be employed to allow the patient to gradually resume the work of breathing. During weaning, the patient is monitored for any evidence of cardiopulmonary instability. The period during which the weaning process takes place is counted as part of the duration time. All of the period of weaning is counted during the process of withdrawing the patient from ventilatory support. The duration includes the time the patient is on the ventilator, as well as the weaning period. The duration ends when the mechanical ventilation is turned off (after the weaning period). Note that some patients do not require this weaning process.

Duration of mechanical ventilation ends with one of the following events:

- Removal of the endotracheal tube (extubation)
- Discontinuance of ventilation for patients with tracheostomy after any weaning period is completed
- Discharge or transfer while still on mechanical ventilation

Occasionally the condition of a patient who has been on ventilation earlier in the hospital stay deteriorates and a subsequent period of mechanical ventilation may be required. Use the guidelines above to calculate this additional period. In such cases, two codes should be assigned to represent the mechanical ventilation.

When mechanical ventilation is used during surgery, it is not normally coded when it is considered a normal part of surgery. However, in the event that the physician documents that the patient has a specific problem and is maintained on the mechanical ventilator longer than expected or if the patient requires mechanical ventilation for an extended period of time postoperatively, it may be coded. If the postoperative mechanical ventilation continues for more than two days, or if the physician has clearly documented an unexpected extended period of mechanical ventilation, the mechanical ventilation may be reported separately. The hours of mechanical ventilation should be counted starting from the point of intubation.

Tracheostomy Complications

Complications of a tracheostomy are classified to subcategory J95.0 in chapter 10 of ICD-10-CM. Infection of a tracheostomy is classified to code J95.02, with an additional code to identify the type of infection and/or a code from category B95–B97 to identify the organism, or sepsis, A40.-, A41.-. Hemorrhage from tracheostomy is coded to J95.01; malfunction complications are coded to J95.03; trachea-esophageal fistula following tracheostomy is assigned to J95.04; unspecified complication is classified to J95.00; other complications are coded to J95.09.

EXERCISE 19.3

The following exercise provides examples of conditions classified in chapter 10 of ICD-10-CM. Code the following diagnoses and procedures. Do not assign External cause of morbidity codes.

1. Chronic left maxillary sinusitis — J32.0
   Open left total maxillary sinusectomy — 09TR0ZZ

2. Acute upper respiratory infection due to *Pneumococcus* — J06.9, B95.3
   Febrile convulsions — R56.00

3. Deviated nasal septum — J34.2
   Allergic rhinitis — J30.9
   Ethmoidal sinusitis — J32.2
   Excision of nasal septum, percutaneous — 09BM3ZZ

4. Chronic pulmonary edema — J81.1

5.	Allergic rhinitis due to tree pollen	J30.1
6.	Congestive heart failure with pleural effusion	I50.9
7.	Acute respiratory failure due to intracerebral hemorrhage	I61.9 J96.00
8.	Acute pharyngitis due to *Staphylococcus aureus* infection	J02.8 B95.61
9.	Chronic chemical bronchitis due to inhalation of chlorine fumes Bronchoscopy with excisional biopsy of right lower bronchus	J68.4 0BB68ZX
10.	Total tension pneumothorax, spontaneous, recurrent, left Video-assisted thoracoscopic surgical pleurodesis, left pleura	J93.0 0B5P4ZZ
11.	Admitted in acute respiratory failure due to acute exacerbation of chronic obstructive bronchitis	J96.00 J44.1
12.	Acute tracheobronchitis due to respiratory syncytial virus infection	J20.5
13.	Gram-negative pneumonia, anaerobic	J15.8
14.	Acute pulmonary insufficiency, due to shock	J80
15.	Acute respiratory distress syndrome due to hantavirus infection	J80 B33.4
16.	Infected tracheostomy due to staphylococcal abscess of the neck	J95.02 L02.11 B95.8

CHAPTER 20

Diseases of the Digestive System

CHAPTER OVERVIEW

- Diseases of the digestive system are found in chapter 11 of ICD-10-CM.
- Many types of gastrointestinal (GI) hemorrhage can be classified. Sometimes documentation may point to bleeding in multiple locations.
- Esophagitis is classified to the digestive system codes, but esophageal varices are coded as a disease of the circulatory system.
- Combination codes are provided for ulcers that indicate bleeding, perforation, or both. Coders should look in the medical record for any indication of site.
- Special notice should be given to conditions involving diverticula because of the similarity of the conditions and names.
- Coding diseases of the biliary system involves determining the location of the calculus.
- Other biliary system conditions revolve around removal of the gallbladder.
- Codes for adhesions include both intestinal and peritoneal. However, minor adhesions are usually not coded.
- Hernias are classified by type and site, and combination codes are used to indicate associated issues.
- Diarrhea can be related to a variety of conditions. It is important to check the Alphabetic Index carefully before coding.
- Other common digestive system issues covered in this chapter of the handbook are appendicitis and constipation.

LEARNING OUTCOMES

After studying this chapter you should be able to:

- Classify a variety of conditions that affect the GI tract.
- Explain the difference in the meaning of terms associated with diverticula.
- Classify diseases of the biliary system.
- Classify common digestive system conditions such as diarrhea, constipation, and appendicitis.
- Correctly code bariatric surgeries and any possible complications related to these procedures.

TERMS TO KNOW

Biliary system
a network including the gallbladder and bile ducts

Calculus
a stone composed of minerals that forms in an organ or duct of the body

Diverticulitis
the inflammation of existing diverticula

Diverticulosis
the presence of one or more diverticula of the designated site

Diverticulum
a small pouch or sac opening from a tubular or saccular organ; considered a medical condition; the plural term is diverticula

Esophagitis
an inflammation of the lining of the esophagus

Esophageal varices
abnormally enlarged veins in the lower part of the esophagus

GI
gastrointestinal; of the stomach and/or intestines

REMEMBER . . .

Many combination codes and exclusion notes are used in chapter 11 of ICD-10-CM.

INTRODUCTION

Diseases of the digestive system are classified in chapter 11 of ICD-10-CM. The coding principles presented in previous chapters of this handbook apply throughout chapter 11. In addition, particular attention should be given to the use of combination codes and to the many exclusion notes in chapter 11.

GASTROINTESTINAL HEMORRHAGE

Gastrointestinal (GI) bleeding manifests itself in several ways:

- Hematemesis (vomiting of blood), which indicates acute upper gastrointestinal hemorrhage
- Melena (presence of dark-colored blood in stool), which indicates upper or lower GI hemorrhage
- Occult bleeding (presence of blood in stool that can be seen only on laboratory examination), which indicates upper or lower GI bleeding
- Hematochezia (presence of bright-colored blood in stool), which indicates lower GI bleeding

The most common causes of GI bleeding are gastric and intestinal ulcers and diverticular disease of the intestine. A diverticular hemorrhage stops spontaneously in approximately 80 percent of cases, with the other 20 percent experiencing a second or third bleeding episode. ICD-10-CM provides specific codes for gastrointestinal tract ulcers, gastritis, angiodysplasia, duodenitis, gastroduodenitis, Crohn's disease, ulcerative colitis, diverticulosis, and diverticulitis to indicate whether there is associated hemorrhage or bleeding. Examples include the following:

K29.01	Acute gastritis with hemorrhage
K57.13	Diverticulitis of small intestine with hemorrhage
K31.811	Angiodysplasia of duodenum with hemorrhage

Codes **K92.0, Hematemesis; K92.1, Melena;** or **K92.2, Gastrointestinal hemorrhage, unspecified,** are not assigned when codes for bleeding of any of the sites mentioned above are available. These codes are acceptable only when the physician's diagnostic statement clearly indicates that the bleeding is due to another condition. Patients with a recent history of GI bleeding are sometimes seen for an endoscopy to determine the site of the bleeding but do not demonstrate any bleeding during the examination. If the physician documents a clinical diagnosis based on the history or other evidence, the fact that no bleeding occurs during the episode of care does not preclude the assignment of a code that includes mention of hemorrhage, or a code from K92.0 through K92.2 when the cause of bleeding could not be determined.

Occasionally, physician documentation may refer to GI bleeding and either single or multiple GI-related endoscopic findings, such as gastritis, duodenitis, esophagitis, diverticulosis (of colon), colon polyp, and so forth. If the physician does not establish a causal relationship between the GI bleeding and the endoscopic findings, code **K92.2, Gastrointestinal hemorrhage, unspecified,** should be reported. In addition, codes for the GI endoscopic findings without hemorrhage should be assigned as additional diagnoses. The physician must identify the source of the bleeding and link the clinical finding from the endoscopy because the finding may be unrelated to the bleeding. The combination codes describing hemorrhage should not be assigned unless the physician identifies a causal relationship. If the documentation provides more specific information and the bleeding is linked to a specific condition, assign the appropriate combination code with bleeding.

Patients may present for a colonoscopy because of rectal bleeding. If the findings include internal and external hemorrhoids with no statement as to whether the rectal bleeding is due to the hemorrhoids, the physician should be queried to determine whether the rectal bleeding is secondary to the hemorrhoids or the hemorrhoids are an incidental finding. If the hemorrhoids are incidental findings and unrelated to the rectal bleeding, code **K62.5, Hemorrhage of anus and rectum,** should be assigned followed by codes for the hemorrhoids without mention of complication. If, however, the physician establishes a causal relationship between the bleeding and the hemorrhoids, assign codes **K64.8, Other hemorrhoids,** and **K64.4, Residual hemorrhoidal skin tags.** "Bleeding" is a nonessential modifier under "hemorrhoids" in the Alphabetic Index and in the inclusion terms for codes K64.0–K64.3; therefore, bleeding is included in the code assignment for the hemorrhoids and should not be coded separately.

FIGURE 20.1 The Digestive System

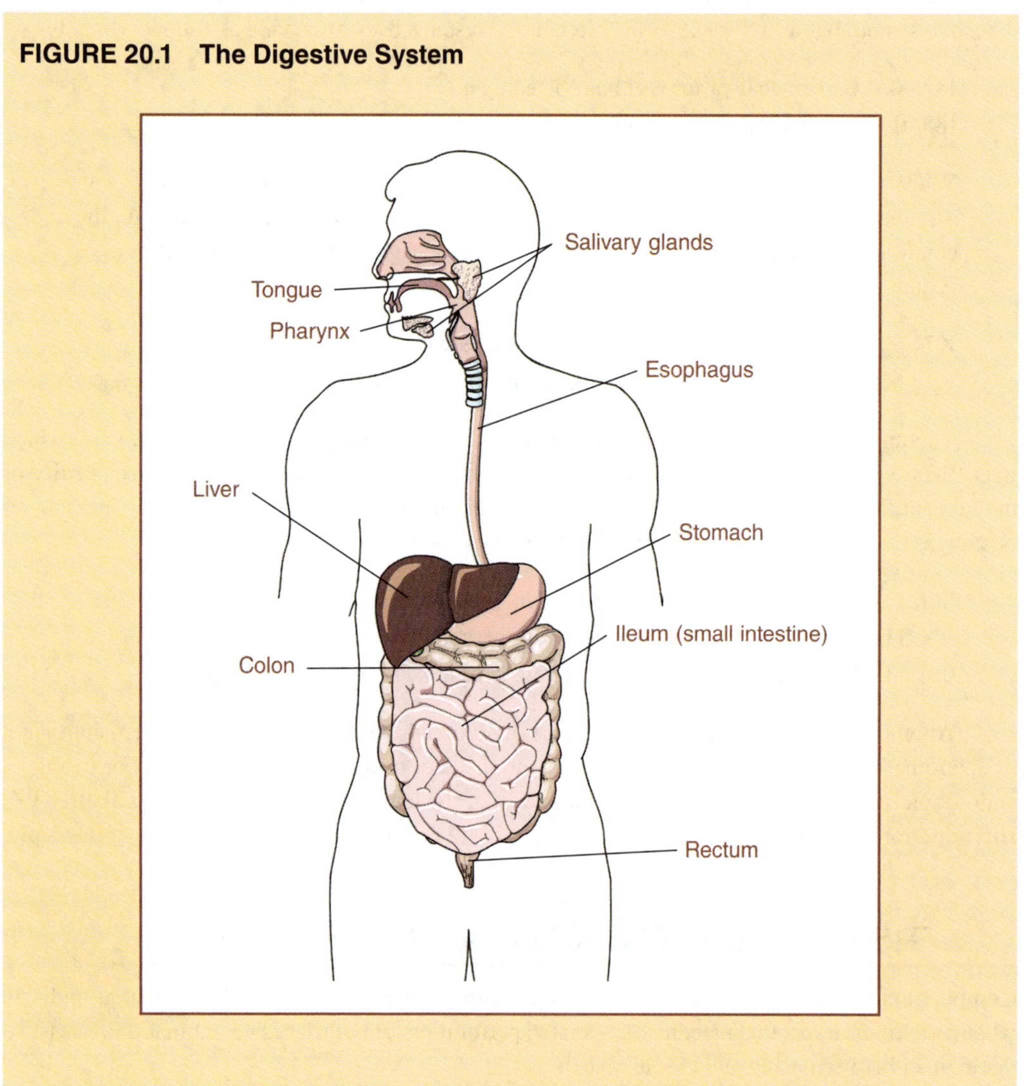

DISEASES OF THE ESOPHAGUS

Esophagitis is classified to category K20, with several different specific conditions. Eosinophilic esophagitis is coded to K20.0, other esophagitis is coded to K20.8, and unspecified esophagitis is coded to K20.9. Esophagitis with gastroesophageal reflux disease is coded to K21.0. Esophagitis with other diseases of the esophagus are classified to category K22 as follows: Ulcerative esophagitis without bleeding is classified to **K22.10, Ulcer of esophagus without bleeding;** ulcerative esophagitis with bleeding is classified to **K22.11, Ulcer of esophagus with bleeding.** Other esophageal conditions classified to category K22 are ulcer of esophagus with bleeding and dyskinesia of esophagus, both of which are classified to K22.4. Barrett's esophagus (codes K22.70 through K22.71-) is a precancerous condition in which the normal cells of the lining of the esophagus are replaced by columnar cells.

Bleeding of the esophagus is coded as **K22.8, Other specified diseases of esophagus,** unless the bleeding is due to esophageal varices. Esophageal varices are not classified as a disease of the digestive system but as a disease of the circulatory system. They are coded as follows:

I85.00 Esophageal varices without bleeding
I85.01 Esophageal varices with bleeding

When esophageal varices are associated with alcoholic liver disease, cirrhosis of the liver, schistosomiasis, toxic liver disease, or portal hypertension, dual coding is required, with the underlying condition coded first and a code for secondary esophageal varices (I85.10–I85.11).

Examples include:

K74.60 + I85.11 Bleeding esophageal varices with cirrhosis of liver
K76.6 + I85.11 Bleeding esophageal varices in portal hypertension

Therapy for esophageal varices consists primarily of ligation of the esophageal vein, which ICD-10-PCS classifies to the root operation "Occlusion," meaning "completely closing an orifice or the lumen of a tubular body part." This procedure may be performed via open approach, percutaneous, or percutaneous endoscopic approach. Examples follow:

06L30ZZ Occlusion of esophageal vein open approach
06L33ZZ Occlusion of esophageal vein percutaneous approach
06L34ZZ Occlusion of esophageal vein percutaneous endoscopic approach

Another treatment for esophageal varices is the endoscopic injection of a sclerosing agent or sclerotherapy, which ICD-10-PCS classifies to the root operation "Introduction." For example, endoscopic injection of sclerosing agent into varix of the lower esophagus is coded to **3E0G8TZ, Introduction of destructive agent into upper GI, via natural or artificial opening endoscopic.**

ULCERS OF THE STOMACH AND SMALL INTESTINE

Combination codes are provided for gastric, gastrojejunal, and duodenal ulcers that indicate whether there is associated bleeding, associated perforation, or both. These combination codes also distinguish between acute and chronic ulcers.

Ulcers of the stomach and the small intestine are often described as peptic without any further identification of the site. The coder should review the medical record for any indication of the site involved; codes from category K27, Peptic ulcer, site unspecified, should not be used when a more specific code can be assigned. Examples of appropriate coding include the following:

K25.5 Chronic gastric ulcer with perforation
K26.3 Acute duodenal ulcer
K25.6 Gastric ulcer with hemorrhage and perforation

DIEULAFOY LESIONS

Dieulafoy lesions are a rare cause of major gastrointestinal bleeding. When gastrointestinal bleeding is present with Dieulafoy lesions, a separate code for the gastrointestinal bleeding is not assigned because it is an integral part of the disease. Assign code K31.82 for Dieulafoy lesion of the stomach and duodenum and code K63.81 for Dieulafoy lesion of the intestine.

Code K22.8 is assigned for Dieulafoy lesions of the esophagus. Dieulafoy lesions of the esophagus typically cause severe bleeding. Endoscopic adrenaline injections can be used to control the bleeding.

COMPLICATIONS OF ARTIFICIAL OPENINGS OF THE DIGESTIVE SYSTEM

Complications of a colostomy, an enterostomy, a gastrostomy, or an esophagostomy are classified to category K94, Complications of artificial openings of the digestive system, rather than complications of surgical and medical care (categories T80–T88).

Complications of Colostomy and Enterostomy

Complications of colostomy are classified to subcategory K94.0, Colostomy complications. Examples include:

K94.01	Colostomy hemorrhage
K94.03	Malfunction of colostomy
K94.12 + L03.311	Cellulitis of abdominal wall due to complication of enterostomy

Complications of Gastrostomy and Esophagostomy

Code K94.32 is assigned for an infection of the esophagostomy. An additional code is assigned to specify the infection. Code K94.33 is assigned for a malfunction of the esophagostomy, such as a mechanical complication.

The mechanical complication of a gastrostomy is assigned code K94.23. Code K94.22 is assigned for an infection of the gastrostomy. Additional codes are assigned to specify the type of infection, such as cellulitis of abdominal wall (L03.311) or sepsis (A40.-, A41.-), if that information is available in the medical record.

DIVERTICULOSIS AND DIVERTICULITIS

A diverticulum is a small pouch or sac opening from a tubular or saccular organ, such as the esophagus, intestine, or urinary bladder. Diverticulosis indicates the presence of one or more diverticula of the designated site; diverticulitis is the inflammation of existing diverticula. A diagnosis of diverticulitis assumes the presence of diverticula; only the code for diverticulitis is assigned, as indicated in the Alphabetic Index, even when both conditions are mentioned in the physician's diagnostic statement. Examples of appropriate coding include the following:

K57.10	Diverticulosis of duodenum
K57.12	Diverticulosis and diverticulitis of duodenum
K57.13	Diverticulitis of jejunum with hemorrhage
K57.20	Diverticulitis of cecum with abscess

ICD-10-CM assumes diverticulosis, not otherwise specified, to be a condition of the intestine.

Congenital versus Acquired Diverticula

Diverticula may be either acquired or congenital. For certain sites, ICD-10-CM assumes that the condition is congenital unless specified otherwise; in other sites, the presumption is that the diverticula are acquired. For example, diverticula of the colon are assumed to be acquired unless specified as congenital; but diverticula of the esophagus are assumed to be congenital unless otherwise specified. The Alphabetic Index (volume 2) lists the following entries for diverticula of the colon and the esophagus:

Diverticulum, diverticula . . . K57.90 . . .
-colon—see Diverticulosis, intestine, large . . .
--congenital Q43.8 . . .
-esophagus (congenital) Q39.6
--acquired (epiphrenic) (pulsion) (traction) K22.5 . . .
-Meckel's (displaced) (hypertrophic) Q43.0

Acquired diverticula of the esophagus are often described by the type of diverticulum (pulsion or traction) or by the portion of the esophagus involved (pharyngoesophageal, midesophageal, or epiphrenic). These qualifications do not affect the code assignment; all are coded **K22.5, Diverticulum of esophagus, acquired.** For example:

K22.5 Epiphrenic diverticula of esophagus
K22.5 Midesophageal traction diverticula of esophagus

DIGESTIVE SYSTEM PROCEDURES

Two ICD-10-PCS guidelines are important to consider when coding procedures of the gastrointestinal system. The first guideline relates to the general body part values "upper intestinal tract" and "lower intestinal tract" provided for the root operations "Change," "Inspection," "Removal," and "Revision." Upper intestinal tract includes the portion of the G.I. tract from the esophagus down to and including the duodenum, and the lower intestinal tract includes the portion of the G.I. tract from the jejunum down to and including the rectum and anus. For example, in the root operation "Inspection" (Table 0DJ), inspection of the jejunum is coded using the body part "lower intestinal tract."

The second guideline of note (not limited to the gastrointestinal system) is a reminder that anastomosis of a tubular body part is not coded separately. As noted in chapter 10 of this handbook, the directive states that "procedural steps necessary to reach the operative site and close the operative site" are not coded separately. For example, when a resection of the sigmoid colon is performed with anastomosis of the descending colon to the rectum, the anastomosis is not coded separately.

EXERCISE 20.1

Code the following diagnoses and procedures. Do not assign External cause of morbidity codes.

1. Acute gastric ulcer with massive gastrointestinal hemorrhage — K25.0
   Exploratory laparotomy with gastric resection, pylorus, with end-to-end anastomosis — 0DT70ZZ

2. Duodenal ulcer, with perforation and hemorrhage	K26.6
3. Penetrating gastric ulcer	K25.5
Open resection of esophageal junction (subtotal	0DT40ZZ
gastrectomy) with esophageal anastomosis	008Q0ZZ
Vagotomy	
4. Bleeding gastric ulcer	K25.4
5. Gastrointestinal ulcerative mucositis due to high-dose	K92.81
chemotherapy for multiple myeloma, subsequent encounter	T45.1x5D
	C90.00
6. Hemorrhage from Dieulafoy lesion of the duodenum	K31.82
Intralesion (endoscopic) injection of epinephrine to control bleeding	3E0G8TZ
7. Clogged feeding jejunostomy. Change of feeding	K94.13
jejunostomy catheter	0D2DXUZ
Malfunction	

DISEASES OF THE BILIARY SYSTEM

Acute and chronic cholecystitis without associated calculus is classified into category K81, with additional characters indicating whether it is acute (K81.0), chronic (K81.1), both acute and chronic (K81.2), or unspecified (K81.9). Combination codes are assigned for cholecystitis, cholelithiasis, and choledocholithiasis to permit reporting these related conditions with a single code. These codes are presented in three groups: calculus of gallbladder (K80.0- through K80.2-), calculus of bile duct (K80.3- through K80.5-), and calculus of both gallbladder and bile ducts (K80.6- through K80.7-).

Within the K80.0-, K80.1-, K80.2-, K80.4-, K80.6- and K80.7- groups, the fourth character indicates whether there is associated cholecystitis. In subcategory K80.3, the fourth character indicates whether there is cholangitis, rather than cholecystitis, whereas the fourth character in subcategory K80.5 indicates that there is neither cholangitis nor cholecystitis. Codes K80.66 and K80.67 are combination codes that include calculus of gallbladder and bile duct with both acute and chronic cholecystitis. Fifth characters in category K80, Cholelithiasis, indicate whether there is associated obstruction.

Codes **K82.0, Obstruction of gallbladder,** and **K83.1, Obstruction of bile duct,** are assigned only when there is obstruction but no calculi are present.

Cholesterolosis

Cholesterolosis is a condition characterized by abnormal deposits of cholesterol and other lipids in the lining of the gallbladder. In its diffuse form, it is known as strawberry gallbladder. This diagnosis is usually made by the pathologist on the basis of tissue examination and is ordinarily an incidental finding without clinical significance. It should not be coded when other gallbladder pathology is present.

Postcholecystectomy Syndrome

Postcholecystectomy syndrome (K91.5) is a condition in which symptoms suggestive of biliary tract disease either persist or develop following cholecystectomy with no demonstrable cause or abnormality found on workup. A postoperative complication code from the T80–T88 series is not assigned with code K91.5.

Cholecystectomy

A cholecystectomy (excision of the gallbladder) can be total (root operation "Resection") or partial (root operation "Excision") and can be performed either as an open procedure (open approach); through a minor incision (percutaneous approach); or through a small, less-invasive laparoscopic incision (percutaneous endoscopic approach). (For illustrations of Medical and Surgical Section approaches, please refer to figure 8.5 on pages 76–77.) When coding a cholecystectomy, the coder should review the operative report to determine whether exploration or incision of the bile ducts was also performed for removal of stones or for other relief of obstruction as well as whether an intraoperative cholangiogram was performed.

Removal of Biliary Calculi

Biliary stones are removed in several ways. A cholecystectomy automatically removes any gallbladder calculus. Alternatively, a cholecystotomy can be carried out for the removal of gallbladder stones without removing the gallbladder. ICD-10-PCS classifies the removal of biliary stones to the root operation "Extirpation" with unique body part (character 4) values for the biliary ducts as shown in figure 20.2.

Stones in the biliary duct can be removed via the open approach, percutaneously, via percutaneous endoscopic approach, via natural or artificial opening, or via natural or artificial opening endoscopic.

Extracorporeal shock wave lithotripsy destroys biliary stones without invasive surgery. The advantages of lithotripsy over conventional surgery for removal of stones include a shorter hospital stay and avoidance of the potential complications associated with surgical intervention. ICD-10-PCS classifies these procedures to the root operation "Fragmentation" with the approach being "external." For example, extracorporeal lithotripsy of the left hepatic duct is coded to **0FF6XZZ, Fragmentation in left hepatic duct, external approach.**

FIGURE 20.2 Excerpt from ICD-10-PCS Table for Hepatobiliary System Extirpation

Section **0** Medical and Surgical
Body System **F** Hepatobiliary System and Pancreas
Operation **C** Extirpation: Taking or cutting out solid matter from a body part

Body Part	Approach	Device	Qualifier
0 Liver **1** Liver, Right Lobe **2** Liver, Left Lobe **4** Gallbladder **G** Pancreas	**0** Open **3** Percutaneous **4** Percutaneous Endoscopic	**Z** No Device	**Z** No Qualifier
5 Hepatic Duct, Right **6** Hepatic Duct, Left **8** Cystic Duct **9** Common Bile Duct **C** Ampulla of Vater **D** Pancreatic Duct **F** Pancreatic Duct, Accessory	**0** Open **3** Percutaneous **4** Percutaneous Endoscopic **7** Via Natural or Artificial Opening **8** Via Natural or Artificial Opening Endoscopic	**Z** No Device	**Z** No Qualifier

EXERCISE 20.2

Code the following diagnoses and procedures. Do not assign External cause of morbidity codes.

1.	Acute cholecystitis with calculus of gallbladder and bile duct	K80.62
	Total laparoscopic cholecystectomy	0FT44ZZ
2.	Chronic cholecystitis with calculus in common duct	K80.44
	Total open cholecystectomy	0FT40ZZ
	Open common bile duct exploration with removal of common bile duct stone	0FC90ZZ
	Intraoperative cholangiogram (gallbladder and bile ducts with high osmolar contrast)	BF030ZZ
	Incidental open appendectomy	0DTJ0ZZ
3.	Biliary obstruction, extrahepatic	K83.1

4. Cholecystitis, acute and chronic, with cholesterolosis — K81.2
   Total cholecystectomy — 0FT40ZZ

5. Acute cholecystitis with choledocholithiasis — K80.42

6. Acute and chronic cholelithiasis with calculi in gallbladder and bile duct — K80.70

7. Acute and chronic cholecystitis with gallbladder and bile duct calculus and obstruction — K80.67

ADHESIONS

Intestinal and peritoneal adhesions are classified as code **K66.0, Peritoneal adhesions (postprocedural) (postinfection),** or **K56.5, Intestinal adhesions [bands] with obstruction (postprocedural) (postinfection),** when obstruction is also present. These codes do not include pelvic peritoneal adhesions; such adhesions are classified as code **N73.6, Female pelvic peritoneal adhesions (postinfective).**

Usually, minor adhesions do not cause symptoms or increase the difficulty of performing an operative procedure. When minor adhesions are easily lysed as part of another procedure, coding a diagnosis of adhesions and a lysis procedure is inappropriate. For example, there are often minor adhesions around the gallbladder that can be pushed aside easily without cutting during gallbladder surgery; coding of adhesions and/or lysis is not appropriate in such situations. Sometimes, however, a strong band of adhesions can cause obstruction or prevent the surgeon from gaining access to the organ to be removed, and a surgical lysis is required before the operation can proceed. In such cases, coding both the adhesions and lysis is appropriate. It is important to note that coders should not code adhesions, and lysis thereof, based solely on mention of adhesions or lysis in an operative report. Documentation of clinical significance by the surgeon may include, but is not limited to, the following language: numerous adhesions requiring a long time to lyse, extensive adhesions involving tedious lysis, extensive lysis, and so forth. If there is any question, the determination of whether the adhesions and the lysis are significant enough to merit coding must be made by the physician. Lysis of adhesions procedures are classified in ICD-10-PCS to the root operation "Release." In the root operation "Release," the body part value coded is the body part being freed and not the tissue being manipulated or cut to free the body part. For example, open lysis of small intestine adhesions are coded to the "small intestine" body part value (8) and reported as 0DN80ZZ.

HERNIAS OF THE ABDOMINAL CAVITY

Hernias are classified by type and site, with combination codes used to indicate any associated gangrene or obstruction. With inguinal and femoral hernias, the codes further subdivide the hernia as unilateral or bilateral and whether it is specified as recurrent; that is, whether it had been repaired during a previous surgery. An incisional hernia is classified as a ventral hernia. Hernias described as incarcerated or strangulated are classified as obstructed. A hernia with both gangrene and obstruction is classified to hernia with gangrene. Careful review of the medical record and attention to instructional notes are important steps in coding these conditions. Coding examples include the following:

K40.00	Bilateral inguinal hernia with obstruction (no mention of gangrene)
K40.41	Unilateral recurrent inguinal hernia with gangrene
K41.11	Gangrenous femoral hernia, recurrent, bilateral
K44.1	Diaphragmatic hernia with gangrene
K42.0	Umbilical hernia with obstruction
K41.30	Incarcerated femoral hernia

Hernia repairs can be performed with a laparoscope inserted through a small incision or through a traditional open surgical approach. When coding hernia repairs, the coder should be careful not to use a bilateral repair code when the hernia itself is described as unilateral. A unilateral repair may be performed even though bilateral hernias are present, but, obviously, it is impossible to repair bilateral hernias when only one hernia exists. Care should be taken to understand how the hernia repair is performed.

While the documentation may refer to herniorrhaphy, or hernia repair, ICD-10-PCS classifies these procedures to two different root operations. Herniorrhaphies are classified to the root operation "Repair," unless the repair is accomplished with the use of a biological or synthetic material such as a mesh or graft, in which case the root operation "Supplement" is used. In addition, herniorrhaphies are classified to the body systems "anatomical regions, lower extremities," or "general" and the appropriate body part where the hernia is located. For example, an open repair of a bilateral inguinal hernia is coded to 0YQA0ZZ, while an open repair of a ventral hernia is coded to 0WQF0ZZ.

Coding examples include:

0YQ50ZZ	Open repair of right inguinal hernia
0YU54JZ	Laparoscopic repair of right inguinal hernia with mesh prosthesis
0YQA3ZZ	Percutaneous repair of bilateral inguinal hernias

EXERCISE 20.3

Code the following diagnoses and procedures. Do not assign External cause of morbidity codes.

1.	Right direct inguinal hernia and left indirect sliding inguinal hernia Open repair of bilateral inguinal hernias	K40.20 0YQA0ZZ
2.	Incarcerated left inguinal hernia Laparoscopic left inguinal herniorrhaphy with mesh prosthesis	K40.30 0YU64JZ
3.	Recurrent left inguinal hernia Percutaneous repair of inguinal hernia, left	K40.91 0YQ63ZZ
4.	Gangrenous umbilical hernia Open repair of umbilical hernia	K42.1 0WQF0ZZ
5.	Strangulated umbilical hernia Laparoscopic repair of umbilical hernia with mesh prosthesis	K42.0 0WUF4JZ
6.	Reflux esophagitis secondary to sliding esophageal hiatal hernia Repair of right esophageal hiatus hernia, open abdominal approach	K21.0 K44.9 0BQR0ZZ
7.	Recurrent ventral incisional hernia with obstruction and gangrene	K43.1

APPENDICITIS

Category K35, Acute appendicitis, uses a fourth character to indicate the presence of either generalized peritonitis (K35.2) or localized peritonitis (K35.3). Unspecified acute appendicitis is coded to K35.80. Occasionally, an appendix ruptures during an appendectomy; this is not classified as a complication of surgery.

Category K37, Unspecified appendicitis, is a vague category that should not be used in an acute care facility. Additional information is almost always available in the medical record.

Surgical removal of the appendix is coded to the root operation "Resection." Incidental appendectomy refers to a procedure performed to remove the appendix as a routine prophylactic measure in the course of other abdominal surgery. ICD-10-PCS does not distinguish between an incidental appendectomy and an appendectomy to remove a diseased appendix.

DIARRHEA

A code from categories A00 through A09 is assigned for infectious diarrhea when the organism has been identified. Code A09 is assigned for infectious diarrhea not otherwise specified, or described only as dysenteric diarrhea, endemic diarrhea, or epidemic diarrhea. Check the Alphabetic Index carefully before coding, because diarrhea can be related to a variety of conditions. Symptom code R19.7 is assigned for diarrhea for which no appropriate subterm can be located. Examples of appropriate code assignments include the following:

A04.7 Diarrhea due to *Clostridium difficile*
R19.7 Acute diarrhea
A07.3 Coccidial diarrhea
K52.9 Chronic diarrhea
R19.7 Infantile diarrhea
K59.1 Functional diarrhea

CONSTIPATION

Unspecified constipation is coded to K59.00, but there are two distinct subtypes of constipation recognized: slow transit constipation (K59.01) and outlet dysfunction constipation (K59.02). The slow transit results from a delay in transit of fecal material throughout the colon secondary to smooth muscle. The latter type of constipation results from difficulty evacuating the rectum during attempts at defecation. Treatment for these two types of constipation is very different. The slow transit type is treated with either laxatives or surgery. Biofeedback is taught for relaxation for the outlet dysfunction constipation.

BARIATRIC SURGERY AND COMPLICATIONS

Bariatric surgery refers to procedures performed on morbidly obese patients for the purpose of weight loss. Several types of restrictive and malabsorptive gastric procedures are performed for weight loss when other methods have failed for severely obese patients. Malabsorptive operations are the most common and restrict food intake and the amount of calories and nutrients the body absorbs. Restrictive operations restrict food intake but do not interfere with the normal digestive process. Restrictive operations for obesity include adjustable gastric banding and vertical banded gastroplasty. (See figure 20.3 for illustrations of these and other procedures.) The weight loss is usually achieved by reducing the size of the stomach (restrictive operations) with an implanted device, such as gastric banding, or through removal of a portion of the stomach or by resecting and rerouting the small intestines to a small stomach pouch (malabsorptive operations), such as gastric bypass surgery. Restrictive operations such as gastric banding are classified to the root operation "Restriction." When coding bypass procedures, it is important to understand the body part bypassed from and the body part bypassed to. The ICD-10-PCS fourth character body part specifies the body part bypassed from (for example, the stomach), and the seventh character qualifier specifies the body part bypassed to (for example, the jejunum).

FIGURE 20.3 Illustrations of Bariatric Surgery

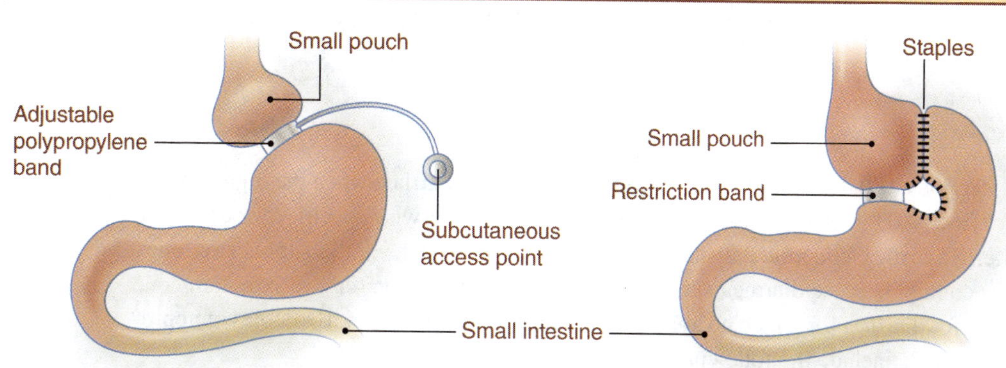

ADJUSTABLE GASTRIC BANDING

VERTICAL BANDED GASTROPLASTY

Adjustable gastric banding and *vertical banded gastroplasty* are gastric surgeries used to restrict and decrease food intake. The adjustable polypropylene band may be tightened or loosened over time to change the size of the gastric passage. The vertical banded gastroplasty utilizes a restriction band and staples to create a small stomach pouch. The band delays the emptying of food from the pouch, causing a feeling of fullness.

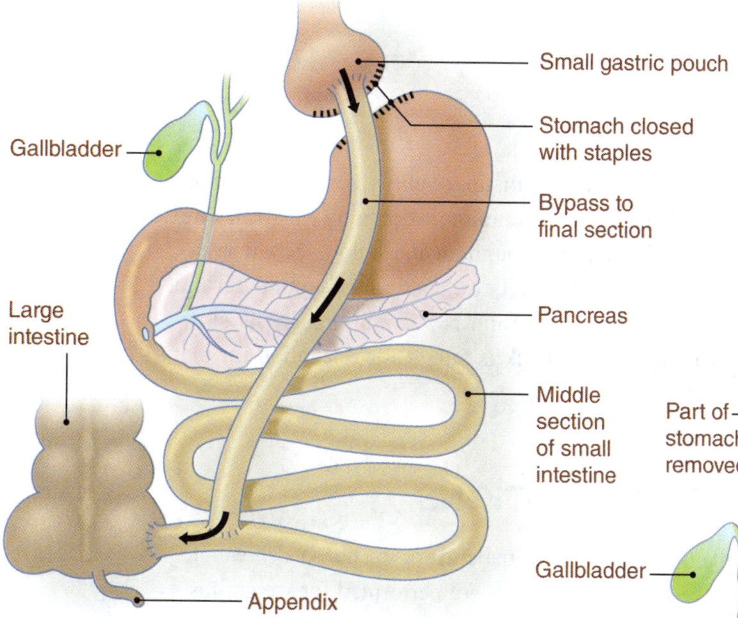

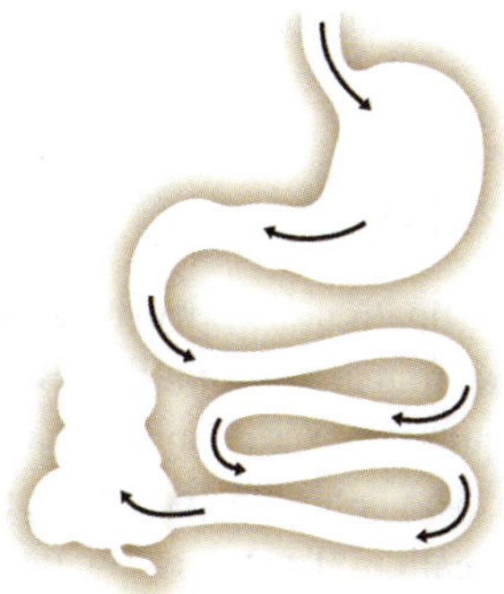

Small gastric pouch
Gallbladder
Stomach closed with staples
Bypass to final section
Large intestine
Pancreas
Middle section of small intestine
Appendix

OPEN GASTRIC BYPASS

Open gastric bypass and *biliopancreatic diversion* are examples of malabsorptive gastric procedures that restrict both food intake and the amount of calories and nutrients the body absorbs. In both these procedures, much of the stomach is bypassed and reconnected to the small intestine either by closing the stomach with staples and creating a small pouch (open gastric bypass) or by removing a portion of the stomach to create a small pouch (biliopancreatic diversion).

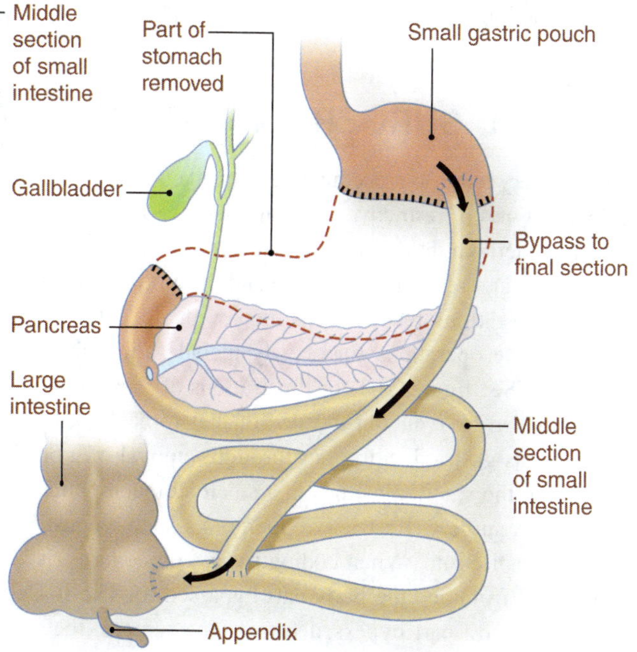

Part of stomach removed
Small gastric pouch
Gallbladder
Bypass to final section
Pancreas
Large intestine
Middle section of small intestine
Appendix

BILIOPANCREATIC DIVERSION

Coding examples include:

0DV64CZ	Laparoscopic gastric restrictive procedure
0DW64CZ	Laparoscopic revision of gastric band
0D160ZB	Open gastric bypass (stomach to ileum)
0DB64Z3	Laparoscopic vertical (sleeve) gastrectomy

Category K95, Complications of bariatric procedures, has been created to uniquely identify complications of bariatric procedures:

K95.01	Infection due to gastric band procedure
K95.09	Other complications of gastric band procedure
K95.81	Infection due to other bariatric procedure
K95.89	Other complications of other bariatric procedure

In the case of infections, additional codes are used to specify the type of infection or organism, such as cellulitis of abdominal wall (L03.311) or sepsis (A40.-, A41.-) and bacterial or viral infectious agents (B95.-, B96.-).

EXERCISE 20.4

Code the following diagnoses and procedures. Do not assign External cause of morbidity codes.

1. Acute ruptured appendicitis with postoperative	K35.2
intestinal obstruction	K91.3
Open appendectomy	0DTJ0ZZ
2. Acute hepatitis and early cirrhosis of the liver	K70.10
due to chronic alcoholism	K70.30
	F10.20
3. Perirectal abscess	K61.1
Atony of colon	K59.8
Percutaneous incision and drainage of perirectal abscess	0D9P3ZZ
4. Hepatic coma with massive ascites secondary to	K72.91
Laennec's cirrhosis	K70.31
Paracentesis	0W9G30Z

5.	Intestinal obstruction due to peritoneal adhesive band Open lysis of adhesive band large intestine	K56.5 0DNE0ZZ
6.	Diverticulosis and diverticulitis of right colon Open right hemicolectomy with end-to-end anastomosis	K57.32 0DTF0ZZ
7.	Infection of gastrostomy with abscess of abdominal wall due to *Streptococcus* B	K94.22 L02.211 B95.1
8.	Polyp of rectum Colonoscopy with polypectomy	K62.1 0DBP8ZZ
9.	Neurogenic bowel	K59.2
10.	Morbid obesity Laparoscopic gastric bypass to ileum	E66.01 0D164ZB

CHAPTER 21

Diseases of the Genitourinary System

CHAPTER OVERVIEW

- Diseases of the genitourinary system are classified in chapter 14 of ICD-10-CM.
  - They are not found in chapter 14 if they are classified by etiology.
  - These diseases include transmissible infections; neoplastic diseases; and conditions complicating pregnancy, childbirth, and the puerperium.
- The term "urinary tract infection" is often used by physicians when referring to conditions such as urethritis, cystitis, or pyelonephritis.
- There are different codes for urinary incontinence depending on the type of incontinence (e.g., stress, functional). When the underlying cause is known, that should be sequenced first.
- Chronic kidney disease develops in conjunction with other conditions. The instructions for sequencing of the code in conjunction with others is found in the Tabular List.
- A relationship is presumed when a patient has both hypertension and kidney disease. Codes extend to the fifth character to cover this condition.
- Renal dialysis codes vary from admission codes to codes for the insertion of catheter without the performance of dialysis. Dialysis codes cover complications such as dialysis dementia.
- Conditions involving the prostate involve a fourth and fifth character. Neoplasms of the prostate are not included within this category of codes.
- Other related codes covered in this chapter are prostatectomy, endometriosis, genital prolapse, dysplasia of the cervix and vulva, and endometrial ablation.
- Neoplasms of the breast are classified in chapter 2 of ICD-10-CM. However, not all conditions and procedures involving the breast are related to neoplasms.

LEARNING OUTCOMES

After studying this chapter you should be able to:

Distinguish among the different conditions often referred to as urinary tract infections.

Code for a variety of kidney diseases and their treatments.

Explain coding for kidney disease in conjunction with hypertension and diabetes.

Classify conditions that affect both male and female genitalia.

TERMS TO KNOW

Acute kidney failure
sudden failure of renal function following a severe insult to the kidneys

Chronic kidney disease
long-term disability of the renal function

Nephropathy
general term indicating that renal disease is present

Ureter
carries urine from the kidneys to the bladder

Urethra
carries urine from the bladder to the outside of the body

REMEMBER . . .

It is important to distinguish between chronic kidney disease, acute kidney failure, and acute kidney injury.

INTRODUCTION

Diseases of the genitourinary system are classified in chapter 14 of ICD-10-CM, except those that are classified by etiology, such as certain easily transmissible infections; neoplastic diseases; and conditions complicating pregnancy, childbirth, and the puerperium. Subterms should be checked carefully in the Alphabetic Index, and special attention should be given to the terms "urethra" and "ureter," which are often confused by coders.

INFECTIONS OF THE GENITOURINARY TRACT

Physicians often use the term "urinary tract infection (UTI)" when referring to conditions such as urethritis, cystitis, or pyelonephritis. Urethritis and cystitis are lower urinary tract infections; pyelonephritis is an infection of the upper urinary tract. The main term for the specific condition should be referred to in the Alphabetic Index before referring to the main term **Infection.** For example, under the main term **Cystitis,** subterms are located for diphtheritic (A36.85) and chlamydial (A56.01) infection. When there is no subterm for the organism, the code for the condition is assigned, with an additional code from categories B95–B97 to indicate the organism. For example, there is no subterm for *Escherichia coli* under the main term for cystitis; therefore, codes N30.90 and B96.20 are assigned for cystitis due to *E. coli.*

The following examples indicate complete coding for such infections:

A59.03	Cystitis due to trichomonas
N30.00 + B96.4	Acute cystitis due to proteus infection
N11.9 + B96.20	Chronic pyelonephritis due to *E. coli*

FIGURE 21.1 The Urinary System

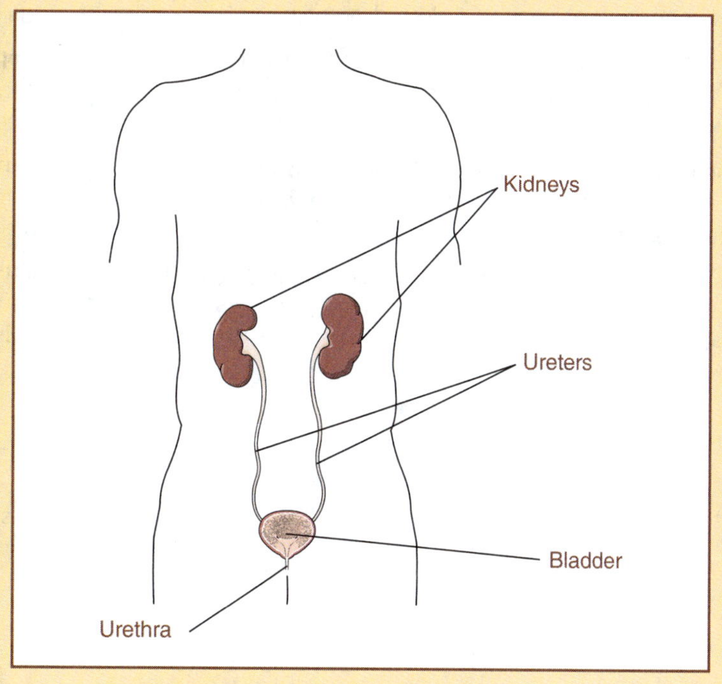

Urinary tract infections that develop following surgery are rarely true postoperative infections and are not usually classified as such. When the operative procedure involves the urinary tract, however, it may be appropriate for the coder to ask the physician whether the infection is related to the procedure. When the infection is related to the presence of an implant, a graft, or a device (such as an indwelling or a suprapubic catheter), code T83.5- or T83.6 is assigned. An additional code may be included to identify the infection. As with all postprocedural complications, code assignment is based on the provider's documentation of the relationship between the infection and the procedure. In the absence of documentation indicating that the infection is due to the surgical procedure, code **N39.0, Urinary tract infection, site not specified,** should be assigned. If the provider states that the UTI is secondary to the indwelling urinary catheter, assign code **T83.51-, Infection and inflammatory reaction due to indwelling urinary catheter,** and code **N39.0, Urinary tract infection, site not specified.**

EXERCISE 21.1

Code the following diagnoses and procedures. Do not assign External cause of morbidity codes.

---

1. Urethral stricture due to gonorrheal infection — A54.01
   Urethral dilation via cystoscope — 0T7D8ZZ

---

2. Abscess of right scrotum due to group B *Streptococcus* — N49.2, B95.1
   Percutaneous incision and drainage of scrotal abscess — 0V953ZZ

---

3. Acute pyelonephritis due to *Helicobacter pylori* infection — N10, B96.81

---

4. Chronic cystitis with hematuria — N30.21
   Pseudomonas infection — B96.5

---

5. Chronic cystitis due to *Monilia* infection — B37.41

---

6. Urinary tract infection due to candidiasis — B37.49

HEMATURIA

Hematuria refers to blood in the urine. Gross hematuria refers to hematuria that is so plentiful that it is visible to the naked eye. Microscopic hematuria refers to blood in the urine visible only under a microscope. ICD-10-CM provides separate codes for gross hematuria (R31.0), benign essential microscopic hematuria (R31.1), other microscopic hematuria (R31.2), and unspecified hematuria (R31.9). Many genitourinary conditions have hematuria as an integral associated symptom. For example, the medical record has a diagnostic statement of hematuria due to renal calculus but only a code of **N20.0, Calculus of kidney,** is assigned. The hematuria is integral to this condition and no additional code is assigned. A certain amount of hematuria is expected following a urinary tract procedure or a prostatectomy. This is not considered a postoperative complication, and no code is assigned unless the bleeding is excessive or persistent.

Microscopic hematuria should not be confused with hemoglobinuria, which is coded as R82.3. Hemoglobinuria is an abnormal finding and refers to the presence of free hemoglobin in the urine on laboratory examination of the urine. It is reported only when the physician has indicated its clinical significance.

Codes in category N30, Cystitis, provide combination codes with a fifth character identifying whether hematuria is present or not.

URINARY INCONTINENCE

Stress incontinence causes involuntary urine loss with physical strain such as coughing or sneezing. Although it occurs in both male and female patients, it occurs more frequently in women, typically as a result of physical changes brought on by earlier childbearing. Prostate surgery is the primary cause of incontinence in men. Stress incontinence is coded as **N39.3, Stress incontinence (female) (male).** Urinary incontinence due to cognitive impairment, severe physical disability, or immobility is coded to **R39.81, Functional urinary incontinence.** Urinary incontinence of nonorganic origin is coded to **F98.0, Enuresis not due to a substance or known physiological condition.**

Other types of incontinence are also classified into subcategory N39.4, Other specified urinary incontinence. When more than one type of incontinence is present, it is classified as **Mixed incontinence (male) (female),** and code **N39.46** is assigned. When the underlying cause of incontinence is known, the code for that condition should be sequenced first. Code N32.81 should also be assigned for any overactive bladder associated with conditions in codes N39.3 and N39.4-.

Treatment for incontinence depends, to a large extent, on the particular type of incontinence present. If it is due to an intrinsic sphincter deficiency, collagen injections are sometimes carried out. Code **3E0K3GC, Introduction of other therapeutic substance into genitourinary tract, percutaneous approach,** is assigned for this therapy.

Other treatments for incontinence are surgical in nature. Codes for repair of incontinence depend on the procedure performed. Typically, these procedures are classified to the root operations "Repair," "Reposition," or "Supplement." Examples of these procedure codes are:

0TSC0ZZ	Reposition bladder neck, open approach
0TSD4ZZ	Reposition urethra, percutaneous endoscopic approach
0TUC7KZ	Supplement bladder neck with nonautologous tissue substitute, via natural or artificial opening
0TQDXZZ	Repair urethra, external approach

RENAL DISEASE

Renal disease is classified into categories N00 through N29. Glomerulonephritis is a type of nephritis in which there is bilateral inflammatory change without infection. Nephrotic syndrome is a complex clinical state characterized by edema, albuminuria, and increased permeability of the glomerular capillary basement membrane. The syndrome may result from an unknown cause or from glomerulonephritis or diseases such as diabetes, systemic lupus erythematosus, hypertension, and amyloidosis. Nephropathy is a general term that indicates that renal disease is present. Infection of the kidney not otherwise specified is classified to N15.9. Kidney disease complicating pregnancy, childbirth, and the puerperium is reclassified in chapter 15 of ICD-10-CM.

Chronic Kidney Disease and End-Stage Renal Disease

Chronic kidney disease (CKD) is considered a more current and precise term than chronic renal failure or chronic renal insufficiency. CKD develops as a complication of other diseases, such as diabetes mellitus, primary hypertension, glomerulonephritis, nephrosis, interstitial nephritis, systemic lupus erythematosus, obstructive uropathy, and polycystic kidney disease. The sequencing of the CKD code in relationship to codes for other contributing conditions is based on the conventions of the Tabular List.

Patients usually live for many years with such chronic kidney disease. When kidney involvement becomes so extensive that kidney function can no longer keep up with the body's needs, dialysis is usually required.

ICD-10-CM classifies CKD on the basis of severity. Based on the glomerular filtration rate (GFR), chronic kidney disease has been categorized into five stages. Category N18, Chronic kidney disease (CKD), has been expanded to the fourth-character subcategory level for further specification of the varying stages of chronic kidney disease. The fourth-character subcategory codes are as follows:

N18.1 Chronic kidney disease, stage 1
N18.2 Chronic kidney disease, stage 2 (mild)
N18.3 Chronic kidney disease, stage 3 (moderate)
N18.4 Chronic kidney disease, stage 4 (severe)
N18.5 Chronic kidney disease, stage 5
N18.6 End stage renal disease
N18.9 Chronic kidney disease, unspecified

Chronic renal disease, chronic renal insufficiency, and chronic renal failure are assigned to code N18.9.

End-stage renal disease (ESRD) (N18.6) is a complex syndrome characterized by a variable and inconsistent group of biochemical and clinical changes that affect volume regulation, acid-base balance, electrolyte balance, excretion of waste products, and several endocrine functions. It is a progression of chronic kidney disease and is defined by clinicians as the point at which regular dialysis sessions or a kidney transplant is required to maintain life. For patients with end-stage renal disease, code **Z99.2**, **Dependence on renal dialysis,** should be assigned as an additional code to report dialysis status.

Chronic renal failure, not otherwise specified, and chronic renal insufficiency are both assigned code **N18.9, Chronic kidney disease, unspecified.** If both a stage of CKD and ESRD are documented for the same patient, only code N18.6 would be assigned.

Kidney transplant may be recommended for patients with severe CKD caused by severe, uncontrollable hypertension, infections, diabetes mellitus, or glomerulonephritis. Patients who have undergone kidney transplant may still have some form of CKD because the kidney transplant may not fully restore kidney function. Code Z94.0 may be assigned with the appropriate CKD code to indicate that a CKD patient is status post kidney transplant. It is incorrect to assume that mild or moderate CKD following a transplant is a transplant failure unless it is documented as such in the medical record.

If transplant complication such as failure or rejection, or other transplant complication is documented in patients with severe CKD or ESRD, code **T86.1-, Complications of kidney transplant,** is assigned. If a post–kidney transplant patient has CKD and the documentation is unclear whether there is transplant failure or rejection, it is necessary to query the provider.

Acute Kidney Failure

Acute kidney failure (N17.-) is very different from chronic kidney disease; it is not a phase of the same condition. Chronic kidney disease is a long-term inability of the kidneys to function adequately; acute kidney failure is the sudden cessation of renal function following severe insult to normal kidneys. Toxic agents, traumatic or surgical shock, tissue destruction due to injury or surgery, or a variety of other conditions can cause acute kidney failure.

Acute renal insufficiency (N28.9) is considered an early stage of renal impairment, evidenced by diminished creatinine clearance or mildly elevated serum creatinine or blood urea nitrogen (BUN). Clinical symptoms or other abnormal laboratory findings may or may not be present but are usually minimal. Treatment varies, depending on the underlying cause, but serious attention is given to prevent its progression to renal failure. Code **N99.89, Other postprocedural complications and disorders of genitorurinary system,** is assigned if renal insufficiency is due to a procedure.

Physicians sometimes use the terms "renal insufficiency" and "renal failure" interchangeably, but ICD-10-CM classifies these terms to different codes. ICD-10-CM classifies unspecified and acute renal insufficiency to code N28.9, whereas acute kidney failure is assigned to category N17. Unspecified renal failure is identified with code **N19, Unspecified kidney failure.** It is important for the coder to be guided by the classification. If the physician uses both terms in the medical record, the physician should be queried for clarification as to the correct diagnosis.

Acute kidney injury is a phrase used by some physicians to refer to acute kidney failure. Care should be taken to determine whether the documentation refers to a traumatic injury to the kidney (which would be assigned to a code in subcategory S37.0) or to a nontraumatic event, which is actually acute kidney failure. Nontraumatic acute kidney injury is assigned to **N17.9, Acute kidney failure, unspecified.** The default for acute kidney injury, unspecified as to traumatic or nontraumatic, is code N17.9.

Kidney Disease with Hypertension

ICD-10-CM presumes a relationship when a patient has both chronic kidney disease or renal sclerosis and hypertension, and category I12, Hypertensive chronic kidney disease, or category I13, Hypertensive heart and chronic kidney disease, should be assigned. The fourth or fifth character indicates the stage of chronic kidney disease as follows:

- Category I12
  —Fourth character of 0 is for "chronic kidney disease stage 5 or end-stage renal disease"
  —Fourth character of 1 is for "chronic kidney disease stage 1 through stage 4, or unspecified chronic kidney disease"
- Category I13
  —Fourth character of 0 is for "with heart failure and chronic kidney disease, stage 1 through 4, or unspecified chronic kidney disease"
  —Fourth character of 1 is for CKD without heart failure with the fifth character indicating the CKD stage as follows:
  –Fifth character of 0 is for "chronic kidney disease stage 1 through stage 4, or unspecified"
  –Fifth character of 1 is for "chronic kidney disease stage 5 or end-stage renal disease"
  —Fourth character of 2 is for "with heart failure and chronic kidney disease, stage 5, or end-stage renal disease"

Codes from categories I12 and I13 require additional codes to identify the stage of CKD as shown on table 21.1.

Acute kidney failure is not caused by hypertension and is not included in the hypertensive kidney disease codes. When acute kidney failure and hypertension are both present, assign a code from category N17, Acute kidney failure, with an additional code for the hypertension.

The use of codes from categories I12 and I13 does not apply in the following situations:

- The renal condition is acute kidney failure.
- The hypertension is described as secondary.
- The kidney disease is specifically stated as due to a cause other than hypertension.

Examples of appropriate codes for kidney disease with hypertension include the following:

I12.9 + N18.9	Hypertensive kidney disease with chronic kidney disease
I13.10 + N18.3	Hypertensive heart and kidney disease with chronic kidney disease, stage 3
I13.2 + N18.5 + I50.9	Hypertensive heart and kidney disease with stage 5 chronic kidney disease and congestive heart failure
N17.9 + I10	Acute kidney failure; hypertension

TABLE 21.1 Hypertensive Chronic Kidney Disease and Hypertensive Heart and Chronic Kidney Disease and the Applicable CKD Stages

	Additional CKD Stage Code Required	
Category I12–I13 Code	N18.1–N18.4 or N18.9	N18.5 or N18.6
I12.00		X
I12.90	X	
I13.00	X	
I13.10	X	
I13.11		X
I13.20		X

Kidney Disease with Diabetes Mellitus

Diabetic kidney complications are coded to E08–E13 with .21 for diabetic nephropathy, .22 for chronic kidney disease, and .29 for other kidney complication. Kidney disease sometimes results from both hypertension and diabetes mellitus. In this situation, the combination code from category I12 or category I13 and a code from subcategory E08–E13 with .2- are assigned. A code from category N18 is assigned to specify the stage of chronic kidney disease.

Examples of appropriate codes for kidney disease due to diabetes include the following:

E11.21	Diabetic nephrosis
I12.9 + E10.22 + N18.4	Chronic kidney disease stage 4 due to hypertension and type 1 diabetes mellitus
E10.22	Chronic kidney disease, unspecified, due to type 1 diabetes

RENAL DIALYSIS

When the kidneys are impaired and unable to function normally, renal dialysis may be started to replace the function of the kidneys. There are basically two types of kidney dialysis to remove waste and excess water from the blood: peritoneal dialysis and hemodialysis.

Patients with end-stage renal disease require a regular schedule of dialysis treatments to manage the symptoms arising from kidney disease. Typically, dialysis is performed as an outpatient service. However, periodically it may be necessary for care to be provided to the renal dialysis catheter, such as toilet or cleansing, or replacement of the catheter. These situations are coded to **Z49.01, Encounter for fitting and adjustment of extracorporeal dialysis catheter,** or code **Z49.02, Encounter for fitting and adjustment of peritoneal dialysis catheter.** Other encounters may be related to adequacy testing for dialysis, which are classified to codes **Z49.31, Encounter for adequacy testing for hemodialysis,** or **Z49.32, Encounter for adequacy testing for peritoneal dialysis.**

If the patient is admitted for other reasons but continues to receive dialysis therapy during the hospital stay or is known to be maintained on renal dialysis, code **Z99.2, Dependence on renal dialysis,** may be assigned as an additional code; the condition responsible for the admission is designated as the principal diagnosis. If the patient is known to be noncompliant with renal dialysis, code **Z91.15, Patient's noncomplicance with renal dialysis,** may be assigned.

Peritoneal Dialysis

Peritoneal dialysis is accomplished by instilling a prepared fluid into the peritoneal cavity and removing the uremic toxins along with the prepared fluid. In peritoneal dialysis, a tube is inserted into the peritoneal cavity. Creation of a cutaneoperitoneal fistula for permanent peritoneal dialysis is coded to bypass, peritoneal cavity to cutaneous, with synthetic substitute. For example, if the procedure is performed using a percutaneous approach, it is coded to **0W1G3J4, Bypass peritoneal cavity to cutaneous with synthetic substitute, percutaneous approach.** Code **3E1M39Z, Irrigation of peritoneal cavity using dialysate, percutaneous approach,** is assigned for the associated dialysis.

Hemodialysis

In hemodialysis, blood is removed from the body and filtered through a dialyzer, or artificial kidney, after which the filtered blood is returned to the body. There are three types of hemodialysis access: catheter, arteriovenous (AV) graft, and arteriovenous fistula. The associated dialysis is coded to the Extracorporeal Assistance and Performance Section, "physiological systems" body system, and root operation "Performance" (completely taking over a physiological function by extracorporeal means). A fifth character is assigned for duration, which distinguishes between a single encounter and multiple encounters. For example, multiple hemodialysis encounters are coded to **5A1D60Z, Performance of urinary filtration, multiple.**

Hemodialysis via Catheter

Hemodialysis via catheter is usually a short-term access, although in some instances it may be used as a permanent access. The catheter is inserted into a large vein in either the neck or the chest. Compared with arteriovenous access, catheters have a greater tendency to become infected, and the blood may not be cleaned as thoroughly.

The coding of hemodialysis catheter access requires the insertion of a venous catheter (ICD-10-PCS code for insertion of infusion device, percutaneous approach, with the appropriate vein) or a totally implantable venous access device (requires two ICD-10-PCS codes, one for the insertion of vascular access device and another for the insertion of reservoir, with the codes being dependent on the site of insertion).

Patients are sometimes admitted for insertion of a catheter or a vascular access device, but no dialysis is performed during the admission. When dialysis is performed during the same episode of care, procedure code 5A1D00Z (single encounter) or 5A1D60Z (multiple encounter) is assigned to specify that the dialysis was actually performed during the encounter. When the admission is for fitting or adjustment of the dialysis catheter, code Z49.01 is assigned for an extracorporeal catheter and Z49.02 for a peritoneal catheter. If concurrent dialysis is performed, procedure code 5A1D00Z (single encounter) or 5A1D60Z (multiple encounter) is assigned. Some coding examples follow:

N18.6 + 05H533Z	Patient with end-stage renal disease admitted for insertion of Hickman catheter into the right subclavian vein for renal dialysis (no dialysis performed)
Z49.01 + N18.5 + 5A1D00Z	Patient with chronic kidney disease, stage 5, admitted for cleansing of hemodialysis catheter, single hemodialysis performed

Arteriovenous Graft

When a tubular graft is used to connect the artery and vein, the connection is known as an arteriovenous graft. After the graft has healed, hemodialysis is performed by puncturing the actual graft to provide access to the blood vessels. One needle is placed in the arterial side of the graft and one in the venous side. When coding the creation of an AV graft, the root operation is "Bypass," with the sixth character assigned to identify the graft. For example, for coding a left brachiocephalic arteriovenous graft, assign code **03180JD, Bypass left brachial artery to upper arm vein with synthetic substitute, open approach.**

Arteriovenous Fistula

Arteriovenous fistulas are indicated when permanent vascular access is required. An artery is surgically joined directly to a vein when creating an AV fistula. As the connection matures, the vein grows larger and stronger until it becomes a reliable point of access, allowing for frequent puncture for hemodialysis.

The AV fistula has fewer complications and lasts longer than other types of access for hemodialysis. When coding the creation of an AV fistula in ICD-10-PCS, the root operation is "Bypass." The fourth character body part represents the body part bypassed "from"; the qualifier specifies the body part bypassed "to." In the context of hemodialysis access, blood flow is generally bypassed from the artery to the vein (high-pressure system to low-pressure system). For example, for coding a left brachiocephalic arteriovenous fistula, assign code **03180ZD, Bypass left brachial artery to upper arm vein, open approach.**

It normally takes two to three months for an AV fistula to mature. A nonmaturing or nondeveloping fistula is considered a mechanical complication and is coded to **T82.590-, Other mechanical complication of surgically created arteriovenous fistula.** Primary causes of a nonmaturing fistula are narrowing of a vein or multiple competing veins. Treatment may consist of performing an arteriovenostomy to create a new AV fistula. Other treatment options may be performed by interventional radiologists—such as balloon angioplasty; revision of AV fistula; and/or closing off competing veins, which can be performed using various techniques.

Other mechanical complications related to the AV fistula are breakdown (T82.510-), displacement (T82.520-), and leakage (T82.530-), while mechanical complications of the vascular dialysis catheter are coded to subcategory T82.4.

COMPLICATIONS OF CYSTOSTOMY

Complications of cystostomy are classified as N99.51-. Code N99.511 is assigned for an infection of the cystostomy. An additional code would be assigned to specify the type of infection, such as abscess of the abdominal wall (L02.211) or cellulitis of the abdominal wall (L03.311), with an additional code to identify the organism. Malfunction of cystostomy is coded as N99.512; other complications of cystostomy, such as fistula, hernia or prolapsed, are coded as N99.518. Note that mechanical complication of indwelling urinary catheter is classified to T83.0- rather than N99.51-.

EXERCISE 21.2

Code the following diagnoses and procedures. Do not assign External cause of morbidity codes.

1.	End-stage renal disease	N18.6
	Peritoneal dialysis	3E1M39Z
2.	Chronic kidney disease, stage 5	N18.5
	Catheter insertion into the left subclavian vein for renal dialysis	05H633Z
	Single hemodialysis performed	5A1D00Z
3.	Stenosis of dialysis arteriovenous fistula, initial encounter	T82.858A
	Percutaneous balloon angioplasty right radial artery	037B3ZZ
4.	Hypertensive end-stage renal disease, dialysis maintenance	I12.0
		N18.6
		Z99.2

CYSTOSCOPY AS OPERATIVE APPROACH

Cystoscopy is used as the approach for many procedures performed in diagnosing and treating urinary tract conditions and is not coded separately when it is the procedural approach. ICD-10-PCS classifies the cystoscopic approach as "via natural or artificial opening endoscopic." (For illustrations of Medical and Surgical Section approaches, please refer to figure 8.5 on pages 76–77.) Procedures described as transurethral should be coded to the approach "via natural or artificial opening," while those described as transurethral ureteroscopic are classified to the "via natural or artificial opening endoscopic" approach. When a cystoscopy is performed to visually and/or manually explore the bladder (without performing another procedure), it is coded to the root operation "Inspection" with code **0TJB8ZZ, Inspection of bladder, via natural or artificial opening endoscopic.**

REMOVAL OF URINARY CALCULUS

Urinary calculi are relatively common and often pass without surgery. Several types of surgical techniques are used when intervention is necessary. Extracorporeal shock wave lithotripsy (ESWL) of the kidney, ureter, and/or bladder (ICD-10-PCS root operation "Fragmentation," external approach) uses shock waves to reduce the stones to a slush that can more easily pass through the urinary tract and be excreted over a short period of time. For example, ESWL of the right ureter is coded to **0TF6XZZ, Fragmentation in right ureter, external approach.**

For stones that are poor candidates for ESWL, endoscopic therapy is indicated. Ureteroscopy is the most common means of visualizing an upper urinary tract calculus. In addition, percutaneous techniques (e.g., percutaneous endourology) can be used.

Ultrasonic lithotripsy requires a rigid endoscope and is commonly performed via a percutaneous renal approach. Ultrasonic lithotriptors are used to treat large bladder stones. Because the ultrasound requires a relatively large, rigid instrument to perform, most stones treated are limited to the lower ureter or the bladder. Lithotripsy with removal of fragments is coded to the root operation "Extirpation."

When the kidney stones are quite large, or in a location that does not allow for effective lithotripsy, the stones can be removed by percutaneous nephrostomy. The procedure is performed with a small incision in the back; a tunnel is created directly into the kidney, and a tube is inserted. The stone is removed through the tube. Percutaneous nephrostomy is coded to the root operation "Extirpation" with percutaneous or percutaneous endoscopic approach.

EXERCISE 21.3

Code the following diagnoses and procedures. Do not assign External cause of morbidity codes.

1.	Right ureteral calculus	N20.1
	Right calyceal diverticulum	N28.89
	Left renal cyst, solitary (acquired)	N28.1
2.	Impacted renal calculus with medullary sponge kidney	N20.0 Q61.5
	Extracorporeal shock wave lithotripsy of left kidney calculus	0TF4XZZ
3.	Calculus in bladder	N21.0
	Lithotripsy of urinary bladder with ultrasonic fragmentation and removal of fragments via percutaneous endoscopic approach	0TCB4ZZ

PROSTATE DISEASE AND THERAPY

Diseases of the male genital organs are classified in categories N40 through N53, with conditions of the prostate using categories N40 through N42. Neoplasms of the prostate are classified as follows:

C61	Malignant neoplasm of the prostate
D29.1	Benign neoplasm of the prostate
D07.5	In situ neoplasm of the prostate

Hyperplasia of the prostate is classified to category N40, Enlarged prostate, with fourth characters providing additional specificity regarding the presence or absence of lower urinary tract symptoms. As indicated by the "use additional code" note under code N40.1, an additional code should be assigned to identify associated symptoms when specified, such as incomplete bladder emptying (R39.14), nocturia (R35.1), straining on urination (R39.16), urinary frequency (R35.0), urinary hesitancy (R39.11), urinary incontinence (N39.4-), urinary obstruction (N13.8), urinary retention (R33.8), urinary urgency (R39.15), or weak urinary stream (R39.12).

Category N41 classifies inflammatory disease of the prostate as follows:

N41.0	Acute prostatitis
N41.1	Chronic prostatitis
N41.2	Abscess of prostate
N41.3	Prostatocystitis
N41.4	Granulomatous prostatitis
N41.8	Other inflammatory diseases of prostate
N41.9	Inflammatory disease of prostate, unspecified

FIGURE 21.2 The Male Reproductive System

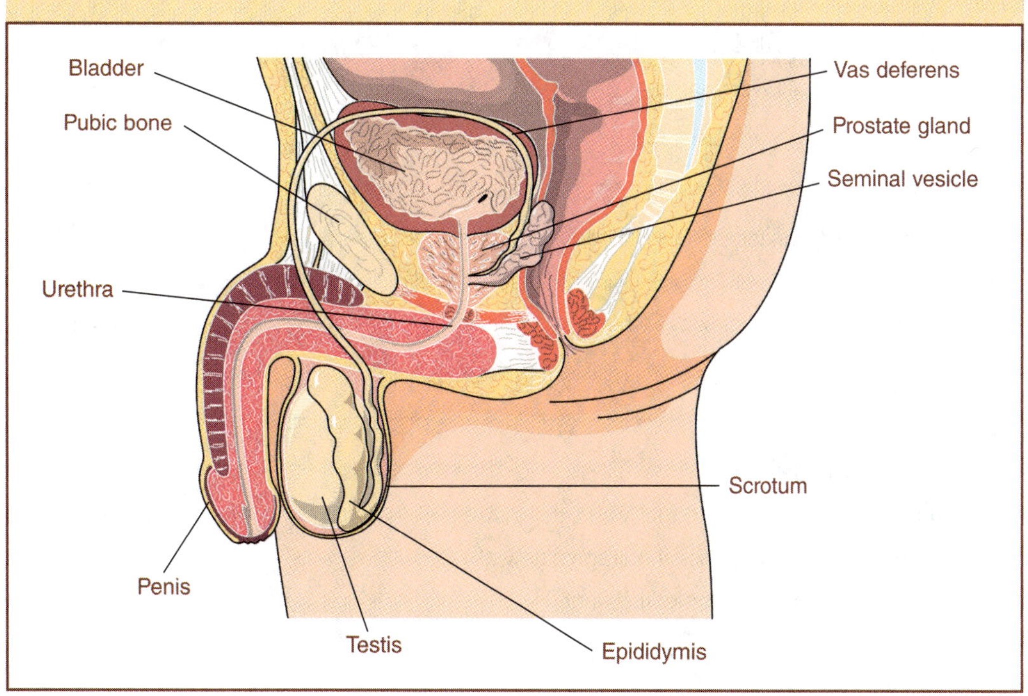

Category N42 classifies other disorders of the prostate with such conditions as follows:

N42.0 Calculus of prostate
N42.1 Congestion and hemorrhage of prostate
N42.3 Dysplasia of prostate
N42.81 Prostatodynia syndrome
N42.82 Prostatosis syndrome
N42.83 Cyst of prostate
N42.89 Other specified disorders of prostate
N42.9 Disorder of prostate, unspecified

In order to code a prostatectomy, it is necessary to determine whether the complete prostate was removed (root operation "Resection"), or only a portion of the prostate was removed (root operation "Excision"), as well as surgical approach (open, percutaneous endoscopic, via natural or artificial opening, or via natural or artificial opening endoscopic). (For illustrations of Medical and Surgical Section approaches, please refer to figure 8.5 on pages 76–77.) For example:

- Total transurethral prostatectomy via cystoscope: 0VT08ZZ, Resection of prostate, via natural or artificial opening endoscopic
- Suprapubic prostatectomy: 0VT00ZZ, Resection of prostate, open approach

In a radical prostatectomy, the seminal vesicles and vas ampullae are excised along with the prostate. This procedure requires two codes: one code for the prostate resection, and a separate code for the resection of bilateral seminal vessels. A prostatectomy performed with a radical cystectomy involves removal of the bladder, prostate, and seminal vessels. Thus, it requires three codes: one for the prostate resection, another for the bladder resection, and a third for the resection of bilateral seminal vessels.

Different types of energy sources may be utilized for the destruction of prostatic tissue such as microwave thermotherapy, radiofrequency thermotherapy, ablation, and cryotherapy. All these different types of energy sources are coded to the same root operation, "Destruction."

ENDOMETRIOSIS

Endometriosis is a condition in which aberrant tissue that almost perfectly resembles the mucous membrane of the uterus is found in various other sites within the pelvic cavity. A code from category N80, Endometriosis, is assigned for this condition, with a fourth character indicating the site in which the aberrant tissue is found. (See figure 21.3 for common sites of endometriosis implantation.) For example:

N80.1 Endometriosis of the ovary
N80.5 Endometriosis of the colon
N80.2 Endometriosis of fallopian tube

GENITAL PROLAPSE

Prolapse of the vagina and/or the uterus is a relatively common condition. In coding genital prolapse, it is first necessary to determine whether the condition involves the vaginal wall, the uterus, or both, and whether the prolapse is complete or incomplete. For example:

N81.2 Incomplete uterovaginal prolapse (uterus descends into introitus, and cervix protrudes slightly beyond)

N81.3 Complete uterovaginal prolapse (entire cervix and uterus protrude beyond the introitus, and vagina is inverted)

FIGURE 21.3 Common Sites of Endometriosis Implantation

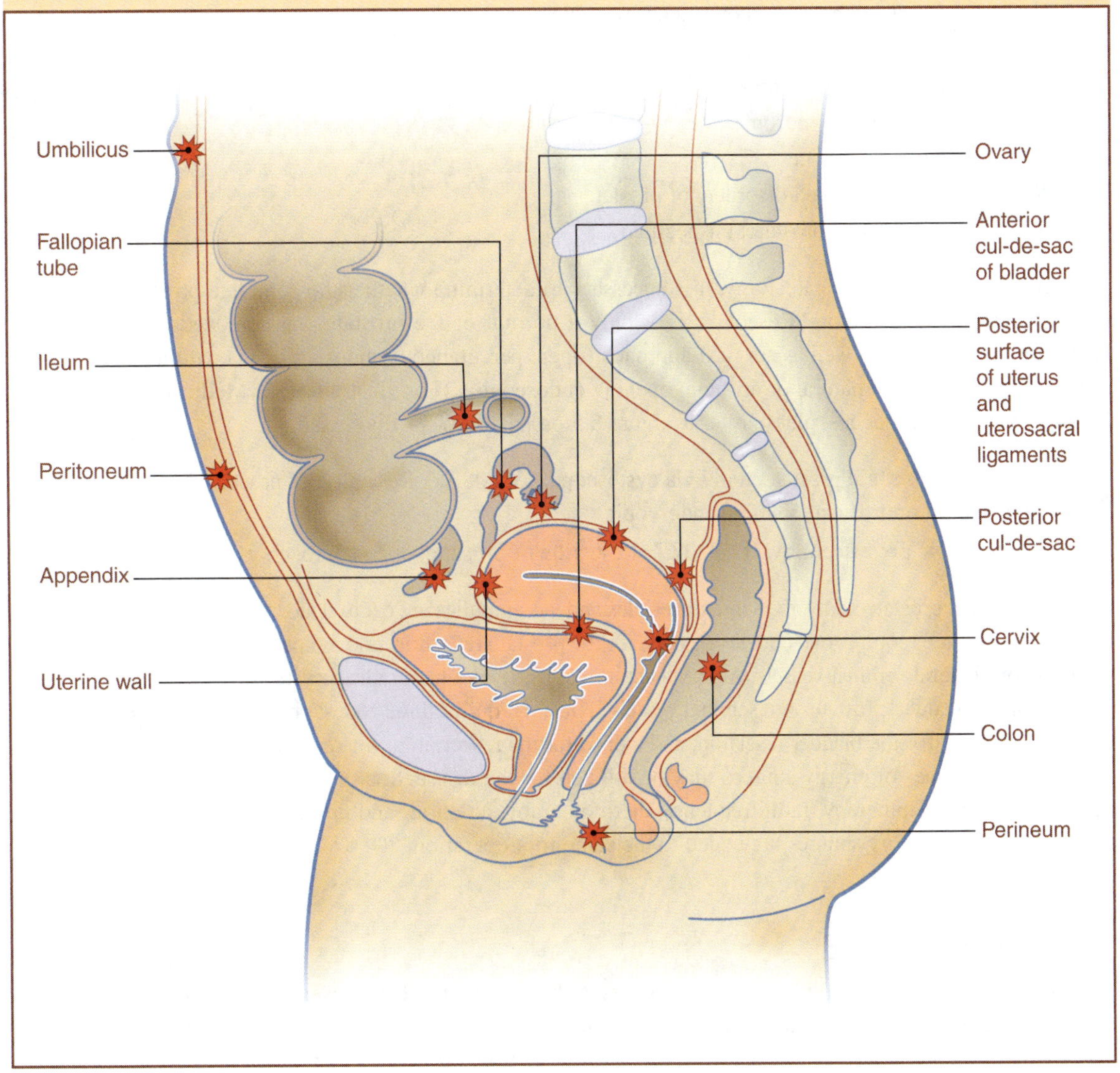

Code N99.3 is assigned for prolapse of vaginal vault occurring after hysterectomy; it is not classified as a surgical complication. This condition may be due to the surgical technique or to the relaxation of supporting structures following surgery. Pelvic or vaginal enterocele, a herniation of the intestine through intact vaginal mucosa, is coded **N81.5, Vaginal enterocele,** whether it is congenital or acquired. Prolapse of the uterus in an obstetric patient is classified in chapter 15 of ICD-10-CM. Examples of appropriate coding for genital prolapse include the following:

N81.4	Prolapse of uterus (no vaginal wall involvement)
N81.5	Vaginal enterocele
N81.85	Prolapse of cervical stump
O34.522	Prolapse of gravid uterus (second trimester)
N81.11	Cystocele, midline
N81.0	Urethrocele
N81.6	Rectocele

ENDOMETRIAL HYPERPLASIA

Endometrial hyperplasia refers to excessive proliferation of the cells of the inner lining of the uterus. It is considered a significant risk factor for endometrial cancer and requires careful monitoring. ICD-10-CM provides the following codes for endometrial hyperplasia:

N85.00	Endometrial hyperplasia, unspecified
N85.01	Benign endometrial hyperplasia
N85.02	Endometrial intraepithelial neoplasia [EIN]

DYSPLASIA OF CERVIX, VAGINA, AND VULVA

Cervical intraepithelial neoplasia (CIN), also known as cervical dysplasia, is the potentially premalignant transformation and abnormal growth (dysplasia) of squamous cells on the surface of the cervix. CIN I is coded to **N87.0, Mild cervical dysplasia,** and CIN II is coded to **N87.1, Moderate cervical dysplasia.** Dysplasia of the cervix specified as CIN III, or severe dysplasia of cervix uteri, however, is carcinoma in situ of the cervix, and code **D06.-, Carcinoma in situ of cervix uteri,** is assigned.

Vaginal intraepithelial neoplasia (VAIN) refers to premalignant histological findings in the vagina characterized by dysplastic changes. It is a rare, generally asymptomatic disorder. Similar to CIN, it is classified in three stages: VAIN I, VAIN II, and VAIN III. Code **N89.0, Mild vaginal dysplasia,** is assigned for VAIN I, while VAIN II is classified to code **N89.1, Moderate vaginal dysplasia.** Similar to CIN III, VAIN III, or severe vaginal dysplasia, is considered to be carcinoma in situ and is coded to **D07.2, Carcinoma in situ of vagina.**

Vulvar intraepithelial neoplasia (VIN) refers to changes that can occur in the skin covering the vulva. In some cases VIN may disappear without treatment. VIN is classified as follows:

- VIN I, or mild dysplasia of vulva—N90.0, Mild vulvar dysplasia
- VIN II, or moderate dysplasia of vulva—N90.1, Moderate vulvar dysplasia
- VIN III is classified to D07.1, Carcinoma in situ of vulva

A diagnosis of CIN III, VAIN III, or VIN III can be made only on the basis of pathological examination of tissues.

Codes from **R87.61-, Abnormal cytological findings in specimens from cervix uteri,** or **R87.62-, Abnormal cytological findings in specimens from vagina,** would be assigned for abnormal results from a cervical or vaginal cytologic examination without histologic confirmation.

HYSTERECTOMY

A hysterectomy to remove the uterus may be performed for different conditions, including symptomatic uterine fibroids, uterine prolapse, endometriosis, and malignant neoplasms of the uterus, cervix, or ovaries. Depending on the indications for surgery, the surgeon may opt to remove all or only part of the uterus. When coding hysterectomies, it is important to clarify whether the cervix is removed, as some of the ICD-10-PCS Tables in the "Female Reproductive System" (e.g., Table 0UT, resection) contain anatomical subdivisions with separate values for "uterus" and "cervix."

- In a supracervical or subtotal hysterectomy, only the upper part of the uterus is removed, keeping the cervix intact. From an ICD-10-PCS perspective, this is coded to the root operation "Resection" and body part value "uterus." For example, for a subtotal laparoscopic hysterectomy, code **0UT94ZZ, Resection of uterus, percutaneous endoscopic approach,** is assigned.

FIGURE 21.4 The Female Reproductive System

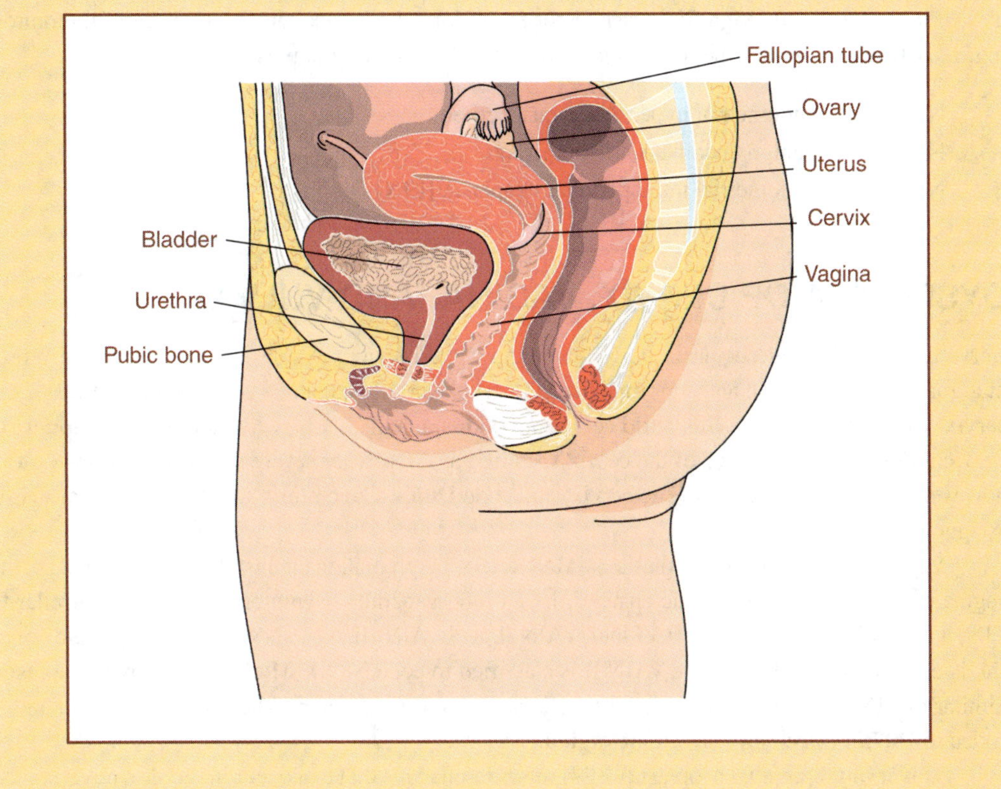

- A total hysterectomy removes the whole uterus and cervix. From an ICD-10-PCS perspective, this procedure requires two separate codes, one for the complete removal of the uterus and another for the complete removal of the cervix, because "uterus" and "cervix" have distinct body part values. This requirement is supported by the ICD-10-PCS guideline for multiple procedures B3.2c, which states that multiple procedures during the same operative episode are coded if "[t]he same root operation is performed on different body parts as defined by distinct values of the body part character." For example, a total laparoscopic hysterectomy is coded as **0UT94ZZ, Resection of uterus, percutaneous endoscopic approach,** along with **0UTC4ZZ, Resection of cervix, percutaneous endoscopic approach.**

ENDOMETRIAL ABLATION

Endometrial ablation is used as an alternative to hysterectomy for women with dysfunctional bleeding that does not respond to hormone therapy. It can also be used to treat women with fibroid tumors or endometrial polyps. A scope equipped with either a roller ball or a u-shaped wire is inserted into the uterus. The lining of the uterus is ablated by laser, radiofrequency electromagnet energy, or electrocoagulation. Endometrial ablation is classified to the root operation "Destruction." For example, **0U5B8ZZ, Destruction of endometrium, via natural or artificial opening, endoscopic,** is assigned for a vaginal endometrial ablation.

DISEASES OF THE BREAST

Neoplasms of the breast are classified in chapter 2 of ICD-10-CM. The coder should be aware, however, that terms such as "growth," "cyst," and "lump" do not necessarily refer to neoplastic disease. When surgery is performed, the pathology report provides more specific information to assist in code assignment. Examples of appropriate coding include the following:

N60.11	Fibrocystic disease of the right breast
D24.9	Benign neoplasm of female breast
D23.5	Benign neoplasm of skin of breast
N62	Gynecomastia
C50.929	Carcinoma of the male breast
C50.919	Carcinoma of the female breast

ICD-10-PCS classifies breast procedures to the body system "skin and breast" with the second character value of "H." Biopsies of the breast are classified to the root operations "Drainage" (value of "9") or "Excision" (value of "B") depending on whether the biopsy involves fluid removal ("Drainage"), as in the case of a cyst, or tissue ("Excision"), as in the case of a mass or lump. Biopsies are coded in ICD-10-PCS with a seventh character qualifier of "X" for diagnostic. When the procedure is described as an excisional biopsy, it usually refers to excision of the entire lesion rather than a simple biopsy, in which case it is coded to the root operation "Excision." The term "lumpectomy" also describes a local excision of a breast lesion.

When surgery on the breast is performed for possible neoplasm, it is customary to perform a biopsy before the definitive surgery begins. A rapid-frozen section is reviewed by a pathologist to determine whether malignancy is present. The code for the definitive procedure is sequenced first, followed by the code for the biopsy. If a diagnostic excision, extraction, or drainage procedure (biopsy) is followed by a more definitive procedure, such as destruction, excision, or resection at the same procedure site, both the biopsy and the more definitive procedure are coded. For example, if a biopsy of the breast is performed first, followed by a partial mastectomy at the same procedure site during the same surgical episode, both the biopsy and the partial mastectomy procedures are coded. The partial mastectomy is sequenced as the principal procedure because it is the procedure performed for definitive treatment most related to the principal diagnosis.

With advances in cancer therapy, radical mastectomy is not performed as often as in the past because a lumpectomy or a modified radical mastectomy appears to be equally effective in most cases. The main distinction between a radical and a modified mastectomy is that all or part of the pectoralis major and all of the pectoralis minor are removed in a radical mastectomy, whereas the pectoralis major is preserved in a modified radical mastectomy. ICD-10-PCS requires separate codes for all components involved in a radical mastectomy. For example, a left radical mastectomy is coded to **0HTU0ZZ, Resection of left breast, open approach; 07T60ZZ, Resection of left axillary lymphatic, open approach;** and **0KTJ0ZZ, Resection of left thorax muscle, open approach.** On the other hand, a left modified radical mastectomy is coded as **0HTU0ZZ, Resection of left breast, open approach;** and **07T60ZZ, Resection of left axillary lymphatic, open approach.** The coder must review the operative report carefully before assigning these procedure codes.

Insertion of tissue expander is another procedure frequently carried out in conjunction with breast surgery. This tissue insertion permits a flap closure of the site, making it unnecessary for the patient to undergo a skin graft. Saline is usually injected into the breast expander at regular intervals following the expander's insertion to gradually enlarge the size of the expander. ICD-10-PCS classifies these procedures to the root operation "Insertion" with the device value of "N" for tissue expander, for example, **0HHT0NZ, Insertion of tissue expander into right breast, open approach.**

BREAST RECONSTRUCTION

Reconstructive breast surgery (figure 21.5) is performed for a variety of reasons. Prostheses are often implanted for patients who have undergone mastectomies. Breast reconstruction can be performed immediately after the surgery or delayed to a later time. When it is known that patients will undergo postoperative radiation, reconstruction is usually delayed. When a patient undergoes a mastectomy and the reconstruction is delayed, code **Z42.1, Encounter for breast reconstruction following mastectomy,** is assigned as the principal or first-listed diagnosis for the return admission for each encounter for a stage of the breast reconstruction.

If the purpose of reconstruction is to increase breast size for improved appearance, prosthetic implants are usually used. Reduction mammoplasty is sometimes performed for patients whose large breast size interferes with normal daily activities or causes significant discomfort, as well as for cosmetic reasons. When mammoplasty is performed to reduce breast size, code **N62, Hypertrophy of breast,** is assigned as the principal diagnosis. When the purpose of the mammoplasty is cosmetic, code **Z41.1, Encounter for cosmetic surgery,** is assigned as the principal diagnosis.

Coding examples for reconstruction include the following:

0HRT0JZ	Replacement of right breast with synthetic substitute, open approach
0HRU075	Replacement of left breast using latissimus dorsi myocutaneous flap, open approach
0HRUX7Z	Replacement of left breast with autologous tissue substitute, external approach
0KXH0ZZ	Transfer right thorax muscle, open approach
0HRV079	Replacement of bilateral breast using gluteal artery perforator flap, open approach
0HRW0JZ	Replacement of right nipple with synthetic substitute, open approach
0HBV0ZZ	Excision of bilateral breast, open approach

Problems related to deformity and disproportion post–breast reconstruction may require patients to seek further medical care. Contour irregularity, excess tissue in reconstructed breast, or misshapen reconstructed breast are assigned to code **N65.0, Deformity of reconstructed breast.** Breast asymmetry, or disproportion between native breast and reconstructed breast, and ptosis (sagging) of native breast in relation to reconstructed breast are assigned to **N65.1, Disproportion of reconstructed breast.**

Sometimes complications develop in patients who have breast implants, making removal of the implants advisable. In such cases, the code for the principal diagnosis depends on the nature of the complication. For example, if the reason for the surgery is that the implant has ruptured, the principal diagnosis is code **T85.41x-, Breakdown (mechanical) of breast prosthesis and implant.** When the reason for removal is that the patient has a capsular contracture of the right breast implant, code **T85.44x-, Capsular contracture of breast implant,** is assigned as the principal diagnosis. Other codes related to problems with breast implants include **T85.42x-, Displacement of breast prosthesis and implant,** which includes malposition of breast prosthesis and implant, and **T85.43x-, Leakage of breast prosthesis and implant.** Removal of the breast implant is classified to the root operation “Removal” and the device “synthetic substitute,” for example: **0HPT0JZ, Removal of synthetic substitute from right breast, open approach.**

FIGURE 21.5 Breast Reconstruction Surgery

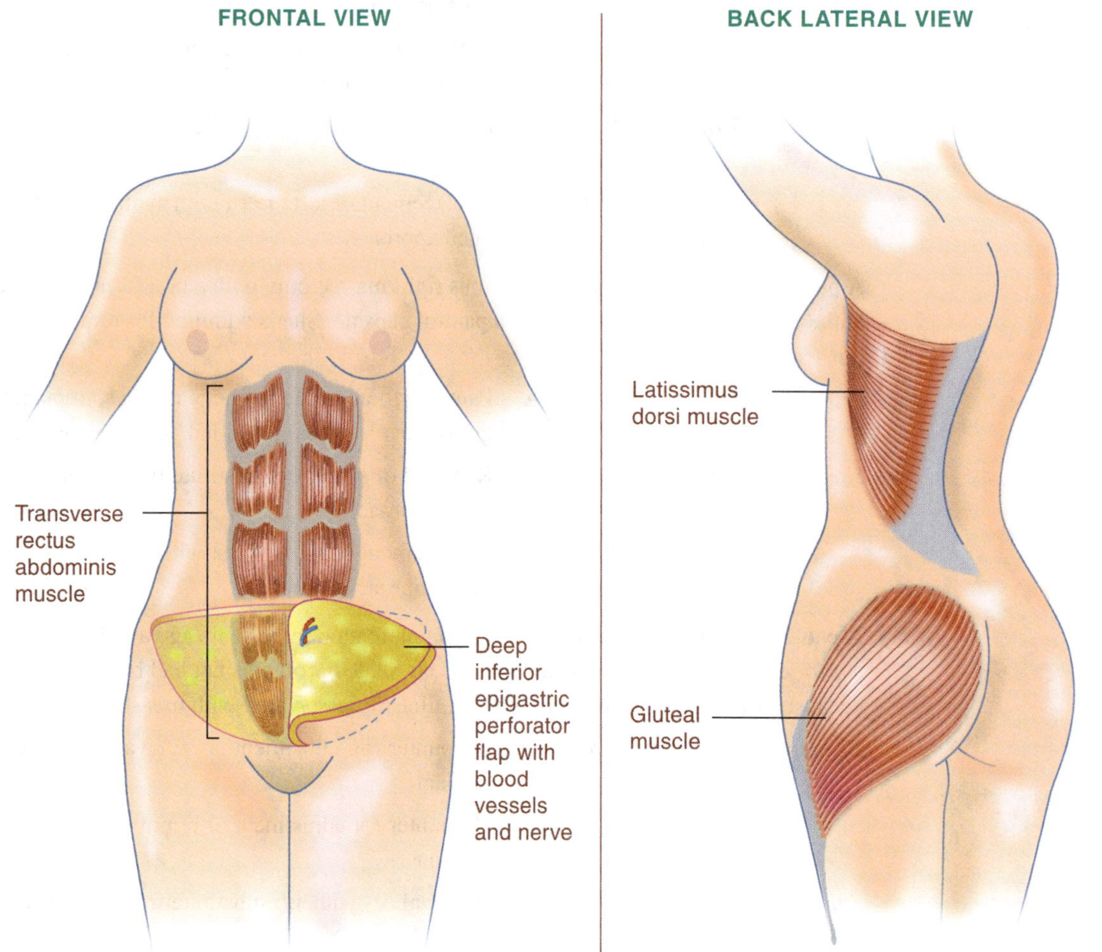

Transverse rectus abdominis muscle (TRAM) flap:
Skin, fat, and transverse rectus abdominis muscle are moved to the chest.

Deep inferior epigastric perforator (DIEP) flap:
Abdominal skin and fat are removed along with the perforator vessel and transplanted to the chest using microsurgery.

Latissimus dorsi flap:
Skin, fat, and latissimus dorsi muscle from the upper back are pulled under the skin to the chest area.

Gluteal free flap:
Skin, fat, and gluteal muscle are removed and transplanted to the chest.

Patients sometimes request removal of an implant because they are concerned that a complication might occur in the future, although there is no problem at present. In this case, assign **Z45.81-, Encounter for adjustment or removal of breast implant.** For example:

- A patient experiences a ruptured breast implant on the left side and is admitted for open removal of the implant and insertion of a new implant.

Principal diagnosis:	T85.41xA	Breakdown (mechanical) of breast prosthesis and implant, initial encounter
Surgery performed:	0HPU0JZ	Removal of synthetic substitute from left breast, open approach
	0HRU0JZ	Replacement of left breast with synthetic substitute, open approach

- A patient who had undergone a previous right mastectomy with a breast implant inserted at the time of surgery suffers from a painful capsule. She is admitted for removal and reinsertion of the implant.

Principal diagnosis:	T85.84xA	Pain due to internal prosthetic devices, implants and grafts, not elsewhere classified, initial encounter
Surgery performed:	0HPT0JZ	Removal of synthetic substitute from right breast, open approach
	0HRT0JZ	Replacement of right breast with synthetic substitute, open approach

- A patient had undergone bilateral breast implantation three years ago and is now admitted for elective implant removal. She had no related problems but had become concerned because of newspaper reports describing illnesses associated with breast implants.

Principal diagnosis:	Z45.811	Encounter for adjustment or removal of right breast implant
	Z45.812	Encounter for adjustment or removal of left breast implant
Surgery performed:	0HPT0JZ	Removal of synthetic substitute from right breast, open
	0HPU0JZ	Removal of synthetic substitute from left breast, open

REVIEW EXERCISE 21.4

Code the following diagnoses and procedures. Do not assign External cause of morbidity codes.

1.	Hydronephrosis with chronic pyelitis	N13.6
	Pyelonephritis, focal, chronic, left	N11.9
2.	Rapidly progressive glomerulonephritis	N01.9
3.	Syphilitic epididymitis	A52.76
4.	Chronic prostatitis due to proteus	N41.1
		B96.4
5.	Phimosis and balanoposthitis	N47.1
		N47.6
6.	Encysted right hydrocele, male	N43.0
	Open hydrocelectomy of hydrocele of spermatic cord	0VBF0ZZ
	Excision	
7.	Benign prostatic hypertrophy with urinary obstruction	N40.1
		N13.8
	Total transurethral prostatectomy via cystoscope	0VT08ZZ
8.	Acute and chronic cervicitis	N72
	Total vaginal hysterectomy	0UT97ZZ
		0UTC7ZZ
9.	Chronic pelvic inflammatory disease	N73.1
	Dysmenorrhea	N94.6

10.	Menometrorrhagia	N92.1
	Endometrial polyp	N84.0
	Corpus luteum cysts of both ovaries	N83.1
	Total abdominal hysterectomy	0UT90ZZ
	Bilateral salpingo-oophorectomy	0UTC0ZZ
		0UT20ZZ
		0UT70ZZ
11.	Cystocele with incomplete uterine prolapse	N81.2
	and stress incontinence	N39.3
		0JQC0ZZ
	Cystocele repair (open approach)	0US90ZZ
	Vaginal suspension of uterus (open approach)	
12.	Pelvic peritoneal endometriosis	N80.3
13.	Dermoid cyst of left ovary	D27.1
	Laparoscopic wedge resection of ovarian cyst	0UB14ZZ
14.	Infertility due to pelvic peritoneal adhesions blocking tubes	N73.6
		N97.1
	Hysterosalpingogram, radiopaque dye	BU18YZZ
	Fluoroscopy	
15.	Psychogenic dysmenorrhea	F45.8
16.	Adhesions of ovary and fallopian tubes	N73.6
	Laparoscopic lysis of adhesions	0UN24ZZ
		0UN74ZZ
17.	Menorrhagia	N92.0
	Dilatation and curettage with vaginal endometrial ablation	0U5B7ZZ
18.	Submucous fibroid of uterus	D25.0
	Laparoscopically assisted partial vaginal hysterectomy (leaving cervix intact)	0UT9FZZ

Coding OF **Diseases** OF THE **Skin** AND **Diseases** OF THE **Musculoskeletal System**

CHAPTER 22

Diseases of the Skin and Subcutaneous Tissue

CHAPTER OVERVIEW

- Diseases of the skin and subcutaneous tissue can be found in chapter 12 of ICD-10-CM.
- Categories L23–L25 classify dermatitis due to plants, food, drugs, and medications in contact with skin.
- Category L27 classifies dermatitis caused by medications taken internally.
    - —The coder must determine whether the condition is an adverse effect of proper administration or a poisoning due to the incorrect use of the drug.
    - —Codes from categories T36 through T65 are used to classify the causation.
- Chronic ulcers of the skin are classified using the fifth character to specify the site.
- The sequencing of the code for cellulitis is dependent on the severity of the wound and the primary goal of the treatment (for cellulitis or for the wound).
- Debridement is classified as either excisional or nonexcisional (brushing, irrigating, scrubbing, or washing).

LEARNING OUTCOMES

After studying this chapter you should be able to:

Know how to classify dermatitis due to contact, food, and ingestion of drug (both correct and incorrect usage).

Code ulcers of the skin.

Explain how to classify cellulitis based on location and the primary goal of the treatment.

Code procedures done on the skin, such as excisions, debridement, and grafting.

TERMS TO KNOW

Cellulitis
an infection of the skin and soft tissues resulting from some sort of break in the skin

Debridement
removal of dead, damaged, or infected tissue

REMEMBER . . .

Chapter 12 of ICD-10-CM includes more than just conditions of the skin. It also includes conditions of the nails, sweat glands, hair, and hair follicles.

INTRODUCTION

Chapter 12 of ICD-10-CM deals with conditions affecting the skin and subcutaneous tissue. The chapter is organized around the following subdivisions:

L00–L08	Infections of skin and subcutaneous tissue
L10–L14	Bullous disorders
L20–L30	Dermatitis and eczema
L40–L45	Papulosquamous disorders
L49–L54	Urticaria and erythema
L55–L59	Radiation-related disorders of the skin and subcutaneous tissue
L60–L75	Disorders of skin appendages
L76	Intraoperative and postprocedural complications of skin and subcutaneous tissue
L80–L99	Other disorders of the skin and subcutaneous tissue

Conditions affecting the nails, sweat glands, hair, and hair follicles are included in this chapter. Congenital conditions of skin, hair, and nails are classified in categories Q80–Q84. Neoplasms of skin are classified in chapter 2 of ICD-10-CM.

DERMATITIS DUE TO DRUGS

ICD-10-CM uses the terms "dermatitis" and "eczema" synonymously and interchangeably in the L20–L30 category range. There are several types of dermatitis, such as atopic (L20.-), seborrheic (L21.-), diaper (L22), allergic contact (L23.-), irritant contact (L24.-), and exfoliative (L26).

Contact dermatitis is a localized rash or irritation of the skin caused by contact with allergens (allergic-contact dermatitis) or irritants (irritant-contact dermatitis). Category L23 is used to classify allergic-contact dermatitis due to metals, adhesive, cosmetics, drugs, dyes, chemical products, food, and plants in contact with skin. Category L24 is assigned for irritant-contact dermatitis caused by irritants in contact with skin, such as detergents, oils and greases, and solvents. Category L25, Unspecified contact dermatitis, is used when the contact dermatitis is not specified as allergic- or irritant-contact dermatitis. Category L27 is for dermatitis due to substances taken internally.

In coding dermatitis caused by medicines, the coder must first determine whether the condition represents an adverse effect due to the proper administration of a drug or poisoning due to the incorrect use of the drug. When the dermatitis is due to a medication used correctly as prescribed, it is considered an adverse effect. When the dermatitis is due to incorrect use of the drug, it is classified as a poisoning by drugs, medicaments, and biological substances.

When coding allergic-contact dermatitis, irritant-contact dermatitis, unspecified contact dermatitis, and dermatitis due to substances taken internally, a code from categories T36 through T65 should be assigned to indicate the way in which the poisoning or adverse effect occurred (e.g., accidental, intentional self-harm) and the type of drug involved. The sequencing of the code from categories T36 through T65 will depend on the circumstances: When the condition is due to poisoning, the T36–T65 code is assigned first; it is assigned as an additional code when the condition is due to adverse effect. (A more detailed discussion of the distinction between adverse effects and poisoning due to drugs and medications is provided in chapter 30 of this handbook.)

Correct coding examples include the following:

L27.0 + T36.0x5A	Initial encounter for dermatitis due to allergic reaction to penicillin tablets, taken as prescribed (adverse reaction)
T36.0x1A + L27.0	Initial encounter for dermatitis due to accidental ingestion of mother's penicillin tablets (poisoning)

In the first example, which indicates an adverse reaction to a prescribed medication taken as directed, the code for the dermatitis is sequenced first, followed by the code for the adverse effect of the penicillin. In the second example, code **T36.0x1A, Poisoning by penicillin, accidental, initial encounter,** is sequenced first, with an additional code to indicate that the effect of the poisoning is dermatitis.

Palmar plantar erythrodysesthesia (PPE), also called hand foot syndrome, is an example of a specific dermatitis that occurs as an adverse reaction to antineoplastic or biologic drugs used for cancer treatment. After the administration of chemotherapy, small amounts of the drug can leak from the capillaries, damaging tissue in the palms of the hands and the soles of the feet. The leakage results in redness, tenderness, and peeling of the palms and soles. The affected area resembles sunburn and may become dry, peeled, and numb. This condition affects the hands and feet because of the increased friction and heat to which the extremities are exposed through normal use. Treatment involves reducing or stopping the drug therapy. Assign code **L27.1, Localized skin eruption due to drugs and medicaments taken internally,** followed by code **T45.1x5A, Adverse effect of antineoplastic and immunosuppressive drugs, initial encounter,** for the PPE due to antineoplastic antibiotics.

ERYTHEMA MULTIFORME

Erythema multiforme is a skin disorder resulting in symmetrical red, raised skin areas all over the body, often resembling targets because they are dark circles with purple-gray centers. In some cases, there are severe systemic symptoms. Erythema multiforme can occur in response to medications, infections, or illness. The exact cause is unknown. If the condition is a drug-induced adverse effect, assign code L51- first. Assign a code from T36–T50 with fifth or sixth character 5 as an additional code to identify the responsible drug.

FIGURE 22.1 The Skin and Subcutaneous Tissue

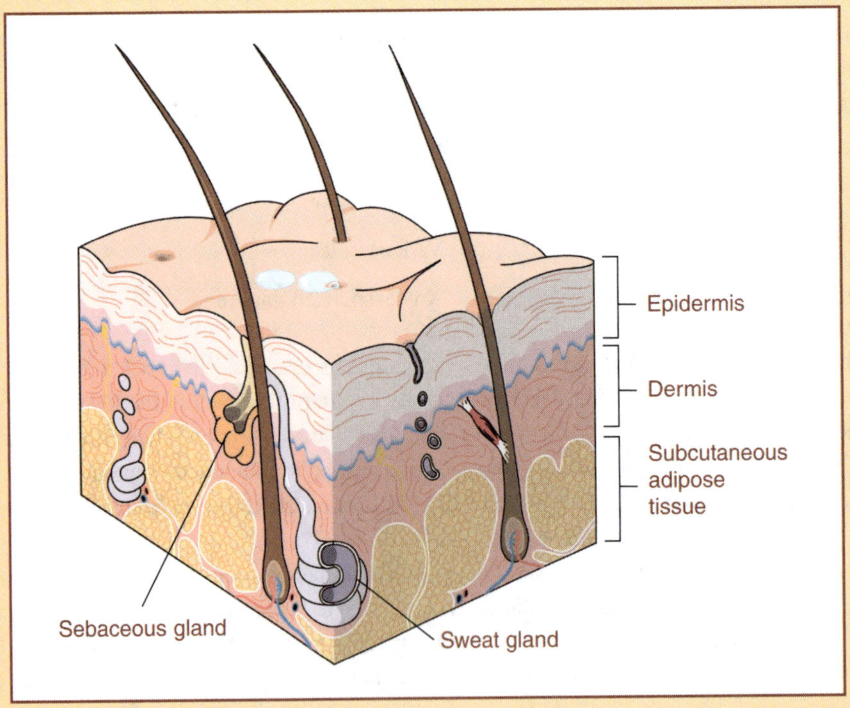

The different types of erythema multiforme are classified as follows:

L51.0	Nonbullous erythema multiforme
L51.1	Stevens-Johnson syndrome
L51.2	Toxic epidermal necrolysis [Lyell]
L51.3	Stevens-Johnson syndrome-toxic epidermal necrolysis overlap syndrome
L51.8	Other erythema multiforme
L51.9	Erythema multiforme, unspecified

Patients with erythema multiforme may also suffer from a variety of other associated manifestations that should be coded separately. The manifestations range from arthropathy (M14.8-) to corneal ulcer (H16.0.-) to stomatitis (K12.-) and several other conditions. In addition, a code from category L49 is reported to reflect the percentage of body surface involved with skin exfoliation.

ULCERS OF THE SKIN

Most chronic ulcers of the skin are classified in categories L89, Pressure ulcer, and L97, Nonpressure chronic ulcer of lower limb, not elsewhere classified, with code I96 assigned first when gangrene is present. A code from L97 may be used as a principal or first-listed code if no underlying condition is documented as the cause of the ulcer. If one of the underlying conditions listed below is documented with a lower-extremity ulcer, a causal condition should be assumed and the underlying condition should be coded first:

I70.23-, I70.24-, I70.33-, I70.34-, I70.43-, I70.44-, I70.53-, I70.54-, I70.63-, I70.64-, I70.73-, I70.74-	Atherosclerosis of the lower extremities
I87.31-, I87.33-	Chronic venous hypertension
E08.621, E08.622, E09.621, E09.622, E10.621, E10.622, E11.621, E11.622, E13.621, E13.622	Diabetic ulcers
I87.01-, I87.03-	Postphlebitic syndrome
I87.01-, I87.03-	Postthrombotic syndrome
I83.0-, I83.2-	Varicose ulcer
I96	Any associated gangrene

Chronic ulcer of the skin, not otherwise specified, is classified to subcategory L98.4, Nonpressure chronic ulcer of skin, not elsewhere classified. Arteriosclerosis of the lower extremities is classified to subcategories I70.2 through I70.7 with fifth characters 3 or 4 when it is associated with ulceration. An additional code from category L97 is assigned to indicate the severity of the ulcer. If gangrene is present, assign code I70.26- or I70.36- with an additional code from L98.49- to identify the severity of any ulcer, if applicable.

Codes from category L89, Pressure ulcer, are combination codes that identify the site of the pressure ulcer as well as the stage of the ulcer. Category L89 provides fifth characters to identify the specific site of the ulcer, such as elbow (L89.0-); back (L89.1-); hip (L89.2-); buttock (L89.3-); contiguous site of back, buttock, and hip (L89.4-); ankle (L89.5-); heel (L89.6-); other site (L89.8-);

and unspecified site (L89.9-). The sixth character for category L89 indicates the severity of the ulcer by identifying the stage of the pressure ulcers, such as unstageable, stage 1, stage 2, stage 3, stage 4, or unspecified.

The code assignment for the pressure ulcer stage may be based on nursing documentation; however, the associated diagnosis of pressure ulcer should be coded on the basis of the provider's documentation (namely, the physician or any qualified health care practitioner who is legally accountable for establishing the patient's diagnosis, as defined in the *ICD-10-CM Official Guidelines for Coding and Reporting*).

Care should be taken not to confuse a pressure ulcer in which the stage is unspecified or not documented (L89.- with a sixth character of "9") with a pressure ulcer documented as unstageable (L89.- with a sixth character of "0"). The staging of pressure ulcers takes into account the depth of tissue loss and the depth of tissue exposed. "Unstageable" refers to pressure ulcers whose stage cannot be clinically determined (e.g., the ulcer is covered by eschar or has been treated with a skin or muscle graft) as well as pressure ulcers documented as deep tissue injury but not documented as due to trauma. The assignment of the pressure ulcer stage code should be guided by clinical documentation of the stage or the terms found in the Alphabetic Index. The provider should be queried if the clinical term cannot be found in the Index or if there is no documentation of the stage.

Documentation of pressure ulcers may sometimes refer to "deep tissue injury." Care should be taken to review the provider documentation to determine whether the term refers to a traumatic injury (such as a contusion) or a pressure ulcer. The Alphabetic Index entry for "Injury, deep tissue" refers the coder to "*see Contusion, by site*"; whereas the entry for "Injury, deep tissue, meaning pressure ulcer" refers the coder to "*see Ulcer, pressure, unstageable, by site*."

If a patient is admitted with a pressure ulcer of one stage, and it progresses to a higher stage, the code for the highest stage reported for that site should be reported. For example, the condition of an individual admitted with stage 2 pressure ulcer of left heel, which advances to stage 3 during the encounter, should be coded to **L89.623, Pressure ulcer of left heel, stage 3.**

Care should be taken to distinguish between pressure ulcers documented as "healed" (no code assigned) and "healing" (assign the appropriate code for the stage documented). If the documentation does not provide information about the stage of the healing pressure ulcer, assign the appropriate code for unspecified stage.

Examples of correct coding for chronic ulcers of the skin include the following:

L89.154	Pressure ulcer, sacral area, stage 4
I96 + L89.153	Pressure ulcer, sacral area, stage 3 with gangrene
L97.909	Ulcer of lower limb, except pressure ulcer
L89.210	Unstageable pressure ulcer of the right hip
L89.149	Pressure ulcer left lower back
L98.499	Chronic ulcer of skin unspecified site

Stasis ulcers are ordinarily due to varicose veins of the lower extremities and are coded to category I83, Varicose veins of lower extremities, rather than to the categories for conditions of the skin. When the physician has used the term "stasis ulcer" but has identified a cause other than varicose veins, code the condition to **I87.2, Venous insufficiency (chronic) (peripheral).** A basic rule of coding is that further research must be done when the title of the code suggested by the Alphabetic Index clearly does not identify the condition correctly. In this case, even though the Index directs the coder to a code involving varicose veins, the code should not be used when no varicosities are present.

CELLULITIS OF THE SKIN

Cellulitis is an acute, diffuse infection of the skin and soft tissues that commonly results from a break in the skin, such as a puncture wound, a laceration, or an ulcer. Occasionally, the break is so small that it cannot be identified by either the patient or the examining physician. Clinically, cellulitis usually presents as an abrupt onset of redness, swelling, pain, or heat in the infected area. Coders should not assume, however, that a reference to redness at the edges of a wound or an ulcer represents cellulitis. The normal hyperemia associated with a wound usually extends a small distance beyond the edges of the wound rather than extending to the diffuse pattern that characterizes cellulitis.

Coding of cellulitis secondary to superficial injury, burn, or frostbite requires two codes, one for the injury and one for the cellulitis. Sequencing of codes depends on the circumstances of the admission. When the patient is seen primarily for treatment of an open wound, the appropriate code for open wound is assigned, with an additional code for the cellulitis. When the wound itself is trivial or when it was treated earlier and the patient is now being seen for treatment of the cellulitis, the code for the cellulitis may be sequenced first, with an additional code for the open wound. For example:

- A patient suffers laceration of the right lower leg while on a hiking trip two days ago and comes to the hospital on his return. By the time he is seen, cellulitis is beginning to develop. The wound is cleansed of the foreign material, nonexcisional debridement is carried out, and antibiotics are started for the cellulitis.

Principal diagnosis:	S81.821A	Laceration with foreign body, right lower leg, initial encounter
Additional diagnosis:	L03.115	Cellulitis of right lower limb
Procedure:	0HDKXZZ	Extraction of right lower leg skin, external approach

- A patient suffers a minor puncture injury to the right finger when removing a staple at the office. Five days later, he is admitted to the hospital because of cellulitis of the finger and is treated with intravenous antibiotics. The wound itself does not require treatment, and therefore no code for injury is assigned.

Principal diagnosis:	L03.011	Cellulitis of right finger

Both cellulitis and lymphangitis of skin are included in category L03. However, separate codes are available for cellulitis and lymphangitis. An additional code should be assigned to indicate the organism responsible (B95–B96), if this information is available. The responsible organism is usually *Streptococcus.*

Cellulitis may also present as a postoperative wound infection or as a result of the penetration of the skin involved in intravenous therapy. For example:

- A patient had an appendectomy six days ago and is now readmitted with evidence of staphylococcal cellulitis of the operative wound.

Principal diagnosis:	T81.4xxA	Infection following procedure
Additional diagnosis:	L03.311	Cellulitis of abdominal wall
Additional diagnosis:	B95.8	*Staphylococcus*

Cellulitis frequently develops as a complication of chronic skin ulcers, in which case it is assigned to a code from category L89 or L97, or subcategory L98.4. These codes do not include any associated cellulitis, so two codes are required to describe these conditions. Designation of the principal diagnosis depends on the circumstances of the admission.

Cellulitis described as gangrenous is classified to code **I96, Gangrene, not elsewhere classified.** When gangrene is present with an ulcer or injury, the gangrene is coded first, with the code for the injury or ulcer assigned as an additional code. This practice follows the instructional notes in the Tabular List to code first any associated gangrene.

OTHER CELLULITIS

Although cellulitis most commonly occurs in the skin and subcutaneous tissue, it also occurs in other areas. In such cases, codes from other chapters of ICD-10-CM are assigned as appropriate.

Cellulitis of female external genital organs is classified as an inflammatory condition and assigned code N76.4. Pelvic cellulitis in women is classified as an inflammatory condition and is assigned to category N73. Occasionally, pelvic cellulitis occurs following abortion, delivery, or molar or ectopic pregnancy, in which case it is classified to chapter 15 of ICD-10-CM. In male patients, pelvic cellulitis is coded as **K65.0, Generalized (acute) peritonitis.**

EXCISION OF LESION

In order to correctly assign a procedure code for the removal of lesions, it is important to first determine whether the procedure was performed on the skin (body system "skin and breast"), or subcutaneous tissue and fascia (body system "subcutaneous tissue and fascia"). Next, determine whether the root operation performed is "Excision" (cutting out or off, without replacement, a portion of a body part) or "Destruction" (physical eradication of all or a portion of a body part by the direct use of energy, force, or a destructive agent). For most skin excisions and destructions, the approach used will be external. For example:

- A simple excision involving only the skin of the face is classified to the root operation "Excision" and coded to **0HB1XZZ, Excision of face skin, external approach.**
- Removal of lesions carried out by cauterization, cryosurgery, fulguration, or laser beam are classified to the root operation "Destruction," such as fulguration of a skin tag of the chest, which is coded to **0H55XZZ, Destruction of chest skin, external approach.**

When the removal of the lesion goes beyond the skin and involves underlying and/or adjacent tissue such as subcutaneous tissue and fascia, the procedure is classified to the "subcutaneous tissue and fascia" body system. The surgeon's description should be followed carefully when assigning these codes in order to determine whether the root operation is "Excision" or "Destruction" and whether the approach was open (cutting through the skin or mucous membrane) or percutaneous (by puncture or minor incision through the skin or mucous membrane). For example:

- Excision of Kaposi's sarcoma of the subcutaneous tissue, right thigh, is classified to the root operation "Excision" and coded to **0JBL0ZZ, Excision of right upper leg subcutaneous tissue and fascia, open approach.**
- Open fulguration of a benign subcutaneous tissue lesion of the right upper arm is classified to the root operation "Destruction" and coded to **0J5D0ZZ, Destruction of right upper arm subcutaneous tissue and fascia, open approach.**

DEBRIDEMENT

Debridement of the skin and subcutaneous tissue is a procedure by which foreign material and devitalized or contaminated tissue are removed from a traumatic or infected lesion until the surrounding healthy tissue is exposed.

Excisional debridement of the skin or subcutaneous tissue is the surgical removal or cutting away of such tissue, necrosis, or slough and is classified to the root operation "Excision." Depending on the availability of a surgical suite or the extent of the area involved, excisional debridement can be performed in the operating room, in the emergency department, or at the patient's bedside. Excisional debridement may be performed by a physician and/or another health care provider and involves an excisional, as opposed to a mechanical (brushing, scrubbing, washing), debridement. Use of a sharp instrument does not always indicate that an excisional debridement was performed. Minor removal of loose fragments with scissors or using a sharp instrument to scrape away tissue is not an excisional debridement. Excisional debridement involves the use of a scalpel to remove devitalized tissue. Documentation of excisional debridement should be specific regarding the type of debridement. If the documentation is not clear or if there is any question about the procedure, the provider should be queried for clarification.

Nonexcisional debridement of the skin is the nonoperative brushing, irrigating, scrubbing, or washing of devitalized tissue, necrosis, slough, or foreign material. Most nonexcisional debridement procedures are classified to the root operation "Extraction" (pulling or stripping out or off all or a portion of a body part by the use of force), except when it is performed by irrigating the devitalized tissue. In that case, the debridement is coded to the Administration Section, root operation "Irrigation." Nonexcisional debridement may be performed by a physician or by other health care personnel. Examples of nonexcisional debridement include Versajet and ultrasonic debridement. The Versajet consists of an ultra-high-pressure generator with a console and disposable attachments. A natural vacuum created by the jet stream removes tissue fragments. Specialized features allow physicians to debride traumatic wounds, chronic wounds, or other soft-tissue lesions and aspirate and remove contaminants or other debris.

When coding for debridement of areas other than skin, excisional debridement is coded to the root operation "Excision" of the specific body part.

When coding multiple-layer debridements of the same site, the coder should assign a code only for the deepest layer of debridement. For example, open excision and debridement of a coccyx wound including bone is coded to **0QBS0ZZ, Excision of coccyx, open approach.** Debridement carried out in conjunction with another procedure is often included in the code for the procedure, but not always.

DERMAL REGENERATIVE GRAFT

Several new technologies that are able to permanently regenerate or replace skin layers are now being used to treat severe burns. Procedures involving the application of grafts are classified to the root operation "Replacement" (putting in or on biological or synthetic material that physically takes the place and/or function of all or a portion of a body part). The approach on all the skin replacement procedures is "external." The root operation "Replacement" identifies through the device character the use of synthetic substitutes (sixth character "J"), autologous tissue substitutes (sixth character "7"), and nonautologous tissue substitute (sixth character "K").

Examples of skin synthetic substitutes include:

- Artificial skin, not otherwise specified
- Creation of "neodermis"
- Decellularized allodermis
- Integumentary matrix implants
- Prosthetic implant of dermal layer of skin
- Regenerate dermal layer of skin

Code **T85.693-, Other mechanical complication of artificial skin graft and decellularized allodermis,** is assigned for failure or rejection of these systems. Codes **T86.820, Skin graft (allograft) rejection,** and **T86.821, Skin graft (allograft) (autograft) failure,** are assigned for complication of other skin graft. Status code Z96.81 is assigned to indicate that the patient has an artificial skin graft.

EXERCISE 22.1

The following exercise provides examples of conditions classified in chapter 12 of ICD-10-CM. Code the following diagnoses and procedures.

1.	Varicose ulcer, lower right leg with severe inflammation	I83.219
2.	Pilonidal fistula with abscess	L05.02
	Excision of pilonidal sinus	0HB8XZZ
3.	Large abscess of trunk due to *Staphylococcus aureus*	L02.219 B95.61
	Infection Incision and drainage of abscess, trunk (chest)	0H95XZZ
4.	Hard corn deformity, right little toe Soft corn deformities, third, fourth, and fifth toes, right	L84
5.	Keloid scar on left hand from previous burn	L91.0 T23.002S
	Excision of scar left hand	0HBGXZZ
6.	Chronic purulent inflamed acne rosacea of lower lip	L71.9
	Wide excision of chronic acne rosacea of lower lip (external) with full-thickness autologous graft over defect, lower lip Replacement	0CR1X7Z
7.	Giant urticaria, initial encounter	T78.3xxA

8.	Contact dermatitis of eyelid	H01.119
9.	Seborrheic keratosis underlying the second metatarsal head, right foot	L82.1
10.	Cellulitis of anus	K61.0
11.	Acute lymphangitis, right upper arm, due to group A streptococcal infection	L03.123 B95.0
12.	Gangrenous diabetic ulcer of right foot due to peripheral circulatory disorder	E11.621 E11.52 L97.519
13.	Surgical (excisional) debridement of skin and fascia of right foot	0JBQ0ZZ
14.	Infected ingrown toenail, right great toe Ablative electrocauterization of toenail	L60.0 0H5RXZZ
15.	Cellulitis, buttock	L03.317
16.	Cellulitis of left upper eyelid	H00.034
17.	Nonexcisional debridement of right diabetic heel ulcer	E11.621 L97.419 0HDMXZZ

CHAPTER 23 Diseases of the Musculoskeletal System and Connective Tissue

CHAPTER OVERVIEW

- Diseases of the musculoskeletal system and connective tissue are covered in chapter 13 of ICD-10-CM.
- Most of the codes within chapter 13 have site and laterality designations referring to the bone, joint, or muscle involved.
- If there is no "multiple sites" code provided and if more than one bone, joint, or muscle is involved, separate codes should be used to indicate the different sites involved.
- Coding back pain is often dependent on the distinction between degeneration and displacement and on the presence or absence of myelopathy.
- Arthritis can be coded independently or in a dual-coding situation if it is a manifestation of another condition.
- Osteoarthritis can be further classified based on whether it is primary or secondary.
- Fractures are considered either stress fractures, pathological fractures, or traumatic fractures.
  - —Fractures that are spontaneous are always considered pathological.
  - —A traumatic fracture should never be coded on the same bone as a pathological fracture.
- Coding joint replacements requires knowledge of the joint involved.
- Coding joint revisions requires information on the removal of any joint-replacement components.
- Coding spinal fusion requires knowing the anatomic portion (column) fused, the approach used (anterior, posterior, or lateral transverse), and whether two or more vertebrae are fused.
- Coding spinal disc prostheses requires knowledge of the type of prosthesis and the segment treated.
- Other conditions coded in chapter 13 include plica syndrome and fasciitis.

LEARNING OUTCOMES

After studying this chapter you should be able to:

Explain the different types of arthritis and what to look for when coding arthritis.

Explain the difference between pathological and traumatic fractures.

Code joint replacements and revisions.

Code back disorders and the variety of procedures for correcting spinal problems.

TERMS TO KNOW

Joint revision
procedure that adjusts, removes, or replaces a joint-replacement component

Myelopathy
damage to the myelinated fiber tracts that carry information to the brain

Osteoarthritis
the most common form of arthritis; a degenerative joint disease

Pathological fracture
fracture that occurs in a bone weakened by disease

REMEMBER . . .

Separate codes are assigned to indicate different sites when no multiple site code is provided.

INTRODUCTION

Chapter 13 of ICD-10-CM is governed by the general coding guidelines already discussed in this handbook. An understanding of the following terms may be helpful to the coder in assigning codes from chapter 13:

- Arthropathy: disorder of the joint
- Arthritis: inflammation of the joint
- Dorsopathy: disorder of the back
- Myelopathy: disorder of the spinal cord
- Radiculopathy: problem in which one or more nerves are affected resulting in pain (radicular pain), weakness, numbness, or difficulty controlling specific muscles.

Most arthropathies are classified in categories M00 through M25 in ICD-10-CM, and most dorsopathies in categories M40 through M54.

Site and Laterality

Most of the codes within chapter 13 have site and laterality designations. The site refers to either the bone, joint, or muscle involved. For some conditions in which more than one bone, joint, or muscle is usually involved (e.g., osteoarthritis), a code is available for "multiple sites." If no multiple sites code is provided and if more than one bone, joint, or muscle is involved, separate codes should be used to indicate the different sites involved.

Bone versus Joint

For certain conditions, the bone may be affected at the upper or lower end (e.g., avascular necrosis of bone, M87, Osteoporosis, M80, M81). Though the portion of the bone affected may be at the joint, the site designation will be the bone, not the joint.

Acute Traumatic versus Chronic or Recurrent Musculoskeletal Conditions

Many musculoskeletal conditions are a result of previous injury or trauma to a site, or are recurrent conditions. Chapter 13 of ICD-10-CM contains bone, joint, or muscle conditions that are the result of a healed injury as well as recurrent conditions of these sites. ICD-10-CM classifies current, acute injuries to chapter 19. Chronic or recurrent conditions should generally be coded with a code from chapter 13. If it is difficult to determine from the documentation in the record which code is best to describe a condition, query the provider.

BACK DISORDERS

Back pain described as lumbago or low back pain, without further qualification, is coded **M54.5, Low back pain.** Back pain not otherwise specified is coded **M54.9, Dorsalgia, unspecified.** Psychogenic back pain is classified under M54.9 and **F45.41, Pain disorder exclusively related to psychological factors.**

Intervertebral disc disorders are classified in categories M50, Cervical disc disorders, and M51, Thoracic, thoracolumbar, and lumbosacral intervertebral disc disorders. Careful attention to the terminology is important in coding these conditions. Degeneration of the disc is not the same condition as displacement (herniation) of the disc, and each requires a different code. For cervical disc disorders (category M50), the code for the most superior level affected should be used.

FIGURE 23.1 The Human Skeleton

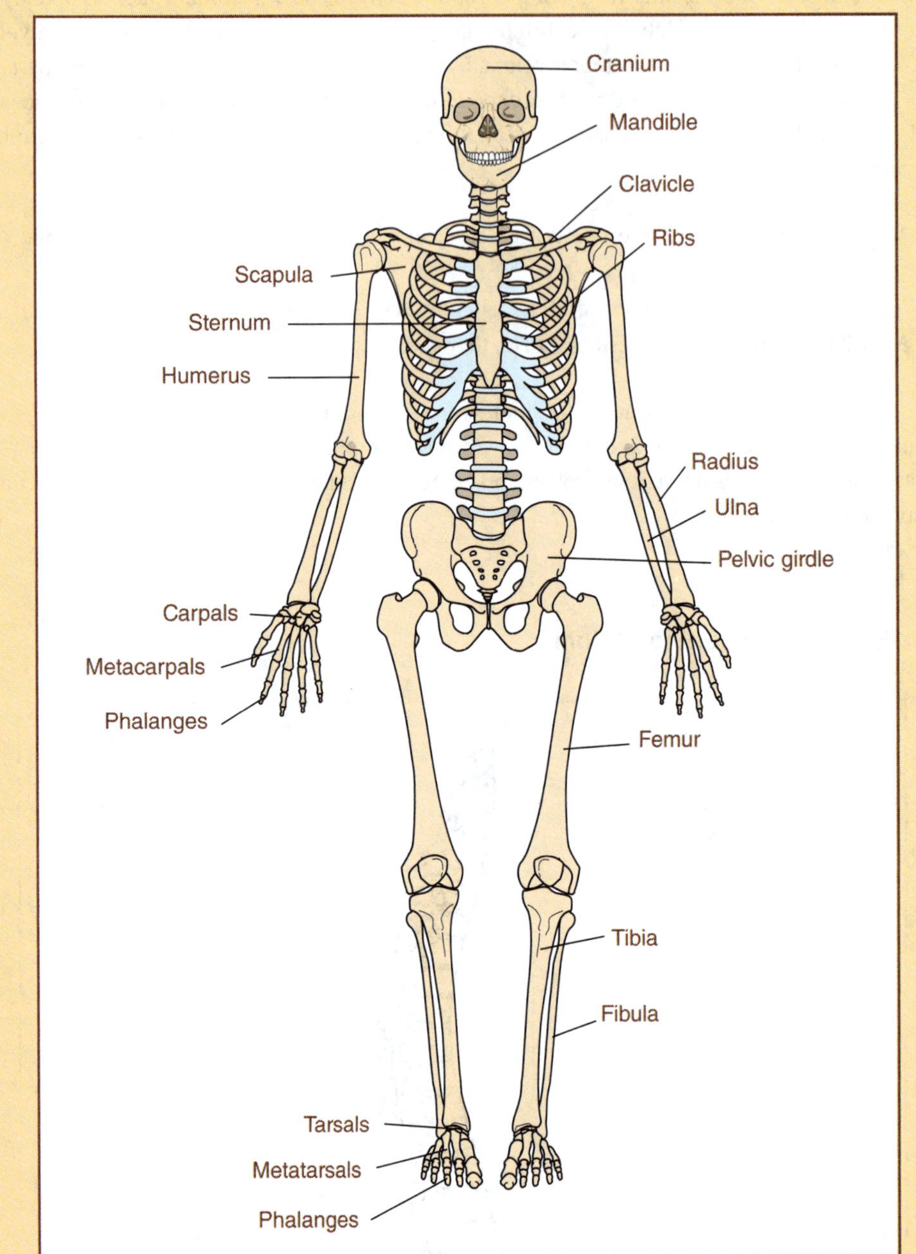

The presence or absence of myelopathy is an important distinction to be made in assigning codes for certain back disorders. Myelopathy is a functional disorder and/or pathological change in the spinal cord that often results from compression. Codes for back disorders such as spondylosis and herniation of the intervertebral disc differentiate between conditions with and without myelopathy. Codes for a herniated disc without myelopathy include those with paresthesia but not paralysis. Terms included in intervertebral disc disorders with myelopathy are classified into subcategories M50.0- and M51.0-, with a fifth character used to indicate the site involved. Examples include the following:

M50.20 Herniated intervertebral disc, cervical, unspecified cervical region, without myelopathy
M51.06 Herniated intervertebral disc, lumbosacral, with myelopathy, lumbar region
M51.24 Herniated intervertebral disc, thoracic, without myelopathy

Categories M50 and M51 are also subclassified, according to whether radiculopathy is present, into subcategories M50.1 and M51.1, with the fifth character indicating the site involved. Radiculopathy refers to a nerve root problem resulting in weakness, numbness, or difficulty controlling specific muscles.

FIGURE 23.2 The Spinal Column

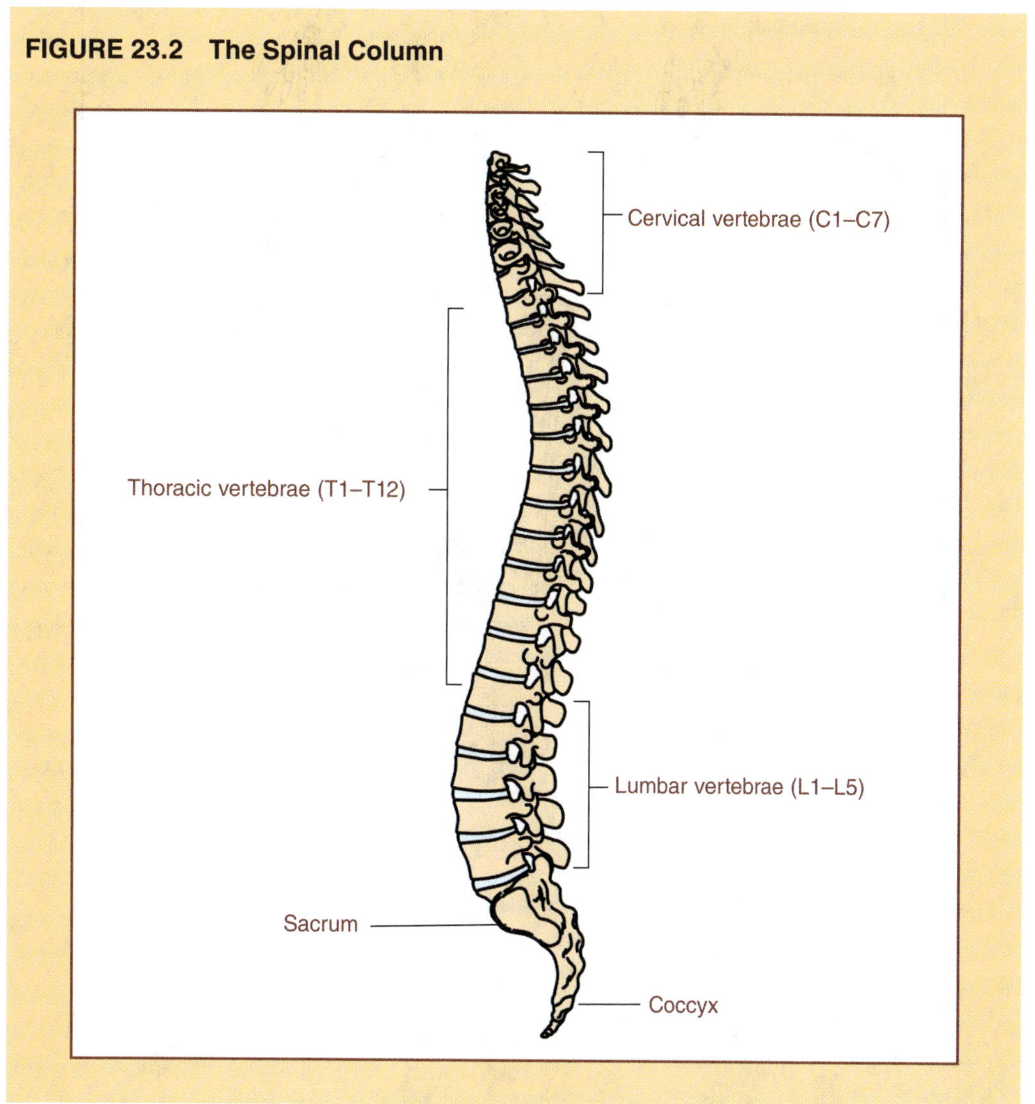

Back pain associated with herniation of an intervertebral disc is included in the code for the herniated disc; no additional code is assigned.

Surgery for the excision or destruction of a herniated disc is classified in ICD-10-PCS by the type of surgery performed. Examples include the following:

0SB40ZZ	Open excision of herniated lumbosacral intervertebral disc
0R5B3ZZ	Destruction of displaced thoracolumbar intervertebral disc by chemonucleolysis, percutaneous approach
0S523ZZ	Percutaneous destruction of lumbar vertebral disc
0RB10ZZ	Open excision of cervical vertebral joint

Code **00JU0ZZ, Inspection of spinal canal, open approach,** is assigned for a laminectomy performed for the purpose of exploration or decompression of the spinal canal. Laminectomy performed for the purpose of excision of herniated disc material, however, represents the operative approach and is not coded separately. Instead, the root operation "Excision" is coded to report the excision of the disc. Occasionally after a decompression laminotomy, Mersilene stabilization may be carried out to reconstitute the intraspinous ligament. The placement of Mersilene sutures is inherent to the total procedure and should not be coded separately.

ARTHRITIS

Arthritis is the common term for a wide variety of conditions that primarily affect the joints, muscles, and connective tissue. The associated symptoms are inflammation, swelling, pain, stiffness, and mobility problems. Arthritis may occur independently, but it is also a common manifestation of a variety of other conditions. Combination codes should be used when available, and dual-coding guidelines should be applied when combination codes are not available. Examples include the following:

M11.811	Arthritis of the right shoulder due to dicalcium phosphate crystals
E11.610	Charcot's arthritis due to type 2 diabetes
C95.90 + M36.1	Arthritis due to leukemia
D66 + M36.2	Hemophilic arthritis
A69.23	Arthritis associated with Lyme disease

Osteoarthritis is the most common form of arthritis; it is also called polyarthritis, degenerative arthritis, and hypertrophic arthritis. It is a degenerative joint disease, usually occurring in older people, with chronic degeneration of the articular cartilage and hypertrophy of the bone. It is characterized by pain and swelling. Codes from categories M15 through M19 are assigned for osteoarthritis, except when the spine is involved, in which case a code from category M47, Spondylosis, is assigned.

The primary axis for coding osteoarthritis is the site, whether it involves multiple sites (M15.-, Osteoarthritis) or single joints. Bilateral involvement of single joint is coded to categories M16 through M19. Codes further specify whether the condition is primary or secondary (for example, posttraumatic). Primary osteoarthritis, also known as polyarticular degenerative arthritis, affects joints in the spine, knee, and hip, as well as certain small joints of the hands and feet. Secondary arthritis, also called monoarticular arthritis, is confined to the joints of one area and results from some external or internal injury or disease. Osteoarthritis that involves multiple sites but is not specified as generalized is coded as **M15.9, Polyosteoarthritis, unspecified.**

Rheumatoid arthritis (categories M05–M06), another fairly common type of arthritis, is an autoimmune disease that affects the entire body. Pyogenic arthritis (M00.-) is due to infection and is classified to the causative organism (*Staphylococcus*, *Pneumococcus*, *Streptococcus*, or other bacteria), with additional characters to indicate the joints involved. An additional code should be assigned for the responsible organism. Category M01 is used to report direct infections of joints in infectious and parasitic diseases. The underlying disease, such as leprosy, mycoses, or parathyroid fever, should be coded first. Gouty arthritis is a recurrent arthritis of the peripheral joints in which excessive uric acid in the blood is deposited in the joints. Gouty arthritis is classified to idiopathic gout. Category M10, Gout, is further subdivided to distinguish whether it is idiopathic (M10.0-), due to lead (M10.1-), drug induced (M10.2-), due to renal impairment (M10.3-), or other secondary gout (M10.4-). Unspecified gout is coded to M10.9. When the gout is specified to be chronic, it is classified to category M1A, Chronic gout, with seventh characters added to specify with or without tophus (crystallized uric acid deposit under the skin).

EXERCISE 23.1

Code the following diagnoses and procedures. Do not assign External cause of morbidity codes.

1. Acute gouty arthritis, right foot	M10.71
2. Chronic nodular rheumatoid arthritis with polyneuropathy	M05.50
3. Traumatic arthritis, left ankle, due to old traumatic dislocation Arthroscopic arthrodesis, left ankle	M12.572 S93.05xS 0SGG4ZZ
4. Herniated intervertebral disc, L4-5 Laminectomy with excision of intervertebral disc, L4-5	M51.26 0SB20ZZ
5. Chronic lumbosacral sprain, subsequent encounter	S33.9xxD

DERANGEMENT

Internal derangement of the knee is classified to category M23; derangement of other specific joints is classified to category M24, with additional characters indicating the site. Recurrent nontraumatic dislocation of the knee is classified to M22.0-, Recurrent dislocation of patella. Recurrent dislocation or subluxation of joints is classified to M24.4-, Recurrent dislocation of joint. Derangement of the knee due to current injury is classified to dislocation under S83.104-, S83.105-, or S83.106-. However, derangement of the meniscus or cartilage of the knee due to current injury is classified to subcategory S83.2-, Tear of meniscus, current injury.

EXERCISE 23.2

Code the following diagnoses. Do not assign External cause of morbidity codes.

1. Recurrent derangement of left ankle	M24.472
2. Recurrent derangement of knee	M23.90
3. Derangement of right knee due to a current fall, initial encounter	S83.104A

OSTEOPOROSIS

Osteoporosis is a systemic condition that affects all bones of the musculoskeletal system and leads to an increased risk of pathological fractures. In osteoporosis, the bones are thinner and weaker than normal. Osteoporosis is classified to categories M80 and M81 depending on whether a current pathological fracture is present or not. Because osteoporosis is a systemic condition, site is not a component of the codes under category M81, Osteoporosis without current pathological fracture. The codes under category M80, Osteoporosis with current pathological fracture, identify the osteoporosis and the site of the pathological fracture.

PATHOLOGICAL FRACTURES

Pathological fractures occur in bones that are weakened by disease. These fractures are usually spontaneous but sometimes occur in connection with slight trauma (such as a minor fall) that ordinarily would not result in a fracture in normal, healthy bone. There are many different underlying causes for pathological fractures, including osteoporosis, metastatic tumor of the bone, osteomyelitis, Paget's disease, disuse atrophy, hyperparathyroidism, and nutritional or congenital disorders.

Fractures described as spontaneous are always pathological fractures. When the fracture is described as a compression fracture, the record should be reviewed to determine whether any significant trauma has been experienced. A fall from a height, such as a diving board, with compression fracture of the spine is classified as an injury, but a compression fracture in an older patient resulting from a slight stumble or another minor injury is usually considered pathological, particularly when the patient also suffers from an underlying condition that frequently causes such fractures. The physician should be asked for clarification.

All pathological fractures are classified to the following categories/subcategories according to the underlying cause:

- Category M80 — Osteoporosis with current pathological fracture
- Subcategory M84.4- — Pathological fracture, not elsewhere classified
- Subcategory M84.5- — Pathological fracture in neoplastic disease (code also the underlying cause)
- Subcategory M84.6- — Pathological fracture in other disease (code also the underlying condition)

Additional characters are used to indicate the bone involved. The following seventh-character values are required when coding pathological fractures:

A Initial encounter for fracture
D Subsequent encounter for fracture with routine healing
G Subsequent encounter for fracture with delayed healing
K Subsequent encounter for fracture with nonunion
P Subsequent encounter for fracture with malunion
S Sequela

The assignment of the seventh-character value for pathological fractures should be performed using the following guidelines:

- "A" is used when the patient is receiving active treatment for the pathological fracture. Examples of active treatment are surgical treatment, emergency department encounter, and evaluation and treatment by a new physician.
- "D" is used for encounters after the patient has completed active treatment and there is routine healing.
- "G," "K," and "P" are used for subsequent encounters for treatment of problems associated with the healing, such as delayed healing, malunions, and nonunions.
- "S" is to be used for encounters for the treatment of sequelae or the residual effect after the acute phase of the fracture has terminated.

Care for complications of surgical treatment for fracture repairs during the healing or recovery phase should be coded with the appropriate complication codes.

Sequencing of codes for pathological fractures depends on the circumstances of admission. A pathological fracture is designated as the principal diagnosis only when the patient is admitted solely for treatment of the pathological fracture. Ordinarily, the code for the underlying condition responsible for the fracture is listed first, with an additional code for the fracture. An example follows.

- Pathological fracture due to neoplasm: If the focus of treatment is the fracture, a code from subcategory M84.5, Pathological fracture in neoplastic disease, should be sequenced first, followed by the code for the neoplasm. If the focus of treatment is the neoplasm with an associated pathological fracture, the neoplasm code should be sequenced first, followed by a code from M84.5 for the pathological fracture. The "code also" note at M84.5 provides this sequencing instruction.

Never assign a code for both a traumatic fracture and a pathological fracture of the same bone; one or the other is assigned. (See chapter 33 of this handbook for a discussion of coding traumatic fractures.)

Appropriate coding examples include the following:

M80.061A + M89.761	Initial encounter for acute fracture of right tibia and major osseous defects due to senile osteoporosis
M84.559D + C79.51+ Z85.43	Subsequent encounter for healing pathological fracture of the hip due to metastatic carcinoma of bone; ovarian cancer five years ago

STRESS FRACTURES

Stress fractures are different from pathological fractures in that they are due to repetitive force applied before the bone and its supporting tissues have had enough time to provide such force, whereas pathological fractures are always due to a physiologic condition, such as cancer or osteoporosis, that results in damage to the bone. Stress fractures usually test negative in an X-ray display, and days or weeks

may pass before the fracture line is visible on an X-ray. Stress fractures are classified to subcategory M84.3. Additional External cause of morbidity codes are used to identify the cause of the stress fracture, for example, code **Y93.01, Activity, walking, marching and hiking.** Other terms classified to stress fractures are fatigue fracture, march fracture, and stress reaction fracture.

MUSCULOSKELETAL BODY PART GUIDELINES

Most ICD-10-PCS body part guidelines are covered in chapter 8 of this handbook, Introduction to ICD-10-PCS and ICD-10-PCS Conventions. However, there is a specific guideline that pertains more closely to this chapter, describing tendons, ligaments, bursae, and fascia near a joint.

Procedures performed on tendons, ligaments, bursae, and fascia supporting a joint are coded to the body part in the respective body system that is the focus of the procedure. Procedures performed on joint structures themselves are coded to the body part in the joint body systems. For example, repair of the anterior cruciate ligament of the knee is coded to the "knee bursae and ligament" body part in the bursae and the "ligaments" body system. Knee arthroscopy with shaving of articular cartilage is coded to the "knee joint" body part in the "lower joints" body system.

REPLACEMENT OF A JOINT

Replacement of a joint is classified in the Medical and Surgical Section to the root operation "Replacement." Code assignment depends on the joint involved. When coding hip replacements, the type of bearing surface is identified by the sixth-character qualifier using the following values:

0 Polyethylene
1 Metal
2 Metal on polyethylene
3 Ceramic
4 Ceramic on polyethylene

The seventh-character qualifier describes whether the prosthesis is cemented or uncemented. A cemented joint replacement attaches the joint to the bone with epoxy cement. An uncemented joint prosthesis has a mesh of holes on its surface that allows the growth of the patient's natural bone to hold the device in place.

If replacement also involves the placement of a bone-growth stimulator, it should be coded separately to the root operation "Insertion" and the device "bone-growth stimulator" (sixth character M). Other examples include the following:

0SRA03Z Replacement of right acetabulum with ceramic prosthesis
0SRG0J9 Total left ankle replacement with synthetic prosthesis, cemented
0SRS01Z Replacement of left femoral head (metal)
0SRA00A Partial replacement (acetabular, polyethylene) of right hip, uncemented
0RRL0JZ Total right elbow replacement (synthetic)

ICD-10-PCS does not provide codes to indicate that a bilateral replacement has been carried out. The procedure code should be assigned twice when the same procedure is performed on bilateral joints. However, if individual codes are available to identify left and right joints, both codes are assigned.

Occasionally, a prosthesis must be removed because of infection, with a new prosthesis placed after a month or two when the infection has completely cleared. The first admission for such a problem is coded T84.5-, Infection and inflammatory reaction due to internal joint prosthesis, with an additional code to identify the infection and a procedure code for removal of the prosthesis (e.g., 0SP90JZ, Removal of synthetic substitute from right hip joint, open approach). Assign code

0SH908Z if a spacer is inserted. On the next admission for joint prosthesis insertion, the principal diagnosis is **Z47.32, Aftercare following explantation of hip joint prosthesis,** with a procedure code for insertion of a new device.

On the other hand, if a malfunctioning device is corrected, assign a code for the root operation "Revision," for example, **0SW90JZ, Revision of synthetic substitute in right hip joint, open approach.**

Any time a joint replacement is adjusted during the same encounter, the procedure is coded as a joint revision. The definition for the root operation "Revision" is "correcting, to the extent possible, a malfunctioning or misplaced device." If a joint prosthesis is removed and replaced during the same encounter, code both the removal and replacement. However, if there is removal of a joint spacer (e.g., cement), a code with the root operation "Removal" is also assigned (e.g., **0SP908Z, Removal of spacer from right hip joint, open approach**) for the removal of the spacer.

Codes for revision of hip replacements identify the specific joint components revised (acetabular surface, femoral surface).

Any time a component of a joint has been previously replaced, the procedure is still considered a replacement even though part of the component is being replaced for the first time. For example, when a patient is admitted for conversion of a previous right hip hemiarthroplasty to a total metal-on-polyethylene right hip replacement, open approach, it should be reported with codes **0SP90JZ, Removal of synthetic substitute from right hip joint, open approach,** and **0SR902Z, Replacement of right hip joint with metal on polyethylene, synthetic substitute, open approach.**

Hip resurfacing involves grinding away the worn surfaces of the femoral head and acetabulum while retaining the femoral neck and majority of the femoral head. The procedure concludes with the placement of new bearing surfaces. Resurfacing arthroplasty is classified to the root operation "Supplement" because the procedure meets the definition of "putting in or on biological or synthetic material that physically reinforces and/or augments the function of a portion of a body part." In addition, character 4 (body part) identifies the specific joint components resurfaced (total resurfacing involves both the acetabular and femoral components; partial involves femoral surface or acetabular surface only), as follows:

0SUR0BZ + 0SUA0BZ	Resurfacing right hip, total, acetabulum and femoral
0SUR0BZ	Resurfacing right hip, partial, femoral head
0SUA0BZ	Resurfacing right hip, partial, acetabulum

Subcategory Z96.6-, Presence of orthopedic joint implants, can be assigned as an additional code when the presence of a joint replacement is significant in terms of patient care.

EXERCISE 23.3

Code the following diagnoses and procedures. Do not assign External cause of morbidity codes.

1. Primary osteoarthritis of right hip — M16.11
   Replacement, total, of hip with ceramic-bearing surface, cemented — 0SR9039

2. Total right knee replacement (synthetic) — 0SRC0JZ

3. Partial replacement (synthetic) of left shoulder (humeral head) — 0PRD0JZ

SPINAL FUSION AND REFUSION

Spinal fusion is a surgical procedure whereby two or more vertebrae are fused to correct problems with the vertebrae. The vertebrae can be fused using bone grafting, genetically engineered bone substitute, and metal devices. The goal of spinal fusion surgery is pain relief after conservative treatments have failed. The procedure is indicated for spinal vertebrae injuries such as protrusion and degeneration of the cushion between vertebrae, curvature of the spine, or weak spine caused by injections or tumors.

The failure of development of solid bone between two or more levels of the spine after spinal fusion is called nonunion or pseudarthrosis. Symptoms may not occur until months or years after the original spinal fusion. Patients can often function relatively normally with pseudarthrosis unless problems develop such as sharp localized pain and tenderness over the fusion, progression of the deformity or disease, or localized motion in the fusion mass. Treatment for symptomatic pseudarthrosis consists of refusion. The procedure involves thorough removal of fibrous tissue from the intended fusion area and the addition of new bone graft.

FIGURE 23.3 Structure of the Spine Involved in Spinal Fusion

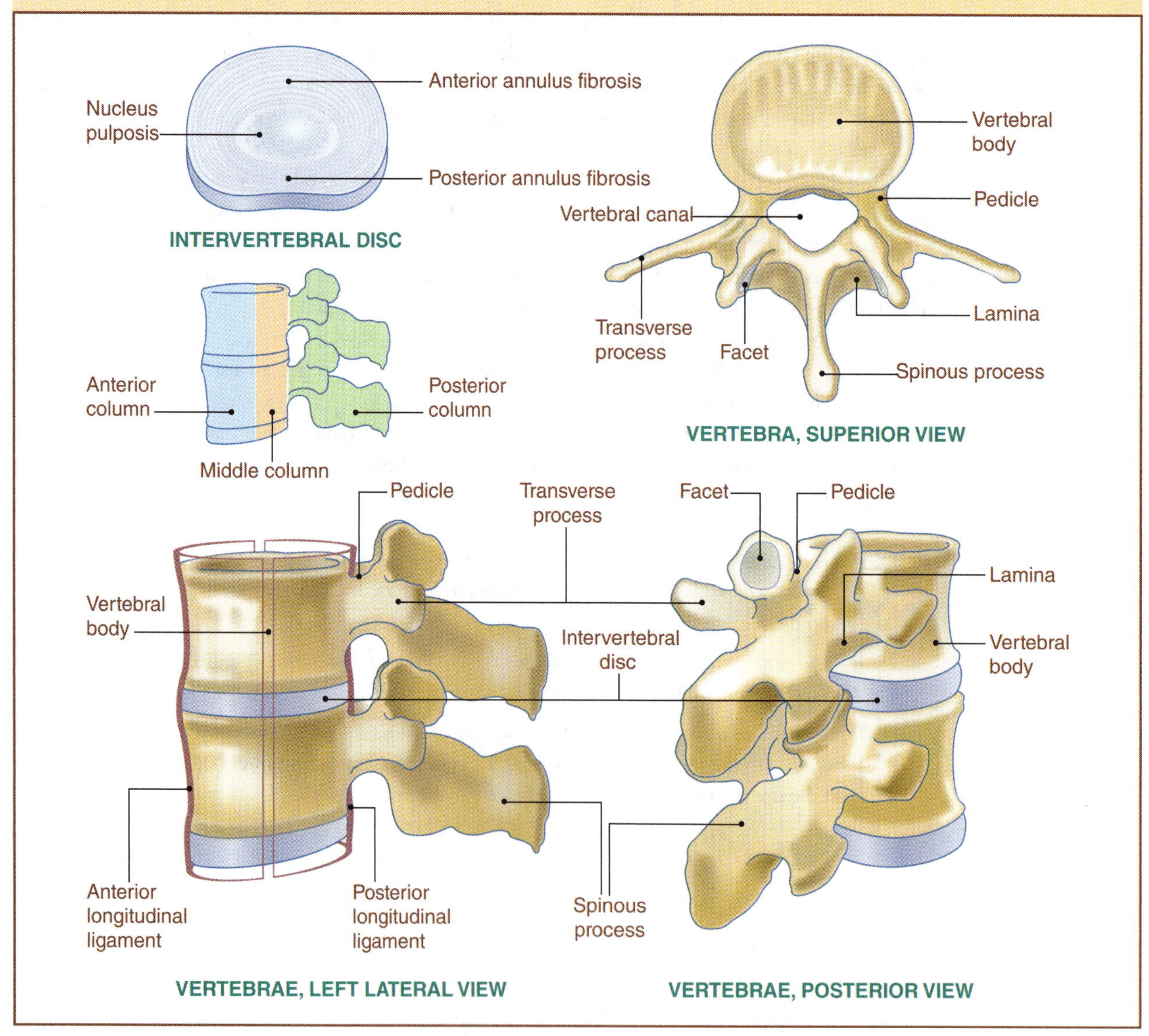

The structure of the spine is considered to be composed of the anterior, middle, and posterior columns. The anterior column is composed of the anterior longitudinal ligament, the anterior annulus, and the anterior portion of the vertebral body. The middle column includes the posterior longitudinal ligament, the posterior annulus, and the posterior portion of the vertebral body. The posterior column includes those spinal structures that are posterior to the posterior longitudinal ligament.

During an anterior column fusion, the body (corpus) of adjacent vertebrae are fused (interbody fusion). The anterior column can be fused using an anterior, lateral, or posterior technique. For the posterior column fusion, posterior structures of adjacent vertebrae are fused (pedicle, lamina, facet, transverse process, or "gutter" fusion). A posterior column fusion can be performed using a posterior, posterolateral, or lateral transverse technique.

Traditionally, three basic approaches have been used for spinal fusion or spinal refusion: anterior, posterior, and lateral transverse. The classic anterior approach requires an incision in the neck or the abdomen, and the fusion is carried out from the front of the vertebrae through the anterior annulus. In the classic posterior approach, the incision is made in the patient's back directly over the vertebrae. Another approach is the lateral transverse, which involves an incision on the patient's side, and the vertebrae are approached through the lamina.

Spinal fusion and refusion procedures are coded to the root operation "Fusion"—joining together portions of an articular body part rendering the articular body part immobile. The body part coded for a spinal vertebral joint(s) rendered immobile by a spinal fusion procedure is classified by the level of the spine, namely, cervical, thoracic, lumbar, lumbosacral, or sacrococcygeal. There are distinct body part values for a single vertebral joint and for multiple vertebral joints at each spinal level. For example, body part values specify "lumbar vertebral joint," "lumbar vertebral joints, 2 or more," and "lumbosacral joint."

If multiple vertebral joints are fused, a separate procedure is coded for each vertebral joint that uses a different device and/or qualifier. For example, **Open fusion of lumbar vertebral joint, posterior approach, anterior column (0SG00ZJ),** and **Open fusion of lumbar vertebral joint, posterior approach, posterior column (0SG00Z1),** are coded separately because the procedures involve different portions of the column (anterior column versus posterior column).

Occasionally, instrumentation called interbody fusion devices are used to stabilize and fuse degenerative disc spaces and to provide an immediately stable segment for fusion and relief of symptoms. These devices are also known as interbody fusion cage, BAK cage, ray-threaded fusion cage, synthetic cage, spacer, or bone dowels. Combinations of devices and materials are often used on a vertebral joint to render the joint immobile. When combinations of devices are used on the same vertebral joint, the device value for the procedure is coded using the following guidelines:

- *If an interbody fusion device is used to render the joint immobile (alone or containing other material like bone graft),* the procedure is coded with the device value "interbody fusion device."
- *If bone graft is the only device used to render the joint immobile,* the procedure is coded with the device value "nonautologous tissue substitute" or "autologous tissue substitute."
- *If a mixture of autologous and nonautologous bone graft (with or without biological or synthetic extenders or binders)* is used to render the joint immobile, code the procedure with the device value "autologous tissue substitute."

Examples include the following:

- Fusion of a vertebral joint using a cage-style interbody fusion device containing morsellized bone graft is coded to the device "interbody fusion device."
- Fusion of a vertebral joint using a bone dowel interbody fusion device made of cadaver bone and packed with a mixture of local morsellized bone and demineralized bone matrix is coded to the device "interbody fusion device."
- Fusion of a vertebral joint using both autologous bone graft and bone bank bone graft is coded to the device "autologous tissue substitute."

Synchronous excision of locally harvested bone graft is reported separately (root operation "Excision"). If recombinant bone morphogenetic protein (a genetically engineered protein) is inserted to help create a bone graft substitute, assign code **3E0V3GB, Introduction of recombinant bone morphogenetic protein into bones, percutaneous approach.**

A 360-degree spinal fusion is a fusion of both the anterior and posterior portions of the spine performed through a single incision (usually via the lateral transverse approach).

A brief explanation of common fusion and refusion procedures is listed below:

- ALIF: The anterior lumbar interbody fusion (ALIF) is an interbody fusion of the anterior and middle columns of the spine through an anterior incision, either transperitoneal or retroperitoneal. It can also be done laparoscopically.
- AxiaLIF: The axial lumbar interbody fusion (AxiaLIF®) is a percutaneous fusion of the anterior column at L5-S1. An AxiaLIF® 360º refers to the combination of an AxiaLIF® procedure of the anterior column performed along with a posterior column fusion, which may include the use of pedicle screws or facet screws. The AxiaLIF® 360º is described as providing a percutaneous 360º fusion.
- DLIF: The direct lateral lumbar interbody fusion (DLIF) is a minimally invasive alternative to conventional spinal fusion. The DLIF is performed through a lateral approach, which allows for limited soft tissue disruption. The procedure can only be performed at L4-L5 or at higher levels and requires dissection through the psoas muscle.
- PLIF: The posterior lumbar interbody fusion (PLIF) involves an anterior and middle column fusion through a posterior approach.
- TLIF: The transforaminal lumbar interbody fusion (TLIF) involves a transverse lateral interbody fusion through a posterior approach.
- XLIF: The extreme lateral interbody fusion (XLIF®) is a less invasive spinal surgery of the anterior column. The fusion may be accomplished either percutaneously or via a circular tube retractor through a lateral approach.

VERTEBROPLASTY AND KYPHOPLASTY

Percutaneous vertebroplasty is a technique used to treat vertebral compression fractures. The procedure involves the insertion of cement glue–like material (polymethylmethacrylate) into the vertebral body to stabilize and strengthen collapsed or crushed bone. ICD-10-PCS classifies this procedure to the root operation "Supplement," with "synthetic substitute" for the device value. For example, percutaneous lumbar vertebroplasty is coded to **0QU03JZ, Supplement lumbar vertebra with synthetic substitute, percutaneous approach.**

The ARCUATE™ XP procedure is a variation of a percutaneous vertebroplasty in which an osteotome is used to cut arcs in the cancellous bone within the vertebral body. The arcs created with the osteotome allow for dispersion of bone cement material when it is subsequently injected into the vertebral body. No bone or bone marrow is removed from, or compacted within, the vertebral body. The ARCUATE™ XP procedure is also coded to the root operation "Supplement."

Percutaneous vertebral augmentation is a procedure using an inflatable balloon that is expanded in order to reestablish vertebral height in compression fractures. After the balloon is removed, the cavity is filled with polymethylmethacrylate, which hardens to further stabilize the bone. Coding of percutaneous vertebroplasty requires two codes, one for the root operation "Reposition" and another for the root operation "Supplement." Other similar procedures coded in the same manner include arcuplasty, kyphoplasty, skyphoplasty, and spineoplasty. For example, percutaneous kyphoplasty of the lumbar spine should be coded to **0QS03ZZ, Reposition lumbar vertebra, percutaneous approach,** and **0QU03JZ, Supplement lumbar vertebra with synthetic substitute, percutaneous approach.**

While these procedures are similar, there is no balloon involved in the vertebroplasty, and no attempt is made to restore vertebral height to reduce the compression fractures of the vertebra; therefore, only the root operation "Supplement" is coded for vertebroplasty and not "Reposition."

If a vertebral biopsy is performed during a kyphoplasty of the lumbar vertebra, assign codes **0QS03ZZ, Reposition lumbar vertebra, percutaneous approach; 0QU03JZ, Supplement lumbar vertebra with synthetic substitute, percutaneous approach;** and **0QB03ZX, Excision of lumbar vertebra, percutaneous approach, diagnostic.** The biopsy is not an inherent part of the kyphoplasty and should be coded separately if performed.

SPINAL DISC PROSTHESES

Minimally invasive arthroplasty procedures are being carried out as an alternative to spinal fusion. These procedures are performed to replace the degenerated disc nucleus and restore or maintain the normal function of the disc by inserting artificial disc prostheses. The prostheses are used to replace the entire spinal disc or replace the disc nucleus.

The insertion of spinal disc prostheses is classified to the root operation "Replacement" and the spinal segment treated, for example, cervical (0RR30JZ), thoracic (0RR90JZ), or lumbosacral (0SR40JZ). ICD-10-PCS does not differentiate between partial and total disc prostheses with unique codes.

Revision/replacement codes are used to report either the repair (root operation "Revision") or the removal of the artificial disc prosthesis with the synchronous insertion of a new prosthesis (two procedure codes, one for root operation "Removal" and another for "Replacement"). These codes specify the part of the spine treated, but they do not distinguish between partial and total prostheses.

SPINAL MOTION PRESERVATION

Patients suffering from spinal stenosis or degenerative disc disease may be treated with conservative measures, including physical therapy and pain management. When conservative care does not provide relief, surgical decompression may be an alternative treatment. Surgical decompression (root operation "Excision") involves removal of the bone and/or tissue causing pressure on the spinal cord or nerve root(s). Common surgical decompression procedures include laminotomy, laminectomy, diskectomy, foraminotomy, and medial facetectomy. The spinal segment may be deemed unstable depending on the extent of bone and tissue removed during the decompression procedure. Stabilization of the spinal segment is primarily accomplished with spinal fusion. However, new spinal motion preservation technologies have been developed to allow for spine stabilization without the motion restriction associated with fusion.

Motion preservation technologies placed in the posterior column of the spine include the following:

- Interspinous process devices (e.g., X-Stop™, Wallis®, and Coflex™ systems)
- Pedicle screw dynamic stabilization devices (e.g., Dynesys® and M-Brace™)
- Facet replacement devices (e.g., The Total Facet Arthroplasty System™ and The Artificial Facet Replacement System™)

Root operation "Insertion," "Revision," or "Replacement" is used for the insertion, revision, or replacement of posterior spinal motion preservation device(s), respectively. These codes include a dynamic stabilization device(s) and any synchronous facetectomy (partial, total) performed at the same level. If a synchronous surgical decompression (foraminotomy, laminectomy, laminotomy) is also performed, it is coded as an additional procedure.

Examples follow.

0RH63BZ	Insertion of interspinous process spinal stabilization device into thoracic vertebral joint, percutaneous approach
0RW104Z	Revision of internal fixation device in cervical vertebral joint, open approach
0SH30CZ	Insertion of pedicle-based spinal stabilization device into lumbosacral joint, open approach
0RW634Z	Revision of internal fixation device in thoracic vertebral joint, percutaneous approach
0SR00JZ	Replacement of lumbar vertebral joint, with synthetic substitute, open approach
0SW30JZ	Revision of synthetic substitute in lumbosacral joint, open approach

PLICA SYNDROME

Although plica syndrome can occasionally be found in other areas, it almost always affects the knee. Plica syndrome occurs when the synovial bands that are present early in fetal development have not combined into one large synovial unit as they develop further. Patients with this syndrome often experience pain and swelling, weakness, and a locking and clicking sensation of the knee. The therapeutic goal is to reduce the inflammation of the synovium and the thickening of the plica. Usual treatment measures attempt to relieve symptoms within three months; if that does not occur, arthroscopic or open surgery to remove the plica may be required. Assign code **M67.5-, Plica syndrome,** for this condition and code for excision of knee joint for the surgery.

FASCIITIS

Necrotizing fasciitis is a fulminating infection that begins with severe or extensive cellulitis that spreads to the superficial and deep fascia, producing thrombosis of the subcutaneous vessels and gangrene of the underlying tissue. Group A *Streptococcus* is the most common organism responsible for this condition, but any bacteria may be the cause. Code M72.6 is assigned for this condition, with an additional code for the organism when this information is known.

EXERCISE 23.4

Code the following diagnoses and procedures. Do not assign External cause of morbidity codes.

1.	Acute polymyositis	M33.20
	Mild thoracogenic scoliosis	M41.30
	Percutaneous biopsy of left trunk muscle	0KBG3ZX
2.	Sclerosing tenosynovitis, left thumb and middle finger	M65.842
3.	Acute osteomyelitis of left distal femur due to type 2 diabetes with diabetic arthropathy	E11.618
		M86.152
	Sequestrectomy (percutaneous) and percutaneous excision of sinus tract, left distal femur	0QCC3ZZ
		0QBC3ZZ
4.	Adhesive capsulitis, left shoulder	M75.02
	Arthroscopic release of coracohumeral ligament	0MN24ZZ
5.	Nonunion of fracture, left femoral neck, subsequent encounter	S72.002K
	Inlay-type iliac bone graft to nonunion of left femoral neck (open approach) Replacement	0QR707Z
	Left iliac crest bone excised for graft (percutaneous) Excision	0QB33ZZ
6.	Recurrent dislocation of patella	M22.00

7.	Deformity of left ring finger, due to old extensor muscle and tendon laceration of left ring finger Laceration	M20.002 S56.426S
	Transfer of flexor tendon from distal phalanx to middle phalanx (open approach)	0LX80ZZ
8.	Cervical spondylosis, C5-6, C6-7	M47.812
	Anterior column cervical spinal fusion, C5-6, C6-7 open, anterior approach, with interbody device	0RG20A0
9.	Dupuytren's contracture (right hand)	M72.0
	Incision and division of palmar fascia (open approach)	0J8J0ZZ
10.	Multiple compression fractures of vertebrae and major osseous defects due to senile osteoporosis (initial encounter)	M80.08xA M89.78
11.	Lumbar spinal stenosis	M48.06
	Decompressive laminectomy with Dynesys stabilization system (open approach)	0SH00CZ OSB00ZZ
12.	Disc herniation and degenerative spondylosis C5-C6	M50.20
	C7 radiculopathy	M47.22
	Arthrodesis C5-C6 anterior interbody fusion device with allograft	0RG10A0
	C7 allograft with titanium plate and screws	0RG104Z

Coding OF Pregnancy AND Childbirth Complications, Abortion, Congenital Anomalies, AND Perinatal Conditions

CHAPTER 24 Complications of Pregnancy, Childbirth, and the Puerperium

CHAPTER OVERVIEW

- Conditions affecting pregnancy, childbirth, and the puerperium are found in chapter 15 of ICD-10-CM.
  - —Codes from chapter 15 take precedence over codes from other chapters.
  - —Codes from chapter 15 are never assigned to the newborn's record.
- Assignment of the final character for trimester should be based on the provider's documentation of the trimester for the current admission/encounter.
- The date of the admission should be used to determine weeks of gestation (category Z3A) for inpatient admissions that encompass more than one gestational week.
- Z codes are used to indicate the outcome of the delivery.
- A normal delivery is contingent on a variety of criteria.
- The Tabular List must be reviewed for assignment of the final character for trimester and the correct seventh character for multiple gestations for some chapter 15 codes.
- Deliveries not deemed normal use as their principal diagnosis code the main circumstance or complication of the delivery.
- When assigning codes from chapter 15, it is important to assess whether a condition was pre-existing prior to pregnancy or developed during or due to the pregnancy in order to assign the correct code.
- Postpartum complications are any complications that occur throughout the six weeks following the delivery.
- There is a sequela code to use for complications that occur after the postpartum period. This code follows the codes for the condition.
- There are codes for delivery assistance procedures, such as fetal head rotation, forceps delivery, vacuum extraction, episiotomy, and cesarean delivery.
- Contraceptive management and procreative management, through both admission and outpatient encounter, are covered by a series of Z codes. These codes can be supplemented by additional codes if an underlying condition is present.

LEARNING OUTCOMES

After studying this chapter you should be able to:

Code complications of pregnancy using the proper fourth and fifth characters.

Use the proper Z codes to assign the outcome of delivery.

Code for other obstetric care besides childbirth.

Know the difference between postpartum complications and late effects of pregnancy, childbirth, and the puerperium.

Differentiate among the procedures assisting delivery.

Code for contraceptive and procreative management.

TERMS TO KNOW

Antepartum
the period of pregnancy from conception to childbirth

Peripartum
the period involving the last month of pregnancy to five months postpartum

Postpartum
the period beginning right after delivery and including the next six weeks

Puerperium
the clinical term for the postpartum period

REMEMBER . . .

If the mother's record does not state the outcome of the delivery, look at the newborn's record.

INTRODUCTION

Conditions that affect the management of pregnancy, childbirth, and the puerperium are classified to categories O00 through O9A in chapter 15 of ICD-10-CM. Conditions from other chapters of ICD-10-CM are usually reclassified in chapter 15 when they are related to or aggravated by the pregnancy, childbirth, or the puerperium. It is the provider's responsibility to state that the condition being treated is not affecting the pregnancy.

Should the provider document that the pregnancy is incidental to the encounter, code **Z33.1, Pregnant state, incidental,** is assigned in place of any chapter 15 codes. Chapter 15 codes take precedence over codes from other chapters, but codes from other chapters may be used as additional codes when needed to provide more specificity. Codes from chapter 15 of ICD-10-CM refer to the mother only and are assigned only on the mother's record. They are never assigned on the newborn's record; other codes are provided for that purpose. (See chapter 27 of this handbook.) Codes from categories O00 through O08 are assigned for pregnancy with abortive outcome, including ectopic pregnancy, molar pregnancy, and abortion. (Code assignments for these conditions are discussed in chapter 25.)

Codes from categories O09 through O9A apply throughout the entire obstetrical experience, which begins at conception and ends six weeks (42 days) after delivery.

ICD-10-CM divides chapter 15 as follows:

O09	Supervision of high-risk pregnancy
O10–O16	Edema, proteinuria, and hypertensive disorders in pregnancy, childbirth, and the puerperium
O20–O29	Other maternal disorders predominantly related to pregnancy
O30–O48	Maternal care related to the fetus and amniotic cavity and possible delivery problems
O60–O77	Complications of labor and delivery
O80, O82	Encounter for delivery
O85–O92	Complications predominantly related to the puerperium
O94–O9A	Other obstetric conditions not elsewhere classified

The process of labor and delivery includes three stages. The first stage begins with the onset of regular uterine contractions and ends when the cervical os is completely dilated. The second stage begins with complete dilation and continues until the infant has been completely expelled. The third stage begins with the expulsion of the infant and continues until the placenta and membranes have been expelled and contraction of the uterus is complete. The puerperium begins at the end of the third stage of labor and continues for six weeks.

Occasionally, a pregnancy continues for a longer term than usual gestation and is considered to be a long pregnancy. The following two codes are used when this occurs:

O48.0	Post-term pregnancy (40 completed weeks to 42 completed weeks of gestation)
O48.1	Prolonged pregnancy (advanced beyond 42 completed weeks of gestation)

FINAL CHARACTER FOR TRIMESTER

The majority of codes in chapter 15 of ICD-10-CM have a final character indicating the trimester of pregnancy. Note that the Tabular List must be reviewed for assignment of the final character for trimester, as the codes in the Alphabetic Index of Diseases and Injuries do not include the complete

FIGURE 24.1 Primary Organs of the Female Reproductive System

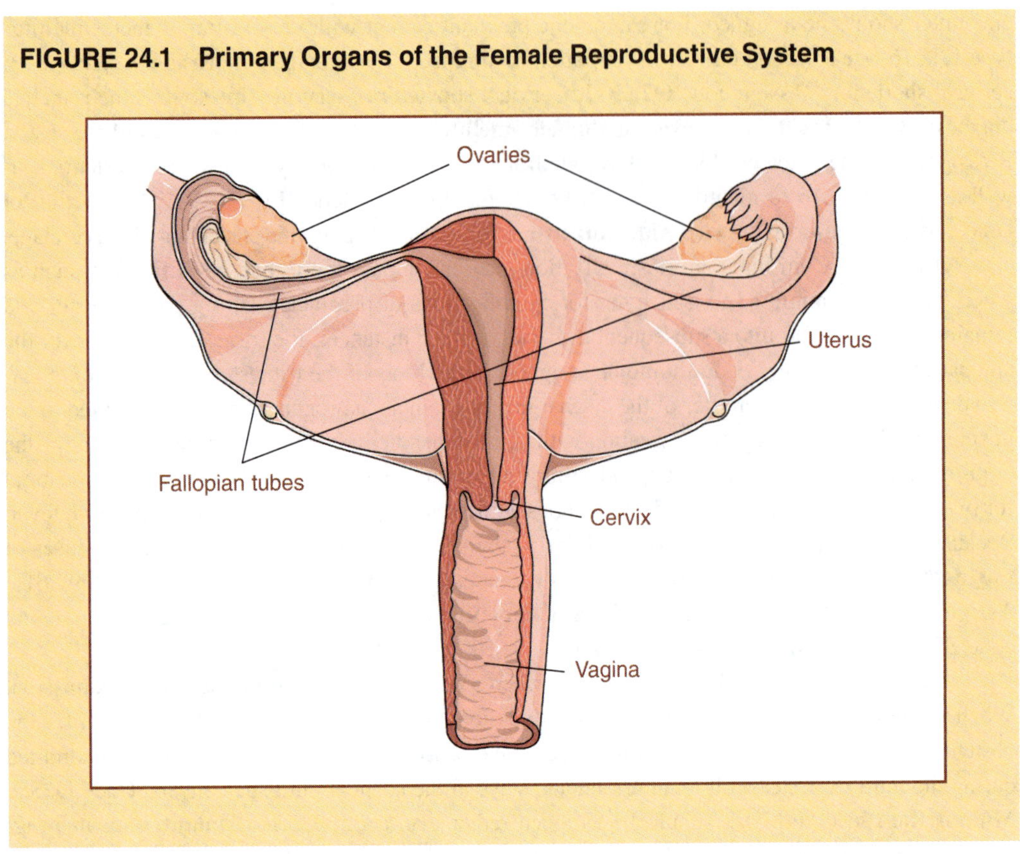

code. The time frames for the trimesters are indicated at the beginning of chapter 15 and are defined by an instructional note as follows:

- First trimester—less than 14 weeks 0 days
- Second trimester—14 weeks 0 days to less than 28 weeks 0 days
- Third trimester—28 weeks 0 days until delivery.

Assignment of the final character for trimester should be based on the provider's documentation of the trimester (or number of weeks) for the current admission/encounter. This refers to the provider as defined in the *ICD-10-CM Official Guidelines for Coding and Reporting:* "Physician or other qualified healthcare practitioner legally accountable for establishing the patient's diagnosis." This definition applies to the assignment of trimester for pre-existing conditions as well as those that develop during or are due to the pregnancy. The provider's documentation of the number of weeks may be used to assign the appropriate final character identifying the trimester. For example, if the documentation refers to the patient having completed 20 weeks, the appropriate code for second trimester may be selected; the provider does not have to explicitly document "second trimester."

Not every single code in chapter 15 has a trimester component. If trimester is not a component of a code, it is because the condition always occurs in a specific trimester or the concept of trimester of pregnancy is not applicable. For example, category O48, Late pregnancy, does not include trimester because, by definition, this category is to be used for pregnancies longer than 40 completed weeks. Certain codes have characters for only certain trimesters because the condition does not occur in all trimesters, but it may occur in more than one. For example, category O60.0, Preterm labor, is for spontaneous onset of labor before 37 completed weeks of gestation, and therefore there are no codes for first trimester, which is less than 14 weeks.

If a condition complicating the pregnancy develops prior to the current admission/encounter or represents a pre-existing condition, the trimester character for the trimester at the time of the admission/

encounter should be assigned. For example, a pregnant patient with pre-existing diabetes mellitus type 1, at 16 weeks (second trimester) gestation is admitted for an emergent transvaginal cerclage for cervical shortening. Assign code **O26.872, Cervical shortening, second trimester,** as the principal diagnosis. Code **O24.012, Pre-existing diabetes mellitus, type 1, in pregnancy, second trimester,** is assigned for the diabetes along with a code from category E10 for any diabetic manifestations, as well as code Z3A.16 to identify weeks of gestation. Also assign code **0UVC7DZ, Restriction of cervix with intraluminal device, via natural or artificial opening,** for the placement of the cerclage.

Occasionally, an inpatient hospitalization may encompass more than one trimester, such as when a patient is admitted to a hospital for complications of pregnancy during one trimester and remains in the hospital into a subsequent trimester. In such instances, the trimester character for the antepartum complication code should be assigned on the basis of the trimester when the complication developed, not the trimester of the discharge. For example, a pregnant female is admitted to the hospital at 27 weeks completed gestation with acute appendicitis complicating her pregnancy. She requires emergency laparoscopic appendectomy, which she tolerates well. She is kept in the hospital for two weeks postoperatively, with intravenous antibiotics administered due to postoperative fever. Because the acute appendicitis developed during the second trimester, code **O99.612, Diseases of the digestive system complicating pregnancy, second trimester,** is assigned rather than O99.613. Assign also code **K35.80, Unspecified acute appendicitis,** to describe the specific condition, and code Z3A.27 to identify weeks of gestation.

The exception to the above guideline is when a delivery occurs during the current admission. Whenever delivery occurs during the current admission and there is an "in childbirth" option for the obstetric complication, the "in childbirth" code should be assigned. For example, a patient is admitted during the third trimester with malnutrition and stays in the hospital until she delivers. Code **O25.2, Malnutrition in childbirth,** should be assigned rather than code **O25.13, Malnutrition in pregnancy, third trimester,** for the malnutrition. If the specific type of malnutrition is documented, assign an additional code from category E40–E46, along with the appropriate code from category Z3A.

It is important to note that although each category in chapter 15 that includes codes for trimester has a code for "unspecified trimester," the "unspecified trimester" code should rarely be used, such as when the documentation in the record is insufficient to determine the trimester and it is not possible to obtain clarification.

Codes in category Z3A, Weeks of gestation, may be used only on the maternal record to provide additional information about the pregnancy. The date of the admission should be used to determine weeks of gestation for inpatient admissions that encompass more than one gestational week. Pregnancy is considered "at term" when gestation attains 37 complete weeks but is less than 42.

OUTCOME OF DELIVERY

Because chapter 15 codes do not indicate the outcome of delivery, a code from category Z37 is assigned as an additional code to provide this information whenever the patient delivers in the hospital. Fourth characters indicate both whether the outcome was single or multiple and whether liveborn or stillborn. For multiple births with more than twins, additional characters indicate the number of outcomes (e.g., triplets, quadruplets) and whether they were all liveborn, some liveborn, or all stillborn. These codes are used only on the mother's record, not the record of the newborn, and are assigned only for the episode of care during which delivery occurred. No code from category Z37 is assigned when delivery occurs outside the hospital prior to admission. Examples of appropriate use of codes from category Z37 include the following:

O80 + Z37.0 + Z3A.40	40 week term pregnancy, spontaneous delivery, vertex presentation; liveborn male infant
O30.003 + O36.4xx0 + Z3A.39 + Z37.3	39 week term pregnancy with spontaneous delivery; twin pregnancy, with one twin liveborn and one stillborn

To locate the code assignment for outcome of delivery, the coder should refer to the main term **Outcome of delivery** in the Alphabetic Index. If the mother's record does not state the outcome, the coder should refer to the newborn's record for this information.

EXERCISE 24.1

For the following exercise, do not assign the delivery codes; assign only the Z codes for outcome of delivery. Remember that in actual practice the delivery code precedes the Z code.

1. Delivery of twins, both stillborn — Z37.4
   Outcome of delivery

2. Delivery of triplets, one stillborn — Z37.61
   Outcome of delivery

3. Delivery of liveborn, female infant — Z37.0
   Outcome of delivery

4. Delivery of single stillborn — Z37.1
   Outcome of delivery

FETAL SEVENTH CHARACTERS

The following subcategories/codes require a seventh character to identify the fetus for which the complication code applies:

O31.00–O31.8x9	Complications specific to multiple gestation
O32.0–O32.9	Maternal care for malpresentation of fetus
O33.3	Maternal care for disproportion due to outlet contraction of pelvis
O33.4	Maternal care for disproportion of mixed maternal and fetal origin
O33.5	Maternal care for disproportion due to unusually large fetus
O33.6	Maternal care for disproportion due to hydrocephalic fetus
O35.0–O35.9	Maternal care for known or suspected fetal abnormality and damage
O36.011–O36.93	Maternal care for other fetal problems
O40.1–O40.9	Polyhydramnios
O41.00–O41.93	Other disorders of amniotic fluid and membranes
O60.10–O60.14	Preterm labor with preterm delivery
O60.20–O60.23	Term delivery with preterm labor
O64.0–O64.9	Obstructed labor due to malposition and malpresentation of fetus
O69.0–O69.9	Labor and delivery complicated by umbilical cord complications

Seventh characters "1" through "9" are for cases of multiple gestations to identify the fetus for which the code applies. The seventh character "0," not applicable or unspecified, is used for the following situations:

- Single gestations
- When the documentation in the record is insufficient to determine the fetus affected and it is not possible to obtain clarification
- When it is not possible to clinically determine which fetus is affected

Note that the Tabular List must be reviewed for assignment of the correct seventh character for multiple gestations for chapter 15 codes, because the seventh characters are not included in the Alphabetic Index.

Some providers prefer to refer to each fetus in multiple gestation cases by alphabetical characters, such as fetus A, fetus B, etc., rather than numbers (fetus 1, fetus 2, etc.). In such cases, fetus A should be equated to fetus 1, fetus B should be equated to fetus 2, and so on. There is no expectation that the same fetus number or alphabetical character be consistently carried over from one admission to another. Identification of the fetus, whether by number or alphabetical character, is based on the provider documentation.

A code from category O30, Multiple gestation, is assigned to provide additional information such as the number of fetuses (e.g., triplet pregnancy), the number of amniotic sacs, and the number of placentas. The risk of complications related to multiple gestations will increase, and the treatment plan will differ, depending on the number of placentas and amniotic sacs.

SELECTION OF FIRST-LISTED AND PRINCIPAL DIAGNOSIS

The selection of first-listed diagnoses or principal diagnoses for encounters/admissions for normal deliveries and other obstetric care is based on the following guidelines.

Routine Outpatient Prenatal Visits

For routine outpatient prenatal visits when no complications are present, a code from category Z34, Encounter for supervision of normal pregnancy, should be used as the first-listed diagnosis. These codes should not be used in conjunction with chapter 15 codes.

Prenatal Outpatient Visits for High-Risk Patients

For routine prenatal outpatient visits for patients with high-risk pregnancies, a code from category O09, Supervision of high risk pregnancy, should be used as the first-listed diagnosis. Secondary chapter 15 codes may be used in conjunction with these codes if appropriate.

ICD-10-CM provides codes for the supervision of the following types of high-risk pregnancies:

O09.00–O09.03	Pregnancy with history of infertility
O09.10–O09.13	Pregnancy with history of ectopic or molar pregnancy
O09.211–O09.299	Pregnancy with other poor reproductive or obstetric history
O09.30–O09.33	Pregnancy with insufficient antenatal care
O09.40–O09.43	Pregnancy with grand multiparity
O09.511–O09.529	Elderly (pregnancy for female 35 years and older at expected date of delivery) primigravida and multigravida
O09.611–O09.629	Young (pregnancy for a female less than 16 years old at expected date of delivery) primigravida and multigravida

O09.70–O09.73	High-risk pregnancy due to social problems
O09.811–O09.899	Supervision of other high-risk pregnancies (includes pregnancy resulting from assisted reproductive technology [O09.81-] and pregnancy with history of in utero procedure during previous pregnancy [O09.82-])

Episodes When No Delivery Occurs

In episodes when no delivery occurs, the principal diagnosis should correspond to the principal complication of the pregnancy that necessitated the encounter. Should more than one complication exist, all of which are treated or monitored, any of the complication codes may be sequenced first.

Admission with Normal Delivery

Code **O80, Encounter for full-term uncomplicated delivery,** is used only when the delivery is entirely normal with a single liveborn outcome. There can be no postpartum complications, and any antepartum complication experienced during pregnancy must have been resolved before the time of delivery. Code O80 is always the principal diagnosis. If there is any complication, code O80 cannot be assigned. Code O80 cannot be used if any other code from chapter 15 is needed to describe a current complication of the antenatal, delivery, or perinatal period. Codes from other chapters may be used as additional codes with code O80 only when the physician has documented that the conditions are not related to, and in no way complicate, the pregnancy.

All of the following criteria must be met in order for code O80 to be used correctly:

- The delivery is entirely normal (requiring minimal or no assistance, with or without episiotomy).
- There is no fetal manipulation (e.g., rotation version) or instrumentation (forceps).
- There is a spontaneous, cephalic, vaginal delivery.
- Presentation at delivery can be only cephalic (head) or occipital. Terms such as "right occipito-anterior (ROA)," "left occipito-anterior (LOA)," "right occipito-posterior (ROP)," "left occipito-posterior (LOP)," and "vertex" describe an occipital presentation. Any other presentation, such as breech, face, or brow, disallows the use of code O80.
- Any antepartum complication experienced during pregnancy must have been resolved before the time of delivery.
- No abnormalities of either labor or delivery can have occurred.
- No postpartum complications can be present.
- No procedures other than the following can have been performed: episiotomy without forceps, episiorrhaphy, amniotomy (artificial rupture of the membranes), manually assisted delivery without forceps, administration of analgesics and/or anesthesia, fetal monitoring, induction of labor (in the absence of medical indications), and sterilization. If any other procedure is performed, code O80 cannot be assigned.
- Outcome of delivery must be single livebirth, Z37.0. When there has been a multiple birth or stillbirth, code O80 cannot be assigned.

Examples include the following:

- A patient who had a completely normal delivery at 38 weeks suffers a postpartum hemorrhage several hours after delivery. Code **O72.1, Other immediate postpartum hemorrhage,** is assigned. Assign also codes Z3A.38 and Z37.0. Although the delivery itself was normal, complications were present during the episode of care; therefore, code O80 cannot be used.

- The prenatal history for a patient who had a completely normal delivery at 40 weeks gestation of a live infant indicates that she had a urinary tract infection at three months' gestation. This was treated with Bactrim on an outpatient basis. There was no recurrence of the infection during the pregnancy, and the patient had no infection at the time of delivery. In this case, code **O80, Encounter for full-term uncomplicated delivery,** is assigned. Codes Z37.0 and Z3A.40 are also assigned to describe the outcome of delivery and the completed weeks of gestation.

EXERCISE 24.2

Write an "X" next to each of the following circumstances of delivery that is assigned code O80, Encounter for full-term uncomplicated delivery.

1.	Liveborn, full-term, breech presentation	______
2.	Liveborn, premature, cephalic presentation	______
3.	Stillborn, full-term, vertex presentation	______
4.	Liveborn, full-term, cephalic presentation; episiotomy with repair	X
5.	Liveborn, full-term, vertex presentation; elective low forceps	______
6.	Liveborn, full-term, vertex presentation; postpartum breast abscess	______
7.	Liveborn, full-term, breech presentation changed to vertex presentation by version prior to delivery	______

Admission with Other Delivery

When a delivery does not meet the criteria for assignment of code **O80, Encounter for full-term uncomplicated delivery,** the principal diagnosis should correspond to the main circumstance or complication of the delivery. In cases of cesarean delivery, the selection of the principal diagnosis should be the condition established after study that was responsible for the patient's admission. If the patient was admitted with a condition that resulted in the performance of a cesarean procedure, that condition should be selected as the principal diagnosis. If the reason for the admission/encounter was unrelated to the condition resulting in the cesarean delivery, the condition related to the reason for the admission/encounter should be selected as the principal diagnosis, even if a cesarean was performed. For example:

- A patient who had a previous cesarean delivery is admitted for a second cesarean delivery at 39 weeks. She also had a pre-existing type 1 diabetes mellitus. Cesarean delivery was accomplished without complication. Code **O34.21 Maternal care for scar from previous cesarean delivery,** is assigned as the principal diagnosis, with an additional code of **O24.02, Pre-existing diabetes mellitus, type 1, in childbirth.** Codes **E10.9, Type 1 diabetes mellitus without complications; Z37.0, Single live birth;** and **Z3A.39, 39 weeks of gestation of pregnancy,** would also be assigned to provide more specificity.

- A patient at 40 weeks gestation is admitted to the hospital in obstructed labor due to a breech presentation. Version is unsuccessful, and the patient delivers by cesarean section several hours later. The principal diagnosis code is **O64.1xx0, Obstructed labor due to breech presentation.** Assign also codes Z37.0 and Z3A.40. There is no need to assign code **O32.1xx0, Maternal care for breech presentation,** as an additional code per the guidance provided with the "excludes1" note at category O32. Code O64.1xx0 already identifies the breech presentation.

Occasionally, a cesarean section may be performed without a medical indication; therefore, there will be no medical condition that resulted in the cesarean delivery. For example, a patient elected to have a low cesarean section due to fear of a vaginal delivery. Assign code **O82, Encounter for cesarean delivery without indication,** as the principal diagnosis.

Code O75.82 is assigned to describe a planned cesarean delivery when the onset of labor occurs after 37, but before 39, completed weeks of gestation. This code allows data to be collected for quality markers for elective cesarean delivery performed between 37 and 39 weeks.

Admission for Other Obstetric Care

When the admission or encounter is for obstetric care other than delivery, the principal diagnosis should correspond to the complication that necessitated the admission or encounter. If more than one complication is present, all of which are treated or monitored, any of the complication codes may be sequenced first. If no obstetric complications are present, the following guidelines govern selection of the principal diagnosis:

- If the reason for admission or encounter is not related to an obstetric condition but the patient is pregnant, code **Z33.1, Pregnant state, incidental,** is assigned as an additional code. This code is never assigned as the principal diagnosis, and no codes from chapter 15 can be assigned.
- When a patient delivers outside a health care facility and is then admitted for routine postpartum care with no complications present, code **Z39.0, Encounter for care and examination of mother immediately after delivery,** is assigned as the principal diagnosis. When a postpartum complication is present, the code for that condition is designated as the principal diagnosis, and code Z39.0 is not assigned.

  For example, a woman is admitted following delivery in the parking lot of the hospital. On admission, it is noted that she had sustained a first-degree perineal laceration. Code **O70.0, First degree laceration during delivery,** is assigned rather than code Z39.0.
- Code **Z39.1, Encounter for care and examination of lactating mother,** is assigned for a visit related to lactation (e.g., supervision, counseling, etc.). However, if the patient presents postpartum with a condition associated with lactation, assign a code from category O92, Other disorders of breast and disorders of lactation associated with pregnancy and the puerperium.
- Occasionally, an expectant mother may visit a pediatrician to receive advice on child care or to evaluate the pediatric office. This is not a visit related to a problem with the pregnancy. Code **Z76.81, Expectant parent(s) prebirth pediatrician visit,** may be assigned for these encounters.

EXERCISE 24.3

Code the following diagnoses.

1. Antepartum supervision of pregnancy in patient with history of three previous stillbirths, 12 weeks gestation — O09.291, Z3A.12
2. Office visit for routine prenatal care, for primigravida patient with no complications, second trimester — Z34.02, Z3A.00
3. Office visit for care of 40-year-old patient who is in the fourth month of her third pregnancy — O09.522, Z3A.00
4. Hospital admission of patient in good condition after delivering a single liveborn infant in taxi on the way to the hospital — Z39.0
   Admission for
5. Admission for intravenous antibiotic therapy of patient who delivered a single liveborn at home three days ago; patient now suffering an abscess of the breast — O91.12
   Puerperal

FETAL CONDITIONS AFFECTING MANAGEMENT OF PREGNANCY

Codes from categories O35, Maternal care for known or suspected fetal abnormality and damage, and O36, Maternal care for other fetal problems, are assigned only when the fetal condition is actually responsible for modifying the mother's care. Such an effect may be documented by additional diagnostic studies based on the fetal problem, additional observation, special care, or termination of the pregnancy. The fact that the fetal condition exists does not in itself justify assigning a code from these categories; this applies only when the condition affects the management of the mother's care. Codes from categories O35 and O36 are used when the listed condition in the fetus is the reason for hospitalization or other obstetric care to the mother, or for termination of pregnancy.

For example, when decreased fetal movements result in a decision to perform a cesarean delivery or early induction of labor in the mother, code **O36.81-, Decreased fetal movements,** is assigned. On the other hand, if no change is made in the mother's care, code O36.81- is not assigned because the decreased fetal movement is not considered to have affected the management of the mother significantly.

Occasionally, it may be difficult to determine fetal viability or nonviability during early pregnancy. Patients previously confirmed as pregnant in the very early weeks may return weeks later for an evaluation. If the fetal heartbeat cannot be heard, an ultrasound may be necessary to confirm that the pregnancy is viable. Assign code O36.80 to describe an encounter to determine fetal viability.

Multiple Gestation

Category O30, Multiple gestation, is used to identify multiple gestation, such as twin (O30.001–O30.099), triplet (O30.101–O30.199), quadruplet (O30.201–O30.299), other specified multiple gestations (O30.801–O30.899), and unspecified (O30.90–O30.93). The risk of complications will increase, and the treatment plan will differ, depending on the number of placentas and amniotic sacs. Fifth characters under category O30 indicate the number of placentas and amniotic sacs, while sixth characters indicate the trimester.

In Utero Surgery

Surgery performed on a fetus in utero (while the fetus is still in the womb) is considered an obstetric encounter. Codes from chapter 16, perinatal codes, should not be used on the mother's record to identify fetal conditions. Instead, when surgery is performed on the fetus in utero, a diagnosis code from category O35, Maternal care for known or suspected fetal abnormality and damage, should be assigned for the fetal condition. Assign the appropriate ICD-10-PCS code for the procedure performed.

Code **O35.7-, Maternal care for (suspected) damage to fetus by other medical procedures,** describes maternal and fetal complications resulting from in utero surgery performed during the current pregnancy. Code O35.7- is used for supervision of pregnancy affected by in utero procedure during current pregnancy. If the newborn experiences any problems or complications because of in utero procedures, assign code **P96.5, Complication to newborn due to (fetal) intrauterine procedure,** on the newborn record.

Code **O09.82-, Supervision of pregnancy with history of in utero procedure during previous pregnancy,** can be used as an additional code assignment with code O35.7- if the patient also has a past history of in utero surgery during a previous pregnancy.

ICD-10-PCS classifies in utero surgeries to the Obstetrics Section, body system "pregnancy," root operation "Repair," body part "products of conception." For example, in utero surgical repair of herniated diaphragm for congenital diaphragmatic hernia is coded to **10Q00ZK, Repair respiratory system in products of conception, open approach.** The diaphragm is classified to the "respiratory" body system in the Medical and Surgical Section.

OTHER CONDITIONS COMPLICATING PREGNANCY, CHILDBIRTH, OR THE PUERPERIUM

Some conditions inevitably complicate the obstetrical experience or are themselves aggravated by pregnancy. Certain categories in chapter 15 of ICD-10-CM distinguish between conditions of the mother that existed prior to pregnancy (pre-existing) and those that are a direct result of pregnancy. When assigning codes from chapter 15, it is important to assess whether a condition was pre-existing prior to pregnancy or developed during or due to the pregnancy in order to assign the correct code. For example, hypertension complicating pregnancy, delivery, and the puerperium is classified to category O10 when it is pre-existing, to category O13 when it is gestational (pregnancy induced), and to category O16 when it is unspecified maternal hypertension.

Categories that do not distinguish between pre-existing and pregnancy-related conditions may be used for either. It is acceptable to use codes specifically for the puerperium with codes complicating pregnancy and childbirth if a condition arises postpartum during the delivery encounter.

Designated conditions, such as edema, proteinuria, and hypertensive disorders in pregnancy, childbirth, and the puerperium are classified to categories O10 through O16. Other maternal disorders, such as hemorrhage, hyperemesis gravidarum, venous complications, genitourinary infections, diabetes mellitus, malnutrition, and liver disorders, are classified to categories O20 through O29 when they complicate the obstetrical experience. Certain infectious diseases such as HIV disease, viral hepatitis, tuberculosis, and venereal disease are classified in category O98.

Some codes for such complications are very specific, and others are rather broad. When a code from chapter 15 describes the condition adequately, only that code is assigned. It is appropriate, however, to assign an additional code when it provides needed specificity. For example, a patient who has a history of vaginal herpes maintained on Valtrex is admitted to the hospital for delivery. At the time of delivery, she is symptom free with no outbreak. Code **O98.32, Other infections with a predominantly sexual mode of transmission complicating childbirth,** is assigned as the principal diagnosis. Codes **A60.04, Herpesviral vulvovaginitis,** and **Z79.899, Other long term (current) drug therapy,** should be assigned as additional diagnoses, along with Z codes for outcome of delivery and for weeks of gestation. Herpes infection during pregnancy poses a risk to the fetus and is appropriately coded as a complication of the pregnancy.

On the other hand, the code for varicose veins of the legs complicating pregnancy (O22.0-) or the puerperium (O87.4) provides complete information, and assignment of an additional code is redundant. Code **O22.3-, Deep thrombophlebitis complicating pregnancy,** requires an additional code to specify whether the deep thrombophlebitis is acute or chronic, and to specify the site.

Other examples of the appropriate use of these codes follow.

O23.12 + Z3A.15	A pregnant patient at 15 weeks gestation has a chronic cystitis and has had recurrent bouts of acute cystitis during her pregnancy, with an acute episode at time of admission
O26.611 + K76.2 + Z3A.10	Necrosis of liver, complicating pregnancy, 10 weeks gestation

Hypertension

Hypertension in pregnancy is always considered a complicating factor in pregnancy, childbirth, or the puerperium. For correct code assignment, it is important to determine whether the hypertension is a pre-existing or a gestational condition. Pre-existing hypertension is classified to category O10, Pre-existing hypertension complicating pregnancy, childbirth and the puerperium, as follows:

O10.01–O10.03	Essential hypertension
O10.111–O10.13	Hypertensive heart disease
O10.211–O10.23	Hypertensive chronic kidney disease
O10.311–O10.33	Hypertensive heart and chronic kidney disease
O10.411–O10.43	Secondary hypertension
O10.911–O10.93	Unspecified

When assigning one of the O10 codes that includes hypertensive heart disease or hypertensive chronic kidney disease, it is necessary to add a secondary code from the appropriate hypertension category to specify the type of hypertensive heart disease (category I11), heart failure (category I50), chronic kidney disease (category I12), or hypertensive heart and chronic kidney disease (category I13).

Patients who do not have pre-existing hypertension may develop transient or gestational or pregnancy-induced hypertension during pregnancy. This condition is essentially an elevated blood pressure and clears relatively quickly once the pregnancy is over. This condition is coded to category O13, Gestational [pregnancy-induced] hypertension without significant proteinuria.

Hypertension in pregnancy sometimes leads to a pathological condition described as eclampsia or preeclampsia. Preeclampsia is a condition marked by high blood pressure accompanied with a high level of protein in the urine. Women with preeclampsia often also have swelling in the feet, legs, and hands. Eclampsia is the final and most severe phase of preeclampsia and occurs when preeclampsia is left untreated. Eclampsia usually results in seizures and causes coma and even death of the mother and baby, and it can occur before, during, or after childbirth. When preeclampsia is superimposed on a pre-existing hypertension, a code from category O11 with an additional code from category O10 to identify the type of hypertension are assigned. When preeclampsia arises without any pre-existing hypertension, it is classified in category O14, Pre-eclampsia. Eclampsia, regardless of whether it is due to pre-existing hypertension, gestational hypertension, or unspecified material hypertension, is classified to category O15, Eclampsia.

Gestational hypertension associated with albuminuria (albumin in urine), edema (abnormal accumulation of fluid in body tissues), or both is generally considered to be preeclampsia or eclampsia. However, codes for eclampsia or preeclampsia are never assigned solely on the basis of an elevated blood pressure, an abnormal albumin level, or the presence of edema. The physician must specify the condition as eclampsia or preeclampsia before any of these codes may be assigned.

When gestational edema, gestational proteinuria, or both gestational edema and gestational proteinuria are present without hypertension, these conditions are classified to category O12, Gestational [pregnancy-induced] edema and proteinuria without hypertension.

Diabetes

Diabetes mellitus is a significant complicating factor in pregnancy. Pregnant women who are diabetic should be assigned a code from category O24, Diabetes mellitus in pregnancy, childbirth, and the puerperium, first, followed by the appropriate diabetes code(s) (E08–E13) from chapter 4 of ICD-10-CM.

Similar to hypertension, category O24 distinguishes between pre-existing diabetes mellitus (including type 1, type 2, other, or unspecified), gestational diabetes, and unspecified diabetes as follows:

O24.011–O24.03	Pre-existing type 1 diabetes mellitus
O24.111–O24.13	Pre-existing type 2 diabetes mellitus
O24.311–O24.319	Unspecified pre-existing diabetes mellitus
O24.410–O24.439	Gestational diabetes mellitus
O24.811–O24.83	Other pre-existing diabetes mellitus
O24.911–O24.93	Unspecified diabetes mellitus

Gestational (pregnancy induced) diabetes can occur during the second and third trimester of pregnancy in women who were not diabetic prior to pregnancy. Gestational diabetes can complicate the pregnancy, and there is an increased risk in women with gestational diabetes to develop diabetes mellitus following delivery. Gestational diabetes can cause complications in the pregnancy similar to those of pre-existing diabetes mellitus. Codes for gestational diabetes are in subcategory O24.4, Gestational diabetes mellitus. No other code from category O24, Diabetes mellitus in pregnancy, childbirth, and the puerperium, should be used with a code from O24.4. The codes under subcategory O24.4 include diet controlled and insulin controlled. If a patient with gestational diabetes is treated with both diet and insulin, only the code for insulin controlled is required.

Code **Z79.4, Long-term (current) use of insulin,** should also be assigned if the pre-existing or unspecified diabetes mellitus is being treated with insulin. However, code Z79.4 should not be assigned with codes from subcategory O24.4, Gestational diabetes. If a patient with gestational diabetes is insulin controlled, the appropriate insulin-controlled code O24.414, O24.424, or O24.434 should be assigned instead of Z79.4. Code **Z86.32, Personal history of gestational diabetes,** is assigned to indicate that a patient has a history of gestational diabetes in a previous pregnancy.

A pregnant patient may have an abnormal glucose tolerance and not be diagnosed with gestational diabetes. In such cases, a code from subcategory O99.81, Abnormal glucose complicating pregnancy, childbirth, and the puerperium, should be assigned instead.

Examples include the following:

O24.113 + E11.620 + Z79.4 + Z3A.29	Pre-existing type 2 diabetes mellitus, with diabetic dermatitis, on insulin, intrauterine pregnancy, 29 weeks gestation
O24.012 + E10.11 + Z3A.26	Pre-existing diabetes mellitus, type 1, ketoacidosis and in coma; intrauterine pregnancy, 26 weeks gestation
O24.414 + Z3A.30	30-weeks-pregnant female seen in physician's office with gestational diabetes. Blood sugar reveals her diabetes is under good control with both diet and insulin

HIV Infection

During pregnancy, childbirth, or the puerperium, a patient admitted because of an HIV-related illness should receive a principal diagnosis from subcategory O98.7-, Human immunodeficiency [HIV] disease complicating pregnancy, childbirth and the puerperium, followed by the code(s) for the HIV-related illness(es). Patients with asymptomatic HIV infection status admitted during pregnancy, childbirth, or the puerperium should receive codes O98.7- and **Z21, Asymptomatic human immunodeficiency virus [HIV] infection status.** For example:

O98.711 + B20 + Z3A.00	First-trimester pregnant female with AIDS
O98.713 + Z21 + Z3A.30	30-weeks-pregnant female with complicating asymptomatic HIV status

Alcohol and Tobacco Use

The Centers for Disease Control and Prevention (CDC) urges pregnant women not to drink alcohol any time during pregnancy. According to the CDC, there is no known safe amount of alcohol to drink while pregnant. Drinking alcohol during pregnancy can cause miscarriage, stillbirth, and a range of lifelong disorders known as fetal alcohol spectrum disorders. According to the United States Surgeon General, alcohol consumed during pregnancy increases the risk of alcohol-related birth defects, including growth deficiencies, facial abnormalities, central nervous system impairment, behavioral disorders, and impaired intellectual development. For any pregnancy case in which the mother uses alcohol during the pregnancy or postpartum, codes from subcategory O99.31, Alcohol use complicating pregnancy, childbirth and the puerperium, should be assigned. A secondary code from category F10, Alcohol related disorders, should also be assigned to identify manifestations of the alcohol use.

Tobacco use also complicates pregnancy. Women who smoke prior to and during pregnancy are at risk for several adverse outcomes, such as premature rupture of membranes, placental abruption, and placenta previa during pregnancy. Babies born to women who smoke during pregnancy also have a higher risk of premature birth and low birth weight and are 1.4 to 3.0 times more likely to die of sudden infant death syndrome (SIDS). Codes from subcategory O99.33, Smoking (tobacco) complicating pregnancy, childbirth, and the puerperium, should be assigned for any pregnancy case in which a mother uses any type of tobacco product during the pregnancy or postpartum. A secondary code from category F17, Nicotine dependence, should also be assigned to identify the type of nicotine dependence.

COMPLICATIONS OF LABOR AND DELIVERY

Complications of labor and delivery are classified to categories O60 through O77. This block of codes contains some of the most important codes for situations when code **O80, Encounter for full-term uncomplicated delivery,** cannot be used.

Category O60, Preterm labor, is defined in ICD-10-CM as "onset (spontaneous) of labor before 37 completed weeks of gestation." This category includes codes for cases with delivery as well as without delivery. Codes from category O60 should not be used with codes from subcategory O47.0- for false or threatened labor.

Failed induction of labor is classified to category O61. Fourth characters distinguish between medical (e.g., intravenous Oxytocin to stimulate contractions), instrumental (e.g., via mechanical or surgical induction, such as with transcervical Foley catheter balloon or laminaria), other, and unspecified methods of induction of labor.

Abnormalities of forces of labor are classified to category O62. Fourth characters specify primary inadequate contractions (O62.0); secondary uterine inertia (O62.1); other uterine inertia (O62.2); precipitate labor (O62.3); hypertonic, incoordinate, and prolonged uterine contractions (O62.4); other abnormalities of labor (O62.8); and unspecified abnormalities of labor (O62.9).

For patients with long labor, ICD-10-CM provides category O63, with the fourth character specifying the stages, such as prolonged first stage (O63.0); prolonged second stage (O63.1); delayed delivery of second twin, triplet, etc. (O63.2); and unspecified (O63.9).

Obstructed Labor

Obstructed labor occurs when the passage of the fetus through the pelvis is mechanically obstructed. The most common cause of obstructed labor is disproportion between the fetus's head and the mother's pelvis. Occasionally, however, obstruction is secondary to malpresentation, malposition, and fetal abnormalities. ICD-10-CM provides categories O64, O65, and O66 for obstructed labor due to different etiologies, as follows:

- Category O64, Obstructed labor due to malposition and malpresentation of fetus, is used to describe situations in which labor may be obstructed due to the position of the fetus. Fetal presentation refers to the part of the fetus that lies closest to or has entered the true pelvis at the time of delivery. Refer to figure 24.2 for examples of fetal presentations. Cephalic presentations are vertex, brow, face, and chin. Breech presentations include frank breech, complete breech, incomplete breech, and single or double footling breech. Shoulder presentations are rare and require cesarean section or turning before vaginal birth. Compound presentation involves the entry of more than one part into the true pelvis, most commonly a hand next to the head. Category O64 provides fourth characters to specify the varying fetal presentations causing the obstruction of labor, such as incomplete rotation of fetal head (O64.0), breech presentation (O64.1), face presentation (O64.2), brow presentation (O64.3), shoulder presentation (O64.4), compound presentation (O64.5), other malpresentation (O64.8), and unspecified malpresentation (O64.9).
- Category O65, Obstructed labor due to maternal pelvic abnormality, is used to report obstructed labor caused by an abnormality in the mother's pelvis, such as deformity (O65.0), generally contracted pelvis (O65.1), pelvic inlet contraction (O65.2), pelvic outlet and mid-cavity contraction (O65.3), unspecified fetopelvic disproportion (O65.4), abnormality of maternal pelvic organs (O65.5), other maternal pelvic abnormalities (O65.8), and unspecified pelvic abnormality (O65.9).

- Category O66, Other obstructed labor, is used to classify other reasons for obstructed labor, such as shoulder dystocia (when the baby's shoulder gets stuck behind the mother's pubic bone) (O66.0), locked twins (a form of malpresentation in which a breech twin and a vertex twin become locked at the chin during labor and attempted delivery) (O66.1), unusually large fetus (O66.2), other abnormalities of fetus (including dystocia due to different etiologies) (O66.3), failed trial of labor (O66.4-), attempted application of vacuum extractor and forceps (O66.5), multiple fetuses (O66.6), other specified obstructed labor (O66.8 with additional code to identify cause of obstruction), and unspecified obstructed labor (O66.9).

ICD-10-CM also provides the following categories for labor and delivery complications caused by different conditions:

O67.0–O67.9	Intrapartum hemorrhage
O68	Abnormality of fetal acid-base balance
O69.0–O69.9	Umbilical cord complications

FIGURE 24.2 Examples of Fetal Presentations

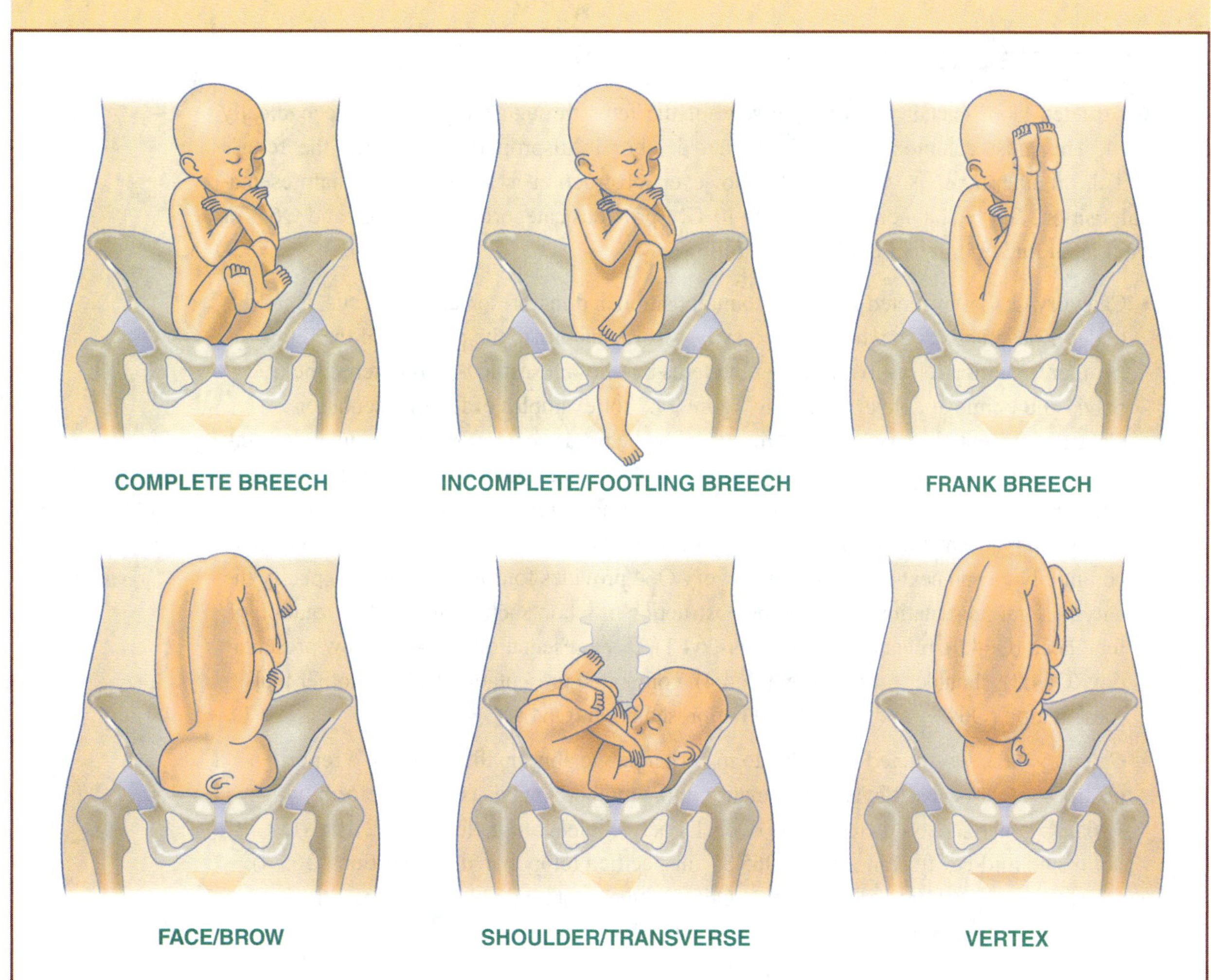

Fetal Stress

Fetal stress is an uncommon complication of labor referring to the presence of signs in a pregnant woman suggesting that the fetus may not be well. It typically occurs when the fetus has not been receiving enough oxygen. Fetal stress may occur when the pregnancy lasts too long (postmaturity) or when complications of pregnancy or labor occur.

ICD-10-CM provides different codes related to fetal problems complicating labor and delivery, such as the following:

- O68, Labor and delivery complicated by abnormality of fetal acid-base balance. This code is used to describe fetal acidemia, fetal acidosis, fetal alkalosis, or fetal metabolic acidemia when these conditions complicate labor and delivery.
- O76, Abnormality in fetal heart rate and rhythm complicating labor and delivery. This code includes fetal problems such as bradycardia, heart rate decelerations, heart rate irregularity, tachycardia, and non-reassuring fetal heart rate or rhythm.
- Category O77, Other fetal stress complicating labor and delivery. This category includes codes for meconium in amniotic fluid (O77.0), fetal stress due to drug administration (O77.1), and other evidence of fetal stress (such as electrocardiographic or ultrasonic evidence) (O77.8). Unspecified fetal stress is classified to code O77.9.

It is important to remember that these codes should only be reported when the above conditions affect the management of the mother.

POSTPARTUM COMPLICATIONS

The postpartum period, clinically termed the "puerperium," begins immediately after delivery and includes the subsequent six weeks. A postpartum complication is defined as any complication that occurs during that six-week period. Postpartum complications are classified to categories O85 through O92.

One type of postpartum complication is a puerperal infection—a bacterial infection following childbirth. An estimated 2 to 4 percent of mothers who deliver vaginally may experience some form of puerperal infection. For cesarean delivery, the figure is five to 10 times higher. The genital tract is the most common site of infection (e.g., endometritis: O86.12). Other types of puerperal infections include infection of obstetrical surgical wound (O86.0), cervicitis (O86.11), vaginitis (O86.13), other infection of genital tract (O86.19), urinary tract infection (O86.20), infection of kidney (O86.21), infection of bladder (O86.22), other urinary infection (O86.29), pyrexia of unknown origin (O86.4), puerperal septic thrombophlebitis (O86.81), and other specified puerperal infections (O86.89).

Code **O85, Puerperal sepsis,** requires a secondary code to identify the causal organism. For example, for a bacterial infection, a code from categories B95 through B97 should be assigned. Codes from category A40, Streptococcal sepsis, or A41, Other sepsis, should not be used for puerperal sepsis. If severe sepsis is also present, code **R65.2-, Severe sepsis,** should be assigned, along with the appropriate code for any associated acute organ dysfunction. Examples include the following:

- A patient who delivered a single healthy baby at 40 weeks develops endometritis two days following cesarean section delivery while still in the hospital. Code **O86.12, Endometritis following delivery,** is assigned. This condition is considered a complication of childbirth and not a complication of pregnancy. In ICD-10-CM, there is an Index entry for "endometritis, puerperal, postpartum, childbirth." Additional codes are assigned to identify the reason for the C-section, the outcome of delivery, and weeks of gestation of pregnancy.

- A patient is admitted three weeks postpartum and treated for acute pyelonephritis due to *Escherichia coli* infection. Code **O86.21, Infection of kidney following delivery,** is assigned as the principal diagnosis. Code **B96.20, Unspecified Escherichia coli [E. coli] as the cause of diseases classified elsewhere,** is assigned as an additional code to provide specificity regarding the infection.

- A patient who delivered via low cervical cesarean section (C-section) six days prior is readmitted with severe sepsis with acute kidney failure due to a methicillin-resistant *Staphylococcus aureus* (MRSA) of the C-section wound. Code **O86.0, Infection of obstetrical surgical wound,** is assigned for the postsurgical wound infection. Codes **O85, Puerperal sepsis; B95.62, Methicillin resistant Staphylococcus aureus as the cause of diseases classified elsewhere; R65.20, Severe sepsis without septic shock;** and **N17.9, Acute kidney failure, unspecified,** are also assigned for the MRSA puerperal sepsis with acute kidney failure.

Uterine atony is a condition that can complicate delivery and refers to failure of the uterine muscle to contract adequately after the delivery. Uterine atony can occur with or without bleeding. Code **O62.2, Other uterine inertia,** is assigned for atony of the uterus without hemorrhage when it occurs immediately following delivery of the baby and placenta. Assign code **O72.1, Other immediate postpartum hemorrhage,** for postpartum uterine atony with hemorrhage when it occurs immediately following delivery of the baby and placenta. Code **O75.89, Other specified complications of labor and delivery,** is assigned for postpartum uterine atony without hemorrhage. For example:

- A patient develops postpartum hemorrhage due to uterine atony immediately after spontaneous vaginal delivery of twins at 38 weeks gestation. The B-Lynch suture is performed to control the bleeding. The B-Lynch suture is a brace suture used to compress the uterus without compromising major vessels in cases of postpartum hemorrhage. Code **O72.1, Other immediate postpartum hemorrhage,** is assigned for postpartum uterine atony with hemorrhage. Codes **O30.003, Twin pregnancy, unspecified number of placenta and unspecified number of amniotic sacs, third trimester; Z3A.38, 38 weeks of gestation of pregnancy;** and **Z37.2, Twins, both liveborn,** are also assigned. Code **0UQ97ZZ, Repair uterus, via natural or artificial opening,** is assigned for the B-Lynch procedure.

- A nulliparous patient had a normal vaginal delivery at 40 weeks gestation. After placental separation, uterine atony was noted, and the patient started to hemorrhage. The atony was unresponsive to bimanual massage, intravenous oxytocin, and intramuscular methylergonovine. The provider evacuated a 50 ml clot from the lower uterine segment (LUS), fundus firm with cessation of bleeding. The appropriate ICD-10-PCS procedure code for evacuation of clot is as follows:

  Assign code **0W3R7ZZ, Control of hemorrhage of general anatomic regions.** The *ICD-10-PCS Official Guidelines* (Section 1C.C1) state that control of postoperative hemorrhage is coded to the root operation "Control" found in the general anatomical regions body systems. The root operation "Control" is defined as: "Stopping, or attempting to stop, postprocedural bleeding." If an attempt to stop postprocedural bleeding is initially unsuccessful, and the procedure to stop the bleeding requires performing any of the definitive root operations "Bypass," "Detachment," "Excision," "Extraction," "Reposition," "Replacement," or "Resection," then that root operation is coded instead of "Control."

Pregnancy associated cardiomyopathy is also referred to as peripartum cardiomyopathy because it may be diagnosed in the third trimester of pregnancy but may continue to progress months after delivery. Code **O90.3, Peripartum cardiomyopathy,** should be used only when the cardiomyopathy develops as a result of pregnancy in women who did not have pre-existing heart disease. For example:

- A patient is admitted due to peripartum cardiomyopathy with ejection fraction of 21 percent and heart failure. The patient is approximately two to three months postpartum. Code **O90.3, Peripartum cardiomyopathy,** is assigned as the principal diagnosis. The peripartum period is defined as the last month of pregnancy to five months postpartum.

For pre-existing heart disease complicating pregnancy and the puerperium, codes from subcategory O99.4, Diseases of the circulatory system complicating pregnancy, childbirth and the puerperium, should be used instead of the pregnancy associated cardiomyopathy code.

OTHER MATERNAL DISEASES

ICD-10-CM provides category O99 to describe other maternal diseases classifiable elsewhere but complicating pregnancy, childbirth, and the puerperium. This category includes conditions that complicate the pregnant state, are aggravated by the pregnancy, or are a main reason for obstetric care. Examples include:

O99.0-	Anemia
O99.1-	Other diseases of the blood and blood-forming organs and certain disorders involving the immune mechanism
O99.2-	Endocrine, nutritional, and metabolic diseases
O99.3-	Mental disorders and diseases of the nervous system
O99.4-	Diseases of the circulatory system
O99.5-	Diseases of the respiratory system
O99.6-	Diseases of the digestive system
O99.7-	Diseases of the skin and subcutaneous tissue
O99.8-	Other specified diseases and conditions

An additional code is used to identify the specific condition. For example:

- A patient is admitted five weeks postpartum with acute cholecystitis and cholelithiasis. Code **O99.63, Diseases of the digestive system complicating the puerperium,** and code **K80.00, Calculus of gallbladder with acute cholecystitis without obstruction,** are assigned.

Malignant neoplasms complicating pregnancy, childbirth, and the puerperium are classified to subcategory O9A.1, with additional code(s) to identify the specific neoplasm. This subcategory is for conditions classified to C00 through C96. Maternal care for benign tumor of corpus uteri is coded to O34.1-, while maternal care for benign tumor of cervix is classified to O34.4-.

Coding of injury, poisoning, physical abuse, sexual abuse, and psychological abuse complicating pregnancy, childbirth, and the puerperium is discussed in chapter 30 of this handbook.

SEQUELAE OF COMPLICATION OF PREGNANCY, CHILDBIRTH, OR THE PUERPERIUM

Code **O94, Sequelae of complication of pregnancy, childbirth, and the puerperium,** is assigned when an initial complication of the obstetrical experience develops a sequela that requires care or treatment at a later date. The sequelae include conditions specified as such, or as late effects, which may occur at any time after the postpartum period. Like all late-effect codes, code O94 is sequenced after the code describing the residual condition. Examples include the following:

- A patient is admitted for repair of postpartal perineum prolapse secondary to traumatic laceration sustained during childbirth two years earlier. Code **N81.89, Other female genital prolapse,** is assigned first, with code **O94, Sequelae of complication of pregnancy, childbirth, and the puerperium,** assigned as an additional code.
- A patient presents with fatigue and cold intolerance. Her history indicates that she had experienced a severe hemorrhage during delivery of a normal liveborn seven months earlier. She was diagnosed with Sheehan's syndrome and treated with replacement hormones. Code **E23.0, Hypopituitarism,** is assigned for Sheehan's syndrome, followed by code **O94, Sequelae of complication of pregnancy, childbirth, and the puerperium.**

EXERCISE 24.4

Code the following diagnoses. Do not code procedures. Assign Z codes where applicable.

	Diagnosis	Codes
1.	Intrauterine pregnancy, spontaneous delivery, single liveborn	O80 Z37.0 Z3A.00
2.	Intrauterine pregnancy, 12 weeks gestation, undelivered, with mild hyperemesis gravidarum	O21.0 Z3A.12
3.	Intrauterine pregnancy, 39 weeks, delivered, left occipitoanterior, single liveborn Primary uterine inertia	O62.0 Z37.0 Z3A.39
4.	Cesarean delivery of stillborn at 38 weeks gestation owing to placental infarction	O43.813 Z37.1 O36.4xx0 Z3A.38
5.	Intrauterine pregnancy, with pernicious anemia, second trimester	O99.012 D51.0 Z3A.00

6. Intrauterine pregnancy, term, 40 weeks gestation — O80
   Spontaneous delivery, left occipitoanterior — Z37.0
   Single liveborn — Z3A.40

7. Intrauterine pregnancy, twins, 33 weeks — O60.14x0
   Premature rupture of membranes, onset of — O42.013
   labor three hours later. Spontaneous delivery of — O30.003
   premature twins, vertex presentation, both liveborn — O88.23
   Postpartum pulmonary embolism — Z37.2
   Z3A.33

8. Premature delivery, third trimester, frank breech — O60.14x0
   presentation, single female liveborn — O32.1xx0
   First-degree tear, vaginal wall — O70.0
   Z37.0
   Z3A.00

9. Term pregnancy, 39 weeks, delivered, single stillborn, — O45.93
   left occipitoanterior — O69.1xx0
   Terminal abruptio placentae — O36.4xx0
   Cord wrapped tightly around neck with compression — Z37.1
   Z3A.39

10. Intrauterine pregnancy, 12 weeks; — O10.011
    long-standing essential hypertension — Z3A.12
    being monitored closely

OBSTETRIC PROCEDURES

When coding obstetrical procedures using ICD-10-PCS, it is important to distinguish whether the procedure is performed on the fetus or on the pregnant female. Procedures performed on the fetus (products of conception) are classified to the Obstetrics Section. Procedures performed on the pregnant female, other than the products of conception, are coded to the appropriate root operation in the Medical and Surgical Section. For example, amniocentesis is coded to the "products of conception" body part in the Obstetrics Section. However, repair of obstetric urethral laceration is coded to the "urethra" body part in the Medical and Surgical Section.

The ICD-10-PCS Obstetrics Section follows the same conventions found in the Medical and Surgical Section, with all seven characters retaining the same meaning as shown in figure 24.3. The body system (character 2) in the Obstetrics Section is always "pregnancy." There are only three values used for body part in this section: "products of conception" (0); "products of conception, retained" (1); and "products of conception, ectopic" (2).

FIGURE 24.3 Structure of Codes in the Obstetrics Section

Character 1	Character 2	Character 3	Character 4	Character 5	Character 6	Character 7
Section	Body System	Root Operation	Body Part	Approach	Device	Qualifier

There are 12 root operations (as shown in figure 24.4) in the Obstetrics Section, 10 of which are also found in the Medical and Surgical Section. The two root operations unique to the Obstetrics Section are defined below:

- Abortion: Artificially terminating a pregnancy
- Delivery: Assisting the passage of the products of conception from the genital tract. This root operation applies only to manually assisted, vaginal delivery.

Cesarean deliveries are coded to the Obstetrics Section to the root operation "Extraction" rather than to the root operation "Delivery." The root operation "Extraction" is also used for vaginal deliveries requiring assistance with forceps, vacuum, or internal version.

Procedures performed following a delivery or an abortion for curettage of the endometrium or evacuation of retained products of conception are all coded in the Obstetrics Section to the root operation "Extraction" and the body part "products of conception, retained." Diagnostic or therapeutic dilation and curettage performed during times other than the postpartum or post-abortion period are all coded in the Medical and Surgical Section to the root operation "Extraction" and the body part "endometrium."

FIGURE 24.4 Root Operations in the Obstetrics Section

Value	Root Operation	Definition
2	Change	Taking out or off a device from a body part and putting back an identical or similar device in or on the same body part without cutting or puncturing the skin or a mucous membrane
9	Drainage	Taking or letting out fluids and/or gases from a body part
A	Abortion	Artificially terminating a pregnancy
D	Extraction	Pulling or stripping out or off all or a portion of a body part
E	Delivery	Assisting the passage of the products of conception from the genital canal
H	Insertion	Putting in a nonbiological appliance that monitors, assists, performs, or prevents a physiological function but does not physically take the place of a body part
J	Inspection	Visually and/or manually exploring a body part
P	Removal	Taking out or off a device from a body part, region, or orifice
Q	Repair	Restoring, to the extent possible, a body part to its normal anatomic structure and function
S	Reposition	Moving to its normal location or other suitable location all or a portion of a body part
T	Resection	Cutting out or off, without replacement, all of a body part
Y	Transplantation	Putting in or on all or a portion of a living body part taken from another individual or animal to physically take the place and/or function of all or a portion of a similar body part

PROCEDURES ASSISTING DELIVERY

Delivery can be assisted in a number of ways. Manually assisted vaginal delivery is coded as follows:

Character 1 Section	Character 2 Body System	Character 3 Root Operation	Character 4 Body Part	Character 5 Approach	Character 6 Device	Character 7 Qualifier
1	0	E	0	X	Z	Z
Obstetrics	Pregnancy	Delivery	Products of conception	External	None	None

Labor may be induced by artificial rupture of membranes (Medical and Surgical Section, root operation "Drainage," body part "amniotic fluid") or by other surgical induction, such as cervical dilatation (0U7C7ZZ). Artificial rupture of membranes may also be performed after labor has begun.

Amnioinfusion (Administration Section, root operation "Introduction") is typically performed during labor via a transcervical approach after rupture of the fetal membranes. An intrauterine pressure catheter is used to infuse a lactated Ringer's or normal saline solution into the amniotic cavity. Alternatively, fluid can be infused through a needle transabdominally. Amnioinfusion is performed as prophylactic treatment of oligohydramnios, for reduction of variable decelerations of the fetal heart rate because of cord compression during labor, or as treatment of preterm premature rupture of membranes.

For example, amnioinfusion of normal saline solution is coded as follows:

Character 1 Section	Character 2 Body System	Character 3 Root Operation	Character 4 Body System	Character 5 Approach	Character 6 Substance	Character 7 Qualifier
3	E	0	E	7	7	Z
Administration	Physiological systems and anatomical regions	Introduction	Products of conception	Via natural or artificial opening	Electrolytic and water balance substance	None

If rotation during delivery is carried out, this procedure is coded to the Obstetrics Section, root operation "Reposition," code **10S07ZZ, Reposition products of conception, via natural or artificial opening.** For a routine delivery, code **10E0XZZ, Delivery of products of conception, external approach,** may be assigned.

Forceps Delivery and Vacuum Extraction

Forceps, vacuum extraction, or internal and combined version may also assist delivery. These are coded to the Obstetrics Section, root operation "Extraction." Codes are provided for low-forceps, mid-forceps, or high-forceps delivery. In a low-forceps delivery (seventh-character qualifier value "3"), forceps are applied to a visible fetal head after it has entered the pelvic floor. Mid-forceps (seventh-character qualifier value "4") are applied to the head during its entry into the pelvic floor, and high forceps (seventh-character qualifier value "5") are applied to the head before it enters the pelvic brim. Breech presentations may require partial or total breech extraction, with or without forceps to the aftercoming head. Vacuum extraction (seventh-character qualifier value "6") uses a traction device rather than forceps applied to the fetal head for extraction of the fetus.

Episiotomy

An episiotomy is a surgical incision in the perineum made just before delivery to enlarge the vaginal opening and assist delivery. Code **0W8NXZZ, Division of female perineum, external approach,** is assigned for a routine episiotomy. The repair (episiorraphy) is not coded separately because the repair is integral to the procedure. When an episiotomy is performed in connection with a forceps delivery, two codes are assigned: a code for the delivery and code 0W8NXZZ for the episiotomy.

Perineal Lacerations

Perineal lacerations are classified as first, second, third, or fourth degree in category O70, Perineal laceration during delivery:

- First-degree tears (O70.0) involve damage to the fourchette and vaginal mucosa, and underlying muscles are exposed but not torn.
- Second-degree tears (O70.1) include the posterior vaginal walls and perineal muscles, but the anal sphincter is intact.
- Third-degree tears (O70.2) extend to the anal sphincter, but the rectal mucosa is intact.
- Fourth-degree tears (O70.3) involve the rectal and anal mucosa.

Code O70.4 describes an anal sphincter tear complicating delivery that is not associated with a third-degree perineal laceration. Code **O70.9, Perineal laceration during delivery, unspecified,** is used when there is no additional information on the degree of the perineal laceration.

Inclusion notes for these codes indicate what is involved in each degree. When more than one degree is mentioned, only the code for the highest degree is assigned. The appropriate surgical repair code is assigned depending on the tissue repaired (e.g., for open repair of the vaginal wall, assign code 0UQG0ZZ) with the body part specifying the deepest layer repaired. For example, repair of a second-degree laceration requires repair of the perineal muscle, mucosa, and skin; therefore, it is coded to the body part "perineum, muscle."

Category O71, Other obstetric trauma, is used for other obstetric trauma, including trauma from instrument for the following injuries: rupture of uterus (spontaneous) before onset of labor (O71.0-) or during labor (O71.1), postpartum inversion of uterus (O71.2), obstetric laceration of cervix (O71.3), obstetric high vaginal laceration alone (O71.4), other obstetric injury to pelvic organs (O71.5), obstetric damage to pelvic joints and ligaments (O71.6), obstetric hematoma of pelvis (O71.7), other obstetric trauma (O71.8-), and unspecified obstetric trauma (O71.9).

Occasionally, an episiotomy extends spontaneously to become a perineal laceration or tear. In this case, assign code **0W8NXZZ, Division of female perineum, external approach,** for the episiotomy, along with code **0WQNXZZ, Repair female perineum, external approach,** for the repair of the tear. Both codes are needed to completely describe this situation. For the diagnosis, assign also the appropriate code from category O70, Perineal laceration during delivery, to specifically describe the laceration or tear.

Fetal Pulse Oximetry

Fetal oxygen monitoring provides the physician with a direct measure of fetal oxygen status when an irregular fetal heart rate is present. The intrapartum fetal oxygen monitor uses a single-use, disposable sensor that is inserted through the birth canal when one of the amniotic membranes has ruptured and the cervix is dilated more than 2 centimeters. The oxygen saturation is displayed on a monitor screen as a percentage. Assign code **10H073Z, Insertion of monitoring electrode into products of conception, via natural or artificial opening,** for this type of fetal monitoring.

Cesarean Delivery

Cesarean delivery is an operative delivery that is carried out when, for some reason, spontaneous delivery is not possible or does not seem advisable. Cesarean sections are classified to the root operation "Extraction," body part "products of conception," and open approach. A classical cesarean section, coded to **10D00Z0, Extraction of products of conception, classical, open approach,** removes the fetus through an incision into the upper part of the uterus using an abdominal peritoneal approach. A low cervical cesarean, coded to **10D00Z1, Extraction of products of conception, low cervical, open approach,** uses an incision into the lower portion of the uterus, with a pelvic cavity or an abdominal peritoneal incision. There is also an extraperitoneal cesarean section (seventh-character qualifier value "2").

EXERCISE 24.5

Code the following procedures.

1. Induction of labor by cervical dilation	0U7C7ZZ
2. Assisted spontaneous delivery	10E0XZZ
3. Vaginal delivery using low forceps Extraction	10D07Z3
4. Extraperitoneal C-section, low transverse incision Delivery	10D00Z2
5. Mid-forceps vaginal delivery with routine episiotomy	10D07Z4 0W8NXZZ

SERVICES RELATED TO CONTRACEPTIVE MANAGEMENT

Category Z30, Encounter for contraceptive management, is assigned as the principal diagnosis for admissions or outpatient encounters for the purpose of contraceptive management. Codes in this category cover services such as initiation of oral contraceptive measures (Z30.011); counseling in natural family planning to avoid pregnancy (Z30.02); insertion of intrauterine contraceptive device (Z30.430); removal of intrauterine contraceptive device (Z30.432); removal and reinsertion of intrauterine contraceptive device (Z30.433); sterilization (Z30.2); and surveillance of injectable contraceptive (Z30.42). Procedure codes must also be assigned when appropriate.

EXERCISE 24.6

Code the following diagnoses and procedures.

1.	Family planning counseling	Z30.09
2.	Encounter for insertion of intrauterine contraceptive device	Z30.430
	Insertion of intrauterine contraceptive device	0UH97HZ
3.	Encounter for removal of intrauterine contraceptive device	Z30.432
	Removal of intrauterine contraceptive device	0UPD7HZ
4.	Encounter for lactation counseling	Z39.1

STERILIZATION

When a patient seeks health care for the purpose of contraceptive sterilization, code **Z30.2, Encounter for sterilization,** is assigned as the principal diagnosis. If there are underlying medical or psychological conditions that led to the decision to undergo sterilization, codes for these conditions may be assigned as additional diagnoses. Because sterilization may be performed as an elective procedure without any predisposing medical or psychological reasons, code Z30.2 can be used as a solo diagnosis code.

When an elective sterilization procedure is performed during a hospital episode in which an obstetrical delivery has occurred, Z30.2 is assigned as a secondary code, with a code from chapter 15 of ICD-10-CM assigned as the principal diagnosis.

Note that code Z30.2 is assigned for both female and male patients for whom a contraceptive sterilization procedure is performed. Sterilization procedures for females are sometimes generically referred to as "tubal ligation." ICD-10-PCS classifies sterilization procedures for females to the female reproductive system to different root operations ("Excision," "Occlusion," or "Destruction") depending on the technique used, for example:

- Partial salpingectomy, whereby the fallopian tubes are cut and tied with suture material: root operation "Excision"
- Clips, external rings, whereby the fallopian tubes are clipped (e.g., Filshie clip, Wolf clip) or blocked with an external ring (e.g., Falope ring, Yoon ring): root operation "Occlusion"
- Electrocoagulation, whereby a small portion of each fallopian tube is burnt or cauterized: root operation "Destruction"

Sterilization procedures for males are classified to the male reproductive system, root operations "Destruction" or "Excision." Code Z30.2 is not assigned as either a principal or a secondary diagnosis when sterilization results from other treatment or when a sterilization procedure is

performed as part of the treatment for another condition. In such cases, the original condition, any complications or comorbidities, and the procedures performed are coded. For example, when a hysterectomy is performed because of injury or damage to the uterus during delivery, only the obstetrical diagnoses and procedures are coded, even though the procedure results in sterility. Code Z30.2 is used only for a sterilization performed specifically for contraception; assigning it when a sterilization is incidental to other treatment is inappropriate.

Other examples of appropriate coding of situations involving sterilization follow.

Z30.2 + F32.9 + Z64.1 + 0UL74ZZ	A patient with multiparity (five children) with reactive depression is admitted for elective sterilization; bilateral endoscopic ligation and division (occlusion) of the fallopian tubes are carried out for sterilization
O32.1xx0 + Z30.2 + Z37.0 + Z3A.38 + 10D07Z6 + 0UL74CZ	Term pregnancy, liveborn delivered; breech presentation; 38 weeks gestation; delivery by partial breech vacuum extraction; endoscopic bilateral tubal ligation with extraluminal device for sterilization

Sterilization procedures are intended to be permanent. However, there may be situations in which a patient may desire a reversal of the sterilization procedure. Admission for a tuboplasty or vasoplasty to reverse a previous sterilization procedure is coded to **Z31.0, Encounter for reversal of previous sterilization.**

EXERCISE 24.7

Code the following diagnostic statements and procedures.

1. Essential hypertension — Z30.2
   Admitted for sterilization — I10
   Laparoscopy with bilateral partial salpingectomy — 0UB74ZZ

2. Endometriosis of uterus — Z30.2
   Admitted for sterilization — N80.0
   Bilateral laparoscopic tubal ligation — 0U574ZZ
   via electrocautery for sterilization

3. Pregnancy, 40 weeks gestation, with breech delivery, — O32.1xx0
   female infant, followed by sterilization — Z30.2
   Z37.0
   Vacuum breech extraction — Z3A.40
   Laparoscopic occlusion of bilateral fallopian tubes — 10D07Z6
   with Falope (external) rings — 0UL74CZ

4. Elective sterilization, patient request	Z30.2
Vasectomy, bilateral (open)	0VBQ0ZZ
5. Elective reversal of previous tubal ligation	Z31.0
Laparoscopic salpingoplasty	0UQ74ZZ

PROCREATIVE MANAGEMENT

A code from category Z31, Encounter for procreative management, is assigned when a patient who is having difficulty becoming pregnant is seen for help in correcting this problem.

Code Z31.61 is assigned as the first-listed diagnosis for an encounter/visit for procreative counseling and advice using natural family planning. Couples seeking natural methods of family planning require training/counseling by a medical professional or a qualified counselor. There are five methods of natural family planning:

- Basal body temperature method
- Ovulation/cervical mucus method
- Symptothermal method
- Calendar method
- Lactational amenorrhea

Therapy for malignant neoplasms or other serious conditions can affect reproductive health and the ability to conceive. Antineoplastic drugs (e.g., alkylating agents) and radiotherapy to the pelvic area may impair ovarian and testicular function, leading to infertility. Depending on the dosage delivered and the length of treatment, healthy sperm cells and ovarian follicles can be destroyed along with cancer cells.

Code **Z31.62, Encounter for fertility preservation counseling,** is assigned for encounters for advice and counseling on available options to conceive a child or maintain pregnancy before the start of cancer treatment or the surgical removal of gonads. The discussion may include whether to conceive before cancer treatment; banking of sperm, eggs, ovarian tissue, or embryos; and/or modification of surgery to spare the uterus.

Code **Z31.84, Encounter for fertility preservation procedure,** is assigned for the fertility preservation encounter. These codes are not limited to those seeking advice prior to cancer treatment or gonad removal. Codes Z31.62 and Z31.84 may be assigned for patients having any treatment (not only cancer treatment) that may affect fertility.

Code **Z31.83, Encounter for assisted reproductive fertility procedure cycle,** is assigned for patients undergoing in vitro fertilization. An additional code should be assigned to identify the type of infertility. Code Z31.83 is not used for encounters for diagnostic testing prior to starting in vitro fertilization. Assign the reason for the encounter when the patient presents for diagnostic testing.

Code **O09.81-, Supervision of pregnancy resulting from assisted reproductive technology,** is assigned for subsequent encounters involving antenatal supervision and/or prenatal care when in vitro fertilization has been successful.

Encounters for investigations such as sperm counts or fallopian tube insufflation are coded to **Z31.41, Encounter for fertility testing.** For encounters for sperm count following sterilization reversal, assign code **Z31.42, Aftercare following sterilization reversal,** instead of Z31.41.

ICD-10-CM provides the following codes to describe encounters for testing and counseling for genetic disease:

Z31.430	Encounter of female for testing for genetic disease carrier status for procreative management
Z31.438	Encounter for other genetic testing of female for procreative management
Z31.440	Encounter of male for testing for genetic disease carrier status for procreative management
Z31.441	Encounter for testing of male partner of patient with recurrent pregnancy loss
Z31.448	Encounter for other genetic testing of male for procreative management
Z31.5	Encounter for genetic counseling

If the encounter is for genetic screening not associated with procreative management, assign a code from subcategory Z13.7, Encounter for screening for genetic and chromosomal anomalies, rather than the Z31.4- series.

SUSPECTED MATERNAL AND FETAL CONDITIONS NOT FOUND

Codes from subcategory Z03.7, Encounter for suspected maternal and fetal conditions ruled out, are to be used in very limited circumstances on a maternal record when an encounter is for a suspected maternal or fetal condition that is ruled out during that encounter (for example, a maternal or fetal condition may be suspected due to an abnormal test result). These codes should not be used when the condition is confirmed. In those cases, the confirmed condition should be coded. These codes should not be used if an illness or any signs or symptoms related to the suspected condition or problem are present. In those cases, the appropriate codes for the diagnosis/sign or symptom should be reported instead.

Codes from subcategory Z03.7 can be used with other codes, but only if they are unrelated to the suspected condition being evaluated. Codes from subcategory Z03.7 may not be used for encounters for antenatal screening of the mother. For encounters for suspected fetal conditions that are inconclusive following testing and evaluation, assign the appropriate code from category O35, O36, O40, or O41.

Codes in subcategory Z03.7 describe suspected fetal/maternal problems not found, as follows:

Z03.71	Encounter for suspected problem with amniotic cavity and membrane ruled out
Z03.72	Encounter for suspected placental problem ruled out
Z03.73	Encounter for suspected fetal anomaly ruled out
Z03.74	Encounter for suspected problem with fetal growth ruled out
Z03.75	Encounter for suspected cervical shortening ruled out

EXERCISE 24.8

Code the following diagnostic statements and procedures. Assign Z codes where applicable.

1.	Elderly primigravida (37 years old); 40 weeks gestation,	O09.513
	spontaneous delivery of living female infant	Z37.0
	Outcome of delivery	Z3A.40
	Manually assisted delivery	10E0XZZ
	Episiotomy and repair	0W8NXZZ
2.	Term pregnancy, 39 weeks gestation, living dichorionic twins	O77.9
	(diamniotic sacs), cesarean delivery	O30.043
	performed because fetal stress noted prior to labor	Z37.2
	Outcome of delivery	Z3A.39
	Low cervical cesarean delivery	10D00Z1
3.	Delivery, 38 weeks gestation, living child,	O80
	ROA presentation	Z37.0
	Outcome of delivery	Z3A.38
	Manually assisted delivery	10E0XZZ
	Fetal cardiac rhythm monitoring during labor	4A1H7FZ
	Episiotomy and episiorrhaphy	0W8NXZZ
4.	Uterine pregnancy, 39 weeks gestation, delivered with	O64.8xx0
	obstructed labor due to transverse lie presentation	O10.02
	Pre-existing hypertension with mild preeclampsia,	O11.3
	single liveborn	Z3A.39
	Outcome of delivery	Z37.0
	Manually assisted delivery	10E0XZZ
5.	Intrauterine pregnancy, 37 weeks gestation, delivered,	O30.033
	spontaneous	O72.0
	Third-stage hemorrhage with anemia	O90.81
	secondary to acute blood loss	D62
	Monochorionic twins, both liveborn, diamniotic placenta	Z37.2
	Outcome of delivery	Z3A.37
		10E0XZZ

6. Pregnancy, 38 weeks gestation, delivered, frank breech	O32.1xx0
presentation with liveborn male infant	Z37.0
Outcome of delivery	Z3A.38
Partial breech extraction with mid-forceps	10D07Z4
to aftercoming head	
7. Pregnancy, 40 weeks gestation, delivered, spontaneous	O80
Liveborn, male infant	Z37.0
Outcome of delivery	Z3A.40
Assisted spontaneous delivery	10E0XZZ
Elective sterilization following delivery	Z30.2
Bilateral endoscopic ligation and crushing of fallopian tubes	0UL78ZZ
8. Intrauterine pregnancy, 26 weeks gestation, with complicating	O34.32
incompetent cervix, undelivered	Z3A.26
Shirodkar cervical cerclage operation	0UVC7ZZ
9. Gestational hypertension	O13.3
Pregnancy, third trimester, 29 weeks gestation, undelivered	Z3A.29
10. Intrauterine pregnancy, 38 weeks gestation, delivered,	O70.1
right occipitoanterior, liveborn male infant	Z37.0
Episiotomy that extended to second-degree	Z3A.38
lacerations, perineum	10907ZC
Outcome of delivery	10D07Z3
Amniotomy for induction of labor	0W8NXZZ
Low-forceps delivery with episiotomy	0KQM0ZZ
Repair of perineal laceration	
11. Delivery, stillborn, male infant, 40 weeks gestation	O64.3xx0
brow presentation; obstructed labor	O36.4xx0
Outcome of delivery	Z37.1
	Z3A.40
Extraction with internal version	10D07Z7
Episiotomy and repair	0W8NXZZ

12.	Twin pregnancy, 38 weeks gestation, with malposition fetus 2 One liveborn twin, one stillborn (fetus 2), two placentae and two amniotic sacs	O32.9xx2 O30.043 O36.4xx2 Z37.3 Z3A.38
	Classical cesarean section	10D00Z0
13.	Postpartum uterine atony without hemorrhage occurring two weeks after delivery	O75.89
14.	Encounter for testing of female for genetic disease carrier status (patient planning on pregnancy)	Z31.430
15.	Encounter for in vitro fertilization (IVF); infertility due to obstructed fallopian tube	Z31.83 N97.1
16.	Visit for procreative counseling using natural family planning	Z31.61
17.	32-year-old gravida 2, para 0, admitted at 39 weeks gestation for an elective primary low cesarean section. The patient had a completely normal prenatal course, a normal pregnancy, and an unremarkable postoperative course. She elected to have a cesarean section because of fear of vaginal delivery. She had a normal single liveborn without complications. Delivery Outcome of delivery	O82 Z37.0 Z3A.39 10D00Z1
18.	Woman is admitted to the hospital and delivers a healthy baby. Four years ago, the woman used heroin and cocaine and currently is receiving prescribed methadone as a result of past dependence. She had a normal single liveborn without complications. The final diagnoses are "Term, 40 weeks gestation, manually assisted delivery, and methadone use." Delivery Outcome of delivery	O99.324 F11.20 Z37.0 Z3A.40 10E0XZZ

CHAPTER 25

Abortion and Ectopic Pregnancy

CHAPTER OVERVIEW

- Codes for pregnancy with an abortive outcome are found in categories O00 through O08 in chapter 15 of ICD-10-CM.
- The primary axis for coding abortion is the type of abortion (spontaneous, induced, or failed).
- Subcategories further specify if the abortion is complete, incomplete, or unspecified and whether a complication is present.
- If the attempted termination of pregnancy results in a liveborn infant, code Z33.2, Encounter for elective termination of pregnancy, is used along with a code from category Z37, Outcome of delivery.
- Molar pregnancies and other abnormal products of conception are also coded to categories O01–O02.
- Codes for ectopic pregnancies have a fourth character to indicate the location (O00.0–O00.9).
- An encounter for an elective abortion without complication is coded Z33.2.

LEARNING OUTCOMES

After studying this chapter you should be able to:

- Classify abortive outcomes by type of abortion.
- Select the appropriate code to indicate whether the abortion is complete, incomplete, or unspecified.
- Code complications to the abortion.
- Understand how to code different types and occurrences of abortions.
- Classify abnormal products of conception (such as molar and ectopic pregnancies).

TERMS TO KNOW

Abortion
the expulsion or extraction of all or part of the placenta with or without an identifiable fetus with less than an estimated 20 weeks gestational age

Biochemical pregnancy
a pregnancy that is too early to confirm except through biochemical means; considered the earliest form of miscarriage

Ectopic pregnancy
a pregnancy in which a fertilized ovum implants and develops outside the uterus

Molar pregnancy
a condition in which an ovum within the uterus develops into a mole or benign tumor

REMEMBER . . .

ICD-10-CM rules may be different from individual state rules when it comes to classifying abortions.

INTRODUCTION

The expulsion or extraction of all or part of the placenta or membrane with an estimated gestation of less than 20 completed weeks is considered an abortive outcome (abortion). Although requirements for fetal death reporting vary from state to state, these requirements should not be confused with ICD-10-CM rules for classifying abortions; they are entirely separate. If an expelled fetus has a period of gestation of more than 20 weeks but less than 37 weeks, it is considered an early delivery and a code from subcategory O60.1, Preterm labor with preterm delivery, is assigned.

Pregnancy with abortive outcome is classified in categories O00 through O08. Note that the term "abortion" in the disease classification of ICD-10-CM refers to a fetal death. It is important to distinguish between an encounter for the purpose of performing an elective abortion versus one for dealing with a spontaneous abortion or a complication of an abortion. Encounters for the purpose of performing an elective abortion are classified to **Z33.2, Encounter for elective termination of pregnancy.** If a procedure to terminate the pregnancy is performed in the hospital, the procedure code is also required.

TYPES OF ABORTION

The primary axis for coding abortion is the type of abortion. Abortive outcome is classified by type in ICD-10-CM as follows:

- *Spontaneous abortion (category O03):* one that occurs without any instrumentation or chemical intervention.
- *Complications following (induced) termination of pregnancy (O04):* Complications after an abortion performed for either therapeutic or elective termination of pregnancy (terms such as "elective abortion," "induced" or "artificial abortion," and "termination of pregnancy" are used when this type of abortion is performed).
- *Failed attempted termination of pregnancy (Category O07):* one in which an induction of termination of pregnancy has failed to evacuate or expel the fetus and the patient is still pregnant. It includes incomplete elective abortion.

COMPLETE VERSUS INCOMPLETE SPONTANEOUS ABORTION

Codes in subcategories O03.0 through O03.4 indicate that the abortion is incomplete, while codes in subcategories O03.5 through O03.9 indicate that the abortion is complete or unspecified. Incomplete abortion refers to retained products of conception—whether from a spontaneous abortion or an elective termination of pregnancy. When the provider documentation does not specify whether the spontaneous abortion is complete or incomplete, ICD-10-CM classifies it to "complete or unspecified." The fact that a follow-up dilatation and curettage (D & C) is performed is not evidence in itself that an abortion is incomplete; the physician makes this determination.

COMPLICATIONS ASSOCIATED WITH ABORTION

Codes in categories O03, O04, and O07 indicate whether a complication is present and the general type of complication, such as a genital or pelvic infection; delayed or excessive hemorrhage; embolism; or other complications including shock, renal failure, venous complications, cardiac arrest, sepsis, or urinary tract infection.

For subsequent encounters when there are retained products of conception following either a spontaneous abortion or an elective termination of pregnancy, assign the appropriate code from category O03, Spontaneous abortion, or code **O07.4, Failed attempted termination of pregnancy without complication,** and code **Z33.2, Encounter for elective termination of pregnancy.** This advice applies even when the patient was discharged previously with a discharge diagnosis of complete abortion. An additional code from category Z3A, Weeks of gestation, along with chapter 15 codes (O00–O9A), is used to identify the specific week of the pregnancy.

For sepsis related to abortion, additional codes may be assigned to identify the infectious organism, and a code from R65.2- to identify severe sepsis, if applicable. Examples follow.

- A patient is admitted with incomplete spontaneous abortion, and a D & C is performed to remove any retained products of conception. There is evidence of pelvic infection. The patient is discharged on the fourth hospital day with the infection cleared. The principal diagnosis is **O03.0, Genital tract and pelvic infection following incomplete spontaneous abortion.** Assign also the appropriate code from category Z3A.
- A patient is readmitted one week following discharge after a termination of pregnancy because she had developed endometritis. Code **O04.5, Genital tract and pelvic infection following (induced) termination of pregnancy,** is assigned as the principal diagnosis, with an additional code for the endometritis and the appropriate code from category Z3A.
- A patient is admitted in renal failure one week after discharge following a complete spontaneous abortion. Code **O03.82, Renal failure following complete or unspecified spontaneous abortion,** is assigned as the principal diagnosis with the appropriate code from category Z3A.
- A patient who underwent an elective abortion one week earlier is admitted because of continued bleeding. A D & C is performed, and the pathology report shows retained products of conception. Code **O04.6, Delayed or excessive hemorrhage following (induced) termination of pregnancy,** is assigned with the appropriate code from category Z3A.
- Five days following discharge for spontaneous abortion, a patient is admitted with a diagnosis of infection due to retained fetal tissue. The retention of fetal tissue indicates that the abortion was not complete, and so code **O03.0, Genital tract and pelvic infection following incomplete spontaneous abortion,** is assigned even though the patient was hospitalized for the abortion previously. Assign also the appropriate code from category Z3A.

EXERCISE 25.1

Code the following diagnoses. Consider the diagnostic statements given below as the only information available in the medical record. Do not assign procedure codes.

1. Failed attempted abortion complicated by hemorrhage	O07.1 Z3A.00
2. Incomplete early abortion (spontaneous)	O03.4 Z3A.00
3. Therapeutic abortion, complete, with electrolyte imbalance	O04.83 Z3A.00
4. Electively induced abortion, complete, with amniotic fluid embolism	O04.7 Z3A.00
5. Patient readmitted with bleeding due to retained placenta one week following previous hospital admission for spontaneous abortion	O03.1 Z3A.00
6. Discharge #1: Electively induced abortion, complete Discharge #2 (same patient): Sepsis following induced abortion during previous admission	Z33.2 O04.87 Z3A.00

MATERNAL CONDITION AS REASON FOR ABORTION

Codes from categories O20 through O29 and O30 through O77 can be assigned as an additional code to indicate a maternal condition that assisted in the decision to proceed with an elective abortion. Pregnancy can be terminated on a purely elective basis, however, and it is not necessary to assign a code to indicate a reason for the abortion. For example:

- A patient who is 12 completed weeks gestation is admitted for elective abortion, based on her physician's advice that her severe heart disease indicates that an abortion might be advisable to prevent cardiac complications. In this case, the principal diagnosis code is **Z33.2, Encounter for elective termination of pregnancy.** Codes **O99.411, Diseases of the circulatory system complicating pregnancy, first trimester,** and **Z3A.12, 12 weeks gestation of pregnancy,** are also assigned, along with an additional code to identify the particular heart disease.

- A patient who had rubella at six weeks gestation requests abortion because of the possibility of fetal abnormality. Code **Z33.2, Encounter for elective termination of pregnancy,** is designated as the principal diagnosis, with codes **O35.3xx0, Maternal care for (suspected) damage to fetus from viral disease in mother,** and **Z3A.01, Less than 8 weeks gestation of pregnancy,** as secondary diagnoses.
- A patient who is 26 weeks pregnant presents for elective termination of pregnancy due to fetal anomalies. Assign code **Z33.2, Encounter for elective termination of pregnancy,** as the principal diagnosis. Codes **O35.9xx0, Maternal care for (suspected) fetal abnormality and damage, unspecified,** and **Z3A.26, 26 weeks gestation of pregnancy,** are assigned as additional diagnoses.
- A first-trimester pregnant patient is admitted with placenta previa. She does not request abortion, but after evaluating various treatment possibilities, her physician concludes that an abortion is necessary. The patient consents, and the abortion is carried out. In this case, the code for placenta previa (O44.01) is sequenced first, followed by the abortion code and the weeks of gestation code.

INADVERTENT ABORTION

When an inadvertent abortion occurs because of surgery, as the result of trauma or other condition unrelated to the pregnancy, the obstetric codes (O00–O9A) are sequenced first. Codes from other chapters may be assigned along with the obstetric codes to further specify the condition. A code from category O03, Spontaneous abortion, is assigned to indicate that an abortion occurred. For example:

- A woman was admitted to the hospital at 12 weeks gestation with acute cholecystitis. The surgeon performed a laparoscopic cholecystectomy. During the stay the patient suffered an inadvertent spontaneous abortion.

Principal diagnosis:	O99.611	Diseases of the digestive system complicating pregnancy, first trimester
Additional diagnoses:	O03.9	Spontaneous abortion
	K81.0	Acute cholecystitis
	Z3A.12	12 weeks of gestation of pregnancy
Principal procedure:	0FT44ZZ	Resection of gallbladder, percutaneous endoscopic approach

- Appendectomy was performed because of acute appendicitis with peritonitis. On the second postoperative day, the patient experienced an inadvertent abortion (complete) at 12 weeks gestation.

Principal diagnosis:	O99.611	Diseases of the digestive system complicating pregnancy, first trimester
Additional diagnoses:	K35.2	Appendicitis with peritonitis
	O03.9	Spontaneous abortion
	Z3A.12	12 weeks of gestation of pregnancy
Principal procedure:	0DTJ0ZZ	Resection of appendix, open approach

EXERCISE 25.2

Code the following diagnoses and procedures.

1.	Therapeutic abortion, complete (10 weeks gestation), performed because of severe reactive psychosis Vaginal vacuum abortion	Z33.2 O99.341 F23 Z3A.10 10A07Z6
2.	Inadvertent abortion (complete) prompted by radiation treatment damage to fetus, necessitating termination of pregnancy (single fetus)	Z33.2 O35.6xx0 Y84.2 Z3A.00
3.	Elective abortion (complete) performed because of chromosomal abnormality of fetus (single fetus) Abortion using laminaria	Z33.2 O35.1xx0 Z3A.00 10A07ZW

ABORTION PROCEDURE RESULTING IN LIVEBORN INFANT

Occasionally, an attempt to terminate a pregnancy results in a liveborn infant. Note that a fetus that has any heartbeat, respiration, or involuntary muscle movement after expulsion is considered to be a live birth, no matter how short a time it survives. In this situation, code **Z33.2, Encounter for elective termination of pregnancy,** and a code from category Z37, Outcome of delivery, are assigned. A code for the procedure used in the attempt to terminate the pregnancy should also be assigned. For example:

- A patient delivers a liveborn infant with extreme immaturity following attempted abortion by insertion of laminaria. Code **Z33.2, Encounter for elective termination of pregnancy,** is assigned, along with code Z37.0 (for the single liveborn). Assign also the procedure code for the insertion of the laminaria.

LOSS OF FETUS WITH REMAINING FETUS

Occasionally, a patient with multiple gestation is admitted for what appears to be a spontaneous abortion during which one or more fetuses are expelled but one or more live fetuses remain in utero. In such cases, no code from category O00–O08 is assigned and a code from subcategories O31.1-, Continuing pregnancy after spontaneous abortion of one fetus or more, and O31.2-, Continuing pregnancy after intrauterine death of one fetus or more, is assigned instead.

MULTIPLE GESTATION FOLLOWING FETAL REDUCTION

Subcategory code O31.3 identifies continuing pregnancy after elective fetal reduction during the current pregnancy. These pregnancies are considered high risk, and there is a need to identify them, even if the pregnancy is reduced to a single fetus. For example, when the woman delivers the single newborn, these codes make it possible to document that this was originally a multiple gestation that underwent fetal reduction. Note that subcategory O31.3 refers to fetal reduction, whereas subcategories O31.1 and O31.2, described in the preceding section, are for spontaneous abortion or involuntary fetal loss.

The subcategories for multiple gestation following fetal reduction are as follows:

O31.30 Continuing pregnancy after elective fetal reduction of one fetus or more, unspecified trimester
O31.31 Continuing pregnancy after elective fetal reduction of one fetus or more, first trimester
O31.32 Continuing pregnancy after elective fetal reduction of one fetus or more, second trimester
O31.33 Continuing pregnancy after elective fetal reduction of one fetus or more, third trimester

Codes in category O31 require a seventh character. Seventh character "0" is for single gestations and multiple gestations where the fetus is unspecified. Seventh characters "1" through "9" are for cases of multiple gestations to identify the fetus for which the code applies. The appropriate code from category O30, Multiple gestation, must also be assigned when assigning a code from category O31 that has a seventh character of "1" through "9."

For example:

- A patient in her 24th week of pregnancy presents with monochorionic (monoamniotic) twin gestation complicated by inter-twin vascular communication. She undergoes elective reduction of the fetus because of inter-twin vascular communication. One fetus had developed polyhydramnios. Code **O31.32x1, Continuing pregnancy after elective fetal reduction of one fetus or more, second trimester, fetus 1,** is assigned as the principal diagnosis. Code **O35.8xx1, Maternal care for other (suspected) fetal abnormality and damage, fetus 1;** code **O40.2xx1, Polyhydramnios, second trimester, fetus 1;** code **O30.012, Twin pregnancy, monoamniotic/monochorionic, second trimester;** and code **Z3A.24, 24 weeks of gestation of pregnancy,** should all be assigned as additional diagnoses.
- A patient with an initial twin pregnancy had previously undergone fetal reduction of one fetus because of suspected chromosomal anomalies. The patient is now in her 38th week and is admitted and delivers a normal single liveborn infant. Code **O31.33x2, Continuing pregnancy after elective fetal reduction of one fetus or more, third trimester,** is assigned as the principal diagnosis. Code **Z37.0, Single live birth;** code **Z3A.38, 38 weeks of gestation of pregnancy;** and code **O30.003, Twin pregnancy, unspecified, third trimester,** should all be assigned as additional diagnoses.

PROCEDURES FOR TERMINATION OF PREGNANCY

ICD-10-PCS classifies procedures performed on the products of conception to the Obstetrics Section. Abortion procedures are coded to the Obstetrics Section, root operation "Abortion," which is defined as "artificially terminating a pregnancy," as shown in the excerpt from the ICD-10-PCS Tables in figure 25.1.

The root operation "Abortion" is subdivided according to whether an additional device, such as a laminaria (a medical product used to dilate the cervix and to induce labor in abortions) or an abortifacient (a substance that causes an abortion), is used, or whether the abortion was performed by mechanical means. If either a laminaria, an abortifacient, or a vacuum is used, then the approach is via natural or artificial opening. All other abortion procedures are those performed by mechanical means (the products of conception are physically removed with the aid of instrumentation), and the device value is Z, no device.

Coding examples follow.

10A07ZZ	Abortion induced by dilatation and curettage
10A07ZW	Transvaginal insertion of laminaria
10A07ZX	Abortion by insertion of prostaglandin suppository

Procedures performed following an abortion for curettage of the endometrium or evacuation of retained products of conception are all coded in the Obstetrics Section to the root operation "Extraction" and the body part "products of conception, retained." For example, dilatation and curettage for an incomplete spontaneous abortion is coded to **10D17ZZ, Extraction of products of conception, retained, via natural or artificial opening.**

FIGURE 25.1 Excerpt of ICD-10-PCS Table for Abortion Procedures

Section	**1**	Obstetrics
Body System	**0**	Pregnancy
Operation	**A**	Abortion: Artificially terminating a pregnancy

Body Part	Approach	Device	Qualifier
0 Products of Conception	**0** Open **2** Open Endoscopic **3** Percutaneous **4** Percutaneous Endoscopic **8** Via Natural or Artificial Opening Endoscopic	**Z** No Device	**Z** No Qualifier
0 Products of Conception	**7** Via Natural or Artificial Opening	**Z** No Device	**Z** Vacuum **W** Laminaria **X** Abortifacient **Z** No Qualifier

ECTOPIC AND MOLAR PREGNANCIES

Ectopic and molar pregnancies and other abnormal products of conception are classified to the following categories, with an additional code from category O08 when any complication occurs:

- O00 Ectopic pregnancy
- O01 Hydatidiform mole
- O02 Other abnormal product of conception

A molar pregnancy occurs when a blighted ovum within the uterus develops into a mole or benign tumor. A blighted ovum typically occurs within the first trimester when a fertilized egg attaches itself to the uterine wall but the embryo does not develop. Cells develop to form the pregnancy sac but not the embryo itself. A high level of chromosome abnormalities can cause a blighted ovum. The hydatidiform mole is a particular type of molar pregnancy and is classified separately (O01.-) in ICD-10-CM. All other molar pregnancies are included in code **O02.0, Blighted ovum and nonhydatidiform mole.**

Human chorionic gonadotropin (hCG) is a hormone produced in the body during pregnancy. An hCG blood test measures the level of hCG detectable in the blood. The test can be qualitative or quantitative. In early pregnancy, the hCG level should double approximately every two to three days. A decrease in the hCG doubling time may be an indication of a miscarriage or ectopic pregnancy. Although the hCG blood level and pregnancy tests will be positive, the gestational sac will not be visible on ultrasound. An ectopic pregnancy must be ruled out when the ultrasound does not demonstrate an intrauterine pregnancy; if it is ruled out, the miscarriage is confirmed. Assign code **O02.81, Inappropriate change in quantitative human chorionic gonadotropin (hCG) in early pregnancy.**

A biochemical pregnancy is the earliest form of miscarriage. The term "biochemical" refers to a situation in which the pregnancy is too early to confirm except through biochemical means. In a biochemical pregnancy, the fertilized egg will not implant properly in the uterus, resulting in an early miscarriage. Biochemical pregnancy is included under code O02.81.

Utilization of assisted technologies has resulted in an increase in multiple gestational pregnancies in which an intrauterine pregnancy may coexist with an ectopic pregnancy. An ectopic pregnancy (O00.-) occurs when a fertilized ovum is implanted and develops anywhere outside the uterus. The fourth character indicates the extrauterine location of the ectopic pregnancy. The codes are as follows:

- O00.0 Abdominal pregnancy
- O00.1 Tubal pregnancy
- O00.2 Ovarian pregnancy
- O00.8 Other ectopic pregnancy
- O00.9 Ectopic pregnancy, unspecified

Patients with a history of an ectopic or molar pregnancy have an increased risk of having another tubal pregnancy. Assign code O09.1- for an encounter involving supervision of an obstetrical patient with a previous history of ectopic or molar pregnancy.

Tubal Pregnancy

Tubal pregnancy is the most common type of ectopic pregnancy. Surgical procedures for removing a tubal ectopic pregnancy include salpingotomy and salpingostomy; in both procedures, the ectopic pregnancy is removed from the tube by means of an incision into the fallopian tube. It can also be removed by salpingectomy (excision of the fallopian tube) with the ectopic pregnancy intact. Removal of ectopic pregnancy is classified to the Obstetrics Section, body system "pregnancy," and body part "product of conception, ectopic." If the removal of the ectopic pregnancy is performed via salpingotomy, the root operation is "Extraction"; if the procedure is performed via salpingectomy, the root operation is "Resection."

Coding examples follow.

O00.1 Tubal pregnancy
10T24ZZ Laparoscopy with resection of ectopic tubal pregnancy

O00.1 Tubal pregnancy
10T20ZZ + 0UB50ZZ Laparotomy, salpingectomy with removal of right tubal pregnancy and excision of portion of right fallopian tube

O00.0 Abdominal pregnancy
10T20ZZ Removal of abdominal pregnancy (open approach)

O00.8 Cornual pregnancy
10T24ZZ Laparoscopic removal of cornual pregnancy

Complications of Molar and Ectopic Pregnancy

Unlike complications of abortions, complications of ectopic and molar pregnancies are classified in category O08, whether they occur during the initial episode of care or during a later episode. When the complication occurs during an episode of care for the purpose of treating the ectopic or molar pregnancy, a code from the O00 through O02 series is sequenced first, followed by a code from category O08. When the patient is readmitted for a complication following treatment of an ectopic or molar pregnancy, assign a code from category O08 as the principal diagnosis. An additional code that describes the complication more specifically can be assigned as needed. Sample codes include the following:

O00.1 + O08.0 Pelvic peritonitis following ectopic tubal pregnancy (this admission)

O08.1 Hemorrhage following ruptured ectopic tubal pregnancy removed on previous admission

MISSED ABORTION

The term "missed abortion" refers to fetal death that occurs prior to the completion of 20 weeks of gestation, with the dead fetus retained for a period of time in the uterus. This condition may be indicated by a cessation of growth, hardening of the uterus, or actual diminution in size of the uterus. Absence of fetal heart tones after they had been previously heard is also indicative of a missed abortion. The retained fetus may be expelled spontaneously, or surgical or chemical intervention may be required. For example:

- A patient in the 19th week of gestation reports that she is no longer feeling any fetal movement. The physician cannot hear any fetal heart tones, although they were present one month ago. On examination, the uterus is hard and possibly smaller than on the last visit. Codes **O02.1, Missed abortion,** and **Z3A.19, 19 weeks of gestation of pregnancy,** are assigned.

When the period of gestation is longer than 20 weeks, retention of a dead fetus is considered a missed intrauterine death (O36.4-). A missed abortion with blighted ovum, nonhydatidiform mole or hydatidiform mole, is not coded to O02.1, but to **O02.0, Blighted ovum and nonhydatidiform mole,** or a code from category O01, Hydatidiform mole, instead.

EXERCISE 25.3

Code the following diagnoses. Do not assign procedure codes.

1. Therapeutic abortion, complete, with embolism	O04.7 Z3A.00
2. Failed attempted induction of abortion	O07.4 Z3A.00
3. Ruptured right tubal pregnancy with peritonitis due to group A *Streptococcus*	O00.1 O08.0 B95.0 Z3A.00
4. Incomplete early abortion at 8 weeks gestation (spontaneous)	O03.4 Z3A.08
5. Eighteen-week spontaneous abortion, complete, with excessive hemorrhage	O03.6 Z3A.18

6. Electively induced abortion with liveborn, 21 weeks	O60.12x0 Z37.0 Z3A.21
7. Electively induced abortion, complete, complicated by shock	O04.81 Z3A.00
8. Ectopic pregnancy, right fallopian tube	O00.1 Z3A.00
9. Carneous mole	O02.0 Z3A.00
10. Hydatidiform mole	O01.9 Z3A.00
11. Missed abortion, 19 weeks gestation	O02.1 Z3A.19
12. Ten-week pregnancy with electively induced abortion, complete Family problems due to multiparity	Z33.2 Z64.1

CHAPTER 26 Congenital Anomalies

CHAPTER OVERVIEW

- Congenital anomalies are classified in chapter 17 of ICD-10-CM.
- Congenital and acquired conditions are often distinguished with a parenthetical note in the main term or subterm of a condition in the Alphabetic Index.
- In a few specific cases, separate codes are provided for the congenital and acquired versions of a condition.
- Congenital anomalies are classified first by the body system involved.
- Although congenital anomalies are present at birth, they may not be recognized until later in life.
- Patient age plays no role in assigning chapter 17 codes. They can be used at any age.
- In the case of newborns, congenital conditions that may have future implications are reported even though they may not be treated during the current episode of care.
- Conditions caused by mechanical factors during gestation are coded to categories Q65–Q79, Congenital malformations and deformations of the musculoskeletal system.
- Conditions due to birth injury are considered perinatal and are not part of the congenital classifications.

LEARNING OUTCOMES

After studying this chapter you should be able to:

Distinguish between congenital and acquired conditions in the Alphabetic Index.

Code for a congenital anomaly even if the classification does not provide a specific code for it.

Explain the relationship of patient age to codes for congenital anomalies.

Explain the difference between congenital and perinatal deformities.

TERM TO KNOW

Congenital anomaly
abnormal condition present at birth, which may not be recognized until later in life

REMEMBER . . .

There are about 4,000 congenital anomalies. Not all have been classified with a specific code.

INTRODUCTION

Congenital anomalies are classified in categories Q00 through Q99 in chapter 17 of ICD-10-CM. Congenital anomalies are abnormal conditions that are present at birth, although they may be recognized later. Codes from chapter 17 may be used throughout the life of the patient. If a congenital anomaly has been corrected, a personal history code should be used to identify the history of the anomaly. Codes in subcategory Z87.7 are used for congenital malformations that may still be present but do not require additional care, as well as corrected anomalies that are no longer present. Many congenital conditions can now be repaired because of medical advances, and patients are left with no residual condition.

LOCATION OF TERMS IN THE ALPHABETIC INDEX

A distinction between acquired and congenital conditions is often noted in the Alphabetic Index by a nonessential modifier associated with the main term or a subterm. When either term appears in parentheses with the main term, the alternative term can ordinarily be located as a subterm.

Note that some conditions are congenital by definition and have no acquired version; others are always considered to be acquired. For many conditions, of course, no distinction is made. When the diagnostic statement does not describe a condition as being either acquired or congenital, ICD-10-CM often makes a presumption that it is one or the other.

The following example from the Alphabetic Index demonstrates this usage:

Deformity . . .
-breast (acquired) N64.89
--congenital Q83.9
--reconstructed N65.0
-bronchus (congenital) Q32.4
--acquired NEC J98.09

In this example, the Alphabetic Index assumes that deformity of the breast without other qualification is classified as acquired, whereas deformity of the bronchus is classified as congenital if not otherwise specified. The Tabular List may offer additional guidance by means of an exclusion note. For example, the entry under category K57, Diverticular disease of intestine, refers the coder elsewhere for congenital diverticulum of intestine, coded **Q43.8, Other specified congenital malformations of intestine.** For code Q43.8, the inclusion note indicates that congenital diverticulum of the colon is appropriately classified here.

ICD-10-CM provides separate codes for congenital hydrocephalus (Q03.-), spina bifida with hydrocephalus (Q05.-), acquired secondary normal pressure hydrocephalus (G91.0), obstructive hydrocephalus (G91.1), and acquired idiopathic normal pressure hydrocephalus (G91.2).

Congenital hydrocephalus is defined as an excessive accumulation of cerebrospinal fluid (CSF) in the brain, which is present at birth. The excessive fluid leads to increased intracranial pressure and possibly brain damage. A code from category Q03, Congenital hydrocephalus, is assigned for this birth defect. ICD-10-CM provides fourth characters to further specify malformation of aqueduct of Sylvius (Q03.0), atresia of foramina of Magendie and Luschka (Q03.1), and other congenital hydrocephalus (Q03.8); when this information is not available, the condition is coded to **Q03.9, Congenital hydrocephalus, unspecified.** If the medical record documentation does not specify whether the hydrocephalus is congenital or acquired, the classification defaults to acquired, code **G91.9, Hydrocephalus, unspecified.**

Spina bifida is a congenital anomaly involving incomplete closure of the embryonic neural tube, resulting in a spinal cord defect. Many individuals with spina bifida have an associated abnormality of the cerebellum, referred to as Chiari II malformation. In affected individuals the back portion of the brain is displaced from the skull into the upper neck. Hydrocephalus develops in approximately 90 percent of individuals with myelomeningocele/spina bifida, because the displaced cerebellum obstructs the flow of CSF. For spina bifida without hydrocephalus, assign a code from Q05.5 through Q05.8, depending on the portion of the spine affected. If spina bifida is present with hydrocephalus, assign a code from Q05.0 through Q05.4 for this type of congenital anomaly, depending on the portion of the spine affected, as follows:

Q05.0 Cervical spina bifida with hydrocephalus
Q05.1 Thoracic spina bifida with hydrocephalus
Q05.2 Lumbar spina bifida with hydrocephalus
Q05.3 Sacral spina bifida with hydrocephalus
Q05.4 Unspecified spina bifida with hydrocephalus

For a diagnostic statement of spina bifida without further specification, assign code **Q05.9, Spina bifida, unspecified.** Use an additional code for any paraplegia or paraparesis (G82.2-) associated with spina bifida.

Congenital anomalies are classified first by the body system involved. Many congenital anomalies have specific codes in ICD-10-CM; others are located under such general terms as "anomaly" and "deformity" rather than under the name of the specific condition. For example:

Q45.8 Congenital malposition of gastrointestinal tract
Q22.5 Ebstein's anomaly
Q40.1 Congenital hiatus hernia
Q82.5 Strawberry nevus
Q03.9 Congenital hydrocephalus

Because approximately 4,000 congenital anomalies have been identified, it is impossible for the classification to provide a specific code for each. When the type of anomaly is specified, but no specific code is provided, the code for other specified anomaly of that type and site should be assigned. Often, only the code for unspecified anomaly of that general type or site can be assigned. When a specific code is not available, additional codes for manifestations of the anomaly should be assigned to the extent possible. Use additional secondary codes from other chapters to specify conditions associated with the anomaly. For example:

- An eight-day-old infant is diagnosed with Finnish-type congenital nephrosis. Finnish-type congenital nephrosis is a minimal change, type I nephrotic disease of childhood, occurring during the first week of life. This condition is caused by mutations in the gene for nephrin on chromosome 19. Proteinuria, hypoalbuminemia, hypogammaglobulinemia, and hyperlipidemia are common lab findings. Codes **Q63.8, Other specified congenital malformations of kidney,** and **N04.0, Nephrotic syndrome, with minor glomerular abnormality,** are assigned for Finnish-type congenital nephrosis.
- A ten-month-old infant is diagnosed with cardiofaciocutaneous (CFC) syndrome. Assign code **Q87.89, Other specified congenital malformation syndromes, not elsewhere classified,** for CFC syndrome. Additional codes may be assigned for any manifestations of the condition as instructed by the guideline on congenital anomalies. CFC syndrome is a genetic condition associated with mutation in four known genes: BRAF, MEK1, MEK2, and KRAS.

RELATIONSHIP OF AGE TO CODES

Codes from chapter 17 can be reported for a patient of any age. Many congenital anomalies, although actually present at birth, do not manifest themselves until later in life. In addition, many cannot be corrected and persist throughout life, and these conditions may be reported for an adult patient. Patient age is not the determining factor in assigning these codes. Following are examples:

- A patient, 30 years of age, with Marfan syndrome was admitted for a heart valve replacement and repair of an abdominal aortic aneurysm. In this case, the code for **Marfan syndrome, Q87.40,** is assigned in spite of the patient's age because the condition is an inherited disorder of the connective tissue that is transmitted as an autosomal dominant trait.
- A patient, age 25, was admitted for brain surgery, which revealed a colloid cyst of the right third ventricle. In this case, code **Q04.6, Congenital cerebral cysts,** is assigned because a colloid cyst of the third ventricle is always congenital and the patient's age does not influence code assignment.

NEWBORN WITH CONGENITAL CONDITIONS

When a diagnosis of a congenital condition is made during the hospital episode in which an infant is born, the appropriate code from chapter 17 of ICD-10-CM should be assigned as an additional code, with the appropriate code from category Z38, Liveborn infants, according to place of birth and type of delivery, used as the principal diagnosis. (See chapter 27 of this handbook.) Examples follow:

Z38.00 + Q36.9	Term birth, single male, vaginal delivery; incomplete cleft lip on right side
Z38.00 + Q54.9	Term birth, single male, vaginal delivery; hypospadias

Note that this is an exception to the guidelines for reporting other conditions. Congenital conditions that may have future health care implications are reported for newborns even though they are not further evaluated or treated during the current episode of care. Therefore, it is appropriate to assign congenital anomalies codes (Q00–Q99) whenever a congenital condition is diagnosed by the physician.

CONGENITAL DEFORMITIES VERSUS PERINATAL DEFORMITIES

Certain musculoskeletal deformities that result from a mechanical factor during gestation, such as intrauterine malposition or pressure, are classified in categories Q65–Q79, Congenital malformations and deformations of the musculoskeletal system. Conditions due to birth injury are classified as perinatal conditions in categories P10–P15, Birth trauma, in chapter 16 of ICD-10-CM, with an additional code assigned to identify the specific condition whenever possible. Examples include the following:

Q65.1	Bilateral congenital dislocation of hip
Q68.2	Congenital dislocation of knee
P13.4	Fracture of clavicle due to birth trauma

PULMONARY ARTERY ANOMALIES

Pulmonary artery atresia (Q25.5) is the incomplete formation of the pulmonary valve (located between the right ventricle and the pulmonary artery), which obstructs the flow of blood through the leaflets and into the lungs. In a newborn, the deoxygenated blood can flow through the patent ductus arteriosus into the pulmonary artery and get to the lungs. However, when the ductus arteriosus closes shortly after birth, the baby will increasingly become cyanotic and will have difficulty breathing because of the defective pulmonary valve.

Pulmonary artery coarctation (Q25.71) refers to narrowing or stenosis of the pulmonary artery. Narrowing of the main pulmonary artery or its branches makes it difficult for blood that is deficient in oxygen to pass from the right ventricle to the lungs to get the oxygen necessary for the body. The heart becomes overworked when it has to pump harder to get the blood into the lungs. A moderate or severe degree of pulmonary artery stenosis can lead to pulmonary hypertension at rest or during exercise. Pulmonary artery stenosis is usually associated with congenital cardiovascular anomalies such as pulmonary valve stenosis and tetralogy of Fallot.

A pulmonary arteriovenous malformation (AVM), referred to as pulmonary arteriovenous aneurysm or pulmonary arteriovenous fistula (Q25.72), is an abnormal communication between the pulmonary artery and the pulmonary vein. The abnormally direct connection between high-pressure arteries and low-pressure veins may be detected via stethoscope as a rhythmic whooshing sound caused by excessively rapid blood flow through the arteries and veins. While pulmonary AVMs are most commonly congenital, they may be acquired through conditions such as hepatic cirrhosis, mitral stenosis, trauma, and metastatic thyroid carcinoma.

NEUROFIBROMATOSIS

Neurofibromatosis (subcategory Q85.0) refers to a group of autosomal dominant genetic disorders that cause tumors to grow along the nerves. Schwannomas (Q85.03) may occur along any nerve of the body, including spinal, cranial, and peripheral nerves, except on the vestibular nerve. As the tumors grow they compress nerves and cause pain, numbness, tingling, weakness, and other neurological symptoms.

CYSTIC KIDNEY DISEASE

There are major differences in the clinical characteristics, pathophysiology, and prognosis of the various types of congenital cystic kidney disease. This fact augments the importance of being as specific as possible about the type when assigning a code. For example, symptoms and problems for polycystic kidney disease, infantile type (Q61.19), progress slowly as more and more cysts develop over the years; this disease is relatively common. Medullary cystic kidney (Q61.5) is a hereditary disorder in which cysts in the center of each kidney cause the kidneys to gradually lose their ability to work; late in the disease, symptoms of chronic kidney disease may develop. When the diagnostic statement does not indicate whether a renal cyst is congenital or acquired, ICD-10-CM presumes that the cyst is acquired.

CONGENITAL MALFORMATIONS OF GENITAL ORGANS

The development of the female reproductive tract is a complex process that involves a highly orchestrated series of events, including cellular differentiation, migration, fusion, and canalization. Failure of any part of the process results in congenital anomalies. Mullerian anomalies refer to all congenital anomalies of the uterus, cervix, and vagina. ICD-10-CM provides unique codes for the spectrum of congenital uterine, cervical, and vaginal anomalies in categories Q50 through Q52:

Q50 Congenital malformations of ovaries, fallopian tubes and broad ligaments
Q51 Congenital malformations of uterus and cervix
Q52 Other congenital malformations of female genitalia

Congenital malformations of male genital organs are classified to categories Q53 through Q55. These categories include conditions such as undescended and ectopic testes, hypospadias, and other congenital malformations of male genital organs.

Cryptorchidism refers to incomplete testicular descent; the condition may be unilateral or bilateral. The term encompasses palpable, nonpalpable, and ectopic testicles. The position of the testis can be abdominal, inguinal, prescrotal, or gliding. ICD-10-CM classifies undescended and ectopic testicle to category Q53. Code Q53.0- describes ectopic testis, and code 053.2- describes undescended testis. In addition, category Q53 specifies whether the undescended testicle is unilateral (Q53.1-) or bilateral (Q53.2-), with the fifth character indicating the location of the undescended testicle (abdominal, ectopic perineal, or unspecified).

Hypospadias is a somewhat common congenital anomaly whereby the opening of the urethra is on the underside, rather than at the end, of the penis. ICD-10-CM classifies hypospadias to category Q54, Hypospadias, with additional fourth characters to specify balanic (Q54.0), penile (Q54.1), penoscrotal (Q54.2), perineal (Q54.3), congenital chordee (ventral curvature of the penis, caused by presence of a fibrous band of tissue instead of normal skin along the corpus spongiosum) (Q54.4), other (Q54.8), or unspecified (Q54.9). Procedures to repair hypospadias are classified to the root operation "Reposition," body part "urethra."

In addition to the above female and male genital malformations, ICD-10-CM provides category Q56, Indeterminate sex and pseudohermaphroditism, which distinguishes among hermaphroditism, not elsewhere classified (Q56.0); male pseudohermaphroditism (Q56.1); female pseudohermaphroditism (Q56.2); pseudohermaphroditism, unspecified (Q56.3); and indeterminate sex, unspecified (Q56.4).

OMPHALOCELE AND GASTROSCHISIS

An omphalocele is a distinct ventral wall defect. The intestines are usually covered by a membranous sac, with the intestine being exposed only if the sac ruptures. An omphalocele is commonly associated with other structural and chromosomal anomalies. Code **Q79.2, Exomphalos,** is assigned for a congenital omphalocele.

Gastroschisis is an anomaly involving a defect of the ventral body wall to the right of the umbilical cord insertion. This anomaly is caused by failure of the developing abdominal wall to completely close, allowing the intestines to protrude from the defect. The exposed intestines are not covered by a membranous sac. Assign code **Q79.3, Gastroschisis,** for congenital gastroschisis.

EXERCISE 26.1

Code the following diagnoses and procedures. Do not assign External cause of morbidity codes.

1. Polycystic kidneys, adult type		Q61.2
2. Hypospadias with congenital chordee Repair of hypospadias and release of chordee (open approach)	Reposition	Q54.4 0TSD0ZZ 0VNS0ZZ
3. Congenital pyloric stenosis Endoscopic dilation of the pylorus		Q40.0 0D778ZZ
4. Congenital dislocation of both hips Closed reduction of dislocation of both hips with immobilization in plaster casts	Reposition	Q65.1 0SS9XZZ 0SSBXZZ
5. Congestive heart failure in patient with congenital interatrial septal defect		I50.9 Q21.1
6. Posterior subcapsular cataract, left eye, congenital		Q12.0
7. Accessory fifth digit, right foot		Q69.2
8. Esophageal web with esophageal spasm and reflux esophagitis		Q39.4 K22.4 K21.0
9. Left trigger thumb, congenital Open tenolysis of flexor sheath of left thumb	Release	Q74.0 0LN80ZZ
10. Urachal cyst and patent urachus		Q64.4

11.	Thoracoabdominal coarctation of aorta	Q25.1
12.	Hallux rigidus, left	M20.22
13.	Down syndrome	Q90.9
14.	Bilateral talipes equinovarus, congenital	Q66.0
15.	Unilateral cleft lip and cleft palate, soft and hard Correction of cleft hard and soft palate via incisions on both sides of the cleft, and repositioning of the tissue and muscles Repair of cleft upper lip	Q37.5 0CS20ZZ 0CS30ZZ 0CQ00ZZ
16.	Cystic lung, congenital	Q33.0
17.	Congenital nevus flammeus	Q82.5
18.	Large congenital atrial septal defect (ASD) and patent foramen ovale (PFO) Repair of ASD/PFO with insertion of synthetic prosthesis across atrial septum via cardiac catheter to reinforce atrial septum Supplement	Q21.1 02U53JZ

CHAPTER 27 Perinatal Conditions

CHAPTER OVERVIEW

- Perinatal conditions other than congenital anomalies are classified in chapter 16 of ICD-10-CM.
- These conditions can be found under the main term Birth or as a subterm under the condition's main term.
- Perinatal conditions are sequenced as the principal diagnosis but behind the appropriate Z38 code for the birth episode.
- Codes for perinatal conditions can be used throughout the patient's life. There is no prohibition due to age.
- Conditions are coded if they meet the definition of reportable conditions or if they have an implication for the newborn's future care.
- Newborn immaturity and prematurity are classified by birth weight. Codes for these conditions are never assigned without a physician's clinical evaluation as indicated in the diagnostic statement.
- Newborn postmaturity is classified by length of gestation.
- The perinatal conditions in chapter 16 cover fetal distress, metabolic abnormalities, difficulties due to aspiration, and more.
- A code is assigned from P00 through P04 when a healthy infant is evaluated for a suspected condition that is not found.
- Infections specific to the perinatal period are considered congenital.
- Infections that occur after birth but within the perinatal period may or may not be classified in chapter 16.
- Z codes are used for routine newborn vaccination and health supervision.

LEARNING OUTCOMES

After studying this chapter you should be able to:

- Locate codes and follow general guidelines with regard to perinatal conditions.
- Use Z codes to classify the birth, and use them with other codes for perinatal conditions.
- Code situations involving newborn immaturity, prematurity, and postmaturity.
- Code for evaluation and observation of newborns and infants.
- Determine what chapter to use to classify a newborn or infant infection.
- Know how and when to assign codes for maternal condition on the newborn record.

TERMS TO KNOW

Newborn immaturity
implies a birth of less than 37 completed weeks gestation

Newborn postmaturity
a gestational period of more than 42 weeks

Newborn low birth weight
implies a birth weight of 1,000–2,499 grams

Newborn extremely low birth weight
implies a birth weight of less than 500–999 grams

REMEMBER . . .

Codes from chapter 16 are never found on a maternal record, and codes from chapter 15 are never found on a newborn's record.

INTRODUCTION

Conditions other than anomalies that originate in the perinatal period are classified in chapter 16 of ICD-10-CM and categories P00 through P96. The perinatal period is defined as before birth through the first 28 days after birth. The perinatal period ends on the 29th day of life because the World Health Organization considers the day of birth as "day zero" for international comparisons.

LOCATING CODES FOR PERINATAL CONDITIONS IN THE ALPHABETIC INDEX

Codes for perinatal conditions are located in the Alphabetic Index by referring to the main term **Birth** or to the main term for the condition and then to such subterms as "newborn," "neonatal," "fetal," "infants," and "infantile." If the Alphabetic Index does not provide a specific code for a perinatal condition, assign code **P96.89, Other specified conditions originating in the perinatal period,** followed by the code from another chapter that specifies the condition.

GENERAL PERINATAL GUIDELINES

Codes from chapter 16 are never used on maternal records. By the same token, codes from chapter 15, Pregnancy, Childbirth and the Puerperium, should never be reported on the newborn record.

Generally, chapter 16 codes are sequenced as the principal or first-listed diagnosis on the newborn record, except for the appropriate code from the Z38 series for the birth episode. Codes from other chapters may be assigned as secondary diagnoses to provide additional detail.

The perinatal guidelines for secondary diagnoses are the same as the general coding guidelines for "additional diagnoses" (refer to chapter 4 of this handbook). In addition, assign codes for any conditions that have been specified by the provider as having implications for future health care needs. Assign codes from chapter 16 only for definitive diagnoses established by the provider. If a definitive diagnosis has not been established, codes for signs and symptoms may be assigned.

Sometimes a newborn may have a condition that may be either due to the birth process or community acquired. If the documentation does not specify which it is, the default code selected should be due to the birth process, and a chapter 16 code should be selected. When the condition is community acquired, do not report a chapter 16 code.

RELATIONSHIP OF AGE TO CODES

Most conditions originating during the perinatal period are transitory in nature. Other conditions that originate during the perinatal period, however, persist, and some do not manifest themselves until later in life. Such conditions are classified in chapter 16, no matter how old the patient is, and may be reported throughout the life of the patient if the condition is still present. For example:

- A 53-year-old woman is admitted for treatment of vaginal carcinoma due to intrauterine exposure to DES (diethylstilbestrol) taken by her mother during pregnancy. Code **C52, Malignant neoplasm of vagina,** and code **P04.8 Newborn (suspected to be) affected by other maternal noxious substances,** are assigned because the intrauterine exposure was still an important element in the patient's condition, even though the problem did not present itself until later in the patient's life.
- An 18-year-old man was admitted for workup because he had begun experiencing respiratory problems. A diagnosis of bronchopulmonary dysplasia was made, and the patient was discharged to be seen in the physician's office in two weeks. Code **P27.1, Bronchopulmonary dysplasia originating in the perinatal period,** is assigned because bronchopulmonary dysplasia is a congenital condition even though it may not become a problem until later in the patient's life.

CLASSIFICATION OF BIRTHS

A code from category Z38 is assigned as the principal diagnosis for any newborn. The first axis for coding is whether the birth is single, twin, or multiple. The codes further specify whether the birth occurred in the hospital, outside the hospital, or unspecified as to place of birth. If the birth occurred in the hospital, additional characters indicate the type of delivery (vaginal or cesarean). The medical record will provide sufficient information regarding the type of delivery to permit selection of the code.

A code from this series is assigned only on the newborn record and is assigned only for the episode in which the birth occurred. If a newborn is discharged and readmitted or transferred to another facility, the code for the condition responsible for the transfer or readmission is designated as the principal diagnosis. For example:

- A single liveborn vaginally delivered in the hospital with an associated diagnosis of subdural hemorrhage due to birth trauma is coded as **Z38.00, Single liveborn infant, delivered vaginally,** and **P10.0, Subdural hemorrhage due to birth injury,** with the Z code sequenced first.
- If the infant is discharged and readmitted or transferred to another facility for treatment of the hemorrhage, the principal diagnosis for that admission is P10.0; no code from category Z38 is assigned.
- If the admission of an infant born outside the hospital is delayed and the newborn is admitted later because of a complication, the complication code is assigned as the principal diagnosis; no code from category Z38 is assigned.

OTHER DIAGNOSES FOR NEWBORNS

A code from category Z38 indicates only that a birth occurred. Additional codes are assigned for all clinically significant conditions noted on the examination of the newborn. A newborn condition is clinically significant when it has implications for the newborn's future health care. This is an exception to the Uniform Hospital Discharge Data Set guidelines.

Insignificant or transient conditions that resolve without treatment are not coded. Medical records of newborns sometimes mention conditions such as fine rashes, molding of the scalp, and minor jaundice. Because these conditions usually resolve without treatment and require no additional workup, they are not coded. For example:

- The physician documents diagnoses of syndactyly and hydrocele on the newborn's diagnostic statement. Even though no treatment is given and no further evaluation is performed during the infant's hospital stay, both of these conditions will require treatment at some time in the future, and so they are reported.
- The physician mentions on the newborn delivery record that the infant has slight jaundice. No further evaluation is performed, and the jaundice clears by the following day. No code for jaundice is assigned.
- The pediatrician documents in the newborn medical record that the baby's heart murmur is benign and most likely due to a patent ductus arteriosus/patent foramen ovale (PDA/PFO). He orders a cardiac consult and an echocardiogram to evaluate the PDA/PFO. Assign code **Q21.1, Atrial septal defect,** for the PFO and code **Q25.0, Patent ductus arteriosus,** for the PDA. These conditions are being evaluated further (e.g., cardiac consultation and echocardiogram); therefore, they can be reported.

PREMATURITY, LOW BIRTH WEIGHT, AND POSTMATURITY

Newborns delivered before full term are defined as either immature or premature by both birth weight and gestational age and are classified in category P07 as follows:

- Extreme low birth weight (P07.0-) implies a birth weight of less than 1,000 grams.
- Low birth weight (P07.1-) implies a birth weight of 1,000–2,499 grams.
- Extreme immaturity (P07.2-) implies less than 28 completed weeks gestation (less than 196 completed days of gestation).
- Preterm (P07.3-) implies 28 completed weeks or more, but less than 37 completed weeks (196 completed days, but less than 259 completed days) of gestation.

When both birth weight and gestational age of the newborn are available, both should be coded, with birth weight sequenced before gestational age. A code from P05 and codes from P07.2- and P07.3- may be used to specify weeks of gestation as documented by the provider in the record. Providers use different criteria in determining prematurity. A code for prematurity should not be assigned unless it is documented.

Even when a newborn is not premature, it may be appropriate to assign a code from category P05, Disorders of newborn related to slow fetal growth and fetal malnutrition. The assigned code does not imply prematurity but indicates that the newborn is smaller than expected for the length of gestation. Occasionally, the obstetrician will document the gestational age in the mother's record, and the pediatrician will document a different gestational age in the infant's chart. For the newborn, the coder assigns the appropriate codes for gestational age based on the attending provider's (e.g., pediatrician's) documentation. Different providers (e.g., obstetrician and pediatrician) may use different criteria in determining weeks of gestation for the mother versus the gestational age of the infant.

To indicate the birth weight, fifth characters are assigned to codes for low birth weight newborns (P07.0- to P07.1-), newborn light for gestational age (P05.0-), and newborn small for gestational age (P05.1-). Note that the weight expressed by the fifth character should be reasonably consistent with the four-character code to which it is applied. For example, a diagnosis of low birth weight newborn would appear to be inconsistent with a fifth character "8" because a birth weight of 2,500 grams falls far outside the criteria for low birth weight even though there is no indication in the manual that the heavier weight is excluded. The physician should be queried when there is a significant discrepancy.

Assignment of codes in categories P05, Disorders of newborn related to slow fetal growth and fetal malnutrition, and P07, Disorders of newborn related to short gestation and low birth weight, not elsewhere classified, should be based on the recorded birth weight and estimated gestational age. For example, an infant born at hospital A at 34 weeks gestation and transferred to hospital B after 14 days for further evaluation of a congenital anomaly could still have a code for prematurity assigned as an additional diagnosis. The fifth character for these codes is always based on birth weight, not the infant's weight at the time of transfer or readmission.

For example, a 12-month-old child who was born preterm is being seen for acute bronchiolitis due to respiratory syncytial virus (RSV). The physician lists "acute bronchiolitis due to RSV, ex-26 week preemie" in the diagnostic statement. Code **J21.0, Acute bronchiolitis due to respiratory syncytial virus,** is assigned as the first-listed diagnosis. Code **P07.25, Extreme immaturity of newborn, gestational age 26 completed weeks,** is assigned to indicate that the child was born at 26 weeks.

As noted earlier, chapter 16 codes may be used regardless of the patient's age if the condition originated in the perinatal period and continued through the life of the patient. Moreover, codes from category P07, Disorders of newborn related to short gestation and low birth weight, not elsewhere classified, may be assigned for a child or an adult if the provider indicates the patient's prematurity and gestational age are contributing conditions affecting the patient's current health status.

Post-term is defined as a gestational period over 40 completed weeks to 42 completed weeks. Prolonged gestation or postmaturity is defined as a gestational period of more than 42 completed weeks. Category P08 classifies a long gestation and/or high birth weight as follows:

P08.0	Exceptionally large newborn baby (usually implies weight of 4,500 grams or more)
P08.1	Other heavy for gestational age newborn (heavy- or large-for-dates newborns, regardless of period of gestation)
P08.21	Post-term newborn
P08.22	Prolonged gestation of newborn

Codes **P08.21, Post-term newborn,** and **P08.22, Prolonged gestation of newborn,** may be assigned based only on the gestational age of the newborn. A specific condition or disorder does not have to be associated with the longer gestational period for these codes to be assigned.

FETAL DISTRESS AND ASPHYXIA

Fetal distress may be defined as signs that indicate a critical response to stress. It implies metabolic abnormalities such as hypoxia and acidosis that affect the functions of vital organs to the point of temporary or permanent injury or even death. ICD-10-CM provides different codes for fetal distress, depending on the specific condition, as follows:

P84	Other problems with newborn Includes the following conditions in newborns without further specification: acidemia, acidosis, anoxia, asphyxia, hypercapnia, hypoxemia, hypoxia, and mixed metabolic and respiratory acidosis
P19.0	Metabolic acidemia in newborn first noted before onset of labor
P19.1	Metabolic acidemia in newborn first noted during labor
P19.2	Metabolic acidemia noted at birth
P19.9	Metabolic acidemia, unspecified

Asphyxia refers to a decreased level of oxygen delivered to the body or an organ with a buildup of carbon dioxide. Birth asphyxia occurs when an infant does not receive enough oxygen before, during, or just after birth, and it can cause decreased heart rate, decreased blood flow, and low blood pressure leading to cellular and organ damage. When the duration of the asphyxia is brief, the infant can recover without any long-lasting injury. If the time period is longer, it may lead to reversible damage, and when prolonged, irreversible injury. Birth asphyxia is classified to code P84.

Hypoxic-ischemic encephalopathy (HIE) is a life-threatening condition that usually results from damage to the cells of the brain and spinal cord secondary to inadequate oxygen during the birth process. HIE is evidence of acute or subacute brain injury due to asphyxia. It is the most common cause of neurologic disease during the neonatal period and is associated with significant mortality and morbidity. Infants with the mild form of HIE are hyper-alert and overreact to the slightest stimulus. This stage usually lasts 24 hours or less. Infants can recover with normal neurologic function. Moderate HIE is associated with lethargy, clinical seizures, suppressed tendon reflexes, bradycardia, and periodic breathing. This stage may last from two to 14 days. A good neurologic prognosis is seen in infants who can recover within five days. Severe HIE is characterized by stupor to coma, primitive to no reflexes, variable heart rate, and apnea. Half of infants with severe HIE die. Eighty percent of those who survive have mental retardation, epilepsy, cerebral palsy, and learning disabilities. Only 10 percent survive with no neurological disability. The codes for HIE distinguish among mild (P91.61), moderate (P91.62), severe (P91.63), and unspecified (P91.60).

Codes for fetal distress or abnormality of heart rate and rhythm are assigned to the newborn record only when the condition is specifically identified by the physician. These codes are never assigned on the basis of other information in the newborn record.

Category P28, Other respiratory conditions originating in the perinatal period, classifies respiratory problems, including atelectasis (P28.0–P28.1-), cyanotic attacks (P28.2), apnea (P28.3–P28.4), respiratory failure (P28.5), respiratory arrest (P28.81), other (P28.89), and unspecified respiratory condition (P28.9), noted after birth.

FETAL AND NEWBORN ASPIRATION

Category P24, Neonatal aspiration, describes meconium aspiration and other types of fetal aspiration in the following subcategories/codes:

P24.0-	Meconium aspiration
P24.1-	Neonatal aspiration of (clear) amniotic fluid and mucus
P24.2-	Neonatal aspiration of blood
P24.3-	Neonatal aspiration of milk and regurgitated food
P24.8-	Other neonatal aspiration
P24.9	Neonatal aspiration, unspecified

Subcategories P24.0- through P24.8- provide an additional fifth character to identify the presence or absence of respiratory symptoms. If applicable, an additional code, I27.2, should be assigned to identify any secondary pulmonary hypertension.

Meconium aspiration in newborns occurs when the fetus gasps while still in the birth canal and inhales meconium-stained amniotic, vaginal, or oropharyngeal fluids. Massive aspiration syndrome is synonymous with massive fetal aspiration. Although meconium aspiration syndrome and massive meconium aspiration are somewhat different conditions with similar clinical presentation and course, code **P24.01, Meconium aspiration with respiratory symptoms,** is assigned for both. Code P96.83 is assigned for meconium staining.

Meconium ileus and meconium plug syndrome (a transient disorder of the newborn's colon with delayed passage of meconium and intestinal dilatation) are coded to **P76.0, Meconium plug syndrome,** except when specified as meconium ileus in cystic fibrosis, which is coded to E84.11 instead. Code P03.82 is assigned for meconium passage (without aspiration) during delivery.

Tachypnea, wheezing, and apnea are sometimes present in meconium aspiration; these conditions may resolve over a short period or may take a more prolonged course. In the milder forms of this condition, dyspnea occurs soon after birth, lasts two or three days, and is followed by rapid recovery. Therapy includes bronchoscopic suction of meconium, oxygen administration, humidity control, and prophylactic antibiotics.

HEMOLYTIC DISEASE OF THE NEWBORN

Infants born to Rh-negative mothers often develop hemolytic disease owing to fetal-maternal blood group incompatibility. These conditions are classified in category P55, Hemolytic disease of newborn. Note that an indication of incompatibility on a routine cord blood test is not conclusive. Do not assign a code from category P55 on the basis of this finding alone; a diagnosis of isoimmunization or hemolytic disease requires provider confirmation.

NECROTIZING ENTEROCOLITIS

Necrotizing enterocolitis (NEC) is a severe gastrointestinal condition that involves injury to the bowel, intestinal mucosal disruption associated with enteric feedings, infectious pathogens, and immature immune response. It is a major cause of morbidity and mortality in premature infants. Although NEC commonly affects premature infants with a birth weight of less than 1,500 grams, it can also occur in infants with low risk factors. The exact etiology of NEC is unknown; however, it is thought that the intestine of the premature infant is weakened by too little oxygen and blood flow. The infant then has an increased risk of developing NEC because of difficulty with blood and oxygen circulation, digestion, and fighting infection. When feedings are started and the food moves into the weakened area of the intestinal tract, bacteria from the food can damage the intestinal tissues. These tissues can develop necrosis and perforation, leading to acute abdominal infection. ICD-10-CM classifies necrotizing enterocolitis according to the following stages:

P77.1 Stage 1 necrotizing enterocolitis in newborn
P77.2 Stage 2 necrotizing enterocolitis in newborn
P77.3 Stage 3 necrotizing enterocolitis in newborn
P77.9 Necrotizing enterocolitis in newborn, unspecified

NEONATAL CEREBRAL LEUKOMALACIA

Periventricular leukomalacia, also known as neonatal cerebral leukomalacia (P91.2), occurs with increasing frequency in infants with very low birth weight. It refers to necrosis of white matter adjacent to lateral ventricles with formation of cyst and is a major risk factor for cerebral palsy and other neurological disorders. Although the cause of this condition is still obscure, recent studies have associated it with intrauterine growth retardation, intrauterine infections, and pregnancies involving monozygotic twins. The condition is frequently associated with severe intraventricular hemorrhage, but it is not necessarily the cause of the problem. An additional code is reported when intraventricular hemorrhage (P52.0, P52.1, P52.21, P52.22, P52.3) is associated with periventricular leukomalacia.

DISORDERS OF STOMACH FUNCTION AND FEEDING PROBLEMS

ICD-10-CM separately classifies vomiting, bilious emesis, failure to thrive, and other feeding problems in newborns. Persistent vomiting in a newborn may be a sign of a very serious condition. These codes are used for newborns experiencing feeding problems (P92.9), bilious vomiting (P92.01), other vomiting (P92.09), regurgitation and rumination (P92.1), slow feeding (P92.2), underfeeding (P92.3), overfeeding (P92.4), neonatal difficulty in feeding at breast (P92.5), failure to thrive (P92.6), and other feeding problems (P92.8) and are only assigned up to the 28th day of life. Codes in the main classification are used for infants and children older than 28 days. For example, a 10-day-old baby presents for weight recheck and feeding problems. Code **Z00.111, Health examination for newborn 8 to 28 days old,** is assigned, along with code **P92.9, Feeding problems of newborn, unspecified.**

OBSERVATION AND EVALUATION OF NEWBORNS AND INFANTS

A code from categories P00–P04, Newborn affected by maternal factors and by complications of pregnancy, labor, and delivery, is assigned when a healthy newborn is evaluated for a suspected condition that is found not to be present when study is complete.

Codes from categories P00–P04 should not be used when the patient has identified signs or symptoms of a suspected problem; in such cases, code the sign or symptom.

A code from categories P00–P04 may also be assigned as the principal diagnosis for a later readmission or encounter when a code from Z38 no longer applies. It is used only for healthy newborns and infants for whom no reportable condition is identified after study and is assigned only during the perinatal period of 28 days. When the newborn presents signs or symptoms of a suspected problem, or when a definite condition is identified, a code for the symptom or condition is assigned; a code from P00–P04 is not assigned. For example:

- The physician is concerned that a vaginally delivered newborn with a drug-dependent mother may have been adversely affected. Drug screens are carried out on the newborn, and the newborn is placed in the intensive care nursery temporarily for closer observation of potential withdrawal symptoms. Drug screens are negative. Codes **Z38.00, Single liveborn infant, delivered vaginally,** and **P04.49, Newborn (suspected to be) affected by maternal use of other drugs of addiction,** are assigned.
- A newborn infant is readmitted two days after discharge because of slight cyanosis and the possibility of a perinatal respiratory problem. Complete workup discloses no problem, including no observable cyanosis, and the newborn is discharged without any diagnosis having been established. Code **P00.3, Newborn (suspected to be) affected by other maternal circulatory and respiratory diseases,** is assigned as the principal diagnosis.
- A newborn infant is readmitted two days after discharge because of cyanosis and the possibility of a perinatal respiratory problem. The infant is diagnosed as having respiratory distress syndrome. Code **P22.0, Respiratory distress syndrome,** is assigned. No code from categories P00–P04 is assigned.

Although ordinarily no additional code is assigned when a condition from categories P00–P04 is the principal diagnosis, codes can be assigned for a perinatal or congenital condition that requires continuing therapy or monitoring during the stay. Codes for congenital conditions that do not receive further evaluation or therapeutic treatment are not assigned when a newborn is admitted for observation. It is inappropriate to assign codes in subcategory Z03.7, Encounter for suspected maternal and fetal conditions ruled out, for the newborn. This code subcategory is only reported on the maternal record.

INFECTIONS ORIGINATING DURING THE PERINATAL PERIOD

Many infections specific to the perinatal period are considered to be congenital and may be classified in chapter 16 of ICD-10-CM when they are acquired before birth via the umbilicus (for example, rubella) or during birth (for example, herpes simplex). Codes are located by referring to the main term for the infection and then identifying subterms, such as "neonatal," "newborn," "congenital," "perinatal," or "maternal," affecting fetus or newborn. Certain perinatal infections (for example, congenital syphilis), however, may appear in chapter 1 of ICD-10-CM, Certain Infectious and Parasitic Diseases.

Infections that occur after birth but appear during the 28-day perinatal period may or may not be classified in chapter 16. When none of the subterms mentioned above is listed, the usual infection code is assigned. If an infection does not appear for a week or more after birth, the record should be reviewed to see whether there is any indication that it may be due to exposure to the infection rather than being congenital. Clarification should be sought from the physician when the record is not completely clear.

If a newborn has sepsis, assign a code from category P36, Bacterial sepsis of newborn. If the P36 code includes the causal organism, do not assign an additional code from category B95, Streptococcus, Staphylococcus, and Enterococcus as the cause of diseases classified elsewhere, or B96, Other bacterial agents as the cause of diseases classified elsewhere. If the P36 code does not include the causal organism, assign an additional code from category B96. If applicable, use additional codes to identify severe sepsis (R65.2-) and any associated acute organ dysfunction, such as acute respiratory failure (P28.5).

As mentioned in chapter 14 of this handbook, ELISA or Western blot tests of newborns with HIV-positive mothers are often positive. This result usually indicates the antibody status of the mother rather than that of the newborn. Code **R75, Inconclusive laboratory evidence of human immunodeficiency virus (HIV),** is assigned to the newborn chart because the HIV antibodies can cross the placenta into the newborn and may persist for as long as 18 months, producing a false positive test result in the newborn. The newborn may later lose these antibodies, which means that there was never any actual HIV infection.

MATERNAL CONDITIONS AFFECTING THE FETUS OR NEWBORN

Codes from categories P00 through P04 are assigned only on the newborn's record and only when the maternal condition is the cause of morbidity or mortality in the newborn. Unless there is an adverse effect, no code from this series is assigned. The fact that the mother has a related medical condition or has experienced a complication of pregnancy, labor, or delivery does not warrant assignment of a code from these categories on the newborn's record. Examples follow.

- A living child born to a diabetic mother in a term birth and delivered by cesarean section is coded as Z38.01. No code from the series P00 through P04 is assigned because the medical record does not document a problem affecting the newborn.
- A newborn delivered of a mother addicted to cocaine shows no sign of dependence, but a drug screen is positive. In this case, code **P04.41, Newborn (suspected to be) affected by maternal use of cocaine,** is assigned as an additional code on the newborn's record.
- A newborn is admitted following cesarean delivery and diagnosed with hypermagnesemia. The provider documents that the infant had developed hypermagnesemia due to the mother's treatment with magnesium sulfate for pregnancy-related eclampsia prior to delivery. Assign codes **P74.4, Other transitory electrolyte disturbances of newborn**, and **P04.1, Newborn (suspected to be) affected by other maternal medication.** Code Z38.01 is assigned as the principal diagnosis.

When a specific condition in the infant that resulted from the mother's condition is identified, a code for that condition is assigned rather than a code from categories P00 through P04. For example, infants born to diabetic mothers sometimes experience a transient abnormally low blood glucose level (hypoglycemia), classified as **P70.1, Syndrome of infant of a diabetic mother.** Others may have a transient diabetic state (hyperglycemia), sometimes referred to as pseudodiabetes, which is coded as **P70.2, Neonatal diabetes mellitus.** When fetal or newborn conditions result in hospitalization or other obstetric care of the mother, codes O35.- and O36.- are assigned on the maternal record.

SURGICAL OPERATION ON MOTHER AND FETUS

ICD-10-CM provides several codes to capture newborns affected by amniocentesis, in utero procedures, surgery performed on the mother during pregnancy, and other maternal factors unrelated to the current pregnancy (i.e., mother's history of surgery not associated with pregnancy). These codes are only assigned on the newborn's record. If the management of the pregnancy is affected because of complications of in utero surgery, assign the appropriate code from subcategory O35.-, Maternal care for (suspected) damage to fetus by other medical procedures, on the mother's record. Obstetric codes from chapter 11 of ICD-10-CM should not be used on the newborn's record.

Specific codes for newborns affected by the above factors are as follows:

P00.7 Newborn (suspected to be) affected by other medical procedures on mother, not elsewhere classified

P00.6 Newborn (suspected to be) affected by surgical procedure on mother

ENDOCRINE AND METABOLIC DISTURBANCES SPECIFIC TO THE FETUS AND NEWBORN

ICD-10-CM provides codes to describe acidosis of newborn and other neonatal endocrine and metabolic disturbances. Causes of respiratory acidosis include, but are not limited to, asphyxia, obstruction to the respiratory tract, respiratory distress syndrome, pneumonia, pulmonary edema, and/or apnea. Metabolic acidosis may be caused by renal failure, septicemia, hypoxia, hypothermia, hypotension, cardiac failure, dehydration, electrolyte disturbances, hyperglycemia, anemia, intraventricular hemorrhage, and/or metabolic disorders. The underlying cause of acidosis must be treated in order to correct the problem. ICD-10-CM classifies transitory endocrine and metabolic disorders specific to newborn to categories P70 through P74. This code range includes transitory endocrine and metabolic disturbances caused by the infant's response to maternal endocrine and metabolic factors or its adjustment to the extrauterine environment.

INFANTILE COLIC

Code **R10.83, Colic,** is assigned for infantile colic. Assign code **R10.84, Generalized abdominal pain,** for colic in an adult or child more than 12 months old. A colicky baby is a healthy, well-fed baby who cries more than three hours a day, three days a week, for more than three weeks. The crying usually occurs at about the same time every day for no apparent reason and may be intense, with the baby having clenched fists and tensed abdominal muscles. The baby may be inconsolable. There is no known cause for colic. It may last from the first few weeks of birth through four months of age.

APPARENT LIFE-THREATENING EVENT

Apparent life-threatening event (ALTE) refers to an episode that may be characterized by any of the following signs: apnea, cyanosis, changes in muscle tone, and/or choking or gagging. It was previously referred to as near-miss sudden infant death syndrome (SIDS) or aborted crib death, but these terms should not be used because they imply an association between ALTE and SIDS. Code **R68.13, Apparent life threatening event in infant,** is assigned for ALTE in a newborn or an infant.

Because of the wide variety of presentations of the ALTE episode, signs and symptoms may be coded as additional diagnoses when:

- No confirmed diagnosis or identifiable cause of the ALTE is established or
- When signs and symptoms are not associated routinely with the confirmed cause of the ALTE or
- When the reporting of signs and symptoms provides additional information about the cause of the ALTE.

ROUTINE VACCINATION OF NEWBORNS

Newborns are vaccinated shortly after birth against hepatitis B and varicella. When the need for vaccination is indicated during the newborn stay, code **Z23, Encounter for immunization,** may be assigned. If the newborn's vaccination is not administered because of parental refusal, assign code **Z28.82, Immunization not carried out because of caregiver refusal.** Procedure codes are required to identify the type of immunization given. In the inpatient setting, the following ICD-10-PCS codes are available to report vaccinations (although most hospitals generally do not code them):

3E0134Z	Introduction of serum, toxoid and vaccine into subcutaneous tissue, percutaneous approach
3E0234Z	Introduction of serum, toxoid and vaccine into muscle, percutaneous approach

HEALTH SUPERVISION OF INFANT OR CHILD

A code from subcategory Z00.1, Encounter for newborn, infant and child health examinations, is assigned for routine encounters of infants and children when no problem has been identified. Codes from subcategory Z00.11, Newborn health examination, are assigned for a routine examination or health check for children under 29 days old, with an additional code to identify any abnormal findings. Code Z00.110 is used for newborns under eight days old, and code Z00.111 is for newborns eight to 28 days old. Code Z00.111 includes newborn weight check. Codes Z00.121 (with abnormal findings) and Z00.129 (without abnormal findings) are used for routine child health examinations for children over 28 days old and include development testing. If any vaccinations are administered during any of these routine examinations, also assign code **Z23, Encounter for immunization.** Codes from subcategory Z00.1 are not assigned for a hospital admission.

EXERCISE 27.1

Code the following diagnoses and procedures as they would be assigned to a newborn's record. Presume that all births were delivered in the hospital and were vaginally delivered unless stated otherwise.

1. Term birth, living male, cesarean delivery, with hemolytic disease due to ABO isoimmunization — Z38.01, P55.1

   Newborn

2. Term birth, living child, vaginal delivery — Z38.00
   Physiological neonatal jaundice — P59.9

   Newborn

3. Normal, full-term female, spontaneous vaginal delivery — Z38.00
   Congenital left hip subluxation — Q65.32

   Newborn

4. Newborn, male, premature (33 weeks gestation, 1,400 grams) — Z38.00
   Hyaline membrane disease — P07.15, P07.36, P22.0

5. Term birth, living male — Z38.00
   Ophthalmitis of newborn due to maternal gonococcal infection — A54.31

   Newborn

6. Near-term birth, living male, delivered by cesarean section with neonatal hypoglycemia — Z38.01, P70.4

   Newborn

7. Term birth, living child — Z38.00
   Intrauterine growth retardation — P05.9

   Newborn

8.	Premature birth, living female infant (27 weeks gestation, 1,850 grams)	Z38.00
	Withdrawal syndrome in infant due to maternal	P07.17
	heroin addiction	P07.26
		P96.1
	Newborn	
9.	Term birth, twin, with fracture of right	Z38.30
	clavicle during birth	P13.4
	Newborn	
10.	Five-year-old child with Erb's palsy secondary to birth trauma	P14.0
11.	Infant with hemolytic disease due to Rh isoimmunization (patient received by transfer from other facility)	P55.0
	Skin phototherapy, single	6A600ZZ
12.	Patient born in Community Hospital, with erythroblastosis fetalis due to ABO incompatibility; transferred immediately after birth to intensive care nursery at University Hospital for further care	
	Newborn	
	a. Codes for Community Hospital stay	Z38.00
		P55.1
	b. Code for University Hospital stay	P55.1
13.	Normal, male infant, delivered by cesarean	Z38.01
	when fetal acidemia was noted early in labor	P19.1
	Fetal distress due to cord compression	P02.5
	Newborn	
14.	Newborn born on the way to hospital	Z38.1
	and admitted directly to newborn nursery	P61.3
	Anemia due to acute blood loss from umbilical stump	P51.9

15.	Term birth with severe sepsis due to *E. coli* caused by amnionitis Newborn	Z38.00 P36.4 P02.7 R65.20
16.	Term birth, delivered with meconium aspiration syndrome due to prolonged labor, first stage Cord around neck of infant two times Newborn	Z38.00 P24.01 P03.89 P02.5
17.	Term birth, living male, with partial facial paralysis Newborn	Z38.00 P11.3
18.	Premature infant (25 weeks, 1,300 grams) transferred from University Hospital's intensive care nursery to Community Hospital for supervision of weight gain with diagnosis of "slow feeding" Newborn	P07.15 P07.24
19.	Newborn twins, #1 delivered in parking lot of hospital, #2 delivered after admission of mother Newborn	#1: Z38.30 #2: Z38.4
20.	Term birth, living child; mother known to be a chronic alcoholic; newborn placed in intensive care nursing for observation for possible alcohol-related problems; none found Observation Newborn	Z38.00 P04.3
21.	Routine visit to well-baby clinic for checkup; healthy 14-day-old infant	Z00.111
22.	Term infant with sickle-cell trait born in hospital Newborn	Z38.00 D57.3

Coding OF Circulatory System Diseases AND Neoplastic Diseases

CHAPTER 28

Diseases of the Circulatory System

CHAPTER OVERVIEW

- Circulatory disorders are classified in chapter 9 of ICD-10-CM.
- Rheumatic fever is classified with and without rheumatic heart disease.
- Ischemic heart disease is a general term for conditions affecting the myocardium.
    - — Myocardial infarctions are classified with a fourth character to indicate the wall involved. They are also classified as to whether there is an ST-segment elevation.
    - — The code for intermediate coronary syndrome includes a range of anginas.
    - — Atherosclerosis is one of the conditions included in the category "other forms of heart disease."
- If a patient is admitted with stable angina (currently a rare practice), the underlying cause is the principal diagnosis.
- There are two main categories of heart failure—systolic and diastolic. It is further classified by left- and right-sided failure.
- The assignment and sequencing of cardiac arrest is dependent on the circumstances of the hospitalization. It does not matter whether the patient is resuscitated or not.
- An aneurysm is diagnosed and then classified according to its location.
    - — Sometimes a term is used to describe its appearance.
    - — A term may also describe its etiology.
- Nontraumatic conditions affecting the cerebral arteries are coded together. These include strokes.
- Hypertension is classified by type (primary or secondary).
- Hypertension can be paired with heart disease, chronic kidney disease, or both.
- Procedures for treating circulatory disorders are varied and appear throughout this chapter of the handbook.

LEARNING OUTCOMES

After studying this chapter you should be able to:

Classify the disorders related to the heart and the rest of the circulatory system.

Distinguish between the different conditions regarded as ischemic heart disease.

Classify heart failure by category and location.

Code for a variety of procedures involving the circulatory system and the heart.

TERMS TO KNOW

Diastolic heart failure
occurs when the heart has a problem relaxing between contractions to allow enough blood into the ventricles

Systolic heart failure
occurs when the ability of the heart to contract decreases

Thrombophlebitis of a vein
a condition indicated by a clot that has become inflamed

Thrombosis of a vein
a condition indicated by the forming of a clot

REMEMBER . . .

The range of circulatory disorders is broad and complex, requiring close attention to instructional terms.

INTRODUCTION

Chapter 9 of ICD-10-CM classifies circulatory disorders except for those that have been reclassified to chapter 15 (obstetrical conditions) or to chapter 17 (congenital anomalies). This chapter covers a broad range of conditions, many of which are commonly seen for patients admitted to acute care hospitals. Because these are complex disorders and many are interrelated, it is particularly important for the coder to be alert to all instructional terms.

FIGURE 28.1 Major Vessels of the Arterial System

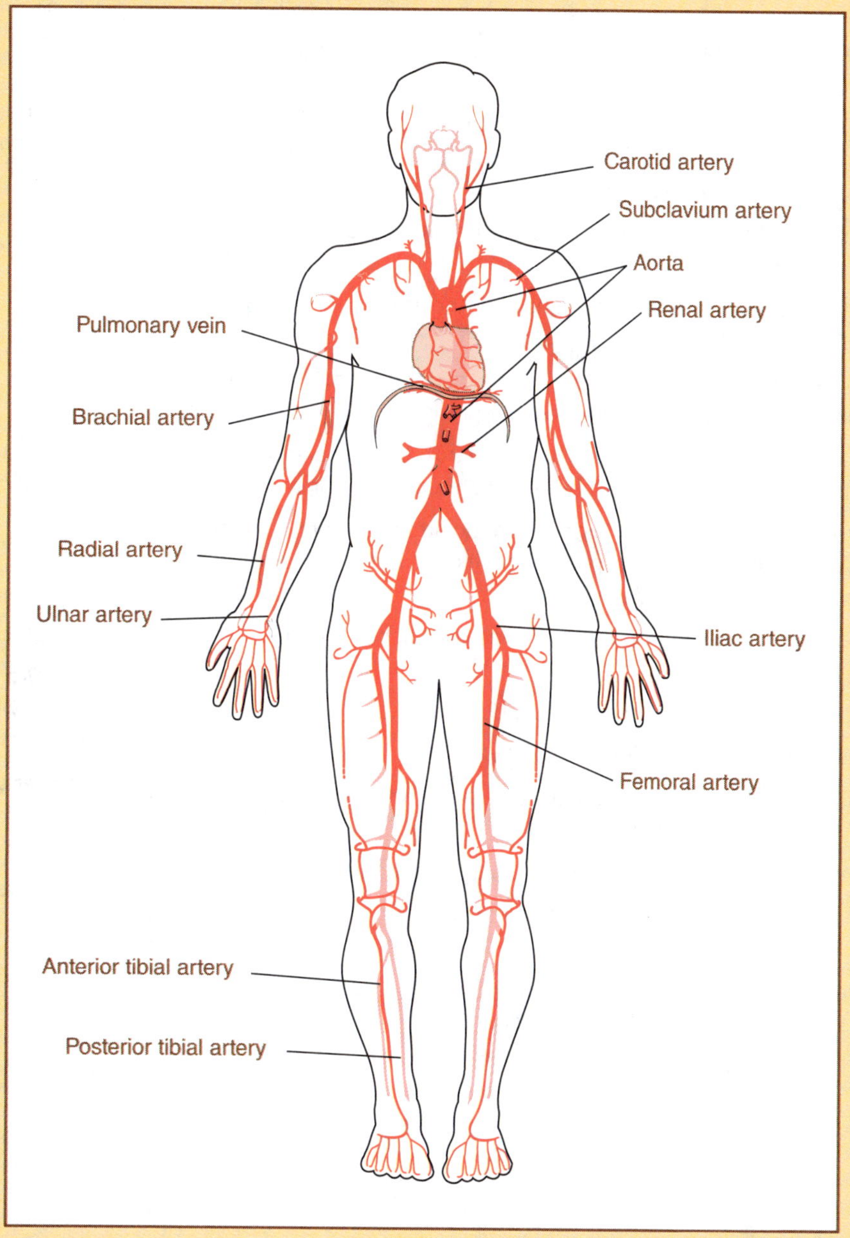

RHEUMATIC HEART DISEASE

Rheumatic heart disease occurs as the result of an infection with group A hemolytic *Streptococcus*. ICD-10-CM classifies rheumatic fever with and without rheumatic heart disease. The first axis distinguishes whether the fever is acute (I00–I02) or inactive (quiescent) (I05–I09), and the second axis determines whether there is heart involvement.

FIGURE 28.2 Major Vessels of the Venous System

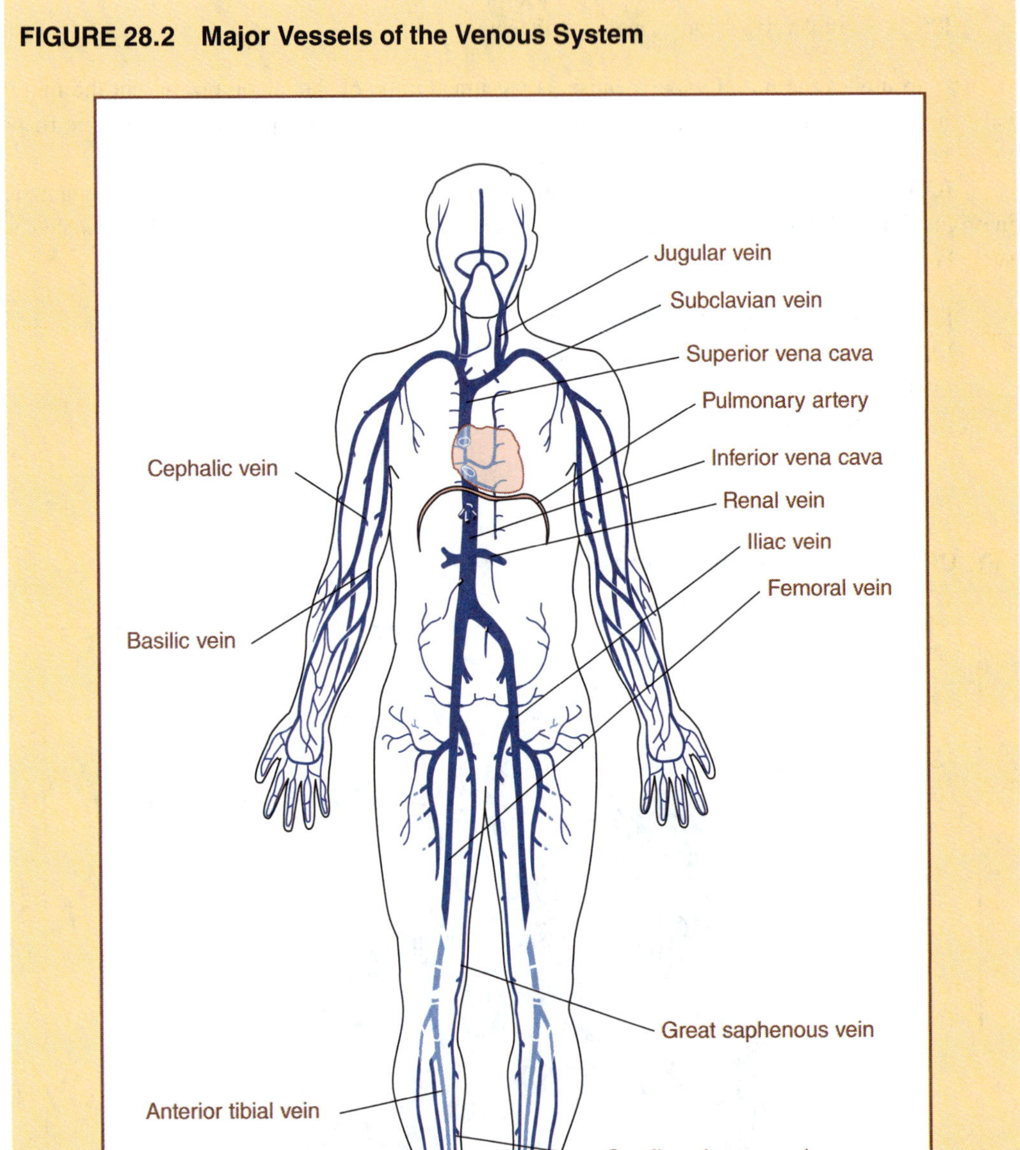

Chronic rheumatic heart disease includes heart disease that has resulted from a previously active rheumatic infection. The heart valves are most often involved. ICD-10-CM presumes that certain mitral valve disorders of unspecified etiology are rheumatic in origin. When the diagnostic statement includes more than one condition affecting the mitral valves, one of which is presumed to be rheumatic, all are classified as rheumatic. For example:

I05.0 Mitral valve stenosis
I34.0 Mitral valve insufficiency
I05.2 Mitral valve stenosis and insufficiency

In these examples the mitral valve stenosis is presumed to be of rheumatic origin, but the mitral valve insufficiency is not. In the third example, the combination code presumes both to be rheumatic because the stenosis is presumed to be rheumatic.

ICD-10-CM presumes that a disorder affecting both the mitral and aortic valves is rheumatic in origin. Otherwise, the aortic condition is classified as rheumatic only when specifically stated as such. For example:

I35.1 Aortic valve insufficiency
I08.0 Mitral valve insufficiency with aortic valve insufficiency
I35.0 Aortic valve stenosis
I06.0 Rheumatic aortic stenosis
I08.0 Mitral stenosis and aortic stenosis

FIGURE 28.3 The Interior of the Heart

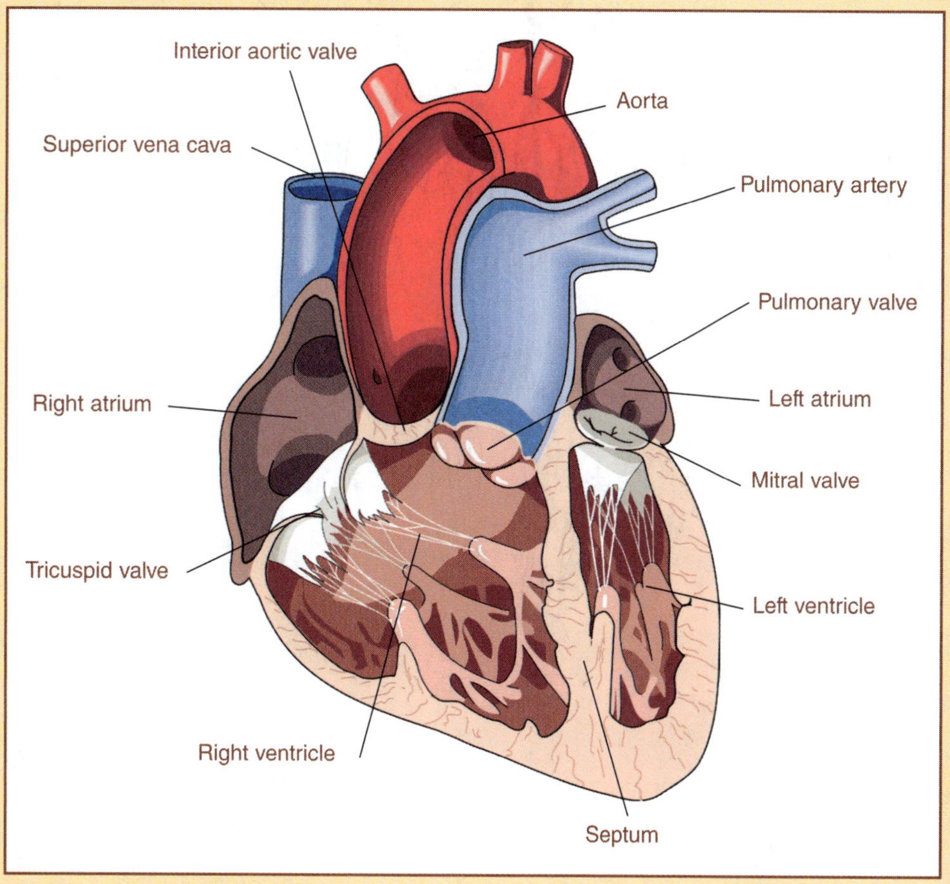

A diagnosis of heart failure in a patient who has rheumatic heart disease is classified as **I09.81, Rheumatic heart failure,** unless the physician specifies a different cause. An additional code from category I50, Heart failure, is assigned to identify the type of heart failure. However, do not make an assumption that congestive heart failure is rheumatic in nature. Unless ICD-10-CM directs the coder to assign the code for "rheumatic," it is inappropriate to assign a code for rheumatic congestive heart failure. For example:

I09.81 + I50.9 + I42.0 + I05.1	End-stage congestive heart failure due to rheumatic heart disease and dilated cardiomyopathy with mitral valve insufficiency
I50.9 + I34.0 + I07.1 + Z95.2	Congestive heart failure, severe mitral valve regurgitation, tricuspid valve regurgitation, and a history of aortic valve stenosis status post valve replacement

EXERCISE 28.1

Code the following diagnoses.

1. Mitral regurgitation	I34.0
2. Mitral valve stenosis with congestive heart failure	I05.0 I50.9
3. Severe mitral stenosis and mild aortic insufficiency	I08.0
4. Aortic and mitral insufficiency Persistent atrial fibrillation	I08.0 I48.1
5. Mitral insufficiency, congenital	Q23.3
6. Mitral valve insufficiency with aortic regurgitation	I08.0
7. Chronic aortic and mitral valve insufficiency, rheumatic, with acute congestive heart failure due to rheumatic heart disease	I08.0 I09.81 I50.9

ISCHEMIC HEART DISEASE

Ischemic heart disease is the general term for a number of disorders affecting the myocardium caused by a decrease in the blood supply to the heart due to coronary insufficiency. The insufficiency is usually caused by deposits of atheromatous material in the epicardial portions of the coronary artery that progressively obstruct its branches so that the lumen of the arteries become either partially or completely occluded. Other common terms for ischemic heart disease are arteriosclerotic heart disease, coronary ischemia, coronary artery disease, and coronary arteriosclerosis (atherosclerosis).

Ischemic heart disease is classified in categories I20 through I25 as follows:

I20 Angina pectoris
I21 Acute myocardial infarction
I22 Subsequent myocardial infarction
I23 Current complications following myocardial infarction
I24 Other acute ischemic heart disease
I25 Chronic ischemic heart disease

An additional code is used to identify hypertension (I10–I15) when present.

Myocardial Infarction

Acute myocardial infarction is an acute ischemic condition that ordinarily appears following prolonged myocardial ischemia. It is usually precipitated by an occlusive coronary thrombosis at the site of an existing arteriosclerotic stenosis. Although ischemic heart disease is a progressive disorder, it is often silent for long periods with no clinical manifestations, and then it can appear suddenly in an acute form without any intervening symptoms having been experienced.

A myocardial infarction (MI) described as acute or with a duration of four weeks or less is classified in category I21, ST elevation (STEMI) and non-ST elevation (NSTEMI) myocardial infarction, with a fourth character indicating the wall involved (such as anterolateral wall or inferior wall). Codes from I21.0- through I21.2- also have a fifth character to indicate the coronary artery involved (e.g., left main coronary artery). Codes I21.0- through I21.3- identify transmural infarctions; code I21.4- identifies subendocardial infarctions that do not extend through the full thickness of the myocardial wall. Diagnostic statements do not always mention the affected wall, but this information can almost always be found in the electrocardiographic report. Code **I21.3, ST elevation (STEMI) myocardial infarction of unspecified site,** should not be assigned unless no information regarding the site is documented in the medical record. If only STEMI or transmural MI without the site is documented, query the provider as to the site, or assign code I21.3.

Myocardial infarctions can also be classified according to whether there is ST-segment elevation (codes I21.0- through I21.3) or non-ST-segment elevation (code I21.4). If there is no information regarding whether there is ST elevation or non-ST elevation, or information regarding the site of the myocardial infarction, coders should assign code I21.3. If a myocardial infarction is documented as nontransmural or subendocardial, but the site is provided, it is still coded as a subendocardial MI. Acute myocardial infarctions specified by site (except subendocardial or nontransmural), and not described as either STEMI or non-STEMI, are coded as acute STEMI by site.

If a non-ST-elevation myocardial infarction (NSTEMI) evolves to ST-elevation myocardial infarction (STEMI), assign the code for the STEMI. If STEMI converts to NSTEMI due to thrombolytic therapy, assign the code for STEMI. Be careful to note that these codes are used for documented acute myocardial infarctions and should not be confused with abnormal findings on electrocardiograms (EKGs) of ST-segment elevation.

When the patient requires continued care for the myocardial infarction, codes from category I21 may continue to be reported for the duration of four weeks (28 days) or less from onset, regardless of the health care setting. This includes patients who are transferred from the acute care setting to the post–acute care setting within the four-week time frame. For encounters after the four-week time frame in which the patient requires continued care related to the myocardial infarction, assign the appropriate aftercare code, rather than a code from category I21. Otherwise, code **I25.2, Old myocardial infarction,** may be assigned for old or healed myocardial infarction not requiring further care.

When a patient suffers a new myocardial infarction within four weeks of an acute myocardial infarction (AMI), a code from category I22, Subsequent ST elevation (STEMI) and non-ST elevation (NSTEMI) myocardial infarction, should be used in conjunction with a code from category I21. The sequencing of the I22 and I21 codes depends on the circumstances of admission.

Figure 28.4 illustrates a process for sequencing AMI and subsequent AMI. Part A shows a decision tree for a patient admitted for AMI. Part B shows a decision tree for a patient admitted due to conditions other than AMI; the patient suffers an AMI during this admission.

FIGURE 28.4 Decision Tree for Coding Acute Myocardial Infarction

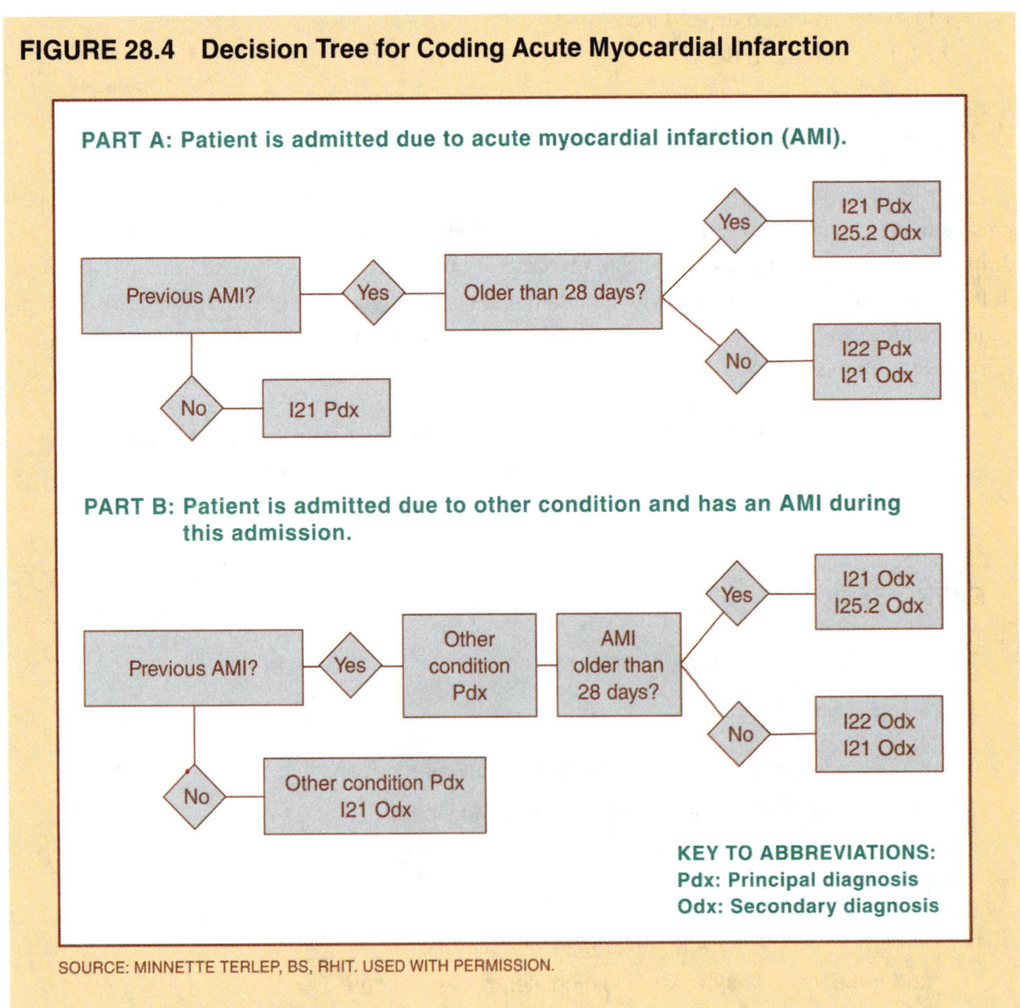

SOURCE: MINNETTE TERLEP, BS, RHIT. USED WITH PERMISSION.

Examples illustrating the sequencing of AMI codes are as follows:

- A patient is admitted to the hospital due to an AMI and has a subsequent AMI within four weeks while still in the hospital. Code I21 is sequenced first as the reason for the admission, with code I22 sequenced as a secondary code.
- A patient suffers a subsequent AMI after discharge for care of an initial AMI. The I22 code should be sequenced first, followed by the I21 code. An I21 code must accompany an I22 code to identify the site of the initial AMI and to indicate that the patient is still within the four-week time frame of healing from the initial AMI.
- The guidelines for assigning the correct code from category I22 are the same as for the initial MI.

An associated postinfarction hypotension is sometimes experienced by patients with acute myocardial infarction. In this situation, the code for the infarction is sequenced first, with an additional code of **I95.89, Other hypotension.**

For both AMIs and subsequent MIs, additional codes may be assigned to identify risk factors, such as the following:

Z77.22	Exposure to environmental tobacco smoke
Z87.891	History of tobacco use
Z57.31	Occupational exposure to environmental tobacco smoke
F17.-	Tobacco dependence
Z72.0	Tobacco use

Evolving Infarction

An evolving myocardial infarction sometimes precipitates right ventricular failure that progresses to congestive heart failure. The patient may then be admitted because of this precursor condition, which then progresses to an acute myocardial infarction. After study, the principal diagnosis in this situation is the infarction, with an additional code assigned for the heart failure. Additional codes should also be assigned for any mention of cardiogenic shock, ventricular arrhythmia, and fibrillation. For example:

I21.09 + I50.9 + I49.01	Congestive heart failure with acute myocardial infarction of anterolateral wall with ventricular fibrillation

EXERCISE 28.2

Code the following diagnoses; do not code procedures.

1. A patient felt well until around 10:00 p.m., when he began having severe chest pain, which continued to increase in severity. He was brought to the emergency department by ambulance. There was no previous history of cardiac disease, but the EKG showed an acute posterolateral myocardial infarction, and the patient was admitted immediately for further care. — I21.29

2. A patient with compensated congestive heart failure on Lasix began to have extreme difficulty in breathing and was brought to the emergency department, where he was found to be in congestive failure. Because it was felt that an impending infarction was possible, a percutaneous transluminal coronary angioplasty (PTCA) was performed, but the patient went on to have an acute inferolateral infarction.	I21.19 I50.9
3. A patient was admitted with acute myocardial infarction involving the left main coronary artery with no history of previous infarction or previous care for this episode. A week later during the hospital stay, he also experienced an acute anterolateral infarction.	I21.01 I22.0
4. A patient was admitted to Community Hospital with severe chest pain, which was identified as an acute anterolateral wall infarction (no history of earlier care). Patient was transferred to University Hospital two days later for angioplasty, returned to Community Hospital after three days at University to continue recovery, and stayed for four days.	
Code for first admission to Community Hospital	I21.09
Code for transfer to University Hospital	I21.09
Code for transfer back to Community Hospital	I21.09
5. The patient in the situation described in item 4 above was readmitted to Community Hospital a week later because he was having severe chest pains and was diagnosed with a new inferior wall MI.	I22.1 I21.09

If the infarction is described as old or healed, the coder should review the medical record to determine whether the infarction is actually old and/or healed or whether the diagnosis refers to a more recent infarction still under care. A diagnosis of old myocardial infarction is usually made on the basis of electrocardiographic findings or some other investigation in a patient who is not experiencing symptoms. Code **I25.2, Old myocardial infarction,** is essentially a history code, even though it is not included in the Z-code chapter of ICD-10-CM. It should not be assigned when current ischemic heart disease is present and should be assigned as an additional code only when it has some significance for the current episode of care.

Current Complications Following Myocardial Infarction

ICD-10-CM provides codes within category I23 to identify current complications following acute myocardial infarctions when they occur within the 28-day period, as follows:

I23.0 Hemopericardium
I23.1 Atrial septal defect
I23.2 Ventricular septal defect
I23.3 Rupture of cardiac wall without hemopericardium
I23.4 Rupture of chordae tendineae
I23.5 Rupture of papillary muscle
I23.6 Thrombosis of atrium, auricular appendage, and ventricle
I23.7 Postinfarction angina
I23.8 Other complications

A code from category I23 must be used in conjunction with a code from category I21 or category I22. Sequencing of the code from category I23 will depend on the circumstances of admission, as follows:

- If the complication of the MI is the reason for the encounter, the I23 code should be sequenced first.
- If the complication of the MI occurs during the encounter for the MI, the I23 code should be sequenced after the I21 or I22 code.

Other Acute and Subacute Ischemic Heart Disease

Code **I20.0, Unstable angina,** includes conditions described as accelerated angina, crescendo angina, de novo effort angina, intermediate coronary syndrome, preinfarction angina, or worsening effort angina. These conditions occur after less exertion has been expended than in angina pectoris; the pain is more severe and is less easily relieved by nitroglycerin. Without treatment, unstable angina often progresses to acute myocardial infarction.

Code I20.0 is designated as the principal diagnosis only when the underlying condition is not identified and there is no surgical intervention. Patients with severe coronary arteriosclerosis and unstable angina may be admitted for cardiac bypass surgery or a percutaneous transluminal coronary angioplasty to prevent further progression to infarction. In such cases, the combination code for coronary arteriosclerosis with unstable angina (I25.110) is assigned as the principal diagnosis. Examples of appropriate coding follow.

- A patient was admitted with unstable angina and underwent right and left heart catheterization, which showed coronary arteriosclerosis. A coronary bypass procedure was recommended, but the patient felt he needed some time to think it over and to discuss it with his family. For this admission, the coronary arteriosclerosis with unstable angina (I25.110) is the principal diagnosis.
- A patient was admitted with unstable angina and a history of myocardial infarction five years ago. She was treated with IV nitroglycerin, and the angina subsided by the end of the first hospital day. No other complications were noted, and no additional diagnostic studies were carried out. In this case, the unstable angina (I20.0) is the principal diagnosis. Assign also code I25.2 to describe the old MI.

A diagnosis of acute ischemic heart disease or acute myocardial ischemia does not always indicate an infarction. It is often possible to prevent infarction by means of surgery and/or the use of thrombolytic agents if the patient is treated promptly. If there is occlusion or thrombosis of the

artery without infarction, code **I24.0, Acute coronary thrombosis not resulting in myocardial infarction,** is assigned. Code **I24.8, Other forms of acute ischemic heart disease,** includes coronary insufficiency and subendocardial ischemia.

Postmyocardial Infarction Syndrome

Patients with acute myocardial infarction sometimes experience postmyocardial infarction syndrome (I24.1) or angina described as postinfarction angina (I23.7). Postmyocardial infarction, also called Dressler's syndrome, is a pericarditis characterized by fever, leukocytosis, pleurisy, pleural effusion, joint pains, and occasionally pneumonia. Codes from category I20, Angina pectoris, cannot be used with code I23.7, Postinfarction angina. Codes from category I23 must be used in conjunction with a code from category I21 or category I22 to identify the acute or subsequent myocardial infarction. Sequencing is dependent on the circumstances of admission. No codes from categories I20, Angina pectoris, nor from category I30, Acute pericarditis, can be used with codes from category I24.

EXERCISE 28.3

Code the following diagnoses.

1. Acute myocardial infarction, inferolateral wall — I21.19
   Third-degree atrioventricular block — I44.2

2. Acute myocardial infarction of inferoposterior wall — I21.11
   Congestive heart failure — I50.9
   Hypertension — I10

3. Impending myocardial infarction (crescendo angina) resulting in occlusion of coronary artery — I24.0

4. Acute coronary insufficiency — I24.8

5. Hemopericardium as a complication of acute myocardial infarction of the inferior wall, which occurred three weeks ago; patient had been discharged a week before — I23.0, I21.19

Chronic Ischemic Heart Disease

Category I25, Chronic ischemic heart disease, includes such conditions as coronary atherosclerosis, old myocardial infarction, coronary artery dissection, chronic coronary insufficiency, myocardial ischemia, and aneurysm of heart. Diagnoses of coronary artery disease or coronary heart disease without any further qualification are too vague to be coded accurately; the physician should be asked to provide a more specific diagnosis. Code **I25.9, Chronic ischemic heart disease, unspecified,** should rarely be assigned in an acute care hospital setting.

Code **I25.1-, Atherosclerotic heart disease of native coronary artery,** includes conditions described as atherosclerotic cardiovascular disease, coronary (artery) atheroma, coronary artery disease, and coronary artery sclerosis. The fifth character indicates the presence or absence of angina pectoris, with a sixth character specifying the type of angina (unstable, with documented spasm, other, or unspecified).

ICD-10-CM has combination codes for atherosclerotic heart disease with angina pectoris, which are included in subcategories I25.11 and I25.7. It is not necessary to use an additional code for angina pectoris when these combination codes are used. A causal relationship can be assumed in a patient with both atherosclerosis and angina pectoris, unless the documentation indicates that the angina is due to a condition other than atherosclerosis. If a patient with coronary artery disease is admitted due to an acute myocardial infarction, the AMI should be sequenced before the coronary artery disease.

Subcategory I25.7, Atherosclerosis of coronary artery bypass graft(s) and coronary artery of transplanted heart with angina pectoris, includes a fifth character to provide additional information on the type of bypass graft (unspecified, autologous vein, autologous artery, nonautologous biological coronary artery bypass graft, native artery of transplanted heart, bypass graft of coronary artery of transplanted heart). A sixth character specifies the type of angina pectoris (unstable, with documented spasm, other, or unspecified). For atherosclerosis of other coronary vessels without angina pectoris, codes from I25.81-, Atherosclerosis of other coronary vessels without angina pectoris, are reported. The sixth character indicates the type of coronary artery (bypass graft, native artery of transplanted heart, or bypass graft of transplanted heart).

For example:

I25.10	Native coronary artery without angina pectoris
I25.710	Autologous vein bypass graft with unstable angina
I25.810	Nonautologous biological bypass graft without angina
I25.810	Artery bypass graft, including internal mammary artery
I25.750	Native coronary artery of transplanted heart with unstable angina
I25.812	Bypass graft (artery) (vein) of transplanted heart
I25.810	Unspecified type of bypass graft
I25.10	Unspecified type of vessel, native or graft

Physicians rarely include information regarding the type of graft in the diagnostic statement, but it is almost always available in the medical record. If the medical record makes it clear that there has been no previous bypass surgery, code **I25.1-, Atherosclerotic heart disease of native coronary artery,** can be assigned. If there is a history of previous bypass, codes I25.70- through I25.73-, I25.79-, or I25.810 should be assigned when information indicating the material used in the bypass is available. Note that arteriosclerosis of a bypass vessel is not classified as a postoperative complication.

When atherosclerosis of a native coronary artery in a transplanted heart is identified in the diagnostic statement, code I25.75- or I25.811 is assigned. Code I25.76- or **I25.812, Atherosclerosis of bypass graft of coronary artery of transplanted heart,** is assigned to identify atherosclerosis of a bypass graft in a transplanted heart.

Chronic Total Occlusion

A chronic total occlusion of coronary artery (I25.82) involves complete blockage of a coronary artery that has been present for an extended period (e.g., months or years). The chronic total occlusion develops when plaque accumulates in the artery, leading to a substantial reduction in blood flow and the development of bypass collateral blood flow. Although well-developed collaterals do not completely compensate for diminished blood flow, they help to preserve the viability of the myocardium and prevent resting ischemia. Patients with chronic total occlusion who present with a change in anginal status that is directly related to physical activity have an increased risk of myocardial infarction or death. Chronic total occlusion of a coronary artery may be treated with angioplasty (root operation "Dilation") or stent placement, usually a drug-eluting stent. These types of obstructions are more resistant to guidewire crossing and are more difficult to treat than other types of coronary stenosis. Advanced methods in treatment have been developed to specifically handle chronic total coronary occlusions.

Code I25.82 should be used as an additional code assignment if coronary atherosclerosis (code series I25.1, I25.7-, I25.81-) is present with a chronic total occlusion of a coronary artery. Code I25.82 should not be assigned if the patient is diagnosed with acute coronary occlusion with or without myocardial infarction.

Code **I25.83, Coronary atherosclerosis due to lipid rich plaque,** describes coronary atherosclerosis with the exact composition of the atherosclerotic plaque. The presence of lipid-rich atherosclerotic plaque can precipitate an acute coronary event. The identification of plaque as lipid rich or non–lipid rich is clinically significant because this information can assist interventional cardiologists in determining the correct treatment (i.e., drug-eluting stent or non-drug-eluting stent). Near infrared spectroscopy (8E023DZ) is a new intravascular diagnostic tool that can detect and differentiate lipid-rich atherosclerotic plaque. When the provider documents lipid-rich plaque, the appropriate code for the coronary atherosclerosis (I25.1-, I25.7-, I25.81-) should be sequenced first, followed by code I25.83 as an additional code assignment.

Code **I25.84, Coronary atherosclerosis due to calcified coronary lesion,** is used to differentiate calcified coronary lesions from other ischemic coronary lesions. The calcium deposits in these types of lesions present a rigid obstacle that can result in an increased risk for complications, such as inadequate stent expansion, acute stent thrombosis, and restenosis when treated by angioplasty with stent placement. When coding a calcified coronary lesion, sequence first the appropriate coronary atherosclerosis code (I25.1-, I25.7-, I25.81-), followed by code I25.84.

ANGINA PECTORIS

Angina pectoris (category I20) is an early manifestation of ischemic heart disease, although in rare instances it occurs as a result of congenital abnormalities of the coronary arteries or such conditions as aortic stenosis, valvular insufficiency, aortic syphilis, and Raynaud's phenomenon. It is characterized by chest pain, usually perceived by the patient as a sensation of tightness, squeezing, pressing, choking, burning; of heartburn or gas; or of an ill-defined discomfort. This type of angina can be produced by any activity or situation that increases the oxygen requirements of the myocardium, such as exercise, walking into the wind, cold weather, consumption of a large meal, emotional stress, and elevation of blood pressure. This type of pain is similar to that of unstable angina, but it is less severe; more easily controlled; and usually relieved in a predictable manner by either rest or the administration of nitroglycerin.

Angina pectoris sometimes occurs even when the patient is at rest, apparently without any stimulation, such as during the night. This condition is referred to as nocturnal or decubitus angina and is classified as I20.8. A variant type that also occurs at rest is known as Prinzmetal angina. Angina described as angiospastic, Prinzmetal, spasm induced, or variant is coded to **I20.1, Angina pectoris**

with documented spasm. Code **I20.8, Other forms of angina pectoris,** includes angina equivalent, angina of effort, and stenocardia. An additional code(s) for symptoms associated with angina equivalent is assigned.

In today's health care environment, it is unlikely that a patient would be admitted to the hospital for treatment of stable angina except for the purpose of undergoing diagnostic studies to determine its underlying cause. In this case, sequence the combination code (I25.1-) for angina with atherosclerotic heart disease (ASHD) as the principal diagnosis when the ASHD is the underlying cause.

EXERCISE 28.4

Code the following diagnoses and procedures.

1.	Crescendo angina due to coronary arteriosclerosis	I25.110
	Right and left cardiac catheterization, percutaneous	4A023N8
2.	Angina pectoris with essential hypertension	I20.9 I10

HEART FAILURE

Heart failure occurs when an abnormality of cardiac function results in the inability of the heart to pump blood at a rate commensurate with the body's needs or the ability to do so only from an abnormal filling pressure. This decrease in blood supply to body tissue results in unmet needs for oxygen as well as in a failure to meet other metabolic requirements. This in turn results in pulmonary and/or systemic circulatory congestion and reduced cardiac output. Precipitating causes of heart failure include cardiac arrhythmias, pulmonary embolism, infections, anemia, thyrotoxicosis, myocarditis, endocarditis, hypertension, and myocardial infarction. All codes for heart failure include any associated pulmonary edema; therefore, no additional code is assigned. A diagnosis of acute pulmonary edema in the absence of underlying heart disease is classified with conditions affecting the respiratory system. (See chapter 19 of this handbook for more information on the respiratory system.)

There are two main categories of heart failure: systolic and diastolic. Systolic heart failure (I50.2-) occurs when the ability of the heart to contract decreases. Diastolic heart failure (I50.3-) occurs when the heart has a problem relaxing between contractions (diastole) to allow enough blood to enter the ventricles. Fifth characters further specify whether the heart failure is unspecified, acute, chronic, or acute on chronic.

When the diagnostic statement lists congestive heart failure along with either systolic or diastolic heart failure, only the code for the type of heart failure is assigned: diastolic and/or systolic. Congestive heart failure is included in the codes for systolic and diastolic heart failure. If congestive heart failure is documented without further specification, it is classified to **I50.9, Heart failure, unspecified.**

Heart dysfunction without mention of heart failure is indexed to **I51.89, Other ill-defined heart diseases.** It is not appropriate for the coder to assume that a patient is in heart failure when only "diastolic dysfunction" or "systolic dysfunction" is documented.

Heart failure is differentiated clinically by whether the right or left ventricle is primarily affected. Left-sided heart failure (left ventricular failure) is due to the accumulation of excess fluid behind the left ventricle. Code **I50.1, Left ventricular failure,** includes associated conditions such as dyspnea, orthopnea, bronchospasm, cardiac asthma, edema of lung with heart disease, edema of lung with heart failure, left heart failure, pulmonary edema with heart disease and with heart failure; therefore, no additional codes are assigned. Heart failure, unspecified, is coded to I50.9. This is a vague code, however, and an effort should be made to determine whether a code from the series I50.1 through I50.4- is more appropriate.

Right-sided failure ordinarily follows left-sided failure and is coded in ICD-10-CM as **I50.9, Heart failure, unspecified.** This code includes any left-sided failure that is present; therefore, codes I50.1 and I50.9 are not assigned for the same episode of care and code I50.9 takes precedence.

The term "congestive heart failure" is often mistakenly used interchangeably with "heart failure." Congestion—pulmonary or systemic fluid buildup—is one feature of heart failure, but it does not occur in all patients.

Hypertensive Heart Disease

Hypertensive heart disease (with or without heart failure) is classified in category I11, with a code from category I50 to identify the type of heart failure (if present) as an additional diagnosis. If chronic kidney disease (N18.-) or unspecified contracted kidney (N26.-) due to hypertension or arteriosclerosis of kidney, arteriosclerotic nephritis, hypertensive nephropathy, or nephrosclerosis is present, a code from category I12 is assigned. The appropriate code from N18.1–N18.4, N18.5, N18.6, or N18.9 is assigned as an additional diagnosis to identify the stage of chronic kidney disease. If hypertensive heart disease and hypertensive chronic kidney disease are present, a code from category I13 is used, with a code from I50.- to identify the type of heart failure (if present), and a code from N18.1–N18.4, N18.5, N18.6, or N18.9 to identify the stage of chronic kidney disease. Category I13 provides different codes to indicate with or without heart failure and/or the stage of the chronic kidney disease. Further information in classifying hypertension and other associated conditions is provided later in this chapter.

Compensated, Decompensated, and Exacerbated Heart Failure

When heart failure occurs, the heart muscle commonly develops compensatory mechanisms such as cardiac hypertrophy, raised arterial pressure, ventricular dilation, or increased force of contraction. When this occurs, the heart failure may be described as *compensated*, permitting near-normal function. When these compensatory mechanisms can no longer meet the increased workload, decompensation of the heart function results; this situation is often described as decompensated heart failure. Code assignment is not affected by the use of these terms; the code for the type of heart failure is assigned. An exacerbation is defined as an increase in the severity of a disease or any of its symptoms. The terms "exacerbated" and "decompensated" indicate that there has been a flare-up (acute phase) of a chronic condition. For example:

- A patient with a known history of congestive heart failure is admitted with an exacerbation of diastolic congestive heart failure. Code **I50.33, Acute on chronic diastolic (congestive) heart failure,** is assigned. An acute exacerbation of a chronic condition (heart failure) is coded as acute on chronic.

CARDIAC TAMPONADE

Cardiac tamponade, also referred to as pericardial tamponade or tamponade (I31.4), is the compression of the heart caused by the accumulation of fluid inside the pericardium. Cardiac tamponade is often associated with viral or bacterial pericarditis. This condition typically occurs as a result of chest trauma, heart rupture, dissecting aortic aneurysm, cancer, cardiac surgery, renal failure, and/or acute myocardial infarction. The underlying cause of the tamponade should be sequenced first, followed by code I31.4.

Cardiac tamponade can be life threatening if left untreated. The goals of therapy are to improve heart function, relieve symptoms, and treat the tamponade. This can be accomplished with pericardiocentesis (root operation "Drainage," body part "pericardial cavity") or creation of a pericardial window (root operation "Drainage," body part "pericardium").

For example, a patient develops increased pericardial effusion and undergoes pericardiocentesis (percutaneous approach) due to rapid pericardial tamponade. Assign code **I31.4, Cardiac tamponade.** For the procedure, assign code **0W9D30Z, Drainage of pericardial cavity with drainage device, percutaneous approach.**

CARDIOMYOPATHY

Cardiomyopathy (I42.-) presents a clinical picture of a dilated heart, flabby heart muscles, and normal coronary arteries. Hypertrophic cardiomyopathy (HCM) is a condition, usually inherited, in which the heart muscle becomes thickened without any obvious cause. It is a known cause of sudden cardiac death in younger athletes, and young people are more likely to develop a more severe form of hypertrophic cardiomyopathy than older adults. HCM can be either obstructive (I42.1) or nonobstructive (I42.2) and is frequently asymptomatic until sudden cardiac death. Other common types of cardiomyopathy are the following:

- I42.0 Dilated cardiomyopathy, which includes congestive cardiomyopathy
- I42.1 Obstructive hypertrophic cardiomyopathy, including idiopathic hypertrophic subaortic stenosis
- I42.2 Other hypertrophic cardiomyopathy, including nonobstructive hypertrophic cardiomyopathy
- I42.3 Endomyocardial (eosinophilic) disease, including endomyocardial (tropical) fibrosis and Löffler's endocarditis
- I42.4 Endocardial fibroelastosis, including congenital cardiomyopathy and elastomyofibrosis
- I42.5 Other restrictive cardiomyopathy, including constrictive cardiomyopathy not otherwise specified
- I42.6 Alcoholic cardiomyopathy due to alcohol consumption; a code for alcoholism (F10.-) is also assigned if present
- I42.7 Cardiomyopathy due to drug and external agent: code first the poisoning due to drug or toxin, if applicable (T36–T65 with fifth or sixth character 1–4 or 6); if caused by an adverse effect, use an additional code, if applicable, to identify the drug (T36–T50 with fifth or sixth character 5)
- I42.8 Other cardiomyopathies
- I42.9 Unspecified

The symptoms of congestive cardiomyopathy (I42.0) are essentially the same as those of congestive heart failure, and the condition is often associated with congestive heart failure. Treatment ordinarily revolves around management of the congestive heart failure, and so the heart failure (I50.-) is designated as the principal diagnosis, with an additional code assigned for the cardiomyopathy.

Two codes may be required for cardiomyopathy due to other underlying conditions; for example, cardiomyopathy due to amyloidosis is coded **E85.9, Amyloidosis, unspecified,** and **I43, Cardiomyopathy in diseases classified elsewhere.** The underlying disease, amyloidosis, is sequenced first. Hypertensive cardiomyopathy should be coded to category I11, Hypertensive heart disease, with an additional code of I43. Assign first code **G71.11, Myotonic muscular dystrophy,** with I43 as an additional code assignment for cardiomyopathy due to myotonia atrophica.

The term "ischemic cardiomyopathy" is sometimes used to designate a condition in which ischemic heart disease causes diffuse fibrosis or multiple infarction, leading to heart failure with left ventricular dilation. This is not a true cardiomyopathy and is coded to **I25.5, Ischemic cardiomyopathy,** when no further clarification is provided by the attending physician. A diagnostic statement of ischemic alcoholic cardiomyopathy is assigned both code I25.5 and code **I42.6, Alcoholic cardiomyopathy,** because these conditions are not related.

TAKOTSUBO SYNDROME

Takotsubo syndrome (I51.81) is a newly recognized reversible form of left ventricular dysfunction, seen in patients without coronary disease. This syndrome is usually precipitated by emotional or physiological stress with sudden onset of chest symptoms, electrocardiographic changes characteristic of myocardial ischemia, transient left ventricular dysfunction, low-grade troponin elevation, and insignificant coronary stenosis by ventriculography. Patients presenting with Takotsubo syndrome are usually monitored and treated for left heart failure, intraventricular obstruction, and/or cardiac arrhythmias if they develop. Other conditions included in code I51.81 are reversible left ventricular dysfunction following sudden emotional stress, stress-induced cardiomyopathy, Takotsubo cardiomyopathy, and transient left ventricular apical ballooning syndrome.

CARDIAC ARREST

Code **I46.9, Cardiac arrest, cause unspecified,** may be assigned as a principal or first-listed diagnosis if the underlying condition is unknown. It does not matter whether the patient is resuscitated. The assignment and sequencing of code I46.9 is dependent on the circumstances of the hospitalization. If the patient is admitted due to cardiac arrest and an underlying cause is not established before the patient is discharged or expires, it is appropriate to assign code I46.9 as the principal or first-listed diagnosis. It may be assigned as a secondary code when cardiac arrest occurs during the hospital episode. If the provider indicates a cardiac cause for the arrest, the underlying cardiac condition is designated as the principal diagnosis, with code **I46.2, Cardiac arrest due to underlying cardiac condition,** as an additional code. If the provider indicates a noncardiac cause, code **I46.8, Cardiac arrest due to other underlying condition,** is assigned as an additional code.

Some providers may document pulseless electrical activity (PEA) rather than cardiac arrest. PEA refers to electrical activity on a monitor without a detectable pulse. It is one of the rhythms that cause a pulseless cardiac arrest. PEA usually has some underlying cause that can be treated; the most common cause in emergency situations is hypovolemia. PEA can be caused by respiratory failure with hypoxia, as in this case the cardiac muscle is unable to generate a sufficient force despite an electrical depolarization. True PEA is the absence of myocardial contraction despite coordinated electrical activity. Code **I46.9, Cardiac arrest, cause unspecified,** may be assigned as a principal or first-listed diagnosis if the underlying condition causing the PEA is unknown. Note that codes are not assigned for symptoms integral to the condition, such as bradycardia and hypotension. Cardiac arrest that occurs as a complication of surgery is coded as **I97.710, Intraoperative cardiac arrest during cardiac surgery,** or **I97.711, Intraoperative cardiac arrest during other surgery,** depending on the type of surgery. Code **O75.4, Other complications of obstetric surgery and procedures,** is assigned for cardiac arrest complicating obstetric surgery or procedures. Note that none of these cardiac arrest codes is assigned to indicate that a patient has died; therefore, do not code cardiac arrest to indicate a patient's death.

ANEURYSM

An aneurysm is a localized abnormal dilation of blood vessels. A dissecting aneurysm is one in which blood enters the wall of the artery and separates the layers of the vessel wall. As the aneurysm progresses, tension increases and the aneurysm is likely to rupture, which usually results in death.

Aneurysms are diagnosed primarily according to their location, such as the following:

I25.41	Coronary artery aneurysm
I71.02	Dissecting aneurysm of abdominal aorta
I71.3	Aneurysm of abdominal aorta with rupture
I71.2	Aneurysm of thoracic artery
I71.1	Ruptured aneurysm of thoracic artery
I71.6	Thoracoabdominal aneurysm

Occasionally, a term describing the aneurysm's appearance is used, such as "berry aneurysm" (I67.1), or a term may describe its etiology, such as "syphilitic aneurysm of aorta" (A52.01) or "traumatic aneurysm" (S25.00-, S25.20-).

AORTIC ECTASIA

Aortic ectasia refers to mild dilation of the aorta—usually less than 3 centimeters in diameter—that is not defined as an aneurysm. In ICD-10-CM, aortic ectasia is classified as follows:

I77.810	Thoracic aortic ectasia
I77.811	Abdominal aortic ectasia
I77.812	Thoracoabdominal aortic ectasia
I77.819	Aortic ectasia, unspecified site

CEREBROVASCULAR DISORDERS

Acute organic (nontraumatic) conditions affecting the cerebral arteries include hemorrhage, occlusion, and thrombosis and are coded in the I60–I68 series. Category I63, Cerebral infarction, is used to describe occlusion and stenosis of cerebral and precerebral arteries resulting in cerebral infarction. Please refer to figure 28.5 for an illustration of the types of cerebral infarction. Category I63 is subdivided on the basis of whether the cerebral infarction is due to thrombosis, embolism, occlusion, or stenosis and whether it is a precerebral or cerebral artery, with sixth characters identifying the artery (e.g., right carotid artery, right middle cerebral artery.) These codes should not be assigned unless cerebral infarction is clearly documented in the medical record and the physician has indicated a relationship between the cerebral artery thrombosis, embolism, occlusion, or stenosis and the infarction. The coder should never assume that infarction has occurred. These codes apply to the current episode of care only; they do not indicate that the patient has had a cerebral infarction in the past.

When there is occlusion and stenosis of precerebral or cerebral arteries without mention of cerebral infarction, codes from category I65, Occlusion and stenosis of precerebral arteries, not resulting in cerebral infarction, or category I66, Occlusion and stenosis of cerebral arteries, not resulting in cerebral infarction, should be used. Other terms classified to these categories are "embolism," "narrowing," "obstruction" (complete) (partial), and "thrombosis." Fifth characters are provided in subcategories I65.0, I65.2, I66.0, I66.1, and I66.2 to indicate whether the condition is present on the right, left, bilateral, or unspecified arteries.

Diagnostic statements often are not specific regarding the site or type of the cerebrovascular condition. When the diagnosis is stated as cerebrovascular accident (CVA) or stroke without any further qualification, it is important for the coder to review the medical record for more definitive information or to consult with the physician. When no further information is available, code **I63.9, Cerebral infarction, unspecified,** is assigned for the diagnosis of stroke or CVA to allow for improved uniformity in coding and statistical data.

Code I63.9 is assigned for an aborted CVA when there is no further specification as to the type of CVA. Patients who present with symptoms of an acute cerebrovascular infarction and are treated with tissue plasminogen activator (tPA) have actually suffered a cerebral infarction. Although brain damage may not be demonstrated by CT (computed tomography) scan, brain damage would be visible microscopically. The administration of tPA is coded to **3E03317, Introduction of other thrombolytic into peripheral vein, percutaneous approach.** It is effective in treating ischemic stroke caused by blood clots that are blocking blood flow to the brain. It is also effective in treating myocardial infarctions.

Code Z92.82 is assigned as an additional code along with category I63, Cerebral infarction, or I21, ST elevation (STEMI) and non-ST elevation (NSTEMI) myocardial infarction, or I22, Subsequent ST elevation (STEMI) and non-ST elevation (NSTEMI) myocardial infarction, to capture the information that the patient is status post administration of tPA at a different facility within the past 24 hours prior to admission to the current facility.

FIGURE 28.5 Types of Cerebral Infarction

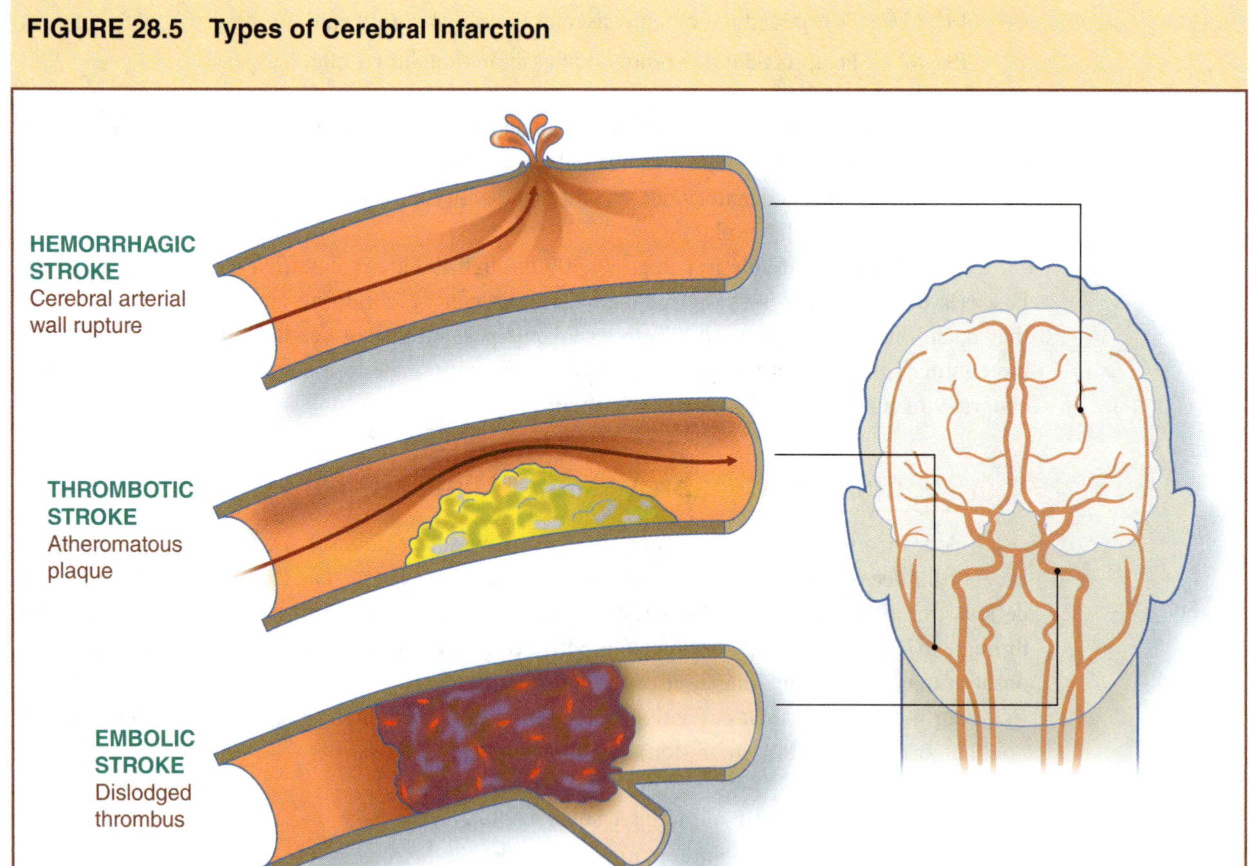

Each component of a diagnostic statement identifying cerebrovascular disease should be coded unless the Alphabetic Index or the Tabular List instructs otherwise. For example:

I60.7 + I67.2	Cerebrovascular arteriosclerosis with subarachnoid hemorrhage due to ruptured berry aneurysm
I61.9 + G93.6	Intracerebral hemorrhage with vasogenic edema
E85.4 + I68.0	Cerebral amyloid angiopathy

ICD-10-CM provides codes to report a postoperative stroke. However, medical record documentation should clearly specify the cause-and-effect relationship between the medical intervention and the cerebrovascular accident in order to assign a code for intraoperative or postprocedural cerebrovascular accident. Proper code assignment depends on whether it was an infarction or a hemorrhage and whether it occurred intraoperatively or postoperatively. If it was a cerebral hemorrhage, code assignment depends on the type of procedure performed. For example:

G97.31	Intraoperative hemorrhage and hematoma of a nervous system organ or structure complicating a nervous system procedure
G97.32	Intraoperative hemorrhage and hematoma of a nervous system organ or structure complicating other procedure
I97.810	Intraoperative cerebrovascular infarction during cardiac surgery
I97.811	Intraoperative cerebrovascular infarction during other surgery
I97.820	Postprocedural cerebrovascular infarction during cardiac surgery
I97.821	Postprocedural cerebrovascular infarction during other surgery

For codes from subcategory I97.8, assign an additional code to identify the specific type of stroke/cerebrovascular accident. The general coding rule for postoperative complications is that when the complication code does not specifically identify the condition, an additional code should be assigned to more fully explain it.

Conditions classifiable in categories I00 through I99 are reclassified in subcategory O99.4, Diseases of the circulatory system complicating pregnancy, childbirth and the puerperium, when they occur during pregnancy, childbirth, or the puerperium. Because code O99.4- does not indicate the nature of the circulatory system condition, it is appropriate to assign an additional code from chapter 9 of ICD-10-CM for greater specificity.

Sequelae of Cerebrovascular Disease

Codes from category I69, Sequelae of cerebrovascular disease, allow for greater specificity in reporting the residual effects of cerebrovascular diseases. These "late effects" include neurologic deficits that persist after initial onset of cerebrovascular conditions classifiable to categories I60 through I67. The neurologic deficits caused by cerebrovascular disease may be present from the onset or may arise at any time after the onset of the condition classifiable to categories I60 through I67. Fourth-character subclassifications indicate the causal condition (e.g., nontraumatic subarachnoid hemorrhage, cerebral infarction), as follows:

I69.0-	Sequelae of nontraumatic subarachnoid hemorrhage
I69.1-	Sequelae of nontraumatic intracerebral hemorrhage
I69.2-	Sequelae of other nontraumatic intracranial hemorrhage
I69.3-	Sequelae of cerebral infarction
I69.8-	Sequelae of other cerebrovascular diseases
I69.9-	Sequelae of unspecified cerebrovascular diseases

Fifth characters provide information regarding the neurological deficits (with some codes having sixth characters for additional specificity). The fifth characters and the corresponding neurological deficits are as follows:

0 Unspecified sequelae
1 Cognitive deficits
2 Speech and language deficits
3 Monoplegia of upper limb
4 Monoplegia of lower limb
5 Hemiplegia/hemiparesis
6 Other paralytic syndrome
9 Other sequelae (includes apraxia, dysphagia, facial weakness, ataxias, and other sequelae)

Codes for other paralytic syndrome following cerebrovascular disease (I69.06, I69.16-, I69.26-, I69.36-, I69.86-, and I69.96-) provide an instructional note to assign additional codes to indicate the type of paralytic syndrome, such as locked in state (G83.5) or quadriplegia (G82.5-). Also, an additional code should be added to codes I69.091, I69.191, I69.291, I69.391, I69.891, and I69.991 to identify the type of dysphagia, if known. For "other sequelae of cerebrovascular disease" (codes I69.098, I69.198, I69.298, I69.398, I69.898, and I69.998), assign additional codes to identify the specific sequelae.

Codes from category I69 are assigned for any remaining deficits when the patient is admitted at a later date. Like other late effect codes, category I69 is assigned only when it is significant for the current episode of care. Code **Z86.73, Personal history of transient ischemic attack (TIA), and cerebral infarction without residual deficits,** should be assigned rather than a code from category I69 when the patient has a history of a cerebrovascular infarction or CVA with no residual conditions, a history of TIA, a history of prolonged reversible ischemic neurological deficit (PRIND), or a history of reversible ischemic neurological deficit (RIND). Codes from category I69 differ from other late effect codes in two ways:

- These codes can be assigned as the principal diagnosis when the purpose of the admission is to deal with the late effect.
- These codes can be assigned as additional codes when a new CVA is present and deficits from an earlier episode remain. This distinction permits the identification of those deficits due to the current CVA and those remaining from an earlier episode.

Unlike other late effects, neurological deficits such as hemiplegia and aphasia due to cerebrovascular accidents are often present from the onset of the disease rather than arising after the original condition itself has cleared. Report any neurological deficits caused by a CVA even if they have resolved at the time of discharge from the hospital. For example, a patient is admitted because of subarachnoid hemorrhage with associated aphasia and hemiplegia that has cleared by the time of discharge. Even though these deficits have cleared at discharge, the following codes are assigned:

I60.9 Nontraumatic subarachnoid hemorrhage, unspecified
R47.01 Aphasia
G81.90 Hemiplegia

Note that codes from category I69 are not assigned for sequelae of traumatic intracranial injuries. Instead, assign codes from category S06, Intracranial injury, with the seventh-character value "S" for sequelae.

EXERCISE 28.5

Code the following diagnoses.

	Diagnosis	Code
1.	Occlusion of right internal carotid artery with cerebral infarction with mild hemiplegia resolved before discharge	I63.231 G81.90
2.	Hemiplegia on right (dominant) side due to old cerebral thrombosis	I69.351
3.	Admission for treatment of new cerebral embolism with cerebral infarction and with aphasia remaining at discharge (patient suffered cerebral embolism one year ago, with residual apraxia and dysphagia) Sequelae	I63.40 R47.01 I69.390 I69.391
4.	Cerebral infarction due to thrombosis with right hemiparesis (dominant) and aphasia	I63.30 G81.91 R47.01
5.	Cerebral embolism right anterior cerebral artery	I66.11
6.	Insufficiency of vertebrobasilar arteries	G45.0
7.	Admission for rehabilitation because of monoplegia of the right arm and right leg, each affecting dominant side (patient suffered a nontraumatic extradural (intracranial) hemorrhage one month ago) Sequelae	I69.231 I69.241
8.	Quadriplegia due to ruptured berry aneurysm five years ago	I69.265 G82.50

HYPERTENSION

ICD-10-CM classifies hypertension by type as essential or primary (code I10) and secondary (category I15). Categories I10 through I13 classify primary hypertension according to a hierarchy of the disease from its vascular origin (I10) to the end-organ involvement of the heart (I11), chronic kidney disease (I12), or heart and chronic kidney disease combined (I13). Essential hypertension is also described as high blood pressure, primary hypertension, hypertensive vascular disease, or systemic hypertension.

Primary, Transient, and Secondary Hypertension

Malignant hypertension is a sudden and rapid development of extremely high blood pressure. The lower (diastolic) blood pressure reading, which is normally around 80 mm Hg, is often above 130 mm Hg. Without effective treatment, malignant hypertension can lead to congestive heart failure, hypertensive encephalopathy, intracerebral hemorrhage, uremia, and even death.

The term "benign hypertension" refers to a relatively mild degree of hypertension of prolonged or chronic duration. Although malignant hypertension is almost always identified in the diagnostic statement, benign hypertension is rarely specified as a diagnosis. From an ICD-10-CM coding perspective, hypertension described as accelerated, benign, essential, idiopathic, malignant, or systemic is assigned to code **I10, Essential (primary) hypertension.**

Occasionally, the hypertension may be described as controlled or uncontrolled. Uncontrolled hypertension usually refers to an existing state of hypertension that is under control by therapy. Uncontrolled hypertension may refer to untreated hypertension or hypertension that does not respond to current therapeutic regimen. However, whether the hypertension is controlled or not does not affect code selection. Assign the appropriate code from categories I10 through I15, Hypertensive disease.

When the hypertension is described as transient, assign code **R03.0, Elevated blood pressure reading without diagnosis of hypertension,** unless the patient has an established diagnosis of hypertension. For transient hypertension of pregnancy, assign code **O13.-, Gestational [pregnancy-induced] hypertension without significant proteinuria** or **O14.-, Pre-eclampsia.**

Secondary hypertension (category I15) is the result of some other primary disease or underlying condition. When the condition causing the hypertension can be cured or brought under reasonable control, the secondary hypertension may stabilize or disappear entirely. Two codes are required to report secondary hypertension: one for the underlying cause and one from category I15 to identify the secondary hypertension. The sequencing of these codes is dependent on the circumstances of admission or encounter. For example:

M32.10 + I15.8	Hypertension due to systemic lupus erythematosus
I15.2 + E22.0	Acromegaly with secondary hypertension seen for hypertension management

Hypertension described as "controlled" or with "history of" usually refers to an existing hypertension that is under control by means of continuing therapy. The coder should review the medical record to determine whether the hypertension is still under treatment; if so, the appropriate code from categories I10 through I15 should be assigned.

Some providers may document hypertensive urgency without further specification. When only hypertensive urgency is documented, query the provider regarding the specific type of hypertension. If, however, upon clarification the hypertension is still not further specified (e.g., essential or secondary), assign code **I10, Essential hypertension.** The coder is directed to "*See* hypertension" when "urgency, hypertensive" is referenced in the Index.

HYPERTENSIVE HEART DISEASE

Certain heart conditions are assigned to category I11, Hypertensive heart disease, when a causal relationship is stated (due to hypertension) or implied (hypertensive). Hypertensive heart disease includes heart failure, myocarditis, cardiomegaly, cardiovascular disease, and degeneration of the myocardium. Category I11 is subdivided to indicate whether heart failure is present. However, an additional code from category I50 is still required to specify the type of heart failure, if known.

A cause-and-effect relationship between hypertension and heart disease cannot be assumed, however, and careful attention must be given to the exact wording of the diagnostic statement. When the diagnostic statement mentions both conditions but does not indicate a causal relationship between them, separate codes are assigned, with sequencing being dependent on the circumstances of the admission/encounter. For example:

I11.0 + I50.9	Congestive heart failure due to hypertension
I11.0 + I50.9	Hypertensive heart disease with congestive heart failure
I50.9 + I10	Congestive heart failure with hypertension

A causal relationship is presumed to exist for a cardiac condition when it is associated with another condition classified as hypertensive heart disease. For example:

I11.0 + I50.9	Hypertensive myocarditis with congestive heart failure
I11.0 + I50.9	Hypertensive cardiovascular disease with congestive heart failure

The coder should review the medical record for any reference to the presence of conditions such as coronary arteriosclerosis or chronic coronary insufficiency that could merit additional code assignments.

HYPERTENSION AND CHRONIC KIDNEY DISEASE

When the diagnostic statement includes both hypertension and chronic kidney disease or renal sclerosis (in contrast to hypertension and heart disease), ICD-10-CM usually assumes that there is a cause-and-effect relationship and a code from category I12, Hypertensive chronic kidney disease, is assigned. A causal relationship need not be indicated in the diagnostic statement. A fourth character is used with category I12 to indicate the stage of the chronic kidney disease. The appropriate code from category N18 should be used as a secondary code to identify the stage of chronic kidney disease.

Note that category I12 does not include acute kidney failure, which is an entirely different condition from chronic kidney disease and is not caused by hypertension. Kidney conditions that are not indexed to hypertensive chronic kidney disease may or may not be hypertensive; if the physician indicates a causal relationship, only the code for hypertensive chronic kidney disease is assigned. Sample codes for cases of hypertensive chronic kidney disease include the following:

I12.9	Hypertensive nephropathy, benign
I12.9	Hypertensive nephrosclerosis
I12.9 + N18.3	Accelerated hypertension with chronic kidney disease stage 3
N17.2 + I10	Acute kidney failure with renal papillary necrosis and hypertension

HYPERTENSIVE HEART AND CHRONIC KIDNEY DISEASE

The codes in category I13, Hypertensive heart and chronic kidney disease, are combination codes that include hypertension, heart disease, and chronic kidney disease. The inclusion note at category I13 specifies that the conditions classified to categories I11 and I12 are included together in I13. Therefore, if a patient has hypertension, heart disease, and chronic kidney disease, then a code from I13 should be used rather than individual codes for hypertension, heart disease, and chronic kidney disease, or codes from I11 or I12.

Fourth and fifth characters indicate with or without heart failure, as well as the stage of the chronic kidney disease. Assume a relationship between the hypertension and the chronic kidney disease, whether or not the condition is so designated. If heart failure is present, assign an additional code from category I50 to identify the type of heart failure. The appropriate code from category N18, Chronic kidney disease, should be used as a secondary code, with a code from category I13 to identify the stage of chronic kidney disease. For patients with both acute renal failure and chronic kidney disease an additional code for acute renal failure is required.

When the diagnostic statement indicates hypertension and diabetes mellitus are both responsible for chronic kidney disease, assign the appropriate code from category I12 along with a code from categories E08 through E13, with fifth character of 2, from the subcategory for diabetes with kidney complications. Sequencing is optional. An additional code is assigned for the stage of chronic kidney disease (N18.-), if known.

HYPERTENSION WITH OTHER CONDITIONS

Although hypertension is often associated with other conditions and may accelerate their development, ICD-10-CM does not provide combination codes. Codes for each condition must be assigned to fully describe the condition. For example:

I70.0 + I10	Atherosclerosis of aorta with essential hypertension
I25.10 + I10	Coronary atherosclerosis and systemic hypertension
I25.10	Arteriosclerotic heart disease
I25.10 + I10	Arteriosclerotic heart disease with essential hypertension

Hypertensive Cerebrovascular Disease

For hypertensive cerebrovascular disease, first assign the appropriate code from categories I60 through I69, followed by the appropriate hypertension code (I10–I15).

Hypertensive Retinopathy

Subcategory H35.0, Background retinopathy and retinal vascular changes, should be used with a code from categories I10–I15, Hypertensive diseases, to include the systemic hypertension. The sequencing is based on the reason for the encounter.

EXERCISE 28.6

Code the following diagnoses.

	Diagnosis	Code
1.	Left heart failure with hypertension	I50.1
		I10
2.	Hypertensive cardiomegaly	I11.9
3.	Congestive heart failure	I50.9
	Cardiomegaly	I51.7
	Hypertension	I10
4.	Acute congestive diastolic heart failure due to	I11.0
	hypertension	I50.31
5.	Hypertensive heart disease	I11.9
	Myocardial degeneration	
6.	Acute cerebrovascular insufficiency	I67.81
7.	Cerebral thrombosis	I66.9
	Moderate arterial hypertension	I10
8.	Arteriosclerotic cerebrovascular disease	I67.2
	Hypertension, primary	I10
9.	Chronic coronary insufficiency	I25.89
	Essential hypertension	I10
10.	Acute coronary insufficiency	I24.8
	Hypertensive heart disease	I11.9

HYPERTENSION COMPLICATING PREGNANCY, CHILDBIRTH, AND THE PUERPERIUM

Hypertension associated with pregnancy, childbirth, or the puerperium is considered to be a complication unless the physician specifically indicates that it is not. This condition includes pre-existing hypertension as well as transient hypertension of pregnancy or hypertension arising during pregnancy. Hypertension complicating pregnancy, childbirth, and the puerperium is reclassified in categories O10 through O11 and O13 through O16. (See chapter 24 of this handbook.)

ELEVATED BLOOD PRESSURE VERSUS HYPERTENSION

Blood pressure readings vary from time to time and tend to increase with age. Because of these variables, a diagnosis of hypertension must be made on the basis of a series of blood pressure readings rather than a single reading. A diagnosis of elevated blood pressure reading, without a diagnosis of hypertension, is assigned code R03.0. This code is never assigned on the basis of a blood pressure reading documented in the medical record; the physician must have specifically documented a diagnosis of elevated blood pressure.

True postoperative hypertension is classified as a complication of surgery, and code **I97.3, Postprocedural hypertension,** is assigned. However, a diagnosis of postoperative hypertension often refers only to an elevated blood pressure that reflects the patient's agitation or inadequate pain control and would be coded to R03.0.

When the patient has a pre-existing hypertension, only a code from categories I10 through I13 is assigned; neither pre-existing hypertension nor simple elevated blood pressure is classified as a postoperative complication. Any other diagnosis of transient hypertension, except that occurring in pregnancy, or a diagnosis of postoperative hypertension not clearly documented in the medical record should be discussed with the physician to determine whether it represents an elevated blood pressure reading or a true hypertension.

ATHEROSCLEROSIS OF EXTREMITIES

Atherosclerosis of the native arteries of the extremities is classified into subcategory I70.2. Fifth characters used with subcategory I70.2, Atherosclerosis of native arteries of the extremities, indicate the progression of the disease as follows:

- Code I70.21- indicates atherosclerosis of the extremities with intermittent claudication.
- Code I70.22- indicates the presence of rest pain; it includes any intermittent claudication.
- Codes I70.23-, I70.24-, and I70.25- indicate a condition that has progressed to ulceration; it includes any rest pain and/or intermittent claudication. Code L97.- is used with I70.23- and I70.24-, and code L98.49- is used with I70.25-, to identify the severity of the ulcer.
- Code I70.26- indicates the presence of gangrene; it includes any or all of the preceding conditions. Code L98.49- is assigned as an additional code to identify the severity of any ulcer, if applicable.

Atherosclerosis of extremities involving a graft is coded to I70.3- through I70.7-, as follows:

I70.3- Unspecified graft
I70.4- Autologous vein bypass graft
I70.5- Nonautologous biological bypass graft
I70.6- Nonbiological bypass graft
I70.7- Other type of bypass graft

Codes from I70.3- through I70.7- provide additional characters to indicate the same progression of disease discussed above under subcategory I70.2, Atherosclerosis of native arteries of the extremities, namely, intermittent claudication, rest pain, ulceration, and gangrene.

A chronic total occlusion of an artery of the extremities (I70.92) develops when hard, calcified plaque accumulates in an artery over an extended period of time, resulting in a clinically significant decrease in blood flow. Approximately 40 percent of patients with peripheral vascular disease present initially with partial occlusion, which progresses to a chronic total occlusion. Intervention with angioplasty and stenting is more complex because passing a guidewire through a total occlusion is extremely difficult.

Code I70.92 should be used as an additional code assignment with subcategories I70.2 through I70.7 when a chronic total occlusion is present with atherosclerosis of the extremities. An acute occlusion of arteries of the extremity is assigned to code series I70.2-, I70.3-, and I70.4-.

PULMONARY EMBOLISM

An embolus is a blood clot that usually occurs in the veins of the legs (deep vein thrombosis, or DVT). Emboli can dislodge and travel to other organs in the body. A pulmonary embolism is a clot that lodges in the lungs, blocking the pulmonary arteries and reducing blood flow to the lungs and heart. Pulmonary embolic disease may be acute or chronic (long-standing, having occurred over many weeks, months, or years). In the majority of cases, acute pulmonary emboli do not cause chronic disease because the body's mechanisms will generally break down the blood clot.

An acute embolus is usually treated with anticoagulants (e.g., intravenous heparin and warfarin or oral Coumadin) to dissolve the clot and prevent new ones. For acute pulmonary embolism, anticoagulant therapy may be carried out for three to six months. Therapy is discontinued when the embolus dissolves. A filter to interrupt the vena cava is another treatment option. The device filters the blood returning to the heart and lungs until the pulmonary embolism dissolves.

The tulip filter device is indicated in cases of recent pulmonary embolism and proximal DVT with a contraindication to anticoagulation, and as prophylaxis following trauma. When the tulip filter is used on a temporary basis, complications of permanent filters (i.e., thrombosis, migration, inferior vena cava occlusion or perforation, filter fragmentation, and increased risk for DVT) can be avoided. The tulip filter device consists of four legs that form the shape of a cone. A small hook at the base of each leg is used for fixation of the device. Filter wires form the shape of tulip petals, giving the device its name. A hook at the apex of the cone allows the filter to be retrieved, although it may be used as a permanent fixture to manage thromboembolic disease. For example:

- A patient with pulmonary embolism (I26.99) undergoes placement of bilateral common femoral vein tulip filters. Code **06H03DZ, Insertion of intraluminal device into inferior vena cava, percutaneous approach,** is assigned for insertion of the femoral tulip filter.

Acute pulmonary embolisms are classified to category I26, Pulmonary embolism, with fourth characters to indicate whether there is acute cor pulmonale, and fifth characters to indicate septic pulmonary embolism. Code **I26.99, Other pulmonary embolism without acute cor pulmonale,** is used for an acute pulmonary embolism not otherwise specified. Code **I27.82, Chronic pulmonary embolism,** is assigned for a chronic or recurrent pulmonary embolism. In addition, assign code **Z79.01, Long-term (current) use of anticoagulants,** along with code I27.82 to describe any associated long-term use of anticoagulant therapy. If the pulmonary embolism has completely resolved and the provider indicates history of pulmonary embolism, assign code **Z86.711, Personal history of pulmonary embolism.**

SADDLE EMBOLISM

Saddle emboli are one of the most severe and life-threatening forms of embolism. Patient survival depends on early diagnosis and treatment. The aorta is the most common site for a saddle embolus, but it can occur at other sites, such as the pulmonary artery at the level of the bifurcation of the pulmonary trunk and extending into the main right and left pulmonary arteries. Treatment can involve various methods, including intravenous (IV) heparin, IV tissue plasminogen activator (TPA), and/or thrombectomy. The following codes are assigned: saddle embolus of pulmonary artery with acute cor pulmonale (I26.02), saddle embolus of pulmonary artery without acute cor pulmonale (I26.92), saddle embolus of abdominal aorta (I74.01), and other arterial embolism and thrombosis of abdominal aorta (I74.09).

THROMBOSIS AND THROMBOPHLEBITIS OF VEINS OF EXTREMITIES

Deep vein thrombosis and thrombophlebitis are two distinct processes that can coexist. A patient can develop a thrombus with or without inflammation. A diagnosis of thrombosis of a vein indicates that a clot has formed; a diagnosis of thrombophlebitis indicates that the clot has become inflamed. When both thrombosis and thrombophlebitis of the lower extremities are documented, assign only the code from subcategories I82.4-, Acute embolism and thrombosis of deep veins of lower extremity; I82.5-, Chronic embolism and thrombosis of deep veins of lower extremity; and I82.81-, Embolism and thrombosis of superficial veins of lower extremities.

Thrombophlebitis of the extremities is classified according to the veins involved, as follows:

I80.0-	Superficial vessels of lower extremities
I80.1-	Femoral vein
I80.20-	Unspecified deep vessels of lower extremities
I80.21-	Iliac vein
I80.22-	Popliteal vein
I80.23-	Tibial vein
I80.29-	Other deep vessels of lower extremities
I80.3-	Lower extremities, unspecified
I80.8	Other
I80.9	Unspecified site

Deep vein thrombosis, also referred to as venous thromboembolism, is a blood clot in a major vein. DVT generally involves the veins of the lower extremity, but it can also occur in the veins of the upper extremity. With the use of catheters for venous access and cardiac devices, there is increased risk of developing DVT in the upper extremities, such as the axillary, subclavian, or

brachiocephalic veins. DVT can occur following orthopedic surgery, pelvic/abdominal surgery, or prolonged inactivity (e.g., long-distance travel, bed rest due to injury or illness, paralysis). Some individuals have a predisposition for developing blood clots due to an abnormality in their blood clotting system (e.g., factor V mutation, protein C or S deficiency, lupus).

Treatment involves anticoagulants to inhibit further development of blood clots or clot-dissolving drugs. In the hospital, heparin is usually administered intravenously. In some cases, a filter is placed in the vena cava to prevent emboli or clots from traveling to the heart and lungs. Following discharge, anticoagulant therapy is recommended for three to six months (or longer). High-risk patients may be maintained on anticoagulant therapy for an indefinite period.

Venous embolism and thrombosis can be of deep vessels or superficial vessels, and it can be acute or chronic, with recurrent episodes. Recurrent deep vein thrombosis can be prevented through prophylactic anticoagulant therapy, venous stasis prevention with gradient elastic stockings, and intermittent pneumatic compression of the legs. When DVT has completely resolved and the provider documentation indicates past history of DVT, assign code **Z86.718, Personal history of other venous thrombosis and embolism.**

ICD-10-CM classifies venous embolism and thrombosis to category I82, Other venous embolism and thrombosis, according to the veins involved, with the codes for veins of the extremities being further specified as acute or chronic, as follows:

I82.0	Budd-Chiari syndrome
I82.1	Thrombophlebitis migrans
I82.2-	Vena cava and other thoracic veins
I82.3	Renal vein
I82.4-	Deep veins of lower extremity (acute)
I82.5-	Deep veins of lower extremity (chronic)
I82.6-	Veins of upper extremity (acute)
I82.7-	Veins of upper extremity (chronic)
I82.a-	Axillary vein (acute and chronic)
I82.b-	Subclavian vein (acute and chronic)
I82.c-	Internal jugular vein (acute and chronic)
I82.81-	Superficial veins of lower extremities
I82.89-	Other specified veins (acute and chronic)
I82.9-	Unspecified veins

Code **Z79.01, Long-term (current) use of anticoagulants,** is reported along with codes in subcategories I82.5 and I82.7 to describe any associated long-term use of anticoagulant therapy.

Atheroembolism is separate and distinct from atherosclerosis, thrombosis, or embolism. Thrombosis and embolism involve true clots, whereas atheroembolism involves cholesterol crystals from atheromatous plaques from vessels like the aorta or the renal artery. Atheroembolism is most commonly associated with the extremities. Category I75 is used to report atheroembolism.

OTHER CIRCULATORY CONDITIONS

In general, the coding principles applicable throughout ICD-10-CM apply to other sections of the ICD-10-CM chapter on circulatory diseases, which are not discussed specifically in this handbook.

EXERCISE 28.7

Code the following diagnoses and procedures.

1. Bleeding third degree hemorrhoids	K64.2
Stasis ulcer, left lower extremity	I83.029
Hemorrhoidectomy	06BY0ZC
2. Chronic venous embolism and thrombosis	I82.B23
of subclavian veins on long-term Coumadin therapy	Z79.01
Chronic orthostatic hypotension	I95.1
3. Arteriosclerosis of legs with intermittent claudication	I70.213
4. Septic embolism pulmonary artery due to *Staphylococcus*	A41.01
Aureus sepsis	I26.90
Saphenous phlebitis, right leg	I80.01
5. Pulmonary hypertension	I27.2
6. Raynaud's syndrome with gangrene	I73.01
7. Esophageal varices, hemorrhagic	I85.01
8. Bleeding esophageal varices due to portal hypertension	K76.6
Ligation of esophageal varices (endoscopic)	I85.11
	06L34ZZ
9. Arteriosclerotic ulcer and gangrene of left	I70.262
lower leg	L97.929

10. Patient was admitted with acute headache and problems with vision; condition deteriorated rapidly, and patient died within four hours of admission; final diagnosis: ruptured berry aneurysm — I60.7

11. Dissecting aneurysm of thoracic aorta — I71.01
Excision of the aneurysm with anastomosis (open approach) — 02BW0ZZ

STATUS Z CODES

ICD-10-CM provides several Z codes to indicate that the patient has a health status related to the circulatory system, such as the following:

Z94.1	Heart transplant status
Z95.0	Presence of cardiac pacemaker
Z95.1	Presence of aortocoronary bypass graft
Z95.2	Presence of prosthetic heart valve
Z95.3	Presence of xenogenic heart valve
Z95.4	Presence of other heart-valve replacement
Z95.5	Presence of coronary angioplasty implant and graft
Z95.8	Presence of other cardiac and vascular implants and grafts
Z95.810	Presence of automatic (implantable) cardiac defibrillator
Z95.811	Presence of heart assist device
Z95.812	Presence of fully implantable artificial heart
Z95.818	Presence of other cardiac implants and grafts
Z95.82	Presence of other vascular implants and grafts
Z95.820	Peripheral vascular angioplasty status with implants and grafts
Z95.828	Presence of other vascular implants and grafts

These codes are assigned only as additional codes and are reportable only when the status affects the patient's care for a given episode.

PROCEDURES INVOLVING THE CIRCULATORY SYSTEM

Several complex diagnostic tests have been developed for evaluating a patient's circulatory status, and several intensive procedures are currently in use for treating diseases of the circulatory system. The coronary artery bypass, used for patients with severe blockage in the coronary arteries, has been augmented by less invasive procedures, such as angioplasty. Some of these tests and procedures are described briefly in this section.

Intravascular Imaging Procedures

A new imaging technique for diagnosing intravascular vessels is known as intravascular vessel imaging. This procedure utilizes a catheter-based ultrasound imaging method that allows viewing of the vessels from within. The codes for the intravascular imaging procedures are found in the Imaging Section; body system "upper arteries," "lower arteries," or "veins"; root type "Ultrasonography" and qualifier "intravascular," as shown in the example below:

Character 1 Section	Character 2 Body System	Character 3 Root Type	Character 4 Body Part	Character 5 Contrast	Character 6 Qualifier	Character 7 Qualifier
B	4	4	0	Z	Z	3
Imaging	Lower arteries	Ultrasonography	Abdominal aorta	None	None	Intravascular

Other examples of codes for intravascular imaging procedures follow.

B343ZZ3 Ultrasonography of right common carotid artery, intravascular
B344ZZ3 Ultrasonography of left common carotid artery, intravascular
B345ZZ3 Ultrasonography of bilateral common carotid arteries, intravascular
B340ZZ3 Ultrasonography of thoracic aorta, intravascular
B341ZZ3 Ultrasonography of right brachiocephalic-subclavian artery, intravascular
B34JZZ3 Ultrasonography of left upper extremity arteries, intravascular
B240ZZ3 Ultrasonography of single coronary artery, intravascular

Diagnostic Cardiac Catheterization

Cardiac catheterization is an invasive diagnostic procedure performed for diagnosing and assessing the severity of cardiovascular disease. The procedure includes recording intracardiac and intravascular pressures, recording tracings, obtaining blood for blood-gas testing, and measuring cardiac output. A number of other tests involve the insertion of cardiac catheters, but they are not classified as diagnostic catheterization unless a separate procedure with a report including the measurements listed in the preceding sentence has been documented.

ICD-10-PCS classifies cardiac catheterizations to the Measurement and Monitoring Section; "physiological systems" body system; function/device (character 6) "sampling and pressure"; and qualifier specifying whether it was a left heart, right heart, or bilateral catheterization, as shown below.

Character 1 Section	Character 2 Body System	Character 3 Root Type	Character 4 Body Part	Character 5 Approach	Character 6 Function/Device	Character 7 Qualifier
4	A	0	2	3	N	7
Measurement and monitoring	Physiological systems	Measurement	Cardiac	Percutaneous	Sampling and pressure	Left heart

Other examples of cardiac catheterization codes include:

4A023N8 Measurement of cardiac sampling and pressure, bilateral, percutaneous approach
4A023N6 Measurement of cardiac sampling and pressure, right heart, percutaneous approach
4A020N7 Measurement of cardiac sampling and pressure, left heart, open approach

Angiocardiography

Cardiac angiography is a diagnostic test ordinarily performed in conjunction with diagnostic cardiac catheterization. Ergovine provocation testing is often performed in association with coronary arteriograms to diagnose coronary spasm and is included in the code for the coronary arteriogram. Angiographies and arteriographies are classified in ICD-10-PCS in the Imaging Section; root type "Plain radiography" or "Fluoroscopy," depending on the imaging modality used; with the body part character identifying the vessel imaged and whether the contrast material used was high osmolar, low osmolar, or other contrast. For cardiac angiographies, ICD-10-PCS distinguishes in the body part character whether it is single or multiple coronary arteries and whether the procedure was performed on a bypass graft. For example:

B2120ZZ Fluoroscopy of single coronary artery bypass graft using high osmolar contrast
B211YZZ Fluoroscopy of multiple coronary arteries using other contrast
B2061ZZ Plain radiography of right and left heart using low osmolar contrast

Intraoperative Fluorescence Vascular Angiography

Intraoperative fluorescence vascular angiography is a new imaging technology that allows real-time evaluation of the coronary vasculature and cardiac chambers during coronary artery bypass graft (CABG) procedures. It is used to assess the quality of the vascular anastomoses and patency of the graft, with results that are similar to selective coronary arteriography and cardiac catheterization. This new imaging technique is accomplished in less time and without the use of potentially harmful contrast material. This procedure is classified in ICD-10-PCS similar to conventional angiographies with fluoroscopy but distinguished by the use of the qualifier "laser" in character 6 and the qualifier "intraoperative" in character 7. For example, compare these codes with the two fluoroscopy examples listed above under angiocardiography:

B212010 Fluoroscopy of single coronary artery bypass graft using high osmolar contrast, laser intraoperative
B211Y10 Fluoroscopy of multiple coronary arteries using other contrast, laser intraoperative

Intraoperative fluorescence vascular angiography (IFVA) can also be used in noncoronary applications, such as breast cancer surgery, pediatric micro and reconstructive surgery, and other types of tissue reconstruction. In addition, IFVA not only visualizes the coronary vasculature but also enables intraoperative visualization of blood perfusion to the heart muscle, allowing surgeons to successfully perform transmyocardial revascularization (TMR).

Electrophysiologic Stimulation and Recording Studies

Electrophysiologic stimulation and recording studies, commonly referred to as EP studies, are performed as part of the diagnosis and therapeutic management of patients with ventricular tachycardia or ventricular fibrillation, both forms of cardiac arrhythmia that carry a high risk of sudden death. Sometimes a bundle of His electrocardiography will be done as part of an EP study. The bundle of His electrocardiography is a test that measures electrical activity in a part of the heart that carries the signals that control the time between heartbeats (contractions).

EP studies are also performed for patients who have unexplained syncope and palpitation or supraventricular tachycardia. The procedure involves inserting a catheter—a narrow, flexible tube—attached to electricity monitoring electrodes, into a blood vessel, often through a site in the groin or neck, and winding the catheter wire up into the heart. After cardiac access is obtained either

percutaneously or via cutdown, specialized electrophysiologic catheter electrodes are inserted and guided into position under fluoroscopy. Once the catheter reaches the heart, electrodes at its tip gather data and a variety of electrical measurements are made. These data pinpoint the location of the faulty electrical site. During this "electrical mapping," the cardiac arrhythmia specialist, an electrophysiologist, may instigate, through pacing (the use of tiny electrical impulses), arrhythmias that are the crux of the problem.

Coding of invasive EP studies requires two codes: **4A023FZ, Measurement of cardiac rhythm, percutaneous approach,** and **3E063KZ, Introduction of other diagnostic substance into central artery, percutaneous approach.**

For noninvasive programmed electrical stimulation, assign code **4A02X4Z, Measurement of cardiac electrical activity, external approach.**

Implant of Automatic Defibrillator/Cardioverter

The automatic implantable cardioverter defibrillator (AICD) is an electronic device designed to detect and treat life-threatening tachyarrhythmias by means of countershocks. Patients receiving this therapy have usually had one or more episodes of life-threatening arrhythmias that cannot be controlled by other therapy.

A total cardioverter defibrillator system implant is usually performed as a single procedure. It includes the formation of a subcutaneous tissue pocket or an abdominal fascia pocket, implantation or replacement of the defibrillator with epicardial patches and any transvenous leads, intraoperative procedures for evaluation of the lead signal, defibrillator threshold measurements, and tests of the implanted device with induction of arrhythmia. During the surgery to implant the AICD, the device is tested by inducing ventricular fibrillation (VF). Shocks are delivered and normal sinus rhythm is restored. A diagnosis of ventricular fibrillation is not coded when it is induced by the use of a defibrillator (shocking) to make sure the AICD recognizes the VF because the arrhythmia is being induced to check the functioning of the device.

The implant is sometimes performed in two stages, however, with the leads implanted first and the generator implanted on a subsequent day during the same hospital admission.

Coding of the insertion of an AICD requires multiple codes, as follows:

1. A code for the insertion of the defibrillator generator into the subcutaneous pocket either into the chest or the abdomen, using either an open approach or a percutaneous approach. Examples of codes:

0JH608Z	Insertion of defibrillator generator into chest subcutaneous tissue and fascia, open approach
0JH838Z	Insertion of defibrillator generator into abdomen subcutaneous tissue and fascia, percutaneous approach

2. A code for the insertion of the defibrillator lead(s). There are multiple possible codes depending on whether the lead is inserted into the right atrium, left atrium, right ventricle, or left ventricle. There are also different codes based on whether the leads were inserted using the open or percutaneous approach. Examples of codes follow.

02H60KZ	Insertion of defibrillator lead into right atrium, open approach
02H73KZ	Insertion of defibrillator lead into left atrium, percutaneous approach
02HK4KZ	Insertion of defibrillator lead into right ventricle, percutaneous endoscopic approach

3. Any extracorporeal circulation (continuous cardiac output) (5A1221Z) or any other concomitant surgical procedure should also be coded.

There are two codes for the revision or relocation of a cardiac device pocket depending on whether an open or percutaneous approach is used:

0JWT0PZ	Revision of cardiac rhythm related device in trunk subcutaneous tissue and fascia, open approach, or
0JWT3PZ	Revision of cardiac rhythm related device in trunk subcutaneous tissue and fascia, percutaneous approach

These codes may be used for the creation of a pocket for a loop recorder or pocket for an implantable, patient-activated cardiac event recorder. Insertion and relocation of both devices are included in these codes.

When a patient is admitted for replacement or adjustment of an automatic cardioverter/defibrillator, code **Z45.02, Encounter for adjustment and management of automatic implantable cardiac defibrillator,** is assigned as the principal diagnosis unless the procedure is being performed because of a mechanical complication, in which case a code from subcategory T82.1, Mechanical complication of cardiac electronic device, is assigned. When only the leads are replaced, code the removal of the old lead, and then the insertion of the new lead. When only the pulse generator is replaced, code the removal of the old generator as well as the insertion of the new generator. For example, if the pulse generator is removed from the chest and replaced with a new one, code both procedures using the open approach:

0JPT0PZ	Removal of cardiac rhythm related device from trunk subcutaneous tissue and fascia, open approach, and
0JH608Z	Insertion of defibrillator generator into chest subcutaneous tissue and fascia, open approach

Automatic implantable cardioverter/defibrillators sometimes require checking of the pacing thresholds or interrogation without arrythmia induction. This procedure is coded to **4B02XTZ, Measurement of cardiac defibrillator, external approach.** For example, a bedside check or interrogation of an AICD device is assigned to code 4B02XTZ.

Cardiac Pacemaker Therapy

Cardiac pacemaker therapy (figure 28.6) involves electrical control of the heart rate. ICD-10-PCS codes differentiate between the insertion of temporary pacemakers and the insertion of permanent pacemakers. In a temporary pacemaker insertion, leads are inserted via a catheter and attached to an external pulse generator. This type of pacemaker is generally used for an acutely ill patient until a permanent pacemaker can be inserted. Another type of temporary pacemaker is used intraoperatively or immediately following surgery, with the leads inserted into the myocardium in an already-opened chest. Temporary pacemaker procedures are classified to **5A1213Z, Performance of cardiac pacing, intermittent,** or **5A1223Z, Performance of cardiac pacing, continuous,** plus the appropriate code for the lead insertion.

A temporary transmyocardial pacemaker, in which a needle is inserted into the chest and into the myocardium with leads fed through the needle directly into the heart muscle and attached to an external pacing device, is sometimes used in an effort at cardiopulmonary resuscitation. This procedure is considered an integral part of cardiopulmonary resuscitation (5A2204Z), and no additional code is assigned.

At least two codes are required for the initial insertion of a permanent pacemaker. One code indicates the type of device, commonly called a pulse generator, which is coded to the Medical and Surgical Section; "subcutaneous tissue and fascia" body system; root operation "Insertion"; with character 6, device, providing information regarding the type of pacemaker (single chamber, single

chamber rate responsive, or dual chamber). Separate codes are used to report the insertion of the leads.

Pacemaker leads (electrodes) can be placed either transvenously into the inside of the heart or epicardially onto the outside of the heart. In order to insert a transvenous lead into the ventricle, an incision is made in the skin and the lead is passed into the subclavian vein, down the superior vena cava, across the right atrium, and into the right ventricle. When transvenous leads are used, the pacemaker device is ordinarily placed in a subcutaneous pocket in the upper chest wall. Code 0JWT0PZ or 0JWT3PZ is assigned for the revision or relocation of a pocket for a pacemaker, defibrillator, or other implanted cardiac device.

No incision into the chest cavity is needed for the insertion of an epicardial lead. The most common site for the pacemaker pocket when epicardial leads are used is the abdominal wall.

There are three types of pacemaker devices on the market—single chamber, single chamber rate responsive, and dual chamber—each of which has a unique ICD-10-PCS sixth-character value for its insertion. For example, for a single-chamber pacemaker inserted into a chest pocket using an open approach, code **0JH604Z, Insertion of single chamber pacemaker into chest subcutaneous tissue and fascia, open approach,** is assigned.

A single-chamber device uses a single lead; a dual-chamber device requires two leads, one in the atrium and one in the ventricle. It is important to be sure that the code for the lead insertion and the code for the pacemaker device are compatible. A rate-responsive device is one in which the pacing rate is determined by physiological variables other than the atrial rate. This type of pacemaker

FIGURE 28.6 Pacemaker Insertion

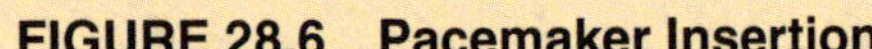

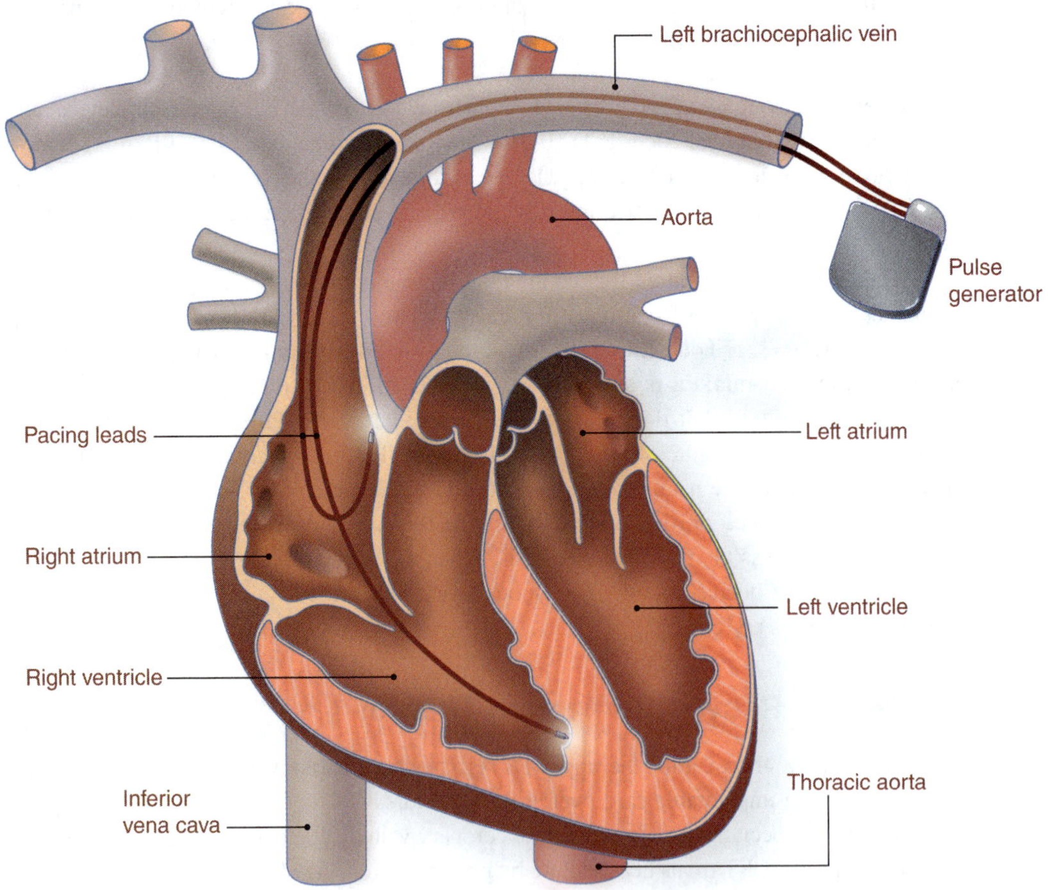

permits patients to lead a more normal life and is strongly preferred for a potentially active patient. Physicians use various terms for this ability to respond and in many cases mention only the device number in documenting an insertion. The coding department should work with the hospital operating room staff and/or physicians to identify the devices commonly used in the facility and how they might be consistently identified in the operative report.

For example, insertion of a dual-chamber permanent pacemaker with electrodes into the right atrium and right ventricle is coded to:

0JH606Z	Insertion of pacemaker, dual chamber into chest subcutaneous tissue and fascia, open approach
02H63JZ	Insertion of pacemaker lead into right atrium, percutaneous approach
02HK3JZ	Insertion of pacemaker lead into right ventricle, percutaneous approach

Sometimes pacemakers require replacement of the pulse generator, or there may be a need to upgrade from a single-chamber pacemaker to a dual-chamber pacemaker. ICD-10-PCS provides individual codes for each component of the procedure. For example, a replacement of the pulse generator alone requires codes for the removal of the old generator and insertion of the new generator. Similarly, if replacement of the existing leads is required, codes will be required for the removal of the old leads, as well as codes for the insertion of the new leads.

For example, if a single-chamber pacemaker is removed from the chest and replaced with a new one, code both procedures using the open approach:

0JPT0PZ	Removal of cardiac rhythm related device from trunk subcutaneous tissue and fascia, open approach, and
0JH604Z	Insertion of pacemaker, single chamber into chest subcutaneous tissue and fascia, open approach

When an existing pacemaker device is replaced with a new device, the type of device removed does not affect the removal code. ICD-10-PCS provides a single code (0JPT0PZ) for removal of cardiac rhythm–related device from the chest or abdomen—whether pacemaker or cardiac defibrillator. However, the codes for device insertion do provide information regarding the type of cardiac rhythm device.

When a patient is admitted for routine removal, replacement, or reprogramming of a cardiac pacemaker, code **Z45.010, Encounter for checking and testing of cardiac pacemaker pulse generator [battery],** or code **Z45.018, Encounter for adjustment and management of other part of cardiac pacemaker,** is assigned as the principal diagnosis. Reprogramming is a simple nonoperative procedure that does not require a procedure code. Physicians sometimes indicate that a patient is being admitted for battery replacement. This is something of a misnomer because pacemakers no longer use batteries and the whole device is actually replaced. When the pacemaker device is being replaced only because it is nearing the end of its expected life, code Z45.010 or Z45.018 is assigned as the principal diagnosis. When it is being replaced because of a mechanical complication of the device, a code from subcategory T82.1, Mechanical complication of cardiac electronic device, is assigned.

Cardiac Resynchronization Therapy

Cardiac resynchronization therapy (CRT) is a newer technology similar to conventional pacemaker therapy and implantable cardioverter defibrillators. CRT is different because it requires the implantation of a special electrode within the coronary vein to attach the device to the exterior wall of the left ventricle. CRT treats heart failure by providing strategic electrical stimulation to the right

atrium, right ventricle, and left ventricle of the heart to recoordinate ventricular contractions and improve cardiac output. CRT is also sometimes referred to as biventricular pacing.

ICD-10-PCS codes distinguish between the insertion of cardiac resynchronization pacemaker without internal cardiac defibrillator (CRT-P) and the insertion of cardiac resynchronization defibrillator (CRT-D). The codes differ in the values for the seventh-character qualifier, which distinguish between "cardiac resynchronization pacemaker pulse generator" and "cardiac resynchronization defibrillator pulse generator," as shown in the examples below, when these pulse generators are inserted using a percutaneous approach:

0JH637Z Insertion of cardiac resynchronization pacemaker pulse generator into chest subcutaneous tissue and fascia, percutaneous approach

0JH639Z Insertion of cardiac resynchronization defibrillator pulse generator into chest subcutaneous tissue and fascia, percutaneous approach

No additional codes are assigned for the creation of the pocket to hold the device, implantation of the device, or intraoperative procedures to evaluate lead signals. However, separate codes are required for the insertion of the transvenous leads.

For the CRT-P, codes are needed for the insertion of pacemaker leads into the right or left ventricle (e.g., **02HK3JZ, Insertion of pacemaker lead into right ventricle, percutaneous approach**). For the CRT-D, codes are needed for the insertion of defibrillator leads (e.g., **02HK3KZ, Insertion of defibrillator lead into right ventricle, percutaneous approach; 02HL3KZ, Insertion of defibrillator lead into left ventricle, percutaneous approach; 02H43KZ, Insertion of defibrillator lead into coronary vein, percutaneous approach**).

Over time, there may be a need to replace the lead into the left ventricular coronary venous system, replace the pacemaker pulse generator on a CRT-P, or replace the defibrillator pulse generator on a CRT-D. In all of these situations, code the removal and insertion of the replacement device separately. When the leads are repositioned only (not replaced), the code for the root operation "Revision" is assigned. For example, code **02WA3MZ, Revision of cardiac lead in heart, percutaneous approach,** is assigned for repositioning of the CRT-D or CRT-P lead only via a percutaneous approach.

Antimicrobial Envelope

The antimicrobial envelope is a large-pore surgical mesh envelope that holds a pacemaker, cardiac resynchronization device, or implantable cardioverter defibrillator (ICD). The surgical mesh contains antibacterial agents to help provide protection from microbial colonization of the device during and immediately after placement. Assign either code **3E0102A, Introduction of anti-infective envelope into subcutaneous tissue, open approach,** or code **3E0132A, Introduction of anti-infective envelope into subcutaneous tissue, percutaneous approach,** in conjunction with the cardiac implantable electronic device codes to provide information about devices used as part of the primary procedure.

Cardiac Contractility Modulation

The cardiac contractility modulation (CCM) system is a new treatment modality for patients with moderate to severe heart failure resulting from either ischemic or nonischemic cardiomyopathy. In cardiac contractility modulation, nonstimulatory impulses are delivered during the absolute refractory period to enhance cardiac function and contractility. The CCM system is dissimilar to a cardiac pacemaker because the signals do not initiate a new heartbeat; instead, they are intended to improve the strength of the heart.

The implantable pulse generator produces signals delivered to the heart via the pacemaker leads. Three leads are implanted in the heart: two leads are placed in the right ventricular septum, and a third lead is placed in the right atrium. The leads are connected to a pulse generator, and the generator is placed in a subcutaneous pectoral pocket. An external programmer allows medical personnel to customize the signal parameters according to the patient's specific needs. The charger allows the patient to recharge the battery of the pulse generator in the comfort of his or her home.

The implantation of the CCM system can occur alone, in the presence of an AICD, or in combination with implantation of both a CCM system and an AICD. Coding for the insertion of the CCM device is similar to the coding of pacemakers and cardiac resynchronization devices. A code is required for the insertion of the device, similar to the pacemaker, CRT-D, and CRT-P, but with a different seventh-character qualifier value for "contractility modulation device" and separate codes for the insertion of the leads. For example:

0JH63AZ	Insertion of contractility modulation device into chest subcutaneous tissue and fascia, percutaneous approach
02HK3MZ	Insertion of cardiac lead into right ventricle, percutaneous approach; assigned only once, even though two leads are inserted into the ventricle, because it does not meet the ICD-10-PCS guideline for reporting of multiple procedures
02H63MZ	Insertion of cardiac lead into right atrium, percutaneous approach

Percutaneous Mitral Valve Repair

The MitraClip® implant is a minimally invasive, closed chest, catheter-based approach for intracardiac repair of mitral regurgitation caused by valve pathology and/or left ventricular dysfunction. The procedure is performed on a beating heart and is an alternative to the open heart surgical approach. Interventional cardiologists can perform the procedure in the cardiac catheterization laboratory or in a hybrid operating suite under general anesthesia. The procedure does not require cardiopulmonary bypass. Insertion of the MitraClip® implant is coded to **02UG3JZ, Supplement mitral valve with synthetic substitute, percutaneous approach.**

Percutaneous Aortic and Pulmonary Valve Repair

Endovascular and transapical replacement of aortic valve and pulmonary valves is a catheter-based procedure that allows for implantation of a prosthetic valve within the diseased native valve without invasive surgery or cardiopulmonary bypass. There are two approaches to transcatheter aortic and pulmonary valve replacement: endovascular and transapical. A bioprosthetic valve is delivered by catheter across the diseased native valve through the femoral artery or vein (endovascular approach) or through the apex of the heart by means of a thoracotomy incision (transapical approach). In both approaches, a balloon valvuloplasty catheter is advanced through the aorta and placed over the diseased native aortic or pulmonary valve. A balloon valvuloplasty is then performed. The delivery catheter is placed over the native valve, and the new bioprosthetic valve is put in place, destroying the native valve underneath it. Endovascular or transapical replacement of the aortic or pulmonary valves is coded to the root operation "Replacement." For example:

02RF3JZ	Replacement of aortic valve with synthetic substitute, percutaneous approach
02RH3JH	Replacement of pulmonary valve with synthetic substitute, transapical, percutaneous approach

Percutaneous Balloon Valvuloplasty

Percutaneous balloon valvuloplasty (027H3ZZ) is a noninvasive treatment for pulmonary valve stenosis. It involves a balloon wedge catheter that is advanced via the femoral vein into the heart and across the stenotic valve. The balloon is then inflated by hand pressure. There is no need for general anesthesia, the hospital stay is short, and no scarring results from the procedure.

Percutaneous Transluminal Coronary Angioplasty

Percutaneous transluminal coronary angioplasty (PTCA) procedures are classified in the Medical and Surgical Section to the root operation "Dilation," percutaneous approach. Code selection is based on the number of coronary artery sites treated using the fourth-character, body part value to indicate coronary artery at one site, two sites, three sites, or four or more sites. Coronary arteries are classified by the number of distinct sites treated rather than the number of coronary arteries or the anatomic name of a coronary artery (e.g., left anterior descending).

When a thrombolytic agent is also administered, assign a separate code, for example, code **3E03317, Introduction of other thrombolytic into peripheral vein, percutaneous approach.**

Because reclosure often occurs following angioplasty, a stent is frequently inserted to prevent reclosure. Please refer to figure 28.7 for an illustration of angioplasty with stent insertion. In

FIGURE 28.7 Angioplasty with Stent Insertion

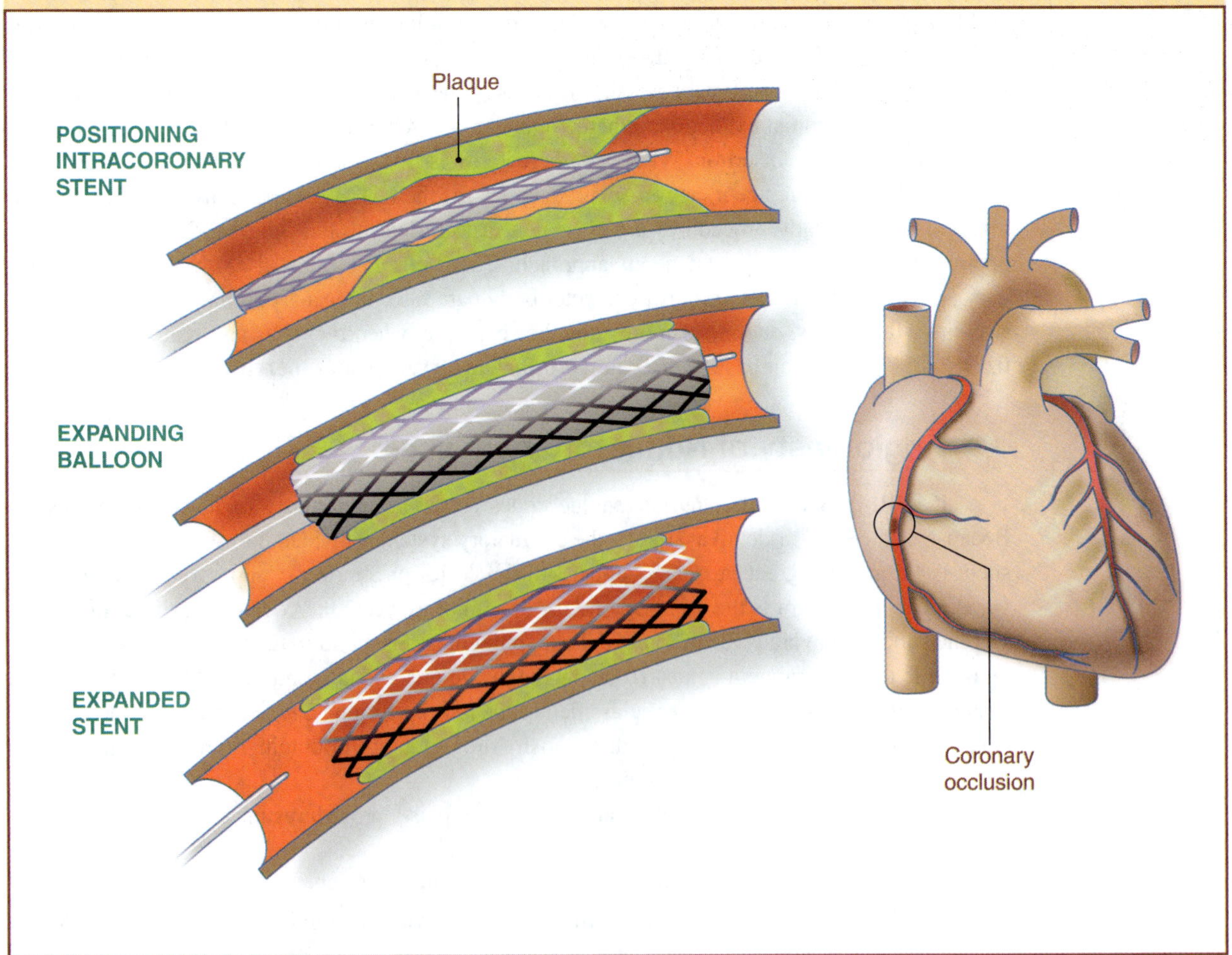

this procedure, a small, stainless steel mesh stent is inserted during angioplasty to prop open the blocked coronary arteries. After the balloon has been threaded into the coronary artery and inflated to squash plaque deposits against the vessel wall, the process is repeated with a second balloon carrying the stent. Expansion of the balloon pushes the stent against the artery wall, where it remains to maintain patency.

ICD-10-PCS provides different values for character 6, device, to identify whether a "drug-eluting intraluminal device (stent)," "intraluminal device (stent)," "radioactive intraluminal device," or no device was used. Note that a separate procedure code is coded for each artery dilated when the device value differs for each artery. For example, when PTCA of two coronary artery sites is performed, one with a drug-eluting stent and the other with a non-drug-eluting stent, code **027034Z, Dilation of coronary artery, one site with drug-eluting intraluminal device, percutaneous approach,** and **02703DZ, Dilation of coronary artery, one site with intraluminal device, percutaneous approach.**

ICD-10-PCS coronary dilation root operations provide a seventh-character qualifier to report when the procedure is performed at a vessel bifurcation. Use of this qualifier captures data regarding the procedural differences between interventional procedures on a straight vessel and a vessel bifurcation. Bifurcation lesions usually involve blockages of a main coronary vessel and an adjacent side vessel, resulting in a lesion that is more complex to treat.

Minor intimal tears often occur during angioplasty or the newer rotational atherectomy procedures; these are considered to be an unavoidable part of the procedure and are not classified as complications.

Transluminal coronary atherectomy is a minimally invasive catheter-based procedure that removes plaque from arteries. This procedure is effective in removing calcification due to plaque build-up and removing blockages in coronary arteries, allowing blood to circulate unobstructed to the heart muscle. Transluminal extraction atherectomy uses a device that cuts plaque off the vessel walls and is used to clear bypass grafts. The types of mechanical atherectomy are rotational, directional, and transluminal extraction. Atherectomy can be used instead of, or along with, angioplasty with or without stent insertion. When an atherectomy is performed along with a PTCA and infusion of a thrombolytic agent, assign separate codes for the PTCA, atherectomy, and thrombolytic infusion. Atherectomy procedures are classified in the Medical and Surgical Section to the root operation "Extirpation," percutaneous approach. Code selection is based on the number of coronary artery sites treated. The fourth-character body part value indicates coronary artery at one site, two sites, three sites, or four or more sites. For example, when two sites are treated, assign code **02C13ZZ, Extirpation of matter from coronary artery, two sites, percutaneous approach.**

Angioplasty of Noncoronary Vessels

ICD-10-PCS provides myriad unique codes to report angioplasty of noncoronary vessels. Because of the level of detail available, the circulatory system is divided into several body systems, such as "heart and great vessels," "upper arteries," "lower arteries," "upper veins," and "lower veins." The diaphragm is the dividing line for determining where the code is classified. For example, the subclavian vein is located above the diaphragm and is found in the "upper veins" body system, while the femoral vein is located below the diaphragm and is found in the "lower veins" body system. Angioplasty procedures are classified to the root operation "Dilation" and include different values for the device character 6 to distinguish "drug-eluting intraluminal device," "intraluminal device (non-drug eluting)," or no device.

Examples of codes for noncoronary vessel angioplasty procedures include:

027V3ZZ	Dilation of superior vena cava, percutaneous approach
047H3DZ	Dilation of right external iliac artery with intraluminal device, percutaneous approach

047P34Z	Dilation of right anterior tibial artery with drug-eluting intraluminal device, percutaneous approach
037J34Z	Dilation of left common carotid artery with drug-eluting intraluminal device, percutaneous approach
037G3ZZ	Dilation of intracranial artery, percutaneous approach

An atherectomy is a minimally invasive catheter-based procedure that can be performed on noncoronary vessels to remove plaque. To treat a blockage, a guide wire is advanced across the area of stenosis/occlusion, and an atherectomy catheter is advanced into the diseased arterial segment. On the tip of the catheter is either a high-speed rotating device (burr) or a sharp blade. The burr grinds the plaque into minute particles, whereas the blade shaves the plaque away. The plaque is ground up or suctioned out. ICD-10-PCS provides procedure codes for atherectomy of noncoronary vessels, such as the common carotid arteries, the internal and external carotid arteries, the vertebral arteries, and the other extracranial arteries. It classifies atherectomy to the root operation "Extirpation." Extirpation is defined as taking or cutting out solid matter from a body part. When an atherectomy is done along with an angioplasty, assign codes for both procedures. Examples of codes describing noncoronary atherectomy procedures include:

03CG3ZZ	Extirpation of matter from intracranial artery, percutaneous approach
03CH3ZZ	Extirpation of matter from right common carotid artery, percutaneous approach

If a thrombolytic agent is used, it should be assigned as an additional code, with the appropriate code from the Administration Section, root type "Introduction." For example:

3E03317	Introduction of other thrombolytic into peripheral vein, percutaneous approach
3E04317	Introduction of other thrombolytic into central vein, percutaneous approach
3E05317	Introduction of other thrombolytic into peripheral artery, percutaneous approach

Coronary Artery Bypass Graft

CABGs are performed to revascularize the myocardium when a blockage in a coronary artery limits the blood supply to the heart. The grafts bypass the obstructions in the coronary arteries. (See figure 28.8.)

Coronary circulation consists of two main arteries, right and left, each with several branches:

- Right coronary artery (RCA)
  —Right marginal
  —Right posterior descending (PDA)
- Left main coronary artery (LMCA)
  —Left anterior descending branch (LAD)
  —Diagonal
  —Septal
  —Circumflex (LCX)
  —Obtuse marginal (OM)
  —Posterior descending
  —Posterolateral

The aortocoronary artery bypass is the one most commonly used. It brings blood from the aorta into the obstructed coronary artery, bypassing the obstruction by means of a segment of the patient's own saphenous vein, nonautologous biological material, or occasionally a segment of the internal mammary artery.

Coronary artery procedures are classified by the number of distinct sites treated rather than the number of coronary arteries or the anatomic name of a coronary artery (e.g., left anterior descending). Coronary artery bypass procedures are coded differently from other bypass procedures. Rather than identifying the body part bypassed from, the body part identifies the number of coronary artery sites bypassed to, and the qualifier specifies the vessel bypassed from. For example, aortocoronary artery bypass of one site on the left anterior descending coronary artery and one site on the obtuse marginal coronary artery is classified in the body part axis of classification as two coronary artery sites, and the qualifier specifies the aorta as the body part bypassed from.

ICD-10-PCS also identifies the type of tissue used in the device character 6 as "autologous venous tissue," "autologous arterial tissue," "synthetic substitute," or "nonautologous tissue substitute."

Examples of aortocoronary bypass procedure codes follow.

021009W Bypass coronary artery, one site from aorta with autologous venous tissue, open approach

02100JW Bypass coronary artery, one site from aorta with synthetic substitute, open approach

02110KW Bypass coronary artery, two sites from aorta with nonautologous tissue substitute, open approach

FIGURE 28.8 Coronary Artery Bypass Graft

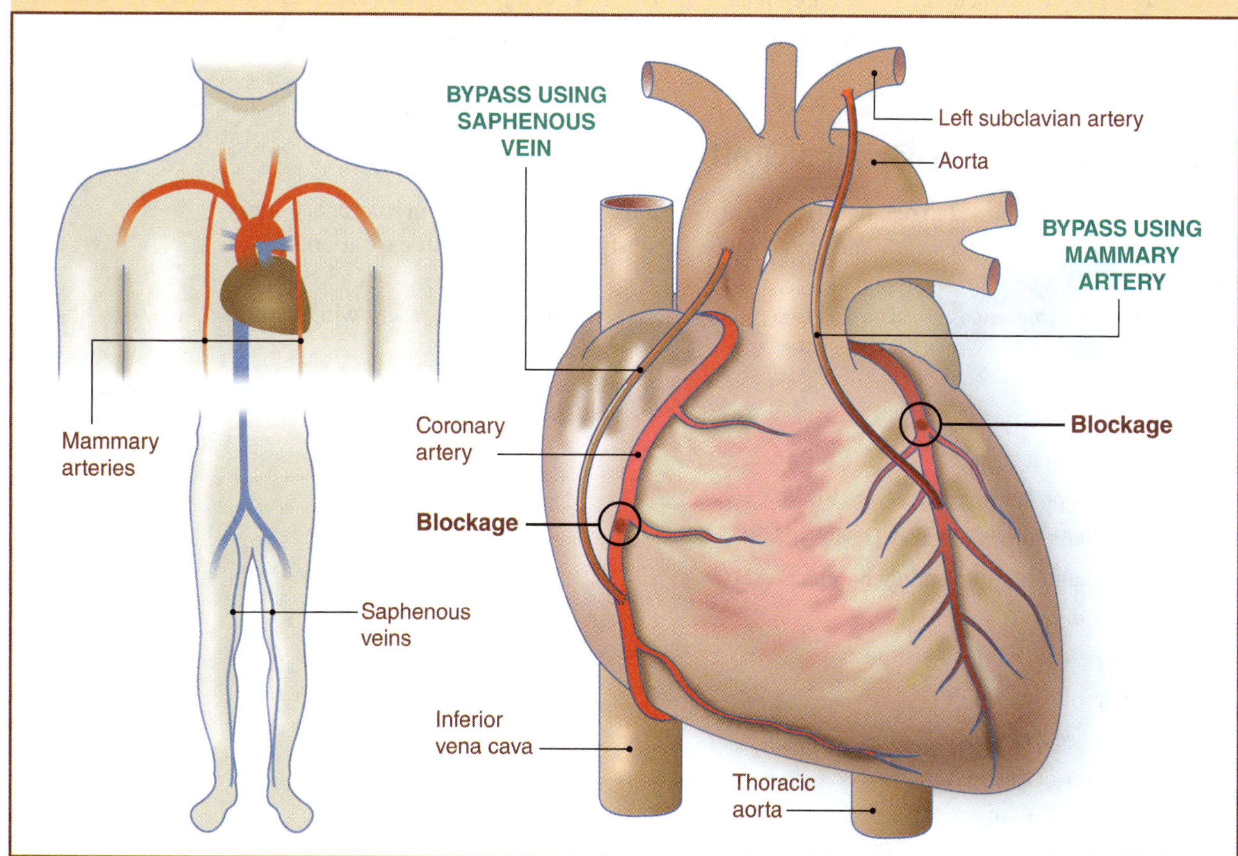

All coronary bypass procedures do not involve the aorta. The internal mammary-coronary artery bypass graft is accomplished by loosening the internal mammary artery from its normal position and using it as a conduit to bring blood from the subclavian artery to the occluded coronary artery. When coding internal mammary-coronary artery bypass grafts, the body part identifies the number of coronary artery sites bypassed to, and the qualifier specifies the vessel bypassed from—namely, the internal mammary artery. ICD-10-PCS also identifies the type of tissue used in the device character 6 as "autologous venous tissue," "autologous arterial tissue," "synthetic substitute," or "nonautologous tissue substitute."

Examples of internal mammary-coronary artery bypass procedure codes follow.

02100Z8 Bypass coronary artery, one site from right internal mammary, open approach

02110J9 Bypass coronary artery, two sites from left internal mammary with synthetic substitute, open approach

The internal mammary artery (IMA) is traditionally used as a pedicle (in situ) graft in coronary artery bypass surgery. This is reflected in ICD-10-PCS by the seventh-character qualifier. However, occasionally the length of the right IMA is not sufficient to reach the desired position on the target artery. In these situations length can be compensated for by excising the right IMA and using it as a free graft or by adding an additional conduit (graft extension). If the right IMA is excised and used as a free graft to bypass the diseased coronary artery, assign an additional procedure code for the excision of the right internal mammary artery as follows:

03B00ZZ Excision of right internal mammary artery, open approach

It is rare for only one coronary artery to be bypassed, and it is also fairly common to perform both an internal mammary-coronary artery bypass and an aortocoronary bypass at the same operative episode. The surgeon's brief statement of the operation performed does not always distinguish the types of bypasses involved, which makes it necessary for the coder to refer to the body of the operative report when the statement is not clear.

When multiple coronary artery sites are bypassed, a separate procedure is coded for each coronary artery site that uses a different device and/or qualifier. For example, aortocoronary artery bypass and internal mammary coronary artery bypass are coded separately.

Other arteries are also used to bypass an obstruction in the coronary artery. ICD-10-PCS distinguishes these procedures by the use of different values for character 7, qualifier, such as thoracic artery and abdominal artery. For example:

02130ZC Bypass coronary artery, four or more sites from thoracic artery, open approach

02130ZF Bypass coronary artery, four or more sites from abdominal artery, open approach

If an autograft is obtained from a different body part in order to complete the objective of the procedure, a separate procedure is coded. For example, coronary bypass with excision of saphenous vein graft, excision of saphenous vein, is coded separately.

An additional code should also be assigned for any use of extracorporeal circulation (continuous cardiac output) (5A1221Z). However, procedures such as hypothermia, cardioplegia, intraoperative pacing, and chest tube insertions are considered to be integral to bypass surgery; no separate codes are assigned.

In coding coronary artery bypass procedures, it is important to keep the following points in mind:

- The fact that a detached segment of the internal mammary artery is used as graft material instead of saphenous vein in performing an aortocoronary bypass does not make it an internal mammary-coronary artery bypass. The internal mammary-coronary artery bypass involves the use of the internal mammary itself as a still vascularized conduit for the blood supply and does not involve the aorta.
- When more than one coronary artery is involved in either type of graft, the anastomosis is sometimes carried out in a sequential manner, bypassing more than one artery. The mention of sequential anastomoses does not affect the code in any way.

The following examples may provide further assistance in coding coronary bypass grafts:

1. Coronary artery vascularization (via thoracotomy) is carried out with four grafts: the aorta to the diagonal branch of the left coronary and in sequential fashion to the obtuse marginal branch of the circumflex, the right coronary artery, and the left anterior descending coronary artery. This procedure involves only the aorta and the coronary arteries. Because four coronary arteries were bypassed, code **02130AW, Bypass coronary artery, four or more sites from aorta with autologous arterial tissue, open approach,** is assigned.
2. During an open procedure, grafts from the aorta to the coronary arteries are carried out by grafting the bifurcated left anterior descending system with a 1.5-millimeter excised section of the left internal mammary artery as a free graft. The first diagonal was then grafted side-to-side with a 4-millimeter section of the saphenous vein. The obtuse marginal was then grafted with a 4-millimeter section of the saphenous vein. The posterior descending was diffusely diseased and was grafted with a 4-millimeter section of the right greater saphenous vein. All four grafts bring blood from the aorta to the coronary arteries. Sections of both the right greater saphenous vein and the left internal mammary artery are used for this purpose. Because four arteries (LAD, diagonal, obtuse marginal, and posterior descending) were bypassed, code **021309W, Bypass coronary artery, four or more sites from aorta with autologous venous tissue, open approach,** code **03B10ZZ, Excision of left internal mammary artery, open approach,** and code **06BP0ZZ, Excision of right greater saphenous vein, open approach,** are assigned.
3. Bypass grafts are performed (via thoracotomy) by bringing the left internal mammary artery to the left anterior ascending; a right greater saphenous vein graft is then used to bring blood from the aorta to the obtuse marginal branch of the circumflex artery, to the diagonal artery, and to the proximal PDA. In this case, a single internal mammary-coronary artery bypass and three aortocoronary bypass grafts are placed (OM, diagonal, PDA). The codes assigned are **02100Z9, Bypass coronary artery, one site from left internal mammary, open approach; 06BP0ZZ, Excision of right greater saphenous vein, open approach;** and **021209W, Bypass coronary artery, three sites from aorta with autologous venous tissue, open approach.** The sequence of the codes is optional.
4. The left internal mammary artery is loosened and used to bypass the left anterior descending artery; grafts of the right great saphenous vein are bypassed to the posterior descending artery and to the obtuse marginal branch of the circumflex. In this case, three coronary arteries are bypassed, one by an internal mammary-coronary artery bypass and two by aortocoronary bypasses. The codes assigned are **02100Z9, Bypass coronary artery, one site from left internal mammary, open approach; 06BP0ZZ, Excision of right greater saphenous vein, open approach;** and **021109W, Bypass coronary artery, two sites from aorta with autologous venous tissue, open approach.**

Heart revascularization is also performed by other techniques. Transmyocardial revascularization is a procedure that uses a laser to bore holes through the myocardium to restore perfusion to areas of the heart where blood flow may be impaired due to diseased or clogged arteries. TMR is coded to the root operation "Repair" (restoring, to the extent possible, a body part to its normal anatomic structure and function). Although TMR does not restore the heart's anatomic structure, the procedure is performed to restore function to the heart. The procedure can be performed by open approach (02QA0ZZ, 02QB0ZZ, or 02QC0ZZ), percutaneous endoscopic approach (02QA4ZZ, 02QB4ZZ, or 02QC4ZZ), and percutaneous or endovascular procedures (02QA3ZZ, 02QB3ZZ, or 02QC3ZZ).

EXERCISE 28.8

Code the following diagnoses and procedures.

1.	A patient was admitted through the emergency department complaining of chest pain with radiation down the left arm increasing in severity over the past three hours. Initial impression was impending myocardial infarction, and the patient was taken directly to the surgical suite, where percutaneous transluminal angioplasty with insertion of coronary stent was carried out on the right coronary artery. Infarction was aborted, and the diagnosis was listed as acute coronary insufficiency.	I24.8 02703DZ
2.	Atherosclerosis of previous coronary artery bypass graft with unstable angina Right greater saphenous vein graft was used to bring blood from the aorta to the right coronary artery, the left coronary artery, and the left anterior descending artery. Intraoperative continuous pacing pacemaker was used during the procedure as well as extracorporeal circulatory assistance. Pacemaker leads were inserted in left atria and ventricle. Bypass	I25.700 021209W 06BP0ZZ 5A1221Z 5A1223Z 02H70JZ 02HL0JZ
3.	Occlusion of the right coronary artery Right and left diagnostic cardiac catheterization	I24.0 4A023N8

4. A patient with known native vessel coronary atherosclerosis and unstable angina underwent percutaneous balloon angioplasty carried out on three coronary arteries with vessel bifurcation
Insertion of two stents
Extracorporeal circulation (continuous cardiac output)
Performance
I25.110
02723D6
5A1221Z

5. A patient with sick sinus syndrome was admitted for initial insertion of dual-chamber pacemaker device into chest, percutaneous approach
Leads right ventricle and right atrium
I49.5
0JH636Z
02H63JZ
02HK3JZ

6. A patient was admitted for replacement of single-chamber pacemaker device because the battery was expected to fail within a short time; device was replaced with single-chamber, rate-responsive pacemaker device.
No leads needed to be replaced.
Z45.010
0JH635Z
0JPT3PZ

7. A patient was admitted for open revision of displaced and protruding pacemaker device with single-chamber, rate-responsive device
Complication, mechanical
T82.121A
0JWT0PZ

8. A patient with ventricular tachycardia underwent catheter-based invasive electrophysiological cardiac study (via femoral artery)
I47.2
4A023FZ
3E053KZ

Exclusion or Excision of the Left Atrial Appendage

Exclusion or excision of the left atrial appendage (LAA) is a component of most operations to treat atrial fibrillation (AF) and reduces late thromboemboli in patients with AF undergoing mitral valve surgery. Code **I51.3, Intracardiac thrombosis, not elsewhere classified,** is assigned for an atrial appendage thrombus. The clot occurs in the heart, not the coronary vessels. Coding of this procedure depends on the technique used, such as "Excision," "Destruction," or "Repair." For example:

02Q74ZZ   Left-sided thoracoscopic stapling of the left atrial appendage

Atrial Fibrillation and Flutter

Atrial fibrillation is a common type of arrhythmia characterized by rapid, irregular heartbeat, which presents with a wide range of symptoms and severity. Atrial fibrillation is classified as paroxysmal (I48.0), persistent (I48.1), permanent/chronic (I48.2), or unspecified (I48.91). Treatment of the various forms of the disorder is based on whether the duration of the arrhythmia is short, medium, long, or unknown; on whether the patient is symptomatic; on the severity of the symptoms; and on whether restoration to sinus rhythm is achievable. Because of the increased risk of thromboembolism and stroke, prevention of thrombus formation is a major goal of therapy.

Atrial flutter is the second most common atrial arrhythmia and is frequently associated with atrial fibrillation. Atrial flutter is caused by a reentrant rhythm in either the right or left atrium. Typically initiated by a premature electrical impulse arising in the atria, atrial flutter is propagated due to differences in refractory periods of atrial tissue. There are two types of atrial flutter: type I, or typical (I48.3), and type II, or atypical (I48.8). Unspecified atrial flutter is classified to I48.92.

Thoracoscopic and Thoracoscopically Assisted Ablation of Heart Tissue (Maze Procedure)

The maze procedure is a surgical treatment used for atrial fibrillation by creating lines of conduction block in the heart itself. The classic maze procedure is performed through an open chest approach, creating the lines with a scalpel by a carefully placed pattern of incisions in the heart tissue. Scar tissue (lesions) forms as the incisions heal, which creates the conduction block. There are variations called maze 1, maze 2, and maze 3, which represent different patterns of incisions. Through the years, various approaches for the maze procedure have been developed.

The open approach (02560ZZ, 02570ZZ) is the traditional method of surgery and is performed via a median sternotomy or thoracotomy. "Cut-and-sew" was the original open technique, involving incisions into the atrial tissue followed by reconstruction of the atria. Because of the difficulties and risks associated with multiple atrial incisions, more recently a series of linear ablations are being performed. There is a variety of energy sources used for ablation (e.g., radiofrequency, cryothermy, microwave, laser, ultrasound). The energy source is delivered via a probe or a clamp instrument and can be applied at strategic locations within the heart or on the heart's surface. The creation of the incisions/ablation lines can be directly visualized with the open approach.

Endovascular (percutaneous) approaches (02563ZZ, 02573ZZ) through peripherally inserted cardiac catheters have also been developed. Endovascular ablations have been very effective in the treatment of arrhythmias, including atrial fibrillation and atrial flutter, resulting from a single abnormal source (i.e., ectopic focus) of electrical stimulation on the right side of the heart.

The thoracoscopic approach (02564ZZ, 02574ZZ) is the newest technique. However, what is commonly referred to as the thoracoscopic approach should more accurately be referred to as "thoracoscopically assisted." The thoracoscope is used for illumination and visualization only, as the actual surgical ablation instruments are inserted via a (mini) thoracotomy or a subxiphoid incision rather than through the scope itself. Just recently, a total thoracoscopic approach has been established. As with the open approach, the thoracoscopically assisted and total thoracoscopic techniques require opening up the pericardium. Significant dissection of the pericardial sinuses and other vital structures is required in order to gain access to target areas of the heart. Additionally, as with the open technique, incisions can be made into the atria thoracoscopically, but most often linear ablations are done. For example:

- A patient with chronic persistent atrial fibrillation underwent a minimally invasive epicardial radiofrequency maze procedure via pericardioscopic assistance (convergent procedure). At surgery, the thorax is entered and a full-thickness ablation of right atrial tissue is accomplished. Code **02564ZZ, Destruction of right atrium, percutaneous endoscopic approach,** is assigned for the minimally invasive epicardial radiofrequency maze procedure.

Heart Assist Devices

Heart circulatory support systems can provide temporary left, right, or biventricular support for patients whose hearts have failed but have the potential for recovery. The device can also be used as a bridge for patients who are awaiting a heart transplant. It involves an electromechanically driven pump the size of a human heart implanted within the abdominal wall. This system provides circulatory support by taking over most of the workload of the left ventricle. Blood enters the pump through an inflow conduit connected to the left ventricle and is ejected through an outflow conduit into the body's arterial system.

The system is monitored by an electronic controller and powered by primary and reserve battery packs worn on a belt around the waist or carried in a shoulder bag. There is also a stationary system that consists of a small bedside monitor. The controller is connected to the implanted pump by a percutaneous lead (a small tube containing control and power wires) through the patient's skin.

The implantation of a total internal biventricular heart replacement system (02RK0JZ and 02RL0JZ) involves substantial removal of part or all of the biological heart. Both ventricles are resected, and the native heart is no longer intact. A ventriculectomy is included in this procedure, so it should not be coded separately. However, any associated procedures performed in conjunction with the placement of the total internal biventricular system, such as combined heart-lung transplantation or heart transplantation, should be reported.

ICD-10-PCS provides the following codes for the implantation, repair, and removal of implantable and nonimplantable single or biventricular external heart assist systems:

Synthetic substitute heart/ventricle

02RK0JZ	Replacement of right ventricle with synthetic substitute, open approach
02RL0JZ	Replacement of left ventricle with synthetic substitute, open approach
02WA0JZ	Revision of synthetic substitute in heart, open approach

Implantable heart assist system

02HA0QZ	Insertion of implantable heart assist system into heart, open approach
02HA3QZ	Insertion of implantable heart assist system into heart, percutaneous approach
02HA4QZ	Insertion of implantable heart assist system into heart, percutaneous endoscopic approach
02WA0QZ	Revision of implantable heart assist system in heart, open approach

02WA3QZ	Revision of implantable heart assist system in heart, percutaneous approach
02WA4QZ	Revision of implantable heart assist system in heart, percutaneous endoscopic approach
02PA0QZ	Removal of implantable heart assist system from heart, open approach
02PA3QZ	Removal of implantable heart assist system from heart, percutaneous approach
02PA4QZ	Removal of implantable heart assist system from heart, percutaneous endoscopic approach

External heart assist system into heart

02HA0RS	Insertion of external heart assist system into heart, open approach
02HA3RS	Insertion of external heart assist system into heart, percutaneous approach
02HA4RS	Insertion of external heart assist system into heart, percutaneous endoscopic approach
02WA0RZ	Revision of external heart assist system in heart, open approach
02WA3RZ	Revision of external heart assist system in heart, percutaneous approach
02WA4RZ	Revision of external heart assist system in heart, percutaneous endoscopic approach
02PA0RZ	Removal of external heart assist system from heart, open approach
02PA3RZ	Removal of external heart assist system from heart, percutaneous approach
02PA4RZ	Removal of external heart assist system from heart, percutaneous endoscopic approach

Implantable Infusion Pump and Vascular Access Devices

Implantable vascular access devices (VADs) and implantable infusion pumps are two distinct catheter systems, each of which can be used to deliver drug therapy. The main difference between them is that the implantable infusion pump is self-contained and completely implanted in the body, whereas the implantable vascular access device is not a pump but a port implanted in the body to provide easy access to the vascular system. These procedures are classified in ICD-10-PCS to the Medical and Surgical Section, "subcutaneous tissue and fascia" body system, root operation "Insertion," and the appropriate body part where the device is inserted. The difference in the code assignment is reflected in the selection of the device (character 6) for "infusion pump" (V) or "vascular access device" (X). For example:

0JHG0VZ	Insertion of infusion pump into right lower arm subcutaneous tissue and fascia, open approach
0JHG0XZ	Insertion of vascular access device into right lower arm subcutaneous tissue and fascia, open approach

The implantable infusion pump is surgically placed in the body, usually under general anesthesia. In certain instances, a catheter is attached to the pump and inserted into an artery for direct infusion of a drug; in such cases, the code for the insertion of the infusion device into the artery (e.g., code **03HY03Z, Insertion of infusion device into upper artery, open approach**) is also assigned. The pump is used to deliver intra-arterial drugs such as chemotherapeutic agents for patients with primary hepatomas or colon cancer with metastasis to the liver, as well as to deliver pain medication for terminal cancer patients. The pump allows the patient greater flexibility and freedom of movement while receiving treatment and also permits treatment on an outpatient basis once the pump has been inserted.

The use of an infusion pump that remains outside the body and infuses medication through a subcutaneous or venous needle is not coded. Only the procedure for placing a venous needle or catheter is coded. The application of this device includes the insertion of a permanent catheter.

An implantable VAD is a sterile catheter system implanted subcutaneously under local anesthesia and used for multiple purposes, such as infusion of total parenteral nutrition and bolus injections of medication. The device is placed in central veins, such as the subclavian, rather than a peripheral vein. VADs are designed to provide repeated access to the vascular system without the trauma or complications of multiple venipunctures. The devices can be left in place for weeks or months, as opposed to days, and are generally placed in patients who require long-term access for chemotherapy, nutrition, or blood withdrawal.

Simple venous catheters are sterile catheter systems that provide repeated access to the vascular system for procedures such as blood withdrawal and medication or fluid administration. The catheter is inserted into a peripheral vein, such as the cephalic vein, by puncturing the skin and then taping the catheter in place. These catheters remain in place for a much shorter period of time than do VADs. Examples of simple venous catheters (also called heparin locks) include Angiocaths, Abbott catheters, and Jelco catheters. For example, code **05HB03Z, Insertion of infusion device into right basilic vein, open approach,** is assigned for insertion of a simple catheter system into the basilic vein in the right arm. Code **0JPVX3Z, Removal of infusion device from upper extremity subcutaneous tissue and fascia, external approach,** is assigned for the removal of an infusion device from the upper extremity, while code **0JPVXXZ, Removal of vascular access device from upper extremity subcutaneous tissue and fascia, external approach,** is assigned for removal of a vascular access device from the upper extremity. Refer to figure 28.9 for a central venous catheter (CVC) and figure 28.10 for a peripherally inserted central catheter (PICC).

Selection of the body part value for insertion of vascular access devices as well as simple venous catheters is based on the site in which the catheter resides after the insertion procedure is completed, meaning the end placement of the device rather than the point of entry. For example, a peripherally inserted central catheter line (PICC) in the right arm with the tip ending in the superior vena cava is coded to **02HV33Z, Insertion of infusion device into superior vena cava, percutaneous approach.**

FIGURE 28.9 Central Venous Catheter (CVC)

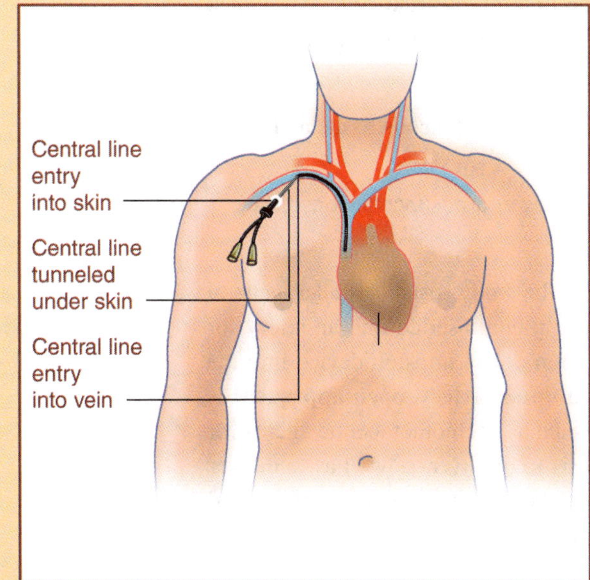

FIGURE 28.10 Peripherally Inserted Central Catheter (PICC)

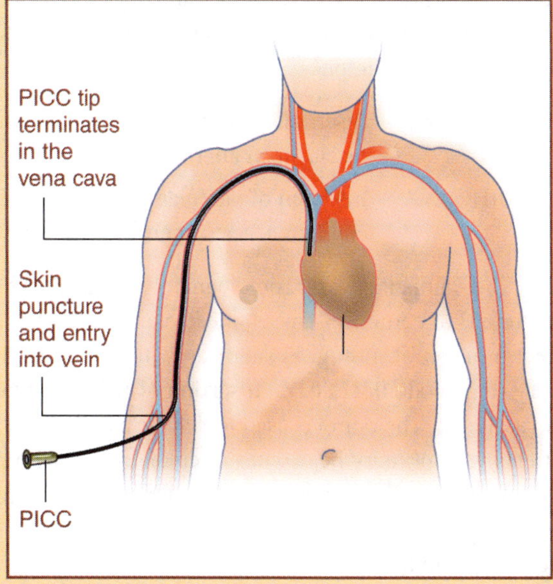

Implantable Hemodynamic Monitor

The implantable hemodynamic monitoring system allows clinicians to identify early signs of volume overload before signs and symptoms of heart failure become apparent. Clinicians can then adjust treatment to prevent acute decompensated heart failure and the need for hospital admission. The device consists of two key components. A lead with a pressure sensor is placed within the right ventricle at the right ventricular outflow tract. The other component is the monitoring device, which includes pressure-sensing circuitry with memory to process and collect the data obtained by the sensor. For example:

02HK00Z Insertion of pressure sensor monitoring device into right ventricle, open approach

0JH600Z Insertion of hemodynamic monitoring device into chest subcutaneous tissue and fascia, open approach

0JH800Z Insertion of hemodynamic monitoring device into abdomen subcutaneous tissue and fascia, percutaneous approach

Intravascular and Intra-Aneurysm Pressure Measurement

Measurement of intra-aneurysm sac pressure during endovascular repair of an abdominal or thoracic aortic aneurysm can help to detect and treat endoleaks during endoluminal grafting. This procedure is classified by ICD-10-PCS to the Medical and Surgical Section, root operation "Insertion," body part either "abdominal aorta" or "thoracic aorta," and pressure sensor device. For example, **02HW30Z, Insertion of pressure sensor monitoring device into thoracic aorta, percutaneous approach:**

Character 1 Section	Character 2 Body System	Character 3 Root Operation	Character 4 Body Part	Character 5 Approach	Character 6 Device	Character 7 Qualifier
0	2	H	W	3	0	Z
Medical and surgical	Heart and great vessels	Insertion	Thoracic aorta	Percutaneous	Monitoring device, pressure sensor	No qualifier

Intravascular pressure measurement of coronary arteries provides physiological assessment of intravascular lesions. The specialized guidewire-mounted pressure sensor measures pressure and flow and can be used during diagnostic cardiac catheterization to determine the significance of a blockage in a coronary artery. Pressure wire measurement can confirm therapeutic results in coronary vessel stenting, identify culprit vessels, assist in developing an individual therapeutic strategy, and provide step-by-step guidance during complex interventional procedures. This procedure is classified to the Measurement and Monitoring Section, "physiological systems" body system, root operation "Measurement," pressure function, coronary qualifier. A code example is **4A033BC, Measurement of arterial pressure, coronary, percutaneous approach:**

Character 1 Section	Character 2 Body System	Character 3 Operation	Character 4 Body System	Character 5 Approach	Character 6 Function/Device	Character 7 Qualifier
4	A	0	3	3	B	C
Measurement and monitoring	Physiological systems	Measurement	Arterial	Percutaneous	Pressure	Coronary

Any other diagnostic or therapeutic procedures performed in conjunction with intravascular pressure measurement of coronary arteries are coded separately.

Intravascular pressure measurement can be performed on other vessels, such as intrathoracic arteries (i.e., assessment of the aorta, aortic arch, and carotid arteries), pulmonary arteries, and peripheral arteries, including assessment of vessels of the arms and legs. Assign additional codes for any synchronous diagnostic or therapeutic procedures performed.

Implantation of Carotid Sinus Stimulation System

The baroreflex system helps to regulate function of the heart, kidneys, and peripheral vasculature to maintain an appropriate blood pressure. The carotid sinus baroreflex activation device is currently the only medical device used to treat refractory hypertension. It consists of an implantable pulse generator, bilateral carotid sinus leads, and a computer programming system. The pulse generator is placed in a subcutaneous pocket in the pectoral region below the collar bone. Electrodes are placed bilaterally on the carotid arteries, two main blood pressure control points, and the leads run under the skin and connect to the pulse generator. Placement of the leads is determined by intraoperative blood pressure responses to test activations. The programming system regulates the activation energy from the device to the leads and can be adjusted based on the needs of the patient.

When the device is activated, the programming system delivers activation energy through the leads to the carotid sinus. The baroreceptors of the carotid arteries send signals through neural pathways to the brain that there is a rise in blood pressure that needs to be corrected. The brain sends signals to other parts of the body to counteract the rise in blood pressure by modulating the nervous system and hormones to dilate blood vessels and allow blood to flow more freely, reduce the heart rate, and influence fluid handling by the kidneys. This results in reduced blood pressure and workload by the heart, improved circulation, and a more optimal neurohormonal balance.

Insertion of a complete system is coded by assigning separate codes for each of the following components of the surgery:

0JH60MZ	Insertion of the stimulator generator into a subcutaneous pocket in the chest
03HK3MZ	Insertion of stimulator lead into right internal carotid artery via percutaneous approach
03HL3MZ	Insertion of stimulator lead into left internal carotid artery via percutaneous approach

In the event that it becomes necessary to revise the leads or the pulse generator, ICD-10-PCS provides separate codes for these procedures as well.

For example:

- A patient who is status post implantation of a carotid sinus baroreflex activation device due to refractory hypertension is admitted to have the lead adjusted and repositioned (via percutaneous approach) within the left carotid sinus for better signal activation. Assign code **Z45.09, Encounter for adjustment and management of other cardiac device,** as the principal diagnosis. Assign code **I10, Essential (primary) hypertension,** as an additional diagnosis. Assign code **03WY3MZ, Revision of stimulator lead in upper artery, percutaneous approach,** for repositioning of the lead.

Implantation of Cardiomyostimulation System

Dynamic cardiomyoplasty is a fairly complicated new surgical technique performed using a two-step open procedure that involves elevating the latissimus dorsi muscle, then wrapping it around the heart. A stimulator similar to a pacemaker is implanted and connected to both the heart and the wrapped muscle. There are a number of components to the procedure, which are all coded separately, as follows:

- Transfer of the trunk muscle either left (0KXG0ZZ) or right (0KXF0ZZ)
- Resection of the rib, either left (0PT20ZZ) or right (0PT10ZZ)
- Insertion of cardiac lead into pericardium, open approach (02HN0MZ)

Heart Transplantation

Heart transplantation is carried out when the heart is failing and does not respond to therapies. The main reasons for heart transplants are cardiomyopathy, severe coronary artery disease, and congenital defects of the heart. Code **02YA0Z0, Transplantation of heart, allogeneic, open approach,** or **02YA0Z1, Transplantation of heart, syngeneic, open approach,** is used to report the transplantation of a heart from a donor. "Allogeneic" refers to transplant from a genetically similar, but not identical, donor; "syngeneic" refers to a transplant from a genetically identical or closely related donor. An insufficient number of organs is available for transplantation to meet the need. A patient may wait months for a transplant, and many patients do not live long enough to receive the organ.

Procedures on Aneurysms

An aneurysm of a vessel is an abnormal dilatation, causing the vessel to become enlarged and weakened, which can lead to rupture. In ICD-10-PCS, the selection of the appropriate root operation for aneurysm repair depends on the primary physical action performed to correct the aneurysm.

The open technique is the gold standard for abdominal aortic aneurysm repair. In this surgery, the aneurysm sac is cut open and repaired by the use of a long tubular (e.g., Dacron or polytetrafluoroethylene) graft. The graft is sutured to the aorta, connecting one end of the aorta at the site of the aneurysm to the other end of the aorta. If the aneurysm is repaired by cutting open the aneurysm and removing the affected section of artery and replacing it with a graft, the root operation is "Replacement." ICD-10-PCS provides distinct values for different types of grafts, such as autologous and nonautologous tissue substitutes, synthetic substitutes, and zooplastic tissue. The following codes are examples of open repair of abdominal aortic aneurysms:

04R007Z	Replacement of abdominal aorta with autologous tissue substitute, open approach
04R00JZ	Replacement of abdominal aorta with synthetic substitute, open approach
04R00KZ	Replacement of abdominal aorta with nonautologous tissue substitute, open approach
02RW08Z	Replacement of thoracic aorta with zooplastic tissue, open approach

Endovascular aneurysm repair is a minimally invasive procedure used to treat an aneurysm. In this type of repair, a stent graft is deployed under radiologic guidance via the femoral artery into the site of the aneurysm. The stent graft restricts the aneurysm from circulating blood, thus preventing its expansion and rupture. If the aneurysm is repaired by putting in a stent graft or other device into the lumen of the artery, the root operation is "Restriction" and the device is "intraluminal." If the aneurysm is repaired by wrapping or otherwise deploying material or a device (e.g., clip, sleeve, and so forth) on or around the outside of the artery, the root operation is "Restriction" and the device is "extraluminal."

The following codes are examples of procedures for endovascular repair of aneurysms:

04V93CZ	Restriction of left renal artery with extraluminal device, percutaneous approach
04V53DZ	Restriction of superior mesenteric artery with intraluminal device, percutaneous approach

At times, an intraoperative intra-aneurysm sac pressure monitoring procedure may be performed in conjunction with an endovascular repair, which may be coded separately along with the endosvascular repair. For example:

02VW3DZ	Restriction of thoracic aorta with intraluminal device, percutaneous approach
02HW30Z	Insertion of pressure sensor monitoring device into thoracic aorta, percutaneous approach

Endovascular embolization uses particulate agents, such as gelfoam, polyvinyl alcohol and spherical embolics, coils, liquid sclerosing agents (such as alcohol and tissue adhesives), and other types of embolic materials. It is important to distinguish between the root operations "Restriction" and "Occlusion" when the documentation refers to embolization.

Embolization procedures are always performed to occlude a vessel. The purpose of the procedure is to terminate blood flow out of the vessel. The selection of the appropriate root operation depends on how the procedure is being defined. For example, if the objective of the procedure is to obliterate the vessel (total occlusion), the root operation is "Occlusion." If only a partial occlusion is being done, the root operation is "Restriction."

For example:

- A patient has a percutaneous coil embolization of the right uterine artery; code **04LE3DT, Occlusion of right uterine artery with intraluminal device, percutaneous approach,** is assigned.

Endovascular implantation of a branching or fenestrated graft into the aorta is a new technology that has been developed as an endovascular repair option for patients who are not anatomical candidates for standard endovascular repair of abdominal aortic aneurysms (AAA). The branching or fenestrated endograft is a tubular fabric graft with supporting metal stents that feature custom-positioned holes (fenestrations) to ensure proper blood flow through the aorta and to the kidneys and nearby organs. Each fenestrated graft is customized for the individual aneurysm. Assign code **04V03DZ, Restriction of abdominal aorta with intraluminal device, percutaneous approach,** for this endovascular repair of AAA.

EXERCISE 28.9

Code the following diagnoses and procedures.

1. Second degree prolapsed hemorrhoids	K64.1
Hemorrhoidectomy by cryosurgery	065Y0ZC
2. Painful varicose veins, right lower leg	I83.811
Right greater saphenous ligation and stripping for varicosities, open	06DP0ZZ
3. Mitral stenosis and aortic insufficiency	I08.0
Atrial fibrillation	I48.91
Hypertension	I10
4. Abdominal aortic aneurysm	I71.4
Hypertensive cardiovascular disease essential	I11.9
Resection of abdominal aortic aneurysm with synthetic graft replacement, percutaneous endoscopic approach	04R04JZ
5. Acute myocardial infarction, anterior wall	I21.09
6. Renovascular hypertension secondary to	I77.3
fibromuscular hyperplasia, right renal artery	I15.0
Nuclear renal scan with Tc-99m	CT131ZZ
7. Congestive heart failure due to	I11.0
hypertensive heart disease	I50.9
8. Acute systolic congestive heart failure	I50.21
End-stage dilated cardiomyopathy	I42.0
Permanent cardiac pacemaker in place	T82.598A
Status	Z95.0
Percutaneous revision of external heart assist device due to exposed wire and device malfunction	02WA3RZ

9.	Cerebral occlusion, thrombotic with cerebral infarction Hypertensive cardiovascular disease	I63.30 I11.9
10.	Hypertension Chronic kidney disease	I12.9 N18.9
11.	Postoperative pulmonary artery infarction, initial encounter	T81.718A I26.99
12.	Hypertensive encephalopathy due to accelerated hypertension	I67.4 I10
13.	Percutaneous insertion of pacemaker leads (right ventricle and right atrium), insertion of dual-chamber pacemaker device in chest pocket (open)	02H63JZ 02HK3JZ 0JH606Z
14.	Arteriosclerosis of autologous vein bypass graft (four-vessel bypass graft with saphenous vein carried out two years ago)	I25.810 Z95.1
15.	Acute pulmonary edema with left ventricular failure	I50.1
16.	Cerebral infarction, acute, with thrombosis Residual hemiplegia, right, dominant side, and aphasia (at discharge) Essential hypertension	I63.30 G81.91 R47.01 I10
17.	Severe stenosis of left main coronary arteries in patient with no previous history of bypass surgery Aortocoronary bypass, left diagonal and left circumflex arteries with right greater saphenous vein graft, open Cardiopulmonary bypass (extracorporeal cardiac) Performance	I25.10 021109W 06BP0ZZ 5A1221Z

CHAPTER 29 Neoplasms

CHAPTER OVERVIEW

- Neoplastic diseases are classified in chapter 2 of ICD-10-CM.
- Neoplasms are categorized by two axes.
  - The first axis for coding is by behavior (malignant, benign, carcinoma in situ, uncertain behavior, and unspecified behavior).
  - The second axis for coding is by anatomical site.
- The morphology of tumor cells is studied for classifying a neoplasm by its tissue origin.
- Neoplastic diseases are indexed by morphological type and common terms.
- The Neoplasm Table lists anatomical sites alphabetically. It uses behavior type to indicate the correct code.
- There are two types of malignant neoplasms.
  - Solid neoplasms have a localized point of origin and are considered to be the primary neoplasm of the site. They often metastasize to secondary sites.
    - The statement "metastatic to" indicates that the site of a metastatic tumor is secondary, while "metastatic from" indicates a primary site.
    - When coding, refer to the morphology type in the Alphabetic Index.
  - Lymphatic and hematopoietic tumors often circulate through the bloodstream and lymphatic system.
    - These tumors do not spread to secondary sites. All sites to which they spread through circulation are considered primary.
    - Special coding requirements are in place for Hodgkin's disease and non-Hodgkin's lymphomas.
- Sometimes treatment can be a guide when selecting a principal diagnosis.
  - When the treatment is directed at the primary site, the malignancy of that site is often the principal diagnosis.
  - When it is directed at a secondary site, the malignancy of the primary site is an additional code.
  - Admission solely for chemotherapy treatment requires a Z code as the principal diagnosis.

LEARNING OUTCOMES

After studying this chapter you should be able to:

Explain the various classifications of neoplasms.

Locate codes for neoplastic diseases.

Code for malignant neoplasms (both solid and hematopoietic or lymphatic).

Code for the treatment of neoplastic diseases.

TERMS TO KNOW

Direct extension
the invasion of adjacent sites by a malignant neoplasm

Invasive
the extension of tumor cells to other adjacent sites

Metastasis
the resulting spread of invasive tumor cells

Neoplasm
a new or abnormal growth

REMEMBER . . .

Morphology codes are optional but are used in tumor registries and pathology indexes.

INTRODUCTION

A neoplasm is a new or abnormal growth. In the ICD-10-CM classification system, neoplastic disease is classified in categories C00 through D49. Certain benign neoplasms, such as prostatic adenomas, may be found in the specific body system chapters.

BEHAVIOR CLASSIFICATION

The first axis for coding neoplasms is behavior; the second axis is the anatomical site. ICD-10-CM classifies neoplasms into five behavior groups and a sixth for unspecified behavior:

C00–C75, C76–C96	Malignant
C7A–C7B, D3A	Neuroendocrine
D00–D09	Carcinoma in situ
D10–D36	Benign
D37–D48	Uncertain behavior
D49	Unspecified behavior

Malignant Neoplasms

Malignant neoplasms are tumor cells that extend beyond the primary site, attaching themselves to adjacent structures or spreading to distant sites. They are characterized by relentless growth and are difficult to cure. The term "invasive" is often used to describe the extension of the tumor cells to other adjacent sites. The resulting spread is called "metastasis."

Certain types of malignant neoplasms are noted for their invasive properties (for example, malignant melanoma of the skin) and usually require excision beyond the primary site because of their potential microinvasiveness. In such cases, a biopsy finding of malignancy on tissue removed during outpatient surgery may indicate the need for more extensive surgery on an inpatient basis. When such further surgery is performed, however, the pathology report may or may not indicate further malignancy. When no further malignancy is found, the physician ordinarily documents the diagnosis as a malignancy in accordance with the findings of the initial biopsy, because that condition is the reason for admission and the primary neoplasm may, in fact, require further treatment. In this situation, the diagnosis provided by the physician should be coded even though the current pathology report does not confirm the diagnosis. A copy of the original pathology report should be obtained and filed with the current medical record if at all possible.

Neuroendocrine Tumors

Neuroendocrine tumors (categories C7A–C7B, D3A) arise from endocrine or neuroendocrine cells scattered throughout the body. The most common sites are the bronchi, stomach, small intestine, appendix, and rectum. These tumors are commonly classified according to the presumed embryonic site of origin, such as the foregut (bronchi and stomach), midgut (small intestine and appendix), and hindgut (colon and rectum).

A carcinoid tumor is a tumor that develops from enterochromaffin cells. These cells produce hormones that normally are found in the small intestine, appendix, colon, rectum, bronchi, pancreas, ovaries, testes, bile ducts, liver, and other organs. Carcinoid tumors are capable of producing these same hormones, often in large quantities, and can cause carcinoid syndrome (E34.0). Carcinoid tumors can be found throughout the body, but the majority are found in the gastrointestinal tract. Approximately 25 percent of carcinoid tumors are found in the bronchial airways and the lung. In some cases, it may not be possible to locate the site of origin of the carcinoid tumors, although symptoms of carcinoid syndrome may be present. Carcinoid tumors can present as a

primary malignancy (category C7A), as a secondary or metastatic tumor (category C7B), or as a benign tumor (category D3A). Codes Z85.020, Z85.030, Z85.040, Z85.060, Z85.110, Z85.230, and Z85.520 are used to describe the history of a malignant neuroendocrine tumor that has been previously excised or eradicated with no further treatment.

When multiple endocrine neoplasia (MEN) syndrome is associated with malignant or benign neuroendocrine tumors, code also the MEN syndrome (E31.2-). However, this code is not assigned when the health record documentation does not support the condition. If there is an associated endocrine syndrome, assign the appropriate additional code, such as carcinoid syndrome (E34.0). For example:

C7A.092 + E31.21 + E34.0	Malignant carcinoid tumor of the stomach, Wermer's syndrome, and carcinoid syndrome

Merkel Cell Carcinoma

Merkel cell carcinoma, also called neuroendocrine carcinoma of the skin, arises from the uncontrolled growth of Merkel cells in the skin. It is a rare skin cancer and potentially life threatening; aggressive therapy may be needed. Merkel cell carcinoma does not have a distinctive appearance and usually develops on sun-exposed skin (e.g., head, neck, arms) as a painless, firm, flesh-colored to red or blue bump. It is diagnosed via skin biopsy. The following subcategories and codes are assigned for Merkel cell carcinoma:

C4A.0	Merkel cell carcinoma of lip
C4A.1-	Merkel cell carcinoma of eyelid, including canthus
C4A.2-	Merkel cell carcinoma of ear and external auricular canal
C4A.3-	Merkel cell carcinoma of other and unspecified parts of face
C4A.4	Merkel cell carcinoma of scalp and neck
C4A.5-	Merkel cell carcinoma of trunk
C4A.6-	Merkel cell carcinoma of upper limb, including shoulder
C4A.7-	Merkel cell carcinoma of lower limb, including hip
C4A.8	Merkel cell carcinoma of overlapping sites
C4A.9	Merkel cell carcinoma, unspecified

Malignant Neoplasms of Ectopic Tissue

Malignant neoplasms of ectopic tissue are coded to the site of origin mentioned in the documentation. For example, ectopic pancreatic malignant neoplasms involving the stomach are coded to **C25.9, Pancreas, unspecified.**

Benign Neoplasms

Benign neoplasms are not invasive and do not spread to either adjacent or distant sites. They may, however, cause local effects such as displacement, pressure on an adjacent structure, impingement on a nerve, or compression of a vessel and therefore require surgery. Uterine myomas, for example, may cause pressure on the urinary bladder, which results in urinary symptoms. Most benign tumors can be cured by total excision.

Carcinoma in Situ

Tumor cells in carcinoma described as in situ are undergoing malignant changes but are still confined to the point of origin without invasion of the surrounding normal tissue. Other terms that

describe carcinoma in situ include "intraepithelial," "noninfiltrating," "noninvasive," and "preinvasive" carcinoma. Severe cervical and vulvar dysplasia described as CIN III or VIN III are classified as carcinoma in situ. (See chapter 21 of this handbook for more information.)

Neoplasms of Uncertain Behavior

The ultimate behavior of certain neoplasms cannot be determined at the time they are discovered, and a firm distinction between benign and malignant tumor cells cannot be made. Certain benign tumors, for example, may be undergoing malignant transformation; as a result, continued study is necessary to arrive at a conclusive diagnosis.

Neurofibromatosis refers to a group of autosomal dominant genetic disorders that cause tumors to grow along the nerves. Code **Q85.00, Neurofibromatosis, unspecified,** is assigned for neurofibromatosis.

Schwannomas may occur along any nerve of the body, including spinal, cranial, and peripheral nerves, except on the vestibular nerve. As the tumors grow, they compress nerves and cause pain, numbness, tingling, weakness, and other neurological symptoms. Code **Q85.03, Schwannomatosis,** is assigned for this condition.

Neoplasms of Unspecified Behavior

Category D49 is provided for those situations in which neither the behavior nor the morphology of the neoplasm is specified in the diagnostic statement or elsewhere in the medical record. This usually occurs when a patient is transferred to another medical care facility for further diagnosis and possible treatment before diagnostic studies are completed, or when a patient is given a working diagnosis in an outpatient setting pending further study. Category D49 includes terms such as "growth," "neoplasm," "new growth," and "tumor" when the neoplasms are not otherwise specified. A code from category D49 would not be used for a neoplasm treated in an acute care facility because more definitive information should always be available.

It is important not to confuse neoplasms of unspecified behavior with those of uncertain behavior. The exception for coding neoplasm of unspecified behavior is when coding dark areas or spots of the retina, which are referred to as neoplasms or suspected melanoma. These spots are often difficult to biopsy and must be continually evaluated. Code **D49.81, Neoplasm of unspecified behavior, retina and choroid,** is assigned for this condition. Because a biopsy of the retina poses a risk to the eye and is only performed if the lesion extends, there is usually no tissue biopsy taken to confirm the diagnosis. Therefore, code D49.81 is appropriately assigned for this condition.

Unspecified Mass or Lesion

It is incorrect to select a code from category D49, Neoplasms of unspecified behavior, when only the terms "mass" or "lesion" are used. When coding diagnoses documented as mass or lesion of a particular site, and when that site is not listed under the main terms **Mass** or **Lesion,** the coder should follow the cross-references under the main term representing the documented diagnosis. If a final diagnosis is documented as "lump," and there is no Index entry for the affected organ or site under "lump," look up the main term **Mass** as directed by the "see" note under the main term **Lump.** If there is no Index entry for the specific site under **Mass,** look up the main term **Disease.** The Index directs the coder to see Disease of specified organ or site for **Mass,** specified organ NEC.

If a final diagnosis is documented as "lesion," and there is no Index entry for the specified organ or site under the main term **Lesion,** look up the main term **Disease.** The Index directs you to see Disease by site for **Lesion,** organ or site NEC.

EXERCISE 29.1

By referring to the following subcategories in the Tabular List, match the codes in the left column with the descriptions listed in the right column.

1. C18.4	Transverse colon	c	a.	Benign
2. D44.10	Adrenal gland	d	b.	Carcinoma in situ
3. C43.0	Lip	c	c.	Malignant
4. D02.1	Trachea	b	d.	Uncertain behavior
5. D49.4	Bladder	e	e.	Unspecified behavior
6. D10.6	Nasopharynx	a		
7. C7A.025	Sigmoid colon	c		

MORPHOLOGY CLASSIFICATION

Morphology of neoplasms refers to the form and structure of tumor cells and is studied in order to classify a neoplasm by its tissue of origin. The tissue of origin and the type of cells that make up a malignant neoplasm often determine the expected rate of growth, the severity of illness, and the type of treatment given. Metastatic neoplasms are identified at the metastatic site by their morphology, which is different from the normal tissue at that site but the same as that at the primary site.

A tumor registry is a cancer data system that provides follow-up on all cancer patients. A tumor registry documents and stores all major aspects of a patient's cancer history and treatment. The registry database includes demographics, medical history, diagnostic findings, primary site, metastasis, histology, stage of disease, treatments, recurrence, subsequent treatment, and end results. Coders may use the completed cancer staging form for coding purposes when it is authenticated by the attending physician. If staging classes are being documented in the hospital medical record, the coding staff should obtain copies of the current classifications for use in decoding the numerical/alphabetic designations.

EXERCISE 29.2

Mark the following statements either true or false.

1. Morphology of neoplasms refers to the study of the form and structure of the tissue and cells from which the neoplasm arises. T
2. Metastatic neoplasms can be identified by their morphology, which is identical to the morphology of the surrounding normal tissue and cells at the metastatic site. F
3. Coders may use the completed cancer staging form for coding purposes when it is authenticated by the attending physician. T

LOCATING CODES FOR NEOPLASTIC DISEASE

The first step in locating the code for a neoplasm is to refer to the main term for the morphological type in the Alphabetic Index of Diseases and Injuries and then to review the subentries. For some types, a specific diagnosis code is provided. For example, for a diagnosis of renal cell carcinoma, the Alphabetic Index lists the main term **Carcinoma** and the subterm "renal cell" as follows:

Carcinoma . . .
-renal cell C64.-

When the site is not listed as a subterm or when a specific code is not given in the Alphabetic Index, a cross-reference to the Neoplasm Table in volume 2 of the Index appears. Cross-references should be followed closely; the following entries indicate the help the coder can receive when the type of neoplasm is referenced in the Alphabetic Index:

Sarcoma . . .
-cerebellar C71.6
-embryonal—*see* Neoplasm, connective tissue, malignant
-Ewing's—*see* Neoplasm, bone, malignant

The Neoplasm Table (part of which is reproduced as table 29.1) lists anatomical sites alphabetically on the far left. (The indention levels have the same significance as those used elsewhere in the Alphabetic Index.) Columns to the right indicate the code for each behavior type for that site.

To use the Table, coders must first locate the anatomical site in the list, move across the page to the behavior type, and then select the appropriate code. For each site there are six possible code numbers according to whether the neoplasm in question is malignant, benign, in situ, of uncertain behavior, or of unspecified nature. The description of the neoplasm will often indicate which of the six columns is appropriate (e.g., malignant melanoma of skin, benign fibroadenoma of breast, carcinoma in situ of cervix uteri). Where such descriptors are not present, the remainder of the Index should be consulted, where guidance is given to the appropriate column for each morphological (histological) variety listed, such as Mesonephroma—*see* Neoplasm, malignant; Embryoma—*see also* Neoplasm, uncertain behavior; Bowen's disease—*see* Neoplasm, skin, in situ. However, the guidance in the Index can be overridden if one of the descriptors mentioned above is present; for example, malignant adenoma of colon is coded to C18.9 and not to D12.6, as the adjective "malignant" overrides the Index entry "Adenoma—*see also* Neoplasm, benign." Codes listed with a dash (-) following the code have a required fifth character for laterality. Codes from the Neoplasm Table should be verified in the Tabular List.

TABLE 29.1 Section of the Neoplasm Table in the Alphabetic Index of Diseases and Injuries

	Malignant Primary	Malignant Secondary	Ca in Situ	Benign	Uncertain Behavior	Unspecified Behavior
Neoplasm, neoplastic—*continued*						
-nostril	C30.0	C78.39	D02.3	D14.0	D38.5	D49.1
-nucleus pulposus	C41.2	C79.51	—	D16.6	D48.0	D49.2
-occipital						
--bone	C41.0	C79.51	—	D16.4-	D48.0	D49.2
--lobe or pole, brain	C71.4	C79.31	—	D33.0	D43.0	D49.6
-odontogenic—see Neoplasm, jaw bone						
-olfactory nerve or bulb	C72.2-	C79.49	—	D33.3	D43.3	D49.7
-olive (brain)	C71.7	C79.31	—	D33.1	D43.1	D49.6
-omentum	C48.1	C78.6	—	D20.1	D48.4	D49.0

EXERCISE 29.3

Assign diagnosis codes to the following diagnoses.

1. Bronchial adenoma — D38.1
2. Burkitt's lymphoma of intrapelvic lymph nodes — C83.76
3. Lipoma of head — D17.0
4. Hairy cell leukemia in remission — C91.41
5. Endometrial sarcoma — C54.1
6. Hodgkin's sarcoma — C81.90

BASIC TYPES OF MALIGNANT NEOPLASMS

There are two basic types of malignant neoplasms:

C00–C75, C76–C80	Solid
C81–C96	Hematopoietic and lymphatic

Solid tumors have a single, localized point of origin and are considered to be primary neoplasms of that site. Solid tumors tend to spread to adjacent or remote sites, with such sites classified as secondary or metastatic neoplasms. For example, a diagnosis of carcinoma of the lung with metastasis to the brain indicates that a primary neoplasm of the lung has metastasized to a secondary site in the brain.

Lymphatic and hematopoietic neoplasms arise in the reticuloendothelial and lymphatic systems and the blood-forming tissues. These neoplasms differ from solid malignant neoplasms in several ways, including the following:

- They may arise in a single site or in several sites simultaneously.
- Tumor cells often circulate in large numbers in the bloodstream and the lymphatic system rather than remaining confined to a single site.
- Spreading to other sites in the hematopoietic and lymphatic system is not considered to be secondary but is also classified as primary neoplasm.

Because of the differences between solid and hematopoietic-lymphatic diseases, this handbook deals with the two types of malignant neoplasms separately. Solid tumors are covered first, and then the discussion moves on to tumors that arise in the hematopoietic and lymphatic systems.

CODING OF SOLID MALIGNANT NEOPLASMS

A solid malignant neoplasm may spread from its site of origin by either direct extension or metastasis. Direct extension is the invasion of adjacent sites; "metastasis" refers to the spread to distant sites and the establishment of a new center of malignancy. ICD-10-CM does not make a distinction between these two types of extension. The terms "metastatic" and "secondary" are generally used interchangeably.

Overlapping Sites

When a primary malignant neoplasm overlaps two or more contiguous (next to each other) sites, it is classified to the subcategory/code ".8," signifying "overlapping lesion," unless the combination is specifically indexed elsewhere. For example, ICD-10-CM provides the following codes for certain malignant neoplasms whose stated sites overlap two or more boundaries:

C00.8	Neoplasm of overlapping sites of the lip whose point of origin cannot be assigned to any other code within category C00
C16.8	Neoplasm of stomach whose point of origin cannot be assigned to any other code within category C16
C34.80	Neoplasm of overlapping sites of lung, bronchus, and trachea whose point of origin cannot be assigned to any other code within category C34

When there are multiple neoplasms of the same site that are not contiguous, such as tumors in different quadrants of the same breast, codes for each site should be assigned.

EXERCISE 29.4

Code the following diagnoses.

1. Carcinoma of upper and middle third of esophagus C15.8
2. Carcinoma of oral cavity and pharynx C14.8
3. Adenocarcinoma of rectum and anus C21.8

Malignancy in Two or More Noncontiguous Sites

A patient may have more than one malignant tumor in the same organ. These tumors may represent different primary cancers or metastatic disease, depending on the site. When the documentation is unclear, the provider should be queried regarding the status of each tumor in order to select the correct codes.

When more than one primary cancer occurs in the same organ system, these are called synchronous primary cancers. This condition can occur in the lungs where the target organ, in this case the respiratory epithelium, is attacked/altered by the inciting agent (e.g., tobacco smoke). However, the physician must make that designation as to whether one of the tumors represents a second primary cancer or a metastasis. For example:

- A patient with stage IV non–small cell lung cancer of the left lower lobe is admitted with extensive peritoneal metastasis and liver metastasis. A CT scan of the lung shows a large tumor in the left lung base with diffuse extension to the right lung. When queried, the provider documents that the tumor had started in the left lung and metastasized to the right lung. Because the provider has clearly documented that the primary malignancy of the left lung had extended to the right lung, assign code **C34.32, Malignant neoplasm of lower lobe, left bronchus or lung,** as the principal diagnosis and code **C78.01, Secondary malignant neoplasm of right lung,** as a secondary diagnosis. In addition, assign codes **C78.6, Secondary malignant neoplasm of retroperitoneum and peritoneum,** and **C78.7, Secondary malignant neoplasm of liver and intrahepatic bile duct.**

Neoplasms Described as Metastatic

The terms "metastatic" and "metastasis" are often used ambiguously in describing neoplastic disease, sometimes meaning that the site named is primary and sometimes meaning that it is secondary. When the diagnostic statement is not clear in this regard, the coder should review the medical record for further information. When none is available, however, the following guidelines apply.

"Metastatic To"

The statement "metastatic to" indicates that the site mentioned is secondary. For example, a diagnosis of metastatic carcinoma to the lung is coded as secondary malignant neoplasm of the lung (C78.0-). A code for the primary neoplastic site should also be assigned when the primary neoplasm is still present; a history code from category Z85, Personal history of malignant neoplasm, should be assigned when the primary neoplasm has been excised or eradicated. The fourth character of category Z85 indicates the body system where the prior neoplasm occurred, and the fifth and sixth characters indicate the specific organ or site involved.

Ordinarily, no history code is assigned when the patient has had a prior benign or in-situ neoplasm or neoplasm of uncertain behavior. The exceptions are a few neoplasms that are included in subcategory Z86.0, as follows:

Z86.000	Personal history of in-situ neoplasm of breast
Z86.001	Personal history of in-situ neoplasm of cervix uteri
Z86.008	Personal history of in-situ neoplasm of other site
Z86.010	Personal history of colonic polyps
Z86.011	Personal history of benign neoplasm of the brain
Z86.012	Personal history of benign carcinoid tumor
Z86.018	Personal history of other benign neoplasm
Z86.03	Personal history of neoplasm of uncertain behavior

"Metastatic From"

The statement "metastatic from" indicates that the site mentioned is the primary site. For example, a diagnosis of metastatic carcinoma from the breast indicates that the breast is the primary site (C50.9-). A code for the metastatic site should also be assigned.

Multiple Metastatic Sites

When two or more sites are described as "metastatic" in the diagnostic statement, each of the stated sites should be coded as secondary or metastatic. A code should also be assigned for the primary site when this information is available; it should be coded C80.1 when it is not.

Single Metastatic Site

When only one site is described as metastatic without any further qualification and no more definitive information can be obtained by reviewing the medical record, the following steps should be followed:

1. Refer first to the morphology type in the Alphabetic Index and code to the primary condition of that site. For example, a diagnosis of metastatic renal cell carcinoma of the lung indicates that the primary site is the kidney and the secondary site is the lung. The correct coding for this is **C64.9, Malignant neoplasm of kidney, except renal pelvis, unspecified side,** and **C78.00, Secondary malignant neoplasm of lung, unspecified side.** When a specific site for the morphology type is not indicated in a code entry or is not indexed, assign the code for unspecified site within that anatomical site. For example, oat cell carcinoma is indexed to **C34.90, Malignant neoplasm of bronchus or lung, unspecified, unspecified side,** when no more specific site is stated.

2. When the morphology type is not stated or the only code that can be obtained is either C80.0 or C80.1, code as a primary malignant neoplasm unless the site is one of the following:
   - Bone
   - Brain
   - Diaphragm
   - Heart
   - Liver
   - Lymph nodes
   - Mediastinum
   - Meninges
   - Peritoneum
   - Pleura
   - Retroperitoneum
   - Spinal cord
   - Sites classifiable to C76

Malignant neoplasms of these sites are classified as secondary when not otherwise specified, except for neoplasm of the liver. ICD-10-CM provides code **C22.9, Malignant neoplasm of liver, not specified as primary or secondary,** for use in this situation.

Examples of coding by this two-step procedure include the following:

C34.90 + C79.9	Metastatic carcinoma of the lung, coded by step 2, with the primary site assigned to the lung: carcinoma of lung; secondary site not specified
C79.51 + C80.1	Metastatic carcinoma of bone, coded by step 2, with the primary site unknown and the bone as the secondary site: carcinoma, site unknown; secondary site bone

No Site Stated

Code **C80.0, Disseminated malignant neoplasm, unspecified,** is for use only in those cases where the patient has advanced metastatic disease and no known primary or secondary sites are specified. It should not be used in place of assigning codes for the primary site and all known secondary sites. Code **C80.1, Malignant (primary) neoplasm, unspecified,** equates to Cancer, unspecified. This code should only be used when no determination can be made as to the primary site of a malignancy. This code should rarely be used in the inpatient setting. Code **C79.9, Secondary malignant neoplasm of unspecified site,** is assigned when no site is identified for the secondary neoplasm.

When no site is indicated in the diagnostic statement but the morphology type is qualified as metastatic, the code provided for that morphological type is assigned for the primary diagnosis along with an additional code for secondary neoplasm of unspecified site. For example, a diagnosis of metastatic apocrine adenocarcinoma with no site specified is coded as a primary malignant neoplasm of the skin, site unspecified (C44.99). An additional code of C79.9 is assigned for the secondary neoplasm. Code C44.99 is obtained by referring to the following main term and subterms in volume 2:

Adenocarcinoma . . .
-apocrine . . .
--unspecified site C44.99

EXERCISE 29.5

Code the following diagnoses.

	Diagnosis	Code
1.	Metastatic carcinoma of right lung	C34.91 C79.9
2.	Metastatic carcinoma to brain	C79.31 C80.1
3.	Metastatic carcinoma from prostate to pelvic bone Previous prostatectomy with no recurrence at primary site History	C79.51 Z85.46
4.	Metastatic carcinoma to brain from lung Previous resection of lung with no recurrence at primary site History	C79.31 Z85.118
5.	Metastatic carcinoma from prostate to pelvic bone	C61 C79.51
6.	Metastatic carcinoma of brain and lung	C79.31 C78.00 C80.1
7.	Metastatic carcinoma of pancreas and omentum	C78.89 C78.6 C80.1

8.	Metastatic adenocarcinoma of transverse colon	C18.4 C79.9
9.	Metastatic carcinoma of bronchus	C34.90 C79.9
10.	Metastatic carcinoma of spinal cord	C79.49 C80.1
11.	Metastatic carcinoma of femur	C79.51 C80.1
12.	Metastatic carcinoma of brain	C79.31 C80.1
13.	Metastatic serous papillary adenocarcinoma of bone	C56.9 C79.51
14.	Metastatic infiltrating duct cell carcinoma, female	C50.919 C79.9
15.	Metastatic odontogenic fibrosarcoma	C41.1 C79.9
16.	Chondroblastic osteosarcoma of limb with metastasis	C40.90 C79.9

CODING OF MALIGNANCIES OF HEMATOPOIETIC AND LYMPHATIC SYSTEMS

Unlike solid tumors, neoplasms that arise in lymphatic and hematopoietic tissues do not spread to secondary sites. Instead, malignant cells circulate and may occur in other sites within these tissues. These sites are considered to be primary neoplasms rather than secondary. Figure 29.1 shows the location of the lymph nodes in the body.

Neoplasms of Lymph Nodes or Glands

Primary malignant neoplasms of lymph nodes or glands are classified in categories C81 through C88, with a fourth character providing more specificity about the particular type of neoplasm and a fifth character indicating the nodes involved (except for categories C86 and C88, which do not specify site). If the neoplasm involves lymph nodes or glands of additional sites, the fifth character "8" is assigned to indicate that the malignancy now involves multiple sites. For example, code **C83.38, Diffuse large B-cell lymphoma, lymph nodes of multiple sites,** is assigned for a diagnosis of diffuse large B-cell lymphoma of intra-abdominal and intrathoracic lymph nodes; individual codes are not assigned.

When a solid tumor has spread to the lymph nodes, a code from category C77 is assigned. For example, adenocarcinoma of right female breast with metastasis to lymph nodes of the axilla is coded to **C50.911, Malignant neoplasm of unspecified site of right female breast,** and **C77.3, Secondary and unspecified malignant neoplasm of axilla and upper limb lymph nodes.** No code from categories C81 through C88 is assigned.

Lymphomas can be malignant or benign. Benign lymphomas are classified to code **D36.0, Benign neoplasm of lymph nodes.** Malignant lymphomas are located by referencing the subterms for the site under the main term **Lymphoma.** When a diagnostic statement of lymphoma does not match any subentry under **Lymphoma** in the Index, the coder may find that the pathology report indicates the neoplasm's behavior. However, the physician should be queried for confirmation before code selection.

Hodgkin's Lymphoma

Hodgkin's lymphoma (category C81) is a type of cancer originating from lymphocytes. Hodgkin's lymphoma is characterized by the orderly spread of disease from one lymph node group to another and by the development of systemic symptoms with advanced disease. Hodgkin's lymphoma may be treated with radiation therapy, chemotherapy, or hematopoietic stem cell transplantation. The choice of treatment depends on the age and sex of the patient and the stage, bulk, and histological subtype of the disease.

Category C81 provides a fourth-character subclassification to identify the pathologic subtype of Hodgkin's lymphoma and fifth characters to identify the lymph nodes affected (e.g., unspecified site; head, face, and neck; intrathoracic; intra-abdominal; axilla and upper limb; inguinal region and lower limb; intrapelvic; spleen; multiple sites; extranodal and solid organ sites). The pathologic subtype is identified in the following subcategories:

C81.0 Nodular lymphocyte predominant Hodgkin's lymphoma (a rare subtype)
C81.1 Nodular sclerosis classical Hodgkin's lymphoma (the most common subtype)
C81.2 Mixed cellularity classical Hodgkin's lymphoma (a common subtype, most often associated with Epstein-Barr virus infection)
C81.3 Lymphocytic depletion classical Hodgkin's lymphoma (a rare subtype)
C81.4 Lymphocyte-rich classical Hodgkin's lymphoma
C81.7 Other classical Hodgkin's lymphoma
C81.9 Hodgkin's lymphoma, unspecified

FIGURE 29.1 Lymphatic System

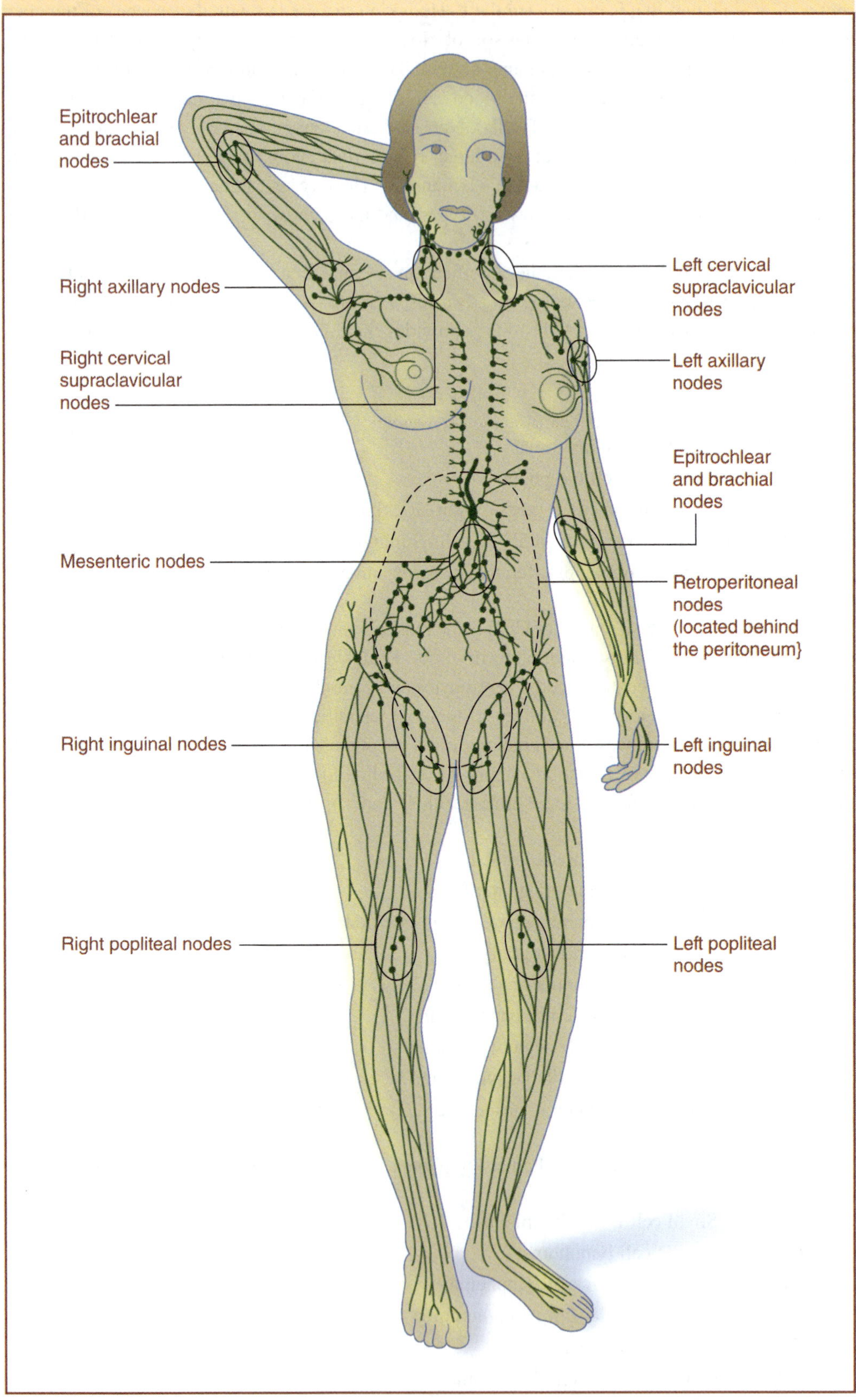
Epitrochlear
and brachial
nodes
Right axillary nodes
Right cervical
supraclavicular
nodes
Mesenteric nodes
Right inguinal nodes
Right popliteal nodes
Left cervical
supraclavicular
nodes
Left axillary
nodes
Epitrochlear
and brachial
nodes
Retroperitoneal
nodes
(located behind
the peritoneum}
Left inguinal
nodes
Left popliteal
nodes

Non-Hodgkin's Lymphomas

Non-Hodgkin's lymphomas are a heterogeneous group of malignant lymphomas that present a clinical picture that is broadly similar to Hodgkin's disease but with the absence of the giant Reed-Sternberg cells that are characteristic of Hodgkin's lymphoma. Lymphomas develop from the lymphoid components of the immune system. The main cell found in lymphoid tissue is the lymphocyte, an infection-fighting white blood cell, of which there are two main types: B lymphocytes (B-cells) and T lymphocytes (T-cells). Non-Hodgkin's lymphomas can occur at any age and are often marked by lymph nodes that are larger than normal and by fever and weight loss. There are many different types of non-Hodgkin's lymphoma. These types can be divided into aggressive (fast-growing) and indolent (slow-growing) types, and they can be formed from either B-cells or T-cells.

Throughout the past 40 years, the classification of lymphoma has changed considerably based on new insights provided by technological advances, as well as advances in the understanding of the clinical behavior of lymphoma. ICD-10-CM provides the following categories for non-Hodgkin's lymphomas:

C82 Follicular lymphoma
C83 Non-follicular lymphoma
C84 MatureT/NK-cell lymphomas
C85 Other and unspecified types of non-Hodgkin's lymphoma
C86 Other specified types of T/NK-cell lymphomas
C88 Malignant immunoproliferative diseases and certain other B-cell lymphomas

Follicular lymphoma (category C82) is the most common of the indolent non-Hodgkin's lymphomas, and the second most common form of non-Hodgkin's lymphomas overall. It is defined as a lymphoma of follicle center B-cells (centrocytes and centroblasts), which has at least a partially follicular pattern. Category C82 utilizes a dual-axis classification to allow the classification to accommodate the differences in terminology often encountered in medical records. Category C82 allows the classification of follicular lymphoma according to morphological grades (e.g., grade I) or the description of the follicle (e.g., diffuse follicle center), as follows:

C82.0- Follicular lymphoma grade I
C82.1- Follicular lymphoma grade II
C82.2- Follicular lymphoma grade III, unspecified
C82.3- Follicular lymphoma grade IIIa
C82.4- Follicular lymphoma grade IIIb
C82.5- Diffuse follicle center lymphoma
C82.6- Cutaneous follicle center lymphoma
C82.8- Other types of follicular lymphoma
C82.9- Follicular lymphoma, unspecified

ICD-10-CM classifies non-follicular lymphoma to category C83, as follows:

C83.0 Small cell B-cell lymphoma
C83.1 Mantle cell lymphoma
C83.3 Diffuse large B-cell lymphoma
C83.5 Lymphoblastic (diffuse) lymphoma
C83.7 Burkitt lymphoma
C83.8 Other non-follicular lymphoma
C83.9 Non-follicular (diffuse) lymphoma, unspecified

Similar to category C81, Hodgkin's lymphoma, categories C82 through C85 provide fifth characters to identify the lymph nodes affected (e.g., unspecified site; head, face, and neck; intra-thoracic; intra-abdominal; axilla and upper limb; inguinal region and lower limb; intrapelvic; spleen; multiple sites; extranodal and solid organ sites).

Multiple Myeloma, Other Immunoproliferative Neoplasms, and Leukemias

Multiple myeloma and malignant plasma cell neoplasms are classified in category C90, with a fourth character indicating the particular type of neoplasm. Leukemias are classified in categories C91 through C95, with the fourth character indicating either the stage of the disease (acute or chronic) or the type of leukemia (e.g., adult T-cell, prolymophocytic leukemia of T-cell type). For all codes in categories C90 through C95, a fifth character is used to indicate the status of the patient, as follows:

0 Not having achieved remission (failed remission)
1 In remission
2 In relapse

Fifth character "0" is assigned if the health record documentation does not indicate that the patient has achieved remission. When the provider documents that the malignancy is in remission, assign fifth character "1." This character is only assigned when the physician specifically describes the neoplasm as being in remission. If the patient experiences a recurrence and the provider documents "relapse," assign fifth character "2." A relapse or recurrence can occur any time during therapy or after completion of treatment, even months or years after remission.

It is important not to confuse "in remission" with personal history. The categories for leukemia, and category C90, Multiple myeloma, have codes indicating whether the leukemia has achieved remission. Relevant personal history codes are **Z85.6, Personal history of leukemia,** and **Z85.79, Personal history of other malignant neoplasms of lymphoid, hematopoietic and related tissues.** Personal history codes explain a patient's past medical condition that no longer exists and is not receiving treatment but has the potential for recurrence, and therefore may require continued monitoring. If the documentation is unclear as to whether the leukemia has achieved remission, the provider should be queried.

EXERCISE 29.6

Code the following diagnoses.

1. Aleukemic myeloid leukemia, in remission — C92.Z1
2. Reticulum cell sarcoma of the spleen — C83.37
3. Sarcoma, reticulum cell, intrathoracic — C83.32

4. Intrapelvic Hodgkin's granuloma C81.96

5. Chronic myeloid leukemia C92.10

6. Plasma cell leukemia C90.10

7. Carcinoma of lung with metastatic carcinoma of intrathoracic lymph nodes C34.90 C77.1

8. Mycosis fungoides of intrathoracic and intra-abdominal lymph nodes C84.08

9. Chlamydial lymphogranuloma A55

10. Adenolymphoma of left female breast D24.2

11. Diffuse large B-cell lymphoma intra-abdominal C83.33

12. Peripheral T-cell lymphoma neck C84.41

SEQUENCING OF CODES FOR NEOPLASTIC DISEASES

The basic rule for designating principal diagnoses is the same for neoplasms as for any other condition; that is, the principal diagnosis is the condition found after study to have occasioned the current admission or encounter. There is no guideline that indicates a code for malignancy takes precedence. Because the principal diagnosis is sometimes difficult to determine in a patient with a malignant neoplasm, however, the thrust of treatment can often be used as a guide to selecting the principal diagnosis.

Some neoplasms are functionally active in that they may affect the activity of endocrine glands. All neoplasms are classified in chapter 2 of ICD-10-CM, whether they are functionally active or not. The code for these primary neoplasms is assigned first, followed by a code from chapter 4 to identify the endocrine dysfunction associated with any neoplasm. For example:

C56.0 + E28.0 Hyperestrogenism due to carcinoma of right ovary
C56.0 + L68.0 Carcinoma of right ovary with hirsutism

Treatment Directed at Primary Site

When treatment is directed toward the primary site, the malignancy of that site is designated as the principal diagnosis, in which case the primary malignancy is coded as the principal diagnosis, followed by any metastatic sites. The only exception to this guideline is if a patient admission/encounter is solely for the administration of chemotherapy, immunotherapy, or radiation therapy, in which case the appropriate Z51.- code is assigned as the first-listed or principal diagnosis, and the diagnosis or problem for which the service is being performed is assigned as a secondary diagnosis. For example:

C18.7 + C78.7	Carcinoma of sigmoid colon with small metastatic nodules on the liver; sigmoid resection of the colon carried out
Z51.11 + C18.7	Carcinoma of sigmoid colon with prior resection; admitted for chemotherapy

Sometimes two primary sites are present; in this case, each is coded as a primary neoplasm. When treatment is directed primarily toward one site, the neoplasm of that site should be designated as the principal diagnosis. When treatment is directed equally toward both, either may be designated as the principal diagnosis.

Occasionally, a patient admitted for surgery to correct a nonneoplastic condition has a pathology report indicating that a microscopic focus of malignancy is also present. In this situation, the condition that occasioned the admission remains the principal diagnosis, with an additional code assigned for the malignancy. For example:

- A patient with severe urinary retention due to hypertrophy of the prostate is admitted for prostatectomy. Transurethral resection of the prostate is carried out, and the patient is discharged with a diagnosis of benign hypertrophy of the prostate. When the pathology report is received, this diagnosis is confirmed, but a microscopic focus of adenocarcinoma is also identified. Code **N40.1, Enlarged prostate with lower urinary tract symptoms,** is assigned as the principal diagnosis, with codes **C61, Malignant neoplasm of prostate,** and **R33.8, Other retention of urine,** as additional diagnoses.
- A patient is admitted for treatment of endometriosis of the uterus, and a total abdominal hysterectomy is carried out. The pathology report confirms the endometriosis but indicates that carcinoma in situ of the cervix is also present. In this case, the endometriosis is the reason for admission and remains the principal diagnosis. An additional code is assigned for the cervical neoplasm.

Treatment Directed at Secondary Site

When a patient is admitted because of a primary neoplasm with metastasis and treatment is directed solely toward the secondary site, the secondary site is designated as the principal diagnosis even though the primary malignancy is still present. A code for the primary malignancy is assigned as an additional diagnosis.

When a patient is admitted because of a primary neoplasm with metastasis and treatment is directed equally toward the primary and secondary sites, the primary malignancy should be designated the principal diagnosis, with an additional code assigned to the secondary neoplasm.

Admission for Complications Associated with a Malignant Neoplasm

Patients with malignant neoplasms often develop complications due to either the malignancy itself or the therapy that they have received. When admission is primarily for treatment of the complication, the complication is coded first, followed by the appropriate code(s) for the neoplasm.

The exception to this guideline is anemia. When the admission/encounter is for management of an anemia associated with the malignancy, and the treatment is only for anemia, the appropriate code for the malignancy is sequenced as the principal or first-listed diagnosis, followed by code **D63.0, Anemia in neoplastic disease.** When the admission/encounter is for management of an anemia associated with an adverse effect of the administration of chemotherapy or immunotherapy, and the only treatment is for the anemia, the anemia code is sequenced first, followed by the appropriate codes for the neoplasm and the adverse effect (T45.1x5-). For example:

- A patient with metastatic, non–small cell lung cancer of the right upper lobe develops anemia following chemotherapy. The patient presents to the oncologist for treatment of anemia of chemotherapy. Codes **D64.81, Anemia due to antineoplastic chemotherapy; C34.11, Malignant neoplasm of upper lobe, right bronchus or lung; C79.9, Secondary malignant neoplasm of unspecified site;** and **T45.1x5-, Adverse effect of antineoplastic and immunosuppressive drugs,** are assigned.

When the admission/encounter is for management of an anemia associated with an adverse effect of radiotherapy, the anemia code should be sequenced first, followed by the appropriate neoplasm code and code **Y84.2, Radiological procedure and radiotherapy as the cause of abnormal reaction of the patient, or of later complication, without mention of misadventure at the time of the procedure.** For example:

- A female patient with cancer of the right breast is seen for treatment of anemia due to radiation therapy. Code **D64.9, Anemia, unspecified,** is assigned first, followed by codes **C50.911, Malignant neoplasm of unspecified site of right female breast,** and **Y84.2, Radiological procedure and radiotherapy as the cause of abnormal reaction of the patient, or of later complication, without mention of misadventure at the time of the procedure.**

When the admission/encounter is for management of an anemia documented as "pancytopenia due to chemotherapy," code D61.810 is assigned for pancytopenia caused by cancer-fighting drugs. In cancer patients, pancytopenia usually occurs due to bone marrow suppression from chemotherapy. Bone marrow suppression (a decreased ability of the bone marrow to manufacture blood cells) is a common side effect of chemotherapy. For example:

- A female patient with cancer of the upper-outer quadrant of the left breast developed pancytopenia following chemotherapy. The patient presents to the oncologist for follow-up of the pancytopenia. The oncologist listed chemotherapy-induced pancytopenia in his diagnostic statement. Assign code **D61.810, Antineoplastic chemotherapy induced pancytopenia,** as the first-listed diagnosis. Assign code **C50.412, Malignant neoplasm of upper-outer quadrant of left female breast,** as an additional diagnosis.

When the admission/encounter is for management of dehydration due to the malignancy or the therapy or a combination of both, and only the dehydration is being treated (intravenous rehydration), the dehydration is sequenced first, followed by the code(s) for the malignancy.

Because the principal diagnosis may be difficult to determine, the focus of treatment can often be used as a guide. For example:

- A patient under treatment for prostate cancer is admitted for gross hematuria. The patient receives 15 units of blood, and bladder irrigation is started and continues until the urine is clear. Code **R31.0, Gross hematuria,** is assigned as principal diagnosis. Assign code **C61, Malignant neoplasm of prostate,** as an additional diagnosis. In this case, the patient was admitted and treated for gross hematuria. Treatment was not directed at the malignancy.

When the admission/encounter is for treatment of a complication resulting from a surgical procedure, designate the complication as the principal or first-listed diagnosis if treatment is directed at resolving the complication. For example:

- A male patient with known adenocarcinoma of the prostate has an outpatient orchiectomy. The physician states that the patient was admitted due to a postoperative complication of postprocedural urethral stricture. Assign code **N99.114, Postprocedural urethral stricture, male, unspecified,** as the principal diagnosis. Assign code **C61, Malignant neoplasm of prostate,** as an additional diagnosis.

Admission or Encounter Involving Administration of Radiotherapy, Immunotherapy, or Chemotherapy

When an episode of care involves the surgical removal of a neoplasm, primary or secondary site, followed by adjunct chemotherapy or radiation treatment during the same episode of care, the code for the neoplasm should be assigned as the first-listed or principal diagnosis.

When a patient admission/encounter is solely for the administration of chemotherapy, immunotherapy, or radiation therapy, assign code **Z51.0, Encounter for antineoplastic radiation therapy,** or **Z51.11, Encounter for antineoplastic chemotherapy,** or **Z51.12, Encounter for antineoplastic immunotherapy,** as the first-listed or principal diagnosis. When the patient receives more than one of these therapies during the same admission, more than one of these codes may be assigned, in any sequence. Because the patient is still under treatment for the malignancy, even though it may have been removed surgically, an additional code for the malignancy is assigned rather than a code from category Z85.

When a patient is admitted for the purpose of radiotherapy, immunotherapy, or chemotherapy and develops complications such as uncontrolled nausea and vomiting or dehydration, the principal or first-listed diagnosis code is **Z51.0, Encounter for antineoplastic radiation therapy,** or **Z51.11, Encounter for antineoplastic chemotherapy,** or **Z51.12, Encounter for antineoplastic immunotherapy,** followed by any codes for the complications.

Tumor lysis syndrome (TLS) is a group of serious, potentially life-threatening metabolic disturbances that can occur after antineoplastic therapy or as a result of radiation or corticosteroid therapy. It is often associated with leukemias and lymphomas but is also seen in other hematologic malignancies and solid tumors. Code **E88.3, Tumor lysis syndrome,** is assigned first, followed by code T45.1x5- to identify the cause when TLS is drug induced. For example:

- A child is diagnosed with acute myeloblastic leukemia and admitted for chemotherapy. Chemotherapy is administered into a peripheral vein and the provider diagnoses tumor lysis syndrome secondary to antineoplastic therapy. Code **Z51.11, Encounter for antineoplastic chemotherapy,** is assigned as the principal diagnosis. Codes **C92.00, Acute myeloblastic leukemia, not having achieved remission; E88.3, Tumor lysis syndrome**; and **T45.1x5A, Adverse effect of antineoplastic and immunosuppressive drugs, initial encounter,** are also assigned. Code **3E03305, Introduction of other antineoplastic into peripheral vein, percutaneous approach,** is assigned for the administration of chemotherapy.

When a patient is admitted for the purpose of inserting a port for later administration of chemotherapy but no chemotherapy is given during the same episode of care, the malignancy is designated as the principal diagnosis and code **Z51.11, Encounter for antineoplastic chemotherapy,** is not assigned. When insertion of the port is followed by chemotherapy during the same episode of care, code Z51.11 is assigned as the principal diagnosis. If an intraperitoneal catheter is inserted for the chemotherapy and chemotherapy is administered during the episode of care, assign code **3E0M305, Introduction of other antineoplastic into peritoneal cavity, percutaneous approach.**

An admission for radium implant insertion or for treatment by radioactive iodine (I-131) is not considered an admission solely for a radiotherapy session. The code for the malignant neoplasm is designated the principal diagnosis; code Z51.0 is not assigned.

Encounter to Determine Extent of Malignancy

When the reason for the admission/encounter is to determine the extent of the malignancy or for a procedure such as paracentesis or thoracentesis, the primary malignancy or appropriate metastatic site is designated as the principal or first-listed diagnosis, even though chemotherapy or radiotherapy is administered.

Current Malignancy versus Personal History of Malignancy

When a primary malignancy has been excised but further treatment, such as an additional surgery for the malignancy, radiation therapy, or chemotherapy is directed to that site, the primary malignancy code should be used until treatment is completed.

Codes from category Z85, Personal history of malignant neoplasm, are assigned only when the primary neoplasm has been previously excised or totally eradicated from its site and is no longer under any type of treatment, and there is no evidence of any existing primary malignancy. This guideline applies to both solid and hematopoietic or lymphatic neoplasms, including leukemia. Note, however, that patients with leukemia are often admitted for a variety of tests or other treatment in addition to chemotherapy. If there is any question about whether the admission is for the sole purpose of chemotherapy, immunotherapy, or radiotherapy, the physician should be consulted.

Malignant Neoplasm Associated with Transplanted Organ

A malignant neoplasm of a transplanted organ should be coded as a transplant complication. A code from category T86.-, Complications of transplanted organs and tissue, is assigned as the principal diagnosis, followed by code **C80.2, Malignant neoplasm associated with transplanted organ.** An additional code is assigned for the specific malignancy.

Malignant Neoplasm in a Pregnant Patient

Codes from chapter 15 of ICD-10-CM, Pregnancy, Childbirth, and the Puerperium, are always sequenced first on a medical record. A code from subcategory O9A.1-, Malignant neoplasm complicating pregnancy, childbirth, and the puerperium, should be used first, followed by the appropriate code from chapter 2 to indicate the type of neoplasm.

Pathologic Fracture Due to a Neoplasm

The sequencing of pathological fractures due to neoplasm is dependent on the focus of treatment, as follows:

- If the focus of treatment is the fracture, a code from subcategory M84.5, Pathological fracture in neoplastic disease, should be sequenced first, followed by the code for the neoplasm.
- If the focus of treatment is the neoplasm with an associated pathological fracture, the neoplasm code should be sequenced first, followed by a code from M84.5 for the pathological fracture. The "code also" note at M84.5 provides this sequencing instruction.

Malignant Ascites

Malignant ascites (R18.0) is the abnormal buildup of fluid in the abdomen caused by malignancy. Diagnostic tests to determine the underlying cause may involve blood tests, ultrasound of the abdomen, and paracentesis. Treatment may include diuretics, therapeutic paracentesis (needle aspiration of the peritoneal cavity), or other therapies directed at the underlying cause. For example:

- A patient is admitted with pancreatic cancer with massive widespread malignant ascites. The final diagnosis is pancreatic cancer with malignant ascites and metastasis to the retroperitoneum. Therapeutic paracentesis is performed. Assign code **C25.9, Malignant neoplasm of pancreas, unspecified,** as the principal diagnosis. Codes **R18.0, Malignant ascites,** and **C78.6, Secondary malignant neoplasm of retroperitoneum and peritoneum,** should be assigned as secondary diagnoses. Assign code **0W9G3ZZ, Drainage of peritoneal cavity, percutaneous approach,** for the paracentesis.

Malignant Pleural Effusion

Malignant pleural effusions (J91.0) can occur due to impaired pleural lymphatic drainage from a mediastinal tumor (especially in lymphomas) and not because of direct tumor invasion into the pleura. The lymphoma is obstructing the drainage system, which is usually caused by disturbance of the normal Starling forces regulating reabsorption of fluid in the pleural space. The code for the malignancy is assigned first, and the code for the malignant pleural effusion is assigned as an additional diagnosis.

Encounter for Prophylactic Organ Removal

For encounters specifically for prophylactic removal of breasts, ovaries, or another organ due to a genetic susceptibility to cancer or a family history of cancer, the principal or first-listed diagnosis should be a code from category Z40, Encounter for prophylactic surgery. The appropriate codes to identify the associated risk factor (such as genetic susceptibility or family history) should be assigned as additional diagnoses.

If the patient has a malignancy of one site and is having prophylactic removal of another site to prevent either a new primary malignancy or metastatic disease, a code for the malignancy should also be assigned in addition to a code from subcategory Z40.0, Encounter for prophylactic surgery for risk factors related to malignant neoplasms. A Z40.0- code should not be assigned if the patient is having organ removal for treatment of a malignancy, such as the removal of testes for the treatment of prostate cancer.

Coding of Admissions or Encounters for Follow-Up Examinations

Once a malignant neoplasm has been excised or eradicated, periodic follow-up examinations are carried out to determine whether there is recurrence of the primary malignancy or any spread to a secondary site. When there is no evidence of recurrence at either a primary site or a metastatic site, code **Z08, Encounter for follow-up examination after completed treatment for malignant neoplasm,** is assigned as the principal diagnosis. Use an additional code to identify the personal history of malignant neoplasm (Z85.-). Use an additional code to identify any acquired absence of organs (Z90.-). Codes should also be assigned for any diagnostic procedures (such as endoscopy and biopsy) that are carried out.

When there is evidence of recurrence at the primary site, the code for the malignancy is designated as the principal diagnosis. For example, a primary carcinoma of the anterior wall of the urinary bladder that was previously excised but has recurred in the lateral wall is coded to **C67.2, Malignant neoplasm of lateral wall of bladder.**

When there is no recurrence at the primary site but there is evidence of metastasis to a secondary site, a code for secondary neoplasm of that site is assigned along with a code from category Z85. Code Z08 is not assigned.

EXERCISE 29.7

Mark the following statements either true or false.

1. The recurrence of an original primary malignant neoplasm that was previously removed is classified to category Z85, Personal history of malignant neoplasm. F
2. If a primary malignant neoplasm was excised previously and the original primary site has not recurred, assign the code for the previous primary malignant neoplasm, using the appropriate code from categories C00 through D49 F
3. Whenever secondary neoplasms are present, the Z code for identifying personal history of malignant neoplasm can never be sequenced as the principal diagnosis code for Uniform Hospital Discharge Data Set purposes. T

TREATMENT OF NEOPLASMS

Treatment of neoplasms consists of surgery, chemotherapy, radiation therapy, and other cancer treatment methods. Surgery generally involves removal of the neoplasm. ICD-10-PCS classifies these procedures to the Medical and Surgical Section, with the most common root operations for these being "Excision," "Resection," "Destruction," and "Extirpation."

Thermal Ablation

New advancements in radiofrequency thermal ablation have expanded treatment options for some cancer patients. Thermal ablative procedures utilize heat to destroy lung, liver, or renal malignancies. Minimally invasive, image-guided thermal ablation provides effective treatment of localized neoplastic disease and can also be used as an adjunct to traditional surgery, chemotherapy, and/or radiation treatment. Under radiological imaging, a needle-electrode is inserted at the site of the tumor; radiofrequency energy is then applied to destroy the tumor. Thermal ablation can be performed by four different methods: open, laparoscopic, thoracoscopic, and percutaneous. ICD-10-PCS classifies thermal ablative procedures to the Medical and Surgical Section, root operation "Destruction." For example, code **0B5M4ZZ, Destruction of bilateral lungs, percutaneous endoscopic approach,** is assigned for thoracoscopic thermal ablation of both lungs.

Chemotherapy and Immunotherapy

Chemotherapy and immunotherapy are coded to the Administration Section, root operation "Introduction," and to the appropriate body system/region where the chemotherapy or immunotherapy agent is administered (e.g., "central vein," "peripheral vein," "peritoneal cavity"), while character 6, substance, identifies whether an antineoplastic or immunotherapeutic substance was administered. Character 7, qualifier, also provides additional information such as whether high-dose interleukin-2 (IL-2), low-dose IL-2, Clofarabine, or monoclonal antibody was administered. For example, the structure of code **3E03305, Infusion of antineoplastic chemotherapy into peripheral vein,** is shown below:

Character 1 Section	Character 2 Body System	Character 3 Root Operation	Character 4 Body System/ Region	Character 5 Approach	Character 6 Substance	Character 7 Qualifier
3	E	0	3	3	0	5
Administration	Physiological systems and anatomical regions	Introduction	Peripheral vein	Percutaneous	Antineoplastic	Other antineoplastic

Bacille Calmette-Guerin is a nonspecific immunotherapy agent used in the treatment of melanoma, cancer of the lung, soft-tissue sarcoma, carcinoma of the colon, and carcinoma of the breast. Interferon is another nonspecific immunotherapy agent used in treating malignancy. Another type of immunotherapy is IL-2, which is used to treat patients with advanced renal cell carcinoma and advanced melanoma. There is a high-dose IL-2 and a low-dose IL-2 therapy. High-dose IL-2 therapy is a hospital inpatient–based regimen usually performed in specialized treatment settings such as the intensive care unit or bone marrow transplant unit. The high-dose IL-2 therapy requires highly specialized oncology professionals to carry out because of the severity of the predictable toxicities, which need extensive monitoring.

Blood brain barrier disruption (BBBD) chemotherapy is a unique option for the delivery of drugs for the treatment of brain tumors and brain metastases. The blood brain barrier (BBB) is an impediment to the delivery of chemotherapy for central nervous system (CNS) malignancies. The BBB is the lining of the small blood vessels in the brain that prevents substances such as toxins or drugs from entering the brain. Patients receiving chemotherapy for brain tumors do not receive adequate doses because antineoplastic drugs cannot cross the BBB through conventional methods of drug delivery. An improved method for drug delivery to the CNS is the infusion of chemotherapy directly into brain arteries through disruption of the BBB. BBBD therapy delivers key drugs and other substances to the brain (i.e., rituximab, trastuzumab, antibodies, or genes), avoiding the long-term cognitive effects of radiotherapy. This technique can deliver five to 10 times the concentration of the drug into the brain without the risks of neurotoxicity. Assign code **Z51.11, Encounter for antineoplastic chemotherapy,** as the principal diagnosis when the admission is for chemotherapy with infusion of a substance to disrupt the blood brain barrier. This procedure is classified by ICD-10-PCS to the Administration Section, root operation "Introduction," and the blood brain barrier disruption is identified by character 7, qualifier. The structure of the code **3E043GN, Introduction of blood brain barrier disruption substance into central vein, percutaneous approach,** is shown below:

Character 1 Section	Character 2 Body System	Character 3 Root Operation	Character 4 Body System/ Region	Character 5 Approach	Character 6 Substance	Character 7 Qualifier
3	E	0	4	3	G	N
Administration	Physiological systems and anatomical regions	Introduction	Central vein	Percutaneous	Other therapeutic substance	Blood brain barrier disruption

The Viadur (leuprolide acetate) implant is used as palliative treatment for advanced prostate cancer. The device is implanted subcutaneously in the arm and delivers leuprolide acetate continuously over a period of 12 months. Leuprolide acetate lowers testosterone, a hormone that is needed by prostate cancer cells. Assign code **3E013VJ, Introduction of other hormone into subcutaneous tissue, percutaneous approach,** for the insertion of the Viadur implant. The code for the prostate malignancy is designated as the principal diagnosis.

Radiation Oncology

Radiation oncology refers to the radiation procedures performed for cancer treatment. ICD-10-PCS classifies these procedures in a special section strictly for radiology oncology procedures. In this section, the characters have the following meanings:

1 Section
2 Body system
3 Modality, which is the basic manner of treatment. Four different modalities are used in this section: "Beam radiation," "Brachytherapy," "Stereotactic radiosurgery," and "Other radiation."
4 Treatment site
5 Modality qualifier, which further specifies the treatment modality. For example, for "Brachytherapy," additional modality qualifiers specify high dose rate or low dose rate.
6 Isotope, which defines the isotope used, if applicable. For example, isotopes used for "Brachytherapy" include cesium-137, iridium-192, iodine-125, palladium-103, and californium-252.
7 Qualifier

The structure of the code **DM1198Z, High dose rate (hdr) brachytherapy of right breast using iridium-192 (Ir-192),** is shown below:

Character 1 Section	Character 2 Body System	Character 3 Modality	Character 4 Treatment Site	Character 5 Modality Qualifier	Character 6 Isotope	Character 7 Qualifier
D	M	1	1	9	8	Z
Radiation oncology	Breast	Brachytherapy	Breast, right	High dose rate	Iridium 192	None

Laser Interstitial Thermal Therapy

Thermal therapy can be used to destroy malignancies involving the brain, breast, liver, prostate, and other organs. The energy sources come in many forms, such as laser, microwave, and radiofrequency. The heat source may be extracorporeal (outside the body), extrastitial (outside the tumor), or interstitial (inside the tumor).

Laser interstitial thermal therapy (LITT) is a surgical procedure in which obliteration of soft tissues in the body is performed through elevated temperatures caused by the local absorption of laser energy under magnetic resonance imaging guidance. With this type of therapy, the energy is applied directly to the tumor rather than passing through surrounding normal tissue. The therapy encompasses the whole target but does not extend to surrounding critical structures. LITT may also be performed to remove cancerous lesions from other sites, such as head and neck, liver, breast, prostate, and lung. ICD-10-PCS classifies LITT to the Radiation Oncology Section, root type "Other radiation," with the character 5, modality qualifier, of "laser interstitial thermal therapy." The structure of the code **D0Y1KZZ, Laser interstitial thermal therapy of brain stem,** is shown below:

Character 1 Section	Character 2 Body System	Character 3 Modality	Character 4 Treatment Site	Character 5 Modality Qualifier	Character 6 Isotope	Character 7 Qualifier
D	0	Y	1	K	Z	Z
Radiation oncology	Central and peripheral nervous system	Other radiation	Brain stem	Laser interstitial thermal therapy	None	None

Intra-Operative Electron Radiation Therapy

Intra-operative electron radiation therapy is a specialized, intensive radiation treatment administered during surgery directly to the cancer tumor or tumor bed. Normal tissue is protected, thereby substantially increasing the effectiveness of the treatment. The code for the malignant neoplasm is designated as the principal diagnosis; code Z51.11 is not assigned. Assign the appropriate code for the radiation provided using a code from the Radiation Oncology Section, root operation "Beam radiation," modality "electrons," and selecting the "intraoperative" value for character 7, qualifier. The structure of the code **DW013Z0, Beam radiation of head and neck using electrons, intraoperative,** is shown below:

Character 1 Section	Character 2 Body System	Character 3 Modality	Character 4 Treatment Site	Character 5 Modality Qualifier	Character 6 Isotope	Character 7 Qualifier
D	W	0	1	3	Z	0
Radiation oncology	Anatomical regions	Beam radiation	Head and neck	Electrons	None	Intraoperative

EXERCISE 29.8

The following exercise provides a review of the material on neoplasms presented in this handbook. For this exercise, assign procedure codes where applicable.

1. Infiltrating papillary transitional cell carcinoma of urinary bladder (neck) — C67.5
   Percutaneous excision of bladder neck tumor — 0TBC3ZZ

2. Carcinoma of midesophagus with spread to celiac lymph nodes — C15.4, C77.2
   Permanent gastrostomy procedure, percutaneous approach with synthetic substitute — 0D163J4
   Radiotherapy to esophagus using photons 1-10 MeV — DD001ZZ

3. Malignant carcinoid tumor of small intestine — C7A.019
   Endoscopic excision of tumor of small intestine — 0DB88ZZ

4. Carcinoma, scirrhous, female left breast, outer portion — C50.812
   Open biopsy with frozen section followed immediately by left radical mastectomy (resection of left breast, left axillary lymph nodes and pectoral muscle) — 0HTU0ZZ, 07T60ZZ, 0KTJ0ZZ, 0HBU0ZX

5.	Intramural leiomyoma of uterus	D25.1
	Total vaginal hysterectomy	0UT97ZZ
		0UTC7ZZ
6.	Multiple myeloma	C90.00
7.	Carcinoma of gallbladder with metastasis	C23
	to abdominal lymph nodes and liver	C77.2
	and peritoneal implants	C78.7
		C78.6
	Exploratory laparotomy with	0FT40ZZ
	cholecystectomy, needle	0DBW3ZX
	biopsy of peritoneal implant, and intra-operative	D7063Z0
	electron radiation therapy abdominal lymph nodes	
8.	Squamous cell carcinoma in situ, floor of mouth	D00.06
	Resection of lesion, floor of mouth (mucosa)	0CB4XZZ
9.	Metastatic malignant melanoma from left	C43.59
	lateral chest wall to axillary lymph node	C77.3
	Neoplasm	
	Excision of malignant melanoma	0WB80ZZ
	of chest wall (open approach) with radical left	07T60ZZ
	axillary lymphadenectomy (open approach)	
10.	Metastatic adenocarcinoma of sacrum,	C79.51
	prostatic in origin	Z85.46
	Previous prostatectomy	
	History	
11.	A 33-year-old female admitted for prophylactic	Z40.01
	removal of both breasts, with documented genetic	
	susceptibility to breast cancer due to extensive family	Z15.01
	history of breast carcinoma	Z80.3
	Bilateral mastectomy	0HTV0ZZ
12.	Seminoma, left testis	C62.92
	Bilateral radical orchiectomy (open approach)	0VTC0ZZ

13. Lipoma, right kidney — D17.71
Percutaneous needle aspiration biopsy of right kidney — 0T903ZX

14. Chronic lymphocytic leukemia (B-cell), in remission — C91.11

15. Admitted for chemotherapy (peripheral vein) following oophorectomy on previous admission for carcinoma of left ovary — Z51.11, C56.2, 3E03305

16. Brain metastasis, admitted for chemotherapy and infusion of substance to disrupt blood brain barrier (peripheral vein, percutaneous) — Z51.11, C79.31, 3E033GN, 3E03305

17. Ovarian carcinoma with malignant ascites and metastasis to the peritoneal cavity
Percutaneous paracentesis peritoneal cavity — C56.9, R18.0, C78.6, 0W9G3ZZ

18. Patient was diagnosed with glioblastoma multiforme (GBM) and admitted for laser interstitial thermal therapy (LITT) under MRI guidance. The patient was taken to the OR, where the neurosurgeon inserted an MRI-compatible laser probe through a guide attached to the cranium and then through a small cranial burr hole. The probe was then advanced into the tumor and positioned under MRI guidance. — C71.9, D0Y0KZZ

19. Patient was diagnosed with a malignant frontal lobe glioblastoma of the brain. She subsequently underwent open surgical resection of the tumor with insertion of the GliaSite® catheter in the cavity created by the tumor excision. The patient was discharged home and three weeks later presented to the hospital for infusion of high dose liquid brachytherapy (I-125) via the cranial catheter. After therapy, the catheter was removed via craniectomy, and the patient was discharged. — C71.1, 00B00ZZ, 00H003Z, D01099Z, 00P003Z

Coding of Injuries, Burns, Poisoning, and Complications of Care

CHAPTER 30

Injuries

CHAPTER OVERVIEW

- Injuries, poisoning, and certain other consequences of external causes are found in chapter 19 of ICD-10-CM.
- The primary axis for classifying injuries is the anatomical site.
- The secondary axis is the type of injury.
- The most severe cause of injury is used as the principal diagnosis.
- External cause of morbidity codes indicate how the injury occurred, the intent (accident or intentional), the place where the injury occurred, the status of the patient at the time the injury occurred, and any activity that may have caused or contributed to the injury.
- An External cause code is never a principal diagnosis.
- Multiple External cause codes can be used. The first corresponds to the most serious diagnosis.
- Code child and adult abuse before the associated injuries or conditions resulting from the abuse.
- Fractures make an extensive use of the seventh-character value, which is more detailed than for other injuries.
- Any fracture not specified as open or closed is classified as closed in ICD-10-CM.
- A fracture not indicated whether displaced or not displaced should be coded to displaced.
- Reduction is the most common treatment for fractures.
- If dislocations accompany fractures, they are included in the fracture code.
- Internal injuries, blood vessel and nerve injuries, open wounds, and amputations are also covered in this chapter.
- An amputation not identified as partial or complete should be coded to complete.

LEARNING OUTCOMES

After studying this chapter you should be able to:

Use External cause codes to assist in the classification of an injury.

Select the correct seventh-character value.

Code for procedures related to fractures.

Code for open wounds and other varieties of injuries.

TERMS TO KNOW

External cause codes
indicate external cause of morbidity; used with injury and poisoning codes

Pathological fracture
a fracture caused by bone weakening associated with conditions such as osteoporosis or neoplastic diseases

REMEMBER . . .

This chapter of ICD-10-CM utilizes extensive inclusion and exclusion notes, which make for some long and complicated codes.

INTRODUCTION

Chapter 19 of ICD-10-CM classifies injuries, poisoning, certain early complications of trauma, complications of surgical and medical care, and certain other consequences of external causes. Because this chapter covers such a broad range of conditions, guidelines for the coding of burns, poisoning, adverse effects, and complications of medical and surgical care will be discussed in subsequent chapters of this handbook.

Injuries are classified in the following sections:

S00–S09	Injuries to the head
S10–S19	Injuries to the neck
S20–S29	Injuries to the thorax
S30–S39	Injuries to the abdomen, lower back, lumbar spine, pelvis, and external genitals
S40–S49	Injuries to the shoulder and upper arm
S50–S59	Injuries to the elbow and forearm
S60–S69	Injuries to the wrist, hand, and fingers
S70–S79	Injuries to the hip and thigh
S80–S89	Injuries to the knee and lower leg
S90–S99	Injuries to the ankle and foot
T07	Injuries involving multiple body regions
T14	Injury of unspecified body region
T15–T19	Effects of foreign body entering through natural orifice
T20–T32	Burns and corrosions
T33–T34	Frostbite
T36–T50	Poisoning by, adverse effect of and underdosing of drugs, medicaments and biological substances
T51–T65	Toxic effects of substances chiefly nonmedicinal as to source
T66–T78	Other and unspecified effects of external causes
T79	Certain early complications of trauma
T80–T88	Complications of surgical and medical care, not elsewhere classified

The primary axis for classifying injuries is the anatomical site as indicated in the preceding list; the second axis is determined by type of injury. Chapter 19 of ICD-10-CM uses the S section for coding different types of injuries related to single body regions, and it uses the T section to cover injuries to unspecified body regions as well as poisoning and certain other consequences of external causes. Inclusion and exclusion notes are used extensively in this chapter, some of them long and complex, and it is important to give careful attention to these if correct code assignments are to be made.

Codes from S00 through T14.9 are for traumatic injuries and should not be used for normal, healing surgical wounds or to identify complications of surgical wounds.

SEVENTH CHARACTERS

Most categories in chapter 19 have seventh-character values that are required for each applicable code. The seventh character must always be the seventh character in the code. For codes that require a seventh character but are not six characters long, a placeholder "x" must be used to fill in the empty characters. Most categories in this chapter have three seventh-character values (with the exception of fractures, which are covered later in this chapter): "A," initial encounter; "D," subsequent encounter; and "S," sequela. Categories for traumatic fractures have additional seventh-character values.

Seventh Character "A"

The seventh-character value "A," initial encounter, should be used while the patient is receiving active treatment for the condition. Examples of active treatment are surgical treatment, emergency department encounter, and evaluation and treatment by a new physician.

Seventh Character "D"

The seventh-character value "D," subsequent encounter, is used for encounters after the patient has received active treatment of the condition and is receiving routine care for the condition during the healing or recovery phase. For aftercare of an injury, assign the acute injury code with the seventh-character "D" (subsequent encounter). Examples of subsequent care are cast change or removal, removal of external or internal fixation device, medication adjustment, other aftercare, and follow-up visits following treatment of the injury or condition.

Seventh Character "S"

The seventh-character value "S," sequela, is used for complications or conditions that arise as a direct result of a condition, such as scar formation after a burn; the scars are sequelae of the burn. When using the seventh character "S," it is necessary to use both the injury code that precipitated the sequela and the code for the sequela itself. The "S" is added only to the injury code, not the sequela code. The "S" value identifies the injury responsible for the sequela. The specific type of sequela (e.g., scar) is sequenced first, followed by the injury code.

MULTIPLE CODING OF INJURIES

When coding multiple injuries, each injury should be coded separately unless a combination code is provided, in which case the combination code is assigned. General codes for multiple injuries are provided for use when there is insufficient detail in the medical record (such as trauma cases transferred promptly to another facility) to assign a more specific code. Code **T07, Unspecified multiple injuries,** should not be assigned in the inpatient setting unless information for a more specific code is not available.

As discussed in chapter 2 of this handbook, the word "with" and the word "and" are used in a specific way in ICD-10-CM, and they are used a great deal in chapter 19 of ICD-10-CM. The word "with" means that both sites mentioned in the diagnostic statement are involved in the injury.

The word "and," when it appears in a code title, is interpreted as meaning "and/or"—that is, that either or both sites are involved. In coding injuries, mention of fingers usually takes into account the thumb, but there are a few separate codes for injuries of the thumb. Terms such as "condyle," "coronoid process," "ramus," and "symphysis" refer to the portion of the bone involved in an injury, not to the bone itself.

SEQUENCING OF INJURY CODES

If admission is due to injury and several injuries are present, the code for the most severe injury, as determined by the provider and the focus of treatment, is designated as the principal diagnosis. If the diagnostic statement is not clear on this point, the physician should be asked to make this determination.

Superficial injuries such as abrasions or contusions are not coded when associated with more severe injuries of the same site—only the severe injury should be coded.

When a primary injury results in minor damage to peripheral nerves or blood vessels, the primary injury is sequenced first, with an additional code(s) for injuries to nerves and spinal cord (such as category S04) and/or injury to blood vessels (such as category S15). When the primary injury is to the blood vessels or nerves, that injury should be sequenced first.

EXTERNAL CAUSE OF MORBIDITY

As mentioned in chapter 12 of this handbook, External cause of morbidity codes (categories V01–Y99) are used with injury codes to provide information about how an injury occurred (cause), the intent (accidental or intentional), the place where the injury occurred, and the status (e.g., military, civilian) of the patient at the time the injury occurred. In the case of a person who seeks care for an injury or other health condition that resulted from an activity, or when an activity contributed to the injury or health condition, activity codes (category Y93) are used to describe the activity.

The codes for poisoning, adverse effect, and underdosing (categories T36–T50) and for toxic effects of substances chiefly nonmedicinal as to source (categories T51–T65) include information on the cause (e.g., the responsible substance) as well as the intent (accidental or intentional). No External cause code from chapter 20 of ICD-10-CM is needed for cause or intent for these codes.

Injuries are a major cause of mortality, morbidity, and disability, and the cost of care related to these conditions contributes significantly to the increased cost of health care. Reporting External cause codes provides data for injury research and evaluation of injury prevention strategies. Although reporting external cause is optional unless mandated by state or insurance carrier regulation, health care providers are strongly encouraged to report External cause codes for all initial treatment of injuries. Guidelines for reporting have been developed, and providers are urged to follow these guidelines so that there is consistency in the data.

Major categories of External cause codes include:

V00–V99	Transport accidents
W00–X58	Other external causes of accidental injury
X71–X83	Intentional self-harm
X92–Y09	Assault
Y21–Y33	Event of undetermined intent
Y35–Y38	Legal intervention, operations of war, military operations, and terrorism
Y62–Y84	Complications of medical and surgical care
Y90–Y99	Supplementary factors related to causes of morbidity classified elsewhere

The selection of appropriate External cause codes for injuries is guided by the Index to External Causes of Injury and by inclusion and exclusion notes in the Tabular List. The codes are found in the Tabular List in alphabetical order.

External Cause Status

A code from category Y99, External cause status, is assigned to indicate the work status of the person at the time the injury occurred. The status code indicates whether the injury occurred during military activity, whether a nonmilitary person was at work, or whether a student or volunteer was involved in a nonwork activity at the time of the causal event. A code from Y99 should be assigned, when applicable, with other External cause codes, such as transport accidents and falls. Category Y99 codes include status codes for activities done as a hobby, for leisure, and for recreation as well as volunteer activity and activity of off-duty military personnel.

The external cause status codes are not applicable to poisonings, adverse effects, misadventures, or late effects. Do not assign a code from category Y99 if no other External cause codes (cause, activity) are applicable for the encounter. Do not assign code **Y99.9, Unspecified external cause status,** if the status is not stated.

Activity Codes

Assign a code from category Y93, Activity codes, to describe the activity of the patient at the time the injury or other health condition occurred. Codes from category Y93 are used only once, at the initial encounter for treatment. Only one code from Y93 should be recorded on a medical record.

If a patient is a student but is injured while performing an activity for income, use seventh character "2," work-related activity. A work-related activity is any activity for which payment or income is received.

The activity codes are not applicable to poisonings, adverse effects, misadventures, or sequela. Coders should not assign code **Y93.9, Activity, unspecified,** if the activity is not stated.

Sequencing of External Cause Codes

An External cause code is never used as the principal diagnosis. If the reporting format limits the number of External cause codes that can be used in reporting clinical data, report the code for the cause/intent most related to the principal diagnosis. If the format permits capture of additional External cause codes, the cause/intent, including medical misadventures, of the additional events should be reported rather than the codes for place, activity, or external status.

If two or more events cause separate injuries, an External cause code should be assigned for each. The first-listed External cause code will be selected using the following sequencing hierarchy:

- External cause codes for child and adult abuse take precedence over all other External cause codes.
- External cause codes for terrorism events take priority over all other External cause codes except child and adult abuse.
- External cause codes for cataclysmic events take priority over all External cause codes except those for child and adult abuse and terrorism. Cataclysmic events include storms, floods, hurricanes, tornadoes, blizzards, volcanic eruptions, and earth surface movements and eruptions.
- Transport accidents take priority over all other External cause codes except those for cataclysmic events, child and adult abuse, and terrorism.
- Activity and external cause status are assigned following all causal (intent) External cause codes.
- The first-listed External cause code should correspond to the cause of the most serious diagnosis due to an assault, an accident, or self-harm, following the order of hierarchy listed above.

Transport and Vehicle Accidents

A transport accident (V00–V99) is one in which the vehicle involved must be moving or running or in use for transport purposes at the time of the accident. A long note at the beginning of this section defines in detail just what is meant by each type of transportation and what vehicles are included. The note also defines the injured person in a motor vehicle accident, such as a passenger, driver, bicyclist, or pedestrian. For example:

S72.309B + V03.10xA + Y93.01 + Y99.8	Open fracture, shaft of femur (pedestrian during recreational walk struck by automobile)

Accidents caused by machines such as agricultural or earth-moving equipment are classified as transport accidents if the pieces of equipment were in operation as transport vehicles when the accidents occurred. Otherwise, they are classified in category W30, Contact with agricultural machinery, or category W31, Contact with other and unspecified machinery, with a fourth character indicating the specific type of equipment.

External Cause of Injury Classified by Intent

Separate External cause codes are provided to classify the external cause of injuries resulting from accident, self-harm, or assault. If the intent is unknown or unspecified, code the intent as accidental intent. All transport accident categories (V00–V99) assume accidental intent. External cause codes for events of undetermined intent should only be used if the record documentation specifies that the intent cannot be determined.

Category Y38, Terrorism, is used to identify injuries and illnesses acquired as a result of terrorism. These codes (Y38.0- through Y38.9-) follow the definition of terrorism established by the U.S. Federal Bureau of Investigation (FBI). Coders are not to classify a death or an injury as terrorist related unless the federal government has designated the incident as terrorism. The definition of terrorism employed by the FBI is found at the inclusion note at the beginning of category Y38: "These codes are for use to identify injuries resulting from the unlawful use of force or violence against persons or property to intimidate or coerce a Government, the civilian population, or any segment thereof, in furtherance of political or social objective." More than one Y38 code may be assigned if the injury is the result of more than one mechanism of terrorism (e.g., destruction of aircraft and firearms). A code from category Y92, Place of occurrence of the external cause, is assigned as an additional code to identify the place of occurrence.

Place of Occurrence

ICD-10-CM provides external cause category Y92, Place of occurrence of the external cause, for use as an additional code to indicate the location of the patient at the time of injury or other condition. A place of occurrence code is used only once, at the initial encounter for treatment. No seventh-character values are used for category Y92.

Only one code from Y92 should be recorded on a medical record. When the place of occurrence is not specified or is not applicable, code **Y92.9, Unspecified place or not applicable,** is not assigned. Note that codes from category Y92 refer only to the location, not to the activity of the injured person. Separate codes are provided for the activity and status. For example:

W10.0xxA + Y92.520	Fall on escalator in airport building
X03.0xxA + X06.2xxA + Y92.096 + Y93.E9 + Y99.8	Clothing caught fire while burning household trash in backyard of home, causing burn

LATE EFFECTS OF EXTERNAL CAUSES

When the condition code from the main classification is a sequela (late effect) of injury, the associated External cause code must also indicate a late effect or sequela. Sequelae are reported using the External cause code with the seventh-character value "S" for sequela. These codes should be used with any report of a late effect or sequela resulting from a previous injury. A sequela External cause code should never be used with a related current nature of injury code. Late effect External cause codes are used for subsequent visits when a late effect of the initial injury is being treated, and not for subsequent visits for follow-up care (e.g., to assess healing, to receive rehabilitative therapy) when no late effect of the injury has been documented.

For example, a diagnosis of extensive scarring of the face due to an old burn is coded as **L90.5, Scar conditions and fibrosis of skin; T20.00xS, Burn of unspecified degree of head, face, and neck, unspecified site, sequela;** and **X08.8xxS, Exposure to other specified smoke, fire and flames, sequela.** In this example, code T20.00xS indicates that the condition is a late effect of burn of eye, face, head, and neck, and code X08.8xxS indicates that it is a late effect of an accident caused by fire. Note that both codes have the same seventh character "S" for sequela.

EXERCISE 30.1

Assign only the External cause codes in the following exercises. Assume initial encounter unless stated otherwise.

1.	Closed fracture, right tibia and fibula, due to fall from bicycle while patient was working as a messenger for a delivery service	V18.0xxA Y93.55 Y99.0
2.	Injury to deliveryman who got off of a moving pick-up truck not on a public highway because he thought the driver was stopping Accident	V58.4xxA Y99.0
3.	Multiple facial lacerations to military police officer driving an automobile while on duty that was in a collision with another automobile on expressway	V43.52xA Y99.1 Y92.411
4.	Anoxic brain damage due to previous head injury, three years ago, when patient was accidentally struck by car while walking along highway Accident	V03.90xS

5. Injury received by crew member of commercial airline when he fell at takeoff — V97.0xxA, Y99.0

 Fall

6. Injury received by guest passenger in hot-air balloon when balloon made unexpected descent — V96.02xA, Y93.89, Y99.8

 Accident

7. Passenger injured when he accidentally collided with another passenger while getting off a streetcar onto road — V82.4xxA, Y92.410

 Accident

8. Railway employee injured by accident involving collision with rolling stock — V81.2xxA, Y99.0

9. Railway employee injured when hit by rolling stock while unloading material — V81.2xxA, Y99.0

 Accident

10. Passenger injured in accidental derailment of train — V81.7xxA

 Accident

11. Motorcyclist injured in accidental collision with train — V25.4xxA

CHILD AND ADULT ABUSE

Expanded codes for child and adult abuse facilitate the gathering of more specific data. Child abuse has become a major concern in the United States. All 50 states, the District of Columbia, and the U.S. territories have mandatory child abuse and neglect reporting laws that require certain professionals and institutions to report suspected maltreatment to a child protective services agency. Each state has its own definitions of child abuse and neglect based on minimum standards set by federal

law. Federal legislation provides a foundation for states by identifying a minimum set of acts or behaviors that define child abuse and neglect. Adult abuse is considered to be both underreported and underdiagnosed.

Keep in mind that codes for child and adult abuse are assigned only when the physician documents abuse; coders should not interpret narrative descriptions as abuse without the physician's confirmation.

ICD-10-CM provides two categories for reporting adult and child abuse, neglect, and other maltreatment. The first axis of classification is whether the abuse is confirmed (category T74) or suspected (T76). The exception to this is code **T74.4, Shaken infant syndrome,** which ICD-10-CM defaults to confirmed abuse. The fourth character for categories T74 and T76 indicates the type of abuse (neglect or abandonment, physical abuse, sexual abuse, emotional abuse, or unspecified maltreatment), while the fifth character specifies whether child or adult abuse is involved. The selection of the code for confirmed or suspected abuse is based on medical record documentation.

ICD-10-CM does not specify the age limit for the assignment of child abuse codes versus adult abuse codes. The age of majority varies among states. If the patient has reached the age of majority per state guidelines, it would be appropriate to assign the adult abuse codes. In some states, an emancipated minor is considered an adult. For example, if a judge declares a minor emancipated, he or she is usually granted majority status at the same time. Other factors may influence the age of majority as well, such as marriage or participation in the armed forces. In some instances when it is not documented, the provider will need to be queried to determine if the patient is an emancipated minor.

Abuse often results in physical injuries and other medical conditions. When this is the case, sequence first the appropriate code from categories T74 or T76, followed by any accompanying mental health or injury code. Use an additional External cause code to identify perpetrator, if known (Y07.-).

ICD-10-CM classifies confirmed adult and child abuse, neglect, and maltreatment as assault. Any of the assault codes (X92–Y09) may be used to indicate the external cause of any physical injury resulting from the confirmed abuse.

For suspected cases of abuse or neglect, do not report External cause or perpetrator codes. If a suspected case of abuse, neglect, or mistreatment is ruled out during an encounter, code **Z04.71, Encounter for examination and observation following alleged adult physical abuse, ruled out,** or code **Z04.72, Encounter for examination and observation following alleged child physical abuse, ruled out,** should be used. If a suspected case of alleged rape or sexual abuse is ruled out during an encounter, code **Z04.41, Encounter for examination and observation following alleged adult rape, ruled out,** or code **Z04.42, Encounter for examination and observation following alleged child rape, ruled out,** should be used. No code from category T76 is used for these encounters.

Incidents of documented adult abuse complicating pregnancy, childbirth, and the puerperium, whether suspected or confirmed, are classified to chapter 15 of ICD-10-CM (rather than to T74.- or T76.-), as follows:

O9A.3- Physical abuse
O9A.4- Sexual abuse
O9A.5- Psychological abuse

Codes from O9A.3-, O9A.4-, and O9A.5 should be sequenced first, followed by the appropriate codes (if applicable) to identify any associated current injury due to physical or sexual abuse, as well as a code to identify the perpetrator of the abuse.

Examples of child and adult abuse include the following:

- A patient is seen in the emergency department with a diagnosis of confirmed battered spouse syndrome and with a laceration of the right forehead. She reports that her husband hit her in the face because he was angry when she was late getting ready to go out

to dinner. The following codes should be assigned: **T74.11xA, Adult physical abuse, confirmed, initial encounter; S01.81xA, Laceration without foreign body of other part of head, initial encounter; Y04.0xxA, Assault by unarmed fight or brawl, initial encounter; Y07.01, Husband as perpetrator of maltreatment and neglect,** and **Y99.8, Other external cause status.**

- A four-month-old infant is seen in the emergency department with a diagnosis of shaken infant syndrome. The baby had been unconscious for approximately two hours after being shaken vigorously by the father when he was unable to make the infant stop crying. The diagnostic statement also includes diagnoses of subdural hematoma and bilateral retinal hemorrhage. The following codes should be assigned: **T74.4xxA, Shaken infant syndrome, initial encounter; S06.5x3A, Traumatic subdural hemorrhage with loss of consciousness of 1 hour to 5 hours 59 minutes, initial encounter; H35.63, Retinal hemorrhage, bilateral; Y07.11, Biological father, perpetrator of maltreatment and neglect;** and **Y99.8, Other external cause status.**
- An elderly woman is brought to the hospital in a state of severe malnutrition. She had been living in an unlicensed care home, where it was suspected she was fed only one meal per day for several months. In the hospital, a gastric feeding tube is placed and high-protein supplements are given for severe caloric deficiency malnutrition. The following codes should be assigned: **T76.01xA, Adult neglect or abandonment, suspected, initial encounter; E41, Nutritional marasmus; Z59.4, Lack of adequate food and safe drinking water; 0DH67UZ, Insertion of feeding device into stomach, via natural or artificial opening;** and **3E0G76Z, Introduction of nutritional substance into upper G.I., via natural or artificial opening.**
- A six-month-old infant with heat prostration is brought to the hospital by her parents, who had left her alone in their car while they did their grocery shopping. The parents stated that the child was asleep and they had felt that she would be all right for the short time they would be gone. The physician documents suspected child abandonment. The following codes should be assigned: **T76.02xA, Child neglect or abandonment, suspected, initial encounter; T67.5xxA, Heat exhaustion, unspecified, initial encounter.**

Subcategory Z62.81, Personal history of abuse in childhood, provides codes to indicate that a patient has a past personal history of abuse in childhood:

Z62.810	History of physical and sexual abuse in childhood
Z62.811	History of psychological abuse in childhood
Z62.812	History of neglect in childhood
Z62.819	History of unspecified abuse in childhood

Codes from category Z91 are also available to indicate that a patient has a past personal history of adult psychological trauma:

Z91.410	History of adult physical and sexual abuse
Z91.411	History of adult psychological abuse
Z91.412	History of adult neglect
Z91.419	History of unspecified adult abuse
Z91.49	History of psychological trauma NEC

There are also counseling codes (category Z69) to provide information regarding encounters for mental health services for the victim or perpetrator of abuse. These codes include counseling for child abuse problems, spousal or partner abuse problems, and other abuse.

FRACTURES

Fractures are classified in different categories or subcategories according to their anatomical locations, as follows:

S02	Fractures of skull and facial bones
S12	Fractures of cervical vertebra and other parts of neck
S22	Fractures of rib(s), sternum, and thoracic spine
S32	Fractures of lumbar spine and pelvis
S42	Fractures of shoulder and upper arm
S49.0–S49.1-	Physeal fractures of shoulder and upper arm
S52	Fracture of forearm
S59.0–S59.2-	Physeal fractures of elbow and forearm
S62	Fracture of wrist and hand level
S72	Fracture of femur
S79.0–S79.1-	Physeal fractures of hip and thigh
S82	Fractures of lower leg, including ankle
S89	Physeal fractures of lower leg
S92.0–S92.3-	Fracture of foot and toe, except ankle

Three-character categories indicate more specific sites within these broad groupings, fourth characters usually indicate the bone (e.g., mandible), and fifth characters usually indicate a more specific portion of the bone (e.g., condylar process of mandible). For fractures of the extremities, fourth characters usually indicate a general part of the bone (e.g., upper end of ulna), fifth characters indicate a more specific part of the bone (e.g., olecranon process with intra-articular extension of ulna), and the sixth characters provide information on laterality (e.g., right, left, or unspecified) as well as whether the fracture is displaced or nondisplaced.

In an open fracture, an open wound that communicates with the bone is present. Terms that indicate open fracture include the following: "compound," "infected," "missile," "puncture," and "with foreign body."

Closed fractures do not produce an open wound. They are described by terms such as "comminuted," "depressed," "elevated," "greenstick," "spiral," "simple," and "transverse." Any fracture not specified as open or closed is classified as closed in ICD-10-CM. A comminuted fracture refers to a fracture in which bone is broken, splintered, or crushed into a number of pieces. A "comminuted fracture" is distinguished from a "compound fracture," an open fracture in which the bone is sticking through the skin. (See figure 30.1 for examples of open and closed fractures.)

A fracture not indicated as either displaced or not displaced should be coded to displaced. Occasionally, a diagnostic statement contains terms that relate to both open and closed fractures. In this case, the code for the open fracture always takes precedence. For example, a diagnosis of compound comminuted fracture uses terms that can indicate both open and closed fractures. However, such a fracture would be coded as open because the term "compound" always carries this meaning, even though the term "comminuted" by itself refers to a closed fracture.

The principles of multiple coding of injuries should be followed in coding fractures. Fractures of specified sites are coded individually by site in accordance with both the provisions within categories S02, S12, S22, S32, S42, S49, S52, S59, S62, S72, S79, S82, S89, S92 and the level of detail furnished by medical record content. Multiple fractures are sequenced in accordance with the severity of the fracture.

Note that a code from category M80, Osteoporosis with current pathological fracture, not a traumatic fracture code, should be used for any patient with known osteoporosis who suffers a fracture—even if the patient had a minor fall or trauma, if that fall or trauma would not usually break a normal, healthy bone.

Seventh-Character Values for Fractures

ICD-10-CM makes extensive use of seventh-character values for fractures. While most categories in chapter 19 have three seventh-character values—"A," initial encounter; "D," subsequent encounter; and "S," sequela—the seventh-character values for fractures are significantly different. More importantly, the actual seventh-character codes vary depending on the bones affected, and therefore it is imperative to review the Tabular List at each category level to determine the appropriate code value. For example, codes in category S02, Fracture of skull and facial bones, have six available seventh-character values. However, category S52, Fracture of forearm, has sixteen different seventh-character values (see figure 30.2).

The greater number of seventh-character values doesn't mean that the concepts of initial encounter, subsequent encounter, and sequela no longer apply. Rather, there are additional axes of classification included in these values. For example, the code values for initial encounter (A, B, C) and subsequent encounter (D–H, J–R) applicable to category S52, Fracture of forearm (figure 30.1), also distinguish between open (B–C, E–F, H–J, M–N, Q–R) and closed (A, D, G, K, P) fractures.

FIGURE 30.1 Examples of Open and Closed Fractures

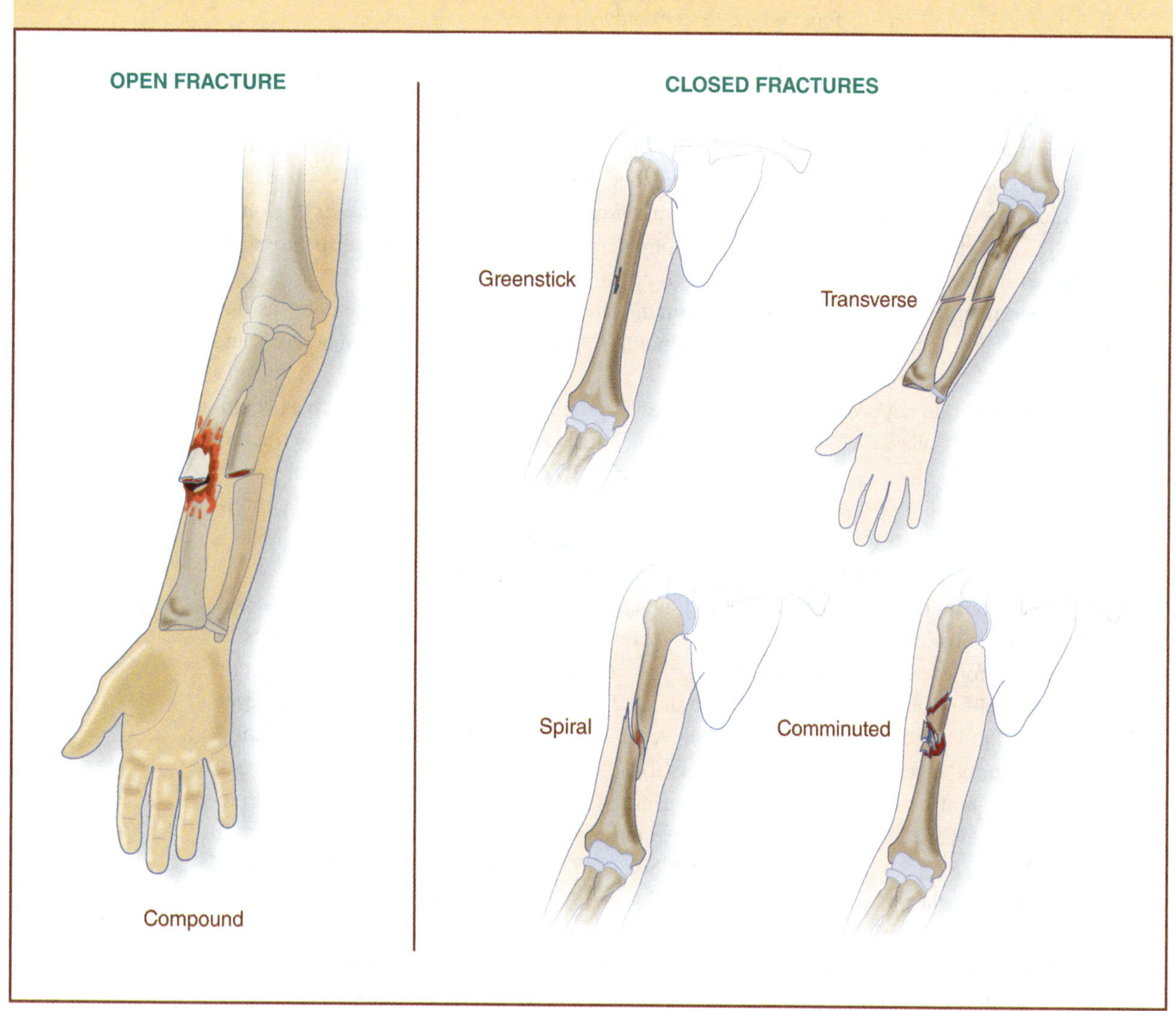

Figure 30.2 Sample Tabular List Seventh-Character Values

S52 Fracture of forearm

Note: A fracture not indicated as displaced or nondisplaced should be coded to displaced
A fracture not indicated as open or closed should be coded to closed
The open fracture designations are based on the Gustilo open fracture classification

Excludes1: traumatic amputation of forearm (S58.-)

Excludes2: fracture at wrist and hand level (S62.-)

The appropriate 7th character is to be added to each code from category S52

A - initial encounter for closed fracture
B - initial encounter for open fracture type I or II; initial encounter for open fracture NOS
C - initial encounter for open fracture type IIIA, IIIB, or IIIC
D - subsequent encounter for closed fracture with routine healing
E - subsequent encounter for open fracture type I or II with routine healing
F - subsequent encounter for open fracture type IIIA, IIIB, or IIIC with routine healing
G - subsequent encounter for closed fracture with delayed healing
H - subsequent encounter for open fracture type I or II with delayed healing
J - subsequent encounter for open fracture type IIIA, IIIB, or IIIC with delayed healing
K - subsequent encounter for closed fracture with nonunion
M - subsequent encounter for open fracture type I or II with nonunion
N - subsequent encounter for open fracture type IIIA, IIIB, or IIIC with nonunion
P - subsequent encounter for closed fracture with malunion
Q - subsequent encounter for open fracture type I or II with malunion
R - subsequent encounter for open fracture type IIIA, IIIB, or IIIC with malunion
S - sequela

In addition, for subsequent encounters, the code values specify whether the fracture is undergoing routine healing (D–F) or if there is a problem such as delayed healing (G–J), nonunion (K–N), or malunion (P–R). For example:

- A patient who suffered a traumatic fracture of the shaft of the left humerus a month earlier is admitted with fever and pain secondary to diverticulitis. The fracture is healing well and is treated minimally.

Principal diagnosis:	K57.92	Diverticulitis of intestine, part unspecified, without perforation or abscess without bleeding
Additional diagnosis:	S42.302D	Unspecified fracture of shaft of humerus, left arm, subsequent encounter for fracture with routine healing

- A young man who fractured the lateral malleolus of the left fibula six weeks previously is admitted for removal of the internal pins under local anesthesia.

Principal diagnosis:	S82.62xD	Displaced fracture of lateral malleolus of left fibula, subsequent encounter for fracture with routine healing

Several different methodologies are used to classify fractures. ICD-10-CM uses the Gustilo classification in the assignment of the seventh-character value for open fractures (see figure 30.2) for categories S52, Fracture of forearm; S72, Fracture of femur; and S82, Fracture of lower leg, including ankle. However, coders should not select the fracture type without provider documentation in the medical record, even though the fracture may be described using the terminology found in the Gustilo classification (figure 30.3). For example, if the documentation reflects an open fracture with a 2-centimeter wound and extensive soft tissue damage, it should not be coded as a Gustilo type III fracture without physician confirmation. When the documentation reflects an initial encounter for an open fracture, but the Gustilo open fracture type is not specified, ICD-10-CM defaults to the seventh-character value "B" for initial encounter for open fracture type I or II.

Initial Care

The seventh-character value for initial encounter (A, B, C) for traumatic fracture is assigned while the patient is receiving active treatment for the fracture. Examples of active treatment are surgical treatment, emergency department encounter, and evaluation and treatment by a new physician.

Subsequent Care

Fractures are coded using the seventh-character value for subsequent care for encounters after the patient has completed active treatment of the fracture and is receiving routine care for the fracture during the healing or recovery phase. Examples of fracture aftercare are cast change or removal, removal of external or internal fixation device, medication adjustment, and follow-up visits following fracture treatment.

Subsequent care for complications of fractures, such as malunion and nonunion, should be reported with the appropriate seventh-character values for subsequent care with nonunion (K, M, N,) or subsequent care with malunion (P, Q, R). However, if a patient delays seeking treatment for a fracture and presents for initial care for a fracture or nonunion, the appropriate seventh character for "initial encounter," rather than "subsequent encounter," should be assigned. Care for complications of surgical treatment for fracture repairs during the healing or recovery phase should be coded with the appropriate complication codes rather than the seventh-character values.

Malunion implies that bony healing has occurred but that the fracture fragments are in poor position. Treatment of malunion ordinarily involves surgical cutting of the bone (osteotomy), repositioning the bone, and adding some type of internal fixation device with or without bone graft. Malunion is frequently diagnosed while the fracture is still in a healing state, but sometimes no surgical intervention is used in the hope that the patient may not have any functional problems as a result of the malunion.

FIGURE 30.3 Gustilo Classification of Open Fractures

I Low energy, wound less than 1 cm

II Wound greater than 1 cm with moderate soft tissue damage

III High energy wound greater than 1 cm with extensive soft tissue damage

- IIIA Adequate soft tissue cover
- IIIB Inadequate soft tissue cover
- IIIC Associated with arterial injury

Nonunion, on the other hand, implies that healing has not occurred and that there is still separation of the bony structures involved in the fracture. Treatment of nonunion usually involves opening the fracture, scraping away intervening soft tissue (usually scar tissue), performing a partial debridement of the bone end, and repositioning the bone. Treating nonunion of a fracture is more complicated and difficult to perform than treating a malunion.

Skull Fractures and Intracranial Injuries

Fractures of skull and facial bones are classified to category S02. Fourth characters indicate the area of the skull (e.g., base) or face (e.g., mandible) fractured. Fifth characters provide additional specificity, such as the specific bone or the type of fracture. Any associated intracranial injury is coded separately using a code from category S06.

If an intracranial injury involves an open wound of the head (S01.-) or a fracture of the skull (S02.-), these are coded separately, as instructed by the notes in the Tabular List. Codes for intracranial injury (S06.-) have additional characters to indicate:

- Whether a loss of consciousness was associated with the injury
- How long the unconscious state lasted
- If the loss of consciousness was greater than 24 hours
  —with return to preexisting level of consciousness
  —without return to preexisting level of consciousness with patient surviving
- Whether there was loss of consciousness of any duration with death due to brain injury or due to any other cause, prior to regaining consciousness

Because the type of information above is rarely included in the diagnostic statement, it usually must be obtained through a review of the medical record, particularly the emergency department record and admitting note.

Category S06, Intracranial injury, which includes traumatic injury, is divided into the following subcategories:

S06.0 Concussion
S06.1 Traumatic cerebral edema
S06.2 Diffuse traumatic brain injury
S06.3 Focal traumatic brain injury (with further subdivisions for unspecified; contusion and laceration of right, left, or unspecified cerebrum; traumatic hemorrhage of right, left, or unspecified cerebrum; and contusion, laceration, and hemorrhage of cerebellum or brainstem)
S06.4 Epidural hemorrhage
S06.5 Traumatic subdural hemorrhage
S06.6 Traumatic subarachnoid hemorrhage
S06.8 Other specified intracranial injuries (including injury of right or left internal carotid artery, intracranial portion, and other intracranial injury)
S06.9 Unspecified intracranial injury

Concussion (S06.0x-) is the most common type of traumatic brain injury. It refers to cerebral bruising that sometimes leads to a transient unconsciousness, often followed by brief amnesia, vertigo, nausea, and weak pulse. The patient may experience severe headache and blurred vision after regaining consciousness. Recovery usually takes place within 24 to 48 hours. Patients with this type of head injury are often dazed, and the physician may have to rely on clinical findings alone to make a diagnosis of concussion. When there is documentation of concussion with other intracranial injuries classified in category S06, the code for the specified intracranial injury should be assigned. When the head injury is further described as a cerebral laceration or a cerebral contusion or when it is associated with subdural, subarachnoid, other intracranial hemorrhage, or other specified condition classifiable in category S06, the code for concussion is not assigned.

Postconcussional syndrome (F07.81) includes a variety of symptoms that may occur for a variable period of time following a concussion, sometimes as long as a few weeks. The symptoms most often associated with postconcussional syndrome are headache, dizziness, vertigo, fatigue, difficulty in concentrating, depression, anxiety, tinnitus, heart palpitations, and apathy. Any of these conditions may cause the patient to seek treatment. Code F07.81 is ordinarily not assigned on the initial admission for treatment of the concussion. When the patient is treated for symptoms within 24 to 48 hours of injury and the physician lists a diagnosis as postconcussional syndrome, postcontusional syndrome, or posttraumatic brain syndrome, the coder should ask the physician whether the concussion is still in the current state. If it is, it should be coded to S06.0x- rather than F07.81. Posttraumatic headache is often associated with postconcussion syndrome. Use an additional code (G44.3-) to capture any associated acute or chronic posttraumatic headache, if applicable, along with code F07.81.

Vertebral Fractures

Vertebral fractures are classified according to the region of the spine affected: cervical spine (S12.-), thoracic spine (S22.0-), and lumbar spine (S32.0-). Fourth characters at category S12 indicate the vertebra (e.g., first cervical vertebra), while fifth and sixth characters provide additional information on the type of fracture (e.g., stable, unstable, displaced, nondisplaced). Fifth characters at subcategories S22.0 and S32.0 indicate the vertebra (e.g., second thoracic vertebra, third lumbar vertebra, etc.), while sixth characters specify the type of fracture (e.g., wedge compression, stable burst). For example:

S12.030-	Displaced posterior arch fracture of first cervical vertebra
S22.020-	Wedge compression fracture of second thoracic vertebra
S32.031-	Stable burst fracture of third lumbar vertebra

Additional codes are used to report any associated spinal cord injuries, as follows:

S14.0, S14.1-	Cervical spinal cord injury
S24.0, S24.1-	Thoracic spinal cord injury
S34.-	Lumbar spinal cord and spinal nerve injury

If the fracture of the ribs, sternum, and thoracic spine also involve injury of intrathoracic organs, these should be coded separately using codes from subcategory S27.

Fractures of the Pelvis

Fractures of the pelvis are classified to category S32. The pelvis is formed by a group of bones (ischium, ilium, pubis, sacrum, and coccyx) that form a circle that supports the spine and connects the trunk to the lower extremities. Any or all of these bones can be fractured; fractures that

involve disruption of the pelvic circle are considered more severe. ICD-10-CM provides codes to identify multiple pelvic fractures with (S32.81-) or without (S32.82-) disruption of the pelvic circle. ICD-10-CM also provides seventh characters to capture whether the fracture is open or closed and whether this is the initial or subsequent encounter for care or sequela.

Fractures of the Extremities

Category codes S42, S49, S52, S59, S62, S72, S79, S82, S89, and S92 classify fractures of the extremities. Fourth characters usually indicate a general part of the bone (e.g., upper end of ulna), fifth characters indicate a more specific part of the bone (e.g., olecranon process with intra-articular extension of ulna), and sixth characters provide information on laterality (e.g., right, left, or unspecified) as well as whether the fracture is displaced or nondisplaced. For example:

S42.142B Displaced fracture of glenoid cavity of scapula, left shoulder, initial encounter for open fracture

S52.044C Nondisplaced fracture of coronoid process of right ulna, initial encounter for open fracture type IIIA, IIIB, or IIIC

Physeal fractures (subcategories S49.0–S49.1-, S59.0–S59.2-, S79.0–S79.1, and S89.0–S89.3-), which include growth plate fractures, refer to a disruption in the cartilaginous physis of long bones that may or may not involve epiphyseal or metaphyseal bone. These fractures account for 15–20 percent of major long-bone fractures and 34 percent of hand fractures in childhood. The large majority of these fractures heal well without any further problems. However, some lead to clinically significant shortening and angulation; others lead to disorders due to destruction of epiphyseal circulation, which inhibits development of growth plate or formation of bone bridge.

There are many different classification systems throughout the world related to physeal fractures, with the Salter-Harris (SH) classification being the preferred system in North America. ICD-10-CM provides fifth characters to capture the SH type of fracture (type I, II, III, or IV), if documented by the physician. For example:

S49.002A Unspecified physeal fracture of upper end of humerus, left arm, initial encounter for closed fracture

S49.011D Salter-Harris Type I physeal fracture of upper end of humerus, right arm, subsequent encounter for fracture with routine healing

Multiple fractures of the same bone(s) classified with different fourth-character or fifth-character subdivisions (bone part) within the same three-character category are coded individually by site. For example:

- Initial encounter for comminuted fracture of the shaft of the right humerus, with nondisplaced closed-fracture dislocation of right shoulder involving the greater tuberosity, is coded **S42.301A, Unspecified fracture of shaft of humerus, right arm, initial encounter for closed fracture,** and **S42.254A, Nondisplaced fracture of greater tuberosity of right humerus, initial encounter for closed fracture.**
- Initial encounter closed fractures of the olecranon process and coronoid process of the left ulna are coded **S52.022A, Displaced fracture of olecranon process without intra-articular extension of left ulna, initial encounter for closed fracture,** and **S52.042A, Displaced fracture of coronoid process of left ulna, initial encounter for closed fracture.**

EXERCISE 30.2

Code the following diagnoses. Assume these are for initial encounters unless otherwise noted. Do not assign External cause codes.

	Diagnosis	Code
1.	Comminuted fracture, upper end of left tibia	S82.102A
2.	Fracture, left ischium	S32.602A
	Fracture, left second, third, fourth, fifth, and sixth ribs	S22.42xA
3.	Closed fracture of vault of skull with subdural hemorrhage; three-hour loss of consciousness	S02.0xxA S06.5x3A
4.	Open Monteggia's fracture, type II	S52.279B
5.	Cerebral concussion Brain stem contusion without open wound Patient unconscious for almost two hours	S06.383A
6.	Trimalleolar fracture, left ankle	S82.852A
7.	Closed fracture, lateral condyle, left humerus	S42.432A
8.	Compound fracture, coronoid process of mandible	S02.63xB
9.	Compound fracture, type II, shaft of tibia and fibula, left	S82.202B S82.832B
10.	Bilateral compound depressed skull fractures Bilateral massive cerebral contusion and laceration	S02.91xB S06.310A S06.320A

Pathological Fractures

Bones weakened by conditions such as osteoporosis or neoplastic disease often develop pathological fractures that occur with no trauma or only minor trauma that would not result in fracture in a healthy bone. This type of fracture is classified with musculoskeletal conditions rather than with injuries and is discussed in chapter 23 of this handbook.

Current pathologic fractures are reported using categories/subcategories M80, M84.4-, M84.5, and M84.6. For example:

- A patient with a chronic vertebral pathological fracture with orders for pain medication is admitted for an unrelated condition. Code **M84.48xA, Pathological fracture, other site, initial encounter for fracture,** is assigned for a chronic vertebral fracture. The seventh-character value "D" is not appropriate because the patient has not completed active treatment.

Compression Fractures

Compression fractures may be due either to disease or to trauma. The coder should search the medical record for any recent significant trauma or for any indication of concurrent bone disease that might point to pathological fracture. If the diagnosis cannot be clarified, the physician should be asked to provide further specificity.

Fractures Due to Birth Injury

Fractures due to birth injury are not classified in the injury chapter of ICD-10-CM but instead are classified as perinatal conditions (category P13) and are discussed in chapter 27 of this handbook.

PROCEDURES RELATED TO FRACTURES

In the treatment of fractures, the primary goal is to achieve correct bone alignment and maintain alignment until healing is completed and normal function can be restored. Procedures include open and closed reduction, simple manipulation, and application of various types of fixation and traction devices. The type of treatment depends on the general condition of the patient, the presence of any associated injuries, and the type and location of the fracture.

Reduction of Fractures

The most common fracture treatment involves moving bone fragments into as nearly normal an anatomic position as possible, with stabilization to maintain the bone in this position until it is sufficiently healed to prevent displacement. ICD-10-PCS classifies reduction of a displaced fracture to the root operation "Reposition." The application of a cast or splint in conjunction with the "Reposition" procedure is not coded separately. Treatment of a nondisplaced fracture is coded to the procedure performed; for example, casting is classified to the root operation "Immobilization" in the Placement Section.

In an open reduction, the surgeon exposes the bone by extending the open wound over the fracture or making a further incision to work directly with the bone for the purpose of restoring correct alignment. Debridement is often necessary to remove debris or other material that has entered an open fracture site. In a closed reduction, alignment is achieved without incision to the fracture site. Debridement of the bone is not needed.

Internal Fixation

Internal fixation includes the use of pins, screws, staples, rods, and plates that are inserted into the bone to maintain alignment. When the fractured bone is in good alignment so that no manipulation is necessary, internal fixation may be used to stabilize the bone without any fracture reduction being performed. Internal fixation is also used without reduction when it is necessary to reinsert an internal fixation device because the original is either displaced or broken. An incision is made for the purpose of inserting the internal fixation wires or pins; a code from the root operation "Insertion" is assigned for fixation that is not associated with fracture reduction. Internal fixation can also be used with closed fracture reduction. The small incision necessary to insert the fixation device does not warrant considering the procedure to be an open reduction.

External Fixation

Unlike internal fixation, external fixation is ordinarily noninvasive and includes "Traction" or "Immobilization" by the use of casts or splints. The classification essentially recognizes four types of external fixation devices: monoplanar (seventh-character qualifier "3"), ring system (seventh-character qualifier "4"), hybrid system (seventh-character qualifier "5"), and limb-lengthening device (seventh-character qualifier "9"). When "Traction" is performed, a code from the Placement Section, root operation "Traction," is used. External fixation devices may later be removed using the root operation "Removal" in the Medical and Surgical Section. "Removal" of splints, casts, and braces are classified to the Placement Section, root operation "Removal."

Although "Traction" devices are usually applied by means of Kirschner wires or Steinmann pins, the use of these materials is not considered an internal fixation. "Traction" devices include the following:

- Skin "Traction," such as tape, foam, or felt traction devices applied directly to the skin, with longitudinal force applied to the limb
- Skeletal "Traction" into or through the bone that applies force directly to the long bones (the wires or pins are drilled transversely through the bone and exit through the skin)
- Cervical spinal "Traction," such as Baron's tongs, Crutchfield tongs, and halo skull "Traction"
- Upper-extremity "Traction," such as Dunlap's skin "Traction"
- Lower-extremity "Traction," such as Buck's extension skin "Traction," Charnley's "Traction" unit, Hamilton-Russell's "Traction," balanced suspension "Traction," and fixed skeletal "Traction"

EXERCISE 30.3

Code the following procedures; do not code diagnoses.

1. Traction to right lower extremity with traction apparatus	2W6LX0Z

2. Open reduction and debridement of Monteggia fracture, right upper extremity, with Rush pin (internal) to stabilize ulna — 0PSK04Z, 0PBK0ZZ
   Reposition
   Excision

---

3. Open reduction of fracture, right tibia, with Knowles pins (internal) and two-inch screw — 0QSG04Z
   Below-the-knee cast applied

---

4. Open reduction and Kirschner wire fixation (internal) of distal to main fragment, fracture of left humerus shaft — 0PSG04Z

---

5. Open reduction of fracture, left hip, with Jewett nail fixation (upper femur) — 0QS704Z

---

6. Reduction, displaced fracture right humerus shaft (external approach) with cast — 0PSFXZZ

---

7. Open reduction and internal fixation, fracture of right mandible — 0NST04Z

---

8. Open reduction, fracture of left maxilla and left zygomatic arch — 0NSS0ZZ, 0NSN0ZZ
   Closed reduction, nasal bone fracture (external approach) — 0NSBXZZ

---

9. Bifrontal craniotomy with reposition and debridement of compound skull fractures — 0NSP0ZZ, 0NS00ZZ
   Open reduction, right orbital fracture — 0NB10ZZ
   Tracheostomy (percutaneous) — 0NB20ZZ, 0B113Z4

ADMISSIONS OR ENCOUNTERS FOR ORTHOPEDIC AFTERCARE

Patients who have had fracture reduction usually require aftercare for removal of wires, pins, plates, or external fixation devices. In addition, patients with orthopedic injuries still in the healing stage may be seen primarily for conditions not related to the injury but with some monitoring or clinical evaluation of the injury carried out during the episode of care. Aftercare for traumatic fractures is coded to the acute fracture with the appropriate seventh-character value for subsequent care. The aftercare Z codes should not be used for aftercare of injuries. For aftercare of an injury, the acute injury code is assigned, with the appropriate seventh-character value for subsequent encounter.

Z codes are provided for admissions or encounters for other (non-fracture related) orthopedic aftercare, as follows:

Z47.1	Aftercare following joint replacement surgery
Z47.2	Encounter for removal of internal fixation device
Z47.81	Encounter for orthopedic aftercare following surgical amputation
Z47.82	Encounter for orthopedic aftercare following scoliosis surgery
Z47.89	Encounter for other orthopedic aftercare

However, code **Z47.2, Encounter for removal of internal fixation device,** should not be used if the encounter is for removal of the internal fixation device due to infection or inflammatory reaction to an internal fixation device (T84.6-) or a mechanical complication of an internal fixation device (T84.1-). The appropriate code from T84.6- or T84.1- should be used instead.

A code from subcategory Z47.3- is assigned for admissions or encounters involving aftercare following explantation of a joint prosthesis. Aftercare includes admissions for joint replacement surgery where it was necessary to stage the procedure, or for joint prosthesis replacement following a prior explantation of the prosthesis. There may be a medical need to remove an existing joint prosthesis (e.g., due to infection or other problem); however, it may not be possible to replace the prosthesis at the same encounter, thereby requiring a return encounter to insert a new prosthesis.

Z codes are also provided to indicate an orthopedic status when it is significant for the episode of care. Orthopedic status codes include **Z89.23, Acquired absence of shoulder joint; Z89.52, Acquired absence of knee joint; Z89.62, Acquired absence of hip joint; Z96.6-, Presence of orthopedic joint implants; Z96.7, Presence of other bone and tendon implants; Z97.1-, Presence of artificial limb (complete) (partial);** and **Z98.1, Arthrodesis status.** Acquired absence of joint codes are assigned when a patient is awaiting implantation of a joint prosthesis. In a common scenario, the prosthesis is removed due to infection to allow the site time to heal, and the patient is readmitted before completing the joint replacement procedure. The acquired absence codes indicate that the patient has had a prosthesis explanted; however, they can also be used when the current encounter is unrelated to implantation of a new prosthesis.

When the aftercare involves replacement of the hip joint prosthesis following previous explantation, assign code Z47.32. For example:

- A patient developed an infection after a left total hip replacement and was admitted for surgical treatment. At surgery, the prosthesis was removed. An antibiotic impregnated cement spacer was inserted. Because the infection had resolved, the patient was readmitted at six weeks for removal of the antibiotic spacer and revision of the total hip replacement with insertion of a new metal hip prosthesis.

For the initial admission in this example, assign code **T84.52xA, Infection and inflammatory reaction due to internal left hip prosthesis, initial encounter,** as the principal diagnosis. Code

Z96.642, Presence of left artificial hip joint, should be assigned as an additional diagnosis. Assign code **0SHB08Z, Insertion of spacer into left hip joint, open approach, no qualifier,** and code **0SPB0JZ, Removal of synthetic substitute from left hip joint, open approach, no qualifier.** For the second admission, assign code **Z47.32, Aftercare following explantation of hip joint prosthesis,** as the principal diagnosis. For the procedures performed, assign code **0SRE01Z, Replacement of left hip joint, acetabular surface with metal synthetic substitute, open approach, no qualifier;** code **0SRS01Z, Replacement of left hip joint, femoral surface with metal synthetic substitute, open approach, no qualifier;** and code **0SPB08Z, Removal of spacer from left hip joint, open approach, no qualifier.**

Aftercare codes should be used in conjunction with any other aftercare codes or other diagnosis codes to provide better detail on the specifics of an aftercare encounter visit, unless otherwise directed by the classification. The sequencing of multiple aftercare codes depends on the circumstances of the encounter. For example:

- A patient had a right intertrochanteric hip fracture that was repaired through a total hip joint replacement. He is now receiving aftercare at the physician's office. Codes **Z47.1, Aftercare following joint replacement surgery,** and **Z96.641, Presence of right artificial hip joint,** are assigned for the encounter. Each code represents a different piece of information regarding the aftercare and is needed to describe the encounter fully. Code **S72.141D, Displaced intertrochanteric fracture of right femur, subsequent encounter for closed fracture with routine healing,** is not appropriate because there is no longer a fracture; the hip has been replaced by a prosthetic joint.

DISLOCATIONS AND SUBLUXATIONS

Joint dislocation occurs when bones in a joint become displaced or misaligned and the ligaments are damaged. A subluxation is a partial or incomplete dislocation. Dislocation or subluxation associated with fracture is included in the fracture code, and reduction of the dislocation is included in the code for the fracture reduction. Dislocation or subluxation of a joint without associated fracture is classified in the following categories:

S03 Dislocation and sprain of joints and ligaments of head
S13 Dislocation and sprain of joints and ligaments at neck level
S23 Dislocation and sprain of joints and ligaments of thorax
S33 Dislocation and sprain of joints and ligaments of lumbar spine and pelvis
S43 Dislocation and sprain of joints and ligaments of shoulder girdle
S53 Dislocation and sprain of joints and ligaments of elbow
S63 Dislocation and sprain of joints and ligaments at wrist and hand level
S73 Dislocation and sprain of joint and ligaments of hip
S83 Dislocation and sprain of joints and ligaments of knee
S93 Dislocation and sprain of joints and ligaments at ankle, foot, and toe level

The first axis is the general site, such as wrist and hand, with the fifth character indicating a more specific site such as midcarpal dislocation of the wrist; the sixth-character axis indicates whether it is a subluxation or dislocation, and laterality. Any associated open wound or spinal cord injury is coded separately.

Reduction of dislocation not associated with fracture is coded to the Medical and Surgical Section, root operation "Reposition," with the body part being the appropriate joint (rather than the actual bone, as with procedures to reduce fractures).

INTERNAL INJURIES OF THE CHEST, ABDOMEN, AND PELVIS

Internal injuries of the chest, abdomen, and pelvis are classified to categories S24–S27 and S34–S37. Any associated open wounds are coded separately. For example:

S27.0-	Pneumothorax (traumatic) without mention of open wound
S27.1- + S21.309-	Hemothorax with open wound front wall of thorax into thoracic cavity
S36.400-	Injury of duodenum without mention of open wound into cavity
S26.91-	Contusion of heart

Codes from subcategory S37.0, Injury of kidney, are used to describe an internal injury of the kidney caused by trauma. A nontraumatic acute kidney injury is coded **N17.9, Acute kidney failure, unspecified.**

BLOOD VESSEL AND NERVE INJURIES

When a primary injury results in minor damage to peripheral nerves or blood vessels, the primary injury is sequenced first, with additional codes for injuries to nerves and spinal cord (such as category S04) and/or injury to blood vessels (such as category S15). When the primary injury is to a blood vessel or nerve, however, the code for that injury should be sequenced first.

For example, an open wound of the abdominal wall without penetration into the peritoneal cavity, but with rupture of the aorta, would be coded **S35.00-, Injury to abdominal aorta,** with S31.109- as an additional code.

OPEN WOUNDS

Open wounds such as lacerations, puncture wounds, cuts, animal bites, avulsions, and traumatic amputations that are not associated with fracture are coded separately in categories S01, S11, S21, S31, S41, S51, S61, S71, S81, and S91. Fourth characters provide more specificity regarding the body area. Fifth and sixth characters indicate the type of wound such as laceration, puncture wound, or open bite, and whether there is a foreign body. Any associated injury to internal organs or wound infection are coded separately.

Both cellulitis and osteomyelitis sometimes occur as complications of open wounds. Sequencing of codes for open wounds with these major infections depends on the circumstances of admission. It is important to determine whether it is the wound that is being addressed or only the resulting infection. For example, a patient who had an open wound of the hand six weeks ago might be seen because osteomyelitis has developed. In this situation, the osteomyelitis would ordinarily be designated as the principal diagnosis, with an additional code for the open wound. A patient who had a slight puncture wound earlier in the week might show evidence of cellulitis at the site. The wound itself did not require any attention. The reason for the encounter is cellulitis, and cellulitis is the principal diagnosis.

AMPUTATIONS

When listed as a diagnosis, traumatic amputation is classified to subcategories S08.1- through S08.8-, S28.1- through S28.2-, S38.1- through S38.2-, S48.0- through S48.9-, S58.0- through S58.9-, S68.0- through S68.7-, S78.0- through S78.9-, S88.0- through S88.9-, and S98.0- through S98.9-, rather than classified as an open wound. ICD-10-CM distinguishes between complete and partial traumatic amputations. An amputation not identified as partial or complete should be coded to complete amputation. For example:

S58.019-	Complete traumatic amputation of arm at elbow
S58.122-	Partial traumatic amputation of left arm below elbow
S88.011-	Complete traumatic amputation of right leg at knee

The term "amputation" is also used for an amputation procedure, which can be performed for a variety of reasons other than the treatment of trauma. Amputation is performed by either disarticulation or cutting through the bone. Amputation procedures are classified in ICD-10-PCS to the Medical and Surgical Section, root operation "Detachment." The body part value is the site of the "Detachment." If applicable, a qualifier is assigned to specify the level where the extremity was detached. "Detachment" procedures are found only in body systems "X" ("anatomical regions, upper extremities") and "Y" ("anatomical regions, lower extremities") because amputations are performed on the extremities, across overlapping body layers (e.g., skin, muscle, bone), and therefore cannot be coded to a specific musculoskeletal body system, such as bones or joints.

The root operation "Detachment" makes use of specific qualifiers that are dependent on the body part value in the "upper extremities" and "lower extremities" body systems. Definitions of the terms used with "Detachment" are shown in table 30.1.

Sample codes include the following:

0X6J0Z0	Disarticulation of right wrist, complete, open
0Y6M0Z0	Complete amputation right foot
0Y6C0Z3	Amputation above right knee, distal shaft of femur
0X680Z2	Mid-shaft amputation, right humerus

TABLE 30.1 Definitions of Terms Used for Qualifiers for "Detachment" Procedures

Body Part	Qualifier Term Definition
Upper arm and upper leg	**High:** Amputation at the proximal portion of the shaft of the humerus or femur
	Mid: Amputation at the middle portion of the shaft of the humerus or femur
	Low: Amputation at the distal portion of the shaft of the humerus or femur
Hand and foot	**Complete:** Amputation through the carpometacarpal joint of the hand or through the tarsometatarsal joint of the foot
	Partial: Amputation anywhere along the shaft or head of the metacarpal bone of the hand or of the metatarsal bone of the foot
Thumb, finger, or toe	**Complete:** Amputation at the metacarpophalangeal/metatarsophalangeal joint
	High: Amputation anywhere along the proximal phalanx
	Mid: Amputation through the proximal interphalangeal joint or anywhere along the middle phalanx
	Low: Amputation through the distal interphalangeal joint or anywhere along the distal phalanx

OTHER INJURIES

Superficial injuries such as contusions, blisters, abrasions, superficial foreign bodies, and insect bites are classified to categories S00, S10, S20, S30, S40, S50, S60, S70, S80, and S90. The fourth and fifth characters indicate a more specific site or type of injury. The sixth character indicates laterality. When these injuries are associated with a major injury, such as fracture of the same site, a code for the superficial injury is usually not assigned. Note that the term "superficial" does not refer to the severity of the injury but to the superficial structures affected, that is, those pertaining to or situated near the surface.

The presence of a foreign body entering through an orifice is classified in categories T15 through T19. When the foreign body is associated with a penetrating wound, it is coded as an open wound, by site, residual foreign body in soft tissue. A splinter without open wound is classified to superficial injury by body region. A foreign body accidentally left during a procedure in an operative wound is considered to be a complication of a procedure and is coded T81.5-. Codes within T15–T19 that include the external cause do not need an additional External cause code.

EARLY COMPLICATIONS OF TRAUMA

Certain early complications of trauma that are not included in the code for the injury are classified in category T79, Certain early complications of trauma, not elsewhere classified. The fourth-character axis indicates the type of complication, such as air or fat embolism, traumatic secondary and recurrent hemorrhage and seroma, traumatic shock, traumatic anuria, traumatic ischemia of muscle, traumatic subcutaneous emphysema, or traumatic compartment syndrome. Ordinarily, codes from category T79 are assigned as secondary codes, with the code for the injury sequenced first. With today's shorter lengths of stay and increased emphasis on outpatient care, however, the complication itself may occasionally be the reason for an outpatient encounter or admission and is the principal diagnosis in such cases.

Subcategory T79.A, Traumatic compartment syndrome, classifies compartment syndrome secondary to trauma. Nontraumatic compartment syndrome is classified to M79.A-. Acute traumatic compartment syndrome is usually a sequela of a serious injury to the lower or upper extremities, abdomen, or other sites and can lead to significant motor and sensory deficits, pain, stiffness, and deformity when untreated. Acute traumatic compartment syndrome is always associated with fractures, dislocations, and/or crush injuries. Other risk factors for the development of acute traumatic compartment syndrome include vascular injuries and coagulopathy. The diagnosis is established by multiple compartment pressure readings. Traumatic compartment syndrome is coded as follows:

T79.A0	Compartment syndrome, unspecified
T79.A11	Traumatic compartment syndrome of right upper extremity
T79.A12	Traumatic compartment syndrome of left upper extremity
T79.A19	Traumatic compartment syndrome of unspecified upper extremity
T79.A21	Traumatic compartment syndrome of right lower extremity
T79.A22	Traumatic compartment syndrome of left lower extremity
T79.A29	Traumatic compartment syndrome of unspecified lower extremity
T79.A3	Traumatic compartment syndrome of abdomen
T79.A9	Traumatic compartment syndrome of other sites

EXERCISE 30.4

Code the following diagnoses. Assume these are for initial encounters unless otherwise noted. Do not assign External cause codes.

1. Stab wound of abdominal wall, infected	S31.119A L08.9
2. Lacerations, left foot, with foreign body	S91.322A
3. Traumatic amputation of left arm and hand above the elbow	S48.112A
4. Traumatic anuria due to injury to kidney	S37.009A T79.5xxA

OTHER EFFECTS OF EXTERNAL CAUSE

Categories T66 through T78 classify other and unspecified effects of external causes resulting from exposure to heat and to cold and a variety of other conditions due to external causes that are not classifiable elsewhere in ICD-10-CM. Codes from these categories are not assigned when a more specific code for the effect is available. For example, colitis due to radiation therapy is coded **K52.0, Gastroenteritis and colitis due to radiation,** because the effect is identified. A diagnosis of complication of radiation therapy not otherwise specified and with no further information documented in the medical record is coded **T66.-, Radiation sickness, unspecified.**

Code T68.- is assigned for hypothermia, with several exceptions. If it is due to anesthesia, code T88.51 is assigned. When the hypothermia is not due to low temperature, code **R68.0, Hypothermia not associated with low environmental temperature,** is assigned. An additional code is used to identify the source of exposure, such as exposure to excessive cold of man-made origin (W93) or of natural origin (X31). Three codes are provided for hypothermia of the newborn: **P80.0, Cold injury syndrome; P80.8, Other hypothermia of newborn;** and **P80.9, Hypothermia of newborn, unspecified.**

Category T78, Adverse effects not elsewhere classified, is used to classify a variety of adverse effects such as anaphylactic reaction/shock, adverse food reactions, angioneurotic edema, unspecified allergy, and Arthus phenomenon.

Anaphylaxis is an immunologic reaction that affects multiple body systems. Reactions can range from mild—with hives, itchiness, swelling of eyes and lips, and some congestion—to life threatening, with airway obstruction and cardiovascular collapse. Shock occurs when there is excessive fluid leakage from the blood vessels into the tissues. Anaphylactic reaction due to an adverse food reaction is coded T78.0, with a fifth character indicating the type of food involved. For example:

- A patient with a known allergy to tree nuts presents to the emergency department with wheezing and urticaria. The patient is diagnosed with an anaphylactic reaction secondary to eating cookies containing walnuts. Assign code **T78.05xA, Anaphylactic reaction due to tree nuts and seeds, initial encounter.** Codes from subcategory T78.0 are assigned for both anaphylactic reaction and anaphylactic shock due to adverse food reaction.

Anaphylactic reaction due to correct medicinal substances properly administered is classified to code **T88.6-, Anaphylactic reaction due to adverse effect of correct drug or medicament properly administered,** followed by a code from T36 through T50, with fifth- or sixth-character "5" to identify the drug. Codes in subcategory T80.5, Anaphylactic reaction due to serum, describe allergic reactions to serum including blood transfusions, vaccination, and other serum. Other serum reactions due to the administration of blood and blood products, vaccination, and other serum are classified to subcategory T80.6. When the anaphylactic reaction is due to an incorrect use of a drug, a medicinal or biological substance, or a toxic material not chiefly medicinal, the reaction is classified as a poisoning, with the poisoning code sequenced first and an additional code of T78.2- assigned to indicate the reaction.

EXERCISE 30.5

Code the following diagnoses and assign External cause codes. Assume these are for initial encounters unless otherwise noted.

1. Heat prostration due to salt and water depletion	T67.4xxA
2. Frostbite, all toes due to cold exposure	T33.831A T33.832A X31.xxxA
3. Radiation cataract	H26.8 W90.8xxA
4. Anaphylactic reaction due to eating peanuts	T78.01xA

LATE EFFECTS OF INJURIES

In coding late effects of injuries, the residual condition or specific type of sequela (such as scar, deformity, or paralysis) is sequenced first, followed by the injury code with the seventh-character value "S," sequela. A seventh-character "S" is also assigned to the External cause of injury code. A current injury code is never used with a late effect code for the same type of injury.

EXERCISE 30.6

Code the following diagnoses and assign External cause codes; sequence the codes according to the principles for coding late effects.

	Diagnosis	Codes
1.	Paralysis of right wrist due to previous accidental self-inflicted laceration of right radial nerve	G56.91 S64.21xS X58.xxxS
2.	Esophageal stricture due to old lye burn of esophagus	K22.2 T28.6xxS
3.	Nonunion fracture of neck of left femur suffered in a bar brawl three months ago	S72.002K Y04.0xxS
4.	Posttraumatic scars of cheek due to old accidental lacerations	L90.5 S01.419S X58.xxxS

EXERCISE 30.7

Code the following diagnoses and procedures. Assume these are for initial encounters unless otherwise noted. Assign External cause codes where information is provided.

1. Anterior dislocation of left shoulder,	S43.015A
patient thrown from horse she was riding	V80.010A
while working as a horse trainer	Y93.52
	Y99.0
Dislocation reduction, external approach	0RSKXZZ
2. Displaced fracture dislocation left humerus,	S42.212A
surgical neck; patient caught in avalanche	X36.1xxA
while on vacation skiing at mountain resort	Y92.838
	Y93.23
	Y99.8
Open reduction and internal fixation	0PSD04Z
with Rush pin and screws	
3. Colles fracture, right	S52.531A
Patient fell from chair at home	W07.xxxA
	Y92.099
	Y99.8
Closed reduction with anterior-posterior	0PSHXZZ
plaster splints (external approach)	
4. Intracapsular fracture, neck of femur, right	S72.011A
Patient fell from in-line skates	V00.111A
	Y93.51
	Y99.8
Closed reduction with insertion of	0QS634Z
Smith-Petersen nail (percutaneous approach)	

5.	Closed fractures of right upper femur and left ilium	S72.001A
	Fat emboli, posttraumatic	S32.302A
	Patient driving motorcycle on highway	T79.1xxA
	lost control and overturned	V28.4xxA
	Loss of control	
	Open reduction with plate fixation, right upper	0QS604Z
	femur, with skeletal traction	2W67X0Z
	for ilium fracture	
6.	Fracture of base of skull, with right	S02.10xA
	subdural hemorrhage without loss of consciousness;	S06.5x0A
	patient fell from parachute in a voluntary descent	V97.29
	during military training	Y99.1
7.	Posttraumatic shortening of left radius	M21.732
	due to previous comminuted fracture of	S52.502S
	distal end of left forearm, broken in	V86.92xS
	accidental crash of snowmobile	
8.	Ruptured spleen, traumatic	S36.09xA
	Major contusion to left kidney	S37.022A
	Traumatic shock	T79.4xxA
	Patient caught in heavy farm machinery	W30.9xxA
	that he was operating on his farm	Y92.79
		Y99.0
	Excretory urography with low osmolar contrast	07TP4ZZ
	Laparoscopic splenectomy	BT141ZZ
9.	Cerebral cortex contusion; patient died	S06.337A
	from brain injury without regaining consciousness;	W13.0xxA
	patient had fallen through balcony from skyscraper	Y92.29
	observation tower while sightseeing	Y93.89
		Y99.8

10.	Confirmed battered wife syndrome due to severe beating of chest wall by husband Multiple contusions over trunk	T74.11xA S20.219A Y04.0xxA Y07.01
11.	Anoxic brain damage due to previous intracranial injury with loss of consciousness three years ago, when patient was accidentally struck by car while walking along highway	G93.1 S06.9x9S V03.90xS
12.	Comminuted fracture of the right distal radius and ulna; child fell from playground equipment; initial treatment is in the physician's office	S52.501A S52.601A W09.8xxA Y93.89 Y99.8
	Two weeks later, patient had open reduction and internal fixation (ORIF) at an acute care hospital	S52.501A S52.601A W09.8xxA 0PSK04Z 0PSH04Z
	Follow-up visit to the physician's office for X-rays and postoperative examination	S52.501D S52.601D
13.	A three-year-old child was brought into the hospital for an evaluation of suspected physical abuse. The child's older sibling had been beaten severely by the stepfather, so it was requested that the younger child be evaluated for abuse. After evaluation, examination, and interviews, it was determined that the younger child had not been abused.	Z04.72

CHAPTER 31 Burns

CHAPTER OVERVIEW

- Categories T20 through T32 are assigned for all burns and corrosions except sunburn and friction burns.
- ICD-10-CM distinguishes between burns and corrosions. Burn codes are assigned to thermal burns from a heat source. Corrosion codes are for burns due to chemicals.
- Burns are first classified by general anatomical site. A fourth character indicates the type of burn according to depth: first, second, or third degree.
- Codes are sequenced to reflect the degree of the burn. The highest degree takes precedence.
  - —Multiple burns on the same site require classification of only the highest degree of burn.
  - —Multiple burns at different sites require sequencing the most severe burn first and using additional codes for the burns of other sites.
- The extent of the body surface involved is estimated using the "rule of nines," a guideline that is also used to help code the burn.
- External cause codes are used to classify the place of occurrence as well as:
  - —The source of the burns and corrosions, such as fire, electric current, and hot liquid
  - —Situations such as accident, assault, and suicide
- Other injuries associated with burns often require additional codes.
- Certain pre-existing conditions might have an impact on the prognosis or care of the patient. These pre-existing conditions should be coded as additional diagnoses.

LEARNING OUTCOMES

After studying this chapter you should be able to:

Understand the difference between first-, second-, and third-degree burns.

Properly sequence the codes of multiple burns and related conditions.

Understand how the extent of burn is calculated using the "rule of nines."

Identify injuries and illnesses that might be coded in association with the burns.

TERM TO KNOW

Rule of nines
a tool to help physicians estimate the amount of body surface involved in a burn

REMEMBER . . .

Burns heal at different rates. It is possible to have both healed and unhealed burns for the same episode of care.

INTRODUCTION

Codes from categories T20 through T32 are assigned for burns and corrosions except sunburn and friction burns, which are classified as dermatitis and superficial injury, respectively. ICD-10-CM distinguishes between burns and corrosions. The burn codes are for thermal burns, except sunburns, that are a result of a heat source (e.g., fire, hot appliance). Burns due to chemicals are classified to corrosion. The guidelines for both burns and corrosions are the same. Nonhealing burns and necrosis of burned skin are coded as acute current burns (categories T20–T28, seventh character "A" for initial encounter or "D" for subsequent encounter). Sequelae (such as scarring or contracture) that remain after a burn has healed are classified as sequela (categories T20–T28, seventh character "S" for sequela). Because burns heal at different rates, a patient may have both healed and unhealed burns during the same episode of care. For this reason, it is possible to use current burn codes as well as late-effect burn codes on the same record (when both a current burn and sequelae of an old burn exist).

ANATOMICAL SITE OF BURN

The first axis for classifying burns is the general anatomical site, with a fifth character or sixth character to indicate a more specific site, as follows:

T20–T25	Burns and corrosions of external body surface, specified by site
T26–T28	Burns and corrosions confined to eye and internal organs
T30–T32	Burns and corrosions of multiple and unspecified body regions

When coding burns, assign separate codes for each burn site. Codes for multiple sites and category T30 should only be used if the location of the burns is not documented. Category T30, Burn and corrosion, body region unspecified, is extremely vague and should rarely be used.

FIGURE 31.1 Skin Layers

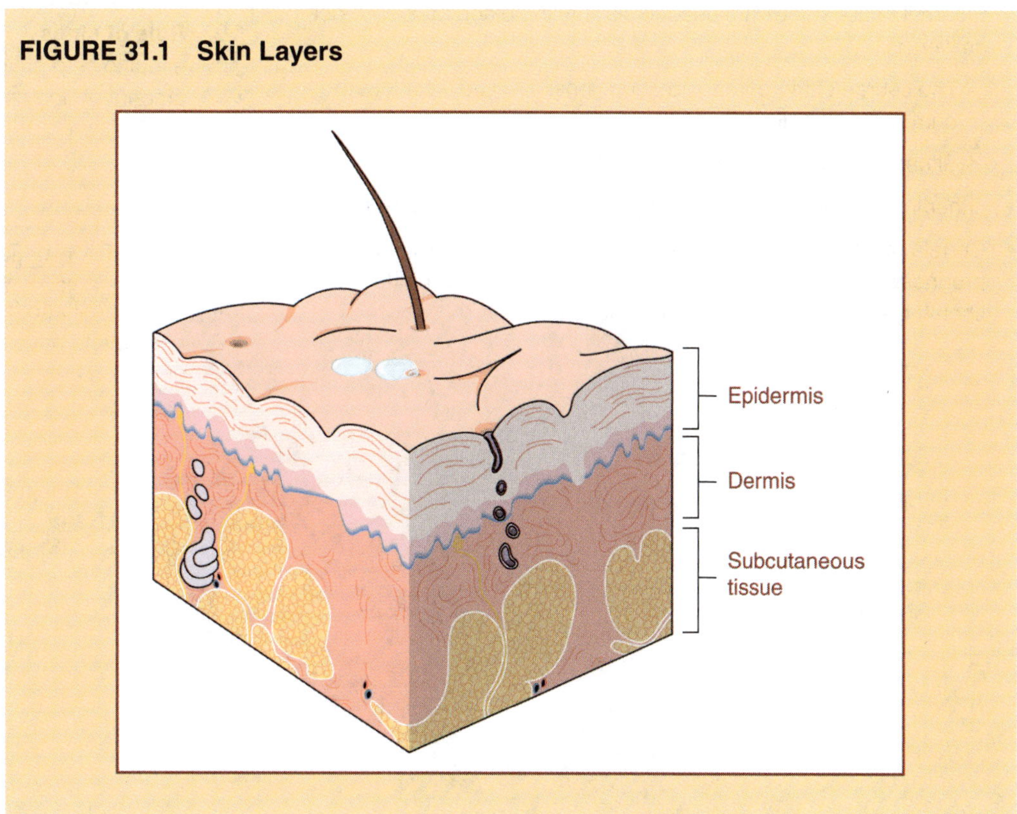

DEPTH OF BURN

For categories T20 through T25, the fourth-character axis indicates the type of burn or corrosion according to depth or degree, as follows:

- First degree (erythema)
- Second degree (blistering)
- Third degree (full-thickness involvement)

First Degree

Damage from first-degree burns is limited to the outer layer of the epidermis, with erythema and increased tenderness. First-degree burns have good capillary refill and do not represent significant injury in terms of fluid replacement needs.

Second Degree

Second-degree burns represent a partial-thickness injury to the dermis, which may be either superficial or deep. Deep second-degree burns heal much more slowly than first-degree burns and are prone to developing infection. The end result of second-degree burns may be hypertrophic scarring.

Third Degree

In third-degree burns, the dermal barrier is lost, and the presence of necrotic tissue creates fluid volume loss with systemic effects on capillaries well away from the burn site. In addition, the burn site establishes an ideal culture medium for infection, which may be life threatening. The critical factor in healing of third-degree burns is blood supply. Areas rich in blood supply, such as hair follicles and sweat glands, have a better chance for reepithelialization.

Deep third-degree burns are characterized by an underlying necrosis with thrombosed vessels. Codes for burns of this depth are assigned only on the basis of a specific diagnosis made by the physician.

Burns of the eye and internal organs (T26–T28) are classified by site, but not by degree. Categories T31 and T32 classify burns and corrosions by the extent of body surface involved and the extent of body surface with third-degree burn or corrosion, but not by specific sites.

SEQUENCING OF CODES FOR BURNS/CORROSIONS AND RELATED CONDITIONS

Burns and corrosions of the same local site at the three-character category level (T20–T28) but of different degrees (depth) are classified to the subcategory identifying the highest degree recorded in the diagnosis. A third-degree burn takes precedence over a second-degree burn, and a second-degree burn takes precedence over a first-degree burn. For example, first-degree and second-degree burns of the leg are classified as second-degree burn of limb (T24.209-); no code is assigned for the first-degree burn.

When coding multiple burns, sequence first the code that reflects the burn of the highest degree (most severe), with additional codes for the burns of other sites. For example, a patient is admitted with third-degree burns of the lower leg and first-degree and second-degree burns of the forearm. The following codes should be assigned:

T24.339- Third-degree burn of leg
T22.219- Second-degree burn of forearm

The circumstances of the admission will determine the principal diagnosis or first-listed diagnosis if a patient has both internal and external burns.

When a patient is admitted for burn injuries and other related conditions such as smoke inhalation and/or respiratory failure, the circumstances of admission govern the selection of the principal or first-listed diagnosis.

Codes for corrosion require that a code from categories T51 through T65, Toxic effects of substances chiefly nonmedicinal as to source, be assigned first to identify chemical and intent.

SEVENTH-CHARACTER VALUES

Categories T20 through T28 require the following seventh-character values:

A Initial encounter
D Subsequent encounter
S Sequela

Value "A" (initial encounter) is used while the patient is receiving active treatment for the injury. Examples of active treatment are surgical treatment, emergency department encounter, and evaluation and treatment by a new physician.

Value "D" (subsequent encounter) is used for encounters after the patient has received active treatment of the injury and is receiving routine care for the injury during the healing or recovery phase. Examples of subsequent care are medication adjustment, other aftercare, and follow-up visits following injury treatment. The aftercare Z codes should not be used for aftercare for injuries. For aftercare of an injury, assign the acute injury code with the seventh character "D" (subsequent encounter).

Value "S" (sequela) is for use for complications or conditions that arise as a direct result of an injury, such as scar formation after a burn; the scars are sequelae of the burn. When using value "S," it is necessary to use both the injury code that precipitated the sequela and the code for the sequela itself. The "S" is added only to the burn or corrosion code, not the sequela code. The "S" value identifies the injury responsible for the sequela. The specific type of sequela (e.g., scar) is sequenced first, followed by the injury code.

Note that using code **Z41.1, Encounter for cosmetic surgery,** is inappropriate for burn patients admitted for repair of scar tissue, skin contracture, or other sequelae. For such patients, a code should be assigned for the condition being treated.

EXTENT OF BURN

Categories T31 and T32 classify burns and corrosions according to the extent of body surface involved. The fourth character indicates the total percentage of body surface involved in all types of burns (T31) or corrosions (T32), including third-degree burns. The fifth character indicates the percentage of the body surface involved in third-degree burns only. Because the fourth character refers to total body surface, the fifth character can never be greater than the total body surface amount. For example, code T31.73 indicates that 70–79 percent of the body surface was involved in some type of burn; the fifth character indicates that third-degree burns were involved in 30–39 percent of the body surface. The fifth character zero (0) is assigned when less than 10 percent of body surface (or no body surface) is involved in a third-degree burn.

The extent of body surface involved in a burn injury is an important factor in burn mortality, and hospitals with burn centers need this information for evaluating patient care management and for preparing statistical data. In addition, third-party payment is often influenced by the extent of

the burn. When more than 20 percent of the body surface is involved in third-degree burns, it is advisable to assign an additional code from category T31. Burn centers sometimes use a code from category T31 as a solo code because many of their patients present with such extensive and severe burns involving many sites that coding them individually is difficult.

Categories T31 and T32 are based on the classic "rule of nines" for estimating the amount of body surface involved in a burn. Physicians may modify the percentage assignments for head and neck in infants and small children because young children have proportionately larger heads than do adults. The percentage may also be modified for adults with large buttocks, abdomen, or thighs. The rule of nines establishes estimates of body surface involved, as follows:

Head and neck	9 percent
Each arm	9 percent
Each leg	18 percent
Anterior trunk	18 percent
Posterior trunk	18 percent
Genitalia	1 percent

For example, based on this rule a physician can calculate that first-degree burns involve 9 percent of the body surface, second-degree burns involve 18 percent, and third-degree burns involve 36 percent. Adding these together, 63 percent of the body was involved in some type of burn. Code T31.63 (burn of any degree involving 60–69 percent of body surface, with 30–39 percent involved in third-degree burn) could then be assigned. Coders are not expected to calculate the extent of a burn, but understanding the rule of nines may help the coder recognize when burns are so extensive that the physician should be asked for additional information.

SUNBURN

Sunburn and other ultraviolet radiation burns are classified in chapter 12, Diseases of Skin and Subcutaneous Tissue. Category L55, Sunburn, is assigned for first-degree (L55.0), second-degree (L55.1), and third-degree sunburns (L55.2) or for an unspecified degree (L55.9). Sunburn due to other ultraviolet radiation exposure, such as a tanning bed, is classified to category L56, Other acute skin changes due to ultraviolet radiation, or category L57, Skin changes due to chronic exposure to nonionizing radiation.

EXTERNAL CAUSES OF BURNS

External cause codes, including codes from category Y92, Place of occurrence of the external cause, are assigned for burns and corrosions, as discussed in chapter 30 of this handbook, which covers other injuries. The following External cause categories should be used to report source and intent:

X00–X08	Exposure to smoke, fire and flames
X10–X19	Contact with heat and hot substances
X75	Intentional self-harm by explosive material
X76	Intentional self-harm by smoke, fire and flames
X77	Intentional self-harm by steam, hot vapors and hot objects
X96	Assault by explosive material
X97	Assault by smoke, fire and flames
X98	Assault by steam, hot vapors and hot objects

ASSOCIATED INJURIES AND ILLNESSES

When a burn is described as infected, two codes are required. The code for the burn is sequenced first, with an additional code for the infection, for example, Initial encounter, *Staphylococcus* infection, second-degree burn of abdominal wall, is coded to T21.22xA + L08.89 + B95.8.

Other injuries frequently occur with burns, and other conditions are sometimes caused by burns. Examples of such injuries include the following:

- Smoke inhalation often occurs in cases of burns due to combustible products (category T59). Certain toxic substances from plastic products may produce hydrogen cyanide (T57.3-). Code J70.5 is assigned to describe a smoke inhalation injury not otherwise specified. Smoke inhalation is caused by inhalation or exposure to hot gaseous products of combustion and can cause serious respiratory complications. Use an additional code to identify any associated respiratory conditions, such as acute respiratory failure. Code J68.9 is assigned for smoke inhalation due to chemical fumes and vapors. When a patient presents with a burn injury and another related condition, such as smoke inhalation or respiratory failure, the circumstances of admission determine the selection of the principal or first-listed diagnosis.

  For example, a child who was rescued from a burning house has no obvious burns, but soot is present about his nose and mouth. The patient is intubated and ventilated for less than 48 hours because of the risk of airway edema from the smoke. The provider diagnoses smoke inhalation. Code **J70.5, Respiratory conditions due to smoke inhalation,** is assigned as the principal diagnosis. Assign code **X00.1xxA, Exposure to smoke in uncontrolled fire in building or structure, initial encounter,** for the external cause of the injury. The patient suffered no obvious burns but was admitted for airway management secondary to the toxic effects of smoke. In addition, assign codes **5A1945Z, Respiratory ventilation, 24-96 consecutive hours,** and **0BH17EZ, Insertion of endotracheal airway into trachea, via natural or artificial opening.**
- Electrical burns, such as those caused by high-tension wires, may cause ventricular arrhythmias (I49.-) that require immediate attention.
- Traumatic shock (T79.4-) is often present at the time of admission or may occur later.

Pre-existing conditions may also have an impact on the burn patient's prognosis and care management and therefore should be coded as additional diagnoses when they otherwise meet criteria for reportable diagnoses. Examples of potentially harmful pre-existing conditions that should be reported include the following:

- Cardiovascular disorders (such as angina, congestive heart failure, or valvular disease) may increase ischemia and precipitate myocardial infarction in a patient with extensive second-degree or third-degree burns. Pulmonary wedge monitoring may be necessary in these cases.
- Asthma, chronic bronchitis, and other chronic obstructive pulmonary diseases may require ventilation therapy.
- Peptic ulcers, either gastric or duodenal, and ulcerative colitis are pre-existing conditions that may lead to gastrointestinal bleeding and require treatment along with the burn.
- Pre-existing kidney disease increases the risk of tubular necrosis and renal failure in patients with third-degree burns or extensive second-degree burns.
- Alcoholism may pose a threat of alcohol withdrawal syndrome, requiring prophylactic treatment for delirium tremens.
- Diabetes mellitus slows the healing process, and diabetes mellitus with stated manifestations can further complicate the management of burn cases.

EXERCISE 31.1

Code the following diagnoses, including External cause codes. Assume that the incidents are for the initial encounter unless otherwise stated.

---

1. First-degree burn of lower left leg and second-degree burns of left foot when adding wood to bonfire at beach resort while on vacation	T25.222A T24.132A X03.8xxA Y93.89 Y99.8 Y92.838
2. First-degree burns of face and both eyes, involving cornea, eyelids, nose, cheeks, and lips, due to accidental lye spill at home	T54.3x1A T26.51xA T26.52xA T26.61xA T26.62xA T20.52xA T20.54xA T20.56xA Y99.8 Y92.099
3. Burns over 38 percent of body, with 10 percent of body involved in third-degree burns and 28 percent involved in second-degree burns; firefighter burned in forest fire	T31.31 X01.8xxA Y99.0 Y92.821
4. Acid burns to left cornea from nitric acid	T54.2x1A T26.62xA
5. Subsequent encounter with nonhealing first- and second-degree burns of back that occurred five weeks ago when patient's clothing caught fire in kitchen accident in his home	T21.23xD X02.0xxD

6. Food service employee sustained first-degree and second-degree burns, thumb and two fingers, right, from kitchen fire in nursing home while cooking, initial encounter	T23.241A X02.8xxA Y93.G3 Y99.0 Y92.120
7. Farm employee admitted with severe shock due to third-degree burns of back due to uncontrolled barn fire, initial encounter	T21.33xA T79.4xxA X00.0xxA Y99.0 Y92.71
8. First-, second-, and third-degree burns of body; 10 percent first degree, 15 percent second degree, and 32 percent (over the trunk) third degree; patient is crew member of ferry boat steamship on which boiler exploded	T21.30xA T31.53 V93.51xA Y99.0 V93.09xA
9. Severe sunburn of face, neck, and shoulders; patient spent most of the day at the beach	L55.9 X32.xxxA Y99.8 Y92.832 Y93.89
10. Infected friction burn of left thigh due to rope burn while water skiing barefoot at Lake Berryessa	S70.312A L08.89 V94.4xxA Y93.17 Y99.8 Y92.828
11. First-degree burns of back of left hand due to hot tap water in home where patient was visiting	T23.162A X11.8xxA Y99.8 Y92.099

12.	Superficial burns (dermatitis) of face and chest from a tanning bed	L56.9 W89.1xxA
13.	Bilateral corneal flash burn due to welding torch	H16.133 W89.0xxA

CHAPTER 32 Poisoning, Toxic Effects, Adverse Effects, and Underdosing of Drugs

CHAPTER OVERVIEW

- A condition caused by drugs or other ingested substances can be considered as an adverse effect, a toxic effect, or a poisoning.
- Underdosing refers to taking less of a medication than is prescribed by a provider or a manufacturer's instruction.
  - Underdosing codes should never be assigned as the principal or first-listed codes.
  - If the reduction in the prescribed dose of the medication results in a relapse or an exacerbation of the medical condition for which the drug is prescribed, then the medical condition itself should be coded first.
- An adverse effect is one caused by a correctly prescribed and used drug.
  - A code indicating the nature of the adverse effect is assigned first.
  - The combination code (T36–T50) that includes the adverse effect and the responsible substance follows.
- Poisoning is a condition caused by the incorrect use of a drug or another substance.
  - A code from categories T36- through T65 is sequenced first.
  - This is followed by the code for the manifestation of the poisoning.
  - When no intent of poisoning is indicated, the code for accidental poisoning should be assigned.
- Interactions of properly used therapeutic drugs and alcohol or nonprescription drugs are considered instances of poisoning.
- Codes for poisoning, adverse effects, and underdosing are found in the ICD-10-CM Table of Drugs and Chemicals.
- No additional External cause code is required for poisoning, toxic effect, adverse effect, and underdosing codes.
- Acute conditions caused by alcohol or drug abuse are considered poisonings, but chronic conditions are not.
- The late effects of poisoning, adverse effects, and underdosing are coded with the seventh character "S" for sequela.

LEARNING OUTCOMES

After studying this chapter you should be able to:

- Differentiate between adverse effects and poisoning.
- Locate codes associated with poisoning and adverse effects.
- Code for poisoning due to substance abuse.
- Code for late effects for adverse reactions and poisoning.

TERMS TO KNOW

Adverse effect
classification of a condition caused by a drug or another substance when used correctly

Poisoning
classification of a condition caused by a drug or another substance when used incorrectly

Toxic effect
classification of a condition caused by ingestion or contact with a harmful substance

Underdosing
classification of a condition caused by taking less of a medication than is prescribed by a provider or a manufacturer's instruction

REMEMBER . . .

A condition caused by the use of a drug may be classified as either an adverse effect or a poisoning. The determination is based only on whether or not the substance was correctly prescribed and properly administered.

INTRODUCTION

Conditions due to drugs and medicinal and biological substances are classified to categories T36 through T50. Codes in these categories are combination codes that specify both the responsible substance and whether it is a poisoning (including the intent, e.g., accidental), an adverse effect, or an underdosing, with the fifth or sixth character used to specify the following:

1 Poisoning, accidental (unintentional)
2 Poisoning, intentional self-harm
3 Poisoning, assault
4 Poisoning, undetermined
5 Adverse effect
6 Underdosing

Toxic effects of substances chiefly nonmedicinal as to source are classified to categories T51 through T65. Similar to categories T35 through T50, codes in categories T51 through T65 are combination codes that specify the responsible substance as well as the intent (e.g., accidental). However, adverse effect and underdosing are not applicable to toxic effects. As with other categories in chapter 19 of ICD-10-CM, categories T30- through T65 require seventh-character values, as follows: "A" for initial encounter, "D" for subsequent encounter, and "S" for sequela. These values are described in more detail in chapter 30 of this handbook.

The condition is classified as an adverse effect when the correct substance was administered as prescribed. When the substance was used incorrectly, it is classified as a poisoning with the appropriate fifth or sixth character of "1" through "4," depending on the intent of the poisoning (e.g., accidental). The condition may be exactly the same and the drug may be the same; the determination of whether it is a poisoning or an adverse effect is based on the manner in which the substance was used. ICD-10-CM makes the distinction between adverse effects of drugs administered correctly and poisoning—to facilitate the collection of data on adverse effects that result from the correct use of drugs, and on the extent to which incorrect use results in patient care problems.

Note that using the prescribed medication less frequently than prescribed, using it in smaller amounts, or not using the medication as instructed by the manufacturer is not coded as poisoning, but rather as underdosing.

When the drug was correctly prescribed and properly administered, a code for the nature of the adverse effect is sequenced first, followed by an additional code(s) for the adverse effect of the drug (T36–T50, with a fifth or sixth character "5"—e.g., T36.0x5). Drug adverse effect manifestations can range from minor or temporary effects to more serious and sometimes permanent damage. Examples of adverse effect manifestations include rash, tachycardia, delirium, gastrointestinal hemorrhage, vomiting, hepatitis, renal failure, and respiratory failure.

When the condition results from the interaction of two or more therapeutic drugs, each used correctly, it is classified as an adverse effect, and each drug is coded individually, unless the combination code is listed in the Table of Drugs and Chemicals.

When the condition is a poisoning, the poisoning code (e.g., T36.0x1-) is sequenced first, followed by additional codes for all manifestations. Poisoning codes have an associated intent, and code selection is based on the circumstance of the poisoning. When no intent of poisoning is indicated, the code for accidental poisoning should be assigned. The codes for undetermined poisoning (fifth or sixth character "4") are reserved for use when there is specific documentation in the record that the intent of the poisoning cannot be determined. For example, a diagnosis of coma due to codeine is coded as follows:

T40.2x1A + R40.20	Coma due to accidental poisoning due to codeine
T40.2x2A + R40.20	Coma due to codeine taken in a suicide attempt
T40.2x4A + R40.20	Coma due to overdose of codeine, cause unknown
T40.2x1A + R40.20	Coma due to poisoning due to codeine

If there is also a diagnosis of abuse of or dependence on the substance, the abuse or dependence is also coded.

Because codes in categories T36 through T65 include the responsible substances as well as the external cause, no additional External cause code is required for these codes. However, if the intent of the underdosing is known, External cause codes may be used to report failure in dosage during medical and surgical care (Y63.6–Y63.9) or patient's underdosing of medication regime (Z91.12- through Z91.13-).

The adverse effects of therapeutic substances correctly prescribed and properly administered (toxicity, synergistic reaction, side effect, and idiosyncratic reaction) may be due to (1) differences among patients, such as age, sex, disease, and genetic factors, and (2) drug-related factors, such as type of drug, route of administration, duration of therapy, dosage, and bioavailability.

Harmful substances ingested or coming into contact with a person are classified as toxic effects. These are assigned to categories T51 through T65, Toxic effects of substances chiefly non-medicinal as to source, except for contact with and (suspected) exposure to toxic substances (Z77.-). Code examples include the following:

T57.2x1-	Chronic manganese toxicity
T57.0x1-	Toxicity due to exposure to arsenical pesticide
Z77.090	Toxicity due to asbestos exposure

Toxic effect codes should be sequenced first, followed by the appropriate code(s) to identify all the associated manifestations of the toxic effect, such as respiratory conditions due to external agents (J60–J70). Similar to the codes for poisoning, toxic effect codes are combination codes that include the substance as well as the associated intent by the use of the following fifth or sixth characters:

1 accidental
2 intentional self-harm
3 assault
4 undetermined

Also similar to the codes for poisoning, when no intent is indicated, the code for accidental intent (fifth or sixth character "1") should be assigned. The codes for undetermined intent (fifth or sixth character "4") are reserved for use when there is specific documentation in the record that the intent of the toxic effect cannot be determined.

A diagnostic statement of toxic effect, toxicity, or intoxication due to a prescription drug, such as digitalis or lithium, without any further qualification usually refers to an adverse effect of a correctly administered prescription drug. The adverse effect should be coded as such unless medical record documentation indicates otherwise. The following terms in the medical record usually indicate correct usage and identify the condition as an adverse effect:

- "Allergic reaction"
- "Cumulative effect of drug" (toxicity)
- "Hypersensitivity to drug"
- "Idiosyncratic reaction"
- "Paradoxical reaction"
- "Synergistic reaction"

When the medical record documents an error in dosage or administration, the condition should be coded as a poisoning. Terms that usually identify the condition as a poisoning include the following:

- "Wrong medication given" or "wrong medication taken"
- "Error made in drug prescription"

- "Wrong dosage given" or "wrong dosage taken" (unless specified as underdosing, or lower dosage than prescribed)
- "Intentional drug overdose"
- "Nonprescribed drug taken with correctly prescribed and properly administered drug"

The poisoning code is sequenced first, followed by the code for the manifestation. This sequencing is based on the chapter-specific guideline providing such direction. Therefore, it applies even if the poisoning may have already been addressed.

For example, a patient is seen in the emergency department in a coma and suffering from acute respiratory failure due to a drug overdose. The patient undergoes a gastric lavage for the drug overdose. The patient is also intubated, connected to an invasive mechanical ventilator, and transferred to another hospital for continued toxicology management and treatment of the acute respiratory failure. The poisoning is still sequenced as the principal diagnosis at the receiving hospital.

When a condition is the result of the interaction of a therapeutic drug used correctly with a nonprescription drug or with alcohol, it is classified as a poisoning. Poisoning codes are also assigned for each drug. For example, a diagnosis of coma identified as an adverse reaction to Valium taken correctly but associated with the intake of two martinis is coded as follows:

T51.0x1A	Poisoning due to alcohol, accidental
T42.4x1A	Poisoning due to Valium, accidental
R40.20	Coma

Taking a larger or more frequent dosage than prescribed is classified as a poisoning. Note that taking a lower amount or discontinuing the use of a prescribed medication is not classified as either a poisoning or an adverse reaction, but rather as underdosing. Underdosing codes should never be assigned as the principal or first-listed code. If the reduction in the prescribed dose of the medication results in a relapse or an exacerbation of the medical condition for which the drug is prescribed, then the medical condition itself should be coded first.

For example, a patient was prescribed Amiodarone to control his atrial fibrillation. The patient quit taking his prescribed medication on his own one week ago, because he said the medication made him nauseous. He is now admitted for control of atrial fibrillation and medication adjustment. The atrial fibrillation is coded as the principal diagnosis and the underdosing code as an additional diagnosis, as follows:

I48.91	Atrial fibrillation
T46.2x6A	Underdosing of Amiodarone
Z91.14	Patient's noncompliance with medication

Figure 32.1 illustrates a process for coding poisoning and adverse effects of drugs.

LOCATION OF CODES ASSOCIATED WITH POISONING, ADVERSE EFFECTS, AND UNDERDOSING

Codes for poisonings, adverse effects, and underdosing are located most easily by referring to the ICD-10-CM Table of Drugs and Chemicals (see figure 32.2). Drugs and other chemicals are listed in alphabetical order at the far left of the Table, with the first column on the right listing the accidental poisoning code for that substance. The remaining columns provide codes for poisoning for the other external circumstances (intentional self-harm, assault, and undetermined), for adverse effect, and for underdosing.

If a specific drug cannot be located in the Table, it can usually be found by either the generic name or the drug class or type (e.g., antibiotic). The hospital pharmacist can also be a valuable source of information.

Codes should not be assigned directly from the Table without verification in the Tabular List. The Table of Drugs and Chemicals is extensive and very detailed, but it does not take into account the instructional notes in the Tabular List. For example, the Table lists codes from category T36, Poisoning by, adverse effect of and underdosing of systemic antibiotics, but the exclusion note at category T36 indicates that codes from subcategory T45.1 should be used for antineoplastic antibiotics.

FIGURE 32.1 Decision Tree for Coding Adverse Effects of Drugs or Poisoning Due to Drugs or Medicinal or Biological Substances

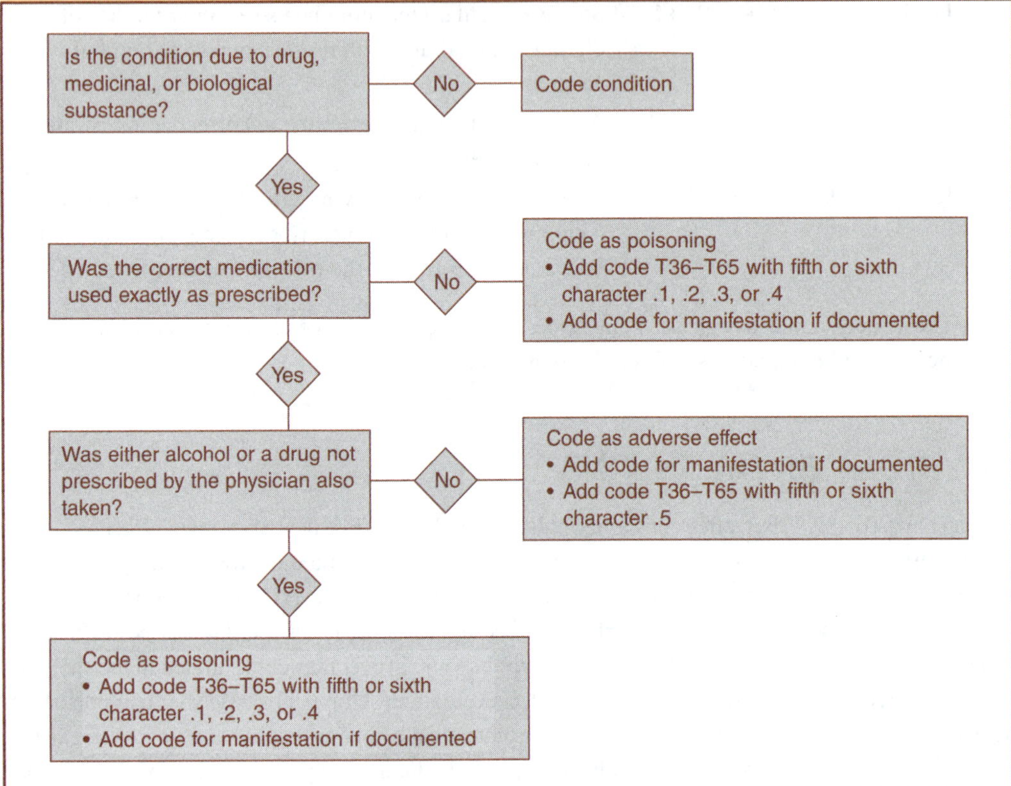

Figure 32.2 Excerpt from ICD-10-CM Table of Drugs and Chemicals

Substance	Poisoning, Accidental (Unintentional)	Poisoning, Intentional Self-Harm	Poisoning, Assault	Poisoning, Undetermined	Adverse Effect	Underdosing
Acetylphenylhydrazine	T39.8x1	T39.8x2	T39.8x3	T39.8x4	T39.8x5	T39.8x6
Acetylsalicylic acid (salts)	T39.011	T39.012	T39.013	T39.014	T39.015	T39.016
-enteric coated	T39.011	T39.012	T39.013	T39.014	T39.015	T39.016
Acetylsulfamethoxypyridazine	T37.0x1	T37.0x2	T37.0x3	T37.0x4	T37.0x5	T37.0x6
Achromycin	T36.4x1	T36.4x2	T36.4x3	T36.4x4	T36.4x5	T36.4x6
-ophthalmic preparation	T49.5x1	T49.5x2	T49.5x3	T49.5x4	T49.5x5	T49.5x6
-topical NEC	T49.0x1	T49.0x2	T49.0x3	T49.0x4	T49.0x5	T49.0x6
Aciclovir	T37.5x1	T37.5x2	T37.5x3	T37.5x4	T37.5x5	T37.5x6

GUIDELINES FOR ASSIGNMENT OF CODES FOR POISONING, ADVERSE EFFECTS, UNDERDOSING, AND TOXIC EFFECTS

When two or more drugs or medicinal or biological substances are reported as being responsible for a poisoning, an adverse effect, an underdosing, or a toxic effect, code each substance individually unless the same code would describe the causative agent for more than one adverse reaction, poisoning, toxic effect, or underdosing. In other words, assign the code only once when the same code identifies more than one responsible substance. For example:

I49.1 + T46.0x5A + T42.4x5A	Supraventricular premature beats secondary to use of digitalis and Valium, both used as prescribed, initial encounter
R50.83 + T50.A15A	An infant with a high fever due to correct administration of DPT vaccine
R68.2 + L29.9 + T42.3x5A	Patient suffering from dry mouth and itching as a result of taking phenobarbital as prescribed by his physician (either R68.2 or L29.9 may be the principal or first-listed code)

The coder should assign as many codes as needed to completely describe all responsible substances for either an adverse effect or a poisoning.

ENVIRONMENTAL TOXINS

Subcategory T65.82, Toxic effect of harmful algae and algae toxins, describes toxic effects of exposure to harmful algae bloom, such as toxic effect of blue-green algae bloom, brown tide, cyanobacteria bloom, Florida red tide, *Pfiesteria piscicida*, and red tide. *Karennia brevis* (*K. brevis*) are microscopic, fast-growing marine algae that create blooms called red tides. *K. brevis* produces a powerful toxin called brevetoxin. When shellfish feed on *K. brevis*, brevetoxin becomes concentrated in the shellfish. Individuals who eat shellfish contaminated with brevetoxin develop neurotoxic shellfish poisoning. This type of food poisoning leads to severe gastrointestinal and neurologic symptoms. Assign code Z77.121 to describe possible contact with and exposure to harmful algae and algae toxins. This code may be assigned when the patient may have been in the vicinity of algae bloom but has not developed symptoms, or when the patient may have symptoms suspicious of exposure to algae bloom, but a definitive cause of the symptoms has not been confirmed.

Environmental exposure to brevetoxin can also affect people who swim in an ocean polluted by brevetoxins or who inhale brevetoxins in the air. Symptoms can include irritation of the eyes, nose, and throat; tingling of the lips and tongue; coughing; wheezing; and shortness of breath. For example, a patient develops severe abdominal pain, vomiting, and a tingling sensation in the fingers after eating shellfish. The patient is diagnosed with neurotoxic shellfish poisoning due to red tides. Assign code **T65.821A, Toxic effect of harmful algae and algae toxins, accidental (unintentional), initial encounter.**

EXERCISE 32.1

Code the following diagnoses, assuming that the drug involved was taken correctly unless otherwise specified. Assume these are initial encounters.

1. Coma due to acute barbiturate intoxication, attempted suicide	T42.3x2A R40.20
2. Two-year-old patient ingested an unknown quantity of mother's Enovid	T38.4x1A
3. Syncope due to hypersensitivity to antidepressant medication Table	R55 T43.205A
4. Hypokalemia resulting from reaction to Diuril given by mistake in physician's office	T50.2x1A E87.6
5. Diplopia due to allergic reaction to antihistamine, taken as prescribed Table	H53.2 T45.0x5A
6. Lethargy due to unintentional overdose of sleeping pills	T42.71xA R53.83
7. Electrolyte imbalance due to interaction between lithium carbonate and Diuril, both taken as prescribed Table	E87.8 T50.2x5A T43.595A
8. Parkinsonism, secondary to correct use of haloperidol Table	G21.11 T43.4x5A

9.	Cerebral anoxia resulting from barbiturate overdose, suicide attempt		T42.3x2A G93.1
10.	Toxic encephalopathy due to excessive use of aspirin		T39.011A G92
11.	Ataxia due to Valium (taken as prescribed) consumed with three martinis	Table, Valium Table, alcohol	T42.4x1A T51.0x1A R27.0
12.	Allergic dermatitis due to slow-acting insulin	Table	L27.0 T38.3x5A
13.	Coumadin intoxication due to accumulative effect resulting in gross hematuria	Table	R31.0 T45.515A
14.	Severe bradycardia due to accidental double dose of digoxin	Table, digoxin	T46.0x1A R00.1
15.	Generalized convulsions due to accidental Darvon overdose		T39.8x1A R56.9
16.	Light-headedness resulting from interaction between Aldomet and peripheral vasodilating agent (both taken as prescribed)	Table	R42 T46.7x5A T46.5x5A
17.	Uncontrolled hypertension due to patient having reduced his anti-hypertensive medication (patient couldn't afford it)		I10 T46.5x6A Z91.120

UNSPECIFIED ADVERSE EFFECT OF DRUGS

ICD-10-CM provides code **T88.7-, Unspecified adverse effect of drug or medicament,** to identify adverse reactions when the nature of the reaction is not specified. Use an additional code from categories T36 through T50, with fifth or sixth character "5" if applicable, to identify the responsible drug. Code T88.7- may be used in the outpatient setting, but only when no sign or symptom of the adverse effect is documented. The use of code T88.7- for inpatient reporting is inappropriate. If the patient is exhibiting symptoms or signs, the code for that condition should be assigned. If the adverse condition cannot be identified, one of the following codes should be assigned:

R82.5	Elevated urine levels of drugs, medicaments and biological substances
R82.6	Abnormal urine levels of substances chiefly nonmedicinal as to source
R89.2	Abnormal level of other drugs, medicaments and biological substances in specimens from other organs, systems and tissues
R89.3	Abnormal level of substances chiefly nonmedicinal as to source in specimens from other organs, systems and tissues

ICD-10-CM provides subcategory T50.90-, Poisoning by, adverse effect of and underdosing of unspecified drugs, medicaments and biological substances, for instances when the drug or substance responsible for the poisoning, adverse effect, or underdosing is not specified.

POISONING DUE TO SUBSTANCE ABUSE OR DEPENDENCE

An acute condition due to a reaction resulting from the interaction of alcohol and a drug(s) or due to a drug involved in abuse or dependence is classified as a poisoning. Additional codes are assigned for both the acute manifestation of the poisoning and the dependence or abuse. For example:

T40.1x1A + J81.0 + F11.20	Acute pulmonary edema due to accidental heroin overdose in a patient who is heroin dependent

Chronic conditions related to alcohol or drug abuse or dependence are not classified as poisoning. The code for the chronic condition is sequenced first, followed by a code for the abuse or dependence. For example:

K70.30 + F10.20	Alcoholic cirrhosis of the liver; chronic alcohol dependence
K70.10 + F10.20	Alcoholic hepatitis; chronic alcohol dependence, episodic
F14.14	Drug-induced depressive state due to cocaine abuse

EXERCISE 32.2

Code the following diagnoses. Assign External cause codes where appropriate. Assume these are initial encounters.

1. Muscle cramps of leg due to occupational use of arsenic pesticide — T57.0x1A, R25.2

   Table, arsenic

2. Systemic hypocalcemia and hypokalemia due to use of lye in household chores	T54.3x1A E83.51 E87.6 Y92.099
Table, lye	
3. Bradycardia due to ingestion of oleander leaves	T62.2x1A R00.1
Table, oleander	
4. Patient, a known cocaine abuser, was admitted with respiratory failure due to crack/cocaine overdose. Patient was placed on mechanical ventilation for 20 hours.	T40.5x1A J96.00 F14.10 5A1935Z
Table, cocaine	
5. Patient admitted with dialysis dementia secondary to aluminum toxicity (aluminum acetate solution) due to renal dialysis therapy	T49.0x5A F03.90 Y84.1
Table, aluminum	

LATE EFFECTS OF POISONING, ADVERSE EFFECTS, AND UNDERDOSING

When coding late effects of a poisoning, the code for the responsible drug or substance is sequenced first (the code from categories T36 through T65), with the seventh character "S" for sequela, followed by the specific type of sequela (e.g., brain damage).

When coding late effects of an adverse effect, assign a code for the nature of the adverse effect (sequela) first, followed by the code for the responsible drug or substance (T36–T50, with fifth or sixth character "5"), with the seventh character "S" for sequela.

Long-term chronic effects of a prescription drug taken over a period of time—and still being taken at the time the chronic effects arise—are coded as current adverse effects. For example, steroid-induced diabetes may be caused by an adverse effect of correctly administered medications, poisoning, or late effect of poisoning. For a patient who develops steroid-induced diabetes and is currently taking steroids as prescribed, his condition is coded as an adverse effect (E09.- + T38.0x5A).

If the patient suffers delayed effects that arose or remain long after the steroid was discontinued, code E09.- is assigned first, followed by code T38.0x5S. For example:

G93.9 + T36.0x5A	Brain damage due to allergic reaction to penicillin (current medication)
G93.9 + T36.0x5S	Brain damage due to allergic reaction to penicillin (use of medication discontinued six months ago)

EXERCISE 32.3

Code the following diagnoses, sequencing the codes correctly. Assign External cause code if appropriate.

1. Extrapyramidal disease resulting from previous overdose of Thorazine in an attempted suicide six months ago	T43.3x2S G25.9
2. Bilateral neural deafness resulting from accidental overdose of streptomycin administered in physician's office two years ago	T36.5x1S H90.3
3. Anoxic brain damage secondary to previous accidental overdose of Nembutal nine months ago	T42.3x1S G93.1
4. Secondary parkinsonism due to poisoning by lithium four years ago	T56.891S G21.8
5. Patient recently discharged from the hospital with diagnosis of acute systolic congestive heart failure. Discharged with a prescription for digoxin 200 mcg once daily, with instructions for a low-fat and low-sodium diet and avoidance of alcohol and caffeine. Two weeks later, patient was seen in the emergency department with shortness of breath on minimal exertion and severe edema. On questioning, patient admitted to having reduced digoxin to every other day because it is too expensive. Diagnosis: Relapse of acute systolic congestive heart failure due to low dose of digoxin.	I50.21 T46.0x6A Z91.120

CHAPTER 33

Complications of Surgery and Medical Care

CHAPTER OVERVIEW

- Categories T80 through T88 in ICD-10-CM cover complications of medical and surgical care that are not already classified elsewhere.
- Complications that occur only in other specified body sites are classified in that chapter of ICD-10-CM.
- Intraoperative and postprocedural complication codes are found within the body system chapters, with codes specific to the organs and structures of that body system.
- Not all postcare conditions are classified as complications.
  - —There must be an unexpected or abnormal occurrence.
  - —There must be a documented relationship between the condition and the care.
  - —There must be an indication that it is a complication.
- There are several instructional notes (in particular, exclusion notes) related to complications.
- When coding, look for a subterm indicating postoperative or iatrogenic condition.
- Look to the main term **Complications** if no subterms are found in the particular entry for the condition.
- Complications involving an internal device, an implant, or a graft are classified first.
- It is important to distinguish between admission for complications and admission for routine and scheduled aftercare.

LEARNING OUTCOMES

After studying this chapter you should be able to:

Understand when and when not to code a condition or an occurrence as a complication.

Locate complication codes.

Use all of the instructional notes present in ICD-10-CM to properly classify a condition caused by a complication of medical or surgical care.

TERM TO KNOW

Iatrogenic condition
condition resulting from the treatment of another condition

REMEMBER . . .

Coders should never make assumptions with regard to complications because of the legal ramifications of these codes.

INTRODUCTION

Categories T80 through T88 are provided in ICD-10-CM for complications of medical and surgical care that are not classified elsewhere. Categories T80 through T85 and T88 require a seventh-character value to specify initial encounter ("A"), subsequent encounter ("D"), or sequela ("S"), similar to other codes in chapter 19 of ICD-10-CM. Note that not all conditions that occur following surgery or other patient care are classified as complications. First, there must be more than a routinely expected condition or occurrence. For example, a major amount of bleeding is expected with joint replacement surgery; hemorrhage should not be considered a complication unless such bleeding is particularly excessive. In addition, there must be a documented cause-and-effect relationship between the care provided and the condition, and some indication must be present that it is a complication, not a postoperative condition in which no complication is present, such as an artificial opening status or an absence of an extremity. In some cases, this is implicit, as in a complication due to the presence of an internal device, an implant, or a graft or due to a transplant. Code assignment for postprocedural complications is based on the provider's documentation of the relationship between the complication and the procedure. The coder cannot make this determination and should always query the provider for clarification when a postprocedural complication is not documented clearly. The guideline regarding a code assignment's being based on the provider's documentation of the relationship between the condition and the care or procedure extends to any complications of care, regardless of the chapter in which the code is located. Note that the term "complication" as used in ICD-10-CM does not imply that improper or inadequate care is responsible for the problem.

No time limit is defined for the development of a complication. It may occur during the hospital episode in which the care was provided, shortly thereafter, or even years later. When it occurs during the episode in which the operation or other care was given, it is assigned as an additional code. When it develops later and is the reason for the hospital admission or encounter, it is designated as the principal or first-listed diagnosis. Complications of surgical and medical care are classified in ICD-10-CM as follows:

- Complications that occur only in other specified body sites are classified in that chapter of ICD-10-CM.
- Complications that affect multiple sites or body systems are generally classified in categories T80 through T88. An additional code(s) is assigned to identify the specific condition resulting from the complication.
- Intraoperative and postprocedural complication codes are found within the body system chapters, with codes specific to the organs and structures of that body system. These codes should be sequenced first, followed by a code(s) for the specific complication, if applicable.
- Complications of abortion, pregnancy, labor, or delivery are classified in chapter 15 of ICD-10-CM.

It is imperative that the coder use the Alphabetic Index carefully and follow all instructional notes. Exclusion notes are fairly extensive in this section and often direct the coder elsewhere. There are several basic exclusions that must be observed:

- Complications of medicinal agents, such as adverse effects, poisoning, and toxic effects of drugs and chemicals
- Any encounters with medical care for postoperative conditions in which no complications are present, such as artificial opening status, closure of external stoma, or fitting and adjustment of external prosthetic device
- Burns and corrosions from local applications and irradiation
- Mechanical complication of respirator or ventilator

- Postprocedural fever
- Complications of the condition for which surgery was performed
- Specified conditions classified elsewhere, such as ostomy complications, postlaminectomy syndrome, postgastric surgery syndromes, or postmastectomy lymphedema syndrome.
- Any condition classified elsewhere in the Alphabetic Index when described as being due to a procedure or medical care, such as disorders of fluid and electrolyte imbalance or functional disturbances during cardiac surgery (Note that the adjective "iatrogenic" is often used to indicate that the condition is a result of treatment.)

When assigning codes in categories T80–T88, Complications of surgical and medical care NEC, use an additional code to identify the specific complication, but only if the additional code provides greater specificity as to the nature of the condition. If, however, the complication code describes the condition fully, no additional code is necessary.

LOCATING COMPLICATION CODES IN THE ALPHABETIC INDEX

The coder should first refer to the main term for the condition and look for a subterm indicating a postoperative or another iatrogenic condition. For example:

Adhesion(s) . . .
-postoperative (gastrointestinal tract) . . . K66.0
--with obstruction K91.3 . . .
--pelvic peritoneal N99.4 . . .
-vagina N99.2
Colostomy . . .
-malfunction K94.03

When no entry can be found under the main term for the condition, the coder should refer to the main term **Complications** and look for an appropriate subterm, such as one of the following:

- Nature of complication, such as "foreign body," "accidental puncture," or "hemorrhage"
- Type of procedure, such as "colostomy," "dialysis," or "shunt"
- Anatomical site or body system affected, such as "respiratory system"
- General terms, such as "mechanical," "infection," or "graft"

Examples include the following entries from the Alphabetic Index:

Complications
-postmastoidectomy . . . H95.19-
Complications
-cardiac . . .
--device, implant or graft T82.9
---infection . . . T82.7-
---mechanical
----breakdown T82.519 . . .
----displacement T82.529

POSTOPERATIVE CONDITIONS NOT CLASSIFIED AS COMPLICATIONS

Certain conditions resulting from medical or surgical care are residual conditions of a procedure, but no complicating factor is involved. For example, postlaminectomy syndrome often occurs following laminectomy, but it is a sequela of the procedure, not a complication. The extensive exclusion list at the beginning of the T80–T88 series is helpful in making some of these distinctions. Other examples include:

K56.5	Postoperative intestinal or peritoneal adhesions with obstruction
K94.12 + B95.4	Infection of enterostomy due to group C *Streptococcus*
N73.6	Postoperative pelvic adhesions (female)

Some conditions that occur postoperatively are not classified as complications, nor do they have special codes to indicate that they are postoperative in nature. Postoperative pain not associated with a specific postoperative complication, for example, is assigned to the appropriate postoperative pain code in category G89 (G89.18, G89.22, G89.28), but **only** if it is not routine or if postoperative pain was not expected immediately after surgery, and only if it meets the guidelines for a reportable diagnosis.

Patients are frequently admitted from outpatient surgery with pain and/or nausea and vomiting, but these are common symptoms during postoperative recovery and are not coded to categories T80 through T88 unless the physician identifies them specifically as complications of the surgery. The principal diagnosis is the symptom or other condition that occasions the postoperative admission.

Sometimes the patient is admitted because of a general concern rather than because of specific symptoms. Although physicians may state that the admission is for observation, this type of situation is ordinarily not coded to category Z03, Encounter for medical observation for suspected diseases and conditions ruled out. If no specific condition is identified, the principal diagnosis is admission for postprocedural aftercare (Z48.-).

Postoperative anemia is rarely considered to be a complication of surgery. When the physician documents postoperative anemia due to blood loss, code **D62, Acute posthemorrhagic anemia,** is assigned, but no complication code is assigned unless the physician documents excessive bleeding as a complication. The fact that blood is administered during a surgical procedure does not indicate a postoperative anemia. Transfusions are sometimes given as a prophylactic replacement to avoid postoperative anemia. Anemia is not assigned solely because the patient received a transfusion; the physician must document the condition.

A diagnosis of postoperative hypertension often means only that the patient has a pre-existing essential hypertension or an elevated blood pressure. If the physician clearly identifies it as a postoperative complication, code **I97.3, Postprocedural hypertension,** is assigned.

EXERCISE 33.1

Code the following diagnoses. Do not assign External cause codes.

1. Postoperative fever	R50.82
2. Postoperative esophagitis	K20.9
3. Colostomy malfunction	K94.03
4. Postleukotomy syndrome	F07.0
5. Postoperative peritoneal adhesions	K66.0
6. Postoperative blind loop syndrome	K91.2

COMPLICATIONS AFFECTING SPECIFIC BODY SYSTEMS

ICD-10-CM classifies many intraoperative and postprocedural complication codes within the body system chapters with codes specific to the organs and structures of that body system. These codes should be sequenced first, followed by a code(s) for the specific complication, if applicable. Intraoperative and postprocedural complications and disorders are classified within body system chapters to the categories listed below:

D78	Spleen
E36 and E89	Endocrine system
G97	Nervous system
H59	Eye and adnexa
H95	Ear and mastoid process
I97	Circulatory system
J95	Respiratory system
K91	Digestive system
L76	Skin and subcutaneous tissue
M96	Musculoskeletal system
N99	Genitourinary system

The above categories (except for E89 and K94) provide additional characters to specify complications such as intraoperative or postprocedural hemorrhage and hematoma, or accidental puncture and laceration (e.g., inadvertent rents, tears, or lacerations) during a procedure. In addition, codes

distinguish whether the conditions resulted from a procedure on the specified organ or from complications of other procedures. For example:

- Hemorrhage after repair of spleen laceration is coded to **D78.21, Postprocedural hemorrhage and hematoma of spleen following a procedure on the spleen.**
- Accidental laceration of the spleen secondary to colectomy is coded to **D78.12, Accidental puncture and laceration of spleen during other procedure.**

Several of the categories listed above provide additional specificity for certain other procedures or other complications besides intraoperative or postprocedural hemorrhage and hematoma, accidental puncture, and laceration. Category E89, Postprocedural endocrine and metabolic complications and disorders, not elsewhere classified, is further subdivided to provide specific codes for the following types of complications:

E89.0	Postprocedural hypothyroidism
E89.1	Postprocedural hypoinsulinemia
E89.2	Postprocedural hypoparathyroidism
E89.3	Postprocedural hypopituitarism
E89.40	Asymptomatic postprocedural ovarian failure
E89.41	Symptomatic postprocedural ovarian failure
E89.5	Postprocedural testicular hypofunction
E89.6	Postprocedural adrenocortical (-medullary) hypofunction
E89.810	Postprocedural hemorrhage and hematoma of an endocrine system organ or structure following an endocrine system procedure
E89.811	Postprocedural hemorrhage and hematoma of an endocrine system organ or structure following other procedure
E89.89	Other postprocedural endocrine and metabolic complications and disorders

Category G97, Intraoperative and postprocedural complications and disorders of nervous system, not elsewhere classified, includes additional codes for problems related to spinal or lumbar puncture and ventricular shunting, such as cerebrospinal fluid leak from spinal puncture (G97.0), other reaction to spinal and lumbar puncture (G97.1), and intracranial hypotension following ventricular shunting (G97.2). Category H95, Intraoperative and postprocedural complications and disorders of ear and mastoid process, not elsewhere classified, provides additional codes for problems related to postmastoidectomy, such as chronic inflammation, granulation, mucosal cyst, and other disorders, as well as postprocedural stenosis of the external ear canal.

Category I97, Intraoperative and postprocedural complications and disorders of circulatory system, not elsewhere classified, also includes codes for conditions such as postcardiotomy syndrome (I97.0), other postprocedural cardiac functional disturbances (I97.11–I97.191), postmastectomy lymphedema syndrome (I97.2), postprocedural hypertension (I97.3), intraoperative cardiac functional disturbances (I97.71–I97.791), and other complications such as intraoperative or postprocedural cerebrovascular infarction (I97.81–I97.821).

Category J95, Intraoperative and postprocedural complications and disorders of respiratory system, not elsewhere classified, includes specific codes for several other complications, such as the following:

J95.00–J95.09	Tracheostomy complications
J95.1, J95.2	Acute pulmonary insufficiency following thoracic surgery (J95.1) and following nonthoracic surgery (J95.2)
J95.3	Chronic pulmonary insufficiency following surgery
J95.4	Chemical pneumonitis due to anesthesia
J95.5	Postprocedural subglottic stenosis
J95.81	Postprocedural pneumothorax
J95.82	Postprocedural respiratory failure
J95.84	Transfusion-related acute lung injury (TRALI)
J95.85-	Complication of respirator, which includes ventilator-associated pneumonia (see chapter 19 of this handbook for a more detailed discussion)

Code J95.4 is assigned for chemical pneumonitis due to anesthesia and includes postprocedural aspiration pneumonia and Mendelson's syndrome when they result from a procedure. An additional code for adverse effect, if applicable, is assigned to identify the anesthesia (T41.-, with fifth or sixth character 5). Do not assign a code from category J69-, Pneumonitis due to solids and liquids, with code J95.4 because J95.4 fully describes the nature of the complication.

Code K91.86 is used to report the retention of gallstones following cholecystectomy. This condition is not uncommon following a laparoscopic cholecystectomy because gallstones may fall into the bile duct, abdominal cavity, or abdominal wall, causing a later obstruction or infection. Code **K91.86, Retained cholelithiasis following cholecystectomy,** is assigned in this situation.

Category M96, Intraoperative and postprocedural complications and disorders of musculoskeletal system, not elsewhere classified, includes specific codes for the following conditions:

M96.0	Pseudarthrosis after fusion or arthrodesis
M96.1	Postlaminectomy syndrome, not elsewhere classified
M96.2, M96.3	Kyphosis post radiation (M96.2) and postlaminectomy (M96.3)
M96.4, M96.5	Lordosis postsurgical (M96.4) or postradiation scoliosis (M96.5)
M96.6-	Fracture of bone following insertion of orthopedic implant, joint prosthesis, or bone plate

ICD-10-CM differentiates between cardiac functional disturbances that occur intraoperatively during cardiac or any type of surgery (I97.7-) and postprocedural cardiac functional effects following cardiac or other surgery (I97.1-). For example:

K81.0 + I97.191 + I49.9	Acute cholecystitis; postoperative cardiac arrhythmia (same admission)
I97.130 + I50.9	Heart failure following cardiac surgery performed during previous admission; patient discharged one month ago
I97.131 + I50.21	Acute systolic heart failure on second postoperative day following cholecystectomy
I97.710	Cardiac arrest during cardiac bypass surgery

EXERCISE 33.2

Code the following diagnoses. Do not assign External cause codes.

1.	Cataract fragments in left eye following cataract surgery Complications	H59.022
2.	Headache due to lumbar puncture	G97.1
3.	Post iridectomy plateau iris syndrome	H21.82
4.	Seroma of transabdominal myocutaneous (TRAM) flap post mastectomy of the left breast	N99.820
5.	Postprocedural hypertension	I97.3
6.	35-year-old female patient presents to physician's office with complaints of flushing, sleeplessness, headache, and lack of concentration after having had uterine artery embolization for uterine leiomyoma a few months ago. Physician diagnoses patient with premature postsurgical menopause.	E89.41

COMPLICATIONS FOLLOWING INFUSION, TRANSFUSION, AND THERAPEUTIC INJECTION

Category T80 includes the following complications following infusion, transfusion, and therapeutic injections:

T80.0-	Air embolism
T80.1-	Vascular complications
T80.2-	Infections
T80.3-	ABO incompatibility reaction due to transfusion
T80.4-	Rh incompatibility reaction
T80.A-	Non-ABO incompatibility reaction
T80.5-	Anaphylactic shock due to serum
T80.6-	Other serum reactions (e.g., intoxication, protein sickness, serum rash, serum sickness, serum urticaria)
T80.81-	Extravasation of vesicant agents
T80.89-	Other complications
T80.9-	Unspecified complication

Extravasation is the accidental infiltration of intravenously infused drugs into the surrounding tissue. Vesicants are chemically active substances that can produce blistering on direct contact with the skin or mucous membrane. Extravasation of antineoplastic drugs during cancer treatment can lead to serious complications. In milder cases, extravasation can cause pain, reddening, or irritation on the arm at the site of the infusion needle. In severe cases, tissue damage may involve tissue necrosis and lead to loss of the limb. The following codes are assigned to describe complications following extravasation of vesicant agent:

T80.810	Extravasation of vesicant antineoplastic chemotherapy
T80.818	Extravasation of other vesicant agent

Code T80.22- describes an acute infection following a transfusion, infusion, or injection of blood and blood products. Transfusion-transmitted infections include any infectious organism (bacteria, virus, parasite, or other) transmitted through transfusion, infusion, or injection of blood or blood products (whole blood, red blood cells [RBCs], plasma, platelets, or other). Code T80.22- should be used for acute infections, not for chronic cases. In addition, if the transfusion-transmitted infection has specifically been identified as human immunodeficiency virus (HIV), assign a code for the HIV disease first.

ICD-10-CM provides codes to report transfusion reactions due to blood or blood product incompatibility, as follows:

T80.30–T80.39	ABO incompatibility reaction due to transfusion of blood or blood products
T80.40–T80.49	Rh incompatibility reaction due to transfusion of blood or blood products
T80.A0–T80.A9	Non-ABO incompatibility reaction due to transfusion of blood or blood products

These codes also provide information on the different types of hemolytic transfusion reactions, including both acute hemolytic transfusion reaction and delayed hemolytic transfusion reaction. A hemolytic transfusion reaction is a systemic response by the body to the administration of blood that is incompatible with the recipient's blood, resulting in destruction of red blood cells. This condition can lead to acute renal failure and/or disseminated intravascular coagulation.

Anaphylactic reactions following transfusion of blood and blood products (T80.51-) are attributed to soluble substances in donor plasma. The most common transfusion reactions are fever, chills, pruitus, or urticaria, which can resolve without specific treatment or complications. For example:

- A patient presents with complaints of dizziness, weakness, and fatigue. The provider documented weakness and fatigue due to acute anemia due to blood loss, and the patient subsequently received two units of packed RBCs into the peripheral vein. During the administration of the second unit, she developed fever, hoarseness, and facial edema and was treated with IV Benadryl. Assign code **D62, Acute posthemorrhagic anemia,** as the principal diagnosis. Codes **T80.51xA, Anaphylactic reaction due to administration of blood and blood products, initial encounter,** and **T45.8x5A, Adverse effect of other primarily systemic and hematological agents, initial encounter,** should be assigned as additional diagnoses. Assign procedure code **30233N1, Transfusion of nonautologous red blood cells into peripheral vein, percutaneous approach.**

Please note that other transfusion-related problems are coded to other chapters, such as hemochromatosis due to repeated blood cell transfusions (E83.111), transfusion-associated circulatory overload (E87.71), post-transfusion purpura (D69.51), and post-transfusion fever (R50.84).

Code T80.52- is used to report anaphylactic reactions due to vaccination, and code T80.59- is reserved for anaphylactic reactions due to other serum. Although an anaphylactic reaction to vaccine is rare, it can develop when a person with preformed IgE antibodies to a vaccine constituent is given a vaccine containing that substance. The IgE-mediated reactions are usually caused by vaccine components other than the immunizing agent. Serum sickness is a reaction similar to an allergy. It involves an immune system reaction to certain medications, injected proteins used to treat immune conditions, or antiserum (the liquid part of blood that contains antibodies that help protect against infectious or poisonous substances). Codes T80.61-, T80.62-, and T80.69- describe other serum reactions due to the administration of blood and blood products, other serum reaction due to vaccination, and other serum reaction, respectively.

COMPLICATIONS DUE TO PRESENCE OF INTERNAL DEVICE, IMPLANT, OR GRAFT

Categories T82 through T85 classify conditions that occur only because an internal device, implant, or graft is present. These complications are classified according to the body system, as follows:

T82 Complications of cardiac and vascular prosthetic devices, implants and grafts
T83 Complications of genitourinary prosthetic devices, implants and grafts
T84 Complications of internal orthopedic prosthetic devices, implants and grafts
T85 Complications of other internal prosthetic devices, implants and grafts

Complications of this type are classified first according to whether they are mechanical or nonmechanical in nature. A mechanical complication is one that results from a failure of the device, implant, or graft, such as breakdown, displacement, leakage, or other malfunction. These are classified by the type of mechanical complication and the type of device involved. For example:

T83.39- Perforation of uterus by intrauterine contraceptive device
T84.195- Protrusion of intramedullary nail in left femur
T85.621- Displacement of peritoneal dialysis catheter
T82.49- Obstruction of arteriovenous dialysis catheter
T82.511- Breakdown of surgically created arteriovenous shunt
T82.111- Defective cardiac pulse generator

Subcategory T84.0, Mechanical complications of internal joint prosthesis, classifies a range of complications involving prosthetic joint implants, with additional characters to identify the specific joint (e.g., right knee, left hip). The specific mechanical complications are indicated as follows:

T84.01 Broken internal joint prosthesis
T84.02 Dislocation of internal joint prosthesis
T84.03 Mechanical loosening of internal prosthetic joint
T84.04 Periprosthetic fracture around internal prosthetic joint
T84.05 Periprosthetic osteolysis of internal prosthetic joint
T84.06 Wear of articular bearing surface of internal prosthetic joint
T84.09 Other mechanical complication of internal joint prosthesis

Infection and inflammatory reactions due to the presence of a device, an implant, or a graft that is functioning properly are classified to the following codes and subcategories:

T82.6	Infection and inflammatory reaction due to cardiac valve prosthesis
T82.7-	Infection and inflammatory reaction due to other cardiac and vascular devices, implants and grafts
T83.6	Infection and inflammatory reaction due to prosthetic device, implant and graft in genital tract
T84.5-	Infection and inflammatory reaction due to internal joint prosthesis
T84.6-	Infection and inflammatory reaction due to internal fixation device
T84.7	Infection and inflammatory reaction due to other internal orthopedic prosthetic devices, implants and grafts
T85.7-	Infection and inflammatory reaction due to other internal prosthetic devices, implants and grafts

Additional codes should be assigned to identify the infection.

Code **T82.7-, Infection and inflammatory reaction due to other cardiac and vascular devices, implants and grafts,** is used for infections due to arterial, dialysis, or peripheral venous catheters or an infusion catheter not otherwise specified. Bloodstream infections due to central venous catheters should be assigned code T80.211 rather than code T82.7-. Examples of central venous catheters include the Hickman catheter, peripherally inserted central catheter (PICC), portacath, umbilical venous catheter, and triple lumen catheter.

Central line–associated bloodstream infections are systemic infections. Codes T80.211 and T80.212 distinguish between local and systemic infections due to a central venous catheter. A local infection due to a central venous catheter is assigned code T80.212. Local infections include exit or insertion site infections, port or reservoir infections, or tunnel infections, which are laboratory-confirmed bloodstream infections not due to an infection at another site. When there is a documented infection due to a central venous catheter, but the infection is not specified as to whether it is systemic or local, assign code T80.219. Code **T83.51-, Infection and inflammatory reaction due to indwelling urinary catheter,** should have additional codes for the specific infection, such as cystitis or sepsis, and for the responsible organism if that information is available. For example:

T82.7xxA	Infected pacemaker pocket, initial encounter
T85.71xA + B96.20	*Escherichia coli* infection due to peritoneal dialysis catheter, initial encounter
T83.51xA + N30.11	Chronic interstitial cystitis with hematuria due to indwelling catheter, initial encounter

Subcategories T82.8, T83.8, T84.8, and T85.8 classify other complications due to the presence of an internal prosthetic device, implant, or graft. This includes nonmechanical complications, with additional characters indicating embolism, fibrosis, hemorrhage, pain, stenosis, or thrombosis. When the complication is documented as postoperative pain due to the presence of a device, an implant, or a graft left in a surgical site, an additional code from category G89 is used to identify acute (G89.18) or chronic (G89.28) pain due to presence of the device, implant, or graft.

Code T82.857 is assigned for occlusion of a coronary bypass graft unless it is identified by the physician as being due to arteriosclerosis. Arteriosclerotic occlusions of a coronary artery bypass graft are classified as codes I25.70 through I25.799, Coronary atherosclerosis. The fifth character indicates the type of graft (autologous vein, autologous artery, nonautologous biological graft, transplanted heart, bypass graft of transplanted heart, and other coronary bypass graft). Occlusion of the coronary artery when there is no history of bypass graft is classified as arteriosclerosis of native coronary arteries (I25.10–I25.119).

TRANSPLANT COMPLICATIONS

Category T86, Complications of transplanted organs and tissue, is reserved for transplant complications such as failure, infection, rejection, or malignancy associated with organ transplant, with the fourth, fifth, or sixth character indicating the organ involved. When infection is present, a code from categories B95 through B97 should be assigned as an additional code. A transplant complication code is assigned only if the complication affects the function of the transplanted organ. Additional codes are assigned to identify other transplant complications, such as acute graft-versus-host disease (D89.810-), malignancy associated with organ transplant (C80.2), or post-transplant lymphoproliferative disorders (D47.z1). Two codes are required to fully describe a transplant complication: the appropriate code from category T86 and a secondary code that identifies the complication. For example:

T86.09 + D89.810	Acute graft-versus-host disease resulting from complications of bone marrow transplant
T86.19 + C80.2 + C64.9	Malignant neoplasm of transplanted kidney
T86.858 + D47.z1	Lymphoproliferative disorder post intestinal transplant

Code T86.5 describes complications of stem cell transplants. Stem cell transplants can be performed using the patient's own stem cells (autologous stem cell transplant) or donor stem cells (allogeneic stem cell transplant). Most stem cell transplantation procedures are performed using stem cells collected from the peripheral blood. Complications can develop from a stem cell transplant, including: graft-versus-host disease, stem cell (graft) failure, organ damage, cataracts, secondary cancers, and death.

Pre-existing conditions or conditions that develop after the transplant are not coded as complications unless they affect the function of the transplanted organs. Post-transplant surgical complications that do not relate to the function of the transplanted organ are classified to the specific complication. For example, a postsurgical infection is coded as a postoperative wound infection, not as a transplant complication. However, infections affecting the function of transplanted organs are classified to category T86, such as **T86.812, Lung transplant infection.** Post-transplant patients who are seen for treatment unrelated to the transplanted organ are assigned a code from category Z94, Transplanted organ and tissue status, to capture the transplant status of the patient. A code from category Z94 should never be used with a code from category T86 for the same organ.

For conditions that affect the function of the transplanted kidney—other than chronic kidney disease (CKD)—a code from subcategory T86.1- should be assigned, along with a secondary code that identifies the condition. Patients with CKD following a transplant should not be assumed to have transplant failure or rejection unless it is documented by the provider. Patients who have undergone kidney transplant may still have some form of CKD because the transplant may not fully restore kidney function. Therefore, the presence of CKD alone does not constitute a transplant complication. If documentation supports the presence of failure, infection, rejection, or another transplant complication, then it is appropriate to assign a code from subcategory T86.1-, Complications of kidney transplant, followed by the appropriate CKD code (N18.-). For patients with CKD following a kidney transplant who do not have a transplant complication such as failure or rejection, code **Z94.0, Kidney transplant status,** should be assigned instead of a code from subcategory T86.1-. For example:

- A patient with end-stage kidney disease due to a congenital anomaly of the urinary tract underwent deceased-donor right renal transplantation. Postoperatively, he had persistent severe hyperkalemia, which required hemodialysis. The patient also experienced delayed graft function. For the principal diagnosis, assign code **T86.19, Other complication of kidney transplant,** for the delayed graft function. Assign codes **N18.6, End stage renal**

disease; Q64.9, Congenital malformation of urinary system, unspecified; and **E87.5, Hyperkalemia,** as additional diagnoses. For the procedures, assign code **0TY00Z0, Transplantation of right kidney, allogeneic, open approach,** and code **5A1D00Z, Performance of urinary filtration, single.**

COMPLICATIONS OF REATTACHMENT AND AMPUTATION

Complications of reattached extremities and amputated stump are classified to category T87. Complications of reattached extremities are classified by whether they relate to the upper extremity (T87.0x-) or the lower extremity (T87.1x-). The sixth character indicates laterality. Complications of other reattached body parts are classified to code T87.2.

Complications of amputated stump include neuroma (T87.30–T87.34), infection (T87.40–T87.44), necrosis (T87.50–T87.54), other complication (T87.8), and unspecified (T87.9). The fifth characters for subcategories T87.3- through T87.5- specify whether the condition is of the upper or lower extremity, as well as laterality. Code **T87.8, Other complications of amputation stump,** includes amputation stump contracture, contracture of next proximal joint, flexion, edema, and hematoma.

Phantom limb syndrome is a condition relatively common in amputees whereby the patient has the perception of sensations, usually including pain, in an arm or a leg after the limb has been amputated. Phantom limb syndrome is not coded to category T87, but to codes G54.6 and G54.7, depending on whether or not there is associated pain.

EXERCISE 33.3

Code the following diagnoses. Do not assign External cause codes. Assume cases are for initial encounters unless otherwise noted.

1. Leakage of breast prosthesis — T85.43xA

2. Intrauterine contraceptive device imbedded in uterine wall — T83.39xA

   Imbedding

3. Erosion of skin by pacemaker electrodes — T821.90A

   Complication

4. Bone marrow transplant with rejection syndrome — T86.01

   Acute graft-versus-host disease — D89.810

   Complication

5.	Displaced lens implant, right eye Complication	T85.22xA
6.	Complication of transplanted intestine Malignant neoplasm of colon related to intestinal transplant	T86.858 C80.2 C18.9
7.	Broken right hip joint prosthesis after fall	T84.010A
8.	A 60-year-old type 2 diabetic woman had a right above-the-knee amputation two months ago due to severe diabetic circulatory problems in the limb. The stump had developed an abscess with *Staphylococcus aureus* cultured.	T87.43 B95.61 L02.415 E11.51
9.	Kidney transplant failure with chronic kidney disease, stage IV	T86.12 N18.4
10.	A patient with severe single-vessel coronary artery disease had cardiac catheterization and angioplasty with attempts to pass a stent into the right coronary artery. During manipulation of the wire, the wire broke off and became stuck in the right coronary artery and in the aorta. A snare was used to catch the wire and pull it out.	I25.10 T82.518A 02703ZZ 4A033BC

COMPLICATIONS OF PROCEDURES NOT CLASSIFIED ELSEWHERE

Category T81, Complications of procedures, not elsewhere classified, is used to classify a miscellaneous group of postoperative complications. Additional codes are not usually required because the complication code itself provides sufficient specificity. Category T81 requires a seventh character to be added to each code to specify initial encounter ("A"), subsequent encounter ("D"), or sequela ("S"). Examples of codes in category T81 include:

T81.31 Disruption of external operation (surgical) wound
T81.83 Persistent postprocedural fistula
T81.11 Postoperative cardiogenic shock

Cardiogenic shock is attributable to a weakened heart that is not able to pump enough blood to organs of the body. Causes of cardiogenic shock include myocardial infarction, pericardial tamponade, and heart failure. Assign code **T81.11, Postprocedural cardiogenic shock,** for cardiogenic shock due to surgery. Postoperative infections originating in the wound, lungs, or blood/vascular catheter may lead to septic shock. Code **T81.12, Postprocedural septic shock,** is assigned for postoperative septic shock. Assign code **T81.19, Other postprocedural shock,** for postsurgical hypovolemic shock (the most common type of postoperative shock), which occurs when large amounts of fluids are lost because of hemorrhage or severe dehydration. For example:

- A patient developed refractory cardiogenic shock, which required temporary extracorporeal membrane oxygenation (ECMO) support, after undergoing aortic valve (mechanical) replacement due to severe aortic stenosis. Assign code **I35.0, Nonrheumatic aortic (valve) stenosis,** as the principal diagnosis. Assign code **T81.11xA, Postprocedural cardiogenic shock, initial encounter,** as an additional diagnosis. Assign codes **02RF0JZ, Replacement of aortic valve with synthetic substitute, open approach,** and **5A15223, Extracorporeal membrane oxygenation, continuous,** for the procedures.

Wound dehiscence involves partial or total disruption of any or all layers of an operative wound site. Common causes of wound dehiscence include excess tension on the sutured edges, necrosis of the wound edges, seroma or hematoma causing pressure on the wound, and wound infection. ICD-10-CM provides codes to distinguish between disruption of internal (T81.32-) and external (T81.31-) surgical wounds as well as a disruption of a traumatic injury wound repair (T81.33-). For example:

- An eight-year-old had a lower leg traumatic laceration that was sutured several weeks ago. The patient was seen in the emergency department two weeks after the sutures were removed because of disruption of the wound repair. Code T81.33xA is assigned for this encounter.

Subcategory T81.5, Complications of foreign body accidentally left in body following procedure, is assigned for situations in which there is an unintended retention of a foreign object (e.g., sponge) in a patient after surgery or another procedure. The occurrence of unintended retention of objects at any point after the surgery ends should be captured regardless of setting or whether the object is removed. Subcategory T81.5 is further subdivided to specify the complication due to the foreign body, such as adhesions (T81.51-), obstruction (T81.52-), perforation (T81.53-), other complication (T81.59-), or unspecified complication (T81.50-). Sixth characters specify whether the foreign body was accidentally left following surgical operation ("0"); following infusion or transfusion ("1"); following kidney dialysis ("2"); following injection or immunization ("3"); following endoscopic examination ("4"); following heart catheterization ("5"); following aspiration,

puncture, or other catheterization ("6"); following removal of catheter or packing ("7"); following other procedure ("8"); or following unspecified procedure ("9"). For example:

- At surgery, a suture broke away from the needle and the needle was lost. Multiple attempts to find it were unsuccessful. An X-ray did not reveal the needle and the chest was closed. Another X-ray showed that the needle was positioned to the right of the aortic valve. The chest was reopened but the needle still could not be located. The surgeon decided that further search for the needle would cause the patient harm, so the chest was closed, and the patient was transferred to the ICU in stable condition. Assign code **T81.500A, Unspecified complication of foreign body accidentally left in body following surgical operation, initial encounter.** Although the surgeon made the decision to leave the needle to avoid harm to the patient, it was not the intent of the original procedure to leave a foreign body behind.

Acute reaction to foreign substance (rather than foreign body) accidentally left during a procedure is coded to subcategory T81.6, rather than subcategory T81.5. Category T81 also provides codes for complications of artery following a procedure, such as mesenteric artery (T81.710), renal artery (T81.711), other artery (T81.718), or unspecified artery (T81.719).

COMPLICATIONS OF SURGICAL AND MEDICAL CARE NOT CLASSIFIED ELSEWHERE

Category T88, Other complications of surgical and medical care, not elsewhere classified, is used to classify a number of specific conditions that may occur following almost any type of procedure. For example:

T88.0	Sepsis following immunization
T88.1	Generalized vaccinia
T88.2	Shock due to anesthesia
T88.4	Failed or difficult intubation

COMPLICATIONS VERSUS AFTERCARE

As discussed earlier, it is important to differentiate between an admission for a complication of surgery or medical care and one for aftercare. An admission for aftercare is usually planned in advance to take care of an expected residual or to carry out follow-up activity, such as removal of pins or plates placed during earlier orthopedic surgery. Aftercare is classified to categories Z42 through Z51. The aftercare Z codes should not be used for aftercare for injuries. For aftercare of an injury, the acute injury code is assigned with the appropriate seventh-character value for subsequent encounter.

Subcategory Z48.0, Encounter for attention to dressings, sutures and drains, distinguishes between encounters for change or removal of nonsurgical wound dressing (Z48.00), for change or removal of surgical wound dressing (Z48.01), for removal of sutures (Z48.02), and for removal of drains (Z48.03).

The coder must be careful not to assign complication codes for routine aftercare encounters. For example:

Z47.2	Admitted for removal of pins from femur
Z47.33	Admitted for replacement of knee prosthesis following explantation of infected joint prosthesis
Z46.89	Patient visit for removal of cast

EXERCISE 33.4

Code the following diagnoses, some of which identify complications and some of which identify aftercare. Assume initial encounter unless otherwise noted. Do not assign External cause codes or procedure codes.

1. Admitted for removal of internal fixation nail in right forearm that has extruded into surrounding tissue, causing severe pain — T84.192A
   Complication, orthopedic
2. Admitted for closure of colostomy — Z43.3
3. Admitted for adjustment of breast prosthesis — Z44.30
4. Admitted for removal of displaced breast prosthesis — T85.42xA
   Complication, surgical, internal

STATUS POST

The term "status post" used in diagnostic statements is sometimes interpreted by coders to mean that there is a postoperative complication; however, the term is rarely intended to carry this meaning. It usually indicates that the patient underwent the procedure at some time in the past. The condition ordinarily would be classified in the Z80–Z87 series but only when it is significant for the current episode of care.

SURGICAL OR MEDICAL CARE AS EXTERNAL CAUSE

As with certain other ICD-10-CM chapter 19 codes, some of the complication of care codes have the external cause included in the code. The code includes the nature of the complication as well as the type of procedure that caused the complication. No External cause code indicating the type of procedure is necessary for these codes. For example, code **M96.621, Fracture of humerus following insertion of orthopedic implant, joint prosthesis, or bone plate, right arm,** includes the nature of the complication (fracture) as well as the type of procedure that caused the complication (insertion of orthopedic implant, joint prosthesis, or bone plate).

In addition, ICD-10-CM provides three sets of External cause codes to indicate medical or surgical care as the cause of a complication:

Y62–Y69	Misadventures to patients during surgical and medical care
Y70–Y82	Medical devices associated with adverse incidents in diagnostic and therapeutic use
Y83–Y84	Surgical and other medical procedures as the cause of abnormal reaction of the patient, or of later complication, without mention of misadventure at the time of the procedure

Codes from categories Y62 through Y69 are used only when the condition is stated to be due to a misadventure of medical or surgical care. These categories include failure of sterile precautions during surgical and medical care (Y62.0–Y62.9), failure in dosage (Y63.0–Y63.9), contaminated medical or biological substances (Y64.0–Y64.9), other misadventures (Y65.0–Y65.53), other specified misadventure (Y65.8), nonadministration of surgical and medical care (Y66), and unspecified misadventure (Y69).

Code Y65.51 is assigned when the wrong operation (procedure) is performed on the correct patient and includes a wrong device implanted into a correct surgical site. Code Y65.52 is assigned for performance of an operation (procedure) on a patient not scheduled for surgery. This includes performance of procedure intended for another patient and performance of procedure on the wrong patient. Code Y65.53 is assigned for performance of the correct operation (procedure) on the wrong side/body part.

Categories Y70–Y82 are used to report breakdown or malfunction of medical devices during use, after implantation, or with ongoing use. The codes are used to report adverse incidents with the following types of devices:

Y70 Anesthesiology devices
Y71 Cardiovascular devices
Y72 Otorhinolaryngological devices
Y73 Gastroenterology and urology devices
Y74 General hospital and personal-use devices
Y75 Neurological devices
Y76 Obstetric and gynecological devices
Y77 Ophthalmic devices
Y78 Radiological devices
Y79 Orthopedic devices
Y80 Physical medicine devices
Y81 General- and plastic-surgery devices
Y82 Other and unspecified medical devices

Codes from categories Y83–Y84 are used when the condition is described as due to medical or surgical care but without mention of misadventure.

Examples include the following:

J70.0 + Y63.2	Radiation pneumonitis due to adverse reaction to overdose of radiotherapy
T81.89x- + Y65.51	Left femoral component inserted into right leg instead of right femoral component during total knee replacement

Because of the potential legal problems that may develop from reporting these codes, the facility should give careful thought to formulating policies and guidelines for their use. Coders should never make an assumption that there has been a misadventure; such codes should be assigned only when there is a clear-cut diagnostic statement to this effect by the physician.

EXERCISE 33.5

Code the following diagnoses. Do not assign External cause or Z codes. Assume initial encounters unless otherwise noted.

1. Infected injection site, left buttock or Complications	T80.29xA
2. Sloughing of skin graft due to rejection of pedicle graft to right arm	T86.820
3. Headache due to lumbar puncture	G97.1
4. Postoperative cardiac arrest occurring in operating room during closure of abdomen, with successful resuscitation	I97.711
5. Persistent vomiting following gastrointestinal surgery	K91.0
6. Air embolism resulting from intravenous infusion	T80.0xxA
7. Thrombophlebitis of antecubital vein of the upper arm resulting from intravenous infusion Postoperative	T80.1xxA I80.8
8. Hypovolemic shock due to surgery this morning Postoperative	T81.19xA
9. Persistent postoperative vesicovaginal fistula	T81.83xA N82.0
10. Cardiac insufficiency resulting from mitral valve prosthesis, in place for three years	I97.110

11.	Perforation of coronary artery by catheter during cardiac catheterization Complication	I97.51
12.	Displacement of cardiac pacemaker electrode Complication, mechanical	T82.120A
13.	Phantom limb with pain following surgical amputation	G54.6
14.	Neuroma of stump following surgical amputation of left leg	T87.34
15.	Methicillin-susceptible *Staphylococcus aureus* infection of transplanted kidney Complication, transplant, organ	T86.13 B95.61
16.	A patient with leukemia is admitted to the hospital after noting feelings of palpitations and shortness of breath. The patient has an infusion catheter in place for the administration of chemotherapy. A chest X-ray shows that the tip of the infusion catheter had broken off and traveled to the pulmonary artery.	T82.514A C95.90
17.	A 13-year-old male status post open reduction internal fixation of a right radial shaft fracture is admitted with bowing and angulation (malunion) of the fracture site secondary to a bent plate (internal fixation device). The physician states that vigorous activity on the child's part caused the plate to break and plans to reinsert a six-hole plate for fixation of the fracture.	T84.112A S52.301P

Final Review Exercise

Final Review Exercise

The final review exercise draws on concepts presented throughout this handbook. Read each brief summary below and assign codes for all diagnoses and procedures, including codes for external causes and locations of occurrence as needed. For purposes of this assignment, accept narrative statements (for example, conditions, procedures, or other therapy) as though listed in a diagnostic statement.

In day-to-day practice, many hospitals have opted through their internal coding policies not to collect data on noninvasive diagnostic services performed in the inpatient setting, such as X-rays, electrocardiograms (EKGs), computed tomography scans (CTs), and ultrasounds. For this reason, codes for these minor diagnostic services have been omitted from the answers. If you are using the *without Answers* version of this handbook, ask your instructor for the answers.

1. A patient was admitted with complaint of a dull ache and occasional acute pain in the right calf. Examination revealed swelling and redness of the calf as well as a slight fever. The patient gave a history of having been on Premarin therapy for the past 20 years and stated that she has always followed the doctor's instructions for its use. Venous plethysmography revealed the presence of a thrombus. The estrogen therapy dosage was modified, and the patient was discharged with a diagnosis of deep vein thrombosis and thrombophlebitis of the right femoral vein due to supplemental estrogen therapy. She will be seen in the physician's office in one week and will be followed regularly over the next several months.

I82.411	Acute embolism and thrombosis of right femoral vein
T38.5x5A	Adverse effect of other estrogens and progestogens, initial encounter
Z79.818	Long term (current) use of other agents affecting estrogen receptors and estrogen levels

Comment: Assign only the code for the thrombosis based on the excludes1 note at category I80. This condition is an adverse effect of estrogen use; therefore, assign the code for the manifestation first, followed by the code for the adverse effect.

2. A patient was admitted to the hospital because he was suffering acute abdominal pain. He was also found to be intoxicated, and his medical history indicated that he has been alcohol dependent for several years with episodic binging every three to four months. The current binge apparently started three days ago. The abdominal pain proved to be due to alcohol-induced acute pancreatitis, and he was treated with nasogastric suction, administration of IV fluids, and pain control. The patient was observed for possible withdrawal reaction with standby orders; multiple vitamins were given.

K85.2	Alcohol induced acute pancreatitis
F10.229	Alcohol dependence with intoxication, unspecified
HZ2ZZZZ	Alcohol detoxification

Comment: The condition responsible for the admission was the acute pancreatitis. No code is assigned for the abdominal pain because it is integral to the acute pancreatitis. The observation for withdrawal, standby orders, and administration of multiple vitamins are sufficient to code detoxification, but no withdrawal delirium occurred and so only the code for acute intoxication in alcoholism is assigned.

3. A patient with a four-year history of anorexia nervosa was seen in the physician's office because of significant weight loss over the past three months, going from 82 pounds down to 53 pounds. She was admitted to increase body weight and to be given nutritional counseling because of her severe malnutrition.

F50.00	Anorexia nervosa
E43	Severe malnutrition

Comment: Code E43, Unspecified severe protein-calorie malnutrition, should be assigned as an additional diagnosis for the severe malnutrition. For some anorexic patients, the weight loss is so severe that it leads to malnutrition. Code E43 further describes the severity of the patient's condition.

4. A patient was admitted through the emergency department following a fall from a ladder while painting the outside of his single-family house. He had contusions of the scalp and face and an open type I intertrochanteric fracture of the right femur. The fracture site was debrided, and an open reduction with internal fixation was carried out.

S72.141B	Displaced intertrochanteric fracture of right femur, initial encounter, for open fracture type I or II
S00.03xA	Contusion of scalp
S00.83xA	Contusion of other part of head
W11.xxxA	Fall from ladder
Y92.018	Other place in single-family (private) house as the place of occurrence of the external cause
Y99.8	Other external cause status
Y93.H9	Other activity involving property and land maintenance, building and construction
0QS604Z	Open reduction with internal fixation (reposition right upper femur)
0QB60ZZ	Debridement (root operation "Excision")

Comment: When several injuries are present, the most severe is designated as the principal diagnosis. When a fracture is not indicated as displaced or nondisplaced, it should be coded to displaced. The seventh-character value for the femur fracture is "B" because initial encounters for open fracture type I are classified to "B." The fracture reduction of the intertrochanteric femur is classified to the root operation "Reposition." The intertrochanteric area is between the greater and lesser trochanter, which is classified to the upper femur.

5. A patient who underwent a modified radical mastectomy of the left breast six months earlier because of carcinoma now has metastasis to the bone. She was admitted for a transfusion of nonautologous packed red blood cells (via peripheral vein) to treat aplastic anemia, probably due to her treatment by chemotherapy. She was discharged with a hemoglobin count of 11.5 and will be followed as an outpatient.

D61.1	Drug-induced aplastic anemia
T45.1x5A	Adverse effect of antineoplastic and immunosuppressive drugs, initial encounter
C79.51	Secondary malignant neoplasm of bone
Z85.3	History of malignant neoplasm of breast
Z90.12	Acquired absence of left breast and nipple
30233N1	Transfusion of red blood cells

Comment: Chemotherapy-induced aplastic anemia requires two codes; code D61.1 is sequenced first, followed by the adverse effect code to identify the drug. A code is assigned for the metastasis to the bone, and a history code is assigned to indicate the previous breast malignancy.

6. A patient was admitted for cholecystectomy because of chronic cholecystitis. Before she went to the operating room the next morning, nursing personnel noted that she had apparently developed a urinary infection, and laboratory tests confirmed a diagnosis of urinary tract infection due to *E. coli*. Because of the infection, the surgery was canceled, antibiotic therapy was instituted, and the patient was discharged on the third hospital day to continue antibiotic therapy at home. She will be seen in the physician's office in three weeks, and surgery will be rescheduled.

K81.1 Chronic cholecystitis

N39.0 Urinary tract infection, site not specified

B96.20 Unspecified Escherichia coli [E. coli] as the cause of diseases classified elsewhere

Z53.09 Surgery not carried out because of contraindication

Comment: The principal diagnosis does not change because the planned treatment was not carried out; therefore, the cholecystitis is the principal diagnosis. Code Z53.09 is assigned to indicate that the planned surgery was canceled because of a contraindication, which was the urinary tract infection.

7. A patient who recently underwent an oophorectomy because of adenocarcinoma of the ovary was admitted to the hospital for chemotherapy. Shortly after administration of the therapy, the patient developed a fever and chills and on the second day she had a productive cough. Chest X-rays indicated an acute pneumonia, and sputum culture was positive for *Klebsiella*. Antibiotics were administered, and the patient was discharged on the fifth hospital day after the chemotherapy was administered via peripheral vein.

Z51.11 Encounter for antineoplastic chemotherapy

C56.9 Malignant neoplasm of unspecified ovary

J15.0 Pneumonia due to Klebsiella pneumoniae

3E03305 Introduction of antineoplastic (chemotherapy) into peripheral vein

Comment: When a patient is receiving therapy for neoplastic disease, a code for that condition is assigned, rather than a history code, even though resection may have been performed previously. Because the patient was admitted solely for chemotherapy, Z51.11 remains the principal diagnosis even though the patient remained in the hospital because of the pneumonia. Code C56.9 is assigned as an additional code, rather than a history code, because the patient is still under treatment.

8. A patient who had noticed significant abdominal enlargement over a period of several weeks without a change in her dietary habits was admitted for exploratory laparotomy. Surgery revealed a large malignant ovarian tumor, and the left ovary was resected. The pelvic cavity was explored thoroughly for any evidence of metastatic spread, but none was noted. Chemotherapy treatments were started (via peripheral vein) on the day prior to discharge, and the patient was scheduled to continue therapy on an outpatient basis.

C56.2 Malignant neoplasm of left ovary

0UT10ZZ Resection left ovary, open approach

3E03305 Introduction of antineoplastic (chemotherapy) into peripheral vein

Comment: When adjunct therapy such as radiotherapy or chemotherapy is given during an admission in which definitive surgery was performed, the code for the neoplasm is designated as the principal diagnosis and no code from category Z51 is assigned. No code is assigned for the laparotomy because it is the operative approach for the oophorectomy.

9. A female patient who had undergone surgery for carcinoma of the right breast two months earlier has since been on a program of chemotherapy. On a routine office visit yesterday, the physician noted that she had become severely dehydrated as a result of this program, and she was admitted for IV therapy for rehydration. Her regular chemotherapy session (via peripheral vein) was carried out on the third day.

E86.0	Dehydration
T45.1x5A	Adverse effect of antineoplastic and immunosuppressive drugs, initial encounter
C50.911	Malignant neoplasm of right female breast
3E03305	Introduction of antineoplastic (chemotherapy) into peripheral vein

Comment: Assign a code for the nature of the adverse effect (dehydration) first, followed by the adverse effect code (e.g., T45.1x5). The guideline regarding the management of dehydration due to the malignancy does not apply because the dehydration was an adverse effect of the therapy, rather than due to the malignancy. The malignant neoplasm is assigned as a secondary diagnosis. Even though she received chemotherapy during her hospital stay, the admission was not solely for that purpose and so Z51.11 is not assigned.

10. A patient was admitted with abdominal pain and complaints of melena noted for the past two days. Examination revealed an acute diverticulitis of the colon. Laboratory studies reported a significant hypokalemia. The provider documented hypokalemia, and the patient was placed on oral potassium. Bleeding from the diverticulitis subsided within a few days on conservative treatment, and the patient was discharged to be followed on an outpatient basis.

K57.33	Diverticulitis of colon with bleeding
E87.6	Hypokalemia

Comment: The presence of melena indicates that bleeding is associated with the diverticulitis. Bleeding in a patient with diverticulitis is presumed to be due to the diverticulitis unless the physician specifies that it is due to a different cause. No code is assigned for the abdominal pain, as it is implicit in the diagnosis. The low potassium was treated and therefore is a reportable diagnosis.

11. A patient was admitted with complaints of severe joint pain affecting both hands and hips. The physician's diagnosis indicated rheumatoid arthritis with sympathetic inflammatory myopathy.

M05.49	Rheumatoid myopathy with rheumatoid arthritis of multiple sites

Comment: No code for the joint pain is assigned because it is a characteristic component of rheumatoid arthritis.

12. A patient who was two months pregnant contracted rubella. On her next prenatal visit to the doctor's office (at 9 weeks gestation), it was decided to admit the patient for therapeutic abortion because of the probability of abnormality of the fetus. Complete abortion was carried out by D & C.

Z33.2	Encounter for elective termination of pregnancy
O35.3xx0	Maternal care for (suspected) damage to fetus from viral disease in mother
Z3A.09	9 weeks gestation of pregnancy
10A07ZZ	Abortion of products of conception, via natural or artificial opening

Comment: Because the fetal condition was responsible for modifying the treatment of the mother, the code for it is assigned to explain the rationale for the abortion.

13. Increasing fetal stress was noted during labor. The patient was transferred to the surgical suite, where a classical cesarean delivery was performed. A full-term normal male was delivered.

O77.9 Fetal stress

Z37.0 Single live birth

10D00Z0 Classical cesarean section

Comment: In this case, the fetal stress affected the management of the mother, leading to the decision to deliver by cesarean. Cesarean section is classified to the Obstetrics Section, root operation "Extraction."

14. A patient was admitted with systolic heart failure, acute on chronic, congestive heart failure, and unstable angina. The unstable angina was treated with nitrates, and IV Lasix was administered to manage the heart failure. Both conditions improved, and the patient was discharged to be followed on an outpatient basis.

I50.23 Acute on chronic systolic (congestive) heart failure

I20.0 Unstable angina

Comment: Because both conditions equally meet the criteria for principal diagnosis, either may be listed first. It is not necessary to assign code I50.9 because I50.23 includes the congestive heart failure.

15. A patient was admitted for observation and evaluation for possible intracranial injury following a collision with another car while he was driving to work. The patient had minor bruises on the upper back and abrasions of the skin of the left upper arm. The bruises did not appear to need any treatment; the abrasions were swabbed with disinfectant, and Neosporin was applied. Intracranial injury was ruled out.

Z04.1 Observation examination and observation following transport accident

S20.229A Contusion of unspecified back wall of thorax

S40.812A Abrasion of left upper arm

V43.52xA Car driver injured in collision with other type car in traffic accident

Comment: When the patient is admitted for observation for a possible serious injury such as an intracranial injury, the Z04 code is assigned as the principal diagnosis even when minor injuries are present. In this case, the purpose of admission was to observe the patient; the minor injuries would not have required hospital admission. Additional codes are assigned for the minor injuries. Code S30.0- should not be used because it refers to the lower back rather than the upper back.

16. A patient was brought to the emergency department following a burn injury experienced in a fire at the garage where he works. He was admitted and treated for first-degree and second-degree burns of the forearm and third-degree burn of the back.

T21.34xA Third-degree burn of back

T22.219A Second-degree burn of forearm

X00.0xxA Exposure to flames in uncontrolled fire in building or structure

Y92.59 Other trade areas as the place of occurrence of the external cause

Y99.0 Civilian activity done for income or pay

Comment: When several burns are present, the burn of the highest degree takes precedence; therefore, the third-degree burn of the back is designated as the principal diagnosis. When more than one degree of burn occurs at the same site, only the code for the highest degree is assigned; therefore, only the second degree of the forearm is coded.

17. A patient was admitted because of suspected carcinoma of the colon. Exploratory laparotomy was carried out, and a significant mass was discovered in the sigmoid colon. The sigmoid colon was resected and end-to-end anastomosis accomplished. Small nodules were noted on the liver, and a needle biopsy of the liver was performed during the procedure. The pathology report confirmed adenocarcinoma of the sigmoid colon with metastasis to the liver.

C18.7	Malignant neoplasm of sigmoid colon
C78.7	Secondary malignant neoplasm of liver
0DTN0ZZ	Resection of sigmoid colon, open approach
0FB03ZX	Needle biopsy of liver

Comment: No code is assigned for the exploratory laparotomy because it is the operative approach for the sigmoidectomy. End-to-end anastomosis is included in the code for the colon resection. A needle biopsy performed during open surgery is coded as a percutaneous biopsy.

18. A patient was discharged following prostate surgery with an indwelling catheter in place. He was readmitted with urinary sepsis due to methicillin-resistant *Staphylococcus aureus* (MRSA) due to the presence of the catheter. The physician confirmed the diagnosis of sepsis due to MRSA. The catheter was removed and the patient started on antibiotic therapy. The patient's condition improved over several days, and he was discharged without an indwelling catheter.

T83.51xA	Urinary sepsis due to indwelling urinary catheter
A41.02	Sepsis due to methicillin-resistant Staphylococcus aureus
N39.0	Urinary tract infection, site not specified
Y84.6	Urinary catheterization as the cause of abnormal reaction of the patient, or of later complication, without mention of misadventure at the time of the procedure
0TPDX0Z	Removal of drainage device from urethra, external approach

Comment: This infection was caused by the presence of the indwelling catheter and is coded as an infection of that device. The physician also confirmed the diagnosis of sepsis. Code A41.02 is assigned for *Staphylococcus aureus* sepsis instead of code A41.9, because the organism is specified. Because the diagnosis code identifies that the infection is resistant, do not assign a code from category Z16 as an additional diagnosis.

19. A patient 25 weeks pregnant was diagnosed as having an iron-deficiency anemia and was admitted for transfusion of nonautologous packed red blood cells.

O99.012	Anemia complicating pregnancy, second trimester
D50.9	Iron-deficiency anemia, unspecified
Z3A.025	25 weeks gestation of pregnancy
30233N1	Transfusion of red blood cells

Comment: Code O99.012 from chapter 15 of ICD-10-CM is assigned as the principal diagnosis because the anemia is complicating the pregnancy. Second trimester is assigned because the patient is 25 weeks pregnant. Code D50.9 is also assigned to provide greater specificity as to the type of anemia.

20. A patient was admitted with occlusion (due to plaque) of the right common carotid artery, and open carotid endarterectomy was carried out with extracorporeal circulation (continuous cardiac output) used throughout the procedure.

I65.21	Occlusion and stenosis of right carotid artery
03CH0ZZ	Extirpation of matter from right common carotid, open approach
5A1221Z	Performance of cardiac output, continuous (extracorporeal circulation)

Comment: The objective of the carotid endarterectomy was to take out or cut out the solid matter (plaque) occluding the carotid artery; therefore, the procedure is coded to the root operation "Extirpation" rather than "Excision" (cutting out or off, without replacement, a portion of a body part). The extracorporeal circulation is classified to the Extracorporeal Assistance and Performance Section, root operation "Performance," because the machine has taken over the patient's cardiac function during the procedure.

21. A patient was admitted in a coma due to acute cerebrovascular thrombosis with cerebral infarction; the coma cleared by the fourth hospital day. Aphasia and hemiparesis were also present. The aphasia had cleared by discharge, but the hemiparesis was still present.

I63.30 Cerebral thrombosis with cerebral infarction

R40.20 Coma

R47.01 Aphasia

G81.90 Hemiplegia, unspecified, affecting unspecified side

Comment: A code for coma is assigned because it is not integral to a diagnosis of cerebral thrombosis. Codes are assigned for aphasia and hemiparesis; any neurological deficits that occur, even if they have resolved by discharge, are coded because they affect the patient's care.

22. A patient was admitted with severe abdominal pain that began two days prior to admission and progressed in severity. Esophagogastroduodenoscopy (EGD) revealed an acute gastric ulcer, but no signs of hemorrhage or malignancy were noted. The provider documented acute gastric ulcer, and the patient was put on a medical regimen, including a bland diet, and was advised not to take aspirin.

K25.3 Acute gastric ulcer without hemorrhage or perforation

0DJ08ZZ Inspection of upper intestinal tract, via natural or artificial opening, endoscopic (esophagogastroduodenoscopy)

Comment: No code is assigned for the abdominal pain because it is integral to gastric ulcer.

23. A patient with type 1 diabetes mellitus with hyperglycemia was admitted for regulation of insulin dosage. The patient had been in the hospital four weeks earlier for an acute ST elevation myocardial infarction of the inferoposterior wall, and an EKG was performed to check its current status.

E10.65 Diabetes mellitus, type 1 with hyperglycemia

I21.19 ST elevation (STEMI) myocardial infarction involving other coronary artery of inferior wall

Comment: A patient admitted four weeks after an acute myocardial infarction will always require clinical evaluation; in this case, a specific diagnostic study was also performed.

24. A patient who was treated seven weeks ago at Community Hospital for an acute anterolateral myocardial infarction is now admitted to University Hospital for surgical repair of an atrial septal defect resulting from the recent infarction. Following thoracotomy, the defect was repaired with a nonautologous tissue graft; cardiopulmonary bypass (extracorporeal circulation, continuous cardiac output) was used during the procedure. The patient was discharged in good condition, to be followed as an outpatient.

I51.0 Atrial septal defect, acquired

I25.2 Old myocardial infarction

02U50KZ Supplement atrial septum with nonautologous tissue substitute, open approach

5A1221Z Performance of cardiac output, continuous (cardiopulmonary bypass)

Comment: Because seven weeks have elapsed since the infarction, neither the acute myocardial infarction nor code I23.1, Atrial septal defect as current complication following acute myocardial infarction, should be reported. Codes from category I23 are used for certain current complications following ST elevation (STEMI) and non-ST elevation (NSTEMI) myocardial infarction, but only within the 28 days post myocardial infarction. Codes from category I21, ST elevation (STEMI) and non-ST elevation (NSTEMI) myocardial infarction, are also used within four weeks (28 days) of onset. Instead, code I25.2, Old myocardial infarction, may be assigned. No code is assigned for the thoracotomy because it is the operative approach for the repair. The objective of the atrial septal repair was to supplement the atrial septum with the graft, so the procedure is coded to the root operation "Supplement."

25. A patient with bilateral mixed conductive and sensorineural hearing loss was admitted for cochlear implantation. Bilateral multiple-channel implants were inserted, and the patient was discharged, to be followed as an outpatient.

H90.6 Mixed conductive and sensorineural hearing loss, bilateral

09HD06Z Insertion of multiple channel cochlear prosthesis into right inner ear, open approach

09HE06Z Insertion of multiple channel cochlear prosthesis into left inner ear, open approach

Comment: Because a combination code including both types of hearing loss is provided, only code H90.6 is assigned rather than individual codes for the hearing loss. Because the prosthetic device was inserted in both ears and a single code is not available for bilateral, two procedure codes are necessary, one for each ear.

26. A patient who underwent a right kidney transplant three months ago is admitted for biopsy because of an increased creatinine level discovered on an outpatient visit. Percutaneous biopsy revealed chronic rejection syndrome. The patient was discharged on a modified medication regimen, to be followed closely as an outpatient.

T86.11 Kidney transplant rejection

0TB03ZX Excision of right kidney, percutaneous approach, diagnostic

Comment: Transplant rejection is coded as a complication of the transplanted organ. A percutaneous biopsy is coded to the root operation "Excision," with the qualifier "diagnostic."

27. A patient was admitted with a displaced fracture of the shaft of the right femur. Closed reduction was carried out and a cast was applied.

S72.301A Unspecified fracture of shaft of right femur

0QS6XZZ Reposition right upper femur, external approach

Comment: When the diagnostic statement does not indicate whether the fracture is open or closed, ICD-10-CM classifies it as closed. Reduction of a dislocated fracture is classified to the root operation "Reposition." Because this was a closed reduction, no incision or skin puncture was performed and the approach is external. Cast application in conjunction with the "Reposition" procedure is not coded separately.

28. A patient who has had recurrent attacks of angina was seen in his physician's office because he felt that the anginal attacks seemed to be occurring more frequently and to be more severe and more difficult to control. He had not had a thorough evaluation previously, and bypass surgery had not been recommended in the past. He was admitted to the hospital for diagnostic studies to determine the underlying cause of this unstable angina. He underwent combined right- and left-heart catheterization, which revealed significant atherosclerotic heart disease. He was advised that coronary artery bypass surgery was indicated, but he did not want to make a decision without further discussion with his family. He was discharged on antianginal medication and will be seen in the doctor's office in one week.

I25.110 Atherosclerotic heart disease of native coronary artery with unstable angina pectoris

4A023N8 Measurement of cardiac sampling and pressure, bilateral, percutaneous approach

Comment: I25.110 is a combination code that includes both the atherosclerosis and the unstable angina pectoris. Because this patient has not had a bypass surgery in the past, the arteriosclerosis is of a native coronary artery. Cardiac catheterization is classified to the Measurement and Monitoring Section, root operation "Measurement," body system "cardiac." Because the catheterization was for both the right and left sides, the qualifier "bilateral" is used.

29. The patient discussed in the preceding case returned to the hospital for bypass surgery. His angina is under control with the antianginal medications he was prescribed. Reverse right greater saphenous vein grafts were brought from the aorta to the obtuse marginal and the right coronary artery; the left internal mammary artery was loosened and brought down to the left anterior descending artery to bypass this obstruction. The gastroepiploic artery was used to bypass the circumflex. Extracorporeal circulation (continuous cardiac output) and intraoperative pacemaker were used during the procedure.

I25.119	Atherosclerotic heart disease of native coronary artery with unspecified angina pectoris
021109W	Bypass coronary artery, two sites from aorta with autologous venous tissue, open approach
02100Z9	Bypass coronary artery, one site from left internal mammary, open approach
02100ZF	Bypass coronary artery, one site from abdominal artery, open approach
06BP0ZZ	Excision of right greater saphenous vein, open approach
5A1221Z	Performance of cardiac output, continuous (cardiopulmonary bypass)
5A1223Z	Performance of cardiac pacing, continuous (intraoperative pacemaker)

Comment: Code I25.110 is not used because his angina is not specified to be unstable. Four coronary artery bypass grafts were placed, two of which were aortocoronary, one a left internal mammary-coronary artery, and one an abdominal-coronary bypass. A code for the "Excision" of the saphenous vein for harvesting of the graft is also assigned. Codes are assigned for the cardiopulmonary bypass and the intraoperative pacemaker.

30. A patient was brought to the hospital by ambulance after a fall from the scaffolding while working on the construction of a new bank building. He had struck his head and experienced a brief period of unconsciousness (approximately 45 minutes). On examination, he was found to have an open skull fracture with cerebral laceration and contusion. The skull fracture was reduced after debridement and the patient was transferred to the intensive care unit, where he stayed for four days. He was discharged on the tenth day in good condition and advised to avoid any strenuous activity and to see his physician in one week.

S02.91xB	Unspecified fracture of skull, initial encounter for open fracture
S06.332A	Contusion and laceration of cerebrum, unspecified, with loss of consciousness of 31 minutes to 59 minutes, initial encounter
W12.xxxA	Fall from scaffolding, initial encounter
Y92.61	Building [any] under construction as the place of occurrence of the external cause
Y99.0	Civilian activity done for income or pay
Y93.H3	Activity, building and construction
0NS00ZZ	Reposition skull, open approach

Comment: Code S02.91 requires the seventh-character value "B" to indicate that this is an open fracture. Any intracranial injury (S06.-) associated with the skull fracture requires a separate code. In this case, code S06.332- is assigned because the patient was documented to have loss of consciousness for less than one hour. Debridement of compound (open) fracture of the skull is included in the code for fracture reduction.

31. A patient was admitted for corrective surgery for a keloid of the left hand due to a burn experienced in a brush fire one year ago. Radical excision of the scar was carried out, and the defect was covered with a full-thickness graft taken from the left upper arm. The patient was discharged in good condition, to be seen in the physician's office in two weeks.

L91.0	Keloid scar
T23.002S	Burn of unspecified degree of left hand, unspecified site, sequela
X01.0xxS	Exposure to flames in uncontrolled fire, not in building or structure, sequela
0HBGXZZ	Excision of left hand skin, external approach
0HRGX73	Replacement of left hand skin with autologous tissue substitute, full thickness, external approach
0HBCXZZ	Excision of left upper arm skin, external approach

Comment: The residual keloid is sequenced first, with code T23.002S indicating that it is a late effect of a burn of the hand. Because the condition is a late effect, the External cause of morbidity code must also be a late effect code; therefore, the seventh-character value "S," for sequela, is assigned. A separate code is assigned for obtaining the autograft (per the ICD-10-PCS Official Coding Guidelines) because the tissue is obtained from a different body part in order to complete the objective of the procedure.

32. A patient was brought to the emergency department by ambulance at 1:00 a.m. by her husband, who stated that they had been to a dinner party at a friend's home earlier in the evening. His wife had two martinis before the meal and several glasses of wine with the meal. At bedtime she took Valium that her physician had ordered prn for nervousness and inability to sleep. Shortly thereafter, the husband noticed that she appeared to be somewhat stuporous, became worried about her condition, and brought her to the emergency department. The provider documented accidental overdose secondary to Valium taken with alcohol.

T51.0x1A	Toxic effect of ethanol, accidental (unintentional), initial encounter
T42.4x1A	Poisoning by benzodiazepines, accidental (unintentional), initial encounter (Valium)
R40.1	Stupor
Y92.099	Unspecified place in other non-institutional residence as the place of occurrence of the external cause

Comment: Although the Valium was used correctly, the fact that alcohol was also taken during the same period makes this a poisoning. Because two substances were involved, two poisoning codes are assigned. Either poisoning code can be designated as the principal diagnosis.

33. A patient was admitted to the hospital with an admitting diagnosis of acute hip pain. There was no history of trauma; she stated that she had simply stood up from her chair, immediately experienced acute pain in the left leg, and fallen back into the chair. She has had osteoporosis for several years and is also a known diabetic. An X-ray revealed a fracture of the lower third of the shaft of the femur. A routine preoperative chest X-ray showed a few strands of atelectasis and a small cloudy area that may have represented mild pleural effusion. A cast was applied to the leg to immobilize the fracture. Her blood sugars were monitored and remained normal throughout the stay. The physician documented spontaneous fracture secondary to osteoporosis.

M80.052A	Age-related osteoporosis with current pathological fracture, left femur, initial encounter
E11.9	Type 2 diabetes mellitus without complications
2W3MX2Z	Immobilization of left lower extremity using cast

Comment: Spontaneous fractures such as this are always classified as pathological. Codes in category M80 are combination codes that include the osteoporosis with current pathological fracture. ICD-10-CM classifies osteoporosis not otherwise specified to age-related osteoporosis. No codes are assigned for the atelectasis or possible pleural effusion because these represent X-ray findings only, without further evaluation or treatment. The diabetes was monitored, and so a code is assigned. Diabetes mellitus unspecified as to type is classified to type 2. Because only a cast was placed on the fracture without the need for reduction ("Reposition"), the procedure is coded to the root operation "Immobilization" in the Placement Section.

34. A patient with a five-year history of emphysema was brought to the hospital's emergency department in acute respiratory failure. Endotracheal intubation was carried out in the emergency department, and the patient was placed on mechanical ventilation. She was then admitted to the ICU, where she remained on the ventilator for three days and then was taken off the ventilator without a weaning period. She was discharged on the fifth hospital day.

J96.00 Acute respiratory failure, unspecified whether with hypoxia or hypercapnia

J43.9 Emphysema, unspecified

5A1945Z Respiratory ventilation, 24-96 consecutive hours

0BH17EZ Insertion of endotracheal airway into trachea, via natural or artificial opening

Comment: Acute respiratory failure associated with chronic pulmonary disease, such as emphysema, can be designated as the principal diagnosis. The patient was on mechanical ventilation only three days, a total of less than 96 hours. A code is assigned for the tube insertion because it was performed in the emergency department of the hospital with immediate admission.

35. A patient in acute respiratory failure was brought to the hospital by ambulance with ventilator in place. In the ambulance, an endotracheal tube was inserted into the patient. He had a long history of congestive heart failure, and studies confirmed that he was in congestive failure, with pleural effusion and acute pulmonary edema. The patient was treated with diuretics, and his cardiac condition was brought back into an acceptable range. He continued on ventilation for four days and was weaned on the fifth day. The physician was questioned regarding the reason for the admission, and she indicated that the patient was admitted for the acute respiratory failure.

J96.00 Acute respiratory failure, unspecified whether with hypoxia or hypercapnia

I50.9 Heart failure, unspecified

5A1955Z Respiratory ventilation, greater than 96 consecutive hours

Comment: When a patient is admitted with respiratory failure and another acute condition (e.g., congestive heart failure), the principal diagnosis will not be the same in every situation. Selection of the principal diagnosis will depend on the circumstances of admission. In this instance, the physician had to be queried to determine whether the congestive heart failure or the respiratory failure was responsible for the admission. Pulmonary edema and pleural effusion with heart condition or heart failure is classified to heart failure; no additional codes are assigned for these conditions. Time counting for mechanical ventilation begins at time of admission when the ventilator is already in use. No code is assigned for the endotracheal tube insertion because it was done in the ambulance and cannot be reported by the hospital.

36. A five-year-old child was brought to the emergency department after the mother found the child playing with an open bottle of her prescription sedatives. She could not tell if the child had taken any pills, but she wanted the child evaluated for possible problems. The child was evaluated, and no evidence of poisoning or any other signs or symptoms were found. The mother was reassured, and the child was taken home.

Z03.6 Encounter for observation for suspected toxic effect from ingested substance ruled out

Comment: It is appropriate to use category Z03 when a patient is seen for evaluation and no diagnosis is made. If the suspected diagnosis or a related diagnosis had been established, including a significant sign or symptom, the code for that condition would be assigned rather than the code from category Z03.

37. A patient with hypertensive and diabetic end-stage renal disease who is on chronic dialysis is admitted because of disequilibrium syndrome (electrolyte imbalance) caused by the dialysis.

E87.8 Other disorders of electrolyte and fluid balance, not elsewhere classified

I12.0 Hypertensive chronic kidney disease with stage 5 chronic kidney disease or end-stage renal disease

N18.6 End-stage renal disease

E11.29 Type 2 diabetes mellitus with other diabetic kidney complication

Z99.2 Dependence on renal dialysis

Y84.1 Kidney dialysis as the cause of abnormal reaction of the patient, or of later complication, without mention of misadventure at the time of the procedure

Comment: When end-stage renal disease is the result of both hypertension and diabetes mellitus, both diabetes and hypertension are coded because they are responsible for the condition (I12.- and E11.29). Because the patient has hypertensive end-stage renal disease and is on chronic dialysis, codes I12.0 and N18.6 are assigned. Code Y84.1 is assigned to indicate the external cause.

38. A patient who has had arteriosclerotic disease of the right lower extremity with intermittent claudication for three years recently progressed to ulceration, and is now admitted with ulceration and gangrene of the toes of the right foot resulting from the arteriosclerosis. A tarsometatarsal amputation of the right foot was performed, and the patient left the operating room in good condition.

I70.261 Atherosclerosis of native arteries of extremities with gangrene, right leg

L97.519 Non-pressure chronic ulcer of other part of right foot with unspecified severity

0Y6M0Z0 Detachment at right foot, complete, open approach

Comment: Code I70.261 includes gangrene. An additional code may be assigned for the ulceration. Amputations are coded to the root operation "Detachment." Amputations through the tarsometatarsal joint of the foot are considered complete; therefore, the qualifier "complete" is selected.

39. A two-year-old child with a severe cough was admitted to the hospital with a history of having experienced malaise, loss of appetite, and cough for several days. In addition to the cough, he was experiencing some shortness of breath, and a chest X-ray showed an acute pneumonia. Sputum cultures showed *B. pertussis*. He was started on IV antibiotics and became afebrile on the fifth hospital day. A repeat chest X-ray was negative on the sixth hospital day, and the cough had partially cleared. He was discharged on the eighth day to be cared for at home and followed as an outpatient.

A37.01 Whooping cough due to Bordetella pertussis with pneumonia

Comment: Whooping cough is the condition resulting from infection by *B. pertussis*. Code A37.01 identifies the pneumonia associated with whooping cough, and no separate code for the pneumonia is assigned.

40. A 10-year-old boy was admitted because of severe cellulitis of the left leg. He had gone on a hiking trip in the nearby forest with his Boy Scout troop a week earlier and now has a painful reddened area on the left leg. He stated that there was a good deal of thorny brush and that he had several minor thorn punctures of the left leg but had experienced no problem with them. The day before admission he had developed a painful swollen area that had become worse during the night. A diagnosis of cellulitis due to *Streptococcus* A was made, and antibiotics were administered. The wound itself was evaluated but did not appear to need specific treatment. The area on the leg progressively healed. The patient was discharged to continue the antibiotic series at home and will be seen in the physician's office in one week.

L03.116 Cellulitis of left lower limb

S81.832A Puncture wound without foreign body, left lower leg

B95.0 Bacterial infection due to group A *Streptococcus*

W60.xxxA Contact with nonvenomous plant thorns and spines and sharp leaves

Y92.821 Forest as the place of occurrence of the external cause

Y93.01 Activity, walking, marching and hiking

Y99.8 Other external cause status

Comment: In this case, the minor puncture wounds did not require treatment at the time they occurred and would not have required hospital care; therefore, the cellulitis is designated as the principal diagnosis. The wounds were evaluated, however, and so a code for the injury is assigned. Although thorn punctures were noted, there was no mention of a thorn in the wounds; therefore, no code for foreign bodies was assigned.

41. An unconscious diving instructor was admitted with concussion and a skull fracture and subdural hematoma after jumping from a high diving board and hitting the side of the pool at the gymnasium where he worked. Drainage of the subdural space was carried out by incision and the fracture reduced. The patient left the operating room in fair condition but died from his brain injury the following day without having ever regained consciousness.

S02.91xA Unspecified fracture of skull, initial encounter for closed fracture

S06.5x7A Traumatic subdural hemorrhage with loss of consciousness of any duration with death due to brain injury before regaining consciousness, initial encounter

W16.532A Jumping or diving into swimming pool striking wall causing other injury, initial encounter

Y92.39 Other specified sports and athletic area as the place of occurrence of the external cause

Y93.12 Springboard and platform diving

Y99.0 Civilian activity done for income or pay

0NS00ZZ Reposition of skull, open approach

00940ZZ Drainage of subdural space, open approach

Comment: No code is assigned for concussion when there is skull fracture with intracranial injury. Code S06.5x7A is used because the patient was unconscious on admission, never regained consciousness, and expired the following day from the brain injury. Two procedure codes are needed, one for the fracture reduction and one for the incision and "Drainage" of the hematoma.

42. A patient was admitted because of increasing confusion and memory loss, which his family was unable to deal with. The patient was disoriented and unable to furnish any information. He was diagnosed as having senile dementia with Alzheimer's disease and was transferred to a nursing home.

G30.9 Alzheimer's disease, unspecified

F02.80 Dementia in other diseases classified elsewhere without behavioral disturbance

Comment: When dementia is associated with Alzheimer's disease, the code for Alzheimer's disease is sequenced first, followed by code F02.80.

43. Newborn twin girls, both living, were delivered in the hospital at 35 completed weeks, with extremely low birth weight of 850 grams for twin #1 and 900 grams for twin #2. Both were transferred to the neonatal intensive care nursery with a diagnosis of extreme immaturity.

Twin #1:
- Z38.30 Twin liveborn infant, delivered vaginally
- P07.03 Extremely low birth weight newborn, 750-999 grams
- P07.38 Preterm newborn, gestational age 35 completed weeks

Twin #2:
- Z38.30 Twin liveborn infant, delivered vaginally
- P07.03 Extremely low birth weight newborn, 750-999 grams
- P07.38 Preterm newborn, gestational age 35 completed weeks

Comment: A code from category Z38 is always designated as the principal diagnosis for the episode in which birth occurs. For babies born in the hospital, the fifth digit indicates whether the delivery was by cesarean; in this case, it was not. When both birth weight and gestational age of the newborn are available, both should be coded, with birth weight sequenced before gestational age.

44. A patient with a long history of angina pectoris came to the emergency department complaining of increasing anginal pain that he could not relieve with nitroglycerin and rest. The pain had occurred again about an hour ago and has been increasing in severity. Cardiac catheterization done recently showed some occlusion of the right coronary artery. It was decided to go ahead with a percutaneous transluminal coronary angioplasty, administering a thrombolytic agent to a coronary artery, in the hope of averting what appeared to be an impending myocardial infarction. The procedure was carried out without incident and the infarction was averted, but the patient did have an occlusion of the coronary artery.

- I24.0 Acute coronary thrombosis not resulting in myocardial infarction
- 02703ZZ Dilation of coronary artery, one site, percutaneous approach
- 3E07317 Introduction of other thrombolytic into coronary artery, percutaneous approach

Comment: The code for unstable angina (I20.0) is not assigned when a code from category I24 is assigned. Code 02703ZZ is assigned for the PTCA on a single site. The infusion of a thrombolytic agent is reported separately using code 3E07317.

45. A patient was admitted to the hospital with unstable angina that had been increasing in severity since the previous day. He was placed on bed rest and telemetry, and IV nitroglycerin was administered. An EKG showed some paroxysmal tachycardia as well, and so IV heparin was added to his medication program. His angina returned to its normal status, and the tachycardia was not shown on repeat studies at the end of one week. The patient was discharged to be seen by a visiting nurse over the next two weeks to supervise his medication regimen, and an appointment with his physician was made for two weeks later.

I20.0 Unstable angina

I47.9 Paroxysmal tachycardia, unspecified

Comment: In this case, no studies were done to identify the underlying pathology and no surgical intervention was undertaken. Therefore, the unstable angina is the principal diagnosis.

46. A patient who had been HIV-positive for several years was seen in his physician's office with skin lesions over his back suggestive of HIV-related Kaposi's sarcoma. He was seen for incisional biopsy, which confirmed the diagnosis.

B20 Human immunodeficiency virus (HIV) disease

C46.0 Kaposi's sarcoma of skin

0HB6XZX Excision of back skin, external approach, diagnostic

Comment: When the patient is admitted for treatment of a condition due to HIV infection, the code for the infection is designated as the principal diagnosis, with an additional code for the related condition.

47. A patient was admitted through the emergency department with acute right flank pain and was taken to surgery for removal of a ruptured appendix. At the time of the appendectomy, generalized peritonitis was observed along with some suspicious nodules on the head of the pancreas. A needle biopsy was performed while the abdomen was open; a diagnosis of carcinoma of the pancreas head was made on the basis of the pathological examination.

K35.2 Acute appendicitis with generalized peritonitis

C25.0 Malignant neoplasm of pancreas, head of pancreas

0DTJ0ZZ Resection of appendix, open approach

0FBG3ZX Excision of pancreas, percutaneous approach, diagnostic

Comment: The code for the appendicitis is designated the principal diagnosis because it was clearly the condition that occasioned the admission. The code for the malignant neoplasm is also assigned, but there is no guideline that suggests that a malignancy takes any precedence in a situation of this type. A needle biopsy done in the course of an open surgical procedure is coded as a closed biopsy.

48. A patient with a long history of type 2 diabetes mellitus was admitted in hyperosmolar coma with blood sugars out of control. Modification of the insulin regimen was instituted, and the patient was monitored carefully throughout her stay. The coma cleared on the first hospital day, and the patient was brought into control over the next four days. In addition to this acute metabolic condition, she also had a diagnosis of diabetic chronic kidney disease with stage 2 chronic kidney disease. The patient was discharged on a modified insulin regimen and will be followed by a visiting nurse until the diabetes stabilizes.

E11.01 Type 2 diabetes mellitus with hyperosmolarity with coma

E11.22 Type 2 diabetes mellitus with diabetic chronic kidney disease

N18.2 Chronic kidney disease, stage 2 (mild)

Comment: The code for diabetes mellitus with hyperosmolarity includes the associated coma. Although a diagnosis of diabetic kidney disease was also established during this episode of care, it was the coma that occasioned the admission; therefore, it is designated as the principal diagnosis. Code N18.2 is assigned as an additional code to specify the stage of chronic kidney disease.

49. A patient was admitted with a severe stage 3 pressure ulcer on the left buttock, with extensive necrotic tissue and gangrene. She was taken to the operating room, where the surgeon carefully excised the necrotic tissue (skin). The ulcer site was then treated with antibiotic ointment and gauze bandage, and the patient was returned to the nursing unit, where the wound was monitored carefully and additional antibiotic treatment was administered. By the fourth day, healing was beginning to close the area, but treatment was continued until discharge on the seventh day. The family was advised to use an egg crate mattress and to turn the patient regularly. The patient was scheduled for an outpatient visit in one week.

I96 Gangrene, not elsewhere classified

L89.323 Pressure ulcer of left buttock, stage 3

0HB8XZZ Excision of buttock skin, external approach

Comment: The code for gangrene must be sequenced first because of the instructional note at category L89 to code first any associated gangrene. Excisional debridement is classified to the root operation "Excision" of the appropriate layer, in this case, skin.

50. A patient with a diagnosis of end-stage renal disease due to type 1 diabetes mellitus was admitted for her first hemodialysis session. A right internal jugular vein catheter was placed and a single hemodialysis session carried out. The patient tolerated the procedure well and will continue receiving hemodialysis on a regular schedule.

Z49.01 Encounter for fitting and adjustment of extracorporeal dialysis catheter

E10.22 Type 1 diabetes mellitus with diabetic chronic kidney disease

N18.6 End-stage renal disease

5A1D00Z Performance of urinary filtration, single

05HM33Z Insertion of infusion device into right internal jugular vein, percutaneous approach

Comment: Code Z49.01 is the principal diagnosis because this admission was solely for the purpose of dialysis. Subcategory Z49.0, Preparatory care for renal dialysis, includes encounters for dialysis instruction and training. The fact that the venous catheter was inserted does not affect principal diagnosis assignment when the catheterization is followed by dialysis. Code E10.22 is assigned for the diabetes mellitus with diabetic chronic kidney disease. The end-stage renal disease is the manifestation of the diabetes and the condition for which the dialysis is performed. Procedure codes are assigned for both the catheter "Insertion" and the hemodialysis.

Appendix A

APPENDIX A Coding and Reimbursement

Clinical coding systems assign a distinct numeric value to medical diagnoses, procedures and surgery, signs and symptoms of disease and ill-defined conditions, poisoning and adverse effects of drugs, and complications of surgery and medical care. They serve an important function for physician reimbursement, hospital payments, quality review, benchmarking measurement, and the collection of general medical statistical data. In addition, coding accuracy is critical for ensuring accurate risk adjustment and, correspondingly, reliable comparative quality ratings.

Reimbursement is based on claims and documentation filed by providers using medical diagnosis and procedure codes. Depending on the type of provider and payer, different combinations of coding systems are used in payment models to reimburse providers for the care rendered to patients. The coding systems in use currently in the United States are the following:

- ICD-9-CM diagnosis codes (to be replaced by ICD-10-CM)
- ICD-9-CM procedure codes (to be replaced by ICD-10-PCS)
- Current Procedural Terminology (CPT)
- Health Care Procedure Coding System (HCPCS) level II codes

Essentially all providers and all payers use the ICD (ICD-9-CM to be replaced by ICD-10-CM) system for diagnosis reporting. For reporting procedures, however, the Health Insurance Portability and Accountability Act (HIPAA) designates different standards. ICD-9-CM volume 3 codes (to be replaced by ICD-10-PCS) are the standard for hospitals when reporting surgery and procedures for inpatients. CPT and HCPCS are the standards for hospital reporting of outpatient procedures, and for reporting all physician and other nonhospital provider services.

MEDICARE AND MEDICAID REIMBURSEMENT

Medicare and Medicaid are federal programs managed by the Centers for Medicare & Medicaid Services (CMS). They have different payment models based on the provider.

Physicians and Nonhospital Providers

Medicare and Medicaid reimburse physicians and other providers/suppliers for services rendered to Medicare beneficiaries on a fee-for-service (FFS) basis. CMS develops fee schedules for physicians, ambulance services, and clinical laboratory services and for durable medical equipment, prosthetics, orthotics, and supplies. These fee schedules are driven by the CPT or HCPCS codes. However, diagnosis codes may also be used to determine coverage or medical necessity for medical items and services that are "reasonable and necessary" for a variety of purposes.

Hospitals

Medicare reimburses hospitals on a prospective payment system (PPS) basis, in which payment is made based on a predetermined, fixed amount. The payment amount for a particular service is derived based on the classification system of that service (for example, diagnosis-related groups

for inpatient hospital services). CMS uses separate PPSs for reimbursement to acute inpatient hospitals, hospital outpatient services, inpatient psychiatric facilities, inpatient rehabilitation facilities, long-term care hospitals, home health agencies, hospice, and skilled nursing facilities.

Acute Inpatient Hospitals

Under the inpatient PPS, each inpatient admission to an acute inpatient hospital is categorized into a diagnosis-related group (DRG). Each DRG has a payment weight assigned to it, based on the average resources used to treat Medicare patients in that DRG. The DRGs use principal diagnosis, secondary diagnoses, and procedures to group clinically similar patients using similar resources. Each inpatient admission can be grouped to only one DRG. As of October 1, 2007, CMS revised the DRG groupings by resequencing the groups and refining the list of secondary diagnoses that were considered to affect the severity of a case. This system is called Medicare Severity Diagnosis Related Groups (MS-DRGs). All secondary diagnoses are classified based on the degree of severity: complication/comorbidity (CC), major complication/comorbidity (MCC), or non-CC/MCC. The presence or absence of CCs or MCCs may affect the DRG classification, so it is crucial that the codes are sequenced correctly to ensure accurate reimbursement.

Hospital Outpatient Services

Under the outpatient PPS (OPPS), hospital outpatient services, certain Part B services furnished to hospital inpatients who have no Part A coverage, and partial hospitalization services furnished by community mental health centers are classified into groups called ambulatory payment classifications (APCs). Services in each APC are similar clinically and in terms of the resources they require. A payment rate is established for each APC. Depending on the services provided, hospitals may be paid for more than one APC for an encounter.

In most cases, the unit of payment under the OPPS is the individual service or procedure (using CPT or HCPCS codes). Services are assigned to APCs based on similar clinical characteristics and similar costs. The payment rate and copayment calculated for an APC apply to each service within the APC. Sometimes new services are assigned to New Technology APCs, which are based solely on similarity of resource use until clinical and cost data are available to permit assignment to a clinical APC.

Most services are paid separately, including, but not limited to, the following:

- Most surgical, diagnostic, and nonsurgical therapeutic procedures
- Blood and blood products
- Most clinic and emergency department visits
- Some drugs, biologicals, and radiopharmaceuticals
- Brachytherapy sources
- Corneal tissue acquisition costs

Partial hospitalization for psychiatric services is paid on a per diem basis, with the payment rates dependent on the number of individual services provided to the patient on one day. The payment represents the expected cost of a day of intensive mental health care in a hospital outpatient department (OPD) or community mental health center (CMHC). Beginning January 1, 2011, there are two APCs for partial hospitalization furnished by hospital OPDs and two APCs for partial hospitalization furnished by CMHCs, all based on intensity of day.

Within each APC, payment for ancillary and supportive items and services is packaged into payment for the primary independent service. Separate payments are not made for a packaged service that is considered an integral part of another service paid under the OPPS.

Inpatient Psychiatric Facilities

Inpatient services furnished in psychiatric hospitals—as well as general hospitals' psychiatric units exempt from prospective payment—are paid by Medicare on a per diem PPS. Patients are classified to MS-DRGs, and a comorbidity adjustment is calculated based on certain diagnosis codes. Note that the list of comorbidities is different from the CC/MCC list for acute care hospital MS-DRGs.

Inpatient Rehabilitation Facilities

The inpatient rehabilitation facility (IRF) PPS uses information from a patient assessment instrument (IRF PAI) to classify patients into distinct groups based on clinical characteristics and expected resource needs. A case-mix adjusted payment for varying numbers of days of IRF care is made using case-mix groups (CMGs). Separate payments are calculated for each group, including the application of case- and facility-level adjustments. Payment is calculated on a per discharge basis. The IRF PAI requires diagnosis codes to report the etiologic diagnosis as well as secondary diagnoses. The etiologic diagnosis refers to the original problem leading up to the condition requiring rehabilitation. Secondary diagnoses considered comorbidities are arrayed into three tiers based on whether the costs associated with that comorbidity are high, medium, or low.

Long-Term Care Hospitals

The Medicare PPS for long-term care hospitals (LTCHs) applies to hospitals that have an average inpatient length of stay greater than 25 days. These hospitals are paid on a per discharge system with a DRG-based patient classification system that reflects the differences in patient resources and costs in LTCHs. These DRGs are referred to as MS-LTC-DRGs. Similar to MS-DRGs, they are driven by the principal diagnosis, secondary diagnoses, and procedures.

Critical Access Hospitals

Critical access hospitals (CAHs) are recognized by Medicare as a separate provider type with its own regulations and a separate payment method from other types of hospitals. To qualify as a CAH, a hospital must meet several criteria, the most important of which are the following:

- Location in a rural area more than a 35-mile drive from the nearest hospital or CAH or more than a 15-mile drive in areas with mountainous terrain or only secondary roads
- No more than 25 inpatient beds
- Average annual length of stay of 96 hours or less per patient for acute care

Critical access hospitals are not subject to the inpatient or outpatient PPS. Instead, CAHs may choose to be paid by Medicare under the "Standard Payment Method" or the "Optional Payment Method." Under the standard method, payments for outpatient CAH facility services are made at 101 percent of reasonable costs, and professional services are billed under the Medicare Physician Fee Schedule (PFS). Under the optional method, the Medicare Administrative Contractor is billed for both facility and professional services furnished to outpatients by a physician or practitioner who has reassigned his or her billing rights to the CAH.

Home Health Agencies

Under prospective payment, Medicare pays home health agencies (HHAs) a predetermined base payment. The payment is adjusted for the health condition and care needs of the beneficiary. The adjustment for the health condition, or clinical characteristics, and service needs of the beneficiary is referred to as the case-mix adjustment. A case-mix adjusted payment for up to 60 days of care is made using one of 80 home health resource groups (HHRGs). The HHRGs are determined based on assessments made using the Outcome and Assessment Information Set (OASIS).

Hospice

Medicare pays hospice agencies a daily rate for each day a beneficiary is enrolled in the hospice benefit. The daily payments are made regardless of the amount of services furnished on a given day and are intended to cover costs that the hospice incurs in furnishing services identified in the beneficiary's plan of care. Payments are made based on the following levels of care required to meet beneficiary and family needs:

- Routine home care
- Continuous home care
- Inpatient respite care
- General inpatient care

Skilled Nursing Facilities

Skilled nursing facilities (SNFs) are paid by Medicare on a per diem PPS covering all costs (routine, ancillary, and capital) related to the services. Per diem payments for each admission are case-mix adjusted using a resident classification system (resource utilization groups, or RUGs) based on data from resident assessments (Minimum Data Set, or MDS) and relative weights developed from staff time data.

COMMERCIAL PAYER REIMBURSEMENT

Commercial payers determine their own rules for payment and reimbursement based on fee schedules or negotiated contracts. Some commercial payers have negotiated contracts that are based on diagnosis codes, procedure codes, a combination of both, or other payment models such as DRGs.

Appendix B

APPENDIX B Reporting of the Present on Admission Indicator

The present on admission (POA) indicator is a data element required for Medicare claims reporting. The POA indicator provides information on whether a diagnosis was present at the time of a patient's admission. The Medicare POA requirement applies to all diagnosis codes involving inpatient admissions to general acute care hospitals (except for critical care access hospitals, Maryland waiver hospitals, long-term care hospitals, cancer hospitals, and children's inpatient facilities). Some states (e.g., Maryland) have additional regulatory requirements for POA reporting. State guidelines for public health and quality reporting may differ from the national Medicare reporting requirements. In addition, several commercial health plans require POA reporting by contractual agreement with the hospital.

It is important that the POA indicator be reported correctly because it is significant in quality-of-care reporting and analysis and potentially significant for medicolegal and reimbursement issues. A select number of hospital-acquired conditions are not recognized by the Medicare severity-adjusted diagnosis-related group (MS-DRG) system if the condition is the only complication/comorbidity (CC) or major complication/comorbidity (MCC).

The POA indicator should be reported for principal and secondary diagnosis codes and External cause of injury codes based on a review of the provider's documentation. Distinguishing between pre-existing conditions and complications enhances the use of administrative data for outcomes reporting. Secondary diagnoses may be chronic illnesses that have been in existence for some time, or they may have developed after admission. Unless the POA indicator is reported, it is not easy to determine the difference between pre-existing conditions and complications when analyzing only the ICD-10-CM codes.

DEFINITION

The term "present on admission" means "present at the time the order for inpatient admission occurs." Conditions or adverse events that occur prior to an inpatient admission are considered to be present on admission, including any conditions occurring in the emergency department, observation, clinic, or outpatient surgery prior to inpatient admission.

DOCUMENTATION

The usefulness of POA data for quality-of-care, medicolegal, and reimbursement issues is dependent on the provider's accurate and complete medical record documentation. "Provider" in this context refers to the physician or any qualified health care practitioner who is legally accountable for establishing the patient's diagnosis, similar to the definition used for code assignment. The coder should not include documentation from nurses or other allied health professionals who are not legally accountable for establishing the patient's diagnosis (except for the reporting of pressure ulcer staging and body mass index).

The provider must resolve any inconsistent, missing, conflicting, or unclear documentation before the appropriate POA indicator may be selected. Resolving inconsistencies may necessitate querying the provider for clarification.

There is no required time frame as to when a provider must identify or document a condition to be present on admission. In some clinical situations, it may not be possible for a provider to make a definitive diagnosis (or a condition may not be recognized or reported by the patient) for a period of time after admission. In some cases it may be several days before the provider arrives at a definitive diagnosis. This does not mean that the condition was not present on admission. Determination of whether the condition was present on admission is based on the applicable POA guideline or the provider's best clinical judgment.

GUIDELINES

Guidelines for the selection of POA indicators are included in the *ICD-10-CM Official Guidelines for Coding and Reporting* as appendix I. The POA guidelines are not intended to replace any guidelines in the main body of the official guidelines, nor are they intended to provide guidance on when a condition should be coded. Rather, the POA guidelines are intended to show how to apply the POA indicator to the final set of diagnosis codes already selected.

The guidelines are not intended to be a substitute for a provider's clinical judgment as to whether a condition was or was not present on admission. Issues related to the linking of signs and symptoms, timing of test results, or findings should be referred to the provider for clarification.

REPORTING OPTIONS

There are five options for reporting all diagnoses:

Code	Definition
Y	Yes (present at the time of inpatient admission)
N	No (not present at the time of inpatient admission)
U	Unknown (documentation is insufficient to determine if condition is present on admission)
W	Clinically undetermined (provider is unable to clinically determine whether condition was present on admission or not)
Unreported/not used	Exempt from POA reporting [This option is the only circumstance in which the POA field is left blank. The condition must be on the list of ICD-10-CM codes for which this field is not applicable.]

Conditions Present on Admission

Assign "Y" as the POA reporting option for the following circumstances:

- Condition explicitly documented as being present on admission.
- Condition diagnosed prior to inpatient admission (e.g., hypertension, diabetes mellitus, asthma).
- Condition diagnosed during the admission but clearly present (but not diagnosed) before admission (e.g., a patient with a lump in her breast is admitted and has a biopsy, and the pathology report reveals carcinoma of the breast).
- Condition diagnosed as possible, probable, suspected, or rule out at the time of discharge and, based on signs, symptoms, or clinical findings, condition is suspected during admission (e.g., a patient is admitted with chest pain, transferred to another facility, and discharged as possible myocardial infarction).

- Condition that developed during an outpatient encounter prior to a written order for inpatient admission (e.g., a patient falls while in the emergency department, sustains a fracture, and is subsequently admitted as an inpatient).
- Condition diagnosed as impending or threatened, based on symptoms or clinical findings that were present on admission (e.g., a patient with a known history of coronary atherosclerosis is now admitted for treatment of impending myocardial infarction; the final diagnosis is documented as "impending" myocardial infarction).
- Condition reported with a combination code, and all parts of the combination code are present on admission (e.g., a patient with acute prostatitis is admitted with hematuria).
- Condition reported with the same ICD-10-CM code representing two or more conditions during the same encounter, and all conditions were present on admission (e.g., bilateral unspecified age-related cataracts).
- Single code that only identifies the chronic condition and not the acute exacerbation (e.g., acute exacerbation of chronic leukemia).
- Chronic condition, even if it is not diagnosed until after admission (e.g., lung cancer is diagnosed during hospitalization).
- Condition in which the final diagnosis includes comparative or contrasting diagnoses, and both are present or suspected at the time of admission (e.g., a patient is admitted with severe abdominal pain, nausea, and vomiting, with the admitting diagnosis of acute pyelonephritis versus diverticulum of the colon; the patient is discharged and sent home).
- Infection codes that include the causal organism, if the infection (or signs of the infection) is present on admission, even though the culture results may not be known until after admission (e.g., a patient is admitted with severe cough, fever, and congestion and his culture of sputum reveals staphylococcal infection; the patient is diagnosed with staphylococcal pneumonia).
- Congenital conditions and anomalies (except for categories Q00–Q99, Congenital anomalies, which are on the exempt list). Congenital conditions are always considered to be present on admission.
- Condition present at birth or that develops in utero, including conditions that occur during delivery (e.g., injury during delivery).
- External cause code representing an external cause of morbidity that occurred prior to inpatient admission (e.g., the patient fell out of bed at home).

Conditions Not Present on Admission

Assign "N" as the POA reporting option for the following circumstances:

- Condition the provider explicitly documents as not present at the time of admission (e.g., a patient develops a vascular catheter infection a few days after the insertion of the catheter).
- Condition reported as an inconclusive final diagnosis based on signs, symptoms, or clinical findings that were not present on admission (e.g., a patient develops a fever after surgery, and the final diagnosis includes "possible postoperative infection").
- Condition diagnosed as impending or threatened and based on symptoms or clinical findings that were not present on admission (e.g., a patient is admitted to the hospital for prostate surgery and postoperatively develops chest pain; the final diagnosis includes "impending myocardial infarction").
- Condition reported with a combination code, and any part of the combination code is not present on admission (e.g., obstructive chronic bronchitis with acute exacerbation, and the exacerbation is not present on admission).

- Conditions reported with the same ICD-10-CM code representing two or more conditions during the same encounter, and any one of the conditions was not present on admission (e.g., traumatic secondary and recurrent hemorrhage and seroma are assigned to a single code, T79.2, but only one of the conditions was present on admission).
- External cause code representing an external cause of morbidity that occurs during inpatient hospitalization (e.g., a patient falls out of the hospital bed during his stay, or he experiences an adverse reaction to a medication administered after inpatient admission).

Unclear Documentation

Assign "U" as the POA indicator when the medical record documentation is unclear as to whether the condition was present on admission. Coding professionals are encouraged to query the providers when the documentation is unclear. It is important to note that "U" should not be routinely assigned but should be used only under very limited circumstances, such as when the provider is not available to provide clarification.

Conditions Clinically Undetermined

Assign "W" as the POA indicator when the medical record documentation indicates that it cannot be clinically determined whether the condition was present on admission. For example, a patient is admitted in active labor, and during the stay a breast abscess is noted when she attempts to breast feed. The provider is unable to determine if the abscess was present on admission.

It is important to distinguish between the reporting options "U" and "W." For example, if the provider is queried and is not able to determine whether the condition was present on admission, report using "W." In contrast, if the documentation is not available and the provider is not queried, or the provider is not available to provide a response, report using "U." Coders should make every attempt to limit the number of "U" options reported, as this may potentially be construed as an error or treated as "N" for Medicare payment purposes.

Conditions Exempt from POA Reporting

A list of categories and codes exempt from the POA requirement may be found in the *ICD-10-CM Official Guidelines for Coding and Reporting* as part of appendix I. These codes are exempt because they indicate circumstances regarding the health care encounter or factors influencing the health status but do not represent a current disease or injury or are always present on admission. Examples include injury, poisoning, and certain other consequences of external causes with the seventh character "S," personal and family history codes, and encounter for immunization Z codes.

The codes and categories on the exempt list are the only codes that are exempt from POA reporting. The list of exempt codes is updated every year based on the new codes implemented for the year.

Special Considerations

For obstetrical patients, whether or not delivery occurs during the current hospitalization does not affect assignment of the POA indicator. The determining factor for POA assignment is whether the pregnancy complication or obstetrical condition described by the code is present at the time of admission. If the obstetrical code includes information that is not a diagnosis, do not consider that information in the POA determination. If the obstetrical code includes more than one diagnosis and any one of the diagnoses identified by the code was not present on admission, assign "N" (e.g., category O11, Pre-existing hypertension with pre-eclampsia).

Newborns are not considered to be admitted until after birth; therefore, any condition that is present at birth or that develops in utero is considered to be present at admission.

EXERCISE B.1

Assign the appropriate POA indicator for the following scenarios:

1. A patient is treated in observation, falls out of bed, and breaks a hip. The patient is subsequently admitted as an inpatient to treat the hip fracture. What is the POA indicator for the fracture? Y
2. A patient is admitted to the hospital for coronary artery bypass surgery. Postoperatively, he develops a pulmonary embolism. What is the POA indicator for the pulmonary embolism? N
3. A patient is admitted in active labor. She is known to have a gastric ulcer under medical management. After delivering the baby, she complains of melena and is noted to have bleeding from the gastric ulcer. What is the POA indicator for bleeding from the gastric ulcer? N
4. A single liveborn infant is delivered in the hospital. The physician documents neonatal tachycardia. What is the POA indicator for the neonatal tachycardia? Y
5. A patient is admitted with fever, weakness, severe malaise, and coughing. She is diagnosed with pneumonia. She deteriorates rapidly and is transferred to the ICU with severe sepsis. On physician query, the physician documents that he cannot determine whether the patient had sepsis on admission because she deteriorated so quickly. What is the POA indicator for the severe sepsis? W

EXERCISE B.2

Locate the POA exempt list in the *ICD-10-CM Official Guidelines for Coding and Reporting.* Write an "X" next to each code below that is exempt from POA reporting.

1.	O80	Encounter for full-term uncomplicated delivery	X
2.	O60.10	Preterm labor with preterm delivery, unspecified trimester	
3.	Z99.2	Dependence on renal dialysis	X
4.	V00.311-	Fall from snowboard	X
5.	Y30.-	Falling, jumping or pushed from a high place, undetermined intent	X

Appendix C

APPENDIX C

Case Summary Exercises

Therese M. Jorwic, MPH, RHIA, CCS, CCS-P, FAHIMA, and Janatha R. Ashton, MS, RHIA

CONTENTS

ABOUT THIS APPENDIX

The case summary exercises in this appendix are based on the actual health records of both inpatients and outpatients. The patients described often have multiple conditions that may or may not be related to the current episode of care. Some exercises include several episodes of care for the same patient in various settings.

How to Use This Appendix

The case summary style of the exercises requires you to consider the patient's condition as well as all relevant information provided: medical history, reason for admission or encounter, laboratory results, procedures performed, and diagnoses listed. In all exercises, you need to apply pertinent coding principles and official coding guidelines in making code assignments and designating the principal diagnosis and procedure for each episode of care.

Each exercise includes a brief summary and a diagnosis statement that should be read carefully. You may assume that all diagnoses and procedures that are mentioned and that should be coded have been approved by the patient's physician. Be sure to sequence the principal diagnosis and principal procedure first.

After referring to the appropriate ICD-10-CM and ICD-10-PCS coding manuals, fill in the codes that you think should be assigned (including any appropriate codes for external causes and locations of occurrence as needed) in the space provided next to each case summary. For inpatient care and the outpatient and ambulatory care settings, assign and sequence codes according to the *ICD-10-CM Official Guidelines for Coding and Reporting* and the *ICD-10-PCS Official Coding Guidelines*.

The sequence of this appendix corresponds to chapters 13 through 33 of the handbook and progresses from simpler to more difficult areas. It is recommended that you will have read all of the chapters (1–33) of the handbook before you begin the case summary exercises in this appendix. You may, however, complete the exercises in any order after you have learned the basic coding principles and understand how to apply official coding guidelines.

About the Answers

Answers are provided in the right-hand column of the *with Answers* version of the handbook. (Ask your instructor for the answers if you are using the *without Answers* version.) The right-hand column lists the appropriate codes for each exercise, with the codes for the principal diagnosis and principal procedure sequenced first. Explanatory comments discuss why certain codes are appropriate while others are not, and why some conditions listed in the case summaries are not coded at all. The comments also indicate how principal diagnosis and procedure codes were designated and which symptoms are inherent to certain conditions and so are not coded separately.

For outpatient encounters, ICD-10-PCS codes are typically not reported when a claim is submitted. According to the Health Insurance Portability and Accountability Act (HIPAA) Standards for Electronic Transactions (published in the *Federal Register,* vol. 65, no. 160, p. 50325, August 17, 2000), "The use of ICD-9-CM procedure codes is restricted to the reporting of inpatient procedures by hospitals." ICD-10-PCS was developed to replace ICD-9-CM procedure codes in whatever setting they are currently used. However, a hospital may choose to collect ICD-10-PCS codes for internal or non-claim-related purposes. In addition, hospitals may report procedure codes for outpatient services for specific payers under contractual agreements or as required by their state data reporting regulations.

In day-to-day practice, many hospitals have opted through their internal coding policies not to collect data on noninvasive (without contrast) diagnostic services performed in the inpatient setting, such as X-rays, electrocardiograms (EKGs), computed tomography scans (CTs), and ultrasounds. For this reason, codes for these minor diagnostic services have been omitted from the answers.

The codes and comments in the answers reflect the latest *ICD-10-CM Official Guidelines for Coding and Reporting* (2013 edition) and *ICD-10-PCS Official Coding Guidelines* (2014 edition). Specific guidelines are referenced in parentheses by section and guideline number. At press time, release of the revised 2014 version of the ICD-10-CM guidelines was anticipated for late summer 2013.

1. SYMPTOMS, SIGNS, AND ILL-DEFINED CONDITIONS

1. **Inpatient admission:** The patient, an elderly man, was admitted through the emergency department for severe urinary retention. In the emergency department, it was also determined that his hypertension was accelerated (210/105). He had been hospitalized three months earlier for identical problems, and he said he had not taken any of his medications since the last hospitalization, as he could not afford the cost. The urinary retention was relieved by placement of a Foley catheter. Medications were started, and the hypertension improved rapidly. The patient was evaluated for the extent of benign prostatic hypertrophy. Transurethral resection of the prostate was recommended, but it was refused by the patient.

   Discharge diagnoses: (1) Malignant hypertension, (2) acute urinary retention secondary to benign hypertrophy of the prostate, (3) noncompliance with treatment program.

N40.1	Enlarged prostate with lower urinary tract symptoms
R33.8	Other retention of urine
I10	Essential (primary) hypertension
T46.5x6A	Underdosing of other antihypertensive drugs, initial encounter
Z91.120	Patient's intentional underdosing of medication regimen due to financial hardship
0T9B70Z	Drainage of bladder with drainage device, via natural or artificial opening

Comments: Codes for symptoms, signs, and ill-defined conditions such as urinary retention (R33.8) are not used as a principal diagnosis when a related definitive diagnosis (prostatic hypertrophy) has been established. However, as indicated by the "use additional code" note at code N40.1, an additional code should be assigned in conjunction with the benign prostatic hypertrophy code to identify other lower urinary tract symptoms. Hypertension is not classified as malignant or benign; all cases are assigned to category I10. Underdosing of medication is coded in ICD-10-CM. Locate the main term **Anti-hypertensive drug NEC** in the Table of Drugs and Chemicals and reference the underdosing column. See the Alphabetic Index under the main term **Noncompliance,** subterms "with," "medication regimen NEC," "underdosing," "intentional," "due to financial hardship of patient." Foley catheter placement is classified to the Medical and Surgical Section, root operation "Drainage."

2. **Inpatient admission:** The patient was admitted for recurrent epistaxis that did not respond to nasal packing in the emergency department. He was status post myocardial infarct seven weeks earlier, with no current symptoms. An EKG was performed to evaluate the status of the MI. The patient also suffered from a deviated nasal septum. Multiple attempts were made to stop the bleeding with more packing, but none was successful for more than a few hours. Therefore, the following procedures were performed: (1) anterior and posterior nasal packing, (2) endoscopic ethmoidal artery ligation, (3) endoscopic septoplasty. He was transfused via central vein with two units of packed red cells during the operation.

   Discharge diagnoses: (1) Severe and recurrent epistaxis, (2) post myocardial infarct, (3) deviated nasal septum.

R04.0	Epistaxis
J34.2	Deviated nasal septum
I25.2	Old myocardial infarction
03LR4ZZ	Occlusion of face artery, percutaneous endoscopic approach
2Y41X5Z	Packing of nasal region using packing material
09QM4ZZ	Repair nasal septum, percutaneous endoscopic approach
30243N1	Transfusion of nonautologous red blood cells into central vein, percutaneous approach

Comments: Following the Uniform Hospital Discharge Data Set (UHDDS) definition of principal diagnosis, epistaxis is the condition established after study to be responsible for occasioning the admission of the patient to the hospital for care. Because no related condition was identified, the symptom code can be designated as the principal diagnosis. Deviated nasal septum is not designated as principal because epistaxis is not specified as being due to this condition. The myocardial infarction occurred more than four weeks ago without any symptoms.

The ethmoid artery originates in the ophthalmic artery, with distribution to the ethmoidal cell and the lateral wall of the nasal cavity, and is therefore classified as an artery of the face. Ligation of the ethmoid artery is classified to the root operation "Occlusion." Nasal packing is classified in the Placement Section, root operation "Packing."

3. **Inpatient admission:** The reason for the patient's admission was substernal chest pain with some arm involvement. A combined right and left selective low osmolar contrast coronary angiography and a bilateral low osmolar contrast pulmonary angiography were performed. No coronary artery disease or pulmonary embolus was found.

   Discharge diagnosis: Chest pain without occlusive coronary artery disease.

R07.2	Precordial pain
B2061ZZ	Plain radiography of right and left heart using low osmolar contrast
B2011ZZ	Plain radiography of multiple coronary arteries using low osmolar contrast
B30S1ZZ	Plain radiography of right pulmonary artery using low osmolar contrast
B30T1ZZ	Plain radiography of left pulmonary artery using low osmolar contrast

Comments: Because no underlying etiology for the substernal chest pain was identified, the symptom is designated as the principal diagnosis. Code both the right and left pulmonary artery for the angiography.

4. **Inpatient admission:** The patient, a 19-year-old man, was transferred from another hospital with intractable headache. The accompanying CT scan was normal, but clinical symptomatology was suggestive of subarachnoid hemorrhage. Lumbar puncture, non-contrast bilateral internal carotid cerebral arteriogram, and contrast cerebral MRI were all normal. When the findings were discussed with the patient, he became increasingly belligerent. Although his headaches were only somewhat improved, he refused further treatment and was discharged for follow-up with his own physician.

   Discharge diagnosis: Headache.

R51	Headache
009U3ZX	Drainage of spinal canal, percutaneous approach, diagnostic
B308ZZZ	Plain radiography of bilateral internal carotid arteries
B33RYZZ	Magnetic resonance imaging (MRI) of intracranial arteries using other contrast

Comments: No cause for the headache was determined because subarachnoid hemorrhage was ruled out through testing. Therefore, the symptom is the principal diagnosis.

5. **Inpatient admission:** The patient has a known diagnosis of prostatic cancer. He started having fevers approximately one week earlier. The fevers did not respond to outpatient antibiotics. Blood and urine cultures showed no growth. He was admitted for workup of the fevers with possible prostatic abscess formation. There were no obvious signs of infection or abscess on a transrectal ultrasound of the prostate. An iodine-123 radioisotope bone scan of the body revealed no skeletal metastases. The antibiotic therapy was changed, and he was given an IV push. He improved and was discharged.

   Discharge diagnoses: (1) Fever of unknown origin, (2) cancer of the prostate.

R50.9	Fever, unspecified
C61	Malignant neoplasm of prostate
CW1NFZZ	Planar nuclear medicine imaging of whole body using iodine 123 (I-123)

6. **Inpatient admission:** The two-year-old patient had an acute onset of fever and some shaking chills at home. He was thought to have experienced a febrile seizure and was admitted for workup and treatment. There was some infiltrate in the right lung per chest X-ray. All laboratory work was within normal limits. He was observed during his stay. No problems were noticed, and he remained afebrile after the first day. He was discharged for office follow-up.

   Discharge diagnosis: Rule out febrile seizure.

R56.00 Simple febrile convulsions

Comments: The "rule out" wording in the final diagnosis means that febrile seizure was suspected. Suspected conditions that have not been ruled out at the end of the stay are coded as if confirmed for inpatients. A separate code for fever is not necessary because code R56.00 includes the fever. Although infiltrate was noticed on the right lung X-ray, no further mention was made of it, and apparently it was not considered significant. (Abnormal findings are not coded and reported unless the physician indicates their clinical significance.)

7. **Inpatient admission:** The patient was admitted through the emergency department with possible acute cholecystitis. She had severe abdominal pain and a markedly elevated white count. A gallbladder ultrasound, cholecystogram, and contrast intravenous pyelogram were all normal. The next day her pain was almost gone, and the white blood count dropped to nearly normal. It was not felt worthwhile to continue the workup.

   Discharge diagnoses: (1) Abdominal pain, (2) leukocytosis.

R10.9	Unspecified abdominal pain
D72.829	Elevated white blood cell count, unspecified
BF12YZZ	Fluoroscopy of gallbladder using other contrast
BT14YZZ	Fluoroscopy of kidneys, ureters and bladder using other contrast

Comments: The symptom, abdominal pain, is the principal diagnosis because no underlying etiology was identified. Leukocytosis should be coded as an additional diagnosis.

8. **Inpatient admission:** The patient, an obese male, was admitted with generalized abdominal pain suggestive of early appendicitis, although he had a normal white count and normal differential. An intravenous pyelogram and X-ray of the lower gastrointestinal tract with barium enema were negative. All laboratory studies were normal. He improved while in the hospital without a definite cause for his pain ever being identified. He was placed on a low-fat, 1,500-calorie diet prior to discharge.

   Discharge diagnoses: (1) Abdominal pain of undetermined origin, generalized; (2) obesity.

R10.84	Generalized abdominal pain
E66.9	Obesity, unspecified
BT14YZZ	Fluoroscopy of kidneys, ureters and bladder using other contrast

Comments: No cause for the abdominal pain could be determined; therefore, it is designated as the principal diagnosis. Although obesity was not responsible for admission, it is coded because it was clinically evaluated and treatment was started. Although the patient was placed on a low-fat diet, code E66.01, Morbid (severe) obesity due to excess calories, is not appropriate because the obesity was not documented as such.

9. **Inpatient admission:** This patient with type 2 diabetes was admitted for evaluation of elevated liver function tests. An abdominal ultrasound showed cholelithiasis. The hepatitis profile was negative. Her sugars stayed within the low normal range throughout hospitalization. At discharge, the physician was unable to determine whether the abnormal liver functions were due to diabetes mellitus or cholelithiasis.

   Discharge diagnosis: Abnormal liver function secondary to either diabetes mellitus or cholelithiasis.

R94.5	Abnormal results of liver function studies
E11.9	Type 2 diabetes mellitus without complications
K80.20	Calculus of gallbladder without cholecystitis without obstruction

Comments: The diagnostic statement represents a symptom followed by contrasting/comparative diagnoses. The symptom is coded and sequenced first, followed by codes for the contrasting/comparative diagnoses.

10. **Inpatient admission:** The patient, a woman with type 1 diabetes, was admitted because of increased swelling of the right foot that was determined to be an abscess. *Staphylococcus aureus* grew from the abscess. She underwent a percutaneous incision and drainage of the foot abscess. Her course in the hospital otherwise was essentially unremarkable. The foot gradually improved with antibiotic therapy, hyperbaric oxygen therapy, and daily whirlpool therapy.

    Discharge diagnoses: (1) Abscess right foot, (2) type 1 diabetes mellitus.

L02.611	Cutaneous abscess of right foot
B95.61	Methicillin susceptible Staphylococcus aureus infection as the cause of diseases classified elsewhere
E10.9	Type 1 diabetes mellitus without complications
0Y9M3ZZ	Drainage of right foot, percutaneous approach
F08G5BZ	Wound management treatment of integumentary system—lower back/lower extremity using physical agents
5A05121	Extracorporeal hyperbaric oxygenation, intermittent

Comments: The symptom, swelling of the foot, is not coded because the swelling was determined to be an abscess. Code L02.611 is assigned as the principal diagnosis. The abscess is not stated as due to the diabetes; therefore, code E10.9 is the appropriate code choice. Incision with drainage is the principal procedure because it was performed as treatment for the abscess. Whirlpool treatment to the wound is classified to the Physical Rehabilitation and Diagnostic Audiology Section, root operation "Activities of daily living," with the qualifier "wound management." Code 5A05121 is assigned for the oxygenation of the surgical wound.

11. **Inpatient admission:** The child was admitted with a fever and lethargy. The admitting diagnosis was "rule out sepsis." When admitted, he was responsive but lethargic. The physical examination was within normal limits except for the left eardrum, which was reddened. He was placed on intravenous antibiotics after the full septic workup was complete. Improvement was evident by the next day, when he was alert, active, and started on feedings. He became afebrile and was discharged on oral antibiotics for otitis media, with sepsis ruled out.

    Discharge diagnoses: (1) Fever, (2) otitis media.

H66.92	Otitis media, unspecified, left ear

Comments: Fever is a symptom and should not be sequenced as the principal diagnosis because the related definitive diagnosis of otitis media has been established as the underlying etiology. Fever is an inherent part of otitis media and does not require a separate code assignment. ICD-10-CM has codes to indicate the ear affected.

12. **Inpatient admission:** The patient, a 10-month-old male, presented with acute stridor and respiratory distress. His mother felt that he had possibly choked on a peach. Nothing was seen on chest X-ray. A rigid bronchoscopy ruled out foreign body, but the findings were consistent with croup. He was discharged on medication to follow up with his pediatrician in one week.

    Discharge diagnosis: Croup.

J05.0	Acute obstructive laryngitis [croup]
0BJ08ZZ	Inspection of tracheobronchial tree, via natural or artificial opening endoscopic

Comments: The symptoms, stridor and respiratory distress, are integral to the diagnosis of croup and are not coded separately.

13. **Emergency department visit:** A 26-year-old male, involved in a car crash, was taken to the local emergency department (ED) in a coma, where he was diagnosed with a traumatic brain injury with loss of consciousness of one hour. Glasgow coma scale (GCS) was 6 on arrival in the ED. Patient was transferred to a trauma center for further care.

    Discharge diagnosis: Traumatic brain injury.

S06.9x3A	Unspecified intracranial injury with loss of consciousness of 1 hour to 5 hours 59 minutes, initial encounter
R40.243	Glasgow coma scale score 3-8
V49.9xxA	Car occupant (driver) (passenger) injured in unspecified traffic accident, initial encounter

Comments: Coma scale codes should be sequenced after the diagnosis code(s). Assign a code from R40.24-, Glasgow coma scale, total score, when only the total score is documented in the medical record.

2. INFECTIOUS AND PARASITIC DISEASES

1. **Inpatient admission:** This HIV-positive patient was admitted with skin lesions on the chest and back. Biopsies were taken, and the pathologic diagnosis was Kaposi's sarcoma. Leukoplakia of the lips and splenomegaly were also noted on physical examination.

   Discharge diagnoses: (1) HIV infection; (2) Kaposi's sarcoma, back and chest; (3) leukoplakia; (4) splenomegaly.

B20	Human immunodeficiency virus [HIV] disease
C46.0	Kaposi's sarcoma of skin
K13.21	Leukoplakia of oral mucosa, including tongue
R16.1	Splenomegaly, not elsewhere classified
0HB5XZX	Excision of chest skin, external approach, diagnostic
0HB6XZX	Excision of back skin, external approach, diagnostic

2. **Inpatient admission:** The patient underwent an outpatient laparoscopic-assisted cholecystectomy for cholecystitis and was admitted the next day because of a flare-up of chronic hepatitis C. The chronic hepatitis C was secondary to intravenous drug use. With medication, the chronic hepatitis C was controlled, and the woman was discharged.

   Discharge diagnoses: (1) Chronic hepatitis C, (2) IV drug dependence.

B18.2	Chronic viral hepatitis C
F19.20	Other psychoactive substance dependence, uncomplicated

Comments: Although an outpatient procedure was performed for cholecystitis, the reason for admission, per the UHDDS definition of principal diagnosis, is chronic hepatitis C.

3. **Inpatient admission:** An elderly male patient with a history of benign hypertension became extremely febrile the day before admission. On admission he was extremely lethargic with a possible septic urinary tract infection. He was pan cultured and started on IV antibiotics and fluids. Pseudomonas showed in the urine culture. The next day, his mind was quite clear and the fever defervesced from an initial 104.6 to 99.0 degrees. However, he had gross hematuria. As the IV fluids were decreased, he resumed his usual hypertensive state. By the third hospital day, the urine had cleared and he was discharged on oral antibiotics, with septicemia ruled out.

   Discharge diagnoses: (1) Urinary tract infection due to *Pseudomonas,* (2) gross hematuria, (3) benign essential hypertension.

N39.0	Urinary tract infection, site not specified
B96.5	Pseudomonas (aeruginosa) (mallei) (pseudomallei) as the cause of diseases classified elsewhere
R31.0	Gross hematuria
I10	Essential (primary) hypertension

Comments: The instruction with code N39.0, "Use additional code to identify organism . . ." must always be followed when the organism is known. Because hematuria is not integral to a urinary tract infection, it is coded. All hypertension is coded to I10.

4. **Inpatient admission:** The patient, with arteriosclerotic coronary heart disease and type 2 diabetes mellitus, came to the hospital with symptoms that were felt to represent sepsis. She was placed on antibiotics, and the symptoms improved. ST- and T-wave changes were evident on an EKG. The patient's glucose showed marked elevation, thought to be secondary to the sepsis. The blood sugars were brought under control with an adjustment of her insulin therapy and an appropriate diet.

   Discharge diagnoses: (1) Arteriosclerotic coronary heart disease, (2) uncontrolled type 2 diabetes mellitus, (3) questionable sepsis.

A41.9	Sepsis, unspecified organism
I25.10	Atherosclerotic heart disease of native coronary artery without angina pectoris
E11.65	Type 2 diabetes mellitus with hyperglycemia
Z79.4	Long term (current) use of insulin

Comments: The admission was necessitated by signs and symptoms of sepsis, which was never ruled out and, therefore, is the principal diagnosis. ICD-10-CM coding guidelines state that for a diagnosis of sepsis, the appropriate code for the underlying systemic infection is assigned. Code A41.9 is assigned if the type of infection or causal organism is not further identified.

For the diabetes code, see the main term **Diabetes** in the Alphabetic Index and the subterm **Inadequately controlled,** with the cross-reference that states "code to Diabetes, by type, with hyperglycemia. See the Index, diabetes, with hyperglycemia, E11.65."

No code is assigned for the ST- and T-wave changes on the EKG because they represent abnormal findings that were not treated or further evaluated.

Code Z79.4 is assigned because the patient is on insulin therapy.

5. **Outpatient clinic visit:** The HIV-infected patient was suffering from an acute lymphadenitis due to his HIV infection. The glands in the neck area were most affected. Antibiotics were prescribed, but the patient refused antiretroviral treatment at this time. He was of the opinion that his religion would eventually make antiretroviral medication unnecessary. Another consideration was his narcotic dependency. He was encouraged to continue participation in both the narcotic addiction and HIV support groups.

   Diagnoses: (1) Acute lymphadenitis secondary to HIV infection, (2) narcotic dependence, (3) refusal of medication due to religious reasons.

B20	Human immunodeficiency virus [HIV] disease
F11.20	Opioid dependence, uncomplicated
Z53.1	Procedure and treatment not carried out because of patient's decision for reasons of belief and group pressure

Comments: Code B20 is assigned for all HIV infections and is designated as the reason for encounter when the patient was seen for HIV infection or a related condition. Code L04.0, Acute lymphadenitis of face, head and neck, should not be assigned along with code B20 because of the exclude1 note at category L04 excluding HIV disease resulting in generalized lymphadenopathy (B20). For the narcotic dependence code, see the main term in the Index **Dependence,** narcotic (drug) NEC, which refers the user to "see Dependence, drug, opioid." Following this instructional note, the user arrives at code F11.20. Code Z53.1 may be assigned to show the refusal of medications for religious reasons.

6. **Inpatient admission:** The patient is an 85-year-old female who presents to the emergency department (ED) with increasing shortness of breath, hypoxia, productive cough, and progressive weakness. She acutely deteriorated in the ED and was emergently sent to the intensive care unit (ICU). In the ICU, the patient was intubated, mechanically ventilated for four days, and started on broad-spectrum antibiotics.

   Diagnoses: (1) Septic shock, (2) acute respiratory failure, (3) Hemophilus influenza pneumonia.

A41.3	Sepsis due to Hemophilus influenzae
J14	Pneumonia due to Hemophilus influenzae
R65.21	Severe sepsis with septic shock
J96.01	Acute respiratory failure with hypoxia
5A1955Z	Respiratory ventilation, greater than 96 consecutive hours

Comments: For cases of severe sepsis, the underlying infection is sequenced first, followed by a code from subcategory R65.2, Severe sepsis. When the reason for admission is both sepsis, or severe sepsis, and a localized infection (e.g., pneumonia), the code for the localized infection should be assigned as a secondary diagnosis.

3. ENDOCRINE, NUTRITIONAL, AND METABOLIC DISEASES AND IMMUNE-SYSTEM DISORDERS

1. **Inpatient admission:** The patient was admitted for an evaluation of her adrenal malfunction. She had a four-year history of hypertension and hypokalemia with evidence of primary aldosteronism. A non-contrast CT scan of the abdomen also suggested a left adrenal mass. She was discharged and was to return for a left adrenalectomy the following week.

   Discharge diagnoses: (1) Probable adrenal mass, left; (2) hypertension and hypokalemia probably due to primary aldosteronism.

E27.8 Other specified disorders of adrenal gland

E26.9 Hyperaldosteronism, unspecified

E87.6 Hypokalemia

I10 Essential (primary) hypertension

Comments: Either of the interrelated diagnoses, adrenal mass or aldosteronism, can be designated as the principal diagnosis because the patient was admitted for evaluation of adrenal malfunction. In the Alphabetic Index, reference the main term **Mass,** specified organ NEC, which directs to disease of specified organ or site. Under disease, adrenal, specified, NEC code E27.8 is located.

2. **Inpatient admission:** The patient was admitted for severe malnutrition and hematuria secondary to amyotrophic lateral sclerosis. Because of her malnutrition, a nasogastric feeding tube was placed under fluoroscopy and nutritional substance administered later. During her stay, the hematuria cleared spontaneously, and she was discharged to home care.

   Discharge diagnoses: (1) Malnutrition, (2) hematuria secondary to amyotrophic lateral sclerosis.

E43 Unspecified severe protein-calorie malnutrition

G12.21 Amyotrophic lateral sclerosis

R31.9 Hematuria, unspecified

0DH67UZ Insertion of feeding device into stomach, via natural or artificial opening

3E0G76Z Introduction of nutritional substance into upper GI, via natural or artificial opening

Comments: Admission was necessitated by malnutrition, not the underlying amyotrophic lateral sclerosis. Therefore, severe malnutrition, the condition requiring placement of a feeding tube, is the principal diagnosis.

3. **Inpatient admission:** The patient fell at his single-family home and was unable to get up. Neighbors found him several hours later, and he does not remember any circumstances surrounding the event. Blood sugars were monitored, and a diagnosis of diabetes mellitus was given. It became rapidly evident to the attending physician that, even with dietary restriction, the patient would need insulin therapy to lower his blood sugar level. Insulin therapy was started. The only other positive finding was beta-*Streptococcus* group B, which grew from the urine culture and was treated with oral antibiotics.

   Discharge diagnoses: (1) New onset type 2 diabetes mellitus, out of control; (2) urinary tract infection with beta-*Streptococcus*.

E11.65 Type 2 diabetes mellitus with hyperglycemia

N39.0 Urinary tract infection, site not specified

B95.1 Streptococcus, group B, as the cause of diseases classified elsewhere

W19.xxxA Unspecified fall, initial encounter

Y92.099 Unspecified place in other non-institutional residence as the place of occurrence of the external cause

Comments: The condition, after study, that necessitated admission was newly diagnosed diabetes out of control. Type 2 diabetic patients often require insulin to bring blood sugar down to an acceptable level, but this does not mean that the diabetes has become insulin dependent. For the diabetes code, see the subterm in the Index **Inadequately controlled,** with the cross-reference that states "code to Diabetes, by type, with hyperglycemia. See the Index, diabetes, with hyperglycemia, E11.65."

The code for Long-term (current) use of insulin is not appropriate because the insulin therapy was just started and there is no information about long-term use. ICD-10-CM does not classify out-of-control diabetes mellitus. An activity code is not reported, as the activity is not stated.

4. **Outpatient clinic visit:** The patient with type 2 diabetes was status post cadaveric kidney and pancreatic transplants. He was being seen for follow-up of a recent below-the-knee amputation (BKA) of the foot and a nonhealing, gangrenous ulcer on his left foot secondary to diabetic peripheral vascular disease. The operative site was healing very nicely, and there was no evidence of infection.

   Diagnoses: (1) Status post left foot amputation, (2) status post kidney and pancreas transplants, (3) diabetes mellitus.

Z09	Encounter for follow-up examination after completed treatment for conditions other than malignant neoplasm
E11.51	Type 2 diabetes mellitus with diabetic peripheral angiopathy without gangrene
Z94.0	Kidney transplant status
Z94.83	Pancreas transplant status
Z89.432	Acquired absence of left foot

Comments: The reason for the encounter was for follow-up examination following surgery. Code Z89.432 indicates the status post amputation of the left foot—the reason follow-up was necessary. Diabetes and complication of peripheral vascular disease are included in one code. The gangrene is not coded as current, as the foot has been amputated and the gangrene is no longer present. Other codes represent conditions that required consideration in evaluating the patient's current status.

5. **Inpatient admission:** The patient, an elderly woman with type 2 diabetes mellitus, developed hypoglycemia at the nursing home and was symptomatic. In the emergency department, her decreased blood sugar was treated with intravenous D5W. A urinary tract infection was also present and was treated with antibiotics. The urine culture grew *Klebsiella,* sensitive to Cipro. She then developed mild congestive heart failure, probably secondary to the hypoglycemic reaction, which responded to oxygen and rest. Her Diabeta was restarted at a lower dosage.

   Discharge diagnoses: (1) Congestive heart failure secondary to hypoglycemia, (2) type 2 diabetes mellitus, (3) urinary tract infection.

E11.649	Type 2 diabetes mellitus with hypoglycemia without coma
I50.9	Heart failure, unspecified
N39.0	Urinary tract infection, site not specified
B96.1	Klebsiella pneumoniae [K. pneumoniae] as the cause of diseases classified elsewhere

Comments: ICD-10-CM has a specific code for type 2 diabetes with hypoglycemia

6. **Inpatient admission:** The patient, a woman with a diagnosis of cell-mediated immune deficiency with thrombocytopenia and eczema, was admitted for incision and drainage of a foot abscess. Her course in the hospital was essentially unremarkable. The foot gradually improved with intermittent hyperbaric oxygen therapy and daily whirlpool therapy. *Staphylococcus aureus* grew from the abscess.

   Discharge diagnoses: (1) Abscess right foot, (2) cell-immune deficiency with thrombocytopenia and eczema.

L02.611	Cutaneous abscess of right foot
D82.0	Wiskott-Aldrich syndrome
B95.61	Methicillin susceptible Staphylococcus aureus infection as the cause of diseases classified elsewhere
0Y9M3ZZ	Drainage of right foot, percutaneous approach
F08G5BZ	Wound management treatment of integumentary system—lower back/lower extremity using physical agents
5A05121	Extracorporeal hyperbaric oxygenation, intermittent

7. **Inpatient admission:** The patient, a young male with type 1 diabetes, was brought in a comatose state to the emergency department by friends. He was admitted in ketoacidosis and was resuscitated with saline hydration via insulin drip. After regaining consciousness, he reported that the morning of admission he was experiencing nausea and vomiting and decided not to take his insulin because he had not eaten. He was treated with intravenous hydration and insulin drip. By the following morning, his laboratory work was within normal range and he was experiencing no symptoms.

   Discharge diagnoses: (1) Diabetic ketoacidosis, (2) juvenile-type diabetes.

E10.641	Type 1 diabetes mellitus with hypoglycemia with coma
T38.3x6A	Underdosing of insulin and oral hypoglycemic [antidiabetic] drugs, initial encounter
Z91.128	Patient's intentional underdosing of medication regimen for other reason

Comments: See the main term **Diabetes,** subterms "type 1," "with," "ketoacidosis," "with coma." In ICD-10-CM there are codes for underdosing. See the Table of Drugs and Chemicals under "insulin" and consult the column for underdosing. Add the seventh-character "A," as this is the initial encounter. Also code for intentional underdosing for other reason by consulting the main term **Noncompliance,** subterms "medication regimen," "intentional NEC."

8. **Inpatient admission:** The patient with type 1 diabetes mellitus seriously out of control was admitted for regulation of insulin dosage. He had a recently abscessed right molar, which was determined, in part, to be responsible for the elevation of his blood sugar. The patient had been in the hospital three weeks earlier for an acute myocardial infarction of the inferoposterior wall, and an EKG was performed to check its current status.

   Discharge diagnoses: (1) Myocardial infarction, (2) abscessed tooth, (3) uncontrolled type 1 diabetes mellitus.

E10.65	Type 1 diabetes mellitus with hyperglycemia
K04.7	Periapical abscess without sinus
I21.11	ST elevation (STEMI) myocardial infarction involving right coronary artery

Comments: Type 1 diabetes is classified to category E10. See the main term **Diabetes,** subterm "inadequately controlled" with the cross-reference that states "code to Diabetes, by, type, with hyperglycemia. See the Index, diabetes, Type 1 with hyperglycemia." The abscessed tooth is significant as a possible etiology of the out-of-control diabetes and was also under treatment during this admission. Code I21.11 is assigned for the myocardial infarction, which occurred less than four weeks ago and was evaluated during this admission.

9. **Outpatient clinic visit:** A 57-year-old Hispanic male presented to the Medical Eye Service clinic for a retinal evaluation of diabetic retinopathy. He reported vision that fluctuated only in the morning and poorer vision in the right eye. He was diagnosed with type 2 diabetes mellitus 15 years ago and is currently taking Glucophage. He was diagnosed with diabetic retinopathy and was advised to schedule grid laser treatment at his earliest convenience.

   Diagnosis: Severe nonproliferative diabetic retinopathy, OD greater than OS.

E11.349	Type 2 diabetes mellitus with severe nonproliferative diabetic retinopathy without macular edema

Comments: Code E11.349 is a combination code that includes all components of the patient's diagnosis. No additional code is required.

4. MENTAL DISORDERS

1. **Outpatient clinic visit:** The patient was seen to evaluate his progress in dealing with his long-standing alcoholism. In addition, he had a passive-aggressive personality and was dependent on Librium. He was actively participating in Alcoholics Anonymous and stated he would continue to participate. He apparently now had some alcoholic liver damage and was referred to an internist for further investigation of that condition.

   Diagnoses: (1) Alcohol dependence; (2) passive-aggressive personality disorder; (3) drug dependence, Librium; (4) alcoholic liver damage.

F10.20 Alcohol dependence, uncomplicated

F13.20 Sedative, hypnotic or anxiolytic dependence, uncomplicated

F60.89 Other specific personality disorders

K70.9 Alcoholic liver disease, unspecified

Comments: ICD-10-CM classifies dependence by uncomplicated, in remission, with intoxication, etc.

2. **Outpatient clinic visit:** The patient, a young female, was brought in by her sister. She has had periods of severe depression for many years. Her medications consisted of Lithium, Synthroid, and Midrin for depression, hypothyroidism, and migraine headaches, respectively. During the past week, however, she became manic, running all her credit cards to the limit, getting inappropriately involved in a woman's suicide attempt, quitting her job, and trying to take over the pulpit at church. On the day of the clinic visit, she threatened to strike the telephone repairman with a lead pipe. She was to be admitted for Lithium adjustment.

   Diagnoses: (1) Bipolar disorder, manic type; (2) hypothyroidism; (3) migraine headaches.

F31.10 Bipolar disorder, current episode manic without psychotic features, unspecified

E03.9 Hypothyroidism, unspecified

G43.909 Migraine, unspecified, not intractable, without status migrainosus

Comments: No code assignment is necessary for depression because depression is a component of bipolar disorder. Although not psychiatric conditions, both hypothyroidism and migraine headaches are coexisting conditions under treatment and should be coded.

3. **Inpatient admission:** The woman was brought in by police for observation of a suspected mental condition. They found her roaming the streets, and she seemed disoriented and confused. She was treated for scabies, body lice, and cellulitis of the right foot. Her mental status cleared rapidly. The only psychiatric disorder found was moderate intellectual disability.

   Discharge diagnoses: (1) Moderate intellectual disability; (2) scabies; (3) body lice; (4) cellulitis, right foot.

F71	Moderate intellectual disabilities
Z91.83	Wandering in diseases classified elsewhere
B86	Scabies
B85.1	Pediculosis due to Pediculus humanus corporis
L03.115	Cellulitis of right lower limb

Comments: Although the scenario indicates that the patient was admitted for observation, a condition (moderate intellectual disabilities) is identified as the etiology for the patient's disorientation and confusion. No code is assigned for observation in the presence of a confirmed condition.

All the nonpsychiatric conditions meet the UHDDS definition of additional diagnoses. They were diagnosed and treated; therefore, codes are assigned.

Code Z91.83 may be used when wandering related to a disease or condition is documented by the provider, and such documentation reflects that the wandering is clinically relevant. Note that the underlying disorder (i.e., intellectual disabilities) should be coded first according to the Tabular List instructions.

ICD-10-CM classifies cellulitis as either the toe or the lower limb, along with laterality. Because the foot is documented as the condition site, the lower limb code is used based on cross-reference under the main term **Cellulitis,** subterm "foot—see Cellulitis, lower limb." The code for the right side is selected.

4. **Outpatient clinic visit:** This 59-year-old male patient with a history of paranoid schizophrenia has had constant conflict with his family and coworkers for years. His wife reported that he was in danger of losing his job because he threatened his supervisor's life. He recently spent the night in jail after an altercation with a neighbor. Medication was prescribed, and he was to return for follow-up in one week.

   Diagnosis: Schizophrenia, paranoid type, chronic with acute exacerbation.

F20.0 Paranoid schizophrenia

Comments: ICD-10-CM does not include codes for acute/chronic remission/exacerbation for schizophrenia.

5. **Outpatient clinic visit:** An 18-year-old teenage patient was described by his mother as recently having periods of depression, throwing temper tantrums, and stealing from neighbors. He has a history of type 1 diabetes and sometimes refuses to take his insulin or follow his diet. His speech, best described as "baby talk," had also become worse during the previous two months. A prescription was to be written for his depression.

   Diagnoses: (1) Depression, (2) borderline personality disorder, (3) delayed speech development, (4) type 1 diabetes mellitus.

F32.9 Major depressive disorder, single episode, unspecified

F60.3 Borderline personality disorder

F80.9 Developmental disorder of speech or language, unspecified

E10.9 Type 1 diabetes mellitus without complications

Z79.4 Long term (current) use of insulin

Comments: Because medication was prescribed for the patient's depression, depression is sequenced first. The insulin use code is not required for type 1 diabetics because these patients require insulin. However, this code may be assigned, if desired, to provide additional information. ICD-10-CM provides a code for underdosing of medication. Although the patient is described as sometimes refusing to take his insulin, the documentation does not indicate that underdosing of insulin was a factor at the present time. Therefore, code T38.3x6A is not assigned.

6. **Inpatient admission:** The patient was brought to the emergency department by the police and admitted to psychiatric service. Police requested an evaluation after the man was disorderly and aggressive at the scene of an automobile accident in which he was involved. He is admitted with a diagnosis of probable dementia.

   Discharge diagnoses: (1) Organic brain syndrome with presenile dementia, (2) probably Alzheimer's disease with dementia.

G30.9 Alzheimer's disease, unspecified

F02.81 Dementia in other diseases classified elsewhere, with behavioral disturbance

Comments: Alzheimer's disease is coded to G30.9 with a "use additional code" note for dementia. The dementia is coded to F02.81, Dementia in other diseases classified elsewhere with behavioral disturbances, due to the disorderly and aggressive behavior.

7. **Inpatient admission:** The patient, with a four-year history of anorexia nervosa, was seen in the physician's office because of significant weight loss over the past three months, going from 82 pounds down to 53 pounds. She was admitted to increase body weight and to be given nutritional counseling because of her severe malnutrition.

   Discharge diagnosis: Anorexia nervosa, severe malnutrition with marasmus.

F50.00 Anorexia nervosa, unspecified

E41 Nutritional marasmus

Comments: Code E41, Nutritional marasmus, should be assigned as an additional diagnosis for the severe malnutrition. For some anorexic patients, the weight loss is so severe that it leads to malnutrition. Code E41 further describes the severity of the patient's condition.

8. **Inpatient admission:** The patient was admitted with possible pyelonephritis. Her complaints were bilateral flank pain and chills. A contrast intravenous pyelogram was normal. Within two days of admission, the character of her pain changed somewhat in that it became primarily in the right upper quadrant. The physician documented in the progress notes that significant features of conversion hysteria were present and accounted for the patient's symptoms. On the third hospital day, the patient's IV was discontinued, liver function tests were rechecked, and antibiotics were discontinued. Later that day, she left abruptly, saying she would not return.

   Discharge diagnoses: (1) Right upper quadrant abdominal pain, (2) conversion disorder.

F44.9	Dissociative and conversion disorder, unspecified
R10.11	Right upper quadrant pain
BT14YZZ	Fluoroscopy of kidneys, ureters and bladder using other contrast

Comments: Codes for symptoms, signs, and ill-defined conditions from chapter 18 of ICD-10-CM are acceptable when a related definitive diagnosis has not been established by the provider. Although the patient was admitted with possible pyelonephritis, this condition was not confirmed and it was determined that conversion hysteria (definitive diagnosis) was the reason for the patient's symptoms and therefore the principal diagnosis.

9. **Psychiatry clinic visit:** The HIV-infected patient, who had a long history of cocaine addiction, started using cocaine again. Several months ago he was admitted for treatment of *Pneumocystis carinii* pneumonia. Presently, severe depression brought him to the clinic. He and the physician had an extensive discussion about returning to Narcotics Anonymous and also joining an AIDS support group. A prescription for Prozac was given for his depression.

   Diagnoses: (1) Depression, (2) cocaine addiction, (3) HIV infection.

F32.9	Major depressive disorder, single episode, unspecified
B20	Human immunodeficiency virus [HIV] disease
F14.20	Cocaine dependence, uncomplicated

Comments: Depression was responsible for the clinic visit and is sequenced as the reason for the encounter. The HIV infection contributed to the patient's depression, but it was the depression that was the reason for the encounter.

10. **Outpatient clinic visit:** Patient is a 34-year-old male who came back from a tour of duty in Iraq. Since his return, his family has noticed he is often anxious, has a short temper, and has been drinking excessively. His family persuaded him to seek professional counseling, during which he was diagnosed with post-traumatic stress disorder, given a prescription for Paxil, and scheduled for once-a-week therapy sessions at the mental health clinic.

    Diagnoses: (1) Acute post-traumatic stress disorder, (2) anxiety disorder due to alcohol abuse.

F43.11	Post-traumatic stress disorder, acute
F10.180	Alcohol abuse with alcohol-induced anxiety disorder

Comments: A separate code for anxiety is not necessary because code F10.180 includes alcohol abuse and the anxiety disorder.

5. DISEASES OF THE BLOOD AND BLOOD-FORMING ORGANS AND CERTAIN DISORDERS INVOLVING THE IMMUNE MECHANISM

1. **Inpatient admission:** The patient had a congenital aplastic anemia that had been responding well to treatment. She was admitted for observation following a full-mouth extraction for multiple dental caries with pulp exposure and pyorrhea in outpatient surgery. She had only minimal bleeding following surgery. However, it was believed to be necessary to admit her for monitoring. She was discharged the next day with her blood counts remaining at acceptable levels.

   Discharge diagnosis: Aplastic anemia.

   D61.09 Other constitutional aplastic anemia

   Comments: Dental caries and pyorrhea are the reasons for the outpatient encounter; however, aplastic anemia represents the reason for inpatient admission, per the UHDDS definition of principal diagnosis. See the main term **Anemia,** subterms "aplastic," "congenital."

2. **Inpatient admission:** The patient, who had sickle-cell anemia, presented to the emergency department with a two- to three-day history of severe right leg and arm pain. After she was admitted, parenteral narcotics were administered and the pain improved. The blood counts returned to a stable level within 24 hours.

   Discharge diagnosis: Sickle-cell pain crisis.

   D57.00 Hb-SS disease with crisis, unspecified

   Comments: Pain is a symptom integral to sickle-cell crisis. Therefore, a separate code assignment for the pain is not necessary.

3. **Inpatient admission:** The patient was an elderly woman visiting her physician with complaints of heart palpitations. A routine office evaluation revealed significant anemia. She had not been eating well because she had recently moved from her home of 30 years. After admission to the hospital, a cardiology consultation suggested that the palpitations were probably due to the anemia. During the gastrointestinal workup, mild gastritis was revealed. After a transfusion of two units of packed red blood cells into the central vein, her hemoglobin returned to normal range. The patient was discharged to the nursing home with a prescription for Zantac to control her gastritis.

   Discharge diagnoses: (1) Nutritional anemia, (2) gastritis.

   D53.9 Nutritional anemia, unspecified
   K29.70 Gastritis, unspecified, without bleeding
   R00.2 Palpitations
   30240N1 Transfusion of nonautologous red blood cells into central vein, open approach

   Comments: Although palpitations were the reason for admission, the underlying cause was determined to be anemia, so the anemia is sequenced as the principal diagnosis. In addition, a code is assigned to identify palpitations that are not inherent in anemia and were worked up by cardiology as a significant condition.

4. **Inpatient admission:** The patient had locally advanced bladder cancer. He had excellent response to chemotherapy treatments administered prior to admission, with only a small amount of residual disease noted in the bladder. He was admitted with increasing nausea, anorexia, fevers, and constipation. His calcium levels were found to be elevated. A slight decrease was achieved with IV hydration, and it continued to fall with IV pamidronate. Because he was asymptomatic, further workup was not indicated, and he was discharged.

   Discharge diagnoses: (1) Hypercalcemia, (2) bladder cancer.

   E83.52 Hypercalcemia

   C67.9 Malignant neoplasm of bladder, unspecified

   Comments: Although the primary site of the neoplasm had been treated in the past, residual disease was still present and under treatment; therefore, the bladder cancer code should be assigned. Nausea, anorexia, fevers, and constipation are inherent to hypercalcemia and are not coded.

5. **Inpatient admission:** The patient was diagnosed with Coombs' negative hemolytic anemia four years earlier. Since diagnosis, her disease course waxed and waned. During some bouts, she had 15 to 20 blood transfusions of two to three units of packed red blood cells each. This admission was for splenectomy. The plan also called for removing a kidney stone on the left side, which was identified on her preadmission workup. Both surgeries, total splenectomy and laparoscopic pyelolithotomy, were performed without incident. Her postoperative recovery also went smoothly.

   Discharge diagnoses: (1) Hypersplenism secondary to acquired hemolytic anemia; (2) stone, left kidney.

   D73.1 Hypersplenism

   D59.9 Acquired hemolytic anemia, unspecified

   N20.0 Calculus of kidney

   07TP0ZZ Resection of spleen, open approach

   0TC44ZZ Extirpation of matter from left kidney pelvis, percutaneous endoscopic approach

   Comments: The spleen was removed because of hypersplenism, which is a further manifestation of hemolytic anemia. Hypersplenism is the principal diagnosis because it was the reason for admission and the condition to which the thrust of treatment was directed. No specific treatment was addressed to the anemia, but it is related to the hypersplenism and therefore is coded. Splenectomy and pyelolithotomy are both therapeutic procedures; however, splenectomy is designated as the principal procedure because it is related to the principal diagnosis. Although the diagnosis refers to stone in the left kidney, a pyelolithotomy refers to removal of stone from the renal pelvis.

6. **Inpatient admission:** A 50-year-old man receiving Coumadin therapy was admitted with hematemesis secondary to acute gastritis. A prolonged prothrombin time was reported, secondary to the anticoagulant effect of the Coumadin therapy.

   Discharge diagnosis: Acute gastritis.

   K29.01 Acute gastritis with bleeding

   Z79.01 Long term (current) use of anticoagulants

   Comments: Code K29.01 includes the acute gastritis with hemorrhage. No code is assigned for the prolonged bleeding time.

7. **Outpatient clinic visit:** A 59-year-old female patient presents to the oncologist with oat cell lung cancer of the right upper lobe and anemia. Patient had recently undergone a chemotherapy treatment.

   Diagnoses: (1) Anemia due to carcinoma, (2) oat cell lung carcinoma.

   C34.11 Malignant neoplasm of upper lobe, right bronchus or lung

   D63.0 Anemia in neoplastic disease

   Comments: The neoplasm responsible for the anemia is coded first for anemia in neoplastic disease. Even though the patient received chemotherapy treatment, it should not be assumed that the chemotherapy caused the anemia.

6. DISEASES OF THE NERVOUS SYSTEM AND SENSE ORGANS

1. **Ophthalmology clinic visit:** The HIV-infected patient complained of difficulty focusing while reading. His examination revealed no evidence of retinopathy. He did have early presbyopia, for which "drugstore readers" were recommended.

   Diagnoses: (1) Presbyopia, (2) HIV infection.

H52.4 Presbyopia

B20 Human immunodeficiency virus [HIV] disease

Comments: Presbyopia is designated as the reason for the encounter because it was chiefly responsible for the services received. The HIV infection was not specified as causing the presbyopia and was not treated. Nevertheless, it is documented as a coexisting condition.

2. **Inpatient admission:** The patient was under medical management for long-standing, bilateral mild stage primary open-angle glaucoma, as well as age-related bilateral macular degeneration. Three days previously, an abnormally high intraocular pressure developed. The patient was treated successfully as an outpatient. The next day, another pressure spike occurred, and the patient was admitted for further management. He was treated medically for two days, and both the pressure and visual acuity improved sufficiently for discharge.

   Discharge diagnoses: (1) Acute primary open-angle glaucoma, (2) macular degeneration, (3) intraocular pressure.

H40.11x1 Primary open-angle glaucoma, mild stage

H35.30 Unspecified macular degeneration

Comments: Glaucoma is coded and sequenced as the principal diagnosis following the UHDDS definition. High intraocular pressure is integral to glaucoma and is not coded. Macular degeneration is under current medical management and meets the UHDDS definition of additional diagnosis.

3. **Inpatient admission:** The patient previously suffered anterior dislocation of the left hip, which was reduced; however, this was followed by numbness and weakness in the left femoral nerve distribution. Evaluation indicated that she would benefit from surgery. A left femoral nerve external neurolysis was carried out successfully.

   Discharge diagnosis: Mononeuritis, femoral nerve.

G57.22 Lesion of femoral nerve, left side

S73.032S Other anterior subluxation of left hip, sequela

01ND3ZZ Release femoral nerve, percutaneous approach

Comments: Mononeuritis is the condition necessitating admission of the patient to the hospital for surgery. Dislocation is not coded because it is a previous condition no longer under treatment, but a code indicating that the mononeuritis is a late effect of the dislocation is assigned. The mononeuritis code allows for laterality. Late effects in ICD-10-CM are coded with the seventh character "S." The neurolysis procedure is classified to the root operation "Release."

4. **Inpatient admission:** The patient, a teenager, was admitted for evaluation and control of his intractable seizures. On days one, three, and four, seizures were recorded per video EEG. His video EEGs were consistent with epileptiform discharges of right temporal lobe origin. Dilantin and phenobarbital dosages were adjusted, and the patient was discharged in satisfactory condition.

   Discharge diagnosis: Partial complex epilepsy localized to the right temporal lobe.

G40.219 Localization-related (focal) (partial) symptomatic epilepsy and epileptic syndromes with complex partial seizures, intractable, without status epilepticus

4A10X4Z Monitoring of central nervous electrical activity, external approach

Comments: In the Alphabetic Index of Diseases and Injuries, the main term **Epilepsy** is searched, with subterms "localization," "symptomatic," "with complex partial seizures," "intractable." Video EEG is classified to the Measurement and Monitoring Section, root operation "Monitoring," "electrical activity" function.

5. **Ambulatory surgery:** The patient was brought in for surgical intervention of a mature, symptomatic cataract in the left eye and high intraocular pressures despite medical therapy. Procedures performed were an external trabeculectomy and phacoemulsification.

   Diagnoses: (1) Primary open-angle glaucoma, severe stage left eye, moderate stage right eye; (2) cataract, left eye.

H40.11x3 Primary open-angle glaucoma, severe stage

H40.11x2 Primary open-angle glaucoma, moderate stage

H26.9 Unspecified cataract

08133Z4 Bypass left anterior chamber to sclera, percutaneous approach

08DK3ZZ Extraction of left lens, percutaneous approach

Comments: Either the glaucoma or the cataract could be designated as the first-listed diagnosis because both were present on admission and both were treated. Because subcategory H40.11 does not distinguish laterality, and the patient has glaucoma of the same type but different stage in each eye, assign a code for the type of glaucoma for each eye with the seventh character for the specific stage. The procedure performed for the definitive treatment of cataract is sequenced as the first procedure. The trabeculectomy is for the glaucoma and is therefore listed first as sequenced above. For the trabeculectomy, see the root operation "Bypass," body part "anterior chamber." For the procedure, in the Index see **Phacoemulsification, Lens,** without IOL implant see Extraction, Eye 08D.

6. **Inpatient admission:** The patient, an 18-month-old boy, was admitted with right orbital cellulitis. He was started on antibiotics and seemed to be improving. However, the day after admission a slight exophthalmos was noticed. A non-contrast CT scan of the head showed increasing edema of the eye orbit with filling of ethmoid sinuses. The medications were changed. A right endoscopic complete ethmoidectomy was performed because the ethmoid sinuses were filled on the right side. The infant improved and was discharged in satisfactory condition.

   Discharge diagnoses: (1) Right orbital abscess, (2) exophthalmos, (3) orbital edema, (4) acute ethmoidal sinusitis.

H05.011 Cellulitis of right orbit

H05.20 Unspecified exophthalmos

J01.20 Acute ethmoidal sinusitis, unspecified

09BU4ZZ Excision of right ethmoid sinus, percutaneous endoscopic approach

Comments: The principal diagnosis is orbital cellulitis/abscess because this was the condition necessitating admission. Orbital edema is integral to orbital cellulitis and should not be coded separately. However, exophthalmos is not integral to orbital cellulitis and should be coded. Ethmoidal sinusitis was qualified as acute.

7. **Inpatient admission:** The elderly male patient, a type 1 diabetic, developed weakness of the right arm and leg. The weakness worsened; eventually he fell and was unable to move. When brought to the emergency department, he was able to speak but unable to use his right arm or leg. A consultation after admission suggested either an acute left-sided cortical stroke or a TIA. Diagnostic radiographic procedures were scheduled; however, he completely recovered before the procedures could be completed and was able to ambulate with no neurological deficits within 24 hours of admission. He was discharged and will have a workup performed for cerebrovascular insufficiency as an outpatient.

   Discharge diagnoses: (1) Probable transient ischemic attack, (2) diabetes mellitus.

G45.9 Transient cerebral ischemic attack, unspecified

E10.9 Type 1 diabetes mellitus without complications

Z79.4 Long term (current) use of insulin

Comments: Acute cerebrovascular attack was ruled out and therefore is not coded. Arm and leg paralysis were transient, focal neurological deficits that completely cleared during the hospitalization; therefore, no code assignments are required. The "probable" condition necessitating admission was TIA. Conditions described as probable on discharge are coded as though confirmed. A code is assigned for diabetes even though no specific treatment was given because it is a condition that always requires clinical evaluation when any other medical problem is present. Code Z79.4 is not required for type 1 diabetics because these patients require insulin. However, this code may be assigned, if desired, to provide additional information.

8. **Inpatient admission:** The patient, an elderly female nursing home resident, was under medical management for chronic senile dementia and postherpetic neuralgia. She also had a history of renal cyst. She was admitted with nausea and emesis, which cleared after several days. She also complained of increasing nasal sinus congestion and headache. She was treated with antibiotics and decongestants for sinusitis. Recovery was uneventful, and she was returned to the nursing home for further care.

   Discharge diagnoses: (1) Postherpetic neuralgia, (2) sinusitis, (3) chronic senile dementia.

J32.9 Chronic sinusitis, unspecified

B02.29 Other postherpetic nervous system involvement

F03.90 Unspecified dementia without behavioral disturbance

Comments: Although postherpetic neuralgia and chronic senile dementia were also present, the condition determined to be responsible for admission was sinusitis. No code is assigned for the renal cyst because it was qualified as "history of" and was not further evaluated or treated during the patient's stay.

9. **Neurology clinic visit:** The patient, a 23-month-old right-handed child, has congenital mitral stenosis. After a cardiac catheterization six months earlier, she had a large middle cerebral artery infarct. She is being followed for left arm paralysis, residuals of the cerebrovascular accident. She appeared to be making progress with weekly physical therapy. The muscle strength, tone, and stretch reflexes were improved, but she had some decrease in light touch sensation.

   Diagnoses: (1) Paralysis, left arm; (2) congenital mitral stenosis.

I69.334 Monoplegia of upper limb following cerebral infarction affecting left non-dominant side

Q23.2 Congenital mitral stenosis

Comments: Monoplegia, as a sequela of the previous stroke, is coded in the I69.3 subcategory. Because the patient is right-handed, the left side is considered nondominant. In coding late effects of cerebrovascular disease, a combination code identifies both the residual and the late effect; therefore, only code I69.334 is required. Because this residual was the reason for her visit, this code is listed as the reason for the encounter.

10. Inpatient admission: A 50-year-old female with terminal metastatic breast cancer is admitted to the hospital because of severe neck pain. The pain has worsened over the past week in spite of increasing amounts of oral pain medications. She is admitted for pain management and is initially given p.o. morphine 10–15 mg q. 4–6 hours p.r.n. for severe pain. During the next morning, she continues to complain of severe pain and is given IV (via peripheral vein) morphine 2 mg, which relieves her pain. Eventually, her pain subsides and the morphine is gradually tapered off. She is discharged and referred to the pain clinic for further outpatient care.

Diagnosis: Severe neck pain due to bone metastasis from malignant neoplasm of right breast.

G89.3	Neoplasm related pain (acute) (chronic)
C50.911	Malignant neoplasm of unspecified site of right female breast
C79.51	Secondary malignant neoplasm of bone
M54.2	Cervicalgia
3E030NZ	Introduction of analgesics, hypnotics, sedatives into peripheral vein, open approach

Comments: The patient was admitted for pain management, rather than for treatment or diagnosis of the breast cancer; therefore, the pain code is assigned as the principal diagnosis. The underlying neoplasm is assigned as an additional diagnosis. Typically, the neoplasm code would provide information regarding the specific site, in which case an additional code for the site of pain should not be assigned. However, in this instance, because the neoplasm codes (breast and bone) do not specify the site of the pain (neck), an additional code is assigned for the neck pain.

7. DISEASES OF THE RESPIRATORY SYSTEM

1. **Inpatient admission:** The patient, a 51-year-old woman with acute respiratory failure secondary to an acute exacerbation of chronic obstructive bronchitis, was brought to the emergency department by emergency medical services. In the emergency department, she was intubated and placed on mechanical ventilation. On admission, it soon became apparent that she had suffered severe, irreversible hypoxic encephalopathy. On day 5, she was weaned from the ventilator and extubated; however, significant neurological function was never regained. In accordance with her advance directive, tube feedings were discontinued. She became febrile and dyspneic. Antibiotics were started to provide comfort and relief of her pneumonia. She expired on day 13.

   Discharge diagnoses: (1) Acute respiratory failure with hypoxia secondary to chronic obstructive bronchitis, (2) pneumonia, (3) encephalopathy.

J96.01	Acute respiratory failure with hypoxia
J44.1	Chronic obstructive pulmonary disease with (acute) exacerbation
G93.1	Anoxic brain damage, not elsewhere classified
J18.9	Pneumonia, unspecified organism
5A1955Z	Respiratory ventilation, greater than 96 consecutive hours
0BH17EZ	Insertion of endotracheal airway into trachea, via natural or artificial opening

Comments: Respiratory failure was responsible for admission and is designated as the principal diagnosis. The patient was intubated in the emergency department and maintained on mechanical ventilation until day 5, more than 96 hours.

2. **Inpatient admission:** The elderly patient came to the emergency department complaining of shortness of breath and nausea. It was apparent that she was suffering from congestive heart failure and respiratory failure, and she was admitted for immediate treatment of the acute respiratory failure. Before any diagnostic work could be accomplished, she died.

   Discharge diagnoses: (1) Acute respiratory failure, (2) congestive heart failure.

J96.00	Acute respiratory failure, unspecified whether with hypoxia or hypercapnia
I50.9	Heart failure, unspecified

Comments: When a patient is admitted with respiratory failure and another acute condition, the principal diagnosis will depend on the circumstances of admission. In this case, the patient was admitted for immediate treatment of the acute respiratory failure; therefore, it is sequenced as the principal diagnosis. Congestive heart failure is coded as an additional diagnosis.

3. **Inpatient admission:** The patient was admitted after visiting the emergency department for shortness of breath, chest pain, hypoxia, and a white cell count of 32,600. The patient had a history of chronic obstructive pulmonary disease. Interstitial infiltrate at the right middle and lower lobes of the lung was seen on chest X-ray. Sputum culture grew *Streptococcus pneumoniae.* He tolerated the antibiotics, and the symptoms improved significantly.

   Discharge diagnoses: (1) Right lower lobe pneumonia due to *Streptococcus pneumoniae,* (2) acute exacerbation of chronic obstructive lung disease.

J13	Pneumonia due to Streptococcus pneumoniae
J44.1	Chronic obstructive pulmonary disease with (acute) exacerbation
R09.02	Hypoxemia

Comments: *Streptococcus pneumoniae* is the causative organism. Because this organism is specified in the title of code J13, an additional code assignment is not necessary. Code J44.1 is assigned for exacerbated chronic obstructive pulmonary disease. Chronic obstructive pulmonary disease is one of the conditions that requires clinical evaluation even if no further treatment is given. Therefore, it is listed as an additional code. Code R09.02, Hypoxemia, is assigned as an additional diagnosis for the hypoxia because it is not inherent in pneumonia.

4. **Inpatient admission:** The patient, a young man, came to the emergency department after being ill for at least three weeks. He initially had a head cold and sore throat, followed by fever, difficulty swallowing, chills, and brown sputum. Because of severe lymphadenopathy in the neck, as well as other stated symptomatology, he was admitted. A huge left tonsil confluent with the surrounding tissues and covered with exudate was also noted on the physical examination. This appeared to represent a peritonsillar abscess and severe tonsillitis. A throat culture showed a heavy growth of beta-*Streptococcus* group C. Intravenous antibiotics were given with success, and he was discharged.

   Discharge diagnoses: (1) Severe tonsillitis with beta-*Streptococcus* group C, (2) probable left peritonsillar abscess.

J36 Peritonsillar abscess

B95.4 Other streptococcus as the cause of diseases classified elsewhere

Comments: Both tonsillitis and peritonsillar abscess were present at admission. Both conditions were treated, and both meet the criteria for principal diagnosis. However, only one of them should be coded because of the excludes1 instructional note at code J36 and category J03 that precludes the coding of both conditions together. Because the abscess is the more severe condition, assign only code J36. Assign also code B95.4 to identify the infectious organism as instructed by the use additional code note at J36.

5. **Inpatient admission:** The type 1 diabetic patient was admitted with a right heel ulcer that had failed a number of outpatient therapies. Also, because the patient was hypoxic on admission with a history of COPD, he was given supplemental oxygen. He coughed up sputum, and a chest X-ray showed a mild increase in interstitial markings. Consequently, he was treated for acute bronchitis with erythromycin, which provided good results. Gradually, the foot ulcer healed. But the hypoxia persisted, and an increase in his oxygen therapy was helpful. He was to be followed by home health services.

   Discharge diagnoses: (1) Diabetic foot ulcer, right heel; (2) acute bronchitis; (3) diabetes mellitus; (4) history of COPD.

E10.621 Type 1 diabetes mellitus with foot ulcer

L97.419 Non-pressure chronic ulcer of right heel and midfoot with unspecified severity

J44.0 Chronic obstructive pulmonary disease with acute lower respiratory infection

J20.9 Acute bronchitis, unspecified

R09.02 Hypoxemia

Z79.4 Long term (current) use of insulin

Comments: The diabetes code includes the ulcer, but an additional code specifies the site of the ulcer. Code J44.0, Chronic obstructive pulmonary disease with acute lower respiratory infection, has a note to use an additional code to identify the infection; code J20.9 is added. There is an excludes2 note under category J20 for acute bronchitis with chronic obstructive pulmonary disease. Because both conditions exist at the same time it is acceptable to use both codes. Code R09.02 is assigned for the hypoxia, which is not inherent in COPD. Code Z79.4 is not required for type 1 diabetics because these patients require insulin. However, this code may be assigned, if desired, to provide additional information.

6. **Inpatient admission:** The patient, a man in extremely poor health due to chronic obstructive pulmonary disease and chronic alcoholism, was admitted for severe shortness of breath, a PO_2 of 42, abdominal pain, and what appeared to be impending delirium tremens. He was placed on Ventolin and Solu-Medrol. Librium was also given to prevent delirium tremens. A colonoscopy was performed because of a past history of polyps, with no recurrence found. It was felt that the patient had mild colitis. On discharge, he was no longer dyspneic at rest. He was to start taking Zantac for colitis and to continue Solu-Medrol.

   Discharge diagnoses: (1) Chronic lung disease with acute bronchospasm, (2) impending delirium tremens, (3) alcohol dependence, (4) colitis, (5) history of colon polyps.

J98.01	Acute bronchospasm
J44.9	Chronic obstructive pulmonary disease, unspecified
F10.231	Alcohol dependence with withdrawal delirium
K52.9	Noninfective gastroenteritis and colitis, unspecified
Z86.010	Personal history of colonic polyps
0DJD8ZZ	Inspection of lower intestinal tract, via natural or artificial opening, endoscopic

Comments: Bronchospasm represents the exacerbation of the COPD and was the reason for admission. ICD-10-CM includes the delirium tremens in alcoholism in one code, F10.231. Code Z86.010 is assigned because the history of polyps was the reason for the colonoscopy.

7. **Inpatient admission:** The patient, a 13-month-old girl, had two apnea alarms within the past few hours. After the last discharge from this hospital for apnea, an apnea alarm was ordered. Because of continued alarms, the mother returned the child to the hospital. She was placed on a cardiac apnea monitor with event record mode and on continuous bioximeter. There were no alarms noted during hospitalization. She was discharged home with an apnea monitor with event record mode in place.

   Discharge diagnosis: Rule out apnea.

R06.81	Apnea, not elsewhere classified
4A12X9Z	Monitoring of cardiac output, external approach

Comments: Rule out apnea as a probable diagnosis. On inpatient discharge, suspected conditions are coded as though confirmed. The apnea monitor is indexed under the main term **Monitoring,** subterm "cardiac output."

8. **Inpatient admission:** The patient, a three-year-old male, was admitted for evaluation of fever, cough, and persistent pulmonary interstitial infiltrate. A chest tube was placed on the right side for drainage. The child's condition was consistent with pneumonia and aspiration of mucus. On the day after chest tube insertion, the chest X-ray was clear, and the chest tube was pulled. He was placed on aspiration precautions and antibiotics. He was to be followed up as an outpatient.

   Discharge diagnosis: Pneumonia secondary to aspiration of mucus.

J69.0	Pneumonitis due to inhalation of food and vomit
0W9930Z	Drainage of right pleural cavity with drainage device, percutaneous approach

Comments: After study, the condition found to be chiefly responsible for the admission of the patient for care was aspiration pneumonia. Code J69.0 includes both the aspiration and the pneumonia. The chest tube insertion was performed for drainage; refer to the Index main term **Drainage,** subterms "cavity," "pleural," "right."

9. Inpatient admission: The patient, a five-year-old male, was seen as an outpatient for chronic asthmatic bronchitis with exacerbation without improvement. He was admitted for further treatment and on physical examination was also found to have bilateral suppurative otitis media. After being placed in a croup tent and treated with antibiotics, his temperature gradually returned to normal, and he improved.

Discharge diagnoses: (1) Asthmatic bronchitis, (2) acute suppurative otitis media.

J44.1	Chronic obstructive pulmonary disease with (acute) exacerbation
J45.901	Unspecified asthma with (acute) exacerbation
H66.003	Acute suppurative otitis media without spontaneous rupture of ear drum, bilateral

Comments: Category J44 is selected for chronic asthmatic bronchitis, with the fourth character denoting the acute exacerbation. There is a "code also" note for asthma at category J44, so the J45.901 code is added. ICD-10-CM has codes for right, left, or bilateral otitis media.

10. Inpatient admission: The patient was admitted after she developed progressive dyspnea and wheezing, intractable to ambulatory care management. The provisional admitting diagnosis was status asthmaticus. Her history showed that she was status post mastectomy for breast cancer and still had some residual lymphedema in the left upper extremity. In the hospital, she received low-flow oxygen, antibiotics, bronchodilators, and IV steroids, as well as her usual medications for hypertension and hypothyroidism.

Discharge diagnoses: (1) Status asthmaticus, (2) hypertension, (3) hypothyroidism, (4) status post breast cancer with lymphedema.

J45.902	Unspecified asthma with status asthmaticus
I97.2	Postmastectomy lymphedema syndrome
I10	Essential (primary) hypertension
E03.9	Hypothyroidism, unspecified
Z85.3	Personal history of malignant neoplasm of breast

Comments: Code J45.902 is used for unspecified asthma with status asthmaticus. Status asthmaticus is usually considered to be present when the condition does not respond to treatment on an ambulatory basis. However, the provider must document status asthmaticus.

11. Inpatient admission: The patient, an elderly woman, was known to have congestive heart failure, arteriosclerotic heart disease, and chronic obstructive pulmonary disease. She has no history of CABG. She developed increased shortness of breath, dyspnea on exertion, temperature elevation, and productive cough. These problems were felt to represent congestive failure and pneumonia. She was admitted for cultures, IV antibiotics, pulmonary toilet, and increased diuresis. Her initial non-contrast chest film showed congestive heart failure and bilateral lung infiltrates. In discussing this case with the pulmonary consultant, the physician felt it was wise to transfer the patient to another hospital so that both pulmonary and cardiology staff could work together with this patient.

Discharge diagnoses: (1) Arteriosclerotic heart disease, (2) congestive heart failure, (3) pneumonia, (4) chronic obstructive lung disease.

I50.9	Heart failure, unspecified
J18.9	Pneumonia, unspecified organism
J44.0	Chronic obstructive pulmonary disease with acute lower respiratory infection
I25.10	Atherosclerotic heart disease of native coronary artery without angina pectoris

Comments: Either congestive heart failure or pneumonia could be designated as the principal diagnosis because both were present on admission and attention was directed to both conditions. Code J44.0, Chronic obstructive pulmonary disease with acute lower respiratory infection, is assigned instead of J44.9 because of the presence of pneumonia. Code I25.10 for arteriosclerosis of native artery, as there is no evidence of bypass surgery in the past.

12. **Inpatient admission:** The patient, a 94-year-old man with known arteriosclerotic coronary artery disease, no history of bypass, and exacerbation of end-stage chronic obstructive bronchitis, was admitted with a provisional diagnosis of acute respiratory failure. He was treated with IV antibiotics and pulmonary toilet. Although his long-term prognosis was poor, he was improved upon discharge.

    Discharge diagnoses: (1) Arteriosclerotic coronary artery disease, (2) end-stage chronic obstructive bronchitis, (3) angina, (4) acute respiratory failure.

J96.00	Acute respiratory failure, unspecified whether with hypoxia or hypercapnia
J44.9	Chronic obstructive pulmonary disease, unspecified
I25.119	Atherosclerotic heart disease of native coronary artery with unspecified angina pectoris

Comments: Respiratory failure is listed as the principal diagnosis because it is the reason for the admission. Code I25.119, for arteriosclerosis of native artery, is assigned because there has been no previous bypass surgery. Angina is included in this code as well.

13. **Inpatient admission:** The patient, a five-week-old infant, had been discharged from the hospital following her birth without any complaints. She was now admitted through the emergency department, where she was found to be febrile and lethargic and to have a weak cry. Dry mucous membranes were also noted. The admission diagnosis was "rule out sepsis." She was given STAT respiratory treatment and IV fluids, followed by intravenous antibiotics. Urine cultures grew *Enterococcus.* Blood cultures were negative. Sputum cultures grew *Mycoplasma pneumoniae.* She gradually improved and was weaned from the oxygen tent. She improved rapidly and was discharged three days following admission.

    Discharge diagnoses: (1) Right lower lobe pneumonitis due to *Mycoplasma pneumoniae,* (2) fever, (3) dehydration, (4) urinary tract infection.

J15.7	Pneumonia due to Mycoplasma pneumoniae
E86.0	Dehydration
N39.0	Urinary tract infection, site not specified
B95.2	Enterococcus as the cause of diseases classified elsewhere

Comments: Any of the conditions could have been designated as the principal diagnosis according to symptoms on admission and treatment rendered. All conditions meet the criteria for additional diagnoses except for fever, which is integral to pneumonia. Code J15.7 is assigned rather than the newborn infection codes because in this case, the infant had previously been discharged in good condition and developed the pneumonitis later, which would mean that it was a community-acquired condition.

14. **Inpatient admission:** The patient, an 18-month-old male, was admitted with reactive airway disease versus viral pneumonia. His symptoms of wheezing and congestion had become increasingly worse over the past few days. He had been healthy since birth except for congenital pulmonary stenosis, which was evaluated during this admission. He was placed on medications and oxygen. Blood culture and viral panel were negative. He was to be followed by the pulmonary clinic.

    Discharge diagnoses: (1) Acute exacerbation of reactive airway disease, (2) mild pulmonary stenosis.

J45.901	Unspecified asthma with (acute) exacerbation
Q25.6	Stenosis of pulmonary artery

Comments: Viral pneumonia was ruled out and should not be coded. The main term **Disease,** reactive airway, in the Alphabetic Index of Diseases and Injuries says, "see Asthma." Although the asthma had not reached the status asthmaticus stage, it had become exacerbated. Congenital pulmonary stenosis is coded because it probably is involved in the reactive airway disease and would have received clinical evaluation during the stay.

15. **Inpatient admission:** A 76-year-old female with known Hodgkin intrathoracic lymphoma was admitted for malignant pleural effusion. She had previously undergone thoracentesis with symptomatic relief. Because of the recurrence of the effusion, video-assisted thoracoscopic (VAT) drainage of the pleural fluid from the left pleural cavity was carried out, along with mechanical abrasion and left pleurodesis via the application of talc.

    Discharge diagnoses: (1) Malignant pleural effusion, (2) Hodgkin intrathoracic lymphoma.

C81.92	Hodgkin lymphoma, unspecified, intrathoracic lymph nodes
J91.0	Malignant pleural effusion
0W9B4ZZ	Drainage of left pleural cavity, percutaneous endoscopic approach
0B5P4ZZ	Destruction of left pleura, percutaneous endoscopic approach

Comment: The patient was admitted for the malignant pleural effusion. However, code J91.0 is assigned as the secondary diagnosis based on the Tabular List note to code first the underlying neoplasm. The "percutaneous endoscopic approach" is used for the thoracoscopic procedure. The pleurodesis and mechanical abrasion are classified to the root operation "Destruction."

8. DISEASES OF THE DIGESTIVE SYSTEM

1. **Inpatient admission:** This patient underwent a gastric bypass three weeks earlier and is now admitted because of continuous vomiting and severe dehydration. Radiologic and laboratory studies provided no indication of problems with the previous surgery or other abnormalities. Rehydration was accomplished. On close observation, it appeared that she was eating too fast and too much.

   Discharge diagnoses: (1) Exogenous morbid obesity with recent gastric bypass, (2) dehydration due to continuous vomiting.

K91.0 Vomiting following gastrointestinal surgery
E86.0 Dehydration
E66.01 Morbid (severe) obesity due to excess calories

Comments: Although the vomiting is not specified as due to the gastric surgery, the Tabular List and Alphabetic Index of Diseases and Injuries instruct the coder to assign K91.0 for any vomiting following gastrointestinal surgery.

2. **Inpatient admission:** The elderly nursing home patient was admitted with aspiration pneumonitis. She was unable to swallow or eat as a result of a stroke, which occurred two months earlier. She was experiencing progressive aspiration and weight loss. It was hoped that anchoring a feeding tube would alleviate the situation. Therefore, a percutaneous gastrostomy with placement of a feeding tube with endoscopic guidance was performed.

   Discharge diagnoses: (1) Difficulty swallowing secondary to cerebrovascular infarction, (2) impending malnutrition, (3) aspiration pneumonia.

J69.0 Pneumonitis due to inhalation of food and vomit
I69.391 Dysphagia following cerebral infarction
R13.10 Dysphagia, unspecified
R63.4 Abnormal weight loss
0DH63UZ Insertion of feeding device into stomach, percutaneous approach

Comments: Aspiration pneumonia is sequenced as the principal diagnosis. Because no code exists for impending malnutrition, code R63.4 is assigned to identify loss of weight, the precursor condition.

Dysphagia is the late effect of the previous cerebrovascular accident. I69.3 is the subcategory for sequelae of stroke not otherwise specified. As indicated by the "use additional code" note at code I69.391, an additional code is assigned to identify the type of dysphagia. Because the type of dysphagia has not been further specified other than as difficulty swallowing, code R13.10 is assigned.

The endoscopic gastrostomy is classified to the Medical and Surgical Section, root operation "Insertion," and the sixth-character value for feeding device. The endoscopic guidance is not coded separately. The approach is "percutaneous" because the tube was inserted percutaneously (rather than via the scope).

3. **Inpatient admission:** The patient was transferred in from facility A, where he experienced 12 hours of hematemesis requiring transfusions with 14 units of red blood cells and six units of fresh-frozen plasma. Upon admission to facility B, a gastroscopic examination revealed a 4- by 2-centimeter gastric ulcer with visible vessels. He was taken to the operating room, where a hemigastrectomy with Billroth I anastomosis of the duodenum was performed.

   Discharge diagnosis: Bleeding gastric ulcer.

K25.4 Chronic or unspecified gastric ulcer with hemorrhage
0DB60ZZ Excision of stomach, open approach
0D160Z9 Bypass stomach to duodenum, open approach
0DJ68ZZ Inspection of stomach, via natural or artificial opening endoscopic

Comments: The ulcer is unspecified as acute or chronic, with hemorrhage and without mention of perforation. Code K25.4 is assigned to identify the bleeding gastric ulcer to the greatest degree of specificity available.

Two codes are required for the hemigastrectomy and Billroth I anastomosis of the stomach to the duodenum. Hemigastrectomy is coded to the root operation "Excision," as a portion of a body part is removed. The Billroth I procedure is classified to the root operation "Bypass." The fourth character identifies the body part bypassed "from," and the seventh-character qualifier specifies the body part bypassed "to." The gastroscopy is coded to the root operation "Inspection."

4. **Inpatient admission:** The patient's admitting diagnosis was acute pancreatitis. Findings on a CT scan performed prior to admission were consistent with acute and chronic pancreatitis and pancreatic duct calculi. Multiple stones were noted on endoscopic retrograde cholangiopancreatography (ERCP); one of them was big enough to occlude the pancreatic duct. There was generalized stenosis of the pancreatic duct. (During ERCP, a stent was put in place to bypass the area of obstruction. The patient improved immediately.) Extracorporeal shock wave lithotripsy (ESWL) then achieved partial fragmentation of the stone. Because of abdominal pain, a second ESWL was required and, again, achieved only partial fragmentation of the stone. The patient underwent another ERCP, which identified multiple stones and pancreatic duct stenosis with occlusion of the previously placed stent. During the procedure, the obstructed area was passed through, but there was still a 2-millimeter area of pancreatic duct stenosis. A balloon was inserted to dilate this area endoscopically. There were multiple stones, and the occluded stent was removed and replaced with a new one beyond the area of obstruction. There was no puncture of the skin or mucous membrane necessary to remove or replace the occluded stent.

   Discharge diagnoses: (1) Acute and chronic pancreatitis, (2) pancreatic calculi.

   Procedures: (1) ERCP with pancreatic duct stent insertion, (2) ESWL (pancreatic stone) on two separate occasions, (3) ERCP with prolonged dilation of pancreatic duct and removal of occluded stent and replacement with a new, single-pigtail stent.

K85.9	Acute pancreatitis, unspecified
K86.1	Other chronic pancreatitis
K86.8	Other specified diseases of pancreas
0F7D8DZ	Dilation of pancreatic duct with intraluminal device, via natural or artificial opening endoscopic
0FPB8DZ	Removal of intraluminal device from hepatobiliary duct, via natural or artificial opening endoscopic
0FFDXZZ	Fragmentation in pancreatic duct, external approach

Comments: Because the patient had both acute and chronic pancreatitis and separate subterms exist in the Alphabetic Index, both codes are assigned, with the acute pancreatitis sequenced first.

ERCP with dilation and stent insertion is included in 0F7D8DZ, with the device value of "D" for "intraluminal device." The root operation "Dilation" is chosen, as this was the objective of the procedure. Code 0FPB8DZ is assigned to identify the removal of the occluded stent. The extracorporeal shock wave lithotripsy is coded to the root operation "Fragmentation" because the objective of the procedure was to break up the stone. The approach for the ESWL is external because the shock waves are delivered through the skin and no incisions are made. The ERCP with stent insertion is sequenced as the principal procedure because it is the procedure most closely related to the principal diagnosis of acute pancreatitis.

5. **Outpatient visit:** The patient came in complaining of severe abdominal pain. Abdominal scout film showed scoliosis and some degenerative changes in the lumbar spine. However, a high osmolar contrast abdominal CT scan showed extensive diverticulosis involving the descending and sigmoid portions of the colon, with obvious evidence of diverticulitis.

   Diagnosis: Diverticulitis.

K57.32	Diverticulitis of large intestine without perforation or abscess without bleeding
BW200ZZ	Computerized tomography (CT scan) of abdomen using high osmolar contrast

6. **Inpatient admission:** The 86-year-old woman was admitted with rectal bleeding. She was also massively dehydrated, with a BUN of 124. On admission, some IV fluids and transfusions of whole blood via a central vein were administered because her initial hemoglobin was 9.5 and later dropped to 7.4. On colonoscopy, multiple ulcers of the rectum, consistent with ulcerative proctitis, were found and biopsies were taken. The tissue was negative for neoplastic disease, and the patient was started on steroid enemas, with resolution.

   Discharge diagnoses: (1) Rectal bleeding, (2) dehydration, (3) acute blood loss anemia, (4) ulcerative proctitis.

K51.211	Ulcerative (chronic) proctitis with rectal bleeding
E86.0	Dehydration
D62	Acute posthemorrhagic anemia
0DBP8ZX	Excision of rectum, via natural or artificial opening endoscopic, diagnostic
30243H1	Transfusion of nonautologous whole blood into central vein, percutaneous approach

Comments: Ulcerative proctitis is sequenced as the principal diagnosis because the workup and treatment were directed at identifying and treating the cause of the bleeding. ICD-10-CM provides a combination code that includes rectal bleeding and proctitis. Acute blood loss anemia, a further manifestation of ulcerative proctitis, and dehydration are also coded because both meet criteria for additional diagnoses.

7. **Inpatient admission:** The patient, a 20-year-old female, presented to the emergency department complaining of bilateral arm and shoulder pain, "yellow eyes," and dark urine. The emergency department evaluation revealed profound jaundice with markedly elevated liver function tests. The patient was admitted for further evaluation. A non-contrast gallbladder ultrasound was negative for gallstones. Hematological studies indicated sickle-cell disease, which could be contributing to the jaundice. Because the liver function gradually improved, it was felt that she could be further evaluated as an outpatient for probable acute hepatitis B.

   Discharge diagnosis: Jaundice secondary to sickle-cell disease versus acute hepatitis B.

R17	Unspecified jaundice
B16.9	Acute hepatitis B without delta-agent and without hepatic coma
D57.1	Sickle-cell disease without crisis

Comments: When a symptom is followed by contrasting or comparative diagnoses, the symptom should be sequenced first.

8. **Inpatient admission:** The patient was admitted for evaluation of guaiac-positive stools. All sites that could be visualized on esophagogastroduodenoscopy (EGD) were within normal limits except a small area in the gastric fundus, which was biopsied. A colonoscope was then inserted to 35 centimeters, and diverticula were noted. Because of narrowing resulting from edema due to diverticulitis, it was not possible to pass the scope farther. The tissue report showed benign acute and chronic gastritis but no ulcer.

   Discharge diagnoses: (1) Occult blood in stool of undetermined origin, (2) diverticulosis with diverticulitis of colon, (3) acute and chronic gastritis.

R19.5	Other fecal abnormalities
K29.00	Acute gastritis without bleeding
K29.50	Unspecified chronic gastritis without bleeding
K57.32	Diverticulitis of large intestine without perforation or abscess without bleeding
0DB68ZX	Excision of stomach, via natural or artificial opening endoscopic, diagnostic
0DJD8ZZ	Inspection of lower intestinal tract, via natural or artificial opening endoscopic

Comments: No cause for the blood in stools was determined; therefore, the symptom is the principal diagnosis. When diverticulitis is present, it is understood that diverticulosis also exists, and an additional code for the latter condition is unnecessary. Two endoscopic procedures were performed: EGD and colonoscopy. When an endoscope is passed through more than one area of the body, the procedure is coded to the farthest site only.

9. **Inpatient admission (episode 1):** Because the patient had a 20-year history of severe complicated ulcerative colitis, he was admitted for surgical intervention. A total abdominal colectomy with ileostomy was performed. The postoperative recovery was without incident.

   Discharge diagnosis: Ulcerative colitis.

K51.919	Ulcerative colitis, unspecified with unspecified complications
0DTE0ZZ	Resection of large intestine, open approach
0D1B0Z4	Bypass ileum to cutaneous, open approach

Comments: The condition necessitating admission and surgery was ulcerative colitis. Colectomy is the definitive treatment for colitis and is therefore designated as the principal procedure. The ileostomy is coded to the root operation "Bypass."

   Inpatient admission (episode 2): Three months after surgery, the patient was again admitted for a percutaneous endoscopic endorectal pull-through with excision of the submucosal portion of the rectum with endoscopic formation of a loop ileostomy via the existing ileostomy. This procedure was further treatment for the long-standing and intractable ulcerative colitis.

   Discharge diagnosis: Ulcerative colitis.

K51.919	Ulcerative colitis, unspecified with unspecified complications
0DBP4ZZ	Excision of rectum, percutaneous endoscopic approach
0D1B8Z4	Bypass ileum to cutaneous, via natural or artificial opening endoscopic

Comments: More extensive surgery was required to further control the patient's ulcerative colitis. Colitis is, again, the condition necessitating admission. Endorectal pull-through, or removal of the submucosal portion of the rectum, is the definitive treatment for ulcerative colitis and is therefore the principal procedure.

Inpatient admission (episode 3): Four months following the second surgery, the patient was admitted for ileostomy closure. He had no symptoms of ulcerative colitis. The postoperative course was uneventful.

Discharge diagnosis: Status post ileostomy closure.

Z43.2 Encounter for attention to ileostomy

0DQB0ZZ Repair ileum, open approach

Comments: The ulcerative colitis responded to the previous surgeries and was no longer present; therefore, it is not coded. The sole purpose for the third admission is ileostomy closure. In the Alphabetic Index to Procedures (ICD-10-PCS), the main term **Closure** has a note to "see Repair." See "Repair, ileum," for the first four characters for the ileostomy closure.

10. **Inpatient admission:** The patient experienced rectal pain for several months due to a 2.5-centimeter mass on the anterior rectal wall. An open excision of the mass was performed, and a frozen section revealed an inflammatory lesion without evidence of malignancy. The final pathology report showed the tissue to represent a granuloma of the rectum.

    Discharge diagnosis: Rectal granuloma.

K62.89 Other specified diseases of anus and rectum

0DBP0ZZ Excision of rectum, open approach

Comments: The condition, established after study, that necessitated the admission of the patient to the hospital for care was rectal granuloma. Although the lesion was not initially identified, the physician was able to further specify the condition as granuloma following "Excision" and pathologic examination.

11. **Inpatient admission:** The patient, a woman with chronic right upper-quadrant abdominal pain, was admitted for possible pancreatitis after two episodes of vomiting clear fluid. Pain medications were started and a nasogastric tube was placed for drainage, with intermittent suction. The NG tube was pulled three days after admission, and the patient was discharged to follow up with her physician one week later.

    Discharge diagnosis: Pancreatitis.

    Principal procedure: Insertion, nasogastric tube.

K85.9 Acute pancreatitis, unspecified

0D9670Z Drainage of stomach with drainage device, via natural or artificial opening

Comments: Pain and vomiting are not coded because they are integral to pancreatitis. Although the pancreatitis is not qualified as acute or chronic, code K85.9 is assigned because this is the code provided in the Alphabetic Index of Diseases and Injuries for pancreatitis that is not further specified. The objective for the insertion of the NG tube is drainage. Therefore, the procedure is coded to the root operation "Drainage."

12. Inpatient admission: The patient, a man with a long history of alcohol dependence with resultant alcoholic cirrhosis, was admitted with red, coffee-ground hematemesis. An emergent esophagogastroduodenoscopy revealed bleeding esophageal varices, which were excised. The varices are secondary to the alcoholic cirrhosis. No problems were identified in the stomach or duodenum. He was transfused via peripheral vein in his left arm with multiple units of packed red cells and frozen plasma, and yet the bleeding continued. He was returned to surgery, and an esophagoscopy was performed to sclerose the bleeding esophageal varices a second time.

Discharge diagnoses: (1) Upper gastrointestinal bleed, (2) esophageal varices, (3) Laennec's cirrhosis, (4) alcohol dependence.

Principal procedure: Control of esophageal bleeding by excision of varices.

K70.30	Alcoholic cirrhosis of liver without ascites
I85.11	Secondary esophageal varices with bleeding
F10.20	Alcohol dependence, uncomplicated
0DB58ZZ	Excision of esophagus, via natural or artificial opening endoscopic
3E0G8TZ	Introduction of destructive agent into upper GI, via natural or artificial opening endoscopic
30233N1	Transfusion of nonautologous red blood cells into peripheral vein, percutaneous approach
30233K1	Transfusion of nonautologous frozen plasma into peripheral vein, percutaneous approach

Comments: The esophageal varices are due to the alcoholic cirrhosis. In the Index, refer to the main term **Varix,** esophagus, in (due to) cirrhosis of the liver, bleeding, I85.11. There is a "code first" note at the I85.1 subcategory instructing that the underlying disease should be coded first. Therefore, the code for the alcoholic cirrhosis is sequenced first.

Code 0DB58ZZ is assigned for the excision of the varices of the esophagus. Code 3E0G8TZ is assigned for the sclerotherapy. The injection of a sclerosing agent into the varices to prevent bleeding is coded to the root operation "Introduction." The "upper intestinal tract" is selected for the body system, which includes the esophagus down to and including the duodenum. Separate codes for the EGD and esophagoscopy are not assigned because these procedures were performed only as the approach to the more definitive procedure.

13. Inpatient admission: The patient, a 35-year-old male, was admitted for possible gastritis. He had undergone a cadaveric renal transplant for end-stage renal disease secondary to focal membranous glomerulonephritis two years earlier. On endoscopic examination of the lower esophagus and stomach, patchy erythemas were seen in the stomach and biopsies of the stomach were taken. A linear erosion was noted at the gastroesophageal junction. The impression was mild reflux esophagitis and mild antral duodenitis. As his dietary intake improved, his physical condition improved as well.

Discharge diagnoses: (1) Reflux esophagitis, (2) duodenitis.

K21.0	Gastro-esophageal reflux disease with esophagitis
K29.80	Duodenitis without bleeding
Z94.0	Kidney transplant status
0DB68ZX	Excision of stomach, via natural or artificial opening endoscopic, diagnostic

Comments: Either esophagitis or duodenitis can be designated as the principal diagnosis because both are consistent with the reason for admission, both were identified during the hospitalization, and both were treated. The previous kidney transplant is coded because it was significant in the patient's current care and treatment.

14. Inpatient admission: The patient recently underwent an ultrasound that showed a filling defect in the gallbladder, thought to represent a cholelithiasis. It was felt that the woman's symptoms were suggestive of cholecystitis and that cholecystectomy was in order. On admission, a laparoscopic cholecystectomy with lysis of adhesions around the gallbladder was carried out, followed by a contrast intraoperative cholangiogram. A proctologist was consulted due to the presence of persistent rectal pain. A mild anal fissure was identified on flexible sigmoidoscopy. A needle biopsy of the liver was performed due to an abnormal liver function study times 3. The pathology report indicated that the liver tissue was normal.

Discharge diagnoses: (1) Chronic cholecystitis and cholelithiasis, (2) anal fissure, (3) abnormal liver function studies.

K80.10	Calculus of gallbladder with chronic cholecystitis without obstruction
K60.2	Anal fissure, unspecified
R94.5	Abnormal results of liver function studies
0FT44ZZ	Resection of gallbladder, percutaneous endoscopic approach
0FB03ZX	Excision of liver, percutaneous approach, diagnostic
BF03YZZ	Plain radiography of gallbladder and bile ducts using other contrast
0DJD8ZZ	Inspection of lower intestinal tract, via natural or artificial opening endoscopic

Comments: Code K80.10 includes both chronic cholecystitis and cholelithiasis. Adhesions and lysis of adhesions are not coded because adhesions were not listed as a discharge diagnosis. Lysis of adhesions is fairly common in cholecystectomy surgery and is not coded unless the significance was specified by the physician. Although the biopsy of the liver was normal, the physician still felt that there was an abnormality in the liver function lab studies, so this was coded. The laparoscopic cholecystectomy is sequenced as the principal procedure because it is the definitive procedure most closely related to the principal diagnosis of cholecystitis.

15. Inpatient admission: The male patient came in complaining of headache, nausea, vomiting, and chest pain. The impression on admission was possible coronary artery disease and probable viral gastroenteritis. Only a small, sliding hiatal hernia was found on air contrast upper GI. No ischemia was found on cardiac evaluation. The patient gradually improved and was discharged two days later to follow up with his family physician in one week for gastroenteritis and further evaluation of the hiatal hernia.

Discharge diagnoses: (1) Probable viral gastroenteritis, (2) hiatal hernia.

A08.4	Viral intestinal infection, unspecified
BD15YZZ	Fluoroscopy of upper GI using other contrast

Comments: The reason for admission was possible coronary artery disease and probable gastroenteritis. Possible coronary artery disease was ruled out by diagnostic evaluation and is not coded. The principal diagnosis is viral gastroenteritis. Probable diagnoses at the time of discharge are coded as though confirmed. No code is assigned for the hiatal hernia because it is an incidental X-ray finding for a condition that was not treated or evaluated further during the current encounter and therefore is not reportable.

16. **Inpatient admission:** The patient, a woman with a long history of Crohn's disease, was admitted with abdominal cramping, vomiting, and diarrhea of sudden onset. Admitting orders included all current medications for Crohn's disease. Her amylase was 241 on admission, and she had a slightly elevated white blood count. Both returned to normal with treatment for pancreatitis, and the abdominal problems also slowed down. She was to be followed as an outpatient.

    Discharge diagnoses: (1) Pancreatitis, (2) Crohn's disease.

K85.9 Acute pancreatitis, unspecified

K50.90 Crohn's disease, unspecified, without complications

Comments: Patient's symptomatology and treatment were related to pancreatitis. Sequence pancreatitis as the principal diagnosis. Crohn's disease, a coexisting condition, is coded because it was also treated.

17. **Physician office visit (episode 1):** The patient, an elderly woman, came in for severe epigastric abdominal pain. She had some nausea but no vomiting. She was referred for further studies to rule out cholecystitis and localized ulcer perforation.

    Diagnosis: Possible cholecystitis and/or perforated gastric ulcer.

R10.13 Epigastric pain

R11.0 Nausea

Comments: Only symptoms can be coded for this visit because questionable diagnoses are coded as if established only for hospital inpatients. Conditions are coded to the highest level of certainty on physician office visits. Either abdominal pain or nausea can be sequenced as the reason for the encounter.

Inpatient admission (episode 2): An ultrasound was negative and an upper GI failed to yield a diagnosis. Therefore, the patient was admitted for further evaluation because of the continued severity of her abdominal pain. An exploratory laparotomy was performed and immediately revealed a perforated appendix lying in a subhepatic space with abscess. An appendectomy was performed. The abscess cleared post-operatively with administration of high doses of intravenous antibiotics.

Discharge diagnosis: Appendicitis with perforation and subhepatic abscess.

K35.3 Acute appendicitis with localized peritonitis

0DTJ0ZZ Resection of appendix, open approach

Comments: The patient's symptomatology was explained by the definitive finding of appendicitis with perforation. Abdominal pain and nausea are inherent to appendicitis and should not be coded separately. Perforation and peritonitis are both included in code K35.3.

18. Inpatient admission: The patient was admitted with vague abdominal pain, and a workup was carried out. All laboratory findings were within normal limits, except for a slightly elevated white blood count. The patient requested transfer to another hospital close to his home for further evaluation. The patient was transferred with a working diagnosis of diverticulitis versus colon tumor.

Discharge diagnosis: Diverticulitis versus tumor of colon.

K57.92 Diverticulitis of intestine, part unspecified, without perforation or abscess without bleeding

D49.0 Neoplasm of unspecified behavior of digestive system

Comments: When diagnoses are stated in a comparative or contrasting manner, both conditions are coded and sequenced according to the circumstances of admission. In this instance, either condition is consistent with abdominal pain, and either can be sequenced as the principal diagnosis.

19. Inpatient admission: The patient, an eight-year-old boy, was brought in from school because of persistent cyclical vomiting with accompanying abdominal pain. He was admitted for observation and monitoring of vital signs. Laboratory work was within normal limits, vital signs remained stable, the abdomen remained flat and soft, and there was no muscle guarding or tenderness. He was discharged the following day in an improved condition.

Discharge diagnoses: (1) Cyclical vomiting, (2) abdominal pain.

G43.A0 Cyclical vomiting, not intractable

R10.9 Unspecified abdominal pain

Comments: Vomiting, not otherwise specified, is coded as a symptom. However, when the vomiting is specified as cyclical, it is classified to code G43.A0.

20. Inpatient admission: The patient had a history of recurrent infections in the perianal area. He was seen two days earlier in the physician's office for a perianal abscess and anal fistula. The prescribed medication and enemas did not alleviate the situation, so he was admitted for surgical intervention. In surgery, an anal fistulotomy was performed on the skin of the perineum with drainage of the perianal abscess. The patient responded to further treatments of antibiotics and diet and was to be followed in the office.

Discharge diagnoses: (1) Perianal abscess, (2) anal fistula.

K61.0 Anal abscess

K60.3 Anal fistula

0D9QXZZ Drainage of anus, external approach

0H89XZZ Division of perineum skin, external approach

21. **Inpatient admission:** The patient is status post heart transplantation six months earlier. Since then, he had been admitted numerous times for fever and diarrhea, presumably due to cytomegalovirus. On this occasion, he was admitted for further evaluation of fever and diarrhea. Stool and blood cultures were negative. A single, shallow erosion in the colon was viewed and biopsied on colonoscopy. Internal, bleeding hemorrhoids were also visualized. The pathology report showed moderate, nonspecific, chronic colitis with no diagnostic evidence of cytomegalovirus. Chronic colitis was determined to be the cause of the patient's symptomatology. The patient was also followed by endocrinology for his diabetes, and no changes were recommended in his medication. His diarrhea improved, medication and diet were prescribed for bleeding hemorrhoids and chronic colitis, and he was released.

    Discharge diagnoses: (1) Chronic colitis; (2) bleeding internal hemorrhoids; (3) diabetes mellitus, type 1; (4) status post heart transplant.

K52.9	Noninfective gastroenteritis and colitis, unspecified
K64.8	Other hemorrhoids
E10.9	Type 1 diabetes mellitus without complications
Z94.1	Heart transplant status
Z79.4	Long term (current) use of insulin
0DBE8ZX	Excision of large intestine, via natural or artificial opening endoscopic, diagnostic

Comments: Chronic colitis is designated as the principal diagnosis because it is the condition, established after study, that necessitated admission. A previous heart transplant is significant to the current care and treatment of the patient. A code for long-term insulin use is not required for type 1 diabetics because these patients require insulin. However, this code may be assigned, if desired, to provide additional information.

The biopsy was performed during the colonoscopy; therefore, the root operation is "Excision," with a qualifier for "diagnostic."

22. **Inpatient admission:** The patient had undergone cardiac transplantation about three years earlier. On this occasion, he came to the emergency department with a three-day history of right lower quadrant pain. The white blood count was elevated, and a small-bowel X-ray examination showed some dilated small bowel loops but no free air. He was admitted, and an abdominal gastrointestinal ultrasound showed a mass measuring about 5 by 5 by 4 centimeters, which was presumed to be an appendiceal cyst. He underwent an ultrasound-directed percutaneous right lower quadrant aspiration; only a few drops of material were collected for diagnostic examination. Blood cultures were sterile, leukocytosis improved, and he remained afebrile with gradually decreasing pain. He was discharged on antibiotics and was to return in a few weeks for an interval appendectomy.

    Discharge diagnoses: (1) Probable appendiceal cyst, (2) status post cardiac transplantation.

    Procedure performed: Ultrasound-directed aspiration of appendiceal mass.

K38.8	Other specified diseases of appendix
Z94.1	Heart transplant status
0D9J3ZX	Drainage of appendix, percutaneous approach, diagnostic

Comments: Probable appendiceal cyst is coded as though confirmed. The fact that the patient had a transplanted heart is important during all subsequent medical care. Aspiration of appendiceal mass for diagnostic examination is coded to the root operation "Drainage," percutaneous approach, with a qualifier for "diagnostic."

9. DISEASES OF THE GENITOURINARY SYSTEM

1. **Inpatient admission:** The patient, an 83-year-old woman, came in through the emergency department complaining of fever, confusion, and lethargy. Urine and blood cultures were positive for *E. coli.* Sepsis and urinary tract infection were diagnosed. The patient slowly responded to IV antibiotic therapy, but she began to experience vomiting episodes with abdominal pain. These episodes were probably related to her hiatal hernia with reflux esophagitis. The vomiting seemed to improve with medications and diet. The patient was discharged one week following admission on oral Keflex and Zantac to follow up as an outpatient.

   Discharge diagnoses: (1) Urinary tract infection, (2) gram-negative sepsis secondary to diagnosis 1, (3) hiatal hernia with reflux esophagitis.

A41.51 Sepsis due to Escherichia coli [E. coli]

N39.0 Urinary tract infection, site not specified

B96.20 Unspecified Escherichia coli [E. coli] as the cause of diseases classified elsewhere

K44.9 Diaphragmatic hernia without obstruction or gangrene

K21.0 Gastro-esophageal reflux disease with esophagitis

Comments: Although sepsis and urinary tract infection (UTI) were both present on admission, sepsis is sequenced as the principal diagnosis as guided by the ICD-10-CM Official Coding Guidelines (Section I.C.1.d.4, Sepsis and severe sepsis with a localized infection). That guideline provides direction to sequence first the code for the underlying systemic infection when the reason for the admission is both sepsis and a localized infection. ICD-10-CM codes both the sepsis and the causative agent in one code. However, because *E. coli* grew in both the urine and blood cultures, code B96.20 is assigned to identify the infectious agent responsible for the UTI. The hiatal hernia is coded because it was treated.

2. **Inpatient admission:** The patient was admitted for abnormal uterine bleeding. An ultrasound performed prior to admission suggested a possible bicornuate uterus. Because of her morbid obesity, a hysteroscopy with dilation and curettage was performed. Findings indicated a single cavity without any septum, polyps, or submucous fibroids. The patient was seen by the dietitian and discharged on a 1,500-calorie diet to reduce her weight.

   Discharge diagnoses: (1) Morbid obesity, (2) abnormal uterine bleeding unrelated to menstruation.

N93.9 Abnormal uterine and vaginal bleeding, unspecified

E66.01 Morbid (severe) obesity due to excess calories

0UDB8ZZ Extraction of endometrium, via natural or artificial opening endoscopic

3. **Inpatient admission:** The patient, a young man with hypertensive heart disease and end-stage renal disease, was admitted for placement of an arteriovenous fistula in his left arm to prepare for hemodialysis. The AV fistula was accomplished between the left radial artery and cephalic antebrachial vein in the lower arm. A single hemodialysis session was provided to treat the end-stage chronic kidney disease.

   Discharge diagnoses: (1) Hypertensive heart disease and nephrosclerosis, (2) end-stage chronic kidney disease.

I13.11	Hypertensive heart and chronic kidney disease without heart failure, with stage 5 chronic kidney disease, or end stage renal disease
N18.6	End stage renal disease
031C0ZF	Bypass left radial artery to lower arm vein, open approach
5A1D00Z	Performance of urinary filtration, single

Comments: When a patient is admitted for placement of a fistula for future dialysis, the condition necessitating the dialysis is coded as the principal diagnosis. Hypertensive heart disease, kidney disease, and chronic kidney disease are classified to the combination code I13.11. Code N18.6 is assigned as an additional code to identify the specific end-stage renal disease. The creation of the AV fistula is classified to the root operation "Bypass." According to the *ICD-10-PCS Official Coding Guidelines* (B3.6a), the fourth-character body part in bypass procedures specifies the body part bypassed "from" (radial artery); and the qualifier specifies the body part bypassed "to" (cephalic antebrachial vein). In the context of hemodialysis access, blood flow is generally bypassed from the artery to the vein (high-pressure system to low-pressure system).

4. **Inpatient admission:** The patient had a history of frequent episodes of severe chronic interstitial cystitis. Despite previous treatment, she has had no resolution of her symptoms. She was admitted for and received an open partial cystectomy and bilateral ileoureterostomy.

   Discharge diagnosis: Severe, chronic interstitial cystitis.

N30.10	Interstitial cystitis (chronic) without hematuria
0TBB0ZZ	Excision of bladder, open approach
0T180ZC	Bypass bilateral ureters to ileocutaneous, open approach

Comments: Because only part of the bladder was removed, the root operation is "Excision." The ileoureterostomy involves both ureters being diverted via the ileum to the outside of the body and is classified to the root operation "Bypass." The partial cystectomy is sequenced as the principal procedure because it is the procedure most closely related to the principal diagnosis of cystitis.

5. **Inpatient admission:** The patient had chronic kidney disease secondary to malignant hypertension and was status post insertion of a left arteriovenous fistula six months earlier. He presented with exacerbation of his renal condition and was admitted for evaluation and hemodialysis. His medications were adjusted, and he received several hemodialysis sessions during this admission. His condition stabilized, and he was discharged in an improved state.

   Discharge diagnoses: (1) End-stage renal disease associated with malignant hypertension, (2) exacerbation of kidney disease.

I12.0	Hypertensive chronic kidney disease with stage 5 chronic kidney disease or end stage renal disease
N18.6	End stage renal disease
Z99.2	Dependence on renal dialysis
5A1D60Z	Performance of urinary filtration, multiple

Comments: Code I12.0 is a combination code that encompasses the hypertension and the patient's chronic kidney disease. ICD-10-CM does not distinguish between malignant and benign forms of hypertension. There is no additional code available to indicate the exacerbation of the renal failure. Acute renal failure is not an exacerbation of chronic kidney disease; it is essentially a different condition. An additional code, N18.6, is assigned to identify the end-stage renal disease. Assign code Z99.2 to identify that the patient is a dialysis patient.

6. **Inpatient admission:** The patient had end-stage renal disease and chronic kidney disease secondary to hypertension. He was admitted for a cadaveric renal transplant. He underwent a single renal hemodialysis session prior to transplant. The left donor kidney was placed in the right iliac fossa. Postoperative recovery was uneventful.

   Discharge diagnosis: End-stage renal disease resulting from hypertension.

I12.0	Hypertensive chronic kidney disease with stage 5 chronic kidney disease or end stage renal disease
N18.6	End stage renal disease
0TY10Z0	Transplantation of left kidney, allogeneic, open approach
5A1D00Z	Performance of urinary filtration, single

Comments: Code I12.0 is a combination code that encompasses the hypertension and the patient's chronic kidney disease. The fact that the kidney transplant is from a cadaver is indicated via the qualifier for allogeneic.

7. **Inpatient admission:** The patient became ill the day before admission with nausea, vomiting, dysuria, and hematuria. Initial laboratory work included a urinalysis report of RBCs too numerous to count, and a repeat urinalysis the following day reported the same results. On contrast retrograde pyelogram of both kidneys, the ureters, and the bladder, hydronephrosis of the right kidney and possibly some secondary hydronephrosis with obstruction of the ureteropelvic junction were seen. Spontaneously, the hematuria and other symptoms cleared. The patient was to be referred to a urologist for follow-up.

   Discharge diagnosis: Hematuria and hydronephrosis possibly due to idiopathic ureteropelvic obstruction.

N13.1	Hydronephrosis with ureteral stricture, not elsewhere classified
R31.9	Hematuria, unspecified
BT14YZZ	Fluoroscopy of kidneys, ureters and bladder using other contrast

Comments: ICD-10-CM has a combination code that identifies both the ureteral obstruction and the hydronephrosis.

8. **Physician office visit (episode 1):** The patient, an elderly man, has had carcinoma of the bladder with numerous recurrences since 2007. On his annual bladder checkup, an obstructive prostate with urinary retention was present, but no evidence of a recurrence of the carcinoma was found. He was to be admitted for further evaluation of the prostatic obstruction.

   Diagnoses: (1) Prostatic obstruction with urinary retention, (2) no evidence of recurrence of bladder carcinoma.

N40.1	Enlarged prostate with lower urinary tract symptoms
R33.8	Other retention of urine
Z85.51	Personal history of malignant neoplasm of bladder

Comments: The patient had not had any recurrence of carcinoma of the bladder. Therefore, code Z85.51 is assigned for history of bladder cancer. Code R33.8 is assigned as an additional code as indicated by the "use additional code" note at code N40.1.

Inpatient admission (episode 2): On cystoscopy, a mild urethral stricture and an obstructive prostate with urinary retention were found. The urethra was dilated, and the patient underwent transurethral prostatectomy (TURP) without complication. The pathology report showed benign prostatic hypertrophy.

Discharge diagnoses: (1) Urethral stricture secondary to benign prostatic hypertrophy (BPH), (2) urinary retention, (3) history of carcinoma of the bladder.

N40.1	Enlarged prostate with lower urinary tract symptoms
N35.8	Other urethral stricture
R33.8	Other retention of urine
Z85.51	Personal history of malignant neoplasm of bladder
0VB08ZZ	Excision of prostate, via natural or artificial opening endoscopic
0T7D8ZZ	Dilation of urethra, via natural or artificial opening endoscopic

Comments: Code N40.1 includes the BPH and lower urinary tract symptoms, but additional codes are needed for the urethral stricture and the urinary retention. Only a part of the prostate is removed in a TURP, so the root operation "Excision" is used.

9. **Inpatient admission:** The nursing home patient had frequent urinary tract infections and numerous courses of antibiotics. The most recent urine culture grew *Pseudomonas aeruginosa,* resistant to all oral antibiotics. The patient was admitted for IV antibiotic therapy. Significant in her history was the placement about three years earlier of a cardiac pacemaker for conduction defects. It was working satisfactorily during her hospitalization. Because the cultures continued to show *Pseudomonas* after IV antibiotics were given, a cystoscopy was performed. The patient still had a bladder infection with erythema of the bladder wall. Urine cultures were obtained at that time, and the report showed a high colony count of *Pseudomonas* that was then susceptible to oral antibiotics. She was discharged on oral Cipro.

   Discharge diagnoses: (1) Bladder infection, resistant to oral antibiotics; (2) pacemaker in situ.

N30.90	Cystitis, unspecified without hematuria
B96.5	Pseudomonas (aeruginosa) (mallei) (pseudomallei) as the cause of diseases classified elsewhere
Z16.24	Resistance to multiple antibiotics
Z95.0	Presence of cardiac pacemaker
0TJB8ZZ	Inspection of bladder, via natural or artificial opening endoscopic

Comments: The cystoscopy specified the urinary tract infection to be of the bladder; therefore, the more specific code of N30.90 is used. Code Z16.24 shows that the *Pseudomonas* was resistant to multiple antibiotics.

10. **Inpatient admission:** The patient was experiencing heavy, abnormal uterine bleeding and abdominal pain. On vaginal examination, there was bright red blood in the vagina and the left adnexa was enlarged. The woman was admitted and taken to surgery, where an exploratory laparotomy revealed a left follicular ovarian cyst. While the surgeon was examining the left ovary, the cyst spontaneously ruptured. An ovarian cystectomy was performed without complication. The postoperative course was uneventful, and the patient was discharged.

    Discharge diagnosis: Ruptured left follicular ovarian cyst.

N83.0 Follicular cyst of ovary

0UB10ZZ Excision of left ovary, open approach

Comments: The laparotomy is the approach to the "Excision" of the cyst.

11. **Inpatient admission:** The male patient was admitted with severe colic secondary to a left ureteral calculus. A cystoscopy was performed, and a stone extracted. On retrograde pyelography, no stone was seen in the ureter or kidney. However, the pathology report indicated that only a small fragment of the stone was retrieved. Postoperatively, the patient did well at first but then began having severe colic again. He was returned to surgery for another cystoscopy. The remainder of the stone was located in the distal left ureter and extracted. The postoperative course was uncomplicated.

    Discharge diagnosis: Left ureteral calculus.

N20.1 Calculus of ureter

0TC78ZZ Extirpation of matter from left ureter, via natural or artificial opening endoscopic

0TC78ZZ Extirpation of matter from left ureter, via natural or artificial opening endoscopic

BT14YZZ Fluoroscopy of kidneys, ureters and bladder using other contrast

Comments: Because the cystoscopic calculus extraction was repeated, the code is assigned twice to identify two separate surgical procedures. The procedure for extraction of ureteral calculus is classified to the root operation "Extirpation," taking or cutting out solid matter from a body part.

12. **Inpatient admission:** The patient, a woman with insignificant past medical and surgical history, was the sister of a patient with end-stage renal disease secondary to hypertension. She was to be a living related kidney donor for her brother. She was prepared for surgery the day of admission, but due to her brother's active hepatitis C infection, the surgery was canceled.

    Discharge diagnoses: (1) Kidney donor, (2) procedure canceled.

Z52.4 Kidney donor

Z53.8 Procedure and treatment not carried out for other reasons

Comments: Code Z52.4 is indexed in the Alphabetic Index of Diseases and Injuries under the main term **Donor,** subterm "kidney." Code Z53.8 is indexed under **Procedure** (surgical), "not done," "specified reason NEC." Because it is the brother's condition and not the donor's that necessitated the decision to cancel the procedure, code Z53.8, not Z53.09, is assigned.

13. **Inpatient admission:** The patient was previously evaluated and found to be a suitable kidney donor for his eight-year-old son. A total unilateral left donor nephrectomy was performed without complication, and the patient was discharged.

Discharge diagnosis: Donor nephrectomy.

Z52.4	Kidney donor
0TT10ZZ	Resection of left kidney, open approach

Comments: Code Z52.4 is indexed in the Alphabetic Index under the main entry **Donor,** subterm "kidney."

14. **Inpatient admission:** The patient, a young woman, was admitted with a two-day history of dysuria, frequency, and urgency, with onset of severe flank pain on the evening prior to admission. A laboratory workup confirmed pyelonephritis, and she was immediately started on intravenous medications and fluid. Urine cultures grew *Enterobacter aerogenes,* which was sensitive to several antibiotics.

Discharge diagnoses: (1) Acute pyelonephritis, (2) abdominal and flank pain.

N10	Acute tubulo-interstitial nephritis
B96.89	Other specified bacterial agents as the cause of diseases classified elsewhere

Comments: All symptoms are integral to pyelonephritis and are not coded. Because the organism is not identified in the title of code N10, code B96.89 is added to provide further specificity.

15. **Inpatient admission:** The patient was admitted for a hysterectomy. Prior to admission, a diagnostic workup showed extensive endometriosis involving the uterus, ovaries, and fallopian tubes. Because the patient had asthma, she was seen by the pulmonary consult service and cleared for surgery. A total abdominal hysterectomy and a bilateral salpingo-oophorectomy were performed without complication. Postoperatively, the patient did well and was discharged.

Discharge diagnoses: (1) Endometriosis of uterus, ovaries, and fallopian tubes; (2) asthma.

N80.0	Endometriosis of uterus
N80.1	Endometriosis of ovary
N80.2	Endometriosis of fallopian tube
J45.909	Unspecified asthma, uncomplicated
0UT90ZZ	Resection of uterus, open approach
0UTC0ZZ	Resection of cervix, open approach
0UT20ZZ	Resection of bilateral ovaries, open approach
0UT70ZZ	Resection of bilateral fallopian tubes, open approach

Comments: Any of the category endometriosis codes can be designated as the principal diagnosis.

The total abdominal hysterectomy (0UT90ZZ) is designated as the principal procedure code because it is most consistent with endometriosis of the uterus. However, if code N80.1 or N80.2 were sequenced as the principal diagnosis, the bilateral removal of either the ovaries or fallopian tubes would have been sequenced as the principal procedure. Separate codes are assigned to reflect the "Resection" of the uterus, cervix, ovaries, and fallopian tubes.

16. **Inpatient admission:** The patient, a young woman, was admitted for treatment of a persistent, symptomatic right adnexal mass. The cystic mass was about 5 centimeters and presumed to be ovarian in origin. An exploratory laparotomy was performed, with right ovarian cystectomy. Pathologic findings confirmed a follicular cyst. The patient's postoperative course was unremarkable, and she was discharged.

    Discharge diagnosis: Follicular cyst, right ovary.

N83.0	Follicular cyst of ovary
0UB00ZZ	Excision of right ovary, open approach

Comments: The laparotomy is the approach to the "Excision" of the cyst.

17. **Inpatient admission:** A patient with irregular but heavy menstruation and hirsute of face and abdomen was seen for an X-ray that was suggestive of ovarian mass. An exploratory laparotomy was performed with wedge biopsy of both ovaries; results were consistent with primary polycystic ovary syndrome. The patient was started on oral contraceptives to decrease testosterone levels.

    Discharge diagnosis: Polycystic ovary syndrome.

E28.2	Polycystic ovarian syndrome
0UB20ZX	Excision of bilateral ovaries, open approach, diagnostic

Comments: The exploratory laparotomy is not coded separately; the inspection of a body part that is integral to the performance of a procedure is not coded separately.

18. **Inpatient admission:** The patient had a four-month history of gross hematuria. A kidney ultrasound showed lesion of bladder. A cystoscopy confirmed lesion of trigone bladder. The patient was then admitted for open radical cystoprostatectomy with urinary diversion due to infiltrative mucinous adenocarcinoma. Once the bladder was removed, an ureteroenteric anastomosis was performed to connect the ureters to a newly created ileostomy.

    Discharge diagnosis: Adenocarcinoma trigone bladder.

C67.0	Malignant neoplasm of trigone of bladder
0TTB0ZZ	Resection of bladder, open approach
0VT00ZZ	Resection of prostate, open approach
0T180ZC	Bypass bilateral ureters to ileocutaneous, open approach

Comments: The radical cystoprostatectomy is coded to the root operation "Resection" for both the bladder and the prostate. Code 0T180ZC is assigned for the anastomosis between the ureters and the ileostomy.

10. DISEASES OF THE SKIN AND SUBCUTANEOUS TISSUE

1. **Inpatient admission:** The female patient was admitted for treatment of an open wound of the scalp with cellulitis of the scalp and left ear. The wound was the result of a cut two days before admission. Excisional debridement of both the scalp and the left ear was carried out in the operating room. The patient was treated with antibiotics during her two-day stay. She was discharged on oral antibiotics in an improved condition.

   Discharge diagnosis: Cellulitis of scalp and ear secondary to scalp laceration.

S01.01xA	Laceration without foreign body of scalp, initial encounter
L03.811	Cellulitis of head [any part, except face]
H60.12	Cellulitis of left external ear
0HB0XZZ	Excision of scalp skin, external approach
0HB3XZZ	Excision of left ear skin, external approach

Comments: The open wound is sequenced as the principal diagnosis based on the circumstances of admission. Also, treatment was directed primarily toward the open wound (excisional debridement).

2. **Inpatient admission:** The patient, a young man with spina bifida of the lumbar region, was admitted for excision of a sacral pressure ulcer. He had a ventriculoperitoneal shunt in place on the right side for hydrocephalus. The lesion was successfully fulgurated without complication.

   Discharge diagnoses: (1) Stage III pressure ulcer, sacrum; (2) lumbar spina bifida; (3) status post placement of a ventriculoperitoneal shunt for hydrocephalus.

L89.153	Pressure ulcer of sacral region, stage 3
Q05.2	Lumbar spina bifida with hydrocephalus
Z98.2	Presence of cerebrospinal fluid drainage device
0H56XZZ	Destruction of back skin, external approach

Comments: The site and the stage of the pressure ulcer are captured in one code. Hydrocephalus and lumbar region spina bifida are included in code Q05.2. The ventriculoperitoneal shunt is present but did not require attention (Z98.2). Fulguration of skin is classified to the root operation "Destruction."

3. **Inpatient admission:** The female patient was admitted from the nursing home with a large stage III sacral pressure ulcer, which was treated with excisional debridement and a flap-graft closure of the back. She had chronic lymphocytic B-cell leukemia, which required peripheral vein transfusions with three units of whole blood. She was stabilized and returned to the nursing home.

   Discharge diagnoses: (1) Pressure ulcer, sacrum; (2) chronic lymphocytic leukemia.

L89.153	Pressure ulcer of sacral region, stage 3
C91.10	Chronic lymphocytic leukemia of B-cell type not having achieved remission
0HB6XZZ	Excision of back skin, external approach
0HX6XZZ	Transfer back skin, external approach
30233H1	Transfusion of nonautologous whole blood into peripheral vein, percutaneous approach

Comments: The site and the stage of the pressure ulcer are captured in one code. After the excisional debridement, closure was accomplished by flap graft, which is synonymous with pedicle graft of skin. This is classified to the root operation "Transfer."

4. **Inpatient admission:** The patient, an elderly man, had an acute onset of swelling, erythema, and tenderness in the left anterior neck. He was admitted for evaluation and IV antibiotic therapy, with provisional diagnoses of thyroiditis and cellulitis. Radiological findings showed a large, mixed-density, soft-tissue mass in the left lower neck compatible with cellulitis. The mass appeared to involve the soft tissue of the neck but not the thyroid gland. Abscess formation could not be excluded, although none was directly visualized. His symptomatology responded well to antibiotic therapy.

   Discharge diagnoses: (1) Cellulitis, (2) possible abscess.

L03.221 Cellulitis of neck

L02.11 Cutaneous abscess of neck

Comments: The thyroiditis is not coded because it was ruled out.

5. **Inpatient admission:** The patient's admitting diagnoses were abdominal pain and ventral wall hernia. The woman presented for hernia repair. At the time of surgery, she was noted to have numerous mid-abdominal adhesions of the peritoneum, mostly in the area of a previous midline scar. Sharp lysis of the extensive adhesions was undertaken, and then the hernia was repaired. Postoperatively, the patient did very well.

   Discharge diagnoses: (1) Ventral wall hernia, (2) abdominal adhesions.

K43.9 Ventral hernia, without obstruction or gangrene

K66.0 Peritoneal adhesions (postprocedural) (postinfection)

0WQF0ZZ Repair abdominal wall, open approach

0DNW0ZZ Release peritoneum, open approach

Comments: The express reason for admission was hernia repair; therefore, the hernia is sequenced as the principal diagnosis. Abdominal adhesions are coded because they required extensive lysis before attention could be directed to the hernia repair and were documented as a discharge diagnosis. The lysis of adhesions is coded to the root operation "Release."

6. **Inpatient admission:** The patient was admitted for intravenous antibiotic treatment of cellulitis of the left leg secondary to a minor scratch. By the third hospital day, the erythema was much improved. During the entire hospitalization, the patient, a known opioid drug abuser, exhibited considerable drug-seeking behavior and requested narcotics, especially IV morphine. All narcotics were discontinued on the third hospital day, and he exhibited no withdrawal symptoms. He was discharged for follow-up in the physician's office.

   Discharge diagnoses: (1) Cellulitis, left leg; (2) drug abuse; (3) scratch, left leg.

L03.116 Cellulitis of left lower limb

F11.10 Opioid abuse, uncomplicated

Comments: No code is assigned for the minor injury (scratch on leg) because it had progressed to cellulitis, and the cellulitis is coded instead.

7. **Inpatient admission:** A patient was diagnosed with radiation recall dermatitis of the right chest after starting Amoxicillin for urinary tract infection due to E. coli. Medical history indicated administration of extra-beam radiation to the area one year ago in treatment of poorly differentiated squamous cell carcinoma of right lung. Provider documented that the dermatitis at the previously irradiated chest was the result of the prescribed antibiotic use. The Amoxicillin was discontinued and the patient was started on a different antibiotic.

   Discharge diagnoses: (1) Dermatitis of right chest, (2) urinary tract infection, (3) current primary carcinoma of right lung, (4) history of radiation.

L27.1	Localized skin eruption due to drugs and medicaments taken internally
T36.0x5A	Adverse effect of penicillins
N39.0	Urinary tract infection, site not specified
B96.20	Unspecified Escherichia coli [E. coli] as the cause of diseases classified elsewhere
C34.90	Malignant neoplasm of unspecified part of unspecified bronchus or lung
Z92.3	Personal history of irradiation

Comments: The provider documentation specifies that the dermatitis was caused by the Amoxicillin, not the radiation therapy. Therefore, code L59.8, Other specified disorders of the skin and subcutaneous tissue related to radiation, is not appropriate unless the dermatitis was actually caused by the radiation therapy.

8. **Inpatient admission:** A patient was admitted for incision and drainage of chin abscess. A blade was used to open the draining area. A small amount of purulent material was expressed. The area was bluntly dissected widely around the abscess pocket, and the wound was drained of fluid.

   Discharge diagnosis: Incision and drainage of MRSA abscess of the skin.

L02.01	Cutaneous abscess of face
B95.62	Methicillin resistant Staphylococcus aureus infection as the cause of diseases classified elsewhere
0H91XZZ	Drainage of face skin, external approach

Comments: Incision and drainage of an abscess is coded to the root operation "Drainage." Drainage of the skin layer of the chin is assigned code 0H91XZZ.

9. **Outpatient visit:** A patient was seen for six-month swelling and tenderness of the left cheek. Biopsy of the skin and subcutaneous tissue of the area resulted in a diagnosis of hyaline necrosis, a hallmark for lupus profundus.

   Discharge diagnosis: Lupus erythematosus profundus.

L93.2	Other local lupus erythematosus
0JB10ZX	Excision of face subcutaneous tissue and fascia, open approach, diagnostic

Comments: Excision of overlapping layers, such as the skin, subcutaneous tissue, and fascia, is coded to the deepest layer. Code 0JB10ZX identifies the biopsy of the subcutaneous layer.

11. DISEASES OF THE MUSCULOSKELETAL SYSTEM AND CONNECTIVE TISSUE

1. **Inpatient admission:** The patient had experienced increasingly severe pain in his left arm, left shoulder, and neck for two months. A magnetic resonance imaging performed prior to admission showed evidence of a C7-T1 disc herniation. His only other health problem was benign hypertension, controlled with medications. He was admitted for a cervical laminotomy and complete cervical discectomy of the cervical thoracic disc, which was performed by oblique, muscle-splitting incision. His postoperative course was unremarkable, and he was discharged after two days.

   Discharge diagnoses: (1) Cervical disc herniation, C7-T1; (2) benign essential hypertension.

M50.23	Other cervical disc displacement, cervicothoracic region
I10	Essential (primary) hypertension
0RT50ZZ	Resection of cervicothoracic vertebral disc, open approach

Comments: The cervical disc herniation is at C7-T1 (between the last cervical disc and the first thoracic disc); therefore, the code for the cervical thoracic region is selected. Hypertension, although under control, is coded because it is a coexisting chronic, systemic condition that meets the UHDDS definition of additional diagnosis. Because the entire disc is removed, "Resection" is the root operation.

2. **Outpatient encounter (episode 1):** The patient's complaints were neck pain that radiated into both arms, hand pain with numbness and clumsiness, and electric shock–type pains down her body when she bent down. A magnetic resonance imaging scan showed marked spinal stenosis at C3-C4 and C5-C6. She was to be admitted for repair of the spinal stenosis.

   Diagnosis: Spinal stenosis.

M48.02	Spinal stenosis, cervical region
BR30ZZZ	Magnetic resonance imaging (MRI) of cervical spine

Comments: The symptoms (pain, numbness, and clumsiness) are integral to the diagnosis of spinal stenosis and therefore are not coded. Code BR30ZZZ is assigned for the magnetic imaging of the spine.

   Inpatient admission (episode 2): The patient was admitted for repair of spinal stenosis. A laminectomy with fusion of C3-C4 and C5-C6 was carried out using an anterior approach with a graft of bone excised from the right iliac crest.

   Discharge diagnosis: Severe cervical spine stenosis.

M48.02	Spinal stenosis, cervical region
0RG2070	Fusion of 2 or more cervical vertebral joints with autologous tissue substitute, anterior approach, anterior column, open approach
0RB30ZZ	Excision of cervical vertebral disc, open approach
0QB20ZZ	Excision of right pelvic bone, open approach

Comments: The procedure code 0RG2070 includes the number of vertebral joints fused: two or more. An anterior approach is used and is indicated in the qualifier character. The bone graft harvesting is classified to the root operation "Excision." The iliac crest is classified to the body part value "pelvic bone."

3. **Inpatient admission:** The patient, a 33-year-old woman, had a history of low back pain. She recently developed intractable left sciatic pain and paresthesia. Lumbar magnetic resonance imaging procedures, performed prior to admission, showed progressive lumbosacral disc herniation on the left. She was also receiving medications for gastric ulcers and asthma, and these were continued during the hospital stay. A lumbosacral microdiscectomy was performed for a protruded lumbosacral disc herniation, which also had a subligamentous extrusion. The patient recovered with resolution of symptoms and was discharged to follow up with her physician in one week.

   Discharge diagnoses: (1) Lumbosacral disc extrusion, (2) gastric ulcers, (3) asthma.

M51.27	Other intervertebral disc displacement, lumbosacral region
K25.9	Gastric ulcer, unspecified as acute or chronic, without hemorrhage or perforation
J45.909	Unspecified asthma, uncomplicated
0SB40ZZ	Excision of lumbosacral disc, open approach

Comments: The term **Extrusion** leads to the note "see Displacement, intervertebral disc" in the Alphabetic Index. Because asthma and ulcers are under current treatment and meet the UHDDS definition of additional diagnoses, they are assigned codes as coexisting conditions. In a microdiscectomy, only a portion of the disc is removed, so the root operation "Excision" is used.

4. **Inpatient admission:** The teenage patient had complained of left hip pain for the past three weeks. The pain started after a fall that occurred while he was playing basketball in a gym. X-rays revealed a grade I, slipped capital femoral epiphysis of the left hip. The hip was pinned percutaneously, and the postoperative course was uneventful.

   Discharge diagnosis: Slipped capital femoral epiphysis, left hip.

S79.012A	Salter-Harris Type I physeal fracture of upper end of left femur, initial encounter for closed fracture
W18.30xA	Fall on same level, unspecified, initial encounter
Y92.39	Other specified sports and athletic area as the place of occurrence of the external cause
Y93.67	Activity, basketball
Y99.8	Other external cause status
0QH734Z	Insertion of internal fixation device into left upper femur, percutaneous approach

Comments: For the slipped epiphysis, refer to the term "slipped" in the Index. See the note for subterm "current traumatic," which says to code as fracture by site. Under the main term **Fracture,** subterm "femur," the subterm "capital epiphyseal" is indexed to S79.01-. ICD-10-CM guidelines for fractures state that a fracture not specified as displaced or not displaced is coded as displaced. Activity and status codes are included for playing basketball as a recreational activity.

There was no reduction of the slipped epiphysis, but an "internal fixation device" was inserted.

5. **Inpatient admission:** An emergency open repair of a right rotator cuff tear was performed on this patient after she was crushed between a sliding patio door and its frame at her apartment. Exploration revealed a torn right rotator cuff and ruptured deltoid muscle, right shoulder. Open repair of the rotator cuff tendon and repair of the ruptured deltoid muscle were accomplished. The patient recovered and was discharged to follow-up in one week.

   Discharge diagnoses: (1) Tear, right rotator cuff; (2) rupture, deltoid muscle.

S46.011A	Strain of muscle and tendons of the rotator cuff of right shoulder, initial encounter
S46.811A	Strain of other muscles, fascia and tendons at shoulder and upper arm level, right arm, initial encounter
W23.0xxA	Caught, crushed, jammed, or pinched between moving objects, initial encounter
Y92.039	Unspecified place in apartment as the place of occurrence of the external cause
0LQ10ZZ	Repair right shoulder tendon, open approach
0KQ50ZZ	Repair right shoulder muscle, open approach

Comments: Either condition (rotator cuff tear or ruptured deltoid muscle) can be sequenced as the principal diagnosis because both were present on admission, both were surgically corrected, and both meet the UHDDS definition of principal diagnosis. The seventh character to indicate initial encounter is assigned. Although code S46.011- includes strain of muscle and tendons of the rotator cuff, the deltoid muscle is not part of the rotator cuff; therefore, a separate code is needed for rupture of the deltoid muscle. For the ruptured deltoid muscle, refer to the Index for the main term **Rupture,** subterm "muscle (traumatic)"; see also the main term **Strain.** Under the main term **Strain,** subterm "muscle," the coder is directed to see **Injury,** muscle, by site, strain. Because a specific entry for the deltoid muscle is not available and the deltoid is in the shoulder area, see **Injury,** muscle, shoulder, strain. The code referenced in the Index is for unspecified muscle. Code S46.811A is selected for strain of other muscle of the shoulder.

Activity is not stated, so no code is assigned.

6. **Inpatient admission:** The patient, status post cadaveric renal and pancreas transplants with type 2 diabetes and diabetic peripheral angiopathy, had a nonhealing ulcer on his left heel with muscle necrosis that had been debrided three weeks earlier. He came to the emergency department complaining of a three-day history of left foot pain, fever, and foul-smelling discharge from the ulcer. He was admitted, and a left below-the-knee amputation of the lower leg at the distal portion of the tibia and fibula was performed.

   Discharge diagnosis: Diabetic gangrene of the left foot.

E11.52	Type 2 diabetes mellitus with diabetic peripheral angiopathy with gangrene
L97.423	Non-pressure chronic ulcer of left heel and midfoot with necrosis of muscle
Z94.0	Kidney transplant status
Z94.83	Pancreas transplant status
0Y6J0Z3	Detachment at left lower leg, low, open approach

Comments: ICD-10-CM allows for the classification of the diabetes along with the manifestations in one code: E11.52 includes type 2 diabetes, peripheral angiopathy, and gangrene. Codes identifying the patient as status post renal and pancreas transplants are significant to the current episode of care and should be included.

For the procedure code, amputation is coded to the root operation "Detachment." The qualifier "low" in the seventh character is defined as amputation at the distal portion of the shaft of the tibia and fibula.

7. **Inpatient admission:** The patient, an elderly man with chest pain, was admitted to rule out acute myocardial infarct. Two weeks prior to admission, he had a respiratory infection that caused excessive coughing. On evaluation, there was no evidence of cardiac problems, and his chest pain was believed to be due to costochondritis secondary to excessive coughing.

   Discharge diagnosis: Costochondritis.

M94.0	Chondrocostal junction syndrome [Tietze]
R05	Cough

Comments: Costochondritis is assigned as the principal diagnosis because suspected conditions are coded as confirmed diagnoses for inpatients. Code R05 is assigned for the excessive coughing, which is the underlying cause of the costochondritis. No code is assigned for the chest pain, which is integral to the costochondritis.

8. **Inpatient admission:** The patient, an elderly woman, had severe pain in her left hip. The pain started after a hip fracture five years ago, when she was injured in an automobile accident. Her admission diagnoses were traumatic arthritis and ankylosis of the left hip. She also had a pacemaker and was a type 2 diabetic. A total hip replacement was performed without complication.

   Discharge diagnoses: (1) Arthritis and ankylosis secondary to old hip fracture, left side; (2) diabetes mellitus.

M12.552	Traumatic arthropathy, left hip
M24.652	Ankylosis, left hip
S72.002S	Fracture of unspecified part of neck of left femur, sequela
E11.9	Type 2 diabetes mellitus without complications
Z95.0	Presence of cardiac pacemaker
V49.9xxS	Car occupant (driver) (passenger) injured in unspecified traffic accident, sequela
0SRB0JZ	Replacement of left hip joint with synthetic substitute, open approach

Comments: ICD-10-CM allows for laterality; in this case, codes M12.552 and M24.652 include the designation of the left hip in the sixth character. In ICD-10-CM late effects of a fracture are coded as fracture, with the seventh-character value "S" to indicate sequelae. The Alphabetic Index instructs that fracture of the hip is coded as neck of the femur, so code S72.002S is selected for the late effect of the left hip fracture. The External cause code with the seventh-character value "S" indicates sequelae.

For the procedure code, the type of prosthesis used for the hip replacement is not specified, so the qualifier "Z" is selected.

9. **Inpatient admission:** The patient's right knee had bothered him for several months. He had a very painful chronic, indolent, septic prepatellar bursa. It was treated with many antibiotics, cleared up, and then recurred. He was currently admitted for surgical intervention. The site was incised and drained, and then the prepatellar bursa was partially excised. He was referred for physical therapy on discharge.

   Discharge diagnosis: Septic joint, right knee.

M00.861	Arthritis due to other bacteria, right knee
0MBN0ZZ	Excision of right knee bursa and ligament, open approach

Comments: A separate code is not assigned to identify the incision and drainage of the knee because it is integral to the procedural process for the bursectomy.

10. Inpatient admission: For two weeks, the patient had been complaining of left sciatica and had failed outpatient management with bed rest and pain medications. A magnetic resonance imaging procedure confirmed L5-S1 disc herniation on the left. She was hospitalized at complete bed rest with conservative management and pain medications as needed. She received good pain relief with IV pain medication and an epidural steroid injection. She was discharged for physical therapy follow-up.

Discharge diagnosis: Intractable pain secondary to herniation of the L5-S1 disc, with S1 radiculopathy.

M51.17	Intervertebral disc disorders with radiculopathy, lumbosacral region
3E0S33Z	Introduction of anti-inflammatory into epidural space, percutaneous approach

Comments: Intractable pain and radiculopathy are integral to the underlying disease and are therefore not coded. The epidural injection of the steroid is covered in code 3E0S33Z. Steroid is an anti-inflammatory; therefore, the sixth character value "3" is selected.

11. Inpatient admission: The patient was admitted with traumatic arthritis and ankylosis of the left hip due to an old fracture of the femoral neck suffered in a car accident. She was in good health except for suffering mild arteriosclerotic heart disease. X-rays were taken before surgery to evaluate the extent of this problem, but it was felt that it did not contradict the planned surgery. Both the femoral head and acetabulum of the left hip were replaced with a prosthesis. The surgery and postoperative course were without complication. She was transferred to a nursing home for rehabilitation therapy.

Discharge diagnoses: (1) Arthritis and ankylosis, left hip; (2) arteriosclerotic cardiovascular disease.

M24.652	Ankylosis, left hip
M12.552	Traumatic arthropathy, left hip
S72.002S	Fracture of unspecified part of neck of left femur, sequela
I25.10	Atherosclerotic heart disease of native coronary artery without angina pectoris
V49.9xxS	Car occupant (driver) (passenger) injured in unspecified traffic accident, sequela
0SRB0JZ	Replacement of left hip joint with synthetic substitute, open approach

Comments: Either ankylosis or arthritis could be designated as the principal diagnosis because both were equally responsible for the admission. Ankylosis and arthritis are late effects of the previous hip fracture, which is reflected in the S72.002S code as a sequela. Replacement of both the femoral head and the acetabulum is classified as a total hip replacement, 0SRB0JZ. The type of bearing surface for the hip replacement is not known, so the qualifier is listed as "Z."

12. Inpatient admission: The patient, a 12-year-old female, had a history of scoliosis secondary to neurofibromatosis, type 1, and had been treated with a brace for four years. She was now admitted for surgical repair of the progressive scoliosis. A posterior lumbar fusion of T2-L3 using Isola instrumentation interbody fusion device and right iliac crest bone grafting was performed. Her postoperative course was uneventful.

Discharge diagnosis: Thoracolumbar scoliosis secondary to neurofibromatosis, type 1.

M41.55	Other secondary scoliosis, thoracolumbar region
Q85.01	Neurofibromatosis, type 1
0RG80A1	Fusion of 8 or more thoracic vertebral joints with interbody fusion device, posterior approach, posterior column, open approach
0SG10A1	Fusion of 2 or more lumbar vertebral joints with interbody fusion device, posterior approach, posterior column, open approach
0QB20ZZ	Excision of right pelvic bone, open approach

Comments: In the Index, scoliosis secondary NEC is coded to M41.50. See the Tabular List to select the more specific code for the site. Q85.01 is listed for the type 1 neurofibromatosis.

The T2-L3 vertebrae were fused, meaning that 11 of the 12 thoracic vertebrae were fused in this area. In addition, three lumbar vertebrae were fused. Therefore, two procedure codes are necessary for the fusion procedure, one for the thoracic and one for the thoracolumbar vertebral joints. The ICD-10-PCS Official Coding Guidelines (B3.10.C) state that if an "interbody fusion device" is used to render the joint immobile (alone or containing other material like bone graft), the procedure is coded with the device value "interbody fusion device." The harvesting of the iliac crest bone for grafting is coded separately to the root operation "Excision."

13. Inpatient admission: A 59-year-old male was admitted for reverse total shoulder arthroplasty to treat severe degenerative joint disease of the right glenohumeral joint and supraspinatus tear of the right shoulder. The glenoid and humeral components were placed after ensuring adequate bone support.

Discharge diagnoses: (1) Supraspinatus tear, (2) degenerative joint disease of shoulder.

M75.101	Unspecified rotator cuff tear or rupture of right shoulder, not specified as traumatic
M19.011	Primary osteoarthritis, right shoulder
0RRJ00Z	Replacement of right shoulder joint with reverse ball and socket, synthetic substitute, open approach

Comments: The root operation "Replacement" is appropriate for the taking out of the native parts of the shoulder to put in synthetic material that will take their place.

14. Inpatient admission: A patient was seen for spontaneous rupture of the flexor digitorum profundus tendon of the left little finger. The area was opened for exploration; the proximal end of the tendon was repaired with sutures.

Discharge diagnosis: Rupture of the tendon of left little finger.

M66.342	Spontaneous rupture of flexor tendons, left hand
0LQ80ZZ	Repair left hand tendon, open approach

Comments: The exploration of the finger is not reported when the inspection is performed in order to achieve the repair.

12. COMPLICATIONS OF PREGNANCY, CHILDBIRTH, AND THE PUERPERIUM

1. **Inpatient admission (episode 1):** The patient was admitted with pregnancy at 38 weeks gestation. A repeat low transverse cervical cesarean section and elective open bilateral tubal ligation were performed. A 3,300-gram male infant was delivered, with Apgar scores of 9 and 10. The postoperative course was unremarkable. On day 3, the mother's staples were removed, and both the mother and the baby were discharged.

   Discharge diagnoses: (1) Term pregnancy delivered, (2) elective tubal ligation.

O34.21	Maternal care for scar from previous cesarean delivery
Z37.0	Single live birth
Z30.2	Encounter for sterilization
Z3A.38	38 weeks gestation of pregnancy
10D00Z1	Extraction of products of conception, low cervical, open approach
0UL70ZZ	Occlusion of bilateral fallopian tubes, open approach

Comments: The *ICD-10-CM Official Guidelines for Coding and Reporting* provide guidance on the selection of the principal or first-listed diagnosis in obstetrical encounters. In cases of cesarean delivery, the principal diagnosis should be the reason for the cesarean—unless the reason for the admission/encounter was unrelated to the condition necessitating the cesarean delivery. The fact that the patient had a previous cesarean delivery (O34.21) is therefore assigned first. The summary does not indicate any other condition requiring cesarean delivery. Code Z30.2 is assigned to indicate that a tubal ligation was performed for elective sterilization. To indicate the outcome of delivery (e.g., single birth, multiple birth), code Z37.0 is assigned. Code Z3A.38 is assigned to indicate the weeks of gestation at delivery.

The C-section delivery is classified to the Obstetrics Section, root operation "Extraction." The tubal ligation procedure is classified to the root operation "Occlusion."

Inpatient admission (episode 2): The patient underwent a cesarean section seven days earlier. She had an infection in the operative wound at the time she was admitted through the emergency department with a temperature of 101 degrees and minimal drainage of the incision. IV Kefzol was started, but she continued to spike up to a temperature of 101.8 degrees. The antibiotic therapy was changed, and the patient defervesced.

Discharge diagnosis: Postoperative wound infection.

O86.0	Infection of obstetric surgical wound

Comments: The postoperative wound infection is classified to the pregnancy chapters of ICD-10-CM because it represents a complication of the postpartum period and is related to an obstetrical wound.

2. **Inpatient admission:** This type 1 diabetic patient on insulin was status post a low transverse cesarean delivery 12 days earlier. The day before admission, she noticed a large amount of bloody discharge from her wound. She was taken to the operating room, where the wound was opened and a very large hematoma was evacuated. The wound was drained and packed. Three days later, a secondary wound closure was accomplished.

   Discharge diagnoses: (1) Postpartum hematoma, (2) diabetes mellitus.

O90.2	Hematoma of obstetric wound
O24.03	Pre-existing diabetes mellitus, type 1, in the puerperium
Z79.4	Long term (current) use of insulin
0JCB0ZZ	Extirpation of matter from perineum subcutaneous tissue and fascia, open approach
0WQFXZZ	Repair abdominal wall, external approach

Comments: The ICD-10-CM code for pre-existing diabetes in pregnancy includes the type of diabetes. Because there are no manifestations, an additional diabetes code is not necessary. The code for long-term insulin use is optional.

3. **Inpatient admission:** The patient, a 39-year-old female, gravida II, para 1, was admitted in active labor at 39 weeks gestation. She was dilated to 5 centimeters approximately six hours following admission. Pitocin augmentation was started, and she progressed to complete dilation. Low forceps were used due to arrested active phase of labor. There was no episiotomy, but there was a second-degree perineal laceration (perineum and vaginal wall) that was repaired with 3-0 Dexon. A male infant was delivered weighing 2,835 grams, with Apgar scores of 9 and 9. The patient had indicated before delivery that she desired a sterilization procedure. Following delivery, a laparoscopic bilateral tubal ligation was accomplished.

   Discharge diagnoses: (1) Delivery at term, (2) perineal laceration, (3) elective sterilization.

O62.1	Secondary uterine inertia
O70.1	Second degree perineal laceration during delivery
Z37.0	Single live birth
Z30.2	Encounter for sterilization
Z3A.39	39 weeks gestation of pregnancy
10D07Z3	Extraction of products of conception, low forceps, via natural or artificial opening
0KQM0ZZ	Repair perineum muscle, open approach
0UL74ZZ	Occlusion of bilateral fallopian tubes, percutaneous endoscopic approach

Comments: The reason for the forceps delivery is coded (i.e., arrested active phase of labor). Code Z30.2 shows that the tubal ligation was performed for the purpose of voluntary sterilization. Chapter 15 has a "use additional" note to assign a code from category Z3A, Weeks of gestation, to identify the specific week of the pregnancy. A second-degree perineal laceration involves repair of the skin and muscle of the perineum and requires suturing of the perineum layer by layer. ICD-10-PCS guideline B3.5 pertaining to overlapping body layers supports assigning the code to repair of the perineal muscle: "If the root operations Excision, Repair or Inspection are performed on overlapping layers of the musculoskeletal system, the body part specifying the deepest layer is coded." Therefore, the repair of the perineal laceration is coded to the body part "perineum, muscle."

4. **Inpatient admission:** The admitting diagnoses were intrauterine pregnancy at 29 weeks gestation, premature rupture of membranes with premature labor 12 days prior to admission, and chorioamnionitis. Radiological findings revealed a vertex right occiput transverse presentation with a compound presentation of a fetal hand. Because the patient had a temperature of 101.4 degrees, chorioamnionitis was presumed and antibiotics were started. On a subsequent examination, the fetus was found to be presenting vertex left occiput anterior with right hand compound presentation. The right hand was reducible and was pushed up toward the left side of the fetal body. Following a prolonged second stage, a female infant with Apgar scores of 5 and 7 was delivered spontaneously over an intact perineum. A prior cesarean section scar was found to be intact with no lacerations.

   Discharge diagnoses: (1) Delayed delivery following premature rupture of membrane, compound presentation, (2) chorioamnionitis.

O60.13x0	Preterm labor second trimester with preterm delivery third trimester
O42.113	Preterm premature rupture of membranes, onset of labor more than 24 hours following rupture, third trimester
O34.21	Maternal care for scar from previous cesarean delivery
O41.1230	Chorioamnionitis, third trimester, not applicable or unspecified
O32.6XX0	Maternal care for compound presentation, not applicable or unspecified
O63.1	Prolonged second stage (of labor)
Z37.0	Single live birth
Z3A.29	29 weeks gestation of pregnancy
10E0XZZ	Delivery of products of conception, external approach

Comments: Premature labor is designated as the principal diagnosis because it necessitated admission. The third trimester is from 28 weeks 0 days until delivery. Ruptured membranes did not necessitate admission because they had been ruptured for 12 days. Code O42.113 indicates a delayed delivery. Although there was malpresentation of the fetus, it was reducible and did not result in obstructed labor, so a code is not assigned for obstructed labor. The seventh character for obstetrics codes, when required, is 0 for single gestations or multiple gestations when the fetus is not specified.

5. **Inpatient admission:** The patient, gravida II, para 1, was admitted in labor with a 27-week pregnancy. The fetus was in a complete breech position. Labor ceased within a few hours after admission, but the patient was observed closely because she had a history of recurrent pregnancy loss. By the second day, contractions recurred and she rapidly progressed to complete dilation. Because the breech presentation resulted in obstruction, an emergent low cervical cesarean section was performed, and a living female infant was delivered. The postpartum course was uneventful, and the patient was discharged in good condition on the third postoperative day.

   Discharge diagnosis: Preterm delivery, complicated by breech presentation.

O60.12x0	Preterm labor second trimester with preterm delivery second trimester
O64.1xx0	Obstructed labor due to breech presentation, not applicable or unspecified
O26.22	Pregnancy care for patient with recurrent pregnancy loss, second trimester
Z37.0	Single live birth
Z3A.27	27 weeks gestation of pregnancy
10D00Z1	Extraction of products of conception, low cervical, open approach

Comments: In this case the breech position resulted in the need for a cesarean delivery. Although the code resulting in a cesarean delivery is ordinarily listed as the principal diagnosis, the threatened early delivery was the reason for admission and therefore is listed first. The seventh character for obstetrics codes, when required, is 0 for single gestations or multiple gestations when the fetus is not specified. The second trimester ends at 28 weeks. ICD-10-CM provides a combination code that combines obstructed labor and the reason for the obstruction into a single code. Subcategory O26.2- is assigned for a patient with a history of recurrent pregnancy loss who is currently pregnant.

6. **Inpatient admission:** The patient, gravida II, para 1, was admitted at 37 weeks gestation with spontaneous rupture of membranes and contractions every two to three minutes. She had a history of congenital heart block with pacemaker, which the physician documented was under control by the pacemaker and was not affecting the pregnancy. Because there was no descent, even though she was pushing adequately, three attempts at forceps delivery were made with no success due to cephalopelvic disproportion. Because of failure of forceps due to bony pelvic obstruction, a primary low transverse cesarean section was performed. A live single male was delivered. The postoperative course was uneventful.

   Discharge diagnosis: Cesarean delivery of term, live infant, complicated by bony pelvis and cephalopelvic disproportion and failed forceps.

O65.4	Obstructed labor due to fetopelvic disproportion, unspecified
O66.5	Attempted application of vacuum extractor and forceps
Z37.0	Single live birth
Z95.0	Presence of cardiac pacemaker
Z3A.37	37 weeks gestation of pregnancy
10D00Z1	Extraction of products of conception, low cervical, open approach

Comments: The condition that required the cesarean delivery was the obstruction due to the cephalopelvic disproportion. ICD-10-CM has a combination code for these conditions. The congenital heart block was under control by the pacemaker and so no code is assigned for the condition, but a status code indicating that the patient had a pacemaker is assigned. Diagnosis code O66.5 is assigned to indicate the failed forceps prior to the cesarean delivery.

7. **Inpatient admission:** The patient was admitted with an intrauterine pregnancy at 34 weeks gestation in preterm labor. The provider determined that the patient had false labor that ceased spontaneously, and she was discharged the next day.

   Discharge diagnosis: Preterm labor.

O47.03	False labor before 37 completed weeks of gestation, third trimester
Z3A.34	34 weeks gestation of pregnancy

Comments: The code for the preterm labor includes the fact that the patient is in the third trimester.

8. **Inpatient admission:** The patient, at 10 weeks gestation, was admitted for severe dehydration due to hyperemesis gravidarum. The patient had glaucoma, and treatment with eye drops was continued during the patient's stay. She responded well to IV fluid hydration and antiemetics. The provider documented that the glaucoma did not affect the pregnancy.

   Discharge diagnoses: (1) Hyperemesis gravidarum with dehydration, (2) glaucoma.

O21.1	Hyperemesis gravidarum with metabolic disturbance
E86.0	Dehydration
H40.9	Unspecified glaucoma
Z3A.10	10 weeks gestation of pregnancy

Comments: Code O21.1 covers the fact that the patient is less than 20 weeks gestation and has a metabolic disturbance (dehydration). Code E86.0 is assigned to add specific information on the nature of the metabolic disturbance. A code is assigned for the glaucoma because it was treated, but there is no evidence that it complicated the pregnancy. Every condition that may coexist with pregnancy is not necessarily a complication of the pregnancy or affected adversely by the pregnancy.

9. **Inpatient admission:** The patient was admitted with a nonviable fetus at 27 1/2 weeks gestation. An ultrasound prior to admission showed severe renal malformations in the dysmorphic fetus. A pediatric urology consult concluded fetal nonviability secondary to severe oligohydramnios, enlarged kidneys, and a nonoperable candidate. A Prostin capsule was placed intravaginally, and the patient went on to have spontaneous expulsion of a stillborn female. The patient was discharged the following day.

   Discharge diagnoses: (1) Spontaneous vaginal delivery of stillborn fetus with multiple congenital anomalies (pregnancy), (2) oligohydramnios.

O36.4xx0	Maternal care for intrauterine death, not applicable or unspecified
O35.8xx0	Maternal care for other (suspected) fetal abnormality and damage, not applicable or unspecified
O41.02x0	Oligohydramnios, second trimester, not applicable or unspecified
Z37.1	Single stillbirth
Z3A.27	27 weeks gestation of pregnancy
10A07ZX	Abortion of products of conception, abortifacient, via natural or artificial opening

Comments: The seventh character is for the fetus, unspecified or not applicable. The code for oligohydramnios includes specification of the trimester; 27 weeks is the second trimester.

10. **Inpatient admission:** When admitted, this woman, with triplet gestation at 28 weeks, was thought to have had premature rupture of membranes. She was placed on magnesium sulfate after rupture of membranes was ruled out. Tocolysis and fetal monitoring were continued until she underwent spontaneous rupture of membranes one week later. She had a rapid vaginal delivery with liveborn triplets.

    Discharge diagnosis: Spontaneous vaginal delivery of liveborn triplets.

O60.14x0	Preterm labor third trimester with preterm delivery third trimester
O30.103	Triplet pregnancy, unspecified number of placenta and unspecified number of amniotic sacs, third trimester
Z37.51	Triplets, all liveborn
Z3A.28	28 weeks gestation of pregnancy
10E0XZZ	Delivery of products of conception, external approach
10H073Z	Insertion of monitoring electrode into products of conception, via natural or artificial opening

Comments: This patient is at 28 weeks pregnancy, which is the beginning point of the third trimester. Because rupture of membranes was ruled out, a code for this condition cannot be assigned. However, she went into labor and delivered one week after admission; code O60.14x0 should be assigned. Code O30.103 is assigned to indicate that this was a triplet gestation, with the number of placenta and amniotic sacs unspecified. Code 10E0XZZ can be assigned for the uncomplicated obstetrics delivery.

11. **Inpatient admission:** The patient, a 44-year-old female, gravida I, para 0, was admitted for management of an intrauterine fetal death at 23 weeks. On a routine office visit 10 days earlier, no fetal heartbeat was heard. An ultrasound confirmed the suspicions. She elected to have medical induction of labor via intravenous infusion via the arm rather than waiting for a spontaneous delivery and was admitted. A Pitocin drip was started and some contractions were obtained, but the cervix remained unchanged. Dilation and curettage were performed, and she was discharged that afternoon.

    Discharge diagnoses: (1) Intrauterine fetal death at 23 weeks, (2) macerated fetus, (3) elderly primigravida.

O36.4xx0	Maternal care for intrauterine death, not applicable or unspecified
O09.512	Supervision of elderly primigravida, second trimester
Z3A.23	23 weeks gestation of pregnancy
10A07ZZ	Abortion of products of conception, via natural or artificial opening
3E033VJ	Introduction of other hormone into peripheral vein, percutaneous approach

Comments: The principal diagnosis and reason for admission are intrauterine fetal death. Weeks of gestation were 23 weeks, so second trimester is selected. Code O09.512, for elderly primigravida, is assigned, which includes women who will be 35 years of age or older at the expected date of delivery. The macerated fetus is not a complication of pregnancy, labor, or delivery and is not coded.

12. **Inpatient admission:** The 14-year-old patient (gravida I, para 0) is pregnant at 25 weeks gestation. She was admitted with abdominal pain and questionable labor. On examination she was 50 percent effaced and tight fingertip dilated with cephalic presentation. She was placed on Terbutaline. By the next day, she was without discomfort or contractions and was discharged.

    Discharge diagnosis: Premature labor.

O60.02	Preterm labor without delivery, second trimester
O09.612	Supervision of young primigravida, second trimester
Z3A.25	25 weeks gestation of pregnancy

Comments: Code O60.02 for premature labor without delivery in the second trimester is assigned as the patient is at 25 weeks gestation. Premature labor was documented, but the labor was arrested and delivery did not occur. Code O09.612 is assigned for a primigravida in the second trimester, less than 16 years of age at expected date of delivery, as the patient is 14 years old.

13. **Inpatient admission:** The young patient, gravida I, para 0, ab 0, at 43 weeks gestation, presented in labor and labored poorly but succeeded in reaching 4 to 5 centimeters. Augmentation with Pitocin resulted in no change after several hours, and a primary lower uterine segmental cesarean section was performed due to prolonged labor, with birth of a 7-pound, 5-ounce female. The patient did well after delivery and was discharged on the fourth postoperative day.

    Discharge diagnoses: (1) Postterm, intrauterine pregnancy; (2) failure to progress in labor, with prolonged first stage.

O63.0	Prolonged first stage (of labor)
O48.1	Prolonged pregnancy
Z37.0	Single live birth
Z3A.49	Greater than 42 weeks gestation of pregnancy
10D00Z1	Extraction of products of conception, low cervical, open approach

Comments: Code O63.0 is assigned for prolonged first stage of labor. Code O48.1 indicates the postterm pregnancy, which is a pregnancy that has advanced beyond 42 completed weeks gestation and is assigned because the patient is at 43 weeks.

14. Inpatient admission: The patient, gravida II, para 1, was admitted at approximately 25 1/2 weeks gestation with a history of contractions for 24 hours. She was contracting every four to six minutes. Radiological findings showed an intrauterine fetal death of fetus 1 of the triplet pregnancy (monochorionic) but also showed that the other two fetuses were progressing normally. The contractions stopped and then started again. The patient was given magnesium sulfate for tocolysis but contracted through the magnesium and was placed on Ritadrine. Because she then developed a fever with suspected chorioamnionitis and was in active labor, a primary low cervical cesarean section delivered three male infants, two liveborn and one fetal death. Postoperatively, she did well on antibiotics.

Discharge diagnoses: (1) Cesarean delivery of triplets (two liveborn and one fetal death) at 25 1/2 weeks, (2) chorioamnionitis.

O60.12x0	Preterm labor second trimester with preterm delivery second trimester
O36.4xx1	Maternal care for intrauterine death, fetus 1
O30.112	Triplet pregnancy with two or more monochorionic fetuses, second trimester, not applicable or unspecified
O41.1220	Chorioamnionitis, second trimester, not applicable or unspecified
Z37.61	Triplets, some liveborn
Z3A.25	25 weeks gestation of pregnancy
10D00Z1	Extraction of products of conception, low cervical, open approach

Comments: The patient was admitted in early labor with a 25-completed-week gestation with subsequent delivery; 25 weeks is in the second trimester. It was noted that one of the triplets, identified as fetus 1, was dead. Code O36.4xx1 is assigned for maternal care for intrauterine death, with the seventh character "1" to indicate the code applies to fetus 1. Code O30.112 is assigned for triplet pregnancy with two or more monochorionic fetuses, second trimester. She developed suspected chorioamnionitis, and suspected conditions on inpatient admissions should be coded as though confirmed. The outcome of delivery was triplets, two liveborn and one fetal death; therefore, code Z37.61 is assigned.

15. Inpatient admission: The young patient in the 37th week of gestation was admitted with contractions occurring every few minutes. The cervix was 25 percent effaced with a 6-centimeter dilation. Although she had undergone a previous cesarean section, she wished a trial at vaginal delivery. The membranes were artificially ruptured. Six hours later, she was tried on Pitocin augmentation via IV in the hand and within the hour progressed to complete dilation and began pushing. She pushed for two hours and was unable to progress satisfactorily due to arrested active phase of labor. She was taken to surgery, where a repeat low cervical cesarean section was performed for obstructed labor due to cephalopelvic disproportion. A healthy, single, liveborn female was delivered. The postpartum course was uneventful.

Discharge diagnoses: (1) Intrauterine pregnancy at term, (2) previous cesarean section, (3) cephalopelvic disproportion (CPD).

O65.4	Obstructed labor due to fetopelvic disproportion, unspecified
O34.21	Maternal care for scar from previous cesarean delivery
O62.1	Secondary uterine inertia
Z37.0	Single live birth
Z3A.37	37 weeks gestation of pregnancy
10D00Z1	Extraction of products of conception, low cervical, open approach
10907ZC	Drainage of amniotic fluid, therapeutic from products of conception, via natural or artificial opening
3E033VJ	Introduction of other hormone into peripheral vein, percutaneous approach

Comments: The obstructed labor due to cephalopelvic disproportion is designated as the principal diagnosis because it necessitated the performance of a cesarean section for delivery. Only one code is needed to reflect the obstruction and the CPD. Code O34.21 is assigned for maternal care for a scar from previous cesarean delivery because the patient had undergone a previous cesarean section. The artificial rupture of membranes is coded to the Obstetrics Section, root operation "Drainage," and the qualifier "amniotic fluid, therapeutic."

16. **Inpatient admission:** The patient, in her 25th week of gestation, was transferred from another hospital with complete effacement, complete dilation, and occasional contractions. She underwent a primary low cervical cesarean section with preoperative diagnoses of preterm labor, advanced cervical dilation, and failed magnesium tocolysis. Findings included a live male infant weighing 880 grams. The patient's postoperative course was uneventful except for the occurrence of hemorrhoids, which were successfully treated with suppositories.

    Discharge diagnoses: (1) Intrauterine pregnancy at 25 weeks, (2) preterm labor.

O60.12x0	Preterm labor second trimester with preterm delivery second trimester
O87.2	Hemorrhoids in the puerperium
Z37.0	Single live birth
Z3A.25	25 weeks gestation of pregnancy
10D00Z1	Extraction of products of conception, low cervical, open approach

Comments: Preterm labor with delivery in the second trimester is coded because the patient is in the 25th week. ICD-10-CM has a specific code for hemorrhoids in the puerperium, so only code O87.2 is required.

17. **Inpatient admission:** The patient was admitted in active labor at term (38 weeks gestation). She had multiple sclerosis, which had been exacerbated by the pregnancy. In the delivery room, she spontaneously delivered a liveborn female infant over a midline episiotomy without complication.

    Discharge diagnoses: (1) Spontaneous vaginal delivery of term, live female; (2) multiple sclerosis.

O99.353	Diseases of the nervous system complicating pregnancy, third trimester
G35	Multiple sclerosis
Z37.0	Single live birth
Z3A.38	38 weeks gestation of pregnancy
10E0XZZ	Delivery of products of conception, external approach
0W8NXZZ	Division of female perineum, external approach

Comments: Multiple sclerosis represents a nonobstetrical condition of the nervous system complicating the pregnancy. An additional code of G35 is assigned to further specify the complication. Both the episiotomy and the delivery require codes in the ICD-10-PCS. The episiotomy is coded in the Medical and Surgical (rather than the Obstetrics) Section, as it is performed on the patient rather than the fetus. The episiotomy is coded to the root operation "Division," body part "female perineum." When an episiotomy is performed, the repair (episiorraphy) is not coded separately because it is integral to the total procedure.

18. **Physician office visit:** The patient came in for her routine prenatal checkup. She was a primigravida in her first trimester. There were no complications.

    Diagnosis: Normal pregnancy at 10 weeks.

Z34.01	Encounter for supervision of normal first pregnancy, first trimester
Z3A.10	10 weeks gestation of pregnancy

Comments: This is the only code assignment necessary because no complications are present.

19. Physician office visit: The patient came in for her routine prenatal checkup. She was a primigravida in her first trimester. She complained of hyperemesis. She had been unable to eat and had lost 2 pounds since her last visit. Medication was prescribed. She was instructed to call the office immediately if there was no improvement within 12 hours. She was to be rescheduled for a return visit the following week.

Diagnosis: First trimester pregnancy complicated by mild hyperemesis gravidarum.

O21.0 Mild hyperemesis gravidarum

Z3A.00 Weeks of gestation of pregnancy not specified

Comments: The hyperemesis gravidarum is before 20 weeks and stated to be mild.

20. Inpatient admission: The patient was admitted in labor with an estimated 39-week gestation. When she was approximately 7 to 8 centimeters dilated, an amniotomy was performed that revealed meconium-stained liquor. She rapidly progressed to complete cervical dilation. Fetal distress due to meconium necessitated delivery. The infant's head was visible and in the occiput anterior position. Low forceps were applied, a midline episiotomy was performed, and the infant was successfully delivered. The midline episiotomy was repaired.

Discharge diagnoses: (1) Term delivery of liveborn infant, (2) meconium-stained liquor, (3) fetal stress.

O77.0	Labor and delivery complicated by meconium in amniotic fluid
Z37.0	Single live birth
Z3A.39	39 weeks gestation of pregnancy
10D07Z3	Extraction of products of conception, low forceps, via natural or artificial opening
0W8NXZZ	Division of female perineum, external approach
10907ZC	Drainage of amniotic fluid, therapeutic from products of conception, via natural or artificial opening

Comments: Fetal stress due to meconium is assigned one code. Category O77 is assigned for other fetal stress. Although Delivery, complicated by, fetal stress, is indexed to code O77.9, it is not necessary to assign both codes because it is not appropriate to assign a specific code with an unspecified code from the same category. The forceps delivery and the episiotomy require separate codes in ICD-10-PCS. The low forceps delivery is coded to the root operation "Extraction," with the seventh-character qualifier "low forceps."

21. Inpatient admission: The patient, a young woman with estimated gestation of 29 weeks, was admitted for gestational diabetes. It was felt that close monitoring of her blood sugars was in order and the possibility of starting insulin should receive consideration. Throughout her stay, she had no problems or complications. She was maintained on an 1,800-calorie diet. Her blood sugars were borderline abnormal, and a trial at diet control was to be instituted before further consideration was given to the use of insulin.

Discharge diagnoses: (1) Gestational diabetes; (2) intrauterine pregnancy, 29 weeks.

O24.410	Gestational diabetes mellitus in pregnancy, diet controlled
Z3A.29	29 weeks gestation of pregnancy

Comments: The gestational diabetes in pregnancy is diet controlled at this point and therefore is coded to O24.410.

22. **Inpatient admission:** The patient, with an estimated 37-week gestation, was admitted in labor. Her prenatal course was uncomplicated, except for mild pre-existing hypertension. The labor was also uneventful, and the membranes spontaneously ruptured. A 7-pound, 3-ounce viable male was delivered. The delivery was spontaneous and vaginal, with a midline episiotomy, which extended into a third-degree laceration. The lacerations of the perineum and the anal sphincter were sutured. Following delivery, the mother was stable, with no apparent complications.

    Discharge diagnoses: (1) Spontaneous vaginal delivery of term male infant, (2) third-degree perineal laceration.

O70.2	Third degree perineal laceration during delivery
O10.013	Pre-existing essential hypertension complicating pregnancy, third trimester
Z37.0	Single live birth
Z3A.37	37 weeks gestation of pregnancy
10E0XZZ	Delivery of products of conception, external approach
0W8NXZZ	Division of female perineum, external approach
0KQM0ZZ	Repair female perineum muscle, open approach
0DQR0ZZ	Repair anal sphincter, open approach

Comments: Either the pre-existing hypertension or the perineal laceration can be assigned as the principal diagnosis. ICD-10-PCS requires a code for the delivery, the episiotomy, and the "Repair" of the perineal muscle and anal sphincter laceration.

23. **Inpatient admission:** The patient, with an estimated gestation of 39.5 weeks, presented with spontaneous rupture of the membranes and irregular contractions. Her previous pregnancy was delivered by cesarean section. At first, labor failed to progress despite irregular contractions, and she was started on Pitocin via peripheral IV. She then moved ahead with labor and pushed for approximately 45 minutes. The baby was delivered spontaneously, with the help of a midline episiotomy.

    Discharge diagnoses: (1) Term pregnancy delivered of liveborn male infant, (2) previous cesarean section.

O34.21	Maternal care for scar from previous cesarean delivery
Z37.0	Single live birth
Z3A.39	39 weeks gestation of pregnancy
10E0XZZ	Delivery of products of conception, external approach
0W8NXZZ	Division of female perineum, external approach

Comments: Previous cesarean is coded. ICD-10-PCS requires a code for the delivery and the episiotomy. Coding of repair of the perineum is integral to the episiotomy procedure.

13. ABORTION AND ECTOPIC PREGNANCY

1. **Inpatient admission:** The 22-year-old patient was at 10 weeks gestation with an intrauterine pregnancy. She believed this pregnancy to be the result of a rape and did not wish to carry it to term. A complete abortion was accomplished with a dilation and curettage. There were no complications.

   Discharge diagnoses: (1) Elective abortion, (2) history of rape.

Z33.2	Encounter for elective termination of pregnancy
Z64.0	Problems related to unwanted pregnancy
T74.21xA	Adult sexual abuse, confirmed, initial encounter
Z3A.10	10 weeks gestation of pregnancy
10A07ZZ	Abortion of products of conception, via natural or artificial opening

Comments: An elective abortion is classified in ICD-10-CM to the Factors Influencing Health Status and Contact with Health Services chapter, rather than the Pregnancy chapter. Because this patient confirmed that she was raped, the code for confirmed rape is used rather than the code for suspected rape. Procedure code 10A07ZZ is assigned for the abortion.

2. **Inpatient admission:** The patient, at 12 weeks gestation, wished to have the pregnancy terminated following studies showing the fetus to be anencephalic. An intrauterine saline injection produced an incomplete abortion. This procedure was followed by a dilation and curettage.

   Discharge diagnosis: Therapeutic abortion secondary to fetal abnormality.

Z33.2	Encounter for elective termination of pregnancy
O35.0xx0	Maternal care for (suspected) central nervous system malformation in fetus, not applicable or unspecified
Z3A.12	12 weeks gestation of pregnancy
10A07ZX	Abortion of products of conception, abortifacient, via natural or artificial opening
10D17ZZ	Extraction of products of conception, retained, via natural or artificial opening

Comments: An elective abortion is classified in ICD-10-CM to the Factors Influencing Health Status and Contact with Health Services chapter, rather than the Pregnancy chapter. The first procedure was the abortion using saline, classified as an abortifacient. It was followed by a dilation and curettage for extraction of the retained products of conception.

3. **Inpatient admission:** The patient was admitted following a spontaneous abortion, which she experienced earlier in the day. On examination, it appeared that the abortion was incomplete, and she was bleeding heavily. A dilation and curettage was performed.

   Discharge diagnosis: Incomplete spontaneous abortion.

O03.1	Delayed or excessive hemorrhage following incomplete spontaneous abortion
10D17ZZ	Extraction of products of conception, retained, via natural or artificial opening

Comments: The abortion was spontaneous, complicated by excessive bleeding, and incomplete, and is coded to O03.1. Code 10D17ZZ is assigned for completion of the spontaneous abortion. The root operation is "Extraction."

4. **Obstetrics clinic visit:** The patient had an elective abortion performed at another facility two days earlier. She visited the clinic because of pelvic pain, fever, and a nonbloody discharge. She was given antibiotics.

   Diagnosis: Acute endometritis following abortion.

O04.5	Genital tract and pelvic infection following (induced) termination of pregnancy
N71.0	Acute inflammatory disease of uterus

Comments: Category O04 is for complications following an induced abortion, with a fourth character indicating that this is an infection of the genital tract. Code N71.0 is assigned as an additional code to provide more specificity regarding the complication.

5. **Obstetrics clinic visit:** The 35-year-old patient wished to electively terminate a pregnancy because of her hyperthyroidism, which has been difficult to control. She was at 10 weeks gestation. A complete abortion resulted from the vacuum aspiration curettage.

   Diagnoses: (1) Therapeutic abortion, complete; (2) hyperthyroidism.

Z33.2	Encounter for elective termination of pregnancy
O99.281	Endocrine, nutritional and metabolic diseases complicating pregnancy, first trimester
E05.90	Thyrotoxicosis, unspecified without thyrotoxic crisis or storm
Z3A.10	10 weeks gestation of pregnancy
10A07Z6	Abortion of products of conception, vacuum, via natural or artificial opening

Comments: An elective abortion is classified in ICD-10-CM to the Factors Influencing Health Status and Contact with Health Services chapter, rather than the Pregnancy chapter. The reason for the abortion was thyroid dysfunction, coded to O99.281, with an additional code, E05.90, to specify the hyperthyroidism. The therapeutic abortion was completed via vacuum aspiration. The root operation is "Abortion," with the vacuum identified through the seventh-character qualifier.

6. **Inpatient admission:** The young patient was transferred in from another hospital, where she had been treated for a cerebrovascular accident. She was making a good recovery at the other hospital until yesterday, when she became agitated and aggressive and complained of abdominal pain without significant findings on examination. Her husband suggested the possibility of pregnancy, and an HCG assay confirmed the condition, with pregnancy estimated at 6 weeks. After a series of discussions with the patient and family, it was decided to proceed with an abortion. She was admitted here for the abortion. A complete abortion was accomplished with vacuum aspiration curettage. Her mental status improved, and she was discharged.

   Discharge diagnosis: Elective abortion, complete, secondary to cerebrovascular accident.

Z33.2	Encounter for elective termination of pregnancy
O99.411	Diseases of the circulatory system complicating pregnancy, first trimester
I63.9	Cerebral infarction, unspecified
Z3A.01	Less than 8 weeks gestation of pregnancy
10A07Z6	Abortion of products of conception, vacuum, via natural or artificial opening

Comments: An elective abortion is classified in ICD-10-CM to the Factors Influencing Health Status and Contact with Health Services chapter, rather than the Pregnancy chapter. The reason for the abortion was an acute cerebrovascular accident, reflected by code O99.411, with the addition of code I63.9 to specify the stroke. Note that subcategory O99.4 is for diseases of the circulatory system complicating pregnancy, childbirth, or the puerperium and includes conditions in categories I00 through I99. The therapeutic abortion was completed via vacuum aspiration.

7. **Inpatient admission:** The patient, known to be in early pregnancy, was admitted with acute abdominal pain. Ultrasound revealed a tubal pregnancy. The tubal pregnancy was removed laparoscopically via a small incision in the abdomen. The patient was discharged the next day in good condition. She was to be seen in the doctor's office in two weeks.

   Discharge diagnosis: Ectopic pregnancy.

O00.1	Tubal pregnancy
Z3A.00	Weeks of gestation of pregnancy not specified
10T24ZZ	Resection of products of conception, ectopic, percutaneous endoscopic approach

Comments: Ectopic pregnancies are classified by site. The removal of the tubal pregnancy is classified to the Obstetrics Section, root operation "Resection." The procedure involved a small incision and a laparoscope, so the approach is percutaneous endoscopic.

14. CONGENITAL ANOMALIES

1. **Inpatient admission:** The 27-year-old patient was admitted for a pacemaker implant for her atrioventricular heart block, presumably congenital. A skin incision into the chest wall was made and a dual-chamber synchronous pacemaker was inserted into a subcutaneous pocket. The right atrioventricular transvenous leads were inserted percutaneously. She was kept on bed rest until she was stable and then discharged.

   Discharge diagnosis: Atrioventricular heart block, probably congenital in origin.

Q24.6	Congenital heart block
0JH606Z	Insertion of pacemaker, dual chamber into chest subcutaneous tissue and fascia, open approach
02HK3JZ	Insertion of pacemaker lead into right ventricle, percutaneous approach
02H63JZ	Insertion of pacemaker lead into right atrium, percutaneous approach

Comments: Congenital anomaly codes apply to both pediatric and adult patients; the patient's age does not preclude the use of these codes. The heart block is suspected to be congenital in origin and is coded as confirmed.

The insertion of the pacemaker requires three codes: one for the insertion of the pacemaker, one for the right atrium lead, and one for the right ventricular lead.

2. **Inpatient admission:** The patient, an infant, was admitted for open repair of bilateral undescended testes. In the operating room, he underwent bilateral orchiopexies. On the second postoperative day, a diffuse paralytic ileus was visualized on a KUB. The infant began vomiting secondary to the obstruction caused by the ileus. A nasogastric tube was placed, and he was maintained on nasogastric suction and IV hydration for the following two days. On postoperative day 4, the tube was manually removed, and the patient was discharged. The postoperative ileus extended this admission by two days.

   Discharge diagnoses: (1) Undescended testes; (2) postoperative ileus, secondary to bilateral orchiopexies.

Q53.20	Undescended testicle, unspecified, bilateral
K91.3	Postprocedural intestinal obstruction
Y83.8	Other surgical procedures as the cause of abnormal reaction of the patient, or of later complication, without mention of misadventure at the time of the procedure
0VSC0ZZ	Reposition bilateral testes, open approach
0D9670Z	Drainage of stomach with drainage device, via natural or artificial opening
0DP6X0Z	Removal of drainage device from stomach, external approach

Comments: Code Q53.20 includes the bilateral undescended testes. Code K91.3 provides information on the obstruction. Code K56.0 is excluded in cases of postoperative intestinal obstruction, coded to K91.3. The operation on the testes was a reposition, so code Y83.8 is selected for other surgical procedures as the cause of abnormal reaction.

The objective of the orchiopexy was to reposition the testes and restore the testes to their correct anatomical position; therefore, the root operation "Reposition" was selected. There is a body part value for "bilateral testes," so only one procedure code is required for the procedure. The NG tube was inserted for drainage. Therefore, the root operation "Drainage" was selected and the approach is "via natural or artificial opening" because the tube is inserted through the nose. For the removal of the NG tube, the procedure is coded to the root operation "Removal," and the approach is "external." However, many hospitals may opt not to code the removal because it is a rather minor procedure. According to the ICD-10-PCS Official Coding Guidelines, "procedures performed within an orifice on structures that are visible without the aid of any instrumentation are coded to the approach External." In this instance, the tube is clearly visible.

3. **Inpatient admission:** The patient, a six-week-old infant, was admitted for evaluation of a fever. She was placed on IV antibiotics, and blood cultures grew out coagulase-negative *Staphylococcus*. The provider documented "Staph sepsis." Because a murmur was noticed on physical examination, an echocardiogram was done. This revealed physiologic peripheral branch pulmonary artery stenosis and a small left-to-right atrial shunt, most likely a patent foramen ovale. Based on these findings, the provider diagnosed patent foramen ovale and pulmonary artery stenosis.

   Discharge diagnoses: (1) Coagulase-negative, community-acquired staphylococcal sepsis; (2) peripheral pulmonary artery stenosis; (3) patent foramen ovale.

A41.1 Sepsis due to other specified staphylococcus

Q21.1 Atrial septal defect (patent foramen ovale)

Q25.6 Stenosis of pulmonary artery

Comments: The causative bacteria for the sepsis, coagulase-negative *Staphylococcus,* is specified as an inclusion term under code A41.1. Because severe sepsis or associated acute organ failure is not documented, a code from subcategory R65.2 is not assigned. Pulmonary artery stenosis is assumed to be congenital unless specified as acquired. Foramen ovale is always congenital in nature.

4. **Inpatient admission:** The patient, a two-month-old infant, was referred for evaluation of a faulty airway. The mother reported that he had had noisy breathing since birth and that it had worsened recently. Severe to moderate laryngomalacia was identified on a flexible bronchoscopy. A supraglottostomy with repair of the larynx was performed without complication during the procedure or afterward. The patient received antibiotics postoperatively and was discharged in good condition.

   Discharge diagnosis: Laryngomalacia.

Q31.5 Congenital laryngomalacia

0CQS0ZZ Repair larynx, open approach

0BJ08ZZ Inspection of tracheobronchial tree, via natural or artificial opening endoscopic

Comments: Laryngomalacia is considered to be a congenital condition whether specified as such or not. The supraglottostomy is not coded because it is only the opening of the operative site. The supraglottis is part of the larynx. The procedure is coded to the root operation "Repair." Repair is defined as restoring, to the extent possible, a body part to its normal anatomic structure and function. The root operation "Repair" is used only when the method to accomplish the repair is not one of the other root operations.

5. **Inpatient admission:** The patient, a 14-year-old male, had congenital honeycomb lung and type 1 diabetes. On admission, congestive heart failure was present. His breathing was labored, and lower extremity edema was evident. Recently, his oxygen requirements increased dramatically, he ran intermittent fevers, and he consumed large amounts of liquids. With diuretics, significant reduction of the pitting edema was achieved. Antidepressants were added to his medications to help his depression, agitation, and anxiety. Humidified oxygen mask, alternating percussion, and postural drainage helped his breathing. The insulin dosage and type were adjusted. He was discharged on a diabetic diet in stable condition.

   Discharge diagnoses: (1) Heart failure, (2) honeycomb lung, (3) type 1 diabetes mellitus, (4) depression.

I50.9 Heart failure, unspecified

Q33.0 Congenital cystic lung

E10.9 Type 1 diabetes mellitus without complications

F32.9 Major depressive disorder, single episode, unspecified

Comments: Honeycomb lung can be acquired or congenital. Documentation must specify congenital to appropriately assign code Q33.0. Honeycomb lung is significant to the care of a patient under treatment for congestive heart failure. The symptoms mentioned (i.e., edema, labored breathing) are integral to the diagnosed conditions. ICD-10-CM guidelines state that code Z79.4 should be assigned for type 2 patients who use insulin on a long-term basis. This patient is type 1, so code Z79.4 is not assigned.

6. **Inpatient admission:** This four-year-old patient has a diverticulum of the left ventricle. She had a pulmonary artery band inserted four years ago for another congenital defect. Shortly after the prior surgery, she had suffered a stroke and now has a residual paralysis of the right arm. She required feeding by nursing staff as the right side is dominant. Currently, she was admitted with labored breathing and shortness of breath. Her lungs showed infiltrates on chest X-ray, and sputum culture showed presence of *Klebsiella*. She was placed on antibiotics and continuous supersaturated oxygen therapy for pneumonia, and she slowly improved. During this admission, her congenital problem was reevaluated by diagnostic testing. She was discharged in satisfactory condition.

   Discharge diagnoses: (1) *Klebsiella* pneumonia; (2) monoplegia; (3) diverticulum, left ventricle.

J15.0	Pneumonia due to Klebsiella pneumoniae
Q24.8	Other specified congenital malformations of heart
I69.331	Monoplegia of upper limb following cerebral infarction affecting right dominant side
Z87.74	Personal history of (corrected) congenital malformations of heart and circulatory system
3E0F7GC	Introduction of other therapeutic substance into respiratory tract via natural or artificial opening

Comments: Diverticulum of the left ventricle is always a congenital defect and should be assigned to code Q24.8. Code I69.331 identifies the monoplegia as a late effect of the earlier stroke affecting the right dominant side. Code Z87.74 is assigned for the repaired congenital anomaly.

7. **Inpatient admission:** The patient, a two-year-old male, had congenital bilateral clubfoot and atretic spinal cord at level T11-L4. He needed a walker to ambulate, using mostly the upper extremities to get around. He was admitted for repair of a left tibial torsion. A tibial rotational osteotomy was performed, with insertion of pins. He was placed in a splint postoperatively and was changed to a long leg cast the next day. The patient was discharged subsequently to follow up with the orthopedic surgeon in one week.

   Discharge diagnosis: Atretic spinal cord at T11-L4 with left tibial torsion.

M21.862	Other specified acquired deformities of left lower leg
Q66.8	Other congenital deformities of feet
Q06.8	Other specified congenital malformations of spinal cord
0Q8H0ZZ	Division of left tibia, open approach
0QHH04Z	Insertion of internal fixation device into left tibia, open approach
2W3RX1Z	Immobilization of left lower leg using splint
2W3RX2Z	Immobilization of left lower leg using cast

Comments: The left tibial torsion is not stated to be congenital and is coded as other specified acquired deformity of the left lower leg. The club foot is specified as congenital. The most specific code for the atretic spinal cord is Q06.8, Other specified congenital malformations of the spinal cord. The root operation for osteotomy is "Division." The cast and splint applications are classified under the Placement Section, root operation "Immobilization."

8. Inpatient admission: The patient, a 20-month-old girl, was admitted for correction of a left talipes equinovarus clubfoot. Shortly after admission, she started running a fever and it became apparent that she had acute otitis media. She was placed on antibiotics and discharged. Surgery was to be rescheduled at a later date.

Discharge diagnoses: (1) Talipes equinovarus, left; (2) bilateral otitis media.

Q66.0	Congenital talipes equinovarus
H66.93	Otitis media, unspecified, bilateral
Z53.09	Procedure and treatment not carried out because of other contraindication

Comments: The clubfoot is documented as the reason for the admission and is therefore listed as the principal diagnosis. Clubfoot can be classified as either congenital or acquired, but ICD-10-CM presumes it to be congenital unless specified otherwise. Surgery was canceled because of other contraindication (Z53.09), namely, the otitis media. ICD-10-CM has a code that denotes the bilateral presentation of the otitis media.

9. Inpatient admission: The patient, a teenage male, was referred by his orthodontist for surgical correction of multiple congenital deformities. Examination revealed maxillary hypoplasia and maxillary asymmetry. He was found to have an excessive crossbite, with the maxillary midline several millimeters to the right. Surgical correction was indicated, and the plan was to perform both maxillary and mandibular osteotomies to achieve the amount of movement needed. During surgery, it was possible to move the left maxilla into its desired position without a mandibular osteotomy being performed. Postoperatively, he did very well, and the occlusion was good.

Discharge diagnoses: (1) Maxillary hypoplasia, (2) maxillary asymmetry, (3) excessive crossbite.

Procedure performed: Segmental maxillary osteotomy.

M26.24	Reverse articulation
M26.02	Maxillary hypoplasia
M26.11	Maxillary asymmetry
0NSS0ZZ	Reposition left maxilla, open approach

Comments: Any of the conditions can be listed as the principal diagnosis in accordance with the guidelines. Although the surgeon did not perform an osteotomy on the mandible, a code for cancelled surgery is not assigned. The mandibular surgery was found to be unnecessary but was not a canceled procedure. The maxillary hypoplasia and asymmetry are located in the Diseases of the Digestive System chapter of ICD-10-CM rather than in the Congenital Anomalies chapter. The objective of the osteotomy was to restore, to the extent possible, a body part to its normal anatomic structure and function. In ICD-10-PCS, the root operation "Reposition" is defined as moving to its normal location or other suitable location all or a portion of a body part. The body part is moved to a new location from an abnormal location, or from a normal location where it is not functioning correctly. The body part may or may not be cut out or off to be moved to the new location.

10. Inpatient admission: The patient, a 10-month-old infant, had congenital extrahepatic biliary atresia. She was admitted for a liver transplant workup and at admission was in chronic liver failure. The workup included a chest X-ray, KUB, Doppler ultrasound of liver, and EKG, as well as an upper GI endoscopy of the esophagus, stomach, and duodenum.

Discharge diagnoses: (1) Extrahepatic biliary atresia; (2) placed on liver transplant list, stage II.

Q44.2	Atresia of bile ducts
K72.10	Chronic hepatic failure without coma
0DJ08ZZ	Inspection of upper intestinal tract, via natural or artificial opening endoscopic

Comments: Both conditions were present on admission and both necessitated the workup for liver transplant. Either condition can be sequenced as the principal diagnosis in accordance with the ICD-10-CM Official Coding Guidelines. The biliary atresia is presumed to be congenital unless specified otherwise.

15. PERINATAL CONDITIONS

1. **Inpatient admission:** The patient, a preterm, newborn male triplet (1,720 grams), was delivered by cesarean section, as were the other two liveborn mates. He initially required supplemental oxygen and a nasal prong CPAP for transient tachypnea. He was weaned five hours after birth. The one-minute Apgar score was 6, and the five-minute score was 8. He was also treated for diaper dermatitis. A circumcision was performed prior to discharge.

   Discharge diagnoses: (1) Premature male triplet, (2) transient tachypnea, (3) diaper dermatitis.

Z38.69	Other multiple liveborn infant, delivered by cesarean
P07.16	Other low birth weight newborn, 1500-1749 grams
P07.30	Preterm newborn, unspecified weeks of gestation
P22.1	Transient tachypnea of newborn
L22	Diaper dermatitis
0VTTXZZ	Resection of prepuce, external approach
5A09357	Assistance with respiratory ventilation, less than 24 consecutive hours, continuous positive airway pressure

Comments: Z38.69 is the principal diagnosis because the liveborn triplet was born on this admission by cesarean section. A code for both the preterm infant in terms of weight and weeks of gestation is assigned. Because the weeks are not specified, P07.30 is assigned. In circumcision, the foreskin, or prepuce, is removed. Because this has its own body part and it is completely removed, the root operation "Resection" is selected.

2. **Inpatient admission:** The patient, a one-day-old, 2,200-gram infant, was born prematurely at 34 weeks gestation. She was transferred from another hospital for evaluation of a right congenital diaphragmatic hernia. At Hospital A, just before transfer, intubation was required due to respiratory distress. The ventilatory support was continued at Hospital B for three days. When she was stabilized, the right diaphragmatic hernia was repaired via an open approach. The infant progressed rapidly and was discharged on the second postoperative day.

   Discharge diagnoses: (1) Prematurity, (2) diaphragmatic hernia, (3) respiratory distress.

Q79.0	Congenital diaphragmatic hernia
P07.18	Other low birth weight newborn, 2000-2499 grams
P07.37	Preterm newborn, gestational age 34 completed weeks
P22.9	Respiratory distress of newborn, unspecified
0BQR0ZZ	Repair right diaphragm, open approach
5A1945Z	Respiratory ventilation, 24-96 consecutive hours

Comments: Because the patient was admitted at one day old, no code from the Z38 category is assigned. The principal diagnosis is the reason for admission, congenital diaphragmatic hernia. Code P07.18 is assigned for the prematurity and birth weight. Code P07.37 is assigned because of the additional note to identify the number of weeks of gestation, 34 weeks in this case. Intubation is not coded because it was performed at the other hospital. The objective of the hernia procedure is "Repair," and the site is the "diaphragm." Mechanical ventilation was continued for three days, or 72 hours, so code 5A1945Z is assigned.

3. **Inpatient admission:** The patient, a newborn female infant, was delivered spontaneously at term. She was noticed to be jaundiced on the initial screening labs. Lab tests showed the total bilirubin was increased, and she was started on a single session of phototherapy under bilirubin lights. She progressed rapidly and was discharged to home with the mother.

   Discharge diagnoses: (1) Term female newborn, (2) neonatal jaundice.

Z38.00	Single liveborn infant, delivered vaginally
P59.9	Neonatal jaundice, unspecified
6A600ZZ	Phototherapy of skin, single

Comments: Z38.00 is the principal diagnosis because the infant was born by spontaneous vaginal delivery during this admission. An additional code is assigned for the jaundice because it was identified as a problem and required treatment.

4. **Inpatient admission:** The patient, a preterm male infant, was delivered vaginally at approximately 29 weeks gestation. He weighed 1,855 grams at birth. Initially he did well; but on the evening of birth, he was noted to have dusky spells when feeding. During that night, he developed tachypnea. Due to abnormal heart sounds, tachypnea, and dusky spells, an echocardiogram was performed. It showed a patent foramen ovale. The next day, the patient did well and was released to follow up with a pediatric cardiologist on an outpatient basis.

   Discharge diagnoses: (1) Premature, single, male newborn; (2) patent foramen ovale.

Z38.00 Single liveborn infant, delivered vaginally

P07.17 Other low birth weight newborn, 1750-1999 grams

P07.32 Preterm newborn, gestational age 29 completed weeks

Q21.1 Atrial septal defect

Comments: Z38.00 is the principal diagnosis because the infant was delivered vaginally on this admission. The birth weight and prematurity are identified by the use of codes P07.17 and P07.32, respectively. A separate code is not assigned to identify tachypnea because this is integral to patent foramen ovale.

5. **Inpatient admission:** The patient, a newborn preterm male infant delivered by cesarean section, weighed 2,300 grams at birth and had Apgar scores of 8 and 9. Shortly after birth, an increased respiratory rate, effort, and grunting required that he be placed on oxygen. A classical hyaline membrane disease then developed, consistent with his 32- to 33-week gestational age and size. A catheter was percutaneously placed in the umbilical vein and advanced into the inferior vena cava immediately to allow ease in administration of IV fluids and medication. A right pneumothorax, identified on chest X-ray, was immediately needle aspirated, and a chest tube was placed. Subsequently, he was transferred to the newborn intensive care nursery at another hospital.

   Discharge diagnoses: (1) Prematurity, (2) hyaline membrane disease, (3) spontaneous right pneumothorax.

   Procedures performed: (1) Umbilical vein catheter placement, (2) right chest tube placement, (3) aspiration of pleural space (thoracentesis).

Z38.01 Single liveborn infant, delivered by cesarean

P07.18 Other low birth weight newborn, 2000-2499 grams

P07.35 Preterm newborn, gestational age 32 completed weeks

P22.0 Respiratory distress syndrome of newborn

P25.1 Pneumothorax originating in the perinatal period

0W9930Z Drainage of right pleural cavity with drainage device, percutaneous approach

06H033T Insertion of infusion device, via umbilical vein, into inferior vena cava, percutaneous approach

0W993ZZ Drainage of right pleural cavity, percutaneous approach

Comments: Z38.01 is the principal diagnosis because the infant was born by cesarean section on this particular admission. The birth weight and prematurity are identified by the use of codes P07.18 and P07.35, respectively. Hyaline membrane disease is always a congenital condition and should be classified only to code P22.0. Pneumothorax is classified to code P25.1 only when it occurs during the perinatal period.

The pneumothorax was relieved by needle aspiration of the pleural cavity, and the chest tube was placed during the same session. Separate codes are assigned for the thoracentesis and insertion of the chest tube for drainage. In ICD-10-PCS, the correct coding of venous catheter placement depends on the end placement of the catheter, meaning the site where the device ended up. In this case, the catheter was placed in the umbilical vein and advanced into the inferior vena cava, the approach was percutaneous, and the catheter serves as an "infusion device."

6. **Inpatient admission:** The patient was delivered prematurely by cesarean section and weighed 1,750 grams. She had multiple problems, including microcephaly and congenital heart disease. This newborn was transferred to another hospital for further evaluation and intensive pediatric care.

   Discharge diagnoses: (1) Prematurity, (2) microcephaly, (3) congenital heart disease.

Z38.01	Single liveborn infant, delivered by cesarean
P07.17	Other low birth weight newborn, 1750-1999 grams
P07.30	Preterm newborn, unspecified weeks of gestation
Q24.9	Congenital malformation of heart, unspecified
Q02	Microcephaly

Comments: Z38.01 is the principal diagnosis because the infant was born by cesarean section on this admission. Congenital malformation of the heart, not otherwise specified, is assigned to code Q24.9.

7. **Inpatient admission:** The patient, a six-day-old female, was admitted with respiratory distress, wheezes, and a heart murmur. She was intubated on admission and improved on the ventilator. She was extubated 48 hours later. Respiratory syncytial viral bronchiolitis was diagnosed. Other treatment included antibiotics and aerosols. An echocardiogram indicated a ventricular septal defect. She was to return at a later date for further evaluation.

   Discharge diagnoses: (1) Respiratory syncytial viral bronchiolitis, (2) ventricular septal defect, (3) respiratory distress.

P39.8	Other specified infections specific to the perinatal period
J21.0	Acute bronchiolitis due to respiratory syncytial virus
P22.8	Other respiratory distress of newborn
Q21.0	Ventricular septal defect
0BH17EZ	Insertion of endotracheal airway into trachea, via natural or artificial opening
5A1945Z	Respiratory ventilation, 24-96 consecutive hours

Comments: The P39.8 code indicates that this is a newborn infection, and the J21.0 code specifies the type of infection. The patient was intubated and placed on a ventilator for 48 hours. This is a form of extracorporeal performance in which the respiratory system is taken over by the ventilator.

8. **Inpatient admission:** The patient, an 11-month-old male infant, had congenital cytomegalovirus infection. Because of distorted, loud, and rattling breathing, he was admitted for evaluation of his hypertrophied tonsils and adenoids. Treatment for congenital cytomegaloviral infection was continued throughout the admission. In surgery, a microrigid laryngoscopy, a microrigid bronchoscopy, and an external adenotonsillectomy were performed. No abnormalities were noted on laryngoscopy or bronchoscopy. The patient's postoperative course was uncomplicated.

   Discharge diagnoses: (1) Hypertrophied adenoids and tonsils, (2) congenital cytomegalovirus infection.

J35.3	Hypertrophy of tonsils with hypertrophy of adenoids
P35.1	Congenital cytomegalovirus infection
0CTPXZZ	Resection of tonsils, external approach
0CTQXZZ	Resection of adenoids, external approach
0BJ08ZZ	Inspection of tracheobronchial tree, via natural or artificial opening endoscopic
0CJS8ZZ	Inspection of larynx, via natural or artificial opening endoscopic

Comments: The condition that occasioned admission is hypertrophy of the tonsils and adenoids. The code for congenital cytomegalovirus infection is assigned because treatment was continued during the hospital stay. The symptoms (i.e., distorted, loud, and rattling breathing) are integral to hypertrophied tonsils and adenoids and should not be coded separately.

Two procedure codes are required for the removal of the tonsils and adenoids, as they each have a unique body part.

9. **Inpatient admission:** The patient, an 11-month-old male, was found to have a dysplastic kidney on the right side. Because the kidney was not functioning, he was admitted to have it removed. A right, simple nephrectomy was performed. The procedure was uncomplicated, as was the postoperative course. The pathology report showed the kidney to be both dysplastic and multicystic.

   Discharge diagnosis: Right multicystic dysplastic kidney.

Q61.4	Renal dysplasia
0TT00ZZ	Resection of right kidney, open approach

Comments: Both dysplastic kidney and multicystic kidney are congenital conditions always classified to chapter 17 of ICD-10-CM regardless of the age of the patient. Both conditions are covered in code Q61.4. ICD-10-PCS allows for coding the removal of the right kidney.

10. **Inpatient admission:** The patient, a 7-pound, 6-ounce male infant, was delivered vaginally to a 31-year-old woman (gravida II, para 0-1) at 43 weeks gestation. The mother's pregnancy was uncomplicated, labor lasted 24 hours, and the delivery was spontaneous. Apgar scores were 5 and 7. Due to transient tachypnea and a continued oxygen requirement, the infant was taken to the special care nursery. His overall condition improved rapidly with oxygen and adjustments in body fluids.

    Discharge diagnoses: (1) Postterm newborn male, (2) transient tachypnea of the newborn.

Z38.00	Single liveborn infant, delivered vaginally
P08.22	Prolonged gestation of newborn
P22.1	Transient tachypnea of newborn
3E0F7GC	Introduction of other therapeutic substance into respiratory tract via natural or artificial opening

Comments: Z38.00 is the principal diagnosis because the infant was born vaginally on this admission. Codes are not assigned for the Apgar scores. Prolonged gestation is more than 42 weeks.

11. **Inpatient admission:** The patient, a three-week-old male, was admitted through the emergency department with a three-day history of upper respiratory tract infection (URI). Following admission, he was observed not breathing for short periods during sleep. Antibiotics were started for the URI, and he was observed closely. He had been followed in the outpatient clinic for failure to thrive. All evaluative workups were negative, and no active disease other than the respiratory infection was found. The upper respiratory infection cleared, but the apneic episodes continued. He was to be transferred to the children's hospital for more detailed studies of his episodic sleep apnea and failure to thrive.

    Discharge diagnoses: (1) Failure to thrive, (2) acute upper respiratory tract infection, (3) apnea.

P39.8	Other specified infections specific to the perinatal period
J06.9	Acute upper respiratory infection, unspecified
R62.51	Failure to thrive (child)
P28.3	Primary sleep apnea of newborn

Comments: Upper respiratory infection was the reason for admission and should be sequenced as the principal diagnosis: Code P39.8 indicates that this is a newborn infection, and code J06.9 specifies that this is an upper respiratory infection.

12. **Inpatient admission:** The infant patient was born in the hospital to a 36-year-old primigravida woman at an estimated 34 weeks gestation. The mother's pregnancy was complicated by maternal hypertension and gestational diabetes. The infant was delivered by a primary cesarean section due to fetal distress and metabolic acidemia resulting from the mother's failure to progress. The infant was placed on oxygen by nasal prong following birth in response to fetal distress. The oxygen was removed when heart rate, breathing, and blood gases returned to normal. The infant's blood sugars were low following birth, and an infusion of intravenous glucose was initiated until the blood sugars stabilized.

    Discharge diagnoses: (1) Premature newborn male with birth weight of 1,880 grams, (2) transient hypoglycemia.

Z38.01	Single liveborn infant, delivered by cesarean
P07.17	Other low birth weight newborn, 1750-1999 grams
P07.37	Preterm newborn, gestational age 34 completed weeks
P70.0	Syndrome of infant of mother with gestational diabetes
P19.1	Metabolic acidemia in newborn first noted during labor
3E0F7GC	Introduction of other therapeutic substance into respiratory tract via natural or artificial opening

Comments: Code P70.0 is used to denote hypoglycemia in an infant with a mother experiencing gestational diabetes. The mother's hypertension, diabetes, and failure to progress at labor were complications of her delivery and are not coded on the newborn record unless there is an adverse effect to the newborn. The fetal distress and metabolic acidemia were first noted in labor and were treated with oxygen and further monitoring following birth, so code P19.1 is assigned as an additional diagnosis code.

13. **Inpatient admission:** The patient, a preterm male infant, was born the day before admission in another hospital. He weighed 2,608 grams and had Apgar scores of 7 and 9. He was noted to have elevated temperature. WBCs were also elevated. He was transferred here for investigative studies. A urinary tract infection was confirmed with a urine culture that was positive for *E. coli*, and the infection was treated with intravenous antibiotics. Left hydronephrosis was confirmed by bilateral renal ultrasound. Suspected septicemia was ruled out when all blood cultures were negative prior to institution of antibiotic therapy.

    Discharge diagnoses: (1) Urinary tract infection, (2) congenital hydronephrosis, (3) prematurity.

P39.3	Neonatal urinary tract infection
B96.20	Unspecified Escherichia coli [E. coli] as the cause of diseases classified elsewhere
P07.30	Preterm newborn, unspecified weeks of gestation
Q62.0	Congenital hydronephrosis

Comments: Code P39.3 is referenced in the Alphabetic Index of Diseases and Injuries under **Infection,** urinary, newborn. Code B96.20 is added to show *E. coli* as the causative organism. ICD-10-CM does not classify a birth weight over 2,500 grams as low birth weight. Congenital hydronephrosis was noted. No code from the Z38 category is assigned because the infant was born in another hospital.

16. DISEASES OF THE CIRCULATORY SYSTEM

1. **Inpatient admission (episode 1):** The reason for this woman's admission was repair of a 4.7-centimeter infrarenal abdominal aortic aneurysm. She also had arterial hypertension. Because of her strong family history of aneurysms, she wished to have her aneurysm removed on an elective basis rather than waiting for it to follow its natural course. At surgery, via an open approach, the aneurysm sac was cut open and a 16-millimeter Dacron graft was placed. The procedure was successful, and the patient was discharged on the fifth postoperative day.

   Discharge diagnoses: (1) Infrarenal abdominal aortic aneurysm, (2) arterial hypertension.

I71.4	Abdominal aortic aneurysm, without rupture
I10	Essential (primary) hypertension
Z82.49	Family history of ischemic heart disease and other diseases of the circulatory system
04R00JZ	Replacement of abdominal aorta with synthetic substitute, open approach

Comments: The Z82.49 code identifies the family history of aneurysms and explains why the repair was performed on an elective basis. The objective of the procedure was "Replacement" of the portion of the aorta that the aneurysm was located within, that is, putting in or on biological or synthetic material that physically takes the place and/or function of all or a portion of a body part.

Physician office visit (episode 2): The patient presented for routine follow-up examination of an abdominal aortic aneurysm repair with graft replacement. She was doing well, with only mild discomfort. The midline incision was well healed. Femoral and distal pulses were palpable bilaterally. She was to return again in three months.

Diagnosis: Status post aortic aneurysm.

Z09	Encounter for follow-up examination after completed treatment for conditions other than malignant neoplasm
Z86.79	Personal history of other diseases of circulatory system
Z98.89	Other specified postprocedural states

Comments: Z09 is assigned because the patient was seen, after the initial care was completed, for the purpose of determining whether there were any problems related to the surgery. Z86.79 is assigned because history codes may be used in conjunction with follow-up codes to provide the full picture of the healed condition and its treatment. The follow-up code is sequenced first, followed by the history code.

2. **Inpatient admission:** The patient was admitted for workup of right carotid artery stenosis. A carotid duplex performed as an outpatient procedure at another facility showed 80 percent stenosis on the right side and 40 percent on the left. A nonselective low osmolar carotid arteriography, conducted the day after admission, showed only a 50 percent stenosis of the right common carotid artery. The external carotids were found to be small, but there was no significant internal carotid disease on either side. Therefore, because the patient was asymptomatic, it was felt that surgery would present a higher risk of stroke than treating her medically.

   Discharge diagnosis: Carotid artery disease.

I65.23	Occlusion and stenosis of bilateral carotid arteries
B3051ZZ	Plain radiography of bilateral common carotid arteries using low osmolar contrast
B30C1ZZ	Plain radiography of bilateral external carotid arteries using low osmolar contrast

Comments: Although only carotid artery disease was documented on discharge, arteriography indicated the specific condition to be stenosis. Code I65.23 indicates that this condition affects both the right and left arteries. Two ICD-10-PCS codes are required to reflect the bilateral common and external carotid arteriography.

3. **Inpatient admission:** This patient was admitted for repair of a left common carotid stenosis. Two months earlier, an endarterectomy of a right carotid stenosis had been performed. Six months earlier, she had suffered a cerebral hemorrhage that resulted in apraxia and oropharyngeal phase dysphagia, both of which required additional nursing assistance. The open left endarterectomy was successfully accomplished, and the patient was discharged on the fourth hospital day.

   Discharge diagnoses: (1) Left carotid stenosis, (2) residuals of old cerebrovascular accident.

I65.23	Occlusion and stenosis of bilateral carotid arteries
I69.390	Apraxia following cerebral infarction
I69.391	Dysphagia following cerebral infarction
R13.12	Dysphagia, oropharyngeal phase
03CJ0ZZ	Extirpation of matter from left common carotid artery, open approach

Comments: The residual apraxia and dysphagia represent late effects of the previous cerebrovascular accident. They are reportable, as they required additional nursing care. Subcategory I69.3 describes sequelae of a stroke not otherwise specified (NOS). As indicated by the "use additional code" note at code I69.391, code R13.1- is assigned to show the type of dysphagia, which in this case is oropharyngeal (R13.12). Endarterectomy refers to the removal of diseased material from the inside of an artery; therefore, this procedure is coded to the root operation "Extirpation": taking or cutting out solid matter from a body part. The procedure does not require excision of the artery.

4. **Inpatient admission:** The patient was admitted with recurrent unstable angina that could not be controlled with sublingual nitroglycerin. There was no history of bypass or angioplasty in the past. On left cardiac catheterization with coronary arteriography with contrast, a narrowing in the left anterior descending coronary artery and a stenotic area in an intermediate branch were identified. A successful percutaneous transluminal coronary angioplasty (PTCA) of both vessels was carried out.

   Discharge diagnosis: (1) Unstable angina secondary to coronary arteriosclerosis, (2) chronic total occlusion of coronary artery.

I25.110	Atherosclerotic heart disease of native coronary artery with unstable angina pectoris
I25.82	Chronic total occlusion of coronary artery
02713ZZ	Dilation of coronary artery, two sites, percutaneous approach
4A023N7	Measurement of cardiac sampling and pressure, left heart, percutaneous approach
B201YZZ	Plain radiography of multiple coronary arteries using other contrast

Comments: In ICD-10-CM the unstable angina and the arteriosclerosis are included in one code. Because there was no mention of previous bypass surgery, the native artery is selected. In the Index, see the main term **Arteriosclerosis,** subterms "coronary," "native vessel," "with," "angina pectoris," "unstable." ICD-10-PCS includes the angioplasty of two vessels without a device in one code; the root operation is "Dilation."

5. **Inpatient admission:** The patient received his first pacing system 15 years earlier because of congenital complete heart block and severe bradycardia. At the time of admission, he was experiencing these conditions again, plus fatigue secondary to pacemaker pulse generator malfunction. He was admitted for insertion of a new generator. After he was prepped for surgery, the old pacemaker was removed via an incision into the subcutaneous pocket, and a new dual-chamber pacing device was inserted and connected to the existing leads. The postoperative period was uncomplicated.

   Discharge diagnosis: Malfunctioning pacemaker.

T82.111A	Breakdown (mechanical) of cardiac pulse generator (battery), initial encounter
Q24.6	Congenital heart block
R00.1	Bradycardia, unspecified
0JPT0PZ	Removal of cardiac rhythm related device from trunk subcutaneous tissue and fascia, open approach
0JH606Z	Insertion of pacemaker, dual chamber into chest subcutaneous tissue and fascia, open approach

Comments: The pacemaker malfunction is the reason for the admission and the principal diagnosis. The reason the patient had the initial pacemaker was to compensate for heart block and bradycardia. These conditions still exist. Therefore, both conditions are coded as secondary diagnoses. Fatigue is not coded because it is integral to severe bradycardia. To reflect the pacemaker replacement procedure, the removal of the pacemaker and the insertion of the new device are coded.

6. **Inpatient admission:** The patient came to the emergency department because she was unable to speak well. She was admitted because she appeared to be somewhat aphasic. Following admission, she was found to be in atrial fibrillation. A CT scan of the head showed only some probable old defects, and the aphasia was thought to probably be due to a recent cerebral embolus. By the fifth day, she was stable and able to go home. The aphasia had cleared, and the fibrillation was controlled with medication.

   Discharge diagnoses: (1) Cerebral embolism, (2) atrial fibrillation.

I66.9	Occlusion and stenosis of unspecified cerebral artery
I48.91	Unspecified atrial fibrillation
R47.01	Aphasia

Comments: The reason for admission was aphasia, which after study was found to be due to a cerebral embolus. Therefore, the embolus is the principal diagnosis. Aphasia is coded because any neurological deficit due to a CVA is coded even if it has resolved by the time of discharge from the hospital.

7. **Inpatient admission:** The patient was admitted for severe aortic valve stenosis and left ventricular hypertrophy. The aortic valve was replaced with a prosthesis. The patient was successfully weaned from the cardiopulmonary bypass (extracorporeal cardiac) machine. An intraoperative echocardiogram revealed appropriate functioning of the prosthesis.

   Discharge diagnoses: (1) Aortic stenosis and calcification, (2) left ventricular hypertrophy.

I35.0	Nonrheumatic aortic (valve) stenosis
I51.7	Cardiomegaly
02RF0JZ	Replacement of aortic valve with synthetic substitute, open approach
5A1221Z	Performance of cardiac output, continuous

Comments: The cardiopulmonary bypass is coded in the Extracorporeal Assistance and Performance Section and can be found by referring to the Index under "Bypass, cardiopulmonary." Although "cardiopulmonary" refers to two separate body system values—"cardiac" and "respiratory"—only one code is assigned for the "cardiac" body system per the directions in the Index.

8. **Inpatient admission:** The admission diagnoses were aortic and mitral insufficiency. The patient also had HIV infection. A bacterial endocarditis, involving the aortic and mitral valves, had developed five months before admission and was treated and resolved with antibiotics. Procedures performed were mitral and aortic valve replacement with prosthesis and cardiopulmonary bypass (extracorporeal cardiac) during the procedure. The patient improved considerably during the next two days with medications and was transferred to the rehabilitation hospital.

   Discharge diagnoses: (1) Aortic and mitral insufficiency, (2) HIV infection.

I08.0	Rheumatic disorders of both mitral and aortic valves
B20	Human immunodeficiency virus [HIV] disease
02RG0JZ	Replacement of mitral valve with synthetic substitute, open approach
02RF0JZ	Replacement of aortic valve with synthetic substitute, open approach
5A1221Z	Performance of cardiac output, continuous

Comments: The HIV infection was not the reason for admission; therefore, it is not the principal diagnosis. The cardiopulmonary bypass is coded in the Extracorporeal Assistance and Performance Section.

9. **Inpatient admission:** The patient was admitted with atypical chest pain and aching of the left upper extremity. Following admission, she had episodic visual blurring and dizziness. A myocardial infarction was ruled out. Neurological checks were unremarkable, except for a questionable small infarct in the left occipital lobe. Her aspirin therapy was increased, and within two days she was fully ambulatory and asymptomatic.

   Discharge diagnoses: (1) Atypical chest pain of unclear etiology, (2) transient ischemic attacks.

R07.89 Other chest pain

G45.9 Transient cerebral ischemic attack, unspecified

Comments: Transient ischemic attacks should not be confused with "transient residuals" of an acute cerebrovascular accident. The neurological symptoms did not appear until after admission; therefore, chest pain is sequenced as the principal diagnosis.

10. **Inpatient admission:** The patient, a young woman, was admitted with pain and edema in the left leg, which had started two days earlier when she drove home from Florida without stopping. Findings on a venous doppler ultrasound of the pelvic and leg region were consistent with thrombosis She was discharged on Coumadin.

    Discharge diagnosis: Iliac vein thrombosis on the left, acute.

I82.422 Acute embolism and thrombosis of left iliac vein

Comments: The symptoms of pain and edema in the leg are integral to the iliac vein thrombosis and should not be coded separately.

11. **Inpatient admission:** The patient was brought to the hospital emergency department with burning, low sternal, epigastric pain. While in the ED, she developed respiratory distress and subsequent acute myocardial infarction with cardiopulmonary arrest. She was resuscitated, and maneuvers involved in this activity included intubation and defibrillation. Chest X-rays confirmed pulmonary edema and congestive heart failure. EKGs confirmed acute subendocardial myocardial infarction in progress. The patient was then admitted and remained on the ventilator for approximately 24 hours, with gradual improvement. She was transferred to another hospital for further workup and treatment.

    Discharge diagnoses: (1) Acute myocardial infarction, (2) pulmonary edema, (3) congestive heart failure, (4) cardiopulmonary arrest.

I21.4	Non-ST elevation (NSTEMI) myocardial infarction
I50.9	Heart failure, unspecified
I46.2	Cardiac arrest due to underlying cardiac condition
5A2204Z	Restoration of cardiac rhythm, single
0BH17EZ	Insertion of endotracheal airway into trachea, via natural or artificial opening
5A1945Z	Respiratory ventilation, 24-96 consecutive hours

Comments: Cardiac arrest due to underlying cardiac condition is coded to I46.2, with the cardiac condition coded first; therefore, in this case, the myocardial infarction is coded first.

12. **Inpatient admission:** The patient was admitted for evaluation of a three-month history of fever, fatigue, and headaches. She received consultation from the rheumatology service, which recommended biopsy of the temporal arteries. The left temporal artery was negative for inflammation. The right temporal artery, however, showed inflammation of the intima. The histologic picture was compatible with arteritis. Prednisone was given, and the headaches subsided.

    Discharge diagnoses: (1) Right temporal arteritis; (2) open biopsy, right and left temporal arteries.

M31.6	Other giant cell arteritis
03BS0ZX	Excision of right temporal artery, open approach, diagnostic
03BT0ZX	Excision of left temporal artery, open approach, diagnostic

Comments: Headaches are integral to inflammation (arteritis) of the temporal artery and are not coded separately. The procedure is classified as "Excision," with the qualifier for "diagnostic" to indicate that this was a biopsy. A code for both the right and left temporal arteries is assigned.

13. **Inpatient admission:** The patient was admitted for treatment of a stroke. She has a history of type 2 diabetes. The major manifestations were ptosis on the right; moderate expressive aphasia; right-to-left disorientation; and a slow, shuffling gait. On a CT scan of the head, a low-density area at the posterior limb of the left internal capsule and the left posterior parietal subcortical white matter was seen. No hemorrhage was viewed. Gradually, the manifestations improved and then resolved. The patient also had a right midfoot ulcer that required bedside debridement (using a Versajet) by the physician. She was discharged to be followed up by a home health nurse.

    Discharge diagnoses: (1) Cerebrovascular infarction of a thromboembolic source, left posterior artery; (2) type 2 diabetes; (3) diabetic foot ulcer.

I63.432	Cerebral infarction due to embolism of left posterior cerebral artery
E11.621	Type 2 diabetes mellitus with foot ulcer
L97.419	Non-pressure chronic ulcer of right heel and midfoot with unspecified severity
R47.01	Aphasia
R26.89	Other abnormalities of gait and mobility
H02.401	Unspecified ptosis of right eyelid
0HDMXZZ	Extraction of right foot skin, external approach

Comments: The CT scan showed the left posterior artery as affected. Refer to the Alphabetic Index, **Infarction,** due to embolism, cerebral arteries, which provides code I63.4-. The foot ulcer and the diabetes are reflected in the E11.621 code, with a "use additional code" note for the site of the ulcer. The neurological deficits and ptosis that resulted from the stroke are coded. The Versajet debridement has as its objective "Extraction," pulling or stripping away or off all or a portion of a body part by the use of force.

14. **Inpatient admission:** The patient had a three-month history of progressive cyanosis of the fingers and toes. Due to sudden and dramatic progression of symptoms, she was admitted. A right upper-extremity arteriogram revealed complete absence of arterial flow to all proximal phalanges. The findings were thought to be consistent with vasculitis. A percutaneous vascular biopsy of the artery of the right hand was performed to confirm this diagnosis. The report indicated changes consistent with chronic inflammation and necrotizing vasculitis. On vascular surgery consultation, it was felt that her gangrene would demarcate without surgical intervention. There was gradual improvement in pain, and she was switched to oral medications.

    Discharge diagnoses: (1) Necrotizing vasculitis, (2) digital gangrene.

I77.6	Arteritis, unspecified
I96	Gangrene, not elsewhere classified
03BD3ZX	Excision of right hand artery, percutaneous approach, diagnostic
B30HZZZ	Plain radiography of right upper extremity arteries

Comments: Gangrene represents a further manifestation of vasculitis and is coded separately. The biopsy of the artery of the right hand is classified as "Excision," with the qualifier "diagnostic" to indicate that this was a biopsy.

15. **Inpatient admission:** The patient was transferred from another hospital for evaluation of a possible recurrent pulmonary embolism and right lower-extremity pain and swelling determined to be DVT (prior to transfer). A pulmonary arteriogram with contrast confirmed an acute left pulmonary embolus, and heparin was started. Ultrasound of the right lower extremity demonstrated an acute thrombosis of the right femoral vein. Bilateral mammograms were taken to evaluate a right breast lump with discharge that was found on physical examination. The finding was a suspicious density of her right breast. The patient was to be referred to the gynecology clinic for follow-up of this problem after discharge. All medications were adjusted, and she showed much improvement.

    Discharge diagnoses: (1) Deep venous thrombosis, right leg; (2) recurrent pulmonary embolism; (3) lump, right breast.

I82.411	Acute embolism and thrombosis of right femoral vein
I26.99	Other pulmonary embolism without acute cor pulmonale
N63	Unspecified lump in breast
B30TYZZ	Plain radiography of left pulmonary artery using other contrast

Comments: Either pulmonary embolism or DVT could be sequenced as the principal diagnosis. The patient was admitted for further evaluation and treatment of both. The right breast lump is not considered an incidental finding. Although it was not treated, it was identified and workup begun, with the patient being referred for further follow-up.

16. **Inpatient admission:** A patient, who had peripheral vascular disease, came in for a second opinion about possible reconstruction of right femorotibial occlusive disease. An angiogram demonstrated a peroneal vessel that would allow reconstruction. Following an evaluation, he was scheduled to undergo the procedure. However, because he had no other significant diseases or active cardiac ischemia, he was felt to be at low risk for a distal reconstruction. The patient was discharged prior to the procedure due to the development of an upper respiratory infection. The procedure was to be rescheduled in two weeks.

    Discharge diagnoses: (1) Right femorotibial occlusion, (2) URI.

I74.3	Embolism and thrombosis of arteries of the lower extremities
J06.9	Acute upper respiratory infection, unspecified
Z53.09	Procedure and treatment not carried out because of other contraindication
B40FYZZ	Plain radiography of right lower extremity arteries using other contrast

Comments: In the Index, under **Occlusion,** artery, the cross-reference is to "see also **Embolism,** artery." See **Embolism,** limb, lower, to find code I74.3.

17. **Inpatient admission:** The patient was admitted with probable acute myocardial infarction. He was admitted to the critical care unit and also found to be in atrial fibrillation. He was given several medications. A cardiology consultation confirmed an acute inferolateral myocardial infarction on echocardiogram, and the patient was transferred to another hospital for cardiac catheterization.

    Discharge diagnoses: (1) Acute myocardial infarction, (2) atrial fibrillation.

I21.19	ST elevation (STEMI) myocardial infarction involving other coronary artery of inferior wall
I48.91	Unspecified atrial fibrillation

Comments: Although the patient had both acute myocardial infarction and atrial fibrillation, the reason for admission was acute myocardial infarction, which is sequenced first.

18. Inpatient admission: The patient, an elderly man, was transferred from a nursing home. He had had nondominant left-sided hemiplegia since suffering a cerebral thrombosis about three months earlier. He was doing well until the day of admission. A CT scan of the head showed an acute cerebral hemorrhage. He was treated and improved somewhat but then had increased problems secondary to extension of the bleeding. Another CT scan showed a large hematoma in the right basal ganglia. With consultation, it was decided that only supportive care was needed, and the patient was returned to the nursing home.

Discharge diagnoses: (1) Acute cerebral hemorrhage, (2) right basal ganglia hematoma, (3) previous cerebral thrombosis with residual left-sided hemiplegia.

I61.9	Nontraumatic intracerebral hemorrhage, unspecified
I69.354	Hemiplegia and hemiparesis following cerebral infarction affecting left non-dominant side

Comments: The reason for admission was acute cerebral hemorrhage. There was an extension of the cerebral hemorrhage, and a hematoma developed in the right basal ganglia, which is also covered by code I61.9. There is a left-sided nondominant residual hemiplegia, which is a late effect (sequela) of a previous cerebral thrombosis.

19. Inpatient admission: The patient, a female resident of a nursing home, was transferred because of nausea and vomiting. She also suffered from type 1 diabetes mellitus and arteriosclerotic cardiovascular disease. An upper GI X-ray showed esophageal obstruction. She was then admitted with provisional diagnoses of esophageal obstruction versus hiatal hernia versus esophagitis. A gastroscopy was performed, and a partial obstruction due to stricture to the level of the distal esophagus was viewed and dilated. The patient improved without further symptoms. Her blood sugar levels rose to 500 on the third day of admission, and the diabetes was diagnosed as out of control. Her insulin was increased twice in an attempt to lower her blood sugar to baseline. The long-term outlook was not good inasmuch as the patient was not a candidate for definitive surgery. The esophageal stricture was thought to have resulted from a previous cerebrovascular accident.

Discharge diagnoses: (1) Esophageal stricture; (2) arteriosclerotic cardiovascular disease; (3) uncontrolled diabetes mellitus, type 1.

I69.398	Other sequelae of cerebral infarction
K22.2	Esophageal obstruction
I25.10	Atherosclerotic heart disease of native coronary artery without angina pectoris
E10.65	Type 1 diabetes mellitus with hyperglycemia
0D758ZZ	Dilation of esophagus, via natural or artificial opening endoscopic
0DJ68ZZ	Inspection of stomach, via natural or artificial opening endoscopic

Comments: The stricture is a late effect of a previous CVA (cerebrovascular accident) or stroke. Code K22.2 is also assigned to provide greater specificity. No code is assigned for the nausea and vomiting because these symptoms are a common finding with esophageal stricture. For diabetes out of control, see the main term **Diabetes,** subterm "inadequately controlled," with the cross-reference that states "code to **Diabetes,** by, type, with hyperglycemia." See the Index entry "**Diabetes,** type 1 with hyperglycemia." A code for long-term use of insulin is optional for type 1 diabetics because these patients require insulin.

20. **Inpatient admission:** The patient was admitted through the emergency department with substernal chest pain, thought to represent unstable angina. He got pain relief with nitroglycerin. The next morning he asked to be discharged because he had no insurance and could not afford to be in the hospital. Because his physician did not agree with his decision, the patient signed himself out against medical advice. He promised to see the cardiologist immediately and take his medications.

    Discharge diagnosis: Angina, probably unstable.

I20.0	Unstable angina
Z91.19	Patient's noncompliance with other medical treatment and regimen

Comments: Because angina is documented at discharge as probably unstable, code I20.0 should be assigned. The patient signed himself out against medical advice (AMA). Code Z91.19 indicates noncompliance with other medical treatment and regimen.

21. **Inpatient admission:** The patient, who had no history of bypass or angioplasty, was admitted with recurrent chest pain, which could not be controlled with medications and ultimately resulted in an acute ST elevation myocardial infarction of the anterior wall. On combined right and left cardiac catheterization with coronary cineangiography, a narrowing in the left anterior descending coronary artery and stenoses in the left circumflex and distal right coronary artery were found. A successful three-vessel coronary artery bypass graft was carried out. The left internal mammary was used to bypass the left anterior descending, and a reverse segment of the left saphenous vein graft was used to bypass the left circumflex and distal right coronary arteries. The saphenous vein was harvested via a percutaneous endoscopic procedure.

    Discharge diagnoses: (1) Anterior acute myocardial infarction, (2) coronary arteriosclerosis.

    Procedure: Three-vessel coronary artery bypass graft.

I21.09	ST elevation (STEMI) myocardial infarction involving other coronary artery of anterior wall
I25.10	Atherosclerotic heart disease of native coronary artery without angina pectoris
021109W	Bypass coronary artery, two sites from aorta with autologous venous tissue, open approach
02100Z9	Bypass coronary artery, one site from left internal mammary, open approach
06BQ4ZZ	Excision of left greater saphenous vein, percutaneous endoscopic approach
4A023N8	Measurement of cardiac sampling and pressure, bilateral, percutaneous approach
B206YZZ	Plain radiography of right and left heart using other contrast

Comments: The left internal mammary was used to bypass the left anterior descending, equaling one bypass. A segment of the left saphenous vein graft was used to bypass the left circumflex and distal right coronary arteries, equaling two aortocoronary bypasses. Coding the bypasses separately is consistent with Official Coding Guideline B3.6c, which states that "if multiple coronary artery sites are bypassed, a separate procedure is coded for each coronary artery site that uses a different device and/or qualifier." A code is added for the harvest of the saphenous vein. The cardiac catheterization and angiography were combined right and left procedures.

22. **Inpatient admission:** The patient was admitted for a planned exploratory laparotomy and a possible excision of a cystic mass in the pelvis. Shortly after admission, however, she developed bigeminal pulse. The anesthesiologist believed that she should not have surgery. The surgery was canceled, and she was referred back to her internist.

    Discharge diagnoses: (1) Bigeminal pulse, (2) pelvic mass.

R19.00	Intra-abdominal and pelvic swelling, mass and lump, unspecified site
R00.8	Other abnormalities of heart beat
Z53.09	Procedure and treatment not carried out because of other contraindication

Comments: The reason for admission was pelvic mass. Even though the treatment plan was not carried out, it should still be sequenced as the principal diagnosis. The complication bigeminal pulse developed after admission and is sequenced as a secondary diagnosis. Code Z53.09 shows that the planned procedure was canceled due to a contraindication.

23. **Inpatient admission:** The patient, an elderly woman, had a rather sudden onset of severe pleuritic chest discomfort that brought her to the emergency department. She had been undergoing a series of radiation therapy treatments for history of endometrial carcinoma. She was admitted for further evaluation. A right pulmonary angiogram with high osmolar contrast confirmed the diagnosis of pulmonary embolism in the right lower lobe. She was treated with heparin and later Coumadin. Coumadin was to be continued on discharge. The patient was to return for her regular radiation therapy treatment as scheduled.

    Discharge diagnoses: (1) Pulmonary embolism, (2) history of endometrial carcinoma of the uterus.

I26.99	Other pulmonary embolism without acute cor pulmonale
C54.3	Malignant neoplasm of fundus uteri
B30S0ZZ	Plain radiography of right pulmonary artery using high osmolar contrast

Comments: Endometrial carcinoma of the uterus is no longer present; however, the site is still under active treatment. Therefore, code C54.3 is assigned rather than a code from personal history of carcinoma.

24. **Inpatient admission:** The patient was transferred from another hospital for treatment of an acute ST elevation inferior wall myocardial infarction. She also suffered from hypercholesterolemia and benign hypertension; treatment of these conditions was continued during the hospital stay. A left cardiac catheterization with coronary angiogram and arteriography was performed and revealed coronary arteriosclerosis. It was determined that she would benefit from a percutaneous transluminal coronary angioplasty. The angioplasty was performed on the left coronary artery. She tolerated the procedure well and was to continue her medical treatment after discharge.

    Discharge diagnoses: (1) Acute inferior myocardial infarction, (2) coronary arteriosclerosis, (3) hypercholesterolemia, (4) benign essential hypertension.

I21.19	ST elevation (STEMI) myocardial infarction involving other coronary artery of inferior wall
I25.10	Atherosclerotic heart disease of native coronary artery without angina pectoris
E78.0	Pure hypercholesterolemia
I10	Essential (primary) hypertension
02703ZZ	Dilation of coronary artery, one site, percutaneous approach
4A023N7	Measurement of cardiac sampling and pressure, left heart, percutaneous approach
B201YZZ	Plain radiography of multiple coronary arteries using other contrast

Comments: Both the transferring hospital and this facility will assign I21.19 for the acute myocardial infarct. ICD-10-PCS codes the angioplasty to the root operation "Dilation."

17. NEOPLASMS

1. **Inpatient admission:** The elderly woman's admitting diagnosis was carcinoma of the stomach with metastasis to the ovaries. An exploratory laparotomy was performed for the purpose of excising the gastric tumor, but it was so densely attached to other structures that it could not be resected. However, a total abdominal hysterectomy and bilateral salpingo-oophorectomy were accomplished and the patient returned to her room in fair condition. Palliative systemic chemotherapy infusions were given. On the third postoperative day, a large right pleural effusion developed, and a chest tube was percutaneously placed in the right pleural cavity for drainage. Cytology for malignant cells in the pleural effusion was negative. The patient remained stable and wanted to return to her home. The chest tube was removed before discharge.

   Discharge diagnoses: (1) Carcinoma of the stomach metastatic to the ovaries, (2) pleural effusion.

C16.9	Malignant neoplasm of stomach, unspecified
C79.60	Secondary malignant neoplasm of unspecified ovary
J90	Pleural effusion, not elsewhere classified
0UT90ZZ	Resection of uterus, open approach
0UTC0ZZ	Resection of cervix, open approach
0UT20ZZ	Resection of bilateral ovaries, open approach
0UT70ZZ	Resection of bilateral fallopian tubes, open approach
0W9930Z	Drainage of right pleural cavity with drainage device, percutaneous approach
3E04305	Introduction of other antineoplastic into central vein, percutaneous approach
0WP9X0Z	Removal of drainage device from right pleural cavity, external approach

Comments: Even though pleural effusion developed following surgery, the physician did not identify it as a complication of the surgery and the cytology for the effusion was negative. The code for the exploratory laparotomy is not assigned because it was the approach for the total abdominal hysterectomy and bilateral salpingo-oophorectomy. Separate ICD-10-PCS codes are necessary for the removal of the uterus, cervix, ovaries, and fallopian tubes to represent a total hysterectomy.

2. **Inpatient admission:** The patient underwent a hemicolectomy and splenectomy a year earlier for excision of a primary adenocarcinoma of the colon. Recently, he developed abdominal pain. He was admitted with a questionable liver lesion. An ultrasound of the liver, a CT scan of the abdomen, and an exploratory laparotomy with needle biopsy of the liver were performed. The findings indicated inoperable adenocarcinoma of the liver.

   Discharge diagnosis: Adenocarcinoma of the colon metastatic to the liver, unresectable.

C78.7	Secondary malignant neoplasm of liver and intrahepatic bile duct
Z85.030	Personal history of malignant carcinoid tumor of large intestine
0FB03ZX	Excision of liver, percutaneous approach, diagnostic
0WJG0ZZ	Inspection of peritoneal cavity, open approach

Comments: A "history of" code is assigned for the adeno-carcinoma of the colon because it had previously been excised. The liver is specified as the secondary site because the neoplasm spread to it from the colon. The patient was admitted with a questionable liver lesion, which after study was diagnosed as a liver metastasis and therefore assigned as the principal diagnosis. The exploratory laparotomy is coded because it was not followed by definitive surgery. Even though the biopsy was performed during the laparotomy, a needle biopsy of the liver is considered a closed biopsy, and therefore the percutaneous approach is used.

3. **Inpatient admission:** The patient was admitted through the emergency department with severe shortness of breath. She had a history of left upper lobe, non–small cell carcinoma, which had been treated with radiation. Recently, a recurrence in the left supraclavicular area of the lung was found, and she received palliative radiation therapy. She also had a history of severe chronic obstructive bronchitis and had used home oxygen for several years. Her medications were increased for the chronic obstructive pulmonary disease, and she improved sufficiently for discharge.

   Discharge diagnoses: (1) Chronic obstructive pulmonary disease with acute exacerbation, (2) recurrent non–small cell lung cancer.

J44.1	Chronic obstructive pulmonary disease with (acute) exacerbation
C34.12	Malignant neoplasm of upper lobe, left bronchus or lung

Comments: The thrust of treatment was toward the chronic obstructive pulmonary disease, and it is therefore designated as the principal diagnosis. Because the chronic obstructive pulmonary disease is described more specifically in the body of the record as chronic obstructive bronchitis with acute exacerbation, code J44.1 is assigned. Recurrence of a neoplasm is coded as a primary neoplasm of that site. ICD-10-CM allows for specifying the left lung.

4. **Inpatient admission:** On a previous admission, the patient was diagnosed with poorly differentiated papillary serous cystadenocarcinoma of the right ovary. She was admitted for, and received, her fifth chemotherapy treatment (into central vein) with Taxol and Cisplatin.

   Discharge diagnosis: Papillary serous cystadenocarcinoma, stage III.

Z51.11	Encounter for antineoplastic chemotherapy
C56.1	Malignant neoplasm of right ovary
3E04305	Introduction of other antineoplastic into central vein, percutaneous approach

Comments: The sole reason for admission was to receive chemotherapy; therefore, code Z51.11 is designated as the principal diagnosis. A code is also assigned for the neoplasm under treatment.

5. **Inpatient admission:** The patient was seen in the outpatient clinic, where an X-ray revealed compression fractures of T6 and T8. He gave no history of trauma. He was admitted for further evaluation to determine the etiology of the pathologic fractures. Bone marrow aspirate from the vertebrae and biopsies revealed multiple myeloma. During the stay, he went into fluid overload and developed some chest heaviness with runs of ventricular tachycardia. The tachycardia necessitated his transfer to cardiac level II to rule out myocardial infarction. Myocardial infarct was ruled out, and he was discharged after stabilization. He was to be followed up by the oncology clinic.

   Discharge diagnoses: (1) Multiple myeloma; (2) compression fractures, T6 and T8; (3) fluid overload; (4) tachycardia.

C90.00	Multiple myeloma not having achieved remission
M84.58xA	Pathological fracture in neoplastic disease, vertebrae, initial encounter for fracture
E87.70	Fluid overload, unspecified
I47.2	Ventricular tachycardia
07DS3ZX	Extraction of vertebral bone marrow, percutaneous approach, diagnostic

Comments: Although the compression fractures might appear to be the reason for admission, the purpose was clearly to determine the cause of these apparently spontaneous fractures. Diagnostic studies revealed that the underlying problem was the multiple myeloma. ICD-10-CM provides subcategory M84.5 for pathological fracture in neoplastic disease, with code M84.58 specifying vertebrae. The placeholder character "x" and the seventh-character value "A" are added to indicate that this is the initial encounter for the fracture.

6. **Physician office visit:** The 63-year-old patient made her annual visit to her gynecologist. She had no complaints. Examination revealed a 6- to 7-centimeter mass at the vaginal apex. She was to be scheduled for an exploratory laparotomy.

   Diagnosis: Vaginal mass.

N89.9 Noninflammatory disorder of vagina, unspecified

Comments: A mass is not classified to the Neoplasm chapter of ICD-10-CM unless it has been evaluated and determined to be neoplastic. There is no Alphabetic Index entry for the specific site under **Mass.** The Index provides direction to "see Disease of specified organ or site for **Mass,** specified organ NEC," which leads to code N89.9.

7. **Inpatient admission:** The patient was admitted for workup of an abdominal mass. An esophagogastroduodenoscopy with ultrasound of the abdomen demonstrated a complex cystic solid mass in the pancreas, which had invaded the portal vein. The mass was most consistent with carcinoma of the pancreas. The patient refused colonoscopy, biopsy, and surgery. Therefore, she was discharged with medication and was to follow up with her local physician for palliative treatment of carcinoma.

   Discharge diagnosis: Probable carcinoma of the pancreas with extension to the portal vein.

C25.9 Malignant neoplasm of pancreas, unspecified

C79.89 Secondary malignant neoplasm of other specified sites

0DJ08ZZ Inspection of upper intestinal tract, via natural or artificial opening endoscopic

Comments: Suspected carcinoma that is under treatment as if proven is coded as confirmed. Once a primary neoplasm spreads/extends beyond the boundary of the organ where it originated into an adjacent structure, it is coded as a secondary neoplasm. Metastatic neoplasms of veins are coded to neoplasms of connective tissue as directed in the Alphabetic Index of Diseases and Injuries.

8. **Inpatient admission (episode 1):** The patient had a rapidly progressing, drug-resistant, primitive melanotic neuroectodermal tumor (PNET) metastatic to the left femur. He was admitted for fixation of a pathologic fracture of the left femur. An open reduction with internal fixation of the left proximal femur with intramedullary nail insertion was performed.

   Discharge diagnoses: (1) PNET metastatic to the femur; (2) pathologic fracture, neck of the left femur.

M84.552A Pathological fracture in neoplastic disease, left femur, initial encounter for fracture

C79.51 Secondary malignant neoplasm of bone

C80.1 Malignant (primary) neoplasm, unspecified

0QS706Z Reposition left upper femur with intramedullary fixation device, open approach

Comments: Because the focus of the encounter is for the pathological fracture due to the neoplasm, the M84.552A code is sequenced first. Although the Alphabetic Index under **Tumor,** melanotic, neuroectodermal, directs the coder to "see **Neoplasm,** by site, benign," this neoplasm is obviously a malignant form because it has metastasized. The primary site is not identified, nor is guidance provided by the Alphabetic Index. Therefore, code C80.1, for an unknown primary site, is assigned.

ICD-10-PCS classifies fracture reduction to the root operation "Reposition."

Inpatient admission (episode 2): The patient was readmitted for management of a right-sided pleural effusion. A right-sided thoracentesis was accomplished, and he had some relief of his breathing. Cytology confirmed the pleural effusion as malignant. A closed biopsy of the right lung confirmed metastasis to the lung. The patient improved and was discharged to follow up in his physician's office.

Discharge diagnoses: (1) Malignant pleural effusion, (2) PNET metastatic to the left femur and right lung.

C78.01	Secondary malignant neoplasm of right lung
C79.51	Secondary malignant neoplasm of bone
C80.1	Malignant (primary) neoplasm, unspecified
J91.0	Malignant pleural effusion
0W993ZZ	Drainage of right pleural cavity, percutaneous approach
0BBK3ZX	Excision of right lung, percutaneous approach, diagnostic

Comments: The malignant pleural effusion is assigned to code J91.0. In addition, when coding malignant pleural effusion, code first the malignant neoplasm, if known. Code C80.1 is assigned to indicate that the primary malignancy has not been identified. The objective of the thoracentesis was drainage of the pleural effusion to assist in breathing.

Inpatient admission (episode 3): The patient was again admitted, this time for terminal care. The admission diagnosis was severe hypoxemia. He had massive bilateral pulmonary metastases. It was hoped that he could be relieved by chest tube drainage; however, it was obvious from his chest X-ray that removing a small amount of lung fluid would not affect the overall clinical situation. He had significant hemoptysis the second day of hospitalization and was in a comatose state until his death that evening.

Discharge diagnoses: (1) Hypoxemia and hemoptysis secondary to malignant pleural effusion, (2) coma, (3) primitive melanotic neuroectodermal tumor metastatic to the left femur and lungs. Primary unknown.

C78.01	Secondary malignant neoplasm of right lung
C79.51	Secondary malignant neoplasm of bone
C80.1	Malignant (primary) neoplasm, unspecified
J91.0	Malignant pleural effusion
R04.2	Hemoptysis
R40.20	Unspecified coma
R09.02	Hypoxemia
Z51.5	Encounter for palliative care

Comments: Although hypoxemia and hemoptysis are related to the pleural effusion, neither is routinely present with this condition, nor is coma integral to the diagnosed conditions. Therefore, symptom codes are assigned as additional diagnoses. Z51.5, Encounter for palliative care, is assigned as a secondary code because this patient was admitted for terminal care. Palliative care is an alternative to aggressive treatment for patients who are in the terminal phase of their illness. Palliative care is focused toward management of pain and symptoms.

9. **Inpatient admission:** The patient was admitted for chemotherapy. She had ovarian papillary serous cystadenocarcinoma, stage III. Three months earlier, diaphragmatic and omental masses were positive as well. She received Taxol and Cisplatin percutaneously via central vein IV without difficulty. She was to return in three weeks for her next treatment.

Discharge diagnosis: Stage III papillary serous cystadenocarcinoma with metastases to the diaphragm and omentum.

Z51.11	Encounter for antineoplastic chemotherapy
C56.9	Malignant neoplasm of unspecified ovary
C79.89	Secondary malignant neoplasm of other specified sites
C78.6	Secondary malignant neoplasm of retroperitoneum and peritoneum
3E04305	Introduction of other antineoplastic into central vein, percutaneous approach

Comments: The sole reason for admission is for administration of chemotherapy; therefore, Z51.11 is the principal diagnosis. Additional codes are assigned for the neoplastic disease under treatment; personal history of malignant neoplasm codes are not assigned when treatment is still in progress.

10. **Inpatient admission:** The patient was admitted for removal of an abdominal aortic aneurysm. When the abdomen was opened, carcinoma of the esophagus was found. Because the patient was elderly and the aneurysm was small, the surgeon decided not to repair it or to excise the neoplasm. Prior to discharge, a percutaneous endoscopic gastrostomy tube was inserted to ensure adequate caloric intake. The patient recovered without difficulty and was discharged to home with family.

    Discharge diagnoses: (1) Aortic aneurysm, (2) carcinoma of esophagus.

I71.4	Abdominal aortic aneurysm, without rupture
C15.9	Malignant neoplasm of esophagus, unspecified
0DH63UZ	Insertion of feeding device into stomach, percutaneous approach

Comments: Even though the initial treatment plan was not carried out, the principal diagnosis remains code I71.4 because the abdominal aneurysm was the condition that occasioned the admission. When only one site for a neoplasm is mentioned, it is assumed to be primary in the absence of any other information to the contrary.

The approach for the feeding tube insertion is "percutaneous." The endoscope is used for guidance and is not coded separately.

11. **Outpatient visit:** The patient complained of dyspnea on exertion, moderate night sweats, and intermittent fevers. On routine chest X-ray, a mass was visualized in the mediastinum. He was to be scheduled for a CT scan.

    Diagnosis: Probable neoplastic disease.

R22.2	Localized swelling, mass and lump, trunk
R06.00	Dyspnea, unspecified
R50.9	Fever, unspecified
R61	Generalized hyperhidrosis

Comments: Suspected conditions are not coded in the ambulatory care setting; therefore, only codes for the presenting symptoms and the mass identified on X-ray are assigned.

12. **Inpatient admission (episode 1):** The patient was admitted for evaluation of a mediastinal mass. On CT scan of the thorax, a large mass was identified in the anterior superior portion. Multiple pulmonary nodules were also seen. Needle biopsies of nodules in the lungs, obtained during an exploratory thoracotomy, were positive for yolk sac tumor. The first of a series of five chemotherapy treatments was administered percutaneously via central vein IV prior to discharge.

    Discharge diagnosis: Yolk sac tumor of mediastinum with metastases to both lungs.

C38.1	Malignant neoplasm of anterior mediastinum
C78.01	Secondary malignant neoplasm of right lung
C78.02	Secondary malignant neoplasm of left lung
0BBM3ZX	Excision of bilateral lungs, percutaneous approach, diagnostic
0WJ90ZZ	Inspection of right pleural cavity, open approach
0WJB0ZZ	Inspection of left pleural cavity, open approach
3E04305	Introduction of other antineoplastic into central vein, percutaneous approach
BP2WYZZ	Computerized tomography (CT scan) of thorax using other contrast

Comments: Even though chemotherapy was administered, the admission was not solely for this purpose; therefore, the procedure code shows that chemotherapy was administered. The code for yolk sac tumor is located by referring to **Tumor,** yolk sac, in the Alphabetic Index, then referring to the Neoplasm Table. Because the metastasis is to both lungs, and ICD-10-CM does not provide a single combination code for both lungs, separate codes are assigned. A code is assigned for the exploratory thoracotomy because no definitive surgery was associated with it. Because this was for both the left and right side, two codes are assigned.

Inpatient admission (episode 2): This admission was for a second cycle of chemotherapy (into central vein) for the yolk sac tumor of the mediastinum. The patient had minimal nausea and vomiting and was discharged following his treatment.

Discharge diagnosis: Yolk sac tumor of mediastinum with metastases to both lungs.

Z51.11	Encounter for antineoplastic chemotherapy
C38.1	Malignant neoplasm of anterior mediastinum
C78.01	Secondary malignant neoplasm of right lung
C78.02	Secondary malignant neoplasm of left lung
3E04305	Introduction of other antineoplastic into central vein, percutaneous approach

Comments: This admission was for the sole purpose of providing chemotherapy; therefore, code Z51.11 is the appropriate principal diagnosis code. The addition of the neoplasm codes indicates the conditions requiring the therapy.

13. **Inpatient admission:** The female patient had suffered from melanoma for a number of years. She had undergone a primary resection 10 years ago without recurrence, but one year ago, melanoma was discovered in her axilla. She underwent axillary dissection but, a few months later, presented with sacral pain, which bone scan revealed to be left femoral neck and right midfemur sites of metastasis. She had hepatic and adrenal metastases as well. She was admitted for the fifth course of chemotherapy, which was given percutaneously into central vein IV.

    Discharge diagnosis: Metastatic melanoma left and right femur, liver, and adrenal gland.

Z51.11	Encounter for antineoplastic chemotherapy
C79.51	Secondary malignant neoplasm of bone
C78.7	Secondary malignant neoplasm of liver and intrahepatic bile duct
C79.70	Secondary malignant neoplasm of unspecified adrenal gland
3E04305	Introduction of other antineoplastic into central vein, percutaneous approach

Comments: The sole reason for this admission was to provide chemotherapy. Codes are assigned for the current metastatic neoplasms; the history code is not assigned because the recurrent secondary neoplasms are the same type of neoplasm as the earlier neoplasms.

14. **Outpatient clinic visit:** The patient, an elderly woman, returned to the clinic for follow-up of her right malignant extramedullary ileal plasmacytoma. On a recent MRI, it was evident that the neoplasm, which was previously irradiated, had grown. Although she had failed current radiotherapy, there was no evidence that the neoplasm had spread outside its original location. She was started on medication and was to be scheduled for pelvic MRI.

    Diagnosis: Malignant ileal plasmacytoma.

C90.20	Extramedullary plasmacytoma not having achieved remission

Comments: **Plasmacytoma** is referenced in the Alphabetic Index, with the subterm "extramedullary." It is necessary to go to the Tabular List to complete the code.

15. **Inpatient admission:** The female patient had had abdominal pain for several months and infertility for three years. On hysterosalpingogram taken before admission, a right tubal occlusion and questionable uterine myoma were visualized. She was admitted for a myomectomy. During the procedure, multiple adhesions were noted from the tubes to a previous myomectomy site, and lysis was carried out. It was felt that the constriction of the tubes by the adhesions might be the cause of the infertility. On the third postoperative day, the staples were removed and the patient went home.

    Discharge diagnoses: (1) Symptomatic leiomyoma, (2) infertility, (3) adhesions.

D25.9	Leiomyoma of uterus, unspecified
N73.6	Female pelvic peritoneal adhesions (postinfective)
N97.1	Female infertility of tubal origin
0UB90ZZ	Excision of uterus, open approach
0UN70ZZ	Release bilateral fallopian tubes, open approach

Comments: The myoma of the uterus is the principal diagnosis because it was the reason for admission; the lysis of the adhesions was secondary to the excision of the myoma and was required in order to remove the leiomyoma. Dual coding is required for the infertility associated with peritubal adhesions. Lysis of adhesions is classified to the root operation "Release."

16. **Inpatient admission:** The patient was admitted for treatment of a moderately differentiated adenocarcinoma of the endometrium and myometrium. The diagnosis was made after a diagnostic D & C performed a month earlier. She was taken to surgery, where a laparotomy was performed through a midline incision. Exploration revealed no palpable nodes. A total abdominal hysterectomy and bilateral salpingo-oophorectomy were performed without incident or complication. Frozen section of the myometrium showed only minimal invasion at less than one-third of the depth. The postoperative course was benign, and the patient was discharged.

    Discharge diagnosis: Adenocarcinoma of the endometrium, moderately well differentiated, with minimal myometrial involvement.

C54.1	Malignant neoplasm of endometrium
C54.2	Malignant neoplasm of myometrium
0UT90ZZ	Resection of uterus, open approach
0UTC0ZZ	Resection of cervix, open approach
0UT20ZZ	Resection of bilateral ovaries, open approach
0UT70ZZ	Resection of bilateral fallopian tubes, open approach

Comments: The endometrium and myometrium are both parts of the uterus and are coded separately (C54.1 and C54.2). No additional code for secondary neoplasm is assigned. The exploratory laparotomy is the operative approach for the hysterectomy and salpingo-oophorectomy; therefore, a separate code for exploratory laparotomy (root operation "Inspection") is not assigned. Separate ICD-10-PCS codes are necessary for the removal of the uterus, cervix, ovaries, and fallopian tubes to represent a total hysterectomy.

17. Outpatient surgery (episode 1): The patient had a persistent left lung infiltrate on X-ray and subsequently had left pleural effusion. Thoracentesis and bronchoscopy with brush biopsy of the left lung were performed. Tissue studies yielded no diagnosis. The patient was to be admitted for further evaluation.

Diagnosis: Left pleural infiltrate on X-ray, pleural effusion.

J90	Pleural effusion, not elsewhere classified
R91.8	Other nonspecific abnormal findings of lung field
0W9B3ZZ	Drainage of left pleural cavity, percutaneous approach
0BBL8ZX	Excision of left lung, via natural or artificial opening endoscopic, diagnostic

Comments: The pleural effusion was the reason for the encounter. A code is assigned for the abnormal X-ray finding because the physician felt it to be significant and listed it as a diagnosis. The objective of the thoracentesis is to drain fluid from the pleural cavity.

Inpatient admission (episode 2): The patient was taken to surgery, where a thoracoscopy with decortication and left pleural biopsy were performed. The final specimen report showed moderately differentiated epidermoid carcinoma of the left lung. The patient's first course of electron beam radiation therapy was given prior to discharge.

Discharge diagnosis: Primary carcinoma of lung.

C34.92	Malignant neoplasm of unspecified part of left bronchus or lung
0BDP4ZZ	Extraction of left pleura, percutaneous endoscopic approach
0BBP4ZX	Excision of left pleura, percutaneous endoscopic approach, diagnostic
DB023ZZ	Beam radiation of lung using electrons

Comments: This admission was for further evaluation of the patient's condition, and surgery for the malignancy was performed. Although radiation therapy was begun during the hospital stay, it was not the purpose for this admission.

18. Inpatient admission: The patient developed right-sided tinnitus two years earlier, followed by a precipitous loss of hearing on the right side. A preadmission MRI scan identified a large acoustic neuroma. Because hearing on the right was totally lost, it was decided to excise the neuroma using an open radiosurgical destruction technique. The tumor was dissected completely. There were no postoperative complications, and the patient was discharged in satisfactory condition.

Discharge diagnosis: Acoustic neuroma on the right.

D33.3	Benign neoplasm of cranial nerves
005N0ZZ	Destruction of acoustic nerve, open approach

Comments: The hearing loss is integral to the neuroma, and so no additional code is assigned. The neuroma was destroyed using radiosurgical technique and therefore coded to the root operation "Destruction."

19. Inpatient admission: The patient, an elderly right-handed woman, was transferred from a nursing home with left hemiparesis and a diagnosis of suspected brain tumor. She underwent a CT-guided stereotactic biopsy without complications. The frozen-section diagnosis was glioblastoma. She was to come back for radiation therapy the following week, and in the meantime she was to be transferred back to the nursing home for further management. She had continued left hemiparesis, which prevents her from being managed at home.

Discharge diagnoses: (1) Primary glioblastoma, right temporal lobe; (2) left hemiparesis.

C71.2	Malignant neoplasm of temporal lobe
G81.94	Hemiplegia, unspecified affecting left nondominant side
0W914ZX	Drainage of cranial cavity, percutaneous endoscopic approach, diagnostic

Comments: The hemiparesis is not considered a late effect of the glioblastoma because glioblastoma is a current condition under treatment. Late effect is defined as "the residual effect that remains after the termination of the acute phase of an illness or injury."

20. Inpatient admission: The patient, an elderly woman, entered the hospital with a history of weight loss, anorexia, dysphagia, and rectal bleeding. She had also fallen many times at home. A fecal impaction was diagnosed from an abdominal CT scan following admission. Preparation for colonoscopy took about three days, and when the colonoscopy was finally accomplished, the impaction had cleared and no abnormalities were seen. A hiatal hernia was found on esophagogastroduodenoscopy, and two meningiomas were identified on magnetic resonance imaging of the head. She was started on Zantac for the hiatal hernia. It seemed that most of her generalized symptoms were secondary to the fecal impaction. The falling episodes are most likely related to the meningiomas, although they showed no mass effect. Neurological consultation was to be obtained as an outpatient. The patient was discharged on stool softeners for prevention of fecal impaction and Zantac for hiatal hernia.

Discharge diagnoses: (1) Meningiomas, (2) fecal impaction, (3) hiatal hernia.

K56.41	Fecal impaction
D32.9	Benign neoplasm of meninges, unspecified
K44.9	Diaphragmatic hernia without obstruction or gangrene
Z91.81	History of falling
0DJD8ZZ	Inspection of lower intestinal tract, via natural or artificial opening endoscopic
0DJ08ZZ	Inspection of upper intestinal tract, via natural or artificial opening endoscopic
BW20ZZZ	Computerized tomography (CT scan) of abdomen
B030ZZZ	Magnetic resonance imaging (MRI) of brain

Comments: Fecal impaction is designated as the principal diagnosis because it was felt to account for most of the admitting symptoms. Both the hiatal hernia and the meningiomas were diagnosed as the result of further evaluation of the patient's symptoms, with both conditions further evaluated and/or treated during this admission. Code Z91.81, History of falling, is assigned because of the patient's history of having fallen at home many times. This code is for patients who have fallen in the past and may be more susceptible to falling in the future. It also includes the concept of a person at risk for falling.

21. **Inpatient admission:** The patient was admitted with severe back pain. He had prostate cancer excised in 2006. An MRI performed prior to admission showed metastasis to the S1, S2, and S3 areas of the spine. A fine-needle aspiration biopsy of the sacrum was performed, and the report confirmed that metastatic adenocarcinoma, consistent with a prostatic primary, was strongly positive. A bilateral open scrotal orchiectomy was performed without complication. Megavoltage beam radiation treatments (photons 9 MeV) to the operative site were started, and the pain came under control with intravenous morphine. The patient was discharged with pain well controlled on oral medications.

    Discharge diagnosis: Metastatic prostate cancer.

C79.51	Secondary malignant neoplasm of bone
G89.3	Neoplasm related pain (acute) (chronic)
Z85.46	Personal history of malignant neoplasm of prostate
0VTC0ZZ	Resection of bilateral testes, open approach
0QB13ZX	Excision of sacrum, percutaneous approach, diagnostic
DV010ZZ	Beam radiation of testis using photons <1 MeV

Comments: The narrative indicates that there are secondary sites of neoplasm in the spine. The primary site (prostate) was removed in 2006, and because there is no mention of any recurrence, history code Z85.46 is assigned. Radiotherapy was begun on this admission, but it was not the sole purpose of the admission. Code G89.3 is assigned as an additional diagnosis because the admission was for management of the neoplasm, and the pain associated with the neoplasm is also documented.

22. **Inpatient admission:** This 14-year-old patient was admitted to the hospital with a diagnosis of glioblastoma multiforme. The patient is now admitted to undergo a blood brain barrier disruption and percutaneous intra-arterial chemotherapy via the right internal carotid artery and, two days later, via the right basilar artery.

    Discharge diagnosis: Glioblastoma multiforme, admit for chemotherapy.

Z51.11	Encounter for antineoplastic chemotherapy
C71.9	Malignant neoplasm of brain, unspecified
3E053GN	Introduction of blood brain barrier disruption substance into peripheral artery, percutaneous approach
3E06305	Introduction of other antineoplastic into central artery, percutaneous approach

Comments: Code Z51.11 is assigned as the principal diagnosis because the patient was admitted for chemotherapy, which was administered through the blood brain barrier for quicker absorption. Both the blood brain barrier disruption and the administration of chemotherapy should be assigned for the procedures.

23. **Outpatient encounter:** A patient presented to the outpatient imaging department for a "high risk" screening mammogram. The physician documented that she is postmenopausal and nulliparous. In addition, the patient has a sister who is currently being treated for breast cancer.

    Diagnoses: (1) Screening mammogram, bilateral; (2) postmenopausal; (3) nulliparous.

Z12.31	Encounter for screening mammogram for malignant neoplasm of breast
Z78.0	Asymptomatic menopausal state
Z80.3	Family history of malignant neoplasm of breast

Comments: There is no code to specifically identify "high risk" screening mammography. However, additional codes are assigned to show the nature of the high-risk factor.

24. **Outpatient encounter:** The patient has small-cell lung cancer that is in complete remission. The patient is now being seen for prophylactic cranial irradiation therapy, using photons 1-10 MeV.

Diagnoses: (1) Small-cell lung cancer, in remission; (2) radiation therapy.

Z51.0	Encounter for antineoplastic radiation therapy
Z85.118	Personal history of other malignant neoplasm of bronchus and lung
DW011ZZ	Beam radiation of head and neck using photons 1 - 10 MeV

Comments: A code for the encounter for radiation therapy is assigned as the first-listed diagnosis for this admission. Assign a code to show the personal history of small-cell lung cancer, as well as a code to show that the patient is receiving the radiation therapy as a prophylactic measure. The appropriate procedure code for the administration of the radiation therapy should also be assigned.

18. INJURIES

1. **Inpatient admission:** The patient was struck in the face with a softball during a recreational ball game with no loss of consciousness. The result was severe compound fractures of the left ethmoid sinus and frontal sinus bones. The fractures were debrided, and open reduction was carried out. Initially, the postoperative course was uneventful, and the nasal packs, sutures, and nasal splint were removed. However, on the eighth day, the patient became confused and combative. A lumbar puncture was grossly positive for submeningitis. Again, improvement was rapid with antibiotics and intravenous steroids.

   Discharge diagnoses: (1) Compound nasal, ethmoid, and frontal sinus fractures; (2) post-operative meningitis.

   Procedures: Open reduction of compound fractures of the ethmoid and frontal sinus bones.

S02.19xB	Other fracture of base of skull, initial encounter for open fracture
G03.9	Meningitis, unspecified
W21.07xA	Struck by softball, initial encounter
Y92.838	Other recreation area as the place of occurrence of the external cause
Y93.64	Baseball
Y99.8	Other external cause status
0NSG0ZZ	Reposition left ethmoid bone, open approach
0NS20ZZ	Reposition left frontal bone, open approach
009U3ZX	Drainage of spinal canal, percutaneous approach, diagnostic

Comments: Compound fractures are open by definition. In ICD-10-CM the fracture code has a seventh-character qualifier. In this case the fractures are open and this is the initial encounter for the fracture. A placeholder "x" is used to allow for the seventh-character qualifier to be applied. When each of the fractured bones is referenced under the main term **Fracture,** there is an instruction to "see **Fracture,** skull, base."

The External cause code W21.07xA shows that the patient was struck by a softball. These codes require a seventh-character qualifier to indicate that this is the initial or subsequent encounter or a sequela. The placeholder "x" is used so that the qualifier character can be applied. The Y92.838 code indicates that the accident occurred in a place for recreation. ICD-10-CM has activity codes and activity status codes that are assigned for the initial encounter. Codes Y93.64 for playing softball and Y99.8 for recreational activity are assigned.

Fracture reduction is coded to the root operation "Reposition" in ICD-10-PCS, for moving to its normal location or other suitable location all or a portion of a body part. Separate codes exist for each bone, and laterality is required. The lumbar puncture is a drainage procedure for diagnostic purposes, so the qualifier character is X.

2. **Inpatient admission:** The patient, an elderly woman, was cleaning the bathroom and fell backward into the bathtub at her home. She was admitted with possible compression fractures of the lumbar spine. She had had several similar falls in the past due to frequent transient ischemic attacks. She lives alone in a single-family residence. X-rays of the spine showed some degenerative disk disease of L4 and L5, but there were no fractures. She was treated for pain and released after two days.

Discharge diagnoses: (1) Lumbar sprain injury to back, (2) probable transient ischemic attack.

S33.5xxA	Sprain of ligaments of lumbar spine, initial encounter
G45.9	Transient cerebral ischemic attack, unspecified
W18.12xA	Fall from or off toilet with subsequent striking against object, initial encounter
Y92.012	Bathroom of single-family (private) house as the place of occurrence of the external cause
Z91.81	History of falling
Y93.E5	Floor mopping and cleaning
Y99.8	Other external cause status

Comments: The compression fractures were ruled out; therefore, no codes are assigned. In ICD-10-CM the injury code has a seventh-character value to indicate the status of the encounter. This is the initial encounter for the injury, so placeholder "x" is used as needed to allow the seventh-character value to be applied. For the External cause of injury code, again the placeholder "x" is used before the seventh character for initial encounter.

The "probable" transient ischemic attack is coded as an established diagnosis because it is listed as a final diagnosis for an inpatient admission, and the summary strongly implies that the fall was probably due to another such attack. The radiology report contained incidental findings of degenerative disk disease that was not treated or further evaluated; therefore, no code is assigned for this condition. Code Z91.81, History of falling, is added because the patient has had several similar falls in the past. An activity code and activity status are added for the case.

Although the fractures were located in the lumbar area, the summary does not specify the area included in the X-ray.

3. **Inpatient admission:** The patient was carrying a bicycle up an outside stairway at his house when he fell from the stairway into the alley. An X-ray of the lumbosacral spine taken in the emergency department showed an L4 fracture, and X-ray of the upper arm revealed a nondisplaced comminuted fracture of the shaft of the right humerus. An L4-L5 bilateral posterior foraminotomy with fusion and a bone graft (obtained from the iliac crest) to the posterior column L4-L5 facet joints were performed. The fracture of the humerus was treated with application of a sling and immobilization for five days.

   Discharge diagnoses: (1) Fracture, L4; (2) nondisplaced fracture, humerus.

S32.049A	Unspecified fracture of fourth lumbar vertebra, initial encounter for closed fracture
S42.354A	Nondisplaced comminuted fracture of shaft of humerus, right arm, initial encounter for closed fracture
W10.9xxA	Fall (on) (from) unspecified stairs and steps, initial encounter
Y92.018	Other place in single-family (private) house as the place of occurrence of the external cause
0SG1071	Fusion of 2 or more lumbar vertebral joints with autologous tissue substitute, posterior approach, posterior column, open approach
0QB20ZZ	Excision of right pelvic bone, open approach
2W38XYZ	Immobilization of right upper extremity using other device

Comments: The vertebral fracture is the more serious injury and received the major thrust of treatment; therefore, it is designated as the principal diagnosis. The ICD-10-CM code is specific for the L4 site, but the type of fracture is not specified. The closed nature of the fracture is reflected in the seventh-character qualifier. The S42.354A code includes the side of the body, nondisplaced, and the specific type of fracture as well as the fact that this is the initial encounter for a closed fracture. The patient was carrying a bicycle and not bicycling at the time of the accident, so no activity code is assigned.

Code 0SG1071 includes the open posterior approach to the posterior column, fusion, and use of bone graft, autologous tissue substitute. Code 0QB20ZZ is assigned to identify the harvesting of bone from the right iliac crest for use as a bone graft. The sling is placed on the entire arm, so the body part "upper extremity, right," is used.

4. **Inpatient admission:** The patient was admitted following a fall from a ladder at home while watering flowerboxes in the garden, in which she sustained numerous injuries. X-rays showed a nondisplaced fracture of the right humeral neck. A splint was applied, but no other treatment was required. There were contusions on her forehead, thighs, and knees, as well as small abrasions of her forehead and right thigh. The patient received pain medications because of the contusions. The abrasions were superficial and healed without treatment and without evidence of infection.

   Discharge diagnoses: (1) Nondisplaced fracture, right humerus; (2) contusions of forehead, thighs, and knees; (3) abrasions on forehead and right thigh.

S42.214A	Unspecified nondisplaced fracture of surgical neck of right humerus, initial encounter for closed fracture
S00.83xA	Contusion of other part of head, initial encounter
S70.11xA	Contusion of right thigh, initial encounter
S70.12xA	Contusion of left thigh, initial encounter
S80.01xA	Contusion of right knee, initial encounter
S80.02xA	Contusion of left knee, initial encounter
W11.xxxA	Fall on and from ladder, initial encounter
Y92.017	Garden or yard in single-family (private) house as the place of occurrence of the external cause
Y93.H2	Activity, gardening and landscaping
Y99.8	Other external cause status
2W3CX1Z	Immobilization of right lower arm using splint

Comments: The fracture is the most severe injury and is therefore designated as the principal diagnosis. Because the fracture was not displaced, no "Reduction" was required. The code is located by referencing the main term **Fracture,** subterms "anatomic neck," "see fracture humerus," "upper end." At this entry subterm "upper end anatomical neck," see "fracture, humerus, upper end, specified NEC, non-displaced" to get to the code S42.21-. Complete the code by checking the Tabular List.

Codes are listed for the contusions of the forehead and for both the left and right thighs and knee, as pain killers were administered for these injuries. No codes are assigned for the abrasions because they required no further evaluation, and no definitive treatment was directed to them.

5. **Inpatient admission:** The patient was admitted with diagnoses of probable rib fractures and pneumonia. She slipped and fell in the bathtub of her single-family home while taking a shower about four days before admission and had experienced increasingly severe upper back and neck pain. Just prior to admission, she began running a fever, felt short of breath, and developed inspiratory chest wall pain. No rib fractures were identified on chest X-ray, but right upper lobe pneumonia was evident. Sputum culture grew *Klebsiella*. The patient was started on antibiotics and the pneumonia improved. Back pain was relieved by pain medication and bed rest.

   Discharge diagnoses: (1) Right upper lobe pneumonia, (2) cervical and thoracic back strain.

J15.0	Pneumonia due to Klebsiella pneumoniae
S13.4xxA	Sprain of ligaments of cervical spine, initial encounter
S23.8xxA	Sprain of other specified parts of thorax, initial encounter
W18.2xxA	Fall in (into) shower or empty bathtub, initial encounter
Y92.012	Bathroom of single-family (private) house as the place of occurrence of the external cause
Y93.E1	Activity, personal bathing and showering
Y99.8	Other external cause status

Comments: The condition responsible for admission, after study, was found to be pneumonia. The back strain occurred four days prior to admission and probably would not have required hospital admission if it had been the only problem. Although this injury happened four days ago, this is still the initial encounter while the patient is receiving active treatment for the condition. The pneumonia was described in the narrative as being due to *Klebsiella;* therefore, code J18.1, Lobar pneumonia, unspecified organism, is not appropriate. In addition, the activity and activity status codes for bathing are also assigned.

6. **Emergency department visit:** The patient and her husband had been drinking heavily, became intoxicated, and had an argument when they got home to their second-floor apartment. During the argument, he shoved her and she fell in the bedroom against the corner of the water bed, striking her left upper back and chest. She came to the emergency department complaining of severe pain and difficulty breathing. She was found to have subcutaneous emphysema due to the fractures of the ninth and tenth ribs. The ribs were strapped, and she was given a prescription for pain medication. She was released to be followed up as an outpatient.

   Diagnoses: (1) Fractured left ribs, ninth and tenth posteriorly; (2) subcutaneous emphysema; (3) alcohol abuse with intoxication.

S22.42xA	Multiple fractures of ribs, left side, initial encounter for closed fracture
T79.7xxA	Traumatic subcutaneous emphysema, initial encounter
F10.129	Alcohol abuse with intoxication, unspecified
W18.09	Striking against other object with subsequent fall, initial encounter
Y92.032	Bedroom in apartment as the place of occurrence of the external cause
Y04.0xxA	Assault by unarmed brawl or fight, initial encounter

Comments: The fractured ribs were the reason for the emergency department encounter. Although the alcohol abuse was not further evaluated or treated, it was closely related to the trauma and should be coded.

7. **Inpatient admission:** The patient, an elderly woman, was admitted following a fall off her porch at her single-family home while sweeping leaves off the porch. A femoral intertrochanteric fracture was diagnosed in the emergency department, and she was admitted. An open reduction with internal fixation was carried out. As anticipated, postoperative transfusions of whole blood via central vein for blood loss were required during surgery. The blood loss resulted in a drop in hemoglobin and hematocrit, which were monitored daily. Her postoperative recovery went smoothly, and she was transferred to the skilled nursing unit for rehabilitation.

   Discharge diagnoses: (1) Closed fracture, right femur; (2) acute blood loss anemia.

S72.141A	Displaced intertrochanteric fracture of right femur, initial encounter for closed fracture
D62	Acute posthemorrhagic anemia
W13.9xxA	Fall from, out of or through building, not otherwise specified, initial encounter
Y92.018	Other place in single-family (private) house as the place of occurrence of the external cause
Y93.H9	Activity, other involving exterior property and land maintenance, building and construction
Y99.8	Other external cause status
0QS604Z	Reposition right upper femur with internal fixation device, open approach
30243H1	Transfusion of nonautologous whole blood into central vein, percutaneous approach

Comments: The fracture is described as intertrochanteric in the narrative and so the more specific code is assigned. Fractures not specified as open or closed are coded as closed. Fractures not specified as displaced or nondisplaced are coded as displaced. The surgery resulted in only an expected amount of blood loss. However, treatment was rendered (transfusions) and monitoring continued (hemoglobin and hematocrit).

8. **Inpatient admission:** Three weeks before admission, the patient, a construction worker, sustained a perilunate dislocation along with closed fractures of the third metacarpal and proximal middle phalanx bones of the left hand in an accident. The accident occurred when he went to sleep at the wheel and the dump truck he was driving overturned in the median of the interstate; no other vehicles were involved. Immediately after the accident, the patient was seen in a local emergency department, where the metacarpal fracture was reduced and casted and the proximal phalanx was reduced and splinted. The perilunate dislocation was not reduced at that time. He was now admitted to this hospital, where a closed reduction of the perilunate dislocation was carried out after X-rays confirmed there was no fracture and the phalangeal and metacarpal fractures remained in good alignment. A short arm cast was applied, and he was discharged.

   Discharge diagnoses: (1) Closed right perilunate dislocation, (2) healing fractures of the metacarpal shaft and proximal phalanx on the right.

S63.092A	Other subluxation of left wrist and hand, initial encounter
S62.323A	Displaced fracture of shaft of third metacarpal bone, left hand, initial encounter for closed fracture
S62.613A	Displaced fracture of proximal phalanx of left middle finger, initial encounter for closed fracture
V85.5xxA	Driver of special construction vehicle injured in nontraffic accident, initial encounter
Y92.411	Interstate highway as the place of occurrence of the external cause
Y93.H9	Activity, other involving exterior property and land maintenance, building and construction
Y99.0	Civilian activity done for income or pay
0RSPXZZ	Reposition left wrist joint, external approach

Comments: The lunate bone is in the wrist. Fractures that are not specified as open or closed are coded as closed; those not specified as nondisplaced or displaced are coded as displaced. Although three weeks old, the fractures have not healed and are current injuries, and the patient is receiving active treatment for the fracture. This qualifies as an initial encounter as the patient is still involved in active treatment of the injury with a new physician. Code V85.5xxA is referenced in the Index to External Causes of Injury under the entry **Accident,** transport, occupant, dump truck—see **Accident,** transport, construction vehicle occupant. Refer to the Tabular List to complete the code. Activity codes are assigned as this is the initial encounter for treatment of this particular injury.

9. **Inpatient admission:** The patient fell from a tree that he was pruning on his farm. He was able to drive himself to the hospital, but it was apparent on admission that his left arm was fractured. He underwent an open reduction and internal fixation of a fracture of the proximal humerus and an open reduction and internal fixation of the comminuted fractures of the radial and ulnar shafts. He recovered without incident and was discharged to follow up in one week.

   Discharge diagnoses: (1) Comminuted left radius and ulnar shaft fractures, (2) displaced left proximal humerus fracture.

S42.202A	Unspecified fracture of upper end of left humerus, initial encounter for closed fracture
S52.252A	Displaced comminuted fracture of shaft of ulna, left arm, initial encounter for closed fracture
S52.352A	Displaced comminuted fracture of shaft of radius, left arm, initial encounter for closed fracture
W14.xxxA	Fall from tree, initial encounter
Y92.79	Other farm location as the place of occurrence of the external cause
Y93.H2	Activity, gardening and landscaping
Y99.0	Civilian activity done for income or pay
0PSG04Z	Reposition left humeral shaft with internal fixation device, open approach
0PSJ04Z	Reposition left radius with internal fixation device, open approach
0PSL04Z	Reposition left ulna with internal fixation device, open approach

Comments: ICD-10-CM requires separate codes for the fractures of the radius and ulna. The narrative provides more specificity as to the location of the fractures, and so the more specific codes are assigned. Either fracture could have been designated as the principal diagnosis because both are essentially equal in severity. ICD-10-PCS codes are assigned for each site repositioned.

10. Inpatient admission: The patient fell in her apartment after tripping over her cat while carrying a laundry basket to the washer. She was brought in by ambulance and admitted with a fracture of the shaft of right femur. An open reduction with internal fixation was performed. A postoperative fever developed, and a chest X-ray showed severe atelectasis as the cause of the fever. Respiratory therapy gave instructions on incentive spirometry, antibiotics were initiated, and the patient was discharged to a nursing home.

Discharge diagnoses: (1) Closed fracture, femur; (2) postoperative fever and atelectasis.

S72.301A	Unspecified fracture of shaft of right femur, initial encounter for closed fracture
J98.11	Atelectasis
J95.89	Other postprocedural complications and disorders of respiratory system, not elsewhere classified
W01.0xxA	Fall on same level from slipping, tripping and stumbling without subsequent striking against object, initial encounter
Y92.039	Unspecified place in apartment as the place of occurrence of the external cause
Y93.E2	Activity, laundry
Y99.8	Other external cause status
0QS804Z	Reposition right femoral shaft with internal fixation device, open approach

Comments: The information in the narrative is used to assign a more specific code for the fracture. Assign codes J98.11 and J95.89 because the fever and atelectasis were specified as postoperative. The fever is a symptom of the atelectasis. Postoperative atelectasis is often an incidental radiographic or physical finding that is frequently a self-limiting condition, in which case it would not be coded or reported. In this case, it was associated with fever and required further diagnostic (e.g., chest X-ray) and therapeutic (e.g., incentive spirometry) workup.

11. Inpatient admission: The patient was admitted after a box fell on his head at the service garage where he works. A CT scan of the head was negative for any abnormalities, but hourly neurological checks were made to rule out an intracranial injury. No injury was found. A small abrasion on his upper right arm, where the box scraped the skin, was cleansed and Neosporin applied.

Discharge diagnosis: Observation for possible intracranial injury.

Z04.2	Encounter for examination and observation following work accident
S40.811A	Abrasion of right upper arm, initial encounter
W20.8xxA	Other cause of strike by thrown, projected or falling object, initial encounter
Y92.524	Gas station as the place of occurrence of the external cause
Y93.89	Activity, other specified
Y99.0	Civilian activity done for income or pay

Comments: The purpose of the admission was to determine whether the patient had suffered any kind of intracranial injury; this was ruled out. Even though there was a minor injury that did not require hospital admission, the observation code is still assigned as the principal diagnosis. This situation is consistent with the inclusion note with category Z04, "when a person without a diagnosis is suspected of having an abnormal condition, without signs or symptoms, which requires study, but after examination and observation, is ruled out."

12. **Inpatient admission:** The patient, a seven-year-old male, sustained a high-velocity gunshot wound in a drive-by shooting. He was riding his bike in his neighborhood street. He was brought to the emergency department with a massive hemorrhage from the left groin due to the gunshot wound. He also sustained major lacerations of the femoral artery and femoral vein at the hip level, in addition to a bullet lodged in the femur. The patient was immediately taken to surgery. The following procedures were performed via incision: (1) left internal iliac to femoral artery bypass graft with reverse saphenous vein graft; (2) left popliteal to femoral vein bypass graft with greater saphenous vein graft; (3) removal of bullet from the femur; (4) insertion of pins in fracture, left femur.

    Discharge diagnoses: (1) Lacerations of left common femoral artery and femoral vein, with massive hemorrhage; (2) gunshot wound to left groin with high-velocity rifle; (3) bullet lodged in femur; (4) open, nondisplaced, type III C nondisplaced subtrochanteric fracture of left femur.

S75.022A	Major laceration of femoral artery, left leg, initial encounter
S75.122A	Major laceration of femoral vein at hip and thigh level, left leg, initial encounter
S31.124A	Laceration of abdominal wall with foreign body, left lower quadrant without penetration into peritoneal cavity, initial encounter
S72.25xC	Nondisplaced subtrochanteric fracture of left femur, initial encounter for open fracture type IIIA, IIIB, or IIIC
X95.8xxA	Assault by other firearm discharge, initial encounter
Y92.414	Local residential or business street as the place of occurrence of the external cause
Y93.55	Activity, bike riding
Y99.8	Other external cause status
041F09J	Bypass left internal iliac artery to left femoral artery with autologous venous tissue, open approach
0QH704Z	Insertion of internal fixation device into left upper femur, open approach
0QC70ZZ	Extirpation of matter from left upper femur, open approach
06BQ0ZZ	Excision of left greater saphenous vein, open approach

Comments: Because the hemorrhage was life threatening, either blood vessel laceration could represent the principal diagnosis. The injury was not incidental to the fracture (did not occur secondary to the fracture) but occurred in addition to the fracture as a result of the gunshot wound. The fracture was stated to be a type IIIC, so the seventh character "C" is used. There were two bypass procedures performed. In ICD-10-PCS the body part value identifies the origin of the bypass and the qualifier identifies the destination. The harvesting of the greater saphenous vein used for the bypass graft is coded separately to the root operation "Excision." Putting a pin into a nondisplaced fracture is coded to the root operation "Insertion." The removal of the bullet from the femur meets the definition of the root procedure "Extirpation": taking or cutting out solid matter from a body part.

13. **Inpatient admission:** The patient, a 10-year-old boy, was admitted through the emergency department after being struck by an automobile while riding his bicycle in the street in front of his home. His injuries were fractures of the left tibia and fibula, a 4-centimeter laceration and superficial abrasions on the left side of head, and a 1-centimeter-deep laceration on the right earlobe. The fractures were reduced via incision, and an intramedullary Rush rod was placed in the left tibia. The earlobe and head lacerations were sutured.

    Discharge diagnoses: (1) Simple fractures, left tibia and fibula; (2) right ear laceration; (3) left parietooccipital laceration.

S82.202A	Unspecified fracture of shaft of left tibia, initial encounter for closed fracture
S82.402A	Unspecified fracture of shaft of left fibula, initial encounter for closed fracture
S01.01xA	Laceration without foreign body of scalp, initial encounter
S01.311A	Laceration without foreign body of right ear, initial encounter
V13.4	Pedal cycle driver injured in collision with car, pick-up truck or van in traffic accident
Y92.414	Local residential or business street as the place of occurrence of the external cause
Y93.55	Activity, bike riding
Y99.8	Other external cause status
0QSH06Z	Reposition left tibia with intramedullary fixation device, open approach
0QSK0ZZ	Reposition left fibula, open approach
0HQ2XZZ	Repair right ear skin, external approach
0HQ0XZZ	Repair scalp skin, external approach

Comments: No code is assigned for the superficial abrasions because they are associated with a more severe injury at the same site. Fractures not specified as open or closed are coded as closed. ICD-10-CM has separate codes for fractures of the tibia and fibula, and ICD-10-PCS has separate codes for the reductions, which qualify as the root procedure "Reposition." A Rush rod is an "intramedullary fixation device."

14. **Emergency department visit (episode 1):** The patient had been drinking heavily in recent weeks. While visiting the area, he reduced his alcohol intake during the past 24 hours and suffered a seizure. In the emergency department, he seemed to be normal. No neurological or physical abnormalities were noted, and he was released after receiving Dilantin.

    Diagnosis: Seizure, probably due to decrease in alcohol consumption.

R56.9 Unspecified convulsions

Comments: Code R56.9 is the appropriate code assignment for this encounter. "Probable" conditions are not coded in the outpatient setting.

Inpatient admission (episode 2): The patient returned to his room at a local motel, had another seizure, and then fell in the bathroom. He was again brought to the emergency department and found to have a dislocated shoulder. Several attempts were made to replace the shoulder to its proper position. Because this reduction was not successful, he was admitted. With medications to control alcohol withdrawal and seizures along with IV fluids, he became mentally clear. A closed reduction of the dislocated shoulder was performed. The injury became a difficult management problem because the patient would not leave the orthopedic appliance on, and the next day a heavy plaster cast was placed on the shoulder to ensure correct positioning and activity reduction.

Discharge diagnoses: (1) Alcohol withdrawal seizure, (2) left shoulder dislocation.

S43.005A	Unspecified dislocation of left shoulder joint, initial encounter
F10.239	Alcohol dependence with withdrawal, unspecified
R56.9	Unspecified convulsions
W18.00XA	Striking against unspecified object with subsequent fall, initial encounter
Y92.59	Other trade areas as the place of occurrence of the external cause
0RSJXZZ	Reposition right shoulder joint, external approach
2W39X2Z	Immobilization of left upper extremity using cast

Comments: Because attempts to reduce the dislocation were unsuccessful in the emergency department, the patient was admitted. Therefore, shoulder dislocation is the principal diagnosis.

15. **Emergency department visit (episode 1):** The 14-year-old patient was brought to the emergency department with severe pain and swelling of his left ankle. He sustained the injury when he fell off his skateboard on the grade school playground. An X-ray showed a simple trimalleolar fracture of his left ankle. The fracture was reduced, and he was placed in a long leg cast.

Diagnosis: Severe pain and swelling, left ankle, associated with trimalleolar fracture.

S82.852A	Displaced trimalleolar fracture of left lower leg, initial encounter for closed fracture
V00.131A	Fall from skateboard, initial encounter
Y92.211	Elementary school as the place of occurrence of the external cause
Y93.51	Activity, roller skating (inline) and skateboarding
Y99.8	Other external cause status
0QSH3ZZ	Reposition left tibia, percutaneous approach

Comments: A trimalleolar fracture involves the medial, lateral, and posterior malleoli of the tibia. A simple fracture is closed. Fractures that are not specified as nondisplaced or displaced are coded as displaced. Reduction of a displaced fracture is coded to the root operation "Reposition," and the application of a cast or splint in conjunction with the "Reposition" procedure is not coded separately.

Orthopedic clinic visit (episode 2): The patient was status post trimalleolar fracture of the left ankle. He had been in the cast since sustaining the injury three weeks earlier. He had no complaints regarding the fracture, but he had worn down the cast. The cast breakdown extended the length of the sole of the foot. The long leg cast was removed, and the skin was intact. X-rays showed a healing fracture with no change in the reduction. Therefore, he was placed back into a short leg walking cast.

Diagnosis: Aftercare, healing left trimalleolar fracture.

S82.852D	Displaced trimalleolar fracture of left lower leg, subsequent encounter for closed fracture with routine healing
V00.131D	Fall from skateboard, subsequent encounter
2W0RX2Z	Change cast on left lower leg

Comments: The fracture is healing, and the patient was seen solely for cast change. In ICD-10-CM, aftercare for fractures is indicated by using the fracture code with a seventh-character value for subsequent encounter. In this case "D" is used, as this is routine healing for a closed fracture. The External cause code is used for each encounter for which the injury or condition is being treated. This code also has the seventh-character value "D," showing that this is a subsequent encounter.

Orthopedic clinic visit (episode 3): The patient is status post trimalleolar fracture of the left ankle. The fracture now appears to be well healed. The cast was removed. There is no swelling or redness. No additional follow-up is anticipated.

Diagnosis: Aftercare, status post left trimalleolar fracture.

S82.852D	Displaced trimalleolar fracture of left lower leg, subsequent encounter for closed fracture with routine healing
V00.131D	Fall from skateboard, subsequent encounter
2W5RX2Z	Removal of cast on left lower leg

Comments: The fracture has healed, and the patient is seen solely for removal of cast. This episode of care qualifies as a subsequent encounter, after the patient has received active treatment of the injury and is receiving routine care during the healing or recovery phase. The External cause code is used for each encounter for which the injury or condition is being treated. Both codes have the qualifier "D," showing that this is a subsequent encounter.

16. **Inpatient admission:** The patient fractured her left knee several years earlier when she was thrown off a horse. Since then she had undergone realignment and debridement procedures of the undersurface of the patella. At the time of admission, she was severely disabled with multiple effusions, pain, crepitation, and inability to bear weight on the leg. She was taken to surgery and underwent an uneventful total patellectomy. The knee was immobilized with a cast, and she was discharged.

    Discharge diagnosis: Left patellofemoral arthritis.

M12.562	Traumatic arthropathy, left knee
S82.002S	Unspecified fracture of left patella, sequela
Z87.81	Personal history of (healed) traumatic fracture
V80.010S	Animal-rider injured by fall from or being thrown from horse in noncollision accident, sequela
0QTF0ZZ	Resection of left patella, open approach

Comments: The current arthritis is a late effect of the previous fracture and is therefore coded as traumatic arthritis. ICD-10-CM has the qualifier character "S," which is added to the fracture code to indicate a late effect of a fracture. Code Z87.81 is assigned to show a history of traumatic fracture. The External cause code is used for each encounter for which the injury or condition is being treated. The seventh-character value "S" is added to indicate that this is a sequela of the injury.

17. **Inpatient admission:** The woman suffered a displaced fracture dislocation of her right ankle. The injury happened when she jumped off her single-family home front porch in an attempt to catch her fleeing dog, who was being given a bath. She underwent an open reduction and internal fixation of the fracture and was treated with elevation, bed rest, analgesics, and antibiotics. She was released in stable condition.

    Discharge diagnosis: Trimalleolar fracture dislocation, right ankle.

S82.851A	Displaced trimalleolar fracture of right lower leg, initial encounter for closed fracture
W13.8xxA	Fall from, out of or through other building or structure, initial encounter
Y92.018	Other place in single-family (private) house as the place of occurrence of the external cause
Y93.K9	Activity, other involving animal care
Y99.8	Other external cause status
0QSG04Z	Reposition right tibia with internal fixation device, open approach

Comments: A trimalleolar fracture involves the medial, lateral, and posterior malleoli of the tibia. A fracture dislocation is coded to fracture. A displaced fracture is a closed fracture.

18. **Inpatient admission:** The patient was shopping at a retail food warehouse when a gallon can of tomatoes fell on his head from a shelf about 15 feet overhead. He was briefly unconscious and disoriented. X-rays of his skull showed a depressed parasagittal skull fracture with considerable parasagittal depression. He was admitted and taken to surgery, where a craniectomy was performed, with elevation of the depressed skull fracture.

    Discharge diagnosis: Depressed skull fracture.

S02.0xxA	Fracture of vault of skull, initial encounter for closed fracture
S06.9x1A	Unspecified intracranial injury with loss of consciousness of 30 minutes or less, initial encounter
W20.8xxA	Other cause of strike by thrown, projected or falling object, initial encounter
Y92.512	Supermarket, store or market as the place of occurrence of the external cause
0NS00ZZ	Reposition skull, open approach

Comments: The parasagittal area is where the two parietal bones come together in the vault of the skull. The patient was briefly unconscious following the injury. In the Alphabetic Index under **Loss,** consciousness, the cross-reference is to **Injury,** intracraninal. S06.9x1A indicates head injury NOS with a loss of consciousness for 30 minutes or less. The accident occurred in a retail store. The procedure had as its objective to "Reposition," moving to its normal location or other suitable location all or a portion of a body part.

19. **Inpatient admission:** The patient fractured her left patella when she suffered a fall into a hole while golfing on the public golf course. She was taken to surgery, where an open reduction and internal fixation were performed without complication. By the second postoperative day, she was ambulatory on crutches and ready for discharge.

    Discharge diagnosis: Closed fracture, left patella.

S82.002A	Unspecified fracture of left patella, initial encounter for closed fracture
W17.2xxA	Fall into hole, initial encounter
Y92.39	Other specified sports and athletic area as the place of occurrence of the external cause
Y93.53	Activity, golf
Y99.8	Other external cause status
0QSF04Z	Reposition left patella with internal fixation device, open approach

Comments: Although the fracture was closed, an open reduction procedure with internal fixation was performed.

20. **Physician office visit:** The patient went to see his physician after falling off a moving motorcycle. He complained of leg pain, and the physician noted swelling in the right lower extremity. The physician felt that a fracture of the tibia was probable and referred the patient for X-ray to confirm or rule out. For reasons unknown, the patient did not report to the hospital radiology department and did not return to see the physician as instructed.

    Diagnosis: Suspected fracture, right tibia.

M79.604	Pain in right leg
M79.89	Other specified soft tissue disorders
V28.4xxA	Motorcycle driver injured in noncollision transport accident in traffic accident, initial encounter

Comments: Conditions are coded only to the highest level of certainty in the physician office setting. Therefore, codes are assigned only for the symptoms of leg pain and swelling. No code is assigned for the possible tibial fracture.

21. Inpatient admission: A six-month-old infant was admitted with listlessness, nausea and vomiting, and extremely pale skin. The physician diagnosed the patient with heat prostration and suspected child abandonment. The baby was admitted and rehydrated with intravenous fluids.

Discharge diagnoses: (1) Heat prostration, (2) suspected child abandonment.

T76.02xA	Child neglect or abandonment, suspected, initial encounter
T67.5xxA	Heat exhaustion, unspecified
R11.2	Nausea with vomiting, unspecified

Comments: Per the *ICD-10-CM Official Guidelines for Coding and Reporting,* the code for abuse, neglect, and other maltreatment is sequenced first, followed by any accompanying mental health or injury code. Because the abuse is documented as "suspected," a code from category T76 is assigned rather than a code from category T74.

19. BURNS

1. **Inpatient admission:** The patient sustained flash burns when his clothing caught fire. Someone had thrown gasoline onto the park cooking grill by which he was cooking. He suffered second-degree burns to the face, neck, and upper chest, with some first- and second-degree burns on the left forearm. All in all, 12 percent of the total body surface area was burned. The wounds were treated with antibiotics and pain medications. Physical therapists debrided the burned areas and provided hydrotherapy. The wounds continued to heal, and the patient was discharged.

   Discharge diagnoses: (1) Second-degree burns, face, neck, and upper chest; (2) first- and second-degree burns, left forearm; (3) 12 percent of body surface affected by burns.

T22.212A	Burn of second degree of left forearm, initial encounter
T20.20xA	Burn of second degree of head, face, and neck, unspecified site, initial encounter
T21.21xA	Burn of second degree of chest wall, initial encounter
T31.10	Burns involving 10-19% of body surface with 0% to 9% third degree burns
X04.xxxA	Exposure to ignition of highly flammable material, initial encounter
Y92.830	Public park as the place of occurrence of the external cause
Y93.G2	Activity, grilling and smoking food
Y99.8	Other external cause status
F08D5BZ	Wound management treatment of integumentary system—head and neck using physical agents
F08F5BZ	Wound management treatment of integumentary system—upper back / upper extremity using physical agents
0HD1XZZ	Extraction of face skin, external approach
0HD4XZZ	Extraction of neck skin, external approach
0HDEXZZ	Extraction of left lower arm skin, external approach
0HD5XZZ	Extraction of chest skin, external approach

Comments: The patient had first- and second-degree burns on the forearm, but only the highest degree is coded. Code T31.10 is assigned to identify 12 percent of the total body surface that was affected by first- and second-degree burns, with no third-degree burns. Code X04.xxxA indicates that the cause was the ignition of highly flammable material, and code Y92.830 indicates that the injury took place in a park. The activity code is assigned for grilling. Hydrotherapy codes are assigned for the two areas treated. See the Alphabetic Index under the main term **Debridement**, subterm "nonexcisional"; the root operation is "Extraction." One code for each site debrided is assigned.

2. **Inpatient admission:** The patient was brought to the emergency department after being burned. He had been clearing and burning brush in a field at his farm when a gust of wind moved the fire to his tractor. There was an explosion because of the gasoline fumes, and he caught fire. He was treated with IV fluids, antibiotics, and pain medications. All in all, 14 percent of the total body surface was affected by the burns, of which 4 percent was third degree. He was transferred to a burn treatment center for surgical debridement and skin grafting.

   Discharge diagnoses: (1) First- and second-degree burns of the face, right ear, right forearm, and right thumb; (2) third-degree burns of the left hand.

T23.302A	Burn of third degree of left hand, unspecified site, initial encounter
T20.20xA	Burn of second degree of head, face, and neck, unspecified site, initial encounter
T20.211A	Burn of second degree of right ear [any part, except ear drum], initial encounter
T22.211A	Burn of second degree of right forearm, initial encounter
T23.211A	Burn of second degree of right thumb (nail), initial encounter
T31.10	Burns involving 10-19% of body surface with 0% to 9% third degree burns
W30.89xA	Contact with other specified agricultural machinery, initial encounter
W40.1xxA	Explosion of explosive gases, initial encounter
Y92.73	Farm field as the place of occurrence of the external cause
Y93.H9	Activity, other involving exterior property and land maintenance, building and construction
Y99.8	Other external cause status

Comments: The first- and second-degree burns are coded to second degree only. The third-degree burns to the left hand are coded T23.302A. The third degree is sequenced first because it reflects the highest degree of burns. Fourteen percent of the body was affected by burns, of which 4 percent was affected by third degree. The fourth character "0" is assigned because there was less than 10 percent third-degree burn. W30.89xA indicates that the accident was caused by farm machinery; W40.1xxA indicates explosion.

3. **Inpatient admission (episode 1):** The patient was admitted with burns of her right hand and fingers up to the wrist. She had reached into hot water, not realizing the temperature, while canning on her farm. She was taken to surgery, where an excisional debridement of the burns was carried out. A split thickness skin graft was applied over the dorsum and volar aspects of the hand. The postoperative recovery was without infection or other complication.

   Discharge diagnosis: Second- and third-degree burns, right hand and fingers (3 percent of total body surface burned, 2 percent affected by third degree).

T23.391A	Burn of third degree of multiple sites of right wrist and hand, initial encounter
X12.xxxA	Contact with other hot fluids, initial encounter
Y92.79	Other farm location as the place of occurrence of the external cause
Y93.G3	Activity, cooking and baking
Y99.8	Other external cause status
0HRFX74	Replacement of right hand skin with autologous tissue substitute, partial thickness, external approach
0HBFXZZ	Excision of right hand skin, external approach

Comments: For burns of more than one degree of the same site, code to the most severe degree. To identify multiple sites of wrist and hands, assign code T23.391A. The skin graft meets the objective of the root operation "Replacement," putting in or on biological or synthetic material that physically takes the place and/or function of all or a portion of a body part.

Physician office visit (episode 2): Both the burns and the surgical site on this woman's hand seem to be healing nicely. There was no evidence of infection. The area was rebandaged. Antibiotics were continued, and she was to return the following week.

Diagnosis: Second- and third-degree burns, right hand and fingers.

T23.391D	Burn of third degree of multiple sites of right wrist and hand, subsequent encounter
X12.xxxD	Contact with other hot fluids, subsequent encounter

Comments: This episode of care qualifies as a subsequent encounter, after the patient has received active treatment of the injury and is receiving routine care during the healing or recovery phase. The External cause code is used for each encounter for which the injury or condition is being treated. Both codes have the qualifier "D," showing that this is a subsequent encounter.

20. POISONING, TOXIC EFFECTS, ADVERSE EFFECTS, AND UNDERDOSING OF DRUGS

1. **Inpatient admission:** The patient, a 33-year-old male, was admitted through the emergency department after an overdose of Dilantin. His gait was ataxic and he had nausea, vomiting, and blurry vision. His Dilantin level was 48. He had AIDS-related complex (ARC), well documented from previous hospitalizations. He also had posttraumatic epilepsy, which resulted from an intracranial injury received in a 1987 motor vehicle accident. On questioning, he admitted to taking an additional 400 milligrams of Dilantin accidentally on the day of admission. Over the next four days, the Dilantin level gradually decreased to 16.1, and the regular dosage was restarted. It was clear that the current dosage was adequate in preventing seizures without significant side effects.

   Discharge diagnoses: (1) Dilantin toxicity, (2) HIV positive, (3) posttraumatic epilepsy.

T42.0x1A	Poisoning by hydantoin derivatives, accidental (unintentional), initial encounter
R26.0	Ataxic gait
R11.2	Nausea with vomiting, unspecified
H53.8	Other visual disturbances
B20	Human immunodeficiency virus [HIV] disease
G40.909	Epilepsy, unspecified, not intractable, without status epilepticus
S06.9x9S	Unspecified intracranial injury with loss of consciousness of unspecified duration, sequela
V89.2xxS	Person injured in unspecified motor-vehicle accident, traffic, sequela

Comments: In ICD-10-CM the poisoning code includes information on the cause (e.g., the responsible substance) as well as the intent (e.g., accidental), and no additional External cause code is required for the poisoning. The late effect of the intracranial Injury is indicated by the code for the injury with the qualifier character "S" for sequelae. The External cause code is used for each encounter for which the injury is being treated. In this case, the "S" for sequelae is used as the seventh-character value.

2. **Outpatient clinic visit:** The patient came in because of a new rash on his trunk. The thrush, previously diagnosed and being treated with Dapsone, is improving.

   Diagnoses: (1) Skin rash due to an allergic reaction to Dapsone taken internally as prescribed, (2) thrush.

L27.0	Generalized skin eruption due to drugs and medicaments taken internally
T37.1x5A	Adverse effect of antimycobacterial drugs, initial encounter
B37.0	Candidal stomatitis

Comments: The reason for this outpatient encounter is the skin rash, which is an adverse reaction to the therapeutic use of Dapsone. Assign the code for any manifestations of the adverse effects first, followed by the code(s) from categories T30 through T50 (with fifth character 5) that indicates adverse effect as an additional code.

3. **Inpatient admission:** The patient underwent an autologous bone marrow transplantation for choriocarcinoma 13 days earlier. He was readmitted four hours after discharge with a rash, which changed character to an urticarial type of eruption. A skin biopsy of the right lower arm revealed superficial perivascular infiltrate consistent with urticaria. The patient had been started on vancomycin the morning prior to admission. Vancomycin was discontinued, and the urticaria cleared spontaneously.

   Discharge diagnoses: (1) Vancomycin allergy with an urticarial reaction, (2) choriocarcinoma.

L40.0	Psoriasis vulgaris
T36.8x5A	Adverse effect of other systemic antibiotics, initial encounter
C62.90	Malignant neoplasm of unspecified testis, unspecified whether descended or undescended
0HBDXZX	Excision of right lower arm skin, external approach, diagnostic

Comments: The manifestation of the adverse reaction (urticaria) was responsible for admission. Assign the code for any manifestations of the adverse effects first, followed by the code(s) from categories T30 through T50 (with fifth character 5) that indicates adverse effect as an additional code.

Choriocarcinoma is referenced under its name, as a main entry, in the Alphabetic Index of Diseases and Injuries. The code for an unspecified site, male patient, is C62.90.

The skin biopsy is coded as "Excision," with a qualifier for diagnostic.

4. **Inpatient admission:** The patient, a 73-year-old male, was admitted for upper and lower gastrointestinal endoscopy for gastrointestinal bleeding. The patient was given Atropine and, shortly thereafter, the preoperative evaluation showed a heart rate on three occasions of 35, 36, and 37. The patient normally had a heart rate in the upper 40s and had never had one in the 30s. The procedure was canceled due to his bradycardia, and a cardiac evaluation was to be obtained prior to rescheduling. The slow heart rate may have been a reaction to atropine because it occurred shortly after administration of the drug.

   Discharge diagnoses: (1) Gastrointestinal bleed, (2) slow heart rate due to atropine correctly administered.

K92.2	Gastrointestinal hemorrhage, unspecified
T44.4x5A	Adverse effect of predominantly alpha-adrenoreceptor agonists, initial encounter
R00.1	Bradycardia, unspecified
Z53.09	Procedure and treatment not carried out because of other contraindication

Comments: The gastrointestinal bleed remains the principal diagnosis even though the planned treatment was not carried out because of the adverse reaction to the atropine. Slow heart rate is bradycardia. T44.4x5A indicates that this is an adverse effect and initial encounter. Code Z53.09 is assigned to indicate that the planned treatment was not carried out because of a contraindication due to the bradycardia.

5. **Inpatient admission:** The patient, a 46-year-old with AIDS, was recently discharged after workups for fever and weight loss, which were negative. He was readmitted because of histoplasmosis. Amphotericin B was started, and he tolerated the treatment well. Because the patient needed to continue treatment with this medication at home over a fairly long period of time, a Hickman catheter was inserted into the superior vena cava to facilitate administration. He also had severe granulocytopenia, thought to be due to AZT, which was discontinued.

   Discharge diagnoses: (1) Acquired immunodeficiency syndrome; (2) disseminated histoplasmosis; (3) granulocytopenia, possibly due to AZT.

B20	Human immunodeficiency virus [HIV] disease
B39.9	Histoplasmosis, unspecified
D70.9	Neutropenia, unspecified
T37.5x5A	Adverse effect of antiviral drugs, initial encounter
02HV33Z	Insertion of infusion device into superior vena cava, percutaneous approach

Comments: Even though histoplasmosis is stated as the current problem, it is related to the patient's AIDS, which is appropriately designated as the principal diagnosis. In the Index under the main term **Granulocytopenia,** see also "agranulocytosis." In this reference, see also **Neutropenia.** Adverse reaction to AZT is referenced in the Table of Drugs and Chemicals. The Hickman catheter is a "vascular access device" that is tunneled percutaneously through the jugular or subclavian vein to the chest and advanced into the superior vena cava.

6. **Inpatient admission:** The patient was admitted in an altered mental state, showing some confusion as well as ataxia, jaundice, and dizziness. Her husband reported that he felt that the problem related to a massive overusage of an herbal tea given to her by a "healer." She was told to use about a tablespoon per day in a cup of tea but instead had been drinking about a gallon a day. She had a fibroid mass diagnosed about one year earlier but refused conventional treatment. Instead, she was trying to cure it with the tea. After checking with the Poison Control Center, it was determined that the phenylbutazone in this particular brand of tea was probably what was causing her problems. Her mental status returned to its baseline state within 48 hours, and the other problems related to herbal tea consumption disappeared in the same time frame. The presence of a huge uterine mass was confirmed on CT scan, and surgery was offered but refused.

   Discharge diagnoses: (1) Central nervous and digestive system problems secondary to herbal tea intoxication, (2) uterine mass.

T39.2x1A	Poisoning by pyrazolone derivatives, accidental (unintentional), initial encounter
R41.82	Altered mental status, unspecified
R27.0	Ataxia, unspecified
R17	Unspecified jaundice
R42	Dizziness and giddiness
N94.89	Other specified conditions associated with female genital organs and menstrual cycle

Comments: The poisoning code is sequenced as the principal diagnosis, with additional codes for each of the individual manifestations. Phenylbutazone is referenced in the Table of Drugs and Chemicals under **Phenyl,** butazone, poisoning, accidental. The T39.2x1A code includes the accidental intent. The uterine mass is not further identified as to type and so code N94.89 is assigned.

7. **Inpatient admission:** The patient, a young man, collapsed on the street after leaving a bar. An ambulance brought him to the emergency department in severe respiratory distress, which escalated to respiratory failure. He was endoscopically intubated, ventilatory support was initiated, and he was admitted. Respiratory arrest ensued. He died within three hours of admission. Autopsy findings indicated lethal levels of Valium, cocaine, marijuana, and ephedrine.

   Discharge diagnosis: Respiratory failure secondary to overdoses of multiple substances.

T42.4x1A	Poisoning by benzodiazepines, accidental (unintentional), initial encounter
T40.5x1A	Poisoning by cocaine, accidental (unintentional), initial encounter
T40.7x1A	Poisoning by cannabis (derivatives), accidental (unintentional), initial encounter
T44.991A	Poisoning by other drug primarily affecting the autonomic nervous system, accidental (unintentional), initial encounter
J96.00	Acute respiratory failure, unspecified whether with hypoxia or hypercapnia
5A1935Z	Respiratory ventilation, less than 24 consecutive hours
0BH18EZ	Insertion of endotracheal airway into trachea, via natural or artificial opening endoscopic

Comments: When multiple drugs are responsible for a poisoning, each is assigned a separate code. Any one of the poisoning codes could have been designated as the principal diagnosis. The accidental intent is included in the poisoning code. Respiratory distress has evolved to acute respiratory failure as the manifestation of the poisoning, but the poisoning codes must be sequenced first. The patient was intubated and remained on ventilatory support, which qualifies as "Performance" for the root operation. This was for less than 24 hours, and so the code is 5A1935Z.

8. **Inpatient admission:** The patient was admitted for a transurethral resection of the prostate (TURP) for benign prostatic hypertrophy. He was taken to the operating room, but immediately following the induction with general anesthesia, atrial fibrillation developed. The procedure was canceled and the atrial fibrillation treated. It was determined that the arrhythmia was due to the anesthetic.

   Discharge diagnoses: (1) Benign prostatic hypertrophy, (2) atrial fibrillation secondary to anesthesia.

N40.0	Enlarged prostate without lower urinary tract symptoms
I48.91	Unspecified atrial fibrillation
T41.45xA	Adverse effect of unspecified anesthetic, initial encounter
Z53.09	Procedure and treatment not carried out because of other contraindication

Comments: The development of a complication, atrial fibrillation, an adverse reaction to anesthesia, does not change the principal diagnosis. Even though the planned TURP was not carried out, the benign hypertrophy of the prostate was the condition responsible for the admission.

9. **Inpatient admission:** The patient was admitted with nausea and vomiting for the past 24 hours. He was found to have an elevated digoxin level, and after adjustment of dosage, the level came down and the nausea and vomiting ceased. On questioning, he seemed to be taking the digoxin correctly. A new prescription was written, and the patient's digoxin level was to be monitored.

   Discharge diagnosis: Digoxin toxicity.

R11.2	Nausea with vomiting, unspecified
T46.0x5A	Adverse effect of cardiac-stimulant glycosides and drugs of similar action, initial encounter

Comments: Assign a code for the manifestation of the adverse effect first, followed by code T46.0x5A to identify that this is an adverse effect.

10. **Inpatient admission:** The patient was admitted with moderate persistent asthma, which had become intractable to management on an ambulatory care basis. The medications consisted of antibiotics, bronchodilators, and IV steroids. Unfortunately, her stay was prolonged because of an allergic reaction to two of the medications. Celestone and prednisone caused jitteriness and anxiety to the extent that Lorazepam was necessary.

    Discharge diagnoses: (1) Severe asthma, (2) medication allergy.

J45.42	Moderate persistent asthma with status asthmaticus
T38.0x5A	Adverse effect of glucocorticoids and synthetic analogues, initial encounter
F41.9	Anxiety disorder, unspecified

Comments: Asthma is assigned to J45.42 to indicate moderate persistent asthma that is intractable, or with status asthmaticus. The allergy to Celestone and prednisone resulted in an anxiety state that represents an adverse reaction to drugs that were administered correctly. "Celestone" and "prednisone" are located in the Table of Drugs and Chemicals and carry the same T code, so it is reported only once.

11. **Inpatient admission:** The patient came to the outpatient area with swelling and discoloration of the right arm. She was admitted with a provisional diagnosis of axillary vein thrombosis. A venogram of the right arm showed nearly complete obstruction of the axillary vein with an intraluminal clot. She gave a history of having started on birth control pills recently, and it was felt that the drug (Orval) was the cause of the thrombosis. She was taken off the birth control pills and started on IV anticoagulation. When discharged, her prothrombin time was in the therapeutic range, and the arm pain and edema were better.

    Discharge diagnosis: Right axillary vein thrombosis.

I82.A11	Acute embolism and thrombosis of right axillary vein
T38.4x5A	Adverse effect of oral contraceptives, initial encounter
B50MYZZ	Plain radiography of right upper extremity veins using other contrast

Comments: The axillary vein thrombosis is an adverse reaction to Orval. The adverse effect code for Orval can be located in the Table of Drugs and Chemicals by referencing **Contraceptives,** oral.

12. Inpatient admission: The patient, an elderly woman, was admitted with shortness of breath, dyspnea on exertion, fever, and productive cough. These problems were felt to represent lobar pneumonia. She was admitted for cultures and intravenous antibiotics. A chest film showed bilateral lung infiltrates. Erythromycin and Bactrim (also known as sulfamethoxazole and trimethoprim) were given intravenously. However, diarrhea resulted. These drugs were discontinued; when she was switched to Ceftin, her condition showed rapid improvement.

Discharge diagnoses: (1) Lobar pneumonia, (2) diarrhea.

J18.1 Lobar pneumonia, unspecified organism

T36.8x5A Adverse effect of other systemic antibiotics, initial encounter

T36.3x5A Adverse effect of macrolides, initial encounter

R19.7 Diarrhea, unspecified

Comments: The admitting symptoms are all integral to a diagnosis of lobar pneumonia. Diarrhea represents an adverse reaction to erythromycin and Bactrim. Separate adverse effect codes are assigned for each drug. Bactrim is not listed in the Table of Drugs and Chemicals, so the generic name, sulfamethoxazole and trimethoprim, is referenced in the Table of Drugs and Chemicals.

13. Inpatient admission: The patient, a young woman, was brought to the emergency department via ambulance. She was suffering from acute alcohol intoxication. She admitted, however, that she had also ingested a handful of Compazine and Advil (an ibuprofen), thinking they were vitamins and aspirin. In the emergency department, she was treated with charcoal and Narcan and admitted for observation. A psychiatric consultation was obtained, and the psychiatrist deemed the patient stable and not dangerous to herself or others. The patient agreed to obtain drug and alcohol treatment and was discharged.

Discharge diagnoses: (1) Acute alcohol intoxication; (2) multiple substance overdose, Compazine, Advil, and alcohol.

T43.3x1A Poisoning by phenothiazine antipsychotics and neuroleptics, accidental (unintentional), initial encounter

T39.311A Poisoning by propionic acid derivatives, accidental (unintentional), initial encounter

T51.91xA Toxic effect of unspecified alcohol, accidental (unintentional), initial encounter

F10.129 Alcohol abuse with intoxication, unspecified

Comments: A poisoning code should be sequenced as the principal diagnosis because it is unlikely that alcohol intoxication alone would have required inpatient attention. This represents an accidental poisoning by Compazine and Advil because the patient thought she was taking vitamins and aspirin. The accidental intent is included in the T code. There is no entry for Advil in the Table of Drugs and Chemicals, but there is one for ibuprofen. Code F10.129 is assigned for acute alcohol abuse with intoxication without a diagnosis of alcoholism.

14. **Inpatient admission:** The patient was admitted with subdural hematoma that appeared to be related to the anticoagulation she had been on for some time. She underwent an initial CT scan of the brain, which confirmed the subdural hematoma. She had been on chronic Coumadin therapy and had also been taking aspirin as prescribed by her physician for a left lower-extremity deep venous thrombosis. Her Coumadin and aspirin were held, and the prothrombin time was measured on a daily basis. The Coumadin was adjusted, and the aspirin was discontinued. Her condition at discharge was good.

    Discharge diagnoses: (1) Subdural hematoma secondary to medications; (2) chronic deep venous thrombosis, left leg.

I62.01	Nontraumatic acute subdural hemorrhage
T45.515A	Adverse effect of anticoagulants, initial encounter
T39.015A	Adverse effect of aspirin, initial encounter
I82.502	Chronic embolism and thrombosis of unspecified deep veins of left lower extremity
Z79.01	Long term (current) use of anticoagulants

Comments: The subdural hematoma is an adverse reaction involving both Coumadin and aspirin. Therefore, adverse effect codes are assigned for each drug from the Table of Drugs and Chemicals. Code Z79.01 is assigned for the long-term use of Coumadin (anticoagulant).

15. **Inpatient admission:** The patient fractured her left patella when she fell down the basement steps in her single-family home. An open reduction was performed with internal fixation yesterday. During recovery, she had problems with nausea, vomiting, and urinary retention secondary to morphine administration. The pain medication was changed to Demerol, and the symptoms subsided by the second day. The patient was discharged in satisfactory condition the same day.

    Discharge diagnoses: (1) Closed fracture, left patella; (2) allergic reaction to morphine.

    Procedure: Open reduction of patellar fracture with internal fixation.

S82.002A	Unspecified fracture of left patella, initial encounter for closed fracture
W10.8xxA	Fall (on) (from) other stairs and steps, initial encounter
Y92.018	Other place in single-family (private) house as the place of occurrence of the external cause
R11.2	Nausea with vomiting, unspecified
R33.9	Retention of urine, unspecified
T40.2x5A	Adverse effect of other opioids, initial encounter
0QSF04Z	Reposition left patella with internal fixation device, open approach

Comments: Nausea and vomiting and urinary retention represent adverse reactions to morphine. These symptoms developed after admission, and the fracture of the patella remains the principal diagnosis.

16. **Inpatient admission:** A patient was scheduled for outpatient knee arthroscopy. The patient had been sedated and anesthesia was started. The surgeon injected the patient's knee with Bupivacaine. However, prior to the insertion of the arthroscopic trocars, the patient began having trouble breathing. The patient subsequently went into cardiopulmonary arrest and a code blue was called. The patient was resuscitated, intubated, and admitted to the ICU, where she continued to receive ventilator support. Twelve hours later, the patient was transferred to Hospital B for further intensive evaluation and consultation.

    Discharge diagnoses: (1) Adverse reaction to Bupivacaine, (2) cardiopulmonary arrest secondary to #1, (3) anoxic encephalopathy, (4) diabetes with neuropathy, (5) hypertension, (6) osteoarthritis, knees.

I46.8	Cardiac arrest due to other underlying condition
T41.3x5A	Adverse effect of local anesthetics, initial encounter
G93.1	Anoxic brain damage, not elsewhere classified
E11.40	Type 2 diabetes mellitus with diabetic neuropathy, unspecified
I10	Essential (primary) hypertension
M17.0	Bilateral primary osteoarthritis of knee
5A1935Z	Respiratory ventilation, less than 24 consecutive hours

Comments: Code I46.8 is assigned as the principal diagnosis because it is specifically stated as an adverse effect of the Bupivacaine. Code T41.3x5A is assigned to show the drug related to the adverse effect.

21. COMPLICATIONS OF SURGERY AND MEDICAL CARE

1. **Inpatient admission:** The patient was suffering an acute rejection episode involving her left cadaveric renal transplant. She had undergone the transplant three months earlier for end-stage renal disease (ESRD) due to focal glomerulonephritis. An endoscopic-guided percutaneous biopsy of the transplanted kidney was performed, and it was deemed suitable for her to go home after a pulse of steroids.

   Discharge diagnosis: Kidney transplant rejection.

T86.11	Kidney transplant rejection
0TB14ZX	Excision of left kidney, percutaneous endoscopic approach, diagnostic

Comments: Although a patient who has undergone kidney transplant may still have some form of chronic kidney disease (the kidney transplant may not fully restore kidney function), ESRD and focal glomerulonephritis should not be coded because there is no mention of these conditions being present during the current admission. The biopsy is a diagnostic "Excision," performed using a percutaneous approach, endoscopically guided.

2. **Inpatient admission:** The admitting diagnosis was revision of hip arthroplasty. The patient had undergone a total left hip arthroplasty five weeks earlier for osteoarthritis. The prosthesis worked well until the previous week, when she heard a pop. X-rays taken on admission showed a superior displacement of the left acetabular cup, which continued to migrate proximally despite bed rest. The left acetabular component of the prosthesis was revised by insertion of a 60-Ganz plate. Three days after surgery, the patient had a hemoglobin of 10.9 and was transfused with two units of packed red blood cells. Hemoglobin count improved, and the patient was discharged on the fifth postoperative day.

   Discharge diagnoses: (1) Superior displacement, left acetabular cup prosthesis; (2) acute blood loss anemia.

T84.021A	Dislocation of internal left hip prosthesis, initial encounter
D62	Acute posthemorrhagic anemia
0SRE0KZ	Replacement of left hip joint, acetabular surface with nonautologous tissue substitute, open approach
30233N1	Transfusion of nonautologous red blood cells into peripheral vein, percutaneous approach

Comments: Displacement of an orthopedic device is classified as a mechanical complication. In the Alphabetic Index under the main term **Displacement,** the coder is directed to "see **Complications,** joint prosthesis mechanical" under the subterm "joint prosthesis." Code 0SRE0KZ is assigned for the revision of the hip replacement acetabular component, by replacing a portion of the acetabular component.

3. Inpatient admission: The patient was admitted for removal of a left knee prosthesis, which had caused persistent pain since it was placed three years earlier. A recurrent thrombophlebitis was also present in the right lower extremity and was currently being treated with Coumadin. The left knee prosthesis was examined via incision, and there was necrotic tissue of the bone ends (tibia and fibula), which was debrided. Components of the prosthesis were noted to be loosened, and the prosthesis was removed and replaced. Physical therapy was started, and the patient was discharged on antibiotics.

Discharge diagnoses: (1) Necrosis, bone; (2) malfunctioning left knee prosthesis; (3) thrombophlebitis, right leg.

T84.54xA	Infection and inflammatory reaction due to internal left knee prosthesis, initial encounter
T84.033A	Mechanical loosening of internal left knee prosthetic joint, initial encounter
Z79.01	Long term (current) use of anticoagulants
0SPD0JZ	Removal of synthetic substitute from left knee joint, open approach
0SRD0JZ	Replacement of left knee joint with synthetic substitute, open approach
0QBH0ZZ	Excision of left tibia, open approach
0QBK0ZZ	Excision of left fibula, open approach
F07L7ZZ	Manual therapy techniques treatment of musculoskeletal system—lower back / lower extremity

Comments: In the left leg, there was a mechanical complication (loose components) of the prosthesis (T84.033A) as well as a nonmechanical complication, necrosis (T84.54xA). Either could be designated as the principal diagnosis. Code Z96.652, Presence of left artificial knee joint, is not assigned in accordance with instructions from the ICD-10-CM Official Coding Guidelines that a status code should not be used with a diagnosis code from one of the body system chapters, if the diagnosis code includes the information provided by the status code. In this case, the complication codes from category T84 indicate the presence of a left knee prosthetic joint, and therefore the status code does not provide additional information. Code Z79.01 is assigned to show the long-term use of Coumadin.

ICD-10-PCS codes are assigned for the "Removal" of the original prosthesis and "Replacement" with a new prosthesis. The debridement of the bone requires two codes, one for each site. Physical therapy is coded in the Physical Rehabilitation and Diagnostic Audiology Section.

4. Inpatient admission: Two months before admission, the patient completed 37 X-ray therapy treatments following resection of his tongue for removal of primary squamous cell carcinoma. He was admitted for evaluation and therapy of spontaneous extraoral drainage from an exposed bone plate of the left mandible. After debridement of the affected site via incision, he was discharged for follow-up care at the referring hospital.

Discharge diagnosis: Osteoradionecrosis of left mandible.

M27.2	Inflammatory conditions of jaws
Z85.810	Personal history of malignant neoplasm of tongue
Y84.2	Radiological procedure and radiotherapy as the cause of abnormal reaction of the patient, or of later complication, without mention of misadventure at the time of the procedure
0NBV0ZZ	Excision of left mandible, open approach

Comments: See the Alphabetic Index under the main term **Osteoradionecrosis,** subterm "jaw." Because the primary site of the neoplasm is no longer present or under active treatment, code Z85.810 is assigned. Code Y84.2 is assigned to identify the adverse effects of radiation therapy. For the procedure code, in the Index under the main term **Debridement,** excisional, see "Excision."

5. **Inpatient admission:** The patient underwent a laryngoscopy with biopsy in the ambulatory surgery area, and a primary neoplasm of the false vocal cords was confirmed. In the recovery room, she developed acute respiratory insufficiency and was placed on oxygen. Because of the severity of the respiratory insufficiency, she was admitted. By the third hospital day, her blood gases returned to normal, and she was discharged.

   Discharge diagnoses: (1) Carcinoma of vocal cords, (2) postoperative respiratory insufficiency.

J95.2	Acute pulmonary insufficiency following nonthoracic surgery
C32.1	Malignant neoplasm of supraglottis
0CBS8ZX	Excision of larynx, via natural or artificial opening endoscopic, diagnostic

Comments: Postoperative respiratory insufficiency is an example of an intraoperative and postprocedural complication of the respiratory system not elsewhere classified, in category J95. The principal diagnosis is the condition necessitating admission as an inpatient, postoperative respiratory insufficiency. Codes for the ambulatory surgery and the condition for which it was performed are generally assigned when patients are admitted from the outpatient surgery unit.

6. **Inpatient admission:** The patient was admitted because of a displaced T tube, which was partially out of the common bile duct. The T tube was blocked by a malignant tumor of the pancreas, which caused the tube to buckle and leak. The patient was transferred to another hospital for care.

   Discharge diagnoses: (1) Bile in peritoneum due to T tube partially out of common duct; (2) tumor, head of pancreas.

T85.520A	Displacement of bile duct prosthesis, initial encounter
C25.0	Malignant neoplasm of head of pancreas

Comments: Code T85.520A is assigned by referencing the main term **Complication** in the Index, subterm "bile duct implant, mechanical, displacement." "Displacement" of a device is a mechanical complication.

7. **Inpatient admission:** The admission diagnoses were possible uterine septum and adnexal mass. A left ovarian cystic mass, which was thought to be an endometrioma and a uterine septum, was confirmed on hysteroscopy and laparoscopy. In the course of evaluation, a perforation of the left uterine horn occurred. Laparotomy was performed, and the cystic mass was excised from the ovary. The abdominal cavity was copiously irrigated and the uterine perforation repaired. Pathologic findings identified the cystic mass as a dermoid cyst of the ovary.

   Discharge diagnoses: (1) Dermoid cyst, left ovary; (2) uterine septum; (3) inadvertent puncture, left uterine horn.

D27.1	Benign neoplasm of left ovary
Q51.2	Other doubling of uterus
N99.71	Accidental puncture and laceration of a genitourinary system organ or structure during a genitourinary system procedure
0UB10ZZ	Excision of left ovary, open approach
0UQ90ZZ	Repair uterus, open approach
0UJD8ZZ	Inspection of uterus and cervix, via natural or artificial opening endoscopic
0WJJ4ZZ	Inspection of pelvic cavity, percutaneous endoscopic approach

Comments: A dermoid cyst is benign per instructions in the Alphabetic Index under the main term **Cyst,** subterm "dermoid." ICD-10-CM has a code for the left and right ovary. The code for uterine septum is located by following the Index, main term **Septum,** subterm "uterus," see **Double,** uterus. For the accidental puncture code, see the Index under the main term **Complication,** subterms "accidental puncture" or "laceration." Follow the cross-reference to **Complications,** intraoperative, puncture or laceration, and then locate the subterm "specified NEC, genitourinary."

Therapeutic procedures are sequenced before diagnostic procedures. The hysteroscopy and laparoscopy were performed first, and then a laparotomy was necessary to remove the cyst and repair the uterine perforation.

8. **Inpatient admission:** The patient underwent a cystoscopy, with endoscopic passage of a stone basket up the left ureter and a contrast retrograde pyelogram of the kidneys, ureters, and bladder the day before admission. After release, she experienced terrible pain in the ureteral area and had to be readmitted for pain control. A repeat intravenous pyelogram was normal, and laboratory studies were all within normal limits. By the end of the second day, her pain was controlled with oral medications, and she was discharged.

   Discharge diagnosis: Postoperative pain of undetermined cause.

G89.18	Other acute postprocedural pain
N23	Unspecified renal colic
0TC78ZZ	Extirpation of matter from left ureter, via natural or artificial opening endoscopic
BT14YZZ	Fluoroscopy of kidneys, ureters and bladder using other contrast

Comments: Assign code G89.18 as the principal diagnosis because the stated reason for the admission is documented as postoperative pain control. The narrative indicates that the pain was in the ureteral area; therefore, code N23 is assigned to provide greater specificity regarding the location of the postoperative pain. Because the surgery was performed the preceding day at the same facility, the diagnosis and procedure codes for the outpatient encounter are added.

9. **Inpatient admission:** The patient underwent a cold conization of the cervix and fractional dilatation and curettage for postmenopausal bleeding in the outpatient surgery center. The surgery was uncomplicated, and the operative site was dry at the conclusion of the procedure. An examination of tissue rendered a pathologic diagnosis of severe cervical dysplasia, CIN-III. Within two hours postoperatively, there was excessive bleeding and a vaginal pack was placed. She bled through the pack and was then admitted for suture repair of site of the previous cervical biopsy. Postoperatively, she remained dry with no further problems and was discharged in good condition.

   Discharge diagnoses: (1) Severe cervical dysplasia, CIN-III; (2) postoperative bleeding.

N99.820	Postprocedural hemorrhage and hematoma of a genitourinary system organ or structure following a genitourinary system procedure
D06.9	Carcinoma in situ of cervix, unspecified
N95.0	Postmenopausal bleeding
0UQC3ZZ	Repair cervix, percutaneous approach
0UBC7ZZ	Excision of cervix, via natural or artificial opening
0UDB7ZZ	Extraction of endometrium, via natural or artificial opening

Comments: The principal diagnosis is postoperative bleeding, the reason for inpatient admission. No additional code is required to describe postoperative bleeding. A diagnosis of CIN-III with severe dysplasia of the cervix is coded to D06.9. An additional code is assigned for the postmenopausal bleeding, which was the reason for the original outpatient surgery, and for the dilatation and curettage as well as the suture of the cervix because they were performed within a brief period of time before admission.

10. **Inpatient admission:** The patient had a subtrochanteric stress fracture of the left femur, which had been repaired with pin insertion three weeks earlier. She returned with an infection of the operative wound site and delayed healing of the fracture. A wide excisional debridement of the infection site of the soft tissue was carried out via incision. No definite infection could be demonstrated within the bone. Cultures of the operative wound grew *Staphylococcus aureus*, sensitive to everything, and the patient was maintained on IV antibiotics until discharge.

    Discharge diagnosis: Deep soft tissue infection, left thigh.

T81.4xxA	Infection following a procedure, initial encounter
M84.352G	Stress fracture, left femur, subsequent encounter for fracture with delayed healing
B95.61	Methicillin susceptible Staphylococcus aureus infection as the cause of diseases classified elsewhere
0JBM0ZZ	Excision of left upper leg subcutaneous tissue and fascia, open approach

Comments: The postoperative wound infection was of the soft tissue incision site only, not of the site of pin insertion into the bone. The wound infection code, T81.4xxA, represents an initial encounter, as this is the first encounter for the infection. The stress fracture code has the seventh-character qualifier to indicate that this is a subsequent encounter for a fracture with delayed healing. Code 0JBM0ZZ is assigned for the wide excisional debridement of the postoperative wound infection of the soft tissue.

11. **Inpatient admission:** The patient underwent a cervical diskectomy and fusion last year. The pain improved for a few months but has recurred. He was readmitted for further surgery. A left C3-C4, C5-C6, and C6-C7 posterior cervical decompressive laminectomy with foraminotomy was performed. There was considerable postoperative pain, well out of proportion to what would be expected for this surgery. He remained in the hospital the week following surgery, primarily to receive intramuscular pain medications.

    Discharge diagnoses: (1) Cervical spondylosis, (2) severe postoperative back pain.

M47.812	Spondylosis without myelopathy or radiculopathy, cervical region
M54.9	Dorsalgia, unspecified
G89.18	Other acute postprocedural pain
0RB30ZZ	Excision of cervical vertebral disc, open approach

Comments: Code G89.18, Other acute postprocedural pain, is assigned to identify an unusual amount of postoperative pain. This is not coded as a postoperative complication. Code M54.9 is coded for additional specificity to identify the site of the pain.

12. **Inpatient admission:** A month earlier, the patient had undergone open reduction and internal fixation of a traumatic fracture of the left femur. She came to the emergency department with a severe and deep infection of the left thigh. She was admitted and taken to surgery immediately, where a wide excisional debridement of the subcutaneous tissue of the infection was carried out and hardware was removed from the upper portion of the femur. Cultures of fixation pins grew *Staphylococcus aureus*, and she was maintained on IV Oxacillin. She was to continue antibiotics at home after discharge.

    Discharge diagnosis: Staphylococcal infection due to orthopedic fixation device.

T84.621A	Infection and inflammatory reaction due to internal fixation device of left femur, initial encounter
B95.61	Methicillin susceptible Staphylococcus aureus infection as the cause of diseases classified elsewhere
Z87.81	Personal history of (healed) traumatic fracture
0JBM0ZZ	Excision of left upper leg subcutaneous tissue and fascia, open approach
0QP704Z	Removal of internal fixation device from left upper femur, open approach

Comments: Because the infection resulted from the presence of an orthopedic device, code T84.621A is used. Z87.81 indicates a history of traumatic fracture.

13. **Inpatient admission:** This acutely ill patient was admitted with fever, weakness, and chills. He had undergone a bilateral herniorrhaphy four days before admission. He is now experiencing some urgency on urination and dysuria. On admission to the hospital, the operative incisions were slightly red and tender and the abdomen somewhat distended. Blood cultures and wound cultures revealed a heavy growth of *Staphylococcus aureus*, which also grew on a urine culture. *Enterococcus faecalis* also grew on the urine culture. The chills and fever receded with IV antibiotics. It was believed that the patient's problems represented postoperative complications of the herniorrhaphy.

    Discharge diagnoses: (1) Postoperative sepsis and urinary tract infection, (2) postoperative wound infection.

T81.4xxA	Infection following a procedure, initial encounter
N99.89	Other postprocedural complications and disorders of genitourinary system
N39.0	Urinary tract infection, site not specified
B95.61	Methicillin susceptible Staphylococcus aureus infection as the cause of diseases classified elsewhere
B95.2	Enterococcus as the cause of diseases classified elsewhere
A41.01	Sepsis due to Methicillin susceptible Staphylococcus aureus
Y83.8	Other surgical procedures as the cause of abnormal reaction of the patient, or of later complication, without mention of misadventure at the time of the procedure

Comments: The reason for the admission is the postoperative infection. The T81.4xxA code shows the postoperative infection. Code N99.89 indicates that this is a postprocedural complication of the genitourinary system, and code N39.0 indicates that this is a UTI. The causative agents are also coded. ICD-10-CM includes the sepsis and causative agent in one code, A41.01. When the documentation does not specify whether the *Staphylococcus* infection is resistant to Methicillin, the classification defaults to Methicillin susceptible.

14. **Inpatient admission:** A patient who is 50 days post stem cell transplant due to multiple myeloma that is currently in remission was admitted with fever, severe nausea and vomiting, splenomegaly, and cervical lymphadenopathy. A left inguinal lymph node needle biopsy was performed when the lymphadenopathy enlarged and spread to the inguinal area.

    Discharge diagnoses: (1) Post stem cell transplant lymphoproliferative disorder, (2) multiple myeloma in remission.

T86.5	Complications of stem cell transplant
D47.Z1	Post-transplant lymphoproliferative disorder (PTLD)
C90.01	Multiple myeloma in remission
07BJ3ZX	Excision of left inguinal lymphatic, percutaneous approach, diagnostic

Comments: Code T86.5 is assigned as the principal diagnosis according to the sequencing instructions provided in the Tabular List. The needle biopsy is coded to the approach value "percutaneous."

Index

A

***Page numbers in color refer to tables, figures, or illustrations.**

D

E

J

K

L

M

N

O

P

S

T

U